New York YANKEES 365

GEORGE HERMAN
(BABE) RUTH
BIG LEAGUE
CHEWING
GUM

JOE DI MAGGIO, Yankees

ROBERT A.
(RED) ROLFE
Lou Gehrig
says...

New York YANKEES 365

By the ASSOCIATED PRESS   Foreword by DON MATTINGLY

ABRAMS, NEW YORK

FOREWORD *by Don Mattingly*

Growing up in Evansville, Indiana, I didn't have a major league team with star players to follow—to see a St. Louis Cardinals game meant about a three-hour drive each way. But I was fortunate to have three older brothers who were athletically gifted. They let me tag along when they played pickup games in the neighborhood. Depending on the season and the sport they were playing, I would chase down the foul balls or out-of-bounds balls, and occasionally they asked me to fill in when one team was short of players.

Of course, our parents were our greatest supporters, driving us to games throughout the state as we grew older. Dad wasn't the type of parent who was loud or jumped on me after a bad game. I always knew he was there for me no matter how I played, and that made all the difference. My dad's encouragement and influence enabled me to play without fear. As a result, I played more aggressively and wasn't afraid to make mistakes.

I've tried to instill those qualities in my own sons.

Baseball became my passion, and I still take pride in my junior year at Reitz Memorial High School—we had a perfect season, winning the Indiana state championships. Most major league scouts expected that, coming out of high school, I would accept a college offer. Florida State University was one of the schools recruiting me to play college baseball, although I was thinking closer to home: Indiana State. But when the New York Yankees took a chance and drafted me in the nineteenth round of the 1979 amateur draft, that was an opportunity I couldn't pass up. I decided to forgo college and sign with the Yankees.

That's how I found myself in a Yankees uniform. Sure, these were the Oneonta Yankees, but I was starting my career with an organization whose former players read like the lineup card of the gods: Babe Ruth, Lou Gehrig, Joe DiMaggio, Mickey Mantle, and Yogi Berra. Not just Yankees legends, but baseball legends and authentic American heroes.

When the big club called me up from Triple-A Columbus late in the 1982 season after a couple of years in the minors, I still had more than a little to prove. As a kid playing sandlot ball with my brothers, I had dreamed about what it would be like to play in the majors, to make "the show." Now I had a shot with the Yankees, on the biggest stage in baseball.

I had been following the careers of Thurman Munson, Lou Piniella, Willie Randolph, Graig Nettles, Bobby Murcer, Goose Gossage, and Ron Guidry, to name just a few. I admired their work ethic and how they approached every aspect of the game. They epitomized what it means to be a New York Yankee: Pride. Tradition. Professionalism. When I put on that pin-striped uniform and stepped onto the Yankee Stadium field for the first time . . . that was truly a dream come true, one of my most memorable lifetime experiences.

I played in just a handful of games that first season—mostly subbing in the outfield—and had even fewer hits, but for a twenty-one-year-old, this was heady stuff. A couple of seasons later, I would be battling teammate Dave Winfield for the 1984 AL batting title, a race that came down to the last game of the season. I felt very fortunate to be the first Yankee to win that title since Mickey Mantle. Some very rewarding seasons followed, and many things stand out for me, not least of all playing with guys like Winfield and Rickey Henderson at

the beginning of my career, then seeing young stars like Bernie Williams and Derek Jeter develop later in my career. That was very special. And of course, playing first base for the Yankees brings with it the honor of playing Lou Gehrig's position. I'm not about to compare myself to the Iron Horse, but I'd like to think he would have appreciated the way I played the game, and I take some pride that we both received a rare honor for a Yankees player: being named team captain.

Certainly one of the biggest thrills of my career came when I stepped out of the dugout for the first game of the 1995 ALDS in New York against the Seattle Mariners. The excitement of playoff baseball and the overwhelming reception of the New York fans at Yankee Stadium was an unforgettable experience I will always deeply appreciate. Those were my last games as a player.

I had the good fortune to play my entire career with the New York Yankees organization. I was always proud to represent the Yankees, both on and off the field, just as I'm proud to have been even a small part of an organization for which I have great respect. Because Dad not only inspired me to play without fear; he taught me respect. The respect I've always had for the Yankees' profound legacy, and the fans who demonstrate so much loyalty and support for the team.

Don Mattingly is one of the most celebrated Yankees of all time. He played first base for the team from 1982 to 1995, and was hitting coach from 2004 to 2006. In 2007 he was Joe Torre's bench coach. He is currently hitting coach for the Los Angeles Dodgers.

PHIL RIZZUTO

Cracker Jack
BALL
PLAYERS
PECKINPAUGH, NEW YORK - AMERICANS

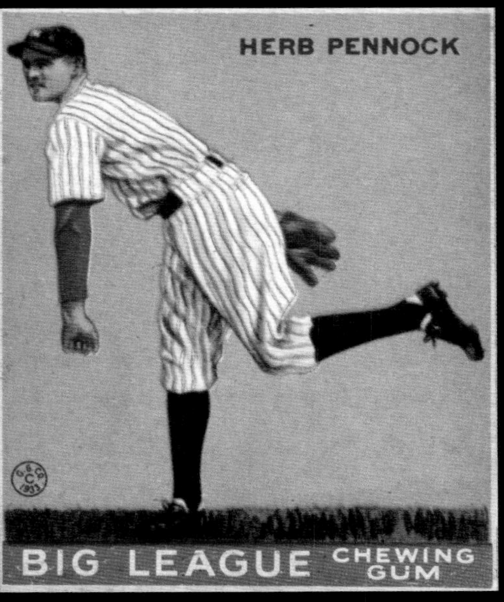
HERB PENNOCK
BIG LEAGUE CHEWING GUM

January

1

THIS JACK IS AN ACE

Before they were known as the Yankees, they were the New York Highlanders. And before that, they were the original American League Baltimore Orioles, bought for $18,000 and moved to New York in 1903. "Happy Jack" Chesbro became the Highlanders' first pitching ace. A spitball specialist when the pitch was still legal, the right-hander started 51 games in 1904 and finished an astonishing 48 complete games while compiling a 41–12 record. Chesbro was one of the premier pitchers of his era; his 41 wins still stand as the American League season record. He was elected to the Baseball Hall of Fame in 1946.

February 6, 1895 George Herman Ruth is born in Baltimore.

January

2

HIGH POINT OF THE SEASON

The Highlanders loosen up at Hilltop Park on Opening Day, April 14, 1908. Built in six weeks in 1903, the ballpark, formally named American League Park, stood in the Washington Heights neighborhood of New York, on the west side of Broadway between 165th and 168th streets. The Highlanders' name referred at least partly to this site, on one of Manhattan's highest points. On this day, the Highlanders would beat the Philadelphia Athletics 1–0, but the New Yorkers would go on to have a dismal 1908 season, finishing 51–103.

April 26, 1901 The Baltimore Orioles—no relation to the current team—begin play as one of the American League's eight original charter teams. They finish their only two seasons in fifth place (68–65) and last place (50–88, thirty-four games out of first), with no viable future.

January

CAN'T WIN FOR LOSING

The Highlanders and the Philadelphia Athletics relax against a billboard before their Opening Day game at Hilltop Park, April 14, 1908. The Highlanders fielded a number of competitive teams, but they never won the American League pennant. In 1908 they had one of their worst seasons, finishing in the cellar of the eight-team American League, thirty-nine and a half games out of first place. The low point may have come on June 30, when forty-one-year-old Cy Young of the Boston Red Sox pitched a no-hitter against the Highlanders at Hilltop Park.

January 9, 1903 Frank Farrell and Bill Devery purchase the Baltimore Orioles for $18,000 and move the team to New York City. The team's first president is Joseph W. Gordon, and the player-manager is Clark Griffith, future owner of the Washington Senators and Hall of Famer.

White Roc

January

4

FORMAL ATTIRE REQUESTED

Uniformly well-dressed men fill the right field stands at Hilltop Park to see the Opening Day game between the Highlanders and the Philadelphia Athletics, April 14, 1908. The ballpark had seating for 16,000, with standing room for another 10,000 or so. Although baseball crowds became far more diverse over the years, appropriately dressed men wearing white shirts and ties in major league parks were not an uncommon sight as late as the 1950s and 1960s. In 1908 the Hoffman & Co. outfield sign offered a box of Havana cigars to any batter who hit it.

March 12, 1903 The American League approves the New York franchise. An all-wood park at Broadway and 168th Street is quickly built to serve as the team's first playing field; it is at one of the highest locations in Manhattan, so the field comes to be known as Hilltop Park and the team as the Highlanders—although other press nicknames, including the increasingly popular "Yankees," appeared at least as early as June 1904.

HIT SCORE BOARD
AND GET BOX
WEBSTER
HIGHEST GRADE
CLEAR HAVANA CIGAR
HOFFMAN & CO
204 W. 125th ST.
A Season Ticket

January

HE HIT 'EM WHERE THEY WASN'T

Right fielder Wee Willie Keeler, shown on a Piedmont cigarette card, probably stood no more than five-foot-four and weighed about 140 pounds, but he compiled Hall of Fame numbers with four teams, including the Highlanders. The Brooklyn native had his best years with the National League Baltimore Orioles and Brooklyn Superbas (later called the Dodgers) before joining the Highlanders in 1903, but he still managed to hit .343 in 1904. The quintessential slap hitter, Keeler held the major league record with base hits in forty-four consecutive games until Joe DiMaggio broke it in 1941. He excelled at bunting and is often credited with the "Baltimore chop": hitting the ball sharply downward, bouncing it so high that the infielders have no play. He also coined the timeless baseball maxim "I hit 'em where they ain't." He did just that.

April 22, 1903 In the first game in the franchise's history, the Highlanders lose to the Washington Senators 3–1; Wee Willie Keeler scores the team's only run. The next day, Harry Howell records the New York team's first win as the Highlanders defeat Washington 7–2.

NEW Y
KEELER, N. Y. AMER.

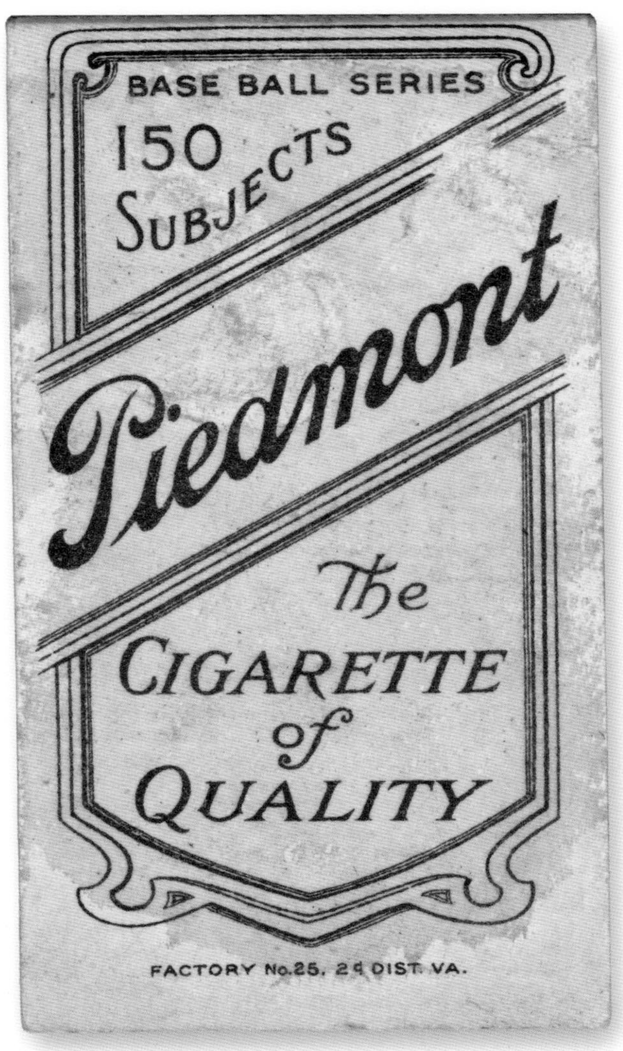
BASE BALL SERIES
150 SUBJECTS
Piedmont
The
CIGARETTE
of
QUALITY
FACTORY No.25. 2d DIST. VA.

January

YANKEES BY ANY OTHER NAME

The Highlanders play at American League Park, commonly known as Hilltop Park, about 1910. When attendance swelled, fans would stand on the field behind home plate, along the foul lines, and around the perimeter of the outfield, as was the practice of the day. By the time this panoramic photo was shot, the Highlanders were commonly known in the press as the Yankees, synonymous with Americans. In 1912 they added the distinctive pinstripes to their uniforms, and in 1913 they abandoned Hilltop Park for the Polo Grounds, home of the Giants, their National League counterparts. With the move, they formally changed the team's name to the New York Yankees.

April 30, 1903 The Highlanders win their first home opener at Hilltop Park, defeating Washington 6–2 before 16,293 fans. The pitcher is "Happy Jack" Chesbro, a 105-game winner in his first four years with the Highlanders and one of the team's first two Hall of Fame pitchers, along with player-manager Clark Griffith.

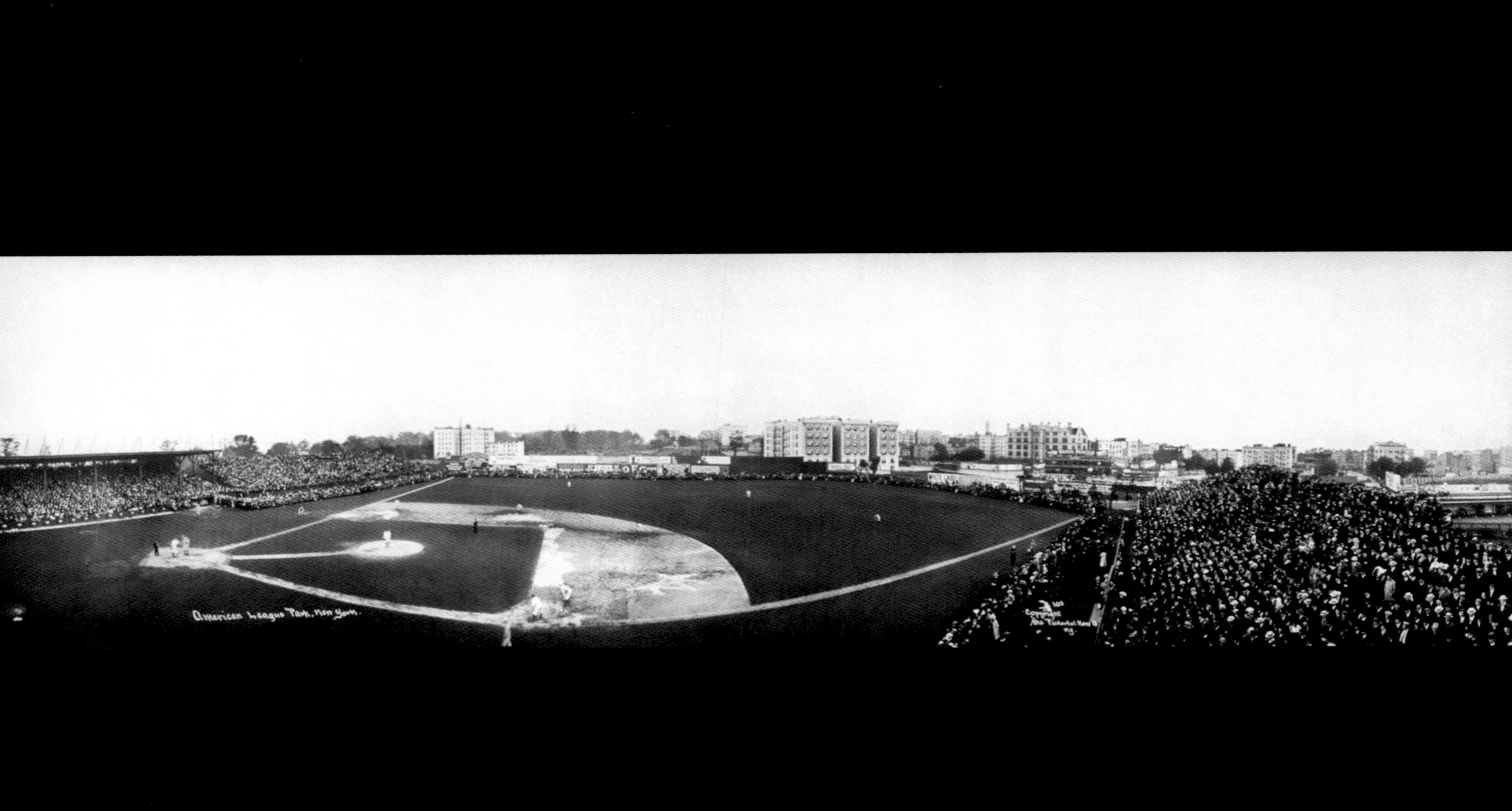
American League Park, New York.
Copyright

January

7

THE DARK PRINCE

"Prince Hal" Chase, left, of the Highlanders poses with legendary New York Giants manager John McGraw about 1910. Chase was the first real star the Highlanders could call their own; by most accounts, he was an outstanding first baseman, and some have called him the smoothest first sacker ever. But his reputation was forever tarnished by allegations of gambling and corruption. When successful Highlanders manager George Stallings charged Chase with fixing games, the league and team management declined to investigate the star first baseman. Instead, the Highlanders forced Stallings to resign and made Chase player-manager with two weeks left in the 1910 season. But after going 76–76 in 1911, Chase stepped down as manager to continue his playing career. After the 1919 season, he was effectively blacklisted from the game.

May 8, 1903 Jack Chesbro pitches a six-hitter as the New York Highlanders defeat the Boston Americans for the first time; the teams will later become officially known as the Yankees and the Red Sox.

January

HELL-RAISER HAL

A 1911 Turkey Red cigarette card features Highlanders first baseman Hal Chase. Cigarette packs of the era were stiffened with promotional cards depicting athletes, actors and actresses, military figures, animals, and other collectible subjects. These were the forerunners of today's baseball cards.

Prince Hal had the distinction of becoming the first captain of the team that would become the Yankees, but his reputation for throwing games and committing suspicious errors overshadowed his accomplishments. On his deathbed, he said, "You note that I am not in the Hall of Fame. . . . I am an outcast, and I haven't a good name. I'm the loser, just like all gamblers are. I lived to make great plays. What did I gain? Nothing. Everything was lost because I raised hell after hours. I was a wise guy, a know-it-all, I guess."

September 29, 1903 The Highlanders finish their first season in fourth place, with a 72–62 record—seventeen games out of first place—and a season home crowd barely topping 200,000. Jack Chesbro goes 21–15, star right fielder Wee Willie Keeler bats .313, and second baseman Jimmy Williams leads the team with eighty-two runs batted in.

No. 6

PROMINENT BASE BALL PLAYERS & ATHLETES

ORDER BY NUMBER ONLY

1 M. Brown, Chicago Nat'l
2 Bergen, Brooklyn
3 Leach, Pittsburg
4 Bresnahan, St. Louis Nat'l
5 Crawford, Detroit
6 Chase, New York American
7 Camnitz, Pittsburg
8 Clarke, Pittsburg
9 Cobb, Detroit
10 Devlin, New York Nat'l
11 Dahlen, Brooklyn
12 Donovan, Detroit
13 Doyle, New York National
14 Dooin, Philadelphia Nat'l
15 Elberfeld, Washington
16 Evers, Chicago National
17 Griffith, Cincinnati
18 Jennings, Detroit
19 Joss, Cleveland
20 Jordan, Brooklyn
21 Kleinow, New York Amer.
22 Krause, Philadelphia Amer.
23 Lajoie, Cleveland
24 Mitchell, Cincinnati
25 M. McIntyre, Detroit
26 McGraw, New York Nat'l
27 Mathewson, N. Y. Nat'l
28 H. McIntyre, Brooklyn
29 McConnell, Boston Amer.
30 Mullin, Detroit
31 Magee, Philadelphia Nat'l
32 Overall, Chicago National
33 Pfeister, Chicago National
34 Rucker, Brooklyn
35 Tinker, Chicago National
36 Speaker, Boston American
37 Sallee, St. Louis National
38 Stahl, Boston American
39 Waddell, St. Louis Amer.
40 Willis, St. Louis National
41 Wiltse, New York National
42 Young, Cleveland
43 Out at Third
44 Trying to Catch Him Nap'g
45 Jordan and Herzog at First
46 Safe at Third
47 Frank Chance at Bat
48 Jack Murray at Bat
49 A Close Play at Second
50 Chief Myers at Bat
51 Jem Driscoll
52 Abe Attell
53 Ad. Wolgast
54 Johnny Coulon
55 James Jeffries
56 Jack (Twin) Sullivan
57 Battling Nelson
58 Packey McFarland
59 Tommy Murphy
60 Owen Moran
61 Johnny Marto
62 Jimmie Gardner
63 Harry Lewis
64 Wm. Papke
65 Sam Langford
66 Knock-out Brown
67 Stanley Ketchel
68 Joe Jeannette
69 Leach Cross
70 Phil. McGovern
71 Battling Hurley
72 Honey Mellody
73 Al Kaufman
74 Willie Lewis
75 Philadelphia Jack O'Brien

Any one of the above named pictures given in exchange for 10 Coupons taken from Turkey Red Cigarettes or 25 Coupons from either Old Mill or Fez Cigarettes. Send coupons by Mail or express, charges prepaid to

BASE BALL AND ATHLETE PICTURE DEPT.

DRAWER S. JERSEY CITY, N.J.

THIS OFFER EXPIRES JUNE 30-1911.

January

THE END OF THE BEGINNING

Fans enter Hilltop Park in 1912, its last season before the Highlanders move to the Polo Grounds. The last major league game was played there Saturday, October 5, 1912, as New York closed its season with an 8–6 win over the Washington Senators. Among the highlights in the ballpark's nine-year history: Legendary pitcher Walter Johnson of the Senators threw shutouts against the Highlanders in three consecutive games in four days in September 1908. Hilltop Park was torn down in 1914, to little fanfare; New York-Presbyterian Hospital/ Columbia University Medical Center now stands on the site. A plaque on the grounds of the medical center marks the approximate location of home plate.

July 4, 1904 Jack Chesbro notches his fourteenth straight win as a Highlander, setting a club and league record. Chesbro goes on to a record-setting forty-one wins, twelve losses, and a 1.82 ERA after pitching an astonishing 454 2/3 innings.

N. Y.
ERICAN LEAGUE.
75
50
50
LINE FORMS ON TH

January

10

NAME A SHORTSTOP WHO BECAME YANKEES CAPTAIN

Roger Peckinpaugh started at shortstop for all nine of his seasons with the Yankees. Described as a natural leader, in 1914 he became the team's second captain, a title he held through 1921. He succeeded Frank Chance as the team's manager for the last few weeks of the 1914 season, making him, at twenty-three, the youngest manager ever in the major leagues, though he did not manage the Yankees the following season. Reliable and proficient both in the field and at the plate, Peckinpaugh was the senior player of the Yankees teams that emerged as contenders in the early 1920s. But after the 1921 season, the captain was traded to the Red Sox and then to the Senators. He was the star of the Senators' 1924 world championship team.

August 24, 1904 Wee Willie "Hit 'em where they ain't" Keeler hits two inside-the-park home runs in a 9–1 win over the St. Louis Browns at Hilltop Park.

January

11

SEASONAL WORK

Coming off his first full season with the World Series champion Red Sox, Babe Ruth, second from right, and his father, far right, tend bar at Ruth's Café at Lombard and Eutaw streets in Baltimore, December 1915. George Herman Ruth Jr. grew up in Baltimore a virtual orphan while his parents struggled to make ends meet. At the age of seven, he was sent to St. Mary's Industrial School for Boys, a boys' home and reformatory, where he flourished as an athlete and honed his baseball skills. As a teenager, George's pitching prowess earned him a contract with the minor league Baltimore Orioles. His teammates reportedly nicknamed the young prospect "Babe." In 1914 he was dealt to the Red Sox, one of baseball's top teams, appearing in five major league games that season for Boston.

October 10, 1904 After blowing both games on October 8 to fall into second place, the Highlanders split a doubleheader on the last day of the regular season and lose the AL pennant to the Boston Americans—thanks to a ninth-inning wild pitch by Highlanders ace Jack Chesbro in the first game. The National League champion New York Giants then refuse to play the champs of the upstart AL, making 1904 the last year without a World Series until the strike of 1994.

STYLE
RAW BAR

January

12

BOSTON'S BABE

Babe Ruth poses in 1919, his last season in a Red Sox uniform. The Babe went 89–46 as a pitcher in his six seasons with Boston, and he was 3–0 with a 0.87 ERA in three World Series starts. He might well have become a Hall of Fame pitcher. But in 1919, playing much of the season in the outfield, he hit .322 with twenty-nine home runs, more than hinting at the greatness to come. Of course, along with the heroics came salary demands and flashes of Ruth's reckless behavior, which may have contributed to Boston's willingness to part with its star. Whatever the reason, by year's end the Babe would be a New York Yankee. The Curse of the Bambino had been born: The Red Sox would not win another World Series in the century.

August 5, 1905 Rookie sensation Hal Chase sets an American League record at first base with thirty-eight putouts in a doubleheader against St. Louis. The speedy defensive standout—a star tarnished by links to gambling throughout his career—will also set a league record with twenty putouts in a nine-inning game on September 21, 1906.

ED SOX

January

13

THE CENTER OF ATTENTION

The 1921 Yankees pose at spring training in Louisiana, with Babe Ruth seated at center, middle row. Led by Ruth's staggering fifty-nine home runs and pitcher Carl Mays's 27–9 record, this was the first Yankees team to win the American League pennant. The Yankees lost the 1921 World Series to the New York Giants, five games to three, the last time the Series was a best-of-nine affair. And it wasn't exactly the first Subway Series; with both teams calling the Polo Grounds home, all eight games were played there.

The Yankees used some far-flung locations for spring training over the years, including Bermuda (1913) and Atlantic City, New Jersey (1944–45). Since 1952, they have trained in Florida.

September 5, 1906 Battling for the pennant, the Highlanders sweep their fifth straight doubleheader and move into first place; however, they end the season three games behind the Chicago White Sox, a weak-hitting team with a superb pitching staff.

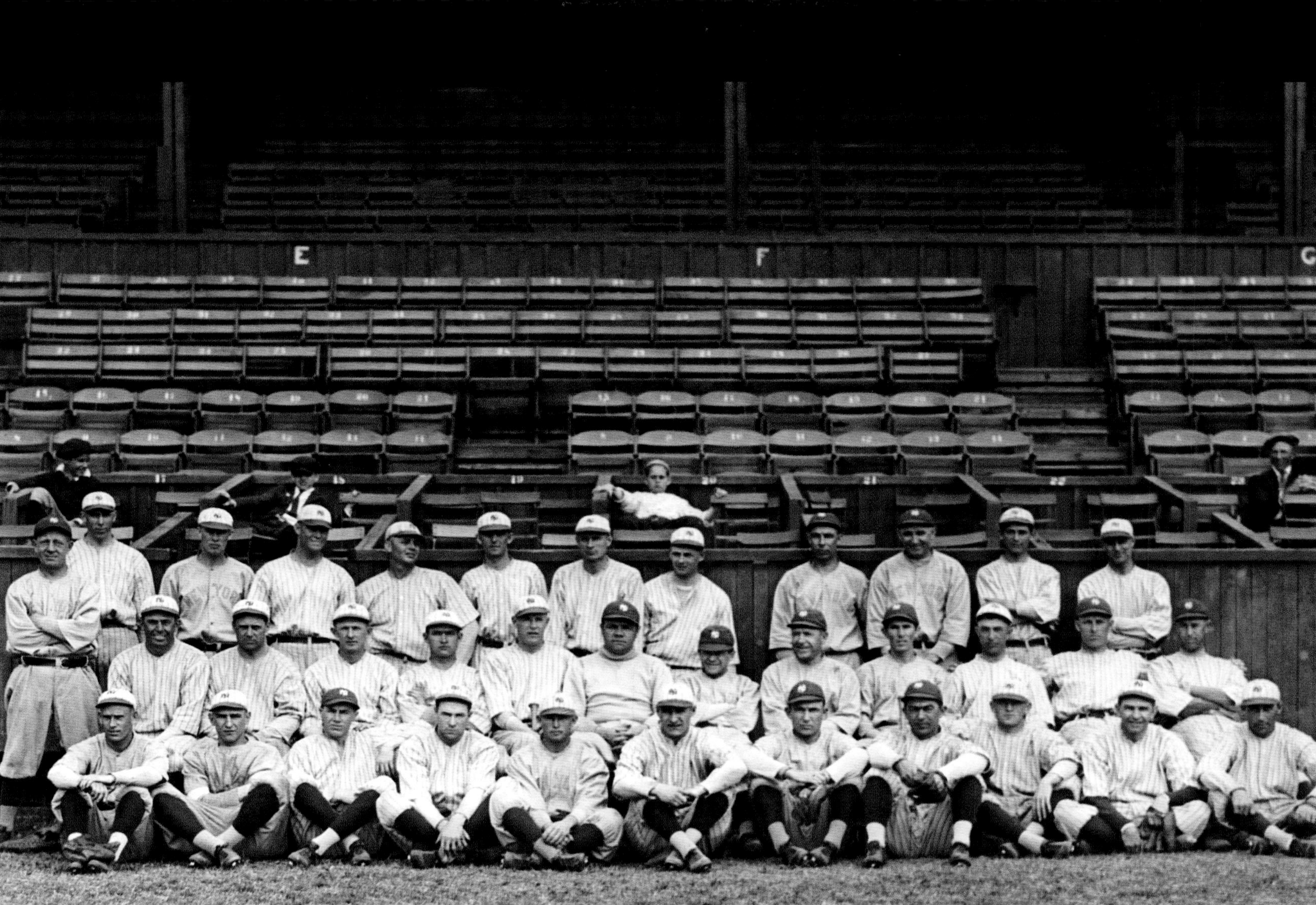
E
F
G

January

14

THE MIGHTY MITE

Yankees manager Miller Huggins handles a camera, about the 1920s. As a second baseman with the Cincinnati Reds and St. Louis Cardinals, Huggins had a knack for getting on base. He joined the Yankees as manager for the 1918 season and presided over one of the most talented teams in baseball history, winning six American League pennants (1921–23 and 1926–28) and three World Series (1923, 1927, and 1928). Not that his players made it easy. Standing just five-foot-six and known as "the Mighty Mite," Huggins had the unenviable task of disciplining Babe Ruth and his band of carousing teammates. But Hug had the temerity to do it. With a reputation for being tough but fair, Huggins earned the respect of most players. And he made them winners. He was inducted into the Hall of Fame in 1964.

June 28, 1907 A young Highlanders catcher, who ends up batting .182 for the season, allows the Washington Senators to steal a league-record thirteen bases off him in a single game; the hapless utility player, who exemplifies the team's woeful fifth-place season, is Branch Rickey, who decades later achieves far greater success integrating baseball.

January

15

LARGER THAN LIFE

Babe Ruth appears on the field with young fans, about 1921. Often described as a child in a man's body, Ruth usually seemed comfortable around kids, and they in turn worshipped him. Ruth's enormous popularity in the Roaring Twenties helped rescue baseball from the malaise of the Black Sox scandal, in which Chicago players conspired to fix the 1919 World Series. Yankees pitcher Waite Hoyt observed: "Babe Ruth found baseball lying in the gutter as a result of the Chicago White Sox World Series scandal in 1919. He reached down with his bat and lifted it to the status of America's national pastime."—baseball-almanac.com

June 24, 1908 The Highlanders' first manager, Clark Griffith, is released after a 24–32 start; under interim manager and star shortstop Kid Elberfeld, the team slumps to 27–71 for the rest of the season and finishes in last place with a team record 103 losses.

January

16

THE CATHEDRAL THAT RUTH BUILT

Barely hinting at the traffic jams of seasons to come, cars line up for the season opener between the Yankees and the Boston Red Sox, April 18, 1923—the first game played at Yankee Stadium. Made possible largely by Babe Ruth's enormous drawing power, the stadium was built in less than a year for $2.5 million. The original configuration seated 58,000, about twice the capacity of a typical ballpark of the period, and Opening Day's standing-room-only crowd was believed to be the largest to attend a baseball game to that date. Most would leave happy, as the Yankees won 4–1.

September 23, 1910 George Stallings, the team's third manager, resigns near the end of a turbulent second season at the helm, though he brings the team up from the basement to a distant second place during the season, following a fifth-place finish in 1909. His nemesis, the popular but ethically questionable Hal Chase, takes over through 1911 (a .500 season with a sixth-place finish) and is generally considered the team's first captain until 1912.

YANKEE STADIUM

January

17

IF YOU BUILD IT, THEY WILL COME

Fans line up at the Yankee Stadium ticket booths, April 19, 1923; grandstand seats were going for $1.10 (a healthy annual salary in 1923 was about $2,000). The Yankees' home attendance at the Polo Grounds had doubled to more than a million fans with the acquisition of Babe Ruth for the 1920 season, and the team continued to lead the league in attendance in 1923. Winning the pennant three straight years didn't hurt, and this year the Yankees would finally beat their rivals across the river, the Giants, for their first World Series title.

April 14, 1911 The Polo Grounds burns down, and the Highlanders, by now commonly but still informally known as the Yankees, allow the New York Giants to share Hilltop Park.

GRAND STAND
GRAND STAND
GRAND STAND
GRAND STAND $1.10
GRAND STAND $1.10
TO

January

18

THE BEGINNING OF A BEAUTIFUL RIVALRY

Boston Red Sox manager Frank Chance, left, poses with Yankees manager Miller Huggins for the first game at Yankee Stadium, April 18, 1923. The Yankees and the Red Sox would wage war here over the next eighty-six years, in one of professional sports' most intense rivalries. The Yankees launched their new stadium with four straight wins over Boston to open the 1923 season. In the ensuing decades, the Yankees would go 484–285 against the Sox at the stadium (through 2008), but Boston would enjoy moments of glory there, too.

Frank Chance managed the Yankees in 1913 and 1914, but he will forever be remembered as the first baseman in the Chicago Cubs' double play combination, Tinker-to-Evers-to-Chance. Like Huggins, he is in the Hall of Fame.

April 11, 1912 Pinstripes appear for the first time on the Highlanders' uniforms, and they return for good in 1915 after a two-year absence, eventually becoming the most famous uniform design in sports. From 1909 the team also experiments off and on with wearing the interlocking "NY"—originally designed by Tiffany & Company in 1877 in honor of a fallen police officer—until it becomes the permanent team logo and cap insignia in 1936. It is not until 1947 that the team adopts Henry "Lon" Keller's logo of an Uncle Sam hat hanging from the barrel of a baseball bat.

RED SOX

January

19

BIG SPENDERS

Yankees owners Jacob Ruppert, left, and Tillinghast L'Hommedieu Huston flank baseball Commissioner Judge Kenesaw Mountain Landis on Opening Day at Yankee Stadium, April 18, 1923. Huston, who made his fortune in engineering and Cuban construction projects, bought the Yankees with Ruppert for $460,000 in 1915. Mark Gallagher's *Yankee Encyclopedia* reports that Til paid his share by slapping 230 $1,000 bills on the table. Huston was instrumental in acquiring Babe Ruth from the Red Sox, and as a construction man he was responsible for the building of Yankee Stadium. But Huston had little use for manager Miller Huggins and often clashed with co-owner Ruppert. By the time this photo was taken, he was about to sell his half of the team to Ruppert for $1.5 million.

April 20, 1912 The Highlanders help the Red Sox open Fenway Park, losing to the Boston team 7–6. The next day back at Hilltop Park, the New York Giants wallop the Highlanders 11–2 in a game to benefit the survivors of the sinking of the *Titanic* one week earlier.

January

WELCOME TO MY HOUSE

Babe Ruth, left, leads the Yankees onto the field for their first game at Yankee Stadium, April 18, 1923. Appropriately, the Bambino christened the stadium with its first home run as the Yankees beat the Red Sox 4–1. It's no secret that Yankee Stadium's dimensions suited Ruth's left-handed power. As generations of lefties would do after him, the Babe took full advantage of the short right field power alley and foul line. The right field foul pole stood just 295 feet from home plate. The left field pole was even shorter at 281 feet, but the bulging expanse of left-center field earned its nickname as "Death Valley."

May 15, 1912 In one of the low points in baseball history, Tigers star Ty Cobb goes into the stands at Hilltop Park to pummel a belligerent fan, leading to a fine and temporary suspension for Cobb and tighter security at ball games.

January

21

CURSES

Harry Frazee and Frank Chance, owner and manager respectively of the Boston Red Sox, huddle at Yankee Stadium in 1923. Frazee famously sold Babe Ruth to the Yankees after the 1919 season for more than $100,000—even then the Yankees had deep pockets. Legend has it that Frazee used the money to finance one of his theatrical productions, which eventually became the musical *No, No, Nanette*. However, he justified the sale to the *Boston Globe*: "I think [the Yankees] are taking a gamble. With this money the Boston club can now go into the market and buy other players and have a stronger and better team in all respects than we would have had if Ruth had remained with us."

July 25, 1912 Highlanders outfielder Bert Daniels, playing at home against the Chicago White Sox, becomes the first player in the franchise's history to hit for the cycle—a single, double, triple, and home run.

January

22

HE'D BURY YOU

The Boston Red Sox, apparently not content with selling Babe Ruth to the Yankees, shipped right-handed pitcher Waite Hoyt to the Yankees one year later. The future Hall of Famer quickly became one of the most consistent winners of the 1920s Yankees dynasty, spending nearly ten years in pinstripes. He led the legendary 1927 team with a 22–7 record. A Brooklyn native, Hoyt was an atypical ballplayer: He enjoyed painting and writing, sang professionally, and occasionally worked as a mortician. He became a close friend of teammate Babe Ruth, and after the Bambino's death, Hoyt proved an invaluable source on all things Ruthian.

October 5, 1912 The team beats the Senators, 8–6, in its last game at Hilltop Park, finishing a disastrous season in last place under manager Harry Wolverton—fifty-five games out of first!—with a 50–102 record and a team-high 386 errors.

January

23

HEAVY HITTER

Babe Ruth pops one up in practice at Yankee Stadium, 1922. A large man of large appetites, Ruth was never exactly svelte, but he was not always the overweight figure depicted later in his career. In 1922 he looked trim and athletic, but his fondness for hot dogs—and just about everything else—remains an enduring part of his legacy. Pitcher Waite Hoyt said of his good friend, "If you cut that big slob in half, most of the concessions in Yankee Stadium would come pouring out."

April 17, 1913 Under new manager and former Chicago Cubs star Frank Chance, the Highlanders—now officially renamed the New York Yankees—play their first home game at the rebuilt Polo Grounds, at Eighth Avenue between 155th and 158th streets, as tenants of the National League's New York Giants. The Yankees end up in seventh place and do not finish better than third until 1921.

January

24

THE FIRST OF MANY

Fans line up for bleacher seats for Game 1 of the 1923 World Series at Yankee Stadium, October 10, 1923. For the third straight year, the Yankees faced their intracity rivals, the Giants, in the World Series, but for the first time the Yankees would be playing home games in their own stadium. The Giants would win this game 5–4 as their center fielder, one Casey Stengel, hit the first-ever World Series home run at the stadium. Attendance for this Wednesday afternoon game was 55,307—not shabby but, curiously, not a sellout.

The stadium's original bleachers were built of wood, later replaced by concrete.

1914 In his sophomore season, shortstop Roger Peckinpaugh becomes the Yankees captain and even replaces Frank Chance as manager for the last seventeen games; he remains captain until he is traded away after the 1921 season.

BLEACHER ENTRANCE
BLEACHER ENTRANCE
BLEACHER ENTRANCE
BLEACHER ENTRANCE
EXIT

January

THIRD TIME'S A CHARM

Babe Ruth slides safely into third on Bob Meusel's single in the second inning of Game 5 of the World Series against the Giants at Yankee Stadium, October 14, 1923. The Yankees banged out fourteen hits—scoring four runs in the second—in defeating their crosstown rivals 8–1. Joe Bush pitched a complete game three-hitter for the Yanks; all three Giants hits were by Irish Meusel, Bob's brother. After losing the World Series to the Giants the previous two years, the Yankees finally broke through in 1923 for their first world championship, winning four games to two. The Babe contributed three home runs (two in Game 2) while batting .368 for the Series.

August 3, 1914 Catcher Les Nunamaker provides the only highlight of a sixth-place season: He throws out three runners trying to steal in the same inning—still a major league record.

| 1890s | 1900s (**1910s**) 1920s | 1930s | 1940s | 1950s | 1960s | 1970s | 1980s | 1990s | 2000s |

January

THE IRON HORSE

Playing in his first full season, Yankees first baseman Lou Gehrig tries to tag Washington Senators base runner Goose Goslin during a 1925 game at Griffith Stadium. The Yankees had an entirely forgettable season in 1925, but there was a bright spot. On June 1, Gehrig pinch-hit for shortstop Pee Wee Wanninger. No one at that game could have known they were witnessing history. Gehrig would not sit out a game until 1939, a stretch of 2,130 consecutive games over fourteen seasons. That record, once thought unbreakable, stood until the Baltimore Orioles' Cal Ripken Jr. broke it in 1995.

January 11, 1915 Colonels Jacob Ruppert and Tillinghast L'Hommedieu Huston purchase the Yankees for $460,000. They hire Wild Bill Donovan to manage for what turns out to be three mediocre seasons, with no better than a fourth-place finish.

January

27

THE WAITER

Center fielder Earle Combs warms up at Yankee Stadium before a game against the Red Sox, September 9, 1926. Modest and unassuming, Combs quietly posted Hall of Fame numbers while leading off the Yankees' fearsome Murderers' Row lineup during the glory years of the late 1920s. The Kentucky Colonel specialized in hitting triples to the outfield gaps, and he was an outstanding contact hitter. Some consider him one of the best leadoff hitters ever. His 231 hits in 1927 stood as the Yankees' season record until Don Mattingly broke it in 1986. When Combs came to the Bronx in 1924, manager Miller Huggins explained his strategy: "We've got a couple of guys named Babe Ruth and Bob Meusel who hit the ball a long way. You get on base and wait for them to knock you in."—Glenn Liebman, *Yankee Shorts*

April 24, 1917 George Mogridge pitches the first Yankees no-hitter, a 2–1 win over Boston at Fenway Park.

January

28

THREE DEEP

With the Yankees down two games to one to the St. Louis Cardinals in the World Series, Babe Ruth responds with a home run to deep center field in Game 4 at Sportsman's Park, October 6, 1926. The Bambino went 3 for 3 on the day, becoming the first person to hit three home runs in a World Series game, as the Yankees won 10–5. The Cards, however, recovered to win the Series 4–3. Improbably, the Babe also hit three homers in Game 4 of the 1928 World Series, also against the Cardinals in Sportsman's Park! Only one other player since has hit three homers in a single game of the Fall Classic. But that would have to wait until 1977.

October 26, 1917 Miller Huggins signs a contract and becomes the Yankees' first great manager, leading the team until late 1929 and finishing with a 1,067–719 record in twelve seasons, including six pennants and three world championships. Huggins will be voted into the Hall of Fame in 1964.

January

DREAMS OF DISTANT GAMES

At a time when there was no major league team west of the Mississippi River, men gather around a chalkboard at a Los Angeles railroad station to hear the play-by-play of Game 3 of the World Series between the Yankees and the St. Louis Cardinals, October 5, 1926. Updates from Sportsman's Park were sent by telegraph line to the terminal, where the plays were called and diagrammed by the man with headphones and a makeshift megaphone. Although about two dozen radio stations in the new NBC network carried play-by-play of the games, live radio broadcasts of the World Series did not become commonplace until the 1930s. The Yankees had just five hits this day, as the Cards won the game 4–0 on their way to the world championship.

January 3, 1920 The Yankees announce their purchase of Boston Red Sox slugger—and former outstanding pitcher—George Herman "Babe" Ruth, for about $125,000 and a $350,000 loan against the mortgage at Fenway Park.

NEW YORK
ST LOUIS
1926

January

CLASS OF THE FIELD

Yankees left-handed pitching ace Herb Pennock poses in September 1927, about a week before the World Series. Pennock was yet another acquisition from Boston that turned to gold; he and teammate Waite Hoyt anchored the Yankees rotation in the mid- to late 1920s. From 1923 to 1928, Pennock never had fewer than sixteen wins in a season. But his Hall of Fame statistics don't describe the style and finesse with which he pitched. He was a thinking man's pitcher, studying and exploiting the weaknesses of each batter. Ironically, the refined and gentlemanly Pennock became a good friend of Babe Ruth, his polar opposite. And like teammate Hoyt, Pennock had diverse interests outside baseball. Pennock came from the horse country west of Philadelphia, where he raised and hunted foxes, earning the nickname "the Knight [or Squire] of Kennett Square."

May 1, 1920 Babe Ruth hits his first home run as a Yankee clear out of the Polo Grounds in a 6–0 win against his former team. Ruth finishes the season batting .376 with fifty-four home runs—more than any other American League *team*, and breaking his previous major league record of twenty-nine—and a league-leading 137 RBIs.

January

31

FLIRTING WITH HISTORY

More than 60,000 fans jam Yankee Stadium for Game 3 of the 1927 World Series between the Yankees and the Pittsburgh Pirates, October 7, 1927. New York left-hander Herb Pennock took a perfect game into the eighth inning, until Pirates third baseman Pie Traynor singled with one out. Pennock finished the game giving up just three hits, as the Yankees won 8–1. They went on to sweep the overmatched Pirates in four games for their second world championship. In his career, Pennock went 5–0 in World Series starts, all with the Yankees.

July 6, 1920 In the fifth inning of an away game against the Washington Senators, the Yankees get seven hits, including a three-run homer, and score a team record fourteen runs, thanks mainly to walks and numerous errors.

February

1

BEST EVER?

The 1927 Yankees, often mentioned in the same breath with "one of the best teams of all time." Lou Gehrig and Babe Ruth are, respectively, first and third from left in the back row. Manager Miller Huggins is at center, middle row. The batting order, better known as Murderers' Row, led nearly every offensive category in the league. Some of the 1927 numbers:

.714—winning percentage (110–44)
19—games ahead of the second-place Philadelphia Athletics
.327—batting average of the first eight hitters in the regular starting lineup
60—home runs by Babe Ruth
175—RBIs by Lou Gehrig
0—games lost in the World Series

August 16, 1920 Yankees ace Carl Mays (26–11 in 1920, 27–9 in 1921) beans Ray Chapman of the Cleveland Indians with a curveball, and Chapman dies the next day—the only fatality resulting from major league play.

February

2

BARNSTORMIN' BUDDIES

Just a few days after sweeping the Pittsburgh Pirates in the World Series, Babe Ruth and Lou Gehrig pose at an exhibition game during a postseason barnstorming tour, October 1927. A furious Commissioner Judge Kenesaw Mountain Landis had suspended Ruth for the first six weeks of the 1922 season for barnstorming in the previous autumn; the practice was outlawed by baseball, largely to preserve the public's interest in the World Series. Landis and the owners feared that players on World Series teams would line their pockets by "restaging" the Series in the off-season. But the ban was subsequently lifted, with some restrictions, freeing the Babe and Lou to tour the country, playing in front of many fans who would never see a major league game. The "Bustin' Babes" and the "Larrupin' Lou's" were the names of their respective barnstorming teams.

September 29, 1920 Having steadily improved under Miller Huggins to a best-ever 95–59 record and a very respectable third-place finish, the Yankees become the first team to draw one million fans. By the end of the season, 1,289,422 fans have attended Yankees games at the Polo Grounds, more than double the team's 1919 record.

BB
BUSTIN
BABES
LL
ARRUPIN'
LOU'S

February

LEANING A LITTLE TO THE LEFT

Although not usually noted for their political interests, the 1928 Yankees line up in support of Democratic presidential nominee Al Smith, the governor of New York, in his campaign against Republican Herbert Hoover. From left are backup catcher Benny Bengough, pitcher Waite Hoyt, first baseman Lou Gehrig, second baseman Tony Lazzeri, third baseman Joe Dugan, shortstop Mark Koenig, and outfielders Bob Meusel, Earle Combs, and Babe Ruth, along with an unidentified team member. These heavy hitters couldn't carry the vote for Smith, however; he even lost New York in Hoover's landslide November victory.

October 29, 1920 Ed Barrow becomes the Yankees' general manager, remaining with the team until 1947. Barrow eventually becomes club president and, finally, chairman of the board. He is a key figure in building the great Yankees clubs of the 1920s to 1940s.

O R A L S M I T H
YANKEES

February

THE YANKEE SKIPPER

Yankees manager Miller Huggins talks with sluggers Babe Ruth, left, and Lou Gehrig at the batting cage during spring training in Florida in the late 1920s. No manager has ever enjoyed two more potent offensive weapons in his lineup. Nevertheless, Huggins bristled at the Babe's flagrant excesses, and despite Hug's slight stature, he could stand up to the slugger. During the miserable 1925 season, Huggins suspended the defiant Ruth for nine days and fined him $5,000. Babe got the point. He later cried when Huggins died of an acute infection at age fifty in 1929. Huggins was the first person honored with a monument in Yankee Stadium's center field, the plaque calling him "a splendid character who made priceless contributions to baseball and on this field brought glory to the New York club of the American League."

May 7, 1921 Outfielder Bob Meusel, a slugger with a great arm for the Yankees through the 1920s, hits for the cycle in a game against the Senators in Washington. He will do it twice more: on July 3, 1922, at Philadelphia and July 26, 1928, at Detroit—the only Yankee to achieve this feat three times.

February

A LEAGUE OF HER OWN

Teammates Lou Gehrig, left, and Babe Ruth study the form of seventeen-year-old Chattanooga Lookouts minor league pitcher Jackie Mitchell, one of the first women to play professional baseball, as the Yankees visited Chattanooga for an exhibition game, April 2, 1931. With a sharp breaking ball, Mitchell thrilled the local fans by striking out both Ruth and Gehrig, back-to-back, in the first inning, a feat some major league pitchers could envy. Judge Kenesaw Mountain Landis, the baseball commissioner, voided Mitchell's contract shortly after the exhibition, saying baseball was "too strenuous" for women.

October 2, 1921 The Yankees clinch their first American League pennant, just before finishing the season with a 98–55 record. Their aces are Carl Mays, Waite Hoyt, and Bob Shawkey; Babe Ruth (.378, a record fifty-nine homers, and 171 RBIs) is supported by an excellent offensive and defensive club.

GANG

February

SULTAN OF SWEAT

Claire Hodgson Ruth, the second wife of Yankees slugger Babe Ruth, spars with Artie McGovern at McGovern's Gymnasium in New York, January 19, 1932. Babe Ruth had turned to McGovern after the dismal 1925 season. Gluttonous, out of shape, and in failing health, Ruth appeared to be nearing the end of his career, but McGovern imposed a rigorous training and diet regimen that restored Ruth's health. Some of the Babe's best years followed, including 107 home runs over the next two seasons. McGovern built a clientele of athletes and celebrities at his Madison Avenue gym.

October 5, 1921 The Yankees make their first World Series appearance, against the Giants, and Carl Mays pitches a 3–0 shutout for the Yankees' first Series win. Days later, however, Babe Ruth is injured in Game 5 of the best-of-nine series, and the Giants take three in a row to win in eight games. Every game takes place at the Polo Grounds, so it does not count as a Subway Series.

February

7

SPRING IN HIS SWING

With newsreel cameramen in the background, Lou Gehrig smiles as he swings through a pitch during spring training at St. Petersburg, Florida, March 2, 1932. Despite batting behind Babe Ruth—who often cleared the bases with a single swing—Gehrig was one of the most prolific RBI men in baseball history, with thirteen consecutive seasons of more than 100 RBIs. In 1932 he drove in 151 runs, giving him a total of 509 RBIs in 1930–32, the most ever in three straight seasons. Gehrig's 184 RBIs in 1931 is still the single season record for a left-hander.

May 5, 1922 After outdrawing the Giants in 1920 and being told to leave the Polo Grounds by 1923, the Yankees break ground and begin construction of their own home. Located just across the Harlem River from the Polo Grounds, between 157th and 161st streets in the Bronx, Yankee Stadium is built in less than a year for about $2.5 million.

February

GIVING 'EM THE BUM'S RUSH

Did he, or didn't he? Babe Ruth is congratulated by Lou Gehrig after the "called shot" home run against the Chicago Cubs in Game 3 of the World Series, October 1, 1932. Cubs catcher Gabby Hartnett and umpire Roy Van Graflan look on. The score was tied 4–4 in the fifth inning; the Cubs' bench was riding Ruth unmercifully; pitcher Charlie Root had a count of two balls and two strikes on the Bambino. What happened next is the stuff of legend. Ruth gestured—some say pointed—but whether at the center field seats, the pitcher, or the bellicose Cubs in the dugout, no one knows for sure. However, he surely drove Root's next pitch into the center field bleachers. As he circled the bases, the Babe laughed and reportedly said to himself, "You lucky, lucky bum." The Yankees went on to sweep the Series, their first world championship under manager Joe McCarthy.

May 20, 1922 Babe Ruth is named cocaptain of the Yankees, but only until May 25; the honor then belongs solely to Everett Scott through 1925.

4
NEW YORK

February

THIS KID LOOKS GOOD IN PINSTRIPES

Eighteen-year-old Joe DiMaggio crosses home plate for the San Francisco Seals of the Pacific Coast League in 1933, his first full year as a professional ballplayer. He hit in a league-record sixty-one consecutive games that season. DiMaggio was considered a blue chip prospect, but a 1934 knee injury off the field scared away most major league teams. The Yankees' scouts thought otherwise, and George Weiss, responsible for developing the talent already in the team's farm system, strongly recommended that the Yankees pay the Seals' asking price. To which general manager Ed Barrow is said to have replied, "This is exactly what you were hired not to do."—Paul Dickson, *Baseball's Greatest Quotations*

Barrow was overruled, and DiMaggio was in Yankees pinstripes for the 1936 season.

September 10, 1922 In their final home game at the Polo Grounds, and just before ending the season with an eighteen-game road trip, the Yankees take both games of a doubleheader against the Philadelphia A's. The overflow crowd is estimated at 40,000, and thousands more are turned away.

SEALS

February

10

NOTHING BUT THE BEST

Babe Ruth arrives in San Francisco from Honolulu aboard the new luxury liner *Lurline* with his wife, Claire Hodgson Ruth, left, and stepdaughter, Julia, November 9, 1933. Ruth had been separated but not divorced from his first wife, Helen Woodford, when she died in a 1929 fire. After Helen's death, Ruth married Claire, a model and occasional actress who had been his close companion for several years. He adopted her daughter, Julia, and Claire adopted Babe's daughter, Dorothy. Both Claire and Julia attended baseball games for years after Babe's death, often as honored guests. In 2008, seventy-five years after this photo was shot, Julia Ruth Stevens threw out the ceremonial first pitch at the last game ever played in the House That Ruth Built.

September 30, 1922 The Yankees clinch their second straight pennant with a 3–1 win over the Red Sox—fitting, since the Yankees' top pitchers and several other players are former Red Sox. But in the World Series, back to a best-of-seven format after a nine-game experiment for three years, the Giants win again, this time in five games, including a tie called—prematurely—on account of darkness.

February

11

YES, THERE WAS A NUMBER 3 BEFORE DALE EARNHARDT

The Bambino. The Sultan of Swat. The Babe. Nearing the end of his Yankees career, Babe Ruth poses while celebrating his thirty-ninth birthday at home in New York, February 1934. Usually cited as the greatest baseball player ever, his prodigious achievements on the field and his outsize persona everywhere else made him a transcendent figure, the first true American sports superstar and a cultural icon. Teammate Joe Dugan said, "When you figure the things he did and the way he lived and the way he played, you got to figure he was more than animal even. There never was anyone like him. He was a god."—Glenn Liebman, *Yankee Shorts*

April 18, 1923 Yankee Stadium opens. Before a crowd of 74,217, Babe Ruth—in his second at bat, in the third inning—hits the first home run in the House That Ruth Built, and the Yankees defeat the Red Sox 4–1.

February

12

POWER FROM THE LEFT AND RIGHT SIDE

Babe Ruth poses with Jimmie Foxx of the Philadelphia Athletics before the season opener, April 17, 1934, at Shibe Park. Double X, as Foxx was known, was one of the few hitters who could challenge the Bambino homer for homer. Many call him the right-handed Babe Ruth. The comparison is apt: Foxx led the league in home runs four times and was a Triple Crown winner in 1933 and a three-time MVP. To date, only Alex Rodriguez of the Yankees has reached 500 home runs at a younger age than Foxx. Ironically, Foxx finished his career the way Ruth started his: pitching. He joined Ruth in the Hall of Fame in 1951.

May 21, 1923 Jacob Ruppert buys out co-owner Til Huston for $1.5 million.

NEW YORK

February

13

A HOBBLED IRON HORSE

Lou Gehrig is helped off the field in Detroit, July 13, 1934, with what was described as a lumbago attack, or what would now be more commonly known as back spasms. In the years since, many have speculated that this episode was one of the early symptoms of the disease that eventually felled the Iron Horse. In the next day's game, Gehrig was penciled into the lineup at shortstop. But after leading off the game with a single—preserving his consecutive game streak—he was quickly replaced by Red Rolfe before taking the field. Despite this setback, Gehrig had a Triple Crown season, batting .363 with forty-nine homers and 165 RBIs.

Any good news at this Friday the 13th game? Well, Babe Ruth hit his 700th home run as the Yankees won 4–2, improving their record to 48–28.

September 4, 1923 Facing the Athletics in Philadelphia, "Sad Sam" Jones (21–8 in 1923) throws the second no-hitter for the Yankees, a 2–0 win.

4

February

14

THE END OF THE GLORY DAYS

Babe Ruth slides safely past the tag of Detroit Tigers catcher Ray Hayworth at Yankee Stadium in mid-August 1934. That same month, the Babe announced what many already suspected: This would be his last season as a full-time player. With his salad days well and truly behind him, he had let it be known that he really wanted to manage; he would continue playing, but only if he could also manage. The Yankees, however, were understandably committed to manager Joe McCarthy. The following season would see the Babe back in Boston, this time with the floundering Braves of the National League. He showed flashes of his old form, but by mid-season he and the team parted ways, his glorious playing days finally at an end.

September 27, 1923 At Fenway Park, twenty-year-old Lou Gehrig, who signed with the Yankees for a $1,500 bonus in the spring, smacks his first of 493 home runs, in one of less than forty at bats in 1923–24.

February

15

HEAVY ON THE TERIYAKI

Babe Ruth receives a hero's welcome from fans in Tokyo, November 1934. Ruth—who had just finished the last of his fifteen seasons with the Yankees—was already well known in Japan, and thousands of people waving Japanese and American flags turned out to greet the Babe's motorcade. He led a contingent of major leaguers on an exhibition tour of the Far East, including seventeen games in Japan. Virtually everywhere he went in Japan, he met worshipful fans. Babe's daughter Julia, who accompanied her parents on the trip, told the *New York Times*'s Dave Anderson in 2000 that "Daddy didn't like the sushi, but he loved the teriyaki." A decade later, Japanese soldiers in the Pacific theater reportedly shouted, "To hell with Babe Ruth!" in combat with U.S. troops. That phrase in turn became the name of an improbable 1969 episode of *Hawaii Five-O* on CBS.

September 28, 1923 The Yankees set an AL record with thirty hits in a game, beating the Red Sox 24–4—including an eleven-run sixth inning.

February

16

MR. CONSISTENCY

Yankees catcher Bill Dickey chases down a foul tip for the photographer during spring training at St. Petersburg, Florida, March 20, 1935. Dickey set a major league record catching one hundred or more games in thirteen straight seasons, and he never played a game at another position. Known as both a slugger and an outstanding defensive catcher, Dickey once commented, "I loved to make a great defensive play; I'd rather do that than hit a home run." Fair enough, but his 1936 batting average of .362 set the record for catchers, a record Dickey now shares with Mike Piazza. He averaged .313 over his seventeen-year career, all with the Yankees. In 1954 he was elected into the Hall of Fame.

October 6, 1923 Pitcher Herb Pennock, acquired from the Red Sox in January, finishes the first of his six excellent seasons with the Yankees, compiling a 19-6 record before going on to win the second and sixth games of the World Series—to be followed by three other Series wins in his career, with no losses. Pennock will join the Hall of Fame in 1948.

February

17

STICKING WITH A WINNER

Yankees owner Colonel Jacob Ruppert, left, congratulates Joe McCarthy at Yankee Stadium, July 16, 1935, following the announcement that McCarthy had been signed as manager of the Yankees—a job Babe Ruth wanted—for two more years. McCarthy soon rewarded Ruppert's confidence with four consecutive world championships, from 1936 to 1939. Marse Joe's seven world championships are a record shared only with another Yankees manager, Casey Stengel, and McCarthy was elected to the Hall of Fame in 1957. Infielder Babe Dahlgren memorably observed, "McCarthy, even drinking, was six innings ahead of everybody else." Pitching ace Lefty Gomez called him "Einstein in flannels."
—Glenn Liebman, *Yankee Shorts*

October 7, 1923 The Yankees finish in first place again, as Babe Ruth bats a career-high and team record .393 and leads the American League in home runs (forty-one) and several other categories. Fittingly, he becomes the first of thirteen Yankees to win the League Award, the precursor to the AL Most Valuable Player Award—and, in the 1920s, given to any player no more than once.

February

PROMISING ROOKIE

Lou Gehrig, left, gets something like a smile from rookie sensation Joe DiMaggio during spring training in St. Petersburg, Florida, March 8, 1936. DiMaggio, purchased from the San Francisco Seals, had earned a reputation for being shy and reserved since joining the Yankees in Florida. He then went on to have one of the outstanding rookie years ever, hitting .323 with twenty-nine home runs and 125 RBIs while playing the outfield with the unshakable poise that became his trademark. For the Yankees, this would also be the year they returned to World Series form, the first of nine world championships during DiMaggio's reign.

October 15, 1923 Facing the Giants for the third straight World Series, the Yankees win Game 6 at the Polo Grounds, 6–4, and finally capture their first world championship. Ironically, the Yankees' 5–4 loss in Game 1, the first World Series game played at Yankee Stadium, is the result of a ninth-inning inside-the-park home run by a Giants outfielder named Casey Stengel.

February

19

WORTH EVERY RED CENT

Yankees manager Joe McCarthy, left, and Charles "Red" Ruffing, his right-handed pitching ace who had recently ended a holdout over salary, pass the time at a spring training game against the Boston Bees (the 1936–40 name for the Boston—later Milwaukee and then Atlanta—Braves) in St. Petersburg, Florida, March 28, 1936. Ruffing was coming off a sixteen-win season in which he also batted .339—and even pinch-hit (something he did more than 200 times with the Yankees). That was good for a $1,000 raise, according to Ruffing, who was said to be getting $12,000 for the season. Ruffing was yet another acquisition from the Red Sox who flourished in the Bronx. In six seasons with Boston, he had never sniffed a winning record, but he developed into a consistent star with the Yankees. Ruffing credited much of his success and longevity as a pitcher to a regimen of running.

June 13, 1924 Hit by a pitch, Bob Meusel charges Tigers pitcher Bert Cole; both teams begin fighting, the Detroit fans then start a riot on the field, and the Yankees are declared the winners by forfeit. They cannot quite fight their way to a fourth straight pennant, though, finishing two games out of first. Babe Ruth, however, wins the AL batting title with a .378 average.

NY
NY
NEW YOR
W YORK

February

FIRST IN WAR, FIRST IN PEACE, THIRD IN THE AMERICAN LEAGUE

President Franklin D. Roosevelt prepares to throw the traditional first pitch in Washington, April 14, 1936, opening the baseball season with a game between the Senators and the Yankees at Griffith Stadium. From left: Roosevelt's son Elliott; Betsy Cushing Roosevelt, wife of FDR's eldest son, James; the president; Yankees manager Joe McCarthy; and Senators manager Bucky Harris (skipper of the Yankees for two years a decade later). The Senators sent their fans home happy with a 1–0 shutout of Lefty Gomez and the Yankees, but they finished the season in third place, twenty games behind the Yanks.

June 1, 1925 Pinch-hitting for Pee Wee Wanninger, Lou Gehrig begins his streak of 2,130 consecutive games played, eventually breaking the record of 1,307 games set by Yankees shortstop Everett Scott (the fading Scott had been replaced on May 6 by none other than Wanninger). On June 2, Gehrig fills in at first base when the veteran Wally Pipp suffers a headache, and the Iron Horse remains there until May 1939.

E PLURIBUS UNUM

February

21

BABE ON THE (BAND)WAGON

Babe Ruth and popular singer Kate Smith rehearse together in New York, September 1936, promoting her new Thursday evening *Bandwagon* series debuting September 17 on the WABC-Columbia radio network. Kate and the Babe were featured in a "comedy sketch of domestic life." Ruth made frequent appearances on radio, sometimes hosting his own shows. The current generation of Yankees fans knows Kate Smith for her vintage recording of Irving Berlin's "God Bless America," which has been played during the seventh-inning stretch at Yankee Stadium ever since the terrorist attacks of September 11, 2001. The Yankees are the only major league team to play the song at every home game. (When tenor Ronan Tynan is in the stadium, he sings a longer live version.)

August 9, 1925 Bobby Veach, who flies out, becomes the only player ever to pinch-hit for Babe Ruth. The Babe's lingering stomach problems and a collapsing pitching staff contribute to a disappointing 69–85 record and seventh-place finish.

February

22

CAPTURE THE FLAG

Manager Joe McCarthy, third from left, and players celebrate in the Cleveland dressing room, September 9, 1936, after sweeping a doubleheader against the Indians to clinch the American League pennant with almost three weeks left in the season. The Yankees went 102–51 to win the pennant by nineteen and a half games over the Detroit Tigers. The Yankees had last been to the World Series in 1932; this season would bring another world championship and mark the start of a Yankees dynasty. Beginning in 1936, the Yankees won six of the next eight World Series under McCarthy.

October 3, 1925 At the end of his first full season, Earle Combs, the Yankees' regular center fielder in 1925–33 and one of the best leadoff hitters ever, leads the team in batting (.342), hits (203), singles, doubles, triples, runs, and walks. With an average of .298 or better in each of these years (.356 in 1927), the best contact hitter of the Murderers' Row years will be voted into the Hall of Fame in 1970.

NEW YORK
NEW YORK
NEW YORK

February

23

PICK YOUR POISON

Yankees batters pose at Yankee Stadium, September 20, 1936. From left: catcher Bill Dickey, first baseman Lou Gehrig, center fielder Joe DiMaggio, and second baseman Tony Lazzeri. With just a week left in the regular season, the Yanks were already looking forward to meeting the Giants in the World Series. On paper, Lazzeri may have been the weakest link in this estimable group, but he drove in five runs (including a grand slam, only the second ever in Series history) in Game 2 of the Fall Classic and contributed three hits in the deciding Game 6 blowout. DiMaggio surprised almost no one by batting .346 for the Series in his rookie year.

October 10, 1926 After bouncing back to win their fourth AL pennant, the Yankees suffer an embarrassing World Series loss to the St. Louis Cardinals. In Game 7, they are still down 3–2 in the ninth inning thanks to Grover Cleveland Alexander's rally-killing strikeout of Tony Lazzeri with the bases loaded in the seventh; with two outs, Babe Ruth, the hero of Game 4 with three home runs and the first Yankee—joined only by Reggie Jackson in 1977—to achieve this feat in a World Series game, is walked and then thrown out trying to steal second.

February

24

WELL, MAYBE NOT THE CLEAN LIVING

Wrapping up a good, but not great, 13–7 season, Yankees pitcher Vernon "Lefty" Gomez warms up on the sidelines of Yankee Stadium, September 23, 1936, in anticipation of his World Series assignment starting nine days later. He went on to win Games 2 and 6 of the Series against the New York Giants, as the Yanks won four games to two; reliever Johnny Murphy got the save in Game 6, as he often did in games that Gomez started. The colorful and quotable Gomez, who was elected to the Hall of Fame in 1972, was an outstanding postseason pitcher. His 6–0 record in World Series starts is still the most wins without a loss in World Series history. Asked how he achieved his postseason success, he said, "Clean living, a fast outfield, and Johnny Murphy."—Paul Dickson, *Baseball's Greatest Quotations*

September 30, 1927 At home on the next-to-last day of the season, Babe Ruth breaks his own single season record with his sixtieth home run, off Tom Zachary of the Washington Senators, and the Yankees end up in first place by nineteen games, setting an AL regular season record (until 1954) of 110 wins to only 44 losses.

February

A RIVER RUNS THROUGH IT

Yankee Stadium, right, sits at the corner of 161st Street and River Avenue in the Bronx, while the Polo Grounds, home to the New York Giants—and the Yankees from 1913 to 1922—lies across the Harlem River in Manhattan. Shortly after this photo was shot in September, both stadiums hosted the 1936 World Series, won by the Yankees 4–2. The Polo Grounds ended up being demolished in 1964; public housing was built on the site.

The ribbon of asphalt running along the river past Yankee Stadium is the then-new Major Deegan Expressway, which has since become the route least likely to get you to the game on time. In 1999, Governor George Pataki proposed renaming the Deegan for Joe DiMaggio, but that honor went instead to the West Side Highway, now known to all New Yorkers as . . . the West Side Highway.

October 8, 1927 Arguably the best team in baseball history—thanks to the Murderers' Row lineup, featuring Babe Ruth, Lou Gehrig, Bob Meusel, Tony Lazzeri, and leadoff hitter Earle Combs, and a superb pitching staff led by Waite Hoyt, Herb Pennock, Urban Shocker, and rookie reliever Wilcy Moore—completes a four-game sweep of the Pittsburgh Pirates for the Yankees' second world championship.

February

ME AND MY GAL

Lou Gehrig, "the Iron Horse," and his wife, Eleanor, who were married in 1933, pose together before Game 1 of the World Series at the Polo Grounds, September 30, 1936. In his famous farewell speech on July 4, 1939, Lou said of Eleanor, "When you have a wife who has been a tower of strength and shown more courage than you dreamed existed, that's the finest I know." Eleanor later echoed his sentiment, saying, "I would not have traded two minutes of the joy and the grief with that man for two decades of anything with another." Eleanor never remarried, and she remained a friend of the Yankees, often attending games with Babe Ruth's widow, Claire. Eleanor Gehrig died on March 6, 1984.

October 11, 1927 Lou Gehrig enjoys his first big season, with forty-seven home runs, 175 RBIs, and a .373 batting average, and wins the AL MVP Award—as he will again in 1936.

YORK

February

27

JUST ONE MORE

Determined fans of Joe DiMaggio crowd their hero for autographs at Game 3 of the World Series at the Polo Grounds, October 8, 1937. The Yankees beat the Giants 5–1 to extend their lead in the Series to 3–0. The 1937 Series was a rematch of the 1936 Fall Classic between the two intracity rivals. DiMaggio, in his second year with the Yankees, had a respectable Series, batting .273 with one home run and four RBIs. That Game 5 homer helped the Yankees cruise to their second of four straight championships, four games to one.

April 20, 1928 The sixth season at Yankee Stadium begins after renovations that include expanding the left field stands to three decks.

NEW YORK

February

HE PUT A JOLT INTO THIS ONE

Joe DiMaggio hits a solo home run off Cliff Melton of the New York Giants in the third inning of Game 5 of the World Series at the Polo Grounds, October 10, 1937. The Yankees clinched the Series with this 4–2 win. In his World Series career, Joltin' Joe had eight home runs. Not surprisingly, the World Series record books are littered with Yankees' names. Of the six men who hit more Series homers than DiMaggio, only one is a non-Yankee: Duke Snider of the Dodgers.

September 9, 1928 After winning forty-nine games in 1925–27 despite severe coronary problems, which force him to retire after pitching only one game in early 1928, Urban Shocker dies of heart failure at age thirty-eight.

March

1

THE OLD MAN AND THE SEA

Giuseppe DiMaggio, a retired fisherman, and his celebrated baseball star son examine the day's catch on the stern of the crab fishing boat operated by Joe's brother Mike in San Francisco, October 28, 1937. Joe hated the smell of dead fish and had no interest in the family business. Baseball was his passion, and that turned out to be a pretty good career move. Ernest Hemingway later made DiMaggio the hero to Santiago, the ancient fisherman in *The Old Man and the Sea*: "Do you believe the great DiMaggio would stay with a fish as long as I will stay with this one? he thought. I am sure he would and more since he is young and strong. Also his father was a fisherman," wrote Papa.

October 9, 1928 The Yankees win 101 games, go to the World Series for the sixth time in the 1920s, and complete a four-game sweep of St. Louis—capped by Babe Ruth's three Game 4 home runs—to win their third world championship in six years. Games 1 and 4 are complete game victories for Waite Hoyt, the icing on his 23–7 season record and the culmination of his great Yankees career from 1921 to 1928, rewarded with entry into the Hall of Fame in 1969.

March

2

THE HEIR APPARENT

Babe Ruth, left, and Joe DiMaggio shake hands as they meet for the first time, January 24, 1938, at a New York sports banquet. Sportswriter Bill Corum, center, introduced the Babe to DiMaggio, who finished second in American League MVP voting to Detroit's Charlie Gehringer. DiMaggio's forty-six homers in 1937 would turn out to be his career high (though only twice in his thirteen seasons did he hit fewer than twenty), but there would be many high points in Joe D's career. With Ruth's retirement and Lou Gehrig's impending decline in health, DiMaggio was poised to become the Yankees' marquee player.

April 16, 1929 The Yankees use numbers as a permanent part of the team's uniform, the first franchise in baseball to do so.

March

SALARYMAN

Joe DiMaggio, left, starting his third season with the Yankees, shakes hands with team owner Colonel Jacob Ruppert in New York, April 25, 1938, as Yankees executive Ed Barrow beams for the press. For many months, DiMaggio had stubbornly held out for $40,000—more than Lou Gehrig was making. A month before the signing, while the rest of the club was at spring training, DiMaggio was still in San Francisco. At that time, he said, "I won't play ball for the Yanks until they meet my demands for more money." The furious Yankees brass held out too, forcing DiMaggio to accept $25,000 and making the signing a media event to leave no doubt who held the upper hand.

May 19, 1929 A sudden rainstorm at Yankee Stadium touches off a stampede for the exits by the standing-room-only crowd in the right field bleachers; two people are killed and sixty-two injured.

March

ROUGH START

In his first game since his salary holdout, Joe DiMaggio is badly shaken up after a collision with second baseman Joe Gordon while chasing down a fly ball at Washington's Griffith Field, April 30, 1938. Joe D was back in the lineup the following day, but he soon found himself the object of booing fans—even at Yankee Stadium—who resented his off-season salary demands. DiMaggio later said the fan reaction shocked and dismayed him. He regained the respect of Yankees fans, at least, by putting together another strong season, leading the team with a .324 batting average, thirty-two home runs, and 140 RBIs. And as Lou Gehrig began to show the effects of the as-yet-undiagnosed disease that would kill him, DiMaggio took over as cleanup hitter in the lineup.

August 11, 1929 Babe Ruth hits his 500th home run, off Cleveland's Willis Hudlin. The following March, a few months after the stock market crash, he will sign a two-year contract for a record $160,000, more than the salary of President Herbert Hoover—but as the Babe notes, "I had a better year than he did."

EW YORK
9
EW
YORK

March

IT'S NOT SKID ROW, BUT IT'S A LONG WAY FROM MURDERERS' ROW

Former Yankees star Bob Meusel works as a gate man at the newly opened Hollywood Park Race Track in Inglewood, California, June 18, 1938. Meusel had been a feared member of Murderers' Row, batting fifth behind Ruth and Gehrig—not a happy prospect for any pitcher. Playing right and then left field, he also had one of the deadliest right arms in baseball history, routinely cutting down runners who dared to test him. But talented as he was, Meusel had a private, carefree air about him, and manager Miller Huggins found him indifferent. Long Bob's contract with the 1927 world championship team paid him some $13,000—quite respectable for the time, but hardly the stuff of dreams. After leaving baseball in the early 1930s, he found himself scratching out a living.

September 25, 1929 Miller Huggins, the manager who led the Yankees to their first six American League pennants and three world championships, suddenly dies of blood poisoning at age fifty, eleven games before the Yankees finish the season in a distant second place.

March

AT THE TOP OF HIS GAME

Red Ruffing warms up at Wrigley Field before pitching the Yankees to a 3–1 complete game win over the Chicago Cubs in Game 1 of the World Series, October 5, 1938. Ruffing compiled a 231–124 record during fifteen seasons in pinstripes, anchoring the rotation with southpaw ace Lefty Gomez from 1930 to 1942. The right-hander had four straight seasons of at least twenty wins in each of the championship years, 1936–39. He also hit thirty-six home runs in his major league career (including five in 1936), fourth all-time among pitchers. Ruffing, who had 273 career wins, might well have been a 300-game winner had he not lost more than two full seasons to World War II. He was inducted into the Hall of Fame in 1967.

October 10, 1930 After a third-place finish managed by former star pitcher Bob Shawkey, the Yankees sign Joe McCarthy to a four-year contract as manager. Lasting just into his sixteenth season, McCarthy will lead the Yankees to an unmatched 1,460 wins, as well as eight World Series and seven world championships, including four straight in 1936–39.

NEW YORK

March

7

LITTLE FLOWER, BIG FAN

Yankees pitcher Lefty Gomez, left, and catcher Bill Dickey huddle with New York City Mayor Fiorello H. La Guardia, the "Little Flower," at Wrigley Field in Chicago for the World Series opener, October 5, 1938. Dickey led the New Yorkers to a 3–1 win with four hits on the day, tying a Series record, while Gomez would win Game 2 against Dizzy Dean the next day. The Yankees were on the fast track to a four-game sweep of the Cubs and their third straight championship. But this was Lou Gehrig's last World Series. He went 4 for 14 with no extra-base hits for the Series, his puzzling decline becoming ever more evident.

September 1, 1931 Lou Gehrig completes a six-game streak, homering in every game, and goes on to finish the Yankees' second-place season with forty-six home runs, tying for the league lead with Babe Ruth, the home run champion for ten years as a Yankee—including six in a row—between 1920 and 1931.

NEW YORK

March

NOW HE'S POOSHING 'EM DOWN

Tony Lazzeri, the spark-plug second baseman of the New York Yankees for twelve seasons (1926–37), shouts down his former teammates during the second game of the World Series as the Yankees met the Chicago Cubs at Wrigley Field, October 6, 1938. Lazzeri did not appear in this game, which the Yankees won 6–3, and he was not a factor in the World Series, as the Yanks swept in four games. Lazzeri was one of the first baseball stars of Italian descent, and he became a hero to Italian Americans. His nickname and trademark cry of "Poosh 'Em Up!" is a loose translation of "hit it out" in Italian. Lazzeri was one of the premier second basemen of his day, as well as a clutch hitter with a lot of power and a key member of five world championship teams. On May 24, 1936, he became the first person to hit two grand slams in one game—in addition to a solo shot and a two-run triple. He finished the day with eleven RBIs, still the American League single game record. Largely underrated, he was elected to the Hall of Fame in 1991.

May 30, 1932 The Yankees unveil a monument in memory of manager Miller Huggins in the deepest part of center field; this marks the beginning of Monument Park.

UBS

March

TWO STRONG CUPS OF JOE

Joe McCarthy, Yankees manager, turns cameraman for distinguished leading man Joe DiMaggio at their St. Petersburg, Florida, training site, March 7, 1939. Where some players chafed at Marse Joe's style, the disciplined DiMaggio and the authoritative manager were well suited to each other. Under McCarthy's tenure, DiMaggio became a center fielder—and a great one. McCarthy was widely recognized for his awareness of everything happening on the field and his attention to detail, qualities he instilled in his players. DiMaggio said, "Never a day went by when you didn't learn something from McCarthy." —BaseballLibrary.com.

June 3, 1932 In a feat still unmatched by any other Yankee, Lou Gehrig hits four home runs in a single game—and a fifth long fly ball comes close to going out—during a 20–13 rout of the Philadelphia Athletics at Shibe Park. In the same game, second baseman Tony Lazzeri hits for the cycle.

March

10

THE PRIDE OF THE YANKEES

New York Yankees first baseman Lou Gehrig watches from the dugout, May 2, 1939, as his teammates warm up for their game against the Tigers in Detroit. The Iron Horse told manager Joe McCarthy he was benching himself for the good of the team, bringing his 2,130-game streak to an end. He was hitting just .143—all singles—and having trouble making routine plays. His teammates worried about his health, but no one, not even McCarthy, would suggest that he sit down. The Briggs Stadium fans gave Gehrig a standing ovation when they learned he would not be in the lineup. The Yankees stormed to a 22–2 win. But the captain never played again.

October 1, 1932 In the fifth inning of Game 3 of the World Series, Babe Ruth answers the vicious heckling from the Chicago Cubs' dugout and fans at Wrigley Field by hitting his legendary "called shot" into the center field bleachers, just after he points to that spot—or maybe he just gestures to pitcher Charlie Root after the second strike. Eyewitnesses and even home movies have never settled the debate.

March

11

TOUGH ACT TO FOLLOW

Yankees first baseman Lou Gehrig puts his arm around the shoulder of teammate Ellsworth "Babe" Dahlgren in the Yankees dugout at Detroit's Briggs Stadium, May 2, 1939, as Gehrig sat out his first game in fourteen years. Dahlgren had the formidable task of replacing Gehrig at first base, and he responded with a home run. For the season, Dahlgren hit .235 with fifteen home runs and eighty-nine RBIs. Dahlgren stayed with the Yankees through the 1940 season, then spent the next six years mostly in the National League.

October 2, 1932 The Yankees complete a four-game sweep and take their fourth world championship, setting a record of twelve consecutive wins in World Series games (in 1927, 1928, and 1932).

March

12

LIVING LEGEND

During a doubleheader against the Washington Senators, Mayor Fiorello H. La Guardia, standing at right of the microphones, speaks for all New Yorkers in paying tribute to the Iron Horse as more than 60,000 people jam Yankee Stadium for Lou Gehrig Appreciation Day, July 4, 1939. The two teams line the infield, with former teammates from the Yankees' famous 1927 team—including Babe Ruth—in the foreground behind the mayor. Shortly after benching himself on May 2, Gehrig was diagnosed with the incurable disease amyotrophic lateral sclerosis, which would forever be known as "Lou Gehrig's disease."

When he retired, Gehrig became the first Yankee whose uniform number, 4, was retired as well, and because of the progressive nature of his illness, he was inducted into the Baseball Hall of Fame the same year, with the normal required waiting period waived.

July 6, 1933 In Chicago's Comiskey Park, Babe Ruth hits a two-run homer to win the first major league All-Star Game. Yankees pitcher Lefty Gomez gets the win.

March

13

CAPTAIN COURAGEOUS

Lou Gehrig wipes away tears during the standing-room-only tribute to him at Yankee Stadium, July 4, 1939. Speaking without notes, Gehrig made the dignified, heartfelt speech that still resonates, not just in sports, but in American culture:

"Fans, for the past two weeks you have been reading about the bad break I got. Yet today I consider myself the luckiest man on the face of this earth. . . .

"Look at these grand men. Which of you wouldn't consider it the highlight of his career just to associate with them for even one day? Sure, I'm lucky. . . .

"When the New York Giants, a team you would give your right arm to beat, and vice versa, sends you a gift—that's something. When everybody down to the groundskeepers and those boys in white coats remember you with trophies—that's something. . . . When you have a father and a mother who work all their lives so you can have an education and build your body—it's a blessing. When you have a wife who has been a tower of strength and shown more courage than you dreamed existed—that's the finest I know.

"So I close in saying that I may have had a tough break, but I have an awful lot to live for."

—Lou Gehrig, July 4, 1939

August 3, 1933 En route to the first of three straight seasons in second place, the Yankees are shut out for the first time since August 2, 1931, ending a 308-game streak in which they scored at least one run in every game.

March

14

REUNITED

Forever third and fourth in the all-time Yankees lineup, Babe Ruth, right, comforts Lou Gehrig, who was visibly moved after addressing the vast throng honoring him at Yankee Stadium, July 4, 1939. Seemingly with little in common aside from their awesome talent, Ruth and Gehrig had once been good friends, but they did not speak for years after a comment Gehrig's mother made about Babe's wife Claire. All was forgiven, however, when Ruth embraced his former teammate on Lou Gehrig Appreciation Day, a moment etched in Yankees history.

August 17, 1933 Lou Gehrig plays in his 1,308th straight game, breaking the major league record set by the Yankees' Everett Scott in 1923—but, of course, the Iron Horse keeps on going.

March

15

ALL TIED UP

Joe DiMaggio slides safely into the plate, scoring the tying run in the ninth inning of the fourth and final game of the World Series against the Cincinnati Reds at Crosley Field, October 8, 1939. DiMaggio scored on Joe Gordon's grounder to third when Ernie Lombardi, the Reds catcher, couldn't hold on to the throw, knotting the score at 4–4. The catcher's lot is not an easy one, and things were about to get worse for Lombardi. Fast-forward to the top of the tenth inning as . . . [*continued on next spread*]

October 1, 1933 Slugger Babe Ruth was also one of the best pitchers in baseball history, based on his record and winning percentage with the Red Sox. With the Yankees well out of contention by the last game, Ruth is allowed to return to the mound for his fifth and last time as a Yankee and his first start in three years; he pitches a twelve-hit complete game and beats Boston 6–5—and even contributes a home run.

NEW YORK

March

SEEING STARS

[*continued from previous spread*] . . . confusion reigns at home plate. Three Yankees—including Joe DiMaggio—ended up scoring on DiMaggio's single to right when right fielder Ival Goodman misplayed the ball as the first run came home. Then Yankees base runner Charlie Keller collided with catcher Ernie Lombardi, leaving Lombardi shaken up at home plate. Finally, DiMaggio scored despite the dazed Lombardi's last-ditch effort to make a tag. Here, DiMaggio, background, walks to the dugout after scoring on his own single, while on-deck batter Bill Dickey (8) gives the "safe" sign. As the dust settled, Lombardi, still on the ground, likely saw the World Series slipping from the Reds' grasp; their comeback attempt in the bottom of the inning fell short, and the Yankees swept the Series.

This was the Yankees' record-breaking fourth consecutive world championship. Since 1936, the Yankees were 16–3 in World Series play.

June 25, 1934 In a home game against Chicago, Lou Gehrig hits for the cycle. He will do it again on August 1, 1937, in a home game against the St. Louis Browns.

March

17

CIVIL SERVANT

Lou Gehrig, retired from baseball, works at his new job with the New York City Parole Commission in 1940. New York Mayor Fiorello H. La Guardia prevailed on the ailing star to work with troubled youths, and Gehrig accepted the position as a public service, declining far more lucrative offers. He took the work seriously, studying parole policy and visiting correctional facilities out of the media glare. Despite his deteriorating health, he worked until about a month before his death, sometimes assisted by his wife, Eleanor.

July 13, 1934 An aging Babe Ruth hits his 700th career home run in the second inning of a game against the Tigers in Detroit.

March

A MOMENT TO REMEMBER

The Yankees stand in silent tribute to Lou Gehrig, joined by Detroit spectators at Briggs Stadium, June 3, 1941. The retired Yankees captain died at his home in the Bronx the previous evening, sixteen years to the day after he replaced Wally Pipp at first base. He was seventeen days shy of his thirty-eighth birthday. Although the Iron Horse's consecutive game record was eventually eclipsed, his name still appears prominently in the record books. His twenty-three career grand slams are still the major league standard, and his four home runs in a single game is a record he shares with fourteen other players. He holds numerous records among first basemen, including the most RBIs in a career and in a single season. A member of six world championship teams, Gehrig is remembered at least as well for the enormous strength and quality of his character.

September 24, 1934 An aging Babe Ruth plays his final game at Yankee Stadium, walking in his only at bat; six days later, he goes 0 for 3 with another walk in his last appearance in any game in a Yankees uniform. During the off-season, he signs with the Boston Braves in a short-lived attempt to continue his career.

NEW YORK

March

19

HEART OF THE LINEUP

Babe Ruth pauses beside the casket of his former friend and Yankees teammate Lou Gehrig at Christ Episcopal Church in the Bronx, June 3, 1941. Gehrig's remains were cremated and the New York native was interred at Kensico Cemetery in Westchester, New York.

In his 1949 verse "Lineup for Yesterday," Ogden Nash wrote in *Sport* magazine:

G is for Gehrig,
The Pride of the Stadium;
His record pure gold,
His courage, pure radium.

September 30, 1934 Lou Gehrig finishes the season as the first of only two Yankees to win the Triple Crown, with a league-leading .363 average, forty-nine home runs, and 165 RBIs.

March

THE STREAK

Joe DiMaggio lines a single to left field in the seventh inning of the second game of a doubleheader against the Washington Senators at Griffith Stadium, June 29, 1941, to set the American League record by hitting safely in forty-two consecutive games. In the first game, DiMaggio had tied George Sisler's modern record of forty-one games, set in 1922. On July 2, DiMaggio broke Wee Willie Keeler's major league record by hitting a home run—his forty-fifth consecutive game with a hit. The Streak finally ended at fifty-six games, a record that has not been seriously challenged since. DiMaggio's streak bridged the All-Star break and the death of former teammate Lou Gehrig in June.

The Yankee Clipper hit .408 during the Streak, and the Yankees went 41–13 (plus two ties), launching them into first place on their way to another world championship.

November 21, 1934 The Yankees acquire Joe DiMaggio from the minor league San Francisco Seals for $50,000.

YORK

March

21

HIT PARADE

Yankees manager Joe McCarthy, center left, and teammates congratulate Joe DiMaggio after he broke the modern record by hitting safely in his forty-second consecutive game, June 29, 1941, at Washington's Griffith Stadium. Joe D's streak began with a single against the Chicago White Sox at Yankee Stadium on May 15. It ended fifty-six games later, on the evening of July 17, when Cleveland Indians third baseman Ken Keltner made two tough backhanded grabs to rob DiMaggio of hits.

More than thirty years later, DiMaggio ran into the cab driver who took him to the ballpark on the day the Streak was finally broken: "The guy said he was that cab driver. He apologized [for telling the ballplayer that he thought the Streak would end that day], and he was serious. I felt awful. He might have been spending his whole life thinking he had jinxed me, but I told him he hadn't. My number was up."—Joe DiMaggio, baseball-almanac.com

April 12, 1935 Lou Gehrig is named captain of the Yankees. That remains true even after his retirement, until his untimely death in 1941.

NEW YORK
NEW YORK
NEW YORK

March

22

TRIBUTE TO THE IRON HORSE

Two years to the day after Lou Gehrig's famous farewell speech, and a little more than a month after the Yankees hero's death, catcher Bill Dickey, left, and manager Joe McCarthy unveil the granite memorial to Lou Gehrig in center field of Yankee Stadium, July 4, 1941, with Gehrig's widow, Eleanor, front left. Dickey was one of Gehrig's closest friends on the Yankees. Looking on at far left is New York City Mayor Fiorello H. La Guardia, who ordered the city's flags flown at half-mast after Gehrig's death. The monument to the late Miller Huggins, Gehrig's first manager with the Yankees, stands at right.

January 29, 1936 Babe Ruth becomes one of the five charter members of the new Baseball Hall of Fame. He will attend the first induction ceremony in Cooperstown, New York, on June 12, 1939, along with Ty Cobb, Walter Johnson, and Honus Wagner (Christy Mathewson died in 1925), as well as the players elected from 1937–39, including the second Yankee elected, Wee Willie Keeler.

HENRY LOUIS GEHRIG
JUNE 19TH 1903 — JUNE 2ND 1941
A MAN, A GENTLEMAN
AND
A GREAT BALL PLAYER
WHOSE AMAZING RECORD
OF 2130 CONSECUTIVE GAMES
SHOULD STAND FOR ALL TIME
THIS MEMORIAL IS A TRIBUTE
FROM THE
YANKEE PLAYERS
TO THEIR BELOVED CAPTAIN AND TEAM MATE
JULY THE FOURTH
1941

March

23

FIVE-STAR LINEUP

Five Yankees players—four of them future Hall of Famers—line up for the All-Star Game in Detroit, July 8, 1941. From left are pitcher Red Ruffing (who didn't get into the game), second baseman Joe Gordon, catcher Bill Dickey, left fielder Charlie Keller, and center fielder Joe DiMaggio. DiMaggio and Gordon figured in the American League's dramatic comeback, both scoring in the bottom of the ninth; Boston's Ted Williams had the walk-off home run that gave the junior circuit a 7–5 win.

Of this group, only five-time All-Star Keller is not in the Hall of Fame. But with teammates DiMaggio and Tommy Henrich, he formed one of the strongest hitting outfields in baseball. In 1941, he joined the elite 30–20–10 club with thirty-three home runs, twenty-four doubles, and ten triples, his first of two such seasons.

May 3, 1936 Before a crowd that includes thousands of jubilant Italian Americans, twenty-one-year-old rookie Joe DiMaggio makes his debut at Yankee Stadium by hitting a triple and two singles against the St. Louis Browns.

March

24

SEEMS LIKE OLD-TIMERS

Three of the greatest hitters who ever played the game—from left, Ty Cobb of the Detroit Tigers, Babe Ruth of the Yankees, and Tris Speaker of the Cleveland Indians (and previously the Boston Red Sox)—don their old team uniforms as they participate in the thirty-second annual Amateur Day of the Cleveland Baseball Federation sandlot group in Cleveland, July 27, 1941. The trio acted as managers and coaches for the tournament. The Cleveland Baseball Federation, which is still active, was formed to give local men and boys the opportunity to play baseball on an organized amateur level. Amateur Day was just one of the association's fundraising efforts.

Speaker and Cobb did not hit with the home run power of Ruth—no one did—but they were more than formidable in their own right. Speaker batted .345 over a twenty-two-year career, and Cobb hit .366 over twenty-four seasons (topping .400 three times)!

May 24, 1936 Tony Lazzeri hits two grand slams, along with a solo shot and a triple, and sets a league record with eleven RBIs in one game.

March

MOST OFTEN, HE WON

Spud Chandler warms up at Yankee Stadium. The Georgia native spent eleven seasons with the Yankees, and he never had a losing season. Despite losing most of two seasons to military service, he posted a career record of 109–43 for a winning percentage of .717, still the major league record for an established pitcher. Spurgeon Ferdinand Chandler remains the only Yankees pitcher to win the AL MVP Award, something even Whitey Ford and Ron Guidry did not achieve. His 1.64 ERA for 1943, his MVP season, remains the Yankees' single season record. For a pitcher, Chandler was also a respectable hitter, with a .201 career average. On July 26, 1940, he hit a grand slam and a second home run, picking up six RBIs in all, in a 10–2 win against the Chicago White Sox at Comiskey Park.

June 24, 1936 In Chicago, Joe DiMaggio becomes the first Yankee to hit two home runs in one inning—a feat not achieved again by a Yankee until 1962; by August, he has taken over in center field, where he will be a fixture for thirteen seasons, with an interruption for military service.

NY
26

March

GREAT EXPECTATIONS

The year of his famous hitting streak and another Yankees championship, Joe DiMaggio and wife Dorothy Arnold admire their son, Joe DiMaggio Jr., at their New York home, December 18, 1941. DiMaggio and Arnold, an actress, married in 1939 after meeting on a film set; they split up in 1943 and later divorced. Joe Jr. was the senior DiMaggio's only child. The son grew up to attend Yale University before dropping out to join the Marines. He had a troubled adulthood marked by substance abuse and homelessness. Although he was estranged from his father for years, he served as a pallbearer when the elder DiMaggio died in 1999. Just five months later, Joe Jr. died of natural causes at fifty-seven.

September 9, 1936 Led by the slugging duo of Gehrig—the league MVP with forty-nine home runs, 152 RBIs, and a .354 average—and DiMaggio—with twenty-nine homers, setting a team record for a rookie, along with 125 RBIs and a .323 average—the Yankees clinch the pennant in record time before going on to win their fifth world championship in six games against the Giants.

March

27

CELLULOID HEROES

Yankees catcher Bill Dickey, left; his wife, the former Violet Arnold; and actor Gary Cooper pose together, February 20, 1942, to promote *The Pride of the Yankees*, the film biography of Lou Gehrig. Dickey played himself in the movie, as did Yankees teammates Babe Ruth, Bob Meusel, and Mark Koenig. Cooper starred as Gehrig and was nominated for an Academy Award as Best Actor, one of eleven nominations the film received, including Best Picture. The film takes some artistic liberties with Gehrig's iconic farewell speech, shortening it and moving the most famous line, "Today I consider myself the luckiest man on the face of the earth," from the beginning of the speech to the end. How did the right-handed Cooper bat convincingly as the left-handed Gehrig? He wore a uniform with a backward number 4 and ran to third base instead of first during the filming. Then the exposed film was printed in reverse, making Cooper appear to be left-handed.

September 27, 1936 Bill Dickey, the Yankees' regular catcher from 1929 to 1941 and one of the best of all time, sets a major league record for a catcher with his team-leading .362 batting average, accompanied by twenty-two home runs and 107 RBIs—the first of his four straight seasons topping .300, twenty home runs, and 100 RBIs. Dickey will be voted into the Hall of Fame in 1954.

YORK

March

LOOKING GOOD

George Stirnweiss, playing for the Newark Bears of the International League, poses in Sebring, Florida, March 14, 1942. The vintage caption for this photo reads: "3rd Baseman George Stirnweiss playing for Newark looks good. He comes from New York City and handles a fast ball." With a medical deferment from military service, Snuffy Stirnweiss was in a Yankees uniform the following season, becoming a premier second baseman during the war years. His 1945 average of .309 led the league in batting, and he had the speed to steal fifty-five bases in 1944. He was also a league leader in fielding. A two-time All-Star, he played on three Yankees championship teams.

In 1958, Stirnweiss, thirty-nine, died tragically when the train he was riding to New York plunged off an open drawbridge into New Jersey's Newark Bay, killing forty-eight people.

April 20, 1937 On Opening Day, fans see the results of a second round of renovations to Yankee Stadium, with the right field stands expanded to three decks, a new concrete structure replacing the wooden bleachers, and the distance to dead center field reduced from 475 feet to 461 feet.

March

YANKEE CLIPPER FOR SPLENDID SPLINTER?

Joe DiMaggio, right, and Boston Red Sox star Ted Williams pose at Fenway Park, August 18, 1942. On this day, the Sox came out on top, 8–7. DiMaggio and Williams were intense competitors. The previous year, Joe D's fifty-six-game hitting streak overshadowed—if that's possible—Williams's .406 season, the last time anyone has hit .400. DiMaggio won the 1941 MVP Award, though Williams had better numbers for the season. Publicly, at least, they were respectful of each other. The Yankee Clipper called Williams "absolutely the best hitter I ever saw," while Williams described DiMaggio as "the best all-around player I ever saw."

At one point, the Yankees and Red Sox reportedly flirted with swapping the two stars. It makes some sense: The right-handed DiMaggio probably would have shelled Fenway's Green Monster, and the lefty Williams could have thrived on Yankee Stadium's short porch in right field. Some say the trade was done over drinks one night, but it fell through in the harsh reality of morning.

July 9, 1937 Joe DiMaggio hits for the cycle in a home game against the Washington Senators. He will do it again on May 20, 1948, in an away game against the Chicago White Sox.

NEW YORK

March

SHAKING OFF THE RUST

Caught on 35mm movie film, Babe Ruth throws during a practice session at Yankee Stadium, August 21, 1942, two days before an exhibition at the stadium. The Bambino would be batting against former Washington Senators pitching star Walter Johnson in a benefit for the Army-Navy Relief Fund. Both men were well beyond their playing days, but the matchup of two living legends captivated fans between games of a Sunday doubleheader. Accounts of the exhibition vary, but Ruth managed at least one towering shot into the right field stands. That the ball hooked just foul did not bother him in the least; he obliged the crowd with another of his trademark home run trots around the bases, tipping his cap as he crossed the plate one more time.

October 10, 1937 After winning 102 games for the second season in a row, the Yankees need only five games to beat the Giants and win their second straight World Series, their first back-to-back world championships since 1927–28.

March

31

TO THE MANNER BORN

Joe DiMaggio poses, September 1942.

"DiMaggio was the closest thing to perfection I ever saw."—Tommy Henrich

"He knew he was Joe DiMaggio, and he knew what that meant to the country." —Lefty Gomez

"[DiMaggio] made the rest of them look like plumbers."—Casey Stengel

"I think there are some players who are born to play ball."—Joe DiMaggio

Glenn Liebman, *Yankee Shorts*, and Paul Dickson, *Baseball's Greatest Quotations*

May 30, 1938 A team record crowd of 81,841 attends Yankee Stadium for a sweep of the Red Sox in a doubleheader.

April

1

G.I. JOE DIMAGGIO

After the 1941 attack on Pearl Harbor, President Roosevelt advised Commissioner Judge Kenesaw Mountain Landis to continue baseball with the nation at war. "I honestly feel it would be best for the country to keep baseball going," FDR wrote. Here, the Yankees bat against the St. Louis Cardinals in Game 2 of the World Series at Sportsman's Park, October 1, 1942. At least 500 major leaguers served in World War II, including 28 now in the Hall of Fame (along with baseball executives, umpires, and a Negro Leagues star). Many players served during the prime of their already brief careers. Meanwhile, teams filled out their rosters with players ineligible for military service.

After losing the first game of the 1942 Series, the Cards reeled off four straight against Joe DiMaggio and the Yanks—the team's first World Series loss in sixteen years. The next three seasons found DiMaggio in uniform for Uncle Sam.

August 27, 1938 Monte Pearson pitches the third no-hitter for the Yankees, and the first at Yankee Stadium, in the second game of a doubleheader against Cleveland (a 13–0 blowout); in the opening game, Joe DiMaggio hits three triples in a row, the last one the game-winning hit. The Yankees' two wins are among twenty-eight in the month, setting a league record.

PERSONAL AUTO LOANS
FILL THE WAR CHEST
Giving is Fighting this Year!
GEM
SINGLEDGE
BLADES
BATTER
BALL STRIKE
OUT
UMPIRES
SOLD IN PARK
FOR "BIG LEAGUE"
COCKTAILS & HIGHBALLS!
Old Quaker
SPECIAL RESERVE
STRAIGHT WHISKEY
5 YEARS OLD

April

2

YOU'RE IN THE NAVY NOW

Yankees shortstop Phil Rizzuto is flanked by his Brooklyn Dodgers counterpart Pee Wee Reese, left, and Dodgers pitcher Hugh Casey as they study *The Bluejacket's Manual,* the bible of naval training, at the Navy base in Norfolk, Virginia, August 10, 1943. Rizzuto and Reese played on a Navy team that visited Hawaii, with Yankees catcher Bill Dickey managing. Dickey moved Rizzuto to third base and had Reese play shortstop, a move that puzzled Rizzuto but one he never questioned. Years later, Scooter savored the experience of those games played on the Kahului Fairgrounds, not least of all because the Navy team beat the Army team seven games out of eight. The center fielder for Army in those games? Joe DiMaggio.

October 9, 1938 After easily taking their third straight pennant with a 99–53 record, the Yankees complete a sweep of the Chicago Cubs to win the World Series again—one of three stretches of three or more consecutive world championships in team history. The winner of Games 1 and 4 is Red Ruffing, capping the first of his two straight 21–7 seasons and four in a row with at least twenty wins (1936–39); an excellent pitcher from 1930–42, he will be voted into the Hall of Fame in 1967.

THE BLUEJACKETS' MANUAL

April

SPUD SHUTS DOWN CARDS

Yankees manager Joe McCarthy, right, gives his ace pitcher, Spud Chandler, a pat on the head in the dressing room after Chandler hurled the Yankees to a 2–0 win over the St. Louis Cardinals in Game 5 of the World Series at Sportsman's Park, October 11, 1943. With the victory, the Yankees clinched the series, avenging their loss to the Cards the previous year. Chandler threw two complete game wins, opening and closing the Series. Known for his slider, Spurgeon Ferdinand Chandler played his entire major league career with the Yankees. This was his best year, going 20–4.

January 13, 1939 Longtime Yankees owner Jacob Ruppert dies at age seventy-one. Ed Barrow succeeds him as team president.

NEW YORK

April

4

GIVE OR TAKE A YEAR OR SO

Was there ever a photo op the Bambino turned down? Babe Ruth wears his "King of Swat" crown as he prepares to cut his birthday cake in celebration of his fifty-first birthday at his home in New York, February 7, 1945. Or was he fifty? Ruth always believed that he was born February 7, 1894, but when applying for a passport not long before his retirement, Ruth realized that his birth certificate listed his date of birth as February 6, 1895. That date is also subject to dispute. For his part, Babe continued to celebrate his birthday on February 7 for the rest of his life. The Babe Ruth Birthplace and Museum in Baltimore throws a birthday bash every year on February 6 in honor of its namesake. He was presented with the crown in 1921 after hitting a record-breaking fifty-nine home runs—a record he broke again, by one, six years later.

May 2, 1939 After opening the season hitting 4 for 28, Lou Gehrig walks the lineup card to home plate, and for the first time since 1925, he is not on it. Gehrig acknowledges what has become painfully obvious—his once magnificent skills are rapidly eroding. A trip to the Mayo Clinic will soon reveal the nature of his incurable illness. He never plays another major league game.

April

FROM CATCHER TO MANAGER IN UNDER SIX INNINGS

Bill Dickey, rookie manager of the Yankees, surveys the field after removing himself from the game as catcher in the sixth inning against the Boston Red Sox at Fenway Park, May 25, 1946. Dickey, having just returned from duty in World War II, had signed on with the Yankees to catch for the season, but one day before this game Joe McCarthy had resigned due to health reasons and disagreements with the new Yankees management. Dickey was quickly named as his replacement. Hailed as one of the best catchers ever, Dickey was instrumental in seven Yankees world championships from 1932 to 1943. But he resigned as manager before the 1946 season was over, as the Boston Red Sox ran away with the pennant. Dickey returned in 1949 as a first base coach and catching instructor, and he became a mentor to Yogi Berra. The Yankees later retired the number 8 in honor of both Dickey and Berra.

June 26, 1939 At Shibe Park in Philadelphia, the Yankees play their first night game, losing to the Athletics 3–2.

April

DOUBLE DAYS

Yankees shortstop Phil Rizzuto slides into home plate to score in the top of the fourth inning in the first game of a doubleheader against the Boston Red Sox at Fenway Park, August 18, 1946. Red Sox catcher Hal Wagner takes the late throw. The Yanks took the first game 5–0, then lost the second half of the twin bill 4–3. Those really were the days: In the space of five days, the Yankees played three doubleheaders (and a seventh game) against three different teams. Now, true doubleheaders—two games for the price of one—are practically extinct as clubs try to maximize their gate receipts. When doubleheaders do occur, usually as the result of a previous rainout, they are often of the day/night variety: The first game is played in the afternoon, and the second game in the evening, several hours later. Fans need a separate ticket for each game.

July 4, 1939 Yankee Stadium is the site of Lou Gehrig Appreciation Day. Gehrig's uniform number, 4, becomes the first to be retired in Major League Baseball, and the beloved Yankees slugger famously tells the 61,808 fans present and everyone listening to the radio that "today I consider myself the luckiest man on the face of the earth."

April

7

THE BIG PICTURE

Washington-based Associated Press (AP) photographer Bill Chaplis, center, shows Yankees center fielder Joe DiMaggio, left, and Cleveland Indians manager Lou Boudreau a telephoto lens camera before a spring training game at Clearwater, Florida, 1946. AP photographers started covering major league baseball in the 1920s, and by 1935 they were transmitting wire photos electronically to newspapers over a network of phone lines. The massive lens seen here was known as a "Big Bertha," and it is fitted to a large-format press camera. After shooting the spring training game, Chaplis would have gone to a makeshift darkroom—often a hotel room—where he developed and printed the photos. Then he would transmit the photos to the AP network, requiring about twelve minutes for each photo. In 1946, that passed for high tech.

July 11, 1939 Yankee Stadium hosts its first All-Star Game; Joe DiMaggio contributes a home run to the 3–1 American League win.

EVELAND

April

HEADED FOR HOME

Babe Ruth finally returns to his Riverside Drive apartment, accompanied by nurse Agnes Kavanaugh, February 15, 1947, after three months in New York's French Hospital. The Babe was reportedly touched by the fans and well-wishers who waited outside the hospital to send him home. Ruth had entered the hospital in November, bothered by eye pain and what was thought to be a toothache or sinus infection. He was diagnosed with a malignant tumor of the upper throat and sinus region, but he was never told he had cancer. He had lost some eighty pounds during this hospital stay. The Bambino was subsequently treated with radiation and an experimental chemotherapy drug, with some improvement, but the cancer persisted.

October 8, 1939 After coasting to a pennant for the fourth straight time, the Yankees—a hitting, pitching, and fielding powerhouse—once again need only four games, this time against the Cincinnati Reds, to win their fourth straight World Series, a feat matched, and exceeded, only in 1949–53.

April

SODA HERE! GET YER ICE-COLD SODA!

A Harry M. Stevens vendor sells 10-cent bottles of soda in the stands at Yankee Stadium, 1947. No game was complete without a bag of Bazzini peanuts, a hot dog, and a cold one. Then as now, vendors could loft a bag of peanuts across the aisles and up a few rows to waiting fans. Some vendors worked the aisles for decades, as much a part of the stadium experience as the players themselves. But with the Yankees now partners in their own hospitality company, those longtime vendors may find that the only way into the new Yankee Stadium is with a ticket. By the way, in 2008, a soda from a vendor set you back $4.75. Keep the change.

October 24, 1939 Joltin' Joe DiMaggio, with a league-leading .381, thirty home runs, and 126 RBIs, wins his first of three MVP Awards, the other two coming in 1941—the year of the Streak—and 1947; he will also win the AL batting title again in 1940.

LONGINES
See the
NEW GEM
10
CENTS

April

10

THE COOKIE GAME

Yankees pitcher Bill Bevens, left, who pitched a one-hitter and lost, 3–2, and center fielder Joe DiMaggio walk down the runway leading to the clubhouse at Ebbets Field after Game 4 of the World Series against the Brooklyn Dodgers, October 3, 1947. With two men on in the bottom of the ninth inning, thanks to walks, Bevens was one out away from pitching the first World Series no-hitter when Dodger pinch hitter Cookie Lavagetto lined a two-run walk-off double to right field. Brooklyn's improbable win evened the Series at 2–2. Lavagetto's dramatic double was his only hit in the Series and the last one of his career. Bevens would pitch two and two-thirds innings of scoreless relief early in the decisive Game 7 of the Series. This was his fourth and last year in the majors.

December 7, 1939 Lou Gehrig is voted into the Hall of Fame in special balloting, with the usual five-year waiting time after retirement waived.

NY
NEW YORK
NY
NEW YORK

April

11

CASEY AT THE BAT

Yankees catcher Yogi Berra faces off with umpire Ed Rommel during the seventh inning of Game 3 of the World Series at Ebbets Field, October 2, 1947. The Yankees claimed that Dodgers pitcher Hugh Casey, background, interfered as Berra tried to catch Casey's foul tip on a bunt attempt. Despite getting the first pinch-hit home run in World Series history, also in Game 3, Berra was having a frustrating Series: He went 3 for 19 at the plate with just two RBIs in this, his first of fourteen trips to the Fall Classic. Casey eventually struck out in this at bat, but the Dodgers won the game 9–8. They were looking to avenge their 1941 World Series loss to the Yankees, but the team from the Bronx went on to win this one in seven games, for an eleventh world championship. This World Series made history with Jackie Robinson's first Series appearance, and it was also the first to be televised.

July 19, 1940 In an otherwise off year for the Yankees, who end up in third place, catcher Buddy Rosar joins an elite club of fewer than a dozen Yankees when he hits for the cycle in a home game against Cleveland. Second baseman Joe Gordon accomplishes the same feat on September 8 in Boston.

B
Dodgers
NEW
9
12

April

12

THE HOLLYWOOD TREATMENT

Babe Ruth gives actor William Bendix some tips on batting form during filming of *The Babe Ruth Story*, May 4, 1948. It didn't help. As a teenager, Bendix was reportedly a Yankees batboy at the Polo Grounds, but despite a superficial resemblance to the Bambino, Bendix had none of Ruth's athleticism. Unfortunately, despite a superficial resemblance to the Bambino, Bendix had none of Ruth's athleticism. Add to that a cliché-ridden, overly melodramatic script, as well as a rushed production schedule to get the film into theaters while Ruth was still alive, and you get a finished product that is practically unwatchable and unintentionally hilarious. *The Pride of the Yankees II* it is not. Author Robert Creamer reported in his biography *Babe* that Ruth attended the premiere on July 26, but he left partway through the movie. There have since been other portrayals of the Babe on the big screen, some better than others, but arguably none have truly captured one of the most iconic figures in American culture.

May 15, 1941 During a 13–1 loss to Chicago at Yankee Stadium, Joe DiMaggio's single off Edgar Smith begins his fifty-six-game hitting streak. He ties and passes George Sisler's AL record of forty-one games in a doubleheader on June 29, then breaks Wee Willie Keeler's major league record of forty-four on July 2.

NY
ANKEES
HILLERICH & BRADSBY Co.
MADE IN U.S.A.
LOUISVILLE, KY.
TRADE MARK

April

13

THE ONCE AND FUTURE KING

Using a bat for support, Babe Ruth stands on the field for the last time as the crowd pays tribute to the ailing hero at ceremonies celebrating the twenty-fifth anniversary of Yankee Stadium, June 13, 1948. Sportswriter W. C. Heinz wrote, "He walked out into the cauldron of sound he must have known better than any other man." After the ceremony, he repaired to the locker room for a drink with friend and former teammate Joe Dugan. As recounted by biographer Robert Creamer, the Babe told Dugan, "Joe, I'm gone. I'm gone, Joe." Then they started crying. Two months later, August 16, 1948, the Bambino was dead.

June 2, 1941 Sixteen years to the day after becoming the Yankees' first baseman, Lou Gehrig dies at age thirty-seven of amyotrophic lateral sclerosis (ALS), which is now known as "Lou Gehrig's disease."

April

14

AMERICAN IDOL

Five young fans of Yankees star Joe DiMaggio invade center field for autographs during the second game of a doubleheader with the Chicago White Sox at Yankee Stadium, July 25, 1948. The game had to be held up in the second, fourth, fifth, and seventh innings as fans hounded their hero. Despite the distractions, the Yanks won 5–3 and 7–3 to go fifteen games over .500. In the line of Yankees succession—and just plain success—DiMaggio links the era of Ruth and Gehrig to the dynasty of Mantle and Berra.

July 17, 1941 Joe DiMaggio's hitting streak ends at fifty-six games, as he goes 0 for 3 against Cleveland—and after Indians third baseman Ken Keltner makes two great fielding plays to rob him of a hit. DiMaggio then goes on a sixteen-game streak, giving him one or more hits in seventy-two games out of seventy-three in a row.

457 FT.

April

15

YOU HAD TO KNOW HIM

As photographers and onlookers crowd the street, the casket containing the body of Babe Ruth, who died at New York's Memorial Hospital of complications due to cancer, is carried from the funeral parlor to a waiting hearse for the trip to Yankee Stadium, August 17, 1948. The Babe's body was to lie in state at the House That Ruth Built until the funeral at St. Patrick's Cathedral. Ruth's former teammates served as pallbearers. At one point, Joe Dugan said to teammate Waite Hoyt something like, "I'd give my right arm for a beer." Hoyt's widely quoted response: "So would the Babe."

September 4, 1941 The Yankees clinch the pennant earlier than any other team before. They finish with a 101–53 record, in first place by seventeen games.

ROAD TEST
PHOTOS
LEARN TO DRIVE
ERNEMAC PHOTOS
COMMERCIAL
PORTRAIT
CANDID
WEDDINGS
ARNEY STONE
597
BONDED MEMBER FTD
Muriel Rock
TOWN FLORIST
-WE- DELIVER
TO ALL PARTS OF THE WORLD

April

16

IF THAT LOCKER COULD TALK

Pete Sheehy, equipment man at Yankee Stadium, views the locker of Babe Ruth on August 17, 1948, the day after the Bambino's death. Sheehy started with the Yankees during the glory days of 1927, with the Babe at his peak; one of his early duties at the stadium was to take care of Ruth's locker. After the Babe's retirement, the dark red locker remained in a place of honor in the clubhouse. In 1949, the Yankees presented his locker and Lou Gehrig's to the Hall of Fame. Joe DiMaggio's locker can now be found there also. Metal locker tags bearing Ruth's name and the number 3 occasionally turn up at auction. One fetched more than $7,000.

October 5, 1941 At Ebbets Field in Game 4 of the World Series, the Brooklyn Dodgers lead 4–3 with two outs in the ninth when catcher Mickey Owen is unable to handle the third strike from pitcher Hugh Casey, the Yankees' Tommy Henrich reaches first, and the Yankees go on to score four runs and win the game. They win their ninth world championship the next day, ending the first of seven World Series between the two New York teams.

BABE RUTH
Nº 3

April

17

BEFITTING A LEGEND

Where once they cheered him, men, women, and children file past the body of Babe Ruth as it lies in state in the rotunda at Yankee Stadium, August 18, 1948. For the better part of two days, people from all walks of life stood in line for hours to pay their respects, with no fewer than 100,000 people passing through the stadium for a moment with their hero. Thousands more lined the funeral route and stood along Fifth Avenue outside St. Patrick's Cathedral. Ruth was buried in the Gate of Heaven Cemetery in Hawthorne, New York.

Teammate Waite Hoyt told Ruth's biographer Robert Creamer: "I am almost convinced that you will never learn the truth on Ruth . . . there was buried in Ruth humanitarianism beyond belief, an intelligence he was never given credit for, a childish desire to be over-virile, living up to credits given his home run power—and yet a need for intimate affection and respect, and a feverish desire to play baseball, perform, act and live a life he didn't and couldn't take time to understand."

October 5, 1942 Despite easily capturing the AL pennant, the Yankees are upset in five games by the young St. Louis Cardinals and lose a World Series for the first time since 1926.

Yankees
Yankees
Yankees

April

18

DOCTOR IN THE HOUSE

Yankees infielders pose on the dugout steps before a game with the Boston Red Sox at Yankee Stadium, September 25, 1948. From left: reserve third baseman Bobby Brown, shortstop Phil Rizzuto, second baseman Snuffy Stirnweiss, and right fielder (and later, first baseman) Tommy Henrich. Brown was primarily a third baseman, but he also played short and second base and even spent a few games in the outfield that season. While solid, if unspectacular, during the regular season, he excelled in the postseason, batting .439 in seventeen World Series games. While he was winning four world championships with the Yankees, he was also studying medicine; today he is known as Dr. Bobby Brown. After a successful career as a physician, he returned to baseball, becoming American League president from 1984 to 1994.

November 3, 1942 Second baseman Joe Gordon, who will finally be voted into the Hall of Fame by the Veterans Committee in December 2008, wins the MVP Award, with a .322 average, eighteen homers, and 103 RBIs.

April

19

THIS GUY'S GONNA MANAGE THE YANKEES?

Yankees manager Casey Stengel poses with a crystal ball at Yankee Stadium, February 17, 1949. Warren Spahn, who pitched for Stengel with the hapless 1942 Boston Braves and the '65 New York Mets, said he played for Stengel "before and after he was a genius." It's true that Stengel came to the Yankees in 1949 with little to recommend him. In his nine years managing in the National League, in 1934–36 and 1938–43 (he had also managed minor league teams since the mid-1920s), Stengel had had only one winning season, never finishing higher than fifth place. What a difference a season makes—that and a roster including DiMaggio, Berra, Reynolds, and Raschi. (And later, Mantle and Ford.) On Stengel's watch, the Yankees dominated the next decade, going to the World Series ten of the next twelve years and winning seven world championships. They didn't call him the Old Perfesser for nothing.

October 11, 1943 Although Joe DiMaggio, Red Ruffing, and others are in the military, the Yankees win their third straight AL pennant and get their revenge on the Cardinals in the World Series, defeating them in five games. Spud Chandler wins the first and last games, his Game 5 shutout stranding eleven Cardinals on the bases.

April

HOT STOVE LEAGUE

Newly hired Yankees manager Casey Stengel, standing behind the stove, gives his squad a pep talk in the team's clubhouse at St. Petersburg, Florida, at the start of the spring training season, March 1, 1949.

The "Hot Stove League" is a league in name only—it refers to all the baseball maneuvering during baseball's off-season, when rumors fly, teams meet to wheel and deal, free agents test the market, and trades are made—or not. In a scene that recalls a Norman Rockwell painting, fans may once have gathered around a hot stove to argue and speculate about the coming season, but now that's more likely to happen in front of a computer screen or on sports talk radio.

November 11, 1943 Pitcher Spud Chandler (20–4 with a team record 1.64 ERA) wins the MVP Award.

KELLER
SANFORD
BROWN 6
HOUK 32
BAUER 25
NEW YOR

April

21

THE BABE PLAYS CENTER FIELD

Claire Ruth unveils the memorial monument to her late husband, Babe Ruth, in deep center field at Yankee Stadium, April 19, 1949. The bronze plaque reads: A GREAT BALL PLAYER / A GREAT MAN / A GREAT AMERICAN. Floral wreaths mark the monuments of the Babe's former teammate Lou Gehrig, left, and his former manager Miller Huggins. It's hard to fathom now, but the three stone monuments were considered "in play" until the stadium was renovated in the 1970s. Deep fly balls could pinball among the monuments, flagpole, and wall, creating an adventure for outfielders. After the renovations, they were relocated to Monument Park, behind the outfield wall.

June 26, 1944 Soon after D-Day, with the tide turning in World War II, the Yankees, Giants, and Dodgers play a three-way, six-inning exhibition game against one another (two innings per pairing) to raise money for war bonds. By the end of the regular season, the wartime-depleted Yankees are down to third place.

NO
HENRY LOUIS GEHRIG
MILLER JAMES HUGGINS
TO THE MEMORY OF
GEORGE HERMAN "BABE" RUTH
1895 - 1948
A GREAT BALL PLAYER
A GREAT MAN
A GREAT AMERICAN
ERECTED BY
THE YANKEES

April

22

WHAT BECOMES A LEGEND MOST?

At 9:00 A.M. on a Saturday, fans pass through the gates at Yankee Stadium to see the Bombers play the Boston Red Sox on Joe DiMaggio Day, October 1, 1949. The gates were opened early as some 4,000 fans waited outside, many of whom had camped out all night to honor their hero. The Yankees great addressed a crowd of about 70,000, ending with the now-famous words, "I want to thank the Good Lord for making me a Yankee." For years since, every Yankee passed under a sign with those words in the tunnel leading to the dugout at the stadium.

The Yankee Clipper was still feeling weak after coming down with viral pneumonia in September; he told manager Casey Stengel he hoped to last three innings. But the Yankees needed wins in both of their last two games against the Red Sox to go to the World Series. Joe stayed in for nine innings—and two hits. The Yankees won this one 5–4. One game to go.

January 25, 1945 Larry MacPhail, Dan Topping, and Del Webb purchase the Yankees—who end the season in fourth place, their worst showing in twenty years—from the estate of Jacob Ruppert for $2.8 million. MacPhail becomes president and general manager; Ed Barrow stays on as chairman of the board for two years, until his retirement.

YANKEE STADIUM
GATE 6
GATE 6
GATE 6

April

23

THE CURSE CONTINUES

Fans rush the field as teammates surround Yankees pitcher Vic Raschi, center, at Yankee Stadium, October 2, 1949. Running in from the background are Gene Woodling, left, and Phil Rizzuto. Raschi had just pitched the Yankees into the World Series with a five-hitter against the Boston Red Sox in the final game of the season. The Yanks won 5–3. After losing three straight to the Red Sox a week earlier, the Yankees—in first place for nearly the entire season—suddenly had to win the last two games of the season against the New England club to capture the pennant. The manager of the Red Sox? Joe McCarthy.

Raschi was near his peak, going 21–10 with twenty-one complete games in the regular season, including this one. This was the first of his three straight twenty-one-win seasons.

May 24, 1946 Early on in what proves to be the third mediocre season in a row for the Yankees, an ailing and stressed-out Joe McCarthy suddenly resigns as manager. Bill Dickey and then Johnny Neun finish out the season.

April

24

THE STENGEL ERA

As a New York Giant, he had hit the first World Series home run at Yankee Stadium twenty-six years earlier. Now, Yankees manager Casey Stengel and his team celebrate in the locker room at the stadium, October 2, 1949, after winning the American League pennant with a 5–3 win over the Boston Red Sox on the last day of the regular season. The Yankees would play the Brooklyn Dodgers in the Fall Classic again, their second meeting in three years. Would anyone have guessed that from 1949 to 1960, Stengel would take the Yankees to a record ten World Series, more than any other manager? Not likely.

May 28, 1946 With 49,917 fans in attendance, the Yankees lose to Washington 2–1 in the first night game at Yankee Stadium.

NY
Yankees

April

WALK-OFF

A Yankee Stadium attendant intercepts Tommy Henrich, who has just hit the first walk-off home run in a World Series game, October 5, 1949. With no score in the bottom of the ninth inning, Henrich took a 2–0 pitch from Brooklyn Dodgers pitcher Don Newcombe (36) to deep right field. Yankees catcher Yogi Berra (8) and coach Bill Dickey (33) wait to congratulate Henrich, as home plate umpire Cal Hubbard looks on. Game 1 of the Fall Classic was a classic pitchers' duel: both teams combined for just seven hits, along with the one run.

August 6, 1946 Tony Lazzeri—the Yankees' regular second baseman in 1926–37 and a great clutch hitter with power in the Murderers' Row lineups and afterward, all despite his having epilepsy—is found dead at age forty-two from a fall at his home, apparently resulting from an epileptic seizure. He will be voted into the Hall of Fame in 1991.

36
8
33

April

WE CAN BE HEROES

Yankees first baseman Tommy Henrich, left, and pitcher Allie Reynolds share the role of hero in the locker room at Yankee Stadium, October 5, 1949, after the Yankees defeated the Brooklyn Dodgers in Game 1 of the 1949 World Series. Reynolds threw a two-hit, complete game shutout of the Dodgers, while Henrich delivered all the offense the Yankees needed: His ninth-inning home run gave the Yankees a 1–0 win. Reynolds would also pick up a save in Game 4 of the Series, pitching three and one-third innings of no-hit ball in relief of Ed Lopat.

September 29, 1946 Despite their poor finish—in third place, seventeen games out—the Yankees enjoy their first two-million-fan season, with 2,265,512 attending games at Yankee Stadium.

NY

April

27

THE JOINT IS JUMPIN'

A panoramic view—actually a composite of three negatives—of Yankee Stadium as the Yankees hosted the Brooklyn Dodgers and 70,053 baseball fans for Game 2 of the 1949 World Series, October 6, 1949. On the mound for the Dodgers is Preacher Roe, who pitched a complete game 1–0 shutout to even the Series.

The trademark scalloped frieze above the upper deck was made of copper, which aged to a green patina until it was painted white in the 1960s. Tom Verducci reported in *Sports Illustrated* that during the 1973–76 renovation, the original frieze was sold for $75,000 and melted down to make piping and the like. The replacement frieze over the bleachers in the post-renovation stadium was cast from concrete.

November 6, 1946 The Yankees announce that the new manager will be Bucky Harris.

LIFEBUOY
GEM
BOTANY TIES
NO BETTING
MARLIN BLADES
BALLANTINE ALE BEER

April

HE'D SEEN IT ALL—OR HAD HE?

Thirty-seven years after he broke into the majors as a player, Casey Stengel could have been forgiven for thinking he'd seen just about everything that could happen in baseball. Here the Old Perfesser shows little reaction to his first world championship as a manager, standing in the dugout with his hands on his hips after his Yankees defeated the Brooklyn Dodgers in Game 5 of the Fall Classic, 10–6, at Ebbets Field, October 9, 1949. In his first season with the Yankees, Stengel had deftly managed a team beset with injuries to key players. Joe DiMaggio had missed much of the first half of the season with heel spurs. However, Stengel used his available players wisely, guiding the team to its twelfth world championship. Impressive—but Stengel was just getting started.

At far left, stepping onto the dugout roof is Associated Press photographer John Lindsay, carrying his Speed Graphic press camera.

April 27, 1947 All of Major League Baseball celebrates Babe Ruth Day. The Babe, already ill with throat cancer and unable to put on his old uniform, speaks briefly to the 60,000 fans at Yankee Stadium.

April

GEORGE I

Yankees shortstop Phil Rizzuto, left, and pitching ace Allie Reynolds make themselves at home after signing new contracts in the downtown Manhattan office of Yankees general manager George Weiss, January 23, 1950. Despite Weiss's tightfisted reputation at contract time, Rizzuto and Reynolds seem pleased. A brilliant, if imperious, baseball executive, Weiss built the Yankees' farm system starting in 1932, before becoming the team's general manager after the 1947 season. In his twenty-nine years with the Yankees, they won nineteen pennants and fifteen world championships. Conservative to the core, Weiss is believed responsible for the Yankees' reluctance to hire black players in the 1950s. When the ownership dumped him after the 1960 World Series loss to the Pirates, he moved to the expansion Mets, laying the foundation for the Amazin's 1969 miracle season. The Yankees, meanwhile, fell on hard times.

October 3, 1947 The pennant-winning Yankees capture their eleventh world championship, beating the Brooklyn Dodgers for the second time, but it takes seven dramatic games. In Game 4, Bill Bevens is one out away from a very sloppy no-hitter (including nine walks) when pinch hitter Cookie Lavagetto doubles in the two men on base, and the Dodgers win 3–2.

April

BAT TO THE BONE

Yankees center fielder Joe DiMaggio bones his bat in the clubhouse at the team's St. Petersburg, Florida, spring training camp, March 6, 1950. The practice of rubbing the bat against a large bone was believed to harden the bat's surface, but any benefit was more than likely in the hitter's mind. Still, it apparently didn't hurt: In the twilight of his playing career that year, the Yankee Clipper would hit .301 with thirty-two home runs.

October 5, 1947 In the sixth inning of Game 6 of the World Series, with two on and the Yankees down 8–5, the usually unruffled Joe DiMaggio famously kicks the dirt at second base as Al Gionfriddo makes an amazing catch of DiMaggio's line drive.

JOHNSON 24
HENRICH 15

May

1

VOICE OF THE YANKEES

Yankees broadcaster Mel Allen, center, receives a B'nai B'rith plaque from comedian Eddie Cantor, right, during Mel Allen Day ceremonies before a game between the Yankees and the Chicago White Sox at Yankee Stadium, August 27, 1950. Colleagues, friends, and fans showered the wildly popular play-by-play man with gifts, including a new black Cadillac sedan, a boat, a television, and cash, which he used to set up scholarships in the name of Babe Ruth and Lou Gehrig. At left is Democratic political boss and former Postmaster General James A. Farley, chair of the event. At far right is Mrs. Asbury Park. Allen called it "the proudest day of my life." His name was synonymous with the Yankees and baseball at a time when the Yankees seemed to be in the World Series every year. He eventually called twenty World Series and twenty-four All-Star games in his career.

October 6, 1947 Capping a long, complicated feud with the Dodgers, the temperamental Larry MacPhail puts a damper on the Yankees' postgame celebrations of their world championship by announcing his retirement as president and general manager. Those roles will be taken on by co-owner Dan Topping and George Weiss, respectively.

RS. ASBURY PARK

May

2

SWEPT AWAY

Yankees catcher Yogi Berra tags out Philadelphia Phillies shortstop Granny Hamner at home to complete a double play in the fourth inning of World Series Game 4 at Yankee Stadium, October 7, 1950. Umpire Charlie Berry makes the call. Yogi had a solo home run and a run-scoring single for two RBIs in the game. The Yankees were on their way to a 5–2 win and a four-game sweep of the Series. This Series-deciding game also made news as the first World Series start by Yankees rookie pitcher Whitey Ford. The New York native held the Phillies scoreless for eight and two-thirds innings before two runs scored on an error. This would be the first of his record ten World Series victories.

June 13, 1948 Babe Ruth, terminally ill and frail, makes his final appearance at Yankee Stadium for its twenty-fifth anniversary. His number, 3, is retired. On August 16, Babe Ruth dies of throat cancer at age fifty-three; two days later, more than 100,000 pass his coffin as he lies in state at the House That Ruth Built.

BOTANY

May

3

DOES A SLUGGER GOOD

Lovell Richardson Mantle pours a glass of milk for her son, promising Yankees rookie Mickey Mantle, at the family's home in Commerce, Oklahoma, April 1951. The original caption says Mantle drank "copious" quantities of milk. The Commerce Comet was at home waiting for word from his local draft board; for a second time, he was classified 4-F, because of a history of osteomyelitis, and was deferred from service in the Korean War. Historic Route 66 passes through the center of Commerce, where it is now named Mickey Mantle Boulevard.

October 12, 1948 Regarded by some as just an eccentric clown with a below-average managerial record, Casey Stengel replaces Bucky Harris as manager after the Yankees finish in third place (despite a 94–60 record). In twelve seasons, Stengel will lead the Yankees to their most successful period ever: ten pennants and seven world championships, including a major league record five in a row and 1,149 wins—the third best behind Joe McCarthy and, later, Joe Torre.

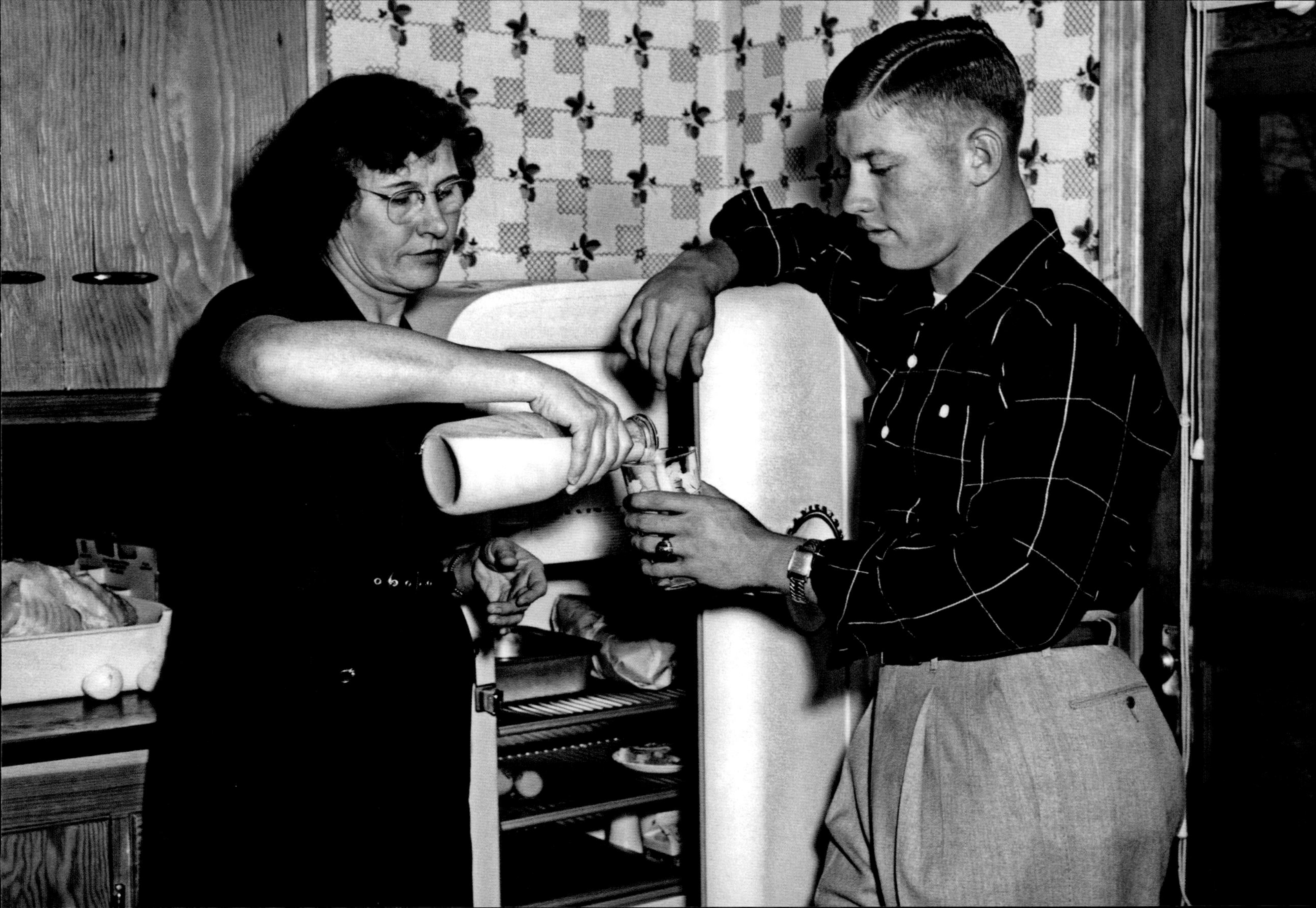

May

THE LEGEND AND THE ROOKIE

Joe DiMaggio, left, the Yankees' star center fielder, and rookie Mickey Mantle shoulder bats at Ebbets Field in Brooklyn, April 14, 1951, as the Yankees met the Dodgers in a short exhibition series that marked Mantle's New York debut. He played right field, going 1 for 4 in this Saturday game, but the following day he was 4 for 4 with a home run in the final game before the regular season. This was DiMaggio's last season, and he did little to make the shy rookie feel welcome; it's said that they barely spoke. And Mantle, who arrived in the big leagues to very high expectations, was slow to adjust to the majors. He struggled, spending part of the season back in the minors, and the New York media hardly embraced the kid from Oklahoma. When he eventually matured as a player, however, he also learned the give-and-take expected by the New York beat reporters, much of the credit for that going to his friend Whitey Ford.

February 7, 1949 Joe DiMaggio signs a $100,000 contract, then misses the first sixty-five games because of a bone spur in his right heel. He returns on June 28 at Fenway Park, the start of a three-game series in which he bats .455, hits four home runs and a single, and drives in nine runs.

AMERICAN
LEAGUE

May

THE OLD FOX

Clark Griffith, player-manager for the New York Highlanders from 1903 to 1908, points out photos of his former teammates to members of the 1951 Yankees at a Touchdown Club dinner in Washington, D.C., August 15, 1951. Clockwise around Griffith: Yankees manager Casey Stengel, second baseman Jerry Coleman, coach Jim Turner, pitcher Vic Raschi, pitcher Art Schallock, first baseman Joe Collins, catcher Yogi Berra, and shortstop Phil Rizzuto. Griffith, a former pitcher, owned the Washington Senators until his death in 1955. Washington's Griffith Stadium bore his name.

October 1–2, 1949 The injury-plagued Yankees are in first place until the last week of the regular season, when they have to battle the surging Red Sox. In the two-day finale at Yankee Stadium, Johnny Lindell homers in the eighth inning to win the first game for the Yankees, on Joe DiMaggio Day; then they clinch the AL pennant on the last day, thanks in large part to second baseman Jerry Coleman's three-run single in the eighth.

May

DOUBLE PLAYS A SPECIALTY

Yankees shortstop Phil Rizzuto leaps over the sliding Bobby Avila of the Cleveland Indians while completing a double play on Larry Doby's ground ball at Yankee Stadium, September 16, 1951. Umpire Bill Grieve calls Avila out at second. The Scooter excelled at defense, and he was a league leader in double plays, fielding percentage, and assists. Pitcher Vic Raschi once said, "My best pitch is anything the batter grounds, lines, or pops in the direction of Rizzuto." —MLB.com

Rizzuto's nickname, "Scooter," is attributed to fellow minor league infielder Billy Hitchcock. Hitchcock took note of Rizzuto's short legs and said, "You ain't runnin', you're scootin'."

October 5, 1949 Vic Raschi, in the first of his three straight years with twenty-one regular season wins, pitches a two-hit shutout, and Tommy Henrich hits a ninth-inning game-winning home run off the otherwise brilliant Don Newcombe, as the Yankees beat the Dodgers in Game 1 of the World Series. The Yankees win the Series in five games—starting an extraordinary sixteen-year run, missing the postseason only twice (1954 and 1959) and capturing the world championship nine times.

May

7

HOLY COW, PHIL!

Joe DiMaggio, right, sprints from third base with the winning run as Phil Rizzuto legs out his squeeze bunt in the ninth inning against the Cleveland Indians at Yankee Stadium, September 17, 1951. Cleveland catcher Jim Hegan watches helplessly. Indians pitcher Bob Lemon, fully expecting the bunt, had thrown a pitch impossibly high, but Rizzuto, a gifted bunter, somehow applied bat to ball, giving the Yankees a 2–1 win and moving the Yanks ahead of Cleveland in the drive to the pennant. Yankees manager Casey Stengel called it simply "the greatest play I ever saw."

October 7, 1950 The Yankees win their second straight World Series by completing a four-game sweep of the Phillies; the victory in the final game goes to a rookie named Edward "Whitey" Ford.

May

YOGI GETS A SPLINTER

Yankees catcher Yogi Berra, the ball in his bare hand, tags out Boston Red Sox slugger Ted Williams at Fenway Park, September 21, 1951. The Splendid Splinter was trying to score from first base on Clyde Vollmer's fourth-inning double off the left field wall. The Yankees won the game 5–1, moving them a game and a half ahead of the Cleveland Indians in the pennant race with just eight games left. The Yankees would finish the season five games out in front of the Tribe, with the Red Sox in third, eleven games out. Williams, a first-ballot Hall of Famer and one of the best pure hitters the game has ever known, played in just one World Series, losing to the St. Louis Cardinals in 1946. Odd fact: Upon his death in 2002, members of Williams's family had his head and body separately frozen in liquid nitrogen at a cryonics facility in Arizona, in hopes of bringing him back to life sometime in the future.

October 27, 1950 The team's spark plug during most of his career (1941–42 and 1946–56), Phil Rizzuto—an outstanding shortstop, base runner, and bunter—wins the AL MVP Award after getting 200 hits, then a team record for shortstops.

May

STOGIE FOR YOGI

Yankees catcher Yogi Berra, right, accepts a light from shortstop Phil Rizzuto after Berra handed out cigars in the Yankees clubhouse, September 25, 1951, to celebrate the birth of his son Tim. Their game against the Philadelphia Athletics was rained out. "Yogi," as Rizzuto referred to him, was one of the few teammates Rizzuto called by his first name. Mickey Mantle and Whitey Ford were reportedly on that short list, too. As a player and broadcaster, Scooter nearly always called teammates and colleagues by their last names—when he wasn't calling them "huckleberries." He once opened a broadcast by reading off the teleprompter, "I'm Bill White . . . ," to which White, the future president of the National League, later said, "That was the only time in eighteen years I heard him mention my first name."—MLB.com

April 17, 1951 With the legendary public-address announcer Bob Sheppard also making his debut, Mickey Mantle goes 1 for 4 in his first major league appearance, a 4–0 win against Boston at home. His first home run comes on May 1 in Chicago, but in mid-July, he is sent back to the minors for five weeks to try to cut down on his strikeouts.

NY

May

10

TOUGH BREAK

Yankees rookie outfielder Mickey Mantle watches Game 3 of the World Series between the Yankees and the New York Giants on television at New York's Lenox Hill Hospital, October 6, 1951. Mantle, playing right field, tore up his knee in the previous day's game as he and center fielder Joe DiMaggio chased down a fly ball from Willie Mays. DiMaggio made the catch as Mantle caught his cleats in the cover of a drain in Yankee Stadium's outfield, severely wrenching his knee. Injuries would dog the Mick throughout his career. Casey Stengel said, "DiMaggio is the best player I ever managed. Mantle is the best one-legged ball player."—Paul Dickson, *Baseball's Greatest Quotations*

This was the first World Series for Mantle and Mays, and the last for DiMaggio. For Mantle, there would be many more.

July 12, 1951 Twenty-three years after the third Yankees no-hitter, Allie Reynolds pitches the fourth, a 1–0 win against the Cleveland Indians at Municipal Stadium. The only Yankees run comes on Gene Woodling's homer off Bob Feller, who gave up just four hits after flirting with a no-hitter himself.

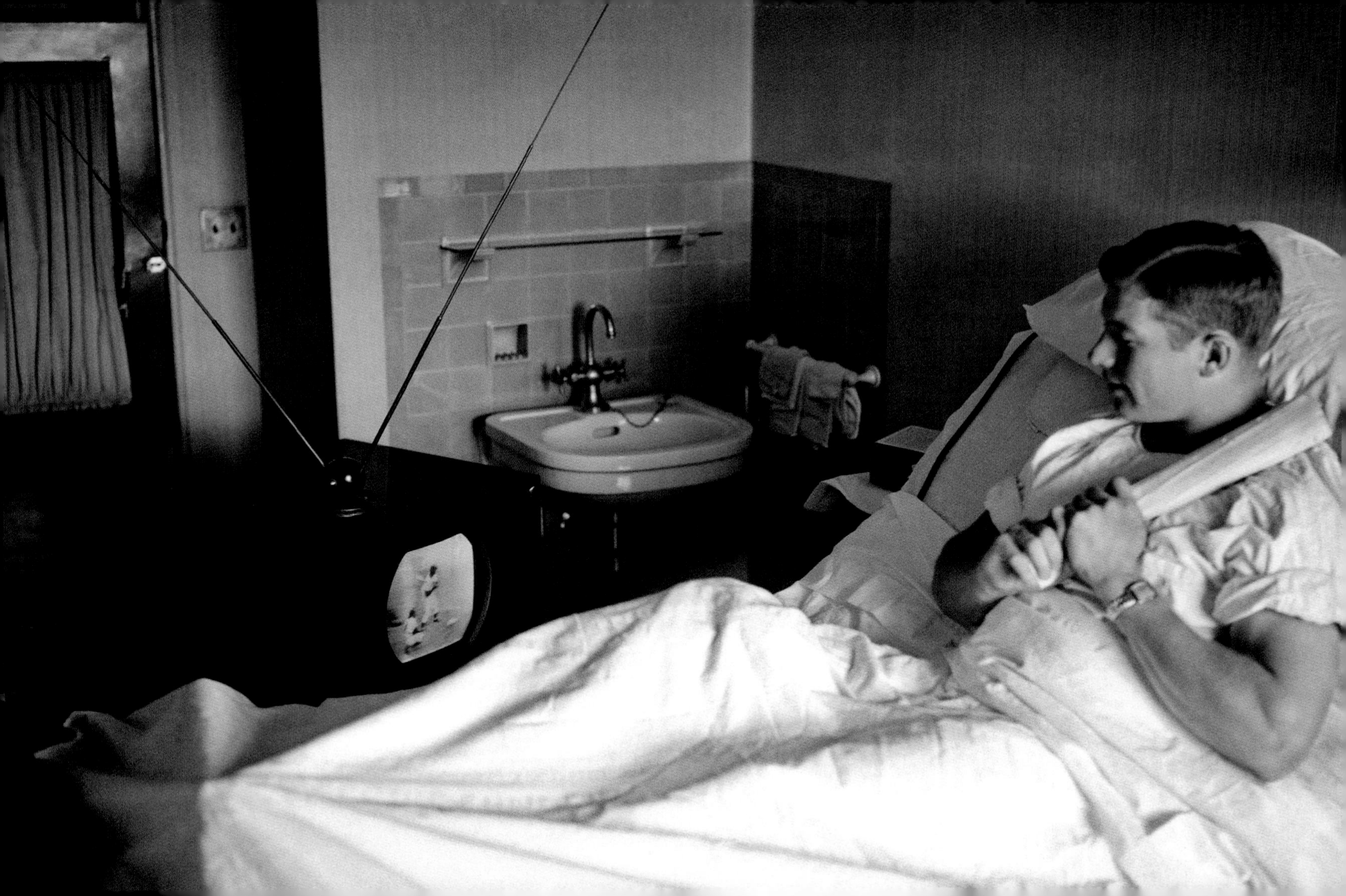

May

11

RASCHI HEARS IT

Vociferous Giants fans in the center field bleachers turn on Yankees pitcher Vic Raschi, who acknowledges their jeers with a wave as he trudges toward the clubhouse after being shelled during the fifth inning of World Series Game 3 at the Polo Grounds, October 6, 1951. The Giants won 6–2 to take a two-games-to-one lead. Raschi came back to win in the sixth and deciding game of the Series. He would finish his career with a 5–3 World Series record.

September 28, 1951 Allie Reynolds throws his second no-hitter of the season—the only Yankee ever to do so—in the first game of a doubleheader against Boston at Yankee Stadium, which the Yankees win 8–0.

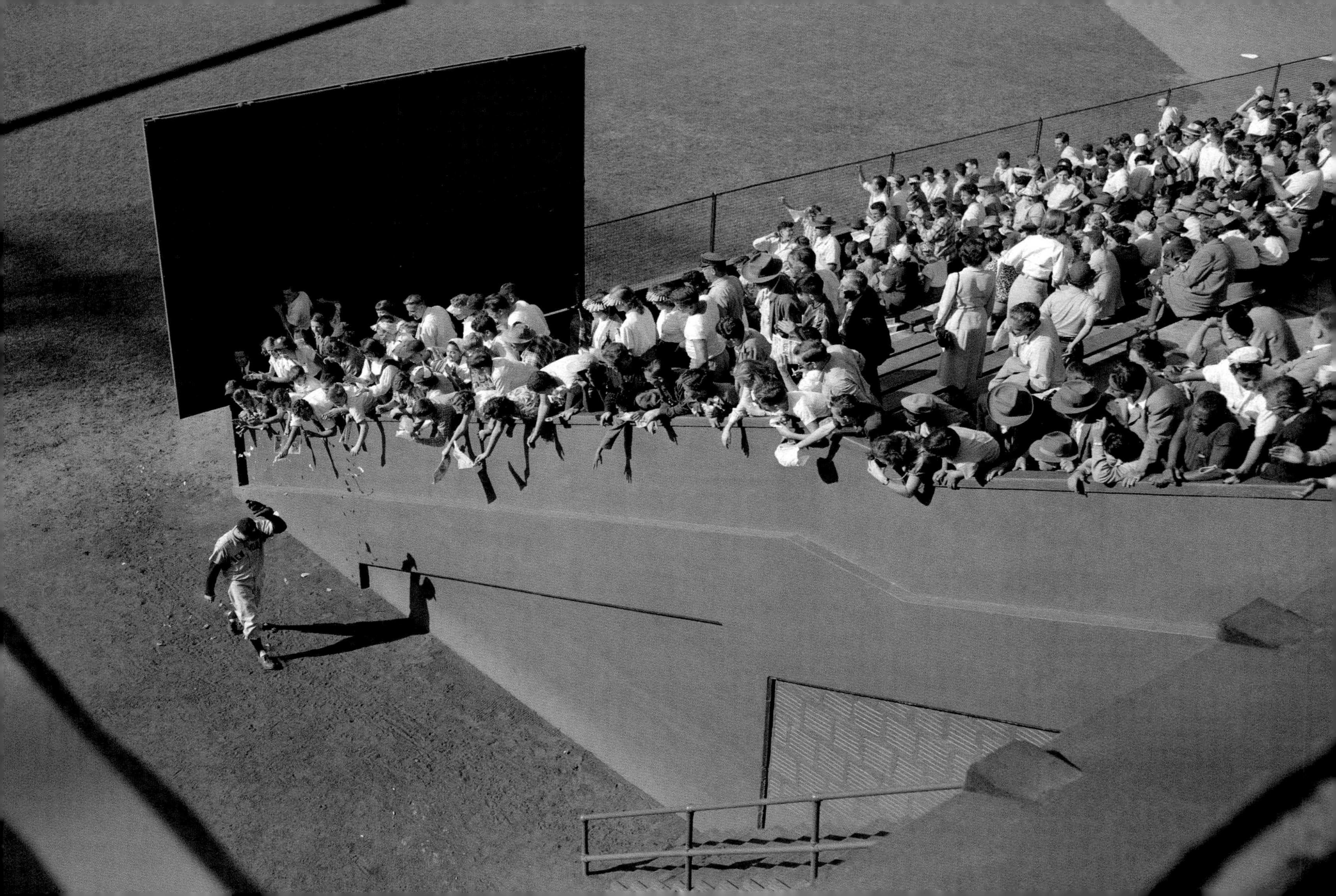

May

12

SUPERCHIEF ON SCHEDULE

Allie Reynolds, second from right in the center group, leaves the field with happy Yankees teammates and news photographers after pitching a complete game 6–2 win over the New York Giants in Game 4 of the World Series at the Polo Grounds, October 8, 1951. From left: shortstop Phil Rizzuto, pitcher Vic Raschi—who seems particularly pleased over Allie's winning effort—Reynolds, and catcher Yogi Berra. Game 4 had been postponed for one day due to rain, giving the Yankees a chance to rest Game 1 loser Reynolds for a comeback on this day. Now the Series was knotted at two games all. Reynolds, who was part Native American, was nicknamed "Superchief," a nod toward his heritage as well as the Santa Fe Railway's high-performance passenger train the Super Chief.

September 30, 1951 It may be Mickey Mantle's first year, but it is Gil McDougald, playing second and third base, who leads the team with a .306 average at the season's close, and he soon becomes the first of eight Yankees to win the Rookie of the Year Award. McDougald's career as a solid hitter and versatile infielder will last a little more than six seasons, but after his line drive on May 7, 1957, smashes Indians pitcher Herb Score near the right eye, McDougald's hitting skills suffer until his retirement in 1960.

Yankees

May

13

GRAND SERIES SLAM

Yankees teammates welcome second baseman Gil McDougald, right, to the dugout after his third-inning grand slam in Game 5 of the World Series against the New York Giants at the Polo Grounds, October 9, 1951. The Yankees romped 13–1 behind Ed Lopat's complete game. Lopat allowed just five hits, a double and four singles. McDougald's rocket off Giants starter Larry Jansen, which broke a 1–1 tie, was only the third World Series grand slam. The first was by the Cleveland Indians' Elmer Smith in 1920, and Tony Lazzeri hit one for the Yanks in 1936. (More than a dozen players, including several other Yankees, have achieved this feat since then.)

October 5, 1951 The Yankees win their third World Series in a row, this time beating the Giants. But in Game 2 of the six-game series, right fielder Mickey Mantle catches his spikes on a protruding drain hole cover as he is chasing a Willie Mays fly ball, causing the first of many major injuries for Mantle throughout his Hall of Fame career.

31
20

May

14

TRIPLE THREAT

Shortstop Phil Rizzuto, left, and catcher Yogi Berra kiss right fielder Hank Bauer in the clubhouse after winning the deciding Game 6 of the World Series at Yankee Stadium, October 10, 1951. Bauer's bases-loaded triple in the sixth inning broke a 1–1 tie and led to a 4–3 Yankees win over the New York Giants. The moment was especially sweet for Bauer, who had slumped badly in previous Fall Classics, batting just .132 in thirty-eight at bats before this game winner. The former Marine also made a spectacular game-ending catch of pinch hitter Sal Yvars's low line drive with the Giants' tying run on base. This was the end of the Giants' storybook season, the year best remembered for Russ Hodges's call of Bobby Thomson's home run, repeatedly shouting: "The Giants win the pennant!" But the Yankees, as expected, won the World Series, their fourteenth world championship against just four Series losses.

November 8, 1951 Catcher Yogi Berra wins the first of three MVP Awards, his others coming in 1954 and 1955—making him one of only three Yankees, along with Mickey Mantle and Roger Maris, to win in consecutive years.

May

15

FOUR ON THE FLOOR

Dapper-looking Associated Press photographer John Rooney sets up his Big Bertha sheet film camera before a game between the Yankees and Detroit Tigers at Yankee Stadium, mid-June 1952. Rooney was using a "gearshift" model—the metal lever resembling a car's stick shift on the side of the telephoto lens allowed the photographer to focus quickly on predetermined locations on the field, such as second base and home plate. That was helpful, but it still required dexterity and split-second timing by the photographer. After the first few innings, a courier or motorcycle messenger would rush Rooney's film back to AP headquarters at 50 Rockefeller Center. There the photos would be processed, printed, and transmitted to newspaper sports editors around the country. Meanwhile, competing wire service photographers would be doing much the same, in a daily race to see who could deliver the best pictures on deadline.

December 12, 1951 Joe DiMaggio, the Yankee Clipper, officially retires after thirteen seasons as one of the game's best all-around players. His number, 5, will be retired in 1952, three years before his entry into the Hall of Fame.

AP

May

16

TIME MACHINE

Leroy "Satchel" Paige of the St. Louis Browns, a first-time All-Star at forty-six—give or take a year or two—describes his pitch selection for some of his American League teammates in the locker room at Philadelphia's Shibe Park, July 8, 1952. From left: Yankees outfielder Mickey Mantle, Yankees pitcher Allie Reynolds, Boston Red Sox outfielder Dom DiMaggio, and Paige. The Yankees had seven players on the AL squad. Yankees manager Casey Stengel had named Paige to the All-Star roster, but the game was cut short after five innings due to rain; Paige, Mantle, and Reynolds never played. Stengel made it up to Paige by taking him to the 1953 All-Star Game, where he pitched the eighth inning. On the subject of age, Paige was often quoted: "I've said it once and I'll say it a hundred times, I'm forty-four years old." However old he was, he may have been as good as anyone who ever took the ball.

July 26, 1952 Mickey Mantle, Joe DiMaggio's successor in center field, blasts his first grand slam, into the upper deck in Detroit.

RASCHI
St. Louis
EW YORK

May

17

WHAT'S MISSING FROM THIS PHOTO?

Fans take in Game 3 of the World Series between the Yankees and the Brooklyn Dodgers from the Yankee Stadium bleachers, October 3, 1952. Announced attendance was 66,698. Dem Bums from Brooklyn won 5–3, but the Yanks came back to win the Series in seven games. This was the fourth World Series meeting between the two clubs, with the Dodgers still trying to break through.

Remember when there were seats in the center field bleachers? In later years, the batter's eye, often called simply "the black," appeared in this section of the renovated Yankee Stadium. The seats were removed and the concrete painted black to provide a clean backdrop in the batter's line of sight. Good for batters, not so good for pitchers, and bad for fans who long to see a packed stadium. A special cachet came with homers into the black—one of the deepest areas of this or any ballpark.

October 7, 1952 The Yankees win four straight world championships for the second time in their history, defeating the Dodgers in another exciting World Series. Climaxing Game 7 and the Series, with two outs and the bases full of Dodgers in the seventh, second baseman Billy Martin makes a dramatic catch of a windblown infield pop-up by Jackie Robinson. The Yankees win 4–2.

De Cicco's
Bon Bon
with the ICE CREAM center
HORTONS
"BOTANY"
500 CLOTHES
TAILORED BY DAROFF
BURMA-SHAVE
Con Edison
IS ON THE BALL
BUY TYDOL
FLYING
GASOLINE
CALL FOR PHILIP MORRIS
What does the catcher tell the pitcher? get
Manhattan
Disosway & Fisher Inc.

May

18

NOT EVEN CLOSE!

Yankees pitcher Johnny Sain is safe at first as Brooklyn Dodgers first baseman Gil Hodges waits for the late throw from second baseman Jackie Robinson in the tenth inning of Game 5 of the World Series at Yankee Stadium, October 5, 1952. At least that's how John Lindsay's camera and some 70,536 fans saw it. But to the person who counts? Umpire Art Passarella called Sain out, and the call stood, despite some choice words from first base coach Bill Dickey (33) and the Yankees dugout. The Dodgers went on to win the game 6–5, but the Yankees ended up prevailing again in another all–New York Fall Classic, taking the Series in seven games.

April 17, 1953 Mickey Mantle hits baseball's first tape measure home run, later declared a 565-footer, off Chuck Stobbs into a row of houses beyond the Washington Senators' Griffith Stadium.

May

19

UNTIL WE MEET AGAIN

With another World Series win over Brooklyn now in the books, Yankees catcher Yogi Berra closes up shop at Yankee Stadium, October 8, 1952, accompanied by his two-year-old son Larry. Berra packed up his shin guards, face masks, and protectors and headed home to Woodcliff Lake, New Jersey, for the off-season. Meanwhile, Brooklyn fans could only "wait 'til next year." Indeed, the 1953 Fall Classic would be a rematch of the Yankees and Dodgers.

Young Larry Berra tried his hand as a player with several minor league clubs in the 1970s, but had little success. His younger brother, Dale Berra, played eleven seasons as an infielder with the Pittsburgh Pirates, Yankees, and Houston Astros.

October 5, 1953 The Yankees set a major league record by winning their fifth consecutive world championship—and all in Casey Stengel's first five years as manager. They do so by beating the Dodgers in six games, Brooklyn's fifth straight Series loss to the Bronx Bombers.

May

20

HOMER'S ODYSSEY

Mickey Mantle holds the ball that he hit for one of his longest home runs, an estimated 565 feet, at Griffith Stadium in Washington, April 17, 1953. Batting righty against Senators left-hander Chuck Stobbs, Mantle launched the ball over the bleachers in left-center, where it glanced off Mr. Boh, the billboard for National Bohemian beer, as it left the stadium. It continued over Fifth Street NW before landing in the yard of Perry Cool at 434 Oakdale Place NW, where Yankees PR man Red Patterson retrieved the ball from a young boy. Patterson later said he calculated that it had traveled 565 feet from home plate, and although he apparently didn't use an actual tape measure, the phrase "tape measure home run" was coined to describe the blast. Mantle, in the locker room after the game, points to the gouge the ball received somewhere between his bat and the Cools' backyard. The Yankees won the game, 7–3.

December 15, 1953 Ed Barrow, former Yankees general manager and a crucial architect of the Yankees dynasties since 1920, dies at age eighty-five.

NEW

May

21

THE LOVE OF HIS LIFE

Screen star Marilyn Monroe kisses retired Yankees star Joe DiMaggio after their wedding at San Francisco City Hall, January 14, 1954. The marriage of two of the country's biggest celebrities seemed like a match made in Hollywood heaven—but it quickly began to unravel. When Marilyn went to perform before U.S. servicemen in Korea during the couple's honeymoon in Tokyo, she reportedly told Joe afterward, "You've never heard such cheering." His terse reply: "Yes I have." The breaking point may have come later that year at Marilyn's famous billowing skirt photo op for the film *The Seven Year Itch*, when she playfully posed over a subway grating as a train passed below. DiMaggio was infuriated by the public display of his wife. A month later, they were divorced; the marriage had lasted nine months. DiMaggio never remarried, and he never discussed Marilyn publicly. After her 1962 death, he arranged for a small, private funeral, and for the next twenty years he had roses regularly delivered to her crypt.

September 21, 1954 Both a starter and reliever, Bob Grim wins his twentieth game, against only six losses, to become the first Yankee to win at least twenty games in his first season since Russ Ford back in 1910. Grim is rewarded with the Rookie of the Year Award.

May

22

FLYING HIGH

Yankees second baseman Jerry Coleman hurdles the bag during a workout with shortstop Phil Rizzuto in St. Petersburg, Florida, March 4, 1954. Coleman, whose career had been interrupted for most of 1952–53 while he served as a Marine fighter pilot in Korea, was slated to take over second base duties from Billy Martin, who had recently been drafted himself. Coleman and Rizzuto were a potent double-play tandem. While no slugger, Coleman is remembered for some clutch hitting. His bases-loaded single on the last day of the 1949 regular season broke the back of the Red Sox and sent the Yankees to the World Series. He was the MVP of the 1950 World Series, and he batted .364 to lead the Yanks in their 1957 Series loss to the Milwaukee Braves. Coleman later became a sports broadcaster for the Yankees and San Diego Padres, as well as Padres manager for one year. As a broadcaster, he earned the nickname "Master of the Malaprop," with phrases such as "He slides into second base with a stand-up double."

September 26, 1954 Despite 103 wins, the Yankees close the season eight games behind the Cleveland Indians, who set a long-standing league record with 111 wins (which will be broken by the Yankees in 1998).

YORK

May

23

ST. LOUIS BLUES

Enos Slaughter, a veteran St. Louis Cardinals outfielder known for his tough, give-no-quarter style on the field, weeps after learning that he was traded to the Yankees, April 11, 1954. At left is Ellis Veech, sports editor of the *East St. Louis (Ill.) Journal*. Slaughter, famous for his Mad Dash from first base to home to win the 1946 World Series, was traded by the Cards after thirteen seasons to make room for promising rookie outfielder Wally Moon. Country Slaughter played two stints with the Yankees, mostly as a reserve outfielder, hitting .350 in the 1956 World Series and adding another world championship in 1958. He had also won two world championships with the Cardinals, who retired his number 9. He was elected to the Hall of Fame in 1985.

November 3, 1954 Several Yankees players meet the All-Japan Stars in Osaka, before a crowd of 64,000, for the first of twenty-five exhibition games in Japan.

May

24

JACKIE SWIPES HOME; BUMS TO STEAL SERIES?

In the fifth Fall Classic between the Bronx and Brooklyn, Dodgers star Jackie Robinson safely steals home plate under the tag attempt of Yankees catcher Yogi Berra in the eighth inning of the World Series opener at Yankee Stadium, September 28, 1955. With pinch hitter Frank Kellert at bat, Robinson just beat the throw from Yankees pitcher Whitey Ford. Berra was apoplectic over the call, turning on home plate umpire Bill Summers in a foot-stomping rage. Despite the daring theft by Robinson, the Yankees won the game 6–5, and they would also win Game 2. The Bombers looked poised for yet another championship . . . until the Dodgers ran off three straight wins. They eventually knocked off the Yanks in seven games, finally bringing a world championship to the loyal fans of Dem Bums. With players like Robinson, Pee Wee Reese, Roy Campanella, Duke Snider, Gil Hodges, and Carl Furillo, even a Yankees fan might grudgingly feel good for the scrappy perennial also-rans from Brooklyn.

April 14, 1955 Elston Howard becomes the first African American to play for the Yankees. He singles in his first game, against the Red Sox.

Dodgers

May

HOME STAND

Mickey Mantle spends some time at home with his wife, Merlyn, and sons Mickey Jr., holding a bat, and David, about 1956. Mickey and Merlyn were hometown sweethearts in Commerce, Oklahoma, but their life together was no fairy tale. The Yankees legend lived as hard as he played. He earned a reputation as a less-than-faithful husband, and eventually both he and Merlyn were treated for alcoholism, as were Mickey Jr., David, and a third son, Danny. A fourth, Billy—said to have been named for Mantle's close friend Billy Martin—died at thirty-six after living for much of his life with Hodgkin's disease, and Mickey Jr. died at forty-seven of non-Hodgkin's lymphoma. Merlyn and Mickey had been separated for years when Mantle himself died of cancer in 1995. But the crypt in Dallas, where the Mick and two of his sons are now interred, also carries her name.

May 13, 1955 Playing the Tigers at home, switch-hitter Mickey Mantle hits three home runs in a game—two batting lefty and one as a right-hander—for the only time; it is the first of ten games in which he hits two homers, one from each side of the plate.

May

HOW ABOUT THAT!

Longtime Yankees play-by-play man Mel Allen calls the game for WPIX-TV between the Yankees and the Baltimore Orioles at Yankee Stadium on May 11, 1956. In 1939, Allen began announcing games for the Yankees, eventually becoming the Voice of the Yankees for all their games. Allen opened each game with "Hello there, everybody!" and his signature call, "How about that!" became a ubiquitous catchphrase. When a Bomber hit a home run, it was a "Ballantine Blast." But when the Yankees suddenly and inexplicably dropped Allen from the broadcast crew before the 1964 World Series, he virtually disappeared overnight. Fans were outraged. The Yankees eventually brought Allen back as an announcer for special events, and finally they called him back to the broadcast booth in the 1970s and '80s. A plaque in Monument Park calls him "A Yankee institution, a national treasure." For fans of a certain age, Mel Allen, WPIX Channel 11, and a black-and-white TV are all one with the Yankees.

June 7, 1955 At Yankee Stadium, Mickey Mantle hits the first home run to reach the black, the seats in center field kept vacant to avoid distracting batters.

wpix 11
wpix 11

May

27

HE GOT ALL OF THAT ONE

Working out in his heyday, Mickey Mantle launches a ball during batting practice at Yankee Stadium, circa 1950s. A few rare players command attention when they step into the batting cage, and not just from the fans; even opposing players can't help but admire the combination of form and raw power. Ruth and Gehrig had it. DiMaggio had it. Later, Reggie had it. And during the steroid era, so many people had it that we lost interest. But Mantle had it in spades. Legit. Did anyone ever hit the ball harder or farther? Not likely. Imagine what he could have done healthy (see page 538).

October 4, 1955 In yet another dramatic seven-game World Series against the Brooklyn Dodgers, the Yankees come up against a Game 7 shutout by Johnny Podres, aided by an unbelievable sixth-inning catch by the speeding Sandy Amoros of a Yogi Berra fly to left. Gil Hodges drives in both Dodgers runs, and the perennial also-rans shock the Yankees in the Bronx—touching off an all-night party throughout Brooklyn.

May

TIE GAME

New York Yankees catcher Yogi Berra, left, gets an assist from his Brooklyn Dodgers counterpart, Roy Campanella, who knots Yogi's tie at Ebbets Field, October 4, 1956, after rain postponed the second game of the 1956 World Series. Ready to leave the park with Campanella is Dodgers pitcher Ralph Branca, center, who was not on the Series roster. Although Campy had a subpar World Series in 1956, he was a perennial All-Star with three NL MVP Awards to his name, as well as a world championship with the Dodgers in 1955. Tragically, he was paralyzed in a January 1958 auto accident. The 1956 World Series was the last to be played at venerable Ebbets Field in Brooklyn. The club broke its deeply loyal fans' hearts when it moved to Los Angeles for the 1958 season.

Lost to obscurity is the fact that Branca—the Dodger who served up the Shot Heard Round the World to the Giants' Bobby Thomson in 1951—pitched in five games for the Yankees in 1954, recording one win with a respectable 2.84 ERA.

May 30, 1956 Mickey Mantle homers off Pedro Ramos of the Senators, and the ball hits the right field facade at the top of Yankee Stadium, just missing its chance to become the first ball ever hit completely out of the stadium.

May

HISTORY IN THE MAKING

Yankees starter Don Larsen delivers a pitch against the Brooklyn Dodgers in Game 5 of the World Series at Yankee Stadium, October 8, 1956. Larsen had a reputation as a carouser; as Jimmy Dykes, his Baltimore manager in 1954, had said, "The only thing he fears is sleep." And he could be erratic on the mound. Despite an 11–5 record in the regular season, he had lasted only one and two-thirds innings in the Series' second game. He claimed to be shocked when he arrived at the stadium for Game 5 and learned that he was pitching. By the fourth inning, when this photo was taken, he was cruising, but it was too early to think seriously that this might be something truly special.

August 25, 1956 Holy cow! Midway through his sixteenth season as a Yankee, the fading star shortstop Phil Rizzuto is abruptly released. Though bitter, he holds his tongue, and the following year the Scooter will begin his second career as a talkative, highly entertaining (if not always analytical or even attentive), and much-loved Yankees broadcaster, until his retirement in 1996.

May

30

NO RUNS, NO HITS, NO NOTHING

The Yankee Stadium scoreboard tells the story after nine innings: no runs and no hits allowed by Yankees pitcher Don Larsen in Game 5 of the World Series, October 8, 1956. In fact, no Brooklyn Dodger had reached base, period: a perfect game. To date, there have been only seventeen perfect games in major league history; Larsen's remains the only postseason perfecto. He was helped along the way by a few defensive gems: In the second inning, a line drive by Jackie Robinson glanced off the glove of third baseman Andy Carey and bounced to shortstop Gil McDougald, who narrowly caught Robinson with a throw to first; there was a spectacular running catch by Mickey Mantle of Gil Hodges's sinking line drive to left-center in the fifth inning; and Hodges hit a liner again in the eighth, but to Carey, who made a great catch. Mantle also homered in the fourth for the Yankees' first run.

September 30, 1956 On the last day of the season, Mickey Mantle edges out Ted Williams for the batting title and wins the Triple Crown (.353, fifty-two home runs, 130 runs batted in)—the only Yankee to do so other than Lou Gehrig in 1934. He is also given the AL MVP Award for the first time, repeating in 1957 and 1962.

OFFICIAL TIME
LONGINES
LONGINES
WITTNAUER
World's Most Honored Watch
ENITH
RADIOS
EVISION
HIGH FIDELITY
R H E
BROOKLYN
YANKEES
YANKEES
BATTING ORDER
VISITORS
BATTING ORDER
NATIONAL
AMERICAN
INNING
INNING
AT BAT OUT
BALL STRIKE
PRO FOOTBALL
GIANTS STEELERS
OCT 21 2 PM
UMPIRES – PLATE 4
BASES 1-5-236
y & Fisher
TERFERING
PLAY
O ARREST
STADIUM
FAVORITE
BALLANTINE
PURITY BODY FLAVOR
ALE
BEER

May

31

PERFECTION

Yankees catcher Yogi Berra leaps into the arms of Don Larsen after the pitcher struck out Brooklyn Dodgers pinch hitter Dale Mitchell on a called third strike to complete his perfect game in Game 5 of the World Series at Yankee Stadium, October 8, 1956. Racing up in the background is first baseman Joe Collins. Larsen had thrown just ninety-seven pitches in retiring all twenty-seven Dodgers batters. Later, both he and Berra would recall how sharp his control was that day. Only once—in the first inning—did he get to a three-ball count against a Dodgers batter.

For the following day's *New York Daily News*, columnist Dick Young provided the famous lead: "The imperfect man pitched the perfect game."

October 8, 1956 Sixteen-year-old fan Joe Torre watches from the Yankee Stadium stands as Don Larsen pitches the only perfect game in World Series history, beating Brooklyn 2–0 in Game 5. Two games later, the Yankees avenge their 1955 World Series loss to the Dodgers, taking back the world championship in the last Subway Series between the two teams.

June

1

WE CAN TALK NOW

Yankees pitcher Don Larsen, center without cap, leaves the field after pitching a perfect game in World Series Game 5 at Yankee Stadium, defeating the Brooklyn Dodgers 2–0, October 8, 1956. To the right of Larsen is catcher Yogi Berra, with shortstop Gil McDougald at left. Larsen says that during the game, he felt little tension on the mound, but the dugout between innings was a "morgue." As prescribed by baseball superstition, his teammates gave him the silent treatment for fear of breaking whatever spell had seized the right-hander that day. With the game now safely in the books, they had plenty to talk about.

Afterward, a reporter asked manager Casey Stengel if this was the best game Larsen had ever pitched. Stengel didn't miss a beat. "So far!" was his oft-quoted reply.

May 16, 1957 Casey Stengel favorite Billy Martin becomes the fall guy when some drunks trigger a brief altercation at the Copacabana nightclub in New York during an outing by several Yankees players and their wives for Martin's birthday. On June 15, George Weiss, the general manager, trades away the fiery second baseman.

Yankees

June

2

FIT FOR A KING

As if we needed more proof that Babe Ruth was larger than life, Yankees slugger Mickey Mantle dons the Babe Ruth Sultan of Swat crown while being honored by the Maryland Professional Baseball Players Association in Baltimore, the Babe's hometown, January 14, 1957. The jewel-studded crown was valued at $3,800. Mantle won baseball's elusive Triple Crown in 1956, leading the majors by batting .353 and hitting fifty-two home runs and 130 RBIs. Mantle remains the last player to lead both leagues in all three categories. No surprise, he was the American League MVP that year, a title he would also win in 1957 and 1962.

July 23, 1957 In a home game against the White Sox, speedy slugger Mickey Mantle hits for the cycle for the only time.

SWAT AWARD
MANTLE

June

3

LAUGHING ALL THE WAY TO THE BANK

Yankees catcher Yogi Berra poses with the "tools of ignorance," his catching gear, during spring training, about the 1950s. With his short, squat build, his gravely voice, and his mangled quotes and malapropisms, he became one of baseball's most amusing personalities. Even the cartoon series *Yogi Bear* seemed a parody of Berra. But those who took him lightly did so at their peril. He didn't just stumble into ten world championships. He was a tough, crafty player on the field, hungry to win. Off the field, Berra could be equally shrewd, parlaying endorsement and business opportunities into a small empire, including his own museum. As Casey Stengel sagely observed, "They say he's funny. Well, he has a lovely wife and family, a beautiful home, money in the bank, and he plays golf with millionaires. What's funny about that?"—Paul Dickson, *Baseball's Greatest Quotations*

October 10, 1957 Milwaukee Braves pitcher Lew Burdette beats the Yankees in Game 7, as he did in Games 2 and 5, and the Bronx Bombers lose the World Series—the first time since 1948 that the world championship leaves New York City. Soon after the Series, so do the Brooklyn Dodgers and the New York Giants, leaving the Yankees as New York's only baseball franchise.

32

June

THE CHAIRMAN IS IN

Hall of Fame left-hander Ed "Whitey" Ford poses at spring training. A native New Yorker, the dominating Chairman of the Board still holds Yankees records for career wins, innings pitched, strikeouts, and shutouts, and his record of ten World Series wins is a benchmark for all major league pitchers. His 1961 season remains one of the finest by a Yankees pitcher, as he went 25–4 to win the Cy Young Award. Of course, it didn't hurt to have Mickey Mantle and Roger Maris hitting home runs in bunches, but Ford was indeed a rare pitcher. Mantle once said of his close friend, "I don't care what the situation was, how high the stakes were—the bases could be loaded and the pennant riding on every pitch, it never bothered Whitey. He pitched his game. . . . Nerves of steel." And Casey Stengel, as usual, had the last word: "If you had one game to win and your life depended on it, you'd want him to pitch it."—Paul Dickson, *Baseball's Greatest Quotations*, and Glenn Liebman, *Yankee Shorts*

December 7, 1957 Splitting his time in the outfield, at shortstop, and at third base before becoming the Yankees' regular shortstop for eight seasons, the versatile Tony Kubek wins the Rookie of the Year Award.

NEW

June

THE WRONG GUYS TO PICK A FIGHT WITH

Veteran Yankees outfielder Hank Bauer, second from right, stands outside a New York courthouse after a grand jury cleared him of felonious assault charges, June 24, 1957. From left are Mickey Mantle, Billy Martin, Bauer, and his wife. The three players were among those at the Copacabana nightclub on May 16 as some Yankees, also including Whitey Ford and Yogi Berra, celebrated Martin's twenty-ninth birthday. When a patron of the club began heckling headliner Sammy Davis Jr. with racial epithets, some of the Yankees stepped in. Who hit whom became the subject of much debate and speculation, but somehow the foul-mouthed delicatessen owner wound up with a broken nose. All charges against Bauer were eventually dropped. He was an ex-Marine who had once been accurately described as having "a face like a clenched fist."

General manager George Weiss used the Copa incident as an excuse to send Martin, whom he didn't like, to Kansas City. In December 1959, Bauer would also go to the Athletics in the trade that brought Roger Maris to the Yankees.

September 28, 1958 Catcher Yogi Berra finishes the season with a perfect fielding record, part of a major league record 148-game streak from July 28, 1957, to May 10, 1959.

June

HARRY SIMPSON?

Obliging the photographer at Yankee Stadium, from left, right fielder Hank Bauer, catcher Elston Howard, center fielder Mickey Mantle, outfielder/first baseman Harry Simpson, and outfielder Enos Slaughter pose together, September 5, 1957. Simpson is little remembered by most Yankees fans. One of the team's earliest African-American players—Howard was the first—Simpson played ninety-nine games in the outfield and at first base for the Yanks during partial seasons in 1957 and 1958, posting modest numbers. He was acquired from the Kansas City Athletics in the multiplayer deal that sent Billy Martin to Kansas City following the Copacabana incident.

October 9, 1958 After capturing their fourth straight pennant, the Yankees win their eighteenth world championship and their seventh in ten years. Taking the last three games, they reclaim the title from the Braves in their second straight seven-game contest.

June

7

SEE YA IN THE SPRING

With a wave of his hat, October 11, 1957, Yankees manager Casey Stengel leaves Yankee Stadium in the hands of the New York Giants football team until next season. The previous day, the Yankees had lost Game 7 of the World Series to pitcher Lew Burdette and the Milwaukee Braves. Don Larsen had started the deciding game for the Yankees just about a year to the day after throwing his perfect game, but he could not get out of the third inning this time, while Burdette went the distance for his third complete game win of the Series. A year later, both teams would meet again in the 1958 World Series, another seven-game affair, but with a reversal of fortunes: This time, Elston Howard would deliver the tie-breaking hit in the eighth, and then Bill "Moose" Skowron would crush a three-run homer to put Game 7 out of reach.

Yankee Stadium was also home to the football New York Giants from 1956 to 1973.

November 12, 1958 Bob Turley (21–7) becomes the first of only five Yankees to win the Cy Young Award since it was introduced in 1956.

ANKE
DIUM
TIME
ES
GATE 6
GATE 4

June

THREE FROM THE DOCK OF THE BAY

The DiMaggio brothers, who emerged from the wharves of San Francisco to become major league outfielders, pose together during Old-Timers' Day at Yankee Stadium, August 9, 1958. Not far removed from their playing days, former Yankees star Joe, center, is flanked by Vince, left, and Dom. Vince, the oldest of the trio, played ten seasons in the National League and had his best years with the Pittsburgh Pirates. He was an All-Star in 1943 and 1944, and he retired with a career batting average of .249. Dom, the youngest, spent eleven seasons in the majors, all with the Boston Red Sox. He was a seven-time All-Star who hit .298 for his career. Dom DiMaggio had a hitting streak of his own, hitting safely in thirty-four consecutive games in 1949. It took a spectacular catch on August 9, 1949—by his brother Joe, who happened to hold the record of fifty-six—to break the streak.

October 13, 1960 One year after injury and illness bring down the Yankees, leaving the team in distant third place, they come back and win their tenth pennant in twelve seasons. But in a World Series in which the Yankees win three games by a combined score of 38–3, they lose a heartbreaking Game 7 and the Series when Bill Mazeroski hits a ninth-inning walk-off home run off Ralph Terry.

NEW YORK

June

THE SPORTING LIFE

Retired Yankees star Joe DiMaggio, second from left, visits the Harwyn Club in New York, February 1959. From left are Harwyn owner Ed Wynne, DiMaggio, restaurateur Toots Shor, and longtime baseball man Leo "the Lip" Durocher. Like many ballplayers, DiMaggio was actually a regular at Toots Shor's eponymous joint at 51 West Fifty-first Street. He and Toots were fast friends, until Toots brought up the delicate subject of Marilyn Monroe—and with a not very delicate comment at that. It's said they never spoke again. Durocher spent several decades in the National League as a player and manager, notably with the Dodgers and Giants, but he started his career playing for the Yankees in the 1920s.

October 18, 1960 One home run negates twelve glorious years: Second-guessed for his pitching decisions throughout the World Series, seventy-year-old manager Casey Stengel is forced out by co-owners Dan Topping and Del Webb. The ax falls on George Weiss, the general manager, on November 2.

June

10

AND THIS WAS AN OFF YEAR

Mickey Mantle gets a hero's welcome from fans as he rounds third base at Yankee Stadium after hitting a walk-off home run to win the game against the Chicago White Sox 5–4, June 18, 1959. The Mick hit a Gerry Staley pitch into the lower right field stands in the bottom of the tenth inning for his fifteenth homer of the season. The 1959 season proved disappointing for Mantle and the Yankees, however. Healthy and poised for a big season, number 7 put up relatively modest numbers. He hit .285 with thirty-one home runs and seventy-five RBIs—one of his worst years during the prime of his career. The Yankees, coming off four straight pennant seasons and a world championship, stumbled to third place, fifteen games behind the Chicago White Sox.

November 2, 1960 Roger Maris, acquired in a trade at the end of 1959, wins the American League MVP Award (his first of two in consecutive years), leading the league in batting average, RBIs, extra-base hits, and total bases while finishing second in home runs to Mickey Mantle.

June

11

WILLIE DRIVES A FORD

Yankees pitcher Whitey Ford delivers his first pitch to Willie Mays of the San Francisco Giants in the twenty-ninth All-Star Game, at Yankee Stadium, July 13, 1960. Mays promptly singled to left field, the start of a rough outing for Ford. He went three innings, giving up three runs and taking the loss. Yankees catcher Yogi Berra also started, with umpire Nestor Chylak behind the plate. This was the second All-Star Game of the 1960 season—from 1959 to 1962, there were two such games each summer. The NL won this one, 6–0. A total of four All-Star games were played at Yankee Stadium: 1939, 1960, 1977, and 2008.

October 1, 1961 Under intense media pressure, Roger Maris passes Babe Ruth's single season home run record, hitting his sixty-first home run into the right field bleachers at Yankee Stadium, off Boston pitcher Tracy Stallard, in the fourth inning of the season's final game. An ailing Mickey Mantle has to settle for second place, with fifty-four homers, in the season-long, good-natured rivalry.

7up
3 3/4 %
WASHINGTON
OFFICES
SPENCER DISPLAY CORP
INSULATED LININGS FOR YEAR ROUND COMFORT
MRS. WAGNER'S PIES
CITIES SERVICE
THE WINNING COMBINATION
GASOLENES
DRINK Coca-Cola
BE REALLY REFRESHED!
smoke
EL PRODUCTO cigars
EXIT
EXIT
457 FT.
461 FT.

June

12

OFFENSIVE DISPLAY

Yankees trot back to the dugout following Bobby Richardson's grand slam in the first inning of World Series Game 3 against the Pittsburgh Pirates at Yankee Stadium, October 8, 1960. Richardson, center with head bowed, shakes hands with the next Yankees batter, Tony Kubek. The Yanks finished the inning with a 6–0 lead, on their way to a 10–0 win and a two-games-to-one lead in the Series. Richardson's six RBIs for the day is a World Series single-game record. His twelve RBIs for this Series is also the record for the Fall Classic. Driven in on Richardson's slam, from far left: third baseman Gil McDougald (followed by a batboy and Richardson); catcher Elston Howard; and first baseman Bill Skowron. With lopsided wins in Games 2, 3, and 6, the Yankees would dominate the Pirates in most offensive categories, and Richardson ended up named the Series MVP. But the Series was far from over.

October 9, 1961 With Ralph Houk managing, and six players belting at least twenty home runs each, the Yankees easily win the pennant with a 109–53 record, then go on to beat the Cincinnati Reds in a five-game World Series. The 1961 team is widely considered one of the very best in baseball history.

June

13

CRUSHED

Pirates fans rush second baseman Bill Mazeroski as he rounds third base on his World Series–winning home run in Game 7 at Pittsburgh's Forbes Field, October 13, 1960. The Yankees were leading 7–4 after the top of the eighth inning—before a flurry of scoring left the score tied 9–9 going into the bottom of the ninth. Mazeroski's homer—the first ever to end a World Series—smashed their hopes of a nineteenth world championship. For the entire Series, the Yankees outscored the Pirates 55–27 (while losing four games by no more than three runs each) and outhit their opponents 91–60. Mickey Mantle had the best World Series of his career, batting .400 with three home runs and eleven RBIs. He later called this Series one of his biggest disappointments. After the bitter loss, the Yankees forced out manager Casey Stengel, his epic twelve-year run at an end. The Yankees reportedly thought that Stengel had grown too old to manage a new generation of players. He was widely quoted as saying, "I'll never make the mistake of turning seventy again."

November 8, 1961 Whitey Ford (25–4) wins the Cy Young Award.

IRATES
4
16
40
42
USHER

June

14

HOME RUNS SERVED DAILY

When Roger Maris joined the Yankees in 1960, he and Mickey Mantle became known as "the M&M Boys." Maris typically batted third, followed by the switch-hitting Mantle in the cleanup spot. Maris went on to win the AL MVP with thirty-nine home runs in 1960; in 1961, when they posed for this photo at Yankee Stadium, both sluggers launched an assault on Babe Ruth's 1927 record of sixty home runs in a season. With four other players who would hit more than twenty homers in 1961, some dubbed this Yankees lineup a latter-day Murderers' Row. The Yankees hit 240 home runs during the regular season, fifty-one more than the next closest team, the Los Angeles Angels. The vaunted 1927 Yankees had 158 home runs in the regular season.

May 23, 1962 In a home game against Kansas City, Joe Pepitone hits two home runs in one inning, as Joe DiMaggio did in 1936.

June

15

ELLIE ON THE MOVE

Yankees catcher Elston Howard throws off his mask as he tracks a bunt attempt turned pop foul by Baltimore Orioles pitcher Hoyt Wilhelm in the third inning at Yankee Stadium, July 29, 1961. Umpire Jim Honochick backs out of the way. Howard made the catch, and the Yanks went on to win 5–4 behind—what else—a complete game from Whitey Ford. With the win (his thirteenth of fourteen straight, tying a league record), Ford was 19–2, and it was still July!

Ellie Howard was an outstanding defensive catcher, especially adept at foul pops. He won the Gold Glove for his position in 1963 and 1964, and he has one of the highest career fielding percentages for catchers.

June 24, 1962 The longest game in Yankees history ends in the twenty-second inning as reserve outfielder Jack Reed hits a two-run home run—his only homer in the major leagues—to defeat the Tigers 9–7 in Detroit.

June

16

TWICE IS NICE

Yankees shortstop Tony Kubek, left, joins right fielder Roger Maris in the locker room after they hit back-to-back home runs off Kansas City Athletics pitcher Jerry Walker at Municipal Stadium, August 26, 1961. Both hit solo shots to deep right in the sixth inning of a game the Yankees won 5–1. Kubek's homer was his sixth of the season, while Maris's was his fifty-first, putting him five ahead of teammate Mickey Mantle, who had hit his last homer on August 20. The home run chase captivated fans as Mantle and Maris slugged their way toward sixty.

September 30, 1962 By the last game of the season, Tom Tresh has demonstrated his skills, substituting at shortstop while Tony Kubek is in military service, then switching in mid-season to left field, all the while hitting twenty home runs and ninety-three RBIs. The effort pays off when Tresh wins the Rookie of the Year Award.

NEW YORK
NEW YORK

June

17

POWER SURGE

Mickey Mantle unleashes the right-handed swing that launched 164 home runs. He had another 372 left-handed. In the 1961 home run race, the Mick was widely considered the favorite to break Babe Ruth's season record of sixty. In 1956, he had come close to the record with fifty-two, and as a career Yankee, he was the sentimental favorite as well. Mantle dueled second-year teammate Roger Maris for much of the season, but as happened so often in his career, injuries sidelined him. He sat out the last part of September with a hip infection, and he had only one home run in the last three weeks of the season. The Mick finished the 1961 campaign with fifty-four, and he was second in that year's AL MVP voting to his friend Maris.

October 16, 1962 The Yankees win their twentieth World Series, and their tenth in sixteen years, against the San Francisco (formerly New York) Giants. Game 7 is a pitchers' duel between the Yankees' Ralph Terry and Jack Sanford; with the Yankees up 1–0 in the ninth, and Giants on second and third, second baseman Bobby Richardson grabs Willie McCovey's line drive for the final out.

7

June

18

FIFTY-TWO AND COUNTING

Roger Maris follows through after hitting his fifty-second homer of the year in the sixth inning against the Detroit Tigers at Yankee Stadium, September 2, 1961. Two innings later, he added number fifty-three, pulling him closer to Babe Ruth's season record of sixty. Already controversy was brewing, because the Babe had hit his sixty in a 154-game season, while Maris was playing a 163-game regular season (as a result of an April 22 tie, which counted in the season statistics). Traditionalists argued that a record by Maris would count only if achieved in 154 games. As the final month of the season advanced, it became obvious that Maris, not the injured Mickey Mantle, had a shot at the record, and the pressure on Maris mounted. After 154 games, he had "only" fifty-nine homers. But to Maris, "A season's a season," and this one wasn't over. —Paul Dickson, *Baseball's Greatest Quotations*

May 22, 1963 About three months after signing a $100,000 contract, Mickey Mantle faces Kansas City's Bill Fischer and hits an eleventh-inning game-winning home run, which strikes the facade of Yankee Stadium at almost the same spot as his May 1956 blast—but this time the ball was still rising, therefore coming even closer to being the only ball ever to be hit out of the stadium.

SEC.
16

June

19

PRESSURE COOKER

Journalists fill the press box at Yankee Stadium during the September 2, 1961, game between the Yankees and the Detroit Tigers. The Yankees beat the Tigers 7–2 as Roger Maris hit home runs fifty-two and fifty-three for the season. Maris, who had been acquired in the trade that sent Don Larsen and Hank Bauer to Kansas City, was playing just his second season with the Yankees. Many fans, and even some sportswriters, did not consider Maris a "true" Yankee. As Maris closed in on Ruth's season home run record, the media attention became relentless—and not all of it positive. Years later, Maris said the press treated him as if he were doing something wrong. Whether or not he was losing patches of his hair due to the pressure, as has often been reported, he was undoubtedly the object of extreme scrutiny that seemed to intensify with each home run he hit.

October 6, 1963 The Yankees win their fourth straight pennant, their third under Ralph Houk, but then are swept in a four-game World Series for the first time, by the Los Angeles (formerly Brooklyn) Dodgers and pitchers Sandy Koufax, Johnny Podres, and Don Drysdale.

June

BUT HOW MANY HOME RUNS DID WHITEY HAVE?

Ace Yankees southpaw Whitey Ford delivers to Baltimore Orioles third baseman Brooks Robinson during the first game of a doubleheader at Memorial Stadium, September 19, 1961. Ford lost this 1–0 game, but he had a pretty good year anyway, going 25–4 and winning the Cy Young Award. This was also the year Ford broke the record for the most consecutive scoreless innings of World Series pitching. The previous record of twenty-nine and two-thirds innings was held by a young Boston Red Sox pitcher named Babe Ruth. Ford eventually went thirty-three and two-thirds straight scoreless innings in the Fall Classic, from 1960 to 1962. When Roger Maris broke the Babe's home run record later this season, Ford quipped, "It was a tough year for the Babe."—Glenn Liebman, *Yankee Shorts*

For the record, Whitey had three home runs in his sixteen seasons.

October 22, 1963 As secretly planned during spring training, the Yankees announce that Ralph Houk will become general manager and Hall of Fame catcher Yogi Berra, a player-coach in 1963, will become manager of the Yankees.

June

21

SIXTY-ONE IN ’61

Phil Rizzuto had the call: “Fastball, hit deep to right! This could be it! Way back there! Holy cow! He did it! Sixty-one for Maris!” Here, Roger Maris watches his record-breaking sixty-first home run, destined for the right field stands at Yankee Stadium on the last day of the season, October 1, 1961. With the stadium less than half full, Maris broke Babe Ruth’s single season total in the fourth inning as he homered off Boston Red Sox right-hander Tracy Stallard, giving the Yankees a 1–0 victory. Maris had played in 161 of the Yankees’ 163 games that season, breaking the 1927 record that Ruth had achieved in 151 of the team’s 155 games (including a tie game in April, which counted in the season’s stats). But, like all new records in the 162-game era, Maris’s record stands in the record books as the single season record for home runs. Period. No asterisk.

November 7, 1963 Elston Howard, the Yankees’ everyday catcher from 1960 to 1966, becomes the first African American to win the American League MVP Award, for his defensive as well as offensive skills.

SEC 17
SEC 15
9

June

22

A KEEPER

Nineteen-year-old Sal Durante, who caught Roger Maris's sixty-first home run ball in the lower right field stands, presents the ball to Maris in a Yankee Stadium runway after the game, October 1, 1961. Maris let Durante keep it, and the Brooklyn teenager sold it to a Sacramento, California, restaurateur for $5,000. Durante, one of the 23,154 fans in attendance, reportedly used the money to pay off some debts and set up housekeeping with his fiancée, whom he married four weeks later. The restaurant owner, Sam Gordon, displayed the ball and eventually gave it to Maris. It now resides in the Hall of Fame.

August 20, 1964 After blowing a four-game series in Chicago, the faltering Yankees are on the team bus when a mischievous Mickey Mantle eggs on utility infielder Phil Linz to play his harmonica louder. The resulting eruption by manager Yogi Berra ends with laughter and a looser team that starts winning two days later—though it takes an 8–3 win over Cleveland on the last day of the season for the Yankees to clinch their fifth consecutive pennant, tying their 1949–53 record.

ONLY
WORKING PRESS
PHOTOGRAPHERS
SPORTSCASTERS
BEYOND THIS POINT

June

23

DALEY DELIVERS

Yankees players congratulate pitcher Bud Daley, left, after he forced the Cincinnati Reds' Vada Pinson, far left, to fly out, ending the fifth and deciding game of the 1961 World Series at Crosley Field, October 9, 1961. The Yankees won the game 13–5 for their nineteenth world championship. The Yankees, from left, are Daley; right fielder Johnny Blanchard, who did not play the ninth inning; first baseman Bill Skowron; and catcher Elston Howard. A batboy runs behind Daley. The pitcher had gone six and two-thirds innings in relief of Yankees starter Ralph Terry, who ran into trouble early. Blanchard was 3 for 4 on the day, with a home run and a double. He hit .400 for the Series.

October 15, 1964 Mickey Mantle hits his record-setting eighteenth—and last—World Series home run, five days after his game-winning shot in Game 3; however, the St. Louis Cardinals edge out the Yankees 7–5 to win Game 7 and the world championship. Manager Yogi Berra is fired almost immediately, a harbinger of bad days to come.

C
28
REDS
EW YORK
NEW

June

24

DAY GAME

Actress Doris Day and actor Cary Grant, standing in the dugout, pose with New York Yankees players—from left, Mickey Mantle, Roger Maris, and Yogi Berra—before a game with the Los Angeles Angels at Dodger Stadium, July 12, 1962. The players appeared as themselves in the romantic comedy movie *That Touch of Mink* with Day and Grant, which was nominated for three Oscars. Mantle and Maris also starred in *Safe at Home!* that same year. A 2008 tell-all biography, *Doris Day: The Untold Story of the Girl Next Door* by David Kaufman, claims that Day and Mantle were romantically involved during the making of their movie.

November 2, 1964 CBS purchases 80 percent ownership of the Yankees for $11.2 million and later becomes the team's sole owner during some of the Yankees' leanest years.

NEW YORK
NEW YORK

June

DICKEY TAUGHT HIM EVERYTHING HE KNEW

Yankees catcher Yogi Berra hauls in a foul pop bunted by pitcher Orlando Pena of the Kansas City Athletics in the eighth inning of a game at Yankee Stadium, September 2, 1962. The Yankees won the game 2–1 after Tony Kubek scored from first on Bobby Richardson's walk-off double in the bottom of the ninth inning. Berra, the former protégé of Yankees Hall of Fame catcher Bill Dickey, was the best all-around catcher of his generation. He was a fifteen-time All-Star (every year from 1948 to 1962) and three-time MVP (in 1951, 1954, and 1955). He was elected to the Hall of Fame in 1972.

October 3, 1965 New manager Johnny Keane takes over an aging and injured Yankees team, with little available in the once prestigious farm system, and the Yankees collapse to 77–85, good only for sixth place, twenty-five games out of first—their worst finish in forty years. Keane will last only twenty games (including four wins) into the 1966 season, to be replaced by Ralph Houk in his second stint as manager.

June

FROM HERE TO ETERNITY

Yankees players celebrate at Candlestick Park after beating the San Francisco Giants 1–0 in Game 7 of the World Series, October 16, 1962. At center, first baseman Bill Skowron, left, and catcher Elston Howard (32) rush winning pitcher Ralph Terry. In the background are shortstop Tony Kubek, left, and second baseman Bobby Richardson, while another teammate rushes in from far left. The Yankees had won nine of the last fourteen World Series. It seemed their birthright to play in, and win, the Fall Classic just about every year. But it would be fifteen years before the Yankees were world champions again. To the Yankees and their fans, that's an eternity.

The Giants were playing in their first World Series since moving from New York's Polo Grounds in 1957 (their first, in fact, since they lost to the Yankees in 1951). More than fifty years later, they're still waiting for their first world championship in San Francisco.

September 11, 1966 John Miller, playing in Boston, becomes the first Yankee to hit a home run in his first major league at bat.

NEW
32
YORK
YORK

June

27

CAREER YEAR

Yankees pitcher Ralph Terry is carried to the clubhouse by teammates after shutting out the San Francisco Giants 1–0 at Candlestick Park, October 16, 1962, to win the World Series. During the 1960 World Series, Terry had given up the famous Series-deciding home run in Game 7 to the Pirates' Bill Mazeroski. Two years later, Terry redeemed himself—and then some. After winning twenty-three games in the regular season, Terry pitched brilliantly in the postseason. He went 2–1 against the Giants, throwing twenty-five innings with an ERA of 1.80, while walking just two batters. That earned him the Series MVP. He had other strong seasons, but none better than this one.

September 20, 1966 After selling off the rest of his shares in the Yankees, Dan Topping departs and Mike Burke, a CBS vice president, becomes president of the Yankees. In October, former Yankees co-owner and president Larry MacPhail's son, Lee MacPhail, is named general manager.

June

28

OH, SO CLOSE!

All those home runs hit by the Bronx Bombers and their opponents over the course of eighty-five years? No one hit a home run out of Yankee Stadium. Not the Babe himself. Not Lou, not Joltin' Joe, not Reggie. You could look it up—no fair ball ever left the stadium during a game. Mickey Mantle may have come closest on May 22, 1963. Batting left-handed against Kansas City A's pitcher Bill Fischer to lead off the bottom of the eleventh inning, Mantle drove a towering shot to right field, hitting the decorative frieze below the roof, just a foot or two from leaving the building. The Mick called it the hardest ball he ever hit. Many witnesses said the ball was still rising when it hit the facade, and teammate Tony Kubek insisted the ball was a high line drive—it had not even begun to drop. Almost overlooked: The homer won the game for the Yankees, 8–7.

This photo illustration shows Mantle hitting against the A's in 1956, with the estimated path of his 1963 home run highlighted. Note the A's defensive shift to the right against the switch-hitting Mantle.

September 25, 1966 Sinking into the basement of an expanded ten-team league—with a 70–89 final record, their first last-place finish since 1912—the Yankees draw a record-low 413 fans, who see the White Sox beat the home team 4–1.

OFFICIAL TIME
LONGINES
BALLANTINE
ALE
BEER
NEW GEM RAZOR
WITHOUT
407 FT.
344 FT.
AT BAT
POS.CF
BALL
STRIKE
OUT

June

YOU COULD WRITE A BOOK

The Yankees celebrate at Metropolitan Stadium in Bloomington, Minnesota, September 13, 1963, after defeating the Minnesota Twins 2–0 to clinch the American League pennant. First baseman Joe Pepitone pours champagne on Jim Bouton, who pitched a complete game shutout for his twentieth win of the season, as catcher Elston Howard and right fielder Johnny Blanchard look on. The Yankees had only four hits on the day, but solo home runs from Pepitone and Blanchard were all they needed. Bulldog Bouton had an outstanding 21–7 season, and in 1964 he won eighteen—plus two in the World Series. But those were his two big seasons. Bouton is best remembered for his 1970 tell-all book *Ball Four*, which details the quirks, flaws, and excesses of his teammates, not least of all Mickey Mantle. The book instantly made Bouton a pariah in baseball circles and a hero to countless readers and fans.

Metropolitan Stadium met the wrecker's ball in 1985. The Mall of America now stands there.

December 8, 1966 After two subpar seasons, due in part to a hand fracture that he says the Yankees misinformed him about, Roger Maris is preparing to retire when the Yankees trade him to the St. Louis Cardinals, where he stays for two years.

NEW YORK
NEW YORK
Yoo-Hoo
CHOCOLATE

June

BRONX BOMBERS? NOT THIS TIME

Roger Maris, left, and Mickey Mantle pose with a bat between them during their workout at Yankee Stadium, September 30, 1963. Hampered by injuries, Maris had played ninety games during the regular season, and Mantle just sixty-five, but both would start in the World Series against the Los Angeles Dodgers in two days. The M&M Boys went hitless in Game 1, and together they would go just 2 for 20 in the Series, with the Mick hitting a single home run and Maris getting injured in Game 2. The Dodgers swept in four games—the first time that ever happened to the Yankees in their sixty-one-year history up to then. While few realized it yet, the Yanks' dynasty that began in 1949 was starting to crumble.

May 14, 1967 Mickey Mantle hits his 500th home run, off Baltimore's Stu Miller in Yankee Stadium, but he bats only .245 for the season.

July

1

A PAIR OF ACES

Yankees twenty-four-game winner Whitey Ford shows Los Angeles Dodgers southpaw Sandy Koufax, himself a twenty-five-game winner, around Yankee Stadium, October 1, 1963, as both teams worked out before the World Series opener the following day. With 104 wins in the regular season, the Yankees were looking for their third straight championship, but Game 1 set the stage for the Dodgers' sweep. Koufax outpitched Ford, striking out fifteen Yankees as the Dodgers won 5–2. Over the course of the entire four-game Series, the Yankees managed a grand total of four runs as Koufax, Johnny Podres, and Don Drysdale virtually shut down the Bombers' bats. As Yogi Berra said of Koufax, "I can see how he won twenty-five games. What I can't understand is how he lost five."

May 30, 1967 Suffering from a circulation problem in his arm ever since 1964, Whitey Ford retires after pitching in only seven games in 1967. His number, 16, will be retired on Opening Day in 1974.

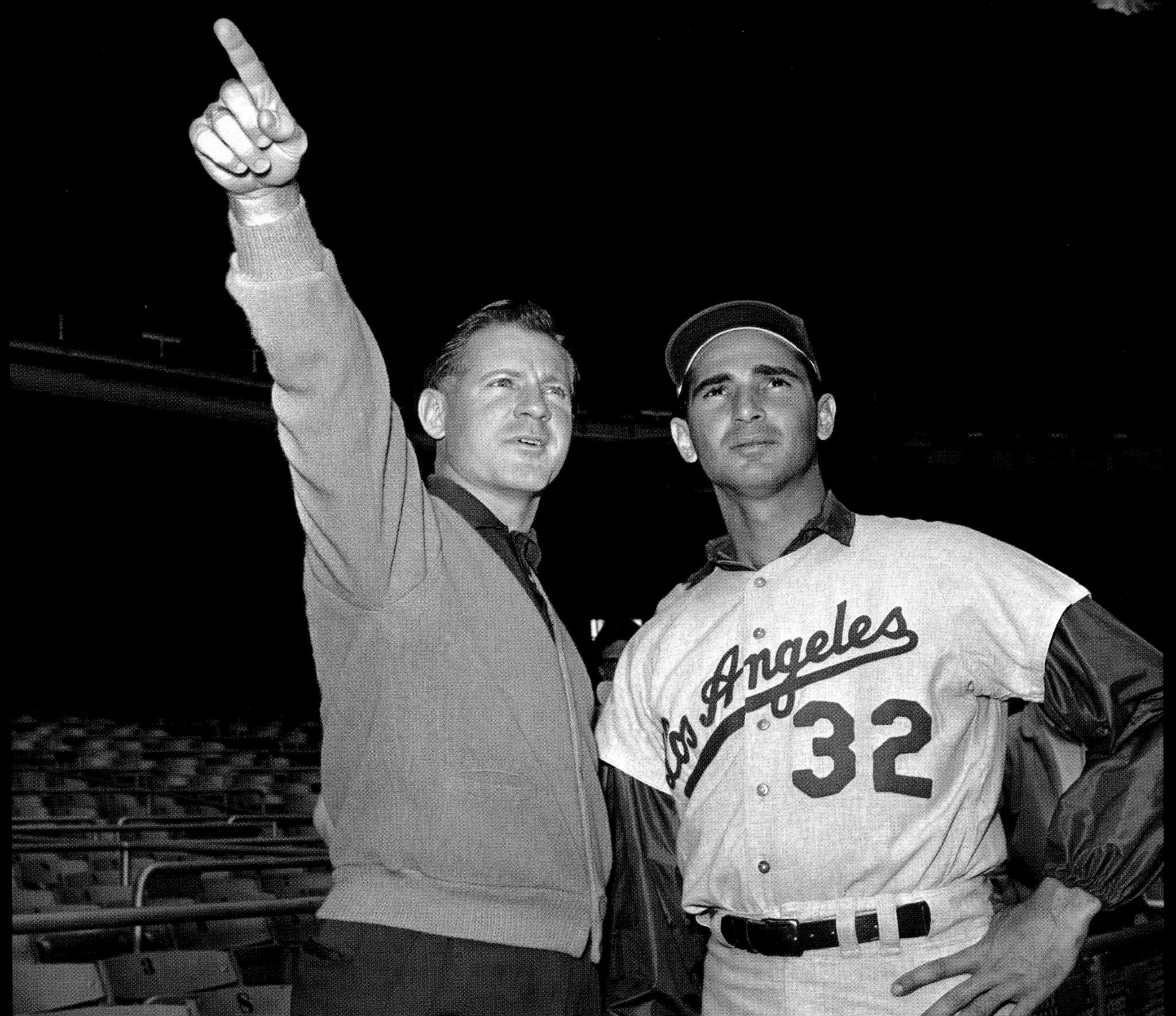
Los Angeles
32

July

2

NOW THEY'RE LEAGUES APART

Two men who had spent a lot of time in dugouts together, Yankees manager Yogi Berra, left, and New York Mets manager Casey Stengel, joke at Shea Stadium, June 15, 1964, as rain washed out the second annual Mayor's Trophy Game between the two teams. After the 1960 World Series loss to the Pittsburgh Pirates, the Yankees had replaced Stengel with manager Ralph Houk. Casey found an Amazin' new home with the expansion Mets, and Yogi was now in his first season as a manager, having taken the Yankees' reins from Houk.

The Mayor's Trophy Game was an annual charity exhibition game between the two clubs. Little importance was attached to the results; it felt more like a spring training game than a Subway Series. When this game was finally played on August 24, the Yankees won 6–4.

September 28, 1968 As manager Ralph Houk continues the slow rebuilding of a younger team, with the Yankees inching up from ninth place in 1967 to a distant fifth, Mickey Mantle plays his 2,401st and final game as a Yankee, in Fenway Park.

NEW YOR
Mets

July

3

THE MANTLE MAGIC RETURNS

Frank Crosetti, the Yankees' star shortstop in the 1930s and then longtime third base coach, congratulates Mickey Mantle as the slugger rounds the bases on a leadoff ninth-inning homer to give the Yankees a 2–1 victory over the St. Louis Cardinals in Game 3 of the World Series at Yankee Stadium, October 10, 1964. Walking back to the dugout is Cardinals third baseman Ken Boyer. The home run, on reliever Barney Schultz's first pitch, was Mantle's sixteenth World Series homer, breaking the previous mark of fifteen held by Babe Ruth. The Mick would go deep twice more against the Cards in this, his twelfth and last Fall Classic.

November 19, 1968 Pitcher Stan Bahnsen (17–12, 2.05 ERA) wins the Rookie of the Year Award.

EXIT
Cardinals
14

July

4

BIG YANK INDEED

Mickey Mantle would hit .333 with three home runs and eight RBIs in the 1964 World Series. His eighteen career World Series home runs remains the record. Not a bad way to be remembered. Here the Yankees slugger leans on his bat as he awaits his turn in the batting cage at Yankee Stadium prior to Game 5 of the Series against the St. Louis Cardinals, October 12, 1964. Only a two-run ninth-inning home run by left fielder Tom Tresh, which temporarily tied the game, prevented the Yankees from being shut out as St. Louis starter Bob Gibson went all ten innings of the game, holding the Yankees to six hits. The Cards won 5–2 on Tim McCarver's three-run homer in the tenth, to take a three-games-to-two lead in the Series.

March 1, 1969 Mickey Mantle announces his retirement. His number, 7, is retired on June 8, Mickey Mantle Day, at Yankee Stadium.

BIG YANK
Esso
FOR
Happy Motoring
Coca-Cola
REFRESHING
7

July

5

THE LAST HURRAH

Elston Howard, left, Tom Tresh (15), and Mickey Mantle (7) greet first baseman Joe Pepitone at home plate after Pepitone's grand slam in the eighth inning of Game 6 of the World Series against the St. Louis Cardinals at Sportsman's Park, October 14, 1964. Pepitone, in his third season as a Yankee, was second only to Mantle in home runs (twenty-eight) and RBIs (one hundred). The Yankees won the game 8–3, as Mantle and Roger Maris also provided solo home runs, back-to-back in the sixth inning, behind the pitching of Jim Bouton and Steve Hamilton. But the Cards came back to win the final game of this Series. The Yankees would not appear in another World Series until 1976, and they would not win one again until 1977.

In his first year as manager, Yogi Berra had taken the Yankees to the seventh game of the World Series against the Cardinals. Naturally, the Yankees fired him. And they hired? Johnny Keane, who had managed the Cardinals in the World Series!

July 21, 1969 Babe Ruth is voted "the Greatest All-Time Player" and Joe DiMaggio "the Greatest Living Player" in balloting announced at the All-Star banquet in Washington, D.C.

NEW YORK
15
7

July

NO TRANSLATION NEEDED

Puerto Rican youngsters plead for Mickey Mantle's autograph from the dugout roof before an exhibition game between the Yankees and the Washington Senators in San Juan, April 5, 1965. Coming off the 1964 World Series loss to the St. Louis Cardinals, the Yankees, under new manager Johnny Keane, stumbled to a sixth-place finish at 77–85, their first losing season since 1925. And in the twilight of his career, the Mick had one of his worst seasons, batting .255 with nineteen home runs and forty-six RBIs in 122 games.

August 10, 1969 Bobby Murcer, late-season call-up Thurman Munson, and Gene Michael hit consecutive home runs, Munson's first in the major leagues. Despite the slugging of Murcer and Joe Pepitone and the pitching of Mel Stottlemyre (later Joe Torre's longtime pitching coach, in his second straight season of at least twenty wins) and Fritz Peterson, the Yankees finish the first season of East and West divisions in fifth place out of six teams.

NEW YORK
YANKEES
NEW YORK

July

7

BIG SHOES TO FILL

In his thirteenth season with the Yankees, catcher Elston Howard walks beside Yankee Stadium with manager Ralph Houk after learning he had been traded to the Boston Red Sox, August 3, 1967. Ellie would join the Red Sox in time to win the 1967 pennant. With the departure of the nine-time All-Star (1957–65) and 1963 American League MVP, Jake Gibbs handled most of the catching duties until Thurman Munson became the Yanks' starting catcher in 1970.

June 24, 1970 Bobby Murcer, who hits at least twenty-two home runs each season from 1969 through 1973, homers in four official at bats in a row during a doubleheader at home against Cleveland. The team ends up in second place in the AL East, with a 93–69 record, though far behind the Orioles.

July

END OF AN ERA

With Mickey Mantle's retirement before the 1969 season, one of the last links to the glory days of the 1950s and early 1960s was gone from the lineup. Here the Mick hangs up his uniform in the Yankee Stadium locker room on Mickey Mantle Day, June 8, 1969. The Yankees retired his number, 7, on this day, and Joe DiMaggio presented Mantle with the plaque that would hang in center field. Mantle, in turn, presented DiMaggio with a plaque and said, "His has got to be hanging just a little bit higher than mine." The plaques were eventually relocated to Monument Park, and in 1996—the year after his death—Mantle's plaque was replaced by a monument that reads in part: "A magnificent Yankee who left a legacy of unequaled courage." The Mick's 536 career home runs remain the record for a switch-hitter. He was elected to the Hall of Fame in his first year of eligibility, 1974.

August 8, 1970 Casey Stengel's number, 37, is retired, four years after he is voted into the Hall of Fame and five years before his death.

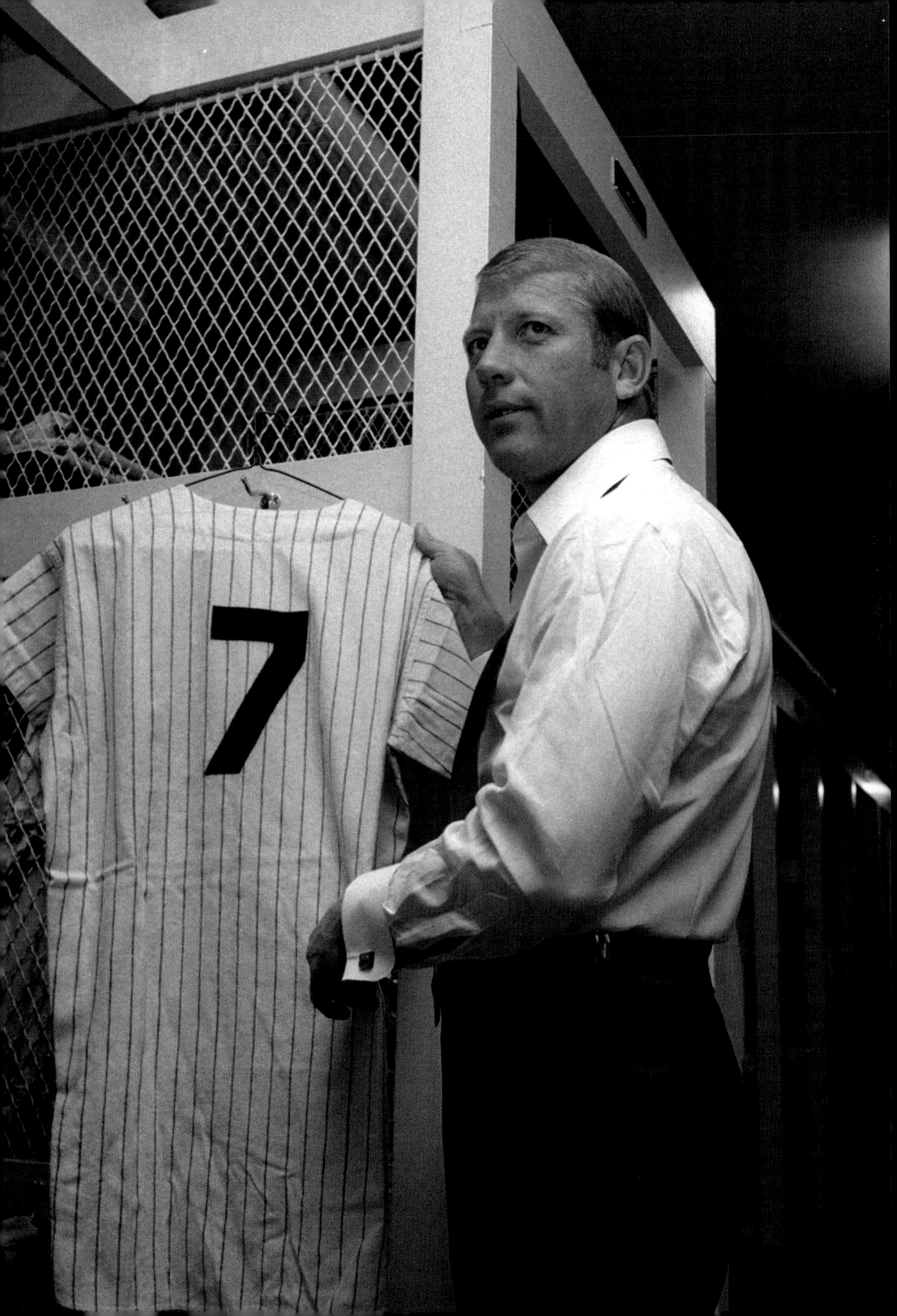
7

July

TAKIN' CARE OF BUSINESS

New York Jets quarterback Joe Namath, right, and retired Yankees star Mickey Mantle introduce their New York employment agency, Mantle Men and Namath Girls, Inc., at a news conference in New York, August 11, 1969. It's unclear why anyone would entrust their career prospects to an agency represented by these two men-about-town, but Mantle was a New York legend and Namath was coming off his Super Bowl III miracle. For sheer star appeal, you'd be hard-pressed to find two better names in 1969. The company, aimed at young job seekers, reported gross revenue of some $2 million in its first year and planned franchises in other cities.

November 25, 1970 Thurman Munson, the Yankees' starting catcher since spring training, wins the Rookie of the Year Award.

"Our people are pros,
just like us."
Men & Namath

July

10

OLD SCHOOL

Center fielder Bobby Murcer slams into Detroit Tigers catcher Tim Hosley in the fifth inning at Yankee Stadium, September 5, 1971. He scored, Hosley was replaced behind the plate, and the Yankees won 6–5. Even with the team eighteen and a half games out of first, Murcer didn't mind taking some hard knocks for the team.

Murcer was billed as a shortstop and spent some time at third base, but his switch to the outfield coincided with the retirement of his fellow Oklahoman Mickey Mantle. By 1970, he was the starting center fielder, prompting no shortage of comparisons to the Commerce Comet. With the Yankees adrift in the early 1970s, Bobby was looked to as the next Mick, but Bobby Murcer would be the first to tell you he was no Mantle. No one was. Murcer was a tough, consistent, and popular teammate, good for about twenty-five home runs and ninety RBIs most seasons. Nothing wrong with that.

September 30, 1971 The Yankees win the last game of a mediocre fourth-place season on a forfeit after Washington Senators fans at RFK Stadium prematurely come onto the field during the home team's last game before moving to Texas.

July

11

HATS OFF

Between games of a doubleheader between the Yankees and the California Angels, Yankees greats Mickey Mantle, left, and Joe DiMaggio doff their caps at Yankee Stadium as they appear for the annual Old-Timers' Game, July 22, 1972. The first official Old-Timers' Day was held in 1946 to give fans an opportunity to see their favorite players put on the pinstripes once again. The tradition began after the memorable visits that both Lou Gehrig and Babe Ruth made to the stadium in their declining health. The Old-Timers' Game is usually a few innings between former players who put the spikes on once a year, if that. A record seventy-two players showed up for Old-Timers' Day on August 2, 2008, the last such day in the old Yankee Stadium.

March 22, 1972 Relief pitcher Sparky Lyle is picked up from the Red Sox in a trade, and his thirty-five saves help the Yankees compete with three other teams before finishing in fourth place, but only six and a half games out of first.

Marlboro Country.

July

12

HE TAKES THE CAKE

Yankees reliever Sparky Lyle leaps the bullpen fence before a game with the Detroit Tigers at Yankee Stadium, August 8, 1972. Prior to the game, Lyle, who regularly emerged from the bullpen to put out fires for the Yankees, in a manner of speaking, received a six-week-old Dalmatian puppy in recognition of his performance, which had seemingly breathed new life into the team and its fans. Lyle pitched three innings in relief of Fritz Peterson on this day to get the win; the final score was 4–2. Lyle had joined the Yankees after five seasons with the Red Sox. In more than one hundred innings of relief this season, he posted a thrifty 1.92 ERA. Among his other claims to fame? He liked to celebrate teammates' birthdays by dropping his pants and sitting on the cake in the clubhouse.

Despite Lyle's valiant efforts, Ralph Houk's Yankees finished in fourth place in 1972, going 79–76.

April 18, 1972 The Yankees retire number 8 for two players on the same day, in honor of Hall of Fame catchers Bill Dickey and Yogi Berra, his protégé.

MONT
CHI
CLEV
BOST
NEW YORK
CINCI
BALT
MILW
NO BETTING
IN STADIUM
TIGERS
BATTING ORDER
YANKEES
Country.
Dr Pepper is making
York.
BALL
STRIKE
OUT

July

13

BLOCKBUSTER TRADE IN THE OFF-SEASON

Yankees pitchers Fritz Peterson, front, and Mike Kekich sit on a schooner's bowsprit with their wives, Marilyn Peterson and Susanne Kekich, on Long Island Sound, August 28, 1972. The two couples were close. Very close. By the time spring training rolled around in 1973, shortly after George Steinbrenner had purchased the team, the two pitchers announced that they had swapped families: wives, kids, and family pets. Baseball officials were mortified; fans were shocked and appalled. Neither player pitched with great success again. Peterson, an accomplished pitcher before the swap (winning at least fifteen games in 1969–72, twenty in 1970), became the target of fans' invective around the league, and his numbers plummeted. He went 8–15 in 1973 and was traded to the Cleveland Indians early in the 1974 season. Kekich, a ten-game winner in each of the previous two years, was only 1–1 when he was dealt to Cleveland in June 1973, and he ended up playing for three different teams, going 6–8 for the rest of his career.

August 7, 1972 Yogi Berra and Lefty Gomez—like his right-handed partner Red Ruffing, a four-time twenty-game winner and Yankees ace through the 1930s—are inducted into the Hall of Fame.

July

14

AN ENDURING LEGACY

Clubhouse attendant and equipment manager Pete Sheehy works in the Yankee Stadium clubhouse at the age of sixty-two, April 12, 1973. The stadium was turning fifty, and Sheehy had been there for almost all of it. He was still a schoolboy of sixteen when he was picked to help with the sweaty shirts and dirt-stained trousers of the New York Yankees in 1927. Sheehy spent the next fifty-eight years with the Yankees, a career that spanned the decades from Babe Ruth's Murderers' Row to Don Mattingly's MVP season. It's said that when Lou Gehrig decided to end his playing days, he flipped his glove to Sheehy, saying, "I'm done, Pete." Sheehy also assigned the number 7 to Mickey Mantle when the struggling rookie, originally given number 6, was recalled from the minors in Kansas City. Although Sheehy had stopped traveling to away games, he remained active with the club until his death in August 1985. As seemed only appropriate, the Yankee Stadium clubhouse was named for him.

August 8, 1972 New York City agrees to buy Yankee Stadium—which the Yankees were actually leasing ever since the stadium was sold to a series of outside owners starting in 1953—and the Yankees schedule renovations, to be completed in 1976, as part of a thirty-year lease with the city.

July

15

LUMBERYARD

Young fans raise their bats in salute as the Yankees take the field against the California Angels at Yankee Stadium, June 3, 1973 (a game the Yankees won, 3–2). Bat Day was always a popular promotion at the stadium; each year, the bat would honor a current player. At one point, an emergency medical group actually published a study on the incidence of blunt force trauma in New York emergency rooms in the days immediately after the 1990 Bat Day. Fortunately, the study found no correlation between the distribution of thousands of Little League bats and emergency room visits.

August 29, 1972 Bobby Murcer hits for the cycle in the first game of a doubleheader at home against the Texas Rangers; it is the first time a Yankee has accomplished the feat since Mickey Mantle in 1957.

SOMERS
LOVES THE
YANKEES

July

16

HISTORY IN THE TAKING

Long before eBay appears on the horizon, fans cart away seats and other pieces of Yankee Stadium on the last day of the season, September 30, 1973, after the Yankees hosted the Detroit Tigers (and lost to them, 8–5) in the last game at the "original" stadium. After this game, the stadium shut down for two years to be gutted and renovated. The renovation included the replacement of all the wooden seats with more contemporary, wider plastic ones. The refurbished stadium opened on April 15, 1976. During the 1974 and 1975 seasons, the Yankees played their home games at Shea Stadium, the Mets' home in Queens. Those original seats now turn up at auction, commanding top dollar. And it is possible to buy jewelry, pens, and other items made from pieces of wood from the seats.

January 3, 1973 With attendance in 1972 dipping below one million for the first time since 1945, a limited partnership led by George M. Steinbrenner III buys the Yankees from CBS for about $10 million. Steinbrenner promises "absentee ownership as far as running the Yankees is concerned."

43

July

17

HALL OF FAMERS ALL

From left, Yankees greats Mickey Mantle, Yogi Berra, Whitey Ford, Joe DiMaggio, and Casey Stengel gather on the steps of Shea Stadium before the annual Old-Timers' Game, August 3, 1974. The game was played at Shea during the Yankee Stadium renovation. Give DiMaggio credit. At fifty-nine, he was still able to bring the crowd of 50,828 to its feet with two long drives: one that just hooked foul and a second that landed on the warning track. The Old-Timers' Game was played before the scheduled Yankees game against the Red Sox, won by the Yankees 6–2.

March 5, 1973 Pitchers Mike Kekich and Fritz Peterson announce at spring training that they have swapped wives, children, and even dogs. After the swap, Kekich and Marilyn Peterson last just a few months as a couple. But Fritz Peterson and Susanne Kekich divorce their spouses, remain together, marry, and have four children.

July

18

HERE'S THE PITCH

Joe DiMaggio demonstrates the Mr. Coffee coffeemaker in a 1970s commercial. Never one to pass up a business opportunity, DiMaggio made a handsome profit for both the company and himself as the dignified and trusted spokesman of Mr. Coffee. New Yorkers also knew him as the face of the Bowery Savings Bank. The Yankee Clipper was highly protective of his image and marketability. He carefully managed the use of his name and the sale of his autographed baseball merchandise, and he made sure he was well compensated for appearing at baseball events, nightspots, and various celebrity functions.

April 6, 1973 Ron Blomberg becomes the first designated hitter in Major League Baseball, going 1 for 3 against the Boston Red Sox after a first-inning walk.

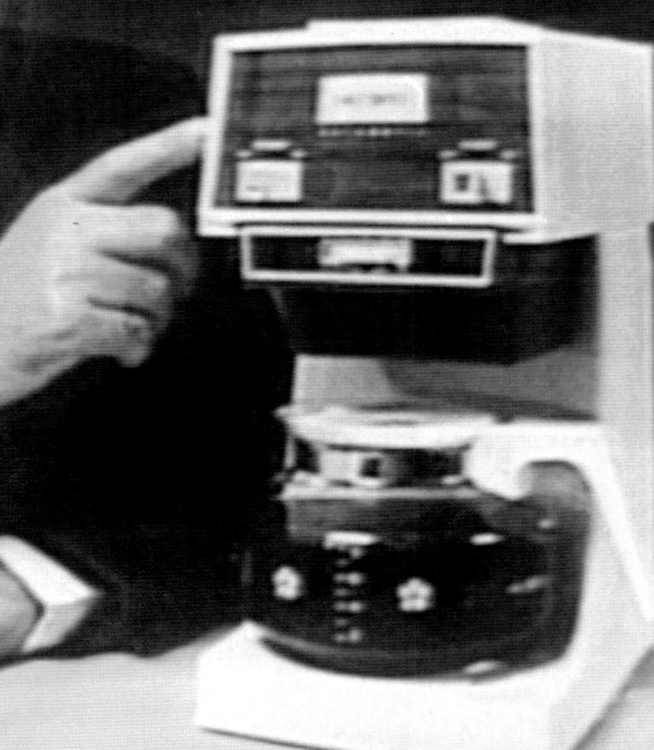
Joe DiMaggio

July

19

WINTER BALL

Jim "Catfish" Hunter tosses a ball for news photographers after the Yankees introduced him at Shea Stadium, January 8, 1975. Hunter, one of baseball's elite pitchers, had been declared a free agent when it was determined that Charlie Finley, the owner of the Oakland A's, had breached Hunter's contract. Coming off a Cy Young Award season, Hunter was up for grabs, and no fewer than twenty teams vied for his services. He eventually signed with the Yankees, in a $3.75 million deal that made him the first of the mega-dollar free agents. The era of free agency had arrived.

September 30, 1973 The Yankees play their final game at Yankee Stadium before two years of major renovations begin, ending the season with another fourth-place finish. Ralph Houk resigns as manager, as does Lee McPhail as general manager.

July

20

PLEASE PARDON OUR APPEARANCE

The overhaul of Yankee Stadium continues, April 18, 1975, with about a year to go until Opening Day. Baseball returned to the stadium on April 15, 1976. Among the changes to the House That Ruth Built, the 118 columns that formerly supported the stadium's grandstand—and obstructed fans' view—were removed. The field was lowered, home plate moved several feet, and the outfield wall repositioned to reduce the expanse of Death Valley in left-center. New seats, lights, and a huge new scoreboard were also installed.

January 3, 1974 With Gabe Paul already installed as George Steinbrenner's choice for both president (to be replaced by Al Rosen in 1978, with Steinbrenner himself assuming the role in 1980) and general manager, Bill Virdon takes over as the first of more than a dozen Yankees managers in the Steinbrenner era, five of them serving two—or more—tours of duty. In his only complete season, the Yankees end up in second place, only two games back—their best finish in a decade.

YANKS AT SHEA
PHONE 592 8200

July

21

DON'T BURST HIS BUBBLE

Catfish Hunter reads fan mail at his locker in Shea Stadium, September 9, 1975. On September 7 in Baltimore, Hunter had pitched a complete game shutout of the Baltimore Orioles for his twentieth win. He finished the season 23–14, with a 2.58 ERA, and joined Hall of Famers Walter Johnson and Lefty Grove as the only American Leaguers with twenty or more wins in at least five straight seasons. In fact, 1975 would be the last season at that level for Hunter, whose 250-plus innings every year in 1970–76 most likely contributed to persistent arm problems. He played four more seasons, with relatively modest numbers, but he remained a positive and popular presence in the clubhouse. Hunter was a eight-time All-Star, twice with the Yankees, and was elected to the Hall of Fame in 1987. He battled diabetes during his career and died in 1999, at just fifty-three, of amyotrophic lateral sclerosis—Lou Gehrig's disease.

April 6, 1974 The Yankees open the first of two seasons sharing Shea Stadium, the home of the New York Mets; it is the Yankees' first home game away from Yankee Stadium since 1922. They enjoy a 90–69 record at Shea in 1974–75.

July

22

I LIKE WHAT YOU'VE DONE WITH THE PLACE

New York Yankees owner George Steinbrenner, right, and Mike Burke, a public relations consultant and former Yankees president, take a look around the newly refurbished Yankee Stadium on April 13, 1976, before ceremonies opening it to the public.

When Steinbrenner bought the team in 1973, he promised, "I won't be active in the day-to-day operations of the club at all." Of course, nothing could have been further from the truth, and the Boss has had a hand in decisions large and small, on and off the field, ever since. One of his first acts was reportedly to stop the daily deliveries of fresh-cut flowers that Burke had ordered for the female assistants in the team offices.

August 12, 1974 Appropriately, teammates and close friends Mickey Mantle and Whitey Ford are inducted into the Hall of Fame together.

July

23

EXTREME MAKEOVER

After a two-year renovation, Yankee Stadium is readied for Opening Day in 1976. This was the golden era of cookie-cutter stadiums, and while Yankee Stadium retained some of its classic ambience, what it gained in amenities it lost in character. After the overhaul, you could make a strong case that this was no longer the House That Ruth Built. However, you could also argue that the DNA of Yankees history, tradition, and pride still infused the place. As it turned out, there was still plenty of history to be played out here.

November 27, 1974 George Steinbrenner is fined $15,000 in court for making illegal contributions to President Richard Nixon's 1972 reelection campaign, and Commissioner Bowie Kuhn then suspends Steinbrenner from baseball for two years, though the suspension is rescinded in March 1976.

YANKEE STADIUM
4 ENTRY
PRESS
HASTINGS

July

24

SUNDAY IN THE PARK WITH GEORGE

I must be in the front row! Not exactly. Yankees principal owner George Steinbrenner, apparently in search of a warm beer and an overpriced hot dog, takes in a Sunday afternoon doubleheader with the regular folks in the bleachers, June 27, 1976. That's him in the aviator shades at center, about four rows from the top. The Boss was rewarded with two wins over the Milwaukee Brewers, 6–2 and 10–2.

December 31, 1974 Pitcher Jim "Catfish" Hunter signs a record five-year, $3.75 million contract, touching off the free agent era of Major League Baseball. The Yankees' ace in 1975–76, he retires in 1979 and will enter the Hall of Fame in 1987.

July

25

SCORING POSITION

Yankees second baseman Willie Randolph scores as Boston Red Sox catcher Carlton Fisk takes Rico Petrocelli's throw in the second inning at Yankee Stadium, July 24, 1976. Mickey Rivers laid down the bunt to bring Randolph home. The Yankees won 4–1 behind a complete game from pitcher Ed Figueroa, leaving the Yanks thirteen games ahead of the second-place Cleveland Indians. Randolph would play thirteen seasons as the starting second baseman for the Yankees, helping the Yanks to five division titles, four AL pennants, and two world championships. A calm, steady, and professional presence in a turbulent Yankees clubhouse, Randolph was the team cocaptain, with pitcher Ron Guidry, from 1986 through 1988. (Guidry remained team captain until he retired in mid-1989.)

August 1, 1975 After the Yankees go 53–51, Billy Martin is hired to replace Bill Virdon as manager, the first of Martin's five separate stints as manager of the Yankees. The Yankees have only a 30–26 record the rest of the season, for a distant third-place finish.

July

THE YANKEES ARE BACK

Yankees first baseman Chris Chambliss celebrates after hitting the game-winning home run in the bottom of the ninth inning during the fifth and deciding game of the AL Championship Series against the Kansas City Royals at Yankee Stadium, October 14, 1976. His home run, off Mark Littell, broke a 6–6 tie to win the American League pennant, propelling the Yankees into their first World Series appearance in twelve years. Although the Yankees would lose the World Series in four straight games to the Cincinnati Reds' Big Red Machine, they had served notice that they were contenders again. The Chambliss home run remains a Yankees highlight, always included on any list of great Yankee Stadium moments.

April 15, 1976 A crowd of 52,613 sees the Minnesota Twins' Dan Ford hit the first home run on Opening Day at the extensively remodeled Yankee Stadium. Renovations include cantilevered upper decks, fewer but wider plastic seats, a new roofline, a relocated Monument Park off the playing field, and a huge new scoreboard with baseball's first state-of-the-art "telescreen"—all for $100 million. The Yankees go on to win 11–4, a sign of far better days ahead.

July

27

BRONX BOMBER

A smoke bomb does little to distract Yankees first baseman Chris Chambliss as he faces Kansas City Royals right-hander Mark Littell in the sixth inning of Game 2 of the AL Championship Series at Yankee Stadium, October 6, 1977. Littell had served up the ball that Chambliss planted in the seats for a walk-off, pennant-winning home run one year earlier. This time, Littell and catcher Darrell Porter were taking no chances. They gave Chambliss an intentional walk, and Littell gave him another in the eighth—but the Yankees won the game anyway, 6–2, to tie the series at one win each. The umpire is Russ Goetz.

April 17, 1976 The year's AL MVP Award winner, Thurman Munson is named captain of the Yankees, the first since Lou Gehrig's death in 1941.

July

28

CY YOUNG SEASON

Yankees catcher Thurman Munson runs to congratulate a leaping Sparky Lyle after the Yankees beat the Royals 5–3 at Royals Stadium to win the AL Championship Series for the second straight year, October 9, 1977. The Yankees had come from behind to score three runs in the top of the ninth inning, and Lyle kept the Royals in check to earn the win. Lyle would appear in relief twice in the World Series against the Los Angeles Dodgers, winning Game 1 and posting a 1.93 ERA for the Series. Lyle won the 1977 Cy Young Award, going 13–5 as a reliever. Although Lyle helped the Yankees win three pennants and two World Series, the relationship soured when the Yankees signed hard-throwing reliever Goose Gossage after the 1977 season. By 1979, Lyle was in a Texas Rangers uniform. Third baseman Graig Nettles had the famous line that Lyle "went from Cy Young to sayonara." In 1979, Lyle detailed his Yankees experiences in *The Bronx Zoo*, a best-selling tell-all book with co-author Peter Golenbock that became the *Ball Four* of its era.

June 15, 1976 The Yankees acquire Vida Blue from Oakland Athletics owner Charlie Finley for $1.5 million—but three days later, Commissioner Bowie Kuhn orders the deal canceled on the grounds that it would be unfairly beneficial to the Yankees.

15
Royals

July

29

ROYAL FLUSH

Graig Nettles, Yankees third baseman, is doused with champagne in the clubhouse at Royals Stadium after the Yankees defeated the Kansas City Royals 5–3, to win the AL Championship Series, October 9, 1977. Although it lacked the drama of Chris Chambliss's 1976 home run, the Yankees had again put the winning run across the plate in their last at bat. This time, Willie Randolph hit a sacrifice fly to score Roy White with the go-ahead run. Pitching in relief, Sparky Lyle earned two of the Yankees' three wins, with a series ERA of 0.96. Thurman Munson led the Yankees' offense with five RBIs. The Yankees would face the Los Angeles Dodgers for the World Series title.

October 2, 1976 Billy Martin's Yankees—the arms of Ed Figueroa, Catfish Hunter, and Dock Ellis; the bats of Graig Nettles, Chris Chambliss, Oscar Gamble, Roy White, and Lou Piniella; the gloves of Thurman Munson, Willie Randolph, and Nettles; and the speed of Mickey Rivers, Randolph, and White—capture the AL East easily with a 97–62 record, snapping their third-longest stretch out of first place (after 1903–20 and 1982–93). Attendance tops two million for the first time since 1950.

July

SO MUCH FOR TEAM CHEMISTRY

The Yankees take the field as starting lineups are announced before Game 3 of the World Series against the Los Angeles Dodgers at Dodger Stadium, October 14, 1977. From left are manager Billy Martin, center fielder Mickey Rivers, second baseman Willie Randolph, catcher Thurman Munson, and right fielder Reggie Jackson. There was little love lost between Munson and Jackson. They developed a tense relationship after Jackson joined the Yankees in 1977 and was quoted by *Sport* magazine as saying: "I'm the straw that stirs the drink. . . . Maybe I should say me and Munson, . . . but he can only stir it bad." Jackson repeatedly denied criticizing the captain and claimed he had been misquoted, but the damage was done. It's said the two rarely spoke.

October 14, 1976 The Yankees win their thirtieth AL pennant on Chris Chambliss's dramatic ninth-inning home run off the Kansas City Royals' Mark Littell, snapping a 6–6 tie in Game 5 of the AL Championship Series. Fans pour onto the field, and Chambliss has to push past them to circle the bases—or where the bases, now souvenirs, were.

EW YORK
EW YORK
NEW YORK
YORK

July

31

WHEN OPPOSITES ATTRACT

Yankees right fielder Reggie Jackson swings manager Billy Martin behind his back before Game 5 of the World Series at Dodger Stadium, October 16, 1977. Martin and Jackson had a volatile relationship. When things were good, they were very good. But when things went badly, these two were at each other's throats. Going into this game, things were good: The Yankees held an imposing three-games-to-one lead in the Series. But the Dodgers rallied to a 10–4 victory behind ace Don Sutton to send the Series back to New York. Of little note: Jackson hit a solo home run on the first pitch he saw from Sutton in the eighth inning of this day's game. That didn't mean much at the time, but it presaged Jackson's epic performance in Game 6.

October 21, 1976 Reaching the World Series for the first time since 1964, the Yankees are no match for Cincinnati's Big Red Machine, and the Reds complete a four-game sweep.

August

1

GOING, GOING, GOING, GONE

World Series Game 6 started off well enough for Yankees right fielder Reggie Jackson at Yankee Stadium, October 18, 1977. In the second inning, he walked on four pitches from Los Angeles Dodgers pitcher Burt Hooton. The Dodgers should have stuck with that game plan. In his next three at bats, Jackson was first-pitch swinging, with the same result every time: three balls in the outfield seats, off three different pitchers.

Here, from left, Jackson goes deep off Hooton in the fourth inning. Then he takes Elias Sosa out of the park in the fifth. And finally, he admires his eighth-inning solo shot off Charlie Hough. Mr. October had five RBIs on the night and hit .450 for the Series. Not to be overlooked: The Yankees won the game 8–4 for their twenty-first world championship, their first since 1962.

November 29, 1976 The Yankees sign free agent Reggie Jackson to a five-year contract.

August

2

REGGIE JACKSON, RUNNING BACK

Yankees slugger Reggie Jackson, center, dodges fans while sprinting for the dugout after the final out of Game 6, as the Yankees clinched the World Series at Yankee Stadium, October 18, 1977. Jackson led his team to an 8–4 win over the Los Angeles Dodgers by hitting three home runs on three consecutive swings at the first pitch. In fact, going back to Game 5 in Los Angeles, he had connected on four straight first-pitch swings. Reggie owned all New York on this night.

June 18, 1977 Billy Martin pulls Reggie Jackson off the field during a game in Fenway Park for not hustling after a ball to right, and the two have to be physically separated during the ensuing dugout and clubhouse shouting match.

PISCATAWAY

August

DROUGHT ENDS IN THE BRONX

Elated fans mob the field, celebrating the first Yankees world championship in fifteen years after an 8–4 victory over the Los Angeles Dodgers at Yankee Stadium in Game 6 of the World Series, October 18, 1977. A member of the beefed-up stadium security detail described a "human wall" of fans descending onto the field.

June 30, 1977 In Toronto, Cliff Johnson becomes only the third Yankee to hit two home runs in a single inning.

SPORTS

August

THAT WINNING FEELING

Yankees manager Billy Martin, left, and his World Series MVP, slugger Reggie Jackson, laugh during a postvictory news conference at Yankee Stadium, October 18, 1977. Jackson clinched the world championship for the Yankees in front of a home crowd of 56,407 at Game 6 against the Los Angeles Dodgers. The postseason display of power earned Jackson the fitting sobriquet "Mr. October." He became only the second player in history to smash three home runs in a single Series game—Babe Ruth did it in 1926 and 1928. That's pretty good company.

October 9, 1977 After winning one hundred regular season games, the Yankees, down 3-2 going into the ninth inning of Game 5, score three runs to edge past Kansas City for the AL pennant in five games.

August

GOOSE IN FLIGHT

Yankees closer Rich "Goose" Gossage flies off the mound as he follows through on a ninth-inning pitch against the Kansas City Royals at Yankee Stadium, May 3, 1978. A high-priced free agent acquisition in the off-season, Gossage saved the game in relief of starter Ed Figueroa as the Yanks won 6–5. Reggie Jackson, Graig Nettles, and Jim Spencer all went deep off Royals starter Dennis Leonard. The Yankees had won four straight, including a three-game sweep of the Royals.

In this, his first season with the Yankees, Gossage won ten games in relief with a 2.01 ERA. Owner of a blistering fastball, he was a prototype of the power-pitching closer, a role that has since become a virtual necessity for a competitive team (but Gossage, who was elected to the Hall of Fame in 2008, often pitched the last two innings or even more).

October 18, 1977 In Game 6 of the World Series, Reggie Jackson enters baseball legend by hitting three first-pitch home runs against the Los Angeles Dodgers' Burt Hooton, Elias Sosa, and Charlie Hough (following another in his last at bat in Game 5), helping to earn him the nickname "Mr. October." The 8–4 win gives the Yankees their twenty-first world championship—their first in fifteen years.

August

URBAN RENEWAL

The home office of baseball appears in its 1976 post-renovation configuration. The bulge of Death Valley in left-center field is not as forbidding as it had been in the original House That Ruth Built, but it would still claim many a long ball. Before the renovation, left-center field was 457 feet, and straightaway center was 461 feet. Post-renovation, left-center stood at 430 feet, and dead center became "only" 417 feet. The outfield wall would be moved in twice more, in 1985 and 1988, giving hitters a little hope, and pitchers less room for error.

At foreground, center, is the smokestack designed to look like a Louisville Slugger, right down to peeling "tape" on the handle. For countless fans, it was the place to meet before the game, hence the common refrain, "Meet me at the bat."

October 26, 1977 With twenty-six saves, Sparky Lyle becomes the first AL relief pitcher to win the Cy Young Award.

YANKEE STADIUM

August

7

COOL CAJUN

Yankees starter Ron Guidry ices his pitching arm as he munches on a sparerib in the locker room following his eighteen-strikeout victory over the California Angels at Yankee Stadium, June 17, 1978. Guidry set the Yankees record for strikeouts in a game while earning his eleventh season victory with a four-hit shutout. The Louisiana southpaw was enjoying one of the greatest pitching seasons in Yankees history. Gator won thirteen games before his first loss, on July 7, and he finished the season at 25–3 with an ERA of 1.74 and a club record of 248 strikeouts. His nine shutouts tied Red Sox pitcher Babe Ruth's record for left-handers. He won the Cy Young Award unanimously, while finishing second to Boston's Jim Rice in the AL MVP voting. And in another claim to fame, Guidry, an amateur drummer in his spare time, once played with the Beach Boys during a postseason concert at the stadium.

January 13, 1978 The great Yankees manager Joe McCarthy dies at age ninety.

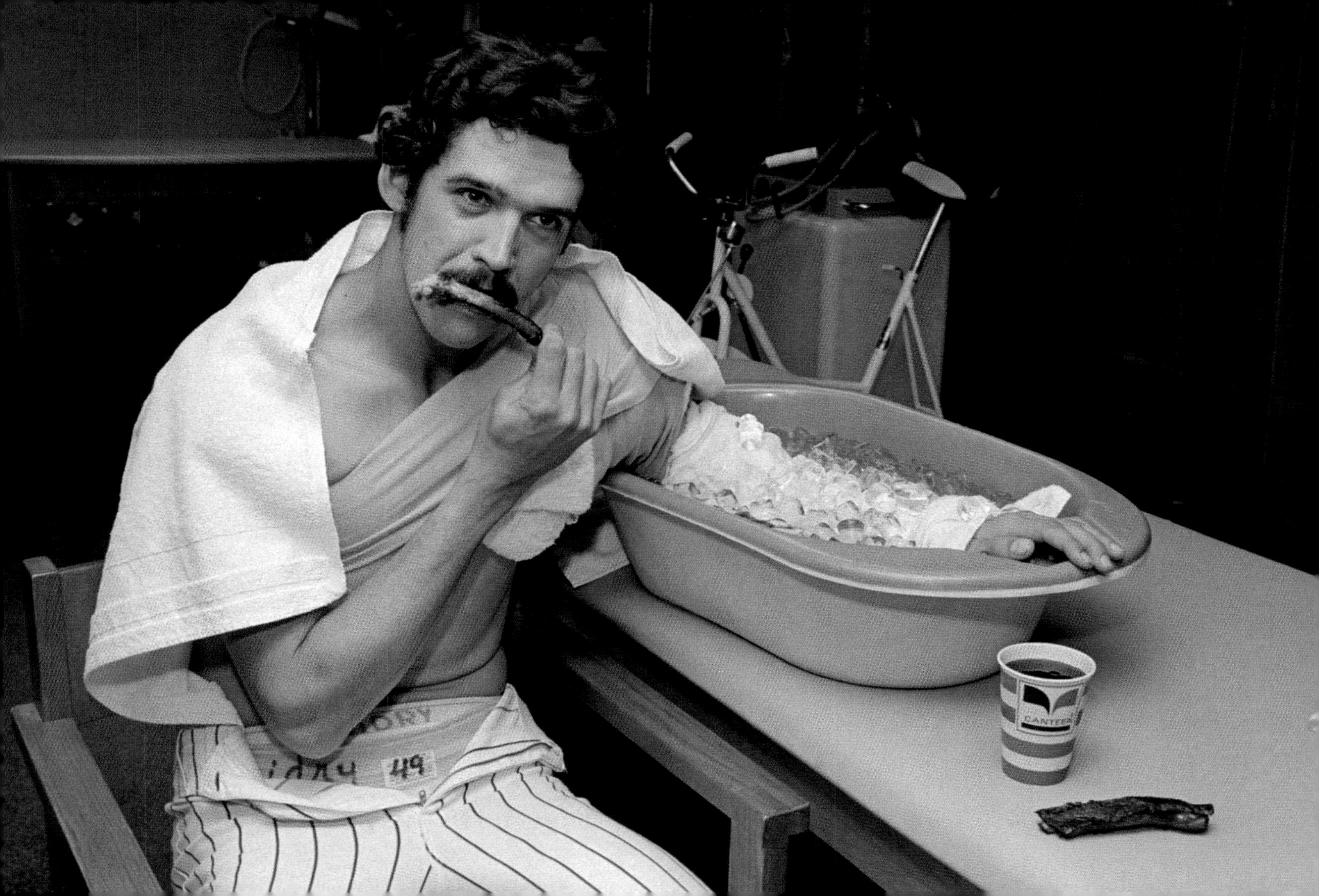
49
CANTEEN

August

FRIENDLY FIRE

Yankees owner George Steinbrenner, left, sits with manager Billy Martin during a break in taping a television commercial for Miller Lite beer at the Lotus Club in New York, July 15, 1978. The script involved a mock argument over the beer, with Steinbrenner finally saying, "Billy, you're fired!" To which Martin replied, "Not again!" Steinbrenner changed managers twenty times in his first twenty-three seasons—he hired and fired Martin alone five times. Reggie Jackson, no stranger to friction with the Boss and Billy, called the tempestuous relationship between Steinbrenner and Martin "a fatal attraction."—Glenn Liebman, *Yankee Shorts*

April 13, 1978 Opening Day at Yankee Stadium is also Reggie Candy Bar Day. When Reggie Jackson hits a three-run home run in the first inning, fans toss the Reggie Bar handouts all over the field.

Lite

August

SORE LOSER

Yankees manager Billy Martin reflects after announcing the "indefinite" suspension of slugger Reggie Jackson following a loss to the Kansas City Royals at Yankee Stadium, July 17, 1978. Jackson was suspended without pay for disobeying Martin's order to hit rather than bunt after the first pitch in the tenth inning, with a runner on base. Jackson bunted a third strike into the catcher's mitt, and the Royals went on to win 9–7 in the eleventh, dropping the Yankees fourteen games behind the Red Sox. In the long, contentious relationship between Martin and Jackson, this incident stood out. When Jackson returned after five games, Martin's comment to reporters regarding Jackson and owner George Steinbrenner—"One's a born liar and the other's convicted"—resulted in his resignation as the Yankees manager. From this low point of the season, the Bombers proceeded to climb into first place in less than two months.

June 17, 1978 Ron Guidry strikes out eighteen batters—including twelve out of thirteen in one stretch—in a 4–0 win against the California Angels, breaking a team record set by Bob Shawkey back in 1919.

August

10

LOUISIANA LIGHTNING

Ron Guidry pitches the fourth inning of a 4–0 win over the Boston Red Sox at Yankee Stadium, September 15, 1978. Once again, Guidry was overpowering, pitching a complete game two-hit shutout for his twenty-second win of the season. Though known for his wicked slider, Guidry was an outstanding all-around athlete who won five straight Gold Gloves. He led the league in victories from 1977 through 1986 with 163 and won more than twenty games three times. The Yankees retired his number, 49, in August 2003, but he has not received serious consideration for the Hall of Fame, despite the fact that he was one of the most dominant pitchers of his era. The obstacle for Guidry may be that he didn't have enough "great" seasons. Arguably, no one was better than Louisiana Lightning at his best, but his career win total, 170 over fourteen seasons, all in pinstripes, is modest by Hall of Fame standards.

July 25, 1978 Even-tempered Bob Lemon is named manager to replace Billy Martin, who won't be fired this time—he has resigned after directing a pointed insult at George Steinbrenner as well as at Reggie Jackson.

August

11

DEEP TO LEFT! YASTRZEMSKI WILL NOT GET IT!

That was the call from Yankees broadcaster Bill White as shortstop Bucky Dent, who had hit all of four home runs in the rest of the season, belted number five off Boston Red Sox starter Mike Torrez in the seventh inning of the one-game divisional playoff at Fenway Park, October 2, 1978. Both teams had finished the season with identical 99–63 records. Dent's shot over the Green Monster with two men on base put the Yankees ahead en route to an eventual 5–4 win and the AL Championship Series against the Kansas City Royals. It's said that after the game, Red Sox manager Don Zimmer coined the nickname by which Dent is still known in Boston: Bucky "F___ing" Dent.

July 29, 1978 The Yankees announce during Old-Timers' Day that the hugely popular Billy Martin will return as manager in 1980, and that Bob Lemon will then become general manager.

21

August

12

NEXT STOP, KANSAS CITY

The Yankees celebrate after winning the one-game playoff against the Boston Red Sox at Fenway Park, October 2, 1978, sending the Yankees to the postseason. Closer Goose Gossage popped up Carl Yastrzemski with two Red Sox on base in the bottom of the ninth, sending the Fenway faithful home stunned. From a fourteen-game Yankees deficit in mid-July, the Yankees and Red Sox had finished the season dead even. The tipping point had been the Boston Massacre of September 7–10, when the Yankees swept four games at Fenway by a combined score of 42–9; the Red Sox actually managed to tally more errors—twelve—than runs. Then came this season-deciding game, sealing the Red Sox's fate for yet another year. But the Yankees had a plane to catch—the American League Championship Series started in Kansas City the following day.

September 7, 1978 The Yankees begin a modern Boston Massacre: a four-day, four-game sweep of the first-place Red Sox by scores of 15–3, 13–2, 7–0, and 7–4. By September 10, the Yankees are in a tie for first.

NEW
27

August

13

TRUE GRIT

Willie Wilson of the Kansas City Royals bounces to his feet after colliding with Yankees catcher Thurman Munson in the seventh inning of Game 2 of the AL Championship Series at Kauffman Stadium in Kansas City, October 4, 1978. Wilson was out on the play, but Kansas City won 10–4 to tie the series at one game all. The Yankees went on to win the pennant in four games and face the Los Angeles Dodgers in the World Series. Munson was known as tough and gritty, both on and off the field, but was beloved by his teammates.

October 2, 1978 The Yankees, having trailed Boston by fourteen games in mid-July, defeat the Red Sox 5–4 in a one-game playoff at Fenway Park to win the AL East title. Capping the incredible comeback, they are down 2–0 in the seventh when light-hitting shortstop Bucky Dent belts a three-run home run over the left field Green Monster, putting the Yankees ahead for good despite a ninth-inning Red Sox threat.

KC

August

14

BRING ON THE DODGERS

Yankees closer Goose Gossage, right, leaps into the arms of Yankees catcher Thurman Munson after defeating the Kansas City Royals 2–1 in Game 4 to win the AL Championship Series at Yankee Stadium, October 7, 1978. Ron Guidry pitched this fourth game despite signs of arm trouble after his performance in the one-game playoff win against Boston five days earlier. Gossage earned the save one day after getting the win in Game 3. The Yanks also mounted a formidable offense in this ALCS, with Chris Chambliss, Reggie Jackson, and Mickey Rivers all hitting .400 or more for the series. On deck: the Dodgers, in a rematch of the 1977 World Series.

October 13, 1978 For the third straight year, the Yankees beat the Royals (in four games this time) to reach the World Series. In Game 3 of the Fall Classic, third baseman Graig Nettles makes four superb fielding plays that are crucial to the Yankees' first win after dropping two games to the Dodgers.

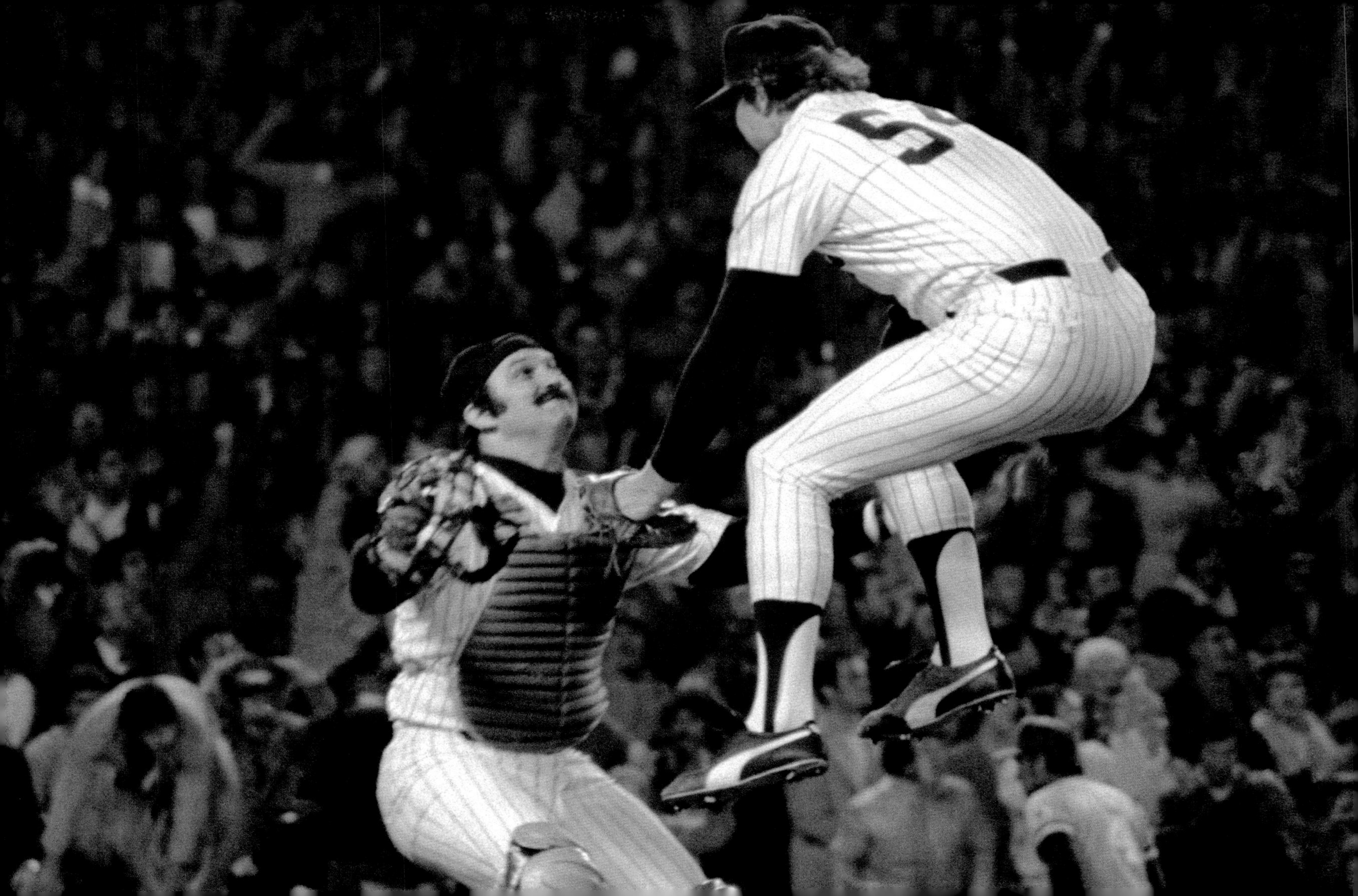

August

15

GREAT BEHIND THE PLATE

The great Yankees teams have been blessed with outstanding catchers. Bill Dickey, Thurman Munson, and Jorge Posada come to mind, along with the two men here: Yankees coaches Yogi Berra, left, and Elston Howard join the celebration after the Yankees clinched the pennant with a 2–1 win over the Kansas City Royals in Game 4 of the AL Championship Series at Yankee Stadium, October 7, 1978.

The first African American to become a Yankee, in 1955, Elston Howard was universally liked and respected as a person of class and dignity, but he was perhaps underrated as a catcher, and he is not in the Hall of Fame. As impressive as his statistics are, they could have been even better: He spent a number of years as Yogi's understudy, waiting for his chance to be Yankees' starting catcher. As Berra phased out of catching, Ellie became a first-tier catcher in his own right. In 1963, he became the first African-American player to win the American League MVP. He died far too early, of heart failure, at age fifty-one.

October 17, 1978 The Yankees beat the Los Angeles Dodgers to become the first team to win the World Series in six games after losing the first two. Their twenty-second world championship gives them back-to-back Series wins for the first time since 1961–62.

August

16

APPEARANCE COUNTS

Yankees pitcher Ed Figueroa checks himself in a mirror before taking the field for practice at Dodger Stadium, October 9, 1978, one day before starting Game 1 of the World Series against the Los Angeles Dodgers. Twenty-game winner Figueroa was ineffective; he didn't even get out of the second inning. The Yanks gave up runs in bunches on the way to an 11–5 loss in the opener.

A hair dryer in the locker room didn't exactly raise eyebrows in 1978. But in the 1960s, when colorful Yankees first baseman Joe Pepitone purportedly became the first player to bring one into the macho domain of the clubhouse, it made news, and the hair dryer became part of Joe Pep's legacy.

November 1, 1978 Ron Guidry earns the Cy Young Award with an incredible season, leading the majors with a 25–3 record, a 1.74 ERA, and nine shutouts. He just misses the pitching Triple Crown, striking out 248 to Nolan Ryan's 260.

YORK
SUN UP

August

17

HAVEN'T WE SEEN THIS BEFORE?

Picking up where he left off the previous October, Yankees designated hitter Reggie Jackson watches his solo home run off Los Angeles Dodgers pitcher Tommy John in the seventh inning of World Series Game 1 (which the Dodgers won 11–5) at Dodger Stadium, October 10, 1978. Mr. October would get a golden opportunity in Game 2 of the Series the next night, with the Yankees down by one run in the ninth inning. Jackson came to bat with two men on base and Dodgers rookie Bob Welch on the mound. The situation seemed made-to-order for a postseason slugger, but with the count full, Welch struck out Jackson swinging to end the game. The rookie won this matchup, but Jackson would have his revenge in Game 6, hitting a two-run homer off Welch.

June 18, 1979 A year earlier than planned, Billy Martin replaces Bob Lemon after a mediocre start by the Yankees.

August

18

GOOD ENOUGH TO WIN

Yankees catcher Thurman Munson congratulates pitcher Ron Guidry after the latter pitched the Yankees to a 5–1 victory over the Los Angeles Dodgers in Game 3 of the World Series at Yankee Stadium, October 13, 1978. The twenty-five-game winner wasn't at his best, giving up eight hits and seven walks, but he allowed only one run. Spectacular fielding from third baseman Graig Nettles killed Dodgers rallies and was credited with turning the Series around for the Bombers.

August 2, 1979 Yankees captain Thurman Munson dies at age thirty-two when the small plane he is piloting crashes at the airport near his home in Canton, Ohio. The Yankees immediately retire his number, 15, and fans filling Yankee Stadium the next night weep and clap for several minutes before the game in honor of the beloved Yankees captain.

August

19

MOST VALUABLE

Yankees shortstop Bucky Dent, World Series MVP, heads for the clubhouse at Dodger Stadium, October 17, 1978, with the arm of closer Goose Gossage, right, around his neck. For the second straight year, the Yankees defeated the Los Angeles Dodgers in the Fall Classic. Dent, the unlikely hero, batted .417 with ten hits and seven RBIs. He just edged out little-heralded second baseman Brian Doyle (subbing for the injured Willie Randolph and batting .438) for the title. The game ended on Thurman Munson's catch of Ron Cey's foul ball for the last out of the Series. That would be Munson's last play in a postseason game. He went out a winner.

August 6, 1979 Sleepless and only hours after delivering a eulogy at Thurman Munson's funeral, close friend Bobby Murcer uses Munson's bat to drive in all five of the Yankees' runs in a 5–4 win against the Orioles.

54

August

REPEAT: WE ARE THE CHAMPIONS

Yankees slugger Reggie Jackson kisses pitcher Ron Guidry after the Yankees won their second consecutive World Series by defeating the Los Angeles Dodgers 7–2 in Game 6 at Dodger Stadium, October 17, 1978. The Dodgers had led the Series two games to none until the Yankees reeled off four straight wins. Although Guidry wasn't at his best during this Series, he pitched a complete game win in Game 3, posting a 1.00 ERA. Reggie, meanwhile, lived up to his "Mr. October" moniker, hitting .391 with two home runs and eight RBIs.

October 28, 1979 The Yankees, shaken by the loss of their captain and by many changes in their championship lineups of 1977–78, drop to fourth place, and Billy Martin is replaced by Dick Howser a few days after getting into a bar fight.

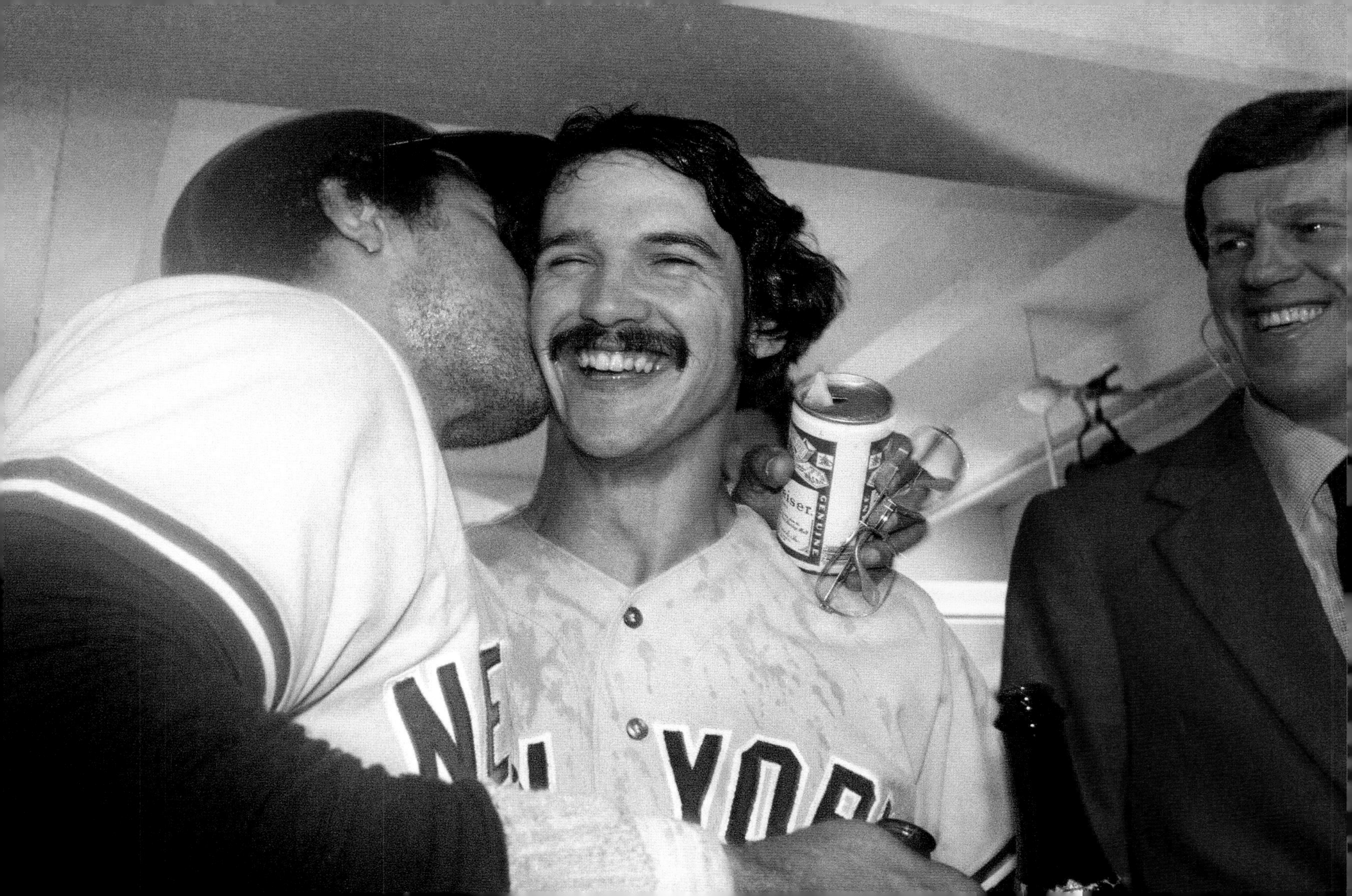
GENUINE

August

21

THE "SLUGGER'S" WIFE

Yankees closer Goose Gossage takes a chocolate offered by Bucky Dent's wife, Stormy, during the team's charter flight back to New York, October 18, 1978, the day after their World Series victory over the Los Angeles Dodgers. Stormy received the candy as a gift and was sharing it with the team. At right is Corna Gossage, Goose's wife. Bucky Dent's storybook season made him a celebrity—except in Boston, maybe—but the demands of the baseball season, personal appearances, and ongoing media attention put a strain on his family life. Dent and Stormy divorced four years later, after eleven years of marriage.

October 10, 1980 Dick Howser leads the Yankees to a 103–59 first-place finish, their most wins since 1963, but they are swept by the Kansas City Royals in three games for the AL pennant. George Brett caps the series with a three-run homer off ace Yankees reliever Goose Gossage in the seventh inning, giving the Royals the lead for good.

August

22

NOW THAT'S A RELIEF

Yankees ace starter Ron Guidry comes in to relieve Jim "Catfish" Hunter, who tosses him the ball in the seventh inning against the Oakland A's at Yankee Stadium, May 6, 1979. Guidry, coming off his Cy Young year, had volunteered to work out of the generally weak bullpen for part of the eleven-week period when injured reliever Goose Gossage was out of action. Gator wound up making three relief appearances, earning two saves. In this game, he went three and two-thirds scoreless innings to get the 6–5 win for the Yanks in ten innings.

November 21, 1980 After repeated feuds with vocal and temperamental owner George Steinbrenner, Dick Howser resigns as manager; he is replaced by Gene "Stick" Michael, a former Yankees infielder, coach, and versatile front office man.

August

23

THE BIONIC MAN

Los Angeles Dodgers manager Tommy Lasorda points out Yankees pitcher Tommy John to fans during the All-Star Game workout at Seattle's Kingdome, July 17, 1979. John had played six successful seasons with the Dodgers before the Yankees picked him up after the 1978 season. John had made a remarkable pitching comeback following experimental elbow surgery in 1974. In what is now known as "Tommy John surgery," doctors replaced a ligament in the elbow of his pitching arm with a tendon from his right forearm. He went on to pitch another fourteen years, including two stints with the Yankees, 1979–82 and 1986–89. In 1979 and 1980, he had two of his best seasons, winning twenty-one and twenty-two games respectively. In 1987, the left-hander went 13–6 during his second tour with the Yanks, leading the team in starts and innings pitched, at age forty-four. In all, John pitched for an incredible twenty-six years in the major leagues.

December 15, 1980 Setting a record at the time, the Yankees sign free agent Dave Winfield to a ten-year, $15 million contract. Winfield will play eight solid seasons for the Yankees, bat .340 in 1984, and hit more than thirty home runs in 1982 and 1983, despite very poor outings in his one AL Championship Series and World Series (1981). He will be voted into the Hall of Fame in 2001.

NY
2

August

24

STREET FIGHTING MEN

In a game against the California Angels, Yankees manager Billy Martin, right, arrives at home plate after umpire Fred Spenn threw catcher Thurman Munson out of the game for arguing a call in the sixth inning at Anaheim Stadium, July 14, 1979. The Angels rallied from a 6–0 deficit in the sixth to win in twelve innings, 8–7.

The Yankees of this era were a tough bunch, but none more than Munson. He'd stand up to anybody, and as the captain, he set the tone for the club. Martin could hold his own, too. As a player and then a manager, he had a reputation as a fighter. When this season ended, he punched out a marshmallow salesman, leading George Steinbrenner to fire him for the second time.

September 6, 1981 During the second portion of a season split in two by a two-month players' strike, Bob Lemon becomes manager for the second time, replacing Gene Michael.

August

THE TOUGHEST LOSS

Rescue workers inspect the wreckage of the Cessna Citation jet that crashed in Akron, Ohio, August 2, 1979, killing the pilot, Yankees catcher Thurman Munson. With two friends aboard, Munson was practicing takeoffs and landings in his new plane when he crashed short of the runway. The two passengers survived. Munson had learned to fly so he could travel back and forth between games to spend more time with his family in Ohio. He was thirty-two. Investigators determined that pilot error caused the crash.

October 28, 1981 The Yankees finish first in the prestrike "First Season," defeat the "Second Season" champion Milwaukee Brewers in five games for the AL East title, and reach the World Series for the first time in three years by sweeping the Oakland Athletics (managed by Billy Martin) in three games. But the Dodgers echo the Yankees' 1978 triumph by winning four straight games after losing the first two. Owner George Steinbrenner issues a much-criticized apology for the team's performance.

August

O CAPTAIN, MY CAPTAIN

With Thurman Munson's photo displayed on the outfield scoreboard, Yankees third baseman Graig Nettles bows his head at Yankee Stadium, August 3, 1979, during ceremonies honoring the memory of the team's catcher and captain, who died piloting his private jet the previous day. Before the game against the Baltimore Orioles (which the Yankees lost, 1–0), the Yankees starters stood at their defensive positions on the field, leaving the catcher's box empty. Munson played his entire career with the Yankees, becoming the team's first captain since Lou Gehrig. He was a seven-time All-Star, the 1970 American League Rookie of the Year, and the American League MVP in 1976.

November 30, 1981 Pitcher Dave Righetti—an excellent starter converted to an outstanding closer in 1984–90—wins the Rookie of the Year Award.

9
417

August

27

BLACK FRIDAY

The Yankees line up on the dugout steps at Yankee Stadium, their sleeves wrapped in black armbands, during a moment of silence, August 3, 1979, for Yankees catcher Thurman Munson, one day after he died piloting his private jet. Coach Yogi Berra is fifth from right, with Bobby Murcer at far right, head bowed. In his book *Number 1,* with Peter Golenbock, Martin wrote, "Thurman's death took a lot out of the ball club, took everything out of the ball club." The Yankees retired Munson's number, 15, and his locker in the Yankees clubhouse remained empty for good.

January 27, 1982 At the end of his contract, Reggie Jackson leaves the Yankees to sign with the California Angels.

August

RISING TO THE OCCASION

Bobby Murcer acknowledges the cheers of fans after his two-run single in the ninth inning defeated the Baltimore Orioles 5–4 at Yankee Stadium, August 6, 1979. Earlier in the day, Murcer had delivered a eulogy at the Canton, Ohio, funeral of his close friend and teammate Thurman Munson. Manager Billy Martin wanted Murcer to sit out that night's game, but Murcer refused. With the Yankees trailing 4–0, he hit a three-run homer in the seventh inning of the nationally televised game. Then his walk-off hit brought the house down. Murcer never used the bat again; he gave it to Munson's widow, Diana.

January 29, 1982 Graig Nettles becomes the captain of the Yankees, until 1984.

August

YOU CAN KICK DIRT; JUST DON'T CALL HIM "NOT CAPABLE"

Yankees manager Billy Martin kicks dirt on rookie home plate umpire Dallas Parks in the eighth inning of a game against the Minnesota Twins at Yankee Stadium, August 16, 1979. The Yankees had given up three runs in the inning before they recorded an out, and Martin was upset with the umpire's calls. When Parks tossed him from the game, Martin responded by kicking dirt at the umpire. Over the course of his managing career, Martin routinely had confrontations with umpires—and just about anybody else, really—for which he was ejected, fined, and suspended. At least Parks didn't sue him over the incident. Parks filed a suit against the Yankees and George Steinbrenner in 1982 when the Yankees' owner issued a press release saying of Parks, "My people tell me that he is not a capable umpire . . . obviously he doesn't measure up." Parks claimed that the Boss's comments went beyond the usual insults hurled at umpires. A judge disagreed and threw out the suit.

April 26, 1982 Gene Michael becomes manager for the second time, replacing Bob Lemon again.

1

August

YOU CAN'T SAVE 'EM ALL

Yankees closer Rich Gossage, right, is congratulated by catcher Rick Cerone after striking out the Detroit Tigers' Richie Hebner at Yankee Stadium to save his thirty-third game of the year, October 4, 1980. The save gave the Yanks a 5–2 win, clinching the AL East Division title for the fourth time in five years. But the Bombers would be swept by the Kansas City Royals in the AL Championship Series. In the deciding third game of that series, the usually unbeatable Gossage blew a save opportunity, giving up a three-run home run to George Brett. That turned out to be the winning hit, and the Royals were in the World Series.

Cerone, a New Jersey native who became popular with fans, was acquired from the Toronto Blue Jays for the 1980 season after the death of catcher Thurman Munson. He wore Phil Rizzuto's number 10 before it was retired by the Yankees. That first Yankees season would be Cerone's best; he batted .277 with fourteen home runs and eighty-five RBIs.

August 3, 1982 Gene Michael is fired after losing a doubleheader, and Steinbrenner adviser Clyde King becomes manager. With three managers and some unfortunate roster changes, the Yankees fall to fifth place and a 79–83 record—their worst since 1967.

August

31

HE CAN BE VERY DEFENSIVE

Third baseman Graig Nettles, center, and Yankees teammates celebrate their 5–3 win over the Milwaukee Brewers in Game 1 of the AL Division Series at County Stadium, October 7, 1981. The Yankees went on to win this series three games to two, then swept the Oakland A's in three games for the pennant. The Los Angeles Dodgers, however, would stop the Yankees' drive for another world championship in a six-game Fall Classic (the Yanks' last appearance in one until 1996).

Nettles started his major league career with the Minnesota Twins in 1967, and he went on to play for five more teams in a career that spanned twenty-two years, but he is best remembered for his eleven seasons with the Yankees. He is often described as the best all-around Yankees third baseman ever. Although Nettles never batted higher than .276 in a full season, he had power, averaging more than twenty home runs a season with the Yankees. For his entire career, he holds the record for AL third basemen with 319 home runs. But in Nettles's case, his glove may have been his biggest weapon.

September 7, 1982 The Yankees bring up four minor leaguers including Don Mattingly, who makes his major league debut in left field the next day and gets his first hit, an eleventh-inning single, on October 1 off Boston's Steve Crawford.

10
28

September

1

HOLDING NOTHING BACK

All-Star games aren't generally played like the seventh game of the World Series, but here Yankees base runner Dave Winfield sends Los Angeles Dodgers second baseman Steve Sax flying during the sixth inning of the interleague matchup at Olympic Stadium in Montreal, July 13, 1982. Winfield was forced out, but Sax was charged with an error that allowed Milwaukee Brewers base runner Robin Yount to advance to second. Winfield was a twelve-time All-Star, playing for both the NL as a San Diego Padre (four times) and the AL as a Yankee (eight times). Sax joined the Yankees from 1989 to 1991, and he made the All-Star team in 1989 and 1990.

January 11, 1983 Fired by Oakland in October, Billy Martin is brought back as Yankees manager for the third time. Fittingly, this marks the beginning of a season full of bizarre episodes, ending with the Yankees in third place.

September

2

CROWD-PLEASER

Reggie Jackson of the California Angels comes out of the dugout to the applause of the Yankee Stadium crowd after his twenty-third home run of the season, July 23, 1982. His ongoing clashes with Billy Martin and George Steinbrenner had driven the free agent to sign with the Angels for the 1982 season. He topped the league that year with thirty-nine home runs and led the Angels to a division title. Many Yankees fans were incensed that the team had let Jackson leave, and they delighted in his home runs, now hit against the Bombers. They cheered his at bats with the familiar "Rehhhh-GIE!" chant, and serenaded the Boss with frequent chants of "Steinbrenner sucks!" George Steinbrenner has since said that not re-signing Jackson was the biggest mistake of his career as Yankees owner. The Boss and Reggie eventually reconciled, and Jackson is now on the Yankees payroll as a special adviser. In 1993, he was inducted into the Hall of Fame wearing a Yankees cap, and the team retired his number, 44.

May 31, 1983 AL President Lee MacPhail, the former Yankees general manager, suspends George Steinbrenner for a week for improper public criticism of umpires.

Angels
44
SONICS

September

NOT-SO-SWEET LOU

Umpire Jim McKean leaves no doubt that Yankees right fielder Lou Piniella is safe at home plate after a double to left by catcher Butch Wynegar in the third inning against the Minnesota Twins at Yankee Stadium, April 23, 1983. Twins catcher Ray Smith can't get the tag down in time. The Yankees scored six runs in the inning and cruised to a 7–4 win behind a complete game by starter Shane Rawley.

Piniella always played with intensity, which was sometimes expressed with his volatile temper. Umpires were often the target of his ire. Phil Rizzuto once said of Sweet Lou, "*Sweet* refers to his swing, not his personality."—Glenn Liebman, *Yankee Shorts*

July 4, 1983 On George Steinbrenner's birthday, Dave Righetti pitches the sixth regular season no-hitter in Yankees history (the first in nearly thirty-two years, and the first by a left-hander in Yankee Stadium), beating the Red Sox 4–0.

AL

September

CLUTCH PLAYER

Dave Winfield, left, grabs Oakland A's catcher Mike Heath by the throat as Heath attempts to keep the Yankee from going after Mike Norris, who sent Winfield to the ground with a first-inning pitch at Yankee Stadium, May 27, 1983. The incident started a bench-clearing melee, and Winfield was ejected from the game (without getting an official at bat), his second time for fighting this season. The Yanks ended up winning the game 4–2. Back in 1973, Heath signed as a shortstop with the Yankees, but he never got to be the man in the middle. He spent much of his time in the Yankees' minor league system, but he did catch the ninth inning (without coming to bat) of Game 5 of the 1978 World Series, a blowout. Heath was traded to the Rangers after the 1978 season and then to the A's in mid-1979.

July 24, 1983 George Brett storms out of the dugout in a frenzy after the umpires disqualify his ninth-inning home run off Goose Gossage in Yankee Stadium, giving Kansas City a 5–4 lead, because his bat violates an obscure rule against applying pine tar, for better gripping, more than eighteen inches from the handle. The Yankees end up declared the winners of the Pine Tar Game, 4–3. But the decision does not stand.

NY
HEATH
2

September

HAPPY BIRTHDAY, BOSS

With two outs in the ninth inning, Yankees left-hander Dave Righetti pitches to Wade Boggs of the Boston Red Sox at Yankee Stadium, July 4, 1983. If you had to pick one batter in the major leagues to break up a no-hitter, you'd look no further than Boggs (the 1983 AL batting champion, with a .361 average). But Righetti made Boggs his ninth strikeout victim of the day, delivering a no-hitter on George Steinbrenner's Independence Day birthday.

Despite his success as a starter, Rags was moved to the bullpen in 1984 to be Goose Gossage's replacement as closer. He proved an excellent reliever for the next seven seasons in New York, averaging thirty-two saves a year. In 1986, he recorded a then record forty-six saves. He is second only to Mariano Rivera in career games pitched as a Yankee. Righetti was originally obtained from Texas in late 1978, in the multiplayer trade that sent Sparky Lyle to the Rangers.

August 4, 1983 Warming up on a Toronto field swarming with seagulls, Dave Winfield casually tosses a ball and hits a bird, killing it. He is later arrested and charged with cruelty to animals, though the charges are subsequently dropped.

SEIKO
4:40
OFFICIAL TIME
1 2 3 4 5 6 7 8 9 10 R H E
RED SOX 0 0 0 0 0 0 0 0 0 0 1
YANKEES 0 0 0 0 1 1 0 2 4 8 0
French's
BIG
430 FT.

September

THE HUMAN HOOVER

Yankees third baseman Graig Nettles dives for a ball hit by Gary Gaetti of the Minnesota Twins in the fifth inning at Yankee Stadium, July 18, 1983. Nettles knocked the ball down, and shortstop Andre Robertson threw to first base for the out. With outstanding range, sure hands, and a good arm, Nettles robbed many batters of hits to the hot corner. In Game 3 of the 1978 World Series, with the Yankees down two games to none, he stopped the Los Angeles Dodgers in their tracks with several spectacular plays. Shortstop Bucky Dent said, "Never saw defense like that in my life. [Nettles] won the World Series for us in that one game."—Glenn Liebman, *Yankee Shorts*

August 18, 1983 The Pine Tar Game resumes in the top of the ninth inning after the AL president upholds the Royals' protest of the umpires' call and restores George Brett's home run; the Royals quickly win, 5–4. On the same day, Yankees shortstop Andre Robertson's career is ended by a nearly fatal car crash.

September

7

DUSTUP AT HOME

Yankees catcher Rick Cerone has words with home plate umpire Dan Morrison, who throws him out of the game for bumping the ump in the fifth inning at Comiskey Park, July 31, 1983. Cerone argued that he had tagged out Chicago White Sox designated hitter Greg Luzinski at home plate. Then Yankees manager Billy Martin was also ejected, for arguing with umpire Dale Ford about how many warm-up tosses Cerone's replacement as catcher, Butch Wynegar, could throw. (After the game, Martin called Ford illiterate and a "stone liar"; as a result, the manager received a two-day suspension, and Ford—who was not selected to umpire in the postseason—later tried to sue Martin for defamation.) The Yankees scored six runs in the top of the eleventh inning to beat the White Sox, 12–6. Cerone played for eight different clubs in an eighteen-year career. After this initial five-year stint with the Yanks, he returned in 1987 and again in 1990.

December 16, 1983 The third Billy Martin era ends with another firing; he is replaced by 1964 manager Yogi Berra, a coach since 1976.

AL
34

September

TAKE A GIANT STEP

Yankees left fielder Dave Winfield tries to outrun California Angels third baseman Ron Jackson while getting caught in a squeeze play at Yankee Stadium, August 20, 1983. Jackson ran down Winfield for the second out in the game's first inning, under the eye of Angels catcher Bob Boone, backing up the play. Nevertheless, the Yankees went on to win the game, 6–2.

Winfield was a superb athlete, also recruited to play professional basketball and football, but baseball was his passion. He and teammate Don Mattingly competed down to the last game of the 1984 season for the AL batting title, with Mattingly going 4 for 5 and ending up with a .343 average; Winfield went 1 for 4 and finished at .340. Despite a miserable postseason, Winfield was one of the league's elite players during his Yankees career, making the All-Star team in each of his eight full seasons in the Bronx. But while his feud with Yankees owner George Steinbrenner may not have affected his play, it sometimes threatened to overshadow his otherwise outstanding career in pinstripes. He was elected to the Hall of Fame in 2001.

July 21, 1984 In Old-Timers' Day ceremonies, the Yankees honor Roger Maris and Elston Howard, retiring their numbers, 9 and 32, respectively.

September

TURNING TWO

After tagging out Milwaukee Brewers runner Robin Yount, background, on a ground ball from Cecil Cooper, Yankees second baseman Willie Randolph fires from one knee to double up Cooper at first in the ninth inning at Yankee Stadium, September 12, 1983. Randolph also drove in the game's only run as the Yankees won 1–0. A five-time All-Star during his thirteen seasons in the Bronx (and once more with the Dodgers), Randolph was patient and consistently productive at the plate, often batting leadoff or second. He had the speed to steal bases, and his outstanding defense made him a key element of this championship era. Later he spent eleven years coaching with the Yankees, until the New York Mets hired him as manager for the 2005 season. Now divorced from the Mets, and still a favorite of Yankees fans, Randolph delighted the crowd when he slid into second base during his introduction before the final game at Yankee Stadium in September 2008.

September 30, 1984 On the last day of his first full season, Don Mattingly gets four hits at home against the Tigers to edge past Dave Winfield in their long competition for the AL batting title. Besides his .343 average, Mattingly plays an almost flawless first base, leads the league in doubles (forty-four) and hits (207), and hits twenty-three home runs and 110 RBIs.

September

10

SWEET LOU

Even Red Sox fans had to respect the way Lou Piniella played the game. Or maybe they were just happy to see him go. Stepping up to bat in the second inning against Boston at Fenway Park, June 14, 1984, Sweet Lou receives a standing ovation from the usually hostile crowd. Before the game, the veteran Yankees outfielder announced that he would retire two days later, after two final games at Yankee Stadium. Piniella went 3 for 3 at Fenway, getting a double, two singles, three runs scored—and three more rounds of cheers. Embraced by Yankees fans for his passion, intensity, and temper, Piniella spent eleven seasons with the team, winning five division titles, four AL pennants, and two world championships. During the one-game playoff against the Red Sox in 1978—the Bucky Dent game—Piniella fought the sun and pulled off shrewd and gutsy defensive plays, on balls hit by Fred Lynn and Jerry Remy, keeping the game in reach for Dent's heroics. Piniella managed the Yanks in 1986 and 1987. He also took over in the mid-season of 1988 when Billy Martin was fired for the fifth and last time.

December 5, 1984 The Yankees acquire Rickey Henderson, the slugger and base-stealing phenomenon, in a trade with the Oakland A's.

NEW YORK

September

11

NIEKRO'S KNUCKLER

Twenty years after he broke into the majors, forty-five-year-old starter Phil Niekro deals a knuckleball against the Chicago White Sox at Yankee Stadium, August 8, 1984. His trademark pitch apparently deserted him on this day, as Niekro was pulled in the third inning after giving up six straight hits—and five runs—without recording an out. The Yankees lost to the White Sox 5–4, on their way to a third-place finish in the division, in this largely forgettable season. Niekro used the knuckler for twenty-four seasons in the major leagues, but he never made an appearance in a World Series. After spending most of his career with the Atlanta Braves, he pitched two years with the Yankees, 1984 and 1985, picking up his 300th win with a complete game shutout of the Toronto Blue Jays on the last day of the 1985 season. Niekro was the first pitcher to reach 300 wins in a Yankees uniform (joined by Roger Clemens in 2003). He was elected to the Hall of Fame in 1997.

April 28, 1985 After a 6–10 start, George Steinbrenner dumps the immensely popular Yogi Berra, replacing him with the fourth installment of Billy Martin as manager. The Yankees get hot starting in July and wind up in second place, only two games out, with a 97–64 record.

September

12

BIG FINISH

Yankees first baseman Don Mattingly follows the flight of his three-run, walk-off home run in the bottom of the ninth inning against the Minnesota Twins at Yankee Stadium, May 13, 1985. The Yanks had trailed 8–0 in the fourth inning, but they scratched their way back to 8–6. With two on and two outs, Mattingly delivered the coup de grâce to Twins reliever Ron Davis, a former Yankee. Little wonder that Mattingly was in his MVP season, batting .324 with thirty-five homers and 145 RBIs. Toss in a Gold Glove, too (his first of nine, including five straight). Batting from 1984 to 1986, Donnie joined Lou Gehrig (in 1930–32) as the only Yankees to have three straight 200-hit seasons. Derek Jeter has since joined that elite group, doing it twice (1998 to 2000 and 2005 to 2007).

August 4, 1985 Phil Rizzuto's number, 10, is retired.

September

13

TAKE THIS JOB AND . . .

Yankees manager Yogi Berra leaves Chicago's Comiskey Park after he was fired and replaced by Billy Martin (starting his fourth of five tours of duty), April 28, 1985. Berra had been hired to replace the volcanic Martin for the 1984 season. The Yankees finished in third place that year, at 87–75. But with this season off to a 6–10 start after three weeks, Steinbrenner, little noted for his patience, dispatched the new general manager, Clyde King (one of three Yankees managers in 1982), to fire Berra. After the 1964 World Series, the Yankees had also abruptly fired Berra, but this time it was personal. Berra was deeply offended and vowed never to set foot in Yankee Stadium as long as Steinbrenner owned the team. It took fourteen years and a 1999 visit by Steinbrenner to the Yogi Berra Museum, on the grounds of Montclair State University in New Jersey, to thaw relations between the two. Since then, Berra has been feted with Yogi Berra Day at the stadium, and he is among the most honored guests on major Yankees occasions.

October 6, 1985 At age forty-six, knuckleball pitcher Phil Niekro wins his 300th game, 8–0, over the Blue Jays in Toronto.

RCA
CHANNEL 5 NEWS

September

14

MAN OF STEAL

Yankees centerfielder Rickey Henderson takes off for a steal of third base in a game with the Oakland Athletics at Yankee Stadium, May 21, 1986. Henderson started his major league career with the Oakland A's back in 1979. This was his second season with the Yankees. He holds the Yankees records for stolen bases in a season (ninety-three in 1988) and in a Yankees career (326 in four and a half seasons). Unfortunately, his Yankees career coincided with some lean years in the Bronx. When the Yankees traded him back to Oakland in 1989, he said, "I don't want to be one of those great players who never made the Series."—Paul Dickson, *Baseball's Greatest Quotations*

Widely acknowledged as the best leadoff hitter and base stealer in baseball history, Henderson is also well known for his eccentricities, including a tendency to refer to himself in the third person. Teammates have reported that before a game he would sometimes repeat "Rickey is the best!" While standing in front of a mirror. Naked.

October 17, 1985 Billy Martin is fired yet again; former Yankees star Lou Piniella becomes manager.

September

15

IF THE UNIFORM FITS . . .

Still cutting an impressive figure, Yankees Hall of Famer Joe DiMaggio tips his cap to the cheers of fans attending Old-Timers' Day at Yankee Stadium, July 11, 1987. During the 1969 centennial of baseball, DiMaggio was voted baseball's greatest living player. Of course, Willie Mays, Mickey Mantle, and Ted Williams were still very much alive, but Joe D was secure in his place in baseball history, and he embraced the title. So much so that at public appearances, for which he was often paid handsomely, he usually insisted on being introduced as just that, our "greatest living ballplayer." He just may have been.

November 20, 1985 Don Mattingly wins the AL MVP Award, the first player on a non-championship team to do so. His forty-eight doubles and 145 RBIs lead the majors, he leads the league in extra-base hits and game-winning RBIs, and he winds up with a .324 average, thirty-five home runs, and 211 hits—the most by a Yankee since 1939.

September

16

SEVEN, GOING ON EIGHT

Third base coach Mike Ferraro congratulates Don Mattingly on his sixth-inning home run against the Texas Rangers at Arlington Stadium, July 17, 1987, Mattingly's seventh straight game with a home run—an AL record. The Yankees won the game 8–4. The following day, Mattingly went deep off Rangers pitcher Jose Guzman, tying Dale Long's major league record of eight straight home run games. Donnie Baseball had ten homers during the eight-game streak, another record. In this 1987 season, he also hit a major league record six grand slams, a mark he now shares with the Cleveland Indians' Travis Hafner. Mattingly, always one of the most popular Yankees, was one of baseball's most dominant and consistent hitters of the mid-1980s, stringing together multiple seasons of 200 hits, thirty or more home runs, and a batting average comfortably over .300, before injuries set in.

December 14, 1985 Roger Maris dies of lymphoma at age fifty-one.

NEW YORK
STRIKE

September

17

HE'S NUMBER ONE. AGAIN.

Five-time Yankees manager Billy Martin holds up his jersey for the 1988 season during a news conference in New York to announce Martin's return to pinstripes, October 22, 1987. Behind the jersey stands Yankees general manager Lou Piniella, who had managed the team for the previous two seasons. This would be Martin's fifth and final stint managing the Yankees. This time he lasted sixty-eight games before being fired, and Piniella stepped back into the breach, finishing the season as manager. Despite Martin's turbulent and troubled Yankees career, both as a player and a manager, few could question his passion for the team. The Yankees retired his number, 1, in August 1986, and his plaque reads, "A Yankee forever. A man who knew only one way to play—to win."

In his various incarnations as Yankees manager, Martin compiled a 556–385 record, while leading the team to three AL pennants and two world championships.

March 4, 1986 Willie Randolph and Ron Guidry become the eighth and ninth Yankee captains, sharing the honor through the 1988 season; Guidry will remain captain until July 12, 1989.

NY
1

September

18

GOOD SEATS STILL AVAILABLE

If you didn't get a foul ball at this game, you weren't trying. Reporters in the press box counted all of 126 fans at the start of this doubleheader between the Milwaukee Brewers and the Yankees, September 21, 1989. The Yanks actually drew more than two million fans to the stadium that year, but by this late-September game, the so-called Bombers were well on their way to the golf course. They finished the season in fifth place, at 74–87. Don Mattingly deserved better.

August 10, 1986 On Billy Martin Day, his number, 1, is retired.

Premium Gasolines
Getty
Rock Solid.
MarketWise.
Prudential-Bache
CASIO
4:04
BREWERS
YANKEES
HITACHI
BIG SCREEN TV
WABC 77AM
MSG
maxell
AB BALL STRIKE OUT
1 0 0 1
Marlboro
Bud
KING OF BEERS
IT'S YOUR CITI
CITIBANK
Bon Ton
399
408
385

September

19

A LONG WAY FROM KALAMAZOO

Derek Jeter, left, eighteen-year-old Yankees first-round draft pick, compares gloves with Yankees backup catcher and designated hitter Jim Leyritz, center, and utility infielder Mike Gallego prior to the Yankees' game against the Kansas City Royals at Yankee Stadium, September 12, 1992. The future Yankees captain was just three months out of Central High School in Kalamazoo, Michigan. He would spend three seasons in the minors before making his major league debut in 1995. His official rookie year was 1996, when he won Rookie of the Year honors.

October 2, 1986 The Yankees end up in second place again, but Don Mattingly has another spectacular year, setting team records for hits (238) and doubles (fifty-three) while also leading the league in slugging percentage and total bases—and hitting .352 with thirty-one home runs and 113 RBIs.

September

WHO'S THE BOSS?

Newly reinstated Yankees owner George Steinbrenner, right, makes himself heard while joining manager Buck Showalter at spring training camp in Fort Lauderdale, Florida, March 1, 1993. In 1990, Steinbrenner had earned a "life" suspension from baseball for paying $40,000 to gambler Howie Spira to discredit Dave Winfield. Steinbrenner and Winfield had a contentious relationship from the start. The Boss thought he had been duped by a cost-of-living clause in Winfield's contract that cost millions more than he had expected. The life suspension was lifted effective in 1993. This wasn't Steinbrenner's first suspension. In 1974, he was suspended for two years for illegal campaign contributions to the Nixon campaign.

Showalter took over a losing club in 1992 and turned the Yankees into contenders by the strike-shortened 1994 season. They made the playoffs in 1995, but Showalter was dropped in favor of Joe Torre for 1996.

July 18, 1987 Don Mattingly hits a home run in his eighth consecutive game, tying him with Dale Long for the major league record. Mattingly hits a ten home runs during his streak.

Canon

September

21

CAPTAIN'S QUARTERS

In the clubhouse at Yankee Stadium, July 2, 1993, the locker stall and number 15 uniform of Yankees team captain Thurman Munson remain undisturbed fourteen years after he was killed in the crash of his private jet. Munson was also honored with a plaque in Monument Park, but Yankees players and coaches observed this tribute in the privacy of the locker room. Before the 2009 season, the locker was moved across the street to a Yankees museum in the new stadium.

September 29, 1987 Don Mattingly sets a major league record by hitting his sixth grand slam of the season, off Boston's Bruce Hurst.

Munson 77 7

September

22

JUST ONE OF THOSE SPECIAL MOMENTS

Pitcher Jim Abbott, left, celebrates his 4–0 no-hit victory over the Cleveland Indians as third baseman Wade Boggs runs to congratulate him at Yankee Stadium, September 4, 1993. Born without a right hand, Abbott pitched with his left hand and wore a right-hander's mitt at the end of his right arm. After delivering each pitch, he would quickly switch the glove to his left hand for fielding. Abbott, who went a modest 11–14 that year, has said, "The truth is, I won't go to the Hall of Fame. But if a career can be measured in special moments, lessons learned, and a connection with people, then I would stack mine up with anyone's."—jimabbott.info

October 19, 1987 For the fifth (and last) time, Billy Martin is hired to manage the Yankees, replacing Lou Piniella.

September

23

"DON'T BE LIKE ME."

Yankees great Mickey Mantle, attending a July 8, 1994, news conference in the New York restaurant that bears his name, said he had special reason to look forward to his fall fantasy baseball camp in Florida—sobriety. "This is the first year I've ever been down there sober," the Hall of Famer said. "I think it's gonna be more fun." Earlier in the year, Mantle had admitted to a serious and prolonged drinking problem, for which he entered treatment at the Betty Ford Center. Less than a year after this news conference, Mantle had a transplant to replace his liver, damaged by years of alcohol abuse, cirrhosis, and hepatitis C. But surgeons also discovered terminal lung cancer. Nine weeks later, he was dead. Before he died, the Mick told the public, "You talk about a role model. This is a role model: Don't be like me."

June 23, 1988 With the Yankees only two games out of first, but Billy Martin getting beaten up in a bar fight and feuding with umpires, he is replaced for the fifth (and last) time, by Lou Piniella (for the second time).

September

24

HIT MAN

Yankees first baseman Don Mattingly acknowledges the crowd's standing ovation after getting his 2,000th career hit in the seventh inning against the California Angels at Anaheim Stadium, July 23, 1994. At the time, the Hit Man was the sixth Yankee to reach 2,000 hits; Bernie Williams and Derek Jeter have since joined that select group. Lou Gehrig currently leads all Yankees with 2,721 hits, a mark Jeter is likely to better (possibly in 2009). Mattingly had a legitimate shot at his first postseason in 1994, but the players' strike led to the cancellation of the playoffs. In 1995, his final season, he finally made it to the postseason, batting .417 with a home run, four doubles, and six RBIs in the five-game AL Division Series loss to the Seattle Mariners. Like Gehrig before him, Mattingly's career ended prematurely due to health concerns, though with less serious consequences. Chronic back problems started to erode Mattingly's production in 1990 and eventually sidelined him for good after the 1995 season. Mattingly is usually cited as the best Yankee never to play in a World Series.

October 7, 1988 After the Yankees finish in fifth place, the Yankees name Dallas Green as the manager in 1989.

YORK

September

PLAYERS UNION SEZ STRIKE

Yankees booster "Freddy Sez" Schuman pumps up the stadium crowd despite an impending baseball strike, August 11, 1994, as the Yankees played the Toronto Blue Jays. Players went out on strike the next day, and baseball was suspended until April 2, 1995 (with the season beginning April 25). The nearly eight-month strike caused the cancellation of more than 900 games and the first cancellation of a World Series since 1904. When the strike shut down baseball, the Yankees were in first place by six and a half games, and Don Mattingly was on the verge of his first postseason appearance in thirteen years in the majors.

Freddy Sez has been a fixture at Yankee Stadium since about 1988. He circulates through the stands carrying a frying pan affixed to a sign. Fans are invited to bang on the pan with a metal spoon to bring the Yankees luck. The distinctive metallic clanging rings through the stadium, and it can often be heard in the background of Yankees TV and radio broadcasts, reassuring evidence that Freddy is in the house.

December 9, 1988 The Yankees and the Madison Square Garden network sign a twelve-year television contract.

FREDDY "SEZ"
YANKEE FANS
THIS IS...
"THE YEAR"
New York

September

THE MICK IS GONE

Although he didn't publicize it, Mickey Mantle knew his days were numbered when doctors found inoperable lung cancer during a routine follow-up exam soon after his liver transplant surgery on June 8, 1995. Before he died on August 13, he encouraged others to practice a healthier lifestyle, using himself as an example of a life lived recklessly. He also promoted awareness of organ donation.

Here, former teammates escort his casket from the Lovers Lane United Methodist Church in Dallas, August 15, 1995. In pairs from left front are Whitey Ford and Yogi Berra, Bill "Moose" Skowron and Hank Bauer, and Johnny Blanchard and Bobby Murcer.

August 18, 1989 After a poor start, Bucky Dent replaces Dallas Green as manager; however, Dent does no better, and the Yankees finish in fifth place again.

September

27

DOC GETS HIS GROOVE BACK

Yankees pitcher Dwight Gooden is carried off the field by his teammates after pitching a no-hitter against the Seattle Mariners at Yankee Stadium, May 14, 1996. The Yankees won 2–0. The Yankees signed the 1985 NL Cy Young Award winner for the season as he was coming off a suspension of nearly two years due to drug problems. He pitched poorly in April and was close to being released before this game. In the first inning, Gerald Williams made a spectacular over-the-shoulder catch (leading to a double play), on a line drive from Alex Rodriguez, that would set the tone for the game. Gooden went face-to-face with the heart of the Mariners lineup in the ninth inning. He walked two batters but survived the inning without giving up a hit or a run. It was an emotionally charged moment for Gooden, who had struggled to regain his form. Doc finished the season at 11–7 with a 5.01 ERA. After 1997, he spent largely forgettable seasons with Cleveland, Houston, and Tampa Bay before finishing his career with the Yankees again. He did not pitch for the Yanks in the 2000 World Series against his former New York Mets club, and he retired after the season.

December 25, 1989 Billy Martin dies at age sixty-one in an automobile accident.

September

FAN OF THE YEAR

Baltimore Orioles right fielder Tony Tarasco stretches for the ball as twelve-year-old Yankees fan Jeffrey Maier deflects it into the stands during Game 1 of the AL Championship Series at Yankee Stadium, October 9, 1996. The hit by Derek Jeter was ruled a home run by right field umpire Rich Garcia, tying the game 4–4 in the eighth inning. Claiming fan interference, Tarasco and Orioles manager Davey Johnson protested the call so vehemently that Garcia ejected Johnson from the game. Garcia later reviewed the play and conceded that it should have been considered fan interference, but he said he still didn't think the ball was catchable. American League president Gene Budig denied Baltimore's protest of the game, and the Yankees went on to win the series. The play seemed emblematic of the Yankees' postseason success: Somehow the breaks would go their way. Maier briefly became a New York celebrity, with an appearance on David Letterman's late-night TV show, and was awarded a key to the city.

June 6, 1990 Stump Merrill becomes manager, replacing Bucky Dent, but the Yankees collapse into last place with a 67–95 record—their lowest winning percentage since 1913 and their most losses since 1912.

eats the

September

BERN, BABY, BERN

Center fielder Bernie Williams (51) is greeted at home plate by teammates, including Derek Jeter, right, and Darryl Strawberry, left, after hitting the game-winning home run in the eleventh inning, lifting the Yankees to a 5–4 win in Game 1 of the AL Championship Series at Yankee Stadium, October 9, 1996. The Yankees went on to win the World Series that year in six games. In 1998, Williams captured the AL batting title to go along with his World Series rings, and was courted by the Red Sox, but signed on with the Yankees for another seven years, earning $85 million. During Williams's career, Yankees broadcaster John Sterling had plenty of opportunities—287 to be exact—to use his home run call, "Bern, Baby, Bern."

July 1, 1990 Hard-luck pitcher Andy Hawkins throws a no-hitter in Chicago (discounted much later by a change in major league rules, because he pitched only an eight-inning game), but loses, 4–0, thanks to three errors and two walks with two outs in the eighth inning. Five days later, he shuts out the Minnesota Twins through two outs in the twelfth—then gives up two runs and loses again.

51

September

GONE WITH THE WIND

Catcher Jim Leyritz watches his eighth-inning three-run home run, along with Atlanta Braves catcher Eddie Perez and plate umpire Steve Rippley, during Game 4 of the World Series, October 23, 1996, in Atlanta. Until Leyritz's homer tied up the game, the Yankees had been in danger of falling behind three games to one in the Series. The Yankees eventually won Game 4 in the tenth inning, 8–6, and never looked back, sweeping the next two games to win the World Series in six, for their first championship since 1978.

July 30, 1990 Commissioner Fay Vincent permanently bans George Steinbrenner from the day-to-day operations of the Yankees for associating with a known gambler to try to get damaging information on the recently traded Dave Winfield, with whom Steinbrenner has long feuded (at one point belittling the slugger, signed to fill Reggie Jackson's shoes, as "Mr. May").

NEW YORK

October

1

LIKE GENERAL SHERMAN, YANKEES TAKE ATLANTA

New York Yankees players surround closer John Wetteland, center, as he celebrates the team's 3–2 win in Game 6 of the World Series against the Atlanta Braves at Yankee Stadium, October 26, 1996. After leaving New York with a two-games-to-none deficit, the Yankees swept three games in Atlanta and came back home to close out the Series. The last time the Yankees had won the World Series, Derek Jeter was four years old.

Wetteland saved all four Yankees wins and was named Series MVP. One of his setup men was a promising pitcher named Mariano Rivera, who would go on to have some success as a Yankees closer, as well.

August 20, 1990 George Steinbrenner resigns as managing general partner of the Yankees; limited partner Robert Nederlander assumes that role, and Gene Michael is named general manager again.

2
NY
24
NY

October

2

RIDE 'EM, BOGGSIE

Wade Boggs, perennial All-Star third baseman, rides a police horse around the field after the Yankees defeated the Atlanta Braves in the sixth and deciding game of the World Series at Yankee Stadium, October 26, 1996. Boggs played fifteen seasons—eleven of them with the Red Sox—before finally winning his only World Series ring. He was one of the most consistent hitters in baseball, eventually retiring with more than 3,000 hits and a .328 career batting average. Ironically, Boggs was pinch-hitting when he had the key bases-loaded walk in the tenth inning of Game 4 to win that pivotal World Series game for the Yankees. Boggs was elected to the Hall of Fame in 2005. The Hall decided that his plaque would show him in a Red Sox cap, apparently over Boggs's objections.

February 28, 1991 Don Mattingly becomes the captain of the Yankees, until 1995.

October

DON LARSEN REDUX

Pitcher David Wells is carried off the field by Bernie Williams, left; Willie Banks, second from left; and Darryl Strawberry after pitching a perfect game against the Minnesota Twins, May 17, 1998, at Yankee Stadium. Wells became the second Yankee to pitch a perfect game, following Don Larsen's perfecto in the 1956 World Series. Larsen and Wells coincidentally graduated from the same high school, Point Loma High, in San Diego. They had something else in common: Neither was known for his discipline, but both achieved perfection on at least one occasion.

October 29, 1991 After another dreadful season (finishing 71–91), the Yankees hire Buck Showalter as manager shortly after firing Stump Merrill. Despite an almost identically poor 1992, Gene Michael stands behind Showalter during their gradually accelerating rebuilding process.

October

AN IMPERFECT GAME

Players from the Baltimore Orioles and New York Yankees engage in a bench-clearing brawl after Orioles reliever Armando Benitez hit Yankees batter Tino Martinez with a pitch at Yankee Stadium, May 19, 1998. Bernie Williams, the first batter to face Benitez, had just hit a three-run home run to give the Yankees a 7–5 lead in the eighth inning when Martinez, who had already been hit earlier in the game, stepped in against the reliever. Benitez promptly drilled him in the upper back. Home plate umpire Drew Coble immediately ejected Benitez, but Darryl Strawberry and Chad Curtis were already leading the charge from the Yankees dugout. Not to be outdone, Yankees reliever Graeme Lloyd rushed from the bullpen to take a swing at Benitez. The ensuing brawl spilled into the Orioles dugout and lasted more than ten minutes. Benitez received an eight-game suspension; Strawberry and Lloyd were each suspended for three games. The Yankees beat the Orioles 9–5 that day and went on to sweep the three-game series, improving their record to a lofty 31–9.

June 1, 1992 With their sixth pick in the amateur draft, the Yankees select a youngster named Derek Jeter. In the off-season, they acquire right fielder Paul O'Neill and pitcher Jim Abbott in trades and sign free agents Jimmy Key and future Hall of Famer Wade Boggs.

50
28
22

October

DIAMOND IN THE ROUGH

Looking west toward Manhattan with Walton Avenue in the foreground, Yankee Stadium sits among apartment buildings in the South Bronx, October 1998. In the 1970s, this area became synonymous with urban blight, and during Game 2 of the 1977 World Series, an ABC camera showed a nearby building engulfed in flames as Howard Cosell intoned, "The Bronx is burning." Years later, as the Yankees' fortunes and attendance reached a low ebb, the club threatened to move to the west side of Manhattan or—get this—New Jersey. But fans started returning in droves when the team found its way back to the postseason in the mid-1990s. And a new stadium ensured that the Bombers stayed put. Some residents say the ballpark brings something special to their corner of the Bronx. "It gives [the neighborhood] more life," said Ana Milagros. On game days, "everyone is happier. . . . You hear the noise, you hear the sirens, everybody's jumping, whether they're watching the game or not."

July 24, 1992 Not long before being forced out as baseball commissioner, Fay Vincent rules that George Steinbrenner can return to running the Yankees starting on March 1, 1993.

853

October

STORYBOOK SEASON

Yankees teammates mob closer Mariano Rivera, foreground, after winning the World Series with a 3–0 victory over the San Diego Padres at Qualcomm Stadium, October 21, 1998. This Yankees team went 114–48 during the regular season, finishing twenty-two games ahead of the second-place Boston Red Sox. In the AL Division Series, the Yankees swept the Texas Rangers in three games before taking the AL Championship four games to two over the Cleveland Indians. Often described as one of the best teams ever, this squad was notable for its relative lack of marquee players; only pitcher David Wells started for the 1998 AL All-Star team. What this Yankees team lacked in outright superstars, however, it more than made up with solid, experienced, and committed role players. This team thrived on a balanced offense, consistent pitching, and an infectious will to win.

January 5, 1993 Reggie Jackson is voted into the Hall of Fame.

NEW YORK
18

October

7

THE BOSS APPROVES

It wasn't Joe Torre's first world championship, and it wouldn't be the last, but this one had to be special. The Yankees manager had just seen his team sweep the San Diego Padres in four games. Here, he and team owner George Steinbrenner, left, share an emotional moment after being presented with the World Series trophy at Qualcomm Stadium, October 21, 1998. Torre had guided his team to one of the most remarkable seasons in baseball history. After the sweep of the Padres, the Yankees' record, including the postseason, stood at 125–50, the most wins ever in a single year. Their winning percentage was .714. Even Boss George could be happy with that.

August 14, 1993 Reggie Jackson's number, 44, is retired during Reggie Jackson Day at Yankee Stadium.

October

GEORGE II

Blustering. Imperious. Overbearing. Meddling. Nixon supporter. Free agent splurger. Serial firer. Turtleneck wearer. Say what you want about George Steinbrenner—and you can say plenty—even his detractors have to admit that the man lives to win. In 1973, he bought a moribund Yankees team for about the same amount of money as four-game winner Carl Pavano's 2008 salary. Steinbrenner then proceeded to build one of the world's most valuable sports franchises, spending a fortune and making an even bigger one. Along the way, he changed Yankees managers twenty times in his first twenty-three seasons, paid a gambler to dig up dirt on future Hall of Famer Dave Winfield, and went mano a mano with two Dodgers fans in a hotel elevator during the 1981 World Series, or so he would have you believe. Oh, and the Yankees won six world championships on his watch, more than anyone else in baseball.

Here, the Boss listens to a reporter's question at a New York news conference, December 4, 1998.

September 4, 1993 Jim Abbott, who was born without a right hand, pitches the Yankees' seventh regular season no-hitter, beating the Cleveland Indians 4–0 at Yankee Stadium.

October

WHERE HAVE YOU GONE, JOE DIMAGGIO?

In the center field once patrolled by Joe DiMaggio, singer-songwriter Paul Simon waves to fans at Yankee Stadium, April 25, 1999, after singing "Mrs. Robinson" as a tribute to the former Yankees center fielder, who died March 8, 1999. The song's lyrics include the melancholy "Joltin' Joe has left and gone away." DiMaggio, one of the greatest baseball players of all time, is still one of only two Yankees right-handers, along with Alex Rodriguez, to hit more than forty home runs in a season. Home runs became routine outs in the Death Valley that was Yankee Stadium's left-center field in 1937, but DiMaggio hit forty-six that year.

October 3, 1993 Moving over .500 ball for the first time since 1988, the Yankees finish in second place for the first time since 1986.

October

10

ON THE SCORECARD? IT'S JUST A FLY BALL TO RIGHT FIELD

Yankees right fielder Paul O'Neill makes a diving catch on a fly ball hit by Montreal Expos center fielder Terry Jones in the first inning at Yankee Stadium, July 18, 1999. Hustling plays by Paulie were not exactly a rarity, but this one would count more than most. Yankees starter David Cone started methodically retiring Expos batters. By the time third baseman Scott Brosius caught Orlando Cabrera's pop fly for the final out, Cone had not allowed a base runner—he'd pitched a perfect game. He threw just eighty-eight pitches—sixty-eight for strikes—and struck out ten. This was only the sixteenth perfect game thrown in baseball history and the third by a Yankee. The Yankees won the game 6–0.

February 25, 1994 After far too long a wait, Phil Rizzuto is voted into the Hall of Fame by the Veterans Committee.

October

11

PERFECT TIMING

New York Yankees pitcher David Cone is lifted onto the shoulders of his teammates by catcher Joe Girardi, left, as manager Joe Torre joins in the celebration after Cone threw a perfect game against the Montreal Expos during Yogi Berra Day at Yankee Stadium, July 18, 1999. Despite the ninety-degree temperatures and a thirty-three-minute rain delay in the third inning, Cone and Girardi teamed up to retire all twenty-seven batters they faced. Before the game, Don Larsen had thrown out the ceremonial first pitch to Yogi Berra, who had caught Larsen's historic 1956 World Series perfect game against the Brooklyn Dodgers. What were the chances of seeing another Yankees perfecto with Larsen and Berra in the stadium? Eerily good, as it turned out. How *do* they do that?

August 12, 1994 The Yankees officially finish the season in first place in the AL East, thanks in part to Paul O'Neill's league-leading .359 average, but a players' strike, countered by owners taking a hard line, cuts the season short and eliminates all playoffs.

October

12

YOU'RE NUMBER ONE

Boston Red Sox legend Carlton Fisk gestures toward the New York Yankees dugout before throwing out the ceremonial first pitch preceding Game 4 of the AL Championship Series, October 17, 1999, at Fenway Park. Fisk may have been feeling confident with Boston coming off a 13–1 win the previous day. The Yankees responded with two convincing wins at Fenway to take the American League pennant, then went on to win the World Series in four straight games over the Atlanta Braves.

May 30, 1995 A day after going 0 for 5 in his major league debut, shortstop Derek Jeter—batting ninth—gets two singles off Tim Belcher of the Mariners in a 7–3 loss at Seattle. Jeter appears in only fifteen games, spending most of the season in the minors, before starting 1996 as the regular shortstop and quickly evolving into the team's best-loved superstar of the era.

October

13

TEAM OF THE CENTURY

Yankees catcher Jorge Posada, left rear, and third baseman Scott Brosius, right, rush pitcher Mariano Rivera as teammates converge on the mound after the Yankees beat the Atlanta Braves 4–1 in Game 4 of the World Series, October 27, 1999, at Yankee Stadium. The Bombers swept the Series, and Rivera was named the Series MVP, further cementing his reputation as baseball's top closer. In six postseason series over the past two years, he had pitched twenty-five and two-thirds innings against the best teams in baseball. His ERA in those innings? Exactly zero.

It seemed only appropriate to close the century with the Bombers' twenty-fifth world championship. This was their third World Series title in four years and their second straight sweep of the Fall Classic. Going back to 1996, the Yankees had won twelve straight World Series games.

August 13, 1995 Mickey Mantle dies of cancer at sixty-three.

October

14

HARD-HEADED ZIM

Yankees bench coach Don Zimmer waves as his float makes its way along the Canyon of Heroes during a ticker-tape parade in lower Manhattan, October 29, 1999, celebrating the Yankees' World Series victory over the Atlanta Braves. Zimmer has on the helmet he wore in the dugout after getting hit by a foul ball off the bat of the Yankees' Chuck Knoblauch during the playoffs. After his time with the Yankees, Zimmer went on to work for the Tampa Bay Rays as a senior adviser. As of 2008, Zimmer was believed to be the only former Brooklyn Dodger active in professional baseball.

September 3, 1995 Shortstop Tony Fernandez becomes the first Yankee in twenty-three years to hit for the cycle, in a home game against the Oakland Athletics.

October

15

STRAW STIRRED

Yankees manager Joe Torre, left, comforts Darryl Strawberry after an emotional moment in Strawberry's speech during the Yankees' victory celebration at New York's City Hall, October 29, 1999. The Yankees clinched a record twenty-fifth World Series title two nights earlier at Yankee Stadium, sweeping the Atlanta Braves in four straight games. Strawberry had just played his last major league game. Challenged by substance abuse, cancer treatment, legal issues, and various other personal problems, the former New York Mets phenom spent his last five major league seasons with the Yankees as a part-time outfielder and designated hitter. Straw was not a factor in his two World Series appearances for the Yankees—1996 and 1999—but Torre must have loved knowing that he had Strawberry's bat in a big spot. During the 1996 AL Championship Series against the Baltimore Orioles, Straw hit .417 with three home runs.

September 6, 1995 Baltimore's Cal Ripken Jr. breaks Lou Gehrig's fifty-six-year record of 2,130 consecutive games. Ripken's streak ended in 1998 at 2,632 games.

World Series

October

16

THE VOICE OF GOD

Public address announcer Bob Sheppard, the iconic voice of the New York Yankees, acknowledges the cheers during a May 7, 2000, ceremony to honor his fiftieth season as the team's announcer. Sheppard, who has announced more than 4,500 Yankees games, is known for his deep, distinguished voice and dramatic style, which Hall of Fame slugger Reggie Jackson once likened to "the voice of God." Before each player's first at bat of the game, the stadium PA system crackles to life with a variation on Sheppard's signature theme: "Now batting . . . for the Yankees . . . number 2 . . . Derek Jeter . . . number 2." Health issues prevented Sheppard from working during the 2008 season, but a recorded version of his voice was still played before Jeter's at bats, at the request of the Yankees captain.

October 4, 1995 With the second-place Yankees the first AL Wild Card team in a revised three-round playoff format, Don Mattingly finally makes it into the postseason after 1,785 games. In Game 2, as fans repeatedly chant his nickname, Donnie Baseball gets a home run and two singles in his final game at Yankee Stadium, and Jim Leyritz's two-run homer in the fifteenth inning gives the Yankees a two-game lead—but then the Mariners win three straight in Seattle and eliminate the Yankees.

Dodge
Official

October

17

DECKED

New York Mets batter Mike Piazza lies in the dirt at Yankee Stadium after being hit by a pitch thrown by New York Yankees pitcher Roger Clemens while leading off the second inning of the second game of the teams' crosstown doubleheader, Saturday, July 8, 2000. Yankees catcher Chris Turner (25) walks over to check on Piazza, who left the game with a concussion and was forced to miss the All-Star Game three days later. Many people (especially Mets fans) suggested that the beaning was intentional and Clemens was seeking revenge following Piazza's grand slam off the pitcher on June 9. After the beaning, the Yankees went on to win the game 4–2—the same score by which they had won the first game, earlier in the day, at Shea Stadium.

November 2, 1995 After Buck Showalter resigns, Joe Torre is named manager. A below-average skipper with three National League clubs up to then, he will lead the Yankees to twelve consecutive seasons in the playoffs, six American League pennants, and four world championships—the greatest period in Yankees history since the Casey Stengel era (and with 1,173 wins, Torre will end up just passing Stengel before heading west).

25

October

18

NO LOVE LOST

New York Mets star Mike Piazza, left, gestures at Roger Clemens with a piece of a broken bat that the Yankees pitcher hurled toward him, as umpire Charlie Reliford stands between the two on October 22, 2000, at Yankee Stadium. The confrontation, one of the most dramatic moments of a pulsating World Series between the Yankees and their crosstown rivals, followed an incident earlier in the year in which Clemens beaned Piazza. This time, a blazing fastball shattered Piazza's bat, sending pieces of it flying toward the mound. As Piazza ran to first, the Yankees pitcher picked up part of the bat and flung it directly in the Mets star's path. Clemens always maintained that he was not trying to hit Piazza, but bad feelings lingered. The Yankees held off a five-run Mets rally to win the game, 6–5, and later the Series.

May 14, 1996 Dwight Gooden, a onetime Mets ace now being given a second chance after problems with drug abuse, pitches the Yankees' eighth regular season no-hitter, defeating the Seattle Mariners 2–0 at Yankee Stadium.

PIAZZA
31

October

19

JOE GETS CARRIED AWAY

Yankees manager Joe Torre is carried off the field by players Bernie Williams, left, and Roger Clemens, after clinching the World Series against the New York Mets on October 26, 2000, at Shea Stadium. The championship was the Yankees' fourth in five years under Torre's steady hand. The 4–2 victory in Game 5 of the all–New York series launched Torre to the pinnacle of his career as skipper. After a skeptical reception from the press when he joined the club in 1996, Torre became one of the most revered managers in Yankees history, a class act with a Midas touch who seemed preternaturally calm and in control. Although Torre led the Yankees to the playoffs in each of his twelve seasons managing the team, the victory against the Mets was the final world championship during his tenure.

June 16, 1996 Mel Allen, the broadcasting Voice of the Yankees from 1939 (taking over as lead announcer a year later) to 1964, dies at age eighty-three. Over the decades, he had many partners on radio and television, including Red Barber and Phil Rizzuto.

ARRIVE HOME SA
FANS DON'T LET FANS DRIVE
REMEMBER, THE NEW YORK
CARE ABOUT YOUR SAFET
STARTER
REUTERS
12:03
Yankees

October

OK, WE'VE GOT THE PARADE THING DOWN

Jubilant Yankees fans celebrate another championship with one of the most dramatic tributes the city can give, a ticker-tape parade through the streets of Manhattan on October 30, 2000. With the Yankees winning four titles in five years, the procession through a stretch of Broadway known as the Canyon of Heroes had become an almost annual event. Still, the Yankees' World Series victory over their crosstown rivals, the Mets, was particularly sweet. The city's first Subway Series since 1956 had captured New Yorkers' imaginations, and they demonstrated their excitement with a blizzard of confetti in honor of the world champions. Mayor Rudolph Giuliani even encouraged parents to keep their children home from school so they could attend the celebration.

September 26, 1996 The Yankees beat the Milwaukee Brewers 19–2 to clinch the AL East title.

New York
CHAMPIONS
Subway Series
THEIR CITY,
THEIR WORLD
26 Rings
Bronx
is in
da house
YAHOO!
Sports

October

21

THE YANKEES MISS HIM. UMPIRES? NOT SO MUCH.

Yankees right fielder Paul O'Neill reacts to being ejected for arguing a third-strike call in the fifth inning of the Yankees' 3–1 victory over the Oakland Athletics on April 29, 2001, at Yankee Stadium. The 2001 season was the last of O'Neill's seventeen-year career, the last half of which was spent with the Yankees. He was the heart and soul of the team, beloved for his rugged style and ability to come through in the clutch. Owner George Steinbrenner, not the easiest man to please in baseball, called the emotional O'Neill "my warrior." During his final game at the stadium, fans serenaded O'Neill with powerful chants of his name, a Bronx thank-you for everything he had done.

October 9, 1996 After defeating the Texas Rangers in the AL Division Series, the Yankees win Game 1 of the AL Championship Series with the help of twelve-year-old fan Jeffrey Maier, when his improper grab for Derek Jeter's fly to right field leads to umpire Rich Garcia incorrectly (as he later admits) calling the ball a home run. The Yankees go on to win the game and the series—their first pennant since 1981.

October

22

THE SANDMAN COMETH

Legendary Yankees closer Mariano Rivera throws to the plate in the ninth inning against the Anaheim Angels on August 25, 2001, in Anaheim, California. The Yankees won the game 7–5, just one of the league-leading fifty saves that the Panamanian-born Rivera notched that season. The soft-spoken pitcher with the out-of-this-world cut fastball is considered by many to be the greatest relief pitcher of all time. He does more than just get batters out: He destroys them, shattering bats at a clip that would keep a fire roaring with kindling late into the night. When Rivera enters a game with the lead, the Yankee Stadium public address system plays the gentle melody of Metallica's heavy metal hit "Enter Sandman," a clear signal that it's lights-out time for the opposition. One bedazzled opponent, Jim Thome, called Rivera's signature fastball "the single best pitch ever in the game."

October 23, 1996 The Yankees are down two games to one in the 1996 World Series, and behind 6–3 in the eighth, when Jim Leyritz brings them back to life with a game-tying three-run home run against Braves closer Mark Wohlers in Atlanta. The Yankees go ahead on a bases-loaded walk to Wade Boggs in the tenth inning and end up the winners.

42

October

23

AMERICA THE BEAUTIFUL

Emotions run high as the Yankees play their first game at the stadium since the September 11 terrorist attacks. In this photo, fan Richard Calderon holds up an American flag during a moment of silence before the start of the game on September 25, 2001. The team honored rescue workers in a ceremony before the first pitch, and New York Mayor Rudolph Giuliani, hailed for his response to the tragedy, received a standing ovation. The Yankees lost the game 4–0 to the Tampa Bay Devil Rays, but they clinched first place in the American League East anyway when the Red Sox lost at Fenway Park. There was no champagne in the Yankees dressing room, with de facto team captain Derek Jeter saying that nobody felt like celebrating.

October 26, 1996 A new Yankees dynasty begins as starter Jimmy Key and closer John Wetteland help the Yankees defeat the Braves, 3–2, in Game 6 of the World Series for their twenty-third world championship. The postgame celebration at Yankee Stadium includes Wade Boggs's memorable ride on a police horse, behind the officer, around the field.

NYSE
adidas
HESS
Bud
Kodak
WILLIAMS
51

October

24

HE'S OUT OF POSITION AND INTO THE HISTORY BOOKS

For most fans, it will forever be remembered as the Flip, and perhaps as Derek Jeter's greatest clutch moment. Leading the Oakland Athletics 1–0 in the seventh inning of Game 3 of the American League Division Series in Oakland, California, on October 13, 2001, Jeter ran from his position at shortstop to a spot in foul territory along the first base line to field an errant throw from Yankees right fielder Shane Spencer. As Oakland's Jeremy Giambi tried to score, Jeter, left, grabbed the ball and flipped it backhand to catcher Jorge Posada, who tagged Giambi out. The Yankees, who were facing elimination, would win the game, then come back and take the series. *Baseball Weekly* would name the play one of the ten most amazing of all time.

November 4, 1996 Shortstop Derek Jeter wins the Rookie of the Year Award.

Athletics
7
2

October

NOW PITCHING, NUMBER 43

President George W. Bush salutes the crowd at Yankee Stadium before Game 3 of the World Series between the New York Yankees and Arizona Diamondbacks on October 30, 2001, in New York. The Yankees' quest for a title in the months after September 11 became a rallying point for New Yorkers coping with the trauma of the terrorist attacks. The Yankees made it to the Series in dramatic fashion, coming back from the brink of elimination to beat Oakland in the AL Division Series, then brushing aside the Seattle Mariners, who had won 116 games that year. But they would come up just short in the end, losing in heartbreaking fashion to the Diamondbacks in the bottom of the ninth inning of Game 7.

December 11 and 24, 1996 Following their World Series win, the Yankees sign left-handed pitchers Mike Stanton and David Wells.

October

DOUBLE TROUBLE

An RBI double by Erubiel Durazo of the Arizona Diamondbacks sails over the outstretched glove of Bernie Williams in deep center field during the eighth inning of Game 4 of the World Series at Yankee Stadium, October 31, 2001. The stadium fell quiet as the D'backs scored twice against Mike Stanton and Ramiro Mendoza in the inning, to take a 3–1 lead. The upstarts from Arizona looked poised to take a lead of three games to one in the Series. The Diamondbacks were playing in the Fall Classic in just their fourth season; the Yankees' organization, dating back to the New York Highlanders, is nine years older than the state of Arizona.

January 22, 1997 Don Mattingly officially retires. His number, 23, is retired on August 31, Don Mattingly Day at Yankee Stadium.

NY

October

27

THE BAMTINO

Yankees first baseman Tino Martinez, nicknamed "the BamTino" (a play on "the Bambino," one of Babe Ruth's nicknames) by Yankees broadcaster John Sterling, is congratulated by teammate Clay Bellinger, left, after hitting a game-tying two-run home run in the bottom of the ninth inning against the Arizona Diamondbacks in Game 4 of the World Series at Yankee Stadium, October 31, 2001. Paul O'Neill, right, scored on the hit. With the Yanks down to their last out of the game, Martinez took the first pitch from Arizona reliever Byung-Hyun Kim to right-center field, tying the game with one swing. The stadium erupted. But the night was still young.

October 6, 1997 The Cleveland Indians—with a much weaker regular season record—stun the defending champions in a five-game AL Division Series, beating the Yankees by a single run in each of the last two games.

Franklin

October

MR. NOVEMBER

Chuck Knoblauch, center, and other Yankees teammates wait at home plate to congratulate Derek Jeter after he hit a game-winning home run in the tenth inning of World Series Game 4 against the Arizona Diamondbacks at Yankee Stadium. The game started Wednesday night, October 31, 2001, but by the time Jeter hit his walk-off homer off closer Byung-Hyun Kim, it was baseball in November. The call by Yankees broadcaster Michael Kay said it all: "See ya! See ya! See ya! A home run for Derek Jeter! He is Mr. November!" In a script even Hollywood would find implausible, the Bombers had come back from the verge of a two-game deficit to tie the Series with a pair of stunning home runs off Kim. You'd have to wait a long time to see another World Series game like that. Right?

February 3, 1998 After a three-year apprenticeship under Gene Michael and Bob Watson, Michael's successor in 1996–97, Brian Cashman is named the Yankees' general manager, at age thirty.

October

DÉJÀ VU ALL OVER AGAIN

Yankees third baseman Scott Brosius celebrates his ninth-inning home run against the Arizona Diamondbacks to tie Game 5 of the World Series at Yankee Stadium, November 1, 2001. Rod Barajas catches for the Diamondbacks, with umpire Jim Joyce behind the plate. It had seemed unlikely that this game could rise to the level of Game 4, which had ended earlier the same day. Pity hapless Diamondbacks closer Byung-Hyun Kim. For the second night in a row, he had a two-run lead with two outs in the bottom of the ninth. Enter Brosius, with Jorge Posada on second. The result? Two runs on the board and pandemonium in the Bronx. That the Yanks would score the winning run in the twelfth inning on an RBI single seemed almost inevitable.

May 17, 1998 With a 4–0 win against the Minnesota Twins at Yankee Stadium, David Wells becomes the first Yankee, and only the fifteenth player in major league history, to pitch a regular-season perfect game.

October

MYSTIQUE AND AURA MISSED THE PLANE

Chuck Knoblauch (11) leaps into the arms of Derek Jeter after Alfonso Soriano singled in Knoblauch for the winning run in the twelfth inning, defeating the Arizona Diamondbacks 3–2 to take Game 5 of the World Series at Yankee Stadium, November 1, 2001. Reflecting a pre-Series put-down of the Yankees by Arizona pitcher Curt Schilling, a sign in the stadium read, "Mystique and Aura, Appearing Nightly."

With the Yankees now one game away from clinching the Series after two miracle wins, there seemed no way the Bombers could lose, even with the final two games in Arizona. But back in Arizona, the D'backs pounded the Yanks 15–2 in Game 6 and also held them to two runs in Game 7. Then, in the ninth inning of the finale, with the Yankees up 2–1, a costly error by the usually sure-handed Mariano Rivera, a game-tying double, and a walk-off bloop single by Arizona's Luis Gonzalez abruptly ended the Yankees' bid for a fourth straight championship.

September 25, 1998 The Yankees win their 112th game of the season, breaking the American League regular season record set by the Cleveland Indians in 1954.

October

31

FLIPPED OUT

Yankees third baseman Robin Ventura falls into the photographers' box while chasing a foul ball during Game 3 of the AL Division Series in Anaheim, California, October 4, 2002. The Angels won the game 9–6, en route to a three-games-to-one drubbing of the Yankees in the series. It was the Yankees' earliest playoff exit since the 1997 ALDS, and a deeply disappointing end to a season that saw the Bronx team win 103 games, tied with Oakland for the most in the majors. But the Yankees' pitching deserted them in the playoffs, posting a horrendous 8.21 ERA while the Angels were hitting a gaudy .376 for the series. "We expected to go to the World Series," pitcher Andy Pettitte lamented after the final game. Not this time.

September 27, 1998 The extraordinary Yankees team—with a lineup starring batting champion Bernie Williams (.339), Derek Jeter (203 hits), Tino Martinez (twenty-eight home runs, 123 RBIs), and Paul O'Neill (forty doubles) and a pitching staff led by starters David Cone (20–7) and David Wells (18–4) and closer Mariano Rivera (thirty-six saves, 1.91 ERA)—finishes the season with its record 114th win (broken by Seattle in 2001 with 116 wins), in first place over the Red Sox by twenty-two games.

November

1

OUT AT THIRD. SIX WEEKS OUT.

The 2003 season gets off to a bad start when Yankees shortstop Derek Jeter dislocates his shoulder during the year's very first game, on March 31, in Toronto. Here, Jeter grimaces after colliding with Blue Jays catcher Ken Huckaby, who had run up the line to cover third as Jeter dived in. Several Yankees complained that the play was dirty and unnecessary, and Jeter reportedly refused to talk to Huckaby when the journeyman tried to apologize. The Yankees superstar would be sidelined for six weeks. Despite the setback, the Yankees would win 101 games and finish first in the American League East. Jeter would be named the team's official captain and end the year batting .324.

October 10, 1998 High-kicking pitcher Orlando "El Duque" Hernandez, who escaped from Cuba the previous December, saves the Yankees from elimination by shutting out the Cleveland Indians in Game 4 of the AL Championship Series. After defeating the Indians in six games, the Yankees cap a record-breaking season with a sweep of the San Diego Padres, giving them their twenty-fourth world championship and a record of 125–50, including 11–2 in the postseason.

BENIK

November

2

BACKSTOP

Yankees catcher Jorge Posada holds up the ball after snagging a foul pop-up behind home plate during a game against the Oakland Athletics on May 3, 2003, in New York. The 2003 campaign was perhaps the Puerto Rico native's best season. He hit thirty home runs and drove in 101 RBIs, both career highs, and was regarded as the team's most valuable player. But Posada also contributed behind the plate, winning kudos for his deft handling of the Yankees' star-studded pitching staff. A fan favorite, Posada is one of a handful of Yankees stars who came up through the team's farm system and who have played their entire careers in New York.

February 19, 1999 The Yankees obtain five-time Cy Young Award winner Roger Clemens, one of the best pitchers in baseball history, from the Toronto Blue Jays in a trade; the players they give up include David Wells.

November

COOPERSTOWN CALLING?

Yankees pitcher Roger Clemens tips his cap to fans at Yankee Stadium, June 13, 2003, after becoming the twenty-first pitcher in history to reach his 300th career win, usually an automatic passport into baseball's Hall of Fame. "The Rocket," as Clemens was known, also notched his 4,000th strikeout in the 5–2 victory over the St. Louis Cardinals, and he even discussed his future Hall of Fame induction after the game—saying he wanted to go in as a Yankee and he hoped his mother would live long enough to see the big day. (She died in 2005.) But a Hall of Fame plaque has become far from certain since the fireballer became one of the highest-profile stars implicated in a major probe of steroids in baseball.

March 8, 1999 Joe DiMaggio dies at age eighty-four.

November

MONSTER PLAYER

A huge portrait of Yankees slugger Hideki Matsui is spotlighted on the fuselage of a Japanese jetliner as part of a "Go, Go, Matsui" campaign by Japan Airlines in Tokyo, June 24, 2003. The photogenic slugger was one of Japanese baseball's biggest stars when he signed a deal with the Yankees before the 2003 season, and Matsui mania gripped his home country, especially during his first season in the big leagues. A huge contingent of Japanese journalists was sent to New York to follow Matsui's every move. Back home, fans snapped up Yankees memorabilia, and some woke up early to catch his at bats live. Matsui did not disappoint, getting an RBI single in his very first big league at bat and smashing a grand slam in his first game at Yankee Stadium, an apt start for the man Japanese fans had nicknamed "Godzilla."

July 18, 1999 David Cone pitches the sixteenth regular season perfect game in baseball history, defeating the Montreal Expos 6–0 on Yogi Berra Day. Both Yogi and Don Larsen—the catcher and pitcher of the only perfect game in World Series history—are present.

Dream
907
JAL

November

HIGH HURDLES

Yankees shortstop Derek Jeter leaps over Doug Mientkiewicz of the Minnesota Twins in the sixth inning of Game 2 of the AL Division Series at Yankee Stadium, October 2, 2003. Jeter was unable to complete the double play, and the Twins' Jacque Jones was safe at first. The Yankees won this game 4–1, en route to winning the series three games to one. After leaving Minnesota midway through the 2004 season, Mientkiewicz joined the Red Sox in time for that fall's miraculous AL pennant and world championship.

September 9, 1999 Jim "Catfish" Hunter dies at age fifty-three of ALS—Lou Gehrig's disease.

November

CHAMPAGNE SHOWERS

Yankees DH Jason Giambi smiles as champagne rains down on him in the clubhouse after New York beat the Minnesota Twins 8–1 in Game 4 of the AL Division Series, October 5, 2003, in Minneapolis. Giambi had a pair of doubles and a walk on the night. The Yankees had finished the season with a league-best 101–61 record, sweeping all seven regular season games against the Twins. The team from Minneapolis shocked the Yankees with a victory in Game 1, but New York returned to form after that, allowing a total of just three runs in the next three games—all victories. The win against the Twins set up an epic clash for the pennant with the archrival Boston Red Sox, one that would live up to its billing as a battle for the ages.

October 3, 1999 The Yankees finish the season with attendance topping more than three million for the first time, as 3,292,736 go to Yankee Stadium.

November

7

BABE RUTH WAS IN THE SEAT NEXT TO ME

A cardboard cutout of legendary slugger Babe Ruth stands among baseball fans during Game 2 of the American League Championship Series between the Yankees and the Boston Red Sox in New York on October 9, 2003, evoking 1918, the last time the Red Sox had won the World Series. Since trading Ruth to the Yankees following the 1919 season, the team from Beantown had failed to win a world championship—often losing in heartbreaking style. The Yankees, meanwhile, became the winningest team in history. Ahead of the 2003 Championship Series, Red Sox players scoffed at the idea of a Curse of the Bambino, but the hex would have the last laugh, with the Yankees breaking Boston's heart in dramatic style.

October 26, 1999 Yankees left fielder Chad Curtis's tenth-inning home run at Yankee Stadium wins Game 3 of the World Series, 6–5; the next day, in the last game of the century, the Yankees finish sweeping the Atlanta Braves for their twenty-fifth world championship. The win is their twelfth straight in Series play, tying the record set by the Yankees in 1927, 1928, and 1932.

1918

November

BAD BLOOD

Yankees pitcher Roger Clemens, left, looks after bench coach Don Zimmer, center, after the venerable Zimmer was thrown to the ground by Boston Red Sox ace Pedro Martinez during an altercation in Game 3 of the AL Championship Series, October 11, 2003, at Fenway Park. The very brief brawl between the burly seventy-two-year-old coach and the thirty-one-year-old pitcher came to exemplify the enmity between the Yankees and their archrival, a deep loathing built up through the better part of the twentieth century. Later in Game 3, two Yankees got into a fight with a Red Sox groundskeeper, prompting Boston officials to have them arrested and charged with assault. Not to be outdone, New York Mayor Michael Bloomberg suggested that Martinez ought to be arrested for throwing the septuagenarian Zimmer to the ground. Oh, and the Yankees won the game, 4–3.

April 23, 2000 Playing the Blue Jays in Toronto, Jorge Posada and Bernie Williams become the first teammates to have switch-hit home runs in a single game (which the Yankees win 10–7).

NEW YOR
NY

November

BUSINESS AS USUAL

Skipper Joe Torre, left, congratulates closer Mariano Rivera after the Yankees defeated the Boston Red Sox, 4–3, in Game 3 of the AL Championship Series, October 11, 2003, in Boston. In a game that would go down as one of the nastiest in Yankees–Red Sox history, it was left to the unflappable Rivera to restore order with a clutch two-inning save. Forget the fourth-inning brawl between Yankees bench coach Don Zimmer and Red Sox ace Pedro Martinez. Ignore the ninth-inning fight that would break out in the bullpen between two Yankees and a Boston groundskeeper. None of that could rattle the unflappable Rivera. The Panamanian retired all six Red Sox batters he faced—the same lights-out result as usual. The win gave New York a 2–1 lead in the best-of-seven series.

June 19, 2000 The Yankees defeat the Red Sox 22–1 at Fenway Park—Boston's worst loss of all time at home.

YORK

November

WAITING GAME

Watching from the Yankees' dugout during the ninth inning, from left, are pitching coach Mel Stottlemyre, bench coach Don Zimmer, manager Joe Torre, and third baseman Aaron Boone, as the Boston Red Sox defeat the Yankees 3–2 in Game 4 of the AL Championship Series at Fenway Park, October 13, 2003. In typical Yankees–Red Sox fashion, this series would go the distance, with Boone providing the Game 7 fireworks.

October 14, 2000 Despite going 3–14 in their final games, the Yankees finish first with a mediocre 87–74 record, beat the Oakland A's in five games, and then go up two games to one against the Seattle Mariners. In Game 4, fastballer Roger Clemens mixes lots of heat with sliders and splitters for a no-hitter through six innings, and he winds up with a complete game, one-hit, fifteen-strikeout victory.

November

11

THE GHOSTS CAME OUT

There have been many great moments in the Yankees–Red Sox rivalry, but one of the very best belongs to Yankees hero Aaron Boone, left. With the Yankees trailing the Red Sox in Game 7 of the 2003 American League Championship Series, Derek Jeter told Boone not to worry—the ghosts of seasons past would come out. The Yankees tied the game with three runs against Pedro Martinez in the eighth inning. Then Boone, the journeyman infielder, smashed an eleventh-inning walk-off home run, sending the Yankees to their thirty-ninth World Series.

The decision by Red Sox manager Grady Little to leave the clearly exhausted Martinez in the game in the pivotal eighth inning would be lambasted by heartbroken Boston fans, and the manager was let go after the season, too late to stop the 2003 Boston team from adding its name to the ghosts of Red Sox past.

October 22, 2000 In Game 2 of the first Subway Series since 1956 (but this time against the New York Mets, not the Brooklyn Dodgers), Mets catcher Mike Piazza shatters his bat in his first time up against Roger Clemens since the Rocket beaned him with a fastball on July 8 during an interleague game. Piazza starts running to first, and Clemens flings a piece of the bat at him—clearing the benches until the umpires rule that it was just a reflex action by the intense Clemens.

November

12

COMEBACK CITY

The Yankees celebrate as they await Aaron Boone (not shown), circling the bases after beating the Boston Red Sox with a solo home run in the bottom of the eleventh inning of Game 7 of the AL Championship Series in New York, October 16, 2003. The Yankees had been five outs away from elimination when they scored three runs in the eighth inning to tie the game against Pedro Martinez.

As crushed Red Sox players exited the field in defeat, Yankees closer Mariano Rivera ran straight to the mound. The legendary reliever, who had worked three scoreless innings in one of the longest relief outings of his career, collapsed in emotion and was embraced by a teammate.

October 26, 2000 The Yankees win their twenty-sixth world championship with a thrilling Game 5 victory against the New York Mets, when utility infielder Luis Sojo's single snaps a tie with two outs in the ninth and ace closer Mariano Rivera gets his second consecutive save. The 2000 team joins the Yankees of 1936–39 and 1949–53, as well as the 1972–74 Oakland Athletics, as the only teams to win at least three consecutive World Series.

November

13

REALLY, WAIT 'TIL NEXT YEAR

Boston Red Sox slugger David Ortiz lies down in the Red Sox clubhouse, reflecting on a bitter 6–5 loss to the Yankees in Game 7 of the AL Championship Series at Yankee Stadium, October 16, 2003. In the background, from left, are bullpen coach Euclides Rojas, backup catcher Bill Haselman, pitcher Jeff Suppan, and starter Derek Lowe (the losing pitcher in Games 2 and 5). After forcing a seventh game in the series, the Red Sox were crushed by Aaron Boone's eleventh-inning home run. Despite losing the series, the Red Sox significantly outhit the Yankees, including an ALCS record twelve home runs. Red Sox Nation would have to wait another year to throw off the Curse of the Bambino, and Ortiz would play a major role in that reversal of fortune.

November 30, 2000 Free agent pitcher Mike Mussina signs a six-year, $88.5 million contract with the Yankees.

37

November

14

POSTSEASON BASEBALL . . . IN JULY

Yankees shortstop Derek Jeter dives headfirst into the stands behind third base to catch a pop fly in the twelfth inning against the Boston Red Sox at Yankee Stadium, July 1, 2004, setting the stage for the Yankees' dramatic 5–4 win an inning later. The Yankees star emerged bloodied and battered, but with the ball firmly in his mitt—just one more clutch play in a career filled with them. Jeter spent an hour in the hospital and received seven stitches. The next day, he sported a purple welt under his right eye and bandages on his chin. Teammate Alex Rodriguez said he "looked like he got punched by Mike Tyson." Still, the Yankees captain insisted on playing, going 0 for 1 with two walks and a stolen base against the Yankees' crosstown rivals, the Mets.

September 2, 2001 Mike Mussina misses a perfect game by one pitch, when pinch hitter Carl Everett of the Red Sox gets a ninth-inning hit on a 1-and-2 count.

13

November

15

HOLY CANNOLI

Former Yankees shortstop Phil Rizzuto tips his cap during Old-Timers' Day ceremonies at Yankee Stadium, July 10, 2004. Throughout his more than sixty years in the Yankees organization, the Scooter's scrappy, idiosyncratic style made him a fan favorite. He played in nine World Series, winning seven world championship rings in a Hall of Fame career. He later became a revered Yankees broadcaster, famous for his meandering asides and his signature call: "Holy cow!" Rizzuto called Roger Maris's sixty-first home run in 1961, and he even provided the play-by-play voice-over for Meatloaf's hit song "Paradise by the Dashboard Light." His love of cannoli and his practice of leaving the broadcast booth early to beat the traffic home to his wife, Cora, in New Jersey became running themes on Yankees radio and television.

September 19, 2001 Roger Clemens beats the Chicago White Sox to become the first pitcher ever to reach 20–1 during a season; he finishes with a 20–3 record and wins his sixth career Cy Young Award (his only one with the Yankees).

November

16

LIGHTNING ROD

Yankees third baseman Alex Rodriguez reacts to taunts from Boston Red Sox fans during a game at Fenway Park in July 2004. A-Rod, the highest-paid player in baseball and considered the best by many, came to personify the Yankees' free-spending ways after they acquired him and his hefty contract from the Texas Rangers during the off-season. Nowhere was the animosity deeper than in Boston, which had also tried to make a deal for the superstar, before having it voided by the players' union. This was just the latest example of the Yankees' deep pockets besting Boston, a tradition that went all the way back to the acquisition of Babe Ruth after the 1919 season.

September 25, 2001 The Yankees play their first home game after the terrorist attacks on the World Trade Center and the Pentagon. The game, which they lose to the Tampa Bay Devil Rays 4–0, follows ceremonies honoring the victims of September 11 and the rescue workers; despite the loss, the Yankees clinch the AL East title when the Boston Red Sox also lose.

November

17

IN YOUR FACE

Boston catcher Jason Varitek, left, shoves Alex Rodriguez in the face after the Yankees star was hit by a pitch in the third inning and began yelling at Red Sox pitcher Bronson Arroyo at Fenway Park, July 24, 2004. Rodriguez later said he "smelled something funny" about Arroyo's inside pitch and thought it was intentional. Even before the incident, Rodriguez had endured merciless taunting from the Boston faithful, a recurring theme throughout A-Rod's Yankees career. Rodriguez and Varitek were both ejected from the game after the benches cleared. The scuffle intensified an already red-hot Yankees–Red Sox rivalry, and it served as a prelude to one of the most dramatic postseason series of all time.

October 13, 2001 The Yankees are down two games to none in the AL Division Series when shortstop Derek Jeter races past the base line between home and first, snatches an errant throw from right fielder Shane Spencer, and—without breaking stride—makes a sidearm, backhanded flip to catcher Jorge Posada in time to stop the Oakland Athletics' Jeremy Giambi from tying the game in the seventh. It's the turning point of the series, which the Yankees take with three straight wins.

ALLSTAR

November

18

PREMATURE CELEBRATION

Yankees fans celebrate a run against the Boston Red Sox in Game 1 of the AL Championship Series in New York, October 12, 2004. The fans' banner refers to remarks by Boston pitcher Pedro Martinez, who had famously said, "I just tip my hat and call the Yankees my daddy," after failing to beat them in a previous matchup. The comment became a sensation, inspiring dozens of clever T-shirt designs and unprintable chants, with which Yankees fans happily serenaded the Boston ace when he took the mound in Game 2 the next night. Some fans even came to that game with baby bottles hanging around their neck. The Yankees won Game 1 with a score of 10–7, en route to a commanding 3–0 lead in the best-of-seven series. Once again, everything seemed to be going the Yankees' way.

October 21, 2001 In the AL Championship Series against the Seattle Mariners, second baseman Alfonso Soriano's game-winning two-run homer in the ninth inning of Game 4 puts the Yankees up three games to one. The next day, also at Yankee Stadium, the Yankees' 12–3 blowout gives them their fourth straight AL pennant, for the first time since the early 1960s.

HEY PEDRO → WHO'S YOUR DADDY?

November

19

BLOOD AND GUTS

With blood visible on his sock, Boston Red Sox pitcher Curt Schilling tends to his injured right ankle during the third inning of Game 6 of the AL Championship Series against the Yankees, October 19, 2004, at Yankee Stadium. Schilling pitched seven gritty innings of one-run ball, and the Red Sox went on to win the game 4–2, tying the ALCS at 3–3. The Red Sox's historic come-from-behind string of four straight victories (the first baseball team to overcome a three-games-to-none deficit to take the league title) created the momentum that led to Boston's sweep of the St. Louis Cardinals in the World Series, the first Red Sox world championship since 1918 and their sixth title overall. The famous bloody sock now resides at the Baseball Hall of Fame in Cooperstown, New York.

October 31, 2001 The Yankees, down two games to one, are trailing the Diamondbacks in Game 4 of the World Series when Tino Martinez hits a two-run homer that sends the game into extra innings. With two outs in the tenth, Derek Jeter earns the nickname "Mr. November" at 12:04 A.M., when he hits his first game-winning home run.

November

DESPERATE MEASURES

Yankees runner Alex Rodriguez knocks the ball out of the glove of Boston Red Sox reliever Bronson Arroyo, left, as first baseman Doug Mientkiewicz avoids a collision during the eighth inning of Game 6 of the AL Championship Series at Yankee Stadium, October 19, 2004. Rodriguez was initially called safe, but after conferring, the umpires ruled that he was out for interference. The decision, which nullified a run, caused fans to rain balls and other debris onto the field. The next inning was played only after helmeted police took position around the diamond. Boston won the game to even the series, then took Game 7 the next night to become the first team in baseball history to win a best-of-seven series after losing the first three games.

November 1, 2001 In Game 5, for the second straight night, Arizona reliever Byung-Hyun Kim gives up a two-run homer—this one to Scott Brosius—that ties the game with two outs in the ninth inning; the exciting marathon lasts until the twelfth, when Alfonso Soriano singles home the Yankees' winning run. Meanwhile, echoing the "Donnie Baseball" farewell to Don Mattingly in 1995, the fans rhythmically chant Paul O'Neill's name and clap, over and over again, during the hard-playing right fielder's final game at Yankee Stadium.

BOSTON
BOSTON

November

21

THE CURSE, REVERSED

Boston Red Sox first baseman Doug Mientkiewicz sprays champagne on Boston fans above the visitors' dugout after the Sox defeated the Yankees 10–3 in the final game of the AL Championship Series, October 20, 2004, at Yankee Stadium. Left for dead after Game 3 of the series, the Red Sox staged a momentous comeback to sweep the final four games of the series. That it ended in the House That Ruth Built, with Frank Sinatra's rendition of "New York, New York" playing over the PA system, could only have added to the sweetness of the moment for the Red Sox and their fans, while leaving the Yankees' faithful to ponder recent events in disbelief.

November 4, 2001 In the heartbreaking Game 7 of the World Series, Alfonso Soriano's eighth-inning home run snaps a tie, and Mariano Rivera—arguably the best relief pitcher in baseball history—strikes out the side. In the ninth, however, Rivera has a very rare bad outing (especially in the postseason), and the Diamondbacks tie the game again and then win the Series on a bloop single.

BankofAmerica

November

22

STRUCK OUT, LOOKING

Yankees center fielder Bernie Williams tosses his helmet and bat after taking a third strike to end the fifth inning against the Texas Rangers, April 23, 2005, at Yankee Stadium. The Yankees got off to a miserable start in 2005, opening the season 11–19—not exactly what owner George Steinbrenner had in mind when he approved a payroll topping $200 million. Williams, the Yankees' star center fielder since 1993, struggled mightily in the early going, hitting an anemic .238 through the end of April. Suffering from tendinitis in his right elbow, Williams was temporarily replaced in center field by Hideki Matsui (and also Tony Womack) as part of an early season shake-up. Williams finished this, his penultimate season, with a subpar .249 average.

May 17, 2002 Jason Giambi, a new Yankee after signing a seven-year contract in December, hits a fourteenth-inning bases-loaded home run to defeat the Twins 13–12, joining Babe Ruth as the only Yankees ever to hit a walk-off grand slam.

November

IN THE ZONE

Alex Rodriguez follows through on a three-run home run off Los Angeles Angels starter Bartolo Colón in the first inning at Yankee Stadium, April 26, 2005. The Yankees third baseman added a two-run homer in the third inning and a grand slam in the fourth, all off Colón, who was watching his ERA balloon every time Rodriguez came up. A-Rod later added an RBI single to make it an even ten RBIs; not bad for a day's work, and just one RBI short of Tony Lazzeri's league record eleven-RBI performance in 1936. But even this game managed to beleaguer A-Rod: Days later, a memorabilia company linked to Alex started selling balls commemorating the game for $399. A-Rod denied knowledge of the souvenir balls, and he broke off ties with the company.

June 10, 2002 Marcus Thames is only the second Yankee—and the first in nearly thirty-six years—to hit a home run in his first major league at bat, during a home game against Arizona.

November

24

BIG UNIT? BIG DEAL

Yankees pitcher Randy Johnson looks to the outfield as he confers with pitching coach Mel Stottlemyre, left, and catcher Jorge Posada during the sixth inning against the New York Mets at Shea Stadium, May 21, 2005. By the next inning, he had left the game after giving up four runs, en route to a 7–1 Yankees loss. Johnson had been a five-time Cy Young Award winner, including four straight from 1999 to 2002 with the Arizona Diamondbacks. And he had owned the Yanks in the 2001 World Series, with three wins and a 1.04 ERA. But he didn't show that form with any consistency in his two years with the Yankees. From the day he arrived in New York, quickly getting into a sidewalk confrontation with a WCBS cameraman, the Big Unit never looked really comfortable in pinstripes. Johnson did win seventeen games each season in New York, but he rarely seemed to string together strong starts, gave up too many home runs, and was a disappointment in the postseason. He went back to Arizona for the 2007 season.

September 21, 2002 The Yankees win their fifth consecutive American League East title, defeating the Detroit Tigers 3–2. This is their sixth title in seven seasons under manager Joe Torre.

EW YORK
20

November

SWEATING IT OUT

Yankees third baseman Alex Rodriguez soaks his face with water beside a fan in the dugout during a game against his former team, the Texas Rangers, at Yankee Stadium, August 13, 2005. With temperatures pushing triple digits, the Yankees won their third straight game, 7–5. After a terrible start, the Yankees ended the season in the playoffs for the eleventh straight year. They went 35–15 in the final 50 games of the regular season, just enough to finish tied with archrival Boston; the Yankees ended up first in their division by virtue of their 10–9 record against the Red Sox during the season. A-Rod was no stranger to hot weather, having played virtually every game during three seasons in Texas. He has since admitted using steroids during that period.

October 5, 2002 In the Yankees' quickest postseason elimination since 1980, the Anaheim Angels win 9–6 in Game 4 to take the AL Division Series.

November

UP AGAINST THE WALL

Yankees outfielders Gary Sheffield (11) and Bubba Crosby collide against the center field wall chasing a two-out line drive by the Los Angeles Angels' Adam Kennedy in the second inning of Game 5 of their AL Division Series in Anaheim, California, October 10, 2005. The ball fell in for a two-run triple, and the Angels ended up winning the game 5–3, clinching the series. With bitter memories of the 2004 AL Championship Series collapse still lingering, this misplay on a seemingly catchable ball seemed to epitomize the Yankees' playoff woes. The team that had always found a way to win when it mattered was now finding ways to lose. Some of the Yankees' biggest names failed to come through in the clutch: Alex Rodriguez had a miserable series, going 2 for 15 with no RBIs; Bernie Williams was 4 for 19 with just one RBI. It was now five years and counting since the last Yankees world championship.

June 3, 2003 Derek Jeter is named captain of the Yankees.

11

November

27

TAKE THE 4 TRAIN

After more than eighty years of drama and history at the House That Ruth Built, the Yankees break ground on a new state-of-the-art stadium on a stretch of public athletic fields directly across the street from the original. The Yankees, never ones to do things in an understated way, erected a small village of canopies, tents, and terraced seating for the August 16, 2006, ground-breaking ceremony, as seen from the number 4 elevated subway platform. The Yankees picked the fifty-eighth anniversary of Babe Ruth's death for the ceremony, a nod to the rich history of the most storied stadium in baseball, if not the world.

June 13, 2003 Roger Clemens wins his 300th game—the first pitcher to do so since Nolan Ryan in 1990—and strikes out the 4,000th batter of his career, in the same game at Yankee Stadium.

Yankee Stadium

November

SCRAMBLED LEGS

The Texas Rangers' Gerald Laird, top, leaps over the tag from Yankees first baseman Doug Mientkiewicz as pitcher Andy Pettitte, left, looks on during the fifth inning at Yankee Stadium, May 8, 2007. Mientkiewicz missed the tag, Laird missed stepping on the bag, and Mientkiewicz then beat Laird to the bag for an out. Mientkiewicz played for a succession of teams after the Red Sox in 2004, platooning at first base for the Yankees in 2007, his only season in pinstripes. He now holds the major league record for the most frequently misspelled name, a record previously held by Al "the Mad Hungarian" Hrabosky.

August 23, 2003 Ron Guidry's number, 49, is retired during a pregame ceremony.

KYOCERA
3

November

PRIDE OF THE YANKEES REVISITED

Yankees broadcaster Bobby Murcer poses before a baseball game between the Yankees and the Texas Rangers (which the Yankees won, 10–1) in Arlington, Texas, May 1, 2007, as he returned to the booth for his first full game behind the mic since having surgery on a malignant brain tumor on December 28, 2006. A five-time All-Star, Murcer spent seventeen seasons in the major leagues between 1965 and 1983, including thirteen with the Yankees; he was the only person to play with both Mickey Mantle and Don Mattingly. Murcer then became a popular Yankees broadcaster and won three Emmy Awards for live sports coverage. Friends said Murcer wanted to attend the final game at the old Yankee Stadium, but he died on July 12, 2008, about ten weeks short of his goal.

September 26, 2003 Andy Pettitte gives up one run in five innings against the Baltimore Orioles at Yankee Stadium to finish his first stint as a Yankee with his second 21–8 season. After going 149–78 in nine years, the clutch lefty joins Roger Clemens with the Houston Astros for three years before returning to the Yankees in 2007 and winning twenty-nine more games over the next two seasons.

Telestrator
adidas

November

A PERFECT 10

A fan holds up a sign referring to Phil Rizzuto during the Yankees game against the Baltimore Orioles at Yankee Stadium, August 14, 2007. The Scooter had died the previous day; at eighty-nine, he had been the oldest living member of the Hall of Fame. Did anyone ever have a bad word to say about Phil? Well, yes. When he first tried out for the Brooklyn Dodgers, manager Casey Stengel took one look and said, "Kid, you're too small. You ought to go out and shine shoes." But Stengel had no complaints when the 5-foot-6 Rizzuto became his star shortstop with the Yankees. The Scooter played his entire career in the Bronx, from 1941 to 1956 (except for 1943–45, spent in the Navy during World War II). The Yankees retired his number, 10, in 1985. Casey surely would have approved.

October 16, 2003 The mutually hostile Yankees and Red Sox meet at Yankee Stadium to finish an especially volatile AL Championship Series, climaxing five days earlier in Game 3, when Yankees bench coach Don Zimmer charges Red Sox pitcher Pedro Martinez—who grabs the seventy-two-year-old's head and flings him to the ground during a bench-clearing brawl. In the eighth inning of Game 7, Martinez is left in longer than usual, and Jorge Posada doubles home Bernie Williams and Hideki Matsui to tie the game; third baseman Aaron Boone then starts the bottom of the eleventh by driving Tim Wakefield's first pitch over the left field wall, giving the Yankees their thirty-ninth AL pennant.

HOLY COW!
IN YANKEES HEAVEN
NOW! #10 SCOOTER

December

1

THE RULES ACCORDING TO JOBA

Yankees pitching sensation Joba Chamberlain reacts after striking out the Boston Red Sox's J. D. Drew to end the eighth inning—stranding the tying runs on base—at Yankee Stadium, August 28, 2007. Chamberlain was called up to the big leagues on August 7, and the big Nebraska native with the blazing fastball and emotional style wasted little time becoming a fan favorite. The Yankees were so protective of the young phenom that they developed a set of guidelines that came to be known as the "Joba Rules," which called for him to be used sparingly and only in certain situations. Chamberlain posted a mind-bending 0.38 ERA in his nineteen appearances, striking out thirty-four batters in just twenty-four innings. But no less an authority than Goose Gossage weighed in on Chamberlain's demonstrative mound celebrations. "There's no place for it in the game," said the Yankees Hall of Famer. "I will stand by that, and I love Joba Chamberlain."

October 25, 2003 The Yankees' postseason ends at Yankee Stadium for the first time since 1981, when the Florida Marlins defeat them in Game 6 of the World Series.

December

A STADIUM GROWS IN THE BRONX

The new Yankee Stadium takes shape across East 161st Street from the existing stadium, August 29, 2007. Yankees fans were deeply torn over the decision to abandon the House That Ruth Built, even for a state-of-the-art facility. The new stadium was completed just ahead of the 2009 season, at a cost well in excess of $1 billion; how much of that was borne by the taxpayers depends on whose accountant you believe. And the fate of the old stadium, the one where Yankees immortals roamed? The one where Joe Louis took the heavyweight title from Max Schmeling? Where the Baltimore Colts' Alan Ameche scored the winning touchdown of the 1958 NFL Championship over New York Giants in "the greatest football game ever played"? Where Notre Dame upset Army in the 1928 "Win one for the Gipper" game? Where Lou Gehrig moved the crowd to tears, and Roger Maris hit number sixty-one? No one was saying exactly, but the smart money was on the city selling off every last seat and fixture, then tearing the place down. It's not like it's a national landmark or anything.

April 11 and 14, 2004 Mike Mussina and Kevin Brown earn their 200th wins in back-to-back games, the first players in major league history to do so.

December

IMPACT PLAYER

Yankees catcher Jorge Posada, right, hangs on to the ball as Boston Red Sox base runner Eric Hinske slams into him in a brutal collision at home plate in the sixth inning at Fenway Park, September 15, 2007. Hinske was out on the play, but the impact knocked Posada out of the game. He was taken to Massachusetts General Hospital, where a CT scan of his head and neck came back negative. The tenacious catcher's play was the only highlight on a dismal day for the Yankees. They were routed 10–1, falling five and a half games behind Boston with little time left to make up the deficit.

July 1, 2004 Running at full speed, Derek Jeter plunges into the seats along the third base line as he makes a spectacular catch of a twelfth-inning pop-up by Trot Nixon of the Red Sox. The Yankees win in the thirteenth and end up with a three-game sweep at home.

RED
20

December

RIPPED

Yankees pinch hitter Jason Giambi breaks his bat on a pitch from Boston Red Sox hurler Curt Schilling in the eighth inning at Fenway Park, September 16, 2007. Giambi would subsequently line a single off the Green Monster as the Yankees held on to win 4–3. When Giambi joined the Yanks in 2002, fans expected big things. And they got that—literally and figuratively. During his seven years in pinstripes, Giambi always seemed to be among the league leaders in slugging and on base percentage. He hit two solo home runs in the wild finale of the 2003 American League Championship, keeping the Yankees in the game. But when the BALCO scandal surfaced, his homers began to look less than heroic. The *San Francisco Chronicle* reported that Giambi testified to using steroids and human growth hormone between 2001 and 2003. At a 2005 news conference, he apologized—though he stopped short of saying for what he was apologizing. Giambi's Yankees career ended with no World Series rings. But he is the answer to this trivia question: Who had the last hit at Yankee Stadium?

September 26, 2004 In Boston, Andy Phillips becomes only the third Yankee to hit a home run in his first major league at bat.

25
TPX.

December

BUGS CHECK IN; THE YANKEES CHECK OUT

New York Yankees catcher Jorge Posada applies bug spray to relief pitcher Mariano Rivera before the bottom of the ninth inning in Game 2 of the AL Division Series against the Cleveland Indians at Jacobs Field, October 5, 2007. It instantly became known as the "Bug Game," as swarms of insects surrounded the players in the later innings. The bugs had already proved the undoing of the Yankees' rookie pitching phenom Joba Chamberlain in the eighth inning. Clearly distracted, Chamberlain walked two batters, hit another, and threw two wild pitches; he allowed the tying run to score without a hit. The Indians won the game 2–1 in eleven innings and went on to win the series 3–1. The Yankees tried to downplay the significance of the aerial invasion. As Alex Rodriguez said after the game, "I've never seen anything like it. But it's certainly not an excuse—we have to be able to go out and play with anything."

September 30, 2004 Bernie Williams's walk-off home run against the Minnesota Twins clinches the Yankees' seventh consecutive American League East title and their tenth straight advance to the playoffs.

POSADA

December

STAYIN' ALIVE

Yankees players—from left, Robinson Cano, Melky Cabrera, Derek Jeter, Johnny Damon, and Bobby Abreu—celebrate after beating the Cleveland Indians 8–4 in a must-win Game 3 of the American League Division Series at Yankee Stadium, October 7, 2007. Cleveland had taken the first two games, putting the Yankees' season in jeopardy. Despite the one-night reprieve, the Yankees would fall in the next game, losing 6–4 after a terrible start by ace Chien-Ming Wang. For the third straight year, the Yankees had not advanced past the first round of the playoffs, and there was a sense of foreboding in the somber clubhouse. After the season, the Yankees had a bitter parting of ways with skipper Joe Torre, marking the end of a glorious era.

October 20, 2004 The Red Sox win Game 7 of the AL Championship Series, and the Yankees become the first team ever to lose a best-of-seven series after winning the first three games.

24
10

December

7

THE ROCKET IS GROUNDED

In sworn testimony before the House Oversight and Government Reform Committee, February 13, 2008, former Yankees pitcher Roger Clemens states that he never used performance-enhancing drugs, contradicting the account of his former personal trainer. Clemens was one of the highest-profile stars named in the Mitchell Report, a landmark investigation into steroids and other performance-enhancing drugs in baseball, but he adamantly denied the charges. As of early 2009, authorities were still deciding whether to indict Clemens for perjury in the case. Regardless, the scandal had tarnished the legacy of one of the best pitchers in baseball history, a man whose induction into the Hall of Fame had once seemed assured.

January 11, 2005 The Yankees acquire five-time Cy Young Award winner Randy Johnson from the Arizona Diamondbacks for Javier Vazquez and two other players; Johnson finishes his first season as a Yankee with a 17–8 record.

MR. CLEMENS

December

ONE-TWO PUNCH

Yankees captain Derek Jeter, left, and outfielder Johnny Damon get ready to hit against the Cincinnati Reds in spring training baseball action in Sarasota, Florida, Friday, March 14, 2008. Damon tormented the Yankees as a member of the Red Sox team that defeated New York in the 2004 AL Championship Series, capped by his grand slam in Game 7 of the ALCS. He then opted to join the team known in Boston as "the Evil Empire," often leading off the Yankees' lineup with Jeter hitting second. To open the 2009 season, manager Joe Girardi reversed the pair, with Jeter batting leadoff.

April 26, 2005 In a 12–4 win over the Angels at home, Alex Rodriguez belts three home runs—including a grand slam—and drives in nine runs in his first three at bats (plus a tenth RBI later), all off Bartolo Colón. Still, it takes a youth movement, with the front office calling up pitcher Chien-Ming Wang and second baseman Robinson Cano and shifting Hideki Matsui to Bernie Williams's spot in center field, to reverse an 11–19 start to the season with a ten-game winning streak from May 7 to 17.

NY
2
NY

NICE TRY

It could have been Boston's twenty-first-century answer to the Curse of the Bambino, but the Yankees were having none of it. After receiving an anonymous tip that construction worker Gino Castignoli, a Red Sox fan, had buried a jersey bearing the name and number of Boston star David Ortiz in two feet of concrete at the new Yankee Stadium, officials brought in jackhammers to have the offensive sportswear removed from a service corridor. Frank Gramarossa, a project executive for the new stadium, holds up the jersey, April 13, 2008. The Yankees even considered bringing criminal charges against Castignoli, proof that hexes and superstition are not taken lightly by followers of the New York–Boston rivalry. The Yankees later donated the shirt to the Jimmy Fund, benefiting a Boston-area cancer institute. It brought $175,000 at auction.

June 9, 2005 With two home runs against the Milwaukee Brewers, Alex Rodriguez becomes the youngest player in major league history to hit 400 homers.

Turner
YANKEES
ORTIZ
34

December

ONE SMALL PITCH FOR A MAN

NASA astronaut Garrett Reisman throws the ceremonial first pitch (figuratively) inside the International Space Station before a game between the Yankees and Boston Red Sox in New York, April 16, 2008. Reisman, seen on the stadium's giant screen, is a lifelong Yankees fan. When he blasted off in March for a three-month stay in space, he carried with him dirt from the Yankee Stadium pitching mound, a Yankees banner, and a hat autographed by owner George Steinbrenner. Floating far above the planet, Reisman drew cheers from the stadium faithful, saying that although there are many nations on earth, "there is only one universe, and it's a Yankee universe." Reisman said he was looking forward to getting back to earth so he could attend a game. Can it get any better? Oh yes: His wife, marine scientist Simone Francis, is an avid fan as well.

August 30, 2005 A-Rod hits his fortieth home run of the season, the first right-handed Yankee to do so since Joe DiMaggio in 1937. He finishes the season with forty-eight home runs, topping Joe D's forty-six, and 130 RBIs, earning him his second AL MVP Award—but the first for a Yankee since Don Mattingly in 1985.

DIAMOND VISION
adidas
43
41

December

11

PILGRIMAGE

Fans line up May 22, 2008, for a glimpse of hallowed ground—the museum and shrine that is Monument Park. It is located between the bullpens beyond the left-center field wall, and if the sports world has a Lourdes, this is it. Receiving a plaque in the park is considered an extraordinary honor for a Yankee, an entry into an ultraexclusive club that includes such immortal names as Babe Ruth, Lou Gehrig, Joe DiMaggio, and Mickey Mantle, as well as more contemporary stars such as Reggie Jackson and Ron Guidry. Other plaques commemorate victims of the September 11 attacks and the several papal addresses at the stadium. When the Yankees moved to their new stadium prior to the 2009 season, Monument Park moved with them, with construction workers carefully disassembling the monuments for the trip across the street.

October 1, 2005 After struggling all season to inch upward, the Yankees defeat the Red Sox at Fenway Park to clinch their eighth consecutive AL East crown. In fact, a loss in the final game the next day drops them into a tie, but the Yankees are awarded the division title because they have a winning record against the Red Sox in the regular season.

RUTH
3
JETER
2
NEW YORK
Yankees

December

12

ON THE FENCE

You would think that Yankee Stadium, in its eighty-five years, had seen almost everything that could happen in a baseball game, but baseball finds a way to invent new things, as it did on July 4, 2008. Yankees left fielder Johnny Damon lies prostrate on the field after a third-inning ball hit by Boston's Kevin Youkilis popped out of his glove and straight onto the top of the outfield wall. The ball bounced and bounced along the thin strip of wall, seemingly unable to decide whether to fall over for a home run. In the end, it trickled back onto the field. Youkilis motored around the bases for a two-run triple, part of a come-from-behind rally that, along with Mike Lowell's three-run homer in the fifth inning, gave Boston a 6–4 win. Damon had to leave the game with a rib injury.

October 2, 2005 The end-of-season good news is an all-time attendance record, with 4,090,696 fans at Yankee Stadium during the regular season. The bad news is that the Angels beat the Yankees in a five-game AL Division Series—the first of three straight first-round eliminations for the Yankees.

December

13

IT'S GONNA TAKE MORE THAN FAKE MUSTACHES

Yankees pitcher Andy Pettitte, left, stands beside fellow hurler Mike Mussina, who wears a fake mustache in support of teammate Jason Giambi, during the National Anthem before a game against the Tampa Bay Rays at Yankee Stadium, July 9, 2008. The Yankees provided 20,000 free mustaches to fans as part of a campaign to get people to vote Giambi into the last position on the AL All-Star team, a promotion the Yankees wryly hyped as the first mustache giveaway in team history. Even the American Mustache Institute took up the cause, putting out a press release that stated "Giambi + Mustache = All-Star." But the fans didn't buy it, and Giambi didn't make the game, which was being played at Yankee Stadium that year. Mussina, meanwhile, was on his way to his first twenty-win season and his best season overall in years.

December 23, 2005 The Yankees poach Johnny Damon from the Red Sox with a four-year, $52 million contract.

December

14

THE HOUSE THAT LUXURY SUITES BUILT

A construction worker stands in front of the field at the new Yankee Stadium, July 11, 2008, while across the street the Yankees prepare to host the All-Star Game. The $1.5 billion new stadium rose steadily as the Bronx Bombers played out their final season at the House That Ruth Built, on pace to open its doors ahead of the 2009 season. The new design is what's now de rigueur for stadiums: state-of-the-art facilities with a retro look. The Yankees decided to keep the same dimensions at the new park, including the short porch in right field, just 314 feet from home plate. Although the new stadium has nearly 5,000 fewer seats than the old one, it boasts fifty-six of the lucrative luxury suites that team officials covet. To say nothing of stratospheric ticket prices.

August 18, 2006 The Yankees begin a four-day, five-game sweep against Boston, outscoring the Red Sox by a total of 49–26, in what the press, referring to the turning point of the 1978 season, calls "Son of Massacre."

YANKEE STADIUM
4591
SAFETY ORIENTATION
UNION IRONWORKERS
LOCAL 580
New York

December

15

THE BOSS IS BACK IN TOWN

Yankees owner George Steinbrenner, right, is hugged by Los Angeles Dodgers special adviser Tommy Lasorda before the All-Star Game at Yankee Stadium on July 15, 2008. The game was Major League Baseball's farewell of sorts to the famous stadium, in its final year before the team's move to new quarters. It was also an emotional night for Steinbrenner, who had recently celebrated his seventy-eighth birthday. This was his last public appearance at the stadium to which he had brought ten pennants and six world championships. The Boss had made fewer and fewer appearances in recent years amid reports of declining health. He had already turned over most responsibility for running the team to his sons, Hank and Hal.

October 1, 2006 After sixteen seasons playing only for the Yankees and quietly but steadily advancing to join the team's career leaders in games played, hits, doubles, home runs, and RBIs, center fielder and fan favorite Bernie Williams pinch-hits a ninth-inning double in his last appearance in a game at Yankee Stadium. He goes 0 for 3 as the designated hitter in Game 3 in Detroit, before the Yankees are eliminated in the fourth game of the AL Division Series; then his career fades away, as the front office of the only team he is willing to play for is no longer interested in him.

December

16

ROOM WITH A VIEW, BUT NOT FOR LONG

Tanisha Cheatam, left, and her friend Asia Saxon watch a Yankees game from Cheatam's living room window in the Bronx, a block away from Yankee Stadium, June 17, 2008. With the Yankees moving to a new facility across the street in 2009, those fans whose homes had even a partial view of the old park may find themselves watching on television. High ticket prices at the new facility effectively block many people in the lower-income Bronx neighborhood from attending games at the new stadium. Others have complained that the community has not benefited enough from the project, and that the neighborhood had lost valuable parkland.

October 11, 2006 Pitcher Cory Lidle dies when the small plane he is copiloting veers away from the East River and strikes an apartment building in Manhattan; he is the second Yankee to die in the crash of a private plane.

December

17

MR. MADONNA

Boston spectators hold up photos of Madonna as the Yankees' Alex Rodriguez waits in the on-deck circle during the eighth inning of a game against the Red Sox at Fenway Park, July 25, 2008. Rumors of a relationship between A-Rod and Madonna swirled shortly after Rodriguez's wife, Cynthia, gave birth to their second daughter. The couple divorced in September 2008. Rodriguez, though often cited as the best player in baseball, is also derisively known as "Mr. April" for his seeming lack of production in the postseason. Following the 2008 season, Rodriguez had still not played in a World Series game.

April 29, 2007 The sizzling Alex Rodriguez starts off his third MVP season—his second as a Yankee—by setting an AL record for the most home runs hit in the month of April, with fourteen (along with a .355 batting average and thirty-four RBIs). He will finish the season with fifty-four, leading the league.

Ninety
Nine
NEW YORK

December

18

SOMEWHERE, THE IRON HORSE WAS SMILING

Shortstop Derek Jeter acknowledges the crowd after his first-inning single in a game against the Chicago White Sox at Yankee Stadium, September 16, 2008. With just a handful of games left at the soon-to-be-shuttered stadium, this was Jeter's 1,270th hit in the Bronx, moving him ahead of Yankees legend Lou Gehrig for the most career hits at the stadium. With the Bombers effectively out of the playoff hunt, Jeter's chase of history became one of the last big milestones at the venerable park. And while records are made to be broken, Jeter's final hit total at the old Yankee Stadium—1,274—is a mark that will never fall.

May 29, 2007 After fifty games, the Yankees are eight below the .500 mark, with a 21–29 record. Then they start turning things around, going an unsurpassed 73–39 for the rest of the season and, as the AL Wild Card, moving into the postseason for the thirteenth consecutive year.

Armitron
2

December

19

THE TRADITIONAL TOUCH

Yankees third baseman Alex Rodriguez taps the sign hanging over the tunnel to the field at Yankee Stadium as he prepares to play the Chicago White Sox in one of the last baseball games ever played there, September 17, 2008. The Yankees won this game 5–1 to start a seven-game winning streak, but it wasn't enough. With the Yankees' playoff hopes virtually extinguished, the realization that the venerable stadium would soon close its doors for the last time had begun to sink in, for players and fans alike. As for the famous sign quoting Joe DiMaggio? It disappeared shortly after the stadium's last home game. No one seemed to mind when the captain, Derek Jeter, admitted it had gone home with him.

June 18, 2007 The Yankees become the first team to sign professional baseball players from the People's Republic of China: Left-handed pitcher Kai Liu and catcher Zhenwang Zhang receive minor league contracts.

"I want to thank the
Good Lord for making
me a Yankee"
— Joe DiMaggio
OCTOBER 1949

December

KEEPING IT IN THE FAMILY

Babe Ruth's adopted daughter, Julia Ruth Stevens, throws out the ceremonial first pitch in the final game ever played at Yankee Stadium, September 21, 2008. The ninety-two-year-old said she was sorry to see the close of the stadium that will always be known as the House That Ruth Built. "I'm very, very sad to think that the Yankee Stadium is not going to be in existence any longer," she said, and others echoed those sentiments during an emotional ceremony. "I feel like I'm losing an old friend," Yankees great Reggie Jackson told the crowd. Late that night, long after Mariano Rivera had thrown the final pitch, a picture of Babe Ruth, winking, beamed from the stadium's big screen. "See You Across the Street!" it read.

July 2, 2007 Roger Clemens wins his 350th game, pitching eight innings of two-hit ball in the Yankees' 5–1 win over the Minnesota Twins at Yankee Stadium. He is the first to reach that plateau since Warren Spahn in 1963.

Yankees

December

21

EVEN YOGI SAYS IT'S OVER

A bevy of Yankees greats toed the dirt one last time before the final game ever played at the grand old stadium. Here, catcher Jorge Posada, left, walks off the field with former catcher Yogi Berra after ceremonies leading up to the September 21, 2008, game. Berra, a beloved figure in baseball and the man who coined the phrase "It ain't over till it's over," acknowledged that the great stadium's time had passed. "I'm sorry to see it over, I'll tell you that," said the eighty-three-year-old Berra, decked out in a vintage uniform similar to the one he wore during his playing days. Berra earned a laugh from the crowd, saying he couldn't recall ever wearing it. But he had no shortage of memories from the stadium where he played, coached, and managed during his Hall of Fame career.

July 31, 2007 The Yankees romp over the Chicago White Sox 16–3; their eight home runs (two by Hideki Matsui) tie a club record set in 1939.

20
8

December

22

THANKS FOR THE MEMORIES

Fans watch from the upper deck as past Yankees heroes are introduced during a ceremony before the last game ever played at Yankee Stadium, September 21, 2008. A magical night at the House That Ruth Built evoked tradition, loyalty, and nostalgia—not just for the ballplayers who performed between the lines, but also for the generations of fans who took memories of the team's exploits home with them. There were tears amid the cheers, and a pyrotechnic burst of camera flashes at nearly every turn. After the game, fans stayed around for the better part of an hour, not wanting to walk through the exits for the last time. One fan held up a makeshift sign that read, "we're not leaving," and the organist played "Goodnight, Sweetheart, Goodnight," as the emotional stragglers finally filed out into the New York night.

August 4, 2007 Alex Rodriguez becomes the youngest player in history to reach 500 career home runs, with a three-run first-inning blast off the Kansas City Royals' Kyle Davies, and the only player to hit his 500th homer at Yankee Stadium since Mickey Mantle.

HESS
BUD LIGHT
Bank of America
SONY
W.B. MASON

December

23

LIKE THERE'S NO TOMORROW

Yankees players, including Bobby Abreu, center, celebrate after beating the Baltimore Orioles 7–3 in the final baseball game at Yankee Stadium, September 21, 2008. The Yankees had hoped to close the stadium with their twenty-seventh world championship, but injuries and off years by key players took their toll, as the team missed the playoffs for the first time in fourteen years. Still, the victory over the O's was a proper sendoff for the stadium, one of the planet's great venues. Since that Yankees win against the Boston Red Sox on April 18, 1923, the building had seen twenty-six World Series victories and countless other historic moments. Nelson Mandela told a packed stadium, "I am a Yankee." Muhammad Ali fought here, and Pele scored improbable goals here. Pink Floyd and U2 rocked the House That Ruth Built. The Philadelphia Eagles' Chuck Bednarik leveled the Giants' Frank Gifford on the same field where three popes celebrated Mass. Legends named Ruth, Gehrig, DiMaggio, and Mantle suited up here. And in the end, the stadium itself became as much a part of Yankees lore as the men who played within its walls.

August 13, 2007 Former Yankees shortstop and then longtime broadcaster Phil Rizzuto dies at age eighty-nine.

December

24

SACRED GROUND

Shortly after throwing the last pitch of the game, Yankees closer Mariano Rivera collects a container full of dirt from the pitcher's mound following the final baseball game at Yankee Stadium, a 7–3 win over the Baltimore Orioles on September 21, 2008. The final out came at 11:41 P.M., the end of an eighty-five-year run for one of the most famous arenas in the world. Afterward, multimillionaire players on both teams knelt to scoop dirt from the mound and home plate area. Rivera took his family out to show them Monument Park, the shrine to Yankeeness being relocated to the new park across the street. Fans lingered long after the game, not wanting the memories to stop, and in the predawn hours, Yankees staffers still romped around the bases of the now-empty stadium.

September 5, 2007 A-Rod, playing on an ankle slightly injured the previous night, hits two home runs in the same inning, the seventh, against the Seattle Mariners—the first Yankee to do so since Cliff Johnson thirty years earlier.

42

December

SEE YOU ACROSS THE STREET

Yankees captain Derek Jeter waves to fans after the Yankees beat the Baltimore Orioles 7–3 in the last game played at Yankee Stadium, Sunday, September 21, 2008. Immediately after the game, Jeter and his teammates gathered on the mound as Jeter addressed the crowd:

"For all of us up here, it's a huge honor to put this uniform on every day and come out here and play. And every member of this organization, past and present, has been calling this place home for eighty-five years. There's a lot of tradition, a lot of history, and a lot of memories. . . . It's pride, it's tradition, and most of all, we have the greatest fans in the world. And we're relying on you to take the memories from this stadium, add them to the new memories that come at the new Yankee Stadium, and continue to pass them on from generation to generation. . . ."

Jeter appeared sincerely moved, and the crowd knew this was a special moment. Then the captain led his team on a lap around the field, acknowledging the cheers of fans, few of whom were ready to leave.

September 30, 2007 The Yankees set an AL record by making more than 500 pitching changes during the season.

December

CASH TALKS

Yankees general manager Brian Cashman steps out for a private phone conversation at Major League Baseball's GM meetings in Dana Point, California, November 4, 2008. Coming off a disappointing season, Cashman and the Yankees plunged into the free agent market with determination—and deep pockets. The Yankees scooped up frontline starting pitchers CC Sabathia and A. J. Burnett, then swooped in to grab first baseman Mark Teixeira, for a combined $423.5 million (in multiyear contracts)—the biggest spending spree in baseball history. The moves sparked the usual criticism that the Yankees were trying to buy a world championship, but the team was making no apologies. With some big contracts falling off their books, the payroll for 2009 (about $201.5 million as of Opening Day), was actually about $7.5 million less than the previous year—a bargain.

October 18, 2007 Ten days after the Yankees' third straight elimination in the AL Division Series, in four games, Joe Torre rejects what he considers an insulting contract offer and resigns as manager, ending an era in New York after twelve seasons. He is succeeded by former Yankees catcher Joe Girardi. Another era is coming to an end as well: after nearly thirty-five years, active control of the Yankees passes from George Steinbrenner, seventy-seven and in declining health, to his sons, Hal and Hank, assisted by Randy Levine and Brian Cashman.

December

27

THE EARTH MOVED

Bronx high school students carry away buckets full of dirt from the original Yankee Stadium during a ceremony, November 8, 2008. On a hushed, rain-soaked field, accompanied by a few former Yankees stars, workers also removed home plate and the pitching rubber. Then the group walked across the street to the Yankees' glittering new park, to mix the old dirt with the fresh soil. One student, fifteen-year-old Gabriel Nieves, described it as a once-in-a-lifetime experience. "It's something you remember forever," he said. Another, seventeen-year-old Omar Liriano, stood proudly on the subway with his shovel and bucket following the ceremony. Inside the bucket was a small mound of Yankee Stadium dirt, which Liriano said he would save forever. "I'm like, wow," he said with a grin. "I'll keep it at home in a jar."

July 12, 2008 Former Yankees slugger and then broadcaster Bobby Murcer dies at age sixty-two of complications related to brain cancer.

NY
NY
NY
TM

December

RITES OF SPRING

Yankees players—from left, Mariano Rivera, Andy Pettitte, Derek Jeter, and Jorge Posada—listen during a news conference by teammate Alex Rodriguez at George M. Steinbrenner Field in Tampa, Florida, February 17, 2009. The presence of the veteran players was seen as a show of support as Rodriguez faced journalists for the first time since admitting steroid use while playing with the Texas Rangers from 2001 to 2003. The three-time American League MVP called using the banned drug a "stupid mistake" that he made when he was young. At one dramatic point during the news conference as he tried to acknowledge his teammates' support, A-Rod paused for about half a minute, blinked several times, took a sip of water, then turned to them and simply said, "Thank you." Pettitte had made a drug-related admission during 2008 spring training, and Jason Giambi made an ambiguous apology on the eve of spring training in 2005.

July 27, 2008 Yankees reliever Rich "Goose" Gossage (1978–83 and 1989) is inducted into the Hall of Fame. He will be joined in 2009 by Rickey Henderson (a Yankee from 1985–89), elected to the Hall of Fame on January 12. Henderson, the major league leader in steals with 1,406 and runs scored with 2,295, is arguably the best leadoff hitter in baseball history.

LACOSTE

December

IF YOU'VE GOT IT, SPEND IT

First baseman Mark Teixeira poses for a photographer on Yankees photo day before a spring training workout in Tampa, Florida, February 19, 2009. Teixeira was one of the three gems the Yankees plucked from the free agent market after failing to make the post-season in 2008. With the economy in a tailspin and most teams looking to trim overhead, the Yankees went shopping, spending $423.5 million to put the slugging first baseman in pinstripes, along with pitchers CC Sabathia and A.J. Burnett. Teixeira wore the number 23 with the Texas Rangers, a number he has favored since he grew up idolizing Don Mattingly. Because the Yankees have retired Mattingly's number, Tex now wears the number 25, previously owned by Jason Giambi.

September 21, 2008 Climaxing an emotional ceremonial farewell to the House That Ruth Built, Derek Jeter addresses the fans and leads his teammates in a last walk around the field after the Yankees play their final regular season game at Yankee Stadium (beating the Baltimore Orioles 7–3). Later, Monument Park, home plate, and other pieces of the stadium are moved to the new home of the Yankees, under construction next door.

December

NUMBERS DON'T LIE?

Yankees third baseman Alex Rodriguez signs autographs during a spring training baseball workout in Tampa, Florida, February 19, 2009, two days after addressing his use of steroids as a Texas Ranger. Rodriguez denies taking any banned substance as a Yankee. But for many fans, his admission of prior use has tainted his remarkable statistics, especially his chase of the all-time home run title now held by Barry Bonds (also questionably, because of steroid accusations). A-Rod—the youngest player to reach 500 home runs—told reporters at his news conference that it's not for him to decide how his numbers should be judged. But many fans felt cheated by the player they had believed was surely "clean." Before spring training was out, A-Rod had surgery for a hip injury, and he missed the beginning of the 2009 season.

September 28, 2008 At Fenway Park, the supposedly over-the-hill Mike Mussina—the unexpected ace of the Yankees' injury-plagued starting rotation—pitches six innings of shutout ball to finish up with a 20–9 record, his first twenty-win season. After 270 wins in eighteen years, eight with the Yankees, Moose decides to retire on a high note.

December

31

FIELD OF DREAMS

A monument to Yankees history and tradition, the new Yankee Stadium hosts its first regular season game, between the Yankees and the Cleveland Indians, April 16, 2009. The Yankees had won two exhibition games at the stadium against the Chicago Cubs earlier in the month, but this home opener didn't follow suit. Despite a pre-game procession of Yankees greats and a ceremonial first pitch by Yogi Berra, the Indians embarrassed the Yankees 10-2 before an announced crowd of 48,271. The new Yankees ace, CC Sabathia, gave up only one run in five and two-thirds innings, but the bullpen had a nine-run meltdown in the seventh, capped by Grady Sizemore's grand slam.

Of course, dreams of summer games—and Fall Classics—wait to be played out here. And the Yankees have a way of making dreams come true.

April 16, 2009 The bat used by Babe Ruth to hit a home run in the first game at the original Yankee Stadium is ceremonially laid across home plate before the first regular season game in the new stadium. Among the few bright spots of the Yankees' 10-2 Opening Day loss to Cleveland: the stadium's first regular season hit (Johnny Damon's first-inning single) and home run (Jorge Posada in the fifth). The Yankees' first win at home, 6–5 against the Indians, will come the next day, with Derek Jeter's tie-breaking solo home run.

Armitron
pepsi
pepsi
pepsi
Ford
at&t
DELTA
KELLY SHOPPACH
CASIO
metlife.com
HESS
Budweiser
TOYOTA
ZALES
Canon
SONY

AFTERWORD

Baseball and The Associated Press grew up together.

The first recorded baseball game was played in Hoboken, New Jersey, in 1846, the same year that AP was founded by five New York newspapers to pool resources for coverage of the Mexican-American War.

The first professional baseball league was established in 1871, and from then through 2008, there would be 387,708 games involving 17,090 players. No news organization covered as many of them as AP, which began carrying stories on every game as early as 1884, and box scores in 1890.

Baseball was hardly the great American pastime in those days, and AP's emphasis on the sport wasn't popular with everyone.

The Washington Post reported on July 16, 1884, that AP carried 15,000 words of baseball news in a single day and quoted a Western newspaper editor as asking indignantly, "For whose benefit is such a colossal piece of nonsense perpetrated?"

The *Post* noted that every team in the country played two games that day, "and it is not unreasonable to suppose that in every reading community there were newspaper patrons anxiously looking for the results of some of the games played."

"Of course," the *Post* added, "no one paper was obliged to print all of the fifteen thousand words, but papers that desire to please their patrons do not make the mistake of supposing that nobody cares for baseball news."

Indeed, interest in baseball exploded after the turn of the century.

On January 9, 1903, Frank Farrell and Bill Devery purchased the defunct Baltimore franchise of the American League for $18,000 and moved the team to Manhattan. The franchise eventually became the New York Yankees, who went on to be the winningest team in the history of professional sports, one that defined dynasties over several decades.

The Associated Press was there to chronicle it all, from the Babe to the Boss.

April 18, 1923: Yankee Stadium, the House That Ruth Built, opened in the Bronx before about 74,200 screaming fans, and Babe Ruth inaugurated it with a clinching home run in a 4–1 victory over the Boston Red Sox, then as now the Yankees' biggest rivals.

It was, AP wrote, "the one touch needed to complete the most picturesque drama in baseball annals. . . . A super world's series atmosphere pervaded in the formal dedication of the huge home of the Yankees. The record crowd, which jammed every nook and corner of the huge triple-decked grandstand and packed all but a few corners of the bleacher sections, far exceeded expectations. Every seat in the mammoth structure could have been filled, but thousands chose to stand in the aisles rather than perch in the few vacant areas of the bleachers."

May 2, 1939: The Yankees beat the Detroit Tigers 22–2 as Lou Gehrig, beginning to lose his battle with ALS, saw his record for consecutive games end after 2,130 games over fourteen years.

"It must have been a cruelly hard decision for the old 'Iron Horse' to make," AP wrote, "when he told Manager Joe McCarthy he was ready to call it a career after 2,130 consecutive games. There was another wrench for both of them yesterday when McCarthy wrote 'Dahlgren, 1B' on a slip of paper and pinned it to the dugout."

July 4, 1939: Lou Gehrig Appreciation Day, as recounted by AP:
"The husky figure climbed slowly up the old wooden stairs back of the Yankees' dugout, shoulders bent, right leg limping and throat torn by sobs. This was Lou Gehrig leaving the most dramatic moment of his life. . . .

"Several times his voice broke and a sob escaped as he announced, 'Today I consider myself the luckiest man on the face of the earth. . . .

"'Just look,' he went on. 'Wouldn't you consider it a privilege to associate yourself with such fine looking men as are standing on this ball field?' . . .

"Then he stumbled, his eyes blinded by tears, back into the clubhouse."

Love 'em or hate 'em, the Yankees are part of Americana.

The Simon and Garfunkel song "Mrs. Robinson" asks, "Where have you gone, Joe DiMaggio?"

The Pride of the Yankees was a hit movie in 1942, starring Gary Cooper as Gehrig.

The Bronx Is Burning was an ESPN miniseries about the 1977 Yankees.

There was even a Broadway musical, *Damn Yankees*, in 1955.

This book is AP's photographic contribution to that cultural phenomenon: 365 pictures, one for each day of the year, of the heroes and the highlights they produced.

Tom Curley

Tom Curley
President
The Associated Press

INDEX

PHOTO CREDITS

Pages 2, 6, 7: Harris Lewine collection via AP
Page 5: Stew Milne/AP
Pages 9, 11, 13, 15, 17, 19, 21, 23, 25, 27, 31, 33, 37, 41, 43, 45, 47, 51, 55, 59: Library of Congress
Page 29: Courtesy of the Babe Ruth Birthplace and Museum, Baltimore
Pages 35, 39, 57, 63, 65, 75, 85, 205: Courtesy of the National Baseball Hall of Fame Library, Cooperstown, New York
Pages 49, 53, 61, 67, 69, 71, 73, 77, 79, 83, 87, 89, 91, 93, 95, 97, 99, 101, 105, 107, 109, 113, 115, 121, 123, 125, 127, 129, 133, 135, 137, 139, 141, 143, 145, 147, 149, 153, 155, 157, 159, 161, 163, 165, 167, 173, 175, 179, 181, 185, 189, 191, 209, 211, 223, 227, 233, 235, 237, 241, 243, 251, 255, 259, 261, 263, 267, 271, 273, 275, 289, 297, 301, 303, 305, 307, 309, 313, 315, 317, 321, 323, 325, 327, 331, 333, 337, 343, 345, 349, 351, 353, 355, 359, 361, 363, 375, 377, 379, 381, 385, 391, 405, 413, 415, 425, 427, 429, 431, 433, 435, 437, 439, 453, 455, 465, 467, 477, 495: AP Photos
Pages 103, 111, 225: Anthony Camerano/AP
Pages 117, 131, 169, 171, 177, 187: Tom Sande/AP
Page 119: Joe Caneva/AP
Page 151: Murray Becker/AP
Pages 183, 199: Abe Fox/AP
Page 193: Edward S. Kitch/AP
Pages 195, 207, 265, 283, 311: John Lindsay/AP
Page 197: Gil Friedberg/AP
Pages 201, 247: Preston Stroup/AP
Pages 203, 219, 295, 329, 347, 383, 393, 397: John Rooney/AP
Pages 213, 215, 245, 249, 269, 279, 291, 319, 335, 339, 371, 387, 389, 399, 417, 419, 461, 487: Harry Harris/AP
Pages 221, 373, 395, 407, 447, 527, 539: Marty Lederhandler/AP
Pages 229, 285: Jacob Harris/AP
Pages 231, 277: Ray Howard/AP
Page 239: Tom Fitzsimmons/AP
Pages 253, 341: William P. Straeter/AP
Page 257: William J. Smith/AP
Page 287: Harvey Georges/AP
Page 299: Robert Kradin/AP
Page 357: Ed Widdis/AP
Page 365: Matty Zimmerman/AP
Page 367: Gene Herrick/AP
Page 369: Eddie Adams/AP
Pages 401, 445, 451, 459, 509, 515: Richard Drew/AP
Pages 403, 411, 421, 423, 441, 449, 463, 469, 473, 475, 489, 491, 497, 501, 503, 511, 517, 521: Ray Stubblebine/AP
Pages 409, 505, 553, 557, 579, 581, 589, 593: Ron Frehm/AP
Page 443: Suzanne Vlamis/AP
Page 457: James P. Finley/AP
Page 479: Lennox McLendon/AP
Page 481: Madeline Drexler/AP
Pages 483, 485, 499: G. Paul Burnett/AP
Page 493: Fred Jewell/AP
Page 507: John Swart/AP
Page 513: Peter Southwick/AP
Page 519: Charles Bennett/AP
Pages 523, 529: Susan Ragan/AP
Page 525: Bill Janscha/AP
Page 531: Richard Harbus/AP
Page 533: Lynne Sladky/AP
Page 535: Mike Albans/AP
Pages 537, 569, 583, 707: Bebeto Matthews/AP
Page 541: Doug Pizac/AP
Pages 543, 563: Adam Nadel/AP
Page 545: David Woo/Dallas Morning News, Pool via AP
Pages 547, 559, 561: Lou Requena/AP
Pages 549, 555, 587, 599, 679: Mark Lennihan/AP
Pages 551, 605: Roberto Borea/AP
Pages 565, 597, 615: Mark J. Terrill/AP
Page 567: Pat Sullivan/AP
Page 571: Steve Crandall/Pool via AP
Page 573: Jeff Zelevansky/AP
Pages 575, 595, 625, 637, 657, 675, 697, 701, 711, 713, 717, 721, 725: Kathy Willens/AP
Pages 577, 635, 641, 651, 653, 683: Charles Krupa/AP
Pages 585, 611, 639, 659: Bill Kostroun/AP
Pages 591, 607, 655, 685: Amy Sancetta/AP
Page 601: Eric Risberg/AP
Page 603: Doug Mills/AP
Pages 609, 613: Rusty Kennedy/AP
Page 617: Aaron Harris/Canadian Press via AP
Pages 619, 723: Ed Betz/AP
Pages 621, 663, 665: Gregory Bull/AP
Page 623: Itsuo Inouye/AP
Page 627: Morry Gash/AP
Pages 629, 631: Al Behrman/AP
Pages 633, 647, 649, 681: Winslow Townson/AP
Pages 643, 677: Frank Franklin II/AP
Page 645: Chad Rachman/AP
Pages 661, 671, 687, 695, 699, 705, 719: Julie Jacobson/AP
Page 667: Chris Carlson/AP
Pages 669, 703, 729: Jason DeCrow/AP
Page 673: Matt Slocum/AP
Page 689: Pablo Martinez Monsivais/AP
Page 691: Gene J. Puskar/AP
Page 693: Frances Roberts/AP
Page 709: Elise Amendola/AP
Page 715: Dick Druckman via AP
Page 727: Lenny Ignelzi/AP
Pages 731, 733, 735: Gene J. Puskar/AP
Page 737: Seth Wenig/AP
Photos credited to Associated Press are available from AP Images at www.apimages.com

Editor: Eric Klopfer
Designer: Darilyn Lowe Carnes
Art Director: Michelle Ishay
Production Manager: Alison Gervais

Library of Congress Cataloging-in-Publication Data:

New York Yankees 365 / by the Associated Press.
p. cm.
ISBN 978-0-8109-8261-1 (harry n. abrams, inc.)
1. New York Yankees (Baseball team) I. Associated Press II.
Title: New York Yankees three hundred sixty five.

GV875.N4N485 2009
796.357'64097471--dc22
2009005573

Printed and bound in China
10 9 8 7 6 5 4 3 2 1

Abrams books are available at special discounts when purchased in quantity for premiums and promotions as well as fundraising or educational use. Special editions can also be created to specification. For details, contact specialmarkets@abramsbooks.com or the address below.

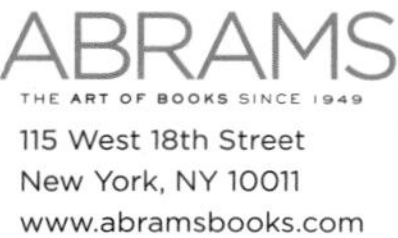

115 West 18th Street
New York, NY 10011
www.abramsbooks.com

ACKNOWLEDGMENTS

Sincere thanks to the following individuals who contributed their valued time and expertise to this project.

At The Associated Press, Chuck Zoeller, creative services director of Corporate Communications, directed every aspect of content creation, from photo selection to caption writing. Other members of the department who participated include Santos Chaparro, Sarah Donna, Ellen Hale, Sam Markham, Amy Silberman, Paula Stone, and Adam Shuck.

Photo research and digital archiving were provided by the staff of AP Images, including manager Erik Klepper, Maggie Bergara, Steve Ciaschi, Wilfred Kolin, Harris Lewine, Althea Morin, Guy Palmiotto, and Sean Thompson.

In addition, AP News staff provided critical assistance. They include Ron Blum, Darrell Christian, Paul Haven, Tom Jory, Peter Morgan, and Terry Taylor. And, of course, current and former AP photographers.

At Abrams, Editor in Chief Eric Himmel initiated and developed this book with Publisher Steve Tager. The book was produced by editor Eric Klopfer, with designer Darilyn Carnes, Andrea Colvin, Alison Gervais, Michael Jacobs, and Richard Slovak.

We also extend deep thanks to: Don Mattingly, Ray Schulte, Niket Chitre and Aparna Naik of Adnet Infosystems, John Horne of the National Baseball Hall of Fame and Museum Library, Cooperstown, New York, and Shawn Herne of the Babe Ruth Birthplace and Museum, Baltimore, Maryland.

Merry Christmas, Judy!
Love, Evie and John

Adult-Gerontology Practice Guidelines

Jill C. Cash, MSN, APN, FNP-BC, is a family nurse practitioner who currently practices at Southern Illinois Rheumatology. Jill has been practicing as a family nurse practitioner for over 18 years. She is a clinical preceptor for nurse practitioner students for various nurse practitioner clinical programs. Her previous experience includes high-risk obstetrics as a clinical nurse specialist in Maternal-Fetal Medicine at Vanderbilt University Medical Center in the Department of Obstetrics-Gynecology. She received her Family Nurse Practitioner Certification from the National Certification Corporation and has a special interest in women's health and rheumatology. Ms. Cash is a member of the Illinois Society for Advanced Practice Nurses, the Association of Rheumatology Health Professionals, the Board of Directors for the Marion Memorial Health Foundation, and Sigma Theta Tau International Honor Society of Nursing. She currently sits on the board of Hospice of Southern Illinois, the board of the American Cancer Society, and the board of Women for Health and Wellness. She has authored several chapters in textbooks and is the coeditor of *Family Practice Guidelines, First, Second,* and *Third Editions*.

Cheryl A. Glass, MSN, WHNP, RN-BC, is a women's health nurse practitioner who currently practices as a clinical research specialist for KEPRO in TennCare's Medical Solutions Unit in Nashville, Tennessee. She is also adjunct faculty at Vanderbilt University School of Nursing. Ms. Glass has been a clinical trainer and trainer manager for Healthways, in Nashville, Tennessee. Her previous nurse practitioner practice was as clinical research coordinator on pharmaceutical clinical trials at Nashville Clinical Research. She also worked in a collaborative clinical obstetrics practice with the director and assistant directors of Maternal–Fetal Medicine at Vanderbilt University Medical Center, Department of Obstetrics-Gynecology. The National Certification Corporation certifies Ms. Glass as a women's health care nurse practitioner. She is a member of the American Association of Nurse Practitioners (AANP) and the National Association of Nurse Practitioners in Women's Health. She is the author of several book chapters and is coeditor of *Family Practice Guidelines, First, Second,* and *Third Editions*. She has published five refereed journal articles. In 1999, Ms. Glass was named Nurse of the Year by the Tennessee chapter of the Association of Women's Health, Obstetric and Neonatal Nurses.

Adult-Gerontology Practice Guidelines

Jill C. Cash, MSN, APN, FNP-BC
Cheryl A. Glass, MSN, WHNP, RN-BC
Editors

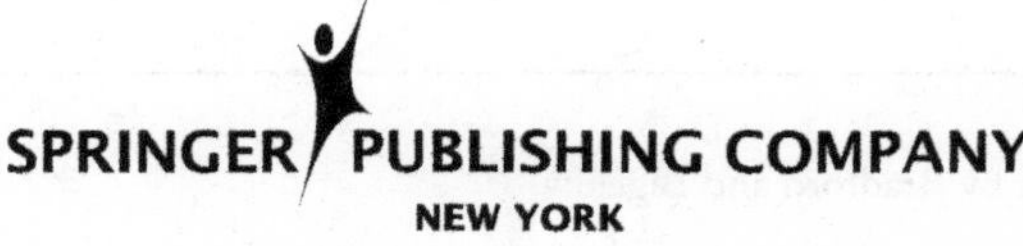

Springer Publishing Company, LLC
11 West 42nd Street
New York, NY 10036
www.springerpub.com

Acquisitions Editor: Margaret Zuccarini
Composition: diacriTech

ISBN: 978-0-8261-2762-4
e-book ISBN: 978-0-8261-2763-1
Patient Teaching Guides ISBN: 978-0-8261-3069-3

Patient Teaching Guides are available from www.springerpub.com/cash-glass-adult-gero

18/ 5 4 3 2

The editors and the publisher of this Work have made every effort to use sources believed to be reliable to provide information that is accurate and compatible with the standards generally accepted at the time of publication. Because medical science is continually advancing, our knowledge base continues to expand. Therefore, as new information becomes available, changes in procedures and drug use and dosages become necessary. We recommend that the reader always consult current research, specific institutional policies, and current drug references before performing any clinical procedure or administering any drug. The author and publisher shall not be liable for any special, consequential, or exemplary damages resulting, in whole or in part, from the readers' use of, or reliance on, the information contained in this book. The publisher has no responsibility for the persistence or accuracy of URLs for external or third-party Internet websites referred to in this publication and does not guarantee that any content on such websites is, or will remain, accurate or appropriate.

Library of Congress Cataloging-in-Publication Data

Adult-gerontology practice guidelines / Jill C. Cash, MSN, APN, FNP-BC Cheryl A. Glass, MSN, WHNP, RN-BC, editors.
pages cm
Includes bibliographical references and index.
ISBN 978-0-8261-2762-4
1. Geriatric nursing. 2. Older people—Medical care. I. Cash, Jill C., editor. II. Glass, Cheryl A. (Cheryl Anne)
RC954.A318 2015
618.97'0231—dc23

2015006471

Printed in the United States of America by Bradford and Bigelow

To my children, Kaitlin and Carsen,
You make me proud! I love you.
—Jill

To my husband, Rob,
Thank you for your patience! I love you.
—Jill

"Always go with your passions. Never ask yourself if [they're] realistic or not."
—Deepak Chopra

This is dedicated to all of the extraordinary women in my life.
—Cheryl

To Ed,
My lifelong partner, I love you.
—Cheryl

"If you have knowledge, let others light their candles in it."
—Margaret Fuller

Contents

APPENDICES

Contributors

Julie Adkins, DNP, APN, FNP-BC
SIMCA Certified Family Nurse Practitioner
West Frankfort, Illinois

Rhonda Arthur, DNP, CNM, WHNP-BC, FNP-BC
Certified Nurse Midwife/Nurse Practitioner
Program Director Family Nursing
Frontier Nursing University
Hyden, Kentucky

Amy C. Bruggmann, MS, APRN-BC, CWS
Director of Clinical Operations
Specialized Wound Management
Chesterfield, Missouri

Beverly R. Byram, MSN, FNP
Clinical Instructor
Vanderbilt University School of Nursing
Director, Ryan White Part D
Comprehensive Care Center
Nashville, Tennessee

Jill C. Cash, MSN, APN, FNP-BC
Family Nurse Practitioner
Southern Illinois Rheumatology
Herrin, Illinois

Moya Cook, MSN, APN, FNP-BC
Certified Family Nurse Practitioner
SIMCA Family Practice
Marion, Illinois

Debbie Croley, MSN, ARNP-C
Certified Geriatric Nurse Practitioner
Clinical Review Coordinator
KEPRO, Tennessee
TennCare Medical Solutions Unit
Nashville, Tennessee

Susan Drummond, RN, MSN, C-EFM
Associate in Obstetrics
Department of Obstetrics and Gynecology
Vanderbilt University Medical Center
Nashville, Tennessee

Brooke Faught, MSN, WHNP-BC-IF
Nurse Practitioner/Clinical Director
Women's Institute for Sexual Health
A Division of Urology Associates
Nashville, Tennessee

Cheryl A. Glass, MSN, WHNP, RN-BC
Clinical Research Specialist
KEPRO, Tennessee
TennCare Medical Solutions Unit
Nashville, Tennessee
Adjunct Faculty
Vanderbilt University School of Nursing
Nashville, Tennessee

Debbie A. Gunter, APRN, FNP-BC, ACHPN
Nurse Practitioner
Emory University
Atlanta, Georgia

Mellisa Hall, DNP, APN-BC, FNP-BC, GNP-BC
Certified Nurse Practitioner
University of Southern Indiana
Evansville, Indiana

Amy Hull, MSN, WHNP-BC
Certified Women's Health Nurse Practitioner
Center for Pelvic Health
Instructor
Vanderbilt University School of Nursing
Nashville, Tennessee

Karen M. Kress, MSN, GNP/ANP
Nurse Practitioner
Emory Geriatrics at St. Joseph's and Domiciliary Care Program
Atlanta, Georgia

Audra C. Malone, DNP, FNP-BC
Assistant Professor
Frontier Nursing University
Hyden, Kentucky

Anne Moore, DNP, APN, FAANP
Nurse Practitioner/Women's Health Clinical Trainer
State of Tennessee. Department of Health
Division of Family Health and Wellness
Nashville, Tennessee

Carol Palmer, PhD, APRN, FNP
Assistant Professor
Frontier Nursing University
Hyden, Kentucky

Laura A. Petty, MSN, GNP-BC
Certified Geriatric Nurse Practitioner
Lebanon, Tennessee

Karla Schroeder, MSN, RN, MHA, ANP-BC, NE-BC
Certified Nurse Practitioner
Palliative Care/Inpatient Medicine Manager
Vanderbilt University Medical Center
Nashville, Tennessee

Angelito Tacderas, MSN, APN, NP-C
Family Nurse Practitioner
Advanced Kidney Institute
Marion, Illinois
By Dezign Healthcare Resources
Carterville, Illinois

Deanna L. Tacderas, MSN, APN, NP-C
Family Nurse Practitioner
River to River Heart Group
Marion, Illinois

Kimberly D. Waltrip, APRN-BC
Certified Nurse Practitioner
PhD Student
University of Missouri
St. Louis, Missouri

Reviewers

Julie Adkins, DNP, APN, FNP-BC
SIMCA Certified Family Nurse Practitioner
West Frankfort, Illinois

Rhonda Arthur, DNP, CNM, WHNP-BC, FNP-BC
Certified Nurse Midwife/Nurse Practitioner
Program Director Family Nursing
Frontier Nursing University
Hyden, Kentucky

Debbie Croley, MSN, ARNP-C
Certified Geriatric Nurse Practitioner
Clinical Review Coordinator
KEPRO, Tennessee
TennCare Medical Solutions Unit
Nashville, Tennessee

Mellisa Hall, DNP, APN-BC, FNP-BC, GNP-BC
Certified Nurse Practitioner
University of Southern Indiana
Evansville, Indiana

Fred Pfalzgraf, MD
Southern Illinois Rheumatology
Herrin, Illinois

Preface

Soon after publishing *Family Practice Guidelines, Third Edition*, a 2014 AJN Book of the Year award recipient, Springer Publishing Company identified the need for a resource suitable for advanced practice students, as well as novice and experienced health care providers, in the adult-gerontology practice setting. *Adult-Gerontology Practice Guidelines* is designed as a complement to *Family Practice Guidelines*.

We again asked our experienced nurse practitioner colleagues for assistance in writing this important resource. *Adult-Gerontology Practice Guidelines* is designed as a practice as well as a reference resource to prepare for certification examinations.

Information is presented in a user-friendly format that is easily accessed using either the table of contents or the book's index. Within the guidelines, emphasis is placed on history taking, on the physical examination, and on key elements of the aging population. Useful website links have been incorporated. Patient Teaching Guides are available, including medication safety and fall prevention. These are presented in perforated tear-out format, making removal from the book easy. **These guides, found in Section III of the book, are also available in PDF format at www.springerpub.com/cash-glass-adult-gero.**

The book is organized into chapters using a body-systems format. The disorders included within each chapter are organized in alphabetical sequence for easy access. Disorders that are more commonly seen in the primary care setting are included.

Bold text or italic text highlights "alerts" for practitioners and educational "clinical pearls."

Organization

The book is organized into three major sections:

- Section I: "Guidelines" presents the 24 chapters containing the individual disorder guidelines.
- Section II: "Procedures" presents 19 procedures that commonly are conducted within the office or clinic setting.
- Section III: "Patient Teaching Guides" presents over 140 Patient Teaching Guides that are perforated for easy distribution to patients as a take-home teaching guide. For ease of reference, the teaching guides are organized by chapter content and can easily be associated with the disorder chapter by matching the teaching guide chapter number and title.

Highlights of *Adult-Gerontology Practice Guidelines*

- Chapter 1, "Normal Physiological Changes in the Aging Adult"
- Chapter 2, "Healthy Living for the Adult-Geriatric Patient"
- Chapter 3, "Adult-Geriatric Assessments"
- Chapter 4, "Caregiver and End-of-Life Issues"
- Chapter 5, "Pain Management Guidelines": Pain Assessment and Management in the Aging Population
- Chapter 6, "Dermatology Guidelines": Bullous Pemphigoid, Cellulitis and Abscess, and Precancerous and Cancerous Skin Lesions
- Chapter 7, "Eye Guidelines": Macular Degeneration, Refractive Disorders, and Retinopathy
- Chapter 8, "Ear Guidelines": Hearing Loss and Presbycusis
- Chapter 10, "Throat and Mouth Guidelines": Dysphagia
- Chapter 12, "Cardiovascular Guidelines": Carotid Artery Stenosis
- Chapter 13, "Gastrointestinal Guidelines": Fecal Incontinence and Hiatal Hernia
- Chapter 14, "Genitourinary Guidelines": Nocturia and Urinary Retention
- Chapter 16, "Gynecologic Guidelines": Pelvic Organ Prolapse and Sexual Health Issues in the Aging Population
- Chapter 19, "Systemic Disorders Guidelines": Cancer Management

- Chapter 20, "Musculoskeletal Guidelines": New Skeletal Disorders
- Chapter 21, "Rheumatology Guidelines": Polymyalgia Rheumatica and Temporal Arteritis/Giant Cell Arteritis
- Chapter 22, "Neurologic Guidelines": Stroke

Procedures

Procedures commonly used in the geriatric population, including the Clock-Draw Test and pessary insertion and management, are present.

We believe you will find that *Adult-Gerontology Practice Guidelines* provides the quick-access reference that you have been searching for to use in your practice setting. You will no longer have to spend valuable office time searching for the information needed to provide quality patient care. It's included here, at your fingertips!

Jill C. Cash
Cheryl A. Glass

Acknowledgments

It has again been a pleasure to work with the editorial staff and team at Springer Publishing Company.

To Margaret Zuccarini, Publisher for Nursing: We are so grateful to work with you again. Your talent, expertise, and continued encouragement and support have been invaluable throughout our journey. We greatly appreciate your suggestions, advice, and patience through it all.

To Jacob Seifert, Assistant Editor at Springer Publishing Company: We appreciate all of your assistance, keeping us organized, and finalizing the manuscript.

To Lindsay Claire, Managing Editor at Springer Publishing Company: Your expertise in editing was greatly appreciated.

To Nandha and Sudheer at diacriTech: It has been a pleasure to work with you again during the production edits.

Jill and Cheryl

SECTION I

Guidelines

- Normal Physiological Changes in the Aging Adult *Jill C. Cash*
- Healthy Living for the Adult-Geriatric Patient *Cheryl A. Glass and Jill C. Cash*
- Adult-Geriatric Assessments *Cheryl A. Glass and Angelito Tacderas*
- Caregiver and End-of-Life Issues *Audra C. Malone and Karla Schroeder*
- Pain Management Guidelines *Moya Cook and Jill C. Cash*
- Dermatology Guidelines *Jill C. Cash, Amy C. Bruggmann, and Cheryl A. Glass*
- Eye Guidelines *Jill C. Cash and Mellisa Hall*
- Ear Guidelines *Jill C. Cash and Carol Palmer*
- Nasal Guidelines *Jill C. Cash*
- Throat and Mouth Guidelines *Jill C. Cash*
- Respiratory Guidelines *Mellisa Hall and Cheryl A. Glass*
- Cardiovascular Guidelines *Debbie A. Gunter, Jill C. Cash, Laura A. Petty, and Cheryl A. Glass*
- Gastrointestinal Guidelines *Cheryl A. Glass*
- Genitourinary Guidelines *Angelito Tacderas, Cheryl A. Glass, and Debbie Croley*
- Obstetrics Guidelines *Jill C. Cash and Susan Drummond*
- Gynecologic Guidelines *Anne Moore, Rhonda Arthur, Amy Hull, Brooke Faught, and Cheryl A. Glass*
- Sexually Transmitted Infections Guidelines *Jill C. Cash and Moya Cook*
- Infectious Disease Guidelines *Cheryl A. Glass and Debbie Croley*
- Systemic Disorders Guidelines *Julie Adkins, Jill C. Cash, Beverly R. Byram, and Cheryl A. Glass*
- Musculoskeletal Guidelines *Julie Adkins and Jill C. Cash*
- Rheumatological Guidelines *Jill C. Cash*
- Neurologic Guidelines *Jill C. Cash, Julie Adkins, Karen M. Kress, Cheryl A. Glass, and Kimberly D. Waltrip*
- Endocrine Guidelines *Julie Adkins, Jill C. Cash, Mellisa Hall, Cheryl A. Glass, and Angelito Tacderas*
- Psychiatric Guidelines *Karen M. Kress, Jill C. Cash, and Cheryl A. Glass*

CHAPTER ONE

Normal Physiological Changes in the Aging Adult

Jill C. Cash

The following is a brief discussion of common changes that occur as one ages.

Brain/Nervous System/Cognition

Beginning in the third decade of life, the brain begins changing (decreasing) in size and function. The blood flow may decrease, and new nerve ending pathways may form to adapt for these changes. The neurons and neurotransmitters decrease in number, and this can cause a loss of muscle mass, as well as muscle tone in the face, neck, and spine. Muscle strength begins to decrease, and impairment in fine motor coordination and agility skills may decrease.

Muscle reflexes may become delayed, such as in the ankle and Achilles reflex, as well as pupillary reflexes. A loss of the degree of reflex activity may lead to slower motor skills reaction time and impairment in balance and coordination, which may then lead to falls and injury. This loss may also contribute to a delay in reaction time to touch and pain, which can also lead to injury.

Muscle tremors in the hands, head, and jaw may also occur due to these neurological changes. These tremors may lead to difficulty with daily activities such as eating, driving, and dressing.

Cognitive processing is expected to slow down with aging; however, the memory should continue to function adequately for the normal life. Expected memory changes may include having a slower memory recall for names and details. Functional status should be monitored closely as one ages, evaluating safety issues and the ability to care for oneself when performing daily tasks.

Acute illness may alter the mental status and can cause confusion and delirium. Assessment for safety should be addressed when illness occurs. Illness causing confusion and delirium may put the patient at risk for injury to himself or herself and/or others.

Breasts

During the postmenopausal years, women will experience breast glandular tissue atrophy due to a decrease in estrogen and progesterone. The breast tissue will become thinner and will be replaced with fibrous connective tissue. Breast size and elasticity decrease, and the breast tissue begins to sag.

In elderly males, there may be a deficiency in testosterone production, which may lead to gynecomastia and excessive fatigue.

Ears/Hearing

After age 55, high-frequency sounds become harder to hear (presbycusis), along with difficulty in hearing the changes in tone and speech. This occurs due to the loss of hair cells and fibrous changes that occur in the cochlea. It becomes more difficult to carry on a conversation in larger, crowded rooms with extraneous noise in the background. Conductive hearing loss occurs from changes in the middle and/or outer ear canal. It is common to see older adults with cerumen accumulation/impaction in the external canal. Otosclerosis occurs from bone remodeling of the middle ear and interferes with sound conduction from the middle ear to the inner ear.

Sensorineural hearing loss occurs from damage to the inner ear, involving the eighth cranial nerve. Conditions that predispose patients to sensorineural hearing loss include hereditary factors, infections, trauma, medications, and chronic medical conditions.

Eyes/Vision

As one ages, the appearance of the eyes may seem sunken due to atrophy of the fatty tissue around the orbit of the eye. The cornea may appear thickened and raised due to fatty deposits on the cornea. Arcus senilis is a common variation in the elderly in which a benign peripheral ring of opacification occurs within the basement membrane. However, this does not interfere with vision.

On physical exam, when examining the eye, the blood vessels may appear pale and narrow. The pupils may become smaller (miosis) during the day time and night time. For example, a 50-year-old patient may have a pupil diameter of 3.5 mm during the day and 5.0 mm at night. Comparatively speaking, the pupil of an 80-year-old patient may only measure 2.3 mm during the day and 2.5 mm at night.

As one ages, common eye changes and complaints include dry eyes and visual changes. Dry eyes may occur due to changes in the lacrimal duct glands, which cause a decrease in tear production and a feeling of burning and dryness of the eyes.

After 40 years of age, it is common to see adults have changes in vision, especially when reading up close, requiring reading glasses. This occurs due to the lens becoming less flexible (presbyopia), causing a decrease in visual sharpness. Other common eye changes that occur with aging include difficulty with depth perception and less precision with color.

Three more complicated conditions commonly seen with aging include cataracts, glaucoma, and macular degeneration. Cataracts develop from having an excessive amount of proteins accumulate in the lens. On exam, cataracts appear as an opacity of the lens and interfere with the presence of the red reflex on exam. Cataracts are commonly removed and implants placed.

Glaucoma occurs when there is an increase in intraocular pressure. The most common form of glaucoma is chronic open-angle glaucoma, which may involve a gradual loss of peripheral vision.

Macular degeneration is a breakdown of the cells in the macula of the retina. This causes a loss of central vision and can lead to blindness. However, peripheral vision is not affected.

Hair

As one ages, two noticeable changes occur to the hair in both women and men. Hair thinning of the scalp, armpits, and pubic area commonly occurs. Fewer functioning melanocytes may cause changes in hair color, such as graying of the hair. In women, facial hair may grow due to a decrease in estrogen and unopposed testosterone levels.

Nail changes may also occur, which includes slow-growing nails, less luster and shine, and the development of longitudinal ridges in the nail beds.

Heart/Blood Circulation

At rest, the cardiac output and heart rate do not change with aging. However, with stress and exercise, a decrease in heart rate is normal. The conduction time of the atrioventricular (AV) node is increased with healthy adults. Therefore, when interpreting an ECG on an adult older than 65 years of age, the P-R interval may range from 210 to 220 milliseconds. However, the QRS interval remains unchanged.

The left ventricular ejection fraction does not decrease with normal aging. However, with exercise, the cardiac output is decreased due to the decrease in maximum heart rate and the inability of the heart to contract (stroke volume) secondary to the beta-adrenergic blockade response that occurs. Older patients may complain of shortness of breath and fatigue, and exhibit a slower recovery time from tachycardia after exercise.

As the heart relaxes and allows for ventricular filling, diastolic function is noted to be prolonged as one ages.

Calcification of the aortic and mitral valves commonly occurs with aging. These are considered normal if the function of the valve is not affected. However, these changes (calcification) may progress and interfere with the normal functioning of the valve; these changes are then considered abnormal.

The arterial and peripheral pulses should remain strong.

The systolic blood pressure may exhibit a gradual rise as one ages. The diastolic blood pressure will remain the same; this leads to a widening pulse pressure with aging. Baroreceptors (which stabilize blood pressure with activity) are less sensitive as one ages, which can lead to orthostatic hypotension. Systolic murmurs are commonly heard in elderly patients.

Immune System

With aging, the immune system becomes less efficient in fighting off disease because the body has less ability to make antibodies against disease. The thymus gland, which produces hormones that activate the T-cells, begins to atrophy and weaken. The peripheral T-cells also decrease in number. These factors increase the risk of developing infections; thus, these infections become more severe and much harder to fight off in the elderly.

Older patients have a much slower recovery time after illness, and the immune system becomes weakened. With a weakened immune system, it is highly recommended that adults receive immunizations that are recommended by the Centers for Disease Control (CDC), such as pneumococcal, influenza, zoster, tetanus, and hepatitis vaccines.

Adults are also much more likely to develop autoimmune disorders with aging.

Kidneys

Renal blood flow decreases as one ages due to the normal age-related changes of the blood vessels and renal system. The renal vessels may get smaller and thicken, which will cause a decrease in renal blood flow. This decrease in blood flow will affect the glomerular filtration rate (GFR) (approximately 10% decrease in function/decade of life after the age of 30 years). A decrease in GFR affects the body's ability to clear waste and medications from the blood.

The kidneys also begin to shrink in size; approximately 20% to 30% of size is lost by the age of 90 years. The bladder, ureters, and urethra all decrease in tone and elasticity as one ages. The bladder capacity shrinks from approximately 500 to 250 mL. This decrease in volume contributes to more frequent urination, as well as less time between urge to urinate and urination; urinary incontinence may then become a problem. However, urinary incontinence does not have to be a normal change with aging. Medication and treatments are available for this condition.

The changes that occur in the kidney put the older patient at risk for renal complications much more quickly than the younger adult. With a reduction in renal blood flow and GFR, the kidneys have to work much harder to maintain electrolyte balance, such as potassium, sodium, calcium, and chloride levels. The levels help the body to maintain stable blood pressure and nerve impulses throughout the body. Therefore, when the kidney function is altered, it puts the patient at greater risk for confusion and blood pressure instability.

Creatinine is a molecule that is created by the skeletal muscles. The kidneys excrete creatinine at the same rate it is produced. By 80 years of age, the kidney's ability to clear creatinine is reduced by 30%. However, as one ages, the body also has a reduction in the amount of skeletal muscle mass. Therefore, the serum creatinine levels should remain stable in the older client since there is less creatinine produced by the skeletal muscle in proportion to less creatinine being cleared by the kidneys.

The kidneys become less efficient in concentrating urine and require more fluids to excrete toxic waste products as one ages. This is why it is common for older patients to have nocturia after drinking beverages that were ingested earlier in the evening. This inefficiency of the kidney may also contribute to a build-up of toxic substances, such as antibiotics, amphetamines, digitalis, and other medications. Medication dosages must be considered when prescribing medications to older patients to avoid toxic accumulation of the medication in the body.

Control of the urinary sphincter weakens with age, which can lead to incontinence and loss of control over voiding. Women may have physical changes (shrinking) of the urethra, which increases the risk of urinary infections. Men may have voiding difficulties secondary to the enlargement of the prostate, compressing the urethra/bladder, which may lead to more frequent and difficult urination.

Lungs

After 50 years of age, the respiratory muscles begin to decline. There is less elasticity of the lung tissue, and it may become more difficult to inflate the lungs in later years. This may cause a decrease in vital capacity (the amount of air exhaled after inhaling at a maximum rate) and an increase in residual volume (the amount of air staying in the lungs after expiration). There may be decreased elasticity that may contribute to enlargement of the pulmonary artery, which will increase the resistance to the blood flow of the lungs, leading to an increase in pulmonary pressure.

The number of functioning alveoli in the respiratory system may also decrease. This may cause thickened capillaries in the lungs and can lead to a decrease in surface area for the oxygen/carbon dioxide exchange; this will lead to a decrease in oxygenation to the vital organs.

There is also a decreased number of cilia and macrophage activity in the nose, mouth, and respiratory system, which can cause a dry mouth and nose. The cough reflex is also diminished, which makes the cough less effective in clearing the respiratory tract from mucus and debris. This can increase the risk of respiratory infections and may lead to bronchospasms with airway obstruction.

The chest anterior/posterior diameter increases as one ages, giving the appearance of round, barrel chest–shaped thorax. The cartilage tissue of the chest may become calcified, which may result in a less mobile thorax.

Metabolism

As one ages, metabolism slows down. The body requires less energy. The hormone changes that occur cause the body to store more body fat and less muscle mass. When muscle mass is reduced, metabolism slows down.

Musculoskeletal

Height

Loss of height is common with aging. Due to poor posture and compression of the joints and spine, by the time one reaches 80 years of age there may be as much as 2 inches of height lost.

Bones

Bone density declines as one ages. Many factors contribute to loss of bone density and strength of the bone. The bones lose calcium and minerals, which cause thinning and weakness of the bone. This increases the risk of bone fracture. Other secondary causes may also contribute to bone density loss, which include certain medication use (steroids, seizure medications, etc.), inadequate intake of calcium and vitamin D, excessive alcohol and tobacco use, as well as decreased weight-bearing exercise/activity.

The joints may also undergo physical changes that may include joint structure change, inflammation, and narrowing of the joint spaces. These changes may cause joint stiffness and pain. This stiffness and pain may contribute to a decrease in mobility and activity, along with slower joint movement and a slower reaction time to changes in position. Decreased physical activity will then lead to weakness.

Oropharyngeal and Gastrointestinal

Throughout the life span, adults are encouraged to maintain a healthy weight by exercising on most days of the week and monitoring their daily dietary intake. The body mass index (BMI) is interpreted by a healthy weight ranging from 18.5 to 24.9 kg/m^2; being overweight from 25 to 29.9 kg/m^2; and obesity as 30 kg/m^2 or greater.

Changes that occur to the oropharyngeal and gastrointestinal system include a decrease in strength of the muscles used for chewing. Salivation is decreased, which causes a dry mouth and a decrease in taste sensation, and thirst perception is diminished. Gastric motility decreases along with a delayed emptying time. The esophageal emptying time is also delayed, along with gastric acid secretion decreasing with age.

Liver size is noted to decrease in size by 25% between 20 and 70 years of age. Liver function tests remain normal. However, by 65 years of age, the liver may not work efficiently when metabolizing drugs. It is common to see a decrease in blood flow throughout the liver by approximately 33% in some older adults.

Constipation is a common problem seen in the older adult. However, constipation is not a normal finding. Common causes of constipation include decrease in activity, a low-fiber diet, and not getting enough fluid intake. Constipation is also a very common side effect from medications, especially from pain medications. Some chronic conditions, such as hypothyroidism, a common disorder seen in older and elderly adults, may contribute to constipation. Other reasons that adults develop constipation may be attributed to inadequate toilet facilities and refraining from use of the facility when the urge to defecate occurs. This practice can be detrimental to the patient and create the potential for complications such as stool impaction. Some patients may also develop an impairment to the sensation to defecate, which also leads to constipation and possibly impaction of stool.

Sexual Function

As adults age, hormone levels begin to decrease. By 50 years of age, lower levels of hormones are produced in men and women. Men produce less sperm and sexual responses are delayed. Penile erections may be delayed along with infrequent orgasm and decrease in sperm count. Impotence in males is not a normal part of aging. However, many medications can contribute to this problem. The male sex drive does not decrease.

Women reach menopause, the cessation of menses, at approximately 35 to 51 years of age. Approximately 1 to 2 years prior to menopause, the ovaries begin declining in function and irregular menses occur, causing menses to become farther apart and lighter in flow. The ovaries will stop producing progesterone and estrogen. When ovulation ceases, reproduction no longer occurrs. These hormonal changes, along with a decrease in blood supply to the vagina, contribute to a decrease in vaginal secretion and lubrication during intercourse and a shorter duration of orgasm. However, sexual pleasure and function do not change in women.

Other changes that can be expected during menopause include diminished size of the uterus and ovaries. The sacral ligaments and pelvic muscles may weaken, causing the uterus to drop down into the vagina. The vagina also shortens and becomes less elastic. The vaginal epithelium may begin to atrophy and become thin, dry, and fragile. Due to the thinning and dryness, intercourse may become painful, as well as having bleeding with sexual activity due to the atrophy of the vaginal epithelium. In addition, the vagina's pH levels become more alkaline during menopause and increase the risk of frequent vaginal infection.

Skin

The skin is the body's protective barrier. As one grows older, the epidermis layer becomes thin, flattens out, and loses elasticity, which leads to the development of fine lines and wrinkles. The sweat, oil, and sebaceous glands become less active, and the skin becomes dry. With less activity of the sweat glands, hydration is difficult to assess by skin alone in the elderly patient. The skin also becomes more fragile. The body's elastin, collagen, and subcutaneous fat tissue diminish and the skin becomes thinner, which increases the risk for shearing and skin tear injuries. When skin breakdown occurs, repair of these cells takes much longer and wound healing is delayed.

Sleep

As one ages, the circadian rhythm changes. The amount of time in rapid eye movement (REM) sleep declines. There is more frequent waking, along with waking earlier in the morning. The time it takes to fall asleep increases and there is increased time spent in lighter stages of sleep than in deep sleep. Sleep fragmentation (waking up during the night) occurs. Research indicates that this change in sleep pattern is related to chronic conditions and medications taken to treat particular conditions.

Snoring is one condition that interferes with sleep. Snoring is linked to obesity and sleep apnea. Studies show that sleep apnea that is not treated increases the risk for cardiovascular disease and other health problems.

Smell

As one ages, the number of olfactory nerve fibers steadily declines, causing a decrease in the sensation of smell. This decline interferes with the ability to smell foods and determine which are healthy or spoiled, as well as distinguish household odors and body odor. The loss of smell becomes a safety issue around the decreased ability to smell smoke.

Taste

After one's fifth decade, taste begins to decline. It is estimated that approximately 50% of the normal taste buds disappear by the age of 80 years. With these changes, one begins to lose an interest in food, which in turn leads to weight loss and malnutrition.

The soft tissue in the oral cavity begins to become atrophic, and the epithelium lining of the cheeks and tongue begins to thin, which is responsible for a loss of taste buds. The atrophic changes also increase the risk of oral ulcers and oral infections.

Along with thinning of the epithelium lining, dental changes also occur. Gums begin to recede, which may lead to hypersensitivity of the teeth and the gums, causing pain with eating and temperature change. Tooth erosion and loss (bone resorption) decreases the tooth structure and support. Missing teeth may interfere with eating.

There also may be a decrease in saliva production, which diminishes the mouth's ability to clean itself. This can also be caused by certain anticholinergic medications, causing a decrease in saliva production.

Bibliography

National Sleep Foundation. Aging and sleep. Retrieved from http://www.sleepfoundation.org/article/sleep-topics/aging-and-sleep

CHAPTER TWO

Healthy Living for the Adult-Geriatric Patient

Cheryl A. Glass and Jill C. Cash

Health Maintenance During the Life Span

Health maintenance involves identifying individuals at risk for health problems and encouraging behaviors that reduce these risks. An important aspect of health maintenance is patient education, including teaching individuals about their risk factors for disease and ways to modify their behaviors to reduce their risks of comorbidities. This book contains Patient Teaching Guides that the practitioner may use for patient education; these forms are found in Section III, Patient Teaching Guides. These are presented in a perforated, tear-out format, making removal from the book easy. They may be photocopied by the practitioner, filled in according to the patient's evaluation and needs, and given to the patient.

Adult Risk-Assessment Form

The Adult Risk-Assessment Form (Exhibit 2.1) should be used for all adult patients to evaluate a patient's risk for particular diseases. The practitioner should interview the patient, assessing for the risk factors listed on the Risk Assessment Form. The family history of first-degree relatives (parents, siblings, and children) should also be discussed, because many diseases are related to genetic factors. Keep a copy of the Risk Assessment Form in the front of the patient's chart, and update yearly or as needed. When complete, this tool can guide the practitioner in determining the assessment needs of each patient. If using electronic medical records, a special section should be identified for risk assessment.

Adult Preventive Health Care

Exhibits 2.2 and 2.3 help the practitioner identify changes in the adult patient's risk factor status, make recommendations for health maintenance (e.g., immunizations, laboratory work, physical exams), and educate patients in prevention. Screening guidelines for each of these can be found in the associated chapters in this book, according to the national association recommendations (i.e., screening recommendations for mammograms were obtained from the American Cancer Society [ACS]). The guide can be used as a quick reference for the practitioner to evaluate the patient's adherence to preventive measures. Keep a copy of this flow sheet and guide in the front of the patient's chart where they can be reviewed routinely and updated as necessary. If using electronic medical records, a special section should be identified as routine health maintenance.

Adult/Geriatric Screening Recommendations

Health promotion includes the utilization of preventative screen testing. Multiple guidelines are available for clinicians to utilize for guidance and discussion of the recommendation with patients. Professional societies, U.S. Public Health Services, and other organizations evaluate the strength of evidence and the weight of clinical research, statistical analysis, and the risk and benefits of testing to make recommendations for screening. Most of the recommendations for this section are from the U.S. Preventive Services Task Force (USPSTF) guidelines.

Eligibility and Medicare coverage for screening are summarized in Table 2.1.

EXHIBIT 2.1 **Adult Risk-Assessment Form**

Name ____________ DOB ____________ Chart # ____________

Allergies ______________________________

Occupation ______________________________

Family History First-degree relatives with remarkable diseases (e.g., hypertension, DM, coronary artery disease [CAD], cancer, and thyroid)	
1.	6.
2.	7.
3.	8.
4.	9.
5.	10.

Assess the Patient for the Following Risk Factors:

A. Coronary Heart Disease
1. High-fat/high-cholesterol diet
2. Obesity
3. Elevated cholesterol level
4. Stroke
5. Hypertension
6. Tobacco use

B. Lung cancer
1. High-fat/high-cholesterol diet
2. Tobacco use

C. Cervical cancer
1. Early age of first intercourse
2. Multiple sexual partners

D. Breast cancer
1. Nulliparous
2. Primigravida after age 35
3. High-fat diet

E. Colon cancer
1. History of polyps
2. High-fat diet

F. Osteoporosis
1. Less than 1 g of calcium per day
2. History of tobacco or alcohol use
3. Sedentary lifestyle
4. Thin, Caucasian
5. Female gender

G. Glaucoma/visual impairment
1. Family history of glaucoma
2. Diabetes mellitus

H. STIs/HIV
1. Alcohol and drug use or abuse
2. Multiple sexual partners
3. Homosexual or bisexual partner
4. History of intravenous drug use
5. History of blood transfusion
6. Exposed to or past history of STI

I. Substance abuse
1. Alcohol or drug use history
2. Family history of substance abuse
3. Stress or poor coping mechanisms
4. Administer the **CAGE** Assessment:
   Have you ever tried to **C**ut down on your alcohol/drug use?
   Do you get **A**nnoyed if someone mentions your use is a problem?
   Do you ever feel **G**uilty about your use?
   Do you ever have an "**E**ye-opener" first thing in the morning after you've been drinking or using the night before?

J. Accidents and suicide
1. Family history of suicide
2. Alcohol or tobacco use
3. History of depression
4. High-stress or "hot-reactor" personality
5. Male gender
6. Alcohol use
7. Previous suicide attempt
8. Poor coping mechanisms or stress

K. Safety
1. Does not use seat belt or car seat
2. Drinks and drives
3. Drives over the speed limit
4. Does not wear safety helmet if driving motorcycle
5. Inadequate number of smoke detectors or none in the home

EXHIBIT 2.2 **Adult Preventive Health Care Flow Sheet**

Immunization Schedule				
Immunization	**Date**	**Date**	**Date**	**Date**
Tetanus/diphtheria				
Measles, mumps, rubella (MMR)				
Tuberculosis (TB) (yearly)				
Hepatitis B (HepB)				
Influenza (yearly)				
Pneumococcal				
Other				
Other				

(*continued*)

EXHIBIT 2.2 Adult Preventive Health Care Flow Sheet (*continued*)

Assess patients for the following behaviors:

Risk Assessment				
Exam	**Date**	**Date**	**Date**	**Date**
Tobacco, amount				
Alcohol, amount				
Substance use				
Domestic violence				

Patients should be educated about any behavior modifications that can reduce their risk factors for health problems. The practitioner should note the date as well as the type of counseling given to a patient.

Patient Education				
Behavior Modification	**Date**	**Date**	**Date**	**Date**
Diet/exercise				
Tobacco/alcohol				
Injury prevention				
Skin protection				
Hormone replacement therapy				
Sexual practices				
Occupational hazards				
Self-exam: breast/testicular				

EXHIBIT 2.3 Adult Health Maintenance Guide

Name ______________________ DOB __________ Chart# ______________

Allergies ______________________ Occupation ______________

The following tests should be performed according to the individual patient's risk factors as part of preventive health care. The practitioner should fill in the date and result of each test and highlight any remarkable results.

Test	Date	Result	Date	Result	Date	Result	Date	Result
Height								
Weight								
BMI								
B/P								
Skin exam								
Oral cavity exam								
EKG								
Thyroid-stimulating hormone (TSH)								
Lipid profile								
Urinalysis								
Rectal exam								
Hemoccult								
Colonoscopy								
PSA								
Testicular exam								
Pelvic exam/Pap smear								
Breast exam								
Mammogram								
Sexually transmitted disease (STD)/HIV								
Additionally, the practitioner should ensure that the patient receives other health care as needed. Assess patient's adherence to other preventive health care exams:								
Dental exam								
Vision/glaucoma exam								

TABLE 2.1 Medicare Coverage and Eligibility for Screening—Current as of 2015

Test/Screen	Medicare Coverage Eligibility
Preventive visit	"Welcome to Medicare" preventive visit is available for Medicare coverage within the first 12 months of obtaining Medicare Part B. • Measurement of height, weight, and blood pressure • Calculation of BMI • Simple vision test • Review of potential risk for depression and level of safety • Offer to talk about creating advance directives • Written plan on which screening, shots, and other preventive services needed.
Yearly "Wellness" visits	Annual "Wellness" visits for Medicare patients with Part B for longer than 12 months (11 full months must have passed since the last visit). The "Wellness" visits are used to develop or update a personalized prevention plan to prevent disease and disability based on current health and risk factors. • Complete a Health Risk Assessment (HRA) • Review medical and family history • Develop or update the list of current providers and prescriptions • Measure height, weight, blood pressure, and other routine measurements • Evaluate cognitive impairment • Personalize health advice • List risk factors and treatment options • Develop screening schedule for appropriate preventive services.
AAA screening	One-time AAA ultrasound if meets eligibility requirements. A referral is required. • Family history of AAA • Male age 65–75 years and have smoked at least 100 cigarettes/lifetime
Bone mass measurement	Covered screen • Once every 24 months • Covered more often if medically necessary who meet the following criteria – Women who are determined to be estrogen deficient based on medical history and other findings – X-rays showing possible osteoporosis, osteopenia, or vertebral fractures – Person taking prednisone or steroid-type drugs or is planning to begin this treatment – Person who has been diagnosed with primary hyperparathyroidism – Person being monitored to evaluate the osteoporosis drug therapy is effective
Cardiovascular disease (behavioral therapy)	One visit per year in primary care physician (PCP) office or primary care clinic • Check blood pressure • Discuss aspirin use (if appropriate) • Discuss dietary information
Cardiovascular disease screening	Every 5 years screening blood tests • Cholesterol • Lipids • Triglycerides
Colorectal screening	Fecal Occult Blood Test (FOBT) • Coverage once every 12 months for ages 50 years or older Multi-target stool DNA test (such as Cologuard™) • Covered once every 3 years if **all conditions** are met – 50–85 years of age – No signs or symptoms of colorectal disease – At average risk for developing colorectal cancer Flexible sigmoidoscopy • Once every 48 months for most people 50 years or older • If not high risk, is covered 120 months after a previous screening colonoscopy Colonoscopy • Once every 24 months if at high risk for colorectal cancer • If not high risk, is covered once every 120 months, or 48 months after a previous flexible sigmoidoscopy Barium enema • When utilized instead of a flexible sigmoidoscopy or colonoscopy – Coverage every 48 months – Coverage every 24 months if older than 50 years old and are at high risk for colorectal cancer
Dental	Medicare does not cover routine dental care or dental procedures such as cleanings, fillings, tooth extractions, dentures, dental plates, or other dental devices
Depression screening	Medicare covers one depression screening per year. The screening must be done in a primary care setting that can provide follow-up treatment and/or referrals

(continued)

TABLE 2.1 Medicare Coverage and Eligibility for Screening—Current as of 2015 (*continued*)

Test/Screen	Medicare Coverage Eligibility
Diabetes	Medicare covers screening to test for diabetes • Based on the screening test, may be eligible for two diabetes screening each year • Covered if any of the following risk factors – Hypertension – History of abnormal cholesterol and triglycerides – Obesity – History of high glucose • Covers these tests if two or more of these apply – Age 65 or older – Overweight – Family history of diabetes (parents, brothers, sisters) – History of gestational diabetes or the delivery of a baby weighing more than 9 pounds
HIV screening	Voluntary HIV screenings, one test once every 12 months • Covered for people at high risk • Anyone who asks for HIV screening Pregnancy HIV screening • Covered for up to three times during pregnancy – Interval testing during pregnancy is not defined by CMS
Immunizations	Flu shot • Normally covers one flu shot per flu season given in the fall or winter Hepatitis B • People at high or medium risk for HepB – Some risk factors noted as increased risk defined by Medicare include hemophilia, end-stage renal disease (ESRD), diabetes, conditions that lower resistance to infection Pneumococcal shot • Once in lifetime
Mammography	Screening mammogram once every 12 months (11 full months must have passed since the last screening) or a diagnostic mammogram when medically necessary • Women with Medicare, 40 years of age or older are covered • Women with Medicare, 35–39 years of age, can get one baseline mammogram
Pap smear/pelvic examination	A clinical breast examination (CBE) is covered as part of the examination with the Pap test and pelvic examination • Once every 24 months for all women • Once every 12 months for women at high risk for cervical or vaginal cancer • Childbearing age and have had an abnormal Pap test in the last 36 months
Prostate cancer screening	All men older than 50 (beginning the day after their 50th birthday) Digital rectal examination • Once every 12 months PSA test • Once every 12 months
STIs screening and counseling	Screening for chlamydia, gonorrhea, syphilis, and/or HepB • Once every 12 months • At certain times during pregnancy HIV screens • Once every 12 months • Up to three times during a pregnancy Medicare also covers up to two individual 20- to 30-minute, face-to-face, high-intensity behavioral counseling sessions each year for sexually active adults at increased risk for STIs.
Vision	Medicare does not cover routine eye examinations for eyeglasses or contact lenses Age-related macular degeneration (AMD) testing is covered Vision screen for glaucoma • Glaucoma test every 12 months for people at high risk for glaucoma – Diabetes – Family history of glaucoma – African Americans and those 50 years or older – Hispanic Americans and those 65 years or older Vision screen for retinopathy • Yearly exam for diabetic retinopathy • People on Medicare who have diabetes

Consult the Medicare website for full coverage information: www.medicare.gov/coverage/preventive-and-screening-services.htm.

Abdominal Aortic Aneurysm

The Centers for Disease Control and Prevention (CDC) notes abdominal aortic aneurysms (AAAs) were the primary cause of death for greater than 10,000 persons in 2009. An AAA is often asymptomatic; however, the symptoms may include throbbing or deep pain in the back or side and/or pain in the buttocks, groin, legs, or syncope.

There are several types of aneurysm: Thoracic aneurysm, abdominal aneurysm, peripheral aneurysm, and those that occur in the brain may cause a stroke. An AAA is an enlarged ballooning area that is more than 50% of the normal diameter of the aorta. In 2014, the USPSTF prereleased its draft update of its 2005 guidelines for AAA. The 2014 update to the USPSTF guidelines is based on additional review of evidence-based guidelines recommendations. The current recommendations for AAA include:

A. **Men ages 65 to 75 who have ever smoked (100 cigarettes in a lifetime) should have a one-time AAA screening.**
   1. Older males who have smoked are at the highest risk of developing an AAA.
   2. Screening for men older than 75 years of age is not recommended. Due to the increase in comorbidities in this population, the benefits of screening and the need for subsequent surgery decrease the likelihood of the benefit. This recommendation should be individualized for males older than 75 years who have a reasonable life expectancy.

B. Health care providers can consider offering AAA screening to men ages 65 to 75 who have never smoked.

C. There is not enough evidence for the USPSTF to recommend that women ages 65 to 75 who have ever smoked should be screened for AAA.

D. **The USPSTF recommends that women who have never smoked should not undergo AAA screening.** This population rarely has an AAA.

E. **The ultrasound is the recommended modality for screening.**

F. Follow-up and surgical treatment depend on the size of the aneurysm. There are currently no recommendation standards for interval surveillance.
   1. Small size is considered 3.0 to 3.9 cm wide.
   2. An intermediate-sized AAA is considered 4.0 to 5.4 cm.
      a. Periodic surveillance has a comparable mortality benefit to routine elective surgery.
      b. **Refer to a vascular specialist if the aortic diameter is greater than 4.5 cm.**
   3. A large AAA is considered 5.5 cm or greater.
      a. Surgery is generally recommended if the AAA is considered large, defined as 5.5 cm, or if the AAA is growing quickly.

G. There are two types of surgical repair.
   1. The open surgical repair is the only proven intervention that has decreased AAA mortality. The open surgical repair of a large AAA has a mortality rate of 4% to 5% and with nearly one third having pulmonary and cardiac complications.
   2. The endovascular aneurysm repair (EVAR) is the surgical-procedure alternative to the open repair. A late conversion to an open repair may be required. The long-term effects of the EVAR devices have not been reported.

Bone Mass Density Measurement for Osteoporosis

The need for screening of bone mass measurement for the presence of osteoporosis becomes apparent because the USPSTF's statistics noted that by 2012 over 12 million Americans older than the age of 50 years are expected to have osteoporosis. Elderly patients have increased susceptibility to fractures due to other medical problems, side effects of medications, and the elderly's tendency to fall. Fractures may cause chronic pain and disability and affect the functional ability and quality of life: mortality and morbidity are highest with a hip fracture.

The fracture risk assessment tool (FRAX) calculates absolute fracture risk or estimates the chance of breaking a bone within the next 10 years. The FRAX score is used to drive decisions for testing and prescribing osteoporosis medications.

The Foundation for Osteoporosis Research and Education (FORE) FRAX score 10-Year Fracture Risk Calculator (FORE FRC) is available at www.riskcalculator.fore.org/default.aspx. The American College of Rheumatology website for FRAX is located at www.rheumatology.org/Practice/Clinical/Clinicianresearchers/Outcomes_Instrumentation/Fracture_Risk_Assessment_Tool_(FRAX).

Screening through the identification of risk factors does not diagnose osteoporosis but identifies people who require further evaluation.

Bone mass measurement screening is done through several tests:

A. A standard x-ray is inadequate for screening for osteoporosis.

B. **The gold standard test for the measurement of bone density is the use of the central dual-energy x-ray absorptiometry (DXA) of the hip and lumbar spine.**
   1. The central DXA of the radius bone and peripheral bone density of the heel or another bone may be required for the morbidly obese patient.

C. The quantitative ultrasonography (QUS) of the calcaneus is also utilized for measurement.
   1. The measurement cutoffs of the QUS and the DXA are not interchangeable.
D. The peripheral quantitative CT (pQCT) is also used for screening, but the cost makes this test for screening prohibitive.

The recommendations for who to screen and screening intervals of 1 to 2 years vary by different organizations, including the National Osteoporosis Foundation, the World Health Organization, and the American College of Obstetricians and Gynecologists. The USPSTF recommends screening for osteoporosis by gender and age:

A. Women
   1. Aged 65 years or older.
   2. The USPSTF does not define the upper age limit for screening in women because the risk of fractures increases in age.
   3. Younger women whose fracture risk is equal to or greater than that of a 65-year-old White woman who has no additional risk factors.
   4. Due to the limits of the precision of testing, a minimum of 2 years may be needed to reliably measure a change in bone mass density (BMD).
B. Men
   1. Routine screening is currently a widespread practice.
   2. Current evidence is insufficient to assess the benefits versus harms of screening for osteoporosis in men. The USPSTF found inadequate evidence that drug therapies reduce the risk of fracture in men who have no previous osteoporotic fracture.

The National Osteoporosis Foundation recommends bone density testing for all men aged 70 years or older and for men aged 50 to 69 years based on their risk-factor profile.

Cardiovascular Disease and Cardiac Screening

The USPSTF has multiple screening and prevention recommendations for cardiac and cardiovascular disease (CVD).

A. Screening Recommendations:
   1. Screen for high blood pressure in adults age 18 years and older.
   2. Screen for lipid disorders by gender and age (see Table 2.2).
   3. Screen for coronary heart disease (CHD) with electrocardiography (ECG):
      a. USPSTF recommends against screening with resting or exercise ECG for the prediction of CHD events in asymptomatic adults at low risk for CHD events.
      b. Currently insufficient evidence to assess the balance of benefits and harms of screening with resting or exercise ECG for the prediction of CHD events in asymptomatic adults at intermediate or high risk for CHD events.
   4. The current evidence is insufficient to assess the balance of benefits and harms of screening for peripheral artery disease and CVD risk assessment with the ankle-brachial index (ABI) in adults.
   5. USPSTF recommends against screening for asymptomatic carotid artery stenosis in the general adult population.
   6. The evidence is insufficient to assess the balance of benefits and harms of using the nontraditional

TABLE 2.2 USPSTF Recommendations for Screening Lipid Disorders in Adults

Females/Age Group	Males/Age Group	Recommendation/Risk
Ages 20 years and older		No recommendation for or against routine screening for lipid disorders if NOT at an increased risk for CHD
Ages 20–45 years		Screen if at increased risk for CHD
Ages 45 years and older		Strong recommendation to screen for lipid disorder if at increased risk for CHD
	Ages 20–35 years	No recommendation for or against routine screening for lipid disorders if NOT at an increased risk for CHD
	Ages 20–35 years	Screen if at increased risk for CHD
	Ages 35 and older	Strong recommendation to screen for lipid disorder if at increased risk for CHD

The USPSTF recommends intensive behavioral dietary counseling for adults with hyperlipidemia and other known risk factors for cardiovascular and diet-related chronic disease. Intensive counseling can be delivered by primary care clinicians or by referral to other specialists, such as nutritionists or dietitians.

risk factors to screen asymptomatic men and women with no history of CHD to prevent CHD events. The nontraditional risk factors included in this recommendation include:

a. High-sensitivity C-reactive protein (hs-CRP)
b. ABI
c. Leukocyte count
d. Fasting blood glucose level
e. Periodontal disease
f. Carotid intima media thickness (carotid IMT)
g. Coronary artery calcification (CAC) score on electron-beam CT (EBCT)
h. Homocysteine level
i. Lipoprotein(a) level

B. Prevention recommendations:

1. Recommendations for the use of aspirin for the prevention of CVD differ by gender and age (see Table 2.3).

Colorectal Screening

See Table 2.4 for the USPSTF recommendations for the screening of colorectal cancer by age ranges.

Dental Care

Research has linked infections from untreated oral care from cavities and gum disease to preterm birth, heart disease, diabetes, and respiratory diseases. Primary care providers are on the front line for performing oral examinations. Alcohol, smoking cigarettes, using pipes, and smokeless tobacco have been identified as among the major causes of poor oral health and the increase in risk of oral cancer.

Medicare does not cover routine dental care or dental procedures such as cleanings, fillings, tooth extractions, dentures, or other dental devices. Medicaid coverage for dental care varies by state. The Affordable Care Act (ACA) expansion of medical insurance coverage for dental services was required for children. It is expected that there will be some expansion of limited dental services for adults through the state Medicaid programs and the health insurance exchanges.

Primary care providers should provide education on good oral hygiene, including brushing, flossing, seeing a dentist at least yearly, and eating a healthy diet. The USPSTF has, however, found inadequate evidence that oral screening examinations accurately detect oral cancer or that treatment of screen-detected oral cancer improves morbidity or mortality.

Many dental schools provide care at reduced costs based on an individual's income. The U.S. Department of Health and Human Services Health Resources and Services Administration (HRSA) has health centers in both cities and rural areas that provide care based on income. HRSA maintains a website to find the nearest health centers at findahealthcenter.hrsa.gov/Search_HCC.aspx.

Depression Screening

Screening for depression in adults (age 18 years and older) is recommended by the USPSTF when staff-assisted depression care supports are in place to ensure accurate diagnosis, effective treatment, and follow-up. Medicare Part B covers an annual depression screening of up to 15 minutes for Medicare beneficiaries in primary care settings when staff-assisted depression care supports are in place to ensure accurate diagnosis, effective treatment, and follow-up, thereby facilitating and coordinating referrals to mental health treatment. Medicare does not identify a specific depression screening tool.

The February 2013 Institute for Clinical System Improvement (ICSI) Adult Depression in Primary Care Guideline is available at www.icsi.org/_asset/fnhdm3/Depr-Interactive0512b.pdf. This document provides practitioners with current information related

TABLE 2.3 USPSTF Recommendations for Aspirin for the Prevention of Cardiovascular Disease

Females/Age Group	Males/Age Group	Recommendation/Risk
Younger than 55 years of age		Recommends against the use of aspirin for stroke prevention
55–79 years of age		Recommends the use of aspirin when the potential benefit of a reduction in ischemic stroke outweighs the potential harm of an increase in gastrointestinal hemorrhage
	Younger than 45 years of age	Recommends against the use of aspirin for myocardial infarction prevention
	45–79 years of age	Recommends the use of aspirin when the potential benefit of a reduction in myocardial infarction outweighs the potential harm of an increase in gastrointestinal hemorrhage
Age 80 years or older	Age 80 years or older	The current evidence is insufficient to assess the balance of benefits and harms of using aspirin for CVD prevention.

TABLE 2.4 Screening for Colorectal Cancer—USPSTF

Age Ranges	Recommendation
Begin screening at 50–75 years of age	Screening detects early-stage cancer and adenomatous polyps. • Screen for colorectal cancer using: ▪ High-sensitivity FOBT - Annual screening test ▪ Multi-target stool DNA test - Every 3 years for persons at average risk for developing colorectal cancer ▪ Sigmoidoscopy - Screening every 5 years combined with high-sensitivity fecal occult blood every 3 years ▪ Colonoscopy ▪ Screening interval test every 10 years • Screening with any of the three recommended tests reduces colorectal cancer mortality in this age range. ▪ Follow-up of positive screening test results requires a colonoscopy. There is high certainty that the net benefit is substantial for ages 50–75 years.
76–85 years of age	Against routine screening for colorectal cancer in the 76–85-year age range There is moderate certainty that the net benefits of screening are small. For adults who have not previously been screened, decisions about first-time screening in this age group should be made in the context of the individual's health status and competing risks, given that the benefit of screening is not seen in trials until at least 7 years later.
Older than 85 years of age	Against screening for colorectal in the older-than-85-years age range. There is moderate certainty that the benefits of screening do not outweigh the harms.
Any age range	There is insufficient evidence to assess the sensitivity and specificity of fecal DNA testing for screening for colorectal neoplasia. There is insufficient evidence to assess the harms related to extracolonic finding utilizing a CT colonography. The balance of benefits and harms cannot be determined.

USPSTF recommendations apply to adults 50 years of age and older, excluding those with specific inherited syndromes (the Lynch syndrome or familial adenomatous polyposis) and those with inflammatory bowel disease. The recommendations do apply to those with first-degree relatives who have had colorectal adenomas or cancer, although for those with first-degree relatives who developed cancer at a younger age or those with multiple affected first-degree relatives, an earlier start to screening may be reasonable. Data suggest that colorectal cancer has a higher mortality rate in African Americans. The reasons for this differential are not well known, and the recommendations are intended to apply to all ethnic and racial groups.
When the screening test results in the diagnosis of clinically significant colorectal adenomas or cancer, the patient will be followed by a surveillance regimen and recommendations for screening are no longer applicable. The USPSTF did not address evidence for the effectiveness of any particular surveillance regimen after diagnosis and/or removal of adenomatous polyps.
The USPSTF recommends against the routine use of aspirin and nonsteroidal anti-inflammatory drugs (NSAIDs) to prevent colorectal cancer for persons at average risk for colorectal cancer.

to screening for depression, including an algorithm for adult depression in the primary care setting, and to the criteria for major depressive episode from the American Psychiatric Association's *Diagnostic and Statistical Manual of Mental Disorders* (5th ed.; *DSM-5;* American Psychiatric Association, 2013).

There are multiple depression screening tools and instructions for scoring in the ICSI guideline, including the following:

A. Patient Health Questionnaire (PHQ-9)
B. Hamilton Rating Scale for Depression (HAM-D) to be administered by a health care professional
C. Cornell Scale for Depression in Dementia (CSDD)
D. Geriatric Depression Scale (GDS)
E. Edinburgh Postnatal Depression Screening (EPDS)

Diabetes Screening

The incidence of type 2 diabetes mellitus (DM) is one of the major health problems facing the United States today and will continue as the population ages and becomes more obese. The tests to be used for the diagnosis of diabetes are also utilized for screening for DM: the fasting plasma glucose, the 2-hour plasma glucose after a 75 g glucose tolerance test, and the hemoglobin A1C tests (see Chapter 23, "Endocrine Guidelines," "Diabetes Mellitus"). The American Diabetes Association (ADA) screening recommendations are:

A. Patient screening should begin at age 45 years.
B. Screening should begin sooner for the overweight or obese with a body mass index equal to or greater than 25 kg/m^2 and with *one or more* of the following risk factors:
   1. Physical inactivity
   2. First-degree relative with diabetes
   3. High-risk race/ethnicity
   4. Women who delivered a baby weighing more than 9 pounds and who were diagnosed with gestational DM (GDM)
   5. Hypertension (> 140/90 mmHg) or receiving therapy for hypertension
   6. High-density lipoprotein (HDL), 35 mg/dL and/or a triglyceride level (NOT) (> 250 mg/dL)
   7. Polycystic ovarian syndrome (POS)

8. A1C more than 5.7%, impaired glucose tolerance (IGT), or impaired fasting glucose on previous testing
9. Other conditions commonly associated with insulin resistance
10. History of CVD

C. If the test results are normal, the ADA recommends retesting at least at 3-year intervals.
D. Patients diagnosed with pre-diabetes should be tested yearly.
E. Testing should also be repeated in the presence of a change in the patient's risk factors.

Hepatitis C Screening

In 2013, the CDC recommended hepatitis C testing for anyone born during 1945 to 1965. The CDC recommends a one-time testing of "baby boomers." Although it is not completely understood, people born between 1945 and 1965 are five times more likely than other adults to be infected with hepatitis C virus (HCV). The CDC notes that one-time testing of everyone born during this period will prevent more than 120,000 deaths from complications of compensated cirrhosis and hepatocellular cancer secondary to HCV infection. HCV is the leading cause of liver cancer.

A test for HCV antibodies is recommended for routine testing of asymptomatic persons. For those with reactive test results, the anti-HCV test should be followed with an additional, supplemental, or confirmatory test for the presence of the virus (see Chapter 13, "Gastrointestinal Guidelines," "Hepatitis C").

HIV Screening

Recommendations for HIV testing is a covered benefit from the Centers for Medicare and Medicaid Services (CMS) as a voluntary test every 12 months for people at increased risk and anyone asking for HIV testing. CMS also covers testing for HIV in pregnancy up to three times. Testing intervals are not defined by CMS.

In 2013, the USPSTF issued a final recommendation statement on HIV screening: Everyone aged 15 to 65 years should be screened for HIV infection. Teens younger than age 15 and adults older than 65 also should be screened if they are at risk for HIV infection (see Chapter 19, "Systemic Disorders Guidelines," "HIV"). USPSTF also recommends that all pregnant women, including women in labor who do not know their HIV status, be screened for HIV infection.

Immunizations

The CDC recommendations for immunizations are presented in Table 2.5.

Immunizations for travel outside of the United States are recommended based on the patient's health status, vaccine history, as well as the area(s) of travel. The presence of the risk of becoming ill from poor sanitary conditions, food and water sources, and endemic diseases are considered in the CDC's recommendations for travel immunizations. The CDC has an interactive tool for immunization recommendations for travel located at wwwnc.cdc.gov/travel/destinations/list.

Mammography

The 2009 USPSTF recommendation to begin screening for breast cancer with a biennial (every other year) screening mammography before age 50 years was quite controversial. The ACA will utilize the 2002 USPSTF recommendation for breast cancer screening. The 2002 guidelines recommend screening mammography with or without clinical breast examination (CBE) every 1 to 2 years for women age 40 years and older.

Newer recommendations were made in 2011 by the American College of Obstetricians and Gynecologists (ACOG) to continue to recommend annual screening with mammography for women beginning at age 40. A breast MRI is not recommended by ACOG as a screening test for women at average risk of developing breast cancer.

Coverage for mammograms for breast cancer screening is mandated by the ACA, which provides that these be given without a co-pay or deductible in plans that started after August 1, 2012.

Although the ACA will utilize the 2002 mammography screening recommendation coverage guidelines, laws on coverage vary slightly from state to state. Of note, state laws don't affect self-insured (self-funded) health plans.

Many states cover a baseline mammogram for women ages 35 to 39 years. The ACA website provides a table of state-by-state coverage laws at www.cancer.org/cancer/breastcancer/moreinformation/breastcancerearlydetection/breast-cancer-early-detection-paying-for-br-ca-screening.

As part of the ACA, Medicare covers the full cost of a mammogram once every 12 months for all women with Medicare aged 40 years and older.

Pap Smear/Pelvic Examination

Human papillomavirus (HPV) increases the risk for cancer, including cervical, vulvar, vaginal, penile, and anal cancer as well as cancer of the oropharynx. The ACA coverage for HPV testing includes high-risk HPV DNA testing in women with normal cytology results. Screening should begin at 30 years of age and should occur no more frequently than every 3 years. See the U.S. Department of Health and Human Services website, HHS.gov/HealthCare. For further information on

TABLE 2.5 2015 Recommended Immunizations for Adults by Age

Note: These recommendations must be read with the footnotes that follow containing number of doses, intervals between doses, and other important information.

Figure 1. Recommended adult immunization schedule, by vaccine and age group[1]

Vaccine ▾ / Age Group ▸	19–21 years	22–26 years	27–49 years	50–59 years	60–64 years	≥ 65 years
Influenza*,2	1 dose annually					
Tetanus, diphtheria, pertussis (Td/Tdap)*,3	Substitute 1-time dose of Tdap for Td booster; then boost with Td every 10 yrs					
Varicella*,4	2 doses					
Human papillomavirus (HPV) Female*,5	3 doses					
Human papillomavirus (HPV) Male*,5	3 doses					
Zoster6					1 dose	
Measles, mumps, rubella (MMR)*,7	1 or 2 doses					
Pneumococcal 13-valent conjugate (PCV13)*,8	1-time dose					
Pneumococcal polysaccharide (PPSV23)8	1 or 2 doses					1 dose
Meningococcal*,9	1 or more doses					
Hepatitis A*,10	2 doses					
Hepatitis B*,11	3 doses					
Haemophilus influenzae type b (Hib)*,12	1 or 3 doses					

*Covered by the Vaccine Injury Compensation Program

For all persons in this category who meet the age requirements and who lack documentation of vaccination or have no evidence of previous infection; zoster vaccine recommended regardless of prior episode of zoster

Recommended if some other risk factor is present (e.g., on the basis of medical, occupational, lifestyle, or other indication)

No recommendation

Report all clinically significant postvaccination reactions to the Vaccine Adverse Event Reporting System (VAERS). Reporting forms and instructions on filing a VAERS report are available at www.vaers.hhs.gov or by telephone, 800-822-7967.

Information on how to file a Vaccine Injury Compensation Program claim is available at www.hrsa.gov/vaccinecompensation or by telephone, 800-338-2382. To file a claim for vaccine injury, contact the U.S. Court of Federal Claims, 717 Madison Place, N.W., Washington, D.C. 20005; telephone, 202-357-6400.

Additional information about the vaccines in this schedule, extent of available data, and contraindications for vaccination is also available at www.cdc.gov/vaccines or from the CDC-INFO Contact Center at 800-CDC-INFO (800-232-4636) in English and Spanish, 8:00 a.m. - 8:00 p.m. Eastern Time, Monday - Friday, excluding holidays.

Use of trade names and commercial sources is for identification only and does not imply endorsement by the U.S. Department of Health and Human Services.

The recommendations in this schedule were approved by the Centers for Disease Control and Prevention's (CDC) Advisory Committee on Immunization Practices (ACIP), the American Academy of Family Physicians (AAFP), the America College of Physicians (ACP), American College of Obstetricians and Gynecologists (ACOG) and American College of Nurse-Midwives (ACNM).

(continued)

TABLE 2.5 **2015 Recommended Immunizations for Adults by Age (*continued*)**

Figure 2. Vaccines that might be indicated for adults based on medical and other indications[1]

Vaccine ▾ / Indication ▸	Pregnancy	Immuno-compromising conditions (excluding human immunodeficiency virus [HIV])[4,6,7,8,13]	HIV infection CD4* T lymphocyte count[4,6,7,8,13]		Men who have sex with men (MSM)	Kidney failure, end-stage renal disease, receipt of hemodialysis	Heart disease, chronic lung disease, chronic alcoholism	Asplenia (including elective splenec-tomy and persistent complement component deficien-cies)[8,12]	Chronic liver disease	Diabetes	Health care personnel
			< 200 cells/μL	≥ 200 cells/μL							
Influenza*[2]	1 dose IIV annually				1 dose IIV or LAIV annually	1 dose IIV annually					1 dose IIV or LAIV annually
Tetanus, diphtheria, pertussis (Td/Tdap)*[3]	1 dose Tdap each pregnancy	Substitute 1-time dose of Tdap for Td booster; then boost with Td every 10 yrs									
Varicella*[4]	Contraindicated			2 doses							
Human papillomavirus (HPV) Female*[5]		3 doses through age 26 yrs				3 doses through age 26 yrs					
Human papillomavirus (HPV) Male*[5]		3 doses through age 26 yrs				3 doses through age 21 yrs					
Zoster[6]	Contraindicated				1 dose						
Measles, mumps, rubella (MMR)*[7]	Contraindicated			1 or 2 doses							
Pneumococcal 13-valent conjugate (PCV13)*[8]						1 dose					
Pneumococcal polysaccharide (PPSV23)[8]						1 or 2 doses					
Meningococcal*[9]	1 or more doses										
Hepatitis A*[10]	2 doses										
Hepatitis B*[11]	3 doses										
Haemophilus influenzae type b (Hib)*[12]		post-HSCT recipients only	1 or 3 doses								

*Covered by the Vaccine Injury Compensation Program

- [dark shading] **For all persons in this category who meet the age requirements and who lack documentation of vaccination or have no evidence of previous infection; zoster vaccine recommended regardless of prior episode of zoster**
- [light shading] **Recommended if some other risk factor is present (e.g., on the basis of medical, occupational, lifestyle, or other indications)**
- [no shading] **No recommendation**

Notes

These schedules indicate the recommended age groups and medical indications for which administration of currently licensed vaccines is commonly recommended for adults ages 19 years and older, as of February 1, 2015, for all vaccines being recommended on the Adult Immunization Schedule: a vaccine series does not need to be restarted, regardless of the time that has elapsed between doses. Licensed combination vaccines may be used whenever any components of the combination are indicated and when the vaccine's other components are not contraindicated. For detailed recommendations on all vaccines, including those used primarily for travelers or that are issued during the year, consult the manufacturers' package inserts and the complete statements from the Advisory Committee on Immunization Practices (www.cdc.gov/vaccines/hcp/acip-recs/index.html). Use of trade names and commercial sources is for identification only and does not imply endorsement by the U.S. Department of Health and Human Services.

Recommended Immunization Schedule for Adults Aged 19 Years or Older: United States, 2015

1. Additional information

- Additional guidance for the use of the vaccines described in this supplement is available at www.cdc.gov/vaccines/hcp/acip-recs/index.html.
- Information on vaccination recommendations when vaccination status is unknown and other general immunization information can be found in the General Recommendations on Immunization at www.cdc.gov/mmwr/preview/mmwrhtml/rr6002a1.htm.
- Information on travel vaccine requirements and recommendations (e.g., for hepatitis A and B, meningococcal, and other vaccines) is available at wwwnc.cdc.gov/travel/destinations/list.
- Additional information and resources regarding vaccination of pregnant women can be found at www.cdc.gov/vaccines/adults/rec-vac/pregnant.html.

2. Influenza vaccination

- Annual vaccination against influenza is recommended for all persons aged 6 months or older.
- Persons aged 6 months or older, including pregnant women and persons with hives-only allergy to eggs can receive the inactivated influenza vaccine (IIV). An age-appropriate IIV formulation should be used.
- Adults aged 18 years or older can receive the recombinant influenza vaccine (RIV) (FluBlok). RIV does not contain any egg protein and can be given to age-appropriate persons with egg allergy of any severity.
- Healthy, nonpregnant persons aged 2 to 49 years without high-risk medical conditions can receive either intranasally administered live, attenuated influenza vaccine (LAIV) (FluMist) or IIV.
- Health care personnel who care for severely immunocompromised persons who require care in a protected environment should receive IIV or RIV; health care personnel who receive LAIV should avoid providing care for severely immunosuppressed persons for 7 days after vaccination.
- The intramuscularly or intradermally administered IIV are options for adults aged 18 through 64 years.
- Adults aged 65 years or older can receive the standard-dose IIV or the high-dose IIV (Fluzone High-Dose).
- A list of currently available influenza vaccines can be found at www.cdc.gov/flu/protect/vaccine/vaccines.htm.

3. Tetanus, diphtheria, and acellular pertussis (Td/Tdap) vaccination

- Administer 1 dose of Tdap vaccine to pregnant women during each pregnancy (preferably during 27 to 36 weeks' gestation) regardless of interval since prior Td or Tdap vaccination.
- Persons aged 11 years or older who have not received Tdap vaccine or for whom vaccine status is unknown should receive a dose of Tdap followed by tetanus and diphtheria toxoids (Td) booster doses every 10 years thereafter. Tdap can be administered regardless of interval since the most recent tetanus or diphtheria-toxoid containing vaccine.
- Adults with an unknown or incomplete history of completing a 3-dose primary vaccination series with Td-containing vaccines should begin or complete a primary vaccination series including a Tdap dose.
- For unvaccinated adults, administer the first 2 doses at least 4 weeks apart and the third dose 6 to 12 months after the second.
- For incompletely vaccinated (i.e., less than 3 doses) adults, administer remaining doses.
- Refer to the ACIP statement for recommendations for administering Td/Tdap as prophylaxis in wound management (see footnote 1).

4. Varicella vaccination

- All adults without evidence of immunity to varicella (as defined below) should receive 2 doses of single-antigen varicella vaccine or a second dose if they have received only 1 dose.
- Vaccination should be emphasized for those who have close contact with persons at high risk for severe disease (e.g., health care personnel and family contacts of persons with immunocompromising conditions) or are at high risk for exposure or transmission (e.g., teachers; child care employees; residents and staff members of institutional settings, including correctional institutions; college students; military personnel; adolescents and adults living in households with children; nonpregnant women of childbearing age; and international travelers).
- Pregnant women should be assessed for evidence of varicella immunity. Women who do not have evidence of immunity should receive the first dose of varicella vaccine upon completion or termination of pregnancy and before discharge from the health care facility. The second dose should be administered 4 to 8 weeks after the first dose.
- Evidence of immunity to varicella in adults includes any of the following:
  - documentation of 2 doses of varicella vaccine at least 4 weeks apart;
  - U.S.-born before 1980, except health care personnel and pregnant women;
  - history of varicella based on diagnosis or verification of varicella disease by a health care provider;
  - history of herpes zoster based on diagnosis or verification of herpes zoster disease by a health care provider; or
  - laboratory evidence of immunity or laboratory confirmation of disease.

5. Human papillomavirus (HPV) vaccination

- Two vaccines are licensed for use in females, bivalent HPV vaccine (HPV2) and quadrivalent HPV vaccine (HPV4), and one HPV vaccine for use in males (HPV4).
- For females, either HPV4 or HPV2 is recommended in a 3-dose series for routine vaccination at age 11 or 12 years and for those aged 13 through 26 years, if not previously vaccinated.
- For males, HPV4 is recommended in a 3-dose series for routine vaccination at age 11 or 12 years and for those aged 13 through 21 years, if not previously vaccinated. Males aged 22 through 26 years may be vaccinated.
- HPV4 is recommended for men who have sex with men through age 26 years for those who did not get any or all doses when they were younger.
- Vaccination is recommended for immunocompromised persons (including those with HIV infection) through age 26 years for those who did not get any or all doses when they were younger.
- A complete series for either HPV4 or HPV2 consists of 3 doses. The second dose should be administered 4 to 8 weeks (minimum interval of 4 weeks) after the first dose; the third dose should be administered 24 weeks after the first dose and 16 weeks after the second dose (minimum interval of at least 12 weeks).
- HPV vaccines are not recommended for use in pregnant women. However, pregnancy testing is not needed before vaccination. If a woman is found to be pregnant after initiating the vaccination series, no intervention is needed; the remainder of the 3-dose series should be delayed until completion or termination of pregnancy.

(continued)

TABLE 2.5 2015 Recommended Immunizations for Adults by Age (*continued*)

6. Zoster vaccination

- A single dose of zoster vaccine is recommended for adults aged 60 years or older regardless of whether they report a prior episode of herpes zoster. Although the vaccine is licensed by the U.S. Food and Drug Administration for use among and can be administered to persons aged 50 years or older, ACIP recommends that vaccination begin at age 60 years.
- Persons aged 60 years or older with chronic medical conditions may be vaccinated unless their condition constitutes a contraindication, such as pregnancy or severe immunodeficiency.

7. Measles, mumps, rubella (MMR) vaccination

- Adults born before 1957 are generally considered immune to measles and mumps. All adults born in 1957 or later should have documentation of 1 or more doses of MMR vaccine unless they have a medical contraindication to the vaccine or laboratory evidence of immunity to each of the three diseases. Documentation of provider-diagnosed disease is not considered acceptable evidence of immunity for measles, mumps, or rubella.

Measles component:

- A routine second dose of MMR vaccine, administered a minimum of 28 days after the first dose, is recommended for adults who:
  - are students in postsecondary educational institutions,
  - work in a health care facility, or
  - plan to travel internationally.
- Persons who received inactivated (killed) measles vaccine or measles vaccine of unknown type during 1963–1967 should be revaccinated with 2 doses of MMR vaccine.

Mumps component:

- A routine second dose of MMR vaccine, administered a minimum of 28 days after the first dose, is recommended for adults who:
  - are students in a postsecondary educational institution,
  - work in a health care facility, or
  - plan to travel internationally.
- Persons vaccinated before 1979 with either killed mumps vaccine or mumps vaccine of unknown type who are at high risk for mumps infection (e.g., persons who are working in a health care facility) should be considered for revaccination with 2 doses of MMR vaccine.

Rubella component:

- For women of childbearing age, regardless of birth year, rubella immunity should be determined. If there is no evidence of immunity, women who are not pregnant should be vaccinated. Pregnant women who do not have evidence of immunity should receive MMR vaccine upon completion or termination of pregnancy and before discharge from the health care facility.

Health care personnel born before 1957:

- For unvaccinated health care personnel born before 1957 who lack laboratory evidence of measles, mumps, and/or rubella immunity or laboratory confirmation of disease, health care facilities should consider vaccinating personnel with 2 doses of MMR vaccine at the appropriate interval for measles and mumps or 1 dose of MMR vaccine for rubella.

8. Pneumococcal (13-valent pneumococcal conjugate vaccine [PCV13] and 23-valent pneumococcal polysaccharide vaccine [PPSV23]) vaccination

- General information
  - When indicated, only a single dose of PCV13 is recommended for adults.
  - No additional dose of PPSV23 is indicated for adults vaccinated with PPSV23 at or after age 65 years.
  - When both PCV13 and PPSV23 are indicated, PCV13 should be administered first; PCV13 and PPSV23 should not be administered during the same visit.
  - When indicated, PCV13 and PPSV23 should be administered to adults whose pneumococcal vaccination history is incomplete or unknown.
- Adults aged 65 years or older who
  - Have not received PCV13 or PPSV23: Administer PCV13 followed by PPSV23 in 6 to 12 months.
  - Have not received PCV13 but have received a dose of PPSV23 at age 65 years or older: Administer PCV13 at least 1 year after the dose of PPSV23 received at age 65 years or older.
  - Have not received PCV13 but have received 1 or more doses of PPSV23 before age 65: Administer PCV13 at least 1 year after the most recent dose of PPSV23; administer a dose of PPSV23 6 to 12 months after PCV13, or as soon as possible if this time window has passed, and at least 5 years after the most recent dose of PPSV23.
  - Have received PCV13 but not PPSV23 before age 65 years: Administer PPSV23 6 to 12 months after PCV13 or as soon as possible if this time window has passed.
  - Have received PCV13 and 1 or more doses of PPSV23 before age 65 years: Administer PPSV23 6 to 12 months after PCV13, or as soon as possible if this time window has passed, and at least 5 years after the most recent dose of PPSV23.
- Adults aged 19 through 64 years with immunocompromising conditions or anatomical or functional asplenia (defined below) who
  - Have not received PCV13 or PPSV23: Administer PCV13 followed by PPSV23 at least 8 weeks after PCV13; administer a second dose of PPSV23 at least 5 years after the first dose of PPSV23.
  - Have not received PCV13 but have received 1 dose of PPSV23: Administer PCV13 at least 1 year after the PPSV23; administer a second dose of PPSV23 at least 8 weeks after PCV13 and at least 5 years after the first dose of PPSV23.
  - Have not received PCV13 but have received 2 doses of PPSV23: Administer PCV13 at least 1 year after the most recent dose of PPSV23.
  - Have received PCV13 but not PPSV23: Administer PPSV23 at least 8 weeks after PCV13; administer a second dose of PPSV23 at least 5 years after the first dose of PPSV23.
  - Have received PCV13 and 1 dose of PPSV23: Administer a second dose of PPSV23 at least 5 years after the first dose of PPSV23.
- Adults aged 19 through 64 years with cerebrospinal fluid leaks or cochlear implants: Administer PCV13 followed by PPSV23 at least 8 weeks after PCV13.
- Adults aged 19 through 64 years with chronic heart disease (including congestive heart failure and cardiomyopathies, excluding hypertension), chronic lung disease (including chronic obstructive lung disease, emphysema, and asthma), chronic liver disease (including cirrhosis), alcoholism, or diabetes mellitus: Administer PPSV23.
- Adults aged 19 through 64 years who smoke cigarettes or reside in nursing home or long-term care facilities: Administer PPSV23.
- Routine pneumococcal vaccination is not recommended for American Indian/Alaska Native or other adults unless they have the indications as above; however, public health authorities may consider recommending the use of pneumococcal vaccines for American Indians/Alaska Natives or other adults who live in areas with increased risk for invasive pneumococcal disease.

- Immunocompromising conditions that are indications for pneumococcal vaccination are: Congenital or acquired immunodeficiency (including B- or T-lymphocyte deficiency, complement deficiencies, and phagocytic disorders excluding chronic granulomatous disease), HIV infection, chronic renal failure, nephrotic syndrome, leukemia, lymphoma, Hodgkin disease, generalized malignancy, multiple myeloma, solid organ transplant, and iatrogenic immunosuppression (including long-term systemic corticosteroids and radiation therapy).
- Anatomical or functional asplenia that are indications for pneumococcal vaccination are: Sickle cell disease and other hemoglobinopathies, congenital or acquired asplenia, splenic dysfunction, and splenectomy. Administer pneumococcal vaccines at least 2 weeks before immunosuppressive therapy or an elective splenectomy, and as soon as possible to adults who are newly diagnosed with asymptomatic or symptomatic HIV infection.

9. Meningococcal vaccination

- Administer 2 doses of quadrivalent meningococcal conjugate vaccine (MenACWY [Menactra, Menveo]) at least 2 months apart to adults of all ages with anatomical or functional asplenia or persistent complement component deficiencies. HIV infection is not an indication for routine vaccination with MenACWY. If an HIV-infected person of any age is vaccinated, 2 doses of MenACWY should be administered at least 2 months apart.
- Administer a single dose of meningococcal vaccine to microbiologists routinely exposed to isolates of Neisseria meningitidis, military recruits, persons at risk during an outbreak attributable to a vaccine serogroup, and persons who travel to or live in countries in which meningococcal disease is hyperendemic or epidemic.
- First-year college students up through age 21 years who are living in residence halls should be vaccinated if they have not received a dose on or after their 16th birthday.
- MenACWY is preferred for adults with any of the preceding indications who are aged 55 years or younger as well as for adults aged 56 years or older who a) were vaccinated previously with MenACWY and are recommended for revaccination, or b) for whom multiple doses are anticipated. Meningococcal polysaccharide vaccine (MPSV4 [Menomune]) is preferred for adults aged 56 years or older who have not received MenACWY previously and who require a single dose only (e.g., travelers).
- Revaccination with MenACWY every 5 years is recommended for adults previously vaccinated with MenACWY or MPSV4 who remain at increased risk for infection (e.g., adults with anatomical or functional asplenia, persistent complement component deficiencies, or microbiologists).

10. Hepatitis A vaccination

- Vaccinate any person seeking protection from hepatitis A virus (HAV) infection and persons with any of the following indications:
  - men who have sex with men and persons who use injection or noninjection illicit drugs;
  - persons working with HAV-infected primates or with HAV in a research laboratory setting;
  - persons with chronic liver disease and persons who receive clotting factor concentrates;
  - persons traveling to or working in countries that have high or intermediate endemicity of hepatitis A; and
  - unvaccinated persons who anticipate close personal contact (e.g., household or regular babysitting) with an international adoptee during the first 60 days after arrival in the United States from a country with high or intermediate endemicity. (See footnote 1 for more information on travel recommendations.) The first dose of the 2-dose hepatitis A vaccine series should be administered as soon as adoption is planned, ideally 2 or more weeks before the arrival of the adoptee.
- Single-antigen vaccine formulations should be administered in a 2-dose schedule at either 0 and 6 to 12 months (Havrix), or 0 and 6 to 18 months (Vaqta). If the combined hepatitis A and hepatitis B vaccine (Twinrix) is used, administer 3 doses at 0, 1, and 6 months; alternatively, a 4-dose schedule may be used, administered on days 0, 7, and 21 to 30 followed by a booster dose at month 12.

11. Hepatitis B vaccination

- Vaccinate persons with any of the following indications and any person seeking protection from hepatitis B virus (HBV) infection:
  - sexually active persons who are not in a long-term, mutually monogamous relationship (e.g., persons with more than 1 sex partner during the previous 6 months); persons seeking evaluation or treatment for a sexually transmitted disease (STD); current or recent injection drug users; and men who have sex with men;
  - health care personnel and public safety workers who are potentially exposed to blood or other infectious body fluids;
  - persons with diabetes who are younger than age 60 years as soon as feasible after diagnosis; persons with diabetes who are age 60 years or older at the discretion of the treating clinician based on the likelihood of acquiring HBV infection, including the risk posed by an increased need for assisted blood glucose monitoring in long-term care facilities, the likelihood of experiencing chronic sequelae if infected with HBV, and the likelihood of immune response to vaccination;
  - persons with end-stage renal disease, including patients receiving hemodialysis, persons with HIV infection, and persons with chronic liver disease;
  - household contacts and sex partners of hepatitis B surface antigen–positive persons, clients and staff members of institutions for persons with developmental disabilities, and international travelers to countries with high or intermediate prevalence of chronic HBV infection; and
  - all adults in the following settings: STD treatment facilities, HIV testing and treatment facilities, facilities providing drug abuse treatment and prevention services, health care settings targeting services to injection drug users or men who have sex with men, correctional facilities, end-stage renal disease programs and facilities for chronic hemodialysis patients, and institutions and nonresidential day care facilities for persons with developmental disabilities.
- Administer missing doses to complete a 3-dose series of hepatitis B vaccine to those persons not vaccinated or not completely vaccinated. The second dose should be administered 1 month after the first dose; the third dose should be given at least 2 months after the second dose (and at least 4 months after the first dose). If the combined hepatitis A and hepatitis B vaccine (Twinrix) is used, give 3 doses at 0, 1, and 6 months; alternatively, a 4-dose Twinrix schedule, administered on days 0, 7, and 21 to 30 followed by a booster dose at month 12 may be used.
- Adult patients receiving hemodialysis or with other immunocompromising conditions should receive 1 dose of 40 mcg/mL (Recombivax HB) administered on a 3-dose schedule at 0, 1, and 6 months or 2 doses of 20 mcg/mL (Engerix-B) administered simultaneously on a 4-dose schedule at 0, 1, 2, and 6 months.

12. *Haemophilus influenzae* type b (Hib) vaccination

- One dose of Hib vaccine should be administered to persons who have anatomical or functional asplenia or sickle cell disease or are undergoing elective splenectomy if they have not previously received Hib vaccine. Hib vaccination 14 or more days before splenectomy is suggested.
- Recipients of a hematopoietic stem cell transplant (HSCT) should be vaccinated with a 3-dose regimen 6 to 12 months after a successful transplant, regardless of vaccination history; at least 4 weeks should separate doses.
- Hib vaccine is not recommended for adults with HIV infection since their risk for Hib infection is low.

13. Immunocompromising conditions

- Inactivated vaccines generally are acceptable (e.g., pneumococcal, meningococcal, and inactivated influenza vaccine) and live vaccines generally are avoided in persons with immune deficiencies or immunocompromising conditions. Information on specific conditions is available at www.cdc.gov/vaccines/hcp/acip-recs/index.html.

TABLE 2.6 Cervical Cancer Screening Guidelines for Average-Risk Women[1]

		ACS, American Society for Colposcopy and Cervical Pathology (ASCCP), and American Society for Clinical Pathology (ASCP)[2]	USPSTF[3]	ACOG[4]
		2012	2012	2012
When to start screening[5]		Age 21. Women aged < 21 years should not be screened regardless of the age of sexual initiation or other risk factors *(Strong recommendation)*	Age 21. *(A recommendation)* Recommend against screening women aged < 21 years *(D recommendation)*	Age 21 regardless of the age of onset of sexual activity. Women aged < 21 years should not be screened regardless of age at sexual initiation and other behavior-related risk factors *(Level A evidence)*
Statement about annual screening		Women of any age should not be screened annually by any screening method *(Strong recommendation)*	Individuals and clinicians can use the annual Pap test screening visit as an opportunity to discuss other health problems and preventive measures. Individuals, clinicians, and health systems should seek effective ways to facilitate the receipt of recommended preventive services at intervals that are beneficial to the patient. Efforts also should be made to ensure that individuals are able to seek care for additional health concerns as they present themselves.	In women aged 30–65 years, should not be performed. *(Level A evidence)* Patients should be counseled that annual well-woman visits are recommended even if cervical cancer screening is not performed at each visit
Screening method and intervals[6]				
Cytology (conventional or liquid based)	21–29 years of age	Every 3 years[7] *(Strong recommendation)*	Every 3 years *(A recommendation)*	Every 3 years *(Level A evidence)*
	30–65 years of age	Every 3 years[7] *(Strong recommendation)*	Every 3 years *(A recommendation)*	Every 3 years *(Level A evidence)*
HPV co-test (cytology + HPV test administered together)	21–29 years of age	HPV co-testing should not be used for women aged < 30 years	Recommend against HPV co-testing women aged < 30 years *(D recommendation)*	HPV co-testing[8] should not be performed in women aged < 30 years *(Level A evidence)*
	30–65 years of age	Every 5 years *(Strong recommendation)*; this is the preferred method *(Weak recommendation)*	For women who want to extend their screening interval, HPV co-testing every 5 years is an option *(A recommendation)*	Every 5 years; this is the preferred method *(Level A evidence)*
Primary HPV testing[9]		For women aged 30–65 years, screening by HPV testing alone is not recommended in most clinical settings *(Weak recommendation)*[10]	Recommend against screening for cervical cancer with HPV testing (alone or in combination with cytology) in women aged < 30 years *(D recommendation)*	Not addressed
When to stop screening		Aged > 65 years with adequate screening history[11,12]	Aged > 65 years with adequate screening history *(D recommendation)*[11]	Aged > 65 years with adequate screening history[11,13] *(Level A evidence)*
Screening post-hysterectomy		Women who have had a total hysterectomy (removal of the uterus and cervix) should stop screening.[14] Women who have had a supra-cervical hysterectomy (cervix intact) should continue screening according to guidelines *(Strong recommendation)*	Recommend against screening in women who have had a hysterectomy (removal of the cervix)[13] *(D recommendation)*	Women who have had a hysterectomy (removal of the cervix) should stop screening and not restart for any reason[13] *(Level A evidence)*[15]

The need for a bimanual pelvic exam	Not addressed in 2012 guidelines but was addressed in 2002 ACS guidelines[16]	Addressed in USPSTF ovarian cancer screening recommendations (draft)[17]	Addressed in 2012 well-woman visit recommendations.[18] **Aged <21 years,** no evidence supports the routine internal examination of the healthy, asymptomatic examination is acceptable. **Aged 21,** no evidence supports **years** or refutes the annual pelvic examination or speculum and bimanual examination. The decision whether or not to perform a complete pelvic examination should be a shared decision after a discussion between the patient and her health care provider. Annual examination of the external genitalia should continue[19]
Screening among those immunized against HPV[16,18]	Women at any age with a history of HPV vaccination should be screened according to the age-specific recommendations for the general population	The possibility that vaccination might reduce the need for screening with cytology alone or in combination with HPV testing is not established. Given these uncertainties, women who have been vaccinated should continue to be screened	Women who have received the HPV vaccine should be screened according to the same guidelines as women who have not been vaccinated *(Level C evidence)*

CIN = cervical intraepithelial neoplasia; HPV = human papillomavirus.

[1]These recommendations do not apply to women who have received a diagnosis of a high-grade precancerous cervical lesion (CIN 2 or 3) or cervical cancer, women with in utero exposure to diethylstilbestrol, or women who are immunocompromised, or are HIV positive.

[2]Saslow D., Solomon D., Lawson H. W., Killackey M., Kulasingam S. L., Cain J., … Myers E.R. (2012). American Cancer Society, American Society for Colposcopy and Cervical Pathology, and American Society for Clinical Pathology screening guidelines for the prevention and early detection of cervical cancer. *CA: A Cancer Journal for Clinicians, 62*(3), 147-172. doi: 10.3322/caac.21139. Available at www.cancer.org/Cancer/CervicalCancer/DetailedGuide/cervical-cancer-prevention

[3]USPSTF. (2012). Screening for Cervical Cancer. Available at www.uspreventiveservicestaskforce.org/uspstf11/cervcancer/cervcancerrs.htm. These recommendations apply to women who have a cervix, regardless of sexual history.

[4]ACOG Committee on Practice Bulletins-Gynecology. (2012). ACOG Practice Bulletin No. 131: Screening for Cervical Cancer. *Obstetrics and Gynecology, 120*(5), 1222-1238. doi: http://10.1097/AOG.0b013e318277c92a

[5]Since cervical cancer is believed to be caused by sexually transmissible HPV infections, women who have not had sexual exposures (e.g., virgins) are likely at low risk. Women aged older than 21 years who have not engaged in sexual intercourse may not need a Pap test depending on circumstances. The decision should be made at the discretion of the women and her physician. Women who have had sex with women are still at risk of cervical cancer. 10%–15% of women aged 21–24 years in the United States report no vaginal intercourse (Saraiya M., Martinez G., Glaser K., & Kulasingam S. Pap testing and sexual activity among young women in the United States. *Obstetrics and Gynecology, 114*(6), 1213-1219. doi: 10.1097/AOG.0b013e3181be3db4.). Providers should also be aware of instances of nonconsensual sex among their patients.

[6]Conventional cytology and liquid-based cytology are equivalent regarding screening guidelines, and no distinction should be made by test when recommending next screening.

[7]There is insufficient evidence to support longer intervals in women aged 30–65 years, even with a screening history of consecutive negative cytology tests.

[8]All ACOG references to HPV testing are for high-risk HPV testing only. Tests for low-risk HPV should not be performed.

[9]Primary HPV testing (HPV testing alone) is defined as conducting the HPV test as the first screening test. It may be followed by other tests (like a Pap) for triage.

[10]No further explanation of which clinical settings HPV testing should be used to screen women aged 30–65 years as a stand-alone test.

[11]Current guidelines define adequate screening as three consecutive negative cytology results or two consecutive negative co-tests within 10 years before cessation of screening, with the most recent test performed within 5 years, and are the same for ACS, ACOG, and USPSTF.

[12]Women aged older than 65 years with a history of CIN2, CIN3, or AIS should continue screening for at least 20 years after spontaneous regression or appropriate management. (Weak recommendation)

[13]And no history of CIN 2 or higher.

[14]Unless the hysterectomy was done as a treatment for cervical precancer or cancer.

[15]Women should continue to be screened if they have had a total hysterectomy and have a history of CIN 2 or higher in the last 20 years or cervical cancer ever. Continued screening for 20 years is recommended in women who still have a cervix and a history of CIN 2 or higher. Therefore, screening with cytology alone every 3 years for 20 years after the initial posttreatment surveillance for women with a hysterectomy is reasonable. (Level B evidence)

[16]2002 guidelines statement: The ACS and others should educate women, particularly teens and young women, that a pelvic exam does not equate to a cytology test and that women who may not need a cytology test still need regular health care visits including gynecologic care. Women should discuss the need for pelvic exams with their providers. Saslow D., Runowicz C. D., Solomon D., Moscicki A. B., Smith R. A., Eyre H. J., & Cohen, C. American Cancer Society guideline for the early detection of cervical neoplasia and cancer. *CA: A Cancer Journal of Clinicians, 52*, 342-362.

[17]The bimanual pelvic examination is usually conducted annually in part to screen for ovarian cancer, although its effectiveness and harms are not well known and were not a focus of this review. No randomized trial has assessed the role of the bimanual pelvic examination for cancer screening. In the PLCO Trial, bimanual examination was discontinued as a screening strategy in the intervention arm because no cases of ovarian cancer were detected solely by this method and a high proportion of women underwent bimanual examination with ovarian palpation in the usual care arm.

[18]Committee on Gynecologic Practice. (2012). ACOG Committee Opinion No. 534: Well-woman visit. *Obstetrics and Gynecology, 120*(2)1, 421-424. doi: 10.1097/AOG.0b013e3182680517.

[19]For women aged 21 years, annual pelvic examination is a routine part of preventive care even if they do not need an internal examination can be left to the patient if she is asymptomatic and has undergone a total hysterectomy and bilateral salpingo–oophorectomy for benign indications, and is of average risk.

women's preventive services guidelines from the ACA, see www.hhs.gov/healthcare/facts/factsheets/2011/08/womensprevention08012011a.html.

In March 2012, the ACA, the USPSTF, and the ACOG released guidelines for cervical cancer screening. Table 2.6 from the CDC summarizes each of their guidelines for cervical cancer screenings.

Prostate Cancer Screening

Prostate cancer is the second most common cancer in men. Prostate cancer is a slow-growing cancer with a lifetime risk of 15.9%. The risk factors for prostate cancer include:

A. Age: Men older than age 50
B. African American men
C. Men who have a family history of prostate cancer
D. Exposure to Agent Orange used in the Vietnam War

Two tests are used for screening: the digital rectal examination and the prostate-specific antigen (PSA) blood test. Screening for prostate cancer with the PSA has been controversial due to the potential of overdiagnosis and overtreatment. The PSA may be elevated with other types of prostate problems other than cancer. Further testing for suspected prostate cancer includes a digital rectal examination, transrectal ultrasound, and/or a needle biopsy.

Watchful waiting with continued observation and physical examinations is a viable management option. Active surveillance includes periodic PSA tests, physical examination, and repeated prostate biopsy. The USPSTF evaluated the evidence and notes that in the United States nearly 90% of men with the PSA-detected prostate cancer have early treatment with one or more treatments, including prostatectomy surgery, radiation, or androgen deprivation therapies. Side effects of these procedures include urinary incontinence, erectile dysfunction, and bowel dysfunction. The use of androgen deprivation therapy for localized prostate cancer is associated with erectile dysfunction, gynecomastia, and hot flashes.

Sexually Transmitted Infections Screening

Taking a thorough sexual history is the basis of identifying high-risk sexual behavior, screening, counseling, and treatment for sexually transmitted infections (STIs). Older men and women should continue to be screened throughout their lifetime for STIs; there is no cutoff on age for the transmission of STIs.

The CDC recommends that persons aged 13 to 64 years of age be screened for HIV. Guidelines and recommendations for HIV/AIDS for clinicians are available at the CDC website located at www.cdc.gov/hiv/guidelines/index.html. For more discussion on sexual health and treatment guidelines for STIs and HIV see Chapter 16, "Gynecologic Guidelines," "Sexual Health Issues in the Aging Population," Chapter 17, "Sexually Transmitted Infections Guidelines," and Chapter 19, "Systemic Disorders Guidelines," "HIV."

Vision Screens

Age-related changes affect the sense of sight and require screening for refractory errors, macular degeneration, glaucoma, and cataracts (see Chapter 7, "Eye Guidelines").

Multiple medical and systemic conditions including genetic, cardiovascular, endocrine, gastrointestinal, nutritional, and metabolic disorders, increase the need for a comprehensive dilated eye examination. The American Optometric Association recommends an examination every 2 years for risk-free adults between 18 and 60 years. For those at risk between 18 and 60 years of age, eye examinations are recommended every 1 to 2 years. For adults who are 61 years of age and older who are risk free, an annual eye examination is recommended. The frequency of a comprehensive eye examination for at-risk adults should occur annually or as recommended.

Bibliography

Allender, J. A., Rector, C., & Warner, K. D. (2010). *Community health nursing* (7th ed.). Philadelphia, PA: Kluwer, Lippincott, Williams & Wilkins.

American Cancer Society. (2014, January 4). *Paying for breast cancer screening.* Retrieved from http://www.cancer.org/cancer/breastcancer/moreinformation/breastcancerearlydetection/breast-cancer-early-detection-paying-for-br-ca-screening

American College of Obstetricians and Gynecologists. (2011, August). Practice bulletin no. 22: Breast cancer screening. *Obstetrics & Gynecology, 118*(2) Part I, 372–382.

American College of Rheumatology. (n.d.). *Fracture risk assessment tool (FRAX).* Retrieved from http://www.rheumatology.org/Practice/Clinical/Clinicianresearchers/Outcomes_Instrumentation/Fracture_Risk_Assessment_Tool_(FRAX)/

American Dental Association. (2013, August 13). *Affordable Care Act, dental benefits examined.* Retrieved from https://www.ada.org/news/8935.aspx

American Optometric Association. (n.d.). *Adult vision: 41 to 60 years of age.* Retrieved from http://www.aoa.org/patients-and-public/good-vision-throughout-life/adult-vision-19-to-40-years-of-age/adult-vision-41-to-60-years-of-age

American Optometric Association. (n.d.). *Recommended eye examination frequency for pediatric patients and adults.* Retrieved from http://www.aoa.org/patients-and-public/caring-for-your-vision/comprehensive-eye-and-vision-examination/recommended-examination-frequency-for-pediatric-patients-and-adults

Andrews, M. M., & Boyle, J. S. (2008). *Transcultural concepts in nursing care* (5th ed.). Philadelphia, PA: Lippincott, Williams & Wilkins.

Benton, J. (2003). Making schools safer and healthier for lesbian, gay, bisexual and questioning students. *Journal of School Nursing, 19*(5), 251–259.

Centers for Disease Control and Prevention. (n.d.a). *Cervical cancer screening guidelines for average-risk women.* Retrieved from http://www.cdc.gov/cancer/cervical/pdf/guidelines.pdf

Centers for Disease Control and Prevention. (n.d.b). *Chronic disease prevention and health promotion: Oral health.* Retrieved from http://www.cdc.gov/chronicdisease/resources/publications/aag/doh.htm

Centers for Disease Control and Prevention. (n.d.c). *Immunization applications for PC/handhelds.* Retrieved from www.cdc.gov/vaccines/pubs/vis/vis-downloads.htm

Centers for Disease Control and Prevention. (2008). *Promoting cultural sensitivity: A practical guide for promoting tuberculosis programs that provide services to Hmong persons from Laos.* Retrieved from http://www.cdc.gov/tb/publications/guidestoolkits/ethnographicguides/hmong/chapters/hmongtbbooklet508_final.pdf

Centers for Disease Control and Prevention. (2011). *Oral health preventing cavities, gum disease, tooth loss, and oral cancers at a glance 2011.* Retrieved from http://www.cdc.gov/chronicdisease/resources/publications/AAG/doh.htm

Centers for Disease Control and Prevention. (2012). *Hepatitis C testing for anyone born during 1945-1965: New CDC recommendations.* Retrieved from http://www.cdc.gov/Features/HepatitisCTesting/

Centers for Disease Control and Prevention. (2013a). *Aortic aneurysm fact sheet.* Retrieved from http://www.cdc.gov/dhdsp/data_statistics/fact_sheets/fs_aortic_aneurysm.htm

Centers for Disease Control and Prevention. (2013b). *CDC catchup immunization schedule for persons aged 4 months through 18 years who start late or who are more than 1 month behind—United States 2013.* Retrieved from http://www.cdc.gov/vaccines/schedules/downloads/child/catchup-schedule-bw.pdf

Centers for Disease Control and Prevention. (2013c). *CDC recommended adult immunization schedule—United States 2013.* Retrieved from http://www.cdc.gov/vaccines/schedules/downloads/adult/adult-schedule-bw.pdf

Centers for Disease Control and Prevention. (2013d). *Information for travelers.* Retrieved from www.cdc.gov/travel/page/traveler-information-center

Centers for Disease Control and Prevention. (2013e). *Vaccines for international travelers.* Retrieved from http://www.cdc.gov/vaccines/adults/rec-vac/travel.html

Cordell, C. B., Borson, S., Boustani, M., Chodosh, J., Reuben, D., Verghese, J., ... Fried, L. B. (2013). Alzheimer's Association recommendation for operationalizing the detection of cognitive impairment during the Medicare annual wellness visit in a primary care setting. *Alzheimer's & Dementia, 9,* 141–150.

Department of Health and Human Services Centers for Medicare and Medicare Services. (2013, February). *Screening for depression. Medicare learning network.* ICN 907799. Retrieved from http://www.cms.gov/Outreach-and-Education/Medicare-Learning-Network-MLN/MLNProducts/Downloads/Screening-for-Depression-Booklet-ICN907799.pdf

Downes, E. A., & Graham, A. R. (2011, March). Healthcare for refugees resettled in the US. *Clinician Review, 21*(3), 25–31.

Ellis, R. L. (2006, May). *Are associate degree nursing graduates adequately prepared to meet the cultural needs of their patients at the end of life?* Paper presented at the meeting of thesis presentation. Retrieved from http://research.wsulibs

Grandfacts. (2010). Retrieved from http://www.grandfactsheets.org

Health Canada. (2009, November 16). *Healthy living the effects of oral health on overall health.* Retrieved from http://www.hc-sc.gc.ca/hl-vs/iyh-vsv/life-vie/dent-eng.php

Huber, D. L. (2010). *Leadership and nursing care management* (4th ed.). St. Louis, MO: Saunders.

Huges, K. H., & Hood, L. J. (2007). Teaching methods and an outcome for measuring cultural sensitivity in undergraduate nursing students. *Journal of Transcultural Nursing, 18*(57), 57–62.

Mitchell, J., Trangle, M., Deganan, B., Gabert, T., Haight, B., Kessler, D., ... Vincent, S. Institute for Clinical Systems Improvement. *Adult Depression in Primary Care.* Updated September 2013. Retrieved from https://www.icsi.org/_asset/fnhdm3/Depr-Interactive0512b.pdf

National Heart Lung and Blood Institute. (n.d.). *Obesity education initiative: BMI calculator.* Retrieved from http://www.nhlbisupport.com/bmi

National Osteoporosis Foundation. (n.d.). *Having a bone density test.* Retrieved from http://nof.org/articles/743

Passel, J. S., & D'Vera, C. (2008). *U.S. population projection 2005–2050.* Washington, DC: Pew Research Center. Retrieved from http://www.pewresearch.org

Purnell, L. D., & Paulanka, B. J. (2008). *Transcultural health care: A culturally competent approach* (3rd ed.). Philadelphia, PA: F.A. Davis.

RESCAN Collaborators, Brown, M. J., Sweeting, M. J., Brown, L. C., Powell, J. T., & Thompson, S. G. (January 2013). Surveillance intervals for small abdominal aortic aneurysms: A meta-analysis. *Journal of the American Medical Association, 309*(8), 806–813.

Ruddock, H. C., & Turner, D. S. (2007). Developing cultural sensitivity: Nursing students' experiences of study abroad program. *Journal of Advance Nursing, 59*(4), 361–369.

SAMHSA-HRSA Center for Integrated Health Solutions. (n.d.). *Screening tools depression.* Retrieved from http://www.integration.samhsa.gov/clinical-practice/screening-tools#depression

Spector, R. E. (2012). *Cultural diversity in health and illness* (8th ed.). Upper Saddle River, NJ: Prentice-Hall.

Stanley, J. M. (2005). *Advanced practice nursing: Emphasizing common roles* (2nd ed.). Philadelphia, PA: F.A. Davis.

Suominen, M. H., Sandelin, E., Soini, H., & Pitkala, K. H. (2009, February). *How well do nurses recognize malnutrition in elderly patients? European Journal of Clinical Nutrition, 63*(2), 292–296.

Tacderas, A. (2009, May). *Examining the level of cultural sensitivity among associate degree student nurses in rural Southern Illinois.* Paper presented at the meeting of the thesis presentation. Southeast Missouri State University, Cape Girardeau, MO, March 2009.

U.S. Census. (n.d.). *Quickfacts.* Retrieved from U.S. Census Bureau website: http://quickfacts.census.gov/qfd/staes/oooo.html

U.S. Department of Agriculture. (n.d.). *Food Pyramid.* Retrieved from http:choosemyplate.gov

U.S. Department of Health and Human Services, Health Resources and Services Administration. *Find a health center.* Retrieved from http://findahealthcenter.hrsa.gov/Search_HCC.aspx

U.S. Department of Health and Human Services, Health Resources and Service Administration. *Women's prevention services guidelines.* Retrieved from http://www.hrsa.gov/womensguidelines/

U.S. Preventive Services Task Force. (2008, March). *Recommendations for STI screening.* Retrieved from http://www.uspreventiveservicestaskforce.org/uspstf08/methods/stinfections.htm#age

U.S. Preventive Services Task Force. (2008, October). *Screening for colorectal cancer recommendation statement*. Retrieved from http://www.uspreventiveservicestaskforce.org/uspstf08/colocancer/colors.htm

U.S. Preventive Services Task Force. (2009, October). Screening for breast cancer. http://www.uspreventiveservicestaskforce.org/uspstf09/breastcancer/brcanrs.htm#clinical

U.S. Preventive Services Task Force. (2012, March). Screening for cervical cancer clinical summary of U.S. Preventive Services Task Force recommendation (AHRQ Publication No. 11-05156-EF-3). Rockville, MD: Author.

U.S. Preventive Services Task Force. (2013, April). *Screening for human immunodeficiency virus (HIV)*. Retrieved from http://www.uspreventiveservicestaskforce.org/uspstf13/hiv/hivfact.pdf

U.S. Preventive Services Task Force. (2013, October). *Aspirin for the prevention of cardiovascular disease*. Retrieved from http://www.uspreventiveservicestaskforce.org/uspstf/uspsasmi.htm

Your Medicare coverage: Abdominal aortic aneurysm screening. Retrieved from http://www.medicare.gov/coverage/ab-aortic-aneurysm-screening.html

Your Medicare coverage: Bone mass measurement (bone density). Retrieved from http://www.medicare.gov/coverage/bone-density.html

Your Medicare coverage: Cardiovascular disease screenings. Retrieved from http://www.medicare.gov/coverage/cardiovascular-disease-screenings.html

Your Medicare coverage: Cervical & vaginal cancer screening. Retrieved from http://www.medicare.gov/coverage/cervical-vaginal-cancer-screenings.html

Your Medicare coverage: Colorectal cancer screening. Retrieved from http://www.medicare.gov/coverage/colorectal-cancer-screenings.html

Your Medicare coverage: Dental services. Retrieved from http://www.medicare.gov/coverage/dental-services.html

Your Medicare coverage: Depression screening. Retrieved from http://www.medicare.gov/coverage/depression-screenings.html

Your Medicare coverage: Diabetes screening. Retrieved from http://www.medicare.gov/coverage/diabetes-screenings.html

Your Medicare coverage: Flu shots. Retrieved from http://www.medicare.gov/coverage/flu-shots.html

Your Medicare coverage: Glaucoma tests. Retrieved from http://www.medicare.gov/coverage/glaucoma-tests.html

Your Medicare coverage: Hepatitis B shots. Retrieved from http://www.medicare.gov/coverage/hepatitis-b-shots.html

Your Medicare coverage: HIV screening. Retrieved from http://www.medicare.gov/coverage/hiv-screening.html

Your Medicare coverage: Macular degeneration. Retrieved from http://www.medicare.gov/coverage/macular-degeneration.html

Your Medicare coverage: Mammograms. Retrieved from http://www.medicare.gov/coverage/mammograms.html

Your Medicare coverage: Pneumococcal shots. Retrieved from http://www.medicare.gov/coverage/pneumococcal-shots.html

Your Medicare coverage: Preventive visit & yearly wellness exams. Retrieved from http://www.medicare.gov/coverage/preventive-visit-and-yearly-wellness-exams.html

Your Medicare coverage: Prostate cancer screening. Retrieved from http://www.medicare.gov/coverage/prostate-cancer-screenings.html

Your Medicare coverage: Sexually transmitted infections (STI) screening and counseling. Retrieved from http://www.medicare.gov/coverage/sexually-transmitted-infections-screening-and-counseling.html

Your Medicare coverage: Yearly eye exam. Retrieved from http://www.medicare.gov/coverage/yearly-eye-exam.html

Wallace, M. P., Weiner, J. S., Almendral, A., Cosiquen, R., Auerbach, C., & Wolf-Klien, G. (2007). Physician's cultural sensitivity in African American advanced care planning: A pilot study. *Journal of Palliative Medicine*, *10*(3), 721-727.

Zawenda, E. (1996). Malnutrition in the elderly. *Postgraduate Medicine*, *100*, 208.

CHAPTER THREE

Adult-Geriatric Assessments

Cheryl A. Glass and Angelito Tacderas

Adult Risk Assessment

Adult and geriatric primary care includes assessment and comprehensive review of physical health/disease states; functional and physical abilities; and cognition, sensory, behavioral health, safety, nutrition, and social needs. Tools may be self-administered, completed by family members, or require staff assistance and/or time testing. Some assessment tools are Internet-based with response-driven tally of scores for clinical interpretation. Other assessment tools are available for purchase for the iPhone and Android phone operating systems.

Besides a physical assessment, independence, quality of life, and safety are evaluated. When impairments are identified, additional questions for clinicians to ask/assess include: Is there an acute identifiable event or is the impairment chronic or reversible? Is the patient able to perform the task safely, slowly, with difficulty, with some assistance, or does the patient have total dependency? History taking and observation of the patient's affect, gait, undressing/dressing, and communication begin the assessment by the examiner.

Functional Capacity and Disability

A basic evaluation includes assessment of a person's dependence/independence in the performance of activities of daily living (ADL), including personal self-care and community interactions with instrumental activities of daily living (IADL). Other terminology for IADL is "executive function." If the patient is unable to perform activities, the identification of family and other support is a vital assessment for social support and needed referrals. The Barthel Index of Activities of Daily Living is an example of an ADL assessment tool. It is located at www.healthcare.uiowa.edu/igec/tools/function/barthelADLs.pdf.

Activities of Daily Living (ADL)

A. ADL evaluation of basic self-care activities include:
   1. Dressing: Use an open-ended question such as "Did you dress yourself today?" Evaluate if the patient is able to dress independently, choose weather-appropriate clothing, use buttons and zippers, and have the physical ability to bend, grasp and, stand.
   2. Eating: Evaluate if the patient is able to use all utensils, cut food, swallow, and eat without choking.
   3. Ambulating: Observation of the patient entering the examination room and movement during the office visit is a key assessment tool to evaluate if the patient is able to walk independently, has gait abnormalities, or has/needs/uses any assistive devices such as a cane, walker, or wheelchair.
   4. Toileting: Evaluate if the patient is continent of urine and/or bowels, or uses disposable undergarment/diapers, bedpan, or bedside commode. What is needed for mobility to get to the toilet? Is the patient able to self-clean?
   5. Hygiene: Evaluate the patient's need for independence or assistance with bathing, showering, shaving, brushing teeth, brushing hair, and other hygiene tasks.

Affective Assessment

Stanford University's website, web.stanford.edu/~yesavage/GDS.html, offers tools to evaluate depression, including the Mood Assessment Scale and the Geriatric Depression Scale (GDS). The Stanford website also offers multilanguage versions of the GDS, including Arabic, Chinese, Creole, Danish, Dutch, Farsi, French, German, Greek, Hebrew, Hindi, Hungarian, Icelandic, Indonesian, Irish,

Italian, Japanese, Korean, Latvian, Lithuanian, Malay, Maltse, Norwegian, Portuguese, Rumanian, Russian, Serbian, Spanish, Swedish, Turkish, Vietnamese, Welsh, and Yiddish.

A. The Mood Assessment Scale for evaluation of depression is located at www.stanford.edu/~yesavage/GDS.english.short.html.

B. The electronic web-based GDS is available at www.medafile.com/GDS15.htm. As of August 2014, Stanford's website notes that there are free iPhone and Android apps for clinicians to perform the 15-item GDS that calculates the results.

Cognitive/Dementia Assessment

A. Vitamin B_{12} deficiency is a common comorbidity in older patients, and routine assessment of vitamin B_{12} levels in older patients diagnosed with dementia is recommended.

B. Alzheimer's disease is the most common form of dementia. The Alzheimer's Association notes that Alzheimer's disease has seven distinct stages.
   1. Stage 1: No impairment
   2. Stage 2: Very mild decline (losing keys; forgetting familiar names)
   3. Stage 3: Mild decline (memory and concentration problems)
   4. Stage 4: Moderate decline (difficulty planning dinner or paying bills on time)
   5. Stage 5: Moderately severe decline (unable to recall events or remember important dates like birthdays, anniversaries, etc.).
   6. Stage 6: Severe decline (needs help getting dressed; personality begins to change)
   7. Stage 7: Very severe decline (late-stage Alzheimer's disease includes trouble eating, swallowing, speaking, and all motor function)

The Alzheimer's Association has published a checklist of warning signs called "Know the 10 Signs: Early Detection Matters." See the following website for full descriptions of the early signs at: www.alz.org/national/documents/checklist_10signs.pdf.
   1. Memory loss that disrupts daily life
   2. Challenges in planning or solving problems
   3. Difficulty completing familiar tasks at home, at work, or at leisure
   4. Confusion with time or place
   5. Trouble understanding visual images and spatial relationships
   6. New problems with words in speaking or writing
   7. Misplacing and losing the ability to retrace steps
   8. Decreased or poor judgment
   9. Withdrawal from work or social activities
   10. Changes in mood and personality

C. There is no "gold standard" tool to evaluate cognitive function and impairment. An initial evaluation provides a baseline for serial surveillance and may also be used to indicate the need for further evaluation. A yearly evaluation can determine and identify a gradual decline over time. Assessments that indicate decline or impairment requires further evaluation. The National Institute on Aging notes someone with Alzheimer's disease may experience the following symptoms:
   1. Getting lost
   2. Trouble handling money and paying bills
   3. Repeating questions
   4. Taking longer to complete normal daily tasks
   5. Poor judgment
   6. Losing things or misplacing them in odd places
   7. Difficulty remembering newly learned information
   8. Unfounded suspicions about family, friends, and professional caregivers
   9. Difficulty speaking, swallowing, and walking

The cognitive assessment does not need to be a lengthy assessment. The Memory Impairment Screen (MIS), the General Practitioner Assessment of Cognition (GPCOG), and the Mini-Cog are noted to be the most useful in the primary care setting. These assessments require 5 minutes to administer and are very similar.

A. The MIS is available on the Alzheimer's Association website: www.alz.org/documents_custom/mis.pdf. The MIS assessment includes:
   1. Evaluation of the patient's ability to recall four words: checkers, saucer, telegram, and red cross.
   2. Administer the Clock-Draw Test (CDT) (refer to the Section II procedure for the CDT).
   3. Recall and associate the four words.

B. The Mini-Cog assessment is a short testing tool used to detect cognitive impairment and the need for further evaluation (see Table 3.1). Administration of the Mini-Cog involves three steps:
   1. Ask the patient to remember three unrelated words (there are six versions of word lists available). Ask the patient to repeat the words to ensure understanding.
   2. Administer the CDT. See the Section II procedure for a copy and instructions for the CDT.
   3. Ask the patient to recall the three words from Step 1.

The Mini-Cog assessment tool is available on the Alzheimer's Association website: www.alz.org/documents_custom/minicog.pdf.

TABLE 3.1 Scoring the Mini-Cog Assessment Test for Cognitive Impairment

3 recalled words	Negative for cognitive impairment
1–2 recalled words + normal CDT	Negative for cognitive impairment
1–2 recalled words + abnormal CDT	Positive for cognitive impairment
0 recalled words	Positive for cognitive impairment

C. An interactive program test for the GPCOG is located on the following website: www.gpcog.com.au.

Environmental Assessment

The environmental evaluation is essential to identify risk factors for falls. Take a "fresh look" at the patients' home for the bathroom, bedroom, kitchen, and general home safety issues. An in-depth review is available in My Falls-Free Plan in Section III, Chapter 3, "Patient Teaching Guides."

Polypharmacy

A. An important step in evaluation of *potential* polypharmacy is the assessment of new symptoms. Typical signs and symptoms suggesting polypharmacy include confusion, gait disturbance, depression, delirium, dementia, anger, forgetfulness, falls, insomnia, drowsiness, and incontinence.

B. The Poly Rx Initiative of the University of Louisville notes the following statistics related to polypharmacy issues in the geriatric population:
   1. 30% of elderly patients use eight or more prescription drugs daily.
   2. The elderly population takes an average of 18 prescription drugs per year.
   3. One in four people ages 65 years and older receive at least 1 of 20 drugs that are potentially inappropriate for elderly patients.
   4. The amount and frequency of alcohol use should be included in medication reviews.

C. Prescribers with insufficient knowledge about geriatric care are a large factor in polypharmacy issues. There are several resources available for the evaluation of polypharmacy issues, including:
   1. Schedule a "brown bag" visit to review medications, and assess the patient and/or family's understanding of medications (see Exhibits 3.1 and 3.2).
   2. The American Geriatric Society (AGS), the Beers Criteria for Potentially Inappropriate Medical Use in Older Adults is located at www.americangeriatrics.org/files/documents/beers/PrintableBeersPocketCard.pdf.
   3. A senior care pharmacist may be available in your local community for a patient referral. Senior care pharmacists are skilled health care professionals who have specialized training in the medication-related needs of seniors. Typically, the senior care pharmacist does a comprehensive consultation through a one-on-one review of all medications. Information on senior care pharmacists is located at the American Society of Consultant Pharmacists (ASCP) website: www.ascp.com/find-senior-care-pharmacist.
   4. The Institute for Save Medication Practices (ISMP) has published the **List of *Confused* Drug Names** that includes look-alike and sound-alike drugs. The List of *Confused* Drug Names is located at www.ismp.org/Tools/confuseddrugnames.pdf.
   5. Provide the patient with the patient teaching sheet on "Safety Issues: Medication Safety" (see Section III for Chapter 3, "Patient Teaching Guides").

D. Suggestions for safeguards to reduce risk in errors when writing a prescription include:
   1. Use both the brand and generic name on prescriptions and labels. Brand names always start with an uppercase letter.
   2. Include the purpose of the medications on prescriptions and labels.
   3. The Food and Drug Administration approved and the ISMP recommend the use of "Tall Man" (mixed case) letters for writing prescriptions. Tall man lettering involves highlighting the dissimilar letters in two names to aid in distinguishing between two drugs, making them less prone to mix-ups. See Table 3.2 for an example of the use of "tall man" letters for medications on the List of *Confused* Drug Names.

E. Multiple websites are available for evaluation of drug interactions, including:
   1. www.drugs.com/drug_interactions.html
   2. reference.medscape.com/drug-interactionchecker
   3. www.healthline.com/druginteractions
   4. www.rxlist.com/drug-interaction-checker.htm
   5. www.rxlist.com/grapefruit-page3/supplements.htm

EXHIBIT 3.1 Checklist for Brown Bag Medication Checkup

What to check for:

- ❑ Indication for each medication
- ❑ Drug interactions between medications and food
- ❑ Adverse drug reactions (esp. which ones to report or how to manage them)
- ❑ Expiration dates of medications
- ❑ How the patient is taking his/her medications
- ❑ Physical disabilities
- ❑ Monitoring tests
- ❑ How the medication is being stored
- ❑ Cultural, reading level, capability
- ❑ Allergies

Make sure the patient understands:

- ❑ What each medication is used for
- ❑ How to take each medication (i.e., with or without food, number of times per day)
- ❑ What to expect from the medication
- ❑ Side effects (esp. which ones to report or how to manage them)

Take home messages for the patient:

- ❑ Stress the importance of properly disposing of expired or discontinued medications
- ❑ Clarify questions on any remaining prescriptions
- ❑ Explain the importance of proper storage with certain medication (i.e., nitroglycerin)
- ❑ Remind patients to communicate with their doctor or pharmacist about any side effects of prescription medications, OTCs, or herbals
- ❑ Suggest medication schedules and the importance of compliance
- ❑ Reinforce lifestyle modifications to promote well-being

Source: Permission to reprint from the Ohio Pharmacists Association. Ohio Patient Safety Institute: www.ohiopatientsafety.org/meds/default.htm.

EXHIBIT 3.2 Medication Review Form—Brown Bag Program

Date: ____________

Patient Name ____ Sex: M F

Telephone Number ____ Age: ____________

Special counseling considerations ____

Reported medicine allergies ____

Please list ALL medications that you are currently taking (prescriptions, OTC medications, other)

________________________ ________________________

________________________ ________________________

________________________ ________________________

____

For Pharmacist Use

	Medicine #1	Medicine #2	Medicine #3	Medicine #4	Medicine #5
Drug name					
Dosage					
SIG on label					

(continued)

EXHIBIT 3.2 Medication Review Form—Brown Bag Program (*continued*)

	Medicine #1	Medicine #2	Medicine #3	Medicine #4	Medicine #5
MD name					
Exp. date					
Reported medical problem					
How long taken?					
Still taken?	Yes/No	Yes/No	Yes/No	Yes/No	Yes/No
Date of last MD visit					
Patient knows purpose of drug	Yes/No	Yes/No	Yes/No	Yes/No	Yes/No
Compliance w/SIG	Yes/No/Partial	Yes/No/Partial	Yes/No/Partial	Yes/No/Partial	Yes/No/Partial
Side effects?					
OTCs					
Improper administration	Yes/No	Yes/No	Yes/No	Yes/No	Yes/No
Over/under use	Yes/No	Yes/No	Yes/No	Yes/No	Yes/No
Expired	Yes/No	Yes/No	Yes/No	Yes/No	Yes/No
Follow-up needed?	Yes/No	Yes/No	Yes/No	Yes/No	Yes/No

Source: Permission to reprint from the Ohio Pharmacists Association. Ohio Patient Safety Institute: www.ohiopatientsafety.org/meds/default.htm.

TABLE 3.2 Examples of "Tall Man" Letters to Prevent Confusion and Decrease Look-Alike Prescription Errors

Drug Name/Tall Man	Confused Drug Name/Tall Man
Bupropion/Tall Man BuPROPion	Buspirone/Tall Man BusPIRone
Clomiphene/Tall Man ClomiPHENE	Clomipramine/Tall Man ClomiPRAMINE
Dobutamine/Tall Man DOBUTamine	Dopamine/Tall Man DOPamine
Glipizide/Tall Man GlipiZIDE	Glyburide/Tall Man GlyBURIDE
Nicardipine/Tall Man NiCARdipine	Nifedipine/Tall Man NIFEdipine
Prednisone/Tall Man PredniSONE	Prednisolone/Tall Man PrednisoLONE

Source: Food and Drug Administration Name Differentiation Project located at: www.fda.gov/Drugs/DrugSafety/MedicationErrors/ucm164587.htm.

Assessment for Continued Driving

A. Consult the Department of Motor Vehicles (DMV) in your state for information related to regulations for older drivers. State laws set standards that may include:
   1. Requirement for a medical evaluation for license renewal
   2. Shorter renewal period for older drivers
   3. Requirement for in-person renewal
   4. Administration of vision, road, or written test for license renewal

B. The decision to "take the keys away" is one of the major changes that impacts adult independence and self-worth. Changes in eyesight, hearing, reflex response, judgment, physical conditions, medications, and memory all impact the decision when to have the patient stop driving. Family members look toward health care providers to assist in determining whether their loved one has the capacity and ability to continue driving.

The assessment begins by asking the patient open-ended questions.

1. How comfortable are you about driving?
   a. Are you able to drive in the evening?
   b. Do you drive in the rain or other bad weather?

c. Do you drive when it is rush hour?
d. Do you avoid driving on the interstate?
e. Do you ever get lost?
f. Have you ever "lost" your car? Have you had problems misplacing your keys, purse, or wallet?
g. Have you had any accidents, including minor "fender benders"?
h. Have you had any recent traffic tickets or warnings?
i. Do other drivers honk their horns when you are driving or stopped at a stop sign or signal light?
j. Do you have anyone help you with errands, including shopping?
k. Do you have any other optional transportation available such as family and friends, senior citizen van services, taxi services, or a church van?

2. Interview family members:
   a. Assess if they discussed the issue about the need to stop driving. A three-module educational tool is available at the AARP website. The modular seminar covers the following subjects: "meaning of driving," "observing driving skills," and "planning conversations." The seminar is located at www.aarp.org/home-garden/transportation/we_need_to_talk.

      The same questions asked to the patient can be used to discuss the patient's ability to continue driving with their family members.
   b. Have they been driven by their loved one, and what did they observe when they were passengers?
   c. Have they noted any memory issues?
   d. How active is their loved one? Have they noted any physical limitations around the home?
   e. Has the family seen any dents or scraped paint on the car?
3. Evaluate alcohol consumption.
4. Review all medications to evaluate polypharmacy issues, drug duplication, and side-effect profiles that would impact driving. Schedule a "brown bag" visit.
5. Rereview all medical diagnoses. The patient may be seeing multiple doctors, and records may not be current.
   a. Vision issues: Glaucoma, cataracts, macular degeneration, retinitis pigmentosa, diabetic retinopathy, abnormality of field of vision (entire spatial area including central and peripheral vision), visual acuity (able to distinguish details and shapes of objects and contrast sensitivity), color vision deficit, need for corrective glasses or contacts
   b. Hearing: Hearing loss
   c. Neurologic disorders: Parkinson's disease, multiple sclerosis, epilepsy (last seizure), syncope, Alzheimer's disease, stroke (hemiparesis), cognitive impairment, Huntington's disease
   d. Heart/vascular: Hypertension, unstable angina, arrhythmia, aortic aneurysm (nonsurgical treatment)
   e. Respiratory issues, including sleep
   f. Sleep issues: Hypersomnia, excessive daytime sleepiness, obstructive sleep apnea
   g. Diabetes: Poorly controlled diabetes/hypoglycemia
   h. Psychiatric disorders and substance abuse: Aggressiveness, behavioral disorders, depression, anxiety, abuse or dependence with alcohol, cannabis, benzodiazepine use
   i. Physical limitations: Amputation, range of motion, manual dexterity, arthritis, difficulties with ADL, hemiparesis
   j. Dementia/cognitive impairment
6. Referrals:
   a. Functional assessment by an occupational therapist
   b. Physical therapy
   c. Medical specialty consultation
   d. On-road assessment by the DMV

Fall Assessment

A. Statistics about falls noted by the National Center for Injury Prevention and Control (NCIPC) are as follows.
   1. One third of people 65 and older fall each year.
   2. Every 29 minutes an older adult dies from a fall. One out of five falls causes a serious injury such as a head trauma or fracture.
   3. Less than half of the Medicare beneficiaries who fell in the previous year talked to their health care provider about it.
   4. The CDC's 2012 Behavioral Risk Factor Surveillance System (BRFSS) research found that adults 45 years and older diagnosed with arthritis were twice as likely to report two or more falls or an injury related to a fall. The CDC also notes the following statistics:
      a. Over 95% of hip fractures are caused by falls.
      b. Men are more likely to die from a fall.
      c. People age 75 and older who fall are four to five times more likely than those age 65 to 74 years to be admitted to a long-term facility for a year or longer.

B. Assess whether the patient had some physical feeling precipitating the fall such as shortness of breath, vertigo, cardiac pain/palpitations, or other signs. Evaluate if other factors such as alcohol, medicines, and over-the-counter (OTC) meds may have been a contributing factor.

1. Did the patient lose consciousness? Was the patient able to get up on his/her own?
2. What injuries occurred in previous fall(s)?
3. Most falls are caused by the interaction of multiple risk factors. The more risk factors a person has, the greater the risk for falls. The clinician's first focus for fall prevention is evaluation of modifiable intrinsic and extrinsic risk factors (see Table 3.3), including:

C. The CDC has developed the Stopping Elderly Accidents, Deaths & Injuries (STEADI) program toolkit of information for health care providers who see older adults in their practice who are at risk of falling or who may have fallen in the past. Information about the STEADI program is located at www.cdc.gov/homeandrecreationalsafety/Falls/steadi/index.html. The CDC (NCIPC) has developed an Algorithm for Fall Risk Assessment & Interventions located at www.cdc.gov/homeandrecreationalsafety/pdf/steadi/pocket_guide_preventing-falls.pdf.

1. The Fall Risk Checklist (see Exhibit 3.3) is one toolkit resource of the CDC NCIPC STEADI program that is available for clinicians.

D. Conduct a focused physical examination of the patient's feet and evaluate the patient's shoes. Evaluate structural abnormalities and neurologic deficits in sensation and proprioception. Refer to a podiatrist or pedorthists if needed.

E. Prescribe exercise as an ongoing need to prevent falls. Suggest working with a group.

1. Suggestions include walking, Tai Chi, swimming, balance exercise, gait training.

F. Discuss the patient's ability to afford a Personal Emergency Response System (PERS) service.

G. Early cataract surgery has been shown to reduce fall rates.

H. Discuss the importance of the need to keep medical information available in the event of a fall. To identify the changing medical history and medications, the Vial of Life is an important resource: www.vialoflife.com/how_to_use_the_vial_of_life.

There are four steps to preparing a Vial of Life:

1. Fill out the Vial of Life form.
2. Place a decal on the front of a baggie to store medical information. The website also suggests the placement of a recent photograph and do not resuscitate and living will documents.
3. Tape the baggie on the outside of the refrigerator.
4. A second decal is placed on the front door for respondents to be able to quickly identify the patient's history.

Consider an occupational and/or physical therapy referral to evaluate the need for any assistive devices, walkers, canes, and wheelchairs.

Gait and Mobility

A. The evaluations of mobility and balance are indicators of the ability to live independently.

B. A basic mobility assessment that includes an evaluation of static and dynamic balance is the Timed Up and Go (TUG). It is a timed evaluation that assesses the ability to stand from a sitting position, walk, turn, stop, and sit down again (see Exhibit 3.4).

1. The items needed include:
   a. A chair with arm rests.
   b. A clock/watch with a sweep second hand.
2. The patient who uses a cane should be assessed in using the assistive device.
3. The patient should be wearing regular shoes.

TABLE 3.3 Intrinsic and Extrinsic Fall Risk Factors

Intrinsic Risk Factors	Extrinsic Risk Factors
Advanced age	Lack of stair handrails
Previous falls	Poor stair design
Muscle weakness	Lack of bathroom grab bars
Gait and balance problems	Dim lighting or glare
Poor vision/cataracts	Obstacles and tripping hazards
Postural hypotension	Slippery or uneven surfaces
Fear of falls	Improper use of assistive device
Chronic conditions including stroke, Parkinson's disease, dementia, arthritis, incontinence (urgent trips to the bathroom), diabetes (proprioception from diabetic peripheral neuropathy), and reduced proximal muscle strength and reaction because of vitamin D deficiency	Psychoactive medications

EXHIBIT 3.3 **Fall Risk Checklist**

Patient: ____________ **Date:** ____________ **Time:** ____________ **a.m./p.m.**

Fall Risk Factor Identified	Factor Present?	Notes
Falls history		
Any falls in past year?	❑ Yes ❑ No	
Worries about falling or feels unsteady when standing or walking?	❑ Yes ❑ No	
Medical conditions		
Problems with heart rate and/or rhythm?	❑ Yes ❑ No	
Cognitive impairment?	❑ Yes ❑ No	
Incontinence?	❑ Yes ❑ No	
Depression?	❑ Yes ❑ No	
Foot problems?	❑ Yes ❑ No	
Other medical conditions (specify)?	❑ Yes ❑ No	
Medications		
Any psychoactive medications, medications with anticholinergic side effects, and/or sedating OTCs? (e.g., Benadryl, Tylenol PM)?	❑ Yes ❑ No	
Gait, strength, and balance		
TUG Test ≥ 12 seconds?	❑ Yes ❑ No	
30-second Chair Stand Test Below average score (see table on back)?	❑ Yes ❑ No	
4-stage balance test full tandem stance less than 10 seconds?	❑ Yes ❑ No	
Vision		
Acuity less than 20/40 OR no eye exam in more than 1 year?	❑ Yes ❑ No	
Postural hypotension		
A decrease in systolic blood pressure (BP) ≥ 20 mmHg or a diastolic BP of ≥ 10 mmHg or light-headedness or dizziness from lying to standing?	❑ Yes ❑ No	
Other risk factors (specify)		
	❑ Yes ❑ No	
	❑ Yes ❑ No	

Chair Stand—Below Average Scores

Age	Men	Women
60–64	< 14	< 12
65–69	< 12	< 11
70–74	< 12	< 10
75–79	< 11	< 10
80–84	< 10	< 9
85–89	< 8	< 8
90–94	< 7	< 4

EXHIBIT 3.4 The TUG Test

Patient: ____________ **Date:** ____________ **Time:** ____________ **a.m./p.m.**

The TUG Test

Purpose: To assess mobility

Equipment: A stopwatch

Directions: Patients wear their regular footwear and can use a walking aid if needed. Begin by having the patient sit back in a standard arm chair and identify a line 3 m or 10 ft away on the floor.

Instructions to the patient:

When I say **Go**, I want you to:

1. Stand up from the chair.
2. Walk to the line on the floor at your normal pace.
3. Turn.
4. Walk back to the chair at your normal pace.
5. Sit down again.

On the word **Go** begin timing

Stop timing after patient has sat back down and record

Time: ________ **seconds**

An older adult who takes ≥ 12 seconds to complete the TUG is at high risk for falling.

Observe the patient's postural stability, gait, stride length, and sway.

Circle all that apply: ■ Slow tentative pace ■ Loss of balance ■ Short strides ■ Little or no arm swing ■ Steadying self on walls ■ Shuffling ■ En bloc turning ■ Not using assistive device properly

Notes: For relevant articles, go to www.cdc.gov/injury/STEADI.

4. Timing
   a. Begin timing when the patient starts to rise from the chair.
   b. Stop timing when the patient is seated again.
5. The patient should be seated in a resting position with both arms on the chair arm rests. The patient is asked to stand up from a chair and walk approximately 10 feet (3 m), turn around, and return to sit down in the chair.
6. Verbal cuing through the test may be needed for a person with cognitive impairment.
7. Evaluation
   a. The normal time to complete the TUG test is between 7 and 10 seconds indicating no balance or mobility issues.
   b. An older adult who takes 12 or more seconds to complete the TUG is at high risk for falling.
   c. Time greater than 20 seconds indicates the need for assistance and for further evaluation for balance.
   d. Taking 30 or more seconds indicates a high risk for falls and higher dependence needs.
8. The TUG test can be repeated periodically to assess ability/decline of gait, mobility, and balance.

C. The Tinetti Assessment Tool measures both balance and gait. This tool is located at consultgerirn.org/uploads/File/Tinetti_Assessment_Balance.pdf.

1. Balance
   a. Individual scores are given for tasks including sitting balance, arising, standing, balance when the examiner nudges the patient, balance with eyes closed, balance ability when turning 360 degrees, and the safety when sitting down.
   b. The maximum score for the balance portion of the Tinetti test is 16 points.
2. Gait
   a. Individual scores are given for tasks/items including the initiation of gait, step length and height of raising the feet to walk, symmetry of stepping, continual stepping, walking straight or a deviation of the path, trunk movement, and walking stance.
   b. The maximum score of the gait portion of the Tinetti test is 12 points.
3. The maximum score for both the balance and gait tests of the Tinetti combined is 28 points.
   a. Scores below 19 are a general indicator of high risk for falls.
   b. Scores between 19 and 24 indicate the patient has a risk for falls.

D. The 30-Second Chair Stand Test is used to test leg strength and endurance (see Exhibit 3.5).

E. Consider a physical therapy and/or an occupational therapy referral for problems with gait and/or balance.

EXHIBIT 3.5 **The 30-Second Chair Stand Test**

Patient: ____________________ **Date:** ____________________ **Time:** ____________________ **a.m./p.m.**

Purpose: To test leg strength and endurance

Equipment:

- A chair with a straight back without arm rests (seat 17-in. high)
- A stopwatch

Instructions to the patient:

1. Sit in the middle of the chair.
2. Place your hands on the opposite shoulder crossed at the wrists.
3. Keep your feet flat on the floor.
4. Keep your back straight and keep your arms against your chest.
5. On **Go**, rise to a full standing position and then sit back down again.
6. Repeat this for 30 seconds.

On **Go**, begin timing.

If the patient must use his or her arms to stand, stop the test. Record 0 for the number and score.

Count the number of times the patient comes to a full standing position in 30 seconds.

If the patient is over halfway to a standing position when 30 seconds have elapsed, count it as a stand.

Record the number of times the patient stands in 30 seconds.

Number: __________ **Score** __________

A below-average score indicates a high risk for falls.

Notes: For relevant articles, go to www.cdc.gov/injury/STEADI

Chair Stand—Below-Average Scores

Age	Men	Women
60–64	< 14	< 12
65–69	< 12	< 11
70–74	< 12	< 10
75–79	< 11	< 10
80–84	< 10	< 9
85–89	< 8	< 8
90–94	< 7	< 4

Instrumental Activities of Daily Living (IADL)

A. The assessment of IADL (executive function) includes the patient's ability to care for himself or herself and interact with the community. IADL includes the ability of the patient to shop and prepare food, handle finances and medications, communicate using the telephone, and perform tasks of housekeeping and laundry. The Lawton & Brody IADL Scale is one of the most widely used and referenced tools (www.abramsoncenter.org/media/1197/instrumental-activities-of-daily-living.pdf).

B. Occupational and physical therapy referrals should be considered.

Cultural Diversity and Sensitivity

Culture is more than nationality or race. It also includes the aged, the illiterate, or those lacking education and persons with physical limitations. Culture influences a person's reasoning, decisions, and actions. It is the accumulation of learned beliefs, values, habits, and practices. Culture influences decision making, thoughts, what is approved or disapproved, what is normal or not, which is acquired from close personal relations (family/members of society) over time.

Cultural diversity exists when groups of different cultures must coexist within an environmental area (family, neighborhood, township, city, or country). Knowing that there are differences in cultures and not assigning values between different cultures reflect cultural sensitivity. However, significant differences may exist in the way health care is perceived and practiced because of the differing values and beliefs regarding health and illness inherent among people of varying cultural backgrounds.

Contributing Factors to Cultural Diversity

- Fewer White non-Hispanic children
- Increasing immigration
- Efficiency in transportation and travel
- Increase in the homeless and the poor population
- Increase in divorce rate
- Increase in single parenting
- Grandparents raising grandchildren
- Substance abuse
- Violence
- Transgender sex changes
- Homosexual acceptance
- Information explosion/high technology
- Illiteracy
- Increase in non-English-proficient health care providers
- Federal regulations
- Physical limitations (handicap)

Cultural sensitivity is the responsibility of all health care providers. Each office visit is an opportunity to gain more knowledge about a client's health beliefs and practices. Inadequate awareness of the client's health beliefs and practices influenced by culture could lead to mistrust. This may result in barriers including inappropriate delivery of care, increased cost, noncompliance, and seeking care elsewhere. Thus, this may eventually lead to even more barriers to health care access. Studies also suggest that there is a correlation between health care illiteracy and increase in noncompliance and medication errors. In addition, those with physical disabilities often have unpleasant experiences with previous health care encounters, which may affect their decisions to seek appropriate care.

Title VI of the Civil Rights Act is very specific about providing services that are less than the existing standard of care to anyone based on race, age, sex, or financial status. According to this document, "No person in the United States shall, on the grounds of race, color or national origin be excluded in the participation in, be denied the benefits of, or be discriminated under any programs or activity receiving federal financing assistance" (U.S. Department of Justice [USDJ], 2015).

Thoughtful Consideration

The provision of care without being sensitive to the needs of a culturally diverse client may suggest that the health care provider's values and beliefs are superior to those of the client's and may lead to disparity of care. Implementing evidence-based guidelines to a culturally diverse population, whose health care practices are not based on scientific studies, remains a constant challenge. The limited patient involvement in care may result in noncompliance, placing patients at greater risk for health-related complications. The delay in provision of health care can result in life-threatening complications.

Numerous resources are available throughout the literature and the Internet. Preferences for educational/assessment tools are within the health care provider's prerogative.

The following are guidelines for promoting cultural sensitivity in the clinical setting.

A. Provide a cultural diversity self-assessment/practice organization.
   1. Online Internet self-assessment tools, for example, Centers for Disease Control and Prevention (CDC) website (see next section).
   2. Download self-assessment tools from public (see next section).
   3. Use existing self-assessment tools and make necessary changes to fit the need (see Exhibit 3.6).

B. Identify the need of the population served.
   1. Understand the community and its health status.
   2. Evaluate resources, attitudes, and barriers inside the communities and practice location.
      a. Access to resources
      b. Notification of assistance
      c. Range of assistance options
         i. Transportation
         ii. Communication; consider an interpreter (personal versus automation)
            1) Identify bilingual staff.
            2) Use family members or personal acquaintance as interpreters (adults only).
            3) Provide multilingual written materials.
         iii. Education (meaningful/multilingual)
            1) User friendly
            2) Friendly technology

C. Educate staff to cultural diversities.
   1. Assessments should include patient's health values and beliefs (see Exhibit 3.7).

EXHIBIT 3.6 Cultural Diversity and Sensitivity Self-Evaluation Form

Using a scale of 1 to 5, with 1 = never and 5 = always, please answer the following questions:

Question	Response Value
1. I am comfortable with my culture and can compromise on situations without sacrificing my integrity.	
2. I think about what I say and how it may affect people with different beliefs and practices.	
3. I am aware that others may stereotype me, and I am willing to proactively get involved and share my beliefs and practices.	
4. I evaluate what the real reasons are when I encounter a conflict with the aged, the handicap, or persons of a different culture.	
5. I am aware of sensitive issues when I am around women and persons of different beliefs and race.	
6. I ask for clarification when I do not understand what others mean.	
7. I am aware of my assumptions about others who are culturally or racially different than myself and I am okay with it.	
8. I object when others use ethnic jokes.	
9. I listen when someone is speaking without interrupting.	
10. I am comfortable forming friendships with people of different cultures.	
11. I find ways to learn more about different cultures and how to communicate effectively.	
12. I realize that flexibility and empathy allow me to evaluate persons of different cultures without imposing any judgments, which allows me to collaborate effectively.	
13. I recognize that there are other ways than mine.	
14. I accept people for who they are regardless of color, educational achievement, financial status, age, physical limitations, or gender.	
15. I don't mind apologizing if I have wronged or offended someone.	
16. I respect that others may have a different interpretation of personal space.	
17. I treat people differently than the biases and prejudices of members of my culture.	
18. I do not look down on people who do not speak English fluently or may have an accent.	
19. I understand that there other ways to communicate.	
20. I use simple and common phrases when around the elderly, those with physical limitations, or someone of diverse culture who may not speak my language proficiently.	
Add up all of the numbers for a Total Score	

Total Score: Outstanding: 95 to 100
Good: 85 to 94
Average: 75 to 84
Needs improvement: 74 or less
(This tool is intended for personal use only. It is designed to be performed as a personal self-assessment. No reliability test that measures stability, equivalence, and homogeneity has been done.)

2. Communication should be meaningful.
   a. Be precise and clear.
   b. Maintain eye contact when speaking.
   c. Use plain language.
   d. Observe facial expressions and body language.
   e. Use short sentences to explain lengthy information.

EXHIBIT 3.7 **Sample: History Form**

Client: Personal, Social, and Family Information

Name ____________________

Date of birth ____________________

1. Today's date ________ 2. Age ____________________

3. Gender: M or F. Is your answer to question number 3 based for those with a transgender sexual change? If no sexual change has taken place, skip questions 4 and 5.

4. Date of procedure ________ 5. Type of procedure ____________________

Medications prescribed ____________________

____

Sexual orientation: heterosexual ________ gay/lesbian ________ other ________

Proficient in speaking English YES NO

Proficient in reading English YES NO

Ability to read lips YES NO

Preferred spoken language ____________________

Most comfortable language when speaking ____________________

Most comfortable language when reading ____________________

Preferred greeting Mr. Mrs. Ms. First name ____________________

Type of nonverbal communication used ____________________

Eye contact ____________________

Need of interpreter ____________________

Relation to interpreter ____________________

Quiet/use of silence ____________________

Use and definition of time ____________________

Use of any common signs (okay, pain, clapping) ____________________

Use of comfort space ____________________

Tactile use ____________________

Use of cultural jargon or slang that may affect evaluation

____

____

Perception of pain ____________________

Cultural ________ Ethnicity ____________________

Family role and function ____________________

Work ____________________

Leisure activities ____________________

Friends ________ Others ____________________

Country of origin ____________________

Country of birth ____________________

Years in the United States ____________________

Did you grow up in a city ________ town ________ suburb ________ rural ________

Ethnicity ____________________

Major support group ____________________

Dominant members of the family ____________________

Decision makers for the family ____________________

Previous work history ____________________

(continued)

EXHIBIT 3.7 **Sample: History Form (*continued*)**

Present work history ______________________________

Education ______________________________

Describe importance of religion ______________________________

Religious beliefs/practices ______________________________

Religious association ______________________________

Cultural/religious practices/restrictions ______________________________

Meaning and use of religious symbols ______________________________

Interaction with family/significant other—describe ______________________________

____

Role of father ______________ Role of mother ______________

Role of elder sibling/siblings ______________________________

Grandparents' role ______________________________

Number of dependents ______________________________

Children/grandchildren ______________________________

Are there any with physical limitations (deaf, mute, or blind)? Yes __________ No __________

If you answered yes to the above, please identify what type ______________________________

Means of communication ______________________________

____

Expectation from this visit ______________________________

Food preferences ______________________________

Beliefs on health promotion ______________________________

____

Family history ______________________________

____

Skin color/hair structure ______________________________

Reason for Visit

Chief complaint ______________________________

Perceived cause ______________________________

Reasons for cause ______________________________

Symptoms of illness ______________________________

____

Onset and severity (pain scale) ______________________________

Effects of illness on activities of daily living (ADL) ______________________________

Fear of the unknown about illness ______________________________

Treatment expectations and results ______________________________

Beliefs/practices about illness ______________________________

Health promotion beliefs and practice ______________________________

Types of healing practices ______________________________

Client's appearance ______________________________

Common diseases and disorders ______________________________

Beliefs and practices regarding traumatic events ______________________________

Beliefs and practices for preventive health ______________________________

____

Surgical history ______________________________

Other medical history ______________________________

Any additional information that may improve client care ______________________________

____

D. Schedule longer appointments if needed.
E. Clarify limitation of health care provider.
F. Clearly identify alternatives offered by health care provider.

Bibliography

Alzheimer's Association. (2009). *Know the 10 signs early detection matters.* Retrieved from http://www.alz.org/national/documents/checklist_10signs.pdf

Alzheimer's Association. (n.d.a). *Memory impairment screen (Mis).* Retrieved from http://www.alz.org/documents_custom/mis.pdf

Alzheimer's Association. (n.d.b). *Mini-Cog.* Retrieved from http://www.alz.org/documents_custom/minicog.pdf

American Academy of Orthopaedic Surgeons. (2012). Guidelines for preventing falls. *Orthoinfo-AAOS.* Retrieved from http://orthoinfo.aaos.org/topic.cfm?topic=A00135

American College of Rheumatology. (n.d.). *Practice management: Timed Up and Go (TUG).* Retrieved from https://www.rheumatology.org/Practice/Clinical/Clinicianresearchers/Outcomes_Instrumentation/Timed_Up_and_Go_(TUG)/

The American Geriatrics Society. (2012). American Geriatrics Society updated Beers criteria for potentially inappropriate medication use in older adults. *Journal of the American Geriatrics Society, 60,* 616–631.

The American Occupational Therapy Association. (2012a). *Behind the wheel: Occupational therapy and older drivers.* Retrieved from https://www.aota.org/about-occupational-therapy/professionals/rdp/articles/older-drivers.aspx

The American Occupational Therapy Association. (2012b). *Driving and transportation alternative for older adults.* Retrieved from http://www.aota.org/About-Occupational-Therapy/Professionals/PA/Facts/Driving-Transportation-Alternatives.aspx

American Society of Consultant Pharmacists (ASCP). (n.d.). *Find a senior care pharmacist.* Retrieved from https://www.ascp.com/find-senior-care-pharmacist

Andrews, M. M., & Boyle, J. S. (2008). *Transcultural concepts in nursing care* (5th ed.). Philadelphia, PA: Lippincott, Williams & Wilkins.

Ard, K. L., & Makadon, H. J. (2012, July 9). *Improving the health care of lesbian, gay, bisexual and transgender people: Understanding and eliminating health disparities.* Boston, MA: The Fenway Institute and The National LGBT Health Education Center. Retrieved from http://www.lgbthealtheducation.org/wp-content/uploads/12-054_LGBTHealtharticle_v3_07-09-12.pdf

Barbour, K. E., Stevens, J. A., Helmick, C. G., Lou, Y-H., Murphy, L. B., Hootman, J. M., … Sugerman, D. E. (2014, May 2). Falls and fall injuries among adults with arthritis-United States, 2012. *MMWR, 63,* 379-383.

Beaton, K., & Grimmer, K. (2013). Tools that assess functional decline: Systematic literature review update. *Clinical Interventions in Aging, 8,* 485–494.

Besdine, R. W. (2013, July). Evaluation of the elderly patient. *The Merck Manual Professional Edition.* Retrieved from http://www.merckmanuals.com/professional/geriatrics/approach_to_the_geriatric_patient/evaluation_of_the_elderly_patient.html?qt=evaluation of the elderly patient&alt=sh

Bradley, S. M. (2011, July-August). Falls in older adults. *Mount Sinai Journal of Medicine, 78,* 590–595.

Centers for Disease Control and Prevention. (2008). *Promoting cultural sensitivity: a practical guide for promoting tuberculosis programs that provide services to Hmong persons from Laos.* Retrieved from http://www.cdc.gov.tb

Centers for Disease Control and Prevention. (2013, September). *Home & recreational safety, falls among older adults: An overview.* Retrieved from http://www.cdc.gov/homeandrecreationalsafety/falls/adultfalls.html

Centers for Disease Control and Prevention. (n.d.). *The Timed Up and Go (TUG) test.* Retrieved from http://www.cdc.gov/homeandrecreationalsafety/pdf/steadi/timed_up_and_go_test.pdf

Chen, G. (2010, August 24). All about aging: Lookout points for safe senior driving. *UCLA Health.* Retrieved from http://www.uclahealth.org/body.cfm?id=502&action=detail&ref=852

Chen, G. (2013, February 12). All about aging: Making homes safer for seniors. *UCLA Health.* Retrieved from http://www.uclahealth.org/body.cfm?xyzpdqabc=0&id=502&action=detail&ref=1163&start=12&issueref=205

Day, J. R., Ramos, L. C., & Hendrix, C. C. (2012). Fall preventions through patient partnerships. *Nurse Practitioner, 37,* 15–19.

Doerflinger, D. M. C. (2013). *Try this: Mental status assessment of the older adults: The Mini-Cog.* Retrieved from http://consultgerirn.org/uploads/File/trythis/try_this_3.pdf

Downes, E. A., & Graham, A. R. (2011, March). Healthcare for refugees resettled in the US. *Clinician Review, 21*(3), 25–31.

Drabkin, A. (2014, April). Stat consult: Falls in older adults. *The Clinical Advisor, 17,* 91–92.

Ellis, R. L. (2006, May). *Are associate degree nursing graduates adequately prepared to meet the cultural needs of their patients at the end of life?* Paper presented at the meeting of thesis presentation. Retrieved from http://research.wsulibs

Elsawy, B., & Higgins, K. E. (2011). The geriatric assessment. *American Family Physician, 83,* 48–56.

Finestone, A.J. (2012). The older driver: When is it time to take away the keys? *Consultant, 52,* 753–760.

Food and Drug Administration. (2013, August 19). *Drugs: Name differentiation project.* Retrieved from http://www.fda.gov/Drugs/DrugSafety/MedicationErrors/ucm164587.htm

Greenberg, S. A. (2012). *Try this: The geriatric depression scale (GDS).* Retrieved from http://consultgerirn.org/uploads/File/trythis/try_this_4.pdf

Hedrich, A. (2013). *Try this: Fall risk assessment for older adults: The Hendrich II fall risk model.* Retrieved from http://consultgerirn.org/uploads/File/trythis/try_this_8.pdf

Hoskins, B. L. (2011). Safe prescribing for the elderly. *Nurse Practitioner, 36,* 47–52.

Huges, K. H., & Hood, L. J. (2007). Teaching methods and an outcome for measuring cultural sensitivity in undergraduate nursing students. *Journal of Transcultural Nursing, 18*(57), 57–62.

Jones, J. H., Treiber, L. A., & Jones, M. C. (2014). Intervening at the intersection of medication adherence and health literacy. *Journal for Nurse Practitioners, 10,* 527–536.

Kostas, T., Paquin, A., & Rudolph, J. L. (2013). Practical geriatric assessment. *Aging Health, 9,* 579–591. Retrieved from http://www.medscape.com/viewarticle/815490

Kristensen, M. T., Foss, N. B., & Kehlet, H. (2007). Timed "Up & Go" test as a predictor of falls within 6 months after hip fracture surgery. *Physical Therapy, 87,* 24–30.

Lach, H. W. (2012, D12). *Try this: Home safety inventory for older adults with dementia.* Retrieved from http://consultgerirn.org/uploads/File/trythis/try_this_d12.pdf

Langan, R. C., & Zawistoski, K. J. (2011). Update on vitamin B_{12} deficiency. *American Family Physician, 83,* 1425–1430.

Mayo, A. M. (2012, D13). *Try this: Use of the functional activities questionnaire in older adults with dementia.* Retrieved from http://consultgerirn.org/uploads/File/trythis/try_this_d13.pdf

McDougall, G. J., Becker, H., Vaughan, P. W., Acee, T. W., & Delville, C. L. (2010). The revised direct assessment of functional status for independent older adults. *The Gerontologist, 50,* 363–370.

National Council on Patient Information and Education. (2008). *Tips on safe storage and disposal of your prescription medicines.* Retrieved from http://www.talkaboutrx.org/documents/safe_storage_BW.pdf

National Chronic Care Consortium. (2003, June). *Tools for early identification, assessment, and treatment for people with Alzheimer's disease and dementia.* Retrieved from http://www.alz.org/national/documents/brochure_toolsforidassesstreat.pdf

The National Institute on Aging. (2010). *Caregiver guide tips for caregivers of people with Alzheimer's disease.* (NIH Publication No. 01-4013). Washington, DC: U.S. Department of Health and Human Services.

Novak, J. (2012). Older adults and driving: NP role in assessment and management. *American Journal for Nurse Practitioners, 16,* 26–32.

Patient.co.uk. (n.d.). *General practitioner assessment of cognition (GPCOG) score.* Retrieved from http://www.patient.co.uk/doctor/general-practitioner-assessment-of-cognition-gpcog-score

Purnell, L. D., & Paulanka, B. J. (2008). *Transcultural health care: A culturally competent approach* (3rd ed.). Philadelphia, PA: F.A. Davis.

Regal, R., & Heatherington, E. (2012). Baseline instrumental activities of daily living and incident dementia. *Journal of the American Geriatrics Society, 60,* 1189–1190.

Rosen, S. L. & Reuben, D. B. (2011). Geriatric assessment tools. *Mount Sinai Journal of Medicine, 78,* 489-497.

Rounds, L., Rappaport, B. A., & Mallary, L. L. (2013). Polypharmacy in senior adults. *Journal for Nurse Practitioners, 17,* 7–14.

Rubenstein, L. Z. (2013, November). Falls in the elderly. *The Merck Manual Professional Edition.* Retrieved from http://www.merckmanuals.com/professional/geriatrics/falls_in_the_elderly/falls_in_the_elderly.html

Ruddock, H. C., & Turner, D. S. (2007). Developing cultural sensitivity: Nursing students' experiences of study abroad program. *Journal of Advance Nursing, 59*(4), 361–369.

Santmyire, A. (2013). Challenges of implementing evidence-based practice in the developing world. *Journal for Nurse Practitioners-JNP, 9,* 306–311.

Shelkey, M.(2012). *Try this: Katz Index of independence in activities of daily living (ADL).* Retrieved from http://consultgerirn.org/uploads/File/trythis/try_this_2.pdf

Shellman, L., Beckstrand, R. L., Callister, L. C., Luthy, K. E., & Freeborn, D. (2014). Postpartum depression in immigrant Hispanic women: A comparative community sample. *Journal of American Association of Nurse Practitioners, 29,* 488-497.

Sheppard, K. (2014). Deaf adults and health care: Giving voice to their stories. *Journal of American Association of Nurse Practitioners, 26,* 504–510.

Spector, R. E. (2012). *Cultural diversity in health and illness* (8th ed.). Upper Saddle River, NJ: Prentice-Hall.

Tacderas, A. (2009). *Examining the level of cultural sensitivity among associate degree student nurses in rural Southern Illinois.* Paper presented at the meeting of the thesis presentation. Southeast Missouri State University, Cape Girardeau, MO, March 2009.

University of Michigan Medical School. (2003). *Geriatric functional assessment an education exercise with a standardized patient instructor emphasizing functional status assessment and communication skills relevant to the care of older patients.* Retrieved from http://www.med.umich.edu/lrc/coursepages/M1/HGD/GeriatricFunctionalAssess.pdf

U.S. Department of Justice. (2015, April 10). Title VI of the Civil Rights Act of 1964. http://www.justice.gov/crt/about/cor/coord/titlevi.php

Wallace, M. P., Weiner, J. S., Almendral, A., Cosiquen, R., Auerbach, C., & Wolf-Klien, G. (2007). Physician's cultural sensitivity in the advance care of African Americans. *Journal of Palliative Medicine, 10*(3), 721–727.

Ward, K. T., & Reuben, D. B. (2013, December 30). Comprehensive geriatric assessment. *UpToDate.* Retrieved from http://www.uptodate.com/contents/comprehensive-geriatric-assessment

Washington State Department of Social and Health Services. (2014, April 23). *My falls-free plan.* Retrieved from http://www.altsa.dshs.wa.gov/pubinfo/falls/documents/Fallfreeplan.pdf

Wolfgram, N. (2012). Medication adherence, what is the prescriber's responsibility? *Advance for NPs and PAs, 3,* 27–28.

Woodruff, K. (2010). Preventing polypharmacy in older adults. *Medscape Nurses.* Retrieved from http://www.medscape.com/viewarticle/732131_1

Young, J., Deagher, D., & MacLullich, A. (2011). Cognitive assessment of older people. *BMJ, 343,* d5042. doi: http://dx.doi.org/10.1136/bmj.d5042

Zagaria, M. A. E. (2012a). Long-distance caregiving: Challenges and tips for success. *American Journal for Nurse Practitioners, 16,* 15.

Zagaria, M. A. E. (2012b). Potentially inappropriate medications for seniors: focus on the 2012 Beers criteria. *American Journal for Nurse Practitioners, 16,* 26–28.

CHAPTER FOUR

Caregiver and End-of-Life Issues

Audra C. Malone and Karla Schroeder

Caregiver Support Issues

It is estimated that 20% of the population in the United States will be older adults by the year 2030. According to the 2010 U.S. Census, 37% of noninstitutionalized older adults have at least one chronic medical condition. Trends indicate that patients living with chronic illness will increase as the population ages, with an estimated 50% of people 65 years of age or older having three or more chronic illnesses. These comorbid conditions are associated with increased utilization of health care services and risk of decreased quality of life (QOL), polypharmacy, adverse reactions, and exacerbations of illness, thus creating a cycle in which health may decline, care becomes more complex, and the patient can no longer manage daily care alone. Trends in health care, including shorter hospital stays, fewer geriatric primary care providers, and limited community resources, have negatively impacted the ability of the patient to maintain living in the community without caregiver support. Therefore, along with the increase in older adults comes an increase in the number of caregivers for older adults. A recent national survey of caregivers estimated that 31% of U.S. households in 2009 had one family member who provided uncompensated care to an elder adult family member in the previous 12 months. The implication for health care providers is that the needs of the patient and the caregiver should be met in order to provide optimal health services. The purpose of this section is to identify and define formal and informal caregivers (IC), review the demographics of caregivers in the United States, examine common caregiver concerns, review assessment of caregiver health and well-being, and identify sources of support.

Formal and Informal Caregivers

Caregivers are categorized as formal or informal. Formal caregivers are those who are paid to provide the care to the recipient. Formal caregivers encompass a wide variety of providers and community resources, including primary and specialty medical providers, home health providers, home aides, social services, and long-term care facilities. It is a myth that most of the care of elderly persons occurs in long-term care, as most caregiving is provided by IC. IC are family, friends, or volunteers who provide uncompensated care to persons with disease or disability. This care ranges from direct care with activities of daily living, instrumental activities of daily living (IADL), transportation, household chores, medication administration, and disease management. It is important for advance practice registered nurses (APRN) to consider that in the current culture of health care, the responsibility for disease management has been transferred from health care professionals to patients and their IC. Additionally, one of the most important predictors of successful disease management for elder adults is the well-being of the caregiver; therefore, the needs of the IC must be identified and included in the plan of care.

Demographics

IC are a heterogeneous group of individuals who have a wide range of caregiving experiences, needs, and resources. The trend to remember is that caregivers and care recipients are getting older and that the demographics will change as the nation ages.

IC Demographics

A. IC provide care for an average total length of 4.6 years, although 31% of IC reported providing care for more than 5 years.
B. The span of caregiving responsibility was 6 months to more than 10 years.
C. The average age of IC is 49.2 years and is increasing.
D. More recent estimates include the mean age of caregivers for patients who have chronic obstructive pulmonary disease (COPD), congestive heart failure (CHF), or cancer as 57 years.

E. The majority of IC are women, and more than 50% of them are working outside of the home.
F. Almost three fourths of the IC who worked outside of the home reported that caregiving influenced their performance at their job, including juggling time at work to meet the demands of caregiving, turning down promotions, losing benefits, and early retirement.
G. Most IC are married (70%), college educated to some degree (62%), and one fourth have trouble paying their bills.
H. The average number of hours per week spent on care provision is 20.4 hours, with a range of less than 8 hours to more than 40 hours.
I. 32% of caregivers reported that they experienced a high burden of care, 17% reported a decline in their health, and 31% indicated that they experienced a high level of stress associated with caregiving.
J. IC are non-Hispanic White (72%), African American (13%), Hispanic (2%), and Asian American (2%).

Care Recipient Demographics

A. The average age of the care recipient is 69 and increasing as the population of elders older than the age of 75 continues to increase.
B. Half of the care recipients live in their own home, and they need assistance with activities of daily living (ADL).
C. In the survey, over three fourths of the IC reported that they desired more information from formal caregivers. The topics of interest include:
   1. Home safety
   2. Balancing caregiving demands and personal needs
   3. Communication and working with health care professionals
   4. End-of-life (EOL) care
   5. Choosing formal caregiving services
   6. More basic information on how to care for their loved one's needs

Interestingly, 30% of the survey recipients said they would turn to their medical provider for this additional information.

IC Concerns

Providing care to a loved one has many benefits. The majority of IC report that they find caregiving meaningful and rewarding; in addition, many report low levels of depression and anxiety and high levels of spiritual well-being. However, this heterogeneous group is also diverse in responses to caregiving. Some IC do not have a positive experience. Some researchers have found that optimal caregiving outcomes are dependent on the amount of physical, emotional, and mental strain experienced by the IC. The need for IC is great, and IC have shown a preference for getting information from their medical providers. Medical providers need to be aware of the potential concerns IC may have. These concerns include work/life balance, financial concerns, and caregiver health.

Work/Life Balance

Caregivers face a monumental task as they are often attempting to provide care to a loved one, understand the disease process and trajectory, manage the health care system, and maintain their own life roles. Additional caregiver roles may include social, occupational, and personal domains. Caregivers have work, family, and community obligations, self-care needs, and leisure activity preferences. All of these should be considered when assessing caregiver response to the caregiving role. Many caregivers have stated that their own health care is of a lesser priority than that of the care recipient. Caregiving was associated with increased risk of negative health behaviors. Hoffman and colleagues proposed that a rationale for the decreased participation in preventive health activities is the demand of providing care and decreased opportunity for health-promoting activities. Therefore, it is important that IC find balance among the multiple demands not only of life but of caregiving responsibilities.

Financial Implications

The financial implications of caregiving affect both caregivers and their employers. Employers of caregivers have reported decreased productivity due to more time missed and interruptions in work flow. Caregivers report increased expenses, decreased resources, and decreased opportunity for advancement in the workplace.

A. Forty percent of caregivers report having to use their savings to provide care needed for their loved one.
B. Forty percent of caregivers reported cutting back on discretionary spending, while 38% reported cutting back on necessary spending.
C. Nearly one third of caregivers report that caregiving is too expensive. Expenses incurred by caregivers include lost time at work, decreased income, and cost of direct care, including transportation, daily needs such as food and supplies, and medical expenditures. The implications of such expenditures are increased burden for the caregiver and fewer resources for caregiving in the community. Lai (2012) found that financial implications were the largest correlating factor for increased caregiving burden.

Caregiver Health

Caregiver health is another concern that APRNs should consider when assisting those who are IC. Hoffman, Lee, and Mendez-Luck (2012) found that caregivers engage in fewer health-promoting activities and more negative health behaviors than their peer noncaregivers.

A. Negative health behaviors include cigarette smoking, drinking regular sodas, and eating fast foods. These findings suggest that the stress associated with caregiving may lead to negative health behaviors, and the demand of caregiving may decrease the opportunity for caregivers to attend to their own health needs.
B. Common health-related sequelae of caregiving include decreased sleep quality, fatigue, poor eating habits, and less exercise.
C. Caregivers are also at risk for decreased psychological well-being. Stress, depression, and social isolation are reported by many caregivers.

Providers' Assistance With the Caregiver

APRNs must actively solicit information about the health and well-being of caregivers, the caregiving requirements, and the burden associated with providing care. This conversation should be a part of routine patient encounters and it can be as easy as asking the question, "Are you a caregiver?"

A. Once the caregiving role has been identified, then APRNs can assess the positive and negative outcomes of caregiving. An integral understanding for the APRN to possess is that the caregiver and care recipient are a unit. The implications are that malfunction of either in this unit can and likely will lead to poor outcomes.
B. Caregivers often report being inadequately prepared for the caregiving role. A particularly vulnerable time for this preparation is during transitions of care. There is a lack of structure and guidance from the medical community to the caregiver when care is being transitioned from a formal caregiving environment to the informal caregiving environment.
C. Caregivers are often engaged at the point of discharge. Therefore, caregivers are informed of a patient's discharge from a facility without planning. Caregivers report frustration and lack of information in providing quality, often technical, care. The high rate of hospital readmission for older adults speaks to this lack of preparation for care provided post-discharge. Caregivers need information, support, and respite.
D. APRNs should seek to engage the caregiver by asking about their frustrations, the caregiving demands, and their preparation for providing the needed care. Common caregiver frustrations include:
   1. Lack of knowledge on how to access resources
   2. How to provide technical care
   3. How to respond to the care recipient's emotional needs
   4. How to anticipate future needs.
E. The APRN will need to have knowledge of the patient in order to adequately inform the caregiver. One goal of this assessment is to collaborate with the caregiver in order to respond to care recipient needs, train caregivers on technical aspects of care, and provide anticipatory guidance for the trajectory of the illness.
F. APRNs should also assess the well-being of the caregiver. There are several tools to assist in assessing the caregiver.
   1. Caregivers should be asked about their basic needs such as sleep, diet, health care, and emotional support.
   2. Caregivers should be asked about their social support networks and if these social supports are adequate. This assessment can be as simple as asking if the caregiver is receiving adequate support or as complex as administering a measurement tool.
   3. Caregivers should be assessed for QOL, stress, and depression. QOL and caregiver burden measurement tools are widely available. It is important for APRNs to use this information to plan tailored interventions that will assist the caregiver.

Providers' Response to Caregiver Needs

A. One strategy that may prove to be beneficial is for medical providers to be aware of assistive technology that will improve the provision of care.
B. 45% of IC used technology to facilitate care, including electronic mobility devices, safety alarms, personal electronic health records, and electronic communication with health care providers.
C. Another resource that health care providers need to identify and promote are health care policies and programs that lessen the burdens of providing care. Health care policies utilized by IC included personal tax credit (56%), a voucher program to pay minimum wage for care provided (30%), and respite services (26%).

Caregiver Resources

Caregiver resources are becoming more widely available. As Medicare and other reimbursement agencies continue to strive to decrease the readmission rates and decrease the cost of care, more attention will be paid to successful interventions that improve the health and well-being of the caregiver and recipient.

A. Interventions that have been most successful include efforts to address physical, emotional, spiritual, and social domains.
B. Potential community resources include the primary care location, respite services, home aid services, palliative care (PC), social services, and support groups.

C. The primary care location is an often overlooked resource; however, this is the ideal site for forming the collaborative connection that will serve the caregiver and care recipient.
D. Respite services may be available through care alliances and organizations. Home aide services may be available to assist the care recipient with activities of daily living; many are utilized through local home health agencies.
E. PC is helpful when learning about how to manage symptoms.
F. Social services may be of assistance to determine if local programs such as Meals on Wheels, as well as financial or housing assistance, are appropriate.
G. Support groups are effective for sharing experiences, problem solving, and building a community of support. There are also several caregiver informational sites accessed by the Internet including the Family Caregiver Alliance (www.caregiver.org) and the National Alliance for Caregiving (www.caregiving.org).

Knowing the impact of family and environment is not new to nursing. Nurses have long acknowledged the significant impact of holistic care that includes not only the patient but those people and places important to the patient. Research about caregiving has been ongoing for decades. The impact, toll, and benefit of caregiving are well documented. What is changing is that reimbursement for care is dependent on quality measures, and these quality measures will make their way measuring the effectiveness of caregiving. APRNs are poised to expand their role to empowering caregivers by providing knowledge, facilitating respite, and supporting caregivers.

Advance Directives

Decision making is an integral concept in health care and has ethical roots. The ethical principle of patient autonomy should be considered when thinking about the role and value of advance directives. Older adults may face a time in which they are unable to make both financial and health care decisions. This creates an ethical dilemma for family members and health care providers. Advance directives should give insight into what the elder would have chosen if he or she could still make decisions. The APRN will need to be familiar with state laws and facility regulations concerning advance directives.

Advance directives are formal documents that enable older adults to make decisions about their future health care when they are no longer capable of making these decisions. The Patient Self-Determination Act of 1990 required that hospitals and other health care facilities provide patients with information on the purpose, execution, and documentation of an advance directive for all patients of the facility. Despite this, many older adults do not have an advance directive. Barriers to completing an advance directive are present for older adults and health care providers. Barriers for older adults include lack of knowledge, fear of burdening family members, and desire to have the health care provider initiate the conversation about advance care planning. Barriers for health care providers include lack of time during an office visit and discomfort in initiating the conversation about advance care planning.

Types of Advance Directives

Decision Making

Decision making includes both financial and health care determinations. **Adults are deemed capable of making decisions until they are proven to be incompetent. The determination of competency is a legal one and must be made by a judge.** Concerned parties may petition the court for a conservatorship (financial) or guardianship (health care) hearing. The court will then investigate; if the older adult is deemed unable to make decisions, then the court will appoint a conservator or a guardian to make decisions regarding finances, health care, or both. **It is important to know the difference between advance directives and conservatorship (guardianship); a primary difference is that the patients determine who will be making decisions on their behalf when executing advance directives.** If there is no advance directive, and the patient is no longer capable of making decisions, then the court may have to decide who will make the decisions for the incapacitated adult.

Power of Attorney

Financial decisions include paying bills, make purchases, and selling, purchasing, or managing assets. **Health care decisions include treatment decisions, EOL care, obtaining medical records, and many others. A competent adult has the option of creating a power of attorney or a durable power of attorney for financial and health care decisions. For both the power of attorney and durable power of attorney, the competent adult selects an agent who will make decisions.**

A. The power of attorney is collaboration between the competent adult and the agent.
   1. The patients retain the rights to make decisions on their own behalf. If the competent adult is subsequently determined to be incompetent, then the power of attorney is often no longer valid and operational.
   2. If the competent adult created a durable power of attorney and is subsequently determined to be incompetent, then the durable power of attorney is still valid and operational. It is important to note that an agent named in a power of attorney, or durable power of attorney, specifically for health care or financial decisions

and not both may be limited in his or her ability to make some decisions. For example, an agent of a financial durable power of attorney may not be able to make health care decisions based on this document alone. A specific document for health care, or financial, decisions must be executed to name an agent for making decisions. These documents may not be interchangeable.

3. It is also important to remember that the rights granted to an agent by the power of attorney or durable power of attorney end when the incapacitated adult dies. Therefore, an agent cannot make decisions about assets or obtain medical records for a deceased person. These rights are granted to the person, or agent, named as the executor of the person's estate.

Living Will

A living will is a document created by a competent adult that specifies what treatment or medical decisions are preferred in the event that the adult becomes unable to make decisions.

A. This document is specific and will likely include preferences for resuscitation, intravenous hydration and nutrition, ventilator support, pain management, and organ donation.
B. The benefit of the document is to assist family members and medical providers in making very difficult decisions by making the wishes of the competent adult known to all parties. However, this document is not always recognized as a legally binding decision.
C. A living will does not name an agent to make health care decisions. A health care power of attorney may be needed in addition to the living will if the living will is not recognized as a legally binding document.
D. The value of a living will should not be understated. The living will acts as a guide to assist decision makers when making very challenging and emotionally charged decisions on the behalf of the loved one.

Do-Not-Resuscitate Orders

A do-not-resuscitate (DNR) order is written by a medical provider in observance of the patient's wishes for EOL care. A competent adult, or the agent for an incompetent adult, can make this decision and communicate it to the medical provider. The order is written by the medical provider and communicated to staff to alert all that the person does not wish to have cardiopulmonary resuscitation (CPR) started should his or her heart or breathing stop. **In the absence of a DNR order, health care personnel may be required to start resuscitation efforts. A living will, in which a competent adult has expressed wishes against resuscitation, does not take the place of a written DNR order.**

MOST Form

Medical orders for the scope of treatment (MOST) forms are written orders that direct medical care based on the patient's wishes. The MOST form is different from a living will because the MOST form is signed by the medical provider and acts as orders to direct patient care. Items included on a MOST form include CPR, antibiotics, fluid, and nutrition. MOST forms are specific, created between the provider and the patient and signed by both parties. The benefit of the MOST form is that the actions and decisions that the patient and their agent have agreed upon are formalized as medical orders.

Resources for Creating an Advance Directive

Once a competent adult has made the decision to execute an advance directive, he or she may need assistance in creating the documents. Advance directives can be created without legal representation. There are many online resources available, including AARP, Caringinfo.org, and state bar associations or agencies for aging. It is important for competent adults to have a conversation with family members or others who may serve as agents to ensure that the agent is willing and able to execute the decisions of the competent adult. The optimal time for such discussions is before a medical condition threatens to incapacitate a person; however, any discussion is better than none. APRNs can assist their patients by initiating the conversation, answering questions, and providing resources.

Overcoming Barriers

Barriers can be characterized as barriers to creation of an advance directive and barriers to implementation of the advance directive. Spoelhof and Elliot (2012) described completion barriers as patient and provider limitations.

A. Patients may have a lack of interest, lack of knowledge, fear of burdening family members, and social isolation. These barriers are aptly addressed by initiating conversations at an early stage, before an illness has occurred. Patients can be approached and asked about their wishes for care should they become incapacitated during a wellness visit, or when discussing screenings for illnesses. This is a nonthreatening time that is well suited for information sharing.
B. Provider barriers include lack of time, lack of reimbursement, and discomfort with the topic. Hoffman, Lee, and Mendez-Luck (2012) found that patients desire to have this discussion with health care providers. In addition, health care providers report greater satisfaction when care is congruent with patient wishes.
C. Barriers to implementation include nonspecific language in the advance directive, agent issues, and advance directive accessibility.

1. The language in an advance directive should be specific and include the patient's wishes for CPR, fluid, and nutrition.
2. An advance directive is also more useful if it is clear in what is meant by incapacitation, as language can make this a difficult determination. For example, it is much clearer to state that the advance directive takes effect in the event of cardiac arrest rather than in the event of no hope for recovery.
3. Agents will need to know that they have been named as health care proxy and to know the wishes of the patient.
4. Advance directives, once completed, should be easily located. The patient, agent, and medical providers should have a copy of all documents. Patients should keep copies of their advance directives in an easily obtainable location at their residence.

There are strategies to help patients and medical providers in completing the process of discussing, creating, and executing advance directives. Interactive, or group, interventions have been more successful than individual encounters for educating on the value and role of advance directives. Having ongoing discussions about the goals of care once a terminal or progressive illness has occurred is another effective means of educating patients and their health care agents. Another strategy is the use of advance directive facilitators to introduce and educate communities. A Values History form may be helpful in assisting the patient to consider his or her own feelings and initiate conversations with potential health care agents. The Values History form was created by the Institute of Public Law and is available online. It is not a substitute for a living will or power of attorney; however, it is a complementary document that examines one's personal beliefs in such a way as to help surrogate decision makers during challenging and emotional EOL decision making.

Palliative Care

PC encompasses a philosophy focused on the prevention and relief of suffering. The goal of PC is to improve QOL for both the patient and family. This includes a highly structured multidisciplinary approach, providing holistic care, while incorporating physical, psychosocial, spiritual, and cultural aspects of care. Communication is essential for collaboration focus on the goals of the patient and family and to ensure dignity at a crucial point of the patient's life. PC is important regardless of the stage of disease. PC is best utilized at the beginning stages and throughout the stages of a serious medical condition, along with aggressive treatment measures. PC does not require the patient to have a DNR or a do-not-intubate (DNI) status.

In the United States, the average life expectancy is 78 years. Approximately 40% of the elderly population has two or more chronic medical conditions. These conditions limit their QOL, render them susceptible to complications including new illnesses, require more frequent hospitalization, and add to their symptom burden. Elderly patients also require a higher level of care provided by family and caregivers.

Special Considerations

All hospice is PC but not all PC is hospice. Hospice, by definition, means a patient must have a terminal diagnosis with a life expectancy of 6 months or less if the disease runs its normal course. Hospice is a Medicare-offered benefit. The following are useful references regarding hospice.

A. Centers for Medicare & Medicaid Services (CMS) guideline for hospice benefit: www.cms.gov/Regulations-and-Guidance/Guidance/Manuals/downloads/bp102c09.pdf
B. Patient teaching handout presented by Medicare: www.medicare.gov/publications/Pubs/pdf/02154.pdf

Best practice reveals seriously ill patients who receive early PC interventions have better management of symptoms, reduced incidence of depression, reduced costs, and survive longer with a better QOL. Nationally, patients are referred to hospice late in the disease trajectory. Patients who have early PC interventions are referred to hospice services in an appropriate time frame.

Key Factors of Care in the Elderly Patient at the EOL

Clear explanation of the plan of care, patient and family wishes, and provision of emotional support are all necessary aspects of care in the elderly patient. Many times children taking care of parents or elder spouses are also taking care of their long-time partners. This adds a level of personal stress to the already emotionally burdensome situation. The following are foundational points to consider when caring for an elderly patient and family at the EOL.

Physical Comfort

A. Proper pain and symptom management: Many times patients are afraid to report pain or other symptoms. Clinicians are afraid to treat elderly patients and to overmedicate; thus, patients do not get adequate pain and symptom management.
B. Decreasing mobility, physical discomfort, and pain may cause difficulty with sitting, standing, and walking. The patient may be embarrassed to ask for general assistance in completing ADL. The more physical mobility decreases, the fewer tasks a person is able to complete independently, and the more the person is dependent on others.

Decision Making

A. Self-determination, also known as autonomy, respects the moral and legal rights of persons with decisional capacity to determine what will be done with their own person.
B. Respect of wishes: Clinicians may have difficulty respecting the wishes of the patient when family has other wishes.
C. Involvement of family/caregiver—Involve the patient, family, and caregiver all together in the decision-making process. It helps for the family and caregivers to hear the patient's request, wishes, and perspective. Many times if the family and caregivers understand and know what the patient wants the decision-making process is much easier for all involved to complete and accept.
D. Clear documentation of goals of care: Guide the patient and family through the goals of the care conversation. Clearly document and communicate the goals to the interdisciplinary group, especially consistency of care, and ensure the patient and families are supported in the decisions that have been reached.

Education

A. Discuss progression of the disease.
B. Explain reasons for medication use, risk versus benefit, and side effects.
C. Give treatment options: Provide an honest discussion of the risk versus benefit for each treatment option.
D. Identify resources available: Utilize the social worker and case manager on the interdisciplinary team (IDT). There are many community resources available for patients. Understanding what types of resources a patient or family may need includes having enough resources for food, medication, housing, and caregiver assistance.
E. Keep the education, goals, and plan centered on the patient and on the family's goals of care. This is very challenging but necessary to build a trusting relationship and validate the individual experience.

Emotional Support

A. Understanding relationship dynamics
B. Social isolation due to effects of their disease process
C. Caregiver fatigue
D. Financial burden
E. Loss of identity

Interdisciplinary Collaborative Practice

The PC IDT may include the clinician, nurse, aide, pharmacist, physical therapist, and nutritionist working as a complementary unit. The IDT works together to address the physical, social, spiritual, and psychological symptoms of patients with serious or life-threatening illness and their families' issues. IDT groups work to improve physical symptoms such as pain, nausea/vomiting, decreased mobility, incontinence, weakness, shortness of breath (SOB), and other distressful symptoms. The goal is always focused on improving patient and family QOL.

The IDT team's initial and regular reassessment of psychological status is imperative, along with continued evolution of treatment methods. The IDT team works collaboratively with psychological and psychiatric team members to address depression, anxiety, delirium, and cognitive impairment as they directly impact patients with serious or life-threatening illness. Recognition of the need for continued social assessment and support for the PC patient and family includes:

A. Initiate support services in a timely manner.
B. Involve case management in assisting with availability of community services, medication issues, financial concerns, or placement concerns.
C. Involve social workers in assisting with availability of community services, counseling, emotional support, and identifying barriers to care.
D. Utilize volunteers to provide social interaction and caregiver relief.
E. Recognition of the cultural implications of care is an important aspect of the patient and family IDT assessment. Each individual has different cultural implications related to his or her specific care. Components of the cultural assessment include:
   1. Birthplace—What is the person's place of birth, and what implication might this have on the patient's care?
   2. Ethnic identity
   3. Community—How does the patient relate to his or her community?
   4. Decision making—Who is the decision maker for the individual: self, spouse, another person?
   5. Language of communication—Does language create a barrier? Consider things like eye contact, gender, position, body language.
   6. Religion or spirituality—How do religion and spirituality specifically affect the individual's plan of care?
   7. Food preferences or prohibitions
   8. Economic situation—Can patients afford medications, food, caregivers? Financial crisis is a major concern at EOL in the elderly population, of whom many have a fixed income.
   9. Health beliefs and practices regarding death, grief, pain, traditional therapies, care of the body, organ donation, caregiver specifications.
      a. Does the patient believe painful suffering is required?
      b. Does the female patient require a female clinician?

c. Is the patient "refusing" an amputation of a part of the body (e.g., gangrenous toe) because the body has to remain intact in his or her culture?

F. Spirituality does not necessarily focus strictly on religion or religious practices but rather promotes an individual's sense of well-being. Collaborative assessment for spiritual distress is completed by the IDT team. Symptoms of spiritual distress include:
1. Feelings of abandonment
2. Anger
3. Feelings of betrayal or mistrust
4. Despair
5. Fear
6. Guilt
7. Regret
8. Sorrow or remorse
9. Depression

G. A chaplain can be an invaluable resource to help the patient focus on spiritual aspects of care, provide support, and allow for a neutral conversation and reminiscence through life's journey.

Physical Aspects of Care

Pain Management

A. Pain is the most common symptom associated with PC. Key concepts of pain management include the subjective nature of pain, an understanding that the symptom may not solely be physical in nature, and knowledge that pain is an experience that greatly affects the whole family unit.

B. Pain is a change to the nervous system and is also reflective of the individual's past pain experiences, making the pain an emotional as well as a physical experience. "Pain is an unpleasant sensory and emotional experience associated with actual or potential tissue damage, or described in terms of such damage" (International Association for the Study of Pain [IASP] definition www.iasp-pain.org/Content/NaviationMenu/GeneralResourceLinks/PainDefinitions/Default.htm). At the EOL, many individuals have difficulty or are unable to communicate their pain. This occurs for several different reasons such as delirium, dementia, aphasia, motor weakness, language barriers, and other factors. Patients who cannot verbally express pain may still be having pain and still require treatment. Often these individuals are either not treated or are inadequately managed for pain.

C. The older adult is at risk for inappropriate pain management. It is estimated that between 25% and 45% of older patients who live in communities do not receive adequate pain management. Research presents several reasons elderly individuals continue to have untreated, undertreated, or unrecognized pain, including an atypical presentation, failure to report, chronic pain, cognitive impairments, lack of clinician knowledge, and fear.

D. Not all pain is treated the same. In order to treat pain appropriately, one must first understand the different types of pain. What follows are different types of pain, with general definitions, and how patients typically describe them.
1. Acute pain
   a. Identified event/acute injury.
   b. Clinically described as pain lasting less than 1 month
2. Chronic pain
   a. The cause of chronic pain may not be easily identified.
   b. Pain persists longer than 1 month.
3. Acute on chronic
   a. Some pain syndromes consist of chronic pain with acute exacerbations or pain crisis.
4. Nociceptive
   a. Usually related to damage to bones, soft tissues, or internal organs
   b. Somatic pain—aching, throbbing
   c. Visceral pain—squeezing, cramping
5. Neuropathic
   a. Usually related to damage of the nervous system
   b. Complaints of burning, tingling, shooting pain

E. Substance abuse issues: 70% to 90% of patients with advanced disease experience pain. The American Pain Society (APS) also reports patients with a pain score of greater than or equal to a "4" on a standard pain scale. This report has great implications for QOL. Assessment of pain is imperative. Pain assessment begins with an in-depth history.
1. History
   a. Identify which drugs the patient has already tried, explain whether these were effective, and state what adverse effect resulted from use.
   b. What medication was prescribed and is it what the patient is actually taking? Compare the patient's information with the family's information. Discrepancies do not always mean noncompliance; there may be a lack of understanding of the medication, financial reasons, fear, or a problem with memory.
   c. Ask patients about over-the-counter medications, recreational drugs, alcohol, and herbal products.
   d. Involve family in conversations. They may have additional or different views/information than that of the patient.
   e. What types of cultural influences on pain exist?
   f. Identify the type of pain.
2. Physical assessment of pain
   a. Identify specific site of pain if possible.
   b. Character of pain: Ask patient to describe pain.

c. Onset: When did the pain begin?
d. Duration and frequency: How long does it last, how often does the pain occur?
e. Exacerbating factors: What makes the pain worse?
f. Associated factors: What symptoms occur with the pain? Examples are anxiety, fear, nausea.
g. Alleviating factors: What makes the pain better? Examples are rest, medication, relaxation, massage.
h. Emotional state: Does the patient feel frustrated, anxious, fearful, or depressed?
i. Existential distress: Does the patient have spiritual distress? Does the patient need to rectify a relationship with a family member?
j. Nonverbal pain cues
   i. Vocal complaints: sighs, gasps, moans, groans, cries
   ii. Facial grimaces/winces, furrowed brow, narrowed eyes, clenched teeth, tightened lips, jaw dropped or clenched, distorted expressions
   iii. Restlessness: constant or intermittent shifting of positions, changes in behavior, combativeness, constant hand motion
k. Physiological cues: tachycardia, tachypnea, hypertension, diaphoresis, insomnia, hyperreflexia, nausea, diarrhea, dilated pupils, anorexia, vasoconstriction, cool extremities
l. Treatment of perceived pain is considered a therapeutic intervention. Treat pain before a procedure is initiated; this could be something as general as turning/repositioning, or bathing at EOL. Instruct families or other caregivers about the importance of proper pain management regarding perceived pain.

3. Pharmacology: **Pharmacological interventions must be tailored to the individual and use the rule "start low and go slow."**
   a. Acetaminophen
      i. Safest for long-term use in elderly
      ii. Good for mild to moderate pain
      iii. May be used in conjunction with opioids: caution that some medications already contain acetaminophen
      iv. Avoid in patients with renal or hepatic insufficiency or alcohol dependence
      v. Maximum daily dose 3 g in 24 hours
   b. Nonsteroidal anti-inflammatory drugs (NSAIDs)
      i. Can be initial therapy for mild to moderate pain
      ii. Adjunct for opioids and nonopioids; when used concurrently, lower doses of opioid may be used
      iii. Useful for the treatment of nociceptive pain
      iv. Should be taken in conjunction with food
      v. Increased risk of gastrointestinal ulceration, renal dysfunction, and impaired platelet aggregation in long-term use
      vi. Use with caution in patients with history of ulcer disease.
   c. Opioids
      i. Used for moderate to severe pain
      ii. Begin with morphine, hypdomorphone, or oxycodone as these medications are easier to titrate appropriately and have fewer side effects.
      iii. Morphine
         1) Patients should be carefully monitored for signs and symptoms of sedation and confusion.
         2) Labs should be closely monitored for renal function.
         3) Morphine should not be used in patients with renal impairment.
         4) Signs of morphine metabolite build-up include sedation, confusion, and respiratory depression. These signs will appear after a few days of therapy; they are not immediate signs. If the signs of metabolite build-up appear, the opioid should be changed.
      iv. Hydromorphone
         1) Metabolite build-up leads to myoclonus, hyperalgesia, and seizures.
         2) Metabolite build-up is most prevalent in patients with renal failure.
         3) Hydromorphine is 1:3 times more potent than morphine.
      v. Oxycodone
         1) Is a synthetic opioid
         2) Long acting and immediate release preparations available
         3) Medication is expensive and may be cost prohibitive for some patients.
         4) 1.5 times more potent than morphine
      vi. Fentanyl
         1) Available in transdermal form, which is useful when patients cannot swallow or have issues with intractable nausea/vomiting
         2) Fever, cachexia, obesity, and ascites will significantly affect absorption of the medication.
         3) **Fentanyl is approximately 80 times more potent than morphine. Do not use Fentanyl on opioid-naïve patients.**

4) Therapy must be monitored closely, and clear education must be provided to patients and family.
5) Therapeutic effects do not begin until 12 hours after initiation.
6) When using long-acting transdermal fentanyl, ensure the patient has adequate medication and plan for breakthrough pain medication.

4. Nonpharmacological interventions for pain
   a. When determining a plan of care for pain management, both pharmacological and nonpharmacological interventions should be incorporated. The plan of care should be tailored to both and meet the needs of the patient and family. Non-pharmacological interventions include:
      i. Massage: This can be completed by a family member or a caregiver. This can increase the therapeutic relationship and provide a sense of control for the family.
      ii. Acupuncture
      iii. Tai chi
      iv. Distraction: This can be anything that distracts; reading, TV, something that is enjoyed.
      v. Relaxation: Teaching deep-breathing techniques can be very useful for both the patient and family and can be completed together.
      vi. Music therapy
      vii. Guided imagery
5. Diagnostic testing
   a. Always evaluate whether tests should be done based on the patient and family goals.
   b. Laboratory data, including complete blood count (CBC) with differential, complete metabolic profile (CMP), and urinalysis labs are useful as a baseline evaluation.
      i. With narcotic use, renal function should be evaluated initially and ongoing.
   c. Radiological testing as indicated
6. Differential diagnosis for pain
   a. Infection
   b. Depression
   c. Anxiety
   d. Constipation
7. Plan
   a. The National Comprehensive Cancer Network (NCCN) has outlined the following goals when assessing and managing pain.
      i. Pain will be controlled at an acceptable level for both the patient and the family.
      ii. Distress caused by pain will be decreased for both the patient and the family.
      iii. The patient will have a sense of control.
      iv. QOL will be optimized for both the patient and family
      v. An interdisciplinary care team can be utilized.
      vi. Assessment is regular and ongoing.
      vii. Identify and address barriers to effective pain management.
      viii. For controlled substances, implement a risk-management plan.
      ix. Refer patients to providers with specialized skills (IDT).
         1) PC
         2) Pain management
         3) Pharmacy for medication management
         4) Physical therapy to promote improved QOL if applicable to goals of care
         5) Occupational therapy to promote improved QOL if applicable to goals of care
         6) Chaplain for existential pain

Symptom Management

Anxiety

A. Anxiety is a common symptom and occurs in approximately 70% of hospice patients. It is often a predisposing factor to another symptom such as pain or SOB.
   1. Causes of anxiety
      a. Fear
      b. Pain—current or unresolved
      c. SOB
      d. Past experiences
      e. Situation
      f. Preexisting anxiety disorder
      g. Delirium
      h. Anticipatory grief
      i. Anxiety has a significant relationship with advance lung disease and periods of hypoxia
      j. Associated with a fear of death
      k. Associated with concerns about religious beliefs, spiritual issues, and existential matters.
   2. Clinical characteristics
      a. Pathological anxiety
         i. Takes on a "life of its own"
         ii. Increases in intensity that exceeds a patient's ability to cope
         iii. Dread or intense worry
         iv. Tension, jitteriness, or restlessness
         v. Treatment nonadherence, social withdrawal, and avoidance

vi. Inability to cope or relax
vii. Symptoms of pathological anxiety are complicated and often exacerbated by insomnia, depression, fatigue, gastrointestinal upset, dyspnea, pain, and dysphagia.

3. Assessment
   a. Begin with a complete history. Identify cause of anxiety if possible.
      i. Understand patient's disease process and progression. Remember anxiety is often complicated by another symptom. Identify disease processes in which symptoms may be present that may produce anxiety: CHF, COPD, cancer, anemia.
      ii. Does the patient have a history of psychological issues?
      iii. Identify key words during conversation such as fear, concern, scared, and worried.
      iv. Utilize tools to help assess anxiety, including the four-item Patient Health Questionnaire for Depression and Anxiety (PHQ-4) available at www.phqscreeners.com/pdfs/08_PHQ-4/English.pdf or the Hospital Anxiety and Depression Scale (HADS) available at: www.abiebr.com/node/410.
      v. Medications such as albuterol and steroids increase anxiety.
      vi. New symptoms
      vii. Patient's knowledge of disease process and progression
      viii. Previous health care and illness experiences both positive and negative
      ix. Evaluate and understand if there are any patterns of the patient's anxiety to determine if there is a cause and effect.
      x. Identify underlying cause of anxiety.
         1) Physical symptoms: inability to sit still, jitteriness, depression, restlessness
         2) Emotional symptoms: edginess, feelings of impending doom, terror
         3) Cognitive difficulties: apprehension, dread, fear, obsession, uncertainty, worry
         4) Behavioral problems: avoidance, compulsions, or psychomotor agitation
         5) Autonomic symptoms: diaphoresis, diarrhea, nausea, dizziness, tachycardia, or tachypnea
4. Diagnostic/laboratory tests: electrolytes, blood cell counts, relevant hormones, toxicology as indicated.
5. Always evaluate diagnostic testing per patient's plan and goals of care.
6. Treatment is based on foundation of the anxiety.
7. **Nonpharmacologic treatment is always the first-line treatment for anxiety.**
   a. Assess and monitor for anxiety.
   b. Offer emotional support.
   c. Reassure when appropriate.
   d. Assess treatment response and side effects frequently.
   e. Provide maximum resolution of anxiety as a goal.
   f. Educate the patient and families on anxiety and treatments.
   g. Provide cognitive and behavioral therapy, relaxation, and distraction.
   h. Encourage chaplaincy if there are spiritual and existential concerns.
   i. Identify underlying cause.
8. **Pharmacologic treatment for anxiety: Consider the individual patient when treating anxiety with medications using the rule "start low and go slow."**
   a. Lorazepam (Ativan) 0.5 mg two to three times a day scheduled as needed. Maximum daily dose is 10 mg per day. May produce paradoxical agitation in elderly, demented, or brain injury patients. Useful to try a small test dose first to see how patient will react to medication. Ativan is short-acting and produces no active metabolites. It is best absorbed when given parenterally.
   b. Haloperidol (Haldol) 0.5 to 1.0 mg two to three times a day scheduled or as needed. Useful if patient is anxious and is unable to tolerate benzodiazepines. May produce extrapyramidal symptoms, including akathisia.
   c. Alprazolam (Xanax) 0.25 mg twice a day scheduled or as needed. Maximum daily dose of 6 mg/day.
   d. Other anxiety medications that may be beneficial include diazepam (Valium), chlorpromazine (thorazine), olanzapine (Zyprexa), and quetiapine (Seroquel).
9. Plan
   a. Complete a detailed history and physical examination.
   b. Discern if the cause of anxiety is psychological or physiological.
   c. If fear is the cause, provide education and reassurance. Do not ignore. Validate and address the concern so that the patient can directly deal with the fear.
   d. Treat the underlying illness or symptom.
   e. Control both the underlying symptom and the anxiety.
   f. Do not assume that anxiety is inevitable and unavoidable.
   g. Educate both the patient and family.

h. Ensure that the goals of the patient and the family are discussed, clear, and followed.
i. Assess and reassess.

10. Differential diagnosis
    a. Depression
    b. Confusion
    c. Delirium
    d. Dementia
11. Potential complications
    a. Difficulty making decisions
    b. Confusion
    c. Inability to intake information
    d. Agitation
    e. Difficulty controlling symptoms

Delirium

A. Delirium can be classified in two different ways: Either as hyperactive or agitated, or hypoactive delirium. Delirium is an acute change in the level of arousal. Accompanying characteristics include altered sleep and wake cycles, mumbling speech, memory and attention disturbances, perceptual disturbances often with delusions, and hallucinations.

1. Clinical characteristics
   a. Clouding of consciousness
   b. Altered ability to maintain attention
   c. Impairment of cognitive function
   d. Daytime sleepiness and nighttime agitation or restlessness
   e. Fluctuation of symptoms by the day or hour
2. Physical examination should be performed to evaluate delirum
3. Useful assessment tool: Delirium Assessment Tool for EOL: **CHIMBOP**
   a. **C**–Constipation
   b. **H**–Hypovolemia, hypoglycemia
   c. **I**–Infection
   d. **M**–Medication withdrawal or side effects
   e. **B**–Bladder, catheter, bladder outlet obstruction, urinary retention
   f. **O**–Oxygen deficiency
   g. **P**–Pain
4. Nonpharmacologic treatments
   a. Identify possible cause of delirium and treat if indicated and part of the plan of care.
   b. Establish safe, soothing, quiet environment.
   c. Decrease stimuli, specifically at night; lights; sounds; and interactions. If in a hospital or facility setting, combine treatments as much as possible.
   d. Ask relatives/friends/visitors to stay by patient for comfort or leave to decrease stimuli.
   e. Make frequent reminders of time and place to reorient if appropriate.
   f. Educate caregivers about delirium, causes, and plan for treatment.
5. Pharmacologic treatments
   a. The agent of choice for most EOL patients with delirium is haloperidol (Haldol).
      i. Haldol has a favorable side-effect profile and can be administered safely both orally and parenterally.
      ii. Starting doses are 0.5 to 1.0 mg orally or IV. Use with caution and base medications on individual patient needs.
      iii. **BLACK BOX Warning, which is a strict warning established by the FDA: Haloperidol is not approved for dementia-related psychosis due to increased mortality in elderly dementia patients on conventional or atypical antipsychotics. Most deaths were due to cardiovascular or infectious events.**
   b. Benzodiazepines should be avoided unless the source of the delirium has been identified as alcohol-sedative drug withdrawal. Benzodiazepines may also be useful when severe agitation is uncontrolled by a neuroleptic medication. Benzodiazepines can cause paradoxical worsening of confusion.
   c. Chlorpromazine (Thorazine) has also been used for dying patients with terminal delirium and may also be useful as an antiemetic. However, that may have higher incidence of side effects such as sedation and hypotension.
   d. Olanzapine (Zyprexa), quetiapine (Seroquel), or risperidone (Risperdal) are also used to treat delirium and are newer atypical neuroleptics. These medications are useful in the treatment of confusion and may be a drug of choice with Parkinson's.
6. Diagnostic tests/evaluation
   a. The degree of workup to seek the cause of delirium is determined by understanding the disease trajectory and overall goals of care.
   b. Always evaluate for the reversible cause of delirium.
   c. Nonpharmacologic treatments should always be used in delirium management.
7. Plan
   a. The most important initial step is to determine the plan and goal of care.
   b. Determine the cause of the delirium.
   c. Determine if the cause is reversible.
   d. Treat the cause if appropriate to the goals of care.
   e. Educate and provide nonpharmacologic treatments.
   f. Provide proper individualized medications
   g. Provide education and support for patient and family.

Dyspnea or SOB

A. Dyspnea is a very distressful symptom defined as distressing SOB or abnormal breathing and is frequently referred to as a feeling of "breathlessness." Dyspnea is a subjective experience of breathing and is described as one of the most distressful symptoms. It is common in many EOL and serious illnesses such as lung disease, stroke, end-stage renal disease, heart disease, dementia, and cancers. Dyspnea can have severe effects on QOL for both the patient and family.
   1. Clinical characteristics
      a. Dyspnea can have a severe effect on functional status, affecting the person's ability to complete ADL.
      b. Breath sounds vary depending on the disease process.
      c. Many factors improve or worsen symptoms: notably, pain, anxiety, movement, and rest.
      d. Dyspnea is a subjective report and a different experience for each individual
   2. Physical examination: evaluate for the following:
      a. Jugular vein distension (JVD)
      b. Bilateral crackles
      c. Respiratory rate and depth
      d. Use of accessory muscles
      e. Does the individual have pain with respiratory movement?
      f. Pursed-lip breathing
      g. Cyanosis
      h. Is the individual unable to speak or only able to speak a few words, and then has to rest to breathe?
      i. Heart rate greater than 90
      j. Respiratory rate greater than 22
      k. Restless or nonpurposeful movements, particularly at EOL or with a change in level of alertness
      l. Abdomen moves in on inspirations; often you can see how hard a patient is working to breathe.
      m. Accessory muscle use
      n. Rise in clavicles during inspiration
      o. Grunting at end of expiration
      p. Guttural sound
      q. Nasal flaring, which is involuntary movement of the nares with breathing
      r. A look of fear
      s. Useful dyspnea scale for assessing SOB
         i. A Respiratory Distress Observation Scale for Patients Unable to Self-Report Dyspnea: homecareinformation.net/handouts/hen/Respiratory_Distress_Observation_Scale.pdf
   3. Common complaints
      a. Suffocation
      b. Inability to breathe
      c. Fear
      d. Impending doom
   4. Other signs and symptoms
      a. Anxiety
      b. Cachexia
      c. Depression
      d. Tachycardia
      e. Pain
   5. Pharmacologic treatment
      a. Medications
         i. Opioids are the first-line treatment for dyspnea. Opioids alter the patient's awareness of SOB, which in turn leads to the lessening of suffering.
         ii. Benzodiazepines may be used as an adjunct medication if anxiety is present with dyspnea. May also be used when opioid medication is not sufficient to treat the feelings of breathlessness.
         iii. In rare cases palliative sedation may be necessary to relieve the symptoms of dyspnea at the EOL. This is only used when all other treatment options have been exhausted and the patient continues to have dyspnea.
      b. Nonpharmacologic treatment for dyspnea
         i. Oxygen
         ii. Counseling
         iii. Teach pursed-lip breathing
         iv. Energy conservation
         v. Elevate head of bed (HOB)
         vi. Good oral care
         vii. Calm, cool, relaxed environment
         viii. Use of fans with movement of cool air reduces the awareness of dyspnea.
         ix. Muscle relaxation
         x. Teach activity grouping to conserve energy
         xi. Small frequent meals to conserve energy
      c. Potential complications
         i. Uncontrolled symptoms
         ii. Cyclical process: SOB produces anxiety which increases SOB, which increases anxiety, which increases SOB and continues in a cyclical motion unless treated appropriately.
         iii. Infection
         iv. Decreased interaction with family and friends, creating isolation and depression
         v. Increased fear or anxiety
      d. Diagnostic testing
         i. Consider disease process and progression
         ii. X-ray if indicated
         iii. Consider lab work if indicated
      e. Differential diagnosis
         i. COPD exacerbation
         ii. Advancement of disease process

iii. Pneumothorax
iv. Anemia
v. CHF exacerbation
vi. Anxiety
vii. Unresolved pain
viii. EOL process

f. Plan
i. Understand and discuss the patient's and family's goals of care.
ii. Evaluate history of illness, disease process, and progression.
iii. Evaluate cause.
iv. Treat cause if indicated relevant to patient and family goals and plan of care.
v. Treat symptoms of SOB based on cause.
vi. Assess and reassess effectiveness of treatment frequently.
vii. Support and educate patient and family.
viii. Validate and identify SOB as a very distressful symptom.

Anorexia/Cachexia

A. Anorexia is defined as a loss of appetite and is usually accompanied by a decrease in intake. Cachexia is defined as a lack of nutrition and wasting. Both anorexia and cachexia are commonly seen in many serious illnesses and EOL processes. Many families find it difficult when a loved one will not or cannot eat and weight loss and muscle wasting continue "even though I'm trying so hard to eat." There are several causes for anorexia and cachexia, including simply not having the energy to take in the required nutrition, lack of appetite, or fullness if taking numerous medications. Lastly, at EOL appetite naturally decreases, and may also be a cause. Investigate the cause of anorexia and cachexia.

1. Common complaints
   a. Nausea
   b. Fatigue
   c. Lack of appetite
   d. Consider whether the patient may feel like he or she is taking in adequate nutrition when that is not the case. Or the patient truly is taking in adequate nutrition and the body is utilizing all of the nutrition and energy for the disease process.
   e. Progressive weight loss and muscle wasting
   f. Cachexia is rarely reversible in advanced illness.
   g. Cachexia may be caused by metabolic abnormalities.
   h. Increases distress for both the patient and family
   i. Negatively impacts body image and causes body image disturbances
   j. Constant reminder of the disease process and progression
2. Causes
   a. Oral/systemic infections
   b. Pain
   c. SOB
   d. Fatigue
   e. Constipation
   f. Nausea/vomiting/diarrhea
   g. Malabsorption
   h. Depression
   i. Medications
3. Potential complications
   a. Fatigue
   b. Weakness
   c. Increased risk for skin breakdown
   d. Increased risk for falls
   e. Increased risk for infections
   f. Metabolic disturbances
   g. Frailty
   h. Isolation
   i. Patient and family distress related to weight loss and lack of intake
4. Physical assessment
   a. Temporal wasting
   b. Significant weight loss (5%–10% of body mass every month)
   c. Decreases intake
   d. Poor skin turgor
   e. Decreased abdominal mass or fat; helpful to measure abdominal girth and track
   f. Decrease in upper arm mass or fat; helpful to measure upper arm circumference and track
5. Pharmacologic treatment
   a. There is no single pharmacologic intervention effective for cachexia.
   b. May be appropriate to try appetite stimulants such as megestrol acetate (MA) (Megace). MA has been used successfully in weight and appetite improvement but has not demonstrated improvement in QOL for patients with AIDS-related cachexia, or in cancer and in COPD patients.
   c. Antioxidant polyphenols from plant foods have been used for cancer-related cachexia. Polyphenols are in fresh and cooked plant foods, particularly those with rich colors, including red, purple, and black. Wine is a polyphenol-rich drink. Wine before meals may be helpful in increasing appetite.
   d. Other medications used in the treatment of anorexia and cachexia include dronabinol (Marinol), corticosteroids, thalidomide, adenosine triphosphate (ATP), omega 3 fatty

acids, TFN (tumor necrosis factor) inhibitor, or oxandrolone (Oxandrin).

e. In some cases, parenteral or enteral nutrition may be useful for patients who cannot swallow. However, consider risk versus benefits and each individual patient, disease process, and progression. Evaluate the patient and family goals and plan of care for cachexia and support these decisions.

6. Nonpharmacologic treatments
   a. Educate the patient and family concerning causes of cachexia.
   b. Eat small frequent meals.
   c. Encourage patient to eat foods that he or she enjoys.
   d. Eat foods that are easy to chew with sauces.
   e. Eliminate dietary restrictions.
   f. Encourage high-calorie foods; nutritional supplements may be useful as tolerated.
7. Plan
   a. Overall, when caring for a seriously ill or EOL individual, the problem of anorexia or cachexia may be one of the most distressing to the patient or family. Eating has many emotional ties; provide support and reassurance to both patient and family.
   b. Constant evaluation and appropriate support and guidance are necessary.
   c. Assess and reassess nutritional status.
   d. Determine patient and family goals and support realistic decisions.
   e. Educate patient and family on risk versus benefit.
   f. Utilize IDT; consult nutritionist if appropriate.
   g. Consider caloric counts.
   h. Educate patients and families about anorexia and cachexia. It is important to listen to their concerns and validate in a respectful manner. Explain that increase in calories does not always equate with weight gain or patient improvement.
   i. Consider palliative or hospice referral; anorexia and cachexia in serious illness is associated with decreased survival.
8. Diagnostic tests/evaluation
   a. Weigh the patient standing or use a bed scale available for bed-bound patients.
   b. Measure arm/abdominal circumferences; this is particularly helpful for patients who cannot be weighed easily. Track the patient's weight measurements.
   c. Evaluate electrolytes as indicated.
   d. Serum albumin decreases as nutritional status declines and also has a prognostic value.
9. Special considerations—Aggressive nutritional treatments in advance illness may cause more discomfort than benefit. Seriously consider risk versus benefit before initiating aggressive nutritional treatments.

Constipation

A. Constipation is defined as the infrequent passage of stool.

The key to constipation in PC is prevention. Patients who are started on opioids should always have a bowel plan in place. If prevention of constipation is not treated seriously, it can lead to more complicated problems such as a preventable bowel obstruction.

1. Common complaints
   a. Rectal pressure
   b. Straining
   c. Cramps/abdominal distension
   d. Nausea
   e. Fullness
2. Causes
   a. Medications
      i. Opioids
      ii. Antidepressants
      iii. Antacids
      iv. Chemotherapy
      v. Overuse of bowel stimulants
   b. Obstructive tumor
   c. Neurological disorders
   d. Decreased or no activity
   e. Hypercalcemia/hypokalemia
   f. Spinal cord compression
   g. Surgical adhesions
   h. Dehydration
   i. Weakness
   j. Pain
   k. Depression
3. Assessment of constipation
   a. History
      i. Characteristics of stool, appearance, and consistency
      ii. Frequency of stool
      iii. History of use of bowel medication
      iv. Fluid intake
      v. Anorexia
      vi. Presence of nausea and/or vomiting
      vii. Review all medications, including over-the-counter and herbal products
   b. Physical assessment
      i. Auscultate, palpate, and percuss the abdomen to evaluate the presence of
         1) Bowel sounds, hyperactive, hypoactive, absent
         2) Bloating
         3) Ascites
         4) Distension

5) Masses
6) Pain and tenderness

ii. Digital rectal examination
1) Avoid in neutropenic patients
2) Digital examination may reveal impaction, tumor, or rectocele
3) Visual examination of rectal area may reveal hemorrhoids, ulcerations, rectal fissures, or skin breakdown, which all make defecation painful.

4. Diagnostic tests
a. Abdominal x-ray to rule out obstruction

5. Differential diagnosis: obstruction

6. Plan
a. Bowel plans for all patients on opioids are necessary due to constipation
b. Prophylactic stool softeners should be used as indicated.
c. Bowel elimination should occur no less than every 3 days regardless of intake.
d. Assess and reassess.
e. Check for impaction and obstruction.
f. Educate the patient and family on constipation/bowel plan.

7. Individual/special considerations
a. May be very embarrassing for patient to address bowel problems; consider privacy, and address the issue respectfully.
b. Encourage patient and/or family to discuss openly and report problems or issues/patterns in bowel elimination and output.

Nausea and Vomiting

A. Nausea is a feeling and will be a subjective report where vomiting will be visible with objective information. Nausea and vomiting (N&V) occurs in up to 70% of terminally ill patients. N&V has negative effects on QOL, causing weight loss, electrolyte disturbances, isolation, frustration, anxiety, and many other associated symptoms.

B. It is important to remember that psychological or emotional factions can also cause N&V, stimulating the emetic receptors in the brain. The clinician must understand the type of N&V to treat it correctly.

1. Causes of N&V
a. Physiological
i. Gastric irritation, constipation, intestinal obstruction
ii. Liver failure, ascites
iii. Autonomic dysfunction
iv. Anxiety—increases gastric acid production
v. Specific treatments such as radiation, chemotherapy, or medications
vi. Infection
vii. Metabolic abnormalities such as renal failure or hepatic failure
viii. Increased intracranial pressure
ix. Vestibular disturbances also cause N&V.

b. Clinical characteristics and pharmacologic treatments
i. Chemoreceptor trigger zone–based N&V
1) Stimulated by chemotherapeutic agents
2) Bacterial toxins caused by infection or viruses
3) Metabolic products such as uremia, hypercalcemia, and infection
4) Opioids
5) Radiotherapy-induced nausea
6) Pharmacologic: The first-line treatment for chemoreceptor trigger zone N&V is a dopamine antagonist such as Haldol or Compazine.

ii. Cerebral cortex–based N&V
1) Anxiety
2) Taste
3) Smell
4) Anticipatory nausea
5) Increased intracranial pressure
6) Pharmacologic—First-line treatment for cerebral cortex N&V is administration of anxiolytics such as lorazepam or hydroxyzine.

iii. Vestibular-based N&V
1) Motion
2) Opioids that sensitize the vestibular center
3) Pharmacologic: First-line treatment for vestibular N&V involves antihistamines and anticholinergics.

iv. Gastrointestinal tract–based N&V
1) Gastric stasis or obstruction
2) Medications
3) Metastatic process
4) Infection
5) Treatments
6) Pharmacologic treatments for gastrointestinal tract N&V
a) First-line treatment for gastric stasis is metoclopramide.
b) Ondansetron is also useful in the treatment of N&V.

c. Assessment
i. Obtain a thorough history that includes clear information so that the clinician can identify what type of N&V the patient is exhibiting. Much like assessment

for pain, the clinician has to ask many questions to properly assess the symptom of N&V.

1) What is the consistency of the emesis?
2) What is the intensity—wrenching, belching acid?
3) Does anything make it better or worse?
4) How often does nausea and/or vomiting occur? Are there any patterns? It may help to have the patient or family keep a symptom diary.
5) How much is the patient vomiting?
6) Are there symptoms or factors that accompany the N&V such as dizziness or low blood sugar? Does it occur when taking medication or eating/smelling certain foods?
7) Evaluate for constipation, impaction, or obstruction.
8) Evaluate for uncontrolled pain, infection, or other processes.
9) Does the patient have anxiety or other emotional or existential concerns leading to N&V?

d. Diagnostic tests
   i. Labs to consider
      1) Renal and liver function tests
      2) Electrolytes: Assess for dehydration
      3) Urinalysis: Assess for infection
      4) X-ray of abdomen: Check for bowel obstruction
      5) CT: Head to assess for brain metastasis

2. Nonpharmacologic treatments for N&V
   a. Educate the patient and family to treat nausea as soon as symptoms start.
   b. Teach relaxation techniques.
   c. Acupuncture may be helpful.
   d. Recommend music therapy.
   e. Teach families and care providers about meals
      i. Serve meals at room temperature with clear fluids.
      ii. Identify and avoid strong smells.
      iii. Avoid large high-bulk meals; instead, eat small, frequent meals.
      iv. Position the patient in an upright position during meals.
      v. Move the patient away from sleeping and cooking prep areas to eat.
   f. At times a nasogastric tube may be needed for intractable nausea and/or vomiting or unrelieved abdominal pressure to alleviate symptoms.

3. Plan for N&V control
   a. Identify the cause and type of N&V.
   b. Assess and reassess the patient as necessary.
   c. Identify patient and family goals and plan of care.
   d. Provide pharmacological interventions.
   e. Educate the patient and family about nonpharmacological interventions.

Xerostomia

A. Xerostomia is defined as dry mouth, together with difficulty in mastication, swallowing, and speech. Xerostomia occurs in up to 97% of patients at EOL and greatly impairs QOL; it can be distressing to the patient and family members. Management is primarily nonpharmacological and can be completed by educating family and caregivers. This provides families and caregivers with a means of control to "do" something often when the individual is feeling helpless at the EOL. Oral care can be a method of bonding or of resolution and is a very important aspect of patient care.

1. Causes
   a. Medications
      i. Anticholinergics
      ii. Opioids
      iii. Diuretics
   b. Radiation
   c. Systemic disease
   d. Oxygen
2. Management
   a. Identify and, if possible, correct the underlying cause.
   b. Educate the patient and family on providing proper and frequent oral care.
      i. Brushing teeth
      ii. Cleaning tongue and lips
      iii. Keeping the mouth and lips moist
   c. Offer frequent sips of liquid, if appropriate, or frequent mouth moistening if patient cannot swallow.
   d. If appropriate, soft moist foods can be offered.
   e. If patient is able, suggest chewing sugarless gum.
   f. Maintain humidity in the room.
   g. Humidify oxygen.
   h. Oral care should continue even if a patient is unresponsive.
3. Plan
   a. Assess for signs and symptoms of xerostomia.
   b. Identify cause and correct if possible.
   c. Educate patient, family, and caregivers regarding proper oral care.
   d. Assess and reassess as needed.

Fatigue

A. Fatigue or a feeling of weariness has been reported to occur in up to 90% of cancer patients. Fatigue is also linked to many other serious illnesses such as COPD, CHF, coronary artery disease (CAD), HIV/AIDS, and advanced renal disease. Much of the treatment for fatigue is nonpharmacologic and requires the clinician to educate the patient and family. Proper assessment to determine the cause of fatigue is imperative.
   1. Causes of fatigue
      a. Disease states such as anemia, electrolyte imbalances, malnutrition, infection, hyperglycemia, fever, pain, organ failure, hypoxia
      b. Depression
      c. Inactivity and immobility
      d. Inadequate rest
      e. Unrelieved symptoms
      f. Medications
      g. Radiation/chemotherapy
      h. Spiritual distress
   2. Assessment
      a. Obtain an adequate history by asking questions to acquire both subjective and objective information.
      b. How do you feel? Are you feeling weak, tired, wiped out?
      c. How long does the fatigue last? Can you see a pattern?
      d. Have you noticed anything that makes the fatigue better or worse?
      e. Have you noticed if any of the medications or treatments make the fatigue better or worse?
      f. Do you feel anxious or depressed?
      g. Do you find it difficult to concentrate?
      h. Tell me how fatigue is affecting your daily life.
      i. Walk me through a typical day.
      j. Tell me how you sleep and what that is like for you.
      k. Monitor vital signs, assessing for fever, increased heart rate, weak pulse, and increased respiratory rate.
      l. Assess as the patient moves and talks; notice if the individual gets short of breath with very simple tasks (stating a few words, standing, walking a few steps).
      m. Evaluate hydration status.
      n. Evaluate muscle status, muscle wasting, muscle strength, and endurance.
      o. Evaluate medications; are there medications that cause sedation and fatigue? Can this be changed; if not, can the time be changed to be taken at bedtime? If not, can the patient and family be instructed on how to group tasks when awake?
   3. Diagnostic testing
      a. Oxygenation status hemoglobin (Hgb), CBC, and differential
      b. Thyroid function
      c. Electrolytes
   4. Treatments
      a. Provide assistance that will help the individual to maintain independence and functional abilities as long as possible such as physical therapy and occupational therapy.
      b. Initiate therapy as appropriate and in alignment with patient goals and plan of care such as transfusions, oxygen, and IV fluids
   5. Plan
      a. Assess for signs and symptoms of fatigue.
      b. Educate patient and family regarding frequent rest periods and grouping activities as much as possible in efforts to conserve energy.
      c. Work with IDT to provide individualized care in efforts to maintain independence and functional ability.
      d. Provide support; suggest home health or hospice aide as appropriate.
      e. Assess and reassess for fatigue.

Depression

A. Depression is noted in many serious illnesses and has been reported in up to 50% of patients in the PC setting. The National Cancer Institute notes that although both depression and anxiety have been frequently reported as comorbid factors in chronic medical conditions, depression is often unrecognized, undertreated, or altogether untreated. Symptoms of depression and anxiety are usually responsive to treatment. Thus, early recognition, assessment, and diagnosis are important to improve outcomes. The patient, family, and clinician should understand that depression and suicidal ideation are not normal at EOL, and symptoms should be aggressively treated.

B. Clinical characteristics
   1. Persistent feelings of helplessness, hopelessness, or inadequacy
   2. Disease-related causes for depression include:
      a. Uncontrolled symptoms such as pain, anorexia, and N&V
      b. Sleep disturbances
      c. Sepsis, abnormal metabolic states, delirium, organic mental disorders, medication reactions
   3. Psychological issues that may lead to depression

a. Existential factors such as fear, loss of independence, loss of control, body image disturbance, impending death
b. History of pre-existing psychological conditions

C. Medications
1. Antihypertensives, analgesics, steroids, hypoglycemics, chemotherapeutics, benzodiazepines, and others
2. Treatments such as radiation

D. Individual situations increase the chance of depression
1. Financial, social, safety, or other issues can increase the chances of depression.
2. Assess and utilize the IDT.

E. Assessment: It may be difficult to assess for depression. Evaluate the patient about mood, fear, withdrawal, and emotional status, including:
1. Complaints of lack of appetite, weight loss with unclear cause
2. Insomnia
3. Decreased sexual interest
4. Decreased interest in activities usually found pleasurable, such as reading, TV, and games
5. Feelings of helplessness and/or hopelessness
6. Psychomotor agitation
7. Fatigue and/or a complaint of diminished energy
8. Ask direct questions when assessing for depression.
   a. Are you depressed?
   b. How would you describe your mood?
   c. How are you sleeping?
   d. What is your energy level?
   e. What do you see in your future?
      i. **Ask "Have you had thoughts of harming yourself?" The patient may need immediate evaluation by a psychiatric professional if the patient has a lethal, precise suicide plan and the ability to carry out the plan.**
9. Pharmacologic treatment
   a. First-line medications for treating depression are selective serotonin reuptake inhibitors (SSRIs) such as fluoxetine, paroxetine, sertraline, or citalopram.
   b. Other medications that may be used to treat depression
      i. Tricyclic antidepressants such as amitriptyline. However, nortriptyline should not be used if the patient has suicidal ideation.
10. Nonpharmacologic treatment measures for depression
   a. Provide mechanisms for patients to remain in control and to maintain autonomy and independence for as long as possible.
   b. Encourage reminiscing; promote focus on life's accomplishments and help with EOL resolutions and closure with family.
   c. Provide anticipatory grief counseling.
   d. Provide adequate symptom relief.
   e. Use cognitive behavioral techniques.
11. Plan
   a. Assess for signs and symptoms of depression.
   b. Understand patient diagnosis, prognosis, progression, goals, and plan of care.
   c. Have clear conversation with patient and family.
   d. Identify depression early.
   e. Treat depression appropriately.
   f. Incorporate nonpharmacologic methods and utilize IDT.
   g. Educate and provide supportive relationship for patient and family.
   h. Ensure patient safety.
   i. Assess and reassess frequently.

Social Aspects of Care

A. Access to care
1. Managing multiple chronic illnesses and disabilities is challenging in the elderly population who require more extensive and in-depth care by providers.
2. Elderly patients require more assistance from caregivers and/or family members.
3. Care for the elderly is often episodic and unplanned. This pattern for chronic and serious illnesses causes patients to access care such as the emergency room (ER). Episodic treatment in the ER is inadequate without a discharge plan. The lack of a comprehensive functional assessment during an ER visit places the elder patient at risk.
4. Fragmented care puts the elder patient at risk for errors caused by polypharmacy, falls, functional decline, untreated symptoms, and increased or undertreated pain and institutionalization. Using an IDT:
   a. Coordinates care; assists with follow-up care and consistency of care
   b. Decreases fragmentation of care
   c. Contains cost of care
   d. Decreases risk of polypharmacy as care is coordinated
   e. Patients who receive appropriate follow-up care have improved quality of life, receive proper education, experience fewer hospitalizations, have lower costs, and experiences less patient and family stress.

5. Other specific considerations when caring for elderly patients in PC
   a. Elderly patients need extensive family and caregiver support and care.
   b. Patients make increased demands on family and caregivers when they lose the ability to drive.
   c. As disease progresses, activities of daily living become progressively more difficult to complete and require significant assistance from others.
6. Special considerations for patient and family feelings
   a. Older spouses may be taking care of their ill older spouses.
   b. Both the patient and family may have feelings of helplessness; they need education on tasks that can be completed, giving them a sense of control.
   c. Children and their parents experience emotional difficulty with role reversal such as bathing their elder parent when they are no longer able to preform general grooming activities. Feelings of resentment and/or guilt as well as depression, anxiety, and frustration may be exhibited.

B. Financial concerns
   1. Many older adults are on a fixed income, with medication expenses accounting for a significant portion of their income.
   2. Older adults may have limited supplemental insurance and be unable to remain in their own homes as their disease progresses and costs rise.
   3. Placement in residential care in the last days of life may require dissolution of all assets.

Spiritual, Religious, Cultural, and Existential Aspects

A. Culture greatly influences how a person and family respond to an illness or crisis, and how decisions are made within the situation. Completion of a cultural assessment is a crucial piece of patient and family care. This assessment addresses many facets of a person's life and how it affects the view of life, illness, interactions, QOL, and death. Culture includes the whole person and how that individual identifies with ethnicity, race, age, national origin, gender, religion, marital status, family, sexual orientation, professional role, current residence, community role, economic status, and educational status. The assessment shows caring to both the patient and family that their culture, beliefs, and practices are important and valid.
   1. Identify who the major support person or people are.
   2. Identify who the decision makers are.
   3. What is the primary or preferred language? Are there language barriers to care?
   4. Is it appropriate to make eye contact, touch?
   5. Are there gender issues associated with communication or care/providers?
   6. Ask about religion or spirituality and how they may affect care.
   7. Are there specific nutritional restrictions or specific religious observations?
   8. Understand the individual's economic situation. This can be an uncomfortable question to ask, however, for it directly affects access to care, medications, safety, living situation, family unit, and other aspects of care.
   9. Ask about health and illness beliefs and practices, traditions, routines, and rituals.
   10. What types of past experiences has the individual and family had?
   11. What do the patient/family know about the disease, prognosis, and progression?
   12. What are the beliefs and practices about pain and suffering?
   13. Ask about traditional therapies, herbal medications, and other therapies.
       a. Make sure to address and include traditional therapy when able and appropriate, as they are a very important part of patient and family-centered care.
       b. Patients/families may not inform clinicians if they do not believe these practices will be taken seriously or included in the plan of care.
       c. Some herbal treatments can interact with medications.
       d. Traditional therapies are often mistaken, misinterpreted, or translated as noncompliance.
   14. To ensure dignity and respect, discuss care of the patient's body as death approaches.
   15. How does the patient and family view organ donation?

Spirituality and Religion

A. Spirituality can be of value even to those who do not consider themselves religious. Spirituality provides a means to forgive and to ask for forgiveness. Religion encompasses beliefs and rituals, and includes the importance of prayer, ceremonies, and other traditions.
   1. Spiritual assessment: Dr. Christina Puchalski developed the FICA spiritual assessment as a tool to evaluate the importance of the patient's personal faith and belief system as a guide for discussion: smhs.gwu.edu/gwish/clinical/fica/spiritual-history-tool
   2. Spiritual symptoms of distress: Spiritual distress often presents as many different symptoms. Often the chaplain from the IDT can be

consulted to assist; other times education, listening, or just being present is needed to ensure the person can validate his or her feelings. Common symptoms of spiritual distress include:

a. Sense of abandonment
b. Direct or indirect anger
c. Sense of betrayal
d. Hopelessness or despair
e. Fear
f. Guilt
g. Need to seek forgiveness
h. Regret
i. Remorse
j. Depression

3. Plan: Ensure cultural and spiritual assessment is completed and addressed specific to the whole person's needs. Utilize the IDT and offer the patient and family appropriate services.

Communication

A. Communication is one of the most complicated and fundamental aspects of PC. Clinicians are uncomfortable with the discussions surrounding death and dying. Often the clinician believes he or she has failed the patient as the disease progresses to the terminal phases. Communication with the patient and family must meet the needs of the patient, be clear and concise, and provide the patient and family with information to make informed decisions.

1. Barriers to effective communication exist for the clinician and the patient/family. These barriers include:
   a. Fear
   b. Lack of experience
   c. Avoidance of emotion
   d. Insensitivity
   e. Guilt
   f. Disagreement with decisions
   g. Lack of understanding of the patient's culture
   h. Lack of understanding of goals
   i. Ethical concerns
2. Communication tips
   a. Build a trusting relationship.
   b. Take time to listen, be silent, and present.
   c. Be honest.
   d. Provide consistency in team communication.
   e. Coordinate care among clinicians and provide a unified clear message.
   f. Validate patient and family concerns.
   g. Understand you can give too much information; ask how much they want to know.
   h. Be sensitive.
   i. Sit down when you speak with patient and family.
   j. Communication isn't all that is "said." Body language accounts for over 80% of nonverbal communication.
3. Communication tools
   a. Use the ask-tell-ask method of communication
      i. Ask the patient/family to describe his or her understanding of the subject.
      ii. Tell the patient/family the information in a clear, concise manner without the use of medical jargon.
      iii. Ask the patient/family if he or she understood the information presented and ask them to repeat the content back or summarize the information.
   b. Recognize and respond to emotion.
   c. Assess the patient's coping style.
   d. Encourage reminiscing.
   e. Don't change the subject.
   f. Use open-ended questions.
   g. Employ useful phrases to encourage communication.
      i. "Tell me more."
      ii. "Tell me what you're hoping for."
      iii. "Sometimes our hopes change; tell me yours."
      iv. "Tell me what questions you have."
         1) "I know your family members from a medical standpoint; tell me about them as persons."
         2) "Tell me what this means for you and your life."
         3) "I know what anxiety feels like for me; tell me what it feels like for you."

Ethics

In 2001 the American Nurses Association presented *The Nursing Code of Ethics,* which establishes ethical standards for the profession. While working in PC, many difficult decisions are made. These decisions often cause clinicians moral or ethical distress. Knowing and utilizing *The Nursing Code of Ethics* allows the nurse to feel confident he or she is following the ethical obligations of the profession. *The Nursing Code of Ethics* with interpretive statements is available at www.nursingworld.org/MainMenuCategories?EthicsStandards?codeofEthicsforNurses/Code-of-Ethics.pdf.

Bibliography

American Academy of Family Physicians. (2011, November). *Principles of neuropathic pain assessment and management: The four-item patient health questionnaire (PHQ-4) for anxiety and depression.* Retrieved from http://staging.aafplearninglink.org/Resources/Upload/File/AAFPLL-Act%201-DL%20Resource%20PHQ-4-11-13-11(1).pdf

American Academy of Hospice and Palliative Care Medicine. (n.d.). *Guide to alleviating physical and psychological pain in patients with serious or life-threating conditions.* Retrieved from aahpm.org

American Association of Colleges of Nursing. (n.d.). *The end-of-life nursing education consortium (NLNEC) projects*. Retrieved from http://www.aacn.nche.edu/elnec

American Geriatrics Society. (2012). *AGS Beers criteria for potentially inappropriate medication in older adults*. Retrieved from http://www.americangeriatrics.org/files/documents/beers/PrintableBeersPocketCard.pdf

American Nurses Association. (2001). *Nursing code of ethics*. Retrieved from http://www/nursingworld.org/MainMenuCategories/EthicsStandards/CodeofEthicsforNurses/Code-of-Ethics.pdf

Anderson, P., Dean, G., & Piech, M. (2010). Fatigue. In B. R. Ferrell, & N. Coyle (Eds.), *Oxford textbook of palliative nursing* (3rd ed., chap. 8, pp. 187–209). New York, NY: Oxford University Press.

Andrews, M. M., & Boyle, J. S. (Eds.). (2011). *Transcultural concepts in nursing care* (6th ed.). Philadelphia, PA: Lippincott Williams & Wilkins.

Beauchamp, T. L., & Childress, J. F. (2008). *Principles of biomedical ethics* (6th ed.). New York, NY: Oxford University Press.

Berry, P., & Griffie, J. (2010). Planning for the actual death. In B. R. Ferrell, & N. Coyle (Eds.), *Oxford textbook of palliative nursing* (3rd ed., chap. 32, pp. 629–644). New York, NY: Oxford University Press.

Berry, P. H. (2010). *Core curriculum for the generalist hospice and palliative nurse* (3rd ed.). Dubuque, IA: Kendall Hunt. Retrieved from http://www.capc.org/tools-for-palliative-care-programs/clinical-tools/

Boreale, K., & Richardson, B. (2011). Communication. In J. T. Panke, & P. J. Conye (Eds.), *Conversations in palliative care: Questions and answers with the experts* (3rd ed., chap. 3). Pittsburg, PA: Hospice and Palliative Nurses Association.

Bradway, C., Trotta, R., Bixby, M. B., McPartland, E., Wollman, M. C., Kapustka, H., … Naylor, M. D. (2011). A qualitative analysis of an advance practice nurse-directed transitional care model intervention. *The Gerontologist, 52*(3), 394–407.

Burton, A. M., Sautter, J. M., Tulsky, J. A., Linquist, J. H., Stat, M., Hayes, J. C., … Steinhauser, K. E. (2012). Burden and well being among a diverse sample of cancer, congestive heart failure, and chronic obstructive pulmonary disease caregivers. *Journal of Pain and Symptom Management, 44*(3), 410–420.

Campbell, M. L., Templin, T., & Walch, J. (2010). A respiratory distress observation scale for patients unable to self-report dyspnea. *Journal of Palliative Medicine, 13*, 285–290.

Casarett, D. J., Inouye, S. K., & American College of Physicians-American Society of Internal Medicine End-of-Life Consensus Panel. (2001). Diagnosis and management of delirium near of the end-of-life. *Annals of Internal Medicine, 3*, 32–40.

Casarett, D. J., & Quill, T. E. (2007). "I'm not ready for hospice": Strategies for timely and effective hospice discussions. *Annals of Internal Medicine, 146*, 443–449.

Clay, O. J., Grant, J. S., Wadley, V. G., Perkins, M. M., Haley, W. E., & Roth, D. L. (2013). Correlates of health related quality of life in African American and Caucasian stroke caregivers. *Rehabilitation Psychology, 58*(1), 28–35.

Dahlin, C. M. (2010). Communication in palliative care: An essential competency for nurses. In B. R. Ferrell, & N. Coyle (Eds.), *Oxford textbook of palliative nursing* (3rd ed., chap. 8, pp. 107–133). New York, NY: Oxford University Press.

Del Fabbro, E. (2011). Cachexia. In S. Yennurajalingam, & E. Burera (Eds.), *Oxford American handbook of hospice and palliative medicine* (chap. 6, pp. 87–91). New York, NY: Oxford University Press.

Derby, S., O'Mahony, S., & Tickoo, R. (2010). Elderly patients. In B.R. Ferrell, & N. Coyle (Eds.), *Oxford textbook of palliative nursing* (3rd ed., chap. 38, pp. 713–743). New York, NY: Oxford University Press.

Dev, R., Fabbro, D., & Bruea, E. (2007, September 17). Association between megestrol acetate treatment and symptomatic adrenal insufficiency with hypogonadism in male patients with cancer. *Cancer, 10*, 1173–1177.

Earthman, C. P., Reid, P. M., Harper, I. T., Ravussin, E., & Howell, W. H. (2002, November–December). Body cell mass repletion and improved quality of life in HIV-infected individuals receiving oxandrolone. *Journal of Parenteral & Enteral Nutrition, 26*, 357–356.

Economou, D. (2010). Bowel management: Constipation, diarrhea, obstruction and ascites. In B. R. Ferrell, & N. Coyle (Eds.), *Oxford textbook of palliative nursing* (3rd ed., chap. 12, pp. 269–289). New York, NY: Oxford University Press.

Ferrell, B., Hanson, J., & Grant, M. (2012). An overview and evaluation of the oncology family caregiver project: Improving quality of life and quality of care for oncology family caregivers. *Psycho-Oncology, 22*, 1645–1652.

Flaherty, J. H., Perry, H. M. 3rd, Lynchard, G. S., & Morley, J. E. (2001). Polypharmacy and hospitalization among older home care patients. *Journals of Gerontology, Series A, Biological Sciences and Medical Sciences, 55*, M554–559.

Frazier, S. C. (2005). Health outcomes and polypharmacy in elderly individuals: An integrated literature review. *Journal of Gerontological Nursing, 31*, 4–11.

Gauer, P., Shuster, J., Protus, B., & Ohio Hospice and Palliative Care Organization. (2010). Guidelines for effective management of symptoms. In *Palliative care consultant: A reference guide for palliative care* (3rd ed.). Dubuque, IA: Kendall Hunt Publishing Company.

Gornick, M., McMillian, A., & Lubitz, J. (1993, Summer). A longitudinal perspective on patterns of medicare payments. *Health Affairs, 12*, 104–150.

Hoffman, G. J., Lee, J., & Mendez-Luck, C. A. (2012). Health behaviors among baby boomer informal caregivers. *The Gerontologist, 52*(2), 219–230.

Honsen, A., Siegler, M., & Winslade, W. (2010, May 26). *Clinical ethics: A practical approach to ethical decisions in clinical medicine* (7th ed.). New York, NY: McGraw-Hill.

Jahan, N. (2013). *Advance care planning/advance directive*. Retrieved from The Joanna Briggs Institute.

Kagawa-Singer, M., Dadia, A. V., Yu, M. C., & Surbone, A. (2010). Cancer, culture, and health disparities: Time to chart a new course? *CA Cancer Journal for Clinicians, 60*, 12–39.

King, C. & Tarcantu, D. (2010). Nausea and vomiting. In B. R. Ferrell, & N. Coyle (Eds.), *Oxford textbook of palliative nursing* (3rd ed., chap. 20, pp. 221–238). New York, NY: Oxford University Press.

Lai, D. W. (2012). Effect of financial costs of caregiving burden of family caregivers of older adults. *Sage Open*. Retrieved from http://sgo.sagepub.com/content/2/4/2158244012470467

Lawang, W., Horey, D., Blackford, J., Sunsern, R., & Riewpaiboon, W. (2013). Support interventions for caregivers of physically disabled adults: A systematic review. *Nursing & Health Sciences, 15*, 534–545.

Lowe, B., Wahi, I., Rose, M., Spitzer, C., Glaesmer, H., Wingenfeld, K, Schneider, A., & Brahler, E. (2010, April). A 4-Item measure of depression and anxiety: Validation and standardization of the patient health questionaire-4 (PHQ-4) in the general population. *Journal of Affective Disorders, 122,* 86–95.

MacDonald, N. (2003). Is there evidence for earlier intervention for cancer-associated weight loss? *Journal of Supportive Oncology, 1,* 279–286.

Mannix, K. A. (2010). Palliation of nausea and vomiting. In B. R. Ferrell, & N. Coyle (Eds.), *Oxford textbook of palliative nursing* (4rd ed., pp. 801–812). Oxford, UK: Oxford University Press.

Mazanec, P., & Panke, J. T. (2010). Cultural considerations in palliative care. In B. R. Ferrell, & Coyle, N. (Eds.), *Oxford textbook of palliative nursing.* (3rd ed., chap. 37, pp. 701–711). New York, NY: Oxford University Press.

McClement, S. E, & Chochinov, H. M. (2010). Spiritual issues in palliative medicine. In G. Hanks, N. I. Cherney, N. A. Christakes, S. Kassa, & R. K. Portenoy (Eds.). *Oxford textbook of palliative medicine* (4th ed., chap. 15.1, pp. 1403–1409). Oxford, UK: Oxford University Press.

National Alliance for Caregiving in collaboration with AARP. (2009). Caregiving in the US. Retrieved from http://www.caregiving.org/pdf/research/CaregivingUSAllAgesExecSum.pdf

National Cancer Institute at the National Institutes of Health. (n.d.). *Cancer information summaries: Fatigue.* Retrieved from http://www.cancer.gov/cancertopics/pdq/supportivecare/fatigue/HealthProfessional

National Cancer Institute at the National Institutes of Health. (n.d.). *Cancer information summaries: Supportive care for depression.* Retrieved from http://www.-cancer.gov/-cancertopics/pdq/suportivecare/depression/HealthProfessional

National Consensus Project for Quality Palliative Care. (2013). *Clinical practice guidelines for quality.* Retrieved from www.nationalconsensusproject.org

Pasacreta, J., Minarik, P., & Neirl-Anderson, L. (2010). Anxiety and depression. In B. R. Ferrell, & N. Coyle (Eds.), *Oxford textbook of palliative nursing* (3rd ed., chap. 20, pp. 425–448). New York, NY: Oxford University Press.

Puchalski, C., Ferrell, B. Virani, R. Otis-Green, S., Baird, P., Bull, J., … Sulmasy. D. (2009, October). Improving the quality of spiritual care as a dimension of palliative care: The report of the consensus conference. *Journal of Palliative Medicine, 12,* 885–904.

Puchalski, C., & Romer, A. L. (2000, Spring). Taking a spiritual history allows clinicians to understand patients more fully. *Journal of Palliative Medicine, 3,* 129–138.

Roshon, P. A., & Gurwitz, J. H. (1997). Optimizing drug treatment for elderly people: The prescribing cascade. *British Medical Journal, 315,* 1096–1099. Retrieved from http://www.ncbi.nlm.nih.gov/pmc/articles/PMC2127690/pdf/9366745.pdf

Sahyoun, N. R., Lentzner, H., Hoyert, D. & Robinson, K. N. (2001, March). *Trends in causes of death among the elderly.* Aging Trends; No.1. Hyattsville, MD: National Center for Health Statistics. Retrieved from http://www.cdc.gov/nchs/data/ahcd/agingtrends/01death.pdf

Snaith, R. P. (2003). The hospital anxiety and depression scale. *Health Quality Life Outcomes.* Retrieved from http://www.ncbi.nlm.nih.gov/pmc/articles/PMC183845/

Spoelhof, G. D., & Elliot, B. (2012). Implementing advance directives in office practice. *American Family Physician, 85*(5), 461–466.

Sykes, N. (2010). Constipation and diarrhea. In G. Hanks, N. I. Cjermeu, N. A. Christakes, M. Fallon, S. Kassa, & R. K. Portenoy (Eds.), *Oxford textbook of palliative nursing* (4th ed., pp. 833–849). Oxford, UK: Oxford University Press.

Taylor, E. J. (2010). Spiritual assessment. In B. R. Ferrell, & N. Coyle (Eds.), *Oxford textbook of palliative nursing* (3rd ed., chap. 33, pp. 647–661). New York, NY: Oxford University Press.

University of Arkansas Medical Sciences. (2014). *Caregiver information.* Retrieved from http://aging.uams.edu/?id=4826&sid=6

U.S. Department of Health and Human Services, National Institutes of Health. (2007). *Patient-centered communication in cancer care promoting healing and reducing suffering.* Retrieved from http://appliedresearch.cancer.gov/areas/pcc/communication/pcc_monograph.pdf

Vachon, M. L. S. (2010). The emotional problems of the patient in palliative medicine. In G. Hanks, N. I. Cherney, N. A. Christakes, S. Kassa, & R. K. Portenoy (Eds.), *Oxford textbook of palliative medicine* (4th ed., chap. 15.1, pp. 1410–1436). Oxford, UK: Oxford University Press.

White, J., & Hammond, L. (2008). Delirium assessment tool for end-of-life: CHIMBOP. *Journal of Palliative Medicine, 11,* 1069.

WHO Pain & Palliative Care Communications Program. (1998). Tolerance, physical dependence and addiction: Definitions, clinical relevance and misconceptions. *11*(3). Retrieved from http://www.whocancerpain.wisc.edu/?q=node/245

Wittenberg-Lyles, E., Goldsmith, J., & Ragan, S. L. (2010, October). The COMFORT initiative: Palliative nursing and the centrality of communication. *Journal of Hospice & Palliative Nursing, 12,* 282–292.

CHAPTER FIVE

Pain Management Guidelines

Moya Cook and Jill C. Cash

Pain Assessment and Management in the Aging Population

Definition

A. Persistent pain occurs quite frequently in the elderly population. However, pain is not a normal part of aging. Chronic pain is defined as having sensory/emotional changes with experience of tissue change/damage for longer than 3 months. Uncontrolled chronic pain may lead to a downward spiral for the patient, progressing to alterations in physical and mental health status. Inadequate assessment and management of chronic pain may lead to a decrease in the quality of life for all patients.

Common Pain Syndromes

A. There are many common pain syndromes that are present in older patients. Assessing for these unidentified pain syndromes may enhance discovering the source of pain for the patient. Common pain syndromes experienced by elderly patients include fibromyalgia, gout, osteoarthritis, unidentified fractures, neuropathies, and vitamin deficiencies, such as vitamin B_{12} deficiency.

Incidence

A. Elderly men and women are the fastest growing population. It is estimated that by the year 2040, there will be more than 1.3 billion people worldwide older than the age of 65. In the United States alone, there will be over 80 million people living in this age group.

Pathogenesis

A. Studies indicate that pain sensitivity changes and pain threshold increase with aging. Therefore, the absence of reportable pain does not mean that pain does not exist in the elderly population. As one ages, the number of neurotransmitter cell receptors in the brain diminishes as brain tissue begins to atrophy. This loss of neurons has a direct impact on pain transmission, which ultimately increases pain tolerance and disguises the presence of pain in the elderly.

Predisposing Factors

A. Aging adult
B. Barriers to effective pain assessment
   1. Cognitive, language impairments
   2. Comorbid chronic condition (depression, anxiety, agitation, illness, dementia, psychological disorders, memory disorders, etc.)
   3. Medications taken by the patient
   4. Ineffective communication to the provider
   5. Ineffective assessment by the provider
   6. Noncompliance of medication regimen

Subjective Data

A. On the initial exam, a comprehensive history is imperative when assessing for pain. Communication is a key ingredient when assessing for pain. Hearing loss, vision loss, and the inability to fill out documents (pain scales) are a few components of the assessment that can interfere with a successful interview. Adjustments should be made to ensure that communication among the patient, family, and provider is clear. Patients who are not able to provide verbal information should be assessed for behaviors and physical signs of pain. Physical signs of pain may include grimacing, moaning, silence, poor eye contact, and so on. Behaviors that may be an indicator of pain may include anxiety, agitation, confusion, depression, isolation, and so on. Other factors to consider when assessing a patient for pain include the patient's age, past medical history, surgical history, current medications, current cognitive status, and functional status. A focused history will assist in establishing a baseline status for the patient.

1. Assess for communication/cognitive impairments that may interfere with the assessment. Consider communication factors, comorbid conditions/illnesses, and current medications.
2. Assess the current mood and physical state of the patient (depression, anxiety, anger, illness).
3. Have the patient describe the duration of pain and what time of day symptoms begin.
4. Ask the patient to describe the pain, for example, crushing, stabbing, or burning.
5. Ask the patient where the sensation begins and in what direction it radiates. Does pain come and go, or is it constant? What makes pain worse? What makes pain better?
6. Have the patient rate pain on a scale of 0 to 10, with 0 being no pain.
7. Ask the patient to complete a functional status form to assess functional abilities. Identify impairments of activities of daily living (ADL) and note limitations.
8. Ask what medications/treatments have been used in the past for pain. Was pain improved?
9. Inquire regarding family/social support, financial resources, and concerns the patient may have regarding social complexities.

Physical Examination

A. Start with vital signs: Check temperature (if applicable), pulse, respirations, and blood pressure.
B. Inspect
   1. Inspect general appearance, noting facial grimaces, frowning, body movement, and response to assisted movement.
   2. Inspect site of pain for swelling and erythema.
C. Palpate
   1. Palpate specific sites of noted discomfort/pain.
   2. Palpate adjacent joints/areas to site of discomfort. (Pain may also be caused from referred pain. A thorough exam of surrounding joints/tissues should be assessed.) Note inflammation, change in skin temperature (warm/cool), and pain with palpation.
   3. Perform a complete musculoskeletal exam, concentrating on the site of pain. Assess range of motion, gait, and mobility. Evaluate strength, noting symmetry of strength, and/or weakness.
   4. Perform a neurological exam on sites involved.
D. Auscultate
   1. Conduct a complete heart exam, checking for dysrhythmias.
   2. Conduct a complete lung exam.
   3. Auscultate abdomen, noting bruits if present.
E. Mental status
   1. Assess for confusion, agitation, change in personality, anxiety, and so forth.

Diagnostic Tests

A. Perform a Mini-Mental State Exam (MMSE). This form is available at www.health.gov.bc.ca/pharmacare/adti/clinician/pdf/ADTI%20SMMSE-GDS%20Reference%20Card.pdf.
B. Perform a functional status assessment. A complete guide to assessing functional status is available at www.med.illinois.edu/depts_programs/sciences/clinical/internal_med/Document/Practical%20Functional%20Assessment%20of%20Elderly%20Persons%208-21-09.pdf.
C. Perform the "Up and Go" test to assess mobility. This form is available at www.cdc.gov/homeandrecreationalsafety/pdf/steadi/timed_up_and_go_test.pdf.
D. Assess for pain using a valid method of testing for elderly patients. The Verbal Descriptor Scales (VDS) is recommended for assessment in the elderly patient. Other available tools include the Faces Pain Scale and the Numeric Rating Scale. These tools may be found at www.consultgerirn.org/uploads/File/trythis/try_this_7.pdf.

Differential Diagnosis

A. Chronic pain

Plan

A. General interventions
   The primary goal is to identify the source of pain. Once the source is noted, then measures to improve pain should be performed.
B. Patient teaching
   1. Educate the patient regarding the source of pain.
   2. Discuss possible sources of improving pain, according to the diagnosis.
   3. Depending on the source of pain, consider nonpharmacological treatments to improve pain.
C. Nonpharmacological treatments: Such treatments may include physical therapy, aquatic therapy, exercise, chiropractic treatments, massage, acupressure, acupuncture, transcutaneous electrical nerve stimulation (TENS), guided imagery, relaxation, hot/cold therapy, and so forth.
D. Pharmaceutical therapy
   1. Body fat, total amount of water/fluid in the body, poor nutritional status, and muscle mass all impact drug metabolism.
   2. Medications, such as diuretics, may influence the impact of drug distribution in the body. These factors should be considered when prescribing medications in the elderly.
      a. Some changes affected by these components include onset of action, availability of the drug, and excretion of the drug.
      b. Use caution when prescribing medications and repeating the dose if no response is

perceived. Repeating the drug dose to obtain therapeutic results can cause adverse events and/or overdose.

c. If the drug has a slow onset, it may build up in the body and cause an overdose of the medication. When prescribing medications to elderly patients, all medications should be started at the lowest dose possible and titrated up slowly as tolerated. Lower doses are better tolerated and potentially will lead to fewer side effects.

3. Mild pain
   a. Nonopiods: Acetaminophen and nonsteroidal anti-inflammatory drugs (NSAIDs) should be discussed and considered for the treatment of mild pain. Assess liver and kidney function prior to administering these medications.
      i. Acetaminophen: Contraindications to acetaminophen include liver failure, hepatic insufficiency, and chronic alcohol use. The maximum recommended dose of acetaminophen is 4 g/24-hr period, which includes all Tylenol products and combination medications that include Tylenol in them.
      ii. NSAIDs: Contraindications to NSAIDs include peptic ulcer disease, chronic kidney disease, and heart failure. Monitor closely if the patient is taking other medications that may interact with the NSAID, such as corticosteroids and SSRIs, Elderly patients should only use one NSAID at a time. Advise the patient to avoid using over-the-counter NSAIDs, along with prescribed NSAIDs. Elderly patients should also be advised to use a proton pump inhibitor along with the NSAID to protect the gastrointestinal system. Patients taking aspirin should not use ibuprofen while also taking aspirin. Patients prescribed these medications should be closely monitored for gastrointestinal problems (ulcers, gastroesophageal reflux), prolonged bleeding times, and adverse change in kidney function. Monitor the current use of other medications (aspirin, NSAIDs, proton pump inhibitors, Coumadin, etc.) that would interact with these medications.
4. Moderate to severe pain
   a. Opioids: Opioids may be considered for the treatment of moderate to severe pain when nonopioids are not effective. Proper education regarding the use of these medications is necessary to avoid misconceptions regarding the use of these drugs. Educate the patient that opioids are safe medications when used properly as prescribed and that with proper use addiction can be prevented.
      i. Opioids treat nociceptive and neuropathic pain.
      ii. Opioids that should not be used in the elderly patient include meperidine and propoxyphene. These agents may cause central nervous system toxicity if poorly metabolized by the liver.
      iii. Side effects can occur with the use of opioids and with proper use can be avoided. Common side effects include constipation, nausea/vomiting, respiratory depression, and somnolence.
5. Other medications
   a. Anticonvulsants, such as gabapentin, have been used successfully to treat neuropathic pain. Starting doses should be low and gradual titration upward can eliminate side effects and be used successfully to treat pain. Studies have shown that doses from 2,400 to 3,600 mg/d decrease pain and improve mood and sleep disturbance.
   b. Tricyclic antidepressants (TCAs): Nortriptyline has been shown to be successful in treating pain in elderly patients. Use caution in patients with known cardiac conditions. Consider ordering a baseline ECG prior to beginning therapy. Avoid use if cardiac/conduction abnormalities are present. The starting dose should begin low, and a gradual increase in dose every 4 to 7 days should be prescribed as tolerated. Amitriptyline, imipramine, and doxepin should be avoided in the elderly due to a higher risk of side effects.
   c. Local anesthetics: Pain patches may be used with discretion. Lidocaine patches are useful for postherpetic neuropathy. Other pain patches may also be trialed, beginning at a low dose and titrate as tolerated. Topical NSAIDs may be used for localized nonneuropathic pain. Capsaicin and menthol topical agents have been shown to improve regional pain syndromes. Epidural injections have also been found useful in alleviating pain in older adults.
   d. Corticosteroids: Steroids may be used for neuropathic pain and pain associated with inflammatory changes or metastatic bone pain. However, great caution should be used in treating patients with steroids. Long-term

use is not recommended. Significant side effects with the use of steroids can occur in the elderly population in a very short period of time (such as muscle wasting). Consider other alternatives for pain control instead of steroids for elderly patients.

e. Cancer pain: The World Health Organization (WHO) recommends around-the-clock pain treatment for patients diagnosed with cancer. Cancer treatment strategies include the following:
   i. Acetaminophen is the first-line treatment for mild pain.
   ii. NSAIDs are recommended for second-line therapy for mild to moderate pain.
   iii. Mild opioids (codeine, hydrocodone, propoxyphene, and oxycodone) are recommended for moderate pain and pain not responding to NSAIDs.
   iv. Morphine may be used for severe pain and pain not responding to mild opioids. Other alternatives to morphine include hydromorphone, fentanyl, and methadone.
   v. Consider adding additional medications for severe pain complicated by anxiety/mood disorders and not controlled on a single agent. Common medications that enhance the effects of analgesics include antidepressants, anticonvulsants (gabapentin), muscle relaxants, antihistamines, corticosteroids, topical creams/gels, antiarrhythmics (beta blockers), and alpha-2 adrenergic agonists (clonidine).

Consultation/Referral

A. Refer all patients to a pain management specialist if considering long-term pain management.

Individual Considerations

A. Pregnancy: Careful consideration should be used when prescribing pain medication to patients who are pregnant. Tylenol is safe during pregnancy. NSAIDs are not recommended during pregnancy. When prescribing medications, refer to the prescribing classification of all medications for safety clarification during pregnancy.

B. Geriatrics
   1. When prescribing medications, consider liver and kidney function and the safety profile of the medication for the patient. Patients with altered kidney function should not be prescribed NSAIDs.
   2. All medication should be started at the lowest dose and then titrated up slowly for efficacy and tolerability.

Acute Pain

Definition

A. Acute pain is defined as pain of a short, limited duration, usually the result of an injury, surgery, or medical illness that usually results from tissue injury; however, it may be experienced even with no identifiable cause. Acute pain usually resolves when the tissue injury improves with the healing process. Most acute pain resolves in less than 6 weeks or less than 3 months.

Incidence

A. Acute pain is the most common reason for self-medication and presentation for treatment in the health care system. Acute pain is very individual, and if not treated properly it can have devastating physiological and psychological effects. Because pain is very subjective, the patient care plan needs to be individualized to meet the patient's needs. Proper treatment of acute pain could prevent the development of some types of chronic pain syndromes.

Pathogenesis

A. Acute pain is usually the result of stimulation of the sympathetic nervous system.

Common Complaints

A. Pain at the specific site
B. Increased heart rate
C. Increased respiratory rate
D. Elevated blood pressure
E. Sweating
F. Nausea

Other Signs and Symptoms

A. Urinary retention
B. Dilated pupils
C. Pallor

Subjective Data

A. Elicit location of pain.
B. Note effects of pain on activities of daily living (ADL).
C. Note intensity of pain at rest and during activity.
D. List precipitating factors.
E. Identify alleviating factors.
F. Note the quality of pain.
G. Is there radiation of pain?
H. Rate pain on a pain scale (usually on the 0–10 scale, with 0 being no pain and 10 being the worst pain).

Physical Examination

A. Check temperature, pulse, respiration, and blood pressure.
B. Inspect
   1. Observe overall appearance.
   2. Note affect and ability to express self and pain.

3. Note facial grimaces with movement.
4. Note gait, stance, and movements.
5. Inspect area at pain site.

C. Auscultate
1. Auscultate heart and lungs.
2. Auscultate neck and abdomen.

D. Palpate: Palpate affected area of pain.

E. Percuss
1. Percuss chest.
2. Percuss abdomen.

F. Perform musculoskeletal exam.

When performing a musculoskeletal exam, identify the location of pain, presence of trigger points, evidence of injury or trauma, edema, erythema, warmth, heat, lesions, petechiae, tenderness, decreased range of motion, pain with movement, crepitus, laxity of ligaments or cords, spasms, or guarding.

1. Perform complete musculoskeletal exam, concentrating on the area of pain.
2. Assess deep tendon reflexes (DTRs).

G. Neurologic exam
1. Perform complete neurologic exam.
2. Identify change in sensory function, skin tenderness, weakness, muscle atrophy, and/or loss of DTRs.

Diagnostic Tests

A. No diagnostic testing is required unless clearly indicated to rule out organic cause of pain. **If organic disease is suspected, diagnostic testing may include:**
1. Computed tomography (CT) imaging
2. MRI
3. Blood chemistries
4. Radiographic x-ray
5. Lumbar puncture
6. Ultrasound
7. Electrocardiogram (EKG)/echocardiogram

Differential Diagnosis

The differential diagnoses depend on the location of the acute pain.

A. Head
1. Migraine
2. Cluster headache/migraine headache
3. Temporal arteritis
4. Intracranial bleeding or stroke
5. Sinusitis
6. Dental abscess

B. Neck
1. Meningitis
2. Muscle strain/sprain
3. Whiplash injury
4. Thyroiditis

C. Chest
1. Pulmonary emboli
2. Myocardial infarction
3. Pneumonia
4. Costochondritis
5. Angina
6. Gastroesophageal reflux disease/esophagitis

D. Abdomen
1. Peritonitis
2. Appendicitis
3. Ectopic pregnancy/uterine pregnancy
4. Endometriosis
5. Pelvic inflammatory disease
6. Peptic ulcer
7. Cholelithiasis
8. Colitis/diverticulitis
9. Constipation
10. Gastroenteritis
11. Irritable bowel syndrome
12. Urinary tract infection, kidney stone, pyelonephritis
13. Prostatitis

E. Musculoskeletal
1. Muscle sprain/strain/tear
2. Skeletal fracture
3. Viral infection
4. Gout
5. Vitamin D deficiency

Plan

A. General interventions
Acute pain is a symptom, not a diagnosis. Try to identify the cause or source of the acute pain, depending on the location. If the pain is organic in nature, make the appropriate referral. The overall goal is to treat the acute pain appropriately.

B. Patient teaching
The pain management plan must include patient and family education regarding preventing and controlling pain, potential medication side effects, and how to prevent the side effects. Discussion must include addiction concerns. Explain addiction that is low when medication is used as directed for a short duration. Explain that complete pain relief may not be achievable initially, but the overall goal is to decrease the pain, thus allowing some daily activities at home to begin recovery.

C. Pharmaceutical therapy
Source of acute pain
1. *Visceral pain:* Treatment of choice is corticosteroids, intraspinal local anesthetic, NSAIDs, and opioids.
2. *Somatic pain:* Acetaminophen, cold packs, corticosteroids, localized anesthetics, NSAIDs, opioids, and tactile stimulation.

3. *Neuropathic pain:* TCAs, using amitriptyline as the first-line treatment for neuropathic pain. Anticonvulsants like carbamazepine (Tegretol), phenytoin (Dilantin), and valproic acid (Depakene) can be useful in treating neuropathic pain but should be reserved for second-line treatment. Carbamazepine and oxcarbazepine can be used for first-line treatment of trigeminal neuralgia. Other treatments include local anesthetics, tramadol (Ultram), and glucocorticoids.

Know each medication's mechanism of action, potential adverse side effects, half-life, and drug–drug interaction potential. Always document that you have advised on potential for sedation, no driving/machinery use, or alcohol while taking medication with these potential adverse side effects.

Follow-Up

A. Once the organic cause of pain has been ruled out, initial follow-up is 48 to 72 hours after onset.
B. Ensure the patient has access to care on a regular schedule.

Consultation/Referral

A. If the acute pain is organic, make the appropriate referral to a specialist.

Individual Considerations

A. Geriatrics: Special consideration must be taken when treating the geriatric patient for acute pain. Failure to treat geriatric patients for pain is inhumane and can increase delirium in this population. Physiological changes, such as decreased body mass, hepatic dysfunction, and renal dysfunction, can cause increased serum drug concentrations. It is appropriate to begin pain medication at 30% to 50% less than the regular adult dose and titrate until pain is relieved. Anti-inflammatory medications are *not* recommended in this population due to the risk of compromised renal function and increased risk of gastrointestinal bleeding.

Ankylosing Spondylitis

Ankylosing spondylitis (AS) is a chronic inflammatory disorder of the axial skeleton. It manifests in the spine but can also involve the hips, shoulders, and peripheral joints. It is usually diagnosed between the ages of 20 and 30 years of age. There is a clear correlation between AS and the human leukocyte antigen (HLA)-B27. These patients may also have elevated C-reactive protein (CRP) and erythrocyte sedimentation rate (ESR). Incidence is usually higher in White males with a ratio of 3 to 1 compared to women. Patients with AS are also found to have a higher incidence of psoriasis, inflammatory bowel disease, acute anterior uveitis, cardiovascular disease, pulmonary disease, osteoporosis, and renal disease. Pain is usually worse in the morning and gets better with movement. If AS is suspected, a referral to rheumatology is recommended.

Chronic Pain

Definition

A. Chronic pain is defined as alteration in comfort that persists longer than 6 weeks (or longer than the anticipated healing time).
B. The pain may be continuous or recurrent and of sufficient duration and intensity. Legitimate chronic pain interferes with a patient's ability to function with normal daily activities and decreases quality of life.

Incidence

A. Pain syndromes are commonly seen in clinical practice and are the third most widespread health problem in the United States. Chronic pain costs the American people about $65 billion a year in health care expenses, disability costs, and lost productivity. Chronic pain patients have a better than 50% chance of becoming addicted to drugs. As the U.S. population continues to age and the average life expectancy is increasing, the primary care provider will be providing care for more chronic diseases and handling more chronic pain patients.
   1. Women are affected more than men by two to one.
   2. Onset is usually in the fourth, fifth, or sixth decades and is often associated with marked functional disability.

Pathogenesis

A. *Skeletal muscle pain* is pain in soft tissue involving the neck, shoulders, trunk, arms, low back, hips, and lower extremities. *Myofascial pain syndrome* relates to the fascia surrounding the muscle tissue.
B. *Inflammatory pain* is caused by chemicals, such as prostaglandins, leading to the stimulation of the pain receptors. Examples include arthritis, infection, tissue injury, and postoperative pain.
C. *Mechanical/compressive pain* is the direct result of the muscle, ligament, and tendon causing strain, leading to the stimulation of the pain receptors. Diagnosis may be based on diagnostic imaging results that may include fracture, obstruction, dislocation, or compression of tissue by tumor, cyst, or bony structure.
D. *Neuropathic pain* involves dysfunction of the somatosensory system. The most common types are diabetic neuropathy, sciatica from nerve root compression, trigeminal neuralgia, and postherpetic neuralgia.

E. *Nociceptive pain* is caused by nociceptors, a type of sensory neuron that receives the pain signal. Mechanical/compressive and inflammatory pain are examples of this type of pain. They both respond well to opioids, with the exception of arthritis.

Predisposing Factors

A. Age 30 to 50 years
B. Female gender
C. History of having seen many physicians
D. Frequent use of several nonspecific medications
E. Depression
F. Personality, including moods, fears, expectations, coping efforts, and resources

Common Complaints

A. Specific to site of pain
B. Emotional distress related to fear, maladaptive or inadequate support systems, and other coping resources
C. Treatment-induced complications
D. Overuse of drugs
E. Inability to work
F. Financial complications
G. Disruption of usual activities
H. Sleep disturbances
I. Pain becomes primary life focus

Other Signs and Symptoms

A. Pain lasts longer than 6 months.
B. There may be anger and loss of faith or trust in the health care system. This type of patient frequently takes too many medications, stays in bed a great deal, has seen many physicians, has lost skills, and experiences little joy in either work or play.

Subjective Data

A. Elicit a clear description of the onset, location, quality, intensity, and time course of pain and any factors that aggravate or relieve it. Use the acronym OLD CARTS-U. O = onset, L = location, D = duration, C = characteristics, A = aggravating triggers, R = relieving triggers, T = timing, S = severity, U = YOU, What do YOU think is going on? What have YOU done to relieve it?
B. *Self-reporting pain assessment tools* should be used early in the process of patient evaluation. Use the tool at each office visit to see progression or regression. Lack of pain assessment is a barrier to good pain control. Consider the age of the patient; his or her physical, emotional, and cognitive status; and preference when choosing the self-reporting pain assessment tool.
   1. Verbal rating scales rate pain as mild, moderate, or severe.
   2. Numeric rating scales rate pain intensity from 0 to 10. They are patient friendly and quick to complete.
   3. The Faces scale is useful for pediatric and cognitively impaired patients. Multicultural translations may be downloaded at www.wongbakerfaces.org.
C. Determine the extent to which the patient is suffering, disabled, and unable to enjoy usual activity. It is important to inquire about ADL and functional limitations.
D. Obtain a complete review of systems, including nausea, numbness, weakness, insomnia, loss of appetite, dysphoria, malaise, fatigue, or depression signs and symptoms.
E. Obtain a complete family and social history. Address spiritual and cultural issues. History of chemical dependency is of interest in this patient population.
F. Obtain the patient's medical history relevant to the pain, including diagnosis, testing, treatments, and outcomes.
G. Obtain a pain history to identify the patient's attitudes, beliefs, level of knowledge, and previous experiences with pain. Are previously used methods for pain control helpful? What is the patient's attitude toward the use of certain pain medications? Often, the patient will discuss certain adverse side effects or allergies from undesired pain medication.

Physical Examination

A. Check temperature, pulse, respirations, and blood pressure.
B. Inspect
   1. Observe overall appearance.
   2. Note affect and ability to express self and pain.
   3. Note facial grimaces with movement.
   4. Note gait, stance, and movements.
   5. Inspect area at pain site.
C. Auscultate
   1. Auscultate heart and lungs.
   2. Auscultate neck and abdomen.
D. Palpate: Palpate affected area of pain.
E. Percuss
   1. Percuss chest.
   2. Percuss abdomen.
F. Perform musculoskeletal exam.

When performing a musculoskeletal exam, identify the location of pain, presence of trigger points, evidence of injury or trauma, edema, erythema, warmth, heat, lesions, petechiae, tenderness, decreased range of motion, pain with movement, crepitus, laxity of ligaments or cords, spasms, or guarding.

1. Perform a complete musculoskeletal exam, concentrating on the area of pain.
2. Note limitations in range of motion.

G. Neurologic exam
1. Perform complete neurologic exam.
2. Note the patient's affect and mood. Is patient cooperative during exam?
3. Identify change in sensory function, skin tenderness, weakness, muscle atrophy, and/or loss of DTRs.

H. Functional assessment
1. The baseline functional assessment provides objective measurable data on a patient's physical abilities and limitations. It can be used to determine if the patient's efforts are valid and complaints are reliable.
2. The information may be used to identify areas of impairment, establish specific functional goals, and measure the effectiveness of treatment interventions.
3. This objective data may be used in worker compensation cases, returning to work status, federal disability, and motor vehicle accident lawsuits.
4. Know the resources in your area that are trained to perform functional assessments. Physical therapists and occupational therapists are the best qualified to perform the assessments.

Diagnostic Tests

A. **None are required unless clearly indicated to rule out the organic cause of pain.**
1. Remember that pain previously diagnosed as chronic pain syndrome can be organic and vice versa. Organic causes must always be evaluated and excluded.
2. Health insurance usually requires plain radiography ordered first for muscle, inflammatory, or skeletal pain. Plain radiography will diagnose a fracture. Additional studies may be recommended by the radiologist if a lesion/abnormality is seen on plain radiography.
3. MRI and CT are ordered if the plain radiography is negative and the patient continues to complain of pain.
4. Electromyography and nerve conduction studies are used to evaluate neuropathic pain. Numerous serum and urine studies should also be considered if the neuropathic pain is undiagnosed.

B. Consider using a depression assessment tool such as the Beck Depression Inventory or Patient Health Questionnaire 9 (PHQ9). These tools can be administered at a subsequent appointment to follow the patient's symptoms. These tools are available at Beck Depression Inventory Scale: www.med.navy.mil/sites/NMCP2/PatientServices/SleepClinicLab/Documents/Beck_Depression_Inventory.pdf.

Differential Diagnosis

A. Pain disorder
B. Pain related to a disease with no cure
C. Somatization disorder
D. Conversion disorder
E. Hypochondriasis
F. Depression
G. Chemical dependency
H. Fibromyalgia

Plan

A. General interventions
1. Treatment is multidimensional and should not be focused on pharmacological treatment alone.
2. Offer hope and potential for improvement of pain control and of function but *not* cure.
3. The pain is real to the patient, and acceptance of the problem must occur before a mutually agreed on treatment plan can be initiated.
4. Depression is a common emotional disturbance in chronic pain patients and is treatable. Consider oral therapy. See Chapter 24 "Psychiatric Guidelines," "Depression."
5. Identify specific and realistic goals for therapy such as having a good night's sleep, going shopping, or returning to work. Patient discussion needs to include the idea that the goal may be decreasing pain intensity, not eliminating pain.
6. Carefully assess the level of pain using available tools such as a daily pain diary or other pain assessment scales.
7. Avoid pain reinforcement such as sympathy and attention to pain. Provide positive response to productive activities. Improving activity tolerance assists in desensitizing the patient to pain.
8. Shift the focus from the pain to accomplishing daily assigned self-help tasks. The accomplishment of these tasks functions as positive reinforcement.

B. Patient teaching: See the Section III Patient Teaching Guide for this chapter, "Chronic Pain."

C. Pharmaceutical interventions
1. Skeletal muscle pain: Treatment should focus on physical rehabilitation and behavioral management. TCAs and muscle relaxants (cyclobenzaprine) may be used. Research is lacking, indicating the need for opioids for treatment of skeletal muscle pain.

2. Inflammatory pain: NSAIDs and corticosteroids are first-line pharmaceutical interventions. Topical creams and solutions have been used in treating arthritis pain.
3. Mechanical/compressive pain: Opioids may be used to manage these symptoms while other measures are being taken.
4. Neuropathic pain
   a. Gabapentin (Neurontin) and pregabalin (Lyrica) have become first-choice treatments in recent years for diabetic neuropathy and postherpetic neuralgia.
   b. TCAs are extremely useful. Patients who are not depressed obtain excellent pain relief with TCAs such as amitriptyline and doxepin.
   c. Anticonvulsants are useful in controlling some neuropathic pain: carbamazepine (Tegretol), phenytoin (Dilantin), and valproic acid (Depakene). **Patients need to be monitored monthly for hepatic dysfunction and hematopoietic suppression.**
   d. Topical agents: Capsaicin applied three to four times per day can be used to reduce pain without significant systemic effects. Topical lidocaine 5% patches are approved for postherpetic neuralgia.
   e. Carbamazepine is used as the first-line treatment for trigeminal neuralgia.
   f. Opioids: Tramadol is considered to be a good choice if an opioid is indicated. In addition to pain control, tramadol also causes serotonin reuptake inhibition similar to that seen with the TCAs.
5. All therapies need a 2- to 3-week trial period to adequately evaluate therapy. Some medications take longer than that to evaluate.
6. NSAIDs should be used for flare-ups of mild to moderate inflammatory or nonneuropathic pain.
7. Opioids require careful patient selection, titration, and monitoring. Avoid long-term, daily treatment with short-acting opioids (Vicodin, Norco, and Percocet). For as-needed use, prescribe small quantities.
8. Smiths Medical received Food and Drug Administration (FDA) approval in February 2013 to market ambulatory infusion pumps in the United States. These pumps can be programmed to administer pain management medication continuously, intermittently, tapered, or patient-controlled.
9. Benzodiazepines and barbiturates are not advised for treatment of chronic pain due to the high risk of substance abuse.
10. Addiction risk interventions when considering opioids
    a. Check your state's prescription monitoring program (PMP) prior to prescribing controlled substances, as needed, and at least annually. PMPs are state-run electronic databases that track dispensing of controlled substances. PMPs provide clinicians with critical information about patient narcotic prescription history and identify seeking behavior patterns.
    b. Contact the patient's pharmacy for a list of current medications. The PMP is not real time, and all current patient prescriptions are available from the pharmacy.
    c. Perform urine drug screen prior to prescribing controlled substances initially, as needed and annually. National guidelines recommend the enzyme immunolinked assay (EIA) and gas chromatography/mass spectroscopy urine screen. Depending on results of urine drug screening, the provider may seek additional consultation, change medication therapy, refer for substance abuse, or discharge the patient.
    d. A written controlled substance treatment agreement between patient, provider, and clinic is recommended. Include expectations of the patient: No other controlled substances will be prescribed by any other provider. One pharmacy only should be used. Medication must be taken as prescribed. There are no early refills on controlled substances. The patient must agree to random drug screens and may be called to report to the clinic for random drug screens and/or pill counts.
    e. Utilize tools such as Addiction Behavior Checklist, DIRE (Diagnosis, Intractability, Risk, Efficacy) score, or CAGE assessment. (Have you ever tried to **c**ut down on your alcohol/drug use? Do you get **a**nnoyed if someone mentions your use is a problem? Do you ever feel **g**uilty about your use? Do you ever have an "**e**ye-opener" first thing in the morning after you've been drinking or using the night before?)
    f. Red flags for misuse, abuse, addiction, and diversion with opioids include:
       i. Psychiatric illness
       ii. Personal history of alcohol or drug abuse
       iii. Family history of alcohol or drug abuse

D. Alternative interventions
1. Cognitive behavioral training: Examples of cognitive behavioral training include problem solving, guided imagery, hypnosis, controlled breathing exercises, attention diversion, meditation, and yoga exercises; progressive muscle relaxation (PMR) is recommended to help relax

major muscle groups. Randomized controlled trials showed significant reduction in pain with alternative interventions such as music, relaxation, distraction, and massage use.

2. Exercise: Examples of exercise include yoga exercises and PMR. PMR is recommended to help relax major muscle groups. Research indicates that yoga decreases bothersome pain after 12 weeks of regular exercise. The benefits of yoga exercise include improved strength, balance, coordination, range of motion, and reduced anxiety. Yoga instruction by a qualified teacher is a low-cost intervention. Yoga is an effective form of self-care and is an affordable way to alleviate pain. Always advise them to start slowly and be prepared for an approach to pain management that may take several weeks of therapy.
3. Alternative therapies: Randomized controlled trials showed significant reduction in pain with alternative interventions such as music, relaxation, distraction, acupuncture, myofascial release treatments, and massage use.
4. Occupational therapy
5. Vocational therapy
6. Physical therapy such as noninvasive techniques, transcutaneous electrical nerve stimulation, hot or cold therapy, hydrotherapy, traction, massage, bracing, and exercise
7. Individual and family therapy or counseling
8. Aesthetic or neurosurgical procedures
9. Patients will inquire about the use of herbal products to treat chronic pain. Advise patients that these products are not regulated by the FDA. Advise the patient that these herbal products may interact with current medications and cause complications. Advise patients to research all herbal products on reputable medically based websites, not blogs or chat rooms. Caution patients regarding devil's claw, feverfew, willow bark, glucosamine, and chondroitin. Discourage any use of dimethylsulfoxide.

Follow-Up

A. See patients every 4 to 6 weeks for evaluation.
B. Ensure the patient has access to care on a regular schedule.
C. These brief visits should be regular so that care is not perceived to be dependent on escalation of symptoms.

Consultation/Referral

A. Consider patient referral to a pain management clinic if pain control is not adequate. Interventions commonly performed at the specialty clinic include facet joint injections, percutaneous radiofrequency neurotomy, epidural corticosteroid injections, transforaminal epidural injections, and sacroiliac joint injections.
B. Consult with a physician if referral is needed for psychological counseling or if substance abuse is suspected.
C. Refer to a certified pain specialist physician if the patient is taking high doses of opioids and detoxification is indicated. Buprenorphine (Suboxone) is the most common medication prescribed by a certified pain specialist physician.
D. Consider rheumatology consult if a rheumatic condition is suspected.

Individual Considerations

A. When prescribing pharmacological agents, consider drug to drug interactions. When administering tramadol with the use of any selective serotonin reuptake inhibitor, educate the patient regarding the possible interactions between the two medications and teach the patient the signs and symptoms of serotonin syndrome and to report these signs if they occur. Avoid using this combination of medications if the patient is known to have problems with metabolizing CYP2D6.

Low Back Pain

Definition

A. Painful conditions of the lower back may be categorized as follows:
   1. Potentially serious disorders: Acute fractures, tumor, progressive neurologic deficit, nerve root compression, and cauda equina syndrome
   2. Degenerative disorders: Aging or repetitive use, degenerative disease, and osteoarthritis
   3. Nonspecific disorders: Benign and self-limiting with unclear etiology

Incidence

A. Lower back pain is commonly seen in patients from ages 20 to 40 years.
B. Approximately 70% to 80% of people experience back pain at one point in their lifetime.
C. The long-term outcome of low back pain is highly favorable.

Pathogenesis

A. Pain arises from fracture, tumor, nerve root compression, degenerative disk, osteoarthritis, and strain of the ligaments and musculature of the lumbosacral area.

Predisposing Factors

A. Trauma causing ligament tearing; stretching of vertebra, muscles, tendons, ligaments, or fascia

B. Repetitive mechanical stress
C. Tumor
D. Exaggerated lumbar lordosis
E. Abnormal, forward-tipped pelvis
F. Uneven leg length
G. Chronic poor posture due to inadequate conditioning of muscle strength and flexibility, improper lifting techniques causing excessive strain, and poor body mechanics
H. Inadequate rest
I. Emotional depression

Common Complaints

A. Pain in the lower back area may range from discomfort to severe back pain, with or without radiation.

Other Signs and Symptoms

A. Ambulating with a limp
B. Limited range of motion
C. Posture normal to guarded

Subjective Data

A. Ask the patient to discuss the origin of pain. How has the pain progressed or changed since the initial injury?
B. Ask the patient to point to an area where pain is felt.
C. Have the patient describe the pain. Is it radiating, with sharp, shooting pain down to the lower leg and feet?
D. Ask: What makes the pain worse or better? Have the patient list current medications or therapies used for pain, noting results of treatment.
E. Investigate occurrence of systemic symptoms such as fever and weight loss.
F. Explore patient's past medical history. Note previous trauma or overuse, tuberculosis, arthritis, cancer, and osteoporosis.
G. **Inquire about symptoms such as dysuria, bowel or bladder incontinence, muscle weakness, paresthesia, and loss of sensation.** Bowel or bladder dysfunction, bilateral sciatica, and saddle compression may be symptoms of severe compression of the cauda equina that necessitates an urgent workup and referral.
H. Ask the patient about precipitating factors such as athletics, heavy lifting, driving, yard work, occupation, sleep habits, or systemic disease.
I. Use a pain scale to describe the worst pain and the best pain levels.

Physical Examination

A. Check temperature, pulse, blood pressure, and respirations.
B. Inspect
   1. Observe general appearance; note discomfort and grimacing on movement and/or examination.
   2. Distraction may distinguish pain behavior from actual pathology.
   3. Note evidence of trauma with bruises, cuts, and fractures.
   4. Note posture and gait.
C. Palpate
   1. Palpate spine and paravertebral structures, noting point tenderness and muscle spasm. Palpation elicits paravertebral tenderness and generalized tenderness over lower back to upper buttocks.
   2. Examine abdomen for masses.
   3. Extremities: Palpate peripheral pulses.
D. Perform neurologic examination
   1. Identify sensation and pain distribution.
   2. Determine motor strength and evaluate whether muscle strength is symmetrical: Upper extremity resistance is equal bilaterally.
   3. Test DTRs and dorsiflexion of big toe.
E. Check sensation of perineum to rule out cauda equina syndrome.
F. Perform traction tests: Straight leg raises, crossed leg raises, Yeoman Guying, Patrick's test. Musculoskeletal findings include the following:
   1. Straight leg raising and dorsiflexion of foot on affected side may reduce lower back discomfort.
   2. Elevate each leg passively with flexion at hip and extension of knee. Positive straight leg raise is radicular pain when leg is raised 30° to 60°.
   3. Crossed leg raises: Test is positive when pain occurs in leg not being raised.
   4. Yeoman Guying: Unilateral hyperextension in prone position identifies lumbosacral mechanical disorder.
   5. Patrick's test: Place heel on opposite knee and apply lateral force; check for hip or sacroiliac disease.
   6. Range of motion: Increased pain with extension often indicates osteoarthritis. Increased pain with flexion often indicates strain or injured disk.
G. Pelvic exam: Consider pelvic and rectal exam, if indicated. If the patient has fallen on the coccyx, a rectal exam is needed to check for stability.

Diagnostic Tests

A. Laboratory: Complete blood count, erythrocyte sedimentation rate, serum calcium, alkaline phosphatase, urinalysis, and serum immunoelectrophoresis when inflammatory, neoplastic, diffuse bone disease, or renal disease is suspected.
B. Radiography of spine
C. Consider the following tests
   1. MRI to rule out disk disease and tumors
   2. Bone scan to rule out cancer

Differential Diagnoses

A. Back pain secondary to musculoskeletal pain
B. Herniated intervertebral disease
C. Sciatica
D. Fracture
E. Tumor
F. Abdominal aneurysm
G. Pyelonephritis
H. Metabolic bone disease
I. Gynecologic disease
J. Peripheral neuropathy
K. Depression
L. Prostatitis
M. Spinal stenosis
N. Osteoarthritis
O. Osteoporosis
P. Ankylosing spondylitis

Plan

A. General interventions
   1. The patient should continue physical activity as tolerated.
   2. For acute muscle strain, have the patient apply local cold packs for 20 to 30 minutes several times a day for the first 24 hours. Heat packs are recommended after the initial 24 hours of injury.
   3. Chronic or recurrent pain may be treated with either ice or heat applications, whichever gives relief.
B. Patient teaching
   1. Give accurate information on the prognosis for quick recovery such as continuing light physical activity, performing back-strengthening exercises, and avoiding overuse of medications.
   2. Improvement occurs in most cases in a few weeks, although mild symptoms may persist.
   3. Joint guidelines by the American College of Physicians and the American Pain Society recommend rehabilitative therapies for patients who do not improve after medications and self-care recommendations. Rehabilitative therapies include exercise therapy, acupuncture, massage therapy, spinal manipulation, cognitive behavioral therapy, and yoga.
   4. Provide educational handouts on back exercises; see the Section III Patient Teaching Guide for this chapter, "Back Stretches."
   5. After intense pain abates, the patient may perform low back exercises for range of motion and strengthening, and isometric tightening exercises of abdominal and gluteal muscles.
   6. Teach patient knee–chest exercises. Recommend to the patient to place his or her back against the wall and contract abdominal and gluteal muscles 5 to 10 repetitions four to six times per day.
   7. Research indicates that yoga is beneficial for many types of back pain. Types of back pain benefited by yoga include musculoskeletal injury, herniated disc, spinal stenosis, spondylolisthesis, piriformis syndrome, arthritis, and sacroiliac joint derangement.
   8. Encourage the patient to perform walking exercise daily.
   9. Teach relaxation techniques.
   10. Encourage the patient to modify work hours and job tasks.
   11. Refer the patient for therapeutic massage or physical therapy as needed.
   12. Obesity is often related to decreased exercise and poor physical fitness with reduced trunk muscle strength and endurance. Obese patients may experience back pain with normal activity.
C. Pharmaceutical therapy
   1. Analgesics: Acetaminophen 325 to 650 mg every 4 to 6 hours. Maximum dose is 4,000 mg a day. Inquire of any other current medications and/or over-the-counter preparations containing acetaminophen.
   2. NSAIDs: Unless contraindicated due to gastrointestinal symptoms or cardiovascular disease
      a. Aspirin: 325 to 650 mg every 4 to 6 hours
      b. Ibuprofen: 200 to 800 mg every 6 to 8 hours. Maximum dose is 3.2 g a day under the care of the provider; otherwise 1.2 g a day.
      c. Naproxen: 500 mg initially, followed by 250 mg every 6 to 8 hours
      d. Piroxicam (Feldene): 20 mg every day
      e. Meloxicam (Mobic): 7.5 to 15 mg daily
      f. Celebrex: 100 to 200 mg twice a day
   3. Muscle relaxants
      a. Cyclobenzaprine HCl (Flexeril): 10 mg three times daily
      b. Carisoprodol (Soma): 350 mg four times daily
      c. Methocarbamol (Robaxin): 1.5 g every day initially, then 750 to 1,000 mg every day
      d. Orphenadrine citrate (Norflex): 100 mg twice a day
      e. Metaxalone (Skelaxin): 800 mg three to four times a day

Follow-Up

A. If pain is severe or unimproved, follow up in 24 hours.
B. If pain is moderate, reevaluate patient in 7 to 10 days.

C. See patient in 2 to 4 weeks to reevaluate condition and behavioral changes.
D. Recurrences are not uncommon but do not indicate a chronic or worsening case.

Consultation/Referral

A. Consult with a physician when considering red-flag diagnoses such as cauda equina syndrome, herniated disk, widespread neurologic involvement, carcinoma, or significant trauma.
B. Referral to a physician is needed for patients who note significant morning stiffness with a gradual onset prior to age 40, with continuing spinal movements in all directions, and involving some peripheral joints, iritis, skin rashes indicating inflammatory disorders such as ankylosing spondylitis and related disorders.

Individual Considerations

A. Pregnancy: Pregnancy is often associated with low back discomfort. This is due to the redistribution of body weight. As weight increases in the abdominal area with the growing fetus, patients tend to compensate by changing posture and tilting the spine back.
B. Adults: For patients older than 50 presenting with no prior history of backache, consider differential diagnosis of neoplasm. The most common metastasis seen is secondary to the primary site of breast cancer, prostate cancer, or multiple myeloma. Pain most prominent in a recumbent position rarely radiates into the buttock or leg.

Bibliography

American Geriatrics Society Panel on Pharmacological Management of Persistent Pain in Older Persons. (2009). Pharmacological management of persistent pain in older persons. *Journal of the American Geriatrics Society, 57*(8), 1331–1346.

Castillo, M., Weiner, D. (2014). *Treatment of persistent pain in older adults.* Retrieved from http://www.uptodate.com/contents/treatment-of-persistent-pain-in-older-adults?source=search_result&search=treatment+of+perisitent+pain+in+older+adults&selectedTitle=1%7E150

Chou, R. (2013). *Subacute and chronic low back pain: Pharmacologic and noninterventional treatment.* Retrieved from http://www.uptodate.com/contents/subacute-and-chronic-low-back-pain-pharmacologic-and-interventional-treatment?source=machineeLearning&search=medication+for+low+back+pain&selectedTitle=1%7E150§ionRank=1&anchor=H6#H6

Chronic Pain Perspectives. (2013). *Ambulatory infusion system gets FDA clearance.* Retrieved from chronicpainperspectives.com

Costead, L., & Banasik, J. (2009). *Pathophysiology* (4th ed.). St. Louis, MO: Elsevier Saunders.

Dunphy, L., Brown, J., Porter, B., & Thomas, D. (2011). *Primary care: The art and science of advanced practice nursing* (3rd ed.). Philadelphia, PA: F. A. Davis.

Fishman, L. (2012). Efficacy and application of yoga for back pain. *Chronic Pain Perspectives.* Retrieved from http://chronicpainperspectives.com/Article.aspx?aid=111&t=Efficacy-andapplication-of-Yoga-for-back-pain

Hughes, R. G. (2008). *Patient safety and quality: An evidence-based handbook for nurses.* Retrieved from http://www.ncbi.nlm.nih.gov/books/NBK2658

Institute for Clinical Systems Improvement. (2011). *Health care guidelines: Assessment and management of chronic pain* (5th ed.). Retrieved from https://www.icsi.org/_asset/bw798b/ChronicPain.pdf

Institute for Clinical Systems Improvement. (2012). *Health care guidelines: Adult acute and subacute low back pain* (15th ed.). Retrieved from https://www.icsi.org/_asset/bjvqrj/LBP.pdf

Kaye, A. D., Baluch, A. R., Kaye, R. J., Niaz, R. S., Kaye, A. J., Liu, H., & Fox, C. J. (2014). Geriatric pain management, pharmacological and nonpharmacological considerations. *Psychology and Neuroscience, 7*(1). Retrieved from http://dx.doi.org/10.3922/j.psns.2014.1.04

Kaye, A. D., Baluch, A., & Scott, J. T. (2010). Pain management in the elderly population. A review. *The Ochsner Journal, 10,* 185.

Michigan Quality Improvement Consortium. (n.d.). *Management of acute low back pain.* Retrieved from www.guidelines.gov

National Guideline Clearinghouse. (2011a). *Assessment and management of chronic pain.* Retrieved from www.guideline.gov

National Guideline Clearinghouse. (2011b). *Guideline for the evidence-informed primary care management of low back pain.* Retrieved from http://www.guideline.gov/content.aspx?id=37954&search=chronic+low+back+pain+and+acute+low+back+pain+and+assessment+and+management+of+pain

National Guideline Clearinghouse. (2011c). *Management of acute low back pain.* Retrieved from http://www.guideline.gov/content.aspx?id=23939&search=chronic+low+back+pain+and+acute+low+back+pain

National Guideline Clearinghouse. (2011d). *Managing chronic non-terminal pain including prescribing controlled substances.* Retrieved from http://www.guideline.gov/content.aspx?id=25657

Nelson, E. M., & Philbrick, A. M. (2012). Avoiding serotonin syndrome: the nature of the interaction between tramadol and selective serotonin reuptake inhibitors. *Annuals of Pharmacotherapy, 46*(12), 1712–1716.

Rastogi, R., & Meek, B. (2013). Management of chronic pain in elderly, frail patients: Finding a suitable, personalized method of control. *Clinical Interventions in Aging.* 37–46. Retrieved from www.ncbi.nlm.nih.gov/pmc/articles/PMC3552607

Rosenquist, E. (2014a). *Definition and pathogenesis of chronic pain.* Retrieved from http://www.uptodate.com/contents/definition-and-pathogenesis-of-chronic-pain?source=search_results&search=definition+and+pathogenesis+of+chronic+pain&sele

Rosenquist, E. (2014b). Evaluation of chronic pain in adults. Retrieved from http://www.uptodate.com/contents/evaluations-of-chronic-pain-in-adults?Source=search_result&search=evaluation+of+chronic+pain+i+adults&selectedTitle=3%&E150

Rosenquist, E., Aronson, M., & Park, L. (2014). *Overview of the treatment of chronic pain.* Retrieved from http://www.uptodate.com/contents/search?search=Overview+of+the+treatment+of+chronic+pain&sp=1&searchType=PLAIN_TEXT&source=HISTORY&searchControl=TOP_PULLDOWN&searchOffset=

Spearling, N., March, L., Bellamy, N., Bodguk, N., & Brooks, P. (2005). Management of acute musculoskeletal pain. *APLR Journal of Rheumatology, 8*. Retrieved from EbscoHost Database.

Tennant, F. (2010). Hormone replacements and treatments in chronic pain. *Practical Pain Management, 10*(1), 36–40.

Yu, D. (2014). *Assessment and treatment of ankylosing spondylitis in adults.* Retrieved from http://www.uptodate.com/contents/assessment-and-treatment-of-ankylosing-spondylitis-in-adults?source=machineLearning&search=ankylosing+spondylitis&selectedTitle=2%7E150§ionRank=2&anchor=H44#H44

CHAPTER SIX

Dermatology Guidelines

Jill C. Cash, Amy C. Bruggmann, and Cheryl A. Glass

Acne Rosacea

Definition

A. A multifactorial vascular skin disorder, acne rosacea is characterized by chronic inflammatory processes in which flushing and dilation of the blood vessels occur on the face. It is manifested in four stages of pathologic events.

Incidence

A. Acne rosacea affects approximately 13 million people in the United States.

Pathogenesis

A. Rosacea is a functional vascular anomaly with a tendency toward recurrent dilation and flushing of the face. This results in inflammatory mediator release, extravasation of inflammatory cells, and the formation of inflammatory papules and pustules.

Predisposing Factors

A. Tendency to flush frequently
B. Exposure to heat, cold, or sunlight
C. Consumption of hot or spicy foods and alcoholic beverages
D. Some topical medications, astringents, or toners

Common Complaints

A. **Papules, pustules, and nodules: Hallmarks for diagnosis are the small papules and papulopustules. Many presenting erythematous papules have a tiny pustule at the crest. No comedones are present.**
B. Periodic reddening or flushing of face
C. Increase in skin temperature of face
D. Face flushing in response to heat stimuli (hot liquids) in mouth

Other Signs and Symptoms

A. Periorbital erythema
B. Telangiectasia, paranasally and on cheeks
C. Rhinophyma
D. Blepharoconjunctivitis with erythematous eyelid margins
E. Conjunctivitis: Diffuse hyperemic type or nodular
F. Keratitis: Lower portion of cornea, associated with pain, photophobia, and foreign body sensation

Subjective Data

A. Ask the patient to describe the location and the onset. Was the onset sudden or gradual? How have the symptoms continued to develop?
B. Assess if the skin is itchy or painful.
C. Assess for any associated discharge (blood or pus).
D. Complete a drug history. Has the patient recently taken any antibiotics or other medications?
E. Determine whether the patient has used any topical medications, astringents, toners, or new skin-care products.
F. Rule out any possible exposure to industrial or domestic toxins, insect bites, and possible contact with venereal disease or HIV.
G. Ask the patient about close contact with others with skin disorders.
H. Identify whether exposure to heat, cold, or sunlight provokes the symptoms.
I. Ask whether eating or drinking hot or spicy foods or consumption of alcoholic beverages provokes the symptoms.

Physical Examination

A. Check temperature, pulse, and blood pressure.
B. Inspect
   1. Inspect skin, focusing on face and scalp.
   2. Inspect nose and paranasal structures.
   3. Inspect eyes, eyelids, conjunctiva, and cornea. **An ocular manifestation, rosacea keratitis, may cause corneal ulcers to develop.**

Diagnostic Tests

A. None
B. Consider skin biopsy to rule out sarcoidosis, if suspected.

Differential Diagnoses

A. Acne rosacea
B. Acne vulgaris
C. Steroid-induced acne
D. Perioral dermatitis
E. Seborrheic dermatitis
F. Lupus erythematosus
G. Cutaneous sarcoidosis

Plan

A. General interventions: Identify any causative or provocative factors: heat, cold, hot or spicy foods, alcoholic beverages, sunlight.
  1. Advise washing face with mild soap such as Cetaphil soap daily.
  2. Steroid creams may be used sparingly on a short-term basis.
  3. Avoid direct sunlight exposure, wearing protective clothing/hats when outdoors. Suggest using a sunscreen of sun protection factor (SPF) 30 when exposed to sunlight.

B. Patient teaching: See the Section III Patient Teaching Guide for this chapter, "Acne Rosacea."
C. Pharmaceutical therapy
  1. Drug of choice: Tetracycline 500 to 1,000 mg twice to four times daily for 2 to 4 weeks.
  2. Others: Erythromycin 500 mg twice daily until clear, minocycline (Minocin), 50 to 200 mg daily divided into two doses, doxycycline (Vibramycin) 100 mg daily, Amoxil, and metronidazole (Flagyl, Protostat). Start at higher dose and taper to maintenance dose.
     a. Topical antibiotics. Apply topical Metrogel twice daily after cleansing skin.
     b. Do not use topical steroids. Topical steroids may worsen irritation.
     c. Other topical antibiotics: Clindamycin (Cleocin-T), erythromycin twice daily.
  3. Refractory cases may respond to isotretinoin (Accutane).

Follow-Up

A. Follow up in 2 weeks to evaluate therapy.
B. See patients monthly for evaluation until maintenance is reached.
C. Relapses are common following discontinuance of antibiotics; repeat treatment.

Consultation/Referral

A. Consult or refer the patient to a dermatologist if there is no improvement, or if the patient is unable to reach maintenance.
B. Provide an immediate referral to an ophthalmologist for treatment and follow up if the eye is involved.

Individual Considerations

A. Adults: Tinted sulfacetamide (Sulfacet-R) lotion may be used by fair-skinned patients to cover erythema.

Acne Vulgaris

Definition

A. Acne vulgaris is a disorder of the sebaceous glands and hair follicles of the skin, which are most numerous on the face, back, and chest. The sebaceous glands become inflamed and form papules, pustules, cysts, open or closed comedones, and/or nodules on an erythemic base. In severe cases, scarring can result.

Incidence

A. Nearly 80% to 90% of all adults experience acne during their lifetime. Acne vulgaris, commonly seen in adolescence, may even extend into the third or fourth decade of life.

Pathogenesis

A. Sebum is overproduced and collects in the sebaceous gland. Sebum, keratinized cells, and hair collect in the follicle. With *Propionibacterium acnes* present, the duct becomes clogged, and lesions (noninflammatory and/or inflammatory) evolve.

Predisposing Factors

A. Age (adolescence)
B. External irritants to skin (makeup, oils, equipment contact on skin)
C. Hormones (oral contraceptives with high progestin content)
D. Medications (lithium, halides, hydantoin derivatives, rifampin)
E. Hot, humid weather

Common Complaints

A. Outbreak of pimples on face, chest, shoulders, and back that do not resolve with over-the-counter (OTC) treatment
B. Acne rosacea: Telangiectasia, flushing, and rhinophyma present

Other Signs and Symptoms

A. Mild: Comedones open (blackhead) and closed (whitehead)
B. Moderate: Comedones with papules and pustules
C. Severe: Nodules, cysts, and scars

Subjective Data

A. Elicit the age of onset of outbreak, duration, and course of symptoms.
B. Determine what makes the lesions worse or better.

C. Ask whether there are certain times of the month or year when lesions are better or worse.
D. Identify the patient's current method of cleanser or moisturizer treatment.
E. Ask if the patient has ever been treated by a provider for this problem. If so, determine the treatment and results of the treatment.
F. Assess whether other family members have this same problem.
G. Ask the patient for a description of the patient's environment and occupation.
H. Explore with the patient any current stress factors in his or her life.

Physical Examination

A. Inspect
   1. Observe skin for location and severity of lesions.
   2. Rate severity of lesions as mild, moderate, or severe.
      a. Mild: Few papules/pustules, no nodules
      b. Moderate: Several papules/pustules, rare nodules
      c. Severe: Many papules/pustules with many nodules
   3. Take a picture of areas of affected skin for chart and document date. Use this for future appointments as a reference to compare results for follow-up visits.

Diagnostic Tests

A. No tests are generally required.
B. Culture lesions to rule out gram-negative folliculitis with patients on antibiotics.
C. Consider hormone testing if other primary causes of acne are considered (follicle-stimulating hormone, luteinizing hormone, testosterone levels).

Differential Diagnoses

A. Acne vulgaris
B. Acne rosacea
C. Steroid rosacea
D. Folliculitis
E. Perioral acne
F. Drug-induced acne

Plan

A. General interventions
   1. Document location and severity of lesions. Assess quality of improvement at each office visit.
   2. The primary goal of treatment is prevention of scarring. Good control of lesions during puberty and early adulthood is required for best results. Anticipate ups and downs during the normal course and treatment.
B. Patient teaching
   1. See the Section III Patient Teaching Guide for this chapter: "Acne Vulgaris."
   2. Instruct the patient on the proper cleansing routine. The patient should wash affected areas with mild soap (Purpose, Cetaphil) twice a day and apply medications as directed.
   3. Warn the patient that washing the face more than two to three times a day can decrease oil production and cause drying.
   4. Discuss current stressors in the patient's life and discuss treatment options.
   5. Recommend exercise routine 3 to 5 days a week.
   6. Recommend oil-free sunscreens. Ultraviolet (UV) light is beneficial; however, there is a need to use with caution when retinoids and tetracycline have been prescribed.
C. Pharmaceutical therapy: **It may take 1 to 3 months before results are visible when using these medications.**
   1. Mild: Treatment of choice is topical. Use one of the following:
      a. Benzoyl peroxide, 2.5%, 5%, 10%; begin with 2.5% at bedtime. May graduate to 5% or 10% twice daily, if needed, as tolerated.
      b. T-Stat, apply to dried areas twice daily. Avoid eyes, nose, and mouth creases.
      c. Topical tretinoin 0.1% (Retin-A Micro); use at bedtime. Apply 20 to 30 minutes after washing skin.
         i. With Retin-A use, the patient may see rapid turnover of keratin plugs.
         ii. Instruct the patient to avoid abrasive soaps.
         iii. Warn the patient regarding photosensitivity.
      d. Desquam E; use at bedtime. Wash face with soap, then apply Desquam E.
   2. Moderate: Use one of the above topical medications in addition to one of the following oral medications:
      a. Tetracycline 500 mg twice daily for 3 to 6 weeks, for adolescents older than 14 years. As condition improves, begin tapering medication to 250 mg twice daily for 6 weeks, then to daily or to every other day.
         i. Instruct the patient to take tetracycline on an empty stomach and to avoid dairy products, antacids, and iron.
         ii. Warn the patient about photosensitivity. This medication may be used as a maintenance dose at 250 mg daily or every other day for those patients who break out after discontinuing antibiotic therapy. No drug resistance is seen with tetracycline.
      b. Erythromycin 250 mg four times per day after meals or topical erythromycin 2%, solution or gel, twice daily or clindamycin

(Cleocin-T), solution, pads, or gel, twice daily. Erythromycin resistance has been seen.

c. Minocycline 100 mg twice daily. When this is effective, taper to 50 mg twice daily.
   i. Have the patient drink plenty of fluids.
   ii. Central nervous system (CNS) side effects (headaches) have been seen.
d. Bactrim single strength twice daily, if the above regimens do not work well. Bactrim works well if others fail because it is effective for gram-negative folliculitis.
e. Oral contraceptives with higher doses of estrogen have also been effective for girls.

3. Severe: Medications as prescribed per dermatologist.

Follow-Up

See patients every 6 to 8 weeks for evaluation.

A. Mild: Adjust dose depending on local irritation.
B. Moderate (oral and topical medications)
   1. Adjust dose according to irritation.
   2. Taper oral antibiotics with discretion and/or continue topical medications.
   3. Oral antibiotics may be tapered and discontinued when inflammatory lesions have resolved.

Consultation/Referral

A. Consult with a physician if treatment is unsuccessful after 10 to 12 weeks of therapy or if acne is severe.
B. The patient may need dermatology consultation.

Individual Considerations

A. Pregnancy
   1. Acne may flare up or improve during pregnancy.
   2. Medications preferred during pregnancy are topical agents.
   3. **Teratogens include tretinoin, tetracycline, and minocycline.**
      a. **When using teratogenic medications, contraception must be practiced to avoid pregnancy to prevent severe fetal malformations.**
      b. **Begin contraception 1 month prior to starting the medication and 1 month after finishing the medication.**

Atopic Dermatitis

Definition

A. This pattern of skin inflammation has clinical features of erythema, itching, scaling, lichenification, papules, and vesicles in various combinations. Currently, the term *eczema* is used interchangeably with *dermatitis.* Most common variants are atopic dermatitis and atopic eczema. Classification is by cause, either endogenous or exogenous.

Incidence

A. Overall prevalence of all forms of eczema is about 18 in 1,000 in the United States.
B. With atopic dermatitis, 60% of those affected become afflicted between infancy and 12 years of age. It is more common in boys.

Pathogenesis

A. Eczema is characterized by a lymphohistiocytic infiltration around the upper dermal vessels. Epidermal spongiosis or intercellular epidermal edema and inflammation is seen.

Predisposing Factors

A. Family history of atopic triad: Dermatitis, asthma, and allergic rhinitis
B. Exposure to allergen
   1. Common foods: Cow's milk, nuts, wheat, soy, and fish
   2. Common environmental allergens: Dust, mold, cat dander, and low humidity (dry air)
C. Exposure to topical medications, most commonly neomycin, lanolin, and topical anesthetics like benzocaine
D. Skin irritants: Harsh soaps, skin-care products with perfumes, chemicals and alcohol, fabrics containing wool, tight clothing
E. Stress

Common Complaints

Skin changes

A. Itching, impossible to relieve
B. Dryness
C. Discoloration, lichenification, and scaling
D. Skin thickening
E. Associated bleeding and oozing skin

Other Signs and Symptoms

A. Primary lesions, papules, and pustules that may lead to excoriation.
B. Adults will have lesions on face, trunk, neck, and genital area.
C. Other common features include infraorbital fold (Dennie sign), increased palmar creases, facial erythema, and scaling.

Subjective Data

A. Determine whether the onset was sudden or gradual.
B. Ask the patient if the skin is itchy or painful.
C. Assess if there is any associated discharge (blood or pus).
D. Ask if the patient has recently taken any antibiotics, other oral drugs, or topical medications.
E. Ask the patient about use of soaps, creams, or lotions.
F. Assess for any preceding systemic symptoms (fever, sore throat, anorexia, vaginal discharge).
G. Ask the patient about recent travel abroad.
H. Rule out insect bites.

I. Rule out any possible exposure to industrial or domestic toxins.
J. Elicit what precipitates itching.
K. Evaluate for increased stress level at home, work, relationships, and so on.

Physical Examination

A. Check temperature (if indicated).
B. Inspect
  1. Inspect skin for lesions.
  2. Recognize bacteria-infected eczema; *S. aureus* is the most common pathogen. It appears with acute weeping dermatitis; crusted, and small, superficial pustules.

Diagnostic Tests

A. Culture skin lesions to determine viral, bacterial, or fungal etiology.
B. Blood work: Serum IgE is elevated with atopic dermatitis.

Differential Diagnoses

A. Atopic dermatitis, acute or chronic
B. Contact dermatitis, acute or chronic
C. Seborrheic dermatitis
D. Ichthyosis vulgaris
E. Bacterial/fungal infections
F. Neoplastic disease
G. Immunologic and metabolic disorders

Plan

A. General interventions
  1. Frequently treat the dry skin with emollients (Aquaphor, Eucerin).
  2. Pat, don't rub skin.
  3. Avoid wool products and lanolin preparations.
  4. Keep fingernails cut short to prevent scratching/scarring skin.
  5. May need to treat secondary bacterial infections as appropriate
  6. Eliminate trigger foods one at a time for 1 month at a time to see improvement. Begin with eliminating cow's milk products. Consider soy-based foods instead.
  7. Allergy testing may be considered if symptoms continue.
  8. Ointments are usually recommended over creams for moisturizing.
B. Patient teaching: See the Section III Patient Teaching Guide for this chapter, "Eczema."
C. Pharmaceutical therapy
  1. Atopic: Acute, adult
    a. Wet dressings with Burow's solution and changed every 2 to 3 hours.
    b. Potent topical corticosteroid: Betamethasone valerate 0.1% two to three times daily
    c. Antihistamine of choice: Cetirizine Hcl (Zyrtec) or diphenhydramine Hcl (Benadryl)
    d. Severe cases: Oral steroid: Prednisone 1 mg/kg (40–60 mg/d) tapered over 2 to 3 weeks
  2. Atopic: Chronic, adult: Short course of potent topical corticosteroid betamethasone dipropionate (Diprolene) or clobetasol propionate (temovate) twice daily for 7 days
  3. Antibacterial treatments for secondary bacterial infections: *S. aureus*
    a. Adults
      i. Augmentin 875 mg by mouth twice a day for 10 to 14 days
      ii. Keflex 500 mg by mouth four times a day for 10 to 14 days
      iii. Erythromycin 500 mg by mouth four times a day for 10 to 14 days *or*
      iv. Dicloxacillin 250 mg every 6 hours for 10 days

Follow-Up

A. See patient in office in 1 to 2 weeks and then every month until condition is stabilized.
B. Monitor the patient for superimposed staphylococcal infection; may use oral erythromycin or dicloxacillin.
C. Patient may be seen every 3 to 6 months thereafter for patient education updates.

Consultation/Referral

A. Eczema herpeticum (herpes simplex type 1) may progress rapidly. Refer the patient to a dermatologist.
B. Refer the patient to a dermatologist if skin eruptions are severe or fail to respond to conservative treatment.

Individual Considerations

A. Pregnancy: Avoid oral steroids.
B. Young adults and elderly: Nummular eczema is commonly seen, characterized by coin-shaped vesicles and papules seen on extremities and/or trunk.

Benign Skin Lesions

Definition

A benign skin lesion is a cutaneous growth with no harmful effects to the body. Benign lesions must be distinguished from the following:

A. Basal cell carcinoma (BCC): Nodular tumor with pearly surface, telangiectasia on surface, and depressed center or rolled edge.
B. Squamous cell carcinoma (SCC): Irregular papule, with scaly, friable, bleeding surface
C. Malignant melanoma: Asymmetric papule, with irregular border, of two or more colors, and greater than 6 mm in diameter.

Incidence

A. Benign lesions are common to all races, and they are seen primarily in the adult and elderly populations.

Pathogenesis

A. The course varies, depending on the specific type of lesion.

Predisposing Factors

A. Sun exposure in the adult and elderly populations
B. Dermatosis papulosa nigra: Common in African Americans and Asians

Common Complaints

A. New lesion of the skin

Other Signs and Symptoms

A. Seborrheic keratosis: Waxy papule with a stuck-on appearance is seen in adults on sun-exposed areas; they appear symmetric, 0.2 to 3.0 cm in size, with a well-demarcated border and of a variety of colors (tan, black, brown).
B. Dermatosis papulosa nigra: Hyperpigmented mole is located on face or neck; a pedunculated papule is symmetric, 1 to 3 mm in diameter.
C. Cherry angioma: Vascular papule, red to purple, is located on trunk in adults; begins in early adulthood; 1- to 3-mm diameter papules that do not blanch.
D. Solar lentigines (liver spots): Tan maculae appear on sun-exposed areas in elders, especially on face and hands; border is irregular, and the size varies.
E. Senile sebaceous hyperplasia: Enlarged sebaceous glands appear as yellow papules on sun-exposed areas, especially on face in elders; papules have central umbilication, and their size varies.
F. Keratoacanthoma: Sun-exposed area lesion, is smooth, skin-colored or reddish in appearance, dome-shaped papule at first, then may turn and grows to 1 to 2 cm in a few weeks, with crusted interior.

Subjective Data

A. Identify when the patient first discovered the lesion.
B. Determine whether the lesion has changed in size, shape, or color.
C. Ask if the patient has discovered more lesions.
D. Elicit information regarding a family history of skin lesions or cancer.

Physical Examination

A. Inspect
   1. Observe skin; note all lesions and evaluate each for asymmetry, border, color, diameter, evolving changes, and/or elevation change.
   2. Note the patient's skin type.

Diagnostic Tests

A. Benign lesions do not require any tests.
B. If unsure regarding possible malignancy, a biopsy is recommended.

Differential Diagnoses

A. Benign skin lesion
   1. Seborrheic keratosis
   2. Dermatosis papulosa nigra
   3. Cherry angioma
   4. Solar lentigines
   5. Senile sebaceous hyperplasia
   6. Keratoacanthoma

Plan

A. General interventions
   1. Reassure the patient that lesions are benign. No treatment is required unless the patient chooses to have the lesion removed for cosmetic purposes.
   2. Lesions may be removed using cryotherapy if they are bothersome for the patient.
B. Patient teaching: See the Section III Patient Teaching Guide for this chapter, "Skin Care Assessment."
C. Pharmaceutical therapy
   1. Topical 5-fluorouracil, 5% imiquimod cream (Aldara), or topical diclofenac gel may be used for benign lesions.

Follow-Up

A. Routine skin exams should be performed yearly.

Consultation/Referral

A. Immediately refer patient to a dermatologist if malignancy is suspected or confirmed by biopsy.

Individual Considerations

A. Adults: Skin lesions begin to appear in early adulthood. Encourage patients to monitor lesions over time.
B. Geriatrics: Benign lesions are commonly seen in the elderly population.

Bites

Animal Bites, Mammalian

Definition

A. A bite from any mammalian animal to a human can be potentially dangerous. Bites from human to human are included.

Incidence

A. Account for 1 to 3.5 million emergency department (ED) visits each year.
B. About 80% to 90% of bites are dog bites.
C. About 6% of bites are cat bites.
D. From 1% to 15% are human bites.
E. The elderly are especially prone to bites.

Pathogenesis

A. Mechanical trauma and break to skin and/or underlying structures
B. Infection from transmission of bacteria
   1. *Pasteurella multocida* is primarily associated with cat bites but may also be associated with dog bites.
   2. *Staphylococcus aureus, Staphylococcus epidermis,* and *Enterobacter* species can be transmitted with dog and cat bites.
   3. *Streptobacillus moniliformis* can be transmitted with rat and mice bites.
   4. *Streptococcus, Staphylococcus,* and *Eikenella* can be transmitted with human bites.
   5. Human bites can transmit diseases such as actinomycosis, syphilis, tuberculosis, hepatitis B, and, potentially, HIV.
C. Rabies, an acute viral infection, may be transmitted by means of infected saliva or by an infected animal licking mucosa from an open wound. It is rarely contracted by means of airborne transmission, but this has been reported to occur in bat-infested caves.

Predisposing Factors

A. Elderly
B. Entering an animal's territorial space and/or surprising an animal

Common Complaints

A. Bitten by an animal
B. Pain
C. Redness
D. Swelling

Subjective Data

A. What person or type of animal bit the patient?
B. Was this a provoked or an unprovoked attack?
C. Did the patient identify and contact the owner of the animal?
D. What was the behavior of the animal; unusual, strange, or ill-appearing?
E. How much time elapsed from being bitten to seeking treatment?
F. Did the patient start any self-treatment?
G. What is the patient's tetanus immunization status?
H. Review history for any prior rabies immunizations.
I. Does the patient know if the animal was a domestic animal? Is the animal's vaccination status known?
J. If the bite is of human origin, determine if it is a closed-fist injury (a human bite/injury that occurs when the closed fist is injured, with teeth penetrating the skin, joint, and possibly bone, over the metacarpal heads) or plain bite.

Physical Examination

A. Check blood pressure, pulse, and respirations; observe overall respiratory status.
B. See Table 6.1.

Diagnostic Tests

A. Refer to Table 6.1.

Differential Diagnoses

A. Animal bite: Dog, cat, human, and so forth
   1. Cat bites more frequently become infected.
   2. Bites on the hand have the highest infection rates. Bites on the face have the lowest infection rates.

TABLE 6.1 Bites

Animal	Signs and Symptoms	Physical Exam (check temperature for all animal bites)	Diagnostic Tests
Dog	Crush injury, lacerations, and abrasions	Inspect site, underlying structures, and distal neurovascular, motor, and sensory function Palpate area. If wound is over 24 hours old, check any signs of cellulitis, lymphangitis	If infected: Laboratory: Complete blood count (CBC), culture and sensitivity for anaerobes and aerobes
Cat	Puncture wounds, may be deep	Determine depth and extent of wound Check for foreign bodies If wound is over 24 hours old, check any signs of cellulitis, lymphangitis	If sepsis suspected: Laboratory: CBC, culture and sensitivity of abscess/tissue site
Rat and squirrel	Laceration, abrasions; more superficial in nature	Check for signs of infection, if wound is over 24 hours old. Check any signs of cellulitis, lymphangitis	If infected: Laboratory: CBC, culture, and sensitivity
Human	Crush injury, laceration; wound of hand (closed-fist wound)	Check for signs of infection, if wound is over 24 hours old Check any signs of cellulitis, lymphangitis. Also, examine for fractures, air in the joint, subchondral bone defects, and osteomyelitis Examine for full range of interphalangeal and metacarpophalangeal joints	As above Also, take x-ray of structures underlying bite

B. Cellulitis and abscesses
C. High-risk potential for rabies from bites from the following:
   1. Skunks, foxes, raccoons, and bats are primary carriers.
   2. Rabbits, squirrels, chipmunks, rats, and mice are seldom infective for rabies.
   3. Properly vaccinated animals seldom are infective.

Plan

A. General interventions
   1. Control bleeding.
   2. Wound care
      a. Immediately wash wound copiously with soap and water.
      b. Irrigate wound with saline, benzalkonium chloride (Zephiran), or 1% povidone-iodine (if the patient is not allergic to iodine).
      c. May use Waterpik.
      d. Use 150 to 1,000 mL of saline solution.
      e. Direct stream on entire wound surface.
      f. Scrub entire surrounding area.
      g. Debride all wounds.
      h. Trim any jagged edges to prevent cosmetic and/or functional complications.
      i. Cover with dry dressing.
   3. Do not suture those wounds with high risk for infection
      a. Hand bites, closed-fist injuries
      b. Bites older than 6 to 12 hours
      c. Deep or puncture wounds
      d. Bites with extensive injury of surface or underlying structures
   4. Rabies control measures
      a. Consult with the local health department regarding risk of rabies in the area.
      b. The domestic animal should be identified, caught, and confined for 10 days of observation. If the animal develops any signs of rabies, it should be destroyed and its brain tissue analyzed. No treatment is necessary if results are negative.
      c. The wild animal should be caught and destroyed for brain tissue analysis. No treatment is necessary if results are negative.
      d. If the bat or wild carnivore cannot be found, rabies prophylaxis is instituted.
B. Patient teaching: Instruct the patient how to keep site free from infection.
C. Pharmaceutical therapy
   1. Antibiotic prophylaxis is controversial, but it is generally recommended for wounds involving subcutaneous tissues and deeper structures.
      a. Prescribe amoxicillin, clavulanic acid (Augmentin) 500 to 875 mg every 12 hours.
      b. Alternatively, prescribe erythromycin (E-Mycin) 250 mg four times daily for 3 to 7 days.
   2. Tetanus prophylaxis
   3. Rabies prophylaxis
      a. Active immunization: Human diploid cell vaccine (HDCV), 1 mL, is given intramuscularly on first day of treatment, and repeat doses are administered on days 3, 7, 14, and 28.
      b. Passive immunization: Rabies immunoglobulin (RIG); (human) should be used simultaneously with first dose of HDCV; recommended dose of RIG is 20 IU/kg. Approximately one-half of RIG is infiltrated into wound, and the remainder is given intramuscularly.

Follow-Up

A. Evaluate wound and change dressing in 24 to 48 hours.
B. Reevaluate as indicated. If the patient is on immunoprophylaxis and has no signs of infection, see in 1 week.
C. Instruct the patient to return immediately for any signs of infection.

Consultation/Referral

A. Refer all patients with bites of ears, face, genitalia, hands, and feet.
B. Consult with a doctor if suspicion of rabies is involved.
C. Contact the local health department.
D. Wounds involving tendon, joint, or bone require hospitalization and surgical consultation.

Individual Considerations

A. Pregnancy: Use appropriate antibiotic management.
B. Elderly: Consider chronic conditions (chronic kidney disease, diabetes, etc.) when prescribing the patient antibiotics.

Insect Bites and Stings

Definition

A. Bites and/or stings on the skin come from commonly encountered insects, bees, hornets, wasps, mosquitoes, chiggers, ticks, fleas, and fire ants.

Incidence

A. Bites are seen in all age groups, more commonly in summer months.

Pathogenesis

A. Some bites elicit local tissue inflammation and destruction due to proteins and enzymes in the poison or venom of the insect.
B. IgE-mediated allergic reactions (immediate or delayed) may occur.
C. Serum-sickness reaction may appear 10 to 14 days after a sting with venom. Toxic reactions can also

occur from multiple stings, yielding large inoculation of poison or venom.

D. With tick bites, exposure to Rocky Mountain Spotted Fever, Lyme disease, ehrlichiosis, and babesiosis disease may occur.

Predisposing Factors

A. Exposure to areas of heavy insect infestations
B. Warm weather months
C. Outdoor exposure with barefoot, bright clothes
D. Use of perfumes and/or colognes
E. Previous sensitization

Common Complaints

A. Local reaction: Pain, swelling, and redness at site after insect bite
B. Toxic reaction: Local reaction plus headache, vertigo, gastrointestinal symptoms (nausea, vomiting, diarrhea), syncope, convulsions, and/or fever

Subjective Data

A. Did patient see what bit or stung him or her?
B. If the patient felt the bite or sting, was he or she bitten or stung once or multiple times?
C. How long ago did it occur?
D. Where was the patient when the injury occurred (environment)?
E. Has the patient ever been bitten or stung before? If so, did he or she have any reaction then? If so, what was the treatment?

Physical Examination

A. Check temperature, pulse, respirations, and blood pressure. Observe overall respiratory status.
B. Inspect
    1. Inspect site of injury for local reaction; note erythema, rash, or edema.
    2. Perform ears, nose, and throat exam.
C. Auscultate: Assess heart and lungs.
D. Palpate
    1. Palpate injured site.
    2. Assess nodes for lymphadenopathy.
    3. Perform abdominal exam, if appropriate.

Diagnostic Tests

A. None are required.
B. Consider taking skin scrapings to evaluate under microscope.
C. Consider culture if infection is suspected.

Differential Diagnoses

A. Insect bite
    1. Bees, hornets, wasps: Local pain, redness, pruritus, and swelling occur at site. Red papules and wheals appear, enlarge, and then subside within hours. Delayed hypersensitivity occurs within 7 days with enlarged, local reaction with fever, malaise, headache, arthralgias, and lymphadenopathy. Toxicity can occur. Anaphylaxis may be seen with generalized warmth and urticaria, erythema, angioedema, intestinal cramping, bronchospasm, laryngospasm, shock, and collapse.
    2. Ticks: Local redness, swelling, itching; enlarged area of redness and swelling may occur.
    3. Mosquitoes and chiggers: Local redness, swelling, and itching occur. Delayed reaction can include edema and burning sensation.
    4. Fleas: Local redness, swelling, and itching occur. Usually, papules are noted in a zigzag pattern, especially on legs and waist. Note hemorrhagic puncta surrounded by erythematous and urticarial patches.
    5. Body lice: Small noninflammatory red spots, intensely pruritic, are found on waist, shoulders, axilla, and neck. Note linear scratch marks. Note secondary bacterial infection.
    6. Scabies: Pruritus is the dominant symptom. Note inflammation and burrows in skin with papules and vesicles, especially in the webs of the hands and feet.
    7. Fire ants: Papules appear and turn to pustules within 6 to 24 hours after bite. Watch for localized necrosis with scarring. Urticaria and angioedema can occur.
B. Allergic reaction

Plan

A. General interventions
    1. **Anaphylaxis: Activate EMS (emergency medical services) immediately.** With all bites and stings, treat anaphylaxis first.
    2. Local reactions: Treat with analgesic of choice. Apply ice packs to site for approximately 10 minutes. Elevate affected extremities.
    3. Delayed reactions: Administer antihistamines as needed. Consider corticosteroid use.
    4. Routine wound care: Cleanse wound. Remove stinger. If it's a painful sting, apply a cotton ball soaked in meat tenderizer or sodium bicarbonate paste.
    5. Debride as necessary.
    6. For embedded insects, apply petroleum jelly, nail polish, or alcohol over the site for 30 minutes and wait for insect or tick to withdraw.
    7. Referral to allergist-immunologist is recommended for patients with a severe systemic reaction for skin testing and to evaluate for candidacy of venom immunotherapy treatment.
    8. Hospitalize the patient with severe reactions.
B. See the Section III Patient Teaching Guide for this chapter, "Insect Bites and Stings."

C. Pharmaceutical therapy
  1. Antihistamines
    a. Adult: Diphenhydramine (Benadryl) 50 mg every 6 hours as needed
  2. Mild anaphylaxis
    a. Epinephrine 1:1000 aqueous solution: 0.3 to 0.5 mL intramuscular (IM). Repeat dosing may be necessary.
  3. Oral antihistamines for next 24 hours (Atarax)
    a. Adults: Hydroxyzine hydrochloride (Atarax) 10 to 25 mg four times daily
  4. Severe anaphylaxis
    a. Epinephrine 1:1000 aqueous solution: 0.3 to 0.5 mL IM. Repeat dosing may be necessary.
    b. Oxygen 2 to 4 L as needed
    c. Albuterol (Ventolin) 5 mg/mL per dose by nebulizer
      i. Adults: 2.5 mg (0.5 mL of 0.5% solution) in 2 mL saline
  5. Self-treatment for anaphylaxis (emergency treatment kits)
    a. Ana-Kit contains a preloaded syringe.
    b. Epipen and Epipen Junior Auto-Injectors are spring-loaded automatic injectors.

Follow-Up
A. Follow up in 2 weeks to evaluate effectiveness of treatment. If symptoms worsen prior to this, evaluation is needed.

Referral/Consultation
A. Consult with physician when anaphylaxis occurs.

Individual Considerations
A. The elderly patient, patients who are immobilized, those with preexisting heart disease or mast cell disorder, those being treated with certain medications (such as beta-adrenergics or angiotensin-converting enzyme [ACE] inhibitors), and those who have had a previous reaction to an insect bite are at the greatest risk for complications when an insect bite occurs. Bites obtained from fire ants, bees, hornets, and wasps may result in severe stings that may even result in death. The honeybee sting is known to present the greatest risk for complications and/or anaphylaxis.

Bullous Pemphigoid

Definition
Bullous pemphigoid is an autoimmune skin condition that occurs primarily in older adults, which is characterized by blisters and/or erosive lesions of the skin or mucosa.

Incidence
Most cases occur in adults older than the age of 60 years. Studies show that during 2000 to 2005, the incidence of bullous pemphigoid was approximately 22 cases per million people, which is three times greater than in previous years.

Pathogenesis
A. The mechanism of the physiological changes that occur in the body to cause bullous pemphigoid is not fully understood. It is believed to be an autoimmune disorder, driven by autoantibody-mediated effects that cause damage to the epithelial basement membrane. Antibodies attach to the antigens on the basement membrane, causing inflammatory changes, resulting in separation of the epidermis from the dermis in the skin and separation of the epithelium from the subepithelial tissue in the mucous membranes, producing blister lesions on the affected tissues.

Predisposing Factors
A. Age (adults older than 60 years)
B. Exposure to certain medications (penicillin, etanercept [Enbrel], sulfasalazine [Azulfidine], and furosemide [Lasix])
C. UV light and radiation therapy

Common Complaints
A. Large, tense blisters commonly located on the arms, legs, or trunk. Commonly seen along skin folds/creases.
B. Blisters may be asymptomatic or may be erythemic and pruritic

Other Signs and Symptoms
A. Irritation to the oral mucosa, mouth sores, and/or bleeding gums
B. Rash in addition to skin blisters
C. Changes in mucous membranes of the eyes, noting redness and discomfort

Potential Complications
A. Bacterial skin infection
B. Sepsis
C. Scarring of the mucous membranes in the mouth or eye

Subjective Data
A. Ask patient if there was any precipitating event prior to the outbreak of the blisters.
B. Have patient describe when the blisters began and the duration of the blisters.
C. Ask patient to describe the onset of the presenting lesions and the progression of the lesions.
D. Ask if the blisters are painful. If so, describe pain, such as stabbing, burning, throbbing, and so on.

E. Rate pain on a scale of 0 to 10, with 0 being no pain.
F. List all medications currently being taken, particularly substances not prescribed. Did the blisters begin after the initiation of any new medications?

Physical Examination

A. Assess vital signs: Check temperature, pulse, respirations, and blood pressure.
B. Inspect
   1. Inspect general appearance of the skin, noting types of blisters/lesions. Note the location of the blisters, along with erythema, inflammation, or weeping. Inspect skin folds carefully.
   2. Inspect the blisters for stages of the blister.
   3. Inspect oral cavity for oral lesions.
   4. Perform ophthalmologic exam: Inspect eyes for erythema, edema, and ulcers.

Diagnostic Tests

A. Biopsy: Skin lesion biopsy for staining and for direct immunofluorescence (DIF) studies. The gold standard for diagnosis is a positive DIF.
B. Blood tests: Peripheral blood smear. Elevated eosinophils and increased IgG levels may be present.

Differential Diagnosis

A. Bullous pemphigoid
B. Cellulitis
C. Dermatitis

Plan

A. General interventions
   1. Promote healing of blisters and prevent secondary bacterial infection.
   2. The goal of treatment is to control blister formation.
B. Patient teaching
   1. Inform patient regarding the course of bullous pemphigoid. This skin condition may last for months or years. Therefore, treatment options are variable for all patients.
   2. Advise the patient to avoid sun exposure directly on the skin.
   3. Skin care: Educate the patient regarding taking care of the fragile skin, avoiding injury to all sites. Tense blisters should be cleansed well with alcohol and carefully ruptured with a sterile needle. The overlying tissue from the blister should remain intact to act as a natural wound cover. Open sores should be covered with a non-adherent bandage to reduce the risk of infection.
   4. Oral blisters should be protected by avoiding spicy or hard foods that would cause more injury to the oral ulcers.
C. Pharmaceutical therapy
   1. First-line therapy suggested is topical steroids. Topical steroids, such as clobetasol propionate 0.05% cream, are applied to the affected area bid until inflammation, new blister formation, and pruritus have resolved for at least 2 weeks. Then gradually taper the steroid cream over the next few weeks to months.
   2. If the topical steroids are not successful, oral steroids may be used. Prednisone 0.5 to 0.75 mg/kg/d may be used as a starting dose. Oral prednisone is used until inflammation, new blister formation, and pruritis have resolved for at least 2 weeks. Then gradually taper the prednisone over the next several weeks to months.
   3. In severe cases, immunosuppressants may be prescribed to help control the lesions. These medications may include methotrexate, azathioprine (Imuran), and mycophenolate mofetil (Cellcept). Using these medications may also allow weaning of the use of corticosteroids.
   4. Medications with anti-inflammatory effects may also be used, such as tetracycline and dapsone.
   5. Antibiotics and niacin may be prescribed for signs of bacterial infection. Tetracycline antibiotics may be used for mild cases. Niacin may also be prescribed, along with tetracycline, to help control gastrointestinal side effects.
   6. Patients who do not respond to steroid treatments may be prescribed biologic therapy such as intravenous rituximab.

Follow-Up

For patients on oral or topical treatments, recommend a follow-up appointment in 1 to 2 weeks, depending on the presentation. If signs of bacterial infection are present, then follow-up would need to be sooner.

Consultation/Referral

A. **Consult with the physician or the dermatologist for all patients who present with signs of bullous pemphigoid for treatment options.**
B. **Consult with the physician if signs of bacterial infection are present. In severe cases, sepsis can develop and become life-threatening for compromised patients.**
C. **The physician or the dermatologist should prescribe potent medications, such as immunosuppressants.**
D. **Refer any patient who presents with any eye involvement to the ophthalmologist.**

Individual Considerations

A. Pregnancy: Rarely seen in this population
B. Geriatrics: Most commonly seen in adults older than 60 years of age. Patients who are compromised or in poor health may develop a secondary bacterial infection, which can be life-threatening.

Candidiasis

Definition

A. A fungal infection of the mucous membranes and/or skin, candidiasis is caused by the *Candida albicans* fungus.

Incidence

A. It occurs frequently in women, children, and the elderly population.

Pathogenesis

A. An overgrowth of *C. albicans* occurs when mucous membranes and/or skin are exposed to moisture, warmth, and an alteration in the membrane barrier.

Predisposing Factors

A. Immunosuppression
B. Use of antibiotics
C. Hyperglycemia
D. Chronic use of steroid
E. Frequent douching by women
F. Adults who wear dentures
G. Urinary/fecal incontinence

Common Complaints

A. Oral: Persistent white patch on the tongue or roof of mouth may be slightly reddened with or without crevices on the tongue.
B. Vaginal: Thick, white, "cottage-cheese-like" vaginal discharge with or without vaginal itching
C. Genital: Bright, red rash with well-demarcated satellite lesions advancing to pustules or erosions in genital or diaper area
D. Males: Erythemic rash that may advance to erosions on the genitalia/scrotal area

Subjective Data

A. Question the patient about onset, duration, and location of lesions.
B. Determine whether the patient has a history of previous infections.
C. Inquire into medical history and current medications.
D. Rule out the presence of any other current medical conditions.

Physical Examination

A. Inspect
   1. Assess skin and mucous membranes for discharge and lesions.
   2. Observe location and severity of lesions.
B. Palpate: Palpate lymph nodes in neck and groin.

Diagnostic Tests

A. Vaginal and genital infections need to be evaluated for sexually transmitted infections (STIs), especially if the patient is sexually active with multiple partners. Vaginal/genital culture specimen should be sent for gonorrhea/chlamydia testing.
B. Other specimens to consider include wet prep/potassium hydroxide (KOH) 10% solution, Gram stain vaginal culture for candida.

Differential Diagnoses

A. Oral candidiasis
   1. Leukoplakia
   2. Stomatitis
B. Genital area
   1. Candidiasis
   2. Bacterial infection
   3. Bacterial vaginosis
   4. Chlamydia
   5. Gonorrhea
   6. Trichomoniasis

Plan

A. Patient teaching
   1. Instruct the patient on applying medication to the skin.
   2. Advise the patient to avoid scratching the site and keep fingernails short.
B. Pharmaceutical therapy: Choose *one* of the following pharmaceutical therapies:
   1. Oral
      a. Nystatin (Mycostatin) oral suspension 100,000 U/mL, four times daily for 7 to 10 days
      b. Gentian violet aqueous solution, 2% for adults, one to two times per day
      c. Lotrimin buccal troches, five times per day for 2 weeks
   2. Topical
      a. Nystatin cream, three to four times per day for 7 to 10 days
      b. Mycolog-II: Apply sparingly to skin twice daily until resolved.
   3. Vaginal
      a. Clotrimazole 1% cream, 5 g intravaginally for 7 to 4 days
      b. Miconazole 2% cream, 5 g intravaginally for 7 days (OTC)
      c. Terconazole 0.8% cream, 5 g intravaginally for 3 days
      d. Terconazole 80 mg vaginal suppository, at bedtime for 3 days
      e. Fluconazole (Diflucan) 150 mg, oral tablet one time

Follow-Up

A. None indicated unless not resolved or complications arise.

Consultation/Referral

A. Consult a physician if not resolved within 2 weeks.

Individual Considerations

A. Pregnancy
  1. Most effective medications for pregnant women are clotrimazole, miconazole, and terconazole.
  2. Recommend a full 7-day course of treatment during pregnancy.

B. Adults
  1. Consider immunosuppression in all adults with oral candidiasis (HIV, diabetes, chemotherapy, leukemia).
  2. Adults with oral lesions need to be assessed for leukoplakia, especially if the patient has a history of smoking or using chewing tobacco.

Cellulitis and Abscess

Abscess

Definition

A. An abscess is a pocket of pus under the skin tissue that may invade deeper skin tissue.

Pathogenesis

A. An abscess develops when a collection of bacteria builds up in the tissue of the body. There may be several types of bacteria present. One common organism is methicillin-resistant *Staphylococcus aureus*.

Common Complaints

A. Painful, swollen, erythemic pocket of pus under the skin tissue

Subjective Data

A. Ask the patient when signs and symptoms of infection, discomfort, redness, or swelling began.

B. Has the patient experienced fever, chills, or other symptoms?

C. What has been used to treat the abscess? Have heat, ice, topical antibiotics, lotions, and so on been used?

D. What treatments make the symptoms worse or better?

Physical Examination

A. Assess site of abscess.

B. Measure length times width.

C. Note erythema, edema, warmth/fever of tissue, tenderness with palpation. Does pain radiate to other areas? If so, where?

D. Is abscess open and draining fluid? If so, note color, consistency, and odor of drainage.

Diagnostic Tests

A. Laboratory testing (complete blood count [CBC], comprehensive metabolic panel [CMP])

B. Open or draining abscess: Culture and sensitivity, and Gram stain

Differential Diagnoses

A. Wound abscess

B. Cellulitis

C. Folliculitis

Plan

A. General interventions
  1. Incision and drainage (I&D) can successfully be performed for an uncomplicated abscess.
  2. Precautions should be considered for contraindications for an I&D. These contraindications include:
     a. Abscess location (perirectal, neck, hand, central area of the face, breasts, and in close proximity to major nerves and blood vessels)
     b. Recurrent abscesses
  3. After completing the I&D, the area should be allowed to close by secondary intention.
  4. Sterile packing should be inserted into the cavity for abscesses larger than 5 cm in diameter, pilonidal abscesses, and for patients with compromised immune systems.

B. Patient teaching
  1. Educate the patient regarding home care for the site of the abscess. If packing is required, instruct patient to return to the physician's office for packing, or consider home health care to perform dressing changes.
  2. New packing should be replaced every 24 to 48 hours until drainage has resolved and until new granulation tissue is present.
  3. Once packing is no longer necessary, the patient will clean the cavity with warm, wet compresses two to three times a day until healed.

C. Pharmaceutical therapy
  1. Oral antibiotic treatments: Antibiotics should be prescribed; using antibiotics that are sensitive to methicillin-resistant *S. aureus* (MRSA). See pharmacological treatment options in this chapter under *Cellulitis*.

Follow-Up

A. The patient should return in 24 to 48 hours to evaluate the cavity and insert new packing as needed.

B. If symptoms worsen prior to follow-up, recommend that the patient to proceed to the emergency department for further assessment.

Consultation/Referral

A. Consult with physician for all abscesses requiring I&D with packing.

B. Consult physician for all abscesses that are not responding to antibiotic treatment for further evaluation.

C. See the entry, Cellulitis, for other treatment options.

Cellulitis

Definition

A. Cellulitis is an acute inflammation and infection of the skin and subcutaneous tissue.

Incidence

A. Cellulitis is not a reportable infection; therefore, the exact incidence is not known. However, some studies show that the incidence of cellulitis is approximately 200 patients per 100,000 patient years.

Pathogenesis

A. Cellulitis occurs when bacteria attacks the skin tissue, which involves the dermis and subcutaneous tissue. The most common organisms causing this bacterial infection include beta-hemolytic Streptococcus (groups A, B, C, G, and F) and *Staphylococcus aureus*.
B. The most common organisms causing an abscess include *S. aureus* (either methicillin-susceptible *S. aureus* or MRSA) that occurs in up to 75% of cases and Group A streptococci.
C. Bacteria may invade healthy tissue but commonly occurs in damaged tissue where there is a break in the skin, allowing invasion of the tissue that can lead to bacterial infection.

Predisposing Factors

A. Age (adults older than 45 years, geriatrics)
B. Immunocompromised immune system
C. Chronic medical conditions (diabetes)
D. History of IV drug abuse
E. Alcoholism
F. Peripheral vascular disease
G. Previous history of cellulitis

Common Complaints

A. Erythema, pain, swelling, and warmth are the classic symptoms.
B. Fever, malaise, and chills
C. Lymphadenopathy of adjacent lymph nodes to site of infection
D. Trauma to skin tissue

Other Signs and Symptoms

A. Drainage/discharge at wound site
B. Erythemic streaks that progress away from the infection site
C. Systemic signs of infection (fever, tachycardia, tachypnea, hypotension, change in mental status)

Potential Complications

A. Sepsis
B. Necrosis of tissue
C. Osteomyelitis

Subjective Data

A. Ask the patient if there was any activity/injury that preceded the episode.
B. Inquire regarding the onset, location, and duration of pain and symptoms. Has the area increased in size or spread to other areas?
C. Ask the patient to describe pain, for example, crushing, stabbing, or burning sensation.
D. Have the patient rate pain on a scale of 0 to 10, with 0 being no pain.
E. Inquire regarding any previous trauma to affected area. Has anyone else had similar symptoms?

Physical Examination

A. Vital signs: Check temperature, pulse, respirations, and blood pressure.
B. Inspect
   1. Inspect general appearance of skin. Note location of involved skin and note erythemic streaking if present.
   2. Measure size (mm/cm) of skin involvement. May include pictures if applicable
   3. Note presence of erythema, edema, and color of skin tissue involved (pink, erythemic, necrotic, pale, etc.).
C. Palpate
   1. Palpate site for warmth, tenderness, firmness, fluctuance.
   2. Palpate adjacent lymph nodes to assess for lymphadenopathy.
D. Auscultate
   1. Heart
   2. Lungs

Diagnostic Tests

A. Laboratory (blood cultures, Gram stain, culture specimen from the abscess, CBC with diff, CRP creatinine, bicarbonate, creatine phosphokinase).
   1. Blood cultures: Recommended for patients presenting with signs of systemic toxicity, extensive skin involvement, a history of comorbid conditions, history of recurrent cellulitis, and/or trauma (dog/cat bite, puncture wounds, etc.).
   2. Culture and sensitivities should be performed on patients with signs of systemic infection, severe skin impairment, history of chronic conditions, recurrent infections, and a history of animal or water injury.
B. Imaging studies
   1. Ultrasound to assess for abscess
   2. X-ray may be performed if suspicious for osteomyelitis.
   3. CT or MRI may be considered when assessing for necrotizing fasciitis.

Differential Diagnosis

A. Cellulitis
B. Abscess
C. Dermatitis

D. Erysipelas (A superficial skin infection that commonly occurs on the face, ears, and/or lower legs. It commonly presents with erythema of the skin with a distinct demarcated border commonly caused by group A streptococcus bacteria. Erysipelas is more commonly seen in older adults.)

Plan

A. General interventions
   1. If there are signs of systemic infection, hospitalization is required.
   2. Educate the patient regarding care for site.
   3. Instruct patient on reporting worsening symptoms as soon as possible to prevent sepsis.

B. Patient teaching
   1. Instruct patient to keep site clean and dry, recommending elevation of extremity if applicable.
   2. Recommend OTC pain medication such as acetaminophen (Tylenol) or ibuprofen (Advil, Motrin) as needed for pain.
   3. Advise patient to notify the primary provider for the following symptoms.
      a. Fever more than 100.0°F
      b. Chills
      c. Increase in size of redness or change in size/consistency of site (i.e., abscess formation)
      d. Erythemic streaks
      e. Lymphadenopathy
      f. Increase in pain
   4. Instruct the patient on use of antibiotics and stress the importance of finishing the full course of prescribed antibiotics.
   5. Once the infection has resolved, stress the importance of notifying the primary provider for reoccurring symptoms.
   6. Recurrent cellulitis should be evaluated for the cause. Chronic underlying conditions, such as edema, should be treated to prevent future episodes. Edema may be treated with compression stocking therapy and/or the use of diuretics.

C. Pharmaceutical therapy
   1. Uncomplicated cellulitis: Oral treatments: cephalexin 500 mg tablet every 6 hours; or dicloxacillin 500 mg tablet every 6 hours; or clindamycin 300 to 450 mg tablet every 6 to 8 hours. Oral medications are prescribed for 5 to 10 days.
      a. Empiric treatment for MRSA should be considered for the following patients:
         i. Patients who do not respond to initial treatment
         ii. Patients with signs of sepsis
         iii. Patients who have recurrent cellulitis
         iv. Patients who have a history of MRSA
   2. Cellulitis MRSA: Oral treatments: doxycycline 100 mg tablet twice a day or clindamycin 300 to 450 mg tablet three times a day or trimethoprim/sulfamethoxazole 1 double strength (DS) tablet twice a day or minocycline 200 mg tablet once then 100 mg tablet twice a day or linezolid 600 mg tablet twice a day or tedizolid 200 mg tablet daily. Oral medications are prescribed for 5 to 10 days.
      a. Dosing should be individualized according the underlying conditions. Obese patients may have a higher failure rate if not prescribed adequate dosing.
      b. Patients with purulent drainage should be treated for MRSA pending culture results.
      c. Patients with renal impairment will require dosage adjustments.
   3. Complicated cellulitis: Intravenous antibiotics should be prescribed for patients with complicated cellulitis and/or erysipelas with signs of sepsis (fever/chills). Antibiotic treatments may include cefazolin, oxacillin, nafcillin, vancomycin, daptomycin, and ceftaroline.

Follow-Up

A. Patient needs to follow up in 24 to 48 hours for reassessment.

B. If worsening symptoms are present, recommend that the patient proceed to the ED for evaluation and treatment.

Consultation/Referral

A. If necrotizing fasciitis is suspected, referral for a surgical consult is imperative.

B. Inpatient hospitalization is recommended for the following:
   1. Hypotension
   2. Elevated creatinine level
   3. Creatine elevated two to three times over normal values
   4. CRP more than 13 mg/L
   5. Low serum bicarbonate level
   6. Elevation in CBC with left shift

Individual Considerations

A. Geriatrics
   1. Suppressive antibiotic therapy is recommended for patients with predisposing risk factors who have a history of recurrent cellulitis.
   2. Geriatric patients are at increased risk of developing thrombophlebitis following an acute episode of cellulitis.

Contact Dermatitis

Definition

A. Contact dermatitis is a cutaneous response to direct exposure of the skin to irritants (irritant contact dermatitis) or allergens (allergic contact dermatitis).
   1. Irritant contact dermatitis is a nonimmunologic response of the epidermis.

2. Allergic contact dermatitis is an immunologic response after one or more exposures to a particular agent.

Incidence

A. Occurs in all ages. People who work with chemicals daily and wash their hands numerous times a day have a higher incidence of irritant dermatitis. Irritant contact dermatitis is seen in the elderly due to dry skin.

Pathogenesis

A. Irritant contact dermatitis is caused by an alteration of the outer layer of the dermis due to exposure to chemicals; lotions; cold, dry air; soaps; detergents; or organic solvents.
B. Allergic contact dermatitis is caused by an alteration in the epidermis when, after exposure to an allergen, the immune system responds by producing inflammation of the cutaneous tissue. Common allergens include poison ivy, poison oak, sumac, nickel jewelry, hair dye, rubber and leather chemicals (latex gloves), cleaning supplies, harsh soaps, detergents, and topical medicines.

Predisposing Factors

A. Occupation (hairdresser, nurse, housecleaner, etc.)
B. Jewelry
C. Activities in yard or woods

Common Complaints

A. Irritation of the skin, ranging from redness to pruritic inflammation, with possible progression of blisters.
   1. Poison oak, ivy, and sumac induce classic presentation: Lesions (vesicles) and papules on an erythemic base presenting in a linear fashion with sharp margins.
   2. Diffuse pattern with erythema may be seen when oleoresin is contracted from pets or smoke from burning fire.
B. Exposure to some type of irritant known to the patient. Round or annular lesions may have an internal cause such as a drug reaction.

Other Signs and Symptoms

A. Chronic
   1. Erythema with thickening
   2. Scaling
   3. Fissures
   4. Inflammation
   5. Lichenification may occur with scales and fissures.
B. Candidiasis diaper rash
   1. Bright red rash with satellite lesions at margins
   2. Inflammation and excoriations present
   3. Creases may be involved.

Subjective Data

A. Ask the patient when irritation began and how it has progressed.
B. Elicit history of exposure to allergens.
C. Question the patient regarding activity and skin contact with irritants prior to outbreak (cleaning agents, walking in woods, hobbies, change in soap/laundry detergent, shaving cream, lotions, etc.).
D. List occupation and family history of allergens.
E. Review medication list, including prescription, OTC, and herbal treatments to evaluate for an interaction.
F. List medications used to relieve symptoms and results.

Physical Examination

A. Check temperature (if indicated).
B. Inspect
   1. Inspect skin, noting types of lesions and location of lesions. **Note the pattern of inflammation. The shape of irritation may mimic the shape of the irritant, such as the skin under a ring or watch, for example.**
   2. Determine progression of lesions.
   3. Differentiate between primary and secondary lesions.

Diagnostic Tests

A. Consider none if source is known.
B. Wet mount (KOH, saline) to rule out fungal infection if candidiasis is suspected.
C. Culture/sensitivity of pustules
D. Patch test to rule out allergic contact dermatitis.

Differential Diagnoses

A. Irritant contact dermatitis
B. Allergic contact dermatitis
C. Candidiasis
D. Tinea pedis, corporis, cruris
E. Drug reactions
F. Pityriasis rosea
G. Scabies

Plan

A. General interventions
   1. Irritant contact dermatitis: Removal of irritating agent
      a. Topical soaks with saline or Burow's solution (1:40 dilution) for weeping areas
      b. Recommend lukewarm baths (not hot), with oatmeal (Aveeno), as needed
      c. For dry erythematous skin, use Eucerin or Aquaphor ointments to rehydrate skin
      d. Remind the patient to avoid scratching skin and to keep nails short.
      e. Suggest use of mild soaps and cleansers.
   2. Allergic contact dermatitis
      a. Instruct the patient to avoid contact with agent.
      b. Have the patient wash with cool water immediately after exposure.

c. Recommend lukewarm baths with oatmeal (Aveeno) three to four times per day.
d. Tell the patient to apply calamine lotion after baths.

B. Patient teaching: See the Section III Patient Teaching Guide for this chapter, "Dermatitis."

C. Pharmaceutical therapy
1. Irritant contact dermatitis: Hydrocortisone 2.5% ointment three to four times per day for 2 weeks
2. Allergic contact dermatitis
a. Low-dose topical steroids: Hydrocortisone 2.5% ointment three to four times per day for 1 to 2 weeks after blistering stage. Triamcinolone acetonide 0.025% (Kenalog) ointment/cream twice daily
b. Intermediate dose topical steroids: Triamcinolone acetonide 0.1% (Kenalog) cream twice daily
c. High-potent topical steroids: Fluocinonide 0.05% (Lidex) ointment three to four times per day. Not to be used on face or skin folds.
d. Hydroxyzine 25 to 50 mg four times daily, diphenhydramine (Benadryl) 25 to 50 mg four times daily.
e. If rash is severe (face, eyes, genitalia, mucous membranes), consider prednisone 60 to 80 mg/d to start and taper over 10 to 14 days.
f. Triamcinolone acetonide (Kenalog) 40 to 60 mg by intramuscular (IM) injection
3. Secondary bacterial infections: Erythromycin 250 mg four times daily or amoxicillin, clavulanate acid (Augmentin) 875 mg twice daily for 10 days
4. Candidiasis
a. Miconazole nitrate 2% cream, miconazole powder, or nystatin cream
b. Clotrimazole (Lotrimin) or ketoconazole (Nizoral) cream three to four times per day for 10 days
c. If inflammation is present along with yeast, use Mycolog II.
d. If secondary bacterial infection is present, use mupirocin (Bactroban) ointment three times daily for 7 to 10 days.

Follow-Up

A. None is required if case is mild.
B. See patient again in 2 to 3 days for severe cases, or phone to assess progress.

Consultation/Referral

A. Consult with a physician when steroid treatment is necessary or if worsening symptoms develop despite adequate therapy.

Individual Considerations

A. Pregnancy: If medications are necessary during pregnancy, consider gestational age of fetus and category of medication.
B. Elderly: Patients may only exhibit scaling as the prominent irritation rather than erythema and inflammation. Topical medications (neomycin, vitamin E, lanolin) and acrylate adhesives are common causes of contact dermatitis.

Erythema Multiforme

Definition

A. This dermal and epidermal inflammatory process is characterized by symmetric eruption of erythematous, iris-shaped papules ("target" lesions) and vesiculobullous lesions.

Incidence

A. Erythema multiforme accounts for up to 1% of dermatology outpatient visits.
B. Adults older than 50 are rarely affected.
C. It may occur in seasonal epidemics.
D. Approximately 90% of cases of erythema multiforme minor follow a recent outbreak of herpes simplex virus (HSV)-1 or mycoplasma infection.

Pathogenesis

A. The disorder is thought to be an immunologic reaction in the skin, possibly triggered by circulating immune complexes.

Predisposing Factors

A. Infections: Recurrent HSV, mycoplasmal infections, and adenoviral infections
B. Drugs: Sulfonamides, phenytoin, barbiturates, phenylbutazone, penicillin
C. Idiopathic: Greater than 50%; consider occult malignancy

Common Complaints

A. Rash with intense pruritus
B. Nonspecific upper respiratory infection followed by rash
C. General malaise, body aches, joint pain
D. Fever

Other Signs and Symptoms

A. Primary: Macules, papules, plaques
B. Secondary: Erythema, dull red target-like lesions blanch to pressure; distribution is symmetric, primarily on flexor surfaces. **Classic target lesions develop abruptly and symmetrically and are heaviest peripherally; they often involve palms and soles.**
C. Swelling of hands and feet
D. Painful oral lesions
E. Eye discomfort (redness, itching, burning, pain, visual changes)

Subjective Data

A. Ask if the patient has ever been diagnosed with erythema multiforme.
B. Determine whether the onset of symptoms was sudden or gradual.
C. Assess for any associated discharge (blood or pus).
D. Identify the location of the symptoms.
E. Complete a drug history. Has the patient recently taken any antibiotics or other drugs? Question the patient regarding use of any topical medications.
F. Determine the presence of any preceding systemic symptoms (fever, sore throat, anorexia, vaginal discharge).
G. Rule out any possible exposure to industrial or domestic toxins.
H. Question the patient concerning any possible contact with venereal disease.
I. Ask the patient about any close physical contact with others with skin disorders.
J. Elicit information concerning any possible exposure to HIV.
K. Rule out sources of chronic infection, neoplasia, or connective tissue disease.

Physical Examination

A. Check temperature, pulse, respirations, and blood pressure.
B. Inspect
   1. Inspect skin for lesions.
   2. Inspect mouth and mucous membranes for lesions.
C. Palpate: Palpate abdomen for masses and tenderness.
D. Auscultate: Auscultate heart, lungs, and abdomen.
E. Neurologic exam

Diagnostic Tests

A. Punch biopsy of skin
B. CBC
C. Urinalysis

Differential Diagnoses

A. Erythema multiforme
   1. Erythema multiforme minor: Pruritus, swelling of hands and feet, painful oral lesions
   2. Erythema multiforme major: Fever, arthralgias, myalgias, cough, oral erosions with severe pain
B. Urticaria
C. Viral exanthems
D. Stevens–Johnson syndrome: **Stevens–Johnson syndrome (SJS) is a severe, life-threatening, systemic reaction with fever, malaise, cough, sore throat, chest pain, vomiting, diarrhea, myalgia, arthralgia, and severe skin manifestations with painful bullous lesions on mucous membranes.**
E. Pemphigus vulgaris
F. Bullous pemphigoid
G. Other bullous diseases
H. Staphylococcal scalded skin syndrome

Plan

A. General interventions
   1. Identify and treat precipitating causes or triggers.
   2. Burow's solution or warm compresses may be used for mild cases as needed.
   3. Oral lesions may be treated with saline solution, warm salt water, and/or Mary's mouth wash (Benadryl, lidocaine, and Kaopectate).
   4. Discontinue any medications suspected of precipitating symptoms.
   5. Provide adequate pain relief if skin or oral lesions are painful. Lesions remain fixed at least 7 days.
   6. Maintain nutrition and fluid replacement for this hypercatabolic state.
   7. Consider chronic viral suppression therapy for recurrent herpes simplex viral infections.
B. Patient teaching: See the Section III Patient Teaching Guide for this chapter, "Erythema Multiforme."
C. Pharmaceutical therapy
   1. Antihistamines such as Benadryl or Claritin may be used for itching.
   2. Acetaminophen may be used to reduce fever and for general discomfort/pain.
   3. Potent topical corticosteroids: Betamethasone dipropionate 0.05% or clobetasol propionate 0.05% twice daily for up to 2 weeks. Avoid use on face and groin.
   4. Open lesions should be treated like open burn wounds. Stop offending medications that may cause blistering of wounds and treat with steroids.
   5. Oral antibiotics may be needed to control secondary bacterial skin infection.
   6. Systemic corticosteroids: Prednisone 50 to 80 mg daily in divided doses, quickly tapered
   7. Hospitalization for severe cases. Intravenous immunoglobulins may be needed.

Follow-Up

A. See the patient in office in 1 to 2 days to evaluate initial treatment.

Consultation/Referral

A. If patient has recurrent or chronic infection, refer him or her to a physician.
B. Immediate consultation and/or hospital admission is critical if SJS is suspected.

Folliculitis

Definition

A. Folliculitis is a bacterial infection of the hair follicle.

Incidence

A. A very common disorder, folliculitis occurs in all ages and is seen more frequently in males.

Pathogenesis

A. Bacterial organisms (most common *S. aureus*) invade the follicle wall and cause an infectious process.

Predisposing Factors

A. Break in the skin tissue
B. Use of razors on skin
C. Poor hygiene
D. Diabetes

Common Complaints

A. Outbreak of pustules on the face, scalp, or extremities that do not resolve despite proper hygiene and care

Other Signs and Symptoms

A. Tenderness and itching at site
B. Furuncle (abscess): A deep pustule, tender, firm or fluctuant, found in groin, axilla, waistline, buttocks
C. Carbuncle: A group of follicles coalescing into one larger, painful, infected area; may see fever and chills
D. Excoriated folliculitis: Chronic thickened, excoriated papules or nodules

Subjective Data

A. Elicit the initial outbreak of lesions and onset and progression of lesions.
B. Identify what makes the lesions better or worse.
C. Ask the patient what medications, soaps, or lotions have been used on the lesions.
D. Complete a medical history. Ask if the patient has had an outbreak similar to this before.
E. Describe systemic symptoms if they have occurred (fever, chills, etc.).
F. Does the patient have a beard, shave his face, or use a razor frequently?
G. Is there a recent history of use of a hot tub? (Commonly seen 1 to 4 days after use of hot tub, whirlpool, or swimming pool use.)
H. Does the patient wear tight pants/jeans or use oils that clog pores in the groin area?
I. Is the patient currently being treated with antibiotics for acne? (May see flare of gram-negative folliculitis with chronic use of antibiotics.)

Physical Examination

A. Check temperature, pulse, respirations, and blood pressure.
B. Inspect: Assess skin for lesions and describe.
C. Palpate: Palpate lesions and associated lymph nodes.

Diagnostic Tests

A. Culture and sensitivity to verify appropriate antibiotic coverage
B. Gram stain
C. KOH/wet prep
D. Fungal culture hair if fungi suspected (Tinea of scalp)

Differential Diagnoses

A. Folliculitis
B. Acne vulgaris
C. Ingrown hair follicle
D. Keratosis pilaris
E. Contact dermatitis

Plan

A. General interventions: Apply warm, moist compresses to site for comfort.
B. Patient teaching
   1. See the Section III Patient Teaching Guide for this chapter, "Folliculitis."
   2. If razors are used on the area, have the patient use clean, sharp razors; throw old razors away; and not share razors. Avoid use of irritating creams or lotions on affected area.
   3. Encourage proper hygiene, such as frequent washing of hands and skin with antibacterial soap.
   4. Warm compresses three to four times a day are encouraged at site for 15 to 20 minutes.
   5. Bleach bath (1/2–1 cup of bleach to 20 L water) reduces spread of staph infection.
C. Pharmaceutical therapy
   1. Mild cases: Apply mupirocin (Bactroban) ointment to affected area three times daily until resolved.
   2. *S. aureus*
      a. Dicloxacillin (Dynapen) 250 mg by mouth four times daily for 10 to 14 days
      b. Erythromycin 250 mg by mouth four times daily for 10 to 14 days
      c. Cephalexin (Keflex) 500 mg by mouth twice daily for 10 to 14 days
   3. *Pseudomonas aeruginosa*
      a. Ciprofloxacin (Cipro) 500 mg by mouth twice daily for 10 days
      b. Ofloxacin 400 mg by mouth twice daily for 10 days
   4. Antistaphylococcal antibiotics
      a. Cephalexin 250 to 500 mg four times a day
      b. Clindamycin 150 to 300 mg four times a day
      c. Dicloxacillin 125 to 500 mg four times a day
      d. Erythromycin 250 to 500 mg four times a day
   5. Bacteria caused by organisms other than *Staphylococcus* may be treated for an extended period of time, 4 to 8 weeks. These areas may include axilla, chest, back, beard, and groin.
   6. Severe cases may be treated with oral antibiotics with topical permethrin every 12 hours every other night for a 6-week period or itraconazole 400 mg daily, isotretinoin 0.5 mg/kg/d for up to 4 to 5 months with UVB light therapy. Consider dermatology referral for severe cases.

Follow-Up

A. If not resolved in 2 weeks, further evaluation is needed.
B. Severe cases, in which carbuncles are not improved with treatment of antibiotic therapy, may warrant incision and drainage.
C. Continue to follow every 2 weeks until resolved.
D. Test for diabetes mellitus if severe cases occur.

Consultation/Referral

A. Refer the patient to a physician for testing for immunodeficiency if severe cases occur or if resistance is seen.
B. Dermatology referral

Herpes Simplex Virus Type 1

Definition

A. HSV-1 viral infection of the cutaneous tissue manifests itself by vesicular lesions on the mucous membranes and skin. HSV-1 is most often associated with oral lesions (mouth, lips), and HSV-2 is associated with genital lesions. The virus appears in three stages:
   1. Primary
   2. Latency
   3. Recurrent infections

Incidence

A. HSV-1 is seen in patients of all ages and in equal numbers of males and females.
B. There are approximately 500,000 new cases of herpes diagnosed annually in the United States.

Pathogenesis

A. Viral infection can be transmitted from a vesicular lesion or fluid (saliva) containing the virus to the skin or mucosa of another person by direct contact, with an incubation period of 2 to 14 days. Trigeminal ganglia are the host of the oral virus. The virus can be reactivated, whereupon it travels along the affected nerve route and produces recurrent lesions. Common sites of infection are the lips, face, buccal mucosa, and throat.

Predisposing Factors

A. Immunocompromised patients
B. Prior HSV infections
C. Exposure to virus

Common Complaints

A. Painful lips, gums, and oral mucosa

Other Signs and Symptoms

A. Primary lesion: Fever, blisters on lips, malaise, and tender gums
B. Recurrent episodes: Fever blisters with prodrome of itching, burning, and tingling sensation at site before vesicles appear

Subjective Data

A. Ask questions regarding location, onset, and duration of lesions.
B. Elicit description of prodromal symptoms.
C. Ask the patient if systemic symptoms occur with vesicular outbreak.
D. Determine when the initial outbreak of lesions occurred (commonly seen in childhood).
E. Inquire whether the patient has been exposed to anyone with similar lesions.
F. If the lesion(s) is recurrent, ask the patient if stress, skin trauma, or sun exposure stimulates outbreak of fever blisters.

Physical Examination

A. Inspect: Inspect skin, note location, appearance, and stage of vesicles.
B. Palpate: Palpate lymph nodes for lymphadenopathy.

Diagnostic Tests

A. Viral cultures

Differential Diagnoses

A. HSV-1
B. Impetigo (Impetigo appears as amber-colored vesicular lesions with crusting.)
C. Stomatitis (Stomatitis appears as erythemic or erosion lesions in the mouth and lips.)
D. Herpes zoster (Herpes zoster causes vesicles that run along a single dermatome.)
E. SJS
F. Herpangina: Vesicles can be noted on the soft palate, tonsillary area, and uvula area, usually caused by the coxsackievirus.

Plan

A. General interventions
   1. Comfort measures. Ice may be used to reduce swelling as needed.
   2. Vaseline or other lip ointments may be applied as needed and lip ointment with SPF 30 or greater when exposed to sunlight.
B. Patient teaching
   1. **Educate the patient regarding the disease process of HSV-1.**
   2. Instruct patient to wash hands frequently.
   3. Suggest proper care of lips to prevent drying and to reduce pain.
   4. Educate regarding transmission of virus to others.
   5. Teach patient to expect recurrences at variable times.
C. Pharmaceutical therapy: **Precautions should be used when administering medication to patients who are immunocompromised and who have a history of renal insufficiency.**
   1. Lidocaine 2% as needed for comfort

2. Diphenhydramine (Benadryl) elixir may be used to rinse mouth as needed.
3. Acetaminophen (Tylenol) as needed for pain
4. Campho-Phenique application as needed
5. Initial episode: Acyclovir 200 mg by mouth five times per day for 7 to 10 days or until resolved
6. Recurrent episodes: Begin one of the following when prodrome begins or within 2 days of onset of lesions to get maximum effect
   a. Acyclovir 200 mg by mouth five times per day for 5 days
   b. Acyclovir 800 mg by mouth twice daily for 5 days
7. Other alternative antivirals: Dosage depends on renal function
   a. Famciclovir (Famvir)
   b. Valacyclovir (Valtrex)
8. Suppressive therapy
   a. Acyclovir 200 mg by mouth two to five times per day for 1 year
   b. Acyclovir 400 mg by mouth twice daily for 1 year

Follow-Up

A. None needed if resolved without complications.

Consultation/Referral

A. Refer the patient to a physician if treatment is unsuccessful or further complications arise.

Individual Considerations

A. Pregnancy: Educate regarding the diagnosis of HSV-1 and precautions to take to avoid transmission to the genital area. Limit the number of sexual contacts, use a latex condom during sexual activity, use water-based lubricants (avoid oil-based lubricants), and avoid spermicides to prevent transmission. Advise the patient that if a lesion in the genital area presents at any time, she is to notify her health care provider for testing.

Herpes Zoster (Shingles)

Definition

A. Herpes zoster is a viral infection manifested by painful, vesicular lesions on the skin, limited to one side of the body, following one body dermatome.

Incidence

A. Infection may occur at any age; however, it is more common in older adults and the elderly. It occurs in 10% to 20% of the U.S. population.

Pathogenesis

A. After the primary episode of chickenpox (varicella-zoster), the virus remains dormant in the body. Herpes zoster occurs when the varicella virus has been stimulated and reactivated in the dorsal root ganglia, producing the clinical manifestations of herpes zoster. Infection usually lasts 14 to 21 days, but may be longer in elderly or debilitated patients.

Predisposing Factors

A. Adulthood
B. Immunocompromised patients
C. Spinal cord trauma or injury

Common Complaints

A. Prodrome: Itching, burning, tingling, or painful sensation at lesion sites
B. Active: Malaise, fever, headache, pruritic rash on the skin

Other Signs and Symptoms

A. Lesions: Clusters of vesicles on an erythemic base that burst and produce crusted lesions; commonly seen on the chest and back area. Distribution of lesions typically appears along a single dermatome.
B. Motor weakness (may be seen in approximately 5% of patients)

Subjective Data

A. Determine onset, location, and progression of rash.
B. Ask the patient about prodromal symptoms: Burning, itching, tingling, or painful sensation at site prior to lesions breaking out.
C. Evaluate patient status regarding immunosuppressive agents, diseases, and so forth.

Physical Examination

A. Check temperature, pulse, respirations, and blood pressure.
B. Inspect
   1. Observe skin for lesions, noting characteristics and distribution.
   2. Inspect ears, nose, and throat.
C. Auscultate: Auscultate heart and lungs.

Diagnostic Tests

A. Usually none
B. Culture vesicular lesions
C. Consider Tzanck smear
D. Young patients with herpes zoster: Consider and test for HIV.

Differential Diagnoses

A. Herpes zoster
B. Varicella
C. Poison ivy
D. HSV
E. Contact dermatitis
F. Coxsackievirus
G. Postherpetic neuralgia

Plan

A. General interventions: Comfort measures. Instruct the patient to apply wet dressings (Burow's solution) on site for 30 to 60 minutes at least four times a day. Calamine lotions may be used as needed; oatmeal (Aveeno) bath for comfort; acetaminophen (Tylenol) as needed for malaise, temperature, and comfort.

B. Patient teaching
   1. See the Section III Patient Teaching Guide for this chapter, "Herpes Zoster (Shingles)."
   2. Tell the patient the rash usually lasts approximately 2 to 3 weeks.
   3. Instruct the patient to monitor for signs/symptoms of postherpetic neuralgia.
   4. Instruct the patient to call if symptoms worsen or do not improve, or if signs of bacterial infection occur.
   5. Emphasize to the patient that the virus is easily transmitted to vulnerable persons.

C. Pharmaceutical therapy
   1. Antiviral medications should be initiated within 24 to 48 hours after outbreak.
      a. Acyclovir (Zovirax) 800 mg every 4 hours while awake for 7 to 10 days
      b. Famciclovir (Famvir) 500 to 750 mg by mouth three times daily for 7 days
      c. Valacyclovir (Valtrex) 1,000 mg by mouth three times daily for 7 days
   2. Acetaminophen (Tylenol) or ibuprofen as needed for pain or discomfort
   3. Narcotics may be used for severe pain as needed.
   4. Postherpetic neuralgia
      a. Postherpetic neuralgia may be treated with narcotics or other pain-relieving medications.
      b. Long-term medications may be needed for control of pain.
         i. Gabapentin 100 to 600 mg three times daily
         ii. Amitriptyline 25 mg every bedtime or other low-dose tricyclic antidepressants
   5. If secondary bacterial infection of the skin occurs, apply silver sulfadiazine (Silvadene) topically to site until resolved.
   6. Use of steroids is controversial. Corticosteroids may be used with caution. May increase risk of dissemination.

Follow-Up

A. As needed for complications

B. Monitor the patient for complications: Postherpetic neuralgia, Guillain–Barré syndrome, motor weakness, secondary infection, meningoencephalitis, ophthalmic and facial palsy, corneal ulceration, and so forth.

Consultation/Referral

A. Consult with physician if secondary infection occurs or if secondary complications arise.

Individual Considerations

A. Pregnancy: Acyclovir is in the category C drug classification. The safety and efficacy of the use of the antiviral medications during pregnancy need to be considered.

B. Elderly
   1. Postherpetic neuralgia occurs in approximately 15% of patients. It is commonly seen in the elderly patient.
   2. The Centers for Disease Control and Prevention recommends the shingles vaccine, Zostavax, for all patients 60 years of age and older, whether you have had the chickenpox or shingles infection in the past. It is also recommended for all immunocompetent persons older than 60 years (whether by disease or drug) with no contraindications. If the patient may become immunocompromised due to anticipated disease or medication, he or she should receive the Zostavax vaccination at the first encounter, or at least 14 days prior to immunosuppressive therapy. For those who have had a recent shingles outbreak, it is recommended that resolution of the rash occur before administering the Zostavax vaccination.
   3. The virus is contagious for those who have not had the chickenpox.

Lice (Pediculosis)

Definition

A. Pediculosis (lice) is an infestation of the louse on human beings in one of three areas:
   1. Head (*pediculosis capitis*)
   2. Pubic area (*pthirus pubis*)
   3. Body (*pediculosis corporis*)

Incidence

A. *Pediculosis capitis* is most common in children. It is estimated that head lice infestations occur in the school systems anywhere from 10% to 40% of the time.

B. *Pthirus pubis* infestation is more common in adults.

C. Lice affect all demographics; all social, racial, and economic groups.

Pathogenesis

A. Head and body lice are transmitted by direct contact from person to person, that is, through sharing hats, combs, brushes, and so forth. The parasite hatches from an egg, or nit. Once hatched, the lice live on humans by sucking blood through the skin. The average adult louse lives 9 to 10 days. The nits appear as small white eggs on the hair shaft. Nits are very difficult to remove and survive up to 3 weeks after removal from the host. Body lice lay nits in the seams of clothing.

B. Pubic lice are found at the base of the hair shaft, where they lay nits. Pubic lice are transmitted through sexual contact.

Predisposing Factors

A. Head and body lice: Exposure to crowded public areas, such as schools; inability to clean and launder clothing, bed linens, and so forth
B. Pubic lice: Sexual contact with infected people
C. Poor hygiene

Common Complaints

A. Head lice: Severe itching and scratching of the head, neck area, and commonly behind the ears
B. Body lice: Severe itching on the body, which may lead to secondary infections of the skin
C. Pubic lice: Severe itching of genital area

Other Signs and Symptoms

A. Excoriated skin from intense scratching
B. Visible lice or nits in hair, body, or clothing
C. Papules with an erythemic base may develop on the genital area, axilla, chest, beard, or eyelashes.

Subjective Data

A. Inquire as to exposure to anyone known to have lice.
B. Identify whether the patient attends a crowded environment such as school, day care, and so forth.
C. Ask if lice and nits have been seen by the patient.
D. Determine onset, duration, and course of symptoms. Ask: When were lice or nits first discovered?
E. Assess whether the patient has been symptomatic (itching, scratching).
F. Inquire about social habits of cleaning, laundry, and so forth.

Physical Examination

A. Check temperature to rule out any secondary infection.
B. Inspect
   1. Inspect hair, body, pubic area, and clothing seams for nits or lice.
   2. Note excoriation of skin.
   3. Examine eyelashes of children.
   4. Examine skin for secondary bacterial infection.

Diagnostic Tests

A. None
B. Culture excoriated area if secondary bacterial infection is suspected.

Differential Diagnoses

A. Lice
B. Scabies

Plan

A. General interventions
   1. Treat immediately with appropriate pediculicides (see Pharmaceutical therapy).
   2. After treatment, it is imperative to remove each nit and louse; use fine-tooth comb for nit removal.
   3. Evaluate entire family for lice.
   4. Treat secondary bacterial infection as needed.
B. Patient teaching
   1. See the Section III Patient Teaching Guide for this chapter, "Lice (Pediculosis)."
   2. Specific instructions need to be given to clients on how to get rid of lice and nits.
   3. Reinforce good hygiene; teach not to share combs, brushes, hats, and hair accessories.
C. Pharmaceutical therapy
   1. Malathion lotion 0.5% (Ovide): Pediculicidal and partially ovicidal
   2. Permethrin lotion 1% (Nix); pediculicidal only. Available OTC.
   3. Synergized pyrethrins (Rid 0.3%). Available OTC.
   4. Apply, repeat in 24 hours, then again in 1 week.
   5. Do not use a shampoo/conditioner or conditioner before using head lice treatments. Do not wash hair for 1 to 2 days after using lice treatment regimen.
   6. *Pthirus pubis:* Lindane (Kwell) or permethrin (Nix); apply to pubic area as directed.
   7. **Lindane (Kwell) toxicity may occur from ingestion or overuse and is exhibited by headaches, dizziness, and convulsions.**
   8. Eyelash manifestation: After removing nits, apply petroleum jelly to lashes three to four times a day for 8 to 10 days. **Eyelashes should never be treated with pediculicides.**

Follow-Up

A. None recommended
B. Some institutions require follow-up to evaluate whether infestation is resolved.

Consultation/Referral

A. If lice are a repeated problem, contact social services or the health department to have a visiting nurse or aide visit the home to evaluate home conditions and to teach the family how to prevent infestations.

Individual Considerations

A. Pregnancy: Lindane (Kwell) is contraindicated during pregnancy.
B. Adults: For adult/elderly patients with the diagnosis of lice, consider self-neglect, unsuitable living conditions, cognitive/psychiatric impairments, and/or abuse/neglect of the elderly. Consider a home visit for evaluation of the patient.

Lichen Planus

Definition

A. Lichen planus is a relatively common acute or chronic inflammatory dermatosis. It affects skin and mucous membranes with characteristic flat-topped, shiny, violaceous (purplish color) pruritic papules with lacy lines on the skin, and milky-white papules in the mouth.

Incidence

A. Lichen planus accounts for 0.1% to 1.2% of office visits to dermatologists.
B. It exhibits no racial preference.

Pathogenesis

A. Etiology is unknown, although it is possibly a cell-mediated immune response. Most cases remit within 7 years. Lesions may heal with significant postinflammatory hyperpigmentation.

Predisposing Factors

A. Severe emotional stress
B. Drugs may induce lichenoid plaques.

Common Complaints

A. Rash with or without pruritus
B. Primary lesions: Small, flat-topped papules that are polygonal, lightly scaly, and violaceous
C. Secondary lesions: Erythema, scales, and erosions

Other Signs and Symptoms

A. Distribution: Volar aspect of wrists, ankles, mouth, genitalia, and lumbar region
B. Wickham's striae (white, lacelike pattern on surface)
C. Scalp: Atrophic skin with alopecia
D. Nails: Destruction of nail fold and bed, especially in large toe
E. Men: Lesions of glans penis
F. Women: Erosive lesions of labia and vulva

Subjective Data

A. Determine whether the onset was sudden or gradual.
B. Ask the patient to describe if the skin is itchy or painful.
C. Assess lesions for any associated discharge (blood or pus).
D. Identify the location(s) of the problem.
E. Complete a drug history. Ask the patient if he or she has recently taken any antibiotics or other drugs. Ask if he or she has used any topical medications, lotions, or other creams.
F. Determine the presence of any preceding systemic symptoms (fever, sore throat, anorexia, or vaginal discharge).
G. Rule out insect bites.
H. Identify any possible exposure to industrial toxins, domestic toxins, or color-film-developing chemicals.
I. Ask if the patient has had any possible sexual contacts with persons with HIV or sexually transmitted infections (STIs).
J. Ask if the patient has had close physical contact with others with skin disorders.

Physical Examination

A. Inspect
   1. Inspect skin and note lesion distribution.
   2. Inspect mucous membranes: Buccal mucosa, tongue, and lips.
   3. Examine hair and nails.
   4. Observe genitalia.

Diagnostic Tests

A. A drop of mineral oil accentuating papule
B. If necessary to confirm diagnosis, deep shave or punch biopsy of developed lesions.
C. HIV or STI testing if indicated

Differential Diagnoses

A. Lichen planus
B. Lichenoid drug eruptions
C. Leukoplakia
D. Chronic graft-versus-host disease
E. Candidiasis (thrush)
F. Lupus erythematosus
G. Contact dermatitis
H. Bite trauma
I. Secondary syphilis

Plan

A. General interventions: Discontinue any suspected drug agent.
B. Patient teaching: See the Section III Patient Teaching Guide for this chapter, "Lichen Planus."
   1. Instruct patients that the disease may be chronic; most cases resolve spontaneously.
   2. Encourage the patient to avoid severe emotional stress.
   3. Encourage the patient to avoid scratching and prevent secondary infection.
   4. Reassure the patient that lichen planus is not contagious.
C. Pharmaceutical therapy
   1. Oral antihistamines: Hydroxyzine hydrochloride 10 to 50 mg four times daily as needed for pruritus, or cetirizine Hcl (Zyrtec) 10 mg daily
   2. Medium- to high-potency topical corticosteroids
      a. Mouth lesions: Fluocinonide 0.05%, ointment or gel, two or three times daily
      b. Body lesions: Betamethasone dipropionate (Diprolene) 0.05%, Triamcinolone (Kenolog) or other class 1 cream or ointment, two times daily. **Caution patients about steroid atrophy.**

c. Genital lesions: Desonide cream 0.05% twice daily initially, although higher-potency creams may be necessary. Topical corticosteroids should be used on genitalia in short bursts only.
d. Hypertrophic lesions: Intralesional injections, such as injecting triamcinolone 5 to 10 mg/mL, 0.5 to 1 mL per 2-cm lesion, are helpful for pruritus relief. Use cautiously in dark-skinned patients because of risk of hypopigmentation.
3. Oral prednisone is rarely used, but if necessary use with a short course only and taper.

Follow-Up

A. See the patient in 1 week for evaluation of treatment.

Consultation/Referral

A. Refer the patient to a dermatologist if there is no response to initial treatment.

Individual Considerations

A. Pregnancy: Use caution with medications prescribed.

Pityriasis Rosea

Definition

A. Pityriasis rosea is an acute, self-limiting, benign skin eruption characterized by a preceding "herald patch" that is followed by widespread papulosquamous lesions.

Incidence

A. Pityriasis rosea is relatively common, with more than 75% of cases in individuals from 10 to 35 years of age.
B. Incidence is slightly higher in women than in men.
C. Incidence is higher during the spring and autumn.

Pathogenesis

A. Disease is idiopathic; some evidence exists to support viral origin or autoimmune disorder.

Predisposing Factors

A. Recent acute infection

Common Complaints

A. Rash: Salmon, pink, or tawny-colored lesions generally concentrated in lower abdominal area, but may develop on arms, legs, and rarely on the face
B. Mild pruritus

Other Signs and Symptoms

A. Earliest lesions may be papular but may progress to 1- to 2-cm oval plaques.
B. Long axes of oval lesions run parallel to each other, hence the term "Christmas tree distribution."
C. Preceding herald patch (2 to 10 cm with central clearing) closely resembles ringworm; usually appears abruptly a few days to several weeks prior to the generalized eruptive phase.

Subjective Data

A. Elicit information about occurrence of initial, single, 2- to 10-cm round-to-oval lesion.
B. Question the patient as to known contacts with similar symptoms. Small epidemics have been identified in fraternity houses and military bases.

Physical Examination

A. Check temperature to rule out any infection.
B. Inspect
   1. Examine all body surfaces with patient unclothed.
   2. Look for characteristic lesions and distribution.
   3. Check the mucous surfaces, palms, and soles, which are usually spared by pityriasis rosea.

Diagnostic Tests

A. Generally none required; however, KOH wet preparation may be useful to distinguish herald patch from tinea corporis.
B. Order serology to rule out syphilis, if applicable.
C. If unable to identify herald patch, a serologic test for syphilis should be ordered because syphilis may be clinically indistinguishable from pityriasis rosea.
D. White blood count normal; no specific lab markers for pityriasis rosea

Differential Diagnoses

A. Pityriasis rosea
B. Nummular eczema
C. Tinea corporis
D. Tinea versicolor
E. Viral exanthems
F. Drug eruptions
   1. Captopril
   2. Bismuth
   3. Barbiturates
   4. Clonidine
   5. Metronidazole
G. Secondary syphilis
H. Lichen planus

Plan

A. General interventions
   1. Direct sunlight to point of minimal erythema hastens disappearance of lesions and decreases itching. UVB light in five consecutive daily exposures can decrease pruritus and shorten rash, particularly if administered within the first week of eruption.
   2. Not proven to be contagious and relatively harmless, so isolation is not required.

B. Patient teaching
   1. See the Section III Patient Teaching Guide for this chapter, "Pityriasis Rosea."
   2. Advise patients disease is self-limiting and clears spontaneously in 1 to 3 months.
C. Pharmaceutical therapy
   1. Generally none is required, but for itching the following recommendations exist: Group V topical steroids and oral antihistamines as per usual dosing.
   2. Prednisone 20 mg twice daily for 1 to 2 weeks in rare cases of intense itching.

Follow-Up

A. None is required unless secondary bacterial infection develops. Disease may recur in approximately 2% of patients.

Consultation/Referral

A. Consult or refer the patient to a physician when disease persists beyond 3 months.

Individual Considerations

A. Pregnancy: Disease has not been shown to affect fetus.
B. Geriatrics: Disease rarely seen in geriatric patients. Strongly consider other differential diagnoses, particularly drug reactions.

Precancerous or Cancerous Skin Lesions

Definition

A. Skin cell changes that occur in the body that may be benign, precancerous, or cancerous.

Incidence

A. Actinic keratosis is the most common precancerous skin disorder that occurs in approximately 58 million Americans, which is an estimate since it is not commonly reported and/or often occurs without diagnosis.
B. BCC is the most common form of skin cancer, with approximately 400,000 new cases per year in the United States. It is often seen in the sixth or seventh decade of life.
C. SCC accounts for 20% of all skin cancers, and it occurs mostly in the middle-aged and elderly populations.
D. Malignant melanoma accounts for less than 5% of all skin cancers. The median age at diagnosis is 61 years of age. The rate of new melanoma skin cases increased to 27.6 per 100,000 in 2008.

Pathogenesis

A. Actinic keratoses: A precancerous skin lesion commonly caused by damage to the skin that is the result of exposure to UV rays or tanning beds. If not treated, these skin lesions may turn into a form of skin cancer, such as SCC.
B. BCC: Skin lesions that result from abnormal cells of the basal layer of the epidermis that progress into the surrounding stroma and support the basal cell growth. UV rays (sunlight) are the major contributor to BCC. BCC is a slow-growing tumor that rarely metastasizes.
C. SCC: Abnormal cells of the epidermis penetrate the basement membrane of the epidermis and move into the dermis, producing SCC. This often begins as actinic keratosis that undergoes malignant change.
D. Malignant melanoma: Abnormal cells proliferate from the melanocyte system. Initially, the cells grow superficially and laterally into the epidermis and papillary dermis. After time, the cells begin moving into the reticular dermis and subcutaneous fat. Malignant tumors occur due to the inability of the damaged cells to protect themselves from the long-term exposure of the UV rays.

Predisposing Factors

A. Advanced age (older than age 50)
B. Median age of 40 years for malignant melanoma
C. Exposure to UV light (sun exposure)
D. Fair complexion (blond or red hair, blue, green or gray eyes)
E. Smokers (damaged lips)
F. Skin damaged by burns and/or chronic inflammation
G. History of blistering sunburns before 18 years of age increases risk

Common Complaints

A. New lesions found on the skin
B. Ulcer/sore that does not heal

Other Signs and Symptoms

A. Actinic keratosis (solar keratosis): Scaly, crusted lesions commonly found on sun-exposed skin areas such as the face, ears, scalp, lips, and hands that are usually rough in texture and appearance.
B. BCC: Tumors arising from the basal cell layer of the epidermis. Tumors may be seen on face and neck; may appear as an open sore, pink growth, or nodule that is greater than 1 cm that appears shiny, pearly in color with telangiectasia; center may cave in.
C. SCC: Skin lesions seen in sun-exposed areas of the skin, or skin damaged by burns or chronic inflammation; lower lip lesions common; firm, irregular papules with scaly, bleeding, friable surface like sandpaper; grows rapidly
D. Malignant melanoma: Asymmetrical tumor of skin with irregular border, variation in color, greater than 6 mm in diameter; can metastasize to any organ

E. Bowen's disease (SCC in situ): Chronic, nonhealing erythemic patch with sharp, irregular borders; occurs on skin and/or the mucocutaneous tissue; resembles eczema but does not respond to steroids

Subjective Data

A. Have the patient identify when lesion was first noted.
B. Ask the patient to describe any changes in size, color, or shape of the lesion.
C. Determine whether the patient has noted any new lesions.
D. Ascertain any family history of malignant melanoma.
E. Determine the patient's history of skin exposure to the sun or any other UV rays.
F. Ask the patient about smoking history. If the patient smokes, ask how many packs per day.

Physical Examination

A. Inspect
   1. Examine skin for lesions.
   2. Note surface, size, shape, border, color, and diameter of lesion.
   3. Examine scalp and ears for lesions.

Diagnostic Tests

A. Biopsy suspicious lesions.

Differential Diagnoses

A. Actinic keratosis
B. BCC
C. SCC
D. Malignant melanoma
E. Solar lentigo
F. Seborrheic keratosis
G. Common nevus
H. Leukoplakia

Plan

A. General interventions
   1. Monitor progress/change of lesions detected.
   2. Biopsy any suspicious lesions. Excise lesion with narrow margins, making sure to include all margins. If biopsy results of specimen are inadequate for accurate histologic diagnosis or staging, repeat biopsy. Include all clinical history information on the pathology report with the specimen when sending to pathology.
B. Patient teaching
   1. See the Section III Patient Teaching Guide for this chapter, "Skin Care Assessment."
   2. Educate patients regarding the importance of early identification of lesions and monthly assessment of skin. The U.S. Preventive Services Task Force (USPSTF) recommends counseling adolescents and young adults less than 24 years of age regarding reducing the amount of UV radiation exposure, especially between the hours of 10 a.m. and 3 p.m. In adults older than 24 years of age, the USPSTF did not find sufficient evidence to determine the effects of counseling these patients regarding the use of sun protection.
   3. Instruct patients on monthly skin evaluation. Teach the "ABCD" method of exam for changes in lesions: **A**symmetry, **B**order, **C**olor, and **D**iameter. A body map may be used to mark skin changes and monitor progress. Mark the site of the lesion on the body map, including measurements and date found. A body map may be found at: www.skincancer.org/skin-cancer-information/early-detection/body-map.
C. Pharmaceutical therapy: None indicated

Follow-Up

A. When a diagnosis is made, follow up according to diagnosis. Differentiate between benign skin lesions and malignant melanoma. Follow-up/treatment depends on diagnosis (nonsurgical versus surgical removal for diagnosis). Surgical removal recommended for recurrent and suspicious lesions.

Consultation/Referral

A. Refer all patients to the dermatologist if skin cancer is suspected.

Individual Considerations

A. Geriatrics: The elderly are at higher risk for skin cancer due to their decreased immune system as they age, as well as their cumulative chronic disease risk factors. Educate these patients regarding their risk factors and teach them how to assess the skin for lesions. Encourage frequent skin assessment and early diagnosis for improved outcomes.

Psoriasis

Definition

A. A common benign, chronic, inflammatory skin disorder, psoriasis is characterized by whitish scaly patches commonly seen on the scalp, knees, and elbows.

Incidence

A. Disease occurs in 1% to 3% of the world population.
B. Psoriasis affects 7.5 million people in the United States, with 80% of them having plaque psoriasis.
C. It occurs at any age.
   1. Peaks of onset seen in adolescence
   2. Young adult (16–22 years old)
   3. Adult (50–60 years old)

Pathogenesis

A. Etiology is unknown; this is a multifactorial disease with a definite genetic component.

Hyperproliferation of the epidermis and inflammation of the epidermis and dermis are seen, with epidermal transit time rapidly increased (six- to ninefold). A T-lymphocyte-mediated dermal immune response may be due to a microbial antigen or autoimmune process.

Predisposing Factors

A. Family history
B. Drugs that exacerbate condition
   1. Lithium
   2. Beta blockers
   3. Nonsteroidal anti-inflammatory drugs
   4. Antimalarials
   5. Sudden withdrawal of systemic or potent topical corticosteroids
C. Stress (common triggering factor)
D. Local trauma or irritation
E. Recent streptococcal infection
F. Alcohol use
G. Tobacco use
H. HIV association; suspected if onset is abrupt

Common Complaints

A. Dry scaly rash

Other Signs and Symptoms

A. Pruritic and/or painful lesions
B. Silvery scales on discrete erythematous plaques
   1. Onset commonly occurs as a guttate form with small, scattered, teardrop-shaped papules and plaques after a streptococcal infection in a young adult.
   2. Larger, chronic plaques occur later in life.
C. Lesions are commonly seen on scalp, elbows, and knees but may involve any area of the body.
D. Glossitis or geographic tongue: Small pits or yellow-brown spots (oil spots)
E. Positive Auspitz sign: Punctate bleeding points with removal of scale.
F. Onycholysis
G. Stippled nails and pitting; approximately 50% of patients have nail involvement.
H. Periarticular swelling of small joints of fingers and toes. **Joint pain and involvement signals psoriatic arthritis.**
I. Pustular variant with predominant involvement of hands and/or feet, including nails

Subjective Data

A. Question the patient regarding any predisposing factors listed above to identify risk factors.
B. Ask the patient if there have been changes in the course of symptoms.
C. Ascertain whether the symptoms worsen in winter and clear in summer.
D. Determine site of lesion and whether the onset is sudden or painful.
E. Ask the patient to describe the skin: Is it itchy or painful?
F. Assess lesions for any associated discharge (blood or pus).
G. Ask if the patient is using any new soaps, creams, or lotions.
H. Rule out any exposure to industrial or domestic toxins.
I. Ask the patient about any possible contact with venereal disease (STIs).
J. Review whether there was close physical contact with others with skin disorders.
K. Elicit information regarding any preceding systemic symptoms (fever, sore throat, and anorexia).

Physical Examination

A. Check temperature (if indicated).
B. Inspect
   1. Inspect skin; note type of lesion and distribution. Assess oral mucosa, nails, and nail beds.
   2. Assess joints for erythema and/or synovitis (inflammation of the synovial membrane).
C. Palpate: Palpate joints for tenderness.

Diagnostic Tests

A. None is indicated unless HIV infection is suspected; order HIV test.
B. If joint inflammation is present, consider rheumatoid factor, erythrocyte sedimentation rate, C-reactive protein, and uric acid.
C. If there is a history of streptococcal infection, order antistreptolysin O titer.

Differential Diagnoses

A. Psoriasis
B. Scalp: Seborrheic dermatitis
C. Body folds: Candidiasis
D. Trunk: Pityriasis rosea, tinea corporis
E. Hand dermatitis
F. SCC
G. Cutaneous lupus erythematosus

Plan

A. General interventions
   1. This is a chronic disorder that requires long-term treatment, a high degree of patient involvement, and therapy that is simple and inexpensive.
   2. Aim of treatment is control, not cure.
   3. Exposure to sunlight may be beneficial. However, a small percentage of patients worsen with exposure to sunlight.
   4. Sequence of agents for involvement of less than 20% body surface is as follows:
      a. Emollients (Eucerin cream or Aquaphor cream)
      b. Keratolytic agents (salicylic acid gel or ointment)

c. Topical corticosteroids: Use lowest potency to control disease.
d. Calcipotriene ointment: Vitamin D analogue (calcipotriene ointment 0.005%)
e. Anthralin: Use as short-contact therapy 1% to 3%.
f. Coal tar (Estar, PsoriGel): Use in conjunction with topical steroids or anthralin. May apply at bedtime or in the morning for 15 minutes and then shower off.
g. Medicated shampoos: Useful for scalp psoriasis, in conjunction with topical steroids and other treatments

B. Patient teaching
1. See the Section III Patient Teaching Guide for this chapter, "Psoriasis."
2. Help the patient understand the chronic nature of this disease characterized by flares and remission. Teach stress monitoring and control. Assist with coping techniques.
3. A trial of a gluten-free diet may be tried to help symptoms. See Appendix B: "Gluten-Free Diet."

C. Pharmaceutical therapy: If disease is not controlled with first agent, then an alternative agent may be tried.
1. Mild to moderate disease: Topical steroids as first-line therapy
2. Emollients to start treatment (e.g., Eucerin Plus lotion or cream, Lubriderm Moisture Plus, Moisturel)
3. Scalp: Use coal tar shampoo (Zetar, T/Gel, Pentrax) in place of regular shampoo two times per week.
   a. Apply lather to scalp, allow to soak for 5 minutes, and then rinse.
   b. If scale is very thick, use P and S Liquid (OTC). Massage in at night and wash out in morning.
4. For additional treatment as needed, apply triamcinolone acetonide 0.1% (Kenalog 0.1%) lotion or equivalent to scaly, stubborn areas once or twice daily until controlled. **Avoid face.**
5. Dovonex scalp solution: Apply on dry scalp as directed.
6. Face and skin folds: Apply hydrocortisone cream 1% sparingly up to 4 weeks, preferably no more than 2 weeks. If lesions are unresponsive, consider increasing to 2.5% and taper quickly with improvement.
7. Body, arms, and legs: Use triamcinolone acetonide 0.025% (Aristocort A) cream twice daily up to 2 weeks. **Avoid normal skin.**
8. For thick plaques, try Keralyt gel (6% salicylic acid), then corticosteroids.
9. Coal tar (Estar gel) once or twice daily in combination with corticosteroids
10. Anthralin (Dritho-Creme) is beneficial as an alternate to steroid lotion for scalp psoriasis. **Avoid sunlight.**
11. Vitamin D_3 analogue: (Calcipotriol), twice daily up to 8 weeks, is comparable to midpotency corticosteroids. **Avoid face and skin folds.**

Follow-Up

A. See patients in 2 to 3 weeks to evaluate treatment.
B. Follow up in 2 months to monitor side effects.
C. Follow-up must be individualized for each patient.

Consultation/Referral

A. Medical management: For involvement greater than 20% of body, refer the patient to a dermatologist for the following:
1. Light therapy with UVA or UVB. UVB light therapy is often used in conjunction with keratolytic agents.
2. Synthetic retinoids: Etretinate or acitretin
3. Low-dose cyclosporine or Azulfidine

B. Refer patients with extensive disease, psoriatic arthritis, or inflammatory disease to a rheumatologist. Medications are used to suppress the immune system's response, and include adalimumab (Humira), alefacept (Amevive), etanercept (Enbrel), infliximab (Remicade), and ustekinumab (Stelara).
C. Cases of generalized pustular psoriasis of exfoliative erythroderma should be referred immediately to a dermatologist.
D. All systemic therapies should be given under supervision of a dermatologist or rheumatologist.

Scabies

Definition

A. Scabies is a contagious skin infestation by the mite *Sarcoptes scabiei.*

Incidence

A. Scabies occurs mainly in individuals in close contact with many other individuals, such as nursing home residents. It is rare among African Americans.

Pathogenesis

A. Scabies is transmitted through close contact with an individual who is infested with the mite *S. scabiei.* Transmission may occur through sexual contact or contact with mite-infested clothing or sheets. The fertilized female mite burrows into the stratum corneum of a host and deposits eggs and fecal pellets. Larvae hatch, mature, and repeat the cycle.
B. A hypersensitivity reaction is responsible for the intense pruritus.

Predisposing Factors

A. Close contact with large numbers of individuals
B. Institutionalization
C. Poverty
D. Sexual promiscuity

Common Complaints

A. Intense itching, worse at night
B. Skin excoriation
C. Generalized pruritus
D. Rash

Other Signs and Symptoms

A. Mites burrow in finger webs, at wrists, in the sides of hands and feet, axilla, buttocks, and in the penis and scrotum in males
B. Discrete vesicles and papules, distributed in linear fashion
C. Erythema
D. Secondary bacterial infections due to scratching (pustules and pinpoint erosions)
E. Nodules in covered areas (buttocks, groin, scrotum, penis, axilla), which may have slightly eroded surfaces that persist for months after mites have been eradicated
F. Diffuse eruption that spares face

Subjective Data

A. Elicit information regarding housing conditions, close contact, or sexual contact with potentially infected individuals.
B. Question the patient regarding onset, duration, and location of itching.

Physical Examination

A. Check temperature.
B. Inspect
   1. Examine all body surfaces with patient unclothed.
   2. Use a magnifying lens to identify characteristic burrows in finger webs, wrists, and penis.
   3. Inspect adult pubic area for lesions.

Diagnostic Tests

A. Three findings are diagnostic of scabies:
   1. Microscopic identification of *S. scabiei* mites
   2. Eggs
   3. Fecal pellets (scybala)
B. Burrow identification: Ink the suspected area with a blue or black felt-tipped pen, then wipe with an alcohol swab. The burrow absorbs the ink, while the surface ink is wiped clean.
C. A tiny black dot may be seen at the end of a burrow, which represents the mite, ova, or feces, and can be transferred by means of a 25-gauge hypodermic needle to immersion oil on a slide for microscopic identification.
D. Place a drop of mineral oil on a suspected lesion, scrape lesion with a #15 blade, and transfer the shaved material to a microscope slide for direct examination of the mite under low power.

Differential Diagnoses

A. Scabies
B. Atopic dermatitis
C. Insect bites
D. Pityriasis rosea
E. Eczema
F. Seborrheic dermatitis
G. Syphilis
H. Pediculosis
I. Allergic or irritant contact dermatitis

Plan

A. General interventions
   1. Implement comfort measures to reduce pruritus.
   2. Treat secondary bacterial infection(s) with antibiotics.
   3. Household members should be treated simultaneously as a prophylactic measure and to reduce the chance of reinfection.
   4. The patient should be advised that pruritus may continue for up to a week even with a successful treatment due to local irritation.
B. Patient teaching: See the Section III Patient Teaching Guide for this chapter, "Scabies."
C. Pharmaceutical therapy
   1. First line of therapy, due to its low toxicity, is 5% permethrin (Elimite cream) applied to all body areas from neck down and washed off in 8 to 14 hours. One application is highly effective, but some dermatologists recommend retreatment in 1 week.
   2. Alternative therapy is lindane (Kwell) cream, applied to all skin surfaces from the neck down and washed off in 8 to 12 hours. Some dermatologists re-treat in 7 days.
   3. A single oral dose of the anthelmintic agent ivermectin (200 mcg/kg) has been shown to be effective and to rapidly control pruritus in healthy patients and HIV patients.
   4. Diphenhydramine (Benadryl) 25 to 50 mg may be given by mouth every 4 to 6 hours if indicated for pruritus. Other nonsedating antihistamines may be used. Toxicity is usually a result of patient overtreatment (failure to follow prescribed regimen). Advise the patient of this danger.

Follow-Up

A. Follow up in 2 weeks to assess treatment response.

Consultation/Referral

A. Consult or refer the patient to the physician if, at 2-week follow-up, pharmaceutical therapy has been ineffective.

Individual Considerations

A. Pregnancy
 1. Permethrin is preferred to lindane in pregnant and/or lactating women due to decreased toxicity.
 2. Patient should be warned of its potential to cause neurotoxicity and convulsions with overuse (more than two treatments).

B. Partners
 1. All intimate contacts within the past month and close household and family members should be treated.

C. Geriatrics
 1. The elderly tend to have more severe pruritus despite fewer lesions.
 2. They are at risk for extensive infections due to an age-related decline in immunity.
 3. The excoriations may become severe and may be complicated by cellulitis.

Seborrheic Dermatitis

Definition

A. A common chronic, erythematous, scaling dermatosis, seborrheic dermatitis occurs in areas of the most active sebaceous glands, such as the face and scalp, body folds, and presternal region.

Incidence

A. Seborrheic dermatitis is very common, affecting approximately 1% to 5% of the general population.
B. Incidence is higher in HIV-infected individuals, ranging from 34% to 83%.

Pathogenesis

A. Etiology is unknown. There is a possibility that it is hormonally dependent, has a fungal *(Pityrosporum ovale* or *Candida albicans)* component, is neurogenic, or may reflect a nutritional deficiency.
B. Currently, it is identified as an inflammatory disorder that most probably results from a dysfunction of sebaceous glands.

Predisposing Factors

A. Possible link between infantile and adult forms
B. Possible familial trend
C. High association with HIV-infected individuals

Common Complaints

A. "Dandruff," dry flaky scalp
B. Rash with "sticky flakes"

Often no presenting complaints are found on a routine physical exam.

Other Signs and Symptoms

A. Variable pruritus, often increased with perspiration and winter
B. Oily, flaking skin on erythemic base around ears, nose, eyebrows, and eyelids
C. Red, cracking skin in body folds; axilla; groin; or anogenital, submammary, or umbilical areas
D. Primary lesions: Plaques
E. Secondary lesions: Erythema, scales, fissures, exudate, and symmetric eyelid involvement
F. Lesions with drainage or crusting may indicate secondary bacterial infection
G. Distribution area in adults: Scalp, eyebrows, paranasal area, nasolabial fold, chin, behind ears, chest, and groin

Subjective Data

A. Identify location, onset, and progression of symptoms.
B. Ask the patient to describe symptoms. Ask if the skin is itchy or painful.
C. Assess lesions for any associated discharge (blood or pus).
D. Elicit information regarding use of topical medications, soaps, creams, or lotions. Quiz patient regarding any oral medications being taken.
E. Determine whether there were any preceding systemic symptoms (fever, sore throat, anorexia, or vaginal discharge).
F. Rule out any possible exposure to industrial or domestic toxins.
G. Ask the patient to identify what improves or worsens this condition.

Physical Examination

A. Inspect
 1. Inspect skin; note areas of lesions and distribution.
 2. Assess eyes for blepharitis.
 3. Inspect ears and nose.
B. Palpate: Palpate skin, noting texture and moisture.

Diagnostic Tests

A. None required
B. May consider possible skin biopsy to rule out other conditions if suspicious

Differential Diagnoses

A. Seborrheic dermatitis
B. Atopic dermatitis
C. Candidiasis
D. Dermatophytosis
E. Histiocytosis X
F. *Psoriasis vulgaris*
G. Rosacea
H. Systemic lupus erythematosus

I. *Tinea capitis*
J. *Tinea versicolor*
K. Vitamin deficiency
L. Impetigo
M. Eczema

Plan

A. General interventions
   1. Shampooing is the foundation of treatment.
      a. Shampoo daily with baby shampoo using a soft brush.
      b. Use medicated shampoos as directed (Selsun Blue, Exsel, or Nizoral).
   2. If scalp does not clear after 1 to 2 weeks of treatment, it is appropriate to use ketoconazole 2% cream.
   3. Seborrheic blepharitis
      a. Hot compresses plus gentle debridement with cotton-tipped applicator and baby shampoo twice a day
      b. For secondary bacterial infection, sulfacetamide sodium 10% (ophthalmic Sodium Sulamyd)
   4. Continue treatment for several days after lesions disappear.

B. Patient teaching: See the Section III Patient Teaching Guide for this chapter, "Seborrheic Dermatitis."

C. Pharmaceutical therapy
   1. Most shampoos should be used two times per week. Those with coal tar can be used three times per week.
   2. Medicated shampoos
      a. Coal tar (Denorex, T/Gel, Pentrax, Tegrin) shampoo; apply as directed.
      b. Salicylic acid (Ionil Plus, P and S) shampoo; apply as directed.
      c. Selenium sulfide (Exsel, Selsun Blue); shampoo daily
      d. Ketoconazole 2% (Nizoral) cream; apply to affected area twice daily for 4 to 6 weeks.
      e. Combination shampoos: Coal tar and salicylic acid (T/Sal); salicylic acid and sulfur (Sebulex). These shampoos may be used one to two times a week, alternating with other shampoos during the week. Always apply corticosteroids as thin layer only; avoid eyes.
   3. Topical corticosteroid lotions or solutions: Use in combination with medicated shampoo if 2 to 3 weeks of treatment with shampoo alone fails.
   4. Adults: Scalp
      a. Start with medium potency, for example, betamethasone valerate 0.1% lotion 20 to 60 mL twice daily.
      b. If treatment is not effective in 2 weeks, increase potency, for example, fluocinonide 0.05% solution 20 to 60 mL twice daily, or fluocinolone acetonide 0.01% oil 120 mL nightly with shower cap.
      c. As dermatitis is controlled, decrease to mild potency, for example, hydrocortisone 1% to 2.5% lotion 60 to 20 mL once or twice daily.
   5. Adults: Face or groin
      a. Low-potency agents, for example, hydrocortisone 1% cream or desonide 0.05% cream once or twice daily
      b. Consider lotion for eyebrows for easier application.
      c. Metronidazole 1% gel on face once or twice daily
   6. Recalcitrant disease
      a. Add ketoconazole 2% cream (15, 30, or 60 g) every day.
      b. Sulfacetamide sodium 10%, with sulfur 5%, lotion 25 g once or twice daily

Follow-Up

A. Advise the patient to call the office in 5 to 6 days to report progress.
B. The patient should return to the office if no improvement is seen.

Consultation/Referral

A. Refer the patient to a dermatologist if the condition does not clear in 10 to 14 days.

Individual Considerations

A. Pregnancy: Ketoconazole is not recommended.

Tinea Corporis (Ringworm)

Definition

A. *Tinea corporis* (ringworm) is a fungal infection of the skin tissue (keratin) commonly seen on the face, trunk, and extremities.

Incidence

A. Ringworm is a fairly common fungal infection seen in adults.

Pathogenesis

A. The causative fungal species varies, depending on the location of the infection. Three common organisms include *Epidermophyton, Microsporum,* and *Trichophyton.*
B. The infection can be obtained from other people, animals (puppies, kittens), and the soil.

Predisposing Factors

A. Exposure to person or facilities (e.g., locker rooms) infected with the fungus
B. Poor nutrition

C. Poor health
D. Poor hygiene
E. Warm climates
F. Immunosuppression

Common Complaints

A. Scaly, itchy patch of skin, often circular in shape

Other Signs and Symptoms

A. *Tinea capitis*: Erythema, scaling of scalp, with hair loss at site asymptomatic
B. *Tinea corporis*: Circular, erythematous, well-demarcated lesion on the skin with hypopigmentation in center of lesion; usually pruritic
C. *Tinea cruris*: Well-demarcated scaling lesions on groin (not scrotum) or thigh; usually pruritic
D. *Tinea pedis*: Scaly, erythemic vesicles on feet, between toes, and in arch, with extreme pruritus
E. *Tinea unguium* (onychomycosis): Thickening and yellowing of toenail or fingernail, often with other fungal infection or alone

Subjective Data

A. Ask the patient about onset, duration, and progression of patch or rash on skin.
B. Assess the patient for other areas of skin involvement.
C. Ask if the lesion is pruritic.
D. Inquire as to the patient's exposure to anyone with similar symptoms.
E. Determine whether the patient has a history of similar lesions.
F. Query the patient regarding predisposing factors.
G. Review with the patient what remedies were used and with what results.

Physical Examination

A. Check temperature (if indicated).
B. Inspect
   1. Examine all areas of skin.
   2. Note type of lesions present.

Diagnostic Tests

A. Obtain scrapings of the border of the lesion for evaluation.
   1. KOH
   2. Wet prep
   3. Fungal cultures

Differential Diagnoses

A. *Tinea corporis*
B. Dermatitis
C. Alopecia areata
D. Psoriasis
E. Contact dermatitis
F. Atopic eczema

Plan

A. General interventions
   1. Identify type of lesion.
   2. Identify other infected family members or sexual partners for treatment.
B. Patient teaching
   1. See the Section III Patient Teaching Guide for this chapter, "Ringworm."
   2. Reinforce medication regimen for a 4- to 8-week period for resolution.
C. Pharmaceutical therapy
   1. *Tinea capitis*
      a. Adults: Griseofulvin 500 mg by mouth per day for 4 to 8 weeks
      b. Ketoconazole (Nizoral) may also be used.
   2. *Tinea corporis, pedis*, and *cruris*: Use wet dressings with Burow's solution along with one of the following:
      a. Clotrimazole 1% (Lotrimin) cream, or econazole nitrate 1% cream, twice daily for 14 to 28 days
      b. Terbinafine 1% cream (Lamisil), topical; apply once or twice daily for 1 to 4 weeks.
   3. Onychomycosis: Successful treatment is difficult.
      a. Itraconazole (Sporanox) 100 mg, two tablets by mouth twice daily for 7 days. Repeat in 1 month, then repeat again in 1 more month.

Monitor liver function tests (LFTs) at 6 weeks after starting medication.

      b. Terbinafine 1% cream (Lamisil)
         i. Fingernail: 250 mg once daily for 6 weeks
         ii. Toenail: 250 mg daily for 12 weeks
      c. Home cure: Apply Vicks VapoRub on toenail bed and cover with a sock every night at bedtime for approximately 4 to 6 months or until resolved. This treatment offers a safe, cost-effective alternative to oral medications.

Follow-Up

A. A 2- to 4-week follow-up is recommended to evaluate progress.
B. When using Sporonox, monitor LFT at 6 weeks. If the medication is continued, monitoring LFTs every 6 to 8 weeks is recommended.

Consultation/Referral

A. Consult a physician if the infection has not improved.

Individual Considerations

A. Pregnancy: Oral antifungal medications are not recommended during pregnancy.

B. Adults
1. *Tinea capitis* is rare in adults.
2. *Tinea cruris* is more common in obese males but rare in females.
3. Transient and/or permanent hearing loss has been documented in some patients with the use of itraconazole. These cases were reported when itraconazole was used with quinidine, which is contraindicated.

C. Elderly
1. Itraconzaole should be used cautiously in the elderly patient.

Tinea Versicolor

Definition

A. Tinea versicolor is a fungal infection of the skin, which may be chronic in nature. It is most commonly seen on the upper trunk; however, it may spread to extremities.

Incidence

A. Tinea versicolor is seen most frequently in adolescents and young adults.

Pathogenesis

A. Tinea versicolor is a fungal infection of the skin caused by an overgrowth of *Pityrosporum orbiculare,* part of the normal skin flora.
B. Discoloration of the skin is seen, forming round or oval maculae, which may become confluent.
C. Maculae range from 1 cm to very large, greater than 30 cm.

Predisposing Factors

A. Immunosuppressive therapy
B. Pregnancy
C. Warm temperatures
D. Corticosteroid therapy

Common Complaints

A. Scaly rash on the upper trunk with occasional mild itching

Other Signs and Symptoms

A. Annular maculae with mild scaling
B. Asymptomatic or pruritic
C. Pink-, white-, or brown-colored rash

Subjective Data

A. Ascertain when and where the rash began.
B. Have the patient describe how the rash has changed.
C. Assess the patient for any associated symptoms with the rash, such as itching and burning.
D. Identify what products the patient has used on the skin to treat rash and with what results.
E. Elicit information regarding a history of similar rashes.
F. Query the patient regarding current medications.
G. Review any medical history for comorbid conditions.

Physical Examination

A. Inspect
1. Inspect skin and note type of lesion.
2. Examine other areas of skin for similar lesions.

Diagnostic Tests

A. Wet prep/KOH
B. Wood's lamp: Wood's light is useful in examining skin to determine the extent of infection. Inspection of fine scales with Wood's lamp reveals scales with a pale yellow-green fluorescence that contains the fungus.
C. Culture lesion: When obtaining a sample scraping, obtain sample from edge of lesion for best sample of hyphae. (Hyphae and spores have a "spaghetti and meatball" appearance.)

Differential Diagnoses

A. Tinea versicolor
B. Tinea corporis
C. Pityriasis alba
D. Pityriasis rosea: Herald patch is clue to diagnosis.
E. Seborrheic dermatitis
F. Vitiligo

Plan

A. General interventions: Apply medication as directed.
B. Patient teaching
1. See the Section III Patient Teaching Guide for this chapter, "Tinea Versicolor."
2. Because causative species is a normal inhabitant of skin flora, recurrence is possible.
3. Skin pigmentation returns after infection is cleared up. This may take several months to resolve.

C. Pharmaceutical therapy
1. Selenium sulfide 2.5% (Selsun Blue)
   a. Advise patient to shower at bedtime. Then apply Selenium sulfide 2.5% cream to skin, covering entire body from chin down to toes. Leave treatment on skin for 8 to 10 hours. Shower off in the morning.
   b. A second treatment option includes applying the Selenium sulfide 2.5% cream to skin lesions daily for 12 days. Leave treatment on skin for 30 minutes, then shower off.
   c. Treatment may be needed monthly until desired results are obtained. **Encourage use of Selsun Blue on entire body surface except for face and head.**
2. Other medications used
   a. Clotrimazole 1% cream twice daily for 4 weeks
   b. Ketoconazole (Nizoral) cream daily for 14 days

c. Ketoconazole (Nizoral) 200 mg orally once daily for 3 days, for adults only. **When using ketoconazole (Nizoral) as treatment, caution the patient regarding liver damage with toxicity.**

Follow-Up

A. None is required if resolution occurs.
B. Monitor LFTs every 6 weeks if patient is on ketoconazole.

Consultation/Referral

A. Consult with a physician if current treatment is unsuccessful.

Individual Considerations

A. Adults: Commonly seen in young adults.

Warts

Definition

A. A wart is an elevation of the epidermal layer of the skin (skin tumor). Warts are caused by the papillomavirus.

Incidence

A. Warts occur in people of all ages, more commonly in children and those in early adulthood.
B. By adulthood, 90% of all people have positive antibodies to the virus.
C. Warts are seen more frequently in females than in males.

Pathogenesis

A. A circumscribed mass develops on the skin that is limited to the epidermal layer. The virus, papillomavirus, is located within the nucleus of the cell.
B. The virus may be transmitted by touch and is commonly seen on the hands and feet.
C. Most warts resolve without treatment within 12 to 24 months.

Predisposing Factors

A. Skin trauma
B. Immunosuppression
C. Exposure to public showers, pools, locker rooms, and so forth

Common Complaints

A. Bump on the skin or specific area of the body (hands, feet, arms, and legs)
B. Usually painless unless present on the bottom of the foot

Other Signs and Symptoms

A. Common wart (*Verruca vulgaris*): Flesh-colored, irregular lesion with rough surface; black dots in center of lesion occasionally seen, which is thrombosed capillaries; can occur on any body part.
B. Filiform wart (*Verruca filiformis*): Thin, threadlike, projected papule on face, lips, nose, or eyelids
C. Flat wart (*Verruca plana*): Flat-topped, flesh- colored papule, 1 to 3 mm in diameter, with smooth surface; seen in clusters or in a line, on face and extremities
D. Plantar wart (*Verruca plantaris*): Firm papula, 2 to 3 cm in diameter, indented into skin with verrucous surface; painful with ambulation, when placed on ball or heel of foot
E. Genital warts: See the sexually transmitted topics on infections in Chapter 17.

Subjective Data

A. Determine onset, location, and duration of tumor.
B. Elicit information regarding a history of previous warts.
C. Identify with the patient what treatment has been used in the past and what the results were. Question the patient regarding length of time OTC medications were used, and how aggressive he or she was with the treatment.

Physical Examination

A. Inspect
   1. Assess skin for lesions, noting location, appearance, size, and surface texture of tumor.
   2. Examine the entire body for other lesions.

Diagnostic Tests

A. None indicated

Differential Diagnoses

A. Wart
   1. *Verruca vulgaris*
   2. Filiform wart
   3. *Verruca plana*
   4. *Verruca plantaris*
B. Seborrheic keratosis
C. Callus
D. *Molluscum contagiosum*: Flesh-colored group of firm papules found on the face, trunk, and/or extremities. A white core may be expressed from lesion. Lesion may be successfully removed by curettage or cryotherapy.

Plan

A. General interventions
   1. Identify type of wart.
   2. Treatment is based on the type of wart.
B. Patient teaching: See the Section III Patient Teaching Guide for this chapter, "Warts."
C. Pharmaceutical therapy
   1. Common wart
      a. After soaking and filing wart with a nail file, apply one of these:
         i. Salicylic acid 17% (Compound W) gel twice daily for up to 12 weeks, if needed.

Keep site covered with adhesive and bandage.

ii. Apply duct tape to site after treatment. Repeat this treatment every night for up to 12 weeks or until resolved.

b. Cryotherapy with liquid nitrogen to site. Repeat every 3 to 4 weeks until resolved. Apply adhesive tape over the site and keep covered.

2. Flat wart or filiform wart
   a. Retinoic acid: Apply to site twice daily for 4 to 6 weeks.
   b. Aldara (imiquimod) 5% cream may be applied by the patient at home. Although labeled use is for genital warts, the patient may consider off-label use at bedtime and wash off after 6 to 8 hours every other day until resolved. Precautions should be stressed regarding caustic nature of cream to healthy skin.
3. Plantar wart: Salicylic acid 40% (Mediplast), apply over wart. Remove in 24 to 48 hours, and remove dead skin with stone or by scraping or using nail file. Repeat every 24 to 48 hours until wart is removed. May take up to 6 to 8 weeks.
4. Educate patient to throw away emory board nail file after each use. If using nail file, cleanse after each use with alcohol.

Follow-Up

A. Follow the patient every 4 to 6 weeks until resolved.

Consultation/Referral

A. If diagnosis is unclear, refer the patient to a dermatologist for surgical excision and biopsy.

Individual Considerations

A. Warts occur in all ages, but are less common in the elderly.

Wound Care

Lower Extremity Ulcer—Amy C. Bruggemann

Definition

A. Vascular ulcer
   1. Arterial/ischemic ulcer
      a. Skin ulcers usually found on the medial or lateral foot or ankle; ulcers are nonhealing due to inadequate arterial flow.
   2. Venous ulcer
      a. Chronic skin and subcutaneous lesions are usually found on lower extremity between the ankle and knee, thought to occur from intracellular edema or inflammatory processes.

B. Diabetic foot ulcer
   1. Skin ulcers usually found on the plantar surface of the foot, most commonly occurring from trauma or plantar pressure

Incidence

A. Diabetic foot ulcers precede over 80% of lower extremity amputations in the United States.
B. The financial burden of venous ulcers is estimated to be $2 billion per year in the United States.
C. Up to 20% of lower extremity ulcers have been shown to have mixed etiology disease.

Pathogenesis

A. An ulcer that is found between the knees and toes constitutes a lower extremity ulcer, and guidelines are based according to the etiology. The thing to remember with lower extremity ulcers is that they may have more than one cause. The most common etiologies are venous insufficiency, arterial insufficiency, diabetic foot ulcer, and/or pressure.

Predisposing Factors

A. Arterial insufficiency
B. Congestive heart failure
C. Coronary heart disease
D. Diabetes
E. Edema
F. Hyperlipidemia
G. Obesity
H. Age: Older than 65 years
I. Venous insufficiency
J. Peripheral neuropathy

Common Complaints

A. Lower extremity or foot pain
B. Bleeding
C. Drainage
D. Hyperglycemia

Subjective Data

A. Ask the patient to describe the location and onset. What does he or she think may have caused an ulcer in that area? Was the onset sudden or gradual? How have the symptoms continued to develop?
B. Assess if the area is pruritic or painful. Does the patient having feeling in the area or is there a decrease in sensation noted?
C. Assess for any associated drainage. Ask about the color and if any odor is present.
D. Complete a drug history. Ask the patient if he or she is taking any steroids or anticoagulants.
E. Has the patient been treated for this location in the past? If so, describe?

F. Determine whether the patient has attempted to treat this at home. If yes, inquire about previous treatments.
G. Does the patient have any numbness or tingling in the lower extremities? Does the patient wake up at night with pain? Does he or she have any pain with ambulation? Does he or she have sensation to his or her feet?
H. Rule out any possible exposure to industrial or domestic toxins, or insect bites.
I. Assess for iodine and sulfa allergies before starting treatment.

Physical Exam

A. Check temperature, pulse, respirations, and blood pressure.
B. Assess the lower extremities, feet, and toes.
   1. Color of the skin
      a. Assess skin, beginning at the top of the legs; move down the legs to the toes for changes in color that may exhibit signs of ischemia.
      b. Hemosiderin staining may exhibit venous insufficiency.
   2. Temperature of the skin
   3. Sensation of the skin
   4. Capillary refill
   5. Pulses
C. Inspect the ulcer.
   1. Measure length times width times depth.
      a. Undermining (destroyed tissue below with wound margin): Measure and note location, using the face of a clock to document the site of undermining: 12 o'clock, 3 o'clock, 6 o'clock, or 9 o'clock.
      b. Tunneling (destroyed tissue pathway that creates dead space underneath the skin): Measure and note location, using the face of a clock to document the site of tunneling: 12 o'clock, 3 o'clock, 6 o'clock, or 9 o'clock.
   2. Describe the wound bed.
      a. Tissue in the wound bed
         i. Necrotic tissue, granulation tissue, epithelial tissue
      b. Color of the tissue (percentage to equal 100%, i.e., 80% pink, 20% yellow)
         i. Red, pink, yellow, brown, black
      c. Drainage
         i. Amount
            1) None, scant, moderate, copious
         ii. Color
            1) Serous, purulent, yellow, serosanguineous, green
      d. Odor
         i. Odor present: Yes
         ii. Odor not present: No
      e. Periwound
         i. Intact
         ii. Not intact
            1) Describe periwound. Note erythema, fever, induration, maceration, excoriation, calloused area, or epiboly

Diagnostic Tests

A. Ankle brachial index (ABI)
B. Arterial Doppler
C. Bone scan
D. CBC
E. Hemoglobin A1C (HGBA1C)
F. MRI
G. Wound culture
H. Wound biopsy
I. Venous Doppler
J. X-ray

Differential Diagnoses

A. Vascular ulcer
   1. Arterial/ischemic ulcer
   2. Venous ulcer
B. Diabetic foot ulcer
C. Abscess
D. Atypical ulcers
E. Dermatological disorder
F. Necrotizing fasciitis
G. Skin cancers
H. Pressure ulcer
I. Trauma
J. *Pyoderma gangrenosum*

Plan

A. Vascular ulcers
   1. Arterial ulcer
      a. Refer to vascular surgery for assessment to improve arterial flow.
      b. Refer to wound care specialist.
   2. Venous ulcer
      a. Establish arterial flow.
         i. Refer to vascular surgeon if deficiency found.
      b. For signs and symptoms of infection, treat the infection first with tissue culture and sensitivity. Treat per pharmaceutical recommendations. Treat with silver alginate to the site for moderate drainage and silver gel to the site for scant drainage.
      c. Once arterial flow has been established as sufficient and infection has been ruled out, compression therapy is the mainstay of treatment for venous ulcers. Compression therapy recommendations:
      i. ABI: 0.8 to 1.0 full compression
         1) Pro-fore
            a) Change in 3 days; if tolerating, then change weekly.

ii. ABI: 0.6 to 0.8 light compression
1) Pro-fore lite
2) Apply calcium alginate to ulcer, then wrap with a Unna Boot and cover with a coban wrap.
a) Change in 3 days; if tolerating well, then change weekly.

B. Diabetic foot ulcer
1. Establish arterial flow.
a. Refer to vascular surgeon if deficiency is found.
2. For signs and symptoms of infection, use a sterile culturette to obtain a tissue culture and sensitivity first to assess what organism is present and to determine sensitivities. Treat per pharmaceutical recommendations. Treat with silver alginate to the site for moderate drainage and silver gel to the site for scant drainage.
3. Initiate offloading to site.
a. Refer to orthotist for assessment if devices are required.
4. Treatment options
a. To debride: NS cleanse, apply santyl and dressing change daily and as needed
b. To granulate an ulcer with scant drainage: NS cleanse, apply hydrogel and dressing change daily and as needed
c. To granulate an ulcer with moderate drainage: NS cleanse, apply calcium alginate and dressing change daily as needed

C. Patient teaching
1. See the Section III Patient Teaching Guide for this chapter, "Wound Care: Lower Extremity Ulcers."

D. Pharmaceutical therapy
1. If culture and sensitivity are performed, antibiotics may be used as recommended per sensitivity.

Follow-Up

A. Follow up in 1 to 2 weeks to evaluate therapy.
B. See patients every 1 to 2 weeks until healing well; then may reduce to 2- to 4-week evaluation until complete closure.

Consultation/Referral

A. Consult or refer the patient to a wound care specialist:
1. Patient has extensive ulcer that you are not comfortable with
a. Visible bone, muscle, or tendon
2. Patient has multiple medical comorbidities (especially diabetes)
3. Patient is not responding to treatment of 2 to 4 weeks
4. Ulcer is showing decrease on follow-up visit
5. Infection is present

Individual Consideration

Adults

A. Ischemic ulcers warrant immediate referral.
B. Complaints of severe pain, lack of pulse, cool digit, or new onset of purplish/bluish discolorations to the feet require immediate workup for arterial clot to lower extremity.

Pressure Ulcers—Amy C. Bruggemann

Definition

A. "A pressure ulcer is localized injury to the skin and/or underlying tissue, usually over a bony prominence, as a result of pressure or pressure in combination with shear. A number of contributing or confounding factors are also associated with pressure ulcers; the significance of the factors has yet to be elucidated" (NPUAP, 2009).

Incidence

A. Acute care 0.4% to 38%
B. Long-term care 2.2% to 23.9%
C. Home care 0% to 17%

Pathogenesis

A. Pressure ulcers occur when an area of tissue remains in surface contact for a period of time. This contact causes occlusion of microvascular vessels, which leads to tissue hypoxia and eventually may cause ischemia. Over time, a pressure ulcer is developed. The amount of time this takes is patient dependent and can be altered by physical and/or environmental factors.

Predisposing Factors

A. Acute illness
B. Fecal/urinary incontinence
C. Malnutrition
D. Weight loss
E. Failure or inability to offload
1. For example, fracture, elevation of head of bed (HOB), lack of education, or noncompliance

Common Complaints

A. Pain
B. Bleeding

Subjective Data

A. Ask the patient to describe the location and onset. What did he or she think may have caused the ulcer in the area? Was the onset sudden or gradual? How have the symptoms continued to develop?
B. Assess if the area is itchy or painful.
C. Assess for any associated drainage. Ask about the color and if any odor is noted.
D. Complete a drug history. Ask the patient if he or she is taking any steroids or anticoagulants.
E. Has the patient been treated for this location before? If so, describe treatments.

F. Determine whether the patient has attempted to treat this problem at home. If yes, ask with what.
G. Rule out any possible exposure to industrial or domestic toxins, or insect bites.
H. Assess for iodine and sulfa allergies before starting treatment.

Physical Exam

A. Check temperature, pulse, respirations, and blood pressure.
B. Inspect the pressure ulcer.
    1. Measure length times width times depth.
        a. Undermining: Measure and note location, using the face of a clock to document site of undermining: 12 o'clock, 3 o'clock, 6 o'clock, or 9 o'clock.
        b. Tunneling: Measure and note location, using the face of a clock to document site of undermining: 12 o'clock, 3 o'clock, 6 o'clock, or 9 o'clock.
    2. Describe the wound bed.
        a. Tissue in the wound bed
            i. Necrotic tissue, granulation tissue, epithelial tissue
        b. Color of the tissue (percentage to equal 100%, i.e., 80% pink, 20% yellow)
            i. Red, pink, yellow, brown, black
        c. Drainage
            i. Amount
                1) None, scant, moderate, copious
            ii. Color
                1) Serous, purulent, yellow, serosanguineous, green
        d. Odor
            i. Odor present: Yes
            ii. Odor not present: No
        e. Periwound
            i. Intact
            ii. Not intact
                1) Erythema, fever, induration, maceration, excoriation, calloused, epiboly

Diagnostic Tests

A. CBC
B. Wound culture
C. Wound biopsy
D. X-ray
E. MRI
F. Bone scan

Diagnosis (NPUAP Guidelines, 2007)

Staging Pressure Ulcers

A. Deep tissue injury
    1. Definition: Purple or maroon localized area of discolored intact skin or blood-filled blister due to damage of underlying soft tissue from pressure and/or shear. The area may be preceded by tissue that is painful, firm, mushy, boggy, warmer, or cooler as compared to adjacent tissue.
    2. Further description: Deep tissue injury may be difficult to detect in individuals with dark skin tones. Evolution may include a thin blister over a dark wound bed. The wound may further evolve and become covered by thin eschar. Evolution may be rapid, exposing additional layers of tissue even with optimal treatment.
B. Stage I pressure areas
    1. Definition: Intact skin with nonblanchable redness of a localized area usually over a bony prominence. Darkly pigmented skin may not have visible blanching; its color may differ from the surrounding area.
    2. Further description: The area may be painful, firm, soft, warmer, or cooler as compared to the adjacent tissue. Stage I may be difficult to detect in individuals with dark skin tones. May indicate "at risk" persons (a heralding sign of risk).
C. Stage II pressure ulcers
    1. Definition: Partial thickness loss of dermis presenting as a shallow open ulcer with a red pink wound bed, without slough. May also present as an intact or open/ruptured serum-filled blister.
    2. Further description: Presents as a shiny or dry, shallow ulcer without slough or bruising. This stage should not be used to describe skin tears, tape burns, perineal dermatitis, maceration, or excoriation.
D. Stage III pressure ulcers
    1. Definition: Full thickness tissue loss. Subcutaneous fat may be visible, but bone, tendon, or muscle are not exposed. Slough may be present but does not obscure the depth of tissue loss. May include undermining and tunneling.
    2. Further description: The depth of a Stage III pressure ulcer varies by anatomical location. The bridge of the nose, ear, occiput, and malleolus do not have subcutaneous tissue. Stage III ulcers can be shallow. In contrast, areas of significant adiposity can develop extremely deep Stage III pressure ulcers. Bone/tendon is not visible or directly palpable.
E. Stage IV pressure ulcers
    1. Definition: Full thickness loss with exposed bone, tendon, or muscle. Slough or eschar may be present on some parts of the wound bed. Often include undermining and tunneling.
    2. Further description: The depth of a Stage IV pressure ulcer varies by anatomical location.

The bridge of the nose, ear, occiput, and malleolus can extend into muscle and/or supporting structures (e.g., fascia, tendon, or joint capsule), making osteomyelitis possible. Exposed bone/tendon is visible or directly palpable.

F. Unstageable pressure ulcers
   1. Definition: Full thickness tissue loss in which the base of the ulcer is covered by slough (yellow, tan, gray, or green) and/or eschar (tan, brown, or black) in the wound bed.
   2. Further description: Until enough slough and/or eschar are removed to expose the base of the wound, the true depth, and therefore stage, cannot be determined. Stable (dry, adherent, intact without erythema or fluctuance) eschar on the heels serves as "the body's natural (biological) cover" and should not be removed.

Differential Diagnoses

A. Abscess
B. Trauma
C. Skin cancer
D. Vascular ulcer
E. Diabetic foot ulcers
F. Dermatological disorder

Plan

A. General interventions: Identify the cause of pressure and alleviate.
B. To debride: Normal saline (NS) cleanse, apply santyl and dressing change daily as needed.
C. To granulate an ulcer with scant drainage: NS cleanse, apply hydrogel and dressing change daily as needed.
D. To granulate an ulcer with moderate drainage: NS cleanse, apply calcium alginate and dressing change daily as needed.

Follow-Up

A. Follow up in 1 to 2 weeks to evaluate therapy.
B. See patients every 1 to 2 weeks until healing well; then may reduce to 2- to 4-week evaluation until complete closure.

Consultation/Referral

A. Consult or refer the patient to a wound care specialist.
   1. Extensive ulcer that you are not comfortable with
   2. Patient with multiple medical comorbidities (especially diabetes)
   3. Patient not responding to treatment of 2 to 4 weeks
   4. Ulcer showing decline on follow-up visit
   5. Infection present

Individual Considerations

Adults

A. Patients at end-of-life may develop pressure ulcers related to the dying process. These patients are treated for comfort.

Wounds of the Skin

Definition

A. Wounds are breaks in the external surface of the body.

Pathogenesis

A. Wounds can be caused by any one of innumerable objects that breach the skin. Lacerations and abrasions typically heal by a three-stage process of clotting, inflammation, and skin cell proliferation. The most common pathogens of wound infections are *S. aureus* and beta hemolytic streptococcus.

Predisposing Factors

A. Exposure to accidental or intentional injury
B. Accident prevention failure
C. High-risk behaviors
D. Conditions that predispose to poor wound healing
   1. Diabetes
   2. Corticosteroid therapy
   3. Immunodeficiency
   4. Advanced age
   5. Undernourishment

Common Complaints

A. Bleeding
B. Pain
C. "Cut" in the skin integrity

Other Signs and Symptoms

A. Signs and symptoms of infection: Deep wounds and dirty wounds have increased risk for infection.
B. Soft tissue damage: Wounds with tissue necrosis have increased risk for infection.

Subjective Data

A. Elicit the patient's description of how the wound occurred, including where and when the injury was sustained.
B. Ascertain how much time elapsed until treatment. If 6 hours have elapsed, bacterial multiplication is likely.
C. Ask if the patient is currently immunized for tetanus.
D. Complete a drug history; include any allergies to medications, anesthetics, or dressings.
E. Ask if the patient is taking any medications, especially steroids or anticoagulants.

F. Assess iodine and sulfa drug allergies before starting treatment.
G. Review with the patient whether anything significant in the past medical history may interfere with the healing process (e.g., immunodeficiency).

Physical Examination

A. Check temperature, pulse, respirations, and blood pressure.
B. Inspect
   1. Inspect wound.
   2. Measure wound for size and depth. Wounds with untidy edges may heal more slowly and with disfigurement.
   3. Assess underlying bony structures.
   4. Inspect for foreign objects.
C. Palpate
   1. Palpate extremities for neurovascular function and sensation.
   2. Palpate tissue distal to wound.
   3. Palpate lymph nodes surrounding injured area.
D. Neurologic exam: Assess motor function distal to wound.

Diagnostic Tests

A. Culture wound site if suspicious of infection.
B. Take x-ray films for deep or crushing wounds.

Differential Diagnoses

A. Wound, minor
B. Accidental self-inflicted injury
C. Self-inflicted injury
D. Domestic violence

Plan

A. General interventions
   1. Wounds that require open-wound management
      a. Abrasions and superficial lacerations
      b. Wounds with great amount of tissue damage
      c. Wounds more than 6 hours old
      d. Contaminated wounds
      e. Large area of superficial skin denudation
      f. Puncture wounds
   2. For wounds that do not require sutures
      a. Cleanse wound well with warm water and soap; remove all dirt and foreign bodies.
      b. Forceful irrigation may be needed; use fine-pore sponge (Optipore) with a surfactant, such as poloxamer 188 (Skin Clens). If wound edges are easily approximate, apply Steri-Strips.
      c. Dry, sterile dressings (Telfa, Duoderm, or Opsite) may be used.
   3. If inflammation is present, soak and wash for 15 to 20 minutes three to four times per day. Cover with clean, dry dressing. **Do not use Steri-Strips.**
   4. For wounds that require sutures:
      a. Clean with warm water and soap. Irrigate with sterile saline solution.
      b. Anesthetize with 1% to 2% lidocaine (xylocaine). Do not use solution with epinephrine at fingertips, nose, or ears. Probe wound for any remaining foreign bodies. Approximate wound edges.
      c. Suture the following with technique appropriate to site.
         i. Skin sutures: Nonabsorbable material (e.g., nylon, Prolene, silk)
         ii. Subcutaneous and mucosal sutures: Absorbable material (e.g., Dexon, Vicryl, or plain or chromic gut)
         iii. Extremities: 4 to 0 nylon
         iv. Soles of feet: 2 to 0 nylon
      d. Cover with clean, dry dressing; change after first 24 hours.
      e. Suture removal is based on location.
         i. Head and trunk: 5 to 7 days
         ii. Extremities: 7 to 10 days
         iii. Soles and palms: 7 to 10 days
      f. Tetanus prophylaxis
B. Patient teaching: See the Section III Patient Teaching Guide for this chapter, "Wound Care: Pressure Ulcers."
C. Pharmaceutical therapy
   1. Control pain with acetaminophen (Tylenol) or ibuprofen, as needed.
   2. Topical antibiotic ointments: Polysporin, bacitracin, and mupirocin
   3. Oral antibiotics for prophylaxis
      a. Amoxicillin, clavulanate acid (Augmentin) 875 mg orally twice a day for 7 to 10 days.
      b. With penicillin allergy, use erthromycin; 500 mg orally twice a day for 7 to 10 days
   4. Other alternatives: Cephalexin (Keflex), cefadroxil (Duricef), ciprofloxacin
   5. Tetanus toxoid 0.5 mL by IM injection in deltoid, if no booster has been administered in the past 5 years
   6. Wounds diagnosed with MRSA should be treated with the following oral antibiotics:
      a. Trimethoprim sulfamethoxazole (Bactrim)
      b. Minocycline or doxycycline
      c. Clindamycin rifampin (should be used in combination with one of the previous antibiotics)
      d. Linezolid
   7. Antibiotics not recommended due to high resistance include:

a. Beta lactams
b. Fluoroquinolones
c. Dicloxacillin
d. Cephalexin

8. Treating the nares with Bactroban ointment twice a day and having the patient use hibiclens soap when showering will help to prevent recurrent infections.
9. For severe cases of infection, the patient requires hospitalization for aggressive antibiotic treatment.

Follow-Up

A. Have the patient return for evaluation and dressing change in 24 to 48 hours.

Consultation/Referral

Refer the patient to a physician for the following wounds.

A. Facial wounds
B. Subcutaneous tissue penetration
C. Functional disturbance of tendons, ligaments, vessels, or nerves
D. Grossly contaminated wounds
E. Wounds requiring hospitalization or aggressive antimicrobial therapy for evidence of pyogenic abscess, cellulitis, and ascending lymphangitis

Individual Considerations

Adults

A. Adults with compromised immune systems and chronic conditions are at greater risk for developing a secondary bacterial infection.

High-Protein Nutrition for Wound Healing—Cheryl A. Glass

A. Nutrition is an essential component in the healing of any wounds. Protein, carbohydrates, fats, vitamins, minerals, and amino acid needs are increased for tissue repair. Table 6.2 summarizes the recommended amount of protein intake needed under different circumstances for tissue repair.
   1. Consult with a dietitian for medical nutrition therapy (MNT).
   2. Evaluate protein intake.
   3. Evaluate the patient's weight.
      a. Serial weights—use same scales
      b. Diet diary or 24-hour recall
      c. The dietary and weight history is used to determine additional needs.
      d. Excessive protein potentially leads to dehydration.
   4. Lab testing
      a. CBC
      b. Basic metabolic panel (BMP)
      c. Protein: Albumin, total protein
      d. Renal: Blood urea nitrogen (BUN) and creatinine
   5. Evaluate wound stage/healing
   6. Supplemental protein supplement may be required.
      a. Sources of protein
         i. **Whole eggs are considered the "gold standard" protein.**
         ii. Meat: Red and white meat
         iii. Fish
         iv. Liver
         v. Dairy: Milk, cheese, yogurt
         vi. Soybeans
         vii. Legumes
         viii. Seeds
         ix. Nuts
         x. Grains
      b. Encourage meals and snacking, double portions of meat and eggs, commercial supplements, and fluids.
         i. Eat five to six smaller meals throughout the day
         ii. Keep ready-to-eat meals and snacks
         iii. Drink shake-type beverages that contain protein, vitamins, and minerals
         iv. Add protein powder to drinks
      c. Consider appetite stimulants
      d. Enteral nutrition should be considered if oral food and fluid intake is not adequate.

TABLE 6.2 Recommended Protein Needs Per Day for Wound Healing

Elderly: Baseline protein needs	1.0–1.2 gm/kg body weight/d
Healthy adults	0.8–1.0 gm/kg body weight/d
Large burns	1.5–3.0 gm/kg body weight/d (varies by extent of the burn)
Postsurgery	1.0–1.5 gm/kg body weight/d (varies by the extent of the surgery)
Pressure ulcers	1.0–2.0 gm/kg body weight/d

Other Considerations

A. The elderly have multiple risk factors for intake of insufficient protein for wound healing.
   1. Financial
      a. Expense of high-protein foods
      b. Expense of oral supplemental nutrition drinks
   2. Difficulty chewing
      a. Dental problems
      b. Loose-fitting dentures
      c. Edentulous
   3. Assistive needs
      a. Inability to prepare foods
      b. Need to have a caregiver feed the elderly person
      c. Given inadequate time to consume food if being fed
   4. Dysphagia
   5. Anorexia
   6. Fatigue
   7. Psychosocial
      a. Depression
      b. Loneliness

B. Consultation with a dietitian for MNT, wound care specialist, social worker, occupational therapist, and behavioral health evaluations is advised.

Xerosis (Winter Itch)

Definition

A. Xerosis, often called "winter itch," is dry skin.

Incidence

A. Xerosis occurs in 48% to 98% of patients with atopic dermatitis.

B. It occurs more frequently in elderly patients.

Pathogenesis

A. Dry skin may fissure, appear shiny and cracked, and leave subsequent inflammatory changes.

Predisposing Factors

A. Frequent bathing with hot water and harsh soaps
B. Cold air
C. Low humidity
D. Central heating or cooling
E. Alcohol use
F. Poor nutrition
G. Cholesterol-lowering drugs
H. Systemic disease manifested by thyroid, renal, or hepatic disease; anemia; diabetes; or malignancy

Common Complaints

A. Dry, rough skin, especially on legs

Other Signs and Symptoms

A. Pruritic, scaling skin, particularly on legs, with cracks and/or fissures

B. Pruritus may be associated with systematic disorders or other infections. **Itching of scabies is particularly intense at night.**

C. Plaques 2 to 5 cm in diameter
D. Erythema
E. Wheal-and-flare response typical of urticaria

Subjective Data

A. Obtain the patient's description of the onset of symptoms and whether it was sudden or gradual.

B. Ask the patient to identify any discomfort. Ask if the skin is itchy or painful.

C. Assess lesions for any associated discharge (blood or pus).

D. Determine whether the patient has recently ingested any new medicines (antibiotics, cholesterol-lowering medications, or other drugs), alcohol, or new foods.

E. Ask the patient about use of any topical medications.

F. Identify any preceding systemic symptoms (fever, sore throat, anorexia, or vaginal discharge).

G. Ask the patient about bathing in hot water and if patient is bathing regularly.

H. Review the patient's full medication history for comorbid conditions.

Physical Examination

A. Inspect: Inspect skin for lesions, noting texture of skin.

B. Palpate
   1. Palpate abdomen for masses and hepatosplenomegaly.
   2. Palpate lymph nodes.

Diagnostic Tests

A. There are no diagnostic tests for xerosis.

Differential Diagnoses

A. Xerosis
B. Scabies
C. Atopic dermatitis

Plan

A. General interventions
   1. Hydration and lubrication of skin.
   2. Assess for and treat secondary infection.

B. Patient teaching
   1. See the Section III Patient Teaching Guide for this chapter, "Xerosis (Winter Itch)."
   2. Avoid alkaline soaps: Use Dove, Basis, mild soap, or soap substitute, such as Cetaphil or Aquanil.

C. Pharmaceutical therapy
   1. Apply emollient cream or lotion (Sarna, Lac-Hydrin, or Eucerin).
   2. Use OTC skin lubricants (petroleum jelly, mineral oil, or cold cream).
   3. Topical corticosteroid
      a. Triamcinolone 0.025% two to four times daily or 0.1% two to three times daily; apply sparingly. Advise not to use steroid treatments any longer than 2 weeks without notifying the primary provider.
      b. Hydrocortisone 1% or 2.5% two to four times daily for no longer than 2 weeks. Recommend applying a thin film and avoiding the face.
   4. Systemic antihistamine to control pruritus, such as diphenhydramine (Benadryl) 25 to 50 mg every 4 to 6 hours as needed

Follow-Up

A. Follow up as indicated until resolved.

Consultation/Referral

A. Consult or refer the patient to a dermatologist if no improvement is seen.

Individual Considerations

A. Geriatrics: Monitor the patient for possible skin breakdown and/or ulceration.

Bibliography

Baddour, L. M. (2014). Cellulitis and erysipelas. *UpToDate.* Retrieved from http://www.uptodate.com/contents/cellulitis-and-erysipelas?source=machineLearning&search=cellulitis&selectedTitle=1~150§ionRank=1&anchor=H6#H6

Bailey, K. J., & Cohen, P. R. (2011). Diagnosis and treatment of "pubic-hair bumps." *Clinical Advisor for Nurse Practitioners, 14*(1), 47.

Baranoski, S., & Ayello, E. (2004). *Wound care essentials: Practice principles.* Philadelphia, PA: Lippincott, Williams, and Wilkins.

Blereau, R. P. (2012). Acneiform folliculitis. *Consultant* (00107069), *52*(6), 469.

Bowden, V. R. (2012). Losing the louse: How to manage this common infestation in children. *Pediatric Nursing, 38*(5), 253–255.

Burns, B. (2013). Insect bites. *Medscape.* Retrieved from http://emedicine.medscape.com/article/769067-overview

Centers for Disease Control and Prevention. (2010). *Sexually transmitted diseases treatment guidelines, 2010. Diseases characterized by vaginal discharge.* Retrieved from www.cdc.gov/std/treatment/2010/vaginal-discharge.htm

Centers for Disease Control and Prevention. (2013a). *Genital herpes—CDC fact sheet.* Retrieved from http://www.cdc.gov/std/herpes/STDFact-Herpes.htm

Centers for Disease Control and Prevention. (2013b). *Vaccines and preventable diseases: shingles vaccination: What you need to know.* Retrieved from http://www.cdc.gov/vaccines/vpdvac/shingles/vacc-need-know.htm

Collins, L., & Seraj, S. (2010). Diagnosis and treatment of venous ulcers. *American Family Physician, 81*(8), 989–996.

Derby, R., Rohal, P., Jackson, C., Beutler, A., & Olsen, C. (2011). Novel treatment of onychomycosis using over-the-counter mentholated ointment: A clinical case series. *Journal of the American Board of Family Medicine, 24*(1), 69–74. Retrieved from www.jabfm.org/content/24/1/69.long

DiZenzo, G., Marazza, G., & Borradori, L. (2007). Bullous pemphigoid: Physiopathology, clinical features and management. *Adv Dermatol, 23,* 257.

Gagliardi, A., Gomes Silva, B., Torloni, M., & Soares, B. (2012). Vaccines for preventing herpes zoster in older adults. *Cochrane Database of Systematic Reviews, 10.* Retrieved from http://summaries.cochrane.org/CD008858/vaccines-for-preventingherpes-zoster-in-older-adults

Gaston, R., & Lewis, D. R. (2010). Animal bites to the hand. *Current Orthopaedic Practice, 21*(6), 559–563.

Gottlieb, A., Korman, N. J., Gordon, K. B., Feldman, S. R., Lebwohl, M., Koo, J. Y., ... Menter, A. (2008). Guidelines for the management of psoriasis and psoriatic arthritis. Section 2. Psoriatic arthritis: Overview and guidelines of care for treatment with an emphasis on biologics. *Journal of the American Academy of Dermatology, 58,* 851–864.

Gunning, K., Pippitt, K., Kiraly, B., & Sayler, M. (2012). Pediculosis and scabies: A treatment update. *American Family Physician, 86*(6), 535–541.

Habif, T. P. (Ed.). (2009). *Clinical dermatology* (5th ed., pp. 710–714). Philadelphia, PA: Mosby Elsevier.

Halevy, S., & Shai, A. (1993). Lichenoid drug eruptions. *Journal of the American Academy of Dermatology, 29,* 249–255.

Hansen, R. C. (1996). Scabies: Tips for diagnosing and cautions about treatment. *Modern Medicine, 64,* 27.

Hazin, R., Abuzetun, J., & Khatri, K. (2009). Derm diagnoses you can't afford to miss. *The Journal of Family Practice, 58,* 298–306.

Herchiline, T. E., Bronze, M. S. et al. (2014). Cellulitis. *Medscape.* Retrieved from http://emedicine.medscape.com/article/214222-overview#a0156

Howlader, N., Noone, A. M., Krapcho, M., Garshell, J., Neyman, N., Altekruse, S. F., ... Cronin, K. A (Eds.). *SEER cancer statistics review, 1975-2010.* Bethesda, MD: National Cancer Institute. Retrieved from http://seer.cancer.gov/csr/1975_2010/, based on November 2012 SEER data submission, posted to the SEER website, April 2013.

Iavazzo, C., Gkegkes, I. D., Zarkada, I. M., & Falagas, M. E. (2011). Boric acid for recurrent vulvovaginal candidiasis: The clinical evidence. *Journal of Women's Health (15409996), 20*(8), 1245–1255.

Johnson, S. R., & Taylor, M. A. (2012). Identification and management of malignant skin lesions among older adults. *Journal for Nurse Practitioners, 8*(8), 610–616.

Klein, R. S. (2013). Epidemiology of herpes simplex virus type 1 infection. *UpToDate.* Wolters-Kluwer Health. May 2014.

Kronfol, R., & Downey, K. A. (2014). Technique of incision and drainage for skin abscess. *UpToDate.* Retrieved from http://www.uptodate.com/contents/technique-of-incision-and-drainage-for-skinabscess?source=machineLearning&search=abscess+incision+and+drainage&selectedTitle=1~150§ionRank=1&anchor=H28#H28

Leiferman, K. M. (2014). Clinical features and diagnosis of bullous pemphigoid and mucous membrane pemphigoid. *UpToDate.* Retrieved from http://www.uptodate.com/contents/clinical-features-and-diagnosis-of-bullous-pemphigoid-and-mucous-Membrane-pemphigoid?source=machineLearning&search=bullous+pemphigoid&selectedTitle=3~60§ionRank=2&anchor=H784094#H784094

Martinez-Diaz, G., & Mancini, A. (2010). CNE series. Head lice: Diagnosis and therapy. *Dermatology Nursing, 22*(4), 2–8.

Menter, A., Gottlieb, A., Feldman, S. R., Voorhees, A. S. V., Leonardi, C. L., Gordon, K. B., … Bhushan, R. (2008). Guidelines for the management of psoriasis and psoriatic arthritis. Section 1. Overview of psoriasis and guidelines of care for the treatment of psoriasis with biologics. *Journal of the American Academy of Dermatology, 5,* 826–850.

Menter, A., Korman, N. J., Elmets, C. A., Feldman, S. R., Gelfand, J. M., Gordon, K. B., … Bhushan, R. (2009). American Academy of Dermatology guidelines of care for the management of psoriasis and psoriatic arthritis. Section 3. Guidelines of care for the management and treatment of psoriasis with topical therapies. *Journal of the American Academy of Dermatology, 60,* 643–659.

Monroe, J. (2012). Papules and plaques from head to foot. *JAAPA: Journal of the American Academy of Physician Assistants, 25*(9), 16.

Moore, S., Mordue Luntz, A., & Logan, J. (2012). Insect bite prevention. *Infectious Disease Clinics, 26*(3), 655–673.

National Clearing House Guidelines. *Guidelines of care for the management of primary cutaneous melanom.* 2001 March (revised 2011 Nov). NGC:009038. American Academy of Dermatology-Medical Specialty Society.

National Pressure Ulcer Advisory Panel and European Pressure Ulcer Advisory Panel. (2009). *Prevention and treatment of pressure ulcers; clinical practice guideline.* Washington, DC: National Pressure Advisory Panel.

Plaza, J. A., et al. (2013). Erythema multiforme. *Medscape Reference. Drugs, Diseases and Procedures.* Retrieved from http://emedicine.medscape.com/article/1122915-overview

Reddy, M., & Sudeep, S. (2006). Preventing pressure ulcers: A systematic review. *Journal of the American Medical Association, 296*(8), 974–984.

Samim, F., Auluck, A., Zed, C., & Williams, P. M. (2013). Erythema multiforme: A review of epidemiology, pathogenesis, clinical features and treatment. *Dental Clinics of North America, 57*(4). 583–596.

Scheinfield, N. (2009). Two generalized red rashes. *The Clinical Advisor, 12,* 75–76, 79–80.

Scheinfield, N. (2010). Skin disorders in older adults. *Consultant, 50,* 60–66.

Schleicher, S. M. (2011). Diagnosis at a glance. *Emergency Medicine (00136654), 43*(1), 13–14.

Selden, S. (2012). Seborrheic dermatitis. *Medscape.* Retrieved from Emedicine.medscape.com/article/1108312-overview

Sokumbi, O., & Wetter, D. A. (2012). Clinical features, diagnosis, and treatment of erythema multiforme: A review for the practicing dermatologist. *International Journal of Dermatology, 51*(8), 889–902. [Medline]

Spentzouris, G., & Labropoulos, N. (2009). The evaluation of lower-extremity ulcers. *Seminars of Interventional Radiology, 26*(4), 286–295.

Stevens, D. L., Bisno, A. L., Chambers, H. F., Everett, E. D., et al. (2005). Practice guidelines for the diagnosis and management of skin and soft-tissue infections. *Clinical Infectious Diseases, 41,* 1373–1406.

Thiboutot, D. M. (1994). Acne rosacea. *American Family Physician, 50,* 1691–1697, 1701–1702.

Tintinalli, J. E., Ruiz, E., & Krome, R. L. (1996). *Emergency medicine: A comprehensive study guide* (pp. 319–321). New York, NY: McGraw-Hill.

U.S. Preventive Services Task Force (2014). *Behavioral counseling to prevent skin cancer.* U.S. Preventive Services Task Force Recommendation Statement. Release Date: May 2012. Retrieved from http://www.uspreventiveservicestaskforce.org/uspstf11/skincancouns/skincancounsrs.htm

Urman, F., & Weinberger, J. (2005). Diagnosing and treating erythema multiforme: This common skin condition, often confused with urticaria, starts with red papules and evolves into pruritic and burning target-like lesions. *Clinical Advisor, 55*(4), 8–12.

Van Onselen, J. (2012). Rosacea: Symptoms and support. *British Journal of Nursing, 21*(12), 1252–1255.

Venables, J. (1995). The management and treatment of eczema. *Nursing Standard, 9,* 25–28.

Watkins, J. (2010a). Pruritis, part 4: Infestations. *Practice Nursing, 21*(5), 247–248, 250, 252 passim.

Watkins, J. (2010b). Treating shingles (herpes zoster) in the older person. *British Journal of Community Nursing, 15*(9), 420–426.

Watkins, J. (2011). Eczema diagnosis and management in the community. *British Journal of Community Nursing, 16*(9), 418–426.

Watkins, J. (2012). Problems with acne vulgaris in adolescence. *Practice Nursing, 23*(11), 562–565.

Weber, D. J., Cohen, M. S., Morrell, D. S., & Rutala, W. A. (2000). The acutely ill patient with fever and rash. In G. L. Mandell, J. E. Bennett, & R. Dolin (Eds.), *Pressure ulcers: A review of pathophysiology, risk factors, and management principals.* Retrieved from www.healthplexus.net

Williams, H., Dellavalle, R., & Garner, S. (2012). Acne vulgaris. *Lancet, 379*(9813), 361–372.

Wilson, J. (2011). Herpes zoster. *Annals of Internal Medicine, 154*(5), ITC3-1–ITC3-16.

Wyndham, M. (2011). Pityriasis rosea. *Practice Nurse, 41*(1), 41.

Zajac, M. H. S., & Jacobson, A. (2009). Impetigo: Taking on a common skin infection. *The Clinical Advisor, 12,* 30–34.

CHAPTER SEVEN

Eye Guidelines

Jill C. Cash and Mellisa Hall

Blepharitis

Definition

A. Blepharitis is dryness and flaking of the eyelashes, resulting from an inflammatory response of the eyelid. Blepharitis is considered a chronic condition exhibiting intermittent exacerbations of worsening redness and irritation of the eyelid.

Incidence

A. The exact incidence is unknown; however, blepharitis is commonly seen.

Pathogenesis

A. Seborrheic: Excessive shedding of skin cells and blockage of glands
B. *Staphylococcus:* Most common bacteria found, responsible for bacterial infection of lid margin
C. Commonly seen with altered lipid protection and increased bacterial colonization of the ocular surface and eyelids.

Predisposing Factors

A. Diabetes
B. Candida
C. Seborrheic dermatitis
D. Acne rosacea
E. Eczema

Common Complaints

A. Burning and itching
B. Lacrimal tearing
C. Photophobia
D. Recurrent eye infections, styes, or chalazions
E. Dry, flaky secretions on lid margins and eyelashes
F. Gritty sensation to both eyes

Other Signs and Symptoms

A. Seborrheic blepharitis: Lid margin swelling and erythema, flaking, nasolabial erythema, and scaling
B. *Staphylococcus aureus* blepharitis: Erythema/edema, scaling, burning, tearing, itching, and recurrent stye or chalazia
C. May have dandruff of scalp and eyebrows

Subjective Data

A. Elicit onset and duration of signs and symptoms.
B. Note sensations of itching, burning, or pain in the eye.
C. Ask: What makes signs and symptoms worse? What makes signs and symptoms better?
D. Any change in soaps, creams, lotions, or shampoos?
E. Has the patient had similar signs and symptoms in the past?
F. **Note any visual change or pain since the last eye exam.**
G. Note contributing factors involved, if present. These should include smoking, allergen exposure, contact lenses, and use of retinoid products.

Physical Examination

A. Inspection
   1. Inspect eyes, noting extraocular eye movements (EOMs) of eyes.
   2. Examine sclera, pupil, iris, and fundus.
   3. Examine eyes for red reflex and corneal light reflex.
   4. Note erythema or edema on lid margin; note dryness, scaling, and flakes.
   5. Assess vision using Snellen chart.

Diagnostic Tests

A. None

Differential Diagnoses

A. Blepharitis
   1. *S. aureus*
   2. Seborrheic
B. Conjunctivitis
C. Squamous cell carcinoma

D. Stye (hordeolum)
E. Chalazion
F. Upper respiratory infection
G. Sinusitis with periorbital involvement

Plan

A. General interventions
 1. Assess patient and rule out bacterial infection and vision changes.
 2. Patients with frequent recurrent blepharitis need further follow-up with an ophthalmologist.
B. Patient teaching
 1. Wash eye with antibacterial soap and water. Should use over-the-counter (OTC) eyelid scrub product or baby shampoo.
 2. Apply warm compresses to eye for comfort daily for approximately 10 to 20 minutes.
 3. Stop use of contacts until the eye is healed.
 4. Encourage good hygiene for prevention of recurrent episodes.
C. Pharmaceutical therapy
 1. Apply erythromycin ophthalmic ointment or azithromycin ophthalmic solution to margin of eye at bedtime, taking care not to contaminate the medication bottle. Bacitracin is an alternative but has been associated with contact dermatitis.
 2. Oral antibiotics: Tetracycline 250 mg by mouth, four times a day for 4 weeks. Alternative: Doxycycline 100 mg by mouth, twice a day, or oxacillin 250 mg four times a day for 4 weeks (contraindicated in pregnancy and lactation).
 3. Consider long-term treatment with doxycycline if infections reoccur.
 4. Topical glucocorticoids, while having a role in treatment, should be prescribed only by an ophthalmologist due to potential side effects.

Follow-Up

A. Recommend follow-up with primary provider in 1 to 2 weeks.
B. Consider referral to eye specialist for recurrent episodes of blepharitis.

Individual Considerations

A. If symptoms are unilateral only, patient should be evaluated by an ophthalmologist, as blepharitis is a bilateral condition. Unilateral cases may be associated with malignancy.

Cataracts

Definition

A. A cataract, opacity of the crystalline lens of the eye, causes progressive, painless loss of vision (functional impairment). Presenile and senile cataract formation is painless and progresses throughout months and years. Cataracts are frequently associated with intraocular inflammation and glaucoma.

Incidence

A. Cataracts are the most common cause of blindness in the world.
B. 95% of people older than age 60 have cataracts without visual disturbance.
C. 50% of people older than age 75 have significant visual loss due to cataracts.

Pathogenesis

A. Age-related changes of the lens of the eye result from protein accumulation, which produces a fibrous thickened lens that obscures vision.

Predisposing Factors

A. Age
B. Trauma
C. Medications (e.g., topical or systemic steroids, major tranquilizers, or some diuretics)
D. Medical diseases (e.g., diabetes mellitus, metabolic syndrome, Wilson's disease, hypoparathyroidism, glaucoma, congenital rubella syndrome, chronic anteri, or uveitis)
E. Chronic exposure to ultraviolet (UV) B light (including sunlight)
F. Down syndrome
G. Low antioxidant vitamin use
H. Alcohol use
I. Smoking
J. Lower educational levels
K. Poor nutrition and sedentary lifestyle
L. Lead exposure

Common Complaints

A. Decreased vision, including reading road signs or small print
B. Blurred or foggy vision, "ghost" images
C. Inability to drive at night

Other Signs and Symptoms

A. Initial visual event can be a shift toward nearsightedness.
B. Visual impairment can be more marked at distances, with abnormal visual acuity exams.
C. Severe difficulty with glare
D. Altered color perception
E. Frequent falls or injuries

Subjective Data

A. Review the onset, course, and duration of visual changes, including altered day or night vision and nearsighted versus farsighted vision. Rule out diplopia or hemianopia.
B. Assess whether involvement is in one or both eyes.

C. Determine what improves vision—use of glasses or use of extra light.
D. Review the patient's medical history and current medications.
E. Review the patient's history for traumatic injury.
F. Discuss the patient's occupation and leisure activities to determine exposure to UV rays.
G. Review lifestyle choices that would identify risk of cataract formation.

Physical Examination

A. Inspect
  1. Conduct a funduscopic examination.
    a. Check red reflex and opacity.
      i. A bright red reflex is seen in the normal eye.
      ii. Cataract formation is seen by the disruption of the red reflex.
      iii. Lens opacities appear as dark areas against the background of the red-orange reflex.
    b. Examine color of opacity. For brunescent cataracts, the nucleus acquires a yellow–brown coloration and becomes progressively more opaque.
    c. Check retinal abnormalities, hemorrhage, scarring, and drusen (small yellow deposits).
    d. Examine extraocular movements and papillary reactivity.

Diagnostic Tests

A. Perform visual acuity exam.
B. Perform peripheral vision exam.
C. Perform slit-lamp exam to determine the exact location and type of cataract.

Differential Diagnoses

A. Cataracts
B. Glaucoma
C. Age-related macular degeneration (MD). MD causes vision loss that is symptomatically similar to cataracts.
D. Diabetic retinopathy
E. Temporal arteritis
F. Cerebral vascular accident

Plan

A. General interventions
  1. Monitor the patient for increased interference of visual impairment on his or her lifestyle.
  2. Cataracts do not need to be removed unless there is impairment of normal, everyday activities.
  3. Surgery is the definitive treatment; however, modification of glasses may improve vision adequately to defer surgery. Contact lenses are optically superior to glasses.

B. Patient teaching
  1. Prevention is important. Teach the patient to use protective eyewear to prevent trauma and sun exposure.
  2. Discuss modifiable lifestyle behaviors that increase the risk of cataract formation.
  3. Wear a hat with a visor to protect eyes when outdoors.
  4. Vitamins: Lutein and zeaxanthin are associated with reduced cataract formation in elderly females.
  5. Patients may not be aware of Medicare coverage for surgical removal. Referring them to Medicare.gov will help them understand costs of surgical intervention.

Follow-Up

A. Surgical removal is indicated if the visual disturbance is interfering with the patient's life, such as causing falls or prohibiting reading.

Consultation/Referral

A. Refer patient for ophthalmologic consultation.
B. Patients should be followed by an ophthalmologist to monitor the cataract for increased size and progressive visual impairment.
C. Contact a social worker or community resources as needed.

Individual Considerations

A. Cataracts are most commonly seen after the age of 60.
B. Patients complaining of visual disturbance should be screened for cataracts.

Chalazion

Definition

A. Chalazion is a chronic inflammatory lesion due to meibomian tear gland obstruction. Chalazions are located in the eyelid margin. A hordeolum (stye) may scar and turn into a chalazion.

Incidence

A. The incidence is unknown.

Pathogenesis

A. Meibomian glands secrete the lipid layer of the tear film that covers and protects the eye. When the glands become blocked, the oil or lipid extrudes into the surrounding tissue, causing the formation of a painless, rubbery nodule.

Predisposing Factors

A. Chalazion may occur as a secondary infection of the surrounding tissues (stye). Chalazions occur more frequently in patients with blepharitis and rosacea.

Common Complaints

A. Swelling, nontender palpable nodule, usually pea-size, inside lid margin or eye
B. Discomfort or irritation due to swelling

Other Signs and Symptoms

A. Tearing
B. Feeling of a foreign body in the eye
C. If infection is present, the entire lid becomes painfully swollen.

Subjective Data

A. Review onset of symptoms, their course and duration, and any concurrent visual disturbance.
B. Question the patient regarding possible foreign body or trauma to the eye.
C. Elicit the quality of pain or tenderness of the eyelid.
D. Review past eye problems and the treatment received.
E. Question for eye tearing, discharge, or matting.
F. Question for employment duties and hobbies predisposing to foreign bodies.

Physical Examination

A. Temperature
B. Inspect
   1. Inspect the eye, sclera, and conjunctiva for a foreign body, erythema, vessel injection, discharge, matting, inflammation of the eyelids, or pterygium.
   2. Check for red- or gray-colored subconjunctival mass in upper and lower eyelid.
C. Palpate
   1. Palpate eyelid for masses, foreign body sensation, and tenderness.
   2. Check for preauricular adenopathy. Usually a hard, nontender nodule is found on the middle portion of the tarsus, away from the lid border; it may develop on the lid margin if the opening of the duct is involved. Some chalazia continue to increase in size and can cause astigmatism by putting pressure on the eye globe.
   3. Chalazia may become acutely tender; however, note the difference between the chalazia and the stye, which is found on the lid margin.

Diagnostic Tests

A. Perform visual acuity exam.

Differential Diagnoses

A. Chalazion
B. Chronic dacryocystitis
C. Hordeolum
D. Blepharitis
E. Xanthelasma

Plan

A. General interventions
   1. Small chalazia do not usually require treatment.
   2. Warm, moist compresses may be applied for 15 minutes four times a day.
B. Patient teaching: Instruct patient regarding warm compresses and hand washing.
C. Pharmaceutical therapy
   1. Antibiotic treatment is not recommended as chalazion is a granulomatous condition.
   2. Intrachalazion corticosteroid injection by an ophthalmologist may be considered.

Follow-Up

A. For large chalazia, follow up with patient in 1 week and then evaluate the patient every 2 to 4 weeks.

Consultation/Referral

A. If the chalazion does not resolve spontaneously, incision and curettage by an ophthalmologist may be necessary.

Conjunctivitis

Definition

A. Conjunctivitis is inflammation of the conjunctiva. All conjunctivitis is erythemic, but not all erythemic eyes are conjunctivitis. Differential diagnosis is key in diagnosis.

Incidence

A. Conjunctivitis may be subdivided into viral, bacterial, allergic, and nonallergic subcategories. Viral conjunctivitis is the most common type of conjunctivitis.

Pathogenesis

Primarily, four types of conjunctivitis are seen:

A. Bacterial (*S. aureus, Haemophilus influenzae, Streptococcus pneumoniae, Neisseria gonorrhoeae,* and *Chlamydia*)
B. Viral (adenovirus, coxsackievirus, herpes zoster ophthalmicus, and enteric cytopathic human orphan [ECHO] viruses)
C. Allergic (seasonal pollens or allergic exposure)
D. Nonallergic (commonly related to mechanical or chemical trauma)

Predisposing Factors

A. Contact to another person with the diagnosis of conjunctivitis
B. Exposure to sexually transmitted infection (STI)
C. Other atopic conditions (allergies)
D. Mechanical or chemical injury

Common Complaints

A. Red eyes
B. Eye drainage

C. Itching (with allergic conjunctivitis)
D. Matting upon awakening

Other Signs and Symptoms

A. Bacterial
 1. Fast onset, 12 to 24 hours of copious purulent or mucopurulent discharge
 2. Burning, stinging, or gritty sensation in eyes
 3. Crusted eyelids upon awakening, with swelling of eyelid
 4. Usually starts out unilaterally; may progress to bacterial infection
 5. Bacterial conjunctivitis may present as beefy red conjunctiva.

B. Viral
 1. Symptoms may begin in one eye and progress to both eyes.
 2. Tearing of eyes
 3. Sensation of foreign body
 4. Systemic symptoms of upper respiratory infection (runny nose, sore throat, sneezing, fever)
 5. Preauricular or submandibular lymphadenopathy
 6. Photophobia, impaired vision
 7. Primary herpetic infection: Vesicular skin lesion, corneal epithelial defect in form of dendrite, uveitis

C. Allergic
 1. Itchy, watery eyes, bilateral
 2. Seasonal symptoms
 3. Edema of eyelids without visual change
 4. With allergic conjunctivitis, hyperemia of eyes is always bilateral, and giant papillae on tarsa may be seen.
 5. May also see eczema, urticaria, and asthma flare

D. Nonallergic (mechanical or chemical)
 1. Itchy, watery eyes; unilateral or bilateral
 2. Frequent causes may include smoke, dust, vapors, and foreign objects
 3. Tearing
 4. Vision obstructed from blurring or tearing

Subjective Data

A. Elicit onset, duration, and course of symptoms.
B. Question patient regarding presence of discharge upon awakening.
C. **Elicit changes in vision since symptoms began.**
D. Determine whether there has been any injury or trauma to the eye.
E. Assess whether these symptoms have appeared before.
F. Rule out exposure to anyone with conjunctivitis.
G. Ask patient about any new events, such as use of contact lenses or change in contact lenses or solutions.
H. Review patient and family history of allergies.
I. Question the patient regarding pain and rate on pain scale.

Physical Examination

A. Check temperature.
B. Inspect
 1. Observe eyes for color and foreign objects. Perform complete eye exam.
 2. Note lid edema.
 3. Assess pupillary reflexes.
 4. Examine eyelids and periorbital skin for erythema, vesicles, inflammation, or tenderness.
 5. Inspect ears, nose, and throat.

C. Auscultate
 1. Auscultate heart and lungs.

D. Palpate
 1. Palpate preauricular lymph nodes and anterior and posterior cervical chain lymph nodes.

Diagnostic Tests

A. Gram stain testing for discharge/exudate extracted from eyes if gonococcal infection is suspected.
B. Culture for chlamydia, if suspected.
C. Perform fluorescein stain of eye if foreign body is suspected or corneal abrasion/ulceration is suspected.
D. Test visual acuity with the Snellen chart. Assess peripheral vision and EOMs.

Differential Diagnoses

A. Conjunctivitis
B. Corneal abrasion
C. Blepharitis
D. Drug-related conjunctivitis
E. Herpetic keratoconjunctivitis
F. Iritis
G. Gonococcal or chlamydial conjunctivitis
H. Angle–closure glaucoma
I. Keratitis

Plan

A. General interventions
 1. Distinguish between bacterial, allergic, nonallergic, or viral infection.
 2. Consider other diagnoses as above if eye pain is noted.

B. Patient education: See the Section III Patient Teaching Guide for this chapter, “How to Administer Eye Medications.”
 1. Cool compresses to affected eye should be applied several times a day.
 2. Clean eyes with warm, moist cloth from inner to outer canthus to prevent spreading infection.
 3. Encourage good hand washing with antibacterial soap.
 4. Instruct on the proper method of instilling medication into eye. Give patient the teaching guide on “How to Administer Eye Medications.”

5. Instruct the female patient to discard all eye makeup, including mascara, eyeliner, and eye shadow, worn at the time of the infection.
6. Teach the patient/parent the difference between bacterial, allergic, nonallergic, and viral infections. Educate according to appropriate diagnosis.
7. If using aminoglycoside or neomycin ointments or drops, use caution and monitor closely for reactive keratoconjunctivitis.
8. Bacterial conjunctivitis is contagious until 24 hours after beginning medication.
9. Viral conjunctivitis is contagious for 48 to 72 hours, but it may last up to 2 weeks.
10. Discuss general eye protection against recurrent exposures or trauma.

C. Pharmaceutical therapy
   1. Bacterial
      a. Aminoglycosides: These should be avoided due to risk of reactive keratoconjunctivitis.
      b. Polymyxin B: Trimethoprim/polymyxin B sulfate (Polytrim) ophthalmic ointment in each eye four times daily for 7 days. Polymyxin B/bacitracin (Polysporin) drops may also be used, 1 gtt every 3 hours for 7 to 10 days
      c. Macrolides: Erythromycin (Ilotycin) ophthalmic ointment 0.5% in each eye four times daily for 7 days
      d. Fluoroquinolones: Ciprofloxacin 0.3%: 1 to 2 gtts every 2 hours for 2 days, then every 4 hours for 5 days. Moxifloxacin (Vigamox) 0.5% 1 gtt three times a day for 7 days. (Due to concerns of resistance, fluoroquinolones should be reserved for treatment of bacterial conjunctivitis primarily in contact wearers.)
   2. Viral
      a. Antiviral medications
         i. Trifluridine 1% drops are indicated for ocular herpes. Patients suspected with ocular herpes should benefit from a same-day referral to an ophthalmologist.
         ii. Oral antiviral medications (trifluridine, valacyclovir) may be used for herpes simplex keratitis. Herpes zoster ophthalmicus is often treated with acyclovir, famciclovir, or valacyclovir and lessens symptoms if started within 72 hours of onset of symptoms. Patients should receive same-day referral for consideration of treatment of ocular herpes.
   3. Allergic
      a. Topical antihistamines/mast cell stabilizer
         i. Azelastine HCl (Optivar): For those older than 3 years, one drop to the affected eye twice a day
         ii. Olopatadine HCl (Pataday) 0.2%: One drop to the affected eye daily
         iii. Olopatadine HCl (Patanol) 0.1%: One drop twice a day to the affected eye
      b. Mast cell stabilizer
         i. *Cromolyn sodium (Crolom) ophthalmic* solution: One to two drops four to six times daily
      c. Topical nonsteroidal anti-inflammatory drug (NSAID)
         i. Ketorolac tromethamine (Acular) 0.5%: One drop four times a day. This is used for severe symptoms of atopic keratoconjunctivitis.
      d. Artificial tears can be used four to five times daily.
      e. Oral antihistamines may be used in severe cases (loratadine or diphenhydramine HCl).
   4. Concurrent conjunctivitis and otitis media should be treated with a systemic antibiotic; no topical eye antibiotic is needed.

Follow-Up

A. If complete resolution occurs within 5 to 7 days after proper treatment, follow-up is not needed.
B. If patient continues to have equal or worsening symptoms after 48 to 72 hours of treatment or if different symptoms appear, then follow-up and a same-day referral to an ophthalmologist are recommended.

Consultation/Referral

A. Consult or refer patient to physician if patient is not responding to treatment within 48 to 72 hours.
B. Same-day referral if patient is suspected of having periorbital cellulitis, iritis, keratitis, herpes zoster ophthalmicus, or acute angle–closure glaucoma.
C. Refer to eye specialist if patient has vision change or eye pain, is not responding to treatment, or if sight-threatening red flags are present.

Individual Considerations

A. Partners: Check partners for gonorrhea and chlamydia when adolescent or adult presents with gonococcal or chlamydial conjunctivitis.
B. Special considerations: Sight-threatening red flags
   1. Reduced visual acuity with onset of symptoms
   2. Observation of a ciliary flush
   3. Photophobia
   4. Severe foreign-body sensation
   5. Corneal opacity
   6. Fixed pupil
   7. Severe headache associated with nausea

Corneal Abrasion

Definition

A. A corneal abrasion is the defect of corneal epithelial tissue, either superficial or deep.

Incidence

A. In the United States, there are 2,000 work-related eye injuries daily.
B. One third of these eye injuries require treatment in an emergency department or by an ophthalmologist.

Pathogenesis

A. Injury from trauma occurs to the epithelial tissue of the cornea.

Predisposing Factors

A. Trauma to the eye caused by a human fingernail, tree branches, wood or metal particles, children's toys, or sports injuries
B. A history of surgical trauma, causing globe weakening
C. A history of spontaneous corneal erosions

Common Complaints

A. Sudden onset of eye pain
B. Foreign-body sensation in the eye
C. Watery eye
D. Mild photophobia

Other Signs and Symptoms

A. Change in vision
B. Redness, swelling, inability to open the eye

Subjective Data

A. Elicit onset, duration, and course of symptoms; note any past history of similar symptoms.
B. Question the patient regarding visual changes (blurred, double, or lost vision, or loss of a portion of the visual field).
C. Question the patient regarding the mechanism of injury and how much time has elapsed since the injury (minutes, hours, or days). Ask: What is his or her occupation, what sports are involved, or what hobbies predispose him or her to injury? Were goggles being worn, and are they routinely worn during the sport or activity?
D. Review the patient's history of exposure to herpetic outbreaks.
E. Determine the degree of pain, if any; headache; photophobia; redness; itching; or tearing.
F. Ascertain whether the patient wears contact lenses or glasses and for what length of time.
G. Ask if the patient has tried any treatments before presentation to the office. If so, what?
H. Rule out the presence of any other infections, such as sinus infection. **Conjunctival discharge signifies an infectious etiology.**
I. Ask about foreign body sensations.
J. Rule out farm injury due to risk of bacterial keratitis.

Physical Examination

A. Vital signs: Blood pressure, pulse, temperature
B. Inspect
   1. Observe *both* eyes.
   2. Test visual acuity and pupil reactivity and symmetry.
   3. Observe cornea surface with direct illumination, noting shadow on surface of iris.
   4. Perform fundoscopic exam.
   5. Evert eyelids for cornea inspection.
   6. Inspect for foreign body and remove if indicated.
   7. Fluorescein stain to visualize changes in epithelial lining. Cobalt blue light or Wood's lamp should be used for visualization.
   8. Consider slit-lamp examination to rule out traumatic hyphema or open globe injuries.

Diagnostic Tests

A. Perform fluorescein stain test: **An epithelial defect that stains with fluorescein is the hallmark symptom.**

Differential Diagnoses

A. Corneal abrasion
B. Corneal foreign body
C. Acute–angle glaucoma
D. Herpetic infection (HSV): HSV is associated with decreased corneal sensation.
E. Recurrent corneal ulceration
F. Ulcerative keratitis
G. Spontaneous corneal erosion

Plan

A. General interventions
   1. Superficial or smaller corneal abrasions should not be patched.
   2. For deeper or larger abrasions and if a foreign body is ruled out, apply a patch that prevents lid motion for 24 hours.
   3. Pressure patch is no longer recommended.
B. Patient teaching
   1. Discuss the use of protective eyewear and prevention of future ocular trauma for the patient with a history of use of power tools or hammering.
   2. See the Section III Patient Teaching Guide for this chapter, "How to Administer Eye Medications."
   3. Advise that the patient should not use/wear contact lenses until the eye is completely healed.
C. Pharmaceutical therapy
   1. Antibiotic drops or ointment. **Never instill antibiotic ointment if there is a possibility of a perforation. Patch the eye and refer the patient to a physician or ophthalmologist.**

a. Erythromycin 0.5% ointment, 1/2-inch ribbon twice a day to four times a day for 7 days.
b. Sulfacetamide sodium ophthalmic solution 10% (Sulamyd), one to two drops instilled into the lower conjunctival sac every 2 to 3 hours during the day; may instill every 6 hours during the night for 5 to 7 days.
c. Sulfacetamide's sodium (Sulamyd) ophthalmic solution or ointment interacts with gentamicin. Avoid using them together.
d. Para-aminobenzoic acid (PABA) derivatives decrease sulfacetamide's action. Wait one half to 1 hour before instilling sulfacetamide.
e. Sulfacetamide precipitates when used with silver preparations. Avoid using them together.
f. Polymyxin B sulfate (Polytrim) 10,000 u, bacitracin zinc 500 u/g ophthalmic ointment (Polysporin), a small ribbon of ointment applied into the conjunctival sac one or more times daily or as needed.
g. Bacitracin 500 u/g ointment, 1/2-inch ribbon twice a day to four times a day for 7 days.

2. Analgesics: Oral NSAIDs or topical analgesics should be used sparingly. Diclofenac (Voltaren) 0.1% solution to eye four times a day as needed, or ketorolac (Acular) 0.5% solution in eye four times a day as needed.
3. Avoid use of home prescriptions that will interfere with the healing process.

Follow-Up

A. Reevaluate the patient **within 24 hours**. Cornea usually heals within 24 to 48 hours.
B. Ophthalmic ointment or drops should be continued for 4 days after re-epithelialization occurs to help in the healing process.
C. If the patient is still symptomatic in 48 hours, consider referral to an ophthalmologist.

Consultation/Referral

Immediate referral to an ophthalmologist is required for large or central lesions or deep or penetrating wounds.

Individual Considerations

A. Pregnancy: Retinal detachment should be considered as a source of eye pain and visual loss, especially in a woman with severe pregnancy-induced hypertension.
B. Encourage protective eyewear for sports (including hockey, soccer, baseball, and basketball) and when using any power equipment or tools.
C. Patients with corneal abrasions secondary to contact lenses are at higher risk for bacterial keratitis. Injuries secondary to contact lenses should be evaluated to rule out a corneal infiltrate or ulcer. If this condition is observed, the patient is at risk for pseudomonas keratitis, an ocular emergency. These patients should never receive an eye patch, should be covered with a topical ophthalmic agent that has pseudomonas coverage, and be evaluated by an ophthalmologist.

Dacryocystitis

Definition

A. Infection or inflammation of the lacrimal sac, or dacryocystitis, can be acute or chronic. Dacryocystitis is more common in children than in adults.
B. Dacryocystitis is usually secondary to obstruction of the nasolacrimal duct.

Incidence

A. The incidence is unknown in adults but occurs in up to 20% of newborns.

Pathogenesis

A. Bacterial infection of the lacrimal sac usually is caused by *Staphylococcus* or *Streptococcus.*

Predisposing Factors

A. Nasal trauma
B. Deviated septum
C. Nasal polyps
D. Congenital dacryostenosis
E. Inferior turbinates

Common Complaints

A. Pain in the eye
B. Redness
C. Swelling
D. Fever
E. Tearing

Other Signs and Symptoms

A. Purulent exudate may be expressed from the lacrimal duct.

Subjective Data

A. Elicit the onset, course, and duration of symptoms. Are symptoms bilateral or unilateral?
B. Review the patient's activity when the symptoms began to determine if etiology is chemical, traumatic, or infectious.
C. Review other presenting symptoms such as fever and discharge.
D. Review the patient's history for previous episodes. Note treatments used in the past.
E. Review history for a recent HSV or fever blister.
F. Review ophthalmologic history.
G. Review medications.

Physical Examination

A. Check temperature, pulse, and blood pressure.
B. Inspect
1. Assess both eyes.
2. Check peripheral fields of vision and sclera.

3. Evaluate conjunctiva for distribution of redness, ciliary flush, and foreign bodies.
4. Inspect lid margins: Evaluate for crusting, ulceration, and masses.

C. Palpate: Palpate lacrimal duct. Discharge can be expressed from the tear duct with the application of pressure.

Diagnostic Tests

A. Check visual acuity.
B. Culture discharge for *Neisseria* if suspected.

Differential Diagnoses

A. Dacryocystitis
B. Chalazion
C. Blepharitis
D. Xanthoma
E. Bacterial conjunctivitis
F. Hordeolum
G. Foreign body

Plan

A. General interventions
   1. Apply warm, moist compresses at least four times per day.
   2. Instruct female patients to discard old makeup, including mascara, eyeliner, and eye shadow used prior to infection.

B. Patient teaching: Application of compresses, hand washing, and proper cleaning. See the Section III Patient Teaching Guide for this chapter, "How to Administer Eye Medications."

C. Pharmaceutical therapy
   1. Dicloxacillin 250 mg by mouth four times daily for 7 days
   2. Erythromycin 250 mg by mouth four times daily for 7 days

Follow-Up

A. Follow up in 2 weeks if symptoms are not resolved.

Consultation/Referral

A. Acute dacryocystitis: Abrupt onset with erythema, warmth, swelling, and pain of the lacrimal duct should be managed on the same day by an ophthalmologist.
B. Chronic dacryocystitis: Refer the patient to an ophthalmologist for irrigation and probing if needed.
C. Lab studies are generally performed by an ophthalmologist.

Dry Eyes

Definition

A. Insufficient lubrication of the eye, or dry eyes, is due to a deficiency of any one of the major components of the tear film.
B. Defects in tear production are uncommon but may occur in conjunction with systemic disease. Presence of systemic disease should be evaluated.

Incidence

A. Increased incidence of dry eyes in the elderly is due to decreased rate of lacrimal gland secretions. It has been estimated as a concern in as many as 30% of people 50 years of age and older.

Pathogenesis

A. Decreased production of one or more components of the tear film results in dry eyes. The tear film comprises three layers:
   1. An outermost lipid layer, excreted by the lid meibomian glands
   2. A middle aqueous layer, secreted by the main and accessory lacrimal glands
   3. An innermost mucinous layer, secreted by conjunctival goblet cells

B. A defect in production of the aqueous phase by lacrimal glands causes dry eyes (keratoconjunctivitis sicca). The condition most often occurs as a physiologic consequence of aging, and it is commonly exacerbated by dry environmental factors. It may also develop in patients with connective tissue disorders.
C. In Sjögren's syndrome, the lacrimal glands become involved in immune-mediated inflammation.
D. Mucin production may decline in the setting of vitamin A deficiency.
E. Loss of goblet cells can occur secondary to chemical burns.

Predisposing Factors

A. History of severe conjunctivitis
B. Eyelid defects such as fifth or seventh cranial nerve palsy, incomplete blinking, exophthalmos, and lid movement hindered by scar formation
C. Drug-induced conditions, including use of anticholinergic agents
   1. Phenothiazine
   2. Tricyclic antidepressants
   3. Antihistamines
   4. Diuretics
   5. Isotretinoin (Accutane)

D. Systemic disease such as rheumatoid disease, Sjögren's syndrome, and neurologic disease
E. Environmental factors such as heat (wood, coal, gas), air conditioners, winter air, and tobacco smoke
F. Use of contacts
G. Increasing age and associated loss of androgens
H. Lipid abnormalities

Common Complaints

A. Ocular fatigue
B. Foreign-body sensation in the eye

C. Itching, burning, irritation, or dryness sensation in the eye

Other Signs and Symptoms

A. Photophobia
B. Cloudy, blurred vision
C. Rainbow of color around lights. Acute angle–closure glaucoma can present with a red, painful eye; cloudy, blurred vision and a rainbow of color around lights; dilatation of the pupil; nausea and vomiting.
D. Bell's palsy, signs of stroke, or other conditions that affect the blinking mechanism

Subjective Data

A. Elicit onset, duration, and frequency of symptoms.
B. Note factors that worsen or alleviate symptoms.
C. Note medical history for systemic conditions and strokes.
D. List current medications, noting anticholinergic drugs and isotretinoin (Accutane) use.
E. Note whether the patient wears contact lenses or glasses, and ask for what length of time.
F. Review occupational and home exposure to irritants, allergens, and fans.
G. Assess whether the patient produces tears. Note eye drainage amount, color, and frequency.
H. Review history of any previous ocular disease, surgeries, or autoimmune disorders.

Physical Examination

A. Check temperature, pulse, respirations, and blood pressure.
B. Inspect
   1. Observe and evaluate *both* eyes.
   2. Conduct a detailed eye exam: Check the eye, lid, and conjunctiva for masses and redness.
   3. Check pupil reactivity and corneal clarity. The corneal reflex should be checked if there is concern about a neuroparalytic keratitis or facial nerve palsy.
   4. Complete a funduscopic exam. Check for completeness of lid closure as well as position of eyelashes.
   5. Examine mouth for dryness.
   6. Inspect skin for butterfly rash.
C. Palpate
   1. Palpate lacrimal ducts for drainage.
   2. Invert upper lid and check for foreign body or chalazion.
   3. Check sinuses for tenderness.
   4. Palpate thyroid.
   5. Palpate joints for warmth and redness or inflammation.

Diagnostic Tests

A. There is no "gold standard" for the diagnosis of dry eye syndrome. Clinical diagnosis using a thorough history and physical exam should be considered. Validated questionnaires include:
   1. Ocular Surface Disease Index (OSDI)
   2. Impact of Dry Eye on Everyday Life (IDEEL)
   3. Salisbury Eye Evaluation Questionnaire (SEE)
B. A Schirmer's test has variable results between examiners. To perform Schirmer's test, use Whatman no. 41 filter paper, 5 mm by 35 mm. A folded end of filter paper is hooked over the lower lid nasally, and the patient is instructed to keep his or her eyes lightly closed during the test. Wetting is measured after 5 minutes; less than 5 mm is usually abnormal.

Differential Diagnoses

A. Dry eyes
B. Stevens–Johnson syndrome
C. Sjögren's syndrome: Chronic dry mouth, dry eyes, and arthritis triad suggest Sjögren's syndrome. Facial telangiectasias, parotid enlargement, Raynaud's syndrome, and dental caries are associated features. Patients complain first of burning and a sandy, gritty, foreign-body sensation, particularly later in the day.
D. Systemic lupus erythematosus
E. Scleroderma
F. Ocular pterygium
G. Superficial pemphigoid
H. Vitamin A deficiency

Plan

A. General interventions
   1. If no ocular disease is present, reduce environmental dryness by use of a room humidifier for a 2-week trial.
   2. Apply artificial tear substitutes and nonprescription drops.
   3. Consider stopping medications being used that may be contributing to the source of dry eye symptoms.
   4. Caution should be used when using OTC allergy medications, if allergy is a contributing cause. Topical antihistamines may exacerbate the condition over time or cause systemic side effects in the elderly.
B. Patient teaching: See the Section III Patient Teaching Guide for this chapter, "How to Administer Eye Medications."
C. Pharmaceutical therapy
   1. Topical artificial tears one or two drops four times daily, preferably one without preservatives (i.e., Thera-tears, Dry Eye Therapy, Tears Naturale)
   2. Drops may be instilled as often as desired.
   3. Cyclosporine ophthalmic drops 0.05% or 0.01% one drop twice daily have been shown

to reduce symptoms of dry eye. Six weeks of treatment may be needed before an effect is appreciated. OTC artificial tears may be used in addition.
4. Oral antioxidants and omega 3 fatty acids have shown some promise in reducing symptoms of dry eye.

Follow-Up

A. Reevaluate the patient in 2 weeks.

Consultation/Referral

A. Refer the patient to an ophthalmologist if symptoms are unrelieved at the 2-week follow-up.
B. Make an immediate referral for red eye, visual disturbance, or eye pain.

Individual Considerations

A. Geriatrics
   1. The rate of lacrimal gland secretions diminishes with aging; therefore, the elderly are at an increased risk for developing dry eye.
   2. Ace-inhibitors may reduce the risk of dry eye syndrome in some patients. Consider treatment with ace-inhibitors for hypertension as appropriate in clients.

Excessive Tears

Definition

A. Excessive tears disorder is an overproduction of tears. Complaints vary from watery eyes to overflowing tears that run down the cheeks, a condition known as epiphora.

Incidence

A. The incidence is unknown.

Pathogenesis

A. The most common cause is reflex overproduction of tears (as occurs in the elderly) due to a deficiency of the tear film.
B. Lacrimal pump failure and obstruction of the nasolacrimal outflow system are other causes of excessive tears.
C. Canalicular infections may be caused by *Actinomyces israelii* (Streptothrix) and *Candida*.

Predisposing Factors

A. Blepharitis (inflammation of the eyelid)
B. Allergic conjunctivitis (infectious or foreign body)
C. Exposure to cold, air conditioning, or dry environment
D. Lid problems: Impaired pumping action of the lid motion due to seventh nerve palsy or conditions that stiffen the lids such as scars or scleroderma
E. Lid laxity from aging or ectropion (sagging of the lower lid)
F. Sinusitis
G. Atopy
H. Age: Increased incidence in the elderly due to an overproduction of tears by the lacrimal gland
I. Congenital obstruction

Common Complaints

A. Watery eyes or tears running down cheeks are common complaints.

Other Signs and Symptoms

A. Unilateral tearing: Obstructive etiology
B. Bilateral tearing: Environmental irritants

Subjective Data

A. Inquire about onset, course, and duration of symptoms. Note frequency of excessive tearing.
B. Ascertain whether this is a new symptom or whether the patient has a past history of similar complaints. Ask how it was treated, and what the response was to treatment(s).
C. Determine severity. Do the tears run down the cheek?
D. Ascertain whether tearing is unilateral or bilateral.
E. Review common environmental predisposing factors.
F. Question the patient regarding vision changes.
G. Review medical history.
H. Review recent history for sinus infections or drainage, facial fractures, and surgery.
I. Confirm no pain associated with condition.

Physical Examination

A. Inspect
   1. Evaluate *both* eyes.
   2. Observe the lid structure and motion.
   3. Conduct a dermal exam to rule out butterfly rash.
   4. Confirm pupil reactivity
   5. Perform a fundoscopic exam for vascular changes.
B. Palpate
   1. Apply gentle pressure over the lacrimal sac to check drainage.
   2. Invert upper lid to check for foreign body.
   3. Palpate face for sinus tenderness.

Diagnostic Tests

A. Culture any drainage expressed from the lacrimal sacs.

Differential Diagnoses

A. Excessive tears
B. Dendritic ulcer: Early symptoms are tears running down cheeks associated with a foreign-body sensation.
C. Congenital glaucoma

D. Dacryocystitis (purulent discharge)
E. Reflex tearing caused by dry eye
F. Blepharitis

Plan

A. General interventions
  1. Eliminate identifiable irritants.
  2. Treatment is aimed mainly at the underlying condition (i.e., ocular infection).
  3. Dacryocystitis is treated with hot compresses at least four times a day and systemic antibiotics.

B. Patient teaching: Instruct the patient on the application of compresses.

C. Pharmaceutical therapy
  1. None is required for diagnosis of excessive tears without infections pathology.
  2. Dacryocystitis
     a. Erythromycin 250 mg four times daily for 7 days.
     b. Dicloxacillin 250 mg four times daily for 7 days.

Follow-Up

A. See patient in 48 to 72 hours to evaluate symptoms, especially if antibiotic therapy was needed.

Consultation/Referral

A. Patients unresponsive to treatment should be promptly referred to an ophthalmologist.
B. Consider referral for lid malposition or nasolacrimal duct obstructions.

Individual Considerations

A. Consider mental health support if condition alters self-image and limits socialization.

Eye Pain

Definition

A. Sensation of pain may affect the eyelid, conjunctiva, or cornea.

Incidence

A. Unknown. Pain in the eye is most often produced by conditions that do not threaten vision.

Pathogenesis

A. The external ocular surfaces and the uveal tract are richly innervated with pain receptors. As a result, lesions or disease processes affecting these surfaces can be acutely painful.
B. Pathology confined to the vitreous, retina, or optic nerve is rarely a source of pain.

Predisposing Factors

A. Eyelids: Inflammation such as hordeolum (stye), trichiasis (in-turned lash), and tarsal foreign bodies.
B. Conjunctiva: Viral and bacterial conjunctivitis or allergic conjunctivitis; toxic, chemical, and mechanical injuries.
C. Cornea: Keratitis (inflammation of the cornea) accompanying trauma, infection, exposure, vascular disease, or decreased lacrimation; microbial keratitis from contact use. If blood vessels invade the normally avascular corneal stroma, vision may become cloudy. Severe pain is a prominent symptom; movement of the lid typically exacerbates symptoms.

Common Complaints

A. Eye pain (sharp, dull, deep): The quality of the pain needs to be considered. Deep pain is suggestive of an intraocular problem. Inflammation and rapidly expanding mass lesions may cause deep pain. Displacement of the globe and diplopia may ensue.
B. Eye movement may cause sharp pain due to meningeal inflammation (the extraocular rectus muscles insert along the dura of the nerve sheath at the orbital apex). Most cases are idiopathic, but 10% to 15% are associated with multiple sclerosis.

Other Signs and Symptoms

These symptoms may be unilateral or bilateral.

A. Eyelids
  1. Tenderness
  2. Sensation of foreign body
  3. Redness
  4. Edema

B. Conjunctiva
  1. Mild burning
  2. Sensation of foreign body
  3. Itching (allergic)

C. Cornea
  1. Burning
  2. Foreign-body sensation
  3. Considerable discomfort
  4. Reflex photophobic tearing
  5. Blinking exacerbates pain.
  6. Pain relieved with pressure holding the lid shut. With a foreign body or a corneal lesion, pain is exacerbated by lid movement and relieved by cessation of lid motion.

D. Sclera: Redness or vessel injection

E. Uveal tract (uveitis or iritis)
  1. Dull, deep-seated ache and photophobia
  2. Profound ocular and orbital pain radiating to the frontal and temporal regions accompanying sudden elevation of pressure (acute angle–closure glaucoma).
  3. Vagal stimulation with high pressure may result in nausea and vomiting.
  4. Usual history of mild intermittent episodes of blurred vision preceding onset of throbbing pain, nausea, vomiting, and decreased visual acuity.
  5. Halos around light

F. Orbit
   1. Deep pain with inflammation and rapidly expanding mass lesions
   2. Eye movement causing sharp pain due to meningeal inflammation
G. Sinusitis: Secondary orbital inflammation and tenderness on extremes of eye movement

Subjective Data

A. Review the onset, duration, and course of symptoms. Inquire regarding the quality of pain.
B. Review any predisposing factors such as trauma or a foreign object. Ask: Was the onset sudden or gradual?
C. Note reported changes in visual acuity or color vision.
D. Note aggravating or alleviating factors.
E. Determine whether the eye pain is bilateral or unilateral.
F. Review history for herpes, infections, and toxic or chemical irritants.
G. Review history for glaucoma and previous eye surgeries or treatments.
H. Assess the patient for any other symptoms such as migraine headache, sinusitis, or tooth abscess.
I. Inquire whether the patient has lost a large amount of sleep.
J. Inquire whether he or she has been exposed to a large amount of UV light or sunlight (vacation, tanning beds).
K. Review history for any other medical problems such as lupus, sarcoidosis, or inflammatory bowel disease.

Physical Examination

A. Inspect
   1. Evaluate *both* eyes.
   2. Test visual acuity and color vision.
   3. Observe for EOMs and visual fields.
   4. Check the eye, lid, and conjunctiva for masses, foreign bodies, and redness.
   5. Check pupil reactivity and corneal clarity.
   6. Conduct a fundoscopic exam for disk abnormalities.
   7. Perform ear, nose, and throat exam.
B. Palpate
   1. Palpate lacrimal ducts for drainage.
   2. Palpate sinuses for tenderness.
   3. Invert upper lid and check for foreign body or chalazion.
   4. Palpate the periorbital skin for tenderness.

Diagnostic Tests

A. Fluorescein stain
B. Measurement of intraocular pressure (IOP)

Differential Diagnoses

A. Eye pain
B. Hordeolum
C. Chalazion
D. Acute dacryocystitis
E. Irritant exposure
F. Conjunctival infection
G. Corneal abrasion
H. Foreign body
I. Ulcers
J. Ingrown lashes
K. Contact lens abuse
L. Scleritis
M. Acute angle–closure glaucoma. With acute angle–closure glaucoma, fixed, midposition pupil, redness, and a hazy cornea may be present.
N. Uveitis
O. Referred pain from extraocular sources such as sinusitis, tooth abscess, tension headache, temporal arteritis, and prodrome of herpes zoster
P. Iritis
Q. Bacterial keratitis
R. Temporal arteritis

Plan

A. General interventions
   1. The initial task is to be sure that there is no threat to vision.
   2. Treatment modality depends on the underlying cause of eye pain.
B. Patient teaching: See the Section III Patient Teaching Guide for this chapter, "How to Administer Eye Medications."
C. Pharmaceutical therapy: Medication depends on the underlying cause.

Follow-Up

A. Follow-up depends on the underlying cause.

Consultation/Referral

A. **Any change in visual acuity or color vision requires an urgent ophthalmologic consultation (same-day referral).**

Glaucoma, Acute Angle–Closure

Definition

A. Acute angle–closure glaucoma is an ocular emergency caused by elevations in IOP that damage the optic nerve, leading to loss of peripheral fields of vision; this leads to loss of central vision, resulting in blindness.

Incidence

A. Acute angle–closure glaucoma is the second leading cause of blindness in the United States. Ten percent of glaucoma cases are due to angle–closure glaucoma. Approximately 5% to 15% of the patient population develops some form of glaucoma.

Pathogenesis

A. The essential pathophysiologic feature of glaucoma is an IOP that is too high for the optic nerve. Increased IOP increases vascular resistance, causing decreased vascular perfusion of the optic nerve and ischemia. Light dilates the pupil, causing the iris to relax and bow forward. As the iris bows forward, it comes into contact with the trabecular meshwork and occludes the outflow of aqueous humor, resulting in increased IOP.

Predisposing Factors

A. Narrow anterior ocular chamber
B. Prolonged periods of darkness
C. Drugs that dilate the pupils (i.e., anticholinergics)
D. Advancing age
E. African American heritage
F. Family history
G. Trauma
H. Neoplasm
I. Corticosteroid therapy
J. Neovascularization
K. Female gender
L. Hyperopia (farsightedness)

Common Complaints

A. Ocular pain
B. Blurred vision, decreased visual acuity, "cloudiness" of vision
C. "Halos" around lights at night
D. Neurologic complaints (headache, nausea, or vomiting)

Other Signs and Symptoms

A. Red eye with ciliary flush
B. "Silent blinder" causes extensive damage before the patient is aware of visual field loss.
C. Dilated pupil
D. Hard orbital globe
E. No pupillary response to light
F. Increased IOP (normal IOP is 10–20 mmHg)

Subjective Data

A. Review the onset, course, and duration of symptoms; note visual changes in one or both eyes. Do symptoms get worse in early evening?
B. Review medical history and medications, including OTC products.
C. Review family history of glaucoma.
D. Determine whether there has been any difficulty with peripheral vision, any headache photophobia, or any visual blurring.
E. Rule out presence of any chemical, trauma, or foreign bodies in the eye.
F. Review any recent history of herpes outbreak.
G. Ask the patient whether this has ever occurred before, and if so, how it was treated.
H. Determine if IOP has been measured in the past.

Physical Examination

A. Blood pressure
B. Inspect
   1. Examine both eyes.
   2. Rule out foreign body.
   3. Inspect for redness, inflammation, and discharge.
   4. Check pupillary response to light.
   5. Redness noted around iris, pupil is dilated, and cornea appears cloudy.
   6. Inspect anterior chamber of eye by holding penlight laterally and direct toward nasal area. Shallow chamber will cast a shadow on the nasal side of the iris.
C. Palpate: Palpate the globe of the eye, which will feel firm on palpation.
D. Funduscopic exam: This may reveal notching of the cup and a difference in cup-to-disk ratio between the two eyes.

Diagnostic Tests

A. Check visual acuity and peripheral fields of vision.
B. Measure IOP with a tonometer. Normal level is 10 to 21 mmHg; acute–angle closure glaucoma IOP is greater than 50 mmHg. Tonometer exam is not recommended if external infection is present.
C. Slit-lamp exam: Edematous and/or cloudy cornea.
D. Gonioscopy (gold standard) using a slit lamp. Exam typically performed by optometrist or ophthalmologist.

Differential Diagnoses

A. Acute angle–closure glaucoma
B. Acute iritis
C. Acute bacterial conjunctivitis
D. Iridocyclitis
E. Corneal injury
F. Foreign body
G. Herpetic keratitis

Plan

A. General interventions
   1. Severe attacks can cause blindness in 2 to 3 days. Same-day referral is critical if angle–closure glaucoma is suspected. **Seek medical attention immediately to prevent permanent vision loss.**
   2. Frequency of attacks is unpredictable.
B. See the Section III Patient Teaching Guide for this chapter, "How to Administer Eye Medications."
C. Pharmaceutical therapy: **Must be instituted by an ophthalmologist.**
   1. Acetazolamide (Diamox) 250 mg orally
   2. Pilocarpine (Pilocar) 4% every 15 minutes during acute attack

D. Surgical intervention
   1. Surgery is indicated if IOP is not maintained within normal limits with medications or if there is progressive visual field loss with optic nerve damage.
   2. Surgical treatment of choice is peripheral iridectomy—excision of a small portion of the iris whereby the aqueous humor can bypass the pupil.

Follow-Up

A. Annual eye exams by an ophthalmologist are necessary to monitor IOP and treatment efficacy.

Consultation/Referral

A. All patients should be referred to an ophthalmologist *immediately* for measurement of IOP, acute management, and possible surgical intervention (laser peripheral iridectomy).

Individual Considerations

A. Adults
   1. Women normally have slightly higher IOPs than men.
   2. Asians may have higher IOPs than African Americans and Caucasians.
   3. Individuals older than age 40 should have their IOP measured periodically. Every 3 to 5 years is sufficient after a stable baseline is established for the patient.

B. Geriatrics: Incidence increases with age, usually in those older than 60.

Hordeolum (Stye)

Definition

A. Hordeolum is an infection of the glands of the eyelids (follicle of an eyelash or the associated gland of Zeis [sebaceous] or Moll's gland [apocrine sweat gland]), usually caused by *S. aureus*.

B. If swelling is under conjunctival side of eyelid, it is an internal hordeolum.

C. If swelling is under the skin of the eyelid, it is an external hordeolum.

Incidence

A. The incidence is unknown; it is more common in children and adolescents than in adults.

Pathogenesis

A. Acute bacterial infection of the meibomian gland (internal hordeolum) or of the eyelash follicle (external hordeolum) is usually caused by *S. aureus*.

Predisposing Factors

A. Age: Commonly seen in adults

B. Meibomian gland dysfunction

C. Rosacea

Common Complaints

A. Eye tenderness

B. Sudden onset of a purulent discharge

C. Painful bump on the edge of the eyelid

Other Signs and Symptoms

A. Redness and swelling of the eye

Subjective Data

A. Review the onset, course, and duration of symptoms.

B. Determine whether there is any visual disturbance.

C. Note whether this is the first occurrence. If not, ask how it was treated before.

D. Evaluate how much pain or discomfort the patient is experiencing.

E. Review the patient's history for chemical, foreign body, and/or trauma etiology.

F. Review the patient's medical history and medications.

G. Does the patient have a history of rosacea or frequent meibomian gland dysfunction?

Physical Examination

A. Inspect
   1. Examine both eyes; note redness, site of swelling, and amount and color of discharge.
   2. Evert the lid and check for pointing.
   3. Assess sclera and conjunctivae for abnormalities.
   4. Inspect ears, nose, and throat.

B. Palpate
   1. Palpate eye for hardness and expression of discharge.
   2. Evaluate for preauricular adenopathy.

Diagnostic Tests

A. Test visual acuity.

B. Discharge can be cultured but is usually treated presumptively.

Differential Diagnoses

A. Hordeolum

B. Chalazion: The main differential diagnosis is chalazia, which point on the conjunctival side of the eyelid and do not usually affect the margin of the eyelid.

C. Blepharitis

D. Xanthoma

E. Bacterial conjunctivitis

F. Foreign body

G. Basal cell carcinoma/sebaceous cell carcinoma

Plan

A. General interventions: Contain the infecting pathogen. Crops occur when the infectious agent spreads from one hair follicle to another.

B. Patient teaching
1. See the Section III Patient Teaching Guide for this chapter, "How to Administer Eye Medications."
2. Apply warm compresses to eye 10 to 15 minutes four times a day for comfort.
3. Instruct on proper eyelid hygiene and good hand washing.
4. Patients should discard all eye makeup, including mascara, eyeliner, and eye shadow.

C. Pharmaceutical therapy
1. Sulfacetamide (Sodium Sulamyd) ophthalmic ointment 10%, 0.5 to 1.0 cm placed in the conjunctival sac four times daily for 7 days
2. Sulfacetamide (Sodium Sulamyd) 10% ophthalmic drops, two drops instilled every 3 to 4 hours for 7 days
3. Polymyxin B sulfate and bacitracin zinc (Polysporin) ophthalmic ointment, 0.5 to 1.0 cm placed in the conjunctival sac four times daily for 7 days
4. If crops of sties occur, some clinicians recommend a course of tetracycline to stop recurrences (consult with a physician).
5. If cellulitis of the surrounding tissue is suspected, oral antibiotics are recommended. Oral antibiotics recommended include Keflex and erythromycin.

Follow-Up
A. Have patient telephone or visit the office in 48 hours to check response.
B. If crops occur, diabetes mellitus must be excluded. Perform blood glucose evaluation.
C. Recommended follow-up appointment in 2 weeks.

Consultation/Referral
A. Hordeolum may produce a diffuse superficial lid infection known as "preseptal cellulitis" that requires referral to an ophthalmologist.
B. If hordeolum does not respond to topical antimicrobial treatment, refer the patient to an ophthalmologist for possible incision and drainage if indicated.
C. Recurrent lesions should be referred to an ophthalmologist for further evaluation and treatment (biopsy) for possible basal cell carcinoma or sebaceous cell carcinoma.

Individual Considerations
A. Recurrent lesions should be referred to a specialist for evaluation and workup for possible carcinoma.
B. Hordeolums are benign infections and usually respond in 1 to 2 weeks with proper treatment. If lesion has not resolved, further workup is recommended.

Macular Degeneration

Definition
A. Macular degeneration (MD) is the result of age-related changes of the macula (central retina) that result in loss of central vision. MD is the leading cause of blindness in the United States.

Incidence
A. The risk of MD increases with age, with risk starting as early as age 50. It is estimated that MD will affect 3.8 million people by 2050. Currently, 14% of people older than the age of 84 years struggle with visual loss due to MD. With progressive MD in one eye, the opposite eye has greater than 40% risk of visual loss within 5 years.

Pathogenesis
A. There are two types of MD: Dry type and wet type.
1. Dry type is secondary to retinal atrophy. The initial cause of the atrophic changes is unclear.
2. Wet type is secondary to abnormal vascular growth in the subretinal space. Immune-mediated inflammation is believed to play a major role in MD.

Predisposing Factors
A. Age
B. Smoking
C. Family history
D. Cardiovascular disease
E. Diet
F. Cataract surgery
G. Aspirin use
H. Excessive alcohol intake (>3 drinks/d)
I. White race

Common Complaints
A. Gradual loss of vision in one or both eyes
B. Scotoma (dark patch in the center of the visual field)
C. Distorted straight edges (appearing curved or irregular)

Potential Complications
A. Blindness resulting in functional impairments
B. Depression secondary to visual loss
C. Isolation

Subjective Data
A. Review the onset, duration, and course of symptoms.
B. Was the change in vision sudden or gradual?
C. Ask if vision loss was unilateral or bilateral?
D. Was distance or near vision affected?
E. Determine family history of MD.
F. Review history of eye disorders and previous eye surgeries or treatments.
G. Review date of last eye exam, including dilation.
H. Review past medical history, including current medications.

I. Determine the amount of change in activities of daily living due to visual impairment.
J. Ask about perceived safety concerns and history of falls.

Physical Examination

A. Vital signs, including blood pressure.
B. Inspect
   1. Symmetry of eyes and obvious deformities
   2. Pupil symmetry and response to light and accommodation
   3. Assessment of fields of vision and extraocular movements
   4. Fundoscopic assessment observing for drusen bodies
   5. Snellen and Rosenbaum screening
   6. Observation of entropion or ectropion
   7. Observation of pterygium

Diagnostics

A. Fluorescein angiogram (performed by an optometrist or ophthalmologist)
B. Optical coherence tomography (performed by an optometrist or ophthalmologist)

Differential Diagnosis

A. MD
B. Presbyopia
C. Cataracts
D. Glaucoma
E. Diabetic retinopathy

Plan

A. General interventions
   1. Referral to eye specialist for formal diagnosis and prescription for corrective lenses
   2. Discussion of eye health, including routine eye exams and prevention of injury
B. Patient teaching
   1. Prevention: Encourage a healthful diet of fruit, green leafy vegetables, fish, and nuts.
   2. Discuss the importance of antioxidants, vitamin C 500 mg, vitamin E 400 IU, lutein 10 mg, zeaxanthin 1 mg, zinc oxide 80 mg, and copper (II) oxide. These supplements are thought to retard the progression of MD.
   3. Stress the importance of routine eye exam.
   4. Emphasize the need to control the blood sugar if diabetic and blood pressure if hypertensive.
   5. Stress the importance of eye protection, including sunglasses.
   6. Healthy lifestyle choices, including an active lifestyle and smoking avoidance, reduce the risk of MD.

Consultation/Referral

A. Referral to an optometrist or ophthalmologist is required for accurate diagnosis.

Individual Considerations

A. Corrective lenses, additional visual aids, good lighting, and visual rehab should all be considered to reduce the functional impairments and isolation from MD.
B. Eye exams are covered, under certain circumstances, by Medicare. Patients can receive up-to-date coverage information at Medicare.gov.

Refractive Disorders

Definition

A. Clear vision occurs when the cornea and the crystalline lens bend (refract) light appropriately onto the retina. Refractive errors occur when any component of the optical system malfunctions. Refraction errors are common and correctable. Refractive errors include ametropia (including myopia, hyperopia, astigmatism) and presbyopia.

Incidence

A. Refractive disorders affect more than one third of people 40 years or older. Myopia and astigmatism are the two most prevalent refractive disorders. Myopia (nearsightedness) is more common in Caucasians and Asians. Astigmatism and presbyopia increase with aging.

Pathogenesis

A. Emmetropia (normal refraction) begins in childhood and continues into early adulthood. The etiology of poorly developed emmetropization is unknown.

Predisposing Factors

A. Myopia
   1. Genetic predisposition
   2. Reading for long periods
   3. Medications (sulfonamides, diuretics and cholinergics) the adverse effects of which are reversible with discontinuing medication.
   4. Diabetes
   5. Trauma
   6. Excessive accommodation
   7. Cataracts
   8. Older maternal age at birth or maternal smoking
B. Hyperopia
   1. Trauma
   2. Anticholinergic medications

Common Complaints

A. Fear of driving or performing usual, common activities due to decreased visual acuity

Potential Complications

A. Motor vehicle accidents
B. Increased risk of falls and hip fractures
C. Isolation due to fear of leaving familiar environment

Subjective Data

A. Review the onset, duration, and course of symptoms.
B. Was the change in vision sudden or gradual?
C. Determine family history of refractive disorders.
D. Review history of eye disorders and previous eye surgeries or treatments.
E. Review date of last eye exam, including dilation.
F. Review past medical history, including current medications and history of diabetes.
G. Determine if patient has used OTC corrective lenses and duration of use.
H. Has there been a change in vision associated with headaches?
I. Ask about the amount of up-close work, including reading, computer use, factory assembly, and sewing.
J. Determine the amount of change in activities of daily living due to visual impairment.
K. Ask about perceived safety concerns and history of falls.

Physical Examination

A. Vital signs, including blood pressure.
B. Inspect
   1. Symmetry of eyes and obvious deformities
   2. Pupil symmetry and response to light and accommodation
   3. Assess fields of vision and extraocular movements
   4. Fundoscopic assessment
   5. Snellen and Rosenbaum screening
   6. Observe for entropion or ectropion
   7. Observe for pterygium

Diagnostics

A. Phoropter (performed by an optometrist or ophthalmologist)

Differential Diagnosis

A. Cranial nerve dysfunction (CN II, III, VI)
B. Transient ischemic attack (TIA)/cerebrovascular accident (CVA)
C. Trauma (if sudden unilateral reduction in acuity)
D. Glaucoma
E. Space-occupying intracranial lesion
F. MD
G. Diabetic retinopathy
H. Cataracts

Plan

A. General interventions
   1. A referral to an eye specialist for formal diagnosis and prescription for corrective lenses
   2. Discuss eye health, including routine eye exams and prevention of injury
B. Patient teaching
   1. Importance of routine eye exam
   2. Importance of control of blood sugars if diabetic and blood pressure if hypertensive
   3. Importance of eye protection, including sunglasses

Consultation/Referral

A. Referral to an eye specialist is required for accurate diagnosis following initial eye screening.

Individual Considerations

A. Refraction errors are more common with aging, especially myopia, presbyopia, and astigmatism. At 40 years of age, patients should expect presbyopic changes.
B. Diabetic retinopathy, though not a refractive error, is a leading cause of blindness. Patients should receive an annual ophthalmic exam.
C. Eye exams are covered under certain circumstances by Medicare. Patients can receive up-to-date coverage information at Medicare.gov.

Retinopathy

Definition

A. Retinopathy is damage of retinal blood vessels most commonly due to pathology secondary to hyperglycemia (diabetic retinopathy). There are two major categories of retinopathy: nonproliferative and proliferative. Retinopathy is further classified into nonproliferative stages—mild, moderate, severe, and very severe—and proliferative stages—early, high risk, and severe. Symptoms do not present until late in the disease process. Retinopathy is a risk marker for higher rates of morbidity and mortality from cardiovascular disease.

Incidence

A. Diabetic retinopathy is the leading cause of blindness of adults between the ages of 25 and 74 years.

Pathogenesis

A. Nonproliferative retinopathy is due to nerve fiber damage, retinal hemorrhages, microaneurysms, or tortuous/dilated retinal vessels.
B. Proliferative retinopathy is due to neovascularization vessel growth that produces harmful changes in the retinal bed, including preretinal or vitreous hemorrhages, fibrosis, and retinal detachment.
C. Macular edema may occur during any stage of retinopathy.

Predisposing Factors

A. Diabetes, including gestational diabetes
B. Uncontrolled hypertension
C. Smoking
D. Chronic kidney disease
E. Dyslipidemia

Common Complaints

A. Visual impairments are not common until pathologic changes are well established.

B. "Curtain falling" or floaters may be mentioned in vitreous hemorrhage

Potential Complications

A. Loss of independence due to visual impairments
B. Loss of employment
C. Motor vehicle accidents
D. Isolation due to fear of leaving familiar environment
E. Depression

Subjective Data

A. Review the onset, duration, and course of symptoms.
B. Was the change in vision sudden or gradual?
C. Discuss home glucose monitoring and results.
D. Review history of eye disorders and previous eye surgeries or treatments.
E. Review date of last eye exam, including dilation.
F. Review past medical history, including current medications and year of onset of diabetes or hypertension.
G. Determine if patient has used OTC corrective lenses for self-treatment and determine duration of use.
H. Determine the level of change in activities of daily living due to visual impairment.

Physical Examination

A. Vital signs, including blood pressure.
B. Inspect
   1. Symmetry of eyes and obvious deformities
   2. Pupil symmetry and response to light and accommodation
   3. Assess fields of vision and extraocular movements
   4. Fundoscopic assessment
   5. Snellen and Rosenbaum screening

Diagnostics

A. Fundoscopic exam, dilated
B. Fluorescein angiography (performed by optometrist or ophthalmologist)
C. Hemoglobin A1c

Differential Diagnosis

A. Diabetic retinopathy
B. Hypertensive retinopathy

Plan

A. General interventions
   1. Identify the possible diagnosis of retinopathy and refer to an eye specialist for formal diagnosis.
   2. Panretinal laser photocoagulation for proliferative retinopathy (ophthalmology)
   3. Vitreous surgery (ophthalmology)
B. Patient teaching
   1. Advise the patient on the importance of routine eye exams.
   2. Discuss the importance of good control of blood sugar if diabetic and blood pressure if hypertensive.

Consultation/Referral

A. Referral is required for accurate diagnosis following initial fundoscopic screening.

Individual Considerations

A. Diabetic retinopathy is the leading cause of blindness between the ages of 25 and 74. Patients should receive an annual ophthalmic exam.
B. Retinopathy can be slowed based on the stage of progression. Early diagnosis is key to sight-saving intervention.

Subconjunctival Hemorrhage

Definition

A. Subconjunctival hemorrhage presents as blood patches in the bulbar conjunctiva.

Incidence

A. Frequently seen in newborns, subconjunctival hemorrhage may also be seen in adults after forceful exertion (coughing, sneezing, childbirth, strenuous lifting).

Pathogenesis

A. This disorder is believed to be secondary to increased intrathoracic pressure that may occur during labor and delivery or with physical exertion.

Predisposing Factors

A. Local trauma
B. Systemic hypertension
C. Acute conjunctivitis
D. Vaginal delivery
E. Severe coughing
F. Severe vomiting

Common Complaints

A. Red-eyed appearance without pain

Other Signs and Symptoms

A. Bright red blood in plane between the conjunctiva and sclera
B. Usually unilateral
C. Normal vision

Subjective Data

A. Identify onset and duration of symptoms.
B. Elicit information about trauma to the eye; is it due to severe coughing or vomiting?
C. Identify history of conjunctivitis or hypertension.

Physical Examination

A. Check temperature, pulse, respirations, and blood pressure (rule out hypertension).
B. Inspect
  1. Observe eyes.
  2. Inspect ears, nose, and mouth.
  3. Inspect skin for bruises or other trauma.
  4. Assess for signs of trauma or abuse. **Blood in the anterior chamber (hyphema) can result from injury or abuse.**
C. Other physical examination components are dependent on etiology.

Diagnostic Tests

A. Perform visual screening.
B. Test EOMs and peripheral vision.

Differential Diagnoses

A. Subconjunctival hemorrhage
B. Systemic hypertension
C. Blood dyscrasia
D. Trauma to eye
E. Conjunctivitis
F. Hyphema
G. Abuse

Plan

A. General interventions: Reassure the patient that the hemorrhage is not damaging to the eye or vision, and that the blood reabsorbs on its own over several weeks.
B. Patient teaching: Teach safety to prevent trauma to the eye.
C. Pharmaceutical therapy: None.

Follow-Up

A. If subconjunctival hemorrhage recurs, evaluate the patient further for systemic hypertension or blood dyscrasia.

Consultation/Referral

A. Consult or refer the patient to a physician if hyphema is noted, if glaucoma is suspected, or if the patient has additional eye injuries.

Individual Considerations

A. Adults
  1. Always measure blood pressure to rule out systemic hypertension.
B. Geriatrics
  1. Always measure blood pressure to rule out systemic hypertension.
  2. Consider evaluation for blood dyscrasia.
  3. Assess clotting times if patient is taking warfarin (Coumadin).

Uveitis

Definition

A. Uveitis, also known as iritis, is inflammation of the uveal tract (iris, ciliary body, and choroid) and is usually accompanied by a dull ache and photophobia due to the irritative spasm of the pupillary sphincter.

Incidence

A. The true incidence is unknown. Approximately 15% of patients with sarcoidosis present with uveitis.

Pathogenesis

A. The cause is unknown. Underlying causes include infections, viruses, and arthritis.

Predisposing Factors

A. Collagen disorders
B. Autoimmune disorders
C. Ankylosing spondylitis
D. Sarcoidosis
E. Juvenile rheumatoid arthritis
F. Lupus
G. Reiter's syndrome
H. Behcet's syndrome
I. Syphilis
J. Tuberculosis
K. AIDS
L. Crohn's disease

Common Complaints

A. Eye pain: Painless to deep-seated ache
B. Photophobia
C. Blurred vision with decreased visual acuity
D. Black spots

Other Signs and Symptoms

A. Unilateral or bilateral symptoms
  1. Unilateral: The pupil is smaller than that of the other eye because of spasm.
B. Ciliary flush
C. Pupillary contraction
D. Nausea and vomiting with vagal stimulation
E. Halos around lights
F. Hypopyon (pus in anterior chamber)
G. Limbal flush with small pupil

Subjective Data

A. Elicit the onset, course, duration, and frequency of symptoms. Are symptoms bilateral or unilateral?
B. Identify the possible causal activity or agent (chemical, traumatic, or infectious etiologies).
C. Review the patient's history of previous uveitis and other ophthalmologic disorders.

D. Review any associated fever, rash, weight loss, joint pain, back pain, oral ulcers, or genital ulcers.
E. Review full medical history for comorbid conditions.

Physical Examination

A. Check temperature, pulse, respirations, and blood pressure.
B. Inspect
   1. Assess both eyes for visual acuity and peripheral fields of vision.
   2. Check sclera and conjunctiva.
C. Other physical components need to be completed related to comorbid conditions.

Diagnostic Tests

A. Slit-lamp test: Slit-lamp examination reveals cells in the anterior chamber and "flare," representing increased aqueous humor protein. Inflammatory cells, called keratic precipitates, can collect in clusters on the posterior cornea.
B. Penlight examination: Flashlight examination shows a slightly cloudy anterior chamber in the uveitic eye.

Differential Diagnoses

A. Uveitis: Uveitis is usually idiopathic, but it may be associated with many systemic and ocular diseases.
B. Acute angle–closure glaucoma
C. Retinal detachment
D. Central retinal artery occlusion
E. Endophthalmitis

Plan

A. General interventions
   1. Treat underlying cause as indicated.
   2. **Provide immediate referral to an ophthalmologist due to possible complications of cataracts and blindness.**
B. Patient teaching
   1. Inform the patient that recurrent attacks are common and also require immediate attention.
   2. Advise the patient to notify the provider if eye pain, change of vision, or other new symptoms occur.
C. Pharmaceutical therapy
   1. **Medications are given by an ophthalmologist.**
   2. Uveitis and colitis often flare simultaneously; oral steroids are effective for both.

Follow-Up

A. The patient with uveitis needs a follow-up with an ophthalmologist.

Consultation/Referral

A. The patient should be referred *immediately* to an ophthalmologist for evaluation and intervention.

Individual Considerations

A. None

Bibliography

Bessette, M. J. (2014). Hordeolum and stye in emergency medicine. *Medscape*. Retrieved from http://emedicine.medscape.com/article/798940-overview

Cronau, H., Kankanala, R. R., & Mauger, T. (2010). Diagnosis and management of red eye in primary care. *American Family Physician, 81*(2), 137–144.

Danforth, D. A. (2008, July). What to do when the "eyes" have it. *The Clinical Advisor, 11*(8). Retrieved from http://www.clinicaladvisor.com/what-to-do-when-the-eyes-have-it/article/121816

Ehrenhaus, M. P. (2014). Hordeolum. *Medscape*. Retrieved from http://emedicine.medscape.com/article/1213080-overview

Ghosh, C., & Ghosh, T. (2014). Eyelid lesions. *UpToDate*. Retrieved from http://www.uptodate.com/contents/eyelid-lesions?source=search_result&search=hordeolum&selectedTitle=1~10

Hom, M. M., Nguyen, A. L., & Bielory, L. (2012). Allergic conjunctivitis and dry eye syndrome. *Annals of Allergy, Asthma & Immunology, 108*(3), 163–166.

Moreno, M. A. (2010). Advice for patients. Strabismus. *Archives of Pediatrics & Adolescent Medicine, 164*(3), 304.

Ortiz, G. (2013). Vasomotor rhinitis and allergic conjunctivitis. *Clinical Advisor for Nurse Practitioners, 16*(1), 24–35.

Spering, K. A. (2011). CME/CE: Therapeutic strategies for bacterial conjunctivitis. *Clinical Advisor for Nurse Practitioners, 14*(8), 31–40.

Watkins, J. (2010). Infective conjunctivitis. *Practice Nursing, 21*(6), 303–304.

CHAPTER EIGHT

Ear Guidelines

Jill C. Cash and Carol Palmer

Acute Otitis Media

Definition

A. Acute otitis media (AOM) is inflammation of the middle ear associated with an acute bacterial infection of the middle ear.

Incidence

A. AOM commonly occurs in children, but it may be seen in adults and geriatric patients.

Pathogenesis

A. Obstruction of the eustachian tube can lead to a middle ear effusion and infection. Contamination of this middle ear fluid often results from a backup of nasopharyngeal secretions. The most common bacterial pathogens in adults are *Streptococcus pneumoniae* and *Haemophilus influenzae.*

Predisposing Factors

A. Recurrent otitis media (three or more episodes in the past 6 months)
B. Previous episode of otitis media or upper respiratory infection (URI) within the last month
C. Medical condition that predisposes to otitis media (i.e., Down syndrome, AIDS, cystic fibrosis, cleft palate, immune disorders, and craniofacial abnormalities)
D. Native American heritage
E. Smoking in the household
F. History of allergies

Common Complaints

A. Ear pain
B. Fever may or may not be present

Other Signs and Symptoms

A. Sleeplessness within past 48 hours
B. Decreased appetite
C. Acute hearing loss
D. URI symptoms
E. Mastoiditis presenting with a swollen and red mastoid
F. Perforated tympanic membrane (sudden severe pain followed by immediate relief of pain with fluid drainage from the ear)
G. Cholesteatoma (saclike structure in the middle ear accompanied by white, shiny, greasy debris)

Subjective Data

A. Elicit onset and duration of symptoms.
B. Inquire whether the patient recently had (or has concurrently) a URI.
C. Determine whether the patient has any change in hearing.
D. Assess the patient for any drainage from the ear(s).
E. Question the patient or his or her caregiver regarding risk factors.
F. Identify the patient's history of otitis media.

Physical Examination

A. Check temperature, pulse, respirations, and blood pressure.
B. Inspect
   1. Observe the canal and auricle for redness, deformity, drainage, or foreign body.
   2. Inspect the tympanic membrane position to determine if it is neutral, whether landmarks are visible, retracted, full, or bulging.
   3. Observe ears for decreased or absent tympanic membrane mobility.
   4. Inspect nose, mouth, and throat.
C. Auscultate: Auscultate heart and lungs.

Diagnostic Tests

A. Tympanogram shows flat or type B curve.
B. Hearing test should be done in patients with persistent otitis media (≥ 3 months duration).

C. Consider complete blood count if the patient appears toxic with a high fever.

Differential Diagnoses

A. AOM
B. Otitis media with effusion (OME)
C. URI
D. Mastoiditis
E. Otitis externa

Plan

A. General intervention: Pain relief with acetaminophen or ibuprofen. Auralgan may be used for a topical pain relief.
B. Patient teaching: Stress the importance of taking antibiotics as prescribed and finishing the prescription as ordered. If pain, fever, or other symptoms do not improve in 48 to 72 hours, then the patient should notify the provider for further evaluation.
C. Pharmaceutical therapy
   1. Drug of choice: With mild infection amoxicillin 500 mg orally every 12 hours or 250 mg orally every 8 hours for 5 to 7 days. For severe infection (fever, severe pain, hearing loss, etc.) amoxicillin 875 mg orally every 12 hours or 500 mg orally every 8 hours for 10 days.
   2. For concerns of amoxil resistance, treatment failure, recent use of antibiotic in the previous 30 days, and/or concurrent other infections, use an antibiotic with beta-lactamase activity such as amoxicillin-clavulanate (Augmentin). Augmentin 500 mg orally every 12 hours or 875 mg orally every 12 hours for 7 to 10 days.
   3. For penicillin allergy: Cefdinir 300 mg orally every 12 hours or 600 mg orally daily for 5 to 7 days.
      a. Cefpodoxime 200 mg orally every 12 hours for 5 to 7 days.
      b. Cefuroxime 500 mg orally every 12 hours for 5 to 7 days.
      c. Ceftriaxone 2 g intramuscularly or intravenously once.
   4. Other alternatives for patients known to have a severe allergy to beta-lactam antibiotics:
      a. Macrolides
      b. Azithromycin 500 mg orally as a single dose on Day 1, then 250 mg orally on Days 2 to 5 or clarithromycin 500 mg orally twice a day for 5 to 7 days; or
      c. Trimethoprim with sulfamethoxazole DS one tablet orally twice a day for 5 to 7 days.
   5. Antibiotic treatment is recommended for all adults and geriatric patients diagnosed with AOM.

Follow-Up

A. Recheck the patient in 2 weeks to evaluate for resolution of the infection. Documentation of the resolution of the ear infection is valuable information if infections are recurrent.
B. If fever, pain, hearing loss, or other new symptoms present or if the patient is not improved in 48 to 72 hours, then a follow-up appointment is recommended.

Consultation/Referral

A. Consult or refer the patient to a physician if the patient appears septic or is diagnosed with mastoiditis.
B. A patient with persistent otitis media with a hearing loss of 20 dB or more should be referred to an otolaryngologist.

Individual Considerations

A. Pregnancy: Do not use sulfa medications (sulfonamides) in pregnant patients.
B. Geriatrics
   1. Elderly patients may present with OME and/or AOM secondary to blocked eustachian tube and/or an URI.
   2. Bullous myringitis is a condition in which blisters are visible on the tympanic membrane that can cause significant pain. Bullous myringitis may be caused by a viral, bacterial, or mycoplasmal infection.

Cerumen Impaction (Earwax)

Definition

A. Cerumen is a protective mechanism of the ear that maintains homeostasis by lubricating the ear canal, removing debris, and providing bactericidal protection. Overproduction of cerumen (earwax) has the potential to produce discomfort and associated conductive hearing loss.

Incidence

A. Certain individuals are at increased risk of excessive earwax due to overproduction or inability of the ear to clear itself. The populations most likely to be diagnosed with cerumen impaction include elders, young children, those with mental disabilities, and institutionalized patients. The incidence in nursing home patients may be as high as 60%.

Pathogenesis

A. Wax builds up in the external canal. With age, the normal self-cleaning mechanisms of the ear fail. Cilia, which have become stiff, cannot remove cerumen and dirt from the ear canal. Placing cotton swabs, paper clips, bobby pins, and so forth into the ear canal may also impact cerumen.

Predisposing Factors

A. Age (decreased function of ear cilia)
B. Use of hearing aids
C. Recurrent otitis externa
D. Dermatologic conditions of the external canal
E. Previous audiologic surgeries
F. Keratosis obturans

Common Complaints

A. Dryness and itching of ear canal
B. Dizziness
C. Ear pain
D. Hearing loss

Other Signs and Symptoms

A. Fullness in the ear
B. Chronic cough
C. Tinnitus

Subjective Data

A. Elicit onset and duration of symptoms.
B. Elicit history of cerumen impaction.
C. Question the patient regarding the method used to clean the ears.
D. Determine personal or family history of anatomic deformity.
E. Assess for any physical barriers to wax extrusion such as cotton swabs, hearing aids, or devices utilized to protect hearing (ear plugs).

Physical Examination

A. Check temperature, pulse, respirations, and blood pressure.
B. Inspect
   1. Observe ears for thick, light to dark brown wax occluding the auditory canal.
   2. Observe tympanic membrane if possible. Perforated tympanic membrane is associated with otitis media.
   3. Inspect nose and throat.

Diagnostic Tests

A. Cerumen impaction is diagnosed with direct visualization of an otoscope.
B. When hearing loss is the primary subjective complaint, you may consider a hearing assessment. Expected outcomes associated with cerumen impaction include conductive hearing loss of 35 to 40 dB and positive Rinne (tuning-fork test reveals bone conduction greater than air conduction in affected ear).

Differential Diagnoses

A. Cerumen impaction
B. Foreign body in the ear canal
C. Otitis externa: White, mucus-like ear discharge is associated with otitis externa.

Plan

A. General interventions
   1. Cerumen removal may be attempted by irrigation with or without cerumenolytics or by manual removal using a curette, forceps, or suction.
   2. Manual removal requires a cooperative patient and involves the use of a metal or plastic loop or spoon. Manual removal does not expose the ear to moisture and therefore may lessen the risk of infection. Manual removal may provide the safest alternative when there is a question of tympanic membrane rupture.
   3. Irrigation may be done with or without pretreatment with a cerumenolytic agent. Irrigation instruments include bulb syringes, 20-mL syringes adapted for irrigation, or oral jet irrigators (ear irrigator tips increase safety). Contraindications include tympanic membrane perforation or myringotomy tube. Also, patients with a history of middle-ear disease, surgery, radiation, vertigo, or potential sharp foreign body should not undergo irrigation.
   4. Cerumenolytics are softening agents that are either water-based or oil-based, or not water- or oil-based. These products are considered to be equally effective. None of these products are considered safe unless the tympanic membrane is intact (no perforations or myringotomy tubes). Cerumenolytics can be used as a standalone treatment for the patient to use at home or utilized as a pretreatment prior to irrigation in the clinic.
B. Patient teaching
   1. See the Section III Patient Teaching Guide for this chapter, "Cerumen Impaction (Earwax)."
C. Pharmaceutical therapy
   1. Research has not identified a specific treatment (manual, irrigation, or cerumenolytic agent) or product (debrox, hydrogen peroxide, and so forth) as the first-line treatment for cerumen impaction, as many patient variables influence the most appropriate treatment option.
   2. Prevention has become a therapy mainstay, and recent research has supported the weekly use of an ear rinse of 70% isopropyl alcohol as safe, effective, and cost efficient.

Follow-Up

A. No follow-up is needed unless indicated. Recurrence is common.

Consultation/Referral

A. Consult or refer the patient to a physician when cerumen cannot be cleared.

Individual Considerations

A. Geriatrics: Cerumen impaction is common in older adult and geriatric patients secondary to the atrophic cilia and dry epithelium of the ear canal.

Hearing Loss

Definition

A. Impaired hearing (complete or partial hearing loss) results from interference with the conduction of sound, its conversion to electrical impulses, or its transmission through the nervous system. There are three types of hearing loss:
   1. Conductive
   2. Sensorineural
   3. Mixed or combined conductive and sensorineural loss

Incidence

A. Hearing loss is present in 10% to 15% of patients; approximately 30 million Americans have some degree of hearing impairment.
B. One in three people older than the age of 60 and half of all people older than the age of 85 have hearing deficits.

Pathogenesis

A. *Conductive hearing loss* occurs when sound is not conducted effectively and presents with a diminution of volume, particularly low tones and vowels. It may be caused by one of the following:
   1. Otologic processes such as chronic or serous otitis media, otitis externa, foreign body, cerumen impaction, or trauma to the middle ear.
   2. Otosclerosis disorder of the architecture of the bony labyrinth, which fixes the footplate of the stapes in the oval window.
   3. Exostoses are bony excrescences of the external auditory canal.
   4. Glomus tumors are benign, highly vascular tumors derived from normally occurring glomera of the middle ear and jugular bulb.

B. *Sensorineural hearing loss* occurs after damage to the inner ear or vestibulocochlear nerve and characteristically produces impairment of the high-tone perception. Affected patients can hear people speaking, but they have difficulty deciphering words because discrimination is poor. It may be caused by one of the following:
   1. Presbycusis is hearing loss associated with aging and is the most common cause of diminished hearing in the elderly; onset is bilateral, symmetric, and gradual.
   2. Noise-induced hearing loss is due to chronic exposure to sound levels in excess of 85 to 90 dB.
   3. Drug-induced hearing loss can be caused by aminoglycoside antibiotics, furosemide, ethacrynic acid, quinidine, and aspirin.
   4. Ménière's disease produces a fluctuating, unilateral, low-frequency impairment usually associated with tinnitus, a sensation of fullness in the ear, and intermittent episodes of vertigo.
   5. Acoustic neuroma is a benign tumor of the eighth cranial nerve (rare).
   6. Sensorineural hearing loss is generally bilateral and symmetric, and it may be genetically determined.
   7. Sudden deafness can derive from head trauma, skull fracture, meningitis, otitis media, scarlet fever, mumps, congenital syphilis, multiple sclerosis, and perilymph leaks or fistulas.

Predisposing Factors

A. Acoustic or physical trauma
B. Ototoxic medications (such as gentamicin and aspirin)
C. Changes in barometric pressures
D. Recent URI
E. Pregnancy
F. Otosclerosis
G. Nasopharyngeal cancer
H. Serous otitis media
I. Cerumen impaction
J. Foreign body in the ear

Common Complaints

A. Partial hearing loss
B. Total hearing loss
C. Difficulty understanding the television, phone conversations, and people talking

Other Signs and Symptoms

A. Unilateral or bilateral hearing loss
B. Hearing noises such as "ringing," "buzzing," and so forth
C. Fullness in ear(s)

Subjective Data

A. Elicit the onset, duration, progression, and severity of symptoms. Note whether symptoms are bilateral or unilateral.
B. Obtain the patient's history of past or recent trauma.
C. Review the patient's occupational and recreational exposure to risk factors.
D. Review the patient's medical history and medications, including over-the-counter (OTC) drugs and prescriptions.
E. Review the patient's history for recent URI or ear infections, especially for chronic ear infections.
F. Elicit data about any previous hearing loss, how it was treated, and how it affected daily activities.

There is often a history of previous ear disease with conductive hearing loss.

G. Review the patient's other symptoms such as dizziness, fullness or pressure in the ears, and noises.
H. Review what causes difficulty with hearing, high tones versus low frequencies. Can patient hear people talking, the television at normal volume, doorbells ringing, telephone ringing, and watch ticking?

Physical Examination

A. Inspect
   1. Examine both ears for comparison.
   2. Externally inspect ears for discharge; note color and odor. Obstruction of the auditory canal by impacted cerumen, a foreign body, exostoses, external otitis, OME, or scarring or perforation of the eardrum due to chronic otitis may be present.
   3. Conduct otoscopic examination to observe the auditory canal for cerumen impaction or foreign body.
   4. Inspect tympanic membrane for color, landmarks, contour, perforation, and AOM. A reddish mass visible through the intact tympanic membrane may indicate a high-riding jugular bulb, an aberrant internal carotid artery, or a glomus tumor.
B. Palpate
   1. Palpate auricle and mastoid area for tenderness, swelling, or nodules.
   2. Check lymph nodes if infection is suspected.
C. Neurologic testing: Weber's and Rinne tests
   1. In the Weber's test, the tuning fork is perceived more loudly in the conductively deaf ear.
   2. The Rinne test shows that bone conduction is better than air conduction (normal is when air conduction is greater than bone conduction).

Diagnostic Tests

A. Audiogram in primary setting
B. Air insufflation for tympanic membrane mobility
C. Tympanometry brain stem—evoked response audiogram
D. Computed tomography (CT) scan or magnetic resonance imaging (MRI) after consultation with an otolaryngologist

Differential Diagnoses

A. Congenital hearing loss
B. Traumatic hearing loss
C. Ototoxicity
D. Presbycusis
E. Ménière's syndrome
F. Acoustic neuroma
G. Cholesteatoma
H. Infection
I. Cerumen impaction
J. Otitis externa
K. Foreign body in the ear
L. Tumors
M. Otosclerosis
N. Perforation of tympanic membrane
O. Serous otitis media
P. Hypothyroidism
Q. Paget's disease

Plan

A. General interventions: Treat any primary cause (i.e., remove impacted cerumen).
B. Patient teaching
   1. Harmful noise levels should be avoided.
   2. Individual hearing protection devices should be utilized in all patients exposed to occupational noise.
C. Pharmaceutical therapy: Treat primary condition if applicable.

Follow-Up

A. If hearing loss is identified and cause is not immediately treatable, refer the patient for further evaluation.

Consultation/Referral

A. Any sudden onset of hearing loss requires immediate referral.
B. The patient should be referred to an otolaryngologist for an extensive workup when the primary cause cannot be identified.
C. Referral should be made to a hearing aid specialist for hearing evaluation and treatment as indicated (i.e., hearing aids).

Individual Considerations

A. Geriatrics
   1. Impaired hearing among the elderly is common and can lower the quality of life.
   2. People with seriously impaired hearing often become withdrawn or appear confused.
   3. Subtle hearing loss may go unrecognized.
   4. Impacted cerumen is very common in the elderly.

Otitis Externa

Definition

A. Otitis externa is an inflammation of the external ear canal, which commonly produces pruritus, pain, and purulent discharge. It may be acute or chronic depending on the underlying pathogenesis.

Incidence

A. Otitis externa is seen in patients of all ages.
B. Both genders are equally affected.
C. Incidence is higher during summer months.
D. Patients with asthma, allergic rhinitis, atopic dermatitis, or other chronic skin disorders are more likely to experience recurrent otitis externa.

Pathogenesis

A. Acute diffuse otitis externa (swimmer's ear): *Pseudomonas* is the most common bacterial infection (67%), followed by *Staphylococcus* and *Streptococcus*. Infection can also be fungal (*Aspergillus*, 90%). Bacterial or fungal invasion is usually preceded by trauma to the ear canal, aggressive cleaning of the naturally bactericidal cerumen, or frequent submersion in water (swimming).
B. Chronic otitis externa: Condition generally results from a persistent, low-grade infection and inflammation with *Pseudomonas*.
C. Eczematous otitis externa: Otitis externa is associated with primary coexistent skin disorder such as atopic dermatitis, seborrheic dermatitis, and psoriasis.
D. Necrotizing or malignant otitis externa: Invasive *Pseudomonas* infection results in skull base osteomyelitis. Cranial nerve palsies (of the VII, IX, and XII cranial nerves) and periostitis of the skull base have been associated with necrotizing otitis externa. Necrotizing or malignant otitis externa is a life-threatening condition that occurs in diabetic or immunocompromised patients. It is most commonly seen in the immunocompromised or diabetic geriatric patient.

Predisposing Factors

A. Exposure to a moist or humid environment (frequently swimming)
B. Ear trauma from scratching, foreign object, or vigorous cleaning
C. Use of a hearing aid or ear plugs
D. Primary skin conditions
E. Immunocompromised, malnourished, or comorbid conditions

Common Complaints

A. Otalgia
B. Itching
C. Erythematous and swollen external canal
D. Purulent discharge
E. Hearing loss from edema and obstruction of canal with drainage

Other Signs and Symptoms

A. Plugged ear sensation (aural fullness)
B. Tenderness to palpation (tragus)

Subjective Data

A. Elicit onset, duration, and intensity of ear discomfort.
B. Inquire into the patient's history of previous ear infections.
C. Determine whether the patient notes any degree of hearing loss.
D. Question the patient about recent exposure to immersion in water (swimming).
E. Determine if the patient wears hearing aids, earplugs, or other devices that may impact the ear canal.
F. Question the patient as to ear canal cleaning practices and any recent trauma to canal.

Physical Examination

A. Temperature
B. Inspect
   1. Carefully examine the ear with otoscope due to extreme tenderness.
   2. Observe the ear for erythematous and edematous external canal; look for otorrhea and debris.
   3. Observe tympanic membrane, which may appear normal.
   4. Inspect nose and throat.
C. Auscultation: Auscultate heart and lungs.
D. Palpate
   1. Apply gentle pressure to tragus and manipulate pinna to assess for tenderness.
   2. Palpate preauricular, postauricular, and lateral cervical lymph nodes.

Diagnostic Tests

A. Examine ear canal scrapings and drainage under microscope for hyphae (if fungal infection is suspected from previous history or ineffective topical therapy).

Differential Diagnoses

A. Otitis externa
B. AOM
C. Chronic suppurative otitis media
D. Cholesteatoma
E. Mastoiditis
F. Referred pain

Plan

A. General interventions
   1. The primary treatment goals are to reduce pain and inflammation and to treat the underlying organism.
   2. In extreme cases, the patient's ear canal may be blocked by edema or drainage, preventing passage of ear drops. Cautiously irrigate the canal and insert a cotton wick (approximately 1 inch long for adults) by gently rotating it to allow passage of drops. Consider referral for abnormal or extensive cases.
B. Patient teaching
   1. See the Section III Patient Teaching Guide for this chapter, "Otitis Externa."
   2. The patient should be advised to keep water out of the ear during treatment, which typically lasts

1 week. During that time, bathing or showering is permitted with earplugs or a cotton ball coated with petroleum jelly inserted into the ear to block water passage into the ear canal.

C. Pharmaceutical therapy
   1. For early, mild cases associated with swimming in which the primary symptom is pruritus, homemade preparations of 50% isopropyl alcohol and 50% vinegar can be used as a drying agent and to create an unsatisfactory environment for *Pseudomonas* growth.
   2. Mild infection: Topical therapy: Use of acidifying agent such as Vosol or Vosol HC, which includes a glucocorticoid therapy: Instill five drops in the ear canal three to four times daily. (Vosol and Vosol HC are contraindicated with perforated eardrum; Vosol HC is contraindicated with viral otic infections.)
   3. Moderate infection: Use of an acidifying agent, antibiotic and glucocorticoid therapy, Cipro HC, and Cortisporin is suggested. The suspension is recommended rather than the solution if the integrity of the tympanic membrane is in question. Other alternatives include ciprofloxacin (Cipro HC), ofloxacin (Floxin), polymyxin B; neomycin (Cortisporin Otic) suspension or solution.
      a. If fungal infection is suspected, Nystatin 100,000 units/mL or clotrimazole topical solutions may be used for candidal or yeast infections.
      b. Acyclovir is the treatment of choice for herpes simplex or herpes zoster.
   4. Severe or resistant infections in healthy patients may require additional management with oral antibiotics and antifungals. In addition, oral antibiotics should be considered as an adjunct to topical therapy in patients who are immunocompromised, malnourished, or have comorbidities.
      a. Ciprofloxacin for pseudomonal infections; dicloxacillin or cephalexin for staphylococcal infections.
      b. Itraconazole (Sporanox) for treatment of otomycosis (fungal otitis externa).
   5. Use of acetaminophen or ibuprofen should be adequate for pain control. Pain uncontrolled by these medications should be a red flag for serious infection and warrants immediate referral.

Follow-Up

A. Follow-up is based on symptom severity and patient comorbidities.
B. If wicking was required, the patient should be seen in 24 hours.
C. Recheck mild to moderate cases in 1 week.

Consultation/Referral

A. Any patient suspected of necrotizing otitis externa requires immediate referral due to potential life-threatening complications of osteomyelitis.

Otitis Media With Effusion

Definition

A. OME is noninfectious asymptomatic middle ear fluid without signs of bacterial infection.

Incidence

A. OME is seen in patients of all ages.
B. OME often follows an acute URI or recent diagnosis of AOM.
C. The middle-ear effusion typically resolves without treatment in more than 80% of all patients. While symptoms can sometimes continue for up to 12 weeks, the majority of patients will have complete symptom resolution by 4 weeks.

Pathogenesis

A. The effusion may be sterile fluid secondary to URI and eustachian tube dysfunction. It may be residual fluid after an episode of AOM.

Predisposing Factors

A. Recent AOM
B. Concurrent or recent URI
C. Chronic sinusitis
D. Allergies
E. Craniofacial predisposition
F. Smoking or exposure to secondhand smoke
G. History of middle-ear infections

Common Complaints

A. Ear pain
B. Increased pressure sensation in the ears
C. Recent hearing loss

Other Signs and Symptoms

A. The patient has a sense of fullness in the ears.
B. Dizziness

Subjective Data

A. Elicit onset and duration of symptoms.
B. Question the patient about recent history of otitis media or URI.
C. Question the patient about hearing loss.
D. Determine if the patient has a past history of frequent otitis media.

Physical Examination

A. Check temperature, pulse, respirations, and blood pressure.

B. Inspect
   1. Inspect ears, noting fluid level, serous middle fluid, and a translucent, amber, gray membrane with decreased mobility.
   2. Inspect nose, mouth, and throat.

C. Auscultation: Auscultate heart and lungs.
D. Palpate: Palpate head, neck, and lymph nodes.
E. Neurologic examination: Give Weber's test and Rinne test with tuning fork.

Diagnostic Tests

A. Pneumatic otoscopy reveals decreased mobility. **Assessment with pneumatic otoscopy is strongly recommended.**
B. Negative pressure on tympanogram.

Differential Diagnoses

A. OME
B. AOM
C. Cerumen impaction or foreign body
D. Otitis externa
E. Cholesteatoma
F. Myringitis
G. Tympanosclerosis

Plan

A. General interventions
   1. Patient should be monitored closely for resolution of effusion without treatment within several weeks.
   2. Patients with persistent OME should be referred to otolaryngologist for a hearing evaluation and possible tympanostomy tubes as indicated.
   3. Although the diagnosis of OME is linked to uncontrolled allergies, antihistamines, decongestants, and nasal steroids are ineffective for treatment.

B. Patient teaching: See the Section III Patient Teaching Guide for this chapter, "Otitis Media With Effusion."
C. Pharmaceutical therapy
   1. The American Academy of Family Physicians and the American Academy of Otolaryngology–Head Neck Surgery do not recommend routine use of antibiotic therapy for OME. However, if subjective history reveals a recent, possibly unresolved AOM, a course of antibiotics (Amoxil) for 10 to 14 days is a viable option.
   2. Intranasal glucocorticoids are not recommended for routine use for OME.
   3. Antihistamines and decongestants are not recommended for the routine use for OME.

Follow-Up

A. Recheck the patient's ears after 4 weeks to monitor for spontaneous resolution. If no resolution is noted, schedule a follow-up appointment.

Consultation/Referral

A. Consult or refer the patient to a physician if treatment is not effective or if the patient has a persistent effusion (at least 3 months) along with a hearing loss of 20 dB or more.
B. Consider referring the patient to an otolaryngologist prior to 12 weeks if the patient does not have the usual underlying risk factors associated with OME.
C. Consider earlier referral to an otolaryngologist when the OME is bilateral due to potential increased hearing loss.

Presbycusis

Definition

A. A neurosensory hearing loss associated with aging.
B. Usually bilateral with a gradual onset.

Incidence

A. Hearing loss is common in elders and increases with age. Presbycusis affects approximately 40% of adults who are 60 to 70 years of age, and roughly 60% of elders up to age 85, and then increases to almost 80% for those older than age 85.
B. Males tend to be affected slightly earlier and experience more impairment.

Pathogenesis

A. Multiple factors of heredity, cumulative noise expo-sure, and age-related physiologic changes to the ear are thought to be factors in the degree of hearing loss. Although presbycusis is multifactorial, physiologic changes in the cochlea have been identified as the primary underlying mechanism of decreased hearing.

Predisposing Factors

A. Age
B. Family history (genetics)
C. Ototoxic medications (such as gentamicin and aspirin)
D. Cumulative noise exposure
E. Cardiovascular disease (hypertension [HTN], hyperlipidemia)
F. Smoking

Common Complaints

A. Partial hearing loss
B. Difficulty understanding the television, phone conversations, and people talking

Subjective Data

A. Elicit the onset, duration, progression, and severity of symptoms. Note whether symptoms are bilateral or unilateral.
B. Review the patient's family history.

C. Review the patient's occupational and recreational exposure to noise.
D. Review the patient's medical history for cardiovascular disease, hypertension, and hyperlipidemia.
E. Ask specifically about all medications, including OTC drugs and prescriptions.
F. Review the patient's history for recent URI or ear infections, especially for chronic ear infections.
G. Elicit data about any previous hearing loss, how it was treated, and how it affected daily activities. There is often a history of previous ear disease with conductive hearing loss.
H. Review the patient's other symptoms, such as dizziness, fullness or pressure in the ears, and noises.
I. Review what causes difficulty with hearing; high tones versus low frequencies. Can patient hear people talking, the television at normal volume, doorbells ringing, telephone ringing, and watch ticking?

Physical Examination

A. Inspect
   1. Examine head, neck, and ears for signs of trauma, asymmetry, masses, or edema.
   2. Externally inspect ears for discharge; note color and odor. Obstruction of the auditory canal by impacted cerumen, a foreign body, exostoses, external otitis, OME, or scarring or perforation of the eardrum due to chronic otitis may be present.
   3. Conduct otoscopic examination to observe the auditory canal for cerumen impaction or foreign body.
   4. Inspect tympanic membrane for color, landmarks, contour, perforation, and AOM. A tympanic membrane that is opaque rather than translucent can be a variation of normal in elders and is not related to hearing loss.
B. Common screening tests
   1. Whispered voice: From 2 feet behind the patient, the examiner whispers words or short phases while occluding one ear at a time.
   2. Patient report: Ask the patient, "Do you have difficulty hearing?"
   3. Screening version of the Hearing Handicap Inventory for the elderly
   4. Weber and Rinne to differentiate conductive from sensorineural hearing loss.

Diagnostic Tests

A. Audiogram in primary setting

Differential Diagnoses

A. Presbycusis
B. Sudden sensorineural hearing loss
C. Ototoxicity
D. Ménière's syndrome
E. Acoustic neuroma
F. Cholesteatoma
G. Chronic otitis media
H. Cerumen impaction

Plan

A. General interventions
   1. All patients with suspected hearing loss should undergo formal testing.
   2. Goals are to prevent further hearing loss and assist the patient in lifestyle changes that increase quality of life.
B. Patient teaching
   1. Let patients know that a follow-up with a specialist is important to identify the correct diagnosis.
   2. Summarize treatment options of aural rehabilitation, hearing aids and, when applicable, cochlear implants.
   3. Assess for and teach patient the consequences of excessive environmental noise; consider protective mechanisms such as earplugs.
C. Nonpharmaceutical therapy
   1. Aggressive management of comorbidities such as HTN and hyperlipidemia may slow progression of hearing loss.
   2. Evaluate for polypharmacy and the role it may play in hearing loss. Specifically assess for ototoxic medications. Eliminate when possible.

Follow-Up

A. Stress the importance of follow-up with the audiologist and otologist. Often the patient does not pursue viable options that would improve quality of life.

Consultation/Referral

A. The patient should be referred to an otolaryngologist immediately for sudden, severe, or rapidly progressing hearing loss and hearing loss that is unilateral; associated with pain, bleeding, or drainage; or hearing loss that involves other neurologic deficits.

Tinnitus

Definition

A. The word "tinnitus" comes from the Latin *tinnire*, which means "to ring." Tinnitus is the perception of an auditory sensation such as hissing, sizzling, or ringing in the absence of external stimuli. Rarely, more complex sounds such as voices or music are heard indistinctly. Sounds can be constant or intermittent and vary in intensity from patient to patient. The tinnitus can also be categorized as rhythmical or pulsatile and corresponding with a heartbeat (this may suggest a vascular origin).

Incidence

A. It is estimated that approximately 10% of the adult population has experienced tinnitus.
B. Prevalence is similar between men and women and is known to increase with age.

Pathogenesis

A. Tinnitus is poorly understood. It is best described as a nonspecific manifestation of pathology of the inner ear, eighth cranial nerve, or the central auditory mechanism.

Predisposing Factors

A. High levels of noise exposure, either recreational or occupational
B. Otological conditions
   1. Neoplasms
   2. Hearing loss
   3. Cerumen impaction
   4. Otitis media
   5. Mastoiditis
   6. Labyrinthitis
C. Neurologic conditions
   1. Vertigo
   2. Migraines
   3. Epilepsy
   4. Meningitis
   5. Multiple sclerosis
D. Trauma to head or neck or issues with temporomandibular joint disorder (TMJ)
E. Immune system disorders such as rheumatoid arthritis, systemic lupus erythematosus, or systemic sclerosis
F. Endocrine influences such as diabetes, hypothyroidism, and pregnancy
G. Psychological disorders
   1. Anxiety
   2. Depression
   3. Posttraumatic stress disorder
H. Hypertension
I. Ototoxic drugs: More than 130 medications are known to cause tinnitus or hearing loss. Patients should be assessed for concurrent use of multiple ototoxic medications, especially when other risk factors are present. The most common broad categories include:
   1. Analgesics
   2. Antibiotics
   3. Antineoplastics and immunosuppressives
   4. Diuretics
   5. Corticosteroids

Common Symptoms

A. Ringing
B. Roaring
C. Buzzing
D. Clicking
E. Hissing
F. Hearing loss

Other Signs and Symptoms

A. "Muffled" hearing
B. Change in own voice, lower pitch

Subjective Data

A. Review the onset, duration, course, and type of symptoms; note whether they are bilateral or unilateral.
B. Determine the frequency and quality of sound; is the ringing constant, intermittent, or pulsating?
C. Review all medications, including OTC drugs and prescriptions.
D. Determine if there is a family history of tinnitus, hearing loss, or neurofibromatosis.
E. Ask whether the patient has experienced recent physical or emotional trauma.
F. Inquire about any past history of ontological disorders, either acute or chronic.
G. Ask about associated symptoms
   1. Headache
   2. Hearing loss
   3. Noise intolerance
   4. TMJ
   5. Vertigo
H. Review work, hobbies, and music habits for noise levels (potential damage).
I. Assess the date of last hearing exam, and determine whether there was any known hearing loss.
J. Review whether patient uses cotton-tipped swabs or other small objects for ear cleaning.

Physical Examination

A. General: The goal of the physical exam is to evaluate for the most common known causes of tinnitus.
B. Inspect
   1. Observe the external ear for discharge; note color and odor.
   2. Conduct otoscopic exam of the auditory canal for cerumen impaction or foreign body.
   3. Inspect tympanic membrane for color, landmarks, contour, perforation, and AOM.
      a. The landmarks (umbo, handle of malleus, and the light reflex) should be visible on a normal exam.
      b. The tympanic membrane should be pearly gray in color and translucent.
      c. A bulging tympanic membrane is more conical, usually with a loss of bony landmarks and a distorted light reflex.
      d. A retracted tympanic membrane is more concave, usually with accentuated bony landmarks and a distorted light reflex (pathologic conditions in the middle ear may be reflected by characteristics of the tympanic membrane).

C. Auscultation: Assess for bruits or murmurs over the ear canal, auricular areas, neck, and chest.
D. Palpate
   1. Palpate auricle and mastoid area for tenderness, swelling, or nodules.
   2. Palpate the TMJ for tenderness or crepitus.
E. Visual exam
   1. Inspect for papilledema.
   2. Assess for visual field changes and for nystagmus.
F. Neurologic exam
   1. Assess all cranial nerves.
   2. First evaluate how the patient responds to your questions.
   3. Patients who speak in a monotone or with erratic volume may have hearing loss.
   4. Check the patient's response to a soft whisper (should respond at least 50% of the time).
   5. Rinne and Weber's testing: The Rinne test is performed by placing the struck tuning fork against the mastoid bone. Begin counting or timing the interval from the start to when the patient can no longer hear. Continue counting or timing the interval to determine the length of time sound is heard by air conduction. Air-conducted sound should be heard twice as long as bone-conducted sound after bone conduction stops.

Diagnostic Tests

A. When tinnitus is acute (< 3 weeks) and has no associated neurologic deficits or hearing loss, consider audiometry. Any focal neurologic findings warrant an MRI and/or prompt physician referral. Tinnitus lasting longer than 3 weeks should be referred to an otolaryngologist. Appropriate diagnostics are influenced by intermittent hearing loss, vertigo, abnormal physical exam findings, pulsatile quality, and unilateral presentation.

Differential Diagnoses

A. Tinnitus
B. Hearing loss that could be related to multiple otologic conditions
   1. Cerumen impaction
   2. Foreign body
   3. AOM
   4. Ménière's disease
   5. Presbycusis
   6. Cholesteatoma
C. Temporomandibular joint syndrome
D. Ototoxicity
E. Central nervous system lesion

Plan

A. General interventions
   1. Assess for underlying cause of tinnitus.
   2. Refer to otolaryngologist for tinnitus lasting longer than 3 weeks.
B. Patient teaching
   1. Educate the patient regarding techniques/therapies to improve symptoms of tinnitus such as sound therapy, interventions to reduce distress such as counseling, and cognitive behavior therapy.
   2. Encourage the patient to attend therapy sessions as indicated.
C. Pharmaceutical therapy
   1. Medications do not have a beneficial role in the treatment of tinnitus.

Follow-Up

A. Length of follow-up depends on whether the patient has an identified and/or treatable cause of tinnitus. A 3-week follow-up to determine chronicity and need for specialist referral is important in the management of tinnitus.

Consultation/Referral

A. Consult with an otolaryngologist as indicated.

Bibliography

Baguley, D., McFerrran, D., & Hall, D. (2013). Tinnitus. *Lancet, 382*, 1600–1607.

Bird, S. (2008). Ear syringing: Minimizing the risks. *Australian Family Physician, 37*(5), 359–360. Retrieved from Proquest Database.

Harmes, K. M., Blackwood, A., Burrows, H. L., Cooke, J. M., Harrison, C. R., & Passamani, P. P. (2013). Otitis media: Diagnosis and treatment. *American Family Physician, 88*(7), 435–440.

Klein, J. O., & Pelton, S. (2013a). Acute otitis media in children: Treatment. In B. Rose (Ed.), *UptoDate*. Retrieved from http://www.uptodateonline.com

Klein, J. O., & Pelton, S. (2013b). Management of otitis media with effusion (serous otitis media) in children. *UpToDate*. Retrieved from http://www.uptodate.com/contents/management-of-otitis-media-with-effusion-serous-otitismedia-in-children?source=search_result&search=otitis+media+with+effusion&selectedTitle=1~48

Lasak, J. M., Allen, P., McVay, T., & Lewis, D. (2014). Hearing loss: Diagnosis and management. *Primary Care Clinic Office, 41*, 19–31.

Limb, C. J., Lustig, L. R., & Klein, J. O. (2014). Acute otitis media in adults (suppurative and serous). *UpToDate*. Retrieved from http://www.uptodate.com/contents/acute-otitis-media-in-adults-suppurative-and-serous#H24

Osguthorpe, J. D., & Nielsen, D. R. (2006). Otitis externa: Review and clinical update. *American Family Physician, 74*, 1510–1516.

Robes, C., & Tillett, J. S. (2013). Pharmacologic therapy for eustachian tube dysfunction. *American Family Physician, 87*(12), 883–884.

Silverstein, H., Wycherly, B. J., Alameda, Y., & Van Ess, M. J. (2012). A prospective study to evaluate the efficacy of isoproplyl alcohol irrigations to prevent cerumen impaction. *Ear, Nose & Throat Journal, 91*(3), E25–E28.

Thibodeau, D., & Lo, B. (2008). Otitis externa: What you need to know. *Clinician Reviews/Convenient Care, 1*(3), 1–8.

Valentino, R. L. (2009). Chronic dysfunction of the eustachian tube. *Clinical Advisor, 12*, 21–25.

Yew, K. S. (2014). Diagnostic approach to patients with tinnitus. *American Family Physician, 89*(2), 106–113.

CHAPTER NINE

Nasal Guidelines

Jill C. Cash

Allergic Rhinitis

Definition

A. Allergic rhinitis is a chronic or recurrent condition characterized by nasal congestion, clear nasal discharge, sneezing, nasal itching, conjunctival itching, and periorbital edema. It usually occurs seasonally after exposure to allergens (same time every year, associated with pollen count), or it may be perennial (year-round, related to indoor inhalants, animal dander, and mold). "Allergic" suggests that a specific IgE antibody mediates the condition.

Incidence

A. Prevalence varies according to geographic region; 20% to 25% of adults have allergic rhinitis.

Pathogenesis

A. This is an IgE-mediated inflammatory disease involving nasal mucosa; IgE antibodies bind to mast cells in the respiratory epithelium, and histamine is released. This results in immediate local vasodilatation, mucosal edema, and increased mucus production.

Predisposing Factors

A. Genetic predisposition to allergy
B. Exposure to allergic stimuli: Pollens, molds, animal dander, dust mites, and indoor inhalants

Common Complaints

A. Nasal congestion
B. Sneezing
C. Clear rhinorrhea
D. Coughing from postnasal drip
E. Sore throat
F. Itchy, puffy eyes with tearing

Other Signs and Symptoms

A. Dry mouth from mouth breathing, snoring
B. Sleep disturbance due to difficulty with breathing, leading to malaise/fatigue
C. Itchy nose
D. Loss of smell and taste
E. Eczema rash
F. Shortness of breath, difficulty breathing, and wheezing
G. Headache
H. Halitosis

Subjective Data

A. Ask about onset, course, and duration of symptoms.
B. Inquire about characteristics of nasal discharge.
C. Inquire about exposure to people with similar symptoms.
D. Ask about seasonal impact on symptoms.
E. Inquire about other diseases caused by allergens, such as asthma, eczema, and urticaria.
F. Rule out pregnancy.
G. Ask female patients about their birth control method, specifically birth control pills.
H. Review exposure to irritants.
I. Ask about any past or recent nasal trauma.

Physical Examination

A. Vital signs: Temperature, blood pressure, pulse, and respirations
B. Inspect
   1. Examine face. Note Dennie's lines (skin folds under eyes) and allergic salute (transverse crease on nose from chronic rubbing of nose).
   2. Examine eyes and conjunctivae.
      a. Tearing; red, swollen eyelids; and allergic shiners (dark circles under eyes from venous congestion in maxillary sinuses) are seen with allergies.
      b. Palpebral conjunctiva pale and swollen, bulbar conjunctiva is injected.
   3. Examine ears, nose, and throat.
      a. Red, dull, bulging, perforated tympanic membrane is seen with otitis media.

b. Nasal redness, swelling, polyps, and enlarged turbinates are seen with upper respiratory infection (URI). Mucosa appears pale blue, boggy with clear discharge in chronic allergy.
c. Cobblestone appearance in pharynx, tonsils, and adenoids seen in chronic allergies
d. Use otoscope light to transilluminate under superior orbital ridge of frontal sinus cavity and also maxillary sinus cavity to assess for fluid in sinus cavity. Healthy sinuses contain air and light up symmetrically.

C. Palpate
1. Palpate face and frontal maxillary sinuses for tenderness.
2. Examine head and neck for enlarged lymph nodes.

D. Percuss
1. Percuss sinus cavities and mastoid bone.
2. Percuss chest for consolidation.

E. Auscultate: Auscultate heart and lungs.

Diagnostic Tests

Diagnosis may be made from history and physical. Other diagnostic tests include:

A. Wright's stain of nasal secretions: Presence of eosinophils confirms allergy, but may be normal
B. Skin testing for allergies
C. Radioallergosorbent test (RAST)
D. Complete blood count (CBC) with increased eosinophils (confirm allergy)

Differential Diagnoses

A. Allergic rhinitis
B. URI
C. Medication-induced rhinitis
D. Sinusitis
E. Otitis media
F. Deviated septum
G. Nasal polyps
H. Endocrine conditions such as hypothyroidism
I. Influenza

Plan

A. General interventions
1. Avoid allergens (most effective treatment).
2. Keep bedroom as allergen-free as possible.

B. Patient teaching: See the Section III Patient Teaching Guide for this chapter, "Allergic Rhinitis."

C. Pharmaceutical therapy
1. Antihistamines (H_1 receptor antagonists) are drugs of choice. Several may need to be tried before an effective one is found. Drugs may also need to be switched occasionally to prevent tolerance.
a. Azelastine HCl (Astelin) metered nasal spray: 137 mcg per metered dose: Adults: Two sprays per nostril twice daily
b. Loratadine (Claritin) 10 mg by mouth daily (adults)
c. Fexofenadine HCl (Allegra) 60 mg capsules orally twice daily or 180 mg daily
d. Cetirizine HCl (Zyrtec)
i. Adults: 5 to 10 mg by mouth daily depending on symptom severity
ii. Lower dose of 5 mg daily for patients with renal or hepatic impairment
e. Montelukast (Singulair): Adults: 10 mg tablet daily
f. Levocetirizine dihydrochloride (Xyzal): Adults: 2.5 to 5 mg daily in p.m. Precautions for renal impairment

2. Topical decongestants for significant congestion of the mucous membranes.

These drugs may also stimulate the sympathetic nervous system and cause insomnia, nervousness, and palpitations. **Use no longer than 3 to 5 days. Discontinuing these drugs after 5 days may result in a rebound effect.**
a. Oxymetazoline hydrochloride (Afrin) spray or drops: Adults: Two to three drops or sprays of 0.05% solution in each nostril twice daily
b. Phenylephrine (Neo-Synephrine) spray or drops: Adults: Two to three drops or one to two sprays in each nostril, or small amount of jelly applied to nasal mucosa, every 4 hours as needed. Do not use for more than 3 to 5 days.

3. Steroid sprays may be used to decrease nasal inflammation. Sprays do not cause significant systemic absorption in usual doses, but occasionally they may cause pharyngeal fungal infections.
a. Beclomethasone dipropionate (Beconase AQ, Vancenase): Adults: One to two sprays in each nostril twice daily
b. Fluticasone propionate (Flonase): Adults: Two sprays daily or one spray twice daily. Maintenance dosing: One spray in each nostril daily
c. Triamcinolone acetonide (Nasacort AQ): Adults: Two sprays daily
d. Mometasone furoate (Nasonex): Adults: Two sprays each nostril once daily
e. Fluticasone furoate (Veramyst):
i. Adults: Two sprays each nostril daily
ii. Maintenance: One spray each nostril daily
f. Budesonide (Rhinocort Aqua): Adults: Two sprays twice daily

g. Qnasl (beclomethasone dipropionate): Adults: Two sprays each nostril once daily; maximum four sprays per day
4. Saline spray
   a. Saline spray is effective in liquefying thick secretions and helps keep mucosa moist.
   b. Use Neti pot or sinus rinse with warm saline water to cleanse inside of nasal mucosa; daily use is suggested.
5. Petroleum jelly applied with Q-tip to inside mucosa of nares three to four times a day helps to provide lubrication and hold in moisture to prevent nasal dryness and bleeding.

Follow-Up

A. Patient should return for follow-up visit in 2 to 3 weeks if necessary; earlier if symptoms worsen after 3 days of treatment.

Consultation/Referral

A. Refer the patient to an allergist if symptoms continue and interfere with daily activities.
B. Allergist may prescribe immunotherapy following identification of offending allergens.

Individual Considerations

A. Pregnancy
   1. Over-the-counter (OTC) antihistimines such as diphenhydramine HCl (Benadryl) may be used for up to 5 days.
   2. OTC decongestants such as oxymetazoline HCl (Afrin) may be used up to 3 days.
B. Geriatrics
   1. Intranasal steroid sprays are best tolerated by the elderly population and offer fewer side effects.
   2. Antihistimines are effective for this population; however, there are more side effects and drug interactions in this group. Consider age and possible drug-to-drug interactions when prescribing medications for allergic rhinitis.

Epistaxis

Definition

A. Epistaxis is a nosebleed or hemorrhage from the nose.

Incidence

A. Nosebleeds occur in approximately 60% of Americans at least once in a lifetime. However, fewer than 10% will seek medical care for a nosebleed.

Pathogenesis

A. Epistaxis is caused by disruption of the nasal mucosa. More than 90% of nosebleeds are related to local irritation rather than underlying anatomic lesions and are self-limiting. Most start in the anterior nasal cavity (Kisselbach's plexus).
B. Posterior nasal bleeding usually originates from the turbinates or lateral nasal wall.
C. Nosebleed more commonly occurs during the winter months. It is commonly associated with other conditions such as URIs, allergic rhinitis, or mucosal changes due to other conditions.

Predisposing Factors

A. Local trauma, usually from nose picking
B. Acute inflammation from a URI (e.g., common cold, acute sinusitis, and allergic rhinitis)
C. Vigorous nose blowing
D. Inhalation of chemical irritants
E. Drying and crusting of nasal septum
F. Trauma
G. Cocaine use
H. Pregnancy
I. Neoplasm
J. Systemic causes
   1. Bleeding disorders (most common)
   2. Hypertension
   3. Arteriosclerosis
   4. Renal disease

Common Complaints

A. Common complaint is unusually severe or frequent nosebleeds.

Other Signs and Symptoms

A. Anterior epistaxis
   1. Unilateral
   2. Continuous, moderate bleeding from septum of nose
B. Posterior epistaxis
   1. Brisk (arterial) bleeding
   2. Blood flowing into pharynx (indicates a more serious problem)

Subjective Data

A. Inquire about amount, duration, and frequency of bleeding.
B. Ask about use of oral anticoagulants, aspirin, or aspirin-containing compounds (e.g., Pepto-Bismol, aspirin, Excedrin).
C. Ask about recent or current URIs, family history of abnormal bleeding, recent surgery, or trauma.
D. Ask the first day of female patient's last menstrual period (if appropriate). Determine if the patient is pregnant.
E. Ask about possible foreign body in the nose.
F. Ask about cocaine use or occupational exposure to irritants or chemicals.

G. If the patient has a history of nosebleeds, how did the patient treat previous nosebleeds?
H. Has the patient ever been evaluated for a blood-clotting abnormality, such as thrombocytopenia or platelet dysfunction?
I. Does the patient complain of bruising easily, melena, or heavy menstrual periods?
J. Ask about family history of bleeding disorders, such as hemophilia or von Willebrand's disease.

Physical Examination

A. Check temperature, blood pressure (check for orthostatic hypertension), pulse, and respirations. **If nasal packing is required, take precaution and monitor patient closely for vasovagal episode during insertion of nasal packing.**
B. Inspect
    1. Check airway patency with patient sitting and leaning forward.
    2. Observe skin, mucous membranes, and conjunctiva for rash, pallor, purpura, petechiae, and telangiectasias.
    3. Perform full eye exam, noting pupillary response.
    4. Examine nose for septal perforation and ulcerations, which indicates cocaine use. Collagen diseases (such as lupus) are occasionally responsible for ulceration. Epistaxis is rare in hemophiliacs without trauma but is characteristic of von Willebrand's disease.
    5. Examine nasal discharge: A unilateral foul discharge with blood indicates a foreign body in the nose.
    6. After bleeding has stopped:
        a. Inspect nasal mucosa for color, discharge, masses, lesions, and swelling of turbinates.
        b. Inspect nasal septum for alignment, septal perforation, and crusting.
C. Auscultate: Auscultate heart and lungs.
D. Palpate: Check for enlarged lymph nodes in the neck to rule out sarcoidosis, tuberculosis, or malignancy.
E. Percuss: Percuss sinuses.

Diagnostic Tests

A. **None is required unless the patient has recurrent or severe blood loss.**
B. Drug screen, if indicated
C. Hematocrit and hemoglobin if bleeding is severe
D. CBC with differential
E. Platelets, prothrombin time (PT), and partial thromboplastin time (PTT) if bleeding disorder is suspected
F. Sinus films if recurrent sinus pain, tenderness, and bleeding

Differential Diagnoses

A. Epistaxis
B. Foreign body
C. Septal deformity
D. Perforated nasal septum
E. Coagulation disorder (von Willebrand's disease)
F. Nasal tumors
G. Drug-induced coagulapathy
H. Hypertension
I. Pregnancy

Plan

A. General interventions: Main goal is to control episodes of bleeding.
B. Patient teaching: See the Section III Patient Teaching Guide for this chapter, "Nosebleeds."
C. Pharmaceutical therapy/medical/surgical management
    1. To control *anterior* septal bleeding.
        a. Have patient sit and lean forward, apply pressure to reduce venous pressure, and prevent swallowing of blood.
        b. Ask patient to blow his or her nose to remove blood clots.
        c. Nares can then be sprayed with oxymetazoline (Afrin).
        d. Ask patient to squeeze nasal septum and hold for approximately 10 minutes.
        e. If bleeding continues, other treatments to perform include:
            i. Anesthetize mucous membrane by applying cotton soaked with a vasoconstrictor, lidocaine 2% or lidocaine (Xylocaine) plus topical epinephrine (1:10,000), or cocaine 4% for 10 to 15 minutes.
            ii. If bleeding continues, cautery may be used by applying a silver nitrate stick to the bleeding site for no longer than 10 seconds to the prominent vessels, until gray eschar appears. Warn the patient that this procedure is painful.
            iii. If bleeding still doesn't stop (rare), nasal packing may be needed, using a nasal tampon. Apply the topical lidocaine to the mucosa, then cover the nasal tampon with bacitracin ointment and insert the tampon into the nasal cavity until the tampon is inside the cavity. Packing may be expanded by applying saline to the packing with a saline filled syringe. Monitor the patient for vasovagal episode during the insertion of packing.
    2. To control *posterior* septal bleeding:
        a. Have the patient sit and lean forward.
        b. Control bleeding: Spray nose with topical anesthetic and vasoconstrictor, and apply pressure to bleeding site.
        c. **Consult a physician. The patient needs emergency room care immediately because of rapid blood loss.**

d. Take blood pressure and pulse; order hematocrit; blood type and cross-match may be needed.

Follow-Up

A. Anterior septal bleeding: Referral to otolaryngologist is recommended for unsuccessful cessation of hemorrhage.
B. For posterior nosebleeds, admit the patient to the hospital and refer to an otolaryngologist.

Consultation/Referral

A. Posterior epistaxis: Refer to a physician and/or otolaryngologist immediately.

Individual Considerations

A. Pregnancy
   1. Nosebleeds are common.
   2. Suggest use of saline spray to keep mucous membranes moist and use humidifier at bedtime.
   3. Follow use of saline spray with Vaseline applied with Q-tip daily to prevent recurrent nosebleeds.
B. Geriatrics
   1. Spontaneous posterior hemorrhage is more common in elderly patients.
   2. Epistaxis is classically associated with hypertension or arteriosclerosis.
   3. Airway obstruction from posterior packing is especially risky in elderly.
   4. Applying water-based lubricant on rims of nostrils to maintain mucosal moisture may cause lipoid pneumonia in elderly.

Nonallergic Rhinitis

Definition

A. Nonallergic rhinitis is an inflammation of nasal mucous membranes, usually accompanied by nasal discharge and mucosal edema. Nonallergic rhinitis disorder has no correlation to specific allergen exposures. It is classified in several ways: Vasomotor, perennial, atrophic, geriatric, drug-induced, or rhinitis of pregnancy.

Incidence

A. Chronic or recurrent nasal congestion occurs in about 10% to 40% of the population.

Pathogenesis

A. Vasomotor and perennial nonallergic rhinitis results from hyperreactive nasal mucosa.
B. Atrophic and geriatric rhinitis results from progressive degeneration and atrophy of the mucus membranes and bones of the nose.
C. Overuse of topical nasal decongestants can worsen symptoms and cause severe rebound congestion.
D. Cocaine abuse causes nasal congestion and discharge.
E. Rhinitis in pregnancy results from hormonal increase; congestion abates with delivery.

Predisposing Factors

A. Adulthood
B. Abrupt changes in temperature, odors, and emotional stress
C. Other predisposing factors depend on type

Common Complaints

A. Nasal congestion
B. Sneezing
C. Clear rhinorrhea
D. Coughing
E. Sore throat
F. Itchy, puffy eyes

Subjective Data

A. Ask about onset, duration, and course of symptoms.
B. Inquire about the color and other characteristics of nasal discharge.
C. Ask about other discomforts and exposure to people with similar symptoms.
D. Inquire about seasonal impact on symptoms, effect of weather changes on symptoms, previous treatments, and results.
E. Rule out pregnancy. Ask female patients about birth control method, specifically contraceptives.
F. Ask about use of prescription drugs, OTC drugs (especially aspirin), and illicit drugs (cocaine).
G. Review medical history for other respiratory problems, such as asthma, emphysema, or chronic bronchitis.

Physical Examination

A. Check temperature and blood pressure.
B. Inspect
   1. Observe general appearance.
   2. Inspect conjunctivae for "allergic shiners" (dark circles under eyes), tearing, and eyelid swelling.
   3. Examine ears for signs of otitis media (red, bulging, perforated tympanic membrane, and purulent drainage).
   4. Examine nose for redness, swelling, polyps (soft, pedunculated, nontender, pale-gray smooth structures), enlarged turbinates, foreign objects, septal deviation, septal perforation (sign of cocaine abuse), ischemia, mucosal injury, atrophy, and "cobblestoned" pharyngeal mucosa (sign of allergy).
C. Auscultate: Auscultate heart and lungs.
D. Percuss
   1. Percuss sinus cavities and mastoid process.
   2. Percuss chest for consolidation.

E. Palpate
   1. Palpate face for sinus tenderness.
   2. Palpate head and neck for enlarged lymph nodes.

Diagnostic Tests

A. Skin testing for allergies may be done.

Differential Diagnoses

A. Nonallergic rhinitis
B. Allergic rhinitis
C. URI
D. Foreign body
E. Sinusitis
F. Otitis media
G. Deviated septum
H. Nasal polyps
I. Endocrine conditions such as hypothyroidism and pregnancy
J. Drug use: Oral contraceptives, aspirin, alpha-adrenergic blockers, cocaine, and nasal decongestant overuse

Plan

A. General interventions
   1. Avoid changes in temperature, odors, and emotional stress.
   2. Identify triggers for condition and address alleviating triggers.
B. Patient teaching
   1. Teach the patient the significance of individual triggers for nonallergic rhinitis. Encourage use of a journal to learn personal triggers.
   2. Avoid triggers such as smoking, smoke-filled rooms, wood-burning stoves/fireplaces, sprays, and perfumes.
   3. Other triggers may include weather changes, hormonal changes, and medications.
   4. Teach methods of treatment and identify treatments that work best for the patient.
   5. Encourage use of Neti pot or nasal flush with warm saline water daily to cleanse sinus cavity. Cleansing the sinus cavity daily will help to remove foreign materials inhaled and will also help with tissue edema. Clean pot after each use and allow to air dry.
C. Pharmaceutical therapy
   1. Vasomotor rhinitis: Physiologic saline solution as nasal spray, thorough cleansing of nares, topical ipratropium bromide, or inhaled ipratropium bromide (Atrovent) three to six puffs every 4 hours, not to exceed 12 inhalations per day
   2. Atrophic rhinitis: Guaifenesin (Guiatuss) 10 mL orally every 4 hours
   3. Physiologic saline nasal spray to nares three times a day
   4. Nasal antihistimines
      a. Azelastine (Astelin): Adults: Two sprays each nostril daily
      b. Olopatadine (Patanase): Adults: Two sprays twice daily
   5. Nasal glucocorticoids: Fluticasone (Flonase): Adults: Two sprays daily or one spray twice daily. Maintenance dosing: One spray in each nostril daily
   6. Mometasone (Nasonex): Adults: Two sprays each nostril once daily
   7. Decongestants: Oral and nasal decongestants are not recommended unless the use of antihistamines and glucocorticoids has failed. Examples may include: Oral pseudoephedrine or nasal oxymetazoline (Afrin) and phenylephrine (Neo-Synephrine). These should not be used longer than 2 to 3 days at a time for congestion due to the effects of rebound congestion with long-term use.

Follow-Up

A. Have patient return in 2 to 3 weeks, and then for biannual exams and/or as needed.

Consultation/Referral

A. Consult with a physician if symptoms continue despite treatment.
B. If treatment fails, refer the patient to an allergist for testing.

Individual Consideration

A. Pregnancy: Reassure pregnant patients that rhinitis is a common hormonal response. Nonallergic rhinitis is not contagious and cannot cross the placenta.

Sinusitis

Definition

Sinusitis is inflammation of the mucous membranes and the paranasal sinuses. It may be acute, subacute, or chronic.

A. Acute sinusitis: Abrupt onset of inflammation and/or infection with symptom resolution after therapy, lasting less than 4 weeks
B. Subacute sinusitis: Persistent purulent nasal discharge despite therapy, lasting 4 to 12 weeks
C. Chronic sinusitis: Episodes of prolonged (>12 weeks) inflammation and/or infection

Incidence

A. Sinusitis is very prevalent. However, true incidence is unknown because people with frontal headaches or congestion self-medicate with OTC decongestants and then request antibiotics if symptoms persist. Incidence increases in spring and fall (allergy seasons) and in winter (cold season).

Pathogenesis

A. Frequent causes:
 1. Obstruction of mucus flow due to edema of nasal mucosa from allergies and URIs
 2. Anatomical abnormalities that interfere with normal mucocilliary clearance mechanism
 3. Exposure to pathogens following URI also causes sinusitis. The most common pathogens include *Haemophilus influenzae, Streptococcus pneumoniae,* and *Moraxella catarrhalis*. The incubation period depends on the pathogen.
 4. Dental abscess is responsible for approximately 10% of cases.
 5. Fungi such as *Mucor, Rhizopus,* and *Aspergillus* can produce invasive sinusitis in patients with poorly controlled diabetes, patients with leukemia, or immunosuppresed patients.
 6. The common cold is a cause in 0.5% to 5.0% of cases.

Predisposing Factors

A. Recent URI
B. Allergens (pollens, molds, smoking, occupational exposure such as coal mining, and animal dander)
C. Nicotine/smoke exposure (first- or secondhand smoke)
D. Air pollutants
E. Deviated septum
F. Adenoidal hypertrophy
G. Dental abscess
H. Diving and swimming
I. Neoplasms
J. Cystic fibrosis
K. Trauma
L. Medical disorders (diabetes, immune disorders, inflammatory disorders, mucosal disorders, cystic fibrosis, and asthma)
M. Flying or rapid changes in altitude

Common Complaints

A. Yellow or green nasal discharge
B. Fever
C. Sore throat
D. Facial pain, frontal pain, or pressure that worsens when patient bends forward
E. Headache
F. Toothache

Other Signs and Symptoms

A. Anosmia (loss of sense of smell)
B. Nasal congestion
C. Cough (worse when lying down); may be chronic
D. Periorbital edema (especially early morning)
E. Malaise or fatigue
F. Halitosis
G. Snoring, mouth breathing
H. Nasal sounding speech

Potential Complications to Consider—Immediate Ear, Nose, and Throat Referral

A. Meningitis: Symptoms are increased fever, stiff neck
B. Subdural and epidural purulent drainage
C. Brain abscess
D. Cavernous sinus thrombosis (acute thrombophlebitis due to infection in area where veins drain into cavernous sinus)
E. Tender periorbital edema (orbital cellulitis)

Subjective Data

A. Elicit onset, duration, and course of symptoms.
B. Inquire whether seasons affect symptoms.
C. Ask the patient about recent URI and how it was treated.
 1. Did the patient receive antibiotics?
 2. Did the patient finish the full course of antibiotics?
D. Ask about allergies.
E. Inquire about recent dental problems, especially dental abscesses.
F. Find out what home therapies and OTC medications the patient tried before the office visit.
G. Ask if the patient took a trip recently, especially by airplane.
H. Inquire whether the patient was swimming or diving recently.
I. Review the patient's medical history for cystic fibrosis, asthma, nasal abnormalities (e.g., deviated septum), and other respiratory problems.

Physical Examination

A. Temperature, blood pressure, pulse, and respirations.
B. Inspect
 1. Observe eyes for periorbital swelling, "allergic shiners" (dark circles under eyes), tearing, and signs of orbital cellulitis (conjunctival edema, drooping lid, decreased extraocular motion, and vision loss).
 2. Examine ears.
 3. Inspect the nose for erythema, edema, discharge, lack of nostril patency, septal deviation and polyps, and presence of a foreign body.
 4. Transilluminate maxillary and frontal sinuses in a darkened room. Absence of light reflection is not definitive.
 5. Examine the mouth and pharynx for erythema and tonsillar enlargement, check teeth for uneven surfaces (sign of grinding), and check retropharynx for evidence of postnasal drip.
C. Auscultate: Auscultate heart and lungs.
D. Palpate
 1. Palpate neck for lymphadenopathy.
 2. Palpate sinuses but do not press on eyes.
  a. Frontal sinusitis: Pain and tenderness over lower forehead (worse when bending

forward) and purulent drainage from middle meatus of nasal turbinates

b. Maxillary sinusitis: Pain and tenderness over cheeks from inner canthus to teeth (referred pain), edematous hard palate (severe cases), and purulent drainage in middle meatus

c. Ethmoid sinusitis: Frontal or orbital headache, tenderness and erythema over upper lateral aspect of nose, drainage from anterior ethmoid cells through middle meatus, drainage of posterior cells through superior meatus

d. Sphenoid sinusitis (uncommon): Frontal or orbital headache or facial pain (headache referred to top of head and deep into eyes), purulent drainage from superior meatus

E. Percuss
 1. Tap maxillary teeth to rule out dental cause.
 2. Percuss maxillary and frontal sinuses.
 3. Percuss over affected area exacerbates pain.
 4. Perform chest percussion, if indicated.

F. Neurologic exam
 1. Evaluate for signs of meningeal irritation, assessing for Brudzinski's sign, Kernig's sign, and nuchal rigidity.

Diagnostic Tests

A. Diagnosis is usually made through history-taking and a physical.

B. Consider sinus x-ray films, which show air-fluid level and thickening of sinus mucous membranes with sinusitis for chronic or recurrent sinusitis or complicated cases.

C. CT of sinus indications include chronic sinusitis, recurrent sinusitis, allergic fungal sinusitis, or osteomeatal complex occlusion.

Differential Diagnoses

A. Sinusitis
B. Headache (cluster, migraine)
C. Rhinitis (allergic or vasomotor)
D. Nasal polyps
E. Tumor
F. URI
G. Trigeminal neuralgia

Plan

A. General interventions
 1. Teach patient to avoid smoking and secondhand smoke.
 2. Drinking extra fluids helps to loosen secretions and hydrate the body.
 3. Encourage patient to use medications as prescribed. OTC medications such as antihistamines and decongestants should be used with caution.
 4. Application of warm, moist compresses to the face several times a day will help with discomfort.
 5. Humidifiers should be used daily. Advise patient to clean humidifiers on a regular basis.
 6. Nasal saline to the nares three times a day will help to keep nasal passages moist.

B. Patient teaching: See the Section III Patient Teaching Guide for this chapter, "Sinusitis."

C. Pharmaceutical therapy
 1. Antibiotics for infection
  a. Drugs of choice for acute sinusitis
   i. Adults
    1) First-line treatment: Augmentin 500 mg orally three times a day or 875 mg orally twice daily for 5 to 7 days.
    2) High-risk patients where non-susceptible *S. pneumonia* is greater than 10% for the following patients: Older than 65 years of age, recent hospitalization, recent use of antibiotics in the past month, or immunocompromised patients; augmentin 2,000 mg (two extended-release tablets) orally every 12 hours for 5 to 7 days
    3) Penicillin/ beta-lactam allergy: Doxycycline 100 mg orally twice daily or 200 mg orally daily for 5 to 7 days; levofloxacin 500 mg orally daily for 5 to 7 days or moxifloxacin 400 mg orally daily for 5 to 7 days.
  b. The same antibiotics can be used for chronic sinusitis, but treatment should last 3 to 4 weeks.

D. Oral and topical decongestants to correct the underlying edematous mucosa (use cautiously with hypertension).
 1. Adults: Pseudoephedrine sulfate (Afrin) 0.05% spray or drops, two to three drops or sprays per nostril twice daily. Maximum for 3 to 5 days
 2. Adults: Phenylephrine (Neo-Synephrine) spray or drops, two to three drops or one to two sprays of 0.25% solution per nostril, or small amount of jelly to nasal mucosa, every 4 hours as needed. Do not use for more than 3 to 5 days.
 3. Pseudoephedrine HCl 30 to 60 mg every 4 to 6 hours as needed for congestion for adults
 4. Nasal saline to nares three times daily as needed for hydrating nasal mucosa 0.25% solution spray or drops, two to three drops or one to two

sprays per nostril every 4 hours as needed. Do not use for more than 3 to 5 days.

E. Steroid sprays may be used to decrease nasal inflammation.
   1. Beclomethasone dipropionate (Beconase AQ, Vancenase AQ); fluticasone (Flonase): Adults: Two sprays daily
   2. Mometasone furoate monohydrate (Nasonex): Two sprays daily

F. Antihistamines are recommended to block histamine production in response to the allergy triggers and prevent allergy symptoms.
   1. Loratadine (Claritin) 10 mg daily
   2. Fexofenadine (Allegra) 180 mg daily
   3. Levocetirizine HCl (Xyzal) 5 mg daily
   4. Leukotriene inhibitors (Singulair, Accolate) for severe allergies and/or asthma 10 mg daily

Follow-Up

A. Recheck the patient in 3 to 4 days if signs and symptoms are not improving with use of treatment prescribed.

B. New recommendations include treating patients with antibiotic therapy for 5 to 7 days. Patients not improving may be resistant to antibiotics and may be switched to a different antibiotic.

Consultation/Referral

A. Admission to hospital is needed if the patient has fever with facial cellulitis and mental changes.

B. Refer chronic sinusitis patients to an otolaryngologist if they do not improve in 4 weeks.

C. Refer patients to a physician or ear, nose, and throat (ENT) specialist for suspected neoplasm, abscess, osteomyelitis, meningitis, or sinus thrombosis.

Individual Considerations

A. Pregnancy
   1. Augmentin is the desired antibiotic for use during pregnancy.
   2. Patients who are allergic to penicillin should be treated with azithromycin.
   3. Doxycycline and fluoroquinolones are *not* recommended during pregnancy.

B. Geriatrics
   1. Precautionary measures should be used for patients with long-term nasogastric tubes. These patients are at higher risk for development of occult sinusitis.
   2. Precautions should be used for patients currently prescribed warfarin (Coumadin).
   3. Avoid use of trimethoprim/sulfamethoxazole (TMP-SMX) with warfarin because the medication can cause a significant increase in PT/international normalized ratio (PT/INR).

Bibliography

Adelson, R., & Adappa, N. (2013). What is the proper role of oral antibiotics in the treatment of patients with chronic sinusitis? *Current Opinion in Otolaryngology & Head & Neck Surgery, 21*(1), 61–68.

Alterk, H. (2014). Approach to the adult with epistaxis. Retrieved from UpToDate. http://www.uptodate.com/contents/approach-to-the-adult-with-epistaxis?source=machineLearning&search=epitaxis&selectedTitle=1~150§ionRank=1&anchor=H17#H17

Bamimore, O., Dronen, S., Silverberg, M., Counselman, F., & Talavera, F. (2011). *Management of acute epistaxis. Medscape reference, drugs, diseases & procedures.* Retrieved from http://emedicine.medscape.com/article/764719-overview#a30

Baroody, F., Mucha, S., Detineo, M., & Naclerio, R. (2012). Evidence of maxillary sinus inflammation in seasonal allergic rhinitis. *Otolaryngology-Head & Neck Surgery, 146*(6), 880–886.

Brook, I., & Hausfeld, J. N. (2011). Microbiology of acute and chronic maxillary sinusitis in smokers and nonsmokers. *Annals of Otology, Rhinology & Laryngology, 120*(11), 707–712.

DeMuri, G., & Wald, E. (2012). Clinical practice. Acute bacterial sinusitis in children. *New England Journal of Medicine, 367*(12), 1128–1134.

deShazo, R. D., & Kemp, S. F. (2014). *Pharmacotherapy of allergic rhinitis.* Retrieved from http://www.uptodate.com/contents/pharmacotherapy-of-allergic-rhinitis?source=search_result&search=allergic+rhinitis&selectedTitle=1~150

Fenn, M. H., & Powrie, K. E. (2011). A patient-centered approach to seasonal allergic rhinitis. *Nursing in Practice: The Journal for Today's Primary Care Nurse, 61,* 57–60.

Greiner, A., Hellings, P., Rotiroti, G., & Scadding, G. (2011). Allergic rhinitis. *Lancet, 378*(9809), 2112–2122.

Hawthorne, M. R., & Ahmad, N. (2010). Acute sinusitis: Pitfalls in diagnosis and management. *Clinical Risk, 16*(6), 209–212.

Holmes, S., & Scullion, J. (2012). Allergic rhinitis: Assessment and treatment. *Nurse Prescribing, 10*(5), 222.

Hwang, P. H., & Getz, A. (2014). *Acute sinusitis and rhinosinusitis in adults: Treatment.* Retrieved from http://www.uptodate.com/contents/acute-sinusitis-and-rhinosinusitis-in-adults-treatment?source=related_link

Lieberman, P. L. (2014). *Chronic nonallergic rhinitis.* Retrieved from UpToDate. http://www.uptodate.com/contents/chronic-nonallergic-rhinitis?source=machineLearning&search=nonallergic+rhinitis&selectedTitle=1~47§ion-Rank=1&anchor=H13#H13

Marple, B., Roberts, C., Frytak, J., Schabert, V., Wegner, J., Bhattacharyya, H., … Sanchez, S. (2010). Azithromycin extended release vs amoxicillin/clavulanate: Symptom resolution in acute sinusitis. *American Journal of Otolaryngology, 31*(1), 1–8.

Mehrtens, J., & Spigarelli, M. (2010). Acute sinusitis. *Adolescent Medicine, 21*(2), 187.

Ramavaram, S., & Jones, S. M. (2012). Natural course and comorbidities of allergic and nonallergic rhinitis in children. *Pediatrics, 130,* S23–S24.

Settipane, R. (2011). Other causes of rhinitis: Mixed rhinitis, rhinitis medicamentosa, hormonal rhinitis, rhinitis of the elderly, and gustatory rhinitis. *Immunology & Allergy Clinics of North America, 31*(3), 457–467. Retrieved from http://dx.doi.org.ezproxy.waterfield.murraystate.edu/10.1016/j.iac.2011.05.011

Slavin, R. G. (2010). Special considerations in treatment of allergic rhinitis in the elderly: Role of intranasal corticosteroids. *Allergy and Asthma Proceedings, 31*(3), 179–184.

Smith, S., Montgomery, L., & Williams, J. (2012). Treatment of mild to moderate sinusitis. *Archives of Internal Medicine, 172*(6), 510–513.

Tan, R., & Corren, J. (2011). The relationship of rhinitis and asthma, sinusitis, food allergy, and eczema. *Immunology & Allergy Clinics of North America, 31*(3), 481–491.

Thorp, B., McKinney, K., Rose, A., & Ebert, C. (2012). Allergic fungal sinusitis in children. *Otolaryngologic Clinics of North America, 45*(3), 631–642.

Ventura, M., Gelardi, M., D'Amato, A., Buquicchio, R., Tummolo, R., Misciagna, G., … Passalacqua, G. (2012). Clinical and cytologic characteristics of allergic rhinitis in elderly patients. *Annals of Allergy, Asthma & Immunology, 108*(3), 141–144.

Wilson, K., Spector, M., & Orlandi, R. (2011). Types of rhinitis. *Otolaryngologic Clinics of North America, 44*(3), 549–559.

CHAPTER TEN

Throat and Mouth Guidelines

Jill C. Cash

Dental Abscess

Definition

A. A dental abscess is a space infection of the gingival or periodontal tissues.

Incidence

A. Incidence is unknown.

Pathogenesis

A. An abscess occurs when bacteria gain access into the gingiva or periodontal tissues. Dental infections are often polymicrobial and usually caused by anaerobic gram-negative rods and gram-positive cocci.

Predisposing Factors

A. Poor dental hygiene
B. Dental caries

Common Complaints

A. Constant, severe jaw pain
B. Swelling
C. Difficulty chewing with tooth due to pain

Other Signs and Symptoms

A. Fever
B. Warmth, redness
C. Loss of appetite
D. Heat and cold sensitivity
E. Halitosis

Potential Complications

Risk of complications increases with valvular disease. The following are complications:

A. Sepsis
B. Leukocytosis associated with facial cellulitis

Subjective Data

A. Elicit information from the patient regarding onset, duration, location, and quality of pain.
B. Note radiation of pain as well as alleviating or aggravating factors.
C. Note if pain is brought on by contact with hot, cold, or sweet substances; this may indicate periapical abscess or dental caries.
D. Ask if the patient has a fever. If so, how high and for how long?
E. Inquire about history of mitral valve prolapse or rheumatic fever.

Physical Examination

A. Check temperature, pulse, respirations, and blood pressure.
B. Inspect
   1. Inspect teeth for caries, mobility of teeth or protrusion from sockets, and gum disease.
   2. Examine teeth for erosion, enamel decalcification, diminished tooth size, discoloration, and sensitivity to temperature changes.
C. Palpate
   1. Palpate neck and submental area for enlarged, tender lymph nodes.
D. Percuss
   1. Percuss all teeth. Tenderness is diagnostic of an abscess.
E. Auscultate
   1. Auscultate heart and lungs.

Diagnostic Tests

A. None usually required.
B. White blood cell (WBC), if cellulitis is suspected.
C. X-rays may be considered.
D. CT with contrast, if cellulitis suspected.

Differential Diagnoses

A. Dental abscess
B. Periodontal disease
C. Cellulitis
D. Peritonsillar abscess

Plan

A. General interventions
   1. Treat immediate infection.
   2. Refer to dentist for immediate evaluation and treatment.

B. Patient teaching
   1. Advise patient to apply a heating pad to painful facial area for comfort.
   2. Advise soft diet until pain resolves.
   3. Review daily dental care and hygiene with patient.

C. Pharmaceutical therapy
   1. Drug of choice: Penicillin V potassium (Pen-Vee-K) 250 to 500 mg orally every 6 hours while the patient awaits dental consultation
   2. Other medications
      a. Cephalexin (Keflex) 500 mg every 6 hours until dental consultation
      b. Clindamycin (Cleocin) 300 mg orally every 6 hours until dental consultation
   3. For discomfort and fever: Ibuprofen (Advil) 400 to 600 mg orally every 6 to 8 hours, not to exceed 1,200 mg/d. Tylenol 500 mg orally every 4 to 6 hours may be used for patients with renal impairment. Consider renal function when prescribing nonsteroidal anti-inflammatory drugs (NSAIDs) to older adults and geriatric patients.

Follow-Up

A. Follow up 2 to 3 days after dental exam to evaluate results.

Consultation/Referral

A. Advise the patient to see a dentist promptly, even if pain resolves.

Individual Considerations

A. Pregnancy
   1. Patients may safely have dental procedures during pregnancy.
   2. X-ray films may be taken with lead shield over patient's abdomen.
   3. Epinephrine and nitrous oxide should not be used during dental procedures.
   4. Tetracycline should not be used; it causes staining of fetal bones and teeth.

Dysphagia

Definition

A. Dysphagia is defined as difficulty swallowing.
   1. Oropharyngeal dysphagia is defined as difficulty with the initial task of swallowing, which can be accompanied by choking, coughing, or a food block in the pharynx.
   2. Esophageal dysphagia is defined as difficulty swallowing after the initiation of swallowing; feeling food lodged in the esophagus. A motor disorder occurs when there is difficulty swallowing solids and/or liquids. This can be intermittent or progressive. A mechanical obstruction occurs when there is difficulty swallowing solids, which may be nonprogressive or progressive.
      a. Nonprogressive disorders include an esophageal ring or eosinophilic esophagitis.
      b. Examples of progressive disorders include peptic stricture (chronic heartburn is present) and esophageal/gastric cardia cancer.
   3. Odynophagia is defined as having pain with swallowing.

Incidence

A. Dysphagia affects approximately 300,000 to 600,000 persons annually.

B. Approximately 15% of the elderly population are affected by dysphagia.

Pathogenesis

A. In advancing age, the muscle strength and the range of motion of swallowing decline, which may impact the effectiveness of swallowing. A decrease in oral secretions, taste changes, and smell acuity may also impact the effectiveness of swallowing.

Predisposing Factors

A. Age (elderly)

B. Stroke

C. Dementia

Common Complaints

A. Difficulty with swallowing

B. Reflux of food/liquid into the nose

Other Signs and Symptoms

A. Weight loss

B. Nutritional deficiency

C. Refusal to eat

Potential Complications

A. Malnutrition

B. Pneumonia

Subjective Data

A. Ask the patient if he or she has difficulty swallowing when initiating the swallow or a few seconds after trying to swallow.

B. Does difficulty swallowing occur at every meal or snack? If so, is it getting worse?

C. Is it difficult to swallow solid foods, liquids, or both? Difficulty swallowing solids and liquids occurs when a motility disorder of the esophagus is present. Difficulty swallowing solids that generally progresses to liquids is commonly caused by a mechanical obstruction.

D. When swallowing occurs, does the patient experience coughing, reflux, or does food go up through the nose?
E. Can the patient identify a site where food commonly gets lodged?
F. Has the patient noticed any change in appetite? Weight loss or weight gain? Nausea, vomiting, diarrhea, constipation, change in stools, heartburn, or chest pain?
G. Has the patient started any new medications that have caused indigestion or reflux?
   1. Common medications that may cause reflux include bisphosphonates, ferrous sulfate, potassium chloride, ascorbic acid, tetracycline, and NSAIDs.

Physical Examination

A. Vital signs: Check temperature, pulse, respirations, and blood pressure.
B. Inspect
   1. Inspect the oral cavity for lesions, ulcers, and poor dentition. Note muscle weakness or paralysis in movement of tongue.
   2. Inspect head and neck for any masses.
   3. Inspect face for muscle weakness and neck for swallowing difficulty.
   4. Assess all cranial nerves, focusing on cranial nerves V, VII, X, XI, and XII.
C. Palpate
   1. Palpate the neck and supraclavicular lymph nodes for adenopathy or palpable masses.
D. Auscultate
   1. Heart
   2. Lungs

Diagnostic Tests

A. Upper endoscopy
B. Barium swallow
C. Motility testing

Differential Diagnosis

A. Oropharyngeal dysphagia
B. Esophageal dysphagia
C. Odynophagia
D. Achalasia (decreased peristalsis in the distal esophagus and loss of relaxation of the lower esophageal sphincter while swallowing)

Plan

A. General interventions: Identify the cause of dysphagia and treat accordingly.
B. Patient teaching
   1. Educate the patient regarding the possible causes of dysphagia.
   2. Stress the importance of nutrition and educate the patient and family about dietary alternatives to maintain nutrition and prevent weight loss.
   3. Discuss potential diagnostic testing necessary to identify the cause of dysphagia.
C. Dietary management
   1. Depending on the diagnosis and treatment, dietary management—solids versus liquids—will need to be discussed with the patient and family.
   2. A modified food diet should be provided for the patient and family, prepared with a nutritionist and dietitian.
D. Pharmaceutical therapy
   1. Proton pump inhibitors may be prescribed to help control acid reflux.
   2. If infection of the esophagus is suspected, antibiotics may be considered.

Follow-Up/Referral

A. Refer to gastroenterology for screening tests required for diagnosis.
B. Refer to a speech or swallowing specialist for assessment and education regarding swallowing exercises.
C. Refer to a dietitian/nutritionist for alternative food options and education on proper nutrition and prevention of weight loss.

Individual Considerations

A. Dysphagia may occur in conditions such as systemic sclerosis and Sjögren's syndrome.
B. Dysphagia is commonly seen after long-term intubation.
C. For the elderly population, consider cancer in the differential diagnosis if the patient is noted to have anemia and/or weight loss.

Epiglottitis

Definition

A. Epiglottitis is inflammation and swelling of the epiglottis and is a medical emergency.

Incidence

A. Epiglottitis usually occurs in children between ages 2 and 8 years, but it may also occur in adults. The incidence of epiglottitis has decreased since the *Haemophilus influenzae* vaccine was introduced.

Pathogenesis

A. Epiglottitis is almost always caused by *H. influenzae*, although *Streptococcus pneumoniae* and *Streptococcus pyogenes* have also been implicated.

Predisposing Factors

A. Upper respiratory infection
B. Trauma to the mucosa in the nasopharynx tissue from a viral infection or from injury from food being swallowed.
C. Hypertension
D. Diabetes mellitus

E. Substance abuse
F. Immune deficiency

Common Complaints

A. Sudden onset of fever
B. Sudden onset of dysphagia
C. Sudden onset of drooling
D. Sudden onset of muffled voice

Other Signs and Symptoms

A. Difficulty with breathing and/or respiratory distress
B. Stridor
C. Very ill appearance
D. Sore throat
E. Change in voice

Subjective Data

A. Determine onset, duration, and course of illness.
B. Has breathing been labored?
C. Is breathing interfering with the patient's ability to eat or drink?
D. Has the patient had a fever?
E. Has the patient had trouble swallowing or talking?

Physical Examination

A. Check temperature, pulse, respirations, and blood pressure.
B. Inspect
   1. Observe overall appearance.
   2. Check nail beds and lips for cyanosis.
   3. Note drooling or difficulty swallowing.
   4. Note breathing pattern and rhythm.
   5. Note cough if present.
   6. Direct exam of the throat can be attempted if there is no concern about compromising the airway. If airway compromise is of concern, do not examine the throat; airway occlusion may result.
C. Auscultate: Auscultate heart and lungs.

Diagnostic Tests

A. Lateral neck radiograph confirms diagnosis. However, this test may delay establishment of airway.

Differential Diagnoses

A. Epiglottitis
B. Foreign body aspiration
C. Retropharyngeal abscess

Plan

A. General interventions
   1. Immediate transfer to the emergency department for evaluation and hospitalization.
   2. While awaiting transport to hospital, establish patent's airway, start oxygen, and assemble airway equipment.
   3. Insert intravenous (IV) access for fluids and antibiotic administration.
   4. If respiratory arrest occurs, you may not be able to see the airway to intubate. An AMBU bag and mask may work temporarily, but nasogastric (NG) tube insertion may be necessary to prevent gastric distension.
   5. Prompt recognition and appropriate treatment usually result in rapid resolution of swelling and inflammation.
B. Patient teaching
   1. Educate patient and family that epiglottitis is a medical emergency.
   2. If patient has drooling and no cough, diagnosis is most likely epiglottitis.
C. Pharmaceutical therapy
   In-hospital treatment:
   1. IV fluids
   2. Antibiotics; IV antibiotics after physician consultation
   3. Blood and epiglottis cultures obtained prior to starting antibiotics
   4. Drug of choice
      a. First-line antibiotic therapy includes the use of third-generation cephalosporins, which include ceftriaxone (Rocephin), ampicillin/sulbactam (Unasyn).
      b. If unable to use these due to allergy, etc., other alternatives include chloramphenicol, cefuroxime (Ceftin), and clindamycin (Cleocin).

Follow-Up

A. Follow-up care occurs in the hospital.
B. An airway specialist should evaluate the patient in the operating room.

Consultation/Referral

A. If you suspect epiglottitis, consult with the physician immediately.
B. The patient should be transferred to the emergency department for treatment and care.
C. Maintain a patent airway while transferring the patient to the emergency department.

Oral Cancer, Leukoplakia

Definition

A. Oral cancer is cancer of the buccal mucosa, tongue, gingiva, hard palate, soft palate, or lips. White patches, known as leukoplakia, or red, velvety patches, known as erythroplakia, on the buccal mucosa may indicate premalignant lesions.

Incidence

A. Oral cancer is primarily seen in the elderly. Approximately 90% of oral cancer is diagnosed as squamous cell carcinoma. Male-to-female predominance is

2 to 1; oral cancer is higher in African American than Caucasian adults. The death rate is fairly high for oral cancer; it is secondary to the cancer being diagnosed in the late stages of development.

B. There are 42,000 Americans diagnosed with new cases of oral cancer, and 8,000 deaths will occur each year.
C. Oral cancer represents 3% of all newly diagnosed cancers and 2% of all cancer-related deaths.
D. The frequency of oral cancer of cheek and gum rises 50-fold among long-term users of smokeless tobacco.
E. Patients diagnosed with oral cancer are at greater risk of developing cancer in another part of the body, such as the lung, larynx, esophagus, or other site. Therefore, follow-up exams are recommended for the remainder of the patient's life.

Pathogenesis

A. Pathogenesis is unknown; 50% of oral cancers already have metastasized at time of diagnosis. The following factors are involved.
    1. Use of tobacco in all its forms is highly correlated with risk of oral cancer.
    2. Risk of oral cancer also is high with heavy alcohol consumption. Whether this is due to a direct effect of alcohol on the oral mucosa or to associated smoking or vitamin deficiency remains unclear.
    3. Chronic iron deficiency leading to Plummer–Vinson syndrome is known to alter mucosal tissues, and this change may be related to increased oral cancer. Research has shown that a diet low in fruits and vegetables contributes to oral cancer.
    4. Epstein–Barr virus and papillomavirus have been found in cells of the tongue manifesting oral hairy leukoplakia, a hyperplastic change found in AIDS patients. Human papillomavirus (HPV) is found in approximately 20% to 30% of cases of oral cancer.
    5. Occupational hazards also exist from sun exposure. It is estimated that 30% of those with oral cancer worked outdoors.

Predisposing Factors

A. Male gender
B. Age older than 40 years for men, older than 50 years for women
C. African American ancestry
D. Smoking or use of other tobacco products, including such smokeless products as snuff and dip
E. Alcohol consumption
F. Sun exposure
G. Poor diet, deficient in vitamins A, C, and E, and high in salted or smoked meats, fats, and oils
H. Previous cancer

Common Complaints

A. Oral sores that do not heal; this is what most commonly leads patients to seek medical care.
B. Poorly fitting dentures
C. Bleeding mucosa or gingiva without apparent cause
D. Difficulty swallowing, usually indicating more advanced disease
E. Altered sensations: Burning or numbness, usually indicating more advanced disease
F. Leukoplakia or erythroplakia

Other Signs and Symptoms

A. No symptoms, possibly
B. Decreased appetite related to altered taste
C. Increased salivation
D. Sore throat
E. Foul breath odor
F. Oral or neck mass
G. Lymphadenopathy

Subjective Data

A. Review onset, course, and duration of symptoms. Question the patient regarding altered taste, sensations, difficulty swallowing, and foul breath.
B. Evaluate for risk factors. See Predisposing Factors.
C. Ask the patient about previous history of cancer and treatments.
D. Review the patient's use of tobacco products, including age of onset, amount of daily use, and quit dates.
E. Evaluate amount of alcohol intake, including age of onset, amount of daily use, and quit dates.
F. Review the patient's general health history for other chronic conditions.
G. Review medication history, including prescription and over-the-counter drug use, especially aspirin.
H. Take dental history, including previous gum surgery, how long ago dentures were fitted, and if they always fit well.
I. Establish usual weight. Is there any weight loss related to altered taste, and if so, how much and in what length of time?

Physical Examination

A. Check temperature, pulse, respirations, blood pressure, and weight.
B. Inspect
    1. Observe general appearance.
    2. Note quality of voice patterns.
    3. Note odor of breath.
    4. Inspect lips, gums, tongue, buccal mucosa for swelling, discoloration, bleeding, asymmetry, texture, limited movement of tongue, abnormal ulcerations, leukoplakia, and erythroplasia. Take out dentures first.

5. Assess for tenderness or pain in mouth/tongue.
   a. Leukoplakia ranges from slightly raised, white, translucent areas to dense, white, opaque plaques, with or without adjacent ulceration. Normal intraoral mucosa is pinkish or salmon-colored.
   b. Mucosal erythroplasia is red, inflammatory, or erythroplastic mucosal changes. It appears smooth, granular, and minimally elevated, with or without leukoplakia, and it persists more than 14 days.
   c. Erythroplakia may mimic inflammatory lesions, but it can be differentiated by failure of the affected area to blanch with light pressure. **Erythroplakia is a malignant change seen as a red, velvety, plaque-like lesion on mucous membrane.**
   d. Other oral lesions appear black, blue, or brown.
   e. Tongue, oropharynx (soft palate, lingual aspect of retro-molar trigone, anterior tonsillar pillar), and floor of mouth.
   f. Cancer of the lip is a lesion that fails to heal.
   g. Signs and symptoms of cancer of tongue are swelling, ulceration, areas of tenderness or bleeding, abnormal texture, and limited movement.

C. Palpate
   1. Palpate mouth for masses. Try to remove or scrape patches.
   2. Palpate lymph nodes: Cervical (anterior/posterior chain), submandibular, sublingual, and submental, pre/postauricular; check nodes for size, firmness, and tenderness.

D. Auscultate lungs and heart. The lungs are the most frequently involved extranodal metastatic site.

Diagnostic Tests

A. Check serum blood for HIV, if indicated.
B. Stain oral lesion with toluidine blue: Lesion stains dark blue after rinsing with acetic acid. Normal tissue does not absorb the stain.
C. Perform biopsy for persistent lesions (> 2 weeks): It is essential to differentiate from blue-black lesion of malignant melanoma.
D. Perform chest radiography to rule out metastasis.
E. Consider computed tomography, magnetic resonance imaging, or bone scan to rule out metastasis.

Differential Diagnoses

A. Oral leukoplakia
B. Actinic keratosis
C. Periapical abscess
D. Gingivitis
E. Periodontitis
F. Lichen planus
G. Oral candidiasis
H. Discoid lupus
I. *Pemphigus vulgaris*

Plan

A. General interventions
   1. If oral cancer is suspected, refer to physician or otolaryngologist/dentist for evaluation.
   2. Suspicious lesions should have biopsy.
   3. Leukoplakia ranges from slightly raised, white, translucent areas to dense, white, opaque plaques, with or without adjacent ulceration. Normal intraoral mucosa is pinkish or salmon-colored.
   4. Mucosal erythroplasia is red, inflammatory, or erythroplastic mucosal changes. It appears smooth, granular, and minimally elevated, with or without leukoplakia, and it persists more than 14 days.
   5. Erythroplakia may mimic inflammatory lesions, but it can be differentiated by failure of the affected area to blanch with light pressure.
   6. Cancer of the lip is a lesion that fails to heal.

B. Patient teaching
   1. Advise the patient to stop smoking and stop using oral tobacco products.
   2. Advise the patient to decrease/eliminate alcohol consumption.
   3. Encourage routine dental care and exams.
   4. Review dietary intake and educate patient regarding benefits of increasing dietary intake of vitamins A, C, and E. Encourage patient to decrease dietary intake of foods that are high in salt, smoked meats, fats, and oils.
   5. Recommend wearing sunscreen/lip balm with sun protection factor (SPF) of 15 or greater.

C. Pharmaceutical therapy
   1. Erythroplakia does not respond to antifungal therapy.
   2. Treatment is based on diagnosis.

Follow-Up

A. If immediate biopsy is not indicated, ask the patient to return for reevaluation in 2 weeks, after eliminating irritants and noxious agents.

Consultation/Referral

A. Refer the patient to an otolaryngologist and/or dentist for immediate biopsy for deeply ulcerative or fungating lesions. Follow-up treatment may include one or more of the following: Wide excision, radical neck dissection, radiation, and chemotherapy.

Individual Considerations

A. Adults: The American Cancer Society recommends that people between age 20 and 40 undergo an oral cancer screening every 3 years, and those older than 40 years be screened every year. Oral screening should be considered annually in adults who use tobacco and/or alcohol.

Resources

American Academy of Family Physicians: www.aafp.org
American Cancer Society: www.cancer.org
National Cancer Institute: www.cancer.gov
Oral Cancer Foundation: www.oralcancer foundation.org

Pharyngitis

Definition

A. Pharyngitis is inflammation of the pharynx and surrounding lymph tissue.

Incidence

A. Pharyngitis is the fourth most common condition seen in medical practice. Group A streptococcus accounts for approximately 5% to 15% of adults who present for evaluation and treatment for pharyngitis.

Pathogenesis

A. Pharyngitis may be due to viral, bacterial, and fungal agents, as well as other atypical agents.
   1. Viral agents include coxsackievirus, enteric cytopathic human orphan (ECHO) viruses, and Epstein–Barr virus.
   2. Bacterial agents include Group A beta-hemolytic streptococcus, *Neisseria gonorrhoeae*, and *Corynebacterium diphtheriae*.
   3. The fungal source is *Candida albicans*.
   4. **Atypical agents include** *Mycoplasma pneumoniae* and *Chlamydia trachomatis (rare)*.
   5. Noninfectious causes include allergic rhinitis, postnasal drip, mouth breathing, and trauma.

Predisposing Factors

A. Cigarette smoking
B. Allergies
C. Upper respiratory infections
D. Oral sex
E. Drugs (antibiotics and immunosuppressants)
F. Debilitating illnesses (such as cancer) that can cause *Candida albicans* to proliferate

Common Complaints

A. Sore and/or scratchy throat
B. Fever
C. Headache
D. Malaise

Other Signs and Symptoms

A. Oral vesicles
B. Exudate on throat
C. Lymphadenopathy
D. Fatigue
E. Dysphasia
F. Abdominal pain
G. Vomiting

Potential Complications

Without proper antimicrobial treatment, streptococcal pharyngitis can lead to serious complications such as:

A. Suppurative adenitis with tender, enlarged lymph nodes
B. Scarlet fever
C. Peritonsillar abscess
D. Glomerulonephritis
E. Rheumatic fever

Subjective Data

A. Ask the patient about onset, course, and duration of symptoms. Ask about dyspnea or dysphagia.
B. Inquire about mouth lesions, rhinorrhea, cough, drooling, and fever.
C. Ask about malaise, headache, fatigue, and fever; these are symptoms of mononucleosis.
D. Take a sexual history, if indicated. Ask if family members or sexual partners have the same signs and symptoms. Pharyngeal gonorrhea has no symptoms, so high-risk patients should be tested.
E. Ask whether symptoms have caused decreased intake of food and fluid.
F. Determine history of heart disease; previous strep pharyngitis; rheumatic fever; and other respiratory diseases, such as asthma, emphysema, and chronic allergies.
G. If rash is present, find out when it first occurred and if it has spread.
H. Ask about signs and symptoms of urinary tract infection and pyelonephritis.
I. Ask about a history of herpes, immunosuppressive disorders, and steroid use.
J. Review immunization history.

Physical Examination

A. Temperature and blood pressure, if indicated.
B. Inspect
   1. Observe general appearance.
   2. Examine the mouth, pharynx, tonsils, and hard and soft palate for vesicles and ulcers, candidal patches, erythema, hypertrophy, exudate, and stomatitis. Check gum and palate for petechiae and tongue for color and inflammation.
   3. Examine the ears, nose, and throat. Assess patency of airway if tonsils are enlarged.
   4. Inspect skin for rashes.
      a. Pastia's lines are petechiae present in a linear pattern along major skin folds in axillae and antecubital fossa that are seen with Group A strep.

b. Erythema marginatum, caused by Group A streptococcus, is an evanescent, nonpruritic, pink rash mainly on the trunk and extremities. It may be brought out by heat application.

C. Auscultate: Auscultate heart and lungs.

D. Percuss
1. Percuss abdomen, especially spleen area.
2. Percuss chest.

E. Palpate
1. Palpate lymph nodes, especially of the anterior and posterior cervical chains, axilla, and groin.
2. Palpate abdomen for organomegaly and suprapubic tenderness.
3. Palpate back for costovertebral angle (CVA) tenderness.

F. Neurologic exam: Check for nuchal rigidity and meningeal irritation.

Diagnostic Tests

A. Rapid strep test; if negative, then perform throat culture and sensitivity. **Throat culture and sensitivity is the gold standard for diagnosis.**
B. Monospot test
C. Complete blood count with differential
D. Gonorrhea culture
E. Blood cultures if sepsis is suspected
F. Radiograph of neck if possible trauma

Differential Diagnoses

A. Pharyngitis
B. Stomatitis
C. Rhinitis
D. Sinusitis with postnasal drip
E. Epiglottis
F. Peritonsillar abscess
G. Mononucleosis
H. Herpes simplex
I. Coxsackie A virus
J. *Corynebacterium diphtheriae*
K. Trench mouth
L. Vincent's angina
M. *Candida albicans*
N. HIV

Plan

A. General interventions
1. Patients with a history of rheumatic fever and those who have a household member with a documented Group A streptococcal infection need immediate treatment without prior testing.
2. Herpangina are small oral vesicles on the fauces and soft palate caused by the coxsackievirus.
3. Herpes causes vesicles and small ulcers (stomatitis) of the buccal mucosa, tongue, and pharynx.
4. Trench mouth (gingivitis) and necrotic tonsillar ulcers (Vincent's angina) cause foul breath, pain, pharyngeal exudate, and a gray membranous inflammation that bleeds easily.
5. *Candida albicans* (thrush) may be painful and causes cheesy, white exudate.
6. Oral candidiasis may be the first symptom of HIV.
7. Peritonsillar cellulitis causes inflamed, edematous tonsils; grayish-white exudate, high fever, rigors, and leukocytosis. Peritonsillar abscess (palpable mass) may also develop.
8. Mononucleosis causes tonsillar exudates in 50% of patients; 33% develop petechiae at junction of hard and soft palate.
9. *Corynebacterium diphtheriae* causes a whitish-blue pharyngeal exudate "pseudomembrane" that covers the pharynx and bleeds if removal is attempted.
10. Do not put instruments in the airway if you suspect epiglottitis.

B. Patient teaching: See the Section III Patient Teaching Guide for this chapter, "Pharyngitis."

C. Pharmaceutical therapy
1. Drug of choice: Prescribe one of the following penicillins for bacterial pharyngitis.
   a. Penicillin V potassium (Pen-Vee-K): 500 mg twice a day for 10 days
   b. Amoxicillin 500 mg twice a day for 10 days
   c. Penicillin G benzathine: 1.2 million units intramuscular injection, one dose
   d. Cephalexin 500 mg twice a day for 10 days
2. If the patient is allergic to penicillin
   a. Clindamycin: 600 mg three times a day for 10 days
   b. Azithromycin: 500 mg on day 1 followed by 250 mg daily on days 2 to 5
   c. Clarithromycin: 250 mg twice a day for 10 days
3. Recurrent bacterial pharyngitis
   a. Clindamycin: 600 mg three times a day for 10 days
   b. Penicillin and rifampin: Penicillin V: 500 mg twice a day for 10 days
   c. Amoxicillin–clavulanic acid: 500 mg every 8 hours or every 12 hours for 10 days; or 875 mg every 12 hours for 10 days; not for use in creatinine clearance less than 30 mL/min
   d. Penicillin G benzathine 1.2 million units intramuscular injection, plus one dose rifampin 600 mg per day orally for 4 days
4. For pharyngeal gonorrhea: ceftriaxone (Rocephin) 500 mg to 1 g by IM injection
5. For *Mycoplasma pneumoniae* and *Chlamydia trachomatis*: Erythromycin (E-Mycin) 250 mg orally three to four times daily for 10 days

6. For pharyngeal candidiasis in the immunocompromised patient:
   a. Oral nystatin suspension (100,000 U/mL) 15 mL by swish-and-swallow method four times a day
   b. Clotrimazole troche 10 mg held in mouth 15 to 30 minutes three times daily

Follow-Up

A. If symptoms do not improve in 3 to 4 days, recheck patient.
B. Treat sexual partners of patients with pharyngeal gonorrhea.

Consultation/Referral

A. Consult physician if patient has severe dysphagia or dyspnea, signaling possible airway obstruction.
B. Refer the patient to an otolaryngologist if peritonsillar abscess is noted.

Individual Considerations

A. **Recommendations include treating patients with oral antibiotics for 10 days to eradicate infection. For patients who are not able to tolerate oral antibiotics, penicillin G benzathine may be given via intramuscular route.**

Stomatitis, Recurrent Aphthous Stomatitis

Definition

A. Stomatitis is tender, round, discrete, oval, shallow, 1- to 5-mm ulcers in the oral cavity. The ulcers are gray-white or yellow, on nonkeratinized skin, and surrounded by erythematous halos. They typically involve the labial and buccal mucosa and tongue, and adjacent tissue appears healthy.
B. Major recurrent aphthous stomatitis (RAS) has larger, deeper ulcers; lasts a longer period of time; usually recurs up to four times a year; and frequently leaves scars. It can cause significant dysphagia.

Incidence

A. Stomatitis affects 20% to 50% of the population. It is very common in North America.

Pathogenesis

A. Cause is poorly understood. Genetic, immunologic, viral, or nutritional causes are possible.

Predisposing Factors

A. Minor trauma
B. History of RAS
C. Possible nutritional deficiency of iron, B12 deficiency, folic acid, or zinc
D. Hormonal changes

Common Complaints

A. Painful sore in mouth

Other Signs and Symptoms

A. Burning sensation in mouth for 24 to 48 hours before lesions appear

Subjective Data

A. Elicit history of aphthous stomatitis.
B. Ask the patient about prodrome of burning or stinging in the mouth.
C. Elicit information regarding previous illness and trauma.

Physical Examination

A. Check temperature, pulse, respirations, and blood pressure.
B. Inspect
   1. Inspect mouth for ulcers.
   2. Inspect ears, nose, and throat.
   3. Inspect skin, especially palms and soles, for lesions; indicates hand-foot-and-mouth disease.
C. Auscultate: Auscultate heart and lungs.

Differential Diagnoses

A. Aphthous stomatitis
B. Herpetic stomatitis
C. Behçet's disease
D. Crohn's disease
E. HIV
F. Kawasaki syndrome
G. Hand-foot-and-mouth disease

Plan

A. General interventions
   1. Avoid spicy, salty, or hot foods.
   2. Encourage cold foods, such as fluids, ice pops, and so on to help with pain.
   3. Avoid hard, sharp food that is difficult to chew.
   4. Recommend using a soft bristle toothbrush when brushing teeth. Sodium lauryl sulfate found in toothpaste may delay healing time.
B. Patient teaching: See the Section III Patient Teaching Guide for this chapter, "Aphthous Stomatitis."
C. Pharmaceutical therapy
   1. Mouthwash made of diphenhydramine (Benadryl), with Kaopectate, or Maalox or sucralfate, and viscous lidocaine three to four times a day. Tell the patient not to swallow medication.
   2. Sucralfate (Carafate) suspension 1 teaspoon four times a day may be used to swish in mouth and spit out for oral comfort.
   3. Glucocorticoid gel such as fluocinonide gel (Lidex) 0.05% two to four times a day, one of which is always at bedtime.
   4. Orabase with or without triamcinolone acetonide (Kenalog) applied to ulcer two to four times a day until healed.

Follow-Up

A. Follow up as needed for treatment of recurrences.

Consultation/Referral

A. Refer the patient to, or consult with, a physician if ulcers are deeper or larger than 1 to 5 mm, if Kawasaki disease is suspected, or if no improvement is seen with adequate treatment.
B. Any lesion lasting longer than 3 weeks should be evaluated by a dentist or oral surgeon to rule out cancer.

Individual Considerations

A. Pregnancy: Avoid use of fluocinonide and triamcinolone acetonide (Kenalog) in pregnant or nursing women.
B. Adults: Consider underlying immunological conditions for patients who have recurrent oral ulcers.

Thrush

Definition

A. Thrush is a fungal infection of the oral cavity and/or the pharynx caused by *Candida*.

Incidence

A. Approximately 9% to 31% of AIDS patients and 20% of patients diagnosed with cancer will have thrush.
B. Healthy adults may also experience an episode of thrush; however, these adults usually have other risk factors, such as the frequent use of inhaled steroids and/or the use of antibiotics.

Pathogenesis

A. Thrush is an overgrowth of yeast cells, *Candida albicans*, on the oral mucosa, which leads to desquamation of the epithelial cells, creating a pseudomembrane over the normal oral mucosa. Other species of yeast cells may include *C. glabrata*, *C. krusei*, and *C. tropicalis*.

Predisposing Factors

A. Use of broad-spectrum antibiotics
B. Human immunodeficiency virus
C. Prolonged steroid use (systemic or inhaled corticosteroids)
D. Cancer treatments (radiation/chemotherapy)
E. Dentures
F. Malnutrition

Common Complaints

A. Soreness, pain of the mouth
B. White plaque coating the buccal mucosa, palate, tongue, or oropharynx

Other Signs and Symptoms

A. Erythemic, sore tongue, buccal mucosa, or oropharynx

Subjective Data

A. Determine onset, duration, and course of illness.
B. Has the patient used antibiotics or other medications in the previous weeks?
C. Does the patient use inhaled or systemic steroid on a daily basis?
D. Has the patient had difficulty swallowing?

Physical Examination

A. Check temperature, pulse, respirations, and blood pressure.
B. Inspect
   1. Inspect oral cavity for white, curdlike plaques that cannot be removed.
   2. Inspect ears, nose, and throat.

Diagnostic Tests

A. Gram stain or KOH performed on scraping specimen of lesions. Confirmed diagnosis with the presence of yeast and pseudohyphae. Gram stain or KOH testing is recommended for recurrent infections.

Differential Diagnoses

A. Thrush
B. Esophageal candidiasis (hallmark symptom is odynophagia or pain with swallowing)
C. Stomatitis
D. Aphthous ulcer
E. Hairy leukoplakia

Plan

A. General interventions
   1. Instruct the patient/family on proper use and cleaning/rinsing of inhalers/dentures to prevent reoccurrence of thrush.
   2. Instruct patient on the use of oral medications to treat thrush.
B. Patient teaching: See the Section III Patient Teaching Guide for this chapter, "Thrush."
C. Pharmaceutical therapy
   1. Oral candidiasis: Nystatin (Mycostatin) oral suspension 1 mL four times a day for 1 week. Place medication in front of mouth on each side. Rub directly on plaques with a cotton swab. Pastilles: 200,000 units lozenge four times a day for 14 days, or swish-and-swallow 500,000 units four times a day for 14 days or two 500,000 unit tablets three times daily for 14 days.
   2. Clotrimazole troche (Mycelex): 10 mg five times daily for 14 days; monitor for side effects.
   3. Fluconazole: Adults: 200 mg × 1, then 100 mg daily for 5 to 7 days
   4. Mary's Magic Mouthwash (diphenhydramine, nystatin, Maalox) may be used for maintenance once thrush has resolved. Swish and spit this mouthwash one to three times a day as needed.

Follow-Up

A. Advise the patient to telephone the office if there is no improvement, if thrush lasts more than 10 days, or if there is unexplained fever.

Consultation/Referral

A. Consult a physician if thrush does not resolve with adequate antifungal treatment.
B. Immunosuppressed patients are at higher risk for developing systemic dissemination and candidal esophagitis. Consult a physician if this is suspected.

Bibliography

American Academy of Pediatrics. (2010). *2009 Red book online: Report of the Committee on Infectious Diseases*. Elk Grove Village, IL: Author.

American Cancer Society. (2013). *Oral cavity and pharyngeal cancer*. Retrieved from http://www.cancer.org/cancer/oral-cavityandoropharyngealcancer/detailedguide/index

Chiocca, E. M. (2011). Action stat. Epiglottitis. *Nursing, 41*(3), 72.

Doshi, D. (2009). Bet 3. Avulsed tooth brought in milk for replantation. *Emergency Medicine Journal, 26*(10), 736–737.

El Fakih, R., Fears, R., & Hansen, L. (2011). Epiglottitis. *Consultant (00107069), 51*(1), 50.

Fine, A., Nizet, V., & Mandl, K. (2011). Improved diagnostic accuracy of group A streptococcal pharyngitis with use of real-time biosurveillance. *Annals of Internal Medicine, 155*(6), 345–352.

Ground, P. (2003). Nurse practitioners' practice guideline for the avulsed tooth. *Clinical Excellence for Nurse Practitioners, 7*(1–2), 14–19.

Grover, C. (2011). Images in clinical medicine. "Thumb sign" of epiglottitis. *New England Journal of Medicine, 365*(5), 447.

Hoyle, C. (2009). Make your strep diagnosis spot on. *Nurse Practitioner, 34*, 46–52.

Kamargiannis, N., Gouveris, H., Katsinelos, P., Katotomichelakis, M., Riga, M., Beltsis, A., & Danielides, V. (2011). Chronic pharyngitis is associated with severe acidic laryngopharyngeal reflux in patients with Reinke's edema. *Annals of Otology, Rhinology and Laryngology, 120*(11), 722–726.

Kauffman, C. A. (2014). Clinical manifestations of oropharyngeal and esophageal candidiasis. *UpToDate*. Retrieved from http://www.uptodate.com/contents/clinical-manifestations-of-oropharyngeal-and-esophageal-candidiasis?source=machineLearning&search=thrush&selectedTitle=2~150§ionRank=2&anchor=H6695891#H6695891

King, J. (2009). Infectious mononucleosis: Update and considerations. *Nurse Practitioner, 34*, 42–45.

Kociolek, L., & Shulman, S. (2012). Pharyngitis. *Annals of Internal Medicine, 157*(5), ITC3-1.

Lembo, A. J. (2014). Oropharyngeal dysphagia: Clinical features, diagnosis, and management. *UpToDate*. Retrieved from http://www.uptodate.com/contents/oropharyngeal-dysphagia-clinical-features-diagnosis-and-management?source=search_result&search=dysphagia+elderly&selectedTitle=2~150

Malpractice Counsel. Undiagnosed epiglottitis blamed for death. (2011). *Emergency Medicine (00136654), 43*(1), 27–28.

Mitchell, M. S., Sorrentino, A., & Centor, R. M. (2011). Adolescent pharyngitis: A review of bacterial causes. *Clinical Pediatrics, 50*(12), 1091–1095.

Pfadt, E., & Carlson, D. S. (2012). Action STAT. Avulsed tooth. *Nursing, 42*(8), 72.

Pichichero, M. E. (2014). Treatment and prevention of streptococcal tonsillopharyngitis. *UpToDate*. Retrieved from http://www.uptodate.com/contents/treatment-and-prevention-of-streptococcal-tonsillopharyngitis?source=see_link

Schams, S., & Goldman, R. (2012). Steroids as adjuvant treatment of sore throat in acute bacterial pharyngitis. *Canadian Family Physician, 58*(1), 52–54.

Scully, C. (2014). Cancers of the oral mucosa workup. *Medscape*. Retrieved from http://emedicine.medscape.com/article/1075729-workup

Shulman, S., Bisno, A., Clegg, H., Gerber, M., Kaplan, E., Lee, G., ... Van Beneden, C. (2012). Clinical practice guideline for the diagnosis and management of group A streptococcal pharyngitis: 2012 update by the Infectious Diseases Society of America. *Clinical Infectious Diseases Advance Access*, 1–17. Retrieved from http://www.uphs.upenn.edu/bugdrug/antibiotic_manual/grpastrepidsa.pdf

Sura, L., Madhavan, A., Carnaby, G., & Crary, M. (2012). Dysphagia in the elderly: Management and nutritional considerations. *Clinical Interventions in Aging, 7*, 287–298. Retrieved from http://www.ncbi.nlm.nih.gov/pmc/articles/PMC3426263/

Syed, I., Odutoye, T., Lee, M. S., & Wong, P. (2011). Management of acute epiglottitis in adults. *British Journal of Hospital Medicine (Lond), 72*, M74–M76.

Tibballs, J., & Watson, T. (2011). Symptoms and signs differentiating croup and epiglottitis. *Journal of Paediatrics and Child Health, 47*(3), 77–82.

Winkeljohn, D. (2010). Adherence to oral cancer therapies. *Clinical Journal of Oncology Nursing, 14*(4), 461–466.

Woods, C. R. (2014). Epiglottitis (supraglottitis): Clinical features and diagnosis. *UpToDate*. Retrieved from http://www.uptodate.com/contents/epiglottitis-supraglottitis-clinical-features-and-diagnosis?source=search_result&search=epiglottitis+adult&selectedTitle=1~41

CHAPTER ELEVEN

Respiratory Guidelines

Mellisa Hall and Cheryl A. Glass

Asthma

Definition

A. Asthma is chronic airway inflammation characterized by recurrent episodes of wheezing, breathlessness, chest tightness, and cough, particularly at night and in the early morning. Episodes are associated with widespread, variable, often reversible airflow obstruction and bronchial hyperresponsiveness when airways are exposed to various stimuli or triggers. Asthma is responsible for lost school days, lost productivity, and presenteeism.

B. Asthma is classified in four ways:
   1. *Step 1—Mild intermittent:* Symptoms less than or equal to two per week; asymptomatic with normal peak expiratory flow rate (PEFR) between attacks; nighttime symptoms less than or equal to two per month; PEFR greater than 80% predicted with variability less than 20%
   2. *Step 2—Mild persistent:* Symptoms greater than two per week but less than one per day; exacerbations may affect activity; nighttime symptoms greater than two per month; PEFR greater than or equal to 80% predicted with variability 20% to 30%
   3. *Step 3—Moderate persistent:* Daily symptoms requiring beta-2 agonist use; attacks affect activity; exacerbations greater than or equal to two per week; nighttime symptoms greater than one per week; PEFR greater than 60% and greater than 80% predicted with variability greater than 30%
   4. *Step 4—Severe persistent:* Continuous symptoms with limited physical activity; frequent exacerbations; frequent nighttime symptoms; PEFR less than or equal to 60% predicted with greater than 30% variability

Incidence

A. Asthma affects 25 million people in the United States.
B. Asthma rates in the general population are increasing, including developed countries.
C. Up to 95% of patients with asthma also suffer from persistent rhinitis.
D. Asthma is often associated with other comorbid conditions, including gastroesophageal reflux disease (GERD) and obesity.
E. The diagnosis is more common in adult females than males.
F. Puerto Ricans, African Americans, Filipinos, and Irish Americans have higher rates than other ethnicities.
G. Asthma control and asthma outcomes are worse for lower socioeconomic groups.

Pathogenesis

A. Asthma arises from a complex cycle of processes initiated by airway inflammation resulting from physical, chemical, and pharmacologic agents (such as environmental—irritants, allergens, furry animals, cockroaches, dust mites, pollens and mold, cold air, viral respiratory infections, and exercise). It progresses to airway hyperresponsiveness, bronchoconstriction, airway wall edema, chronic mucus plug formation, and chronic airway remodeling.

Predisposing Factors

A. Family history
B. Coexisting sinusitis, nasal polyps, and sensitivity to aspirin or other nonsteroidal anti-inflammatory drugs (NSAIDs)
C. Exposure in workplace to wood dust, metals, and animal products

D. Premenstrual asthma (PMA)
E. Smoking
F. Early menarche
G. Obesity
H. Postmenopausal hormone replacement therapy
I. Viral respiratory infections
J. Gastroesophageal reflux

Common Complaints

A. Recurrent cough (worse at night and early morning)
B. Recurrent wheezing
C. Recurrent shortness of breath (SOB)
D. Recurrent chest tightness (may worsen with moderate activity)

Other Signs and Symptoms

A. Nocturnal awakening from symptoms
B. Variation of symptoms with seasons or environment
C. Chest discomfort, tightness with moderate activity

Subjective Data

A. Ask about onset, duration, and course of symptoms.
B. Inquire about sudden severe episodes of coughing, wheezing, and SOB and whether precipitating factors can be identified.
C. Ask whether the patient has chest colds that take more than 10 days to resolve.
D. Ask if the patient is a smoker, how much, and for how long he or she has smoked.
E. Ask whether symptoms seem to occur during certain seasons or during exposure to the following environmental irritants:
   1. Tobacco smoke
   2. Perfume
   3. Household pets
   4. Fireplaces
   5. Woodburning stoves
   6. Mold
   7. Dust mites
   8. Cockroaches
F. Find out how often coughing, wheezing, or SOB awakens the patient.
G. Ask if symptoms are caused or exacerbated by moderate exercise or physical activity.
H. Determine the family history of asthma, allergies, and eczema.
I. Determine if the patient is pregnant or has medical problems. If so, do not prescribe beta 2 adrenergics and use NSAIDs cautiously. The safest medications are cromolyn sodium and anticholinergic drugs. Leukotriene inhibitors should be prescribed in pregnancy only if clearly needed.
J. Administer the asthma control test. The test is available online from www.asthmacontrol.com. A score greater than 20 points indicates the patient's asthma is well controlled. Scores of 16 to 19 points indicates the patient is not well controlled.
K. Evaluate if the patient has ever been tested for allergies.
L. Ask if the patient has ever needed to go to the emergency room or had to be hospitalized for an asthmatic attack.
M. Review all medications including over-the-counter (OTC) and herbal supplements.
N. Ask if prescription or OTC inhalers are used and to what extent.

Physical Examination

A. Check temperature (if indicated), blood pressure, pulse, respirations, and pulse oximetry. Measure the patient's height and weight to calculate body mass index (BMI) since obesity is associated with asthma.
B. Inspect
   1. Observe for hyperexpansion of thorax and signs that accessory muscles are being used (retractions, nasal flaring) or stridor.
   2. Note appearance of hunched shoulders and/or chest deformity.
   3. Inspect ears, nose, and throat. Evaluate the presence of enlarged tonsils and adenoids, and nasal polyps.
   4. Inspect skin for eczema, dermatitis, or other irritation that might signal allergy.
   5. Observe for allergic shiners and pebbled conjunctiva.
   6. Observe for digital clubbing.
C. Auscultate
   1. Auscultate lung sounds. Note wheezing during normal expiration and prolonged expiration, which is seen with asthma.
   2. Listen to all lung fields for an asymmetric wheeze.
   3. Auscultate heart rate.
D. Percuss: Percuss lung fields.

Diagnostic Tests

A. **Spirometry is the gold standard.** Peak flow meter measurements are not a substitute for spirometry. Evaluate the forced vital capacity (FVC) and forced expiratory volume in 1 second (FEV_1) before and after the patient inhales a short-acting bronchodilator.
B. Chest radiograph (CXR) and complete blood count (CBC) to exclude other diagnoses and infection.
C. Check PEFR after inhalation of short-acting beta 2 agonist. Diagnosis is confirmed if:
   1. There is a 15% increase in PEFR after 15 to 20 minutes.
   2. PEFR varies more than 20% between arising and 12 hours later in patients taking bronchodilators (or 10% without bronchodilators).

3. There is a greater than 15% decrease in PEFR after 6 minutes of running or exercise.

D. Consider a bronchial provocation test with histamine or methacholine for nondiagnostic spirometry.

Differential Diagnoses

A. Asthma
B. Chronic obstructive pulmonary disease (COPD)
C. GERD
D. Congestive heart failure (CHF)
E. Cough secondary to medications such as an angiotensin-converting enzyme (ACE) inhibitor or beta blockers
F. Pneumonia
G. Pulmonary embolism
H. Laryngeal dysfunction
I. Benign and malignant tumors
J. Vocal cord dysfunction
K. Obstructive sleep apnea (OSA)
L. Tuberculosis (TB)
M. Postviral syndrome
N. Obesity
O. Allergic rhinitis

Plan

A. General interventions
   1. Review proper medication dosages. Short- and long-term agents come in several formulations; nebulizer, metered-dose inhaler (MDI), and a dry powder inhaler (DPI).
   2. Demonstrate correct use of inhalers, spacers, and nebulizers. If the patient does not use correct technique when using these devices, medication does not get delivered to the bronchioles, and therefore the patient may believe the medication does not work. Most often the medication works well when delivered to the bronchioles correctly. See the Section III Patient Teaching Guide for this chapter, "How to Use a Metered-Dose Inhaler." The easiest delivery mechanism should be considered for the elderly.
   3. Stress the importance of using a peak flow monitor at home to monitor progress of the disease. See the Section III Patient Teaching Guide for this chapter, "Asthma Action Plan and Peak Flow Monitoring."
   4. Short-acting beta-2 agonists (SABA) are used for rescue from acute symptoms. Ask the patient to state or identify which inhaler he or she uses for rescue.
   5. Use of a SABA more than twice a week for symptom relief indicates the patient has inadequate asthma control and needs an inhaled corticosteroid (ICS) as controller therapy.
   6. Stress the need for an asthma action plan. See the Section III Patient Teaching Guide for this chapter, "Asthma Action Plan and Peak Flow Monitoring."

B. Patient teaching: See the Section III Patient Teaching Guide for this chapter, "Asthma."

C. Pharmaceutical therapy: Drugs are prescribed in a stepwise fashion for the type of asthma. The amount of medication used depends on the severity of asthma (Steps 1–6). **Prior to any medication/dosage changes, monitor the patient's compliance** (see Table 11.1). The following treatments are recommended:
   1. Mild intermittent asthma (Step 1)
      a. No long-term preventive medications are needed.
      b. Use SABAs as rescue medication. May be used up to four times a day to treat exacerbation.
      c. Alternative medications include cromolyn, nedocromil, and leukotriene modifier.
   2. Mild persistent asthma (Step 2)
      a. Low-dose ICS are used daily as a long-term preventive medication.
      b. Alternative medications include an ICS plus either cromolyn or a leukotriene modifier.
   3. Moderate persistent asthma (Step 3)
      a. Low-dose ICS plus a long-acting beta-2 agonist (LABA) *or* a medium-dose ICS
      b. ICS plus either a leukotriene modifier or theophylline or zileuton
   4. Severe persistent asthma (Step 4)
      a. Medium- to high-dose ICS plus either a LABA or montelukast
      b. Medium-dose ICS plus either a leukotriene modifier or theophylline
      c. Second alternative: Medium-dose ICS plus either leukotriene modifier, theophylline, or zileuton
      d. Consider omalizumab for patients with allergies for severe persistent asthma
   5. Step 5: Preferred agents are high-dose ICS plus either LABA or montelukast
   6. Step 6: Preferred agents are high-dose ICS plus either LABA or montelukast and oral systemic corticosteroids
   7. Mild to moderate asthma: Leukotriene modifiers are used to reduce the need for short-acting, inhaled beta-2 agonists. They are also an alternative to low-dose ICS for patients with mild persistent asthma.
   8. Exercise-induced bronchospasm
      a. Short-acting inhaled beta-2 agonist, two inhalations shortly before exercise are effective for 2 to 3 hours.
      b. LABA, two inhalations are effective 10 to 12 hours.

TABLE 11.1 Medications for Asthma and COPD (by Class/Alphabetical Order)

Brand	Generic	Drug Classification	Availability
(SABA) Short-acting beta-2 agonist, for rescue/fast-acting rescue			
Accuneb	Albuterol	Beta-2 agonist	Nebulizer
Albuterol	Albuterol sulfate	Beta-2 agonist	Inhaler, solution Nebulizer Syrup
Combivent	Ipratropium + albuterol	Combination anticholinergic + beta-2 agonist	MDI
Fenoterol	Ipratropium + fenoterol	Beta-2 agonist	Inhaler, MDI, and oral syrup
Maxair Autohaler	Pirbuterol acetate	Beta-2 agonist	
ProAir HFA inhaler	Albuterol	Beta-2 agonist	MDI
Proventil HFA inhaler	Albuterol	Beta-2 agonist	MDI
Terbutaline sulfate	Brethine	Beta-2 agonist	Tablet
Ventolin HFA	Albuterol sustained release	Beta-2 agonist	MDI
Vospire ER	Albuterol	Beta-2 agonist	Extended-release (ER) tablet
Xopenex	Levalbuterol Tartrate	Beta-2 agonist	HFA inhaler Concentrate solution for nebulizer
(LABA) Long-acting beta-2 agonist, for maintenance/long-acting control			
Advair Diskus	Fluticasone + Salmeterol	Combination-steroid + LABA	Dry powder diskus MDI-HFA inhaler
Arcapta	Indacaterol	Long-acting beta-1 agonist	Nebulizer
Brovana	Arformoterol	Beta-2 agonist	Nebulizer
Foradil Aerolizer	Formoterol fumarate	LABA	Nebulizer Dry powder diskus
Perforomist	Formoterol solution	Beta-2 agonist	Nebulizer
Serevent Diskus	Salmeterol	LABA	Dry powder diskus
(ICS) Inhaled corticosteroid anti-inflammatory, for maintenance or long-term control			
Aerobid and Aerobid M	Flunisolide	ICS	MDI MDI with menthol
Alvesco	Ciclesonide	ICS	MDI
Asmanex	Mometasone	ICS	Twist-haler dry powder
Beclovent	Beclomethasone Dipropionate	ICS	Dipro powder Inhaler
Dulera Flovent HFA	Mometasone furoate + Formoterol Fluticasone	Combination corticosteroid + LABA ICS	MDI MDI (also available as a DPI as Flovent diskus)
Pulmicort	Budesonide	ICS	Flexhaler and respules
QVAR	Beclomethasone	ICS	MDI
Symbicort	Budesonide + Formoterol	Combination corticosteroid + LABA	MDI
Breo Ellipta	Fluticasone + Vilanterol	Combined corticosteroid + Long-acting muscarinic antagonist	DPI
Leukotriene modifiers—nonsteroidal anti-inflammatory			
Accolate	Zafirkalast	Leukotriene modifier	Tablet
Singulair	Montelukast	Leukotriene modifier	Chew tablet and granules
Zyflo	Zileuton	Leukotriene modifier	Filmtab

(continued)

TABLE 11.1 Medications for Asthma and COPD (by Class/Alphabetical Order) (*continued*)

Brand	Generic	Drug Classification	Availability
Anticholinergics			
Anoro Ellipta	Umeclidinium + vilanterol	Anticholinergic/LABA	DPI
Atrovent HFA	Ipratropium	Antimuscarinic/antispasmodic	MDI and nebulizer
DuoNeb	Ipratropium + Albuterol	Combination antimuscarinic/antispasmodic + beta-2 agonist	Nebulizer
Spiriva with HandiHaler	Tiotropium	Antimuscarinic/antispasmodic	Dry powder diskus
Tudorza	Aclidinium	Anticholinergic	DPI
Mast cell stabilizer			
Intal	Cromolyn sodium	Mast cell stabilizer	MDI
Tilade	Nedocromil	Mast cell stabilizer	MDI
Methylxanthine			
Aminophylline	Theophylline	Methylxanthines respiratory smooth muscle relaxant	Tablet
Theo-24	Theophylline sustained-release	Methylxanthines respiratory smooth muscle relaxant	Tablet
Anti-IgE (IgE blocker) monoclonal antibody			
Xolair	Omalizumab	IgE blocker-immunomodulator	Subcutaneous injection
Systemic corticosteroids—used as a short-term "burst" for control			
Deltasone	Prednisone	Systemic corticosteroid	Tablet
Medrol	Methylprednisolone	Systemic corticosteroid	Tablet
Prelone	Prednisolone	Systemic corticosteroid	Tablet
Phosphodiesterase-4 inhibitors (PDE4)			
Ariflo	Cilomilast	Selective PDE4	Tablet
Daliresp	Roflumilast	Selective PDE4	Tablet

DPI, dry powder inhaler; HFA, hydrofluoroalkanes; MDI, metered-dose inhaler.

9. Hypertension and asthma: Drug of choice is a calcium channel blocker. Asthmatics also tolerate diuretics well.
10. Theophylline can cause cardiac arrhythmias; therefore, use it with caution and always follow up with theophylline levels.
11. Vaccinations
    a. Influenza vaccine should be administered annually to asthmatics.
    b. Pneumococcal vaccine is recommended for patients 19 and older with chronic lung disease, including asthma.

Follow-Up

A. After acute episodes, follow up within 1 to 2 hours or next day to monitor improvement until patient is stable.
B. For patients with mild intermittent or mild persistent asthma under control for at least 3 months, assess and follow up at least every 6 months to provide education and reinforce positive behaviors.
C. Gradually reduce medication dosage. If control is not achieved, consider increasing dosage after reviewing medication technique, compliance, and environmental control.

Consultation/Referral

A. Consider hospitalization for patients with acute episodes who do not completely respond to treatment within 1 to 2 hours.
B. If all therapies fail—including a short burst of prednisone—refer patient to an asthma specialist.
C. Consult with a physician when the patient is pregnant or has other medical problems, or when standard treatment is ineffective.
D. Refer if the patient presents with atypical symptoms.

Individual Considerations

A. Pregnancy
    1. Risks of uncontrolled asthma far outweigh risks to mother or fetus from drugs used to control the disease.

2. Most drugs used to treat asthma and rhinitis, with the exception of brompheniramine and epinephrine, pose little increased risk to the fetus.
3. Classes of drugs that do cause risk include decongestants, antibiotics (tetracycline, sulfonamides, and ciprofloxacin), live virus vaccines, immunotherapy (if doses are increased), and iodides. Always weigh benefits against risks because adequate fetal oxygen supply is essential. The obstetrician should be consulted.
4. If corticosteroids are necessary, recommend aerosolized forms due to their lower systemic effects. Prednisone or methylprednisolone are preferred and should be prescribed at minimum effective doses.
5. Do not prescribe inhaled triamcinolone because it is teratogenic.
6. Drugs recommended during pregnancy
   a. A beta-2 agonist, such as terbutaline, is preferred; two inhalations every 4 hours as needed up to eight inhalations per day. Regular daily use suggests a need for additional medications.
   b. Cromolyn, two inhalations four times daily as initial therapy for patients needing regular medication.
   c. Regular inhaled beclomethasone if cromolyn is not effective.
   d. Regular oral theophylline if beclomethasone is not effective.
   e. Oral prednisone if all other therapies fail; 1 week of 40 mg/d, followed by 1 to 2 weeks of tapering
7. Leukotrine inhibitors should be prescribed in pregnancy only if clearly needed.
   a. Accolate is excreted in the breast milk and should not be prescribed to mothers who are breastfeeding.
   b. Fetal anomalies have been reported with Zyflo.

B. Geriatrics
1. Asthma in the elderly is often associated with other comorbidities such as cardiac conditions.
2. Half of elderly patients with asthma have first onset after age 65. Respiratory viruses are a common trigger.
3. Recurrent episodes of SOB may be the primary symptom.
4. Treatment is the same as with younger patients, with inhaled steroids the mainstay and oral steroids reserved for severe episodes. The elderly have more adverse effects from inhaled ICS.
5. If steroids are prescribed, carefully monitor the patient for complications, including cataracts, increased intraocular pressure, hyperglycemia, and accelerated loss of bone mass.
6. Inhaled anticholinergics and beta-2 agonists are second-line treatment.
7. The elderly may have difficulty with inhaling medications and may require a nebulizer.
8. Theophylline is rarely effective in the elderly. Asthma medications may have increased adverse effects in the elderly or may aggravate coexisting medical conditions, requiring medication adjustments. Also consider drug interactions and drug and disease interactions.
9. Spacing chambers assist in proper delivery of inhaled medications.

Resources

Adult and Children Asthma Control tests: www.asthmacontrol.com

American Lung Association: www.lungusa.org

Asthma & Allergy Foundation of America: www.aafa.org

Global Initiative for Asthma (GINA) Instructions for Inhaler and Spacer Use: www.ginasthma.com

National Heart Lung and Blood Institute (NHLBI): www.nhlbi.nih.gov

Bronchitis, Acute

Definition

A. Acute bronchitis is inflammation of the tracheobronchial tree. Bronchitis is nearly always self-limited in the otherwise healthy individual. Generally, the clinical course of acute bronchitis lasts 10 to 14 days. The cause is usually infectious, but allergens and irritants may also produce a similar clinical profile. Asthma can be mistaken as acute bronchitis if the patient has no prior history of asthma.

Incidence

A. Bronchitis is more common in fall and winter in relation to the common cold or other respiratory illness. It occurs in men more frequently than in women. Fewer than 5% of patients with bronchitis develop pneumonia. It is one of the most common conditions seen in outpatients.

Pathogenesis

A. Most attacks are caused by viral agents, such as adenovirus, influenza, parainfluenza viruses, and respiratory syncytial virus (RSV).

B. Bacterial causes include *Bordetella pertussis, Mycobacterium tuberculosis, Corynebacterium diphtheriae,* and *Mycoplasma pneumoniae. B. pertussis* should be considered in adults with persistent coughs.

Predisposing Factors

A. Viral infection

B. Upper respiratory infection

C. Exposure to cigarette smoke
D. Exposure to other irritants
E. Allergens
F. Chronic aspiration/GERD
G. Immunocompromise and frailty

Common Complaints

A. The most common symptom initially is a dry, hacking, or raspy-sounding cough. The cough then loosens and becomes productive.

Other Signs and Symptoms

A. Sore throat
B. Rhinorrhea or nasal congestion
C. Rhonchi during respiration
D. Low-grade fever
E. Malaise
F. Retrosternal pain during deep breathing and coughing
G. Decreased/lack of appetite

Subjective Data

A. Ask about onset, duration, and course of symptoms.
B. Is cough productive?
C. Is there substernal discomfort?
D. Is there malaise or fatigue?
E. Has patient had a fever?
F. Does patient smoke? (Smoking aggravates bronchitis.)
G. A review of occupational history may be important in determining whether irritants play a role in symptoms.
H. Assess for symptoms of gastroesophageal reflux.
I. If diabetic, ask about home blood glucose readings.

Physical Examination

A. Check temperature, pulse, and blood pressure. Consider pulse oximetry.
B. Inspect
   1. Observe overall appearance, including level of consciousness (LOC).
   2. Inspect eyes, ears, nose, and throat (pharynx may be injected).
   3. Transilluminate sinuses.
C. Palpate: Palpate lymph nodes, maxillary, and frontal sinuses.
D. Auscultate: Auscultate in all lung fields for crackles, wheezing, and rhonchi.

Diagnostic Tests

A. Consider chest x-ray to exclude pneumonia.

Differential Diagnoses

A. Bronchitis
B. Upper respiratory infection
C. Asthma
D. Sinusitis
E. Cystic fibrosis (CF)
F. Aspiration
G. Respiratory tract anomalies
H. Foreign-body aspiration
I. Pneumonia
J. COPD and emphysema
K. Pertussis

Plan

A. General interventions—primarily supportive and should ensure the patient is adequately oxygenating.
   1. Tell the patient to increase fluid intake.
   2. Suggest humidity and mist therapy.
   3. Avoid irritants, such as smoke.
B. Patient teaching: See the Section III Patient Teaching Guide for this chapter, "Bronchitis, Acute."
C. Pharmaceutical therapy
   1. Acetaminophen (Tylenol) for fever and malaise.
      a. Adults: 625 to 1,000 mg orally every 4 hours; not to exceed 4 g/d
   2. Expectorants such as guaifenesin with dextromethorphan (Robitussin DM, Humibid DM, Mytussin) to treat minor cough from bronchial/throat irritation
   3. Among otherwise healthy individuals, antibiotics have not demonstrated to be beneficial for acute bronchitis and are against current Centers for Disease Control and Prevention (CDC) recommendations. However, oral antibiotics should be considered if symptoms persist for 2 weeks with supportive treatment (long-term persistence indicates bacterial infection).
      a. Amoxicillin-clavulanic acid (Augmentin) 250 to 500 mg by mouth every 8 hours
      b. Doxycyline 100 mg by mouth every 12 hours
      c. Trimethoprim-sulfamethoxazole 80 to 160 one tablet by mouth every 12 hours
      d. Sputum cultures prior to antibiotic therapy help isolate causative pathogen.
   4. Albuterol (Ventolin) for patients with wheezes or rhonchi, or for patients with a history of bronchoconstriction
      a. Two puffs every 4 to 6 hours *or* 2 to 4 mg by mouth three to four times a day

Follow-Up

A. Follow up if patient does not improve in 48 hours.
B. Recommend yearly influenza vaccinations.

Consultation/Referral

A. In uncomplicated cases, mucus production decreases and cough disappears in 7 to 10 days. If symptoms persist, refer the patient to a physician.

B. Refer the patient if you note respiratory distress or if he or she appears ill and you suspect pneumonia.

Individual Considerations

A. Geriatrics: Monitor elderly patients for complications such as pneumonia. The elderly have a greater morbidity and mortality rate.

Bronchitis, Chronic

Definition

A. Chronic bronchitis is excessive mucus secretion with chronic or recurrent productive cough occurring 3 successive months a year for 2 consecutive years.
B. Others limit the definition to a productive cough that lasts more than 2 weeks despite therapy.
C. Patients with chronic bronchitis have more mucus than normal because of either increased production or decreased clearance. Coughing is the mechanism for clearing excess secretion.

Incidence

A. The incidence of chronic bronchitis is uncertain. There is a lack of definitive diagnostic criteria, and there is considerable overlap with asthma. Visits for bronchitis are second only to visits for otitis media and are slightly more common than for asthma.
B. Chronic bronchitis is more prevalent in females than males.
C. Chronic bronchitis prevalence increases with age.
D. Chronic bronchitis rates are highest in African American and Caucasian ethnicities.

Pathogenesis

A. Mucociliary clearance is delayed because of excess mucus production and loss of ciliated cells, leading to a productive cough.
B. Bacteria most often implicated are *Streptococcus pneumoniae, Haemophilus influenzae, M. pneumoniae,* and *Moraxella catarrhalis.*
C. Specific occupational exposures are associated with symptoms of chronic bronchitis, including coal, cement, welding fumes, organic dusts, engine exhausts, fire smoke, and secondhand smoke.

Predisposing Factors

A. Cigarette smoking
B. Cold weather
C. Acute viral infection
D. COPD/emphysema
E. Occupational exposure to other airborne irritants
F. Chronic, recurrent aspiration or gastroesophageal reflux
G. Allergies

Common Complaints

A. Worsening cough: Hacking, harsh, or raspy sounding
B. Changes in color (yellow, white, or greenish), amount, and viscosity of sputum
C. "Rattling" sound in chest
D. Dyspnea/breathlessness
E. Wheezing

Other Signs and Symptoms

A. Difficulty breathing, retrosternal pain during a deep breath or cough
B. Rapid respirations
C. Fatigue
D. Headache
E. Loss of appetite
F. Fever
G. Myalgias
H. Arthralgias
I. Sleep disturbance due to cough

Subjective Data

A. Determine the onset, course, and duration of illness.
B. Is the patient having trouble breathing?
C. Has there been a fever?
D. How is the patient's appetite? Is the patient drinking enough fluids?
E. Does the patient smoke, or is the patient exposed to secondhand smoke?
F. Review occupational history to evaluate exposure to irritants.
G. Does the patient have a history of asthma?

Chronic bronchitis has a long history of a productive cough and late-onset wheezing. Patients with asthma with a chronic obstruction have a long history of wheezing with a late-onset of productive cough.

H. Chest pain in any certain area?
I. When was the patient's last illness?
J. Blood glucose levels if diabetic
K. Frequency of SABA inhaler use and effectiveness
L. Any confusion (especially in advanced age)

Physical Examination

A. Check temperature, pulse, blood pressure, respirations, and pulse oximetry.
B. Inspect
   1. Observe overall appearance including signs of respiratory distress.
   2. Inspect eyes, ears, nose, and throat.
      a. Pharynx may be injected.
      b. Conjunctivitis suggests adenovirus.

3. Transilluminate sinuses.
4. Assess skin turgor and mucous membranes for dehydration.

C. Auscultation
1. Ausculate lungs in all fields. Lung sounds may sound normal to scattered, bilateral crackles, rhonchi, or large airway wheezing.
2. Ausculate heart.

D. Percuss chest.

E. Palpate
1. Lymph nodes
2. Maxillary and frontal sinuses

Diagnostic Tests

A. **Patients with uncomplicated respiratory illness need little, if any, laboratory evaluation.**
B. Pulse oximetry
C. Sputum culture to identify bacteria
D. CXR may help exclude other diseases or complications.
E. Pulmonary function studies may be indicated.
F. EKG and pulmonary function tests (PFTs) may be required for COPD patients.
G. Sweat test may be necessary to rule out CF.

Differential Diagnoses

A. Chronic bronchitis
B. Acute bronchitis
C. Asthma
D. Sinusitis
E. CF
F. Bronchiectasis
G. Central airway obstruction
H. Pneumonia
I. Lung cancer
J. Aspiration syndrome
K. Gastroesophageal reflux
L. TB
M. Foreign body

Plan

A. General interventions
1. Rest during early phase of illness.
2. Encourage stopping smoking and staying away from secondhand smoke.
3. Suggest exercise for patients with COPD.
4. The patient's goal is to improve symptoms and to decrease cough and production of sputum.
5. Inform patients that increased sputum production may occur after smoking cessation and the patient may have airway reactivity (wheezing), especially seen in asthmatics.
6. Discuss patient's choices of advance directives preferably before exacerbation occurs.

B. Patient teaching: See the Section III Patient Teaching Guide for this chapter, "Bronchitis, Chronic."

C. Dietary management
1. Increase fluids.
2. Eat nutritious food.

D. Pharmaceutical therapy
1. Bronchodilators should be considered for bronchospasm.
   a. Albuterol sulfate (Proventil, Ventolin)
      i. Adults: MDI-2 actuations (90 mcg/actuation) inhaled every 4 to 6 hours
2. Analgesics and antipyretics are used to control fever, myalgias, and arthralgias.
3. Consider oral steroids to decrease inflammation.
   a. Adults: 5 to 60 mg/d by mouth
   b. Tapering steroids is not necessary with short courses.
4. ICS may be effective.
   a. Beclomethasone (QVAR) available as an MDI that delivers 40 or 80 mcg/actuation.
      i. 40 to 80 mcg inhaled by mouth twice a day, not to exceed 320 mcg twice a day.
   b. Fluticasone (Flovent HFA, Flovent diskus). Available as MDI (44 mcg, 110 mcg, or 220 mcg per actuation) and diskus power for inhalation (50 mcg, 100 mcg, or 250 mcg per actuation).
      i. Adults
         1) MDI: 88 mcg inhaled by mouth twice a day, not to exceed 440 mcg twice a day
         2) Diskus: 100 mcg inhaled by mouth twice a day, not to exceed 500 mcg twice a day
5. Antibiotics for bacterial infection
   a. Amoxicillin-clavulanic acid (Augmentin)
      i. 250 to 500 mg by mouth every 8 hours
   b. Doxycyline 100 mg by mouth every 12 hours
   c. Trimethoprim-sulfamethoxazole 80 to 160 one tablet by mouth every 12 hours
   d. Suspected pseudomonas coverage: Levofloxacin 500 mg daily

Follow-Up

A. Follow up if there is no improvement in 3 to 4 days after starting therapy.
B. Recommend yearly influenza vaccinations.

Consultation/Referral

A. Refer patients with respiratory distress to a physician. If respiratory failure occurs (rare), hospitalization may be needed.
B. Refer patients with COPD to a physician or pulmonary specialist.

Individual Considerations

A. Elderly
  1. Follow-up may be needed every 24 hours to ensure improvement and to assess for septic changes.
  2. Use of hand-held bronchodilator should be demonstrated.

Chronic Obstructive Pulmonary Disease

Definition

A. COPD is progressive, chronic, expiratory airway obstruction due to chronic bronchitis or emphysema. The relief of bronchoconstriction due to inflammation has some reversibility. Chronic bronchitis is a chronic productive cough lasting 3 months during 2 consecutive years, after all causes of chronic cough have been excluded. Emphysema is an abnormal, permanent enlargement (hyperinflation) of the air sacs, as well as the destruction of the elastic recoil. Many patients have both types of air restriction symptoms of chronic bronchitis and emphysematous destruction leading to COPD. Patients with asthma whose airflow obstruction is completely reversible are not considered to have COPD. When asthmatic patients do not have complete reversible airflow obstruction, they are considered to have COPD.

B. Irreversible airflow obstruction is a key factor in the patient's disability. The goal of COPD management is to improve daily quality of life (QOL) and the recurrence of exacerbations. Smoking cessation continues to be the most important therapeutic intervention.

C. The Global Initiative for Chronic Obstructive Lung Disease (GOLD) staging criteria are as follows:
  1. Stage I—Mild obstruction: FEV_1 greater than 80% of predicted value, some sputum, and chronic cough.
  2. Stage II—Moderate obstruction: FEV_1 between 50% and 80% of predicted value, SOB on exertion, and chronic symptoms.
  3. Stage III—Severe obstruction: FEV_1 between 30% and 50% of predicted value, dyspnea, reduced exercise tolerance, exacerbations affecting QOL.
  4. Stage IV—Very severe obstruction chronic respiratory failure: FEV_1 less than 30% of predicted value or moderate obstruction FEV_1 less than 50% of the predicted value and chronic respiratory failure.
  5. Comorbidities commonly seen with COPD include hypertension, cardiac disorders including atrial fibrillation and heart failure, diabetes/metabolic syndrome, gastrointestinal disorders, lung cancer, depression, and osteoporosis.

Incidence

A. Approximately 24 million people in the United States have been diagnosed with COPD. It is the third leading cause of death in the United States. Since 2011, COPD has been more commonly seen in females than in males. The exact worldwide prevalence is unknown.

Pathogenesis

A. Chronic bronchitis leads to the narrowing of the airway caliber and increase in airway resistance. Mucus gland enlargement is the histological hallmark of chronic bronchitis.

B. In emphysema, loss of the air sac's elastic recoil causes air limitation. Emphysema caused by smoking is the most severe in the upper lobes. Most patients with COPD have smoked one pack of cigarettes a day for 20 or more years before the symptomatic dyspnea, cough, and sputum appear.

Predisposing Factors

A. Cigarette smoking
B. Occupational, environmental, or atmospheric pollutants
  1. Dust
  2. Chemical fumes
  3. Secondhand smoke
  4. Air pollution
C. Genetic factor: Alpha 1-antitrypsin (AAT) deficiency
D. Recurrent or chronic lower respiratory infections or disease (childhood and as adult)
E. Age (most common in fifth decade of life)

Common Complaints

A. Chronic cough and colorless sputum, usually worse in morning
B. Dyspnea with exertion, progressing to dyspnea at rest
C. Wheezing
D. Difficulty speaking or performing tasks
E. Weight loss (decrease in fat-free mass)

Other Signs and Symptoms

A. Pursed-lip breathing
B. Use of accessory muscles
C. Tripod position
D. Barrel chest
E. Cyanosis (fingertips, tip of nose, around lips)
F. Tachypnea
G. Tachycardia
H. Difficulty speaking or performing tasks
I. Distended neck veins

J. Abnormal, diminished, or absent lung sounds
K. Mental status changes
L. Anxiety and depression
M. Pulmonary hypertension
N. Cor pulmonale
O. Left-sided heart failure

Subjective Data

A. Ask the patient about past respiratory problems and infections. Does he or she currently have fever, chills, or other signs of infection?
B. Ask about onset of cough and characteristics of sputum (amount, color, and presence of blood).
C. Determine cigar use and cigarette pack-year history (pack/day times the number of years smoked).
D. Inquire about exposure to occupational or environmental irritants.
E. How far can the patient walk before becoming breathless? Is there more breathlessness when the patient walks on a slight incline?
F. Does the patient become breathless or tired when performing activities of daily living (ADL)?
G. Ask about insomnia, anxiety, restlessness, edema, and weight change.
H. How many pillows does the patient sleep on? Does he or she have to sleep in a recliner or sitting up?
I. Assess the patient's ability to perform ADL and instrumental activities of daily living (IADL), including grooming and personal hygiene, performing chores around the house, shopping, cooking, and driving.
J. Ask about alcohol use.
K. Review all medications, including OTC and herbal products.
L. Review further assessment questions based on existing comorbidities.
M. Depression screening

Physical Examination

A. Record temperature (if indicated), blood pressure, pulse, respirations, and pulse oximetry. The respiratory rate increases proportionally to disease severity. Take height and weight to calculate the BMI. **The patient may have a fairly normal examination early in the disease.**
B. Inspect
    1. Observe general appearance: Skin color, affect, posture, gait, amount of respiratory effort when walking; note increased anterior–posterior chest diameter.
    2. Examine sputum: Frothy pink signals pulmonary edema. Hemoptysis as seen in TB.
    3. Examine lips, fingertips, and nose for cyanosis. (Finger clubbing is not characteristic of COPD.)
    4. Observe the neck for distended veins and peripheral edema (advanced disease).
    5. Check for pursed-lip breathing and use of accessory muscles.
C. Auscultate
    1. Auscultate the heart.
    2. Auscultate lungs for wheezes, crackles, decreased breath sounds, and prolonged forced expiratory rate.
    3. Assess for vocal fremitus (vibration) and egophony (increased resonance and high-pitched bleating quality). Air trapping causes air pockets that don't transmit sound well. Absent vesicular lung sounds are a distinctive characteristic of COPD.
    4. Auscultate the carotids.
D. Percuss: Percuss chest for presence of hyperresonance and for signs of consolidation.
E. Palpation
    1. Palpate the neck for lymphadenopathy.
    2. Palpate the chest.
    3. Evaluate abdomen for organomegaly.
    4. Evaluate pedal edema.
F. Mental status: Assess for decreased LOC.
G. Perform 6-minute walking distance (6MWD) testing to evaluate oxygen desaturation.
H. Further physical examinations are dependent on comorbidities.

Diagnostic Tests

A. **Spirometry is the gold standard for diagnosing COPD. PFTs are used to diagnose, determine severity, and follow the disease progression of COPD. Spirometry before and after using bronchodilator.**
    1. FEV_1 is used as an index to airflow obstruction and evaluates the prognosis in emphysema.
    2. FVC
    3. FEV_1/FVC ratios less than 0.70
B. CXR (not required to diagnose COPD but rules out other diagnoses)
C. CBC-evaluate polycythemia due to chronic hypoxia
D. Sputum specimen for culture
E. If the patient is younger than 40 years of age or has a family history of early onset of emphysema, measure AAT levels.
F. Arterial blood gas (ABG) for baseline
G. EKG: Note sinus tachycardia, atrial arrhythmias
H. Two-dimensional echocardiogram is used to evaluate secondary pulmonary hypertension.
I. Chest CT is an alternative imaging study for emphysema; however, it is not required as a diagnostic tool.
J. Perform a purified protein derivative (PPD) test if TB is suspected.
K. Brain natriuretic peptide (BNP)
L. Theophylline level (if applicable)

Differential Diagnoses

A. COPD
B. Asthma
C. Heart failure
D. Bronchiectasis
E. Pulmonary edema
F. TB
G. AAT deficiency
H. Pneumonia
I. Pulmonary embolism
J. CF
K. Cancers
L. Central airway stenosis
M. Panbronchiolitis

Plan

A. General interventions
   1. Educate and encourage active participation in the plan of care, including medication adherence.
   2. A smoking cessation plan is an essential part of a comprehensive treatment plan. Develop a smoking cessation plan; assess readiness to quit. Set a quit date; encourage a group smoking cessation program. **Discuss smoking at every subsequent visit.** (see the Section III Patient Teaching Guide for this chapter, "Nicotine Dependence.")
   3. Advise to stay away from secondhand smoke and limit exposure to other pulmonary irritants, including extreme temperature changes.
   4. Advise exercise with provider approval.
   5. Educate and counsel patients regarding advance directives.
   6. Consider pulmonary rehabilitation for all stages of COPD.
   7. The selection of inhalers is dependent on the patient's age and ability to use the inhaler. Patients should be evaluated as to their coordination and inspiration abilities necessary to use inhalers; otherwise, aerosol medication via nebulizer is the best delivery method.
   8. Have patients bring in their medication/spacers to demonstrate correct use.
   9. Consider group visits for teaching sessions.

B. Patient teaching: See the Section III Patient Teaching Guide for this chapter, "Chronic Obstructive Pulmonary Disease (COPD)."

C. Dietary management
   1. About 25% of COPD patients are malnourished because of coexisting medical conditions, depression, and inability to shop for or prepare food.
   2. Suggest a low-carbohydrate diet. High-carbohydrate intake may increase respiratory work by increasing CO_2 production.

D. **Pharmaceutical therapy: Treatment guidelines are based on spirometry.**

Peak flow meters should not be used to diagnose or monitor COPD.

   1. Stage I (Mild FEV_1 80% or greater)—The patient may be unaware he or she has COPD. Give influenza vaccine and use anticholinergics or SABA bronchodilators as needed.
   2. Stage II (Moderate FEV_1 between 50% and 79%)—Give influenza vaccine, plus SABA bronchodilators as needed, plus long-acting anticholinergics or beta-2 bronchodilator(s) plus cardiopulmonary rehabilitation.
   3. Stage III (Severe FEV_1 between 30% and 49%)—Give influenza vaccine, plus SABA bronchodilators as needed, plus long-acting anticholinergic or beta-2 bronchodilator(s), plus cardiopulmonary rehabilitation, plus inhaled glucocorticoid steroids if patient has repeated exacerbations.
   4. Stage IV (Very Severe FEV_1 less than 30%)—Give influenza vaccine, plus SABA bronchodilator as needed, plus long-acting anticholinergic or beta-2 bronchodilator(s), plus cardiopulmonary rehabilitation, plus inhaled glucocorticoid steroids if repeated exacerbations plus long-term oxygen therapy (if the patient meet criteria for O_2). Medicare guidelines require a patient's PaO_2 to be less than 55 mmHg or his or her resting oxygen saturation to be below 88% on room air.
   5. Utilization of a spacer/holding chamber for inhalers should be encouraged, especially in elderly or those with difficulty activating MDIs.
   6. Administer pneumonia vaccine for patients 65 years and older, or beginning at age 19 if immunocompromised or chronic respiratory condition is present. Consider revaccination every 5 to 10 years for high-risk patients.

Administer yearly flu vaccine. Trivalent influenza vaccine is essential for all COPD patients. Give the patient the vaccine in late September, at least 6 weeks before the flu season.

   7. Prescribe pharmacologic agents/nicotine replacement therapy for smoking cessation.
      a. Nicotine chewing gum produces better quit rates than counseling alone.
      b. Transdermal nicotine patches have a long-term success rate of 22% to 42%.

c. Use of an antidepressant, such as Zyban (150 mg twice a day), has been shown to be effective for smoking cessation and may be used in combination with nicotine replacement therapy.
d. Chantix is a partial agonist selective for alpha-4, beta-2 nicotinic acetylcholine receptors.

8. Antibiotics are not recommended in COPD patients except with acute exacerbation; with symptoms of increased dyspnea, increased sputum volume, and increased sputum purulence; or changes in cough, fever, or other evidence of an infection such as an infiltrate on CXR. Antibiotics are prescribed for COPD patients on mechanical ventilation.
9. Consider phosphodiesterase-4 (PDE-4) inhibitors (roflumilast or cilomilast) as needed when necessary.
10. Mucolytic agents have small benefits and are not usually recommended.
11. Antitussives are not recommended.
12. Long-term oxygen has been shown to increase survival in patients with severe resting hypoxemia. Target oxygen saturation is 88% to 92%.
13. **Cardioselective beta blockers are not contraindicated in COPD. A noncardioselective beta blocker may contribute to bronchospasm.**

Follow-Up

A. For acute exacerbations, follow up same day or following day.
B. Follow up stable, chronic COPD every 1 to 2 months, depending on the patient's needs.
C. Serial PFTs may help guide therapy and offer prognostic information.
D. Monitor serum theophylline levels if theophylline is used. Theophylline has a narrow therapeutic window and the potential for toxicity. Adverse effects including nausea and nervousness are the most common. Other adverse effects include abdominal pain with cramps, anorexia, tremors, insomnia, cardiac arrhythmia, and seizures.
E. Reevaluate patients on oxygen therapy in 1 to 3 months after starting oxygen.
F. Evaluate for osteoporosis; bone mineral density is lower in COPD patients, and they are at risk for vertebral fractures.
G. Monitor the patient's body weight.

Consultation/Referral

A. Consult with a physician if the patient has acute respiratory decompensation, severe cor pulmonale (distended neck veins, hepatomegaly, dependent peripheral edema, ascites, and pleural effusion).
B. Refer the patient to a pulmonary specialist for rehabilitation, if available.
   1. Outpatient education for the patient and family
   2. Exercise training
   3. Breathing retraining, that is, pursed-lip breathing, huff coughing
   4. Correct administration of medications
C. Refer to a registered dietitian (RD) to provide medical nutrition therapy (MNT). RDs focus on the prevention and treatment of weight loss associated with COPD and other comorbidities.
D. Send to a pulmonologist for evaluation for continuous positive airway pressure (CPAP) or bi-level positive airway pressure (BiPAP).
E. Send to a pulmonologist to evaluate for surgical intervention such as bullectomy, lung volume reduction surgery, or lung transplantation.

Individual Considerations

A. Pregnancy
   1. COPD is rare except in AAT deficiency.
   2. Monitor drug treatment for potential teratogenic effects.
B. Adults: Sexual dysfunction is common in patients with COPD; encourage other ways to display affection.
C. Geriatrics
   1. Presentation may be atypical.
   2. Patients should have annual flu vaccinations and pneumococcal vaccination every 5 years (according to adult immunization guidelines).
   3. Patients may not have the ability to use inhaler devices due to tremors, muscle weakness, poor hand–eye coordination, and/or poor memory.
   4. Theophylline is on the Beers list of drugs to use with caution in the geriatric population related to cardiovascular, renal, hepatic, insomnia, peptic ulcers, and drug–drug interactions.
   5. Discuss the course of disease, living wills, advanced directives, and resuscitation status early, before a crisis occurs.

Resource

Global Initiative for Chronic Obstructive Lung Disease (GOLD) guidelines: www.goldcopd.org

Common Cold/Upper Respiratory Infection

Definition

A. The common cold is a self-limiting acute respiratory tract infection (ARTI) resulting from viral infection of the upper respiratory tract. It is also called acute nasopharyngitis. ARTI is characterized by mild coryzal symptoms, rhinorrhea, nasal obstruction, and sneezing.

Incidence

A. Upper respiratory tract infections are among the most frequent reasons for office visits. However, the true incidence is not known because patients treat themselves with OTC and home remedies, as well as the seasonal and geographic variability. Most adults have two to four colds a year.

Pathogenesis

A. Over 25% to 80% of ARTIs are caused by a rhinovirus (> 100 antigenic serotypes). Other viral agents include coronavirus (10%–20%), RSV, adenoviruses (5%), influenza viruses (10%–15%), and parainfluenza viruses. Incubation period is 1 to 5 days with viral shedding lasting up to 2 weeks.
B. Rhinoviral infections are chiefly limited to the upper respiratory tract but may cause otitis media and sinusitis.

Predisposing Factors

A. Exposure to airborne droplets
B. Direct contact with virus by touching hands or skin of infected people, or by touching surfaces they touched and then touching eyes or nose
C. Very young or old ages
D. Smoking, which increases risk by 50%
E. Crowded conditions such as long-term care facilities and college dormitories

Common Complaints

A. Low-grade fever
B. Generalized malaise
C. Nasal congestion and discharge (initially clear, then yellow and thick)
D. Sneezing
E. Sore throat or hoarseness
F. Watery and/or inflamed eyes

Other Signs and Symptoms

A. Headache
B. Cough

Subjective Data

A. Elicit the onset, course, and duration of symptoms.
B. Inquire about color and other characteristics of nasal discharge and sputum. **Purulent nasal discharge after 14 days signals bacterial sinusitis.**
C. Inquire about other discomforts and exposure to people with similar symptoms.
D. Review allergens, seasonal problems, and exposure to irritants and smoke.
E. Review history for other respiratory problems, such as asthma, chronic bronchitis, and emphysema.

Physical Examination

A. Check temperature, pulse, respirations, and blood pressure. Check pulse oximetry if difficult respiratory symptoms are noted.
B. Inspect
   1. Observe general appearance.
   2. Inspect eyes. Note "allergic shiners," tearing, and eyelid swelling.
   3. Observe ears, throat, and mouth. Otitis media is indicated by redness and bulging of tympanic membrane, or by membrane perforation with drainage.
   4. Inspect nose for nasal redness, swelling, polyps, enlarged turbinates, septal deviation, and foreign bodies.
   5. Transilluminate sinuses.
      a. Group A streptococci: Tonsillar enlargement, exudates, palatine petechiae
      b. Allergies: "Cobblestoned" pharyngeal mucosa
      c. Mononucleosis: About half of patients with mononucleosis develop tonsillar exudates, and about one third develop petechiae at the junction of the hard and soft palate, which is highly suggestive of the disease.
C. Auscultate
   1. Auscultate all lung fields.
   2. Auscultate heart.
D. Percuss
   1. Percuss sinus cavities and mastoid process of temporal bone to rule out otitis media.
   2. Percuss chest for consolidation.
E. Palpate
   1. Palpate face for sinus tenderness.
   2. Examine head and neck for enlarged, tender lymph nodes.

Diagnostic Tests

A. Diagnosis may be made from history and physical. Because common cold manifestations are so prevalent, an aggressive workup is rarely necessary.
B. Consider rapid strep test if the patient has symptoms or was exposed to Group A streptococcus.
C. Consider throat culture if the patient has negative rapid strep and is symptomatic.
D. Consider testing for influenzas A and B

Differential Diagnoses

A. Upper respiratory infection
B. Allergic rhinitis
C. Foreign body
D. Sinusitis
E. Influenza
F. Group A strep pharyngitis
G. Otitis media
H. Pneumonia
I. Acute bronchitis

Plan

A. General interventions: No specific treatment.

B. Controlled trials reveal minimal therapeutic benefits of vitamin C for the treatment and prevention of colds. Zinc has no proven benefit. Echinacea has not shown any differences in rates of infection or severity of symptoms when compared with placebo. Validation and standardization of herbal products have not been completed.
C. Patient teaching: See the Section III Patient Teaching Guide for this chapter, "Common Cold."
D. Pharmaceutical therapy
   1. **The American College of Chest Physicians released clinical practice guidelines in 2006 for the management of cough.**
   2. **Antibiotics are ineffective in treating viral infection.**
   3. Corticosteroids may actually increase viral replication and have no impact on cold symptoms.
   4. Topical decongestants for rhinorrhea and nasal congestion
      a. Intranasal ipratropium bromide 0.06% two sprays, each nostril, three to four times daily
      b. Intranasal cromolyn sodium one spray, each nostril, three to four times daily
      c. Pseudoephedrine (Afrin) nasal spray 0.05% two to three sprays per nostril twice daily, or phenylephrine (Neo-Synephrine) nasal spray 0.25% to 1% two to three sprays per nostril every 4 hours as needed. Limit use to 3 to 4 days maximum.
   5. Oral decongestants such as pseudoephedrine (Sudafed) have no proven benefits, and the side effects can be problematic in the elderly.
   6. Analgesics, such as acetaminophen (Tylenol) and ibuprofen (Advil), may be used for headache relief.
   7. Cough suppressants are not recommended, as side effects outweigh benefits.
   8. Colds have no allergic mechanism, so antihistamines are ineffective. The atropine-like drying effect from antihistamines may exacerbate congestion and obstruct the upper airway by impairing mucus flow.

Follow-Up

A. None is recommended unless symptoms persist longer than 7 days from onset or the patient develops symptoms of lower respiratory infection.

Consultation/Referral

A. Consult a physician if the patient has been reevaluated and given a new treatment plan but still has symptoms.
B. Make a same-day referral to an otolaryngologist if tonsillar abscess is suspected.

Individual Considerations

A. Adolescents: May use dextromethorphan as a recreational drug with potential for abuse
B. Elderly: Potential benefits from cold preparations do not outweigh the risks.

Cough

Definition

A. Coughing is a mechanism that clears the airway of secretions and inhaled particles. The act of coughing has the potential to traumatize the upper airway (e.g., vocal cords). A chronic cough is one that lasts longer than 8 weeks.
B. Because coughing can be an effective behavior, psychological issues must be considered as a cause or effect of coughing.

Incidence

A. Data on the incidence of coughing is not available. However, most healthy people do not cough, and the main reason for coughing is airway clearance. A chronic cough is the most common presenting symptoms in adults who seek medical treatment in an ambulatory setting.
B. The incidence of pertussis is increasing in adults secondary to the lack of booster vaccination.

Pathogenesis

A. Stimulation of mucosal neural receptors in the nasopharynx, ears, larynx, trachea, and bronchi can produce a cough, as can acute inflammation and/or irritation of the respiratory tract. Cough is a reflex response that is mediated by the medulla but is subject to voluntary control. There is clear evidence that vagal afferent nerves regulate involuntary coughing.
B. Pertussis (whooping cough) is caused by the bacterium *B. pertussis*.
C. The **pathogenic triad of chronic cough** responsible for 92% to 100% of chronic cough is as follows.
   1. Upper airway cough syndrome (UACS), previously referred to as postnasal drip syndrome
   2. Asthma
   3. GERD

Predisposing Factors

A. Pharyngeal irritants
B. Foreign-body aspiration
C. TB (persons in prisons and nursing homes and immigrants from endemic areas of TB)
D. Psychogenic factors
E. Mediastinal or pulmonary masses
F. CHF

G. CF
H. Congenital malformations
I. Viral bronchitis
J. Asthma (sole symptom in 28%)
K. Mycoplasma infection
L. Upper airways cough syndrome, previously referred to as postnasal drip
M. Chronic sinusitis
N. Allergic rhinitis
O. Environmental irritants
P. GERD
Q. Chronic bronchitis
R. Pulmonary edema
S. Medications, including ACE inhibitors
T. Impacted cerumen and external otitis
U. Nonasthmatic eosinophilic bronchitis (NAEB, 13%–33%)

Common Complaints

A. Common complaint is a cough that interferes with ADL and sleeping, leading to a decrease in a patient's QOL.
B. The pertussis cough is uncontrollable and violent. Following coughing, a "whooping" sound follows with a deep breath.

Other Signs and Symptoms

A. Fatigue
B. Rhinitis
C. Epistaxis
D. Tickle in throat
E. Pharyngitis
F. Night sweats
G. Dyspnea
H. Fever
I. Sputum production
J. Hoarseness

Subjective Data

A. Elicit information about onset, duration, and course of the cough. Was onset recent or gradual? Does the cough occur at night? **Nocturnal cough may be caused by chronic interstitial pulmonary edema and may signal left-sided heart failure. Cough caused by asthma is also worse at night. Morning cough with sputum suggests bronchitis.**
B. Inquire about the cough's characteristics. For example, is it productive, dry, bronchospastic, brassy, wheezy, strong, or weak? If it is productive, is it bloody or mucoid? What are the color, consistency, odor, and amount of sputum or mucus? Dry, irritative cough suggests viral respiratory infection. Severe or changing cough should be evaluated for bronchogenic carcinoma. Rusty-colored sputum suggests bacterial pneumonia. Green or very purulent sputum is due to degeneration of white cells. HIV cough also produces purulent sputum.
C. Inquire whether the cough is associated with eating and choking episodes. Wheezing or stridor with coughing may indicate a foreign body or aspiration.
D. Ask whether the cough is associated with postnasal drip, which produces a chronic cough, clear sputum, edematous nasal mucosa, and a "cobblestoned" pharyngeal mucosa.
E. Find out if the cough is associated with heartburn or a sour taste in the mouth, indicating GERD.
F. **Ask about precipitating factors, such as exercise, cold air, or laughing. Also ask about alleviating factors. Cough from asthma can be triggered or exacerbated by exposure to environmental irritants, allergens, cold, or exercise.**
G. Ask about current and previous work. Is the patient exposed to occupational and environmental irritants, such as dust, fumes, or gases? If so, what are the type, level, and duration of exposures?
H. Ask about family history of respiratory illness, such as CF or asthma.
I. Is the patient a smoker? If so, how much does he or she smoke, and how long has he or she smoked? Is he or she exposed to secondhand smoke? How much of the day? **Smoking is the main cause of chronic cough.**
J. Find out the date of the patient's last tuberculin skin test. Note recent exposure to TB.
K. Inquire about any exposure to the flu.
L. Does the patient have a history of heart problems?
M. Does the patient have a history of respiratory problems or other medical problems? Chronic bronchitis is a major cause of chronic cough and sputum production. Cough may also be an early sign of lung cancer; in late stages, cough occurs along with weight loss, anorexia, and dyspnea.
N. Review medications such as ACE inhibitors. Cough related to ACE inhibitors usually subsides within 2 weeks, but the median time is up to 26 days.
O. Weight loss or worsening dyspnea?
P. Exposure to TB (confined living conditions? Incarceration?)
Q. Ask about pain in back or bony skeleton.

Physical Examination

A. Record temperature, blood pressure, and weight. Compare previous changes in weight.
B. Inspect
   1. Observe general appearance for cyanosis, difficulty breathing, use of axillary muscles, and finger clubbing.
   2. Examine ears, nose, and throat.
C. Auscultate: Auscultate heart and lungs.

D. Percuss
  1. Percuss sinus cavities and mastoid process.
  2. Percuss chest and lungs for consolidation.
E. Palpate
  1. Palpate face for sinus tenderness.
  2. Examine head and neck for lymph nodes, masses, and jugular vein distension (JVD).

Diagnostic Tests

Testing can be held to a minimum by careful review of history and physical exam.

A. White blood cell (WBC) if infection suspected
B. HIV test if suspected
C. Sputum for eosinophils, Gram stain, and/or culture
D. Mantoux test if indicated
E. CXR
F. Pulmonary function testing/spirometry
G. Methacholine challenge to rule out asthma
H. Esophageal pH monitoring to rule out GERD
I. CT with consideration of contrast scan if necessary (radiologist may need to determine)

Differential Diagnoses

A. Environmental irritants
  1. Cigarette, cigar, or pipe smoking
  2. Pollutants (wood smoke, smog, burning leaves, etc.)
  3. Dust
  4. Lack of humidity
  5. Chemical exposure in home or workplace, including illicit substances
B. Lower respiratory tract problems
  1. Lung cancer
  2. Asthma
  3. Chronic obstructive lung disease (includes bronchitis)
  4. Interstitial lung disease
  5. CHF
  6. Pneumonitis
  7. Bronchiectasis
  8. Foreign body or aspiration
  9. Tracheal-esophageal fistula
  10. Pulmonary embolism
  11. Pulmonary edema
  12. Pneumonia
C. Upper respiratory tract problems
  1. Chronic rhinitis
  2. Chronic sinusitis
  3. Disease of external auditory canal
  4. Pharyngitis
D. Medication-induced cough from ACE inhibitors
E. Extrinsic compression lesions
  1. Adenopathy
  2. Malignancy
  3. Aortic aneurysm
F. Psychogenic factors
G. Gastrointestinal problems such as reflux esophagitis
H. Genetic problems such as CF

Plan

A. General intervention: If sputum is purulent, obtain a sample for examination.
B. Patients with COPD and CF should be taught huffing as an adjunct to other methods of sputum clearance.
C. Patient teaching: See the Section III Patient Teaching Guide for this chapter, "Cough."
D. Pharmaceutical therapy
  1. The risk of cough suppressants outweighs the benefits of use.
  2. Antibiotics should not be prescribed for coughs unless a bacterial infection is suspected.
  3. Therapy depends on various acute inflammatory and chronic irritating processes and on cause of cough. Refer to applicable sections of this chapter, such as "Asthma" and "Tuberculosis," and see Chapter 13, "Gastrointestinal Guidelines."
  4. Inhaled or oral antihistamines could be considered if cough is related to allergic rhinitis. Potential side effects versus benefits should be considered, especially in the elderly.

Follow-Up

A. The patient with a normal CXR and no risk factors for lung cancer (e.g., smoking or occupational exposure) can be followed expectantly without further testing.
B. In patients whose cough resolves after the cessation of ACE inhibitors, and for whom there is a compelling reason to treat with these agents, a repeat trial of ACE inhibitors may be attempted.
C. See applicable sections for specific diagnoses.
D. Pertussis vaccination should be administered to all adults according to CDC adult vaccine guidelines. Pertussis cases should be reported to the local health department.

Consultation/Referral

A. Consult a physician if symptoms persist after treatment. Reevaluate patient in 2 weeks if he or she is no better.
B. When a cough lasts more than 2 weeks without another apparent cause and it is accompanied by paroxysms of coughing, post-tussive vomiting, and/or an inspiratory whooping sound, the diagnosis of a *B. pertussis* infection should be made unless another diagnosis is proven.
C. Patients whose condition remains undiagnosed after a workup and therapy may need referral to a cough specialist.

Individual Considerations

A. Pregnancy: Cough may be an early symptom of pulmonary edema. Watch intrapartum patients for signs of edema.
B. Adolescents: Dextromethorphan has been associated with abuse potential.
C. Elderly: The risk of side effects from OTC cough suppressants should be discussed with the patient.

Dyspnea

Definition

A. Dyspnea occurs when a patient experiences any level of breathing discomfort. The symptom is often associated with pulmonary disorders and cardiac ischemia and is a significant predictor of mortality. The risk of experiencing dyspnea increases with age. Up to 37% of people older than the age of 70 experience dyspnea. Treatment is directed at identifying and managing the underlying pathologic concern.

Incidence

A. Dyspnea affects up to one half of patients seen in hospitals and up to one fourth of patients seeking outpatient care.
B. Millions of patients living at home experience chronic dyspnea related to pulmonary and cardiac morbidities.
C. Between 3 and 4 million emergency room visits annually are due to some level of dyspnea.
D. Dyspnea is associated with cardiovascular disease (leading cause of death in the United States) and pulmonary disease (asthma and COPD, affecting more than 25 million).

Pathogenesis

A. Respiration is controlled by peripheral chemoreceptors in the carotid bodies and aortic arch, and central chemoreceptors in the medulla.
B. Chemoreceptors are stimulated by a drop in partial pressure of oxygen in arterial blood, a drop in pH, and a change in pCO_2 levels.
C. Additional receptors play a role in maintaining oxygenation including mechanoreceptors in the upper airway, pulmonary receptors, and chest wall receptors.
D. Breathing discomfort occurs when a patient recognizes hypoxia and hypercapnia. Dyspnea is experienced due to physical, psychologic, social, and environmental factors.
E. In order for adequate gas exchange to occur, oxygen must reach the alveoli from the environment. If any part of the airway is compromised, including the alveolar beds, the process is dysfunctional to some degree.
F. In addition to intact respiratory receptors and a clear airway for gas exchange, the act of breathing also requires muscular strength and adequate hemoglobin levels to transport oxygen.

Predisposing Factors

A. Asthma
B. COPD
C. Interstitial lung disease
D. Cardiovascular disease
E. Deconditioning/obesity

Common Complaints

A. Difficulty breathing or the sensation of "air hunger"
B. Change in respiratory pattern
C. Potential wheezing
D. Weakness
E. Fatigue
F. Functional disability

Other Signs and Symptoms

A. Chest tightness
B. Rapid or shallow breathing
C. Breathing feels "heavy"
D. Chronic dyspnea is associated with depression
E. Severe, acute dyspnea is associated with a sensation of impending death
F. Headache
G. Anorexia

Potential Complications

A. Hypoxemia
B. pH imbalance
C. Cardiac dysrhythmias

Subjective Data

A. Determine the onset, duration, and course of dyspnea.
B. Determine if any SABA (rescue) inhaler was used, the name, quantity used, and when last used.
C. Establish medical history, including pulmonary, cardiac, neuromuscular, or hematologic impairments.
D. Determine smoking history, including inhalation of illicit substances (methamphetamines).
E. Rate the degree of dyspnea on a dyspnea scale.
F. Ask patient to list all medications currently being taken, including oral or aerosolized herbal products.
G. Ask about exposures to caustic substances, including fumes, smoke, carbon monoxide in the home or workplace, and occupational exposures to inhaled toxins.
H. Is there associated cough or wheezing?
I. Pain in chest wall, mental confusion, or extreme fatigue?
J. Determine if there is a history of anxiety or panic episodes.
K. Consider if the patient has established advance directives and made any change from previous directives.

Physical Examination

A. Check temperature (if applicable), blood pressure, pulse, pulse oximetry, LOC, and ability to speak in complete sentences without obvious air hunger.
B. Inspect
   1. Inspect general appearance, noting degree of dyspnea, respiratory pattern.
   2. Check trachea for deviations.
   3. Inspect for use of accessory muscles of breathing.
   4. Inspect skin for pallor, cyanosis, bruising, open wounds, and turgor.
   5. Inspect facial features for fear or lethargy.
   6. Inspect legs for edema.
   7. Capillary refill
C. Palpate
   1. Palpate chest wall for tenderness/injury.
   2. Palpate radial and peripheral pulses for amplitude and rhythm.
   3. Palpate chest wall for crepitus.
D. Auscultate
   1. Cardiac for rhythm, S3/S4
   2. Lungs in all fields for adventitious sounds
   3. Abdomen for distension

Diagnostic Tests

A. EKG: Shows inverted T waves, ST segment elevation, and Q waves. One normal EKG initially does not always rule out MI; perform serial EKGs if MI suspected.
B. ABG
C. Chest x-ray
D. CBC with differential
E. Comprehensive metabolic panel (glucose, electrolytes, renal and hepatic functions)
F. BNP
G. Thyroid-stimulating hormone (TSH)
H. PFTs

Differential Diagnosis

A. Acute myocardial infarction
B. Pulmonary embolus
C. Aortic dissection
D. Pneumothorax
E. Poisoning (secondary to inhaled elicit substances or unintentional: Carbon monoxide)
F. Asthma, uncontrolled
G. COPD exacerbation
H. Pulmonary fibrosis
I. Pulmonary edema
J. Neuromuscular dysfunction
K. Respiratory suppression secondary to medication overdose
L. Anemia
M. Anxiety/panic episode
N. Developing pregnancy with gravid uterus
O. End-stage heart failure
P. Pulmonary hypertension
Q. Lung cancer
R. Progression of morbid obesity and deconditioning
S. Aspiration or foreign body

Plan

A. Patient teaching
   1. Educate patient about modifying controllable risk factors for pulmonary and cardiovascular disease. Smoking cessation should be addressed at each patient encounter.
   2. Discuss the benefits of cardiovascular exercise.
   3. The treatment of dyspnea is determined by the underlying etiology.
   4. If coronary heart disease (CHD) is present:
      a. Make sure patient is aware of signs and symptoms of MI.
      b. Make sure patient knows to seek medical attention or dial 911 if signs and symptoms occur.
      c. Encourage cardiopulmonary resuscitation (CPR) training for family and/or close friends.
      d. Patient should carry nitroglycerin at all times and know how to use it.
B. Dietary management: If applicable, counsel patient on benefits of weight loss to comfort of breathing. Encourage well-balanced meals and adequate fluid intake.
C. Pharmaceutical therapy
   1. Oxygen should be delivered based on patient status. For conscious patients in outpatient settings, oxygen is most effectively delivered through a nonrebreather mask. The Hypoxic Drive is not a consideration for limiting oxygenation in acute emergencies.
   2. When MI is suspected: Aspirin 160 to 325 mg (four 81 mg baby aspirin) chewed or swallowed as soon as possible. Enteric-coated aspirin delays absorption and therefore is not recommended.
   3. For bronchodilatation a SABA should be delivered by inhaler or nebulization.
   4. Further intervention must be under the direction of a clinician after a full evaluation.

Follow-Up

A. Follow-up is determined by the patient's condition and primary diagnosis. Timely follow-up is essential and is based on individual patient considerations. In elderly who live alone, next day follow-up should be considered if the patient will not be hospitalized.

Consultation/Referral

A. **If you suspect MI as the cause of dyspnea, refer patient through emergency medical services (EMS) for immediate emergency department evaluation.**
B. **For suspected pulmonary emboli or dissecting aneurysms, patients should be transported by EMS.**

C. Consultation for chronic dyspnea with a pulmonologist if lung disorder
D. Consultation with appropriate specialist if cardiac, neuromuscular, or hematologic disorder
E. Referral to pulmonary and/or cardiac rehabilitation services
F. Referral to medical supply company if long-term oxygen or assistive devices needed
G. Referral to occupational therapy for functional rehabilitation

Individual Considerations

A. Pregnancy
   1. For optimal oxygenation, patients with a gravid uterus should be placed on their left side while they are receiving supplemental oxygen.
   2. Obstetric referral is recommended for significant dyspnea during pregnancy.
   3. Control of asthma or any chronic lung disorder is crucial as the mother must maintain adequate oxygenation to sustain the fetus.
B. Adolescents
   1. Consideration should be made to risk-taking and use of illicit substances.
   2. Smoking prevention
C. Geriatrics
   1. Frailty is a risk marker for morbidity and mortality for all causes of dyspnea.
   2. Adult vaccination guidelines (CDC) should be followed for prevention.
   3. The primary care provider should be aware of the patient's choices in worsening dyspnea. Advance directives should be available on the outpatient medical record.
   4. Consideration for hospice or palliative care services should be recommended to support the patient and family early in the course of chronic illness.

Emphysema

Definition

A. Emphysema is an abnormal dilation and destruction of alveolar ducts and airspaces distal to the terminal bronchioles. Lung function slowly deteriorates over many years before the illness develops. Emphysema is one of the COPDs—a term that refers to conditions characterized by continued increased resistance to expiratory airflow. Chronic bronchitis, emphysema, and asthma comprise COPD. Chronic bronchitis and emphysema with airflow obstruction commonly occur together.
B. There are three morphological types of emphysema.
   1. Centriacinar emphysema: Associated with long-term smoking; primarily involves the upper half of the lungs.
   2. Panacinar emphysema found predominantly in the lower half of the lungs. Panacinar emphysema is observed in patients with AAT deficiency.
   3. Paraseptal emphysema involves the distal airway.

Incidence

A. Emphysema typically occurs in people older than age 50, with peak occurrence after the age of 65.
B. The prevalence of emphysema is 20.2 cases per 1,000.
C. The prevalence is greater in Caucasians than other ethnicities.
D. Emphysema is slightly greater in females (21.4/1,000) than males (19.0/1,000).

Pathogenesis

A. Decreased gas exchange occurs due to focal destruction limited to the airspaces distal to the respiratory bronchioles, causing airway obstruction, hyperinflation, loss of lung recoil, and destruction of alveolar–capillary interface.

Predisposing Factors

A. Long-term cigarette smoking
B. Occupational and environmental exposure to toxic agents
   1. Dust
   2. Chemical fumes
   3. Secondhand smoke
   4. Air pollution
   5. Gases
C. Alpha 1-protease inhibitor deficiency
D. Intravenous drug use secondary to pulmonary vascular damage from the insoluble fillers (e.g., cornstarch, cotton fibers, cellulose, talc)
E. Connective tissue disorders (e.g., Marfan syndrome and Ehlers-Danlos)
F. HIV

Common Complaints

A. Gradually progressing exertional dyspnea
B. Chronic cough
C. Wheezing
D. Fatigue
E. Weight loss

Other Signs and Symptoms

A. Cough with mild to moderate sputum production and clear to mucoid sputum
B. Early-morning cough
C. SOB
D. Tachypnea
E. Use of accessory muscles for breathing; pursed-lip breathing; *prolonged* expiration
F. Barrel chest (increased anterior to posterior chest diameter)
G. Flushed skin

H. Clubbed fingers
I. Decreased libido
J. Thin, wasted appearance
K. Wheezing, particularly during exertion and exacerbations of emphysema
L. Functional impairment related to dyspnea
M. Depression

Subjective Data

A. Elicit information about onset, duration, and course of symptoms.
B. Determine if the patient is a smoker. If so, how much and for how long? Evaluate exposure to secondhand smoke. How much of the day?
C. Ask about current and previous work. Is the patient exposed to occupational and environmental irritants, such as dust, fumes, or gases? If so, what are the type, level, and duration of exposures?
D. Inquire about the cough's characteristics. Is it productive, dry, bronchospastic, brassy, wheezy, strong, or weak?
E. Question the patient about episodes of tachypnea, frequency of respiratory infections, and incidence of angina during exertion.
F. Does the patient have a hereditary disease (e.g., CF or AAT deficiency), asthma, nasal abnormalities (e.g., deviated septum), or other respiratory problems?
G. When was his or her last tuberculin skin test and risk for TB exposure?
H. Find out the patient's usual weight, and assess how much weight loss has occurred and over what time period.
I. Evaluate current vaccination status for pneumonia and influenza.
J. Review all medications, including OTC and herbal products.
K. Assess the patient's ability to perform ADL and IADL, including grooming and personal hygiene, performing chores around the home, shopping, cooking, and driving.
L. Ask about alcohol use.
M. Screen for depression
N. Ask about frequency of use of SABA.

Physical Examination

A. Temperature (if indicated), pulse, respirations, blood pressure, and weight for changes. Consider pulse oximetry.
B. Inspect
    1. Observe general appearance; note flushed skin color, use of accessory muscles, pallor around lips, pursed-lip breathing, barrel chest (lung hyperinflation), and thinness.
    2. Assess for peripheral edema.
    3. Dermal examination: Note finger clubbing and cyanosis.
    4. Observe mental status and psychiatric concerns including depression
C. Auscultate
    1. Auscultate heart.
    2. Auscultate lungs for wheezes, crackles, decreased breath sounds (generally diffuse decreased breath sound).
    3. Assess for vocal fremitus (vibration) and egophony (increased resonance and high-pitch bleating quality). Air trapping causes air pockets that don't transmit sound well.
D. Percuss: Percuss chest for presence of hyperresonance and signs of consolidation.
E. Palpate
    1. Palpate abdomen.
    2. Evaluate pedal edema.
    3. Evaluate the abdomen for organomegaly.
F. Further physical examinations are dependent on comorbidities.

Diagnostic Tests

A. Pulse oximetry: Blood gases if indicated. Baseline should be considered as early in disease process as patient presents.
B. AAT to rule out hereditary deficiency
C. Tuberculin skin test
D. **PFTs reveal increased total lung capacity with poor respiratory expulsion and increased respiratory volume.**
E. EKG reveals sinus or supraventricular tachycardia.
F. CXR reveals hyperinflation, flat diaphragm, and enlarged heart.
G. Sputum evaluation and/or culture

Differential Diagnoses

A. Emphysema
B. Chronic bronchitis
C. Chronic asthma
D. Bronchiectasis
E. CF
F. Chronic asthmatic bronchitis
G. TB
H. AAT deficiency
I. CHF

Plan

A. Medical management: Supplemental oxygen therapy is indicated if the patient has a resting PaO_2 less than 55 mmHg or a PaO_2 less than 60 mmHg, along with right heart failure or secondary polycythemia. Goals are to achieve a PaO_2 of greater than 55 mmHg (usually 1–3 L/min).
B. Patient teaching: See the Section III Patient Teaching Guide for this chapter, "Emphysema."

C. Develop a smoking-cessation plan: Assess readiness to quit. Set a quit date, and encourage a group smoking-cessation program. A smoking-cessation plan is an essential part of a comprehensive treatment plan.
   1. Nicotine chewing gum produces better quit rates than counseling alone.
   2. Transdermal nicotine patches have a long-term success rate of 22% to 42%.
   3. The use of an antidepressant such as Zyban (150 mg twice a day) has been shown to be effective for smoking cessation and may be used in combination with nicotine replacement therapy.
   4. Chantix is a partial agonist selective for alpha-4, beta-2 nicotinic acetylcholine receptors.

D. Pharmaceutical therapy
   1. Drugs of choice are inhaled beta-2 agonist and anticholinergics. Beta-2 agonists are used primarily for relief of symptoms and, in stable patients, have an additive effect when used with an anticholinergic agent (e.g., ipratropium bromide). A spacer/chamber device should be used to improve delivery and reduce adverse effects. The following inhaled preparations have rapid action and fewer cardiac side effects:
      a. Ipratropium bromide (Atrovent) has bronchodilatory activity with minimum side effects.
         i. MDI: Two to four puffs every 4 to 6 hours
         ii. Nebulizer: 250 mcg diluted with 2.5 mL normal saline every 4 to 6 hours
      b. Tiotropium (Spiriva) is a bronchodilator similar to Ipratropium. Available in a capsule form containing a dry powder or oral inhalation via HandiHaler inhalation device. Adults: One capsule (18 mcg) inhaled every day via the inhaler device.
      c. Metaproterenol sulfate (Alupent) is available as a liquid for nebulizer and MDI.
         i. MDI: Two puffs every 3 to 4 hours
         ii. Nebulizer: 0.2 to 0.3 mL of 5% solution diluted to 2.5 mL with normal saline three to four times a day
      d. Albuterol (Proventil, Ventolin) is available as a liquid for nebulizer, MDI, and DPI.
         i. MDI: One to four puffs every 3 to 4 hours
         ii. Nebulizer: 0.2 to 0.3 mL of 5% solution diluted to 2.5 mL with normal saline three to four times a day
   2. If improvement is not satisfactory or tachyphylaxis occurs, consider trial of theophylline. Theophylline improves respiratory muscle function and stimulates the respiratory center as well as bronchodilates.
      a. Initial dose: 10 mg/kg daily divided in oral doses every 8 to 12 hours
      b. Maintenance: 10 mg/kg daily divided in oral doses every day or twice a day. Adjust doses in 25% increments to maintain serum theophylline level of 5 to 15 mcg/mL; not to exceed 800 mg/d.
   3. Oral steroids should be used to treat outpatients with acute exacerbations. Corticosteroids reduce mucosal edema, inhibit prostaglandins that cause bronchoconstriction, and increase responsiveness to bronchodilators. Taper dose as soon as bronchospasm is controlled. A minority of patients who respond to oral steroids can be maintained on long-term inhaled steroids.
   4. In patients with COPD, chronic infection or colonization of the lower airways is common. The goal of antibiotic therapy is not to eliminate organisms, but to treat acute exacerbations. If infection is present, give one of the following.
      a. Augmentin 500 mg orally twice daily
      b. Doxycycline 100 mg orally twice daily
      c. Trimethoprim-sulfamethoxazole 80 to 160 mg orally every 12 hours
      d. If pseudomonas is considered: Levofloxacin 500 mg daily
   5. Mucolytic agents in clinical practice are not recommended currently because of a lack of evidence for their benefit.
   6. Trivalent influenza vaccine is essential for all COPD patients. Give the patient the vaccine each mid-September, at least 6 weeks before onset of flu season.
   7. Pneumococcal vaccine is essential for COPD patients. Give as a single intramuscular injection of 0.5 mL.
   8. AAT is needed for significant antitrypsin deficiency (less than 80 mg/dL). Patients get weekly or monthly infusions. Consult with a physician before therapy. A history of smoking rules out candidacy.

Follow-Up

A. If the patient is acute, contact by phone in 24 to 48 hours and consider immediate referral.

B. Monitor the patient's body weight.

C. Serial PFTs may help guide therapy and offer prognostic information.

D. Monitor theophylline levels because of the drug's potential for toxicity. Adverse effects, including nausea and nervousness, are the most common. Other adverse effects include abdominal pain with cramps, anorexia, tremors, insomnia, cardiac arrhythmia, and seizures. Theophylline doses: 100 to 200 mg every 6 to 8 hours.

Consultation/Referral

A. If the patient's condition remains acute after 48 hours of treatment, consider immediate referral to a physician.
B. Refer the patient to a social worker for help in getting Meals on Wheels, handicapped parking, and finding other community resources.
C. A consultation with a pulmonary specialist is recommended.

Individual Considerations

A. Adults: Sexual dysfunction is common in patients with COPD; encourage other ways to display affection.
B. Geriatrics
   1. Discuss course of disease, living wills, advanced directives, and resuscitation status early, before a crisis occurs.
   2. Theophylline is on the Beers list of drugs to use with caution in the geriatric population related to cardiovascular, renal, hepatic, insomnia, and peptic ulcers.

Resources

A patient's guide to aerosol drug delivery is available at www.aarc.org/headlines/10/11/patient aerosol/Patient_aerosol_guide.pdf

Global Initiative for Chronic Obstructive Lung Disease (GOLD) guidelines: www.goldcopd.org

Guide to aerosol devices for physicians, nurses, pharmacists, and other health care professionals is available at aarc.org/resources/aersol_nnrts.pdf

National Emphysema Foundation: www.emphysemafoundation.org

H1N1 Influenza A (Swine Flu)

Definition

A. H1N1 influenza A, swine flu, is an influenza A virus that causes a highly contagious respiratory disease. H1N1 has been reported worldwide and was designated a phase 6 global pandemic status by the World Health Organization (WHO) in 2009.
B. Persons with flulike symptoms should promptly contact their health care providers. If an antiviral is warranted, it should ideally be started within 48 hours from the onset of symptoms. Viral pneumonia is the primary sign of clinical deterioration.

Incidence

A. The WHO declared the 2009 H1N1 pandemic over as of August 2010. However, this strain of flu still continues to circulate with other seasonal flu strains.

Pathogenesis

A. H1N1 is a new subtype of influenza A (A/H1N1) virus that is spread by human-to-human transmission. The swine flu is also transmitted by pig to person; however, persons cannot be infected with the H1N1 virus from consuming pork.
B. The primary mode of spread is through exposure to viral strain respiratory secretions from respiratory droplets (coughing or sneezing) and direct contact with contaminated surfaces. H1N1 can also be spread through contaminated diarrhea stools.
C. The infectious period is considered to be 1 day prior to the onset of fever until 24 hours after fever ends.

Predisposing Factors

A. Age
   1. Adults 25 to 64 years who have medical conditions that place them at high risk for influenza-related complications
   2. Adults age 65 years or older
B. Pregnant women
C. Women up to 2 weeks postpartum
D. Crowded conditions
E. Institutions such as nursing homes
F. Occupational exposure: Teachers and health care workers

Common Complaints

A. Clinical manifestations of H1N1 influenza depend on the age and previous experience with the influenza virus. Rapid onset respiratory illness is the most common complaint.
   1. Cough
   2. Sore throat
   3. Dyspnea/wheezing
   4. Rhinorrhea
B. Abrupt onset of fever and/or chills (temperature of 100°F [37.8°C] or greater)
C. Headache
D. Body aches
E. Altered mental status

Other Signs and Symptoms

A. Joint pain
B. Diarrhea
C. Vomiting

Subjective Data

A. Review the onset, course, and duration of symptoms, especially fever and respiratory symptoms.
B. Review symptoms of other family members or coworkers who are also ill. Is the onset of acute febrile respiratory illness within 7 days of close contact with a person with a confirmed case of H1N1?
C. If pregnant, establish gestational age.

D. Review for recent travel location and use of cruise ships or planes.
E. Evaluate living conditions for exposure risks.
F. Is the patient a smoker?
G. Review all medications, including OTC and herbal products. Has the patient taken any medications for the symptoms?
H. Does the patient have a history of asthma or COPD?
I. Is the patient immunocompromised (i.e., HIV, transplant recipient, chemotherapy)?
J. What other medical comorbidities, such as diabetes, does the patient have?

Physical Examination

A. Check temperature, pulse, respirations, and blood pressure.
B. Inspect
    1. Observe general overall appearance for pallor and for any respiratory distress.
    2. Assess hydration status.
    3. Conduct an eye, ear, nose, and throat exam.
C. Auscultate
    1. Auscultate all lung fields, observing for wheezing and crackles.
    2. Auscultate the heart.
D. Palpate: Palpate the neck and lymph nodes: Preauricular, posterior auricular, submental and sublingual, anterior cervical chain, and supraclavicular nodes.
E. Neurologic exam
    1. Assess LOC.
    2. Assess for nuchal rigidity.
    3. Assess for meningeal signs.
        a. Signs of meningeal irritation include nuchal rigidity.
        b. Positive Brudzinski's and Kernig's signs (refer to Figures 11.1 and 11.2)
            i. Brudzinski's sign: Place the patient supine and flex the head upward. Resulting flexion of both hips, knees, and ankles with neck flexion indicates meningeal irritation.
            ii. Kernig's sign: Place the patient supine. Keeping one leg straight, flex the other hip and knee to a bent knee to form a 90° angle. Slowly extend the lower leg. This places a stretch on the meninges, resulting in pain and spasm for the hamstring muscle. Resistance to further extension can be felt.

Diagnostic Tests

A. Testing is not necessary for all patients who present with influenza-type symptoms.

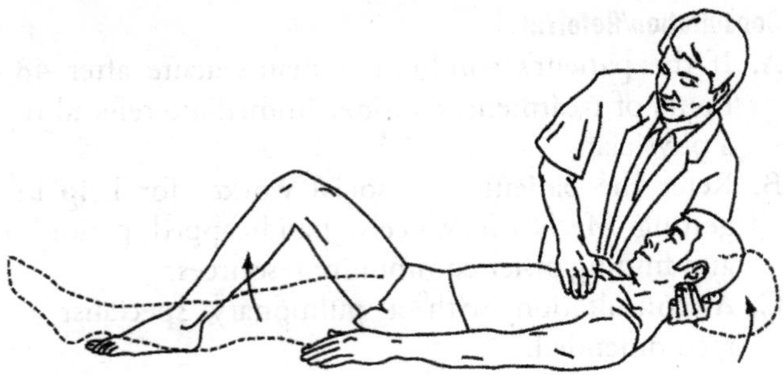

FIGURE 11.1 Brudzinski's sign.

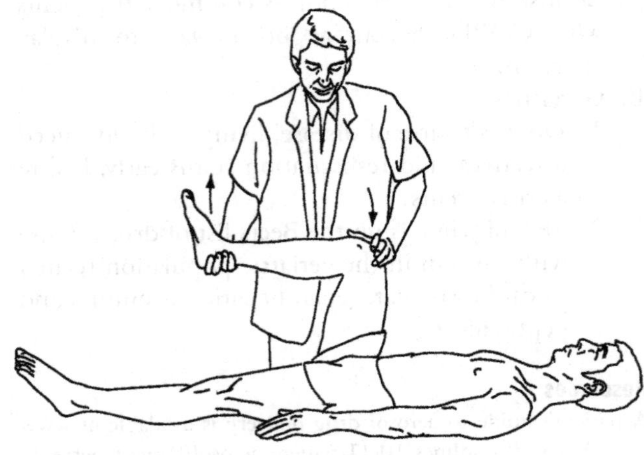

FIGURE 11.2 Kernig's sign.

    1. Rapid influenza antigen testing
    2. Respiratory swab for H1N1 testing for detection by real-time reverse transcriptase PCR.
    3. Viral culture
    4. CBC with differential (not a required test)
    5. Imaging (rule out complications)
        a. Chest x-ray
        b. CT chest imaging for complications

Differential Diagnoses

A. Influenza
    1. H1N1 A (swine flu)
    2. Influenza A
    3. Influenza B
    4. Avian flu (H5N1)
B. Pneumonia
C. Bronchitis
D. Mononucleosis
E. Early HIV
F. Severe acute respiratory syndrome (SARS)
G. Meningitis

Plan

A. General interventions
    1. Management usually focuses on treatment of symptoms and is supportive.
        a. Bed rest
        b. Increased fluids

c. Antipyretics and analgesics for fever and myalgias
d. Encourage patients to stay home (self-isolate) if they become ill and avoid touching the eyes, nose, and mouth.

2. Community precautions
a. Avoid close contact with those who are sick.
b. Wash hands often or use alcohol-based hand gels.
c. Use of face masks may be advisable or required.
d. Droplet precautions should be used and maintained for 7 days after onset of illness or until symptoms have resolved.

B. Pharmaceutical therapy
1. Coverage for the H1N1 swine flu is now included in the seasonal influenza vaccination available in both an inactivated influenza vaccine (IIV), previously called trivalent inactivated vaccine (TIV), and a live attenuated influenza vaccine (LAIV). The influenza vaccine should be administered as prophylaxis prior to flu season (generally October–March). Patients should be encouraged to receive an annual flu vaccine.
a. The live, attenuated influenza vaccine available as a nasal mist is available for target-age populations for adults up to 49 years of age.
b. A high-dose influenza vaccine is available for adults older than 65 years.
c. The most current information available on the flu vaccines is noted on the CDC website (www.cdc.gov).

2. Antiviral therapy

Antivirals started within the first 48 hours confer the greatest benefit.

a. Neuraminidase inhibitors oseltamivir (Tamiflu) and zanamivir (Relenza) are used for both treatment and chemoprophylaxis of the H1N1 influenza A virus.
b. Amantadine and rimantadine antivirals are not recommended for H1N1 because of resistance to other influenza strains.
c. The WHO recommends that patients with underlying medical conditions and pregnant women should receive treatment with oseltamivir (oral) or zanamivir (inhaled) as soon as possible after symptom onset without waiting for laboratory test results.
d. Antiviral therapy recommendations vary by type of influenza, age group, renal function, and risk factor. In order to prescribe the most current antiviral therapy, refer to the CDC website for the most up-to-date recommendations www.cdc.gov/flu/professionals/antivirals/antiviral-summary-clinicians.htm.
e. Oseltamivir should not be administered with a LAIV within 2 weeks prior to or 48 hours after treatment.

3. Acetaminophen or ibuprofen as needed for fever and myalgia

Follow-Up

A. Schedule a follow-up visit within 7 to 10 days if symptoms do not improve.
B. Monitor patient for pulmonary and neurologic complications.
C. The local and state health departments are the point of contact for information about current influenza activity.

Consultation/Referral

A. Refer the patient to a physician or neurologist for any complications.

Individual Considerations

A. Pregnancy
1. Pregnancy predisposes the patient to an increased risk for influenzal pneumonia.
2. Flu vaccine may be given to patients in high-risk populations. Because of the risk of influenzal pneumonia, many physicians recommend that pregnant women be vaccinated when an epidemic threatens.
3. Immunization of pregnant women is considered safe at any stage of pregnancy.
4. Zanamivir is the antiviral of choice for pregnancy because of limited systemic absorption.
5. Oseltamivir is used in pregnancy for women with asthma secondary to a higher risk for complications.
6. Both oseltamivir and zanamivir are pregnancy category C drugs.
7. Breastfeeding is not contraindicated during influenza.

B. Adults: Persons with high-exposure occupations, such as teachers, health care workers, police, and firefighters, should consider yearly immunization. Vaccine should be offered/administered to persons with chronic metabolic diseases, renal dysfunction, HIV infection, and immunosuppression.

Resource

Centers for Disease and Control and Prevention: www.cdc.gov/flu/professionals

Influenza (Flu)

Definition

A. Influenza is a common, acute, viral infection that is a self-limiting, febrile illness of the respiratory tract. Illness is spread person to person, primarily by respiratory secretions that can be spread from infected persons through sneezing, coughing, talking, and self-inoculation of secretions through direct contact routes. Influenza is one of the top 10 causes of death in the United States when it occurs with pneumonia.

Incidence

A. Epidemics occur yearly, primarily in the winter months, in both the northern and southern hemispheres. Travelers should be reminded that the flu season is different by hemisphere and can occur on cruise ships. Attack rates may be as high as 10% to 20% of the population. Mortality is highest in the geriatric population older than 65 years of age, except during pandemics when 50% of influenza deaths occur in individuals younger than 65 years of age. Extraordinarily high attacks have occurred in the institutionalized and semiclosed populations.

Pathogenesis

A. Influenza A and B are viruses that have the ability to undergo periodic antigenic changes of their envelope glycoproteins, the hemagglutinin and neuraminidase. Among influenza A viruses that infect humans, there are three major subtypes of hemagglutinins (H1, H2, and H3) and two subtypes of neuraminidases (N1 and N2). Influenza A outbreaks typically start abruptly, peak over 2 to 3 weeks, and last approximately 2 to 3 months. H1N1 (swine flu) is an influenza A virus.
B. The avian flu was the N5N1 and H7N7 viral infection associated with recent exposure to dead or ill poultry. Following exposure, the incubation period for human H5N1 infection was 7 days or less. Clusters of human-to-human transmission of avian flu had a typical incubation period of 3 to 5 days.
C. Influenza B outbreaks are generally less extensive and less severe. Outbreaks associated with the B virus have been reported in schools, military camps, nursing homes, and cruise ships.
D. *H. influenzae* is a gram-negative coccobacillus. *H. influenzae* is an invasive bacterial disease that can cause meningitis, otitis media, sinusitis, epiglottitis, septic arthritis, occult febrile bacteremia, cellulitis, pneumonia, and empyema; occasionally, this virulent organism causes neonatal meningitis.
E. The incubation period for *H. influenzae* is from between 18 and 72 hours to 5 days after exposure. The exact period of communicability for *H. influenzae* is unknown, but it may be for as long as the organism is present in the upper respiratory tract.

Predisposing Factors

A. The primary mode of spread is via exposure to viral strain respiratory secretions from respiratory droplets (coughing or sneezing) and direct contact of contaminated surfaces.
   1. Adults
      a. Aged older than 65 years (dependent on the viral strain)
      b. Pregnancy
      c. High-exposure jobs: Teachers, health care workers, police, and firefighters
      d. Recent illnesses or state that has lowered resistance (stress, excessive fatigue, poor nutrition)
      e. Immunosuppression from drugs, illness, or chronic illness (transplant recipients, lung disease, heart disease)
      f. Crowded living conditions, including military camps and institutions such as nursing homes
      g. Travel in endemic areas
      h. Avian flu: Exposure to dead or ill poultry

Common Complaints

A. Clinical manifestations of influenza depend on age and previous experience with the influenza virus.
B. Rapid-onset respiratory illness is the most common complaint.
C. Abrupt onset of fever and/or chills
D. Joint pain
E. Headache
F. Conjunctivitis (avian flu)

Other Signs and Symptoms

A. Upper respiratory congestion (watery eyes, clear nasal drainage, headache, sore throat, and hoarseness)
B. Malaise or fatigue
C. Anorexia
D. Swollen lymph nodes
E. Nonproductive cough (persisting for weeks)
F. Muscle aches
G. Gastrointestinal symptoms
H. Febrile seizures
I. Otitis media

Subjective Data

A. Review the onset, course, and duration of symptoms, especially myalgia and malaise.
B. Query the patient if they have had a flu shot and when the last flu vaccination was received.
C. Review symptoms of other family members or coworkers who are also ill.

D. Review for recent travel location and use of cruise ships or planes.
E. Evaluate living conditions for exposure risks.
F. Is the patient a smoker?
G. Review all medications, including OTC and herbal products. Has the patient taken any medications for the symptoms?
H. Does the patient have a history of asthma or COPD?
I. Is the patient immunocompromised (i.e., has HIV, is a transplant recipient, is on chemotherapy)?
J. What other medical comorbidities, such as diabetes, does the patient have?

Physical Examination

A. Check temperature, pulse, respirations, and blood pressure.
B. Inspect
   1. Observe overall appearance for pallor and for any respiratory distress.
   2. Assess hydration status.
   3. Conduct an eye, ear, nose, and throat exam.
C. Auscultate
   1. Auscultate the lung fields, observing for wheezing and crackles.
   2. Auscultate the heart.
D. Palpate: Palpate the neck and lymph nodes: Preauricular, posterior auricular, submental and sublingual, anterior cervical chain, and supraclavicular nodes.
E. Neurologic exam
   1. Assess LOC.
   2. Assess for nuchal rigidity.
   3. Assess for meningeal signs:
      a. Signs of meningeal irritation include nuchal rigidity.
      b. Positive Brudzinski's and Kernig's signs (refer to Figures 11.1 and 11.2)
         i. Brudzinski's sign: Place the patient supine and flex the head upward. Resulting flexion of both hips, knees, and ankles with neck flexion indicates meningeal irritation.
         ii. Kernig's sign: Place the patient supine. Keeping one leg straight, flex the other hip and knee to a bent knee to form a 90° angle. Slowly extend the lower leg. This places a stretch on the meninges, resulting in pain and spasm for the hamstring muscle. Resistance to further extension can be felt.

Diagnostic Tests

A. Usually none is required. However, if the patient appears ill, consider the following:
   1. WBC and CBC
   2. Viral RNA cultures: Obtain during the first 72 hours of illness because the quality of virus shed subsequently decreases rapidly. There is some evidence that a throat sampling yields an improved specimen. Nasopharyngeal secretions obtained by swab or aspirate should be placed in an appropriate transport medium for culture.
   3. Rapid antigen test (usually less sensitive in the detection of influenza A than the PCR; a negative rapid diagnostic test should be confirmed with a viral culture or other means).
   4. Monospot test: **Monospot test is negative with the flu and positive with mononucleosis.**
   5. CXR (only if pneumonia suspected)
   6. Sputum culture (complications only)
   7. Lumbar puncture (complications only)
   8. Rapid plasma reagin (RPR) test (for high-risk HIV factors): Negative RPR to rule out syphilis
   9. PCR assay (It can differentiate between influenza subtypes; it offers high sensitivity and specificity but is not readily available for clinical use.)

Differential Diagnoses

A. Influenza
   1. Influenza A
   2. Influenza B
   3. Avian flu (H5N1)
   4. H1N1 (swine flu)
B. Pneumonia
C. Bronchitis
D. Mononucleosis
E. Early HIV
F. SARS
G. Meningitis

Plan

A. General interventions
   1. Management is usually treatment of symptoms.
   2. Encourage flu vaccine for patients in susceptible populations prior to flu season.
   3. **Patients should expect to have a persistent cough and malaise after initial acute phase.**
B. Patient teaching: See the Section III Patient Teaching Guide for this chapter, "Influenza (Flu)."
C. Pharmaceutical therapy

Influenza can alter the metabolism of certain medications, especially theophylline, possibly resulting in the development of toxicity from high serum concentrations.

   1. Acetaminophen (Tylenol) as needed for fever
   2. NSAIDs as needed for body aches
   3. Amantadine and rimantadine (class of medications known as adamantanes) are

not recommended for antiviral treatment or chemoprophylaxis of currently circulating influenza A virus strains.

4. **Antivirals started within the first 48 hours confer the greatest benefit.** Antiviral therapy recommendations vary by type of influenza, age group, renal function, and risk factor. In order to prescribe the most current antiviral therapy, refer to the CDC website for the most up-to-date recommendations: www.cdc.gov/flu/professionals/antivirals/antiviral-summary-clinicians.htm.
5. The recommended duration of treatment is 5 days. Longer treatment regimens may be necessary in persons with immunosuppression for hospitalized patients.
6. Zanamivir (Relenza)
   a. Not recommended for persons with underlying airways disease, including asthma or COPD.
   b. Zanamivir is for uncomplicated acute illness due to influenza A or B in adults who have been symptomatic for no more than 2 days.
   c. See Table 11.2 for the recommended dosage and schedule of influenza antivirals for treatment and chemoprophylaxis.
7. Oseltamivir (Tamiflu)
   a. For adults and adolescents 13 years of age or older who have been symptomatic for no more than 2 days
   b. Preferred treatment for pregnant women. Pregnant women are recommended to receive the same antiviral dosing as nonpregnant women.
   c. See Table 11.2 for the recommended dosage and schedule of influenza antivirals for treatment and chemoprophylaxis.
8. Vaccination
   a. Flu vaccine should not be administered to persons allergic to eggs.
   b. The vaccine should be administered in the autumn prior to the flu season, at least 6 weeks before the onset of the season.
   c. Influenza vaccines may be administered concurrently with other live or inactivated vaccines.
   d. **Immunization is the major means of influenza prevention.** Each year the vaccine is produced with influenza strains. The vaccine may be trivalent or quadrivalent formulations.
   e. Two types of administration of the vaccine are available.
      i. IIV, previously called TIV, is administered intramuscularly.
      ii. LAIV is administered intranasally. The LAIV is available for adults up to 49 years of age.
   f. A high-dose influenza vaccine is also available for adults older than 65 years.
   g. The recommended site of vaccination in adults is the deltoid muscle.
   h. Oseltamivir (Tamiflu) should not be administered with a LAIV within 2 weeks prior to or 48 hours after treatment.

TABLE 11.2 Recommended Dosage and Schedule of Influenza Antiviral Medications* for Treatment† and Chemoprophylaxis§

Antiviral Agent		Age Group (Years) 13–64	≥ 65
Zanamivir	Treatment, influenza A and B	10 mg (2 inhalations) twice daily	10 mg (2 inhalations) twice daily
	Chemoprophylaxis, influenza A and B	10 mg (2 inhalations) once daily	10 mg (2 inhalations) once daily
Oseltamivir	Treatment, influenza A and B	75 mg twice daily	75 mg twice daily
	Chemoprophylaxis, influenza A and B	75 mg once daily	75 mg once daily

NA, not approved.

*Zanamivir is manufactured by GlaxoSmithKline (Relenza–inhaled powder). Zanamivir is approved for treatment of persons age older than 7 years and approved for chemoprophylaxis of persons age older than 5 years. Zanamivir is administered through oral inhalation by using a plastic device included in the medication package. Patients will benefit from instruction and demonstration of the correct use of the device. Zanamivir is not recommended for those persons with underlying airway disease. Oseltamivir is manufactured by Roche Pharmaceuticals (Tamiflu – tablet). Oseltamivir is approved for treatment or chemoprophylaxis of persons aged older than or equal to 1 year. Oseltamivir is available for oral administration in 30 mg, 45 mg, and 75 mg capsules and liquid suspension. This information is based on data published by the Food and Drug Administration (FDA), available at http://www.fda.gov/Drugs/DrugSafety/InformationbyDrugClass/ucm100228.htm.

†Recommended duration for antiviral treatment is 5 days. Longer treatment courses can be considered for patients who remain severely ill after 5 days of treatment.

§Recommended duration is 10 days when administered after a household exposure and 7 days after the most recent known exposure in other situations. For control of outbreaks in long-term care facilities and hospitals, CDC recommends antiviral chemoprophylaxis for a minimum of 2 weeks and up to 1 week after the most recent known case was identified.

Follow-Up

A. Schedule a follow-up visit within 7 to 10 days if symptoms do not improve.
   1. People at highest risk for influenza complications
      a. All persons 50 years of age and older
      b. Anyone with chronic pulmonary (including asthma) or cardiovascular (except isolated hypertension), renal, hepatic, neurologic, hematologic, or metabolic disorders, including diabetes mellitus
      c. Persons who have immunosuppression, including immunosuppression caused by medications or HIV infection
      d. Women who are or will be pregnant during the influenza season
      e. Residents of nursing homes and other long-term care facilities
      f. American Indians and Alaska Natives
      g. Persons who are morbidly obese (BMI ≥ 40)

B. Monitor the patient for pulmonary and neurologic complications.

C. Because antiviral resistance patterns can change over time, clinicians should monitor local antiviral resistance surveillance data. Local and state health departments are the points of contact for information about current influenza.

Consultation/Referral

A. Refer the patient to a physician or neurologist for any complications.

Individual Considerations

A. Pregnancy
   1. The American College of Obstetricians and Gynecologists (ACOG) in their 2014 Committee Opinion note that the flu vaccine is an essential element of preconception, prenatal, and postpartum care.
   2. Pregnancy predisposes the patient to an increased risk for influenzal pneumonia.
   3. Immunization of pregnant women is considered safe at any stage of pregnancy with the IIV.
   4. LAIV available as an intranasal spray is not recommended for pregnant women but is safe for postpartum women.
   5. The inactivated vaccine is safe for breastfeeding mothers and their infants.
   6. Zanamivir is the antiviral of choice for pregnancy because of limited systemic absorption.
   7. Oseltamivir is used in pregnancy for women with asthma secondary to a higher risk for complications.

B. Adults: Persons with high-exposure occupations such as teachers, health care workers, police, and firefighters should consider yearly immunization. Vaccine should be offered/administered to persons with chronic metabolic diseases, renal dysfunction, HIV infection, and immunosuppression.

C. Geriatrics
   1. Ninety percent of flu-related deaths and half of flu-related hospitalization occur in people age 65 and older.
   2. Factors that contribute to more severe infections include weakened immune systems due to aging, decreased lung compliance, and decreased respiration muscle strength.
   3. Influenza vaccine is recommended yearly for patients older than the age of 60. The vaccine should be offered to nursing home residents, especially those with a history of cardiopulmonary disease.
   4. Pneumococcal pneumonia and influenza are significant causes of mortality and morbidity in the elderly.

Resource

Centers for Disease and Control and Prevention: www.cdc.gov/flu/professionals

Obstructive Sleep Apnea

Definition

A. OSA is the periodic reduction (hypopnea) or cessation (apnea) of breathing due to a narrowing or occlusion of the upper airway during sleep. OSA has been linked to traffic accidents, cardiac diseases, stroke, diabetes, and visceral obesity. OSA is also associated with nocturnal cardiac arrhythmias and chronic and acute cardiac events, and is a risk factor for strokes. OSA worsens in the supine sleeping position. The following are diagnostic criteria for OSA if either of these two conditions exists:
   1. The presence of 15 or more apneas, hypopneas, or respiratory effort-related arousals per hour of sleep in an asymptomatic patient. More than 75% of the apneas and hypopneas must be obstructive.
   2. Five or more obstructive apneas, obstructive hypopneas, or respiratory effort-related arousals per hour of sleep in a patient with symptoms or signs of disturbed sleep. More than 75% of the apneas or hypopneas must be obstructive.

Incidence

A. The incidence of OSA in the morbidly obese population is between 38% and 88%.

B. Obesity adds a fourfold added risk for disordered breathing.

C. OSA is the most common sleep-related breathing disorder and is increasing in prevalence due to increasing obesity rates.

D. OSA is more common in males than females.
E. Ethnicity and geographic distribution have no effect on OSA incidence.

Pathogenesis

A. Increased tissue thickness of the structures of the tongue and soft tissues in the pharyngeal cavity that decreases the passageway for air to the trachea is thought to be the mechanism of OSA. During the night the muscles of the oropharynx relax and results in the relative obstruction of the airway. Obesity and hypertrophy of tonsils and/or adenoids play a major role in OSA. Patients with severe OSA left untreated have a two- to threefold risk for all-cause mortalities.

Predisposing Factors

A. Obesity
B. Increased neck circumference
C. Age: Increases with age and plateaus in the sixth decade
D. Gender: Males
E. Postmenopause females
F. Hypothyroidism
G. Tonsillar hypertrophy
H. Alcohol
I. Craniofacial abnormalities
J. Medications
   1. Benzodiazepines
   2. Antipsychotics
   3. Opioid analgesics
   4. Beta blockers
   5. Barbiturates
   6. Antihistamines
   7. Sedative antidepressants
K. Allergic rhinitis
L. Genetic conditions (e.g., Down syndrome, Pierre Robin anomalies, Marfan's syndrome, etc.)
M. Ethnic (e.g., African American, Asian, Hispanic)
N. Acromegaly

Common Complaints

A. Daytime sleepiness
B. Loud snoring, gasping, or snorting during sleep
C. Fatigue
D. Insomnia

Other Signs and Symptoms

A. Adults
   1. Asymptomatic: Patients may not recognize they have OSA since they are able to go to sleep anytime.
   2. Restless sleep
   3. Dry mouth or sore throat
   4. Lack of physical or mental energy
   5. Falling asleep when watching TV, reading, or driving/riding in a car
   6. Morning headaches
   7. Decreased libido and impotence
   8. Cognitive deficits
   9. Depression
   10. Mood disorders

Subjective Data

A. Does the patient feel sleepy during the day? Is daytime sleepiness a problem?
B. Does the patient struggle to stay awake during the day?
C. Does the patient take naps? How often, and for how long?
D. Does the patient feel physically and mentally exhausted?
E. Does the patient's bed partner complain about snoring, gasping, or snorting?
F. Ask the Epworth Sleepiness Scale questions related to how often the patient dozes off or falls asleep (in contrast to just feeling tired). Each situation is scored from 0 = would never doze, to 1 = a slight chance of dozing, 2 = moderate chance of dozing, and 3 = a high chance of dozing. There are eight situations to which the patient responds:
   1. Sitting and reading
   2. Watching TV
   3. Sitting inactive in a public place (e.g., a theater or meeting)
   4. As a passenger in a car for an hour without a break
   5. Lying down to rest during the day when circumstances permit
   6. Sitting and talking to someone
   7. Sitting quietly after lunch without alcohol
   8. In a car, while stopped for a few minutes in traffic
G. Ask patient to list all medications currently being taken, particularly substances not prescribed, including OTC and herbal products.
H. Review alcohol use.
I. Men who present with sleep disorders should also be questioned about the presence of erectile dysfunction.

Physical Examination

A. Blood pressure, pulse, respirations, height and weight to calculate BMI, and waist measurement
B. Inspect
   1. Oropharynx examination for:
      a. Peritonsillar narrowing or hypertrophy
      b. Tongue (evaluate for macroglossia)
      c. Elongated or enlarged uvula
      d. Palate (high arch or narrow palate)
      e. Measure neck circumference (> 16 inches in a female or 17 inches in a male)
   2. Nasal examination; Look for septal deviation and nasal polyps.
   3. Inspect for signs of pulmonary hypertension or cor pulmonale.
      a. Jugular venous distension
      b. Peripheral edema

C. Palpate thyroid gland.
D. Auscultate heart and lungs.
E. Mental status: Assess for confusion, flat affect, and somnolence.

Diagnostic Tests

A. Polysomnography (PSG) is the standard method of diagnosis. The apnea hypopnea index (AHI) or the respiratory disturbance index (RDI) is used to quantify hypopneas and classify the degree of sleep disturbance.
    1. Full-night PSG (gold standard)
    2. Split-night PSG
    3. Home testing with portable monitors

Patients with cardiac, respiratory, or neurologic disease may be at the greatest risk for central sleep apnea, and the American Academy of Sleep Medicine (AASM) does not recommend the use of portable monitors for diagnosis in these patients.

B. Routine lab work is not helpful in the confirmation or exclusion of OSA.

Differential Diagnosis

A. OSA
B. Primary snoring
C. Narcolepsy
D. Restless leg syndrome
E. Swallowing disorder
F. Nocturnal seizures
G. GERD
H. Obesity hypoventilation syndrome
I. Sleep deprivation, including shift-work disorder
J. Neurodegenerative disease (e.g., Parkinson's, dementia, Alzheimer)
K. Substance abuse
L. Alcoholism
M. Asthma
N. Central sleep apnea

Plan

A. Patient teaching
    1. Educate patient about modifying controllable risk factors such as keeping diabetes and hypertension under control, diet, exercise, and stopping smoking.
    2. Treatment with CPAP and BiPAP is required at all times during the night and during naps.
    3. Behavioral strategies include sleeping in a nonsupine position using a positioning device (e.g., alarm, pillow, backpack, tennis ball are used for positional therapy).
    4. Give patient teaching sheet on sleep apnea. See the Section III Patient Teaching Guide for this chapter, "Sleep Apnea."

B. **CPAP or BiPAP is the mainstay of treatment for moderate to severe OSA.**
C. Dietary management: Even a modest weight loss of 10% to 20% has been associated with an improvement.
D. Nonsurgical treatment
    1. Oral appliances (OAs): Require a thorough dental examination
        a. Custom-made OAs may improve airway patency during sleep by enlarging the upper airway and/or by decreasing the upper airway collapse.
        b. Mandibular repositioning appliances (MRAs) cover the upper and lower teeth and hold the mandible in an advance position.
        c. Tongue-retaining devices (TRDs) hold the tongue in a forward position without mandibular repositioning.
E. Surgical treatment
    1. Tracheostomy can eliminate OSA but not central hypoventilation syndromes. This procedure should be considered only when other options have failed or when it is considered necessary by clinical urgency.
    2. Maxillary-mandibular advancement (MMA) is indicated when the patient cannot tolerate/refuses CPAP and an OA is not appropriate/effective.
    3. Multilevel or stepwise surgery (MLS) is a combined procedure or serves as a stepwise multiple surgery.
    4. Bariatric surgery's weight loss has been effective in improving sleep efficiency and increasing rapid eye movement (REM) sleep. The severity of presurgical OSA determines the degree to which OSA improves postbariatric surgery.
    5. Radiofrequency ablation (RFA) is for treatment of mild to moderate OSA when the patient cannot tolerate/refuses CPAP and an OA is not appropriate/effective.
    6. Laser-assisted uvulopalatoplasty is not recommended for OSA.

Follow-Up

A. There is no standard for recommending repeat PSG testing or a CPAP titration study after significant weight loss.

Consultation/Referral

A. Refer to a dentist for an OA.
B. Refer to a pulmonologist for management of therapy and/or surgical treatment.
C. Refer patient to a cardiologist as needed.
D. If patient is uninsured, refer to social worker for assistance in treatment purchases as needed.

Pneumonia (Bacterial)

Definition

A. Pneumonia is inflammation and consolidation of lung tissue due to a bacterial pathogen. The causative agent and the anatomic location classify pneumonia. It is not uncommon to have acute viral and bacterial pneumonia concurrently.
B. Other types of pneumonia and pulmonary inflammation occur secondary to smoking, exposure to chemicals, fungi, near drowning, and recurrent aspiration with gastroesophageal reflux.
C. **Hospitalization is recommended in severe cases of pneumonia.**
D. The Pneumonia Severity Index Calculator is a tool to estimate pneumonia mortality and assist in determining whether the patient should best be treated in the inpatient or outpatient setting. Website: www.pda.ahrq.gov/clinic/psi/psicalc.asp

Incidence

A. Pneumonia is a leading cause of death for patients older than 65 years.
B. Bacterial pneumonia is more prevalent in the very old and very young.
C. A higher mortality rate occurs in persons with immunodeficiency, comorbid conditions, abnormal vital signs, and virulent pathogens.
D. The incidence rate also varies by pathogens.

Pathogenesis

A. Pneumonia results from inflammation of the alveolar space. Lobar pneumonia has four stages:
   1. Vascular congestion and alveolar edema within the first 24 hours of infection
   2. Red hepatization (2–3 days), characterized by erythrocytes, neutrophils, and fibrin within the alveoli
   3. Gray hepatization (2–3 days), characterized by a gray-brown to yellow color secondary to exudate
   4. Resorption and restoration of the pulmonary architecture. A rub may still be auscultated due to the fibrinous inflammation
B. Bacterial causes include *S. pneumoniae* (the most common pathogen), Hib (the second most common pathogen), *Staphylococcus aureus, Legionella, Chlamydia trachomatis, Chlamydia pneumoniae, M. pneumoniae, Pseudomonas, Klebsiella,* and *Pneumocystis jiroveci* pneumonia (PCP) in patients with HIV.

Predisposing Factors

A. Advanced age
B. Impaired mentation
C. Smoking
D. COPD
E. Alcoholism
F. Aspiration
G. Heart failure
H. Diabetes
I. Heart disease
J. Crowded conditions (dormitories, long-term care centers)
K. Immunodeficiency
L. Congenital anomalies
M. Abnormal mucus clearance
N. Lack of immunization
O. Measles
P. Indoor air pollutants from cooking or heating with wood
Q. History of pneumonia
R. Lung cancer

Common Complaints

Acute onset of these symptoms

A. Fever
B. Shaking chills
C. Dyspnea, rapid, labored breathing
D. Cough
E. Rust-colored sputum

Other Signs and Symptoms

A. Increased respiratory rate (tachypnea)
B. Chest pain, localized
C. URI symptoms such as pharyngitis
D. Headache
E. Nausea
F. Vomiting
G. Vague abdominal pain
H. Diarrhea
I. Myalgia
J. Arthralgias
K. Anorexia
L. Change in LOC, including confusion

Subjective Data

A. Determine the onset, duration, and course of illness.
B. Has the patient had fever or shaking chills?
C. Has there been breathing trouble? Are the breathing problems interfering with eating and drinking?
D. If diabetic, take home blood sugar readings.
E. Is there a cough? Is the cough productive? What color is the sputum?
F. Are any other family members ill?
G. Has the patient ever been hospitalized for pneumonia or respiratory distress before?
H. Review the history for any chronic diseases.
I. Has the patient ever been immunized for influenza or pneumonia?
J. Review all medications, including OTC and herbal products. Specifically review whether the patient has been on any antibiotics in the past 3 months.

Recent exposure to an antibiotic is a risk factor for antibiotic resistance. Continued or repeated use of that class of antibiotics is not recommended.

K. Ask about change in sexual partners (including elderly) for risk of HIV or chlamydia infections.

Physical Examination

A. Temperature, blood pressure, pulse, and weight
   1. **In the elderly the blood pressure can be low; this is a consideration for sepsis.**
B. Inspect
   1. Observe overall appearance. Does the patient appear ill? Consider the clinical presentation, age of the person, and history.
   2. Observe breathing pattern and the use of accessory muscles, grunting, retractions, and tachypnea.
   3. Obtain a pulse oximetry to assess oxygen saturation. **An O_2 saturation less than 92% is an indicator of severity and the need for oxygen therapy.**
   4. Check nail beds and lips for cyanosis.
   5. Examine the eyes, nose, ears, and throat.
   6. Examine skin for turgor and mucous membranes for dehydration.
C. Auscultate
   1. Auscultate heart.
   2. Auscultate lungs for the following (auscultate bases first in geriatric patients):
      a. Crackles (present in 80% of patients), wheezes, and decreased breath sounds
      b. Whispered pectoriloquy (increased loudness of whisper during auscultation)
      c. Egophony (patient's "e" sounds like "a" during auscultation)
      d. Bronchophony (voice sounds louder than usual)
   3. Auscultate abdomen (usually hypoactive bowel sounds).
D. Percuss chest to identify areas of consolidation.
E. Palpate
   1. Palpate chest for tactile fremitus (increased conduction when patient says "99").
   2. Palpate lymph nodes for adenopathy.
   3. Palpate sinuses for tenderness. Sinusitis is a sign of *Mycoplasma* infection.

Diagnostic Tests

A. WHO defines pneumonia solely on the basis of clinical findings observed by inspection and timing of respirations.
B. CXR
   1. Infiltrates confirm diagnosis. False negatives result from dehydration, evaluation in first 24 hours, and infection.
   2. Ordering a posterior, anterior, and lateral CXR ensures adequate visualization for diagnosis.
C. CBC with differential
D. BUN, creatinine level, and GFR if acute renal failure secondary to dehydration or sepsis is a concern
E. Cultures
   1. Blood cultures if critically ill, immunocompromised, or for persistent symptoms
   2. Sputum cultures are reserved for very ill patients for unusual presentations
F. Consider rapid viral testing.
G. Consider skin testing for TB for high-risk exposure risk.

Differential Diagnoses

A. Pneumonia
   1. Bacterial pneumonia
   2. Viral pneumonia
   3. Aspiration pneumonia
   4. Chemical-induced pneumonia
   5. Fungal pneumonias (especially in immunocompromised or diabetes out of control)
B. Asthma
C. Bronchitis/bronchiolitis
D. Pertussis
E. Heart failure
F. Pulmonary embolus
G. Empyema and abscess
H. Aspiration of foreign body

Plan

A. General interventions
   1. Encourage rest during acute phase.
   2. Encourage patients to avoid smoking/secondhand smoke.
   3. A vaporizer may be used to increase humidity.
   4. Encourage good hand washing or use of hand sanitizer.
B. Patient teaching: See the Section III Patient Teaching Guide for this chapter, "Bacterial Pneumonia."
C. Dietary management: Encourage a nutritious diet with increased fluid intake.
D. Chest physiotherapy is not prescribed for pneumonia.
E. Pharmaceutical therapy
   1. ***S. pneumonia*** **is the most common bacterial pathogen, and resistance against antibiotics is a concern.** Resistance is seen more commonly in:
      a. Age greater than 65 years
      b. Use of a beta-lactam antibiotic or fluoroquinolones in the past 6 months
      c. Alcoholism
      d. Chronic illness/comorbidities
      e. Immunosuppression therapy or illness
      f. Exposure to a child at a day care center
   2. The Pneumonia Severity Calculator should be used prior to initiation of antibiotic therapy; it is available at www.pda.ahrq.gov/clinic/psi/psicalc.asp.

3. Treatment with antibiotics is empirical. Oral therapy should continue 7 to 10 days.
   a. If antimicrobials have not been used in the past 3 months:
      i. Macrolide antibiotics *or*
      ii. Doxycycline
   b. If antimicrobials have been used in the past 3 months:
      i. Respiratory quinolones
      ii. Augmentin or high-dose Amoxicillin
4. Administer acetaminophen (Tylenol) for fever.
5. Avoid cough suppressants. Suppression of a cough may interfere with airway clearance.
6. Vaccines
   a. Pneumococcal vaccine is recommended for anyone older than the age of 19 with chronic lung disease, including asthma; immunocompromised adults; and in the elderly 65 years and older.

Follow-Up

A. Patients should know the signs of increasing respiratory distress and seek immediate medical attention.
B. Follow up by telephone in 24 hours.
C. If there is no improvement after 48 hours on antibiotics, the patient is advised to call back.
D. Schedule a return visit in 2 weeks for evaluation, unless elderly and living alone: Follow up in person within a week.
E. Follow up with a CXR in 4 to 6 weeks for patients older than 60 years and for those who smoke. However, if the patient is younger than 60 years, a nonsmoker, and feels well at 6-week follow-up, there is no need to follow up with a CXR.

Consultation/Referral

A. Patients who are immunocompromised or have signs of toxicity or hypoxia may need hospitalization. Refer them to a physician.
B. If the patient is in any level of respiratory distress, dehydrated, or hypoxemic, consult with or refer the patient to a physician/hospital.
C. Poor prognostic signs that require referral are age older than 65 years, respiration rate greater than or equal to 30 breaths per minute, systolic BP less than 90 or diastolic BP less than 60, temperature greater than 101°F, altered mental status, extrapulmonary infection, and WBC less than 4,000 or greater than 30,000.
D. Physician consultation is needed for suspected PCP.

Individual Considerations

A. Pregnancy
   1. The annual U.S. rate of antepartum CAP is 0.5 to 1.5 per 1,000 pregnancies.
   2. Perinatal mortality may increase slightly due to associated increase in prematurity. Pneumonia puts older mothers at high risk of maternal death.
   3. The symptoms of bacterial pneumonia are the same in pregnancy.
   4. CXRs are acceptable in pregnancy to diagnose pneumonia.

Pneumonia (Viral)

Definition

A. Viral pneumonia is inflammation and consolidation of lung tissue due to a viral pathogen.
B. **Hospitalization is recommended in patients who are significantly immunocompromised and frail elderly.**

Incidence

A. Viral pneumonia accounts for only 2% up to 15% of pneumonia cases in adult pneumonia. It is not uncommon to have concurrent viral and bacterial infections.
B. Elderly persons have the highest rate of influenza-associated hospitalizations.

Pathogenesis

A. Pneumonia results from inflammation of the alveolar space and may compromise air exchange. Viral pneumonia is caused by influenza viruses, parainfluenza virus, adenovirus, and RSV.
B. Influenza is the most common cause of viral pneumonia in adults.
C. Viruses and bacteria are spread from a cough or sneeze.
D. Pneumonia can also be spread via blood.

Predisposing Factors

A. Age extremes
B. Frailty or immunocompromised conditions
C. Exposure to viral illness
D. Lack of immunization

Common Complaints

A. Fever
B. Cough
C. Dyspnea
D. Tachypnea
E. Wheezing (more common in viral pneumonia)

Other Signs and Symptoms

A. Upper respiratory prodrome
B. Poor appetite
C. Malaise/lethargy
D. Myalgia
E. Muscle aches
F. Headache
G. Fatigue
H. Chest pain/tightness

Subjective Data

A. Determine onset, duration, and course of illness.
B. Has the patient had fever, cough, and upper respiratory infection?
C. Have there been any flulike symptoms?
D. Has there been any labored breathing?
E. Has there been a cough? Is it a productive cough? What color is the sputum?
F. Are the breathing problems affecting the ability to eat or drink?
G. Has the patient had nausea, vomiting, or diarrhea?
H. Review if the patient is up to date on immunizations.
I. Review all medications, including OTC and herbal products.
J. If diabetic, ask about home blood glucose readings/control
K. Is there localized pain in chest?
L. Pneumonia history

Physical Examination

A. Temperature, blood pressure, pulse, respirations, and pulse oximetry. **Observe LOC.**
B. Inspect
   1. Observe overall appearance. Does the patient appear ill? Consider the clinical presentation, age of person, and history.
   2. Observe respiratory pattern, grunting, nasal flaring, retractions, and use of accessory muscles.
   3. Check pulse oximetry. **An O_2 saturation less than 92% is an indicator of severity and the need for oxygen therapy.**
   4. Check nail beds and lips for cyanosis.
   5. Examine eyes, ears, nose, and throat.
C. Auscultate
   1. Auscultate heart.
   2. Auscultate lungs for the following (auscultate bases first in geriatric patients):
      a. Crackles, decreased breath sounds
      b. Whispered pectoriloquy (patient's whispered sounds are louder than normal)
      c. Egophony (patient's "e" sounds like "a")
      d. Bronchophony (voice sounds louder than usual)
D. Percuss: Percuss chest for dull sound (consolidation).
E. Palpate
   1. Palpate lymph nodes for swelling.
   2. Palpate chest for tactile fremitus (increased conduction when patient says "99").
   3. Palpate sinuses.

Diagnostic Tests

A. CXR that reveals interstitial, perihilar, or diffuse infiltrates
B. CBC with differential
C. Rapid viral tests per nasal swab
D. Sputum Gram stain if indicated

Differential Diagnoses

A. Viral pneumonia
B. Bacterial pneumonia
C. Varicella pneumonia
D. Herpes pneumonia
E. Cytomegalovirus pneumonia
F. Pertussis
G. Asthma
H. Bronchitis/bronchiolitis
I. Sinusitis
J. Foreign-body obstruction
K. Aspiration
L. Fungal pneumonias (especially in the immunocompromised)
M. SARS
N. Middle East respiratory syndrome coronovirus (MERS-CoV)
O. Avian flu
P. Pulmonary TB

Plan

A. General interventions
   1. Tell the patient to rest during acute phase.
   2. Avoid smoking or secondhand smoke.
   3. Require respiratory isolation; may use facial masks.
   4. Encourage good hand washing or use of hand sanitizer.
B. Patient teaching: See the Section III Patient Teaching Guide for this chapter, "Pneumonia, Viral."
C. Dietary management: Encourage fluids and nutritious diet.
D. Chest physiotherapy is not prescribed for pneumonia.
E. Pharmaceutical therapy: Antiviral agents have limited support for efficacy. Treatment should be targeted based on viral etiology.
   1. Zanamivir (Relenza) is the recommended initial choice when influenza A infection or exposure is suspected. Zanamivir is administered by an MDI. Zanamivir is effective only if it is started within 24 to 48 hours of onset of fever and symptoms.
   2. The combination of oseltamivir (Tamiflu) and rimantadine, an adamantane, is considered a second-line alternative. Tamiflu resistance emerged in the United States during the 2008 to 2009 influenza season.
   3. Amantadine or rimantadine started within 24 hours of the onset of viral symptoms decreases fever and other symptoms by 1 day in uncomplicated cases.
   4. Acyclovir (Zovirax) for herpes viruses is administered as an IV infusion.

5. Ribavirin (Virazole) for RSV is administered as an aerosol. Synagis has also been used in conjunction with ribavirin for high-risk patients.

F. Patients with viral pneumonia who are superinfected with bacterial organisms require antibiotic therapy.
G. Avoid cough suppressants. The suppression of a cough may interfere with airway clearance.
H. Give acetaminophen (Tylenol) for fever
I. Immunizations
   1. **Recommend the influenza vaccine for prevention.**
   2. The measles vaccine is recommended except during pregnancy and with immunocompromised patients.

Follow-Up

A. Signs and symptoms may vary greatly according to the viral pathogen, severity of disease, and patient's age.
   1. Tell the patient to return to the clinic if no improvement is seen after 48 hours on antiviral agents.
   2. Follow up by phone in 24 hours.
   3. Consider follow-up at 2 weeks if bronchoconstriction is noted on exam.

Consultation/Referral

A. Consult a physician if viral pneumonia is strongly suspected.
B. Consult a physician if the patient is pregnant.
C. Consult a physician or transfer to the hospital if patient is in respiratory distress, dehydrated, or hypoxemic.
D. Consider consultation with a pulmonologist.

Individual Considerations

A. Pregnancy
   1. Ribavirin is contraindicated in pregnancy, class X drug.
   2. Acyclovir is given in the third trimester at 10 mg/kg IV every 8 hours for 5 days.
   3. The varicella-zoster immune globulin (VZIG) may be considered in pregnancy.
   4. The measles virus is a live-attenuated virus and should not be given during pregnancy.
   5. Pneumonia in pregnancy is associated with higher morbidity rates. Physician consultation is advised.

Tuberculosis

Definition

A. TB is an infectious disease. It is a granulomatous disease caused by *M. tuberculosis, Mycobacterium bovis,* and other mycobacteria. Humans are the only reservoirs for *M. tuberculosis.* TB may involve multiple organs, including the lungs, liver, spleen, kidney, brain, spine, and bone.
B. In most immunocompetent individuals, macrophages are successful in containing the bacilli, and the infection is self-limited and often subclinical. As many as 5% of adults with primary TB are asymptomatic. When the pulmonary macrophages are unable to contain the bacilli, it leads to clinically apparent infection-progressive primary TB.
C. Postprimary (reactivation) TB occurs when the initial infection is successfully contained by the pulmonary macrophages, with bacilli remaining viable within the macrophages. Infection results when the host's immune status (T cells) is compromised.
D. **Patients with fever of unknown origin, failure to thrive, significant weight loss, or unexplained lymphadenopathy should be evaluated for TB.**
E. The lungs are the most common site for the development of TB; 85% of symptomatic patients present with pulmonary complaints.

Incidence

A. TB is a worldwide infection and is considered a global public health emergency by the WHO. One third of the world population is infected.
   1. The WHO reports more than 9 million new cases of TB every year.
   2. TB can affect any age group. Over 60% of the cases are 25 to 40 years old.
   3. TB is the leading cause of death for those infected with HIV.
   4. The incidence of TB in the United States is 3.2 cases per 100,000 population.
   5. Due to the high risk among immigrants, California, New York, Texas, and Florida accounted for half of the TB cases reported in the United States.

B. Postprimary TB is a significant cause of worldwide morbidity and mortality. Pulmonary morbidity results from a chronic cough, hemoptysis, fibrosis, superinfection, bronchial stenosis, repeated pulmonary infections, or empyema. Morbidity also arises from chronic TB osteomyelitis, chronic renal insufficiency, and central nervous system (CNS) TB.

Pathogenesis

A. Mycobacteria are nonspore-forming, slow-growing bacilli. TB infection occurs by means of inhalation of airborne bacillus droplets from an infected host. The development of an infection depends on prolonged exposure (weeks) to an individual with active pulmonary TB. Bacilli travel through the pulmonary lymphatics or enter the vascular system and are disseminated to the brain, meninges, eyes, bones, joints, lymph nodes, kidneys, intestines, larynx, and skin. The incubation period from infection to positive skin test reaction is 2 to 10 weeks, although disease may not occur for many years or may never occur. The risk of disease is greatest within 2 years following infection.

Predisposing Factors

A. Exposure to someone with active disease
B. High-risk groups: Minorities, foreign-born people, prisoners, nursing home residents, teachers, indigents, migrant workers, and health care providers
C. HIV infection is one of the most significant risk factors for TB.
D. Steroid therapy, cancer chemotherapy, and hematologic malignancies increase the risk of TB.
E. Tumor necrosis factor-alpha (TNF-alpha) antagonist used for rheumatoid arthritis, psoriasis, and other autoimmune disease is associated with a significant risk for TB. **Prior to beginning any TNF-alpha treatment, a TB skin test should be administered.**
F. Non-TB infections such as measles, varicella, and pertussis may activate quiescent TB.
G. Smoking
H. Malnutrition
I. Alcoholism
J. IV drug abuse
K. Congenital TB (rare)

Common Complaints

A. Fever (usually low grade at onset but becoming marked with progression of disease)
B. Malaise
C. Weight loss/difficulty gaining weight
D. Cough
E. Night sweats
F. Chills
G. Occasional hemoptysis
H. Fatigue

Other Signs and Symptoms

A. Pulmonary TB: Fatigue, irritability, undernutrition, with or without fever and cough
B. Glandular TB: Chronic cervical adenitis
C. Meningeal TB: Fever and meningeal signs, positive cerebrospinal fluid
D. Failure to thrive
E. Anorexia

Subjective Data

A. Determine onset, duration, and course of illness.
B. Review symptom history: Fever, night sweats, chills, or cough
C. Review history of weight loss.
D. Review exposure history to someone who has TB.
E. What is the patient's living situation?
F. Review travel history to endemic areas with TB, including China, Pakistan, the Philippines, Thailand, Indonesia, Bangladesh, and the Democratic Republic of Congo.
G. Review HIV status or need for testing.

Physical Examination

A complete physical examination is mandatory. Physical findings of pulmonary TB are not specific and usually are absent in mild or moderate disease.

A. Record temperature, respirations, pulse, blood pressure, and weight.
B. Inspect
    1. Observe overall appearance.
    2. Check skin for pallor.
    3. Inspect eyes, ears, nose, and throat.
C. Auscultate
    1. Auscultate heart.
    2. Auscultate lungs and chest for the following:
        a. Rales in upper posterior chest
        b. Bronchophony (voice sounds louder than usual)
        c. Whispered pectoriloquy: Patient's whispered sounds are louder than normal.
D. Percuss chest.
E. Palpate
    1. Palpate for lymphadenopathy, usually anterior or posterior cervical and supraclavicular nodes. Less commonly involved lymph nodes include submandibular, axillary, and inguinal lymph nodes.
    2. Palpate to evaluate hepatosplenomegaly.
F. Neurologic examination
    1. Evaluate the presence of nuchal rigidity.
    2. Assess deep tendon reflexes.

Diagnostic Tests

Diagnosis is based on a combination of tuberculin skin testing, PPD testing, and sputum cultures. Bronchoscopy may be required to obtain specimens. Patients with primary TB may not undergo imaging; however, conventional CXR may be performed, and 15% of patients with primary TB have normal CXR findings.

Patients with progressive primary or postprimary TB may need a CT to evaluate parenchymal involvement, satellite lesions, bronchogenic spread, and miliary disease. MRI may be ordered to evaluate complications, such as the extent of thoracic wall involvement with empyema.

A. Tuberculin skin test using the Mantoux test is the recommended method. The dosage of 0.1 mL or 5 tuberculin units (TU) of PPD should be injected intradermally into the volar aspect of the forearm using a 27-gauge needle. A wheel should be raised and should measure approximately 6 to 10 mm in diameter. Skilled personnel should read the test in 48 to 72 hours after administration. Measure the amount of induration and not the erythema.

Measure transverse to the long axis of the forearm (see Table 11.3).

B. The FDA has approved QuantiFERON-TB Gold as an alternative TB test for detecting both TB and latent TB infection.
C. Annual Mantoux tests for those at high risk. There is no need to repeat PPD once the patient has reacted and had a positive PPD. A two-step is recommended for initial screening only.
D. AP and lateral CXR films: "Snowstorm" appearance indicates miliary TB; segmental consolidation and hilar adenopathy are common; pleural effusion may be present.
E. CBC with differential
F. **Sputum culture with acid-fast smear; nasopharyngeal secretions and saliva are not acceptable.**
G. IFN-gamma release assay (IGRAs) test
H. HIV testing as indicated by risk factors to guide management
I. Pregnancy test (if indicated) to guide management

Differential Diagnoses

A. TB
B. Bronchiectasis
C. Asthma
D. Histoplasmosis
E. Coccidioidomycosis
F. Blastomycosis
G. Malignancies
H. Other pulmonary infections
I. Aspiration pneumonia

Plan

A. General interventions
   1. **Report all suspected and confirmed cases of TB to the local health department.**
   2. **Directly observed therapy (DOT) is mandatory for the treatment of patients with coexistent HIV disease, those with multidrug-resistant (MDR) TB, and those who may be noncompliant.**
   3. Educate patients regarding compliance to therapy, adverse effect of medications, and follow-up care.

B. Pharmaceutical therapy: The American Thoracic Society (ATS) and the CDC provide the standard guidelines for therapy.
   1. Refer to the CDC for up-to-date guidelines on treatment: www.cdc.gov/tb/publications/guidelines/treatment.htm. Medication protocols vary and include the following first-line agents: Isoniazid (INH), rifampin (Rifadin), pyrazinamide (Tebrazid), and ethambutol (Etibi).
      a. Isoniazid (Laniazid, Nydrazid) dosing
         i. Adults: 5 to 10 mg/kg by mouth (not to exceed 300 mg/d)
      b. Rifampin (Rifadin) dosing
         i. Adults: 600 mg by mouth every day
      c. Pyrazinamide (Tebrazid) dosing
         i. Adults: 15 to 30 mg/kg by mouth every day; not to exceed 2 g/d
      d. Ethambutol (Myambutol) dosing
         i. Adults with no previous anti-TB therapy: 15 mg/kg by mouth every day
         ii. Adults with previous therapy: 25 mg/kg by mouth every day
   2. Compliance with drug regimen is most important.
   3. Drug resistance averages 5% to 10% nationally and is increasing.
   4. The bacilli Calmette-Guerin (BCG) vaccine is available for the prevention of disseminated TB. BCG is a live vaccine. BCG does not prevent infection with *M. tuberculosis.*

Follow-Up

A. Regular follow-up every 4 to 8 weeks to ensure compliance and to monitor the adverse effects and response of the medications.
B. Repeat CXR may be performed after 2 to 3 months of therapy to observe the response to treatment for patients with pulmonary TB.
C. Consider monitoring liver enzymes monthly in the following patients:
   1. Severe or disseminated TB
   2. Concurrent or recent hepatic disease or hepatobiliary tract disease from other causes

TABLE 11.3 Interpretation of Mantoux Tuberculin Skin Test

Positive Reaction—Induration Size	Risk Factors
5 mm or more	Close contact with a known or suspected TB; immunosuppressive conditions (e.g., HIV); on immunosuppressive medications; or an abnormal chest x-ray—consistent with active TB, previously active TB, or clinical evidence of the disease.
10 mm or more	High-risk categories (i.e., homeless, HIV infected, users of illicit drugs, residents in nursing homes, incarcerated, or institutionalized); travel histories to high-prevalence areas of world.
15 mm or more	Any age without any risk factors for TB.

3. Those receiving high doses of INH (10 mg/kg/d) in combination with rifampin, pyrazinamide, or both drugs
4. Women who are pregnant or within the first 6 weeks postpartum
5. Clinical evidence of hepatotoxic effects

Consultation/Referral

A. An infectious diseases consultation for the management of affected patients
B. Reportable illness to the county health department

Individual Considerations

A. Pregnancy
    1. Manage TB on a case-by-case basis with a physician.
    2. Chemotherapy must be started immediately after the first trimester to protect both mother and fetus.
        a. First-line agents recommended by the AAP include INH, rifampin, and ethambutol.
        b. Streptomycin is contraindicated in pregnancy.
    3. All pregnant women on INH therapy should receive pyridoxine.
    4. The mother who has current disease but is noncontagious at delivery does not require separation from her infant. These mothers can also breastfeed.
    5. The mother who has current disease and is contagious at delivery requires separation from her infant until the mother is noncontagious.

Bibliography

Agency for Healthcare Research and Quality. (2009). Clinical guideline for the evaluation, management and long-term care of obstructive sleep apnea. *National Guideline Clearing House Guideline Summary NGC-7517*. Retrieved from guideline.gov/content.aspx?id=15298

Agency for Healthcare Research and Quality. (2012). Diagnosis and management of asthma. *National Guideline Clearing House Guideline Summary NGC-009282*. Retrieved from http://www.guideline.gov/content.aspx?id=38255&search=asthma

Agency for Healthcare Research and Quality. (2014). Diagnosis and management of chronic obstructive pulmonary disease (COPD). *National Guideline Clearing House Guideline Summary*. Retrieved from http://www.guideline.gov/syntheses/synthesis.aspx?id=48263&search=copd

American College of Obstetricians and Gynecologists (ACOG). (2014, September). Committee Opinion No. 608 influenza vaccination during pregnancy. *Obstretics and Gynecology, 124*, 648–650.

American Dietetic Association. (2009). *American Dietetic Association chronic obstructive pulmonary disease (COPD) evidence-based nutrition practice guideline*. Retrieved from http://www.adaevidencelibrary.com/tmp/prn6D80E0CAFE734D8FC127FB5D0FBB7BEB.pdf

American Lung Association. (n.d). *Tuberculosis fast sheet*. Retrieved from www.lung.org/lung-disease/tuberculosis/tuberculosis-fact-sheet.html

American Lung Association. (2014, May). *Chronic Obstructive Pulmonary Disease fact sheet*. Retrieved from http://www.lung.org/lung-disease/copd/resources/facts-figures/COPD-Fact-Sheet.html

American Society for Metabolic and Bariatric Surgery. (2012, March). *Peri-operative management of obstructive sleep apnea*. Retrieved from asmbs.org/2012/03/peri-operative-management-of-obstructive-sleep-apnea

American Thoracic Society. (2012). *An official American Thoracic Society statement: An Update on the mechanisms, assessment, and management of dyspnea*. Retrieved from http://www.thoracic.org/search.php?cx=007982365765420951334%3A7u3jtkdzuqu&cof=FORID%3A10&ie=UTF-8&q=dyspnea&sa.x=0&sa.y=0&siteurl=www.thoracic.org%2Fstatements%2F&ref=www.uptodate.com.lib-proxy.usi.edu%2Fcontents%2Fapproach-to-the-patient-with-dyspnea%3Fsource%3Dpreview%26search%3Ddyspnea%26selectedTitle%3D1%257E150%26language%3Den-US%26anchor%3DH1&ss=1531j407531j7

Bronze, M. S. (2014, April 17). H1N1 influenza (swine flu). *Medscape Reference*. Retrieved from emedicine.medscape.com/article/1807048-overview

Centers for Disease Control and Prevention. (2009, July). *Clinical signs and symptoms of influenza*. Retrieved from www.cdc.gov/flu/professionals/acip/clinical.htm

Centers for Disease and Control and Prevention. (2011, January 21). Antiviral agents for the treatment and chemoprophylaxis of influenza recommendations of the Advisory Committee on Immunization Practices (ACIP). *MMWR Report, 60*(1): 1–24. Retrieved from www.cdc.gov/mmwr/preview/mmwrhtml/rr6001a1.htm

Centers for Disease Control and Prevention. (2012, March 13). *Tuberculosis (TB)*. Retrieved from http://www.cdc.gov/tb/topic/basics/default.htm

Centers for Disease Control and Prevention. (2012, August 16). *Pertussis (whooping cough) surveillance & reporting*. Retrieved from www.cdc.gov/pertussis/surv-reporting.html

Centers for Disease Control and Prevention. (2012, September 1). *Fact sheet: Tuberculin skin testing*. Retrieved from http://www.cdc.gov/tb/publications/factsheets/testing/skintesting.htm

Centers for Disease Control and Prevention. (2012, September 1). *Treatment for TB disease*. Retrieved from http://www.cdc.gov/tb/topic/treatment/tbdisease.htm

Centers for Disease Control and Prevention. (2013, January 11). *FastStats asthma*. Retrieved from www.cdc.gov/nchs/fastats/asthma.htm

Centers for Disease Control and Prevention. (2013, January 11). *FastStats chronic obstructive pulmonary disease (COPD) includes: chronic bronchitis and emphysema*. Retrieved from www.cdc.gov/nchs/fastats/copd.htm

Centers for Disease Control and Prevention. (2013, February 8). *Pertussis (whooping cough)*. Retrieved from www.cdc.gov/pertussis

Centers for Disease Control and Prevention. (2013, August 20). *Summary recommendations: Prevention and control of influenza with vaccines: Recommendations of the Advisory Committee on Immunization Practices (ACIP), 2013–14*. Retrieved from www.cdc.gov/flu/professionas/acip/2013-interim-recommendations.htm

Centers for Disease Control and Prevention. (2013, September 30). *Bronchitis (Chest cold)*. Retrieved from http://www.cdc.gov/getsmart/antibiotic-use/URI/bronchitis.html

Centers for Disease Control and Prevention. (2013, October 3). *What you should know about the 2014–2015 influenza season.* Retrieved from www.cdc.gov/flu/season/flu-season-2014-2015.htm

Centers for Disease Control and Prevention. (2014, September 9). *People at high risk of developing flu-related complications.* Retrieved from http://www.cdc.gov/flu/about/disease/high_risk.htm

Centers for Disease Control and Prevention. (2014). *Recommended adult immunization schedule – United States, 2014.* Retrieved from http://www.cdc.gov/vaccines/schedules/downloads/adult/adult-schedule.pdf

Centers for Disease Control and Prevention. (2014, March 7). *Data and Statistics.* Retrieved from http://www.cdc.gov/TB/statistics

Chen, H. H. (2014 May 13). Chronic cough. *Medscape Reference.* Retrieved from emedicine.medscape.com/article/1048560-overview

Demirjian, B. G. (2012, September 17). Emphysema. *Medscape Reference.* Retrieved from emedicine.medscape.com/article/298283-overview

Deng, J. C., & Nguyen, C. D. (2011). 2009 influenza A (H1N1) virus. *Epocrates online.* Retrieved from https://online.epocrates.com/dx/indexprint.jsp?entire=true&iid=1178&sid-21

Downey, R. (2014, May 12). Obstructive sleep apnea. *Medscape Reference.* Retrieved from http://emedicine.medscape.com/article/295807-overview

Epocrates. (2014). *Epocrates Essential (version 14.1), IOS.* Retrieved from http://epocrates.com

Fanta, C. H. (2014, July 8). An overview of asthma management. *UpToDate.* Retrieved from http://www.uptodate.com/home

Fayyaz, J. (2014, March 28). Bronchitis. *Medscape Reference.* Retrieved from emedicine.medscape.com/article/297108-overview

File, T. M. (2014, May 27). Acute bronchitis in adults. *UpToDate.* Retrieved from http://www.uptodate.com/home

File, T. M. (2014, July 7). Treatment of community-acquired pneumonia in adults in the outpatient setting. *UpToDate.* Retrieved from http://www.uptodate.com/home

Global Initiative for Chronic Obstructive Lung Disease. (2014). *Pocket guide to COPD diagnosis, management, and prevention: A guide for health care professionals.* Retrieved from www.goldcopd.org/upload http://www.goldcopd.org/guidelines-pocket-guide-to-copd-diagnosis.html

Herchline, T. E. (2013). Tuberculosis treatment and management. *Medscape Reference.* Retrieved from emedicine.medscape.com/article/230802-treatment

Herchline, T. E. (2014, June 9). Tuberculosis. *Medscape Reference.* Retrieved from emedicine.medscape.com/article/230802-overview

Horsburgh, C. R. (2014, July 14). The epidemiology of tuberculosis. *UpToDate.* Retrieved from http://www.uptodate.com/home

Journal Watch Specialities. (n.d.). *FluMist: Intranasal flu vaccine.* Retrieved from infectious-diseases.jwatch.org/cgi/content/full/2003/808/3

Ledbetter, E. (2009). Quick care tips: Assessment and treatment of influenza. *Advance for Nurse Practitioners, 17,* 40.

Medscape Drug Reference. (n.d.). Theophylline oral. *Medscape.* Retrieved from http://www.medscape.com/druginfo/dosage?drugid=3591&drugname=Theophylline+Oral&monotype=default

Mosenifar, Z. (2014, May 2). Viral pneumonia treatment & management. *Medscape Reference.* Retrieved from emedicine.medscape.com/article/300455-overview

MPR Nurse Practitioner Edition (2014, Summer). *Haymark Media Publication.* Retrieved from www.eMPR.com

O'Laughlen, M. C., & Rance, K. (2012, November). Update on asthma management in primary care. *The Nurse Practitioner, 37,* 32–40.

Pozniak, A. (2014, June 18). Clinical manifestations and evaluation of pulmonary tuberculosis. *UpToDate.* Retrieved from http://www.uptodate.com/home

Qaseem A., Dallas, P., Owens, D. K., Starkey, M., Holty, J. E. C., & Shekelle, P. (2014). Diagnosis of obstructive sleep apnea in adults: A clinical practice guideline from the American College of Physicians. *Annals of Internal Medicine, 161,* 210–220.

Rajnik, M. (2014, April 28). Rhinovirus infection. *Medscape Reference.* Retrieved from http://emedicine.medscape.com/article/227820-overview

Rennard, S. I. (2014, May 31). Chronic obstructive pulmonary disease: Definition, clinical manifestations, diagnosis, and staging. *UpToDate.* Retrieved from http://www.uptodate.com/online/contents/chronic-obstructivepulmonary-disease-definition-clinical-manifestationsdiagnosis-and-staging?topickey=PULM%2F15455

Schwartzstein, R. M. (2014, January 14). Approach to the patient with dyspnea. *UpToDate.* Retrieved from http://www.uptodate.com/home

Schwartzstein, R. M. (2014, January 14). Physiology of dyspnea. *UpToDate.* Retrieved from http://www.uptodate.com/home

Search Medica Rx. (n.d.). *Zyflo-detailed prescribing information.* Retrieved from www.mims.com/USA/drug/info/Zyflo/Zyflo tablet%2cfilm Coated?q=zylfo&type=full

Sexton, D. J., & McClain, M. T. (2014, January 10). The common cold in adults: Treatment and Prevention. *UpToDate.* Retrieved from http://www.uptodate.com/home

Silvestri, R. C., & Weinberger, S. E. (2014, July 11). Evaluation of subactue and chronic cough in adults. *UpToDate.* Retrieved from http://www.uptodate.com/home

Stanley, T., Gordon, J. S., & Pilon, B. A. (2013, January). Patient and provider attributes association with chronic obstructive pulmonary disease exacerbations. *Journal for Nurse Practitioners, 9,* 34–39.

Sterling, T. R. (2014, July 2). Treatment of pulmonary tuberculosis in HIV-negative patients. *UpToDate.* Retrieved from http://www.uptodate.com/home

Strohl, K. P. (2014, April 24). Overview of obstructive sleep apnea in adults. *UpToDate.* Retrieved from http://www.uptodate.com/home

World Health Organization. (2012, November). *Pneumonia fact sheet N331.* Retrieved from www.who.int/mediacentre/factsheets/fs331/en

CHAPTER TWELVE

Cardiovascular Guidelines

Debbie A. Gunter, Jill C. Cash, Laura A. Petty, and Cheryl A. Glass

Acute Myocardial Infarction

Definition

A. Acute myocardial infarction (MI) is a prolonged lack of myocardial oxygenation leading to necrosis of a portion of the heart muscle. It is caused by atherosclerotic coronary artery disease (CAD), which alone or in association with other factors causes complete blockage of one of the coronary arteries.

Incidence

A. Approximately 1.5 million Americans sustain an acute MI annually in the United States. Despite a marked decrease in incidence and mortality during the past three decades, MI continues to be the leading cause of death in this country, accounting for one fourth of all fatalities. More women die from heart disease than men.

Pathogenesis

A. Abrupt coronary artery occlusion is the primary cause of most MIs. Occlusions can result from atherosclerotic plaque, intracoronary thrombus formation, or arterial spasm.

Predisposing Factors

A. Hypercholesterolemia: Increased low-density lipoprotein (LDL), decreased high-density lipoprotein (HDL)
B. Hypertriglyceridemia
C. Premature familial onset of coronary heart disease (CHD), formerly called CAD, before age 55
D. Smoking
E. Hypertension (HTN)
F. Obesity
G. Sedentary lifestyle
H. Diabetes mellitus
I. Aging
J. Stress

Common Complaints

A. Primary complaint: Pain somewhere in chest, described as worst pain ever experienced
B. Nausea
C. Vomiting
D. Diaphoresis
E. Indigestion

Other Signs and Symptoms

A. Pain in abdomen, arm, back, jaw, and neck
B. Chest heaviness or tightness
C. Anxiety
D. Cough
E. Dyspnea
F. HTN or hypotension
G. Weakness, lightheadedness, syncope
H. Pallor
I. Orthopnea
J. Fatigue
K. Malaise

Potential Complications

A. Arrhythmias
B. Heart failure (HF)
C. Cardiogenic shock
D. Rupture of left ventricular (LV) papillary muscle
E. Ventricular septal rupture
F. Pericarditis or Dressler's syndrome
G. Ventricular aneurysm
H. Thromboembolism
I. Death

Subjective Data

A. Ask the patient what activity brought about or preceded the episode of chest pain.
B. Ask the patient to describe the duration of pain and what time of day symptoms began.
C. Ask the patient to describe pain, for example, crushing, stabbing, or burning.

D. Ask the patient where sensation began and in what direction it radiates.
E. Identify the degree of pain by using a pain scale of 0 to 10, with 0 being no pain.
F. Ask the patient to list all medications currently being taken, particularly substances not prescribed and illicit drugs such as cocaine.

Physical Examination

Patients presenting with acute chest pain should be quickly assessed for the need to call emergency services/911 for immediate transport to the hospital.

A. Check pulse, respirations, blood pressure (BP), and pulse oxygenation.
B. Inspect
   1. Inspect general appearance, noting dyspnea and weakness.
   2. Inspect skin for pallor and diaphoresis.
   3. Inspect legs for edema.
   4. Inspect chest wall for visible pulsations.
   5. Inspect neck for jugular vein distension.
   6. Observe nail beds for signs of cyanosis and note capillary filling time.
C. Palpate
   1. Palpate abdomen for organomegaly.
   2. Palpate peripheral pulses in legs.
   3. Palpate femoral pulses.
D. Auscultate
   1. Auscultate carotid arteries.
   2. Auscultate abdomen.
   3. Conduct a complete heart exam, checking for dysrhythmias.
   4. Conduct a complete lung exam.
E. Mental status: Assess for confusion and anxiety.

Diagnostic Tests

A. EKG: Shows inverted T waves, ST segment elevation, and Q waves. **One normal EKG initially does not always rule out MI; perform serial EKGs if MI suspected.**
B. Laboratory testing
   1. Cardiac biomarkers/enzymes
   2. Troponin levels: A protein that is released when necrosis of the cardiac muscles occurs
   3. Creatine kinase (CK): CK-MB levels increase 3 to 12 hours after the chest pain begins, peaks at 24 hours, and returns to normal in 48 to 72 hours.
   4. Myoglobin: Urine myoglobin levels rise 1 to 4 hours after the chest pain begins.
   5. Complete blood count (CBC)
   6. Chemistry profile
   7. Lipid profile
   8. C-reactive protein (CRP) and inflammatory markers
C. Cardiac imaging: coronary angiogram

Differential Diagnoses

A. Acute MI
B. Unstable angina pectoris
C. Aortic dissection
D. Pulmonary embolism (PE)
E. Pericarditis
F. Esophageal spasm
G. Pancreatitis
H. Biliary tract disease

Plan

A. General interventions
   1. Educating the patient and family regarding the signs and symptoms of an acute MI should be performed.
   2. Long-term care and treatment should be reinforced at each patient visit.
B. Patient teaching
   1. Educate the patient about modifying controllable risk factors such as keeping diabetes and HTN under control, diet, exercise, and smoking cessation.
   2. If known CHD is present
      a. Instruct the patient on signs and symptoms of an acute MI.
      b. Advise the patient to have a plan in seeking medical attention or dialing 911 if signs and symptoms occur.
      c. Advise the patient to carry nitroglycerin at all times and to take the nitroglycerin at the first sign of chest pain. If there is no relief after 5 minutes, 911 should be called. Nitroglycerin may be repeated every 5 minutes times three doses.
      d. Encourage cardiopulmonary resuscitation (CPR) training for family members and close friends.
      e. Exercise regimen: Encourage routine exercise for the patient most days of the week, such as walking, treadmill use, and so on, once released by the cardiologist.
      f. Advise smoking cessation as indicated. Encourage support groups, classes, and smoking cessation aids as indicated (see the Section III Patient Teaching Guide for Chapter 11, "Nicotine Dependence").
C. Dietary management: Counsel the patient on nutrition and low-fat, low-cholesterol, low-sodium diets. Recommend the dietary approaches to stop hypertension (DASH) diet and lifestyle changes. Provide dietary handouts on the DASH diet and low-fat/low-cholesterol/low-sodium diet. See Appendix B for the DASH diet.
D. Pharmaceutical therapy
   1. When MI is suspected: Aspirin 160 to 325 mg (four 81 mg baby aspirin) chewed or swallowed

as soon as possible. Enteric-coated aspirin delays absorption and therefore is not recommended.

2. Instruct the patient on how to take sublingual nitroglycerin tablets and other medications.
3. Nitrates: Nitroglycerin sublingual 0.2 to 0.6 mg every 5 minutes for ischemic chest pain in the absence of hypotension
4. If pain persists after three doses of nitroglycerin:
   a. Morphine sulfate IV; 2 to 4 mg IV, repeating every 5 minutes until pain resolves. Dose may be increased at 2 to 8 mg per dose as tolerated. Monitor side effects: Nausea/vomiting, dizziness, hypotension, respiratory distress.
5. Oxygen therapy: 2 to 4 L per nasal cannula
6. If there are no contraindications (bradycardia, HF, second or third degree heart block, asthma, shock), beta blockers may be started IV during the acute phase and changed to oral therapy during course of the treatment.
7. Fibrinolytic therapy may be used for patients with suspected MI with ST-elevation myocardial infarction (STEMI) or non-ST-elevation myocardial infarction (NSTEMI) with left bundle branch block.
8. After an MI, if the patient is not currently on a statin, a statin should be started.

Follow-Up

A. Follow-up is determined by patient's needs, severity of acute MI, and whether complications are present.

Consultation/Referral

A. If MI is suspected, refer patient for immediate hospitalization.
B. According to the 2013 American College of Cardiology/American Heart Association (ACC/AHA) guidelines for the management of a patient who is a candidate for reperfusion who is seen at a percutaneous coronary intervention (PCI)-capable hospital, this patient should be sent to the cath lab for primary PCI in less than or equal to 90 minutes. If the patient is at a facility that is non-PCI capable, then a transfer should be made to a PCI facility as soon as possible and in less than or equal to 120 minutes. If the time lapse will be greater than 120 minutes, then it is recommended to administer fibrinolytic therapy within 30 minutes of arrival.
C. Follow up with cardiologist as scheduled when discharged from the hospital.

Individual Considerations

A. Geriatrics
   1. In the first hours of MI, the elderly are more likely to complain about symptoms other than typical coronary chest pain. They often describe dyspnea, fatigue, and dizziness. Confusion or altered mental status may be the presenting manifestation of acute MI in up to 20% of patients older than 85 years of age.
   2. Even when classic ischemic precordial discomfort is present, it tends to be less severe and less well defined. The elderly appear to have reduced pain perception.
   3. Older patients are also more likely to have "silent" or unrecognized MIs compared to younger patients. These facts often result in delays in MI diagnosis in the elderly. The length of time from symptom onset to hospital admission is significantly longer for the elderly compared to the younger patient.

Arrhythmias

Definition

Arrhythmias are abnormal heart rhythms. Common types are the following:

A. Bradycardia: Heart rate less than 60 bpm; impulse originates in SA node
B. Tachycardia: Heart rate greater than 100 to 160 bpm; impulse originates in SA node
C. Supraventricular tachydysrhythmias (SVTs): Heart rate greater than 100 bpm; originates in
   1. Atrioventricular (AV) nodal reentrant tachycardia (NRT), which is intranodal reentry by means of fast and slow conduction pathways within the AV junction
   2. Orthodromic atrioventricular reentrant tachycardia (AVRT), which is tachycardia across accessory pathways associated with preexcitation
D. Atrial fibrillation (AF): Chaotic electrical activity caused by rapid discharges from numerous ectopic foci in atria. Atrial rate is difficult to count. There are three types of AF.
   1. Paroxysmal AF occurs in patients who usually have normal sinus rhythm (NSR).
   2. Chronic AF occurs in patients who have a permanent fibrillation rather than brief episodes of symptoms.
   3. Premature ventricular contractions (PVCs) are impulses that form within the Purkinje network (see "Atrial Fibrillation" in this chapter).

Incidence

A. SVTs are the most common cardiac arrhythmias presenting to health care providers.
B. Atrioventricular nodal reentrant tachycardia (AVNRT) accounts for 60% to 70% of all SVTs.
C. AVRTs account for 30% to 40%.
D. AF is the most common cardiac tachydysrhythmia, affecting approximately 2% of the general

population. Prevalence increases with age to 5% of those older than age 69. The presence of AF is associated with a fivefold increase in risk of morbidity, a twofold increase in mortality, and an increased incidence of embolic stroke.

E. PVCs are common, and their frequency increases with age.

Pathogenesis

A. Bradycardia: Dominance of the parasympathetic nervous system, with excessive vagal stimulation to the heart, causes a decreased heart rate of sinus node discharge.

B. Tachycardia: Dominant sympathetic nervous system stimulation of the heart or vagal inhibition results in positive chronotropic, dromotropic, and inotropic effects.

C. AVRT: The most classic form of this SVT is Wolff–Parkinson–White (WPW) syndrome. Reentry occurs in a loop using atrial myocardium, AV node-His-Purkinje system, ventricular myocardium, and an accessory AV connection. During sinus rhythm, antegrade conduction through the accessory connection depolarizes the myocardium earlier than would occur by conduction through the AV node-His-Purkinje system, preexcitation is present, and a delta wave (slurring of initial deflection of the QRS complex) is usually seen on the surface 12-lead EKG.

D. AVNRT: The most common form is antegrade conduction, which occurs through a pathway with a short effective refractory period (ERP) and a longer conduction time. This pathway is often referred to as the slow pathway.

E. AF: Multiple, rapid impulses from many foci depolarize the atria in a totally disorganized manner. In the chaos, no P waves, no atrial contraction, loss of atrial kick, and a totally irregular ventricular response occur. The atria quiver, which leads to formation of mural thrombi and potential embolic events.

F. PVCs: These originate in the ventricles as a result of increased irritability in those cells.

Predisposing Factors

A. Bradycardia
   1. Increased vagal tone
   2. Decreased sympathetic drive
   3. Ischemia to SA node
   4. Drugs: Digitalis, propranolol, sedatives, propylthiouracil (PTU) or Tapazole, aminophylline, caffeine, alcohol, nicotine, and sympathomimetics
   5. Normal variant in athletes
   6. Normal body response to insult
   7. Atrial enlargement
   8. Acute MI
   9. Congestive heart failure (CHF)
   10. Rheumatic heart disease
   11. Hypertensive heart disease
   12. Thyroid disease
   13. Hypothermia
   14. Electrolyte abnormality
   15. Acidosis
   16. Infection

B. Tachycardia
   1. Decreased vagal tone
   2. Increased sympathetic tone
   3. MI

C. SVT
   1. Digitalis toxicity
   2. Catecholamines

D. AF
   1. Myocardial ischemia
   2. Thyrotoxicosis

E. PVC
   1. Stress
   2. Myocardial ischemia

Common Complaints

A. Symptoms may not be present; however, patient may note irregular heartbeat.

B. Palpitations

C. Chest discomfort

D. Shortness of breath (SOB)

E. Dizziness

F. Diaphoresis

G. Weakness

H. Syncope

I. Nausea

Subjective Data

A. Obtain an accurate health and medical history.

B. Explore precipitating factors, such as emotional stress, alcohol or drug use, hot tub, or bath use.

C. Inquire about onset and duration of symptoms, also noting the age of the patient when symptoms began.

D. Explore whether the patient has had concomitant weight loss, mood changes, and tremor, which are often associated with hyperthyroidism.

E. Carefully determine the number of previous episodes of palpitations or symptoms and what treatment, if any, was initiated.

F. Review all medications including prescription, over-the-counter (OTC), and herbal products.

Physical Examination

A. Check pulse, respirations, BP, and weight.
   1. Sinus bradycardia: Pulse rate decreased
   2. EKG: Normal

3. Sinus tachycardia
   a. Pulse regular
   b. Systolic BP (SBP) constant
4. AF
   a. Pulse irregular
   b. SBP changing
5. AVNRT
   a. Pulse regular; AV block usual
   b. SBP constant; electrical alternans rare
6. AVRT
   a. Pulse regular; AV block not present
   b. SBP constant; electrical alternans common, especially at high heart rates
7. PVC: Pulse diminished or absent

B. Inspect
1. General appearance
   a. Is the patient in respiratory distress? Note SOB, chest pain, dyspnea.
   b. Does the patient look apathetic? This is a sign of a thyroid problem.
2. Inspect the skin for flushing or pallor.
3. Examine the eyes, noting lid lag.
4. Assess the neck for jugular vein distension or thyromegaly.
   a. With sinus tachycardia, neck vein pulsation is normal.
   b. With AF, neck vein pulsation is irregular; assess for thyromegaly.
   c. AVNRT: Assess the neck veins for "frog sign," in which the atria contract against closed AV valves, producing rapid, regular, expansive venous pulsation in the neck, resembling the rhythmic puffing motion of a frog.
   d. AVRT: Assess for frog sign.

C. Auscultate the neck for carotid artery bruits and the heart for abnormal heart sounds. Heart rhythm may be regular or irregular, depending on type of dysrhythmia. Have the patient perform vagal maneuver (Valsalva's maneuver). If the vagal maneuver responds to rapid heart rate and the cycle is broken, it is likely the patient has AVRT. If it does not respond, it is possible the patient has AVNRT.
1. Sinus bradycardia
   a. Rate less than 60 bpm
   b. Rhythm regular
2. Sinus tachycardia
   a. Rate equals 160 to 200 bpm
   b. Rhythm regular; gradual onset and cessation
   c. Constant loudness of first heart sound
3. AF
   a. Rate: Atrial rate is nonmeasurable, ventricular rate is variable, usually rapid at onset.
   b. Rhythm: Atrial and ventricular rhythms are irregular.
   c. Loudness of first heart sound changes.
4. AVNRT
   a. AV block is usually present.
   b. Loudness of first heart sound is constant.
5. AVRT
   a. AV block is not present.
   b. Constant loudness of first heart sound
6. PVC
   a. Rate depends on underlying rhythm.
   b. Rhythm: Prematurity interrupts regularity of rhythm.

Diagnostic Tests

A. EKG

B. Drug screen
1. Digitalis
2. Aminophylline
3. Illicit drugs

C. Electrolytes

D. Arterial blood gases (ABGs) if indicated

Differential Diagnoses

A. Multifocal atrial tachycardia

B. Sinus tachycardia with multiple premature atrial contractions

C. Atrial flutter

D. Ventricular tachycardia

E. AV blocks

Plan

A. General interventions
1. Remove as many predisposing factors as possible.
2. Stop smoking.

B. Patient teaching
1. Teach relaxation techniques.
2. Teach the patient and his or her family signs of hemodynamic compromise, including rapid heart rate, unexplained weight gain, worsening dyspnea on exertion, and decreased exercise tolerance.
3. Teach and reassure the patient about long-term medication therapy and its side effects.
4. Educate the patient and family regarding safety, dietary restrictions and complications that may occur (bleeding) with the use of anticoagulant therapy.
5. Discuss the need for a pacemaker/defibrillator or surgical ablation.

C. Pharmaceutical therapy
1. Initial treatment usually is prescribed by a physician.
2. Selection of treatment modality should be based on underlying pathophysiology.
3. For reentrant cases (AVNRT, AVRT), agents that block the reentrant circuit are more effective.
   a. Digitalis
   b. Beta blockers
   c. Calcium channel blockers (CCBs)

4. Episodes caused by increased automaticity are treated with the following:
   a. Quinidine gluconate (Quinaglute)
   b. Procainamide HCl (Procan SR)
   c. Disopyramide phosphate (Norpace CR)
5. Chronic AF is treated with anticoagulants such as warfarin sodium (Coumadin).
   a. Start therapy as soon as possible if a history of underlying heart disease is present.
   b. Evaluate prothrombin time/international normalized ratio (PT/INR) on a regular basis to monitor for therapeutic response to warfarin sodium treatment.

Follow-Up

A. Patients who have their first episode of AF should return to the clinic within 24 to 48 hours for reevaluation.
B. Patients on antiarrhythmic agents should have liver enzymes measured during the first 4 to 8 weeks of therapy.
C. Patients with risk factors for developing cardiac complications to therapy should have EKGs during the first weeks of therapy and every 3 to 6 months thereafter.
D. Monitor patients on digoxin carefully for digitalis toxicity.
E. Caution the patient regarding interactions of medication with digitalis.

Consultation/Referral

A. Consult a physician when questions arise about the difference between a narrow and wide QRS complex.
B. Consult a physician if the patient has an abnormal EKG pattern, refractory AF, suspicion of WPW syndrome, or sick sinus syndrome.
C. Patients with hemodynamic instability should be referred to a hospital or call 911 immediately.
D. Patients unable to tolerate their dysrhythmia should be hospitalized immediately.

Individual Considerations

A. Pregnancy: Digitalis is safe during pregnancy.
B. Geriatrics
   1. Over 50% of AF occurs in the percentage (6%) of the population older than 75 years of age.
   2. Prevalence of AF increases with age.
   3. Advanced age and female gender are potent risk factors for stroke.
   4. New-to-the-market anticoagulants provide alternatives to warfarin but are not without limitations.
   5. The role of mechanical interventions and devices in older AF patients remains to be established.
   6. Lenient rate control with concomitant anticoagulation is a reasonable therapeutic strategy in older patients with limited symptoms.

Atherosclerosis and Hyperlipidemia

Definition

A. Atherosclerosis is a systemic disease characterized by lipid deposition and smooth muscle cell migration and proliferation in the intima of the larger arteries. Atheromatous changes lead to thrombotic stroke, peripheral vascular disease (PVD), atherosclerosis cardiovascular disease (ASCVD), and MI.
B. Hyperlipidemia is an elevation in serum lipoproteins and a major risk factor in the development of CVD. The two main lipids in blood are cholesterol and triglyceride. Cholesterol is a relatively insoluble lipid that is necessary for cell membrane formation, steroid and bile salt production, and the development of nerve sheaths. Cholesterol is composed of three clinically significant components: HDL-C, LDL-C, and very-low-density lipoprotein (VLDL). Triglyceride is found in VLDL particles, but its role in atherosclerosis is not clear.
C. The atherosclerotic build-up of lipids, cholesterol, calcium, and cellular debris within the intima of the blood vessels causes plaque formation, vascular remodeling, and acute and chronic obstruction of the lumen of the blood vessels, which in turn decreases blood flow, causing myocardial ischemia and decreased oxygen to other vital organs.
D. In 2013 the ACC and the AHA published guidelines on the assessment of cardiovascular risk, lifestyle management, and treatment of cholesterol to reduce ASCVD risks. A downloadable spreadsheet enabling estimation of 10-year and lifetime risk for ASCVD, and a web-based calculator, are available at my.americanheart.org/cvriskcalculator and www.cardiosource.org/science-and-quality/practice-guidelines-and-quality-standards/2013-prevention-guideline-tools.aspx. These risk tools are used to drive conversations on patient risk factors for ASCVD, potential benefits, negative aspects of risk, and patient preferences regarding initiation of relevant therapies. The assessment of ASCVD risk factors is recommended every 4 to 6 years in adults 20 to 79 years of age who are free from ASCVD. Long-term and lifetime risk information may be used to motivate therapeutic lifestyle changes (TLCs) and to encourage adherence to these changes and pharmacological therapies.

Incidence

A. Atherosclerosis begins in childhood with the development of fatty streaks. The incidence of atherosclerotic diseases increases with age. CVD causes one in three deaths reported each year in the United States. The annual direct cost of CVD is estimated at $273 billion and the overall cost of CVD is estimated at $444 billion annually.

B. The leading risk factors for CVD are HTN, high cholesterol, and smoking.
   1. HTN can increase arterial wall tension, potentially leading to disturbed repair processes and aneurysm formation.
   2. Cigarette smoking is associated with an increase in multiple inflammatory markers, including CRP, interleukin-6, and tumor necrosis factor.

Pathogenesis

A. Atherosclerosis is in part attributed to the deposition of cholesterol and lipoproteins in arterial smooth muscle cells. Dietary factors, obesity, drugs, and genetic defects in lipoprotein particle metabolism influence lipid and lipoprotein concentrations in blood.

B. Primary hyperlipoproteinemias are either due to single-gene disorders transmitted by simple dominant or recessive mechanisms, or to multifactorial disorders with complicated inheritance patterns.

C. Secondary hyperlipoproteinemias (such as in thyroid disease and diabetes mellitus) occur as part of a constellation of abnormalities in certain metabolic pathways. The association between atherosclerosis, CVD, and hypercholesterolemia is well documented. HDL-C comprises about one fourth of the total serum cholesterol and acts as a scavenger, removing cholesterol from peripheral tissues and returning it to the liver, which produces a favorable cardioprotective effect. Elevated HDL-C levels are desirable. HDL-C levels more than 60 mg/dL are a negative risk factor for CVD; those below 35 mg/dL are a major risk factor for CVD.

D. LDL-C constitutes 70% of the total serum cholesterol. It is the most atherogenic cholesterol subgroup. LDL-C particles interact with platelets, damaged arterial endothelium, and smooth muscle cells in the process of plaque formation. LDL-C levels of 160 mg/dL or greater are associated with an increased number of cardiac events.

E. VLDL accounts for a small amount of total serum cholesterol and is responsible for carrying triglycerides from the liver. Its role in atherogenesis is uncertain, but an inverse relationship has been observed between VLDL and HDL-C.

Predisposing Factors

A. High-risk factors for cardiovascular disease (CVD) events (CVD risk equivalent)
   1. Clinical CVD
   2. Symptomatic carotid artery disease
   3. Peripheral arterial disease (PAD)
   4. Abdominal aortic aneurysm

B. Presence of major risk factors (other than LDL-C)
   1. **Age is the strongest risk factor for the development of cardiovascular disease.**
      a. Age older than 45 years for men, older than 55 years for women
      b. Elderly persons experience a higher morbidity and mortality.
   2. Cigarette smoking
   3. Low HDL-C level, less than 40 mg/dL
   4. Family history of early CVD: MI or sudden cardiac death younger than 55 years in father or other male first-degree relative, before age 65 in mother or other female first-degree relative
   5. HTN (BP > 140/90 mmHg or on antihypertensive medication).
   6. Sedentary lifestyle
   7. Obesity
   8. Metabolic syndrome
   9. Diabetes
   10. Chronic inflammation

HDL-C cholesterol of greater than 60 mg/dL is equal to "negative" risk factor and removes one risk factor from the total count.

Common Complaints

A. There are no complaints or symptoms associated with atherosclerosis and hyperlipidemia. Most lipid abnormalities are detected by routine laboratory testing or as part of a cardiovascular evaluation.

Subjective Data

A. Ask the patient if there is a history of CVD.
B. Discuss his or her past medical history, including predisposing factors for CVD.
C. Have the patient list current medications, including OTC and herbal products.
D. Have the patient discuss his or her current diet and exercise routine.
E. Explore the patient's social habits, including use of alcohol and tobacco.

Physical Examination

A. Check pulse, respirations, BP, height, and weight. Calculate body mass index (BMI) at each subsequent visit. An adult BMI calculator and teen BMI calculator are located at www.cdc.gov/healthyweight/assessing/bmi.
B. Inspect
   1. Funduscopic exam: Examine eyes for premature arcus cornealis, which is a gray opaque line around the cornea caused by lipoid degeneration, and for lipemia retinalis, which is a pale retina with white blood vessels caused by excess serum lipids due to VLDL of more than 2,000 mg/dL or alcoholism.

2. Inspect skin for xanthomas, which appear as red-brown or yellow papules, nodules, or plaque, caused by lipid deposits from high VLDL. Tendinous xanthomas are found on Achilles tendons, patellae, and hands.
3. Inspect joints for Achilles tendonitis and arthritis.

C. Palpate
1. Palpate abdomen for hepatomegaly or splenomegaly.
2. Palpate neck and thyroid.

D. Auscultate
1. Perform a complete heart exam.
2. Perform a complete vascular exam.

Diagnostic Tests

A. Laboratory testing
1. Lipid profile and lipoprotein analysis (see Table 12.1)
2. CBC
3. Complete metabolic panel (CMP)
4. Thyroid function studies to exclude disorders of the thyroid
5. CRP
6. Hemoglobin A1C (if appropriate)

B. Tests/imaging
1. Treadmill stress test
2. Nuclear stress test
3. Echocardiogram
4. Ultrasound
5. CT
6. Coronary angioplasty

Differential Diagnoses

Assess patient for the following secondary causes of ASCVD and hyperlipidemia:

A. Atherosclerosis
B. Hyperlipidemia
C. Diabetes mellitus
D. Hypothyroidism
E. Nephrotic syndrome
F. Porphyria
G. Obesity
H. Obstructive liver disease
I. Diuretic use

Plan

A. General interventions
1. TLCs, including exercise, diet, and weight management, are recommended for all patients.
2. Increased physical activity. The 2013 ACC/AHA guidelines on lifestyle management outline the newest physical activity recommendations advising adults to engage in 40 minutes of aerobic physical activity three to four times a week. The aerobic exercise should involve moderate-to-vigorous intensity to reduce BP, LDL-C, and non-HDL-C.

B. Dietary management
1. Advise the patient that diet modification is the first line of therapy for hyperlipidemia.
2. Explain the cholesterol-lowering diet. Give dietary recommendation sheets. See Appendix B for low-fat/low-cholesterol and DASH dietary approaches to stop HTN.

C. Weight reduction
1. Explain that weight reduction in patients who are more than 20% over ideal body weight can lower LDL-C and triglyceride levels.

D. Other key dietary recommendations include:
1. Reduce intake of saturated fats and trans fats. Aim for 5% to 6% of calories from saturated fat.
2. Increase intake of poly- and monounsaturated fats.

TABLE 12.1 ATP III Classification of LDL-C, Total, and HDL-C Cholesterol (mg/dL)

Determine lipoprotein levels. Obtain complete lipoprotein profile after 9- to 12-hour fast.

- **LDL-C Cholesterol-Primary Target of Therapy**

< 100	Optimal
100–129	Near optimal/above optimal
130–159	Borderline high
160–189	High
> 190	Very high

- **Total Cholesterol**

< 200	Desirable
200–239	Borderline high
> 240	High

- **HDL-C Cholesterol**

< 40	Low
> 60	High

3. Increase intake of soluble fiber (psyllium supplement).
4. Limit intake of alcohol: One drink per day for women and two drinks per day for men
5. Increase intake of plant stanols and sterols (1 oz of Promise Activ or Benecol spread per day).
6. Increase intake of omega-3 fatty acids from marine sources (salmon or tuna twice a week or supplements).
7. Follow the DASH, Mediterranean, or AHA diet.
8. Lower sodium intake. Consume no more than 2,400 mg/d of sodium. Further reduction to 1,500 mg/d of sodium is associated with greater reduction in BP.

E. Discuss smoking cessation (see the Section III Patient Teaching Guide for Chapter 11, "Nicotine Dependence").

F. Pharmaceutical therapy: **Use clinical judgment when deciding potential benefits, possible side effects, and costs of drug treatment.**

1. Drug of choice: HMG-CoA reductase inhibitors (statins)
   a. Statins suppress the activity of the key enzyme in cholesterol synthesis in liver; they are highly effective in lowering LDL-C but can cause liver toxicity, myositis, rhabdomyolysis, and low HDL-C.
   b. There are four major statin benefit groups:
      i. Individuals with the presence of clinical ASCVD, including acute coronary syndromes, a history of MI, stable or unstable angina, coronary or other arterial revascularization, stroke, transient ischemic attack (TIA), or PAD.
      ii. Individuals with primary elevations of LDL-C greater than 190 mg/dL
      iii. Individuals 40 to 75 years of age with diabetes and LDL-C 70 to 189 mg/dL and without clinical ASCVD (refer to Chapter 23 "Endocrine Guidelines" for statin therapy for diabetes).
      iv. Individuals without clinical ASCVD or diabetes who are 40 to 75 years of age with an LDL-C 70 to 189 mg/dL and an estimated 10-year ASCVD risk of 7.5% or higher.
   c. **ASCVD events are reduced by using the maximum tolerated statin intensity in those groups shown to benefit. The expert panel defines intensity of statin therapy on the basis of the average expected LDL-C response to a specific statin and dose. The intensity levels are "high-intensity," "moderate-intensity," and "lower-intensity" statin therapy. Full statin treatment recommendations for primary and secondary prevention as well as the high-moderate-low-intensity statin therapy from the 2013 ACC/AHA guidelines on the treatment of cholesterol are available at content.onlinejacc.org/article.aspx?articleid=1770217.**
   d. Monitor liver function tests (LFTs) before therapy begins, 4 to 6 weeks after starting drug therapy. Then check at 6- to 12-month intervals or more frequently, if necessary.
   e. Discontinue medications if abnormal lab values or adverse symptoms appear.
   f. Use caution with the use of statins and other medications. Avoid concomitant drugs such as erythromycin, nicotine, azole antifungals, clofibrate, and gemfibrozil.
2. Category X drugs
   a. **Statins are category X drugs and are contraindicated in pregnancy.**
3. Non-statin drug therapy (see Table 12.2 for the non-statin drugs that affect cholesterol).
   a. Bile acid sequestrants bind bile acids in the gastrointestinal (GI) tract; lower moderately elevated LDL-C by 20%; and may cause constipation, bloating, and poor absorption of other drugs. Bile acid sequestrant therapy is not recommended if triglycerides are greater than 300 mg/dL.
   b. Nicotinic acid or niacin: Broad-spectrum lipid regulating agent. Niacin has been documented to exhibit anti-inflammatory properties (reduction of lipoprotein associated phospholipase A_2 and CRP). Discuss possibilities of flushing. Niacin is contraindicated with chronic liver disease and severe gout. The niacin-treated subjects in the Atherothrombosis Intervention in Metabolic Syndrome with Low HDL/High Triglycerides: Impact on Global Health (AIM-HIGH) clinical trial had a trend toward increased stroke incidence.
   c. Fibric acid derivatives: Highly effective in lowering triglycerides; lowers VLDL-C, causes modest reduction in LDL-C, and raises HDL-C.
      i. The combination of niacin with other lipid-lowering drugs has been shown to reduce progression and promote regression of coronary and carotid atherosclerosis and improve clinical outcomes.
      ii. Fibrates may cause GI distress, rash, pain, blurred vision, anemia, and gallstones.
      iii. Fibrates may inhibit insulin and oral hypoglycemic absorption, and potentiates oral anticoagulants.

TABLE 12.2 Non-Statin Drugs Affecting Lipoprotein Metabolism

Drug Class	Agents and Daily Doses	Lipid/Lipoprotein Effects	Side Effects	Contraindications
Bile acid sequestrants	Cholestyramine (4–16 g) Colestipol (5–30 g) Colesevelam (1,875–3,750 mg)	LDL-C-C ↓15%–30% HDL-C ↑3%–5% TG No change or increase	Gastrointestinal distress Constipation Decreased absorption of other drugs	Absolute: • Dysbeta-lipoproteinemia • TG > 400 mg/dL Relative: • TG > 200 mg/dL
Nicotinic acid	Immediate release (crystalline) nicotinic acid (1.5–3 g), extended release nicotinic acid (Niaspan®) (500 mg–2 g), sustained release nicotinic acid (1–2 g)	LDL-C-C ↓5%–25% HDL-C ↑15%–35% TG ↓20%–50%	Flushing Hyperglycemia Hyperuricemia (or gout) Upper GI distress Hepatotoxicity	Absolute: • Chronic liver disease • Severe gout Relative: • Diabetes • Hyperuricemia • Peptic ulcer disease
Fibric acids	Gemfibrozil (600 mg BID) Fenofibrate (145–200 mg) Clofibrate (500–2,000 mg)	LDL-C-C ↓5%–20% (may be increased in patients with high TG) HDL-C ↑10%–20% TG ↓20%–50%	Dyspepsia Gallstones Myopathy	Absolute: • Severe renal disease • Severe hepatic disease

Follow-Up

A. Measure patient's total cholesterol 4 weeks after initiation of diet and then at 3- to 4-month intervals.

B. If initiating medication therapy, obtain baseline blood work, including fasting lipid profile with LFTs and a CBC. Recheck tests 4 to 6 weeks after starting drug therapy. Then check at 6- to 12-month intervals or more frequently, if necessary.

Individual Considerations

A. Patients with high cholesterol who are otherwise at low risk for ASCVD (particularly men older than age 35 and premenopausal women) are candidates for primary prevention emphasizing diet modification and increased physical activity. It is recommended that drug therapy be used sparingly in these patients.

B. Lowering serum cholesterol reduces morbidity and mortality in patients with ASCVD, and it also reduces the number of new cardiac events in those without known ASCVD.

C. Elevated triglycerides increase the risk of pancreatitis and diabetes.

Atrial Fibrillation—*Laura A. Petty*

Definition

A. AF is the irregular and rapid heart rhythm caused by abnormal electrical impulses. These impulses make the heart's upper chambers (the atria) beat chaotically and out of sync with the heart's lower chambers (the ventricles), resulting in poor circulation of blood throughout the body.

B. Classification of AF
  1. Paroxysmal AF
     a. Also called intermittent AF
     b. AF that ends spontaneously or with intervention within 7 days of onset.
  2. Persistent AF
     a. AF that is sustained greater than 7 days.
     b. Usually requires pharmacologic and/or cardioversion to restore sinus rhythm.
  3. Long-standing persistent AF
     a. Continuous AF for greater than 12 months
  4. Permanent AF
     a. Term used when a patient and his or her clinician have reached a joint decision to cease further attempts to restore and/or maintain a sinus rhythm.
     b. This represents a therapeutic attitude rather than an inherent pathophysiological characteristic of a patient's AF.
  5. Nonvalvular AF
     a. The term used to reference patients with paroxysmal, persistent, or permanent AF who do not have valvular heart disease (e.g., rheumatic mitral stenosis, a mechanical or prosthetic heart valve, or mitral valve prolapse [MVP]).
  6. "Lone" AF
     a. The term used historically to refer to younger patients without clinical or echocardiographic evidence of cardiopulmonary disease, HTN, or diabetes.

Incidence

A. More than 467,000 hospitalizations in the United States annually list AF as the primary admitting diagnosis. An estimated 99,000+ deaths per year in the United States are attributed to AF. Patients with AF are hospitalized twice as often and are three times more likely to have multiple admissions. As of 2014, between 2.7 million and 6.1 million American adults have AF, with the incidence expected to double over the next 25 years. AF is more common in men than in women. AF is more common in Caucasians.

Pathogenesis

A. Multiple impulses travel throughout the atria, yielding continuous electrical activity and an atrial rate in excess of 300 bpm. The impulses enter the AV node in a completely random manner. A small percentage of the impulses are conducted to the ventricle, which results in a lower ventricular rate, usually 100 to 180 bpm, and an irregularly irregular rhythm. This leads to ineffective atrial contractions, a decrease in cardiac output, and an increased risk of thrombus formation.

Predisposing Factors

A. Increased age
   1. Approximately 1% of all AF patients are less than 60 years of age.
   2. Approximately one third of all AF patients are older than 80 years old.
B. HTN
C. Valvular heart disease
   1. Mitral valve stenosis
   2. Mitral regurgitation
   3. Tricuspid regurgitation
   4. LV hypertrophy
D. HF
E. MI
F. Hyperthyroidism
G. Obstructive sleep apnea (OSA)
H. Obesity
I. Pericarditis
J. Myocarditis
K. Electrocution
L. Pneumonia
M. PE
N. Cardiothoracic surgery
O. Diabetes mellitus
P. Smoking
Q. Excessive alcohol use

Common Complaints

A. Palpitations
B. Angina
C. Fatigue
D. Dyspnea at rest or on exertion
E. Vertigo or dizziness
F. Disorientation
G. Confusion
H. Syncope
I. Headache
J. Urinary frequency or urgency
K. Anxiety
L. Asymptomatic presentation, most often seen in the elderly and in patients with permanent AF

Potential Complications

A. **Stroke**
   1. **The risk for stroke increases five times during an episode of AF.**
   2. **An AF-related stroke is more likely to be severe than a non-AF-related stroke.**
B. **HF**
   1. **The risk of HF increases three times in the presence of AF.**
C. **Dementia**
   1. **The risk of dementia increases two times in the presence of AF.**
D. **Mortality**
   1. **Overall mortality increases two times in the presence of AF.**
E. PE
F. Peripheral emboli
   1. May present as an ischemic extremity or ischemic bowel

Subjective Data

A. Ask the patient what activity brought about or preceded the episode.
B. Have the patient describe the duration of symptoms and what time of day the symptoms began.
C. Ask the patient to describe his or her symptoms.
D. Ask the patient whether any previous episodes have occurred.
E. Ask the patient to list all medications, OTC, and herbal products currently being taken or recently stopped.
   1. Medications with links to AF
      a. Common complication with AF
         i. Theophylline (theophylline anhydrous, Theo-24, Elixophyllin)
         ii. Digoxin (Lanoxin)
         iii. Quinidine (quinidine gluconate, Nuedexta)
         iv. Tricyclic antidepressants (TCAs)
      b. Rare complication with AF
         i. Aricept (donepezil hydrochloride)
      c. Questionable complication with AF
         i. Bisphosphonates (alendronate, risedronate, etidronate)
F. Ask patient to quantify his or her smoking history, alcohol history, and caffeine intake.

Physical Examination

A. **Patients presenting with acute cardiovascular episode should be quickly assessed for the need to call emergency services/911 for immediate transport to the hospital.**

B. Vital signs: Check BP, pulse, and respirations. Count heart rate for 1 full minute.
   1. Check orthostatic BP: Sitting, standing, and lying down.
C. Inspect
   1. Inspect overall physical appearance, noting any distress.
   2. Inspect the neck: Check jugular vein distension and pulsations.
      a. **Provoking maneuvers (i.e., carotid massage) should only be performed by a cardiologist.**
   3. Inspect extremities: Note edema, pallor, and cyanosis.
   4. Perform a fundoscopic exam: Note hemorrhage, exudates, and papilledema to determine the presence of malignant HTN.
D. Palpate
   1. Palpate extremities for peripheral pulses in arm and groin; determine rate and regularity.
   2. Assess capillary refill.
   3. Palpate carotid arteries for thrills and heaves.
E. Auscultate
   1. Auscultate heart: While patient is sitting, standing, and in left lateral recumbent positions, noting normal and extra heart sounds (S3 and S4).
      a. S4 is not present during AF.
   2. Auscultate neck for carotid bruits.
   3. Auscultate lungs: Note the presence of wheezing and crackles.
F. Additional areas for physical examination
   1. Assess for focal neurologic deficits (orientation, unilateral weakness, dysarthria).

Diagnostic Tests

A. CBC, basic metabolic panel (BMP) (including electrolytes, blood glucose, blood urea nitrogen [BUN], creatinine), magnesium, and LFTs
B. Thyroid profile and lipid profile
C. Brain natriuretic peptide (BNP) and NT-proBNP
D. Cardiac profile (including troponin, creatine phosphokinase test [CPK], CK-MB)
E. Serum drug levels, digoxin, amiodarone, quinidine (if applicable)
F. INR, if applicable
G. Creatinine clearance (CrCl)
H. EKG
I. 2-D Echo
J. Transesophageal echocardiogram (TEE), most sensitive and specific test to detect left atrial (LA) thrombi and identify features associated with an increased risk of LA thrombus formation and subsequent systemic embolism
K. Chest x-ray
L. Exercise stress test or thallium stress test, if exercise-induced arrhythmia or CAD is suspected
M. Holter monitoring
N. Evaluation of sleep apnea

Differential Diagnosis

A. AF
B. MI
C. CAD
D. HF
E. Mitral stenosis
F. HTN
G. Hyperthyroidism
H. Digitalis intoxication
I. Acute infections

Plan

A. General interventions
   1. The goal of therapy is to improve the patient's quality of life by reducing morbidity and prolonging survival.
B. Patient teaching
   1. Encourage weight loss, smoking cessation, and stress management. See the Section III Patient Teaching Guide for this chapter, "Atrial Fibrillation."
   2. Educate patients about the adverse effects of their anticoagulant and antiarrhythmic medications.
   3. Instruct patients taking Coumadin (warfarin) to take steps to lessen their risk of falls.
   4. Educate patients with implanted defibrillators and pacemakers about their susceptibility for external electrical fields and avoidance of exposure.
C. Prevention
   1. Control other chronic medical conditions, that is, HTN, diabetes, HF, pulmonary diseases, and hyperlipidemia.
D. Dietary management
   1. Counsel patient on proper nutrition, specifically a low-fat, low-cholesterol, low-sodium diet. Give diet handouts.
   2. Educate patients taking Coumadin (warfarin) regarding dietary modifications to prevent variations in INR levels.
E. Pharmaceutical therapy
   1. Anticoagulant therapy
      a. Goal of therapy: Prevention of thromboembolism
         i. Coumadin (warfarin sodium, Jantoven)
            1) Doses: 1, 2, 2.5, 3, 4, 5, 6, 7.5, and 10 mg tablets
            2) Warfarin Dose Calculator is located at www.globalrph.com/warfarin_calc.htm

3) Review all medications that may affect the anticoagulant effects of warfarin. Globalrph is a resource with a list of medications that both increase and decrease the INR (www.globalrph.com/warfarin_drug_interactions.htm).

ii. Pradaxa (dabigatran)
    1) 75 and 150 mg tablets
        a) Dosage indications based on CrCl
            i) CrCl greater than 30 mL/min: 150 mg, taken twice a day
            ii) CrCl of 15 to 30 mL/min: 75 mg, taken twice a day

iii. Xarelto (rivaroxaban)
    1) 10, 15, and 20 mg tablets
        a) Dosage indications based on CrCl
            i) CrCl greater than 50 mL/min: 20 mg with evening meal
            ii) CrCl of 15 to 50 mL/min: 15 mg with evening meal

iv. Eliquis (apixaban)
    1) 2.5 and 5 mg tablets
        a) Dosage indications: Recommended dose is 2.5 mg, taken twice a day in patients who fit any of the following criteria:
            i) 80 years of age or older
            ii) Weight greater than or equal to 60 kg (132 lbs)
            iii) Serum creatinine greater than or equal to 1.5 mg/dL

2. Antiplatelet therapy
    a. Goal of therapy: Prevention of thromboembolism; modest preventative effect
        i. Aspirin
            1) 81 and 325 mg tablets
        ii. Plavix (clopidogrel bisulfate)
            1) 75 and 300 mg

3. Combined anticoagulant and antiplatelet therapies
    a. Prescription of both antiplatelet medications (Plavix and aspirin) in addition to an anticoagulant is referred to as triple therapy. Triple therapy is commonly used to prevent complications when two or more of the following conditions are present:
        i. AF
        ii. Mechanical valve prosthesis
        iii. Drug-eluting coronary stent
    b. Triple therapy is linked to an increase in bleeding complications ranging from mild to life threatening.

4. Heart rate control therapy
    a. Goal of therapy: Varies based on patient age but typically involves achieving a ventricular rate between 60 and 80 bpm at rest and 90 and 115 bpm during moderate exercise.
    b. Beta blockers
        i. Acebutolol (Sectral, acebutolol hydrochloride)
            1) 200 and 400 mg capsules
        ii. Atenolol (Tenormin)
            1) 25, 50 (scored), and 100 mg tablets
        iii. Betaxolol (Betoptic, Betoptic S, betaxolol hydrochloride)
            1) 10 and 20 mg tablets, all scored
        iv. Bisoprolol (Zebeta, bisoprolol fumarate)
            1) 5 (scored) and 10 mg tablets
        v. Metoprolol (Lopressor, Toprol-XL, metoprolol tartrate)
            1) 50 and 100 mg tablets, all scored
        vi. Nadolol (Corgard)
            1) 20, 40, and 80 mg tablets, all scored
        vii. Propranolol (propranolol hydrochloride)
            1) 10, 20, 40, 60, and 80 mg tablets, all scored
        viii. Sotalol (Betapace, sotalol hydrochloride)
            1) 80, 120, and 160 mg tablets, all scored
        ix. Timolol (timolol maleate)
            1) 5, 10 (scored), and 20 mg (scored) tablets
    c. CCBs
        i. Amlodipine (Norvasc, amlodipine besylate)
            1) 2.5, 5, and 10 mg tablets
        ii. Diltiazem (Cardizem, diltiazem hydrochloride)
            1) 30, 60 (scored), 90 (scored), and 120 mg (scored) tablets
        iii. Felodipine
            1) 2.5, 5, and 10 mg tablets
        iv. Isradipine
            1) 2.5 and 5 mg tablets
        v. Nicardipine (nicardipine hydrochloride)
            1) 20 and 30 mg capsules
            2) Cardene SR: 30, 45, and 60 mg capsules
        vi. Nifedipine (Procardia)
            1) 10 and 20 mg capsules
        vii. Nimodipine
            1) 30 mg capsules
        viii. Verapamil (Calan, verapamil hydrochloride, Tarka)
            1) 40, 80 (scored), and 120 mg (scored) tablets

d. Digoxin
   i. Digoxin (Lanoxin)
      1) 0.125 and 0.25 mg tablets, all scored
5. Heart rhythm control therapy
   a. Goal of therapy: The maintenance of a normal rhythm and suppression of AF
      i. Sodium channel blockers
         1) Disopyramide (Norpace)
            a) 100 and 150 mg capsules
         2) Quinidine (quinidine gluconate)
            a) 200 and 300 mg tablets, all scored
      ii. Potassium channel blockers
         1) Amiodarone (Cordarone, Pacerone, Nexterone, amiodarone hydrochloride)
            a) 200 mg tablet, scored
         2) Dofetilide (Tikosyn)
            a) 125, 250, and 500 mcg capsules
         3) Dronedarone (Multaq)
            a) 400 mg tablet
         4) Sotalol (Betapace, sotalol hydrochloride)
            a) 80, 120, and 160 mg tablets, all scored.

F. Surgical therapies
1. Ablation therapy
   a. Goal of therapy: Prevention of recurrent AF
   b. Preferred clinical characteristics include the following:
      i. Symptomatic paroxysmal AF
      ii. Failure of one or more antiarrhythmic medications
      iii. Normal to mildly dilated atria
      iv. Normal to mildly reduced ventricular function
      v. Absence of severe pulmonary disease
   c. The long-term efficacy of ablation therapy requires further study, especially with regard to patients with HF and structural heart disease.

Follow-Up

A. **AF patients should be comanaged with a physician.**

B. **AF that is resistant to routine therapy should always be followed by a cardiologist.**

C. Lab monitoring as indicated by the patient's anticoagulant and antiarrhythmic medications
1. CrCl for patients taking Pradaxa and Xarelto
2. INR for patients taking Coumadin. Multiple medications affect the anticoagulant property of Coumadin.
   a. The INR labs are located on Globalrph at www.globalrph.com/warfarin_drug_interactions.htm

D. Follow-up is determined by patient's needs, frequency of AF reoccurrence, and the presence of other medical conditions.

E. After defibrillator or pacemaker placement, monitor patient utilizing regular follow-up appointments and EKGs to identify failure of implanted device, thromboembolism, lead dislodgement, infection, and complicating arrhythmias.

Consultation/Referral

A. **If you suspect an acute cardiovascular episode, refer patient for immediate hospitalization in order to initiate thrombolytic therapy, cardioversion, hypertensive management, and additional diagnostic testing.**

B. Referral to cardiology as indicated by patient's clinical situation, specifically the frequency of AF reoccurrence and the presence of other complex medical conditions.

C. AF that is resistant to routine therapy should always be followed by a cardiologist.

Resources

The 2014 AHA/ACC/HRS Guidelines for the Management of Patients With Atrial Fibrillation is available at: http://content.onlinejacc.org/article.aspx?articleid=1854230

Warfarin dose calculator is available at www.globalrph.com/warfarin_calc.htm

Carotid Artery Stenosis

Definition

A. Carotid artery stenosis is the narrowing of one or both of the carotid arteries.

B. Classification of carotid artery stenosis:
1. Moderate
   a. Less than 69% narrowing
2. Severe
   a. 70% to 99% narrowing

Incidence

A. Moderate carotid artery stenosis
1. Prior to age 70: Male, 4.8%; female, 2.2%
2. After age 70: Male, 12.5%; female, 6.9%

B. Severe carotid artery stenosis
1. All ages, both genders: 1.7%

C. Severe asymptomatic carotid artery stenosis
1. After age 80: Male, 3.1%; female, 0.9%

Pathogenesis

A. As the human body ages the artery walls become thicker and less flexible (atherosclerosis). The plaques, also known as atheromas, can develop on the interior artery wall. Over time, the build-up of plaque reduces blood flow to the brain. The arterial narrowing also increases the risk of thrombus formation and subsequent stroke risk.

Predisposing Factors

A. Nonmodifiable factors
1. Age
   a. Male: increased risk prior to age 75
   b. Female: increased risk after age 75

2. Personal or family history of any of the following:
   a. Stroke
   b. Angina
   c. MI
   d. PAD

B. Modifiable factors
   1. HTN
   2. Hypercholesterolemia
   3. Diabetes mellitus
   4. Obesity
   5. Tobacco abuse
   6. Sedentary lifestyle

Common Complaints

A. Asymptomatic carotid artery stenosis
   1. Often there are no symptoms.

B. Symptomatic carotid artery stenosis
   1. Focal neurologic symptoms, acute onset
      a. Monoparesis or hemiparesis
      b. Sensory alterations
         i. Paresthesias
      c. Speech disturbance
         i. Expressive aphasia
         ii. Receptive aphasia
         iii. Changes in speech pattern or vocal quality (dysprosody)
      d. Visual changes
         i. Blurred vision
         ii. Blindness in one eye, partial or complete
         iii. Visual field loss: Specifically contralateral homonymous hemianopsia
         iv. Dimming of vision
      e. Constructional apraxia (i.e., inability to perform purposeful movements)
   2. Vertigo and syncope are symptoms not generally caused by carotid artery stenosis.

Potential Complications

A. Cerebrovascular accident (CVA)

B. TIA

C. Death

D. Comorbidities that increase complication risk
   1. Age: Older than 80 years
   2. New York Heart Association (NYHA) III or IV HF
   3. Left ventricular ejection fraction (LVEF): Less than 30%
   4. Class III or IV angina pectoris
   5. CAD: Left main coronary artery
   6. CAD: Multivessel
   7. Planned cardiac surgery within 30 days
   8. History of MI within 4 weeks
   9. Severe chronic lung disease (i.e., COPD, bronchitis, emphysema, asthma)

Subjective Data

A. Ask patient to describe any new neurologic symptoms.
   1. Further determine the frequency, intensity, and duration of the symptoms

B. Ask patient to list all medications currently being taken, including OTC substances.

Physical Examination

A. **Patients presenting with acute neurologic symptoms indicative of a stroke (paresis, speech or swallowing difficulty, visual field loss, etc.) should be quickly assessed for the need to call emergency services/911 for immediate transport to the hospital.**

B. Vital signs: Check BP, pulse, and respirations.

C. Inspect
   1. Inspect overall physical appearance, noting any distress.
   2. Eyes: Assess papillary reflex bilaterally and perform a funduscopic exam noting arterial occlusions or ischemic retinal damage

D. Auscultate
   1. Neck: Carotid bruits, bilaterally
      a. Studies have shown that carotid bruits have a poor predictive value in asymptomatic patients but are more indicative of CAD. However, the presence of a bruit should still be documented.

Diagnostic Tests

A. Noninvasive testing
   1. Carotid Doppler/duplex ultrasound
   2. Carotid magnetic resonance angiogram (MRA)
   3. Computed tomographic angiography (CTA)

B. Invasive testing
   1. **Cerebral angiography with contrast**
      a. **The gold standard for determination of carotid artery stenosis**

Differential Diagnosis

A. Monoparesis
   1. TIA
   2. CVA/stroke
   3. Multiple sclerosis
   4. Separated shoulder
   5. Fractured limb

B. Hemiparesis
   1. TIA
   2. CVA/stroke
   3. Multiple sclerosis
   4. Spinal tumor

C. Sensory alterations (paresthesias)
   1. TIA
   2. CVA/stroke
   3. Peripheral neuropathy
   4. Cervical spinal stenosis
   5. Lead poisoning

6. Lyme disease
7. Wernicke syndrome
8. Multiple sclerosis

D. Speech disturbance (aphasia)
1. TIA
2. CVA/stroke
3. Myasthenia gravis
4. Brain tumor

E. Speech disturbance (speech pattern or vocal quality, i.e., dysprosody)
1. TIA
2. CVA/stroke
3. Brain tumor

F. Visual changes
1. TIA
2. CVA/stroke
3. Retinal detachment
4. Ocular migraine
5. Cataracts
6. Giant cell arteritis
7. HTN
8. Macular degeneration
9. Sarcoidosis
10. Glaucoma
11. Brain tumor

G. Constructional apraxia
1. TIA
2. CVA/stroke
3. Brain tumor

Plan

A. General interventions
1. The goal of therapy is to improve the patient's quality of life by reducing morbidity and prolonging survival.
2. The estimated risk of stroke within 5 years when utilizing medical management is 11.8% versus the risk of perioperative death, which is 6.4%.

B. Patient teaching
1. Educate patient about modifying controllable risk factors such as HTN, diabetes, hypercholesterolemia, obesity, tobacco abuse, and sedentary lifestyles.
2. If known carotid artery stenosis is present:
   a. Make sure patient is aware of signs and symptoms of TIA and stroke.
   b. Make sure patient knows to seek medical attention or dial 911 if signs and symptoms occur.

C. Dietary management
1. Counsel patient regarding appropriate change to his or her diet (i.e., low-fat, low-cholesterol, low-sodium diet if applicable).
2. Reinforce teaching with nutrition/diet handouts.
3. Consider referral to a registered dietitian.

D. Pharmaceutical therapy
1. Antiplatelet therapy
   a. Aspirin
      i. Taken prior to carotid endarterectomy (CEA) surgery and for at least 3 months postoperatively
      ii. Dosage: 81 to 325 mg/d
2. Additional pharmaceutical therapies
   a. Hypertensive therapy
      i. BP goal: Less than 140/90
   b. Hyperlipidemia therapy
      i. LDL cholesterol goal (primary): Less than 100 mg/dL
      ii. LDL cholesterol goal (secondary): Less than 70 mg/dL
   c. Tobacco cessation therapy

E. Surgical therapies
1. CEA
   a. Goal of therapy: Stroke risk reduction
   b. Preferred clinical characteristics
      i. Recent TIA or CVA within 6 months and ipsilateral stenosis between 70% and 99% (severe).
         1) CEA is recommended.
         2) Morbidity/mortality: Less than 6%
      ii. Recent TIA or CVA within 6 months and ipsilateral stenosis between 50% and 69% (moderate).
         1) CEA is recommended after analysis of other factors that include age, gender, and comorbidities.
         2) Morbidity/mortality: Less than 6%
      iii. Ipislateral stenosis less than 50%
         1) No indication for CEA surgery
   c. Pharmaceutical therapy and CEA
      i. Aspirin
         1) Recommendations: Take prior to CEA surgery and for at least 3 months postoperatively unless contraindicated.
         2) Dosage: 81 to 325 mg/d
      ii. Other available antiplatelet agents do not have standardized dosage or frequency regimens established for postoperative CEA patients.
2. Carotid angioplasty/stenting (CAS)
   a. Goal of therapy: Stroke risk reduction
   b. Preferred clinical characteristics
      i. Symptomatic patients with stenosis less than 70% as determined by noninvasive imaging or less than 50% as determined by conventional contrast angiography.
      ii. Symptomatic patients with stenosis greater than 70% in which surgical

access via CEA would be difficult or prior history indicates an increased complication risk (i.e., radiation-induced stenosis and restenosis of a prior CEA)

iii. Ipsilateral stenosis less than 50%
   1) No indication for CAS surgery

c. Pharmaceutical therapy and CAS
   i. Acetaminophen (aspirin)
      1) Recommendations: Take prior to CEA surgery and for at least 3 months postoperatively unless contraindicated.
      2) Dosage: 81 to 325 mg/d
   ii. Clopidogrel (Plavix)
      1) Recommendations: 300 mg loading dose on operative day and 75 mg a day after stenting
   iii. Other available antiplatelet agents do not have standardized dosage or frequency regimens established for postoperative CAS patients.

3. Contraindications to carotid surgery
   a. Chronic total occlusion of the stenosed artery
   b. Patients with severe disability related to prior CVA

Follow-Up

A. Follow up with cardiology and vascular surgery is determined by patient's needs and the presence of other medical conditions.

Consultation/Referral

A. Referral to a registered dietitian is indicated for additional teaching regarding dietary modifications.

Chest Pain

Definition

A. Chest pain is a localized sensation of distress or discomfort that may or may not be associated with actual tissue damage.

Incidence

A. Chest pain is one of the most common complaints of adult patients. Causes can range from minor disorders to life-threatening diseases, so every patient must be assessed carefully.

Pathogenesis

A. Cardiac etiology: Ischemia, atherosclerosis, inflammation, or valvular problems due to angina, MI, pericarditis, endocarditis, dissecting aortic aneurysm, or mitral valve prolapse (MVP) (see Table 12.3).

B. Musculoskeletal etiology: Muscle strain and inflammation due to costochondritis, chest wall syndrome, cervicodorsal arthritis, or intercostal myositis

C. Neurologic etiology: Nerve inflammation and/or compression due to herpes zoster and nerve root compression

D. GI etiology: Structural defects, inflammation, or infection due to gastroesophageal reflux disease (GERD), hiatal hernia, esophageal spasm, pancreatitis, cholecystitis, or peptic ulcer disease (PUD)

E. Pleural etiology: Inflammation, distension, or compression of pleural membranes due to pneumonia, pulmonary embolus, pulmonary HTN, spontaneous pneumothorax, and lung and mediastinal tumors

F. Psychogenic etiology: Stress due to anxiety, depression, or panic disorders

Predisposing Factors

A. These vary depending on the etiology of pain.

Common Complaints

A. Primary complaint: Pain somewhere in the chest
B. "Levine sign": Placing the fist to the center of the chest to demonstrate pain
C. Fatigue
D. Cough
E. Indigestion
F. Dyspnea
G. Syncope
H. Palpitations
I. Profound fatigue

Other Signs and Symptoms

A. Pain may be typical of angina and MI.
B. Musculoskeletal pain may be relieved by position change, aggravated by body movement, reproducible, or caused by injury or trauma.
C. Neurologic pain is associated with skin lesion if herpes zoster is the causative agent.
D. GI pain may be associated with meals, certain positions, belching, or an acid "brash" taste in mouth, or it may be referred to other sites.
E. Pleural pain is usually accompanied by cough, upper respiratory infection (URI) symptoms, or SOB.
F. Psychogenic pain or pressure along with SOB and dizziness may be associated with a specific event or time.

Subjective Data

A. How long has the patient had chest pain?
B. Has the patient ever been treated for chest pain? What treatment, tests, and medications (such as nitroglycerin) were used?

TABLE 12.3 Comparison of Common Chest Pain Etiologies

Condition	Pain Findings	Associated Symptoms	Precipitating Factors	Relieving Factors	Physical Findings	Diagnostic Tests	Treatment Modalities
Cardiac-stable angina	Substernal, tight, dull pressure, usually lasts longer than 15 minutes		Exertion, cold, emotional stress	Rest, nitroglycerin Valsalva's maneuver	Sinus tach. bradycardia xanthomas, signs of HF	Resting EKG, stress EKG, cardiac enzymes, Echo angiogram	ASA BB Nitrate CCB
Prinzmetal's angina (variant)	Substernal, achy, tight, dull pressure		Often occurs at rest; may awaken from sleep	Nitroglycerin	Same as stable angina	Resting EKG, angiogram	ASA Nitrates CCB
MI	Precordial, substernal, severe, crushing, squeezing, lasts > 15 minutes	Dyspnea, sweating, dizzy, radiation to neck/arm/ jaw N&V, cough fever unstable V/S	Oxygen	Not relieved by nitroglycerin	S3 or S4 murmur, tachycardia, bradycardia pericardia friction rub, hyper/ hypotension	EKG, serial CK enzymes, Echo, radionuclide studies	Analgesia, reperfusion, prevention, and treatment complications limit infarcts Thrombolytic therapy for acute MI
MVP	Usually not substernal, often knifelike, may last 1–3 hours	Palpitations, fatigue, lightheaded, arrhythmia, syncope		Recumbent position, BB, nitroglycerine	Midsystolic click and/ or murmur, thin body status, SOB	Echo, EKG	Usually none, BB if palpitations or ventricular ectopy becomes disabling
Hypertrophic cardiomegaly	Similar to angina	Dyspnea with exertion, arrhythmias, lightheaded syncope	May be increased by nitroglycerin, exertion	BB, squatting	Systolic murmur, increased upright position, Valsalva's maneuver, more forceful PMI	EKG, CXR, Echo, Doppler, Cardiac Cath	BB CCB Possible pacing and myomectomy, exercise restriction
Pericarditis	Retrosternal, sharp or dull, sudden onset, long duration, radiates to one side of the trapezius	Fever, myalgia, anorexia, anxiety, recent viral infection		Sitting up, leaning forward	Friction rub, SVT1, tachypnea, crackles, signs of cardiac tamponade	EKG, Echo CBC, ESR	Hospitalize rule out purulent process analgesics
Endocarditis	Usually dull, retrosternal, may radiate to back	Fever, night sweats, joint pain, back pain, weight loss, headache, murmur			Systolic-diastolic murmur, petechiae, Osler's modes, Roth spots, neck vein distension, pleural or pericardia rub, pain in extremities, splenomegaly hematuria	CBC, ESR blood cultures, Echo	Hospitalize, for antibiotic therapy
GI-esophageal spasm	May be identical to angina		Alcohol or cold liquids	May be relieved by nitroglycerin		Esophageal manometry	Nitroglycerin anticholinergics esophageal dilation
Esophagitis	Burning, tightness	Heartburn, water brash	Overeating, alcohol, recumbent position	Antacids	May have slight to moderate epigastric tenderness	Esophagoscopy	Lifestyle modification, antacid, H2 blocker, PPI, promotility agent
Musculoskeletal costochondritis	Sharp, sometimes pleuritic, parasternal costochondral pain		Sneezing, cough on deep inspiration, or twisting motions, reaching overhead		Erythema at sites of tenderness; positive pinpoint tenderness at costochondral junctions	CXR to r/o other causes	NSAIDs, ASA, Ibuprofen, Naproxen, heat application

ASA, aspirin; BB, beta blocker; CXR, chest x-ray; ESR, eosinophilic sedimentation rate; NSAIDs, nonsteroidal anti-inflammatory drugs; N&V, nausea and vomiting; PPI, proton pump inhibitor.

C. What precipitates and relieves the patient's chest pain?
   1. Precipitating factors: Exertion, taking a deep breath, eating, cold, stress, and sexual intercourse
   2. Alleviating factors: Resting, eating, taking an antacid, taking nitroglycerin, and positional change
D. Inquire about character of pain
   1. Location: Neck, throat, chest, epigastric area, and shoulder
   2. Radiation: Neck, throat, shoulder, lower jaw, and upper extremity
      a. **Radiation to one or both arms is a predictor of acute MI.**
      b. **Chest pain that radiates between the scapulae may be due to aortic dissection.**
   3. Quality: Squeezing, pressure, strangling, fullness, heavy weight, tightening, constriction, and ripping/tearing (acute aortic dissection)
   4. Intensity: Abrupt onset, gradually getting worse, dull, or insidious
   5. Duration: Seconds, minutes, hours, or years
   6. Frequency: Intermittent, occurs every morning/evening
E. Are other associated symptoms present?
F. Discuss any risk factors the patient may have for cardiac disease: Smoking, hyperlipidemia, HTN, sedentary lifestyle, diabetes, and family history.
G. Review medical history as noted above.
H. Review all medications, including prescription (such as sildenafil), OTC, and herbal product.
I. Review recreational/illicit drug use.
J. Inquire about any new physical labor if musculoskeletal etiology is suspected.
K. Has the patient had any trauma (including domestic violence)?
L. Has the patient had a recent infection?

Physical Examination

A. Check temperature (if infection is suspected), pulse, respirations, BP, and pulse oximetry.
B. Inspect
   1. Inspect general appearance.
      a. Appearance of discomfort/distress
      b. Any appearance of respiratory distress
      c. Evaluate jugular venous distention (JVD).
      d. Note patient position: Sitting, lying, squatting. Relief of chest pain with recumbency suggests MVP; relief with squatting suggests hypertrophic cardiomyopathy. Noncardiac chest pain may be present along with cardiac chest pain.
   2. Inspect skin for diaphoresis, jaundice, pallor, herpes zoster lesions, rash, or cyanosis.
   3. Inspect chest wall for herpes zoster lesions or signs of trauma.
   4. Inspect eyes by performing funduscopic exam.
   5. Inspect legs for signs of phlebitis: Unilateral swelling, cyanosis, venous stasis, and diminished pulses.
   6. Inspect neck for enlarged thyroid and lymph nodes, midline trachea, and JVD.
C. Palpate
   1. Palpate chest wall for tenderness and swelling. Chest pain present in only one body position is usually not cardiac in origin.
   2. Palpate abdomen for masses, tenderness, bounding pulses, organomegaly, and ascites.
   3. Palpate femoral and distal pulses.
D. Auscultate
   1. Auscultate carotid arteries for bruits.
   2. Auscultate lungs for crackles, wheezes, equal breath sounds, and pleural rub.
   3. Auscultate abdomen for bruits and bowel sounds.
   4. Auscultate heart for murmurs, rubs, clicks, irregularities, or extra sounds.
E. Neurologic exam: Perform this exam if neurologic etiology is suspected.

Diagnostic Tests

A. **Testing depends on information collected in the exam. A normal physical exam, EKG, and/or lab test results in a patient with chest pain but does not rule out CHD.** Typical tests include the following:
   1. EKG
   2. Chest radiography, whenever diagnosis of chest pain is not clear
   3. Echocardiogram
   4. Stress test
   5. Cardiac catheterization
   6. Barium tests
   7. Endoscopy to rule out GI etiology
   8. Esophageal pH, low
   9. Lab tests
      a. Troponin I or T
      b. Myoglobin
      c. CK
      d. CK MD isoenzyme (CKMB)—may be useful if the initial troponin determination is abnormal for suspected reinfarction
      e. C-reactive protein (CPP)
      f. B-type natriuretic peptide (BNP) for clinical findings/risk of HF
      g. D-dimer for suspected venous thrombotic event (deep vein thrombosis [DVT] or PE)

Differential Diagnoses

A. Cardiac causes
   1. CHD
      a. Acute MI: Chest pain lasting more than 15 minutes
      b. Unstable angina pectoris
      c. Stable angina pectoris
      d. Prinzmetal's, or variant, angina

2. Valvular heart disease
   a. MVP
   b. Aortic stenosis
3. Cardiomyopathies
   a. Hypertrophic
   b. Dilated
   c. Restrictive
4. Pericarditis
5. Endocarditis
6. Aortic dissection

B. Noncardiac causes
1. Pulmonary causes
   a. Pneumonia
   b. Pleurisy
   c. PE
   d. Pulmonary HTN
   e. Pneumothorax
   f. Tracheobronchitis
   g. Lung cancer
2. GI causes
   a. GERD
   b. Esophageal spasm
   c. PUD
   d. Pancreatitis
   e. Cholecystitis
   f. Flatulence
3. Rheumatology causes
   a. Fibromyalgia
   b. Costochondritis
   c. Arthritis
4. Chest wall causes
   a. Rib fracture
   b. Muscle strain
   c. Cervical or thoracic spine disease
   d. Metastatic bone disease
   e. Breast conditions
5. Neurologic causes
   a. Herpes zoster
   b. Postherpetic pain syndrome
   c. Nerve root compression
6. Psychogenic causes
   a. Panic disorder
   b. Generalized anxiety
   c. Depression
   d. Somatoform disorders

Plan

A. General interventions: Direct management toward primary disorder causing the symptom

B. Patient teaching
1. Teach the patient about medications.
2. Encourage CPR training for the patient's family and/or close friends.
3. Explain to the patient and family when and how to call 911 and the importance of going to the ER immediately so that thrombolytic therapy can be considered. A positive response to nitroglycerin does not confirm the presence of CAD.

C. Pharmaceutical therapy
1. Cardiac pain: Nitroglycerin
2. GI pain: H2 blocker, proton pump inhibitors (PPIs)
3. Musculoskeletal pain: Nonsteroidal anti-inflammatory drugs (NSAIDs)
4. Psychogenic pain
   a. Selective serotonin reuptake inhibitors (SSRIs)
   b. TCAs
   c. Benzodiazepines

Follow-Up

A. Follow patients with CAD for an indefinite period of time to detect the recurrence or progression of disease.

B. Other follow-up depends on the etiology of chest pain.

Consultation/Referral

A. Consult a physician when chest pain is cardiac in origin. If a cardiac origin is found in a pregnant patient, schedule a cardiology consultation as soon as possible for comanagement.

Individual Considerations

A. Pregnancy
1. Evaluate chest pain in the same manner as in nonpregnant patients.
2. Rule out pregnancy-induced hypertension (PIH) and HELLP (hemolysis, elevated liver enzymes, low platelets) syndrome when a third-trimester patient presents with upper epigastric/chest pain.

B. Geriatrics
1. Frail elderly patients often do not present with the "typical" symptom complex of chest pain. Frequently, the only symptoms of acute MI are lethargy, decreased level of consciousness (LOC), crackles, CHF, persistent cough, or hypotension.
2. The following signs and symptoms may be the primary presentation in the frail older person for many acute illness states:
   a. Confusion
   b. Self-neglect
   c. Falling
   d. Incontinence
   e. Apathy
   f. Anorexia
   g. Dyspnea
   h. Fatigue
3. Prescribe medications for frail elderly patients based on their creatinine clearance and then slowly taper upward to the desired effect.

Chronic Venous Insufficiency and Varicose Veins—*Laura A. Petty*

Definition

A. PVD is a general term that encompasses all occlusive or inflammatory diseases that occur within the peripheral arteries, veins, and lymphatics. These conditions include PAD, DVT, superficial thrombophlebitis, lymphedema, and chronic venous diseases. Chronic venous diseases include chronic venous insufficiency (CVI) and varicose veins.

1. CVI
   a. It is estimated that 6 to 7 million adults in the United States have CVI. CVI is twice as common in females as in males.
   b. Peak incidence is seen in women between 40 and 50 years of age.
2. Varicose veins
   a. The Vascular Disease Foundation states that more than 24 million Americans have varicose veins. They are usually thought to be more common in females; however, there is a higher incidence in males, especially African American males.

Pathogenesis

A. CVI: Venous insufficiency is caused by incompetent valves that allow valvular reflux and subsequently venous HTN. In CVI, venous HTN leads to obstruction of venous flow, which produces local tissue anoxia, inflammation, and at times even tissue necrosis. This process eventually causes subcutaneous fibrosing panniculitis and additional venous and lymphatic outlet obstruction.

B. Varicose veins: Varicose veins are a form of CVI. The same incompetent valves that cause valvular reflux and subsequently venous HTN in CVI also cause varicose veins. This influx of volume and pressure causes the vessels to dilate, twist, and bulge.

Predisposing Factors

A. CVI
   1. Age
   2. Gender, being female
   3. Prolonged standing or sitting
   4. Prior history of DVT
   5. Stature, more common in tall persons
   6. Obesity

B. Varicose veins
   1. Genetics
      a. Risk increases to 90% if both parents have varicose veins.
      b. If one parent is affected, the risk increases by 25% for men and 62% for women.
   2. Age
   3. Pregnancy
   4. Prolonged standing
   5. Restrictive clothing
   6. Obesity
   7. Ligamentous laxity
      a. A history of hernia(s)
      b. Flat feet
   8. Smoking

Common Complaints

A. CVI
   1. Extremity edema
   2. Pain worse when standing, usually dull, aching, or cramping
   3. Pain improved with elevation
   4. Itching sensation
   5. Feeling of heaviness in extremity
   6. Hyperpigmentation
   7. Thickening and hardening of the skin
   8. Ulcerations

B. Varicose veins
   1. Pain, usually burning, aching, or itching
   2. Blue veins that protrude above the surface of the skin
   3. Leg fatigue
   4. Edema
   5. Symptoms worsening toward the end of the day

Potential Complications

A. CVI
   1. Cellulitis
   2. Peripheral neuropathy
   3. Varicose veins
   4. Abscess
   5. Ulceration
   6. Stasis dermatitis
   7. DVT

B. Varicose veins
   1. Stasis dermatitis
   2. Stasis ulceration
   3. Petechial hemorrhage
   4. Chronic edema
   5. Superficial thrombophlebitis
   6. Hyperpigmentation
   7. Eczema

Subjective Data

A. Ask patient when the symptom(s) were first noticed.

B. Have patient describe duration of symptoms.

C. Ask patient to describe pain, for example, crushing, stabbing, or burning.

D. Ask the patient what makes the symptoms better and what makes them worse.

E. Have patient rate pain on a scale of 0 to 10, with 0 being no pain.

F. Ask patient to list all medications currently being taken, particularly substances not prescribed and illicit drugs such as cocaine.

G. Review recent history of invasive procedures or surgery.

H. Review medical history for heart disease, diabetes, HTN, and DVT.

I. Ask patient if he or she has an increase in the size of lower extremities after being on his or her feet. Discern if his or her one leg is worse than the other.

Physical Examination

A. CVI
1. Vital signs
   a. Check BP and document resting heart rate, respirations, temperature (if indicated), height, and weight.
2. Inspect
   a. Inspect extremity for edema, hyperpigmentation, erythema, difference in temperature.
   b. Inspect and document any varicosities.
3. Palpate
   a. Palpate distended veins, noting tenderness.
   b. Perform the cough impulse test to determine turbulent retrograde flow.
   c. Perform the tap test to determine if the great saphenous vein is distended with blood.
4. Auscultate
   a. Auscultate heart: Rate, rhythm, heart sounds, murmur, and gallops
   b. Auscultate lungs: Lung sounds in all fields

B. Varicose veins
1. **Patient presenting with any of the following should be quickly assessed for the need to call emergency services/911 for immediate transport to the hospital:**
   a. **A bleeding varicosity with eroded surrounding skin**
   b. **A varicosity that has bled and is at risk for bleeding again**
   c. **An ulceration that is worsening and/or painful despite treatment**
2. Vital signs
   a. Check BP and document resting heart rate, respirations, temperature (if indicated), height, and weight.
3. Inspect
   a. Inspect skin for superficial veins that are raised above the skin's surface; patient should be standing.
   b. Inspect extremity for edema, hyperpigmentation, and eczema.
4. Palpate
   a. Palpate distended veins, noting tenderness.
5. Auscultate
   a. Auscultate heart: Rate, rhythm, heart sounds, murmur, and gallops.
   b. Auscultate lungs: Assess lung sounds.

Diagnostic Tests

A. CVI
1. Trendelenburg test
2. Perthes test
3. Doppler ankle/brachial index (ABI)
4. Duplex ultrasound
5. Venography, not utilized often due to expense and risk of phlebitis

B. Varicose veins
1. Trendelenburg test
2. Perthes test
3. Duplex ultrasound

Differential Diagnosis

A. CVI
1. DVT
2. Ulceration
3. Infection
4. PAD
5. Varicose veins with risk of hemorrhage

B. Varicose veins
1. Arthritis
2. Peripheral neuritis
3. Nerve root compression
4. Telangiectasia
5. DVT
6. Inflammatory liposclerosis

Plan

A. Prevention: General
1. Avoid prolonged standing or sitting.
2. Exercise on a regular basis.
3. Encourage smoking cessation, weight loss, and exercise, if applicable.
4. Encourage strategies to better manage other chronic medical conditions that directly affect the progression of PAD, that is, diabetes, dyslipidemia, obesity, and HTN.

B. CVI
1. Nonpharmaceutical therapy
   a. Extremity elevation
   b. Compression stockings
   c. Exercise
   d. Venous ulcerations treated with wound care and compression therapy
2. Pharmaceutical therapy
   a. Diuretics: Management of edema, short-term administration
      i. Hydrochlorothiazide
      ii. Antiplatelet: May increase the speed of healing to ulcerations
         1) Aspirin: 325 mg tablet
         2) Systemic antibiotics: Management of infection in persons demonstrating an increase in pain, erythema, or increase in size of ulceration
3. Surgery
   a. Venous ablation, for patients who continue to be symptomatic after 6 months of nonpharmacologic therapies. Types of ablation: Chemical, thermal, and mechanical

C. Varicose veins
   1. Patient teaching. See the Section III Patient Teaching Guides for this chapter, "Chronic Venus Insufficiency" and "Varicose Veins."
      a. If prolonged standing is required, shift weight from one leg to the other.
      b. Do not sit with legs dependent.
   2. Nonpharmaceutical therapy
      a. Extremity elevation
      b. Compression stockings
      c. Exercise
   3. Surgery
      a. Radiofrequency ablation
      b. Endovenous laser therapy
      c. Phlebectomy
      d. Foam sclerotherapy
      e. Vein litigation

Follow-Up

A. Follow-up is determined by patient's needs, frequency and intensity of symptoms, and the presence of other medical conditions.
B. PVD manifesting persistent symptoms should always be followed by a cardiologist.

Consultation/Referral

A. If you suspect acute limb ischemia, refer patient for immediate hospitalization in order to obtain diagnostic testing to determine the presence of a thrombus and restore circulation to the affected extremity.
B. If chronic limb ischemia has led to ulceration and/or superimposed infection, hospitalization is indicated to initiate a wound care consultation and diagnostic testing to determine the degree of arterial occlusion.
C. Referral to a cardiologist is indicated in the presence of persistent PVD symptoms.
D. Referral to a podiatrist becomes necessary to trim toenails and assess patient for properly fitting shoes.
E. Referral to pain management is indicated if pain is resistant to treatment.

Individual Considerations

A. Nonambulatory patients
   1. Using rocking chairs is a possible substitute for persons unable to participate in a walking program.
B. Geriatrics
   1. Be alert to signs and symptoms of depression related to immobility and pain.

Deep Vein Thrombosis—*Laura A. Petty*

Definition

A. PVD is a general term that encompasses all occlusive or inflammatory diseases that occur within the peripheral arteries, veins, and lymphatics. PVD includes DVT. DVT is a condition in which a thrombus forms in one or more veins. DVT greatly increases the risk of PE.

Incidence

A. The CDC estimates that between 300,000 and 900,000 Americans are diagnosed with a DVT annually. Of those, between 60,000 and 100,000 persons die from complications from DVT, usually PE.
B. The Vascular Disease Foundation states that approximately 5% of the world's population will have a DVT during their lifetime.

Pathogenesis

A. Changes within the venous system precipitate the formation of a DVT. These changes are formally called Virchow's triad. This triad includes hypercoagulability, venous stasis, and injury to the vessel wall. At least two of the triad must be present for a DVT to form. Essentially, an injury to the vessel wall causes inflammation that attracts platelets, especially in a state of altered coagulation. The thrombus that forms spreads in the direction of blood flow and additional layers of platelets are added to the thrombus as time progresses. As it grows, the vessel becomes more occluded and symptoms worsen.

Predisposing Factors

A. Age, 60 years and older
B. Hip or femur fracture
C. Recent surgery, especially cardiac or extremity surgery
D. Prolonged inactivity/immobility
E. Pregnancy
F. Medication
   1. Hormone replacement therapy (HRT)
   2. Oral contraceptives
   3. Tamoxifen
G. Smoking
H. Obesity
I. Cancer
J. Inherited hypercoagulable conditions

Common Complaints

Symptoms of a DVT are usually unilateral and have a sudden onset.

A. Extremity edema
B. Extremity pain
C. Increased temperature of extremity
D. Change in color or extremity
E. Asymptomatic, depending on the size and location of the thrombus

Potential Complications

A. PE
B. Arterial embolism with AV shunting
C. MI
D. CVI

E. Postphlebitic syndrome
F. Phlegmasia cerulea dolens

Subjective Data

A. Ask patient when the symptom(s) were first noticed.
B. Have patient describe duration of symptoms.
C. Ask patient to describe pain, for example, crushing, stabbing, or burning.
D. Ask the patient what makes the symptoms better and what makes them worse.
E. Have patient rate pain on a scale of 0 to 10, with 0 being no pain.
F. Ask patient to list all medications currently being taken, particularly substances not prescribed and illicit drugs such as cocaine.
G. Review recent history of invasive procedures or surgery.

Physical Examination

Patients presenting with acute SOB and/or chest pain should be quickly assessed for the need to call emergency services/911 for immediate transport to the hospital. Patients presenting with symptoms of DVT that include cyanosis of the distal extremity should be quickly assessed for the need to call emergency services/911 for immediate transport to the hospital.

A. Vital signs
  1. Check BP and document resting heart rate, respirations, height, and weight.
B. Inspect
  1. Assess for signs of erythema, increased temperature, and edema.
  2. Assess for a Homans' sign (i.e., calf pain with forced plantar flexion).
  3. Assess for Moses' or Bancroft's sign (i.e., pain when calf muscle is compressed forward against the tibia).
  4. Assess the Lisker sign (i.e., pain upon tibial percussion).
C. Palpate
  1. Palpate pulses distal to affected area, noting symmetry.
  2. Palpate capillary refill.
  3. Palpate extremity for tenderness. Do not perform deep palpation.
D. Auscultate
  1. Auscultate heart: Rate, rhythm, heart sounds, murmur, and gallops
  2. Auscultate lungs: Lung sounds in all fields

Diagnostic Tests

A. DVT
  1. Serum laboratory testing
    a. D-dimer
    b. CBC with differential
    c. Coagulation panel (PT, partial thromboplastin time [PTT], INR)
    d. Testing for idiopathic DVT: Add Factor V Leiden, homocysteine, G20210A Prothrombin, Factor VIII, lupus anticoagulant, protein C&S levels, anticardiolipin antibodies, and antithrombin.
  2. Compression ultrasound
  3. MRI, if thrombus is suspected in the pelvic veins or vena cava
  4. Venography, not utilized often due to expense and risk of phlebitis

Differential Diagnosis

A. DVT
B. Cellulitis
C. Fracture
D. Lymphedema
E. CHF
F. Vein compression (caused by enlarged lymph nodes or mass)
G. Filariasis (parasitic disease)
H. Allergic reaction, localized
I. Compartment syndrome

Plan

A. Patient teaching. See the Section III Patient Teaching Guide for this chapter, "Deep Vein Thrombosis."
  1. Patients taking Coumadin should be educated regarding foods that are high in vitamin K.
  2. Avoid prolonged standing or sitting.
  3. Avoid crossing the legs.
  4. Gradually resume normal activity.
  5. Avoid immobility.
  6. Exercise on a regular basis.
  7. Stop smoking.
  8. Encourage strategies to better manage other chronic medical conditions that directly affect the progression of PAD, that is, diabetes, dyslipidemia, obesity, and HTN.
B. Nonpharmaceutical therapy
  1. Compression stockings
C. Pharmaceutical therapy
  1. Thrombolytics: Administered in the inpatient setting
  2. Anticoagulants
    a. Heparin, intravenous, administered in the inpatient setting
    b. Coumadin (warfarin sodium, Jantoven)
      i. Doses: 1, 2, 2.5, 3, 4, 5, 6, 7.5, and 10 mg tablets
      ii. See "Atrial Fibrillation" section for specifics on Coumadin therapy.

3. Low-molecular-weight heparin (LMWH)
   a. Lovenox (enoxaparin sodium)
      i. Doses: 300 mg/3 mL multidose vial
      ii. Doses: 30 mg/0.3 mL, 40 mg/0.4 mL, 60 mg/0.6 mL, 80 mg/0.8 mL, 100 mg/mL, 120 mg/0.8 mL, and 150 mg/mL prefilled syringes
   b. Fragmin (dalteparin sodium)
      i. Doses: 95,000 IU/9.5 mL multidose vial
      ii. Doses: 2,500 IU/0.2 mL, 5,000 IU/0.2 mL, 7,500 IU/0.3 mL, 10,000 IU/0.4 mL, 10,000 IU/mL, 12,500 IU/0.5 mL, 15,000 IU/0.6 mL, 18,000 IU/0.72 mL by injection
4. Specific factor Xa inhibitor
   a. Arixtra (fondaparinux sodium)
      i. Doses: 2.5 mg/0.5 mL, 5 mg/0.4 mL, 7.5 mg/0.6 mL, and 10 mg/0.8 mL by injection

D. Surgery
   1. Insertion of vena cava filter to prevent PE
   2. Venous thrombectomy

Follow-Up

A. Follow-up is determined by patient's needs, frequency and intensity of symptoms, and presence of other medical conditions.
B. DVT manifesting persistent symptoms should always be followed by a cardiologist.
C. Patients taking anticoagulants are best followed by an anticoagulant clinic and/or cardiologist.

Consultation/Referral

A. If you suspect acute limb ischemia, refer patient for immediate hospitalization in order to obtain diagnostic testing to determine the presence of a thrombus and restore circulation to the affected extremity.
B. If chronic limb ischemia has led to ulceration and/or superimposed infection, hospitalization is indicated to initiate a wound care consultation and diagnostic testing to determine the degree of arterial occlusion.
C. Referral to a cardiologist is indicated in the presence of persistent PVD symptoms.
D. Refer to pain management if pain is resistant to treatment.
E. Refer to a registered dietitian as indicated by the patient's understanding of dietary modification necessary to improve status of risk factors.

Individual Considerations

A. Nonambulatory patients
   1. Using rocking chairs is a possible substitute for persons unable to participate in a walking program.
B. Geriatrics
   1. Be alert to signs and symptoms of depression related to immobility and pain.

Heart Failure

Definition

HF is failure of the heart to pump sufficient blood to meet the metabolic demands of the tissues. The previous guidelines, published in 1999, defined HF according to primary dysfunction and clinical manifestations. However, the 2013 guidelines from the ACC/AHA address management of HF with reduced ejection fraction (HFrEF) and preserved ejection fraction (HFpEF).

The 2013 ACC/AHA guidelines for HF are available at circ.ahajournals.org/content/early/2013/06/03/CIR.0b013e31829e8776. These guidelines include:

A. HFrEF
   1. EF less than 40%, due to weak, inefficient systolic contractions. The LVEF is a measurement of systolic failure.
   2. S3 ventricular gallop rhythm commonly occurs.
   3. Systolic failure is often the result of CHD and/or MI.
   4. It can result from right- or left-sided failure, or both.
B. HFpEF
   1. EF greater than 50%, but with poor compliance of the ventricle, which impedes ventricular diastolic filling (the ventricle is unable to relax).
   2. There are two subgroups.
      a. HFpEF borderline (or intermediate): Patients with an EF of 41% to 49%
      b. HFpEF with EF greater than 40% who previously had HFrEF (EF < 40%) but improvement or recovery was noted in EF
   3. The patient may be asymptomatic for years.
   4. HF presents with the same symptoms of systolic failure, pulmonary congestion, and peripheral edema.
   5. S4 atrial gallop rhythm commonly occurs.

Incidence

A. HFrEF incidence is higher in older women, chronic HTN, obesity, LV hypertrophy, cardiomyopathy, excessive alcohol use, end-stage COPD, valvular disorders, anemia, renal failure, AF, CAD, or diabetes.
B. Approximately 5.7 million people in the United States have HF. By the year 2030, the AHA estimates that there will be a 46% increase in HF in patients with chronic diseases.

C. It is also estimated that the costs of direct patient care (health care services, hospitalization, medications, etc.) for these patients with chronic disease will increase to approximately $53 billion by the year 2030.

Pathogenesis

A. Injuries to the myocardium may cause loss of functioning muscle. Compensatory mechanisms, including cardiac hypertrophy and neurohumoral processes, lead to adverse long-term effects. An inotropic insult results in incomplete emptying (systolic failure), and a compliance abnormality results in incomplete filling (diastolic failure). Most HF has some degree of both abnormalities.

Predisposing Factors

A. Atherosclerotic heart disease
B. MI
C. Rheumatic heart disease involving mitral and aortic valves
D. Cardiomyopathies
E. Hypertensive heart disease
F. Aortic stenosis or regurgitation
G. Thyrotoxicosis
H. Pregnancy-related disorders, such as multiple births with preexisting heart disease
I. Volume overload
J. Beta blockers or other cardiac depressants
K. PE
L. Systemic infection
M. Arrhythmias
N. Renal disease

Common Complaints

Patients are assigned the New York Heart Association classifications by their tolerance of physical activity and SOB. This classification may change according to their progression or regression of their CVD (see Table 12.4).

A. Dyspnea on exertion
B. Hemoptysis
C. Fatigue
D. Cough
E. Orthopnea
F. Edema/weight gain
G. Paroxysmal nocturnal dyspnea
H. Nausea
I. Right upper abdominal pain or fullness
J. Chest pain
K. Palpitations

Other Signs and Symptoms

A. Hemoptysis
B. Bibasilar crackles
C. S3 gallop
D. Murmurs
E. Exercise intolerance
F. Weakness
G. Cough
H. Orthopnea
I. Nocturnal dyspnea
J. Tachycardia
K. Pallor
L. Cyanosis
M. Anorexia
N. Constipation
O. JVD
P. Hepatomegaly
Q. Hepatojugular reflux (HJR)
R. Murmurs
S. Exercise intolerance

Subjective Data

A. Ask the patient if he or she has difficulty breathing.
B. Ask how many pillows he or she sleeps on. Does the patient need to sit up in a recliner to sleep?
C. Inquire about how often he or she wakes up at night with SOB.
D. Inquire about how far the patient can walk without getting SOB. Have the patient describe his or her routine activities of daily living and how well he or she tolerates each activity.
E. Discuss the patient's history of heart disease, heart attack, HTN, or hyperlipidemia.

TABLE 12.4 Functional Classification for Heart Failure

Functional Class	Activities	Objective Assessment
Functional Capacity Class I Objective Assessment A	No limitation. Ordinary activity does not cause undue fatigue, palpitation, dyspnea, or angina.	No objective evidence of CV disease
Functional Capacity Class II Objective Assessment B	Slight limitations. Fatigue, palpitation, SOB, angina with ordinary physical activity.	Objective evidence—minimal CV disease
Functional Capacity Class III Objective Assessment Stage C	Marked limitations. No discomfort at rest. Fatigue, palpitation, SOB, and angina with less than usual activities.	Objective evidence—moderately severe CV disease
Functional Capacity Class IV Objective Assessment Stage D	Inability to do physical activity without discomfort. Symptoms are present at rest and become worse with activity.	Objective evidence—moderately severe CV disease

F. Ask the patient about current medications, as well as prescription, OTC, and herbal products.
G. Question the patient regarding all symptoms found in the Common Complaints section.
H. Discuss drug and alcohol history.
I. Has the patient ever been treated for cancer/chemotherapy, and how long ago?
J. What is the patient's usual weight? Has he or she experienced more symptoms if the patient has pedal edema?
K. Does the patient have a cough? (Consider ACE [angiotensin-converting enzyme] inhibitors as the cause.)

Physical Examination

A. Check pulse respirations, BP, pulse oximetry, height, and weight.
   1. Check BP sitting, standing, and lying down.
   2. Be alert for abnormal vital signs: Hypotension, narrow or wide pulse pressure, tachycardia, bradycardia, and tachypnea.
   3. Calculate BMI.
   4. On all subsequent visits, note weight gain of more than 1 pound per day over 3 consecutive days or 3 pounds in 1 day.
B. Inspect
   1. Inspect overall physical appearance. Is the patient in distress?
   2. Inspect skin: Note pallor, cyanosis, and temperature.
   3. Inspect neck: Check jugular veins for distension.
   4. Inspect extremities: Note edema, cyanosis, pallor, and ulcers.
C. Palpate
   1. Palpate abdomen for hepatomegaly and HJR.
   2. Palpate extremities for peripheral pulses.
   3. Palpate chest wall for displaced point of maximal impulse (PMI), lifts, heaves, and thrills.
D. Auscultate
   1. Auscultate heart for murmurs; tachycardia; S1, S3, or S4 gallops; and other abnormalities.
   2. Auscultate lungs: Note moderate-to-severe crackles/rales and other abnormal sounds.
   3. Auscultate neck and carotid arteries.
E. Mental status: Check mental status because confusion may occur, especially in the elderly.

Diagnostic Tests

A. Two-dimensional echocardiography with Doppler to evaluate LVEF.
B. Radionuclide ventriculography may be used to measure LVEF and LV volumes.
C. Coronary angiography
D. Anterior/posterior chest x-ray
E. EKG for patients with suspected arrhythmia, ischemia, or cardiac disease. Identify acute and old EKG changes to rule out pathologic Q wave, ST segment elevation, and LV hypertrophy.
F. Natriuretic peptides (BNP or NT-proBNP)

Differential Diagnoses

A. HF
   1. HFrEF
   2. HFpEF
      a. HFpEF borderline patients with an EF of 41% to 49%
      b. HFpEF patients with an EF greater than 40% who previously had HFrEF (EF, 40%) with improvement noted in EF
B. Renal disease or nephrotic syndrome
C. Liver disease
D. Asthma
E. COPD: To distinguish between progressing HF and a COPD exacerbation when both conditions are present, the presence of weight gain and an S3 gallop indicates HF, not COPD.

Plan

A. General interventions
   1. Determine the etiology of the failure state and treat appropriately.
   2. Treat HF stages.
      a. Stage A: Treat/manage the patient's underlying conditions (HTN, AF, hyperlipidemia, diabetes, tobacco cessation, obesity, substance abuse [alcohol, cocaine, etc.])
      b. Stage B: Begin ACE inhibitors with beta blockers for patients with HFrEF. Add statin therapy if patient has a history of MI.
      c. Stage C: HFrEF: Implantable cardioverter defibrillators and cardiac resynchronization therapy
         i. Digoxin may be used to manage symptoms. Hydralazine and isosorbide dinitrate are indicated for African American patients with HFrEF, patients with kidney dysfunction, or patients who cannot take ACE inhibitors or angiotensin receptor blocker (ARB) therapy. A diuretic agent is also recommended.
      d. Stage D: Advanced treatment such as cardiac transplant, mechanical support, and/or palliative care
   3. The goals of therapy are to improve the patient's quality of life by reducing symptoms, decreasing morbidity, and prolonging survival.
B. Patient teaching
   1. Teach the patient to weigh daily at the same time, on the same scale, and in the same clothing. The patient is to call if there are gains of more than 3 pounds in 1 day or more than 1 pound a day over a 3-day period.

a. Develop a plan of care for the increase of diuretic dosing for edema/weight gain in order to decrease dyspnea and prevent hospitalization.
2. Encourage weight loss.
3. Recommend regular, moderate exercise as long as dyspnea is not induced. Encourage exercise even though the patient may only tolerate a few minutes of walking to increase endurance and strengthen muscles.
4. Encourage smoking cessation.
5. Encourage medication adherence. Instruct the patient about all medications and possible side effects. Do not use OTC medicines without consulting the provider. NSAIDs are contraindicated in HF.
6. Utilize continuous positive airway pressure (CPAP) or bilevel positive airway pressure (BiPAP) for nighttime sleep and naps for treatment of OSA.

C. Dietary management
1. Read food labels for sodium content.
2. Teach dietary modifications, especially salt restriction of 2,000 to 3,000 mg/d for HFrEF and HFpEF. Less than 2,000 mg sodium per day is recommended in patients with moderate to severe HF symptoms.
3. Fluid restriction is not recommended unless the patient is classified as Stage D or is diagnosed with hyponatremia with sodium levels less than 130 mEq/L. Restrict fluid intake to 2,000 mL/d or less for patients with chronic fluid retention despite use of diuretics and sodium restrictions.
4. Alcohol consumption should be limited to one glass of beer or wine per day. This amount should be counted in the daily fluid restriction.
5. See Appendix B for the DASH diet (Tables B.1–B.5).
6. Other diet changes include low-fat/low-cholesterol and the use of
a. Monounsaturated fats, which decrease cholesterol
i. Canola oil
ii. Olive oil
b. Polyunsaturated fats, which decrease cholesterol but not as well as monounsaturated
i. Vegetable and fish oils
ii. Corn, safflower, peanut, and soybean oils
c. Avoid saturated fats.
i. Animal fats and some plant fats
ii. Butter and lard
iii. Coconut oil and palm oil

D. Pharmaceutical therapy
1. Therapy is based on extent of cardiac impairment and severity of symptoms. Medication regimens include a combination of the following classes: Diuretics, ACE inhibitor (ARB if unable to tolerate ACEI), cardioselective beta blockers, inotropic agents such as Digoxin, vasodilators, nitrates, and anticoagulants if there is an increased risk of thrombus formation. In general, CCBs are not used in HF management.
2. Drug classifications for antihypertensive and cardiac medication are noted in Table 12.5.

TABLE 12.5 Antihypertensive and Cardiac Medications (Sorted Alphabetically)

Brand Name	Generic Name	Drug Class
Accupril	Quinapril	ACE inhibitor
Aceon	Perindopril erbumine	ACE inhibitor
Adalat CC	Dihydropyridine/Nifedipine	CCB
Aldactazide	Spironolactone + HCTZ	Combination-K + sparing + thiazide
Aldactone	Spironolactone	Diuretic-K + sparing
Altace	Ramipril	ACE inhibitor
Amiloride/HCTZ	Amiloride/HCTZ	Combination + diuretic
Atacand	Candesartan Cilexetil	Angiotensin II receptor blocker (ARB)
Atacand HCT	Candesartan + HCTZ	Combination-ARB + diuretic
Avalide	Irbesartan + HCTZ	Combination-ARB + diuretic
Avalide Avapro	Irbesartan + HCTZ Irbesartan	Combination ARB + diuretic angiotensin II receptor blocker (ARB)
Azor	Amlodipine + Olmesartan	CCB + ARB
Benicar	Olmesartan medoxomil	Angiotensin II receptor blocker (ARB)
Benicar HCT	Olmesartan + HCTZ	Combination-ARB + diuretic

(*continued*)

TABLE 12.5 Antihypertensive and Cardiac Medications (Sorted Alphabetically) (*continued*)

Brand Name	Generic Name	Drug Class
Betapace	Sotalol	Beta blocker/class II and III antiarrhythmic
Betapace AF	Sotalol	Class II and III antiarrhythmics
Betaxolol Bidil	Betaxolol HCL Isosorbide dinitrate + Hydralazine	Beta blocker-cardioselective nitrate + diuretic
Bumex	Bumetanide	LOOP diuretic
Bystolic	Nebivolol	Beta blocker-cardioselective
Caduet	Amlodipine + atorvastatin	CCB/amlodipine/atorvastatin
Calan	Verapamil	CCB/antianginal
Calan SR	Verapamil	CCBr
Capoten	Captopril	ACE inhibitor/CHF
Capozide	Captopril + HCTZ	Combination-ace + diuretic
Cardizem LA	Diltiazem	CCB
Cardura	Doxazosin	Alpha-2 blocker AAB
Catapres	Clonidine	Central alpha agonist
Chlorothiazide	Various	Thiazide diuretic
Chlorthalidone	Various	Monosulfamyl diuretic
Cleviprex	Dihydropyridine	CCB
Cordarone	Amiodarone	Class II and III antiarrhythmics
Coreg CR	Carvedilol	Beta blocker-noncardioselective/CHF
Corgard	Nadolol	Beta blocker-noncardioselective/antianginal
Corzide	Nadolol + HCTZ	Combination-beta blocker (noncardioselective) + diuretic
Covera HS	Verapamil	CCB/antianginal
Cozaar	Losartan	Angiotensin II receptor blocker (ARB)
Demadex	Torsemide	LOOP diuretic
Digoxin	Digoxin	Cardiac glycoside/antiarrhythmic
Dilacor XR	Diltiazem	CCB/antianginal
Dilatrate SR	Isosorbide dinitrate	Nitrate
Diovan	Valsartan	Angiotensin II receptor blocker (ARB)/CHF Class II–IV
Diovan HCT	Valsartan + HCTZ	Combination-ARB + diuretic
Diuril	Chlorothiazide	Thiazide diuretic
Dutoprol Dyazide	Metoprolol ext. release + HCTZ triamterene + HCTZ	Beta blocker (cardioselective) + thiazide combination-K + sparing + thiazide
Dynacirc CR	Isradipine controlled release	CCBr
Edarbi	Azilsartan	Angiotensin II receptor blocker
Edarbyclor	Azilsartan + chlorthalidone	Angiotensin II receptor blocker + diuretic
Edecrin	Ethacrynic acid	LOOP diuretic
Exforge	Dihydropyridine + amlodipine	CCB + ARB
Fosinopril HCTZ	Various hydrochlorothiazide	ACE inhibitor thiazide diuretic
Hytrin	Terazosin	Alpha-1 blocker
Hyzaar	Losartan potassium + HCTZ	Combination-ARB + diuretic
Imdur	Isosorbide dinitrate	Nitrate
Inderal	Propranolol	Beta blocker-noncardioselective/antianginal/ antiarrhythmic
Inderide	Propranolol + HCTZ	Combination-beta blocker (noncardioselective) + diuretic

(*continued*)

TABLE 12.5 Antihypertensive and Cardiac Medications (Sorted Alphabetically) (*continued*)

Brand Name	Generic Name	Drug Class
Innopran XL	Propranolol HCL ext release	Beta blocker-noncardioselective
Inspra	Eplerenone	Aldosterone receptor blocker-mineralocorticoid selective/CHF
ISMO	Isosorbide dinitrate	Nitrate
Isoptin SR	Verapamil	CCB
Isosorbide dinitrate	Various	Nitrate
Isosorbide mononitrate	Various	Nitrate
Kerlone	Betaxolol	Beta blocker-cardioselective
Lanoxin	Digoxin	Cardiac glycoside/antiarrhythmic
Lasix	Furosemide	LOOP diuretic
Levatol	Penbutolol sulfate	Beta blocker-noncardioselective
Lopressor	Metoprolol tartrate	Beta blocker-cardioselective/antianginal
Lopressor HCT	Metoprolol + HCTZ	Combination-beta blocker (cardioselective) + diuretic
Lotensin	Benazepril	ACE inhibitor
Lotensin HCT	Benazepril + HCTZ	Combination-ACE + diuretic
Lotrel	Amlodipine + Benazepril	Combination-CCB + ACE inhibitor
Mavik	Trandolapril	ACE inhibitor/CHF
Maxzide	Triamterene + HCTZ	Combination-K + sparing + thiazide
Mexiletine	Various	Class IB antiarrhythmic
Micardis	Telmisartan	Angiotensin II receptor blocker (ARB)
Micardis HCT	Telmisartan + HCTZ	Combination-ARB + diuretic
Microzide	Hydrochlorothiazide (HCTZ)	Diuretic
Minitran	Nitroglycerin	Nitrate
Monoket	Isosorbide dinitrate	Nitrate
Monopril	Fosinopril	ACE inhibitor/CHF
Multaq	Dronedarone	Antiarrhythmic
Nicardipine	Various	CCB
Nitro-BID	Nitroglycerin	Nitrate
Nitro-Dur	Nitroglycerin	Nitrate
Nitrolingual	Nitroglycerin	Nitrate
Nitrostat	Nitroglycerin	Nitrate
Normodyne	Labetalol	Beta blocker
Norpace	Disopyramide	Antiarrhythmics-class 1-ventricular
Norvasc	Amlodipine	CCB/antianginal
Pindolol	Pindolol	Beta blocker-noncardioselective
Plendil	Felodipine	CCB
Prinivil	Lisinopril	ACE inhibitor/CHF
Prinzide	Lisinopril + HCTZ	Combination-ACE inhibitor + thiazide diuretic
Procanbid	Procainamide	Antiarrhythmics-class Ia-ventricular
Procardia XL	Nifedipine	CCB/antianginal
Quinidine gluconate	Various	Antiarrhythmics-class 1 atrial and ventricular
Quinidine sulfate	Various	Antiarrhythmics-class 1 atrial and ventricular
Ranexa	Ranolazine	Antianginal
Rythmol	Propafenone	Antiarrhythmics-class Ic-ventricular

(*continued*)

TABLE 12.5 Antihypertensive and Cardiac Medications (Sorted Alphabetically) (*continued*)

Brand Name	Generic Name	Drug Class
Sectral	Acebutolol	Beta blocker-cardioselective
Sular	Nisoldipine	CCBr
Tambocor	Flecainide	Antiarrhythmics-class Ic-ventricular
Tarka	Trandolapril + verapamil	Combination-ACE + CCB
Tekamlo	Aliskiren + amlodipine	Direct renin inhibitor + dihydropyridine (DHP) CCBr
Tekturna	Aliskiren	Direct renin inhibitor
Tekturna HCT	Aliskiren + HCTZ	Direct renin inhibitor + thiazide diuretic
Tenex	Guanfacine	Central alpha agonist
Tenoretic	Atenolol + chlorthalidone	Combination-beta blocker (cardioselective) + diuretic
Tenormin	Atenolol	Beta blocker-cardioselective/antianginal
Teveten	Eprosartan	Angiotensin II receptor blocker (ARB)
Teveten HCT	Eprosartan + HCTZ	Combination-ARB + diuretic
Thalitone	Chlorthalidone	Antihypertensive/diuretic
Tiazac	Diltiazem	CCB/antianginal
Tikosyn	Dofetilide	Class III antiarrhythmic
Timolide	Timolol maleate + HCTZ	Combination-beta blocker (noncardioselective) + diuretic
Toprol XL	Metoprolol	Beta blocker-cardioselective/antianginal/CHF class II or III
Trandate	Labetalol	Beta blocker-noncardioselective
Tribenzor	Olmesartan + amlodipine + HCTZ	ARB + CCB+ thiazide diuretic
Twynsta	Telmisartan + amlodipine	ARB + CCB
Uniretic	Moexipril + HCTZ	Combination-ACE + diuretic
Univasc	Meoxipril	ACE inhibitor
Valturna	Aliskiren + valsartan	Direct renin inhibitor + ARB
Vaseretic	Enalapril + HCTZ	Combination-ACE + diuretic
Vasotec	Enalapril	ACE inhibitor/CHF with digitalis and diuretics
Verelan PM	Verapamil	CCB
Zaroxolyn	Metolazone	Diuretic-Quinazoline
Zebeta	Bisoprolol	Beta blocker-cardioselective
Zestoretic	Lisinopril + HCTZ	Combination-ace + diuretic
Zestril	Lisinopril	ACE inhibitor/CHF with digitalis and diuretics
Ziac	Bisoprolol + HCTZ	Combination-beta blocker (cardioselective) + diuretic

E. Drugs that should be avoided and/or used with caution in HF because they cause exacerbations or are at high risk for adverse reactions include:
   1. NSAIDs: Increased renal dysfunction, edema, impaired response to ACEI
   2. Cyclooxygenase (COX-2) inhibitors: Increased rate of HF and increased mortality
   3. Aspirin: Interaction between ASA and ACEI and interference with benefits of beta blockers on LVEF
   4. Metformin: Increased risk of lethal lactic acidosis
   5. Thiazolidinediones: Fluid retention that may precipitate HF
   6. CCBs: Some data on possible effect on systolic dysfunction
   7. Antidepressants TCAs and SSRIs: Major adverse cardiovascular events including HF, MI, stroke, and cardiovascular death
   8. Phosphodiesterase inhibitors (PDE-3, PDE-4, and PDE-5): Increased mortality

9. Antiarrhythmic: Negative inotropic activity and further reduction in LV function can impair the elimination and result in toxicity of the antiarrhythmic.
10. Chemotherapy: Many are cardiotoxic.
11. Androgens-testosterone patch: Edema that may increase the rate of HF
12. Theophylline-serum levels may increase and cause toxicity due to acute decompensation of HF.
13. Sodium bicarbonate and Fleet Phospho soda contain significant quantities of sodium.
14. Herbal/supplements may also affect HF.

F. Biventricular pacing or an implantable defibrillator may be necessary for advanced HF.

G. Advanced HF therapies can include:
1. Inotropic therapy in hospital and in home
2. Implanted mechanical-assist devices as a bridge to transplantation or as a destination therapy
3. Heart transplantation

H. Discuss the patient's desire for an evaluation as a heart transplant candidate.

I. The pneumonia vaccination as well as yearly influenza immunization should be encouraged.

J. Discuss the need for compassionate care/hospice when HF does not respond despite maximal therapy.

Follow-Up

A. HF patients should be comanaged with a physician.
B. Close follow-up is essential if the patient is to be maintained as an outpatient.
C. Appointments every 1 to 2 weeks may be necessary, with additional appointments depending on the patient's symptoms, such as increasing SOB, inability to lie flat to sleep, nocturnal moist cough, and increase in daily weight.
D. Lab monitoring is required for electrolytes, BUN, creatinine, proteinuria, and digoxin level.

Consultation/Referral

A. Consult a physician when the patient requires the next level up in pharmacologic management.
B. Consult a cardiologist for staging and hospital management.

Individual Considerations

A. Pregnancy
1. HF is uncommon in healthy women without coexisting heart disease.
2. Pregnancy in a patient with heart disease is considered high risk.
3. Refer to a high-risk obstetrician.

B. Adults
1. The 5-year survival rate is 25% for men and 38% for women.
2. Predictors of poor outcome include an EF of less than 25%, ischemic etiology, ventricular arrhythmias, serum sodium greater than 130 mEq/L, poor functional class, low cardiac index, and high filling pressures.

C. Geriatrics
1. Common signs and symptoms of HF are less specific in older adults, and atypical symptoms may predominate.
2. Age-associated changes in pharmacokinetics must be taken into account when prescribing drugs for HF.
3. Effective communication among health professionals, patients, and families is necessary.
4. Given the life-limiting nature of HF in frail older adults, it is critical for clinicians to discuss end-of-life issues with patients and their families as soon as possible. The Medicare hospice benefit is granted to patients who have been certified by two physicians to have a life expectancy of 6 months or less if their terminal illness runs its natural course. The criteria for determining that HF is terminal are:
   a. New York Heart Association Class III (symptomatic with less than ordinary activities) or IV (symptomatic at rest)
   b. LVEF less than or equal to 20%
   c. Persistent symptoms despite optimal medical management
   d. Inability to tolerate optional management due to hypotension with or without renal failure

Hypertension

Definition

A. HTN is considered a SBP of 140 mmHg or more, or a diastolic blood pressure (DBP) of 90 mmHg or more, or taking antihypertensive medications. The Joint National Committee (JNC) VII defines HTN in adults as follows (see Table 12.6).

B. Resistant HTN is defined as:
1. BP that is not at target despite a three-drug regimen, including an ACE inhibitor or an ARB + a CCB + a diuretic appropriate for the patient's glomerular filtration rate (GFR).
2. Controlled BP while taking four or more medications is also considered resistant HTN.

C. Standing and supine BPs should be measured before the initiation of combination antihypertensive therapy. Orthostatic (postural) hypotension is diagnosed when, within 2 to 5 minutes of quiet standing, one or more of the following is present:
1. At least a 20 mmHg fall in systolic pressure
2. At least a 10 mmHg fall in diastolic pressure
3. Symptoms of cerebral hypoperfusion, such as dizziness.

TABLE 12.6 JNC VII Classification of BP in Adults 18 Years or Older

BP Classification	SBP (mmHg)	DBP (mmHg)
Normal	< 120	and < 80
Pre-HTN	120–139	or 80–89
Stage 1 HTN	140–159	or 90–99
Stage 2 HTN	> 160	or > 100

Seventh Report of the Joint National Committee (JNC VII) Prevention, Detection, Evaluation, and Treatment of High BP, 2003: www.nhlbi.nih.gov/guidelines/HTN/express.pdf

D. The average nocturnal BP is approximately 15% lower than daytime values. Failure of BP to fall by at least 10% during sleep is called "nondipping" and is a stronger predictor of adverse cardiovascular outcomes than daytime BP.
E. Isolated systolic HTN (ISH) is defined when the SBP is greater than or equal to 140 with the DBP normal or below normal (< 90 mmHg). ISH usually affects the elderly, increasing their risk of stroke or MI.
F. Isolated diastolic hypertension (IDH) is defined as a diastolic pressure greater than or equal to 90 mmHg with a systolic pressure less than 140 mmHg. IDH is more common in younger men who are overweight/obese and in individuals younger than 40 years.
G. Malignant HTN is marked HTN with retinal hemorrhages, exudates, or papilledema. Malignant HTN is usually associated with diastolic pressures above 120 mmHg.

Incidence

A. Worldwide, HTN affects about 1 billion people.
B. Approximately one in three adults in the United States have HTN.
C. The incidence of resistant HTN is rising. The data indicates a 21.7% incidence.
D. African American women have the highest death related from HTN 37.7 deaths per 100,000 population.

Pathogenesis

Over 90% of cases have no identifiable cause, thus constituting the category of primary or essential HTN. The remaining 10% of cases have the following secondary causes.

A. Renal causes
   1. Glomerulonephritis
   2. Pyelonephritis
   3. Polycystic kidney disease
B. Endocrine causes
   1. Primary hyperaldosteronism
   2. Pheochromocytoma
   3. Hyperthyroidism
   4. Cushing's syndrome
C. Vascular causes
   1. Coarctation of aorta
   2. Renal artery stenosis
D. OSA
E. Chemical/medication induced HTNs
   1. Oral contraceptives
   2. NSAIDs
   3. Decongestants
   4. Antidepressants
   5. Sympathomimetics
   6. Corticosteroids
   7. Lithium
   8. Ergotamine alkaloids
   9. Cyclosporine
   10. Monoamine oxidase inhibitors (MAOIs), in combination with certain drugs or foods
   11. Appetite suppressants, in combination with certain drugs or foods
   12. Cocaine
   13. Amphetamines

Predisposing Factors

When making a diagnosis, consider not only the absolute BP reading, but also the presence or absence of other cardiovascular risk factors. Factors include the following:

A. Family history of HTN
B. Obesity
C. Alcohol consumption
D. Stress
E. Sedentary lifestyle
F. African American ancestry
G. Male gender
H. Age older than 30 years
I. Excessive salt intake
J. Medications
K. Drug use

Common Complaints

A. HTN is asymptomatic in the majority of patients.

Other Signs and Symptoms

A. Headaches
B. Advanced disease: Organ-specific complaints with end-organ damage
C. Retinopathy

Potential Complications

A. CVA
B. MI
C. Renal failure
D. HF
E. PAD

Subjective Data

A. Ask the patient about any family history of HTN or cardiac or renal disease.
B. Ask if the patient has ever been diagnosed with HTN or cardiac or renal disease.
C. Ask if the patient ever had any high BP readings.
D. Ask if the patient has ever been treated for any of the above problems.
E. Ask about other risk factors, such as smoking, drinking, high fat intake, obesity, and/or diabetes.
F. Inquire about the patient's lifestyle, exercise regimen, work environment, and stress level.
G. Ask the patient about symptoms that suggest secondary etiology.
   1. Palpitations, headache, diaphoresis (pheochromocytoma)
   2. Anxiety, weight gain or loss (thyroid abnormality)
   3. Muscle weakness, polyuria (primary aldosteronism)
H. Find out if the patient is taking drugs that elevate BP (noted under Pathogenesis).
I. Ask if the patient feels nervous when having his or her BP taken in the office ("white coat HTN").
J. Review current medications, including prescription, OTC, and herbal products.
K. Review current recreational/illicit drug use.

Physical Examination

A. Check pulse, BP, height, weight, waist circumference, and distribution of body fat. Calculate BMI.
   1. The diagnosis of HTN is made after averaging two or more properly measured readings at each of two or more visits after an initial screen.
   2. When patient's SBP and DBP fall into two different categories, use the higher category to classify his or her BP.
   3. For accurate measurement, use correct size cuff for patient (adult, large adult, or thigh cuff).
B. Inspect
   1. Observe overall appearance.
   2. Conduct funduscopic exam; look for papilledema, exudates, AV nicking, anterior nicking.
   3. Inspect the neck for jugular vein distension.
   4. Observe for pedal edema.
C. Palpate
   1. Palpate the neck; check thyroid for enlargement.
   2. Palpate the abdomen for masses or organomegaly.
   3. Palpate the extremities; assess peripheral pulses and note edema.
   4. Assess deep tendon reflexes (DTRs).
D. Auscultate
   1. Auscultate heart, noting the PMI.
   2. Auscultate lungs; check for bronchospasm and rales.
   3. Auscultate neck; assess carotid arteries for bruits.

Diagnostic Tests

A. Hematocrit
B. LFTs, LDH (lactate dehydrogenase), uric acid
C. Chemistry profile
D. Lipid profile (total and HDL-cholesterol and triglycerides)
E. Urinalysis for proteinuria
F. Estimated GFR
G. EKG
H. If history, physical exam, or lab tests indicate the need, obtain the following:
   1. Intravenous pyelography (IVP)
   2. Renal arteriogram
   3. Plasma renin
   4. Catecholamines
   5. Chest radiography
   6. Aortogram
   7. Ultrasonography
   8. Sleep study
I. Monitor potassium levels if on ACEI/ARBs or Spironolactone

Differential Diagnoses

A. Primary HTN
B. Secondary HTN
C. Drug-induced HTN
D. White coat syndrome

Plan

A. General interventions (see Table 12.7)
   1. Advise overweight patients to lose weight. Loss of as little as 10 pounds reduces BP in many patients.
   2. Advise the patient to limit or discontinue alcohol intake.
   3. Encourage the patient to stop smoking.
   4. Encourage increased physical activity. The 2013 ACC/AHA guidelines on lifestyle management outline the newest physical activity recommendation, which advises adults to engage in 40 minutes of aerobic physical activity three to four times a week. The aerobic exercise should involve moderate to vigorous intensity.
   5. Encourage some form of relaxation technique.

TABLE 12.7 Modifiable and Nonmodifiable Risk for Control of Hypertension

Modifiable	Nonmodifiable
Sedentary lifestyle	Age
Smoking	Gender
Diet	Ethnicity
Lipid control	Diabetes
Sodium intake	Postmenopausal
Alcohol intake	Family history
Obesity	

B. Patient teaching
   1. Stress asymptomatic nature of disease.
   2. Stress importance of ongoing monitoring and treatment under the direction of a health care provider.
   3. Review risk factors for cardiac, renal, and cerebrovascular disease and possible preventive measures.
   4. The ACC maintains the CardioSmart Patient Education Portal for an online BP and other heart conditions management tool to educate and motivate patients. ACC's CardioSmart is a free resource located at www.cardiosmart.org. CardioSmartTXT *PREVENT* is a 6-month program of health tips and reminders sent via two text messages a week. CardioSmartTXT *QUIT* is a 2-month program to assist patients in smoking cessation. Four text messages are sent a day with information and assistance with smoking cessation.

C. Dietary management: Review specific dietary measures. Give dietary recommendation sheets. See Appendix B for low-fat/low-cholesterol and DASH dietary approaches to stop HTN.
   1. Diet alone will only make the lowest incremental change in BP; therefore, it should be combined with lifestyle modification and lower sodium intake; stopping smoking, weight loss, and exercise are essential.
   2. It is essential for the patient/family to read labels for sodium, fat content, and serving sizes.
   3. Other dietary changes include low-fat/low-cholesterol diets and limiting fats.
      a. Use monounsaturated fats to decrease cholesterol.
         i. Canola oil
         ii. Olive oil
      b. Use in limited quantities: Polyunsaturated fats decrease cholesterol but not as well as monounsaturated.
         i. Vegetable and fish oils
         ii. Corn, safflower, peanut, and soybean oils
      c. Limit saturated fats.
         i. Animal fats and some plant fats
         ii. Butter and lard
         iii. Coconut oil and palm oil

D. Pharmaceutical therapy
   1. If lifestyle changes alone are not adequate to control HTN, consider drug therapy. Medication doses are dependent on age, ethnicity, and comorbid conditions. Most patients will require two or more medications to control their BP. Consider starting antihypertensives and/or diuretics (see Table12.5 for drugs and classifications). The Eighth Joint National Committee (JNC VIII) recommendations were released in 2014 for the initiation and BP goals (see Table 12.8). The JNC VIII published an extensive algorithm for the treatment of HTN. The algorithm is available at jama.jamanetwork.com/solr/searchresults.aspx?q=jnc8&fd_JournalID=67&f_JournalDisplayName=JAMA&SearchSourceType=3
   2. The 2013 Science Advisory recommendations from the AHA, the ACC, and the CDC

TABLE 12.8 Eighth Joint National Committee (JNC VIII) Recommendations for the Management of Hypertension

Ethnicity/Population	Age	Begin Initiation of Pharmacologic Treatment to Lower Blood Pressure	Blood Pressure Goals for Treatment	Other Comments
General population	> 60 years of age	Initiate therapy for SBP > 150 mmHg **OR** DBP > 90 mmHg	Treat to goal of SBP < 150 mmHg **AND** DBP < 90 mmHg	If pharmacologic treatment results in a lower achieved SBP and treatment is well tolerated, treatment does not need to be adjusted
General population	< 60 years of age	Initiate therapy to lower BP **at** SBP > 140 mmHg	Treat to goal of SBP < 140 mmHg	

(continued)

TABLE 12.8 Eighth Joint National Committee (JNC VIII) Recommendations for the Management of Hypertension (*continued*)

Ethnicity/Population	Age	Begin Initiation of Pharmacologic Treatment to Lower Blood Pressure	Blood Pressure Goals for Treatment	Other Comments
General population	< 60 years of age	Initiate therapy to lower BP **at** DBP > 90 mmHg	Treat to goal of DBP < 90 mmHg	
Patients with chronic kidney disease	> 18 years of age	Initiate therapy to lower the SBP > 140 mmHg **OR** DBP > 90 mmHg	Treat to goal of SBP < 140 mmHg **AND** DBP < 90 mmHg	
Patients with chronic kidney disease (regardless of race or diabetes status)	> 18 years of age			Initial or add-on antihypertensive therapy should include an ACEI **or** ARB to improve kidney outcomes
Patients with diabetes	> 18 years of age	Initiate therapy to lower BP at SBP > 140 mmHg, **OR** DBP > 90 mmHg	Treat to goal of SBP < 140 mmHg **AND** DBP < 90 mmHg	The American Diabetes Association recommends diabetics with hypertension should be treated to an SBP goal of < 140 mmHg and to a DBP of < 80 mmHg
General non-Black population including those with diabetes				Initial antihypertensive therapy should include a thiazide-type diuretic, CCB, ACEI, **OR** ARB
General Black population including those with diabetes				Initial antihypertensive therapy should include a thiazide-type diuretic **OR** CCB

ACEI, angiotensin-converting enzyme inhibitor; ARB, angiotensin receptor blocker; CCB, calcium channel blocker; DBP, diastolic blood pressure; SBP, systolic blood pressure.

recommend medication classifications for the treatment of HTN in the presence of medical conditions (see Table 12.9).

3. Antihypertensive/diuretics should be started low and increased if there is inadequate response to initial therapy and nonadherence is ruled out. Consider the following:
   a. Increasing drug dose
   b. Substituting another drug
   c. Adding a second drug from another class; a diuretic is recommended if one is not already being used.
   d. **Beta blockers are no longer first-line antihypertensive agents. Atenolol may increase central aortic pressure.**
   e. **ACEIs and ARBs are critical medications to prescribe and titrate to maximum dose as a first-line medication in people with renal disease, diabetes, and proteinuria.**
4. If response is still inadequate, add a second or third drug or diuretic if one has not already been tried.
5. Evaluate the patient for secondary causes if severe HTN is resistant to therapy.
6. Resistant HTN; rule out all inadequate response to the three-drug therapy (ACEI or ARB or CCB + diuretic):
   a. "White-coat" HTN: Have the patient begin to take and record his or her BP at home and report the values.
   b. Use of size-appropriate BP cuffs on obese patients
   c. Nonadherence to therapy, including side effects, medication regimen too complex, and/or cost/affordability
   d. Volume overload due to excessive salt intake, progressive renal damage, fluid retention from BP reduction, and inadequate diuretic therapy
   e. Drug problems: Dose too low, wrong type of diuretic, inappropriate combinations, rapid inactivation, drug actions, and interactions
   f. Associated conditions: Smoking, obesity, sleep apnea, insulin resistance, ethanol intake greater than 30 mL (1 oz) per day, panic attacks, chronic pain, and organic brain syndrome
   g. Adding spironolactone can decrease SBP by 25 mmHg average and DBP an average of 12 mmHg in resistant hypertensive patients.
7. Treat with decongestants very cautiously. Pseudoephedrine HCl (Sudafed) has the least cardiovascular effect.
8. Diuretics may worsen gout and diabetes.

TABLE 12.9 AHA, ACC, and CDC 2013 Suggested Hypertensive Medications by Medical Condition

Medical Condition	BB	ACEI or ARB	ALDO ANTAG	Thiazide	CCB
CAD/post-MI	X	X			
Systolic HF	X	X	X	X	
Diastolic HF	X	X		X	
Diabetes	X	X		X	X
Kidney disease		X			
Stroke or TIA		ACEI		X	

ACEI, angiotensin-converting-enzyme inhibitor; ALDO ANTAG, aldosterone antagonist; ARB, angiotensin II blocker; BB, beta blocker; CDC, Centers for Disease Control.

9. Beta blockers are contraindicated in asthma, HF, and heart block.
10. Use diltiazem HCl (Cardizem) and verapamil HCl (Calan) cautiously in HF or block.
11. ACE inhibitors may cause coughing.
12. **Abrupt cessation of therapy with a short-acting beta blocker, such as propranolol, or the short-acting alpha-2-agonist clonidine can lead to a potentially fatal withdrawal syndrome. Gradual discontinuation of these agents over a period of weeks should prevent this syndrome.**

Follow-Up

A. If drug therapy is initiated, see the patient again in 2 to 4 weeks for follow-up.
B. Once the patient is stable, see him or her every 3 to 6 months.
C. Evaluate the patient yearly, including uric acid, creatinine, and potassium.
D. Review and discuss drug therapy compliance, effectiveness, and adverse reactions (including effect on sexual activity) at each visit.
E. Home and ambulatory blood pressure monitoring (ABPM) is an adjunctive tool for the management of HTN.
   1. BP tracking apps are available on iTunes for the iPhone, iPod touch, and iPad.
   2. BP tracking apps for Androids are available on Google Play and Amazon Appstore.
   3. A printable BP tracker log is located at organizedhome.com/sites/default/files/image/pdf/health_blood_pressure_tracker.pdf
F. Consider sleep study for diagnosis of OSA (see Chapter 11, "Respiratory Guidelines," "Obstructive Sleep Apnea").
G. Patients with pre-HTN without diabetes, CKD, or CV disease should be treated by nonpharmacologic therapy (i.e., diet, sodium reduction, weight loss, exercise, smoking cessation) and should be evaluated annually.

Consultation/Referral

A. If the patient is pregnant, consult a physician before prescribing medications. Many antihypertensive drugs are harmful to the fetus.
B. Consult a physician if the patient is having an acute hypertensive emergency: DBP greater than 130 mmHg.
C. Consult/comanage with a physician if the patient needs more than three drugs for therapy.

Individual Considerations

A. Pregnancy. Refer to Chapter 15, "Obstetrics Guidelines."
   1. HTN may be either chronic- or pregnancy-induced.
   2. HTN is considered chronic if it is present before pregnancy or diagnosed prior to the 20th week of gestation.
   3. PIH is diagnosed if SBP increases 30 mmHg or more, or if DBP increases 15 mmHg or more, compared with BP readings before the 20th week of gestation. When BP readings are not known, a reading of 140/90 or higher is considered abnormal.
   4. Maternal as well as fetal mortality and morbidity improve with treatment.
B. Geriatrics
   1. The JNC VIII general guideline for patients older than 60 is to treat when BP is greater than 150/90. HTN in the elderly places the patient at risk for coronary events, stroke, HF, and PAD.
   2. Elderly persons with HTN are more likely to develop orthostatic and postprandial hypotension, which may result in falls or syncope.
      a. Evaluate side effects including dizziness and sedation. Beta blockers may cause depression or confusion in the elderly.
      b. Check for orthostatic BP changes.
      c. Avoid SBP less than 130 mmHg and DBP less than 60 mmHg due to effects on cerebral perfusion.

3. The general approach to drug therapy in the geriatric population is to start low and go slow. Specific drug choices should be determined by comorbidities, side effects, and costs.
   a. Start at low doses, with slow titration up to goal.
4. Check the Beers list for harmful drugs in the geriatric population. The 2012 American Geriatrics Society Updated Beers Criteria for Potentially Inappropriate Medication Use in Older Adults is available at www.americangeriatrics.org/files/documents/beers/2012BeersCriteria_JAGS.pdf. A printable pocketcard is available for download at www.americangeriatrics.org/files/documents/beers/PrintableBeersPocketCard.pdf.
5. To avoid hyperkalemia in the elderly, potassium-sparing diuretics should not be given with ACEI or ARBs.

Resources

The National Kidney Foundation provides online calculators at http://www.kidney.org/search_results.cfm?q=calculators

Lymphedema—*Laura A. Petty*

Definition

A. PVD is a general term that encompasses all occlusive or inflammatory diseases that occur within the peripheral arteries, veins, and lymphatics. Lymphedema is a chronic condition caused by the accumulation of lymphatic fluid in the interstitial tissue.

Incidence

A. The Vascular Disease Foundation reports that almost 1 million Americans have lymphedema, and the incidence worldwide is projected to approach 100 million.

Pathogenesis

A. Lymphedema occurs when lymph fluid is unable to flow in a normal manner and accumulates in an extremity. The propensity for lymphedema can be inherited or caused by another condition such as lymphangitis, malignancy, filariasis, or prior removal of lymph nodes.

Predisposing Factors

A. Cancer
B. Radiation therapy
C. Surgical removal of lymph nodes
D. Infection
E. Congenital disorder involving the structure of the lymph system
   1. Milroy's disease
   2. Meige's disease

Common Complaints

A. Severe edema that is consistent with the distal aspect of the extremity
B. Hard skin over edematous area
C. Loss of range of motion

Potential Complications

A. Infection, including lymphangitis and cellulitis
B. Lymphangiosarcoma

Subjective Data

A. Ask patient when the symptom(s) were first noticed.
B. Have patient describe duration of symptoms.
C. Review any history of cancer, radiation, and chemotherapy.
D. Review recent history of invasive procedures or surgery.
E. Ask patient to list all medications currently being taken, particularly substances not prescribed and illicit drugs such as cocaine.
F. Ask patient to describe any pain.
G. Ask the patient what makes the symptoms better and what makes them worse.
H. Have patient rate discomfort on a scale of 0 to 10, with 0 being comfortable.

Physical Examination

A. Vital signs
   1. Check BP and document resting heart rate, respirations, temperature, height, and weight.
B. Inspect
   1. Assess for signs of erythema, increased temperature, and edema.
C. Palpate
   1. Palpate lymph nodes distal and proximal to the site.
   2. Palpate pulses distal and proximal in all extremities.
   3. Palpate extremity for tenderness.
D. Auscultate
   1. Auscultate heart: Rate, rhythm, heart sounds, murmur, and gallops
   2. Auscultate lungs: Lung sounds in all fields

Diagnostic Tests

A. CBC with differential
B. CT
C. Doppler ultrasound
D. MRI
E. Lymphoscintigraphy

Differential Diagnosis

A. Lymphedema
B. Venous insufficiency
C. CHF
D. Lipiderma
E. DVT

Plan

A. Patient teaching. See the Section III Patient Teaching Guide for this chapter, "Lymphedema."
   1. Protect your arm or leg while recovering from cancer treatment.
   2. Avoid heavy lifting, if it's an arm.
   3. Avoid strenuous exercise.
   4. Avoid heat on your arm or leg.
   5. Avoid tight clothing.
   6. Inspect the affected limb daily, noting any cracks or cuts.
   7. Apply lotion daily to protect and prevent dry skin.

B. Nonpharmaceutical therapy
   1. Extremity elevation
   2. Compression stockings or wrapping of affected limb
   3. Pneumatic compression boot
   4. Therapeutic massage, specifically manual lymph drainage
   5. Referral to a lymphedema therapist
   6. Referral to physical therapy for home exercise program

C. Surgery
   1. Lymphaticovenular bypass
   2. Lymphovenous bypass

Follow-Up

A. Follow-up is determined by patient's needs, frequency and intensity of symptoms, and presence of other medical conditions.

B. PVD manifesting persistent symptoms should always be followed by a cardiologist.

Consultation/Referral

A. **If you suspect acute limb ischemia, refer patient for immediate hospitalization in order to obtain diagnostic testing to determine the presence of a thrombus and restore circulation to the affected extremity.**

B. If chronic limb ischemia has led to ulceration and/or superimposed infection, hospitalization is indicated to initiate a wound care consultation and diagnostic testing to determine the degree of arterial occlusion.

C. Referral to a cardiologist is indicated in the presence of persistent PVD symptoms.

D. Referral to a lymphedema therapist and physical therapist is indicated to best manage chronic lymphedema.

Murmurs

Definition

A murmur is turbulent blood flow through the heart as a result of one or more of the following etiologies:

A. Narrow valve opening, stenosis

B. Incomplete valve closure, regurgitant or insufficient blood flow

C. Abnormal opening through chambers, atrial or ventricular septal defect

D. Rapid blood flow through normal valve structures; occurs during pregnancy, with increased physiologic demand states, such as thyrotoxicosis

E. No abnormality; occurs in patients with thin chest walls

Incidence

A. Innocent heart murmurs are quite common. They affect 40% to 45% of children and about 10% of adults at some point during their lifetimes. Innocent heart murmurs are more common in women during pregnancy. Abnormal heart murmurs occur most often in people who have certain heart conditions, such as a defective heart valve (e.g., aortic stenosis, mitral regurgitation).

Pathogenesis

A. Pathogenesis depends on specific etiology, but rheumatic heart disease, calcific changes, ischemic insults, congenital abnormalities, and degenerative diseases can all contribute to the development of a murmur.

Common Complaints

A. Often no symptoms are present, and murmur is found on routine examination.

B. Complaints with advanced valvular disease
   1. Chest pain
   2. Dyspnea
   3. Palpitations
   4. SOB
   5. Exercise intolerance
   6. Postural lightheadedness

Subjective Data

A. Has the patient ever been diagnosed with a murmur?

B. Did the patient have frequent strep infections as a child?

C. Ask the patient about any recent viral infections.

D. Question the patient about chest pain; SOB; palpitations; diaphoresis; lightheadedness; or syncope, especially with exertion.

E. Ask the patient if any family members had sudden cardiac death before age 55.

Physical Examination

A. Check temperature, if indicated, pulse, respirations, and BP.

B. Inspect the chest for lifts and heaves.

C. Palpate the chest for lifts, heaves, and thrills.

D. Auscultate
   1. Auscultate heart for splitting of heart sounds, clicks, rubs, and murmurs; use bell and diaphragm of stethoscope to auscultate patient in left lateral, supine, standing, sitting (and leaning forward), and squatting positions and

after having patient run in place or do jumping jacks for 2 to 3 minutes.

a. A new, systolic, regurgitant murmur in the setting of an acute MI may indicate a ruptured papillary muscle and possible cardiogenic shock.
b. When a new murmur is audible, differentiate location, timing, quality, intensity, and duration. Note if radiation to neck, axilla, or back is present.
c. Note location of murmur.
    i. Aortic: Second right intercostal space (ICS) next to sternum
    ii. Pulmonic: Second left ICS next to sternum
    iii. Tricuspid: Fifth left ICS next to sternum
    iv. Mitral: Fifth left ICS at midclavicular line
d. If murmur is heard, have the patient squat, stand, and/or perform Valsalva maneuver. Squatting will increase the blood to the heart and increase the left ventricle blood volume and stroke volume that will increase the sound of the murmur. Standing and the Valsalva maneuver will provide the opposite, in which the venous return will drop and decrease the ventricle size and stroke volume and soften the sound of the murmur.
e. If the sound of the murmur occurs in the opposite action, softer when squatting and louder when standing or during the Valsalva maneuver, consider hypertrophic cardiomyopathy or MVP as the diagnosis.

2. Auscultate the neck and axilla for radiation.

Diagnostic Tests

A. EKG
B. Echocardiogram
C. Chest radiography

Differential Diagnoses

Major differentiation should be in the description of murmur, as this aids in identification of the murmur.

A. Timing
    1. Identify when the murmur occurs in the cardiac cycle.
    2. Systolic murmurs may or may not be normal.
        a. Occurs between the "S1" lub and the "S2" dub
    3. Diastolic murmurs are always abnormal.
        a. Occurs between the "S2" dub and the "S1" lub
B. Quality: Is the sound harsh, blowing, musical, rumbling, vibratory, or soft?
C. Intensity: Murmurs are usually graded on a six-point scale:
    1. Grade I. Barely audible
    2. Grade II. Audible but soft
    3. Grade III. Easily audible without thrill
    4. Grade IV. Easily audible, thrill usually palpable
    5. Grade V. Audible with only the rim of the stethoscope on the chest wall
    6. Grade VI. Audible with the stethoscope barely off the chest wall; thrill present
D. Duration: Identify location and timing in the specific phase of the cardiac cycle:
    1. Holosystolic: Throughout systole
    2. Holodiastolic: Throughout diastole
    3. Midsystolic: Midway between S1 and S3
    4. Mid-diastolic: Midway between S2 and S1
    5. Decrescendo: Starts loud at the beginning, then tapers off
    6. Crescendo: Starts soft at the beginning, then gets louder
E. Radiation: Murmur can be heard in another place, such as the neck, back, left axilla, or across precordium. Sound usually radiates in the direction of blood flow.
F. Location: Identify location on chest wall where murmur is heard the best. Identify site: Apex, pulmonary area, tricuspid, and aortic areas. Radiation murmur may also include axilla, left fourth ICS, or base of heart.
G. Configuration: The intensity of the murmur over time: Does it plateau, crescendo, decrescendo, or crescendo-decrescendo?
H. Systolic murmurs: Systolic murmurs are benign or pathologic.
    1. Early systolic murmurs
        a. Mitral regurgitation: Holosystolic, blowing may be loud. Located at fifth ICS and radiates to left axilla/back. Heard best in left lateral position and sudden squatting; intensity decreases with the Valsalva maneuver and standing.
        b. Tricuspid regurgitation: Holosystolic, heard left lower sternal border or apex when right ventricle is enlarged. Intensity increases with inspiration and decreases with expiration. Straight leg raises may increase intensity. May also see HJR.
        c. Physiologic: Early to midsystolic, low-pitch normal S1 to S2, located at left lower sternal edge at third to fourth ICS. Heard best with bell and supine and disappears when sitting up or holding breath. Commonly seen in pregnancy and infection.
    2. Midsystolic to late systolic murmurs
        a. Aortic stenosis: Loud, hard crescendo-decrescendo at second right ICS and radiates to neck. Heard best leaning forward, increases with leg raise and lying flat. Decreases with Valsalva and handgrip standing.

b. Pulmonic stenosis: Prolonged, loud S2 or crescendo-decrescendo, usually greater than 3/6 at second ICS and radiates to neck; increases with inspiration.

c. Hypertrophic cardiomyopathy (aortic outflow obstruction): Peaks at midsystole; loud, harsh tone at left, lower sternal border that may radiate to neck. Increases with Valsalva maneuver and standing, decreases with sudden squatting. Note carotid upstroke brisk.

3. Late systolic murmurs
   a. MVP: Midsystolic click heard before late systolic murmur, heard best at fifth left ICS. Heard best with diaphragm; sitting or squatting may increase intensity.
   b. Tricuspid valve prolapse: Heard over the left lower sternal border, delayed onset of murmur with inspiration secondary to an increase in the right ventricular volume.

I. Diastolic murmurs: Murmurs are always pathologic.
   1. Early diastolic murmur
      a. Aortic regurgitation: High-pitch faint, decrescendo may start with S2, at third left ICS and radiates down sternal edge. Heard best leaning forward, holding breath. Increases with sudden squatting or handgrip. May hear displaced point maximal intensity, S3, bounding pulse.
      b. Pulmonary regurgitation: Valvular, dilation of valve annulus, congenital defect (tetralogy of Fallot VSD), pulmonic stenosis. Best heard over left second/third ICS. May sound high pitched with "blowing" sound in patients with HTN. May be pansystolic, having decrescendo configuration.
   2. Mid-diastolic murmur
      a. Mitral stenosis: Rumbling extends beyond mid-diastole at fifth ICS, heard best using the bell of the stethoscope. Increases with left lateral position. May hear snap after S2.
      b. Tricuspid stenosis: Increased flow across the tricuspid valve, heard best at the left sternal border. Identified by its increase in intensity of the murmur with inspiration (Carvallo's sign). Commonly seen with mitral stenosis.

Plan

A. General interventions
   1. Major therapeutic goals are to preserve quality of life, increase life expectancy and exercise capacity, and reduce risk of complications.
   2. Activity restriction is not necessary in patients with asymptomatic valvular disease.

B. Patient teaching: Reassure the patient regarding specific diagnosis. Counsel the patient regarding his or her specific condition. Teach the patient signs and symptoms to report to the health provider, including chest pain, SOB, difficulty breathing, and so forth.

C. Medical and surgical management: Patients who need progressive increases in medications to control symptoms may be candidates for valve replacement surgery.

D. Pharmaceutical therapy
   1. The 2007 AHA Guidelines do not recommend endocarditis antimicrobial prophylaxis treatment for common valvular lesions that include bicuspid aortic valve, acquired aortic or mitral valve disease (including MVP with regurgitation), and hypertrophic cardiomyopathy with latent or resting obstruction.

E. Endocarditis prophylaxis treatment: Cardiac conditions
   1. Prophylactic treatment is recommended for high-risk cardiac condition abnormalities. Specific cardiac conditions include:
      a. Prosthetic cardiac valve or prosthetic material used for cardiac valve repair
      b. Previous infective endocarditis
      c. Certain congenital heart diseases, such as cyanotic congenital heart disease that has not been repaired; a congenital heart disease that has been repaired with an artificial material or device for 6 months after repair; and repaired congenital heart defects with continued problems such as leaks or insufficient flow at the prosthetic device or adjacent to the repair.
      d. Postcardiac transplant valvulopathy
   2. Procedures for high-risk patients previously mentioned who require prophylaxis treatment
      a. All dental procedures with manipulation of gingival tissue or periapical region of teeth or perforation of oral mucosa
      b. Incision or biopsy of respiratory mucosa or any invasive procedure of the respiratory tract system
      c. Procedures that include infected skin or musculoskeletal tissue
      d. Preventative treatment with antibiotics is not recommended for procedures that include the reproductive tract, urinary tract, or GI tract.
   3. Antibiotic prophylactic regimens include single dose 30 to 60 minutes prior to procedure:
      a. Amoxicillin 2 g by mouth, IM, or IV for adults
      b. Ampicillin 2 g IM or IV or 50 mg/kg IM or IV

c. Allergy to PCN: Cephalexin 2 g by mouth for adults
d. Azithromycin or clarithromycin 500 g for adults
e. Allergic to these: Consider cefazolin or ceftriaxone 1 g IM or IV or clindamycin 600 mg IM or IV for adults
4. Other pharmaceutical treatments depend on the specific valvular abnormality.
a. Mitral stenosis: The mitral valve has a narrowing that does not allow adequate blood to the left ventricle during diastole, usually due to rheumatic heart disease. Mitral heart disease is the most commonly seen valve effect with rheumatic heart disease.
b. Diuretics such as furosemide (Lasix) or hydrochlorothiazide (HydroDiuril) are used to control edema.
c. Digoxin (Lanoxin) or beta blockers are used to control AF and irregular heart rate.
d. Warfarin (Coumadin) and the antiplatelet agent aspirin (Bayer) are used to prevent clotting.
e. MVP: The echocardiogram is the recommended test for diagnosis of MVP. Usually no medications are recommended except when symptomatic and required.
i. Beta blockers (such as Atenolol) may be used for palpitations.
ii. Diuretics should be avoided in patients who are volume reserved.
iii. Oral contraceptives should be avoided in women who exhibit neurologic symptoms.
f. Mitral regurgitation: Diuretics, digitalis, and afterload-reducing agents for CHF
i. Aortic stenosis
ii. Diuretics are used for CHF.
iii. Avoid vasodilators; they may result in profound, irreversible hypotension.
iv. Echocardiograms should be performed every 6 to 12 months to follow progression of narrowing of the left ventricle across the aortic valve.
g. Aortic regurgitation: Afterload-reducing agents, digitalis, and diuretics are recommended.

Follow-Up

A. Most patients with valvular disease should be evaluated at least once a year.
B. Patients on oral anticoagulation drugs need monthly follow-up or as needed PT/INRs.

Consultation/Referral

A. Consult a physician if the patient is diagnosed with a new murmur or exercise-induced symptoms during a sports physical.
B. Refer patients with newly diagnosed murmurs to a cardiologist after obtaining echocardiogram results.
C. Drug therapy should be initiated according to diagnosis and symptoms.
D. Onset of AF with rapid ventricular response is an indication for immediate hospitalization.
E. Refer patients with systemic embolization to a physician for emergent anticoagulation therapy and chronic oral anticoagulant therapy. Discuss the possibility of valve replacement with a cardiologist.
F. If a new murmur is diagnosed in a pregnant patient with a history of cardiac disease, refer her to a physician immediately.

Individual Considerations

A. Pregnancy: The development of a new, "high-flow" murmur in a healthy woman is not uncommon due to physiologic changes occurring during pregnancy.
B. Geriatrics
1. Aortic stenosis, which is a systolic murmur, occurs in about 2% of people older than the age of 65. It occurs more often in men than in women.
2. Symptoms of aortic stenosis in the elderly may include:
a. Chest discomfort: The chest pain may get worse with activity and reach into the arm, neck, or jaw. The chest may also feel tight or squeezed.
b. Cough, possibly bloody
c. Breathing problems when exercising
d. Becoming easily tired
e. Feeling the heart beat (palpitations)
f. Fainting, weakness, or dizziness with activity
3. Sometimes a systolic murmur heard best in the aortic area may indicate aortic sclerosis due to aging of the aortic valve rather than true aortic stenosis.

Palpitations

Definition

A. Palpitations are a feeling or an unpleasant awareness of the heartbeat in the chest. It may be described as feeling a sensation of the heart "flip-flopping" or feeling a "rapid flutter" of the heart.

Incidence

A. The incidence of palpitations may range from 1% to 8% of patients in a general practice setting.

Pathogenesis

Palpitations may be caused by the following

A. Increase in stroke volume or contractility
B. Sudden change in heart rate or rhythm
C. Unusual cardiac movement within thorax
D. Hyperkinetic states, which cause constant pounding
E. Valvular heart disease that produces large stroke volumes
F. Catecholamine release during anxiety or panic attacks

Predisposing Factors

A. Cardiac defects
B. Severe anemia
C. Hyperthyroidism
D. Pregnancy
E. Fever
F. Anxiety
G. Stimulants, such as caffeine and certain drugs
H. Emotions, such as fear
I. Exertion
J. Diabetes mellitus and insulin reaction

Common Complaints

A. Palpitations are often described as a turning over or flopping sensation in the chest, but symptoms vary enormously.
B. Most patients are free of palpitations at the time of the exam.

Other Signs and Symptoms

A. Fluttering in the chest
B. SOB
C. Pounding in the chest and neck
D. Diaphoresis
E. Lightheadedness
F. Anxiety or fear

Subjective Data

A. Ask the patient when symptoms first presented, including age, and how they have changed.
B. Have the patient describe the characteristics of the palpitations, such as rapid, regular, irregular, or slow.
C. Ask the patient what precipitates the palpitations. Does anything terminate them, or do they go away on their own?
D. Inquire whether symptoms occur or change with position (standing, bending over, lying down, left lateral decubitus position) and/or exercise.
E. Ask the patient about other symptoms associated with the palpitations such as dizziness or syncope.
F. Ask how often the episodes occur and how long each lasts.
G. Discuss any previous treatments for this condition and the results.
H. Ask the patient about risk factors for CHD and prior cardiac history.
I. Obtain a complete list of medications the patient is currently taking, including OTC and herbal products.
   1. Specifically question the patient's use of OTC decongestants and diet pills.
   2. Are there any new medications or changes in routine medications?

Physical Examination

A. Check pulse (count the pulse for one full minute), respirations, and BP.
B. Inspect
   1. Inspect overall appearance.
   2. Inspect the skin for diaphoresis and pallor.
   3. Inspect the neck for thyromegaly or jugular vein distension.
   4. Inspect the legs for edema.
C. Palpate
   1. Palpate the skin for temperature and dryness.
   2. Palpate the lower extremities for edema and calf tenderness.
   3. Palpate the neck for thyroid enlargement.
D. Auscultate
   1. Auscultate the heart for abnormal rhythms. Auscultate heart sitting, standing, and left lateral decubitus position. Ask patient to walk quickly down the hallway and back and then auscultate heart in all positions again.
   2. Auscultate the lungs.
   3. Auscultate the neck and carotid arteries for bruits.
E. Mental status: Does the patient appear lightheaded, anxious, or fearful?

Diagnostic Tests

A. Diagnostic testing is highly recommended for patients with an arrhythmia, at risk for an arrhythmia, and patients who are anxious and want to explore causes for their symptoms. The following testing is recommended.
   1. Hgb to rule out anemia, if suggestive on exam
   2. Thyroid-stimulating hormone (TSH) to rule out hyperthyroidism, if suggestive on exam
   3. EKG during episode, if possible
   4. Ambulatory monitoring if symptoms continue, either 24-hour Holter monitor or patient-activated transtelephonic monitoring
   5. Treadmill test if palpitations are provoked by exercise

Differential Diagnoses

A. Palpitations are secondary to the underlying problem, such as anxiety, medications, or cardiac or pulmonary origin.

Plan

A. General interventions: Provide reassurance if the palpitations result from a neurotic concern.
B. Patient teaching
  1. Caution the patient to avoid any factors that trigger episodes. Factors may include stress, exercise, foods, and medications.
  2. Teach the patient the vagal maneuver, which is effective in halting palpitations.
C. Medical and surgical management
  1. Correct any underlying problem (e.g., cardiac or pulmonary).
  2. Treat medical conditions accordingly.
  3. Management of arrhythmias should be monitored by a cardiologist.
D. Pharmaceutical therapy: Discontinue all nonessential medications that could cause palpitations.

Follow-Up

A. Depending on the etiology of palpitations and the existence of comorbid conditions, the prognosis in patients with no underlying cardiac disease is generally favorable.

Consultation/Referral

A. Consult a physician if the patient has a history of palpitations leading to syncope or near syncope, angina-like chest pain, or dyspnea. These patients are candidates for referral to a cardiologist and/or inpatient evaluation. Refer any patient with an arrhythmia to a cardiologist.
B. Hemodynamically compromised patients need prompt hospital admission.

Individual Considerations

A. Geriatric
  1. Elderly patients are at increased risk for adverse effects from antiarrhythmic medications.
  2. If drug treatment is necessary, lower doses should be used. Use the rule of thumb of "start low and go slow."

Peripheral Arterial Disease—*Laura A. Petty*

Definition

A. PAD is a circulatory disorder generally characterized by the build-up of plaque on the interior surface of arteries. These plaques harden and narrow the diameter of the arteries, which reduces the volume of blood circulating to internal organs and extremities. The arteries affected by PAD include all arteries in the body, with the exception of the cerebral and coronary arteries. The decreased circulation seen in PAD can also be caused by nonatherosclerotic conditions. Some of these conditions are arteritis, trauma, radiation damage, and fibromuscular dysplasia. Symptoms of PAD can occur in upper or lower extremities.
B. Classification of PAD
  1. Asymptomatic PAD
    a. No symptoms but the presence of risk factors or a new diagnosis of a common coexisting disease (CAD or cerebrovascular disease) should prompt further evaluation.
  2. Intermittent claudication (IC)
    a. Discomfort with physical exertion that remits a few minutes after activity ceases.
  3. Chronic limb ischemia
    a. Pain at rest and/or skin ulceration
  4. Acute limb ischemia
    a. Pain at rest with a pulseless extremity
C. Other conditions contained within PAD
  1. Buerger's disease (thromboangiitis obliterans): A disease manifested by inflammation, peripheral edema, and micro thrombi leading to gangrene of the hands and feet. Usually caused by tobacco abuse, and patients are thought to have a genetic predisposition to develop this condition.
  2. Raynaud's syndrome: A vasospastic disorder manifested by a response in the extremities to cold temperatures or stress where pallor, cyanosis, numbness, and/or pain are experienced
  3. Leriche syndrome: The triad of claudication, absent or diminished femoral pulses, and erectile dysfunction.

Incidence

A. In 2012, the Vascular Disease Foundation estimated that 8 to 12 million adults in the United States had PAD. This correlates to between 12% and 20% of Americans older than 65 years of age.
B. PAD is more common in men than in women.
C. PAD is more common in patients of African and Hispanic descent.

Pathogenesis

A. PAD is most commonly precipitated by atherosclerosis. An atherosclerotic plaque develops in response to turbulent blood flow on the endothelial cells of the vessel wall. The plaque contains inflammatory cells and a thrombogenic lipid core that is covered by a fibrous cap. When the fibrous cap is disturbed, the lipid core can precipitate to development of a thrombus and lead to occlusion of the vessel.

Predisposing Factors

A. Smoking
B. Diabetes
C. Dyslipidemia
D. HTN

E. Obesity
F. Age, increased occurrence after age 60

Common Complaints

A. Pain with activity is commonly characterized as cramping and/or aching
   1. Upper extremity pain in the forearm, hand, and digits.
   2. Lower extremity pain in the foot, calf, hip, thigh, and/or buttocks
      a. Foot pain is most common in tibial or peroneal artery stenosis.
      b. Calf pain is most common with superficial femoral or popliteal artery stenosis.
      c. Thigh pain is most common in aortoiliac and common femoral artery stenosis.
      d. Hip and buttock pain are most common with aortoiliac arterial stenosis.

B. Pain at rest
C. Calf weakness or fatigue
D. Numbness or tingling
E. Dizziness with upper extremity exertion
F. Syncope with upper extremity exertion
G. Extremity ulceration

Other Signs and Symptoms

A. Decreased peripheral pulses
B. Blanching of the affected limb with elevation
C. Ulcerations or infection on distal aspects of extremities
D. Erectile dysfunction

Potential Complications

A. Nonhealing lower extremity ulcerations
B. Infection
C. Amputation
D. Common coexisting diseases
   1. CAD; also known as CHD
   2. Cerebrovascular disease

Subjective Data

A. Ask patient what activity brought about or preceded the episode or whether it occurs at rest. If ambulation was the precipitating factor, how far was the patient able to walk?
B. Have patient describe duration of pain and what time of day symptoms began.
C. Ask patient what alleviates his or her pain.
D. Ask patient whether any previous episodes have occurred.
E. Ask patient to list all medications, including OTC and herbal products currently being taken or recently stopped.
F. Ask patient to quantify his or her smoking history.
G. Ask patient if he or she has had a past medical history of an MI or CVA.
H. If patient is male, ask if he has any history of impotence or erectile dysfunction.

Physical Examination

A. **Patients presenting with acute limb ischemia should be quickly assessed for the need to call emergency services/911 for immediate transport to the hospital.**
   1. **Symptoms of acute limb ischemia as evidenced by the six Ps—pain, pallor, paresthesia, paralysis, pulseness, and poikilothermia (the inability to maintain a constant core temperature).**

B. Vital signs
   1. Check BP in both upper extremities.
      a. A difference in SBP of 10 mmHg or greater in upper extremities is associated with upper extremity PAD and cerebrovascular disease.
      b. A difference in SBP of 15 mmHg or greater in upper extremities is associated with lower extremity PAD.
   2. Check BP in both lower extremities.
   3. Document resting heart rate, respirations, height, and weight.

C. Inspect
   1. Perform a fundoscopic exam: Check for retinal vascular changes.
   2. Inspect abdomen for a pulsating abdominal mass.
   3. Inspect extremities. Note edema, pallor, and cyanosis. Note color of extremities in dependent and elevated positions.
   4. Inspect distal skin, hair, and nails. Note any temperature discrepancies or trophic changes that are indicative of ischemia.
   5. Assess lower extremities for any ulcerations or diffuse erythema.
   6. Assess for Homans' sign (i.e., calf pain with forced dorsiflexion).
   7. Assess whether pain occurs when affected limb is elevated.

D. Palpate
   1. Palpate pulses, noting symmetry.
      a. Bilateral upper extremities (brachial and radial)
      b. Abdominal (aorta)
      c. Bilateral groin (femoral)
      d. Bilateral lower extremity pulses (popliteal, dorsalis pedis, and posterior tibialis)
   2. Palpate capillary refill.
   3. Perform an Allen test: Occlude the radial and ulnar arteries with the fist closed. Open the hand and then release one of the occluded arteries. Repeat but release the other artery. Each time, prompt capillary refill should occur.
   4. Palpate neck for carotid bruits.
   5. Palpate the abdominal aorta, noting any lateral pulsation, which is indicative of an aortic aneurysm.

E. Auscultate
   1. Auscultate heart: Assess rate, rhythm, heart sounds, murmur, and gallops.
   2. Auscultate carotids, abdomen, and bilateral groin for bruits.
   3. Auscultate lungs: Assess lung sounds, noting any sign of HF.

Diagnostic Tests

A. Doppler ABI
   1. Interpretation of ABI ratios
      a. 1.00 to 1.29 normal
      b. 0.91 to 0.99 borderline PAD
      c. 0.41 to 0.90 mild to moderate PAD
      d. 0.00 to 0.40 severe PAD
B. BMP (including BUN, creatinine, sodium, and potassium)
C. Lipid profile
D. CRP, homocysteine, D-dimer
E. EKG (12 lead)
F. Doppler ultrasound
G. Abdominal ultrasound
H. Treadmill testing
I. CTA
J. MRA
K. Arteriography, ordered and performed by surgeon

Differential Diagnosis

A. PAD
B. Venous stasis
C. Venous obstruction/claudication
D. Spinal stenosis
E. Nerve root compression
F. Arthritis of the hip
G. Peripheral neuropathy
H. Arteritis

Plan

A. General interventions
   1. The goal of therapy is to improve the patient's quality of life by reducing morbidity and prolonging survival.
B. Patient teaching. See the Section III Patient Teaching Guide for this chapter, "Peripheral Arterial Disease."
   1. Encourage smoking cessation, weight loss, and exercise, if applicable.
   2. Encourage strategies to better manage other chronic medical conditions that directly affect the progression of PAD, that is, diabetes, dyslipidemia, obesity, and HTN.
   3. Proper foot care
      a. Instruct patient to wear proper-fitting shoes that protect the feet.
      b. Inspect inside of shoes before donning.
      c. Encourage patient to inspect feet daily for signs of trauma or infection.
      d. Instruct patient to dry feet well, including between toes, after bathing.
C. Prevention
   1. Control other chronic medical conditions, that is, diabetes, dyslipidemia, HTN, and obesity.
D. Dietary management
   1. To manage dyslipidemia and HTN: Counsel patient on nutrition and low-fat, low-cholesterol, low-sodium diet.
   2. To manage diabetes: Counsel patient on diabetic diet and carbohydrate counting.
   3. To manage infection related to PAD: Counsel patient on high-calorie, high-protein diet. Consider the addition of vitamins and minerals to promote wound healing, specifically zinc, and vitamins C and A.
   4. Give diet handouts and/or refer to a registered dietitian.
E. Pharmaceutical therapy
   1. Goal of therapy: Prevention of thromboembolism
      a. Trental (pentoxifylline)
         i. 400 mg tablet
            1) Dosage indications based on CrCl
               a) CrCl less than 10 mL/min: 400 mg, taken once a day
               b) CrCl = 10 to 50 mL/min: 400 mg, taken twice daily
               c) CrCl greater than 50 mg/min: 400 mg, taken three times a day
      b. Pletal (cilostazol)
         i. 50 and 100 mg tablets
            1) **Warning: Metabolites of Pletal are inhibitors of phosphodiesterase III and are contraindicated in patients with CHF of any severity.**
            2) Dosage indications
               a) 50 mg, taken twice daily if taken in coadministration with ketoconazole, itraconazole, erythromycin, and diltiazem
               b) 100 mg, taken twice daily at least half an hour before or 2 hours after breakfast and dinner
      c. Aspirin (acetylsalicylic acid, ecotrin)
         i. 81 mg, 325 mg, tablets, taken once daily
      d. Plavix (clopidogrel bisulfate)
         i. 75 mg, taken once daily
   2. Risk-factor reduction
      a. Manage dyslipidemia
         i. LDL cholesterol goal: Less than 100 mg/dL and less than 70 mg/dL for patients at high risk for CAD

b. Manage HTN
  i. BP goal in patients without diabetes: Less than 140/90 mmHg
  ii. BP goal in patients with diabetes or CKD: Less than 130/80 mmHg
c. Manage diabetes
  i. Hemoglobin A1C goal: Less than 7.0%

F. Surgical therapies: Considered in patients with pain at rest, tissue loss, or significant physical limitations that prevent exercise
  1. Bypass
  2. Stenting
  3. Angioplasty/percutaneous transluminal angioplasty

G. Nonsurgical therapies
  1. Smoking cessation program
  2. Daily walking program
    a. Instruct patient to walk to the point of pain, then stop and resume walking when pain remits.
    b. May need to obtain medical clearance for the patient to exercise.

Follow-Up

A. PAD manifesting persistent symptoms should always be followed by a cardiologist.
B. Follow-up is determined by patient's needs, frequency and intensity of symptoms, and the presence of other medical conditions.

Consultation/Referral

A. **If you suspect acute limb ischemia, refer patient for immediate hospitalization in order to obtain diagnostic testing to determine the presence of a thrombus and restore circulation to the affected extremity.**
B. If chronic limb ischemia has led to ulceration and/or superimposed infection, hospitalization is indicated to initiate a wound care consultation and diagnostic testing to determine the degree of arterial occlusion.
C. Referral to a cardiologist in the presence of persistent PAD symptoms
D. Referral to a vascular surgeon for further evaluation of angioplasty, stenting, or bypass surgery
E. Referral to a podiatrist to trim toenails and assess patient for proper-fitting shoes
F. Referral to pain management if pain is resistant to treatment
G. Referral to a registered dietitian as indicated by the patient's understanding of dietary modification necessary to improve status of risk factors

Individual Considerations

A. Nonambulatory patients
  1. Using rocking chairs is a possible substitute for persons unable to participate in a walking program.
B. Geriatrics
  1. Be alert to signs and symptoms of depression related to immobility and pain.

Superficial Thrombophlebitis—*Laura A. Petty*

Definition

A. Superficial thrombophlebitis is inflammation of a vessel wall accompanied by blood stasis in varicose veins, which may also have clot formation in a vein close to the surface.
  1. Most superficial thrombophlebitis occurs in the lower extremity but may also occur in the breast and in the penis (Mondor disease).
  2. A superficial thrombophlebitis may also occur in the upper extremities and in the neck after invasive intravenous catheters used in medical procedures.
  3. Generally superficial thrombophlebitis is self-limiting but may persist for a period of time (3–4 weeks or longer) before resolution.
B. Superficial phlebitis with an infection is referred to as a septic thrombophlebitis.

Incidence

A. With pregnancy, there is approximately a four- to fivefold increase of phlebitis over a nonpregnant female. Eighty percent of thromboembolic events in pregnancy are venous (0.5–2.0 per 1,000). The incidence of PE in pregnancy accounts for 1.1 deaths per 100,000 deliveries.
B. The prevalence of superficial thrombophlebitis ranges from 4% to 8% of patients with an indwelling catheter.
C. Superficial phlebitis after a vein radiofrequency or laser ablation is common.

Pathogenesis

A. Superficial thrombosis is caused by infection, abuse of IV drugs, chemical irritation from overuse of IV route for diagnostic tests and drugs, and/or trauma. Several episodes can signal an underlying problem, such as carcinoma of the pancreas.
B. A common cause of varicose veins is blood-flow stasis, basically due to valvular incompetence and/or dilation of the vessel lumen.
C. Thrombi in the upper extremities commonly have iatrogenic causes, such as IV catheters.
D. Thrombophlebitis during pregnancy through the first 6 weeks postpartum is linked to a reduced fibrinolytic state.

Predisposing Factors

A. **Previous thrombophlebitis is the highest risk factor for recurrence.**
B. Hypercoagulability such as pregnancy (50% of events) through 6 weeks postpartum (50% of events)
C. Hemoglobinopathies
  1. Factor V Leiden mutation
  2. Protein C deficiency

3. Protein S deficiency
4. Prothrombin gene mutation
5. Antithrombin III deficiency
6. Factor XII deficiency

D. Estrogen therapy
1. Oral contraceptives
2. High-dose HRT

E. Malignancy (especially in the tail of the pancreas)
F. Lupus, positive anticardiolipin antibody
G. Sepsis
H. Surgery
I. Long bone trauma
J. Recent IV catheter access
K. Prolonged immobilization
L. Obesity
M. Varicose veins
N. Age older than 60
O. Stroke
P. MI
Q. Family history of DVT
R. Smoking
S. HTN
T. Infection

Common Complaints

A. Warm, tender, inflamed vessel with palpable cord
B. Redness along the course of the superficial vein
C. Tenderness or pain localized to the affected vein

Other Signs and Symptoms

A. Fever/no fever
B. Localized edema

Potential Complications

A. Superficial thrombophlebitis extending into the deep venous system
B. DVT
C. Conversion to suppurative thrombophlebitis
1. Metastatic abscess formation
2. Septicemia
3. Septic emboli

Subjective Data

A. Query the patient regarding onset, duration, and intensity of symptoms.
B. Ask the patient about fever or other related symptoms.
C. Obtain a thorough medical history and account of recent physical activity.
D. Ask the patient about any recent experience of any type of injury.
E. Inquire whether the patient has ever had similar symptoms or history of previous thrombophlebitis. If so, discuss previous treatment and therapy used and the results.
F. Review current medications: Prescription, OTC, and herbal products.
1. **Ask specifically about oral contraceptives and hormone therapy.**

G. Review the patient's occupation for sedentary lifestyle.
H. Review any recent plane travel.
I. Review history for recent invasive procedures.

Physical Examination

A. Check temperature (if indicated with inflammation), pulse, respirations, and BP
B. Inspect
1. Assess overall appearance. Evaluate for the presence of respiratory distress.
2. Inspect extremities, noting erythema and edema.
3. Assess for increased warmth over the affected vein.

C. Auscultate
1. Auscultate heart, noting rate, rhythm, heart sounds, murmurs, and gallops.
2. Auscultate lungs for lung sounds in all fields.

D. Palpate
1. Palpate extremities; check all pulses, including femoral, posttibial, pedal, and radial.
2. Palpate extremities for tenderness and palpable cord.
3. Palpate lymph nodes distal and proximal to the site.
4. Test for Homans' sign in lower extremities bilaterally if DVT is suspected.

Diagnostic Tests

A. **Duplex ultrasound identifies the presence, location, and extent of venous thrombosis.**
B. Doppler ultrasound
C. Laboratory tests are ordered dependent on the clinical situation.
1. CBC with differential
2. Screening for hypercoagulability should not be considered for one episode of superficial thrombophlebitis.
3. Screening for hypercoagulability should be considered for recurrent superficial thrombophlebitis.
4. Blood cultures

Differential Diagnoses

A. Thrombophlebitis
B. Varicose veins
C. Cellulitis
D. Strained muscle
E. Insect bites
F. Erythema nodosum
G. Cutaneous polyarteritis nodosa
H. Kaposi's sarcoma
I. Hyperalgesic pseudothrombophlebitis

Plan

A. General interventions
  1. Advise all patients to stop smoking.
  2. Tell the patient to avoid prolonged sitting or standing and not to cross or massage legs. See the Section III Patient Teaching Guides for this chapter, "Superficial Thrombophlebitis" and "Varicose Veins."
  3. Advise the patient to avoid constrictive clothing such as knee-high hosiery.
  4. Prescribe supportive hose/compression stockings.
  5. Have the patient apply heat and elevate extremity for varicose veins or superficial thrombophlebitis.
  6. Prescribe bed rest for superficial thrombophlebitis.
  7. DVT: Hospitalization is required.
  8. Tell patients with thrombophlebitis to discontinue oral contraceptives and hormone replacement.
  9. Alternative forms of birth control recommended by the American College of Obstetricians and Gynecologists (ACOG) include
     a. Intrauterine device (IUD), including IUDs that contain progestin
     b. Progestin-only oral contraceptives
     c. Progestin-only implants
     d. Barrier methods
     e. Surgical procedures: Vasectomy and tubal ligation

B. Patient teaching: See the Section III Patient Teaching Guide for this chapter, "Superficial Thrombophlebitis."

C. Pharmaceutical therapy for superficial thrombophlebitis
  1. NSAIDs are used for treatment of pain. No NSAID has been identified as superior for treatment.
  2. The use of anticoagulation therapy for the treatment of lower extremity superficial thrombophlebitis is controversial. Unfractionated heparin and LMWH are both used for treatment to reduce risk of DVT and/or recurrent phlebitis.
  3. The American College of Chest Physicians recommends anticoagulation for patients with lower extremity superficial thrombophlebitis at increased risk of thromboembolism. This is defined as the affected venous segment greater than or equal to 5 cm in proximity (< 5 cm) to deep venous system and positive medical risk factors. The American College of Chest Physicians' full evidence-based clinical practice guidelines on antithrombotic therapy are available at journal.publications.chestnet.org/pdfaccess.ashx?ResourceID=3130711&PDFSource=13.
  4. Antibiotics, if infection is suspected

D. Surgery
  1. Biopsy
  2. Vein ablation, only if symptoms are significant and persistent
  3. Vein ligation, only if symptoms are significant and persistent

Follow-Up

A. Schedule an appointment for patients with superficial thrombophlebitis to return in 7 to 10 days, or earlier as needed. Repeat physical examination as needed to evaluate resolution or progression of the thrombophlebitis.

B. Periodic follow-up is needed to monitor patients on anticoagulation therapy.

C. After acute problem is resolved, consider laboratory evaluation for hypercoagulation syndrome (protein C, protein S, and antithrombin III).

D. Monitor bone loss with DEXA scan with prolonged use of heparin.

E. Screening all women for thrombophilias before starting oral contraceptives is not recommended by the ACOG.

F. Women with a history of thrombosis who have not had a complete evaluation should be tested for both antiphospholipid antibodies and inherited thrombophilias.

Consultation/Referral

A. If septic thrombophlebitis or DVT is diagnosed, refer the patient to a physician.

B. Hospitalization is required to initiate heparin therapy.

C. Comanage pregnancy with an obstetrician.

Individual Considerations

A. Pregnancy
  1. **Routine anticoagulation therapy for all pregnant women is not recommended. Therapeutic anticoagulation is recommended for women with acute thromboembolism during the current pregnancy or those at high risk of thrombosis, such as women with mechanical heart valves.**
  2. Warfarin and NSAIDs are contraindicated.
  3. Heparin is the preferred anticoagulant in pregnancy. Neither unfractionated heparin nor LMWH crosses the placenta.
  4. Warfarin, LMWH, and unfractionated heparin do not accumulate in breast milk and do not induce an anticoagulant effect in the infant and therefore are considered compatible with breastfeeding.

B. Geriatrics
   1. Prognosis is poor for patients with septic thrombophlebitis.
   2. Using a rocking chair is a possible substitute for persons unable to participate in a walking program.
   3. Be alert to signs and symptoms of depression related to immobility and pain.

Syncope

Definition

A. Syncope is a brief, sudden loss of consciousness and muscle tone secondary to cerebral ischemia, or inadequate oxygen or glucose delivery to brain tissue. Recovery is spontaneous.

Incidence

A. Syncope is a common problem in all age groups. Between 12% and 48% of healthy young adults have lost consciousness (one third following trauma), but most do not seek medical attention. Adults older than age 75 in long-term care facilities have a 6% annual incidence of syncope, and 23% have had previous episodes. Syncopal episodes account for approximately 1% to 6% of hospital admissions and 3% of emergency room visits.

Pathogenesis

The most common cause of syncope is inadequate cerebral perfusion caused by one of the following:

A. Vasomotor instability associated with a decrease in systemic vascular resistance and/or venous return. The following may cause syncope:
   1. Vasovagal episodes
   2. Situational syncope, from coughing, micturition, and defecation
   3. Medications
      a. Vasodilators
      b. Antiarrhythmics
      c. Diuretics
      d. Neurologic agents
      e. Glucose-regulating drugs
      f. Impotence therapy

B. Decrease in cardiac output caused by blood-flow obstruction within the heart or pulmonary circulation or by arrhythmias. This may be caused by the following:
   1. Aortic, pulmonic, and mitral stenosis
   2. Idiopathic hypertrophic subaortic stenosis (IHSS) or hypertrophic obstructive cardiomyopathy (HOCM)
   3. Pump failure
   4. Subclavian steal syndrome
   5. Seizures

C. Focal or generalized decrease in cerebral perfusion leading to transient ischemia due to cerebrovascular disease.
   1. Carotid arterial disease

D. Metabolic abnormalities
   1. Hypoglycemia
   2. Hypocarbia and hypoxia usually do not result in syncope unless they are profound, although consciousness may be altered.

E. Psychiatric illnesses associated with syncope include:
   1. Generalized anxiety
   2. Panic attacks
   3. Major depressive disorders

F. Unexplained cause

Predisposing Factors

A. Advanced age, caused by altered regulation of cerebral blood flow and/or systemic arterial pressure due to aging process and increased medication use
B. Other factors, depending on etiology
C. Medication use (previously noted)

Common Complaints

A. Dizziness
B. Lightheadedness
C. Fainting with no memory of events

Other Signs and Symptoms

A. Neuroautonomic regulations
   1. Event triggered by changing position, turning head, wearing tight collars
   2. Nausea, warmth, diaphoresis, weakness 1 hour after eating
B. Cardiac causes: Exercise-induced palpitations, chest pain, SOB with no warning prior to episode
C. Neurologic causes
   1. Vertigo
   2. Diplopia
   3. Facial paresthesias
   4. Ataxia
   5. Auditory, visual, or vestibular disturbances
D. Metabolic or endocrine causes
   1. Restlessness
   2. Anxiety
   3. Confusion
   4. No recent food intake, low glucose level
E. Psychiatric: Graceful fainting in presence of an audience

Subjective Data

A. Inquire if the patient ever experienced similar symptoms or episodes before. If so, when and at what age did it begin?
B. Ask the patient or witness of the episode to give a detailed description of loss of consciousness. Was loss of consciousness complete, and if so for how long? What was the posture of the patient

before, during, and after the event? Did it occur abruptly, or were there symptoms leading up to the event?

C. Question the patient regarding events leading up to the episode, noting prodromal symptoms such as headache, aura, nausea/vomiting, lightheadedness, diaphoresis, feeling, or warmth.

D. Obtain a detailed account of symptoms during and after the episode, noting mental status. Did the patient recover on his or her own, or did patient require assistance? Were there any associated symptoms that occurred during the event? SOB, chest pain, loss of bowel, or bladder control?

E. If syncope has occurred in the past, are there any events that precipitate an episode? Exertion, exercise, coughing, standing quickly?

F. Obtain a detailed medication history, addressing prescribed and OTC drugs, alcohol, and illicit preparations.

G. Review the patient's past medical history.

Physical Examination

A. Check temperature, if indicated, pulse, respirations, and BP.
   1. Measure BP and pulse in both arms and legs. Note BP differences between the arms.
   2. Measure BP several times during a 2-minute period with the patient standing.
   3. Check for orthostatic hypotension, which is defined as a drop of 20 mmHg or more in SBP on standing.
      a. First, measure BP after the patient lies supine for 5 to 10 minutes.
      b. Then have the patient stand, and measure BP several times during a 2-minute period.

B. Inspect the range of motion in the neck.

C. Palpate the abdomen, noting pulsatile expansion.

D. Auscultate
   1. Auscultate the heart with position changes. Note murmurs or extra heart sounds to rule out structural disease. Identify dysrhythmias such as bradycardia, supraventricular tachycardia, tachycardia, AV blocks, AF, bundle branch blocks, and sinus pauses or arrests.
   2. Auscultate the carotid arteries.
   3. Auscultate the abdomen for bruits.

E. Neurologic exam: Perform a complete exam, if indicated, including assessing 2nd to 12th cranial nerves, Babinski's reflex, and gait.

F. Mental status: Assess mental health, if indicated.

Diagnostic Tests

The following tests are performed depending on history and physical exam results. The 2009 European Society of Cardiology (ESC) guidelines recommend the following testing:

A. Carotid sinus massage in patients older than 40 years of age. Avoid in patients with history of TIA or stroke in the past 3 months and in patients with carotid bruits. Recommend physician or cardiology specialist assistance when performing carotid massage. Use caution when performing carotid sinus massage. Please consider contraindications, complications, and guidelines for performing procedure.

B. Echocardiogram for patients with a history of heart disease, structural heart disease, or syncope secondary to cardiovascular cause (known heart disease), family history of unexplained sudden death in the family, syncope with exertion or supine, abnormal ECG, sudden onset of palpitation prior to syncope, or arrhythmia on ECG.

C. ECG for patients with suspected arrhythmia or cardiac disease. Identify acute and old EKG changes to rule out pathologic Q wave, ST segment elevation, and LV hypertrophy.

D. Orthostatic challenge test if syncope is related to position change or suspect reflex mechanism

E. Neurological/serum laboratory testing for other concerns of nonsyncopal loss of consciousness. Laboratory testing includes chemistry profile, TSH, and Free T4. Consider a glucose tolerance if diabetes is suspected. BNP may be useful to evaluate cardiac versus noncardiac cause for syncope.

F. Chest radiography, for essential baseline data. Wide mediastinum signals aortic dissection.

G. In-hospital monitoring is recommended for unstable, life-threatening patients.

H. Holter monitor for 24 to 48 hours

I. External event monitor

J. Exercise testing is recommended for patients with syncope that occurs during, or quickly after, cessation of exercise. Echocardiogram is recommended prior to this testing.

K. Cardiac catheterization

L. Lung scan

M. Treadmill test

N. Electrophysiologic studies are recommended for patients with unexplained syncope.

Differential Diagnoses

A. Irregular neuroautonomic regulations
   1. Neurocardiogenic causes
   2. Situational causes, such as coughing, defecation, diving, micturition, sneezing, swallowing, trumpet playing, vagal stimulation, weight lifting, postprandial state

3. Orthostatic causes
   a. Hyperadrenergic state
   b. Hypoadrenergic state, primary or secondary autonomic insufficiency
   c. Carotid sinus syncope
   d. Cardioinhibitory state
   e. Vasodepressor stimulation
   f. Mixed

B. Cardiac causes
   1. Mechanical causes, such as aortic dissection, aortic stenosis, atrial myxoma, cardiac tamponade, global myocardial ischemia, hypertrophic cardiomyopathy, mitral stenosis, MI, prosthetic valve dysfunction, PE, pulmonary HTN, pulmonary stenosis, and Takayasu's arteritis
   2. Electrical causes, such as AV block, long QT syndrome, pacemaker, sick sinus syndrome, supraventricular tachyarrhythmias, and ventricular tachyarrhythmias

C. Neurologic causes
   1. Neuralgias: Glossopharyngeal, trigeminal
   2. Normal pressure hydrocephalus
   3. Subclavian steal
   4. Vertebrobasilar artery disease: Compression, migraine, TIA

D. Metabolic or endocrine causes: Hypoadrenalism, hypoglycemia, hyponatremia, hypothyroidism, and hypoxia

E. Psychiatric causes: Anxiety, hysteria, major depression, panic disorder, somatization, and hyperventilation syndrome

Plan

A. General interventions: Management is directed at primary cause for the episode.

B. Patient teaching
   1. If the patient has orthostatic hypotension, suggest that he or she wear elastic stockings, change positions slowly, sleep with the head of the bed elevated, and exercise legs before standing.
   2. If syncope is induced by situations, warn the patient to avoid or alter his or her approach to such precipitating events.
   3. If the patient has prodromal symptoms, such as nausea, lightheadedness, pallor, sweating, or palpitations, advise him or her to lie down when they occur.
   4. If the patient has hypersensitive carotid sinus reflex, recommend that he or she loosen his or her collar.
   5. Tell patients to avoid prolonged standing. If they can't avoid it, they should contract their calf muscles to increase venous blood flow.
   6. Some driving restrictions exist for patients at risk for recurrent syncope. Driving restrictions are enforced by the state law. Review restrictions with the patient and family as indicated by diagnosis.

C. Dietary management: If not contraindicated, instruct patients with orthostatic hypotension to use salt liberally.

D. Pharmaceutical therapy
   Therapy for neurocardiogenic syncope includes the following:
   1. Nonpharmacologic methods suggested:
      a. Avoid volume depletion.
      b. Maintain adequate sodium levels by increasing salt intake in the diet.
      c. Wear thigh-high elastic support hose with 30 to 40 mmHg pressure.
      d. Orthostatic training is also recommended two times a day.
   2. Drugs of choice: Beta blockers (Inderal 80–160 mg/d, metoprolol 50–100 mg/d)
   3. Fludrocortisone acetate (Florinef Acetate), a corticosteroid, may be used alone or with beta blockers. Initial dosage is 0.1 to 0.4 mg/d; this may be increased gradually to 1.0 to 2.0 mg/d.
   4. Other drugs include anticholinergic agents (Disopyramide 100–200 mg twice daily sustained release), and SSRIs (Zoloft 50 mg/d, Prozac 20 mg/d, Paxil 20 mg/d).

Follow-Up

A. Scheduling of return visits depends on the etiology and severity of syncope and on whether the patient has been placed on medications.

Consultation/Referral

A. Consult with or refer the patient to a physician when cardiac or neurologic involvement is suspected.

B. Consult with or refer the patient to a physician if medication therapy is required.

Individual Considerations

A. Adults
   1. In young adult athletes, be aware of symptoms of Marfan syndrome.
   2. In older adults, coronary atherosclerosis may present along with syncope.

B. Geriatrics
   1. The most common cause of syncope in the elderly is postural hypotension, which can be due to a combination of factors, both intrinsic and extrinsic.
   2. Intrinsic factors can include noncompliant arteries, reduced skeletal muscle pumping action of venous return due to physical inactivity, and aging of the sinoatrial node and conduction system due to progressive atherosclerosis and/or structural heart disease.

3. The most common extrinsic factor involves medications that lower BP and cause vasodilation of blood vessels.
4. In the elderly, syncope often has more than one cause. For example, the combination of taking several heart and BP drugs and standing for a long period of time may lead to syncope even though no single factor might cause syncope.

Bibliography

AHA 2009 Writing Group. (2009). 2009 Focused update: ACCF/AHA guidelines for the diagnosis and management of HF in adults. *Circulation, 119,* 1977–2016.

Alguire, P. C., & Mathes, B. M. (2013, June 13). *Diagnostic evaluation of chronic venous insufficiency. UpToDate.* Retrieved from http://www.uptodate.com/contents/diagnostic-evaluation-of-chronic-venous-insufficiency?source=search_result&search=Diagnostic+evaluation+of+chronic+venous&selectedTitle=1%7E143

Alguire, P. C., & Scovell, S. (2013, May 5). *Overview and management of lower extremity chronic venous disease. UpToDate.* Retrieved from http://www.uptodate.com/contents/overview-and-management-of-lower-extremity-chronic-venous-disease?source=search_result&search=overview+and+management+of+lower+extremity+chronic&selectedTitle=1%7E150

Allison, M. A., Ho, E., Denenberg, J. O., Lander, R. D., Newman, A. B., Fabsitz, R. R., & Criqui, M. H. (2007). Ethnic-specific prevalence of peripheral arterial disease in the United States. *American Journal of Preventive Medicine, 32,* 328–333.

American College of Obstetricians and Gynecologists. (2011, September). Practice bulletin No. 123: Thromboembolism in pregnancy. *Obstetrics & Gynecology, 118,* 718–729.

American Diabetes Association. (2013). Executive summary: Standards of medical care in Diabetes-2013. *Diabetes Care, 36*(Suppl. 1), S4–S10.

American Geriatrics Society 2012 Beers Criteria Update Expert Panel. (2012). American Geriatrics Society updated Beers criteria for potentially inappropriate medication use in older adults. *Journal of American Geriatric Society, 60,* 616–631.

American Heart Association. (2013). *Infective endocarditis.* Retrieved from http://www.heart.org/HEARTORG/Conditions/CongenitalHeartDefects/TheImpactofCongenitalHeartDefects/Infective-Endocarditis_UCM_307108_Article.jsp

Amsterdam, E. A., Kirk, J. D., Bluemke, D. A., Diercks, D., Farkouth, M. E., Garvey, J. E., ... Thompson, P. D. (2010). Testing of low-risk patients presenting to the emergency department with chest pain: A scientific statement from the American Heart Association. *Circulation, 122,* 1756–1776.

Aronow, W. S. (2012, January). Hypertension: Treatment in elders. *Consultant,* 70–78. Retrieved from www.Consultant360.com

Aschenbrenner, D. (2012). Drug watch: New indication for anticoagulants. *American Journal of Nursing, 112,* 23.

Bodi, F. B. (2013, December 5). *Coronary artery atherosclerosis. Medscape Reference.* Retrieved from emedicine.medscape.com/article153647-overview

Boltz, M., Capezuti, L., Flumer, T., & Zwicker, D. (Eds.). (2012). *Evidence-based geriatric nursing protocols for best practice* (4th ed.). New York, NY: Springer Publishing Company.

Bowers, M. T. (2013, November). Managing patients with heart failure. *Journal for Nurse Practitioners, 9,* 621–628.

Brazziel, T., Cox, L., Drury, C., & Guerra, M. (2011). Stopping the wave of PAD. *The Nurse Practitioner, 36,* 29–33.

Cannon, C. P. (2008). Updated strategies and therapies for reducing ischemic and vascular events (STRIVE) ST-segment elevation myocardial infarction critical pathway toolkit. *Critical Pathways in Cardiology, 7,* 223–231.

Carey, S. A., Cink, C., Hall, S., Kuiper, J., Hardaway, B., Theleman, K., & Sass, D. (2013). The impact of a comprehensive inpatient nurse practitioner led heart failure (HF) program. *Journal of Cardiac Failure, 19,* S90.

Carro, A., & Kaski, J. (2011, April). Myocardial infarction in the elderly. *Aging and Disease, 2,* 116–137.

Centers for Disease Control and Prevention. (2011, September 16). Million hearts: Strategies to reduce the prevalence of leading cardiovascular disease risk factors—United States, 2011. *Morbidity and Mortality Weekly Report (MMWR).* Retrieved from http://www.cdc.gov/mmwr/preview/mmwrhtml/mm6036a4.htm?s_cid=mm6036a4_w

Centers for Disease Control and Prevention. (2012, June 8). *Deep vein thrombosis (DVT)/pulmonary embolism (PE)—blood clot forming in a vein.* Retrieved from www.cdc.gov/ncbddd/dvt/data.html

Centers for Disease Control and Prevention. (2012, October 17). *Heart failure fact sheet.* Retrieved from http://www.cdc.gov/dhdsp/data_statistics/fact_sheets/fs_heart_failure.htm

Cheng, A., & Kumar, K. (2013, July 2). *Overview of atrial fibrillation. UpToDate.* Retrieved from http://www.uptodate.com/contents/overview-of-atrial-fibrillation?source=search_result&search=overview+of+atrial+fibrillation&selectedTitle=1%7E150

Chobanian, A. V., Bakris, G. L., Black, H. R., Cushman, W. C., Green, L. A., Izzo, J. L., Jr., ... Roccella, E. J. (2003). Seventh report of the Joint National Committee on prevention, detection, evaluation, and treatment high blood pressure. *Hypertension, 42,* 1206–1252. Retrieved from http://hyper.ahajournals.org/cgi/content/full/42/6/1206

Colucci, W. S. (2014, March 25). *Drugs that should be avoided or used with caution in patients with heart failure. UpToDate.* Retrieved from http://www.uptodate.com/contents/drugs-that-should-be-avoided-or-used-with-caution-in-patients-with-heart-failure?source=search_result&search=Durgs+that+should+be+avoided+or+used+with+caution&selectedTitle=1%7E150

Colucci, W. S. (2014, June 20). *Evaluation of the patient with suspected heart failure. UpToDate.* Retrieved from http://www.uptodate.com/contents/evaluation-of-the-patient-with-suspected-heart-failure?source=search_result&search=evaluation+of+the+patient+with+suspected+heart+failure&selectedTitle=1%7E150

Conn, R. D., & O'Keefe, J. H. (2009). Cardiac physical diagnosis in the digital age: An important but increasingly neglected skill (from stethoscopes to microchips). *American Journal of Cardiology, 104,* 590–595.

Davis, L. L. (2013, November). Using the latest evidence to manage hypertension. *The Journal for Nurse Practitioners, 9,* 621–628.

Dewar, C., Selby, C., Jamieson, K., & Rogers, S. (2008, July). Emergency department nurse-based outpatient diagnosis of DVT using an evidence-based protocol. *Emergency Medicine Journal, 25,* 411–416.

Dumitru, I. (2013, May 6). *Heart failure medication. Medscape Reference.* Retrieved from emedicine.medscape.com/article/163062-medication

Eckel, R. H., Jakicie, J. M., Ard, J. D., Hubbard, V. S., de Jesus, J. M., Lee, I-Min., … Yanovsk, S. Z. (2013, November 12). AHA/ACC guideline on lifestyle management to reduce cardiovascular risk: A report of the American College of Cardiology/American Heart Association Task Force on practice guidelines. *Circulation*. Retrieved from http://circ.ahajournals.org

Enomoto, Y., & Yoshimura, S. (2012). Antiplatelet therapy for carotid stenting. *Interventional Neurology, 1*, 151–163.

Fernandez, L., & Scovell, S. (2014, August 15). *Superficial thrombophlebitis of the lower extremity. UpToDate*. Retrieved from http://www.uptodate.com/contents/superficial-thrombophlebitis-of-the-lower-extremity?source=search_result&search=superficial+thrombophlebitis+of+the+lower+extra&selectedTitle=1%7E150

Forman, D. E., Rich, M. W., Alexander, K. P., Zieman, S., Maurer, M. S., Najjar, S. S., Cleveland, J. C., Jr., Krumholz, H. M., & Wenger, N. K. (2011, May). Cardiac care of older adults: Time for a new paradigm. *Journal of American College of Cardiology, 57*, 1801–1810.

Furie, K. L. (2013, September 18). *Pathophysiology of symptoms for carotid atherosclerosis. UpToDate*. Retrieved from http://www.uptodate.com/contents/pathophysiology-of-symptoms-from-carotid-atherosclerosis?source=search_result&search=pathophysiology+and+carotid+ather&selectedTitle=2%7E150

Ganz, L. (2014, June 11). *Epidemiology of and risk factors for atrial fibrillation. UpToDate*. Retrieved from http://www.uptodate.com/contents/epidemiology-of-and-risk-factors-for-atrial-fibrillation?source=search_result&search=epidemilogy+of+the+rrik+factors+of+atrial&selectedTitle=1%7E150

GlobalRPh. Retrieved from www.global rph.com

Go, A. S., Bauman, M., King, S. M. C., Fonarow, G. C., Lawrence, W., Williams, K. A., & Sanchez, E. (2013, November 15). An effective approach to high blood pressure control: A science advisory from the American Heart Association, the American College of Cardiology, and the Centers for Disease Control and Prevention. *Hypertension*, [epub ahead of print]. Retrieved from http://hyper.ahajournals.org/content/early/2013/11/14/HYP.0000000000000003.reprint

Goff, D. C., Lloyd-Jones, D. M., Bennett, G., Coady, S., D'Agostino, Sr., R. B., Gibbons, R., … Wilson, P. W. F. (2013, November 12). ACC/AHA guideline on the assessment of cardiovascular risk: A report of the American College of Cardiology/American Heart Association Task Force on practice guidelines. *Circulation*. Retrieved from http://circ.ahajournals.org

Gopalakrishnan, P. P., Shukla, S. K., & Tak, T. (2010, July). Antibiotic prophylaxis and anaphylaxis. *Clinical Medicine and Research, 8*, 80–81.

Guyatt, G. H., Akl, E. A., Crowther, M., Gutterman, D. D., & Schunemann, H. J. (2012). Executive Summary antithrombotic therapy and prevention of thrombosis, 9th ed: American College of Chest Physicians evidence-based clinical practice guidelines. *Chest, 141*, 7S–47S.

Hanifin, C. (2010, April). Cardiac auscultation 101: A basic science approach to diagnosing heart murmurs: Applying anatomy and physiology fundamentals to where and when heart sounds are heard best in an effective method for auscultation of cardiac valve pathology. *JAAPA-Journal American Academy of Physician Assistants, 23*, 44.

Heller, J. (2011, October). Treatment of chronic venous insufficiency. *Endovascular Today*, (*Suppl*), 12–15. Retrieved from http://evtoday.com/pdfs/supp_1011_5.pdf

Holroyd-Leduc, J. & Reddy, Madhuri. (Eds). *Evidence-based geriatric medicine*. Oxford, UK: Wiley Publishing.

Jackson, S. M. (2013, February). Diastolic heart failure. *ADVANCE for NPs & PAs, 4*, 23–25, 34.

James, P. A., Oparil, S., Carter, B. L., Cushman, W. C., Dennison-Himmelfarb, C., Handler, J., … Ortiz, E. (2013, December 18). 2014 Evidence-based guidelines for the management of high blood pressure in adults report from the panel members appointed to the eighth Joint National Committee (JNC 8). *Journal of the American Medical Association*. Retrieved from http://jama.jamanetwork.com

Kaplan, N. M., & Domino, F. J. (2014, January 14). *Overview of hypertension in adults. UpToDate*. Retrieved from http://www.uptodate.com/contents/overview-of-hypertension-in-adults?source=search_result&search=overview+of+hypertension+in+adults&selectedTitle=1%7E150

Kelly, R. B. (2010, May 1). Diet and exercise in the management of hyperlipidemia. *American Family Physician, 81*, 1097–1102.

Klever, R. G. (2012, October 26). *Superficial thrombophlebitis. Medscape Reference*. Retrieved from emedicine.medscape.com/article/463256-overview

Lab Tests Online. Retrieved from labtestsonline.org

Languasco, A., Galante, M., Marin, J., Soler, C., Lopez Saubidet, C., & Milbert, M. (2011, December 15). Adherence to local guidelines for venous thromboprophylaxis: A cross-sectional study of medical inpatients in Argentina. *Thrombosis Journal, 9*, 1–8.

Lavigne, P. M., & Karas, R. H. (2013, January 29). The current state of niacin in cardiovascular disease prevention. *Journal of the American College of Cardiology, 61*, 440–446.

Levine, G. N., Steinke, E. E., Bakaeen, F. G., Bozkury, B., Cheitlin, M. D., Conti, J. B., … Stewart, W. J. (2012). Sexual activity and cardiovascular disease: A scientific statement from the American Heart Association. *Circulation, 125*, 1058–1072.

Madhur, M. S. (2013, December 3). Hypertension. *Medscape Reference*. Retrieved from emedicine.medscape.com/article/241381-overview

Mann, F. E., & Hilgers, K. F. (2014, January 21). *Hypertension: Who should be treated? UpToDate*. Retrieved from http://www.uptodate.com/contents/hypertension-who-should-be-treated?source=search_result&search=hypertension+who+should+be+treated&selectedTitle=1%7E150

Mann, J. F. E. (2014, January 7). *Choice of therapy in primary (essential) hypertension: Recommendations. UpToDate*. Retrieved from http://www.uptodate.com/contents/choice-of-therapy-in-primary-essential-hypertension-recommendations?source=search_result&search=choice+of+therapy+in+primary++hypertension&selectedTitle=1%7E150

McCabe, P. (2011). Living with atrial fibrillation: A qualitative study. *Journal of Cardiovascular Nursing, 26*, 336–344.

McCarron, M. O., Goldstein, L. B., & Matchar, D. B. (2013, November 12). *Screening for asymptomatic carotid artery stenosis. UpToDate*. Retrieved from http://www.uptodate.com/contents/screening-for-asymptomatic-carotid-artery-stenosis?source=search_result&search=screening+for+carotin+artery+stenosis&selectedTitle=1%7E150

McLafferty, R. B., Lohr, J. M., Caprini, J. A., Passman, M. A., Padberg, F. T., Rooke, T. W., … Wakefield, T. W. (2007, January). Results of the national pilot screening program for venous disease by the American Venous Forum. *Journal of Vascular Surgery, 45*, 142–148.

Meisel, J. L. (2013, September 12). *Diagnostic approach to chest pain in adults. UpToDate*. Retrieved from http://www

.uptodate.com/contents/diagnostic-approach-to-chest-pain-in-adults?source=search_result&search=diagnostic+approach+to+chest+pain+in+adults&selectedTitle=1%7E150

Mohler III, E. (2013, August 21). *Overview of upper extremity peripheral artery disease. UpToDate.* Retrieved from http://www.uptodate.com/contents/overview-of-upper-extremity-peripheral-artery-disease?source=search_result&search=overview+of+upper+exremity+peripheral+artery&selectedTitle=1%7E150

Mohler, E. R., & Fairman, R. M. (2013, October 7). *Management of asymptomatic carotid atherosclerotic disease. UpToDate.* Retrieved from http://www.uptodate.com/contents/management-of-symptomatic-carotid-atherosclerotic-disease?source=search_result&search=management+of+symptomatic+carotid&selectedTitle=1%7E150

Mohler III, E., & Mitchell, E. (2013, July). *Noninvasive diagnosis of arterial disease. UpToDate.* Retrieved from http://www.uptodate.com/contents/noninvasive-diagnosis-of-arterial-disease?source=search_result&search=noninvasive+diagnosis+of+arterial+disease&selectedTitle=1%7E150

Murdaca, G., Cagnati, P., Gulli, R., Spano, F., Puppo, F., Campisi, C., & Boccardo, F. (2012, February). Current views on diagnostic approach and treatment of lymphedema. *American Journal of Medicine, 125,* 134–140.

Neschis, D. G., & Golden, M. A. (2014, June 12) *Clinical feature, diagnosis, and natural history of lower extremity peripheral artery disease. UpToDate.* Retrieved from http://www.uptodate.com/contents/clinical-features-and-diagnosis-of-lower-extremity-peripheral-artery-disease?source=search_result&search=moher+and+clinical+features+and+lower+extremity&selectedTitle=5%7E150

Nguyen, T., Yacoup, M., Chan, T., & Quach, K. (2012). Atrial fibrillation: Focus on anticoagulant pharmacotherapy. *The Journal for Nurse Practitioners, 8,* 560–565.

O'Gara, P. T., Kushner, F. G., Ascheim, D. D., Casey, D. E., Chung, M. K., de Lemos, J. A., … Yancy, C. W. (2013, January). 2013 ACCF/AHA guideline for the management of ST-Elevation myocardial infarction. *Journal of the American College of Cardiology,* Retrieved from http://content.onlinejacc.org/article.aspx?articleid=1486115

Physicians' Desk Reference: *Drug information.* (2014). Retrieved from www.pdr.net

Pignone, M. (2014, May 2). *Treatment of lipids (including hypercholesterolemia) in primary prevention. UpToDate.* Retrieved from http://www.uptodate.com/contents/treatment-of-lipids-including-hypercholesterolemia-in-primary-prevention?source=search_result&search=treatment+of+lipids&selectedTitle=1%7E150

Prasun, M. (2012). Providing best practice in the management of atrial fibrillation in the United States. *Journal of Cardiovascular Nursing, 27,* 445–456.

Rich, W. M., & Shen, W-K. (Eds.). (2012). Cardiac rhythm disorders in older adults. *Clinics in Geriatric Medicine, 28* (4), 539–750.

Ricotta, J. J., Aburahma, A., Ascher, E., Eskandari, M., Faries, P. & Lal, B. K. (2011, September). Updated society for vascular surgery guidelines for management of extracranial carotid disease. *Journal of Vascular Surgery, 55* (3), 1–31.

Robert, L. (2013, May 15). *Hypertension meeting has primary care track* [Web blog]. Retrieved from www.consultantlive.comp/print/article/10162/2142634

Rooke, T. (2012). *Lymphedema.* Retrieved from vasculardisease.org/lymphedema

Rubenfire, M., Brook, R. D., & Rosenson, R. S. (2010). Treating mixed hyperlipidemia and the atherogenic lipid phenotype for prevention of cardiovascular events. *The American Journal of Medicine, 123,* 892–898.

Rutecki, G. W. (2013, May 22). *Reflections on ASH 2013: Lessons in quality improvement* [Web blog]. Retrieved from http://www.consultantlive.com/conference-reports/ash2013/content/article/10162/2143452

Rutecki, G. W. (2013, May 16). *Some do's and don'ts for tough-to-treat hypertensives* [Web blog]. Retrieved from www.consultantlive.com/print/article/10162/2142822?printable=true

Spencer, A., Jablonski, R., & Loeb, S. J. (2012, February). Hypertensive African American women and the DASH diet. *The Nurse Practitioner, 37,* 41–46.

Spodick, D. H. (2010). Heart sounds: Important and neglected. *The American Journal of Cardiology, 105,* 1040.

Stone, N. J., Robinson, J., Lichtenstein, A. H., Bairey Merz, C. N., Lloyd-Jones, D. M., Blum, C. B., … Wilson, P. W. (2013, November 7). 2013 ACC/AHA guidelines on the treatment of blood cholesterol to reduce atherosclerotic cardiovascular risk in adults: A report of the American College of Cardiology/American Heart Association Task Force on practice guidelines. *Journal of the American College of Cardiology, pii,* S0735–1097.

Suaya, J. A., Stason, W. B., Ades, P. A., Normand, S. L., & Shepard, D. S. (2009, June 30). Cardiac rehabilitation and survival in older coronary patients. *Journal of the American College of Cardiology, 54,* 25–33.

Summary of the Second Report of the National Cholesterol Education Program Expert Panel on Detection, Evaluation, and Treatment of High Blood Cholesterol in Adults (Adult Treatment Panel II). (1993). *Journal of the American Medical Association, 269,* 3015–3023.

U.S. Department of Health and Human Services. (2004). *ATP III update 2004: Implications of recent clinical trials for the ATP III Guidelines.* Retrieved from http://www.nhlbi.nih.gov/guidelines/cholesterol/atp3upd04.htm

U.S. Department of Health and Human Services. (2006). *Your guide to lowering your blood pressure with DASH. NIH Publications No. 06-4082.* Retrieved from http://www.nhlbi.nih.gov/health/public/heart/hbp/dash/new_dash.pdf

Vascular Disease Foundation. (2012). *Carotid artery disease.* Retrieved February 13, 2013, from http://vasculardisease.org/flyers/carotid-artery-disease-flyer.pdf

Vascular Disease Foundation. (2012, May 4). *Vascular disease statistics.* Retrieved from vasculardisease.org/education-prevention/knowledge-is-power/vascular-disease-statistics

Wiley, M., & Kumar, A. (2012, September). Peripheral arterial disease: Diagnosis and treatment. *Consultant, 52,* 601–608.

Wright, A. A., Zhang, B., Ray, A., Mack, J. W., Trice, E., Balboni, T., … Prigerson, H. G. (2008). Associations between end-of-life discussions, patient mental health, medical care near death, and caregiver bereavement adjustment. *JAMA, 300,* 1665–1673.

Wright, B. M., Rutecki, G. W., & Bellone, J. (2013, January). Resistant hypertension: An approach to diagnosis and treatment. *Consultant,* 9–16. Retrieved from www.Consultant360.com

Yancy, C. W., Jessup, M., Bozkurt, B., Butler, J., Casey, Jr. D. E., Drazner, M. H., … Wilkoff, B. L.; American College of Cardiology Foundation; American Heart Association Task Force on Practice Guidelines. (2013, October). 2013 ACCF/AHA guideline for the management of heart failure: A report of the American College of Cardiology Foundation/American Heart Association Task

Force on practice guidelines. *Journal of the American College of Cardiology, 62*, e147–239.

Yao, S., & Tong, L. (2012). Comparison of anticoagulants used for stroke prevention in patients with atrial fibrillation. *The American Journal for Nurse Practitioners, 16*, 29–34.

Zhao, X-O. (2013, September 3). *Pathogenesis of atherosclerosis. UpToDate*. Retrieved from http://www.uptodate.com/contents/pathogenesis-of-atherosclerosis?source=search_result&search=pathogenesis+of+atherosclerosis&selectedTitle=1%7E150

CHAPTER THIRTEEN

Gastrointestinal Guidelines

Cheryl A. Glass

Abdominal Pain

Definition

A. Abdominal pain is a common nonspecific complaint. The responsibility is for clinicians to determine that patients can be safely observed and treated symptomatically and that they require further investigation or a specialist referral. Pain in the abdomen is secondary to problems relating to abdominal organs, and it is categorized as follows:
   1. Acute pain: Pain of less than a few days that has worsened progressively until presentation.
   2. Chronic pain: Interval of 12 weeks can be used to separate acute from chronic pain, that is, it has remained unchanged for months or years.
   3. Emergent: Pain that lasts 3 hours or longer, accompanied by a fever or vomiting.

B. Pain may be categorized by the following description.
   1. Visceral pain is usually dull and aching in character.
   2. Parietal pain is sharp and well localized.
   3. Referred pain is aching and perceived to be near the surface of the body.

Incidence

A. Abdominal pain is very common. Abdominal pain is present in 75% of adolescent students and in about 50% of all adults. Gastroenteritis and irritable bowel syndrome (IBS) are the most common causes of acute pain, and chronic stool retention is the most common cause of chronic pain. Other causes of abdominal pain include the following.
   1. Acute appendicitis: Occurs 10:100,000
   2. Acute cholecystitis: Varies according to age and ethnic origin
   3. Intestinal obstruction, usually small intestines: Accounts for 20% of acute abdominal conditions
   4. Abdominal pain associated with pregnancy: Ectopic pregnancy (1:200 pregnancies), miscarriage, and abruptio placenta

Pathogenesis

A. Pathogenesis depends on the origin of pain. Pain may result from inflammation, ischemia, distension, altered motility, obstruction, or ulceration.

Predisposing Factors

A. Abdominal trauma
B. Motor vehicle accidents
C. Lactose intolerance
D. Pregnancy
E. Torsion
F. Psychogenic pain
G. Sickle cell disease
H. Infection

Common Complaints

Clinical presentation of abdominal pain is determined in part by the site of the involvement.

A. Acute or chronic onset of pain
B. Vomiting
C. Diarrhea

Other Signs and Symptoms

A. Bleeding
B. Referred shoulder pain
C. Fever
D. Nausea and/or projectile vomiting
E. Rigid abdomen
F. Changes in vital signs
G. Abdominal distension
H. Constipation or diarrhea
I. Guarding
J. Rebound tenderness
K. Biliary pain and right subcostal tenderness

L. Anorexia
M. Periumbilical discomfort; consider appendicitis if, within 2 to 12 hours, pain localizes in right lower quadrant (RLQ) at McBurney's point.
N. Dysuria
O. Abdominal mass; do not overlook the possibility of pregnancy as the cause of a mass.
P. Melena (most common in peptic ulcer disease [PUD])

Subjective Data

Evaluate for a "surgical abdomen," defined as a rapidly worsening prognosis in the absence of surgical intervention. Patients should not eat or drink while a diagnosis of a surgical abdomen remains under consideration. Once a surgical abdomen has been excluded, the remainder of the evaluation will be guided by the chronicity of symptoms along with the location of pain.

A. Review onset, duration, course, and quality of pain.
   1. When did the pain start?
   2. What were you doing when the pain started?
   3. Has this ever occurred before?
   4. What was the primary diagnosis?
   5. What was the previous treatment, and was it effective?
   6. Is there anyone else having the same symptoms in your home?
   7. Review the progression of pain.
B. Determine pain rating on a 10-point scale, with 0 being no pain and 10 being equivalent to the worst pain the patient has ever felt.
C. Qualify the duration of pain in minutes, hours, days, weeks, or months. Does the pain interfere with sleep?
D. Review the pattern of pain.
   1. Review aggravating factors.
   2. Review alleviating factors.
   3. Does the pain radiate?
   4. Does the pain have any relationship to food intake?
E. Question specific to females
   1. Determine the patient's last missed menses (LMP).
   2. Has she had a hysterectomy or tubal ligation?
   3. Does she have a recent history of dyspareunia or dysmenorrhea that suggests pelvic pathology?
   4. Is there any history of physical abuse?
   5. **What type of contraception is used? Specifically evaluate for an intrauterine device (IUD).**
F. Review the patient's current medications and drug history, especially antibiotic, laxative, acetaminophen, aspirin, and nonsteroidal anti-inflammatory drug (NSAID) use. Patients taking corticosteroids may have a significant masking of pain.
G. Rule out abdominal trauma from domestic violence, motor vehicle accidents, falls, or assaults.
H. Review bowel habits and note changes: Constipation, diarrhea, anorexia, food intolerance, nausea, vomiting, or bloating.
I. Review the patient's history for sickle cell disease. Any individual of African American or Mediterranean descent presenting with leg or abdominal pain should be questioned regarding sickle cell disease or trait.
J. Review urinary function. Is there any urinary frequency, urgency, dysuria, flank pain, or back pain? If the patient is male, does he have any hesitancy, difficulty starting the urine stream, nocturia, low urinary volume, or any lower abdominal distension indicating urinary retention?
K. Review alcohol intake/history.
L. Has the patient had any unexplained weight loss?
M. Evaluate sexual activity to rule out potential sexually transmitted infection (STI).
   1. Evaluate if patients have new partners.
   2. Are their partners experiencing any symptoms?

Physical Examination

A. Check temperature, pulse, respirations, and blood pressure; include orthostatic blood pressure.

Tachycardia or hypotension may be signs of a ruptured aortic aneurysm, septic shock, gastrointestinal (GI) hemorrhage, or volume depletion. Absence of a fever in the elderly or immunosuppressed does not exclude a serious illness.

B. Inspect
   1. Observe general appearance: Facial expressions, walk, skin turgor; refusal to move/writhing, note grimace during exam.
   2. Perform eye and mouth exam to rule out iritis and aphthous ulcers of the mouth (extraintestinal manifestations of inflammatory bowel disease [IBD]).
   3. Examine the abdomen for the presence of a hernia at the umbilicus, groin, or near the site of prior surgical incisions.
   4. Examine the abdomen for overt masses or pulsations.
   5. Examine the eyes and skin for jaundice.
   6. Observe for any bruising or other signs of domestic violence in the "bathing suit" areas: Breasts, abdomen, back that would be easily covered with clothes.
C. Auscultate
   1. Auscultate for bowel sounds in all four quadrants of the abdomen.
   2. Evaluate heart and lungs.
   3. Check for bruits of aorta, iliac, and renal bruits.
D. Percuss abdomen for tympanic and dullness sounds.

E. Palpate
  1. Palpate abdomen for masses, rebound tenderness, and peritoneal signs.
    a. Before palpating the abdomen, ask the patient to bend the knees to help with relaxation of the wall musculature.
    b. Elderly patients may lack classical peritoneal signs of rebound and guarding.
  2. Check the abdomen for tender pulsatile mass at midline; it may indicate abdominal aortic aneurysm (AAA).
  3. Palpate back; check for cerebrovascular accident (CVA) tenderness.
  4. Perform a bimanual examination in women regardless of whether the patient has had a hysterectomy or is postmenopausal.
    a. Evaluate the size and symmetry of the uterus.
    b. Evaluate the adnexal areas for presence of appropriately sized, mobile ovaries. A fixed, painful adnexal mass is suggestive of an endometrioma or tubo-ovarian abscess.
    c. Endometriosis is suggested by localized tenderness in the cul-de-sac or uterosacral ligaments, palpable tender nodules, pain with uterine movement or tender fixation of adnexal or uterus in a retroverted position.
  5. Check for obturator sign, which is abdominal pain in response to passive internal rotation of the right hip from the 90° angle knee–hip flexion position.
  6. Check for iliopsoas sign; perform this when an inflamed appendix is suspected. Positive psoas sign is the presence of lower quadrant pain, noted as the supine patient raises his or her right leg from the hip while the examiner pushes downward against his or her lower thigh.

F. Perform a rectal exam, including testing of stool for occult blood. **Failure to perform a rectal examination in patients with abdominal pain may be associated with an increased rate of misdiagnosis and should be considered a medicolegal pitfall.**

Diagnostic Tests

A. **In all women of childbearing age, assume the woman is pregnant until proven otherwise. Vaginal bleeding with or without abdominal pain should prompt a transvaginal ultrasound and a serum human chorionic gonadotropin (HCG).**
B. Complete blood count (CBC) with differential
C. Electrolytes
D. SMA 12
E. Chemistry 20
F. Blood urea nitrogen (BUN)
G. Amylase
H. Aminotransferases, alkaline phosphatase (ALP), and bilirubin
I. Lipase
J. Urinalysis; save sample for culture.
K. Coproporphyrin, if lead poisoning is suspected
L. Plain x-ray films of abdomen; consider computed tomography (CT) of abdomen.
M. Abdominal ultrasonography
N. GI series radiography
O. Endoscopy; consider *Helicobacter pylori* testing.
P. Sigmoidoscopy
Q. Barium enema (BE): Avoid with suspected obstruction.
R. Consider endoscopic retrograde cholangiopancreatography (ERCP) to visualize the distal common bile duct.
S. Electrocardiography (EKG) to rule out cardiac pain.
T. Consider blood cultures for elderly that present with abdominal pain associated with either fever or hypothermia or when sepsis is suspected.
U. Chest radiography
V. Guaiac stool for occult blood

Differential Diagnoses

Location and duration of abdominal pain can often help significantly in narrowing the differential diagnosis.

A. Right upper quadrant (RUQ) pain
  1. Acute cholecystitis and biliary colic
    a. Biliary tract: Increased serum amylase
    b. Ascending cholangitis presents with fever and jaundice in a patient with RUQ pain.
    c. In acute cholecystitis, the typical pain is maximal in the RUQ or epigastrium, radiating to the scapular region, and is accompanied by nausea, vomiting, and fever without jaundice. "Murphy's sign," or inspiratory arrest in response to upper quadrant palpation, may be seen with acute cholecystitis. RUQ tenderness to percussion or pressure of the gallbladder is also a suggestive finding.
    d. Ketoacidosis has been found to present with severe abdominal pain in 8% of instances and may be accompanied by emesis and an elevated white cell count. Acute intra-abdominal events such as cholecystitis may be the precipitant of ketoacidosis.
  2. Acute hepatitis
  3. Hepatic abscess
  4. Hepatomegaly due to congestive heart failure (CHF)
  5. Perforated duodenal ulcer (DU)

A perforated ulcer is accompanied by an increased serum amylase.

  6. Acute pancreatitis; bilateral pain

Pancreatitis is accompanied by an increased serum amylase.

7. Herpes zoster
8. Myocardial ischemia
9. Pleural or pulmonary pathology (e.g., pneumonia, pulmonary embolism, or empyema)

B. RLQ pain
1. Appendicitis often begins with symptoms of dull, steady, periumbilical pain and anorexia before localizing to the RLQ at McBurney's point.
2. Regional enteritis
3. Leaking aneurysm
4. Ruptured ectopic pregnancy
5. Twisted ovarian cyst
6. Pelvic inflammatory disease (PID)
7. Ureteral calculi
8. Incarcerated, strangulated inguinal hernia
9. Endometriosis
10. Meckel's diverticulitis
11. Abdominal wall hematoma

C. Left upper quadrant (LUQ) pain
1. Gastritis
2. Acute pancreatitis: Epigastric pain that is relatively sudden, boring to the back, and is associated with nausea, vomiting, and anorexia.
3. Splenic enlargement, rupture, infarction, aneurysm
4. Myocardial ischemia
5. Left lower lobe pneumonia
6. Renal colic: Radiates to the groin

D. Left lower quadrant (LLQ) pain
1. Sigmoid diverticulitis
2. Regional enteritis
3. Leaking aneurysm

AAA may present with a tender pulsatile mass at the abdominal midline. Vascular disorders such as acute arterial insufficiency, due to atherosclerosis or embolus, may present with severe abdominal pain, although mild, constant pain may be the only symptom for several days. Dissection or rupture of an AAA produces severe acute abdominal pain and often radiates to the back or genitalia.

4. Ruptured ectopic pregnancy

Rupture of the fallopian tube generally causes sudden, acute, and localized abdominal pain. Internal hemorrhage causes syncope and referred shoulder pain, caused by phrenic nerve irritation. Diagnosis before tubal rupture may be difficult because symptoms and physical findings mimic other conditions such as appendicitis.

5. Twisted ovarian cyst
6. PID
7. Ureteral calculi
8. Incarcerated, strangulated inguinal hernia

E. Generalized abdominal pain
1. Trauma
   a. **Any person with a possible blow to the abdomen should have orthostatic blood pressure taken, careful palpation of the abdomen, serial abdominal circumferences measured, and be considered for abdominal imaging. Serial hemoglobin and hematocrit (Hct) measurements should be obtained, if necessary.**
   b. In abdominal trauma, the spleen is the most commonly injured organ, especially in blunt abdominal trauma; the onset can be immediate or delayed.
   c. Nontraumatic splenic rupture is often associated with acute infectious mononucleosis.
2. Intestinal obstruction: Obstruction that develops slowly over weeks to months may be relatively subtle in presentation.

Acute obstruction presents with severe "colicky" pain or pain that is wavelike in nature; it makes the pain relentless.

3. Peritoneal irritation: Severe pain due to the rich innervation of the parietal peritoneum. Focal injury results in well-localized discomfort that is described as a sharp aching or burning.
4. Metabolic disturbances may mimic intra-abdominal etiologies.

Porphyria and lead poisoning sometimes simulate bowel obstruction because they can cause cramping, abdominal pain, and hyperperistalsis.

5. Nonspecific dysfunctional abdominal pain and psychogenic abdominal pain are diagnoses of exclusion.

Plan

A. General interventions
1. If necessary, prepare the patient for emergency transport and hospitalization.
2. Management and follow-up of other causes of abdominal pain are variable and depend on diagnosis.

B. Patient teaching
1. See the Section III Patient Teaching Guide for this chapter, "Abdominal Pain."
2. Counsel the patient to keep a pain diary to include activity, foods, and other pain triggers; duration of pain; and what provides relief of symptoms.

C. Pharmaceutical therapy: Treatment depends on the findings from the history, physical, and testing, as well as the clinical diagnosis.

Follow-Up

A. Variable, depending on diagnosis
B. Review pain diary.

Consultation/Referral

A. Consult the physician for the patient with acute abdominal pain and pain related to abdominal trauma.
B. For the obstetric patient, consult a physician for any bleeding or abdominal pain.

Individual Considerations

A. Pregnancy: There is no evidence that acute intra-abdominal surgical emergencies are more common during pregnancy if ectopic pregnancy is excluded.
   1. The presence of peritoneal signs, rebound tenderness, and abdominal guarding is never normal in pregnancy.
   2. Bleeding complications include the following.
      a. First trimester: Miscarriage and ectopic pregnancy
      b. Second and third trimester: Abruptio placenta
   3. Physiologic changes of pregnancy may affect the presentation and evaluation of abdominal pain. The enlargement of the uterus can impede physical examination, affect the normal location of pelvic and abdominal organs, and mask or delay peritoneal signs. (Refer to the entry on "Appendicitis" in this chapter.)
   4. Severe preeclampsia: The clinical manifestations of liver involvement include RUQ or midepigastric pain, elevated transaminases, and, in severe cases, subcapsular hemorrhage or hepatic rupture.
B. Adults
   1. Obesity distorts the abdominal exam, making organ palpation or pelvic examination difficult.
   2. With men older than age 40 and women older than age 50, suspect cardiac origin when presenting with epigastric pain. Consider obtaining EKG for patients in this age group.

While myocardial infarction (MI) "classically" presents with anterior chest pressure or pain, the patient may also have a gastritis or heartburn sensation, coupled with nausea and diaphoresis.

C. Geriatrics
   1. Elderly patients may have a vague or atypical presentation of pain, including fatigue and chest pain, varying in location, severity, and presence of a fever or nonspecific findings on examination.
      a. Classic findings of acute peritonitis, rebound tenderness, and local rigidity occur less in the elderly.
   2. Elderly patients have a diminished sensorium, allowing pathology to advance to a dangerous point prior to symptom development.
      a. The level of pain is much less severe at presentation and continues to be at a lower level of pain.
      b. The elderly may present with altered mental status.
   3. In an older patient, a similar presentation to IBD with abdominal pain and a change in bowel habits can be the first sign of colon cancer.
   4. AAA is observed almost exclusively in elderly patients.
      a. Approximately 5% of men 65 years and older have an AAA.
      b. Maintain a high index of suspension in patients who present with a clinical picture suggestive of renal colic or musculoskeletal back pain.
   5. Elderly patients with urinary tract infection (UTI) are less likely to have dysuria, frequency, or urgency.
   6. Patients older than 65 years have a 30% to 50% risk of gallstones and may not present with significant pain; less than half have fever, vomiting, or leukocytosis.
   7. Fever, an elevated white blood cell (WBC) count occurs in less than half of the elderly patients with diverticulitis. Only about 25% of the elderly with diverticulitis present with a guaiac positive stool.
   8. The incidence of PUD is more common in the elderly due to the availability and use of NSAIDs. The most common presenting symptom with PUD in the elderly is melena.

Resource

Rome Foundation: http://romecriteria.org/criteria

Appendicitis

Definition

A. Appendicitis is acute inflammation of the appendix caused by the obstruction of the appendiceal lumen. There is no single sign, symptom, or diagnostic test that accurately confirms the diagnosis of inflammation. Perforation is rare in the first 12 hours, but the rate of perforation increases after 72 hours. Prompt, early diagnosis and operative intervention is the goal of treatment. The differential diagnoses for appendicitis include all abdominal sources of pain.

Incidence

A. Acute appendicitis occurs at a rate of 10:100,000. It is the most common condition in children (1% to 8%) and during pregnancy (0.06% to 0.1%) that requires emergency abdominal surgery. One in every 2,000 adults older than age 65 will develop appendicitis.

Pathogenesis

A. Foreign bodies, fecal material, tissue hypertrophy, strictures, or a bend or twist on the organ may cause obstruction of the appendix. The obstruction causes colicky pain. Bacterial invasion causes inflammation and leads to gangrene and perforation. The most common bacteria are *E. coli*, pseudomonas, *B. fragilis*, and *Peptostreptococcus* species.

Predisposing Factors

A. Pregnancy
B. Torsion
C. Abdominal trauma
D. Male gender, age 10 to 30

Common Complaints

> *The classic history of anorexia and periumbilical pain followed by nausea, RLQ pain, and vomiting occurs in only 50% of cases.*

A. Adults
   1. Generalized or localized abdominal pain in the epigastric or periumbilical areas. Within 2 to 12 hours, pain localizes in RLQ at McBurney's point, and intensity increases.
   2. The location of the appendix is altered in pregnancy.
   3. Pain typically develops before vomiting.
   4. Nausea and/or vomiting (may be projectile).
   5. Anorexia signals organic cause of abdominal pain.

B. Elderly patients are less likely to present with anorexia, RLQ pain, fever, or leukocytosis.

Other Signs and Symptoms

A. Rigid abdomen
B. Changes in pulse (tachycardia), breathing (tachypnea), or skin temperature
C. Involuntary guarding
D. Rebound tenderness

Subjective Data

Evaluate for a "surgical abdomen," defined as a rapidly worsening prognosis in the absence of surgical intervention. Patients should not eat or drink while a diagnosis of a surgical abdomen remains under consideration. Once a surgical abdomen has been excluded, the remainder of the evaluation will be guided by the chronicity of symptoms along with the location of pain.

A. Review onset, duration, course, and quality of pain. Has pain ever occurred before? If so, what was the primary diagnosis? What was previous treatment, and was it effective?

B. Qualify the duration of pain in minutes, hours, days, weeks, or months. Does it interfere with sleep? Is there a pattern to the pain?

C. Have the patient rate the pain on a 10-point pain scale, with 0 being no pain and 10 being the worst pain the patient has ever felt.

D. Review the pattern of pain.
   1. Review aggravating factors.
   2. Review alleviating factors.
   3. Does the pain radiate?
   4. Does the pain have any relationship to food?

E. Questions specific to females:
   1. Determine the patient's last menstrual period (LMP) to rule out pregnancy.
   2. **What type of contraception is used? Specifically evaluate for an IUD.**
   3. Has she had a hysterectomy or tubal ligation?
   4. Does she have a recent history of dyspareunia or dysmenorrhea that suggests pelvic pathology?

F. Review current medications and drug history, especially antibiotic and laxative use. Patients taking corticosteroids may have a significant masking of pain.

G. Rule out abdominal trauma, motor vehicle accidents, falls, and assault.

H. Discuss bowel habits, including any changes, such as constipation or diarrhea, anorexia, food intolerance, nausea and vomiting, bloating.

I. Ask the patient about urinary frequency, urgency, dysuria, flank pain, and back pain. In males, ask about hesitancy, difficulty starting the urine stream, nocturia, low urinary volume, or lower abdominal distension (urinary retention).

Physical Examination

A. Check temperature, pulse, respirations, and blood pressure, including orthostatic BP.

B. Inspect
   1. Observe general appearance: Facial expressions (grimace during exam), walk, skin color and turgor, level of consciousness, and acuity level of pain.
   2. Inspect abdomen for surgical scars.
   3. Observe for any bruising or other signs of domestic violence in the "bathing suit" area: breasts, abdomen, or back that would be easily covered by clothes.

C. Auscultate
   1. Auscultate the abdomen for bowel sounds in all quadrants.
   2. Auscultate heart and lungs.

D. Palpate: Note guarding with exam.
   1. Palpate the abdomen.
      a. Ask the patient to bend his or her knees to help relax the abdominal wall musculature. Note any rebound tenderness. *Perform at*

the end of the exam because positive response produces pain and muscle spasm that can interfere with subsequent exam.
   b. Check for Murphy's sign, which is inspiratory arrest in response to RUQ palpation, seen with acute cholecystitis.
2. Palpate back; note CVA tenderness.
3. Check for rebound tenderness.
4. Check for obturator sign, or abdominal pain in response to passive internal rotation of right hip from 90° angle hip–knee flexion position. A positive sign indicates pain secondary to irritation of obturator muscle with inflamed appendix.
5. Assess psoas sign or increased abdominal pain occurring when the patient attempts to raise his or her right thigh against the pressure of your hand placed over his or her right knee. Pain is caused by inflammation of the psoas muscle in acute appendicitis.
6. Check for the Apley rule; the farther from the navel the pain, the more likely it is organic in origin.
7. Check for Rovsing's sign, or pain in the RLQ on palpation of the left side.
8. The location of the appendix and pain is altered during pregnancy (see Figure 13.1).

E. Percuss abdomen.
F. Perform rectal exam.

Diagnostic Tests

A. **Serum HCG: Pregnancy should be excluded in all women of childbearing age. Assume the woman is pregnant until proven otherwise.**
B. CBC with differential
C. C-reactive protein (CRP)

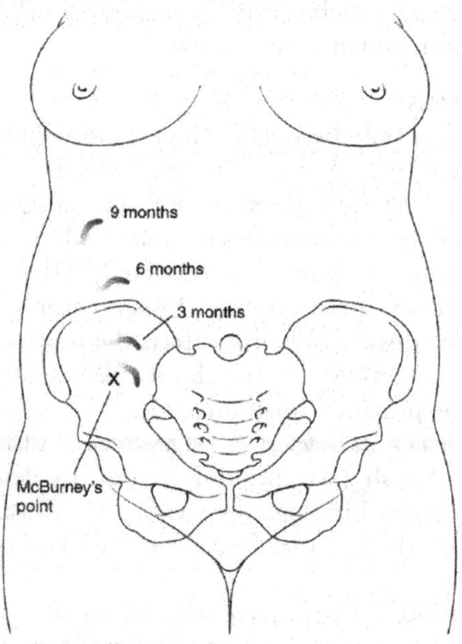

FIGURE 13.1 The position of the appendix alters during pregnancy, and so must the site of incision to gain access.

D. Urinalysis, to rule out urinary disorders
E. Abdominal ultrasonography; any person with trauma to abdomen should have abdominal ultrasound.
F. CT scan
G. Magnetic resonance imaging (MRI) may be used as an alternative diagnostic test in pregnancy to avoid exposure to ionizing radiation.
H. Guaiac stool for occult blood

Differential Diagnoses

The appendix has no fixed position. Duration of pain can help significantly in narrowing differential diagnosis. Nonspecific dysfunctional abdominal pain and psychogenic abdominal pain are diagnoses of exclusion.

A. Appendicitis
B. Regional enteritis
C. Leaking aneurysm
D. Ruptured ectopic pregnancy
E. Twisted ovarian cyst
F. PID
G. Mittelschmerz, or ovulatory bleeding or pain
H. Endometriosis
I. Ureteral calculi
J. Incarcerated, strangulated groin hernia
K. Meckel's diverticulitis
L. Abdominal wall hematoma
M. Bowel obstruction
N. Intestinal malrotation
O. Intussusception
P. Testicular torsion
Q. IBD/Crohn's
R. Parasites
S. IUD
T. Constipation

Plan

A. See the Section III Patient Teaching Guide for this chapter, "Abdominal Pain."
B. Medical and surgical management: Appendectomy may need to be performed.
C. Pharmaceutical therapy
   1. Antibiotics are currently used to treat uncomplicated, nonsurgical appendicitis; however, more studies are needed to determine the efficacy of antibiotic therapy alone.
   2. Do not give antipyretics to mask fever.
   3. Do not administer cathartics because they may cause rupture.

Follow-Up

A. Postoperative follow-up is with the surgeon.

Consultation/Referral

A. Physician consultation and possible emergency transport and hospitalization are often required.

Individual Considerations

A. Pregnancy
   1. Any abdominal pain or bleeding in the first 8 weeks after a missed menstrual period must be considered a symptom of possible *ectopic pregnancy*.
   2. The identification of intra-abdominal masses may be compromised by the enlarged uterus, but this problem may be partially obviated by examining the woman in the lateral position.
   3. The intestinal tract is progressively displaced upward, outward, and backward during pregnancy; bowel sounds are best heard lateral or superior to the uterus.

B. Adults
   1. Obesity distorts abdominal exam, making organ palpation or pelvic exam difficult.
   2. Immunocompromised patients are susceptive to infection. They may not exhibit the typical signs and symptoms of appendicitis; only mild tenderness on exam.
   3. The CT exam is useful in the immunocompromised patient for diagnosis.

C. Geriatrics
   1. The elderly tend to have a diminished inflammatory response, resulting in a less remarkable history and physical examination. Be aware of vague symptoms, such as milder pain, less pronounced fever, and leukocytosis with shift to left on differential.
   2. A redundant sigmoid colon may also cause right-sided pain from sigmoid disease.
   3. Prompt CT scanning is used for diagnosis and differential.

Celiac Disease

Definition

A. Celiac disease, previously known as celiac sprue, is an autoimmune disorder triggered by a well-defined environmental factor, gluten. Celiac disease is a permanent sensitivity to gluten, specifically; the people are unable to tolerate gliadin, the alcohol-soluble fraction of gluten. Three cereals contain gluten and are considered toxic for patients with celiac disease: wheat, rye, and barley. The disease primarily affects the small intestine. Onset of symptoms depends on the amount of gluten in the diet. Dietary nonadherence is the chief cause of persistent or recurrent symptoms (see Appendix B, Table B.6).

B. Celiac disease is one of the most common causes of chronic malabsorption as a result of injury to the small intestine with loss of absorptive surface area, reduction of digestive enzymes, and consequential impaired absorption of micronutrients such as fat-soluble vitamins, iron, and potentially vitamin B_{12} and folic acid.

C. Celiac disease is strongly associated with autoimmune conditions, including type 1 diabetes, Addison's disease, and thyroiditis as well as genetic syndromes, including Down syndrome, Williams syndrome, and Turner's syndrome. The complications from celiac disease include osteopenia, osteoporosis, infertility, short stature, delayed puberty, anemia, and GI malignancies and non-Hodgkin's lymphoma (NHL).

D. After GI symptoms, the second most common manifestation of celiac disease in patients with type 1 diabetes is diminished or impaired bone mineralization.

E. Celiac disease is the most common cause of steatorrhea in people older than 50 years of age and the second most common cause in people older than 65 years.

F. A substantial number of patients are misdiagnosed as having IBS for years prior to the diagnosis of celiac disease.

Incidence

A. Celiac disease can occur at any stage of life. Its prevalence is approximately 1% of the general population in North America. The highest incidence (5%) is noted in the Sub-Saharan African population. The true incidence is undetermined due to asymptomatic disease and underdiagnosis.

B. **Screening of the general population is not recommended.**

C. Newly diagnosed patients with celiac disease should inform their first-degree family members for their increased risk of celiac disease and the American College of Gastroenterology (ACG) recommendation for testing.

Pathogenesis

A. Interactions between gluten and immune and genetic factors result in celiac disease. Gluten is poorly digested. The enzyme tissue transglutaminase (tTG) is the autoantigen against which abnormal immune response is directed. The immune responses promote an inflammatory reaction. Celiac disease primarily affects the mucosal layer of the small intestine. The classic celiac lesion is noted in the proximal small intestine.

B. **A hallmark on histology is the presence of villous atrophy.** The Marsh Classification is used to describe the progressive histological stages of celiac disease. Marsh 1 and Marsh 2 may be seen in sow's and cow's milk allergies.

   Marsh 0: Preinfiltrative stage (normal)

   Marsh 1: Infiltrative lesion (increased intraepithelial lymphocytes)

Marsh 2: Hyperplastic lesion (type 1 plus hyperplastic crypts)

Marsh 3: Destructive lesion (type 2 plus villous atrophy of progressively more severe degrees [termed 3a, 3b, and 3c])

Marsh 4: (atrophic-hypoplastic) Total villous atrophy, crypt hypoplasia

Predisposing Factors

A. Female gender
B. May be precipitated by an infectious diarrheal episode or other intestinal disease (e.g., rotavirus)
C. Genetic disorders
    1. Down syndrome (8% to 12%)
    2. Type 1 diabetes (10%)
    3. Turner's syndrome (2% to 10%)
    4. Williams syndrome (8.2%)
D. Strong hereditary component (10% in first-degree relatives)
E. The introduction of gluten before 4 months of age is associated with an increased development of disease.
F. Autoimmune thyroid disorders (Hashimoto thyroiditis and Graves' disease)
G. Selective IgA deficiency

Common Complaints

A. Asymptomatic
B. Chronic diarrhea or explosive watery diarrhea
C. Foul-smelling voluminous stools
D. Anorexia
E. Abdominal distension
F. Abdominal pain
G. Poor weight gain or weight loss
H. Vomiting
I. Steatorrhea (malabsorption of ingested fat)

Other Symptoms

A. Behavioral changes, including irritability
B. Dehydration
C. Lethargy
D. Constipation
E. Failure to thrive (FTT)
F. Short stature and delayed puberty
G. Dermatitis herpetiformis
H. Arthritis
I. Seizures
J. Weakness and fatigue
K. Dental enamel hypoplasia of permanent teeth
L. Iron-deficiency anemia unresponsive to treatment
M. Bruising/bleeding tendency
N. Osteopenia/osteoporosis
O. Hair loss
P. Lactose intolerance
Q. Aphthous stomatitis

Subjective Data

A. Review the onset, duration, course, and type of symptoms.
B. Review the patient's weight history.
C. Evaluate family history for celiac disease or members with similar histories.
D. Review current medications and drug history, especially antibiotic, laxative, and herbal products.
E. Review bowel habits and note changes: Constipation, diarrhea, anorexia, and/or food intolerance.
F. Review the patient's tolerance to lactose products.

Physical Examination

A. Check vital signs, including height and weight. Follow serial changes in weight.
B. Inspect
    1. Observe general overall appearance.
    2. Oral examination to evaluate glossitis, dry mucosal membranes (dehydration), and the presence of oral aphthae.
    3. Examine the skin for the presence of dermatitis herpetiformis: A blistering rash involving the scalp, neck, elbows, knees, and buttocks.
    4. Evaluate the abdomen for the presence of bloating and protuberant "potbelly."
    5. Evaluate the patient's weight loss, including muscle wasting.
C. Auscultate
    1. Auscultate for bowel sounds in all four quadrants of the abdomen.
D. Percuss abdomen.
E. Palpate
    1. Palpate the abdomen for masses, rebound tenderness, and peritoneal signs.
        a. Before palpating the abdomen, ask the patient to bend his or her knees to help with relaxation of the wall musculature.
    2. Perform a rectal examination, including testing stool for occult blood.

Diagnostic Tests

The confirmation of a diagnosis of celiac disease is based on the combination of findings from the medical history, physical examination, serology, and upper endoscopy, with histological analysis of multiple biopsies of the duodenum. **All testing should be performed while patients are following a gluten-rich diet.**

A. **Endoscopy for duodenal biopsies is the standard and a critical component for diagnosing celiac disease.**
B. Screening and monitoring test for celiac disease (see Table 13.1 for celiac disease tests and possible results).
    1. Tissue transglutaminase antibody (tTG), IgA class
        a. Primary test ordered to screen for celiac disease
        b. Used for monitoring and evaluating the effectiveness of treatment
        c. Antibody levels should fall when gluten is removed from the diet

TABLE 13.1 What Does the Test Result Mean? Some Celiac Disease Tests and Positive Results

Anti-TTG Antibodies, IgA	Total IgA	Anti-TTG Antibodies, IgG	Anti-DGP, IgA	AGAs, IgG	Diagnosis
Positive	Normal				Presumptive celiac disease
Negative	Normal	Negative	Negative	Negative	Symptoms not likely due to celiac disease
Negative	Low	Positive	Negative	Positive	Possible celiac disease (false negative anti-tTG, IgA, and anti-DGP are due to a total IgA deficiency)
Negative	Normal	Negative	Positive	Positive/ negative	Possible celiac disease (may be seen in children younger than 3 years old)

2. Anti-tTG antibodies, immunoglobulin G (IgG)
3. Anti-tTG, IgG class
4. Deamidated gliadin peptide antibodies (anti-DGP, immunoglobulin A [IgA])
5. Antigliadin antibodies (AGAs) IgG (gliadin is a component of wheat storage protein gluten)
6. AGA IgA
7. IgA endomysial antibody (EMA)—less frequently ordered, measures same as the anti-tTG
8. Antireticulin antibody (ARA)—rarely ordered
9. Anti-F-actin-ordered if the disease has been diagnosed; evaluates the severity of intestinal damage. May be used for monitoring.

C. CBC and electrolytes
D. Aspartate transaminase (AST) and alanine transaminase (ALT) (liver enzymes normalize on a gluten-free diet)
E. Prothrombin time (PT) may be prolonged with malabsorption of vitamin K.
F. CRP
G. Erythrocyte sedimentation rate (ESR)
H. Total protein
I. Albumin
J. Calcium
K. Iron, transferrin and ferritin
L. Vitamin B_{12} and folate levels
M. Stool culture, ova, and parasites
N. Fecal fat
O. Bone density (bone mineral density improves on gluten-free diet)
P. Human leukocyte antigen (HLA) haplotypes
Q. Colonoscopy if bloody stools or symptoms of colitis
R. Sweat test to exclude cystic fibrosis (CF)
S. Other testing specific to nutritional deficiencies as needed (vitamin D, B_{12}, folate)
T. Radiograph, including barium swallow study with a small bowel followthrough, is usually nonspecific and is not indicated.

Differential Diagnoses

A. Celiac disease
B. FTT
C. Food allergies
D. IBD
   1. Crohn's disease (CD)
   2. Ulcerative colitis (UC)
E. Immunodeficiency disorders
F. Gastroenteritis (viral or bacterial)
G. Parasites
H. Fungal infection
I. IBS
J. Malabsorption
K. Lymphomas of the small intestine

Plan

A. Nutrition therapy is the only accepted treatment for celiac disease.
   1. Gluten-free dietary instructions should be given and reinforced.
   2. Reinforce the need to read all food labels.
   3. Stress that wheat-free is not the same as gluten-free.
   4. The gluten-free diet must continue throughout the patient's life span.
B. The ACG recommends a referral to a registered dietitian in order to receive a thorough nutritional assessment and education on a gluten-free diet. A gluten-free diet should be maintained for life. Nutritiguides applications are available from the iTunes Store for the iPhone and iPad and from the Google Store for Android products.
C. Genetic testing does not diagnose celiac disease.
D. Monitor for iron and vitamin deficiencies because substitute flours are not fortified with B vitamins. Supplement with iron, folate, and vitamin B_{12} as needed.
E. Screen for osteoporosis.
F. Keep a food/symptom diary in order to eliminate trigger foods. See Appendix B, Table B.6, "Examples

of Foods That Are Allowed and Avoided on a Gluten-Free Diet."

G. Gluten has been identified in dietary supplements, over-the-counter (OTC) medications, nonfood items such as lipstick and envelope adhesive, and in food items with gluten additives such as condiments. Gluten is also found in the fillers of pill capsules.

H. Gluten rechallenge is not generally recommended unless the diagnosis remains uncertain.
   1. The gluten rechallenge is not mandatory for patients with good improvement of symptoms.
   2. HLA-DQ2/DQ8 genotyping for genetic risk factors should be used to try to exclude celiac disease prior to a formal gluten challenge.

I. Pharmacology
   1. Vitamin and calcium supplements
   2. Bisphosphonates for osteoporosis
   3. Corticosteroids may be prescribed for rapid control of symptoms.

Follow-Up

A. After the diagnosis of celiac disease and a strict diet has been started, follow up in 4 to 8 weeks or earlier if the patient has other comorbidities.

B. The Celiac Disease Guideline Committee recommends the measurement of tTGA after 6 months of a gluten-free diet.

C. Newly diagnosed patients with celiac disease should undergo testing and treatment for micronutrient deficiencies. Deficiency testing should include, but not be limited to, iron, folic acid, vitamin D, and vitamin B_{12}.

D. Refer for dietary consultation with a nutritionist with experience in gluten-free diets.

E. Consider allergy testing.

Consultation/Referral

A. If the gluten-free diet fails or the patient experiences new symptoms, a systematic evaluation is required.

B. Endocrine consultation for patients with Hashimoto thyroiditis and celiac disease

Individual Considerations

A. Pregnancy: Women with untreated celiac disease are at risk for preterm birth, low-birth-weight babies, recurrent loss, and reduced fertility.

B. Geriatrics
   1. The elderly may present with nonspecific GI symptoms, abdominal discomfort, bloating, constipation, or dyspepsia.
   2. Diarrhea may be mild or intermittent in the elderly.
   3. Iron-deficiency anemia may also be a presenting symptom. Anemia is present in 60% to 80% of elderly patients with celiac disease.
   4. Up to 70% of adult and elderly patients with celiac disease have osteopenia and, therefore, are at increased risk for fractures.
   5. Ataxia and neuropathy are two main neurologic complications of celiac disease, placing patients at a higher risk for falls.
   6. Autoimmune thyroid disorders are common with elderly celiac patients. The majority present with hypothyroidism.
   7. The risk for NHL is increased in people with celiac disease age 50 years and older.

Resources

www.celiac.com

www.celiac.com: gluten-free recipes

www.celiac.org

www.glutenfreedrugs.com

The 2013 ACG Clinical Guideline: Diagnosis and Management of Celiac Disease is available at http://d2j7fjepcxuj0a.cloudfront.net/wp-content/uploads/2013/05/ACG_Guideline_CeliacDisease_May_2013.pdf

The Academy of Nutrition and Dietetic evidence-based guidelines for treatment of celiac disease is available at http://andevidencelibrary.com/topic.cfm?cat=3677&auth=1

Cholecystitis

Definition

A. Cholecystitis is the acute or chronic inflammation of the gallbladder. Acute cholecystitis has associated stone formation (cholelithiasis) in 90% of all cases, causing obstruction and inflammation. Biliary sludge is a feature of chronic cholecystitis.

B. Following a cholecystectomy, stones may recur in the bile duct.

Incidence

A. Gallbladder disease afflicts more than 20 million (10% to 20% of adults) in the United States. Most patients with an acute attack of cholecystitis have complete remission in 1 to 5 days; however, approximately 20% require surgical intervention. Mortality related to acute cholecystitis is 5% to 10%, with the highest risk for patients older than age 60. The most common complication is the development of gallbladder gangrene with the potential for subsequent perforation (2%). Gangrenous cholecystitis is most common in older patients, diabetics, or patients who delay treatment.

Pathogenesis

A. Cholecystitis occurs subsequent to bile stasis, bacterial infection, ischemia, or cystic obstruction by a gallstone. Acute cholecystitis is related to the

impaction of a calculus in the neck of the gallbladder in approximately 90% of cases. Spontaneous resolution may occur after the reestablishment of cystic duct patency.
B. *Escherichia coli* is the primary microorganism in 80% of cholecystitis infections.
C. Estrogen-induced alteration in bile salts may favor stone formation. Stones occur when cholesterol supersaturates the bile in the gallbladder and precipitates out of the bile. Cholesterol stones are the most common type of gallstones in the United States.
D. Pigment stones occur when free bilirubin combines with calcium. Pigment stones are found in patients with cirrhosis, hemolysis, and infections in the biliary tree.
E. Acalculous cholecystitis is associated with infection and local inflammation. Formation of gallstones is not necessary for the obstruction of the bile duct.

Predisposing Factors

A. Female gender
B. Sudden starvation/prolonged fasting
C. Medications
   1. Cholesterol-lowering drugs: Stone formation increases in users of cholesterol-lowering drugs, which are known to increase biliary cholesterol saturation.
   2. Thiazide diuretics
   3. Ceftriaxone
   4. Cyclosporine
   5. Opiate narcotic analgesics
   6. Estrogen usage (oral contraceptives [OCPs] and hormone replacement therapy [HRT]): Stone formation increases in users of contraceptives and estrogens, which are known to increase biliary cholesterol saturation.
   7. Octreotide
D. Bile acid malabsorption
E. Genetic predisposition: Native Americans and those of Chinese or Japanese descent have a high incidence.
F. Total parenteral nutrition (TPN)
G. Obesity
H. Status post–bariatric surgery. (Patients who have had either the Roux-en-Y or laparoscopic banding surgeries are at increased risk for gallstones.)
I. Pregnancy secondary to elevated progesterone
J. Increasing age
K. Hemolytic anemia
L. Diabetes
M. Hepatic cirrhosis
N. Biliary tree infections

Common Complaints

A. Abrupt, severe abdominal pain lasting 24 hours
B. Constant aching pain or gnawing pain in the RUQ, right subcostal region, with radiation to the back and right shoulder
C. Nausea and vomiting

Other Signs and Symptoms

A. Anorexia
B. Heartburn
C. Upper abdominal fullness
D. Biliary colic: Sudden onset of severe pain in the epigastrium or right hypochondrium that subsides relatively slowly. Tenderness may remain for days.
E. Fat intolerance
F. Fever (low-grade)
G. Mild jaundice (20%)
H. Complicated disease such as an abscess or perforation symptoms includes more severe localized persistent pain, tenderness, fever, chills, and leukocytosis.
I. Chronic diarrhea (4 to 10 bowel movements [BMs] every day for at least 3 months)

Subjective Data

A. Review the onset, location, duration, course, and quality of pain.
B. Use a pain-rating scale, such as a 10-point pain scale, with 0 being no pain and 10 being equivalent to the worst pain the patient has ever felt. Determine progression of the pain as well.
C. Review any alleviating factors, such as antacids, and any worsening factors, such as deep inspiration.
D. Review any pain radiating to the jaw, neck, shoulder, or arm.
E. Review onset of pain in relation to last meal and foods ingested.
F. Ask the patient about recurrent history of epigastric pain.
G. Obtain history and demographic data that may indicate the risk factors for biliary disease.
H. Review the date of the patient's LMP, and if she is pregnant, establish gestational age.

Physical Examination

A. Check temperature, pulse, respirations, and blood pressure. Tachycardia, increased fever and elevated WBC are markers of inflammatory disease.
B. Inspect: Observe general appearance, facial expressions, walk, skin color (15% have jaundice) and turgor, and grimace during exam. Overall appearance is generally unremarkable between attacks; ill appearance occurs during acute attack.
C. Auscultate
   1. Heart
   2. Lung fields
   3. Abdomen for bowel sounds in all four quadrants

D. Percuss abdomen.
E. Palpate
   1. Palpate the abdomen; check for tenderness in the RUQ, especially with inspiration; assess for guarding and rebound tenderness.
   2. Check Murphy's sign. Positive Murphy's sign is inspiratory arrest secondary to extreme tenderness when subhepatic area is palpated during deep inspiration.
F. Perform rectal exam, if indicated.

Diagnostic Tests

A. Laboratory tests
   1. Amylase
   2. CBC with differential
   3. Alkaline phosphate
   4. Bilirubin
   5. AST
   6. ALT
   7. Urinalysis to rule out pyelonephritis and renal calculi
   8. Pregnancy test if childbearing age
   9. Stool for occult blood to rule out bleeding
B. Radiography
   1. **Ultrasonography: Study of choice and can often establish the diagnosis.**
   2. Cholescintigraphy (hepatobiliary [HIDA]) scan is indicated if the diagnosis is uncertain after an ultrasound.
   3. Magnetic resonance (MR) cholangiography
   4. CT scan
   5. Endoscopic retrograde choliangiopancreatography (ERCP) and percutaneous transhepatic cholangiography (PTC)
   6. Chest radiography to rule out pneumonia
C. EKG to rule out MI

Differential Diagnoses

A. Acute cholecystitis
B. Biliary colic
C. Acute pancreatitis
D. Appendicitis
E. PUD/perforation
F. Acute hepatitis
G. Pneumonia or pleurisy
H. MI
I. Renal calculi
J. Gastroesophageal reflux disease (GERD)
K. Pregnancy: Urolithiasis, pyelonephritis

Plan

A. General interventions: Patients with a single episode of biliary colic are reasonable candidates for expectant management, as long as they continue to be free of recurrent pain.
B. Patient teaching
   1. No activity restriction is required.
   2. Treatment depends on acuteness of attack. Heat may be used as needed for pain. If pain continues to worsen, have the patient contact his or her health care provider. Hospitalization and/or surgery may be required depending on the severity of the attack.
C. Dietary management
   1. Counsel the patient to avoid fatty foods.
   2. Encourage the patient to avoid fasting and starvation diets, which make the bile even more lithogenic.
D. Surgical management
   1. Cholecystectomy may be recommended for symptomatic patients. **The standard of care is the laparoscopic cholecystectomy.** Conversion from a laparoscopic procedure to an open surgical procedure is approximately 5%.
   2. Conservative treatment includes IV antibiotics, bowel rest, and an interventional cholecystectomy 6 to 8 weeks later.
   3. A WBC count above 15,000 cells/μL indicates a nonresolving inflammation and is a predictor of treatment failure after 24 to 48 hours of conservative observation. Other predictive factors of failed conservative treatment include:
      a. Age greater than 70 years
      b. Diabetes
      c. Distended gallbladder
   4. Percutaneous drainage (cholecystostomy) is reserved for patients who fail conservative treatment, or as a salvage procedure for high-risk patients.
   5. Extracorporeal shockwave lithotripsy
E. Pharmaceutical therapy
   1. Acetaminophen (Tylenol) may be used as needed for pain.
   2. Anticholinergics are not helpful.
   3. Oral bile acid therapy decreases the amount of cholesterol produced by the liver and absorbed by the intestines. Not for calcified radio-opaque or radiolucent bile pigment stones or urgent need for surgery.
      a. Actigall (Ursodiol)
         i. Dissolution of stones: 8 to 10 mg/kg/d in two to three divided doses
         ii. Prevention therapy 300 mg twice a day
      b. Urso (Ursodiol) 250 mg tablets also available as Urso Forte 500 mg tablets
         i. 13 to 15 mg/kg/d in two to four divided doses

Follow-Up

A. See the patient at next pain attack to reevaluate.
B. Surgical follow-up in 2 weeks

C. Patients on oral bile-acid therapy should follow-up with serial ultrasound at 6 and 12 months, and 1 to 3 months after dissolution of the stone. AST and ALT should be measured at the start of therapy and every 6 months thereafter.

Consultation/Referral

A. For acute attack, consult a physician for possible surgical consultation referral.
B. Refer the patient for elective cholecystectomy when he or she has documented gallstones and recurrent biliary colic or a history of complications from gallstone disease, such as pancreatitis.
C. Refer to a gastroenterologist for consideration of ERCP. The ERCP is the most common procedure for detecting and managing bile-duct stones and may be performed before, during, or after gallbladder removal.

Individual Considerations

A. Pregnancy
   1. RUQ pain in pregnancy differential includes preeclampsia, pancreatitis, and appendicitis.
   2. In the absence of pancreatitis, maternal mortality should be rare, and fetal loss is generally estimated to be no more than 5%. However, if secondary pancreatitis is present, maternal mortality is 15%, and fetal loss is reported as high as 60%.
B. Geriatrics
   1. Signs and symptoms may be nonspecific and vague.
   2. Localized tenderness may be the only presenting sign.
   3. The response of Murphy's sign may be diminished in the elderly.
   4. Persistent elevated WBC more than 15,000 suggests refractory disease and should play a central role in clinical follow-up for elderly patients with acute cholecystitis.
   5. Early cholecystectomy is advocated for elderly patients with gallstone disease. The most important risk factor for postoperative morbidity and mortality is advanced age.
   6. Gallstones occur in nearly 25% of women in the United States by the age of 60 and as many as 50% by age 75. Only about 20% of men have gallstones by their 70s.

Colorectal Cancer Screening

Definition

A. Screening for colorectal cancer has increased early detection and the ability for early intervention of premalignant localized cancer. There are multiple screening guidelines; the U.S. Preventive Services Task Force (USPSTF) recommendations are presented in this review. Screening is done for men and women between the ages of 50 and 75 years. There are two categories of screening:
   1. Stool-based testing
   2. Endoscopic and radiologic testing

Incidence

A. In the United States, colorectal cancer is the second leading cause of cancer-related death in both men and women.
B. Americans have a 5% lifetime risk of colorectal cancer.
C. Colorectal cancer is rare before age 40 years.
D. 90% of the cases of colorectal cancer occur after 50 years.
E. Up to 20% of colorectal cancer in the United States is associated with smoking.
F. Obesity is associated with colon cancer but not increases in rectal cancer. Abdominal obesity is a stronger risk factor than truncal obesity or body mass index (BMI).

Pathogenesis

A. The usual pathogenesis is an adenomatous polyp that grows slowly, followed by dysplasia and final cancerous cells.

Predisposing Factors

A. Age: 50 years and older
B. African American (screening is recommended at age 45)
C. IBD (CD and UC)
D. Family history/genetic
   1. Familial adenomatous polyposis (FAP)
   2. Nonpolyposis colorectal cancer
E. Smoking
F. Obesity
G. Diet high in red meat and fats

Common Complaints

A. Asymptomatic screening

Subjective Data

A. Review the patient's age and risk factors to discuss screening for colorectal cancer.
B. Review family history of colorectal cancer.
C. Review smoking history.
D. Review the patient's diet evaluating red meat, processed meats, and lack of grains, fruits, and vegetables.
E. Review all medications currently being taken, including OTC and herbal products.

Physical Examination

A. Examinations are not required for discussion on colorectal screening testing.
B. A physical examination and vital signs should be taken as indicated for other presenting complaints.

Diagnostic Tests

A. Refer to Chapter 2, Table 2.4, Screening for Colorectal Cancer for testing by age groups
B. Stool-based testing
  1. Guaiac-based fecal occult blood test (FOBT)
  2. **Fecal immunochemical test (FIT) is replacing the FOBT as the preferred cancer detection test.**
  3. Stool DNA (SDNA) panel
C. Endoscopic and radiological
  1. Flexible sigmoidoscopy
  2. **Colonoscopy: The ACG recommends the colonoscopy as the preferred strategy for screening.**
  3. **Double-contrast barium enema (DCBE): The ACG recommends the DCBE as a screening test; however, it has limited effectiveness for polyp detection.**
  4. Computed tomography colonography (CTC)

Differential Diagnosis

A. None related to screening

Plan

A. Patient teaching
  1. Educate patient about modifying controllable risk factors with diet, exercise, and stopping smoking.
  2. Discuss the procedures and the preparation needed for each test.
B. Pharmaceutical therapy
  1. Bowel prep for flexible sigmoidoscopy and colonoscopy depends on the test, patient's age, and other comorbidities.

Follow-Up

A. Follow-up and consultations are determined by patient's needs, severity, and whether complications are present.
B. Patients with classic FAP (> 100 adenomas) should be advised to have genetic counseling
C. **NSAIDs have been associated with a decrease in the risk of developing colorectal cancer. There is insufficient evidence to recommend the use of NSAIDs as a prevention strategy.**

Consultation/Referral

A. Refer to a gastroenterologist and/or surgeon as indicated.

Individual Considerations

A. Geriatrics
  1. Screening after age 75 years should be made on and individual basis.
  2. Medicare Part B covers several colorectal screening tests.
    a. Medicare covers a BE when used instead of a flexible sigmoidoscopy or colonoscopy once every 48 months. Coverage every 24 months if 50 years or older and at high risk for colorectal cancer.
    b. Colonoscopy is covered every 24 months if at high risk for colorectal cancer. If not at high risk, Medicare covers the colonoscopy once every 10 years (120 months), or 48 months after a previous flexible sigmoidoscopy.
  3. FOBT is covered by Medicare once every 12 months for those 50 years of age or older.
  4. Flexible sigmoidoscopy is covered by Medicare every 48 months for most people older than age 50. If not at high risk, Medicare covers the flexible sigmoidoscopy every 10 years after a previous screening colonoscopy.

Resources

www.cdc.gov/cancer/colorectal/pdf/SFL_inserts_screening.pdf CDC website—Screening Tests At-a-Glance includes the 2008 Screening for Colorectal Cancer from the USPTF website

www.cancer.gov/cancertopics/pdq/treatment/rectal/HealthProfessional National Cancer Institute at the National Institutes of Health Rectal Cancer Treatment (PDQ®)

www.cancer.gov/cancertopics/types/colon-and-rectal National Cancer Institutes at the National Institutes of Health Colon and Rectal Cancer

Medicare.gov Your Medicare Care Colorectal Cancer screenings. Retrieved from http://www.medicare.gov/coverage/colorectal-cancer-screenings.html

National Cancer Institute. Tests to detect colorectal cancer and polyps. Retrieved from http://www.cancer.gov/cancertopics/factsheet/Detection/colorectal-screening

National Comprehensive Cancer Network website http://www.nccn.org/professionals/physician_gls/f_guidelines_nojava.asp

Constipation

Definition

A. Constipation means infrequent and difficult defecation of hard stools, and a sensation of incomplete evacuation or straining. Constipation may also refer to a decrease in the volume or weight of stool, and the need for enemas, suppositories, or laxatives to maintain bowel regularity. Constipation is a symptom, not a disease.
B. The lower limit of normal stool frequency is three BMs a week. The Rome consensus criterion defines constipation as two or fewer stools weekly, lumpy/hard stools, straining, sensation of incomplete evacuation/obstruction or blockage, and/or the need for digital removal of stool.
C. Classification of constipation includes:
  1. Normal-transit constipation (most common)
  2. Functional constipation (slow transit)
  3. IBS (constipation dominant)
  4. Outlet obstruction (sudden onset)
  5. Defecatory disorders

Incidence

A. The incidence of constipation is unknown due to frequent self-treatment. Constipation is commonly self-reported. Constipation occurs in more than 50% of patients with colorectal cancers; it is usually a symptom of advanced disease, but it may be the presenting complaint.

Pathogenesis

A. Constipation can be caused by an alteration of the filling of the rectum by colonic transportation and/or reflex defecation of stool.
B. Lack of exercise and prolonged bed rest decreases propulsion of bowel contents.
C. During pregnancy, progesterone has a relaxing effect on the muscles of the GI tract and causes a decrease in peristalsis. The compression of the intestines by the enlarging uterus causes constipation during pregnancy.
D. Habitual use of laxatives is associated with impaired motor activity and has the potential of producing hypokalemia.
E. Hypokalemia can produce a generalized ileus and is most often seen in patients who take diuretics.
F. Psychiatric disease and psychosocial distress have important roles. The exact mechanisms by which emotional difficulties lead to constipation remain unclear, but their contribution is widely recognized.
G. Drugs (see Table 13.2).

Predisposing Factors

A. Insufficient nutrition
   1. Low-fiber diet
   2. Low-fluid intake
B. Neurologic causes
   1. Spinal cord injury
   2. Parkinson's disease
   3. Multiple sclerosis
   4. Aganglionosis (Hirschsprung's disease)
   5. Sacral nerve trauma/tumor
C. Sedentary lifestyle
D. Laxative abuse
E. Travel
F. Ignoring urge to defecate
G. Drug use (individual medications and polypharmacy)
H. Pregnancy, especially third trimester
I. Psychosocial problems
   1. Depression
   2. Sexual abuse
   3. Unusual attitudes to food and bowel function
   4. Obsessive/compulsive
J. Extremes of ages: Infants and geriatrics
K. Hypothyroidism
L. Colorectal cancer
M. IBS
N. Pelvic floor disorders
   1. Impaired function of the pelvic floor and/or external sphincter
   2. Pelvic floor obstruction
   3. Rectal prolapse
   4. Enterocele and/or rectocele
   5. Rectal intussusception

Common Complaints

A. Hard, infrequent stools
B. Straining
C. Inability to defecate when desired
D. Need for digital manipulation to facilitate evacuation

Other Signs and Symptoms

A. Hard, pebbly, rocklike stools
B. Painful defecation
C. Abdominal pain
D. Weight loss
E. Blood in stools

Potential Complications

A. A rectal prolapse of the mucosa is pink and looks like a doughnut or rosette. Complete prolapse involving the muscular wall is larger and red, and it has circular folds.

Subjective Data

A. Review the onset, duration, and course of symptoms.
   1. Is constipation a chronic or acute problem?

TABLE 13.2 Drugs and Classifications That Cause and Increase Constipation

Anticholinergics (atropine, antidepressants, neuroleptics, antiparkinsonian drugs, antispasmodics)	Opiates
Antipsychotics	Cholestyramine (binds bile salts)
Anticonvulsants	Antacids (aluminum hydroxide and calcium carbonate)
Antihistamines	Iron supplements
Antihypertensives (calcium channel blockers, clonidine, hydralazine, monoamine inhibitors oxidase [MOAI], methyldopa)	Nonsteroidal anti-inflammatory drugs (NSAIDs)
Diuretics	Ganglionic blockers

2. If there has been a change in bowel habits, was it gradual or sudden?
3. What feature does the patient rate most distressing?

B. Review bowel habits.
1. Does the patient have a regular time for defecation?
2. Review size, color, consistency, and frequency of stools.
3. Is there any blood?
4. Are there any periods of diarrhea?
5. How often are laxatives being used, and what doses?
6. Are suppositories and enemas also required?
7. Does the patient have the urge to defecate?
8. Does the patient have a sensation of incomplete evacuation?
9. Does the patient need to digitally remove stool?

C. Review the patient's daily diet and fluid intake. Has there been any dietary change?
D. Review the patient's medication history: Prescription and OTC (refer to Table 13.2).
E. Review the patient's daily physical activity.
F. Review the patient's psychosocial history of stress, depression, anxiety, and coping mechanisms.
G. Review the patient's other health problems such as diabetes, depression, hypothyroidism, and hypercalcemia.
H. Review family history of constipation and colorectal cancer.
I. Review surgical history.

Physical Examination

A. Check pulse, respirations, blood pressure, and weight. Check temperature if indicated.
B. Inspect
1. General overall assessment of nutritional status
2. Examine the skin, especially the rectum, for pallor and signs of dehydration and hypothyroidism.
3. Evaluate for the presence of hernias.
4. Inspect anus, including the position, presence of perianal erythema, hemorrhoids, and skin tags.
5. Observe for signs of fecal soiling.
6. Examine the lower back to rule out spinal lesions—hairy or hyperpigmented patches, gluteal fold asymmetry, cutaneous dimples, sinus tracts, and lipomas.
7. The American Gastroenterology Association (AGA) notes that the patient should be in the left lateral position with the buttocks separated to evaluate.
   a. Observe the descent of the perineum during simulated bowel evacuation.
   b. Observe the elevation during a squeeze aimed at retention of stool.
   c. During the simulated defecation, the anal verge should be observed for any patulous opening or prolapse of anorectal mucosa.

C. Auscultate: Auscultate all four abdominal quadrants for bowel sounds. Bowel sounds may be high-pitched or absent.
D. Percuss: Percuss the abdomen.
E. Palpate
1. Palpate the abdomen for masses, tenderness, distension, and fecal mass.
2. Palpate the liver and spleen.

F. Digital rectal exam
1. Examine the rectum for masses, hemorrhoids, fissures, fistula, prolapse, inflammation, and anal warts.
2. Evaluate for impaction, hard stool in ampulla.
3. Perform an anal "wink" reflex test by a light pinprick or scratch.
4. Evaluate sphincter tone.
   a. Disordered innervation of the anus is indicated by finding that the anal canal opens wide when the puborectalis muscle is pulled posteriorly.
   b. Evaluate the resting tone of the sphincter and squeezing effort.
   c. Instruct the patient to "expel the examination finger" to evaluate the force of expulsion.

G. Perform a neurologic examination for tone, strength, and reflexes to search for focal deficits and delayed relaxation phase of the ankle jerks, suggestive of hypothyroidism.
H. Perform pelvic examination to evaluate a prolapse or rectocele. Evaluate when the patient is at rest and with straining.
I. Perform mental status examination, checking for signs of depression and somatization.

Diagnostic Studies

A. No tests are required for common constipation.
B. Tests to rule out differential diagnoses
1. CBC
2. Thyroid studies
3. Potassium and calcium. **Patients taking diuretics should have serum potassium checked. Hypokalemia may reduce bowel contractility and produce an ileus.**
4. Serum glucose to rule out diabetes
5. Barium enema (BE) to evaluate megacolon and redundant sigmoid colon.
6. Flexible sigmoid
7. Colonoscopy (especially if the patient is older than 50 or has had abrupt onset of constipation)
8. CT colonography

9. Stool for occult blood
10. Anorectal function tests if there is no response to a trial of laxatives
    a. Manometry
    b. Electromyography (EMG)

Differential Diagnoses

A. Constipation
B. Intestinal obstruction: Acute onset of constipation requires ruling out an ileus, especially when accompanied by abdominal discomfort.
C. Hypothyroidism
D. Psychosocial dysfunction
E. Fecal impaction
F. Neurologic disorders
G. Multiple sclerosis
H. Spinal cord injury
I. Cancer
J. Drug use
K. CD: Constipation is often the presenting complaint in CD.
L. Diabetes (chronic dysmotility)
M. IBS or constipation

Plan

A. Patient teaching
    1. See the Section III Patient Teaching Guide for this chapter, "Tips to Relieve Constipation."
    2. Encourage the patient to exercise. Both exercise and dietary fiber stimulate the natural wavelike contraction of the colon that triggers the urge to defecate.
    3. Reassure the patient that recommended dietary changes and exercise help with constipation.
    4. Warn chronic laxative users that it may take 4 to 6 weeks before spontaneous BMs return.
    5. Teach the patient regarding potential complications of long-term constipation.
    6. Ask the patient to keep a stool diary to bring to his or her next appointment. (Refer to the Patient Teaching Guide for this chapter "Fetal Incontinence," Table III.3.)
B. Dietary management: See Appendix B.
C. Surgical and medical management
    1. Treatment of constipation is symptomatic and should begin with lifestyle and dietary changes.
    2. Evaluate and stop medications, if possible, that cause constipation.
    3. Mineral oil, also known as liquid paraffin, should be used with caution if the patient is at risk for aspiration or accidental inhalation secondary to the risk of aspiration pneumonia or mineral oil interacts with fat-soluble vitamins and anticoagulants.
    4. Fecal impaction may require enemas or manual removal to relieve the situation. Enemas should not be given routinely to treat constipation because they disrupt normal defecation reflexes and the patient becomes dependent. Disimpaction by enemas treatment includes three enemas per day:
        a. The first enema of the day includes the use of a phosphate-based enema.
            i. Patients older than 12 years: One adult phosphate-based enema, plus 1 L of saline solution.
        b. The second and third enema of the day include only the saline solution and no phosphate-based enema.
        c. **Patients should never receive more than 1 phosphate enema per day because of the risk of phosphate intoxication, hypoglycemia, and hyponatremia.**
    5. Pelvic floor physiotherapy may be offered. The pelvic floor retraining involves teaching the patient to relax his or her pelvic floor muscles during straining and to correlate relaxation and pushing to achieve defecation.
    6. Biofeedback has been effective for short-term treatment of intractable constipation and for the treatment of fecal incontinence (FI). Biofeedback has been shown to improve rectoanal coordination during defecation and symptoms of constipating despite reduced laxative use.
    7. Manual removal of fecal impaction can stimulate the vagus nerve and cause syncope and tachycardia. It is contraindicated in the following conditions:
        a. Pregnancy
        b. After genitourinary, rectal, perineal, abdominal, or gynecologic surgery
        c. MI, coronary insufficiency, pulmonary embolus, CHF, or heart block
        d. GI or vaginal bleeding
        e. Blood dyscrasias or bleeding disorders
        f. Hemorrhoids, fissures, and rectal polyps
D. Pharmaceutical therapy
    1. Bulk-forming agents (see Table 13.3) decrease abdominal pain and improve stool consistency. These should be used if an increase in dietary fiber does not work. They act by causing retention of fluid and increasing fecal mass. They must be taken with plenty of fluids to prevent formation of an obstructing bolus. Flatulence and abdominal distension may occur, but long-term use is safe.
    2. Stimulant laxatives (see Table 13.3) act by directly stimulating the colonic nerves. Suppositories are faster (20–60 minutes) versus oral laxatives (8–12 hours).

TABLE 13.3 Laxatives

Bulk laxatives	Psyllium (Konsyl, Metamucil) Polycarbophil
Saline laxatives	Methylcellulose (Citrucel)
	Calcium polycarbophil (FiberCon)
	Wheat dextrin (Benefiber)
	Magnesium hydroxide (Milk of Magnesia)
Lubricating agents (Emollient)	Magnesium citrate
	Mineral oil
Stimulant laxatives	Docusate
	Bile acids
	Bisacodyl (Dulcolax)
	Castor oil
	Senna
	Cascara
	Aloes
	Rhubarb
	Ex-Lax
	Senokot
Osmotic agents	Magnesium and phosphate salts
	Lactulose (Kristalose)
	Sorbitol
	Polyethylene glycol (Colyte, Glycolax, Miralax)
	Glycerin suppositories

3. Osmotic laxatives (see Table 13.3) act by retaining fluid in the bowel by osmosis, changing the water distribution in the feces. Good hydration is important.
4. When severe depression requires the use of antidepressants, the least constipating agent should be selected (i.e., one with minimal anticholinergic activity).
5. Treat other identified causes, for example, hypothyroidism.
6. The treatment for IBS-constipation is discussed later in this chapter.

Follow-Up

A. Repeat assessment in 4 to 6 weeks. Ask the patient to keep a stool diary and bring it in for subsequent appointments.

B. If there is no evidence of obstruction, anemia, or occult blood loss, follow the patient expectantly for a few weeks on a conservative program that includes increased dietary fiber and increased exercise, and follow stool guaiac.

C. Failure to improve may indicate a serious underlying cause and need for referral.

Consultation/Referral

A. Consider consultations with a gastroenterologist (adult), gynecologist, or psychologist/psychiatrist as indicated.

B. Surgical consultation may be required for slow transit constipation. Total colectomy with ileorectal anastomosis may be required when there is failure of aggressive, prolonged trials of laxatives, fiber, and prokinetic agents.

Individual Considerations

A. Pregnancy
1. Constipation is very common in pregnancy secondary to progesterone and the enlarging uterus (see "Pathogenesis").
2. Constipation that results from iron supplementation can be avoided by increasing the intake of fluid and high-fiber foods, and increasing physical activity such as walking.
3. Bulking agents and lactulose will not enter breast milk. Senna, in large doses, will enter breast milk and may cause diarrhea and colic in infants.

B. Adults
1. The most common cause of chronic constipation in adults is failure to initiate defecation.
2. Diabetics should avoid stimulant laxatives such as lactulose and sorbitol. Their metabolites may influence blood glucose levels.

C. Geriatrics
1. Constipation in old people is not a result of aging; it is usually related to an increase in constipating factors such as chronic illnesses, immobility, dietary factors, medications, neurologic factors, and psychiatric conditions. **Acute onset of constipation is considered a red flag in the geriatric population.**
2. An important diagnostic concern in the elderly is the possibility of constipation being due to a colonic neoplasm. More than 25% of patients with colorectal carcinomas present with constipation.
3. Check for a fecal impaction, especially in elderly patients with a history of chronic constipation. Fecal impaction ranks as one of the major sources of anorectal discomfort among the elderly and bedridden. Chronic, incomplete evacuation leads to formation of an obstructing bolus of desiccated hard stool in the rectum.
4. Diarrhea rather than constipation is sometimes the only complaint because of the collection of liquid stool distending the proximal colon and passing around the obstructing bolus.

Resource

Rome Foundation: http://romecriteria.org/criteria

Crohn's Disease

Definition

A. Crohn's disease (CD) is a chronic IBD of the GI tract that produces ulceration, fibrosis, and malabsorption. CD can involve any segment of the GI tract from the mouth to the anus; the terminal ileum and colon are the most common sites.
   1. In 2003 CD was subclassified based on age, location (ileal, colonic, ileocolonic, or upper GI), and clinical presentation (nonstricturing/nonpenetrating to penetrating) using the Montreal classification.
   2. Elderly patients with IBD can be subdivided into two groups.
      a. Elderly patients with onset of IBD at a late age (late-onset IBD)
      b. Elderly patients with long-standing IBD; first diagnosed as having IBD at a younger age (long-standing IBD)

B. The disease is chronic, relapsing, and incurable. CD is characterized by episodes of remission and exacerbation. The most frequent cause of death in persons with IBD is the primary disease, followed by malignancy and thromboembolic disease. In most cases, symptoms correspond well with the degree of inflammation present. The diagnosis is usually established with endoscopic finding in a patient with a compatible clinical history. Objective evidence for disease activity should be sought before administering medication that may have significant adverse effects.

C. More than 70% of patients with CD undergo surgery within 20 years of the diagnosis. Indications for surgery include stricture, intractable or fulminant disease, anorectal disease, and intra-abdominal abscess. Surgical procedures include bowel resection and ileal pouch–anal anastomosis (IPAA). Approximately 30% of patients who have surgery for CD have a recurrence within 3 years, and up to 60% will have a recurrence within 10 years.

D. The lifetime risk of fistula development is 20% to 40%.

E. The incidence of adenocarcinoma in patients with CD is higher than in the general population. Lymphoma is also increased, especially for patients with IBD treated with azathioprine (AZA) (6-mercaptopurine [6-MP]).

Incidence

A. The incidence rate ranges from 3.1 cases per 100,000 to 20.2 cases per 100,000. An estimated 1 to 2 million people in the United States have UC or CD. The incidence of IBD has been reported to be highest in Jewish populations. IBD is very prevalent among the American Jewish population—four to five times that of the general population.

B. The peak incidence of CD is most common in late adolescence to the third decade of life: elderly persons aged 70 to 80 years. Ten percent to 15% of cases of IBD are diagnosed in patients older than 60 years of age. CD may involve the entire GI tract; note the incidence according to the location.
   1. 80% have small bowel involvement, usually in the distal ileum. In severe cases of ileitis, complications may include fistulas or an abscess in the RLQ of the abdomen.
   2. 50% have ileocolitis (involving both the ileum and colon). This type is associated with significant weight loss.
   3. 20% have disease limited to the colon, with roughly one-half having sparing of the rectum.
   4. A small percentage has predominant involvement of the mouth (aphthous ulcers) or gastroduodenal area; fewer have involvement of the esophagus (odynophagia and dysphagia) and proximal small bowel.
   5. One third have perianal disease (perianal pain, drainage from large skin tags, anal fissures, perirectal abscesses, and anorectal fistulae).
   6. 15% to 20% have arthralgias. Arthritis is the most common complication.

Pathogenesis

Pathogenesis is unknown. The common end pathway is inflammation of the mucosal lining of the intestinal tract, causing ulceration, edema, bleeding, and fluid and electrolyte loss. Speculation for the pathogenesis includes:

A. Pathogenic organism (remains unidentified)
B. Immunologic response
C. Autoimmune process
D. Potential genes linked to IBD
   1. Chromosome 16 (*IBD1* gene).
   2. *CARD15* gene, which is noted to be a susceptibility gene for CD
   3. Susceptibility genes on chromosomes 5 (5q31) and 6 (6p21 and 19p)

Predisposing Factors

A. Age between 15 and 35 years
B. Genetic predisposition/family history of CD
   1. First-degree relatives 5- to 20-fold increased risk
   2. 70% incidence in identical twins versus 5% to 10% in nonidentical twins
   3. Jewish populations
C. Smoking (increased risk for CD but reduces risk in UC)

Common Complaints

The following cardinal symptoms occur in about 80% of patients.

A. Chronic or nocturnal diarrhea
B. Abdominal pain, the classic location being in the RLQ (appendicitis like)
C. Fatigue, commonly related to pain, inflammation, and anemia

Other Signs and Symptoms

Symptoms vary, depending on the location of the intestinal tract and extent of disease:

A. Constipation: Early sign
B. Weight loss
C. Abdominal mass
D. Cramping with BM
E. Rectal bleeding or blood in stools
F. Perianal discomfort or soft or semiliquid irritating rectal discharge
G. Vomiting
H. Low-grade fever
I. Folate deficiency
J. Anorexia
K. Fissures and fistulas, abscesses sometimes extending to skin
L. Extraintestinal symptoms
   1. Erythema nodosum (correlates well with the activity of disease)
   2. Inflammation of the eyes
   3. Inflammation of the skin
M. Urgent need to move bowels
N. Loss of normal menstrual cycle

Subjective Data

A. Ask about onset, duration, and course of symptoms. Have any of the presenting symptoms occurred at any time in the past (flares of CD may have gone undiagnosed in the past)?
B. Review the patient's history and extent of diarrhea, including frequency, consistency, color, quantity, and odor of stools. Evaluate if there is blood, mucus, pus, or food particles in the stools.
C. Inquire about recent travel to foreign countries.
D. Ask the patient if diarrhea represents a change in bowel habits. Is there nocturnal diarrhea?
E. Ask the patient what makes the diarrhea worse or better.
F. Inquire about previous GI surgery.
G. Review the patient's usual weight and any history of weight loss. If weight loss has occurred, how many pounds? How is the patient's appetite?
H. Review family history of CD, colon cancer, UC, and malabsorption syndrome.
I. How has the duration of current complaints affected the patient's work or usual social activities?
J. Review for duration and extraintestinal symptoms, including:
   1. Urinary complications: Renal calculi
   2. Sclerosing cholangitis: Fatigue and jaundice
   3. Skin diseases
      a. Erythema nodosum: Painful, tender, raised, purple lesion on the tibia
      b. Pyoderma gangrenosum: Inflamed patch of skin that has progressed to ulceration
      c. Herpetic lesions related to immune suppression
   4. Arthritic symptoms
K. Review medications, especially antibiotics and NSAIDs.
L. Review the patient's current tobacco/cigarette use.

Physical Examination

A. Check temperature, pulse, respirations, blood pressure, and weight. Record serial weights.
B. Inspect
   1. Observe general appearance, noting pallor, wasting, apathetic appearance, ecchymosis, skin ulcerations, jaundice, and signs of Kaposi's sarcoma.
   2. Inspect the head and neck for aphthous ulcers, glossitis, stomatitis, and poor dentition.
   3. Inspect the abdomen for surgical scars.
   4. Order eye examination for uveitis.
   5. Inspect joints for warmth and redness.
C. Auscultate the abdomen in all quadrants for altered bowel sounds (obstruction).
D. Palpate
   1. Palpate the neck for goiter and lymphadenopathy.
   2. Palpate the abdomen for distension, ascites, tenderness rebound, guarding, and masses.
   3. Palpate for hepatomegaly in RLQ.
   4. Palpate the joints for tenderness.
E. Rectal exam
   1. Check anal sphincter for tags, control, and discharge.
   2. Palpate for masses, fissures, fistulas, and inflammation.
   3. Perform digital rectal examination to assess for anal strictures and rectal mass.
F. Neurologic exam: Assess for signs of vitamin B_{12} deficiency, including tingling sensation and numbness in hands or feet.

Diagnostic Tests

A. Laboratory tests
   1. CBC with differential
   2. Electrolytes and albumin
   3. ESR
   4. Serum cobalamin (vitamin B_{12})
   5. Serum iron studies
   6. Folate

7. Liver enzymes and functioning tests (international normalized ratio [INR]) and bilirubin
8. HIV
9. Celiac antibody testing should be considered.
10. Thiopurine methyltransferase (TPMT) activity should be assessed before AZA or mercaptopurine.

B. Stool studies
1. Guaiac
2. Stool culture
3. *Clostridium difficile* toxin assay
4. Ova and parasites

C. Imaging
1. Abdominal flat plate
2. BE
   a. Classic "string sign": Narrow band of barium flowing through an inflamed or scarred area in terminal ileum; differentiates CD from UC
   b. "Rectal sparing": Suggests CD in the presence of inflammatory changes in other parts of the colon
   c. "Thumbprinting": Indicates mucosal inflammation (may be seen on flat plate of abdomen)
   d. "Skip lesions": Areas of inflammation with normal-appearing areas
3. Small bowel follow-through GI series
4. Fistulogram: Used to guide the surgical correction
5. CT scan of the abdomen and pelvis (limited use in IBD but may detect fistulae)

D. Procedures with/without biopsy
1. Colonoscopy: Mucosa has characteristic cobblestone appearance.
2. Flexible sigmoidoscopy with biopsy: Reveals "skip areas" in colon, significant small bowel involvement, fistulas, and granulomas
3. Upper endoscopy: Aphthous ulcerations occur in the stomach and duodenum in 5% to 10% of patients.
4. Capsule enteroscopy: The major risk is the potential for the camera to become lodged at the point of stricture and require operative intervention.
5. Skin biopsy

E. Tuberculin purified protein derivative (PPD) skin test

Differential Diagnoses

A. CD
B. UC
C. Appendicitis
D. Colon cancer
E. IBS
F. Anorexia nervosa
G. Perianal abscess
H. Intestinal protozoan and bacterial etiologies
I. Food poisoning
J. Cytomegalovirus (CMV)
K. Intestinal tuberculosis (TB)

Plan

A. **CD should be managed jointly with a gastroenterologist, colorectal surgeon, and specialists such as a rheumatologist and nutritionist.**

B. Patient teaching: See the Section III Patient Teaching Guide for this chapter, "Crohn's Disease."

C. Dietary management
1. Adequate nutrition is critical to promotion of healing. Sufficient protein and calories limit the stress on an inflamed and often strictured bowel.
2. Patients with cramps and diarrhea should alter the fiber content of their diets. Diet should include high fiber, low fat (see Appendix B).
3. Those with steatorrhea benefit from decrease in fat intake to less than 80 g/d. Give the patient a copy of the low-fat/low-cholesterol diet (see Appendix B).
4. An empiric trial of restricting milk products may terminate diarrhea due to lactase deficiency.
5. Patients with severe diarrhea may require partial bowel rest, which removes the stimulus that food has on bowel motility and secretion.
6. Elemental diet preparations, such as Ensure, Sustacal, or Isocal, have been found to induce remission, improve symptoms, and decrease disease activity in patients with acute disease.
7. TPN is used when the patient's oral intake is not adequate or when surgery is indicated.
8. Pretreatment screening for TB, using Mantoux (a PPD) skin testing, is needed prior to initiation of immunomodulators and thiopurines.
9. Immunization status
   a. Immunizations with inactivated vaccines should be brought up to date and rigorously maintained during treatment, including influenza, meningococcus, and pneumococcus.
   b. Check varicella titers prior to treatment with immunomodulators and re-immunize if titers are low.
   c. The risk of administering live vaccines (polio, rubella, and yellow fever) to patients on immunomodulators has not been established; however, most experts avoid live vaccines during treatment.

D. Medical and surgical management
1. Surgery does not cure the patient and is reserved for intractable disease, perforation, obstruction, or severe bleeding.

2. The objective of surgery is to remove grossly involved bowel and to spare as much normal-appearing bowel as possible.
3. Postoperative recurrence rates are estimated at 30% to 50% per decade and are inversely related to preoperative disease duration.

E. Pharmaceutical therapy: The medical management of CD can be divided into treatment of an acute exacerbation and maintenance of remission. In acute exacerbation, triggers such as underlying infection, fistula, perforation, and other pathology must be ruled out prior to the intravenous (IV) administration of glucocorticoids. The goal of chronic therapy is the remission of bowel inflammation. Therapies include the following.
   1. Vitamin, mineral, and folic acid supplements are necessary for proper healing and avoidance of secondary complications, such as bone disease and anemia.
      a. Patient should take a multiple vitamin containing about five times the normal daily vitamin requirements.
      b. Folic acid supplementation is required for patients on sulfasalazine because it impairs folic acid absorption.
      c. Vitamin B_{12} replacement is required for patients who have ileal surgery.
      d. Vitamin D, 4,000 IU, is required for patients with steatorrhea.
   2. Opiates provide symptomatic relief of diarrhea during acute phases of illness and chronic active colitis. Diphenoxylate and atropine (Lomotil), codeine, tincture of opium (Paregoric), and loperamide (Imodium A–D) all limit the number of BMs. Tincture of belladonna and other anticholinergics help control cramping.
   3. Stepwise medication approach (see Table 13.4)
      a. Aminosalicylates (5-ASA) are a mainstay of therapy because of their anti-inflammatory activities and rapid absorption throughout the small intestines. Several formulations are available for targeting a specific region of the bowel.
      b. Corticosteroids are used if IBD fails to respond to 5-ASA. Corticosteroids should be tapered as rapidly as possible as they do not have a role in maintaining remission.
      c. Immunomodulatory agents may be initiated for IBD refractory to corticosteroids or frequent flares that require steroids. These agents require monitoring of blood counts due to hematological toxicity. A 3% incidence of pancreatitis, allergic reactions, infections, and marrow toxicity is associated with their use. The main drawback to the use of AZA and 6-MP is their slow onset. The effect of therapy is noted after 3 to 6 months of treatment. The Food and Drug Adminstration (FDA) recommends that individuals should have TPMT genotype or phenotype assessment before initiation of therapy with AZA or 6-MP to detect individuals who have low-enzyme activity or who are homozygous deficient in TPMT.
      d. Tumor necrosis factor (TNF)–alpha blocker
      e. Antibiotics are utilized in adults for perianal disease or inflammatory mass.
      f. Thalidomide, an inhibitor of both TNF and angiogenesis, has been used off-label to treat refractory IBD.

Follow-Up

A. Have the patient record his or her weight daily to monitor changes.
B. Assess frequency and consistency of stools to evaluate volume losses and effectiveness of therapy.
C. Instruct patients on self-medication and to call a physician if fever develops, diarrhea worsens, bleeding occurs, or abdominal pain becomes marked.
D. Monitoring patients on 5-ASA should include CBC at least twice a year and urinalysis at least annually.
E. Monitoring patients on 6-MP requires frequent monitoring, including CBC and aminotransferase levels (ALT and AST) before treatment, and again at 2, 3, 8, and 12 weeks after initiating therapy. When stable, monitor every 3 months thereafter, and 2 to 3 weeks after a change in dosage.
F. Monitoring patients on MTX includes a CBC and aminotransferases as with 6-MP/thiopurine therapies.
G. Periodic bone mineral density assessment is recommended for patients on long-term corticosteroid therapy (longer than 3 months). Osteopenia should be treated aggressively. The primary intervention includes dietary counseling and supplementation to ensure adequate intake of vitamin D and calcium.
H. Annual ophthalmologic examinations are recommended for patients on long-term corticosteroids.
I. Patients who are using corticosteroids should be monitored for glucose intolerance and other metabolic abnormalities.

Consultation/Referral

A. Refer the patient to a gastroenterologist initially for evaluation. Treatment requires multidisciplinary management with a gastroenterologist and other subspecialists, including a nutritionist, surgeon, rheumatologist, ophthalmologist, and social workers.

TABLE 13.4 Medications for Crohn's Disease (CD) and Ulcerative Colitis (UC)

Aminosalicylates (5-ASA) anti-inflammatory activities, and rapid absorption throughout the GI tract. The 5-ASA drugs are not specifically approved by the Food and Drug Administration (FDA) for CD.

		Induction Therapy	Maintenance Therapy
Sulfasalazine (Azulfidine)	Treatment of mild to moderate UC, and as adjunctive therapy in severe UC. Converted to mesalamine in the colon.	**Ulcerative Colitis and Crohn's** Initial 1–2 g/d in divided doses. Gradual increase to 3–4 g/d in divided doses	**Ulcerative Colitis** For the prolongation of the remission period between acute attacks 2–4 g/d in divided doses
Balsalazide (Colazal)	Mild to moderately active CD. Release is delayed until the terminal ileum and cecum. Converted to mesalamine in the colon.	**Ulcerative Colitis and Crohn's** 6.75 g/d in divided doses Duration 8–12 weeks	**Ulcerative Colitis and Crohn's** Safety and effectiveness has not been established beyond 12 weeks
Mesalamine (Asacol)	Targeted for release in the distal ileum and colon	**Ulcerative Colitis and Crohn's** 2.4–4.8 g/d in divided doses	**Ulcerative Colitis and Crohn's** Maintenance: 2.4–4.8 g/d in divided doses
Mesalamine (Pentasa)	Mild to moderate disease. Released in the duodenum to the distal colon	**Ulcerative Colitis and Crohn's** 4 g/d in divided doses for up to 8 weeks	**Ulcerative Colitis and Crohn's** 2–4 g/d in divided doses
Mesalamine (Apriso)	Locally acting aminosalicylates 24 hour delayed and extended release. Release occurs at a pH ≥6, then prolonged throughout the colon	**Ulcerative Colitis** 1.5–3 g/d in divided doses	**Maintenance of Remission of UC**. 1.5 g/d.
Mesalamine Suppository (Canasa)	Specific to the rectum and distal colon	**Ulcerative Proctitis Rectal Suppository** One, 500 mg suppository rectally twice a day **OR** One 1,000 mg rectally at night. Suppositories should be retained 1–3 hours to achieve maximal benefit.	**Maintenance of Remission of Ulcerative Proctitis Rectal Suppository** One, 500 mg suppository rectally twice a day **OR** One 1,000 mg rectally at night. Suppositories should be retained 1–3 hours to achieve maximal benefit.
Mesalamine Retention enema (Rowasa)	Specific to the rectum and distal colon	**Retention Enema**—60 mL (4 g) at bedtime, retained overnight (8 hours)	**Retention Enema**—60 mL (4 g) at bedtime, retained overnight (8 hours)
Corticosteroids—Nonspecifically suppress the immune system. Mainstay of treatment for active flares.			
Budesonide (Uceris) (Entocort EC)	Treatment of mild to moderate CD involving the ileum and/or ascending colon Released in the distal small intestine and right colon	**Ulcerative Colitis and Crohn's** 9 mg daily for up to 8 weeks TAPER to 6 mg daily for 2 weeks prior to complete cessation. For recurring episodes of active CD, a repeat 8 week course can be given.	**Ulcerative Colitis and Crohn's** Maintenance of clinical remission of mild to moderate CD of ileum and/or ascending colon 6 mg/d up to 3 months Maintenance treatment beyond 3 months has no proven substantial clinical benefit.
Prednisone (most common oral steroid used) Methylprednisolone (IV)	Used in acute treatment but are not preventative IV steroids are used in patients in severe disease that requires hospitalization.	**Ulcerative Colitis and Crohn's** Dosage and length of treatment vary Steroids should not be stopped abruptly, tapering should begin concomitantly with initiating other treatments to maintain remission	**Ulcerative Colitis and Crohn's** Not for maintenance therapy

(continued)

TABLE 13.4 Medications for Crohn's Disease (CD) and Ulcerative Colitis (UC) (*continued*)

Hydrocortisone enemas (Cortenema) Hydrocortisone acetate foam and steroid suppositories (Cortifoam, ProctoFoam-HC)	Colonic disease–proctitis requiring topical/rectal formulations	**Ulcerative Colitis and Crohn's** **Enema**—1 nightly at HS; usual length of treatment 2–3 weeks **Suppository**—1 twice a day (a.m. and p.m.). Severe proctitis may require using a suppository 3 times a day or using 2 suppositories twice a day. **Foam**—1 applicator once daily or every 12 hours for 2–3 weeks, then 1 applicator every other day if needed.	**Ulcerative Colitis and Crohn's** Dosage and length of treatment are based on medical treatment and response to treatment.

Immunomodulatory Agents:

- **Thiopurines—The 2013 American Gastroenterology Association (AGA) recommends against using thiopurine monotherapy to induce remission with patients with moderately severe Crohn's disease. Because of the delay in the onset of action of 6-thiopurines, concomitant therapy with systemic corticosteroids or an anti-TNF-α drug is required for rapid system relief with moderately severe CD.**
- **AGA suggests against using MTX to induce remission in patients with moderately severe CD.**
- **AGA suggests using MTX over no immunomodulator therapy to maintain corticosteroid-induced remission in patients with CD.**

6-Mercaptopurine (6-MP) (Purinethol)	Slow onset—the onset of therapy is noted after 3–6 months.	**Crohn's Disease** Weight-based dosage and response to therapy 1.5 mg/kg/d	**Crohn's Disease** Weight-based dosage and response to therapy 1.5 mg/kg/d
Azathioprine (Imuran) Used off-label for UC and CD	Converts to its active form 6-MP Slow acting and can take up to 3 months to work	**Ulcerative Colitis and Crohn's** Weight-based dosage and response to therapy 2.5 mg/kg/d	**Ulcerative Colitis and Crohn's** Weight-based dosage and response to therapy 2.5 mg/kg/d
Methotrexate (MTX) Folic Acid Antagonist	Improvement generally in 3–6 weeks; however, full benefit may not be seen for 12 weeks.	**Crohn's Disease** 15–25 mg once a week by injection. Patients also need to take folic acid 1 mg/d.	**Crohn's Disease** 15 mg per week Patients also need to take folic acid 1 mg/d

Biologics—Tumor necrosis factor (TNF)-alpha blocker

- **The AGA recommends using anti-TNF-α *monotherapy* to induce remission in patients with moderately severe CD.**
- **The AGA recommends using anti-TNF-α with thiopurines over *thiopurines monotherapy* to induce remission in patients with moderately severe CD.**
- **The AGA recommends using anti-TNF-α over no anti-TNF-α to maintain corticosteroid- or anti-TNF-α induced remission in patients with CD.**

Infliximab Remicade IV infusion	Moderate to severe CD with fistulizing CD or resistance to steroids and conventional therapy	**Crohn's Disease** 5 mg/kg IV over 2 hours at 0, 2, and 6 weeks	**Crohn's Disease** 5 mg/kg every 8 weeks thereafter. If no response by week 14, consider discontinuing therapy.
Certolizumab Pegol (Cimzia) Subcutaneous (subq) in the abdomen or thigh	Moderate to severe CD resistance to steroids and conventional therapy	**Crohn's Disease** 400 mg (two 200 mg) subq injections on day 1, then 2 weeks and at 4 weeks	**Crohn's Disease** 400 mg every 4 weeks
Adalimumab (Humira) Subcutaneous in the abdomen or thigh	Moderate to severe CD resistance to steroids and conventional therapy	**Crohn's Disease** Prefilled syringes. On day 1, four injections are self-administered. On day 15, two injections are self-administered	**Crohn's Disease** 1 injection every 2 weeks
Golimumab (Simponi)	Moderate to severe UC resistant to steroid and conventional therapy	**Ulcerative Colitis** 200 mg injections are self-administered at initiation, 100 mg subq at week 2	**Ulcerative Colitis** 100 mg injection every 4 weeks

(*continued*)

TABLE 13.4 Medications for Crohn's Disease (CD) and Ulcerative Colitis (UC) (*continued*)

Vedolizumab (Entyvio) FDA approved 2014	Moderate to severe CD and UC resistance to steroids and conventional therapy	**Ulcerative Colitis and Crohn's** 300 mg IV infused over 30 minutes at initiation, week 2 and week 6	**Ulcerative Colitis and Crohn's** 300 mg IV every 8 weeks
Anti-Adhesion Molecule			
Natalizumab (Tysabri) Distribution is restricted and is available only through a close monitored program known as TOUCH	Moderate to severe CD for patients who failed anti-TNF therapy.	Crohn's disease 300 mg every 4 weeks. Given by IV infusion over 1 hour. Discontinuation after 12 weeks based on individual response/ protocol	Crohn's disease 300 mg IV monthly—Restricted distribution
Antibiotics—Used for treatment of bacterial infections that cause abscesses and can be helpful with treatment of fistulas			
Ciprofloxacin (Cipro)		**Ulcerative Colitis and Crohn's** Dosage and length of treatment varies	**Ulcerative Colitis and Crohn's** Dosage and length of treatment varies
Metronidazole (Flagyl)		**Ulcerative Colitis and Crohn's** Dosage and length of treatment varies	**Ulcerative Colitis and Crohn's** Dosage and length of treatment varies

Adapted from 2013 American College of Gastroenterology Guidelines http://gi.org.

B. Promptly hospitalize for parenteral management patients who are toxic, bleeding heavily, in severe pain, or too sick to obtain adequate nutrition orally.
C. Consider a referral for genetic testing.

Individual Considerations

A. Pregnancy
   1. Active disease at time of conception is associated with increased incidence of miscarriage and postpartum exacerbation. It may also predispose the patient to other maternal and prenatal risks, such as premature labor, small-for-gestational-age babies, and stillbirth.
   2. Sulfasalazine and steroids are safe and effective during nursing or pregnancy.
   3. Women on prednisone should receive supplementary steroids during labor and delivery as well as during other highly stressful times.
   4. Counsel women to attempt pregnancy only when the disease has been quiescent for several months.
   5. Withholding sulfasalazine for 2 to 3 days before delivery may be advisable to minimize neonatal jaundice due to bilirubin displacement.
   6. MTX is a FDA category X drug.
B. Geriatrics
   1. **Unexplained diarrhea, weight loss, and perianal disease in the elderly should arouse suspicions regarding CD. Elderly patients have worse outcomes because of delayed presentation and comorbid conditions.**
   2. Diagnostic delay is more common in the elderly. The differential diagnosis for older patients includes:
      a. Diverticulitis and diverticular bleeding
      b. Ischemic colitis
      c. Microsocopic colitis
      d. Infectious colitis
      e. NSAID-induced ulcerations, strictures, and perforation
      f. Radiation colitis (most commonly gynecological, rectal, and prostate cancers)
   3. Elderly patients tend to have CD confined to the distal colon, with only 40% having proctitis.
   4. With an increase in cancers in elder patients with CD, it is imperative to evaluate and exclude cancer before beginning immunosuppressant or biologic therapies. Older patients with CD are at increased risk for cancers, including those cancers found in the following.
      a. Small intestines
      b. Pancreas
      c. Endocrine glands
      d. Kidney
      e. Stomach
      f. Lung and NHL and nonmelanoma skin cancer
   5. Review CD therapies, with comorbid conditions in mind, due to side effects, interactions between medications, need for increased laboratory

monitoring (e.g., INR, as well as digoxin levels and phenytoin levels), and risk of infections.
6. Anti-TNF-α agents are contraindicated in patients with New York Heart Association (NYHA) class III and IV heart failure (HF).
7. Age is currently not a contraindication for performing an IPAA. Elderly patients with good anal sphincter function and adequate cognitive ability are better surgical candidates for the IPAA procedure.
8. The incidence of a deep vein thrombosis is higher in the elderly.

Resource

Crohn's and Colitis Foundation of America: www.ccfa.org

Cyclosporiasis

Definition

A. Cyclosporiasis is a one-cell parasite that infects the upper small intestines. Causes of cyclosporiasis include drinking infected water or produce (fresh fruits, especially raspberries, and vegetables) or exposure to the organism during travel to countries where it is endemic.
B. It manifests as protracted and relapsing gastroenteritis. The clinical syndrome consists of explosive watery diarrhea, nausea, anorexia, weight loss, fatigue, and abdominal cramps that may persist for 7 days to several weeks, with a waxing and waning course.
C. In an immunocompromised host, onset is insidious, and the condition becomes chronic with symptoms; the shedding of oocysts continues indefinitely. Symptoms associated with cyclosporiasis are more severe in HIV/AIDS patients.
D. The oocysts are resistant to most disinfectants used in food and water processing and can remain viable for prolonged periods.

Incidence

A. The incidence of infection is unknown, although it is common around the world.
B. Most outbreaks in the United States and Canada have been associated with consumption of imported fresh produce.
C. It affects all ages.

Pathogenesis

A. Infection is caused by an 8- to 10-μm, spore-forming coccidian protozoan called *Cyclospora cayetanensis*. Transmission of oocysts is by the oral-fecal route. The incubation period ranges from 2 days to 2 weeks after excretion, depending on temperature and humidity.

Predisposing Factors

A. Incompetent or compromised immune system (e.g., infection with AIDS)
B. Travel to underdeveloped or tropical countries
C. Ingestion of contaminated food or water
D. Contact with animals that carry the parasite

Common Complaints

A. Abrupt, profuse, malodorous, watery diarrhea
B. Nausea
C. Vomiting
D. Anorexia
E. Substantial weight loss
F. Flulike symptoms
G. Abdominal cramps and bloating

Other Signs and Symptoms

A. Asymptomatic
B. Low-grade fever
C. Nausea and vomiting
D. Profound fatigue
E. Yellow-to-khaki-green stools
F. Flatus
G. Dehydration

Subjective Data

A. Review onset, duration, and course of symptoms. Is diarrhea acute or chronic?
B. Question the patient about travel to areas known for cyclospora, such as Haiti, Puerto Rico, Pakistan, India, Mexico, Nepal, New Guinea, and Peru. It has also been seen in Chicago, Los Angeles, New York, Florida, and Massachusetts.
C. Review the patient's intake of medications and other substances that can cause diarrhea, especially antibiotics, laxatives, quinidine, magnesium-containing antacids, digitalis, loop diuretics, antihypertensives, alcohol, caffeine, herbal teas, and sorbitol-containing (sugar-free) gum and mints.
D. Ask about the nature of the patient's BMs, including frequency; consistency; volume; and presence of blood, pus, or mucus.
E. Review associated symptoms that need evaluation: Fever, abdominal pain, and anorexia.
F. Ask the patient if other family members or sexual contacts are also ill.
G. Establish the patient's normal weight and any recent weight loss. How much weight was lost and over what period of time?

Physical Examination

A. Check temperature, pulse, respirations, blood pressure, and weight (vital signs are normal in most cases).
B. Inspect
   1. Inspect general appearance for signs of illness and dehydration.
      a. Inspect mucous membranes.
      b. Note the presence of decreased skin turgor.

C. Auscultate the abdomen for bowel sounds in all quadrants.
D. Palpate
   1. Palpate the abdomen for masses, rebound tenderness, guarding; may exhibit RUQ pain (biliary disease).
   2. Palpate lymph nodes for enlargement.
E. Perform rectal exam.

Diagnostic Tests

Identification may be made by microscopic examination under ultraviolet light, by modified acid-fast staining, or by review of wet mounts of stool by experienced microscopists. Finding large numbers of white cells suggests an inflammatory or invasive diarrhea. The following tests are done.

A. Acid-fast Ziehl–Neelsen stained slide of stool
B. Stool culture for ova and parasites: Parasites are passed intermittently, so three or more stools on alternating days should be examined.
C. Endoscopy with small bowel biopsy

Differential Diagnoses

A. Cyclospora infection
B. Giardiasis
C. Malabsorption
D. *E. coli* infection: *E. coli* causes diarrhea within hours of ingesting contaminated food. Confirm by checking if others were affected.
E. IBS: Leukocyte-free mucus is the hallmark of IBS.
F. Viral diarrhea
G. Lactose intolerance
H. Other bacterial infections, for example, *Shigella, Salmonella,* and *Campylobacter*
I. Cholera
J. IBD (CD or UC)

Plan

A. General interventions
   1. Advise the patient to tell household members and sexual contacts to seek medical examination and treatment.
   2. Children and caregivers with diarrhea should be excluded from childcare centers until they become asymptomatic.
   3. Fresh produce should always be washed thoroughly before it is eaten.
B. Patient teaching: See the Section III Patient Teaching Guide for this chapter, "Diarrhea."
   1. Discuss safe sexual practices.
   2. Teach contact precautions to those caring for diapered and/or incontinent children.
C. Dietary management
   1. Tell the patient to increase fluids. Fluid replacement is the basic approach to prevent dehydration from diarrhea.
   2. Tell the patient to restrict milk products to rule out lactose intolerance.
   3. Give the patient a copy of a diet to control nausea and vomiting.
D. Pharmaceutical therapy
   1. Drugs of choice are trimethoprim-sulfamethoxazole (TMP-SMZ). They can reduce shedding, and they stop diarrhea within 2 days.
      a. Adults
         i. Immunocompetent host: TMP 160 mg/SMZ 800 mg tablet orally twice a day for 7 to 10 days
         ii. Immunocompromised host: TMP 160 mg/SMZ 800 mg tablet orally four times a day for 10 days, followed by prophylaxis with TMP 160 mg/SMZ 800 mg orally three times per week
   2. Ciprofloxacin (Cipro) is the alternative treatment for patients with allergies to sulfamethoxazole.
      a. Adults: Cipro 500 mg orally twice a day for 7 to 10 days for acute infection
      b. Adults: Prophylaxis in HIV: Cipro 500 mg orally three times a week

Follow-Up

A. See the patient in 1 week to verify continuing clinical improvement.
B. If diarrhea persists 2 weeks or more, a second evaluation is indicated.
C. Retest stools for blood and leukocytes; do a stool culture for ova and parasites.
D. Report cases of cyclosporiasis to the health department.

Consultation/Referral

A. Consult an infectious disease specialist and/or gastroenterologist if the patient has no symptom relief after completing therapies or has a prolonged or severe case.

Individual Considerations

A. Pregnancy
   1. TMP-SMX is a pregnancy category C drug. Use during pregnancy if the potential benefit outweighs the risk to the fetus.
   2. TMP-SMX should be avoided near term because of the potential for hyperbilirubinemia and kernicterus in the newborn.

Diarrhea

Definition

A. Diarrhea is an abnormally high fluid content in the stool. Generally, diarrhea also involves an increase in the frequency of BMs, which can range from 4 to 5 to more than 20 times a day. Diarrhea may be an acute onset or chronic/persistent diarrhea.

B. Acute diarrhea is usually self-limited; the most common complication of diarrhea is dehydration.
C. Chronic diarrhea is defined as lasting longer than 14 days.

Incidence

A. The incidence of diarrhea is unknown.
B. The incidence of *C. difficile* infection is approximately 7%, and 28% of patients who were hospitalized have positive cultures for the organism. *C. difficile*-associated diarrhea has a mortality rate as high as 25% in the frail elderly.
C. Be aware that *C. difficile* can occur among patients in the community who have been treated with antibiotic therapy or antineoplastic agents with antibacterial activity.

Pathogenesis

A. The increased water content in diarrhea stools is due to an imbalance in the physiology of the small and large intestinal processes. See Table 13.5 for organisms that cause diarrhea.

Predisposing Factors

A. Enteric infections
B. Females have a higher incidence of *Campylobacter* species infections.
C. Institutional: Day care and skilled nursing facilities
D. Food: Raw or contaminated food
E. Contaminated water or inadequate chlorinated water supply
F. Travel
G. Chemotherapy or radiation induced
H. Vitamin deficiencies (niacin and folate)
I. Vitamin toxicity (C, niacin, and vitamin B_3)
J. Ingestion of heavy metals (copper, tin, or zinc) or toxins
K. Ingestion of plants, mistletoe, or mushrooms
L. Antibiotics

Common Complaints

A. Frequent watery stool
B. Foul-smelling stools (fat malabsorption)
C. Flatulence
D. Abdominal cramping

Other Signs and Symptoms

A. Lethargy
B. Fever
C. Nausea and vomiting
D. Currant jelly stool (blood and mucus)
E. Anorexia
F. Dehydration in adults
   1. Thirst
   2. Less frequent urination

TABLE 13.5 Organisms That Cause Diarrhea

Viral organisms	Rotavirus
	Norovirus
	Adenovirus
	Calicivirus
	Astrovirus
	Ebola
Invasive bacteria	*Escherichia Coli*
	Klebsiella
	Clostridium difficile
	Clostridium perfringens
	Shigella
	Salmonella
	Campylobacter
	Cholera
	Yersinia
	Plesiomonas
	Aeromonas
Parasites	*Giardia*
	Entamoeba organisms
	Cryptosporidium
	G. lamblia

   3. Dark urine
   4. Dry skin
   5. Fatigue
   6. Dizziness
   7. Lightheadedness

Subjective Data

A. Review the onset of diarrhea stools. What is the normal stool pattern?
B. Review the consistency, color, volume, and frequency of the stools.
C. Review dietary intake of raw foods, contaminated food, and nonabsorbable sugars, including lactulose or lactose in lactose malabsorbers.
D. Review any contact with others who may have the same symptoms.
E. Have any of the stools contained blood?
F. Review travel history, including camping vacations.
G. Review medication history, including vitamins, herbal production, laxatives, antacids that contain magnesium, opiate withdrawal, Olestra, and methylxanthines (caffeine, theobromine, and theophylline).
   1. Specifically inquire about the use of antibiotics in the previous 2 to 3 months (*C. difficile* may develop as late as 10 weeks after stopping antibiotics).

H. Review any food allergies and history of lactose intolerance.
I. Evaluate the presence of other symptoms such as fever and abdominal pain.

Physical Examination

A. Check temperature, pulse, respirations, blood pressure (standing and sitting), and weight.
B. Inspect
   1. Observe the patient's general overall appearance, the presence of lethargy or depressed consciousness, or grimace during exam.
   2. Evaluate muscle tone, skin turgor, reduced muscle, and fat mass.
   3. Examine mouth, lips, and mucous membranes for signs, symptoms, and severity of dehydration.
   4. Perianal examination for skin breakdown, erythema, and fissures.
C. Auscultation
   1. Assess heart and lungs.
   2. Auscultate the abdomen in all four quadrants.
   3. Assess the presence of borborygmi (significant increase in peristaltic action that may be audible and/or palpable).
D. Percuss abdomen.
E. Palpate
   1. Palpate the abdomen for masses, guarding, rebound tenderness, and peritoneal signs.
   2. Palpate for lymphadenopathy.
   3. Perform a rectal examination, including testing of stool for occult blood.

Diagnostic Tests

A. Stool specimens for the evaluation of
   1. *C. difficile*
      a. PCR assays: Several FDA-approved assays for testing for *C. difficile*
      b. Toxin detection EIA detects toxin A, toxin B, or both for *C difficile*
      c. Tissue cytotoxin assay: Previously the gold standard test; however, the test has a limitation of being a slow turnaround.
      d. Antigen detection by latex agglutination or immunochromatographic assay
      e. Polymerase chain reaction (PCR)
      f. *C. difficile* glutamate dehydrogenase antigen detection
   2. Fecal leukocytes
   3. Blood
   4. Culture
   5. Ova and parasites
   6. Fecal alpha-1 antitrypsin levels
   7. Viral antigen testing
B. Specific enzyme immunoassay (EIA) and direct florescence antibody (DFA) assays are becoming the standard for the diagnosis of giardiasis.
C. CBC: WBC may be elevated.
D. Albumin
E. Electrolytes
F. A colonoscopy for intestinal biopsy for chronic or protracted diarrhea or patients with AIDS should be done. A sigmoidoscopy alone may not reveal any abnormality.
G. Abdominal ultrasound to identify intussusception
H. Abdominal CT
I. Hydrogen breath test for lactose/fructose intolerance

Differential Diagnoses

A. Diarrhea: Infectious etiology
B. IBD
   1. CD
   2. UC
C. CF
D. Giardiasis
E. Protozoan
F. Malabsorption syndromes
G. Intussusception
H. Stool impaction
I. IBS
J. Meckel's diverticulum
K. Intolerance to lactose, carbohydrates, and protein
L. Antibiotic-associated diarrhea
M. Pseudomembranous colitis
N. Toxic megacolon
O. Appendicitis

Plan

A. See the Section III Patient Teaching Guide for this chapter, "Diarrhea."
B. Examination of stools for ova and parasites should be done every other day or every 3 days.
C. Rehydration with oral fluids for each diarrhea stool. Administer small amounts at frequent intervals.
D. Hold foods until hydration is completed. No evidence shows that bananas, rice, applesauce, and toast (BRAT) are useful, and they are not currently recommended.
E. Use antibiotics (or the discontinuation of antibiotics in the case of *C. difficile)* or use antiparasitic agents, depending on the etiology.
F. The use of probiotics, *Lactobacillus GG* (I, A) and *S. boulardii* (II, B), has been found to be effective and may reduce the spread of rotavirus.
G. Encourage proper hygiene and food preparation to prevent spread and future infections.

H. Water should be boiled for at least 1 minute if contamination is suspected.
I. Anitprotozal: Nitazoxande (Alinia) 500 mg every 12 hours for 3 days.
J. HIV/AIDS: Crofelemer (Fulyzaq) for noninfectious diarrhea in adults on antiretroviral therapy; 125 mg tablet twice per day
K. Antidiarrheals
   1. Loperamide (Imodium)
      a. Initially 4 mg, then 2 mg after each loose stool. Maximum dose 16 mg/d. Stop in 48 hours if diarrhea is not relieved.
      b. Chronic diarrhea: Initially 4 mg, maintenance 4 to 8 mg/d; reevaluate if no improvement in diarrhea in 10 days at 16 mg/d.
   2. Bismuth subsalicylate (Kaopectate) 262 mg/15 mL, take 30 mL every 30 to 60 minutes if needed; maximum four doses per day
   3. Diphenoxylate HCL (Lomotil) 2 tablets or 10 mL four times daily until diarrhea is controlled; maintenance, 2 tablets or 10 mL per day
L. *C. difficile* treatment
   1. Stop antibiotics.
   2. Avoid antiperistaltic agents.
   3. If mild symptoms or first occurrence: metronidazole 500 mg three times per day for 10 to 14 days
   4. If the first occurence of infection is moderate to severe use vancomycin 125 mg four times a day for 10 to 14 days
   5. Second recurrence: Tapered and pulsed doses of vancomycin
      a. Vancomycin 125 mg four times a day for 14 days
      b. 125 mg twice a day for 7 days
      c. 125 mg once every 2 days for 8 days
      d. 125 mg once every 3 days for 15 days
   6. Fidaxomicin (Dificid) 200 mg orally twice a day for 10 days is an alternative treatment for a second recurrence.
   7. Third recurrence
      a. Vancomycin: Taper as noted previously followed by rifaximin 400 mg twice a day for 14 days
      b. IV immunoglobulin 400 mg/kg once every 3 weeks for a total of two to three doses
      c. Fecal transplantation (fecal bacteriotherapy)

Follow-Up

A. Follow-up depends on the severity of diarrhea and the age of the patient.
B. Leukocytosis of increasing severity in hospitalized patients should prompt a clinical evaluation for *C. difficile* infection.

Consultation/Referral

A. Evaluate the need for a surgical consultation (fulminant colitis, peritonitis, or toxic megacolon) or one with an infectious-disease specialist or a gastroenterologist.

Individual Considerations

A. Geriatrics
   1. Review any hospitalizations within the past 72 hours as a cause of diarrhea. Traditionally *C. difficile* infections occurred in an institutional setting; however, community-acquired infection is not uncommon.
   2. Advanced age is a risk factor for *C. difficile* infection.
   3. Diarrhea may be related to fecal impaction.
   4. Dehydration is more common in the elderly. Signs of dehydration include:
      a. Confusion
      b. Muscle weakness
      c. Fever
      d. Dizziness
      e. Poor skin turgor
      f. Hypotension
      g. Tachycardia
   5. Due to polypharmacy in the elderly, review all medications for drug-to-drug interaction.

Resources

Drugs.com Drug Interactions Checker: www.drugs.com/drug_interactions.html

Medscape Drug Interaction Checker: reference.medscape.com/drug-interactionchecker

RxList Drug Interactions Checker: www.rxlist.com/drug-interaction-checker.htm

Diverticulosis and Diverticulitis

Definition

A. Diverticulum is the saclike protrusion of mucosa through the muscular colonic wall. Protrusions can occur in weakened areas of the bowel wall and blood vessels. Diverticulosis is the presence of diverticula, but it does not imply a pathologic condition. Diverticulitis occurs when the diverticula become plugged and inflamed. Surgery is often the treatment of choice for young symptomatic patients. Diverticular disease is one of the most common causes of lower GI hemorrhage and a leading consideration in patients who present with brisk rectal bleeding.
B. There is no evidence of a relationship between the development of diverticula and smoking, caffeine,

and alcohol consumption. However, an increased risk of developing diverticular disease is associated with a diet that is high in red meat and total fat content. This risk can be reduced by a diet high in fiber content, especially with fruits and vegetables (cellulose) (see Appendix B, Table B.7, "Fiber Recommendations by Age").

C. Diverticulosis is often diagnosed as an incidental finding on a BE or sigmoid/colonoscopy.
D. Recurrent attacks of diverticulitis can result in the formation of scar tissue, leading to narrowing and obstruction of the colonic lumen.

Incidence

Diverticulosis is very common and increases with age.

A. Prevalence by age
    1. Age 40: 5%
    2. Age 60: 30%
    3. Age 80: 65%
B. No significant difference in prevalence by gender

Diverticulosis is symptomatic in 70% of cases. It leads to diverticulitis in 5% to 25% and is associated with bleeding in 5% to 15%. The sigmoid colon is commonly affected. There are two types of diverticular disease and diverticulitis.

A. Simple, with no complications; responds to treatment such as dietary changes without the need for surgery
B. Complicated, with abscesses, fistula, obstruction, perforation, and peritonitis leading to sepsis; usually requires surgery

Pathogenesis

A. The present theory that fiber is a protective agent against the development of diverticula and subsequent diverticulitis holds that insoluble fiber causes the formation of more bulky stool, which leads to decreased effectiveness in colonic segmentation. The overall result is that intracolonic pressure remains close to the normal range during colonic peristalsis. The diverticular sac can become inflamed when undigested food residues and bacteria get trapped in the thin-walled sacs. If this occurs, blood supply is mechanically compromised and bacterial invasion ensues.

Predisposing Factors

A. Advanced age
B. Obesity (84% to 96%)
C. Dietary factors
    1. Low residue
    2. High red meat and total fat content
D. Complicated diverticular disease is increased
    1. Smokers
    2. NSAID use
    3. Acetaminophen use (especially paracetamol)
E. Indication that genetics are a predisposing factor
    1. Left-sided diverticula is predominant in the United States.
    2. Right-sided (cecal) diverticula is predominant in Asia.

Common Complaints

A. Diverticulosis is usually asymptomatic.
B. Painless rectal bleeding is the hallmark of diverticular bleeding, with intermittent passage of maroon or bright red blood.
C. Common diverticulitis symptoms
    1. LLQ pain
    2. Constipation

Other Signs and Symptoms

A. Back pain
B. Flatulence
C. Periodic abdominal distension
D. Borborygmi, or loud, prolonged gurgles caused by hyperactive intestinal peristalsis
E. Diarrhea
F. Nausea or vomiting
G. Dysuria
H. Tenderness on palpation, possible guarding
I. Low-grade fever

Subjective Data

A. Review onset, duration, and course of symptoms, including size, color, consistency, and frequency of stools.
B. Ask the patient if constipation is a chronic or acute problem, and if it alternates with diarrhea.
C. Review the patient's daily diet and fluid intake.
D. Ask the patient about medication use, including iron supplements, NSAIDs, and acetaminophen.
E. Inquire about the color, amount, and frequency of rectal bleeding. Does the patient strain when having a BM?
F. Review the patient's history of pain with defecation.

Physical Examination

A. Check temperature, pulse, respirations, blood pressure, and weight.
B. The physical examination may be relatively unremarkable but most commonly reveals abdominal tenderness or a mass.
C. Inspection
    1. Observe the general overall appearance for signs of pain.
    2. Inspect the abdomen in detail, assessing for distension.
D. Auscultate all four quadrants of the abdomen. Absent bowel sounds suggest peritoneal inflammation.
E. Percuss the abdomen.

F. Palpate
 1. Palpate the abdomen for rebound tenderness or masses signaling possible abscess and tenderness.
 2. Palpate beneath right costal arch, checking for Murphy's sign or pain on deep inspiration.
G. Rectal exam: Evaluate for hemorrhoids, masses, fissures, fistulas, inflammation, and stool in ampulla.

Diagnostic Tests

A. The diagnosis of diverticular colitis is made endoscopically and histologically.
B. CT scan is becoming the optimal method of investigation for suspected acute diverticulitis.
C. CBC with differential: WBC may show leukocytosis with a shift to the left; hemoglobin and Hct may be low with chronic or acute bleeding.
D. CRP
E. Radiography: Flat plate and upright films of abdomen to evaluate ileus or obstruction, free air, and perforation
F. Abdominal ultrasonography to evaluate masses or abscess
G. Proctosigmoidoscopy
H. BE after infection subsides. Caution: A BE during the acute phase may increase intraluminal pressure and cause bowel perforation.
I. Hemoccult: Stool
J. Pregnancy test if there is possibility of pregnancy

Differential Diagnoses

A. Diverticulitis
B. Diverticulosis
C. Acute appendicitis
D. Bowel obstruction
E. Ischemic colitis
F. Colon cancer
G. Hemorrhoids
H. Constipation or impaction
I. IBD
J. Urologic disorder: Pyelonephritis
K. PID
L. Ectopic pregnancy

Plan

A. Stress the importance of strict adherence to diet.
B. Dietary management
 1. NPO (nothing by mouth) status for acute treatment
 2. Full-liquid diet or low-fiber diet if not on bowel rest
 3. Long-term dietary management
  a. High-fiber diet, including bran, beans, fruits, and vegetables
  b. Bulk agents if unable to tolerate bran
  c. Note foods to avoid, such as nuts.
C. Medical and surgical management: Acute treatment has not been well defined in diverticular disease.
 1. Acute treatment may include the following:
  a. NG tube placement
  b. IV fluids
 2. Surgical intervention is required for abscess, peritonitis, obstruction, fistula, and failure to improve after several days of medical management, or recurrence after successful medical management.
D. Pharmaceutical therapy: Optimal treatment has not been defined.
 1. Conservative management of diverticulosis: Psyllium (Metamucil) one to three teaspoons in 8 oz of liquid three times a day.
 2. Diverticulitis initial attack: Ciprofloxacin (Cipro) 500 mg orally twice daily and metronidazole (Flagyl) 500 mg orally three times a day for 7 to 14 days. Amoxicillin/clavulanic or sulfamethoxazole-trimethoprim may also be used with metronidazole.
 3. 5-ASA may be added if there is a lack of response.
 4. Relapse: May repeat with the same antibiotic regimen for 1 month
 5. Chronic disease: Utilize long-term ciprofloxacin but not metronidazole.
 6. Avoid laxatives, enemas, and opiates.

Follow-Up

A. Follow up in 1 to 2 weeks. Continue conservative management if the patient has no signs of complications.
B. A colonoscopy should be performed from 2 to 6 weeks after recovery to evaluate the extent of the diverticulosis/rule out other manifestations.

Consultation/Referral

A. Consult a physician if the patient has mild diverticulitis: Temperature less than 101°F; WBC less than 13,000 to 15,000.
B. Arrange for prompt hospitalization and surgical consultation if the patient's temperature rises above 101.0°F, the patient's pain worsens, peritoneal signs develop, or WBC continues to rise. Surgery consultation is required for abscess, peritonitis, obstruction, fistula, or failure to improve after several days of medical management.

Elevated Liver Enzymes

Definition

Liver function tests (LFTs) used to determine the health of the liver are not direct measures of its function. The liver has excretory, metabolic, protective, detoxification, hematologic, and circulatory functions. LFTs may be abnormal even in patients with a healthy liver. Normal laboratory chemistry values may vary according to age, gender, ethnicity, blood group, and postprandial state, as well as other factors such as exercise and pregnancy. Common liver chemistry tests (see Table 13.6) include the following.

A. Making differential diagnosis of the different types of jaundice
B. Assessing the severity of hepatocellular injury
C. Following the trend of the disease
D. Diagnosing for the presence of latent liver disease (i.e., differential diagnosis of ascites or hematemesis)
E. Screening the suspected case during outbreaks of infective hepatitis
F. Screening the persons exposed to hepatotoxic drugs
G. Evaluating cholestatic problems

Incidence

A. The incidence of elevated liver enzymes is undetermined. Abnormal elevations of serum liver chemistries may occur in 1% to 4% of the asymptomatic population.

Pathogenesis

A. Pathogenesis varies by diagnosis.

Predisposing Factors

A. Predisposing factors are dependent on the suspected or known medical diagnosis.

Common Complaints

A. Asymptomatic
B. Pruritus
C. Jaundice
D. Ascites
E. Fatigue
F. Weight loss
G. Change in the color of urine (dark) or stools (clay-colored)

Subjective Data

A complete medical history is the single most important part of the evaluation of the patient with elevated LFTs.

Review medications, including prescription, statins, and OTC medications, as well as herbal therapies.

A. Determine the duration of LFT abnormalities (if known).
B. Review the presence of accompanying symptoms, including arthralgias, myalgias, rash, abdominal

TABLE 13.6 Liver Chemistry Tests and Implications

Liver Chemistry Test	Clinical Implication of Abnormality
ALT	Hepatocellular damage
AST	Hepatocellular damage
ALP	Cholestasis, infiltrative disease, or biliary obstruction
Albumin	Synthetic function
Alpha-fetoprotein	Cancer marker when elevated
Bile acids: Urine bile salts, bile pigments, and urobilinogen	Cholestasis or biliary obstruction, impaired hepatic update or secretion, or portal-systemic shunting
Bilirubin: Serum total, direct and indirect bilirubin	Cholestasis, impaired conjugation, or biliary obstruction
Cholesterol, serum triglycerides	Lipoprotein production and metabolism, chronic cholestasis
Fibrinogen	Liver damage/cirrhosis, acute liver insufficiency, poisoning
Gamma-glutamyl transpeptidase (GGT)	Cholestasis or biliary obstruction, malignant involvement in hepatocellular disease, more sensitive than other enzymes in alcoholism
Hepatitis surface antigen, IGM, antibody, RNA, genotype, viral load	Differentiation of type of hepatitis
Lactate dehydrogenase (LDH)	Hepatocellular damage not specific for hepatic disease
Total proteins, albumin globulin, (A/C ratio)	Hepatitis, advanced liver disease
PT	Synthesis function in hepatocellular disease, fulminate hepatitis
Plasma ammonia	Central nervous system (CNS) dysfunction/toxicity or end-stage liver disease
5′-Nucleotidase (5NT)	Cholestasis or biliary obstruction
Urea	End-stage liver disease

pain, fever, pruritus, and changes in the color of urine or stool.

C. Has the patient experienced any anorexia or weight loss? Over what period of time did weight loss occur?
D. Review parenteral exposures, including transfusions, IV and intranasal drug use, tattoos, and sexual history.
E. Review the patient's recent travel history and possible exposure to contaminated foods.
F. Review the patient's exposure to people with jaundice.
G. Review the patient's occupational history and exposure to hepatotoxins.
H. Review the patient's history of alcohol consumption.
I. Evaluate the gestational age of pregnancy. Hemolysis, elevated liver enzymes, and low platelets (HELLP) syndrome is generally present in the third trimester of pregnancy.

Physical Examination

A. Temperature, pulse, respirations, and blood pressure
B. Observation
   1. Observe for temporal and proximal muscle wasting.
   2. Perform eye and mouth (mucous membranes) examination for icterus.
   3. Perform dermal examination for icterus, spider nevi, palmar erythema, presence of caput medusae (the presence of dilated veins seen on the abdomen; noted with cirrhosis of the liver and portal hypertension)
   4. Evaluate the presence of gynecomastia.
   5. Observe for the presence of jugular venous distension (JVD), a sign of right-sided HF that suggests hepatic congestion.
C. Auscultate heart and lungs.
D. Percuss abdomen.
E. Palpate
   1. Abdominal examination
      a. Evaluate the presence of hepatomegaly; focus on the size and consistency of the liver.
      b. Evaluate the presence of splenomegaly; focus on the size of the spleen. An enlarged spleen is most easily appreciated with the patient in the right lateral decubitus position.
      c. Assess for ascites: Note presence of a fluid wave or shifting dullness.
      d. Assess for an abdominal mass.
   2. Lymph nodes: Evaluate lymphadenopathy.
   3. Conduct testicular examination for testicular atrophy (increased estrogen/reduced testosterone).

Diagnostic Tests

A. The particular LFT tests ordered are related to the suspected or identified medical diagnosis. Table 13.7 shows common serologic tests for viral hepatitis.

Differential Diagnoses

A. Table 13.8 shows differential diagnoses with elevated liver enzymes.

TABLE 13.7 Serologic Tests for Hepatitis

Virologic Test	Usual Clinical Implication of a Positive Test
Hepatitis A-IgM	Positive in acute hepatitis A
Hepatitis A-IgG	Positive in response to previous hepatitis A infection or vaccination
Hepatitis B surface antigen (HBsAg)	Positive during active hepatitis B infection
Hepatitis B surface antibody	Positive in response to previous hepatitis B infection or vaccination
Hepatitis B core antibody-IgM	Positive during active hepatitis B infection
Hepatitis B core antibody-IgG	Positive in response to current or prior hepatitis B infection
Hepatitis B virus (HBV)-DNA	Positive during active hepatitis B infection
Hepatitis Be antigen	Positive test indicates replicative state of wild-type hepatitis B infection
Hepatitis Be antibody	Positive after replicative state of wild-type hepatitis B infection
HBV viral load	Assess hepatitis B virology
Hepatitis C virus (HCV)-antibody enzyme-linked immunosorbent assay (ELISA)	Positive during or after hepatitis C infection
HCV-immunoblot assay (RIBA)	Positive during or after hepatitis C infection
HCV-RNA	Positive during hepatitis C infection
HCV viral load	Assess hepatitis C virology
HCV genotype	Genotyping is used for evaluation of the length of therapy

TABLE 13.8 Differential Diagnosis With Elevated Liver Enzymes

Infiltrating diseases of the liver • Sarcoidosis • TB • Fungal infection • Amyloidosis • Lymphoma • Metastatic malignancy • Hepatocellular carcinoma (HCC)	
Acute viral hepatitis (A-E, EBV, CMV, herpes)	Wilson's disease (genetic disorder of biliary copper excretion)
Cholestasis disease	Acute bile duct obstruction
Chronic hepatitis B, C	Hemolysis
Steatosis/nonalcoholic steatohepatitis (NASH)	Rhabdomyolysis m
Hereditary hemochromatosis (HH)	Thyroid disorders
Medication/herbal-induced	Strenuous exercise-induced changes
Alpha-1-antitrypsin deficiency	Pregnancy—HELLP syndrome
Cirrhosis	Toxin(s) exposure
Celiac disease	Acute Budd–Chiari syndrome
Alcohol-related liver injury	Anorexia nervosa

Plan

A. **The clinical significance of any liver chemistry test abnormality must be interpreted in the context of the clinical situation.** The plan of care is dependent on the suspected or identified medical diagnosis. Lifestyle modifications, including discontinuance of medications and alcohol, weight loss, and dietary changes, can be recommended as appropriate.

B. Patients with marked abnormalities of liver tests, or with signs and symptoms of chronic liver disease or hepatic decompensation (i.e., ascites, encephalopathy, coagulopathy, or portal hypertension), should be evaluated and treated in a more expeditious manner than asymptomatic patients.

Follow-Up

A. Follow-up testing for elevated LFTs, including abdominal/liver ultrasonography, CT, MRI, and liver biopsy, is dependent on the risk factors for disease, symptoms and history, and physical finding of the suspected or identified medical diagnosis. A liver chemistry test that is normal does not ensure that the patient is free of liver disease. If a laboratory error is suspected, the laboratory test should be repeated.

Consultation/Referral

A. Consider a consultation or referral to a hepatologist, gastroenterologist, or infectious disease specialist.

Individual Considerations

Pregnancy: HELLP syndrome is a severe form of pregnancy-induced hypertension (PIH or preeclampsia). It may occur anywhere from the mid-second trimester to immediate postpartum. The HELLP syndrome occurs in 0.2% to 0.6% of pregnancies. The etiology is unknown. The presence of laboratory abnormalities confirms the diagnosis. Treatment of the HELLP syndrome will not be covered. However, the laboratory abnormalities that are noted include the following.

A. Hemolytic anemia
B. Proteinuria
C. Serum AST level (> 70 IU/L)
D. Low platelet count (< 10,000 cells/mL)
E. Serum LDH level (> 600 IU/L)
F. Total bilirubin level (> 1.2 mg/dL)

Fecal Incontinence

Definition

A. FI is the involuntary loss of bowel function, ranging from an occasional leakage of mucus or stool when passing flatus to complete loss of bowel control. FI also occurs during exertion and inability to hold a BM when trying to get to the toilet. There are three classifications of FI.
   1. Overflow incontinence secondary to fecal impaction
   2. Reservoir secondary to diminished colonic or rectal capacity
   3. Rectosphincteric dysfunction: Structural or neurologic damage to the anal sphincter

Incidence

A. The true incidence is unknown; however, the ACG estimates that more than 18 million Americans have FI.
B. Up to 21% of institutional patients have FI.
C. Greater incidence of FI in women
D. Greater incidence in the elderly
E. Literature notes a 4% to 7% incidence of fecal and urinary incontinence

Pathogenesis

A. Stool continence requires the ability to hold stool, the ability to sense the presence of stool in the rectum (rectal sensation), the ability to relax and hold the stool (rectal compliance) when a toilet is not convenient, the physical and mental capabilities to recognize the urge, and the ability to go to the toilet. The rectum, anus, and nervous system also need to be working normally.

Predisposing Factors

A. Fecal impaction/constipation
B. Diarrhea (viral/bacteria etiology)
C. Obstetrics
   1. Forceps delivery
   2. Episiotomy
   3. Vaginal tears
   4. Large baby (> 9.5 pounds)
D. Neurologic/spinal etiology of rectosphincter dysfunction
   1. Lumbar disc herniation with subsequent cauda equina syndrome
   2. Spinal cord injury
   3. Multiple sclerosis
   4. Spina bifida
   5. Meningocele/myelomeningocele
   6. Imperforated anus
   7. Diabetes
   8. Stroke
E. Trauma
F. Hemorrhoids
G. Rectocele
H. Rectal prolapse
I. Dementia
J. Radiation for rectal/pelvic cancer
K. IBD
L. Inactivity (constipated-related bowel control problems)
M. Vitamin B_{12} deficiency
N. Hypothyroidism
O. Severe learning disability

Common Complaints

A. Leakage of mucus/stool when passing flatus
B. Uncontrolled passing of stool

Other Signs and Symptoms

A. Inability to get to the toilet in time

Subjective Data

A. Ask about the following bowel-related issues:
   1. When did the FI start and how often does the patient have bowel control problems?
   2. Is the patient incontinent of mucus, liquid, and/or solid stools? Does he or she leak a little or have full incontinence?
   3. Is the patient able to control passing gas?
   4. Does he or she have an urge to have a BM or just have loss of control?
   5. Are hemorrhoids present?
   6. What foods make the FI worse?
   7. Does the patient have to do a self-rectal evacuation of stool? How often?
   8. Does the patient have anal intercourse? How often? Use of penetrating objects?
   9. Is there a history of impaction?
   10. Does the patient wear a pad or an adult diaper?
B. Obtain a detailed obstetrical history
   1. Number of vaginal deliveries
   2. Use of forceps
   3. Infant birth weights
   4. Need for episiotomy for each vaginal delivery
   5. Presence of vaginal tears
   6. Stool incontinence after deliveries
C. Has the patient been diagnosed with Crohn's or UC? Is the patient currently under treatment? In compliance with his or her treatments?
D. Review full medical history, especially for diabetes, pelvic radiation, neurologic disease, and back injury.
E. Inquire about urinary incontinence.
F. Review surgical history, including pelvic/rectal surgeries.
G. Review all medications currently being taken, including OTC and herbal products. Specifically, evaluate for laxative abuse and recent antibiotic use.
H. Are any other family members ill?
I. Has the patient recently traveled or gone camping, which would identify infectious causes? (Refer to entries on diarrhea and infectious diseases.)

Physical Examination

A. Check temperature (if applicable), pulse, respirations, blood pressure, and weight.
B. Inspect
   1. Inspect general appearance.
   2. Examine the back and lower limbs.
   3. Inspect the perianal area for fecal matter, dermatitis, excoriation, fistula, abscess, rectal prolapse, hemorrhoids, and scars.
   4. Evaluate if the anal sphincter is open or closed at rest.
C. Auscultate
   1. Auscultate all four quadrants of the abdomen.
D. Palpate
   1. Palpate all quadrants of the abdomen to evaluate distension, tenderness, and masses.
E. **Anorectal examination: A negative digital rectal examination does not rule out proximal impaction.**
   1. Evaluate anal stenosis, resting tone
   2. Check presence of impacted stool

3. Assess the puborectalis muscle by palpating the posterior anal canal.
   a. Ask the patient to bear down as if having a BM. (An intact puborectalis displaces the examining finger anteriorly.)
   b. Ask the patient to squeeze the provider's finger.
4. Stroke the perinanal skin bilaterally to check for an anal "wink" anocutaneous reflex.

F. Give a pelvic examination to evaluate the presence of a cystocele, rectocele, enterocele, vaginal prolapse, and fistula.

G. Mental status
   1. Make a cognitive assessment, such as the Mini-Mental State Examination (MMSE).
   2. Assess for depression.

Diagnostic Tests

A. Stool specimens to rule out infectious etiology (refer to the entry on Diarrhea in this chapter)
B. Abdominal x-ray
C. Rectal manometry
D. Anorectal ultrasound
E. Defecography
F. MRI
G. Sigmoidoscopy/colonoscopy
H. Anal EMG
I. Thyroid function tests
J. Hydrogen breath tests to evaluate lactose/fructose intolerance

Differential Diagnosis

A. FI
B. Constipation/fecal impaction
C. Diarrhea secondary to infectious etiology
D. IBD
E. Postradiation therapy

Plan

A. **Fecal impaction treatment involves a three-step program.**
   1. **Disimpaction**
      a. **Manual removal**
      b. **Removal with/without enemas**
   2. **Oral polyethylene glycol**
   3. **Maintenance therapy to reduce the risk of reoccurrence.**

B. Patient teaching
   1. Discuss keeping a stool diary for a week (see Section III, Table III.1).
   2. Discuss keeping a food diary for a week to assist in identifying any foods that cause, trigger, or worsen FI such as coffee, fatty greasy foods, dairy products (lactose intolerance), sugar-free gum, and cured/smoked meats.
   3. Discuss a high-fiber diet. Give patient a dietary sheet on a high-fiber diet (see Appendix B, "High-Fiber Diet")
   4. Discuss the need for additional fluids, 8 to 10 glasses of water, to help prevent constipation. Caffeine, carbonated beverages, alcohol, and milk may cause diarrhea.
   5. Discuss the need for manual disimpaction.
   6. Remove physical barriers that prevent getting to the bathroom.
   7. Discuss tips to help deal with bowel incontinence/hygienic measures.
      a. Use the toilet before leaving home.
      b. Identify public restrooms before they are needed.
      c. Carry a bag of supplies and change clothes as soon as possible.
      d. Pants with elastic are easier to pull down than pants that have buttons.
      e. Wear disposable underwear/absorbent pads.
      f. Use water without soap; soap dries and irritates.
      g. Use baby wipes.
      h. Use a moisture-barrier cream, such as zinc oxide.
      i. Use fecal deodorant.

C. Conservative treatment
   1. Bowel retraining program
      a. Schedule defecation throughout the day, especially after meals.
   2. Biofeedback
      a. **Biofeedback requires the ability to comprehend and follow directions, motivation, and cooperation.**
         i. Auditory or visual feedback for re-education of the pelvic floor muscles
         ii. Rectal sensitivity training utilizing a rectal balloon
         iii. Anal sphincter exercises
   3. Pelvic floor exercises
   4. Anal plug

D. Dietary management: Counsel patient on nutrition and low-fat, low-cholesterol, low-sodium diets. Give diet handouts.

E. Pharmaceutical therapy

Solutions containing magnesium, phosphate, or citrate should be used with caution or avoided, especially with patients who have hypertension, HF, or chronic renal failure secondary to the absorption of these electrolytes increases fecal impaction.

   1. Loperamide hydrochloride (Imodium): 2 to 4 mg two or three times a day to control symptoms. Maximum daily dose for loperamide is 16 mg.
   2. Diphenoxylate hydrochloride/atropine (Lomotil)
      a. Contains an opioid-Schedule V medication under the Controlled Substance Act.

b. Two tablets four times a day until diarrhea is controlled.
c. Maintenance dose two tablets per day
3. Bulking agents to increase formed stools (used for diarrhea and constipation)
a. Methylcellulose (Citrucel)
b. Psyllium (Metamucil)
4. Fecal impaction
a. Polyethylene glycol (Miralax)
b. Enemas (predictable and have a timely response)
c. Suppositories
d. Laxatives
5. Manage and treat underlying disease(s) if present, including *C. difficile* and IBD (see related entries).

F. Medical management
1. Sacral nerve stimulator: In 2013 the FDA approved the Medtronic InterStim Therapy System.
2. Nonabsorbable bulking agent: Hyaluronic acid/dextranomer (SOLESTA)-tissue bulking agent given by submucosal injection.
a. Indicated as an option for FI treatment for patients older than 18 years of age having failed conservative treatment.
b. Administered by trained providers who hold a certification on the SOLESTA procedure.

G. Surgical management is dependent on the findings of the history, physical, diagnostic testing, failure of conventional therapies, and patient consent.

Follow-Up

A. Follow-up is determined by patient's needs, severity of acute MI, and whether complications are present.

Consultation/Referral

A. Refer to a gastroenterologist for a endoscopy and if diagnosis is still in question.
B. Refer to a colorectal surgeon.

Individual Considerations

A. Geriatrics
1. **FI is the second leading cause of institutionalization of the elderly.**
2. Polypharmacy with constipating drugs and laxative overuse in the elderly are common reasons for FI in the elderly.
3. Diphenoxylate hydrochloride/atropine predispose the elderly with significant side effects, including mental status changes and urinary retention.
4. Reduced fluid intake is a common factor for constipation in the elderly.
a. Impaired thirst perception
b. Urinary incontinence
c. Limited access to liquids due to immobility

Gastroenteritis, Bacterial and Viral

Definition

A. Bacterial and viral gastroenteritis is an acute inflammation of the GI mucosa of the middle or lower intestine. It is primarily an acute, self-limited illness. Immunocompromised patients can develop unremitting or fatal symptoms from gastroenteritis.

Incidence

A. Gastroenteritis is very common, occurring in all age groups. Epidemic outbreaks of bacterial gastroenteritis occur in groups who have ingested contaminated food. Viral excretion can begin before symptoms. Gastroenteritis is responsible for an estimated 8 million health care visits and 250,000 hospitalization a year.

Pathogenesis

A. Gastroenteritis is commonly due to infectious agents—viruses, bacteria, and parasites (see Table 13.9). There are four viral agents: rotavirus, norovirus, enteric adenovirus, and astrovirus. Exotoxins produced by some organisms induce hypersecretion or increased peristalsis, resulting in diarrhea or vomiting. Bacteria such as *E. coli* and *Salmonella* penetrate and invade the gastric mucosa and lead to diarrhea accompanied by fever and fecal leukocytes. Viruses destroy enterocytes of the upper jejunal villi, often producing secondary lactose intolerance.

TABLE 13.9 Infectious Agents Causing Gastroenteritis

Causative Agent	Incubation Period
Noroviruses	12 hours to 2 days
E. coli	24–72 hour
Campylobacter	2–5 days
Staphylococcus	1–6 hours
Shigella	8–24 hours
Botulism	12–36 hours
Giardia lamblia	7–21 days
Salmonella	6–72 hours
Rotaviruses	1–3 days
Adenovirus	5–8 days
Clostridium perfringens	10–12 hours
C. difficile	Variable
Listeria species	20 hours

Predisposing Factors

A. Travel to areas where cholera or *Giardia* is epidemic
   1. Ingestion of raw or undercooked seafood or drinks containing cholera-contaminated ice or water
   2. Ingestion of *Giardia*-contaminated water supplies
B. Ingestion of food contaminated with *Salmonella* or *Shigella*. Foods that are often implicated are domestic fowl and eggs, custard-filled pastries, processed meats, foods warmed on steam tables, poultry, red meat, raw seafood, raw milk, rice, and bean sprouts due to the following.
   1. Inadequate cooking time and temperatures
   2. Poor hygiene, lack of hand washing
   3. Improper storage of food
   4. Ingestion of fruits and vegetables contaminated by an infected person or by animal products
C. Infection by person-to-person spread
   1. Day care centers: Rotavirus can be found on toys and hard surfaces.
   2. Overcrowded environment, inadequate health care or education.
   3. Schools/dormitories
   4. Nursing homes
   5. Banquet halls, cruise ships
D. Contact with *Salmonella*-infected turtles, iguanas, and other reptiles.
E. Seasonal outbreaks
   1. Rotavirus and astrovirus occur from October to April.
   2. Adenovirus occurs throughout the year.
   3. Norovirus occurs throughout the year but tends to increase in cooler months.

Common Complaints

A. Abrupt onset of nausea and vomiting
B. Abrupt onset of diarrhea
C. Fever, sometimes

Other Signs and Symptoms

A. Explosive flatulence
B. Cramping abdominal pain
C. Abdominal tenderness
D. Frequent watery diarrhea
E. Mucoid stools with or without blood
F. Tenesmus
G. Myalgia
H. Headache
I. Weakness
J. Malaise

Subjective Data

A. Review onset, duration, and course of symptoms, including presence of abdominal pain and frequency of BMs. Ask the patient if anyone else in the family has the same symptoms.
B. Ask the patient about travel history, including travel by cruise ships or travel to foreign countries and camping with ingestion of water from streams, springs, or untreated wells.
C. Ask the patient about crowded or unsanitary living conditions, use of day care centers, and institutional living.
D. Take a 24-hour diet history, including ingestion of prunes or beans.
E. Review diarrhea history.
   1. How many stools?
   2. How frequent are the diarrhea stools?
   3. What color is the stool?
   4. Does the stool contain mucus?
   5. Has there been blood in the stool?
   6. Does the patient have tenesmus (constant feeling for the need to pass stool)?
F. Inquire about other symptoms, such as fever or respiratory problems.
G. If the patient is an infant, ask caregiver about activity level, irritability, sleep pattern, fluid intake, and number of wet diapers.
H. Review drug history intake, including laxatives, antacids, antibiotics, quinine, or anticancer medications.
I. Has the patient been vaccinated with the rotavirus vaccine?

Physical Examination

A. Check temperature, pulse, respirations, blood pressure, and weight.
   1. Bacterial infections: Temperatures between 101°F and 102°F
   2. Viral infections: Temperatures of 103°F and above
   3. Note hypotension and tachycardia.
B. Inspect
   1. Inspect general appearance; note if the patient is very ill.
   2. Assess hydration status. Signs of dehydration:
      a. Mild: Slightly dry buccal mucous membranes, increased thirst, decreased urine output
      b. Moderate: Sunken eyes, loss of skin turgor, dry buccal mucous membranes, decreased urine output
      c. Severe: Signs of moderate dehydration and one or more of the following: rapid thready pulse, tachypnea, lethargy, and postural hypotension
C. Auscultate the abdomen in all quadrants for bowel sounds; note hyperactive bowel sounds, absent or hypoactive bowel sounds (common with botulism), and borborygmi.
D. Palpate the abdomen for diffuse tenderness, slight distension, masses, rebound tenderness, and spasm.

E. Rectal exam: Check for masses, fissures, inflammation, perianal erythema, or stool in ampulla.
F. Neurologic exam
   1. Check for dizziness, difficulty swallowing, and other neurologic signs.
   2. Neurologic signs and symptoms indicate botulism and require emergency intervention.

Diagnostic Tests

A. No immediate lab tests are required if dehydration is absent or mild and the patient feels well except for frequent diarrhea.
B. CBC with differential: Serologic studies can detect viral pathogens.
C. Sedimentation rate: Elevated with infections or inflammation
D. Electrolytes, sodium, chlorides, potassium, and BUN
E. Blood gases to assess acid–base balance, if indicated.
F. Blood cultures, if indicated
G. Stool for guaiac, leukocytes, ova, and parasites; test specimens three times, every other day. Stool guaiac is usually negative in viral infections, positive in invasive bacterial infections. Large numbers of white cells in stool suggest inflammatory or invasive diarrhea, such as occurs with *Shigella, Salmonella, Campylobacter,* invasive *E. coli,* or *Entamoeba.* Mononuclear cells in stool are characteristic of salmonellosis.
H. Stool culture if blood or mucus, fever more than 24 hours, or leukocytes are present
I. Special cultures for *Campylobacter* and cholera are required.
J. Urinalysis: Excludes UTI as cause of nonspecific diarrhea; urine specific gravity to assess dehydration
K. Sigmoidoscopy: Skip bowel prep with gross blood, large numbers of leukocytes in stool, or severe illness.
L. Culture food from suspected foci for *Salmonella.*
M. Real-time reverse transcriptase-polymerase chain reaction (RT-qPCR) is the most widely used assay for detecting norovirus in stool, vomitus, and environmental specimens. The best detection is in stool specimens.

Differential Diagnoses

A. Gastroenteritis, bacterial and viral
B. Acute viral hepatitis
C. Acute appendicitis
D. Cholecystitis
E. IBD
F. PID
G. Bowel obstruction for other causes

Plan

A. General interventions
   1. **Meticulous hand washing is the single most important measure to decrease transmission. Hand sanitizers are an option when access to soap or clean water is limited.**
   2. Advise the patient to begin bed rest with progression to regular activities.
   3. If the patient is diapered and/or incontinent, tell the patient or caregiver to adhere strictly to contact precautions. Alcohol-based hand washing may decrease the spread.
   4. Diaper-changing areas should be separate from food preparation areas.
   5. Chlorine-based disinfectants inactivate rotavirus and may prevent disease transmission from contact with environmental surfaces.
B. Patient teaching: See the Section III Patient Teaching Guide for this chapter, "Diarrhea."
C. Dietary management
   1. Patients should remain NPO and then slowly add clear liquids to maintain hydration.
   2. Hydration is one of the most important factors in the prevention of complications.
   3. Recommend the BRAT diet until the patient is able to tolerate other solids. See Appendix B for "Nausea and Vomiting Diet Suggestions"
D. Pharmaceutical therapy
   1. The primary treatment for viral gastroenteritis is fluid replacement. There are no specific antiviral pharmaceutical therapies. IV rehydration of fluids and electrolytes may be required in severe dehydration.
   2. Antibiotics may or may not be prescribed according to the bacterial source. Antimicrobial therapy is not indicated for uncomplicated (noninvasive) gastroenteritis because therapy does not shorten duration of the disease and can prolong duration of excretion of *Salmonella* organisms.
   3. **Antidiarrheal therapy delays transit time and can reduce the severity and duration of abdominal cramping; however, it may prolong the course of some bacterial diarrhea such as *Shigella* and *E. coli.***
   4. Stop other medications that may be triggering diarrhea.

Follow-Up

A. Tell the patient to return if the condition worsens or if signs and symptoms have not abated in 48 to 72 hours. However, diarrhea due to *Salmonella* may be expected to persist for up to 2 weeks.
B. If diarrhea persists for 2 weeks or more, see the patient for a secondary evaluation.
C. Reporting surveillance systems
   1. In 2009 the Centers for Disease Control and Prevention (CDC) launched the National Outbreak Reporting System (NORS) to collect information on outbreaks of foodborne,

waterborne, and enteric disease that is spread from person to person, animals, environmental surfaces, and other ways by public health agencies.
2. In 2009 the CDC developed CaliciNet for public health and food regulator laboratories to submit outbreaks to a national database.
3. New Vaccine Surveillance Network (NVSN)
4. Foodborne Disease Active Surveillance Network (FoodNet)

Consultation/Referral

A. Refer patients to a physician immediately if they have dehydration, rebound tenderness, severe abdominal pain, neurologic symptoms, and intussusception.
B. Refer any patient with diarrhea longer than 7 days that has had no response to usual treatment.
C. Refer an immunocompromised patient.

Individual Considerations

A. Adults: Those with concomitant chronic debilitating disease are at a higher risk of mortality.
B. Geriatrics
  1. Elderly are at a higher risk of mortality secondary to dehydration.
     a. Confusion
     b. Muscle weakness
     c. Fever
     d. Dizziness
     e. Poor skin turgor
     f. Hypotension
     g. Tachycardia
  2. Diminished thirst mechanism and decreased body water exacerbate dehydration.
  3. New residents to nursing/group homes should be isolated from ill patients.

Resource

Centers for Disease Control and Prevention: www.cdc.gov

Gastroesophageal Reflux Disease

Definition

A. The ACG defines GERD as symptoms or complications resulting from the reflux of gastric contents into the esophagus or beyond, into the oral cavity (including larynx) or lung.
B. GER is considered a normal physiologic process in healthy infants, children, and adults. Most episodes last less than 3 minutes, and most often occur 30 to 60 minutes after meals and with reclining positions. GERD is present when the episodes, more than twice a week, cause troublesome symptoms or complications.
C. A very large population of patients will present after self-medicating with antacids, bicarbonate soda, and OTC medications. Management of GERD should be tailored to the frequency, severity, and duration of symptoms.

Incidence

A. GERD is very common. Daily heartburn typically occurring postprandially has been estimated to affect 17% to 65% of the normal adult population. Reflux esophagitis affects over 50% of women at some time during pregnancy. It is estimated that 30% to 90% of asthmatics have GERD. Barrett's esophagus, which affects fewer than 1% of adults, is commonly associated with GERD.

Pathogenesis

A. GERD is relaxation or incompetence of the lower esophagus persisting beyond the newborn period. Relaxation of the lower esophageal sphincter (LES) allows reflux of gastric acid and pepsin into the distal esophagus. Heartburn occurs when reverse peristaltic waves cause regurgitation of acidic stomach contents into the esophagus. Anatomical abnormalities such as a hiatal hernia predispose persons to GERD. Improper diet and nervous tension are also precipitating factors.
B. GER has been identified as a trigger for asthma, possibly by the activation of vagal reflexes and/or microaspiration. Asthma may promote GERD, and GERD may provoke asthma. Some asthma medications may reduce LES tone, further complicating the picture. Conversely, a patient with GERD may experience pulmonary disease as a response to the esophageal acid exposure.

Predisposing Factors

A. Obesity
B. Consuming large meals
C. Pregnancy
D. Emotional stress
E. Increased abdominal pressure from tight clothes, straining to lift or defecate, or swallowing air
F. Ingesting drugs that promote LES relaxation; slow gastric emptying can directly affect the mucosal lining (see Table 13.10).
G. Foods that promote LES relaxation
  1. Alcohol
  2. Chocolate
  3. Peppermint
H. Smoking: Increases stomach acid and LES pressure
I. Ingestion of caustic agents such as lye
J. Infection by agents, such as *Candida,* herpes simplex, or CMV, which directly attack the esophageal mucosa
K. Compromised immunity, from AIDS, diabetes, or chemotherapy
L. Asthma

TABLE 13.10 Commonly Used Medications That Can Impede Esophageal Function, Retard Gastric Emptying, or Cause Direct Esophageal Mucosal Injury

Impede Esophageal Function	Retard Gastric Emptying	Direct Esophageal Mucosal Injury
Calcium channel blockers	Calcium channel blockers	Nonsteroidal anti-inflammatory drugs (NSAIDs)
Theophylline	Narcotics	Aspirin
Nitrates	Anticholinergics	Tetracycline
Diazepam	Clonidine	Trimethoprim-sulfamethoxazole
Narcotics	Dopamine agents	Antiretroviral agents
Beta-agonists	Lithium	Ascorbic acid
Anticholinergics	Nicotine	Ferrous sulfate
Progesterone	Progesterone	Phenytoin
		Potassium chloride
		Propanolol
		Quinidine
		Theophylline
		Bisphosphonate

From Poh et al. (2010). Reprinted with permission.

Common Complaints

A. Heartburn
B. Regurgitation of fluid or food
C. Chest pain

Alarm Symptoms

A. Dysphagia (difficulty swallowing)
B. Unintentional weight loss
C. Predominant upper abdominal pain
D. Hematemesis (vomiting blood)
E. Melena (black feces/blood stool)
F. Odynophagia (painful swallowing)
G. Severe symptoms

Other Signs and Symptoms

A. Retrosternal aching or burning
B. Nocturnal aspiration, water or "acid" brash
C. Harsh taste in the mouth upon awakening
D. Chronic cough, especially at bedtime
E. Hoarseness
F. Globus sensation
G. Nausea
H. Dental erosion

Subjective Data

A. Review onset, duration, and course of heartburn or other symptoms.
B. Review medication history, including OTC medication and herbals.
   1. Has the patient been taking OTC antacids, H_2 blockers, or OTC proton pump inhibitors (PPIs)?
   2. How long has the patient been using these OTCs?
   3. Is the patient taking drugs that induce symptoms (refer to Table 13.10)?
C. Ask the patient about alleviating and aggravating factors.
D. Review the patient's habits, including smoking and alcohol intake.
E. Inquire about other symptoms, such as weight loss, dysphagia, blood loss, regurgitation, and diarrhea.
F. Establish the patient's usual weight to determine extent of problem.
G. Ask the patient about any history of asthma and CD.
H. Review the patient's dietary history for bulimia.

Physical Examination

A. Check pulse, respirations, blood pressure, and weight.
B. General observation of respiratory distress
C. Inspect
   1. Examine throat and evaluate mouth for dental erosion
   2. Assess swallowing ability.
D. Auscultate
   1. Evaluate the presence of wheezing in the lungs.
   2. Auscultate the heart.
   3. Evaluate the abdomen in all four quadrants.
E. Palpate
   1. Palpate abdomen for the presence of hepatosplenomegaly and masses.
   2. Assess the abdomen for tenderness or distension.
F. Perform rectal exam (if indicated for any history of hematemesis).

Diagnostic Tests

A. Clinical findings and history alone usually confirm the diagnosis in the vast majority of reflux sufferers.
B. Rule out cardiac/noncardiac chest pain before institution of therapy (see Chapter 12, section on Chest Pain).
C. Endoscopy is not required for the presence of typical GERD symptoms but is recommended for the presence of alarm symptoms or for screening patients at high risk for complications.

D. Endoscopy with biopsy is usually the first diagnostic tool in cases of caustic ingestion or suspected infectious etiology. The ACG does not recommend an endoscopy to establish the diagnosis of GERD-related asthma, chronic cough, or laryngitis.
E. Ambulatory 24-hour pH monitoring: Prolonged monitoring is the best clinical tool for diagnosing GERD in asthmatics. However, it is very expensive and not universally available.
F. Upper GI series or barium contrast radiography is not used to diagnose GERD but rules out anatomic abnormalities of the upper digestive tract.
G. Esophageal manometry is not used for the diagnosis of GERD; rather it is used to evaluate patients who have failed to respond to an empiric trial of PPIs.
H. Guaiac test for occult blood. Bleeding may accompany reflux esophagitis and be slow and chronic, resulting in iron-deficiency anemia, or brisk, resulting in hematemesis. GERD may not be obvious to the clinician when obtaining a patient history, especially in an asthma patient with confounding respiratory symptoms.
I. Consider *H. pylori* testing.

Differential Diagnoses

A. GERD
B. MI/angina
C. Esophageal spasm
D. Gallbladder disease
E. Cancer—gastric or esophageal
F. Infections: CMV, herpes simplex virus, and *Candida*
G. Peptic ulcer
H. Ingestion of caustic substance
I. Self-induced vomiting/bulimia
J. Pyloric stenosis
K. Food allergy
L. Eosinophilic esophagitis (EE)
M. Autoimmune skin disorders affecting the esophagus

Plan

A. General interventions: Management depends on cause and severity of symptoms.
B. Patient teaching: See the Section III Patient Teaching Guide for this chapter, "Gastroesophageal Reflux Disease (GERD)."
C. Dietary management
   1. Weight loss is advised for overweight or obese patients with GERD symptoms.
   2. At present, there is no supporting data for special dietary precautions; however, a dietary elimination of foods helps to identify triggers.
D. Medical and surgical management
   1. The Nissen fundoplication is a surgical procedure used to treat GERD in asthmatics. It improves the antireflux barrier and provides a lasting solution. Because it is not always successful, it is reserved for severe cases. The Nissen operation is often performed as a laparoscopic procedure.
   2. **Surgical therapy is not recommended for patients who do not respond to PPI therapy.**
   3. **The ACG guidelines note that surgical therapy is as effective as medical therapy for carefully selected patients with chronic GERD when performed by an experienced surgeon.**
   4. **Patients on NSAIDs who experience upper gastric pain including reflux need to be referred for endoscopy as soon as possible.**
E. Pharmaceutical therapy
   1. The potential adverse effects of acid suppression include the increased risk of community-acquired pneumonia and GI infections, including *C. difficile*-associated diarrhea.
   2. Long-term use of acid suppression therapy without a diagnosis is not advised.
   3. The target of pharmaceutical therapy is improvement in quality of life by the reduction/relief of symptoms and healing of erosive esophagitis (EE).
   4. On-demand or self-directed therapy has been shown to be effective; however, patient's use and response should be evaluated.
   5. Histamine-2 receptor antagonists (H_2 blockers) are effective in managing milder, infrequent GI symptoms. Tolerance occurs with chronic use of H_2 blockers. Several H_2 blockers are currently available as prescription and OTC: nizatidine (Axid), famotidine (Pepcid), cimetidine (Tagamet), and ranitidine (Zantac).
   6. **PPIs are used for both GERD and EE and are considered the "gold standard" of treatment.**
      a. Initiation of a PPI should be prescribed once a day, before the first meal of the day. For maximal pH control, the traditional delayed-release PPI should be administered 30 to 60 minutes before a meal.
      b. Avoid the concomitant use of clopidogrel (Plavix) with omeprazole or esomeprazole because of the significant reduction of the antiplatelet activity of Plavix. This is an FDA safety labeling change.
      c. Dosages are age- and weight-based.
      d. Long-term therapy should be titrated down to the lowest effective dose based on symptom control.
      e. Patients may experience a relapse in their GERD symptoms after discontinuance and therefore may need to be tapered off or use a stepdown approach with an antacid or an H_2 blocker.

f. No PPI is approved for use in infants younger than 1 year.
g. PPIs are currently available by prescription and OTC (see Table 13.11).

Follow-Up

A. Noncardiac chest pain due to GERD should have a diagnostic evaluation before institution of therapy.
B. Empiric treatment with a PPI may be attempted for a short period except for patients presenting with any alarm symptoms. Schedule a return visit in 1 to 2 weeks to evaluate the relief of symptoms.
C. Patients having frequent relapses and failure to adequately respond to long-term OTC H_2 blockers and PPI use should have an endoscopic evaluation.
D. The need for prescribed long-term PPI treatment or the presence of alarm symptoms requires a gastroenterology consultation.
E. Consider bone density studies for patients with long-term PPI use.

Consultations

A. Referral is necessary if the patient fails to improve after trying two different medications, or if the patient has dysphagia, recent weight loss, or blood loss.
B. PPI nonresponders need to be referred for evaluation.

Individual Considerations

A. Pregnancy
   1. Underlying causes in pregnancy are diminished gastric motility and displacement of stomach by enlarging uterus.
   2. Rule out pregnancy-induced hypertension (PIH); evaluate the patient immediately for signs and symptoms of sudden onset discomfort with no relief from antacids (PIH or HELLP syndrome).
B. Geriatrics
   1. GERD prevalence increases with age and may be associated with a hiatal hernia.
   2. Prolonged reflux results in esophagitis and may lead to stricture development. Chronic recurrence may develop into Barrett's syndrome.
   3. Treatment of GERD is the same as for general adults; however, do diagnostic testing in short-time sequence secondary to stricture and cancer in the elderly.
   4. Atypical symptoms are common presentations in the elderly.
      a. Vomiting
      b. Anorexia
      c. Dysphagia
      d. Respiratory symptoms
      e. Belching
      f. Hoarseness
      g. Postprandial fullness
   5. PPIs are the mainstay treatment in the elderly. Most elderly patients will need long-term maintenance therapy.
   6. PPIs interact with medications that are commonly taken in the older population, including warfarin, phenytoin, and diazepam. PPIs also reduce the antiplatelet effect of clopidogrel.
      a. Monitor the therapeutic effect of warfarin and phenytoin.

TABLE 13.11 Proton Pump Inhibitors

PPI	Available Dosages	Over the Counter
Omeprazole (Prilosec)	Capsules 10 mg, 20 mg, and 40 mg	Tablet 20 mg
Lansoprazole (Prevacid)	Capsules 15 mg and 30 mg Oral suspension and Solu Tab 15 mg and 30 mg IV (30 mg)	Capsule 15 mg
Rabeprazole (Aciphex)	Capsules 20 mg and Sprinkles 5 mg and 10 mg	Not available
Pantoprazole (Protonix)	Capsules 20 mg and 40 mg Oral suspension 30 mg IV 40 mg	Not available
Esomeprazole (Nexium)	Capsules 20 mg and 40 mg Oral suspension 20 mg and 40 mg IV 20 mg and 40 mg	22.3 mg (24 hour caps)
Dexlansoprazole (Dexilant)	Capsules 30 mg and 60 mg	Not available
Omeprazole + sodium bicarbonate (Zegerid)	Capsules Omeprazole 20 mg and 20 mg plus 300 mg Na+ Oral suspension Omeprazole 20 mg and 40 mg plus 460 mg Na+	Capsule 20 mg

Resources

American Gastroenterological Association: www.gastro.org
Rome Foundation: http://romecriteria.org/criteria
The 2013 guidelines for the diagnosis and management of gastroesophageal reflux disease is available online at http://gi.org/guideline/diagnosis-and-managemen-of-gastroesophageal-reflux-disease

Giardiasis Intestinalis

Definition

A. *Giardiasis intestinalis* (formerly *Giardia lamblia)* is the leading parasitic cause of diarrhea. Infestation can lead to malabsorption by coating large areas of the small bowel, particularly the lower duodenum and upper jejunum. Most people infected with *G. intestinalis* remain asymptomatic, and most infections are self-limited.

Incidence

A. Giardiasis has a worldwide distribution and is especially prevalent in the United States and overseas. It is common in areas where water supplies are contaminated by human sewage. The age-specific prevalence of giardiasis is highest in children 1 to 9 years and in adults 35 to 44 years of age. The peak onset occurs annually during early summer through early fall.

Pathogenesis

A. *Giardiasis intestinalis* is a flagellated protozoan. The infective form is the cyst. Humans are the principal reservoir of infection, but *Giardia* can infect dogs, cats, beavers, and other animals that can contaminate water with feces containing cysts.
B. People become infected either directly, by hand-to-mouth transfer of cysts from feces of an infected person (e.g., childcare), or indirectly, by ingestion of fecal-contaminated water or food. Most community-wide epidemics result from contaminated water supplies.
C. The incubation period is 1 to 3 weeks, with an average of 7 to 10 days. The infective form is the cyst with infection limited to the small intestine and the biliary tract. Disease is communicable for as long as the infected person excretes cysts.

Predisposing Factors

A. **50% to 75% of outbreaks occur in childcare settings.**
B. Travel to endemic areas
C. Subjection to unsanitary food handling
D. Exposure to contaminated water supplies
E. Male homosexuality
F. CF
G. Immunocompromised individuals are at high risk.

Common Complaints

Acute Complaints

A. Explosive, foul-smelling diarrhea
B. Mucus in stools, bulky stools
C. Upper abdominal pain or discomfort
D. Flatulence
E. Nausea
F. Anorexia
G. Weight loss

Other Signs and Symptoms

Chronic Complaints

A. Intermittent loose stools (but not diarrhea)
B. Steatorrhea
C. Increased flatulence or distension
D. Vague abdominal discomfort
E. Fatigue related to anemia
F. Profound weight loss (10%–20% of body weight)
G. Malabsorption
H. Urticaria

Subjective Data

A. Review onset, duration, and course of symptoms. Is diarrhea acute or chronic?
B. Ask the patient about travel to areas known for giardiasis.
C. Review the patient's intake of medications and other substances that can cause diarrhea, especially antibiotics, laxatives, quinidine, magnesium-containing antacids, excess alcohol, caffeine, herbal teas, digitalis, loop diuretics, antihypertensive agents, and sorbitol-containing (sugar-free) gums and mints.
D. Review the nature of the patient's BMs, including frequency; consistency; volume; and presence of blood, pus, or mucus.
E. Does diarrhea have any relationship to meals? Onset of diarrhea within hours of ingesting a potentially contaminated food is suggestive of bacterial infection such as *E. coli;* this is confirmed by checking if others were similarly affected.
F. Ask the patient about associated symptoms that need evaluation, such as fever, abdominal pain, or rash.
G. Ask the patient if other family members or sexual contacts are also ill.
H. Establish the patient's normal weight, and if any weight has recently been lost, review amount and over what period of time.

Physical Examination

The physical examination may reveal no specific finding.

A. Check temperature, pulse, respirations, blood pressure, and weight.
B. Inspect: General appearance for signs of dehydration; include evaluation of mucous membranes.

C. Auscultate: Abdomen for bowel sounds in all quadrants.
D. Palpate
   1. Palpate the abdomen for masses, tenderness, guarding, and rebound. Patients with periumbilical or RLQ pain and copious volumes of watery stool are likely to have a small bowel etiology.
   2. Palpate lymph nodes for enlargement.
E. Perform rectal exam.

Diagnostic Tests

A. EIA and direct fluorescence antibody (DFA) are becoming the standard for diagnosis of giardiasis in the United States.
B. Stool bacteria culture and sensitivity
C. Mucus stool for leukocytes: Mucus free of leukocytes is the hallmark of IBS; a large number of white cells suggests inflammatory or invasive diarrhea.
D. Stool for ova and parasites; test three times on alternate days. **Parasites are passed intermittently, so examine stools on alternating days.**
E. Stool for occult blood
F. Endoscopy to identify cyst in duodenal fluid or small bowel tissue

Differential Diagnoses

A. Giardiasis
B. Malabsorption
C. *E. coli* infection
D. IBS
E. Viral diarrhea
F. Lactose intolerance
G. Other bacterial infections, such as *Shigella*, *Salmonella*, and *Campylobacter*
H. CD
I. Sprue

Plan

A. General interventions
   1. Advise adult workers with diarrhea to stay away from day care centers until they become asymptomatic.
   2. Advise the patient's household and sexual contacts to seek medical examination and treatment.
B. Patient teaching
   1. See the Section III Patient Teaching Guide for this chapter, "Diarrhea."
   2. Discuss safe sexual practices. Avoiding oral-anal and oral-genital sex can decrease venereal transmission.
   3. Recommend contact precautions for duration of illness for diapered and/or incontinent children.
   4. People with diarrhea caused by giardia should not use recreational water venues, including swimming pools and water slides, for 2 weeks after symptoms resolve.
C. Dietary management
   1. Tell the patient or caregiver to prevent dehydration from diarrhea by increasing fluids.
   2. Advise restricting milk products to rule out lactose intolerance. Postgiardia lactose occurs in 20% to 40% of patients.
   3. Tell backpackers, campers, and people likely to be exposed to contaminated water to avoid drinking directly from streams. To make water safe for drinking, boil the water, or use chemical disinfection or filtration. Boiling water is the most reliable method to make water safe for drinking.
D. Pharmaceutical therapy
   1. Treatment of asymptomatic carriers is not generally recommended.
   2. **Metronidazole, tinidazole, and nitazoxanide are the drugs of choice for treatment.**
      a. Metronidazole (Flagyl) is the principal agent used to treat giardiasis in the United States.
         i. Adults: 250 mg orally three times daily for 5 to 7 days
      b. Tinidazole (Tindamax) has fewer side effects than metronidazole.
         i. Adults: 2 g single dose
      c. Nitazoxanide (Alinia) oral suspension has similar efficacy to metronidazole and has the advantage of treating other intestinal parasites
         i. Age 12 years and older: 500 mg tablet every 12 hours or 25 mL oral suspension every 12 hours with food for 3 days
   3. Paromomycin (Humatin), a nonabsorbable aminoglycoside, is recommended for treatment of symptomatic infection in pregnant women in the second and third trimesters.
      a. Adults: 500 mg three times daily for 5 to 10 days

Follow-Up

A. Relapses after treatment are common, especially in immunocompromised patients.
B. Schedule follow-ups at 6 weeks and 6 months after treatment, as indicated.
C. If diarrhea persists for 2 weeks or more, secondary evaluation is indicated. Stools should be examined again for blood, leukocytes, and parasites.
D. Patients who remain undiagnosed after an extensive evaluation and trial of metronidazole (Flagyl) often turn out to have IBS or surreptitious laxative abuse.

Consultation/Referral

A. Consult a physician if the patient has no relief of symptoms after completion of therapies.

Individual Considerations

A. Pregnancy
   1. Treatment of patients during pregnancy is recommended. Giardiasis in pregnancy is associated with dehydration, malabsorption, or severe symptoms.
   2. Malabsorptive symptoms may persist since regeneration of functioning intestinal mucosa requires time.
   3. Breastfeeding appears to protect infants from *Giardiasis intestinalis.*

B. Geriatrics
   1. Anemia, weight loss, and anorexia have been the most prominent signs in the elderly.

Hemorrhoids

Definition

A. Hemorrhoids are clusters of vascular tissues, smooth muscle, and connective tissue of the anal canal. Internal hemorrhoids are above the anorectal line and covered by rectal mucosa. Hemorrhoids can be found at any position of the rectum. Internal hemorrhoids are graded by severity (see Table 13.12).

B. External hemorrhoids are below the anorectal line, covered by anal skin, and appear as painless, flaccid skin tags (see Figure 13.2).

C. When blood within the hemorrhoid becomes clotted due to obstruction, the hemorrhoids are referred to as thrombosed and appear as blue, shiny masses.

D. **Although rectal bleeding is commonly associated with hemorrhoids, it may be a symptom of other disease processes, such as colorectal cancer, IBD, other colitides, diverticular disease, and angiodysplasia.**

Incidence

A. The incidence of hemorrhoids is unknown. Patients tend to present after utilization and failure of OTC treatments. Hemorrhoids are common in people between 20 and 65 years of age. They are uncommon in people younger than age 20 except secondary to pregnancy.

TABLE 13.12 Severity of Hemorrhoids Used to Guide Treatment Options

Grade	Severity
I	The hemorrhoids bleed but do not prolapse.
II	The hemorrhoids prolapse upon defecation but reduce spontaneously.
III	The hemorrhoids prolapse upon defecation and must be reduced manually.
IV	The hemorrhoids are prolapsed and cannot be reduced manually.

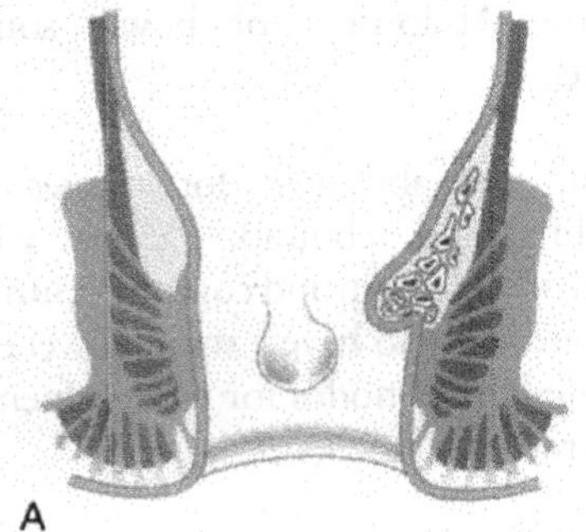

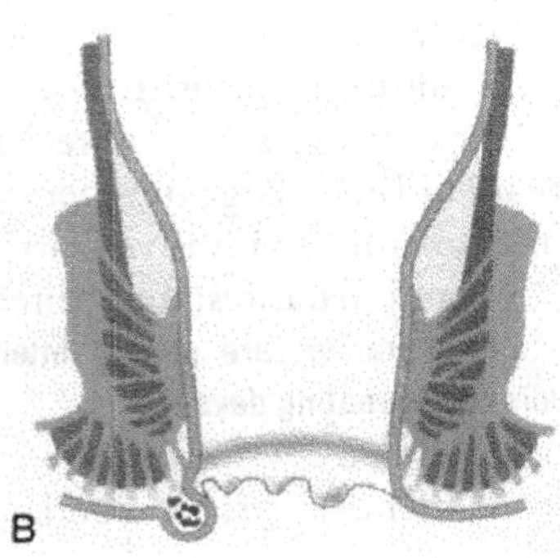

FIGURE 13.2 Internal and external hemorrhoids. A. Internal hemorrhoid: Covered by a thin sheet of tissue called mucous membrane, an internal hemorrhoid bulges into the rectal opening and may sink a bit during bowel movements. B. External hemorrhoid: Covered by skin, an external hemorrhoid protrudes from the rectum.

Pathogenesis

A. Mechanism is unknown. Prolapse may be initiated by shearing force from passage of large firm stool, by increased venous pressure from HF or pregnancy, or by straining that occurs with lifting or defecation.

Predisposing Factors

A. Pressure associated with constipation
B. Pelvic congestion
C. Poor pelvic musculature
D. Pregnancy
E. Constipation or straining with stool
F. Portal hypertension, cirrhosis
G. Low-fiber diet
H. Sedentary jobs, such as driving trucks, piloting planes
I. Loss of muscle tone due to advanced age
J. Anal intercourse
K. Obesity
L. Colon malignancy
M. Rectal surgery
N. IBD

Common Complaints

A. Cardinal features
   1. Bleeding: Painless, bright red bleeding with defecation (internal)
   2. Anal pruritus
   3. Prolapse
   4. Pain related to thrombosis

Other Signs and Symptoms

A. Visible prolapsed mass
B. Incomplete defecation
C. Leakage of feces (internal hemorrhoids)
D. Excessive moisture
E. Weakness or fatigue, with anemia

Subjective Data

A. Review onset and duration of symptoms, especially the history of rectal bleeding, prolapse, issues of hygiene and pain.
B. Review the patient's history of hemorrhoids and treatments, including surgery.
C. Ask the patient about recent pregnancy, liver disease, and constipation.
D. Inquire about the patient's job and level of daily activity.
E. Review the patient's sexual practices for anal intercourse.
F. Review the patient's dietary history for fluid intake and sources/amount of fiber.
G. Ask about bowel habits, including frequency, consistency, and ease of evacuation.
H. Review a detailed family history, with emphasis on intestinal disease.

Physical Examination

A. Check temperature (if indicated), pulse, respirations, blood pressure, and weight.
B. Inspection
   1. Observation of rectal area for skin tags, prolapse, irritation, fissures, and condyloma.
      a. Internal hemorrhoids are usually not visible unless prolapsed.
      b. External hemorrhoids protrude with straining or standing.
   2. Using anoscopy: Visualize internal rectum for hemorrhoids, fissures, or masses.
C. Palpate
   1. Palpate abdomen for masses.
   2. Internal hemorrhoids are usually not palpable unless thrombosed.
   3. Perform digital rectal examination.

Diagnostic Tests

A. Hematocrit and hemoglobin, if bleeding present
B. Anoscopy: Reveals internal hemorrhoids as bright red to purplish bulges. **Digital rectal examination alone can neither diagnose nor exclude internal hemorrhoids; anoscopy is required.**
C. Sigmoidoscopy or colonoscopy (geriatric population)
D. Stool for guaiac testing
E. Air-contrast BE for atypical bleeding

Differential Diagnoses

A. Hemorrhoids
B. Condyloma acuminata
C. Rectal prolapse
D. Rectal bleeding due to one of the following
   1. Colorectal cancer
   2. Polyps
   3. Anal fissure
   4. Fistula
   5. Perianal abscess
   6. IBD, including UC and CD
   7. Diverticulitis
   8. Pelvic tumor

Plan

A. General interventions: No treatment is necessary if the patient is asymptomatic except for maintaining regular bowel habits and performing comfort measures.
B. Patient teaching: See the Section III Patient Teaching Guide for this chapter, "Hemorrhoids."
C. Dietary management: High-fiber diet and an adequate fluid intake should be continued indefinitely in order to maintain a soft bulky stool that can be passed without straining (see Appendix B, Table B.7 "Fiber Recommendations by Age").
D. Medical and surgical management
   1. Use warm sitz baths up to three times a day for irritation and pruritus.
   2. Conservative treatment for thrombosed hemorrhoid includes lying prone and applying ice pack to area.
   3. Incision and evacuation of thrombosis or clot may be performed under local anesthesia. Other treatments for thrombosed hemorrhoids noted in clinical trials have included the following.
      a. Topical nitroglycerin 0.2% topical ointment for temporary analgesia. The most common side effect was headache.
      b. Topical nifedipine
      c. In a small study, one intrasphincter injection of botulinum toxin relieved pain within 24 hours.
   4. Symptomatic Grade I, Grade II, and some Grade III hemorrhoids may be treated by the following.
      a. Rubber band ligation is the treatment of choice for Grades I and II hemorrhoids. Rubber band ligation is the most widely used and is associated with fewer complications than surgery.

b. Bipolar, infrared, and laser coagulation (may require more than one treatment)
c. Sclerotherapy
d. Stapled hemorrhoidopexy can be performed in patients with Grade III hemorrhoids.

5. External hemorrhoids usually do not require surgical therapy except in cases of thrombosis. For selective Grade III and Grade IV internal and strangulated hemorrhoids that fail medical and nonoperative therapies, surgical treatment is required. **Stapled hemorrhoidopexy has a faster recovery but has a higher recurrence rate. Hemorrhoidectomy is the treatment of last choice because it requires hospitalization and an extended recovery period, and it risks compromising competence of the anal sphincter.** Hemorrhoidectomy complications include:
a. Urinary retention
b. UTI
c. Fecal impaction
d. Pain
e. Hemorrhage
f. Stricture formation (1%) or sphincter damage (rare)
g. Nonhealing wound
h. Fistula formation
i. Anal leakage

E. Pharmaceutical therapy
1. Drug of choice: Bulk-forming agents such as psyllium seed (Metamucil), methylcellulose (Citrucel), or calcium polycarbophil (Fibercon), 1 to 3 teaspoons in 8 oz of liquid three times a day. Maintenance dose is 1 to 3 teaspoons after dinner.
2. Stool softener: Docusate sodium (Colace) or docusate calcium (Doxidan) 100 mg three times daily.
3. For irritation and pruritus, topical creams and anesthetics are found in OTC products such as Anusol, pramoxine HCl (Tronolane Cream), Preparation H, and topical hydrocortisone preparations.
4. NSAIDs supplemented with narcotics. An oral analgesic such as codeine may be prescribed for thrombosed hemorrhoids. However, codeine causes constipation.

Follow-Up

A. None is necessary if resolution occurs and the patient is asymptomatic.
B. Reevaluate the patient in 2 weeks for further treatment if symptoms persist.
C. Evaluate the patient with an intervention in 7 to 10 days.

Consultation/Referral

A. **The onset of urinary retention and fever immediately after an office-based procedure may be the initial sign of perianal sepsis and mandates emergent patient evaluation.**
B. Refer the patient with acute thrombosis of external hemorrhoids to a physician.
C. Refer the patient to a surgeon if hemorrhoids bleed repeatedly, prolapse, produce intractable pain, or are thrombosed, and if 3 to 5 consecutive days of treatment do not provide relief.

Individual Considerations

A. Pregnancy
1. Labor, which results in pressure on the pelvic floor by the presenting part of the fetus and the expulsive efforts of the woman, may aggravate hemorrhoids, causing protrusion and inflammation during the puerperium. Hemorrhoids may be pushed back after delivery to prevent them from becoming swollen and painful.
2. Surgical treatment is contraindicated in pregnancy because of the risk of inducing labor.
3. Conservative treatment is recommended with excision of thrombosed external hemorrhoids if necessary.

B. Geriatrics
1. Prolapse of rectal mucosa is more common in the elderly.
2. Colonoscopy is recommended in the geriatric population to exclude malignancy or other underlying disease.

Hepatitis A

Definition

A. Hepatitis A is an acute self-limited illness with inflammation of the liver caused by a viral infection. Hepatitis A virus (HAV) is spread by viral shedding. All cases of hepatitis A are reportable to the public health department.
B. The highest titers of HAV in the stool of infected patients occur 1 to 2 weeks before onset of illness (jaundice or elevation of liver enzymes), during which time patients are most likely to transmit infection. Risk subsequently diminishes and is minimal in the week after onset of jaundice. Up to 70% of adults will have jaundice. Fulminant hepatitis is rare, and chronic infectious and carrier states do not occur.
C. Duration of HAV infection is typically 8 weeks, but prolonged disease, as long as 6 months, can occur in 10% to 15% of symptomatic patients.
D. The major methods of prevention include improved sanitation of water sources, improved hygiene

practice prior to food preparation and diaper changes, immunization with the hepatitis A vaccine, and administration of immune globulin (IG).

E. Hepatitis A does not reoccur because IgG antibodies to HAV provide lifelong protection.

Incidence

A. From 30% to 35% of acute hepatitis cases in the United States are due to HAV. In developing countries, where infection is endemic, most people are infected during the first decade of life. In the United States, the incidence of HAV has declined since 1995 due to the administration of the HAV vaccine.
B. Outbreak in custodial institutions accounts for about 10% to 15% of reported HAV in the United States. No appreciable seasonal variation in incidence has been noted.
C. The incidence of mortality from HAV is 0% to 1%. The single most important determinant of illness severity is age; a direct correlation between increasing age and the likelihood of adverse events is present.

Pathogenesis

A. HAV is a small, RNA enterovirus classified as a member of the picornavirus group. Viral replication depends on hepatocyte uptake and synthesis, and assembly occurs exclusively in liver cells. Transmission of HAV is person-to-person, primarily by the fecal–oral route and parenterally. The incubation period is 15 to 50 days, with an average of 25 to 30 days.
B. Common-source, food- and waterborne epidemics have occurred, including several caused by shellfish contaminated with human sewage. Nosocomial outbreaks have occurred as a result of shedding of HAV from infected, asymptomatic neonates, children, or adults.

Predisposing Factors

A. Ingestion of infected water, food, and shellfish
B. Close personal contact with an HAV-infected person
   1. Contact with a child who attends a child care center (especially with children in diapers)
   2. Male homosexual activity
   3. Vertical transmission from mother to fetus (limited)
   4. Personal contact with a newly arriving international adoptee
C. Poor sanitation or personal hygiene
D. Crowded living conditions
E. International travel
F. IV drug abuse

Common Complaints

A. Malaise
B. Anorexia
C. Nausea
D. Low-grade fever
E. Jaundice-icteric phase (70% of older children and adults)
   1. Tea-colored urine
   2. Clay-colored stool
   3. Abdominal pain
   4. Pruritus
   5. Enlarged liver
F. Fatigue
G. Joint pain

Other Signs and Symptoms

A. Adults: Severe, prolonged course with fatigue, headache, vomiting, and symptoms noted earlier.
B. Relapsing hepatitis A is more common in the elderly. There generally has been a protracted course of symptoms and a relapse of symptoms following an apparent resolution.

Subjective Data

A. Review duration, onset, and severity of symptoms, including specifics about urine or stool color changes.
B. Ask the patient about family members and sexual contacts with similar symptoms.
C. Review the patient's history of blood transfusions, IV drug use, and alcohol abuse.
D. Inquire about occupational exposure.
E. Ask the patient about recent international travel or exposure to newly arrived international adoptees.
F. Review immunization status.
G. Review medications for a possible Tylenol overdose or Ecstasy use as a cause for acute drug-induced liver injury.

Physical Examination

A. Check temperature (acute illness), pulse, respirations, blood pressure, and weight.
B. Inspect
   1. Note general appearance.
   2. Inspect the skin for slight jaundice or rash.
   3. Inspect mucous membranes and nail beds.
   4. Inspect eyes for yellow sclera.
C. Auscultate lung fields, all quadrants of the abdomen, and the heart.
D. Percuss the abdomen.
E. Palpate
   1. Palpate all quadrants of the abdomen for masses, liver tenderness, and hepatosplenomegaly (about 10% of cases).

Diagnostic Tests

A. Viral serology for typing HAV, IgG, and IgM. **Serum IgM presents at onset of illness and disappears within 4 months, generally indicating current or recent infection. However, it may persist for 6 months or longer. Presence of IgG anti-HAV antibodies without virus-specific IgM indicates past infection and immunity.**
B. Liver function studies, including ALT, AST, LDH, and ALP.
C. Bilirubin, direct and indirect
D. CBC
E. PT
F. Urinalysis: Reveals proteinuria and bilirubinuria
G. Imaging studies are usually not indicated for hepatitis A infection. An ultrasound may be used to exclude other pathology.

Differential Diagnoses

A. HAV
B. Mononucleosis
C. Cancer
D. Obstructive jaundice
E. Alcoholic hepatitis or cirrhosis
F. Hepatotoxic drug use
   1. Drug-induced liver injury (e.g., Tylenol, Ecstasy)
   2. Drug-induced hypersensitivity reaction (e.g., sulfasalazine hypersensitivity)
G. Food poisoning
H. Exclusion of other hepatitis types
I. CMV
J. Acute HIV infection

Plan

A. General interventions
   1. Contact precautions are recommended for diapered and/or incontinent patients for 1 week after onset of symptoms.
   2. Children and adults with acute HAV infection should be excluded from school, work, and childcare centers for 1 week after onset of illness.
   3. Hepatitis is self-limiting and does not require therapy. Treatment is supportive.
      a. Limit activities secondary to malaise.
      b. OCPs and HRT should be stopped to avoid cholestasis.
      c. Alcohol consumption is not advised.
      d. Adults who work as food handlers should not work for 1 week after onset of the illness.
   4. Encourage strict hand washing.
B. Patient teaching
   1. See the Section III Patient Teaching Guide for this chapter, "Jaundice and Hepatitis."
   2. Teach the patient that major methods for prevention are improved sanitation (e.g., of water sources and in food preparation) and personal hygiene.
   3. Food and travel precautions include the following:
      a. Avoid uncontrolled water resources: Use bottled water, boil water, or add iodine to inactivate the virus.
      b. Avoid raw shellfish.
      c. Avoid uncooked foods.
      d. All fruit should be washed and peeled.
C. Dietary management: Encourage optimum nutrition.
D. Pharmaceutical therapy
   1. IG (Gamastan, Gammar-P): Preexposure administration is 0.02 mL/kg, two doses IM. HAV vaccine preexposure is preferred in all populations unless contraindicated.
   2. Postexposure IG administration given IM within 2 weeks of HAV exposure is 80% to 90% effective in preventing symptomatic infection.
      a. Time of exposure: 2 weeks or less
         i. Younger than 12 months: 0.02 mL/kg of IG given IM into a large muscle.
         ii. 12 months to 40 years: Hepatitis A vaccine.
         iii. 41 years and older: 0.02 mL/kg IG given IM into a large muscle. No more than 5 mL should be administered into one site for an adult or large child.
      b. Postexposure prophylaxis with IG is recommended for the following:
         i. Household and sexual contacts of infected persons
         ii. Newborn infants of HAV-infected mothers
         iii. Childcare center staff, children, and their household contacts
         iv. Students when transmission within school is documented
         v. Staff in institutions and hospitals
         vi. People who ingested HAV-contaminated food or water within 2 weeks of last exposure
   3. Vaccines
      a. Two inactivated HAV vaccines, Havrix and Vaqta, are available in the United States.
      b. Twinrix is a combination hepatitis A (Havrix) and hepatitis B (Engerix-B) vaccine available in the United States for ages 18 years or older (see Table 13.13).
   4. HAV vaccine is recommended for the following.
      a. Children 2 years and older in defined and circumscribed communities with high endemic rates and/or periodic outbreaks of HAV infection
      b. Patients with chronic liver disease
      c. Homosexual and bisexual men
      d. Users of injections and illicit drugs

TABLE 13.13 Dosages and Schedules for Hepatitis A Vaccines

A. HAVRIX

Licensed dosages and schedules for HAVRIX[a]				
Age	**Dose (ELISA units)[b]**	**Volume (mL)**	**No. of Doses**	**Schedule (months)[c]**
12 months to 18 years	720	0.5	2	0, 6–12
≥ 19 years	1,440	1.0	2	0, 6–12

[a]Hepatitis A vaccine, inactivated, GlaxoSmithKline.
[b]Enzyme-linked immunosorbent assay units.
[c]0 months represents timing of the initial dose; subsequent numbers represent months after the initial dose.

B. VAQTA

Licensed dosages and schedules for VAQTA[a]				
Age	**Dose (U.)[b]**	**Volume (mL)**	**No. of Doses**	**Schedule (months)[c]**
12 months to 18 years	25	0.5	2	0, 6–18
≥ 19 years	50	1.0	2	0, 6–18

[a]Hepatitis A vaccine, inactivated, Merck & Co., Inc.
[b]Units.
[c]0 months represents timing of the initial dose; subsequent numbers represent months after the initial dose.

C. TWINRIX

Licensed dosages and schedules for TWINRIX[a]				
Age	**Dose (ELISA units)[b]**	**Volume (mL)**	**No. of Doses**	**Schedule[c]**
≥ 18 years	720	1.0	3	0, 1, 6 months
≥ 18 years	720	1.0	4	0, 7, 21–30 days + 12 months

[a]Combined hepatitis A and hepatitis B vaccine, inactivated, GlaxoSmithKline.
[b]Enzyme-linked immunosorbent assay units.
[c]This 4-dose schedule enables patients to receive 3 doses in 21 days; this schedule is used prior to planned exposure with short notice and requires a fourth dose at 12 months.

From Centers for Disease Control and Prevention: www.cdc.gov/hepatitis/HAV/HAVfaq.htm.

   e. Those with occupational risk of exposure, such as handlers of nonhuman primates and persons working with HAV in a laboratory setting
   f. Travelers who need preexposure immunoprophylaxis.
   g. Patients with clotting-factor disorders such as hemophilia.
5. HAV vaccine is potentially indicated for the following.
   a. Childcare center staff and children
   b. Patients and staff in custodial care institutions
   c. Hospital personnel
   d. Food handlers; **however, routine HAV for food handlers is not recommended.**
   e. Patients with hemophilia
6. HAV vaccine may be administered simultaneously with other vaccines, but it should be given in a separate syringe and at a separate site.
7. The need for an additional hepatitis A booster beyond the two-dose primary immunizations has not been established.
8. Immune response in immunocompromised patients such as those with HIV may be suboptimal. The vaccine is inactivated; therefore, no special precautions are needed when vaccinating immunocompromised patients.
9. Vaccine side effects are generally mild and may include
   a. Local pain at the immunization site
   b. Localized induration at the injection site
10. Tylenol may be administered for fever and arthralgia but is strictly limited to a maximum dose of 3 to 4 g/d in adults.

Follow-Up

A. Dehydration may require hospital admission.
B. Follow up in 2 weeks for reevaluation.
C. Check for hepatitis B immunity and vaccinate.
D. Hepatitis A is reportable to the public health department.

Consultation/Referral

A. Consult a physician if necessary.

Individual Considerations

A. Pregnancy
   1. Pregnant women recently exposed to HAV should receive prophylactic gamma globulin.

2. HAV is an inactivated vaccine and is considered safe during pregnancy.
3. HAV infection during pregnancy is associated with increased risk of premature labor and delivery.

B. Adults: In the United States, the lowest rate of HAV infection is in people older than 40.

C. Geriatrics
1. The elderly have greater numbers of HAV antibodies, resulting in fewer cases.
2. Symptoms are usually vague. Fatigue; pruritus; and the classic symptoms of jaundice, hepatomegaly, and liver tenderness are commonly absent in the elderly.
3. Diagnostic test results in the elderly include elevated bilirubin, lower or normal transaminase and ALP, and normal ultrasonography.
4. Treatment is supportive. Corticosteroids may relieve symptoms but prolong the disease state due to prolonged viral replication.

D. Special populations
1. People with chronic liver disease are at risk of fulminant hepatitis and should be immunized.
2. People who are awaiting or have received liver transplants should be immunized.

Hepatitis B

Definition

A. Hepatitis B is inflammation of the liver caused by HBV. Acute HBV infection cannot be distinguished from other forms of acute viral hepatitis on the basis of clinical signs and symptoms or nonspecific laboratory findings. Acutely infected patients may be asymptomatic or symptomatic. The likelihood of developing symptoms of acute hepatitis is age dependent.

B. Chronic HBV infection is defined as the presence of HBsAg in serum for at least 6 months or by the presence of HBsAg in a person who tests negative for antibody of the immunoglobulin (Ig) M subclass to hepatitis B core antigen (IgM anti-HBc).

C. HBV is the main cause of cirrhosis and HCC worldwide. For selected candidates, liver transplantation currently seems to be the only viable treatment for the latest stages of hepatitis B.

D. Antiviral treatment may be effective in approximately one third of the patients who receive it. Eight different genotypes (A through H) have been identified. The progression of the disease seems to be more accelerated, and the response to treatment with antiviral agents is less favorable for patients infected by genotype C compared with those infected by genotype B. Genotypes A or B have a better response to interferon (IFN) treatment compared with patients infected by genotype C or D.

E. Acute HBV is undistinguishable from other forms of hepatitis in the acute viral stage on the basis of clinical symptoms.

F. In 2012 the CDC recommended testing for the following.
a. All pregnant women
b. Persons born in regions with intermediate or high rates of hepatitis B (HBsAg prevalence of $\geq$ 2%)
c. U.S.-born persons not vaccinated as infants whose parents were born in regions with high rates of hepatitis B (HBsAg prevalence of $\geq$ 8%)
d. Infants born to HBsAg-positive mothers
e. Household, needle-sharing, or sex contacts of HBsAg-positive persons
f. Men who have sex with men
g. Injection drug users
h. Patients with elevated liver enzymes (ALT/AST) of unknown etiology
i. Hemodialysis patients
j. Persons needing immunosuppressive or cytotoxic therapy
k. HIV-infected persons
l. Donors of blood, plasma, organs, tissues, or semen

Incidence

A. An estimated one third of the global population has been infected with HBV. Approximately 350 million people are lifelong carriers, and only 2% spontaneously seroconvert annually. Of chronically infected patients, 15% to 40% will develop cirrhosis, progressing to liver failure and/or HCC.

B. Acute hepatitis B occurs in 1 to 2 out of every 1,000 pregnancies in the United States, and chronic infection occurs in 5 to 15 out of every 1,000 pregnancies. The course of maternal HBV infections does not seem to be affected by coexistent pregnancy. However, premature labor and delivery is increased.

Pathogenesis

A. HBV is a hepadnavirus. HBV-related liver injury is largely caused by immune-mediated mechanisms mediated via cytotoxic T-lymphocyte lysis of infected hepatocytes. The virus is transmitted through blood or body fluids, such as wound exudates, semen, cervical secretions, and saliva that are HBsAg positive. It is not transmitted by the fecal–oral route or by water. Blood and serum contain the highest concentration of virus; saliva contains the lowest.

B. The incubation period is 45 to 160 days (2 to 5 months), with an average of 120 days. An infected person can infect others 4 to 6 weeks before symptoms appear and for an unpredictable time thereafter.

C. The production of antibodies against HBsAg confers protective immunity and can be detected in patients who have recovered from HBV or in those patients who have been vaccinated. The immunoglobulin M (IgM) subtype indicates an acute infection or reactivation. IgG subtype indicates chronic infection.

Predisposing Factors

A. Higher prevalence in African Americans and other populations
   1. Hispanic origin
   2. Asian origin
   3. Alaskan Eskimos
   4. Asian Pacific islanders
   5. Australian aborigines

B. Sexual contact is the major mode of transmission.
   1. High number of sexual partners
   2. An early age of first intercourse
   3. Homosexuality/bisexuality

C. IV drug use, sharing needles

D. Work in health care profession

E. Household exposure

F. Perinatal exposure, by vertical infection

G. Receiving blood transfusions or blood products for hemophilia and hemodialysis

H. Breastfeeding, by transmission in breast milk

I. Staffing or residing in institutions

J. International travel

K. Incarceration in long-term correction facilities

L. Percutaneous contact with inanimate objects contaminated with HBV; virus can survive 1 week or longer.

Common Complaints

A. The following symptoms occur in the acute phase of HBV.
   1. Anicteric hepatitis: Asymptomatic (majority of patients)
   2. Icteric hepatitis: Associated with a prodromal period
      a. Anorexia
      b. Nausea and vomiting
      c. Low-grade fever
      d. Myalgia
      e. Fatigue
      f. Aversion to food and cigarettes
      g. Intermittent, mild to moderate RUQ and epigastric pain
   3. Hyperacute, acute, and subacute hepatitis symptoms
      a. Hepatic encephalopathy
      b. Somnolence
      c. Disturbances in sleep pattern
      d. Mental confusion
      e. Coma

B. The following symptoms occur in the chronic phase of HBV:
   1. Asymptomatic: May be healthy carriers without any evidence of active disease
   2. During the replicative state, common symptoms are:
      a. Fatigue
      b. Anorexia
      c. Nausea
      d. Mild upper quadrant pain or discomfort
      e. Hepatic decompensation

Other Signs and Symptoms

A. Icteric phase (10 days after the appearance of constitutional symptoms and lasts for 1 to 3 months)
   1. Jaundice of sclera and skin
   2. Tea-colored urine
   3. Clay-colored stools, often precede jaundice
   4. RUQ tenderness
   5. Enlarged liver

Subjective Data

A. Review onset, duration, course, and severity of symptoms. Ask the patient for specifics about urine and stool color.

B. Ask the patient about other family members and sexual contacts with similar symptoms.

C. Discuss the patient's history of blood transfusions, IV drug use, and alcohol abuse.

D. Review the patient's occupational exposure.

E. Inquire about recent international travel.

F. Establish the patient's usual weight; note amount of any weight lost and over what length of time.

G. Review for a history of variceal bleeding.

Physical Examination

A. Check temperature, pulse, respirations, blood pressure, and weight.

B. Inspect
   1. Observe general appearance, muscle wasting, ascites, and peripheral edema.
   2. Inspect the skin for jaundice, palmar erythema, rash, spider nevi, spider angioma, and dehydration.
   3. Inspect the eyes for yellow sclera.
   4. Inspect the mucous membranes and nail beds.
   5. Evaluate for the presence of gynecomastia.

C. Auscultate
   1. Auscultate lung fields and the heart.
   2. Auscultate all quadrants of the abdomen.

D. Percuss abdomen.
E. Palpate
 1. Palpate all quadrants of the abdomen for masses, liver enlargement or tenderness, hepatomegaly, and splenomegaly.
 2. Palpate the lymph nodes for lymphadenopathy.
 3. Palpate for testicular atrophy.

Diagnostic Tests

A. Diagnostic test for HBV antigens and antibodies (see Table 13.14).
B. CBC with differential
C. Complete liver panel
 1. AST/ALT
 2. Bilirubin
 3. PT
 4. Albumin
D. Other viral infection markers: HCV and HDV
E. ALP
F. Serum iron levels
G. GGT
H. HBV genotype
I. HBV DNA viral load
J. Imaging
 1. Abdominal ultrasound
 2. CT or MRI to help exclude biliary obstruction
K. Liver biopsy to assess the severity of disease
L. Pregnancy testing before antiviral therapy
M. Before oral antiviral therapy is introduced, all patients should be screened for HIV.

Differential Diagnoses

A. Hepatitis B
B. Exclusion of other types of hepatitis (A, C, D, E, viral, or autoimmune hepatitis)
C. Infectious mononucleosis
D. Hepatotoxic drug ingestion, for example, chloramphenicol, acetaminophen, or methyldopa
E. Carcinoma
F. Alcoholic cirrhosis
G. Hemochromatosis
H. Wilson's disease

Plan

A. General interventions
 1. No specific therapy for acute HBV infection is available.
 2. Before any form of HBV therapy is started, and optimally at the first presentation, the patient needs to be provided with information about the natural history of chronic hepatitis B infection and the fact that most infections remain entirely without symptoms even in those with severe disease, so that there is a need for regular lifelong monitoring.
 3. Hepatitis B immune globulin (HBIG) and corticosteroids are not effective treatment.
B. Patient teaching
 1. See the Section III Patient Teaching Guide for this chapter, "Jaundice and Hepatitis."
 2. Tell the patient to avoid sexual activity until he or she is free of HBsAg.
 3. History of anaphylactic reaction to common baker's yeast is a contraindication to HBV vaccination.
 4. There are no dietary restrictions with acute and chronic hepatitis (without cirrhosis). Decompensated cirrhosis, portal hypertension, or encephalopathy are prescribed.
  a. Low-sodium diet (1.5 g/d)
  b. High-protein diet (white-meat protein, e.g., pork, turkey, and fish)
  c. Fluid restriction of 1.5 L/d in the presence of hyponatremia
C. Pharmaceutical therapy: The goal of treatment is to prevent progression to cirrhosis, hepatic failure, and hepatocellular cancer.
 1. Primary prevention includes vaccination of high-risk individuals, including teens. Vaccination is up to 95% effective.
 2. HBV vaccine is the recommended preexposure for the following groups:
  a. All adolescents
  b. IV drug users

TABLE 13.14 Diagnostic Tests for HBV Antigens and Antibodies

Factors to Be Tested	HBV Antigen or Antibody	Indication
HBsAg	HBsAg	Detects acutely or chronically infected; antigen used in hepatitis B vaccine
Anti-HBs	Antibody to HBsAg	Identifies resolved HBV infections; determines immunity after immunization
HBeAg	Hepatitis B e antigen	Identifies at risk of transmitting HBV
Anti-HBe	Antibody to HBeAg	Identifies lower risk of transmitting HBV
Anti-HBc	Antibody to hepatitis B core antigen; IgM (HBcAg)	Identifies acute, resolved, or chronic HBV infection. Anti-HBc is not present after immunization.
IgM anti HBc	IgM antibody to HBcAg	Identifies acute or recent HBV infections (includes HBsAg-negative during the window phase of infection)

c. Sexually active heterosexuals with more than one sex partner in the previous 6 months or those who have an STI
d. Health care workers and others at occupational risk
e. Residents and staff of institutions for developmentally disabled persons
f. Staff of nonresidential childcare centers
g. Patients undergoing hemodialysis
h. Patients with bleeding disorders who receive clotting factor concentrates
i. Household contacts and sexual partners of HBV carriers
j. Members of households with adoptees who are HBsAg positive
k. International travelers to areas of high or intermediate endemicity
l. Inmates of long-term correctional facilities

3. Hepatitis B vaccine can be given concurrently with other vaccines.
4. Early prophylaxis is paramount after an HBsAg needle stick (see Table 13.15). H-BIG should be administered immediately, no later than 48 hours, after exposure. Postexposure prophylaxis HBV vaccine is recommended.
5. Currently, IFN alfa-2b (Intron A) or alfa-2a (Roferon-A), pegylated IFN alfa-2a (Pegasys), lamivudine (Epivir), telbivudine (Tyzeka), adefovir dipivoxil (Hepsera), entecavir (Baraclude), and tenofovir (Viread) are the main treatment drugs approved globally (see Table 13.16).
   a. Tenofovir, entecavir, and pegylated IFN (PEG-IFN) alfa-2a are preferred in adults as first-tine therapy.
   b. All antivirals require close monitoring due to side-effect profiles.
   c. Dose adjustment is required in the presence of renal impairment, dialysis, and is used with caution in patients with a history of pancreatitis.

TABLE 13.15 Postexposure Hepatitis B Prophylaxis After Percutaneous Exposure

Exposed Person	HBsAg Negative	Unknown or Not Tested	Treatment When Source Is HBsAg Positive
Unimmunized	Initiate hepatitis B vaccine series	Initiate hepatitis B vaccine series	Administer 1 dose of HBIG 0.06 mL/kg IM; then initiate hepatitis B vaccine series
Previously immunized: known responder	No treatment	No treatment	No treatment
Previously immunized: known nonresponder	No treatment	If known high-risk source, treat as if source was HBsAg positive	Administer 1 dose of HBIG 0.06 mL/kg IM; then initiate reimmunization or HBIG (2 doses) hepatitis B vaccine series
Previously immunized: response unknown	No treatment	Test exposed person for anti-HBs. If adequate, no treatment. If inadequate, administer vaccine booster	Test exposed person for anti-HBs and administer vaccine booster dose. Two additional doses should be administered to complete a 3-dose reimmunization series

TABLE 13.16 Comparisons of Approved Treatments for Chronic Hepatitis B

	HBeAg Positive Normal ALT	HBeAg Negative Positive Chronic Hepatitis	HBeAg Negative Chronic Hepatitis
IFN or peginterferon alfa	No therapy	Indicated	Indicated
Lamivudine	No therapy	Indicated: high rate of resistance	Indicated: high rate of resistance
Adefovir	No therapy	Indicated	Indicated
Entecavir	No therapy	Indicated	Indicated
Telbivudine	No therapy	Indicated: high rate of resistance	Indicated: high rate of resistance
Tenofovir	No therapy	Indicated	Indicated

6. Orthotopic liver transplantation (OLT) is the treatment of choice for patients with fulminant hepatic failure who do not recover and for patients with end-stage liver disease.

Follow-Up

A. Laboratory monitoring
   1. Monitor liver function (ALT) every 3 to 6 months for active disease.
   2. Monitor HBeAg every 3 to 6 months dependent on ALT levels.
   3. Monitor CBC and creatinine every month (1 to 2 days prior to treatment).
   4. Monitor HBV DNA every 3 to 6 months when the patient is on treatment in the reactivation phase.

B. Risk of exposure to HBsAg ceases when antigen disappears from the bloodstream, usually within 6 to 8 weeks of infection. Repeated serum determinations of HBsAg can help define when precautions may be relaxed.

C. Laboratory, physical examination, and psychosocial evaluation are required for antiviral therapy.

D. The American Association for the Study of Liver Disease (AASLD) recommends HCC surveillance using ultrasound in the following types of patients with chronic HBV.
   1. Asian men older than 40 and Asian women older than 50
   2. All patients with cirrhosis, regardless of age
   3. Patients with a family history of HCC; any age
   4. Africans older than the age of 20 and any carriers older than 40 years with persistent or intermittent ALT evaluation and/or HBV DNA level greater than 2,000 IU/mL should be screened with an ultrasound every 6 to 12 months.
   5. Any individual with HBV/HIV coinfection.

E. Routine booster doses of hepatitis B vaccine are not recommended for children or adults with normal immune status.

Consultation/Referral

A. Patients with persistently elevated serum transaminase concentrations (exceeding twice the upper limits of normal), as well as those with elevated serum alpha-fetoprotein concentrations or abnormal ultrasounds, should be referred to a gastroenterologist for further management.

Individual Considerations

A. Pregnancy
   1. No adverse effect on developing fetus has been observed when pregnant women are vaccinated against HBV.
   2. Many antivirals are pregnancy category X drugs.
   3. Pregnancy and lactation are not a contraindication to vaccination.
   4. Prenatal HBsAg testing of all pregnant women is recommended to identify newborns who require immediate postexposure prophylaxis.
   5. Breastfeeding by an HBsAg-positive mother poses no additional risk for acquisition of HBV infection by infant.

B. Adults
   1. Most HBV infections are acquired in adolescence or adulthood, largely as a result of IV drug use, sexual contact, or occupational or household exposure. HBV infection is associated with other sexually transmitted diseases, including syphilis.
   2. Patients who have received a blood transfusion should refrain from blood donation for 6 months, the incubation period for HBV. Blood should never be donated if the patient is a hepatitis B carrier or was infected with hepatitis C.

C. Geriatrics
   1. The elderly have fewer cases of HBV due to diminished immune response; however, they tend to be asymptomatic HBV carriers.
   2. Those who do develop the disease have a greater tendency to deteriorate into chronic liver failure or chronic hepatitis.

Resources

American Association for the Study of Liver Diseases: www.aasld.org
American Liver Foundation: www.liverfoundation.org
Centers for Disease Control and Prevention: www.cdc.gov/hepatitis
Hepatitis and HIV: www.hivandhepatitis.com
Hepatitis B Foundation: www.hepb.org
Hepatitis Foundation International: www.hepfi.org
Immunization Action Coalition: www.immunize.org
National Institute of Diabetes and Digestive and Kidney Diseases: www2.niddk.nih.gov
United Network for Organ Sharing: www.unos.org

Hepatitis C

Definition

A. Hepatitis C is an inflammation of the liver caused by the hepatitis C virus (HCV). HCV has signs and symptoms often undistinguishable from those of hepatitis A or B (HAV or HBV). The disease tends to be asymptomatic to mild and has an insidious onset. Acute fulminate infection is rare. The major feature of HCV is its propensity to become chronic. Persistent infection occurs in at least 75% to 85% of patients, even in the absence of biochemical evidence of liver disease. Approximately 60% to

70% of patients develop chronic hepatitis, and 5% to 20% develop cirrhosis.

B. **15% to 45% of people infected with HCV spontaneously clear the infection by a strong immune response without the need for treatment. Although they are no longer infected, they will still test positive for anti-HCV antibodies.**

C. Multiple (6) HCV genotypes and subtypes exist. The genotype is a major factor in the effectiveness of the patient's response to therapy. Approximately 50% of patients infected with genotype 1 and approximately 80% of patients with genotypes 2 and 3 achieve a sustained virologic response (SVR). SVR is defined as undetectable HCV RNA 12 months or more after treatment cessation.

D. The development of chronic hepatitis and its complications increase with several factors, including older age at acquisition, HIV infection, excessive alcohol consumption, and male gender.

E. HCV is the leading cause of nonalcoholic hepatic failure and cirrhosis, and the cause of 90% of post-transfusion hepatitis. Primary HCC also occurs in these patients.

Incidence

A. The World Health Organization (WHO) estimates that more than 185 million individuals are chronically infected with HCV worldwide.

B. Seroprevalence rates among individuals vary according to their associated risk factors. The highest rates occur in persons with large or repeated direct percutaneous exposure to blood or blood products, such as IV drug users and patients with hemophilia who have received multiple blood transfusions.

C. Seroprevalence among pregnant women in the United States has been estimated at 1% to 2%. Maternal–fetal (vertical) transmission is only 5% from women who are HCV RNA positive at the time of delivery. Maternal coinfection with HIV has been associated with increased risk of perinatal transmission of HCV RNA.

D. Serum anti-HCV antibody and HCV RNA have been detected in colostrum. However, although only a limited number of patients have been studied, the rate of transmission among breastfed infants is the same as among bottle-fed infants.

E. More than 30% of adults with chronic infection progress to cirrhosis an average of 20 years after their initial infection. Patients with cirrhosis have a secondary risk of portal hypertension, liver failure, and other complications. HCV is the leading indication for liver transplantation among adults in the United States.

F. HCC is diagnosed an average of 30 years after initial HCV infection in 1% to 5% of patients, most of whom have underlying cirrhosis.

Pathogenesis

A. HCV is a small, single-stranded RNA virus with a lipid envelope and is a member of the Flavivirus family. Infection is spread primarily by parenteral exposure to blood and blood products from HCV-infected persons. In the United States, the current risk of HCV infection following blood transfusion is estimated at 0.1% or less because of exclusion of high-risk individuals from the pool of blood donors and screening for HCV. Sexual transmission of HCV is uncommon except with high-risk behavior.

B. The incubation period averages 6 to 7 weeks, with a range of 2 weeks to 6 months. The time from exposure to the development of viremia generally is 1 to 2 weeks.

Predisposing Factors

All people with HCV-RNA in their blood are considered to be infectious. The following groups are at high risk for HCV infection and should be tested:

A. IV drug users who have shared needles
B. Intranasal cocaine users, presumably resulting from epistaxis and shared equipment
C. Hemophiliacs, hemodialysis patients, and those who received blood transfusions before 1992
D. Recipients of solid organ transplants prior to 1992
E. Health care workers with percutaneous exposures
F. Individuals with multiple sexual partners
G. Transmission among contacts living with infected persons may occur with percutaneous or mucosal exposure to blood.
H. Infants of infected mothers, by vertical transmission
I. HCV is more common in males than females.
J. Tattooing, body piercing, and acupuncture with unsterile equipment
K. HIV

Common Complaints

A. Chronic HCV-asymptomatic unless there is progressive inflammation and complications from cirrhosis
B. Malaise
C. Anorexia
D. Nausea
E. Myalgia
F. Fever
G. Abdominal pain

Other Signs and Symptoms

A. Jaundice (occurs in fewer than 20% of patients).

B. Hepatomegaly is present in one third of patients with an acute infection.
C. Ascites
D. Spider nevi
E. Dark urine
F. Clay-colored stools

Subjective Data

A. Review duration, onset, and severity of symptoms.
B. Ask the patient about other family members and sexual contacts with similar symptoms.
C. Review the patient's history of blood transfusions, IV drug use, and alcohol abuse.
D. Ask the patient about occupational exposure.
E. Ask about high-risk sexual practices.
F. Has the patient had any testing for cirrhosis? What testing and when?
G. Review HIV status.

Physical Examination

A. Check temperature (acute infection), pulse, respirations, blood pressure, and weight.
B. Inspect
   1. Observe general appearance, muscle wasting, edema, and demeanor. **Administer a depression self-assessment tool at each visit when on HCV therapy.**
   2. Inspect the skin for jaundice, rash, dehydration, palmar erythema, excoriations, spider nevi, and tattoos/piercings.
   3. Inspect the eyes for yellow sclera.
   4. Inspect mucous membranes and nail beds for clubbing and cyanosis.
   5. Inspect for gynecomastia and small testes.
C. Auscultate
   1. Auscultate lung fields and heart.
   2. Auscultate all quadrants of the abdomen and evaluate for abdominal bruit.
D. Percuss the abdomen.
E. Palpate
   1. Palpate all quadrants of the abdomen for masses; liver enlargement or tenderness; characteristics of cirrhosis; and hepatosplenomegaly, which occurs in about 10% of cases.
   2. Palpate the lymph nodes for lymphadenopathy and enlarged parotid.

Diagnostic Tests

A. Laboratory tests
   1. IgG antibody ELISAs for HCV. If positive, a nucleic acid testing (NAT) test should be done to detect HCV RNA to confirm chronic HCV (see Table 13.17).
   2. HCV genotyping
   3. HCV viral load: Quantitative assay used as a prognostic indicator for patients undergoing antiviral therapy
   4. ALT and AST
   5. Hepatitis A IgM and IgG
   6. HBsAg and antibody, core antibody
   7. CMV IgM and IgG (and/or CMV in urine culture)
   8. Epstein-Barr virus IgM and IgG
   9. HIV IgG enzyme-linked immunoassay (ELISA)
   10. Alpha-fetoprotein
B. Ultrasonography is used for monitoring HCV-related complications.
C. Assessment of the degree of liver fibrosis and cirrhosis
   1. Aminotransferase/platelet ratio index (APRI)
   2. FIB4 test
   3. Fibrotest
   4. Transient elastography (ultrasound-based technique)

TABLE 13.17 Results of Screening Tests for Hepatitis C Virus and Usual Interpretation

ELISA Results	RIBA Results	PCR Results	Interpretation
Positive	Positive or Indeterminate	Positive	Active or chronic HCV infection
Positive	Positive	Negative	Cleared HCV infection of PCR persistently negative
Positive	Negative, Intermediate, or not performed	Negative	Cleared HCV infection or false-positive results on ELISA
Positive	Negative	Not usually done if RIBA results are negative	False-positive results on ELISA
Negative	Not performed if ELISA results are negative	Not usually done if RIBA results are negative (unless suspicion for acute infection is high)	No evidence of past exposure to HCV
Negative	Not performed if ELISA results are negative	Positive (test is not usually done in clinic setting unless suspicion for infection is high)	Early (< 7–8 weeks) of HCV infection or false-negative results

Source: U.S. Preventive Services Task Force: www.uspreventiveservicestaskforce.org/3rduspstf/hepcscr/hepcrevtaba.htm.

5. Liver biopsy is no longer considered to be the gold standard for determining the histologic grade and stage of fibrosis/cirrhosis.

D. Patients with advanced fibrosis and cirrhosis (METAVIR stages F3 and F4) should be prioritized for treatment due to their higher risk of developing cirrhosis and hepatocellular cancer.

E. Prior to the institution/during antiviral therapy, perform the following tests:
   1. CBC with platelets
   2. Viral load
   3. Liver function (ALT/AST)
   4. Pregnancy test
   5. Thyroid profile
   6. Blood glucose/A1C
   7. Consider a dilated retinal examination.
   8. Consider a stress test.
   9. Screen for alcohol abuse, drug abuse, and/or depression.

Differential Diagnoses

A. Hepatitis C
B. Hepatitis A
C. Hepatitis B
D. Alcoholic liver disease
E. Drug toxicities
F. Opportunistic infections associated with HIV infection

Plan

A. Patient teaching
   1. See the Section III Patient Teaching Guide for this chapter, "Jaundice and Hepatitis."
   2. Discuss the possibility of transmission to others, and tell the patient to refrain from donating blood, organs, tissues, or semen and from sharing toothbrushes and razors.
   3. All patients with chronic HCV should be immunized against hepatitis A and hepatitis B.
   4. Counsel the patient to avoid hepatotoxic medications and alcohol. The WHO recommends that alcohol screening and behavioral interventions for people with moderate to high alcohol intake should be instituted.
   5. Immunoprophylaxis for postexposure prophylaxis with IG is not recommended.
   6. The CDC recommends that anyone born between the years of 1945 and 1965 be tested for HCV one time.

B. Because of the risk of fetal anomalies with the treatment of ribravirin, **patients and their partners should be counseled not to become pregnant while on therapy and for 6 months after the completion of treatment. Two forms of contraception are recommended; one of which should be a barrier method. Pregnancy tests should be done prior to institution of HCV therapy and monthly thereafter.**

C. Pharmaceutical therapy is aimed at inhibiting HCV replication and eradicating infection. Pharmaceutical regimens are quickly evolving as new medications come to the market. Choice of therapy may, however, be cost prohibitive.
   1. Treatment for HCV infection includes:
      a. Pegylated and standard interferon alpha (IFN)
      b. Nucleoside analogue: Ribavirin (RBV)
      c. Protease inhibitors: Direct acting antivirals
         i. Boceprevir (Victrelis)
         ii. Telaprevir (Incivek)
         iii. Simeprevir (Olysio)
      d. NS5B nucleotide polymerase inhibitor sofosbuvir (Sovaldi)
      e. In October 2014, the U.S. FDA approved Harvoni (ledipasvir and sofosbuvir). Harvoni is the first combination pill approved to treat chronic HCV genotype 1.
   2. The 2014 WHO recommendations include:
      a. PEG-IFN combined with RBV is recommended for treatment of chronic HCV, rather than standard IFN and RBV.
         i. PEG-IFN +RBV should be used to increase the likelihood of a sustained virological response without increasing the side-effect profile.
      b. Treatment with telaprevir or boceprevir given in combination with PEG-IFN and RBV is suggested for genotype 1, rather than PEG-IFN and RBV alone.
      c. Treatment with sofosbuvir, given in combination with RBV with or without PEG-IFN (depending on the HCV genotype), is recommended in genotypes 1, 2, 3, and 4 HCV rather than PEG-IFN and RBV alone (no treatment for persons who cannot tolerate IFN). (The cost of sofosbuvir in the United States may be prohibitive as a general treatment modality.)
      d. Treatment with simeprevir given in combination with PEG-IFN and RBV is recommended for persons with genotype 1b HCV and for persons with genotype 1a HCV infection without the Q80K polymorphism rather than PEG-IFN and RBV alone.
   3. The length of therapy is dependent on the genotype and treatment.
      a. Persons with genotypes 1 and 4 are treated with PEG-IFN/RBV for 42 to 72 weeks.
      b. Persons with genotypes 2 and 3 are treated with PEG-IFN/RBV for 24 to 48 weeks.

c. The longer treatment durations are recommended for:
   i. Advance fibrosis or cirrhosis (METAVIR F3 and F4)
   ii. Coinfection with HIV
   iii. Slow early virological response
d. Interferon-containing regimens are contraindicated in person with decompensated cirrhosis because of the risk of accelerated decompensation. Consideration of a liver transplant is indicated.
e. For genotypes 1 and 4, sofosbuvir + RBV + PEG-IFN may be given for 12 weeks.

4. AASLD and the Infectious Diseases Society of America (IDSA) guidelines break down therapy in detail by genotype, length of therapy, and medications. The guidelines are located at www.hcvguidelines.org/full-report-view
5. Regular monitoring of toxicity and efficacy should be done by laboratory testing and clinical review of symptoms and side-effect profiles.

Follow-Up

A. Refer to current guidelines on institution for contraindications in drug therapy, adverse outcomes, laboratory testing, and frequency.
   1. The 2014 WHO Guidelines are located at www.who.int/hiv/pub/hepatitis/hepatitis-c-guidelines/en.
   2. AASLD and IDSA recommendations for testing, managing, and treating hepatitis C are located at www.hcvguidelines.org/full-report-view.

Consultation/Referral

A. Referrals include gastroenterologist, psychiatrist, endocrinologist, neurologist, hematologist, dietitian, and social workers.
B. Patients who are coinfected with HBV or HIV or have end-stage renal disease should be referred for treatment.

Individual Considerations

A. Pregnancy
   1. No data currently exist to support counseling a woman against pregnancy (unless under active treatment) as previously noted with the treatment of Ribvarin.
      a. RBV is a pregnancy category X drug with abortifacients potential.
      b. IFN is a pregnancy category C drug and should be used only if the benefits outweigh the risk to the fetus. IFN is a pregnancy category X when combined with RBV.
   2. Routine serologic testing of pregnant women for HCV infection is not recommended. Women with significant risk factors for HCV should be offered antibody screening.
   3. According to current guidelines of the U.S. Public Health Service and the American Academy of Pediatrics, maternal HCV infection is not a contraindication to breastfeeding. HCV-positive mothers should consider abstaining from breastfeeding if their nipples are cracked or bleeding.
   4. The method of delivery has not been shown to increase the risk of vertical transmission of HCV. Cesarean delivery is reserved for obstetric indications.
B. Adults
   1. Infected persons with steady partners do not need to change their sexual practices. However, they should be informed of the possible risk of transmission and of what precautions to use to prevent transmission.
   2. Persons with multiple partners should be advised to reduce the number of partners and to use condoms to prevent transmission.
   3. The best means of limiting transfusion-associated HCV is to rely exclusively on volunteer rather than commercial blood donors and to screen donors for anti-HCV antibodies.
C. Geriatrics: As the population ages the cases of HCV will increase more in the elderly than in other age groups.

Resources

American Association for the Study of Liver Diseases: www.aasld.org

American Liver Foundation: www.liverfoundation.org

Centers for Disease Control and Prevention: www.cdc.gov/hepatitis

Hepatitis and HIV: www.hivandhepatitis.com

Hepatitis Foundation International: www.hepfi.org

Immunization Action Coalition: www.immunize.org

National Institute of Diabetes and Digestive and Kidney Diseases: www2.niddk.nih.gov

Project Inform Information, Inspiration, and Advocacy for People with HIV/AIDS and Hepatitis C: http://www.projectinform.org/ (Includes Spanish resources)

United Network for Organ Sharing: www.unos.org

World Health Organization Guidelines for the screening, care, and treatment of persons with hepatitis C infection: http://www.who.int/hiv/pub/hepatitis/hepatitis-c-guidelines/en

Hernias, Abdominal

Definition

A hernia is the protrusion of a peritoneum-lined sac through some defect in the abdominal wall. Abdominal wall hernias are the most common surgical procedure.

Hernias are a leading cause of disability and work loss. Types include the following:

A. Umbilical hernia: Occurs when the intestinal muscles fail to close around the umbilicus, allowing the omentum and/or intestines to protrude into the weaker area
B. Incisional hernia: Caused by a defect in the abdominal musculature that develops after a surgical incision
C. Epigastric hernia: Protrusion of fat or omentum through the linea alba between the umbilicus and the xiphoid. Epigastric hernias are generally less than 2 cm in diameter.
D. Diastasis recti: Acquired hernia most often due to pregnancy and obesity. The right and left rectus muscles separate, but there is no facial defect.
E. Obturator hernia: Follows the path of the obturator nerves and muscles

Incidence

A. Umbilical hernias are more common in African American infants, women, and the elderly. This type of hernia has a higher risk of incarceration and strangulation and therefore a greater mortality because the large bowel is frequently entrapped.
B. Epigastric hernias are most common in men 20 to 50 years old.
C. Incisional hernias typically are noted in the early postoperative period; however, there is an increase in incisional hernias during pregnancy. These iatrogenic hernias occur in 2% to 10% of abdominal operations. In addition to hernias, separation of the recti abdominis muscles (diastasis recti) is often caused by pregnancy or obesity.
D. Obturator hernias occur more commonly in females. Females have a larger canal diameter, which is noted predominantly in thin elderly women.

Pathogenesis

A. Incisional hernias are due to failure of fascial tissues to heal and close.
B. Epigastric hernias are defects in the abdominal midline between the umbilicus and the xiphoid process. They are usually related to a congenital weakness, increased intra-abdominal pressure, surrounding muscle weakness, or chronic abdominal wall strain.
C. An umbilical hernia is caused by failure of the umbilical ring to obliterate after birth. In the infant, the umbilical ring often closes spontaneously within the first 1 to 2 years of life. Increased abdominal pressure or congenital defects cause abdominal hernias that allow abdominal contents to protrude through the opening defect. In adults with an umbilical hernia, obesity increases the danger of incarceration.

Predisposing Factors

A. Congenital predisposition
B. Gender
C. Obesity
D. Multiparity
E. Cirrhosis and ascites
F. Trauma or straining
G. African American ancestry
H. Chronic cough; can precipitate or worsen herniation
I. Previous abdominal surgery
J. Straining, coughing, and sneezing
K. Straining with chronic constipation
L. Incisional hernia factors
    1. Smoking
    2. Connective tissue disorder
    3. Infection
    4. Malnutrition
    5. Immunosuppressive medications
M. Age: Obturator hernias occur predominantly in the elderly.
N. Maternal smoking is associated with an increased prevalence of omphalocele and gastroschisis.

Common Complaints

A. Bulge of abdomen or of a previous scar
B. Symptoms aggravated by cough and straining
C. Varying degrees of discomfort
D. The only sign of a hernia may be increased irritability.

Other Signs and Symptoms

A. Incisional: Bulge through incision wall (may be intermittent)
B. Epigastric: Small, usually painless subcutaneous mass
C. Umbilical
    1. Adult: Vague, intermittent pain; palpable mass
D. Reducible or irreducible: Signs and symptoms are related to the degree of pressure of their contents rather than to size. Most patients are asymptomatic or complain of only mild pain.
E. Strangulated: Colicky abdominal pain, nausea, vomiting, abdominal distension, hyperperistalsis

Subjective Data

A. Review onset, duration, and course of symptoms.
B. Ask the patient about previous abdominal surgeries, wound infection, and pregnancies.
C. Review history of straining, trauma, or physical labor.
D. Determine if the patient has signs and symptoms of strangulation of entrapped bowel: Pain, nausea, vomiting, distension, and fever.
E. Determine if the patient can reduce hernia.

F. Ask the patient whether the hernia is enlarging and uncomfortable.
G. Review the patient's bowel history, specifically constipation.
H. Review the patient's history for chronic obstructive pulmonary disease (COPD)/chronic cough.
I. Review the patient's history for symptoms of obstructive uropathy.
J. Review how the hernia affects the patient's activities of daily living (ADL).

Physical Examination

Examination is the same for all types of abdominal hernias. Perform exam while the patient is standing and supine. History and physical examination are the best means of diagnosing hernias.

A. Check temperature (if indicated), pulse, respirations, and blood pressure.
B. Inspect
    1. Inspect contour and symmetry of the abdomen for bulges or masses. The bulge may be asymmetric.
    2. Inspect irreducible hernias for discoloration, edema, and ascites.
    3. Assess
        a. Have the patient perform Valsalva's maneuver while standing.
        b. Have the patient lie supine, lift head from exam table, and then bear down to tense abdomen.
C. Auscultate all quadrants of the abdomen for bowel sounds.
D. Percuss liver, spleen, and abdomen.
E. Palpate
    1. Palpate the entire abdomen for masses, hepatomegaly, and ascites. Umbilical hernias may be obscured by subcutaneous fat.
    2. Palpate the groin.
    3. Palpate the hernia in order to try to gently reduce it.

Diagnostic Tests

A. None is required if the hernia is easily reducible (depending on the type of hernia).
B. CBC: WBC increased, Hematocrit increased
C. Electrolytes: Na+ increased or decreased
D. Abdominal radiography: Reveals abnormally high levels of gas in bowel
E. Ultrasonography, if strangulation is suspected
F. CT scan of the abdomen and pelvic may be indicated.

Differential Diagnoses

A. Abdominal hernia
B. Diastasis recti
C. Ascites
D. Abdominal wall tumor or cyst
E. Bowel obstruction

Plan

A. Patient teaching
    1. Discuss the hernia and available options for treatment.
    2. Teach the patient signs and symptoms of strangulation.
    3. Instruct the patient to refrain from heavy lifting.
    4. Advise the patient to wear a support garment.
B. Medical and surgical management

Reduction should not be attempted if there are signs of inflammation or obstruction.

    1. Try to reduce hernia unless strangulated. See the Section II Procedure, "Hernia Reduction (Inguinal/Groin)."
        a. Easily reducible: Abdominal contents can be easily returned to their original compartment. Allows symptomatic relief.
        b. Incarcerated: Cannot be returned to its original compartment. The incarcerated tissue may be bowel, omentum, or other abdominal contents.
        c. Strangulated: Surgical emergency—blood supply to the herniated tissue is compromised.
    2. Do not try to reduce strangulated hernias because reduction can cause gangrenous bowel to enter peritoneal cavity.
    3. A truss fits snugly over a hernia to prevent abdominal contents from entering the hernial sac. It does not cure a hernia and is used only when the patient is not a surgical candidate.
    4. Surgery may be done laparoscopically or through an open procedure and by sutured or mesh repair, depending on the age of the person, type and size of the hernia, and the presence of strangulation.

Follow-Up

A. Instruct the patient to call the office if fever or severe pain occurs. Otherwise, no follow-up is required unless for postoperative repair. Postoperative follow-up is with the physician who performed the surgery.

Consultation/Referral

Consult a physician if the patient has abdominal tenderness, discoloration, or edema at the site; fever; or signs of bowel obstruction.

A. Pregnancy
    1. Incisional hernias are more common during pregnancy because of increased intra-abdominal pressure.

2. Bowel obstruction secondary to previous scarring may also be seen and is most common when the uterus emerges from the pelvis early in the second trimester, when the uterus is maximally distended at term, and in immediate puerperium when the uterus promptly decreases in size.

B. Geriatrics
   1. Because of the anatomic position of the obturator hernia, the presentation is more common as a bowel obstruction than as a protrusion of bowel contents.
      a. The geriatric population is more prone to develop electrolyte and acid–base imbalances from obstruction.
   2. The geriatric population has a higher rate of ventral hernias attributed to the loss of muscle strength in the anterior abdominal wall and the prevalence of comorbidities that lead to an increased intra-abdominal pressure.

Hernias, Pelvic

Definition

A hernia is the protrusion of a peritoneum-lined sac through some defect from one anatomical space to another. As shown in Figure 13.3, there are three types of pelvic (inguinal) hernias distinguished by presentation:

A. Indirect: Protrudes through internal inguinal ring; can remain in canal, exit external ring, or pass into scrotum; unilateral or bilateral
B. Direct: Protrudes through external inguinal ring; located in region of Hesselbach's triangle; rarely enters scrotum
C. Femoral: Protrudes through femoral ring, femoral canal, and fossa ovalis

Incidence

A. Indirect inguinal hernias are the most common type of hernia. They affect both sexes, but most

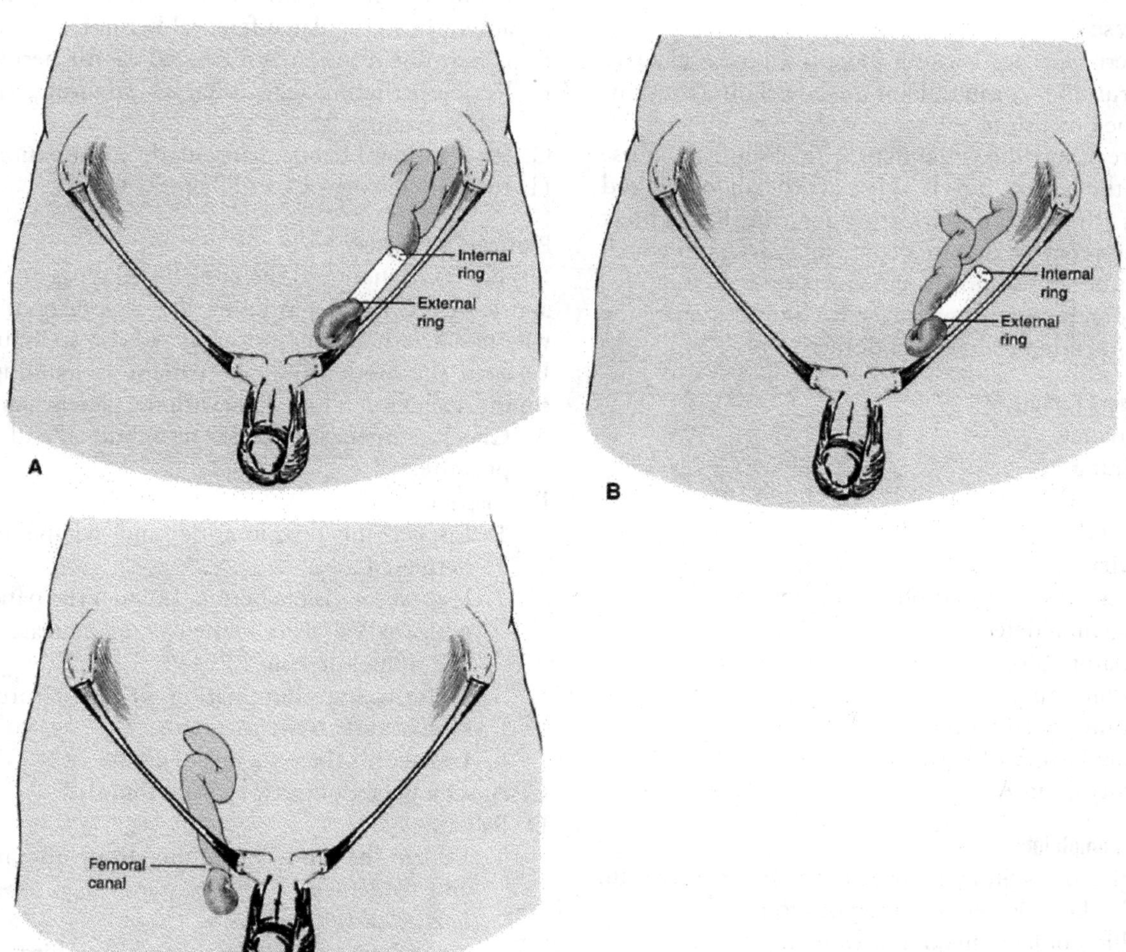

FIGURE 13.3 Pelvic hernias. A. Indirect hernia comes down canal and touches the fingertip on exam. B. Direct hernia bulges anteriorly, pushes against the side of the finger on exam. C. Femoral hernia protrudes through femoral ring, femoral canal, and fossa ovalis, so the inguinal canal is empty on exam.

often are seen in children and young males (7:1 male-to-female ratio). Incidence increases with age.

B. Direct inguinal hernias are less common than indirect inguinal hernias. They occur more often in males and are more common in those older than age 40. Primary inguinal hernias occur in 1% to 5% of infants and in 9% to 10% of those born prematurely.

C. Femoral hernias are the least common type of hernia. They occur more often in females (1.8:1 female-to-male ratio). Right-side presentation is more common than left.

D. Among inguinal hernias, a sliding component is found in 3%; they are overwhelmingly on the left side (left-to-right ratio, 4.5:1). Sliding hernias are much more common in men than in women, and the predominance increases with age.

E. Primary perineal hernias occur most often in elderly multiparous women.

Pathogenesis

Pelvic hernias occur because there is a potential space for protrusion—commonly of the bowel but occasionally of the omentum.

A. Indirect and direct hernias arise along the course that the testicle travels as it exits the abdomen and enters the scrotum during intrauterine life. Indirect hernias may be due to a congenital defect in which the processus vaginalis remains patent.

B. Femoral hernias occur at the fossa ovalis, where the femoral artery exits the abdomen.

Predisposing Factors

A. Pregnancy
B. Straining
C. Age
D. Obesity
E. Gender
F. Repetitive stress/hard physical labor
G. Congenital defect
H. Premature birth
I. Chronic cough
J. Chronic constipation
K. Family history of hernia
L. History of an AAA

Common Complaints

A. Bulging or swelling localized in the groin or scrotum
B. Dull ache in lower abdomen or groin
C. Swelling of labia majora in women
D. Bowel obstruction

Other Signs and Symptoms

A. Ability to reduce hernia
B. Exacerbation on standing, straining, or coughing
C. Strangulation
   1. Colicky abdominal pain
   2. Nausea or vomiting
   3. Hyperperistalsis
   4. Fever
   5. Edema
   6. Discoloration
   7. Tenderness

Subjective Data

A. Review time of onset, duration, course of hernia, and swelling.

B. Review any symptoms and quality of pain. Outright pain with hernias is unusual, and its presence should raise the possibility of incarceration or strangulation.

C. Ask the patient about history of straining, trauma, physical labor, and pregnancy.

D. Inquire about symptoms of obstruction or strangulation of entrapped bowel: pain, nausea, and vomiting. Groin pain and tenderness are generally absent in strangulated femoral hernias.

E. Determine if the patient can reduce the hernia.

F. Review irritating (e.g., exercise, straining, cough) and alleviating factors.

G. Review bowel habits, particularly constipation.

H. Evaluate history of COPD and cough.

Physical Examination

Physical examination is the same for all types of hernias and is directed at determining the type of hernia and whether it is reducible, incarcerated, or strangulated. Perform the exam while the patient is standing and supine. Palpation is best done with the patient standing.

A. Check temperature, pulse, respirations, and blood pressure.

B. Inspect
   1. Inspect for discoloration and edema of the herniated area.
   2. Inspect for visible hernia. Instruct the patient to perform Valsalva's maneuver to increase intra-abdominal pressure.
   3. Preform transillumination of the scrotum to evaluate any bowel contents.
   4. Inspect for the presence of ascites.

C. Auscultate abdomen for bowel sounds.

D. Palpate
   1. Palpate the groin for lymphadenopathy, masses, and tenderness. *The right side is more commonly affected in both genders.*
      a. Males: Using the second or third finger, invaginate the scrotal skin, with and without cough and strain. There will be some degree of pressure with this maneuver, but a true hernia can typically be felt as a "silky" impulse tapping

against the finger. Palpate the scrotum: scrotal lump is either soft or unusually firm.

b. Females: Visually examine for a bulge, and then place two or three fingers across the inguinal canal and ask the patient to bear down or cough to elicit the characteristic bulge or impulse. Palpate the labia for swelling: either soft or unusually firm.

Diagnostic Tests

A. History and physical examination remain the best means of diagnosing hernias.
B. Perform ultrasonography for abdominal masses and strangulation.
C. MRI appears to be able to differentiate inguinal and femoral hernias with a high sensitivity.
D. Sigmoidoscopy is not recommended as a screening test.
E. Plain abdominal x-rays are of limited value in evaluating an incarcerated hernia.
F. Karyotyping should be considered when a testicle is palpable in the inguinal canal or found at herniorrhaphy in phenotypic females.
G. Routine laboratory work is not recommended.

Differential Diagnoses

A. Inguinal or pelvic hernia
B. Acute conditions
   1. Testicular torsion causes sudden, excruciating pain in or around the testicle, which may spread to the lower abdomen; the pain may get worse with standing. Other signs and symptoms include swelling, rising of the affected testicle, nausea, vomiting, fever, and fainting or lightheadedness.
   2. Epididymitis
C. Nonacute conditions
   1. Testicular tumor
   2. Muscle strain
   3. Hip arthritis
   4. Undescended testicle
   5. Hydrocele
   6. Varicocele
   7. Spermatocele
D. Bowel obstruction

Plan

A. Patient teaching
   1. Tell the patient to call the office right away if he finds a lump or swelling in the scrotum, even if it is small or painless. Testicular tumors are usually painless.
   2. Discuss condition and treatment options with the patient.
      a. Surgery is the only effective treatment.
      b. Watchful waiting rather than surgical repair is an option if the patient is asymptomatic as long as he is aware of the risk and understands the need for prompt attention should symptoms of complication occur.
      c. Nonsurgical therapy for groin hernias is the use of a truss. There is insufficient data to determine the efficacy of trusses in controlling symptoms. A truss has the potential risk of bowel constriction; prolonged use of a truss can lead to atrophy of the spermatic cord or fusion to the hernial sac.
   3. Teach the patient signs of strangulation.
   4. Instruct the patient to avoid heavy lifting.
B. Medical and surgical management: Gently reduce a groin hernia while the patient lies supine with hips slightly flexed to relax the abdominal muscles.

Follow-Up

A. Tell the patient to return to the office if fever, severe pain, or strangulation occurs.
B. Postoperative evaluation for hernia recurrences as needed
   1. Immediately from repair
   2. Greater than 6 months and up to 5 years from repair
   3. Late recurrences beyond 5 years from the repair

Consultation/Referral

A. Refer patients with femoral hernias to a physician. These hernias need to be repaired as soon as possible because of increased risk of incarceration and strangulation.
B. Strangulated hernias are nonreducible, and blood supply to protruded tissue is compromised. Refer patients for immediate surgical intervention.

Individual Considerations

A. Pregnancy: Preexisting groin hernias may become more symptomatic during the first trimester of pregnancy. The symptoms must be differentiated from round ligament pain.
B. Geriatrics
   1. Groin hernias are one of the most frequently encountered pathologies occurring in old age, secondary to the presence of constipation, coughing, abdominal fat deposit, and loss of strength of the abdominal wall.
   2. Signs and symptoms of prostatism are frequently present in men with hernias and may require relief before herniorrhaphy.
   3. Excessive waiting time for elective repair increase the risk of strangulation, bowel resection, and mortality, especially with older patients.
   4. The higher rate of comorbidities and the usage of general anesthesia increase the risk of complications in the older patient.

Hiatal Hernia

Definition

A. The hiatal hernia occurs when portions of the stomach or other abdominal cavity organs herniate through the esophageal hiatal of the diaphragm. The patient may be asymptomic, and the herniation may be found incidentally in the diagnostic evaluation of other problems. There are four types of hiatal hernia:
   1. Type I: Sliding hernia. A portion of the stomach, gastroesophageal (GE) junction, slides in and out of the hiatus. The fundus of the stomach remains below the GE junction.
   2. Type II: Paraesophageal hernia. The gastric fundus of the stomach slides through the hiatus and lies next to the esophagus.
   3. Type III: Combined. Combination of sliding and paraesophageal hiatus hernia
   4. Type IV: Complex paraesophageal hernia. The stomach, small and large bowels, spleen, pancreas, or liver are pushed up into the chest through a large defect.

Incidence

A. The most common hiatal hernia is the type I sliding hernia (95%).
B. Type II through type IV hernias make up the remaining 5% and are referred to as paraesophageal hernias (PEH).
C. The least common herniation is type II.

Pathogenesis

A. The exact cause of a hiatal hernia is unknown It is known for the widening of the GE junction and/or laxity of the phrenoesophageal (gastrosplenic and gastrocolic ligaments). A hiatal hernia may also be a congenital defect.

Predisposing Factors

A. Obesity
B. Pregnancy

Common Complaints

A. Asymptomic (found incidentally)
B. Heartburn
C. Upper abdominal pain
D. Vague, intermittent chest discomfort or pain
E. GE reflux or "acid brash"
F. Trouble swallowing
G. Choking

Other Signs and Symptoms

A. Burping
B. Hiccups
C. Coughing
D. Vomiting blood
E. Blood in stools
F. Weight loss

Potential Complications

A. Strangulation/incarceration
B. Gastric volvulus
C. Perforation
D. Respiratory compromise secondary to the hernia

Subjective Data

A. Ask patient what activity brought about or preceded the episode.
B. What are alleviating and aggravating factors?
C. Review medical history for a diagnosis of GERD.
   1. If the patient has a diagnosis of GERD, has the patient been prescribed and is he or she taking PPIs?
   2. Has the patient had an esophageal-gastroendoscopy (EGD)? Was a hiatal hernia noted at the time of the procedure?
D. Review medical history for cardiac diagnosis.
E. Ask patient to list all medications currently being taken, including herbals and OTC medications. Specifically review whether the patient is taking OTC antacids, H_2 blockers, or OTC PPIs.

Physical Examination

A. Check pulse, respirations, and blood pressure.
B. Inspect
   1. Inspect general appearance and observation of respiration, noting any distress.
   2. Assess swallowing ability.
C. Auscultate
   1. Auscultate abdomen in all four quadrants.
   2. Conduct a complete heart and lung exam.
D. Palpate
   1. Palpate upper gastric region for tenderness or distension
   2. Palpate abdomen for organomegaly or masses.
E. Perform a rectal examination (if indicated for hematemesis or blood in the stool).

Diagnostic Tests

A. Barium swallow (identifies anatomy and size of hernia)
B. EGD
C. High-resolution manometry
D. Large hiatal hernias may cause iron-deficiency anemia.
   1. CBC
   2. Iron
   3. Ferritin

Differential Diagnosis

A. Hiatal hernia
B. GERD
C. Cholecystitis
D. Esophageal spasm
E. Coronary artery disease
F. Cancer (gastric or esophageal)

Plan

A. General interventions
  1. Management depends on the cause and severity of symptoms.

B. Patient teaching
  1. Educate patient about modifying controllable risk factors such as keeping diabetes and hypertension under control, diet, exercise, and stopping smoking.

C. Dietary management
  1. There is no specific diet for a hiatus hernia; however, dietary recommendations for GERD apply.
  2. Cut up food into small bite-size pieces.

D. Pharmaceutical therapy
  1. There is no medication specific for a hiatal hernia.

E. Medical and surgical management
  1. Surgical repair is not indicated in the absence of reflux disease.
  2. Age and patient comorbidities should be considered in the routine elective repair of completely asymptomatic PEH.
  3. The Society of American Gastrointestinal and Endoscopic Surgeons guidelines recommend that, during operations for Roux-en-Y gastric bypass (RYGB), sleeve gastrectomy, and placement of adjustable gastric bands, all hiatal hernias should be repaired.
  4. All symptomatic PEH should be repaired.
     a. Surgical repair includes a Nissen fundoplication.
     b. **An emergent surgical repair of a hiatal hernia is required in patients with a gastric volvulus, uncontrolled bleeding, obstruction, strangulation, perforation, and respiratory compromise.**

Follow-Up

A. Follow-up is determined by patient's needs, severity of symptoms, and whether complications are present.

Consultation/Referral

A. Consider a surgical consultation for hiatus repair for:
  1. Patients who have no relief from PPIs.
  2. Pulmonary complications that are linked to GERD, including asthma and recurrent aspiration pneumonia.

Irritable Bowel Syndrome

Definition

IBS is the most common of the GI motility disorders. IBS is responsible for significant direct and indirect health care costs. It is a chronic relapsing functional disturbance of intestinal motility marked by a common symptom complex that includes bloating and abdominal pain or discomfort associated with defecation. The ACG defines IBS as abdominal pain or discomfort that occurs in association with altered bowel habits over a period of at least 3 months. Bladder dysfunction has been identified in 50% of patients with IBS. Patients commonly transition between subgroups.

A. IBS is defined by symptom-based diagnostic criteria, in the absence of detectable organic causes. Rome III criteria for IBS is related to stool characteristics.

B. There are four IBS bowel patterns.
  1. IBS with diarrhea predominant (IBS-D): Loose stools (small volume, pasty/mushy or watery) more than 25% of the time and hard stools less than 25% of the time
  2. IBS with constipation (small, hard, pellet-like stools) predominant (IBS-C): Hard stools more than 25% of the time and loose stools less than 25% of the time
  3. IBS with alternating bouts of constipation and diarrhea
  4. Mixed or cyclic pattern (IBS-M): Both hard and soft stools more than 25% of the time

C. On clinical grounds, other subclassifications are used.
  1. Based on symptoms
     a. IBS with predominant bowel dysfunction
     b. IBS with predominant pain
     c. IBS with predominant bloating
  2. Based on precipitating factors
     a. Postinfectious (PI-IBS)
     b. Food-induced (meal-induced)
     c. Stress-related

Incidence

A. IBS is common, accounting for about 50% of GI complaints seen by health care professionals, and is a major cause of morbidity in the United States. Studies suggest that nearly 20% of all adults suffer from some form of the condition; however, only a fraction seeks medical help.

B. The ACG has recognized IBS as a key component of the Gulf War syndrome.

Pathogenesis

A. IBS has an absence of detectable pathology, and laboratory tests are unrevealing. The understanding of IBS has evolved from a disturbance in bowel motor activity to a more integrated understanding of visceral hypersensitivity and brain–gut interaction. It is thought to be both a normal response to severe stress and a learned visceral response to stress leading to the following.
  1. Nonpropulsive colonic contractions lead to IBS-C predominant

2. Increased contraction in the small bowel and proximal colon with diminished activity in the distal colon, leading to IBS-D predominant
3. Most patients with functional disorders appear to have inappropriate perception of physiologic events and altered reflex responses in different gut regions.
4. The brain–gut transmitters act at different sites in the brain and gut and lead to varied effects on GI motility, pain control, emotional behavior, and immunity. Serotonin plays a critical role in the regulation of GI motility, secretion, and sensation. Studies have shown that IBS may be related to an imbalance in mucosal serotonin and 5-hydroxytryptamine (5-HT) availability caused by defects in 5-HT production, serotonin receptors, or serotonin transport.

Predisposing Factors

A. Age
   1. 50% of IBS occurs prior to age 35.
   2. 40% of IBS occurs between ages 35 and 50.
B. Gender
   1. Women are two to three times more likely to have IBS.
C. Emotional factors and situational stress
D. Prior GI infection–induced IBS
E. Genetics is considered a factor.
F. Carbohydrate intolerance may produce significant symptoms.

Common Complaints

A. Chronic relapsing stool pattern
   1. Diarrhea, over three loose stools per day, *or*
   2. Alternation of diarrhea with constipation. Diarrhea is typically small in volume, has visible mucus, and may follow a hard movement by a few hours, *or*
   3. Constipation: Less than three BMs per week
B. Feeling of incomplete evacuation
C. Abdominal distension and bloating
D. Straining with BMs
E. Aching or cramps in periumbilical or lower abdominal region
F. Pain relief with BM

Other Signs and Symptoms

A. Change in bowel function
B. Clear mucous stool
C. Pain may be precipitated by meals.
D. Pain radiates to left chest or arm, from gas in splenic flexure. Nocturnal pain is unusual and is considered a warning sign.
E. Flatulence
F. Nausea
G. Anxiety
H. Depression
I. Preoccupation with bowel symptoms.
J. Extraintestinal symptoms
   1. Dysmenorrhea
   2. Urinary frequency, urgency, and incomplete bladder emptying
   3. Impaired sexual function and dyspareunia
   4. Fibromyalgia
K. Menses may exacerbate IBS symptoms
L. **Red-flag symptoms** (see Table 13.18)

Subjective Data

A. Review pattern of main symptoms, including onset, duration, and usual course.
B. Ask the patient what are the predominant symptoms—abdominal pain, diarrhea, or constipation.

TABLE 13.18 Common and Red-Flag Differential Diagnoses for IBS

Disorder	Signs and Symptoms	Diagnostic Tests
UC	Peaks at ages 15–35 Bloody diarrhea with mucus, fever, abdominal pain, tenesmus, weight loss	Sigmoidoscopy, colonoscopy, BE
CD	Onset at ages 15–35 or 70–80 Fever, abdominal pain, diarrhea, fatigue, weight loss, anorectal fissures, fistulae, abscesses	Sigmoidoscopy, colonoscopy, BE
Infectious diarrhea	Chronic diarrhea with cramps with or without blood and mucus	Microscopy, stool studies, sigmoidoscopy
Diverticulitis	Lower left abdominal pain, fever, altered bowel habits	CBC, CT, BE
Colorectal malignancy	Age 50 or older Rectal bleeding, altered bowel habits, abdominal or back pain, anemia, occult blood in stool, weight loss	Colonoscopy
Medication side effects	Antacids, laxatives, selective serotonin reuptake inhibitors (SSRIs), thyroid hormones, metformin, narcotics, calcium channel blockers, anticholinergics	History of concordance of symptoms with medication initiation; trial of drug holiday or reducing dosage; rechallenge confirms

Adapted from Anderson (2012). Permission by Merion Publications.

C. Review the patient's history for stress factors, and ask if recurrent symptoms occur in relation to them.
D. Ask what other symptoms occur with the pain, diarrhea, or constipation, such as bloating, blood in stool, or nighttime BMs. **Bleeding, weight loss, and nocturnal diarrhea are not characteristic of IBS. IBS symptoms disappear during sleep.**
E. Establish patient's normal weight history, and determine amount of weight loss, if any, over what time period.
F. Review the patient's diet, including
 1. Response to milk or lactose products
 2. Artificial sweeteners
 3. Alcohol intake
 4. Irregular or inadequate meals
 5. Insufficient fluid intake
 6. Excessive fiber intake
 7. Obsession with dietary hygiene
 8. Response to gluten (wheat, barley, rye) ingestion
G. Inquire about the patient's prescription, herbal, and OTC medications. Ask specifically about the use of laxatives.
H. Review travel and food history for dominant history of diarrhea.
I. Ask the patient if there is a family history of colon cancer, UC, CD, or malabsorption.
J. Is there any fever accompanying lower abdominal pain?
K. What is the relation of symptoms to menstruation?

Physical Examination

A. Check temperature (if indicated), pulse, respirations, blood pressure, and weight.
B. Inspect
 1. Observe general appearance. Does the patient appear anxious or depressed?
 2. Inspect abdominal contour for masses and bulges.
C. Auscultate all quadrants of the abdomen for bowel sounds; note whether they are normal or mildly hyperactive.
D. Percuss the abdomen for tympany or dullness.
E. Palpate the abdomen.
 1. Evaluate the abdomen for mild tenderness, rigidity, guarding, and masses.
 2. Evaluate for hepatosplenomegaly.
 3. Evaluate for lymphadenopathy.
F. Rectal exam
 1. Check for masses and tenderness.
 2. Obtain stool for diagnostic tests.
 3. Rectal exam is normal with IBS.

Diagnostic Tests

A. **The ACG Task Force on IBS recommends that patients younger than 50 years of age who do not have alarm features need not undergo routine colonic imaging. Patients with IBS symptoms who have alarm features, such as anemia or weight loss, or those who are older than 60 years of age, should undergo colonic imaging to exclude organic disease.**
B. Diagnosis of IBS is usually suspected on the basis of the patient's history and physical examination without additional tests (see Table 13.19).
C. Diagnostic tests are performed to exclude organic disease that may masquerade as IBS.
 1. CBC
 2. Sedimentation rate or CRP
 3. Serum potassium, if the patient is on diuretics; hypokalemia may reduce bowel contractility and produce an ileus.
 4. Blood glucose, if diarrhea predominates; rule out diabetes mellitus, which may present as diarrhea due to diabetic gastroenteropathy.
 5. Thyroid function study
 6. Stool specimen: Culture for leukocytes and fat, ova and parasites, and occult blood. Leukocyte-free mucus is a hallmark of IBS.
 7. Stool cultures for *C. difficile* toxin assay, if clinically indicated
 8. BE and/or proctosigmoidoscopy for severe signs and symptoms, after consultation or referral
 9. Celiac serology, if appropriate
 10. A mucosal biopsy is appropriate if a colonoscopy or sigmoidoscopy is performed.

Differential Diagnoses

A. IBS
B. IBD (Crohn's/UC)
C. Viral or bacterial gastroenteritis
D. GI neoplasm
E. Acute diarrhea due to protozoa or bacteria
F. Lactose insufficiency/deficiency
G. Laxative abuse
H. Drug side effect
I. Diabetes
J. Celiac spruce/gluten etiology
K. Diverticulitis
L. Endometriosis/PID
M. Zollinger–Ellison syndrome
N. Diverticulitis

Plan

A. General interventions
 1. Advise the patient to keep a diary of events of BMs and precipitating factors.

TABLE 13.19 Rome III Diagnostic Criteria for IBS

Onset of symptoms at least 6 months before diagnosis
Recurrent abdominal pain or discomfort for more than 3 days per month during the past 3 months
At least two of the following features:
 A. Improvement with defecation
 B. Association with a change in frequency of stool
 C. Association with a change in stool form

2. Encourage the patient to quit smoking because nicotine may aggravate symptoms.
3. Recommend daily exercise to reduce stress.
4. Stress management should be encouraged, including counseling, tapes, meditation, and yoga.

B. Patient teaching: See the Section III Patient Teaching Guide for this chapter, "Irritable Bowel Syndrome."

C. Dietary management
1. Prescribe a high-fiber diet.
2. Tell the patient to avoid foods that aggravate the bowel. Avoid gas-producing foods, such as broccoli, beans, onions, garlic, and so forth. When diarrhea predominates, dietary review is essential for clues of intolerance to lactose or sorbitol.

D. Pharmaceutical therapy
1. Stop all nonessential medications that may affect bowel function, especially irritant laxatives. Avoid narcotics, depressants, and other long-term drug use if possible.
2. Recommend eliminating sorbitol-containing candy and restricting lactose-containing milk products.
3. Drug of choice: Psyllium hydrophilic mucilloid (Metamucil) 1 tablespoon per day in 8 oz of juice or water, followed with another 8 oz of liquid. This treats both diarrhea and constipation.
4. Pain relief
   a. Opiates should be avoided due to the risk of dependence and addiction in chronic conditions.
   b. NSAIDs have an undesirable side effect on the GI tract.
   c. Antispasmodics and anticholinergic agents (IBS-D predominant)
      i. Hyoscyamine (Levsin, Levbid)
         1) Levsin 0.125 to 0.25 mg (1 to 2 tablets) orally or sublingual every 4 hours; not to exceed 12 tablets a day
         2) Levbid 0.375 to 0.75 mg orally twice a day
      ii. Dicyclomine (Bentyl) 20 to 40 mg four times a day; discontinue if not effective within 2 weeks or if 80 mg daily is associated with adverse effects.
   d. Tricyclic antidepressants for diarrhea-predominant IBS. Tricyclics should be avoided for constipated patients.
      i. Amitriptyline (Elavil) 10 mg every bedtime initially, titrate up slowly to 75 mg/d at bedtime as needed
      ii. Desipramine (Norpramin) 10 mg every bedtime initially, titrate up slowly up to 75 mg/d
      iii. Imipramine (Tofranil) 10 to 50 mg orally every bedtime
5. SSRIs
   a. Paroxetine (Paxil) 10 to 60 mg/d
   b. Citalopram (Celexa) 5 to 60 mg/d
6. Antidiarrheals
   a. Opiate-derived antidiarrheals are reserved for very severe cases secondary to the potential for abuse.
   b. Loperamide (Imodium)
      i. Adults: 2 to 12 mg orally divided into twice a day/three times daily doses; doses differ greatly among individuals.
   c. Alosetron (Lotronex), a 5-hydroxytryptamine-3 (5-HT_3) receptor antagonist, is indicated for women with severe IBS-D predominant.
7. Laxatives and stool softeners (IBS-C predominant)
   a. Mineral oil 15 to 45 mL orally daily or divided into three times daily dosing.
   b. Stimulant laxatives may be necessary intermittently for short periods, but prolonged use of stimulant laxatives should be avoided.
8. Lubiprostone (Amitiza), a selective C-2 chloride-channel activator, is indicated for women 18 years and over with IBS-C predominant. 8-μL doses twice a day with food and water.
   a. Lubiprostone should not be used in patients with mechanical bowel obstruction or preexisting diarrhea.
   b. Women should have a documented negative pregnancy test before starting therapy and should be advised to use contraception when taking lubiprostone.
9. Probiotics
10. Linaclotide (LINZESS), guanylate cyclase-C (GC-C) agonist was recently released to market for both IBS-C and chronic idiopathic constipation (CIC).

Follow-Up

A. Reevaluate the effectiveness of treatment in 2 weeks. Treatment may be challenging for symptom management and numerous tests that are inconclusive, but rule out pathology.

B. If symptoms persist without relief, have the patient return as needed.

C. Return if diarrhea lasts more than 2 weeks.

Consultation/Referral

A. Refer to a gastroenterologist for red-flag symptoms.

B. Alosetron (Lotronex) is prescribed under a restricted distribution program through a gastroenterologist.

C. Consult a physician if all treatment options fail.

D. Consider a psychiatric consultation, if indicated, for anxiety, depression, somatization, and symptom-related fears.

Individual Considerations

A. Adults
  1. Annual rectal examination and sigmoidoscopy are recommended after age 50.
  2. When constipation predominates, rule out malignancy, particularly in patients older than age 40 who have weight loss or a family history of colon cancer.

Resource

Rome Foundation: http://romecriteria.org/criteria

Jaundice

Definition

A. Jaundice is a yellow tinge of the skin or mucous membranes. It is a symptom, not a disease. The diagnostic approach begins with gathering a comprehensive history, physical examination, and screening labs. The differential diagnosis is formulated, and further testing may be warranted. The onset of jaundice usually prompts the patient or family to seek medical attention. Jaundice can reflect a medical emergency secondary to massive hemolysis, ascending cholangitis, unconjugated hyperbilirubinemia in the neonatal period, and fulminant liver failure.

Incidence

A. Incidence is variable according to pathogenesis, age, and population.

Pathogenesis

A. The mechanism responsible for jaundice includes excess bilirubin production, decreased hepatic uptake, impaired conjugation, intrahepatic cholestasis, extra-hepatic obstruction, and hepatocellular injury (see Table 13.20).
B. However, it is important to recognize that more than one mechanism can be operating in a given case (i.e., sickle cell anemia and HIV).
  1. Excess bilirubin production results from accelerated red cell destruction. The excessive amounts of hemoglobin and resultant bilirubin released into the bloodstream overwhelm the liver's normal capacity for uptake, and an unconjugated hyperbilirubinemia ensues.
  2. With decreased uptake and conjugation, there is often a concurrent, acquired illness such as infection, cardiac disease, or cancer. Hereditary conditions, such as Gilbert and Crigler–Najjar syndromes, are responsible.
  3. Intrahepatic cholestasis may occur at a number of levels: Intracellularly (e.g., hepatitis), at the canalicular level (when estrogen-induced), at the ductule (phenothiazine exposure), at the septal ducts (primary biliary cirrhosis), and at the intralobular ducts (cholangiocarcinoma).
  4. Extrahepatic obstruction occurs when stone, stricture, or tumor blocks the flow of bile within the extrahepatic biliary tree. A history of gallstones, biliary tract surgery, or malignancy may be elicited.

Predisposing Factors

A. Previous blood transfusion
B. Travel to an area endemic for hepatitis
C. Raw shellfish consumption
D. IV drug abuse
E. High-risk sexual practices
F. Family history of episodic jaundice
G. History of gallstones
H. Previous biliary tract surgery
I. Alcoholism
J. Chemical exposure
K. Working in the health care profession
L. Sickle cell disease
M. Pregnancy (intrahepatic cholestasis)
N. Cancer

Common Complaints

A. Pruritus
B. Dark, tea-colored urine, from conjugated bilirubinuria
C. Light, clay-colored stools, from absence of bile
D. Fatigue
E. RUQ pain

Other Signs and Symptoms

A. Enlarged liver
B. Splenomegaly
C. Fever
D. Chills
E. GI: Appetite loss, weight loss, abdominal pain, nausea, or vomiting
F. Ascites
G. Shortness of breath
H. Palpitations
I. Ecchymosis

TABLE 13.20 Classification of Jaundice According to Bile Pigment and by Mechanism

Unconjugated Hyperbilirubinemia	Conjugated Hyperbilirubinemia
Increased/overproduction of bilirubin	Hepatocellular injury/disease
Impaired/decreased hepatic uptake of bilirubin	Intrahepatic cholestasis
Impaired/decreased conjugation	Extrahepatic cholestasis (biliary obstruction)

J. Steatorrhea, severe
K. Asterixis (tremor)
L. Myalgias
M. Malaise

Subjective Data

A. Review onset, duration, and course of symptoms.
B. Review medication history for drugs/herbals that may induce jaundice (see Table 13.21).
C. Inquire about recent blood transfusions. Are there any known blood disorders in the patient's family history?
D. Ask about contact with a person who has an infection, such as infectious hepatitis.
E. Ask about unprotected sexual activity/HIV status.
F. Review ingestion of potentially contaminated food or water, including *Amanita* mushrooms, milk, or shellfish.
G. Ask about the patient's exposure to any toxic chemicals, such as carbon tetrachloride, chloroform, phosphorus, arsenic, ethanol, or halothane (Fluothane).
H. Review the patient's history of nonsterile needle punctures.
I. Review the patient's medical/surgical history for gallstones, hepatitis, tumor, pancreatitis, Wilson's disease, Budd–Chiari syndrome, liver surgery, or transplantation. Is there a family history of gallstones?
J. Ask how much alcohol the patient has ingested over the years.
K. Ask about dark urine or white or clay-colored stool.
L. Inquire about dyspepsia, anorexia, nausea, vomiting, RUQ or epigastric pain, or pain radiating to the back or shoulder blade. Ask what is the relationship of pain to eating?
M. Inquire about fever, fatigue, malaise, loss of vigor and strength, easy bruising, and weight loss.
N. Review travel history.

TABLE 13.21 Drugs and Herbals Associated With Jaundice

ACE inhibitors
Acetaminophen (Tylenol)
Alkylated steroids
Aminobenzoic acid
Antibiotics
Antidiabetic drugs
Arsenic
Barbiturates
Chlorpromazine
Ethinyl estradiol/OCPs/hormone replacement
Herbal medications (e.g., Jamaican bush tea)
Isoniazid (INH)
Mercaptopurine (Purinethol)
Methyldopa (Aldomet)
Monoamine oxidase inhibitors
Paracetamol (Acetaminophen)
Perphenazine (Trilafon)
Phenothiazine derivatives
Propylthiouracil (PTU)
Rifampin
Sulfonamides
Tamoxifen
TPN

Physical Examination

A. Check temperature, pulse, respirations, blood pressure, and weight. Marked weight loss accompanied by jaundice suggests carcinoma of the head of the pancreas or metastatic disease obstructing the common duct.
B. Inspect
   1. Inspect skin, mouth, palms, and sclera for yellow tinge. Severe jaundice may cause greenish tinge from oxidation of bilirubin to biliverdin.
      a. In fair-skinned people, discoloration is most evident on the face, trunk, and sclera (sclera icterus).
      b. In dark-skinned people, discoloration is most evident in sclera and roof of mouth.
      c. Jaundice is most noticeable in natural sunlight. In artificial or poor light, it may be hard to detect.
   2. Inspect the skin for spider angiomata, rashes, or scratches from severe itching due to pruritus, and for bruising or petechiae.
   3. Inspect the palms for erythema or overt bleeding.
   4. Inspect the chest for gynecomastia.
C. Palpate the abdomen for tenderness, masses, liver enlargement in RUQ, and ascites.
   1. Extrahepatic obstruction and intrahepatic cholestasis may be identical in presentation.
   2. Tenderness is minimal unless cholangitis or rapid distension occurs.
   3. Splenomegaly is unlikely except in primary biliary cirrhosis.
   4. Gallbladder may be palpable (Courvoisier sign) when there is gradual development of the biliary tree. Sudden onset of pain results from passage of stone that becomes wedged into common duct; fever and sepsis shortly thereafter indicate cholangitis.
   5. Malignancy usually presents as a rock-hard mass.
   6. Absence of abdominal pain does not rule out obstruction, especially when it develops slowly from tumor growth or primary biliary cirrhosis.
   7. Advanced hepatocellular disease is indicated by a small liver, signs of portal hypertension

(ascites, splenomegaly, prominent abdominal venous pattern), asterixis, peripheral edema (from hypoalbuminemia), spider angiomata, gynecomastia, palmar erythema, and testicular atrophy.

D. Percuss the abdomen.
E. Auscultate the heart, lungs, and abdomen for bowel sounds.
F. Neurologic exam
   1. Note level of consciousness.
   2. Note asterixis, or flapping tremor elicited when arms are extended and wrists are dorsiflexed.
G. Rectal exam: Check for masses.

Diagnostic Tests

The diagnostic approach begins with a careful history and physician examination, and screening laboratory studies. A differential is formulated, and appropriate further testing is performed to narrow the diagnosis.

A. Initial laboratory tests
   1. Serum bilirubin: Direct, indirect (unconjugated), and total; clinically, jaundice becomes noticeable when levels reach 2.0 to 2.5 mg/dL.
      a. Intrahepatic cholestasis and extrahepatic obstruction: Elevated conjugated bilirubin, elevated serum ALP, mild to moderate rise in transaminase
      b. Gilbert's syndrome is the most common cause of decreased uptake and unconjugated hyperbilirubinemia. It is a benign disorder that produces recurrent self-limited episodes of mild jaundice. Typically, the unconjugated fraction rises to no more than 1.5 to 3.0 mg/100 mL. In Gilbert's syndrome, fasting and minor illness can precipitate jaundice.
   2. ALP
   3. AST/ALT
      a. Elevation of ALT and AST may indicate liver cell damage or may be caused by opiates and aspirin.
      b. Aspirin may also decrease AST and ALT.
   4. PT
      a. PT may be prolonged due to malabsorption, but it is reversible by vitamin K injection.
      b. Prolonged PT unresponsive to parenteral vitamin K strongly suggests hepatocellular failure.
      c. Cholestasis and obstruction may also produce prolongation of PT but can be reversed by vitamin K.
      d. Phenazopyridine (Pyridium) may cause a false-positive bilirubin result.
B. Other laboratory testing as needed
   1. Total serum protein
   2. Serum albumin and globulin
      a. Albumin decreases with cirrhosis and chronic hepatitis.
      b. Globulin increases with cirrhosis, chronic obstructive jaundice, and viral hepatitis.
      c. To interpret albumin level, consider dietary intake and sources of possible protein loss.
   3. Cholesterol
   4. LDH
   5. GGT
   6. Serum ammonia
   7. Bile acids radioimmunoassay: Elevated levels indicate hepatic disease.
   8. Serologic tests for viral hepatitis
   9. Serum iron, transferrin, and ferritin to evaluate hemochromatosis
   10. Serum ceruloplasmin levels to evaluate Wilson's disease
   11. Alpha-1 antitrypsin activity to evaluate alpha-1 antitrypsin deficiency
   12. Urine for bilirubin—bilirubinuria may be an early sign of liver disease.
      a. Collect specimens over a 2-hour period after lunch.
      b. Place specimen in a dark brown container and send to lab immediately to prevent decomposition.
C. **Abdominal ultrasound is considered the screening procedure of choice. More selective imaging procedures are ordered based on clinical evaluation.**
D. Other imaging procedures
   1. Endoscopic ultrasound
   2. HIDA scan: Uses radioactive isotopes
   3. Oral cholecystography
   4. ERCP
   5. PTC
   6. Helical CT
   7. Magnetic resonance cholangiopancreatography (MRCP) is an alternative to ERCP.
   8. Liver biopsy may be indicated for definitive diagnosis.

Differential Diagnoses

A. Jaundice is a symptom, not a diagnosis.
B. Cancer of pancreas
C. Obstruction of biliary tract
D. Icteric phase of hepatitis
E. Cirrhosis
F. Right-sided HF
G. Chronic hemolysis from prosthetic heart valve

Plan

A. Management depends on primary diagnosis. Most patients can be managed on an ambulatory basis, unless they are unable to maintain hydration or unless they begin to show evidence of severe hepatocellular failure.

Follow-Up

A. See the patient 2 to 4 weeks after initial diagnosis and referral.
B. Subsequent routine evaluations are related to primary diagnosis.

Consultation/Referral

A. Consult with a gastroenterologist familiar with liver disease and needle biopsy techniques when hepatocellular disease is suspected; when there is evidence of hepatic failure, portal hypertension, or encephalopathy; or when jaundice persists longer than 3 months.
B. Consultation with a gastroenterologist, surgeon, or radiologist experienced in evaluation of jaundice can be very useful when there is clinical suspicion of extrahepatic obstruction.
C. Admission is mandatory when jaundice is complicated by a fever and peritoneal signs are indicative of cholangitis. IV antibiotics and prompt surgical consultation are required.

Individual Considerations

A. Pregnancy
   1. Viral hepatitis is the most frequent cause of jaundice in pregnancy.
   2. Intrahepatic cholestasis in pregnancy is associated with modest maternal risks, including increased risk of peripartum bleeding and increased likelihood of subsequent cholelithiasis.
   3. Cholestyramine resin, generally 4 g every 4 to 6 hours, has been reported to afford some relief of pruritus in 50% of affected women, presumably by removing a portion of the bile acids by irreversible binding in the gut.
   4. Pregnant women who take cholestyramine are at increased risk for depletion of vitamin K–dependent coagulation factors and should be followed with serial PT times. Such women should also receive prophylactic vitamin K supplementation. If PT becomes prolonged, medication should be discontinued.
B. Geriatrics
   1. The most frequent cause of jaundice in patients older than 65 years is *cholelithiasis*.
   2. The second most frequent cause of jaundice for patients 65 years and older is cancer, especially of the gallbladder.

Malabsorption

Definition

A. Malabsorption syndrome is a group of signs and symptoms occurring as a result of digestive problems and absorption of nutrients. There may be a resultant decrease in absorption of fat-soluble vitamins A, D, E, and K. Poor absorption of carbohydrates, minerals, and proteins may also occur.
B. The presentation of malabsorption varies from severe overt symptoms with weight loss to discrete oligosymptomatic changes in hematologic/laboratory tests that are found incidentally. Malabsorption can result from congenital defects or from acquired defects, such as bariatric surgery, and may be either global or partial. The degree of nutrient malabsorption from bariatric surgery is dependent on the type of bariatric procedure.

Incidence

A. Incidence is unknown.

Pathogenesis

A. Deficiency of intestinal enzymes: Lactase deficiency
B. Inadequate digestion caused by disease of the pancreas (such as CF), gallbladder, or liver
C. Change in bacteria that normally live in the intestinal tract
D. Disease of intestinal walls, such as helminthes (worms) or parasites, tropical sprue, and celiac disease
E. Surgery that reduces the intestinal tract, decreasing the area for absorption such as bariatric surgery
F. Intolerance to gluten, or celiac sprue
G. Atrophic gastritis results in hypochlorhydria and achlorhydria. The body does not produce enough pepsin and hydrochloric acid to release the food-bound vitamin B_{12} from protein.

Predisposing Factors

A. Lactose deficiency
   1. Incidence is increased in African Americans, Indians, and Asians.
   2. Jews typically have onset in adulthood.
B. Family history of malabsorption or CF
C. Use of drugs, such as mineral oil or other laxatives
D. Excess alcohol consumption
E. Travel to foreign countries
F. Intestinal surgery
   1. Partial or total gastrectomy
   2. Small bowel resections (jejunum, ileum, ileocecal)
   3. Partial or total resection of the pancreas
G. Chronic pancreatitis
H. Advanced age (increased risk for malabsorption and malnutrition)
I. Long-term adherence to a strict vegetarian or vegan diet (exclusion of all forms of animal protein, including eggs and dairy products)
J. HIV infection

Common Complaints

A. Diarrhea, stools pale, greasy, and copious
B. Foul-smelling stools, frequently with mucus
C. Weight loss despite adequate food intake
D. Gas or vague abdominal discomfort

E. Anorexia
F. Fatigue secondary to anemia

Other Signs and Symptoms

A. Early malabsorption
   1. Minimal weight loss
   2. Softer, more frequent stools
   3. Steatorrhea; stools "float" because of increased trapped gas
   4. Abdominal discomfort
   5. Bloating
B. Later signs: Symptoms mentioned plus the following.
   1. Marked weight loss
   2. Foul-smelling, bulky, greasy stools
C. Malabsorption of fats and carbohydrates: Previous symptoms plus the following.
   1. Foul-smelling, bulky, greasy, "sticky" stools that may be difficult to flush down the toilet
   2. Ecchymosis
   3. Bone pain
   4. Glossitis
   5. Muscle tenderness
   6. Cramping in lower abdomen after BM
D. Malabsorption of lactose
   1. Nausea and bloating
   2. Cramps
   3. Diarrhea after ingesting more than customary intake of milk products
   4. Absent or mild weight loss and steatorrhea
   5. Good appetite
E. Edema: With severe protein depletion/calorie malnutrition
F. Ecchymosis and bleeding disorders secondary to vitamin K malabsorption

Subjective Data

A. Review onset, duration, and course of symptoms. Are there any other family members with the same history/symptoms?
B. Ask the patient about dietary intake history.
C. Review any changes in BMs and stool characteristics.
D. Inquire about recent travel to areas known for giardiasis or other parasites.
E. Document weight loss, how much, and over what period of time.
F. Review previous GI surgery, including the bariatric procedures and reversals, small bowel resections, and partial or total resection of the pancreas.
G. Ask the patient about signs and symptoms of IBD, such as easy bruising, paresthesia, and sore tongue.
H. Ask about any irradiation treatment.

Physical Examination

A. Check pulse, respirations, blood pressure (may have orthostatic hypotension), and weight. Follow serial weight loss and plot on growth charts.
B. Inspect
   1. Observe general appearance, noting wasting and apathetic appearance.
   2. If the patient experiences a BM after the examination, observe the stool for volume, appearance, presence of blood, mucus, and the presence of gross worms/parasites.
   3. Inspect the skin for ecchymosis, jaundice, pallor, surgical scars, stigmata of hyperthyroidism or hepatocellular failure, or signs of Kaposi's sarcoma. Alopecia or seborrheic dermatitis may be present.
   4. Inspect the ears, nose, and throat for glossitis, stomatitis, aphthous ulcers, poor dentition, and goiter.
C. Auscultate
   1. Auscultate the heart for tachycardia.
   2. Auscultate the abdomen in all four quadrants for bowel sounds, noting borborygmi.
D. Percuss abdomen.
E. Palpate
   1. Palpate all lymph nodes; look for lymphadenopathy.
   2. Palpate the abdomen for organomegaly, focal tenderness, masses, distension, and ascites.
F. Neurologic exam: Assess for signs of vitamin B_{12} deficiency, including motor weakness, peripheral neuropathy, or ataxia.
G. Rectal exam: Note tenderness, discharge, blood, and stool.

Diagnostic Tests

A. Assessment of stool fat: Qualitative assessment on a single specimen
B. Quantitative assessment of a 72-hour stool collection while the patient is following a 100 g of fat diet.
C. Increased fecal fat: Test for celiac disease.
D. Abdominal ultrasound
E. Colonoscopy to evaluate and obtain biopsies
F. Endoscopy to evaluate and obtain biopsies
G. Barium studies
H. Consider CT of the abdomen
I. ERCP helps to document malabsorption due to pancreatic or biliary-related disorders.
J. Breath tests for carbohydrate malabsorption
K. CBC and electrolytes
L. Serum iron, vitamin B_{12}, and folate concentrations
M. PT: May be prolonged due to vitamin K deficiency
N. Vitamin levels: Vitamins A, D, E, and K may be decreased.
O. Total protein: May be decreased
P. Albumin: May be decreased
Q. Serum amylase

R. Stool for ova and parasites; obtain on alternate days for three or more specimens because parasites are passed intermittently.

Differential Diagnoses

A. Malabsorption
B. AIDS
C. Alcoholism
D. Worms or parasites
E. CF
F. CD
G. Tropical sprue
H. Side effect from bariatric surgery
I. Disaccharidase deficiencies (lactase)
J. Fructose intolerance
K. Milk or protein allergy
L. Whipple's disease
M. Zollinger–Ellison syndrome

Plan

A. General interventions: Treatment depends on underlying cause.
B. Patient teaching: See the Section III Patient Teaching Guide for this chapter, "Lactose Intolerance and Malabsorption."
C. Dietary management: In most patients, diet modification or dietary supplements restore health.
D. Pharmaceutical therapy
   1. Vitamin supplements: Fat-soluble vitamins A, D, and K are most likely to be depleted. Supplements help prevent malnutrition, even though caloric intake may be replenished.
      a. Vitamin A: 25,000 to 50,000 U/d orally
      b. Vitamin D: 30,000 U/d orally
      c. Vitamin K: 4 to 12 mg/d orally
      d. Vitamin B_{12}: 1,000 g/mo by IM injection
   2. Enzyme replacements: These replace endogenous exocrine pancreatic enzymes and aid in digestion of starches, fat, and proteins. Pancreatic supplements are typically expressed in U.S. Pharmacopeia Convention (USP) units. One international unit (IU) is equivalent to approximately 2 to 3 USP units.
      a. Pancreatin: Doses vary with the condition being treated. Oral doses are given before or with meals or each snack. They may also be given in divided doses at 1- to 2-hour intervals throughout the day.
      b. Pancrelipase (Creon, Pancrease, Ultrase, Viokase): This must be given with each meal or snack.
         i. Adults: One to three capsules or tablets orally with meals; titrate dose to desired clinical response.
   3. Antispasmodics
      a. Anticholinergic agents are used to reduce the cholinergic stimulation of colonic activity that occurs in response to a meal.
      b. Drug of choice: Dicyclomine hydrochloride (Antispas), 10 to 20 mg orally before meals
   4. Iron and folic acid supplementation are usually required for celiac disease.
   5. Calcium and magnesium supplementation are required after extensive small intestinal resection.

Follow-Up

A. If exam is normal, observe the patient for 1 month and have the patient keep a diary of food intake and weight.
B. For persistent malabsorption, monitor for osteoporosis/bone mass with a DEXA scan.

Consultation/Referral

A. Any patient with weight loss of 15 kg is likely to have a life-threatening condition and requires prompt consultation and hospitalization.
B. Consult a gastroenterologist when malabsorption is documented by 72-hour stool fat assessment.
C. Consider a dietary consultation.
D. Refer back to the bariatric surgeon/center, depending on surgical complications from bariatric surgery.
E. Consider a referral for allergy testing for milk and proteins.

Individual Considerations

A. Geriatrics
   1. Individuals 65 years of age and older are more likely to develop a vitamin B_{12} deficiency because they are at risk for both malabsorption and malnutrition.
   2. The frail elderly may have dietary insufficiency due to:
      a. Cognitive disabilities
      b. Social isolation, depression, bereavement
      c. Physical impairment/mobility limitations
      d. Poor dentition
         i. Poor-fitting dentures
         ii. Edentulous
      e. Poverty
      f. Loss of the sense of taste
      g. Inability to prepare meals
      h. Lack of assistance feeding
      i. Too little time to eat/be fed

Nausea and Vomiting

Definition

Nausea and vomiting are common symptoms for many conditions and diseases; and several terms describe the symptoms (see Table 13.22).

TABLE 13.22 Definitions of Terminology Used to Describe Nausea and Vomiting

Term	Definition
Anorexia	Loss of desire to eat; a true loss of appetite
Early satiety	Fear of being full after eating an unusually small quantity of food
Nausea	The unpleasant sensation of the imminent need to vomit, usually referred to the throat or epigastrium; a sensation that may or may not ultimately lead to vomiting
Regurgitation	The act by which food is brought back into the mouth without the abdominal and diaphragmatic muscular activity that characterizes vomiting
Retching	Spasmodic respiratory movements against a closed glottis with contraction of the abdominal musculature without expulsion of any gastric contents, referred to as "dry heaves"
Rumination	Chewing and swallowing of regurgitated food that has come back into the mouth through voluntary increase in abdominal pressure within minutes of eating or during eating; rumination may be accompanied by weight loss and bulimia
Sitophobia	Fear of eating because of subsequent or associated discomfort
Vomiting	Forceful oral expulsion of gastric contents associated with contraction of the abdominal and chest wall musculature

A. Hyperemesis gravidarum is a condition of persistent, uncontrollable vomiting that begins in the first weeks of pregnancy and may continue throughout pregnancy.
B. Chronic nausea and vomiting is defined as at least 1 month in duration.
C. Complications of nausea and vomiting include fluid depletion, hypokalemia, and metabolic alkalosis.
D. Vomiting is also considered a protective mechanism to remove harmful ingested substances.

Incidence

A. Nausea and vomiting are very common, and the etiology is dependent on the disease/condition.
B. During pregnancy, 70% to 85% of women experience nausea and/or vomiting; 50% have both nausea and vomiting. Onset after the initial 9 weeks of pregnancy should direct especially careful evaluation for another cause within the differential diagnoses of nausea and vomiting in nonpregnant patients. *Hyperemesis gravidarum* occurs in 1 in every 0.5% to 2% of pregnancies.
C. Approximately one third of surgical patients have nausea and/or vomiting after general anesthesia.
D. The incidence of nausea and/or vomiting subsequent to cancer treatment is high.

Pathogenesis

A. Protective mechanisms are activated by numerous GI and non-GI causes. Normal function of the upper GI tract involves an interaction between the gut and the CNS. Nausea and vomiting in pregnancy are related to increased hormones, including HCG, estrogen, and progesterone, as well as decreased gastric motility and relative hypoglycemia that results from a night-long fast.

Predisposing Factors

A. Acute nausea and vomiting
    1. Medications: Digitalis toxicity, opiate use, anesthetic, chemotherapy agents, drug withdrawal, nicotine/ nicotine patches, antibiotics, hormones, and antivirals
    2. Ketoacidosis
    3. Pregnancy or hormones
    4. Binge drinking
    5. Hepatitis
B. Recurrent or chronic nausea and vomiting
    1. Psychogenic vomiting
    2. Metabolic disturbances
    3. Gastric retention
    4. Bile reflux
    5. Pregnancy
    6. Radiation
    7. Gastroparesis
C. Nausea and vomiting with abdominal pain
    1. Viral gastroenteritis
    2. Acute gastritis
    3. Food poisoning
    4. PUD
    5. Acute pancreatitis
    6. Small bowel obstruction
    7. Acute appendicitis
    8. Acute cholecystitis
    9. Acute cholangitis
    10. Acute pyelonephritis
    11. Inferior MI
D. Nausea and vomiting with neurologic symptoms
    1. Increased ICP
    2. Midline cerebellar hemorrhage
    3. Vestibular disturbances
    4. Migraine headaches
    5. Autonomic dysfunction

6. Head trauma
7. Multiple sclerosis

Common Complaints

A. "Queasy" sensation
B. Food aversion
C. Inability to retain food or liquids

Other Signs and Symptoms

A. Increased salivation
B. Bitter taste, "acid brash": Indicates ulcer or small bowel obstruction
C. Weight loss
D. Dehydration
E. Sweating
F. Fast pulse
G. Pale skin
H. Rapid breathing
I. Lightheadedness

Subjective Data

A. Review onset, duration (acute or chronic problem?), and course of symptoms, including the quality (projectile?) and quantity of emesis. What were the color, taste, and consistency of the emesis? Was blood present?
   1. Vomiting bright red blood indicates a hemorrhage—*peptic ulcer*.
   2. Dark red blood indicates a hemorrhage—*esophageal or gastric varices*.
   3. Coffee grounds material is indicative of digested blood from a slowly bleeding gastric ulcer or DU.
   4. Vomiting fecal material is a sign of distal *small-bowel obstruction* and blind-loop syndrome.
   5. Explosive projectile vomiting is associated with increased intracranial pressure such as with meningitis.
B. Ask the patient about other symptoms, including pain, fever, diarrhea, and headache.
C. Inquire if other family members are also ill and what are their symptoms.
D. Review the timing of vomiting in relation to meals, time of day, odors, and activity. Does vomiting occur before or after food intake?
E. Ask the patient about medication intake such as antibiotics, chemotherapy, herbals, digitalis, opiates, and birth control pills.
F. Ask about self-image, binge eating, and self-induced emesis.
G. Review any exposure to hepatitis or travel to places with poor sanitation and outbreaks of cholera.
H. Review the patient's medical history for vertigo, head injury, jaundice, diabetes, hypertension, and pregnancy.
I. Inquire about first day of last period and birth control method used.
J. Establish usual weight. Has there been any recent weight change, how many pounds, and over what period of time?
K. Ask about the patient's history of diabetes, gallbladder disease, ulcer disease, or cancer.

Physical Examination

A. Check temperature (if indicated), pulse, respirations, blood pressure, and weight.
B. Inspect
   1. Observe general overall appearance of skin for pallor and signs of dehydration. Tenting of skin when it is rolled between your thumb and index finger may indicate dehydration.
   2. Inspect for signs of autonomic insufficiency. Postural hypotension, lack of sweat, or blunted pulse and blood pressure responses to Valsalva's maneuver suggest autonomic dysfunction and a bowel motility problem as the underlying etiology of nausea and vomiting. Postural hypotension indicates marked volume depletion or circulatory collapse.
   3. Oral exam: Inspect mouth, teeth, and gums. Pay particular attention for dental enamel erosion as a sign of bulimia.
C. Palpate
   1. Palpate the abdomen for masses, distension, tenderness, signs of peritonitis, and organomegaly.
   2. Palpate the back; note CVA tenderness.
D. Percuss the abdomen.
E. Auscultate
   1. Auscultate the abdomen for bowel sounds in all quadrants.
   2. Auscultate the heart and lungs.
F. Perform rectal exam (if indicated).
G. Perform a neurologic examination (if indicated).

Diagnostic Tests

The cause of an acute episode of nausea and vomiting is typically determined through a detailed history and physical examination. Only if the cause is unclear should further diagnostic tests be performed.

A. Urine: Ketones, urinalysis, pregnancy test, culture and sensitivity, if indicated
B. Serum labs: Multiple chemistry profile, including amylase, electrolytes, BUN, creatinine, glucose, and transaminase
C. Drug screen
D. Upper GI
E. Ultrasonography, to rule out molar pregnancy if persistent nausea and vomiting, especially after 16 weeks gestation
F. Stool for occult blood
G. Endoscopy
H. Head CT scan, if indicated

I. Gastric scintigraphy, to rule out gastroparesis if indicated
J. EKG if chest pain/MI is suspected

Differential Diagnoses

A. See Predisposing Factors.

Plan

A. General interventions: Assess hydration status. Proceed to IV hydration and antiemetics until ketones clear.
B. Dietary management: See Appendix B, "Nausea and Vomiting Diet Suggestions."
C. Pharmaceutical therapy (not an exhaustive list)
   1. Antiemetics
      a. Dextrose/fructose/phosphoric acid solution (Emetrol); available OTC
         i. Adults: 15 to 30 mL by mouth at 15-minute intervals (not to exceed five doses)
         ii. Tell the patient not to dilute the drug or take fluids 15 minutes before or after taking the medication.
         iii. Diabetics should be instructed not to use without consulting their provider
         iv. If nausea continues despite medication, contact health care provider
      b. Promethazine (Phenergan)
         i. Drug of choice for gastroenteritis.
         ii. Adults: 25 to 50 mg by mouth or per rectum every 4 to 6 hours
      c. Trimethobenzamide (Tigan)
         i. Used for gastroenteritis and motion sickness
         ii. Adults: 300 mg orally three or four times daily
         iii. Adults: 200 mg IM three or four times daily
      d. Prochlorperazine (Compazine)
         i. Adults: 5 to 10 mg three or four times daily; spansules 15 mg every 12 hours; suppositories 25 mg twice daily
   2. Outpatient IV hydration in pregnancy: 1 L lactated Ringer's solution to correct dehydration and restore electrolyte balance. Check urine ketones after first liter to determine if additional liter is necessary to clear ketones.
   3. 5-HT_3 antagonists are utilized for nausea related to chemotherapy therapy and postoperative nausea and vomiting. 5-HT_3 drugs are available in oral, IV, and transdermal formulations. Consult a prescribing reference for current dosing/formulations
      a. Ondansetron (Zofran)
      b. Granisetron (Sancuso and Kytril)
      c. Palonosetron (Aloxi)
      d. Dolasetron mesylate (Anzemet)

Follow-Up

A. Tell the patient to call or visit the office in 24 hours to check response and nutritional intake.

Consultation/Referral

A. **First priority is to rule out acute surgical etiology such as bowel obstruction and peritonitis.**
B. Consult a physician and hospitalize the patient promptly if there is evidence of bowel obstruction; increased ICP; or another GI, neurologic, or metabolic emergency.
C. Hyperemesis gravidarum may require hospitalization to correct fluid and electrolyte imbalance.
D. Call for a psychiatric consultation for suspected psychogenic nausea and vomiting.
E. If postural hypotension occurs, especially in elderly patients, hospital admission for parenteral fluid and electrolyte replacement is indicated.
F. Endocrinologist, gastroenterologist, and surgical consultations for treatment, consideration, and placement of a gastric stimulator for diabetic gastroparesis.

Individual Considerations

A. Pregnancy
   1. Determine whether the woman is ingesting nonfood substances, such as starch, clay, or toothpaste, which would indicate pica.
   2. Intractable nausea and vomiting require ultrasonography to rule out hydatidiform mole.
   3. Emetrol, promethazine (Phenergan), and prochlorperazine (Compazine) may be used during pregnancy.
   4. Uncorrected hyperemesis gravidarum can result in severe electrolyte imbalance and possible hepatic and renal damage. The major concern for fetal well-being is uncorrected ketosis, which may result in fetal abnormalities or death in early pregnancy.
   5. Tell the patient to eat toast or a dry cracker; to eat small, frequent meals and snacks; to drink fluids separately from meals; and to avoid fatty, fried, greasy, or spicy foods and foods with strong odors.
B. Geriatrics
   1. There should be a low threshold for hospitalization of the elderly to treat dehydration and correction of fluid and electrolyte imbalance.

Resources

American Cancer Society: www.cancer.org
Rome Foundation: http://romecriteria.org/criteria

Peptic Ulcer Disease

Definition

A. PUD is circumscribed ulceration of the GI mucosa occurring in areas exposed to acid and pepsin. The patient's prior ulcer history tends to predict future behavior and risk of future complications. Complications include bleeding ulcer, perforation, and obstruction.

B. The stomach is divided on the basis of its physiologic functions into two main portions. The proximal two thirds, the fundic gland area, acts as a receptacle for ingested food and secretes acid and pepsin. The distal third, the pyloric gland area, mixes and propels food into the duodenum and produces the hormone gastrin. "Peptic" lesions may occur in the esophagus (esophagitis), stomach (gastritis), or duodenum (duodenitis).

C. There is often no correlation between the presence of an active ulcer, noted by endoscopy, and symptoms. The disappearance of symptoms does not guarantee ulcer healing.

Incidence

A. The annual incidence of peptic ulcer is estimated to range from 0.1% to 1.8%. The ulcer incidence in *H. pylori-infected* individuals is about 1% per year. The recurrence rate is 50% to 80% during the 6 to 12 months following the initial ulcer healing, although relapses are not always symptomatic. Some peptic ulcers heal spontaneously, and 2% to 20% of patients have multiple simultaneous ulcers.

B. From 16% to 31% of ulcers are caused by NSAIDs. Epidemiologic studies show that risks of peptic ulcer and death are three to six times higher among people who take NSAIDs.

C. Cigarette smokers are twice as likely to develop ulcers as nonsmokers.

Pathogenesis

A. Although the precise mechanisms of ulcer formation remain incompletely understood, the process appears to involve the interplay of acid production, pepsin secretion, bacterial infection, and mucosal defense mechanisms. Excess acid production is the hallmark of DU disease. Pepsin secretion is also elevated in DU disease.

B. The relation of aspirin and other NSAIDs to ulcer disease is due largely to the drugs' potent inhibition of gastric mucosal prostaglandin synthesis. In addition to prostaglandin inhibition, many NSAID preparations produce acute diffuse mucosal injury by means of a direct erosive effect.

Predisposing Factors

A. ***H. pylori* infection is the most common cause of ulceration.**

B. **Use of NSAIDs, especially aspirin, ibuprofen, and naproxen, is associated with acute erosive gastritis.**

C. Smoking

D. Genetic factors: Family history of ulcer disease

E. Age
   1. DU occurs between ages 25 and 75.
   2. Gastric ulcer (GU) occurs between ages 55 and 65.

F. Gender
   1. The ratio of male-to-female for gastritis is 1:1.
   2. The ratio of male-to-female for peptic ulcers is 2:1.

G. Excessive alcohol consumption, which stimulates acid secretion

H. Medications
   1. Corticosteroids
   2. Warfarin
   3. Bisphosphonates
   4. Spironolactone
   5. SSRIs

I. Improper diet, irregular meals, and skipped meals

J. Severe physiologic stress
   1. Burns
   2. CNS trauma
   3. Surgery
   4. Severe medical illness
      a. Cirrhosis
      b. COPD
      c. Renal failure
      d. Organ transplantation

K. Other causes
   1. Radiation-induced ulcer
   2. Chemotherapy-induced ulcer
   3. Vascular insufficiency
   4. Duodenal obstruction

L. Zollinger–Ellison syndrome

M. Bile reflux

N. Illicit drugs: Crack cocaine

Common Complaints

A. Pain described as aching, boring, gnawing, or burning feeling.

B. Epigastric pain in RUQ and LUQ of the abdomen or occasionally below breast

C. Pain that awakens the patient at night or in early morning

D. **Perforated peptic ulcer presents with a sudden severe onset of sharp abdominal pain.**

Other Signs and Symptoms

A. Asymptomatic

B. GI distress 1 to 3 hours after a meal, on an empty stomach

C. Pain relieved by food, antacids, or vomiting

D. Nausea and vomiting

E. Hematemesis

F. Chest discomfort

G. Blood in stools, "grape jelly" or maroon-colored stools

H. Loss of appetite or weight

I. Weight gain; those with DU may eat more to ease pain.
J. Anemia

Other Signs and Symptoms

A. Massive bleeding
   1. Acute, bright red hematemesis or large amount of melena with clots in the stool, or "grape jelly" stool
   2. Rapid pulse, drop in blood pressure, hypovolemia, and shock
B. Subacute bleeding
   1. Intermittent melena or coffee-ground emesis
   2. Hypotension
   3. Weakness and dizziness
C. Chronic bleeding
   1. Intermittent appearance of blood
   2. Increased weakness, paleness, or shortness of breath
   3. Occult blood

Subjective Data

A. Ask the patient to describe onset, duration, type, and location of pain. Does it occur at any special time, for example, before meals, after meals, or during the night?
B. Has the patient had a previous ulcer? What was the treatment; if oral treatment was prescribed, did the patient complete the therapy?
C. Have the patient describe what alleviates pain, such as taking antacids, and what worsens pain, such as use of aspirin, oral steroids, or NSAIDs.
D. Review associated symptoms, such as nausea, vomiting, and heartburn.
E. Ask the patient if any first-degree relatives have ulcers.
F. Inquire whether the patient is a smoker. If so, how much and for how long?
G. Ask the patient about alcohol consumption: How much and for how long?
H. Inquire whether any blood has ever been vomited or passed in stool. If so, have the patient describe it.
I. Take the patient's dietary history, including time of meals, frequency of skipped meals, weight loss, and so forth.
J. Review all medications, including a review of OTC and herbal products such as ginkgo biloba; special attention should be taken to inquire about aspirin and NSAIDs.
K. Obtain past medical history of associated diseases, such as cirrhosis, pancreatitis, arthritis, COPD, and hyperparathyroidism.
L. If the patient suspects blood in stool, ask if there has been a change in bowel pattern, presence of abdominal pain or tenderness, and what kind of food, such as red beets, the patient recently ingested.

Physical Examination

A. Check temperature (if indicated), pulse, respirations, blood pressure, and weight.
B. Palpate the abdomen for tenderness, rigidity, masses, and liver or spleen enlargement.
C. Percuss the abdomen for hepatosplenomegaly.
D. Auscultate the abdomen for bowel sounds in all quadrants.
E. Rectal exam
   1. Check for tenderness and masses.
   2. Take stool specimen.

Diagnostic Tests

A. CBC
B. Stool for occult blood
C. Coagulation studies
D. Testing for *H. pylori*
   1. **Endoscopy with biopsy is the most accurate test.**
   2. Urea breath test (UBT)
   3. Serum test for *H. pylori* antibodies
   4. Stool *H. pylori* antigen testing
E. Radiography with barium meal
F. Mucosal biopsy, after GI consultation, to rule out cancer.
G. Fasting gastrin level (screening for Zollinger–Ellison)

Differential Diagnoses

A. PUD
B. GERD
C. Zollinger–Ellison syndrome: Fasting serum gastrin level 500 pg/mL in the presence of acid hypersecretion is diagnostic.
D. Cancer
   1. Gastric lymphoma
   2. Gastric cancer
   3. Pancreatic cancer
E. Pancreatitis (acute or chronic)
F. Myocardial ischemia
G. Abdominal aneurysm
H. Diverticulitis
I. Drug-induced dyspepsia
   1. Theophylline
   2. Digitalis
J. CD involving the stomach or duodenum
K. Gastric infections

Plan

A. General interventions: Goals are to alleviate pain, promote healing, limit complications, and prevent recurrences while minimizing the costs and side effects of treatment.
   1. Encourage the patient to stop taking NSAIDs, unless medically indicated.
      a. If NSAID use is unavoidable, the lowest possible dose and duration and cotherapy with a PPI or misoprostol are recommended.

2. Smoking cessation should be highly encouraged at each visit.

B. Patient teaching: See the Section III Patient Teaching Guide for this chapter, "Management of Ulcers."

C. Dietary management: Advise the patient to avoid alcohol; coffee, including decaffeinated; and other caffeine-containing beverages because they stimulate acid secretion (see Appendix B, "Bland Diet").

D. Medical and surgical management

1. Diagnostic evaluation of the ulcer is by means of endoscopy.
2. Test for *H. pylori* (carbon isotope-urea breath test [UBT], blood test for antibodies to *H. pylori*, stool test, or gastric biopsy at the time of EGD).
   a. A single negative *H. pylori* test should be interpreted cautiously, especially in the face of active bleeding. Blood in the stomach can alter the pH indicator in the rapid urease test. False negatives are likely, and additional testing for *H. pylori* is essential.
   b. Concurrent use of a PPI, antibiotics, or bismuth will cause a false negative test.
3. Surgery remains an option for treatment of refractory disease and complications. The most serious indications for surgery include brisk bleeding of 6 to 8 units of blood in 24 hours, recurrent bleeding episodes, perforation, gastric outlet obstruction refractory to medical therapy, and failure of a benign GU to heal after 15 weeks. Emergency intervention may be required, such as withholding food and oral fluids, starting an IV, placing a nasogastric (NG) tube, providing oxygen therapy, or performing a blood transfusion. If life-threatening bleeding occurs, treat shock.

E. Pharmaceutical therapy

1. The treatment of a peptic ulcer begins with the eradication of *H. pylori* in infected individuals. Empiric therapy for the infection is reasonable for uncomplicated cases in the absence of NSAID use. Documenting infection, even in patients with known ulcers, is an essential step prior to initiating antimicrobial therapy.
   a. Triple therapy anti-*H. pylori* regimen PPI + amoxicillin + clarithromycin
      i. PPI-based regimen (choose one)
         1) Rabeprazole (Aciphex) 20 mg twice a day–total treatment duration 7 days
         2) Esomeprazole (Nexium) 40 mg once a day–total treatment duration 10 days
         3) Lansoprazole (Prevacid) 30 mg twice a day–total treatment duration 10 to 104 days
      ii. Amoxicillin 1,000 mg twice a day
      iii. Clarithromycin 500 mg twice a day
   b. Quadruple therapy–Helidac therapy (sold in a combination pack), oral doses four times a day for 14 days
      i. Choose an H_2 receptor antagonist.
      ii. Metronidazole (Flagyl) 250 mg four times a day
      iii. Tetracycline 500 mg four times a day
      iv. Bismuth subsalicylate two chew tablets four times a day
2. Antisecretory therapy is the mainstay of therapy in uninfected patients and is used for maintenance therapy in selected cases. Full doses of H_2 receptor antagonist provide effective initial therapy; however, PPIs are more effective.

   Patients with uncomplicated, small (< 1 cm) DU or GU who have received adequate treatment for *H. pylori* probably are asymptomatic and do not need any further therapy directed at ulcer healing. Maintenance acid suppression following *H. pyloric* eradication is recommended for patients with a complicated DU.

   If the ulcer is giant (> 2 cm), showing densely fibrosed ulcer beds, or if the patient is a high-risk patient with a protracted prior history, then the patient should be kept on a PPI until a follow-up endoscopy is performed.
   a. H_2 receptor antagonist-based therapy: Split dose, evening, and nighttime therapy are all effective. In the United States, cimetidine, ranitidine, and famotidine are approved for GU healing. Choose one antibiotic combination (Amoxicillin + Clarithromycin OR Metronidazole + Tetracycline as noted above) for 2 weeks and add one of the following:
      i. Cimetidine (Tagamet) 800 mg at bedtime for 4 to 8 weeks
      ii. Ranitidine (Zantac) 300 mg in the a.m. or at bedtime for 4 to 8 weeks
      iii. Famotidine (Pepcid) 40 mg at bedtime for 4 to 8 weeks
      iv. Nizatidine 300 mg at bedtime for 4 to 8 weeks
   b. PPIs are effective in inducing ulcer healing. The PPIs are the most potent inhibitors of gastric acid secretion. Once-daily dosing is generally sufficient for acid inhibition; however, a second dose may be necessary and should be given before the evening meal. Once-daily PPI dosing inhibits acid output

by 66% after 5 days. Optimal dosing is immediately before breakfast.

i. Omeprazole (Prilosec/Zegerid) 20 to 40 mg every morning for 4 weeks
ii. Esomeprazole (Nexium) 20 to 40 mg every morning for 4 to 8 weeks
iii. Lansoprazole (Prevacid) 15 to 30 mg every morning for 4 weeks
iv. Dexlansoprazole (Kapidex) 30 to 60 mg every morning for 4 to 8 weeks
v. Pantoprazole (Protonix) 20 to 40 mg every morning for 4 weeks
vi. Rabeprazole (Aciphex) 20 mg every morning for 4 weeks
vii. Dexlansoprazole (Dexilant) 60 mg every morning for 8 weeks; PPIs should not be given concomitantly with prostaglandins, or other antisecretory agents because of the marked reduction in their effects.

3. An H2 antagonist can be used with a PPI if given after a sufficient interval between their administrations; the minimal times have not been established. The H2 antagonist could be given at bedtime for breakthrough symptoms after a morning dose of a PPI.
4. Sucralfate (Carafate) 1 g orally four times daily, 1 hour before meals and at bedtime; maintenance therapy is 1 g twice daily. Sucralfate is not recommended for *H. pylori* or NSAID ulcers.
5. Misoprostol (Cytotec, a prostaglandin analogue) is effective for peptic ulcers due to NSAID use; peptic ulcers respond well to misoprostol 100 to 200 mcg orally four times a day.

Follow-Up

A. Therapeutic trial of lifestyle changes combined with an H_2 receptor antagonist, sucralfate, or omeprazole for 1 to 2 weeks should provide relief. Reevaluate the patient after 2 weeks, and if symptoms are improved, prescribe a full course of 6 to 8 weeks.
B. Reevaluate the patient again at 8 weeks, after the full course of therapy is completed.
C. Consider repeating breath test to confirm eradication of *H. pylori.*
D. Some authorities advocate routine endoscopic or radiological documentation of healing. However, no studies show this to be cost-effective in uncomplicated cases in which symptoms resolve within 4 to 6 weeks and do not recur.
E. For refractory GU—that is, persistent pain after 8 weeks despite a full medical regimen or unresponsive to treatment for *H. pylori*—endoscopic examination and biopsy are needed, especially in patients older than age 40 who are at increased risk of gastric cancer. Barium study is not sufficient because even malignant ulcers may shrink in size in response to therapy.
F. Evaluate refractory cases for Zollinger–Ellison syndrome, especially when there are multiple ulcers, occurrences in unusual places, marked abdominal pain, or a secretory diarrhea.
G. There is an increased risk of osteoporotic fracture from the long-term use of PPIs.

Consultation/Referral

A. Consult both a surgeon and a gastroenterologist and admit the patient to a hospital when symptoms of hemorrhage, penetration, perforation, or gastric outlet obstruction are present.
B. Refer patients with recurrences or refractory disease to a physician for evaluation for *H. pylori* infection by endoscopy or breath test. If present, eradicate with a 2-week course of triple therapy.

Individual Considerations

A. Pregnancy: The drugs misoprostol and ranitidine are abortifacients. They cross the placental barrier and are excreted in breast milk and are contraindicated in pregnancy or suspected pregnancy. Use in sexually active women of childbearing age should be done with proper warning and detailed patient education.
B. Adults
   1. DUs are more common in people between ages 45 and 54; GUs, between 55 and 64 years.
   2. Patients older than age 40 are at greater risk of gastric cancer and should undergo either an upper GI series or endoscopy to document the nature and location of lesions when there is strong clinical suspicion of ulcer disease.
   3. Gastritis not associated with reflux is present in 75% of people older than age 50.
C. Geriatrics
   1. Silent disease is particularly common among the elderly and those using NSAIDs.
   2. Lethargy, confusion, slurred speech, agitation, and visual hallucinations have been reported with cimetidine, particularly in the elderly.
   3. In the elderly, DU symptoms remain classic with early morning awakening to pain, then quick relief by food or antacids. GU symptoms are less obvious, with burning or gnawing pain experienced in less than 50% of elderly patients.
   4. Anemia may be the only symptom of gastric cancer. Cancer must always be considered and confirmed by endoscopy with biopsy.
   5. When prescribing an NSAID to the elderly, use the lowest dose, for the shortest period of time,

and avoid prescribing a long-acting NSAID, such as indomethacin (Indocin) and piroxicam (Feldene).

6. Due to other medications they take for comorbid health conditions, the elderly are especially at risk with the combination of NSAIDs and the following.
   a. Aspirin
   b. Clopidogrel (Plavix)
   c. Dabigatran (Pradaxa)
   d. Dipyridamole (Persantine)
   e. Prasugrel (Effient)
   f. Ticlopidine (Ticlid)
   g. Warfarin (Coumadin)

Post–Bariatric Surgery Management

Definition

A. The optimal management of overweight and obesity starts with a combination of diet, exercise, and behavior modification. Some patients eventually require bariatric surgery. Bariatric surgery is a therapeutic option for the management of carefully selected patients who are morbidly obese (BMI > 40 kg/m^2), super obese (BMI > 50 kg/m^2), and patients who are severely obese (> 35 kg/m^2) with one significant comorbidity. Several types of bariatric procedures help promote weight loss by restricting food intake either by limiting the amount of food that can be ingested and/or by decreasing the absorption of nutrients from the gut (see Table 13.23).

B. Restrictive procedures limit caloric intake by downsizing the stomach's reservoir capacity, leaving the absorptive function of the small intestine intact. The primary mechanism of malabsorptive procedures is to decrease the effectiveness of nutrient absorption by shortening the length of functional small intestine. Some procedures have both a restrictive and malabsorptive component. The laparoscopic adjustable gastric banding (LAGB), for example, is primarily a restrictive operation in which a small gastric pouch limits oral intake whereas the RYGB is both a restrictive and a malabsorption procedure.

Incidence

A. The CDC notes that more than one third of the U.S. adult population and 17% of U.S. children and adolescents aged 2 to 19 years are obese.

B. Obesity-related conditions include heart disease, stroke, type 2 diabetes, and some cancers. Obesity is one of the leading causes of preventable death.

C. Approximately 25% of bariatric surgery patients have surgical complications. Currently, the most commonly performed gastric bypass procedure is the laparoscopic RYGB, representing 70% to 75% of the procedures.

Pathogenesis

The pathogenesis of obesity is reviewed under "Obesity" in Chapter 23, "Endocrine Guidelines." The incidences of complications vary by surgical procedure and by whether the surgery was performed laparoscopically or by an open surgical procedure. Postoperative complications may occur immediately or may occur long term after surgery.

A. The LAGB, though simpler than malabsorptive procedures, tends to produce more gradual weight loss, and patients may experience band slippage. Deficiency of fat-soluble vitamins, thiamine, and folate has been observed, especially if the patient develops frequent vomiting.

B. Profound weight loss can be achieved by the malabsorption operations (e.g., BPD, Sleeve procedure, or BPD-DS), depending on the effective length of the functional small bowel segment. The benefit of superior weight loss is often offset by the significant metabolic complications such as protein caloric malnutrition and various micronutrient deficiencies.

C. The small bowel reconfiguration of the RYGB provides additional mechanisms favoring weight loss but includes side effects such as dumping physiology and malabsorption. Deficiency of iron, vitamin B_{12}, folate, calcium, and vitamin D has been frequently observed after RYGB surgery.

TABLE 13.23 Bariatric Surgeries and Mechanism of Action

Restrictive Procedures	Malabsorptive Procedures	Restrictive and Malabsorptive Combination Procedure
Vertical banded gastroplasty (VBG)—Not currently performed	Biliopancreatic diversion (BPD)	Roux-en-Y (RYGB)
Laparoscopic adjustable gastric banding (LAGB)	Duodenal switch (DS)	
Gastric sleeve (GS)	BPD-DS	

Common Complaints

A. Metabolic alteration
   1. Vitamin deficiencies
      a. Vitamin B_1 (Thiamine): Loss of appetite, nausea, and vomiting. Neurologic symptoms, including mental confusion, abnormal eye movement, hearing loss, weakness, and paraesthesia, may occur if left unidentified.
      b. Vitamin B_{12}: Pernicious anemia, fatigue, sore tongue, anorexia, paraesthesia, impaired sense of smell, positive Babinski's sign, loss of deep tendon reflexes (DTRs), and unsteady gait
      c. Fat-soluble vitamins (A, D, E, and K): Night blindness, delayed healing, gait disturbance, and petechiae
   2. Iron deficiency: Fatigue, pallor, and picas
   3. Calcium deficiency: Osteoporosis and hyperparathyroidism
   4. Protein deficiency: Hair loss
   5. Folate deficiency: Folate deficiency anemia, sore tongue, increase in neural tube defects

B. Surgical complications
   1. GI bleeding
   2. Dumping syndrome occurs in approximately 50% of patients after RYGB. Dumping syndrome is characterized by symptoms of nausea, shaking, diaphoresis, and diarrhea shortly after eating foods containing high amounts of refined sugars.
   3. Gastric leakage
   4. Bowel obstruction
   5. Bowel stricture
   6. Band slippage leading to gastric prolapse
   7. Infection
   8. Deep vein thrombus (DVT)
   9. Ulcers
   10. Prolonged vomiting
   11. Cholelithiasis. Patients who have the Roux-en-Y or laparoscopic banding surgeries are at increased risk for gallstones.
   12. Watery diarrhea with foul, extremely foul flatus and abdominal cramping need to be evaluated for *C. difficile.*
   13. Dysphagia

Other Signs and Symptoms

A. Excessive nausea and vomiting after a LAGB may require band adjustment, relieving the tension of the gastric band to reduce or resolve the symptoms.

B. The postsurgical gastric bypass patient may express disappointment and depression if weight is not lost fast enough, or as expected.
   1. Weight loss from the RYGB generally levels off in 1 to 2 years. A weight regain of up to 20 pounds from the weight loss nadir to a long-term plateau is common.
   2. Weight loss after the LAGB is about 50% of the excess body weight and about 25% of the BMI at 2 years postsurgery.
   3. Weight loss after the sleeve procedure is between 6.7% and 130% of excess weight. Patients who experience less than 25% loss of excess weight are considered failures and may be revised to a RYGB or BPD-DS.
   4. Weight loss from the BPD or duodenal switch is about 66.3% to 73.9% of the excess body weight. Significant weight loss is primarily due to malabsorption, and therefore the patients experience more complications because of decreased absorption of food, vitamins, and minerals, as well as protein deficiency.
   5. Diarrhea or constipation occurs, dependent on the type of bariatric procedure.

Subjective Data

A. Review onset and duration of symptoms.

B. Elicit the date of the gastric bypass surgical procedure and any history of reoperations for band slippages, failure to lose weight, or surgical reversals.

C. Elicit a history of any surgical complications.

D. Ask the patient about other symptoms (noted above) depending on the type of surgical procedure.

E. Evaluate the location and level of pain/discomfort.

F. Evaluate the overall psychosocial changes since surgery.

G. Review a 24-hour food recall, choices of healthy foods, skipping meals, food aversion (e.g., red meat), and intolerance.

Physical Examination

A. Check height, weight, waist, and hip circumference. Calculate BMI (follow serial weights), pulse, respirations, and blood pressure. Check temperature if infection is suspected.

B. Inspect
   1. Examine the skin, evaluate surgical site(s), evaluate redness and tenderness.
   2. Oral/dental examination
   3. Evaluate for dehydration.
   4. Eye examination: Evaluate eye movement (thiamine deficiency).
   5. Evaluate gait.
   6. General overview of personal presence and affect
   7. Check for positive Homans' sign (dorsiflexion in the foot).

C. Auscultate
   1. Auscultate the heart and lungs.
   2. Auscultate the abdomen for bowel sounds.

D. Palpate
   1. Palpate abdomen
   2. Evaluate the presence of tenderness.
   3. Evaluate for masses.

E. Neurologic examination: Perform neurological exam, including checking DTRs, sense of smell, and checking for Babinski reflex (vitamin B_{12} deficiency).

Diagnostic Tests

A. Monitor HgA1c and blood glucose closely since diabetes has been resolved in postsurgical procedures.
B. CBC with differential
C. Electrolyte
D. Reticulocyte count
E. Serum vitamin B_{12} level
F. Iron and ferritin
G. Aminotransferases (ALT and AST) and ALP tests
H. Bilirubin
I. Albumin
J. Lipid profile
K. Thiamine
L. Folate
M. Zinc and copper
N. 25-hydroxvitamin D, parathyroid hormone (PTH)
O. Abdominal ultrasound
P. CT scan
Q. Doppler ultrasound of limb for suspected DVT
R. Pulmonary ventilation/perfusion scan for suspected pulmonary embolus
S. Dexa scan
T. Endoscopy

Differential Diagnoses

A. Postoperative surgical complication(s)
   1. Infection
   2. Abdominal pain
   3. Fascial dehiscence
   4. Deep vein thrombosis
   5. Bowel obstruction
   6. Band slippage
   7. Anastomosis leakage
   8. Stomal stenosis/stricture
B. Cholecystitis
C. Dumping syndrome
D. Food intolerance
E. GU
F. Gastroenteritis
G. Vitamin deficiency
H. Malnutrition/protein deficiency
I. Incisional hernia
J. Osteoporosis

Plan

A. General interventions: Postbariatric surgery requires a lifelong follow-up to evaluate micronutritional deficiencies as well as psychosocial changes.
B. Patient teaching
   1. Avoid foods, such as sweets, that provoke dumping syndrome. The patient may need to keep a food diary to identify all triggers.
   2. Supplementing vitamins and iron (if indicated) is a lifelong requirement. Take iron supplements with food.
   3. Surgery does not replace the need for a balanced diet and exercise.
   4. Diabetics may need to check their blood glucose more frequently.
   5. Chew food well, consume food slowly, and avoid liquids when eating. Drink liquids approximately 30 minutes after meals.
   6. Lifelong follow-up is required.
   7. OCPs are not absorbed/as effective, and fertility may increase after bariatric surgery.
C. Pharmaceutical therapy
   1. Evaluate the need for adjusting antidiabetic and antihypertensive medications.
   2. Prescription medications need review for current routes of absorption related to the type of gastric surgery; evaluate for delayed, enteric-coated, extended release medications. Crushed, chewable, liquid, patch, IM, and subq formulations may need to be substituted.
   3. Vitamin B_{12} 1,000 mcg IM every month for life, or take vitamin B_{12} 1,000 to 2,000 mcg sublingual daily. The dose may be reduced if long-term monitoring shows elevated vitamin B_{12} levels.
   4. The patient needs one daily multiple vitamin containing B vitamins and vitamin C and fat-soluble vitamins and minerals. Some patients require a liquid vitamin preparation because the stomach pouch does not tolerate pills.
   5. Prenatal vitamins are useful for those at risk for iron deficiency or for those whose diets put them at risk for folic acid deficiency.
   6. Vitamin D 800 IU daily. Most multivitamin supplements contain 400 IU of vitamin D. Additional supplementation is recommended by taking a second multivitamin or by ingesting a second supplement containing calcium and vitamin D.
   7. Vitamin A 30,000 IU daily for 1 week
   8. Calcium 1,200 to 1,500 mg daily. Calcium citrate may be better absorbed than calcium carbonate after gastric bypass.
   9. Osteopenia and metabolic bone disease after RYGB have been reported. Calcium 1,200 to 1,500 mg with vitamin D 800 IU will prevent metabolic bone disease.
   10. Iron supplementation of 640 mg/d, especially for menstruating women, those patients intolerant to iron-containing foods, and those who

develop iron-deficiency anemia. Iron absorption is improved when iron is administered with vitamin C.

11. Patients with persistent vomiting or other cause of inadequate nutrient intake should receive thiamin 50 mg daily.
12. Long-term anticoagulation may be required for DVT/PE (pulmonary embolism).
13. Metformin is the safest oral drug in the postoperative period, and sliding scale insulin may be needed.
14. If possible, NSAIDs should be discontinued to avoid the risk of gastric bleeding.

Follow-Up

A. Reevaluation depends on the complication and side-effect profiles.
B. If there are no surgical complications, reevaluate on a schedule:
   1. Every 3 months: CBC, glucose, and creatinine
   2. Every 6 months: Protein and albumin, liver functions, iron, ferritin, total iron binding capacity (TIBC), B_{12}, folic acid, and calcium
   3. Annually: CBC, glucose, protein and albumin, creatinine, liver functions, B_{12}, folic acid, calcium, and iron, ferritin, and TIBC
   4. Consider Dexa scan to evaluate osteopenia/osteoporosis.

Consultation/Referral

A. Physician referrals as indicated
   1. Gastroenterology consultation
   2. Bariatric surgeon for surgical complications and revisions
   3. Surgeon for cholecystectomy or panniculectomy
   4. Nutrition consultation
   5. Psychologist consultation
   6. Early consultation with a bariatric surgeon is recommended for pregnancy.

Individual Considerations

A. Women
   1. Contraception and preconception counseling should be given to women of childbearing age.
   2. OCPs are not as effective postsurgery due to the change in absorption.
   3. Women should be counseled to delay pregnancy for 12 to 24 months during the period of rapid weight loss. Increased folic acid is needed preconception in order to decrease the risk of neural tube defects.
B. Pregnancy
   1. Increased vitamin supplements may be needed during pregnancy. Vitamin A supplementation should be limited to 5,000 IU/d.
   2. The gastric band may need to be adjusted during pregnancy.
   3. Serial ultrasounds need to be done to follow fetal growth.

Ulcerative Colitis

Definition

A. UC is one of the two IBDs, along with CD. UC is limited to the colon; it extends proximally from the anal verge in an uninterrupted pattern to a part of or the entire colon. Neither UC nor CD should be confused with IBS, which affects the motility of the colon. Smoking is negatively associated with UC; the relationship is reversed in CD. The general course of UC is intermittent exacerbations and remissions. In severe cases, surgery may be required. The choice of treatment depends on disease activity and extent of pathology, patient acceptability, and mode of drug delivery.
B. Histologically, most of the pathology of UC is limited to the mucosa and submucosa. The severity of UC is defined from mild to fulminant (see Table 13.24). The extent of UC is defined by the following.
   1. Pan-ulcerative (total colitis): Extensive disease with evidence of UC proximal to the splenic flexure. Massive dilation of the colon (toxic megacolon) may lead to bowel perforation.
   2. Left-sided disease: Continuous UC that is present from the rectum, the descending colon up to, but not proximal to, the splenic flexure
   3. Proctosigmoiditis: Disease is limited to the rectum and sigmoid colon involvement.
   4. Ulcerative proctitis: Disease is limited to the rectum–usually less than the full rectum.

Incidence

A. The annual incidence of UC is 8 to 12 per 100,000, depending on the country.
B. UC is three times more common than CD.
C. The most common cause of death in patients with UC is toxic megacolon.
D. Adenocarcinoma of the colon develops in 0.5% to 1% of patients with UC; the risk increases with the duration of the disease.

Pathogenesis

A. UC may be considered an autoimmune disease. Persons with UC often have pantineutrophil cytoplasmic antibodies. Abnormalities of humoral and cell-mediated immunity and/or generalized enhanced reactivity against intestinal bacterial antigen may also be causes of UC.

Predisposing Factors

A. Caucasian
B. Jewish descent

TABLE 13.24 Definition of Severity of Ulcerative Colitis

Mild UC	• ≤ 4 bloody stools/d with or without blood • No systemic toxicity • Normal ESR • Mild abdominal pain or cramping
Moderate UC	• > 4 bloody stools/d • No signs of systemic toxicity • Pulse < 90 beats per minute • Temperature < 37.5°C (99.5°F) • Hemoglobin > 10.5 g/dL • ESR < 30 mm/hr • Moderate abdominal pain
Acute Severe UC[a]	• ≥ 6 bloody stools/d or observable massive and significant blood BM *AND* • 1 or more symptoms of systemic toxicity • Tachycardia > 90 beats per minute • Temperature > 37.8°C (100.4°F) • Hemoglobin < 10.5 g/dL • Increased ESR (> 30 mm/hr)
Fulminant UC	• > 10 stools/d • Continuous rectal bleeding • Systemic toxicity • Tachycardia > 90 beats per minute • Fever > 37.8°C (100.4°F) • Anemia requiring blood transfusions • Abdominal tenderness and distension • Colonic dilation on radiography • May lead to toxic megacolon or colonic perforation

[a]Acute severe colitis is defined by Truelove and Witts Criteria (1955).

C. 30% more females than males
D. Genetic susceptibility (chromosomes 12 and 16)

Common Complaints

A. Frequent small-volume diarrhea
B. Bloody diarrhea with or without mucus
C. Severe bowel urgency
D. Abdominal cramps and pain with BM
E. Constipation
F. Anorexia
G. Anemia
H. Nocturnal BMs

Other Signs and Symptoms

A. Tenesmus (rectal urgency/constant feeling of need to pass stool)
B. Abdominal tenderness
C. Arthralgias
D. Fatigue secondary to anemia
E. Severe UC
   1. Fever
   2. Tachycardia
   3. Significant abdominal tenderness
   4. Signs of volume depletion

Subjective Data

A. Review the onset, duration, signs, and symptoms (number of stools, presence/absence of blood in the stool, fever, and abdominal pain).
B. Review the patient's recent travel history or camping for the presence of intestinal infection.
C. Review the patient's medication history, including antibiotics and NSAIDs.
D. Review family history for IBD, celiac disease, and colorectal cancer.
E. Review the patient's smoking status.
F. Review the patient's history or contact related to TB (testing required prior to biologic therapy).

Physical Examination

A. Check temperature (if indicated), pulse, blood pressure, and weight. Follow serial weights.
B. Inspection
   1. Observe the general overall appearance for nutritional status, cachexia, and pallor.
   2. Observe the perianal region for the presence of tags, fissures, fistulas, and abscess.
   3. Observe the abdomen for distension and presence of surgical scars.
   4. Eye examination for ocular complications (episcleritis, scleritis and uvetis)
   5. Evaluate for the presence of dermatological findings, including erythema nodosum and pyoderma gangrenosum.
C. Auscultation
   1. Auscultate the heart and lungs.
   2. Auscultate all four quadrants of the abdomen.

D. Palpation
   1. Palpate all four quadrants of the abdomen, observing for tenderness, rebound, and guarding.
   2. Evaluate the presence of hepatomegaly.
   3. Evaluate the joints for tenderness, swelling, and effusion
   4. Perform digital rectal examination to assess for anal strictures and rectal masses.

Diagnostic Tests

A. Laboratory tests
   1. CBC with electrolytes
   2. Platelet count
   3. Sedimentation rate
   4. CRP
   5. CMV (chronic immunosuppressive steroids)
   6. HIV
B. Stool testing
   1. Evaluate bacterial, viral, or parasitic causes of diarrhea
   2. Occult blood
   3. Fecal leukocytes
C. Proctosigmoidoscopy or colonoscopy with biopsy
D. Plain abdominal radiograph
E. CT scan
F. Celiac antibody testing should be considered.
G. Intestinal TB testing should be considered.

Differential Diagnoses

A. UC (see Table 13.25)
B. Ischemic colitis (especially in the elderly)
C. Toxic megacolon
D. Colon cancer
E. Adenocarcinoma
F. Rectal cancer
G. Radiation colitis
H. Intestinal infections
I. Intestinal lymphoma
J. Chronic diverticulitis

Plan

A. **Severe UC should be managed jointly by a gastroenterologist in conjunction with a colorectal surgeon.**
B. Dietary considerations
   1. Many patients with UC have concurrent lactose intolerance (see Appendix B for lactose-intolerance dietary recommendations).
   2. Decrease dietary fiber during increased disease activity.
   3. Low-residue diet may decrease the frequency of BMs.
   4. High-residue diet may be helpful in ulcerative proctitis when constipation is the dominant symptom (see Appendix B, Table B.7, "Fiber Recommendations by Age").
   5. Vitamin and nutritional supplements may be recommended.
C. Stress reduction and stress management may improve symptoms.
D. Patients with CD who smoke should be encouraged and offered help to stop smoking at each office visit.
E. Pharmacologic treatment. **Refer to the ACG Practice Guidelines for full treatment algorithms at www.gi.org/guideline/ulcerative-colitis-in-adults.**
   1. The choice of topical agents is guided by the proximal distribution of UC into the bowel, as well as patient preference (see Table 13.25).
   2. Refer to Table 13.4, "Medications for Crohn's Disease (CD) and Ulcerative Colitis (UC)" for a stepwise medication approach for both of the IBDs.
      a. The 5-ASA class of anti-inflammatory drugs is the most common treatment for patients with mild (< 4 bloody stools per day) or moderate active disease (> 4 bloody stools a day without systemic toxicity).
      b. Corticosteroids suppress the immune system and are used for moderate to severe UC.
      c. Biologic therapy (anti-TNF agents): **A tuberculin skin test is recommended prior to therapy. Patients started on Infliximab should also be screened for hepatitis B before initiating therapy.**
F. Indications for consideration of a total colectomy.
   1. Failed medical therapy: Refractory UC
   2. Severe hemorrhage
   3. Fulminate colitis not responsive to treatment
   4. Toxic megacolon
   5. Obstruction or stricture
G. Anxiety and depression are higher in patients with IBD. Screen for depression at each visit.

Follow-Up

A. Screening colonoscopy are recommended for all patients with UC for 8 to 10 years after the onset of symptoms due to the increase in colonic neoplasia.
B. Patients with extensive UC or left-sided colitis with negative findings on the screening colonoscopy should begin surveillance colonoscopy in 1 to 2 years.

TABLE 13.25 Management of Mild to Moderate Distal UC With Topical Agents

Topical agent	Proximal extent/distribution of agent
Suppository	10 cm
Hydrocortisone foam	15–20 cm
Enema	As far as the splenic flexure

Adapted from the AGA Ulcerative Colitis in Adults Practice Guidelines (2010).

C. Steroids should not be used as maintenance therapy. Patients who require long-term steroids are at increased risk of osteoporosis.
D. Subsequent laboratory monitoring tests are dependent on the prescribed therapy.

Consultation/Referral

A. Gastroenterologist for confirmatory diagnosis with a colonoscopy
B. Consultation with a surgeon for severe or fulminant colitis. Toxic megacolon is a life-threatening complication and requires urgent surgical intervention.
C. Patients with ocular complications require an urgent consultation.
D. Patients who have had UC for 8 to 10 years are at risk for colon cancer; therefore, colonoscopy for surveillance is recommended.

Individual Considerations

A. Live vaccinations should not be administered to immunocompromised patients. If required, vaccines should be administered at the time of UC diagnosis.
    1. The flu and pneumonia should be routinely administered.
    2. Consider administering the human papillomavirus vaccine.
B. Women with IBD have been reported to have a high incidence of abnormal Pap smears. Adherence to Pap smear guidelines is recommended by the ACG.
C. Abnormal sperm counts, motility, and morphology are seen with sulfasalazine.

Resources

American College of Gastroenterology (ACG): http://gi.org
Crohn's and Colitis Foundation of America (CCFA): www.ccfa.org

Bibliography

Academy of Nutrition and Dietetics. (n.d.). Celiac disease evidence-bases nutrition practice guideline. Retrieved from http://www.adaevidencelibrary.com/topic.cfm?cat=3677

American Association for Clinical Chemistry. (2013, September 16). Celiac disease tests. *Lab Tests Online.* Retrieved from labtestsonlin.org/understanding/analytes/celiac-disease/tab/test

American College of Gastroenterology. (2013, July). Fecal incontinence. Retrieved from http://patients.gi.org/topics/fecal-incontinence

American College of Obstetricians and Gynecologists. (2009, June). ACOG practice bulletin bariatric surgery and pregnancy. *Obstetrics & Gynecology, 113,* 1405–1413.

American Gastroenterological Association. (2001). American Gastroenterological Association medical position statement: Nausea and vomiting. *Gastroenterology, 120,* 261–262.

American Gastroenterological Association. (2004). American Gastroenterological Association Institute medical position statement: Diagnosis and treatment of hemorrhoids. *Gastroenterology, 126,* 1461–1462.

American Gastroenterological Association. (2006a). American Gastroenterological Association Institute medical position statement on corticosteroids, immunomodulators, and Infliximab in inflammatory bowel disease. *Gastroenterology, 130,* 935–939.

American Gastroenterological Association. (2006b). American Gastroenterological Association Institute medical position statement on the diagnosis and management of celiac disease. *Gastroenterology, 131,* 1977–1980.

American Gastroenterological Association. (2006c). American Gastroenterological Association Institute medical position statement on the management of hepatitis C. *Gastroenterology, 130,* 225–230.

American Gastroenterological Association. (2008). American Gastroenterological Association Institute medical position statement on the management of gastroesophageal reflux disease. *Gastroenterology, 135,* 1383–1391.

American Gastroenterological Association. (2012, April 23). Understanding peptic ulcer disease. Retrieved from http://www.gastro.org/patient-center/digestive-conditions/peptic-ulcer-disease

American Gastroenterological Association. (2013, January). American Gastroenterological Association medical position statement on constipation. *Gastroenterology, 144,* 211–217.

American Gastroenterological Association Clinical Practice Committee. (2002). AGA technical review on the evaluation of liver chemistry tests. *Gastroenterology, 123,* 1367–1384.

American Geriatrics Society (AGS) Foundation for Health in Aging. (2012, April). Ten medications older adults should avoid or use with caution. Retrieved from http://www.americangeriatrics.org/files/documents/beers/FHATipMEDS.pdf

American Society of Colon & Rectal Surgeons. (2012, October). Constipation. Retrieved from www.fascrs.org/patients/conditons/constipation

American Society for Metabolic & Bariatric Surgery. (2008, February). Bariatric surgery: postoperative concerns. Retrieved from http://s3amazonaws.com/publicASMBS/GuidelinesStatement/GeneralStatement/asbs_bspc.pdf

Anand, B. S. (2012, June 7). Peptic ulcer disease. *Medscape Reference.* Retrieved from http://emedicine.medscape.com/article/181753-overview

Andersen, S. (2012, August). Beware the irritable bowel deciphering the overlap of symptoms. *ADVANCE for NPs & PAs,* 21–24(3), 32.

Ansari, P. (2013, November). Fecal incontinence. *The Merck Manual for Health Care Professionals.* Retrieved from http://www.merckmanuals.com/professional/gastrointestinal_disorders/anorectal_disorders/fecal_incontinence.html

Barak, O., Elazary, R., Applebaum, L., Rivkind, A., & Almogy, G. (2009). Conservative treatment for acute cholecystitis: clinical and radiographic predictors of failure. *Israel Medical Association Journal, 11,* 743–793.

Basson, M. D. (2014, January 21). Constipation. *Medscape Reference.* Retrieved from http://emedicine.medscape.com/article/184704-overview

Basson, M. D. (2014, May 22). Ulcerative colitis. *Medscape Reference.* Retrieved from http://emedicine.medscape.com/article/183084-overview

Beltrán, B. (2011, June 14). Old-age inflammatory bowel disease onset: A different problem? *World Journal of Gastroenterology.* 17, 2734–2739.

Beth Israel Deaconess Medical Center. (2013). What are the treatments for Crohn's disease? Retrieved from http://www.bidmc.org/CentersandDepartments/Departments/DigestiveDiseaseCenter/InflammatoryBowelDisease

Program/CrohnsDisease/WhatarethetreatmentsforCrohnsdisease.aspx

Blacklow, N. R. (2009, January). Prevention and treatment of viral gastroenteritis in adults. *UpToDate.* Retrieved from http://www.uptodate.com/online/content/topic.do?topicKey=gi_infec/12064&view=print

Bleday, R. (2013, January). Patient information: Hemorrhoids (Beyond the basics). *UpToDate.* http://www.uptodate.com/contents/hemorrhoids-beyond-the-basics?source=search_result&search=patient+information+and+hemorrhoids&selectedTitle=1%7E76

Bleday, R., & Breen, E. (2013, October). Treatment of hemorrhoids. *UpToDate.* Retrieved from http://www.uptodate.com/contents/treatment-of-hemorrhoids?source=search_result&search=hemorrhoids&selectedTitle=1%7E76

Bloom, A. A. (2014, April 1). Cholecystitis clinical presentation. *Medscape Reference.* Retrieved from http://emedicine.medscape.com/article/171886-clinical

Bonheur, J. L. (2013, February 15). Bacterial gastroenteritis. *Medscape Reference.* Retrieved from http://emedicine.medscape.com/article/176400-overview

Brandt, L. J., Chey, W. D., Foxx-Orenstein, A. E., Schiller, L. R., Schoenfeld, P. S., Spiegel, B. M., Talley, N. J., Quigley, E. M. M., & Moayyedi, P. (2009, January). An evidence-based systematic review on the management of irritable bowel syndrome. American College of Gastroenterology Task Force on IBS. *American Journal of Gastroenterology, 104*, Supp 1, 1–35.

Brooks, D. C. (2012, October 9). Overview of abdominal hernias. *UpToDate.* Retrieved from http://www.uptodate.com/contents/overview-of-abdominal-hernias?source=search_result&search=abdominal+wall+hernia&selectedTitle=1%7E40

Brooks, D. C. (2013, October). Overview and treatment for inguinal and femoral hernia in adults. *UpToDate.* Retrieved from http://www.uptodate.com/contents/overview-of-treatment-for-inguinal-and-femoral-hernia-in-adults?source=search_result&search=groin+hernia&selectedTitle=2%7E68

Brooks, D. C., Obeid, A., & Hawn, M. (2013, January 25). Classification, clinical features and diagnosis of inguinal and femoral hernias in adults. *UpToDate.* Retrieved from www.uptodate.com/contents/classification-clinical-features-and-diagnosis-of-inguinal-and-femoral-hernias-in-adults?topicKey=SURG%2F3686

Bryan, E. D. (2013, May 13). Abdominal pain in the elderly persons. *Medscape Reference.* Retrieved from http://emedicine.medscape.com/article/776663-overview

Buchwald, H. (2005). Consensus conference statement on bariatric surgery for morbid obesity: Health implications for patients, health professionals, and third-party payers. *Surgery for Obesity and Related Diseases, 1*, 371–381.

Buchwald, H., Avidor, Y., Braunwald, Y., Jensen, E., Pories, W., Fahrback, K., & Schoelles, K. (2004). Bariatric surgery: A systematic review and meta-analysis. *Journal of the American Medical Association, 292*, 1724–1737.

Budd, G. M., & Falkenstein, K. (2009). Bariatric surgery: Putting the squeeze on obesity. *The Nurse Practitioner, 34*, 39–45.

Burger, D., & Travis, S. (2011). Conventional medical management of inflammatory bowel disease. *Gastroenterology, 140*, 1827–1837.

Carter, M. J., Lobo, A. J., & Ravis, S. P. L. (2004). Guidelines for the management of inflammatory bowel disease in adults. *Gut.* Retrieved from http://gut.bmj.com/content/53/suppl_5/vl.extract

Casella, S., Zanini B., Lanzarotto, F., Villanacci, V., Ricci, C., & Lanzini, A. (2012). Celiac disease in elderly adults: clinical, serological, and histological characteristics and the effect of a gluten-free diet. *Journal of American Geriatrics Society, 60*, 1064–1069.

Centers for Disease Control and Prevention. (n.d.). Screening tests at-a-glance. Retrieved from http://www.cdc.gov/cancer/colorectal/pdf/SFL_inserts_screening.pdf.

Centers for Disease Control and Prevention. (2009, June 29). Risk factors for vitamin B12 deficiency. Retrieved from http://www.cdc.gov/ncbddd/b12/risks.html

Centers for Disease Control and Prevention. (2010, November 2). Parasites-cyclosporiasis (Cyclospora infection). Retrieved from http://www.cdc.gov/parasites/cyclosporiasis

Centers for Disease Control and Prevention. (2011, April 11). Rotavirus. Retrieved from www.cdc.gov/rotavirus/index.html

Centers for Disease Control and Prevention. (2011, August 4). Hepatitis A faqs for health professions. Retrieved from http://www.cdc.gov/hepatitis/HAV/HAVfaq.htm

Centers for Disease Control and Prevention Vaccines & Immunizations. (2011, November 3). Statement regarding Rotarix® and RotaTeq® rotavirus vaccines and intussusception. Retrieved from www.cdc.gov/vaccines/vpd-vac/rotavirus/intussesception-studies-acip.htm

Centers for Disease Control and Prevention. (2012, August 17). Recommendations for the identification of chronic hepatitis C virus infection among persons born during 1945–1965.

Centers for Disease Control and Prevention. (2012, October 22). Hepatitis C faqs for the public. Retrieved from http://www.cdc.gov/hepatitis/c/cfaq.htm#cFAQ21

Centers for Disease Control and Prevention Vaccines & Immunizations. (2012, November 30). Vaccines and preventable diseases: Rotavirus vaccination. Retrieved from www.cdc.gov/vaccines/vpd-vac/rotavirus/default.htm#ed

Centers for Disease Control and Prevention. (2013, January 10). Treatment of cyclosporiasis. Retrieved from http://www.cdc.gov/parasites/cyclosporiasis/health_professionals/tx.html

Centers for Disease Control and Prevention. (2014, March 28). Adult obesity facts: Obesity is common, serious and costly. Retrieved from http://www.cdc.gov/obesity/data/adult.html

Centers for Disease Control and Prevention National Center for Immunization and Respiratory Diseases Division of Viral Diseases. (n.d). Viral gastroenteritis. Retrieved from www.cdc.gov/ncidod/dvrd/revb/gastro/faq.htm

Chatoor, D., & Emmnauel, A. (2009). Constipation and evacuation disorders. *Best Practice & Research Clinical Gastroenterology, 23*, 517–530.

Chou, R., & Wasson, N. (2013, June 4). Blood tests to diagnose fibrosis or cirrhosis in patients with chronic hepatitis C infection. *Annals of Internal Medicine*, 158, 807–820 and W-328–W330.

Chowdhury, N. R., & Chowdhury, J. R. (2013, June 19). Diagnostic approach to the patient with jaundice or asymptomatic hyperbilirubinemia. *UpToDate.* Retrieved from http://www.uptodate.com/contents/diagnostic-approach-to-the-adult-with-jaundice-or-asymptomatic-hyperbilirubinemia?source=search_result&search=jaundice&selectedTitle=1%7E150

Ciclitira, P. J. (2013, June 24). Management of celiac disease in adults. *UpToDate.* Retrieved from http://www.uptodate.com/contents/management-of-celiac-disease-in-adults?source=search_result&search=celiac&selectedTitle=4%7E150

Craig, S. (2014, July 21). Appendicitis. *Medscape Reference.* Retrieved from http://emedicine.medscape.com/article/773895-overview

Crocket, J. R., Bastian, L. A., & Chireau, M. V. (2013). Does this woman have an ectopic pregnancy? The rational clinical examination systematic review. *JAMA. 309,* 1722–1729.

Crohn's and Colitis Foundation of America. (n.d.a). Crohn's disease medication options. Retrieved from http://www.ccfa.org/what-are-crohns-and-colitis/what-is-crohns-disease/crohn-medication.html

Crohn's and Colitis Foundation of America. (n.d.b). Crohn's treatment options. Retrieved from http://www.ccfa.org/what-are-crohns-and-colitis/what-is-crohns-disease/crohns-treatment-options.html

Crohn's and Colitis Foundation of America. (n.d.c). Types of Crohn's disease and associated symptoms. Retrieved from http://www.ccfa.org/what-are-crohns-and-colitis/what-is-crohns-disease/types of crohns-disease.html

Crohn's and Colitis Foundation of America. (n.d.d). Types of ulcerative colitis. Retrieved from http://www.ccfa.org/what-are-crohns-and-colitis/what is ulcerative-colitis/types-of-ulcerative-colitis.html

Crohn's and Colitis Foundation of America. (n.d.e). What is ulcerative colitis? Retrieved from http://www.ccfa.org/what-are-crohns-and-colitis/what-is-ulcerative-colitis/

Dhawan, V. K. (2014, May 2). Hepatitis C. *Medscape Reference.* Retrieved from http://emedicine.medscape.com/article/177792-overview

Dinning, P. G., & Di Lorenzo, C. (2011). Colonic dysmotility in constipation. *Best Practice & Research Clinical Gastroenterology, 25,* 89–101.

Drugs.com. (n.d.a). Gallbladder disease medications. Retrieved from http://www.drugs.com/condition/gallbladder-disease.html

Drugs.com. (n.d.b). Hiatal hernia. Retrieved from http://www.drugs.com/cg/hiatal-hernia.html

Erickson, K. M. (2014, July 16). Abdominal hernias. *Medscape Reference.* Retrieved from http://emedicine.med-scape.com/article/1989563-overview

Fargo, M. V., & Latimer, K. M. (2012). Evaluation and management of common anorectal conditions. *American Family Physician, 85,* 624–630.

Farrell, R. J., & Peppercorn, M. A. (2013, April 23). Overview of the medical management of mild to moderate Crohn's disease in adults. *UpToDate.* Retrieved from http://www.uptodate.com/contents/overview-of-the-medical-management-of-mild-to-moderate-crohn-disease-in-adults?source=search_result&search=moderate+crohn+disease&selectedTitle=1%7E150

Felberbauer, F. X., Langer, F., Shakeri-Manesch, S., Schmaldienst, E., Kees, M., Kriwanek, S., & Prager, G. (2008). Laparoscopic sleeve gastrectomy as an isolated bariatric procedure: Intermediate-term results from a large series in three Austrian centers. *Obesity Surgery, 18,* 814–818.

Fishman, M. B., & Aronson, M. D. (2013, June 24). History and physical examination in adults with abdominal pain. *UpToDate.* Retrieved from http://www.uptodate.com/contents/history-and-physical-examination-in-adults-with-abdominal-pain?source=search_result&search=abdominal+pain+adult&selectedTitle=5%7E150

Freeman, H. J. (2008). Adult celiac disease in the elderly. *World Journal of Gastroenterology, 14,* 6911–6914.

Gainer, C. L. (2011, September). Helping patients live gluten-free. *The Nurse Practitioner, 36,* 14–20.

Gardner, T. B., & Hill, D. R. (2001). Treatment of giardiasis. *Clinical Microbiology Reviews,* 14(1), 114–128.

Ghany, M. G., Nelson, D. R., Strader, D. B., Thomas, D. L., & Seeff, L. B. (2011, October). An update on treatment of genotype 1 chronic hepatitis C virus infection: 2011 practice guideline by the American Association for the Study of Liver Diseases. *Hepatology, 54,* 1433–1444.

Gisbert, J. P., & Chaparro, M. (2014). Inflammatory bowel disease in the elderly. *Medscape Reference.* Retrieved from http://www.medscape.com/viewarticle/820753

GlobalRPH. (n.d.). Inflammatory bowel disease-common medications. Retrieved from http://www.globalrph.com/bowel.htm

Goebel, S. U. (2014, July 14). Celiac spruce. *Medscape Reference.* Retrieved from http://emedicine.medscape.com/article/171805-overview

Green, P. H. R., & Cellier, C. (2007). Celiac disease medical progress. *New England Journal of Medicine,* 357(17), 1731–1744.

Greenberger, N. J. (2013, November). Constipation. *The Merck Manual for Health Care Professionals.* Retrieved from http://www.merckmanuals.com/professional/gastrointestinal_disorders/symptoms_of_gi_disorders/constipation.html

Gurney, S., Carvalho, L, Gonzalez, C., Galaviz, E., & Sonstein. F. (2014, January). An efficacious and cost-effective pharmacologic treatment for *Helicobacer pylori. The Journal for Nurse Practitioners,* 10, 22–29.

Hayden, D. M., & Weiss, E. G. (2011). Fecal incontinence: Etiology, evaluation, and treatment. *Clinics in Colon and Rectal Surgery,* 24, 64–70.

Hepatitis B. Foundation. (2012, February 3). Approved drugs for adults. Retrieved from http://www.hepb.org/patients/hepatitis_b_treatment.htm

HepCnet. (2003, March 7). Drugs & liver damage. Retrieved from http://www.hepcnet.net/drugsandliverdamage.html

Heuman, D. M. (2014, April 2). Cholelithiasis. *Medscape Reference.* Retrieved from http://emedicine.medscape.com/article/175667-overview

Hofmann, W. P., & Zeuzem, S. (2011, May). A new standard of care for the treatment of chronic HCV infection. *Nature Reviews Gastroenterology & Hepatology, 8,* 257–264.

Hvas, A. M., & Nexo, E. (2006). Diagnosis and treatment of vitamin B12 deficiency. An update. *Haematological/The Hematology Journal, 91,* 1506–1512.

Iannelli, A., Dainese, R., Piche, T., Facchiano, E., & Gugenheim, J. (2008). Laparoscopic sleeve gastrectomy for morbid obesity. *World Journal of Gastroenterology, 14,* 821–827.

Kahrilas, P. J., Shaheen, N. J., & Vaezi, M. F. (2008, October). American Gastroenterological Association Medical Position Statement on the Management of Gastroesophageal Reflux Disease. *Gastroenterology,* 135, 1383–1391. Retrieved from http://www.gastrojournal.org/issues?_key-S0016-5085(08)%20X0010–1

Kahrilas, P. J. (2014, March 14). Hiatus hernia. *UpToDate.* Retrieved from http://www.uptodate.com/contents/hiatus-hernia?source=search_result&search=hiatus+hernia&selectedTitle=1%7E51

Katz, P. O., Gerson, L. B., & Vela, M. F. (2013, February). Guidelines for the diagnosis and management of gastroesophageal reflux disease. *American Journal of Gastroenterology, 108,* 308–328.

Kelly, C. P. (2013, June 25). Diagnosis of celiac disease. *UpToDate.* Retrieved from http://www.uptodate.com/contents/diagnosis-of-celiac-disease?source=search_result&search=diagnosis+of+celiac+disease&selectedTitle=1%7E150

Klapproth, J. M. A. (2012, January 5). Malabsorption. *Medscape Reference.* Retrieved from http://emedicine.medscape.com/article/180785-overview

Kohn, G. P., Price, R. R., Demeester, S. R., Zehetner, J., Muensterer, O. J., Awad, Z. T., Mittal, S. K., Richardson,

W. S., Stefanidis, D., Fanelli, R. D., & the SAGES Guideline Committee. (n.d.). Guidelines for the management of hiatal hernia. Retrieved from http://www.sages.org/publications/guidelines/guidelines-for-the-management-of-hiatal-hernia

Kornbluth, A., Sachar, D. B., & The Practice Parameters Committee of the American College of Gastroenterology. (2010). Ulcerative colitis practice guidelines in adults: American College of Gastroenterology, practice parameters committee. *American Journal of Gastroenterology, 105*, 501–523.

Kushner, R. F., & Cummings, S. (2014, February). Medical management of patients after bariatric surgery. *UpToDate.* Retrieved from http://www.uptodate.com/contents/overview-of-medical-management-of-patients-after-bariatric-surgery?source=search_result&search=bariatric+surgery&selectedTitle=1%7E107

Leder, K., & Weller, P. F. (2013, July 30). Treatment and prevention of giardiasis in adults. *UpToDate.* Retrieved from http://www.uptodate.com/contents/treatment-and-prevention-of-giardiasis?source=search_result&search=giardiasis+adult&selectedTitle=1%7E73

Leder, K., & Weller, P. F. (2013, September 13). Epidemiology, clinical manifestations, and diagnosis of giardiasis. *UpToDate.* Retrieved from http://www.uptodate.com/contents/epidemiology-clinical-manifestations-and-diagnosis-of-giardiasis?source=search_result&search=giardiasis+adult&selectedTitle=2%7E73

Lehrer, J. K. (2014, April 22). Irritable bowel sydrome. *Medscape Reference.* Retrieved from http://emedicine.medscape.com/article/180389-overview

Lichtenstein, G. R., Hanauer, S. B., Sandborn, W. J., & The Practice Parameters Committee of the American College of Gastroenterology. (2009). Management of Crohn's disease in adults. *American Journal of Gastroenterology.* Retrieved from http://s3.gi.org/physicians/guidelines/CrohnsDiseaseinAdults2009.pdf

Lin, M. V., Blonski, W., & Lichtenstein. G. R. (2010). What is the optimal therapy for Crohn's disease: Step-up or top-down? *Expert Review Gastroenterology Hepatology*, 42, 167–180.

Loc, S. F., & McMahon, B. J. (2009). AASLD practice guideline update chronic hepatitis B: Update 2009. Retrieved from www.aasld.org/practiceguidelines/Documents/Bookmarked%20Practice%Guidelines/Chronic_Hep_B_Update_2009%208_24_2009.pdf

Longstreth, G. F. (2013, April 5). Approach to the adult with nausea and vomiting. *UpToDate.* Retrieved from http://www.uptodate.com/contents/approach-to-the-adult-with-nausea-and-vomiting

Madoff, R. D., & Fleshman, J. W. (2004). American Gastroenterological Association technical review on the diagnosis and treatment of hemorrhoids. *Gastroenterology, 126*(5), 1463–1473.

Maggard, M. A., Shugarman, L. R., Suttorp, M., Maglione, M., Sugerman, H. J., Livingston, E. H., & Shekelle, P. G. (2005). Meta-analysis: Surgical treatment of obesity. *Annals of Internal Medicine, 142*, 547–559.

Mason, J. B., & Milovic, V. (2014, April 14). Overview of the treatment of malabsorption. *UpToDate.* Retrieved from http://www.uptodate.com/contents/overview-of-the-treatment-of-malabsorption?source=search_result&search=malabsorption+adult&selectedTitle=2%7E150

Medical Letter®. (March, 2012). Treatment guidelines from the medical letter. Drugs for inflammatory bowel disease. *The Medical Letter,* 10(*15*), 19–30.

Medicare.gov. (n.d.). Your Medicare coverage, colorectal cancer screening. Retrieved from www.medicare.gov/coverage/colorectal-cancer-screenings.html

Milovic, V., & Mason, J. B. (2012, October 31). Clinical features and diagnosis of malabsorption. *UpToDate.* Retrieved from http://www.uptodate.com/contents/clinical-features-and-diagnosis-of-malabsorption?source=search_result&search=malabsorption+adult&selectedTitle=1%7E150

Moses, S. (2014, May 17). Chronic constipation. Retrieved from http://www.fpnotebook.com/GI/Constipation/ChrncCnstptn.htm

Mounsey, A. L., Halladay, J., & Sadiq, T. S. (2011). Hemorrhoids. *American Family Physician,* 84(2), 204–210.

MMWR. Retrieved from http://www.cdc.gov/mmwr/preview/mmwrhtml/rr6104a1.htm?s_cid=rr6104a1_w

MPR Nurse Practitioners' Edition. (2014, Spring). New York, NY: Haymark Media Publications.

National Center for HIV/AIDS, Viral Hepatitis, STD & TB Prevention. Division of Viral Hepatitis. *Viral hepatitis surveillance United States, 2011.* Retrieved from http://www.cdc.gov/hepatitis/Statistics/2011Surveillance/PDFs/2011HepSurveillanceRpt.pdf

National Digestive Diseases Information Clearinghouse (NDDIC). (2011, January). *Diarrhea.* NIH Publication No. 11-2749. Retrieved from http://digestive.niddk.nih.gov/ddiseases/pubs/diarrhea/Diarrhea_208.pdf

National Digestive Diseases Information Clearinghouse (NDDIC). (2012, December). NIH Publication No.13-6513. Retrieved from http://digestive.niddk.nih.gov/ddiseases/pubs/bowelcontrol_ez/index.aspx

National Digestive Disease Information Clearinghouse (NDDIC). (2014, March 5). *Ulcerative colitis.* Retrieved from http://digestive.niddk.nih.gov/DDISEASES/PUBS/colitis/index.aspx

National Institute of Diabetes and Digestive and Kidney Diseases (NIDDK), National Institutes of Health (NIH). (2001, July 1). Let's talk about bowel control. Retrieved from http://www.bowelcontrol.nih.gov

National Institute of Diabetes and Digestive and Kidney Diseases (NIDDK), National Institutes of Health (NIH). (2013, February 20). Living with bowel control problems. Retrieved from http://www.bowelcontrol.nih.gov/lbc.aspx

National Institute for Health and Clinical Excellence. (2012, October). Crohn's disease, management in adults, children, and young people. *NICE Clinical Guideline 152.* Retrieved from guidance.nice.org.uh/cg152

Nazer, H. (2013, January 3). Giardiasis. *Medscape Reference.* Retrieved from http://emedicine.medscape.com/article/176718-overview

Nettina, S. (2010). *The Lippincott manual of nursing practice* (9th ed.). Philadelphia, PA: Wolters Kluwer Health/Lippincott Williams & Wilkins.

NHS Choices. (n.d.). Constipation. Retrieved from http://www.nhs.uk/Conditions/constipation/Pages/Introduction.aspx

Nicks, B. A. (2012, June 6). Hernias. *Medscape Reference.* Retrieved from http/www.emedicine.medscape.com/article/775630-overview

Orzano, A. J., & Scott, J. G. (2004). Diagnosis and treatment of obesity in adults: An applied evidence-based review. *Journal American Board Family Practice, 17*, 359–369.

Page, J. (2012). Recent developments in the treatment of chronic hepatitis C. *Journal for Nurse Practitioners, 8*, 225–230.

Peppercorn, M. A., & Cheifetz, A. S. (2013, December 12). Definition, epidemiology, and risk factors in inflammatory bowel disease. *UpToDate.* Retrieved from http://www.uptodate.com/contents/definition-epidemiology-and-risk-factors-in-inflammatory-bowel-disease?source=search_result&search=inflammatory+bowel+disease+adult&selectedTitle=4%7E150

Peppercorn, M. A., & Farrell, R. J. (2014, June 11). Management of severe ulcerative colitis. *UpToDate.* Retrieved from http://www.uptodate.com/contents/management-of-severe-ulcerative-colitis?topicKey=GAST%2F4068&elapsedTimeMs=0&view=print&displayedView=full#

Poh, C. H., Navarro-Rodriguez, T., & Fass, R. (2010). Review: Treatment of gastroesophageal reflux disease in the elderly. *The American Journal of Medicine, 123,* 496–501.

Porter, R. F., & Gyawali, C. P. (2010, January). Nausea and vomiting. Retrieved from http://patients.gi.org/topics/nausea-and-vomiting

Qaseem, A., Denberg, T. D., Hopkins, R. H., Humphrey, L. L., Levine, J., Sweet, D. E., & Shekelle, P. (2012). Screening for colorectal cancer: A guidance statement from the American College of Physicians. *Annals of Internal Medicine, 156,* 378–386.

Qureshi, W. A. (2013, July 15a). Hiatal hernia. *Medscape Reference.* Retrieved from http://emedicine.medscape.com/article/178393-overview

Qureshi, W. A. (2013, July 15b). Hiatal hernia treatment and management. *Medscape Reference.* Retrieved from http://emedicine.medscape.com/article/178393-treatment

Radhtak, S., & Murray, J. A. (2009). Celiac disease in the elderly. *Gastroenterlogy Clinics of North America, 38,* 433–446.

Ranganath, S. (2012, October 26). Fecal incontinence treatment & management. *Medscape Reference.* Retrieved from http://emedicine.medscape.com/article/268674-treatment

Rao, S. S. (2004). Diagnosis and management of fecal incontinence. American College of Gastroenterology Practice Parameters. *American Journal of Gastroenterology, 99,* 1585–1604.

Rao, S. S. C., & Meduri, K. (2011). What is necessary to diagnose constipation? *Best Practice & Research Clinical Gastroenterology, 25,* 127–140.

Reddy, S. (2009). An evidence-based review of obesity and bariatric surgery. *The Journal for Nurse Practitioners, 5,* 22–28.

Ren, C. J., & Fielding, G. A. (2003). Laparoscopic adjustable gastric banding: Surgical technique. *Journal of Laparoendoscopic & Advanced Surgical Techniques, 13,* 257–263.

Rex, D. K., Johnson, D. A., Adnerson, J. C., Schoenfeld, P. S., Burke, C. A., & Inadomi J. M. (2009). American College of Gastroenterology guidelines for colorectal cancer screening 2008. *American Journal of Gastroenterology.* Retrieved from www.amjgasro.com

Rivadeneira, D. E., Steele, S. R., Ternent, C., Chalasani, S., Buie, W. D., & Rafferty, J. L. (2011). Practice parameters for the management of hemorrhoids (revised 2010). *Diseases of the Colon & Rectum,* 54, 1059–1064.

Robson, K., & Lembo, A. J. (2014, April 21). Fecal incontinence in adults. *UpToDate.* Retrieved from http://www.uptodate.com/contents/fecal-incontinence-in-adults?source=search_result&search=fecal+incontinence+adult&selectedTitle=1%7E123

Rowe, W. A. (2014, June 2). Inflammatory bowel disease. *Medscape Reference.* Retrieved from http://emedicine.medscape.com/article/179037-overview

Rubio-Tapia, A., Hill, I. D., Kelly, C. P., Calderwood, A. H., & Murray, J. A. (2013, May). ACG clinical guidelines: Diagnosis and management of celiac disease. *American Journal of Gastroenterology, 108,* 656–676.

Ruiz, A. R. (2014, May). Overview of malabsorption. *The Merck Manual for Health Care Professionals.* Retrieved from http://www.merckmanuals.com/professional/gastrointestinal_disorders/malabsorption_syndromes/overview_of_malabsorption.html

RxList. (n.d.) Rebetol. Retrieved from http://www.rxlist.com/rebetol-drug/indications-dosage.htm

Saad, R. J., & Chey, W. D. (2014, February). First-line treatment strategies for *Helicobacter pylori* infection. *Gastroenterology & Endoscopy News,* 1–8.

Salix Pharmaceuticals, Inc. (n.d.). Solesta. Retrieved from http://www.solestainfo.com/hcp/home.aspx

Sarles, H. (2014, January). Approach to hemorrhoids a primer for gastroenterologists. *Gastroenterology & Endoscopy News,* 1–4.

Satsangi, J., Silverberg, M. S., Vermeire, S., & Colombel, J.-F. (2006). The Montreal classification of inflammatory bowel disease: Controversies, consensus, and implications. *Gut, 55,* 749–753.

Shah, M., Simha, V., & Garg, A. (2006). Review: Long-term impact of bariatric surgery on body weight, comorbidities, and nutritional status. *Journal of Clinical Endocrinology & Metabolism, 91,* 4223–4231.

Shahedi, K. (2014, April 10). Diverticulitis. *Medscape Reference.* Retrieved from http://emedicine.medscape.com/article/173388-overview

Sharma, G. D. (2014, April 14). Cystic fibrosis. *Medscape Reference.* Retrieved from http://emedicine.medscape.com/article/1001602-overview

Shoff, W. H. (2012, November 16). Cyclospora. *Medscape Reference.* Retrieved from http://emedicine.medscape.com/article/236105-overview

Smith, B. R., Schauer, P., & Nguyen, N. T. (2008). Surgical approaches to the treatment of obesity: Bariatric surgery. *Endocrinology & Metabolism Clinic of North America, 37,* 943–964.

Snyder, J. A., Gurevitz, S. L., Rush, L. S., McKeague, L. C., & Houpt, C. G. (2012, January). Appendicitis review. *Clinician Reviews, 22,* 23–28.

Stevens, T. K., Soffer, E. E., & Palmer, R. M. (2003, May). Fecal incontinence in elderly patients: Common, treatable, yet often undiagnosed. *Cleveland Clinic Journal of Medicine,* 70, 441–448. Retrieved from http://www.merckmanuals.com/professional/gastrointestinal_disorders/symptoms_of_gi_disorders/constipation.html

Surawicz, C. M., Brandt, L. J., Binion, D. G., Ananthakrishnan, A. N., Curry, S. R., Gilligan, P. H., McFarland, L. V., Mellow. M, Zuckerbraun, B. S. (2013). Guidelines for diagnosis, treatment, and prevention of *clostridium difficile* infections. *American Journal of Gastroenterology, 108,* 478–498.

Tack, J., Müller-Lissner, S., Stanghellini, V., Boeckxstaens, G., Kamm, M. A., Simren, M., … Fried, M. (2011). Diagnosis and treatment of chronic constipation—a European perspective. *Neurogastroenterology and Motility, 23,* 697–710.

Terdiman, J. P., Gruss, C. B., Heidelbaugh, J. J., Sultan, S., & Falck-Ytter, V. T. (2013). American Gastroenterological Association Instituite Guideline on the use of thiopurines, methotrexate, and anti-TNF-α biologic drugs for the induction and maintenance of remission in inflammatory Crohn's disease. *Gastroenterology,* 145, 459–1463.

The Center for Food Security & Public Health. (2012, December). *Giardiasis.* Retrieved from http://www.cfsph.iastate.edu/Factsheets/pdfs/giardiasis.pdf

Thornton, S. C. (2012, September 12). Hemorrhoids. *Medscape Reference.* Retrieved from http://emedicine.medscape.com/article/775407-overview

Truelove, S. C., & Witts, L. J. (1955). Cortisone in ulcerative colitis final report on a therapeutic trial. *British Medical Journal,* 2, 1041–1048.

Tyler-Evans, M. E., & Meyer, B. (2009). Post-bariatric surgery: Management considerations for NPs. *American Journal for Nurse Practitioners, 13,* 29–33.

University of Chicago Celiac Disease Center. (n.d.). Gluten free diet. Retrieved from http://www.celiacdisease.net/gluten-free-diet

University of Maryland Medical Center. (2013, June 27). Gallstones and gallbladder disease. Retrieved from http://umm.edu/health/medical/reports/articles/gallstones-and-gallbladder-disease

U.S. Food and Drug Administration. (2011, December). Plavix (clopidogrel bisulfate) tablet detailed view: Safety labeling changes approved by FDA Center for Drug Evaluation and Research (CDER). Retrieved from http://www.fda.gov/Safety/MedWatch/SafetyInformation/ucm225843.htm

U.S. Food and Drug Administration. (2013, September). Medtronic® InterStim® Therapy System-P080025.

U.S. Food and Drug Administration. (2014, October 14). FDA approves first combination pill to treat hepatitis C. Retrieved from http://www.fda.gov/NewsEvents/Newsroom/PressAnnouncements/ucm418365.htm

Utah Library of Medicine. (n.d.). Hepatitic pathology: Caput medusae. Retrieved from http://library.med.utah.edu/WebPath/LIVEHTML/LIVER061.html

Wald, A. (2013, June 22). Patient information: Constipation in adults (beyond the basics). *UpToDate.* Retrieved from http://www.uptodate.com/contents/constipation-in-adults-beyond-the-basics

Wehbi, M. (2013, May 15). Acute gastritis. *Medscape Reference.* Retrieved from http://emedicine.medscape.com/article/175909-overview

World Gastroenterology Organisation Practice Guidelines. (2007). *Diverticular disease.* Retrieved from http://www.worldgastroenterology.org/assets/downloads/en/pdf/guidelines/07_diverticular_disease.pdf

World Gastroenterology Organisation. (n.d.). *WGO practice guideline: Malabsorption.* Retrieved from http://www.worldgastroenterology.org/assets/downloads/en/pdf/guidelines/13_malabsorption_en.pdf

World Gastroenterology Organisation Global Guidelines. (2009, June). *Inflammatory bowel disease: A global perspective.* Retrieved from http://www.worldgastroenterology.org/assets/downloads/en/pdf/guidelines/21_inflammatory_bowel_disease.pdf

World Health Organization. (2014, April). Hepatitis C, Fact sheet No. 164. Retrieved from http://www.who.int/mediacentre/factsheets/fs164/en/

Yitzhak, A., Mizrahi, S., & Aninoach, E. (2006). Laparoscopic gastric banding in Adolescents. *Obesity Surgery, 16,* 1318–1322.

Young-Fadok, T., & Pemberton, J. H. (2012, November 15). Treatment of acute diverticulitis. *UpToDate.* Retrieved from http://www.uptodate.com/contents/treatment-of-acute-diverticulitis?topicKey

Young-Fadok, T., & Pemberton, J. H. (2014, July 10). Management of acute complicated diverticulitis. *UpToDate.* Retrieved from http://www.uptodate.com/contents/management-of-acute-complicated-diverticulitis?source=search_result&search=acute+diverticulitis&selectedTitle=2%7E16

Zakko, S. F., & Afdhal, N. H. (2012, September 11). Pathogenesis, clinical features, and diagnosis of acute cholecystitis. *UpToDate.* Retrieved from http://www.uptodate.com/contents/acute-cholecystitis-pathogenesis-clinical-features-and-diagnosis?source=search_result&search=acute+cholecystitis&selectedTitle=1%7E60

CHAPTER FOURTEEN

Genitourinary Guidelines

Angelito Tacderas, Cheryl A. Glass, and Debbie Croley

Benign Prostatic Hypertrophy

Definition

A. Benign prostatic hypertrophy (BPH) is enlargement of the prostate gland that constricts the urethra, causing urinary symptoms. BPH is not believed to be a risk factor for prostate cancer. BPH occurs primarily in the central or transitional zone of the prostate, while prostate cancer originates primarily in the peripheral part of the prostate.
B. The voiding dysfunction that results from prostate enlargement and bladder outlet obstruction (BOO) is termed lower urinary tract symptoms (LUTS).

Incidence

A. BPH increases progressively with age. The prevalence of prostatic hyperplasia increases from 8% in men aged 31 to 40 years to 40% to 50% in men aged 51 to 60 years to over 90% in men older than 80 years.

Pathogenesis

A. The exact cause is unknown; BPH may be a response to the androgen hormone. The process of aging and the presence of circulating androgens are required for the development of BPH. Hyperplasia, in which the normally thin and fibrous outer capsule of the prostate becomes spongy and thick, and the contraction of muscle fibers cause pressure on the urethra. This requires the bladder musculature to work harder to empty urine.

Predisposing Factors

A. Advancing age
B. Race: African American men younger than 65 years of age may need treatment more often than White men.
C. Genetic predisposition: Increases with a positive family history of BPH having moderate to severe LUTS.
D. Obesity
E. Diabetes
F. High levels of alcohol consumption
G. Physical inactivity

Common Complaints

The clinical manifestations of BPH are LUTS that typically appear slowly and progress gradually over a period of years.

A. Difficulty starting urine flow
B. Dribbling
C. Bladder that does not feel it completely empties
D. Frequency of urination

Other Signs and Symptoms

A. Obstructive symptoms
   1. Hesitancy
   2. Diminution in size and force of urinary stream
   3. Stream interruption (double voiding)
   4. Urinary retention
   5. Straining/Valsalva maneuver to fully empty the bladder
B. Irritative voiding symptoms
   1. Urgency
   2. Frequency
   3. Nocturia
   4. Painless hematuria: An early symptom; may also indicate malignancy
C. Severe late symptoms with untreated BPH
   1. Acute urinary retention
   2. Recurrent urinary tract infections (UTIs)
   3. Hydronephrosis
   4. Loss of renal concentrating ability
   5. Systemic acidosis and renal failure

Subjective Data

A. Have the patient complete the American Urologic Association Symptom Score (AUASS) assessment tool at each visit to track symptoms. The AUASS (see Table 14.1) is used to assess the severity of symptoms of BPH.

B. Review the onset, duration, and course of symptoms. The AUASS assessment tool can be used to quantitatively assess BPH symptoms over time.

TABLE 14.1 American Urologic Association Symptom Score

PATIENT NAME: ______________________ **TODAY'S DATE:** ____________

(Circle One Number on Each Line)	Not at All	Less Than 1 Time in 5	Less Than Half the Time	About Half the Time	More Than Half the Time	Almost Always
Over the past month or so, how often have you had a sensation of not emptying your bladder completely after you finished urinating?	0	1	2	3	4	5
During the past month or so, how often have you had to urinate again less than 2 hours after you finished urinating?	0	1	2	3	4	5
During the past month or so, how often have you found you stopped and started again several times when you urinated?	0	1	2	3	4	5
During the past month or so, how often have you found it difficult to postpone urination?	0	1	2	3	4	5
During the past month or so, how often have you had a weak urinary stream?	0	1	2	3	4	5
During the past month or so, how often have you had to push or strain to begin urination?	0	1	2	3	4	5
	None	**1 Time**	**2 Times**	**3 Times**	**4 Times**	**5 or More Times**
Over the past month, how many times per night did you most typically get up to urinate from the time you went to bed at night until the time you got up in the morning?	0	1	2	3	4	5

Add the score for each number above and write the total in the space to the right. **TOTAL:** ____________

SYMPTOM SCORE: 1–7 (Mild) 8–19 (Moderate) 20–35 (Severe)

QUALITY OF LIFE (QOL)

	Delighted	Pleased	Mostly Satisfied	Mixed	Mostly Dissatisfied	Unhappy	Terrible
How would you feel if you had to live with your urinary condition the way it is now, no better, no worse, for the rest of your life?	0	1	2	3	4	5	6

Used with permission from Associates in Urology, West Orange, NJ (www.njurology.com).

C. Does the patient have signs of a UTI?
D. Is there any blood in the urine or pain in the bladder region? (Evaluate bladder tumor or calculi.)
E. Does the patient have new symptoms such as bone or back pain, loss of appetite, or weight loss (rules out cancer)?
F. Review the patient's history for medical illness, including diabetes and neurologic problems.
G. Review previous urinary problems, surgeries, infections, treatments, success of treatments, and testing.
H. Review the patient's history of sexual dysfunction and any new sexual partners (sexually transmitted infections [STIs]).
I. Review the patient's history of urethral trauma, urethritis, or urethral instrumentation that could have led to urethral stricture.
J. Review medications, both prescription and over-the-counter (OTC) drugs, including sinus or cold products, anticholinergic drugs (for impaired bladder function), and sympathomimetic drugs (to increase outflow resistance).
K. Review family history of BPH and prostate cancer.
L. Review fluid intake, especially caffeinated/carbonated drinks.
M. Evaluate how bothersome the symptoms are to the patient's quality of life.
    1. How often does he have interrupted sleep to get up to go to the bathroom?
    2. How often does he urinate?
    3. Does he have to wear an absorptive underwear pad?

Physical Examination

A. Check temperature (if indicated), blood pressure, and weight (if indicated).
B. Inspect
    1. General appearance for discomfort or acute discomfort with urinary retention.
    2. Consider having the patient void: Normal urination for a man is the ability to empty the bladder of 300 mL of urine in 12 to 15 seconds.
    3. Examine the urethral meatus for discharge.
    4. Retract foreskin (if present) and assess for hygiene and smegma.
    5. Check the shaft of the penis, glans, and prepuce for lesions.
    6. Check inguinal and femoral areas for bulges or hernias; have the patient bear down and cough, and reexamine him.
    7. Perform a neurological examination (evaluate sensory and motor deficits).
C. Palpate
    1. Palpate the abdomen for masses or bladder distension.
    2. Palpate lymph nodes in the groin for enlargement.
    3. Check costovertebral angle (CVA) tenderness.
    4. Palpate the testes and epididymides for inflammation, tenderness, and masses.
    5. Palpate the scrotum for hydrocele or varicocele.
D. Digital rectal exam (DRE): Use the index finger of the dominant hand for the DRE.
    1. Note sphincter tone, nodules or masses, and tenderness. **Decreased anal sphincter tone or the lack of muscle reflex may indicate an underlying neurological disorder.**
    2. Palpate the two lateral lobes of the prostate gland and its median sulcus for irregularities, nodules, induration, swelling, or tenderness just above the prostate anteriorly; determine whether the rectum lies adjacent to the peritoneal cavity. If possible, palpate this region for peritoneal masses and tenderness.

Diagnostic Tests

A. Urinalysis: Evaluate for infection and hematuria.
B. Urine culture if indicated (patients with BPH are more susceptible to UTIs)
C. Optional studies
    1. Prostate-specific antigen (PSA): Reference ranges vary by age and ethnicity and may be elevated with BPH.
    2. Urodynamic testing, including maximal urinary flow rate.
    3. Postvoid residual (PVR) (as shown by in—out catheterization, radiography, or ultrasound).
    4. Cystourethroscopy (assists in planning for surgical therapy).
D. The AUA recommends that the routine measurement of serum creatinine levels is *not* indicated in the initial evaluation.

Differential Diagnoses

A. BPH: Classifications of BPH from the score of the AUA symptom assessment tool:
    1. Mild = total AUASS 0 to 7
    2. Moderate = total AUASS 8 to 19
    3. Severe = total AUASS 20 to 35
B. Other obstructive causes: Prostate cancer, urethral obstruction, urethral stricture, and vesical neck obstruction
C. Neurogenic bladder
D. Cystitis
E. Prostatitis
F. Bladder calculi

Plan

A. General interventions
    1. Have the patient complete a 24-hour voiding chart with assessment of frequency and volume.

2. Any patient with other than mild symptoms needs referral to a urologist to discuss treatment options (surgery or drugs).
3. Monitor the patient with mild symptoms every 3 to 6 months to determine the progression of symptoms. Imaging studies are not routinely necessary in typical cases of BPH unless there is hematuria, an elevated creatinine, or another indication.
4. Treat concurrent UTI and STIs.

B. Patient teaching
1. See the Section III Patient Teaching Guide for this chapter, "Benign Prostatic Hypertrophy (BPH)."
2. Patients should be instructed about the hypotensive effect, asthenia, nasal congestion, and effect on ejaculation of the long-acting alpha-1-antagonists. The hypotensive effects can be potentiated by concomitant use of phosphodiesterase-5 (PDE-5) inhibitors sildenafil (Viagra), stendra (Avanafil), tadalafil (Cialis), or vardenafil (Levitra).
3. Alpha-1-antagonists have been associated with intraoperative floppy iris syndrome. Patients need to discuss using these meds with their ophthalmologist prior to eye surgery (i.e., cataract).

C. Pharmaceutical therapy
1. Five long-acting alpha-1-antagonists are Food and Drug Administration (FDA) approved for treatment of BPH.
   a. Terazosin (Hytrin) 1 to 20 mg/d. Side effect increases hypotensive effect with PDE-5 inhibitor. Terazosin requires dose titration to minimize side effects.
   b. Doxazosin (Cardura) 1 to 8 mg/d. Side effect increases hypotensive effect with PDE-5 inhibitor. Doxazosin requires dose titration to minimize side effects.
   c. Tamsulosin (Flomax) 0.4 to 0.8 mg/d. Side effect decreases ejaculate volume.
   d. Alfuzosin (Uroxatral) 10 mg/d. It generally does not cause ejaculation problems.
   e. Silodosin (Rapaflo) 8 mg/d. Side effect may produce retrograde ejaculation.
2. Prazosin (Minipress), a short-acting alpha-1-antagonist approved for the treatment of hypertension (HTN). It improves urine flow rates and may be considered for a patient with HTN and urinary symptoms.
3. Two 5-alpha-reductase inhibitors are FDA approved for BPH with an enlarged prostate. The major side effects of these drugs are decreased libido and ejaculatory or erectile dysfunction (ED).
   a. **The FDA has advised about safety information for the use of the 5-alpha-reductase inhibitors due to an increased risk of being diagnosed with a more serious form of prostate cancer (high-grade prostate cancer).**
   b. **Women who are, or may become, pregnant should not handle the 5-alpha-reductase inhibitors. They are pregnancy category X, known to cause birth defects.**
   c. Finasteride (Proscar) 5 mg/d
   d. Dutasteride (Avodart) 0.5 mg/d
   e. Dutasteride-tamsulosin (Jalyn): Each capsule contains 0.5 mg dutasteride and 0.4 mg tamsulosin.
4. Dual-drug combination
5. There are no herbal supplements that have been approved by the FDA for the treatment of BPH; however, patients may report taking saw palmetto. The AUA does not endorse supplements.

Follow-Up

A. See the patient in 2 to 3 weeks to monitor symptoms after specialty referral.
B. PSA testing: Baseline testing should begin at age 40. The U.S. Preventative Services Task Force (USPSTF) recommends that PSA testing be discontinued at age 75.
C. PSA is an amino acid glycoprotein specific to prostate disease, but not exclusive to prostate cancer. **Once the patient has exhibited an elevated PSA level, repeat the test yearly. Patients who have undergone treatment for prostate cancer are monitored for recurrence by the PSA levels.**
D. The concept of "watchful waiting" may be appropriate for patients with mild symptoms. The patient should be seen yearly for evaluation and an examination.

Consultation

A. Refer to a urologist for any complicated LUTS, including:
1. History of prostate cancer
2. Elevated PSA
3. Urethral stricture
4. Spinal cord injury
5. Stroke
6. Recurrent/persistent UTI

B. The presence of microscopic hematuria requires an evaluation of the complete urinary system and needs a referral to a urologist.
C. Refer for a procedure after failed medication therapy.
1. Minimally invasive therapy
   a. Transurethral microwave therapy (TUMT)
   b. Transurethral incision of the prostate (TUIP)

2. Surgical therapies
   a. **Transurethral resection of the prostate (TURP) is considered the gold standard of surgical treatment of BPH.** Sexual dysfunction may occur after a TURP, including decreased libido, impotence, and ejaculatory difficulties. Balloon dilation may be used to reduce symptoms; however, relapse is common.
   b. Open prostatectomy
   c. Laser procedures
      i. Laser vaporization of the prostate
      ii. Laser enucleation of the prostate
   d. Transurethral needle ablation (TUNA)
   e. Photoselective vaporization of the prostate (PVP)

Individual Considerations

A. Geriatrics: Elderly men require special attention because their symptoms may be poorly expressed or confusing.

Resources

American Urological Association (AUA): www.auanet.org
National Kidney Urologic Diseases Information Clearinghouse (KNUDIC): kidney.niddk.nih.gov

Chronic Kidney Disease—*Debbie Croley*

Definition

Chronic kidney disease (CKD) is specifically defined as follows.

A. The persistent and usually progressive reduction in glomerular filtration rate (GFR) less than 60 mL/min/1.73 m^2, and/or
B. Albuminuria more than 30 mg of urinary albumin per gram of urinary creatinine
C. CKD is a disorder that leads to progressive kidney damage from a variety of causes, including diabetes, HTN, cardiovascular disease, urinary obstructions, prolonged use of nephrotoxic medications, and inherited diseases such as polycystic kidney disease. Associated comorbidities of CKD include renal osteodystrophy, anemia, metabolic acidosis, and malnutrition. Early recognition of CKD as well as treatment of complications can improve long-term outcomes.

Stages of CKD

A. Stage 1 disease is defined by a normal GFR (> 90 mL/min per 1.73 m^2) and persistent albuminuria.
B. Stage 2 disease is a GFR between 60 and 89 mL/min per 1.73 m^2 and persistent albuminuria.
C. Stage 3 disease is a GFR between 30 and 59 mL/min per 1.73 m^2.
D. Stage 4 disease is a GFR between 15 and 29 mL/min per 1.73 m^2.
E. Stage 5 disease is a GFR of less than 15 mL/min per 1.73 m^2 or end-stage renal disease (ESRD).

Incidence

A. Kidney disease is the ninth leading cause of death in the United States. It is estimated that 80,000 new cases of nondialysis-dependent CKD are diagnosed annually; the incidence of CKD and ESRD has doubled every decade since 1980. The 2006 National Health and Nutrition Examination Survey (NHANES) estimated that the prevalence of CKD for adults older than 20 years in the United States was 16.8%.
B. By age group, CKD was more prevalent among older persons aged above 60 (39.4%) than among younger persons aged 40 to 59 (12.6%) or ages 20 to 39 (8.5%). CKD prevalence was greater among persons with diabetes than among those without diabetes (40.2% versus 15.4%), and among persons with cardiovascular disease than among those without cardiovascular disease (28.2% versus 15.4%). CKD is higher among persons with HTN than among those without HTN (24.6% versus 12.5%). In addition, CKD prevalence was greater among non-Hispanic Blacks (19.9%) and Mexican Americans (18.7%) than among non-Hispanic Whites (16.1%).

Pathogenesis

Blood from the renal arteries and their subdivisions is delivered to the glomeruli. The glomeruli form an ultrafiltrate, nearly free of protein and blood elements, which subsequently flows into the renal tubules. The tubules reabsorb and secrete solute and/or water from the ultrafiltrate. The final tubular fluid, the urine, leaves the kidney, draining sequentially into the renal pelvis, ureter, and bladder, from which it is excreted through the urethra. The causes of CKD are traditionally classified by which portion of the renal anatomy is most affected by the disorder.

A. Vascular disease: Vascular disorders of the kidneys may involve partial or complete occlusion of large, medium, or small renal vessels. Examples of macrovascular or large renal vessel disease are renal artery stenosis and atherosclerotic disease. Benign HTN arteriolar nephrosclerosis results when chronic HTN damages small blood vessels, glomeruli, renal tubules, and interstitial tissues. Glomerulosclerosis is a severe microvascular or small vessel kidney disease caused by diabetes and uncontrolled HTN in which glomerular function of blood filtration is lost as fibrous scar tissue replaces the glomeruli. Loss of glomerular function leads to proteinuria, hematuria, HTN, and nephrosis, with variable progression to ESRD. Proteinuria occurs because of changes to capillary endothelial cells, the glomerular basement membrane (GBM), or podocytes, which normally filter serum protein selectively by size and charge.

B. Tubular and interstitial disease: As with vascular disease, chronic tubulointerstitial nephritis (CTIN) can be primary or secondary to glomerular damage and renovascular vascular disease. CTIN arises when chronic tubular insults cause gradual interstitial infiltration and fibrosis, tubular atrophy and dysfunction, and a gradual deterioration of renal function, usually over years. Causes of CTIN are immune disorders, infections, reflux or obstructive nephropathy, and drugs. Analgesic abuse nephropathy (AAN) is a type of CTIN caused by cumulative lifetime use of large amounts of certain analgesics such as nonsteroidal anti-inflammatory drugs (NSAIDs).

Predisposing Factors

A. Diabetes
B. HTN
C. Cardiovascular disease
D. Chronic use of analgesics such as NSAIDs
E. Autoimmune disorder
F. Polycystic kidney disease
G. Urinary tract obstructions such as BPH or kidney stones
H. Recurrent UTIs
I. Older than 60 years of age
J. African American, Native American, or Hispanic ethnicity
K. Smoking
L. Exposure to toxins
M. Family history of kidney disease

Common Complaints

A. For CKD Stages 1 and 2 there are usually no presenting complaints; however, HTN is usually present. CKD is usually identified through routine screening of kidney function and urine tests for microalbumin.

Signs and Symptoms

A. In CKD Stage 3, the person will develop CKD complications but will still not usually have identifiable signs/symptoms.
   1. HTN
   2. Decreased dietary calcium absorption
   3. Reduced renal phosphate excretion
   4. Elevation of parathyroid hormone
   5. Altered lipoprotein metabolism
   6. Reduced spontaneous protein intake
   7. Anemia
   8. Left ventricular hypertrophy
   9. Salt and water retention
   10. Decreased renal potassium excretion

B. These complications gradually worsen as the person moves to Stage 4 CKD. The person will begin to display signs and symptoms of complications.
   1. Changes in bone density
   2. Fatigue and pallor related to anemia
   3. Edema
   4. Decreases in muscle mass

C. As the CKD progresses to Stage 5, in addition to gradual worsening of the signs/symptoms noted in Stages 3 and 4, the person will experience symptoms indicating chronic uremia.
   1. Impaired sleep
   2. Nocturia
   3. Fatigue
   4. Anorexia, nausea, vomiting, and weight change
   5. Decreased mental acuity
   6. Pruritus
   7. Edema
   8. Respiratory symptoms, including orthopnea and dyspnea
   9. Muscle cramps, twitching, and restless legs
   10. Peripheral neuropathy

Subjective Data

A. Review the patient's medical history to identify risk factors for CKD (previously noted in Predisposing Factors).
B. Elicit information about how well risk factors such as diabetes mellitus (DM) and HTN are controlled.
C. Review onset and duration of signs/symptoms of CKD complications and uremia.
D. Review all medications—including all OTC medications, especially NSAIDs, and supplements. Obtain specific information about dosing and length of time the drug was used.
E. Elicit smoking history.

Physical Exam

A. Observe general demeanor, attentiveness, and signs of fatigue.
B. Measure
   1. Height, weight, and body mass index (BMI)
   2. Vital signs, including orthostatic blood pressure and pulse
C. Inspect
   1. Inspect skin for color, moisture, turgor, and signs of scratching due to chronic pruritus.
   2. Inspect the neck for jugular venous distension.
   3. Inspect the abdomen for distension.
   4. Inspect the extremities for edema, muscle mass, and signs of pain disorders such as arthritis.
D. Auscultate
   1. Auscultate the lungs for rales.
   2. Auscultate the heart for cardiac heave, gallop, or rub.
   3. Auscultate for abdominal or femoral bruit.

E. Palpate abdomen for masses, distension, palpable bladder, or flank tenderness.
F. Neurological exam for sensation and vibratory sense on both feet

Diagnostic Tests

Laboratory testing is critical in ascertaining the stage, course, chronicity, and complications (and associated comorbid conditions) of CKD.

A. Routine kidney function tests
    1. Serum creatinine
    2. Blood urea nitrogen (BUN)
    3. Urinalysis
    4. Measuring GFR: The severity of CKD should be classified based on the level of the estimated glomerular filtration rate (eGFR). Serum creatinine alone should *not* be used as a measure of kidney function. Kidney function in patients with CKD should be assessed by formula-based estimation of GFR (eGFR), preferably using the four-variable Modification of Diet in Renal Disease (MDRD) equation. Clinicians who do not have access to an automated tool may use a web-based tool at www.nkdep.nih.gov/professionals/gfr_calculators/index.htm. Calculate eGFRs using the actual MDRD equation:

$$\text{eGFR} = 186 \times [\text{SCr}] - 1.154 \times [\text{age}] - 0.203 \times [0.742 \text{ if female}] \times [1.210 \text{ if Black}]$$

(SCr, serum creatinine concentration)

B. Assessing proteinuria
    1. When screening adults at increased risk for CKD, albumin in the urine should be measured in a spot urine sample using either:
        a. Albumin-specific dipstick
        b. Albumin-to-creatinine ratio (ACR)
            i. It is usually not necessary to obtain a timed urine collection (overnight or 24 hour).
            ii. First morning specimens are preferred, but random specimens are acceptable if first morning specimens are not available.
            iii. In most cases, screening with urine sticks is acceptable for detecting proteinuria.
            iv. Standard urine dipsticks are acceptable for detecting increased total urine protein.
            v. Albumin-specific dipsticks are acceptable for detecting albuminuria.
    2. Patients with a positive dipstick test (1 or greater) should undergo confirmation of proteinuria by a quantitative measurement (protein-to-creatinine ratio [PCR] or [ACR]) within 3 months.
    3. Patients with two or more positive quantitative tests spaced apart by 1 to 2 weeks should be diagnosed as having persistent proteinuria and undergo further evaluation and management for CKD.

Other Tests to Determine CKD Complications

A. Complete blood count (CBC)
B. If hemoglobin (Hgb) level is less than 12 g/dL in females, and Hgb levels are less than 13.5 g/dL in adult males, also do blood cell indices, absolute reticulocyte count, serum iron, total iron-binding capacity, percent transferrin saturation, serum ferritin, white blood cell (WBC) count and differential, platelet count, and testing for blood in stool.
C. Lipid profile and triglycerides
D. Comprehensive metabolic profile (serum total protein, serum albumin, glucose, calcium, sodium, potassium, chloride, bicarbonate, BUN, creatinine, alkaline phosphatase, alanine amino transferase [ALT], aspartate amino transferase [AST], bilirubin).
E. Prealbumin
F. Phosphorus
G. Parathyroid hormone
H. Urine immunofixation study
I. Ana, anca, c3-c4
    1. Test is done to rule out autoimmune disorder, lupus, vasculitis, and cancer.
    2. No fasting is needed.
J. Hepatitis B surface antigen and hepatitis C antibody
K. Anti-GBM antibody
L. Renal ultrasound to rule out postobstructive uropathy
M. Renal Doppler to rule out renal artery stenosis

Differential Diagnosis

Evaluation is meant to determine whether kidney disease is acute or chronic and to determine prerenal, intrarenal, or postrenal causation.

A. CKD
B. Acute kidney disease

Plan

The treatment plan will focus on patients in earlier stages of CKD—Stages 1, 2, and 3. Persons with Stages 4 and 5 CKD need specialized interventions provided by nephrologists and should be referred immediately.

A. General interventions
    1. Provide support to the patient.
    2. Initiate appropriate referrals for a nephrologist, patient education, and social and financial support as soon as possible.
    3. For Stage 4 or 5 CKD, access devices for hemodialysis such as a primary arteriovenous fistula or graft require months to mature and should be in place for 6 months prior to the start of dialysis.

B. Patient teaching. See the Section III Patient Teaching Guide for this chapter, "Chronic Kidney Disease (CKD)."
  1. Instruct the patient in how kidneys work and how his or her body is affected by the CKD.
  2. Emphasize the importance of following instructions to prevent further kidney damage.
     a. Follow medication management instructions as carefully as possible.
     b. No OTC medications should be taken that are not approved by the provider.
     c. Keeping diabetes and HTN under control is crucial to maintaining kidney function.
     d. Preventing cardiovascular complications by lowering cholesterol and BP is more important when you have CKD.
     e. Smoking cessation is an important way to prevent worsening kidney function.
     f. Routine follow-ups with provider are necessary to monitor kidney function. Patients should be educated and encouraged to keep all appointments.
     g. Follow dietary instructions regarding protein, fats, sodium, and minerals.
     h. Dietary intake of protein is usually restricted to 0.8 to 1.0 g/kg/d of high biologic value protein.
     i. Dietary sodium should be restricted to no more than 2 g daily.
     j. Potassium should be restricted to 40 to 70 meq/d.
     k. Calories should be restricted to 35 kcal/kg/d; if the body weight is greater than 120% of normal or the patient is older than 60 years of age, a lower amount may be prescribed.
     l. Fat intake should be about 30% to 40% of total daily caloric intake.
     m. Phosphorus should be restricted to 600 to 800 mg/d.
     n. Calcium should be restricted to 1,400 to 1,600 mg/d.
     o. Magnesium should be restricted to 200 to 300 mg/d.
  3. Instruct when to notify the provider with urgent signs/symptoms or changes in kidney function.
     a. Changes in urine volume
     b. Anorexia, nausea, and vomiting
     c. Increased edema
     d. Shortness of breath (SOB)
     e. Increased fatigue
     f. Difficulty concentrating
     g. Muscle weakness, cramping, or twitching
     h. Fever
     i. Chest pain

C. Pharmaceutical therapy

D. General principles of medications used to prevent progression of CKD and to manage symptoms of complications of CKD.
  1. Always prescribe the smallest effective dose of any medication.
  2. Start with a low dose and gradually increase. Dosage intervals may need to be extended.
  3. Monitor the effect of any new medication on kidney function with appropriate follow-up with following lab results.
  4. Provide education to the patient of signs/symptoms to report to the provider immediately regarding drug therapy.
  5. Avoid use of nephrotoxic radiographic contrast materials to prevent nephrogenic systemic fibrosis. If radiocontrast material use cannot be avoided because the benefit outweighs the risks, protect the kidney with acetylcysteine (mucomyst) 600 mg orally twice daily on the day of intravenous (IV) contrast.
  6. **For patients with an extensive list of drugs, evaluate the need for dosage adjustment, contraindications, or nephrotoxicity. There are several classifications of the medications requiring dose adjustment. Classes may be used with the mnemonic BANDD CAMP.**

     B: Beta blockers
     A: Ace inhibitors/angiotensin II receptor blockers (ACE/ARBs)
     N: NSAIDs, opioids
     D: Diuretics
     D: Diabetic medications
     C: Cholesterol medications
     A: Antibiotics
     M: Miscellaneous
     P: Psychotropics
  7. Immunizations: Some vaccines in usual doses provide protection, whereas other vaccines require more frequent dosing, or larger doses to achieve and maintain protective antibodies. Protective antibody titers may fall and booster doses should be given if appropriate. In general the recommendations are:
     a. Annual influenza vaccination
     b. Pneumococcal vaccine with a single booster dose 5 years after the initial dose
     c. Hepatitis B vaccine series for patients prior to starting dialysis
  8. HTN control and kidney protection: It is recommended that HTN therapy achieve a goal of blood pressure of 130/80 or less. Use of an angiotensin converting enzyme (ACE) inhibitor or ARB therapy in early stages of CKD with persons who have proteinuria can

preserve kidney function. The clinician should monitor serum potassium upon initiation of the therapy. It is common for the serum potassium to initially rise, then return to normal levels in 2 to 3 months. Follow-up serum potassium levels are recommended. In the early stages of CKD, with no proteinuria, the ACE inhibitors and ARBs have not been shown to be effective in protecting kidney function. HTN control can still be achieved with the ACE/ARB drugs, but other antihypertensive drugs can be used as well.

9. Fluid overload: Occurs when sodium intake exceeds sodium excretion. The combination of sodium restrictions and a loop diuretic such as furosemide (Lasix) can lower intraglomerular pressure and provide some kidney protection.
10. Hyperkalemia: Hyperkalemia is managed with a low potassium diet in combination with prescribing a loop diuretic such as furosemide. If a patient is on an ACE or ARB, the addition of the loop diuretic will compensate for the elevation of serum potassium related to the ACE/ARB treatment.
11. Metabolic acidosis: Build-up of hydrogen ions causes bicarbonate levels to fall below acceptable levels. Sodium bicarbonate in a daily dose of 0.5 to 1 meq/kg/d is often given. This prevents the symptoms of metabolic acidosis, which can increase muscle mass loss and worsen bone disease.
12. Renal osteodystrophy: The development of renal osteodystrophy is caused by hyperphosphatemia and hypocalcemia that are secondary to the decreased kidney function. In order to compensate, the patient will develop secondary hyperparathyroidism. Dietary restriction of phosphate to 800 mg/d is recommended. In Stage 3 CKD, the patient will usually require an oral phosphate binder like calcium carbonate or calcium acetate to prevent hyperphosphatemia. Oral phosphate binders must be taken with meals to be effective. It is imperative to avoid phosphate binders that contain aluminum or magnesium. To suppress parathyroid hormone secretion, the patient is given Calcitriol, a vitamin D analogue.
13. Anemia: Use of elemental iron 200 mg such as ferrous sulfate 325 mg three times daily (65 mg elemental iron per dose) is recommended to maintain the percent transferrin saturation greater than 20%, and the serum ferritin level to be greater than 100 ng/mL. Although primarily used in patients with ESRD, erythropoietic agents (EPO), such as Epoetin Alfa (Procrit), Epogen, and darbepoetin alfa (Aranesp), are also used to correct the anemia in those with CKD who do not yet require dialysis. Dosages of the EPO agents should be prescribed in order to maintain Hgb levels in the range of 11 to 12 g/dL in predialysis patients with CKD.
14. Dyslipidemia: Management of dyslipidemia has been shown to slow progression of CKD. Statins and fibrates are commonly prescribed to lower total cholesterol, low-density lipoprotein (LDL), and triglycerides. The incidence of untoward side effects with statins and fibrates is increased in persons with CKD; therefore, lower dosages and careful monitoring are required.

Follow-Up

A. Regular, consistent follow-up appointments to monitor progression of CKD, management of complications of CKD, and management of comorbidities such as DM and HTN are recommended.

Consultation/Referral

A. Early referral to a nephrologist is recommended for anyone who has CKD. Referral to a nephrologist must be done as quickly as possible for symptomatic patients with Stage 4 or 5. Consultation with an endocrinologist or HTN specialist may be helpful in cases where DM and HTN continue to be poorly controlled.
B. Counseling on renal transplantation should be completed by a nephrologist, after the patient is evaluated as a candidate for kidney transplantation, on what types of transplant are available and how the transplant process works.
C. Referral to a dietitian for nutritional counseling and education to assist the patient to understand and follow complex dietary instructions is recommended.
D. Patients with Stage 4 or 5 CKD need counseling regarding the psychosocial and financial impact of progressive renal disease. Referral to a renal social worker or case manager can help the patient understand his or her health insurance benefits, how the transition to Medicare occurs after the health insurance benefit changes, and to help the patient deal with concerns about work or family life.
E. Patients should be referred to educational and support organizations for further education regarding CKD.

Individual Considerations

A. Although renal replacement therapy is widely available, some patients, especially the more debilitated elderly or those who have a terminal illness, may request end-of-life counseling, including advance directives.

B. In some men, serum creatinine may be elevated after intense exercise or heavy intake of protein in the form of meat. Instruct patients who exercise vigorously to withhold strenuous exercise and large intake of meat protein at least 24 hours prior to evaluation of serum creatinine.

Resources

GlobalRPh

- Commonly used agents for renal failure: http://www.globalrph.com/renalfx.htm
- Creatinine Clearance and CKD staging: http://www.globalrph.com/multiple_crcl_2012.htm
- Medications with general dosing statements: http://www.globalrph.com/special-comments-renal.htm
- Renal Dosing Database: http://www.globalrph.com/index_renal.htm

National Kidney Disease Education Program: www.nkdep.nih.gov

National Kidney Foundation: www.kidney.org

Epididymitis

Definition

Epididymitis is acute infection of the epididymis, the coiled segment of the spermatic duct that connects the efferent duct from the posterior aspect of the testicle to the vas deferens. Epididymitis is commonly found to develop during strenuous exertion in conjunction with a full bladder. **Testicular torsion should be considered in all cases—this is a surgical emergency.**

A. Acute epididymis lasts less than 6 weeks duration of symptoms.
   1. Acute epididymitis often involves the testis (epididymo-orchitis).
B. Chronic epididymis lasts more than 6 weeks duration of symptoms.
   1. Inflammation chronic
   2. Obstructive chronic
   3. Chronic epididymalgia

Incidence

A. Epididymitis is the fifth most common urologic diagnosis in men aged 18 to 50 years. There are approximately 600,000 medical visits per year related to epididymitis. An estimated 1 in 1,000 men develops epididymitis annually. Chronic epididymitis may account for up to 80% of scrotal pain noted in the outpatient setting.

Pathogenesis

A. The exact pathophysiology is unclear. The cause may be the retrograde passage of infected urine from the prostatic urethra to the epididymis from the ejaculatory ducts and vas deferens. Reflux may be induced by having the patient perform Valsalva or may be from strenuous exertion. Pathogens include *Chlamydia trachomatis, Neisseria gonorrhea, Escherichia coli, Proteus* species, *Klebsiella* species, *Pseudomonas, Mycoplasma* species, and *Treponema pallidum.*

Predisposing Factors

A. Age
   1. Age younger than 35 years is generally associated with urethritis with the following organisms.
      a. *C. trachomatis* (chlamydia)
      b. *N. gonorrhoeae* (gonorrhea)
   2. BPH is more common for men older than 35 years.
   3. The older population of men usually has nonsexual epididymitis related to urinary tract instrumentation, surgery, and immunosuppression.
B. Men having sex with men (MSM) who are the insertive partner during anal intercourse have epididymitis with the following organisms:
   1. *E. coli*
   2. *Pseudomonas*
   3. Coliform bacteria
C. UTIs
D. Tuberculosis (TB; should be considered if there is a history of or recent exposure to)
E. Vasectomy
F. Indwelling urethral catheter
G. Urethral stricture
H. Amiodarone—high drug concentrations (dose-dependent)
I. Prolonged sitting (sedentary job, travel)
J. Mumps

Common Complaints

A. Swelling and tenderness of the scrotum (usually located on one side)
B. Fever
C. Chronic epididymitis
   1. Epididymal pain and inflammation that last more than 6 weeks
   2. May be accompanied by scrotal induration

Other Signs and Symptoms

A. Gradual onset of localized, unilateral testicular pain. The patient may get relief with elevation of the scrotum, which *is* a positive Prehn's sign.
B. Urethral discharge
C. Dysuria
D. Hematuria

Subjective Data

A. Elicit the onset, duration, and course of the patient's symptoms.

B. Review the patient's history for vasectomy or trauma to the groin.
C. Are there any other symptoms, including fever, dysuria, or discharge?
D. What helps relieve the pain? Ask about elevating the scrotum.
E. Does the patient's sexual partner(s) have any symptoms or discharge?
F. Has there been any recent instrumentation or catheterization?
G. Is the pain unilateral or bilateral?
H. Review medication history for amiodarone.
I. Does the patient have a recent TB exposure?

Physical Examination

A. Check temperature, blood pressure, and pulse.
B. Inspection
   1. Examine the patient generally for discomfort before and during examination.
   2. Check the urethral meatus for discharge. Retract foreskin (if present) and assess for hygiene and smegma. Check the shaft of the penis, glans, and prepuce for lesions.
   3. Check the inguinal and femoral areas for bulges and hernias; have the patient bear down and cough, and reexamine him.
C. Palpate
   1. Palpate testes and epididymides for inflammation, tenderness, and masses. In chronic cases, epididymis feels firm and lumpy. Vas deferens may be beaded.
   2. Check Prehn's sign by elevating the affected hemiscrotum. This action relieves the pain of epididymitis but exacerbates the pain of torsion.
   3. Elicit a cremasteric reflex. Stroking the inner thigh should result in rise of the testicle and scrotum on the affected side. A normal cremasteric reflex indicates that testicular torsion is less likely.
   4. Palpate scrotum for hydrocele or varicocele.
   5. Check for CVA tenderness.
   6. Examine the abdomen for masses, urinary distension, tenderness, and organomegaly.
   7. Palpate lymph nodes in the groin.
   8. Evaluate for an inguinal hernia.
D. Rectal exam: Check for symmetry, swelling, tenderness, and enlarged prostate.

Diagnostic Tests

A. Gram stain of urethral secretions
B. Urinalysis and urine cultures
C. Urethra swab (before void, after prostate massage) for gonorrhea and chlamydia culture
D. In patients older than 40: Express prostatic secretions
E. TB skin test to rule out TB

Differential Diagnoses

A. Epididymitis
   1. Bacterial
   2. Viral epididymo-orchitis (mumps and *Haemophilus influenzae*)
B. Testicular torsion *(surgical emergency)*
C. Testicular tumor
D. Prostatitis
E. Incarcerated inguinal hernia
F. Orchitis (occurs with parotitis)
G. Trauma
H. Vasectomy side effect
I. Folliculitis
J. Herpes outbreak

Plan

A. Patient teaching for supportive therapy: See the Section III Patient Teaching Guide for this chapter, "Epididymitis."
B. Pharmaceutical therapy
   1. Antibiotic therapy (both partners must be treated for an STI). Treat empirically until laboratory test results are available.
   2. Acute epididymitis should be treated for 10 days (see Table 14.2).
   3. Chronic epididymitis should be treated for 4 to 6 weeks for bacterial pathogens, especially chlamydia
   4. NSAIDs for pain management
   5. Antitubercular triple therapy consists of rifampin, isoniazid, and pyrazinamide for 6 months.
      a. Rifampin (Rifadin) 450 mg orally every day for 2 months; then 900 mg orally every day for an additional 4 months
      b. Isoniazid (Laniazid) 300 mg orally every day for 2 months; then 600 mg orally every day for an additional 4 months
      c. Pyrazinamide 25 mg/kg/d orally for 2 months only
   6. Amiodarone epididymitis usually responds to a dosage reduction or discontinuation.

Follow-Up

A. See the patient in 2 to 7 days depending on severity of infection.
   1. Pain typically improves within 1 to 3 days but may take up to 2 to 4 weeks.
   2. Inadequate treatment can result in abscess formation and decreased fertility.
B. Culture urine at the end of treatment (test of cure).
C. Failure to recognize and treat both partners for STIs is a potential legal pitfall; test for all STIs and do not just focus on chlamydia and gonorrhea.
D. Consider testing for HIV.

TABLE 14.2 The 2010 Centers for Disease Control (CDC) Recommendation Regimens for Acute Epididymitis

For acute epididymitis all patients should receive:
Ceftriaxone 250 mg IM in a single dose
PLUS
Doxycycline 100 mg orally twice a day for 10 days

For acute epididymitis most likely caused by enteric organisms, additional therapy can include:
Levofloxacin 500 mg orally once a day for 10 days
PLUS
Ofloxacin 300 mg orally twice a day for 10 days

For MSM who report insertive anal intercourse and are at risk for both STI and enteric organisms, ceftriaxone with a fluoroquinolone is recommended.

E. Tuberculous epididymitis should be suspected if clinical signs worsen despite appropriate antibiotic therapy.
F. Men older than 50 years should be evaluated for urethral obstruction secondary to prostatic enlargement.

Consultation/Referral

A. **Obtain an immediate consultation with a urologist if testicular torsion, scrotal abscess, or failed medical treatment is suspected.**
B. Consult a physician for the following.
   1. Intravenous pyelography (IVP)
   2. Doppler ultrasonography
   3. Scrotal ultrasonography
   4. Radionuclide scrotal imaging

Individual Considerations

A. Partner: Treat sexual partners for STI. Consider testing for HIV.

Erectile Dysfunction

Definition

A. ED, also known as impotence, is the persistent inability to achieve or maintain penile erection sufficient for satisfactory sexual performance. ED occurs with reduced blood flow to the penis or nerve damage as well as psychological triggers. Low self-esteem, performance anxiety, depression, stress, and effects to quality of life occur secondary to ED. ED is noted to be a precursor to symptomatic coronary artery disease (CAD).
B. Age-associated changes in sexual function in men include delay in erection, diminished intensity and duration of orgasm, and decreased force of seminal emission. ED lasting 3 months or longer should have further evaluation and consideration of treatment.
C. Multiple male sexual dysfunction questionnaires are available for order through the website www.oabq.org/edescrip.html#edits sponsored by Pfizer, Inc. The website notes the questionnaires may be ordered free of charge and are available in several translations. Questionnaires include:
   1. Erectile dysfunction inventory of treatment satisfaction (EDITS) used in the evaluation of satisfaction with medical treatment modalities for ED.
   2. Erectile hardness scale (EHS).
   3. International Index of Erectile Function (IIEF) is available in two versions. Version 1 is applicable to heterosexual men. Version 2 is edited so that it is applicable to heterosexual and homosexual men. The IIEF assesses five dimensions relevant to sexual function:
      a. Erectile function (six items)
      b. Orgasmic function (two items)
      c. Sexual desire (two items)
      d. Intercourse satisfaction (three items)
      e. Overall satisfaction (two items)
   4. Index of premature ejaculation (IPE) assesses control over ejaculation, sexual satisfaction, and distress.
   5. Premature ejaculation diagnostic (PED) tool was developed to screen for premature ejaculation, including control, frequency, minimal sexual stimulation, distress, and interpersonal difficulty.
   6. Quality of erection questionnaire (QEQ) evaluates satisfaction with the quality of erections, including hardness, onset, and duration.
   7. Self-esteem and relationship (SEAR) questionnaire assesses confidence, SEARs.
   8. Sexual health inventory for men (SHIM) is a five-item abridged version of the 15-item IIEF.
   9. Sexual quality of life-men (SQOL-M) was devel-oped to assess sexual confidence, emotional well-being, and relationship issues. This questionnaire has been validated for men with ED and premature ejaculation.

Incidence

A. ED can occur at any age; however, it is more common in men older than 60 years.
B. It is estimated that 15 to 30 million American men have ED.
C. By 2025 it is estimated that 322 million men worldwide will have ED.
D. Men with ED have a 65% to 85% increased risk of subsequent CAD.
E. Reduced libido is estimated as affecting 5% to 15% of men.

Pathogenesis

A. ED is caused by chronic diseases, including cardiovascular disease, HTN, dyslipidemia, obesity, and hypogonadism.
B. ED is also a side effect of multiple medications.
C. The vasoconstrictive effect of smoking is a contributing factor in ED, especially in the presence of existing cardiovascular disease.
D. Psychological factors also are related to ED, including depression, marital/family discord, job instability, and performance anxiety.
E. Cavernosal dysfunction (venous leak) refers to the inability to retain blood in the penis and therefore sustain an erection.

Predisposing Factors

A. Cardiovascular disease
B. Diabetes (neurological and vascular problems)
C. HTN
D. Hyperlipidemia
E. Advanced age (> 60 years)
F. Peripheral neuropathy
G. Obesity
H. Neurologic disorders
   1. Spinal cord injuries
   2. Brain injuries
   3. Multiple sclerosis (MS)
   4. Parkinson's disease
I. Alcohol abuse
J. Drug abuse
   1. Heroin
   2. Cocaine
   3. Marijuana
K. Side effect of medication (e.g., serotonin reuptake inhibitors)
L. Surgical/radiation therapy for cancers of the pelvis
M. Hypogonadism (hypoadrogenism/ hypoestrogenism)
N. Psychological and psychiatric disorders
O. Peyronie's disease (deformity of the penis)
P. Obstructive sleep apnea
Q. Physical inactivity

Common Complaints

A. Inability to achieve an erection
B. Erection is not firm enough for penetration
C. Inability to maintain an erection

Subjective Data

History taking for ED includes sexual, medical, surgical, emotional, and medication evaluations.

A. Sexual history
   1. Did the onset of ED coincide with a specific event?
   2. How long has the patient had trouble attaining or maintaining an erection?
   3. Is he able to obtain an erection in order to penetrate? On a scale of 0 to 10, how hard is the erection?
   4. Is the ED getting worse?
   5. Is he about to achieve orgasm and ejaculate?
   6. How long is the patient able to have intercourse prior to ejaculation?
   7. Is there pain or discomfort with ejaculation?
   8. Does the patient have nocturnal or morning erections?
   9. How frequently does the patient have sexual activity?
      a. Is the activity planned, or does it occur spontaneously?
      b. How much foreplay occurs?
      c. Do the patient and partner agree on the frequency of intercourse?
      d. Is the patient's partner satisfied?
   10. Has the patient tried any treatment(s) for ED?
      a. What treatments have been tried?
      b. Inquire about his desire to try any particular therapy. Is he opposed to try any particular therapy?
B. Medical history
   1. Does the patient have HTN? When was HTN diagnosed? What is his usual blood pressure?
   2. Does the patient have diabetes?
      a. Is he insulin dependent?
      b. Does he have any peripheral neuropathy?
   3. Does the patient have heart disease? When was his heart disease diagnosed?
   4. Has the patient ever had cancer, including any surgery, chemotherapy, and radiation?
   5. Does the patient have dyslipidemia? What were the results of his last laboratory tests?
   6. Does the patient smoke? How much, including the number of pack-years?
   7. Does the patient drink? How much, how often?
   8. Does the patient have penile curvature (Peyronie's disease)?
   9. Does the patient have any neurological disorders?

C. Surgical history
   1. Has the patient had any prior surgeries, including pelvic or prostate, or experienced trauma?
   2. Has the patient had any invasive cardiac procedures or surgery?
D. Emotional history
   1. Has the patient ever had any traumatic sexual experience?
   2. Has the patient had a loss of libido?
   3. Does the patient have a history of depression or mood disorders?
   4. Is the patient experiencing any problems related to work and/or family?
   5. Does the patient have any intrapartner problems such as separation or divorce?
E. Medication history: Ask the patient to list all medications currently being taken, particularly substances not prescribed, including herbal products and illicit drugs. Multiple drug classifications include medications that contribute to ED. Review medications from these drug classes:
   1. Nitrates
   2. Antihypertensives (particularly alpha blockers)
   3. Antiulcer medications
   4. Lipid-lowering medications
   5. 5-alpha reductase inhibitors (e.g., finasteride or dutasteride)
   6. Antidepressants
   7. Herbal products
   8. Illicit drugs
   9. Caffeine

Physical Examination

A. Check blood pressure, height, and weight. Calculate BMI.
B. Inspect
   1. Inspect general appearance, noting dyspnea and weakness.
   2. Inspect skin for jaundice, pallor, and diaphoresis.
   3. Inspect legs for edema, cyanosis, and venous stasis.
   4. Perform a fundoscopic examination.
   5. Evaluate visual field defects (present in hypogonadal men with pituitary tumors).
   6. Inspect for penile plaques (indicates Peyronie's disease).
   7. Inspect the testicles.
      a. Check for presence of atrophy.
      b. Assess asymmetry.
      c. Evaluate the cremasteric reflex by stroking the inner thighs and observe ipsilateral contraction of the scrotum.
C. Palpate
   1. Palpate abdomen for masses, tenderness, bounding pulses, and organomegaly.
   2. Palpate peripheral pulses in legs.
   3. Palpate femoral pulses.
   4. Examine breast to detect gynecomastia.
   5. Palpate the testicles for masses.
   6. Perform a rectal exam to evaluate the prostate.
D. Auscultate
   1. Auscultate carotid arteries for bruits.
   2. Auscultate abdomen for bruits and bowel sounds.
   3. Auscultate heart for murmurs, rubs, clicks, irregularities, or extra sounds.
   4. Auscultate for femoral bruits (possible pelvic blood occlusion).
   5. Auscultate all lung fields.
E. Mental status: Assess for depression.
F. Perform a neurologic examination if neurologic etiology is suspected.

Diagnostic Tests

A. Laboratory tests
   1. Lipid profile
   2. Triglycerides
   3. Glucose or Hgb A1C
   4. PSA testing (if on testosterone replacement)
   5. Hematocrit (if on testosterone replacement)
B. Urinalysis for protein and glucose
C. Duplex ultrasound of the cavernous arteries and other vascular testing as indicated
D. Nocturnal penile tumescence (NPT)
E. Total testosterone: Hormonal testing and treatment in ED should be individualized based on clinical presentation, including libido, premature ejaculation, fatigue, testicular atrophy, and muscle atrophy that suggests a hormonal abnormality. Free testosterone is considered more reliable according to the Endocrine Society.
F. Other tests as indicated for abnormal findings on physical examination

Plan

A. Patient teaching
   1. **A prolonged erection (priapism) lasting more than 4 hours is a medical emergency often requiring immediate urologic attention.**
   2. Educate patient about modifying controllable risk factors such as keeping diabetes and HTN under control, diet, exercise, and stopping smoking.
   3. Failure to respond to PDE-5 inhibitor treatment may be from improper instructions or an inadequate dosage of medication (see Table 14.3 for dosing and side effects).
   4. The initial administration of an alprostadil intraurethral suppository should be done in the office in order to demonstrate correct administration.
   5. The initial intrapenile administration of alprostadil should be done in the office in order to demonstrate correct administration.

TABLE 14.3 Dosing and Side Effects of Oral PDE-5 Inhibitors

	Sildenafil Citrate (Viagra)	Vardenafil HCL (Levitra)	Tadalafil (Cialis)	Stendra (Avanafil)
Doses	25 mg, 50 mg, and 100 mg doses	5 mg, 10 mg, and 20 mg doses	2.5 mg and 5 mg—available for continuous daily use 10 mg and 20 mg doses	50 mg, 100 mg, and 200 mg doses
Instructions	• Recommended starting dose is 50 mg. • Take on an empty stomach. • Maximum dosing once a day. • Titrate according to patient response/side effects. • Effective 30–60 minutes from administration. • A heavy fatty meal may reduce or prolong absorption.	• Recommended starting dose is 10 mg (5 mg initial dose for elderly). • Take on an empty stomach. • Titrate according to patient response/side effects. • Effective 60 minutes from administration. • A fatty meal reduces its effect.	• Recommended starting dose is 10 mg. • Titrate according to patient response. • Maximum dosing once a day. • Effective from 30–60 min. from administration. • Peak efficacy occurs after 2 hours. Efficacy is maintained for up to 36 hours. • Not affected by food. • Has been approved for continuous, daily use in 2.5 mg and 5 mg doses. • Also prescribed for BPH.	• Recommended starting dose is 100 mg, • Titrate according to patient response/side effects. • May be taken with or without food. • Effective 15 to 30 minutes from administration. • Maximum dosing once a day.
Common Side Effects	**Sildenafil Citrate (Viagra)**	**Vardenafil HCL (Levitra)**	**Tadalafil (Cialis)**	**Stendra (Avanafil)**
Headache	X	X	X	X
Flushing	X	X	X	X
Nasal congestion/rhinitis	X	X	X	X
Dyspepsia	X	X	X	
Priapism	X	Rare	Rare	X
Myalgia			X	
Sinusitis		X		X
Backache			X	X
Limb pain			X	
Prolonged erection	X			X
Tachycardia		X		
Visual disturbance	Blue-green color tinge to vision, light sensitivity and blurred vision (lasts 2–3 hours)			
Hypotension with alpha blockers	Should be stable on alpha blocker prior to initiating a PDE-5 inhibitor. Use lowest recommended PDE-5 inhibitor dose.	Should be stable on alpha blocker prior to initiating a PDE-5 inhibitor. Use lowest recommended PDE-5 inhibitor dose.	Should be stable on alpha blocker prior to initiating a PDE-5 inhibitor. Use lowest recommended PDE-5 inhibitor dose.	Should be stable on alpha blocker prior to initiating a PDE-5 inhibitor. Use lowest recommended PDE-5 inhibitor dose.
Sudden vision loss	Discontinue if vision loss occurs	Discontinue if vision loss occurs	Discontinue if vision loss occurs	Discontinue if vision loss occurs
Sudden hearing loss	Discontinue if hearing loss occurs	Discontinue if hearing loss occurs	Discontinue if hearing loss occurs	Discontinue if hearing loss occurs
Use with nitrates (includes nitroglycerin, isosorbide dinitrate, amyl nitrate, and sodium nitroprusside)	Contraindicated due to hypotension	Contraindicated due to hypotension	Contraindicated due to hypotension	Contraindicated due to hypotension

B. Stepwise therapy for ED includes the following treatment modalities:
   1. Pharmaceutical therapy with PDE-5 inhibitors is the first-line therapy for the treatment of ED. PDE-5 inhibitors are not initiators of erection and require sexual stimulation for an erection to occur. The evidence shows that the PDE-5 inhibitors improve erections and successful intercourse with an approximately 80% success rate. The use of PDE-5 inhibitors has been extensively studied; however, they are not without side effects (see Table 14.3 for dosing and side effects).
      a. **Contraindications to PDE-5 inhibitors include high-risk conditions and the concomitant use of nitrites. If the patient develops angina while using a PDE-5 Inhibitor, other antianginal agents should be used instead of nitroglycerin.**
      b. High-risk patients/conditions are defined as:
         i. Unstable or refractory angina
         ii. Refractory angina
         iii. Uncontrolled HTN
         iv. Congestive heart failure (CHF) (New York Heart Association classes III and IV)
         v. Myocardial infarction (MI) or a cardiovascular accident within the previous 2 weeks
         vi. High-risk arrhythmias
         vii. Hypertrophic obstructive and other cardiomyopathies
      c. Prior to proceeding to other ED therapies, patients reporting failure of PDE-5 inhibitors should be evaluated to determine whether the medication trial was adequate.
         i. Evaluate food/drug interactions.
         ii. Timing and frequency of dosing
         iii. Lack of adequate sexual stimulation
         iv. Heavy alcohol use
         v. Relationship issues
         vi. Using a licensed PDE-5 inhibitor medication
      d. After evaluation, reeducation, counseling on the medications, and partner–partner expectations a different PDE-5 inhibitor may be needed, or titrate the patient's current dosing for a change if needed.
      e. Discuss other options for ED if the patient has a contraindication to, or an unsuccessful trial of, PDE-5 inhibitors.
   2. Pharmaceutical therapy with intracavernous injection is the second-line therapy for the treatment of ED. Penile injection therapy involves injection of alprostadil, a vasoactive drug, into the corpora cavernosa of the penis to expand the blood vessels and increase the blood flow to produce an erection. The most common side effects of alprostadil are burning and a prolonged erection lasting more than 4 hours. Prolonged erections require medical intervention to reverse the erection.
   3. A penile implant is the third-line therapy for the treatment of ED. Penile prostheses (implants) are surgically implanted, semirigid rods or a hydraulic device to ensure a rigid erection. The prosthesis does not usually affect urination, sex drive, orgasm, or ejaculation. Pain and/or reduced sensation, infection, or mechanical failure may occur from the prosthesis.
   4. Vacuum erection devices are external cylinders used to pump the penis into the cylinder and produce an erection by drawing blood into the penis. An occluding band is then placed at the base of the penis in order to prevent the blood from leaving with subsequent loss of the erection. **Only vacuum constrictor devices containing a vacuum limiter should be used. The occluding band to maintain the erection should be limited to 30 minutes.**
   5. Penile arterial revascularization is indicated for young men (younger than 45 years) with no known risk factors for atherosclerosis. The goal of the surgery is to correct injury by rerouting the blood vessel around a blockage or injured blood vessel. Men with insulin-dependent diabetes or widespread atherosclerosis are not candidates for this surgery.
   6. Venous ligation surgery is rarely used. Men with insulin-dependent diabetes or widespread atherosclerosis are also not candidates for venous surgery.

Follow-Up

A. At the time of prescription renewal, patients prescribed PDE-5 inhibitors should have a review of the effectiveness, side effects, and any significant change in health status, including all medications.

B. A mild prolongation of the QT interval has been observed with vardenafil. The product labeling for vardenafil recommends that caution be used in patients with a known history of QT prolongation or in patients who are on current medications that prolong the QT interval.

C. Testosterone therapy is not indicated in the treatment of ED if the patient has a normal serum testosterone level.

D. Men who present with sleep disorders should also be questioned about the presence of ED.

Consultation/Referral

A. **Patients whose risk is indetermined for PDE-5 inhibitors should undergo further evaluation by a cardiologist before receiving therapies for sexual dysfunction.**
B. Surgical consultation: Men with penile deformities may require surgical correction.
C. Urologist consultation
D. Endocrinology consultation for complex endocrine disorders
E. Psychosexual counseling

Hematuria

Definition

A. Hematuria is blood in the urine. Hematuria is a symptom of an underlying disease/condition; however, routine screening is not recommended. Microscopic hematuria is defined as three or more red blood cells (RBCs) per high-power microscope field (HPF) in urinary sediment from two of three properly collected, clean-catch midstream urine specimens.
B. Asymptomatic microscopic hematuria can range from minor findings that do not require treatment to highly significant, life-threatening lesions. Microscopic hematuria is an incidental finding. The AUA recommends an appropriate renal or urologic evaluation with asymptomatic microscopic hematuria for patients who are at risk for urologic disease or primary renal disease.
C. If the excretion rate exceeds one million RBCs, macroscopic or gross hematuria is noted. Gross hematuria (macroscopic hematuria) is suspected when red or brown urine is present. Glomerulonephritis is associated with brown urine, whereas bleeding from the lower urinary tract is suggested by pink or red urine. Gross hematuria with passage of clots almost always indicates a lower urinary tract source.

Incidence

A. The prevalence of asymptomatic hematuria is from 0.19% to 21% of the general population. Less than 3% excrete 10 RBC/HPF. Every disease of the genitourinary (GU) tract can produce hematuria.

Pathogenesis

A. Prerenal pathology
   1. Coagulopathy: Hemophilia or idiopathic thrombocytopenia purpura (ITP)
   2. Drugs: Anticoagulants, aspirin
   3. Sickle cell disease or trait
   4. Collagen vascular disease; lupus
   5. Wilms' tumor
B. Renal pathology
   1. Nonglomerular pathology
      a. Pyelonephritis
      b. Polycystic kidney disease
      c. Granulomatous disease; TB
      d. Malignant neoplasm
      e. Congenital and vascular anomalies
   2. Glomerular pathology
      a. Glomerulonephritis
      b. Berger's disease
      c. Lupus nephritis
      d. Benign familial hematuria
      e. Vascular abnormalities; vasculitis
      f. Alport's syndrome; familial nephritis
C. Postrenal pathology
   1. Renal calculi
   2. Ureteritis
   3. Cystitis
   4. Prostatitis
   5. BPH
   6. Epididymitis
   7. Urethritis
   8. Malignant neoplasm
D. False hematuria
   1. Vaginal bleeding
   2. Recent circumcision
   3. Pigmentation
      a. Food: Beets, blackberries
      b. Medications: Quinine sulfate, phenazopyridine, and rifampin
E. Other causes
   1. Trauma
   2. Strenuous exercise (marathons)
   3. Fever

Predisposing Factors

A. See Pathogenesis.
B. Risk factors for malignancy
   1. Age older than 35
   2. Smoking (current use or past history)
   3. Chemical exposure
   4. History of pelvic irradiation
   5. Chronic analgesic abuse
   6. Chronic UTIs

Common Complaints

A. Pink or red urine (clots may be present) or brown cola-colored urine on toilet tissue is the common complaint.

Other Signs and Symptoms

A. Pain may or may not be present. Colicky flank pain radiating to the groin suggests a kidney stone. Significant flank pain of renal colic is usually secondary to renal calculi but may occasionally be associated with passage of clots.

B. Frequency, dysuria, urgency, and suprapubic pain occur with cystitis and inflammatory lesions of the lower urinary tract.
C. Dull flank pain with fever and chills may accompany pyelonephritis.
D. Hesitancy and dribbling of the urine suggest BPH.

Subjective Data

A. Elicit onset, duration, and occurrence (beginning, ending, or during voiding) of hematuria. Describe the color and amount: Is it "pink on tissue" or bright red in the toilet and tissue?
B. Question the patient regarding past medical history of renal disease, systemic disease such as lupus, or sickle cell disease.
C. Review all medications including OTC and herbal products. Evaluate specifically for the use of aspirin, ibuprofen, warfarin (Coumadin), and laxatives containing phenolphthalein. Rifampin and phenazopyridine HCL (Pyridium) can change the color of urine to orange or red.
D. Review other symptoms, such as dysuria, fever, chills, pain, and hesitancy with voiding.
E. Female patients
   1. Establish whether the blood was urinary or from the vagina (after intercourse or during menstruation).
   2. Is the patient postpartum?
   3. Is there a history of endometriosis?
F. Does the patient bruise easily? Does the patient have bleeding noted when flossing teeth or with brushing?
G. Has the patient had a recent bout of pharyngitis with a rash, hematuria, edema, or HTN (glomerulonephritis)?
H. Has he or she had any recent trauma, car accident, or strenuous exercise (i.e., running a marathon)?
I. Does the patient know if he or she has had any exposure to TB?
J. Is there any family history of kidney disease, stones, and familial nephritis?
K. Does the patient have any current outbreaks of herpes or other STI?
L. Review the patient's smoking history.
M. Review occupation exposure to chemicals or dyes (benzenes or aromatic amines).
N. Review food intake of foods such as beets and blackberries.
O. Does the male patient have any hesitancy and dribbling (signs of prostatic obstruction)?
P. Evaluate if there is rectal bleeding from hemorrhoids for strain with a bowel movement (BM).

Physical Examination

A. Check temperature, blood pressure, and weight in the presence of recent weight gain or edema.
B. Male or female patients
   1. Inspect
      a. Inspect mouth: Check tonsils for enlargement and check gums for petechiae.
      b. Examine skin for signs of bleeding or bruises and pallor.
      c. Examine for edema.
   2. Palpate
      a. Check the back and abdomen for CVA tenderness.
      b. Check the abdomen for masses, urinary distension, tenderness, and organomegaly.
      c. Palpate groin lymph nodes for enlargement.
   3. Auscultate
      a. Auscultate the heart and lungs.
      b. Auscultate for abdominal bruits.
C. Female patients
   1. Inspect
      a. Direct visualization of the external genitalia for inflammation, ulcerations, nodules, lesions, and hemorrhoids.
      b. Ask the patient to bear down to check for cystocele and rectocele.
      c. Speculum exam: Observe for atrophic vaginitis, torn tissue, discharge, and friable cervix.
   2. Palpate
      a. Milk urethra for discharge.
      b. Bimanual exam: Check for cervical motion tenderness and adnexal masses.
      c. Rectal exam: Check for the presence of hemorrhoids.
D. Male patients
   1. Inspect
      a. Direct visualization of the genitals; check the urethral meatus for discharge.
      b. Retract the foreskin (if present) and assess for hygiene and smegma. Check the shaft of the penis, glans, and prepuce for lesions or urethral meatal erosion.
   2. Palpate
      a. Palpate the testes and epididymides for inflammation, tenderness, and masses; palpate the scrotum for hydrocele or varicocele.
      b. Check the inguinal and femoral areas for bulges and hernias; have the patient bear down and cough, and reexamine patient.
      c. Rectal exam
         i. Check for swollen or tender prostate.
         ii. Check for the presence of hemorrhoids.

Diagnostic Tests

A. Urinalysis
   1. Centrifuge the urine specimen to see if the red or brown color is in the urine sediment or supernatant.

2. If the supernatant is red to brown, test for heme (Hgb or myoglobin) with a urine dipstick. Semen is in urine after ejaculation and may cause a positive heme reaction on the dipstick.
3. A positive dipstick must always be confirmed with a microscopic examination.
4. Urine culture and sensitivity
5. Urine cytology

B. After the physical exam and consultation, consider the following.
1. CBC with differential
2. BUN
3. Creatinine
4. Prothrombin time (PT), partial thromboplastin time (PTT) platelet count, and bleeding time (if indicated)
5. Sickle cell testing (if indicated)
6. The Nickel premassage and postmassage 2-glass test for the male patient (see the Section II Procedure, "Prostatic Massage Technique: 2-Glass Test").
7. Collect 24-hour urine for calcium, uric acid, protein, and creatinine. Follow with a 24-hour urine collection for creatinine and protein to assess renal function and quantitatively assess the degree of proteinuria.
8. Culture for gonorrhea and chlamydia.
9. Urine culture for acid-fast bacillus.
10. CT urography (CTU) is considered the preferred initial imaging in most patients for any unexplained persistent hematuria. CT is considered the best imaging modality for the evaluation of urinary stones, renal and perirenal infections, and associated complications. IVP and ultrasound are not as sensitive in the evaluation.
11. Cystoscopy (The combination of a CTU and the cystoscopy provides a complete evaluation.)
12. A CT scan of the abdomen or pelvis should be considered with a history of trauma to determine the source of blood.

C. Based on history, consider the following tests:
1. Strep testing to detect poststreptococcal glomerulonephritis
2. Antinuclear antibody to detect lupus nephritis

D. Urological referral testing includes
1. CTU and cystoscopy
2. MRI if a mass is suspected
3. Renal biopsy

Differential Diagnoses

A. See Pathogenesis for differential diagnoses.

Plan

A. General interventions
1. Investigate and diagnose cause(s). Only a limited workup (electrolytes, CBC) is needed in patients younger than 35 with normal physical exam. Patients older than 35 need a detailed investigation and referral.
2. Microhematuria with patients on an anticoagulant requires a urologic/nephrology workup regardless of the type or level of anticoagulation.
3. Repeat urinalysis in 2 weeks.

B. Pharmaceutical therapy: None is recommended for hematuria unless an infection is diagnosed.

Follow-Up

A. For patients who are at risk for malignancy and have a negative workup
1. Evaluate in 1 year.
2. After two consecutive negative urinalyses, discontinue the follow-up.
3. Gross hematuria after the initial negative urinalysis—repeat a full evaluation.

B. For patients with HTN, proteinuria, an increase in creatinine, needs to be reevaluated for renal disease.

C. For persistent asymptomatic microhematuria—after a negative workup, a yearly urinalysis is needed.

D. For persistent or recurrent asymptomatic microhematuria after the initial negative workup, consider repeating the evaluation within 3 to 5 years.

E. Culture urine for acid-fast bacillus if sterile pyuria and hematuria persist.

Consultation/Referral

A. The presence of significant proteinuria (excretion of more than 1,000 mg per 24 hours), red cell cast or renal insufficiency, or a predominance of dysmorphic RBCs in the urine should prompt an evaluation for renal parenchymal disease by a nephrologist. Red cell casts are considered virtually pathognomonic for glomerular bleeding.

B. New gross hematuria should be promptly reevaluated.

Individual Considerations

A. Women
1. Nonpregnant: Rule out menstruation and sexual activity.
2. Pregnant: Rule out vaginal bleeding such as threatened abortion, abruption, or placenta previa.
3. Ultrasound can be used to evaluate the pregnant woman. CTU should not be used secondary to the radiation exposure.

B. Geriatrics: The risk of malignancy increases among older individuals with a significant history of smoking or analgesic abuse.

Resources

Algorithms for hematuria workup and treatment

- American Urology Association: https://www.auanet.org/common/pdf/education/clinical-guidance/Asymptomatic-Microhematuria-Algorithm.pdf

- British Columbia Ministry of Health Guidelines & Protocols Advisory Committee: Macroscopic Hematuria (Persistent) http://www.bcguidelines.ca/pdf/hematuria.pdf
- http://emedicine.medscape.com/article/981898

Interstitial Cystitis

Definition

A. Interstitial cystitis (IC) is a chronic condition that results in recurring discomfort or suprapubic pain, as well as pressure in the bladder and surrounding pelvic region related to bladder filling. IC is also commonly known as painful bladder syndrome (PBS). IC/PBS includes all cases of urinary pain with persistent urge to void or urinary frequency that cannot be attributed to other causes (i.e., infection, stones, or other pathology).

B. The persistent urge to void helps to distinguish the symptoms of IC/PBS from those of overactive bladder (OAB). IC/PBS affects quality of life related to social activities, lost work productivity, sleep deprivation due to urinary frequency, fatigue, and even depression.

C. The Society for Urodynamics and Female Urology (SUFU) has stated that the symptoms should last more than 6 weeks in order for therapy to begin.

D. IC/PBS patients void to avoid or relieve pain, whereas patients with OAB void to avoid incontinence.

Incidence

A. Actual prevalence is unknown because of the variability of diagnostic criteria. It is not uncommon for patients to experience a lag time of 5 to 7 years before diagnosis. It is estimated that in the United States, IC/PBS affects 700,000 to 1 million people. The majority of the affected persons are women (10:1 rated over males). The symptom complex is the same for males.

Pathogenesis

A. The pathophysiology of IC/PBS remains unclear. It is not established whether IC/PBS is a localized condition just involving the bladder or whether it is a systemic disease that affects the bladder.

Predisposing Factors

A. In both genders, with a higher prevalence in females
B. Mean age of diagnosis is 42 to 45 years.
C. UTI
D. Prostatitis
E. Chronic yeast infections
F. Posthysterectomy or other pelvic surgery
G. Medications
   1. Calcium channel blockers
   2. Cardiac glycosides
H. Other hypersensitivity conditions that coexist with IC
   1. Fibromyalgia
   2. Irritable bowel syndrome (IBS)
   3. Chronic headaches
   4. Vulvodynia
   5. Sjögren's syndrome

Common Complaints

A. **Mild discomfort to intense pain with bladder filling and/or emptying is the hallmark symptom. The pain is not limited to the bladder/suprapubic area but includes symptoms throughout the pelvic area, lower abdomen, and back.**
B. Persistent urge to void
C. Frequency
D. Urgency
E. Nocturia

Other Signs and Symptoms

A. Combination of urgency and frequency
B. Pressure
C. Increase in symptoms during menstruation
D. Pain during vaginal intercourse
E. Low back pain with bladder filling

Subjective Data

A. Review onset, frequency, duration, and severity of symptoms.
B. Evaluate if the pain of bladder filling is partially or completely relieved by voiding.
C. Does the patient void frequently in order to maintain a low bladder volume and avoid discomfort versus voiding frequently to avoid urge incontinence (OAB)?
D. Are there any OAB triggers (e.g., citrus, beer, coffee) that exacerbate symptoms?
E. Are symptoms increased after stress, exercise, intercourse, being seated for long periods of time, or during the menstrual cycle?
F. How much do the symptoms affect the patient's quality of life (e.g., sleep disturbance, loss of work, avoiding activities)?
G. Does the patient have any other chronic pain syndromes such as IBS, chronic fatigue, dyspareunia, or fibromyalgia?
H. Review the patient's surgical history and history of GU cancers.
I. Any GU trauma or falls onto the coccyx?
J. Review the patient's history of UTIs, urinary retention, and urinary tract stones.
K. Review all medications, including OTC and herbal products.

L. Administer a pain/symptom evaluation tool at each visit.
   1. The Pelvic Pain and Urgency/Frequency Patient Symptom Scale (PUF) is available at http://www.ichelp.org/document.doc?id=16.5
   2. The Interstitial Cystitis Symptom Index (ICSI) is available at www.essic.eu/pdf/ICSIandICPI.pdf

Physical Examination

A. Temperature (if indicated to rule out infection; fever is not associated with IC) and blood pressure
B. Inspect
   1. Note general appearance for signs of depression and discomfort before and during examination.
   2. Inspect the male external genitalia for redness, edema, lesions, and discharge.
   3. Inspect female genitalia for discharge, lesions, fissures; inspect cervix for cervicitis.
C. Auscultate
   1. Auscultate the heart and lungs.
   2. Auscultate bowel sounds in all four quadrants.
D. Palpate
   1. Palpate back; note CVA tenderness.
   2. Palpate the abdomen for suprapubic tenderness, rebound masses, or pain.
   3. Females: Perform bimanual exam to rule out other infections and pelvic inflammatory disease (PID) (tenderness of the cervix, uterus, and adnexal should be absent). During the pelvic examination, evaluate locations of tenderness and trigger points.
   4. Males: Complete palpation of external genitalia, prostate, and rectal exam.
E. Percuss: Percuss the bladder and CVAs for tenderness.
F. Perform a limited neurological examination to rule out an occult problem.

Diagnostic Tests

A. Urinalysis with microscopy to exclude hematuria.
B. Urine culture and sensitivity may be ordered even with a negative urinalysis to evaluate low levels of bacteria.
C. PVR volume by straight catheter or ultrasound
D. Urodynamic testing is not currently considered to have a role in the diagnosis of IC/PBS; however, urodynamic testing should be used for complex presentations.
E. Cystoscopy is usually reserved for gross or microscopic hematuria.
F. Hydrodistension is not required for diagnosis or treatment.
G. Bladder biopsy is not required for diagnosis; however, it is used for exclusion of other disorders.
H. The potassium sensitivity test is not recommended for routine use since results are nonspecific for IC/PBS.

Differential Diagnoses

A. IC
B. UTI
C. IBS
D. Females
   1. Endometriosis
   2. Vulvodynia
E. Males
   1. Chronic prostatitis
   2. BPH

Plan

A. Behavioral modifications
   1. Restrict fluids to 64 ounces/d, divided into 16 ounces per meal and 8 ounces between meals.
   2. Progressive timed voiding on a 2- to 3-hour schedule. If the patient is unable to hold urine for this interval, progressively increase urine storage time between voids by 15 minutes per week until the goal of a 2- to 3-hour interval is reached.
   3. **Kegel exercises should be avoided with IC.**
   4. Psychosocial support is an integral part of chronic pain disorders.
   5. Several foods have been identified as bladder irritants, including foods rich in potassium. Patients may try to eliminate foods/drinks and reintroduce them one at a time to identify any items that make their symptoms worse. Examples:
      a. Alcohol
      b. Tomatoes
      c. Spices/spicy foods
      d. Chocolate
      e. Caffeinated beverages
      f. Coffee
      g. Artificial sweeteners
      h. Citrus: Lemons, limes, and oranges (including citrus-flavored beverages)
      i. Cranberry/cranberry juice
B. Pharmacological therapies
   1. Pentosan polysulfate sodium (Elmiron) is the only oral medication approved by the FDA for the treatment of IC.
      a. Dosage: 100 mg orally three times daily
   2. Amitriptyline (Elavil) is used in the treatment of other pain syndromes, including IC. May utilize a self-titration dose of 25 mg orally every night and increase in increments of 25 mg every week to a maximum dose of 100 mg orally per day.

3. Bladder instillation
   a. Intravesical dimethyl sulfoxide (DMSO) (Rimso-50) is the only drug approved by the FDA for bladder instillation.
   b. Heparin instillation
   c. Lidocaine instillation
   d. "Bladder cocktail" combination of sodium bicarbonate, heparin, lidocaine, and/or triamcinolone. There are various formulas/combinations.
4. Treat any comorbid depression.
5. Treat any comorbid infections (e.g., UTIs, STIs), inflammatory bowel disease, or endometriosis.
6. Other medications that have been used for symptomatic relief.
   a. Hydroxyzine hydrochloride (Vistaril, Atarax) 25 to 75 mg orally at bedtime
   b. Gabapentin 300 mg up to 2,400 mg in divided doses. Gabapentin requires careful dose titration due to sedation.
   c. Uro-blue medications for short-term bladder spasms
   d. NSAIDs
7. Cyclosporine A has been utilized when other treatments have not provided relief or control of symptoms

C. Intradetrusor botulinum toxin a (BTX-A)—this therapy may require posttreatment intermittent self-catheterization.
D. Laser or electrocautery if Hunner's ulcers are present.
E. Surgical options are available if all other therapies have failed.
F. Some alternative treatments such as guided imagery and acupuncture have shown some success but have not been studied.
G. **Therapies that are not recommended/should not be offered include:**
   1. Long-term antibiotics
   2. High-pressure, long-duration hydrodistension
   3. Systemic steroids
   4. Intravesical resiniferatoxin (ultrapotent capsaicin analogue)
   5. Intravesical Bacillus Calmette Guerin (BCG)
   6. Potassium sensitivity test—not recommended for routine use. It is a nonspecific and painful test.

Follow-Up

A. Allodynia, the perception of nonnoxious stimuli such as touch being noxious or painful, may be present; therefore, an adequate pelvic examination may not be possible. Consider empiric treatment and have the patient return for a pelvic examination to finish the evaluation.
B. Have the patient keep a 1-day bladder diary prior to visits to evaluate a pattern of low urine volume frequency characteristic of IC/PBS.
C. As with all medications, start at the lowest dose and titrate/increase doses if there is an improvement in symptoms.

Consultation/Referral

A. Refer to a urologist for more thorough workup and testing.
B. Refer to a pain management specialist if indicated.
C. Electrical stimulation therapy may be considered. The implanted sacral neuromodulation device is FDA approved for the treatment of urinary urgency and frequency but not specifically for the treatment of IC/PBS.

Resources

Adult Pediatric Urology and Urogynecology: www.adultpediatricuro.com
American Urological Association (AUA): www.auanet.org
International Painful Bladder Foundation: www.painful-bladder.org
Interstitial Cystitis: http://www.mayoclinic.org/diseases-conditions/interstitial-cystitis
Interstitial Cystitis Association (ICA): www.ichelp.org
Interstitial Cystitis Network: www.ic-network.com
Pelvic Pain and Urgency/Frequency Patient Symptom Scale available at www.ichelp.org/document.doc?id=16
Society of Urodynamics, Female Pelvic Medicine & Urogenital Reconstruction: www.sufuorg.com

Nocturia

Definition

Nocturia is frequent wakefulness at night to urinate. The AUA and the International Continence Society (ICS) define nocturia as "the need to awake in order to urinate at least once or twice during the night." Nocturia in the older population is associated with higher rates of falls and fractures.

Incidence

A. The prevalence of nocturia increases with age.
B. Some studies suggest that nocturia is present in 50% of both men and women older than 50 years of age.
C. Among those 18 to 49 years old, more women than men experienced nocturia.
D. Men older than 60 years of age experience nocturia more than women.

Pathogenesis

Aging is a major factor, and nocturia occurs more commonly in the elderly than in younger individuals. In both women and men, the occurrence is much different because of the dissimilarity of the respective anatomy. In women, nocturia is generally experienced as a result of childbirth, menopause, and pelvic organ prolapse. Nocturia in men, however, can be directly attributed to enlarged prostate, also known as BPH.

Predisposing Factors

Multiple factors could cause nocturia in both men and women, including:

A. Chronic diseases
   1. Diabetes
   2. Heart failure/venous status
   3. Diabetes insipidus (Polyuria)
   4. CKD
   5. Obstructive sleep apnea (OSA)
   6. Neurologic diseases
   7. Obesity
B. Medications
   1. Diuretics
   2. Calcium channel blockers
   3. Beta blockers
   4. Xanthines
   5. Selective serotonin reuptake inhibitors (SSRIs)
   6. Cholinesterase inhibitors
C. Caffeine
D. Alcohol
E. Nocturnal polyuria
F. Low nocturnal bladder capacity
G. Combination of the nocturnal polyuria and low nocturnal bladder capacity
H. OAB
I. Gender
   1. Males: BPH
   2. Females:
      a. Pregnancy
      b. Estrogen deficiency
      c. Pelvic floor laxity (e.g., cystocele, uterine prolapse)
J. Excessive fluid intake in the evening
K. IC/PBS
L. Chronic or recurrent UTIs
M. Idiopathic
N. Fecal Impaction

Common Complaints

A. Morning fatigue
B. Frequent wakefulness
C. Insomnia
D. Urinary frequency
E. Urinary urgency
F. Geriatrics
   1. May not present with classic symptoms
   2. Incontinence
   3. Mental confusion
   4. History of falls

Other Signs and Symptom

A. Asymptomatic
B. Bladder spasms
C. Suprapubic pain or suprapubic discomfort
D. Depression

Potential Complications

A. Poor quality of life
B. Sleep deprivation
C. Depression
D. Fractures/mortality due to complications of falls

Subjective Data

A. Review the onset, course, and duration of symptoms.
B. Review the number of sleep interruptions or frequent wakefulness.
C. Are there any other genital problems such as herpes lesions or vaginal discharge?
D. Review all medications, prescriptions, OTC, and herbals for how often and what time of the day they are taken.
E. Does the patient have a fever and chills or back or flank pain (unilateral or bilateral)?
F. Is the patient pregnant? If not, what type of birth control does she use?
G. Is there any history of previous UTIs? How often, and how were they treated? Were any tests performed in a workup by a urologist?
H. Is there any history of IC? Were any tests performed in a workup by a urologist? What treatments?
I. In the postmenopausal woman, review whether she has a known prolapse and/or vaginal atrophy. Does she use any systemic or local estrogen medications?
J. How much liquid or water does the patient drink every day?
   1. Note the amount of caffeine and alcohol.
   2. Note the total amount of fluids.
   3. At what time in the evening are the last fluids taken?
   4. Does the patient awaken at night and drink more liquids?
K. In older men, review the strength of the urinary flow, dribbling, hesitancy, and so on.
L. Is there any history of other medical diseases (noted in the Predisposing Factors section).
M. Does the patient have a mobility issue; use of any aids, such as a cane or a walker?
N. In the elderly, what is their ability to toilet independently?

Physical Examination

A. Both genders
   1. Check temperature (if an infection is suspected), pulse, blood pressure, and respirations. Measure height and weight to calculate BMI.

2. Inspection begins as the patient comes into the examination room.
   a. Assess cognitive and functional status.
   b. Observe mobility (using aids, including walkers and canes).
   c. Assess for risk of falls.
   d. Observe patient to transfer.
   e. Assess manual dexterity (ability to use buttons and zippers).
   f. Inspect for evidence of cardiac overload: pedal edema.
3. Auscultate
   a. Auscultate the lungs for evidence of fluid overload: Rales.
4. Palpate
   a. Palpate the abdomen.
   b. Palpate suprapubic and back for CVA tenderness.
   c. Palpate inguinal nodes and CVA tenderness.
   d. Palpate bladder fullness and need for catherization.
   e. Perform a neurologic examination to determine presence of sensation.
5. Screen for depression.

B. Females
1. Inspect perineal skin for irritation, thinning, vaginal atrophy, and vaginal discharge.
2. Perform a bimanual pelvic exam for prolapse, masses, or tenderness.
   a. Remove the top blade of the speculum and evaluate the vaginal wall support.
   b. Ask the woman to cough to reevaluate the vaginal wall support.
3. Palpate
   a. Perform rectal exam for sphincter tone, masses, and fecal impaction.

C. Males
1. Inspect
   a. Inspect the glans penis for abnormalities in urethral meatus. (Hypospadias may cause postvoid dribbling.)
   b. Uncircumcised men should be evaluated for phimosis and balanitis.
2. Palpate
   a. Perform rectal exam for sphincter tone, masses, fecal impaction, prostate size, and contour.
   b. Palpate the scrotum to evaluate masses.
   c. Evaluate the presence of an inguinal hernia since straining with a partial urinary obstruction can worsen an inguinal hernia.

Diagnostic Tests

History, physical examination, and urinalysis may be sufficient to guide initial therapy and to rule out other causative factors. Other tests include the following.

A. Urine culture and sensitivity if infection is suspected
B. Urine cytology if hematuria or pelvic pain is present
C. Urodynamic testing is strongly recommended.
D. A PSA should be considered.
E. Cystoscopy/ureteroscopy
F. Renal ultrasound with Doppler
G. Chemistry study with Hgb AIC
H. Sleep study may be indicated, especially if positive for nocturnal hypoxemia.
I. Depression screen
J. Neurological evaluation may be needed to include, but not be limited to, CT studies.
K. Nocturnal pulse oximetry study

Differential Diagnosis

A. Nocturia (idiopathic)
B. Nocturnal polyuria
C. Low nocturnal bladder capacity
D. DM/insipidus
E. Medication(s) side effect
F. Fluid intake near bedtime (includes caffeine and alcohol)
G. Chronic or recurrent UTI
H. Enlarged prostate
I. Pregnancy
J. IC/PBS
K. CHF/vascular stasis
L. Heart disease
M. Sleep disturbance

Plan

A. Patient education
1. Give the patient the Section III Patient Teaching Guide for Chapter 3, "Safety Issues: Fall Prevention."
2. Give the patient the Section III Patient Teaching Guide, for this chapter, "Nocturia."

B. 24-hour voiding diary: See the Section III Patient Teaching Guide for this chapter, "Urinary Incontinence: Women."

C. Nonpharmacological treatments
1. Limit fluid intake at night, especially alcohol and caffeine.
2. If edema and venous stasis in the lower extremities are a problem, have patients wear compression stockings and elevate legs during the waking hours and remove stockings prior to retiring.
3. Blood glucose control
4. Evaluate proper usage of CPAP machine if sleep apnea is present.
5. Percutaneous tibial nerve stimulator (PTNS): Has been used for OAB. The use for nocturia remains unclear.
6. Implantable neuromodulation therapy (InterStim): Has been helpful
7. Electrical stimulation may be used to teach the proper use of pelvic muscles.

D. Pharmaceutical therapy
1. Oxybutynin (Ditropan): 5 to 15 mg tablets, anticholinergic medicine that relaxes the detrusor muscle of the bladder. May be combined with bladder volume training. It reduces wet nights in those with nocturnal enuresis. It is available in time-release tablets, as a syrup, as well as in transdermal patches.
2. Trospium chloride: 20 mg tablet, anticholinergic medication blocks cholinergic receptors that are found on muscle cells in the wall of the bladder. Use to treat OAB.
3. Solifenacin (VESIcare): 5 mg and 10 mg tablet, anticholinergic and selective antimuscarinic with fewer anticholinergic side-effects.
4. Darifenacin (Enablex): 7.5 to 15 mg extended release (ER), anticholinergic medication relieves bladder spasms and treats OAB. Decreases bladder contractions and increases bladder capacity. The effects of darifenacin for nocturia vary.
5. Tolterodine (Detrol): 2 mg tabs, anticholinergic/antimuscarinic functions much like oxybutynin antagonist that is available in both short- and long-acting form.
6. Fesoterodine (Toviaz): 4 mg, 8 mg: Anticholinergic, muscarinic receptor antagonist
7. Trospium chloride (Sanctura): 20 mg twice a day or 60 mg ER daily.
8. DDAVP (Desmopressin): 0.1 to 0.4 mg tablets, subcutaneous (SC), IV, and nasal spray. Antidiuretic, use for nocturnal polyuria and vasopressin disorder. Immediate reassessment for effectiveness is recommended.
9. HCTZ and Furosemide antidiuretics: Use if patient is unable to tolerate DDAVP. Used as a second-line treatment option. Give 6 to 8 hours before bedtime.
10. Cyclooxygenase-inhibitor 2 has been used occasionally because of its effect on urine production.
11. Botulinum toxin: Use only as refractory to first-line treatment. Further adjuvant therapy must be under direction after a full evaluation.
12. Melatonin OTC: Using a combination treatment may mitigate rather than reduce symptoms.

Follow-Up
A. Follow-up is determined by the patient's needs, severity of symptoms, and whether complications are present. Adequate time should be allowed for treatments involving the nonpharmacological and pharmacological approach.

Consultation/Referral
A. Consider referral to urologist.
B. Refer to pulmonologist if patient is positive for nocturnal hypoxemia.
C. Urogynecologist: For women with a structural problem and pregnancy
D. Neurology
E. Endocrinology

Individual Considerations
A. Adults/Geriatrics
1. 5-alpha-reductase inhibitors have been known to cause ED.
2. Avoid the use of anticholinergics if GFR is less than 30.
3. Melatonin secretion is impaired in the elderly, which can contribute to disruption of the circadian rhythm of micturition, leading to nocturia.

Resource
National Association for Continence (NAFC): http://www.nafc.org/bladder-bowel-health/nocturia

Prostatitis

Definition
Prostatitis is acute or chronic infection of the prostate gland. Prostatitis is the most important cause of urinary infection in men. Prostatitis accounts for about 2 million office visits a year to urologists and primary care providers.

There are four types of prostatitis:
A. Acute bacterial prostatitis (least common)
B. Chronic bacterial prostatitis
C. Chronic prostatitis/chronic pelvic pain syndrome (common in men of any age)
1. Inflammatory (presence of white cells in the semen-expressed prostatic secretions [EPS], or voided bladder urine postprostatic massage)
2. Noninflammatory (absence of white cells)
D. Asymptomatic inflammatory prostatitis (usually diagnosed when evaluating for other urologic evaluations, including seminal fluid analysis for infertility)

Incidence
A. About 50% of adult men in the United States will be treated for prostate conditions during their lifetime.
B. Acute and chronic bacterial prostatitis occurs in about 1 in 10 men.
C. Nonbacterial prostatitis occurs in about 6 in 10 men.
D. Prostatodynia occurs in about 3 in 10 men.

Predisposing Factors
A. More common in younger and middle-aged men
B. Sexual transmission of bacteria
C. Neuromuscular dysfunction
D. Structural voiding dysfunction

E. BPH
F. History of allergies and asthma (increase in nonbacterial prostatitis)

Pathogenesis

A. Nonbacterial prostatitis is an inflammatory condition with an unknown etiology. Infection results in prostatitis in four ways:
   1. Ascending infection of urethra
   2. Reflux of infected urine into the prostate through ejaculatory and prostatic ducts that empty into the prostatic urethra
   3. Hematogenous spread causing bacterial prostatitis
   4. Invasion by rectal bacteria through direct extension or lymph system spread
B. Causative organisms: *E. coli, Klebsiella, Pseudomonas, Enterococci, Ureaplasma, Gardnerella vaginalis, Trichomonas vaginalis, Chlamydia trachomatis, Chlamydia, Mycoplasma,* or *Neisseria gonorrhoeae. Cytomegalovirus (CMV), Mycobacterium tuberculosis,* and fungi have been associated with prostatitis in HIV-infected patients.
C. Incubation period depends on pathogen.

Common Complaints

A. Dysuria
B. Perineal, rectal, or suprapubic pain (chronic pain syndrome)
C. Less urine flow
D. Spiking fever
E. Back pain
F. Sexual dysfunction

Other Signs and Symptoms

A. Acute bacterial prostatitis
   1. Fever and chills, malaise
   2. Acute onset of dysuria
   3. Hesitancy
   4. Urinary frequency and low back pain
   5. Pain with intercourse and with defecation
   6. Initial or terminal hematuria and edema with acute urinary retention
   7. Arthralgia or myalgia
   8. Nocturia
B. Chronic bacterial prostatitis
   1. Usually presents with recurrent UTI
   2. May be asymptomatic between acute episodes; some men have large fluctuation in symptom severity.
   3. Perineal, inguinal, or suprapubic pain, or irritative symptoms on voiding such as frequency and urgency
   4. Hematuria, hematospermia, or painful ejaculations
   5. Prostatic calculi
C. Nonbacterial prostatitis (most common)
   1. Vague discomfort to pain: Prostatic, lower back, perineum, groin, scrotum, or suprapubic pain; ejaculatory pain
   2. Dysuria, urinary frequency, urgency, hesitancy, and decreased urine flow
   3. Penile discharge, especially noted during the first BM of the day
   4. Sexual difficulty
   5. Low sperm count
   6. Blood or urine in ejaculate
D. Asymptomatic inflammatory prostatitis is found when looking for causes of infertility and testing for prostate cancer.
E. Prostatodynia (cause is unknown)
   1. Prostate irritation
   2. Pain and discomfort in the prostate, testicles, penis, and urethra
   3. Difficulty urinating

Subjective Data

A. Ask the patient to complete the National Institutes of Health Chronic Prostatitis Symptom Index (NIH-CPSI) self-evaluation form (see Table 14.4). The assessment tool evaluates pain, urinary symptoms, and the impact on quality of life.
   1. Mild = 0 to 14 total score
   2. Moderate = 15 to 29 total score
   3. Severe = 30 to 43 total score
      An online NIH symptom index that self-scores is available at www.prostatitis.org/symptomindex.html
B. Review the onset, duration, and course of symptoms.
C. Are there any other symptoms such as discharge, pain, hematuria, hesitancy, back pain, or weight loss?
D. Has the patient ever had the same symptoms? If so, how were they treated?
E. Does any sexual partner(s) have any symptoms, lesions, or known STIs?
F. Does the patient engage in anal intercourse?
G. Has the patient noted any impaired urinary flow?
H. Has the patient required any recent urethral catheterization or instrumentation?

Physical Examination

A. Check temperature and blood pressure.
B. Inspect
   1. Examine the patient generally for discomfort before and during examination.
   2. Check the urethral meatus for discharge.
   3. Retract foreskin (if present) and assess for hygiene and smegma.
   4. Check the shaft of the penis, glans, and prepuce for lesions.

TABLE 14.4 NIH Chronic Prostatitis Symptoms Index (NIH-CPSI)

Pain or Discomfort

1. In the past week, have you experienced any pain or discomfort in the following areas?

	Yes	No
a. Area between rectum and testicles (perineum)	❑ 1	❑ 0
b. Testicles	❑ 1	❑ 0
c. Tip of the penis (not related to urination)	❑ 1	❑ 0
d. Below your waist, in your pubic or bladder area	❑ 1	❑ 0

2. In the past week, have you experienced:

	Yes	No
a. Pain or burning during urination?	❑ 1	❑ 0
b. Pain or discomfort during or after sexual climax (ejaculation)?	❑ 1	❑ 0

3. How often have you had pain or discomfort in any of these areas over the past week?

❑ 0 Never
❑ 1 Rarely
❑ 2 Sometimes
❑ 3 Often
❑ 4 Usually
❑ 5 Always

4. Which number best describes your **average** pain or discomfort on the days that you had it, over the past week?

❑	❑	❑	❑	❑	❑	❑	❑	❑	❑	❑
0	1	2	3	4	5	6	7	8	9	10
No Pain										Pain as bad as you can imagine

Urination

5. How often have you had a sensation of not emptying your bladder completely after you finished urinating, over the past week?

❑ 0 Not at all
❑ 1 Less than 1 time in 5
❑ 2 Less than half the time
❑ 3 About half the time
❑ 4 More than half the time
❑ 5 Almost always

6. How often have you had to urinate again less than 2 hours after you finished urinating, over the past week?

❑ 0 Not at all
❑ 1 Less than 1 time in 5
❑ 2 Less than half the time
❑ 3 About half the time
❑ 4 More than half the time
❑ 5 Almost always

Impact of Symptoms

7. How much have your symptoms kept you from doing the kinds of things you would usually do, over the past week?

❑ 0 None
❑ 1 Only a little
❑ 2 Some
❑ 3 A lot

8. How much did you think about your symptoms, over the past week?

❑ 0 None
❑ 1 Only a little
❑ 2 Some
❑ 3 A lot

Quality of Life

9. If you were to spend the rest of your life with your symptoms just the way they have been during the past week, how would you feel about that?

❑ 0 Delighted
❑ 1 Pleased
❑ 2 Mostly satisfied
❑ 3 Mixed (about equally satisfied and dissatisfied)
❑ 4 Mostly dissatisfied
❑ 5 Unhappy
❑ 6 Terrible

Scoring the NIH-Chronic Prostatitis Symptom Index Domains

Pain: Total of items 1a, 1b, 1c, 1d, 2a, 2b, 3, and 4 = ____

Urinary symptoms: Total of items 5 and 6 = ____

Quality-of-life impact: Total of items 7, 8, and 9 = ____

C. Palpate
1. Palpate testes and epididymides for inflammation, tenderness, and masses; palpate scrotum for hydrocele or varicocele.
2. Check back for CVA tenderness.
3. Evaluate for an enlarged tender bladder due to urinary retention.
4. Palpate the abdomen for masses, urinary distension, suprapubic tenderness, and organomegaly.
5. Palpate inguinal lymph nodes; check the inguinal and femoral areas for bulges and hernias; have the patient bear down and cough, and reexamine him.

6. Rectal exam
   a. Prior to the rectal examination, have the patient obtain a clean-catch urine specimen for culture. Check for symmetry, swelling, tenderness, and enlarged prostate.
   b. In acute prostatitis, rectal examination reveals the prostate gland to be exquisitely tender and boggy.
   c. A fluctuant prostatic mass suggests an abscess that may require surgical intervention.
   d. Perform prostate massage for postmassage urine sample (see the Section II Procedure "Prostatic Massage Technique: 2-Glass Test").

Diagnostic Tests

A. Acute infection
   1. CBC with differential
   2. Urinalysis and urine culture
   3. Culture for STIs
   4. Gram stain, culture of EPS
      a. **Avoid vigorous massage when obtaining specimen because of the risk of inducing bacteremia.**
      b. Gram stain of EPS demonstrates infectious organisms or WBCs typical of an immune response (> 10 WBC/HPF is abnormal). Patients with abnormal WBC but no bacterial growth may have chlamydial or *Ureaplasma* infection and need to be tested or treated empirically.
B. Chronic infection
   1. BUN
   2. CBC with differential
   3. Creatinine
C. Chronic bacterial prostatitis
   1. If recurrent infections are confirmed, evaluate for structural or functional abnormality with CT scan.
   2. Measure residual urine after voiding.
   3. If no urologic abnormalities are found and repeated cultures indicate the same bacterial strain, chronic bacterial prostatitis is likely.
D. Other tests such as ultrasound, MRI, and biopsies as required to rule out other pathology

Differential Diagnoses

A. Prostatitis
   1. Acute: Readily evident by clinical presentation and exam
   2. Chronic: More difficult to diagnose. The hallmark symptom is recurrent UTI. It often resembles prostatic hypertrophy, strictures, and prostatic carcinoma.
   3. Chronic pelvic pain syndrome
B. Pyelonephritis
C. Epididymitis
D. Anal fistulas and fissures
E. BPH causes urinary retention due to obstruction.
F. Urethral stricture or stone
G. Chronic pain syndromes/back pain

Plan

A. General interventions
   1. Patients with acute prostatitis may need hospitalization and IV therapy for severe infection (high fever, increased WBC, dehydration). Less toxic patients may be treated on an outpatient basis.
   2. Older men without evidence of infection with lower tract symptoms should have urine cytology to rule out malignancy.
B. Patient teaching
   1. See the Section III Patient Teaching Guide for this chapter, "Prostatitis."
   2. Having the patient self-massage to reduce symptoms is questionable; the massage of an acutely infected gland is contraindicated because of the risk of bacteremia.
   3. Recommend sitz baths two to three times daily.
C. Dietary management
   1. Increase fluid intake.
   2. Decrease caffeine and alcohol, which can irritate the urethra.
D. Pharmaceutical therapy
   1. Analgesics (NSAIDs) and stool softeners may be needed.
   2. Discontinue or reduce the dosage (if possible) of the patient's anticholinergics, sedatives, and antidepressants because they may impair bladder function.
   3. Inpatient: Broad-spectrum penicillin, third-generation cephalosporins with or without aminoglycosides, or fluoroquinolones.
   4. Acute outpatient therapy: The usual course of treatment is 14 to 28 days. Chronic bacterial prostatitis and chronic pain may require 4 to 6 weeks of antibiotic therapy, including fluoroquinolones, trimethoprim, tetracyclines, or macrolides.
   5. Low-dose suppressive therapy with an agent that has been shown to be effective may be considered.
   6. There are no formal guidelines for the management of chronic bacterial prostatitis or chronic pelvic pain syndrome. Strategies are currently focused on symptomatic relief.
   7. Alpha blockers may be used to control symptoms by reducing BOO.

Follow-Up

A. See the patient in 2 to 10 days depending on the patient's symptoms and course.
B. Culture urine at completion of drug therapy. Test of cure for antibiotics requires elimination of bacteria

from prostatic fluid to prevent chronic flares. Some patients may not achieve cure even after 6 to 12 weeks of therapy.

C. Patients who achieve a partial response may be given a second course of antibiotics. Those failing to demonstrate an organism may benefit from a course of doxycycline or erythromycin for *Chlamydia* and/or *Ureaplasma* coverage.

D. Notify the health department for reportable STIs.

Consultation/Referral

A. Obtain a referral to a urologist for recurrent acute bacterial prostatic infections or infections that persist.

B. Cystoscopy may be required to rule out IC.

C. Urinary retention concomitant with acute prostatitis may require hospitalization.

Resources

American Urological Association (AUA): www.auanet.org
National Institute of Diabetes and Digestive and Kidney Diseases (NIDDK): www.niddknih.org
The Prostatitis Foundation: www.prostatitis.org

Proteinuria

Definition

A. Proteinuria is excess protein (albumin) in urine. Proteinuria may be an incidental finding and have no symptoms. Use of a urine dipstick for screening is acceptable for first detecting proteinuria (see Table 14.5); however, the dipstick should not be used to quantify the amount of urinary protein. Protein concentration is a function of urine volume as well as the quantity of protein present.

B. The measurement of protein excretion is used to establish the diagnosis and to follow the course of glomerular disease. The normal rate of albumin excretion is less than 20 mg/d; the rate is about 4 to 7 mg/d in healthy young adults and increases with age and an increase in body weight. Persistent albumin excretion between 30 and 300 mg/d is called microalbuminuria. Values of 300 mg/d of protein are considered overt proteinuria or macroalbuminuria.

TABLE 14.5 Dipstick Analysis—Detecting and Quantifying Proteinuria

Dipstick Grade	Quantity of Protein
Negative	<10 mg/dL
Trace	10–20 mg/dL
1+	30 mg/dL
2+	100 mg/dL
3+	300 mg/dL
4+	1,000 mg/dL

C. **When proteinuria coexists with hematuria, the likelihood of clinically significant renal disease is high.** In patients with diabetes, microalbuminuria usually indicates incipient diabetic nephropathy. In nondiabetics, the presence of microalbuminuria is associated with cardiovascular disease. Protein is also the cardinal sign of pregnancy-induced hypertension (PIH).

D. Functional/transient proteinuria is associated with fever, exercise, dehydration, cold exposure, and stress and is not associated with underlying renal disease. Orthostatic proteinuria, a transient proteinuria condition, is related to postural changes that affect the glomerular hemodynamics. Orthostatic proteinuria rarely exceeds 1 g/d. Significant renal disease is not usually found upon further testing and workup.

E. Persistent proteinuria is defined as greater than 4 mg/m^2/hr of protein in a 24-hour urine collection or greater than 0.02 mg/mg of protein creatinine ratio on a spot urine. Persistent proteinuria requires further evaluation to rule out underlying renal pathology. There are three types of mechanisms of persistent proteinuria:

1. Glomerular proteinuria (albuminuria): Due to increased filtration of macromolecules across the glomerular capillary wall. The standard urine dipstick is able to detect glomerular proteinuria. Some causes of glomerular proteinuria include diabetes; HTN; nephrotic syndrome; infections including hepatitis, HIV, CMV, malaria, syphilis, and streptococcal infections; chemotherapeutic agents; Alport syndrome; and hemolytic uremic syndrome.
2. Tubular proteinuria: Related to interference with proximal tubular reabsorption. A urinary dipstick is unable to detect tubular proteinuria. Some causes of tubulointerstitial proteinuria include toxins, pyelonephritis, NSAIDs, antibiotics, and inherited causes such as Lowe syndrome and Wilson disease.
3. Secretory (overflow) proteinuria: Increased excretion from the tubules secondary to an overproduction of a particular protein, most commonly noted in interstitial nephritis. A urinary dipstick is unable to detect overflow protein.
4. It is currently recommended that a diagnosis of kidney damage can only be made if at least two measurements are elevated.

Incidence

A. Approximately 4% of males and 7% of females have proteinuria detected by a single routine dipstick test.

B. The prevalence of proteinuria is higher in the elderly and in patients with comorbidities.

Pathogenesis

A. Pathogenesis depends on the underlying etiology. An alteration in glomerular filtration that increases excretion (filtration) of plasma proteins occurs. Increased glomerular permeability, increased production of abnormal proteins (Bence Jones protein), decreased tubular reabsorption, surgical traumas, and infections may increase urinary protein. Urinary protein may also be affected by dietary protein intake.

Predisposing Factors

A. Fever
B. Increased exercise
C. UTI/pyelonephritis
D. Medications
   1. Penicillamine
   2. NSAIDs
   3. ACE inhibitors
   4. Aminoglycosides
   5. Cisplatin
   6. Amphotericin B
   7. Quinolones
   8. Sulfonamides
   9. Cimetidine (Tagamet)
   10. Allopurinol (Zyloprim)
   11. Antiretroviral drugs can be nephrotoxic.
E. Heavy metal exposure
   1. Gold
   2. Cadmium
   3. Mercury
   4. Lead
   5. Copper
F. Collagen vascular disease or vasculitis
G. Family history of proteinuria or pyelonephritis
H. HTN
I. Renal disease
J. CHF or endocarditis
K. Diabetes
L. Lupus
M. Infections
   1. HIV
   2. Syphilis
   3. Hepatitis B and C
   4. Group A beta-hemolytic streptococcus
   5. Viral infection (e.g., mononucleosis)
   6. Malaria
N. Malignancy
   1. Lymphoma
   2. Hodgkin's disease
   3. Breast tumor
   4. Lung tumor
   5. Colon tumor
O. Heroin use
P. PIH
Q. Radiocontrast media

Common Complaints

A. Asymptomatic
B. Increased weight
C. Decreased urine output

Other Signs and Symptoms

A. Edema: Periorbital, presacral, genital, or ankle
B. Nephrotic syndrome: Hypercholesterolemia and hypertriglyceridemia
C. Protein malnutrition: Anorexia and vomiting
D. "Frothy" urine

Subjective Data

A. Review the onset, course, and duration of presenting complaints.
B. Question the patient concerning urinary output, thirst or fluid intake, edema, increase in weight. Establish usual weight history.
C. If a woman, establish the first day of the patient's last period. Is she pregnant? If so, what is the fetus's gestational age? Is there edema, HTN, headache, visual changes (scotoma), hyperreflexia, and/or right upper quadrant pain?
D. Review the patient's past medical history for renal disease, diabetes, CHF, systemic disorders such as lupus, and substance abuse.
E. Does the patient have signs or symptoms of a UTI or pyelonephritis?
F. Review the patient's recent history for exertion, emotional stress, surgical trauma, fever, and any acute illness.
G. When was the patient's last evaluation for cholesterol? Is he or she on any special diet?
H. Review medication list, including prescribed and OTC medications and herbal products.
I. Review the patient's occupational exposure, smoking history, and risk factors for infectious diseases.

Physical Examination

The patient's physical examination may have few abnormalities unless there are features of multisystem disease.

A. Check temperature (if indicated), blood pressure, pulse, respirations, and weight.
B. Inspect
   1. Inspect overall general appearance for edema (pedal, hand, facial, or periorbital edema), butterfly rash [lupus], or ascites.
   2. Evaluate for protein wasting.
   3. Evaluate for jugular vein distension.
   4. Funduscopic exam: Evaluate for retinopathy.
   5. Inspect for pharyngitis.
C. Auscultate: Auscultate the heart and lungs.
D. Palpate
   1. Examine the abdomen; evaluate bladder distension, suprapubic tenderness, masses, or ascites; abdominal tenderness.
   2. Palpate for CVA tenderness.

3. Check deep tendon reflexes, especially in pregnant women.

Diagnostic Tests

A. Urine dipstick is a good screening tool in the outpatient setting.
B. Single void "spot" urine testing
   1. The first urine specimen of the morning is optimal and is guideline recommended. Evaluation of the first morning specimen excludes any postural effect on the protein component.
   2. The gold standard for measurement of protein excretion is a 24-hour urine collection but is now being replaced by the easier to obtain and less complicated spot test. The 24-hour urine is considered impractical for generalized testing.
C. PCR test or ACR test on a first morning or a random spot specimen. The PCR or ACR is useful in following trends in the patient's proteinuria.
D. CBC and serum electrolytes
E. Serum creatinine (if renal disease is suspected)
F. Lipid profile
G. BUN: Serves as an index of renal excretory capacity. Urea is the nitrogenous end product of protein metabolism.
H. Urinalysis, urine culture, and sensitivity (if indicated)
I. Ultrasound of the full urinary tract
J. Screen for diabetes and other testing related to physical findings.
K. Renal biopsy is required to establish the diagnosis in most cases.

Differential Diagnoses

A. See Predisposing Factors.

Plan

A. Current guidelines for screening for evaluation of albuminuria/proteinuria vary by country, but recommendations include at-risk individuals with diabetes, HTN, obesity, smokers, indigenous populations, family history of CKD, age older than 50 years, structural renal tract disease, renal calculi, prostatic hypertrophy, vascular disease, and autoimmune disease.
B. Management for nephrotic syndrome includes diet with sodium and protein restriction, loop and distal-acting diuretics, control of cholesterol (low-saturated-fat, low-cholesterol diet), lipid-lowering agents, pneumococcal and influenza vaccines to prevent infections, and use of steroids and immunosuppressive agents as necessary.
C. Patients with hematuria and proteinuria need a 24-hour urine collection for protein and creatinine clearance.
D. Patient teaching
   1. Encourage low-fat/low-cholesterol diet if hyperlipidemia is present.
   2. Encourage sodium- and protein-restricted diet for nephrotic syndrome.
E. Pharmaceutical therapy: There is no specific drug therapy for excess protein. Use drug therapy appropriate to the underlying medical disease causing proteinuria. In patients with CKD, the administration of ACE inhibitors and/or ARBs is aimed at reducing the degree of proteinuria.

Follow-Up

A. If proteinuria is found on a dipstick and the first morning test results are trace or negative for protein, repeat a first morning test in 1 year.
B. There is no consensus on how often to screen for proteinuria. Guidelines include annual screening, every 5 years for patients older than 50 years or smokers, and every 3 years for patients who have HTN, obesity, or a family history of kidney disease. Monitoring should always include blood pressure, quantitative testing by PCR or ACR, and a serum creatinine.
C. Assess for vasculitic skin changes, rashes, retinopathy, lymphadenopathy, signs of heart failure, abdominal masses, organomegaly, guaiac stools, prostatic enlargement, and joint inflammation.

Consultation/Referral

A. Consider patient referral if kidney damage is progressing from medical disease (systemic lupus erythematosus, HTN, diabetes).
B. Refer the patient as necessary; HTN is a poor prognostic sign for significant renal impairment.
C. Consultation for diagnostic tests to be considered: Kidney, ureter, and bladder (KUB); IVP; renal ultrasonography; renal biopsy
D. Referral to a nephrologist should be considered if a definitive diagnosis is required or a renal biopsy is considered.

Individual Considerations

A. Pregnancy
   1. Protein excretion is considered abnormal in pregnancy when it exceeds 300 mg/24 hr or greater than 0.2 g of protein per gram of creatinine in a random urine specimen.
   2. The gestational age at which proteinuria is first documented is important in establishing the likelihood of PIH versus other renal disease. Proteinuria prior to or early in pregnancy suggests preexisting renal disease.
   3. Monitor urine protein and BP at each prenatal visit and refer the patient if urinary protein remains elevated.

4. Monitor for intrauterine growth restriction (IUGR).
5. Proteinuria (or HTN) that persists longer than 3 months after delivery should be followed closely.

B. Geriatrics: Renal function deteriorates in the elderly who may also have coexisting medical conditions (HTN, diabetes) that may cause nephropathy.

Pyelonephritis

Definition

A. Pyelonephritis is an acute infection and inflammatory disease of the upper urinary tract (renal pelvis, tubules, and interstitial tissue) of one or both kidneys. Acute pyelonephritis is an ascending UTI that has progressed from the lower urinary tract.
B. Fever has been strongly correlated with the diagnosis of acute pyelonephritis; therefore, patients with clinical symptoms of pyelonephritis in the absence of fever should be evaluated for alternative diagnoses.
C. Acute pyelonephritis characteristically causes some scarring to the kidney and may lead to significant damage, kidney failure, abscess formation, and sepsis. Antibiotic therapy is essential to prevent the progression of pyelonephritis.

Incidence

A. 30% of the female population has at least one UTI in their lifetime. Males demonstrate a gradual increase at age 35 and peak at 85 years old.
B. The incidence of pyelonephritis in pregnancy is 2%. Most cases develop as a consequence of undiagnosed or inadequately treated lower UTI.
C. Upper tract infections are less common and more serious than lower tract infections. After puberty, the prevalence of UTIs increases slightly in females but remains low in males.
D. After age 65, UTIs are more common, with an equal incidence in both sexes.
E. Race is not a predisposing factor.

Pathogenesis

A. Pyelonephritis is due to ascending infection from the bladder usually caused by *E. coli* (75% to 90%) and other gram-negative bacteria including *Proteus mirabilis* (5%), *Klebsiella pneumoniae* (5%), *Enterobacter* (3%), and Group B *Streptococcus* (GBS: 1%). Gram-positive causative agents are less common; 10% to 15% of cases are due to *Staphylococcus saprophyticus.*
B. Bacteria can also reach the kidneys through the bloodstream from IV drug abuse and endocarditis.
C. In women, the short urethra in close proximity to the perirectal area makes colonization possible. In pregnancy, the increased glycosuria, increase in urinary amino acids, urinary stasis, and the presence of vesicoureteral reflux facilitate bacterial growth.
D. In men, BPH causing bladder obstruction is a common pathology.
E. Indwelling catheters increase ascending infections and pyelonephritis.

Predisposing Factors

A. Previous UTI, cystitis, and pyelonephritis
B. Sickle cell disease
C. Diabetes
D. Urinary catheterization
E. Obstruction: Calculi, tumors, and urethral strictures
F. Neurogenic bladder disease: Strokes, MS, and spinal cord injuries
G. Urinary reflux
H. HIV
I. Trauma
J. Chronic constipation
K. Incomplete bladder emptying related to medications (e.g., anticholinergics)
L. Gender
   1. Females
      a. Increased sexual activity, failure to void after intercourse, diaphragms, and spermicides
      b. Pregnancy
      c. Atrophic vaginal mucosa predisposes to the colonization of pathogens and UTIs.
   2. Males
      a. Homosexuality
      b. Uncircumcised penis
      c. Sexual partner with colonization
      d. Obstruction: Prostatic hypertrophy
      e. Age 50 years or older
      f. Acute or chronic bacterial prostatitis

Common Complaints

A. Shaking, chills, and fever
B. Flank pain or tenderness
C. Urinary frequency or urgency
D. CVA tenderness
E. Guarding
F. Urinary frequency, nocturia, hematuria, and dysuria (not always present in upper tract infections)
G. Blood in urine secondary to hemorrhagic cystitis (unusual in males with pyelonephritis)

Other Signs and Symptoms

A. Adults (particularly the elderly): May be asymptomatic with cystitis
B. Abdominal pain and suprapubic heaviness
C. Pregnancy: Uterine contractions

D. SOB
E. Anorexia
F. Elderly
   1. Mental status change
   2. Generalized deterioration

Subjective Data

A. Review the onset, course, and duration of symptoms.
B. Are there any problems with voiding such as frequency, urgency, and dysuria?
C. Review the patient's history of fever and any treatment.
D. Are there any other symptoms, odor, and nausea?
E. Have the patient point to the area of the backache. Is it unilateral or bilateral? What makes the backache better?
F. In women, rule out pregnancy; review first day of last menses.
G. Rule out sickle cell disease, diabetes, and MS.
H. Review the patient's previous history of GU tract problems, stones, UTIs, previous pyelonephritis, any previous testing, and any previous anomalies.
I. Review the strength and character of the urinary stream, especially in older men. Ask if the man has ever been diagnosed with BPH.
J. Review the patient's history for active herpes lesion. Does urine flow hurt when urine stream begins? Or is the pain noted when urine passes over the lesion?
K. Review drug allergies.
L. Review all medications including OTC and herbal products. Review medications for a recent history of an incomplete course of antibiotics and current use of anticholinergics.

Physical Examination

A. Check temperature, pulse, and blood pressure; note orthostatic hypotension. Tachycardia may or may not be present, depending on associated fever, dehydration, and sepsis.
B. Inspect
   1. Note general appearance for respiratory distress and dehydration.
   2. Inspect the male external genitalia for redness, edema, lesions, and discharge.
   3. Inspect the female genitalia for discharge, lesions, and fissures; inspect cervix for cervicitis.
C. Palpate
   1. Palpate the back; check CVA tenderness (usually unilateral over the involved kidney).
   2. Palpate the abdomen for suprapubic tenderness, rebound masses, or pain.
   3. Perform a pelvic examination to rule out other infections and PID (tenderness of the cervix, uterus, and adnexal should be absent).
D. Auscultate: Auscultate the lungs and heart.
E. Pregnancy
   1. Check fetal heart rate; fetal tachycardia may be present with fever.
   2. Palpate for uterine tenderness and contractions.
   3. Pelvic examination for cervical dilation, if indicated for increased risk of preterm labor.
F. Males: Complete palpation of external genitalia, prostate, and rectal exam.

Diagnostic Tests

A. **Urine culture and sensitivity should always be performed before initial empiric treatment with antibiotics.**
B. **Urinalysis for evaluation of pyuria. Pyuria is present in almost all women with acute cystitis and pyelonephritis; its absence strongly suggests an alternative diagnosis.**
   1. Leukocyte esterase on dipstick detects pyuria or WBCs.
   2. Significant pyuria is greater than two to five leukocytes per HPF.
   3. Urine may need to be obtained from straight in-and-out catheterization if the patient is incontinent or has dementia.
C. CBC with differential or WBC, especially with systemic symptoms
D. Blood culture, if indicated
E. Arterial blood gases (ABGs), if indicated
F. Consider sedimentation rate, especially with severe illness and in the elderly.
G. Culture for gonorrhea and chlamydia, if symptoms are associated with STI.
H. Wet prep, if symptoms are associated with STI
I. Imaging studies are not routinely required for the diagnosis of acute pyelonephritis but can be helpful.
   1. CT scan to identify altered parenchymal perfusion, hemorrhage, nonrenal disease, inflammatory masses, and obstruction. CT with contrast medium is considered the imaging modality of choice for nonpregnant women.
   2. MRI to rule out masses or obstruction
   3. Renal ultrasonography with Doppler study
   4. Scintigraphy to detect focal renal abnormalities
   5. Voiding cystourethrogram
   6. IVP, if indicated

Differential Diagnoses

A. Pyelonephritis
B. Appendicitis/acute abdomen
C. Cholecystitis
D. Pancreatitis
E. Diverticulitis
F. Pneumonia
G. Prostatitis
H. Epididymitis
I. PID
J. Nephrolithiasis

Plan

A. General interventions
   1. Optimal therapy for acute uncomplicated nephritis depends on the severity of the illness at presentation.
   2. Many severe infections (increased WBC, dehydration or vomiting, high fever) may need hospital admission for IV therapy. Risk factors include older adult, coexisting illness, pregnancy, and uncontrolled vomiting.

B. Give instruction on early recognition of UTIs. See the Section III Patient Teaching Guide for this chapter, "Urinary Tract Infection (UTI)."

C. Dietary management
   1. Increase fluids; have the patient drink at least one large glass of water every hour while awake.
   2. Encourage the patient to drink cranberry juice to help fight and prevent UTIs. If the taste is objectionable, he or she may mix cranberry juice 1:1 with another juice such as grape juice.
   3. There are no dietary restrictions with pyelonephritis.

D. Pharmaceutical therapy
   1. Acetaminophen (Tylenol) for fever
   2. Urinary analgesic as needed to relieve dysuria. Dysuria is usually diminished fairly quickly after the start of antibiotics.
   3. Antiemetics as needed; however, if the patient is not able to tolerate oral fluids, he or she should be hospitalized.
   4. Antibiotics: Empiric antibiotic selection should be guided by local antibiotics resistance patterns, allergies, and culture results. Patients with delayed response to therapy should also receive a longer course of antibiotics of 14 to 21 days.
      a. Adults
         i. First-line therapy: Ciprofloxacin (Cipro) 500 mg twice daily for 7 days, *or* extended release Cipro XR 1,000 mg once a day for 7 days
         ii. First-line therapy: Levofloxacin (Levaquin) 750 mg once daily for 5 to 7 days
         iii. Second-line therapy: Trimethoprim and sulfamethoxazole (TMP-SMX) (Sep-tra DS, Bactrim DS) 160 mg and 800 mg, respectively, one tablet twice daily for 7 to 10 days. Because of the high rate of resistance of *E. coli*, the empirical use of TMP-SMX should be avoided in patients who require hospitalization.
         iv. Alternative therapy: Amoxicillin-clavulanate (Augmentin) 500 mg/125 mg orally twice a day for 14 days OR Augmentin 250 mg/125 mg orally three times a day for 3 to 7 days.
      b. **Antibiotics that should not be utilized for pyelonephritis**
         i. **Nitrofurantoin (Macrodantin) and fosfomycin (Monurol) should not be used to treat pyelonephritis in adults. It is excreted in the urine but does not achieve therapeutic serum levels.**
         ii. **Ampicillin or amoxicillin should not be used for enterococcal infections in hospitalized and other institutionalized patients.**
         iii. **Fluoroquinolones are not used in pregnancy due to the risk of auditory and vestibular toxicity in the fetus.**
         iv. **Aminoglycosides are contraindicated in pregnancy due to the risk of permanent ototoxicity to the fetus.**

Follow-Up

A. Follow up with the patient in 24 to 48 hours depending on the evaluation of the initial severity of symptoms.
   1. Patients with persistent fever or clinical symptoms after 48 to 72 hours of appropriate antibiotic therapy should undergo initiation of another class of antibiotics and consider radiological evaluation.
   2. If the patient feels that he or she is not progressing well or is getting worse, evaluate the patient emergently and consider hospital admission and IV antibiotics.

B. Urine cultures are not needed for patients with acute cystitis or pyelonephritis if symptoms resolved on antibiotics. However, repeat cultures are in order for patients with recurrent symptoms or any complicated course of illness.

C. Women with recurrence of pyelonephritis need further urologic investigation.

Consultation/Referral

A. Consult or refer the patient to a physician if he or she requires IVP, cystoscopy, or renal biopsy.

B. Males with persistent bladder infections need a urologic consultation.

C. Pyelonephritis in men suggests structural problems and needs hospitalization and further evaluation (IVP).

D. Consult an infectious disease specialist for patients with unusual or resistant pathogens.

E. For pregnancy, consultation with an obstetrician is required.

Individual Considerations

A. Pregnancy
   1. Pyelonephritis is the most common urinary tract complication in pregnancy.
   2. Untreated asymptomatic bacteriuria (ASB) is a risk factor for acute cystitis and pyelonephritis in pregnancy.

3. Based on the higher risk of complications in pregnancy, pyelonephritis has traditionally been treated with hospitalization and intravenous antibiotics until the woman is afebrile for 48 hours and symptoms improve.
4. Once the pregnant patient is discharged from the hospital, oral antibiotics should continue for 10 to 14 days of treatment.
5. A urine culture should be obtained 1 to 2 weeks after completion of therapy and monthly thereafter to monitor for recurrent infection.
6. Aminoglycosides should be avoided due to the potential risk of ototoxicity following prolonged fetal exposure.
7. Fluoroquinolones are contraindicated during pregnancy due to the risk of auditory and vestibular toxicity in the fetus.

B. Males
1. Consider ordering renal function tests (BUN and creatinine).
2. Men older than 50 years of age: Consider urologic consultation and IVP.

C. Geriatrics
1. Patients may need hospitalization for IV antibiotics and hydration.
2. Bladder or kidney infections may be common in patients with long-term urinary catheters and can lead to septicemia if untreated or unrecognized.
3. Fluoroquinolone use in the elderly has the potential to cause neuropsychiatric symptoms, including seizures to worsening dementia.

Renal Calculi, or Kidney Stones (Nephrolithiasis)

Definition

A. Renal calculi, or kidney stones, are due to the formation of crystals in the urinary system from the kidneys to the bladder. Nephrolithiasis refers to renal stone disease; urolithiasis refers to the presence of stones in the urinary system. The majority of stones (80%) consist of calcium usually as calcium oxalate, but they can contain uric acid, struvite (magnesium, ammonium, and phosphate), oxalic acid, phosphate salts, or the amino acid cystine. Spontaneous passage of a stone is related to the stone size and location. Approximately one-half of symptomatic patients require intervention for stone removal. An untreated staghorn (branch-shaped) with persistent renal obstruction can destroy renal tissue with potential for life-threatening sepsis.

Incidence

A. Renal calculi are very common, with a higher incidence noted in males. At least 12% of men and 7% of women have at least one symptomatic stone by age 70. Initial cases typically occur between ages 30 and 40, and the prevalence increases with age. Idiopathic nephrolithiasis is common in males, whereas primary hyperparathyroidism is more common in females.

B. Most kidney stones pass spontaneously; however, 10% to 30% do not pass and can cause continuing pain, infection, or obstruction.

C. Stones due to infection (struvite) are more common in women.

D. The incidence of stones in pregnancy is one in every 1,500 to 3,000 pregnancies.

E. The recurrence rate for calculi is 50% within 5 years.

Pathogenesis

A. The formation of uric acid stones requires continued and excessive oversaturation of urine with stone-forming constituents, uric acid, calcium, and oxalate. Dehydration, hyperuricosuria, and significantly acidic urine contribute to uric acid supersaturation and stone formation. Struvite stones form only when the urinary tract is infected with urea-splitting organisms such as *Proteus* species.

B. Hydroureteronephrosis is the most significant renal alteration in pregnancy. Dilatation is greater on the right side than the left because of pressure due to physiological engorgement of the right ovarian vein and dextrorotation of the uterus.

Predisposing Factors

A. Male
B. Dehydration (poor intake and immobility)
C. Chronic obstruction with stasis of urine
D. Hypercalcemia caused by hyperparathyroidism; renal tubular acidosis; multiple myeloma; or excessive intake of vitamin D, milk, and alkali
E. Diet high in purines and abnormal purine metabolism (gout)
F. Pregnancy (1 per 1,500)
G. Chronic infections
H. Foreign bodies
I. Excessive oxalate absorption in inflammatory bowel disease, bowel resection, or ileostomy
J. Previous stone formation
K. Family history of nephrolithiasis
L. Medications
1. Vitamins A, C, and D
2. Loop diuretics
3. Acetazolamide
4. Ammonium chloride
5. Calcium-containing medications, including alkali and antacids
6. Indinavir

7. Sulfadiazine
8. Atazanavir
9. Guaifenesin
10. Sulfa drugs
11. Topiramate
12. Acyclovir

M. Obesity
N. Gastric bypass/bariatric surgical procedures
O. Diabetes

Common Complaints

A. Severe flank and groin pain
B. Blood in urine
C. Asymptomatic (dependent on the size of the stone)

Other Signs and Symptoms

A. Unilateral flank pain that radiates to the groin.
B. Sudden onset of colicky pain
C. Hematuria
D. Nausea and vomiting

The timing and appearance of hematuria are both important. Hematuria seen at the beginning of the urine stream may indicate bleeding in the urethra. Terminal hematuria, or blood in the end of the urine stream, denotes bladder neck or the prostate as the source. Lastly, blood throughout the entire urination suggests a lesion.

E. Restlessness
F. Symptoms common with cystitis or inflammatory lesions of the lower tract are usually absent: Frequency, dysuria, urgency, and suprapubic pain.

Subjective Data

A. Review the onset, duration, and course of symptoms.
B. Review other signs and symptoms of UTI or pyelonephritis: Frequency, dysuria, and fever.
C. Have the patient describe pain (colicky); note intensity (use a 0- to 10-point scale, 10 being the worst pain) and the characteristics of pain (constant, intermittent).
D. Has the patient ever had a stone before? How was it treated? What tests were performed? Has the patient ever seen a urologist?
E. Review dietary intake of high animal protein in the diet, milk, and other calcium-containing products for excessive intake.
F. Review the patient's medication history including excessive vitamin C or D supplements, antacids that contain calcium, and other medications noted in the predisposing factors.
G. Ask the patient to describe any hematuria or blood clots passed.
H. Ask about recent trauma to the back or abdomen.
I. Is there a family history of stone formation?
J. Is the patient pregnant?

Physical Examination

A. Check temperature, blood pressure, and pulse (may have tachycardia).
B. Inspect
   1. Inspect general appearance for discomfort before and during exam. Patients with renal colic are extremely restless and exhibit active movement on presentation.
   2. During the examination, evaluate voluntary guarding of the abdominal musculature.
   3. Inspect external genitalia (male or female) for lesions, discharge, inflammation, and ulcerations.
   4. Assess for peripheral edema.
C. Auscultate
   1. Auscultate the abdomen, noting bruits if present.
   2. Auscultate bowel sounds.
D. Palpate
   1. "Milk" the urethra for discharge.
   2. Palpate the abdomen for masses and tenderness, organomegaly, and suprapubic tenderness.
   3. Palpate the groin; check lymph nodes.
   4. Palpate the back and abdomen.
   5. Check for the presence of CVA tenderness.
E. Perform pelvic or bimanual exam, if indicated, to rule out PID.

Diagnostic Tests

The diagnosis of nephrolithiasis can be made on the basis of clinical symptoms alone, but diagnostic testing is needed to confirm.

A. Laboratory tests
   1. Serum BUN
   2. Creatinine
   3. Calcium
   4. Uric acid
   5. Serum electrolytes; consider fasting serum calcium and phosphorus and parathyroid hormone
   6. Pregnancy test (if indicated) to rule out an ectopic pregnancy
B. Stone for analysis
C. Urinalysis
   1. Urine dipstick for a gross screen
   2. pH determination (pH > 7.5 is compatible with infection lithiasis, and a pH of < 5.5 favors uric acid lithiasis.)
   3. Red cell casts strongly suggest glomerulonephritis.
   4. Evaluate urine sediment for crystalluria.
D. Urine culture, if indicated
E. 24-hour urine for creatinine, calcium, uric acid, oxalate, pH, and sodium measurement
   1. Patient should be on his or her usual diet before taking 24-hour specimen.
   2. Collection should be 1 to 2 months after any interventions, including shock-wave lithotripsy, uretoscopy, or percutaneous stone removal.

F. **Noncontrast helical CT scan is the imaging standard to assess the urinary tract in acute renal colic.**
G. Renal ultrasound is the procedure of choice for pregnancy.
H. KUB x-ray is often ordered with the pelvic CT or ultrasound.
I. IVP
J. Nuclear renal scan

Differential Diagnoses

A. Kidney stone(s): Associated with colicky flank pain radiating to the groin. Significant flank pain of renal colic is usually secondary to renal calculi but may occasionally be associated with passage of clots.
B. UTI: Passage of large, bulky blood clots implicates the bladder as the source, whereas long, shoestring-shaped specks or thin, stringy clots suggest an upper urinary tract or ureteral origin.
C. Acute abdomen/appendicitis
D. Cholecystitis
E. Pyelonephritis: Associated with dull flank pain with fever and chills. In evaluating urine sediment, the presence of white cells and bacteria favors a diagnosis of pyelonephritis or interstitial nephritis.
F. PID
G. Inflammatory bowel disease
H. Urinary tract obstruction
I. Constipation
J. Ectopic pregnancy

Plan

A. General interventions
   1. Increase fluids to allow passage of stone. Strain all urine to recover stone for analysis.
   2. Reduce possibility of recurrence with dietary modifications.
   3. Patient is usually referred for imaging after evaluation of creatinine.
   4. Patients can be managed on an outpatient basis with close follow-up if stones are small (< 6 mm).
B. Dietary management
   1. Force fluids to maintain a daily output of 2 to 3 L of urine. Fluid intake that increases urinary production of at least 2 L of urine per day increases the flow rate and lowers the urine solute concentration.
   2. Dietary consultation may be needed secondary to stone analysis.
C. Pharmaceutical therapy
   1. Pain medication (narcotic and nonnarcotic) is a priority.
      a. NSAIDs should be discontinued 3 days prior to shock-wave lithotripsy to decrease the risk of bleeding.
   2. Antibiotics should be given for infection.
   3. Give antiemetics if needed.
   4. Other medical/pharmaceutical management depends on the etiology of the stone.
D. Surgical options are dependent on stone size and location.
   1. Percutaneous nephrolithotomy is the first treatment option for most patients and is considered the treatment of choice for patients with staghorn calculi.
   2. Extracorporeal shock-wave lithotripsy is the least invasive of the surgical methods.
   3. Percutaneous nephrostomy (should be the last procedure for most patients)
   4. Open nephrostomy

Follow-Up

A. Reevaluate the patient in 24 hours by phone or in the clinic.
B. Evaluate sooner if pain increases, due to potential to progress to complete obstruction.
C. Recurrent stone formation is a manifestation of a systemic disease; evaluate for the management of the metabolic abnormality.

Consultation/Referral

A. Patients with severe pain, nausea, and vomiting need hospitalization for IV hydration and pain control. Consult with a physician.
B. Patients with severe symptoms and persistent obstruction beyond 3 to 4 days should be referred for urologic evaluation.
C. Refer for surgical interventions: Lithotripsy, urethroscope interventions, extracorporeal shockwave lithotripsy, and percutaneous ultrasonic lithotripsy may be indicated. Treatment varies based on the location and size of the stone. Laparoscopy may be indicated for the removal of a large or severely impacted ureteral calculi.

Individual Considerations

A. Pregnancy
   1. Urolithiasis is the most common cause of nonobstetrical abdominal pain that requires hospitalization in pregnancy.
   2. 80% to 90% are diagnosed in the first trimester.
   3. Renal ultrasound is the first-line screening test for pregnant patients. A transvaginal ultrasound may also be performed.
   4. Low-dose CT is reserved for complex cases in the second and third trimesters.
   5. Conservative treatment is used: Bed rest, hydration, and analgesia.
   6. Invasive measures include stent placement, ureteroscopy, and percutaneous nephrostomy.

7. Upon presentation, rule out
   a. Ectopic pregnancy
   b. Abruptio placenta
   c. Preterm labor

Testicular Torsion

Definition

A. Testicular torsion is twisting of the testicle around the vas deferens, with compromise in the blood supply and possible necrosis to the testicles. Testicular torsion is a urologic emergency and is the most frequent cause of testicle loss in the adolescent male population. Approximately 40% of all cases of acute scrotal pain and swelling are diagnosed with testicular torsion. There is often a history of recurrent episodes of testicular pain before torsion.
B. Testicular torsion is most commonly misdiagnosed as epididymitis.
   1. Epididymitis usually presents with gradual onset of pain that is localized posterior to the testis that gradually radiates to the lower abdomen.
   2. These symptoms are rare with torsion.

Incidence

A. Incidence in males younger than 25 years old is approximately 1 in 4,000. Although torsion can occur at any age, the largest number of cases occur during adolescence.
B. The bell clapper congenital anomaly is present in approximately 12% of males, and 40% have the abnormality in the contralateral testicle.

Pathogenesis

A. Testicular torsion and torsion of the spermatic cord are due to abnormal fixation of the testicle to the scrotum, allowing free rotation. The bell clapper deformity allows the testicle to twist spontaneously on the spermatic cord. Venous occlusion and engorgement cause arterial ischemia and infarction of the testicle.

Predisposing Factors

A. Age: More common in adolescence
B. Trauma to testicle
C. Spontaneous occurrence
D. Congenital bell clapper anomaly
E. Exercise
F. Undescended testicle
G. Active cremasteric reflex

Common Complaints

A. Sudden onset of severe unilateral scrotal pain (less than 24 hours)
B. Swelling of scrotal sac
C. High position of the testicle
D. Abnormal cremasteric reflex

Other Signs and Symptoms

A. Sudden onset of testicular pain, may radiate to groin
B. Possible edema
C. Abdominal pain (20% to 30%)
D. Nausea and vomiting (50% of cases)
E. Fever (16%)
F. Urinary frequency (4%)

Subjective Data

A. Review the onset, duration, and course of symptoms.
B. Review for a history of prior episodes of intermittent testicular pain that resolved spontaneously.
C. Review abdominal symptoms such as pain, nausea and vomiting, and fever.
D. Review urethral discharge (possible STI) and dysuria.
E. Review the patient's history for trauma to the scrotum or testicle.

Physical Examination

A. Check temperature, blood pressure, pulse, and respirations.
B. Inspect
   1. Observe the patient generally for pain before and during examination.
   2. Visualize the scrotal sac for edema, symmetry, lesions, discharge, and color (especially for blue dot superior to the affected testicle). Testis is located high in the scrotum as a result of shortening of the cord by twisting.
   3. Check the inguinal and femoral areas for bulges and hernias.
C. Auscultate
   1. Auscultate all four quadrants of the abdomen; note bowel sounds.
   2. Assess the scrotum for bowel noise.
D. Palpate
   1. Palpate the abdomen for masses, rebound, and tenderness or guarding.
   2. Palpate the groin; check the lymph nodes.
   3. Examine for an inguinal hernia.
   4. Genital exam
      a. Check warmth, tenderness, swelling, and any nodularity; if a mass is present, check if it is solid or cystic. The testes should be sensitive to gentle compression but not tender. They should feel smooth, rubbery, and free of nodules.
      b. Elicit a cremasteric reflex by stroking the inner thigh with a blunt object (reflex hammer or ink pen). The testicle and scrotum should rise on the stroked side. **Cremasteric reflex is usually absent in testicular torsion.**
      c. Elevate the scrotum; there is usually no relief in pain with torsion. Elevation of the scrotum may improve the pain of epididymitis (Prehn's sign).

Diagnostic Tests

A. Urinalysis: Normal in 90% of cases of testicular torsion
B. Doppler ultrasonography for blood flow and scrotal ultrasonography

Differential Diagnoses

A. **Testicular torsion: Firm, tender mass of acute onset in an afebrile young man with a history of prior episodes must be considered to represent torsion until proven otherwise.**
B. Epididymitis
C. Orchitis
D. Hydrocele
E. Testicular tumor: Usually a hard, enlarged, painless testicle
F. Acute appendicitis
G. Scrotal/testicular trauma
H. Varicocele

Plan

A. **Testicular torsion is a urologic emergency requiring surgery.**
B. Immediately refer the patient to a urologist.
C. Symptoms lasting *more than 6 hours* can indicate testicular necrosis.
D. The opposite testicle is usually stabilized during the same surgery.

Pharmaceutical Therapy

None

Follow-Up

A. Patient should follow up with the urologist as directed.

Consultation/Referral

A. All patients with suspected testicular torsion need to be immediately evaluated by a physician and referred to a urologist.

Individual Considerations

A. Geriatrics: In older males, rule out epididymitis, especially with new sexual partners or with symptoms of dysuria and urethral discharge.

Urinary Incontinence

Definition

A. Urinary incontinence (UI) is the involuntary loss of urine severe enough to have unpleasant social or hygienic consequences. UI is diagnosed primarily on history; inquire about UI at every interview. UI is a symptom of an underlying disease process in most cases; some cases are reversible with appropriate treatment.
B. Incontinence is not considered a part of normal aging. Morbidity related to incontinence includes UTIs, indwelling catheters, falls/fractures, sleep interruption, social withdrawal, and depression.
C. Successful toileting depends on ready access to facilities, motivation to remain dry, mobility and manual dexterity, and the cognitive ability to recognize/react to the urge to void.
D. UI can be divided into the following categories: Functional, urge, overflow, stress, and mixed. Each category has a unique etiology, pathophysiology, symptoms, and management.

Incidence

A. The exact incidence of UI is unknown. The prevalence of incontinence increases with age.
B. The incidence of women identified with the definition of any leakage at least once in the past year ranges from 25% to 51%. The incidence is reported to be 10% when identified with weekly urinary leakage. The 2014 American College of Physicians guideline notes the following incidence of UI in women:
   1. In young women (aged 14 to 21 years), incidence is approximately 25%.
   2. Incidence of middle-age and postmenopausal women (aged 40 to 60 years) is approximately 44% to 57%.
   3. Elderly (≥ 75 years of age) have approximately a 75% incidence of UI.
C. The prevalence of UI in men is approximately half that of women. The incidence of UI is affected by treatment of prostate disease. Men with incontinence have a higher risk of institutionalization compared to men without UI.
D. **The elderly are more frequently affected with UI; 6% to 10% of admissions to long-term care facilities are related to incontinence.**

Pathogenesis

UI can be caused by pathologic, anatomic, or physiologic factors and differs by type of incontinence.

A. Functional incontinence: Loss of urine due to the inability to get to the bathroom, either due to problems of mobility or cognition.
B. Urge incontinence/OAB: Inability to delay voiding after the sensation of fullness is perceived. Common causes are detrusor hyperactivity or hyperreflexia associated with disorders of the lower urinary tract, tumors, stones, uterine prolapse, cystitis, urethritis, or impaired bladder contractility. Central nervous system (CNS) disorders such as stroke, dementia, parkinsonism, or spinal cord injury also can be causative factors.
C. Overflow incontinence: Loss of urine associated with an overdistension of the bladder. Common causes are anatomic obstruction by an enlarged prostate, a prolapsed cystocele, a contractile bladder due to diabetes, spinal cord injury, MS, or suprasacral cord lesions.
D. Stress incontinence: Involuntary loss of urine during coughing, sneezing, laughing, bending

over, or other physical activity that increases intra-abdominal pressure. Prostate surgery is the most common cause of stress incontinence in men.

Predisposing Factors

A. Age for both males and females
B. Female: 85% of cases are in women.
C. Increased parity
D. Previous GU surgeries (e.g., prostate surgery and hysterectomy)
E. Restricted mobility
F. Menopause
G. Infections
H. Chronic illnesses (e.g., diabetes)
I. Fecal impactions
J. Excessive urinary output
K. Delirium
L. Dementia
M. Neurologic disorders (e.g., stroke, spinal cord injury)
N. Variety of medications (e.g., antihypertensive medicines, diuretics, sedatives)
O. Pelvic trauma (e.g., episiotomy, forceps delivery)
P. Obesity
Q. Sleep apnea
R. Depression
S. High-impact exercise

Common Complaints

A. Urgency: Sudden and compelling desire to pass urine
B. Urge incontinence: Involuntary leakage accompanied by urgency with the following precipitating factors.
   1. Hearing running water
   2. Placing hands in water
   3. Trying to unlock the door when returning home
   4. Exposure to a cold environment
C. Stress incontinence: Involuntary leakage with the following precipitating factors.
   1. Exertion
   2. Sneezing/coughing
   3. May experience leakage with little or no activity
D. OAB: Symptoms may occur with or without urge incontinence.
   1. Urgency
   2. Frequency
   3. Nocturia

Other Signs and Symptoms

A. Mixed incontinence: Urge and stress leakage
B. Experiencing leakage with little or no activity
C. Continuous leakage (i.e., dribbling)
D. Daytime frequency
E. Nocturia: Up one or more times a night to void
F. Slow urine stream, intermittent stream, or hesitancy
G. Need to strain to start, maintain, or improve voiding.
H. Incomplete emptying sensation

Subjective Data

A. Question the patient regarding onset, duration, and severity of the incontinence.
   1. Do you ever leak urine/water when you don't want to?
   2. Do you ever leak urine when you cough, laugh, or exercise?
   3. Do you ever leak urine on the way to the bathroom (urgency)?
   4. Do you ever use pads, tissue, or cloth in your underwear to catch urine?
B. Elicit situations when UI is worse, when it is improved, and what stimuli are associated with increasing UI (high fluid intake, high caffeine intake, agitation).
C. Review whether the female patient is pre- or postmenopausal.
D. Review other LUTS such as nocturia.
E. Review the patient's history of bowel function (i.e., fecal incontinence). If constipation is a problem, abdominal pressure from a large retained stool can cause symptoms, including retention.
F. Review medications, including OTC drugs and herbals.
   1. Review if the presence of medications, such as ACE inhibitors, can trigger a chronic cough.
   2. Review medications prescribed for UI.
      a. Evaluate their effectiveness
      b. Evaluate if the medications were discontinued due to side effects:
         i. Dry mouth (oxybutynin)
         ii. Constipation
         iii. Dizziness (tropium)
         iv. Blurred vision
         v. Insomnia (oxybutynin)
         vi. Hallucinations (Tolterodine)
G. Preview previous continence therapy and its effectiveness
   1. Pelvic floor muscle training (PFMT), first-line therapy with stress incontinence.
   2. Bladder training, including timed voiding for urge incontinence
   3. PFMT + bladder training for mixed UI
   4. Weight loss and exercise in obese women
   5. Lifestyle changes, including timed urination, dietary changes, and fluid limitation
   6. Abobotulinumtoxin A therapy (BXT)
   7. Percutaneous nerve, magnetic, or electrical stimulation
H. Review the impact of incontinence on quality of life, including work impairment, sexual dysfunction,

activities of daily living, sleep, recreational activity, social interaction, and depression.

I. Assess whether the elderly patient has incontinence despite toileting.

J. Review sexual function.

K. Review history and previous treatment for prostate disease.

L. Review other comorbid medical diagnoses such as neurologic disabilities, narrow-angle glaucoma, and diabetes.
   1. Do not prescribe a muscarinic medication in a patient with narrow-angle glaucoma unless approved by the treating ophthalmologist.
   2. Use caution when prescribing antimuscarinic for OAB with a frail patient.

M. What is the diabetic patient's blood glucose averages (polyuria is increased with uncontrolled diabetes)?

Physical Examination

A. Both sexes
   1. Check temperature (if an infection is suspected), pulse, blood pressure, and respirations.
   2. Inspect for evidence of cardiac overload: Pedal edema.
   3. Auscultate the lungs for evidence of fluid overload: Rales.
   4. Perform neurologic examination to determine the presence of sensation.
   5. Palpate the abdomen for masses, fullness over bladder, and tenderness.
   6. Assess cognitive and functional status, including mobility, transfers, manual dexterity, and ability to toilet in the elderly.
   7. Screen for depression.

B. Females
   1. Inspect perineal skin for irritation, thinning, vaginal atrophy, and vaginal discharge.
   2. Remove the top blade of the speculum and evaluate the vaginal wall support.
   3. Ask the woman to cough to reevaluate the vaginal wall support.
   4. Ask the patient to perform a Kegel to evaluate the pelvic floor muscular.
   5. Palpate
      a. Perform a bimanual pelvic exam for prolapse, masses, or tenderness.
      b. Perform rectal exam for sphincter tone, masses, and fecal impaction.

C. Males
   1. Inspect
      a. Inspect the glans penis for abnormalities in urethral meatus. (Hypospadias may cause postvoid dribbling.)
      b. Uncircumcised men should be evaluated for phimosis and balanitis.
   2. Palpate
      a. Perform rectal exam for sphincter tone, masses, fecal impaction, prostate size, and contour.
      b. Palpate the scrotum to evaluate masses.
      c. Evaluate the presence of an inguinal hernia since straining with a partial urinary obstruction can worsen an inguinal hernia.

Diagnostic Tests

The history, physical examination, and urinalysis are sufficient to guide initial therapy. Other tests include the following.

A. Urine culture and sensitivity if infection is suspected.

B. Urine cytology if hematuria or pelvic pain is present.

C. Cystometry. See the Section II Procedure, "Cystometry."

D. PVR by catheterization or ultrasound. A PVR of less than 50 mL is considered adequate emptying, and greater than 200 mL is considered inadequate, suggesting either detrusor weakness or obstruction. Indications for PVR:
   1. Men with mild to moderate lower urinary symptoms
   2. Men with OAB (urgency)
   3. Persons with spinal cord injury or Parkinson's disease
   4. Persons with prior episodes of urinary retention
   5. Persons with severe constipation

E. A PSA should be considered.

F. Routine urodynamic testing is not recommended.

G. Cystoscopy is not required for incontinence; however, it is indicated for hematuria.

Differential Diagnoses

A. Eight reversible causes of transient incontinence can be remembered by using the mnemonic DIAPPERS.

Delirium
Infection (urinary)
Atrophic urethritis and vaginitis
Pharmaceuticals
Psychologic disorders, especially depression
Excessive urine output
Restricted mobility
Stool impaction

Plan

A. Functional UI: Therapy is directed at the cause of the condition, such as overdiuresis, inability to go to the toilet, or poor access to toilet facilities.

B. Behavioral interventions
   1. A bladder diary (see Table 14.6) may provide information on usual timing and circumstances of UI.
   2. Timed scheduled voiding and/or prompted caregiver-scheduled toileting

TABLE 14.6 **Bladder-Control Diary**

Your Daily Bladder Diary

This diary will help you and your health care team figure out the causes of your bladder-control trouble. The **sample** line shows you how to use the diary. Use this sheet as a master for making copies that you can use as a bladder diary for as many days as you need.

Your name: ______________________

Date: ______________________

Time	Drinks		Trips to the bathroom		Accidental leaks	Did you feel a strong urge to go?	What were you doing at the time?
	What kind?	*How much?*	*How many times?*	*How much urine? (circle one)*	*How much? (circle one)*	*Circle one*	*Sneezing, exercising, having sex, lifting, etc.*
Sample	Coffee	2 cups	✓✓	(○) ○ ○ sm med lg	○ (○) ○ sm med lg	Yes (No)	Running
6–7 a.m.				○ ○ ○	○ ○ ○	Yes No	
7–8 a.m.				○ ○ ○	○ ○ ○	Yes No	
8–9 a.m.				○ ○ ○	○ ○ ○	Yes No	
9–10 a.m.				○ ○ ○	○ ○ ○	Yes No	
10–11 a.m.				○ ○ ○	○ ○ ○	Yes No	
11–12 noon				○ ○ ○	○ ○ ○	Yes No	
12–1 p.m.				○ ○ ○	○ ○ ○	Yes No	
1–2 p.m.				○ ○ ○	○ ○ ○	Yes No	
2–3 p.m.				○ ○ ○	○ ○ ○	Yes No	
3–4 p.m.				○ ○ ○	○ ○ ○	Yes No	
4–5 p.m				○ ○ ○	○ ○ ○	Yes No	
5–6 p.m.				○ ○ ○	○ ○ ○	Yes No	
6–7 p.m.				○ ○ ○	○ ○ ○	Yes No	
7–8 p.m.				○ ○ ○	○ ○ ○	Yes No	
8–9 p.m.				○ ○ ○	○ ○ ○	Yes No	
9–10 p.m.				○ ○ ○	○ ○ ○	Yes No	
10–11 p.m.				○ ○ ○	○ ○ ○	Yes No	
11–12 midnight				○ ○ ○	○ ○ ○	Yes No	
12–1 a.m.				○ ○ ○	○ ○ ○	Yes No	
1–2 a.m.				○ ○ ○	○ ○ ○	Yes No	
2–3 a.m.				○ ○ ○	○ ○ ○	Yes No	
3–4 a.m.				○ ○ ○	○ ○ ○	Yes No	
4–5 a.m.				○ ○ ○	○ ○ ○	Yes No	
5–6 a.m.				○ ○ ○	○ ○ ○	Yes No	

(continued)

TABLE 14.6 Bladder-Control Diary (*continued*)

I used ____ pads today. I used ____ diapers today (write number).

Questions to ask my health care team: ______________________________

Let's Talk About Bladder Control for Women is a public health awareness campaign conducted by the National Kidney and Urologic Diseases Information Clearinghouse (NKUDIC), an information dissemination service of the National Institute of Diabetes and Digestive and Kidney Diseases (NIDDK), National Institutes of Health.

From NKUDIC, NIH. http://kidney.niddk.nih.gov/kudiseases/pubs/bcw_ez/insertB.htm.
Please see Section III Patient Teaching Guide this chapter, "Genitourinary Disorders," for a copy of this table to hand out to patients.

3. Bladder training by systematic ability to delay voiding through the use of urge of inhibition.
4. Stress incontinence: Kegel perineal exercises may improve UI by 30% to 90%. Exercises using graduated vaginal cones or weights induce pelvic muscle tone and strength, reducing UI.
5. Overflow UI: Crede's method is used for expressing the bladder, by applying pressure with the hands placed in the suprapubic area after voiding to assist in emptying.
6. Intermittent catheterization is an option frequently utilized after other measures have failed or overflow UI occurs.
7. Weight loss
8. Dietary changes including elimination of bladder irritants: caffeine, citrus/acidic foods, alcohol, and carbonated drinks
9. Avoid constipation.
10. Reduce excessive fluid intake, with no fluid intake 3 to 4 hours before bedtime if nocturia is a problem.

C. Patient education: See the Section III Patient Teaching Guide for this chapter, "Urinary Incontinence: Women."

D. Surgical treatment is based on the cause of incontinence.

E. Continence pessaries may benefit women with stress UI.

F. Electrical stimulation may be prescribed to inhibit bladder instability and improve striated and levator contractility and efficiency.

G. Treatment of concomitant constipation is an important step in the treatment of incontinence.

H. Treatment of vaginal atrophy is another important step in the treatment of incontinence.

I. Injection of BTX (botox) is an option for treatment of urge incontinence in selected patients.

J. Transurethral bulking agents injected into the submucosal tissues of the urethra or bladder neck is an option for women and men with UI due to BPH.

K. Indwelling catheters are not recommended as a management strategy for OAB.

L. Pharmaceutical therapy
1. Do not prescribe a muscarinic medication with patients when they are currently on other medications with anticholinergic properties.
2. Use anticholinergic and antispasmodic drugs to decrease reflex bladder contractions and increase bladder capacity (contraindicated in uncontrolled narrow-angle glaucoma, urinary retention, or gastric retention and frail patients).
3. The choice of pharmacologic therapy should be based on the patient's age, co-morbidities, concurrent medications, adverse effect profile, tolerability, ease of use, and cost of the medication.
4. The FDA has not approved any medications for stress incontinence.
5. The American College of Physicians (ACP) recommends against *systemic* pharmacologic therapy for stress UI.
   a. Oxybutynin chloride (Ditropan): Tablets and syrup formulation
      i. Adults: 5 mg orally two to three times per day (maximum of 20 mg/d)
   b. Oxybutynin chloride (Ditropan XL): Extended release tablets
      i. Adults: Initially 5 to 10 mg once a day. May increase the dosage weekly in 5 mg increments (maximum of 30 mg/d)
   c. Oxybutynin chloride (Gelnique): Topical gel
      i. Apply 1 g gel sachet once a day to intact skin.
   d. Tolterodine tartrate (Detrol LA)
      i. 2 to 4 mg orally per day

e. Fesoterodine (Toviaz): Extended release capsule
   i. 4 mg once a day (maximum of 8 mg/d)
f. Trospium (Sanctura XR): Extended releasecapsule
   i. Taken on an empty stomach, 60 mg orally every morning
g. Darifenacin (Enablex)
   i. 7.5 mg oral once a day
   ii. May increase to 15 mg once a day
h. Solifenacin (VESIcare)
   i. Initially 5 mg orally once a day
   ii. May increase to 10 mg daily

6. Alpha-adrenergic antagonists stimulate urethral smooth muscle contraction.
7. Beta-3 adrenergic agonist: Mirabegron (Myrbetriq)
   a. Initially 25 mg once a day
   b. May increase to 50 mg once a day
8. For postmenopausal women, vaginal estrogen may restore urethral mucosa; use the same type, dosage, and patient selection criteria as with estrogen therapy (ET). Systemic estrogen such as the estrogen patch should not be prescribed for UI.

Follow-Up

A. Follow-up is based on the type and cause of UI.

Consultation/Referral

A. When to consult a physician for UI depends on the type and cause of UI. UI is a problem that can be successfully treated.
B. Refer to a specialist for incontinence with abdominal and/or pelvic pain or hematuria in the absence of a UTI, or when surgical treatment is desired.
C. Refer for urodynamic testing, which is considered the gold standard. Testing requires special equipment and training.
D. Refer to a gynecologist or urology clinic experienced in fitting a continence pessary.
E. Refer to a urologist for hematuria and/or risk factors of bladder cancer.

Individual Considerations

A. Pregnancy: Stress incontinence is frequently associated with pregnancy and is treated with pelvic exercises.
B. Geriatrics
   1. Incontinence in the elderly is a risk factor for falls. Many falls occur en route to the bathroom, especially at night.
   2. Incontinence increases social isolation and depression.
   3. Functional incontinence is common in older adults with arthritis or Parkinson's or Alzheimer's diseases. Patients are unable to hold their urine until they reach the bathroom and undress. A toileting program usually assists in this situation.
   4. Durable medical equipment such as a bedside commode should be considered.
   5. Antimuscarinic medications may increase confusion.

Urinary Retention

Definition

Urinary retention is the inability to empty the bladder completely. It can be acute or chronic with symptoms such as total inability to urinate or simply inability to empty the bladder completely.

A. Acute urinary retention can cause great discomfort or pain and is sudden in onset and involves inability to urinate at all even when the bladder is full. It is the most common urologic emergency in men. The duration may be short, but it can also be potentially life-threatening, requiring immediate emergency intervention.
B. Chronic urinary retention presents with the inability to empty the bladder and is long term. Most of the time, chronic urinary retention is diagnosed with other associated GU conditions such as UTI, UI, and OAB.

Incidence

A. Urinary retention occurs less frequently in women than in men.
B. The overall incidence in men ages 40 to 83 years old is less than 7 per 1,000.
C. At age 70, the rate increases to 100 per 1,000.
D. By the age of 80 years, the incidence is up to 300 per 1,000

Pathogenesis

Urinary retention can be caused by three different factors:

A. Detrusor underactivity (DU) is defined by the International Continence Society as a contraction of reduced strength and/or duration resulting in prolonged or incomplete emptying of the bladder. Both neurogenic and myogenic factors are involved in DU and may be influenced by pharmacotherapy or by primary disorder inhibiting the detrusor and altering urethral sphincter relaxation.
B. BOO caused by tumors (GU, GI, or intestinal), bladder neck stenosis, calculi, structural malformation, or previous surgical interventions are classified as mechanical-anatomical. Little is known of the functional (nonmechanical–nonanatomical) cause but may include dyssynergia of the bladder neck and sphincter detrusor or dysfunction of the ureteral sphincter.
C. Combination of these mentioned.

Predisposing Factors

There are multiple factors that could cause urinary retention for both men and women, including:

A. Neurologic
   1. Peripheral neuropathy
      a. DM
      b. Infections
      c. Guillain–Barré syndrome
      d. Radiations and postsurgical interventions of the pelvis
   2. CNS
      a. CVA
      b. Parkinson's
      c. Hydrocephalus—normal pressure
      d. MS
      e. Shy–Drage syndrome
   3. Spinal cord
      a. Mass or trauma
      b. Cauda equina syndrome
      c. Spinal dysraphism

B. Ureteral strictures
C. Bladder calculi
D. Medications
   1. Antihistamines
   2. Anticholinergics/antispasmodics for bowel and bladder
   3. Tricyclic antidepressants
   4. Decongestants
   5. Nifedipine
   6. Antiseizure medications (AEDs)
   7. NSAIDs
   8. Opioids

E. Constipation/fecal impaction
F. Low nocturnal bladder capacity
G. Combination of the nocturnal polyuria and low nocturnal bladder capacity
H. OAB
I. Ureteral disruption secondary to trauma
J. Obstructions for men
   1. BPH: most common
   2. Phimosis
   3. Cancer of the prostate
   4. Stenosis of the penile meatal
   5. UTIs
      a. Acute prostatitis
      b. Abscess
      c. Balanitis

K. Obstructions for women
   1. Uterine: Prolapse, cystocele/rectocele
   2. Uterine fibroid
   3. Ovarian cyst
   4. Ureteral sphincter dysfunction
   5. Pelvic malignancy
   6. GU infections
   7. Inflammations or dermatitis

L. Abdominal mass
M. Diabetes especially with peripheral neuropathy
N. Postoperative urinary retention

Common Complaints

A. Acute symptoms
   1. Inability to urinate
   2. Dysuria with pain and urgency

B. Dysuria with poor or weak stream
C. Urinary frequency
D. Urinary urgency
E. Geriatrics
   1. May not present with classic symptoms
   2. Incontinence
   3. Mental confusion
   4. History of falls

Other Signs and Symptoms

A. Asymptomatic
B. Bladder spasms.
C. Suprapubic pain or suprapubic discomfort
D. Depression
E. Morning fatigue
F. Frequent wakefulness
G. Insomnia

Potential Complications

A. UTIs
B. CKD
C. Poor quality of life

Subjective Data

A. Review the onset, course, and duration of symptoms.
B. Review all medications, OTC medicines, and herbal products with notation of the medication/classes that cause urinary retention (see Predisposing Factors)
C. Does the patient have a fever and chills or back or flank pain (unilateral or bilateral)?
D. Is there any history of previous UTIs? How often and how were they treated? Were any tests performed in a workup by a urologist?
E. Males: Review the strength of the urinary flow, dribbling, and hesitancy.
F. Females
   1. Postmenopausal woman: Review whether she has a known prolapse and/or vaginal atrophy.
   2. Does she use any systemic or local estrogen medications?

G. Is there any history of other medical diseases noted in predisposing factors?
H. Review for the presence of neurologic disorders, including spinal cord injury or MS.
I. Review if there are other active problems or a history of genital problems such as herpes.
J. Has the patient had any recent surgical procedures?

Physical Examination

A. Both sexes
  1. Check temperature (if an infection is suspected), pulse, blood pressure, and respirations.
  2. Inspect for evidence of cardiac overload: Pedal edema.
  3. Auscultate the lungs for evidence of fluid overload: Rales.
  4. Perform neurologic examination to determine the presence of sensation and neurogenic bladder. Check anal reflex and sphincter tone.
  5. Palpate the abdomen, suprapubic, and back for masses, fullness over bladder, inguinal nodes, and CVA tenderness (bladder is percussible with 150 mL and palpable > 200 mL of urine).
  6. Assess cognitive and functional status, including mobility, transfers, manual dexterity, and ability to toilet in the elderly.
  7. Screen for depression.
  8. Assess for falls and possible healing fractures.
  9. Evaluate for obesity.

B. Females
  1. Inspect perineal skin for irritation, thinning, vaginal atrophy, herpetic lesion, or vaginal discharge.
  2. Remove the top blade of the speculum and evaluate the vaginal wall support.
  3. Ask the woman to cough to reevaluate the vaginal wall support.
  4. Palpate
     a. Perform a bimanual pelvic exam for prolapse, masses, or tenderness.
     b. Perform rectal exam for sphincter tone, masses, and fecal impaction.

C. Males
  1. Inspect
     a. Inspect the glans of the penis for abnormalities in urethral meatus. (Hypospadias may cause postvoid dribbling.)
     b. Uncircumcised men should be evaluated for phimosis and balanitis.
     c. Inspect for active herpetic lesions.
  2. Palpate
     a. Perform rectal exam for sphincter tone, masses, fecal impaction, prostate size, and contour.
     b. Palpate the scrotum to evaluate masses.
     c. Evaluate the presence of an inguinal hernia since straining with a partial urinary obstruction can worsen an inguinal hernia.

Diagnostic Tests

The history, physical examination, and urinalysis may be sufficient to guide initial therapy and to rule out other causative factors. Other tests include the following

A. Urine culture and sensitivity if infection is suspected.
B. Urine cytology if hematuria or pelvic pain is present.
C. A PSA should be considered.
D. Cystoscopy/ureteroscopy
E. Urodynamic testing is strongly recommended.
F. PVR measurement
G. CT scans
H. Electromyography
I. Depression screen
J. Neurological evaluation may be needed to include, but is not limited to, CT studies.
K. Chemistry study with Hgb A1C
L. Nocturnal pulse oximetry study
M. Sleep study may be indicated, especially in those positive for nocturnal hypoxemia.
N. Ultrasound of the kidneys with Doppler

Differential Diagnosis

A. Urinary retention
B. Urinary obstruction
  1. Bladder calculi
  2. Ureteral stricture
C. Medication(s) side effect
D. Neurologic etiology
E. Male-related etiologies as noted in the predisposing factors
F. Female-related etiologies as noted in the predisposing factors
G. Fecal impaction
H. Abdominal mass
I. CKD

Plan

A. **Acute urinary retention is considered a medical emergency that should be managed by immediate catheterization.**
B. Patient teaching
  1. Behavior training includes:
     a. Doing a "double void" by emptying the bladder; wait and try again to empty the bladder.
     b. Biofeedback
     c. Bladder and pelvic muscle retraining
  2. Train for self-catherization if indicated.
  3. Keep a 24-hour voiding diary (a voiding diary is present in the Section III Patient Teaching Guideline for this chapter, "Urinary Incontinence: Women").
  4. Avoid constipation/fecal impaction
  5. Evaluate the need for an indwelling catheter (e.g., postsurgical).
  6. Implantable neuromodulation therapy to the sacral nerves (InterStim) has been helpful.
C. Pharmacological
  1. Review all medications and herbals to evaluate what may be discontinued.
  2. Medications may need to be started to treat an enlarged prostate.

a. Dutasteride (Avodart): 0.5 mg daily
b. Finasteride (Proscar): 5 mg daily
3. Evaluate the need to prescribe medications to relax the bladder outlet and prostate to help relieve blockage
a. Doxazosin (Cardura): 1 to 4 mg daily
b. Silodosin (Rapaflo): 8 mg daily (give with food)
c. Tadalafil (Cialis): 5 mg daily
d. Tamsulosin (Flomax): 0.4 mg daily
e. Terazosin (Hytrin): 1 to 10 mg daily at H.S.

Follow-Up

A. Follow-up is determined by patient's needs, severity of symptoms, and whether complications are present. Adequate time should be allowed for treatments involving nonpharmacological and pharmacological approaches.

Consultation/Referral

A. Refer to a urologist for consideration of:
1. Treatment with a urethral dilation, urethral stents
2. Surgical intervention
3. Suprapubic

B. Urogynecologist: For women with structural problem and pregnancy
C. Neurology
D. Endocrinology

Individual Considerations

A. Adults/Geriatrics
1. Use caution with medications for ED 5-alpha-reductase inhibitors, which have been known to cause ED.
2. Avoid and/or use caution with women, especially if pregnancy is a possibility.
3. Caution is needed when used with medications for ED.

Urinary Tract Infection (Acute Cystitis)

Definition

A. UTI is an infection of the urinary bladder. UTI is defined as the presence of at least 100,000 organisms per mL of urine in an asymptomatic patient or more than 100 organisms per mL of urine with accompanying pyuria (> 7 WBC/mL) in a symptomatic patient. ASB when left untreated is a risk factor for acute cystitis (40%) and pyelonephritis in 25% to 30% of pregnant women.

B. UTIs can be divided anatomically into upper and lower tract (cystitis) infections. For a discussion of upper tract infection, see the section in this chapter, "Pyelonephritis."

C. UTIs may be considered uncomplicated or complicated.
1. An uncomplicated UTI is noted in a healthy person with a normal urinary tract system and may be treated with oral antibiotics.
2. A UTI noted in a person with a structural or functional urinary tract system or in a person who is immunocompromised is considered complicated. It may require parental therapy until afebrile.

Incidence

A. Incidence depends on age and gender. The prevalence of UTI in males varies according to age.
1. Young men aged 15 to 50 years rarely develop a UTI.
2. The incidence of a UTI in geriatric males may be as high as in geriatric females (up to 15%).

B. Over 50% of women will have one UTI in their lifetime.
1. Prevalence for females increases by 1% per decade and 2% to 4% throughout childbearing years.
2. The incidence of UTIs in pregnancy ranges from 4% to 7%. In pregnancy, the increased incidence is related to both hormonal influence and anatomic changes that increase the risk of urinary stasis and vesicoureteral reflux.
3. By age 30, approximately 25% of women have experienced symptoms of a UTI.

Pathogenesis

A. Bacteria ascend from the perineum through the urethra. The greater susceptibility of younger women and girls is related to a shorter urethra. In older women, it is related to estrogen-mediated dilation of the urethra.

B. The normal male urinary tract has many natural defenses to infection. The greater susceptibility of elderly males is related to problems with the prostate and other urologic disease and can be linked to the instrumentation required for therapy.

C. Gram-negative bacilli are the most common pathogens; 80% to 90% of cases are related to coliform bacteria (*E. coli*). It originates from fecal floras that colonize the periurethral area.

D. Other gram-negative bacteria include *K. pneumonia* or *P. mirabilis*. *S. saprophyticus* (gram-positive coccus) accounts for about 10% to 15% of UTIs.

E. Other pathogens include *Enterobacter, Pseudomonas, Enterococci,* and *Staphylococci.*

F. The incubation period depends on the pathogen.

Predisposing Factors

A. Female (until elderly, then equal frequency in males and females)
B. Pregnancy
C. Poor hygiene
D. Trauma
E. Instrumentation
F. Sexual intercourse
G. Oral contraceptive or diaphragm use

H. Diabetic female (there is no increased risk for diabetic males)
I. Anomalies of the GU tract
J. Neurologic factors
K. Vesicoureteral reflux
L. Obstruction: Stones
M. Foreign bodies
N. Bubble baths and hot tubs
O. Douching
P. Anal intercourse
Q. HIV
R. Uncircumcised penis
S. Catheterization
T. Nosocomial infection
U. Phimosis

Common Complaints

A. Burning on urination
B. Frequency
C. Cloudy or bloody urine
D. Urgency
E. Geriatrics
  1. May not present with classic symptoms
  2. Fever
  3. Incontinence
  4. Mental confusion

Other Signs and Symptoms

A. Asymptomatic
B. Frequency, dysuria, bladder spasms, suprapubic discomfort, urgency, and nocturia
C. Suprapubic pain
D. Fever
E. CVA tenderness
F. Hematuria

Subjective Data

A. Review the onset, course, and duration of symptoms.
B. Does the patient have a fever and chills or back or flank pain (unilateral or bilateral)?
C. Are there any other genital problems such as herpes lesions or vaginal discharge?
D. Review the associated factors: Sexual intercourse (specifically review for anal intercourse), douching, or bubble bath.
E. Ask female patients if they use appropriate hygiene practices after urination and BMs.
  1. Wiping from front to back
  2. Frequent changes of hygienic products
  3. Hand washing
F. Is the patient pregnant? If not, what type of birth control does she use?
G. Is there any history of previous UTIs? How often, and how were they treated? Were any tests performed in a workup by a urologist?
H. How much liquid or water does the patient drink every day? Note the amount of caffeine.
I. In older men, review the strength of the urinary flow, dribbling, hesitancy, and so forth.
J. In the postmenopausal woman, review whether she has a known prolapse and/or vaginal atrophy. Does she use any systemic or local estrogen medications?
K. Is there any history of other medical diseases, including diabetes or sickle cell disease?
L. Review for the presence of neurologic disorders, including spinal cord injury or MS.
M. Does the patient require self-catheterization?

Physical Examination

A. Check temperature, blood pressure, pulse, and respirations. **The absence of a fever does not exclude the presence of an infective process.**
B. General observation of general appearance for discomfort before and during examination.
C. Auscultation of the heart and all lung fields.
D. Palpate
  1. Palpate the abdomen: Kidneys, masses; assess for suprapubic tenderness.
  2. Palpate the back; note CVA tenderness.
  3. Check for inguinal lymph node enlargement.
  4. Palpate the suprapubic area.
E. Percuss: Percuss over the bladder and the CVA area for tenderness.
F. Females
  1. Inspect external genitalia for lesions, Bartholin's gland cysts, irritation, and discharge.
  2. Milk urethra for discharge.
  3. Assess rectal area.
  4. Speculum exam: Evaluate vaginal vault for discharge, cervicitis, and inflammation; evaluate for atrophic vaginal changes and torn tissue.
  5. Bimanual exam: Check for cervical motion, tenderness, and masses.
G. Males
  1. Inspect the penis/urinary meatus for phimosis, lesions, signs of inflammation, and discharge. Retract the foreskin (if present) and assess for hygiene and smegma.
  2. Palpate the testes and epididymides for inflammation, tenderness, and masses.
  3. **Rectal examination is mandatory in males.** Check for swollen and tender prostate. In patients with suspected acute bacterial prostatitis, palpation should be very gentle due to the potential for bacteremia.

Diagnostic Tests

The diagnosis of a UTI can often be made based on a focused history and the presenting symptoms.

A. Urinalysis: A catheterization or suprapubic aspiration may need to be obtained for elderly, obese, microscopic hematuria, or for functionally impaired patients.
   1. Appearance: Should be clear. Cloudy urine may indicate presence of pyuria, pus, blood, cells, phosphate, or lymph fluid.
   2. Odor: Usually faint aromatic odor; ammonia odor indicates *Proteus*, which is related to food changes; offensive odor indicates bacterial infection.
   3. pH: Normal is around 6 (acid); may normally vary from 4.6 to 7.5.
   4. Specific gravity: Reflects the kidney's ability to concentrate urine and the body's hydration or dehydration status. Normal is 1.005 to 1.025.
   5. Color: Shows concentration; usually yellow or amber.
      a. Straw color = dilute urine
      b. Dark color = concentrated (dehydrated)
      c. Red or red-brown to blood = transfusion reaction, drugs, and bleeding lesions
      d. Yellow brown = bile duct disease, jaundice
      e. Dark brown or black = melanoma or leukemia
B. Cystitis: Positive results
   1. Urinalysis dipstick findings: pH greater than 7.0, positive for leukocyte esterase and positive for nitrites. *A negative urine dipstick does not rule out an infection.*
   2. Microscopic exam of urine findings: WBC greater than 2 to 5, WBC/HPF, bacteria, positive Gram stain for cocci or rods, yeast, and blood.
   3. Urine culture and sensitivity
      a. Positive culture standard 10^5 colony-forming units; symptomatic female 10^2; symptomatic males 10^3.
      b. Screening for asymptomatic bacteria is recommended for patients in pregnancy, for elderly males with documented prostatic or urologic abnormalities, for patients with a recent catheterization, and for patients with known stones or documented structural abnormalities.
      c. Clean-catch urinalysis: Catheterization or suprapubic aspiration may be necessary depending on patient's age and condition. Catheterization should be reserved for patients with an obstruction or for those who cannot cooperate or collect a clean-catch urine specimen.
      d. Culture for STIs if suspected
      e. Wet prep for female, if indicated
C. Imaging
   1. Ultrasound
   2. Conventional voiding cystourethrography
   3. Urodynamic evaluation

Differential Diagnoses

A. UTI: Watch for systemic symptoms of pyelonephritis.
B. Vaginal or pelvic infection
C. Prostatitis or epididymitis: Tender, enlarged prostate; tender testicle or scrotum
D. Bladder tumor
E. IC
F. Urinary calculi
G. BPH: Changes in urinary stream and nocturia
H. OAB/Urge incontinence
I. Pelvic organ prolapse
J. Irritant urethritis
K. Consider the possibility that chronic, asymptomatic infections are a potential source of disseminated infection, such as endocarditis. This is particularly likely in the male patient with prostate disease and infection requiring instrumentation.

Plan

A. Patient education: See the Section III Patient Teaching Guide for this chapter, "Urinary Tract Infection (UTI)."
B. Dietary management
   1. Instruct the patient to increase fluids and drink at least one large glass of liquid every hour.
   2. Instruct the patient to avoid foods that irritate the bladder: caffeine, alcohol, tomatoes, citrus, and spicy foods.
   3. Encourage the patient to drink cranberry juice to help fight bladder infections. If the patient dislikes the taste of plain cranberry juice, it can be mixed 1:1 with another juice, such as orange juice.
C. Pharmacologic therapy
   1. Antibiotics: 3-day course may be efficacious and is less expensive than the traditional 7- to 10-day course of therapy for uncomplicated infections.
   2. The antibiotic of choice depends on the specific bacteria found upon culture. Empiric antimicrobial therapy should cover all likely pathogens.
   3. Trimethoprim and sulfamethoxazole (Septra, Bactrim DS) 160 mg and 800 mg, respectively, one tablet twice daily for 3 to 5 days.
      a. Give above dosage for 3 to 5 days for uncomplicated cystitis in females.
      b. Give above dosage for 7 to 10 days to patients who are male, are elderly, or have recurrent UTI, or for complicated cases.

4. Other antibiotics
   a. Trimethoprim (Trimpex): 100 mg twice daily for 10 days
   b. Nitrofurantoin (Macrobid): 100 mg tablet: One tablet twice daily for 7 days
   c. Lomefloxacin hydrochloride (Maxaquin): 400 mg every day for 3 days for uncomplicated case; 10 to 14 days for complicated
   d. Amoxicillin (Amoxil): 500 mg three times daily for 7 days
5. Urinary analgesic if needed
   a. Phenazopyridine HCL (Pyridium): 100 to 200 mg three times daily for 1 to 2 days only when given with an antibiotic. Educate the patient that this drug turns urine orange.
   b. Multiple Uroblue medications are available; take one orally four times a day. Educate the patient that this drug turns the urine blue/green.
6. Drugs of choice for UTI or pyelonephritis in pregnancy
   a. Nitrofurantoin (Macrobid) 100 mg: One tablet orally every 12 hours for 5 days
   b. Amoxicillin: 500 mg orally every 12 hours for 3 to 7 days
   c. Amoxicillin-clavulanate (Augmentin): 500 mg orally every 12 hours for 3 to 7 days
   d. Cephalexin (Keflex): 500 mg orally every 12 hours for 3 to 7 days
   e. If dysuria is present: phenazopyridine HCL (Pyridium) 200 mg orally three times daily for 2 days when given with an antibiotic.
7. **Antibiotics that should not be utilized in pregnancy are**
   a. **Fluoroquinolones are not used in children because of potential concerns about sustained injury to developing joints.**
   b. **Fluoroquinolones (FDA Class C) are contraindicated during pregnancy because of auditory and vestibular toxicity in the fetus.**
   c. **Tetracyclines should not be used in pregnancy (FDA Class D) or in children because of tooth staining.**
8. Consider prophylactic therapy for patients with chronic conditions/recurrent infections.
   a. Low-dose antibiotics daily for 3 to 6 months
   b. Self-start antibiotics
   c. Postcoital antibiotics
9. Quinolones, cephalosporins, and macrolides should be reserved for complicated or resistant infections.
10. Vaginal estrogen should be considered in postmenopausal women with urogenital atrophic changes.

Follow-Up

A. Routine posttreatment urinalysis/culture is not indicated in asymptomatic patients.
B. Have the patient return if symptoms do not resolve at the end of treatment.
C. Have the patient return if the symptoms reoccur within 2 weeks of treatment for a urine culture. Retreatment with a 7-day course of antibiotics using a different agent should be considered.

Consultation/Referral

A. Young men do not have UTIs very often; a urologic workup may be needed if etiology such as a STI cannot be determined.
B. Patients with bacteriuria are also more likely to have identifiable abnormalities on an IVP, including small kidneys, delayed excretion, caliceal dilation and blunting, ureteral reflux, stones, and obstructive lesions.
C. Consultation with a urologist is essential in all forms of prostatitis or in all but the most clear-cut cases of acute scrotum.

Individual Considerations

A. Women
   1. Recurrent infections are common in females.
   2. Repeat urine cultures and sensitivity after an antibiotic course is complete (approximately 2 to 4 weeks after therapy is completed).
   3. If the patient is perimenopausal and has two or fewer UTIs a year, consider patient-initiated therapy to start when symptomatic. Consider topical estradiol cream for atrophic vaginitis. If the patient has three UTIs a year, prescribe a prophylactic single-dose regimen after intercourse. If infections are not related to intercourse, consider urine cultures every 2 months, with extended antibiotic therapy.
B. Pregnancy
   1. The incidence of pyelonephritis in pregnancy is 1% to 2%. Most cases develop as a consequence of undiagnosed or inadequately treated lower UTI.
      a. In the presumptive diagnosis of pyelonephritis in pregnancy, ultrasound of the kidneys and urinary tract should be considered.
   2. Approximately 75% to 80% of pyelonephritis cases occur on the right side, with a 10% to 15% incidence on the left side. A small percentage of cases are bilateral.
   3. GBS (Group B *Streptococcus*) colonization has important implications during pregnancy, contributing to maternal pyelonephritis and preterm birth. Intrapartum transmission may lead to neonatal GBS infection.
      a. Women with documented Group B streptococcal bacteriuria in the current pregnancy should be treated at the time of labor or rupture of membranes with

appropriate IV antibiotics for the prevention of early-onset neonatal GBS disease.

b. **Asymptomatic women with urinary GBS in pregnancy should not be treated with antibiotics for the prevention of adverse maternal and perinatal outcomes.**
c. **Women with documented GBS bacteriuria should not be rescreened by genital tract culture or urinary culture in the third trimester, as they are presumed to be GBS colonized.**

4. Current guidelines recommend universal vaginal and rectal screening in all pregnant women at 35 to 37 weeks gestation rather than treatment based on risk factors.
5. A urine culture screening is recommended for all pregnant women at their first prenatal visit.
6. Suppressive antibiotic therapy should be instituted in pregnant patients who develop acute cystitis, recurrent or persistent ASB, or pyelonephritis.
7. Patients with sickle cell hemoglobinopathies are at increased risk for UTI and should be screened more aggressively, possibly benefiting from antibiotic prophylaxis.
8. **Antibiotics that should not be used during pregnancy include**
   a. **Tetracyclines (adverse effects on fetal teeth/bones and congenital defects)**
   b. **Quinolones (congenital defects)**
   c. **Trimethoprim in the first trimester (facial defects and cardiac abnormalities)**
   d. **Sulfonamides in the last trimester (kernicterus)**
   e. **Aminoglycosides (permanent ototoxicity in the fetus)**

C. Geriatrics: Patients may not have classic symptoms. Consider UTI if the patient presents with increased UI, fever, and mental confusion.

Varicocele

Definition

A. Varicocele is engorgement of the internal spermatic veins above the testes. This vascular abnormality is a cause of decreased testicular function. Some varicoceles are easy to identify and may be surgically corrected. The presence of a varicocele does not mean that surgical correction is a necessity.

Incidence

A. Varicocele may occur in 15% to 20% of normal males; 80% to 90% of cases occur on the left side. Up to 35% to 40% of men with a palpable left-sided varicocele may actually have bilateral varicoceles that are identified upon physical examination.
B. Right-sided varicocele is uncommon and can indicate retroperitoneal malignancy. Varicocele is the leading known cause of male infertility (40%). Decreased sperm counts, infertility, and testicular atrophy occur in 65% to 75% of varicocele cases. There is no correlation between size of the varicocele and the degree of infertility.

Pathogenesis

A. The exact pathophysiologic mechanisms for varicoceles are not fully identified. Varicoceles may be due to valvular incompetence or elevated hydrostatic pressure in the spermatic veins. Testicular temperature elevation also appears to play a role in varicocele-induced dysfunction. **New varicoceles in older men may be secondary to renal tumors.**

Predisposing Factors

A. Varicoceles generally manifest at the time of puberty.

Common Complaints

A. Asymptomatic
B. Infertility
C. Pain or discomfort in the scrotum

Other Signs and Symptoms

A. Pain or aching and heaviness in the scrotum
A. Feels like "worms"; scrotum may have bluish discoloration.

Subjective Data

A. Note the onset, course, and duration of symptoms. When was the varicocele first noted?
B. Has the scrotum enlarged? If there is enlargement, over what time span? Does it collapse with lying or sitting down?
C. Is there any pain or discomfort?
D. Has there been any history of infertility?

Physical Examination

A. Check vital signs, temperature as indicated.
B. Inspect
   1. The examination should be done when the patient is lying or standing in a warm room. Warm temperature promotes relaxation of the scrotum.
   2. Examine the general appearance of the penis; note scrotal size, shape, and rugae. Varicocele tends to collapse with the patient sitting or supine.
   3. Transilluminate the scrotum to visualize the varicocele.
   4. A large varicocele can easily be identified by inspection.
C. Palpate
   1. Palpate each side of the scrotum for testicular size, presence of varicocele (Valsalva maneuver performed while the patient stands helps to reveal a small varicocele), and absence of vas deferens.
      a. A moderate-size varicocele can be identified by palpation without having the patient perform the Valsalva maneuver.

2. Palpate the spermatic cord between the thumb and forefingers while the patient performs a Valsalva maneuver.
   a. A small varicocele is identified only when the patient bears down, increasing the intra-abdominal pressure.
   b. Varicocele should significantly diminish in size when the patient assumes the supine position.
3. Evaluate whether the varicocele can be reduced while the patient is supine.
4. Palpate the abdomen for hernias, masses, and tenderness.
5. Rectal exam: Palpate the prostate and seminal vesicles for tenderness and other signs of infection.

D. Auscultate: Listen over the scrotum to assess bowel sounds to rule out hernia.

Diagnostic Tests

A. Scrotal ultrasound with a high-resolution color-flow Doppler is the diagnostic method of choice when clinical exams are equivocal but are not indicated for standard evaluation.
B. Semen analysis times two, if indicated
C. CT to evaluate retroperitoneal pathology (e.g., renal cell carcinoma) for
   1. Sudden onset of varicocele
   2. Single right-sided varicocele
   3. Any varicocele that is not reducible in the supine position

Differential Diagnosis

A. Varicocele classifications
   1. Grade I (small): Palpable only on Valsalva maneuver, which increases intra-abdominal pressure and therefore impedes drainage and increases the varicocele size.
   2. Grade II (medium): Palpable when standing and bearing down (Valsalva maneuver)
   3. Grade III (large): Visible on inspection alone
   4. Subclinical: Not palpable; vein larger than 3 mm on ultrasound; Doppler reflux on Valsalva maneuver
B. Hernia
C. Epididymitis
D. Hydrocele
E. Testicular tumor: **Consider retroperitoneal tumor, especially if presenting symptoms have a sudden onset.**

Plan

A. Urologic consultation for diagnosis and possible surgery. Surgery should be considered when all of the following conditions are met.
   1. Palpable varicocele found upon physical examination
   2. Couple with known infertility
   3. Female with normal fertility or potential treatable cause of infertility
   4. Male partner with abnormal semen parameters or abnormal results from sperm function tests
B. Athletic supporter for comfort
C. Patient teaching: See the Section III Patient Teaching Guide for this chapter, "Testicular Self-Examination."
D. Pharmaceutical therapy: None is recommended.

Follow-Up

A. After surgery, no follow-up is necessary if the patient is taught scrotal self-exam.
B. If no surgery is performed, the patient should be taught self-exam and instructed to return for pain or change in size and shape.
C. Adolescents with varicoceles should be followed with annual objective measurements of testis size and/or semen analyses in order to detect the earliest sign of varicocele-related testicular injury.

Consultation/Referral

A. Refer the patient to a urologist for surgical evaluation. Varicocelectomy is recommended in cases of pain and infertility, and it may be offered in the preadolescent to ensure proper testicular development.

Bibliography

Adult and Pediatric Urology and Urogynecology. (n.d.). *Prostatitis.* Retrieved from www.adultpediatricuro.com/prostatitis.shtml

Allen, V. M., & Yudin, M. H. (2012, May). SOGC Clinical practice guideline: Management of group B streptococcal bacteriuria in pregnancy. *Journal Obstetrics Gynaecology Canada, 276,* 482–486.

Allison, M. (2012, April). Evaluation of insomnia in the adult client. *The Journal for Nurse Practitioners-JNP, 8,* 330–331.

American Society of Nephrology. (2009). *Chapter 5: Rate of decline in eGFR and clinical evaluation of the elderly with low eGFR.* Retrieved from www.asn-online.org/education/distancelearning/curricula/geriatrics/Chapter5.pdf

American Urological Association. (2005). *Chapter 1: AUA guideline on the management of staghorn calculi: Diagnosis and treatment recommendations.* Retrieved from www.auanet.org/content/clinical-practice-guidelines/clinical-guidelines/main-reports/staghorn calculi/chapter1.pdf

American Urological Association. (2007). *Chapter 1: The management of ureteral calculi: Diagnosis and treatment recommendations.* Retrieved from www.auanet.org/content/clinical-practice-guidelines/clinical-guidelines/main-report/uretcal07/chapter1.pdf

American Urological Association. (2007, June). *The management of erectile dysfunction: An update.* Retrieved from www.auanet.org/common/pdf/education/clinical-guidelines/Erectile-Dysfunction.pdf

American Urological Association. (2009). *Prostate-specific antigen best practice: 2009 update.* Retrieved from www.auanet.org/content/media/psa09.pdf

American Urological Association. (2010). *Management of BPH. Chapter 1: Guideline on the management of benign prostatic hyperplasia (BPH).* Retrieved from http://www.auanet.org/content/clinical-practice-guidelines/clinical-guidelines.cfm?sub=bph

American Urological Association. (2011, January). *Diagnosis and treatment of interstitial cystitis/bladder pain syndrome.* Retrieved from http://www.auanet.org/content/clinical-practice-guidelines/clinical-guidelines/main-reports/ic-bps/diagnosis_and_treatment_ic-bps.pdf

Anastasi, J. K., Chang, M., & Capili, B. (2011, January). Herbal supplements, talking with your patients. *Journal for Nurse Practitioners-JNP, 7*(1), 29–35.

Anger, J. T., Scott, V. C. S., Kiyosaki, K., Khan, A. A., Weinberg, A., Connor, S. E., ... Litwin, M. S. (2013). Development of quality indicators for women with urinary incontinence. *Neurology and Urodynamics, 32,* 1058–1063.

Associates in Urology. (n.d.). *Patient questionnaire: AUA symptom score (AUASS).* Retrieved from www.njurology.com/_forms/auass.pdf

Associates in Urology. (n.d.). *Quality of life questionnaire.* Retrieved from http://www.njurology.com/_forms/qualityoflife.php

Associates in Urology. (n.d.) *Sexual health inventory for men (SHIM).* Retrieved from http://www.njurology.com/_forms/ shim.pdf

Barron, M. L. (2013, March). Fertility literacy for men in primary care settings. *Journal for Nurse Practitioners-JNP, 9,* 155–160.

Browne, O. T., & Bhandari, S. (2012, April 5). Interpreting and investigating proteinuria. *British Medical Journal, 344,* e2339. Retrieved from http://www.bmj.com

Buttaro, T. M., Koeniger-Donohue, R., & Hawkins, J. (2014, May). Sexuality and quality of life in aging: Implications for practice. *Journal for Nurse Practitioners-JNP, 10,* 480–485.

Carran, M., & Shaw, I. (2012, July). New Zealand Malayan war veterans' exposure to dibutylphthalate is associated with increased incidence of cryptorchidism, hypospadias and breast cancer in their children. *New Zealand Medical Journal, 125,* 52–63.

Carroll, M. F., & Temte, J. L. (2000, September 15). Proteinuria in adults: A diagnostic approach. *American Family Physician, 62,* 1333–1340. Retrieved from www.aafp.org/ aft/2000/0915/p1333.html?printable=afp

Centers for Disease Control and Prevention. (2011, January 28). *Sexually transmitted diseases treatment guidelines, 2010, epididymitis.* Retrieved from http://www.cdc.gov/std/ treatment/2010/epididymitis.htm

Chen, S., & Vijayan, A. (Eds.). (2012). *The Washington manual of nephrology subspecialty consult.* (3rd ed.). Philadelphia, PA: Wolters Kluwer Health, Lippincott, Williams & Wilkins.

Ching, C. B. (2013, March 21). Epididymitis treatment & management. *Medscape Reference.* Retrieved from emedicine.medscape.com/article/436154-treatment

Chutka, D. S. (2012, September). Urinary incontinence: Is there effective therapy? *Consultant, 53,* 617–624. Retrieved from www.Consultant360.com

Clemens, J. Q. (2013, February 6). Urinary incontinence in men. *UpToDate.* Retrieved from www.uptodate.com/contents/urinary-incontinence-in-men?topicKey=PC%2F14611

Clemens, J. Q. (2013, July 11). Pathogenesis, clinical features, and diagnosis of interstitial cystitis/bladder pain syndrome. *UpToDate.* Retrieved from http://www.uptodate.com/contents/pathogenesis-clinical-features-and-diagnosis-of-interstitial-cystitis-bladder-pain-syndrome?source=search_result&search=interstitial+cystitis&selectedTitle=1%7E150

Clemens, J. Q., Calhoun, E. A., Litwin, M. S., McNaughton-Collins, M., Dunn, R. L., Crowley, E. M., & Landis, J. R. (2009). Rescoring the NIH chronic prostatitis symptom index (NIH-CPSI): Nothing new. *Prostate Cancer Prostatitis Diseases, 12,* 285–287.

Cleveland Clinic. (n.d.). *Nocturia.* Retrieved from http://my.clevelandclinic.org/health/diseases_conditions/hic_Bladder_Irritating_Foods/hic_nocturia

The Clinical Advisor. (2013, February 6). *Kidney guide features albuminuria testing.* Retrieved from www.clinicaladvisor.com/ kidney-guide-features-albuminuria-testing/article/279307

Clinical Key. (n.d.). *Pyelonephritis.* Retrieved from https://www.clinicalkey.com/topics/urology/pyelonephritis.html

Colgan, R., Williams, M., & Johnson, J. R. (2011, September 1). Diagnosis and treatment of acute pyelonephritis in women. *American Family Physician, 84,* 519–526.

Collins, M. (2013, September). To dip or not? That is the question. *The Journal for Nurse Practitioners-JNP, 9,* 544–545.

Consensus Group. (2007). A multidisciplinary consensus meeting on IC/PBS. *Reviews in Urology, 9,* 81–83.

Cunningham, G. R., & Rosen, R. C. (2014, June 2). Overview of male sexual dysfunction. *UpToDate.* Retrieved from http://www.uptodate.com/contents/overview-of-male-sexual-dysfunction?source=search_result&search=overview+of+male+sexual+dysfunction&selectedTitle=1%7E150

Cunningham, G. R., & Seftel, A. D. (2014, March 31). Treatment of male sexual dysfunction. *UpToDate.* Retrieved from http://www.uptodate.com/contents/treatment-of-male-sexual-dysfunction?source=search_result&search=treatment+of+male+sexual+dysfunction&selectedTitle=1%7E150

Curhan, G. C., Aronson, M. D., & Preminger, G. M. (2014, May 20). Diagnosis and acute management of suspected nephrolithiasis in adults. *UpToDate.* Retrieved from http://www.uptodate.com/contents/diagnosis-and-acute-management-of-suspected-nephrolithiasis-in-adults?source=search_result&search=diagnosis+and+acute+management+of+suspected+nephrolithiasis&selectedTitle=1%7E150

Datta, S. N., Chaliha, C., Singh, A., Gonzales, G., Mishra, V. C., Kavia, R. B.C., ... Elneil, E. (2007). Sacral neurostimulation for urinary retention: 10-year experience from on UK centre. *BJU International, 101,* 192–196.

Davis, L. L. (2013, November/December). Using the latest evidence to manage hypertension. *Journal of Nurse Practitioners-JNP,* 9, 321–328.

Davis, R., Jones, J. S., Barcocas, D. A., Castle, E. P., Lang, E. K., Leveillee, R. J., ... American Urological Association. (2012). Diagnosis, evaluation, and follow-up of asymptomatic microhematuria (AMH) in adults: AUA guideline. *American Urological Association (AUA).* Retrieved from www.auanet.org/content/media/asymptomic_microhematuria_ guidelien.pdf

De Ridder, D., Ost, D., & Bruyninckx, F. (2007). The presence of Fowler's syndrome predicts successful long-term outcome of sacral nerve stimulation in women with urinary retention. *European Urology, 51,* 229–234.

Department of Veterans Affairs, Department of Defense. (2008). *The VA/DoD clinical practice guideline for management of chronic kidney disease in primary care.* Retrieved from www.healthquality.va.gov/ckd/ckd_v478_sums.pdf

Deters, L. A. (2014a, March 28). Benign prostatic hypertrophy. *Medscape Reference.* Retrieved from emedicine.medscape.com/article/437359-overview

Deters, L. A. (2014b, March 28). Benign prostatic hypertrophy clinical presentation. *Medscape Reference.* Retrieved from emedicine.medscape.com/article/427359-clinical

Deters, L. A. (2014c, March 28). Benign prostatic hypertrophy medication. *Medscape Reference.* Retrieved from emedicine.medscape.com/article/437359-medication

Dmochowski, R. R., Peters, K. M., Morrow, J. D., Guan, Z., Gong J., Sun, F., ... Staskin, D. R. (2010). Randomized, double-blind, placebo-controlled trial of flexible-dose fesoterodine in subjects with overactive bladder. *Urology, 75,* 62–68.

DuBeau, C. E. (2011, July 31). Epidemiology, risk factors, and pathogenesis of urinary incontinence. *UpToDate.* Retrieved from http://www.uptodate.com/contents/epidemiology-risk-factors-and-pathogenesis-of-urinary-incontinence?source=search_result&search=epidemiology+risk+factors+and+pathogenesis+of+urinary+incontinence&selectedTitle=1%7E150

Early, A., Miskulin, D., Lamb, E. J., Levey, A. S., & Uhlig, K. (2012). Estimating equations for glomerular filtration rate in the era of creatinine standardization. *Annals of Internal Medicine, 156,* 785–795.

Edinburgh Royan Infirmary Renal Unit. (n.d.). *Proteinuria.* Retrieved from www.edren.org/pages/gpino/proteinuria.php

Eneanya, A., & Lin, J. (2011, October/November). Dietary factors and chronic kidney disease. *Kidney News, 3,* 32–34.

Fuller, K. (2014, June). Diagnosis of testicular cancer. *Journal for Nurse Practitioners-JNP, 10,* 437–438.

Fulop, T. (2014a, April 18). Acute pyelonephritis. *Medscape Reference.* Retrieved from emedicine.medscape.com/article/245559-overview

Fulop, T. (2014b, April 18). Acute pyelonephritis treatment and management. *Medscape Reference.* Retrieved from emedicine.medscape.com/article/245559-treatment

Gerfen, A., & Frick, L. (2012, June). Acute uncomplicated cystitis and pyelonephritis in women. *The Journal for Nurse Practitioners-JNP, 8,* 484–485.

Gleich, P. (2012, January). Bladder outlet obstruction: Diagnosis and medical management. *Consultant, 52,* 33–37.

Gormley, E. A., Lightner, D. J., Burgio, K. L., Chal, T. C., Clemens, J. Q., Culkin, D. J., ... Vasavada, S. P. (2012). Diagnosis and treatment of overactive bladder (non-neurogenic) in adults: AUA/SUFU guideline. *American Urological Association.* Retrieved from www.auanet.org/content/media/OAB_guideline.pdf

Grabe, M., Bjerklund-Johansen, T. E., Botto, H., Cek, M., Naber, K. G., Pickard, R. S., ... Wullt, B. (2013). Guidelines on urological infections. *European Association of Urology.* Retrieved from www.uroweb.org/guidelines/on-line-guidelines

Grossfeld, G. D., Wolfe, J. S., Jr., Litwin, M. S., Hricak, H., Shuler, C. L., Agerterh, D. C., & Carroll, P.R. (2001). *Asymptomatic microscopic hematuria in adults: Summary of the AUA best practice policy recommendations.* Retrieved from http://www.aafp.org/afp/2001/0315/p1145.pdf

Gulati, S. (2014, May 14). Hematuria workup. *Medscape Reference.* Retrieved from http://emedicine.medscape.com/article/981898-workup

Gupta, K., Hooton, T. M., Naber, K. G., Wultz, B., Colgan, R., Miller, L. G., ... European Society for Microbiology and Infectious Diseases. (2011, March 1). International clinical practice guidelines for the treatment of acute uncomplicated cystitis and pyelonephritis in women: A 2010 update by the Infectious Disease Society of American and the European Society for Microbiology and Infectious Diseases. *Clinical Infectious Diseases, 52,* e103–e120.

Hampton, T. (2011, September). A simple urine test detects rapid kidney function decline. *Kidney News, 3,* 1–3.

Harrington, D. H., & Kinchen, L. (2014). Vascular complications in maternal care. *The Journal of Nurse Practitioners-JNP, 10,* 360–361e.1.

Hatzimouratidis, K., Amar, E., Eardley, I., Giuliano, F., Hatzichristou, D., Montorsi, F., ... European Association of Urology. (2010). Guidelines on male sexual dysfunction: Erectile dysfunction and premature ejaculation. *European Urology, 57,* 804–814.

Hooton, T. M., & Gupta, K. (2014, August 4). Acute uncomplicated cystitis and pyelonephritis in women. *UpToDate.* Retrieved from http://www.uptodate.com/contents/acute-uncomplicated-cystitis-and-pyelonephritis-in-women?source=search_result&search=acute+uncomplicated+cystitis&selectedTitle=1%7E78

Johnson D. W. (2011, May). Global proteinuria guidelines: Are we nearly there yet? *Clinical Biochemistry Reviews, 32,* 89–95.

Johnson, T. M. (2014, August). Nocturia: Clinical presentation, diagnosis, and treatment. *UpToDate.* Retrieved from http://www.uptodate.com/contents/nocturia-clinical-presentation-diagnosis-and-treatment?source=search_result& search=nocturia+and+clinical+presentation&selectedTitle=1%7E150

Johnson, T. M., Abbasi, A., Ehrlich, S. A., Kleris, R. S., Raison, C. L., & Master, V. A. (2010). *Urology, 77,* 183–186.

Käkkinen, J. T., Hakama, M., Shiri, R., Auvinen, A., Tammela, T. L. J., & Koskimäki, J. (2006, December). Incidence of nocturia in 50-80-year-old Finnish men. *The Journal of Urology, 176,* 2541–2545.

Kapustin, J. (2008, October). Latent autoimmune diabetes in adults. *The Journal of Nurse Practitioner-JNP, 4,* 681–687.

Kellogg-Spate, S. (2012). Treatment for the genitourinary symptoms of vaginal atrophy: A perspective for nurse practitioners. *Women's Health Care Annual Conference Issue, 11,* 33–39.

Kessler, T. M., Buchser, E., Meyer, S., Engeler, D. S., Al-Khodairy, A-W., Bersch, U., ... Burkhard, F. C. (2007). Sacral neuromodulation for refractory lower urinary tract dysfunction: Results of a nationwide registry in Switzerland. *European Urology, 51,* 1357–1363.

Keyock, K. L., & Newman, D. K. (2011, October). Understanding stress urinary incontinence. *The Nurse Practitioner, 36,* 25–37.

Khan, F. R., Younis, A., Alosta, A., & Khan, S. A. A. (2011, September/October). Management of nocturia. *Trends in Urology & Men's Health, 2,* 35–37.

Kim, E. D. (2014, August 21a). Erectile dysfunction. *Medscape Reference.* Retrieved from http://emedicine.medscape.com/article/444220-overview

Kim, E. D. (2014, August 21b). Erectile dysfunction treatment & management. *Medscape Reference.* Retrieved from http://emedicine.medscape.com/article /444220-treatment

Kruger, D. (2012, April 2). *The pathophysiology, diagnosis, and management of proteinuria.* Retrieved from www.jaap.com/the-pathophysiology-diagnosis-and-management-of-proteinuria/printarticle/234025.

Krystal, A. D., Rogers, S., & Fitzgerald, M. A. (2006). Long-term pharmacotherapy in the management of chronic insomnia. *The Journal of Nurse Practitioners–JNP, 2,* S621–S632.

Kupelian, V., Wei, J. T., O'Leary, M. P., Norgaard, J. P., Rosen, R. C., & McKinlay, J. B. (2012). Nocturia and quality of life: Results from the Boston area community health survey. *European Urology, 61,* 78–84.

Landford, C. (2012, November). Clinical features and diagnosis of small-vessel vasculitis. *Cleveland Clinic Journal of Medicine, 79,* S3–S26.

Laureanno, P., & Ellsworth, P. (2010, September-October). Demystifying nocturia: Identifying the casue and tailoring the treatment. *Urologic Nursing, 30,* 276–287.

Lee, S. L. (2014, September 29). Hydrocele. *Medscape Reference.* Retrieved from emedicine.medscape.com/article/438724-overview

Lerma, E. V. (2012a, September 13). Proteinuria. *Medscape Reference.* Retrieved from emedicine.medscape.com/article/238158-overview

Lerma, E. V. (2012b, September 13). Proteinuria, treatment & management. *Medscape Reference.* Retrieved from emedicine.medscape.com/article/238158-treatment

Martin, K. A. (2014, June 17). Evaluation of male sexual dysfunction. *UpToDate.* Retrieved from http://www.uptodate.com/contents/evaluation-of-male-sexual-dysfunction?source=search_result&search=evaluation+of+male+sexual+dysfunction&selectedTitle=1%7E150

MedlinePlus. (2012a). *Self catheterization-female.* Retrieved from http://www.nlm.nih.gov/medlineplus/ency/patientinstructions/000144.htm

MedlinePlus. (2012b). *Self catheterization-male.* Retrieved from http://www.nlm.nih.gov/medlineplus/ency/patientinstructions/000143.htm

National Association for Continence. (n.d.). *Nocturia.* Retrieved from http://www.nafc.org/bladder-bowel-health/nocturia

National Institute of Diabetes and Digestive and Kidney Diseases. (2014, July). *Urinary retention.* NIH Publication No. 14-6089. Retrieved from http://kidney.niddk.nih.gov/Kudiseases/pubs/UrinaryRetention/UrinaryRetention_508.pdf

National Kidney Disease Education Program. (n.d.). *GFR calculators.* Retrieved from http://www.nkdep.nih.gov/professionals/gfr_calculators/index.htm

National Kidney Foundation. (2002). *KDOQI clinical practice guidelines for chronic kidney disease: Evaluation, classification, and stratification.* Retrieved from www.kidney.org/professionals/kdoqi/guidelines_ckd/p5_g5.htm

National Kidney Foundation. (2014). Kidney stones. Retrieved from http://www.kidney.org/atoz/content/kidneystones

Osman, N. I., & Chapple, C. R. (2013). Focus on nocturia in the elderly. *Medscape Nurses.* Retrieved from http://www.medscape.com/viewarticle/809746

Palone, D. R. (2010). Benign prostatic hyperplasia. *Clinics of Geriatric Medicine, 26,* 223–239.

Practice Committee of the American Society for Reproductive Medicine. (2008). Report on varicocele and infertility. *Fertility and Sterility, 90,* S247–S249.

Preminger, G. M., & Curhan, G. C. (2013, September 17). Nephrolithiasis during pregnancy. *UpToDate.* Retrieved from http://www.uptodate.com/contents/nephrolithiasis-during-pregnancy?source=search_result&search=nephrolithiasis+during+pregnancy&selectedTitle=1%7E150

Qaseem, A., Dallas, P., Forciea, M. A., Starkey, M., Denberg, T., & Shekelle, P. (2014). Nonsurgical management of urinary incontinence in women: A clinical practice guideline from the American College of Physicians. *Annals of Internal Medicine, 161,* 429–440.

Qaseem, A., Snow, V., Denberg, T. D., Casey, D. E., Forciea, M. A., Owens, D. K., & Shekelle, P. (2009). Hormonal testing and pharmacologic treatment of erectile dysfunction: A clinical practice guideline from the American College of Physicians. *Annals of Internal Medicine, 151,* 639–649.

Reynolds, W. S., & Bales, G. T. (2007). Results of sacral neuromodulation therapy for urinary voiding dysfunction: Outcomes of a prospective, worldwide clinical study. P. E. van Kerrebroeck , A. C. van Voskuilen, J. P. Heesakkers, A. A. Lycklama á Nijholt, S. Siegel, U. Jonas, C. J., Fowler, M. Fall, J. B. Gajewski, M. M. Hassouna, F. Cappellano, M. M. Elhilali, D. F. Milam, A. K. Das, H. E. Dijkema and U. van den Hombergh. *Journal of Urology, 178,* 2029–2034.

Rosenberg, M. T., Newman, D. K., & Page, S. A. (2007). Interstitial cystitis/painful bladder syndrome: Symptom recognition is key to early identification, treatment. *Cleveland Clinic Journal of Medicine, 74,* S54–S62.

Rovner, E. S. (2014, April 10). Interstitial cystitis. *Medscape Reference.* Retrieved from emedicine.medscape.com/article/2055505-overview

Rupp, T. J. (2013, April 18). Testicular torsion in emergency medicine. *Medscape Reference.* Retrieved from emedicine.medscape.com/article/778086-overview

Sarma, A. V., & Wei, J. T. (2012, July 19). Benign prostatic hyperplasia and lower urinary tract symptoms. *New England Journal of Medicine, 367,* 248–257.

Schaefer, A. J. (2006). Chronic prostatitis and the chronic pelvic pain syndrome. *New England Journal of Medicine, 355,* 1690–1701.

Sheikh, F., & Venyo, A. (2012, November 11). Proteinuria in pregnancy: A review of the literature. *Obstetrics and Gynaecology.* Retrieved from http://www.webmedcentral.com

Smith, D. A., Chini, E., & Buntin, F. (2009). Incontinence in older adults: Options for realistic, effective treatment. *Advance for Nurse Practitioners, 71,* 41–44.

Soda, T., Masui, K., Okuno, H., Terai, A., Ogawa, O., & Yoshibura, K. (2010). Efficacy of nondrug lifestyle measures for the treatment of nocturia. *The Journal of Urology,* 184, 1000–1004.

Srinath, H. (2013, November). Acute scrotal pain. *Australian Family Physician,* 42, 790–792. Retrieved from http://www.racgp.org.au/download/Documents/AFP/2013/November/201311srinath.pdf

STENDRA. (n.d.). Highlights of prescribing information. Retrieved from https://www.stendra.com/wp-content/uploads/STENDRA-avanafil-tablets-full-PI.pdf?accessed=20140930222139

Sumfest, J. M. (2012, January 20). Cryptorchidism. *Medscape Reference.* Retrieved from emedicine.medscape.com/article/438378-overview

Summers, A. (2014, July). Fournier's gangrene. *The Journal for Nurse Practitioners-JNP,* 10, 582–587.

Sutherland, S. E., Lavers, A., Carlson, A., Holtz, C., Kesha, I., & Siegel, S. W. (2007). Sacral nerve stimulation for voiding dysfunction: One institutions's 11 year experience. *Neurourology and Urodynamics, 26,* 19–28.

Tartavoulle, T. M., & Porche, D. (2012, November). Low testosterone. *The Journal for Nurse Practitioners-JNP, 8,* 778–786.

The Merck Manual. (2014, March). Prostatitis. Retrieved from http://www.merckmanuals.com/professional/genitourinary_disorders/benign_prostate_disease/prostatitis.html

The Testicular Cancer Resource Center. (2009, March 16). *How to do a testicular self examination.* Retrieved from http://tcrc.acor.org/tcexam.html

Tikkinen, K. A. O., Johnson II, T. M., Tammela, T. J. L., Sintonen, H., Haukka, J., Huhtala, H., & Auvinen, A. (2010). Nocturia frequency, bother, and quality of life: How often is too often? A population-based study in Finland. *European Urology, 57,* 488–498.

Trojian, T. H., Lishnak, T. S., & Heiman, D. (2009, April). Epididymitis and orchitis: An overview. *American Family Physician, 79,* 583–587.

Turek, P. J. (2013, March 8). Prostatitis treatment & management. *Medscape Reference.* Retrieved from emedicine.medscape.com/article/785418-treatment

Urology Care Foundation. (2013a). ED: Non-surgical management (erectile dysfunction). Retrieved from http://www.urologyhealth.org/urology/index.cfm?article=60

Urology Care Foundation. (2013b). ED: Surgical management (erectile dysfunction). Retrieved from http://www.urologyhealth.org/urology/index.cfm?article=28

Urology Care Foundation. (2014). Testicular torsion. Retrieved from http://www.urologyhealth.org/urology/index.cfm?article=34

U.S. Department of Health and Human Services, National Institutes of Health. (2012). National Kidney and Urological Diseases Information Clearinghouse: *Hematuria: Blood in the urine.* (NIH Publication 12-4559). Retrieved from http://kidney.niddk.nih.gov/kudiseases/pubs/hematuria

U.S. Department of Health and Human Services, National Institutes of Health. (2014). National Kidney and Urological Disease Information Clearinghouse: *Kidney and Urologic Diseases.* (NIH Publication 14-4553). Retrieved from http://kidney.niddk.nih.gov/kudiseases/pubs/prostatitis

U.S. Department of Health and Human Services, National Institutes of Health. (2007). National Kidney and Urological Diseases Information Clearinghouse: *Urinary incontinence in women.* (NIH Publication No. 08–4132). Retrieved from http://kidney.niddk.nih.gov/kudiseases/pubs/pdf/UI-Women.pdf

U.S. Department of Health and Human Services, National Institutes of Health. (2008a, April). National Kidney and Urological Disease Information Clearinghouse: *Interstitial cystitis/painful bladder syndrome.* (NIH Publication No. 08–3220). Retrieved from http://kidney.niddk.nih.gov/kudiseases/pubs/pdf/interstitialcystitis.pdf

U.S. Department of Health and Human Services, National Institutes of Health. (2008b). National Kidney and Urological Diseases Information Clearinghouse: *Prostatitis: Disorders of the prostate.* (NIH Publication No. 08–4553). Retrieved from http://kidney.niddk.nih.gov/Kudiseases/pubs/pdf/Prostatitis.pdf

U.S. Department of Health and Human Services, National Institutes of Health. (n.d.). National Kidney and Urological Diseases Information Clearinghouse: *Bladder control diary.* Retrieved from http://kidney.niddk.nih.gov/kudiseases/pubs/bladdercontrol/index.htm

van Doorn, B., Blanker, M. H., Kok, E. T., Westers, P., & Bosch., J. L. H. (2013). Prevalence, incidence, and resolution of nocturnal polyuria in a longitudinal community-based study in older men: the Krumpen study. *European Urology, 63,* 542–547.

van Koeveringe, G. A., Vahibi, B., Anderson, K. E., Kirschner-Herrmans, R., & Oelke, M. (2011). Detrusor underactivity: a plea for new approaches to a common bladder dysfunction. *Neurology and Urodynamics, 30,* 723–728.

Vaughn, C. P., Junco, J. L., Trotti, L. M., Johnson II, T. M., & Bliwise, D. L. (2013). Nocturia and overnight polysomnography in Parkinson disease. *Neurourology and Urodynamics, 32,* 1080–1085.

Vitton, V., Abysique, A., Gaigé S., Leroi, A.-M., & Bouvier, M. (2008). Colonosphincteric electromyographic responses to sacral root stimulation: evidence for a somatosympathetic reflex. *Neurogastroenterology Motility, 20,* 407–416.

Wada, N., Kita, M., Hashizume, K., Matsumoto, S., & Kakizaki, H. (2013). Urodynamic effects of dutasteride add-on therapy to alpha-adrenergic antagonist for patients with benign prostatic enlargement: prospective pressure-flow study. *Neurourology and Urodynamics, 32,* 1123–1127.

Wayment, R. O. (2012, March 15). Pregnancy and urolithiasis. *Medscape Reference.* Retrieved from emedicine.medscape.com/article/455830-overview.

Web, M. D. (2009). Testicular self-exam. *Medicinehealth.* Retrieved from http://www.emedicinehealth.com/testicular_ self-exam/page7_em.htm#Physician%20Treatment

Weiss, J. P., Blaivas, J. G., Bliwise, D. L., Dmochowski, R. R., DuBeau, C. E., Lowe, F. C., ... Wein, A. J. (2011). The evaluation and treatment of nocturia: a consensus statement. *BJU International, 108,* 6–21.

Weiss, J. R., Moysich, K. B., & Swede, H. (2005). Epidemiology of male breast cancer. *Cancer Epidemiology, Biomarkers & Prevention, 14,* 20–26.

Werner, K. T., & Perez, S. T. (2012, November/December). The role of nurse practitioners in the management of cirrhotic patients. *The Journal for Nurse Practitioners-JNP,* 8, 816-821.

White, W. M., (2012, January 3). Varicocele. *Medscape Reference.* Retrieved from emedicine.medscape.com/article/438591-overview

Wolfe, J. S. (2014a, April 28). Nephrolithiasis. *Medscape Reference.* Retrieved from emedicine.medscape.com/article/437096-overview

Wolfe, J. S. (2014b, April 28). Nephrolithiasis treatment & management. *Medscape Reference.* Retrieved from emedicine.medscape.com/article/437096-treatment

Yokoyama, O., Yamaguchi, O., Kakizaki, H., Itoh, N., Yokota, T., Okada, H., ... Yamada, S. (2011, July). Efficacy of solifenacin on nocturia in Japanese patients with overactive bladder: impact of sleep evaluated by bladder diary. *The Journal of Urology, 186,* 170–174.

Zaccardi, J. E. (2013, January). Managing urinary tract infections in women. *The Clinical Advisor.* Retrieved from http://www.clinicaladvisor.com/managing-utis-in-women/article/276373

CHAPTER FIFTEEN

Obstetrics Guidelines

Jill C. Cash and Susan Drummond

Antepartum

Preconception Counseling: Identifying Patients at Risk

A woman's health before conception influences her ability not only to conceive, but also to maintain pregnancy and to achieve a healthy outcome. Some women are unaware that their medical conditions, medications, occupational exposure, or social practices may have negative consequences in the earliest weeks of pregnancy, before the pregnancy test is positive. They don't know that organogenesis begins around 17 days after fertilization. Steps to provide the ideal environment for the developing fetus are most likely to be effective if they precede the traditional initiation of prenatal care.

The goal of preconceptional care is to reduce perinatal mortality and morbidity. Targeting only self-referred women who are planning their next conception or women referred with risk factors can result in a significant number of missed opportunities for primary prevention. Nurses working with women of childbearing age and their families have a responsibility to promote reproductive health during every health encounter. Even among married women in the United States, the unintended pregnancy rate is nearly 40%; 85% of teen pregnancies are unintended.

During the antepartum period, assessment for routine screening exams should be performed to promote a healthy pregnancy. Topics of discussion should include status on current immunizations, assessing rubella immunity, determining hepatitis status, Pap smears, cultures for sexually transmitted infections (STIs), and reviewing the history for chronic diseases, such as diabetes, hypertension, lupus, and so forth.

When discussing preconception plans, the patient's history, as well as that of her partner, should be evaluated for poor health habits (alcohol, smoking, drug use), exposure to toxic substances (radiation and chemicals), multiple sexual partners (risk of HIV, hepatitis, and STIs), and racial or ethnic origin. Preconceptional evaluation should include the following:

A. Maternal age: Pregnancy-induced hypertension (PIH) occurs at the extreme of ages, insulin-dependent diabetes increases with maternal age, and the risks of Down syndrome and other chromosomal abnormalities increase with maternal age. Advanced maternal age is defined as 35 years of age at delivery. The American College of Obstetricians and Gynecologists (ACOG) requires counseling on genetic screening/testing options for women of advanced maternal age.
B. Universal carrier screening is available for women who desire to know if they are carriers for an autosomal recessive disorder such as Tay–Sachs disease, sickle cell anemia, or cystic fibrosis. Ideally, this blood test should be done preconceptionally, but it can be performed at any time during the pregnancy. If the screening test is positive, the woman's partner can then be tested.
C. Social issues: Screen every woman for intimate partner violence. Research indicates that most abused women continue to be victimized during pregnancy and that the violence may escalate. Child abuse is also common in homes where there is abuse of adults. This assessment should be done only if the partner is not present. Information should be given to the patient concerning available community, social, and legal resources, and her immediate safety, the safety of her children, and an escape plan should be assessed.
D. Financial: Discuss insurance, maternity benefits, work-leave policy, and contingency plans for lost wages due to pregnancy complications with the patient.
E. Environmental and occupational considerations: Routine assessment of hobbies and home and employment environments may identify exposures that have been associated with adverse reproductive

consequences that can be minimized in the preconceptual period.

F. Fetal effects are dependent on dose(s) and gestational age at exposure related to the following:
   1. Radiation: Fetal effects include microcephaly, mental retardation, eye anomalies, intrauterine growth retardation (IUGR), and visceral malformations. Lead aprons should be used to protect the patient from any radiation exposures.
   2. Heavy metals: Mercury exposure is related to brain damage and neuromuscular defects. Lead exposure is related to increased spontaneous abortion, low birth weight, brain damage, and increased premature rupture of membranes (PROM). Cadmium is retained by the fetal liver and kidney and is also associated with fetal craniofacial defects. Nickel is associated with neonatal deaths.
   3. Pesticides: Occupations at risk for pesticide exposure include, but are not limited to, the following: ranch and farm workers (including migrant workers); gardeners (home and professional); groundskeepers; florists; structural pest control workers; hunting and fishing guides; health care workers who deal with contamination; and people employed in pesticide production, mixing, and application. Dioxin is associated with an increased rate of spontaneous abortion, myelomeningocele, and limb defects. The pesticides dichlorodiphenyltrichloroethane (DDT) and dichlorodiphenyldichloroethylene (DDE) are associated with increased abortion, prematurity, low birth weight, and PIH.
   4. Other: Carbon monoxide is associated with increased stillbirths, neurologic deficits, seizures, spasticity, and retarded psychomotor development. Ozone is associated with increased spontaneous abortion and increased structural defects. Anesthetic gases are associated with increased abortion, birth defects, low birth weight, and infertility.

G. Infectious diseases: See Chapter 17, "Sexually Transmitted Infections Guidelines" and Chapter 18, "Infectious Disease Guidelines."

H. Medications: Assess and minimize the risk of exposure to medications by reviewing the patient's use of prescription and nonprescription drugs. Provide the patient with information on the safest choices and avoiding drugs associated with fetal risks. Identify all prescription and nonprescription medications taken by the mother and partner to assess for risks to the fetus associated with current medications. Teratogenic defects linked to certain medications may include cleft lip and palate, congenital heart disease, microcephaly, caudal dysplasia, and caudal regression syndrome.

I. Medical problems: Health assessment of potential risk not only to the fetus but also to the woman, should she become pregnant, should be discussed. Care must be taken to identify and counsel all women whose life expectancy could be markedly reduced by pregnancy or whose fetus would have a high likelihood of complications. For example, women with known cardiac problems, epilepsy, transplanted organs, or uncontrolled diabetes and hypertension should be told of the risks associated with pregnancy.
   1. Diabetes: Researchers have demonstrated a dose-related response between glycosylated hemoglobin (Hgb A1c) during the first trimester of pregnancy and the incidence of congenital defects: The better the glycemic control, the lower the risk for birth defects. The preconceptional plan for diabetes includes the following:
      a. Change all patients on oral agents to insulin therapy before pregnancy is attempted.
      b. Achieve strict plasma glucose control. The ACOG recommends self blood glucose monitoring during pregnancy with the following glucose levels to be met.
         i. Fasting: Less than or equal to 95 mg/dL
         ii. Preprandial glucose values less than 100 mg/dL
         iii. 1-hour postprandial glucose levels less than 140 mg/dL
         iv. 2-hour postprandial glucose levels less than 120 mg/dL
         v. Nighttime glucose levels should not drop below 60 mg/dL. Care should be taken to avoid hypoglycemia during pregnancy.
      c. Reduce the Hgb A1c to 6% or less.
      d. Assess the patient for vasculopathy, neuropathy, nephropathy, and retinopathy.
      e. Refer the patient for genetic and nutritional counseling.
      f. Enhance the woman's knowledge of diabetes during pregnancy.

J. Nutrition: Dietary evaluation and recommendations of alternatives that may benefit the fetus's development are important components of preconceptional counseling. Evaluation of nutritional status should include assessment of the appropriate weight for the patient's height as well as a discussion of eating habits such as vegetarianism, fasting for religious or personal reasons, eating disorders, and the use of megavitamins.

K. Obstetric considerations: Preconceptional reproductive history is an important tool for identifying factors that may be amenable to intervention. Review term, preterm, aborted (elective, spontaneous, and therapeutic) pregnancies, as well as a short history on living children. Review the gestational age at delivery of each neonate and any pregnancy and delivery complications. Preterm labor (PTL) has a 30% recurrence risk, and preeclampsia has a 5% to 70% recurrence rate in subsequent pregnancies. Women who developed severe features of preeclampsia and were delivered before 30 weeks gestation have the highest risk of preeclampsia in future pregnancies. In some instances, after preconceptual and genetic counseling, the couple may decide to forgo pregnancy or to use assisted reproductive technologies such as donor eggs and/or sperm.

L. Recurrent loss: The workup and counseling for recurrent losses include evaluation for a uterine defect (septal or bicornuate uterus or uterus didelphys), endocrine problem (luteal phase defect or hypothyroidism), chromosomal defect, or presence of antiphospholipid syndrome. Antiphospholipid syndrome is defined as the presence of maternal anticardiolipin antibodies and/or lupus anticoagulant in association with recurrent pregnancy loss, thrombotic events, and/or thrombocytopenia. Approximately 10% of women with unexplained recurrent pregnancy loss test positive for anticardiolipin antibodies and/or lupus anticoagulant. In the nonpregnant patient, thrombosis of a single vessel is the most common complication associated with antiphospholipid syndrome.

M. Lifestyle: Queries regarding a woman's social lifestyle history should seek to identify behaviors and exposures that may compromise reproductive outcome. While environmental exposures are a frequent concern of couples considering pregnancy, women should be informed that, in general, maternal use of alcohol, tobacco, and other mood-altering drugs is more hazardous for a fetus than most other lifestyle choices.

1. Alcohol: Alcohol is a known teratogen. There is no safe limit of alcohol use during pregnancy. Women should be informed that prenatal alcohol consumption is a preventable cause of birth defects including neurodevelopmental deficits and intellectual disability. Research indicates that as many as 73% of 12- to 34-year-old women expose their fetuses to alcohol at some time during pregnancy.
2. Smoking: Fetal effects of smoking are also related to the dose-response effect. Smoking is associated with an increase in bleeding in pregnancy (abruption and placenta previa), IUGR, preterm birth, low birth weight, stillbirth, respiratory distress in the neonate, and sudden infant death syndrome. Counsel the patient on smoking cessation. Suggestions of ways to quit include tapering the use of nicotine (tapering and brand switching to lower tar and nicotine), monitoring smoking behavior, setting a contract to quit smoking, identifying social support or a buddy, and restricting area(s) such as a no smoking zone. Give the patient positive reinforcement for behavior change and cessation of the use of tobacco. Nicotine replacement therapy may be considered but only under close supervision with careful discussions with the patient, as the U.S. Preventive Services Task Force has concluded that nicotine replacement products during pregnancy have not been sufficiently evaluated for safety or efficacy.
3. Substance use: If substance exposure is complicated by addiction, structured recovery programs are usually needed to effect behavioral change. Substance use/abuse is teratogenic to the fetus, and cessation of all substances is imperative before, during, and after pregnancy.

N. Exercise: Exercise and recreational activities should be reviewed and discussed relative to safety, including the use of bike helmets, avoiding strenuous exercise, and hyperthermia. The ACOG recommends that maternal heart rate (for pregnant women) not exceed 140 beats per minute (bpm). If the woman is not currently exercising, walking and swimming can be suggested. Heat exposure appears to be teratogenic. Use of saunas or hot tubs and high fevers in the first trimester have been associated with an increased risk of neural tube defects (NTDs).

Preconception counseling helps to identify high-risk patients who need intensive care during pregnancy and delivery, and it identifies women who need referral for medical management, nutritional counseling, genetic counseling, or behavior modification. Prescribe a prenatal vitamin daily for any woman considering pregnancy.

Routine Prenatal Care

Initial Prenatal Visit

The initial prenatal visit is a very important visit. A comprehensive health history is obtained; blood is drawn for baseline prenatal laboratory values to be established; and depending on the time, the physical examination may also be performed. Many practitioners have the patient return in 1 to 2 weeks to perform the physical exam due to the amount of time taken for history and for collecting blood for laboratory tests. Another variation is to obtain the baseline lab tests (except blood type and Rh factor) after the first trimester (to avoid unnecessary testing in the event the patient should have a miscarriage).

The initial visit is also a time for teaching the pregnant patient (see Exhibit 15.1). Literature and

EXHIBIT 15.1 Routine Prenatal Patient Education Topics

Topic	Dates
Prenatal care in your practice (office visits, blood tests)/Prenatal handouts	______
Diet/nutrition/weight gain	______
Enrolled in women, infants, and children (WIC)	______
Substance use (alcohol, smoking, drugs)	______
Domestic violence (history, type of injuries)	______
Over-the-counter (OTC) medication use	______
Activity: work and exercise	______
Travel	______
Clothing	______
Personal hygiene	______
Cats	______
Sexual activity	______
Physiologic changes during pregnancy	______
Fetal development	______
Father's role during pregnancy	______
Common discomforts/treatments	______
Symptoms to report immediately	______
Fetal kick counts	______
Prenatal classes	______
Breastfeeding/bottle feeding	______
Circumcision	______
Infant supply preparation	______
Safety/car safety	______
Preparing for delivery	______
When to come to the hospital	______
Labor and delivery expectations	______
Postpartum care	______
First days with baby	______
Postpartum birth control	______
TESTS	
Quad screen	______
Noninvasive Prenatal Screening	______
1-hour DM screen	______
Ultrasonography	______
Glucose tolerance test if applicable	______
Amniocentesis/chorionic villus sampling (CVS) if applicable	______
Group B strep	______

Fetal monitoring: Kick counts: ______

NST: ______ BPP: ______

(Content discussed can be found in patient handout provided to patient at first prenatal visit.)

BPP, biophysical profile; NST, nonstress test.

brochures on health promotion (i.e., breast self-exam, dietary recommendation, exercise, and smoking cessation) and information regarding the normal changes, discomforts, and concerns during pregnancy should be provided. The after-hours contact information should also be provided, along with contact information for the labor and delivery. Reassure the patient that as the pregnancy progresses you will answer questions she may have; however, outside resources may also be beneficial for the patient and her family. Encourage the patient to enroll in childbirth education, sibling classes (if applicable), breastfeeding classes, and any other classes of interest to her and her partner.

Important information to cover is the patient's medical and surgical history (including previous obstetric history), family genetic history, psychiatric disorders, contraception history, medications taken since the last menstrual period, menstrual history, social habits (smoking, substance abuse, alcohol), environmental exposures (job, hobbies, and so on), exposure to abuse (mental, physical, sexual), and sources of social support and health promotion (immunizations up to date, etc.).

Laboratory tests that are ordered at the initial exam include the following: complete blood count (CBC), rubella titer, HIV (with the patient's consent), syphilis (rapid plasma reagin [RPR] or Venereal Disease Research Laboratory [VDRL]), hepatitis B surface antigen, blood type and Rh factor, antibody screen, tuberculosis testing, urine culture and sensitivity, and bacterial vaginosis screen.

Optional tests include Hgb A1c, sickle cell screening, thyroid profile, and hepatitis C. Other tests performed with the physical examination include Pap smear and cultures for chlamydia and gonorrhea. Additional tests may be ordered throughout the pregnancy.

A. 15 to 20 weeks gestation: Maternal serum multiple marker screening (quad screen) (optional test per patient wishes and father of baby and other family history)
B. 18 to 20 weeks gestation: Obstetric ultrasonography
C. 24 to 28 weeks gestation: Screen all women for gestational diabetes by performing the 1-hour glucola test, by patient history, or clinical risk factors. Diagnosis of gestational diabetes is determined by the results of the 100 g 3-hour oral glucose tolerance test (GTT). A positive diagnosis requires that two or more of the diagnostic criteria for the 100 g, 3-hour tolerance test for gestational diabetes mellitus (GDM) tolerance test be met or higher (ACOG Committee Opinion, 2011).
D. 35 to 37 weeks gestation: Vaginal culture for Group B *Streptococcus* infection

The American Academy of Pediatrics recommends universal screening for Group B *Streptococcus* infection at 36 weeks gestation.

E. Special tests: Even with the best preconceptional plan and modifications, about 2% to 3% of all babies have a major congenital malformation.

Neural Tube Defects

In about 90% of the cases, NTDs are not expected on the basis of past history. NTDs are associated with multifactorial causes, including environmental factors, undernutrition (lack of folic acid), chromosomal defects, maternal hyperthermia, diabetes, clomiphene citrate (Clomid) induction, and maternal obesity.

In 1996, the Food and Drug Administration (FDA) approved a population-based strategy, effective January 1998, to fortify grain food sources with folic acid. The recurrence risk of NTD is 2% to 3% without the use of preconceptional doses of folic acid. Even with the FDA strategy, folic acid supplement of 0.4 mg (400 mcg) per day at least 1 month before conception and during the first trimester of pregnancy is recommended. Women who have had a child with an NTD require higher doses of folic acid, 4 mg daily.

Genetic Screening

Genetic screening is recommended for all women. Genetic counseling for discussion of testing options is recommended if the mother is 35 years or older at the time of delivery, or if she has a family history of any abnormal genetic disorders, such as Down syndrome. The parents choose whether they would like to have genetic testing performed to evaluate the fetus for abnormal chromosomes. The following tests can be performed for genetic screening:

A. Chorionic villus sampling (CVS): Performed at 10 to 12 weeks gestation
B. Amniocentesis: Performed at 15 to 18 weeks gestation, ideally, but can be performed later in pregnancy.
C. Amniocentesis can also be performed to assess for spinal cord defects. Amniocentesis can detect elevated protein levels (alpha-fetoprotein and the presence of acetyl cholinesterase) in the amniotic fluid that is present in the event of a spinal cord defect. Therefore, if performing an amniocentesis, information regarding both genetic makeup and spinal cord defects can be determined during the single procedure of the amniocentesis.
D. Noninvasive prenatal screening: Cell-free DNA from the fetus is found in maternal serum and can lead to prenatal identification of pregnancies at high risk for Trisomy 13, 18, and 21, as well as detect gender. This screen is a maternal blood test and can be done as early as 10 weeks. A positive screen should be confirmed with a diagnostic test such as CVS or amniocentesis.

The routine schedule of appointments includes a visit every 4 weeks until 28 weeks gestation, every

2 weeks until 36 weeks gestation, then weekly until delivered.

A. Each visit should document
   1. Weight
   2. Blood pressure (BP)
   3. Fundal height, fetal heart tones, and fetal movement (should be detected by the patient by 20 weeks)
   4. Urine: Protein and glucose

B. Each visit should evaluate and discuss possible problems of pregnancy, such as PTL, vaginal bleeding, and so on. A few questions to ask at each visit include the following.
   1. Have you had any blurred vision, spots before your eyes, or epigastric pain?
   2. Have you had any headaches? If so, evaluate and note source of relief.
   3. Have you had any nausea or vomiting? If so, note source of relief.
   4. Have you had any abdominal pain, contractions, backache, pelvic pressure, or other pain?
   5. Have you had any vaginal bleeding, discharge, or leakage of fluid?
   6. Evaluate fetal movement, noting when movement was first felt (quickening) and daily fetal movement.
   7. Evaluate social support at home and in the work environment.
   8. Assess for substance use/abuse. If the patient smokes, ask about current habits. Teach the patient the effects of smoking on herself and the fetus (bleeding, IUGR, increased risk of miscarriage), and encourage smoking cessation.
   9. Assess nutrition and dietary intake of recommended calories during pregnancy.
   10. Ask the patient about her routine exercise program and tolerance of increased exercise during pregnancy.

Anemia, Iron Deficiency

Definition

A. Anemia in pregnancy results from decreased serum iron. The iron-binding capacity is increased. Red blood cells (RBCs) are microcytic and hypochromic. The Centers for Disease Control and the ACOG define first- and third-trimester anemia as a Hgb of less than 11.0 g/dL, hematocrit (Hct) of less than 33%, and second trimester as a Hgb of less than 10.5 g/dL, Hct of less than 32%.

Incidence

A. Anemia is a common medical complication of pregnancy. Iron-deficiency anemia constitutes 75% to 95% of pregnancy-related anemias.

Pathogenesis

A. Increased demand for iron during pregnancy occurs because of increased maternal blood volume. Hgb and Hct decrease during the first and second trimesters due to a greater expansion of plasma volume relative to the increase in RBC mass and usually increase during the third trimester when plasma expansion has ceased

B. Another 0.5 to 1.0 mg/d of iron is needed for lactation. During most pregnancies, diet alone does not provide the necessary iron.

Predisposing Factors

A. Failure to take oral iron; often due to inability to tolerate oral iron supplements

B. Multiple gestation; increases iron requirement and may contribute to increased blood loss at delivery

C. Diet high in phosphorus or foods such as tea, coffee, milk, or soy

D. Low iron and protein diet, eating nonfood items (pica)

E. Not eating foods that help with absorption of iron (orange juice, broccoli, strawberries)

F. History of gastrointestinal surgery may cause iron malabsorption (i.e., gastrectomy)

G. Chronic bleeding during pregnancy (i.e., placenta previa, marginal sinus separation of placenta, hemorrhoidal bleeding)

H. Short intervals between pregnancies

I. Race: Non-Hispanic Black females

J. Age: Teenage girls

Common Complaints

A. Tiredness

B. Inability to take prenatal vitamins because of nausea

C. Bleeding problems (see section "Predisposing Factors")

D. Pica

Other Signs and Symptoms

A. Fatigue

B. Pale mucous membranes and skin

C. Tachycardia

Subjective Data

A. Elicit the onset, duration, and course of presenting symptoms.

B. Elicit information about the patient's "typical" dietary intake for meals and snacks, and review pica (eating clay, starch, ice, and other nonnutritive substances).

C. Review the patient's intake of prenatal vitamins and supplemental iron. How often does she take iron? Elicit the reason for skipping the supplemental iron (nausea, constipation), if applicable.

D. Review the patient's history of gastrointestinal surgeries, irritable bowel syndrome (IBS), and Crohn's disease.

E. Review the patient's history for any type of anemia and previous treatment, including blood transfusions.
F. Review pregnancy history for closely spaced pregnancies (two in a calendar year) and multiple gestation.
G. Review the patient's intake of medications for the use of aspirin and other nonsteroidal anti-inflammatory drugs (NSAIDs).

Physical Examination

A. Check pulse and BP: Note postural hypotension and tachycardia.
B. Inspect: General appearance
   1. Inspect the skin, mucous membranes, and conjunctivae for pallor.
   2. Observe the mouth and tongue: Note atrophy of papillae and smooth, beefy red appearance of tongue with anemia.
   3. Note dryness of skin. Inspect texture of nails (brittle, spoon-shaped, concave); inspect the hair for brittleness.
C. Palpate: Palpate the abdomen for masses; assess fundal height.
D. Auscultate: Auscultate the heart for systolic flow murmurs; auscultate lungs.

Diagnostic Tests

A. Blood work: Hgb/Hct
   1. First trimester: Less than 11 g/dL Hgb or less than 33% Hct
   2. Second trimester: Less than 10.5 g/dL Hgb or less than 32% Hct
   3. Third trimester: Less than 11 g/dL Hgb or less than 33% Hct
B. Peripheral blood smear: Note microcytic and hypochromic RBCs on peripheral smear.
C. Sickle cell screen, if applicable
D. Serum iron: Low with anemia
E. Iron-binding capacity: High iron-binding capacity with anemia
F. Transferrin: Saturation less than 15%
G. Stool for occult blood, if applicable
H. Emesis for presence of blood, if applicable

Differential Diagnoses

A. Iron-deficiency anemia
B. Normal physiologic anemia of pregnancy: During normal pregnancy, concentrations of erythrocytes and Hgb usually fall because of the greater increase in plasma volume (increased by 45%) relative to the increase in erythrocyte volume (increased by 25%).
C. Megaloblastic anemia: This condition is commonly associated with iron-deficiency anemia and is rarely seen alone.
D. Hemolytic anemia: Sickle cell anemia, thalassemia, hereditary spherocytosis, and erythrocyte enzyme deficiency
E. Aplastic anemia: Bone marrow failure
F. Hematologic malignancies: Leukemia and lymphoma
G. Clotting factor or other hemostatic deficiencies: von Willebrand's disease, idiopathic thrombocytopenia (ITP), and disseminated intravascular coagulation (DIC)

Plan

A. General interventions
   1. Perform initial evaluation of Hgb and Hct at first prenatal visit; repeat at 24- to 28-week blood draw with diabetes testing.
   2. Diet counseling and nutrition consultation
   3. The patient may be eligible for the Women, Infants, and Children (WIC) program that provides supplemental foods for pregnant women and young children. Ask your local health department for information available in your community.
      a. Advise the patient to take supplemental iron in addition to prenatal vitamins. If she is unable to tolerate prenatal vitamins, suggest a children's chewable vitamin, two tablets daily.
      b. Encourage the patient to continue iron supplementation through the first month postpartum and throughout breastfeeding.
B. Patient teaching: See the Section III Patient Teaching Guide for this chapter, "Iron-Deficiency Anemia (Pregnancy)."
C. Pharmaceutical therapy
   1. Prophylaxis: Oral iron supplements are recommended for all gestations with usual dose of 60 mg/d elemental iron, or 325 mg/d ferrous sulfate. Time-released tablets may help but are more expensive.
   2. Most prenatal vitamins contain supplemental iron. Therefore, if the woman is taking one vitamin daily, she may only need to take two iron tablets. Nausea and vomiting occur in 20% to 25% of patients. These side effects are dose-related. Have the patient alter times of administration of the iron supplement to determine when the iron is best tolerated.
   3. Treatment: With iron-deficiency anemia, three times the prophylactic dose of iron should be given, or 325 mg ferrous sulfate three times daily.
   4. Intramuscular (IM) or intravenous (IV) iron may be ordered for the small proportion of patients who do not tolerate oral iron due to gastrointestinal complaints, malabsorption syndrome, or non-compliance with the oral iron regimen.

Follow-Up

A. Carry out routine prenatal and postpartum follow-up care. When the patient begins taking the recommended dose of supplemental iron, the RBC response can be measured in 2 weeks by an elevation in her reticulocyte count.
B. Repeat Hct after 4 to 6 weeks of therapy.
C. If no improvement is seen in reticulocyte count or Hct after 4 weeks of therapy and the patient has been compliant, another cause of anemia should be investigated.

Consultation/Referral

A. Consider consult with a physician if Hgb is less than 9 g/dL or Hct is less than or equal to 27% and does not improve with the above treatments.

Gestational Diabetes Mellitus

Definition

A. GDM is a carbohydrate intolerance with onset or recognition during pregnancy.

Incidence

A. It is estimated that up to 6% to 7% of pregnancies are complicated by diabetes mellitus (DM) and approximately 90% of these cases represent women with GDM. It usually resolves after pregnancy.

Pathogenesis

A. Insulin antagonism caused by the placental hormones leads to gestational diabetes. As greater amounts of these hormones are produced with advancing gestation, the diabetogenic effect of pregnancy becomes more pronounced, reaching significant levels in the second trimester. Women with GDM are at risk for later development of type 1 and, more commonly, type 2 diabetes. GDM may actually be the expression of pregnancy-induced stresses on carbohydrate metabolism in the genetically predisposed patient. It is estimated that up to 50% of women with GDM will develop DM within approximately 25 years of the pregnancy. Some women have undiagnosed type 2 diabetes prior to pregnancy.

Predisposing Factors

A. Members of any of the following ethnic groups:
   1. Hispanic American
   2. African American
   3. Native American
   4. South or East Asian
   5. Pacific Islander
B. Maternal age older than 25 years
C. Obesity (body mass index [BMI] > 30)
D. Family history of diabetes
E. Previous birth of a macrosomic, malformed, or stillborn baby
F. Hypertension
G. Glycosuria at first prenatal visit
H. Gestational diabetes in a previous pregnancy

Common Complaints

A. Common complaints of hyperglycemia include polydipsia, polyuria, nocturia, fatigue, and blurred vision. However, gestational diabetes is often asymptomatic.

Other Signs and Symptoms

A. Glycosuria
B. Fundal height measurement greater than gestational age in weeks
C. Frequent candidal infections
D. Rapid weight gain

Potential Complications

A. Ketoacidosis
   1. May develop in GDM
   2. More common in insulin-dependent diabetes
   3. May develop with glucose levels as low as 200 mg/dL
   4. May be present in an undiagnosed diabetic woman receiving beta-mimetic agents (such as terbutaline) for tocolysis or steroids to enhance fetal lung maturity. **Fetal mortality rate is 10% in women who come to the hospital in diabetic ketoacidosis (DKA). Glucose and ketones cross the placenta.**
   5. Therapy hinges on timely, aggressive volume resuscitation, insulin administration, and correction of maternal electrolyte imbalance.
B. Polyhydramnios
C. Increased risk for neonatal morbidity such as hypoglycemia, hyperbilirubinemia, polycythemia, respiratory distress due to delayed lung maturity, and/or traumatic birth injury related to shoulder dystocia, which is associated with macrosomia.
D. Increased risk for stillbirth—risk is related primarily to poor glycemic control

Subjective Data

A. Review previous pregnancy history for two or more spontaneous abortions, previous stillbirths, or unexplained neonatal deaths.
B. Review birth weight (macrosomia) and gestational age of previous children.
C. Review previous pregnancy history for polyhydramnios and/or congenital anomalies.
D. Review the patient's history for a predisposition to infections, especially urinary tract infections (UTIs) and candidal vaginitis and for family history of diabetes
E. Review previous pregnancy history for gestational diabetes, diet restrictions, and need for insulin therapy.

Physical Examination

A. Check BP, pulse, and weight.
B. Inspect: Perform speculum exam for wet prep, if indicated.

C. Palpate: Check the patient's fundal height each visit after 20 weeks.
D. Auscultate fetal heart tones after 10 to 12 weeks gestation.

Screening/Diagnostic Tests

Women who have risk factors for type 2 diabetes should be screened at the initial prenatal visit.

A. Perform "one-step" 2-hour 75 g (fasting) oral glucose tolerance test (OGTT) or "two-step" 1-hour 50 g (nonfasting) followed by a 3-hour 100 g (fasting) OGTT for positive results.
B. Day curves (fasting blood sugar [FBS] and pre- and postprandial blood glucose testing)
C. HgbA1c
D. Urine dipstick for glucose: Early glycosuria needs further evaluation (i.e., HgbA1c, urine culture, random glucose "finger stick").
E. Ultrasonography if fetal size is greater than average for gestational date to rule out twins, congenital anomaly such as atresia, and polyhydramnios.

Differential Diagnoses

A. Gestational diabetes
    1. DM (type 1)
    2. DM (type 2)

Plan

A. General interventions
    1. The American Diabetes Association (ADA) recommends that all pregnant women be screened.
        a. Diabetes mellitus screen (DMS): "Two-step" 1-hour 50 g (nonfasting) OGTT followed by a 3-hour 100 g OGTT for positive results
            i. Administer 50-g oral glucose load (fasting not required).
            ii. Draw blood for glucose assessment 1 hour after glucose load is given.
            iii. Typically performed between 24 and 28 weeks gestation; performed earlier if the patient has glycosuria, risk factors, advanced maternal age, or if fetal size is greater than average for gestational date by fundal height measurement.
            iv. Abnormal result is a glucose level 130 to 140 mg/dL (use your institutional limits).
            v. Follow up all abnormal results with a 3-hour GTT; if DMS is more than 200 mg/dL, the patient may skip GTT and begin dietary modifications and glucose evaluation for insulin needs.
        b. Three-hour GTT
            i. Draw fasting blood glucose first.
            ii. Administer 100-g glucose load.
            iii. Draw blood for glucose assessment 1 hour, 2 hours, and 3 hours after glucose load is given.
            iv. Plasma or serum glucose results (Carpenter/Coustan criteria)
                1) Fasting = 95 mg/dL
                2) 1 hour = 180 mg/dL
                3) 2 hours = 155 mg/dL
                4) 3 hours = 140 mg/dL
            v. If two or more values of 3-hour GTT are elevated:
                1) Refer the patient for nutritional counseling. Once the patient is on the ADA diet, begin testing her weekly for fasting and 2-hour postprandial blood glucose measurements.
        c. "One-step" 2-hour 75 mg OGTT may be performed instead of the "two-step" approach.
    2. Antepartum testing
        a. For women with well-controlled GDM, there is no national consensus with respect to criteria for initiation and timing of testing. Options include weekly or twice weekly testing with either the nonstress test (NST) or biophysical profile (BPP) beginning at 32 to 34 weeks.
        b. For women with insulin-dependent gestational diabetes or whose condition is *not* well controlled, manage as if the patient had pregestational diabetes. Administer twice weekly NSTs beginning by 32 weeks. If a patient's diabetes is poorly controlled, consider fetal assessment earlier and more frequently.
    3. Serial ultrasonography
        a. Evaluate fetal growth, estimate fetal weight, and detect polyhydramnios and malformations.
        b. Repeat at 4- to 6-week intervals to assess growth.
        c. Macrosomia is a leading risk factor for shoulder dystocia at vaginal delivery and cephalopelvic disproportion. Women with GDM should be counseled regarding the option of a scheduled cesarean delivery when the external fetal monitor (EFM) is more than or equal to 4,500 g.
    4. Postpartum contraception
        a. Low-dose oral contraceptives (OCs) may be used in women with GDM who do not have other risk factors.
        b. Rate of subsequent diabetes in OC users is not significantly different from those who do not use OCs.
        c. Consider serial measurement of total cholesterol, low-density lipoprotein, high-density lipoprotein, and triglycerides.

5. Notify nursery staff of perinatal diabetes history, especially if the patient has a history of insulin-dependent diabetes, so that the neonate can be carefully monitored for hypoglycemia.

B. Patient teaching: GDM requires intensive patient and family education to help reduce perinatal complications.
   1. Exercise
      a. If the patient had an active lifestyle prior to pregnancy, encourage her to continue a program of exercise approved for pregnancy such as walking or swimming for 20 minutes per day.
      b. Upper extremity exercise in previously sedentary women with GDM may improve glycemic control.
   2. Instruct the patient in self-monitoring blood glucose.
      a. Have her take measurement pre- or postprandially, or both. Preprandial values are typically taken if on insulin. Fasting and postprandial values may be taken if patient is diet-controlled. FBS should be less than 95 mg/dL. Postprandial values should be less than 140 mg/L 1 hour postprandial and less than 120 mg/L at 2 hours postprandial. The HgbA1c goal is less than 6%. Nighttime levels should not decrease lower than 60 mg/dL.
      b. If the patient is taking multiple doses of insulin, she may need to take measurements more frequently.
   3. See the Section III Patient Teaching Guides for this chapter, "Gestational Diabetes" and "Insulin Therapy During Pregnancy."

C. Dietary management: Place the patient on a diet that is prescribed for preexisting diabetes in pregnancy, such as the ADA diet, in the following amounts:
   1. Current weight less than 80% ideal body weight (IBW): 35 to 40 kcal/kg/d
   2. Current weight 80% to 120% IBW: 30 kcal/kg/d
   3. Current weight 120% to 150% IBW: 24 kcal/kg/d
   4. Current weight more than 150% IBW: 12 to 15 kcal/kg/d
   5. Dietary consumption 40% to 50% carbohydrate, 20% protein, 30% to 40% fat

D. Pharmaceutical therapy
   1. Insulin therapy is recommended if dietary management does not consistently maintain fasting glucose levels of less than 95 mg/dL. Two-hour postprandial values should be less than 120 mg/dL (see Figure 15.1).
   2. Oral antidiabetic medications (Glyburide and Metformin) are being increasingly used in women with GDM, although they are not yet approved by the U.S. FDA for this indication. Glyburide results in increased insulin secretion and insulin sensitivity at the tissue level. Metformin inhibits hepatic gluconeogenesis and glucose absorption and stimulates glucose uptake in peripheral tissues.

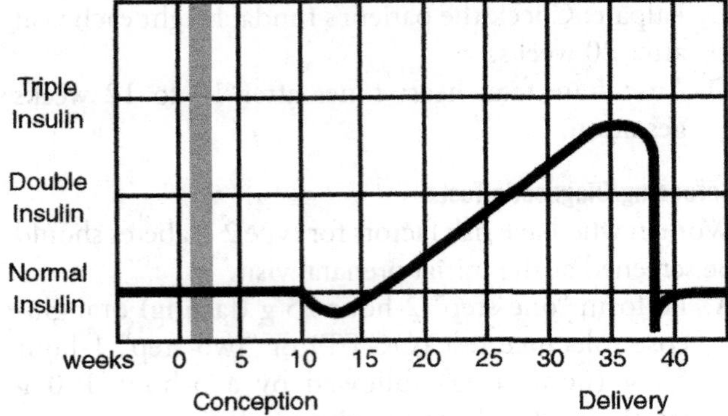

Figure 15.1 Insulin requirement during pregnancy.

   3. In general, insulin therapy in pregnancy is no different from vigorous management of diabetes with insulin in nonpregnant women. Insulin does not cross the placenta.
   4. Therapy must respond to the changing insulin requirements during pregnancy; typical starting dosage is 0.7 to 1.0 units/kg/day in divided doses.
      a. Women with relatively simple insulin programs may require more complex regimens as the pregnancy progresses.
   5. Intensive insulin therapy (as opposed to conventional therapy) is often required in pregnancy.
   6. Human insulin (Humulin) is preferred to animal or synthetic insulin.
   7. Instruct the patient to report glucose values on at least a weekly basis. Some monitors have a USB port for uploading to a computer where they may be viewed on a website or emailed to the provider. Alternatively, patients may opt to fax or telephone in their values.
   8. The blood glucose values should be evaluated at least weekly to adjust to the patient's changing needs.

Follow-Up

A. Weekly evaluation of day curves

B. Fetal testing schedule

C. For women who develop diabetes during pregnancy, give the patient 75-g glucose load to evaluate for the development of type 2 diabetes at the return postpartum visit at 6 weeks after delivery. These women should be screened at least every 3 years from then on. Encourage lifestyle changes to prevent the development of diabetes.

Consultation/Referral

A. Consult or comanage the patient with a physician as indicated and if GDM is not controlled by diet and exercise.
B. **Refer to a dietician for nutritional consult for carbohydrate counting and teaching the patient dietary and lifestyle changes needed for tight glucose control.**

Preeclampsia

Definition

A. Preeclampsia (antiquated term *toxemia*) is hypertension with proteinuria that develops during pregnancy and lasts or develops up to 6 weeks postpartum. In the absence of proteinuria, any of the following can establish the diagnosis: new-onset thrombocytopenia, impaired liver function, renal insufficiency, pulmonary edema, or visual or cerebral disturbances.
B. Hypertension is defined as the following:
   1. Either a systolic BP more than 140 mmHg or a diastolic BP more than 90 mmHg, or both. The values must be elevated on at least two separate occasions at least 4 hours apart. **Severity of hypertension is not necessarily associated with the severity of preeclampsia.**
   2. Eclampsia is the occurrence of grand mal seizures in a patient with preeclampsia.
   3. Chronic hypertension in pregnancy is often complicated by superimposed preeclampsia.

Incidence

A. Hypertensive disorders are the most common medical complication of pregnancy, with a reported incidence of up to 10% worldwide. Incidence varies among different regions and countries. The incidence of preeclampsia has increased by 25% in the United States during the past two decades. The risk of recurrent preeclampsia is between 5% and 70%. Women who develop severe features of preeclampsia prior to 30 weeks gestation have the highest risk of preeclampsia in future pregnancies.

Pathogenesis

A. The etiology of preeclampsia is unknown, although several theories exist. Generalized vascular endothelial damage is a hallmark of the pathophysiologic responses.

Predisposing Factors

A. Nulliparity
B. Chronic hypertension
C. Age extreme (< 18 years and > 35 years)
D. Race (African American women are at higher risk.)
E. DM
F. Renal disease
G. Family history of preeclampsia in a sister or mother
H. Previous pregnancy with PIH
I. Multiple gestation
J. Hydatidiform mole
K. Obesity

Common Complaints

A. Headache unrelieved by analgesics
B. Right upper quadrant (RUQ) pain
C. Severe heartburn unrelieved by antacids
D. Nausea and vomiting
E. Edema: Peripheral and/or facial
F. Visual disturbances
G. Photophobia

Other Signs and Symptoms

A. Hypertension (BP of 140 mmHg systolic or greater or 90 mmHg diastolic or greater that occurs after 20 weeks gestation in a woman without a previous history of hypertension).

First-trimester signs of PIH need ultrasonographic evaluation for the presence of a gestational trophoblastic disease (molar pregnancy) as well as the other differential diagnoses.

B. Proteinuria: Urinary excretion of 0.3 g protein or greater in 24-hour urine specimen
C. Brisk deep tendon reflexes (DTRs) or clonus

Potential Complications

A. Multiple organ involvement
B. HELLP syndrome (hemolysis, elevated liver enzymes, and low platelets)
C. Eclampsia, which may lead to maternal demise
D. Fetal complications: IUGR, oligohydramnios, abruptio placenta

Subjective Data

A. Elicit information about headaches, their onset and duration, the progression of headache, and/or other symptoms.
B. What part of the head hurts? Differentiate headache from sinus headache. Note severity and any relief measure tried (acetaminophen, massage, sleep).
C. Is the headache "new"? Does the patient have a previous history of migraines? Is this like a previous migraine?
D. What are other concurrent symptoms: Nausea, vomiting, RUQ pain, and visual changes?
E. Question the patient about edema. If edema is present, has it significantly worsened over the past few days? Has she been able to wear rings up to this point? Has she had to wear different shoes due to pedal edema?
F. What are her usual weight and today's weight (on the same scales). Has she gained more than 2 pounds in 1 week?

G. Ask specifics about RUQ pain, sometimes identified as "severe heartburn." Note the duration, severity, and relief measures tried. Have the patient point to the area of discomfort (midsternum or under right breast).
H. Are there any visual disturbances, such as black dots she can't see through?
I. Review other gastrointestinal symptoms such as diarrhea, abdominal pain, and gallbladder attack.
J. Review for signs of fever and thyroid storm.
K. Review the patient's history for seizures.

Physical Examination

A. Check temperature, BP, pulse and respirations, weight, and fetal heart tones.
B. Inspect
   1. Check pedal, hand, and facial edema.
   2. Check fundal height.
C. Palpate
   1. Palpate the abdomen, noting any hepatosplenomegaly and RUQ tenderness to the palpation.
   2. Palpate the lower extremities for pitting edema.
D. Percuss
   1. Gently check for liver enlargement.
   2. Perform neurologic exam for hyperreflexia: Check DTR and clonus.
E. Auscultate
   1. Auscultate the heart and lungs.
   2. Auscultate the fetal heart tone.

Diagnostic Tests

A. CBC and platelets
B. Liver profile (alanine aminotransferase [ALT] and aspartate aminotransferase [AST])
C. Renal workup
   1. Uric acid, serum creatinine, and urine protein
   2. Urine culture if proteinuria is present to rule out urinary tract infection (UTI).
   3. Collect 24-hour urine for total protein and creatinine clearance.
D. Ultrasonography, if indicated, to rule out IUGR and/or oligohydramnios

Differential Diagnoses

A. Preeclampsia
B. Hyperemesis gravidarum
C. Infection: Appendicitis, gastroenteritis, pyelonephritis, glomerulonephritis, hepatitis, and pancreatitis
D. Acute fatty liver of pregnancy
E. Systemic lupus erythematosus
F. Hemolytic uremic syndrome
G. Hepatic encephalopathy
H. Gastrointestinal disorder: Peptic ulcer and heartburn
I. Thrombotic or ITP
J. Gallbladder disease
K. Chronic hypertension
L. Thyroid storm
M. Gestational hypertension

Plan

A. General interventions
   1. Any patient with an elevated BP should be reassessed in the lateral recumbent position, using proper cuff size, after the patient is allowed to relax for several minutes prior to BP measurement.
   2. If the patient's BP begins to rise above baseline values:
      a. Advise the patient to maintain a modified bed rest schedule (stop working).
      b. Recommend frequent BP evaluation at home.
      c. See the patient weekly or biweekly for further maternal and neonatal assessment; administer NST and take BPP if appropriate.
   3. If hypertension and proteinuria are present, refer the patient to an obstetrician or perinatologist for further assessment and management. She may need immediate admission to the hospital for inpatient management or delivery.
   4. If the patient has a grand mal seizure, the primary consideration is to protect her. Monitor seizure type and duration. Call for immediate transport to the hospital labor and delivery unit. Place the patient in the lateral recumbent position following the seizure.
   5. Immediately transfer the patient to a hospital for eclampsia after stabilization.
B. Dietary management: Salt restriction does not stop swelling and high BP problems in pregnancy.
C. Pharmaceutical therapy
   1. Diuretics are *not* prescribed during pregnancy for edema.
   2. Angiotensin-converting enzyme (ACE) inhibitors and angiotensin II receptor blockers (ARBs) are not recommended during pregnancy due to the teratogenic effects on the fetus that may occur, such as renal dysgenesis and/or fetal death.
   3. Aldomet is commonly used during pregnancy to control chronic or superimposed hypertension during pregnancy.
   4. Inpatient therapy is determined by a physician and may include
      a. Magnesium sulfate for seizure prophylaxis
      b. Hydralazine or labetalol, which are first-line antihypertensive agents if a patient's diastolic BP is more than 110 mmHg.
      c. Corticosteroids, which may be given to enhance fetal lung maturity prior to delivery in patients between 24 and 34 weeks gestation.
      d. In severe preeclampsia, therapy may include cervical ripening agents such as prostaglandins

or misoprostol and/or oxytocin induction of labor.

e. Narcotics may be used for severe headaches.
f. Diazepam (Valium) and phenytoin (Dilantin) are not recommended for seizures in pregnancy There is increased risk of recurrent seizures.

Follow-Up

A. The only "cure" for preeclampsia is delivery. See the patient in 1 week after delivery for BP assessment, or sooner if symptoms persist.

Consultation/Referral

A. If the patient is diagnosed with preeclampsia, refer her to a physician for continued care and delivery.

Preterm Labor (PTL)

Definition

A. PTL is labor that produces documented cervical changes after 20 weeks and prior to 37 completed weeks of gestation.

Incidence

A. PTL occurs in approximately 11% live births in the United States and precedes 50% of the preterm births. It accounts for more than 70% of neonatal mortality.

Pathogenesis

A. Infection and ischemia are common causes of PTL. Infection may originate from several sites, including the bladder, kidney(s), cervix, uterus, gastrointestinal tract, and upper respiratory tract. Ischemia may be caused by decreased oxygen delivery to the uterus due to maternal hypoxia, hypovolemia, or vena caval compression. Overdistension of the uterus in the presence of polyhydramnios or multiple gestation may cause PTL symptoms. However, in most cases, the cause is unknown.

Predisposing Factors

A. Previous PTL or preterm delivery
B. Preterm rupture of membranes
C. Uterine anomalies, surgery, and fibroids
D. Multiple gestations
E. History of second-trimester abortion(s)
F. Incompetent cervix
G. History of cone biopsy
H. Recurrent urinary tract and kidney infections
I. Polyhydramnios
J. Macrosomatic fetus
K. Maternal age extremes
L. Placenta previa
M. Abruptio placentae
N. Poor nutritional status and low prepregnancy weight
O. Maternal dehydration
P. Maternal race (occurs more frequently in African American population)
Q. Low socioeconomic status
R. Inadequate prenatal care
S. Anemia
T. Substance use/abuse (smoking, drug, alcohol)
U. Vaginal infection
V. Presence of fetal fibronectin, a protein produced by the trophoblast and other fetal tissues, has been noted in cervical-vaginal secretions between 24 and 34 weeks gestation in a subgroup of women who are at increased risk for preterm birth.
W. Short cervical length
X. Short interpregnancy interval

Common Complaints

A. Abdominal pain or cramping
B. Low backache
C. Increase or change in vaginal discharge, "gush" of fluid, loss of mucus plug, and bloody show or vaginal spotting
D. Diarrhea
E. "Something's not right"

Other Signs and Symptoms

A. Pelvic pressure
B. Contractions or period-like cramps

Subjective Data

A. Elicit information about the onset, frequency, duration, and course of cramps; presence or absence of backache; how long these symptoms have existed; and whether symptoms began subsequent to a certain event or activity. What, if anything, makes these symptoms better or worse?
B. Question the patient about color, odor, consistency, and amount of vaginal discharge or bleeding: Was there a spot the size of a quarter or a half-dollar? Has she been wearing a perineal pad? How often does she have to change the pad? Is the pad soaked with blood when she changes it?
C. For fetuses older than 18 weeks gestation, question the patient about frequency of fetal movements.
D. Question the patient about urinary frequency, presence of urgency, or dysuria.
E. Question the patient about recent sexual activity (i.e., has there been recent intercourse?)
F. If the patient complains of diarrhea, ask her if she has a fever and if anyone else in the family is ill.

Physical Examination

A. Check temperature, BP, and fetal heart tones.
B. Inspect: Note general appearance of discomfort.
C. Palpate
   1. Abdomen: Note presence, frequency, intensity of uterine contractions, and resting tone. Measure fundal height.
   2. Back: Check for costovertebral angle (CVA) tenderness.

D. Auscultate: Auscultate the heart and lungs (especially if the patient is on tocolysis).
E. Pelvic exam
   1. Sterile speculum exam: Evaluate rupture of membranes and vaginal discharge or bleeding. **If meconium-stained amniotic fluid is noted, immediately consult a physician and transfer the patient to a hospital. Note if meconium is thin or thick (thick meconium may be associated with breech presentation).**
   2. Bimanual exam: If membranes are not ruptured, perform gentle bimanual examination. Note cervical dilation, effacement, station, cervical position, and softness of cervix.
   3. Cervical exam during pregnancy: See the Section II Procedure, "Bimanual Examination: Cervical Evaluation During Pregnancy." **Do not perform a digital examination of the cervix if PROM is present without active labor.**

Diagnostic Tests

A. White blood cell (WBC), if indicated
B. Urine dipstick for ketones, leukocyte, esterase, protein, and nitrite
C. Evaluate vaginal discharge for pH with phenaphthazine (nitrazine) tape.
D. Check ferning, if discharge is nitrazine positive or if PROM is suspected.
E. Wet prep, if indicated
F. Cervical cultures for STDs
G. Cervical and rectal culture for Group B strep
H. Fetal fibronectin, where available. Candidates for fetal fibronectin testing must meet the following criteria:
   1. Intact fetal membranes
   2. Cervical dilatation less than 3 cm
   3. Gestational age 24 0/7th weeks to 34 6/7th weeks
   4. No sexual intercourse in preceding 24 hours
I. Urine culture
J. Ultrasonography: Fetal biometry and dating, cervical length, amniotic fluid volume, BPP, placental location, fetal presentation, ruling out fetal anomalies
K. Electronic fetal monitoring (EFM) for contractions

Differential Diagnoses

A. PTL
B. Preterm (or Braxton Hicks) contractions, with no cervical change
C. Incompetent cervix
D. Preterm rupture of membranes
E. Low back muscle strain
F. Pyelonephritis or UTI
G. Placenta previa
H. Abruptio placentae
I. Gastroenteritis
J. Vaginal infection
K. Maternal dehydration
L. Ketoacidosis

Plan

A. General interventions
   1. Regular uterine contractions with cervical dilation or effacement, with pressure on the lower uterine segment, strongly indicates PTL.
   2. If the cervix is dilated more than 3 cm with contractions upon presentation, the patient is probably having PTL. Consult with a physician for hospital admission and tocolysis candidacy.
   3. If the patient is symptomatic with a positive fetal fibronectin test, consult with a physician for maternal transfer to a hospital equipped to care for preterm infants.
   4. Second trimester: If the patient shows signs and symptoms of PTL, consider diagnosis of incompetent cervix. Refer the patient to a physician for ultrasonography for cervical length and possible cerclage placement.
B. Outpatient management
   1. Education: See the Section III Patient Teaching Guide for this chapter, "Preterm Labor."
   2. Outpatient bed rest
   3. Prophylactic treatment against infection
   4. Administer corticosteroids to enhance fetal lung maturity if less than 34 weeks gestation. Observe the patient for contractions in the office.
   5. Fetal fibronectin testing, where available, using ACOG Guidelines
C. Inpatient management of PTL
   1. Observation, possibly with IV hydration
   2. Cervical cerclage
   3. Prophylactic treatment against infection (Group B *Streptococci)* until urine and cervical culture results are available
   4. Parenteral tocolysis either to stop PTL or delay delivery long enough to allow transfer to a facility with the ability to care for preterm infants. According to numerous clinical studies, predelivery administration of magnesium sulfate reduces the occurrence of cerebral palsy and, therefore, may be the drug of choice for parenteral tocolysis in the hospital setting.
   5. Administer corticosteroids to enhance fetal lung maturity if less than 34 weeks.
   6. Transport the patient to a perinatal center for neonatal care.
D. Patient teaching: See the Section III Patient Teaching Guide for this chapter, "Preterm Labor."
E. Pharmaceutical therapy
   1. Tocolytics may be utilized between 24 and 34 weeks gestation Maintenance therapy with tocolytics is generally ineffective, while short-term use is recommended mainly to allow for the

administration of antenatal steroids. Recently, the FDA posted warnings cautioning against the use of maintenance oral terbutaline during pregnancy due to lack of efficacy and potential maternal cardiac risks and death; it should not be prescribed on an outpatient basis. Injectable terbutaline may be used on a short-term basis (48 to 72 hours) in a hospital setting.

2. Corticosteroids
   a. Steroids are given to enhance lung maturity in the fetus.
   b. A single rescue course may be considered if the antecedent treatment was given more than 2 weeks prior and the patient is judged to be likely to deliver within the next week.

Follow-Up

A. Depending on the clinical scenario, the patient may need to be seen weekly or biweekly. Fetal fibronectin test may be repeated every 2 weeks, but positive results alone should not be used to exclusively direct management. Repeat cultures as indicated, discontinuing antibiotics if cultures are negative. Encourage close phone contact with the patient regarding questions or concerns.

Pyelonephritis in Pregnancy

Definition

A. Pyelonephritis is an infection in one or both kidneys, usually involving the entire urinary tract. **Pyelonephritis may evolve into acute respiratory distress syndrome (ARDS) in pregnancy.**

Incidence

A. The incidence of pyelonephritis in pregnancy is 1% to 2%. Most cases develop as a consequence of undiagnosed or inadequately treated lower UTI. Approximately 75% to 80% of pyelonephritis cases occur on the right side, with a 10% to 15% incidence on the left side. A small percentage of cases are bilateral.

Pathogenesis

A. *E. coli* is the main pathogen in pyelonephritis, though *Klebsiella pneumoniae* and *Proteus* species are also important causes of infection. Occasionally highly virulent gram-negative bacilli, such as *Pseudomonas*, *Enterobacter*, and *Serratia*, are responsible (more commonly noted in immunocompromised patients). Gram-positive group B Streptococcus may also be responsible. Anaerobes also are unlikely pathogens in pyelonephritis except in cases of chronic obstruction or instrumentation.

Predisposing Factors

A. Pregnancy: Due to pregnancy-related anatomic changes in the urinary tract, such as dilated ureters due to smooth muscle relaxation and pressure on the bladder from the enlarging uterus. The immunosuppression of pregnancy may also contribute.
B. History of UTI, cystitis, and pyelonephritis
C. Sickle cell disease

Common Complaints

A. Fever
B. Chills
C. Flank pain or tenderness
D. Urinary frequency or urgency
E. Hematuria and dysuria

Other Signs and Symptoms

A. UTI is associated with urinary frequency, urgency, and dysuria; hematuria; and suprapubic pain.
   1. Chemical reactions to deodorant or douches can affect urination.
   2. Patients with frequent pyelonephritis do *not* complain of frequency and dysuria.
B. Pyelonephritis is associated with fever, palpitations, dizziness, backache, and urinary frequency.
   1. Hematuria may be present, especially if the patient has a history of a previous stone.
   2. Dysuria is not always present in upper tract infections.
C. Abdominal pain and uterine contractions, risk of PTL and birth
D. Shortness of breath

Potential Complications

A. Sepsis and septic shock
B. ARDS: Mortality rate 50% to 70%
C. Pulmonary embolus, usually presents as sudden-onset CVA tenderness

Subjective Data

A. Elicit information on the onset, duration, and progression of symptoms.
B. Elicit problems with voiding. Ask the patient about urinary frequency, urgency, and dysuria.
C. Ask the patient if she has experienced preterm contractions.
D. Ask if the patient is complaining of fever or chills.
E. Ask the patient if her urine has a bad odor.
F. Ask the patient if she has felt more tired than usual.
G. Ask the patient if she has felt more nauseated than usual or if she has been vomiting.
H. Does she have a backache? Note location (unilateral or bilateral) and what, if anything, makes the backache better or worse.
I. Review the patient's history for sickle cell disease, if appropriate; has she been tested?
J. Review prenatal history for recurrent UTIs, previous pyelonephritis, and any abnormalities of the genitourinary (GU) tract.

Physical Examination

A. Check temperature, pulse, respirations, and BP: Fever more than 100.4°F, tachycardia, tachypnea, hypotension associated with sepsis, septic shock, and ARDS.
B. Inspect: Note general appearance for respiratory distress.
C. Palpate
   1. Back: Check CVA tenderness (right CVA tenderness is more common in pregnancy).
   2. Abdomen
      a. Palpate for uterine tenderness and contractions.
      b. Palpate for suprapubic tenderness.
D. Auscultate
   1. The lungs and heart
   2. The fetal heart rate (FHR)
E. Bimanual exam: Check for cervical dilation.

Diagnostic Tests

A. CBC with differential or WBC: Leukocytosis with left shift on differential seen
B. Blood culture, if indicated
C. Respiratory function
   1. Arterial blood gases (ABGs), if indicated
   2. Pulse oximetry, if indicated
D. Renal function
   1. Urinalysis
      a. Check urinalysis for WBCs, RBCs, leukocyte esterase, and/or nitrites.
      b. Glucosuria may be normal in pregnancy due to decreased tubular capacity to reabsorb glucose. If it is consistently noted, further testing is needed.
      c. Proteinuria is *not* normal during pregnancy. All cases warrant further investigation.
   2. Urine culture and sensitivity: More than 100,000 colonies/mL indicates UTI.
   3. Intravenous pyelogram (IVP), if indicated
   4. Renal ultrasonography, if indicated

Differential Diagnoses

A. Pyelonephritis
B. Cystitis
C. Urethritis
D. Urethral stricture
E. Urolithiasis
F. Genital infection
G. Chorioamnionitis
H. Septic abortion
I. Postpartum endometritis
J. Muscular strain
K. Pulmonary embolus
L. Severe upper respiratory tract infection
M. Postprocedural dysuria or urinary frequency (i.e., following bladder catheterization or cystoscopy)
N. Chemical irritants
O. Postpartum septic pelvic thrombophlebitis
P. Renal calculi

Plan

A. General interventions
   1. Rule out other sources of infection.
   2. Assess for PTL.
B. Patient education: See the Section III Patient Teaching Guide for this chapter, "Urinary Tract Infection During Pregnancy: Pyelonephritis."
C. Dietary management
   1. Advise the patient to eat a regular diet as tolerated.
   2. Encourage her to drink 8 to 10 glasses of water a day.
   3. Warn the patient to avoid beverages with caffeine. 100% cranberry juice and cranberry and blueberry capsules are good for urinary tract problems.
D. Pharmaceutical therapy
   1. Broad-spectrum antibiotic coverage until cultures and sensitivity results are back
   2. Drug of choice
      a. Nitrofurantoin (Macrobid) 100 mg orally every 12 hours for 7 to 10 days
      b. Amoxicillin 500 mg orally every 12 hours for 7 days
      c. Augmentin 500 mg orally every 12 hours for 7 days
   3. If dysuria is present: Phenazopyridine (Pyridium) 200 mg orally three times daily after meals for 3 days. Warn the patient that phenazopyridine (Pyridium) turns urine orange.
   4. Alternative medications
      a. Cephalexin (Keflex) 500 mg orally every 12 hours for 7 days

Follow-Up

A. Once antibiotic therapy is initiated, most patients have a decrease in symptoms within 48 hours. By the end of 72 hours, almost 95% of patients are afebrile and asymptomatic. Stress to patients the importance of completing the course of antibiotics regardless of the absence of symptoms.
B. The most likely causes of treatment failure are a resistant microorganism or obstruction; common causes of obstruction in pregnancy are urolithiasis or compression of the ureter by the gravid uterus.
C. Repeat a urine culture at a 2-week follow-up visit.
D. Recurrence rates are very high. After the initial antibiotic therapy course is completed, consider a daily prophylactic dose of an antibiotic, such as nitrofurantoin (Macrodantin) 50 to 100 mg by mouth at bedtime for recurrent infections.

E. Patients receiving prophylactic antibiotics should have their urine screened for bacteria at each subsequent office visit and be questioned about the recurrence of symptoms.
F. If no prophylactic treatment is undertaken, obtain a urine culture if symptoms recur or if urine dipstick is positive for leukocyte esterase or nitrites.

Vaginal Bleeding: First Trimester

Definition

Vaginal bleeding during the first trimester of pregnancy may range from spotting to massive hemorrhage (spontaneous abortion). Types of abortion are:

A. Threatened abortion: Vaginal bleeding with absent or minimal pain *and* a closed, long, thick cervix
B. Inevitable abortion: Vaginal bleeding with pain and cervical dilation and/or effacement
C. Spontaneous abortion: The nonviable products of conception are expelled from the uterus spontaneously. This process may be complete or incomplete.
D. Vaginal bleeding may also be related to ectopic pregnancy, implantation of the pregnancy, or cervical inflammation/infection.

Incidence

A. Vaginal bleeding is a common event in pregnancy. Spontaneous abortion, a primary concern in the first trimester, occurs in about 30% of all pregnancies; most occur before the 16th week. Ectopic pregnancy occurs in 1 of every 200 pregnancies; 75% of pregnancies occurring after failure of tubal sterilization are likely to be ectopic.

Pathogenesis

A. Spontaneous abortion: The pathogenesis varies according to cause. In most cases, it is due to embryonic death, with resultant decrease in hormone levels and subsequent sloughing of the uterine decidua. Many of the embryonic deaths occur due to chromosomal abnormalities that are incompatible with life.
B. Ectopic pregnancy: Fertilized ovum is prevented or slowed in its progress down the fallopian tube. Pregnancy is implanted outside of the uterus, most commonly in the fallopian tube.

Predisposing Factors

A. Spontaneous abortion: In most cases, the cause is unknown.
   1. Advanced maternal age (occurs more often in older women), suggesting that a chromosomal abnormality in the embryo may contribute
   2. Abnormal uterine environment
   3. Systemic disease
   4. Weight extremes (BMI < 18.5 or > 25)
   5. Immunologic deficiencies
   6. Substance use, including caffeine, alcohol, cigarettes, and cocaine.
   7. Trauma
   8. Previous spontaneous AB
B. Ectopic pregnancy: Caused by previous damage to the fallopian tube; frequently caused by pelvic inflammatory disease, tubal surgery for infertility, or bilateral tubal ligation.

Common Complaints

A. Spontaneous abortion: Vaginal bleeding occurs that may or may not be associated with cramping or uterine contractions. When a pregnancy is more than 8 weeks gestation, the presence of uterine bleeding, uterine contractions, and/or pain are indications of a threatened abortion until proven otherwise.
B. Ectopic pregnancy: Vaginal bleeding and pelvic pain occur soon after the first missed period; the patient may be unaware of pregnancy. Sudden, acute, localized abdominal pain is associated with fallopian tube rupture.

Other Signs and Symptoms

A. Threatened abortion: Slight bleeding may be present over several weeks; cramping; no passage of tissue; positive pregnancy symptoms present, including nausea, vomiting, fatigue, breast tenderness, and urinary frequency.
B. Inevitable abortion: Moderate to profuse vaginal bleeding occurs. Tissue may or may not be passed, uterine cramps or abdominal pain are present, symptoms of pregnancy may be decreased or absent.
C. Incomplete abortion: Moderate to profuse vaginal bleeding, sometimes for several weeks, occurs; reports of passage of tissue; painful uterine cramping or "contractions;" and symptoms of pregnancy often absent.
D. Complete abortion: Patient experiences profuse bleeding, passage of tissue and large clots, abdominal cramping, or uterine contractions.
E. Ectopic pregnancy: Amenorrhea or irregular vaginal bleeding; abdominal pain is usually present, may be unilateral or generalized and may be associated with vertigo and syncope; shoulder pain, with irritation of phrenic nerve, may be present. Anxiety or palpitations are often noted.

Subjective Data

A. Elicit information about the onset, duration, and progression of symptoms.
B. Ask the patient about vaginal bleeding. When did it start? Is it continuous bleeding, "like a period," or is it spotting? How much bleeding has occurred? How

many pads have been saturated? What is the size of the blood spots? Determine amount of bleeding: How much blood is on peri-pad? (a) Scant amount: less than 1-inch diameter, (b) light amount: less than a 4-inch diameter, (c) moderate amount: less than a 6-inch diameter, (d) heavy amount: saturates the peri-pad within 1 hour.

C. What is her current method of birth control? Was the birth control method used consistently? Has she had a tubal ligation, or has she recently used an intrauterine contraceptive device (IUD)?
D. Ask the patient the first day of her last menstrual period to date the pregnancy. Did she have a positive pregnancy test? If so, when?
E. Does she have a history of ectopic pregnancy or pelvic inflammatory disease?
F. Question the patient regarding the presence or absence of abdominal and/or back pain. If present, is it a continuous discomfort, or is it intermittent cramping? Was the onset sudden? How severe is the pain?
G. Is the patient experiencing shoulder pain? This may be referred pain from phrenic nerve irritation due to intraperitoneal bleeding.

Physical Examination

A. Check temperature, pulse, respirations, and BP: Note postural hypotension and tachycardia. Hemodynamic instability may be noted in cases of profuse bleeding; assess vital signs and be alert for hypotension, tachycardia, tachypnea, and/or labored breathing.
B. Inspect
   1. Note general overall appearance of discomfort or pain before, during, and after examination.
   2. Examine peri-pad to determine amount of bleeding, if available.
C. Palpate
   1. Perform abdominal examination for rebound tenderness, masses, softness, tenderness, or abdominal wall distension. Sudden, acute, localized abdominal pain with signs of internal hemorrhage suggest rupture of the fallopian tube.
   2. Palpate uterine size. Measure fundal height for consistency with pregnancy dates. If fundal height suggests pregnancy has advanced beyond first trimester, bleeding may be caused by abruption, placenta previa, or rupture of membranes with heavy bloody show.
   3. Check iliopsoas and obturator muscle tests.
D. Auscultate: Auscultate the heart, lungs, and bowel sounds to rule out other abdominal problems.
E. Pelvic examination
   1. Perform sterile speculum examination: Assess color and amount of bleeding. Tissue and the products of conception may be noted at cervical os or in vaginal vault. Assess for Chadwick's sign. The entire fetus may be noted in the vaginal vault; tissues that remain in the uterus may include portions of fetal membranes or placenta. Look for vaginitis/cervicitis and other signs and symptoms of infection that could be causing the bleeding.
   2. Bimanual examination: Check Hegar's sign; elicit this sign cautiously, as a false positive result may be related to a rough examination. Evaluate cervical dilation; cervical motion tenderness, often present with ectopic pregnancy; bulging cul-de-sac, which represents a hemoperitoneum. Adnexal mass is present in 50% of ectopic pregnancies.

Diagnostic Tests

A. Pregnancy test: Quantitative serum beta human chorionic gonadotropin (HCG); serial tests at least 48 hours apart, making sure to perform test at same lab for accurate results
B. CBC with differential and platelet
C. Blood type, Rh, antibody screen, and cross match if indicated
D. Prothrombin time (PT) and partial thromboplastin time (PTT)
E. Doppler ultrasonography for fetal heart tones, for fetuses older than 11 weeks
F. Ultrasonography: Transvaginal and/or abdominal scan

Differential Diagnoses

A. First-trimester vaginal bleeding secondary to
   1. Threatened abortion
   2. Inevitable abortion
   3. Incomplete abortion
   4. Complete abortion
   5. Septic abortion
   6. Ectopic pregnancy: There is strong suspicion of ectopic pregnancy or fallopian tube rupture if symptoms present with history of fallopian tube damage (i.e., tubal surgery for infertility, previous ectopic pregnancy), pelvic infection, or IUD use.
   7. Hydatidiform mole
   8. Anovulatory bleeding with an antecedent period of amenorrhea
   9. Benign or malignant genital tract lesion
   10. Menstrual bleeding
   11. Genital trauma
   12. Advanced pregnancy with placenta previa or abruptio placentae
   13. Salpingitis
   14. Appendicitis
   15. IUD-related symptoms
   16. Pelvic inflammatory disease

Plan

A. General interventions: Stabilize maternal condition and then determine the cause of bleeding.
   1. Threatened abortion: Expectant management. Bed rest is often prescribed. Symptoms either subside, leading to normal gestation, or worsen, leading to inevitable abortion. If bleeding persists without leading to spontaneous abortion, the patient should be evaluated frequently, usually on a weekly basis, by means of ultrasonography to assess fetal viability. The patient should avoid intercourse and should not use tampons to absorb bleeding.
   2. Inevitable abortion: Care may include expectant management or preparation for dilation and curettage (D&C).
   3. Incomplete abortion: Prepare for suction and possible D&C.
   4. Complete abortion: If abortion is complete and the products of conception are delivered with complete membranes present and cessation of bleeding has occurred, no surgical intervention is indicated. In these cases, the tissue specimens must be carefully examined for completeness. Send all specimens to the laboratory for further examination. If there is any question regarding complete passing of the placenta, do serial quantitative HCGs until back to nonpregnant levels.
   5. Ectopic pregnancy: Consult with a physician regarding possible medical management with methotrexate or refer the patient to a physician for surgical intervention. The physician may perform culdocentesis to assess for hemoperitoneum. If the patient is in shock, resuscitation with IV fluids should be started immediately by means of two large-bore angiocatheters. IV fluids such as lactated Ringer's solution or normal saline should be infused at a rapid rate. The patient is taken to the operating room, where the indicated procedure is one that controls hemorrhage in the shortest period of time. Salpingectomy and/or hysterectomy may be included.

B. Patient teaching: See the Section III Patient Teaching Guide for this chapter, "First-Trimester Vaginal Bleeding."

C. Pharmaceutical therapy
   1. Rh_O(D) immune globulin should be administered to any Rh-negative patient.
   2. Acetaminophen (Tylenol) or ibuprofen as needed for discomfort
   3. Ectopic pregnancy: Methotrexate is a folic acid antagonist that has been used to inhibit the growth of trophoblastic cells. This chemotherapy is the treatment of choice for ectopic pregnancy when surgery is contraindicated, or in the management of postoperative persistent trophoblast. Refer the patient to a physician to evaluate her for methotrexate or operative intervention. In most cases, operative intervention is required.

Follow-Up

A. Threatened abortion: Follow the patient weekly to assess for interval growth and presence of fetal cardiac motion. Instruct the patient on peri-pad count.
B. Spontaneous abortion: Once the uterine contents have been evacuated, follow up with a 6-week postabortion visit, unless the situation warrants an earlier follow-up visit. Contraception needs to be discussed with the patient. Advise her that it is best to wait for two or three menstrual cycles before becoming pregnant again.
C. Ectopic pregnancy: Once the ectopic pregnancy has been removed, the patient should be seen in 2 to 6 weeks for a postoperative examination, unless the situation warrants an earlier follow-up visit. If methotrexate is used, do serial quantitative HCGs until they return to nonpregnant levels.

Consultation/Referral

A. Consult with a physician if the patient has any frank bleeding, signs of fetal compromise, or maternal shock, or if the cause of bleeding cannot be determined.

Vaginal Bleeding: Second and Third Trimester

Definition

Bright or dark red vaginal bleeding during the second or third trimester (> 12 weeks gestation) may be painless, or it may be associated with uterine contractions or severe abdominal pain. Antepartum bleeding (uterine bleeding after 20 weeks gestation that is unrelated to labor and delivery) occurs in 4% to 5% of pregnancies. Common causes of bleeding include:

A. Low-lying placenta: The edge of the placenta grows into the area of the lower uterine segment near the cervical os.
B. Placenta previa: Implantation of the blastocyst occurs in the lower uterine segment, followed by placental growth. Eventually, the placenta may partially or completely cover the cervix.
C. Abruptio placentae: Partial or premature separation of the placenta takes place.
D. Uterine rupture: Complete uterine rupture extends through the entire uterine wall, and the uterine contents are extruded into the abdominal cavity. Incomplete rupture extends through the endometrium and myometrium, but the peritoneum remains intact. This occurs almost exclusively during labor and/or delivery.

E. Uterine dehiscence: separation of an old surgical scar
F. Bloody discharge is *not* normal prior to 37 weeks gestation unless associated with recent sexual intercourse or pelvic exam. Light spotting or bleeding may be caused by recent sexual intercourse, PTL, rupture of membranes, or cervicitis.
Note: The evaluation of vaginal bleeding prior to 20 weeks is similar to that in the first trimester.

Incidence

A. Placenta previa: Approximately 1:200 pregnancies, more common in parous women
B. Abruptio placenta: Approximately 1:250 pregnancies
C. Uterine rupture: If uterus is unscarred, incidence is approximately 1:6,000 to 20,000 pregnancies. If uterus has a scar, the incidence varies depending on the type and location of the prior uterine incision. If the prior incision was low transverse, the incidence is approximately 0.7% to 2.0%, and if the prior incision was classical, the incidence is approximately 1% to 12%.

Pathogenesis

A. Placenta previa: The pathogenesis of placenta previa is unknown. One hypothesis is that the presence of areas of suboptimal endometrium in the upper uterine cavity due to previous surgery or pregnancies promotes implantation of trophoblast in or toward the lower uterine segment. Another hypothesis is that a particularly large placental surface area, as in multiple gestation or in response to reduced uteroplacental perfusion, increases the likelihood that the placenta will cover or encroach upon the cervical os.
B. Abruptio placenta: Abruptio placenta is initiated by bleeding into the decidua basalis. The decidua then splits, and the placenta is sheared off, either partially or totally. Blood may move into and through the myometrium, leading to a board-like uterus.
C. Uterine rupture: Uterine rupture may occur from uterine injury, due to previous surgery or trauma.

Predisposing Factors

A. Placenta previa: Late fertilization with delayed implantation, previous uterine scar, advanced maternal age, multiple gestation, large placenta, previous previa, and smoking
B. Abruptio placenta: Hypertension (chronic, gestational, or preeclampsia), cocaine use, trauma, high parity, sudden decompression of overdistended uterus (i.e., when membranes rupture), smoking, chorioamnionitis, abdominal trauma, and cephalic version
C. Uterine rupture: Multiparity, previous uterine incision, tetanic contractions, or prolonged labor, especially with excessive use of oxytocin.

Common Complaints

A. Placenta previa: Painless vaginal bleeding, usually in amounts of spotting to frank hemorrhage. Bleeding occasionally is accompanied by cramping or uterine contractions. A "gush" of fluid associated with sudden onset of massive vaginal bleeding may be reported. Painless vaginal bleeding should be treated as a placenta previa until proven otherwise.
B. Abruptio placentae: Firm, tender uterus; high-frequency, low-amplitude uterine contractions
   1. Marginal abruption: Vaginal bleeding may be absent or minimal and bright red; there may be some old, dark blood. Abdominal pain is usually mild.

Vaginal bleeding with abdominal pain should be treated as an abruption until proven otherwise.

   2. Moderate abruption: Vaginal bleeding may be moderate or absent. Abdominal pain is usually significant and associated with contractions.
   3. Severe abruption: Vaginal bleeding may be moderate, severe, or absent. Abdominal pain is severe. **The patient may have a concealed placental abruption without vaginal bleeding.**
C. Uterine rupture: Vaginal bleeding is moderate, severe, or absent. The patient may experience a sudden onset of extreme abdominal pain (commonly at the previous uterine scar site).

Other Signs and Symptoms

A. EFM tracings: May exhibit characteristics that are associated with anemia or hypoxemia, such as decreased or absent variability, bradycardia, tachycardia, recurrent late or prolonged decelerations, or a sinusoidal pattern.
B. Placenta previa: Uterine resting tone usually relaxed. Fetal status at first exam is usually stable. Recurrence of bleeding is common. First bleeding episode in placenta previa is rarely significant. Second or third bleeding episode is often associated with significant vaginal bleeding.
C. Abruptio placentae: Rupture of membranes has bloody show with copious amounts of clear or greenish-brown fluid; the fluid is probably meconium-stained, which signifies fetal distress.
   1. Marginal abruption: Uterine resting tone is usually relaxed. Fetal status on the fetal monitor at first exam is usually stable. Labor progresses rapidly with vaginal bleeding or large amounts of bloody show.
   2. Moderate abruption: Uterine resting tone is hypertonic. At first exam, the fetus is usually alive. FHR may exhibit characteristics that are associated with hypoxemia or anemia such as decreased/absent variability, tachycardia,

bradycardia, recurrent late or prolonged decelerations, or a sinusoidal pattern. Labor progresses rapidly with vaginal bleeding or large amounts of bloody show.
3. Severe abruption: Uterine resting tone is hypertonic or "board-like." At first exam, fetus may be dead. If fetus is alive, EFM is consistent with hypoxemia or anemia as listed above.

D. Uterine rupture: Uterine resting tone may be normal or hypertonic. At first exam, fetus may be dead or FHR pattern is consistent with hypoxemia or anemia as listed above.

Subjective Data

A. Elicit information about onset, duration, and progression of vaginal bleeding. When did it start? Is it continuous bleeding, "like a period," or is it spotting?
B. Ask: How much bleeding has occurred? How many pads have been saturated? What is the size of the blood spots—the size of a quarter or a half dollar?
C. Elicit information regarding the presence or absence of abdominal pain. If present, review the onset, duration, and progression of pain. Is it a continuous discomfort or intermittent cramping? How severe is the pain? Did it have a sudden onset?
D. Is the patient experiencing shoulder pain? This is likely to be referred pain from phrenic nerve irritation due to intraperitoneal bleeding.
E. Elicit the first day of the patient's last menstrual cycle, to date pregnancy.
F. Ask the patient if she feels the baby move and if the movement has been normal this day, if more than 18 weeks gestation.

Physical Examination

A. Check temperature, pulse, respirations, and BP; include FHR.
1. A pregnant patient does not demonstrate signs and symptoms of hypovolemic shock until she has lost 30% of her circulating volume.
2. Prepare the patient for emergency transport to a hospital even if she is hemodynamically stable.

B. Inspect: Inspect the patient's general appearance related to discomfort and pain. Observe bleeding characteristics and pooling.

C. Palpate
1. Check for palpable fetal parts on abdominal wall; note fetal movement.
2. Palpate the uterus for relaxed or hypertonic uterus. Check for contractions. If present, note frequency, duration, and intensity and resting tone to palpation

D. Auscultate
1. Auscultate the abdomen; check fetal heart tones, or EFM, for baseline and periodic FHR patterns. Verify FHR versus maternal heart rate.
2. Auscultate the maternal heart and lungs.

E. Perform sterile speculum exam to look for the source of bleeding. **Do not perform vaginal bimanual exam until placenta previa is ruled out.**

Diagnostic Tests

A. CBC and platelets
B. PT, PTT, and fibrinogen
C. Blood type, Rh status, and type and cross match if indicated
D. Fetal cell stain, Kleihauer-Betke test. Fetal cell stain can determine the amount of fetal blood in the maternal circulation.
E. Determine if $Rh_O(D)$ immune globulin (Rh_OGAM) is indicated.
F. Ultrasonography/BPP
G. NST/EFM

Differential Diagnoses

A. Placenta previa
B. Abruptio placentae
C. Uterine rupture
D. Ruptured vasa previa
E. Rupture of membranes
F. Normal bloody show
G. Rectal hemorrhoidal bleeding

Plan

A. General interventions
1. Tocolysis may be considered if the patient has no active hemorrhage and reassuring FHR pattern.
2. If significant vaginal bleeding is present, the primary goal is to maintain oxygen delivery to the mother and fetus while preparing them for transport. Interventions include lateral maternal positioning to avoid vena caval compression; administering supplemental oxygen; initiating large-bore IV line; delivery of fluid bolus of normal saline or lactated Ringer's solution; keeping flow sheet of vital signs, assessments, actions, and responses; maintaining continuous recording of FHR and uterine activity on EFM; and providing emotional support and anticipatory guidance.
3. If vaginal bleeding is minimal and home management is being considered, discuss risks with the patient and assess her ability to maintain bed rest. Also assess patient's access to telephone and transportation in case of major bleeding episode. Consider the distance from the patient's home to the nearest hospital.

B. Patient teaching: See the Section III Patient Teaching Guide for this chapter, "Vaginal Bleeding: Second and Third Trimester."

C. Pharmaceutical therapy for preterm placenta previa with preterm contractions
   1. Tocolysis options
      a. Terbutaline sulfate (Brethine) 0.25 mg by subcutaneous injection every 15 minutes times three doses if maternal heart rate less than 120.
      b. Indomethacin 50 mg per rectum followed by 25 mg orally every 6 hours. **Note: Indomethacin should not be given after 32 weeks gestation, and duration of indomethacin therapy should not exceed 72 hours.**
      c. The patient may be admitted to inpatient antepartum unit for parenteral tocolysis such as magnesium sulfate.
   2. Antenatal corticosteroids may be given if preterm delivery is a possibility within the next week and the estimated gestational age (EGA) is less than 34 weeks.
      a. Betamethasone 12 mg may be given by IM injection every 24 hours times two doses.
      b. Dexamethasone 6 mg IM may be given every 12 hours times four doses.
      c. A single "rescue" course of repeat antenatal steroids should be considered in women at less than 34 weeks gestation whose prior course was administered at least 7 days previously and who remain at risk of delivering.
   3. If the patient is Rh-negative, give her Rh_O(D) immune globulin (Rh_OGAM) IM by injection after each vaginal bleeding episode.
      a. Full-dose Rh_O(D) IM immune globulin, which is adequate

Follow-Up

A. Follow-up depends on patient diagnosis and on whether patient hospitalization is needed.

Consultation/Referral

A. Consult a physician for all patients noted to have second- and third-trimester vaginal bleeding.

B. Consult with a physician if the patient has any frank, bright red bleeding, signs of fetal compromise, or maternal shock, or if the cause of bleeding cannot be determined and/or treated by the practitioner.

Postpartum

Breast Engorgement

Definition

A. Breast engorgement is swollen, tender breasts caused by overfilling of milk, increased blood flow, and fluids in the breasts.

Incidence

A. Breast engorgement may affect 40% of postpartum mothers.

Pathogenesis

A. *Primary engorgement* is the result of distension and stasis of the vascular and lymphatic circulations occurring 2 to 4 days following delivery. It is prompted by the decrease in progesterone levels after the placenta is delivered.

B. *Secondary engorgement* is due to distension of the lobules and alveoli with milk as lactation is established. It may occur from excessive stimulation of milk production via pumping, taking medications to increase milk supply, or decreased milk extraction from not feeding the baby as often. Without stimulation by suckling and removal of milk, secretion of prolactin decreases and milk production decreases and finally ceases.

Predisposing Factors

A. Engorgement often develops if early feedings are not frequent enough, suckling is inadequate, or breastfeeding is not conducted in a relaxed atmosphere. Engorgement is more likely to develop sooner and more intensely in mothers who have breastfed a prior child.

Common Complaints

A. Swollen, tender breasts
B. Discomfort when breastfeeding
C. A low-grade fever lasting between 4 and 16 hours

Other Signs and Symptoms

A. Pain, tenderness, and redness in one area of the breast is associated with mastitis.

B. Physical examination should not be focused just on breast symptoms but should include a general ruling out of other potential problems, such as coexistent UTI.

Subjective Data

A. Elicit onset, duration, and course of symptoms. Review the frequency of breastfeeding and/or use of breast pump. Is the patient still breastfeeding, or has she stopped due to the discomfort?

B. Exclude other causes of fever, such as UTI, wound infection, and red streaks on one or both breasts, to rule out mastitis.

C. Quantify pain symptoms and relief measures, including heat packs, ice packs, breast binder, and analgesics such as Tylenol.

Physical Examination

A. Check temperature, BP, and pulse.

B. Inspect: Examine the breasts for erythemic streaks on breasts. Check episiotomy or abdominal incision, if indicated.

C. Palpate
   1. Examine the breasts for tenderness, hardness, warmth, and lumps.
   2. Palpate axilla for lymphadenopathy.
   3. Check back for CVA tenderness.

Diagnostic Tests

A. Tests generally are not indicated for breast engorgement.
B. Urine culture or wound culture, if applicable.

Differential Diagnoses

A. Breast engorgement
B. Mastitis

Plan

A. General interventions
   1. Encourage the patient to take analgesics prior to breastfeeding and continue breastfeeding.
   2. Encourage ice packs for discomfort and frequent breastfeeding. There should be *no stimulation* to the breasts other than that provided by the baby when nursing, and the patient should take analgesics for discomfort. Reassure her that engorgement is temporary and usually resolves within 24 to 48 hours.
B. Patient teaching: See the Section III Patient Teaching Guide for this chapter, "Breast Engorgement and Sore Nipples."
   1. Educate the patient regarding milk production.
   2. Advise the patient to breastfeed frequently to reduce chances of engorgement.
   3. Provide reassurance and support for the patient to continue breastfeeding through this temporary period of discomfort. Engorgement may last 2 to 3 days before milk supply meets demand; continuation of breastfeeding will resolve discomfort and problem.
C. Pharmaceutical therapy: Acetaminophen (Tylenol) two tablets 500 to 1,000 mg every 4 to 6 hours, or ibuprofen 400 to 600 mg orally 30 to 45 minutes prior to breastfeeding and as needed.

Follow-Up

A. Follow-up may not be required for engorgement.
B. Lactation consultation if indicated

Individual Considerations

A. Pregnancy loss: It is imperative to discuss breast care and engorgement with women who have a second-trimester termination of pregnancy, have a stillbirth, or experience a neonatal loss.

Endometritis

Definition

A. Endometritis is an infection of the endometrium (the interior lining of the uterus) that occurs postpartum. Endometritis is the most common cause of puerperal fever in obstetrics.

Incidence

A. The incidence of endometritis has been noted to be as high as 38.5% after cesarean section; the incidence is 1.2% after vaginal delivery.

Pathogenesis

A. During labor and delivery, indigenous cervicovaginal flora enter the uterine cavity. Onset is usually 3 to 5 days after delivery, unless it is caused by beta-hemolytic streptococcus, in which case the onset is earlier and more precipitous. Infection is usually polymicrobial in nature. Undiagnosed or unsuccessfully treated infection of the endomyometrium can progress to involve the entire uterus and may spread to accessory pelvic structures. The main pathway for spread of the infection is the broad ligament. Sources of bacteria may be any one or a combination of the following:
   1. Indigenous vaginal bacteria, usually pathogenic only when tissue is damaged
      a. Beta-hemolytic streptococcus
      b. *Streptococcus viridans*
      c. *Neisseria gonorrhoeae*
      d. *Gardnerella*
   2. Contamination by normal bowel bacteria
      a. *Clostridium perfringens*
      b. *E. coli*
      c. *Proteus mirabilis*
      d. *Aerobacter aerogenes*
      e. *Enterococcus*
      f. *Pseudomonas aeruginosa*
      g. *Klebsiella pneumoniae*
   3. Contamination from environment; staphylococcus is a common organism.

Predisposing Factors

A. Operative delivery: Cesarean section is the major predisposing factor for pelvic infection. The most important determinant of infection for patients undergoing cesarean delivery is the duration of labor.
B. Intrapartum: Prolonged rupture of membranes, numerous vaginal exams in labor, use of internal monitoring devices during labor, use of instruments in delivery, prolonged labor, intrauterine manipulation such as internal rotation or manual removal of placenta can all lead to endometritis
C. Postpartum: Retained placental fragments or membranes, improper perineal care, and host resistance also predispose a patient to infection
D. Anemia: This probably represents a marker for poor nutrition.
E. Obesity

Common Complaints

A. "Feeling ill" with fever or chills
B. Muscle aches
C. Headache
D. Uterine pain and tenderness
E. Foul-smelling lochia

Other Signs and Symptoms

A. Fever (100.4°F–104.0°F)
B. Subinvolution
C. Uterus may be atonic.
D. Abnormalities of lochia
   1. May be scant and odorless if anaerobic infection
   2. May be moderately heavy, foul, bloody, or seropurulent if aerobic infection
E. Tachycardia

Subjective Data

A. Elicit onset, duration, and course of symptoms.
B. Review the color, odor, and amount of lochia.
C. Review the patient's pain or discomfort and the relief measures used.
D. Review other body symptoms to rule out other infections such as UTI, breast engorgement, or mastitis.
E. Review labor and delivery events for complications (see section Predisposing Factors).

Physical Examination

A. Check temperature, pulse, and BP: The patient may be tachycardic with heart rate 100 to 140 bpm.
B. Inspect: Observe color, amount, and odor of lochia. Check abdominal incision, if applicable. Check the perineum for lacerations, breakdown of incision, redness, and drainage.
C. Palpate
   1. Palpate the abdomen; check uterine tenderness.
   2. Palpate the back; check CVA tenderness.
D. Auscultate: Auscultate the heart and lungs.
E. Pelvic exam
   1. Speculum exam: Inspect the cervix for lacerations, drainage, or redness.
   2. Bimanual exam: Check for cervical motion tenderness; palpate adnexa for masses and tenderness; note "heat" of the pelvis.

Diagnostic Tests

A. CBC with differential
B. Blood and urine cultures
C. Cervical cultures, to rule out a STI, if indicated
D. Wet prep, if indicated

Differential Diagnoses

A. Endometritis
B. STDs, such as chlamydia, gonorrhea, or trichomoniasis
C. Septic pelvic thrombophlebitis
D. UTI/pyelonephritis
E. Pneumonitis
F. Extreme breast engorgement—"milk fever"
G. Wound infection

Plan

A. General interventions
   1. Instruct on proper hygiene. Teach the patient proper techniques to prevent infection (perineal area, incision site, breast).
   2. Acetaminophen (Tylenol) for fever as needed
B. Patient teaching: See the Section III Patient Teaching Guide for this chapter, "Endometritis."
C. Pharmaceutical therapy
   1. Antibiotic therapy
      a. Augmentin 500 mg orally four times daily for 10 days
      b. If the patient is allergic to penicillin and not breastfeeding, doxycycline 100 mg orally every 12 hours for 7 days
      c. If the patient is allergic to penicillin and breastfeeding, cephalexin (Keflex) 500 mg orally four times daily for 7 days
      d. Rocephin/ceftriaxone 250 mg IM times one with Flagyl 500 mg by mouth twice a day for 7 days (if breastfeeding, pump and dispose of breast milk during treatment)
   2. If uterus is boggy and/or bleeding is excessive: Methylergonovine maleate (Methergine) 0.2 mg orally every 4 hours for six doses. (Do not give if the patient is hypertensive.)

Follow-Up

A. Call the patient in 24 to 48 hours to evaluate her status.
B. Instruct the patient to call if symptoms do not resolve within 24 hours or if they worsen.

Consultation/Referral

A. Consult with physician if symptoms do not resolve, if they worsen within 24 hours, or if the patient's temperature does not go below 100.0°F after 48 hours on antibiotics. If no significant improvement is seen within 2 to 3 days, the patient may need to be admitted to the hospital.

Mastitis

Definition

A. Mastitis is an infection of breast tissue with potential for abscess formation.

Incidence

A. Mastitis has been estimated to occur in 2% to 10% of breastfeeding mothers. Less than 1% of these require hospitalization. Symptoms seldom appear before the end of the first week postpartum and are most often seen during the first 2 months postpartum.

Pathogenesis

A. During the period of lactation, the breast changes from an essentially nonfunctioning organ to a complex functioning organ of the body. The developing multiductal system becomes a rich environment for the growth of bacteria. The most common offending organism is *Staphylococcus aureus* (95%). The immediate source of the organisms that cause mastitis is almost always the nursing infant's nose and mouth.

Predisposing Factors

Invasion of bacteria in the presence of breast injury, including:

A. Bruising from rough manipulation (pumping) or failing to break the neonate's attachment to the areola and nipple before removing from breast
B. Prolonged breast engorgement
C. Milk stasis in a duct
D. Cracking or fissures of the nipple
E. Poor hand washing

Common Complaints

A. Breast engorgement, usually bilateral
B. Pain in the breast, usually unilateral
C. Fever
D. Red streak(s)
E. Flu-like symptoms: Body aches, headache, malaise, and chills

Other Signs and Symptoms

A. Fever 100.0°F to 104.0°F, rapid rise
B. Exquisitely tender breast tissue
C. Hard mass in the breast
D. Tachycardia and tachypnea
E. Axillary lymphadenopathy

Subjective Data

A. Elicit the onset, duration, and course of symptoms.
B. Note the frequency and length of time of the feeding or pumping.
C. Are there any red streaks on the breasts?
D. Are the nipples cracked and bleeding?
E. Quantify pain symptoms, relief measures tried, and results.
F. Review other symptoms to rule out other infections, such as wound infection, episiotomy breakdown, and UTI.

Physical Examination

A. Check temperature and BP, pulse, and respirations.
B. Physical exam should not be focused just on breast symptoms but should include a general ruling out of other potential problems, such as coexistent UTI or endometritis.
C. Inspect
   1. Visually inspect breasts.
   2. Perform breast exam.
   3. Check episiotomy or abdominal incision to rule out infection.
D. Palpate
   1. Perform breast exam. Observe breastfeeding for adequacy of latch, suck, swallow, jaw glide, and any clicking.
   2. Palpate lymph modes of the neck and axilla.
   3. Palpate the abdomen.
   4. Check CVA tenderness.
E. Auscultate: Auscultate the heart and lungs.

Diagnostic Tests

A. Treatment usually initiated based on symptoms and exam
B. CBC: Leukocytosis in peripheral smear
C. WBC, culture, and sensitivity of breast milk to identify bacteria for persistent signs of infection or if antibiotic treatment is unsuccessful
D. Urine or wound cultures, if applicable
E. Ultrasound considered if breast is not responding to treatment to evaluate for breast abscess

Differential Diagnoses

A. Mastitis: Fever, chills, and malaise in conjunction with unilateral breast pain
B. Breast engorgement: Bilateral presentation of breast discomfort
C. Breast abscess: Discharge of purulent exudate from nipple, masses, or reddened areas that develop a bluish hue of the skin over the area of abscess
D. Clogged milk duct
E. Viral syndrome
F. Inflammatory breast cancer

Plan

A. General interventions
   Encourage self-care and support. Advise the family to assist the patient with self-care and infant care during this acute period. The woman may feel extremely ill for the first 24 to 48 hours of therapy and may find it difficult to continue breastfeeding, as well as perform self-care and newborn care activities.
B. Patient education
   1. See the Section III Patient Teaching Guides for this chapter, "Mastitis" and "Breast Engorgement and Sore Nipples."
   2. Advise the patient to continue to breastfeed or pump to maintain milk supply.
   3. Stress the importance of continuation of breastfeeding or pumping despite infection.
C. Dietary management
   1. There are no dietary restrictions.
   2. Have the patient increase fluid intake with increased temperature (at least 10 to 12 glasses a day).
   3. Encourage her to eliminate caffeine, if possible, or use in moderation.

D. Pharmaceutical therapy
1. Antibiotics
a. Drug of choice: Dicloxacillin 500 mg by mouth every 6 hours for 10 days
2. Alternative drug therapy
a. Cephalexin (Keflex) 500 mg by mouth should be taken four times daily for 10 days.
b. Concerning methicillin-resistant *Staphylococcus aureus* (MRSA), trimethoprim-sulfamethoxazole one to two tablets twice a day or clindamycin 300 mg orally four times a day for 10 days. Linezolid 600 mg orally twice a day for 10 days may also be used.
c. Severe infection, inpatient treatment with vancomycin 30 mg/kg IV twice daily should be used.
3. Advise the patient to complete the full course of antibiotics even if symptoms are improved sooner.
4. Candidal vaginitis may develop secondary to antibiotic therapy. The patient should be aware of the signs, symptoms, and treatment plan if it should occur. Use the probiotics *Lactobacillus fermentum* or *Lactobacillus salivarius* with use of antibiotics.
5. Acetaminophen (Tylenol) or ibuprofen for pain management
6. The patient may require pain medication if acetaminophen (Tylenol) or ibuprofen is not effective. Use acetaminophen with codeine phosphate (Tylenol No. 3) or other narcotic as needed for pain.

Follow-Up

A. Evaluate the patient in 48 hours if a breast abscess is suspected; assess need for surgical consultation.

Consultation/Referral

A. Consult a physician if a breast abscess is suspected, for persistent signs of infection, or if antibiotic treatment is unsuccessful. Treatment of a breast abscess may include surgical incision and drainage of the abscess.
B. Notify the pediatrician if mastitis is diagnosed.

Postpartum Depression

Definition

A. Postpartum depression is a mood disorder characterized by unexplained tearfulness, sadness, irritability, and disturbances in appetite and sleep patterns, as well as an inability to care for self or baby, usually presenting within 2 weeks to 3 months postpartum.

Incidence

A. Reported incidence in the United States is between 8% and 15%.

Pathogenesis

A. It is believed that postpartum depression may be related to psychological, physiologic, and cultural factors. The extreme hormonal changes that occur during the postpartum period may contribute. Postpartum thyroiditis is also a suspected factor. However, no confirmed biologic cause has been found. Some authorities have suggested that the mother's feeling of "loss of control" over her own life is the underlying precipitating factor.

Predisposing Factors

The following may make a mother more likely to experience postpartum depression.
A. Preterm infant
B. Multiple gestation
C. History of postpartum depression or mental illness
D. Social stressors: Dissatisfaction in the marriage, financial difficulties, and lack of support in the home
E. Age younger than 20 years
F. Single parent
G. Poor relationship with the father of the baby
H. Evidence of significant emotional problems in the past
I. Having experienced separation from one or both parents during childhood or adolescence
J. Having received poor parental support and attention in childhood or having limited social support in adulthood
K. Low self-esteem

Common Complaints

A. Insomnia
B. Poor appetite
C. Tearfulness
D. Fatigue
E. Anxiety
F. Headaches
G. Difficulty concentrating or confusion
H. Feelings of excessive guilt or worthlessness
I. Possible suicidal ideations

Other Signs and Symptoms

A. Mood swings
B. Despondency, social withdrawal, and feeling of inadequacy
C. Guilt
D. Impaired memory
E. Ambivalence about motherhood and baby
F. Inability to care for self and baby
G. Poor grooming of self and/or baby

Subjective Data

A. Elicit onset, duration, and course of symptoms.
B. Review the patient's medical history for predisposing factors.

C. Question the patient regarding her ability to care for her infant, herself, and other family members at home.
D. Review the amount of support in the home. Is she the primary caregiver? Are there any family members or friends who help in the household management, sibling child care, and newborn care?
E. Does the patient get out of bed and dress herself daily?
F. Does the patient have thoughts of harming the infant, herself, or others?

Physical Examination

A. Check temperature, pulse, respirations, and BP.
B. Inspect
   1. Note general overall appearance, including dress, makeup, neatness of hair, tearfulness, and apathy.
   2. Observe her interaction with the baby, for example, talking to the baby and tone of voice, eye contact, and so on.
C. Postpartum examination (see Exhibit 15.2).

Diagnostic Tests

A. Diagnostic tools are available on the Internet, including the Edinburgh Postnatal Depression Scale: www.fresno.ucsf.edu/pediatrics/downloads/edinburghscale.pdf
B. If depression is diagnosed, a thyroid profile should be ordered.

EXHIBIT 15.2 Postpartum Examination

Date: ____________

History: Age: ______ G ______ PT ______ P ______ A ______ L ______

Labs: Blood type & Rh: ______ If negative, was Rh_0GAM workup done and Rh_0GAM given in the hospital, if needed?

Rubella: ______ If nonimmune, was she immunized before hospital discharge? ____________

Discharge HCT: ____________

Medical and antepartum complications: ____________

Intrapartum course/complications: ____________

Delivery: Date: ______ Type: ______ Sex: ______ Birth weight: ______

Apgars: 1 minute: ______ 5 minutes: ______ Neonatal: Gestational age: ______

Complications: ____________

Feeding: Breast/bottle: ______ Current infant status: ______

Surgery: Bilateral tubal ligation (BTL): Yes/No ____________

If yes, pathology report reviewed: Postpartum complications: ____________

Current status: Medical problems: ____________

Sexual intercourse since delivery/problems: ____________

Psychosocial/postpartum depression: ____________

Medications: ____________

Physical exam: BP: ______ Pulse: ______ Resp: ______ Weight: ______

Breasts: ____________

Pelvic: Episiotomy or laceration: ____________

Abdomen: ____________

Adnexa: ____________

Uterus: ____________

Vagina: ____________

Cervix: ____________

Pap smear: Date/results: ____________

Plan: Contraception: ____________

Referrals: Labs: ____________

New prescriptions: ______ Patient Teaching Guides: ______

Other: ____________

Signature: ____________

Differential Diagnoses

A. Postpartum depression
B. Baby blues: Tearfulness, insomnia, fatigue, headaches, poor appetite, and so on; appearing between the birth and 14 postpartum days
C. Postpartum psychosis: Extreme emotional lability, agitation, delusions, hallucinations, and sleep disturbances
D. Postpartum panic disorder: Extreme anxiety, fear, tightness in the chest, and increased heart rate
E. Postpartum obsessive-compulsive disorder: Obsessive thoughts of harming the child, exaggerated fear of being left alone with the infant, anxiety, depression, and/or unnecessarily vigilant protectiveness of the infant
F. Bipolar disorder

Plan

A. General interventions
   1. Assess all patients for mood disorders at postpartum and all postpartum contacts (see Exhibit 15.3).
   2. Early assessment and treatment is very important. Symptoms that are not treated for several weeks may get progressively worse. Patients with severe depression, characterized by suicidal or homicidal ideation, aggressive behavior, delusions, hallucinations, catatonia, poor judgment, or grossly impaired functioning, are typically hospitalized.
   3. Encourage involvement of the patient's partner and immediate family members in the counseling sessions to assist them in learning ways to assist the patient effectively.
   4. If postpartum depression is diagnosed, perform serum thyroid levels.
B. Patient teaching
   1. Advise the patient that she is not to blame for the condition, that it is not uncommon, and that successful treatment is likely.
   2. Discuss participation in a support group, interpersonal psychotherapy, and cognitive behavioral therapy.
   3. If antidepressants are prescribed, advise the patient that the medication may take 4 to 6 weeks for peak effect. Review benefits/risks/side effects of the medication prescribed. The risk of suicide may increase after beginning antidepressants; therefore, a follow-up appointment in 1 to 2 weeks is recommended.
C. Pharmaceutical therapy
   1. Antidepressants may be ordered for women with moderate to severe symptoms of depression when physical and emotional functioning has been compromised. (Refer to the section "Depression" in Chapter 24, "Psychiatric Guidelines.")
   2. Base selection of medication on whether or not the patient is breastfeeding. Selective serotonin reuptake inhibitors (SSRIs) and tricyclic antidepressants are commonly used and generally considered safe for breastfeeding infants.
      a. Citalopram (Lexapro) in a single daily dose, usually taken in the morning. Initial dose 10 mg/d; dosage can be increased at intervals of 1 week to 20 mg.
      b. Sertraline (Zoloft) 50 mg in a single dose at bedtime. Dosage can be increased up to 200 mg/d.
      c. Amitriptyline (Elavil) 75 mg/d in divided doses. Dosage can be increased up to 150 mg/d.

Follow-Up

A. If the patient had risk factors for depression noted prior to delivery, a follow-up office visit 3 to 4 days after hospital discharge is suggested.
B. Frequent telephone contact, or several repeat visits, may be necessary during the course of the depression until the symptoms have improved.
C. The risk of suicide may increase after beginning antidepressants; therefore, a follow-up appointment in 1 to 2 weeks is recommended.
D. Assess the patient for suicidal ideation and child neglect at every contact.

Consultation/Referral

A. Assess the need to refer the patient to a psychiatrist, psychologist, or family counselor.
B. Refer to group therapy, interpersonal psychotherapy, and/or cognitive behavioral therapy.
C. Consult a psychiatrist about alternative treatments if no change in signs and symptoms is seen.

Resources

Pacific Postpartum Support Society: www.postpartum.org
Postpartum Support International: www.postpartum.net or 1-805-967-7636
Postpartum Support Line: (604) 255-7999

Secondary Postpartum Hemorrhage

Definition

A. Secondary-postpartum hemorrhage is defined as blood loss of 500 mL or more after the first 24 hours of delivery and within 6 to 12 weeks of delivery.

Incidence

A. Incidence is approximately 0.5% to 2% of women in developed countries.

Pathogenesis

A. Hemorrhage may result from retained placental fragments, subinvolution of the uterus, intrauterine infection, or inherited coagulation defects.

EXHIBIT 15.3 Blues Questionnaire: Kennerley

Name:__________ **Days Postpartum:**__________ **Date:**__________

Below is a list of words that newly delivered mothers have used to describe how they are feeling. Please indicate HOW YOU HAVE BEEN FEELING TODAY by ticking NO or YES. Then please mark the box that best describes how much variance there is, if any, from your usual self.

	NO	YES	IS THIS	Much less than usual	Less than usual	No difference	More than usual	Much more than usual
Tearful			Is this					
Mentally tense			Is this					
Able to concentrate			Is this					
Low spirited			Is this					
Elated			Is this					
Helpless			Is this					
Finding it difficult to show your feelings			Is this					
Alert			Is this					
Forgetful, muddled			Is this					
Anxious			Is this					
Wishing you were alone			Is this					
Mentally relaxed			Is this					
Brooding on things			Is this					
Feeling sorry for yourself			Is this					
Emotionally numb, without feelings			Is this					
Depressed			Is this					
Overemotional			Is this					
Happy			Is this					
Confident			Is this					
Changeable in your spirits			Is this					
Tired			Is this					
Irritable			Is this					
Crying without being able to stop			Is this					
Lively			Is this					
Oversensitive			Is this					
Up and down in your mood			Is this					
Restlessness			Is this					
Calm, tranquil			Is this					

Used with permission. Kennerley and Gath (1989).

Predisposing Factors

A. Abnormally adherent placenta
B. Prolonged rupture of membranes leading to infection
C. Overdistended uterus from multiple gestation, and polyhydramnios
D. Hematoma

Common Complaints

A. Heavy red bleeding or slow reddish-brown oozing
B. Abdominal pain
C. Loss of appetite
D. Fatigue; cannot get enough rest and is unable to complete self-care and infant care activities

Other Signs and Symptoms

A. Lochia rubra is bright-red discharge immediately after delivery (1 to 3 days) and may contain a few small clots. A continuous trickle of bright-red blood suggests a laceration of the cervix or vagina.

Saturation of one peri-pad in less than 15 minutes (two pads in 30 minutes, or rapid pooling of blood under the buttocks) is considered excessive bleeding and requires immediate attention.
B. Foul odor: Lochia should not be malodorous. Lochia usually has a "fleshy" odor.
C. Boggy uterus: Check the consistency of the uterus, whether it is firm or boggy. If atony is present, support the lower uterine segment, and massage the uterus or do bimanual compression.
D. Faintness
E. Tachycardia
F. Hypotension

Subjective Data

A. Elicit onset, duration, and course of symptoms.
B. Elicit the amount and color of lochia, including size of blood clot(s).
C. Review symptoms of infection including fever and malodorous lochia.
D. Review labor and delivery events, including the date of delivery, use of forceps or vacuum, weight of baby, manual removal of placenta, complications, and postpartum course.
E. Review pregnancy for predisposing factors such as multiple gestation and polyhydramnios (as previously noted).

Physical Examination

A. Check temperature, BP, pulse, and respirations.
B. Inspect
   1. Note color and amount of vaginal bleeding.

Lochia may appear heavier when the woman first stands up because the lochia pools in the vagina while she is recumbent. Once the pooled blood is discharged, lochial flow should return to normal.

   2. Inspect episiotomy or abdominal incision.
C. Palpate
   1. Check for consistency of uterus, massaging uterus if boggy.
   2. Express clots, if applicable.
   3. By 2 weeks postpartum, the uterus should have involuted and once again be a "pelvic organ."
   4. Check abdominal tension.
D. Pelvic exam
   1. Speculum exam: Assess cervical lacerations.
   2. Bimanual exam: Rule out retroperitoneal hemorrhage.

Diagnostic Tests

A. Hct or CBC with differential
B. If bleeding is not under control, type and cross match blood
C. Coagulation test, if DIC is suspected
D. Blood cultures to rule out infection
E. Possible evaluation for a coagulation disorder such as von Willebrand's disease

Differential Diagnoses

A. Late postpartum bleeding
B. Normal postpartum bleeding
C. Postpartum infection

Plan

A. General interventions
   1. Perform uterine massage: Support the lower uterine segment during massage to prevent uterine prolapse.
   2. Give IV hydration for hypovolemic shock: hypotension, tachycardia, and faintness.
   3. Hospitalization is usually required for postpartum hemorrhage.
   4. Encourage breastfeeding (if applicable) to increase uterine contraction.
   5. Advise the patient to rest and increase oral fluids.
B. Pharmaceutical therapy
   1. Methylergonovine maleate (Methergine) 0.2 mg orally every 4 hours for six doses. **Do not give if the patient is hypertensive.**
   2. For severe hemorrhage
      a. Oxytocin (Pitocin) 10 to 20 units to 1,000 mL IV fluids.
      b. Methylergonovine maleate (Methergine) 0.2 mg by IM injection, if the patient has no history of hypertension. Advise the patient to take full course of Methergine even if bleeding stops.
      c. **Hemabate: 250 mcg, may repeat every 15 to 90 minutes as needed**
      d. Misoprostol (Cytotec, PGE1): 800 to 1,000 mcg, pr
      e. Continue bimanual compression, and notify a physician.
   3. If infection is suspected or confirmed, antibiotics are prescribed.

Follow-Up

A. Reevaluate the patient 1 week from the date of discharge from the hospital.
B. Repeat Hct at postpartum visit.
C. The patient may need iron replacement therapy, if not already prescribed. If stable at 1-week follow-up visit, have the patient return in 4 to 6 weeks postpartum for routine postpartum exam.

Consultation/Referral

Immediately consult or refer the patient to a physician for possible hospitalization for D&C and/or blood product replacement.

Six Weeks Postpartum Exam

History

A. Chart review
   1. Antepartum course, including prenatal laboratory data: Pap smear, cervical cultures, maternal blood type and Rh, rubella and syphilis screen, and CBC
   2. Intrapartum course: Length of labor, type of delivery, and any maternal complications
   3. Neonatal course: Gestational age, weight, length, cord gases, admission to normal or intensive care nursery, length of stay in the intensive care nursery, and any neonatal complications
   4. Immediate postpartum course: Postpartum recovery, any postpartum complications, laboratory data, and length of hospital stay

B. Interval history
   1. Number of weeks postpartum
   2. General maternal health and well-being, including diet or appetite, bowel and bladder function, level of activity, sleep patterns, and pain or discomfort
   3. Interval problems: Calls to health care provider, visits to emergency room, fever, or illness
   4. Adjustment and role adaptation to the baby: Motherhood, fatherhood, sibling rivalry, psychosocial assessment of depression, family support, housing or financial issues
   5. Resumption of sexual activity: When problems encountered, comfort measures used, and type of contraception used
   6. Family planning: Previous method of contraception used, success of method, plans to resume contraception, and options for contraception
   7. Status of infant: Breastfeeding or bottle feeding, consolability, sleep patterns, voiding, and stool patterns
   8. Establishment of health care follow-up: Pediatrician appointment, immunizations; referral to WIC, public health, and so on, if applicable, or follow up with nurse practitioner or nurse–midwife

C. Review of relevant systems
   1. Breasts: Cracked or sore nipples, clogged ducts, engorgement, mastitis; breast care practiced
   2. Bladder function: Stress incontinence, dysuria, urinary frequency, and flank pain
   3. Bowel function: Constipation; discomfort, especially if the patient has a history of third- or fourth-degree laceration; relief measures used and results
   4. Perineum: Problems or discomfort at episiotomy site, problems with wound healing, and signs of infection
   5. Lochia: Duration, type, odor, presence of clots; or resumption of menses: date, duration, and amount
   6. Abdomen: If cesarean delivery, healing of wound, signs of infection; exercises initiated
   7. Legs: Varicosities, heat, swelling, and calf tenderness

Physical Examination

A. BP and pulse; temperature
B. Weight
C. Auscultate: Auscultate the heart and lungs.
D. Breast exam: Examine nipple integrity, masses, inflammation, and engorgement.
E. Palpate: Palpate the abdomen for tenderness, masses, involution of uterus; examine cesarean section incision for wound integrity and signs of infection.
F. Examine legs for varicosities and signs of thrombophlebitis.
G. Examine perineum, healing of episiotomy or lacerations, and abnormalities of Bartholin's gland.
H. Speculum exam: Note lesions or lacerations of cervix, discharge, signs of infection; obtain Pap smear.
I. Bimanual exam: Check for abnormalities of cervix, uterus, adnexa; status of involution; presence of cystocele or rectocele; and vaginal muscle tone.
J. Rectovaginal exam: Check for integrity of episotomy or laceration if indicated.

Laboratory Data

A. Pap smear
B. Other tests as indicated; CBC if anemia or hemorrhage is documented or suspected

Patient Teaching

This visit may be the last contact the woman has with the health care delivery system for some time. The practitioner should evaluate any problems and provide appropriate consultations, referrals, interventions, counseling, and teaching.

A. Explain the necessity of a yearly gynecologic exam.
B. Encourage regular aerobic, abdominal, and Kegel exercises.
C. Counsel the patient on choice of contraception including failure rates with typical use
   1. Abstinence
   2. Natural family planning, calendar method
   3. Spermicides

4. Barrier methods: Condoms, cervical caps, diaphragm
5. Intrauterine devices
6. Oral contraceptives
7. Tubal ligation
8. Vasectomy
9. Depo-Provera injection
10. Contraceptive implants

D. Explain the benefits of a healthy diet, especially if the patient is breastfeeding.
E. Discuss breastfeeding, if applicable; answer any questions, and address concerns.
F. Instruct the patient in breast self-exam, and explain the importance of performing this monthly.
G. Explain the benefits of an inter-pregnancy interval of 1 to 2 years.

Follow-Up

A. Administer rubella vaccination if the patient has nonimmune status and administration of vaccine was missed in the hospital stay and she has not had unprotected intercourse since delivery.
B. If a woman's physical exam and laboratory and Pap tests are normal, she does not require a physical for 1 year.
C. Establish a plan for the woman to obtain Pap smear results (follow-up phone call or letter with results). See the Postpartum Examination sheet (Exhibit 15.2) to use for documentation in the patient's chart.

Wound Infection

Definition

A. Infection may occur at the site of the cesarean section incision or episiotomy or genital tract laceration. Most wound infections become clinically apparent 5 to 6 days after delivery.

Incidence

A. Rates of infection after cesarean delivery range from 5 to 30 times more than vaginal delivery.

Pathogenesis

A. A variety of organisms may be responsible. Examples include *Staphylococcus* or *Streptococcus* species and gram-negative organisms, gram-positive cocci and *Bacteroides*, *Clostridium* species, or *E. coli*.

Predisposing Factors

A. Obesity
B. Anemia
C. Malnutrition
D. Smoking
E. Diabetes
F. Substance abuse
G. Susceptible to infection
H. Poor hygiene
I. Lower socioeconomic status
J. Lack of preoperative prophylactic antibiotics

Common Complaints

A. Redness, heat, swelling, and tenderness at site
B. Foul-smelling drainage
C. Elevated temperature

Other Signs and Symptoms

A. Fever and chills
B. Edema
C. Foul-smelling discharge and pus

Subjective Data

A. Elicit onset, duration, and course of symptoms.
B. Review medical history (see section "Predisposing Factors"); antepartum history for complications such as diabetes; intrapartum complications for prolonged rupture of membranes, fever in labor, use of internal monitoring devices, length of labor, or frequent cervical examinations.
C. Question the patient regarding hygiene at wound site since delivery, including the frequency of changing peri-pads, use of sitz baths, and showering.
D. Question the patient regarding drainage from wound or episiotomy, noting color, amount, and odor.
E. Review signs and symptoms of breast engorgement and UTI.
F. Review vaginal delivery for third- and fourth-degree episiotomy.

Physical Examination

A. Check temperature, pulse, respirations, and BP.
B. **Examination should not be limited to the incision site. A complete physical is needed to evaluate breasts, lungs, hematomas, and concurrent UTIs.**
C. Inspect: Examine the incision site (episiotomy or abdomen) for drainage, redness or edema, and intactness.
D. Palpate
   1. Perform breast examination.
   2. Palpate suture line (episiotomy or abdomen). Probe incision with cotton-tipped swab to evaluate for hematoma, cellulitis, and/or pus.
   3. Palpate all abdominal quadrants.
   4. Palpate the vagina to rule out concealed hematoma.
E. Auscultate: Auscultate the heart and lungs.
F. Percuss: Percuss the back to assess CVA tenderness.

Diagnostic Tests

A. CBC with differential
B. Blood culture (optional)

C. Culture of infected area
D. Urinalysis, culture and sensitivity, if indicated

Differential Diagnoses

A. Wound infection
B. Impending dehiscence. If serosanguinous drainage is noted after the first 24 hours, dehiscence is possible.
C. Episiotomy breakdown

Plan

A. General interventions
   1. The wound may need to be opened and cleaned.
   2. For an infection at a cesarean section site, wound irrigation and dressing changes several times a day may be necessary.
   3. Home health referral may be needed.
B. Patient teaching: See the Section III Patient Teaching Guide for this chapter, "Wound Infection: Episiotomy and Cesarean Section."
C. Dietary management
   1. No dietary restrictions are recommended; encourage the patient to eat well-balanced meals. Increase protein in diet for wound healing.
   2. Instruct the patient to increase fluid intake; have her drink at least 10 to 12 glasses of liquid a day.
D. Pharmaceutical therapy
   1. Augmentin 875 mg twice a day for 7 to 10 days
   2. Clindamycin 450 mg every 6 hours for 7 to 10 days; safe for breastfeeding
   3. Cefoxitin 1 to 2 g by IM injection or IV infusion every 6 to 8 hours; safe for breastfeeding
   4. Acetaminophen (Tylenol) when required for elevated temperature

Follow-Up

A. Reevaluate the patient in 48 hours to assess wound healing.

Consultation/Referral

A. **Consult a physician for evaluation and possible surgical closure.**

Bibliography

American Academy of Pediatrics/American College of Obstetricians and Gynecologists, ACOG Committee on Obstetric Practice (Author) Laura Riley, MD FACOG (Editor), Ann R. Stark MD FAAP (Editor), Sarah J. Kilpatrick MD PhD FACOG (Editor), & Lu-Ann Papile MD FAAP. (2012). *Guidelines for perinatal care* (7th ed.). Elk Grove Village, IL, and Washington, DC.

American College of Obstetricians and Gynecologists. (1998). Vitamin A supplementation during pregnancy. *ACOG Committee Opinion*, Number 196.

American College of Obstetricians and Gynecologists. (2003). Exercise during pregnancy and the postpartum period. *Clinical Obstetrics and Gynecology, 42(2)*, 496–499.

American College of Obstetricians and Gynecologists. (2004). Nausea and vomiting in pregnancy. *ACOG Practice Bulletin*, Number 52.

American College of Obstetricians and Gynecologists. (2005). The importance of preconception care in the continuum of women's health care. *ACOG Committee Opinion*, Number 313, September 2005, Reaffirmed 2012.

American College of Obstetricians and Gynecologists. (2006). Postpartum hemorrhage. *ACOG Practice Bulletin*, Number 76, 1–9. Reaffirmed 2012.

American College of Obstetricians and Gynecologists. (2008a). Anemia in pregnancy. *ACOG Practice Bulletin*, Number 95.

American College of Obstetricians and Gynecologists. (2008b). Medical management of ectopic pregnancy. *ACOG Practice Bulletin*, Number 94.

American College of Obstetricians and Gynecologists. (2010). Moderate caffeine consumption during pregnancy. *ACOG Committee Opinion*, Number 462.

American College of Obstetricians and Gynecologists. (2011). Antenatal corticosteroid therapy for fetal maturation. *ACOG Committee Opinion*, Number 475, 1–2.

American College of Obstetricians and Gynecologists. (2012a). Chronic hypertension in pregnancy. *ACOG Practice Bulletin*, Number 125.

American College of Obstetricians and Gynecologists. (2012b). Management of preterm labor. *ACOG Practice Bulletin*, Number 127.

American College of Obstetricians and Gynecologists. (2012c). Prediction and prevention of preterm birth. *ACOG Practice Bulletin*, Number 31, 1–11.

American College of Obstetricians and Gynecologists. (2013a). Gestational diabetes mellitus. *Practice Bulletin 137*, 1–11.

American College of Obstetricians and Gynecologists. (2013b). Hypertension in pregnancy. *Obstetrics and Gynecology, 122*(5), 1122–1131.

American College of Obstetricians and Gynecologists. (2014). Antepartum fetal surveillance. *ACOG Practice Bulletin*, Number 145, 1–11.

American Diabetes Association. (2004). Preconception care of women with diabetes. *Diabetes Care, 27*(Suppl. 1), S76.

American Diabetes Association. (2014). Standards of medical care in diabetes. *Diabetes Care, 37*(Suppl. 1), s18–s20.

Anderson, F. W., Hogan, J. G., & Ansbacher, R. (2004). Sudden death: Ectopic pregnancy mortality. *Obstetrics and Gynecology, 103*(6), 1218–1223.

Association of Women's Health, Obstetric & Neonatal Nursing and Johnson & Johnson Consumer Products. (1996). *Compendium of postpartum care* (pp. 1.17, 1.26–1.29, 1.32–1.33, 4.08–4.09, 5.08). Skillman, NJ: Johnson & Johnson.

Atterbury, J. L., Munn, M. B., Groome, L. J., & Yarnell, J. A. (1997). The antiphospholipid antibody syndrome: An overview. *Journal of Obstetric, Gynecologic, and Neonatal Nursing, 26*(5), 522–530.

Bell, R., Glinianaia, S. V., Tennant, P. W., Rankin, J., & Bilous, R. W. (2012). Peri-conception hyperglycaemia and nephropathy are associated with risk of congenital anomaly in women with pre-existing diabetes: A population-based cohort study. *Diabetologia, 55*, 936–947.

Byrne, J., Flagaard-Tillery, K., Johnson, S., Wright, L., & Silver, R. (2009). Group A streptococcai puerperal sepsis: Initial characterization of virulence factors in association with clinical parameters. *Journal of Reproductive Immunology, 82*(1), 74–83.

Cash, J. C. (2014). Assessment of the childbearing woman. In J. Weber & J. Kelley (Eds.), *Health assessment in nursing* (5th ed., pp. 665–692). Philadelphia, PA: Lippincott-Raven.

Catalano, P. (2007). Management of obesity in pregnancy. *Obstetrics and Gynecology, 109(2,* Pt. 1), 419–433.

Centers for Disease Control and Prevention. (2010). Prevention of perinatal group B streptococcal disease. Revised guidelines from CDC. *MMWR Recommendations and Reports, 59*(RR-10), 1–36.

Committee on Health Care of Underserved Women, American College of Obstetricians and Gynecologists. (2007). ACOG Committee Opinion 361: Breastfeeding: Maternal and infant aspects. *Obstetrics and Gynecology, 109,* 479.

Committee on Practice Bulletins—Obstetrics, The American College of Obstetricians and Gynecologists. (2012). Practice bulletin no. 130: Prediction and prevention of preterm birth. *Obstetrics and Gynecology, 120,* 964.

Cook, C., Henderson, J. J., Kent, J. C., Lai, C. T., & Hartmann, P. E. (2007). Hormonal control of the lactation cycle. In T. W. Hale & P. F. Hartman (Eds.), *Textbook of human lactation* (1st ed., p. 90). Amarillo, TX: Hale Publishing.

de Weerd, S., Thomas, C., Cikot, R., Steegors-Theunissen, R., deBoo, T., & Steegers, E. (2002). Preconception counseling improves folate status for women planning pregnancy. *Obstetrics and Gynecology, 99*(1), 45–50.

Evans, M., Elixa, L., Landsverger, E., Olbrien, J., & Harrison, H. (2004). Impact of folic acid fortification in the United States: Markedly diminished high maternal serum alpha-fetoprotein values. *Obstetrics and Gynecology, 103*(3), 474–479.

Hale, T. W. (2006). *Medications and mother's milk* (12th ed.). Amarillo, TX: Hale Publishing.

Hoveyda, F., & MacKenzie, I. Z. (2001). Secondary postpartum haemorrhage: Incidence, morbidity and current management. *British Journal of Obstetrics and Gynaecology, 108*(9), 927.

Iams, J. D. (2014). Identification of candidates for progesterone. *Obstetetrics and Gynecology, 123*(6), 1317–1326.

Jovanovic, L., Savas, H., Mehta, M., Trujillo, A., & Pettitt, D. (2011). Frequent monitoring of A1C during pregnancy as a treatment tool to guide therapy. *Diabetes Care, 34*(1), 53–54.

Keeler, S. M., Roman, A. S., Coletta, J. M., Kiefer, D. G., Feuerman, M., & Rust, O. A. (2009). Fetal fibronectin testing in patients with short cervix in the midtrimester: Can it identify optimal candidates for ultrasound-indicated cerclage? *American Journal of Obstetrics and Gynecology, 200,* 158.

Kennerley, H., & Gath, D. (1989). Maternity blues. I. Detection and measurement by questionnaire. *British Journal of Psychiatry, 155,* 356–362.

Marchesi, D., Bertoni, S., & Maggini, C. (2009). Major and minor depression in pregnancy. *Obstetrics and Gynecology, 113*(6), 1292–1298.

Mathiesen, E. R., Ringholm, L., & Damm, P. (2011). Pregnancy management of women with pregestational diabetes. *Endocrinology and Metabolism Clinics of North America, 40,* 727.

McCance, D. R. (2011). Pregnancy and diabetes. *Best Practice & Research: Clinical Endocrinology & Metabolism, 25,* 945.

Morbidity and Mortality Weekly Trend. (2013). Preterm births—United States 2006 and 2010. Retrieved from www.cdc.gov

Nettina, S. (Ed.). (2010). *Lippincott manual of nursing practice* (9th ed.). Philadelphia, PA: Wolters Kluwer Health/Lippincott Williams & Wilkins.

Paramsothy, P., Lin, Y., Kernic, M., & Foster-Schubert, K. (2009). Interpregnancy weight gain and caesarean delivery risk in women with a history of gestational diabetes. *Obstetrics and Gynecology, 113*(4), 817–823.

Peaceman, A. M., Andrews, W. W., Thorp, J. M., Cliver, S. I. P., Lukes, A., Iams, J. D., ... Pietrantoni, M. (1997). Fetal fibronectin as a predictor of preterm birth in patients with symptoms: A multicenter trial. *American Journal of Obstetrics and Gynecology, 177*(1), 13–18.

Staff. (2009a). *Anemia in pregnancy.* Retrieved from http://www.cdc.org

Staff. (2009b). *Gestational diabetes.* Retrieved from http://www.diabetes.org

Varney, H., Kriebs, J. M., & Gregor, C. L. (2004). *Varney's midwifery* (4th ed.). Sudbury, MA: Jones & Bartlett.

Villers, M., Jamison, M., Castro, L., & James, A. (2008). Morbidity associated with sickle cell disease in pregnancy. *American Journal of Obstetrics and Gynecology, 199*(2), 125, e1–125:e5.

Wong, A., Blumenfield, Y., El-Sayed, Y., & Druzin, M. (2008). 834: NST surveillance in a large university cohort-rates of nonreassuring tracings by indication. *American Journal of Obstetrics and Gynecology, 199*(6, Suppl. A), S35.

CHAPTER SIXTEEN

Gynecologic Guidelines

Anne Moore, Rhonda Arthur, Amy Hull, Brooke Faught, and Cheryl A. Glass

Amenorrhea

Definition

Amenorrhea is the absence of menstruation when menstrual periods should occur.

A. Primary amenorrhea
   1. No menstrual period by age 14 in the absence of growth or development of secondary sexual characteristics
   2. No menstrual period by age 16 regardless of the presence of normal growth and development with the appearance of secondary sexual characteristics

B. Secondary amenorrhea: No menstrual period for 6 months in a woman who usually has normal periods, or for a length of time equal to three cycle intervals in a woman with less frequent cycles

Incidence

A. Amenorrhea in a woman who has had menstrual periods is quite common at some time during her reproductive life. Amenorrhea that is a result of agenesis of part of the reproductive system or a chromosomal anomaly is quite rare.

Pathogenesis

A. Physiologic: Pregnancy, breastfeeding, and menopause. Pregnancy is the most common cause of secondary amenorrhea and must be ruled out.

B. Disorders of the central nervous system (hypothalamic): Hypothalamic amenorrhea is one of the most common types of secondary amenorrhea. There is a deficiency in the pulsatile secretion of gonadotropin-releasing hormone (Gn-RH). Examples include a stressful lifestyle; weight loss, as in anorexia or bulimia; extreme exercise; medications such as hormones; hypothyroidism; and major medical disease such as Crohn's disease, celiac disease, or systemic lupus erythematosus.

C. Disorders of the ovary. Examples include abnormal chromosomes such as Turner's syndrome; gonadal dysgenesis or agenesis (there may be no or very delayed Tanner stage); premature ovarian failure (POF; premature menopause, before age 40); effect of radiation or chemotherapy; and polycystic ovarian (PCO) disease.

D. Disorders of the outflow tract or uterine target organ: Abnormalities in the systems of this compartment are uncommon. Examples include Asherman's syndrome from inadvertent endometrial ablation during dilatation and curettage (D&C) and agenesis or structural anomalies of the uterus, tubes, or vagina.

E. Disorders of the anterior pituitary. Examples include prolactin tumors.

Predisposing Factors

A. The disorder can affect any female between the ages of 14 and 55 years.

Common Complaints

A. "I haven't had a period in months."

B. "I have periods only a few times each year."

C. "I have nipple discharge."

Other Signs and Symptoms

A. Irregular, infrequent menstrual periods

B. Galactorrhea

C. Pregnancy

D. Excessive hair growth

Subjective Data

A. Review complete menstrual history, including age of onset, duration, frequency, regularity, and dysmenorrhea.

B. Review the patient's pregnancy history.

C. Review the patient's contraception history.

D. Note other medications the patient is taking, such as hormones or antidepressants.
E. Ask the patient if she has had a major medical disease or treatment such as chemotherapy for a childhood cancer.
F. Inquire about any breast discharge.
G. Review the patient's weight pattern.
H. Ask the patient to describe her physical self-image. Does she consider herself obese or fat?
I. Review sources of stress in her life.
J. Discuss exercise pattern and history.

Physical Examination

A. Check height, weight, blood pressure, and pulse.
B. Inspect
   1. Note overall appearance. Look at the neck (thyroid).
   2. Skin assessment: Check for central hair growth, which is androgen responsive. Areas to inspect for coarse hair include the upper lip, chin, sideburns, neck, chest, lower abdomen, and perineum.
C. Palpate
   1. Palpate the neck for thyroid enlargement.
   2. Palpate the abdomen for enlarged organs or uterine enlargement compatible with pregnancy.
D. Auscultate
   1. Auscultate the heart and lungs.
   2. If pregnancy is suspected, consider auscultating for fetal heart tones.
E. Pelvic examination
   1. Inspect external genitalia. Note pubic hair pattern for Tanner staging. Note any lesions, masses, or discharge.
   2. Speculum examination: Inspect vagina and cervix. Note bluish color, which is Chadwick's sign with pregnancy.
   3. Bimanual examination: Palpate for softening of the cervical isthmus, which is Hegar's sign for pregnancy. Palpate for size of uterus and for adnexal masses.

Diagnostic Tests

A. Urine: Pregnancy test
B. Serum
   1. Serum human chorionic gonadotropin (HCG)
   2. Thyroid-stimulating hormone (TSH) to rule out thyroid disease
   3. Prolactin: Normal less than 20 ng/mL
   4. Follicle-stimulating hormone (FSH): Greater than 40 IU/mL indicates ovarian failure
   5. Consider luteinizing hormone (LH):FSH ratio to rule out polycystic ovaries.
C. Vaginal and/or pelvic ultrasonography
D. Consider genetic testing/karotype analysis in primary amenorrhea.

Differential Diagnoses

A. Amenorrhea
B. Pregnancy
C. Constitutional delay
D. Hypothyroidism
E. Polycystic ovary syndrome
F. POF, or early menopause
G. Perimenopause
H. Menopause
I. Pituitary adenoma
J. Androgen insensitivity syndrome

Plan

A. General interventions
   1. If laboratory values are normal, proceed to progesterone challenge test to rule out hypothalamic amenorrhea.
   2. If the patient is pregnant, counsel regarding pregnancy and begin antepartum care.
   3. If other laboratory information points to an underlying cause for amenorrhea, treat as appropriate.
B. Patient teaching: See the Section III Patient Teaching Guide for this chapter, "Amenorrhea."
C. Pharmaceutical therapy
   1. Progesterone challenge
      a. Medroxyprogesterone acetate (Provera, Cycrin) 10 mg each day for 5 to 10 days. Alternatively, progesterone in oil 200 mg by intramuscular (IM) injection.
      b. Positive test is any vaginal bleeding. Bleeding usually occurs in 2 to 7 days after finishing the medicine. A late vaginal bleed may be associated with ovulation.
      c. In the absence of galactorrhea, with a normal prolactin level, normal TSH, and positive progesterone challenge, further evaluation is unnecessary.

All anovulatory patients require therapeutic management. There is a risk of endometrial cancer with unopposed estrogen. There is a short latent period in progression from a normal endometrium to atypia to cancer, even in a young woman.

A negative withdrawal bleed may be associated with polycystic ovarian syndrome (PCOS).

   2. Progesterone therapy for hypothalamic amenorrhea
      a. Medroxyprogesterone acetate (Provera, Cycrin) 10 mg for 10 days each month
      b. Low-dose oral contraceptive pills
      c. Clomiphene citrate for women desiring pregnancy
      d. Hormone replacement therapy (HRT) for perimenopausal women

Follow-Up

A. Reproductive age: The patient should return after 6 months of treatment with progesterone or oral contraceptive pills. Discontinue the hormones and assess for return of normal periods. If this does not occur, reinstitute progesterone or oral contraceptive therapy.

B. Perimenopausal: Maintain hormonal therapy. The patient should return annually for evaluation.

Consultation/Referral

A. Refer the patient to a physician if there is no withdrawal bleeding from progesterone challenge. The problem is either with the outflow track, which is rare, or with the ovarian production of estrogen or hypothalamic production of gonadotropins. This is usually beyond the scope of the nurse practitioner.

B. Refer the patient to a physician if her prolactin level is elevated (> 20 mg/mL) for further workup to rule out pituitary adenoma.

Atrophic Vaginitis

Definition

A. Atrophic vaginitis is inflammation of the vaginal epithelium due to a lack of estrogen support. Anything that lowers estrogen levels after puberty can result in a loss of vaginal thickness and rugosity and a decrease in the elasticity of the vaginal tissues.

Incidence

A. Atrophic vaginitis is very common. It may occur in three stages of a woman's life: Preadolescence, when breastfeeding a baby, and postmenopause.

Pathogenesis

A. Estrogen maintains the vaginal pH in an acidic range. Lack of sufficient estrogen promotes an increase in vaginal pH that supports the development of bacterial infections. Estrogen loss also results in a decrease in vaginal glycogen and a thin-walled epithelium, promoting friability and inflammation.

Predisposing Factors

A. Preadolescence
B. Breastfeeding
C. Postmenopause
D. Ovarian failure

Common Complaints

A. Vaginal dryness, irritation, and/or bleeding
B. Dyspareunia
C. Dysuria

Other Signs and Symptoms

A. Postcoital bleeding
B. Thin vaginal discharge
C. Vaginal itching

Subjective Data

Because patients may be reluctant to volunteer information about vulvovaginal symptoms, ask specific questions about the presence and severity of symptoms.

A. Question the patient regarding onset, duration, and course of symptoms.

B. Is this a new problem? If so, review the use of a new soap, laundry detergent, or hygiene products.

C. Describe the color, amount, and odor of vaginal discharge or bleeding.

D. Determine existence of coexisting vasomotor symptoms, such as hot flashes.

E. Is she experiencing dysuria, urinary frequency, vulvar dryness and itching, or dyspareunia? With dyspareunia, question the patient whether discomfort is due to irritation or pain with deep penetration, or both.

F. Determine if the patient is breastfeeding and for what length of time.

G. Ask the patient the date of her last menses and if she is having irregular cycles. Determine if the patient had a hysterectomy with oophorectomy or ovarian failure.

H. Review the number of the patient's sexual partners and any new sexual practices.

I. Review the patient's current medications, including antidepressants.

J. Explore whether she has stopped HRT.

K. Has the patient tried any self-help measures? Was there any relief?

L. When was the last Pap smear, and what were the results?

Physical Examination

A. Check temperature (if infection is suspected), blood pressure, pulse, and respirations.

B. Inspect: Observe the patient generally for discomfort before, during, and after pelvic examination.

C. Palpate: Back: Check for costovertebral angle (CVA) tenderness. Abdomen: Note suprapubic tenderness.

Pelvic Examination

A. Inspect
1. Examine external genitalia for friability, erythema, lesions, condyloma, and amount and color of discharge.
2. Sparse and brittle pubic hair, shrinking of the labia minora, and inflammation of the vulva may be noted in menopausal women.
3. The vulva may appear erythematous, and there may be labial edema.
4. Excoriation may be present if the woman has complained of pruritus.

B. Palpate: "Milk" urethra for discharge to rule out infection.
C. Speculum examination
   1. Check rugae, friability of vaginal epithelium, and color and amount of discharge; evaluate cervix for lesions, friability, and erythema.
   2. Typical atrophic symptoms on inspection: Thin, friable vaginal epithelium; decreased or absent vaginal rugae; scant vaginal discharge
   3. A pediatric speculum may be needed for geriatric women.
D. Bimanual examination
   1. Check for cervical motion tenderness (CMT), uterine size, and position (if no hysterectomy).
   2. Check adnexa for masses.

Diagnostic Tests

A. Serum FSH level: FSH greater than 40 in IU/mL (check with specific labs) indicates menopause or ovarian failure.
B. Serum estradiol level: Estradiol less than 30 pg/mL denotes hypoestrogenemia.
C. Urine culture, if applicable
D. Vaginal pH; normal pH range in premenopausal women is 4 to 4.5.
E. Pap smear with maturation index. (Vaginal wall maturation index evaluation is controversial.)
F. Wet prep
   1. Multiple white blood cells (WBCs) indicate inflammation, may show increased bacteria, and may have decreased lactobacillus suggesting atrophic vaginitis.
   2. Test should be negative for *Trichomonas*. Bacterial vaginosis (BV): Whiff test should be negative.
G. Cultures for gonorrhea and chlamydia, if applicable.
H. Ultrasound for uterine lining thickness (< 4 or 5 mm suggest loss of estrogenic stimulation)
I. Endometrial biopsy, if indicated

Postmenopausal vaginal bleeding must be thoroughly investigated to rule out the possibility of endometrial hyperplasia or endometrial cancer.

Differential Diagnoses

A. Atrophic vaginitis
B. Trauma
C. Foreign body in the vagina
D. Urinary tract infection (UTI)
E. Vaginitis from infective cause: Fungus, bacteria, or virus
F. Contact irritation: Latex (condom); spermicide; lubricant
G. Menopause

Plan

A. General interventions: Treat any underlying infections (gonorrhea, chlamydia, vaginitis) as diagnosed.
B. Patient teaching: See the Section III Patient Teaching Guide for this chapter, "Atrophic Vaginitis."
   1. Women should be reassured that this problem is physical, not emotional.
   2. Discuss the benefits of regular sexual activity to decrease problems of atrophic vaginitis. An important reason for decreased sexual activity is unavailability of partner. Masturbation also facilitates the natural resumption of the production of lubricating secretions by the body. Decline in sexuality is influenced by culture and attitudes as well as physical problems.
   3. Symptomatic relief of dryness during sexual activity may be obtained with the use of water-soluble lubricants and adequate foreplay. Lubricants are used to reduce friction and dyspareunia related to vaginal dryness.
   4. Vaginal moisturizer for relief of symptoms
   5. Discuss pregnancy prevention and inform that perimenopausal symptoms do not ensure lack of fertility.
C. Pharmaceutical therapy
   1. Calamine lotion may be applied externally for local symptomatic relief.
   2. Estrogen therapy (ET)
      a. Vaginal hormonal therapy

Absolute contraindications for use of ET also apply to use of topical estrogen (breast cancer, active liver disease, history of recent thromboembolic event). Vaginal estrogen creams are systemically absorbed. As with use of oral and transdermal estrogen, a progestin must be administered to women who have an intact uterus, secondary to the risk of endometrial hyperplasia or cancer.

         i. Conjugated estrogen (Premarin) cream 0.625 mg/g; use 0.5 to 1.0-g applicator inserted intravaginally at bedtime every night for 1 to 2 weeks, then every other night for 1 to 2 weeks, then as needed. **Not for daily use if the patient has an intact uterus.**
         ii. Estradiol (Estrace) 0.1 mg/g, one-half (2 g) to one (4 g) applicator inserted intravaginally at bedtime every night for 1 to 2 weeks. When vaginal mucosa is restored, maintenance dose is one-quarter

applicator (1 g) one to three times weekly in a cyclic regimen. **Not for daily use if the patient has an intact uterus.**

iii. Estradiol acetate transvaginal ring (Femring) 0.5 mg a day to 0.1 mg a day. Insert one ring per vagina and replace every 90 days.

iv. Estradiol (Estring) 7.5 mcg/24 hr, insert one ring per vagina and replace every 90 days.

v. Estradiol hemihydrate (Vagifem) vaginal tablets 25 mg one tablet per vagina each day for 14 days, the one tablet twice weekly for 10 weeks

b. Oral estrogen replacement therapy

i. Conjugated estrogen (Premarin) 0.625 mg orally every day from days 1 through 25 of month. Plus conjugated estrogen (Provera) 10 mg orally on days 13 through 25

ii. See "Menopause" section for other regimens of HRT.

For long-term ET, consider use of oral or patch methods of delivery if the patient shows additional symptoms of hypoestrogenemia (i.e., hot flashes, night sweats).

c. Ospemifene (Osphena) is an estrogen agonist/antagonist that was approved by the Food and Drug Administration (FDA) in 2013 for the treatment of moderate-to-severe dyspareunia secondary to vulvar and vaginal atrophy due to menopause.

i. Dosage 60 mg daily with food

ii. Use for the shortest duration consistent with treatment goals and risk for the individual patient

iii. Contraindications for the use of ospemifene:

1) Undiagnosed abnormal genital bleeding

2) Known or suspected estrogen-dependent neoplasia

3) History of or active deep vein thrombosis (DVT) or pulmonary embolism (PE)

4) History of or active arterial thromboembolic disease (i.e., stroke, myocardial infarction [MI])

5) **Ospemifene is a category X associated with embryo-fetal harm and/or death. It should not be prescribed for women who are or may become pregnant.**

Ospemifene has estrogenic agonistic effects on the endometrium. As with use of oral, vaginal, and transdermal estrogen, a progestin must be administered to women who have an intact uterus, secondary to the risk of endometrial hyperplasia or cancer.

Follow-Up

A. Breastfeeding women should be reevaluated following weaning, especially if symptoms persist (i.e., alternate etiology is suspected).

B. Postmenopausal women should be evaluated for additional etiologies (i.e., endometrial hyperplasia) if vaginal bleeding persists beyond 3 to 6 months following treatment.

C. The patient should return to clinic 1 to 2 months after beginning oral or vaginal drug therapy; the patient then needs to be seen in 3 to 6 months to check side effects, blood pressure, and response to therapy.

D. Perform Pap smears and physical examination per patient health history or risks and symptoms.

Consultation/Referral

A. If bleeding is a symptom in a postmenopausal woman, the practitioner *must* rule out bleeding of uterine origin. If there is *any* doubt, consultation for endometrial biopsy or dilatation and curettage (D&C) must be obtained.

Individual Considerations

A. Breastfeeding women have amelioration of symptoms as weaning progresses unless an alternate etiology exists.

B. Postmenopausal women

1. Evaluate the patient for other risks of hypoestrogenemia, such as cardiovascular disease and osteoporosis. Continuous systemic ET may be indicated.

2. Evaluate need for continuous systemic estrogen replacement therapy.

3. Vaginitis in the postmenopausal woman is rarely due to any of the organisms responsible for vaginitis in the premenopausal woman (unless she has new sexual partners). *Candidiasis, trichomoniasis,* and BV are uncommon after the menstruating years.

C. Geriatrics

1. The pelvic examination may be more difficult related to the lack of hip mobility.

2. The examination may need to be performed on the patient turned to her left side.

Bacterial Vaginosis (*Gardnerella*)

Definition

A. BV is an infection of the vagina caused by an alteration in the normal flora of the vagina, with an increase in anaerobes and gram-negative bacilli as well as a decrease in the *Lactobacillus* flora.

Incidence

A. According to the Centers for Disease Control and Prevention (CDC), BV is the most common vaginal infection in women of childbearing age and is common in pregnant women. It is not considered exclusively a sexually transmitted infections (STIs).

Pathogenesis

A. The main etiologic agent in BV is an increase in anaerobes in the vagina. The reason this occurs is unknown. The normal lactobacilli of the vagina decrease, and vaginal pH is increased in BV. The organisms present in BV cause the level of vaginal amines to be high. These amines are volatilized when the pH is increased, causing the characteristic "fishy" odor.
B. Bacterial vaginitis is primarily polymicrobial, and the pathogens seen include *Bacteroides* species, *Peptostreptococcus* species, *Eubacterium* species, *Mobiluncus* species, *Gardnerella*, and *Mycoplasma hominis*. The incubation period is unknown.

Predisposing Factors

A. History of STIs
B. Multiple sexual partners
C. Intrauterine device (IUD) use
D. Factors that change the normal vaginal flora
   1. Hormonal changes (menses, pregnancy)
   2. Medications: Oral contraceptive use and antibiotic therapy
   3. Foreign bodies in the vagina (tampons, IUDs), semen, and douching

Common Complaints

A. Vaginal discharge (thin, white, gray, or milky)
B. Fishy vaginal odor
C. Postcoital odor

Other Signs and Symptoms

A. Asymptomatic
B. Increase in odor after menses
C. Itching and burning, occasional

Subjective Data

A. Elicit onset, duration, and course of presenting symptoms.
B. Review any changes in the characteristics and color of vaginal discharge. Does the patient's partner(s) have any symptoms?
C. Review any symptoms of pruritus, perineal excoriation, burning; signs of UTI.
D. Review medication and medical history.
E. Determine if the patient is pregnant; note date of last menstrual period (LMP).
F. Question the patient for a history of STIs or other vaginal infections.
G. Review previous infection, treatment, compliance with treatment, and results.
H. Note last intercourse date.
I. Elicit information about possible foreign body.
J. Review use of vaginal deodorants or sprays, scented toilet paper, tampons, pads, and douching habits.
K. Review change in laundry detergent, soaps, and fabric softeners.
L. Review use of tight restrictive clothing, tight jeans, and nylon panties.
M. Review history for seizures and anticoagulant therapy.

Physical Examination

A. Check temperature, pulse, and respirations.
B. Inspect: Examine external vulva and introitus for discharge, irritation, fissures, lesions, rashes, and condyloma.
C. Palpate
   1. Palpate the abdomen for masses or tenderness. Note enlarged or tender inguinal lymph nodes.
   2. Palpate the external perineal area for vulvar masses.
   3. "Milk" the urethra for discharge.
   4. Check for CVA tenderness.
D. Pelvic examination
   1. Inspect
      a. Note the color, amount, and odor of discharge.
      b. Inspect the cervix.
         i. BV is a vaginosis rather than vaginitis. There is usually little or no inflammation of the vaginal epithelium associated with BV.
         ii. BV is associated with a pink, healthy cervix; "strawberry cervix" is seen with cervicitis due to *Trichomonas vaginalis (TV)*.
         iii. A red, edematous, friable cervix is seen with *Chlamydia trachomatis*.
   2. Speculum examination
      a. Inspect side walls for adhering discharge.
      b. The clinical diagnosis of BV requires the presence of three of the following four signs:
         i. Homogeneous, white, adherent vaginal discharge
         ii. Vaginal fluid pH greater than 4.5. Take smear for testing from the lateral walls of the vagina, not from the cervix, for accurate pH.

iii. A fishy, amine-like odor from vaginal fluid before or after mixing it with 10% potassium hydroxide (positive whiff test). Semen releases the vaginal amines; therefore, there is an increase in odor after intercourse.

iv. Presence of "clue cells" (squamous vaginal epithelial cells covered with bacteria, causing a stippled or granular appearance and ragged, "moth-eaten" borders) or coccobacilli forms both in the fluid and adhering to the epithelial cells.

3. Bimanual examination: Check for CMT and adnexal masses. **BV may be a risk factor for pelvic inflammatory disease (PID).**

Diagnostic Tests

A. Vaginal pH: Greater than 4.5 with BV; normal vaginal pH range is 4 to 4.5
B. Wet prep with 10% potassium hydroxide and normal saline prep; microscopic examination of vaginal secretions should always be done.
C. Rapid chromogenic test to detect sialidase enzyme producing flora is a rapid reliable test that aids in diagnosis in absence of microscopy.
D. Herpes culture, if indicated
E. Urinalysis and culture, if indicated

Differential Diagnoses

A. BV
B. Vulvovaginal candidiasis
C. Trichomoniasis
D. Gonorrhea
E. Chlamydia
F. Presence of foreign body
G. Normal physiologic discharge

Plan

A. General interventions: Inform the patient regarding other modalities for treating BV. These methods include the following:
   1. Vinegar and water douches: One tablespoon of white vinegar in 1 pint of water. Douche one to two times a week.
   2. *Lactobacillus* and *Acidophilus* culture four to six tablets orally daily.
   3. Garlic suppositories: One peeled clove of garlic wrapped in a cloth dipped in olive oil inserted vaginally overnight and changed daily.
B. Patient teaching: See the Section III Patient Teaching Guide for this chapter, "Bacterial Vaginosis." BV is *not* considered a STI.
C. Pharmaceutical therapy
   1. Drug of choice
      a. Metronidazole (Flagyl) 500 mg orally twice daily for 7 days *or*
      b. Metronidazole gel 0.75% one applicator (5 g) per vagina at bedtime for 5 days
         i. Metronidazole is less expensive, easier to use, and associated with greater compliance.
         ii. Side effects of metronidazole include sharp, unpleasant metallic taste in the mouth; furry tongue; central nervous system reactions, including seizures; and urinary tract disturbances. Advise patients to avoid alcohol while taking metronidazole and 24 hours after completing the medication, or they will experience the severe side effects of abdominal distress, nausea, vomiting, and headache.
         iii. Metronidazole may prolong prothrombin time in patients taking oral anticoagulants.
   2. Other medications if the patient is unable to use oral metronidazole
      a. Clindamycin 300 mg orally twice daily for 7 days
      b. Metronidazole gel (MetroGel) 0.75% one applicator vaginally twice daily for 5 days
      c. Clindamycin 2% cream one applicator vaginally at bedtime for 7 days

Clindamycin cream is oil-based and may weaken latex condoms for at least 72 hours after terminating therapy.

   3. Special considerations: Pregnancy: BV has been associated with adverse pregnancy outcomes; therefore, all symptomatic pregnant women and asymptomatic high risk for preterm delivery women require treatment.
      a. Metronidazole 500 mg orally twice a day for 7 days or 0.75% metronidazole gel 5 g per vagina once daily for 5 days
      b. Clindamycin 300 mg orally twice a day for 7 days

Follow-Up

A. Nonpregnant women: No follow-up is recommended unless indicated. Recurrence is common.
B. High risk for preterm delivery; pregnant women should be reevaluated 1 month after treatment.
C. Recommendations for treatment of BV in females infected with HIV are the same as for noninfected patients.
D. Consider treatment of the patient's partner(s) in women with recurrent disease.

Consultation/Referral

A. Refer the patient to a physician for recurrence that is unresponsive to therapies.

Individual Considerations

A. Pregnancy: Clindamycin cream may be associated with increased adverse events in newborns and should not be used during the second half of pregnancy.
B. Partners: Routine treatment of a patient's partner(s) is not recommended at this time because it does not influence relapse or recurrence rates.

Bartholin Cyst or Abscess

Definition

A. The Bartholin's glands are small, round, nonpalpable mucous-secreting organs. They are located bilaterally in the posterolateral vaginal orifice. Obstruction of the duct causes the gland to swell with mucus and form a Bartholin's cyst. The cause of obstruction is usually unknown but may be due to mechanical trauma, thickened mucus, neoplasm, stenosis of the duct, or infectious organisms not limited to STIs. The cyst may become infected, resulting in an abscess. Cysts develop more commonly in younger women, and occurrence decreases with aging; therefore, it is important to rule out neoplasm in women over 40 experiencing Bartholin's cyst.
B. The majority of women with Bartholin's cyst are asymptomatic, but large cysts can cause pressure and interfere with walking and sexual intercourse. Abscesses generally develop rapidly over a 2- to 3-day period and are painful. Some abscesses may spontaneously rupture and often reoccur.

Predisposing Factors

A. History of STIs
B. Local trauma

Common Complaints

A. Cysts can be asymptomatic and are found incidentally on physical exam.
B. Localized pain/irritation
C. Dyspareunia
D. Difficulty walking or sitting due to edema

Subjective Data

A. Elicit onset, duration, and course of presenting symptoms
B. Review any changes in the characteristics and color of vaginal discharge. Does the patient's partner(s) have any symptoms?
C. Review any symptoms of pruritus, perineal excoriation, burning; signs of UTI.
D. Review the patient's medication and medical history.
E. Determine if the patient is pregnant; note the date of LMP.
F. Question the patient for a history of STIs or other vaginal infections.
G. Review previous infection, treatment, compliance with treatment, and results.
H. Note last intercourse date.

Physical Examination

A. Inspect: Examine external vulva and introitus for discharge, irritation, fissures, lesions, and rashes. Bartholin's cyst will appear as a round mass, usually near the vaginal orifice causing vulvar asymmetry. Cysts are usually unilateral, tense, nontender, and without erythema. An abscess is usually unilateral, tense, painful, and erythematous.
B. Palpate: Palpate the external labia and lateral posterior introitus for enlarged cyst, mass, or tenderness; note discharge if present.

Diagnostic Tests

A. Culture and sensitivity of purulent abscess fluid
B. Cervical culture for STI (*Neisseria gonorrhea* and *Chlamydia trachomatis*)
C. Excisional biopsy in women older than 40

Differential Diagnoses

A. Bartholin's cyst
B. Bartholin's abscess
C. Neoplasm
D. STI
E. Sebaceuos cyst

Plan

A. General interventions: Reassurance is indicated for women younger than 40 with asymptomatic cysts. Incision and drainage (I&D) with culture and sensitivity is often required for symptomatic cysts and abscesses. Because cysts and abscesses often reoccur, surgery to create a permanent opening from the duct to the exterior is often the definitive treatment. Two such surgical methods are placement of a wards catheter or marsupialization. Referral is indicated for I&D and other surgical intervention if the provider is not experienced with the procedures.

Women older than 40 must be referred for surgical exploration and excision biopsy.

B. Warm sitz baths three or four times a day may encourage spontaneous rupture of abscess and provide comfort.
C. Pharmaceutical therapy
   1. Recurrent abscesses are treated with oral broad-spectrum antibiotics such as cefixime 400 mg three times a day for 7 days and clindamycin 300 mg every day for 7 days. If STI is present, treat according to CDC STI treatment guidelines.

Follow-Up

A. Report to health care provider if symptoms reoccur.

Consultation/Referral

A. Refer the patient to a physician for recurrence that is unresponsive to therapies. Refer women older than 40 with cyst for excisional biopsy.

Breast Pain

Definition

A. Benign breast disorders such as mastalgia, mastodynia, and fibrocystic breast changes are characterized by lumps or pain. The lumps may be physiologic nodularity, a ropy thickening, or distended fluid-filled cysts that are mobile. The pain may be cyclic or noncyclic, and it may be unilateral or bilateral.

Incidence

A. This is a very common problem. Fifty percent or more of menstruating women experience breast pain. Two thirds of breast pain is cyclic and occurs in women in their 30s; one third is noncyclic and may occur in women at any age, but it tends to occur in women closer to menopause.

Pathogenesis

A. Dysplastic, benign histologic changes occur in the breast such as hyperplasia of the breast epithelium, adenosis, microcysts and macrocysts, duct ectasia, and apocrine metaplasia.

Predisposing Factors

A. Menstruation
B. Ingesting substances containing methylxanthines (coffee, tea, chocolate, and cola drinks). Methylxanthines have been noted to contribute to breast pain by clinical observation only.

Common Complaints

A. "My breasts are painful, particularly just before my period."
B. "I have lumps in my breasts, and they hurt."

Other Signs and Symptoms

A. Tender breasts with palpation
B. Ropelike masses, usually bilateral, with mobile, well-circumscribed masses that are cystic or rubbery

Subjective Data

A. Elicit history of pain. Note onset, duration, location, and relation to menstrual period. Ask: Is pain constant or intermittent?
B. What has the patient tried to alleviate the pain? Note what has worked, such as nonsteroidal anti-inflammatory drugs (NSAIDs).
C. Note the patient's family history of breast pain, lumps, or cancer.
D. Has there been trauma such as being hit or having a rough sexual experience?
E. Do her breasts hurt during or after exercise such as running, aerobics, soccer, or basketball?
F. Does she wear a good, supporting, properly fitted bra generally and for sports?
G. Has she had any breast surgery or biopsy?
H. Note medication history such as oral contraceptives or phenytoin.

Physical Examination

A. Inspect: Examine the breasts, and note masses; dimples; changes in the skin; changes in the way the nipples are pointed while the patient is in the sitting position with arms in neutral position in lap, above the head, or pressing in on hips.
B. Palpate: Palpate the breasts; look for hard, fixed, or cystic masses in the breast, under the nipple, in the tail of the breast, and in the axilla. Use a standardized breast examination technique. Compress the nipple for discharge. Measure masses, and describe them in the patient's record. Use a clock face to describe their location.

Diagnostic Tests

A. Mammogram: May be difficult to interpret in women younger than 35 years
B. Ultrasonography to differentiate cystic from solid masses
C. Magnetic resonance imaging (MRI) useful for detecting tissues with increased blood flow but limited by false positive results
D. Fine-needle aspiration and biopsy
E. Excisional biopsy for solid lumps
F. Pregnancy test

Differential Diagnoses

A. Fibrocystic breast changes with mastalgia
B. Benign breast masses: Fibroadenoma and duct ectasia
C. Nipple discharge: Duct ectasia, prolactin-secreting pituitary tumors
D. Pain: Costal chondritis, chest wall muscle pain, neuralgia, herpes zoster infection, and fibromyalgia
E. Heart: Angina pectoris
F. Gastrointestinal (GI): Gastroesophageal reflux disease
G. Psychologic: Anxiety and depression

Plan

A. General interventions: Once malignancy is excluded, reassure the patient. Use the term *fibrocystic changes* rather than *fibrocystic disease* to stress the functional nature of the problem. Stress that the pain is real but not a disease state.
B. Patient teaching: See the Section III Teaching Guide for this chapter, "Fibrocystic Breast Changes and Breast Pain."
   1. Teach the patient breast self-examination. Encourage monthly breast self-exam. Continue clinical breast exams annually.

2. "Lumpiness" that varies with the menstrual cycle is not abnormal. Breasts may normally be of different sizes. It is a change that is significant.
3. Consider changing dose or discontinuing HRT for women on HRT with mastalgia.
4. Symptomatic measures to relieve discomfort
   a. Good supporting bra, properly fitted. Adolescents whose breasts are maturing and perimenopausal women whose body is changing are two groups who often wear improperly fitted bras.
   b. Local heat or ice application (whatever works best)

C. Diet: Elimination of methylxanthines is a good idea, but the relationship of methylxanthines to breast pain is unproven in research studies. Sodium intake restriction has also been advocated but has not been supported by research.

D. Pharmaceutical therapy
1. Diuretic: Spironolactone (Aldactone) 10 mg twice daily premenstrually
2. Oral contraceptive pills: Low-dose estrogen (20 mcg) pills are recommended.
3. Topical nonsteroidal anti-inflammatory gel can be used for local mastalgia.
4. Anti-estrogen treatment
   a. Danazol (Danocrine) 200 mg daily for 6 months. *Note:* Doses below 400 mg daily may not inhibit ovulation. The patient must use a barrier contraceptive or IUD contraceptive measure. Although the side-effect profile is significant, long-term symptomatic relief and histologic changes may be achieved.
   b. Tamoxifen citrate 10 mg per day for 3 to 6 months for severe cyclic breast pain
5. Vitamins
   a. Vitamin E is no longer recommended for treatment of mastalgia.
   b. Research has demonstrated mixed results on the benefits of vitamin B_6 and vitamin A.
6. Herbs
   a. Flaxseed 25 mg daily may show benefit in the treatment of cyclic mastalgia.
   b. Evening primrose oil (EPO): There is insufficient evidence to recommend EPO for the treatment of mastalgia.

Follow-Up

A. Women with fibrocystic changes need to be seen after 1 to 2 months of pharmacologic therapy to assess for complications and efficacy.

B. Women with atypical hyperplasia on biopsy need close follow-up every 3 to 6 months by a physician.

Consultation/Referral

A. Consult or refer the patient to a physician when breast masses are identified.

B. Consult with a physician and refer the patient to a surgeon if findings include a suspicious mammographic study, an abnormal needle biopsy, or a solid mass per ultrasonogram.

Individual Considerations

A. Pregnancy: Consider blocked duct or mastitis.

B. Adults: Mammography is indicated annually for women at average risk from age 40 to 69, and women should be informed of the risks, benefits, and limitations of regular screening. Older women should be individualized considering potential risks, benefits, and limitations of screening. High-risk women may benefit from additional screening, including earlier initiation of screening and additional screening modalities such as ultrasound and MRI. When clinical breast examination, mammography, and needle aspiration biopsy are used, breast cancer detection rates are 93% to 100%.

C. Geriatric: Breast pain should be worked up as possible cancer.

D. Partners: Pain may inhibit sexual activity involving the breast.

Cervicitis

Definition

A. Cervicitis is acute or chronic inflammation of the cervix that is visible to the examiner.

Incidence

A. Incidence is unknown due to multiple etiologies.

Pathogenesis

A. Acute cervicitis is primarily due to infection from the following organisms:
1. Bacteria
   a. *C. trachomatis*
   b. *N. gonorrhoeae*
   c. *Mycoplasma*
   d. Ureaplasma
2. Viruses
   a. Herpes simplex virus (HSV) type 2
   b. Human papillomavirus (HPV)
3. *T. vaginalis*

B. Chronic cervicitis is primarily due to the following
1. Trauma occurring during childbirth or instrumentation
2. Infection
3. Presence of foreign bodies (i.e., IUDs)

Predisposing Factors

A. Vaginal delivery

B. Cervical procedures: Laser, loop, or other excision procedures

C. IUD

D. STIs

Common Complaints

A. Copious mucopurulent vaginal discharge
B. Postcoital bleeding

Other Signs and Symptoms

A. Asymptomatic; may be found on routine gynecologic exam
B. Thick yellow vaginal discharge
C. Dysuria
D. Dyspareunia
E. Vulvovaginal irritation or pruritus

Subjective Data

A. Determine onset, duration, and course of symptoms. Is there any dyspareunia, pelvic pain, fever, or urinary symptoms?
B. Determine characteristics of the vaginal discharge.
C. Review the patient's history of STIs.
D. Review the patient's sexual history to include number of partners and partner symptoms (if any), use of sex toys, and sexual lifestyle.
E. Note last Pap smear and results. Has the patient ever had an abnormal Pap, and if so, how was it treated?
F. Note date of LMP, use of contraception, and type(s) of contraception.
G. If the patient has recently been pregnant, review her records for cervical cerclage, vaginal delivery with cervical laceration, or other complications.

Physical Examination

A. Check temperature, pulse, and respirations.
B. Inspect: Observe generally for discomfort before, during, and after exam.
   1. Observe the external vulva for Bartholin's gland enlargement (Bartholin's gland abscess is due primarily to infection by chlamydia), lesions, irritation, fissures, and condyloma.
   2. Note color, amount, and odor of vaginal discharge.
C. Palpate: Back: Note CVA tenderness. Abdomen: Palpate for enlarged or tender inguinal lymph nodes.
D. Pelvic examination
E. Speculum examination: Inspect cervix for inflammation and ectropion.
   1. **Cervical ectropion is found in 15% to 20% of healthy young women (especially in teens and with the use of oral contraceptives). It represents columnar epithelium that is found farther out on the ectocervix, causing the cervix to appear granular and red. Presence of cervical erosion, however, suggests advanced cervical pathology. A "strawberry cervix" (petechiae) is highly suggestive of *T. vaginalis*.**
   2. Check cervix for friability and bleeding when the cervix is touched with a cotton-tipped swab.
   3. Assess the vagina and cervix for leukoplakia, lesions, polyps, and discharge. Assess vaginal walls for discharge and rugae.
   4. **Vesicular or ulcerated cervical lesions warrant testing for HSV, syphilis, and/or chancroid.**
F. Bimanual examination: Check CMT; adnexal masses; uterine size, consistency, and tenderness.
   1. Milk urethra for discharge
   2. Palpate Bartholin's glands

Diagnostic Tests

A. WBC, if indicated
B. Consider testing for syphilis (rapid plasma reagin [RPR] or Venereal Disease Research Laboratory test)
C. Wet prep
D. Cervical cultures for gonorrhea and chlamydia
E. Pap smear
F. Urine culture and sensitivity, if indicated
G. Herpes culture, if indicated

Differential Diagnoses

A. Cervicitis
B. Chlamydia
C. Gonorrhea
D. Bartholin's gland abscess
E. Cervical neoplasm
F. Cervical polyps
G. HSV type 2
H. UTI
I. Cervical ulceration, or erosion, from trauma: Fingernail, cervical biopsy, postpartum, or sex toys
J. PID

Plan

A. General interventions: Patients whose culture is negative generally respond to a round of doxycycline therapy, which is the drug of choice for nonchlamydial, nongonorrheal cervicitis.
B. Patient teaching
   1. Women should be encouraged to obtain routine, annual examinations and Pap smears in accordance with Pap smear guidelines.
   2. Patients should be cautioned to avoid alcohol consumption during and 24 hours after the completion of oral metronidazole due to a disulfiram-like reaction (nausea, vomiting, headache, cramps, and flushing).
   3. Patient should have no sexual intercourse for 1 week.
   4. Avoid tampons and douches until antibiotics are completed.
   5. Give the patient teaching sheet. See the Section III Patient Teaching Guide for this chapter, "Cervicitis."

C. Pharmaceutical therapy
  1. Drug of choice for chlamydia: Doxycycline 100 mg twice daily for 7 days or azithromycin 1 g orally in a single dose. Treat all partners.
  2. Drug of choice for gonorrhea: Ceftriaxone (Rocephin) 125 mg by IM injection plus either a single dose of azithromycin 1 g orally or doxycycline 100 mg orally twice a day for 7 days
  3. Drug of choice for HSV: Acyclovir 400 mg three times daily for 7 to 10 days for initial outbreak, acyclovir 400 mg three times a day for 5 days for recurrent outbreak, or acyclovir 400 mg twice a day for suppression
  4. Drug of choice for *Trichomonas:* Metronidazole 500 mg twice daily for 7 days (treat all partners), or 2 g orally in a single dose
  5. Drug of choice for UTI: See the section "Urinary Tract Infection (Acute Cystitis)" in Chapter 14, "Genitourinary Guidelines."

Follow-Up

A. Recommend "test of cure": Reculture 1 to 2 weeks following completion of pharmacologic therapy.
B. Follow up with Pap smear as mandated by result.

Consultation/Referral

A. Refer the patient to a physician for suspected neoplasm and for cervicitis unresponsive to treatment.
B. If the cervix has a suspicious lesion, the patient should be referred for colposcopy and/or biopsy regardless of cytology results. **On physical examination, the cervix may be edematous and erythematous and may show exposed columnar epithelium. It may be friable. Reddened areas of the cervix may be seen around the cervical os. The irregularity and friability sometimes differentiate them from eversion; other times, colposcopy is required to make the distinction.**

Individual Considerations

A. Pregnancy: Cervical inflammation is common in early pregnancy. If an STI is diagnosed, nonteratogenic pharmacologic therapies must be implemented.
B. Partners: A positive STI result warrants treatment of each sexual partner in accordance with CDC STI treatment guidelines.

Contraception

Definition

A. Contraception is the intentional prevention of pregnancy by either or both sexual partners. Contraception can be mechanical, chemical, or surgical and is either reversible or nonreversible. Considerations in counseling regarding contraceptive choices include cost, efficacy, safety, and personal considerations such as personal belief systems and ability to use selected method.

The CDC's U.S. Medical Eligibility Criteria for Contraceptive Use is a formal adaptation of the 1996 World Health Organization's Medical Eligibility Criteria for Contraceptive Use. This valuable document assists health care providers in counseling women and men and assists health care providers to determine safe and effective contraceptive methods individualized to patient preferences and individual health issues. The CDC summary can be especially valuable for the busy clinician. Find the link to the summary charts at **www.cdc.gov/reproductivehealth/UnintendedPregnancy/Contraception_Guidance.htm.**

Incidence

A. Women frequently visit primary care providers to request contraception and family planning education. Over 11 million women in the United States use oral contraceptive pills. Ninety-eight percent of women aged 15 to 44 have used at least one contraceptive method. Unfortunately, approximately 50% of all pregnancies in the United States are unintended. Consistent use of a reliable and effective contraceptive method can greatly reduce the unintended pregnancy rate. Easy access and education regarding contraceptive use is a keystone in the prevention of unintended pregnancy.

Subjective Data

A. Review complete menstrual history, including age of onset, duration, frequency, regularity, and dysmenorrhea. Review date of LMP.
B. Review the patient's pregnancy history.
C. Review the patient's contraception and sexual history.
D. Note other medications the patient is taking, including over-the-counter (OTC) medications and supplements.
E. Ask the patient if she has had a major medical disease, including hypertension, cardiovascular incident, thromboembolic disease, diabetes, migraine headaches, gallbladder disease, or liver disease.
F. Review substance abuse/use history.
G. Review childhood illness and immunization record.
H. Note allergies.
I. Review pertinent family medical history.

Physical Examination

A. Check height, weight, blood pressure, pulse, and body mass index (BMI).
B. Inspect

1. Note overall appearance. Look at neck (thyroid). Inspect breast/genitalia for Tanner staging.
2. Skin assessment: Check for central hair growth, which is androgen responsive. Areas to inspect for coarse hair include the upper lip, chin, sideburns, neck, chest, lower abdomen, and perineum.

C. Palpate
1. Palpate the neck for thyroid enlargement.
2. Palpate the abdomen for enlarged organs or uterine enlargement compatible with pregnancy.

D. Auscultate
1. Auscultate the heart and lungs.
2. If pregnancy is suspected, consider auscultating for fetal heart tones.

E. Breast examination

F. Pelvic examination
1. Inspect external genitalia. Note pubic hair pattern for Tanner staging. Note any lesions, masses, or discharge.
2. Speculum examination: Inspect vagina and cervix. Note any vaginal discharge. Obtain Pap smear and cervical/vaginal cultures according to Pap smear guidelines.
3. Bimanual examination: Palpate the cervix and check for CMT. Palpate the size of the uterus and assess for adnexal masses.
4. Consider rectal examination as indicated.

Diagnostic Tests

A. Urine: Pregnancy test as indicated/urinalysis as indicated

B. Serum: Complete blood count (CBC) if indicated by history

C. Pap smear according to American Society for Clinical Pathology guidelines

D. Vaginal/cervical cultures for STIs as indicated

Plan

A. General interventions
1. Review all methods of contraception available with the patient and partner, if available.
2. Consider all aspects of the client's history and make recommendations as appropriate.

B. Patient teaching
1. Review anatomy and physiology of the menstrual cycle and reproduction with all patients.
2. Review the risks, benefits, costs, use, and efficacy of contraceptive methods. Review perfect use versus typical use of method selected.
3. Review STI prevention and limitations of STI prevention as related to each method.
4. Assist the patient in selecting the most appropriate method of contraception with regard to cost, efficacy, health status of the patient, ability to use correctly and consistently, and the patient's personal values.
5. Warning signs and information on when to call the care provider should be provided to all patients.
6. All women of childbearing age should be educated on the availability and proper use of emergency contraceptives.
7. Provide all patients information on the prevention of STIs.

Methods of Contraception

A. Abstinence: Refraining from sexual intercourse
1. Advantages: Easily accessible and inexpensive. Perfect use offers protection against STIs and pregnancy.
2. Disadvantages: User dependent

B. Barrier methods
1. Male condom
   a. Advantages: Male condoms are easily accessible (OTC with no prescription needed) and relatively inexpensive. Condoms do not require daily intervention and offer some protections against STIs.
   b. Disadvantages: Male condoms are technique dependent for efficacy. Breakage and spillage can occur. Some condoms are made from latex, and those with latex allergies need to be aware and carefully check the label for latex content. Nonlatex condoms are available. Male condoms are intended for one-time use only.
   c. Efficacy with perfect use of male condoms: Approximately 2 in 100 women will become pregnant each year. With typical use of male condoms, approximately 15 in 100 women will become pregnant each year.
2. Female condom
   a. Advantages: Female condoms are easily accessible (OTC with no prescription needed) and relatively inexpensive. Condoms do not require daily intervention and offer some protections against STIs.
   b. Disadvantages: Female condoms are technique dependent for efficacy. Slippage and spillage can occur. The female condom is intended for one-time use only and may be inserted up to 8 hours prior to intercourse.
   c. Efficacy with perfect use of the female condom: Approximately 5 in 100 women will become pregnant each year. With typical use of the female condom, approximately 21 in 100 women will become pregnant each year.

3. Diaphragm
   a. Advantages: Diaphragms are nonhormonal and can be used for years with proper care. May be inserted up to 6 hours prior to intercourse.
   b. Disadvantages: Diaphragms must be properly fitted by an experienced health care provider and are user controlled. Placement is crucial to contraceptive benefit and spermicide must be used. Must be removed within 24 hours due to risk of toxic shock syndrome (TSS). The patient must have fit checked after childbirth and weight gain or loss. UTIs may be more frequent in diaphragm users, and some women may experience sensitivity or allergy to spermicide. Avoid use during menses.
   c. Efficacy with perfect use of the diaphragm: 6 in 100 women will become pregnant each year. With typical use of the diaphragm, 16 in 100 women will become pregnant each year.
4. Cervical cap
   a. Advantages: Cervical caps are nonhormonal and can be used for years with proper care. The cervical cap may be inserted and left in place up to 48 hours.
   b. Disadvantages: Cervical caps must be properly fitted by an experienced health care provider and are user controlled. Placement is crucial to contraceptive benefit, and spermicide must be used. It must be removed within 48 hours due to risk of TSS. The FemCap is made of latex and is not appropriate for latex-allergic patients. Some women may experience sensitivity or allergy to spermicide. Avoid use during menses.
   c. Efficacy with use of the cervical cap is similar to the diaphragm.
5. Vaginal sponge
   a. Advantages: The vaginal sponge is a nonhormonal OTC polyurethane sponge that releases the spermicide nonoxynol-9. It can be used for multiple acts of intercourse over 24 hours.
   b. Disadvantages: The vaginal sponge is user controlled. Some women may experience sensitivity or allergy to the spermicide. Avoid use during menses.
   c. Efficacy with use perfects use of the vaginal sponge: Among parous women, 20 in 100 will become pregnant each year, and nine nulliparous women will become pregnant each year. With typical use, 32 in 100 parous women and 16 nulliparous women will become pregnant each year.

C. Surgical
1. Male sterilization
   a. Advantages: Sterilization is a very effective form of contraception. User does not have to remember to do anything prior to intercourse, and it is not user dependent. Sterilization is permanent.
   b. Disadvantages: Sterilization involves a surgical procedure. Insurance may not cover the cost of the procedure.
   c. Efficacy with perfect use of male sterilization; 0.1 in 100 women will become pregnant each year. With typical use of male sterilization 0.15 in 100 women will become pregnant each year.
2. Female sterilization is the second most often used contraceptive method in the United States.
   a. Advantages: Sterilization is a very effective form of contraception. User does not have to remember to do anything prior to intercourse, and it is not user dependent. Sterilization is permanent.
   b. Disadvantages: Sterilization involves a surgical procedure. If pregnancy does occur, there is a higher incidence of ectopic pregnancy. Insurance may not cover the cost of the procedure.
   c. Efficacy with both perfect and typical use of female sterilization: 0.5 in 100 will become pregnant each year.

D. IUD
1. Hormonal (Mirena)
   a. Advantages: Mirena is a very effective form of contraception. Mirena may be left in place for 5 years. User does not have to remember to use prior to intercourse. Mirena may reduce menstrual flow.
   b. Disadvantages: Risks of any IUD include uterine perforation; increased spontaneous abortion; ectopic pregnancy; and pelvic pain and infection. Mirena must be inserted by a qualified health care professional. IUD may be spontaneously expelled.
   c. Efficacy with both perfect and typical use of the Mirena: 0.2 in 100 will become pregnant each year.
2. Nonhormonal (ParaGard)
   a. Advantages: ParaGard is a very effective form of contraception. ParaGard may be left in place for 10 years. User does not have to remember to use prior to intercourse.
   b. Disadvantages: Risks of any IUD include uterine perforation; increased spontaneous abortion, ectopic pregnancy, and pelvic pain and infection. ParaGard must be inserted by

a qualified health care professional. IUD may be spontaneously expelled.

c. Efficacy with perfect use of the ParaGard: 0.6 in 100 women will become pregnant each year. With typical use of the ParaGard, 0.8 in 100 women will become pregnant each year.

Women who are not appropriate candidates for an IUD include those with recent pelvic infections, anatomical uterine abnormalities, and pregnancy. Caution should be exercised when considering an IUD in women who have multiple sexual partners; FID; immunosuppression; undiagnosed, irregular, or heavy menstrual bleeding; abnormal Pap smear; and difficulty obtaining follow-up care. See World Health Organization's IUD Toolkit at www .k4health.org/ toolkits/iud

E. Pharmaceutical therapy
   1. Progestin only pills (POPs) (also known as mini pill).
      a. Advantages: The POP is a safe hormonal alternative for women who cannot take estrogen. It is preferred to combined oral contraceptives (COCs) for lactating women as it is not as likely to decrease milk supply. POPs are rapidly reversible and controlled by women.
      b. Disadvantages: The POP cannot be taken if the patient has any contraindications to progestin use. POPs are less effective than COCs and must be taken daily at the same time, requiring strict adherence to regime.
      c. Efficacy with perfect use of POPs: 0.3 in 100 women per year will become pregnant. With typical use, 8 in 100 women per year will become pregnant.
   2. Injection of Depo-Provera long-acting depot medroxyprogesterone acetate (DMPA).
      a. Advantages: Easy to use. The user only has to remember the injection every 3 months. May decrease vaginal bleeding. DMPA is a safe hormonal alternative for women who cannot take estrogen.
      b. Disadvantages: Women cannot use DMPA if they have any contraindications to progesterone use. May cause amenorrhea or irregular vaginal bleeding. May cause increased weight gain. Requires routine (3 months) visits to the provider's office for IM injections. DMPA does not provide protection against STIs. DMPA is associated with reversible decreased bone mineral density.
      c. Efficacy with perfect use of DMPA: 0.3 in 100 women per year will become pregnant. With typical use, 3 in 100 women per year will become pregnant.
      d. Depo-Provera should be administered during the first 5 days of the menstrual cycle, or postpartum prior to resumption of intercourse (preferably after lactation has been established). If this is not possible or if a woman is late for injection, administer pregnancy test and have the patient use condoms for at least 1 week after injection.
   3. Contraceptive implant (Nexplanon): Long-acting reversible etonogestrel implant
      a. A single-rod subdermal radiopaque implant
      b. Advantages: Progestin implant is a safe hormonal alternative for women who cannot take estrogen. This is a long-acting (3 years) reversible contraceptive.
      c. Disadvantages: Women cannot use Nexplanon if they have any contraindications to progestin use. Possible insertion and removal complications exist.
      d. The manufacturer strongly recommends that care providers who wish to insert and/ or remove Nexplanon participate in training sessions. Only clinicians who have completed the training program are eligible to purchase the product. The link to request this training is www.nexplanon-usa.com/en/hcp/services-and-support/request-training/index.asp
      e. **Absolute contraindications to progestogen therapy**
         i. Active thrombophlebitis or thromboembolic disorders
         ii. Acute liver disease
         iii. Known or suspected cancer of the breast
         iv. Pregnancy
         v. Undiagnosed, abnormal vaginal bleeding
   4. Combined estrogen/progesterone contraceptives: Combined estrogen/progesterone contraceptives come in three delivery methods: oral pills, a transdermal patch, and a vaginal ring. Advantages and disadvantages and efficacy are similar regarding hormones, but there are some differences in delivery method.
      a. Advantages: Combined contraceptives are easy to use, convenient, rapidly reversible, and controlled by women. The transdermal patch is only changed weekly, and the vaginal ring is left in place for 3 weeks. In addition to predictable menses, combined contraceptives decrease menstrual flow and length of menses.
      b. Disadvantages: Dependent on user, and oral pills must be taken daily. Exposure to

hormones may not be suitable for certain women based on health status and risk. See absolute and relative contraindications that are not appropriate for some women in a prescriber's reference guide. Smoking in conjunction with use of combined contraceptive use increases cardiovascular risk and should be considered. Does not protect against STIs. Other medications, such as anticonvulsants and antibiotics, may interfere with the effectiveness of combined hormonal contraceptives and should be considered in prescribing.

c. Efficacy with perfect use of combined hormonal contraceptive: 0.3 in 100 women per year will become pregnant. With typical use, 8 in 100 women per year will become pregnant.

d. Prescribing considerations: Oral contraceptives come in combination extended cycle, combination monophasic, combination biphasic, combination triphasic, and progestin-only formulations. Side effects can be managed in consideration of pill composition (see prescribing reference guides such as the Monthly Prescribing Reference at www.empr.com). General considerations for pill selection include age, health history/status, and the patient's preference. Because POPs are highly sensitive to consistency in timing, reserve prescriptions of them for women who have contraindications to estrogen. Alternatives for COCs should be considered in women older than 35 who smoke due to increased risks of thrombolytic events. In asymptomatic adolescents, it is acceptable to prescribe COCs without an initial pelvic exam. For adolescents or anyone who may have difficulty remembering to take a daily pill, consideration should be given to prescription of the vaginal ring, patch, or other methods. See the office's prescriber's reference for complete information on safety side effects and contraindications.

e. **Absolute contraindications to ET**
   i. Acute liver disease
   ii. Cerebral vascular or coronary artery disease, MI, or stroke
   iii. History of or active thrombophlebitis or thromboembolic disorders
   iv. History of uterine or ovarian cancer
   v. Known or suspected cancer of the breast
   vi. Known or suspected estrogen-dependent neoplasm
   vii. Pregnancy
   viii. Undiagnosed, abnormal vaginal bleeding

f. **Relative contraindications to ET**
   i. Active gallbladder disease
   ii. Familial hyperlipidemia

5. Spermicide (foam, film, gel, tablets, and suppositories)
   a. Advantages: Spermicide is a nonhormonal OTC preparation and contains nonoxynol-9. It is inexpensive and easily accessible.
   b. Disadvantages: Spermicide is user controlled and if not used consistently will lead to contraception failure. Some may experience sensitivity or allergy to spermicide. Spermicide has a high failure rate.
   c. Efficacy with perfect use of spermicide: 18 in 100 women will become pregnant each year. With typical use of spermicide, 29 of 100 women will become pregnant each year.

F. Natural family planning (NFP)
   1. Advantages: NFP is nonhormonal. It is inexpensive and easily accessible.
   2. Disadvantages: NFP is user controlled and depends on regularity of cycle and avoidance of intercourse. Can be complex for user and has a high failure rate. Does not protect against STIs.
   3. Efficacy with use: With typical use of the fertility awareness method, 25 in 100 women will become pregnant each year.

Additional information, training, and patient teaching may be found at the following websites: Association of Reproductive Health Professionals: www.arhp.org/Publications-and-Resources/Quick-Reference-Guide-for-Clinicians/choosing/Fertility-awareness; Institute for Reproductive Health: www.irh.org; Planned Parenthood: www.plannedparenthood.org

G. Withdrawal
   1. Advantages: Withdrawal is nonhormonal. It is inexpensive and easily accessible.
   2. Disadvantages: Withdrawal is user controlled. Withdrawal has a high failure rate and does not protect against STIs.
   3. Efficacy with use: With typical use of withdrawal method 85 in 100 women will become pregnant each year.

Follow-Up

A. The patient should return in 3 months of initiation of oral contraceptives, ring, and patch to assess blood pressure, use, side effects, and satisfaction. Then yearly visits are recommended for health maintenance.

B. Patients on Depo-Provera injections should return every 3 months for follow-up injection and weight evaluation and then yearly for health maintenance.
C. Patients with a diaphragm should return for refitting with change in weight or postpartum and for routine health maintenance.

Consultation/Referral

A. If the contraceptive method selected is one the practitioner is not experienced in providing (diaphragm, implant, IUD, surgical sterilization), refer to an experienced appropriate provider.

Dysmenorrhea

Definition

Dysmenorrhea is painful uterine cramping felt primarily in the lower abdomen but also in the lower back and upper thighs.

A. Primary dysmenorrhea: Not associated with pelvic pathology; usually associated with ovulatory cycles. Occurs first day or two of the menstrual period. Usually worse the first day. Affects teens and women in their 20s. Often associated with prostaglandin-induced symptoms of diarrhea, nausea, vomiting, and/or headache.
B. Secondary dysmenorrhea: Painful uterine contractions due to a pathologic etiology such as endometriosis or PID. Occurs in women primarily after menstruation has been established for several years, occurring in their 20s, 30s, and 40s. This type of pain is usually a progressive pain that intensifies over time.

Incidence

A. Primary dysmenorrhea is very common, affecting virtually 100% of young women to some extent at some time. It is the leading cause of absenteeism from work or school in women younger than 30. A smaller, but significant group, perhaps 10%, miss days of school or work each month because of the incapacitating pain. The incidence of endometriosis is 8% to 30% of women of reproductive age.

Pathogenesis

A. Primary dysmenorrhea is due to myometrial contractions that are caused by prostaglandins in the secretory endometrium. The prostaglandins cause uterine ischemia through platelet aggregation, vasoconstriction, and dysrhythmic contractions.
B. Secondary dysmenorrhea is associated with pathologic conditions such as endometriosis, cervical stenosis, tumors, adhesions, adenomyosis, myomas, polyps, infection (PID), IUD malposition, retained products of conception, or nongynecologic causes. The pain of secondary dysmenorrhea may also be unrelated to menses.
C. In endometriosis, there are islands of endometrium found on peritoneal surfaces of the bladder, broad ligaments, fallopian tubes, ovaries, bowel, and cul-de-sac, as well as distant sites on the abdominal wall, vagina, lung, or other sites.

Predisposing Factors

A. Female
B. Reproductive age
C. Ovulatory menstrual cycles
D. Cervical stenosis, possibly

Common Complaints

A. "I have painful periods."
B. "My menstrual cramps are terrible, particularly the first day of my cycle."
C. "My cramps are so bad I feel sick to my stomach and have diarrhea."

Other Signs and Symptoms

A. History of menstrual cramps just prior to the onset of the menstrual period and for the first 24 to 48 hours
B. Pain beginning earlier; associated with intercourse, defecation, and urination; and lasting throughout the menstrual period is associated with endometriosis or adenomyosis.
C. Acute pain may be associated with infection (PID) or ectopic pregnancy.

Subjective Data

A. Obtain a complete menstrual history: Age at menarche; frequency, duration, and regularity of periods; amount of flow, measured in the number of perineal pads or tampons used.
B. Ask the patient about the location of the pain; note radiation and associated symptoms such as nausea, vomiting, or diarrhea.
C. Is pain rhythmic or spasmodic?
D. How old was the patient when the pain began? Primary dysmenorrhea usually begins 2 to 3 years after menarche, with the onset of ovulatory cycles.
E. Inquire about the type of contraception used.
F. Obtain obstetric history.
G. Is the pain related to the menstrual period, or does it occur prior to or independent of the menstrual period?
H. Does the patient have dyspareunia?
I. Does she have UTI symptoms?
J. What treatments have been tried, and which were effective?

Physical Examination

A. Check height and weight, temperature, blood pressure, and pulse.

B. Inspect
   1. Examine the general body habitus for female adipose distribution on the buttocks and thighs.
   2. Note breast development.
   3. Observe the abdomen for distension.
C. Palpate and percuss: Examine the abdomen for masses or tenderness.
D. Auscultate: Auscultate the heart, lungs, and abdomen for bowel sounds.
E. Pelvic examination
   1. Inspection: Inspect the external genitalia for pubic hair pattern, lesions, discharge, and odor.
   2. Palpation: Palpate the external genitalia for masses or areas of tenderness.
F. Speculum examination: Inspect the cervix and vagina for discharge, lesions, ectropion, cervical erosion, and IUD string.
G. Bimanual examination
   1. Palpate the vagina and cul-de-sac areas for tenderness or masses.
   2. Check:
      a. Cervical position, mobility, and pain with mobility
      b. Uterine size, mobility, shape, regularity, masses, position, and tenderness
      c. Adnexa for masses (cystic or solid) and tenderness
   3. A normal pelvic examination is a significant finding in primary dysmenorrhea and often in endometriosis.

Diagnostic Tests

A. Perform stat quantitative serum pregnancy test if suggested by history/physical exam.
B. Consider pelvic ultrasonography to rule out pelvic pathology.
C. Laboratory studies: Urinalysis, hemoglobin, hematocrit, and WBC
D. Consider vaginal and cervical cultures for chlamydia and gonorrhea, if infection is suspected.

Differential Diagnoses

A. Dysmenorrhea: The patient's history and a normal pelvic examination are used to diagnose primary dysmenorrhea.
B. Complication of pregnancy: Missed or incomplete abortion or ectopic pregnancy
C. Endometriosis or adenomyosis
D. Ruptured/ovarian cyst
E. Infection: Endometritis, salpingitis, PID, or pelvic adhesions
F. Fibroid tumors
G. Adhesions
H. UTI
I. Bowel disease: Irritable bowel disease, inflammatory or diverticular bowel disease

Plan

A. General interventions: Support patient concerns and identify reality of discomfort. Identify primary source of pain if other diagnoses exist.
B. Patient education: See the Section III Patient Teaching Guides for this chapter, "Dysmenorrhea (Painful Menstrual Cramps or Periods)" and "Contraception: How to Take Birth Control Pills (for a 28-Day Cycle)."
   1. Educate the patient about the physiology of menstruation.
   2. Teach the patient that endometriosis is one of the leading causes of infertility. Discuss the consequences that may occur with chronic pelvic pain/endometriosis, which includes compromised fertility issues.
   3. Encourage activity and exercise, such as walking or swimming.
   4. Advise warm baths or heating pads to help relieve some pain.
C. Pharmaceutical therapy
   1. NSAIDs
      a. They inhibit prostaglandin synthesis in the endometrium, thus decreasing uterine cramping while providing an analgesic effect.
      b. The drugs should be started as the menstrual period begins. It is no longer considered the standard of care to begin the drugs a few days prior to onset of the menstrual period.
      c. Prostaglandin inhibitors relieve dysmenorrhea in 80% of women.
      d. Take NSAIDs with food to avoid GI upset and irritation.
   2. Medications of choice for dysmenorrhea
      a. NSAIDs
         i. Arylacetic acid derivatives: Naproxen sodium (Aleve) 200 mg every 8 to 10 hours; naproxen sodium (Anaprox) 275 mg every 6 to 8 hours, or 550 mg every 12 hours; and naproxen sodium (Naprelan) 1 to 1.5 g once daily
         ii. Propionic acid derivatives: Ibuprofen (Advil, Motrin, Nuprin) 200 to 800 mg every 4 to 6 hours; ketoprofen (Orudis) 12.5 to 25 mg every 4 to 6 hours. These are OTC medications.
      b. Hormonal contraception
      c. Combined estrogen/progestin contraception
         i. Oral contraceptive pills: Any combination pill is efficacious. Consider extended cycle dosing to prevent having monthly periods.
         ii. Nuvaring
         iii. Progestin-only contraception
         iv. Depo-Provera
         v. Mirena
         vi. Nexplanon

3. Medications of choice for endometriosis
   a. NSAIDs
   b. Combined hormonal contraception
   c. With physician consultation or referral, danazol (Danocrine)
   d. With physician consultation or referral, Gn-RH agonists such as nafarelin (Synarel), leuprolide acetate (Lupron, Lupron Depot), and goserelin acetate (Zoladex).

Follow-Up

A. Have the patient return in 3 months. Encourage the patient to give the treatment 3 months to determine effectiveness.

Consultation/Referral

A. Consult with a physician if dysmenorrhea does not respond to NSAIDs or oral contraceptives for further workup to determine the source of the pain.
B. Consider consultation with OB/GYN for laparoscopy or hysteroscopy to diagnose endometriosis; however, empirical treatment is recommended.

Individual Considerations

A. Pregnancy: Uterine contractions in pregnancy could be preterm labor.
B. Adolescents: Remember that endometriosis can occur in this age group. It is not an extremely rare finding.
C. Adults: Endometriosis can be a disabling condition interfering with work and sexual relationships. It may continue into the perimenopausal period.

Dyspareunia

Definition

A. Dyspareunia is genital or pelvic discomfort associated with sexual intercourse (entry or deep penetration) and interferes with sexual satisfaction. Dyspareunia may be superficial relating to vulvar and vaginal pain, or it may be deep relating to deep pelvic pain.

Incidence

A. 60% of women have dyspareunia at some time in their life. Up to 30% of women experience chronic dyspareunia.

Pathogenesis

Physical and psychosocial etiologies have been identified.

A. Physical causes
   1. Vulvovaginal anomalies
      a. Thick imperforate hymen
      b. Short vagina
      c. Vaginal agenesis
      d. Vaginal septum
   2. Organic dyspareunia
      a. Episiotomy scars (trauma from childbirth)
      b. Bartholin's gland cyst
      c. Vulvar dystrophy
      d. Inflammation or infection, STI
      e. Vulvovaginal cancer
      f. Pelvic pathology
         i. PID
         ii. Uterine or ovarian tumors
         iii. Adenomyosis
         iv. Endometriosis
   3. Musculoskeletal anomalies
      a. Disk disease
      b. Myofascial pain
      c. Coccygodynia
   4. Extensive prolapse or organ displacement
   5. Urethral syndrome or other urinary tract disorders
   6. Vulvodynia
   7. GI anomalies
      a. Constipation
      b. Irritable bowel syndrome
      c. Inflammatory bowel disease
      d. Anorexia
   8. Hypoestrogenism/atrophic vulvovaginitis
B. Psychosocial causes
   1. Childhood molestation
   2. Fear of pain, infection, or pregnancy
   3. Pelvic congestion syndrome
   4. Poor partner communication
   5. History of sexual assault
   6. Previous trauma during intercourse
   7. Domestic violence

Common Complaints

A. Irritation or burning with intercourse
B. Lack of vaginal lubrication
C. Pain with vulvar or vaginal contact
D. Pain with deep penetration
E. Postcoital bleeding

Other Signs and Symptoms

A. Vulvar pain
B. Vaginal pain or burning
C. Vaginal dryness

Subjective Data

A. Review the onset, duration, and course of presenting symptoms.
B. Review the patient's medical or surgical history for physical causes (see Pathogenesis).
C. Ask: How often does pain occur: With every intercourse, near periods, in certain sexual positions? What relief measures have been tried? Is there improvement with using extra lubrication? How much relief was obtained with each measure?

D. Obtain a complete sexual history, including:
   1. Sexual practices
   2. Sexual satisfaction
   3. Orgasm
   4. Perception of partner satisfaction
   5. Age at first coitus
   6. History of sexual abuse, molestation, rape
   7. Perceptions regarding sexuality
   8. Number of sexual partners and preferences
   9. Time spent on foreplay
   10. History of recent delivery and breastfeeding
   11. Age at onset of puberty, date of last menses, and cycle history
   12. Current method of birth control and satisfaction with method; previous methods and why they were discontinued
   13. Presence of vaginal discharge, odor, dysuria, or other physical symptoms before or after intercourse
   14. Medications, including prescription and OTC drugs
   15. Can the woman insert a tampon without pain?

Physical Examination

A. Check temperature, pulse, respirations, and blood pressure.
B. Inspection: Observe generally for discomfort before, during, and after examination.

Look for signs of physical or sexual abuse, abrasions, bruises, and lacerations. For pain greatest upon deep penile penetration, suspect PID, ovarian cyst, endometriosis, pelvic adhesions, relaxation of pelvic support, or uterine fibroids.

C. Auscultate: Auscultate the abdomen for bowel sounds in all quadrants. Auscultation of the abdomen should precede any palpation or percussion due to the changes in intensity and frequency of sounds after manipulation.
D. Palpate
   1. Palpate the abdomen for masses; check for suprapubic tenderness.
   2. Examine the back for range of motion.
E. Pelvic examination
   1. Inspect: Perform perineal exam for atrophic vaginitis. Atrophic vaginitis presents as red, shiny, smooth vaginal sidewalls (loss of rugae); vaginal thinning; decreased elasticity of vaginal tissues. Vulvar inflammation may be present. Assess discharge and rugae for hormonal support.
   2. Evaluate the patient for vulvovaginitis. Perform vulvar exam for Bartholin's/Skene's gland enlargement, fissures, lesions. Inspect for anatomic variants: Narrowed introitus, congenital malformations (septum), and pelvic relaxation (cystocele and rectocele).
F. Speculum examination: Inspect for cervicitis, friability, and discharge. If the woman can insert a tampon without pain, a mechanical obstruction is unlikely.
G. Bimanual examination: Check CMT; adnexal masses; and uterine size, consistency, and position.
H. Rectovaginal examination: Palpate uterosacral ligaments for pain and nodularity and other signs of PID and endometriosis. **In cases of rectal trauma/intercourse, cultures may be needed to rule out STIs.**

Diagnostic Tests

A. CBC
B. Sedimentation rate, if indicated by physical
C. Hormonal assays: FSH, estradiol
D. Wet prep to rule out candidiasis, trichomoniasis, and BV
E. Vaginal/urine cultures for chlamydia, gonorrhea
F. Viral cultures of lesions, if any
G. Urine culture, if applicable
H. Stool culture, if applicable
I. Pelvic ultrasonography, if indicated
J. Fecal occult blood test

Differential Diagnoses

A. Dyspareunia
B. See Pathogenesis

Plan

A. General interventions
   1. Detailed physical examination after a thorough history.
   2. Patients should be encouraged to involve their partner(s) in assessment, diagnosis, and treatment of dyspareunia.
   3. A secure, trusting relationship must be established with the care provider before many patients feel comfortable discussing sexuality issues. Continuity with one provider is essential.
   4. Patients with dyspareunia should be evaluated for multiple etiologies. Treat underlying pathologies such as musculoskeletal anomalies, pelvic infection, UTI, STIs, hormonal deficiencies, and GI etiologies (see specific chapters for treatment plans and drug therapy).
B. Patient teaching: See the Section III Patient Teaching Guide for this chapter, "Dyspareunia (Pain With Intercourse)."
C. Pharmacologic therapy
   1. Refer to specific chapter for therapies related to etiology.
   2. Vulvodynia: Consider the use of topical agents applied to the vulva or vestibule, antihistamine therapy, and/or tricyclic antidepressants.

3. Lidocaine (Xylocaine) 2% gel applied to vulva, vestibule, and fourchette
4. Diphenhydramine (Benadryl) 25 to 50 mg orally at bedtime, or 0.1% triamcinolone acetonide cream twice daily for pruritus
5. Amitriptyline 10 mg orally at bedtime

Follow-Up

A. Perform test of cure for all diagnosed infections, if indicated (see specific infection and therapy).
B. Refer to follow-up plans for specific etiology.

Consultation/Referral

A. Treat/refer the patient for removal of cysts, endometriomas.
B. Refer the patient to a gynecologist for vulvovaginal anomalies, including thickened imperforate hymen, shortened vagina, and vaginal agenesis. Vaginal dilator therapy may be instituted.
C. Refer the patient for sexual therapy consultation for continued complaints without an identifiable physical cause.

Individual Considerations

A. Pregnancy or postpartum: Sexual intercourse may continue throughout pregnancy unless there is pain, bleeding, preterm labor, or premature rupture of the membranes. Alternate positions should be suggested by the provider. Sexual intercourse may resume in the postpartum period when the bleeding has decreased or stopped, incision or episiotomy is healed, and the woman is comfortable upon finger insertion and test of vaginal discomfort. Breastfeeding causes hormonal changes that may produce a menopause-like state, and extra lubrication is usually required.
B. Partners: Encourage the patient to have partner(s) participate in sexual health counseling.

Emergency Contraception

Definition

A. Emergency contraception is a prospective method of pregnancy prevention when unprotected intercourse occurs.

Incidence

A. Presently, emergency contraception has been used by only 1% of American women. The intent is to increase the use of emergency contraception to reduce the number of unintended pregnancies and thus reduce the number of abortions and deliveries of truly unwanted children. Over 3 million women are not using birth control and are at risk for unintended pregnancy.

Pathophysiology

A. Hormones in oral contraceptive pills temporarily disrupt ovarian hormone production and cause an absent or dysfunctional luteal phase hormone pattern. This results in an out-of-phase endometrium that is unsuitable for implantation. Hormone disruption may likewise interfere with fertilization and cause disordered tubal transport. Hormones or minerals (copper) in an IUD as well as an inflammatory response occur, which makes the endometrium unsuitable for implantation and interferes with fertilization and transport.

Predisposing Factors

A. Rape
B. Failure of other means of birth control, including broken condom, dislodged diaphragm or cervical cap, expelled IUD, lost or forgotten pills
C. Unprotected intercourse

Common Complaints

A. "I'm worried that I might get pregnant because the condom broke."
B. "My diaphragm slipped."
C. "I went on vacation and forgot my pills."

Other Signs and Symptoms

A. Unprotected intercourse

Subjective Data

A. Elicit a menstrual history. When was the patient's LMP? Are her periods regular?
B. What form of contraception was used, if any?
C. Has the patient experienced any early signs of pregnancy? If so, discuss.
D. Ask about early symptoms of pregnancy such as frequency of urination, nausea, breast tenderness, and late or missed period.
E. Ask the patient about her feelings or plans if she should get pregnant.

Physical Examination

A. Check blood pressure, pulse, and weight.
B. Inspect abdomen for enlargement compatible with pregnancy.
C. Palpate abdomen for uterine size; if fundus is palpable, measure for fundal height.
D. Auscultate heart, lungs, abdomen. If the uterus is enlarged and is measured to be greater than 11 weeks gestation, attempt to hear fetal heart tones with fetal Doppler.
E. Pelvic exam
   1. Inspect the external genitalia for lesions; note female pubic hair pattern.
   2. Speculum exam: Observe for bluish color of cervix (Chadwick's sign). Observe vaginal discharge; note color and odor.
   3. Bimanual exam: Palpate the cervix for softening associated with early pregnancy. Palpate uterine size.

Diagnostic Tests

A. Pregnancy test: Urine or serum HCG

Differential Diagnoses

A. Unprotected intercourse, potential for pregnancy
B. Pregnancy
C. Dysfunctional uterine bleeding (DUB)
D. Amenorrhea from anovulation
E. PCOS
F. Perimenopause

Plan

A. General interventions
   1. Review the patient's past medical history, contraceptive history, date of LMP, estimated date of ovulation, date of unprotected intercourse, and number of hours since the first and most recent unprotected intercourse.
   2. Discuss the likely risk of pregnancy.
   3. Explore the patient's feeling about continuing pregnancy.
   4. Decide whether a physical exam and pregnancy test are needed if there is a possibility of a pregnancy from the previous month.
B. Patient teaching: See the Section III Patient Teaching Guide for this chapter, "Emergency Contraception."
   1. Discuss options, risks, failure rates, necessary follow-up, alteration of menstrual period, and warning signs of complications.
   2. Discuss interim plan for contraception.
   3. Advise the patient to take oral contraceptive pills as prescribed or have IUD inserted within 96 hours of unprotected intercourse.
   4. Treatment is most effective if taken within 12 to 24 hours for progestin estrogen methods and within 120 hours for progestin antagonist/antagonist.
   5. Treatment is *not effective* in an already established pregnancy.
   6. Educate the patient about the possibility of menstrual cycle disturbance with the next menstrual period.
   7. If menstrual bleeding does not begin within 3 weeks, evaluate for possible pregnancy.
   8. Emergency contraception is not associated with an increased incidence of abnormal outcome of pregnancy should pregnancy not be averted. Emergency contraception does not always work.
   9. This is *not* to be used as a primary contraceptive method.
   10. Have prescription or pack of pills available for an emergency situation.
   11. The IUD should be used only for women at low risk for PID and when the woman intends to continue use of the IUD for contraception.
C. Pharmaceutical therapy
   1. Emergency contraception oral formulations
      a. Levonorgestrel emergency contraceptive is available under the brand names Next Choice, Plan B, and Plan B One-Step. Plan B, commonly called the "morning after pill," is available in one-dose (1.5 mg tablet of levonorgestrel) or two-dose (0.75 mg tablets each) packaging. Progestin-only emergency contraception is now available in the United States without age restrictions.
         i. Plan B One-Step (levonorgestrel 1.5 mg tablet) should be taken as soon as possible after unprotected sex (no later than 72 hours).
         ii. Plan B two dose (levonorgestrel 0.75 mg tablet): Patients should take the first dose as soon as possible after unprotected intercourse (no later than 72 hours) and the second dose 12 hours after the first dose.
      b. Using a standard packet of oral contraceptives; two doses of a combination of ethinyl estradiol and norgestrel or levonorgestrel, 12 hours apart. Table 16.1 provides the equivalent dosing that may be utilized as an emergency contraceptive.
         i. Method must be utilized within 72 hours of unprotected intercourse. Treatment is most effective if taken within 12 to 24 hours.
         ii. Side effects of nausea and vomiting with emergency contraception are common. Take each dose with food. Take antiemetic, dimenhydrinate (Dramamine) 50 mg orally, 30 minutes before dose of medication.
         iii. If vomiting occurs within 1 to 3 hours of taking a dose, take another dose.
         iv. Educate the patient about common side effects such as breast tenderness, abdominal pain, headache, and dizziness.
      c. Ella (ulipristal acetate) is a progesterone antagonist/antagonist that is available only by prescription.
         i. One tablet is taken orally as soon as possible after unprotected intercourse within 120 hours (5 days).
         ii. Common side effects are headaches, abdominal pain, and nausea. Less common side effects include dysmenorrhea, fatigue, and dizziness.
         iii. Repeated use of Ella within the same menstrual cycle is not recommended.
         iv. If vomiting occurs within 1 to 3 hours of taking a dose, take another dose.
         v. Educate the patient about common side effects such as breast tenderness, abdominal pain, headache, and dizziness.

TABLE 16.1 Emergency Contraception

Brand	Number of Pills per Dose	Ethinyl Estradiol (mcg)/Dose	Levonorgestrel (mg)/Dose
Antiprogestin Emergency Contraception Pill			
Directions for antiprogestin pills: Take one pill within 120 hours.			
Brand	**Number of Pills per Dose**		
Ella	1 white pill		
Progestin-Only Emergency Contraceptive Pill			
Directions for progestin-only pills: Take one dose within 72 hours.			
Brand	**Number of Pills per Dose**	**Ethinyl Estradiol (mcg)/Dose**	**Levonorgestrel (mg)/Dose**
Plan B One-Step	1 white pill	0	1.5
Plan B Two Dose	2 white pills	0	0.75
Next Choice	2 peach pills	0	1.5
Combine Oral Contraceptive Pills for Emergency Contraception			
Directions for COC pills: Take first dose within 72 hours and repeat dose in 12 hours.			
Brand	**Number of Pills per Dose**	**Ethinyl Estradiol (mcg)/Dose**	**Levonorgestrel (mg)/Dose**
Ovral	2 white pills	100	0.50
Lo/Ovral	4 white pills	120	0.60
Nordette	4 orange pills	120	0.60
Levlen	4 orange pills	120	0.60
Triphasil	4 yellow pills	120	0.50
Tri-Levlen	4 yellow pills	120	0.50
Alesse	5 pink pills	100	0.50

2. IUD
   a. Copper IUD (ParaGard's CUT 380, Ortho Pharmaceuticals) must be inserted within 5 to 7 days after ovulation in a cycle when unprotected intercourse has occurred. The advantage is that the IUD may be left in place for continuing contraception for 10 years.
   b. Mechanism of action: Two ideas have been proposed.
      i. IUD leads to endometrial changes that prohibit implantation.
      ii. The copper ions have a direct toxic effect on the embryo.

Consultation/Referral

A. Consult with a physician if there is no withdrawal bleed within 4 weeks.
B. Consult with or refer the patient to a physician if necessary to insert IUDs.
C. Here are several ways patients can find emergency contraception.
   1. Not 2 Late is operated by the Office of Population Research at Princeton University and the Association of Reproductive Health Professionals: 888-NOT-2-LATE.
   2. Websites
      a. Emergency contraception (you can be included as a provider): ec.princeton.edu
      b. Planned Parenthood: www.ppfa.org

Follow-Up

A. Have the patient return in 3 to 4 weeks if she does not have a menstrual period. If she has a menstrual period, recommend that she return in 1 month to assess contraceptive use and offer options.

Special Considerations

A. Pregnancy: There is no increased incidence of anomalies if pregnancy does occur.

Endometriosis

Definition

A. Endometriosis is ectopic endometrial tissue that exhibits hormonal responsiveness but is located outside the uterine cavity. Bleeding from this ectopic endometrial tissue causes pelvic inflammation and scarring, resulting in chronic pelvic pain and infertility. Endometrial lesions have been found in the vagina, GI tract (especially the sigmoid colon), thoracic cavity, limbs, and gallbladder.

Incidence

A. The true incidence of endometriosis is unknown. Ranges of 5% to 30% have been cited. Positive family history (mother or sister) increases the risk tenfold. Endometriosis does not have a higher incidence for any particular race or socioeconomic group.

Pathogenesis

A. Retrograde menstruation is the most popular theory for the etiology of endometriosis. Menses are suspected of "flowing backward" through the fallopian tubes, resulting in the "seeding" of endometrial tissue outside the uterus.

Predisposing Factors

A. Positive family history, mother and/or sister
B. History of progressive dysmenorrhea
C. History of prolonged uninterrupted menstrual cycles; first pregnancy at a late age
D. Limited or no prior use of hormonal contraceptives

Common Complaints

A. Pain prior to period, pain with menstrual periods that increases over time (dysmenorrheal)
B. Pain with intercourse (dyspareunia)
C. Pain with bowel movements, may include constipation from the fear or pain of having a bowel movement (dyschezia)
D. Spotting and bleeding

Other Signs and Symptoms

A. Dyspareunia and/or pain that radiates to the thigh and back
B. Chronic, noncyclic pelvic pain
C. Abnormal vaginal bleeding: Premenstrual spotting and DUB
D. Other bowel symptoms: Diarrhea and rectal bleeding
E. Urinary symptoms: Dysuria, urgency, and hematuria

Subjective Data

A. Review the onset, duration, and course of complaints.
B. Obtain a menstrual history: Interval and duration of menstrual cycles and history of dysmenorrhea.
C. Obtain a contraceptive history.
D. Question the patient regarding change in bowel patterns or habits or pain with defecation.
E. Obtain a sexual history, including incidence of dyspareunia.
F. Note patient parity and/or history of infertility.

Physical Examination

A. Temperature, pulse, respirations, and blood pressure.
B. Inspect
 1. Note general appearance for discomfort before, during, and after examination.
 2. Perform detailed external genitalia exam.
C. Auscultate: Auscultate abdomen for bowel sounds in all quadrants. Auscultation of the abdomen should precede any palpation or percussion due to the changes in intensity and frequency of sounds after manipulation.
D. Palpate
 1. Palpate abdomen for masses.
 2. Check for suprapubic tenderness.
 3. Back: Check for CVA tenderness.
E. Pelvic examination
 1. Speculum examination: Inspect the cervix for cervicitis; friability; and discharge color, odor, and amount. Note any cutaneous lesions of the vagina, cervix, and perineum that resemble "powder burn or chocolate spots."
 2. Bimanual examination: Check for CMT, adnexal masses; check uterine size, consistency, position, and mobility.
 3. Rectovaginal examination: Palpate uterosacral ligaments for pain and nodularity. Evaluate for masses and polyps of rectum.

The most common indicator for endometriosis is a fixed retroverted uterus with nodularity. Palpation of endometrial implants may result in exquisite pain for the patient.

Diagnostic Tests

There are no specific diagnostic tests for endometriosis. Diagnosis may be done by laparoscopy. However, this is no longer recommended. Treat empirically.

A. Serum beta HCG, to rule out ectopic pregnancy
B. CBC to rule out infection
C. Cervical culture for chlamydia, gonorrhea, to rule out STI and PID
D. Urine culture, if indicated
E. Transvaginal ultrasonography, to rule out cysts and masses
F. GI series or barium enema, if indicated

Differential Diagnoses

A. Endometriosis
B. Dysmenorrhea
C. Ovarian cysts
D. PID
E. Premenstrual syndrome (PMS)
F. Mittelschmerz
G. Trauma
H. Appendicitis
I. Pregnancy: Normal, missed abortion, or ectopic
J. GI or GU complaints: Diverticular disease, spastic colon, or UTI

Plan

A. General interventions
 1. The patient may be managed empirically if she is suspected of having endometriosis with pharmacologic and nonpharmacologic therapies.
B. Patient teaching
 1. Treatment goals include prevention of disease progression, alleviation of pain, and preservation of fertility. Treatment options include the following:
  a. Observation alone
  b. Medical therapy or pharmacologic therapy

c. Referral or consultation for laparoscopic therapy, including laser vaporization and removal of adhesions if other treatment strategies are unsuccessful

2. Continuation or recurrence of pelvic pain may necessitate assisting the woman to manage her chronic pelvic pain and dysmenorrhea with NSAIDs, hormonal options, and/or other nonnarcotic chronic pain therapies, such as visualization and biofeedback.

3. **Hysterectomy and bilateral salpingo-oophorectomy are the only definitive cures for women who do not wish to conserve their reproductive capacity. This should be considered only as a last resort for failed conservative treatment.**

C. Pharmaceutical therapy

1. Mild endometriosis

a. Combined hormonal contraception is considered the first-line therapy. If the patient experiences pain during the week of withdrawal bleeding, she may take active pills/use ring continuously, omitting the placebo days.

Combination oral contraceptives are being used to produce a state of pseudo-pregnancy that should induce regression of the disease.

b. Medroxyprogesterone acetate 10 mg daily for up to 6 months, or a long-acting progestin (Depo-Provera) 100 to 200 mg by IM injection each month for 6 months

2. Moderate to severe complaints

a. Gn-RH agonist

i. Leuprolide acetate (Lupron) 3.75 mg by IM injection every month

ii. Nafarelin (Synarel) nasal spray twice daily

Use of Gn-RH agonist, which acts to suppress ovulation, can result in side effects, including hot flashes, mood changes, and other menopausal symptoms. Use is restricted to 6 months to avoid decrease in bone density. Expense of this therapy may preclude its use.

b. Danazol 200 to 400 mg twice daily for up to 6 months

i. **Use of danazol, which acts to produce anovulation and hypogonadotropism, can result in androgenic side effects, including acne, hirsutism, weight gain, and voice changes that may not be reversible.**

ii. Other side effects, which are reversible, include decreased breast size, atrophic vaginitis, dyspareunia, hot flashes, and emotional liability.

Follow-Up

A. Patients must return monthly while receiving Gn-RH agonist or danazol therapies to assess for symptom relief and side-effect profile.

Consultation/Referral

A. The workup, evaluation, and medications for endometriosis are expensive. Refer to a gynecologist for initial management. A prudent approach is recommended with a conservative treatment option; evaluate the results before trying another.

B. Refer the patient for a surgical consultation for definitive diagnosis. Endometriosis may be suspected based on symptoms and physical examination. It cannot, however, be confirmed unless actually visualized by laparoscopy.

Individual Considerations

A. Pregnancy: Infertility may be a presenting symptom. Treatment may, therefore, be focused on endometriosis abatement and fertility support.

Resource

Endometriosis Association 8585 North 76th Place Milwaukee, WI 53223 800-992-3636 800-426-2363 (Canada) www.endometriosisassn.org

Infertility

Definition

A. Infertility is defined as the inability of a couple to conceive within 12 months of unprotected intercourse. Many clinicians use a 6-month time frame if the woman is 35 years of age and older.

B. A woman who has never been pregnant or a man who has never initiated a pregnancy is said to have "primary infertility."

C. If a previous pregnancy has been achieved and the couple is unable to conceive a subsequent pregnancy, the term "secondary infertility" is applied.

Incidence

A. It is estimated that approximately 2.5 million couples may be classified as infertile. PID is the leading cause of infertility in the world. Between 5% and 20% of infertility is unexplained.

Pathogenesis

Infertility may occur in the male or female. Evaluate both partners.

A. Infrequent intercourse

B. Interpersonal problems

C. Medical (see Table 16.2)

Predisposing Factors

A. Predisposing factors depend on the etiology.

TABLE 16.2 Pathogenesis of Infertility

Male Pathogenesis	Female Pathogenesis
A. Faulty sperm production	A. Advanced maternal age
1. Azoospermia from	B. Disorder of ovulation/hypothalamic dysfunction
a. Cancer therapy	1. Anovulation
b. Adult mumps	2. Amenorrhea
c. Sertoli-cell-only syndrome	3. Polycystic ovary triad
d. Hypogonadism	a. Acne
e. Retrograde ejaculation	b. Obesity
2. Oligospermia from	c. Hirsutism
a. Varicocele	4. Premature ovarian failure
b. Small testicular size	a. Autoimmune
B. Reproductive tract anomaly	b. Idiopathic
1. Blocked vas deferens	c. Cancer therapy
2. Varicocele	5. Luteal phase insufficiency
3. Congenital obstruction of epididymis	6. Prolactinoma
C. Klinefelter's syndrome	C. Ovarian factors
D. Physical and chemical agent exposure	1. Cysts or tumor
1. Coal tar	2. Irradiation
2. Radiation	D. Tubal disorders/damage/blocked
E. Endocrine disorders	1. PID
1. Diabetes	2. Chlamydia trachomatis
2. Low serum testosterone	3. Postpartum infection
3. Pituitary tumors	4. Pelvic trauma (motor vehicle accident)
4. Hyperprolactinemia	5. Inflammatory bowel disease
F. Testicular infection	6. Endometriosis
G. Injury to reproductive organs/tract	7. Adhesions
H. Nerve damage/neurologic disease: Spinal cord injury	E. Uterine pathology
I. Impotence/erectile difficulty: Performance anxiety	1. Congenital anomalies: duplication
J. Premature ejaculation	2. Septate
K. Early withdrawal	3. Fibroids
L. Lifestyle factors	4. IUD
1. Drugs	5. Asherman's syndrome
2. Smoking	6. Synechiae
3. Alcohol	F. Cervical factors
4. Malnutrition	1. Anatomic abnormalities (hood)
M. Antispermatozoa antibodies	2. Previous cervical surgery (i.e., conization, which leads to mucus depletion)
N. Medications	3. Hostile cervical mucus
1. Antihypertensives	4. Presence of sperm antibodies in the cervix
2. Antidepressants	5. Infections
3. Antipsychotics	G. Lifestyle factors
4. Antiulcer agents/antacids	6. Drugs
5. Muscle relaxants	7. Smoking
	H. Vaginal factors
	1. Intact hymen
	2. Septum
	3. Absent vagina
	4. Infection
	a. Trichomonas
	b. Candida
	c. Chlamydia

(continued)

TABLE 16.2 Pathogenesis of Infertility (*continued*)

Male Pathogenesis	Female Pathogenesis
	d. Mycoplasma e. Bacterial vaginosis f. Gonorrhea g. Streptococci I. Medications: Oral contraceptives J. Medical problems 1. Lupus 2. Hypothyroidism 3. Diabetes 4. Antiphospholipid syndrome

Common Complaints

A. The common complaint is an inability to achieve pregnancy despite frequent acts of intercourse.

Other Signs and Symptoms

A. Dependent on the pathogenesis and history

Subjective Data

A. Obtain a complete health history, including the following.
   1. Age of both partners
   2. General health of both partners
   3. Complete pregnancy history of the female
      a. Number of pregnancies, term and preterm
      b. Vaginal deliveries or cesarean sections
      c. Recurrent miscarriages, gestational age(s)
      d. Stillbirths
      e. D&C for abortions or miscarriages
      f. Cerclage for incompetent cervix
   4. Paternity history of the male
   5. Length of infertility, including prior workup, if any
   6. Coital history
      a. Frequency
      b. Timing and adequacy
      c. Use of lubricants; some may be spermicidal
      d. Postcoital habits: Douching or voiding
   7. Adequacy of intercourse
      a. Penetration of the vagina
      b. Ejaculation by the male
B. Obtain a complete menstrual history, including
   1. Age at puberty
   2. Regularity of cycles
   3. Discomfort during menses
   4. Date of LMP
C. Obtain a complete gynecologic history, including
   1. Contraceptive use
   2. Medical and surgical interventions
      a. D&C
      b. Laparoscopy or endometriosis
   3. Anomalies
D. Take a complete nutritional and exercise history; note eating disorders.
   1. Anorexia nervosa
   2. Bulimia
E. Review female *and* male reproductive tract infections and treatments for past and present partners.
F. Review each individual's habits.
   1. Smoking: How much, how often, how long
   2. Drugs: How much, how often, how long for each drug
   3. Alcohol: How much, how often, how long
   4. Use of saunas or hot tubs
   5. Exercise, including cycling
G. Take a complete medication history, specifically review for
   1. Antihypertensives
   2. Antidepressants
   3. Antipsychotics
   4. Antiulcer agents or antacids
   5. Muscle relaxants
H. Review for exposure to toxic chemicals, radiation, or known teratogens
   1. Military war exposure
   2. Employment exposure
   3. Residential exposure
      a. Microwaves
      b. Pesticides
I. Inquire about diethylstilbestrol (DES) exposure in utero (for either partner).
J. Review for symptoms of thyroid dysfunction
   1. Weight gain or loss
   2. Change of bowel habits
   3. Intolerance to heat or cold
   4. Appetite changes
K. Review for systemic diseases
   1. Cardiac
   2. Collagen vascular diseases
   3. Diabetes

L. Assess the psychosocial context of the infertility, including personal, emotional, and economic factors; family pressures for children; expectations; timing of pregnancy; consideration of adoption; and stress from failure to conceive.

Other Signs and Symptoms

A. See Pathogenesis and information obtained in Subjective Data regarding past medical history.
B. History of not being able to get pregnant over the past 6 to 12 months.

Physical Examination: Male

A. Check temperature, pulse, respirations, and blood pressure. Obtain height, weight, and BMI.
B. Inspect
   1. Note general signs and appearance of underandrogenization: Decreased body hair, gynecomastia, and eunuchoid proportions.
   2. Test the patient's visual field for possible mass lesion.
   3. Examine the penis for hypospadias. Observe urethra for discharge.
C. Percuss: Check deep tendon reflexes (DTRs) for signs of hypothyroidism.
D. Palpate
   1. Neck: Examine thyroid.
   2. Genitals: Examine the scrotum for testicular size, absence of vas deferens, and presence of varicocele.
E. Rectal examination: Check prostate and seminal vesicles for tenderness and other signs of infection.

Valsalva's maneuver performed while the patient stands helps to reveal small varicocele. Varicocele feels like "a bag of worms" with bluish discoloration visible through the scrotum. Approximately 23% to 30% of infertile males have varicocele (usually present on the left side). No treatment is necessary if the semen analysis is normal.

Physical Examination: Female

A. Check temperature, pulse, respirations, and blood pressure. Obtain height, weight, and BMI.
B. Inspect
   1. Examine breasts for presence of nipple discharge.
   2. Note general signs and appearance of PCOS.

PCOS triad includes acne, obesity, and hirsutism.

C. Auscultate: Abdomen for bowel sounds in all quadrants. Auscultation of the abdomen should precede any palpation or percussion due to the changes in intensity and frequency of sounds after manipulation.
D. Palpate
   1. Neck: Examine the thyroid.
   2. Check abdomen for tenderness and masses.
   3. Back: Check CVA tenderness.
E. Percuss: Check DTRs.
F. Pelvic examination
   1. Inspect: Perform detailed external peritoneal exam for signs of infection; lesions; or anomalies of clitoris, labia, Skene's gland, Bartholin's gland, vulva, and perineum.
   2. Speculum examination
      a. Observe length of vagina, position and characteristic of cervix, and any anomalies.
      b. Sound the uterus and cervix for stenosis. Observe the characteristics of cervical mucus: Thin and watery or thick and cloudy, odor, or evidence of infection.
   3. Bimanual examination: Check uterine size, consistency, contour, mobility, CMT, and adnexal masses.

A fixed, immobile uterus determined on bimanual exam indicates the presence of pelvic scarring resulting from "old disease" such as endometriosis and PID.

   4. Rectovaginal examination: Palpate uterosacral ligaments for pain and nodularity; evaluate masses and polyps of rectum.

Diagnostic Tests

A. Male factor
   1. Semen analysis
   2. Sperm penetration assay
B. Ovarian factor
   1. Basal body temperature (BBT)
   2. Serum progesterone: Serum progesterone greater than 15 ng/mL indicates ovulation.
   3. Urinary LH for surge
   4. FSH: A high FSH, greater than 40 m IU/mL, indicates ovarian failure.
   5. TSH
   6. Serum prolactin

When nipple discharge is present, check serum prolactin and TSH to rule out hyperprolactinemia and hypothyroidism.

C. Cervical factor
   1. Postcoital test (PCT), at LH surge
   2. Assess for ferning of the cervical mucus
   3. Assess for spinnbarkeit, during midcycle

Ferning of cervical mucus, determined by microscopy, indicates preovulatory estrogen. Spinnbarkeit demonstrates that estrogenic mucus is thin, clear, and copious in amount and can stretch to introitus from the cervical os.

Just prior to ovulation, the mucus is the thinnest; mucus threads of 6 to 10 cm from the endocervix are normal.

D. Pelvic or uterine factor
   1. Endometrial biopsy
   2. Hysterosalpingogram (HSG); also done for tubal factor
   3. Ultrasonography
   4. Laparoscopy

E. Other tests
   1. Pap smear with maturation index
   2. Cultures for gonorrhea and chlamydia
   3. Pregnancy test, if amenorrhea is present
   4. CBC, sedimentation rate
   5. *Mycoplasma* culture
   6. Wet mount

Differential Diagnoses

A. Infertility
B. Sexual dysfunction
C. Hypothyroidism
D. Hypothalamic dysfunction: Amenorrhea
E. Hyperprolactinemia
F. Menopause
G. Ovarian failure
H. PCOS
I. Asherman's syndrome
J. Tubal occlusion
K. Antisperm antibodies
L. Endometriosis
M. Oligo-ovulation
N. Uterine anomalies: Fibroids, synechiae, and septa
O. Pelvic adhesions

Plan

A. General interventions
   1. Semen analysis is the first step in an infertility workup. Semen analysis should be performed in a reputable laboratory. If the first evaluation is abnormal, it should be repeated one time. Normal semen analysis includes the following.
      a. Sperm count: Greater than 20 million/mL
      b. Volume: 2.6 mL
      c. Motility: Greater than 50%
      d. Morphology: Greater than 60%
      e. Liquefaction: Within 20 to 30 minutes of ejaculation
   2. The male physical examination is generally done if semen analysis is abnormal.
   3. **The male should always be evaluated first before a long and expensive female evaluation is begun.**
   4. Female evaluation
      a. BBT: Followed for several months to evaluate ovulation. Some patients' temperatures dip just before the day of ovulation and then rise. Ovulation and the development of the corpus luteum manifest as an increase in BBT by 0.6°F to 1°F above the patient's baseline temperature (LH surge). The BBT provides presumptive evidence of normal oocyte production and related hormonal change, as well as guidance for the frequency and timing of intercourse.
      b. PCT: Evaluates the character, quality, and spinnbarkeit of the cervical mucus. The presence of at least 5 to 10 motile sperm per high-power field is normal. The PCT should be performed on about day 14 or around the time of expected LH surge as determined by the patient's BBT chart. Poor timing of the PCT is a cause of suboptimal mucus. The test should then be repeated.
      c. Endometrial biopsy: Sampling of the uterine lining late in the luteal phase. The test is scheduled 10 days after the BBT increase, or 2 to 3 days before the onset of the next menses. A normal secretory endometrium and the absence of inflammation indicate that implantation is feasible.
      d. HSG (performed in radiology): Evaluates tubal patency and rules out uterine anomalies. The HSG should be scheduled for the interval between cessation of menstrual flow and ovulation to avoid retrograde flow of menstrual tissue into the tubes and the abdominal cavity.
      e. Laparoscopy: Diagnostic if used as the final screening examination for infertility. Performed by a gynecologist, it is usually done in the first 2 weeks of the menstrual cycle to ensure that the patient is not pregnant. Direct visualization of the pelvic organs provides data about the degree of adhesion formation, presence of endometriosis or fibroids, and the possibility of surgical repair of damaged tubes.

B. Patient teaching
   1. Infertile couples often require extensive counseling, including grief counseling for failure to achieve pregnancy.
   2. See the Section III Patient Teaching Guide for this chapter, "Instructions for Postcoital Testing."
   3. Teach the patient to take BBT measurements.

C. Pharmaceutical therapy
   1. Treatment depends on causative factor(s).
   2. Prescription medications must be supervised by physician and/or specialist due to possible complications such as ovarian hyperstimulation.

Follow-Up

A. Follow-up depends on causative factor(s).

Consultation/Referral

A. Consultation and referral is required for special testing, surgery, and assisted reproductive therapy.
B. Immediate referral to a physician is necessary for ovarian hyperstimulation.

Menopause

Definition

A. Physiologic or natural menopause is the cessation of menses for 12 consecutive months due to the loss of ovarian follicular activity. Natural or physiologic menopause is a retrospective diagnosis recognized 12 months after the final menses. Natural menopause is generally experienced in women between 45 and 55 years of age.
B. Natural menopause before the age of 40 is considered premature.
C. POF is the full or intermittent loss of ovarian function before the age of 40. POF is thought to be caused by genetics, autoimmune disorders, or surgical or chemical interventions.
D. Induced menopause is the abrupt cessation of menses related to chemical or surgical interventions.
E. Perimenopause is caused by fluctuations in ovarian function in the years preceding menopause. The average onset is usually in a woman's 40s but may occur earlier. Due to fluctuations in ovarian function, pregnancy may still occur and unintended pregnancy should be avoided. Perimenopausal symptoms often last several years, with the average duration being 5 years.

Incidence

A. Currently, 30 million American women are menopausal, with another 6 million to become menopausal in the next 10 years. Two million women enter menopause each year—6,000 every day.

Pathogenesis

A. Physiologic menopause is due to failure of ovarian follicular development and ovarian hormone depletion. The major endocrine changes include the decreasing negative feedback on the hypothalamic-pituitary system with increasing FSH and LH. When the ovaries cease to produce estrogen, they become unable to respond to FSH, resulting in the cessation of ovulation and menstruation.

Common Symptoms

A. Insomnia
B. Absence of menses
C. Urogenital atrophy
   1. Vaginal dryness
   2. Dyspareunia
   3. Dysuria/frequency
D. Vasomotor symptoms such as hot flashes/night sweats
E. **All postmenopausal spotting/bleeding should be evaluated for pathologic causes.**

Subjective Data

A. Determine onset, duration, and course of presenting symptoms.
B. Obtain complete medical history, including medications, and assess for risk of osteoporosis, cardiovascular disease, and breast and endometrial cancer.
C. Obtain complete gynecologic history, including menarche, interval and duration of menstrual cycles, history of dysmenorrhea, and pregnancy history. Question the patient regarding sexual history and contraceptives use (condoms, pills, diaphragm, IUD).
D. What is the patient's current menstrual pattern? Is pregnancy a possibility?
E. Review associated symptoms (hot flashes, insomnia, genitourinary symptoms), onset, timing, duration, and impact on daily life.
F. Assess for mood swings and dysphoria.

Physical Examination

A. Check temperature, pulse, respirations, and blood pressure.
B. Inspect: Observe general overall appearance and obtain height, weight, and BMI.
C. Auscultate heart, lungs, and abdomen.
D. Percuss: Percuss the abdomen for organomegaly.
E. Palpate
   1. Palpate thyroid gland.
   2. Perform clinical breast exam, including supra/infraclavicular and axillary lymph node assessment.
   3. Palpate groin for lymphadenopathy.
   4. Palpate the abdomen for masses.
F. Pelvic examination
   1. Inspect: External genitalia for fissures, lesions (external genital warts, genital ulcers), and atrophy.
   2. Palpate: For tenderness, cysts, lesions, "milk" the urethra for discharge.

3. Speculum examination
    a. Inspect vagina for presence of discharge (amount, color, odor), rugae, foreign bodies, signs of trauma, inflammation
    b. Inspect cervix for presence of inflammation, friability, discharge.
    c. Perform vaginal/cervical cultures and Pap test as indicated.
4. Bimanual examination if indicated (pain, bleeding)
    a. Check CMT; evaluate the size, contour, mobility, and tenderness of uterus. An enlarged or irregular uterus requires additional evaluation.

Over time it is normal for the postmenopausal uterus to decrease in size.

    b. Palpate the adnexa for tenderness and masses.

Ovaries should not be palpable in postmenopausal women and require further evaluation if masses or ovaries are appreciated.

5. Rectovaginal examination: With stool for occult blood in women age 50 and older.

Diagnostic Tests

A. No laboratory tests are diagnostic for menopause.
B. Consider TSH.
C. Consider qualitative beta HCG if amenorrhea is sudden
D. CBC if excessive vaginal bleeding
E. Obtain Pap smear as indicated.
F. Endometrial biopsy as indicated for postmenpausal spotting or bleeding
G. Transvaginal ultrasonography for enlarged or irregular uterus or inadequate exam due to body habitus
H. Additional screening as indicated, such as mammogram, hemoccult, cholesterol, and bone mineral density.

Differential Diagnoses

A. Menopause
B. Perimenopause
C. Anemia
D. Leukemia or other cancer
E. Menstrual irregularity for any cause of secondary amenorrhea
F. Pregnancy
G. Psychosomatic illness
H. Thyroid disorders

Plan

A. Patient education
    1. Provide reassurance as to the cause of the absence of menses.
    2. Discuss common symptoms of menopause.
    3. Provide education regarding healthy lifestyle changes: Regular exercise, weight control, smoking cessation, limiting use of drugs and alcohol, and stress reduction.
    4. Encourage a healthy diet rich in vitamin D and calcium.
        a. Supplement diet with calcium to achieve: 1,000 mg a day for women age 19 to 50; 1,200 mg a day for women 50 years of age and older.
        b. Vitamin D supplements to achieve:
            i. 600 IU/d until the age of 70 and then
            ii. 800 IU/d for 71 years of age and older
    5. Encourage vaginal lubricants as needed for vaginal dryness, including water-soluble options and coconut oil. See section on "Atrophic Vaginitis."
    6. Avoid warm environments, caffeine, alcohol, spicy food, and emotional upset; these may trigger hot flashes.
    7. Encourage sleep hygiene and adequate rest.
    8. Discuss the risks and benefits of exogenous hormone therapy.
    9. Assess and manage women at increased risk for osteoporosis according to current osteoporosis guidelines.
    10. Assess and treat cardiac risk factors, including hypertension and dyslipidemia as indicated.
    11. Give the patient the relevant teaching guide. See the Section III Patient Teaching Guide for this chapter, "Menopause."
B. Pharmaceutical therapy
    1. HRT
        a. ET and estrogen plus progestogen therapy (HRT) may be a strategy for management of menopausal symptoms. All women should be counseled regarding the indications, risk, and benefits of HRT. HRT is indicated for treatment of vasomotor symptoms: hot flashes and night sweats, and vulvo-vaginal atrophy and painful intercourse. Use of exogenous ET prevents bone loss when used for symptom management but is not indicated for treatment of osteoporosis. It may be used as a strategy for women with osteopenia if other pharmacologic methods are insufficient or inadequate. (see "Osteoporosis/Kyphosis/Fracture" in Chapter 21, "Rheumatological Guidelines").

            Risks of HRT include an increased risk of venous thromboembolism (VTE) and breast cancer. Long-term unopposed ET increases the risk of endometrial cancer; that is why all women using ET must be prescribed a progestogen concomitantly. Potential areas of concern with the use of HRT include gallbladder disease and cardiovascular events. ET should not be prescribed for women with a history of significant cardiovascular disease warranting procedures such as coronary artery bypass graft surgery (CABG) or percutaneous transluminal coronary angioplasty (PTCA). The provider should carefully screen and educate the patient prior to initiating HRT (see Table 16.3).

b. Postmenopausal women without an intact uterus generally are not prescribed progesterone and are treated with estrogen alone.

c. Oral HRT may be given either sequentially or continuously. The sequential regimen is given daily, with progesterone given 12 to 14 days of the month. It is common to have withdrawal bleeding with this regimen. An alternative to this is the continuous regimen in which both estrogen and progesterone are taken daily.

2. Transdermal estrogen: Patches, creams, sprays, lotions. Generally considered safer than oral medications with respect to VTE risk as the first-pass metabolism effect is avoided and lower doses can achieve a therapeutic effect (see Table 16.4).
3. Transvaginal estrogen (see Table 16.5)
4. **Absolute contraindications to use of ET also apply to use of oral and topical estrogen (breast cancer, active liver disease, and/or history of recent thromboembolic event). Vaginal estrogen creams are minimally systemically absorbed. Screening for endometrial hyperplasia and/or use of a progestogen episodically should be considered on an individual basis.**
5. **Absolute contraindications to ET**
   a. Acute liver disease
   b. Cerebral vascular or coronary artery disease, MI, or stroke
   c. History of or active thrombophlebitis or thromboembolic disorders
   d. History of uterine or ovarian cancer
   e. Known or suspected cancer of the breast
   f. Known or suspected estrogen-dependent neoplasm
   g. Pregnancy
   h. Undiagnosed, abnormal vaginal bleeding
6. Relative contraindications to ET
   a. Active gallbladder disease
   b. Familial hyperlipidemia

TABLE 16.3 Hormone Replacement Therapy

Name	Active Ingredient	Dosage
Estrogen Sequential or Continuous Combined		
Premarin	Conjugated estrogen	0.625 mg/d
Estratab	Esterified estrogen	0.625 mg/d
Menest	Esterified estrogen	0.625 mg/d
Estrace	Micronized estradiol	1.0 mg/d
Ortho-est	Estropipate	0.625 mg/d
Progestin Only for Sequential Regimen		
Amen	Medroxyprogesterone	5–10 mg added to estrogen the first 10–14 days of month
Cycrin	Medroxyprogesterone	5–10 mg added to estrogen the first 10–14 days of month
Provera	Medroxyprogesterone	5–10 mg added to estrogen the first 10–14 days of month
Prometrium	Micronized progesterone	100–200 mg added to estrogen the first 10–14 days of month
Progestin Only for Continuous Combined Regimen		
Cycrin	Medroxyprogesterone	2.5 mg a day
Provera	Medroxyprogesterone	2.5 mg a day
Combination Packet for Continuous Combined Regimen		
Prempro	0.625 mg conjugated equine estrogen and 2.5 mg medroxyprogesterone	1 tablet orally each day
Activella	1 mg 17-beta estradiol and 0.5 mg norethindrone	1 tablet orally each day
FemHrt	5 mcg ethinyl estradiol and 1 mg norethindrone	1 tablet orally each day

See complete prescribing reference or package insert for dosing, titration, contraindications, and side effects.

TABLE 16.4 Transdermal Replacement Therapy

Delivery	Name	Active Ingredient	Dosage
Transdermal patch	Climara	Estradiol	0.25 mg/d 0.0375 mg/d 0.05 mg/d 0.06 mg/d 0.075 mg/d Apply one patch weekly (lower abdomen or upper buttocks)
Transdermal patch	Combipatch	Estradiol 0.05 mg and norethindrone acetate 0.14 mg/d Or estradiol 0.05 mg and norethindrone acetate 0.0.25 mg/d	Continuous combined regimen one patch twice weekly for 28-day cycle (lower abdomen)
Transdermal patch	Vivelle		One patch twice weekly to trunk
Gel-pump	Elestrin	Estradiol	0.06% gel, one pump daily to clean dry skin of upper arm
Gel-pump	Estrogel	Estradiol	0.75 mg/1.25 g gel, one pump daily to clean dry skin of upper arm
Spray	Evamist	Estradiol	1.53 mg/spray, one spray daily to inside of arm
	Vivelle	Estradiol	0.05/d, 0.1 mg/d

See complete prescribing reference or package insert for dosing, titration, contraindications, and side effects.

TABLE 16.5 Transvaginal Replacement Therapy

Delivery	Name	Active Ingredient	Dosage
Cream	Estrace	Micronized 17-beta estradiol	0.1 mg/g, one-half (2 g) to one (4 g) applicator intravaginally at bedtime every night for 1–2 weeks. When vaginal mucosa is restored, maintenance dose is one-quarter applicator (1 g) one to three times weekly in a cyclic regimen.
	Premarin	Conjugated equine estrogen	0.625 mg/g, use 0.5- to 1.0-g applicator inserted intravaginally at bedtime every night for 1–2 weeks, then every other night for 1–2 weeks, then as needed
Ring	Estring	Micronized 17-beta estradiol	7.5 mg/24 hr insert new ring every 90 days
	Femring	Estradiol acetate	0.05–0.1 mg/d insert new ring every 90 days
Vaginal tablet	Vagifem	Estradiol acetate	25 mcg once daily for 2 weeks then twice weekly
IUD	Mirena	Levonorgestrel	20 mcg daily

See complete prescribing reference or package insert for dosing, titration, contraindications, and side effects.

7. Absolute contraindications to progesterone therapy
   a. Active thrombophlebitis or thromboembolic disorders
   b. Acute liver disease
   c. Known or suspected cancer of the breast
   d. Pregnancy
   e. Undiagnosed, abnormal vaginal bleeding

Educate the patient to notify care provider if unusual vaginal bleeding, calf pain, chest pain, shortness of breath, hemoptysis, severe headaches, visual disturbances, breast pain, abdominal pain, or jaundice occur while being prescribed HRT.

C. Nonhormonal pharmacological therapy for vasomotor symptoms
1. Antidepressants
   a. Fluoxetine (Prozac) 20 mg/d
   b. Venlafaxine (Effexor) 37.5 to 75 mg/d
   c. Paroxetine (Paxil) 12.5 to 25 mg/d
   d. Paroxetine (Brisdelle) 7.5 mg/d at bedtime
2. Anticonvulsant
   a. Gabapentin (Neurontin) 300 mg/d and titrate to three or four a day
3. Antihypertensive
   a. Clonidine 0.05 to 0.1 mg/twice a day. For nonhormonal pharmacologic therapies, review prescribing literature for side effects, titrations, and discontinuation regimens.

D. Nonprescription remedies/herbals
   1. Many nonprescription remedies have been used for the treatment of menopausal symptoms. These remedies include isoflavones (soy and red clover), black cohosh, dong quai, EPO, ginseng, licorice, and vitamin E and vitamin C. Data is lacking regarding safety and efficacy of any of these alternatives.
   2. The provider should review with the patient the lack of standardization and evidence regarding the safety and efficacy of these products. Currently, results of research have been insufficient to support or refute the use of these remedies for the treatment of menopausal symptoms.

Follow-Up

A. Follow up in 3 to 6 months to assess response to treatment, and then yearly for annual exam (as indicated) and mammogram.
B. Consider discontinuation of HRT in 5 years based on patient response and risks and benefits.

Consultation/Referral

A. Consult a gynecologist if the patient experiences symptoms resistant to treatment or vaginal bleeding from an unknown source.

Pap Smear Interpretation

A. The Pap smear is a sample of cells taken from the cervix for cytological evaluation. The Pap smear is a *screening test* designed to increase detection and treatment of precancerous and early cancerous lesions, and to decrease morbidity and mortality from cases of invasive cervical cancer.
B. In the United States, approximately 14,500 new cases of cervical cancer occur annually. Of these cases, approximately 4,800 deaths occur. Cervical cancer is the seventh most common cancer in women. There has been a 70% reduction in the incidence of cervical cancer due to the use of Pap smear screening.
C. The following are risk factors for development of cervical cancer:
   1. Early age at first intercourse: Younger than 18 years
   2. Multiple sexual partners: More than three in a lifetime
   3. High parity
   4. Lower socioeconomic status
   5. Advanced age
   6. Compromised immune system: Infection with HIV
   7. Smoking
   8. Male partner with a history of multiple partners or STIs
   9. History of STI, especially HPV

   Sexually transmitted agents, particularly the HPV strains 16, 18, 31, 33, 39, and 42, are strongly associated with the development of cervical cancer. HPV DNA is present in 93% of cervical cancer and precursor lesions.

   10. DES exposure in utero
   11. Cervical dysplasia: The risk of carcinoma is 100 times greater in women with dysplasia than in those with a normal cervix.
D. The Pap smear should include sampling from both the ectocervix and the endocervix to be considered "adequate for interpretation." The ectocervix is the cervical portion extending outward from the external cervical os. The endocervix extends upward from the external os to the internal os, where the cervical epithelium meets the uterine endometrium.
E. Cervical epithelium is composed of squamous and columnar cells. Squamous epithelium, appearing smooth and pink, lines the vagina and continues upward to cover variable amounts of the ectocervix. Columnar epithelium, darker red and more granular in appearance, lines the endometrium and continues downward to the cervix, lining the endocervical canal. The boundary between squamous and columnar epithelium is called the squamocolumnar junction (or transformation zone) and may occur anywhere on the ectocervix or endocervix.
F. The squamocolumnar junction may regress at various times as a result of hormonal variation, particularly with sexual activity and during pregnancy, through processes known as epidermidalization and squamous metaplasia. Epidermidalization is an upward growth of squamous cells that replace columnar cells. Squamous metaplasia is the differentiation of columnar cells into squamous cells. The area between the original and new squamocolumnar junction is called the transformation zone. When columnar epithelium is visible on the ectocervix, appearing as a granular, red area, it is referred to as eversion, ectropion, or ectopy. This is often seen in pregnancy or with oral contraceptive use.
G. Cervical cancer is a progressive disease with a number of histologically definable stages. Invasive cancer of the cervix and its precursors are detectable by cytology before becoming symptomatic and before gross clinical signs appear. When symptoms are present, they usually include (in order of frequency) postcoital spotting; intermenstrual bleeding, especially after exertion; and increased menstrual bleeding. Patients with invasive cancer may experience serosanguineous or yellowish vaginal discharge, which may be foul smelling and intermixed with blood.

H. Advanced disease may cause urinary or rectal symptoms, including bleeding. On speculum examination, advanced lesions appear as necrotic ulcers; in invasive disease they may extend upward or protrude into the vagina.
I. See the Section II Procedure, "Pap Smear and Maturation Index Procedures."

Bethesda System

The 2001 Bethesda system is the most current classification system used to interpret cytological findings. It includes the following evaluations.

A. Adequacy of the specimen
   1. Satisfactory for evaluation
   2. Presence or absence of endocervical or transformational zone components
   3. Quality indicators such as obscuring blood or inflammation
   4. Unsatisfactory for evaluation and specific reason
B. General categorization
   1. Negative for intraepithelial lesion or malignancy
   2. Epithelial cell abnormality
   3. Other, such as infection

If an infection is indicated as a Pap smear finding, evaluate the patient and treat her accordingly. Pap smears are not diagnostic of vaginal or cervical infection. Institute therapy for infections confirmed through the use of wet prep and/or cultures as guided by cytological reading. For example, if Candida is identified on Pap smear results, evaluate the patient in the office, confirm finding, and treat the patient with appropriate antifungal therapy.

C. Interpretation/result
   1. Squamous cell abnormalities
      a. Atypical squamous cells of undetermined significance (ASCUS): Indicates some abnormality but cause is unclear (infection common)
      b. Atypical squamous cells: Cannot exclude high-grade squamous intraepithelial lesion (HSIL) (ASC-H)
      c. Low-grade squamous intraepithelial lesion (LSIL): Indicates HPV, mild dysplasia, or cervical intraepithelial neoplasia (CIN) I
      d. HSILs: Moderate and severe dysplasia, carcinoma in situ or CIN II, and CIN III
      e. Squamous cell carcinoma
   2. Glandular cell
      a. Atypical glandular cells (AGCs)
      b. AGCs favor neoplastic
      c. Adenocarcinoma
   3. Other
      a. Endometrial cells in women older than 40

Initial Management of Abnormal Pap Smears

A. ASCUS or LSIL in women age 21 to 24
   1. Repeat cytology in 12 months for the next 2 years, with colposcopy after 1 year for HSIL and colposcopy after 2 years if ASCUS or LSIL remains.
   2. HPV: Not recommended but if performed:
      a. HPV negative, continue routine screen with Pap test in 3 years
      b. HPV positive, annual Pap smear for 2 years with colposcopy after 1 year if HSIL and after 2 years if ASCUS or LSIL continues
B. ASC-H is managed with colposcopy.
C. LSIL
   1. HPV negative can be managed with repeat co-testing in 1 year or colposcopy.
   2. LSIL with positive or no HPV test is managed with colposcopy.
   3. Pregnant women with LSIL can be managed with colposcopy or can defer colposcopy until 6 weeks postpartum.
D. HSIL management in women includes either immediate loop excision or colposcopy.
E. AGC management for all subcategories except atypical endometrial cells includes colposcopy. For women age 35 and older with risk of endometrial neoplasm, endometrial sampling is also indicated.
   1. Atypical endometrial cell management includes endometrial and endocervical sampling.
F. Cytology negative but absent or insufficient endocervical/transitional zone component
   1. Age 21 to 29 or 30 and older with HPV negative: Conduct routine screening cytology in 3 years.
   2. Age 30 and older and HPV unknown: HPV testing is preferred.
   3. Age 30 and older and HPV positive: Conduct cytology + HPV testing in 1 year or immediate genotyping for HPV.
   4. See and download American Society for Colposcopy and Cervical Pathology (ASCCP) algorithms* for complete management options at www.asccp.org

ASCCP has a mobile device application: ASCCP Mobile ASCCP Abnormal Cervical Cancer Screening Guidelines available at iTunes.

* Reprinted from *Journal of Lower Genital Tract Disease* Volume 17, Number 5, with the permission of ASCCP© American Society for Colposcopy and Cervical Pathology 2013. No copies for the algorithms may be made without the prior consent of ASCCP.

Recommendations

A. According to the American Cancer Society (ACS), the U.S. Preventative Task Force, ASCCP, and the American College of Obstetricians and Gynecologists guidelines, all women should begin cervical cancer screening at age 21.
B. Women younger than 21 should not be screened regardless of the age of sexual initiation. Screening should be performed every 3 years. No woman should be screened annually. Highlights of the recommendations include:
   1. Begin screening at age 21 years.
   2. Women from age 21 to 29 years should have conventional or liquid-based cytology every 3 years, and no HPV testing should be performed.
   3. Women from age 30 to 65 years should have conventional or liquid-based cytology every 3 years or, to extend testing time, use conventional or liquid-based cytology plus HPV co-test every 5 years. HPV co-testing should not be used in women younger than 30.
   4. Stop screening at age older than 65 with adequate screening history. Negative history includes having three consecutive negative cytology results or two consecutive tests with co-testing results in the past 5 years for the patient.
   5. Continued regular screening is recommended for women who have had a history of CIN2, CIN3, or adenocarcinoma.
   6. Posthysterectomy: Stop screening for total hysterectomy. However, if the patient had a history of high-grade lesions prior to surgery, then cytology screening every 3 years for the next 20 years is recommended.
   7. HPV vaccination screen according to age-specific recommendation.
   8. Women who have a high-risk medical history (immunocompromised, HIV positive, DES exposed in utero, or a history of cervical cancer) are not included in the updated routine guidelines.
C. The Advisory Committee on Immunization practices recommends routine vaccination of females and males aged 11 to 12 with three doses of quadrivalent HPV vaccine and states the series can be started as young as 9 years of age. Catch-up vaccination is recommended for adolescents and young adults aged 13 to 26.
D. Patient education regarding the prevention of cervical cancer by avoiding exposure to HPV should include reduction or elimination of high-risk activities. These high-risk activities include having sexual intercourse at an early age, having multiple sexual partners, having partners with multiple partners, and having sex with uncircumcised males. Use of condoms can reduce the risk of HPV as well as other STIs. Smoking cessation can also reduce the risk of cervical cancer. Identification and treatment of precancerous lesions can reduce the risk of invasive cervical cancer, so screening according to ACS guidelines should be encouraged.

Treatment Modalities

Treatment is instituted based on the severity of the lesion and the presence of pathology within the columnar epithelium of the endocervix. Treatment options include

A. Observation and repeat cytology
B. Cryotherapy
C. Loop excision of the transformation zone
D. Laser of the transformation zone
E. Cold-knife conization
F. Observation and repeat cytology

Pelvic Inflammatory Disease

Definition

A. Pelvic inflammatory disease (PID) is an inflammation caused by an infection of the upper genital tract. This inflammation can involve the uterine endometrium (endometritis), fallopian tubes (salpingitis), ovaries (oophoritis), broad ligament or uterine serosa (parametritis), and the pelvic vascular system or pelvic connective tissue.

Incidence

A. Annual incidence is estimated to be approximately 1 million cases in the United States. In women aged 15 to 24 years, the incidence is projected at 1% annually in the United States.
B. PID is the leading cause of infertility in the world.

Pathogenesis

A. PID is caused by organisms that ascend from the vagina and cervix into the uterus. Menses facilitates gonococcal invasion of the upper genital tract as the luteal phase stimulates gonococcal growth and the cervical mucus barrier is removed. Infection and inflammation spread throughout the endometrium to the fallopian tubes. From there, it extends to the ovaries and peritoneal cavity.
B. The most common organisms cultured from patients with PID are *C. trachomatis, N. gonorrhoeae, M. hominis, Ureaplasma urealyticum, Bacteroides, Peptostreptococcus, Escherichia coli*, and some endogenous aerobes and anaerobes.
C. The incubation period varies with the infective organism.

Predisposing Factors

A. Age: Rates of PID are higher for women at younger ages. It is highest in the younger than 30-year-old age group (70% incidence younger than age 25). Teens are particularly susceptible because they have an immature immune system and larger zones of cervical ectopy with thinner cervical mucus.

B. Sexual activity: Women with multiple sexual partners are three times more likely to develop PID when compared to women with only one partner.
C. Intrauterine contraceptive device (IUC): IUCs can lead to an iatrogenic development of PID and can promote the spread of vaginal or cervical organisms into the uterus by means of the IUC string.
D. History of PID
E. Menstruation: Supports the development and spread of PID. Women who are *not* currently menstruating have a decreased risk.
F. History of invasive procedures: These procedures may result in iatrogenic PID. PID is usually seen within 4 weeks of the procedure (D&C, IUC insertion, HSG, and vacuum curettage abortion).
G. There is an increased incidence of PID in African Americans, non-White women, and women in lower socioeconomic groups.
H. Cigarette smoking
I. Frequent vaginal douching

Common Complaints

A. Lower abdominal pain
B. Fever or chills
C. Increased vaginal discharge
D. Nausea and vomiting
E. Low back pain

Other Signs and Symptoms

A. Asymptomatic; vague and nonspecific symptoms
B. Minimal to severe pelvic pain
C. Right upper quadrant pain (25%)
D. Abnormal vaginal bleeding

Subjective Data

A. Determine onset, duration, and course of presenting symptoms.
B. Review the character of vaginal discharge (if any); history of recent dysmenorrhea and/or dyspareunia; any intestinal or bladder symptoms.
C. Question the patient regarding sexual history: Current number of sexual partners; current or most recent sexual activity; and contraceptive used (condoms, pills, diaphragm, IUC) and frequency of method used.
D. Question the patient as to whether her current sexual partner has experienced any symptoms.
E. What is the patient's current menstrual pattern? Does she think she is pregnant? When did the pain begin in relation to her cycle?
F. Review prior pelvic or abdominal surgeries and procedures (HSG, abortion) and when they were done.
G. Review the history and quality of pain, how long, bilateral or unilateral, what makes it better, and what makes it worse (intercourse, Valsalva's maneuver with bowel movement, activity).

Physical Examination

A. Check temperature, pulse, respirations, and blood pressure.
B. Inspect: Observe general overall appearance for discomfort before, during, and after exam.
C. Auscultate: Auscultate the abdomen for bowel sounds in all quadrants. Auscultation of the abdomen should precede any palpation or percussion due to the changes in intensity and frequency of sounds after manipulation.
D. Percuss: Percuss the abdomen for organomegaly.
E. Palpate.
   1. Palpate the groin for lymphadenopathy.
   2. Palpate the abdomen for masses.
   3. Palpate the levator ani muscle left and right, the urethra, and trigone of the bladder.
   4. Perform rebound, involuntary guarding, and jar tests. **The jar test is performed by intentionally hitting or jarring the examination table and watching for a pain response. Pelvic discomfort is exacerbated by the Valsalva's maneuver, intercourse, or movement. Abdominal or pelvic pain with PID is usually bilateral. About 25% of patients complain of right upper quadrant pain; the pain usually occurs within 7 to 10 days of menses, remains continuously, and is most severe in the lower quadrants.**
F. Pelvic examination
   1. Inspect: Examine the vulva for Bartholin's gland enlargement, fissures, condyloma, herpes, and pelvic relaxation.
   2. Palpate: "Milk" the urethra for discharge.
   3. Speculum examination: Inspect for cervicitis and friability. Evaluate vaginal discharge and bleeding for color, amount, and odor. Lower abdominal or pelvic pain is the most common symptom of PID and typically is moderate to severe. However, many women may have subtle or mild symptoms that are not readily recognizable as PID, including abnormal bleeding, dyspareunia, or vaginal discharge.
G. Bimanual examination
   1. Check CMT; evaluate the size, contour, mobility, and tenderness of the uterus.
   2. Palpate the adnexa for tenderness and masses. Classic PID presentation is lower abdominal and adnexal tenderness and CMT (chandelier sign). The pelvic area may feel hot.
H. Rectovaginal examination: Assess for adnexal thickening and masses.

Diagnostic Tests

A. CBC with differential; WBC greater than 10,500 cell/mm^3
B. Sedimentation rate or C-reactive protein
C. Quantitative beta HCG
D. RPR, hepatitis B surface antigen, and HIV
E. Cultures for gonorrhea and chlamydia
F. Transvaginal ultrasonography
G. Laparoscopy, by referral

Always test the patient for quantitative beta HCG even if she claims her menses are regular and she is using reliable contraception because of the extreme risk of ectopic pregnancy. Cultures must always be done; lab work (such as HIV) may be done as indicated, depending on the patient's history and presentation. Eliciting data in the health history about hysterectomy, previous appendectomy, abortions, and procedures such as HSG may provide exclusionary diagnoses.

H. Diagnostic criteria (DC) for clinical diagnosis of PID
   1. Minimal criteria
      a. Lower abdominal tenderness
      b. Adnexal tenderness
      c. CMT
   2. Additional routine criteria
      a. Oral temperature greater than 101°F
      b. Abnormal cervical or vaginal discharge
      c. Elevated erythrocyte sedimentation rate (> 15 mm/hr)
      d. Elevated C-reactive protein
      e. Laboratory documentation of cervical infection with *N. gonorrhoeae* or *C. trachomatis*
   3. Elaborate criteria for diagnosing PID
      a. Tubo-ovarian abscess on ultrasound or radiologic tests
      b. Laparoscopic abnormalities consistent with PID

Differential Diagnoses

A. Gynecologic factors
   1. PID
   2. Ectopic pregnancy
   3. Pelvic endometriosis
   4. Dysmenorrhea
   5. Adenomyosis
   6. Functional ovarian cysts
   7. Endometrial polyps or fibroid
   8. Pelvic relaxation
   9. Anatomic abnormalities
B. GI factors
   1. Acute appendicitis
   2. Irritable bowel syndrome
   3. Ulcerative colitis, Crohn's disease
   4. Diverticulitis
   5. Hernia
C. Genitourinary factors
   1. Cystitis, urethritis interstitial cystitis
   2. Ureteral obstruction
   3. Carcinoma of bladder
D. Musculoskeletal factors
   1. Myofascial pain
   2. Pelvic floor myalgia
   3. Spinal injuries or degenerative disease
E. Neurologic factor: Nerve entrapment syndrome

Plan

A. General interventions
   1. A low threshold is needed for diagnosis of PID because of the risk of damage to reproductive health. Early treatment with the use of antibiotics of an upper genital tract infection is imperative. Other causes of lower abdominal pain, such as irritable bowel syndrome and endometriosis, are not likely to be impaired by empiric antibiotic therapy. The risk of ectopic pregnancy is 6 to 10 times greater in women with PID compared with uninfected women.
   2. Antibiotic therapy should be instituted promptly, based on clinical diagnosis without awaiting culture results, to minimize the risk of progression of the infection and risk of transmission of the organisms to other sexual partners.
   3. If the patient has an IUC in place, it should be promptly removed.
   4. Ambulatory patients should be monitored closely and reevaluated within 3 days of initiating antibiotic therapy. A decrease in pelvic tenderness should be observed within 3 to 5 days of initiation of therapy; if not, additional evaluation is warranted.
B. Patient teaching
   1. See the Section III Patient Teaching Guide for this chapter, "Pelvic Inflammatory Disease."
   2. Male sexual partners (and all partners) of patients with PID must be examined, cultured when possible, and treated empirically for presumptive gonorrheal and chlamydial infection.
   3. Women who do not use any contraception are at the greatest risk. Transmission of STIs can be minimized with effective use of condoms.
C. Pharmaceutical therapy (see Table 16.6)

Follow-Up

A. Because of the high risk of reinfection, many clinicians recommend reevaluation in 4 to 6 weeks after completion of therapy. Patients with positive cultures for gonorrhea and chlamydia should be

TABLE 16.6 CDC Recommendations for Treating PID

Inpatient Therapy	Ambulatory Therapy
Regimen A[a]	**Regimen A**
Cefotetan 2 g IV every 12 hours or cefoxitin 2 g plus doxycycline 100 mg IV or orally every 12 hours	Ceftriaxone 250 mg IM in a single dose plus doxycycline 100 mg orally twice a day for 14 days
	With or Without
This regimen is continued for at least 48 hours after clinical improvement and followed by doxycycline 100 mg orally twice daily to complete 14-day total course.	Metronidazole 500 mg orally twice daily for 14 days
Regimen B[a]	**Or**
Clindamycin 900 mg IV every 8 hours (15–40 mg/kg/d)	Cefoxitin 2 g IM in a single dose and probenecid, 1 g orally administered concurrently in a single dose plus doxycycline 100 mg orally twice a day for 14 days with or without metronidazole 500 mg orally twice a day for 14 days
Plus	**Or**
Gentamicin, loading dose 2.0 mg/kg IV, followed by maintenance 1.5 mg/kg IV every 8 hours. Single daily dosing may be substituted.	Other parenteral third-generation cephalosporin (e.g., ceftizoxime or cefotaxime) plus doxycycline 100 mg orally twice a day for 14 days with or without metronidazole 500 mg orally twice a day for 14 days
This regimen is continued for at least 48 hours after significant clinical improvement is demonstrated, and it is followed by doxycycline 100 mg orally twice daily to complete a 14-day total course. Alternatively, clindamycin 600 mg orally three times daily may be given to complete a 14-day total course.	

[a]When tubo-C is present, many clinicians use clindamycin because it provides more effective anaerobic coverage than doxycycline.
Note: For women or their partners who cannot tolerate doxycycline or tetracycline, erythromycin 500 mg orally four times daily may be used for 10 to 14 days.

recultured in 7 to 10 days after completing therapy. "Test of cure" is necessary.

B. Hepatitis B immunization should be initiated in previously unvaccinated persons.

Consultation/Referral

Consult a gynecologist if the patient diagnosis is atypical, evidence for a presumptive diagnosis is present, or hospitalization is required. General criteria for hospitalization are the following.

A. Diagnosis is uncertain.
B. Pelvic or tubo-ovarian abscess is suspected.
C. IUC in situ
D. The patient is pregnant.
E. The patient is an adolescent or is believed to be incapable of adhering to outpatient regimen.
F. Outpatient therapy fails; the patient is not better in 48 to 72 hours.
G. The patient cannot be reevaluated in 48 to 72 hours.
H. The patient is HIV positive.
I. There is generalized peritonitis or severe illness.
J. The patient cannot tolerate oral medication therapies.
K. Surgical emergencies cannot be ruled out.

Individual Considerations

A. Pregnancy: Fluoroquinolones are generally contraindicated for pregnant and nursing mothers.
B. Partners: Sexual partners should be evaluated and treated for STIs.

Pelvic Organ Prolapse

Definition

A. Many terms have been used to describe pelvic organ prolapse (POP), the protrusion or downward movement of the pelvic organs through the vaginal introitus. Frequently used descriptors include cystocele, urethrocele, rectocele, enterocele, vaginal prolapse, and uterine prolapse. Each term describes a specific organ that has been displaced and, while frequently used by clinicians, these descriptors do not accurately and completely describe the extent of what is actually occurring. Thus, it is recommended that when describing what is seen on exam, one may define prolapse by using anatomical definitions, such as anterior vaginal wall prolapse, apical prolapse, posterior vaginal wall prolapse, vault eversion, cervical prolapse, or rectal prolapse (see Table 16.7).

TABLE 16.7 Anatomical Description of POP

Previous Descriptors for POP	Current Anatomical Definitions
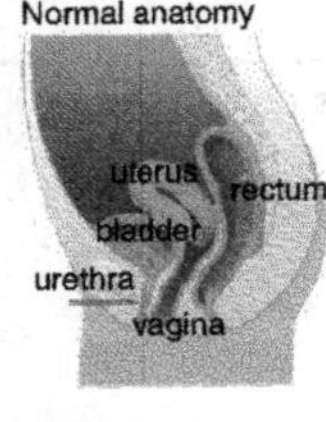	Normal pelvic floor support with bladder located anteriorly. Uterus is located superior to the bladder.
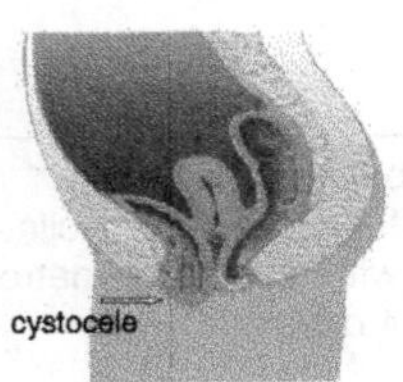	Anterior vaginal wall prolapse
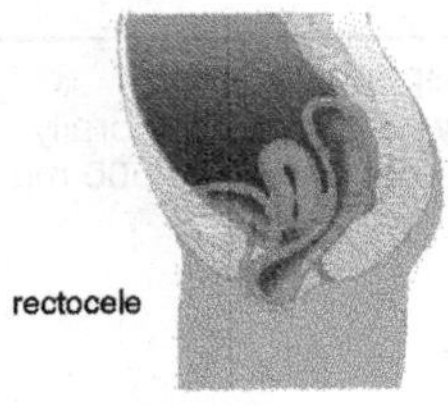	Posterior vaginal wall prolapse
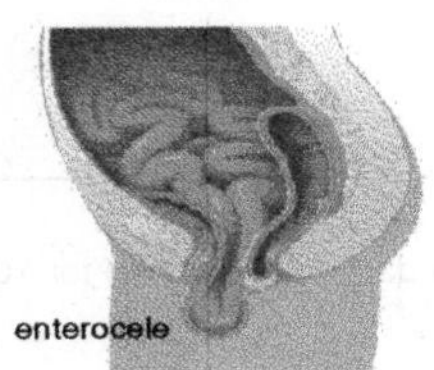	Vaginal vault prolapse

Used with permission from Steven Goldwasser, M.D., Urogynecology Clinic, Jacksonville, FL: http://bladderdoc.com.

B. POP is also defined by stages of descent.
   1. Stage 0: No evidence of descent
   2. Stage 1: Very minimal and usually asymptomatic descent
   3. Stage 2: Protruding to the vaginal hymen and slightly beyond
   4. Stage 3: Protruding well beyond the hymen
   5. Stage 4: Being complete or almost complete descensus

Incidence

A. POP is a common problem affecting women of all ages, races, and ethnicities.

B. Most authorities describe the incidence as somewhere between 10% and 30% of the female population, with increased incidence observed with advancing age. The Women's Health Initiative (WHI) found a 41% incidence of POP among women aged 50 to 79, with the most commonly observed compartment being the anterior wall. Interestingly, researchers from the Pelvic Organ Support Study (POSST) saw that on routine gynecologic exams of asymptomatic women, 35% experienced stage 2 POP and 2% had descent that measured to stage 3.

C. It is believed that as the U.S. population continues to age and to expand, the incidence and prevalence of prolapse will continue to grow.

Pathogenesis

A. Though not fully understood, some logical pathologic factors may create the occurrence of POP.

B. Some evidence suggests that weakness of the pelvic floor muscles (PFM) creates a more vertical angle for the vagina, thus no longer supporting the vagina and the pelvic organs in a slightly horizontal fashion.
   1. This loss of a "backboard" increases the chance for the pelvic organs to be affected by gravity and descend downward through the canal.
   2. Weakness of the muscles may also create an inability of the vaginal introitus to contract or close during periods of increased intra-abdominal pressure, such as during a cough.
   3. Over time this can also allow the pelvic organs to descend through the widened opening.

C. Much research is ongoing into the role of connective tissue injuries that may occur to increase the risk of POP.
   1. Direct injury to the muscles and connective tissue of the pelvic floor, such as during childbirth, may combine to encourage a herniation of the pelvic organs through the tear or tears in the fascia.
   2. A more novel and very interesting theory involves the observation of possible familial or hereditary causes for prolapse.
   3. Studies have indicated both "structural and biochemical" changes observed in the collagen of microscopically analyzed prolapsed tissue.
   4. Other research has shown a weakening of collagen with increasing age. Over time the collagen becomes weaker, and faster degradation is observed, thus increasing the prevalence of POP. This raises the question regarding whether this is a "normal" process of aging versus an actual hereditary cause for the hastening of the collagen deprivation and resulting prolapse.
   5. Research into all these theories of pathology continues to expand as we try to understand the root causes for prolapse and possible means for prevention.

Predisposing Factors

Many external and some potentially preventable risk factors can combine to create the risk for POP. Yet, it is not fully understood which of these factors creates the greatest risk.

A. Pregnancy and vaginal childbirth: Evidence supports the lack of consensus regarding pregnancy versus delivery as the predisposing risk factor. Other obstetric factors considered include:
   1. Macrosomia
   2. Length of second stage of labor
   3. Midline episiotomy
   4. Forceps-assisted vaginal delivery
   5. Anal sphincter laceration
   6. Oxytocin use for labor initiation
   7. Epidural analgesia
   8. Higher gravidity
B. Age and menopausal status
   1. The risk of POP doubles with each decade of life.
   2. It is unclear how the loss of estrogen and the effects of age can be differentiated.
   3. Questions remain regarding age, menopause, and collagen loss with aging.
C. Race
   1. African American and Asian women have the lowest risk for POP.
   2. Hispanic women appear to have the highest risk, with White women directly following.
D. Hysterectomy
   1. Route of hysterectomy does not appear to influence risk, although some evidence exists regarding the benefit of keeping the cervix for prevention of POP after hysterectomy.
   2. POP after a hysterectomy performed for the indication of prolapse appears to be a greater risk than hysterectomy for other causes.
E. Connective tissue disease
   1. Ehler–Danlos syndrome
   2. Marfan's syndrome
F. Increases in intra-abdominal pressure
   1. Obesity
   2. Chronic constipation
   3. Chronic lifting
   4. Chronic coughing
   5. Chronic obstructive pulmonary disease (COPD)
   6. Cigarette smoking

Common Complaints

Patients may experience a plethora of symptoms that may or may not be connected to the POP. Furthermore, research has shown a direct correlation between increased stage of prolapse and symptom occurrence. Many of the complaints are more noticeable to the patient as the prolapse advances beyond the hymen. It is also important to note that while many of these complaints may be identified by the patient as being caused by the POP, they may not be directly related to the problem at all. This is noted in the inconsistencies of prolapse symptoms in the literature.

A. Feeling of a bulge or ball in the vagina
B. Vaginal or pelvic pressure
C. Rubbing of bulge against undergarments and/or vaginal bleeding
D. Concurrent urinary incontinence (UI)
E. Urinary urgency or frequency
F. Urinary hesitancy
G. Constipation and/or anal incontinence (AI)
H. Incomplete rectal evacuation/stool trapping
I. Low back pain
J. Sexual dysfunction/dyspareunia
K. Pelvic pain

When determining the severity of symptoms, the clinician may find it helpful to use validated prolapse symptom questionnaires, including the Pelvic Floor Distress Inventory (PFDI), Urinary Distress Inventory 6 (UDI-6), Colorectal-Anal Distress Inventory 8 (CRADI-8), the Pelvic Organ Prolapse Distress Inventory 6 (POPDI-6) and the Pelvic Floor Impact Questionnaire (PFIQ) (see Table 16.8). http://www.fpminstitute.com/download.phtml/166/pelvic_floor_distress_inventory.pdf.

TABLE 16.8 The Institute for Female Pelvic Medicine & Reconstructive Surgery

PELVIC FLOOR DISTRESS INVENTORY

NAME ______________________________ DATE __________

Please answer each question by checking the best response. While answering these questions, please consider your symptoms over the past 3 months. We realize that you may not be having problems in some of these areas but please fill out both sides of this form as completely as possible.

URINARY DISTRESS INVENTORY 6 (UDI-6)

Do you experience, and, if so, how much are you bothered by	Not at all	Somewhat	Moderately	Quite a bit
Usually experience frequent urination?	☐	☐	☐	☐
Usually experience urine leakage associated with a feeling of urgency, that is, a strong sensation of needing to go to the bathroom?	☐	☐	☐	☐
Usually experience urine leakage related to coughing, sneezing, or laughing?	☐	☐	☐	☐
Usually experience small amounts of urine leakage (that is, drops)?	☐	☐	☐	☐
Usually experience difficulty emptying your bladder?	☐	☐	☐	☐
Usually experience pain or discomfort in the lower abdomen or genital region?	☐	☐	☐	☐

COLORECTAL-ANAL DISTRESS INVENTORY 8 (CRADI-8)

Do you experience, and, if so, how much are you bothered by	Not at all	Somewhat	Moderately	Quite a bit
Feel you need to strain too hard to have a bowel movement?	☐	☐	☐	☐
Feel you have not completely emptied your bowel at the end of a bowel movement?	☐	☐	☐	☐
Usually lose stool beyond your control if your stool is well formed?	☐	☐	☐	☐
Usually lose stool beyond your control if your stool is loose?	☐	☐	☐	☐
Usually lose gas from the rectum beyond your control?	☐	☐	☐	☐
Do you usually have pain when you pass your stool?	☐	☐	☐	☐
Experience a strong sense of urgency and have to rush to the bathroom to have a bowel movement?	☐	☐	☐	☐
Does part of your bowel ever pass through the rectum and bulge outside during or after a bowel movement?	☐	☐	☐	☐

Reviewed With Patient _____/___/___

Dr.'s Initials & Date ______________

PELVIC ORGAN PROLAPSE DISTRESS INVENTORY 6 (POPDI-6)

Do you experience, and, if so, how much are you bothered by.....	Not at all	Somewhat	Moderately	Quite a bit
Usually experience pressure in the lower abdomen?	☐	☐	☐	☐
Usually experience heaviness or dullness in the pelvic area?	☐	☐	☐	☐
Usually have a bulge or something falling out that you can see or feel in your vaginal area?	☐	☐	☐	☐
Ever have to push on the vagina or around the rectum to have or complete a bowel movement?	☐	☐	☐	☐
Usually experience a feeling of incomplete bladder emptying?	☐	☐	☐	☐
Ever have to push up on the bulge in the vaginal area with your fingers to start or complete urination?	☐	☐	☐	☐

PELVIC FLOOR IMPACT QUESTIONNAIRE

Instructions: Some women find that bladder, bowel, or vaginal symptoms affect their activities, relationships, and feelings. For each question, place an **X** in the response that best describes how much your activities, relationships, or feelings have been affected by your bladder, bowel, or vaginal symptoms or conditions **over the past 3 months**. Please make sure you mark an answer in **all 3 columns** for each question.

(*continued*)

TABLE 16.8 The Institute for Female Pelvic Medicine & Reconstructive Surgery (*continued*)

How do symptoms or conditions relate to the following usually affect your	*Bladder or Urine*	*Bowel or Rectum*	*Vagina or Pelvis*
1. Ability to do household chores (cooking, housecleaning, laundry)?	☐ Not at all ☐ Somewhat ☐ Moderately ☐ Quite a bit	☐ Not at all ☐ Somewhat ☐ Moderately ☐ Quite a bit	☐ Not at all ☐ Somewhat ☐ Moderately ☐ Quite a bit
2. Ability to do physical activities such as walking, swimming, or other exercise?	☐ Not at all ☐ Somewhat ☐ Moderately ☐ Quite a bit	☐ Not at all ☐ Somewhat ☐ Moderately ☐ Quite a bit	☐ Not at all ☐ Somewhat ☐ Moderately ☐ Quite a bit
3. Entertainment activities such as going to a movie or concert?	☐ Not at all ☐ Somewhat ☐ Moderately ☐ Quite a bit	☐ Not at all ☐ Somewhat ☐ Moderately ☐ Quite a bit	☐ Not at all ☐ Somewhat ☐ Moderately ☐ Quite a bit
4. Ability to travel by car or bus for a distance greater that 30 minutes away from home?	☐ Not at all ☐ Somewhat ☐ Moderately ☐ Quite a bit	☐ Not at all ☐ Somewhat ☐ Moderately ☐ Quite a bit	☐ Not at all ☐ Somewhat ☐ Moderately ☐ Quite a bit
5. Participating in social activities outside your home?	☐ Not at all ☐ Somewhat ☐ Moderately ☐ Quite a bit	☐ Not at all ☐ Somewhat ☐ Moderately ☐ Quite a bit	☐ Not at all ☐ Somewhat ☐ Moderately ☐ Quite a bit
6. Emotional health (nervousness, depression, etc)?	☐ Not at all ☐ Somewhat ☐ Moderately ☐ Quite a bit	☐ Not at all ☐ Somewhat ☐ Moderately ☐ Quite a bit	☐ Not at all ☐ Somewhat ☐ Moderately ☐ Quite a bit
7. Feeling frustrated?	☐ Not at all ☐ Somewhat ☐ Moderately ☐ Quite a bit	☐ Not at all ☐ Somewhat ☐ Moderately ☐ Quite a bit	☐ Not at all ☐ Somewhat ☐ Moderately ☐ Quite a bit

Reviewed With Patient ____________/___/___

Dr.'s Initials and Date ____________________

Used with permission by Dr. Vincent Lucente, FACOG, from The Institute for Female Pelvic Medicine & Reconstructive Surgery http://www.fpminstitute.com.

Potential Complications

Most prolapse complications center around the impact on the woman's quality of life. However, some researchers and clinicians believe some direct, serious complications may occur as a result of increasing stages of POP, including:

A. Urinary retention, with resulting increased risk for hydronephrosis and hydroureter
B. Vaginal ulcers/sores/infection and vaginal bleeding
C. Recurrent UTI

Subjective Data

A. Ask the patient if she feels a bulge or a feeling of pressure in the vagina.
B. Does the patient feel as if she is sitting on something, much like a ball?
C. Ask the patient if she feels something rubbing against her undergarments.
D. Have the patient describe whether symptoms worsen when standing.
E. Ask patient to describe if she needs to manually assist herself to empty her bowel or bladder. Does she need to maneuver on the toilet?
F. Determine if the patient has had any prior treatments for the prolapse, surgical or conservative.
G. Ask about progression of the bulge; has it become more pronounced over time?
H. Is it difficult to have sex, as if something is blocking the opening of the vagina?
I. Review her full obstetric history specifically for factors as noted above.
J. Review her medical history with specific queries about COPD and smoking.
K. Review all medications, including OTC and herbal products. Evaluate problems such as chronic cough secondary to ace inhibitors.

Physical Examination

As patients with POP may have other conditions caused by pelvic floor dysfunction, it is important for the clinician to perform a thorough examination to evaluate the full spectrum of problems and the resulting impact on function and quality of life.

A. General inspection of external genitalia performed with patient in lithotomy position
   1. Evaluate the perineal area for skin rash, such as with changes consistent with atrophy, as well as bowel or bladder incontinence.
   2. Evaluate for other skin changes indicative of vulvar dermatoses or yeast infections.
   3. Evaluate for allodynia—a positive pain response to light touch.
   4. Evaluate the urethra for discharge, masses, or atrophy.
   5. Perform a cough stress test (CST) to evaluate for stress urinary incontinence (SUI)
      a. This test is positive if leakage is noted during the cough.
      b. A positive result may indicate a significant weakness of the urethral sphincter or a poorly supported urethra.
      c. While performing the test, look to see if the urethra is hypermobile as this may indicate SUI, even if the CST is negative for leakage.

B. Neurologic exam of sacral reflexes
   1. Evaluate S2 to S4 dermatomes.
      a. Evaluate for symmetry of sensation.
      b. Evaluate soft sensation with cotton-tipped end of Q-tip.
      c. Evaluate sharp sensation with wooden end of Q-tip.
   2. Bulbocavernosus reflex
      a. Elicit the reflex response by using a cotton swab; gently stroke the bilateral labia majora looking for a positive reflex response by observing subtle contraction or movement of the labial tissue (see Figure 16.1).
      b. No movement of the tissue is a negative response, which may indicate nerve damage to the pelvic floor.
      c. Up to 20% of normal patients may have a negative response.
      d. Neurologic testing for the bulbocavernosus reflex is also useful in evaluating a cauda equina lesion.
   3. Anal reflex, "wink"
      a. Using the cotton-tipped end of Q-tip, strike bilateral sides of the anal meatus, observing for contraction (see Figure 16.1).
      b. Up to 25% of normal patients may have absent response.

C. Pelvic organ prolapse quantification (POPq) exam
   1. System of measurement of prolapse defined by the International Continence Society (ICS).
   2. The prolapse is measured in specific segments or sections, with all measured points in relation to the hymen.
   3. Exam is performed with the patient in either lithotomy or standing positions.
   4. A split speculum and measuring stick are used to visualize and measure the extent of the prolapse (see Figure 16.2).
   5. All points of measurement are performed during valsalva with exception of one: Total vaginal length (TVL), which is a resting measurement.
   6. Measured points are plotted on a "Tic-Tac-Toe" grid (see Figure 16.3).
      a. Point Aa: Anterior wall; this point can be 3 cm from the hymen to its fullest extent, +3 cm beyond the hymen.
      b. Point Ba: This is the more proximal or deeper portion of measurement of the anterior wall located from the vaginal cuff/cervix or anterior vaginal fornix to point Aa. In the absence of prolapse, the value would be −3 cm from point Aa and with prolapse it can fall anywhere from −2 cm from the hymen to

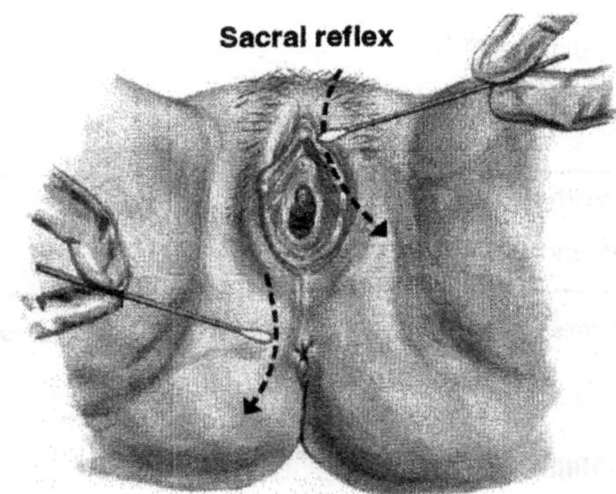

Figure 16.1 Pelvic floor neurologic testing—bulbocavernosus and anal "wink" reflexes.

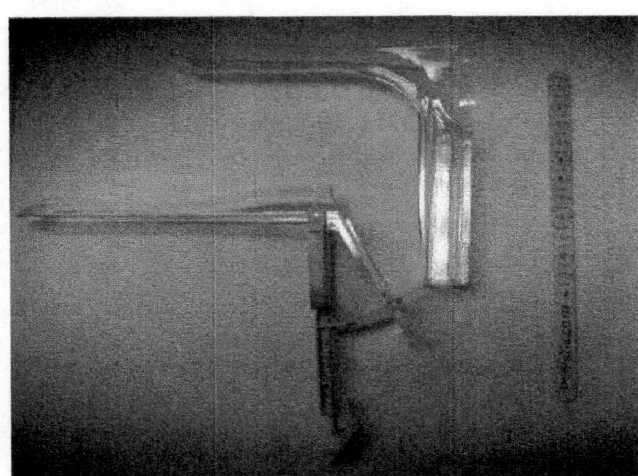

Figure 16.2 Split speculum and measuring stick.

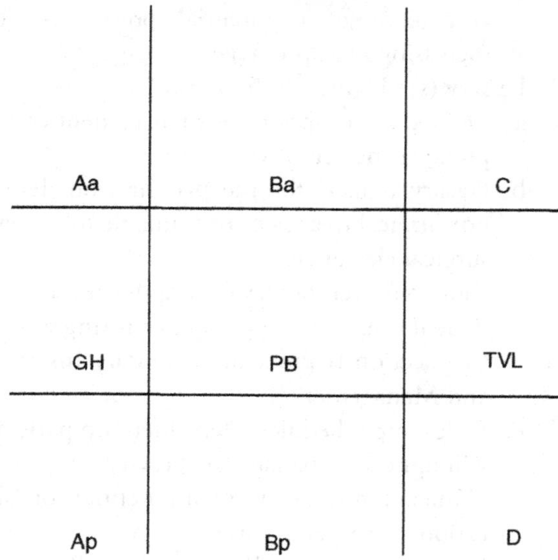

Figure 16.3 Measurement points on the "Tic-Tac-Toe" grid.

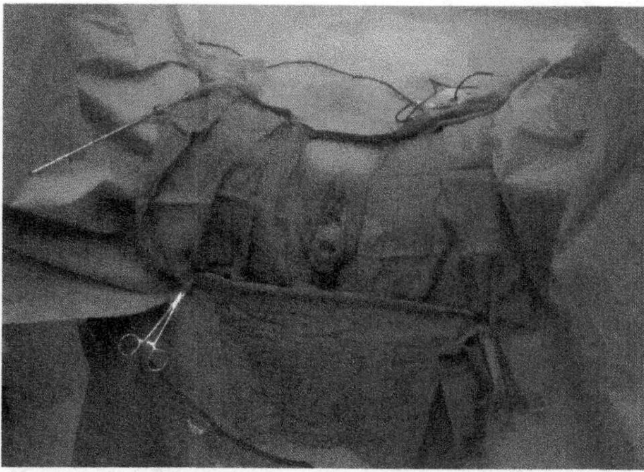

Figure 16.4 Complete prolapse.

Used with permission of Barry Jernigan, MD, Center for Pelvic Health http://www.centerforpelvichealth.org.

a positive value that can be equal to the cuff's length. For example, point Ba can be −3 to +10, depending on the length of the anterior wall to the cuff.

c. Point C: This point represents the most distal edge of the cervix or vaginal cuff if no uterus is present.

d. Point D: This measurement is not included in the POPq measurement if the patient has had a hysterectomy; this point differentiates a well-supported uterus from true uterine prolapse, and measurement is taken from the posterior fornix in the patient with a cervix. This point represents the level of the uterosacral ligament. Point D can be −10 to as much as +10.

e. Point Ap: This point is a measurement of the posterior wall, and, like the anterior wall, this point can be −3 cm from the hymen to +3 cm beyond the hymen.

f. Point Bp: This is the more proximal or deeper portion of measurement of the posterior wall located from the vaginal cuff or posterior fornix to point Ap. In the absence of prolapse, the value would be −3 cm from point Ap and with prolapse it can fall anywhere from −2 cm from the hymen to a positive value that can be equal to the cuff's length. For example, point Bp can be −3 to +10, depending on the length of the posterior wall to the cuff/fornix.

D. Stages of prolapse
1. Stage 0: No prolapse
2. Stage 1: Leading edge of POP comes to within 2 cm of hymen.
3. Stage 2: Leading edge of POP moves from −1 cm above to +1 cm beyond hymen.
4. Stage 3: Leading edge of POP is +2 cm beyond the hymen but is still 2 cm less than the total length of the vagina (TVL).
5. Stage 4: Complete prolapse (see Figure 16.4)

Diagnostic Tests

A. Obtain a clean catch urinalysis to screen the urine for clarity, hematuria, and infection.
1. Send the urine for culture and sensitivity to evaluate for the presence of infection.
2. Urine for cytology is recommended for evaluation of hematuria.

B. Immediately after void, obtain a post-void residual (PVR) by inserting a catheter into the bladder or use a bladder scanner.

C. Blood urea nitrogen (BUN), creatinine, for evaluation of kidney function

D. Pelvic ultrasound for evaluation of uterus and ovaries if there is vaginal bleeding. Consider an endometrial biopsy if ultrasound shows an abnormal endometrium.

E. Pap smear

F. Urodynamic testing for evaluation of bladder function and UI

G. Cystoscopy for evaluation of bladder structure and hematuria. CT scan to evaluate for hydronephrosis and hydroureter (important to assess if patient is experiencing increased PVRs)

Differential Diagnosis

A. Prolapsed uterine fibroid
B. Anterior or posterior vaginal wall cyst
C. Ureterocele
D. Rectal prolapse

Plan

A. Patient teaching
   1. Educate patient about proper body mechanics and avoidance of repetitive, chronic strain.
   2. Smoking cessation
   3. Discuss perineal hygiene to avoid irritation to the vulva and prolapsing vagina.

B. Treatment options
   1. Observation
      a. Expectant management can be an option if the patient is not bothered by the prolapse and only desires the confirmation that the prolapse is not progressing in stage.
      b. Follow-up can be every 6 months or annually, depending on the patient's preference.
   2. Pelvic floor muscle exercises (PFME)
      a. Little research exists to indicate that Kegel exercises can reduce prolapse stage.
      b. Primary goals for pelvic floor physical therapy (PFPT) serve to improve symptoms of prolapse, enhance proper body mechanics, and serve as a potential prevention for increasing prolapse stage.
   3. Pessary (see Figures 16.5 to 16.8)
      a. Offered as an option for management of the prolapse, not curative.
      b. Pessary is used for the patient who desires nonsurgical treatment or is unable to achieve surgical clearance.
      c. Can be for temporary or long-term use.
      d. Patient must undergo a pessary-fitting session (see Section II Procedure, "Pessary Insertion and Management").
      e. Follow-up schedule is dependent on patient's willingness to manage the pessary.
      f. Clinician must be aware of potential complications with pessary use.
         i. Pain may occur if pessary is too large.
         ii. Pessary may fall out if it is too small.
         iii. Vaginal bleeding
         iv. Erosion or ulcer

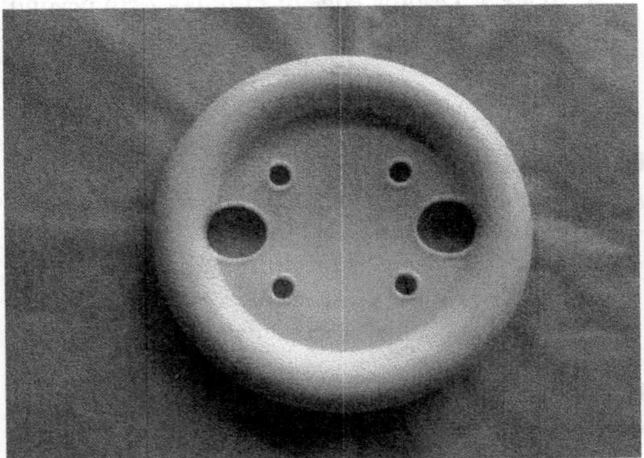

Figure 16.5 Ring with support pessary.
Used with permission from CooperSurgical. coopersurgical.com.

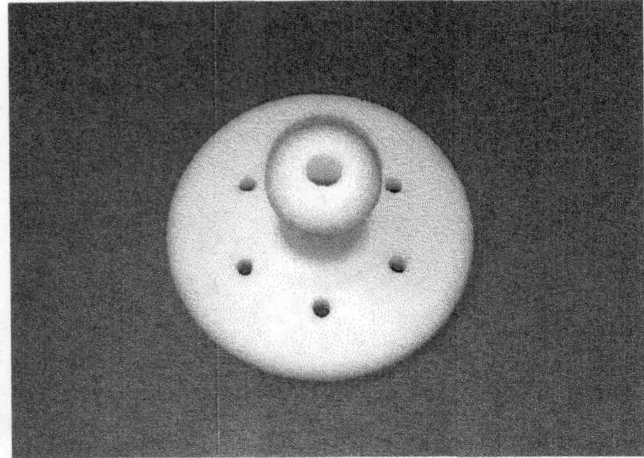

Figure 16.6 Gellhorn pessary.
Used with permission from CooperSurgical. coopersurgical.com.

Figure 16.7 Donut pessary.
Used with permission from CooperSurgical. coopersurgical.com.

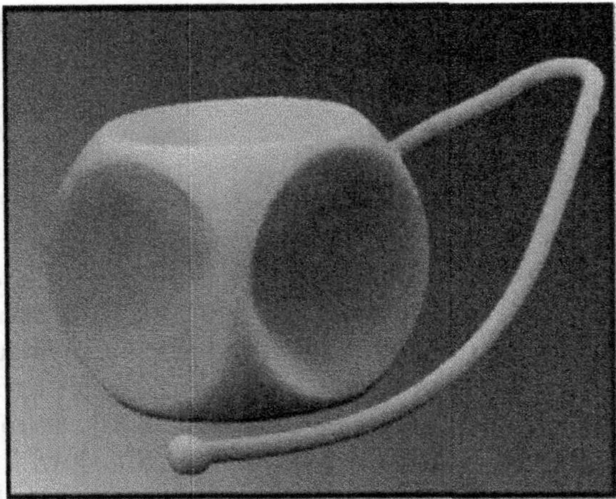

Figure 16.8 Cube pessary.
Used with permission from CooperSurgical. coopersurgical.com.

4. Surgery
    a. Surgical correction techniques will not be discussed in this chapter and require the evaluation of a subspecialist physician.

Individual Considerations

A. Pregnancy and reproductive-age women
    1. Pregnancy is not a contraindication for pessary use.
    2. Practice of PFME is acceptable during pregnancy.
    3. In the absence of large prolapse, no treatment is necessary during pregnancy if the patient and baby are stable.
    4. If the patient has not completed childbearing, surgical correction is not recommended. Offer a pessary or PFME to this patient until she is past this stage.
B. Geriatrics
    1. Must consider the geriatric patient's ability to manage her pessary.
        a. Frailty and decreased mobility may prevent the patient's personal management of a pessary.
        b. Dementia may inhibit the geriatric patient's ability to perform a regimen of PFME.
        c. Close family involvement is important to ensure proper management and follow-up for the geriatric patient with dementia.
        d. If surgical correction is desired in this patient, preoperative clearance must be obtained. In cases of dementia, family members must provide consent.

Premenstrual Syndrome

Definition

A. PMS is a psychoneuroendocrine disorder with a constellation of symptoms that occur in the luteal phase, days 18 to 21, and interfere with a woman's life. This is followed by a symptom-free period. The American Psychiatric Association (APA) diagnosis is "luteal phase dysphoric disorder."

Incidence

A. Virtually every menstruating woman experiences some symptoms at some time. Twenty percent of menstruating women have symptoms serious enough to interfere with their lives, but only a small percentage have disabling symptoms. Symptoms occur more commonly in women in their 30s and 40s.

Pathogenesis

The basis of PMS is presumably hormonal. During the luteal phase, progesterone levels increase and estrogen levels decrease, causing a shift in the ratio of these hormones; this contributes to causing symptoms experienced during PMS. These hormones are also known to interact with neurotransmitters in the brain, such as serotonin; these interactions are thought to cause some of the symptoms experienced, such as mood changes and pain thresholds, during PMS.

Predisposing Factors

A. Female of reproductive age

Common Complaints

The following are APA DC for luteal phase dysphoric disorder.

A. Symptoms are temporally related to the menstrual cycle, beginning during the past week of the luteal phase and remitting after the onset of menses.
B. The diagnosis requires at least five of the following, and one of the symptoms must be one of the first four.
    1. Affective lability, for example, sudden onset of being sad, tearful, irritable, or angry (mood swings)
    2. Persistent and marked anger or irritability
    3. Marked anxiety or tension
    4. Markedly depressed mood and feelings of hopelessness
    5. Decreased interest in usual activities
    6. Easily fatigued or marked lack of energy
    7. Subjective sense of difficulty in concentrating
    8. Hypersomnia or insomnia
    9. Physical symptoms such as breast tenderness, headaches, edema, abdominal bloating, joint or muscle pain, and weight gain
C. The symptoms interfere with work, usual activities, or relationships.
D. The symptoms are not an exacerbation of another psychiatric disorder.
E. "I've got PMS; I'm so miserable."
F. Feelings of irritability and emotional lability

Subjective Data

A. Obtain a complete menstrual history.
    1. Menarche; frequency, duration, and regularity of periods
    2. Ask about premenstrual symptoms that are physical: Weight gain, edema, acne, nausea, vomiting, constipation, backache, headache, migraine, syncope, breast tenderness, breast swelling, hot flashes, paresthesia of hands or feet, aggravation of convulsive disorder, increased appetite, food cravings (sweets, salt, or food in general), and fatigue.
    3. Ask about premenstrual symptoms that are emotional: Irritability, emotional lability, anxiety, depression, crying, palpitations, fatigue, aggression, lethargy, and sleep disturbances.

4. Ask particularly about the timing of the symptoms. When do the symptoms begin and end in relationship to the menstrual period? Has the patient kept a calendar of symptoms?

B. Ask about symptoms of dysmenorrhea. Some women confuse menstrual cramps and PMS.
C. Note type of contraception the patient uses.
D. Review her obstetric history, if applicable.
E. Elicit the types of treatment the patient has tried and efficacy of treatment.
F. Ask the patient about the amount and type of exercise she gets. Women with PMS often get little exercise.

Physical Examination

A. Check height, weight, and blood pressure.
B. Inspect: Note overall appearance; inspect thyroid.
C. Palpate: Palpate the neck, noting thyroid enlargement or nodules. Palpate the abdomen, noting enlargement, masses, or tenderness.
D. Auscultate: Auscultate the heart, lungs, and abdomen.
E. Pelvic examination
   1. Inspect the external genitalia for pubic hair pattern, lesions, or discharge.
   2. Speculum examination: Check for discharge and lesions.
   3. Bimanual examination: Check for size, mobility, shape, and tenderness of the uterus and adnexal area.
   4. No physical abnormality or changes are consistent with PMS.

Diagnostic Tests

A. Consider Pap smear and screening for STIs.
B. TSH

Differential Diagnoses

A. PMS
B. Major depression
C. Dysmenorrhea
D. Substance abuse
E. Perimenopausal symptoms
F. Sexual dysfunction
G. Fibromyalgia
H. There are rarely major medical problems, but hypothyroidism, hyperthyroidism, anemia, and autoimmune disorders (such as systemic lupus erythematosus) must be kept in mind.

Plan

A. General interventions
   1. Have the patient keep a menstrual calendar or diary for at least 3 months to document occurrence of symptoms in the luteal phase.
   2. Symptomatic treatments: Treatment must be individualized.

B. Patient teaching: See the Section III Patient Teaching Guide for this chapter, "Premenstrual Syndrome."
   1. Diet: Have the patient eat six small meals a day to even out glucose load. Have her avoid caffeine to decrease irritability and facilitate sleep. Encourage her to avoid simple sugars and eat complex carbohydrates to provide a slow, steady source of energy. She should avoid salt to decrease edema.
   2. Activity: Instruct the patient to increase exercise, preferably aerobic exercise. Suggest exercising every day (walking, swimming, and stretching). Encourage stress reduction activities such as imagery or yoga, as well as support or counseling groups. Encourage smoking cessation as well as adequate sleep and rest.
C. Pharmaceutical therapy
   1. Nonsteroidal anti-inflammatory drugs (NSAIDs) for relief of muscular aches, headaches, and menstrual cramps. Follow directions for the particular NSAIDs, whether OTC or prescription.
   2. Minerals
      a. Magnesium 360 mg/d for 14 days
      b. Calcium 1,200 to 1,600 mg/d
   3. Vitamins used to decrease anxiety and irritability, food cravings, painful breasts, depression, fatigue, and lethargy.
      a. Vitamin B_6 (pyridoxine) 50 to 150 mg each day
      b. Multiple vitamin one each day
      c. Vitamin E 400 IU's each day
   4. See Table 16.9, "Medications Used With PMS," for other therapies used for PMS.

Follow-Up

A. Follow up every 3 to 4 months to assess or alter treatment and/or therapy.

Consultation/Referral

A. Consult a physician if symptoms are severe or not relieved by first-line measures.

Individual Considerations

A. Partners: Encourage the patient to have her partner come to a visit. Partner education and support are helpful.

Sexual Health Issues in the Aging Population

Definition

A. The World Health Organization has declared that sexual health is an integral part of overall health. Sexuality is an aspect of the human species that begins at birth and ends at death despite socially

TABLE 16.9 Medications Used With PMS

Drug	Dose	Purpose
Diuretics		Decreases edema peripherally and, perhaps, centrally
Spironolactone (Aldactone)	100 mg from day 12 until first day of next menses	
Antidepressants		Decreases depression and anxiety and improves mood
Fluoxetine (Prozac)	10–40 mg every day or during the luteal phase (individual dose may vary)	
Paroxetine (Paxil)	10–30 mg every day or during the luteal phase (individual dose may vary)	
Sertraline hydrochloride (Zoloft)	50–150 mg every day or during the luteal phase (individual dose may vary)	
Citalopram	10–30 mg daily	
Venlafaxine XR	75–150 mg daily	
Antianxiety drugs		Decreases anxiety
Alprazolam (Xanax)	0.25 mg three or four times daily during luteal phase as needed	
Buspirone (BuSpar)	7.5–15 mg twice daily	
Miscellaneous drugs		
Bromocriptine mesylate (Parlodel)	2.5 mg three times daily during breast luteal phase	Used to decrease tenderness; works slowly
Oral contraceptive pills (Yaz[a])	Take on a daily basis	Evens the hormonal milieu, blocks ovulation
Danazol (Danocrine)		Has antiestrogenic effects. *Consult with a physician.*

[a]Has drospirenone and ethinyl estradiol.

Source: Steiner and Li (2014).

accepted stereotypes. Sexuality is not strictly a component of procreation, but also an element of the entire individual, intertwined with religious, cultural, and spiritual beliefs. It frequently binds individuals into romantic relationships.

B. According to a survey conducted by AARP in 2009, of 1,670 individuals older than 45, 32% of women and 41% of men reported having sex at least once a week. From the same survey, 45% of men and 8% of women said they think about sex at least once daily.

C. In 2013 the *Diagnostic and Statistical Manual of Mental Disorders* (*DSM*) released the 5th edition with significant changes to sexual dysfunction diagnoses.
   1. One of the biggest changes was the combination of sexual interest and arousal disorders into one category with gender specificity.
   2. Sexual aversion disorder was eliminated during the transition from the *DSM-IV-TR* to the *DSM-5*.
   3. Genital arousal disorder has yet to be classified in the *DSM*.

Incidence

A. The prevalence of sexual problems in the geriatric population is also frequently underestimated. According to the Global Study of Sexual Attitudes and Behaviors (GSSAB), nearly half of all sexually active respondents aged 40 to 80 reported at least one sexual complaint including erectile dysfunction, premature ejaculation, lack of sexual interest, lack of sexual pleasure, inability to reach orgasm, and lubrication difficulties. Despite this, less than 19% sought medical attention for such issues.

B. Medical providers frequently underestimate the commonality of sexual activity in the older population.

C. While sexual complaints are frequently considered specific to certain population genres, most of these diagnoses are actually age bimodal due to the variety of causative etiologies.

D. Although many older adults remain sexually active, they rarely bring up the topic of sexual health with their health care providers.
   1. While 20% of individuals aged 60 to 94 report having had intercourse within the previous 3 months, only 38% of men and 22% of women

have discussed sexual behavior with their health care provider after the age of 50.

2. Barriers to pursuing medical care for sexual complaints include:
   a. Believing that the problem is not serious
   b. Not being bothered by the problem
   c. Lack of awareness of available treatments
   d. Lack of access or affordability of medical care

E. Across the globe, only 9% of men and women are asked about their sexual health by their health care providers, yet more than half of men and women consistently report sexual activity in the previous year. Of a random sample of 500 U.S. nurse practitioners regarding taking a sexual history in the 50+-year-old patient population, only 2% reported they always conducted a sexual history and 23.4% never or seldom did. Barriers to sexual health history taking were:
   1. Lack of time
   2. Interruptions
   3. Limited communication skills
   4. Inability to cope with issues that arise with sexual history response
   5. Embarrassment
   6. Feeling that taking such a history in the older population is not appropriate

Pathogenesis

A. Although sexuality transforms throughout the life span and varies among individuals, we are typically born with similar constituents: reproductive organs, sex hormones, and a brain wired to receive nerve impulses from erogenous parts of the body.

B. At a very young age, individuals often identify areas of the body that induce pleasure with physical stimulation. Over the course of the first few decades of life, sexual structures and hormones mature, sexual functioning develops, and integration of partnered sexuality and intimacy often occurs.

C. After child-bearing years, the aging process can complicate sexual functioning for both men and women. Unfortunately, this frequently terminates sexual activity despite medical capabilities to prevent and treat sexual disorders. If these changes are acknowledged and embraced, individuals can find themselves in just as satisfying a sexual point in their lives as ever. Some even report improvement from past years.

Predisposing Factors

A. Chronic health conditions
   1. Cardiovascular disease
   2. Diabetes
   3. Obstructive sleep apnea
   4. Dementia/Alzheimer's disease
   5. Parkinson's disease
   6. Multiple sclerosis
   7. Cancer

B. Depression

C. Intra-partner violence

D. Postsurgical condition/complication

E. Physical disabilities

F. Side effects from medications

Common Complaints

A. Sexual dysfunction in men encompasses the following problems:
   1. Lack of desire/arousal
   2. Erectile dysfunction
      a. Inability to achieve or maintain an erection sufficient for satisfactory sexual performance
      b. Curvature of the penis with erection (Peyronie's disease)
      c. Problems with penetration
      d. Orgasmic disorder
   3. Ejaculation

B. Alternately, in women sexual complaints occur in the realms of:
   1. Lack of desire/arousal
   2. Lack of orgasm
   3. Sexual/genital pain
      a. Lack of vaginal lubrication

Subjective Data

A. Sexuality integrates into many layers of the individual and nearly always requires collaboration with a multidisciplinary team. Functioning as a sort of "gatekeeper" in this realm of medicine can help manage treatment recommendations from multiple providers for complicated, multifaceted, and sensitive health matters.

B. When addressing patients with potential sexual issues, a variety of questionnaires and assessment tools can help facilitate efficient communication in a busy medical setting. They can also aid in "breaking the ice" with potential uncomfortable topics. A study conducted in Great Britain identified that general practitioners do not discuss sexual health with their older patients because they feel it is not appropriate to discuss such issues with this age group and because they feel sexual health equates with younger people. Interestingly, these beliefs were found to be based on stereotypes versus actual patient experience. In this circumstance, questionnaires would not only identify the presence of sexual complaints irrespective of age, but also foster patient–provider communication. See Table 16.10 for a list of questionnaires that can help to identify sexual dysfunction in men and women.

C. Mailing the questionnaire prior to the appointment
   1. Not all questions are pertinent to each patient and it is important to identify this in the cover letter.

TABLE 16.10 Validated Sexual Health Questionnaires for Men and Women

Men	Women
Erectile Dysfunction Inventory of Treatment Satisfaction (EDITS)	Female Sexual Function Index (FSFI)
Erection Hardness Scale (EHS)	Female Sexual Distress Scale Revised (FSDS-R)
International Index of Erectile Function (IIEF)	Decreased Sexual Desire Screener (DSDS)
Index of Premature Ejaculation (IPE)	Hypoactive Sexual Desire Disorder Screener (HSDD)
Premature Ejaculation Diagnostic Tool (PEDT)	Sexual Function Questionnaire (SFQ28),
Quality of Erection Questionnaire (QEQ)	Abbreviated Sexual Function Questionnaire (ASFQ)
Self-Esteem and Relationship Questionnaire (SEAR)	Sexual Quality of Life-Female (SQOL-F)
Sexual Health Inventory for Men (SHIM)	
Sexual Quality of Life-Men (SQOL-M)	
Ageing Male Symptoms (AMS) scale	

2. Mailed questionnaires offer the opportunities for:
   a. Answering sensitive questions in a private setting
   b. Some patients like to include their partners' input in the answering of questions, which is also helpful when paperwork is mailed prior to the appointment.
3. Allowing patients to leave questions blank indicates:
   a. The question does not pertain to their situation.
   b. They do not understand the question.
   c. They would rather discuss in the office.

D. In your interview, it is important to be considerate of the patient's comfort level when addressing sensitive topics such as this, and potentially modify assessment techniques and terminology.

E. During the patient interview, consider factors that play a role in the patient's potential belief structure regarding sexuality such as age, culture, ethnicity, religious affiliation, and sexual orientation.

Physical Examination

A. Physical examination is dependent on the type of sexual dysfunction and other chronic medical conditions.

Diagnostic Tests

A. Diagnostic testing is dependent on the type of sexual dysfunction and other chronic medical conditions.

Plan

A. It is incredibly important to consider the entire individual when evaluating sexual health, utilizing a holistic approach inclusive of the mind, body, and spirit when addressing concerns and implementing treatment plans. An individualized approach includes consideration of age-related factors. It is also critical to involve partner(s) when appropriate and agreed upon by the patient.

B. Elderly lesbian, gay, bisexual, and transgender (LGBT)
   1. More than 2 million older adults identify as LGBT. In addition, the National Social Life, Health and Aging Project (NSHAP) indicated approximately 4% of the 3,005 respondents reported at least one same-sex sexual relationship (SSSR). Although the age of the respondents fell between 57 and 85 years of age, those reporting at least one SSSR tended to be younger, more educated, in better health, and more likely to be actively working.
   2. Rates of the LGBT population are generally considered to be underestimated, especially in the elderly population, due to fears of social stigmas and discrimination. Keeping in mind the age of this population, it is important to remember that up until the early 1970s homosexuality was considered a mental disorder in the *DSM* of the APA. In addition, many individuals may identify as heterosexual but still partake in some same-sex sexual contact.
   3. Use of nonspecific and non-offensive terms on paperwork and in an office encounter can help to facilitate rapport between a medical provider and patient. Considering that a patient experience begins in the waiting room, medical providers should make sure to include posters, handouts, books, magazines, and television shows that do not convey derogatory opinions of any patient population. Also, use of patient questionnaires that can be filled out privately prior to a face to face encounter

allows patients to share personal details in a safe manner.

4. In the older LGBT community, most respondents identify as gay men (61%), followed by lesbian (33%), transgender (7%), bisexual men (3%), bisexual women (2%), and "queer" (1%).
5. As previously stated, homosexual contact is the most commonly reported STI risk behavior in individuals older than 50. Although age differences in gay men do not seem to make a significant difference in likelihood of engaging in sexual or risk behavior, those with significantly older partners tend to take the receptive position more during anal intercourse.

C. Use of aids/toys /products
1. Use of sexual aids and toys may be a taboo subject for many older persons. At the same time, changes that occur to sexual functioning with age often warrant modification and inclusion of products into sexual activity that may not have been necessary in the past. The conversation of such products with patients should be approached with sensitivity.
2. It can be helpful to compare use of sexual aids to other more socially acceptable therapies used on the body, such as weights to strengthen weak muscles. This analogy can normalize a previously uncomfortable concept.
3. As previously reviewed, changes occur to vaginal mucosa with age, including tissue thinning, dryness, and inelasticity.
    a. Vaginal moisturizers and lubricants can drastically improve the quality of sexual encounters and potentially alleviate vaginal discomfort.
    b. Women should be instructed to avoid products with flavoring, dyes, and perfumes because many of these ingredients can irritate sensitive vulvovaginal mucosa.
4. Women should be aware of personal allergies and sensitivities. Available lubricant and moisturizing products contain a variety of potential irritants that should be reviewed by the patient before purchasing and using.
5. For men with problems getting and maintaining erections, there are OTC options such as constrictive rings that fit at the base of the penis and help to hold blood in the erect penis, There are also masturbation sleeves that assist in enhancing sensation during self-stimulation and partnered manual stimulation. OTC penis pumps enhance blood flow in the penis although the prescription versions are of better quality and sometimes covered by insurance.
6. Vibrators are a popular choice for enhancing vulvovaginal sexual response for women reporting arousal and orgasm difficulties. There are many different shapes, sizes, speeds, colors, and compositions, which can be daunting for a woman looking for her first vibrator. If possible, it can be helpful to have some examples to show patients in the office or even a safe website to view together so that an explanation of each type can be reviewed.
7. For women in heterosexual relationships, there are constrictive penis rings with small vibrators attached to provide clitoral stimulation during penetration. There are also a variety of arousal creams, gels, oils, and so forth, available, although once again, they should be used with caution as there is always a potential for contact dermatitis.
8. Many elderly individuals are either not going to have transportation to get to a store that sells sexual aids and toys or they are not going to feel comfortable making that trip. Providing patients with resources such as safe, online websites or a local product representative can help facilitate ease of purchase. Another option that some clinics utilize is selling these products on site. This is a mutually beneficial endeavor as it offers an additional revenue stream while providing patients the opportunity to purchase sensitive items in a safe and private manner.
9. Older patients will not be familiar with use of certain sexual aids and toys. Drawings and demonstrations on anatomical models in the medical office setting can help with proper use at home.

Differential Diagnosis

A. Sexual dysfunction in the elderly
1. Currently, there are 26 FDA-approved pharmaceutical agents that treat male sexual dysfunction, including PDE5 inhibitors and testosterone replacement.
2. The FDA has yet to approve a single medication for the treatment of female sexual dysfunction outside of two medications used to treat dyspareunia related to menopausal changes: conjugated estrogen creams and ospemifene oral tablets.
3. Female sexual complaints involving interest, arousal, and orgasm must be addressed with alternative and off-label options.

B. Sexual interest/arousal disorders in men and women
1. Consider a variety of etiologies in patients reporting bothersome sexual dysfunction

including physical health, relationship status, and psychosocial factors in order to best individualize the treatment regimen.

   a. While 33% of mature adult women in the United States (defined as 40-80 years of age) report decreased sexual interest, only 18% of men report the same complaint.
   b. Similarly, more women (21%) report vaginal lubrication difficulties than inability to reach orgasm or non-pleasurable, and painful sex. This is consistent with the general female population.

2. Depression consistently coincides with interest/arousal disorders in both men and women. Approximately 40% of individuals with a sexual disorder have depression. Unfortunately, the most common treatment for depression, selective serotonin reuptake inhibitors (SSRIs) frequently result in sexual side effects in both men and women. Although men report higher rates of sexual dysfunction related to SSRIs, women tend to experience more severe dysfunction.
3. There is no current FDA-approved pharmaceutical agent specifically for sexual interest/arousal disorder in either men or women; treating underlying cause(s) will frequently improve sexual functioning.
4. Consider collaboration with a multidisciplinary team such as sex therapists, sexuality educators, medical specialists and subspecialists, physical therapists, and alternative health providers in order to capture all aspects of these conditions.

C. Erectile dysfunction

1. Male erectile dysfunction (ED) is the inability to achieve or maintain an erection sufficient for satisfactory sexual performance.
2. Frequency of ED increases with age and comorbidities
3. ED can be a symptom of more concerning etiologies, including diabetes and cardiovascular disease, and should be considered when evaluating male patients.
4. Erectile dysfunction is a known comorbidity of testosterone deficiency. Additional comorbidities of testosterone deficiency include increased body weight, adiposity and increased waist circumference, insulin resistance, type 2 diabetes mellitus, hypertension, inflammation, atherosclerosis/cardiovascular disease, and increased incidence of mortality. More severe testosterone deficiency–related symptoms correlate with higher cardiovascular risk in men.
5. Common prescriptive treatment for ED includes:
   a. Phosphodiesterase-5 inhibitors (PDE-5i)
      i. Despite available options, only about 25% of men with ED are treated and PDE-5is are the most frequently utilized medication. Interestingly, men older than the age of 60 are much less likely to be treated than men age 40 to 59.
   b. Injectable or urethral prostaglandins
   c. Exogenous testosterone replacement when applicable
   d. Additional treatment options include constrictive penis rings, vacuum erection devices (VED), and surgical placement of penile prostheses.
   e. Some literature even suggests the benefit of pelvic floor muscle physical therapy for men experiencing ED.

D. Orgasmic disorder

1. Of women between 57 and 85 years of age, 35% to 38.2% were unable to achieve orgasm, comparable to 16.1% to 33% of men in the same age category. Both men and women experienced more of a prevalence with advancing age. In women, this complaint ranked second only to low desire and trouble lubricating. In men, inability to achieve orgasm ranked fifth to lack of interest in sex, anxiety about performance, trouble maintaining or achieving an erection, and climaxing too early.
2. For men or women to be diagnosed with orgasmic dysfunction a delay in, or absence of, orgasm must happen following sufficient sexual stimulation.
3. Simple explanation of sexual physiology and average time to orgasm can help some patients identify a misunderstanding of expectations
4. In cases of true orgasmic dysfunction, especially acute onset, patients should be worked up for underlying causes such as cardiovascular and/or neurologic etiologies.
5. Visual examination of the genitals can help to rule out skin changes that can impede sensation.

E. Premature ejaculation

1. Premature ejaculation (PE) occurs in approximately 21% to 30% of men, with less prevalence in older men. This data coincides with worsening incidences of erectile dysfunction with advancing age.
2. The consensus on the definition of premature ejaculation as stated by the International Society for Sexual Medicine is "ejaculation which always or nearly always occurs prior to or within about 1 minute." The typical ejaculatory latency in men is between 4 and 8 minutes.
3. While there is no clearly defined cause for PE, some research suggests a correlation

with multiple causes, including genetic predisposition, serotonin receptor activity, elevated penile sensitivity, and nerve conduction atypias. More recent evidence has shown a connection with PE, ED, and folate deficiency, possibly due to the effect of folic acid on the metabolism of nitric oxide.

4. Men with PE often report embarrassment over their condition and frequently avoid sexual relationships because of it. Pharmaceutical treatment options utilized over the years include topical anesthetics, PDE-5is, and anti-depressant medications.
5. Combining pharmaceutical intervention with behavioral, cognitive, and sex therapy techniques is the most likely regimen to prove efficacious for premature ejaculation.

F. Genito-pelvic pain/penetration disorder

1. In the general female population, anywhere from 7% to 58% of women report pain with intercourse. Specifically in the older population, 12.7% of women between the ages of 40 to 80 report pain with sex, comparable to only 3.1% of men.
2. There are many potential causes for painful intercourse in older women including:
   a. Vulvovaginal atrophy
   b. Disuse atrophy
   c. Pelvic floor dysfunction
   d. Changes to vaginal anatomy due to surgery, such as vaginal hysterectomy
   e. Vulvovaginal skin conditions and infections
   f. In addition, physical disabilities, chronic pain, and cognitive changes can negatively impact the sexual response cycle, leading to pain during vaginal penetration.
3. Estrogen plays a direct role in vulvovaginal epithelial cell maturation, which subsequently maintains healthy vulvovaginal pH and appropriate vaginal flora. During the perimenopausal period and following both natural and surgical menopause, significant changes occur to the vaginal microbiota in response to loss of endogenous estrogen. Symptoms of vulvovaginal atrophy occur in approximately 50% of postmenopausal women, including burning with urination, painful intercourse, bleeding with intercourse, vaginal discharge, vulvovaginal soreness, itching, and burning. Given the prevalence of this condition in older women, this population should be screened for signs and symptoms of vulvovaginal atrophy.
4. There are many FDA-approved treatment options for vulvovaginal atrophy including local estrogen replacement and an oral selective estrogen receptor modulator (SERM).
   a. Not all women are candidates for treatment with hormones and/or estrogen agonists. Patients should be counseled and treated on a case by case basis, taking into consideration their medical history.
   b. In certain situations, collaboration with the patient's other health care providers can help weigh risk versus benefit of traditional hormonal treatment for vulvovaginal atrophy.
5. Vaginal surgeries such as hysterectomies and prolapse repairs can lead to scarring, strictures, and shortening of the vaginal canal. These surgical complications combined with vulvovaginal atrophy can result in tremendous pain with vaginal penetration, including intercourse, use of sexual aids and toys, and even pelvic examinations.
   a. If appropriate, 6 weeks of preoperative local vaginal estrogen can improve tissue integrity including synthesis of mature collagen, decreased degradative enzyme activity, and increased thickness of the vaginal wall. This suggests improved tolerance for suturing and maintenance of connective tissue integrity for prolapse repair without significant changes to circulating estrogen levels.
6. Pain with intercourse for any reason can result in avoidance of sexual contact.
   a. Avoidance of sexual contact can lead to disuse atrophy, further worsening painful sex.
   b. Fear of pain further compounds the problem and frequently the pelvic floor muscles become involved. Muscle tension is a natural guarding response that occurs as a protective mechanism in the presence of pain. Pelvic floor muscle dysfunction frequently accompanies pelvic pain and painful intercourse.
   c. Incorporation of pelvic floor muscle rehabilitation with a trained pelvic floor physical therapist is crucial to properly addressing these issues.
   d. Although sexual pain for men is not classified in the *DSM*, pelvic floor physical therapy can benefit men with pelvic floor dysfunction as well.
7. Given recent changes to the recommendations for annual Pap testing in the older female population, many women are receiving less frequent routine pelvic medical care.
   a. Because the vulva and vagina are not overtly visible without intentional inspection, this area of the body can easily be missed, especially if conditions occur that are asymptomatic. For example, vulvar skin

changes, vaginal ph shifts, and asymptomatic vaginal infections will not be identified without medical evaluation.

b. It is important to maintain vulvovaginal inspection and pelvic examination in older women at least on an annual basis in order to identify changes from baseline.
   i. Use of colposcopy for the vulva and vagina can be helpful to better visualize mild skin changes.
   ii. If consent is obtained, photography is a great way to document anatomical variances for future reference.
   iii. There should be a low threshold for performing a biopsy with any concerning and grossly unidentifiable tissue findings.

G. Peyronie's disease
   1. Although male sexual pain is not classified in the *DSM*, Peyronie's disease is an incurable condition involving fibrotic plaques of the penis that can result in a palpable plaque, curvature of the penis with erection, and pain with sexual activity. Penetrative intercourse can also result in partner discomfort due to the curvature.
   2. In addition to the physical sequelae, men frequently report embarrassment and psychological distress over the aesthetic changes and sexual implications. Younger men are prone to this condition due to the frequency and intensity of intercourse, although there is a peak of incidence in older men likely due to weaker erections; this causes more opportunity for tunical trauma secondary to erectile dysfunction.
   3. Treatment is available including injectable therapies, interferon alpha-2b and collagenase clostridium histolyticum as well as surgery although efficacy varies based on the severity of symptoms.

H. STIs
   1. The medical provider should never assume potential for STIs based on patient age. It has been stated that sexual activity does not terminate at a certain age. Therefore, it is important to consider the fact that most sexually active individuals will contract an STI at some point in their lives.
   2. Many cases of STIs remain undiagnosed and many STIs can have long-term sequelae especially if left undiagnosed and untreated. The most common risk behaviors in individuals older than 50 include:
      a. Homosexual contact
      b. Intravenous drug use
   3. While STIs predominately occur in the younger population, rates of STI episodes in the older population have been on the rise.
      a. More than 20% of STIs reported in the United States occur in the 15- to 24–year-old age group, yet British researchers found that STI rates have doubled in less than 10 years in the 45 and older patient population. In the British study of STI trends in older people, rates of all five chosen STIs—chlamydia, genital herpes, genital warts, gonorrhea, and syphilis increased. With nearly 4,500 reported episodes, genital warts and genital herpes were identified as the most common STIs, accounting for 45% and 19% of reported infections, respectively. The age group between 55 and 59 was most likely to be affected, and men were more likely than women.
      b. Among the general U.S. population, there was only a slight increase in STI incidents between 2000 and 2008, from 18.8 million to 19.7 million. HPV and trichomoniasis were the two STIs showing the sharpest increase in estimates of incidence. Trichomoniasis has the highest prevalence in women over the age of 40 while chlamydia and gonorrhea have the lowest prevalence in this age category.
         i. HPV
            a. Although the prevalence rates of new HPV infection decline with age, there is still a significant prevalence in the older population (see Table 16.11).
            b. The rate of progression from new infection to CIN 2+ or CIN 3+ was not higher for women aged 34 years and older comparable to younger women after 3 years of follow-up. Newly detected HPV infection does not typically persist or progress onto CIN 2 or worse disease regardless of age.
            c. Refer to the Section III Patient Teaching Guide for Chapter 17, "Herpes Simplex Virus."

TABLE 16.11 Rates of Newly Acquired HPV Infection by Age

Ages	Rates
18–25	35.9%
26–33	30.6%
34–41	18.1%
> 42	13.5%

Reprinted by permission from Rodriguez et al. (2010).

ii. Trichomoniasis

a. Approximately 50% to 60% of trichomonas infections are asymptomatic in women.

b. While some of the adverse health outcomes from infection with trichomonas vaginalis (TV) are not a concern in the older patient population, such as preterm birth and low birth weight infants, trichomoniasis has been shown to increase the risk of HIV infection.

c. Refer to the Chapter 17 Patient Teaching Guide, "Trichomoniasis."

iii. HIV

a. Despite comparable rates of reported sexual risk factors in the younger versus older population, late middle-age (50–59 years old) and old adults (60–75 years old) are less likely to use condoms and to have ever had an HIV test (see Table 16.12). HIV/AIDS knowledge and risk perception, perceived behavioral control, and behavioral intentions toward condom use are lower among older adults compared to their younger counterparts.

b. Adults older than 60 are less likely to discuss HIV/AIDS with family, friends, and medical providers.

TABLE 16.12 HIV/AIDS Prevalence Increase by Age in 2011

Age at Diagnosis	No. Diagnosis of HIV Infection
< 13	165
13–14	44
15–19	1,936
20–24	6,943
25–29	6,397
30–34	5,311
35–39	4,515
40–44	4,909
45–49	4,734
50–54	3,383
55–59	1,979
60–64	1,057
> 65	808

Source: Centers for Disease Control and Prevention, 2011 HIV Surveillance Report.

c. Refer to the Section III Patient Teaching Guide for Chapter 19, "Reference Resources for Patients With HIV/AIDS."

iv. HSV

a. Painful ulcers result from HSV presentation; asymptomatic HSV type 2 shedding can contribute to chronic inflammation in the genital tract and painful intercourse.

b. The social stigma associated with HSV infection complicates those entering into new sexual relationships. Older patients with clinically diagnosed genital herpes should be counseled on preventive measures as well as ways to approach the topic with potential partners. Informing patients of the prevalence of this STI can help to lessen the fear and shame often associated with HSV.

c. Refer to the Chapter 17 Patient Teaching Guide, "Herpes Simplex Virus."

Sexuality and Chronic Health Conditions

Lifestyle and genetics play a role in the ageing process of each unique individual. Medical intervention for age-related ailments varies widely across different patient populations. With advancing medical technology and research, humans are living longer; with that, a larger proportion of the life span is spent with chronic health ailments and conditions. Medications, surgeries, and other medical interventions can further complicate sexuality in the aging population.

A. Cancers.

1. In the United States, the leading cancer sites in women by prevalence are breast, lung, and colon/rectum, although lung cancer death rates supersede breast cancer death rates in women. In men, the leading cancers occur in the prostate, lung, and colon/rectum.
2. Many treatments for cancer can have a significant impact on sexual functioning in both men and women. These effects can persist throughout the remainder of the individual's life.
3. The psychological burden of a potential life-threatening condition impacts every facet of life including sexuality and intimacy. This is relevant for both the patient as well as his or her partner.
4. Although there has been a tremendous amount of research in the area of nerve-sparing surgeries for prostate cancer, urologic and sexual side effects remain a significant concern. Common

side effects of radical prostatectomy include orgasmic dysfunction, urinary incontinence during sexual activity, penile sensory changes, penile shortening, and penile deformity.

5. Among women following mastectomy, significantly more report problems with sexual desire, arousal, the ability to achieve an orgasm, and intensity of the orgasm.
6. Both prostate and breast cancer treatment regimens frequently involve endocrine therapy that suppresses or eliminates circulating estrogen and/or testosterone.
   a. Although these individuals may have already experienced a decline in hormone levels depending upon age at initiation of suppressive treatment, the abrupt shift can prove quite detrimental to overall quality of life.
   b. With androgen deprivation therapy for prostate cancer, men frequently experience symptoms similar to women in menopause, including hot flashes, cognitive dysfunction, and sexual complaints such as erectile dysfunction, orgasmic difficulty, and loss of sexual desire.
   c. In women, aromatase inhibitor-treated breast cancer patients report more sexual complaints than tamoxifen-treated patients and controls. While only 31% of tamoxifen-treated patients reported painful intercourse, 57% of aromatase-inhibitor-treated patients reported the same. Aromatase inhibitor-treated patients also reported a 74% incidence of insufficient lubrication.

B. Diabetes

1. Diabetes (DM) is on the rise in the United States. In men with recently diagnosed type 2 diabetes mellitus, there is a high prevalence of sexual dysfunction. In this population, erectile dysfunction was classified as either mild, mild-moderate, moderate, or severe, with a cumulative prevalence of nearly 67%. More than 21% described their ED as severe.
2. Additional sexual comorbidities include premature ejaculation, delayed ejaculation, and hypoactive sexual desire. Considering the progressive nature of diabetes, early diagnosis, counseling, and management can aid in preservation of sexual functioning.
3. Sexual dysfunction is more prevalent in women with all types of diabetes, although more so in those with type 2 DM. In women with diagnosed diabetes, nearly one in four experience sexual dysfunction, although degree of severity varies based on type of diabetes, diabetic complications, hemoglobin A1C value, and presence of depression.
4. Low Female Sexual Function Index (FSFI) values correlate with high body mass index (BMI). This is of note with type 2 DM patients given the comorbidity of obesity.
5. Among studies of sexual functioning in both men and women with diabetes, patients consistently have a higher prevalence of depression, which further negatively impacts sexual functioning.
6. Refer to the Section III Patient Teaching Guide for Chapter 23, "Diabetes."

C. Sleep apnea

1. Sleep apnea is a chronic breathing disorder that disrupts sleep. In addition to the physical impact on the individual, partners are often bothered by the sound of heavy breathing and loud snoring. Because of this, sleep dynamics may change and result in the couple sleeping in separate beds and/or rooms.
2. Approximately 60% of men with diagnosed obstructive sleep apnea (OSA) have concomitant erectile dysfunction. Although the use of continuous positive airway pressure (CPAP) is effective at managing OSA, only about 29% of men report improvement in erectile dysfunction.
   a. Use of PDE-5is has been shown helpful in this patient population, even when CPAP is not included in the treatment regimen.
3. There is limited understanding of sexual health in women with obstructive sleep apnea, although multiple studies have shown an increase in sexual dysfunction concurrent with OSA. Some evidence suggests that sexual dysfunction correlates with OSA in obese women only if nocturnal hypoxia is present. Other than this, severity of OSA has not consistently been linked with degree of Female Sexual Distress (FDS).
4. Refer to Chapter 11, "Respiratory Guidelines" for further detailed information on OSA.

D. Cardiovascular disease

1. After a cardiac event, patients are frequently left with uncertainty of their ability to resume sexual activity. While patients turn to their health care professionals for guidance, most medical providers do not address the topic of sexuality after a cardiovascular event, specifically myocardial infarctions.
2. Many individuals with a history of cardiovascular event(s) are fearful of resuming regular physical activity, including sexual activity, due to fear of recurrence or even death.
   a. A study intended to observe changes in blood pressure and heart rate during sexual activity

showed that these measurements increase just slightly for a short time and recover their baseline level soon after sexual activity for healthy adults.

b. Given this knowledge, many medical providers are comfortable allowing patients to resume some form of sexual activity within a reasonable amount of time following a cardiovascular event. This decision needs to be made on a case by case basis.

3. While cholesterol lowering medications can benefit erectile function in men with concomitant ED and hypercholesterolemia, many of the medications used to treat and manage cardiovascular health conditions can have a negative effect on sexuality.
4. There has been some data to suggest a correlation with HMG-CoA-reductase-inhibitor medications, otherwise known as "statins," and low libido in men. Gender-specific research regarding the effect of statins on the sexual health of women is lacking.
5. Hypertension in women can lead to sexual dysfunction in the areas of libido, arousal, and orgasm more so than men. While beta blockers are known to produce sexual side effects, treatment with alternative medications and lifestyle modifications can potentially reduce sexual dysfunction in this population.
6. Refer to Chapter 12, "Cardiovascular Guidelines" for further detailed information on cardiovascular conditions.

E. Dementia/Alzheimer's disease
1. Sexuality can be significantly impacted by dementia and Alzheimer's. The most commonly reported sexual dysfunction is disinterest due to apathy and blunted affect. Spouses can develop disinterest and poor sexual functioning in response to worsening of partner's cognitive decline.
2. In severe cases, hypersexual tendencies occur as a manifestation of disinhibition in patients with dementia and Alzheimer's. Examples of this include sexual comments, public exposure masturbation, and unwarranted sexual proposals.
3. Refer to Chapter 22, "Neurologic Guidelines" for further detailed information on dementia/Alzheimer's.

Sexuality and End of Life

A. Many couples maintain sexual activity even in the presence of terminal illness. Sexual functioning should be acknowledged and included in end-of-life planning with the medical provider with the understanding that sexuality and intimacy extend beyond penetrative intercourse.

B. Physical limitations warrant modification, not termination, of sexual activity if both partners desire continued sexual contact.

C. By initiating the conversation with the patient and his or her partner, the medical provider normalizes this concept and establishes an open communication forum. Subsequently, patients may be more open to appropriate sexual health recommendations and referrals.

Sexuality and Physical Disabilities

A. Physical health problems are one of the most commonly reported reasons for sexual inactivity. With the increasing incidence of physical ailments that occur with aging, most elderly individuals will experience an acute or chronic disability at some point that impacts sexual functioning.

B. When a couple in a sexual relationship encounters independent changes in their physical health, sexual functioning becomes complicated twofold. Acknowledging and addressing these changes can help alleviate stress surrounding individual and partnered sexual functioning.

C. In many cases, certain sexual positions are not possible to maintain with physical disabilities. At the same time, sexually active individuals may not be familiar with alternative sexual positions and practices. Older men and women may not be comfortable with certain aspects of sexuality. According to the 2009 AARP survey, 20% of men and 12% of women have oral sex at least once a week. While cunnilingus and fellatio may not have been a form of sexual activity included in the practices of older couples prior to the onset of a disability, inclusion of this practice can help to maintain or even resurrect sexual activity in the cases of erectile dysfunction, premature ejaculation, diminished arousal/orgasm, painful intercourse, physical disabilities, and so on.

D. In addition to oral sex, patients can frequently benefit from education on alternative sexual practices, positions, and use of aids and toys. Referral to a certified sex therapist and/or a sexuality educator can benefit patients in this situation.

E. Because neurologic functioning is so critical to the sexual response cycle in both men and women, neurologic conditions can significantly impede sexual functioning. Lower urinary tract symptoms are common in patients with multiple sclerosis, and detrusor over-activity is an independent predictor of erectile dysfunction and female sexual dysfunction. This same study further supported the connection with depression and sexual dysfunction in both male and female patients.

F. In men with multiple sclerosis, erectile dysfunction is the most common sexual complaint, with prevalence over 50%, followed by decreased sexual desire, then difficulty reaching orgasm and ejaculation. Despite this prevalence and negative impact on sexual quality of life, few men with multiple sclerosis report sexual complaints to their health care providers. The length of disease does not seem to play a role in male sexual complaints although it does with women.

G. Parkinson's disease is another progressive disease of the neurologic system that can impact sexual functioning. Over 60% of both men and women with Parkinson's report fatigue. Other commonly reported symptoms include changes to bowel and bladder habits, nervousness, feelings of sadness, restless legs, pain, dribbling saliva, and excessive sweating.
   1. In men with Parkinson's disease, sexual dysfunction is a common symptom that also correlates with depression.
   2. In women with Parkinson's, the most influential factors on sexuality are depression as well as anxiety. Women with this disease report more problems with mood and apathy, whereas men report more sexual dysfunction.

Consultation/Referral

A. Despite the prevalence of sexual activity in the older population and the quality of life impact of sexual dysfunction, few medical programs incorporate sexual health training into their curriculum outside of STIs and reproduction. Even fewer address specific considerations for the geriatric population. Because of this, it is up to the medical provider to seek the latest information on caring for sexual health issues.
   1. Providers should acknowledge sexuality as an important component of overall health when caring for our older patients. It is also necessary for providers to either manage sexual dysfunction or refer out when appropriate.
   2. Collaboration with outside health care providers fosters a multidisciplinary approach to a complex medical entity. Sexual dysfunction, especially in the elderly population, is nearly nonexistent in medical training.
   3. Although few medical programs incorporate sexual health training into their curriculum, especially in relation to the older patient population, there are a variety of organizations available to help foster medical research and clinical practice in the realm of sexual medicine.
   4. It is helpful to establish a network of referral sources in the local area with which to collaborate, including pelvic floor physical therapists, sex therapist, sexuality educators, and medical specialists such as urologists, gynecologists, and oncologists.
   5. Some key organizations to consider becoming involved in include the International Society for Sexual Medicine (ISSM), International Society for the Study of Women's Sexual Health (ISSWSH), Sexual Medicine Society of North America (SMSNA), American Association of Sexuality Educators, Counselors and Therapists (AASECT), and the Society for Sex Therapy and Research (STAR).

Individual Considerations

A. Divorcees/widows/widowers
   1. The United States has the highest rate of divorce in the world with approximately 45% of marriages expected to end in divorce. According to the U.S. Census Bureau, 17.5 percent of people age 50 and older were either divorced or separated as of 2011. This age group is the only population where divorce rates are rising which further supports the need for sexuality education with older patients.
   2. Infidelity is a fairly common occurrence in U.S. marriages, from which older couples most certainly are not immune. From the AARP Sex, Romance, and Relationships survey, 21% of male respondents and 11% of female respondents admitted that they cheated during a current or recent long-term relationship, yet only 12% of both sexes say that their partner cheated on them. This identifies a discrepancy between true infidelity in this population and partner awareness.
      a. Social media allows individuals to connect who previously may not have had contact. Interactions via technology allow for private communication that facilitates loss of inhibitions that may play more of a role in face-to-face encounters. As younger generations age, social media will likely become even more commonplace with advancing technology.
      b. Younger couples are adhering less to some of the strict beliefs, values, and morals that prevented many older couples from having premarital sexual activity. As this younger population ages, men and women are more likely to have had multiple sexual partners prior to their marriage, potentially leading to difficulty with long-term monogamy.

c. Physical changes including disabilities, chronic health conditions, and aesthetic transitions can impact sexual attraction, leading partners to possibly seek out something "better."
d. Despite the potential increase in infidelity in coming years within the older population, only about 6% of respondents from the AARP survey reported that infidelity was the cause of their breakup. Some respondents actually reported that infidelity enhanced their relationship; 25% of cheaters reported that their infidelity improved their sex lives and 11% of the partners agreed.
e. Marital status does not seem to play a role in the prevalence of male erectile dysfunction although having never been married and widowhood are predictors of low sexual desire in men.
f. Older widowers are more likely to remarry than older widowed women. Younger age correlates with increased likelihood of becoming involved in a new relationship for women, although higher monthly income and level of education were better predictors for men.

3. There is minimal research in the realm of sexuality after spousal loss. Widows report a lower incidence of sexual intercourse than widowers and they are more likely to report lack of sexual desire.
   a. Recent partner loss has been shown to be a significant risk factor for depression in the elderly, which is a known correlating factor for sexual dysfunction in both men and women.
   b. For sexually active widows and widowers, four key needs reported to maintain sexual desire are:
      i. Good health
      ii. Good sexual functioning
      iii. Positive sexual self-esteem
      iv. Sexually skillful partner

B. Survivors
   1. The emotional burden of losing a spouse or partner is frequently compounded by survivor's guilt. It is not uncommon for the surviving partner to feel uncomfortable or uneasy about developing feelings toward new partner(s). There is the guilt of disrespecting the memory of the deceased, the social stigma of being perceived as "moving on too fast," and the fear of the unknown.
   2. Many older widows and widowers have been in a monogamous relationship for an extended period of time and are unfamiliar with modern day dating practices. In addition, it is completely normal for a widow/widower to inadvertently compare new intimate and sexual partners with the deceased spouse. This makes for potential interpersonal conflict as well as partner discomfort.
   3. Many spouses take on the role of caregiver in the situation of a chronic illness. Caretaker guilt can develop during this period of time, which hinders the caregiver's psychosocial and somatic adjustment of this role. The abrupt change in role from caregiver to grieving widow following spousal death has the potential to be extremely psychologically taxing and should be acknowledged by the medical provider. Referral to a grief counselor familiar with such situations can be very helpful in this circumstance.
   4. For spousal loss related to suicide, there is the added sensitivity of the situation. The bereavement group postvention (BGP) therapy has been shown to reduce anger, guilt, and despair. Because of the stigma attached to suicide, surviving partners may find it difficult to bring up their experience with future partners.

Vulvovaginal Candidiasis

Definition

A. Candidiasis (also known as moniliasis) is a common, yeast-like fungal infection of the vulva and vagina. In 90% of the cases, the cause is *Candida albicans* infection.

Incidence

A. Approximately 75% of all women have at least one episode of candidiasis. It is estimated that 50% of these women have recurrences. Yeast has been identified with circumcised males, but symptomatic complaints are more common with uncircumcised males.

Pathogenesis

A. Multiple fungal species cause candidiasis, including *C. albicans* (90%), *C. tropicalis, Torulopsis glabrata* (10%), *Candida parapsilosis*, and *Candida krusei.*
B. *C. albicans, C. tropicalis*, or *T. glabrata* are part of the normal flora of the mouth, GI tract, and vagina. They may become pathogenic with changes in the vaginal pH that encourage the overgrowth of the fungus.
C. The incubation period is 96 hours.

Predisposing Factors

A. Diabetes
B. Systemic antibiotic use

C. Pregnancy
D. Oral contraceptive pill use
E. Obesity
F. Warm climate
G. Immunocompromised
H. HIV
I. Wearing tight, restrictive clothing
J. Corticosteroid use
K. Tub bathing
L. Frequent use of hot tubs or whirlpools

Common Complaints

A. Thick white "cheesy" vaginal discharge
B. Itching, mild to intense vulvar pruritus
C. Vaginal or vulvar irritation, red and swollen
D. Discomfort during and after sexual intercourse

Other Signs and Symptoms

A. Vulvar excoriation
B. Vaginal swelling or inflammation
C. Burning with urination
D. Burning with or during intercourse
E. Increased symptoms near menses

Subjective Data

A. Determine onset, course, and duration of symptoms; note if infection is first occurrence, recurrent, persistent, or chronic.
B. Obtain medication history; include antibiotics, steroids, and birth control pills.
C. Review the patient's past medical history, and review systems for evidence of diabetes, HIV, or any immunocompromise.
D. Review hobbies that include the use of hot tubs, whirlpools, frequent swimming, or tight exercise clothing.
E. Review the patient's history of wearing polyester underwear, wearing underwear to bed, or wearing tight jeans.
F. Review previous treatment, self-treatment measures, and compliance with previous treatments.
G. Determine if the patient is pregnant; note first day of LMP.
H. Review sexual activity and partners. Do the partner(s) have any of the same symptoms, "jock itch," or oral candidiasis?
I. Review the use of vaginal deodorants or spray, scented toilet paper, tampons, pads, and douching.
J. Has there been any change in soaps, laundry detergent, or fabric softeners?
K. Review diet for high sugar content.

Physical Examination

A. Check temperature, pulse, and blood pressure.
B. Inspect
   1. Inspect the vulva for inflammation, fissures, lesions, excoriation, rashes, and condyloma.
   2. Examine the hair (Hart's) line and skin folds for inflammation, irritation, or skin breakdown.
   3. Note skin changes that suggest secondary bacterial infection (erythema, drainage).

Inflammation that spares the skin folds is consistent with contact irritation. Inflammation that is within the skin folds suggests Candida.

C. Palpate
   1. Perform external exam for enlarged or tender inguinal lymph nodes, vulvar masses, and lesions.
   2. Back: Assess for CVA tenderness.
D. Pelvic examination
   1. Inspect: Observe side walls of vagina. Note amount, smell, and color of the discharge.

Typical discharge with Candida *is adherent to vaginal side walls and characteristically thick, white, and curd-like (resembles cottage cheese). Side walls may exhibit erythema. The discharge has a musty odor.*

   2. **Speculum examination: Inspect the cervix for discharge and friability.**
   3. Bimanual examination: Check for CMT. Palpate for the size of the uterus and for adnexal masses or tenderness.

Diagnostic Tests

A. Wet prep with 10% potassium hydroxide and normal saline prep.

Yeast hyphae and/or spores are determined by microscopic examination of vaginal discharge prepared with 10% potassium hydroxide or normal saline. A positive whiff test indicates BV.

B. Test discharge with nitrazine paper.

The pH with candidiasis remains in the normal range of less than 4.5.

C. Consider 2-hour glucose testing.
D. Consider testing for gonorrhea and chlamydia.
E. Herpes culture, if lesions present
F. Urinalysis and culture, if indicated

Differential Diagnoses

A. Vulvovaginal candidiasis
B. Vulvar dystrophy
C. Allergic vulvitis

D. BV
E. UTI
F. Chlamydia
G. Gonorrhea
H. *Trichomonas*
I. HSV type 2
J. Chemical vaginitis
K. Normal physiologic discharge

Plan

A. General interventions
 1. Although vaginal candidiasis is treated using OTC products, encourage patients with initial presenting symptoms to have an evaluation to rule out other vaginal infections prior to self-treatment.
 2. Consider treating partners.

While candidiasis is not considered an STI, it can be sexually transmitted. The partner should be treated in cases of recurrent infections, even if the partner is asymptomatic.

 3. For recurrent infections, consider fasting and 2-hour postprandial glucose tests for chronic yeast infections.
 4. Consider testing for HIV for chronic yeast infections.

B. Patient teaching
 1. See the Section III Patient Teaching Guide for this chapter, "Vaginal Yeast Infection."
 2. Patients should be encouraged to present for evaluation if, after appropriate therapy has been instituted, they continue to have symptoms.
 3. Treatment should continue even during menstruation.

C. Pharmaceutical therapy
 1. Vaginal antifungal creams: Mild cases may respond to 3 days of therapy; severe cases may require 10 to 14 days. Some of these preparations are available in vaginal suppository form for a one- or three-night regimen with proven efficacy. Most OTC "zoles" are effective.
  a. Clotrimazole (Gyne-Lotrimin, Lotrimin, Mycelex, Mycelex-G): One applicator full at bedtime for 7 days
  b. Miconazole (Monistat): One applicator full at bedtime for 7 days
  c. Butoconazole nitrate (Femstat): One applicator full at bedtime for 7 days
  d. Terconazole (Terazol): One applicator full at bedtime for 7 days
  e. Terconazole vaginal antifungal cream is not available OTC. Imidazole drugs (miconazole, clotrimazole, econazole, butoconazole) are not as effective for non-*C. albicans* infections as are triazole compounds.
 2. Oral antifungal agents
  a. Fluconazole (Diflucan) 150 mg orally once. If treatment is not successful, prescription may be refilled one time; if it is still unsuccessful, consider treating the patient's partner and/or glucose testing for diabetes.
  b. Nystatin one tablet (100,000 units) orally or vaginally for 14 days. Nystatin may be taken twice a day or at bedtime.

Follow-Up

A. The patient who presents with recurrent candidiasis should be evaluated for HIV and/or other immunocompromised etiologies and diabetes.
B. If fasting and 2-hour blood glucose testing are normal, other options for recurrent candidiasis include treatment with clotrimazole one applicator every other week for 2 months. If the patient remains symptom-free, reduce treatment to once each month, in the week prior to menstrual period.
C. If recurrent candidiasis persists, request laboratory produce a yeast culture *Candida* for *T. glabrata* or *C. tropicalis*. Gentian violet, which disrupts the chitin cell wall, has been found to be effective as an office-based option for some patients.

Consultation/Referral

A. Consult or refer the patient to a physician if there is no response to the previous treatments and/or in presence of concurrent systemic disease.

Individual Considerations

A. Pregnancy may lead to an increase in vulvovaginal candidiasis because of the increased glycogen content of the vagina and to the stimulatory effects of estrogen and progesterone on candidal growth. OTC antifungal creams are appropriate for use in this population if there is no rupture of membranes. Candidiasis may be transmitted from the infected mother to the newborn at delivery.
B. Partners should be evaluated if the patient presents with recurrences. OTC antifungal creams are appropriate for use in this population.

Bibliography

Aerts, L., Christiaens, M. R., Enzlin, P., Neven, P., & Amant, F. (2014). Sexual functioning in women after mastectomy versus breast conserving therapy for early-stage breast cancer: A prospective controlled study. *Breast, 23*(5), 629–636. doi:10.1016/j.breast.2014.06.012

Allsworth, J. E., Ratner, J. A., & Peipert, J. F. (2009). Trichomoniasis and other sexually transmitted infections: Results from the 2001–2004 National Health and Nutrition Examination Surveys. *Sexually Transmitted Diseases, 36,* 738–744.

Althof, S. E. (2007). Treatment of rapid ejaculation: Psychotherapy, pharmacotherapy, and combined therapy. In S. R. Leiblum (Ed.), *Principles and practice of sex therapy* (4th ed., pp. 212–240). New York, NY: Guilford.

American Cancer Society. (2012). *Cervical cancer: Prevention and early detection.* Retrieved from http://www.cancer.org/cancer/cervicalcancer/moreinformation/cervicalcancerpreventionandearlydetection/cervical-cancer-prevention-and-early-detection-find-pre-cancer-changes

American College of Obstetricians and Gynecologists Committee on Practice Bulletins-Gynecology. (2006). ACOG practice bulletin. No. 73: Use of hormonal contraception in women with coexisting medical conditions. *Obstetrics and Gynecology, 107,* 1453–1472.

American College of Obstetricians and Gynecologists Committee on Practice Bulletins–Gynecology. (2014). ACOG practice bulletin. No. 141: Management of menopausal symptoms. *Obstetrics and Gynecology, 123,* 202–216.

American Psychiatric Association. (2013). *Diagnostic and statistical manual of mental disorders: DSM-5* (5th ed.). Washington, DC: Author.

American Society for Colposcopy and Cervical Pathology. (2012). 2012 Updated consensus guidelines for the management of abnormal cervical cancer screening tests and cancer precursors. *Journal of Lower Genital Tract Disease, 17*(5), S1–S27.

Archer, J., & Lloyd, B. B. (2002). *Sex and gender* (2nd ed.). Cambridge, UK: Cambridge University Press.

Ashtari, F., Rezvani, R., & Afshar, H. (2014). Sexual dysfunction in women with multiple sclerosis: Dimensions and contributory factors. *Journal of Research in Medical Sciences, 19*(3), 228–233.

Atnip, S., & O'Dell. (2012). Vaginal support pessaries: Indications for use and fitting strategies. *Urologic Nursing, 32*(5), 114–124.

Bagrodia, A., Diblasio, C. J., Wake, R. W., & Derweesh, I. H. (2009). Adverse effects of androgen deprivation therapy in prostate cancer: Current management issues. *Indian Journal of Urology, 25*(2), 169–176.

Barber, M. D. (2005). Symptoms and outcome measures of pelvic organ prolapse. *Clinical Obstetrics and Gynecology, 48*(3), 648–661.

Barnes, T., & Eardley, I. (2007). Premature ejaculation: The scope of the problem. *Journal of Sex and Marital Therapy, 33*(3), 151.

Bartelet, M., Waterink, W., & van Hooren, S. (2014). Extreme sexual behavior in dementia as a specific manifestation of disinhibition. *Journal of Alzheimer's Disease, 42*(3), S119–S124. doi:10.3233/JAD-132378

Basson, R. (2001). Using a different model for female sexual response to address women's problematic low sexual desire. *Journal of Sex & Marital Therapy, 27,* 395–403.

Baumgart, J., Nilsson, K., Evers, A. S., Kallak, T. K., & Poromass, I. S. (2013). Sexual dysfunction in women on adjuvant endocrine therapy after breast cancer. *Menopause, 20*(2), 162–168.

Bennett, K. M., Arnott, L., & Soulsby, L. K. (2013). "You're not getting married for the moon and the stars": British widowers about the idea of new romantic relationships. *Journal of Aging Studies, 27*(4), 499–506.

Besdine, R. (2013). Evaluation of the elderly patient. *The Merck Manual for Health Care Professionals.* Retrieved from http://www.merckmanuals.com/professional/geriatrics/approach_to_the_geriatric_patient/evaluation_of_the_elderly_patient.html

Bodley-Tickell, A. T., Olowokure, B., Bhaduri, S., White, D. J., Ward, D., Ross, J. D. C., . . . Goold, P. (2008). Trends in sexually transmitted infections (other than HIV) in older people: Analysis of data from an enhanced surveillance system. *Sexually Transmitted Infections. 84,* 312–317. doi:10.1136/sti.2007.027847

Brown, M. T., & Grossman, B. R. (2014). Same-sex sexual relationships in the national social life, health and aging project: Making a case for data collection. *Journal of Gerontological Social Work, 57*(2–4), 108–129.

Brown, S. L., & I-Fen, L. (2012). The gray divorce revolution: Rising divorce among middle-aged and older adults, 1990–2010. *Journals of Gerontology B Psychol Sci Soc Sci, 67*(6), 731–741.

Bugge, C., Hagen, S., & Thakar, R. (2013). Vaginal pessaries for pelvic organ prolapse and urinary incontinence: A multiprofessional survey of practice. *International Urogynecology Journal, 24,* 1017–1024.

Bump, R., Bo, K., Brubaker, L., DeLancey, J., Klarskov, P., Shull, B., & Smith, A. (1996). Final draft: The standardization of terminology of female pelvic organ prolapse and pelvic floor dysfunction. *Pelvic Organ Prolapse & Pelvic Floor Dysfunction,* 1–10.

Bump, R. C., Mattiasson, A., Bo, K., Brubaker, L. P., DeLancey, J. O., Klarskov, P., . . . & Smith, A. R. (1996). The standardization of terminology of female pelvic organ prolapse and pelvic floor dysfunction. *American Journal of Obstetrics & Gynecology, 175,* 1, 10–17.

Burrows, L. J., Meyn, L. A., Walters, M. D., & Weber, A. M. (2004). Pelvic symptoms in women with pelvic organ prolapse. *Obstetrics and Gynecology, 104*(5), 982–988.

Carcia-Cruz, E., Leibar-Tarnavo, A., Romero-Otero, J., Asiain, I., Carrión, A., Castañeda, R., . . . Alcaraz, A. (2014). Marked testosterone deficiency-related symptoms may be associated to higher metabolic risk in men with low testosterone levels. *Journal of Sexual Medicine, 11*(9), 2292–2301. doi:10.1111/jsm.12615

Centers for Disease Control and Prevention. (2008). *Bacterial vaginosis: CDC fact sheet.* Retrieved from http://www.cdc.gov/std/bv/STDFact-Bacterial-Vaginosis.htm

Centers for Disease Control and Prevention. (2009). *Bacterial vaginosis: CDC fact sheet.* Retrieved from http://www.cdc.gov/std/bv/STDFact-Bacterial-Vaginosis.htm

Centers for Disease Control and Prevention. (2010). Sexually transmitted diseases treatment guidelines, 2010. *Morbidity and Mortality Weekly Report, 59*(RR-12), 1–94.

Centers for Disease Control and Prevention. (2011). HIV surveillance report. Retrieved from http://www.cdc.gov/hiv/library/reports/surveillance/2011/surveillance_report_vol_23.html

Centers for Disease Control and Prevention. (2012). Update to CDC's Sexually Transmitted Diseases Treatment Guidelines, 2012: Oral cephalosporins no longer a recommended treatment for Gonococcal infections. *Morbidity and Mortality Weekly Report, 61*(31), 590–594.

Centers for Disease Control and Prevention. (2013). HPV vaccine for preteens and teens. Retrieved from http://www.cdc.gov/vaccines/who/teens/vaccines/hpv.html

Cherlin, A. J. (2010). Demographic trends in the United States: A review of research in the 2000s. *Journal of Marriage and Family, 72,* 403–419.

Clayton, A. H., Pradko, J. F., Croft, H. A., Montano, C. B., Leadbetter, R. A., Bolden-Watson, C., . . . Metz., A. (2002). Prevalence of sexual dysfunction among newer antidepressants. *Journal of Clinical Psychiatry, 63,* 357–366.

Constantino, R. E., & Bricker, P. L. (1996). Nursing postvention for spousal survivors of suicide. *Issues in Mental Health Nursing, 17*(2), 131–152.

Contraceptive Technology Update. (2008, September 1). Increase the radar for STDs in seniors (sexually transmitted disease). *Contraceptive Technology Update.*

Corona, G., Giorda, C. B., Cucinotta, D., Guida, P., Nada, E., & Gruppo di studio BUBITO-DE. (2014). Sexual dysfunction at the onset of type 2 diabetes: The interplay of depression, hormonal and cardiovascular factors. *The Journal of Sexual Medicine, 11*(8), 2065–2073.

Corton, M. M. (2009). Anatomy of pelvic floor dysfunction. *Obstetrics and Gynecology Clinics, 36*, 3, 401–419.

Cundiff, G. W., & Fenner, D. (2004). Evaluation and treatment of women with rectocele: Focus on associated defecatory and sexual dysfunction. *Obstetrics & Gynecology, 104*(6), 1403–1421.

De Graaf, L., Brouwers, A. H., & Diemont, W. L. (2004). Is decreased libido associated with the use of HMG-CoA-reductase inhibitors? *British Journal of Clinical Pharmacology, 58*(3), 326–328.

Derouesne, C. (2005). Sexuality and dementia. *Psychologie & Neuropsychiatrie du Viellissement, 3*(4), 281–289.

Doumas, M., Tsiodras, S., Tsakiris, A., Douma, S., Chounta, A., Papadopoulos, A., . . . Giamarellou, H. (2006). Female sexual dysfunction in essential hypertension: A common problem being uncovered. *Journal of Hypertension, 24*(12), 2387–2392.

Duman, N. B. (2014). Frequency of sexual dysfunction and its causative factors among diabetic women in Turkey. *Pakistan Journal of Medical Sciences, 30*(3), 558–563.

Efantis, J., & Simon, T. (2008). Menopause. In T. M. Buttaro, J. Trybulski, P. P. Bailey, & J. Sandberg-Cook (Eds.), *Primary care: A collaborative practice* (3rd ed., pp. 877–886). St. Louis, MO: Mosby Elsevier.

Einstin, M. H., & Cox, J. T. (2013). Cervical disease. *OBG Management, 25*(5), 43–49.

Fanfulla, F., Camera, A., Fulgoni, P., Chiovanto, L., & Nappi, R. E. (2013). Sexual dysfunction in obese women: Does obstructive sleep apnea play a role? *Sleep Medicine, 14*(3), 252–256.

Fernando, R. J., Thakar, R., Sultan, A. H., Shah, S. M., & Jones, P. W. (2006). Effect of vaginal pessaries on symptoms associated with pelvic organ prolapse. *Obstetrics & Gynecology, 108*(1), 93–99.

Flynn, M. K., & Amundsen, C. L. (2006). Diagnosis of pelvic organ prolapse. In C. R. Chapple, P. E. Zimmern, L. Brubaker, A. R. B. Smith, & K. Bo (Eds.), *Multidisplinary management of female pelvic floor disorders* (p. 118). Philadelphia, PA: Churchill Livingstone Elsevier.

Frederick, L. R., Cakir, O. O., Arora, H., Helfand, B. T., & McVary, K. T. (2014). Undertreatment of erectile dysfunction: Claims analysis of 6.2 million patients. *Journal of Sexual Medicine.* doi:10.1111/jsm.12647

Fredriksen-Goldsen, K. I., Kim, H. J., Emlet, C. A., Muraco, A., Erosheva, E. A., Hoy-Ellis, C. P., . . . & Petry, H. (2011). *The aging and health report: Disparities and resilience among lesbian, gay, bisexual, and transgender older adults.* Retrieved from http://caringandaging.org/wordpress/wp-content/uploads/2011/05/Full-Report-FINAL-11-16-11.pdf

Frey, A., Sonksen, J., Jakobsen, H., & Fode, M. (2014). Prevalence and predicting factors for commonly neglected sexual side effects to radical prostatectomies: Results from a cross-sectional questionnaire-based study. *The Journal of Sexual Medicine.* doi:10.1111/jsm.12624.

Geraci, R. (2010, January 1). Sex survey on sexual relationships & aging, single & married sex life. *AARP.* Retrieved July 1, 2014, from http://www.aarp.org/relationships/love-sex/info-05-2010/2009-aarp-sex-survey.html

German, D., & Lee, A. (Eds.). (2012). *Nurse practitioner's prescribing reference.* New York, NY: Haymarket Media.

Ginocchio, C. C., Chapin, K., Smith, J. S., Aslanzadeh, J., Snook, J., Hill, C. S., & Gaydos, C. A. (2012). Prevalence of trichomonas vaginalis and coinfection with *chlamydia trachomatis* and *Neisseria gonorrhoeae* in the United States as determined by the Aptima Trichomonas vaginalis Nucleic Acid Amplification Assay. *Journal of Clinical Microbiology, 50*, 2601–2608.

Gokkaya, S. C., Ozden, C., Levent-Ozdal, O., Koyuncu, H., & Memis, A. (2008). Effect of correcting serum cholesterol levels on erectile function in patients with vasculogenic erectile dysfunction. *Scandinavian Journal of Urology and Nephrology, 42*(5), 437–440.

Gott, M., Hinchliff, S., & Galena, E. (2004). General practitioner attitudes to discussing sexual health issues with older people. *Social Science & Medicine, 58*, 2093–2103.

Gravitt, P., Rositch, A., Silver, M. I., Marks, M. A., Chang, K., Burke, A. E., & Viscidi, R. P. (2013). A cohort effect of the sexual revolution may be masking an increase in human papillomavirus detection at menopause in the United States. *Journal of Infectious Diseases, 207*, 272–280.

Haber, D. (2009). Gay aging. *Gerontology & Geriatrics Education, 30*, 267–280.

Handa, V. L., Blomquist, J. L., McDermott, K. C., Friedman, S., & Munoz A. (2012). Pelvic floor disorders after vaginal birth: Effect of episiotomy, perineal laceration, and operative birth. *Obstetrics & Gynecology, 119*(2, pt 1), 233–239.

Hatcher, R. A., Trussell, J., Nelson, A. L., Cates, W., Kowal, D., & Policar, M. S. (Eds.). (2011). *Contraceptive technology* (20th ed.). New York, NY: Ardent Media.

Hayes, R. D., Bennett, C. M., Fairley, C. K., & Dennerstein, L. (2006). What can prevalence studies tell us about female sexual difficulty and dysfunction? *Journal of Sexual Medicine. 3*, 589–595.

Haylen, B. T., de Ridder, D., Freeman, R. M., Swift, S. E., Berghamans, B., Lee, J., . . . Schaer, G. N. (2010). An International Urogynecological Association (IUGA)/International Continence Society (ICS) joint report on the terminology for female pelvic floor dysfunction. *Neurourology and Urodynamics, 29*, 4–20.

Heit, M., Rosenquist, C., Culligan, P., Graham, C., Murphy, M., & Shott, S. (2003). Predicting treatment choice for patients with pelvic organ prolapse. *Obstetrics & Gynecology, 101*(6), 1279–1284.

Hensley, P. L., & Numberg, H. G. (2002). SSRI sexual dysfunction: A female perspective. *Journal of Sexual and Marital Therapy, 28*(Suppl 1):143–153.

Hu, X., Liu, W. G., & Yan, F. L. (2013). Male sexual dysfunction and Parkinson's disease: A preliminary investigation. *Zhonghua Nan Ke Xue, 19*(6), 518–521.

Institute of Medicine. (2011). *Dietary reference intakes for calcium and vitamin D.* Washington, DC: National Academies Press.

Irvine, J. (2010). *Disorders of desire: Sexuality and gender in modern American sexology.* Philadelphia, PA: Temple University Press.

IsHak, W. W., & Tobia, G. (2013). DSM-5 Changes in diagnostic criteria of sexual dysfunctions. *Reproductive System & Sexual Disorders, 2*, 122. doi:10.4172/2161-038X.1000122

Johannes, C. B., Clayton, A. H., Odom, D. M., Rosen, R. C., Russo, P. A., Shifren, J. L., & Monz, B. U. (2009).

Distressing sexual problems in United States women revisited. *Journal of Clinical Psychiatry, 70*(12), 1698–1706.

Johnston, C., Zhu, J., Jing, L., Laing, K. J., McClurkan, C. M., Klock, A., . . . Corey L. (2014). Virologic and immunologic evidence of multifocal genital herpes simplex virus 2 infection. *Journal of Virology, 88*(9), 4921–4931.

Jones, K., Yang, L., Lowder, J. L., Meyn, L., Ellison, R., Zyczynski, H. M., . . . & Lee, T. (2008). Effect of pessary use on genital hiatus measurements in women with pelvic organ prolapse. *Obstetrics & Gynecology, 112*(3), 630–636.

Kaplan, H. S. (1979). *Disorders of sexual desire and other new concepts and techniques in sex therapy.* New York, NY: Simon and Schuster.

Kerkhof, M. H., Hendriks, L., & Brölmann, H. A. M. (2009). Changes in connective tissue in patients with pelvic organ prolapse—A review of the current literature. *International Urogynecology Journal, 20*, 461–474.

Kingsberg, S. A., & Krychman, M. L. (2013). Resistance and barriers to local estrogen therapy in women with atrophic vaginitis. *The Journal of Sexual Medicine. 10*, 1567–1574.

Kinsey, A. C., Pomeroy, W. B., & Martin, C. E. (1948). *Sexual behavior in the human male.* Philadelphia, PA: W. B. Saunders Co.

Kinsey, A. C., Pomeroy, W. B., Martin, C. E., & Gebhard, P. H. (1953). *Sexual behavior in the human female.* Philadelphia, PA: W. B. Saunders Co.

Kleinplatz, P. J. (2008). Sexuality and older people. *British Medical Journal, 337*, 121–122.

Kontula, O., & Haavio-Mannila, E. (2009). The impact of aging on human sexual activity and sexual desire. *Journal of Sex Research, 46*(1), 46–56.

Kotkova, P., & Weiss, P. (2013). Psychiatric factors related to sexual functioning in patients with Parkinson's disease. *Clinical Neurology and Neurosurgery, 115*(4), 419–424.

Langston, J. P., & Carson, C. C. (2014). Peyronie's disease: Review and recent advances. *Maturitas, 78*(4), 341–343.

Laumann, E. O. (1999). Sexual dysfunction in the United States: Prevalence and predictors. *Journal of the American Medical Association, 281*, 537–544.

Laumann, E., Das, A., & Waite, L. (2008). Sexual dysfunction among older adults: Prevalence and risk factors from a nationally representative U.S. probability sample of men and women 57–85 years of age. *Journal of Sexual Medicine, 5*, 2300–2311.

Laumann, E. O., Glasser, D. B., Neves, R. C., & Moreira Jr, E. D. (2009). A population-based survey of sexual activity, sexual problems and associated help-seeking behavior patterns in mature adults in the United States of America. *International Journal of Impotence Research, 21*, 171–178.

Lavoisier, P., Roy, P., Dantony, E., Watrelot, A., Ruggeri, J., & Dumoulin, S. (2014). Pelvic-floor muscle rehabilitation in erectile dysfunction and premature ejaculation. *Physical Therapy.* doi:10.2522/ptj.20130354

Lew-Starowicz, M., & Rola, R. (2014). Sexual dysfunctions and sexual quality of life in men with multiple sclerosis. *The Journal of Sexual Medicine, 11*(5), 1294–1301.

Lewthwaite, B. J., Staley, D., Girouard, L., & Maslow, K. (2013). Characteristics of women with continued use of vaginal pessaries. *Urologic Nursing, 33*(4), 171–176.

Lindau, S. T., Schumm, L. P., Laumann, E. O., Levinson, W., O'Muircheartaigh, C. A., & Waite, L. J. (2007). A study of sexuality and health among older adults in the United States. *New England Journal of Medicine, 357*(8), 762–774.

Lunelli, R. P., Rabello, E. R., Stein, R., Goldmeier, S., & Moraes, M. A (2008). Sexual activity after myocardial infarction: Taboo or lack of knowledge? *Arquivos Brasileiros de Cardiologia, 90*(3), 156–159.

MacBride, M. B., Rhodes D. J., & Shuster L. T. (2010). Vulvovaginal atrophy. *Mayo Clinic Proceedings, 85*, 87–94.

Maes, C. A., & Louis, M. (2011). Nurse practitioners' sexual history-taking practices with adults 50 and older. *Journal for Nurse Practitioners, 7*, 216–222.

Manchana, T., & Bunyavejchevin, S. (2012). Impact on quality of life after ring pessary use for pelvic organ prolapse. *International Urogynecology Journal, 23*, 873–877.

Markle, D., Skoczylas, L., Goldsmith, C., & Noblett, K. (2011). Patient characteristics associated with a successful pessary fitting. *Female Pelvic Medicine & Reconstructive Surgery, 17*(5), 249–252.

Master-Hunter, T., & Heiman, D. (2006). Amenorrhea: Evaluation and treatment. *American Family Physician, 73*(8), 1374–1382.

McNeeley, S. (2008). *Bartholin's gland cysts. The Merck Manuals Online Medical Library.* Retrieved from http://www.merck.com/mmpe/sec18/ch249/ch249c.html

Mertz, G. J. (2008). Asymptomatic shedding of herpes simplex-virus 1 and 2: Implications for prevention of transmission. *Journal of Infectious Diseases. 198*(8), 1098–1100.

Miller, K. L., & Baraldi, C. A. (2012). Geriatric gynecology: Promoting health and avoiding harm. *American Journal of Obstetrics & Gynecology, 207*(5), 355–367.

Montgomery, S. A., Baldwin, D. S., & Riley, A. (2002). Antidepressant medications: A review of the evidence for drug-induced sexual dysfunction. *Journal of Affective Disorders, 69*, 119–140.

Moreira, E. J., Brock, G., Glasser, D., Nicolosi, A., Laumann, E., Paik, A., . . . Gingell, C., GSSAB Investigator' Group. (2005). Help-seeking behaviour for sexual problems: The global study of sexual attitudes and behaviors. *International Journal of Clinical Practice, 59*(1), 6–16.

Mosher, W. D., Martinez, G. M., Chandra, A., Abma, J. C., & Willson, S. J. (2004). Use of contraception and use of family planning services in the United States: 1982–2002. *Advanced Data from Vital and Health Statistics, 350, National Center for Health Statistics.* Retrieved from http://www.cdc.gov/nchs/data/ad/ad350.pdf

Nappi, R. E., & Kokot-Kierepa, M. (2012) Vaginal health: Insights, views & attitudes (VIVA): Results from an international survey. *Climacteric, 15*, 36–44.

National Institute of Health. (1992, December 7–9). Impotence. *NIH Consensus Statement. 10*(4), 1–33.

Nguyen, J. N., & Jones, C. R. (2005). Pessary treatment of pelvic relaxation: Factors affecting successful fitting and continued use. *Journal of Wound, Ostomy and Continence Nurses Society, 32*(4), 255–261.

North American Menopause Society. (2012). The 2012 hormone therapy position statement of the North American Menopause Society. *Menopause: The Journal of the North American Menopause Society, 19*(3), 257–271.

North American Menopause Society. (2013). Management of symptomatic vulvovaginal atrophy position statement of the North American Menopause Society. *Menopause: The Journal of the North American Menopause Society, 20*(9), 888–902.

O'Dell, K., & Atnip, S. (2012). Pessary care: Follow up and management of complications. *Urologic Nursing, 32*(3), 126–145.

O'Dell, K., Wooldridge, L. S., & Atnip, S. (2012). Managing a pessary business. *Urologic Nursing, 32*(3), 138–145.

Otcenasek, M., Baca, V., Krofta, L., & Feyereisl, J. (2008). Endopelvic fascia in women shape and relation to parietal pelvic structures. *Obstetrics and Gynecology, 111*(3), 622–630.

Parish, S. J., & Shindel, A. (2013). Sexuality education in North American medical schools: Current status and future directions (CME). *Journal of Sexual Medicine*, 3–18.

Pastore, A. L., Palleschi, G., Ripoli, A., Silvestri, L, Maggioni, C., Pagliuca, G., . . . Carbone, A. (2014). Severe obstructive sleep apnea syndrome and erectile dysfunction: A prospective randomised study to compare sildenafil vs. nasal continuous positive airway pressure. *International Journal of Clinical Practice, 68*(8), 995–1000.

Patel, M. S., Mellen. C., O'Sullivan, D. M., & LaSala, C. A. (2011). Pessary use and impact on quality of life and body image. *Female Pelvic Medicine & Reconstructive Surgery, 17*(6), 298–301.

Pedraza, R., Nieto, J., Ibarra, S., & Haas, E. M. (2014). Pelvic muscle rehabilitation: A standardized protocol for pelvic floor dysfunction. *Advances in Urology*. doi:10.1155/2014/487436

Pontiroli, A. E., Cortelazzi, D., & Morabito, A. (2013). Female sexual dysfunction and diabetes: A systematic review and meta-analysis. *Journal of Sexual Medicine. 10*(4), 1044–1051.

Prati, G., Mazzoni, D., & Zani, B. (2014, June 19). Psychosocial predictors and HIV-related behaviors of old adults versus late middle-aged and younger adults. *Journal of Aging and Health, 27*(1), 123–139. doi:10.1177/0898264314538664.

Prestage, G., Jin, F., Bavinton, B., Scott, S. A., & Hurley, M. (2013). Do differences in age between sexual partners affect sexual risk behavior among Australian gay and bisexual men? *Sexually Transmitted Infections, 89*(8), 653–658. doi:10.1136/sextrans-2012-050947.

Rahn, D. D., Good, M. M., Roshanravan, S. M., Shi, H., Schaffer, J. I., Singh, R. J., & Word, R. A. (2014). Effects of preoperative local estrogen in postmenopausal women with prolapse: a randomized trial. *Journal of Clinical Endocrinology and Metabolism*. doi:10.1210/jc.2014-1216

Rodríguez, A., Schiffman, M., Herrero, R., Hildesheim, A., Bratti, C., Sherman, . . . , Burk, R. D. (2010, March 3). Longitudinal study of human papillomavirus persistence and cervical intraepithelial neoplasia grade 2/3: Critical role of duration of infection. *Journal of the National Cancer Institute, 102*, 315–324.

Rortveit, G., Brown, J. S., Thom, D. H., Van Den Eeden, S. K., Creasman, J. M., & Subak, L. L. (2007). Symptomatic pelvic organ prolapse: Prevalence and risk factors in a population-based, racially diverse cohort. *Obstetrics & Gynecology, 109*(6), 1396–1403.

Rosolowich, V., Saettler, E., Szuck, B., Leah, R., Levesque, P., Weisberg, F., . . ., Rosolowich, V. (2006). Mastalgia. *Journal of Obstetric and Gynaecology Canada, 28*(1), 49–57.

Saslow, D., Boetes, C., Burke, W., Harms, S., O'Leach, M., Lehman, D., & Russell, C. A. (2007). American Cancer Society guidelines for breast cancer screening with MRI as an adjunct to mammography. *CA: A Cancer Journal for Clinicians, 57*(2), 75–89.

Sasso, K. (2003). Case study: Challenges of pessary management. *Journal of Wound and Ostomy Care Nursing, 30*(3), 152–158.

Satterwhite, L. S., Torrone, E., Meites, E., Dunne, E., Mahajan, R., Ocfemia, C. B., . . ., Weinstock, H. (2013). Sexually transmitted infections among US women and men. *Sexually Transmitted Diseases, 40*, 187–193.

Schneider, D. S., Sledge, P. A., Schuchter, S. R., & Zisook, S. (1996). Dating and remarriage over the first two years of widowhood. *Annals of Clinical Psychiatry, 8*(2), 51–57.

Schwarzer, U., Sommer, F., Klotz, T., Braun, M., Reifenrath, B., & Engelmann, U. (2001). The prevalence of Peyronie's disease: Results of a large survey. *British Journal of Urology International, 88*(7), 727–730.

Seftel, A. D. (2013). Can simvastatin improve erectile function and health-related quality of life in men aged ≥ 40 years with erectile dysfunction? Results of the erectile dysfunction and statins trial. *Journal of Urology, 188*(5), 1871–1872.

Sharlip, I. D., Hellstrom, W. J., & Broderick, G. A. (2008). The ISSM definition of premature ejaculation: A contemporary, evidence-based definition. *Journal of Urology, 179*(Suppl.), 340, abstract 988.

Sharon, P. (2010). Doctor-patient communication about desire with women who have distressing low desire in primary care and general OB/GYN practice. Paper presented at the *International Society for the Study of Women's Sexual Health Conference*, St. Petersburg, Florida.

Simon, J. A. & Reape, K. Z. (2009). Understanding the menopausal experiences of professional women. *Menopause, 16*, 73–76.

Soddoqui, N. Y., & Edenfield, A. L. (2014). Clinical challenges in the management of vaginal prolapse. *International Journal of Women's Health, 6*, 83–94.

Solomon, D., Davey, D., Kurman, R., Moriarty, A., O'Connor, D., Prey, M., . . ., Young, N. (2002). The 2001 Bethesda System: Terminology for reporting results of cervical cytology. *Journal of the American Medical Association, 287*(16), 2114–2119.

Spillers, R. L., Wellisch, D. K., Kim, Y., Matthews, B. A., & Baker, F. (2008). Family caregivers and guilt in the context of cancer care. *Psychosomatics, 49*(6), 511–519.

Stær-Jensen, J., Siafarikas, F., Hilde, G., Bø, K., & Ellström Engh, M. (2013). Ultrasonographic evaluation of pelvic organ support during pregnancy. *Obstetrics and Gynecology, 122*(2), 329–336.

Stavaras, C., Pastaka, C., & Papala, M. (2012). Sexual function in pre- and post-menopausal women with obstructive sleep apnea syndrome. *International Journal of Impotence Research, 24*(6), 228–233.

Steiner, M., & Li, T. (2014). Premenstrual syndromes. In M. Curtis, S. Linares, & T. Antoniewicz (Eds.), *Glass' office gynecology*. Philadelphia, PA: Lippincott.

Strachan, E., Saracino, M., Selke, S., Magaret, A., Buchwald, D., & Wald, A. (2011). The effects of daily distress and personality on genital HSV shedding and lesions in a randomized, double-blind, placebo-controlled, crossover trial of acyclovir in HSV-2 seropositive women. *Brain, Behavior and Immunity, 25*(7), 1475–1481.

Strassberg, D. S., & Perelman, M. A. (2009). Sexual dysfunctions. In P. H. Blaney & T. Millon (Eds.), *Oxford textbook of psychopathology* (2nd ed., pp. 399–430). New York, NY: Oxford University Press.

Sturdee, D. W. & Panay, N. (2010). Recommendations for the management of postmenopausal vaginal atrophy. *Climacteric, 13*, 509–522.

Subramanian, S., Bopparaju, S., Desai, A., Wiggins, T., Rambaud, C., & Surani, S. (2010). Sexual dysfunction in women with obstructive sleep apnea. *Sleep & Breathing, 14*(1), 59–62.

Sungur, M. Z., & Gündüz, A. (2014). A comparison of DSM-IV-TR and DSM-5 definitions for sexual dysfunctions: Critiques and challenges. *Journal of Sexual Medicine, 11*, 364–373.

Swift, S. (2000). The distribution of pelvic organ support in a population of female subjects seen for routine gynecologic care. *American Journal of Obstetrics and Gynecology, 183*(2), 277–285.

Swift, S., Tate, S., & Nicholas, J. (2003). Correlation of symptoms with degree of pelvic organ support in a general population of women: What is pelvic organ prolapse? *American Journal of Obstetrics and Gynecology, 189*(2), 372–377.

Swift, S., Woodman, P., O'Boyle, A., Kahn, M. Valley, M., Bland, D., Wang, W., . . . Schaffer, J. (2005). Pelvic Organ Support Study (POSST): The distribution, clinical de?nition, and epidemiologic condition of pelvic organ support defects. *American Journal of Obstetrics and Gynecology, 192*, 795–806.

Tan, O., Bradshaw, K., & Carr, B. R. (2012). Management of vulvovaginal atrophy related sexual dysfunction in postmenopausal women: An up-to-date review. *Menopause, 19*, 109–117.

Tangredi, L. A., Danvers, K., Molony, S. L., & Williams, A. (2008). New CDC recommendations for HIV testing in older adults (2008). *The Nurse Practitioner, 33*(6), 37–44.

The Kinsey Institute—History—Origins [About the Institute]. (2006). *The Kinsey Institute—History—Origins [About the Institute]*. Retrieved July 22, 2014, from http://www.kinseyinstitute.org/about/origins.html

Traish, A. M. (2014). Adverse health effects of testosterone deficiency (TD) in men. *Steroids*. doi:10.1016/j.steroids.2014.05.010

Trichomoniasis—what is trichomoniasis? (2005, January 1). *Trichomoniasis*. Retrieved from http://www.std-gov.org/stds/trichomoniasis.htm

Tronstein, E., Johnston, C., Huang, M. L., Selke, S., Magaret, A., Warren, T, . . ., Wald, A. (2011). Genital shedding of herpes simplex virus among symptomatic and asymptomatic persons with HSV-2 infection. *Journal of the American Medical Association, 305*(14), 1441–1449.

Trowbridge, E. R., & Fenner, D. E. (2007). Practicalities and pitfalls of pessaries in older women. *Clinical Obstetrics and Gynecology, 50*(3), 709–719.

Tsimtsiou, Z., Hatzimouratidis, K., Nakopoulou, E., Kyrana, E., Salpigidis, G., & Hatzichristou, D. (2006). Predictors of physicians' involvement in addressing sexual health issues. *Journal of Sexual Medicine, 3*, 583–588.

Turvey, C. L., Carney, C., Arndt, S., Wallace, R. B., & Herzog, R. (1999). Conjugal loss and syndromal depression in a sample of elders aged 70 years or older. *American Journal of Psychiatry, 156*(10), 1596–1601.

U.S. Cancer Statistics Working Group (2013). *United States Cancer Statistics: 1999–2010 Incidence and Mortality Web-Based Report.* Atlanta, GA: Department of Health and Human Services, Centers for Disease Control and Prevention, and National Cancer Institute.

U.S. Department of Health and Human Services, U.S. Preventive Task Force. *Screening for cervical cancer.* Retrieved from http://www.uspreventiveservicestaskforce.org/3rduspstf/cervcan/cervcanrr.htm

U.S. Full Prescribing Information. (2013). Osphena™ (Ospemifen). [Packet Insert]. Shionogi, Inc. Retrieved from http://www.shionogi.com/pdf/PI/Osphena-PI.pdf

Wald, A., Zeh, J., Selke, S., Warren, T., Ryncarz, A. J., Ashley, R., . . ., Corey, L. (2000). Reactivation of genital herpes simplex virus type 2 infection in asymptomatic seropositive persons. *New England Journal of Medicine, 342*(12), 844–850.

Weber, A. M., & Richter, H. E. (2005). Pelvic organ prolapse. *Obstetrics & Genecology, 106*(3), 615–634.

Whitcomb, E. L., Rortveit, G., Brown, J. S., Creasman, J. M., Thom, D. H., Van Den Eeden, S. K., & Subak, L. L. (2009). Racial differences in pelvic organ prolapse. *Obstetrics and Gynecology, 114*(6), 1271–1277.

World Health Organization. (2011a). Global atlas on cardiovascular disease prevention and control. Geneva, Switzerland: WHO.

World Health Organization. (2011b). Global status report on noncommunicable diseases 2010. Geneva, Switzerland: WHO.

Wiegersma, M., Panman, C. M., Kollen, B. J., Vermeulen, K. M., Schram, A. J., Messelink, E. J., . . . Dekker, J. H. (2014). Pelvic floor muscle training versus watchful waiting or pessary treatment for pelvic organ prolapse (POPPS): Design and participant baseline characteristics of two parallel pragmatic randomized controlled trials in primary care. *Maturitas, 77*, 168–173.

Wohlrab, K., & Pragana, M. (2013). Pessaries for pelvic organ prolapse. *Postgraduate Obstetrics & Gynecology, 33*(21), 1–7.

Wu, J. M., Vaughan, C. P., Goode, P. S., Redden, D. T., Burgio, K. L., Richter, H. E., & Markland, A. D. (2014). Prevalence and trends of symptomatic pelvic floor disorders in U.S. women. *Obstetrics and Gynecology, 123*(1), 141–148.

Xue-Rui, T., Ying, L., Da-Zhong, Y., & Xiao-Jun, C. (2008). Changes of blood pressure and heart rate during sexual activity in healthy adults. *Blood Pressure Monitoring, 13*, 211–217.

Yan, W. J., Yu, N., Yin, T. L., Zou, Y. J., & Yang, J. (2014). A new potential risk factor in patients with erectile dysfunction and premature ejaculation: Folate deficiency. *Asian Journal of Andrology*. doi:10.4103/1008-682X

Sexually Transmitted Infections Guidelines

Jill C. Cash and Moya Cook

Chlamydia

Definition

A. Chlamydia is a sexually transmitted infection (STI) caused by the *Chlamydia trachomatis* bacterium.

Incidence

A. The World Health Organization (WHO) estimates 50 million cases worldwide with more than 4 million cases annually. *Chlamydia* is the most common sexually transmitted organism in the United States. In 2010, the Centers for Disease Control and Prevention (CDC) reported 1,307,893 cases of chlamydia, which is approximately 426 cases per 100,000 population. It is not a CDC reportable infection; however, local health department notification is required. **The United States Preventive Services Task Force is recommending all sexually active women 24 years and younger undergo screening for chlamydia and gonorrhea. These recommendations also apply to older women who previously tested negative, but have developed new risk factors. Pregnant women who tested positive for chlamydia or gonorrhea in the first trimester and have been treated for 3 months should also undergo screening.**

Pathogenesis

A. *Chlamydia trachomatis* is an intracellular bacterium with parasitic properties. It is transmitted by sexual contact or perinatally when a vaginal delivery occurs through an infected birth canal.

Predisposing Factors

A. History of STIs
B. Multiple sexual partners
C. Early age at first coitus
D. Unprotected intercourse

Common Complaints

A. Up to 80% of those infected are asymptomatic
B. Mucopurulent cervical, vaginal, or urethral discharge
C. Dysuria
D. Urinary frequency and urgency
E. Pelvic pain (dull or severe)

Other Signs and Symptoms

A. Cervical friability
B. Cervical motion tenderness
C. Uterine and/or adnexal tenderness

Subjective Data

A. Elicit history of onset of symptoms, location, frequency, duration, aggravating and alleviating factors, and associated symptomatology.
B. Question the patient about the history of other STIs and sexual habits.

Physical Examination

A. Inspect
   1. Males: Observe for anal and/or urethral discharge.
   2. Female pelvic exam: Observe for anal and/or vaginal discharge.
   3. Female speculum exam: Inspect vaginal wall and cervix for discharge and irritation.
B. Palpate
   1. Males
      a. Palpate inguinal lymph nodes.
      b. Milk penis for discharge.
      c. Palpate the groin.
   2. Females
      a. Palpate the inguinal lymph nodes.
      b. Bimanual exam
         i. Milk urethra
         ii. Palpate periurethral and Bartholin glands for exudate.

iii. Assess for cervical motion tenderness.
iv. Assess for uterine and adnexal tenderness.

Diagnostic Tests

A. Culture samples from urethra, endocervix, rectum, pharynx, conjunctiva; culture is gold standard for diagnosis.
   1. Insert brush or swab 1 to 2 cm into endocervix, urethra, or rectum.
   2. Rotate for 30 seconds, withdraw, and place in appropriate culture media for transport.

Differential Diagnoses

A. Chlamydia
B. Gonorrhea
C. Urethritis

Plan

A. General interventions
   1. Culture samples immediately for timely treatment. Consider testing for other STIs such as gonorrhea and trichomoniasis.
B. Patient teaching
   1. See the Section III Patient Teaching Guide for this chapter, "Chlamydia."
   2. Inform the patient of the need for partner notification and treatment. Notification is recommended for any partner with whom the patient has had sexual contact within 30 days of the onset of symptoms or 60 days if asymptomatic.
   3. Stress the importance of completing treatment regimen.
   4. Advise the patient to avoid sexual intercourse during treatment and for 7 more days following the last day of antibiotic treatment.
C. Pharmaceutical therapy
   1. The CDC recommends the following regimens:
      a. Doxycycline 100 mg by mouth twice daily for 7 days
      b. Azithromycin 1 g by mouth in a single dose
   2. Alternative regimen
      a. Levofloxacin 500 mg orally once daily for 7 days
      b. Erythromycin base 500 mg by mouth four times daily for 7 days
      c. Erythromycin ethylsuccinate 800 mg by mouth four times daily for 7 days
      d. Ofloxacin 300 mg by mouth twice daily for 7 days

Follow-Up

A. **The CDC now recommends that all patients follow up in 3 months for repeat culture.**

Consultation/Referral

A. Consult or refer the patient to a physician when treatment with the recommended dosage fails if patient noncompliance and reexposure have been ruled out.

Individual Considerations

A. Pregnancy
   1. Doxycycline, ofloxacin, and levofloxacin are contraindicated during pregnancy.
   2. All pregnant women diagnosed with chlamydial infection should be retested in 3 weeks following treatment.
   3. For women older than 25 years of age, those with new partners, and/or those at high risk for infection, repeat chlamydial testing during the third trimester should be performed.
   4. All pregnant women diagnosed with chlamydial infection during the first trimester should be retested at 3 weeks following treatment, and again in 3 months after treatment.
   5. The CDC recommends the following regimens for pregnant women.
      a. Azithromycin 1 g orally in a single dose or amoxicillin 500 mg orally three times a day for 7 days
      b. For those women intolerant to the recommended regimens:
         i. Erythromycin base 500 mg by mouth four times daily for 7 days
         ii. Erythromycin base 250 mg by mouth four times daily for 14 days
         iii. Erythromycin ethylsuccinate 800 mg by mouth four times daily for 7 days
         iv. Erythromycin ethylsuccinate 400 mg by mouth four times daily for 14 days
B. Adult: Untreated or long-standing chlamydial infection in women may lead to infertility.

Gonorrhea

Definition

A. Gonorrhea is an STI caused by the *Neisseria gonorrheae* organism.

Incidence

A. The WHO estimates 2.5 million cases worldwide. Gonorrhea is a CDC reportable infection. In 2010, the CDC reported that there were 309,341 cases reported in the United States, which is 100.8 cases per 100,000 population. Male-to-female transmission is estimated at 50% to 90%, while female-to-male transmission is estimated at only 20% to 25%. Women account for two-thirds of disseminated gonorrhea with joint infection.

Pathogenesis

A. *Neisseria gonorrhoeae*, a gram-negative diplococcus, is the causative organism. The infection begins with adherence of *N. gonorrhoeae* to the mucosal cells in the genitourinary tract or endocervix. The incubation period is typically 2 to 5 days for urethritis and 5 to 10 days for cervical infection. Rectal and pharyngeal infections are usually asymptomatic. Transmission during vaginal birth is possible and may result in conjunctivitis and blindness in neonates.

Predisposing Factors

A. History of STIs
B. Multiple sexual partners
C. Early age at first coitus

Common Complaints

A. Dysuria
B. Yellow, white, or mucoid urethral discharge in males
C. Greenish, irritating vaginal discharge in females
D. Menstrual irregularities
E. Pelvic pain
F. Fever

Other Signs and Symptoms

A. Asymptomatic
B. Uterine or adnexal tenderness
C. Mucopurulent discharge from endocervix
D. Polyarthralgias
E. Necrotic skin lesions

Subjective Data

A. Elicit history of onset, duration, and location of symptoms. Note aggravating and alleviating factors and associated symptomatology.
B. Question the patient about the history of other STIs and sexual habits.

Physical Examination

A. Check temperature.
B. Inspect
    1. Inspect the skin for necrotic skin lesions.
    2. Males: Inspect for anal and/or urethral discharge; elicit latter by milking penis.
    3. Females
        a. Inspect anus and introitus for discharge; milk urethra.
        b. Speculum exam: Inspect vaginal walls and cervix for discharge and irritation.
C. Palpate
    1. Examine joints for effusion and swelling.
    2. Males: Palpate inguinal lymph nodes.
    3. Females
        a. Palpate inguinal lymph nodes.
        b. Palpate periurethral and Bartholin glands for exudate.
        c. Bimanual exam
            i. Assess for cervical motion, tenderness, and friability.
            ii. Assess for uterine and adnexal tenderness.

Diagnostic Tests

A. Testing of vaginal, endocervical, urethral (men only), or urine specimens
    1. Thayer-Martin and Genprobe are two of the most commonly used culture media.
    2. Collect exudate with cotton-tipped applicator for Thayer-Martin culture.
    3. Use dacron-tipped applicator for Genprobe culture.
    4. Obtain endocervix culture samples by rotating swab in endocervix for a full 30 seconds.
    5. Nucleic acid amplification tests (NAAT)
    6. For persons diagnosed with gonorrhea, testing should also be performed for chlamydia, syphilis, and HIV.
B. During septic joint stage, gonococci can be recovered from the joint by aspiration for culture.

Differential Diagnoses

A. Gonorrhea
B. Chlamydia
C. Arthritis (rheumatoid or septic)

Plan

A. General interventions
    1. The United States Preventive Services Task Force recommendations include:
        a. **All sexually active women 24 years and younger undergo screening for chlamydia and gonorrhea. These recommendations also apply to older women who previously tested negative, but have developed new risk factors. Pregnant women who test positive for gonorrhea in the first trimester and have been treated should undergo screening again in 3 months.**
        b. Prompt diagnosis is needed to begin treatment.
    2. Report positive test results to the health department.
B. Patient teaching
    1. See the Section III Patient Teaching Guide for this chapter, "Gonorrhea."
    2. Stress the importance of completing the medication regimen.
    3. Inform the patient of the need for partner notification and treatment. Notification is recommended for any partner with whom the patient has had sexual contact within 60 days of the onset of symptoms.
C. Pharmaceutical therapy
    1. CDC recommendation: Ceftriaxone 250 mg by intramuscular (IM) injection of a single dose, *or*
    2. If ceftriaxone is not available, CDC recommends: Cefixime 400 mg by mouth in a single dose, *or*

3. Single-dose injectable cephalosporin plus azithromycin 1 g orally single dose or doxycycline 100 mg orally twice daily for 7 days
4. For patients with severe allergy to cephalosporins, the CDC recommends azithromycin 2 g dose orally.
5. The CDC advises that quinolones no longer be used for treatment of gonorrhea due to the increased bacterial resistance.

Follow-Up

A. The CDC no longer recommends a test of cure; however, patients who continue to exhibit symptoms should have culture performed.
B. All individuals should be closely monitored for treatment failure.
C. Reinforce treatment of all sexual partners within the past 60 days of diagnosis.
D. Providers are advised to report all treatment failures to the local or state public health department within 24 hours.

Consultation/Referral

A. Consult with a physician or refer the patient if treatment with the recommended dosage fails and patient noncompliance and reexposure have been ruled out.

Individual Considerations

A. Pregnancy
   1. Treatment with cephalosporins is advised.
   2. If unable to tolerate cephalosporins, azithromycin 2 g orally can be considered.
   3. Presumed or diagnosed coinfections with chlamydia should be treated with azithromycin or amoxicillin.
   4. Pregnant women who test positive for gonorrhea in the first trimester and have been treated should undergo screening again in 3 months.
B. Adults
   1. Untreated or long-standing gonorrheal infection in women can lead to infertility.
   2. For patients with allergies to cephalosporins, using azithromycin treatment is recommended.

Herpes Simplex Virus Type 2

Definition

A. Herpes simplex is a recurring viral disease that is transmitted by direct contact with the secretions or mucosa of an infected individual who is shedding the virus. The virus is usually characterized by painful vesicular lesions that form an ulcer, crust over, then dry without scarring.

Incidence

A. It is estimated that approximately 776,000 people in the United States are infected with the herpes virus annually. Approximately 16.2%, or one out of six, people from 14 to 49 years of age have genital herpes.

Pathogenesis

A. Herpes simplex virus (HSV) is the causative organism. HSV-1 produces oral lesions, and HSV-2 produces genital lesions. Kissing, sexual contact, vaginal delivery, and autoinoculation are all possible routes of transmission. The virus remains dormant, and outbreaks can be stimulated by several factors, including stress, illness, sunlight exposure, and menstruation. A prior infection with HSV-1 can increase the incidence of an asymptomatic HSV-2 infection by threefold.

Predisposing Factors

A. Early age at first coitus
B. Multiple sexual partners
C. History of STIs

Common Complaints

A. Dysuria
B. Pruritus
C. Burning
D. Swelling sensation

Other Signs and Symptoms

A. Primary episode
   1. Painful, vesicular, ulcerated, or crusted oral or genital lesion, singly or in clusters
   2. Flulike syndrome: Fever, chills, headache, malaise, and myalgia
B. Recurrent episode: Less painful lesions and little or no systemic symptoms

Subjective Data

A. Elicit history of onset of symptoms; their location, frequency, and duration; aggravating and alleviating factors; and associated symptomatology.
B. Question the patient about the history of other STIs and sexual habits.

Physical Examination

A. Check temperature.
B. Inspect: Inspect the head, eyes, ears, nose, throat, and mucous membranes for lesions.
C. Palpate: Palpate the neck and abdomen for lymphadenopathy.
D. Pelvic exam
   1. Assess external genitalia, perineum, and anus for lesions.
   2. Assess for inguinal lymphadenopathy.

Diagnostic Tests

A. Viral culture

Clinical diagnosis is often reliable, but confirmation with viral culture should be attempted. Vesicles should be unroofed or crust removed for most reliable sample.

1. Viral isolation: Obtain vesicular fluid by swabbing lesion with cotton- or dacron-tipped applicator.
2. Place applicator in appropriate transport viral medium before drying.
3. Refrigerate until ready for transport.

B. Serology: HSV-specific glycoprotein G2 (HSV-2) and glycoprotein G1 (HSV-1). **Pap smear is not a sensitive test for HSV-2.**

Differential Diagnoses

A. HSV
B. Primary syphilis
C. Chancroid
D. Lymphogranuloma venereum
E. Folliculitis
F. Candidal fissure
G. Vestibular vulvitis
H. Mucocutaneous manifestations of Crohn's disease

Plan

A. General interventions
1. Culture samples immediately to begin treatment.

B. Patient teaching
1. See the Section III Patient Teaching Guide for this chapter, "Herpes Simplex Virus."
2. Advise patients to abstain from sexual activity during prodrome or while lesions are present.
3. Condom use should be encouraged when sexually active.

C. Pharmaceutical therapy: The CDC recommends the following treatment regimens.
1. Primary episode
   a. Acyclovir 200 mg by mouth five times a day for 7 to 10 days or until clinical resolution
   b. Acyclovir 400 mg by mouth three times a day for 7 to 10 days or until clinical resolution
   c. Famciclovir 250 mg by mouth three times a day for 7 to 10 days or until clinical resolution
   d. Valacyclovir 1 g by mouth twice a day for 7 to 10 days or until clinical resolution
2. Recurrent episode: Begin during prodrome.
   a. Acyclovir 400 mg by mouth three times a day for 5 days
   b. Acyclovir 800 mg by mouth twice a day for 5 days
   c. Acyclovir 800 mg by mouth three times a day for 2 days
   d. Famciclovir 125 mg by mouth two times a day for 5 days
   e. Famciclovir 1,000 mg by mouth two times a day for 1 day
   f. Famciclovir 500 mg once, followed by 250 mg two times a day for 2 days
   g. Valacyclovir 500 mg by mouth two times a day for 3 days
   h. Valacyclovir 1 g by mouth once daily for 5 days
3. Daily suppressive therapy
   a. Acyclovir 400 mg by mouth twice daily, famciclovir 250 mg by mouth twice a day, or valacyclovir 500 mg by mouth once a day or 1 g by mouth once a day
   b. Discontinue after 1 year of continuous use to reassess recurrence rate.

Clients receiving daily suppressive therapy of acyclovir 200 mg should use the lowest dose that provides relief from symptoms. Suppressive therapy has been shown to reduce frequency of recurrences by 75% in clients with more than six recurrences per year. It does not eliminate symptomatic or asymptomatic viral shedding or the potential for transmission.

4. Topical acyclovir, famciclovir (Famvir), and valacyclovir (Valtrex) have had mixed results in clinical trials and are not currently recommended by the CDC.

Follow-Up

A. Follow-up is not recommended unless it is warranted by clinical presentation.

Consultation/Referral

A. Consult or refer the patient to a physician when there is prolonged ulceration unresponsive to therapy.

Individual Considerations

A. Pregnancy
1. Acyclovir and valacyclovir are category B for pregnancy and considered safe to use during pregnancy. These medications can be used for treatment as well as for suppression during pregnancy. The American College of Obstetricians and Gynecologists recommends that suppressive therapy begin at approximately 36 weeks gestation to prevent an outbreak of lesions and to increase the chance of having a vaginal delivery (see Table 17.1).
2. Culture lesions if outbreak occurs. Lesion must be crusted for 7 days for vaginal delivery to be an option; otherwise, a cesarean delivery is recommended to avoid transmission of virus to newborn.
3. Pregnant women without genital herpes should be advised to avoid intercourse during the third trimester with partners known or suspected of having genital herpes.
4. Acyclovir allergy: No effective alternatives to acyclovir have been identified.

TABLE 17.1 Pharmacological Treatment of Herpes in Pregnancy

Antiviral	Acyclovir Dosage	Valacyclovir Dosage
Initial lesion outbreak	400 mg tid for 7–10 days	1 g bid for 7–10 days
Recurrent lesions	400 mg tid for 5 days or 800 mg for 5 days	500 mg bid for 3 days
Daily suppression from 36-week gestation until delivery	400 mg tid	500 mg bid

bid, twice a day; tid, three times a day.

B. Partners: Symptomatic partners should be evaluated and treated in the same manner as any patient with genital lesions.
C. Geriatric: Genital herpes is rarely seen in the elderly. Recurrent infection of the buttocks region is not uncommon, especially in females.

Human Papillomavirus

Definition

A. The human papillomavirus (HPV) is an STI. Condylomata acuminata, genital warts, and venereal warts are other names for HPV.

Incidence

A. It is estimated that approximately 79 million Americans are infected with HPV. There are approximately 14 million new infections each year. It is estimated that annually there are 360,000 new cases of genital warts in the United States. Certain strains of HPV are associated with cancer. Annually, in the United States, there are approximately 12,000 women diagnosed with cervical cancer, 2,100 cases of vulvar cancer, 500 cases of vaginal cancer, 600 cases of penile cancer, 2,800 cases of anal cancer in women, 1,500 cases of anal cancer in men, 1,700 oropharyngeal cancers in women, and 6,700 oropharyngeal cancers in men.

Pathogenesis

A. The HPV, a slow-growing DNA virus of the papovavirus family, is the causative organism. Over 70 strains of the virus have been identified, and types 6 and 11 are most associated with genital warts. Types 16, 18, 31, 33, and 35 are high risk and are associated with cervical neoplasia. Warts may appear as early as 1 to 2 months after exposure, but most infections remain subclinical.

Predisposing Factors

A. Early first coitus
B. Multiple sexual partners
C. History of transmitted infections

Common Complaints

A. Painless genital "bumps" or warts
B. Pruritus
C. Bleeding during or after coitus
D. Malodorous vaginal discharge
E. Dysuria

Other Signs and Symptoms

A. Wart-like growths on the genital area, which are elevated and rough or flat and smooth
B. Lesions occurring singly or in clusters, from less than 1 mm to cauliflower-like aggregates
C. Papillomas that are pale pink in color

Subjective Data

A. Elicit history of onset of symptoms, location, frequency, duration, aggravating and alleviating factors, and associated symptomatology.
B. Question the patient about the history of other STIs, sexual behaviors, recent change in sexual partner, and partner's history of STIs.

Physical Examination

A. Inspect
  1. Inspect external genitalia, perineum, and anus for lesions.
  2. Females, speculum exam: Inspect vaginal walls and cervix for lesions.
  3. Application of 3% acetic acid whitens lesions.

Diagnostic Tests

A. Visual identification is adequate in most cases.
B. Cytology: Pap smears are useful for screening. Pap results of koilocytosis, dyskeratosis, keratinizing atypia, atypical inflammation, and parakeratosis are all suggestive of HPV.
C. Histology: Colposcopy with directed biopsy is diagnostic for subclinical lesions, dysplasia, and malignancy.
D. DNA typing: Determination of specific strains is useful in diagnosing subclinical infections (the test is costly and false negatives occur).

Differential Diagnoses

A. HPV
B. Condylomata
C. Molluscum contagiosum
D. Carcinoma

Plan

A. General interventions: Make diagnosis promptly to begin treatment.
B. Patient teaching
   1. See the Section III Patient Teaching Guide for this chapter, "Human Papillomavirus (HPV)."
   2. Explain to the patient that therapy eliminates visible warts but does not eradicate the virus. No therapy has been shown to be effective in eradication of HPV. Ablation of warts may decrease viral load and transmissibility.
   3. Advise the patient to abstain from genital contact while lesions are present.
   4. Education regarding Gardasil vaccine is recommended for girls and boys 9 to 25 years of age for prevention of HPV. The vaccination may help to prevent contracting four of the viruses (6, 11, 16, and 17), which increase the risk of cervical cancer for women.
C. Pharmaceutical therapy
   1. Therapy is not recommended for subclinical infections (absence of exophytic warts).
   2. Trichloroacetic acid (TCA) 80% to 90% solution is applied weekly to visible warts by clinician until warts resolve. If unresolved after six applications, consider other therapy. See the Section II Procedure, "Trichloroacetic Acid (TCA)/Podophyllin Therapy."
   3. Podophyllum resin (Podophyllin) 10% to 25% in tincture of benzoin compound applied weekly to visible warts by clinician until warts resolve.
      a. Application of petroleum jelly on surrounding skin may be used for protection of unaffected areas.
      b. Advise the patient to wash off resin after 4 hours. If unresolved after six applications, consider other therapy.
   4. Apply TCA 80% to 90% to the warts and allow to dry weekly by clinician until warts resolve.
   5. Podofilox 0.5% solution for home treatment, applied to visible warts by the patient twice daily for three consecutive days, followed by 4 days without treatment. Cycle is repeated up to four times.
   6. Imiquimod 5% (Aldara) cream applied to wart, left on for 6 to 10 hours, then washed with mild soap. Use daily, three times a week (Monday, Wednesday, Friday), until wart resolves or up to 16 weeks.
D. Medical/surgical management: Cryotherapy, electrodessication, electrocautery, carbon dioxide laser, and surgical excision are options to be considered for patients with large or extensive lesions or refractory disease.

Follow-Up

A. Short-term follow-up is not recommended if the patient is asymptomatic after treatment.
B. **The CDC does not recommend more frequent Pap smears for women with external warts.**
C. Long-term follow-up should include annual Pap smears and pelvic exams. Encourage the patient to self-examine genitalia.

Consultation/Referral

A. Consult or refer the patient to a physician when lesions persist after six consecutive treatments or when cervical or rectal warts are diagnosed.

Individual Considerations

A. Pregnancy: Podophyllum and podofilox are contraindicated during pregnancy.
B. Partners: Treatment is recommended if visible lesions are present.
C. Geriatric
   1. Verrucous carcinoma and vulvar intraepithelial neoplasia (VIN) can be indistinguishable from condyloma. Older women are more likely to have VIN or carcinoma.
   2. Diagnosis made by biopsy; colposcopy is strongly advised.
   3. Immunocompetence should be investigated in new or recurrent condyloma.

Syphilis

Definition

A. Syphilis is an STI characterized by distinct primary, secondary, and tertiary stages that occur over several years or decades. Latent or inactive periods occur between the stages. Early latent is less than 1 year after infection; late latent is more than 1 year after infection. **Health department notification of infection is required by law in all states.**

Incidence

A. In 2000, syphilis was virtually nonexistent. Between 2005 and 2013 the CDC reported that the number of primary and secondary cases of syphilis reported each year more than doubled. The annual rate increased from 2.5 to 5.3 cases per 100,000. The increase in cases among men was 5.1 in 2005 to 9.8 in 2013. The reported cases of primary and secondary syphilis remain highest in homosexual and bisexual men.

Pathogenesis

A. *Treponema pallidum*, a spirochete bacterium, is the causative organism that infects the mucous membrane through microscopic abrasions during intercourse. The growth characteristics and metabolism of *T. palladium* are due to the inability to grow the organism in a culture.

Predisposing Factors

A. History of STIs
B. Multiple sexual partners
C. Illicit drug use
D. Prostitution

Common Complaints

A. Genital lesion, generalized rash involving palms and soles, mucous patches, and condyloma latum are common.

Other Signs and Symptoms

A. Primary syphilis
   1. Chancre that is painless or minimally painful
   2. Round, indurated lesion with little or no purulent exudate
   3. Regional bilateral lymphadenopathy
B. Secondary syphilis
   1. Generalized maculopapular rash that is nonpruritic and copper colored, on palms or soles; may be erythematous or scaly
   2. Mucous patches; painless, white, mucous membrane lesions
   3. Generalized lymphadenopathy; flulike syndrome including fever, headache, sore throat, and malaise
   4. Patchy alopecia
C. Tertiary syphilis
   1. Gumma: Locally destructive granulomatous tumors involving various organs or systems; commonly seen on liver but can occur on other organs (heart, brain, skin, bone, testis).
   2. Cardiovascular: Aortic involvement, aneurysms, and valve insufficiency
   3. Neurologic: Tabes dorsalis and general paresis
D. Latent syphilis: Asymptomatic

Latent-phase syphilis manifests itself after treatment failure or no history of treatment. Spirochete can lie dormant for years.

E. Congenital syphilis: Symptoms range from asymptomatic to fatal.

Subjective Data

A. Elicit history of onset, location, frequency, duration of symptoms; aggravating and alleviating factors; and associated symptomatology.
B. Question the patient about history of other STIs, illicit drug use, and sexual habits.

Physical Examination

A. Check temperature, pulse, respirations, and blood pressure.
B. Inspect
   1. Inspect the skin; note lesions and rashes.
   2. Observe the head; note patchy alopecia.
   3. Examine the mouth and throat; note lesions.
   4. Inspect the genital and rectal area; note lesions and rashes.
C. Palpate: Palpate the lymph nodes (neck, supraclavicular, axillary, epitrochlear, and inguinal regions).
D. Auscultate: Auscultate heart and lungs.
E. Neurologic exam
   1. Assess sensory functioning.
   2. Test cranial nerves, first through twelfth.

Diagnostic Tests

Evaluate for other STIs for patients presenting with syphilis.

A. Serology: Nontreponemal tests
   1. Venereal Disease Research Laboratory (VDRL) test
   2. Rapid plasma reagin (RPR) tests
   3. HIV

Results are reactive (positive) or nonreactive (negative). Titers correlate with active disease and should be quantitative. These tests are equally valid but cannot be compared because of titer differences (RPR is slightly higher than VDRL). All reactive results require confirmation with treponemal tests.

B. Serology: Treponemal tests
   1. Fluorescent treponemal antibody absorption (FTA-ABS) test
   2. Microhemagglutination assay for antibody to *T. pallidum*

Once FTA-ABS for antibody to T. pallidum, *VDRL, and RPR are reactive, these tests usually remain reactive for life.*

C. Cerebrospinal fluid (CSF) culture to detect neurosyphilis
D. Microscopy: *T. pallidum* cannot be seen with light microscopy; dark-field microscopy exam of the serous exudate from lesions is the definitive test for syphilis. Properly equipped labs with specially trained personnel must be available for this test.

Differential Diagnoses

A. Syphilis
B. HSV

Plan

A. General interventions: Staging of the disease may be difficult but guides management decisions.

B. Patient teaching
   1. See the Section III Patient Teaching Guide for this chapter, "Syphilis."
   2. Advise the patient to abstain from sexual activity until treatment is completed.
   3. Inform the patient of Jarisch–Herxheimer reaction (fever, headache, myalgia) that may occur within the first 24 hours of treatment. Antipyretics may be prescribed.
   4. Discuss the importance of partner notification.
   5. Stress the importance of complying with follow-up regimen
C. Pharmaceutical therapy: The CDC recommends the following treatment regimens.
   1. Primary syphilis, secondary syphilis, early latent syphilis.
      a. Adults: Benzathine penicillin G 2.4 million units injected IM in a single dose
   2. Late latent syphilis, latent syphilis of unknown duration, late syphilis (manage with expert consultation)
      a. Adults: Benzathine penicillin G 7.2 million units total, administered as three doses (2.4 million units each) injected IM at 1-week intervals
   3. Neurosyphilis (manage with expert consultation)
      a. Adults: Aqueous crystalline penicillin G, 18 to 24 million units daily, 2 to 4 million units administered by intravenous (IV) every 4 hours for 10 to 14 days
      b. Adults: Procaine penicillin 2 to 4 million units injected IM daily plus probenecid 500 mg by mouth four times a day, both for 10 to 14 days
   4. Primary syphilis, secondary syphilis, latent syphilis, late latent syphilis in (nonpregnant) patient with penicillin allergy: Doxycycline 100 mg by mouth twice daily for 2 weeks.
   5. Latent syphilis of unknown duration, late syphilis: Treat with above regimen for infections of less than 1 year duration. If greater than 1 year, treat with above regimen for 4 weeks.
   6. For pregnant patients with penicillin allergy, penicillin treatment after desensitization is recommended for the following reasons:
      a. Penicillin is effective for preventing transmission and treating the infected fetus.
      b. Doxycycline and tetracycline are contraindicated in pregnancy.
      c. Erythromycin may not cure the infected fetus.

Follow-Up

A. Primary and secondary syphilis: Clinical and serologic exams should be conducted at 6 and 12 months. Absence of fourfold decrease at 3 months is indicative of treatment failure.
B. Latent syphilis: Clinical and serologic exams should be conducted at 6, 12, and 24 months. Absence of fourfold decrease within 12 to 24 months is indicative of treatment failure.
C. Tertiary syphilis: Minimal evidence regarding follow-up exists. Follow-up largely depends on nature of lesions.
D. Neurosyphilis: CSF examination should take place every 6 months until cell count is normal.

Consultation/Referral

A. Consult or refer the patient to a physician when the recommended treatment fails and patient noncompliance and reexposure have been ruled out, or when neurosyphilis is diagnosed.

Individual Considerations

A. Pregnancy
   1. Draw blood samples for RPR/VDRL from all prenatal patients.
   2. Administer appropriate regimen of penicillin for the patient's stage of syphilis. Consider a second dose of penicillin 1 week after the initial treatment.
   3. Patients who are allergic to penicillin should be desensitized and treated with penicillin during pregnancy.
   4. Follow-up: Perform serologic tests monthly until adequacy of treatment has been ensured.
   5. The Jarisch–Herxheimer reaction may predispose women to premature labor or fetal distress if treatment occurs in the second half of the pregnancy. Advise these patients to immediately seek medical attention if they experience uterine contractions or changes in fetal movement.
   6. Abortions and stillbirths are common.
B. Partners: Identify at-risk partners who have had sexual contact with the patient within these time frames:
   1. Primary syphilis: 3 months plus duration of symptoms
   2. Secondary syphilis: 6 months plus duration of symptoms
   3. Early latent syphilis: 1 year
C. Geriatric
   1. Dementia, tremors, and pupillary changes are the result of long-term untreated syphilis.
   2. The CSF should be tested using the FTA-ABS test. The VDRL is usually not adequate.
   3. Syphilis is uncommon in the elderly in developed countries; however, it is very common worldwide.

Trichomoniasis

Definition

A. Trichomoniasis is an STI caused by the *Trichomonas vaginalist* protozoan. Nonsexual transmission by means of fomites is possible but rare.

Incidence

A. Trichomoniasis is not a CDC reportable infection. Therefore, exact incidence is unavailable. The CDC estimates that 3.7 million people have the infection.

Pathogenesis

A. *Trichomonas vaginalis*, a flagellated protozoan, is the causative organism.

Predisposing Factors

A. History of STIs
B. Multiple sexual partners

Common Complaints

A. Copious, yellow-green, or watery gray vaginal discharge
B. Vaginal odor
C. Dysuria
D. Dyspareunia
E. Postcoital spotting or bleeding
F. Abdominal discomfort
G. Pruritus

Other Signs and Symptoms

A. Asymptomatic
B. Perineal irritation

Subjective Data

A. Elicit history of onset, location, frequency, duration of symptoms, and aggravating and alleviating factors; note associated symptomatology.
B. Question the patient about history of other STIs or vaginal infections, changes and characteristics of vaginal discharge, and recent change in sexual partner.

Physical Examination

A. Check temperature.
B. Inspect: Inspect introitus for discharge and irritation.
C. Speculum exam
   1. Inspect the vaginal walls for discharge and irritation.
   2. Inspect the cervix for discharge, erythema, punctate hemorrhages (strawberry-patch cervix), and friability.
D. Bimanual exam
   1. Assess for cervical motion tenderness.
   2. Palpate for uterine and adnexal tenderness.

Diagnostic Tests

A. Wet prep: Presence of motile, flagellated trichomonads. Increased number of white blood cells (> 0.10 per high-power field) may be present.
B. Culture sample in Diamond's or Kupferberg's medium.
   1. This is the most sensitive and specific diagnostic method.
   2. It is expensive, and culture sample is not widely available.
C. Pap smear: Report may include trichomonads, but sensitivity is low.
   1. If trichomonads are noted on Pap smear, the patient should be reexamined and diagnosis confirmed with a wet prep.
D. Vaginal pH is usually greater than 4.5.
E. The potassium hydroxide/wet prep "whiff test" may be positive.

Differential Diagnoses

A. Trichomoniasis
B. Bacterial vaginosis
C. Vulvovaginal candidiasis
D. Chlamydia
E. Gonorrhea
F. Pelvic inflammatory disease
G. Foreign-body vaginitis

Plan

A. General interventions: Prompt diagnosis helps to initiate treatment.
B. Patient teaching
   1. See the Section III Patient Teaching Guide for this chapter, "Trichomoniasis."
   2. Advise the patient to abstain from sexual activity until treatment is complete.
   3. Advise the patient to avoid alcohol consumption during and 24 hours after metronidazole treatment due to the possible Antabuse effect from the medication.
   4. Inform the patient that urine may darken in color during treatment.
   5. Inform the patient of a possible metallic taste in the mouth during treatment.
C. Pharmaceutical therapy
   1. **Drug of choice: Metronidazole 2 g orally in a single dose or tinidazole 2 g orally in a single dose**
   2. Alternative regimen: Metronidazole 500 mg by mouth twice daily for 7 days. Expected cure rate from either regimen is 95%.
   3. Treatment failure: The CDC recommends retreatment with metronidazole 500 mg by mouth twice daily for 7 days.
   4. If repeated failure occurs, treat with metronidazole 2 g by mouth four times daily for 3 to 5 days.
   5. Metronidazole gel is unlikely to achieve therapeutic levels in the urethra or perivaginal glands. It is a considerably less efficacious treatment than oral preparations and is *not* recommended for use.

Follow-Up

A. Immediate follow-up is not recommended if the patient is initially asymptomatic or symptoms are relieved by treatment. Due to concern of resistance, a 3-month follow-up for sexually active women is recommended.

Consultation/Referral

A. Consult or refer the patient to a physician when recommended treatment fails and patient noncompliance and reexposure have been ruled out.
B. The CDC guidelines recommend consultation and susceptibility testing for treatment failures.

Individual Considerations

A. Pregnancy
   1. First trimester: Metronidazole is contraindicated.
   2. Palliative treatment: Clotrimazole 1% vaginal cream one applicator full daily at bedtime for 7 days
   3. Second and third trimester: Metronidazole 2 g by mouth one time
   4. Lactation: Metronidazole 2 g by mouth one time; discontinue breastfeeding during and 24 hours after treatment. Pumping and discarding milk is recommended.
B. Partners: Recommended treatment is metronidazole 2 g orally one time.
C. Geriatric
   1. Uncommon pathogen in postmenopausal women
   2. Symptoms are vulvar irritation with discharge.
   3. Diagnose with wet prep
   4. Treat with metronidazole 1 g in the morning and 1 g in the evening
D. Patients with HIV
   1. Screen all women at first visit and annually for trichomoniasis. Treatment for trichomoniasis: Multiple dose therapy: Metronidazole 500 mg twice a day for 7 days

Bibliography

AANP SmartBrief. (2014). *USPSTF recommends wider STD screening for women.* Retrieved from http://r.smartbrief.com/resp/gdzoDRcmAYIVaCfMfDlgfMfCAhxQ

Albrecht, M. (2014). *Epidemiology, clinical manifestations, and diagnosis of genital herpes simplex virus infection.* Retrieved from http://www.uptodate.com/contents/epidemiology-clinical-manifestations-and-diagnosis-of-genital-herpes-simplex-virus-infection?source=search_results&search=herpes+simplex+2&selectedTitle=1%7E68

American College of Obstetricians and Gynecologists Committee on Practice Bulletins. (2007). ACOG Practice Bulletin. *Clinical management guidelines for obstetrician-gynecologists.* No. 82 June 2007. Management of herpes in pregnancy. *Obstetrics and Gynecology, 109*(6), 1489–1498.

Borhart, J., & Birnbaumer, D. (2011). Emergency department management of sexually transmitted infections. *Emergency Medicine Clinics of North America, 29*(3), 587–603.

Centers for Disease Control and Prevention. (2011a). *Sexually transmitted diseases treatment guidelines, 2010.* Retrieved from www.cdc.gove/std/treatment/2010/vaginal-discharge.htm

Centers for Disease Control and Prevention. (2011b). *Sexually transmitted diseases treatment guidelines, 2010.* Retrieved from http://www.cdc.gov/std/treatment/2010/genital-ulcers.htm#hsv

Centers for Disease Control and Prevention. (2013a). *Gonorrhea.* Retrieved from www.cdc.gov/std/gonorrhea/default.htm

Centers for Disease Control and Prevention. (2013b). *Chlamydia.* Retrieved from www.cdc.gov/std/chlamydia/default.htm

Centers for Disease Control and Prevention. (2013c). *Genital herpes—CDC fact sheet.* Retrieved from http://www.cdc.gov/std/herpes/stdfact-herpes.htm

Centers for Disease Control and Prevention. (2013d). *Incidence, prevalence, and cost of sexually transmitted infections in the United States.* Retrieved from www.cdc.gov/std/stats/STI-Estimates_fact-Sheet- Reb-2013.pdf

Centers for Disease Control and Prevention. (2013e). *Genital HPV infection—Fact sheet.* Retrieved from www.cdc.gov/std/HPV/STDFact-HPV.htm

Fantasia, H., Fontenot, H. B., Sutherland, M., & Harris, A. L. (2011). Sexually transmitted infections in women. *Nursing for Women's Health, 15*(1), 46–58. doi:10.1111/j.1751-486X.2011.01610.x. Retrieved from http://dx.doi.org.ezproxy.waterfield.murraystate.edu

Hoover, K., & Tao, G. (2008). Missed opportunities for chlamydia screening of young women in the United States. *Obstetrics and Gynecology, 111*(5), 1097–1102.

Kao, T., & Manczak, M. (2013). Family influences on adolescents' birth control and condom use, likelihood of sexually transmitted infections. *Journal of School Nursing, 29*(1), 61–70.

Mark, H., Jordan, E. T., Cruz, J., & Warren, N. (2012). What's new in sexually transmitted infection management: Changes in the 2010 guidelines from the Centers for Disease Control and Prevention. *Journal of Midwifery & Women's Health, 57*(3), 276–284.

O'Connor, C., & Shubkin, C. (2012). Adolescent STIs for primary care providers. *Current Opinion in Pediatrics, 24*(5), 647–655.

Peate, I. (2011). Managing sexually transmitted infections. *Practice Nursing, 22*(6), 285–289.

Richardson, K. K., & Shannon, M. T. (2012). STI screening & treatment in pregnancy. *Nurse Practitioner, 37*(12), 30–37.

Schreiber, C., Meyer, C., Creinin, M., Barnart, K., & Hillier, S. (2006). Effects of long-term use of nonoxynol-9 on vaginal-flora. *Obstetrics and Gynecology, 111*(5), 1097–1102.

CHAPTER EIGHTEEN

Infectious Disease Guidelines

Cheryl A. Glass and Debbie Croley

Cytomegalovirus

Definition

A. Cytomegalovirus (CMV) is in the herpesvirus family, which includes varicella-zoster (chickenpox) and infectious mononucleosis (Epstein–Barr virus [EBV]). Differences in CMV genotypes may be associated with differences in virulence. CMV is responsible for a viral infection with a high rate of asymptomatic excretion. Shedding of the virus takes place intermittently. CMV can be isolated in cell culture from urine, pharynx, respiratory secretions, human milk, tears, saliva, semen, cervical secretions, and body fluids such as blood and amniotic fluid. Cytomegalic cells can be found in tissue, including the lung, liver, kidney, intestine, adrenal gland, and the central nervous system (CNS).

B. CMV persists in latent form after a primary infection, and reactivation can occur years later, particularly under conditions of immunosuppression, transplantation, and pregnancy. CMV is one of the **TORCH** infections (**T**oxoplasmosis, **O**ther [i.e., hepatitis and syphilis], **R**ubella, **C**MV, and **H**erpes infections).

C. The most common illness caused by CMV is retinitis.

Incidence

A. CMV is found worldwide in all ages, races, and ethnic groups. Seropositivity increases with age, ranging from 40% to 100% depending on geography, cultures, childrearing practices, and socioeconomic status. Approximately 50% of blood donors have been exposed to CMV, and 10% carry CMV in white blood cells (WBCs). The incidence of horizontal transmission of CMV occurring in settings such as day care ranges from 10% to over 80% from the exposure to saliva and urine. Another increase in CMV is noted in adolescence secondary to sexual activity.

B. This invasive disease is most notable in immunocompromised patients.
   1. End-stage renal disease
   2. Solid-organ transplant
   3. Bone marrow transplant
   4. Long-term corticosteroids
   5. HIV
      a. Combination antiretroviral therapy (ART) has reduced the risk of CMV in people with HIV by 75%.
      b. The risk of CMV is the highest in HIV patients when their CD4 cell counts are below 50 cells/μL. CMV is rare if the CD4 count is more than 100 cells/μL.

C. CMV is the most common congenital infection in the United States. The incidence of congenital vertical transmission of CMV ranges from 0.2% to 2.5%. Most newborns appear normal and are asymptomatic; however, 5% to 15% congenitally infected newborns will have symptoms at delivery. Prenatal CMV infections occur from contact with maternal cervicovaginal secretions during delivery or from breast milk ingestion. Preterm infants are at the greatest risk to acquire CMV from breast milk.

Pathogenesis

A. Human CMV, a DNA virus, is a member of the herpesvirus group. This virus is transmitted both horizontally (by direct person-to-person contact with virus-containing secretions) and vertically (from mother to infant before, during, or after birth). Infections have no seasonal correlation.

B. The incubation period for horizontally transmitted CMV infections in households is unknown. Primary CMV infection usually manifests itself in 4 to 7 weeks and may persist as long as 16 to 20 weeks after initial infection. CMV disease is most likely 30 to 60 days after transplant.

C. The CMV remains in a person for life; there is no treatment that will permanently eliminate CMV infection.

Predisposing Factors

A. Exposure to young children (especially those in day care centers)
B. Sexual contact (cervicovaginal secretions and semen)
C. Blood transfusions: **Patients with impaired immune function (e.g., bone marrow and organ transplant recipients, premature babies) are at risk for CMV infection from contaminated transfused blood.**
D. Hospital or occupational exposure: Universal precautions are considered adequate to prevent transmission of CMV within hospitals. Nosocomial transmission from person to person has not been documented. Isolation is not recommended.
E. Pregnancy: Pregnant health care workers are not restricted from caring for CMV-infected patients and should follow universal precautions.
F. Transplacental transmission
G. Ascending infection from the cervix
H. Tissue or organ transplantation
I. Household spread among family members
J. Breast milk

Common Complaints

A. Mononucleosis-like syndrome
B. Fever
C. Overwhelming fatigue
D. Pharyngitis
E. Ulcerative lesions in the mouth
F. Loss of vision (retinal detachment may occur up to 50% to 60% in the first year after diagnosis)

Other Signs and Symptoms

A. Mothers: Asymptomatic or mononucleosis-like syndrome
B. Adults
   1. Visual changes: Floaters or loss of visual fields on one side
   2. Retinitis
   3. Arthralgias
   4. Nausea, abdominal cramping, and vomiting (includes hematemesis)
   5. Prolonged fever
   6. Mild hepatitis
   7. Headache
   8. Gastritis presents with abdominal pain and colitis present as a diarrheal illness. CMV may infect the gastrointestinal (GI) tract from the oral cavity through the colon. The typical manifestation of disease is ulcerative lesions. In the mouth, these may be indistinguishable from ulcers caused by herpes simplex virus (HSV) or aphthous ulceration.
C. Immunocompromised persons
   1. Bacterial: Pneumonia, retinitis, myocarditis, and aseptic meningitis
   2. Anemia
   3. Thrombocytopenia

Subjective Data

A. Review onset of presenting signs, symptoms, and their duration.
B. Review the patient's history for recent upper respiratory infection (URI) and mononucleosis like symptoms.
C. Elicit information concerning contact with any person known to be CMV infected.
D. Review history for other family members with similar symptoms.
E. Ask the patient about any occupational exposure.
F. Review the patient's exposure to children in day care centers.
G. Review recent blood transfusions and/or organ transplantation.
H. Determine the patient's history for risk factors or presence of HIV.
   1. If known HIV, does the patient know his or her last viral load CD4 count?
   2. Is the patient taking ART? When were the antivirals started?
I. Ask family members if the patient has been confused, lethargic, or withdrawn, or has exhibited personality changes (CMV encephalitis, dementia).

Physical Examination

A. Check temperature, pulse, respirations, blood pressure, and weight (document serial weight loss).
B. Inspect
   1. Inspect skin for jaundice and petechiae.
   2. Conduct a detailed eye exam.
      a. **CMV infection may appear as yellow-white areas with perivascular exudates and hemorrhage, having a "cottage cheese and ketchup" appearance at either the periphery or the center of the fundus.**
         i. Differentiating suspected CMV retinitis and cotton wool spots is essential. Cotton wool spots appear as small, fluffy white lesions with indistinct margins and are not associated with exudates or hemorrhages.
      b. Evaluate field of vision.
   3. Perform ear and nasal exam.
   4. Perform an oral/throat exam. In the mouth, ulcerative lesions may be indistinguishable from ulcers caused by HSV or aphthous ulcers.

5. Conduct hearing test.
6. Evaluate thoroughly for lymphadenopathy

C. Auscultate
1. Auscultate the heart.
2. Auscultate the lungs.

D. Palpate
1. Palpate the abdomen.
   a. Note organomegaly
   b. Mild to moderate abdominal pain and tenderness associated with GI colitis.
2. Pregnancy: Palpate fundal height and evaluate for suspected intrauterine growth restriction (IUGR).

E. Neurologic exam
1. Assess all cranial nerves.
2. Sensation (deficits may occur without loss of vibratory sense and proprioception).
3. Deep tendon reflexes
4. Motor skills and coordination
5. Gait

Diagnostic Tests

A. **Viral culture of specimen from urine, cervix, vagina, nasopharynx, and saliva.**
1. **Viral culture is the best means of diagnosing acute CMV infections, although it does not distinguish between primary and recurrent disease. Urine contains high titers of the virus because CMV is relatively stable in urine.**

B. Complete blood count (CBC) with differential: Differential WBC count reveals increased lymphocytes, many of which are atypical.

C. Total direct and indirect serum bilirubin

D. Liver function: Alanine aminotransferase (ALT) and aspartate aminotransferase (AST)

E. Colonoscopy with biopsy

F. Serology for CMV immunoglobulin G (IgG) and IgM: **Only the recovery of the virus from a target organ provides unequivocal evidence that the disease is caused by CMV infection. However, a fourfold or greater rise in IgG-specific antibody titer is usually considered evidence of acute infection.**

G. Amniocentesis for PCR to detect CMV DNA is the preferred diagnostic approach for detecting the infected fetus.

H. Immunocompromised patients, especially transplant recipients, may be monitored for viral surveillance weekly using surrogate markers for viremia-PCR.

I. Chest x-ray if indicated

J. CT scan if indicated to evaluate abnormalities of the brain in the presence of an abnormal neurologic examination, seizures, and microcephaly.

K. Sensorineural hearing evaluation

L. **Routine maternal screening for CMV infection is not recommended during pregnancy. Lab tests that are currently available generally cannot conclusively determine whether a primary CMV infection has occurred during the pregnancy.**

Differential Diagnoses

A. CMV
B. Other TORCH infections
C. HIV
D. Viral: Autoimmune hepatitis or hepatitis A to E
E. Enteroviruses
F. Fever of unknown origin (FUO)

Plan

A. General interventions
1. Provide support for the patient and family.
2. Contact social services if long-term support will be required for these infants/families.
3. Rest is vital.

B. Patient teaching
1. Patients with splenomegaly should avoid activity that may increase the risk of injury to the spleen, such as contact sports and heavy lifting.
2. Mothers infected with CMV should be discouraged from breastfeeding because CMV is secreted in breast milk. CMV-specific IgM antibodies are present in only 80% of patients with primary CMV infections and in 20% of patients with recurrent infections. Therefore, a negative result does not exclude the diagnosis of CMV.
3. Isolation is not required.
4. Use universal precautions, especially good hand washing.
5. Do not share eating or drinking utensils, drinks, or food with toddlers or young children.
6. Educate about the importance of ART in treating CMV.
   a. Patients with CMV retinitis may require lifelong suppressive therapy to prevent blindness. Vision loss will not return to pre-CMV status.
   b. Report visual deterioration immediately.

C. Pharmaceutical therapy
1. Drug of choice: Ganciclovir (Cytovene) for CMV retinitis; treatment is divided into an induction and a maintenance phase.
   a. The safety of ganciclovir in pregnancy has not been established.
   b. Patients receiving ganciclovir should have blood counts monitored closely due to dose-dependent bone marrow suppression. Monitor for leukopenia, neutropenia, anemia, or thrombocytopenia. Stop ganciclovir when neutrophil counts are less than 500/mm^3. Growth factors may be necessary.

c. The dose should be decreased in patients with impaired renal function. Monitor creatinine.
d. Ganciclovir induction: 5 mg/kg per dose intravenously (IV) administered over 1 hour every 12 hours for 14 to 21 days, depending on the clinical and virologic response. Oral ganciclovir should not be used for induction.
e. Ganciclovir maintenance
    i. A single daily dose of 5 mg/kg may be administered IV every other day or 5 days a week, skipping the weekend.
    ii. Oral ganciclovir 1 g orally three times a day may be used for maintenance/prophylaxis in some patients, but poor oral availability makes it less effective than IV administration.
f. Although ganciclovir has appeared to be beneficial in the treatment of some congenitally infected infants, its use is controversial and is considered mainly for high-risk patients with severe congenital CMV.

2. Alternative drug therapy: Foscarnet (Foscavir)
    a. Used in ganciclovir-resistant CMV retinitis and herpes simplex disease.
    b. The safety of foscarnet in pregnancy has not been established.
    c. Foscarnet is nephrotoxic. Meticulous attention must be paid to renal function. Small changes in creatinine require new calculation for renal clearance. Obtain a 24-hour serum creatinine at baseline and discontinue if serum creatinine is less than 0.4 gL/min/kg.
    d. Patients must be well hydrated.
    e. Foscarnet
        i. Foscarnet induction: 60 mg/kg IV every 8 hours or 90 to 120 mg/kg IV every 12 hours for 14 to 21 days for the induction of CMV retinitis
        ii. Foscarnet maintenance: 90 to 120 mg/kg IV per day as a single infusion. Infusion rate should not exceed 1 mg/kg/min.
3. Cidofovir (S)
    a. Cidofovir induction: 5 mg/kg IV once a week for 2 weeks
    b. Cidofovir maintenance: 5 mg/kg IV every 2 weeks
    c. Probenecid is given on the day of the IV infusion in order to reduce the renal uptake of cidofovir.
4. CMV immunoglobulin IV: Initial dose is 150 mg/kg and is followed by gradually reduced doses once every 2 weeks for 16 weeks. Currently available antiviral agents do not cure CMV disease in HIV-infected patients.
5. Immune globulin (IG) or CMV hyperimmune globulin CytoGam may be utilized for passive immunoprophylaxis, especially in bone marrow and organ transplant recipients, to help develop antibodies and protect against CMV infection.
6. CMV vaccines are currently in clinical trials.

Follow-Up

A. **Because retinitis is the most common manifestation of CMV disease, patients with CNS, GI, or pulmonary disease should be assessed with a dilated retinal examination to detect subclinical retinal disease.**
B. Monitor CBC, serum creatinine, and electrolytes (especially calcium and magnesium) every week.
C. The patient should be seen for reports of excessive bruising or bleeding, jaundice, or abnormal CNS functioning.

Consultation/Referral

A. Consultation with an infectious disease specialist is indicated for acute infection, especially for immunocompromised patients.
B. Antivirals have many adverse effects and are best managed by the physician who has experience using these drugs.
C. Consultation with a hematologist is needed in severe cases, especially with hemolytic anemia and thrombocytopenia.
D. Consultation with a neurologist is indicated for meningitis, encephalitis, polyneuritis, and Guillain–Barré syndrome
E. Consultation with an ophthalmologist is needed on an emergent basis for a dilated retinal examination due to the risks of blindness. Serial dilated retinal examinations should be done after ART induction therapy and monthly thereafter.
F. Consultation with a perinatologist is indicated for pregnant patients. Evaluation may include ultrasonography, amniocentesis, and percutaneous umbilical blood sampling (PUBS).
G. Refer to a gastroenterologist for an endoscopic evaluation with tissue biopsies.

Individual Considerations

A. Pregnancy
    1. Between 55% and 85% of pregnant women are immune to CMV, with a higher prevalence of immunity in lower socioeconomic populations.
    2. Susceptible pregnant women have a 2% to 2.5% risk of acquiring primary CMV during pregnancy. Those with prior immunity have a 1% chance of reactivation of latent infection.

3. Recovery of CMV from the cervix or urine of women at or before the time of delivery does not warrant a cesarean section.

B. Perinatal transmission of CMV occurs by four routes:
   1. In utero transplacental infections
   2. Ascending infections from the cervix
   3. Exposure to infected secretions from the lower genital tract during delivery
   4. Ingestion of infected breast milk

Because CMV is spread by intimate contact with infectious secretions, hand washing after exposure to secretions is particularly important for pregnant health care workers.

C. Adults
   1. Occupational exposure: **Risk often appears to be greatest for childcare personnel who care for children younger than 2 years of age.**
   2. Routine serologic screening for childcare staff is not currently recommended.
   3. Pregnant personnel who may be in contact with CMV-infected patients should be counseled regarding the risk of acquiring CMV infection and about the need to practice good hygiene, particularly hand washing. There is no need for routinely transferring personnel to other work situations.

D. Geriatrics
   1. CMV infection increases the mortality rate in healthy older people based on an excess—a near doubling—of vascular deaths.
   2. Although uncommon, CMV colitis in the elderly immunocompromised person is potentially life-threatening, particularly in persons with chronic renal disease.
      a. The symptoms of CMV colitis are nonspecific.
         i. The most common presentation is bloody diarrhea.
         ii. Colonoscopy findings are variable and nonspecific; therefore, a biopsy is critical for the diagnosis.

Encephalitis

Definition

A. Encephalitis is the inflammation of cerebral tissue caused by viral agents or other toxins. The syndrome of acute encephalitis shares many clinical features with acute meningitis. Patients with either syndrome present with fever, headache, and altered states of consciousness. In most cases of encephalitis, there is some concomitant meningeal inflammation, in addition to the cephalitic component, a condition commonly referred to as meningoencephalitis.

Incidence

A. Incidence is unknown. Japanese encephalitis (JE) occurs in annual epidemics in Asia during the rainy season. The prevalence of JE (arbovirus) is related to ecologic and climatic conditions that affect the natural transmission cycles during summer months (June–September).

B. Arboviruses (Eastern or Western equine, St. Louis, and West Nile virus [WNV]) cause disease when mosquitoes are active, whereas walking in the woods or marshy areas with high tick populations might suggest other viral encephalitides such as Colorado tick fever or nonviral etiologies such as Lyme disease or Rocky Mountain Spotted Fever (RMSF).

C. Herpes encephalitis has the highest morbidity and mortality of the common viral encephalitides and may occur at any time. The mortality rate for untreated patients is 70%; less than 5% of survivors have normal neurologic function. Herpes simplex type 1 is the most common cause of sporadic encephalitis. The most important viral etiology to rule out is HSV, since this clinical entity is usually fatal if left untreated. Survival and recovery from neurologic sequelae are related to the mental status at the time of acyclovir initiation.

D. Encephalopathy is the most common CNS manifestation of HIV infection, occurring in 65% of patients with HIV/AIDS.

E. Mortality depends on the etiological agent. Morbidity related to the severity of sequelae also varies according to the causative agent.

Pathogenesis

A. JE is the most common form of epidemic viral encephalitis. For the past several years, WNV has been the most common cause of proved viral encephalitis in the United States. Encephalitis may occur as a secondary infection from mumps, varicella (chickenpox), rubella, rubeola, rabies, herpes simplex types 1 and 2, EBV, HIV, and influenza. Postinfectious encephalitis, in contrast to viral encephalitis, typically occurs either as the initial infection is resolving or may appear following subclinical illness that was not appreciated by the patient.

B. The incubation period depends on the pathogen.

C. Tick-borne diseases include Russian spring–summer encephalitis and Powassan encephalitis.

Predisposing Factors

A. Military personnel and travelers
B. Age extremes are highest risk
C. Exposure to vectors
   1. Mosquitoes
   2. Ticks

3. Bat
4. Raccoon
5. Feral dogs/cats
6. Sandflies

D. HIV positive
E. Herpes
F. Rodent-borne arenavirus: Exposure to the secretions of mice, rats, and hamsters
G. Occupational exposure
1. Laboratory workers
2. Health care workers
3. Veterinarians

H. Recreational activities (camping/hunting)
I. Recent vaccination

Common Complaints

A. Severe headache. **A person with encephalitis has a severe headache throughout the entire head. Over the course of about 48 hours, the person may show a lack of energy and then lapse into a coma.**
B. Stiff neck
C. Mental changes: Altered mental status, altered behavior, and personality changes
D. Decreased level of consciousness (LOC)
E. Fever

Other Signs and Symptoms

A. CNS symptoms
1. Nuchal rigidity
2. Irritability
3. Hemiparesis: Weakness or paralysis on one side of body
4. Flaccid paralysis
5. Seizures
6. Exaggerated deep tendon reflexes
7. Ataxia
8. Nystagmus

B. Photosensitivity
C. Swollen or protruding eyes
D. Malaise
E. Nausea and/or vomiting
F. Dysphagia with rabies

Subjective Data

A. Review the onset, duration, and course of all symptoms.
B. Rule out recent history of chickenpox, rubeola, herpes, or other infections.
C. Ask the patient about recent travel.
D. Question the patient regarding recent mosquito or animal bites (rule out rabies).
E. Elicit a detailed sexual history.
F. Does the patient have HIV?
G. Ask about recent recreational activities, including camping, spelunking, or hunting.

Physical Examination

A. Check temperature, pulse, respirations, and blood pressure.
B. Inspect
1. Observe general overall appearance.
2. Conduct an eye exam.
3. Examine the skin for rash, vesicles, or bites.
a. Maculopapular rash is seen in approximately half of patients with WNV.
b. Grouped vesicles in a dermatomal pattern suggest varicella-zoster.
c. Classic herpetic skin lesions suggest herpes encephalitis.
4. Assess dehydration status.
5. Observe for seizure activity.
6. Observe for tremors of the eyelids, tongue, lips, and extremities, which may suggest the possibility of St. Louis encephalitis or West Nile encephalitis.

C. Auscultate: Auscultate the lungs and monitor breathing pattern. Auscultate the heart.
D. Palpate
1. Palpate the lymph nodes: Preauricular, posterior auricular, submental and sublingual, anterior cervical chains, and supraclavicular nodes
2. Palpate the mastoid bone.

E. Neurologic exam
1. Assess LOC.
2. Assess the patient for personality changes.
3. Assess for meningeal signs.
a. Signs of meningeal irritation include nuchal rigidity.
b. Positive Brudzinski's and Kernig's signs (see Figures 18.1 and 18.2).
i. Brudzinski's sign: Place the patient supine and flex the head upward. Resulting flexion of both hips, knees, and ankles with neck flexion indicates meningeal irritation.
ii. Kernig's sign: Place the patient supine. Keeping one leg straight, flex the other hip and knee to a bent knee to form a 90° angle. Slowly extend the lower leg. This places a stretch on the meninges, resulting in pain and spasm for the hamstring muscle. Resistance to further extension can be felt.
4. Check deep tendon reflexes (exaggerated and/or pathologic reflexes).

Diagnostic Tests

A. CBC with differential, electrolytes, glucose, blood urea nitrogen (BUN), and creatinine
B. PCR tests for viruses
C. Serology for arboviruses

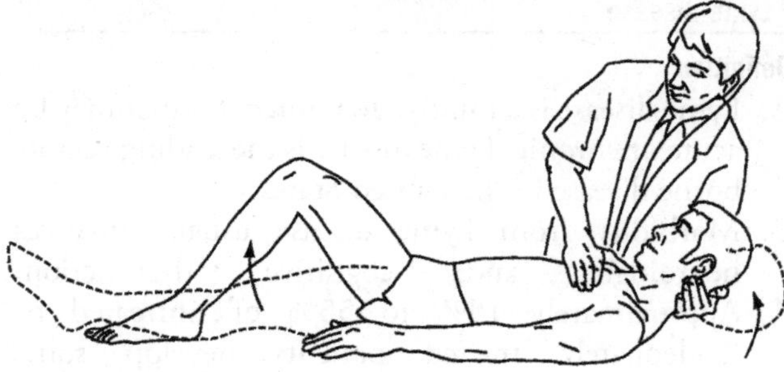

Figure 18.1 Brudzinski's sign.

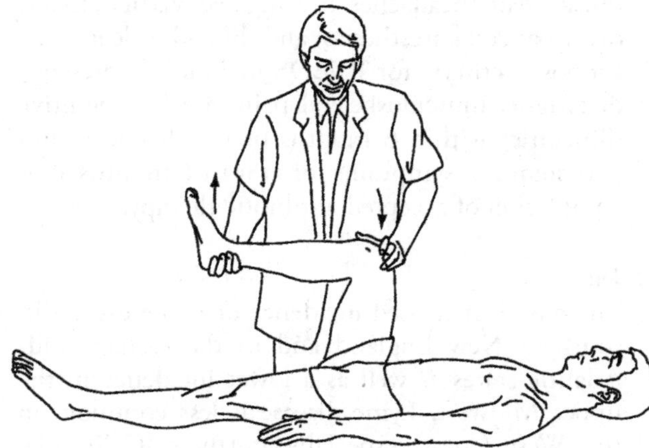

Figure 18.2 Kernig's sign.

D. Lumbar puncture for the following:
   1. Protein (elevated)
   2. Glucose (usually normal)
   3. White cell count (increased)
   4. Red cell count (usually negative in a nontraumatic tap)
   5. Culture (viral and bacterial): **Detection of virus-specific IgM antibody in cerebrospinal fluid (CSF) is diagnostic.**
E. Electroencephalogram (EEG)
F. CT scan: Useful to rule out space-occupying lesions or brain abscess
G. MRI: Sensitive in detecting demyelination
H. Brain scan: Imaging studies (CT scan, MRI, brain scan) may be normal early; later, nonspecific abnormalities are seen.
I. Stool or throat cultures may be helpful if enteroviruses are suspected.
J. Skin lesions and urine may be cultured for herpes simplex and CMV.
K. Brain biopsy is the diagnostic standard.

Differential Diagnoses

A. Encephalitis
B. WNV
C. St. Louis virus
D. Chickenpox
E. Measles: Rubeola or rubella
F. Herpes
G. Rabies
H. Influenza
I. Mumps
J. Meningitis
K. Brain abscess
L. Tuberculosis
M. Syphilis
N. Intracranial hemorrhage
O. Head trauma
P. Toxic ingestion
Q. Fungal meningitis
R. RMSF/tick-borne diseases
S. Cerebral bacterial infections
T. Toxoplasmosis
U. Lyme disease
V. Cat-scratch disease (CSD)
W. CMV
X. Nonparalytic poliomyelitis
Y. Epilepsy

Plan

A. General interventions: If encephalitis is suspected, hospitalization is recommended for further diagnostic studies and evaluation.
B. Patient teaching
   1. Prevention for vector-borne encephalitis involves mosquito and tick avoidance, use of insect repellents, and vaccination.
   2. The JE vaccine is an inactivated vaccine derived from infected mouse brain and is recommended for expatriates living in Asia and for certain travelers. It is also recommended for the following:
      a. Persons who will be residing in areas where JE virus is endemic or epidemic
      b. Travelers planning prolonged stays (more than 30 days) in endemic areas during the transmission season, especially with activities such as bicycling, camping, or other unprotected outdoor activities in rural areas.
      c. Inactivated JE vaccine series
         i. Adults: Three doses of 1.0 mL each, administered subcutaneously on days 0, 7, and 30. An abbreviated schedule of 0, 7, and 14 days can be used when the longer schedule is precluded by time constraints.
   3. If rabies is suspected, the domestic animal should be observed for 10 days to detect rabid behavior. If there is no indication of rabies, the animal should be immunized. Animals that show rabid

behavior or wild animals should be sacrificed and their brains submitted to the local/state health department for pathology testing.

C. Pharmaceutical therapy
   1. Empiric treatment for HSV-1 should always be initiated as soon as possible if the patient has encephalitis without explanation due to the high mortality and morbidity. Acyclovir 10 mg/kg administered IV (given over 1 hour) every 8 hours for 14 to 21 days.
   2. Antibiotics for bacterial etiology (refer to diagnosis-specific chapters)
   3. Anticonvulsants for seizures
   4. Other pharmaceutical therapies depend on specific causal agent.
   5. Initiate short courses of corticosteroids to control brain edema.
   6. If rabies is suspected: Human rabies IG should be given 20 U/kg dose.

Follow-Up

A. Follow-up varies and is specific to causal agent.
B. Long-term management of patients with neurologic sequelae includes rehabilitation services, home care, or nursing home placement for convalescent care.

Consultation/Referral

A. Refer the patient to a physician and/or hospital. Consultations include a neurologist, infectious disease specialist, and neurosurgeon for managing elevated intracranial pressure.

Individual Considerations

A. Adult travelers: Advise patient to take mosquito bed nets and aerosol insecticide sprays to reduce the risk of mosquito bites at night.
B. Geriatrics
   1. Elderly patients may be at risk for a severe form of the disease. Mortality is significantly higher in persons older than age 70.
   2. **Encephalitis should be considered in all elderly patients who have progressive mental confusion.**
   3. WNV encephalitis occurs primarily in patients older than 65 years of age.
   4. HSV is the main cause of encephalitis in individuals older than 60 years of age, in whom it has a more severe clinical course.
   5. Herpes simplex encephalitis in the elderly presents with atypical clinical symptoms.
      i. Progressive amnestic cognitive disorder
      ii. Behavioral changes
      iii. Progressive mental confusion
      iv. Focal neurologic deficits, which mimics stroke

Lyme Disease

Definition

A. Lyme disease is a multisystem infection that may be acute or chronic. Lyme disease is the leading vector-borne disease in the United States.
B. Morbidity from Lyme disease usually involves neurologic and cognitive dysfunction. Approximately 15% to 55% of untreated or inadequately treated patients develop some symptoms of post-Lyme disease symptoms. Posttreatment Lyme disease syndrome (PTLDS) includes cognitive disturbances, fatigue, joint/muscle pain, headaches, hearing loss, vertigo, mood disturbances, paresthesias, and difficulty sleeping.
C. Proposed criteria for PTLDS include the presence of fatigue, musculoskeletal pain, and/or cognitive difficulties within 6 months of the diagnosis and persistence of symptoms for at least 6 months after completion of accepted antibiotic therapy.

Incidence

A. There is an increased incidence of Lyme disease in southern New England and in the eastern mid-Atlantic states as well as a lower incidence in the upper Midwest. Lyme disease is less common on the West Coast, especially northern California. There is a seasonal increase between the months of April and October; more than 50% of cases occur in June and July. In the United States the incidence is highest among children ages 5 to 9 years and in adults ages 45 to 54 years.

Pathogenesis

A. *Borrelia burgdorferi,* a spirochete bacterium, is an infectious agent carried by the *Ixodes dammini* deer tick on the East Coast and midwestern areas of the United States. Vector transmission is usually from the deer tick to humans. Rodents and pets can also harbor deer ticks.
B. The spirochete enters the bloodstream at the time of tick feeding. The incubation period is 3 to 32 days, or about 1 to 3 weeks after bite. Late manifestations occur several months to more than 1 year later.

Predisposing Factors

A. People of all ages are affected.
B. Recreational exposure
   1. Hiking
   2. Golfing
   3. Hunting
   4. Soccer
C. Gardening
D. Exposure to rodents such as field mice and domestic pets, which may also carry the ticks.

Common Complaints

A. Flulike symptoms
B. Fatigue
C. Headache
D. Joint pain

Other Signs and Symptoms

A. Stage 1: Acute (early localized)
   1. Rash: Erythema migrans

About 80% of infected persons develop a characteristic expanding erythematous rash, erythema migrans. It usually begins as a red macule at the site of the tick bite and spreads out to form a large annular lesion with red secondary outer rings, an intense red outer border (measuring at least 5 cm), and some clearing at the site of the bite. Appearance is a "bull's-eye" shape. The lesion is generally painless and not pruritic.

   2. Body aches
   3. Fever or chills
   4. Swollen lymph nodes
B. Stage 2: Disseminated infection (early disseminated)
   1. Malaise, debilitating fatigue
   2. Headache
   3. Photophobia
   4. Mild neck stiffness
   5. Joint or muscle pain
   6. Migratory arthralgia
   7. Rash: Diffuse erythema
   8. Itching
   9. Transient heart block
      a. In 5% to 10% of cases, patients have cardiac involvement: A transient heart block ranging from asymptomatic, first-degree atrioventricular (AV) block to complete heart block with fainting. The cardiac phase lasts 3 to 6 weeks.
   10. Bell's palsy
      a. A unilateral or bilateral Bell's palsy is the most common cranial nerve deficit.
   11. Mild encephalopathy
C. Stage 3: Chronic (late disease)
   1. Prolonged arthritis
      a. Approximately 60% of complaints evolve into frank arthritis. Onset of arthritis is variable but averages 6 months from the time of initial infection. The knee is the most common site and the pattern continues to be oligoarticular.
   2. Chronic neurologic deficits
   3. Distal paresthesia
   4. Radicular pain
   5. Memory loss

Subjective Data

A. Review the onset, course, and duration of symptoms.
B. Ask the patient about any recent outdoor activities, such as camping, hiking, gardening, or other activities. Less than half of the people infected remember a tick bite. A history of a tick bite is not necessary for diagnosis.
C. Have other family members had similar symptoms?
D. Review thorough history of medications.
E. Review any history of rash and course of spread.
F. Rule out late symptoms associated with Lyme disease such as arthritis, memory loss, and distal paresthesia.
G. Has the patient been previously treated for Lyme disease or RMSF?

Physical Examination

A. Check temperature, pulse, respirations, and blood pressure.
B. Inspect
   1. Observe general overall appearance.
   2. Observe rash pattern and type.
   3. Inspect the skin; observe for target-like pattern.
C. Palpate
   1. Palpate the lymph nodes and mastoid bones.
   2. Examine the joints for tenderness, swelling, and range of motion.
D. Auscultate: Auscultate the heart and lungs.
E. Neurologic exam: Evaluate for signs of meningeal irritation by means of Brudzinski's sign and Kernig's signs (see Figures 18.1 and 18.2).
   1. Brudzinski's sign: Place the patient supine and flex the head upward. Resulting flexion of both hips, knees, and ankles with neck flexion indicates meningeal irritation.
   2. Kernig's sign: Place the patient supine. Keeping one leg straight, flex the other hip and knee to a bent knee to form a 90° angle. Slowly extend the lower leg. This places a stretch on the meninges, resulting in pain and spasm for the hamstring muscle. Resistance to further extension can be felt.

Diagnostic Tests

A. CBC with differential
B. Sedimentation rate
C. Serum antibody (enzyme-linked immunosorbent assay [ELISA]) testing for *B. burgdorferi* (not present for several weeks)
D. Western blot if ELISA is positive
E. Lyme titer or culture for spirochete (after 20 days of signs and symptoms)
F. Arthrocentesis for joint effusion
G. PCR testing

H. ALT and AST (may be mildly elevated)
I. Creatine phosphokinase
J. Lumbar puncture indicated for the presence of manifestations of meningitis

Differential Diagnoses

A. Lyme disease
B. Insect or spider bite
C. RMSF
D. Cellulitis
E. Arthritis
F. Bacterial meningitis
G. Chronic fatigue syndrome (CFS)
H. Viral syndrome
I. Nummular eczema
J. Tinea corporis (ringworm)

Plan

A. General interventions
   1. **Prophylactic therapy after a tick bite is generally not advised.** It takes 24 hours from the time of tick contact with the skin to transmit the spirochete.
   2. **Start prophylactic treatment with doxycycline for tick bites that are "swollen."**
   3. Wait for the development of symptoms (e.g., erythema migrans) and treat promptly if the patient becomes symptomatic.
B. Patient teaching
   1. See the Section III Patient Teaching Guide for this chapter, "Lyme Disease and Removal of a Tick."
   2. Not all neurologic signs and symptoms may completely resolve (such as headache, photophobia, Bell's palsy, and third-stage symptoms).
   3. Patients with active Lyme disease should not donate blood because spirochetemia occurs in early Lyme disease. Patients who have been treated for Lyme disease in the past can be considered for blood donation.
   4. Currently there is no vaccine for Lyme disease. The vaccine was withdrawn in early 2002. Previously vaccinated patients are not protected against Lyme disease.
   5. Nonspecific symptoms may persist for months after treatment of Lyme disease. There is no evidence that the complaints represent ongoing active infection or need repeated antibiotics.
      a. Headache
      b. Fatigue
      c. Arthralgias
C. Pharmaceutical therapy
   1. Early localized Lyme disease
      a. Doxycycline: 14- to 21-day antibiotic course (Warn patient regarding photosensitivity.)
         i. Adults: 100 mg, orally, twice daily
      b. Amoxicillin: 14- to 21-day antibiotic course
         i. Adults: 500 mg orally three times a day
      c. Cefuroxime (Ceftin): 14- to 21-day antibiotic course
         i. Adults: 500 mg twice a day
   2. Lyme carditis
      a. Ceftriaxone (Rocephin): 75 to 100 mg/kg (maximum of 2 g/d), IM or IV infusion for 14 to 28 days
      b. Penicillin: 18 to 24 million U/d given by IV infusion in divided doses every 4 hours for 14 to 28 days
   3. Neurologic manifestations
      a. Facial nerve paralysis: Use oral regimen for early disease for 21 to 28 days.
      b. Lyme meningitis
         i. Ceftriaxone (Rocephin): 14- to 28-day antibiotic course
            1) Adults: 2 g IM or IV infusion once a day
         ii. Penicillin: 14- to 28-day antibiotic course
            1) Adults: 18 to 24 million U/d IV divided into 6 daily doses
      c. Possible alternatives for Lyme meningitis: Doxycycline 100 mg by mouth or IV infusion for 14 to 21 days
   4. Lyme arthritis
      a. Same oral regimen as early localized Lyme disease for a total of 28 days
      b. Ceftriaxone (Rocephin): 75 to 100 mg/kg (maximum of 2 g/d), IM or IV infusion for 14 to 28 days
      c. Penicillin: 300,000 U/kg (maximum of 20 million U/d) given by IV infusion in divided doses every 4 hours for 14 to 28 days.
   5. Pregnant women
      a. For localized early Lyme disease, amoxicillin 500 mg three times daily for 21 days
      b. For disseminated early Lyme disease or any manifestation of late disease, penicillin G 20 million units daily for 14 to 21 days
      c. For asymptomatic seropositivity, no treatment is necessary.
   6. The Jarisch–Herxheimer reaction, with increased fever, chills, and malaise, can occur transiently when antibiotic therapy is initiated. NSAIDs may be beneficial, and the antimicrobial agent should be continued.

Follow-Up

A. Follow-up depends on the stage of disease.
B. Repeat Lyme titer in 1 to 2 months to determine the need for continuation of antibiotic therapy.

Consultation/Referral

A. Referral to a physician is indicated when the patient with strong clinical evidence of Lyme disease fails to respond to prescribed antibiotics.

B. Consultation with a neurologist is particularly important for those patients with refractory neurologic deficits.
C. Consultation with a rheumatologist is needed for patients with persistent or debilitating arthritis or fibromyalgia occurring after Lyme disease.

Individual Considerations

A. Pregnancy
   1. Maternal–fetal transmission of infection with subsequent injury to the fetus has been reported. Antibiotic treatment should be instituted promptly in symptomatic patients.
   2. Tetracyclines are contraindicated in pregnancy. Otherwise, therapy is the same as for nonpregnant persons.
   3. There is no causal relationship between maternal Lyme disease and congenital malformations.
   4. There is no evidence that Lyme disease can be transmitted in breast milk.

Resources

ALDF iPhone application on "Lyme Disease Tick Map": http://www.aldf.com/ALDF_iPhone_Application.shtml
American Lyme Disease Foundation, Inc. (ALDF) website: http://aldf.com

Meningitis

Definition

A. Meningitis is an acute inflammation of the meninges, or membranes lining the brain and spinal cord. A virus or noninfectious insult, such as blood in the subarachnoid space, causes aseptic meningitis. Three baseline clinical features have been independently associated with an adverse outcome—hypotension, altered mental status, and seizures.
B. Vaccines are available for three types of bacteria that cause meningitis:
   1. *Neisseria meningitidis:* Polysaccharide or *conjugate vaccines are available.*
   2. *Streptococcus pneumonia:* Pneumococcus vaccine
   3. *Haemophilus influenza* type b (Hib) vaccine
C. Bacterial meningitis is a severe infection with associated complications including brain damage, hearing loss, neurologic/learning disabilities, and digit or limb amputations. Mortality rate varies in part with the organism and if it is a nosocomial or a community-acquired infection.

Incidence

The attack rate of bacterial meningitis in the United States is 0.6 to 4 cases per 1,000,000 persons. The most common organisms causing bacterial meningitis are presented here.

A. Adults up to age 60
   1. *S. pneumoniae*
   2. *N. meningitidis*
   3. *H. influenzae*
   4. *L. monocytogenes*
   5. Group B *streptococcus*
B. Adults 60 years and older
   1. *S. pneumoniae*
   2. *L. monocytogenes*
   3. *N. meningitidis*

Acute meningitis due to infectious causes usually does not recur. However, a small number of patients with acute meningitis may develop recurrent attacks between intervals of good health. Chronic meningitis is arbitrarily defined as meningitis lasting 4 weeks or more.

Pathogenesis

A. An acute inflammation of the meninges can be caused by *S. pneumoniae,* Group B streptococci, *H. influenzae, L. monocytogenes, N. meningitidis,* gonococci (rare), *Mycobacterium tuberculosis, E. coli,* herpes, gram-positive anaerobes, and *Bacteroides,* and as a sequelae of Lyme disease and varicella (chickenpox).
B. The incubation period is variable, depending on the pathogen, usually 1 to 10 days. Transmission occurs from person to person through droplets from the respiratory tract and requires close contact.

Predisposing Factors

A. Peak demographics
   1. Adolescents
   2. Freshman college students living in dormitories
B. Attendance in the military
C. Sequela of Lyme disease
D. Odontogenic infection
E. Sequela of otitis media, bacterial sinusitis, *H. influenzae* type B infection, and varicella
F. Sickle cell disease, asplenia, Hodgkin's disease, and antibody deficiencies
G. Review history for sexually transmitted and HIV infection.
H. Penetrating wound, head trauma, spinal tap, surgery, or anatomic abnormality
I. Occupational exposure such as laboratory personnel
J. Travel exposure
K. Maternal infection and fever at the time of delivery
L. Lumbar epidural steroid injections
M. Immunosuppression

Common Complaints

A. Classic triad
   1. Nuchal rigidity
   2. Fever
   3. Altered mental status

Other Signs and Symptoms

A. Adults
   1. Sudden onset of a severe, constant headache affecting the entire head that worsens with movement; CNS symptoms (nuchal rigidity, nausea and/or vomiting, confusion, lethargy, decreased LOC)
   2. Fever or chills
   3. Backache
   4. Photophobia
   5. Difficulty swallowing
   6. Facial and eye weakness and sagging eyelids
   7. Seizures
   8. Rash: The type of rash—macular, maculopapular, petechial, or purpuric—is dependent on the virus/organism.
   9. Anorexia
B. Chronic meningitis: Usually have subacute onset of symptoms, including fever, headache, and vomiting.

Subjective Data

A. Review the onset, course, and duration of symptoms, including a progressive petechial or ecchymotic rash.
B. Determine current or recent history of ear infections, URI, sinus infection, and chickenpox exposure.
C. Ask the patient about any recent dental procedures, extractions, and gum procedures.
D. Review the patient's recent history of tick bite and any treatments.
E. Review the patient's recent history of Hib immunization.
F. Evaluate a history of serious drug allergies.
G. Evaluate a history of recent head trauma/fracture.
H. Evaluate full history for ventriculoperitoneal shunt and other cranial surgery/procedures.
I. Review history for use of lumbar epidural steroid injections for pain.
J. Review all medications, including OTC and herbal products. Determine recent use of antibiotics.
K. Review for a history of illicit drug use, especially the IV route.
L. Review any recent travel locations.

Physical Examination

A. Check temperature, pulse, respirations, and blood pressure.
B. Inspect
   1. Observe general overall appearance.
   2. Examine the skin for the presence of a petechial or ecchymotic rash.
   3. Complete an ear, nose, and throat exam.
   4. Examine mouth and teeth for dental diseases and disorders.
   5. Assess the patient for dehydration.
   6. Observe the patient for seizure activity.
   7. Assess level of pain.
   8. Inspect for cranial nerve palsies.
C. Auscultate: Auscultate the lungs, monitor breathing pattern, and auscultate heart.
D. Palpate
   1. Neck: Palpate the lymph nodes.
   2. Palpate the mastoid bones.
   3. Abdominal examination: Hepatosplenomegaly
E. Neurologic exam
   1. Perform a complete neurologic examination.
   2. Evaluate for signs of meningeal irritation by means of Brudzinski's and Kernig's signs (see Figures 18.1 and 18.2). Positive Brudzinski's and Kernig's signs:
      a. Brudzinski's sign: Place the patient supine and flex the head upward. Resulting flexion of both hips, knees, and ankles with neck flexion indicates meningeal irritation.
      b. Kernig's sign: Place the patient supine. Keeping one leg straight, flex the other hip and knee to a bent knee to form a 90° angle. Slowly extend the lower leg. This places a stretch on the meninges, resulting in pain and spasm for the hamstring muscle. Resistance to further extension can be felt.

Diagnostic Tests

The definitive diagnosis is from bacteria isolated from CSF and the presence of elevated protein and low glucose in the CSF.

A. Lumbar puncture to obtain CSF for analysis
   1. Gram stain
   2. Absolute neutrophil count
   3. CSF protein
   4. CSF glucose
   5. Culture and sensitivity
   6. WBCs (pleocytosis)
B. Laboratory tests
   1. CBC with differential
   2. Metabolic panel, including electrolytes, glucose, BUN, and liver profile
   3. Coagulation profile
   4. Platelet count
   5. Blood cultures × 2
C. Cultures of petechial or purpuric lesion scraping and synovial fluid
D. MRI or CT scan, with and without contrast (a screening CT is not necessary in the majority of the patients)

Differential Diagnoses

A. Meningitis
   1. Bacterial etiology
   2. Viral etiology
   3. Fungal etiology
   4. Aseptic meningitis
   5. Chronic meningitis

B. Lyme disease
C. Herpes
D. Dementia
E. Gonorrhea
F. Otitis media
G. Dental abscess
H. Chickenpox
I. Sinusitis
J. Mastoiditis
K. Intracranial abscess
L. Encephalitis
M. Subarachnoid hemorrhage

Plan

A. General interventions
   1. Treat aggressively because the progression of disease is often rapid. Antibiotic therapy should be initiated immediately after blood cultures are drawn and after the results of the lumbar puncture if the clinical suspicion is high.
   2. Dexamethasone should be given shortly before or at the same time as the antibiotics if clinical/laboratory evidence suggest bacterial meningitis.
   3. Maintain hydration.
   4. In addition to standard precautions, droplet precautions are recommended until 24 hours after initiation of effective antimicrobial therapy.
   5. Chemoprophylaxis is warranted for people who have been exposed directly to a patient's oral secretions through close social contact, such as sharing toothbrushes or eating utensils as well as childcare and preschool contact within 7 days before the onset of the disease in the index case. Throat and nasopharyngeal cultures are of no value in deciding who should receive chemoprophylaxis and are not recommended.
   6. Airline travelers with 8 hours of contact, who are seated directly next to an infected person, should receive prophylaxis.

B. Patient teaching
   1. Advise close contacts of the patient with meningococcal and *H. influenzae* meningitis that prophylactic treatment with rifampin (Rifadin) may be indicated; they should check with their health care providers or the local public health department.

C. Pharmaceutical therapy
   1. Antibiotic therapy: Broad-spectrum coverage should be initiated until culture results are available. The doses vary by the organism. All antibiotics should be administered IV for at least 7 days. Empiric therapy may require adjustment after the culture results.
      a. Cefotaxime and ceftriaxone are commonly used as empiric therapy with *S. pneumoniae, N. meningitidis,* and *H. influenzae.* Vancomycin may be added to cefotaxime or ceftriaxone if renal function is normal until culture and susceptibility results are available.
      b. Listeria has traditionally been treated with ampicillin or penicillin G, and gentamicin may be added for its synergistic effect.
      c. *Pseudomonas aeruginosa* is often resistant to most commonly used antibiotics. Ceftazidime has been the most consistently effective cephalosporin therapy.
   2. Chemoprophylaxis in adults includes rifampin, ceftriaxone, ciprofloxacin, and azithromycin.
   3. Vaccinations: Polysaccharide alone or conjugate meningococcal vaccines are licensed in the United States.
      a. Meningococcal polysaccharide vaccine (MPSV4) is administered in a single 0.5 mL dose intramuscularly. MPSV4 is the only meningococcal vaccine licensed for people older than age 55 years.
      b. Meningococcal conjugate vaccine (MCV4) is given to all military recruits in the United States. MCV4 is the preferred vaccine for people ages 9 months to 55 years of age.
      c. In June 2012, the FDA licensed the meningococcal serogroups C and Y and *Haemophilus* b tetanus toxoid conjugate (Hib-MenCY-TT) vaccine for the prevention of invasive Hib and serogroups C and Y meningococcal disease in children. This vaccine is not recommended for routine administration for persons age 9 months through 55 years of age.
      d. No vaccine is available in the United States for the prevention of serogroup B meningococcal disease.
      e. Immunizations with the pneumococcus, Hib, and influenzae vaccines also protect against bacterial meningitis.

Follow-Up

A. Have the patient return to the clinic in 2 to 3 days if conditions (i.e., otitis media) are not significantly improved with antibiotic therapy.
B. Follow-up is dependent on symptoms. Schedule return visit after completion of antibiotics, or 2 to 3 weeks after initial examination.
C. Sequelae associated with meningococcal disease occur in 11% to 19% of patients.
   1. Hearing loss
   2. Neurologic disability
   3. Digit or limb amputations
   4. Skin scarring

D. **Bacterial meningitis is a notifiable disease to the local health department. All presumptive, probable, and confirmed cases should be reported.**

Consultation/Referral

A. The patient needs immediate consultation with a physician if lethargic.

Individual Considerations

A. Pregnancy
   1. The American Academy of Pediatrics (AAP) lists the following indications for selective intrapartum chemoprophylaxis in GBS-positive women:
      a. Preterm labor and delivery
      b. Preterm rupture of membranes
      c. Rupture of membranes greater than 18 hours before delivery
      d. Intrapartum fever
      e. Multiple gestation
      f. Previous offspring with invasive GBS disease
   2. Maternal: Culture introital or vaginal and anorectal samples for GBS, using a selective medium such as Todd-Hewitt broth. Vaginal colonization of Group B *streptococcus* occurs in 5% to 40% of pregnant women, of which 40% to 70% transmit GBS to their offspring.
   3. The most significant problem associated with pregnancy is exposure of the fetus to GBS in the maternal genital tract. In 2002, the CDC, the AAP, and the American College of Obstetricians and Gynecologists recommended universal perinatal screening for vaginal and rectal GBS colonization at 35 to 37 weeks gestation.
   4. Treat patients with positive urine culture only because recolonization occurs frequently. Antibiotics should be administered to women for preterm labor, premature rupture of membranes (including preterm), and positive GBS cultures (past or present).

B. Adults
   1. Immunization with the pneumococcal vaccination has been shown to decrease the incidence of bacterial meningitis.

C. Geriatrics
   1. The overall mortality rate is higher for elderly patients, in part because of the high prevalence of comorbid conditions.

Mononucleosis (Epstein-Barr)

Definition

A. Infectious mononucleosis is an acute, infectious viral disease caused by EBV, with three classic symptoms: Fever, pharyngitis, and lymphadenopathy. The spread is via intimate contact between susceptible persons and asymptomatic EBV shedders through the passage of saliva.

B. Oral shedding may occur for 6 months after the onset of symptoms prior to its latency phase.

C. Epstein-Barr is not related to CFS; however, the fatigue related to EBV may last several months.

Incidence

A. Antibodies to EBV have been demonstrated in all population groups with a worldwide distribution. Approximately 90% to 95% of adults are EBV-seropositive.

Pathogenesis

A. EBV, human herpesvirus 4, is the primary agent of infectious mononucleosis. EBV persists asymptomatically for life in nearly all adults and is associated with the development of B cell lymphomas, T cell lymphomas, and Hodgkin's lymphoma in certain patients.

B. The incubation period is 30 to 50 days, with an average of 11 days; it is communicable during the acute phase, which may be prolonged. Acute symptoms resolve in 1 to 2 weeks. Pharyngeal excretion may persist for up to 18 months following clinical recovery. It is estimated that once infected with EBV, the virus may be intermittently shed in the oropharynx for decades.

C. EBV has also been isolated both in the cervix and in male seminal fluid, suggesting the possibility of sexual transmission.

D. EBV has also been noted in breast milk.

Predisposing Factors

A. Exposure through oropharyngeal secretions (kiss, cough, shared food)

B. Roommates

C. Intrafamilial transmission to siblings

Common Complaints

A. Infectious mononucleosis is characterized by the following triad of symptoms:
   1. Fever
   2. Tonsillar pharyngitis (with exudate may possibly have a white, gray-green, or necrotic appearance)
   3. Lymphadenopathy (usually posterior cervical chains—typically symmetric)

Other Signs and Symptoms

A. Fatigue: May be persistent and severe

B. Generalized aches

C. Appetite loss

D. Headache

E. Hepatosplenomegaly: Mild hepatitis is encountered in approximately 90% of individuals; splenomegaly is noted in approximately 50%. Jaundice is uncommon.

F. Rash may be present in approximately one third of patients with CMV mononucleosis.
  1. Macular
  2. Papular
  3. Maculopapular
  4. Rubelliform
  5. Morbilliform
  6. Scariantiniform

Subjective Data

A. Review signs, symptoms, and course and duration of symptoms, specifically the triad of pharyngitis, fever, and lymphadenopathy.
B. Assess the patient for recent URI and sore throat.
C. Inquire about any contact with persons known to have mononucleosis and other infections such as strep infections.
D. Review the patient's history for other family members with similar symptoms.
E. Carefully review medications. A mononucleosis syndrome with atypical lymphocytosis can be induced by drugs, including:
  1. Phenytoin
  2. Carbamazepine
  3. Antibiotics such as isoniazid and minocycline

Physical Examination

A. Check temperature, pulse, respirations, and blood pressure.
B. Inspect
  1. Conduct ear, nose, and throat exam, especially tonsils and palate.
    a. Pharynx shows lymphoid hyperplasia, erythema, and edema.
    b. Tonsillar exudate is present in about 50% of cases.
    c. Tonsillar pillars may touch "kissing tonsils" and may lead to airway compromise.
    d. Evaluate for petechiae at the junction of the hard and soft palate.
    e. Evaluate for oral hairy leukoplakia (OHL) on the lateral portions of the tongue. OHL appears as white corrugated painless plaques that cannot be scraped from the surface. (EBV-related malignancies as well as HIV may present with OHL.)
C. Auscultate: Auscultate the heart and lungs.
D. Palpate
  1. Palpate the lymph nodes, especially anterior and posterior cervical chains, axilla, and groin. **Firm, tender, and mobile lymph nodes are indicative of mononucleosis; lymphadenopathy is usually symmetric and presents in the posterior cervical chain more than the anterior chain.**
  2. Palpate the abdomen, especially the spleen. Splenomegaly is noted in 50% of cases. Hepatomegaly and tenderness are noted in 10% of cases.
E. Percuss: Percuss the abdomen, especially the spleen area.
F. Neurologic exam: Evaluate for facial nerve palsy or symptoms of meningitis.

Diagnostic Tests

A. WBC count with differential and a heterophile test

A positive heterophile antibody test is diagnostic for EBV.

B. Throat swab for rapid strep; if negative, send for culture.
C. Monospot test
D. EBV IgM and IgG
E. Cold agglutinin titer: **Cold agglutinin titer is markedly elevated in the setting of hemolysis (> 1:1,000).**
F. Liver function tests: Abnormal liver function tests in a patient with pharyngitis strongly suggest the diagnosis of infectious mononucleosis. (80% to 90% of cases have elevated liver enzymes.)
G. Abdominal ultrasound if indicated for splenomegaly

Differential Diagnoses

A. Mononucleosis
B. Streptococcal pharyngitis (Group A beta-hemolytic streptococcus)
C. Viral syndrome
D. Hodgkin's disease
E. Hepatitis
F. CMV
G. Secondary syphilis
H. CFS
I. Acute HIV
J. Toxoplasmosis
K. Adenovirus
L. Rubella
M. Acute HIV
N. Human herpesvirus type 6 (HHV-6) (Roseola)
O. Human herpesvirus type 7 (HHV-7)

Plan

A. General interventions
  1. **Make certain that the patient does not have an upper airway obstruction from enlarged tonsils and lymphoid tissue.**
  2. Treat concurrent infections.
  3. Isolation is not required with good hand washing and prevention of the spread of pharyngeal secretions.
  4. Bed rest is unnecessary.
  5. There is no commercially available vaccine to prevent EBV infection.
  6. Splenic rupture is rare but potentially life-threatening, occurring in one to two cases

per thousand. It occurs between the 4th and 21st day of symptomatic illness, but it can be the presenting symptom. The typical manifestations are abdominal pain and/or a falling hematocrit.

B. Patient teaching
   1. See the Section III Patient Teaching Guide for this chapter, "Mononucleosis."
   2. Prolonged communicability may persist for up to 1 year.
C. Pharmaceutical therapy
   1. Acyclovir is not recommended for infectious mononucleosis.
   2. Antibiotic therapy is reserved for concurrent infections such as streptococcal pharyngitis.
   3. Administer analgesics, such as acetaminophen or NSAIDs, for fever, body aches, and malaise.
   4. Corticosteroids may be considered in the presence of overwhelming infections, including mononucleosis-related airway obstruction or other complications, such as severe hemolytic or aplastic anemia.

Follow-Up

A. Examine patient every 1 to 2 weeks.
B. Initial monospot test may be negative; repeat in 7 to 10 days.
C. If splenomegaly is present, schedule an appointment to reevaluate the patient prior to the release for contact sports. **Splenomegaly puts patients at risk for rupture secondary to blunt trauma (i.e., sports and motor vehicle accidents).**
D. Patients with the classic triad of symptoms of mononucleosis should also have a diagnostic test for strep since the presenting symptoms are so similar.

Consultation/Referral

A. Consult a physician for marked tonsil enlargement and difficulty swallowing or symptoms lasting longer than 2 weeks. An emergent consultation with an otolaryngologist may be required.

Individual Considerations

A. Pregnancy: Intrauterine infection with EBV is rare.
B. Geriatrics: Older adults may not present with the classic triad of symptoms.
   1. Lymphadenopathy is not as common with older patients.
   2. Pharyngitis and myalgia are the most frequent complaints.
   3. Fever may be prolonged, lasting several weeks.

Rheumatic Fever

Definition

A. Acute rheumatic fever (ARF) is an autoimmune inflammatory process that occurs as sequelae of a Group A beta-hemolytic streptococcal (GAS) tonsillopharyngitis. Rheumatic fever is a preventable disease through the detection and adequate treatment of streptococcal pharyngitis.
B. The individual who has had an attack of rheumatic fever is at very high risk of developing recurrences after subsequent GAS pharyngitis and needs continuous antimicrobial prophylaxis to prevent such recurrences (secondary prevention). The most significant complication of ARF is rheumatic heart disease, which occurs after repeated bouts of acute illness.
C. Rheumatic heart disease is the predominant cause of mitral stenosis.

Incidence

A. The incidence of rheumatic fever is between 0.3% and 3.0% following ineffectively treated cases of Group A streptococcal URIs.
   1. About 20% diagnosed with rheumatic fever have a positive history of pharyngitis or recall any upper respiratory symptoms within the preceding 3 months.
   2. The incidence of first episodes falls steadily after adolescence and is rare after 30 years of age.
   3. The disease does not seem to have a major racial predisposition.
   4. ARF has been uncommon since the 1970s, but there has been an increase of RF since 1987.
B. Cardiac involvement is the most serious complication due to valvular fibrosis leading to stenosis and/or insufficiency. Morbidity due to congestive heart failure (CHF), strokes, and endocarditis is common among individuals with rheumatic heart disease, and about 1.5% of persons with rheumatic carditis die of the disease annually. Mitral stenosis and Sydenham chorea are more common in females who have gone through puberty. People who have had a previous attack of RF are at high risk for a recurrent attack, which worsens the damage to the heart.

Pathogenesis

A. Rheumatic fever is caused by a preceding infection with Group A streptococcus and *S. pyogenes.* Nonsuppurative inflammatory lesions of the joints, heart, subcutaneous tissue, and CNS characterize ARF. The incubation period is between 1 and 5 weeks and 6 months after a Group A strep pharyngitis.

Predisposing Factors

A. Group A pharyngitis, untreated or inadequately treated
B. Crowded living conditions
C. Occupational exposure: Teachers, health care providers, and military personnel

D. Most common in tropical countries
E. Gender: More common in females

Common Complaints

A. Sore throat (generally of sudden onset), pain on swallowing
B. Joint pain/arthralgias to frank polyarthritis is usually symmetrical and involves large joints such as knees, ankles, elbows, and wrists. Joints feel warm, swollen, and inflamed. **Polyarthritis is the most common manifestation. Both synovitis and periarticular inflammation occur, especially in the knees and ankles. There may be erythema of the overlying skin.**
C. Fever varies from 101°F to 104°F.

Other Signs and Symptoms

A. Fatigue
B. Appetite loss
C. Sydenham chorea (more common in women): Chorea, a CNS disorder lasting 1 to 3 months, is purposeless, involuntary, rapid movements often associated with muscle weakness, involuntary facial grimaces, speech disturbance, and emotional liability. Sydenham chorea usually resolves with permanent damage but occasionally lasts 2 to 3 years.
D. Subcutaneous nodules are firm, painless nodules that are seen or felt over the extensor surface of certain joints, particularly elbows, knees, and wrists; in the occipital region; or over the spinous processes of the thoracic and lumbar vertebrae. The skin overlying them moves freely and is not inflamed.
E. Erythema marginatum is an evanescent, nonpruritic, pink rash with pale centers and round or wavy margins; lesions vary greatly in size and occur mainly on the trunk and extremities, and are usually not seen on the face. Erythema is transient, migrates from place to place, and may be brought out by the application of heat.
F. Enlarged lymph nodes
G. Headache
H. Carditis: Development of new heart murmurs, cardiomegaly, and CHF
I. Pericarditis, pericardial friction rub, and/or pericardial effusion
J. Aortic regurgitation, manifested by
   1. Palpitations
   2. Dyspnea on exertion
   3. Angina at rest

Subjective Data

A. Review a recent history (1 to 3 months) of sore throat and the onset, duration, severity, and treatment of symptoms.
B. Complete a drug history. Did the patient finish the prescribed antibiotics? Does the patient take aspirin? **Use of aspirin can mask signs of inflammation and tends to prolong the course of the disease.**
C. Assess the patient for signs and symptoms of rheumatic and scarlet fever.
D. Discuss the patient's history of heart problems, chest pain, or shortness of breath.
E. Evaluate the onset and complaints of chorea: Fidgety, clumsy, uncoordinated erratic facial movements, including grimaces, grins, and frowns. Tongue movements. Ask if the movements and other symptoms disappear with sleep.
F. Review symptoms of joint pain.

Physical Examination

A. Check temperature, pulse, respirations, and blood pressure.
B. Inspect
   1. Inspect joints for swelling and warmth.
   2. Observe for signs of chorea (symptoms noted above).
   3. Conduct a dermal exam, especially the trunk and proximal aspects of the extremities. Individual lesions of erythema marginatum are evanescent, moving over the skin in wavy patterns or with indented margins. The lesions may be macular and can develop and disappear in minutes, appearing to change shape while being examined.
   4. Complete an ear, nose, oral, and throat exam. Evaluate tonsillopharyngeal erythema with or without exudates. Observe for beefy, red, swollen uvula.
C. Auscultate
   1. Auscultate heart. Note heart murmur, pericardial friction rub, or effusion. Characteristic murmurs of acute carditis include the high-pitched, blowing, holosystolic, apical murmur of mitral regurgitation and a high-pitched, decrescendo, diastolic murmur of aortic regurgitation heard in the aortic area. The features of CHF include tachycardia, a third heart sound, rales, and edema.
   2. Auscultate all lung fields. Note shortness of breath.
D. Palpate
   1. Palpate the neck lymph nodes.
   2. Palpate the extremities: Apical and radial pulses.
   3. Palpate the abdomen.
E. Neuromuscular examination for chorea
   1. Have the patient stick out his or her tongue for observation of a "bag of worms" when protruded.
   2. Have the patient grip your hand—with chorea, he or she will be unable to maintain a grip; rhythmical squeezing results.

3. Observe for the spooning sign—a flexion at the wrist with finger extension when the hand is extended.
4. Observe for the pronator sign—the palms turn outward when held above the head.

Diagnostic Tests

A. No single specific laboratory test can confirm the diagnosis of ARF. The throat culture remains the criterion for confirmation of Group A streptococcal infection.
   1. If a rapid antigen detection test is negative, obtain a throat culture.
   2. Because of the high specificity, a positive rapid antigen test confirms a streptococcal infection.
B. Erythrocyte sedimentation rate (ESR) is usually elevated at the onset of ARF.
C. C-reactive protein (CRP) is usually elevated at the onset of ARF.
D. EKG or echocardiography. **Note prolonged PR interval.**
E. Chest radiograph can reveal cardiomegaly and CHF.
F. Echocardiology may demonstrate valvular regurgitant lesions.
G. Tests that may rule out differential diagnoses include RF, ANA, Lyme serology, blood cultures, and evaluation for gonorrhea.

Differential Diagnoses

A. Rheumatic fever: Jones Criteria (updated in 1992)
   1. Major criteria
      a. Carditis (based on clinical criteria)
      b. Polyarthritis
      c. Chorea (rare in adults)
      d. Erythema marginatum (uncommon, rare in adults)
      e. Subcutaneous nodules (uncommon, rare in adults)
   2. Minor criteria
      a. Arthralgia
      b. Fever
      c. Elevated ESR or CRP level
      d. Prolonged PR interval
B. Juvenile rheumatoid arthritis
C. Rheumatoid arthritis
D. Gonococcal arthritis
E. Septic arthritis
F. Sickle cell anemia
G. Infective endocarditis
H. Leukemia
I. Gout
J. Huntington chorea
K. KD
L. Systemic lupus erythematous
M. Lyme disease
N. Reiter's syndrome
O. Scarlet fever

Plan

A. General interventions: Bed rest is a traditional part of ARF therapy and is especially important with carditis. Bed rest is needed throughout the acute illness and should continue until the ESR has returned to normal for 2 weeks.
B. Patient teaching
   1. Reinforce the need to take the complete prescribed course of antibiotics for strep infections.
   2. Adequate treatment for a streptococcal pharyngitis or skin infection is the best prevention against rheumatic fever. Strep infections are contagious, but rheumatic fever is not.
   3. Chorea is usually managed conservatively in a quiet nonstimulatory environment. Valproic acid is the preferred agent if sedation is needed. Although there is no conclusive evidence of their efficacy, IVIG, steroids, and plasmapheresis have all been used successfully in refractory chorea.
   4. Diuretics are the mainstay of carditis/heart failure.
C. Pharmaceutical therapy
   1. Antibiotic treatment in patients who present with ARF is necessary regardless of the throat culture results to minimize the possible transmission of the rheumatogenic streptococcal strain. The drug of choice is penicillin, but erythromycin or sulfadiazine may be used in patients who are allergic to penicillin. Use of long-acting intramuscular penicillin G avoids compliance problems of oral regimens.
      a. Benzathine penicillin G
         i. Adults
            1) Primary prophylaxis for treatment of Group A streptococcal pharyngitis: 1.2 million units IM in a single dose.
            2) Secondary prevention of RF is 1.2 million units IM every 4 weeks.
      b. Penicillin VK
         i. Adults
            1) Primary prophylaxis: 500 mg by mouth two to three times a day for 10 days
      c. Amoxicillin
         i. Adults: Primary prophylaxis: 875 mg orally in two divided doses for 10 days
      d. Erythromycin base
         i. Adults
            1) Primary prophylaxis: 250 to 500 mg orally four times a day for 10 days
      e. Azithromycin
         i. Adults: 500 mg orally once a day for 5 days
      f. Clarithromycin
         i. Adults: 250 mg orally twice a day for 10 days

2. Codeine is the analgesic of choice for arthritis symptoms.
3. Aspirin (Anacin, Ascriptin, Bayer, and Bayer Buffered aspirin) is used in patients with moderate to severe arthritis and carditis without heart failure. Treatment is administered for 1 to 2 weeks but may be administered for 6 to 8 weeks.
   a. Adults: 4,000 mg/kg/d divided every 4 to 6 hours for 1 to 2 weeks. Treatment may be extended if needed.
4. Cardiac involvement with confirmed rheumatic fever
   a. Heart failure—antibiotics + diuretic + angiotensin-converting enzyme inhibitors + steroid therapy
   b. Atrial fibrillation—antibiotics + digoxin
   c. Valve leaflet or chordae tendineae rupture—antibiotics + requires full assessment for an emergent valve replacement
5. Severe chorea—antibiotics + anticonvulsants
6. Secondary antibiotic prophylaxis for procedures for chronic established changes of the heart valves

Follow-Up

A. The test of cure is a negative throat culture.
B. Pharyngitis patients with a history of rheumatic fever and those who are symptomatic and have a household member with documented Group A streptococcal infection should receive immediate treatment without need for prior testing.
C. **The AHA no longer recommends prophylaxis for infective endocarditis (IE) in most patients.** The 2014 AHA/ACC Guidelines for the Management of Patients With Valvular Heart Disease is located at www.content.onlinejacc.org/article.aspx?articleid=1838843. The AHA/ACC Guidelines note that prophylaxis is reasonable for patients at highest risk of IE:
   1. Before dental procedures that involve the manipulation of gingival tissue, manipulation of the periapical region of the teeth, or perforation of the oral mucosa.
      a. Patients with prosthetic cardiac valves
      b. Patients with previous IE
      c. Cardiac transplant recipients with valvular regurgitation due to a structurally abnormal valve
      d. Patients with congenital heart disease (CHD) and:
         i. Unrepaired cyanotic CHD, including palliative shunts and conduits
         ii. Completely repaired congenital heart defect repaired with prosthetic material or device, whether placed by surgery or catheter intervention, during the first 6 months after the procedure
         iii. Repaired CHD with residual defects at the site or adjacent to the site of prosthetic patch or prosthetic device.
   2. Prophylaxis against IE is not recommended in patients with valvular heart disease who are at risk of IE for nondental procedures, for example, transesophageal echocardiogram (TEE), colonoscopy, cystoscopy, or esophagogastroduodenoscopy (EGD) in the absence of active infection.
D. The major complication is cardiac valve disease. Rheumatic fever accounts for the largest number of aortic regurgitation cases. Continuous streptococcus prophylaxis in patients with prior rheumatic fever is the major means of preventing cardiac sequelae.
E. The patient with carditis should be followed every 6 months by a cardiologist, with an echocardiography every 1 to 2 years.

Consultation/Referral

A. Consult and comanage the patient with a physician.
B. Consult an ear, nose, and throat (ENT) specialist if indicated for patients with intact tonsils and recurrent symptomatic strep infections for consideration of tonsillectomy.
C. Consultation with a cardiologist may be required to manage heart blocks and CHF.
D. Consultation with a neurologist or psychiatrist may be required to confirm the diagnosis of chorea and to assist in its management.

Individual Considerations

A. Adults: Cases are rare for patients older than age 40.
B. Pregnancy
   1. Penicillin G is pregnancy category B. Fetal risk is not confirmed in humans but has been shown in some studies in animals.
   2. Erythromycin is pregnancy category B.
   3. Aspirin products are pregnancy category D. As fetal risk has been shown in humans, use only if the benefits outweigh the risk to the fetus.

Rocky Mountain Spotted Fever

Definition

A. RMSF is a systemic febrile illness with characteristic rash from the bite of an infected tick. It can involve the skin; central nervous, cardiac, and pulmonary systems; GI tract; and muscles. Ticks need 6 to 10 hours of feeding to transmit RMSF; therefore, early discovery and removal of ticks is a preventative measure.

B. In the United States, RMSF is a reportable disease.
C. Long-term sequelae are common with severe RMSF, including
   1. Paraparesis
   2. Hearing loss
   3. Peripheral neuropathy
   4. Seizures
   5. Bowel and bowel incontinence
   6. Cerebellar and vestibular dysfunction
   7. Blindness

Incidence

A. RMSF is the most common rickettsial infection in the United States. The prevalence of RMSF is in the southeastern and southern central states. Although RMSF is more common in rural and suburban locations, it does occur in urban areas. The incidence varies by geographic area. RMSF is more common in the spring and early summer, but has been seen in the cold weather months in the southern United States.
B. People of all ages can be infected.
C. African Americans have a higher case-fatality rate, possibly due to the difficulty of distinguishing the rash in highly pigmented skin.

Pathogenesis

A. *Rickettsia rickettsii* is the infectious agent and is transmitted by a tick vector. Rickettsia also infects rodents, squirrels, and chipmunks. Up to one third of patients with proven RMSF do not recall a recent tick bite or tick contact. RMSF is not transmitted by person-to-person contact.
B. The incubation period is usually about 1 week, but it ranges from 2 to 14 days after the tick bite. It appears to be related to the size of the rickettsial inoculum.
C. Principal recognized vectors
   1. *Dermacentor variabilis* (American dog tick)
   2. *Dermacentor andersoni* (Rocky Mountain wood tick)
   3. *Amblyomma americanum* (Lone Star tick)
   4. *Rhipicephalus sanguineus* (brown dog tick)

Predisposing Factors

A. Outdoor activities (hunting, hiking, camping)
B. Tick bite: The tick must attach and feed for 6 to 10 hours before transmitting the infection.
C. Age is not a predisposing factor, but the disease is more common in children and young adults.
D. Exposure to heavy brush areas
E. Contact with dogs and other animals with ticks
F. Transmission has occurred on rare occasion by blood transfusion.
G. Blood transmission is rare.

Common Complaints

In early phase, most patients have nonspecific signs and symptoms. Less than 5% of patients have the classic triad of symptoms of fever, headache, and rash.

A. Fever (> 102°F)
B. Sudden onset of severe headache
C. Rash usually (90%) occurs between 3 and 5 days of illness. The typical RMSF rash begins as a pink maculopapular eruption on the ankles and wrists. The rash then spreads both centrally and to the palms of hands and soles of the feet. By the fourth day, the rash spreads centripetally and becomes petechial and papular. Hemorrhagic, ulcerated lesions may follow. In a small percentage, onset of the rash is delayed (past 5 days) and/or is atypical (e.g., confined to one body region). **Urticaria and pruritus are not characteristic of RMSF, and their presence makes the diagnosis unlikely.**

Other Signs and Symptoms

A. Myalgias
B. Deep nonproductive cough at the time of the rash
C. Edema
D. Bleeding
E. Conjunctivitis with or without photophobia
F. Retinal abnormalities
G. EKG abnormalities
H. Seizures
I. Dehydration
J. Malaise
K. Nausea without vomiting
L. Altered mental status

Potential Complications

A. Disseminated intravascular coagulation (DIC)
B. Acute renal failure
C. Myocarditis/Heart failure: Usually a cause of death
D. Skin necrosis and gangrene (fingers, toes, elbows, ears, and scrotum)
E. Seizures
F. Encephalopathy
G. Peripheral neuropathy
H. Hearing loss
I. Cerebellar and vestibular dysfunction

Subjective Data

A. Review the onset, course, and duration of symptoms.
B. Elicit information about a recent tick bite or removal.
C. Ask the patient about any recent outdoor activities such as camping, hiking, and so on.
D. Rule out similar symptoms in other family members.
E. Review any history of rash and course of spread.
F. Elicit a history of mental or neurologic changes including seizures.

G. Rule out other symptoms associated with Lyme disease such as arthritis, memory loss, and distal paraesthesia.
H. Review the patient's recent history of blood transfusion.

Physical Examination

A. Check temperature, pulse, respirations, and blood pressure.
B. Inspect
   1. Conduct an ear, nose, and throat exam.
   2. Inspect the skin, especially on the wrist, palms, ankles, and soles of the feet. The face is generally spared from the rash.
   3. Note the presence of petechiae. The rash may blanch and appear macular in the early phase.
   4. Conduct an eye examination; evaluate periorbital edema and petechial conjunctivitis.
C. Auscultate
   1. Perform complete heart evaluation.
   2. Auscultate all lung fields.
D. Palpate
   1. Palpate all lymph nodes.
   2. Palpate the mastoid bones.
E. Neurologic examination
   1. Assess LOC.
   2. Evaluate the patient for signs of meningeal irritation, such as nuchal rigidity and positive Brudzinski's and Kernig's signs (see Figures 18.1 and 18.2).

Diagnostic Tests

A. **Antibody titers: A fourfold rise in antibody titer is the diagnostic gold standard for RMSF. Antibodies typically appear 7 to 10 days after the onset of the illness.**
B. CBC with differential
C. Platelet count: As the illness progresses, thrombocytopenia becomes more prevalent and may be severe.
D. Electrolytes
E. Liver function studies
F. Bilirubin
G. Skin biopsy: 3 mm punch biopsy
H. Lumbar puncture may be indicated.
I. Rickettsial blood cultures are highly sensitive and specific; however, they require specialized laboratories.

Differential Diagnoses

A. RMSF
B. RMSF is commonly mistaken for an undifferentiated viral illness during the first few days of illness. Consider RMSF if other signs and symptoms support a diagnosis, even if a rash is not present.
C. Viral meningitis
D. Lyme disease
E. Mononucleosis
F. Atypical measles
G. Viral hepatitis
H. Parvovirus B19 (fifth disease)

Plan

A. General interventions
   1. **Early treatment is necessary; never delay initiation of antimicrobial treatment to confirm clinical suspicion of the disease. This is a life-threatening disease. Antibiotics are less likely to prevent fatal outcome from RMSF if started after day 5 of symptoms.**
   2. **Antibiotic therapy (see Pharmaceutical therapy). If penicillin or a cephalosporin is administered empirically in the first few days of the illness, the subsequent rash may be incorrectly diagnosed as a drug reaction.**
   3. Hospitalization should be considered for most patients.
B. Patient teaching
   1. See the Section III Patient Teaching Guide for this chapter, "Rocky Mountain Spotted Fever and Removal of a Tick," and the Section II Procedure, "Removal of a Tick."
   2. RMSF is not transmissible by person-to-person contact; therefore, isolation is not necessary.
   3. Relapse of the illness may occur; the patient should report recurrence of symptoms immediately.
   4. Patients who report tick bites should be advised to inform their health care provider if any systemic symptoms, especially fever and headache, occur in the following 14 days.
   5. All pets should be treated for ticks.
C. Pharmaceutical therapy

The diagnosis of RMSF can rarely be confirmed or disproved in its early phase; the cornerstone of management is empiric therapy based on clinical judgment and the epidemiologic setting.

   1. Drug of choice: Doxycycline 100 mg orally or IV every 12 hours for 5 to 7 days for adults
      a. Doxycycline 200 mg initial loading dose IV may be given for critically ill patients.
      b. Doxycycline is the drug of choice in adults except for pregnant women.
      c. Most experts consider the risk of morbidity from rickettsial diseases greater than the minimal risk of dental staining from one short course of doxycycline.
   2. Alternative drug therapy: Chloramphenicol (Chloromycetin)
      a. Chloramphenicol requires frequent serum platelet counts and CBCs.
      b. Not available in oral form in the United States.
      c. Use of chloramphenicol should be considered only in rare cases, such as severe allergy to

doxycycline or in pregnancy if the mother's life is in danger.
   d. Use of chloramphenicol is associated with a higher risk of fatal outcome.
3. Prophylactic therapy with doxycycline or another tetracycline is not recommended following tick exposure.

Follow-Up

A. See the patient 24 to 48 hours after initial visit and again at the end of antibiotic therapy (unless following lab for chloramphenicol therapy). RMSF progresses rapidly. Approximately 10% of outpatients are subsequently admitted to the hospital.
B. The patient must be seen for any alteration in mental status, stiff neck, severe headaches, nausea and vomiting, severe weakness, dizziness, or high fever.
C. Hospitalization is indicated in patients who are severely ill or have complications, such as seizures, hypotension, or marked GI symptoms.
D. Several rickettsial diseases, including RMSF, are nationally notifiable diseases and should be reported to state and local health departments.

Consultation/Referral

A. Consult a physician for any suspected signs of RMSF because the patient is in danger of vascular collapse and disseminated intravascular collapse.
B. Consultation with an infectious disease is advised.

Individual Considerations

A. Pregnancy: Tetracyclines should not be used in pregnancy.
B. Geriatrics
   1. In older patients and in severe or fatal cases of RMSF, the rash tends to appear later and with less frequency.
   2. Age and decreased platelet count at presentation have been independently associated with the development of ARF.
   3. Acute renal failure development increases the odds ratio of dying by a factor of 17.

Toxoplasmosis

Definition

A. Toxoplasmosis is caused by an intracellular protozoan parasite, *Toxoplasma gondii.* Cats are the primary host in which *T. gondii* can complete its reproductive cycle. Humans are the intermediate host. Toxoplasmosis is acquired through contact with infected cat feces, by eating raw or undercooked meat, and by eating soil-contaminated fruit or vegetables. In less developed countries, contaminated unfiltered water is an important source of infection, as is a transfusion or organ transplantation from an infected donor (rare).
B. Emphasis should not be placed on prior exposure to cats, since patients can acquire toxoplasma without direct contact with felines. Toxoplasmosis is one of the TORCH infections. Toxoplasmosis causes CNS disease in patients with AIDS and has perinatal consequences. Latent infection can persist for the life of the host.
C. There are three genotypes of *T. gondii*: types I, II, and III. Genotype II is generally responsible for congenital toxoplasmosis in the United States.
D. There is no vaccination available for the prevention of toxoplasmosis.

Incidence

A. Toxoplasmosis has a worldwide distribution. There is no association with cat ownership. The incidence of seropositivity in adults ranges from 9% (United States) to 85% (Europe). Adults most commonly acquire toxoplasmosis by environmental exposure, that is, through ingestion of infectious oocysts, usually from soil contamination with feline feces.
B. Once a person is infected, the parasite lies dormant in neural and muscle tissue and will never be eliminated. Approximately 50% of all pregnant women in the United States have been previously infected and are immune, whereas those who keep cats as pets have a higher seropositivity rate. The rate of primary infection during pregnancy ranges from 1 to 8 per 1,000.
C. The severity of congenital infection is dependent on the gestation age at the vertical transmission. The greatest risk to the fetus is vertical transmission in the first trimester. Thirty percent of exposed fetuses acquire the infection; however, 85% of live infants appear normal at birth.
D. Approximately 225,000 cases of toxoplasmosis are reported each year in the United States.
E. ***T. gondii* is the third most common lethal foodborne disease in the United States.**

Pathogenesis

A. *T. gondii* is the causative agent and an intracellular protozoan parasite. *T. gondii* is worldwide in distribution; cats, birds, and domesticated animals serve as reservoirs. *T. gondii* is recognized as a major cause of opportunistic infection in AIDS.
B. The incubation period is estimated to be on average 7 days (4- /21-day range).
C. Routine screening for toxoplasmosis in pregnancy is not currently recommended.
   1. Maternal toxoplasmosis infection is acquired orally.
   2. Fetal infection results from transmission of parasites via the placenta (vertical transmission).
   3. Neonatal infection may also occur during vaginal delivery.

Predisposing Factors

A. Food sources
   1. Eating raw or undercooked meats, especially mutton, lamb, and pork
   2. Drinking unpasteurized goat milk
   3. Eating raw shellfish
B. Exposure to contaminated soil or gardens, kitty litter, and cats.
C. Immunocompromised state
   1. HIV-infected/AIDS
   2. Cancer therapy
   3. Transplant recipients
   4. Prescribed immunosuppressive drugs
D. *T. gondii* has been documented as being acquired from blood or blood product transfusion and organ (i.e., heart) or bone-marrow transplant from a seropositive donor with latent infection.
E. Poor sanitary conditions
F. Consumption of contaminated unfiltered water
G. Occupational exposure
   1. Working with meat
   2. Landscaping
H. Travel to underdeveloped country

Common Complaints

A. 80% to 90% of acute *T. gondii* infectious hosts are asymptomatic.
B. Bilateral, symmetrical, nontender cervical adenopathy
C. 30% of symptomatic patients have generalized lymphadenopathy.

Other Signs and Symptoms

A. Usually subclinical infection
   1. Fever
   2. Arthralgia, malaise, and myalgia
   3. Headache
   4. Sore throat/pharyngitis
   5. Skin rash: Diffuse nonpruritic maculopapular rash
   6. Hepatosplenomegaly
   7. Chorioretinitis: Ocular pain and loss of visual acuity (most frequent, permanent manifestation of toxoplasmic infection)
B. Pregnancy
   1. IUGR or low birth weight
   2. Hydrocephaly
   3. Microcephaly
   4. Anemia
C. CNS toxoplasmosis
   1. **Headache, dull and constant, is an almost universal symptom of cerebral lesions in AIDS patients.**
   2. Fever
   3. Lethargy
   4. Altered mental state
   5. Seizures
   6. Weakness
   7. Hemiparesis
   8. Cranial nerve disturbances
   9. Sensory abnormalities
   10. Movement disorders
   11. Neuropsychiatric manifestations: Toxoplasmosis is a significant factor in the causation of mental retardation and blindness.

Subjective Data

A. Review onset, course, and duration of symptoms.
B. Determine if the patient is pregnant.
C. Review presence of indoor cat and contact with kitty litter.
D. Rule out other illness with review of symptoms such as pharyngitis (mononucleosis).
E. Elicit initial site of rash and progression to other body areas.
F. Determine any new medications and contact exposures.
G. Rule out other family members with similar symptoms.
H. Review HIV status.
I. Review ingestion of raw/rare or undercooked meats, raw shellfish, and unpasteurized goat's milk.
J. Review recent travel to an underdeveloped country (untreated water).
K. Review occupational exposure.

Physical Examination

A. Check temperature, pulse, respirations, and blood pressure.
B. Inspect
   1. Conduct ear, nose, and throat exam and careful funduscopic exam.

A funduscopic exam may reveal yellow-white areas of retinitis with fluffy borders. Diagnosis of ocular toxoplasmosis is based on observation of characteristic retinal lesions in conjunction with toxoplasma-specific serum IgG or IgM antibodies.

   2. Complete a dermal exam.
C. Auscultate: Auscultate lungs and heart.
D. Palpate
   1. Palpate all lymph nodes, especially cervical nodes. Lymph nodes are usually smaller than 3 cm in size and nonfluctuant.
   2. Palpate the abdomen.
   3. Palpate the joints.
E. Neurologic exam: Conduct a mental status evaluation.

Diagnostic Tests

A. ELISA is the most commonly employed test due to overall performance and cost for toxoplasmosis IgG and IgM antibody titer. Maternal infections usually are confirmed by a fourfold rise in the serum IgG.
B. Serial titers: No single level of IgG antibody can be used to determine the duration of the infection.

IgG specific antibodies achieve peak concentration 1 to 2 months after exposure and remain positive indefinitely.

C. CBC with differential
D. HIV (rule out)
E. Pregnancy test if indicated
F. CT scan or MRI (usually superior to CT scan)

Differential Diagnoses

A. Toxoplasmosis
B. EBV
C. CMV (CMV retinitis)
D. CSD
E. Tuberculosis
F. Syphilis
G. Sarcoidosis
H. Hodgkin's disease
I. Lymphoma
J. Viral syndrome
K. HIV
L. Mononucleosis
M. *Pneumocystis carinii* pneumonia
N. Varicella-zoster
O. Fungal infection of eye

Plan

A. Patient teaching: **Hand washing is the single most important measure to reduce transmission of *T. gondii*.**
   See the Section III Patient Teaching Guide for this chapter, "Toxoplasmosis."
B. Pharmaceutical therapy
   1. Treatment is rarely necessary since most clinical illness resolves spontaneously; the exception is during pregnancy.
   2. Treatment is usually given for 2 to 4 weeks.
      a. Nonpregnant adults: One of two regimens is typically prescribed.
         i. Pyrimethamine: 100 mg loading dose then 25 to 50 mg by mouth daily; *plus* sulfadiazine 2 to 4 g/d by mouth in divided doses; *plus* leucovorin calcium (folinic acid) 10 to 25 mg by mouth daily.
         ii. Pyrimethamine: 100 mg loading dose, then 25 to 50 mg by mouth daily; *plus* clindamycin 300 mg by mouth four times a day; *plus* leucovorin calcium (folinic acid) 10 to 25 mg by mouth daily.
      b. Pregnancy: Despite the lack of evidence of treatment efficacy, prenatal treatment is usually offered to pregnant women who are diagnosed with toxoplasmosis.
         i. Spiramycin alone: 1 g orally every 8 hours without food. The drug is available in the United States for use in pregnancy from Rhone-Poulenc (Montreal, Quebec) if an Investigation New Drug number is obtained from the FDA under the "compassionate use" pathway.
         ii. Three-week course of pyrimethamine 50 mg once a day orally or 25 mg twice a day; and Sulfadiazine 3 g/d orally divided in two or three doses; *alternating* with a 3-week course of spiramycin 1 g orally three times a day until delivery.
         iii. Pyrimethamine 25 mg once per day by mouth *and* sulfadiazine 4 g/d orally divided into two to four doses until term.
         iv. Leucovorin calcium (folinic acid) 10 to 25 mg/d orally is added during pyrimethamine and sulfadiazine administration to prevent bone marrow suppression.
      c. Persons with compromised immune system:
         i. Trimethoprim 10 mg/kg/daily *plus* sulfamethoxazole 50 mg/kg/daily by mouth. May be considered as a nonpyrimethamine alternative for AIDS patients if unable to tolerate usual adult therapy noted above.
         ii. **Administering dapsone with pyrimethamine appears to provide effective chemoprophylaxis in HIV patients seropositive for *T. gondii* who have CD4 cell counts lower than 200. However, rash, fever, and hemolytic anemia are common adverse effects, often necessitating cessation of therapy.**
         iii. For AIDS patients, after primary therapy, lifelong prophylaxis for recurrence of toxoplasmosis is required for as long as they are immunosuppressed.

Follow-Up

A. Follow up in 1 week to evaluate for secondary complications.
B. Pyrimethamine is a folic acid antagonist that can cause dose-related bone marrow suppression with resultant anemia, leukopenia, and thrombocytopenia. Sulfadiazine is another folic acid antagonist; it works synergistically with pyrimethamine, and it can cause bone marrow suppression and reversible ARF. Patients should return for laboratory monitoring (CBC and platelet counts) weekly.

Consultation/Referral

A. Consultation is needed for all patients; comanage with a physician/specialist.
B. Refer the patient to an obstetrician if pregnant.
C. Ophthalmologist-medication recommendation depends on the size of the eye lesion, the location, and the characteristics of the lesion (active acute versus chronic not progressing).

Individual Considerations

A. Pregnancy
   1. Routine prenatal screening is not the standard of care secondary to costs. Many women have antibodies prior to pregnancy that protect the fetus.
   2. Transplacental infection increases the incidence of first-trimester spontaneous abortion, IUGR, preterm birth, neonatal anomalies, and stillbirth.
   3. Pyrimethamine is a folic acid antagonist and should not be given in the first trimester.
   4. Sulfadiazine should not be given in the third trimester secondary to the increased incidence of jaundice in the neonate.
   5. Transmission of toxoplasmosis in breast milk has not been demonstrated. Pyrimethamine is excreted in the breast milk; however, the WHO and the AAP classify it as compatible with breastfeeding.

B. AIDS patients
   1. Patients with AIDS who have antibodies to *T. gondii* and a CD4 count of 100 cells/mm^3 should be considered at high risk for development of clinical disease. Reactivation of latent infection in the CNS is a common HIV- and AIDS-related complication.
   2. Patients with a CD4 count less than 100 cells/mm^3 should receive prophylaxis against toxoplasmosis.
   3. Serology in HIV-infected patients is used mainly to identify those at risk for developing toxoplasmosis. Therefore, all HIV-positive patients should be tested for the presence of IgG antibodies.

Varicella (Chickenpox)

Definition

A. Varicella, commonly called chickenpox, is a viral disease with a vesicular rash that occurs in crops. It manifests as a generalized, pruritic, vesicular rash. Varicella-zoster virus (VZV) infection causes two clinically distinct forms of disease: Varicella (chickenpox) and herpes zoster (shingles).
   1. Primary VZV results in the diffuse vesicular rash of chickenpox.
   2. VZV remains dormant in the sensory nerve roots for life. Reactivation of the virus is known as shingles.
      a. With shingles, the virus migrates along the sensory nerve via dermatomes. The symptoms include pain, sensory loss, and neurologic complications.
      b. A diagnostic clue of shingles is sensory symptoms that do not cross the midline.
      c. Postherpetic neuralgia is a prolonged complication from shingles.

B. There are two available vaccines for the prevention of varicella: the MMRV and a monovalent varicella vaccine.
   1. Both the monovalent and the quadrivalent immunizations carry a risk of febrile seizures. A personal or family history of seizures is considered a precaution for the administration of the MMRV.

Incidence

A. Seasonal incidence of VZV peaks in the months of March through May.
B. The rate of chickenpox is 5 persons per 1,000.
C. After the primary infection, the risk of shingles increases with age. The lifetime risk of herpes zoster infection is 15% to 20%.
D. The incidence of congenital varicella is 1% to 2% if the maternal infection occurs before 20 weeks gestation.

Pathogenesis

A. VZV, herpesvirus 3, is a member of the herpesvirus family. Humans are the only source of infection for this highly contagious virus infecting over 90% of susceptible household contacts. Person-to-person transmission occurs primarily by direct contact with a patient with varicella or zoster, and it occasionally occurs by airborne droplet spread, from respiratory secretions spread onto the conjunctival or nasal/oral mucosal, and from direct contact with vesicular zoster lesions. In utero infections also occur from transplacental passage of the virus during maternal varicella infection.
B. The incubation period is 14 to 16 days. It is communicable 1 to 2 days to 1 week before macular eruption and until lesions crust over (about 1 week).

Predisposing Factors

A. Exposure to someone with the varicella virus
   1. Direct contact with skin lesions or by respiratory tract secretions
   2. Direct contact with patients with shingles can induce chickenpox in susceptible health care workers.
B. Compromised immune system
C. Late winter and early spring

Common Complaints

A. Low-grade fever
B. Mild malaise
C. Skin lesions or rash: Characteristic rash is pruritic, vesicular exanthem occurring in crops that begin on the head and neck and progress to involve the

trunk and extremities. Blisters collapse within 24 hours to 1 week and crust over to form scabs. Skin eruptions appear almost anywhere on the body, including the scalp; penis; and inside the mouth, nose, throat, and vagina.
D. Itching
E. Myalgia 1 to 4 days before onset of rash

Other Signs and Symptoms

A. Adults may develop varicella pneumonitis. (The risk of pneumonitis is higher in smokers than nonsmokers.)
B. Cough
C. Headache
D. Respiratory symptoms: Cough and chest discomfort. Respiratory symptoms usually develop shortly after cutaneous eruption. Respiratory failure in pregnancy can be rapid.
E. Abdominal pain lasting 1 to 2 days

Subjective Data

A. Review the onset, duration, and course of symptoms.
B. Elicit exposure information when noting characteristic rash, the time it started, spread of the rash or lesions, and characteristic changes.
C. Review any pulmonary or nervous system problems, such as seizures, that occur as complications.
D. Determine if the person has HIV, is immunocompromised, or is pregnant.
E. Determine the caregiver's immunity status to varicella.
F. Review the patient's immunization history.
G. Review all medications, including OTC and herbal products.

Physical Examination

A. Check temperature, pulse, respirations, and blood pressure.
B. Inspect
   1. Conduct a dermal exam, especially the hairline.
   2. Inspect the buccal mucosa.
   3. Conduct an ear, nose, and throat exam, and a detailed eye exam.
   4. Shingles: Note location of lesions; they usually involve only one to three dermatomes.
C. Auscultate: Auscultate the heart and lungs.
D. Palpate: Palpate the neck and lymph nodes.

Diagnostic Tests

A. Diagnosis is usually determined by the appearance of the skin eruptions, and laboratory tests are not necessary.
B. ELISA
C. Tissue culture of vesicular fluid or tissue biopsy (requires up to a week for result).
D. Varicella IgG and IgM: VZV-specific IgM is present within 5 days of onset of the rash and lasts 4 to 5 weeks. A significant increase in varicella IgG antibody by standard serologic assay can confirm a diagnosis retrospectively. These antibody tests are not as reliable in immunocompromised people.
E. Pregnancy test if indicated; if positive, order the following:
   1. Anti-VZV IgG to establish immunity
   2. Tzanck smear of suspicious lesions
   3. Culture lesion for herpes simplex
F. PCR of vesicular swabs or scrapings, scabs for crusted lesions, or tissue biopsy
G. Chest x-ray, if indicated, to rule out pneumonia
H. Genotyping of the virus is available free of charge through a specialized CDC reference lab. The CDC reference lab contact number is 404-639-0066. Merck & Company also performs genotyping through a safety research program. The Merck & Company contact number is 1-800-672-6372.

Differential Diagnoses

A. Varicella (chickenpox)
B. Herpes simplex
C. Scabies
D. Impetigo
E. Coxsackievirus
F. Insect or spider bite
G. Drug reaction
H. Secondary syphilis
I. Measles
J. Rubella
K. RMSF
L. Scabies

Plan

A. General interventions
   1. Avoid contact with persons infected with chickenpox. Patients with varicella should avoid contact with others. Health care workers should be immune to varicella. Determine immunity status with varicella IgG antibody titer if status is unknown.
   2. Strict isolation should be enforced. Varicella is contagious 1 week before outbreak and until the lesions crust over (about 1 week). Isolation is a precaution until the vesicles dry.
   3. Order oatmeal baths (Aveeno) for comfort. Spray starch may also be sprayed on lesions to assist with severe itching.
B. Patient teaching
   1. Lesions that can be covered pose little risk to a susceptible person because transmission usually occurs from direct contact with the fluid from the lesion. Clothing or a dressing should cover lesions until they have crusted.

2. Scarring can occur from secondary infection of lesions; encourage good hand washing and no scratching.

C. Pharmaceutical therapy
   1. If therapy can be initiated within the first 24 hours of rash onset, prescribe oral acyclovir 20 mg/kg/dose in four divided doses for 5 days (maximum dose is 800 mg per dose four times daily); the usual dose for adults is 800 mg four times a day. **Patients on oral acyclovir should be well hydrated during therapy.**
   2. Acyclovir by IV infusion is recommended for treatment of immunocompromised patients and patients with serious complications such as varicella pneumonia or encephalitis. Acyclovir IV dosage is 10 mg/kg every 8 hours for 7 days.
   3. Varicella-zoster immune globulin (VZIG) is no longer available. The only manufacturer of this product has ceased production.
   4. Systemic antipruritic: Diphenhydramine HCl (Benadryl)
      a. Adults: 25 to 50 mg every 4 to 6 hours (maximum adult dosage 300 mg/d)
   5. Varicella vaccine may be given simultaneously with MMR vaccine, but separate syringes and injection sites must be used. If not given simultaneously, the interval between administration of varicella vaccine and MMR should be at least 1 month.
   6. Antihistamines are helpful in the symptomatic treatment of pruritus.
   7. The use of corticosteroids for patients with shingles to prevent postherpetic neuralgia is controversial.
   8. Treatment for postherpetic neuralgia includes gabapentin, pregabalin, tricyclic antidepressants, phenytoin, carbamazepine, cimetidine, and topical capsaicin.

Follow-Up

A. No follow-up is necessary in uncomplicated cases.
B. Have the patient return to the office for any secondary skin infections, conjunctival involvement, CNS problems such as encephalitis and meningitis, or pneumonia.

Consultation/Referral

A. Refer the patient to a physician if pregnant; varicella pneumonia in pregnancy is a medical emergency.

Individual Considerations

A. Pregnancy
   1. Varicella vaccine should not be administered to pregnant women.
      a. Women are advised not to get pregnant for at least 1 month following the varicella immunization.
      b. A pregnant mother or household member is not a contraindication for immunization for a child in the household.
   2. When postpubertal females are immunized, pregnancy should be avoided for at least 1 month after immunization.
   3. VZIG: Maternal therapy's aim is to reduce maternal morbidity; whether it protects the fetus is unknown.
   4. Reporting by telephone of inadvertent immunization when the varicella-zoster-containing vaccine is given during pregnancy is encouraged: 1-800-986-8999 or via the Internet at www.merckpregnancyregistries.com/varivax.html.
   5. Maternal complications of active varicella infection may include preterm labor, encephalitis, and varicella pneumonia. The mortality rate in gravid females is 10%. The profound maternal hypoxia that occurs in varicella pneumonia is associated with increased risk of spontaneous abortion and stillbirth.
   6. Fetal complications of active varicella infection may include IUGR, limb reduction defects, and eye defects.
   7. Acyclovir is a category B drug based on FDA drug classification in pregnancy. IV acyclovir is recommended for the pregnant patient with serious complications of varicella. VariZIG or IVIG can be used during pregnancy for susceptible women who are exposed to VZV.

B. Adults
   1. Adult patients usually have a prodrome and more severe illness. Adults have 25% increased risk of mortality.
   2. Shingles (reactivated chickenpox) appears as grouped vesicular lesions distributed in one to three sensory dermatomes, sometimes accompanied by pain localized to the area. Systemic symptoms are few.
   3. A recommendation for varicella vaccination includes persons at high risk for exposure, which include adolescents and adults who live in households with children.
   4. The herpes zoster "shingles" vaccine was recently approved for adults older than age 50 years. The CDC, however, does not have a recommendation for routine use of shingles vaccine for people between 50 and 59 years old (refer to Chapter 6, "Dermatology Guidelines").

C. Immunocompromised: IV antiviral therapy is recommended for immunocompromised patients, including patients being treated with chronic corticosteroids. Therapy initiated early in the course of illness, especially within 24 hours of rash onset, maximizes efficacy.

West Nile Virus—*Debbie Croley*

Definition

WNV disease is a mosquito-borne viral illness caused by one of the most widely distributed anthropod-borne (arbovirus) viruses. WNV is a member of the genus Flavivirus group. That is, it is a single-strand RNA virus. WNV is transmitted from infected animal hosts, typically wild birds, to humans via the most common types of mosquitoes. Once a patient recovers from WNV disease, he or she is thought to have a lifelong immunity to the disease. There is no immunization for WNV. The two categories of WNV disease are non-neuroinvasive and neuroinvasive.

A. Non-neuroinvasive disease is less severe and often presents as a febrile illness.
B. Neuroinvasive disease leads to encephalitis, meningitis, and flaccid paralysis and requires much more intensive treatment.

Incidence

A. **WNV is a reportable disease that allows the CDC to maintain significant surveillance data and statistics.** As of January 7, 2014, 48 states and the District of Columbia reported WNV. In 2013 a total of 2,374 cases of WNV in people were reported to the CDC. There were 114 deaths in this population. Fifty-one percent of the cases were classified as neuroinvasive and 49% were classified as non-neuroinvasive.
B. Approximately 20,000 new cases occur in North America each year, with 1 in 150 patients developing severe neurological disease; 3% to 15% of those developing severe neurological disease will die.
C. WNV was first noted in North America in 1999. WNV is endemic in the Middle East, Africa, and Asia.
D. Human WNV infections usually begin in midsummer and decline in September, correlating with peak mosquito activity. Mosquito bites are most likely to occur during peak feeding times during dawn and dusk. Prolonged contact or multiple mosquito bites increase the risk of developing WNV.

Pathogenesis

A. Mosquitoes are infected with WNV when feeding on an infected animal host. Wild birds are the most common source of infection, although other animals such as horses and chickens can be animal hosts. The virus is delivered to the human via mosquito bite when the mosquito's saliva is deposited in the human skin cells. The virus replicates in the skin cells and migrates to the lymph nodes and various organs. Infected immune cells are able to transverse the blood–brain barrier and infect the brain parenchyma, leading to encephalitis and meningitis. The typical incubation period for WNV is 3 to 14 days.

Predisposing Factors

A. Time of year: Late summer and early fall
B. Region: Living in or traveling to a region with a higher number of reported cases
C. Work or recreational outdoor exposure
D. Homelessness
E. Age: Most serious disease occurring in the elderly and infants
F. Blood transfusion
G. Organ transplant

Common Complaints

A. Non-neuroinvasive WNV
  1. Up to 80% of persons are asymptomatic.
  2. Fever (> 100.4°F or 38°C)
  3. Headache
  4. Myalgia
  5. Arthralgias
  6. Fatigue
  7. GI symptoms: Nausea, vomiting, and diarrhea
  8. Maculopapular rash: Usually noted on chest, back, and arms; occurs in 20% to 50% of patients. The presence of the rash represents a decreased risk of neuroinvasive disease.

Other Signs and Symptoms

A. Abdominal pain
B. Eye pain
C. Irregular heart rhythm

Potential Complications: Neuroinvasive Disease

A. Meningitis: Stiff neck, photophobia, focal neurological deficits, and higher fever (to 104°F)
B. Encephalitis: Mental status changes, stupor, confusion, coma, movement disorders, focal neurological deficits, personality changes, higher fever (to 104°F), and seizures
C. Flaccid paralysis: Cranial nerve palsy, vertigo, dysarthria, dysphagia, respiratory failure
D. Other rare complications
  1. Cardiac dysrhythmia
  2. Myocarditis
  3. Rhabdomyolysis
  4. Optic neuritis
  5. Uveitis
  6. Chorioretinitis
  7. Orchitis
  8. Pancreatitis
  9. Hepatitis

Subjective Data

A. Review the onset, course, and duration of symptoms, especially fever, rash, headache, and myalgia.
B. Ask patient to describe any neurological symptoms, changes in mental status, stiff neck, photophobia, and seizures.
C. Review symptoms of other family members or coworkers who are also ill.

D. Ask the patient to recall what activity brought about or preceded his or her symptoms.
E. Ask patient what steps he or she has taken to treat symptoms at home.
F. Review the patient's medical history for any chronic illnesses.
G. Review all medications, including OTC and herbal products.
H. Review history of mosquito bites and any preventive steps taken such as use of insect repellent.
   1. Outdoor work activities
   2. Outdoor recreational activities
   3. Review recent travel
I. Evaluate living conditions for exposure risks

Physical Examination

Patients presenting with neurological symptoms should be quickly assessed and referred to a neurologist for immediate evaluation of symptoms.

A. Check temperature, pulse, blood pressure, and respirations.
B. Inspect
   1. Observe general overall appearance, noting weakness, difficulty breathing, or changes in affect, speech, or LOC.
   2. Assess hydration status.
   3. Ophthalmic examination: Assess the presence of papilledema.
   4. Inspect face for muscle weakness or drooping.
   5. Dermal inspection for the presence of a maculopapular rash, especially on the abdomen, back, and arms.
C. Auscultate
   1. Ausculate heart for dysrhythmias.
   2. Ausculate all lung fields for adventitious breath sounds.
D. Palpate
   1. Palpate skin for signs of dehydration—poor skin turgor.
   2. Palpate the neck and lymph nodes: Preauricular, posterior auricular, submental and sublingual, anterior cervical chain, and supraclavicular nodes
   3. Palpate abdomen for tenderness and/or organomegaly.
E. Mental status and neurologic examination
   1. Administer mental status exam to look for confusion, stupor, and changes in LOC.
   2. Complete cranial nerve testing: Focus on visual fields, extraocular movement (EOM) of a transient downbeat nystagmus, facial muscle movement and strength, and gag reflex.
   3. Muscle strength testing and testing for sensation in all extremities
   4. Test reflexes.
      a. Deep tendon reflexes
      b. Babinski reflex is performed by running the reflex hammer up the midline of the sole of the foot from heel to the base of the toes (both feet are tested).
         i. A normal reaction is for the toes to either remain still or else to curl downward.
         ii. A positive Babinski is noted when the big toe points upward and the other toes fan out.
   5. Assess for meningeal signs.
      a. Signs of meningeal irritation include nuchal rigidity
      b. Assess for positive Brudzinski's and Kernig's signs (refer to Figures 18.1 and 18.2)
   6. Brudzinski's sign: Place the patient supine and flex the head upward. Resulting flexion of both hips, knees, and ankles with neck flexion indicates meningeal irritation.
   7. Kernig's sign: Place the patient supine, keeping one leg straight; flex the other hip and knee to a bent knee to form a 90° angle. Slowly extend the lower leg. This places a stretch on the meninges, resulting in pain and spasm for the hamstring muscle. Resistance to further extension can be felt.

Diagnostic Tests

A. **WNV IGM antibody capture enzyme-linked immunoassay (MAC-ELISA) is the gold standard diagnostic test.** A positive result would indicate WNV.
B. If there is concern that the illness could have been caused by another type of flavivirus, an additional test, the plaque reduction neutralization test, is used to identify false positive MAC-ELISA test results.
C. CBC with differential: Will show increased leukocytes
D. For patients with neuroinvasive disease
   1. Lumbar puncture—positive for WNV—will show pleocytosis, increased lymphocytes, increased protein, and normal glucose. The MAC-ELISA test should be performed on CSF when lumbar puncture is completed.
   2. Imaging: MRI of the brain and spinal cord is the preferred imaging test. MRI may show meningeal inflammation and bilateral lesions.
   3. EEG: May show generalized slowness

Differential Diagnoses

A. Non-neuroinvasive WNV
   1. WNV
   2. Other viral causes of febrile illness
B. Neuroinvasive WNV
   1. Other viral causes of encephalitis: St. Louis equine encephalitis, California encephalitis, Western and Eastern encephalitis

2. Acute poliomyelitis
3. Post-polio syndrome
4. Guillain–Barré syndrome
5. Multiple sclerosis
6. Vertebrobasilar stroke

Plan

A. Non-neuroinvasive disease
 1. Patient teaching
  a. Educate about expected signs and symptoms of WNV acute febrile illness.
  b. Explain signs and symptoms that would require immediate medical evaluation such as mental status changes, stiff neck, and neurological symptoms.
  c. Instruct the patient to rest as needed. The patient may expect fatigue to continue for up to 3 weeks.
  d. Instruct that WNV disease will be reported to the health department for surveillance purposes. Special populations may be subject to follow-up.
  e. Prevention strategies for WNV include ways to avoid mosquito bites.
   i. Use mosquito repellent containing DEEP, picaridin, FR3535, or oil of lemon eucalyptus.
   ii. Mosquitoes are most active from dusk to dawn; stay indoors during these peak times.
   iii. Wear long sleeves and pants.
   iv. Remove mosquito breeding sites; dump standing water in flower pots and buckets.
   v. Change the water in bird baths weekly.
  f. Finding dead birds may be a sign that WNV is circulated between birds and mosquitoes.
   i. Do not handle a dead bird with bare hands.
   ii. Report finding dead birds to the local health department for testing.
 2. Dietary management
  a. There are no specific dietary recommendations for WNV.
  b. Encourage the patient to drink plenty of fluids to prevent dehydration.
  c. If the patient is experiencing nausea and vomiting, meals should be light and nonspicy, and should be taken in smaller amounts more frequently.
 3. Pharmaceutical therapy
  a. Utilize supportive therapy such as acetaminophen for fever, antiemetics for nausea and vomiting, and antidiarrheal medications for diarrhea.
 4. There are no WNV vaccines licensed for use in humans.

B. Neuroinvasive disease
 1. **Patients presenting with neurological symptoms should be quickly assessed and referred to a neurologist for immediate evaluation and treatment of acute symptoms.**

Follow-Up

A. Follow-up would be determined by the patient's needs, severity of acute symptoms, and risk of complications.
B. WNV disease is a reportable disease to the health department for surveillance purposes.

Consultation/Referral

A. Neuroinvasive disease: Refer to neurologist immediately.
 1. For longer term needs from neuroinvasive disease, the patient may benefit from a referral to a neuropsychologist, rehabilitation specialist, physical therapist, occupational therapist, and/or speech therapist.
B. Consider an infectious disease specialist if there is difficulty with identifying the infectious agent.

Individual Considerations

A. Pregnancy
 1. There has been no causal relationship found between WNV during pregnancy and fetal abnormalities. A small number of infants, born to women who developed WNV within 3 weeks prior to delivery, were found to have symptomatic WNV disease shortly after birth.
 2. If WNV is diagnosed during the last few weeks of pregnancy, a detailed examination of the newborn should be completed and steps taken to monitor for signs and symptoms of the disease in the days and weeks after the birth.
 3. All cases of WNV in pregnant women should be reported to the health department so that the cases can be followed to determine the outcome of the pregnancies.
 4. The virus has been found in breast milk, and, in rare cases, breastfeeding has been linked to development of WNV in infants. The benefits of breastfeeding outweigh the risks of WNV disease; therefore, mothers should be encouraged to breastfeed.
 5. Pregnant women can use insect repellent products containing DEET without adverse effects.
B. Geriatrics
 1. Adults older than age 50 are more likely to suffer more serious illness and are more likely to develop neuroinvasive disease. Close attention should be given to the mental status

exam and neurological examination of the elderly.

a. Frank encephalitis occurs more in the elderly and manifests with fever, altered mental status, seizures, focal neurologic deficits, or movement disorders such as tremor parkinsonism.

Bibliography

Akhter, K. (2014, April 7). Cytomegalovirus clinical presentation. *Medscape Reference.* Retrieved from http.//emedicine.medscape.com/article/215702-clinical

Albrecht, M. A. (2012). Prevention of varicella-zoster virus infection: Herpes zoster. *UpToDate.* Retrieved from http://www.uptodate.com/contents/prevention-of-faricella-zoster-virus-infection-herpes-zoster

American Academy of Pediatrics. (2012). Epstein–Barr virus infections (infectious mononucleosis). In L. K. Pickering (Ed.), *Red book: 2012 report of the committee on infectious diseases* (29th ed., pp. 318–321). Elk Grove Village, IL: Author. Retrieved from http://aapredbook.aappublications.org.proxy.library.vanderbilt.edu/content/1/SEC131/SEC178.body?sid=4caab2bl-b2d1-455d-89a8-29988bb296a4

American Heart Association/American College of Cardiology. (2014). Practice guideline, 2014 AHA/ACC guideline for the management of patients with valvular heart disease. *Journal of the American College of Cardiology, 63*, e57–e185. Retrieved from http://content.onlinejacc.org/article.aspx?articleid=1838843

Anderson, W. E. (2014, March 20). Varicella-zoster virus. *Medscape Reference.* Retrieved from emedicine.medscape.com/article/231927-overview

Armstrong, C. (2010). Practice guidelines: AHA guidelines on prevention of rheumatic fever and diagnosis and treatment of acute streptococcal pharyngitis. *American Family Physician.* Retrieved from www.aafp.org/afp/2010/0201/p346.html

Bi, Z., Liu, K., & Liu, H. Y. (2012, August 19). West Nile virus infection in older adults. *Clinical Geriatrics.* Retrieved from http://www.clinicalgeriatrics.com/articles/West-Nile-Virus-Infection-Older-Adults

Burke, A. P. (2013, September 9). *Pathology of rheumatic heart disease.* Retrieved from http://emedicine.medscape.com/article/1962779-overview#a30

Centers for Disease Control and Prevention. (2006). *Epstein Barr virus and infectious mononucleosis.* Retrieved from www.cdc.gov/ncidod/diseases/ebv.htm

Centers for Disease Control and Prevention. (2008). *Chickenpox vaccine, what you need to know.* Retrieved from www.cdc.gov/vaccines/pubs/vis/downloads/vis-varicella.pdf

Centers for Disease Control and Prevention. (2011a). *Tick removal.* Retrieved from www.cdc.gov/lyme/removal/index.html

Centers for Disease Control and Prevention. (2011c). *Chapter 3 infectious diseases related to travel.* Retrieved from www.cdc.gov/yellowbook/2012chapter-3-infectious-diseasesrelated-to-travel/measles-rubeola.htm

Centers for Disease Control and Prevention. (2011d). *Vaccine information statement: Meningococcal vaccines.* Retrieved from www.cdc.gov/vaccines/pubs/vis/downloads/vis-mening.pdf

Centers for Disease Control and Prevention. (2012a). *Fifth disease.* Retrieved from www.cdc.gov/parvovirusb19/fifthdisease.html

Centers for Disease Control and Prevention. (2012b). *Bacterial meningitis.* Retrieved from www.cdc.gov/meningitis/bacterial.html

Centers for Disease Control and Prevention. (2012c). *Symptoms—Bartonella.* Retrieved from www.cdc.gov/bartonella/symptoms/index.html

Centers for Disease Control and Prevention. (2012d). *Transmission—Bartonella.* Retrieved from www.cdc.gov/bartonella/transmission/index.html

Centers for Disease Control and Prevention. (2013a). Prevention and control of meningococcal disease recommendations of the Advisory Committee on Immunization Practices (ACIP). *MMWR Report, 62*(2). Retrieved from www.cdc.gov/mmwr/preview/mmwrhtml/rr6202a1.htm

Centers for Disease Control and Prevention. (2013b). *West Nile virus clinical evaluation & disease* retrieved from http://www.cdc.gov/westnile/healthCareProviders/healthCareProviders-ClinLabEval.html

Centers for Disease Control and Prevention. (2013c). *West Nile virus treatment and prevention.* Retrieved from http://www.cdc.gov/westnile/healthCareProviders/healthCareProviders-TreatmentPrevention.html

Centers for Disease Control and Prevention Division of Vector-Borne Diseases. (2013). *West Nile virus in the United States: Guidelines for surveillance, prevention, and control.* Retrieved from http://www.cdc.gov/westnile/resources/pdfs/wnvguidelines.pdf

Centers for Disease Control and Prevention. (2014, January 7). *West Nile virus preliminary maps & data for 2013.* Retrieved from http://www.cdc.gov/westnile/statsMaps/preliminaryMapsData/index.html

Centers for Disease Control and Prevention. (2014, May 1). *Shingles prevention & treatment.* Retrieved from http://www.cdc.gov/shingles/about/prevention-treatment.html

Centers for Disease Control and Prevention. (n.d.). *Toxoplasmosis.* Retrieved from www.cdc.gov/parasites/toxoplasmosis/health_professionals/index.html

Centers for Disease Control and Prevention National Center for Emerging and Zoonotic Infectious Diseases Division of Vector-Borne Diseases. (n.d.). *West Nile virus (WNF) fact sheet.* Retrieved from http://www.cdc.gov/westnile/resources/pdfs/wnvFactsheet_508.pdf

Clinical Key. (n.d.). Encephalitis causes, diagnosis & treatments. Retrieved from https://www.clinicalkey.com/topics/neurology/encephalitis.html

Cunha, B. A. (2013, January 31). Rocky Mountain spotted fever. *Medscape Reference.* Retrieved from emedicine.medscape.com/article/228042-overview

Cunha, B. A. (2014, March 30). Infectious mononucleosis. *Medscape Reference.* Retrieved from emedicine.medscape.com/article/222040-overview

Domingo, P., Pomar, V., de Benito, N., & Coll, P. (2013). The spectrum of acute bacterial meningitis in elderly patients. *BMC Infectious Diseases.* Retrieved from http://www.ncbi.nlm.nih.gov/pmc/articles/PMC3599144

Drew, W. L., & Lalezari, J. P. (2006). Cytomegalovirus and HIV. *HIV InSite, UCSF University of California, San Fransico.* Retrieved from hivinsite.ucsf.edu/InSite?page=kb-05-03-03#S5.2X

Erlich, K. S. (2011). Varicella-zoster virus and HIV. *HIV InSite, UCSF University of California, San Francisco.* Retrieved from hivinsite.ucsf.edu/insite?page=kb-00&doc=kb-05-03-01

Family Practice Notebook. (2013). *Meningitis.* Retrieved from www.fpnotebook.com/neuro/ID/Mngts.htm

Farrar, F. (2013). West Nile virus: An infectious viral agent to the central nervous system. *Critical Care Nursing Clinics of North America, 25,* 191–203.

Ferri, F. F. (Ed.). (2012). Encephalitis, acute viral. In *Ferri's Clinical Advisor 2013* (1st ed.). St. Louis, MO: Mosby.

FLU.gov. (n.d.). Who is at risk, seniors. Retrieved from http://www.flu.gov/at-risk/seniors/

fpnotebook. (2013). *West Nile virus encephalitis.* Retrieved from www.fpnotebook.com/neuro/ID/WstNIVrsEnchitis.htm

Gilbert, R., & Petersen, E. (2013, November 20). Toxoplasmosis and pregnancy. *UpToDate.* Retrieved from http://www.uptodate.com/contents/toxoplasmosis-and-pregnancy?source=search_result&search=toxoplasmosis+in+pregnancy&selectedTitle=1%7E150

Goodman, D. M., & Livingston, E. H. (2012). West Nile virus. *Journal of the American Medical Association.* Retrieved from http://jama.jamanetwork.com/article.aspx?articleid=1355345

Haley, R. W. (2012). West Nile virus. *Journal of the American Medical Association.* Retrieved from http://jama.jamanetwork.com/article/aspx?

Hasbun, R. (2014, April 23). Meningitis. *Medscape Reference.* Retrieved from emedicine.medscape.com/article/232915-overview

HealthyChildren.org. (2012). *Insect repellents.* Retrieved from www.healthychildren.org/English/safety-revention/at-play/pages/Insect-Repellents.aspx

Hökelek, M. (2013, May 3). Toxoplasmosis. *Medscape Reference.* Retrieved from emedicine.medscape.com/article/229969-overview

Immunization Action Coalition. (n.d.). *Healthcare personnel vaccination recommendations.* Retrieved from www.vaccineinformation.org

Larkin, J. A. (2001). CMV colitis in the elderly patient. *Medscape Reference.* Retrieved from http://www.medscape.com/viewarticle/410184

MD Consult. (2011). *Encephalitis.* Retrieved from www.mdconsult.com

Meyerhoff, J. O. (2014, July). Lyme disease. *Medscape Reference.* Retrieved from emedicine.medscape.com/article/330178-overview

MRP Nurse Practitioner's Edition. (Summer, 2014). New York, NY: Haymark Media. Inc.

Petersen, L. R. (2013, October 9). Epidemiology and pathogenesis of West Nile virus infection. *UpToDate.* Retrieved from http://www.uptodate.com/contents/epidemiology-and-pathogenesis-of-west-nile-virus-infection?source=search_result&search=west+nile+virus&selectedTitle=2%7E59

Rowley, A. H., & Ryan. S. F. (2013). Kawasaki disease. *Clinician Reviews, 23,* 34–38.

Saccomano, S. J., & Ferrara, L. R. (2013). Infectious mononucleosis. *Clinician Reviews, 23,* 42–49.

Salinas, J. D. (2014, July 21). West Nile virus. *Medscape Reference.* Retrieved from http://emedicine.medscape.com/article/312210-overview

Salvaggio, M. R. (2013, October 18). Human herpesvirus 6 infection differential diagnoses. *Medscape Reference.* Retrieved from emedicine.medscape.com/article/219019-differential

Savva, G. M., Pachnio, A., Kaul, B., Morgan, K., Huppert, F. A. Brayne, C., & Moss, P. A. (2013, June). Cytomegalovirus infection is associated with increased mortality in the older population. *Aging Cell, 12,* 381–387.

Şerefnur, Ö., & Fahretttin, E. (2011). Encephalitis in elderly population, pathogenesis of encephalitis. Hayasaka, D. (Ed.). InTech. Retrieved from http://www.intechopen.com/books/pathogenesis-of-encephalitis/encephalitis-in-elderly-population

Tunkel, A. R., Glaser, C. A., Bloch, K. C., Sejvar, J. J., Marra, C. M., Roose, K. L., ... Infectious Diseases Society of America. (2008). The management of encephalitis: Clinical practice guidelines by the Infectious Diseases Society of America. *Clinical Infectious Diseases, 47,* 303–325.

U.S. Department of Health and Human Services Centers for Disease Control and Prevention. (2014). *Tickborne diseases of the United States: A reference manual for health care providers* (2nd ed.). Fort Collins, CO: Centers for Disease Control and Prevention Division of Vector-Borne Diseases.

Wallace, M. R. (2014, March 14). Rheumatic fever. *Medscape Reference.* Retrieved from http://emedicine.medscape.com/article/236582-overview

Wellesl, M. R. (2011). Streptococcal pharyngitis. *New England Journal of Medicine, 364,* 648–655.

World Heart Federation. (2014). Rheumatic heart disease. Retried from http://www.world-heart-federation.org/press/fact-sheets/rheumatic-heart-disease

CHAPTER NINETEEN

Systemic Disorders Guidelines

Julie Adkins, Jill C. Cash, Beverly R. Byram, and Cheryl A. Glass

Anemia

Iron-Deficiency Anemia (Microcytic, Hypochromic)

Definition

A. Microcytic anemia is characterized by small, pale red blood cells (RBCs) and depletion of iron (Fe) stores. The hematocrit (HCT) is less than 41% in males, with a hemoglobin (Hgb) less than 13.5 g/dL. In females, the HCT is less than 37% with a Hgb less than 12 g/dL. Usually mild, it can become moderate or severe.

Incidence

A. Iron deficiency is the most common cause of anemia worldwide; it is particularly prevalent in women of childbearing age. It is estimated to occur in 20% of adult women, 50% of pregnant women, and 3% of adult males in the United States.

Pathogenesis

A. Anemia is acquired; it develops slowly and in stages. Iron loss exceeds intake so that stored iron is progressively depleted. As stored iron is depleted, a compensatory increase in absorption of dietary iron and in the concentration of transferrin occurs. Iron stores can no longer meet the needs of the erythroid marrow; the plasma transferrin level increases and the serum iron concentration declines, resulting in a decrease in iron available for RBC formation.

Predisposing Factors

A. Female with history of heavy menses
B. Chronic blood loss, gastrointestinal (GI) blood loss
C. Family history or personal history of anemia
D. Poor diet, including strict vegetarian diets
E. Closely spaced pregnancies
F. Pica
G. Chronic hemoglobinuria due to an abnormally functioning cardiac valve
H. Chronic aspirin use, anticoagulants or nonsteroidal anti-inflammatory drug (NSAID) use
I. Repeated blood donation
J. Decreased iron absorption due to gastric surgery
K. Taking too many antacids that contain calcium
L. Postgastric bypass surgery

Common Complaints

A. Fatigued all of the time
B. Heart feels like it is racing, beating hard
C. Out of breath on exertion
D. Loss of appetite, nausea, and vomiting
E. Headaches throughout day
F. Weak and dizzy

Other Signs and Symptoms

Clinical presentation depends on severity, patient's age, and the ability of the cardiovascular and pulmonary systems to compensate for the decreasing oxygen-carrying capacity of the blood.

A. Initial: Exercise-induced dyspnea and mild fatigue symptoms may be minimal until the patient has significant anemia.
B. As HCT falls, dyspnea and fatigue increase.
   1. Malaise
   2. Drowsiness
   3. Sore tongue and mouth
   4. Skin pallor
   5. Pale mucous membranes and conjunctiva
   6. Pale fingernail beds
   7. Tachycardia
   8. Palpitations
   9. Tinnitus
C. Severe anemia
   1. Atrophic glossitis, cheilitis (lesions at the corner of the mouth)

2. Koilonychia (thin concave fingernails with raised edges)

Subjective Data

A. Inquire about onset, course, and duration of symptoms.
B. Ask the patient about past history of GI bleeding.
C. Take careful history of GI complaints that might suggest gastritis, peptic ulcer disease, or other conditions that might produce GI bleeding.
D. Ask if there has been a change in stool color or bleeding from hemorrhoids.
E. In menstruating women, ask about blood loss during menses.
F. Ask about dietary intake of iron-rich foods and pica.
G. Obtain medication history, especially use of aspirin, anticoagulants, and other NSAIDs.
H. Rule out history of anemia, blood-clotting problems, sickle cell disease, glucose-6-phosphate dehydrogenase (G6PD) deficiency, or other hereditary hemolytic disease.
I. Review occupation and activities with exposure to lead or lead paint.
J. Has the patient experienced palpitations, chest pain, dizziness, or shortness of breath, especially on exertion or activity?

Physical Examination

A. Check temperature, pulse, respirations, blood pressure, and weight. Check for postural hypotension.
B. Inspect
   1. Inspect general appearance; the patient may be pale, lethargic, or without overt signs if anemia is mild.
   2. Conduct eye exam; check conjunctivae for paleness.
   3. Examine oral mucosa, corners of the mouth (for cheilitis); note appearance of the tongue (atrophy of the papillae; smooth, shiny, beefy red appearance), angular stomatitis, or pale gums.
   4. Examine the skin for dryness and perfusion.
   5. Examine nails for brittleness, flattening, ridges, and concave or spoon shape.
C. Palpate: Palpate the abdomen for tenderness and enlargement of the liver and spleen.
D. Percuss: Percuss the abdomen.
E. Auscultate: Auscultate the heart for systolic flow murmurs.
F. Rectal exam: Assess for masses and obtain stool for occult blood.

Diagnostic tests

A. Initial
   1. Complete blood count (CBC) with differential and peripheral smear
   2. Serum ferritin level, serum iron, total iron-binding capacity (TIBC), retic count, RBC indices
   3. Serum iron concentration: Absent iron stores equal ferritin value less than 30 ng/mL.
   4. Urinalysis
   5. Stool for occult blood
B. Follow-up
   1. TIBC: Serum ferritin, TIBC rises.
   2. HCT 3 to 4 weeks after treatment. Treatment should continue for at least 4 to 6 months after the HCT returns to normal.
   3. GI series, if indicated.
   4. Upper and lower endoscope, if indicated.
   5. Ultrasonography or CT scan, if indicated.

Differential Diagnoses

A. Iron-deficiency anemia
B. Inadequate intake of iron
C. Any condition that causes acute or chronic blood loss
D. Hemolytic diseases such as sickle cell and G6PD deficiency
E. Anemia of chronic disease, thalassemia, and sideroblastic anemias
F. Lead poisoning
G. Neoplasm

Plan

A. General interventions: Identify source of anemia. Discuss dietary sources of iron-rich foods.
B. Patient teaching
   1. See the Section III Patient Teaching Guide for this chapter, "Iron-Deficiency Anemia."
   2. Stress the importance of dietary intake of foods high in iron, which is absorbed better than most vitamins. Orange juice increases absorption of iron. Tea and milk reduce iron absorption.
   3. Provide iron supplements. Dose according to iron lab values.
   4. Encourage the patient to stop smoking.
C. Pharmaceutical therapy
   1. Oral iron replacement
      a. Adult
         i. Begin 6-month trial of ferrous sulfate tablets 300 to 325 mg three times daily before meals or with orange juice 1 hour before meals. Food decreases iron delivery by 50%.
         ii. Iron supplement (Slow Fe) one time-release capsule daily
         iii. Niferex 150 Forte one daily or more as required by follow-up iron levels
   2. Alternative drug therapy: Parenteral iron is indicated if the patient cannot tolerate or absorb oral iron or if iron loss exceeds oral replacement.
      a. Iron dextran injection (Imferon)

b. Iron sorbitex injection (Jectofer)
  i. Parenteral iron therapy is expensive.
  ii. It is associated with significant side effects: Anaphylaxis, phlebitis, regional adenopathy, serum sickness-type reaction, and staining of intramuscular (IM) injection sites.
  iii. Dose is based on the patient's weight.
  iv. Do not administer parenteral iron along with oral iron.

Follow-Up

A. Follow-up of adults is variable, depending on source of blood loss. Manage signs of anemia.
B. It is advisable to see the patient after 3 to 4 weeks, both to monitor the hematologic response and to answer questions about the medication, which may result in improved compliance.
C. If the patient's Hgb level has increased by 1.0 g/dL in 3 to 4 weeks, continue iron supplementation for an additional 3 to 6 months. The HCT should return to normal after 2 months of iron therapy. However, keep taking iron supplements for another 6 to 12 months to replace the body's iron stores in the bone marrow.
D. Determine the effectiveness of iron replacement therapy during the first 2 weeks of therapy by checking the reticulocyte count.

Consultation/Referral

A. Refer the patient to a physician for the following.
  1. Hgb is not increased by 1.0 g/dL after 1 month of treatment.
  2. The therapeutic trial should not be continued beyond 1 month because the Hgb concentration has not increased and patient compliance with recommended regimen is not a factor.
  3. There is a steady downward trend in HCT despite treatment.
  4. There is a significant drop in HCT over previous readings (rule out lab error first).
  5. Lab findings show Hgb less than 9.0 g/dL or HCT less than 27%. Suspect underlying inflammatory, infectious, or malignant disease.
B. Refer the patient for nutrition consultation, if indicated.

Individual Considerations

A. Pregnancy
  1. Check HCT at initial prenatal visit, 28 weeks, and 4 weeks after initiating therapy.
  2. Lab findings of Hgb greater than 13 g/dL and HCT greater than 40% may indicate hypovolemia. Be alert for signs of dehydration and preeclampsia.
  3. Counsel the patient on proper diet and refer to a dietitian.
  4. Recommend one to two iron tablets a day in addition to prenatal vitamins containing iron.
  5. If unable to tolerate vitamins, recommend children's Chewable Flintstones vitamins with iron, two orally, daily.
B. Adults
  1. Bleeding is the usual cause of anemia in adults. In adult men and postmenopausal women, bleeding is usually from the GI tract.
  2. In premenopausal women, menstrual loss may be the underlying cause of anemia.
  3. Smokers may have higher Hgb levels; therefore, anemia may be masked if standard Hgb levels are used.

Pernicious Anemia (Megaloblastic Anemia)

Definition

A. Pernicious anemia is a megaloblastic, macrocytic, normochromic anemia caused by a deficiency of intrinsic factor in the gastric juices produced by the stomach, which results in malabsorption of vitamin B_{12} necessary for DNA synthesis and maturation of RBCs. There is the production of abnormally large and oval red cells with a mean corpuscular volume (MCV) in excess of 100 fL (femtoliters). The anemia can be severe, with HCT as low as 10% to 15%.

Incidence

A. Pernicious anemia is common in people of northern European descent. Both sexes are equally affected. It is most prevalent in Scandinavian and English-speaking populations. It usually occurs in the fifth and sixth decades of life; it is rarely seen in persons younger than 35 years, but it can occur in individuals in their 20s. There is an increased incidence in those with other immunologic diseases. The average age of diagnosis is age 60. Rarely is pernicious anemia passed down through families.

Pathogenesis

A. Pernicious anemia is possibly due to an autoimmune reaction involving the gastric parietal cell that results in nonproduction of intrinsic factor and atrophy of gastric mucosa. Vitamin B_{12} deficiency can result from inadequate intake, impaired absorption, increased requirements as in pregnancy, or faulty utilization. Poor intake is rare, occurring most often in strict vegetarians. You get this vitamin from eating foods such as meat, poultry, shellfish, eggs, and dairy products.

Predisposing Factors

A. People of northern European descent
B. Ages 50 to 60 years
C. Immunologic disease
D. Loss of parietal cells following gastrectomy

E. Overgrowth of intestinal organisms
F. Crohn's disease
G. Ileal resection or abnormalities
H. Fish tapeworm
I. Congenital enzyme deficiencies
J. Diet: Strict vegetarian diets
K. Medications such as aminosalicylate sodium
L. Alcoholism
M. Hashimoto's thyroiditis
N. Addison's disease, Graves' disease, myasthenia gravis, or type 1 diabetes
O. History of gastric bypass or banding surgery

Common Complaints

A. Weakness and dizziness
B. Tongue is sore, red, and shiny
C. Numbness, burning, tingling sensation of arms or legs
D. Feel heart "jumping out of skin"
E. Edema of lower extremities
F. Anorexia
G. Diarrhea

Other Signs and Symptoms

A. Dyspnea on exertion
B. Pallor
C. Fatigue
D. Tachycardia
E. Exercise intolerance
F. Angina
G. Glossitis
H. Mucositis
I. Peripheral paresthesia
J. Palpitations
K. Abdominal tenderness, organomegaly
L. Advanced stages: Dementia and spinal cord degeneration

Classic presentation involves sore tongue and numbness and tingling in the extremities, hands, or feet.

Subjective Data

A. Inquire about onset, duration, and course of presenting symptoms.
B. Ask the patient to describe usual bowel habits. Has there been any blood in stools?
C. If GI complaints are present, inquire about presence of red, burning tongue; abdominal complaints; presence of diarrhea or constipation.
D. If neurologic complaints are present, inquire about presence of pins-and-needles paresthesia and weakness, unsteadiness due to proprioceptive difficulties, lethargy, and fatigue.
E. Inquire about dietary intake, using 24-hour recall.
F. Ask about alcohol consumption: How much? How long?
G. Obtain medication history: Over-the-counter (OTC) and prescription drugs.
H. Obtain past medical history, specifically if the patient has a history of gastrectomy, gastric bypass/banding, resection of ileum, or other GI disorders.
I. Review usual weight and recent loss.

Physical Examination

A. Check temperature, pulse, respirations, blood pressure, weight.
B. Inspect
    1. Observe general, overall appearance; observe walking.
    2. Conduct oral exam for characteristic red, shiny tongue.
    3. Conduct dermal and eye exams for color: Affected patients are slightly icteric.
    4. Evaluate the look of the person related to age: Affected patients show premature aging or graying.
C. Palpate
    1. Palpate the abdomen for masses.
    2. Evaluate pedal edema.
D. Percuss: Percuss the abdomen
E. Auscultate
    1. Auscultate heart sounds and lungs.
    2. Auscultate the abdomen for bowel sounds.
F. Neurologic exam: Assess deep tendon reflexes (DTRs) and mental status.
    1. Look for paresthesia involving hands and feet, gait disturbances, or memory loss (mild forgetfulness to dementia or altered thought processes). Poor finger–nose coordination may be seen; positive Romberg's and Babinski's signs may be present.

Diagnostic Tests

A. CBC with differential and peripheral smear: **Macroovalocytes and hypersegmented neutrophils may be present on peripheral blood smear. (They are absent in the setting of concurrent iron deficiency.)**
B. Serum vitamin B_{12} level: Less than 100 pg/mL
C. Serum folic acid levels, serum iron, serum ferritin, and TIBC
D. Serum intrinsic factor antibody
E. Lactate dehydrogenase (LDH)
F. Urinalysis
G. Stool for occult blood
H. GI radiographic studies
I. Gastric analysis: Achlorhydria is found on stimulation testing
J. Bone marrow aspiration
K. A woman with low B_{12} levels may have a false positive Pap smear due to vitamin B_{12} effects on the epithelial cells.

Differential Diagnoses

Differential diagnosis of anemia by red cell morphology can be undertaken (MCV, mean corpuscular hemoglobin concentration [MCHC]). Common causes of each type of anemia are as follows:

A. Normochromic, normocytic: Normal MCV = 80 to 100, MCHC = 32% to 36%
   1. Aplastic anemia
   2. Chronic disease
   3. Early iron deficiency
   4. Hemolysis
   5. Hemorrhage
B. Microcytic: MCV = 50 to 82, MCHC = 24 to 32
   1. Chronic disease
   2. Iron deficiency
   3. Thalassemia
C. Macrocytic: MCV greater than 100, MCHC greater than 36
   1. Antimetabolites
   2. Folic acid deficiencies
   3. Vitamin B_{12} deficiencies
   4. Chronic alcoholism

Plan

A. General interventions
   1. Most common method of determining vitamin B_{12} deficiency is by serum vitamin B_{12} assay.
   2. Most common method of demonstrating folate deficiency is by measurement of serum folic acid levels.
   3. Red cell indices and peripheral smear should be done to determine classification of anemia to facilitate workup.
   4. Red cell distribution width (RDW) determination can assist in detecting red cell heterogeneity previously available only by exam of the peripheral smear. The RDW determination overcomes the problems of detecting coexisting microcytic and macrocytic anemias.
B. Patient teaching
   1. See the Section III Patient Teaching Guide for this chapter, "Pernicious Anemia."
   2. Neurologic symptoms usually improve with treatment; however, some neurologic deficits may not be reversible.
C. Pharmaceutical therapy
   1. Vitamin B_{12} (cyanocobalamin or hydroxocobalamin) 100 mg intramuscularly or subcutaneous administration daily for 1 week.
      a. Decrease frequency and administer a total of 2,000 mg during the first 6 weeks of therapy (weekly for 1 month).
      b. **Maintenance treatment requires lifelong administration of 100 mg intramuscular injection monthly depending on B_{12} levels. Some people may require lifelong administration at different intervals such as every 2 weeks.**
      c. Nascobal (intranasal cyanocobalamin) one spray in one nostril one time per week.
   2. Recommended daily allowance for vitamin B_{12}
      a. Adults: 2.0 mcg/d
      b. Pregnant women: 2.2 mcg/d
      c. Breastfeeding women: 2.6 mcg/d
   3. Concomitant iron supplementation during first month of therapy. Rapid blood cell regeneration increases iron requirements and can lead to iron deficiency.

Follow-Up

A. The patient must be seen in 2 weeks to determine response to treatment: Increased reticulocyte count and increased HCT; diminution in neurologic signs and symptoms.
B. Evaluate the patient monthly when giving vitamin B_{12} injections.
C. **Endoscopy every 5 years is used to rule out gastric carcinoma. People with pernicious anemia may have gastric polyps and are more likely to develop gastric cancer and gastric carcinoid tumors.**
D. Check the patient every 6 months for HCT, and check his or her stool for occult blood.
E. HCT value rises 4% to 5% per week in uncomplicated cases.

Consultation/Referral

A. Refer the patient to a dietitian.
B. Rapid reticulocytosis should be seen following treatment; it peaks in 7 to 10 days.
C. Consult a physician if no change is seen.

Individual Considerations

A. Pregnancy
   1. Lactovegetarians and ovolactovegetarians do well in pregnancy.
   2. Vegetarian women who eat neither eggs nor milk products should take vitamin B_{12} supplements during pregnancy and lactation.
B. Adults: Disorder rarely is seen in patients younger than age 35 years.
C. Geriatrics
   1. Disorder most commonly is seen in the geriatric population.
   2. Follow up elderly patients with assessment of cardiovascular symptoms 48 hours after initiating therapy.
   3. Rapid blood cell regeneration increases iron requirements and can lead to iron deficiency.

Cancer Management—*Jill C. Cash and Cheryl A. Glass*

Definition

A. Cancer is a disease in which cells in the body divide in an abnormal fashion, invading normal cells and tissues. These abnormal cells proliferate and spread to other parts of the body by means of the blood and of the lymphatic systems. Cancer cells generally begin in one area of the body, causing "cancer" in that particular organ of the body. However, with invasion of other tissues/organs, the cancer cells can spread to other organs, causing "cancer" in other parts of the body.

Incidence

There are over 100 different types of cancer. The different cancers are broken down into five broad categories.

A. Carcinoma: Cancer of the skin and/or tissue covering major internal organs
B. Sarcoma: Cancer of the bone, cartilage, muscle, fat, connective tissue, and blood vessels
C. Leukemia: Cancer of the bone marrow and blood forming tissues
D. Lymphoma and myeloma: Cancer of the immune system
E. Central nervous system: Cancer of the brain and spinal cord system
F. It has been estimated that in the year 2014 there were approximately 1,665,540 new cases of cancer reported, approximately 585,720 cancer-related deaths expected in the United States. The cancers that are expected to be the most frequent include the following:
   1. Bladder cancer
   2. Breast cancer
   3. Lung cancer
   4. Melanoma
   5. Colon/rectal cancer
   6. Non-Hodgkin's lymphoma
   7. Endometrial cancer
   8. Pancreatic cancer
   9. Kidney (renal cell) cancer
   10. Prostate cancer
   11. Leukemia
   12. Thyroid cancer
G. Breast cancer is expected to be the most common type of cancer, followed by prostate cancer and lung cancer.

Pathogenesis

A. Cell division occurs by the body producing new cell formation in a controlled order, producing the appropriate amount of cells to keep the body healthy. Once the cell grows and divides properly, the cell will die and new cells will replace the old cells. However, when cancer occurs, cell division does not occur properly, and mutations occur that affect normal cell growth and division. The existing cells do not die while new cells are being produced, and the overproduction/accumulation of cells form a mass, which is known as a tumor. Tumors may be benign or malignant. Benign tumors are not hazardous to the body. Malignant tumors are cancerous and may spread to other parts of the body, known as metastasis.

Predisposing Factors

A. Predisposing risk factors for each type of cancer depend on the type of cancer present.

Common Complaints

Many complaints and side effects may occur prior to the diagnosis of cancer as well as during cancer treatment. A few common complaints include:

A. Fatigue
B. Nausea and vomiting
C. Constipation
D. Diarrhea

Subjective Data

A. Inquire about onset, duration, and course of presenting symptoms.
B. What measures has the patient used to relieve the symptoms?
C. What makes the symptoms worse or better?
D. What medications, OTC or prescription, have been used to treat the symptoms? What were the results?
E. Over the past week, how have symptoms changed?
F. Is patient sleeping well? If not, what has the patient tried to do to assist sleeping?
G. Has patient lost or gained weight over the past few weeks?

Physical Examination

A. Check temperature, pulse, respirations, blood pressure, and weight.
B. Inspect
   1. Observe overall appearance.
   2. Inspect skin for color and hydration.
C. Palpate
   1. If abdominal symptoms exist, palpate abdomen for tenderness and masses.
   2. Evaluate for tissue swelling.
D. Percuss
   1. Percuss abdomen
E. Ausculate
   1. Auscultate heart and lung sounds.
   2. Ausculate abdomen for bowel sounds.
F. Neurologic exam
   1. Assess DTRs and mental status.

Diagnostic Tests

A. CBC with differential
B. Comprehensive metabolic profile (CMP)
C. Bone mineral density (BMD): Consider assessing for osteoporosis in patients who are at risk for fracture. Long-term use of steroids, chemotherapy treatment, and advanced age contribute to an increase risk in bone loss leading to osteoporosis.

Differential Diagnosis

A. Cancer being the primary diagnosis, the secondary diagnosis is made according to the presenting symptoms which may include:
   1. Dehydration
   2. Fatigue
   3. Nausea and vomiting
   4. Constipation
   5. Diarrhea
   6. Osteoporosis
   7. Anemia

Plan

A. General interventions for the common side effects of cancer treatment may include:
   1. Fatigue (NCCN website, www.nccn.org/professionals/physician_gls/f_guidelines.asp)
      a. Advise taking several naps during the day in the chair or bed, whichever is most comfortable.
      b. Encourage daily exercise or activities as tolerated. Short periods of exercise and activity help to increase energy levels and also help with anxiety/depression.
      c. Encourage the patient to ask family and friends for help when needed. During this time, the patient should not feel guilty for needing help with certain activities.
      d. Encourage the patient to keep a schedule and block off times when he or she will need to perform certain activities. Saving energy for these tasks/time blocks will help the patient complete the task and feel better when performing the task.
   2. Nausea and vomiting (NCCN website www.nccn.org/professionals/physician_gls/f_guidelines.asp)
      a. Several medications are used to prevent and treat nausea and vomiting. Some medications may be used prior to the start of chemotherapy to prevent nausea and vomiting. The medication used may depend on the type of chemotherapy being prescribed. Stress the importance of the patient notifying the oncologist about the severity of nausea/vomiting and treatment success with medications being prescribed.
      b. Other suggestions to improve nausea and vomiting include:
         i. Eat small, frequent meals during the day. Eating meals at a slower pace can also improve symptoms.
         ii. Bland foods are best tolerated. Avoid spicy foods, alcohol, and caffeine.
         iii. Wear comfortable clothing that does not restrict breathing or interfere with comfort around the abdomen.
         iv. Encourage frequent oral hygiene to eliminate bad tastes in the mouth.
         v. Eat foods that have ginger in them, such as ginger tea. Ginger has been shown to reduce nausea.
         vi. Hydration must be maintained. Encourage the patient to drink plenty of liquids in whatever form the patient is able to tolerate. Water, Gatorade, Pedialyte, and other bland liquids are suggested. Some patients may also tolerate liquids that are cold; however, drinking liquids that are close to room temperature may be easier for some patients to keep down.
   3. Constipation/diarrhea
      a. Constipation can be experienced as a side effect of some chemotherapy medications.
      b. Encourage the patient to notify the oncologist if severe constipation is experienced.
      c. Encourage good dietary habits, such as increasing liquids, and eating foods high in fiber for prevention/treatment of constipation.
      d. Healthy dietary choices include foods high in protein (eggs, meat, fish, poultry, peanut butter, beans), an assortment of fruits and cooked vegetables, and foods low in fat and lactose. Avoid fatty/fried foods, raw vegetables, and dried fruits.
      e. Daily exercise is recommended to improve constipation.
      f. Diarrhea may occur as a side effect and can cause dehydration and loss of electrolytes from the body. Hydration should be maintained by drinking plenty of water, Gatorade, or Pedialyte. OTC medications may be used, such as loperamide (Imodium). If medications are needed to control the diarrhea, the primary provider or oncologist should be notified. If diarrhea is not controlled by diet and OTC medications, prescription medications may be given. For severe diarrhea not controlled by dietary changes and oral medications, intravenous hydration and medications should be prescribed.
   4. Bone loss can be a side effect of patients treated with radiation. Radiation breaks down the bone-building cells and increases the risk of fracture. Steroids are given to some patients with cancer. Steroids are known to increase the production of osteoclasts, which are cells that break down bone tissue. Other chemotherapy agents are known to suppress bone marrow growth. Therefore, all patients should have a baseline bone density screening test (Dexascan). Vitamin D and calcium should also be taken daily. Counsel the

patient regarding daily weight-bearing activities to increase bone strength. See Chapter 21, "Rheumatological Guidelines," for evaluation and treatment of osteoporosis.

5. Anemia should also be evaluated for in patients receiving medications for cancer. Anemia can be caused by the cancer, radiation, chemotherapy, iron deficiency, or a combination of these. Symptoms of anemia include fatigue, pale skin, shortness of breath, tachycardia, dizziness, and so on. See this chapter entry on Anemia.

B. Caregiver support, advance directives, and palliative care should also be addressed. See Chapter 4, "Caregiver and End-of-Life Issues," for information on this content.

C. Reference websites for clinicians and patients
1. The National Comprehensive Cancer Network (NCCN) comprises 25 designated cancer centers that have world-class, state-of-the art research programs. The National Cancer Institute (NCI) is a U.S. federal agency for cancer research and clinician and family information. NCCN mobile apps are available for free for smartphones and tablets from the App Store for iPad or iPhone (search NCCN) or from the Google Play Store for the Android tablet or smartphone (search NCCN).
   a. Clinician resources: National Comprehensive Cancer Network Guidelines www.nccn.org/professionals/physician_gls/f_guidelines.asp
2. NCCN patient and caregiver resources
   a. NCCN guides for patients: www.nccn.org/patients/guidelines/default.aspx covers .guidelines by cancer type, including breast cancer, caring for adolescents and young adults, colon cancer, melanomas, and others. The site also covers lung cancer screening.
   b. Dictionary of terms: www.nccn.org/patients/resources/dictionary/default.aspx
   c. Cancer staging guide: www.nccn.org/patients/resources/diagnosis/staging.aspx
3. NCI
   a. Prostate cancer treatment: www.cancer.gov/cancertopics/pdq/treatment/prostate/Patient/page4
   b. NCI dictionary of cancer terms: www.cancer.gov/dictionary
   c. NCI drug dictionary: www.cancer.gov/drugdictionary
4. American Cancer Society
   a. Colon/rectum cancer: www.cancer.org/cancer/colonandrectumcancer
   b. Breast cancer: www.cancer.org/cancer/breastcancer
   c. Ovarian cancer: www.cancer.org/cancer/ovariancancer
   d. Cervical cancer: www.cancer.org/cancer/%20cervicalcancer/index
5. National Breast Cancer Foundation, Inc.
   a. Breast cancer www.nationalbreastcancer.org/about-breast-cancer

Follow-Up

A. Follow-up will be based on the presenting symptoms and testing results.

Consultation/ Referral

A. Refer the patient to the oncologist or physician if side effects are not controlled with treatments offered.

B. For extreme cases of dehydration/illness, hospitalization may be required.

Individual Considerations

A. Geriatrics
1. Geriatric patients who are immunocompromised deteriorate more quickly. The threshold for hospitalization and/or referral to the specialist should be lower for these patients along with more aggressive treatment options.

Chronic Fatigue

Definition

A. Fatigue is one of the most common symptoms confronting the practitioner in an office practice. A patient with chronic fatigue is characterized as having fatigue with multiple associated symptoms for longer than 6 months in which these symptoms have a profound impact on daily activities.

Incidence

A. Fatigue accounts for 1% to 3% of visits to generalists as an isolated symptom or diagnosis. Psychiatric disorders are involved in less than 50% of cases. Chronic fatigue has a reported frequency in excess of 20%. Fatigue is seen predominantly in women, four times more than in men, and the highest prevalence is among people aged 40 to 59; however, it can affect people of all ages, including teens and children.

Pathogenesis

A. Fatigue is a sensitive but nonspecific indicator of underlying medical and/or psychological pathology. It is reportedly more often due to unknown cause or to psychiatric illness than to physical illness, injury, medications, drugs, or alcohol.

Predisposing Factors

A. Hyperthyroidism

B. Hypothyroidism

C. Cardiac disease: Congestive heart failure

D. Neurally mediated hypotension

E. Infections: Endocarditis, hepatitis
F. Respiratory disorders: Chronic obstructive pulmonary disease (COPD) and sleep apnea
G. Anemia
H. Arthritides and related disorders
I. Cancer
J. Alcoholism
K. Side effects from drugs such as sedatives and beta blockers
L. Psychologic conditions such as insomnia, depression, anxiety, and somatization disorder
M. Female gender
N. Epstein-Barr virus

Common Complaints

A. Lack of energy
B. Listlessness
C. Fatigue that interferes with participation in family, work, or even leisure activities

Other Signs and Symptoms

A. Weakness
B. Overexertion
C. Poor physical conditioning
D. Inadequate quality or quantity of sleep
E. Undernutrition and poor appetite
F. Stress
G. Obesity
H. Emotional problems: Depression, anxiety, and somatization disorder
I. Fibromyalgia

Subjective Data

A. Review history for onset, duration, and course description of the fatigue.
B. Ask the patient about significant losses, low self-esteem, and occurrence of crying spells and suicidal thoughts. **High prevalence of depression and suicide is present in this patient population.**
C. Ask the patient about a history of any abuse of hypnotic drugs, alcohol, or tranquilizers.
D. Review medications, both OTC and prescription drugs.
E. Review the patient's medical history for cardiac, thyroid, and other medical conditions.
F. Review sleep and insomnia history.
G. Review history for family illness, new baby, or postpartum.
H. Establish last menses to rule out pregnancy.
I. Review exercise patterns.
J. Review diet with 24-hour recall.
K. Elicit history of fever, night sweats, weight loss, and enlarged lymph node(s).
L. Inquire about recent major life changes, such as moving or a change in job.
M. Establish usual weight, and review recent weight gain or loss, over what period.
N. Review any recent infections, flu, or mononucleosis.
O. Review high-risk sexual practices and intravenous drug use to rule out human immunodeficiency virus (HIV) exposure.
P. Review recent history for transfusion of blood products to rule out hepatitis or HIV exposure.
Q. Obtain history of the patient's daily living and working habits.

Physical Examination

A. Check temperature, pulse, respirations, blood pressure, and weight; check for postural hypotension.
B. Inspect
   1. Observe general overall appearance. Skin: Conduct dermal exam for changes in pigmentation, purpura, dryness, rashes, jaundice, pallor, splinter hemorrhages, or petechiae.
   2. Eyes: Conduct a funduscopic exam to rule out Roth's spots and tuberculoma.
   3. Check sclerae for icterus.
   4. Throat: Inspect pharynx for petechiae at the junction of the hard and soft palate to rule out mononucleosis.
   5. Extremities: Inspect joints for inflammation.
C. Palpate
   1. Palpate the neck to rule out goiter.
   2. Palpate all lymph nodes (neck, axilla, and groin) for size, degree of tenderness, and distribution.
   3. Complete clinical breast exam for masses.
   4. Palpate the abdomen for organomegaly, masses, and ascites.
   5. Palpate the joints for tenderness.
   6. Assess the genitalia for masses and tenderness, to rule out infection.
D. Percuss: Percuss the abdomen for organomegaly, masses, ascites, and hepatic tenderness.
E. Auscultate: Auscultate the heart and lungs.
F. Neurologic exam: Complete mental status assessment.
G. Rectal exam: Assess for masses, prostatic pathology, and occult blood.

Diagnostic Tests

A. CBC with differential and peripheral smear
B. Erythrocyte sedimentation rate (ESR)
C. Calcium, albumin, blood urea nitrogen (BUN), and creatinine
D. Glucose
E. Transaminase (aminotransferase): Viral hepatitis is associated with elevation in transaminase.
F. HIV serum test
G. Thyroid panel to rule out hyperthyroidism or hypothyroidism
H. Heterophile test to rule out acute mononucleosis
I. Monospot
J. Epstein–Barr virus
K. Sleep study

Differential Diagnoses

A. Chronic fatigue syndrome
   1. The Centers for Disease Control and Prevention (CDC) include these two criteria for chronic fatigue syndrome diagnosis:
      a. "Unexplained, persistent fatigue present for 6 months or more that is not due to ongoing exertion; is not substantially relieved by rest, is of new onset (not lifelong) and results in a significant reduction in previous levels of activity.
      b. Four or more of the following symptoms present for 6 months or more:
         i. Impaired memory or concentration
         ii. Postexertional malaise (extreme, prolonged exhaustion and sickness following physical or mental activity)
         iii. Unrefreshing sleep
         iv. Muscle pain
         v. Multi-joint pain without swelling or redness
         vi. Headaches of a new type or severity
         vii. Sore throat that's frequent or recurring
         viii. Tender cervical or axillary lymph nodes

B. Hypercalcemia
C. Mild renal failure
D. Early diabetes mellitus
E. Hypothyroid or hyperthyroidism
F. Cardiac disease
G. Anemia
H. Anicteric hepatitis
I. Connective tissue disease
J. Immune hyperactivity
K. Disturbed sleep or obstructive sleep apnea
L. Occult neoplasm
M. Infection: History of fever, sweats, weight loss, and diffuse adenopathy. These symptoms also suggest HIV, especially with high-risk behaviors (see the entry on HIV in this chapter).
N. Mononucleosis

Plan

A. General interventions
   1. Find out the patient's view of his or her illness before proceeding with patient education.
   2. Manage underlying disease (refer to specific chapters).
   3. Treat the patient with nutritional or vitamin supplementation, as indicated.
   4. There are no therapies that provide prompt relief from symptoms.
   5. Strong patient–provider alliance is essential.
   6. Evaluate the patient for the possibility that he or she is confusing focal neuromuscular disease with generalized lassitude.
   7. Consider having a sleep study performed if obstructive sleep apnea is a possibility.

B. Patient teaching
   1. Discuss and review the evidence for the diagnosis, and offer a careful explanation of symptoms. Many patients think they have a medical problem producing fatigue symptoms.
   2. Review the diagnostic criteria for depression (see Chapter 24, "Psychiatric Guidelines"), and describe the neurochemical mechanisms by which depression leads to fatigue. Refer the patient for individual counseling or group therapy.
   3. Review the idiopathic nature of chronic fatigue syndrome and its nonprogressive nature. Inform the patient that it has a gradually improving clinical course and has the chance of full recovery. Symptoms are self-limited, usually clearing within 12 to 18 months. Research shows that people with chronic fatigue for 2 years or less are more likely to improve than the person whose diagnosis has taken longer.
   4. Encourage the patient to begin a gentle exercise program and to engage in life's activities.
   5. Provide nutritional education.

C. Pharmaceutical therapy
   1. For postural hypotension
      a. Increase dietary sodium.
      b. Antihypotensive agent: Fludrocortisone 0.1 mg daily.
   2. Low-dose antidepressant therapy for disordered sleep
      a. Amitriptyline HCl 25 mg every bedtime
      b. Imipramine HCl 25 to 50 mg at bedtime; may increase dosage up to 300 mg daily
      c. Doxepin HCl 10 to 20 mg every bedtime
      d. Short-term hypnotic: Zolpidem (Ambien) 5 to 10 mg at bedtime
   3. NSAIDs for symptomatic relief of myalgia, arthralgia, or headache.
   4. Correct anemia with iron supplements, if applicable.

Follow-Up

A. **Follow up in 2 weeks to reevaluate status and then monthly, depending on signs and symptoms.**
B. Follow closely if the patient is depressed.

Consultation/Referral

A. Consult a physician if no improvement is seen with therapies. Emphasize the legitimacy of the patient's symptoms and summarize the workup, its rationale, and its findings.
B. Refer the patient to a mental health professional as indicated by depression and/or suicidality.

Individual Considerations

A. Adults: Fatigue is most often explained by common factors such as overexertion, poor physical conditioning, inadequate quantity or quality of sleep, obesity, malnutrition, stress, obstructive sleep apnea, and emotional problems.

B. Geriatrics: Prescribing medications should be tailored for the patient, using low-dose medications. Give precautions about falls if the patient is using medications to aid in sleep.

RESOURCE

ME/CFS Initiative (formerly the Chronic Fatigue Syndrome) http://solvecfs.org/

Fevers of Unknown Origin

Definition

A. The criteria for fevers of unknown origin (FUO) are an illness of at least 3-weeks duration, fever over 101.0°F (38.3°C) on several occasions, and undiagnosed FUO after 1 week of study in the hospital. Because of cost factors, the criterion requiring 1 week of hospitalization is often bypassed.

Incidence

A. In adults, infections account for 20% to 40% of the cases, whereas cancer accounts for 7% to 20% of FUO cases. Autoimmune disorders occur with equal frequency in adults and children. Infection, cancer, and autoimmune disorders combined account for 20% to 25% of FUO in patients who have been febrile for 6 months or longer. Various miscellaneous diseases account for another 25%. Approximately 50% of FUO remain undiagnosed but have a benign course, with symptoms eventually resolving.

Pathogenesis

There are five categories of FUO causes.

A. Infection: Most common systemic infections are tuberculosis (TB) and endocarditis.

B. Neoplasms: Most common are lymphoma and leukemia.

C. Autoimmune disorders: Most common are Still's disease, systemic lupus erythematosus (SLE), and polyarteritis nodosa.

D. Miscellaneous causes: Hyperthyroidism, thyroiditis, sarcoidosis, Whipple's disease, familial Mediterranean fever, recurrent pulmonary emboli, alcoholic hepatitis, drug fever, factitious fever, and others

E. Undiagnosed FUO

Predisposing Factors

A. Upper respiratory infection

B. Urinary tract infection

C. Viral illnesses

D. Drug allergy, especially to antibiotics

E. Connective tissue disease

Common Complaints

A. The patient feels "sick all over," with malaise and fatigue.

B. The patient has chills all over the body with high fever.

Other Signs and Symptoms

A. Tachycardia

B. Sensation of warmth or flushing

C. Piloerection

D. Myalgias

E. Mild inability to concentrate, confusion, delirium, or even stupor

F. Labial herpes simplex outbreak, or fever blisters

Subjective Data

A. Review the onset, course, and duration of symptoms.

B. Review family, occupational, and social history.

C. Review sexual practices, including monogamy and oral, rectal, and vaginal sexual habits, recreational habits, and any new changes.

D. Elicit information regarding use of intravenous drugs.

E. Review if the patient has had this illness before. How was it treated?

F. Review travel during the past month.

G. Review any new hobbies, changes at home or work, or other new events.

H. Review the patient's history for contact with any friends or family members who have been sick and do not seem to be getting any better.

I. Review the patient's history for eating any uncooked meat and dietary changes during the past month.

J. Review for risk factors for thrombophlebitis (see Chapter 12, "Cardiovascular Guidelines").

Physical Examination

A. Check temperature, pulse, respirations, blood pressure, weight, and height.

B. Inspect

1. Conduct funduscopic exam to rule out retinopathy, Roth's spots, and choroidal tubercles.
2. Examine the ears, nose, and throat. Inspect the mouth.
3. Observe the skin and mucous membranes.

C. Palpate

1. Palpate the neck, axilla, and groin for lymphadenopathy.
2. Elderly: Palpate the scalp for tender arteries of cranial arteritis.
3. Palpate the thyroid gland.
4. Palpate the abdomen for organomegaly, masses, tenderness, guarding, rebound, suprapubic

tenderness, and costovertebral angle (CVA) tenderness.

5. Palpate the musculoskeletal system for bone or joint swelling, tenderness, increased warmth; check lower extremities for evidence of phlebitis, asymmetrical swelling, calf tenderness, and palpable cord.

D. Percuss
   1. Percuss the sinuses for tenderness, and transilluminate for evidence of sinusitis.
   2. Percuss the chest for consolidation.
   3. Percuss the abdomen.
E. Auscultate
   1. Auscultate the heart for murmurs and rubs.
   2. Auscultate the lungs for rales, consolidation, and effusion.
F. Neurologic exam
   1. Assess for signs of meningeal irritation (Brudzinski's and Kernig's signs), and presence of focal deficits.
   2. Conduct mental status exam.
G. Genitorectal exam, if applicable
   1. Female: Conduct pelvic exam for cervical discharge, adnexal masses, lesions, and pelvic inflammatory disease (PID) symptoms.
   2. Male: Conduct prostate and testicular exam for tenderness and masses; check penis for discharge, rash, and lesions.
   3. Both: Conduct rectal exam for discharge, tenderness, and masses; check stool for occult blood specimen.
   4. Check the skin for rashes or wounds.

Diagnostic Tests

A. CBC with differential
B. ESR
C. Urinalysis and urine culture
D. Blood glucose
E. Liver function test
F. Blood cultures
G. Consider serology for suspected infections or pathology (refer to Chapter 18, "Infectious Disease Guidelines"). Suspected infections include Epstein-Barr virus, Q fever, Lyme disease or other tick-borne diseases, hepatitis, syphilis, and cytomegalovirus (CMV).
H. Suspected collagen disease: Antinuclear antibodies (ANA) and rheumatoid factor
I. Suspected TB: Tuberculin skin test, sputum, and urine cultures
J. Immunologic studies: ELISA, Western blot test, and antistreptolysin O (ASLO) titer
K. Suspected mononucleosis: Heterophile antibody test
L. Suspected *Salmonella:* Widal's test
M. Suspected thyroiditis: Thyroid profile
N. Suspected malaria or relapsing fever: Direct examination of blood smears
O. Imaging: Depends on suspected infection
   1. Chest, sinus radiographic films
   2. GI studies: Proctosigmoidoscopy, evaluation of gallbladder function
   3. CT scan of abdomen and pelvis, abdominal ultrasonography
   4. MRI is better than CT scan for detecting lesions of the nervous system.
P. Suspected embolism: Ventilation-perfusion (V/Q) scan
Q. Suspected endocarditis or atrial myxoma: Echocardiography
R. Radionuclide studies: Gallium scan and radium-labeled immunoglobulin useful in detecting infection and neoplasm.
S. Laparotomy in the deteriorating patient if the diagnosis is elusive despite extensive evaluation. Any abnormal finding should be aggressively evaluated: Headache necessitates a lumbar puncture to rule out meningitis; biopsy any skin from an area of rash to look for cutaneous manifestations of collagen vascular disease or infection; enlarged lymph nodes should be aspirated or biopsied and examined for cytologic features to rule out neoplasm and send for culture.

Differential Diagnoses

A. FUO
B. Systemic and localized infections
C. Neoplasms
D. Autoimmune disorders
E. Thrombophlebitis
F. Miscellaneous causes (see Definition)

Plan

A. General interventions: Observe the patient taking own temperature to document the presence of a fever to make sure the temperature is not self-induced.
B. Patient teaching
   1. Instruct the patient to keep a record of temperatures, preferably rectal, taken each evening, when elevations are most likely to occur.
   2. Reassure the patient that there is nothing abnormal about temperatures in the range of 97.0°F to 99.3°F.
   3. Instruct the patient on use of physical cooling aids, such as exposure of skin to cool ambient temperature, bedside fan, and sponging with cool water or alcohol.
   4. Explain to the patient that immersion in an ice water bath may be indicated for hyperthermic emergencies.
C. Pharmaceutical therapy
   1. Start therapeutic trials if a diagnosis is strongly suspected.

   a. Antituberculous drugs for TB
   b. Tetracycline for brucellosis
   c. If the patient shows no clinical response in 2 weeks, stop therapy and reevaluate.
2. Symptomatic antipyretic therapy: Salicylates or acetaminophen every 4 hours if not contraindicated

Follow-Up

A. Follow up in 24 to 48 hours.
B. Indications for admission to the hospital: Fever remains elevated beyond 101°F for weeks, and ambulatory diagnostic efforts have been unsuccessful.

Consultation/Referral

A. Consult with a physician for diagnosis and comanagement if indicated.
B. Refer the patient to a specialist if unable to differentiate definitive diagnosis.

Individual Considerations

A. Pregnancy
   1. Refer the patient for perinatal consultation.
   2. High fevers early in the first trimester have been associated with an increase in neural tube defects.
   3. Maternal fevers may cause fetal tachycardia.
B. Geriatrics
   1. Common causes of FUO include TB, Hodgkin's lymphoma, and temporal arteritis.
   2. Elderly patients commonly present with nonspecific symptoms.

HIV—*Beverly R. Byram*

Definition

A. AIDS is a chronic, life-threatening condition caused by HIV. HIV is a retrovirus that targets helper T (CD4) cells and contains a viral enzyme called reverse transcriptase that allows the virus to convert its RNA to DNA, then integrate and take over the cell's own genetic material. Once taken over, the new cell begins to produce new HIV retrovirus. This process kills the CD4 cells that are the body's main defense against illness. This interferes with the body's ability to fight off infection—bacteria, viruses, and fungi—that cause disease. AIDS is the term used to define a severely compromised immune system.

Epidemiology

A. Recent estimates show that 1 in 6 persons infected with HIV are now older than 50 years of age. This is due to longer survival of HIV-positive patients on antiretroviral therapy and increased diagnoses with wider HIV testing recommendations. The older population does not see itself as high risk, and there is little HIV prevention geared toward people older than 50. Perception among providers is that older adults are not a high-risk population and are not screened for HIV as often as younger adults. In 2009, the American College of Physicians (ACP) suggested that the age range of routine HIV screening be extended to 75 years.
B. The widespread use of antiretroviral therapy has altered the course of HIV disease. In 2012, HIV was reclassified as a chronic illness. More than 50% of deaths in HIV-positive persons on highly active antiretroviral therapy (HAART) are related to conditions other than AIDS.

Risk Factors

A. Gay or bisexual men or prostitutes
B. Needle sharing by IV drug users (IVDU)
C. Heterosexual contact with an infected partner
D. Perinatal infection: Mother-to-child transmission
E. Open wound and mucous membrane exposure to body fluids of infected person
F. Recipients of transfusion of contaminated blood or blood products (rare since 1985)

Pathogenesis

A. HIV belongs to a subgroup of retroviruses called lentiviruses or "slow" viruses. The course of infection of the virus is characterized by a long interval between infection and the onset of serious symptoms. CD4 cells are the primary target of the HIV.
B. Primary HIV infection is followed by a burst of viremia during which the virus is easily detected in peripheral blood per HIV PCR viral load. During the "window period," the first 2 to 6 weeks following infection, persons may test negative for the HIV antibody with the enzyme-linked immunosorbent assay (ELISA) and Western Blot tests. During this time, the person can be highly infectious to sexual partners. In this time of early infection with high viral load, the CD4 cells can decrease by 20% to 40%. Within 2 to 4 weeks after exposure to the virus, up to 70% of infected patients experience a flulike illness related to acute infection. The immune system fights back to reduce the HIV levels with killer T cells (CD8) that attack and kill the infected cells. The patient's CD4 cell count may rebound by 80% to 90%. A patient can remain symptom-free for a long time, often years. During this time there is low-level replication of HIV but ongoing deterioration of the immune system. Enough of the immune system remains intact to prevent most infections. The patient is infectious during this time.

C. The final phase of HIV occurs when a sufficient number of CD4 cells are destroyed and when production of new CD4 cells cannot match destruction. Patients exhibit fatigue, fever, and weight loss. This failure of the immune system leads to AIDS.
D. An HIV-infected person can live an average of 8 to 10 years before developing clinical symptoms. HIV disease is not uniformly expressed in all people. A small portion of patients develop AIDS and die within months of infection. Approximately 5% of infected patients, known as "long-term nonprogressors," have no signs of disease after 12 or more years.
E. Most AIDS-defining conditions are marked by a CD4 count of less than 200 cells or the appearance of one or more of the opportunistic infections (OI). Bacteria, viruses, or fungi that would not cause illness in a healthy immune system cause OI. These infections are often severe and sometimes fatal.
F. Research shows age-related immune system dysfunction associated with decreased CD4 cell response to antiretroviral therapy due to thymus involution.
G. Untreated HIV in patients older than age 50 show a more rapid progression toward AIDS and poor overall survival.

Common Complaints

A. Fatigue: Often severe
B. Fever: Longer than 1 month
C. Night sweats: Drenching
D. Loss of appetite
E. Weight loss
F. Rash

Other Signs and Symptoms

A. Lymphadenopathy: Enlarged lymph nodes often involving at least two noncontiguous sites
B. Anemia
C. Neutropenia
D. Thrombocytopenia
E. Cough
F. Dyspnea
G. Asymptomatic whitish patches on sides of tongue: Hairy leukoplakia
H. Thrush: Oral candidiasis
I. Odynophagia: Esophageal candidiasis, CMV esophagitis
J. Chronic vaginal candidiasis
K. Skin changes: Rashes, dry skin, and seborrheic dermatitis
L. Purplish, nonblanching nodules found on the skin, mucous membranes, and viscera: Kaposi's sarcoma
M. Muscle wasting
N. Chronic diarrhea: Longer than 1 month
O. Hepatosplenomegaly
P. Cardiomyopathy
Q. Chronic bacterial infections, including community-acquired pneumonias
R. TB
S. Sexually transmitted infections (STIs)
T. Peripheral neuropathy
U. Dementia

Subjective Data

A. Review symptoms: Onset, course, and duration.
B. Ask about previous HIV testing: Dates and reasons for testing.
C. Past medical history review: Hospitalizations, comorbidities, immunizations, normal weight, pain, chronic lymph node disorders, and any changes of skin overlying lymph nodes.
D. Past surgical history review.
E. Sexual history: Number of partners in the past year, number of lifetime partners, any previous partner known to be HIV positive or have STIs, and any previous partners known to have been incarcerated
   1. Women: History of abnormal Pap smears, contraception, and condom use with partner.
   2. Men: Men having sex with men (MSM), heterosexual, bisexual, receptive anal intercourse, and condom use.
F. Past mental health history: Past and current mental health diagnosis and treatment.
G. Substance use: Tobacco, alcohol, and drugs
H. History of IVDU: Needle sharing and when last used drugs
I. Transfusion or blood product history prior to 1985.
J. Lived or traveled outside of the United States: When and for how long.
K. Assess the presence of persistent fever with no localizing symptoms.
L. Assess the patient's support system: Who knows about their diagnosis?

Physical Examination

A. Height, weight, blood pressure, pulse, respiratory rate, and temperature
B. General observation: General appearance, including fat distribution, signs of wasting
C. Inspect
   1. Skin: Evaluate for rashes, seborrhea, folliculitis, moles, Kaposi's sarcoma, warts, herpes, dry skin, skin cancer, fungal infections, molluscum contagiosum, jaundice, and needle marks.
   2. Head and neck; eyes, ears, nose, and throat (HEENT)
      a. Assess visual acuity.
      b. Retina exam for CMV
      c. Evaluate sclera for icterus.

d. Oral exam for thrush, hairy leukoplakia, mucosal Kaposi's sarcoma, gingivitis, aphthous ulcers, and dental health

D. Auscultate
   1. Pulmonary auscultation for air movement and abnormal breath sounds
   2. Cardiac evaluation for normal and abnormal heart sounds

E. Palpate
   1. Palpate the thyroid.
   2. Lymphatic evaluation of regional versus generalized swelling: Specific location, size, and texture of nodes.
   3. Palpate the abdomen to evaluate the presence of hepatosplenomegaly, masses, tenderness, pain, or rebound tenderness.
   4. Breast examination

F. Rectal/vaginal examination
   1. Both genders: Inspect for the presence of ulcers and warts in the vagina, perineum, and rectum.
   2. Females: Perform bimanual examination, Pap smear with HPV testing, obtain specimens for STI testing, and perform a digital rectal exam and anal Pap smear, if indicated.
   3. Males: Perform testicular exam, digital rectal exam; consider an anal Pap if indicated.

G. Neurologic examination
   1. Assess mental status.
   2. Assess cranial nerves, including gait, strength, DTRs; evaluate proprioception, vibration, pinprick, temperature, and sensation in distal extremities.

H. Psychiatric examination: Screen for depression.

Diagnostic Tests

A. Repeat HIV ELISA and Western blot
B. CBC, with differential, including platelets
C. Complete chemistry profile
D. Fasting lipid profile
E. Venereal disease research laboratory and rapid plasma reagin
F. Serologies for toxoplasmosis
G. CD4/CD8 cells and CD4/CD8 ratio
H. HIV RNA viral load
I. HIV resistance genotype
J. HLA-B 5701 (risk for Abacavir hypersensitivity reaction syndrome)
K. Tropism testing: If considering using CCR5 antagonist
L. Hepatitis serologies: Hepatitis A virus (HAV) serology (antibody); hepatitis B virus (HBV) serology (HBsAb, HBeAb, HBsAb); and hepatitis C virus (HCV) serology (antibody)
M. Cultures for STIs: Anal, vaginal (culture pharynx if history indicates oral sex)
N. Urinalysis
O. Pap smear with HPV testing
P. TB screening

Differential Diagnoses

A. HIV
B. Other diseases that lead to immune suppression or are related to symptoms
C. Cancer
D. Chronic infections
E. TORCH infections
F. Syphilis
G. TB
H. Endocarditis
I. Infectious enterocolitis
J. Bowel disorders: Antibiotic-associated colitis, inflammatory bowel disease, or malabsorptive symptoms
K. Endocrine diseases
L. Neuropathy
M. Alcoholism
N. Liver disease
O. Renal disease
P. Thyroid disease
Q. Vitamin deficiency
R. Chronic meningitis

Plan

A. General interventions
   1. Refer and comanage the patient with HIV/AIDS clinician.
   2. Identify and refer for treatment of substance abuse.
   3. Explain to the patient that each visit will include a review of history, a physical exam, and laboratory studies to assess health status.
   4. Discuss health habits: Smoking, nutrition, and exercise.
   5. Discuss treatment plan.
      a. HAART
      b. Therapy for OI and malignancies
      c. Prophylaxis for OI: PCP and MAC
      d. Management of side effects of medications and comorbidities
      e. Immunizations

B. Patient teaching
   1. Discuss living with HIV disease.
   2. Discuss transmission prevention strategies: Safer sex practices and condom use.
   3. Provide contact information for AIDS social service organizations (ASO).
   4. Discuss the patient's concerns, including notification of sexual partner(s) and needle-sharing partner(s).
   5. See the Section III Patient Teaching Guide for this chapter, "Reference Resources for Patients With HIV/AIDS."

C. Pharmaceutical therapy
   1. Treatment with HAART. The Department of Health and Human Services (DHHS) guidelines on the treatment of HIV/AIDS recommended HAART for all HIV-infected patients regardless of CD4 cell count.
   2. Polypharmacy is one of the biggest challenges in caring for the aging population. The average HIV-negative patient older than 50 years old takes an average of 5 medications. These added to 3 to 5 or more HIV medications complicates monitoring for medication interaction and side effects. Comorbidities, existing medications, and potential organ toxicities should all be considered in choosing a HAART regimen.
   3. HAART (Public Health Service Task Force Guidelines for the Use of Antiretroviral Agents in HIV-1 Infected Adults and Adolescents) classes:
      a. Nucleoside/nucleotide reverse transcriptase inhibitors (NRTIs)
      b. Non-nucleoside reverse transcriptase inhibitors (NNRTIs)
      c. Protease inhibitors (PIs)
      d. Integrase inhibitors (INIs)
      e. Fusion inhibitors (FIs)
      f. CCR5 inhibitors (CIs)
      g. Combination antiretrovirals—pill formulations with multiple antiretroviral medications
   4. Prophylaxis and treatment for OIs. May discontinue prophylaxis if sustained immune reconstitution on HAART.
      a. Pneumocystis pneumonia (PCP). Prophylaxis if CD4 count is less than 200 or if the patient has oral candidiasis.
         i. First line: Bactrim DS (TMP-SMZ), one tablet three times weekly or one tablet daily (if toxoplasmosis is positive)
         ii. Alternatives: Dapsone, atovaquone, and aerosolized pentamidine
      b. Mycobacterium avium complex (MAC) Prophylaxis if CD4 count is less than 75.
         i. First line: Zithromax 1,200 mg weekly
         ii. Alternative: Clarithromycin
   5. Managing the side effects of HAART, complications of HIV therapy, and aging population: There are multiple complications of long-term HIV infection and treatment with HAART. Age-related decrease in renal and hepatic function should be considered when choosing a HAART regimen. These problems can lead to higher levels of HIV medications and increased toxicities. There are no guidelines for dose adjustment based on age but renal and hepatic function should be monitored on an ongoing basis and adjustments made accordingly. Other considerations for HAART choices include immunizations—(live virus vaccines contraindicated unless CD4 count > 200—varicella, MMR)
      a. Hepatitis A and B series
      b. Tetanus
      c. Pneumococcal vaccine
      d. Yearly influenza vaccines
      e. Tdap booster as needed
      f. Shingles vaccine contraindicated in HIV patients

D. Complications associated with both HIV-positive and with older populations requiring diligent monitoring.
   1. Osteoporosis—HIV/AIDS patients are at high risk for decreased bone density
   2. Hypogonadism—common in men with AIDS
   3. Neuropsychiatric disorders—depression, anxiety, and substance use are common in the HIV population.
      There is increased risk for HIV-related dementia.
   4. Peripheral neuropathy—common side effect with older HIV medications
   5. Cardiovascular disease (CVD)—HIV-related disorders such as insulin metabolism, diabetes, lipodystrophy, dyslipidemia, and hypertension. CVD complications are among the leading cause of death in HIV disease.
   6. Malignancies—liver, anal, cervical, and lung cancers are common in HIV/AIDS patients.
   7. Menopause—early menopause has been described, and the use of hormone replacement therapy has not been adequately studied in the HIV population

Follow-Up

A. Schedule return visit 4 to 6 weeks after initial visit to discuss staging HIV/AIDS and living with HIV/AIDS.

   More frequent visits are needed with a new diagnosis and initiation of HAART. Once HIV is suppressed, less frequent visits are required, generally every 4 to 6 months.

B. TB screening annually

C. Pap smear
   1. Initially, if normal, repeat in 6 months, then yearly if it remains normal.
   2. If abnormal, follow guidelines by the American Society of Colposcopy and Cervical Pathology (ASCCP).

D. Annual Pap smears for patients as indicated.

E. Urinalysis yearly if taking a tenofovir-containing regimen

F. STI screening initially, then yearly if high risk

G. Other annual screening as per the U.S. Preventive Services Task Force (USPSTF) and HIV/AIDS Treatment Guidelines (AIDSinfo.NIH.gov/guidelines)

Consultation/Referral

A. Refer the patient to a specialist in HIV for management of continued care and pharmacologic therapy.
B. Refer the patient to a nutritionist for baseline evaluation and diet counseling.
C. Perform vision screening yearly
D. Require dental care every 6 months
E. Make hepatology referral if chronic, active hepatitis B and/or C. Truvada is approved for HBV treatment.

Individual Considerations

A. Preexposure prophylaxis (PrEP) is a prevention method for HIV-negative partners.
   1. Truvada is Food and Drug Administration (FDA) approved for use as PrEP among heterosexual and MSM HIV-negative partners. One tablet is taken daily to reduce the risk of infection. Those taking PrEP should be monitored for potential side effects.
B. Postexposure prophylaxis (PEP)
   1. PEP—Depending on exposure type and severity, postexposure antiretroviral treatment (ART) should be started as quickly as possible and be taken for 4 weeks.
      a. Expert consultation should be obtained as quickly as possible, (National HIV/AIDS Clinician's Consultation Center PEPline, 1-888-448-4911).
      b. Follow with occupational health for regular clinical assessment and labs.
      c. Perform HIV testing with HIV RNA, viral load, if an illness compatible with seroconversion illness occurs (fever, lymphadenopathy, pharyngitis, and rash).
      d. Advise transmission precautions during first 3 to 6 months postexposure (use condoms, refrain from donating blood, etc.).

Idiopathic (Autoimmune) Thrombocytopenic Purpura

Definition

A. Idiopathic thrombocytopenic purpura (ITP) is an autoimmune disorder in which an IgG autoantibody is formed that binds to platelets. Platelets help your blood clot by clumping together to plug small holes in damaged blood vessels. The platelet count is less than 150,000 mm^3.

Incidence

A. Acute ITP commonly occurs in childhood, frequently precipitated by a viral infection. Peak age of incidence is between 20 and 50 years. There is a 2:1 female-to-male predominance. The adult form is usually a chronic disease (> 6 months) and it seldom follows a viral infection.

Pathogenesis

A. ITP is due to production of antiplatelet antibodies that lead to peripheral destruction and sequestration of platelets. It is not clear which antigen on the platelet surface is involved. Platelets are not destroyed by direct lysis even if the antiplatelet antibody binds complement. Destruction takes place in the spleen, where splenic macrophages with Fc receptors bind to antibody-coated platelets.

Predisposing Factors

A. Infections
B. Chronic alcoholism
C. Sepsis
D. AIDS
E. Immune disorders, such as SLE
F. Drug use
G. Chronic lymphocytic leukemia (CLL)
H. Pregnancy

Common Complaints

A. Purple spots and bruises on skin
B. Nosebleeds
C. Mouth and gums bleeding

Other Signs and Symptoms

A. Purpura, petechiae, and hemorrhagic bullae in the mouth
B. Tendency to bleed easily—easy bruising
C. Menorrhagia—abnormal heavy menstruation
D. No systemic illness: The patient feels well and is not febrile.

Subjective Data

A. Determine when the patient or caregiver first noticed symptoms; note if the symptoms have changed or progressed.
B. Rule out pregnancy as cause of nosebleeds.
C. Ask if the patient is feeling well except for the bleeding or bruising.
D. Determine if the patient has a fever.
E. Obtain medication history for OTC and prescribed medications.
F. Determine the patient's history of immune disorders, recent infections, alcoholism, and pregnancy.
G. Establish usual weight and any recent weight loss.

Physical Examination

A. Check temperature, pulse, respirations, blood pressure, and weight.
B. Inspect
   1. Observe general appearance.

2. Conduct dermal exam for purpura and petechiae.
3. Conduct eye exam; check sclera for hemorrhages.
4. Examine the mouth for dental carries and poor hygiene, mouth petechiae, and hemorrhagic bullae.

C. Palpate

Normally, the spleen should not be palpable.

1. Palpate the abdomen, liver, and spleen.
2. Palpate the cervical, axillary, and groin lymph nodes for adenopathy.

D. Percuss: Percuss the abdomen, liver, and spleen.

E. Auscultate
1. Auscultate the heart and lungs.
2. Auscultate the abdomen for bowel sounds and bruits.

Diagnostic Tests

A. Platelet count

The major concern during the initial phase is risk of cerebral hemorrhage when platelet count is less than 5,000 platelets/fiL.

B. IgG

Increased levels of IgG appear on the platelet count in the presence of thrombocytopenia.

C. CBC with differential and peripheral smear

Peripheral smear shows normal WBCs and red blood cells (RBCs), platelets low in count with large size.

D. Bleeding time is prolonged.

E. Coagulation tests: Prothrombin time (PT), partial thromboplastin time (PTT), and fibrinogen are usually normal. Platelet-associated antibodies may be detected.

Coagulation studies are normal.

F. Referral for bone marrow aspiration

Bone marrow may appear normal or have increased megakaryocytes (early form of platelets) with thrombocytopenia.

Differential Diagnoses

Thrombocytopenia may be produced in two ways: By abnormal bone marrow function or by peripheral destruction of platelets.

A. Abnormal bone marrow function
1. Aplastic anemia
2. Hematologic malignancies
3. Myelodysplasia: This can only be ruled out by examining the bone marrow.
4. Megaloblastic anemia
5. Chronic alcoholism

B. Non–bone marrow disorders
1. Immune disorders
   a. ITP
   b. Drug induced from medications being taken
   c. Secondary to CLL and SLE
   d. Posttransfusion purpura
2. Hypersplenism resulting from liver disease
3. Disseminated intravascular coagulation (DIC)
4. Thrombotic thrombocytopenic purpura
5. Sepsis
6. Hemangiomas
7. Viral infection, AIDS
8. Pregnancy
9. Hypothyroidism

Plan

A. General interventions: Comanage the patient with a physician for medication therapy.

B. Patient teaching
1. Instruct the patient to avoid trauma; advise *no contact sports.*
2. Instruct the patient to avoid salicylates, which impair platelet function.
3. Prednisone therapy benefits
   a. Prednisone increases platelet count by increasing platelet production.
   b. Long-term therapy may decrease antibody production.
   c. Bleeding often diminishes 1 day after beginning prednisone.
   d. Platelet count usually begins to rise within a week; responses are almost always seen within 3 weeks.
   e. About 80% of patients respond, and the platelet count usually returns to normal.

C. Medical or surgical management
1. Splenectomy is the most definitive treatment. Most adults ultimately undergo splenectomy.
2. Splenectomy is indicated if patients do not respond to prednisone initially or require unacceptably high doses to maintain an adequate platelet count.

D. Pharmaceutical therapy
1. Initial treatment
   a. Prednisone 1 to 2 mg/kg/d.
   b. High-dose therapy should be continued until the platelet count is normal, and the dose should then be gradually tapered.
2. In most patients, thrombocytopenia recurs if prednisone is completely withdrawn.

3. High-dose therapy should not be continued indefinitely in an attempt to avoid surgery.
4. Alternative drug therapy
   a. High-dose intravenous immunoglobulin 400 mg/kg/d for 3 to 5 days is highly effective in rapidly raising the platelet count.
      i. This treatment is expensive, costing approximately $5,000.
      ii. The beneficial effect lasts only 1 to 2 weeks.
      iii. This therapy should be reserved for emergency situations such as preparing a severely thrombocytopenic patient for surgery.
5. Danazol 600 mg/d
   a. Danazol is used for patients who fail to respond to prednisone and splenectomy.
6. Platelet transfusions are an option rarely used.
7. Avoid aspirin, NSAIDs, and warfarin, which interfere with platelet function and blood clotting. Be aware if the patient is also taking any new selective inhibitors of factor Xa such as Xarelto, Pradaxa or Eliquis, and so on.

Exogenous platelets survive no better than the patient's own platelets. In many cases, platelets survive less than a few hours. This therapy is reserved for cases of life-threatening bleeding in which enhanced hemostasis for even an hour may be of benefit.

Follow-Up

A. The patient must be monitored very closely. Platelet counts should be drawn daily to weekly; frequency depends on the severity and course.
B. Prognosis for acute ITP: 80% respond and fully recover within 2 months; 15% to 20% progress to chronic ITP.
C. Prognosis for chronic ITP: 10% to 20% recover fully; remainder continue to have low platelet counts and may see a remission or relapses over time.
D. The principal cause of death from ITP is intracranial hemorrhage.

Consultation/Referral

A. After diagnosis, refer the patient to a hematologist.

Individual Considerations

A. Pregnancy
   1. Rule out hemolysis, elevated liver enzymes, low platelets (HELLP) syndrome, infection, and DIC as causes of thrombocytopenia.
   2. There is an increased incidence of spontaneous abortions and hemorrhage at the time of delivery from genital tract injury.
   3. Antepartum management: Conduct fetal blood sampling and testing when the mother has a known history of ITP.
   4. Intrapartum management
      a. Avoid fetal hypoxia, which can decrease the fetal platelet count.
      b. Avoid prolonged labor.
      c. Conduct continuous fetal monitoring.
      d. Epidural anesthesia may be used if the platelet count is at least 100,000 cells/mm^3.
   5. Postpartum management: Breastfeeding is not recommended because of the possible transmission of antiplatelet antibodies through breast milk.
B. Geriatrics: ITP is uncommon in this population; there is usually another cause for low platelets Avoid medications that impede platelet function.

Lymphadenopathy

Definition

Lymphadenopathy is enlargement of a lymph node, manifested in benign, self-limiting diseases and in those that are incurable and fatal. Only small lymph nodes in the neck, axilla, and groin are palpable in normal individuals. Palpable nodes in other regions, or any node exceeding 0.5 cm in size, are potentially abnormal. The body has approximately 600 lymph nodes. There are different categories of lymphadenopathy.

A. Localized adenopathy
B. Hilar adenopathy
C. Generalized lymphadenopathy
D. Other lymphatic abnormalities that present in other ways, such as lymphangitis, lymphadenitis, and lymphedema

Incidence

A. Lymphadenopathy is a very common presenting symptom. Age is an important diagnostic factor: In patients younger than age 30, the cause proves to be benign in 80% of cases; in patients older than age 50, the rate of benign disease falls to 40%. In primary care patients with unexplained lymphadenopathy, approximately three fourths of patients will present with localized lymphadenopathy and one fourth with generalized lymphadenopathy.

Pathogenesis

A. Inflammation and infiltration are responsible for pathologic enlargement. Localized lymphadenopathy may represent the spread of disease from an area of drainage. The left supraclavicular node is referred to as the "sentinel" node, which is in contact with the thoracic duct and drains much of the abdominal cavity. The right supraclavicular node drains the mediastinum, lungs, and esophagus. Generalized lymphadenopathy often results from infection, malignancy, hypersensitivity, and metabolic disease.

Predisposing Factors

A. Factors posing high risk for HIV infection
   1. Homosexuality and bisexuality
   2. Intravenous drug abuse
   3. Hemophilia, conditions requiring multiple transfusions
   4. Prostitution
   5. Haitian ancestry
B. Occupational exposure
C. History of pharyngitis, upper body infections (head and neck), or intraoral infection
D. Exposure to animals: Cats, sheep, cattle, rodents, deer ticks
E. Travel to the southwest United States
F. Exposure to bird droppings
G. Lacerations sustained from gardening
H. Exposure to TB
I. History of sexual exposure resulting in STIs
J. History of tobacco abuse
K. Cancer
L. Anticonvulsant drugs that cause skin rash, fever, hepatosplenomegaly, and eosinophilia; for example, phenytoin (Dilantin)
M. Other medications
   1. Hydralazine
   2. Para-aminosalicylic acid
   3. Allopurinol

Common Complaints

A. Sore throat
B. Fever
C. Fatigue and malaise
D. Loss of appetite
E. Loss of weight
F. Swollen, painless lumps in neck

Other Signs and Symptoms

A. May feel "good" except for finding enlarged lymph node.
B. Node location(s): For inguinal enlargement, rule out conditions that may resemble inguinal or femoral lymphadenopathy: Hernias; ectopic testicular, endometrial, or splenic tissue; lipomas; varices; and aneurysms. If inguinal area is painful and tender, it is most frequently caused by STIs.
C. Skin rash
D. Bruising or petechiae
E. Pruritus
F. Erythema of skin or scalp
G. Skin eruption
H. Night sweats
I. Enlarged and tender abdomen, abdominal pain
J. Joint pain

Subjective Data

A. A comprehensive and detailed history is necessary for diagnosis (see Predisposing Factors). Review the onset, course, and duration of symptoms.
B. What does the patient note with respect to location, tenderness or painfulness, softness or hardness, and mobility of lymph nodes? Has the patient noticed more than one enlarged lymph node?
C. Review the patient's history of intravenous drug use. Review risk factors for HIV.
D. Review history for hobbies, specifically gardening and camping, and occupation (see "Toxoplasmosis" and "Lyme Disease" in Chapter 18, "Infectious Disease Guidelines").
E. Review medications: Prescription, OTC, and herbal remedies.
F. Determine whether the patient has a fever or a known valvular heart disease.
G. Review any other associated symptoms or signs.
H. Review any recent exposure to family and friends with infections. Has the patient had recent immunizations?
I. Review recent dental problems or abscessed teeth.
J. Note whether the patient is a smoker. If so, how much, for how long, and when did the patient quit smoking?
K. Review the patient's history for recent cat scratches.
L. Review the patient's history for recent travel.
M. Review the patient's history for new sexual partners, to rule out STIs.
N. Review usual weight and any recent weight loss, noting how much over what period of time.
O. Elicit information about similar symptoms in the past, when they occurred, how they were treated (antibiotics, biopsy), and the success of the treatment.
P. Elicit information about alcohol intake, noting how much, how long, and, if the patient has quit, how long ago.

Physical Examination

A. Check temperature, pulse, respirations, blood pressure, and weight.
B. Inspect
   1. Conduct a funduscopic exam.
   2. Examine the eyes, ears, nose, and throat.
   3. Conduct a dermal exam, and check mucous membranes for a primary inoculation site; this may be a clue to a diagnosis of cat-scratch disease (CSD).
C. Palpate
   1. Palpate the abdomen.
   2. Conduct a clinical breast exam. Palpate mass to determine if it is a lymph node, if applicable.

3. Palpate all nodal areas for localized and generalized lymphadenopathy.
   a. Hard, fixed nodes suggest metastasis, and a biopsy should be taken promptly. Size alone is not itself diagnostic; any node larger than 3 cm suggests neoplastic disease.
4. Palpate the scalp in the elderly for the tender arteries of cranial arteritis.
5. Palpate the neck for thyroid gland tenderness.

D. Percuss: Percuss sinuses for tenderness, and transilluminate for evidence of sinusitis.
E. Auscultate: Auscultate the heart and lungs.
F. Musculoskeletal system exam
   1. Assess for bone or joint swelling, tenderness, and increased warmth.
   2. Examine lower extremities for evidence of phlebitis: Asymmetric swelling, calf tenderness, and palpable cord.
G. Genitorectal exam
   1. Conduct careful external evaluation for herpetic lesions, masses, discharge, erythema, chancroid, scabies, and pediculosis.
   2. "Milk" urethra for discharge.
   3. Note any folliculitis if the patient regularly shaves genital area.
   4. Female pelvic exam: Look for cervical discharge, cervical motion tenderness, adnexal tenderness, and mass or "heat" in the pelvis.
   5. Males: Examine the prostate and testicles for tenderness and masses, as well as the penis for discharge and rash.
   6. Examine the rectum for discharge, tenderness, masses, and fistulas.

Diagnostic Tests

A. CBC with differential
B. Peripheral blood smear: The most useful laboratory test; may be helpful in the diagnosis of chronic leukemia, infectious mononucleosis, and other viral illnesses
C. Blood chemistries
D. Liver function tests, especially alkaline phosphatase
E. Angiotensin-converting enzyme (ACE) test
F. ANA and rheumatoid factor
G. RPR and microhemagglutination assay for antibody to *T. pallidum* (MHA-TP), to rule out syphilis
H. Heterophile test, to rule out mononucleosis
I. ELISA and Western blot, to rule out HIV
J. Uric acid: Elevations may reflect lymphoma or other hematologic malignancies.
K. Blood cultures
L. Urethral or cervical cultures and smears
M. Throat culture
N. Chest x-ray
O. Mammogram with ultrasonography of suspicious breast area, if indicated
P. After consultation
   1. Abdominal ultrasonography or CT scan, if indicated
   2. Biopsy or fine-needle aspiration: Fine-needle aspiration is used to obtain a cytologic diagnosis of a suspected cancer. False negative results may occasionally occur.
   3. Lymph node biopsy: Lymph node biopsy is the definitive test to confirm or rule out a suspected neoplastic process.
   4. Mediastinoscopy
Q. Tuberculin skin testing (PPD) and the ACE determination can facilitate assessment.
   1. If the patient tests *negative for ACE and PPD* and is Caucasian, then bronchoscopy and mediastinoscopy may be necessary to rule out lymphoma. If the patient tests *positive for ACE but negative for PPD,* then the probability is very high that sarcoidosis is the cause.
   2. If the patient tests *negative for ACE but positive for PPD*, then primary TB is likely.

Differential Diagnoses

A. There are four general categories for lymphadenopathy.
   1. Infections
      a. Mononucleosis
      b. AIDS or AIDS-related complex (ARC): Generalized adenopathy in an asymptomatic HIV-infected patient indicates a high risk of progression to AIDS. The lymphadenopathy represents follicular hyperplasia in response to HIV infection.
      c. Toxoplasmosis
      d. Secondary syphilis
   2. Hypersensitivity reactions
      a. Serum sickness
      b. Phenytoin and other drugs
      c. Vasculitis: Lupus and rheumatoid arthritis (RA)
   3. Metabolic diseases
      a. Hyperthyroidism
      b. Lipidoses
   4. Neoplasia
      a. Leukemia
      b. Hodgkin's disease, advanced stages
      c. Non-Hodgkin's lymphoma
B. Causes can be isolated by site of the enlarged nodes (see Table 19.1).

Plan

A. General interventions
   1. Pay careful attention to nodal history and characteristics on physical examination.

TABLE 19.1 Causes of Lymphadenopathy by Site of Enlarged Nodes

Anterior Auricular Viral conjunctivitis Trachoma Posterior auricular Rubella scalp infection	**Submandibular or Cervical (Unilateral)** Buccal cavity infection Pharyngitis (can be bilateral) Nasopharyngeal tumor Thyroid malignancy
Axillary Breast malignancy Breast infection Upper extremity infection	**Supraclavicular (Left)** Intra-abdominal malignancy Renal malignancy Testicular or ovarian malignancy
Cervical (Bilateral) Mononucleosis sarcoidosis Toxoplasmosis pharyngitis	**Supraclavicular (Right)** Pulmonary malignancy Mediastinal malignancy Esophageal malignancy
Epitrochlear Syphilis (bilateral) Hand infection (unilateral)	**Any Region** Cat-scratch fever Hodgkin's disease Leukemia Metastatic cancer Sarcoidosis Granulomatous infections
Hilar Adenopathy Sarcoidosis (unilateral or bilateral) Fungal infection (histoplasmosis, coccidioidomycosis) Lymphoma (unilateral or bilateral) Bronchogenic carcinoma (unilateral or bilateral) TB (unilateral or bilateral)	
Inguinal Syphilis Genital herpes Lymphogranuloma venereum chancroid Lower extremity or local infection	

2. Make a careful assessment to establish that the palpable mass is a lymph node. Chronicity alone is not always serious.

B. Patient teaching: As indicated by the particular disease process causing the lymphadenopathy. See the relevant guidelines.

C. Pharmaceutical therapy: Dependent on the diagnosis

Follow-Up

A. Follow the patient closely to evaluate resolution of lymphadenopathy and disease process.

B. Follow-up depends on the diagnosis.

Consultation/Referral

A. Consultation with a physician may be useful if a period of observation is needed.

B. Refer the patient to a specialist after initial workup, if indicated.

C. Refer the patient to an oncologist or oncologic surgeon if the patient is suspected of having a malignancy, to consider the need for biopsy or best approach to obtaining a tissue diagnosis.

Individual Considerations

A. Geriatrics: Regional lymphadenopathy occurs often when carcinomas metastasize to lymph nodes in the elderly.

Bibliography

Aberg, J. A., Gallant, J. E., Ghanem K. G., Emmanuel, P., Zingman, & B. S., Horberg, M. A. (2014). Primary care guidelines for the management of persons infected with HIV: 2013 update by the HIV medicine association of the Infectious Diseases Society of America. *Clinical Infectious Diseases, 58*, e1–34.

AIDSINFO. (2012, July 31). *Recommendations for use of antiretroviral drugs in pregnant HIV-l-infected women for maternal health and interventions to reduce perinatal HIV transmission in the United States.* Retrieved from http://aidsinfo,nih.gov/contentfiles/lvguidelines/perinatalgl.pdf

AIDSINFO. (2012, November 5). Offering information on HIV/AIDS treatment, presentation, and research. *Guidelines for the use of antiretroviral agents in pediatric HIV infection.* Retrieved from http://aidsinfo.nih.gov/guidelines/html/2/pediatric-arv-guidelines/0

AIDSINFO. (2013, February 12). Offering information on HIV/AIDS treatment, presentation, and research. *Guidelines for the use of antiretroviral agents in HIV-l-infected adults and adolescents.* Retrieved from http://aidsinfo.nih.govguidelines/html/1/adult-and-adolescent-arv-guidelines/0

AIDSINFO. (2013, May 7). Offering information on HIV/AIDS treatment, presentation, and research. *Guidelines for the prevention and treatment of opportunistic infections in HIV-infected adults and adolescents.* Retrieved from http://aidsinfo.ninh.gov/guidelines/html/4/adult-and-adolescent-oi-prevention-and-treatment-guidelines/0

The AIDS Infonet. (2013). *Reliable, up-to-date treatment information.* Retrieved from http://www.aidsinfonet.org

AIDSmeds. (2012, August 28). *Treatment for HIV & AIDS.* Retrieved from http://www.aidsmeds.com/list.shtml

AIDSmeds. (2012, November 13). *Currently approved drugs for HIV: A comparative chart.* Retrieved from http://www.aidsmeds.com/articles/DrugChart_10632.shtml

American Academy of HIV Medicine. (2007). *Fundamentals of HIV medicine for the HIV specialist.* Washington, DC: Author. Retrieved from http://www.AAHIVM.org

American Congress of Obstetricians and Oncologists. (2012). *New cervical cancer screening recommendations for the U.S. Preventive Services Task Force and the American Cancer Society/American Society for Clinical Pathology.* Retrieved from http://www.acog.org/About%20ACOG/Announcements/New%20Cervical%Cancer%Screening%20Recommendations.aspx

American Geriatrics Society 2012 Beers Criteria Update Expert Panel. (2012). American Geriatrics Society updated Beers Criteria for potentially inappropriate medication use in older adults. *Journal of American Geriatrics Society, 60*(4), 616–631.

American Society for Colposcopy and Cervical Pathology. (2012). *Updated consensus guidelines for the management of abnormal cervical cancer precursors.* Retrieved from http://www.asccp.org/ConsensusGuidelines/UpdatedConsensusGuidelines/tabid14181/Default.aspx

Angeline, M. E., Gee, A. O., Shindle, M., Warren, R. F., & Rodeo, S. A. (2013). The effects of vitamin D deficiency in athletes. *American Journal of Sports Medicine, 41*(2), 461–464.

The Body. (n.d.a). *Approved HIV medications by class.* Retrieved from http://www.thebody.com/index/treat/classes.html

The Body. (n.d.b). *First steps to HIV/AIDS treatment.* Retrieved from http://www.thebody.com/index/treat/first.html

The Body. (n.d.c). *HIV/AIDS medication basics.* Retrieved from http://www.thebody.com/content/art40488.html

The Body. (n.d.d). *HIV drug-drug interactions.* Retrieved from http://www.thebody.com/index/treat/interactions.html

The Body. (n.d.e). *Side effects of HIV/AIDS and HIV medications.* Retrieved from http://www.thebody.com/index/treat/side_effects.html#general

Bonnie, M. A., & Ledbetter, C. (2011). Fever of unknown origin: An evidence-based approach. *Nurse Practitioner, 36(8),* 46–52.

Brady, V. (2012). Vitamin deficiency: Beyond bone health. *Clinical Advisor for Nurse Practitioners, 15*(9), 20–26.

Brown, H. (2013). Managing pernicious anemia. *Independent Nurse, 18*(02), 22–24.

Cadogan, M. (2010). Functional implications of vitamin B12 deficiency. *Journal of Gerontological Nursing, 36*(6), 12–16.

Cazanave, C., Dupon, M., Lavignolle-Aurillac, V., Barthe, N., Lawson-Ayayi, S., Mehsen, N., … Dabis, F. (2008). Reduced bone mineral density in HIV-infected patients: Prevalence and associated factors. *AIDS, 22,* 395–405.

Centers for Disease Control and Prevention. (2003, July 18). *MMWR recommendations and reports: Incorporating HIV prevention into the medical care of persons living with HIV.* Retrieved from http://aidsinfo.nih.gov/contentfiles/HIVpreventioninmedcare_TB.pdf

Centers for Disease Control and Prevention. (2005, September 30). *MMWR recommendations and reports: Management of occupational exposures to HIV and recommendations for post-exposure prophylaxis.* Retrieved from http://aidsinfo.nih.govcontentfiles/healthcareoccupexpoGL.pdf

Centers for Disease Control and Prevention. (2006, October 19). *Questions and answers: Men on the down low.* Retrieved from http://www.cdc.gov/hiv/topics/aa/resources/qa/print downlow.htm

Centers for Disease Control and Prevention. (2007, June 28). *HIV/AIDS and African Americans.* Retrieved from http://www.cdc.gov/hiv/topics/aa/print/index.htm

Centers for Disease Control and Prevention. (2012, June). Monitoring selected National HIV prevention and care objectives by using HIV surveillance data—United States and 6 U.S. dependent areas—2010. *HIV Surveillance Supplemental Report.* Retrieved from http://www.cdc.gov/hiv/topicssurveillance/resources/reports

Centers for Disease Control and Prevention. (2012, August 10). Interim guidance for clinicians considering the use of pre-exposure prophylaxis for the prevention of HIV infection in heterosexually active adults. *Morbidity and Mortality Weekly Report (MMWR).* Retrieved from http://www.cdc.gov/mmwrpreview/mmwrhtml/mm6131a2.htm?s_cid=mm6131a2_w

Centers for Disease Control and Prevention. (2013, January). *HIV testing trends in the United States, 2000–2011.* Retrieved from http://www.cdc.gov/hiv/pdf/testing_trends.pdf

Centers for Disease Control and Prevention. (2013, April 15) *Diagnoses of HIV infection in the United States and Dependent Areas, 2011.* Division of HIV/AIDS Prevention, National Center for HIV/AIDS, Viral Hepatitis, Sexual Transmitted Diseases and Tuberculosis Prevention, Centers for Disease Control and Prevention. Retrieved from http://www.cdc.gov/hiv/library/reports/surveillance/2011/surveillance_Report_vol_23.html

Centers for Disease Control and Prevention. (2013, April 23). *HIV in the United States: At a glance.* Division of HIV/AIDS Prevention, National Center for HIV/AIDS, Viral Hepatitis, Sexual Transmitted Diseases and Tuberculosis Prevention, Centers for Disease Control and Prevention. Retrieved from http://cdc.gov.hiv.statistics.basics.ataglance.html

Centers for Disease Control and Prevention. (2013, May 13). *HIV among Black/African American gay, bisexual, and other men who have sex with men.* Division of HIV/AIDS Prevention, National Center for HIV/AIDS, Viral Hepatitis, Sexual Transmitted Diseases and Tuberculosis Prevention, Centers for Disease Control and Prevention. Retrieved from http://www.cdc.gov/hiv/risk/racialethnic/bmsm/facts/index.html

Centers for Disease Control and Prevention. (2010) *STD Treatment Guidelines 2010.* Retrieved from http://www.cdc.gov/std/treatment/2010/default.htm

Centers for Disease Control and Prevention. (n.d.). *CDC CFS Toolkit* (Updated 2011, September 6). Atlanta, GA: Author. Retrieved from www.cdc.gov/cfs/toolkit/index.html

Christley, Y. J., & Martin, C. R. (2012). Perinatal perspective on chronic fatigue syndrome. *British Journal of Midwifery, 20*(6), 389–393.

Correia, L., Sodre, F., Garcia, G., Sabino, M., Brito, M., Kalil, F., & Noya-Rabelo, M. (2013). Relation of severe deficiency of vitamin D to cardiovascular mortality during acute coronary syndromes. *American Journal of Cardiology, 111*(3), 324–327.

Cuzin, L., Depierre, C., Gerard, S., et al. (2007). Immunologic and clinical responses to highly active antiretroviral therapy in patients with HIV infection aged >50 years. *Clinical Infectious Diseases, 45,* 654.

Deighton, K. (2011). Pernicious anemia (B12 deficiency). *Evidence-Based Practice, 14*(10), 14.

Engsig, F. N., Zangerle, R., Katsarou, O., Dabis, F., Reiss, P., Gill, J.,… Obel, N. (2014). Long-term mortality in HIV positive individuals virally suppressed for >3 years with incomplete CD4 recovery. *Clinical Infectious Diseases, 58,* 1312

Friedman, J. J., Chen, Z., Ford, P., Johnson, C., Lopez, A., Shander, A., & van Wyck, D. (2012). Iron deficiency anemia in women across the life span. *Journal of Women's Health, 21*(12), 1282–1289.

Greene, M., Justice, A. C., Lampiris, H. W., & Valcour, V. (2013). Management of human immunodeficiency virus infection in advanced age. *JAMA, 309*(13), 1397–1405.

Horn, T., & Urbina, A. (2013, February). *The POZ and AIDSmeds drug chart.* Retrieved from http://www.aidsmeds.com/lessons/DrugChartHighRes.pdf

Horowitz, H. (2013). Fever of unknown origin or fever of too many origins? *New England Journal of Medicine, 368*(3), 197–199.

Institute of Medicine. (2011). *HIV screening and access to care: Health care system capacity for increased HIV testing and provision of care.* Washington, DC: The National Academies Press.

International AIDS Society-USA. (2013). *New guidelines, strategies, and drugs for initiation of antiretroviral.* Retrieved from https://www.iasusa.org/content/new-guidelines-strategies-and-drugs-initiation-antiretroviral-2013

Kahanov, L., Eberman, L. E., & Grammer, S. (2012). Diagnosis and treatment of idiopathic thrombocytopenic purpura. *International Journal of Athletic Therapy & Training, 17*(2), 25–28.

Lalani, S., Pope, J., de Leon, F., & Peschken, C. (2010). Clinical features and prognosis of late-onset systemic pupus erythematosus: Results from the 1000 faces of lupus study. *Journal of Rheumatology, 37*(1), 38–44.

Mctigue, J., & Croker, B. (2012). Lupus and the autoimmune process: The view from 2012. *Clinical Advisor for Nurse Practitioners, 15*(1), 25–33.

Motyckova, G., & Steensma, D. (2012). Why does my patient have lymphadenopathy or spleenomegaly? *Hematology Oncology Clinics of North America, 26*(2), 395–408.

National HIV/AIDS Clinician's Consultation Center. (2013). *Warmline 800-933-3413. PEPline 888-448-4911. Perinatal HIV Hotline 888-448-8765.* Retrieved from www.ncc.ucsf.edu

National Institute of Health. (2013). *Pernicious anemia.* Retrieved from http://www.ncbi.nlm.nih.gov/pubmedhealth/PMH1595

Panel on Antiretroviral Guidelines for Adults and Adolescents. *Guidelines for the use of antiretroviral agents in HIV-1-infected adults and adolescents.* Department of Health and Human Services. http://www.aidsinfo.nih.gov/guidelines/html/1/adult-and-adolescent-treatment-guidelines/0

Park, S., Kang, J., Roh, J., Huh, H., Yeo, J., & Kim, D. (2013). Secondary syphilis presenting as a generalized lymphadenopathy: Clinical mimicry of malignant lymphoma. *Sexually Transmitted Diseases, 40*(6), 490–492.

Robinson, M., Sheets Cook, S., & Currie, L. M. (2011). Systemic lupus erythematosus: A genetic review for advanced practice nurses. *Journal of the American Academy of Nurse Practitioners, 23*(12), 629–637.

Schambelan, M., Benson, C. A., Carr, A., Currier, J. S., Dubé, M. P., Gerber, J. G.,... Saag, M. S. (2002). Management of metabolic complications associated with antiretroviral therapy for HIV-1 infection: Recommendations of an International AIDS Society-USA panel. *Journal of Acquired Immune Deficiency Syndromes, 31*: 257.

Short, M., & Domagalski, J. (2013). Iron deficiency anemia: Evaluation and management. *American Family Physician, 87*(2), 98–104.

Siddiqui, Z., & Osayande, A. (2011). Selected disorders of malabsorption. *Primary Care,* 38(3), 395–414.

Stabler, S. (2013). Clinical practice: Vitamin B12 deficiency. *New England Journal of Medicine, 368*(2), 149–160.

Teitelbaum, J. (2011). Effective treatment of chronic fatigue syndrome. *Integrative Medicine: A Clinician's Journal, 10*(6), 44–48.

Theander, K., & Unosson, M. (2011). No gender differences in fatigue and functional limitations due to fatigue among patients with COPD. *Journal of Clinical Nursing, 20*(9/10), 1303–1310.

Tsokos, G. (2011). Systemic lupus erythematosus. *New England Journal of Medicine, 365*(22), 2110–2121.

U.S. Food and Drug Administration. (n.d.). *Antiretroviral drugs used in the treatment of HIV infection.* Retrieved from http://www.fda.gov/ForConsumers/byAudience/ForThe patient Advocates/HIVandAIDSActivities/ucm118915.html

U.S. National Library of Medicine. (2013a, March 12). *Iron deficiency anemia.* Retrieved from http://www.ncblinmnih.gov/pubmedhealth/pmh00001610

U.S. National Library of Medicine. (2013b, March 12). *Pernicious anemia.* Retrieved from http://www.ncbinlmnih.gov/pubmedhealth/pmh00001595

U.S. Preventive Services Task Force Recommendation Statement. (2013, April) *Screening for HIV.* Retrieved from http://www.uspreventiveservicestaskforce.org/uspstf13/hivhivfinalrs.htm

Warren, E. (2012). Chronic fatigue syndrome. *Practice Nurse, 42*(6), 14–18.

Weiss, S. (2012). Oral involvement of systemic diseases. *Clinical Advisor for Nurse Practitioners, 15*(6), 25–30.

Winkeljohn, D. (2010). Idiopathic thrombocytic purpura. *Clinical Journal of Oncology Nursing, 14*(4), 411–413.

Womack, J. A., Brandt, C. A., & Justice, A. C. (2014). Women, aging, and HIV: Clinical issues and management strategies. *Journal of Nurse Practioners, 10,* 409.

World Health Organization. (2012, July). *Guidance on oral pre-exposure prophylaxis (PrEP) for serodiscordant couples, men and transgender women who have sex with men at high risk for HIV.* Retrieved from http://www.who.int/hiv/pub/gidance_prep/en/index.html

Yancey, J., & Thomas, S. (2012). Chronic fatigue syndrome: Diagnosis and treatment. *American Family Physician, 86*(8), 741–746.

CHAPTER TWENTY

Musculoskeletal Guidelines

Julie Adkins and Jill C. Cash

Aging Knee/Knee Pain

Definition

A. The knee is the largest joint of the body. The knee is not protected by layers of fat or muscle; exposure may lead to a high incidence of trauma. The articular cartilage is a firm, rubbery protein material covering the end of a bone. It acts as a cushion between the bones so that the bones do not grind together. When this articular cartilage breaks down, symptoms such as knee pain, swelling, bone spur formation, and decreased motion develop. Over a period of years, the joint slowly changes where normal activity becomes painful and difficult.
B. There is a loose relationship between knee pain and osteoarthritis of the knee. Many older people are pain free with radiological arthritis of the knee, whereas many people with knee pain have little evidence of osteoarthritis.

Incidence

A. One fourth of people aged 50 and older report chronic knee pain; for two thirds of these, the pain is severe and disabling. Osteoarthritis of the knee is one of the five leading causes of disability among elderly men and women.

Pathogenesis

A. Knee pain in patients without inflammatory arthritis may have crepitus, bony tenderness, bony enlargement, effusion, or muscle wasting. Depending on the cause of the problem, knee pain occurs due to problems such as bone rubbing bone, and extra fluid in joint space that causes pressure, irregularities of the bone, and torn cartilage.

Predisposing Factors

A. Heredity
B. Weight gain: Increases pressure on the knee joints
C. Age: The ability of the cartilage to heal itself decreases with age.
D. Gender: Occurs more frequently in women than in men.
E. Trauma history of previous injury to the knee
F. Repetitive injuries in sports or other trauma
G. Activity: Requires long periods of standing, poor posture/gait
H. Chronic conditions: Metabolic disorders, muscle weakness, poor fitness, vitamin C deficiency, vitamin D deficiency

Common Complaints

A. Knee pain at rest and with activity
B. Inability or decreased ability to perform certain daily functions
C. Knee gives way while walking, standing, or moving
D. Difficulty with getting up out of a chair
E. Need for assistive devices to ambulate

Other Signs and Symptoms

A. Inability to stand, walk, or sit for long periods of time
B. Pain may increase with exposure to cold or heat
C. Pain at rest

Potential Complications

A. Falls
B. Fractures

Subjective Data

A. Inquire regarding onset, duration, and frequency of knee pain.
B. Did trauma precipitate the pain, either recently or long ago?
C. Elicit a clear description of the pain and factors that aggravate or relieve it.
D. Does knee swell, feel warm to touch, or turn red at any time?

E. Does pain increase or worsen with rest/activity?
F. Ask patient to report a pain scale with rest and with activity.
G. How does pain interfere with daily living activities? Is patient unable to work? Does knee pain waken the patient at night? Does he or she have difficulty with walking, climbing steps, or getting into the car?
H. What has the patient used for pain? Over-the-counter (OTC) products and prescription products? Heat/ice/brace and so on?
I. Has the patient experienced any type of pain like this in the past?

Physical Examination

A. Inspect
   1. Gait: Observe for any abnormal movement used to compensate for the pain in the knee.
   2. Note symmetry of muscles above the knee for atrophy.
   3. Assess the knee for swelling, redness, or gross deformity. Swelling is classified as either localized (bursa) or generalized (intra-articular). A bursal swelling is most frequently found over the patella or over the tibial tubercle. Occasionally a bursal swelling may present in the popliteal area due to a cyst. Intra-articular swelling is usually due to an irritation of the synovium and can cause a generalized swelling of the entire knee.
B. Palpate
   1. Palpate the knee for points of tenderness, effusion, or changes in skin temperature. The knee is easier to palpate when it is flexed, making the skeletal landmarks more distinct. Palpate both the medial and lateral aspect of the knee.
   2. Test for joint stability involving the collateral ligaments and cruciate ligaments.
   3. Assess range of motion (ROM) actively and passively—flexion, extension, and internal and external rotation.

Diagnostic Tests

A. **X-ray of affected knee or both knees for comparison. Perform knee x-rays while the patient is standing. Possible MRI or CT as necessary.**
B. **Laboratory values to consider: Complete blood count (CBC), erythrocyte sedimentation rate, uric acid, rheumatoid factor.**

Differential Diagnosis

A. Knee pain
B. Sepsis
C. Gout
D. Malignancy/avascular necrosis
E. Meniscal tears
F. Bursitis
G. Fibromyalgia
H. Arthritis (rheumatoid arthritis, psoriatic arthritis, reactive arthritis)
I. Referred pain from the hip or back

Plan

A. General interventions
   1. Knee exercises and bracing, if necessary
   2. Activity modifications should be discussed with the patient to reduce pain.
   3. Nonsurgical management includes appropriate footwear and assistive devices.
   4. Complementary and alternative modalities include glucosamine chondroitin, acupuncture, osteopathy, and chiropractic interventions.
   5. Joint aspiration, if indicated.
B. Patient teaching
   1. Weight loss education should be discussed and encouraged. Dietary management along with exercise routine should be considered. Approximately 4 to 5 pounds of pressure on the knee are relieved with every one pound of weight loss.
C. Pharmacological therapy
   1. Acetaminophen
   2. Cox-2 Inhibitors (Celebrex)
   3. Nonsteroidal anti-inflammatory drugs (NSAIDs) (Naproxen, ibuprofen, Mobic, etc.)
   4. Topical medication such as Capsaicin, topical NSAIDs, or lidocaine patches may be considered.
   5. Intra-articular treatments include:
      a. Steroid injections (Depomedrol), which may provide short-term relief (1–4 weeks)
      b. Hyaluronan injections (viscosupplementation), which may provide relief for approximately 6 to 12 months.

Follow-Up

A. Follow up in 1 to 2 weeks for evaluation of knee pain and prescribed modality effectiveness.
B. Evaluate for side effects of pharmacologic treatment.

Consultation/Referral

A. Refer to physical therapy for exercise regimens or physiotherapy. May include knee taping and water therapy.
B. Surgical consultation if there is no relief from pharmacologic or physical therapy methods. May include arthroscopy versus partial or total knee replacement, dependent on the objective findings.

Individual Considerations

A. Evaluate patient individually for renal, gastrointestinal, or hepatic disorders in regards to pharmacologic preparations.
B. Ensure access to proper eyeglasses, hearing aids, and assistive devices such as canes, walkers, elevated toilet seats, grab bars, and shower chairs.

C. Take all measures to prevent falls, which adds to morbidity and functional decline.
D. Evaluate poly-pharmacy and other comorbidities and possible drug interactions.
E. Evaluate for medication compliance and level of alertness before starting drugs with potentially hazardous side effects.

Bunion

Definition

A. A bunion is a bony enlargement at the base of the great toe.

Incidence

A. Approximately nine out of ten bunions occur in women. Nine out of ten women wear shoes that are too small and/or too tight, and/or are too narrow.

Pathogenesis

A. The bony prominence and abnormal angle at the base of the great toe gets larger, and the skin over it may be red and tender, causing pain when wearing any type of shoe. The great toe may angle toward the second toe or move all the way under it, causing the skin under the foot to become thicker and more painful. This may force the second toe out of alignment and overlap the third toe. The pain may become chronic.

Predisposing Factors

A. Wearing shoes too small and/or too narrow for the feet
B. Wearing heels higher than 1¼ inches

Common Complaints

A. Pain in the great toe at rest and with walking/movement
B. Difficulty wearing shoes
C. Great toe looks deformed due to hallux valgus deformity

Other Signs and Symptoms

A. Metatarsophalangeal (MTP) joint is tender and enlarged.
B. Patient can't walk normally due to pain.
C. It hurts to bend the toe.

Potential Complications

A. Acute arthritic pain

Subjective Data

A. Ask the patient what activity brought about or preceded the episode of pain.
B. Ask the patient to describe the pain; note duration of pain and impairment of activity.
C. Inquire regarding any limited ROM of toe/toes.
D. Ask the patient if there is any evidence of sores, calluses, or open areas of skin.
E. Ask the patient what treatments have been used and what makes the pain better or worse.
F. Ask the patient to list all medications currently being taken, including OTC preparations.

Physical Examination

A. Vital signs: Temperature, pulse, respirations, and blood pressure
B. Inspect
   1. Inspect the MTP joint for tenderness and enlargement.
   2. Inspect skin for skin irritations, open sores, drainage, and calluses.
   3. Evaluate ROM of MTP joint, plantar-flexion, and dorsiflexion.
   4. Evaluate for other toe involvement.
C. Palpate
   1. Palpate the MTP joint for tenderness
   2. Palpate peripheral pulses in legs.
   3. Check passive ROM for rigidity and crepitation and degree of pain on movement

Diagnostic Tests

A. None
   Advanced cases are easily diagnosed by inspection and exam.
B. X-rays may be used to confirm the diagnosis and to assess for inflammation and joint changes.

Differential Diagnosis

A. Bunion
B. Morton's neuroma
C. Bursitis

Plan

A. General interventions
   1. Recommend the use of a bunion shield.
   2. Advise using ice over the side and top of the toe for comfort and elevation.
   3. Encourage performing stretching exercises of extensor and flexor tendons.
   4. **Moderate cases (4–6 weeks)** may require an NSAID for pain relief, dependent on renal function of the patient. They may require a local intra-articular injection for pain/inflammation relief.
   5. **Chronic cases (8–10 weeks)** may require a referral to an orthopedist or podiatrist.
B. Patient teaching
   1. Educate the patient on the most common cause (tight-fitting shoes). Encourage the patient to wear wide-toed shoes.
   2. Educate the patient on use of a cotton or rubber spacer to be worn between first and second toe.

C. Pharmaceutical therapy
   1. NSAIDs may be taken in moderate cases, dependent on patient history of gastrointestinal or renal disorders.
   2. Further adjuvant therapy may be considered for chronic conditions/severe pain.

Follow-Up

A. Follow-up is determined by the patient's needs and by whether complications are present. All treatments, including surgery, are palliative.

Consultation/Referral

A. Orthopedist or podiatrist referral for chronic cases; possible bunionectomy
B. Physical therapy for stretching exercises of the extensor and flexor tendons before deformity becomes permanent
C. All treatments, including surgery, are palliative.

Individual Considerations

A. Geriatrics
   1. Use precautionary measures when using NSAID therapy in the geriatric population due to possible gastrointestinal or renal disorders.

Degenerative Disk Disease (Neck/Lumbar)

Definition

A. Degenerative disk disease is a general term for the gradual deterioration of the disks between the vertebrae of the spine that can occur naturally or through a twisting injury where portions of the disk may tear, resulting in thinner and more fragile cartilage. Any level of the spine can be affected. The disk itself has very few nerve endings and no blood supply. The disk has no way to repair itself and the pain created by the damaged disk can either be a chronic condition or have periodic flare-ups.

Incidence

A. In the United States, back pain is the second leading symptom that prompts visits to the health care provider. As many as 80% of adults experience at least one episode of back pain during their lifetime, and 5% experience chronic problems with their back. Cervical degenerative disk disease is much less common than disk degeneration of the lumbar spine. After a patient reaches the age of 60, some level of disk degeneration is a normal finding rather than an exception.

Pathogenesis

The degenerative changes of the spine can be subdivided into three stages:

A. Dysfunction: May involve outer annular tears, separation of the endplate, cartilage destruction, and facet synovial reaction
B. Instability: Disk resorption and loss of disk space height, possibly leading to subluxation
C. Restabilization: Progressive changes leading to osteophyte formation or bone spurs and stenosis

Predisposing Factors

A. Injury/inflammation
B. Age related, occurs more commonly as one ages
C. Slight genetic component

Common Complaints

A. Pain that is usually related to activity; flares up at times but then returns to a low-grade pain level or pain will go away entirely. Cervical disk degeneration is most frequently felt as a stiff neck. Lumbar symptoms may include local tenderness, hypomobility, and painful extension of the lumbar back.
B. Muscle spasms of the neck, arms, or shoulders due to cervical nerve inflammation or impingement. Lumbar symptoms may include a "giving away or catch in the back," pain with standing and/or flexion.
C. Headache, muscle tenderness, stiffness, and reduced movement. Pain in buttocks or upper thighs.

Other Signs and Symptoms

A. Paresthesia of upper extremities and hands with decreased strength and hand grip.
B. Referred pain to hips, knees, ankles, and feet
C. Progression to chronic pain (pain lasting over 3 months)

Potential Complications

A. Presence of bowel and bladder symptoms
B. Cauda equina syndrome
C. Disability

Subjective Data

A. When did the pain begin?
B. Ask the patient what activity brought about or preceded the episode. Was there an injury that could be related to the pain? Activity modification?
C. Have the patient rate the pain on a scale of 0 to 10, with 0 being no pain, or on the visual analogue scale, a series of faces of varying intensity.
D. Does the pain radiate to any other point of the body?
E. What factors make the pain better or worse?
F. Ask if the patient has had any problems with bladder or bowels.
G. Ask the patient to list all medications currently being taken, including OTC and herbal. Any current modalities tried?
H. Ask the patient if there is any family history of osteoporosis or degenerative disk disease

Physical Examination

A. **Vital signs: Weight, blood pressure, temperature, pulse, respirations.**
   Notice red flags such as weight loss, fever, elevated pulse.
B. Start with a general physical examination to determine the source of the problem, dependent on where there is pain—neck, lower back, arms, legs, and so forth.
C. Inspect
   1. Inspect general appearance, skin rashes, or deformities.
   2. Observe gait, assistive device use
D. Palpate
   1. Assess the motion of spine and neck. Assess for pain with twisting, bending, or moving.
   2. Assess muscle strength or weakness.
   3. Palpate areas of tenderness or muscle spasms.
   4. Sensory changes—assess increased or decreased sensation associated with point of tenderness.
   5. Check deep tendon reflexes (DTRs).
   6. Assess motor skills such as toe or heel walk.
E. Auscultate
   1. Auscultate carotid arteries.
   2. Auscultate abdomen.
   3. Conduct a complete heart exam.
   4. Conduct a complete lung exam.

Diagnostic Tests

A. X-ray of affected area may reveal a decrease in the height space between disks, bone spurs, sclerosis, facet hypertrophy (enlargement), and instability during flexion or extension of limbs. X-ray will show fracture, infections, or tumors if suspected.
B. MRI or CT scan is used for more severe causes, such as loss of water in a disk, stenosis, or herniated disk, as well as to rule out differential diagnoses.

Differential Diagnosis

A. Degenerative disk disease
B. Infection
C. Fracture
D. Tumor

Plan

A. General interventions
   1. Initial decisions are made according to the seriousness of the findings. Some problems need immediate attention, possibly even surgery. The vast majority of problems; however, do not require immediate surgery.
B. Patient teaching
   1. Educate the patient about avoiding actions that aggravate the condition.
      a. Modify activities to avoid lifting heavy objects and playing sports or other activities that require rotating the back or neck.
      b. Teach correct ergonomics, such as how to lift heavy objects, how to sit in a chair, and how to correct sleep postures.
   2. Nonsurgical interventions
      a. Rest
      b. An exercise program or physical therapy that may strengthen the back and avoid further inflammation or injury.
      c. Alternating heat and ice to the affected site
C. Pharmaceutical therapy
   1. Mild pain medications can reduce inflammation and pain. These medications will not stop degeneration, but they will help with pain control.
      a. NSAIDs block the inflammatory response in joints. Caution of use can decrease renal function, and excessive use can lead to kidney problems.
      b. Non-narcotic pain relievers: Most commonly used are Tylenol and aspirin, but they must be avoided in patients with gastrointestinal disorders or liver problems.
      c. Narcotic pain medications: Narcotics relieve pain by acting as a numbing anesthetic to the central nervous system. Narcotics can cause many side effects such as nausea, vomiting, constipation, sedation, or drowsiness. Precautions about falls are paramount with these types of medications.
      d. Muscle relaxants can help relieve pain but have been shown to be only marginally effective. There is a significant risk for drowsiness and falls. Fall precautions and driving restrictions must be advised while using narcotics and muscle relaxants.

Follow-Up

A. Follow-up is determined by the patient's response to conservative measures for pain relief, impact on activities of daily living (ADL), ability to carry out work duties, or worsening of symptoms.

Consultation/Referral

A. **Physical therapy**: May include modalities of heat and ice, massage, ultrasound, and electric stimulation. Other treatments may include bracing, flexibility and strength training, pool therapy, and/or posture training.
B. **Referral for epidural steroid injections**: A combination of steroid and a local anesthetic given through the back into the epidural space. Injections are used when conservative treatments options have failed. Referral should be made to a pain control specialist for epidural steroid injections.

C. **Referral to a neurosurgeon if immediate, emergent findings are found on evaluation or if symptoms last over 6 months without any relief.**

Individual Considerations

A. Geriatrics
   1. Assess current living conditions, support systems, transportation issues, and impact on ADL. Educate the patient to enhance an understanding of the disease process and review possible treatment options available.
   2. Assess all medications the patient is currently taking for interactions and review precautions with the patient regarding pain control medications used.
   3. Review assistance that is available to avoid aggravating activities.
   4. When prescribing pain medications or muscle relaxants, discuss ways to avoid falls and injuries, noting side effects of medications, such as drowsiness that may occur when performing activities of daily living.
   5. Special considerations are needed if surgery is necessary: Family support, rehabilitation, transportation, and home health care.

Hammer Toe

Definition

A. A hammer toe is a deformity of the second, third, or fourth toe. The toe is bent at the middle joint, resembling a hammer.

Pathogenesis

A. Hammer toe results from shoes that don't fit properly or a muscle imbalance. Muscles work to straighten and bend the toes. If the toe is bent for long periods, the muscles tighten and can't stretch out.

Predisposing Factors

A. Shoes that narrow at the toe push the toes into a bent position, making the toes rub against the shoe. Eventually, the toe muscles are unable to straighten the toe with any shoe or barefoot.

Common Complaints

A. "My toe is bent."
B. "I can't find shoes to fit due to my bent toe."
C. "I have a sore or callus on my toe because it won't straighten out."

Other Signs and Symptoms

A. Formation of corns and calluses on the middle joint of the toe or on the tip of the toe
B. Pain in the toes and feet
C. Difficulty finding shoes to fit feet

Potential Complications

A. Ulcers of the middle joint of the toe may develop, possibly leading to infection or osteomyelitis.
B. Patient may have chronic pain of the toe. Abscesses of corns and calluses may develop.

Subjective Data

A. Pain over the ball of the foot.
B. Toe rubbing on shoes.
C. Skin over top of toe is starting to thicken.
D. Toe/toes are crooked.

Physical Examination

A. Inspect
   1. Examine the extensor tendons of the toes for flexibility. It should be tight when the ankle is placed in plantar-flexion position.
   2. Examine the MTP joints for irritation and thickening.
   3. Note corns and calluses on top of the toe if present.
B. Palpate
   1. Palpate over MTP joints. Note tenderness over the MTP joint and a positive MTP joint squeeze.
   2. Note ROM of all toes and ankle.

Diagnostic Tests

A. X-rays
   1. X-rays are not routinely recommended. X-rays rarely provide any additional information not found on physical examination.
   2. X-rays should be performed if severe swelling, unusual color, or unequal movement/ROM of toes is present.

Differential Diagnosis

A. Hammer toe
B. Rheumatoid arthritis
C. Osteoarthritis
D. Reflex sympathetic dystrophy—consider if there is extensive swelling and discoloration.

Plan

A. General interventions
   1. Conservative treatment consists of new shoes with soft, roomy toe areas. Shoes should be one-half inch longer than the longest toe. Sandals may help as long as they do not pinch or rub the affected area of the toe. Toe exercises can stretch and strengthen the muscles, and toes can be gently stretched manually. Advise using corn pads or cushions to cover calluses or thickened skin. Consider paring the large corns and calluses with sharp dissection. Toe spacers may also be suggested to use for comfort.

B. Pharmaceutical therapy
   1. Local steroid injection at the most painful MTP head may be considered, with reemphasis on passive stretching exercises.

Follow-Up

A. Consider injection of the joint if the case is severe. Aftercare treatment involves resting the foot for 3 days, wearing loose-fitting shoes, using a toe spacer, and applying ice for approximately 15 minutes every 4 to 6 hours.
B. Restart passive stretching of the foot after 3 to 4 weeks.
C. If pain recurs or persists, repeat injection at 6 weeks.

Consultation/Referral

A. Physical therapy for active assessment and treatment. Increasing the flexibility of the MTP joints and toes will prevent hammer toe.
B. Consider referral to a surgeon/podiatrist for evaluation for arthroplasty with or without fusion with K wires.

Individual Considerations

A. Evaluate the patient's ability to perform passive stretching exercises due to other comorbidities.
B. Assess the patient with diabetes for corns and calluses. Monitor for infection, poor circulation, and/or decreased sensation in the feet.
C. Fall precautions should be discussed with patients at risk for falls who have pain/numbness of the foot or who wear adaptive footwear.

Morton's Neuroma

Definition

A. A neuroma is a benign tumor of a nerve. Morton's neuroma is not actually a tumor, but a chronic irritation/inflammation and thickening of the tissue that surrounds the digital nerve leading to the toes. This neuroma occurs as the nerve passes under the ligament of the metatarsals.

Incidence

A. The neuroma usually occurs between the third and fourth toes.
B. It occurs in women eight to ten times more frequently than men.

Pathogenesis

A. Morton's neuroma occurs when pressure is exerted from the bottom of the foot from walking on hard surfaces with poorly padded shoes or barefoot, and/or pressure from the sides of ill-fitting tight shoes. It may also develop from chronic irritation and/or trauma.

Predisposing Factors

A. Poor padded shoes or walking barefoot
B. Tight shoes or high heels
C. Trauma

Common Complaints

A. Burning pain in the ball of the foot radiating to the toes. Pain intensifies with activity or wearing shoes. Night pain is rare.
B. Possible numbness or unpleasant feeling in toes
C. Sharp pain between toes, dead feeling of toes

Other Signs and Symptoms

A. Symptoms may be worse with tight shoes or activity.
B. Selective shoes are worn for comfort.

Subjective Data

A. Ask the patient to describe the pain in the foot. Is it a burning, stabbing sensation in the toes?
B. Assess pain intensity. Ask regarding dull or sharp pain between toes.
C. Where does pain occur in the foot?
D. Does the patient have difficulty walking due to pain or numbness?
E. Does the patient take certain measures to improve pain, such as wearing specific shoes, avoiding shoes, or not going barefoot?

Physical Examination

A. Inspect
   1. Inspect foot for redness, swelling, or pain.
   2. Inspect for color change, bruising, rash, or other changes in skin.
B. Palpate
   1. Palpate affected foot for palpable mass or a "click" between toes.
   2. Apply pressure to area to reproduce pain for local tenderness.
   3. Assess ROM of toes and foot.

Diagnostic Tests

A. X-ray of the foot to rule out other pathology such as fracture

Differential Diagnosis

A. Morton's neuroma
B. Fracture or stress fracture
C. Arthritis

Plan

A. General interventions
   1. Recommend the use of orthoses to help relieve irritation by lifting and separating the bones to eliminate pressure on the nerve.

B. Patient teaching
   1. Make a change in footwear. Avoid high heels or tight shoes. Use of toe spacers may improve symptoms.
C. Pharmaceutical therapy
   1. Injection: Local digital nerve block may be trialed.
   2. NSAIDs are ineffective due to poor penetration to these tissues.

Follow-Up

A. One month or sooner to evaluate pain relief and/or exacerbating symptoms such as numbness or gait instability
B. Steroid injection to the point of tenderness if there is no relief from conservative treatments. Steroid injection may be repeated in 6 weeks if pain recurs or persists.

Consultation/Referral

A. Referral to an orthopedist or podiatrist for possible neurectomy if other treatment modalities are unsuccessful or if pain continues after two steroid injections.

Individual Considerations

A. Injection: Aftercare to include rest for several days and avoidance of all unnecessary weight bearing
B. Ice for soreness: Ice to site for 15 minutes every 4 to 6 hours. Tylenol may be used for pain.
C. Encourage taking extra time in walking due to irritation.
D. Encourage the use of assistive walking devices to decrease pressure on foot.
E. Surgery may cause secondary problems, such as numbness in adjacent toes.

Neck and Upper Back Disorders

Definition

A. Nonspecific disorders: Self-limited, usually benign disorders with unclear etiology, such as regional upper back and neck pain and shoulder pain adjacent to the neck.
B. Degenerative disorders: Consequences of aging or repetitive use, or a combination thereof, such as degenerative disk disease and osteoarthritis.
C. Potentially serious neck or upper back disorders: Fractures, dislocation, infection, tumor, progressive neurologic deficit, or cord compression.

Incidence

A. Exact numbers are unknown.

Pathogenesis

A. Cervical strain is irritation and spasm of the upper back and cervical muscles. The upper portion of the trapezius and the levator scapulae muscles, rhomboid major and minor muscles, and the long cervical muscles are most often affected.

Predisposing Factors

A. Whiplash-like injuries
B. Cervical strain
C. Cervical arthritis
D. Holding your head in a forward posture or odd position. Frequently seen in patients who regularly use computers, cell phones/texting, laptops, and iPads
E. Sleeping on a pillow too high or too flat
F. Stress/tension

Common Complaints

A. Aching neck
B. Tightness and tenderness in neck area
C. Stiffness and tightness in shoulders
D. Stiff neck and a headache upon awakening

Other Signs and Symptoms

A. Limited range of motion (ROM)
B. Back pain: Guarding with cervical motion
C. Numbness in upper extremities
D. Muscle weakness

Subjective Data

A. What are presenting symptoms? Note pain, numbness, weakness, or stiffness.
B. Was there any type of injury, either recently or in the past?
C. Is the pain located primarily in the neck, upper back, or shoulder? Is there any radiation noted?
D. How do these symptoms limit the patient's activity?
E. How long can the patient sit, stand, walk, or do overhead work?
F. Is the patient able to lift? If so, how much weight is bearable? Compare to normal weight.
G. How long has the patient had these symptoms?
H. How have the symptoms evolved, from the beginning of discomfort until now?
I. If the patient has a previous history of similar or the same pain, what therapy was used in the past and what were the results?
J. Does the patient have any medical problems?

Physical Examination

Infection may include severe cervical spasms (nuchal rigidity), elevated temperature, chills, hypotension, and tachycardia.

A. Check temperature, blood pressure, and pulse.
B. Inspect: Observe stance and gait. Note the patient's coordination and use of extremities.

C. Palpate
   1. Palpate trigger points in upper back, paracervical, and rhomboid muscles.
   2. Palpate for any bony tenderness in neck, shoulders, and upper back.
   3. Perform ROM tests.
   4. Assess the patient for reduced ipsilateral and contralateral bending of the neck.
   5. Check for fracture, or inability to move neck due to pain, and severe cervical midline vertebral pain. Note tenderness, the patient holding head for stability; look for possible neurologic deficits.

D. Assess DTRs bilaterally.
   1. Biceps reflex tests fifth and sixth cervical nerve root.
   2. Brachioradialis reflex tests fifth and sixth cervical nerve root.
   3. Triceps reflex tests seventh and eighth cervical nerve root.

E. Test muscle strength in shoulders.

F. Abduction, elbow flexion, or supination tests fourth and fifth cervical disks.

G. Check for weakness of radial wrist extension, indicating fifth and sixth cervical disk problems. Check for weakness of elbow extension and ulnar wrist flexion, indicating seventh cervical nerve impairment. Check weak finger abduction and adduction, indicating seventh and eighth cervical nerve impairment. Measure circumference at forearm and upper arm for muscle atrophy. Dominant arm is 1/4 inch greater than nondominant arm.

H. Sensory: Test light touch, pinprick, pressure sensations in forearm and hand. Possible cervical spinal cord compromise is indicated by paresthesia of upper extremities, weakness of upper or lower extremities, and difficulty walking.

I. Percuss back, spine, and neck areas. Tumor is indicated by tenderness to vertebral percussion, cachexia.

J. Auscultate heart and lungs.

Diagnostic Tests

A. Radiography of cervical spine

Differential Diagnoses

A. Regional neck pain
B. Cervical strain
C. Cervical arthritis
D. Cervical nerve root compression with radiculopathy
E. Rotator cuff tendinitis
F. Rotator cuff tendon tear
G. Postlaminectomy syndrome
H. Spinal stenosis
I. Torticollis (which may be present at birth or caused by injury or disease)

Plan

A. General interventions
   1. Correct posture and lifestyle modifications (exercise, strengthening, etc.) are imperative for the patient to remain free of pain. Patient education and therapy depend on individual diagnosis.

B. Patient teaching
   1. Teach the patient to use local applications of cold packs during the first 3 days of acute complaints and hot pack applications thereafter.
   2. Encourage the following changes in lifestyle:
      a. Sitting straight with shoulders held high.
      b. Sleeping with the head and neck aligned with the body and a small pillow under the neck.
      c. Driving with arms slightly shrugged, using arm rests.
      d. Avoiding carrying objects with a strap over shoulders.
      e. Making ergonomic changes in computer, cell phone, iPad use, and so on.
   3. Suggest adjustments in tasks at work and at home.
   4. Encourage daily stretching exercises, including shoulder roll, scapular pinch, and neck stretches.
   5. Have the patient perform ROM exercises daily.
   6. Tell the patient to avoid extremes of ROM, prolonged periods in one position, and any other aggravating activity.
   7. Explain relaxation techniques and stress reduction.
   8. Give the patient the Section III Patient Teaching Guide for this chapter, "RICE Therapy and Exercise Therapy," if applicable.

C. Pharmaceutical therapy
   1. Nonprescription medications: Acetaminophen or NSAIDs.
   2. Prescription medications: NSAIDs and/or muscle relaxants for nighttime use

Follow-Up

A. Evaluate the patient after 2 weeks of conservative treatment. If pain continues after 2 to 3 weeks despite adequate therapy, order radiography, and physical therapy, including ultrasonography, massage, and gentle cervical traction beginning at 5 pounds for 5 to 10 minutes once a day. Soft cervical collar may be worn while doing physical work.

Consultation/Referral

A. Consult or refer the patient to a physician if there is still no improvement after adequate time for healing and no relief is noted with physical therapy and medications.

Plantar Fasciitis and Bone Spurs

Definition

A. Plantar fasciitis is an inflammatory condition in the plantar fascia (foot) that causes pain in the arch of the foot and radiates to the heel. The plantar fascia is a long, thin ligament lying directly beneath the skin on the bottom of the foot. It connects the heel to the front of the foot and supports the arch. Even though many people with plantar fasciitis have heel spurs, the spurs are not the cause of plantar fasciitis pain.

Incidence

A. Plantar fasciitis is the most common cause of heel pain in the United States. Plantar fasciitis is seen in both men and women and most often affect active men ages 40 to 70 (U.S. National Library of Medicine, 2013). Approximately 2 million patients are treated for this condition every year. One out of ten people have heel spurs, but only 1 out of 20 people with heel spurs has foot pain.

Pathogenesis

A. Repetitive small tears in the plantar fascia causing collagen breakdown at the medial tubercle of the calcaneus

Predisposing Factors

A. Athletes: Overuse injury from running
B. Tight or weak muscles/tendons (Achilles tendon, heel cord, gastrocnemius, soleus muscle)
C. Poor arch support/improper footwear (poor support in shoes)
D. Anatomic abnormalities (low arch support, flat foot, high arch, tibial torsion, overpronated foot, leg-length discrepancy, forefoot varus, thinning of fat pad)
E. Obesity

Common Complaints

A. Severe foot pain in the bottom of the foot, especially first thing in the morning
B. Burning pain when walking
C. Stiffness in foot/heel
D. May be worse in the morning, improve during day, and then get painful at the end of day

Other Signs and Symptoms

A. Both heels may be affected.
B. Pain is located in the medial tubercle of the calcaneus, medial of the longitudinal arch.
C. Heel spurs may or may not be present.
D. Pain worsens with standing for long periods of time.

Subjective Data

A. Ask the patient when pain began and how long it lasts.
B. Does pain occur with walking, running, and standing?
C. Does pain begin on the first few steps after getting out of bed or after long periods of sitting or resting? Pain may subside after a few minutes of walking.
D. Is pain constant, stabbing pain? Rate pain on scale of 0 to 10.
E. Locate pain site; does pain radiate into toes or leg?

Physical Examination

A. Check pulse and blood pressure.
B. Inspect
   1. Examine feet bilaterally. Assess for high arch.
   2. Note swelling, discoloration, or rash.
C. Palpate
   1. Palpate both feet, noting tenderness at point tenderness. Point tenderness will be noted over insertion on medial heel (calcaneus medial tubercle).
   2. Perform passive dorsiflexion of toes and ankle. Have the patient stand on tips of toes to see if this elicits pain.
D. Auscultate the heart and lungs.

Diagnostic Tests

A. X-ray may be performed but is often normal and not needed. Perform if tumor, spur, or fracture is suspected.
B. MRI may be ordered if thickening of proximal plantar fascia is noted or rupture of proximal fascia is suspected.

Differential Diagnoses

A. Plantar fasciitis
B. Heel pain
C. Heel spur
D. Fracture

Plan

A. General interventions
   1. Conservative treatment includes no long periods of standing for the next 6 to 8 weeks.
B. Patient education
   1. Arch support: Encourage the patient to get a pair of shoes with good arch supports. Arch supports are imperative for relief and shoes may need arch support in addition to new shoes.
   2. Shoe inserts are suggested. Suggest getting proper shoe fitting for running if the patient is an athlete.
   3. The patient should avoid walking on hard surfaces and never go barefoot. The patient should also avoid wearing sandals and flip-flops.
   4. Ice therapy may help with pain control and swelling.

5. Exercises
   a. Roll foot arch with a tennis ball for 20 to 30 minutes each evening to help stretch plantar fascia.
   b. Perform calf stretches against a wall, leaning forward against the wall, extending one leg behind you, one leg in front of you, stretch the leg, and reverse.

C. Pharmaceutical therapy
   1. NSAIDs such as ibuprofen (Motrin) 800 mg three times daily or naproxen (Naprosyn) 500 mg by mouth twice a day for comfort
   2. Cortisone injections may be attempted for severe cases. A corticosteroid lidocaine 1 to 1.5 mL injected directly into the most tender area on the sole of the foot may be helpful.

Follow-Up

A. Recommend follow-up in 4 weeks following treatment. Pain should slowly improve with aggressive treatment management. The patient must be compliant with instructions given for improvement. May take 6 to 12 months for complete resolution.
B. If pain worsens, consider diagnostic workup (x-ray or MRI).
C. Use caution with steroid injections. Multiple injections can cause the plantar fascia to rupture, resulting in flat foot and chronic pain.

Consultation/Referral

A. Refer to a podiatrist if conservative treatment therapy failed after 6 weeks.
B. Recommend physical therapy to stretch calf muscles and plantar fascia, using specialized ice treatments and/or massage.
C. Surgical treatment: Only after 12 months of aggressive nonsurgical treatments. Possible surgery may be recommended to lengthen the calf muscle (gastrocnemius) or to have a plantar fascia release procedure whereby the ligament is partially cut to relieve tension in the tissue. Large bone spurs may be surgically removed with open incision if indicated.

Individual Considerations

A. Use caution when using NSAIDs in the geriatric population due to gastrointestinal or kidney disorders.
B. Fall precautions should be discussed when having severe pain and difficulty walking.
C. Evaluate support systems for transportation to physical therapy if patient is unable to drive.

Sciatica

Definition

A. Sciatica is a sharp or burning pain, usually associated with numbness that radiates down the posterior or lateral leg that can result in neurosensory and/or motor deficits. Sciatica indicates abnormal function of the lumbosacral nerve roots or one of the nerves in the lumbosacral plexus.

Incidence

A. The prevalence of sciatica in the general population is 40%, though only 1% have any neurosensory or motor deficits. The most common cause of sciatica is herniated disks, 95% of which occur at the L4 to L5 or L5 to S1 level.

Pathogenesis

A. Pressure on the nerve from a herniated disk, bony osteophytes, a compression fracture, or any other extrinsic pressure (e.g., pelvic mass or epidural process, "wallet sciatica") causes progressive sensory, sensorimotor, or sensorimotor visceral loss. Typically, sciatica affects only one side of the body.

Predisposing Factors

A. Inflexibility
B. Obesity
C. Trauma
D. Bony osteophytes

Common Complaints

A. Pain around the buttock area
B. Pain often associated with numbness traveling down the lateral or posterior leg
C. Numbness
D. Paresthesia

Other Signs and Symptoms

A. Difficulty walking with affected leg
B. Positive straight leg raises, positive Patrick's sign
C. Decreased sensation

Subjective Data

A. Elicit onset of symptoms, duration, and what makes pain better or worse.
B. Inquire about previous episodes of pain or trauma.
C. Have the patient point to the area of pain, numbness, or tingling.
D. Are symptoms unilateral or bilateral?
E. Question the patient about loss of bowel or bladder control or other deficits and/or changes.
F. Does the patient notice leg weakness or difficulty walking?

Physical Examination

A. Check pulse and blood pressure.
B. Inspect gait and movement of back and extremities.
C. Palpate spinous processes.
D. Examine flexion and extension of spine. Assess sensation, DTRs, muscle strength, and motor weakness of lower extremities.

E. Examine neurologic function of back and lower extremity.
   1. Straight leg raising sign is positive.
   2. Dorsiflexion of ankle is positive.
   3. Check for loss of sensation in radicular pattern. Light touch pinprick and two point discrimination are not present.
   4. Look for decrease or loss of DTRs
   5. Check muscle strength of lower extremities.
   6. Check motor weakness.
   7. Check for cauda equina syndrome, indicated by urinary retention, radicular symptoms, and saddle anesthesia.

Cauda equina syndrome is a surgical emergency, characterized by bowel and bladder dysfunction; saddle anesthesia at the anus, perineum, or genitals; and widespread or progressive loss of strength in the legs or gait disturbances.

F. Percuss for tenderness over the spinous processes.

Diagnostic Tests

A. Radiography, when red flags for fracture, cancer, or infection are present.
B. CT scan or MRI, when cauda equina, tumor, infection, or fracture is suspected; MRI is test of choice for patients with prior back surgery.

Differential Diagnoses

A. Sciatica of unknown etiology
B. Lumbosacral strain
C. Herniated disk
D. Bony osteophytes, spinal stenosis
E. Compression fracture
F. Neoplasm of spine
G. Pelvic mass
H. Epidural process causing progressive sensory, sensorimotor, or sensorimotor visceral loss
I. Meralgia paresthetica

Plan

A. General interventions: Care for these patients should evolve over a three-step process.
   1. Step 1 (2–4 days)
      a. Bed rest for severe radiculopathy only.
      b. Limit walking and standing to 30 to 40 minutes each day.
      c. Recommend application of heat or cold packs to site as needed.
   2. Step 2 (7–14 days)
      a. Reevaluate neurologic and back exam; tell the patient "Let pain be your guide" when resuming normal daily activities.
      b. Have him or her perform gentle stretching exercises.
      c. Encourage walking on flat surfaces.
      d. Educate him or her regarding proper care of the back, with regard to exercises, posture, and so forth.
      e. Provide handouts on back exercises/stretches for the patient. See Section III Patient Teaching Guide for Chapter 5, "Back Stretches."
      f. Physical therapy may be implemented at this time if no significant improvement is noted.
   3. Step 3 (2–3 weeks)
      a. Reevaluate the patient, noting degree of improvement with exam.
      b. Continue muscle toning and reconditioning exercises.
      c. If improvement is noted, gradually increase physical activities.
      d. Reinforce healthy care of the back.
      e. Continue physical therapy until the patient can perform exercises without assistance or until released by the physical therapist.

B. Pharmaceutical therapy
   1. NSAIDs as needed: Naproxen (Naprosyn) 500 mg initially, followed by 250 mg every 6 to 8 hours.
   2. Acetaminophen may also be used as needed, especially if the patient is not able to tolerate ibuprofen.
   3. For more severe pain not relieved by NSAIDs, consider acetaminophen (Tylenol) with codeine for short duration. Narcotics should not be used for more than 2 weeks.
   4. Muscle relaxants: Muscle relaxants should not be used for more than 2 weeks.
      a. Cyclobenzaprine (Flexeril) 10 mg one to three times daily.
      b. Muscle relaxants place patients at risk for drowsiness. Warn the patient not to mix medications with alcohol because it may potentiate the medication.

Follow-Up

A. Initial follow-up is needed in 1 to 2 weeks.

Consultation/Referral

A. If cauda equina syndrome is suspected, prompt referral to a physician is necessary.
B. If bilateral sciatica is associated with vertebral collapse, osteoporosis, neoplasia, and/or vascular disease, consult with a physician.

Individual Considerations

A. Pregnancy: Sciatica pain is common due to physiologic changes of the pelvis as pregnancy progresses to term. Avoid use of NSAIDs. Physical therapy may be used as indicated.
B. Adults: **For older than 50, presenting with no prior history of backache, consider differential diagnosis of**

neoplasm. Most common metastasis is secondary to the primary site of breast or prostate, or to multiple myeloma. Pain is most prominent in recumbent position and rarely radiates into buttock or leg.

C. Geriatrics: Bilateral sciatica is associated with vertebral collapse, osteoporosis, neoplasia, and/or vascular disease. Refer the patient to a physician immediately. Use caution when prescribing medication to the elderly due to the risk for drowsiness and potential falls.

Shoulder Pain

Definition

A. The shoulder is the most mobile joint in the body. The shoulder can abduct, adduct, rotate, be raised in front and back of torso and move through a full 360 degree plane. Due to its full ROM, the shoulder is more prone to injury than any other joint.

B. Anatomy of the shoulder
   1. The shoulder joint is made up of bones held in place by tendons, ligaments, and muscles.
   2. The shoulder joint has three joints.
      a. Glenohumeral joint (the main joint of the shoulder)
      b. Acromioclavicular joint
      c. Sternoclavicular joint
   3. Unlike other joints, all joints work together to permit a universal motion of the shoulder.
   4. Types of cartilage in the shoulder
      a. White cartilage is present on the ends of the bones and allows the bones to glide and move on each other (articular cartilage).
      b. Labrum cartilage is fibrous cartilage found only around the shoulder socket.
   5. Multiple muscles are responsible for movement in the shoulder. These muscles attach to the scapula, humerus, and clavicle forming the shoulder cap and underarm. These muscles include:
      a. Serratus anterior
      b. Subclavius
      c. Pectoralis minor
      d. Sternocleidomastoid
      e. Levator scapulae
      f. Rhomboid major and minor
      g. Trapezius
      h. Deltoid

Incidence

A. According to the Centers for Disease Control and Prevention, in 2010 nearly 1.2 million people in the United States visited an emergency room for shoulder problems.

B. A community survey of 644 elderly people over the age of 70 (318 male and 326 female) revealed a prevalence of shoulder disorders as being approximately 21%.

C. Shoulder disorders were more common in women (25% versus 17%).

D. 70% of the cases involved the rotator cuff.

E. Fewer than 40% of the subjects sought medical attention for their symptoms.

F. Studies confirm that shoulder pain is a chronic problem that interferes with daily care and activities for the elderly population.

Pathogenesis

A. The shoulder is an unstable joint due to the joint's ROM, which increases the likelihood of joint injury and degenerative changes. Major injuries to the shoulder include rotator cuff tears and bone fractures involving the clavicle, scapula, and proximal humerus.

B. The most common shoulder problems are dislocation, separation, rotator cuff disease, rotator cuff tear, frozen shoulder, fracture, and arthritis.

Predisposing Factors

A. Overuse of the shoulder and/or frequent overhead reaching
B. Manual labor
C. Sports
D. Injury
E. Arthritis
F. Tendon inflammation or tear
G. Fracture
H. Instability

Common Complaints

A. Pain on movement of the shoulder or arm
B. Limitation of movement of the shoulder
C. Stiffness of the shoulder

Other Signs and Symptoms

A. Swelling of the shoulder
B. Difficulty lifting the arm and getting dressed
C. Difficulty with routine ADL

Potential Complications

A. Fracture
B. Gallbladder disease
C. Heart disease/myocardial infarction (MI)
D. Disease of the cervical spine
E. Tumors
F. Infection
G. Nerve-related disorders

Subjective Data

A. Ask patient what activity brought about or preceded the episode. Any falls? Any direct blow injuries?

B. Inquire about the duration of pain, what makes it worse, what makes it better.

C. Ask patient to describe pain, for example, dull, aching, or burning. Any numbness or tingling?
D. Does pain radiate to other areas of the back, arm, or neck?
E. Have patient rate pain on a scale of 0 to 10, with 0 being no pain.
F. Note a list of all medications currently being taken, particularly any OTC preparations, rubs/creams, splints/sling, or electrical stimulation devices.

Physical Examination

A. Vital signs: Check temperature (if applicable), pulse, respirations, and blood pressure
B. Inspect
   1. Always compare each area bilaterally for comparison and contour of anatomy.
   2. Inspect general appearance and gait, noting evenness and symmetry of motion, as well as wing arm in tandem with opposite lower extremity.
   3. Observe shoulder movement as patient disrobes—normal is smooth, natural, and bilateral. Abnormal findings are jerkiness and patient's attempt to move in order to decrease pain.
   4. Inspect skin for discoloration, abrasions, scars, or evidence of previous pathology.
   5. Inspect the clavicle for distortion or abnormality, possibly indicating a fractured clavicle
   6. Inspect the deltoid portion of the shoulder, which should be rounded as a result of the draping of the deltoid muscle over the greater tuberosity of the humerus. Normally, the area is full and round and the two sides are symmetrical. Inspect for atrophy or asymmetry, possibly representing a dislocation.
   7. Inspect the posterior shoulder: The scapula. In the resting position, the scapula is positioned over ribs 2 to 7 and medial border is approximately 2 inches from the spinous processes. The triangular area of the scapula is opposite T3. Inspect for winged effect, which may indicate weakness or atrophy of the serratus anterior muscle. Scapular asymmetry also occurs when the scapula has only partially descended from the neck to the thorax, causing a webbing or shortening of the neck (Sprengel's deformity).
C. Auscultate
   1. Auscultate carotid arteries.
   2. Auscultate abdomen.
   3. Conduct a complete heart exam and lung exam.
D. Palpate
   (The provider should position self behind the seated patient with cupped hands on the deltoid and acromion.)
   1. Palpate the suprasternal notch and the joint that holds the clavicle in place
   2. Palpate in a sliding motion the anterior superior surface of the clavicle.
   3. Palpate the acromioclavicular joint by pushing in a medial direction against the thickness end of the clavicle. Then ask the patient to flex and extend the shoulder. Movement of the joint will be palpated under the fingers. Note any crepitation which may indicate osteoarthritis or dislocation of the lateral end of the clavicle.
   4. Palpate the acromion and the greater tuberosity of the humerus
   5. Palpate the bicipital groove, which is located anterior and medial to the greater tuberosity. It is more easily palpable if the arm is externally rotated, providing for a more exposed position for palpation. This requires gentle palpation because the long head of the biceps lies within it, and too much pressure may elicit pain, causing difficulty with further evaluation.
   6. Palpate the scapula. It is clinically important to palpate this area, for it is frequently a site of referred pain from the cervical spine.
   7. Palpate the soft tissues of the shoulder, which is divided into four clinical zones:
      a. Rotator cuff (the supraspinatus, infraspinatus, subscapularis, and the teres minor muscles). Note tenderness during palpation. This may be due to defects, tears, or tendon detachment. The supraspinatus muscle is the most commonly ruptured muscle, especially near its insertion. Passive extension of the shoulder moves the rotator cuff into a palpable position. Hold the patient's arm and lift the elbow posteriorly.
      b. Subacromial and subdeltoid bursa can be very tender if bursitis is present. Palpate for thickening, masses, specific tenderness, or crepitation.
      c. Axilla—Abduct the arm with one hand as you gently insert your index and middle fingers into the axilla. Then return the patient's arm to the side to relax the skin; your fingers will be able to penetrate higher into the axilla. Palpate for lymph node enlargement or tenderness. Palpate the anterior wall, medial wall, and posterior walls of the axilla.
      d. Prominent muscles of the shoulder girdle—Palpate the muscles bilaterally for size, shape, consistency, and tone. Palpate the sternocleidomastoid, the pectoralis major, bicep, deltoid, trapezius, rhomboid minor and major, latissimus dorsi, and serratus anterior.

8. Evaluate the ROM, both active and passive. The shoulder girdle involves six motions: abduction, adduction, extension, flexion, internal rotation, and external rotation.
9. Two useful tests to help to diagnose a rotator cuff tear are:
   a. Empty can test for detecting a supraspinatus tear—Arm is elevated to 90 degrees and angled forward 30 degrees to place the humerus in line with the scapula. The shoulder is internally rotated by pointing the thumb down to the ground. The clinician applies a downward force as the patient attempts to resist. Pain and/or weakness are deemed a positive test.
   b. Drop arm test—the arm is abducted to at least 90 degrees. Lower the arm slowly and control the descent. The inability to perform this task slowly and with control is a positive test. The patient may still have a tear even if this test is negative.

E. Mental status: Assess for confusion.

Diagnostic Tests

A. Plain x-rays of the shoulder—will show any injuries or fractures to the bones.
B. MRI and/or ultrasound—these tests create a better picture of soft tissues, identifying injuries to the ligaments and tendons.
C. Arthrogram—a dye is injected into the shoulder to visualize the joint, muscles, and tendons.
D. Arthroscopy—a surgical procedure using a fiber-optic camera to inspect the joint. This procedure may show injuries that may not be apparent on exam or other tests. Sometimes arthroscopy may be used to correct the problem.
E. Electromyogram (EMG) can be used to evaluate nerve function, if indicated.

Differential Diagnosis

A. Shoulder pain
B. Heart disease
C. Gallbladder disease
D. Liver disease
E. Disease of the cervical spine

Plan

A. General interventions
   1. Educate the patient regarding proper treatment and care for the injured shoulder.

B. Patient teaching
   1. Educate the patient on rest, altering activities to avoid overexertion or overdoing activities to prevent shoulder pain.
   2. Educate the patient on sling use, if indicated.
   3. Educate the patient on RICE: Rest, Ice, Compression, and Elevation.
   4. Educate the patient on ROM, strengthening exercises.

C. Pharmaceutical therapy
   1. NSAIDs or aspirin as indicated. Consider kidney function and other chronic conditions.
   2. Injection of corticosteroid drug if shoulder doesn't get better or injection of lidocaine for numbing effect.
   3. Oral prednisone therapy to reduce inflammation, short term only.
   4. Cautionary use of opioid analgesics for pain

Follow-Up

A. Approximately 23% of all new episodes of shoulder pain completely resolve within 1 month and 44% within 3 months of onset.
B. Approximately 50% of patients with an acute shoulder who are treated conservatively recover within 5 months, and approximately 60% recover within 12 months.
C. The patient's personality traits, coping styles, and occupational factors may determine otherwise.
D. Follow-up should be in 1 to 2 weeks to reevaluate shoulder function, pain status, and impact of daily life abilities.

Consultation/Referral

Acute fracture or dislocation requires immediate referral to orthopedic surgeons. Urgent referral as needed for any red flag diagnoses.

A. Referral to orthopedic surgeon if there are positive imaging findings or surgical interventions are needed.
B. Referral to physical therapy or physiotherapist for exercise, strengthening, strapping, immobility devices, or ultrasound therapy as well as prevention of further injuries.

Individual Considerations

A. Geriatrics
   1. Consider acute versus chronic shoulder interventions.
   2. NSAID use is dependent on comorbid diseases such as gastrointestinal, cardiac, or renal disease.
   3. Cautionary use of opioid analgesics due to fall risk. If using analgesics, educate the patient regarding fall risk prevention.
   4. Need for ADL support to avoid injury. Special attention is given to patients using mobility devices requiring use of the affected shoulder.
   5. Consider fluoroquinolone-associated tendinopathy, including tendon rupture, in patients who complain of shoulder pain after the use of fluoroquinolone antibiotics (ofloxacin, ciprofloxacin, Levofloxacin). Perform an MRI for assessment/evaluation. Refer to orthopedics as indicated.

Resource

Exercise: A Guide From the National Institute on Aging. www.nia.nih.gov/search/site/shoulder%20exercises

Spinal Stenosis

Definition

Spinal stenosis is a narrowing of the spaces in the spine that result in pressure on the spinal canal and/or the nerve roots. The narrowing may involve a small or large area of the spine. In the lumbar area, pressure may elicit pain or numbness in the legs. In the cervical area, it may produce pain or numbness in the shoulders and arms/hands. The stenosis occurs in up to three areas.

A. The canal in the center of the column where the nerve roots run
B. The canals at the base of the nerves branching out from the spine
C. The openings of the vertebrae through which the nerves pass and go to other areas of the body.

Incidence

A. Spinal stenosis is most common in men and women older than the age of 50.
B. The incidence of lumbar spinal stenosis in the United States has been estimated at 8% to 11% of the population, and an estimated 2.4 million Americans will be affected by 2021. Lumbar stenosis accounts for 75% of the cases.

Pathogenesis

A. Spine
  1. The spine consists of 26 bones that extend in a line from the base of the skull to the pelvis. Twenty-four of those bones are called vertebrae.
     a. 7 cervical vertebrae
     b. 12 thoracic vertebrae
     c. 5 lumbar vertebrae
  2. The sacrum consists of five fused vertebrae between the hip bones.
  3. The coccyx has three to five bones at the lower tip of the vertebral column, which are linked together and cushioned by shock-absorbing disks.
B. Narrowing of the spinal canal may be inherited or acquired. Spinal stenosis most often results from a gradual, degenerative aging process where the ligaments of the spine may thicken and calcify. The bones and joints enlarge where surfaces of the bone begin to project from the body (called osteophytes or bone spurs), thereby decreasing the space (neural foramen) for nerve roots leaving the spine. Disk degeneration causes the same narrowing of the vertebral space.

Predisposing Factors

A. Aging with secondary changes (narrowing of the spinal canal)
B. Osteoarthritis (the most common cause of spinal stenosis)
C. Herniated disk (places pressure on the spinal cord and nerve root)
D. Trauma to the spine
E. Bone disease such as Paget's disease of the bone (may see structural narrowing of the spinal canal)
F. Tumors of the spine
G. Ossification occurs when calcium deposits form, turning the fibrous tissues of the ligament into bone and in turn pressing on the nerves of the spinal canal.
H. Rheumatoid arthritis
I. Spinal surgery

Common Complaints

The neck or back may not be painful, but if the narrowed space is pushing on a nerve root, symptoms will associate with the nerve root in the arms or legs.

A. Numbness in arms or legs
B. Weakness in arms or legs
C. Cramping in arms or legs
D. Pain radiating down the leg (sciatica), causing difficulty in walking

Other Signs and Symptoms

A. Symptoms develop slowly over time.
B. Pain comes and goes, generally not continuous.
C. Pain worsens during certain activities such as walking or change of position.
D. Some symptom relief by rest and/or any flexed forward position (lumbar)

Potential Complications

A. Incontinence
B. Paralysis
C. Unresolved presenting symptoms or worsening of symptoms
D. Surgical risks include infection, tear in the membrane covering the spinal cord, blood clot formation, and neurological deterioration.

Subjective Data

A. When were the symptoms first noticed? Ask patient what brought about or preceded the episode.
B. Have the symptoms worsened over time? Describe the pain and note certain times of the day that symptoms were more prominent.
C. Describe pain, as well as radiation of pain, or effect (numbness or tingling) on other body parts—hips, thighs, knees, calves, ankles, feet, arms, hands, fingers.

D. What makes the pain worse? What makes the pain better?
E. Have the patient rate pain on a scale of 0 to 10, with 0 being no pain.
F. Ask the patient to list all medications currently being taken, particularly substances not prescribed and illicit drugs.
G. Are there any other medical problems or chronic conditions that may contribute to symptoms?
H. Any incontinence issues with bowel or bladder? If so, when did symptoms begin, and how are they changing?

Physical Examination

A. **Symptoms of cauda equina are a rare form of spinal stenosis. It occurs because of the compression of the cauda equina, and symptoms may include loss of control of bowel, bladder or sexual dysfunction, pain, or weakness or loss of feeling in one or both legs. Cauda equina syndrome is serious and requires urgent medical attention. Patients should be transported to the hospital immediately.**
B. **Spinal stenosis of the cervical spine can be far more dangerous by compressing the spinal cord, leading to major body weakness or even paralysis, and requires urgent medical attention. Patients should be transported to the hospital immediately.**
C. Vital signs: Check temperature, pulse, respirations, and blood pressure.
D. Inspect
   1. Inspect and observe general appearance, gait, assistive devices used, positioning of affected portion of the spine, and overall appearance of pain.
   2. Inspect for gross abnormalities of weakness of arms or legs, foot drop or drag.
   3. Inspect legs for edema/swelling, skin rashes or discolorations of skin of arms/hands or leg/feet, skin temperature changes or symptoms of stasis, and fatty masses (lipomas) in the area of the low back, which may be a sign of spina bifida.
E. Auscultate
   1. Heart
   2. Lungs
F. Palpate: Cervical spine and lumbar spine
   1. Neck
      a. Palpate the neck with the patient in the supine position; the muscles of the neck are relaxed in this position and the bony structures are more defined.
      b. Palpate the anterior neck while supporting the base of the neck.
      c. Palpate the hyoid bone (situated above the thyroid cartilage), which is opposite the C3 vertebral body.
      d. Palpate the "Adam's apple," which marks the C4 body, whereas the lower portion of the Adam's apple is the C5 level. The first cricoid ring, inferior to the sharp lower edge of the thyroid, is opposite the C6 body. This ring is immediately above the site for an emergency tracheostomy. Too much pressure on palpation may cause the patient to gag. The carotid tubercles are at the horizontal level of C6 and located laterally about one inch from the first cricoid ring. The carotid tubercles should be palpated separately to avoid restriction of flow to both carotid arteries at the same time. C1 can be located as a small hard bump which lies between the angle of the jaw and the styloid process.
      e. Palpate the posterior neck while standing behind the patient, cupping the anterior neck to avoid tension on the muscles. The posterior aspect includes the occiput, spinous processes, mastoid process, and the facet joints. Begin at the base of the skull, palpating C2 (C1 lies deep). Palpate from C2 to T1 for normal curvature of the spine. If the vertebra is uncertain, it can be determined with the anterior structures of the anterior neck.
      f. Palpate the lumbar spine while sitting on a stool behind the standing patient. Place the fingers on the top of the iliac crest with the thumbs on the midline of the back (L4–L5) and palpate spinous processes downward. Pain referred from the spine may be reproduced in the back of the legs during palpation. Pain with palpation of the coccyx is usually the result of direct blow trauma. Palpate the anterior aspect of the spine, with the patient lying supine with knees bent to relax the abdominal muscles. The umbilicus lies at L3 to L4. L4 to S1 are palpable below the aorta's division into the common iliacs. L5 to S1 may be palpated when palpating below the umbilicus and pushing into the abdomen with abdominal relaxation.
      g. Palpate the soft tissues of the neck and lumbar spine
         i. The anterior triangle: This is made up of the two sternocleidomastoid muscles, superior by the mandible and inferior by the suprasternal notch.
         ii. The posterior aspect involves the trapezius muscles and the greater occipital nerves at the base of the skull, as well as the superior nuchal ligament that extends to the C7 process.

iii. Soft tissue palpation of the lumbar spine involves:
   a) The midline raphe (supraspinous and interspinous ligaments and the paraspinal muscles)
   b) The iliac crest (gluteal muscles)
   c) The posterior superior iliac spine (sacral triangle)
   d) The sciatic area (sciatic nerve—the largest nerve in the body runs vertically down the midline of the posterior thigh, giving off branches to the hamstring muscles, and then divides into the tibial and peroneal areas)
   e) The anterior abdominal wall and inguinal areas. Pain in the inguinal area usually indicates disorders of the hip joint.

h. Assess the ROM of the cervical and lumbar spine with basic movements of flexion, extension, lateral rotation to the left and right, and lateral bending to the left and right.
   i. Rotation: Ask the patient to shake his head from side to side.
   ii. Flexion and extension: Ask the patient to touch his chin to his chest and to look up at the ceiling.
   iii. Lateral bending is assessed by having the patient try to touch his ear to his shoulder without lifting the shoulder to his ear.
   iv. Normal lateral bending is 45 degrees toward each shoulder.
   v. Vertebral motion is greatest where the disk is the thickest and larger joint surfaces are present (L4, L5, S1) so motion taking place is greater than between L1 and L2.
   vi. ROM of the lumbar spine includes flexion (bend as far forward as patient can with knees straight and try to touch toes—measure the distance from floor to fingertips), extension (place palm on his back and have patient bend backward as far as possible—estimate the range of extension), lateral bending (lean to the left and then lean to the right as far as possible—estimate the degree and compare sides), and rotation (rotate the pelvis and compare ranges of rotation).

i. Perform a neurological exam that includes muscle testing and examination of the entire upper extremities for weakness or disorders of sensation. There are eight nerves exiting the cervical spine. Stenosis or disorders such as a herniated disk frequently reflected to the upper extremity usually originate from the C5 to T1. The primary nerves involved in the sensory distribution of the upper extremities are:
   i. C5—lateral arm, axillary nerve
   ii. C6—lateral forearm, thumb, index and half of middle finger, musculoskeletal nerve
   iii. C7—middle finger
   iv. C8—ring and little finger, medial forearm, medial antebrachial-cutaneous nerve
   v. T1—medial arm, medial brachial cutaneous nerve

The neurological exam of the lumbar spine is completed by performing an assessment of the ROM.

j. Assess reflexes and sensation: Biceps reflex and lateral arm axillary nerve indicates primarily origination from C5 to C6.
   i. Assess C6 by the brachioradialis reflex tested proximal to the wrist. C6 supplies sensation to the lateral forearm, the thumb, the index, and half of the middle finger. To assess, form the number six with your thumb, index, and middle finger by pinching your thumb and index finger and extending the middle finger.
   ii. Access C7 (radial nerve) by having the patient begin extension of the tricep/elbow from a position of flexion as motion is resisted. C7 also involves the median and ulnar nerves. To test wrist flexion, ask the patient to make a fist and flex the wrist as you resist against the palmar aspect of the closed fist. To test the radial nerve (C7), press on the dorsum of the patient's extended fingers. To test the reflex of C7—tap the triceps tendon where it crosses the olecranon fossa at the elbow. Sensation testing is supplied to the middle finger by C7.
   iii. C8 has no reflex, muscle strength or sensation test to determine integrity.
   iv. To test nerves emanating from T12, L1, L2, and L3—the iliopsoas is the main flexor of the hip—have patient sit on a table, place hand over the iliac crest, and ask the patient to actively raise his thigh from the table.
   v. Sensation testing of L1, L2, and L3 is over the area of the anterior thigh between the inguinal ligament and the knee.

vi. Muscle testing of L2, L3, and L4—femoral nerve—is performed by having the patient sit on the edge of the table, stabilizing the distal end of the thigh, and instructing the patient to extend his knee while offering resistance to the motion.

vii. To test the obturator nerve (hip adductors)—instruct the patient to abduct the legs after placing a hand on the medial sides of the knee and ask to abduct knees to resistance.

viii. *L4* muscle testing involves the tibialis anterior tested by resistance to dorsiflexion and inversion by pushing against the dorsal medial aspect of the first metatarsal bone.

ix. Reflex testing of L4 involves the patellar reflex and sensation testing of the medial side of the leg below the knee.

x. Neurological muscle testing of *L5* involves the deep peroneal nerve by placing your thumb on the dorsal surface of the foot so that the patient must dorsiflex his great toe to reach it. Oppose this motion by pushing on the nailbed of the great toe. To test the superior gluteal nerve (L5)—have the patient lie on his side and instruct him to abduct his leg and then push against the lateral side of the thigh for resistance. Reflex testing of L5—test the tibialis posterior reflex.

xi. Muscle testing of S1 involves the superficial peroneal nerve and is performed by securing the patient's ankle and having him plantar flex and evert the foot and oppose the motion by resistance pushing. The inferior gluteal nerve is tested by having the patient flex the knees and extend the hips as resistance is applied to hip extension while palpating the gluteus maximus for tone.

xii. The Achilles tendon reflex is the tendon reflex mediated by the S1, S2 tibial nerve. Sensation of the S2 dermatomes includes the lateral malleolus and lateral side and plantar aspect of the foot. S2, S3, S4 are the principal nerves of the bladder and supply the intrinsic muscles of the foot. There is no deep reflex for S2, S3, and S4. The dermatomes around the anus receive innervation from S2, S3, and S4. The abdominal (lie supine and stroke each quadrant of the abdomen with the sharp edge of a reflex hammer), cremasteric (stroke the inner side of the upper thigh with the sharp end of the reflex hammer) and anal reflex (simply touch the perianal skin, causing contraction as response) are superficial and require skin, stimulation.

xiii. Pathological reflexes (the significance of their presence or absence is the reverse of the normal reflexes). These include:

a) The Babinski test: Run a sharp instrument across the plantar surface of the foot from the calcaneus to forefoot—if negative, the toes either do not move or bunch up uniformly. If positive, the great toe extends while the other toes plantar flex and splay. Results should be negative in adults.

b) The Oppenheim test: Run your fingernail along the crest of the tibia. Normally, there should be either no reaction, or the patient should complain of pain; if abnormal, the great toe extends while the other toes plantar flex and splay.

k. Perform complete abdominal exam.

G. Mental status: Assess for any psychopathological component impacting symptomology and diagnosis.

Diagnostic Tests

A. Diagnostic imaging: MRI scan or a CT scan with and without myelogram. Plain CT scans are of limited value unless they are made with very fine segmental scan slices.

B. Bone density or DEXA scan testing are used to assess for osteopenia and/or osteoporosis.

C. Electrophysiological studies are mainly used to rule out differential diagnosis of spinal cord lesions or disorders of the nervous system, but may be helpful when the patient presents with multisegmental symptoms. These studies are often complicated with coexisting conditions such as diabetes mellitus or polyneuropathy affecting the nerves.

D. Laboratory tests can help to rule out inflammatory processes: CBC, C-reactive protein (CRP), renal function test, basic metabolic panel (BMP), erythrocyte sedimentation rate.

Differential Diagnosis

A. Spinal stenosis

B. Conditions that may mimic cauda equina (ruptured abdominal aortic or iliac aneurysms, acute aortic dissection, acute leg ischemia, or deep vein thrombosis [DVT]).

C. Claudication
(Presentation of intermittent leg pain may indicate claudication—arterial, peripheral, or neurogenic.)
D. Diabetic polyneuropathy
E. Paget's disease
   1. Paget's disease is a chronic disorder typically resulting in enlarged and abnormal bones—the spine is one of the most common sites affected by this disease. The lumbar spine is affected in at least half of the cases. Paget's disease may present symptoms of disk prolapse with nerve root entrapment and with the increased vascularity of the Pagetic vertebrae, which may diminish the spinal cord or nerve root blood supply; this causes pain.
F. Amyloidosis associated with hemodialysis or amyloid tumors may cause spinal stenosis or even cauda equina syndrome.

Plan

A. General interventions
   1. Physical therapy
      a. Build strength and endurance.
      b. Maintain flexibility and stability of spine.
      c. Improve balance and gait.
      d. Reduce pain.
   2. Alternative therapies (chiropractic treatment and/or acupuncture)
   3. Bracing may be used for lumbar stenosis to help support those patients with weak abdominal muscles or multilevel degeneration and also help regain or maintain stability.
B. Patient teaching
   1. Home treatments may include hot or cold packs as necessary.
   2. Assistive ambulatory devices such as canes or walkers may be used to relieve pain and provide stability and fall prevention. Instruct patient on the proper use of these devices.
   3. Encourage the use of home exercises. Provide patient with proper back exercises.
C. Pharmaceutical therapy
   1. Pain control
      a. NSAIDs if not contraindicated
      b. Muscle relaxants to treat the muscle spasms associated with spinal stenosis.
      c. Antidepressants such as amitriptyline can help ease chronic pain.
      d. Antiseizure medications such as Neurontin or Lyrica may be used to reduce pain caused by damaged nerves.
      e. Opioids may be considered to control severe pain. All patients must be assessed individually for comorbid conditions, as well as medication interactions and precautions, before prescribing medications. Fall risk assessment; independence of activities, including driving; and mental capabilities should also be evaluated.
   2. Steroid trigger injections to decrease irritated and swollen areas may help reduce inflammation and relieve pain. Repeated steroid injections can weaken bones and connective tissue, so injections should be limited.

Follow-Up

A. Follow-up is determined by patient's needs: Complications from surgery, continued pain and inflammation, or assessment of functional status with nonsurgical therapies interventions.

Consultation/Referral

A. Refer to a neurosurgeon if nonsurgical modalities fail. The extent of the patient's pain and the patient's preferences all factor into whether to have surgery.
B. **Surgical consult should be obtained immediately if a patient has numbness or weakness that interferes with walking, impaired bowel or bladder function, or other neurological involvement.**
C. Pain management specialists should be considered if conservative measures are not meeting patient's needs.
D. Refer to physical/occupational therapy for evaluation and treatment.

Individual Considerations

A. Geriatrics
   1. When the elderly patient can no longer walk sufficiently to care for himself or herself and perform essential tasks, then surgery is usually recommended. The priority of surgery is to increase the patient's activity tolerance with lessened pain.
   2. Booklet for exercise: A Guide from the National Institute on Aging is available free of charge to educate patients on exercises-motivation-safety, along with self-tests, benefits, and nutrition. This booklet can be obtained from NIA Information Center, PO Box 8057, Gaithersburg, MD 20898-8057.

Sprains: Ankle and Knee

Definition

Sprains are ligament stretching or partial tearing from forceful stress on the joint. Sprains are categorized as:
A. Grade 1: Microscopic tears without ligament tearing or joint instability
B. Grade 2: Partial tearing of involved ligaments and laxity of joint with moderate function loss
C. Grade 3: Ligament tearing with severe function loss and joint instability

Incidence

A. *Ankle* sprains are among the most common injuries seen in primary care.

B. *Knee* injuries are among the 10 most common causes of occupational injury and worker compensation claims.

Pathogenesis

A. Sudden stress to a supporting ligament causes ligament stretching or tearing. Sprains are usually the result of jumping, falling, or rotating a joint.

B. Ankle sprains are most often inversion sprains, with symptoms on the lateral side of the joint.

C. Eversion injuries affect the medial side.

D. Knee sprains most often involve the patellofemoral joint.

Predisposing Factors

A. Previous injury to ankle or knee

B. Athletic activities

C. Patellofemoral instability

Common Complaints

A. "I twisted my ankle or knee."

B. "I stepped off of a step and came down on the side of my foot."

C. Swelling, pain, weakness of ankle or knee from a previous injury.

Other Signs and Symptoms

A. First degree: Minimal pain; mild to moderate pain with stress, little swelling; minimal tenderness with palpation; little functional loss; unimpaired weight bearing or walking; internal microdamage with full continuity

B. Second degree: Moderate pain with ROM; swelling; marked tenderness on palpation; moderate loss of function; difficulty with weight bearing or walking; mechanical dissociation with partial loss of continuity

C. Third degree: Severe pain, especially with passive inversion; severe swelling, marked tenderness; marked decrease in ROM; intolerant of weight bearing or walking; joint instability; discoloration of skin; complete rupture of a ligament

Subjective Data

A. Inquire about history of trauma.

B. Have the patient describe the injury: Time, place, activity, predisposing factors, and time symptoms developed.

C. Determine if the symptoms are acute or chronic.

D. Inquire about the type and location of the pain.

E. Have the patient describe the pain and what conditions aggravate or relieve pain.

F. Ask if there are symptoms of popping, clicking, locking, recurrent swelling, or giving way of joint.

G. Ask if there is pain or other symptoms elsewhere, such as low back, hip, or leg.

H. Explore history of any previous ankle or knee injury.

I. Determine if the current injury was evaluated and treated previously.

J. Have the patient describe the ability to bear weight on the extremity and to tolerate ROM.

K. Review the patient's medical history for arthritis, gout, cancer, autoimmune disorders, or metabolic disease.

Physical Examination

A. Check temperature, pulse, respirations, and blood pressure.

B. Inspect
   1. Observe ambulation. Note overall appearance and facial grimaces during exam.
   2. Inspect injured area for swelling, discoloration, and deformity. Compare injured side to uninjured side.

C. Palpate
   1. Palpate the injured site for tenderness.
   2. Palpate the joints above and below the injured site.
   3. Perform ROM (active and passive), resisted range of motion to evaluate strength.
   4. Check for catching or locking of the knee on extension.
   5. Assess the neurovascular status of the knee or ankle and distal extremity.
   6. *Ankle*: Palpate for tender sulcus in anterolateral aspect on inversion of the ankle. Assess for pain aggravated by forced ankle inversion. Perform isometric test of plantar flexion and eversion. Perform anterior drawer test, talar tilt test.
   7. *Knee*: Palpate for tenderness on the medial and lateral joint line. Perform McMurray's test to detect a torn meniscus (see Section II Procedure, "Evaluation of Sprains"). Symptoms of sprained knees:
      a. Meniscus tear: Locking of knee with flexion and giving way of knee
      b. Collateral ligament tear or strain: Pain at lateral or medial sides
      c. Anterior cruciate tear: Popping sound at injury site and immediate swelling
      d. Posterior cruciate tear or strain: Pain in interior knee
      e. Patellofemoral syndrome: Popping or snapping, pain under patella with motion, and pain on stairs or hills
      f. Tendinitis: Pain over patellar tendon
      g. Prepatellar bursitis: Swelling over patella with inability to kneel due to swelling
      h. Nonspecific effusion: Effusion worse with exercise
   8. See the Section II Procedure, "Evaluation of Sprains."

Diagnostic Tests

A. Radiography of extremity, if fracture is suspected.
B. MRI, if mechanical symptoms and effusion persist.
C. Bone scans or MRI are usually reserved for those who have failed to respond after 6 to 12 weeks of therapy.

Differential Diagnoses

A. Ankle sprain
  1. Fracture
  2. Acute dislocation
  3. Infection
  4. Ligament strain
  5. Tendinitis or tenosynovitis
  6. Nonspecific foot or ankle pain
B. Knee sprain
  1. Fracture
  2. Dislocation
  3. Septic arthritis
  4. Infected prepatellar bursitis
  5. Inflammation
  6. Tumor
  7. Meniscus tear
  8. Collateral ligament tear
  9. Anterior cruciate tear
  10. Posterior cruciate tear
  11. Collateral ligament strain
  12. Cruciate ligament strain
  13. Patellofemoral syndrome or chondromalacia
  14. Effusion, nonspecific
  15. Patellar tendinitis
  16. Prepatellar bursitis
  17. Nonspecific knee pain

Plan

A. General interventions: Reinforce the degree of injury and the need to take care of extremity to prevent further damage.
B. Patient teaching
  1. See the Section III Patient Teaching Guide for this chapter, "RICE Therapy and Exercise Therapy."
  2. Give the patient the Section III Patient Teaching Guides for this chapter, "Ankle Exercises" or "Knee Exercises."
C. Pharmaceutical therapy
  1. Drug of choice
    a. NSAIDs to reduce pain and inflammation
    b. Consider one of the following: aspirin, ibuprofen, indomethacin, or piroxicam.
    c. If there is increased risk for bleeding, acetaminophen with codeine may be used for pain.
  2. Injectable medication
    a. Methylprednisolone acetate (Depo-Medrol) may be used if symptoms continue to be present 6 to 8 weeks after injury.
    b. Repeat injection in 4 to 6 weeks if symptoms have not been reduced by 50%.

Follow-Up

A. Schedule initial follow-up in 2 weeks to evaluate current therapy or sooner if problems arise.

Consultation/Referral

A. Refer the patient to a physician if fracture is suspected.
B. Refer the patient to a physician or orthopedic surgeon if therapy is unproductive and symptoms have not begun to regress within 6 weeks.

Individual Considerations

A. Medication log of the geriatric patients should be available for interaction and consideration to this population for gastrointestinal, renal, cardiovascular, and endocrine disorders.

Bibliography

American Academy of Orthopedic Surgeons. (n.d.a). *Arthritis of the foot and ankle.* Retrieved from http://orthoinfo.aaos.org

American Academy of Orthopedic Surgeons. (n.d.b). *Bunions.* Retrieved from http://orthoinfo.aaos.org

American Academy of Orthopedic Surgeons. (n.d.c). *Hammer toe.* Retrieved from http://orthoinfo.aaos.org

American Academy of Orthopedic Surgeons. (n.d.d). *Morton's neuroma.* Retrieved from http://orthoinfo.aaos.org

American Academy of Orthopedic Surgeons. (2010). *Shoulder pain and common shoulder problems.* Retrieved from http://orthoinfo.aaos.org/topic.cfm?topic=A00065

American College of Obstetricians and Gynecologists. (2004). ACOG practice bulletin. Clinical management guidelines for obstetrician-gynecologists. Number 50, January 2003. *Obstetrics and Gynecology, 103,* 203–216.

American College of Rheumatology. (2010). *2010 Fibromyalgia diagnostic criteria.* Retrieved from https://www.rheumatology.org/practice/clinical/classification/fibromyalgia

Anderson, B. (1999). *Office orthopedics for primary care: Diagnosis and treatment* (2nd ed.). Philadelphia, PA: W.B. Saunders.

Bellantoni, M. (1996). Osteoporosis prevention and treatment. *American Family Physician, 1,* 986–991.

Bigos, S., et al. (1994). *Acute low back problems in adults: Clinical Practice Guideline Number 14,* AHCPR Publication No. 95-0642. Rockville, MD: Agency for Health Care Policy and Research, Public Health Service, U.S. Department of Health and Human Services.

Birrer, R. B., Bordelon, R. L., & Sammarco, G. J. (1992, February 29). Ankle: Don't miss a sprain. *Patient Care, 26,* 6–28.

Brun, S. (2012). Shoulder injuries: Management in general practice. *Australian Family Physician, 42*(4), 188–194.

Chard, M. D., Hazelman, R., Hazelman, B., King, R., & Reiss, B. (1991). Shoulder disorders in the elderly: A community survey. *Arthritis Rheumatology, 34*(6), 766–769.

Chow, R., et al. (2007). Clinical guidelines: Diagnosis and treatment of low back pain. A joint clinical practice guideline from the American College of Physicians and the American Pain Society. *Annals of Internal Medicine, 147*(7), 478–491.

Current Reviews in Musculoskeletal Medicine. (2011a). Agents used in the non-surgical management of osteoarthritis, *4*(3), 113–122. doi:10.1007/s12178-011-9084-9

Current Reviews in Musculoskeletal Medicine. (2011b). Recommendations for OA treatment with specific consideration of elderly patients, *4*(3), 113–122. doi:10.1007/s12178-011-9084-9

Daily, P., Bishop, G., Russell, I., & Fletcher, E. M. (1990). Psychological stress and the fibrosistic/fibromyalgia syndrome. *Journal of Rheumatology, 17,* 1380.

Daniels, J. (1997). Treatment of occupationally acquired low back pain. *American Family Physician, 2,* 587–596.

Degenerative Disc Disease Definition. (2014). *Spine-Health.* Retrieved from http://www.spine-health.com/glossary/degenerative-disc-disease

Deyo, R. A., Loeser, J. D., & Bigos, S. J. (1990). Herniated lumbar intervertebral disc. *Annals of Internal Medicine, 112,* 598–603.

Emkey, G., & Reginato, A. (2009). All about gout and pseudogout: Meeting a growing challenge. *Journal of Musculoskeletal Medicine,* S17–S23.

Ernst, D., & Lee, A. (Eds.). (2009). *NPPR: Nurse practitioners' prescribing reference.* New York, NY: A Haymarket Media Publication.

Hoppenfeld, S. (1976). *Physical examination of the spine and extremities* (pp. 2–34, 171–198). Norwalk, CT: Appleton & Lange.

Jones, A. (1997). Primary care management of acute low back pain. *Nurse Practitioner, 22*(7), 50–68.

Kalaci, A., Cakici, H., Hapa, O., Yanat, A. N., & Sevinc, T. T. (2009). Treatment of plantar fasciitis using four different local injection modalities: A randomized prospective clinical trial. *Journal of the American Podiatric Medical Association, 99*(2), 108–113.

Kalff, R., Washchke, C., Gobisch, A., & Hopf, C. (2012). *Degenerative lumbar spinal stenosis in older people: Current treatment options.* Retrieved from https://www.aerzteblatt.de/int/archive/article/145981/Degenertative_lumbar-Stenosis

Kelly, J. (2013). *Fibromyalgia guidelines trigger changes for FPS.* Retrieved from http://www.medscape.com/viewarticle/804011_print

Kinkade, S. (2007). Evaluation and treatment of acute low back pain. *American Family Physician, 75*(8), 1181–1188.

Kishner, S. (2012). Degenerative disk disease. *Medscape Reference.* Retrieved from http://www.emedicine.medscape.com/article/1265463-overview

Lewiecki, E. M., & Watts, N. B. (2009). New guidelines for the prevention and treatment of osteoporosis. *Southern Medical Journal, 102*(2), 175–179.

Mayo Clinic. (2012). *Diseases and conditions: Spinal stenosis.* Retrieved from http://www.mayoclinic.org/diseases-conditions/spinal-stenosis/basics/definition

Mayo Clinic. (2013). *Gout.* Retrieved from http://www.mahoclinic.com/health/gout/DS00090?METHOD=print

McGee, C. (1997). Secondary amenorrhea leading to osteoporosis. *Nurse Practitioner, 22*(5), 22, 38, 41–45, 48.

Medline Plus. *Foot injuries and disorders.* Retrieved from http://www.nlm.nih.gov/medlineplus/footinjuriesanddisorders.html

Mufson, M., & Regestein, Q. (1993). The spectrum of fibromyalgia disorders. *Arthritis and Rheumatism, 35*(5), 647–649.

Muma, R., Lyons, B., Newman, T., & Carnes, B. (1996). *Patient education: A practical approach.* Stamford, CT: Appleton & Lange.

National Fibromyalgia Association. (n.d.). *Fibromyalgia fact sheet.* Retrieved from http://www.fmaware.org

National Institute of Arthritis and Musculoskeletal and Skin Diseases. (2010). *What are shoulder problems?* Retrieved from www.niams.nih.gov

National Institute of Arthritis and Musculoskeletal and Skin Diseases. (2013). *Spinal stenosis.* Retrieved from http://www.niams.nih.gov/Health_info/Spinal_Stenosis/

National Institute of Arthritis and Musculoskeletal and Skin Diseases. (2014). *Questions and answers about shoulder problems.* Retrieved from http://www.niams.nih.gov/Health_Info/Shoulder_Problems?

National Osteoporosis Foundation. (1998). *Physician's guide to prevention and treatment of osteoporosis.* Retrieved from http://www.nof.org/professionals/clinicals-Guide

National Osteoporosis Foundation. (n.d.a). *Medications to prevent & treat osteoporosis.* Retrieved from http://www.nof.org/patientinfo/medications.htm#Raloxifene

National Osteoporosis Foundation. (n.d.b). *Prevention: Vitamin D.* Retrieved from http://www.nof.org/prevention/vitaminD.htm

Neufeld, S. K., & Cerrato, R. (2008). Plantar fasciitis: Evaluation and treatment. *Journal of the American Academy of Orthopaedic Surgeons, 16*(6), 338–346.

Noble, J. (1996). *Textbook of primary care medicine* (2nd ed.). St. Louis, MO: Mosby.

PDR Health. (2009). Retrieved from www.pdrhealth.com

Pham, A. N., Colon-Emeric, C. S., & Weber, T. J. (2009). Osteoporosis in older women. *Clinical Geriatrics, 17*(10), 20–28.

Ray, C. (2014). *What is spinal stenosis.* Retrieved from http://www.spine-health.com/conditions/apinal-stenosis/what-spinal-stenosis

Ross, C. (1997). A comparison of osteoarthritis and rheumatoid arthritis: Diagnosis and treatment. *Nurse Practitioner, 22*(9), 20–39.

Rubin Institute for Advanced Orthopedics. (n.d.). *Aging knee.* Retrieved from http://lifebridgehelath.org/RIAO/AgingKnee.aspx

Shamie, N. (2011). *Lumbar spinal stenosis: The growing epidemic.* Retrieved from http://www.aaos.org/news/aaosnow/may11/clinical10.asp

Szpalski, M., & Gunzburg, R. (2003). Lumbar spinal stenosis in the elderly: An overview. Retrieved from http://www.ncbi.nlm.nih.gov.pmc/articles/PMC3591819

Sweet, M. G., Sweet, J. M., Jeremiah, M. P., & Galazka, S. S. (2009). Diagnosis and treatment of osteoporosis. *American Family Physician, 79*(3), 193–200.

Tierney, L., McPhe, S., & Papadakis, M. (2007). *Current medical diagnosis and treatment* (46th ed.). New York, NY: McGraw-Hill.

Turk, D., & Wilson, H. (2009). Managing fibromyalgia: An update on diagnosis and treatment. *Journal of Musculoskeletal Medicine,* S1–S7.

Ullrich, P. F. (2014a). Cervical degenerative disc disease. *Spine-Health.* Retrieved from http://www.spine-health.com/conditions/degenerative-disc-disease/Cervical-degenerative-disease

Ullrich, P. F. (2014b). Common symptoms of degenerative disc disease. *Spine-Health.* Retrieved from http://www.spine-health.com/conditions/degenerative-disc-disease/common-symptoms

Ullrich, P. F. (2014c). Degenerative disc disease treatment guidelines. *Spine-Health.* Retrieved from http://www.spine-health.com/conditions/degenerative-disc-disease

Ullrich, P. F. (2014d). Lumbar degenerative disc disease treatments. *Spine-Health.* Retrieved from http://www.spine-health.com/degenerative-disc-disease/lumbar-degenerative-disc-disease

Underwood, M. (2005). *Chronic knee pain in the elderly.* London, UK: Arthritis Research Campaign.

University of Maryland Medical Center Medical Center. (2013). *Degenerative disc disease: A patient's guide to degenerative disc disease.* Retrieved from www.unm.edu/programs/spine/health/guides/degenerative-disc-disease

U.S. Department of Health and Human Services. (2004). *Bone health and osteoporosis: A report of the Surgeon General.* Retrieved from http://www.surgeongeneralgov/library/bonehealth/content.html

U.S. National Library of Medicine. (2013). *Plantar fasciitis.* Retrieved from http://www.ncbi.nlm.nih.gov/pubmedhealth/PMH0004438

Vecchio, P., Kavanagh, R., Hazelman, B., & King, R. (1995). Community survey of shoulder disorders in the elderly to assess the natural history and effects of treatment. *Annals of Rheumatic Disorders, 54*(2), 152–154.

Wikipedia. (2013). *Fibromyalgia.* Retrieved from http://en.wikipedia.org/wiki/Fibromyalgia

Wolfe, F., Smythe, H., Yunus, M., Bennett, R. M., Bombardier, C., Goldenberg, D. L., et al. (1990). The American College of Rheumatology 1990 criteria for the classification of fibromyalgia: Report of the Multicenter Criteria Committee. *Arthritis and Rheumatism, 33*, 160–173.

CHAPTER TWENTY-ONE

Rheumatological Guidelines

Jill C. Cash

Fibromyalgia

Definition

A. Fibromyalgia syndrome is a clinical soft tissue condition characterized by generalized aching and stiffness of the muscles, soft tissue, tendons, and ligaments associated with the finding of numerous tender points in characteristic locations.

B. **The American College of Rheumatology (ACR) 2010 has developed criteria to use for diagnosing fibromyalgia. These criteria include characteristic symptoms of pain at specific trigger point locations that are displayed by the patient for the past 3 months when there is no other reason or explanation for the associated pain.**

C. **Trigger point locations are found primarily in the back, neck, jaw, shoulders, chest, abdomen, arms, hips, and legs.**

D. **Somatic symptoms are also assessed for and present with fibromyalgia. Somatic complaints may include cognitive problems, sleeping difficulties, fatigue, headaches, and other associated symptoms. These criteria can be found at the ACR website** www.rheumatology.org.

E. Fibromyalgia affects females more than males at a ratio of 10:1, and patients with an average age of 47 years; 5% of the population is affected by fibromyalgia. Its usual onset is between 20 and 50 years; however, it has also been diagnosed in the young as well as the elderly. Often patients have symptoms longer than 5 years before finally being diagnosed. The prevalence of fibromyalgia in rheumatology practice is 20%.

Pathogenesis

A. The cause is unclear. Studies of sleep physiology, neurohormonal function, muscular function, and psychological factors support a central mechanism for the disorder linked to depression.

B. Other research suggests a pathophysiologic and psychological disorder.

C. Researchers believe that repeated nerve stimulation causes the brain to change, which involves an abnormal increase in levels of neurotransmitters. The brain's pain receptors become more sensitive, meaning they can overreact to pain signals.

D. Fibromyalgia symptoms fluctuate over time and seldom disappear.

Predisposing Factors

A. Life stress
B. Depression
C. Female gender
D. Age: Mid-30s and older

Common Complaints

A. Common complaints are multifocal pain present longer than 3 months, moderate to extreme fatigue, morning stiffness, nonrestorative sleep, and pain worsening with stress, inactivity or overactivity, exposure to cold, sensitivity to touch, light, and sound.

Other Signs and Symptoms

A. Numbness
B. Swelling
C. Reactive hyperemia of skin
D. Raynaud's syndrome (RS)
E. Irritable bowel syndrome and bladder symptoms
F. Headaches (migraine and tension headaches)
G. Restless leg syndrome
H. Mood disorder (depression/anxiety)
I. Cognitive difficulties
J. Changes in the barometric pressure

Subjective Data

A. Determine onset, duration, and course of complaints.
B. Does fatigue interfere with the patient's daily activity?
C. Note sleep quality. Does the patient feel rested after sleeping?
D. Do exacerbations of discomfort occur with stress, activity, and cold?
E. Has the patient experienced stress and/or depression in the past?
F. Does she have a family history of rheumatoid disease?
G. Has she ever been diagnosed with chronic fatigue syndrome, Lyme disease, or thyroid disease?

Physical Examination

A. Check temperature, pulse, and blood pressure (BP).
B. Inspect
   1. Observe overall appearance.
   2. Observe the nails, skin, mucous membranes, eyes, joints, and spine. If clubbing is noted and tender points are minimal, consider hypertrophic osteoarthropathy.
C. Palpate: Palpate the muscles as outlined in the above criteria for classification of fibromyalgia. Note the following when palpating for tender points.
   1. Pressure should be insufficient to produce pain in normal patients or at uninvolved sites in affected patients.
   2. Pain on digital palpation must be present in at least 11 of 18 tender point sites.
   3. "Positive pain reaction" is related to the patient stating that palpation causes pain. Tenderness is not to be considered as pain.
   4. Painful points must be differentiated from trigger points of myofascial syndrome, which produce referred pain on compression.
   5. Control areas not expected to be tender in fibromyalgia, such as the middle of the forehead and fingertips, should be examined to exclude psychological pain or malingering.
D. Auscultate the heart and lungs.

Diagnostic Tests

A. Laboratory studies are normal with fibromyalgia.
B. Testing to consider assessing for other conditions include:
   1. Complete blood count (CBC)
   2. Erythrocyte sedimentation rate (ESR)
   3. C-reactive protein (CRP)
C. If the history and physical suggest some type of inflammatory, rheumatic condition, also order:
   1. Antinuclear antibody (ANA)
   2. Rheumatoid factor (RF)
D. If there are concerns regarding a possible thyroid or muscle condition, also order:
   1. Thyroid-stimulating hormone (TSH)
   2. Creatinine phosphokinase
E. Assessment for a sleep disorder should include ordering a sleep study.

Differential Diagnoses

A. Fibromyalgia
B. Rheumatoid arthritis (RA)
C. Osteoarthritis (OA)
D. Polymyalgia rheumatica
E. Ankylosing spondylitis
F. Myositis
G. Systemic lupus erythematous
H. Hypothyroidism
I. Chronic fatigue syndrome
J. Obstructive sleep apnea

Plan

A. General interventions: Multiple therapies may be beneficial for controlling symptoms. Stress importance of daily exercises and therapy to control pain. Support groups are beneficial for patients and families.
B. Patient teaching: See the Section III Patient Teaching Guide for this chapter, "Fibromyalgia." Teach the patient that fibromyalgia is a recognizable syndrome that does not progress or cripple and does not warrant further testing. The patient can be assured that it is not "all in her head."
   1. Exercise: Encourage the patient to exercise daily, including stretching programs along with walking, low-impact cardiovascular conditioning such as cycling, and low-impact aerobics. Initially, pain may increase with the first 2 weeks of exercise; then it improves with a routine exercise program.
   2. Pain control: Pain may improve with exercise, hot baths, heating pads, warm weather, and stress reduction.
C. Pharmaceutical therapy
   1. Amitriptyline 10 to 50 mg at bedtime for sleep
   2. Cyclobenzaprine 10 to 40 mg daily or other muscle relaxants
   3. Nonsteroidal anti-inflammatory drugs (NSAIDs) 200 to 600 mg every 4 to 6 hours. Maximum dose is 1.2 g a day. Use precautions and consider patients with contraindications to NSAIDs, such as gastrointestinal (GI), renal, cardiovascular, and other medication interactions.
   4. Analgesics such as acetaminophen (Tylenol) as needed
   5. Selective serotonin reuptake inhibitors (SSRIs) if depression is present.

6. Lyrica 75 mg twice a day to 150 mg twice a day; maximum dose of 450 mg a day
7. Cymbalta 30 to 60 mg once a day. Give precautions of nausea with medication. If nausea is severe, consider prescribing zofran 8 mg 30 minutes prior to cymbalta dose. Advise patient that nausea will resolve after 3 to 4 weeks.
8. Savella titrated dose 12.5 mg on Day 1, 12.5 mg twice a day for 2 days, Days 4 to 7, 25 mg twice a day, then 50 mg twice a day (recommended dose). Maximum dose 100 mg twice a day. Withdraw gradually. Precautions should be considered with renal impairment.
9. Opioids have not been studied in randomized controlled trials and should be considered only after all other medicinal therapies have been exhausted. Tramadol, a centrally acting analgesic with atypical opioid and antidepressant-like activity, is moderately effective in treating fibromyalgia pain.
10. Antiseizure medication, neurontin, is approved for use in the treatment of neuropathic pain but not fibromyalgia. Neurontin 300 mg orally three times a day should be the starting dose, with titrations upward as tolerated.

Follow-Up

A. Schedule regular visits in initial 2 to 4 weeks to evaluate how therapy is helping. Educate the patient each visit, and stress positive reinforcement and supervision of treatment regimen. Visits may then be scheduled every 3 months to monitor progress.

Consultation/Referral

A. Consult with a physician if the patient has abnormal laboratory results.
B. Consult or refer the patient to a physician/psychiatrist if depression is suspected and current medication therapy is unsuccessful.

Gout

Definition

A. Gout is an acute, sudden inflammatory disease of the joint, caused by high concentrations of uric acid in the joints and bones.
B. Three stages of gout
   1. Acute gouty arthritis: Acute attack exhibiting severe pain, redness, and swelling of a joint, which may last from days to weeks, even if left untreated
   2. Intercritical gout: Period of time without flares
   3. Chronic/tophaceous gout: The progression of gout that has been inadequately treated, resulting in urate crystal deposits (tophaceous deposits) in the joints that can cause deformity and disability of the joint

Incidence

A. Gout is most common in men from ages 30 to 60. It occurs less often in women; women become increasingly susceptible to gout after menopause (Mayo Clinic, 2013). The most commonly affected joint is the first metatarsophalangeal joint, followed by the ankle, knees, and other joints.

Pathogenesis

A. Primary: High levels of uric acid result from either increased production or decreased excretion rates of uric acid.
B. Secondary: Hyperuricemia results from primary disease processes (such as hypertension, renal failure, kidney disorders, enzyme deficiencies, and skin disorders) or medications/toxins.

Predisposing Factors

A. Chronic conditions: Renal disease, hypertension, skin disorders, blood disorders, diabetes, hyperlipidemia, OA, arteriosclerosis, obesity
B. Medications (diuretics, acetylsalicylic acid, nicotinic acid, ethambutol, pyrazinamide)
C. Age: Men older than 30, postmenopausal women
D. Lead poison
E. Family history of gout
F. Diet (high intake of beer and meat/seafood products)

Common Complaints

A. Redness, swelling, warmth, and/or pain in one joint (commonly seen in the first metatarsophalangeal joint-podagra). The pain is likely to be the most severe in the first 12 to 24 hours.
B. History having joint pain in other joints, followed by pain-free episodes.

Other Signs and Symptoms

A. Tophi is seen from several years of untreated gout.
B. Fever may be present in acute stages.

Subjective Data

A. Note when initial symptoms began.
B. Review patient history of gout.
C. Determine what makes the symptoms worse or better.
D. List medications/therapies used and the result of the different therapies used.

Physical Examination

A. Check temperature, pulse, respirations, and BP.
B. Inspect
   1. Inspect the joints for redness and swelling.
   2. Note the presence of tophi on other joints.
C. Palpate: Palpate the joints for tenderness, pain, and increase in temperature (warmth).

Diagnostic Tests

A. Joint aspiration: The gold standard in diagnosing gout is to perform synovial fluid aspiration of the joint, examine the fluid with a polarized light microscopy, and identify uric acid crystals.

B. CBC: White blood cell (WBC) count elevated
C. ESR: Elevated in gout
D. Serum uric acid level: Uric acid greater than 7.0 mg/dL. Serum uric acid level may be normal during acute attacks. Perform test 2 weeks after acute attack.
E. 24-hour urine uric acid excretion: Greater than 900 mg/24 hr
F. RF titer
G. X-ray or MRI: Identify bone cysts/gouty tophi.

Differential Diagnoses

A. Gout
B. Infectious arthritis
C. RA
D. Hyperparathyroidism
E. Pseudogout (calcium pyrophosphate deposition disease)—commonly occurs in the knee, wrist, or other joints
F. Bursitis
G. Cellulitis

Plan

A. General interventions
   1. Rest the joint area; perform no heavy lifting or weight-bearing activity.
   2. **Aspirin products should not be used.**
B. Patient teaching
   1. Increase fluid intake to at least eight glasses of water daily.
   2. Avoid alcohol intake and excessive meat and seafood products.
   3. Medication treatment and compliance of taking the prescribed medications can be very effective in preventing the development of the chronic tophaceous gout stage.
   4. See the Section III Patient Teaching Guide for this chapter, "Gout."
C. Pharmaceutical therapy
   1. Analgesia
      a. NSAIDs
         i. Indocin 50 mg every 8 hours for eight doses, then 25 mg every 8 hours until pain free for 1 to 2 days. Normal course is 5 to 7 days therapy.
         ii. Naproxen, 750 mg initially, followed by 500 mg every 12 hours
         iii. NSAIDs are contraindicated for patients with the diagnosis of renal insufficiency, heart failure, ulcer disease, NSAID allergy, and anticoagulation therapy.
      b. Colchicine (Colcrys): Colchicine 1.5 to 1.8 mg in two to three divided doses. Taper dose during attack until resolution for 1 to 2 days. Colchicine must be taken within 12 to 24 hours of acute attack to be effective. Colchicine warnings: Be aware of contraindications. Colchicine is contraindicated in patients with advanced renal and liver disease. Caution regarding drug interactions. Intolerable side effects of colchicine include nausea, vomiting, and diarrhea. Probenecid effects with other drugs include penicillin and methotrexate (MTX).

For long-term use, colchicine 0.6 mg/d may be used for patients who have more than one attack per year. See package insert for recommendations for more frequent use.

      c. Corticosteroids
         i. Intra-articular steroids: For patients who cannot tolerate oral medications, consider steroid injection into the joint for pain relief (triamcinolone acetonide or methylprednisolone acetate).
         ii. Oral steroids: Oral steroids may also be used for patients who cannot take NSAIDs or colchicine and who cannot have an intra-articular steroid injection. Prednisone is safe and effective. Be aware of rebound effects.
   2. For hypersecretion of uric acid, long-term therapy is needed to decrease uric acid production: Allopurinol (Zyloprim) is the drug of choice. Starting dose 100 mg/d and titrate up over several weeks to a maximum of 300 mg/d. The goal is to keep the uric acid level under 6.5 mg/dL. Uloric is also used to lower blood uric acid levels. The recommended dose is 40 mg/d with or without food; maximum dose is 80 mg/d. Initial laboratory studies include liver enzymes prior to beginning Uloric. Common side effects include liver problems, nausea, gout flares, joint pain, and rash.
   3. For reduced excretion rates of uric acid, consider probenecid (Benemid) 250 mg by mouth twice a day for 1 week, then increase to 500 mg by mouth twice a day. Increased consumption of fluids must be encouraged.
   4. Chronic gout: If patients have three or more attacks per year, consider long-term therapy; low dose of NSAIDs, or allopurinol for 2 to 12 months.
   5. Alternative medications for intolerance, renal insufficiency, and extensive tophi production include oxypurinol, febuxostat, and uricase. Refer these patients to a rheumatology specialist.

Follow-Up

A. The patient should be contacted within 24 hours for evaluation.

B. Schedule a follow-up visit in 1 month to reevaluate status.
C. Chronic gout: Obtain yearly uric acid levels; before initiating long-term therapy, obtain baseline blood urea nitrogen (BUN), serum lipid profile, and CBC and periodic liver enzymes.

Consultation/Referral

A. Consult and refer to physician or rheumatologist for aspiration of joint fluid and treatment options.

Individual Considerations

A. Pregnancy: Colchicine is not recommended.
B. Geriatrics
    1. Reformation in joint areas may be seen in patients who have a history of gout from the uric acid deposits.
    2. Complications for chronic gout include nephrolithiasis and chronic urate nephropathy.
    3. Avoid Indocin in elderly patients due to the increased risk of adverse effects with other medications when compared to other NSAIDs in this population.
    4. NSAIDs are not recommended in elderly patients with a history of heart failure, GI ulcers/disease, and renal impairment.
    5. Individual considerations must be given in this population regarding GI, cardiac, renal, and liver disease.

Osteoarthritis

Definition

A. OA, formerly known as degenerative joint disease, is a chronic noninflammatory disease that affects the movable joints. OA is characterized by destruction of the cartilage with resultant decrease in the joint spaces and bony overgrowth. OA is considered to be primary when there are no underlying conditions, and secondary to conditions such as trauma, septic arthritis, inflammatory arthritis, metabolic disorders, or congenital or acquired joint abnormalities.

Incidence

A. It is estimated that up to 12% of the general population between the ages of 25 and 74 have OA.
B. The incidence clearly increases with age as up to 85% of the general population over the age of 65 has radiographic changes suggestive of OA; 90% of all people have radiographic features of OA on weight-bearing joints by age 40.

Pathogenesis

A. Damage to the articular cartilage and subchondral bone may be due to local trauma and results in chondrocyte injury.
B. Chondrocytes release proteolytic enzymes that assist in repair of the cartilage.
C. In OA, the remodeling process of chondrocytes and release of enzymes is impaired and results in a loss of strength and greater trauma and destruction of the subchondral bone. The end result is joint destruction and bony overgrowth.

Predisposing Factors

A. Increasing age: Among patients older than 55 years
B. Gender: Women are more commonly affected and exhibit greater disease severity.
C. Genetic predisposition; distal interphalangeal (DIP) joint involvement
D. Trauma, such as previous fractures or ligamentous injuries; occupationally related repetitive stress on the joint
E. Altered joint anatomy or instability
F. Obesity: Mechanical injury in the knee may increase OA.
G. Secondary inflammation such as infections, inflammatory arthropathies, and metabolic disorders

Common Complaints

A. Unilateral joint pain frequently involving the joints of the hands, neck, lower back, knees, and hips
B. Morning stiffness lasting less than 1 hour

Other Signs and Symptoms

A. Unilateral joint pain involving the DIP and proximal interphalangeal (PIP) joints, first carpometacarpal joint, hips, knees, cervical and lumbar spine, and first metatarsophalangeal joint
B. Mild OA, or early disease, pain that increases with joint use and decreases with rest
C. Severe OA, or late disease, pain that is present with rest

Subjective Data

A. Elicit the patient's age at onset of pain.
B. Has the pain gradually gotten worse over the months or years?
C. How long does the pain last in the morning? Does the pain get worse with joint use and better with rest?
D. What joints are involved?
E. Is the joint pain described as "aching"?
F. What does the patient take to relieve the pain?
G. Is there any joint deformity, redness, swelling, or warmth?
H. Is there any decrease in range of motion (ROM) of the joint?
I. Is there any family history of OA?

Physical Examination

A. Check temperature, pulse, and BP.
B. Inspect the joints for enlargement, edema, and erythema.

C. Palpate
1. Palpate the joints, noting temperature, edema, and tenderness. Joints are cool; bony enlargement may be present in the PIP (Bouchard's nodes) or DIP joints (Heberden's nodes) and other weight-bearing joints.
2. Palpate extremities. Perform assisted and active ROM exercises. With exam, limited ROM of the joint and/or pain on palpation may be present, along with crepitus.

Diagnostic Tests

A. ESR: OA does not cause an increase of the ESR
B. Chemistry profile
C. CBC
D. RF
E. Routine radiography: Confirms disease severity and presence of joint space narrowing
F. Computed tomography (CT) scan or magnetic resonance imaging (MRI): Considered with nerve impingement syndrome (spine) or spinal stenosis

Differential Diagnoses

A. Inflammatory OA
B. RA
C. Gout or pseudogout
D. Septic arthritis
E. Bursitis or tendonitis
F. Systemic lupus erythematous
G. Fracture or trauma

Plan

A. General interventions
1. Confirm diagnosis.
2. Provide the patient support and education to improve patient well-being and reduce discomfort.
3. Physical therapy and/or occupational therapy should be initiated, if indicated.

B. Patient teaching
1. See the Section III Patient Teaching Guide for this chapter, "Osteoarthritis."
2. Reinforce the importance of joint protection; avoid repetitive stress or trauma.
3. Encourage daily exercises and strengthening exercises.
4. Encourage weight loss if the patient is obese.

C. Pharmaceutical therapy
1. First-line agents: The goal of treatment is to preserve joint mobility. First-line agents should be used in a stepwise approach.
a. Acetaminophen up to 1 g four times daily. In early disease, this may be given on an as-needed basis.
b. NSAIDs if acetaminophen has failed to control the pain. Use with caution. Consider renal function and risk factors for peptic ulcer disease (PUD) and cardiovascular disease.
i. Naproxen 220 to 375 mg one to two times daily.
ii. Inflammatory OA: Consider naproxen 375 to 500 mg twice a day. Recommend taking this medication for 2 to 4 weeks for maximum effects.
iii. Ibuprofen 200 to 400 mg three times a day may also be considered. Doses may be increased at a gradual pace for maximum benefit as tolerated. If one NSAID does not work, consider other NSAIDs.
a) Cox-2 inhibitors, such as celecoxib (Celebrex), may also be considered. Celebrex 200 mg daily to twice a day as tolerated.
b) Meloxicam (Mobic) 7.5 to 15 mg daily
c. For high-risk patients, an H_2 receptor blocker may decrease gastritis and be helpful in preventing duodenal ulcers. Consider Arthrotec 50: One tablet three times a day.
d. **Misoprostol may be considered in patients who are at high risk for gastric ulcers. It reduces the risk of the development of stomach ulcers. It should not be used by pregnant women. It is considered high risk for fetal death and possible congenital abnormalities.**
e. Topical creams
i. Diclofenac gel, applied to the affected area are recommended for patients with severe pain who are not able to tolerate oral NSAIDs.
ii. Capsaicin cream may be applied to the joint. Capsaicin creams may cause local burning at the site of application for the first several days.
2. Second-line agents: Second-line agents, such as intra-articular corticosteroid injections, may prevent some joint erosion and decrease pain. The same joint should not be injected more than three to four times a year, injecting at 3-month intervals. If the joint is injected at this frequency for more than 1 year, alternative options, such as surgery, should be considered. Narcotics may provide relief from more severe OA pain, but they carry a risk of dependence.
3. The use of glucosamine and chondroitin has not been established and is not recommended for patients. There does not appear to be any risks associated with using glucosamine and chondroitin. If the patient does not notice any relief within the first 6 months of use, then recommendations are to discontinue this product.
4. Physical therapy to create an individualized exercise regimen to strengthen muscles, increase ROM, and reduce pain

5. Lubrication injections (Hyalgan or Synvisc) may also be considered. Referral to the rheumatologist should be considered for this treatment.

Follow-Up

A. Follow-up is based on disease severity and treatment. If the patient is treated with first-line agents, follow up on pain control, nonpharmacologic interventions, and possible side effects of medications within 2 to 4 weeks.

Consultation/Referral

A. Referral to an orthopedic surgeon may be considered for moderate to severe pain as indicated.

Individual Considerations

A. Pregnancy: NSAIDs should not be used in pregnancy unless clearly indicated.
B. Adults and geriatrics: Patients on chronic NSAIDs should be monitored closely for toxicity such as renal insufficiency, gastritis, and PUD. This is especially true for the elderly and those with preexisting GI disease, diabetes, congestive heart failure, and cirrhosis.

Osteoporosis/Kyphosis/Fracture

Definition

A. Osteoporosis is a condition of reduced bone mass resulting in bone fragility and fracture. The World Health Organization (WHO) has defined it as "spinal or hip bone mineral density (BMD) of 2.5 standard deviations or more below the mean for healthy, young women (T-score of –2.5 or below) as measured by dual energy x-ray absorptiometry." BMD is performed on the lumbar spine, hip, and/or forearm.
B. Osteopenia is defined as a spinal or hip BMD between 1 and 2.5 standard deviations below the mean (T-Score between –1 and –2.5).
C. Kyphosis (dowager's hump) is the forward curvature of the thoracic spine. It is estimated that kyphosis occurs in approximately 20% to 40% of patients older than 60 years of age. Kyphosis may occur due to many different causes, including vertebral fractures, muscle weakness, degenerative disk disease, postural changes, and genetic/metabolic changes. Kyphosis is associated with other conditions such as decreased pulmonary function, back pain, increased risk of fracture of the spine, limited mobility, and an increase in mortality.
D. Osteoporotic fracture occurs from a fall that occurs while standing at normal height or less, without any type of trauma and/or while performing daily activities. A vertebral compression fracture is the most common type of osteoporotic fracture.
E. Vertebral fractures: There are three primary types of vertebral fractures:
   1. Biconcave deformity
   2. Wedge fracture and compression fracture
   3. Compression fracture is a fracture most commonly seen in the midthoracic or thoracolumbar spine. Common complaints of a compression fracture include low back pain and difficulty performing routine daily activities. However, some compression fractures may be asymptomatic. Each compression fracture may contribute to approximately one centimeter of height loss.
   4. Pain control should be addressed with oral analgesics such as acetaminophen, ibuprofen, or naproxen.
      a. Precautions should be considered for patients with compromised kidney function.
      b. Opioids and nasal calcitonin, 200 units (one spray) daily for 2 to 4 weeks, has been shown to provide effective relief for mild-to-moderate pain when analgesics are not effective.
      c. Pain control and activity changes should be addressed with the patient to promote healing of the fracture and prevention of more fractures.
      d. Treatment options for compression fractures include vertebral augmentation and kyphoplasty.
      e. Long-term management of compression fracture and osteoporosis should be addressed with the use of medications.

Incidence

A. Approximately 50% to 60% of 50-year-old women sustain osteoporosis-related fractures during their remaining life. Spinal fractures occur in 25% of White women by age 65, causing pain, deformity, and disability. Most common fractures include 25% at distal radius (Colles fracture), 50% in the vertebrae, and 25% in the hip.
B. One third of all women and 17% of men suffer a hip fracture before age 90, and 20% of those who sustain a fracture die within 3 months of the event.

Pathogenesis

A. Osteoporosis is due to bone reabsorption being greater than bone formation.

Predisposing Factors

A. Hypogonadal states, particularly menopause
B. Small body frame
C. Smoking
D. Low calcium intake
E. Lack of weight-bearing exercise
F. Family history
G. Excessive alcohol intake
H. Asian or Caucasian
I. Secondary causes
   1. Hyperparathyroidism
   2. Hyperthyroidism

3. Cushing's syndrome
4. Multiple myeloma
5. Thyroid replacement therapy
6. Corticosteroid therapy
7. Renal disease

Common Complaints

A. Loss of height
B. Kyphosis, or dowager's hump
C. Back pain as a result of a compression fracture

Other Signs and Symptoms

A. Cervical lordosis
B. Fracture with little or no trauma
C. Crush fracture of vertebra
D. Pain

Subjective Data

A. Explore history of the following:
   1. Loss of height. If the patient is unsure of his or her height, compare present height to the height written on the driver's license.
   2. Low initial bone mass
   3. Early menopause, oophorectomy, postmenopause, or amenorrhea
   4. European or Asian family origin
   5. Family history of spinal fractures and osteoporosis
   6. Sedentary lifestyle with little weight-bearing activity
   7. Endocrine disorders
   8. Medications taken, specifically corticosteroids, barbiturates, heparin, and thyroid hormone
   9. Low calcium and vitamin D intake
   10. Increased alcohol, caffeine, and protein intake
   11. Renal disease/dialysis
B. Determine onset, duration, location, and characteristic of pain.
C. Has the patient had any recent falls?

Physical Examination

A. Check pulse, BP, height, and weight.
B. Inspect
   1. Compare present height to previous height. If the patient is not aware of his or her normal height, then ask what height was most recent on his or her driver's license.
   2. Observe presence of dorsal kyphosis.
   3. Observe physical abnormalities that interfere with mobility.
C. Palpate the joints and over bone for pain.

Diagnostic Test

A. Laboratory studies
   1. Women: Comprehensive Metabolic Profile (calcium, phosphorus, albumin, total protein, creatinine, liver enzymes, alkaline phosphatase, electrolytes) and 25-hydroxyvitamin D level
   2. Men: Comprehensive Metabolic Profile (calcium, phosphorus, albumin, total protein, creatinine, liver enzymes, alkaline phosphatase, electrolytes) and 25-hydroxyvitamin D level, testosterone level.
B. CBC, ESR, and serum protein electrophoresis, to rule out multiple myeloma and leukemia.
C. A BMD or a DEXA scan measures bone density of the spine and/or hip. The result of the BMD is read in "T-scores" or "Z-scores." "T-scores" are evaluated for postmenopausal women and older men. A "T-score" is a number given to identify the amount of bone present when compared to other healthy adults. "Z-scores" are recommended for premenopausal women. A "Z-score" is a score given to identify the amount of bone present when compared to other people the same age, sex, and weight.
D. The WHO Fracture Risk Assessment Tool (FRAX), was developed to determine the absolute fracture risk of breaking a bone in the next 10 years. This tool may be used with the BMD results to determine who needs to be treated with medication for prevention of fracture when treatment is unclear. This resource should be used on women who have not previously been treated with antiresorptive therapy and when T-scores are between −1.5 and −2.5.
E. Radiography: X-ray for suspected vertebral fracture. Consider a CT to assess for instability of a wedge fracture. An MRI is recommended to assess for the extent of a compression fracture and possible malignancy.

Differential Diagnoses

A. Osteoporosis
B. OA
C. Secondary causes
   1. Thyroid disease
   2. Glucocorticoid therapy
   3. Malabsorption syndromes
   4. Renal or collagen diseases
   5. Vitamin D deficiency
   6. Metastatic cancer
   7. Multiple myeloma

Plan

A. General interventions: Lifestyle changes should be introduced to the patient.
B. Patient teaching
   1. Calcium: Educate the patient regarding calcium intake in the diet.
      a. Dietary intake of calcium is recommended for the following:
         i. Men younger than 50 years of age: 1,000 mg/d
         ii. Men 50 to 69 years: 1,000 mg/d

iii. Men older than 70 years: 1,200 mg/d
iv. Women younger than or equal to 50 years: 1,000 mg/d
v. Women older than 50 years: 1,200 mg/d
vi. Sources high in calcium include salmon or sardines with bones, low-fat yogurt and skim milk, green vegetables, and cheese.

2. Vitamin D: Educate the patient regarding vitamin D intake in the diet.
   a. Dietary intake of vitamin D is recommended for the following:
      i. Men younger than 50 years: 400 to 800 IU/d
      ii. Men 50 to 69 years: 800 to 1,000 IU/d
      iii. Men older than 70 years: 800 to 1,000 IU/d
      iv. Women younger than or equal to 50 years: 400 to 800 IU/d
      v. Women older than 50 years: 800 to 1,000 IU/d
      vi. Sources high in vitamin D include vitamin D fortified milk and vitamin D fortified cereals, fish liver oils, cod liver oil, mushrooms, herring, catfish, salmon, sardines, egg yolks, cheese, and beef liver.
3. Encourage the patient to eliminate alcohol and caffeine from the diet.
4. Encourage the patient to eliminate cigarette smoking.
5. Prescribe regular moderate exercise, such as 30 minutes of walking at least three times per week. Walking 50 to 60 minutes three times per week provides optimal benefits.
6. Tell the patient to avoid medications that may cause drowsiness and may precipitate falls.
7. Use extra light at night in the bathroom to help prevent falls.
8. Discuss fall prevention. See the Section III, Patient Teaching Guide for Chapter 3, "Safety Issues: Fall Prevention."
9. Remove all scatter rugs and clutter. Make the home safer, including installing handrails on steps.

C. Pharmaceutical therapy
   1. Calcium supplements

Calcium supplements may be contraindicated in patients who have a history of renal stones.

   a. Calcium carbonate (Os-Cal) 500 mg orally one to two times per day, or Tums 1 tablet orally two to three times a day. See above for recommendations.
2. Vitamin D supplements: See Plan for recommended dosing. Patients who are vitamin D deficient should ingest an increased dosage, according to the deficiency.
3. Bisphosphonates—First-line therapy recommended for osteoporosis.
   a. Acts by reducing bone resorption and bone loss by preventing osteoclast activity
   b. May be given daily, weekly, or monthly
      i. Alendronate sodium (Fosamax): Available in 5 mg, 10 mg, 35 mg, 40 mg, and 70 mg tablets, 70 mg liquid, 70 mg tablet + 2,800 IU vitamin D tablet
      ii. Risedronate (Actonel): Available 5 mg daily, 35 mg weekly, or 150 mg monthly; Boniva (Ibandronate) 150 mg monthly
      iii. Zoledronic (Reclast) 5 mg/100 mL (intravenous [IV]) infusion once yearly. IV infusion given once a year over 15-minute infusion. The creatinine and calcium must be checked prior to infusion.
   c. Give the patient instructions to take medication with 6 to 8 ounces of water one-half hour before breakfast or any medication for the day. Have her stand or sit upright after taking medication. Tell her not to eat food for 30 minutes after taking the medication. Precautions should be used for patients who have upper GI side effects.
   d. Studies support the efficacy of treatment with bisphosphonates for up to 5 years. After 5 years of treatment, reassess the patient. Treatment beyond 5 years of bisphosphonate therapy is highly individualized.
4. Receptor activator of nuclear factor kappaB ligand (RANKL)
   a. Acts by inhibiting osteoclast formation, decreasing bone resorption, reducing bone fracture, and increasing bone density.
      i. Denosumab (Prolia) 60 mg subcutaneous injection once every 6 months.

Patients with chronic kidney disease and/or a risk of hypocalcemia should have a serum calcium level checked 10 days after the administration.

5. Selective estrogen receptor modulator (SERM):
   a. Raloxifene (Evista) 60 mg orally daily.
   b. For postmenopausal women: Prevents osteoporosis, is cardio-protective, and appears to decrease estrogen-recepted breast cancer by 65% over 8 years. May note side effect of increased vasomotor symptoms and increased risk of venous thromboembolism.

6. Calcitonin
   a. Intranasal calcitonin (Miacalcin) 200 IU 1 puff in alternating nostrils daily
   b. Calcitonin injections (Calcimar) 100 IU by subcutaneous injection three times per week at bedtime
   c. Fortical (Calcitonin-salmon) 200 U/spray: Nasal spray; one spray in nostril daily, alternate nostrils.
7. Parathyroid hormone
   a. Recombinant human parathyroid hormone (PTH) rebuilds bone density and increases strength of bone. Approved for severe osteoporosis for postmenopausal women and men with the diagnosis of osteoporosis who have failed antiresorptive therapy and are not able to tolerate bisphosphonates. See package insert for contraindications.
   b. Forteo (Teriparatide) 20 mcg prefilled, 28 day pen/syringe; subcutaneous injection daily. Taken for a maximum of 2 years. Check calcium and renal function before prescribing.
8. HRT

Estrogen therapy and estrogen/progesterone therapy are available as a tablet or a transdermal patch and come in a wide variety of doses. HRT is approved for prevention of bone loss but not approved for the treatment of osteoporosis.

   a. Postmenopausal women with intact uterus should take conjugated estrogen (Premarin) 0.625 mg orally daily, or medroxyprogesterone (Provera) 10 mg orally daily. Premarin in doses less than 0.625 mg may not be protective against osteoporosis.
   b. Postmenopausal women without a uterus should take conjugated estrogen (Premarin) 0.625 mg orally daily.
   c. Women with progressive disease should be given HRT plus calcium supplementation up to 2,000 mg/d.
   d. Evaluate women closely based on history and risk factor for needed benefit of HRT for the prevention of bone loss. The Women's Health Initiative study indicated significant increased risk of cardiovascular events and breast cancer for women taking estrogen and progestin therapy combined (American College of Obstetricians and Gynecologists [ACOG], 2004). The benefit/risk ratio must be evaluated for each patient, and the use of hormone therapy must be used in the lowest dose possible and for the shortest length of time.

Follow-Up

A. If the patient is on calcium supplements, check urinary calcium excretion two times per year. If it is below 250 mg/d, nephrocalcinosis and the risk of renal stones is decreased.
B. Bone density test is recommended every 2 years to evaluate the effectiveness of medical plan.

Consultation/Referral

A. If fracture is suspected, consult with a physician.

Individual Considerations

A. Geriatrics
   1. Assessment and treatment for osteoporosis must be performed routinely to prevent the risk of fracture, which may increase the risk of morbidity and mortality rates in this population.
   2. Medicare will pay for a screening bone density test every 2 years.

Polymyalgia Rheumatica

Definition

A. Polymyalgia rheumatica (PMR) is an inflammatory condition, with an insidious or abrupt onset, that causes morning muscle stiffness, pain, and decreased ROM, primarily in the hips, shoulders, and neck.

Incidence

A. PMR occurs in all racial groups; however, it is rarely seen in the African American and Latino populations.
B. It is commonly seen in adults older than 50 years of age, with an increased incidence in the 70- to 80-year-old population.
C. Women are affected two to three times more often than men.
D. PMR is occasionally associated with giant cell arteritis (GCA).
E. Approximately 15% of diagnosed patients with PMR will also have GCA.
F. Approximately half of patients diagnosed with GCA will be diagnosed with PMR.

Pathogenesis

A. The cause of PMR is unknown. Environmental and genetic factors have been shown to play a role in PMR. Studies speculate that environmental triggers, such as viruses, may cause the onset of symptoms.
B. There are common similarities between PMR and GCA.

Predisposing Factors

A. Age (older than 50 years of age)
B. Sex (women are affected two to three times more often than men)
C. Ethnicity (people of Northern European origin have a higher rate of PMR)

Common Complaints

A. Early morning joint stiffness and pain, lasting for approximately 20 to 30 minutes after waking for at least 2 weeks
B. Stiffness and pain commonly occur in the shoulders, hips, and neck.
C. Decreased ROM of joints
D. Muscle pain
E. Weakness of joints and muscles

Other Signs and Symptoms

A. Fever
B. Fatigue
C. Malaise

Potential Complications

A. Difficulty performing daily activities, such as getting up out of a chair, dressing, and bathing
B. Decreased activity
C. Overall, a decrease in general health due to limitations

Subjective Data

A. Ask patient if there was an activity that brought about or preceded the episode of joint pain.
B. Has the patient had any recent illness or injury?
C. Ask patient to describe the onset, duration, and intensity of pain, noting what particular joints are involved.
D. How long do pain and stiffness last in the morning?
E. Does the patient notice a decrease in ROM? Are there activities that the patient is not able to perform?
F. Ask patient to list all medications currently being taken, particularly substances not prescribed and over-the-counter (OTC) products. What medications improve pain?
G. Has the patient noticed a problem with sleeping since the symptoms began?

Physical Examination

A. Vital signs: Check temperature, pulse, respirations, and BP
B. Inspect
  1. Hands, wrists, elbows, shoulders, hips, and neck for erythema and synovitis
C. Palpate
  1. Palpate joints for swelling and pain. Marked swelling is not usually seen in patients with PMR.
  2. Assess ROM of the shoulders, hips, back, neck. Perform passive ROM of the shoulders and hips.
  3. Assess trigger points for tenderness, assessing for symptoms of fibromyalgia.
  4. Assess muscle strength of upper and lower extremities and neck.
  5. Assess temporal arteries for signs of inflammation.
D. Auscultate
  1. Heart
  2. Lungs

Diagnostic Tests

A. CBC—normocytic anemia common
B. ESR—elevation
C. CRP, noncardiac—elevation
D. RF—negative
E. X-rays or MRI of the affected joints

Differential Diagnosis

A. PMR
B. RA
C. GCA
D. Fibromyalgia (symptoms will have been present for years)

Plan

A. General interventions
  1. Treat the patient with steroid therapy to improve symptoms, starting at an adequate dose to resolve symptoms. Treatment will include slowly tapering the steroids over a period of weeks/months to keep the patient symptom free until off of steroids.
B. Patient teaching
  1. See the Section III Patient Teaching Guide for this chapter, "Polymyalgia Rheumatica."
  2. Educate the patient and family that PMR is primarily a self-limiting condition that will improve slowly over time.
  3. Treatment will include several weeks/months of low-dose prednisone therapy, tapering slowly until completion of steroid therapy. Tapering slowly and patience will prevent recurrent attacks and rebound flares.
C. Pharmaceutical therapy
  1. Low-dose prednisone is used to treat the symptoms. Steroids should be given to relieve symptoms (starting dose may be 10 to 20 mg orally daily) and then will be tapered slowly over the next 6 months. Gradually decreasing the steroid dose by very small increments over time has the best results, minimizing the possibility of relapse.

Follow-Up

A. **A follow-up appointment is recommended 2 weeks after the initial appointment.**
B. **If symptoms are improving with the steroid therapy, a follow-up appointment is recommended every 1 to 2 months until there are not any flares of symptoms and the patient has completed the steroid therapy. This treatment may take several months and even up to greater than 1 year.**

Individual Considerations

A. Another condition to consider with the symptoms is remitting seronegative symmetrical synovitis with pitting edema. This condition presents with hand and distal extremity swelling, noting marked pitting edema in extremities. It is commonly seen in patients older than 50 years of age with an acute onset of swelling and pain. Symptoms respond quickly to the use of low-dose steroids. Laboratory testing for RA is negative.

B. Patients on long-term steroids should have a BMD performed to evaluate for osteoporosis.

Raynaud's Syndrome

Definition

A. Raynaud's syndrome (RS) is an idiopathic disease in which an exaggerated vascular response occurs in extreme measures (heat, cold, and stress) and is manifested by bilateral blanching, pallor, and discomfort in the fingers, followed by cyanosis, then erythema after warming the digits.

B. Having cold hands and feet are very common complaints. RS involves both cutaneous color change and cool skin temperature. Although the hands are the most common area of attacks, it also can occur in the toes, ears, nose, face, knees, and nipples.

C. A Raynaud attack typically begins in a single finger and spreads symmetrically; however, the thumb is often spared.

D. RS may be either primary or secondary. Spontaneous remission may occur with primary RS.

E. Criteria for diagnosis of primary RS
   1. Symmetric episodic attacks
   2. No evidence of peripheral vascular disease
   3. No tissue gangrene, digital pitting, or tissue injury
   4. Negative nailfold capillary examination
   5. Negative ANA test
   6. Normal ESR

F. Indications of secondary RS
   1. Age of onset older than 40 years
   2. Painful severe attacks with signs of ulceration/ischemia
   3. Ischemic signs/symptoms proximal to the fingers or toes
   4. Asymmetric attacks
   5. Abnormal laboratory, suggesting vascular or autoimmune disorders

Incidence

A. 3% to 20% in women
B. 3% to 14% in men
C. 3% in African Americans
D. Wide global differences from the United States

Pathogenesis

A. Primary RS: Speculated theories include digital microvascular vasospasm due to increased response of alpha 2-adrenergic receptors and a high sympathetic vascular tone.

B. Secondary RS: Symptoms occur as a secondary manifestation from other diseases such as connective tissue disorders, systemic sclerosis, atherosclerotic diseases, and neurovascular disorders such as carpal tunnel syndrome.
   1. Symptoms may be unilateral and may only affect one or two fingers.
   2. Secondary RS usually has poorer morbidity than the primary disease.

Predisposing Factors

A. Primary Raynaud
   1. Female
   2. Onset of symptoms after menarche (15–30 years)
   3. Smoking
   4. Emotional stress

B. Secondary Raynaud
   1. Onset after age 40
   2. Occurs in females also with systemic diseases (rheumatic diseases, primary biliary cirrhosis, thyroid disease)

C. Family history: Multiple family members
D. Frostbite
E. Vascular trauma (distal ulnar artery)
F. Vibration-induced/occupation exposure (jack-hammers, pneumatic drills)
G. Medication-associated RS (see Table 21.1).

Common Complaints

A. Paleness of the fingertips after exposure to cold temperatures, followed by redness and discomfort after warming fingers
B. "White attack": Sharp, demarcated color of skin pallor
C. "Blue attack": Cyanotic skin
D. White or blue attack, usually lasting 15 to 20 minutes

Other Signs and Symptoms

A. Paresthesias and numbness
B. Clumsiness of the aching hand/finger
C. Loss of pulp in pads of fingers (severe cases) which is usually associated with systemic disease

Subjective Data

A. Determine the age of onset, time, duration, and course of presenting symptoms.
B. Question the patient regarding location and symptoms, noting blanching, followed by erythema and pain after hands are warm.
C. Note frequency of attacks.
D. Review the presence of any other skin alterations that have occurred. Do they also note skin mottling of

TABLE 21.1 Drugs That Induce Raynaud's Syndrome

Amphetamines	Clonidine	Interferon-alpha
Beta blockers	Cocaine	Nicotine
Bleomycin	Cyclosporine	Vinblastine
Cisplatin	Ergot	Vinyl chloride

the arms and legs? Livedo reticularis is a lilac or violet mottling or reticular pattern during a cold response.

E. Ask the patient to identify any events that precipitate occurrences and what makes symptoms worse or better.
   1. Air conditioning
   2. Grocery cold/freezer food sections
   3. Cold weather
   4. Cold water
   5. Emotional stress
   6. Sudden startling
F. Identify any other symptoms that occur at the same time, such as migraine headaches.
G. Review the patient's health history for underlying disorders such as hypothyroidism and connective tissue disease.
H. Review current or past occupation (especially those that include the use of vibratory tools).
I. Review current medications, stimulants, herbals, and over-the-counter (OTC) medications. See Table 21.1.

Physical Examination

A. Check pulse, respirations, and BP.
B. Inspect
   1. Dermal examination: Note malar/petechial rash, telangiectasias, digital pallor, or erythema. Examine for any ulceration or signs of ischemia.
   2. Inspect joints for swelling or redness and overall ischemic changes.
   3. Examine several fingernails using a microscope or ophthalmoscope; examine capillaries at nailfold.
      a. Normal: Fine red capillaries, lined in the same direction
      b. Abnormal: Capillaries dilated, tortuous, irregularly spaced. Avoid using the index finger for evaluation.
C. Auscultate the heart and lung fields.
D. Palpate joints for tenderness and peripheral pulses bilaterally.
E. Neurologic examination: Sensory function
   1. Sensory discrimination (hot/cold, sharp/dull)
   2. Location of sensation (proximal/distal to previous stimuli)
   3. Vibratory sensation with tuning fork (distal to proximal joints)
   4. Graphesthesia (draw a number or letter in palm of the hand with a blunt object such as a pencil, applicator stick, or pen and have the patient identify the letter/number).

Diagnostic Tests

A. There is no gold standard diagnostic test.
B. History alone is accepted as diagnostic since no office test application consistently triggers an attack. A history of at least two color changes, pallor, and cyanosis after cold exposure is adequate for the diagnosis of RP.
C. The cold water challenge test is no longer recommended.
D. Tools to assess vascular response (usually not readily available)
   1. Nailfold capillaroscopy
   2. Video microscopy
   3. Thermography
   4. Angiography
   5. Laser Doppler
   6. Direct measures of the skin temperature and local blood flow
E. Laboratory tests
   1. Antinuclear antibody (ANA)
   2. Erythrocyte sedimentation rate (ESR)
   3. Thyroid profile if hypothyroidism is suspected
   4. Other tests, depending on suspected etiology
      a. CBC
      b. Chemistry profile with renal and liver function
      c. Urinalysis
      d. RF
      e. Complement (C3 and C4)
      f. ANA

Differential Diagnoses

A. RP (primary vs. secondary)
B. Scleroderma
C. Systemic lupus erythematosus (SLE)
D. Occupational trauma
E. Medication induced
F. Peripheral vascular disease
G. Neurovascular processes (diabetes, atherosclerosis, thrombosis obliterans)

Plan

A. General interventions
   1. If ulcerations are present, monitor for secondary infections. Consider topical/systemic antibiotics if secondary infection. Debridement may be necessary.
   2. Biofeedback and relaxation techniques are frequently used for treatment.
B. Patient teaching
   1. Stress the importance of not smoking.
   2. Keep the body warm.
      a. If in extreme temperatures, wear extra clothing (thermal underwear) to maintain core body temperature.
      b. Wear mittens instead of gloves to protect hands and keep them warm.
      c. Wear a hat to conserve heat.
   3. If possible, stop all medications that could be inducing symptoms. Other drugs that should be avoided include:
      a. Decongestants
      b. Herbs that contain ephedra

4. If vibrator injury is present, stop the repetitive activity that induces symptoms. Consider alternative methods of work. If unable to totally stop the activity, decrease time spent using the vibratory equipment.

C. Surgical therapy
   1. Temporary sympathectomy involving a local chemical block with lidocaine or bupivacaine (without epinephrine) relieves the pain.
   2. Botulinum toxin A has been used for chemical sympathectomy.
   3. Cervical sympathectomy (primary RS)
   4. Localized digital sympathectomy
   5. Vascular reconstruction

D. Pharmaceutical therapy
   1. Therapy may be required only during the winter months.
   2. Long-acting calcium channel blockers are used.
      a. Nifedipine 30 to 180 mg/d
      b. Amlodipine 5 to 20 mg/d
   3. Low-dose aspirin antiplatelet therapy 75 to 81 mg/d may be considered in secondary RP with a history of ischemic ulcers or other thrombotic events.
   4. Vasodilators (sildenafil) and endothelin receptor antagonists (bosentan) may be useful in refractory cases with associated digital ulcers/infarcts. However, these medications are not FDA approved for this treatment.

Follow-Up

A. Follow up in 1 month or as needed by patient symptoms.

Consultation/Referral

A. Consult a physician if signs of ischemia and/or if refractory symptoms are present.
B. Refer to a rheumatologist if there is a moderate/high suspicion of secondary RP.
C. Refer for surgical therapies.

Individual Considerations

A. Adults: The onset of Raynaud after age 40 is commonly associated with an underlying disease.

Rheumatoid Arthritis

Definition

A. RA is a chronic systemic disease that involves articular inflammation of the joints. The disease is generally insidious, and symmetrical involvement of joints is a characteristic feature. Typically, inflammation occurs in the PIP and metacarpophalangeal (MCP) joints of the fingers and thumbs; however, other joints that may also be involved include the elbows, shoulders, ankles, knees, and toes.
B. RA is not limited to the joints; extra-articular features of RA include anemia, pleuropericarditis, neuropathy, myopathy, splenomegaly, Sjögren's syndrome, scleritis, vasculitis, and renal disease. Most patients with extra-articular symptoms also have the classic RA joint symptoms. Patients with RA are at increased risk for development of carpal tunnel syndrome, stroke, an osteoporotic fracture, and renal disease (secondary to drug toxicity).
C. The ACR criteria for RA requires that an algorithm be used to assess for criteria to meet the diagnosis for RA. A score of greater than or equal to 6/10 is recommended for the patient to be diagnosed with RA based on the working algorithm. Patients who should be screened for RA include those who have had at least one swollen joint, with the joint swelling not being caused by any other known etiology.
D. Classification criteria for screening for RA:
   1. Joint involvement
   2. Serology: RF and ACPA
   3. Acute-phase reactants: CRP and ESR
   4. Duration of symptoms
E. Scoring for this algorithm may be found at www.rheumatology.org/ACR/practice/clinical/classification/ra/ra_2010.asp
F. There are four stages of RA.
   1. Stage 1: No symptoms or signs, normal activity. RF and/or cyclic citrullinated peptide (CCP) antibody is present.
   2. Stage 2: Morning stiffness, warmth at joint, normal activities of daily living (ADL), minimal limitation in joint use. Increased T cells, B cells, antibody production, and synovial cells.
   3. Stage 3: Morning stiffness, warmth at joint, and extra-articular manifestations. Marked limitation in ADL. Increased T cells, B cells, antibody production, and synovial cells.
   4. Stage 4: Same as stage 3 plus proliferating synovial membrane involved, causing injury to the bone, tendons, and cartilage. Patient is now incapacitated or confined to wheelchair.

Incidence

A. RA occurs in approximately 1% to 2% of the population.

Pathogenesis

A. The cause is unknown. Articular inflammation results in joint damage. Antibody formation in the joint area results in inflammation in the joint area.

Predisposing Factors

A. Family history, including 15% prevalence in monozygotic twins
B. Female gender (3:1 women to men ratio)
C. Ages 20 to 50 years
D. Recent systemic illness or trauma

Common Complaints

A. Joint pain
B. Morning stiffness in joints for at least 1 hour that has been present for more than 6 weeks.
C. Swelling in at least three joints or more for at least 6 weeks. Common joints affected include the wrists, MCP joints, PIP joints.

Other Signs and Symptoms

A. Fatigue
B. Malaise
C. Subcutaneous nodules
D. Joint deformities
   1. PIP joints: Boutonniere deformities
   2. Fingers: Swan neck contractures, ulnar deviation
   3. Wrists: Loss of extension
   4. Hips: Loss of internal rotation, followed by flexion contractures
   5. Knees: Suprapatellar pouch distension
   6. Elbows: Decreased extension, olecranon bursitis
   7. Shoulders: Limited movement
   8. Cervical spine: Subluxation rare
   9. Temporomandibular joint: Pain when biting
E. Depression
F. Low-grade fever
G. Weight loss
H. Myalgia
I. Anemia
J. Carpal tunnel syndrome

Subjective Data

A. Review when joint pains began and identify the joints involved.
B. Elicit the patient's description of pain and a description of how the pain interferes with ADL (walking, climbing stairs, using the toilet, getting up from a chair, opening a jar).
C. Review the family history of RA.
D. Has the patient ever had any type of injury to the specific joint area? Rule out recent injuries.
E. Identify what makes the pain worse and name alleviating factors. In patients with RA, activity typically alleviates symptoms, which is indicative of inflammation.
F. Review list of medications, including herbal and OTC. What therapies have specifically been used, and what were the results?
G. Review the patient's history for recent infections.
H. Does the patient use any assistive devices, including cane, crutches, walker, wheelchair/power mobility device, kitchen devices/grips, and so forth?

Physical Examination

A. Check temperature, if indicated, pulse, respirations, BP, and weight.
B. General observation
   1. Observe the patient getting up and down in the chair.
   2. Observe the patient walking (may have a tendency to bear weight on heels and hyperextend toes secondary to tenderness to the metatarsophalangeal joints).
   3. Observe the patient handling objects in his or her hands.
   4. Observe for signs of depression.
C. Inspect
   1. Inspect all joints, noting deformities, erythema, and temperature. (Heat and redness are not prominent features of RA.)
   2. Evaluate for pitting edema in the hand (may have a "boxing glove" appearance).
   3. Inspect for subcutaneous rheumatoid nodules (elbow is most common site).
   4. Evaluate skin for ulcerative lesions (secondary from venous stasis and neutrophilic infiltration), skin atrophy and ecchymosed from glucocorticoids, and petechiae (side effect from medications causing thrombocytopenia).
   5. Eye examination
      a. Episcleritis: Acute redness and pain without discharge
      b. Scleritis: Deep ocular pain with dark red discoloration
D. Auscultate
   1. Auscultate the heart.
   2. Auscultate the lungs (at risk for infectious complications from immunosuppression)
E. Percuss
   1. Patellar tap to evaluate synovial thickening/effusion of the knee
F. Palpate
   1. Palpate the lymph nodes.
   2. Oral exam to palpate the salivary glands (may have lymphocytic infiltration).
   3. Palpate all joints to evaluate for tenderness with pressure, pain with movement of the joint, and "bogginess" of the joint (synovial thickening).
   4. Palpate the popliteal fossa for evidence of a popliteal (Baker's) cyst.
   5. Examine abdomen for splenomegaly.
G. Musculoskeletal examination
   1. Assess grip (a reduced grip is a useful parameter in evaluating disease activity and progression).
   2. Assess the strength of the extremities.
   3. Assess ROM (active and passive) and flexion.

Diagnostic Tests

A. CBC and platelets
B. ESR
C. RF

D. CCP antibody
E. CRP
F. Uric acid level
G. Synovial fluid aspiration (optional)
H. Plain film radiography of hands, wrists and feet, and other affected joints as a baseline and to monitor disease progression

Differential Diagnoses

A. RA
B. OA
C. Psoriatic arthritis
D. Palindromic rheumatism
E. Crystalline arthritis (gout and pseudogout)
F. Polyarthritis
G. Reactive arthritis
H. Acute viral/infectious process
 1. Lyme disease
 2. Hepatitis B
 3. Hepatitis C
 4. Parvovirus B19 (acute infection)
I. Sjögren's syndrome: Keratoconjunctivitis sicca, splenomegaly, and lymphadenopathy
J. Sarcoidosis
K. Polymyositis

Plan

A. General interventions
 1. Focus on exercise and joint mobility to maintain functional abilities.
 2. Encourage smoking cessation, especially females on glucocorticoids due to the risk of increased bone loss/fracture.
B. Patient teaching
 1. Counsel patients that alcohol should be avoided when using MTX due to the risk of hepatotoxicity.
 2. Stress the importance of returning for laboratory follow-up while on disease-modifying antirheumatic drugs (DMARDs).
 3. Discuss vaccinations, especially pneumonia and influenza vaccines.
C. Pharmaceutical therapy
 1. Early disease
  a. Daily NSAIDs and pain-relieving medications.
   i. Ibuprofen 600 to 800 mg every 6 to 8 hours as needed
   ii. Naproxen 500 mg orally every 12 hours as needed
   iii. Celecoxib (Celebrex) 200 mg by mouth daily
   iv. Acetaminophen (Tylenol) 500 to 1,000 mg orally every 4 to 6 hours as needed
  b. Comorbid conditions, such as a history of heart failure, renal disease, and peptic ulcers should be considered before starting NSAID therapy.
  c. Be aware of other medications and consider possible drug-to-drug interactions with NSAIDs and other medications such as antacids, anticoagulants, oral hypoglycemic agents, antihypertensive/diuretics, lithium, MTX, and diphenylhydantoin (Dilantin).
 2. Moderate to severe RA disease
  a. Oral glucocorticoids, prednisone up to 5 to 10 mg/d may be added for active joint inflammation. Prednisone may be used up to 6 months and should be tapered over a period of a few months and then completely discontinued if possible.
  b. Intra-articular long-acting glucocorticoid injections are used for the reduction of synovitis in inflamed joints.
  c. DMARDs are recommended by the ACR if early RA manifestations have been present for less than 6 months. Adding DMARDs depends on the number of inflamed joints, severity of inflammation, functional impairment, and the number of poor prognostic signs (bony erosions and extra-articular disease). Nonbiologic DMARDs include:
   i. MTX is given on a weekly basis starting with 7.5 mg/wk and is increased as tolerated to control symptoms. Titration: Increase the dose after 4 weeks at a rate of 2.5 mg/wk to a maximum of 25 mg/wk. MTX should not be given to patients who desire to become or who are pregnant or patients with liver disease.
   ii. Sulfasalazine (Azulfidine) 500 to 1,000 mg a day initially
   iii. Hydroxychloroquine (Plaquenil; 6.5 mg/kg dosing) 200 to 400 mg daily to bid dosing. May reduce risk for DM in RA patients
   iv. Leflunomide (Arava) 10 to 20 mg/d.
  d. Biologic DMARDS: If response is not adequate, biologic agents, tumor necrosis factor (TNF), and alpha inhibitors may be instituted. Due to the associated side effects, rheumatology consult is recommended for treatment. Examples of TNFs:
   i. Infliximab (Remicade) 3 to 10 mg/kg every 4 weeks; IV infusion
   ii. Adalimumab (Humira) 0.8 mL (40 mg) subcutaneous injection into abdomen or thigh every 2 weeks
   iii. Etanercept (Enbrel) 50 mg subcutaneous injection weekly.
   iv. Simponi 50 mg subcutaneous injection monthly
   v. Cimzia 200 mg subcutaneous injection every other week.

vi. Other biologics available for treatment for moderate to severe RA: Abatacept (Orencia), rituximab (Rituxan), actemra, and xeljanz.

e. In patients who may be resistant to DMARD therapy, combination therapy may also be initiated. Examples of this include using MTX plus a TNF inhibitor or sulfasalazine, and so forth.

f. Patients receiving treatment with pharmacological agents should be evaluated at routine intervals (every 3 months) regarding their functional status to identify if treatment therapies are improving the symptoms. There are several functional forms that are available for use. The Stanford Health Assessment Questionnaire (HAQ) is a well-known questionnaire that is recommended for use.

g. Drug monitoring, by performing serum blood work, is also recommended at routine intervals when prescribing pharmacological agents to avoid adverse effects of the medications being prescribed.

3. Osteopenia/osteoporosis: Initiate bisphosphonate therapy as indicated for signs of bone loss unless the patient is premenopausal. Use a low threshold for starting medications with postmenopausal women with RA.

Follow-Up

A. Follow-up will be guided by medication therapy. Disease activity and response to therapy should be reassessed every 4 to 6 weeks.
B. Follow laboratory values with certain medications, including MTX, with liver function testing, kidney assessment (albumin), CBC, platelets, and urinalysis monthly.
C. Assume all patients with RA are at risk for osteoporosis. Perform DEXA scan to evaluate bone loss secondary to glucocorticoid-induced osteopenia.
D. Anti-TNF agents are contraindicated in patients with an active infection and in those who are at high risk for reactivation of tuberculosis. A TB skin test is required before administration. Patients with a positive skin test should be treated with prophylactic antituberculosis therapy 1 month prior to therapy with anti-TNF agents.
E. Patients should receive a baseline ophthalmologic exam before starting antimalarial drugs, and then follow-up eye exams every 6 to 12 months while on therapy.

Consultation/Referral

A. Refer all patients to a rheumatologist with early inflammatory arthritis if RA is a suspected disease. Early intervention may prevent bone joint destruction and improve long-term outcomes for the patient.
B. Patients with a history of chronic swelling and pain of the joints should be referred to a rheumatologist.
C. Refer all patients to the rheumatologist, orthopedist, or emergency room if a septic joint is suspected.

Individual Considerations

A. Pregnancy
   1. RA activity improves substantially in pregnancy.
      a. 70% to 80% improved during pregnancy.
      b. Approximately 90% of women will have a flare during the postpartum period. Flares usually occur within the first 3 months postpartum.
   2. Leflunomide, etanercept, adalimumab, and infliximab are contraindicated in pregnancy and while breastfeeding.
   3. Pregnancy should be avoided with the use of MTX and Arava. Women need to have one normal menstrual cycle following discontinuation of MTX before attempting pregnancy. Men should wait at least 3 months after discontinuing MTX before attempting to conceive.
   4. Therapy during pregnancy should be coordinated with the perinatologist and rheumatologist.
B. Geriatrics
   1. Use NSAIDs with caution. Consider age, weight, and chronic conditions when prescribing NSAIDs. NSAIDs are not recommended in patients with renal conditions.

Systemic Lupus Erythematosus

Definition

A. SLE is a chronic, inflammatory autoimmune disorder. It may affect multiple organ systems. The body's immune system forms antibodies that attack healthy tissues and organs. The clinical course is marked by spontaneous remission and relapses. Severity varies from a mild episodic disorder to a rapidly fulminating fatal disease. The three types of lupus are as follows.
   1. Discoid lupus erythematosus (DLE) affects the skin, causing a rash, lesions, or both.
   2. SLE attacks body organs and systems, such as joints, kidneys, brain, heart, and lungs. SLE is usually more severe than DLE and can be life-threatening.
   3. Drug-induced lupus symptoms usually disappear when medication is discontinued.

Incidence

A. The incidence of SLE in relation to gender, ancestry, and familial history has been repeatedly documented. About 85% of patients with SLE are women; it affects mainly young women after menarche and before menopause. The majority of patients who develop SLE during childhood or after age 50 are also women. SLE occurs in 1:1,000 Caucasian women and in 1:250 African American women. The disorder is concordant in 25% to 75% of identical twins. The risk of developing the disease if a mother has SLE is 1:40 for a daughter and 1:250 for a son. A positive ANA is seen in up to 25% of asymptomatic family members, and the prevalence of other rheumatic diseases is increased among close relatives of patients. There is a high frequency of specific genes in SLE. Only 10% to 15% of DLE patients will have or will develop SLE.

Pathogenesis

A. The exact cause of SLE is still unknown, but clinical manifestations of SLE are secondary to the trapping of antigen–antibody complexes in capillaries of visceral structures, or to autoantibody-mediated destruction of host cells such as thrombocytopenia. SLE is commonly precipitated by recent exposure to illness, infections, ultraviolet light, surgery, pregnancy, and stress.

Predisposing Factors

A. Female gender
B. African, Asian, Hispanic ancestry
C. Childbearing age
D. Positive family history of SLE
E. Drug use
   1. Procainamide
   2. Hydralazine
   3. Isoniazid

Common Complaints

A. Joint pain: Joint symptoms occur in 90% of patients.
B. Fever
C. Loss of appetite, weight loss
D. Fatigue
E. Oral or nasal ulcers
F. Hair loss
G. Photosensitive skin rash and skin lesions over areas exposed to sunlight
H. RP

Other Signs and Symptoms

A. DLE
   1. Rash: Erythematous, round, scaling papules 5 to 10 mm in diameter, appearing as "butterfly" shape across bridge of nose, typically sparing the nasolabial folds
   2. Rash, commonly on the trunk, extremities, scalp, external ear, and neck
B. SLE: The ACR 1997 Criteria for diagnosis must include four or more of the first eleven of the following criteria:
   1. Malar rash
   2. Discoid rash
   3. Photosensitivity
   4. Oral ulcers
   5. Arthritis (generally bilateral, symmetric, especially in hands and wrists)
   6. Serositis
   7. Renal disorder: Chronic renal problems as indicated by proteinuria (>0.5 g/d of protein or >3+ protein) or cellular casts
   8. Neurologic disorder (seizures or personality changes, psychosis)
   9. Hematologic disorder
   10. Immunologic disorder
   11. Positive ANA (abnormal titer of ANA)
   12. Other signs and symptoms
      a. Weight loss
      b. Fatigue
      c. Acute abdominal pain
      d. Alopecia
      e. Tendon involvement
      f. Urinalysis: Active urine sediment [blood or protein without urinary tract infections (UTI)]
      g. Fever and malaise
      h. Lymphadenopathy
      i. Edema of lower extremities seen with renal involvement
   13. Other complications

   (Probable SLE: Have two or three of the first eleven ACR guidelines criteria, along with one other feature.)

   (Possible SLE: Have one of the first eleven ACR guidelines, along with one other feature.)
      a. Hashimoto's thyroiditis
      b. Hemolytic anemia
      c. Thrombocytopenia purpura
      d. Arterial and venous thrombosis in the presence of antiphospholipid antibodies
      e. Recurrent pleurisy
      f. Pleural effusion, pneumonitis
      g. Pulmonary embolism
      h. Pericarditis, endocarditis, myocarditis
      i. Hypertension
      j. Splenomegaly
      k. Recurrent miscarriages in the presence of antiphospholipid antibodies.
      l. RP
C. Central nervous system (CNS) problems
   1. Chronic headaches (migraine)
   2. Seizures or epilepsy
   3. Personality changes, chronic brain syndrome
D. Decreased Hgb, WBC, and platelets

Subjective Data

A. Determine systemic features and onset, course, and duration of symptoms (inquire regarding other signs and symptoms).

B. Obtain medication history (see Predisposing Factors).
C. Determine family history of rheumatoid diseases.
D. Review the patient's recent history for possible allergen exposure.

Physical Examination

A. Check temperature, pulse, respirations, and BP.
B. Inspect
  1. Observe general overall appearance and generalized movement of extremities.
  2. Conduct dermal exam for color, petechiae, rashes and lesions, and hair loss.
  3. Conduct funduscopic exam; note photosensitivity.

Funduscopic exam: Cotton–wool exudates are the most common eye lesion.

  4. Examine mouth and nose for oral ulcers.
  5. Observe for pericardial lifts and heaves.
  6. Inspect joints for subluxation of the metacarpal phalangeal joints and swan neck deformities of the hands
C. Palpate
  1. Palpate the back for tactile fremitus; palpate the heart for lifts, heaves, and thrills.
  2. Palpate the neck for thyroid enlargement.
  3. Palpate the neck, axilla, and groin for lymphadenopathy.
  4. Palpate the abdomen for organomegaly, masses, and tenderness; check suprapubic tenderness and cerebral vascular accident (CVA) tenderness.
D. Percuss
  1. Percuss the chest, anterior and posterior lung fields for consolidation.
  2. Percuss the abdomen for splenomegaly.
E. Auscultate
  1. Auscultate the heart.
  2. Auscultate the abdomen.
  3. Auscultate the lungs.
F. Musculoskeletal exam
  1. Examine for bone or joint swelling, tenderness, and increased warmth.
  2. Check lower extremities for evidence of phlebitis, asymmetrical swelling, calf tenderness, and palpable cord.
G. Neurologic exam: Complete neurologic exam with mental status exam.

Diagnostic Examination

A. CBC with differential
B. Platelets
C. ANA: Indirect immunofluorescence assay (IFA) positive. This finding is clinically significant. In patients with SLE, the ANA will typically be positive with a high titer ANA. A negative ANA by the IFA method dramatically decreases the risk of SLE.
D. Complement levels (decreased C3 and C4)
E. RF can also be positive in patients with SLE.
F. Anti-DNA antibodies, seen in approximately 30% with renal disease
G. Thyroid profile
H. Antiphospholipid antibodies: Lupus anticoagulant, IgA, IgG, and IgM anticardiolipin antibodies, IgA, IgG, and IgM anti-beta2-glycoprotein
I. ESR
J. Urinalysis for hematuria, proteinuria and cellular casts, and urine culture for infection
K. Collection of 24-hour urine for protein and creatinine clearance
L. Skin biopsy
M. Follow-up Coombs' test: Positive
N. MHA-TP to confirm reactive syphilis for positive RPR: False positive serologic test for syphilis needs follow-up.
O. Chest x-ray film may show changes.
P. X-ray of joints for nondestructive arthritis

Differential Diagnoses

A. SLE
B. DLE
C. Undifferentiated connective tissue disease
D. Drug-induced lupus
E. RA: Lupus can resemble RA, especially early in the course of SLE. Unlike RA, the arthritis is nonerosive: There is no joint destruction.
F. Vasculitis
G. Scleroderma
H. Chronic active hepatitis
I. Acute drug reactions
J. Polyarteritis
K. Infection
L. Influenza
M. Rosacea
N. Neoplasm

Plan

A. General interventions: After diagnosis, refer the patient to a rheumatologist and comanage with a physician.
B. Patient teaching: See the Section III Patient Teaching Guide for this chapter, "Systemic Lupus Erythematosus (SLE)."
C. Pharmaceutical therapy
  1. NSAIDs for arthritis symptoms
  2. Prednisone 40 to 60 mg initially for the control of thrombocytopenic purpura, hemolytic anemia, myocarditis, pericarditis, convulsions, and nephritis
  3. Always give the lowest dose that controls the condition.

4. Corticosteroids can usually be tapered to low doses, 10 to 15 mg/d, during disease inactivity.
5. The antimalarial drug, hydroxychloroquine sulfate, daily may help treat lupus rashes and joint symptoms that do not respond to NSAIDs. Do not exceed 400 mg/d. *Consult with a rheumatology specialist.*
6. Alternative drug therapy: Immunosuppressive agents such as cyclophosphamide, chlorambucil, and azathioprine are used in cases resistant to corticosteroids. The exact role of immunosuppressive agents is controversial.

Follow-Up

A. Very close follow-up by a physician specialist is needed when immunosuppressants are employed.
B. If fever is present on exam, explore for cause of fever to rule out infection. Monitor closely for infections, especially with opportunistic organisms.
C. Preventive heart care is important due to the presence of premature atherosclerosis seen in these patients.
D. Up-to-date immunizations
E. Osteoporosis screening

> *Infections are the leading cause of death secondary to the depression of WBCs, followed by active SLE, chiefly due to renal or CNS disease.*

Consultation/Referral

A. After diagnosis, refer the patient to a medical specialist, a rheumatologist.
B. Refer the patient to a perinatologist for pregnancy management.
C. Referral to a specialist for a biopsy of the skin or kidney may be necessary to confirm the diagnosis.

Individual Considerations

A. Pregnancy
   1. Infertility: 25% of patients have a problem getting pregnant.
   2. Patients with SLE experience frequent miscarriages and stillbirths.
   3. Patients are considered high risk, and consultation and management with a perinatologist are needed.
   4. Approximately 33% of patients have an antibody (anticardiolipin) associated with early failure of the placenta. Approximately 10% have a related antibody (lupus anticoagulant) that allows early pregnancy but compromises fetal growth as the placenta fails. The remaining 25% of pregnancies deliver prematurely.
   5. Family planning
      a. Barrier methods or intrauterine devices (IUDs) are best and safest.
      b. Birth control pills may exacerbate lupus. Avoid use of estrogen birth control pills with active SLE. Consider alternate methods of birth control.
   6. Exacerbations of lupus are sometimes caused by pregnancy.

B. Geriatrics: Males are affected more than females.

Temporal Arteritis/Giant Cell Arteritis

Definition

A. Temporal arteritis, also known as GCA, is a vascular illness that can affect the entire body; however, it primarily affects the blood vessels. There is inflammation of the arteries that begins in the aortic arch and branches out to the cranial arteries.

Incidence

A. GCA occurs in approximately 1 in 500 individuals over the age of 50 years. GCA rarely occurs in individuals younger than 50 and is more commonly seen during later years (older than 70 years). It can also be seen in patients diagnosed with PMR. Approximately 50% of patients diagnosed with GCA will also have PMR.

Pathogenesis

A. The cause of GCA is unknown. The immune system attacks the body and causes inflammation of the medium and large arteries, which causes thickening of the arterial walls and narrowing of the lumen. When these changes occur, the result is a decrease in blood flow and it can potentially cause an occlusion in the artery, leading to ischemia. Arteries commonly involved include the temporal artery, medium and large vessels, and the vessels of the eyes. Blindness is the major feared acute morbidity with GCA.

Predisposing Factors

A. Age (older than 50 years old)
B. Ethnicity (Scandinavian) Northern European descent
C. Sex (women more than men)

Common Complaints

A. Abrupt onset of headaches
B. Visual impairment
C. Joint pain (PMR)

Other Signs and Symptoms

A. Fever
B. Anemia
C. Jaw or arm claudication
D. Fatigue
E. Weight loss

Potential Complications

A. Visual loss, blindness
B. Joint pain

Subjective Data

A. Ask the patient when presenting symptoms began. Discuss the course of new-onset symptoms. Note systemic symptoms such as fever, weight loss, fatigue, headache, vision changes, jaw/arm pain.
B. Have patient describe the presenting complaints. What makes it better or worse?
C. Ask patient to describe pain as crushing, stabbing, or burning.
D. Have patient rate pain on a scale of 0 to 10, with 0 being no pain.
E. What has the patient taken to relieve the pain or symptoms?
F. Note any visual disturbance or changes. Is vision change constant, or does it occur when headache is present? What makes the headache worse? What makes the headache better?

Physical Examination

A. Vital signs: Check temperature, pulse, respirations, and BP (Take BP in both arms and note discrepancies.)
B. Inspect
   1. Inspect overall general appearance. Patients with GCA usually appear chronically ill.
   2. Perform fundoscopic exam, looking for a pale disk and blurred margins of the disk. Assess PERRLA, extraocular movements (EOMs), and visual acuity.
C. Palpate
   1. Palpate pulses (carotid, brachial, radial, pedal, and femoral pulses).
   2. Perform ROM of all joints (shoulders, neck, hips, extremities), noting limitations due to pain and/or swelling.
   3. Assess joints for swelling and pain. (Note symptoms of PMR.)
D. Auscultate
   1. Heart for murmurs
   2. Carotid, brachial, femoral arteries for bruits
   3. Abdomen, noting any bruits

Diagnostic Tests

A. Serum laboratory studies (ESR, CBC, CRP, Comprehensive Metabolic Profile)
B. Temporal artery biopsy (Any patient suspected of having temporal arteritis should have a temporal artery biopsy performed. This is the gold standard for diagnosing GCA. The recommended sample size of the artery for biopsy should be greater than or equal to 4 cm. False negative biopsy results may be up to 20%.

Differential Diagnosis

A. Temporal arteritis/GCA
B. Vasculitis

Plan

A. General interventions
   1. Educate the patient and family regarding the disease process of GCA.
B. Patient teaching
   1. Educate the patient and family that common symptoms of GCA include headaches, vision change, and jaw/arm joint pain.
   2. Teach the patient that GCA causes inflammation of the blood vessels in the head and neck, but not the blood vessels in the brain.
   3. Advise the patient that PMR may also occur in some patients, in which joint pain may be present.
   4. Medications commonly used for GCA are steroids. Steroids will improve the inflammation, which in return will improve pain. The steroids are commonly used for the duration of treatment and will be tapered down over several months. Steroids are the only medication that has proven to prevent blindness. Any side effects or problems should be reported to the primary provider.
   5. A baby aspirin is commonly used daily.
   6. Any vision changes should be immediately reported to the primary provider. Vision loss/blindness is one of the greatest risks of GCA.
C. Pharmaceutical therapy
   1. If GCA is suspected, consult with the collaborating physician and begin steroids immediately. Prednisone dosage is 40 to 60 mg daily. Do not wait for biopsyresults. Steroids suppress the manifestations of symptoms and decrease the risk of blindness. Steroids will eventually be tapered when symptoms begin to improve, commonly after 1 month or so.
   2. Aspirin 81 to 325 mg/d is recommended.

Follow-Up

A. Follow up with physician/surgeon/rheumatologist as recommended.

Consultation/Referral

A. Consultation with the collaborating physician or surgeon should be obtained regarding any patient suspected of having temporal arteritis.
B. Refer all patients to a rheumatologist within one week of diagnosis to manage the patient with GCA.
C. All patients suspicious of having temporal arteritis should be referred to a general surgeon for a temporal artery biopsy within 2 to 3 days after beginning steroids.
D. Refer the patient to the ophthalmologist for evaluation and treatment.

Individual Considerations

A. Geriatrics
  1. Most commonly seen in older patients. Symptoms may occur after the age of 50 years; however, GCA is most commonly seen in patients older than 70 years.

Vitamin D Deficiency

Definition

A. Vitamin D deficiency is defined as having a serum 25-hydroxyvitamin D (25(OH)D or calcidiol) level lower than 15 ng/mL. Vitamin D insufficiency is defined as having a serum 25(OH)D level lower than 30 ng/mL. Recommended normal levels of 25-hydroxyvitamin D are 30 to 40 ng/mL.
B. Vitamin D deficiency is also known as hypovitaminosis D.

Incidence

A. Vitamin D deficiency is seen in all ages. It is most commonly seen in the elderly, institutionalized populations, and/or patients who have recently been hospitalized. It is found to be more common in women than in men (83% vs. 48%), the difference most likely being less skin exposure to the sun. There also is a higher incidence of deficiency in the winter months, again due to less sun exposure in the winter months.

Pathogenesis

A. The best source of vitamin D is obtained from direct sunlight exposure to the skin. It is also absorbed by ingesting foods that are rich in vitamin D. The liver is responsible for breaking it down. It hydroxylates the vitamin D to storage form, 25-hydroxyvitamin D (25[OH]D), which then breaks down during the next step in the kidney into the bioactive form, 1,25-dihydroxyvitamin D (1,25[OH]2D). The 1,25(OH)2D is regulated by the PTH and causes calcium absorption to occur in the intestine, which in return affects bone metabolism and muscle function. When any part of this cascade is interrupted, the cascade is broken and vitamin D deficiency occurs.

Predisposing Factors

A. Race (darker skin population)
B. Age: Elderly population is at highest risk
C. Long-term institutionalized individuals (nursing home)
D. Obese individuals
E. Decreased sun exposure (individuals who spend very little time outdoors in the sun)
F. People with serious renal or digestive disorders (chronic kidney disease and malabsorption problems)
G. Medications: Drugs such as dilantin, phenobarbital, and rifampin induce hepatic p450 enzymes and accelerate catabolism of vitamin D.

Common Complaints

A. Complaints vary from none to severe.
B. Chronic muscle aches/pain/fatigue/weakness
C. Joint pain and bone pain

Other Signs and Symptoms

A. Fracture of bone
B. Frequent falls and muscle weakness
C. The most severe form of vitamin D deficiency can cause nutritional rickets.

Subjective Data

A. With patients presenting with complaints, assess onset, duration, and course of complaints.
B. Assess daily nutritional habits. Does the patient get enough calcium and vitamin D in current diet?
C. Does the patient live in the home or an institution? Is the patient allowed to spend time outdoors in sunlight? What time of the season/year is it? Is 20 to 30 minutes in the sun without sunscreen reasonable?
D. Is the patient currently taking any vitamin supplements? If so, review vitamins and ingredients in that particular vitamin.
E. Review the patient history and determine if the patient has a chronic condition, malabsorption condition, chronic kidney condition, or takes medications interfering with absorption. If there is no current diagnosis of a GI problem, inquire regarding food intolerances, stool patterns, constipation, and diarrhea history.
F. Does the patient currently take a vitamin D and/or calcium supplement?
G. Has the patient had a recent vitamin D level drawn?
H. Inquire regarding the patient's fatigue level.
I. Assess for muscle weakness and frequent falls, especially if a pattern of more falls in the winter months is noticed.
J. Has the patient been diagnosed with osteoporosis? If so, the patient needs to be screened for vitamin D deficiency.

Physical Examination

A. Check pulse and BP.
B. Inspect
  1. Observe the patient walk in the room and assess for stability.
  2. Observe the skin color and overall appearance and type of skin texture.
  3. Note any deformities in the spine.
    a. Kyphosis
    b. Bowing of the legs
    c. Waddling of gait

C. Palpate
  1. Palpate joints or areas of complained tenderness that the patient presented with.
  2. Palpate the abdomen if intestinal absorption problems are suspected and workup is needed.
D. Auscultate the heart and lungs.

Diagnostic Tests

A. Serum 25(OH)D: Normal (30–80 ng/mL)
B. PTH: Normal (14–72 pg/mL)
C. Calcium level: Normal (8.5–10.2 mg/dL)

Differential Diagnoses

A. Vitamin D deficiency
B. Osteoporosis
C. Rickets
D. Cystic fibrosis
E. Malabsorption syndrome
F. Chronic kidney disease

Plan

A. General interventions
   Educate the patient regarding vitamin D deficiency. Reinforce the importance of taking vitamin D as prescribed and keeping a follow-up appointment to reassess values as recommended.
B. Patient teaching
  1. Diet with foods high in vitamin D must be increased. A few foods high in vitamin D include fish oil, cod liver, salmon, milk fortified with vitamin D, and cereals fortified with vitamin D.
  2. Calcium should also be taken with vitamin D on a daily basis for the prevention of osteoporosis.
  3. Inadequate sun exposure: Recommend 20 to 30 minutes of sunlight during summer months without use of sunscreen.
C. Pharmaceutical therapy
  1. For vitamin D levels less than 20 ng/mL: Vitamin D_2 or D_3: 50,000 IU weekly for 6 to 8 weeks. It is recommended to recheck vitamin D level, and if the vitamin D level is still less than 30 ng/mL, repeat the prescribed dose for another 8 weeks.
  2. For vitamin D levels 20 to 30 ng/mL: Vitamin D_3 600 to 800 IU daily
  3. Cholecalciferol (vitamin D_3) is preferred to ergocalciferol (vitamin D_2) for supplementation when available.
  4. Calcium levels should also be maintained with a recommended dietary intake of 1,000 to 1,200 mg daily.

Follow-Up

A. Follow-up should be performed according to recommendations based on laboratory results. Initial laboratory results should be repeated in 3 to 4 months after the initial treatment. As soon as vitamin D levels are stable, repeat labwork to confirm that levels remain within normal range. If levels continue to fall, refer to a specialist.

Consultation/Referral

A. Consult with a physician or refer to a GI specialist for patients who consistently have low vitamin D levels. For malabsorption problems, these patients should be referred to a GI specialist for workup.

Individual Considerations

A. Pregnancy: No contraindications for treatment during pregnancy. The same prescribing dose is safe for pregnancy and breastfeeding patients.
B. Geriatrics
  1. Vitamin D deficiency is commonly seen in this population.
  2. All patients diagnosed with osteoporosis should be assessed for vitamin D deficiency.
  3. Patients with a serum 25(OH)D level of less than 10 are at risk for developing osteomalacia.

Bibliography

AIDSINFO. (2012, July 31). Offering information on HIV/AIDS treatment, presentation, and research. *Recommendations for use of antiretroviral drugs in pregnant HIV-l-infected women for maternal health and interventions to reduce perinatal HIV transmission in the United States.* Retrieved from http://aidsinfo,nih.gov/contentfiles/lvguidelines/perinatalgl.pdf

AIDSINFO. (2012, November 5). Offering information on HIV/AIDS treatment, presentation, and research. *Guidelines for the use of antiretroviral agents in pediatric HIV infection.* Retrieved from http://aidsinfo.nih.gov/guidelines/html/2/pediatric-arv-guidelines/0

AIDSINFO. (2013, February 12). Offering information on HIV/AIDS treatment, presentation, and research. *Guidelines for the use of antiretroviral agents in HIV-l-infected adults and adolescents.* Retrieved from http://aidsinfo.nih.govguidelines/html/1/adult-and-adolescent-arv-guidelines/0

AIDSINFO. (2013, May 7). Offering information on HIV/AIDS treatment, presentation, and research. *Guidelines for the prevention and treatment of opportunistic infections in HIV-infected adults and adolescents.* Retrieved from http://aidsinfo.ninh.gov/guidelines/html/4/adult-and-adolescent-oi-prevention-and-treatment-guidelines/0

AIDS Infonet. (2013). *Reliable, up-to-date treatment information.* Retrieved from www.aidsinfonet.org

AIDSMEDS. (2012, August 28). *Treatment for HIV & AIDS.* Retrieved from http://www.aidsmeds.com/list.shtml

AIDSMEDS. (2012, November 13). *Currently approved drugs for HIV: A comparative chart. Retrieved* from http://www.aidsmeds.com/articles/DrugChart_10632.shtml

American Academy of HIV Medicine. (2007). *Fundamentals of HIV medicine for the HIV specialist.* Washington, DC: Author. Retrieved from http://www.AAHIVM.org

American College of Obstetricians and Gynecologists. (2004). ACOG practice bulletin. Clinical management guidelines for obstetrician-gynecologists. Number 50, January 2003. *Obstetrics and Gynecology, 103,* 203–216.

American College of Rheumatology (2010). *2010 Fibromyalgia diagnostic criteria*. Retrieved from https://www.rheumatology.org/practice/clinical/classification/fibromyalgia

American Congress of Obstetricians and Oncologists. (2012). *New cervical cancer screening recommendations for the U.S. Preventive Services Task Force and the American Cancer Society/American Society for Clinical Pathology*. Retrieved from http://www.acog.org/About%20ACOG/Announcements/New%20Cervical%Cancer%Screening%20Recommendations.aspx

American Society for Colposcopy and Cervical Pathology. (2012). *Updated consensus guidelines for the management of abnormal cervical cancer precursors*. Retrieved from http://www.asccp.org/ConsensusGuidelines/UpdatedConsensusGuidelines/tabid14181/Default.aspx

Angeline, M. E., Gee, A. O., Shindle, M., Warren, R. F., & Rodeo, S. A. (2013). The effects of vitamin D deficiency in athletes. *American Journal of Sports Medicine, 41*(2), 461–464.

Becker, M. A. (2014a). Clinical manifestations and diagnosis of gout. *UpToDate*. Retrieved from http://www.uptodate.com/contents/clinical-manifestations-and-diagnosis-of-gout?source=search_result&search=gout&selectedTitle=2~150

Becker, M. A. (2014b). *Treatment of acute gout. UpToDate*. http://www.uptodate.com/contents/treatment-of-acute-gout?source=machineLearning&search=gout&selectedTitle=1~150§ionRank=1&anchor=H85444272#H85444272

The Body. (n.d.a). *Approved HIV medications by class*. Retrieved from http://www.thebody.com/index/treat/classes.html

The Body. (n.d.b). *First steps to HIV/AIDS treatment*. Retrieved from http://www.thebody.com/index/treat/first.html

The Body. (n.d.c). *HIV/AIDS medication basics*. Retrieved from http://www.thebody.com/content/art40488.html

The Body. (n.d.d). *HIV drug-drug interactions*. Retrieved from http://www.thebody.com/index/treat/interactions.html

The Body. (n.d.e). *Side effects of HIV/AIDS and HIV medications*. Retrieved from http://www.thebody.com/index/treat/side_effects.html#general

Bonnie, M. A., & Ledbetter, C. (2011). Fever of unknown origin: An evidence-based approach. *Nurse Practitioner, 36*(8), 46–52.

Brady, V. (2012). Vitamin deficiency: Beyond bone health. *Clinical Advisor for Nurse Practitioners, 15*(9), 20–26.

Brown, H. (2013). Managing pernicious anemia. *Independent Nurse*, (18-02), 22–24.

Cadogan, M. (2010). Functional implications of vitamin B12 deficiency. *Journal of Gerontological Nursing, 36*(6), 12–16.

Centers for Disease Control and Prevention. (2003, July 18). *MMWR recommendations and reports: Incorporating HIV prevention into the medical care of persons living with HIV*. Retrieved from http://aidsinfo.nih.gov/contentfiles/HIVpreventioninmedcare_TB.pdf

Centers for Disease Control and Prevention. (2005, September 30). *MMWR recommendations and reports: Management of occupational exposures to HIV and recommendations for post-exposure prophylaxis*. Retrieved from http://aidsinfo.nih.govcontentfiles/healthcareoccupexpoGL.pdf

Centers for Disease Control and Prevention. (2006, October 19). *Questions and answers: Men on the down low*. Retrieved from http://www.cdc.gov/hiv/topics/aa/resources/qa/printdownlow.htm

Centers for Disease Control and Prevention. (2007, June 28). *HIV/AIDS and African Americans*. Retrieved from http:/www.cdc.gov/hiv/topics/aa/print/index.htm

Centers for Disease Control and Prevention. (2012, June). Monitoring selected National HIV prevention and care objectives by using HIV surveillance data—United States and 6 U.S. dependent areas—2010. *HIV Surveillance Supplemental Report*. Retrieved from http://www.cdc.gov/hiv/topicssurveillance/resources/reports

Centers for Disease Control and Prevention. (2012, August 10). Interim guidance for clinicians considering the use of preexposure prophylaxis for the prevention of HIV infection in heterosexually active adults. *Morbidity and Mortality Weekly Report (MMWR)*. Retrieved from http://www.cdc.gov/mmwrpreview/mmwrhtml/mm6131a2.htm?s_cid=mm6131a2_w

Centers for Disease Control and Prevention. (2013, January). *HIV testing trends in the United States, 2000–2011*. Retrieved from http://www.cdc.gov/hiv/pdf/testing_trends.pdf

Centers for Disease Control and Prevention. (2013, April 15) *Diagnoses of HIV infection in the United States and Dependent Areas, 2011*. Division of HIV/AIDS Prevention, National Center for HIV/AIDS, Viral Hepatitis, Sexual Transmitted Diseases and Tuberculosis Prevention, Centers for Disease Control and Prevention. Retrieved from http://www.cdc.govhiv/library/reports/surveillance/2011/surveillance_Report_vol_23.html

Centers for Disease Control and Prevention. (2013, April 23). *HIV in the United States: At a glance*. Division of HIV/AIDS Prevention, National Center for HIV/AIDS, Viral Hepatitis, Sexual Transmitted Diseases and Tuberculosis Prevention, Centers for Disease Control and Prevention. Retrieved from http://cdc.gov.hiv.statistics.basics.ataglance.html

Centers for Disease Control and Prevention. (2013, May 13). *HIV among Black/African American gay, bisexual, and other men who have sex with men*. Division of HIV/AIDS Prevention, National Center for HIV/AIDS, Viral Hepatitis, Sexual Transmitted Diseases and Tuberculosis Prevention, Centers for Disease Control and Prevention. Retrieved from http:/www.cdc.gov/hiv/risk/racialethnic/bmsm/facts/index.html

Chou, R., Qaseem, A., Snow, V., Casey, D., Cross, T., Jr., Shekelle, P., & Owens, D. K. (2007). Clinical guidelines: Diagnosis and treatment of low back pain: A joint clinical practice guideline from the American College of Physicians and the American Pain Society. *Annals of Internal Medicine, 147*(7), 478–491.

Christley, Y. J., & Martin, C. R. (2012). Perinatal perspective on chronic fatigue syndrome. *British Journal of Midwifery, 20*(6), 389–393.

Correia, L., Sodre, F., Garcia, G., Sabino, M., Brito, M., Kalil, F., & Noya-Rabelo, M. (2013). Relation of severe deficiency of vitamin D to cardiovascular mortality during acute coronary syndromes. *American Journal of Cardiology, 111*(3), 324–327.

Dawson-Hughes, B. (2014). Vitamin D deficiency in adults: Definition, clinical manifestations, and treatment. *UpToDate*. Retrieved from http://www.uptodate.com/contents/vitamin-d-deficiency-in-adults-definition-clinical-manifestations-and-treatment?source=search_result&search=vitamin+d+deficiency&selectedTitle=1~150

Deighton, K. (2011). Pernicious anemia (B12 deficiency). *Evidence-Based Practice, 14*(10), 14.

Emkey, G., & Reginato, A. (2009, October). All about gout and pseudogout: Meeting a growing challenge. *Journal of Musculoskeletal Medicine*, S17–S23.

Ernst, D., & Lee, A. (Eds.). (2009). *NPPR: Nurse practitioners' prescribing reference*. New York, NY: A Haymarket Media Publication.

Friedman, J. J., Chen, Z., Ford, P., Johnson, C., Lopez, A., Shander, A., & van Wyck, D. (2012). Iron deficiency anemia in women across the life span. *Journal of Women's Health, 21*(12), 1282–1289.

Horn, T., & Urbina, A. (2013, February). *The POZ and AIDSMEDS drug chart.* Retrieved from http://www.aidsmeds.com/lessons/DrugChartHighRes.pdf

Horowitz, H. (2013). Fever of unknown origin or fever of too many origins? *New England Journal of Medicine, 368*(3), 197–199.

Hunder, G. G. (2014). Clinical manifestations of giant cell (temporal) arteritis. *UpToDate.* Retrieved from http://www.uptodate.com/contents/clinical-manifestations-of-giant-cell-temporal-arteritis?source=search_result&search=temporal+arteritis&selectedTitle=3~103

International AIDS Society. (n.d.). *Antiretroviral treatment of adult HIV infection.* Retrieved from http://www.iasusa.org/content/antiretroviral-treatment-adult-hiv-infection-0

Kado, D. M. (2014). Overview of hyperkyphosis in older persons. *UpToDate.* Retrieved from http://www.uptodate.com/contents/overview-of-hyperkyphosis-in-older-persons?source=search_result&search=kyphosis&selectedTitle=1~59

Kahanov, L., Eberman, L. E., & Grammer, S. (2012). Diagnosis and treatment of idiopathic thrombocytopenic purpura. *International Journal of Athletic Therapy & Training, 17*(2), 25–28.

Kalaci, A., Cakici, H., Hapa, O., Yanat, A. N., & Sevinc, T. T. (2009). Treatment of plantar fasciitis using four different local injection modalities: A randomized prospective clinical trial. *Journal of the American Podiatric Medical Association, 99*(2), 108–113.

Kalunian, K. C. (2014). Diagnosis and classification of osteoarthritis. *UpToDate.* Retrieved from http://www.uptodate.com/contents/diagnosis-and-classification-of-osteoarthritis?source=search_result&search=osteoarthritis&selectedTitle=1~150

Kinkade, S. (2007). Evaluation and treatment of acute low back pain. *American Family Physician, 75*(8), 1181–1188.

Klippel, J. H. (2008). *Primer on the rheumatic diseases.* New York, NY: Springer.

Lalani, S., Pope, J., de Leon, F., & Peschken, C. (2010). Clinical features and prognosis of late-onset systemic pupus erythematosus: Results from the 1000 faces of lupus study. *Journal of Rheumatology, 37*(1), 38–44.

Lewiecki, E. M., & Watts, N. B. (2009). New guidelines for the prevention and treatment of osteoporosis. *Southern Medical Journal, 102*(2), 175–179.

Mayo Clinic. (2013). *Gout.* Retrieved from http://www.mayoclinic.com/health/gout/DS00090?METHOD=print

Mctigue, J., & Croker, B. (2012). Lupus and the autoimmune process: The view from 2012. *Clinical Advisor for Nurse Practitioners, 15*(1), 25–33.

Motyckova, G., & Steensma, D. (2012). Why does my patient have lymphadenopathy or splenomegaly? *Hematology Oncology Clinics of North America, 26*(2), 395–408.

National HIV/AIDS Clinician's Consultation Center. (2013). *Warmline 800-933-3413. PEPline 888-448-4911. Perinatal HIV Hotline 888-448-8765.* Retrieved from www.ncc.ucsf.edu

National Osteoporosis Foundation. (n.d.a). *Medications to prevent & treat osteoporosis.* Retrieved from http://www.nof.org/patientinfo/medications.htm#Raloxifene

National Osteoporosis Foundation. (n.d.b). *Prevention: Vitamin D.* Retrieved from http://www.nof.org/prevention/vitaminD.htm

National Osteoporosis Foundation. (1998). *Physician's guide to prevention and treatment of osteoporosis.* Retrieved from http://www.nof.org/professionals/clinicals-Guide

Neufeld, S. K., & Cerrato, R. (2008). Plantar fasciitis: Evaluation and treatment. *Journal of the American Academy of Orthopaedic Surgeons, 16*(6), 338–346.

Park, S., Kang, J., Roh, J., Huh, H., Yeo, J., & Kim, D. (2013). Secondary syphilis presenting as a generalized lymphadenopathy: Clinical mimicry of malignant lymphoma. *Sexually Transmitted Diseases, 40*(6), 490–492.

Pham, A. N., Colon-Emeric, C. S., & Weber, T. J. (2009). Osteoporosis in older women. *Clinical Geriatrics, 17*(10), 20–28.

Robinson, M., Sheets Cook, S., & Currie, L. M. (2011). Systemic lupus erythematosus: A genetic review for advanced practice nurses. *Journal of the American Academy of Nurse Practitioners, 23*(12), 629–637.

Rosen, H. N., & Walega, D. R. (2014). Osteoporotic thoracolumbar vertebral compression fractures: Clinical manifestations and treatment. Retrieved from http://www.uptodate.com/contents/osteoporotic-thoracolumbar-vertebral-compression-fractures-clinical-manifestations-and-treatment?source=search_result&search=compression+fracture&selectedTitle=1~150

Short, M., & Domagalski, J. (2013). Iron deficiency anemia: Evaluation and management. *American Family Physician, 87*(2), 98–104.

Shur, P. H., & Wallace, D. J. (2014). Diagnosis and differential diagnosis of systemic lupus erythematosus in adults. *UpToDate.* Retrieved from www.uptodate.com/contents/diagnosis-and-differential-diagnosis-of-systemic-lupus-erythematous-in-adults?topicKey=RHEUM%2F4668&elapsedTimeMs

Siddiqui, Z., & Osayande, A. (2011). Selected disorders of malabsorption. *Primary Care, 38*(3), 395–414.

Solomon, D. H. (2014). Overview of selective COX-2 inhibitors. *UpToDate.* Retrieved from http://www.uptodate.com/contents/overview-of-selective-cox-2-inhibitors?source=see_link&anchor=H10#H10

Stabler, S. (2013). Clinical practice: Vitamin B12 deficiency. *New England Journal of Medicine, 368*(2), 149–160.

Sweet, M. G., Sweet, J. M., Jeremiah, M. P., & Galazka, S. S. (2009). Diagnosis and treatment of osteoporosis. *American Family Physician, 79*(3), 193–200.

Teitelbaum, J. (2011). Effective treatment of chronic fatigue syndrome. *Integrative Medicine: A Clinician's Journal, 10*(6), 44–48.

Theander, K., & Unosson, M. (2011). No gender differences in fatigue and functional limitations due to fatigue among patients with COPD. *Journal of Clinical Nursing, 20*(9/10), 1303–1310.

Tierney, L., McPhe, S., & Papadakis, M. (2007). *Current medical diagnosis and treatment* (46th ed.). New York, NY: McGraw-Hill.

Tsokos, G. (2011). Systemic lupus erythematosus. *New England Journal of Medicine, 365*(22), 2110–2121.

Turk, D., & Wilson, H. (2009). Managing fibromyalgia: An update on diagnosis and treatment. *Journal of Musculoskeletal Medicine,* S1–S7.

U.S. Department of Health and Human Services. (2004). *Bone health and osteoporosis: A report of the Surgeon General.* Retrieved from http://www.surgeongeneralgov/library/bonehealth/content.html

U.S. Food and Drug Administration. (n.d.). *Antiretroviral drugs used in the treatment of HIV infection.* Retrieved from http://

www.fda.gov/ForConsumers/byAudience/ForThepatient Advocates/HIVandAIDSActivities/ucm118915.html
U.S. National Library of Medicine. (2013a, March 12). *Iron deficiency anemia.* Retrieved from http://www.ncblinmnih .gov/pubmedhealth/pmh00001610
U.S. National Library of Medicine. (2013b, March 12). *Pernicious anemia.* Retrieved from http://www.ncbinlmnih .gov/pubmedhealth/pmh00001595
U.S. National Library of Medicine (2013c). *Plantar fasciitis.* Retrieved from http://www.ncbi.nlm.nih.gov/pubmed-health/PMH0004438
U.S. Preventive Services Task Force Recommendation Statement. (2013, April). *Screening for HIV.* Retrieved from http://www.uspreventiveservicestaskforce.org/uspstf13/ hivhivfinalrs.htm
Warren, E. (2012). Chronic fatigue syndrome. *Practice Nurse, 42*(6), 14–18.
Weiss, S. (2012). Oral involvement of systemic diseases. *Clinical Advisor for Nurse Practitioners, 15*(6), 25–30.
Wikipedia. (2013). *Fibromyalgia.* Retrieved from http:// en.wikipedia.org/wiki/Fibromyalgia
Winkeljohn, D. (2010). Idiopathic thrombocytic purpura. *Clinical Journal of Oncology Nursing, 14*(4), 411–413.
Wolfe, F., Smythe, H. A., Yunus, M. B., Bennett, R. M., Bombardier, C., Goldenberg, D. L., ... Sheon, R. P. (1990). The American College of Rheumatology 1990 Criteria for the Classification of Fibromyalgia. *Arthritis Rheum, 33,* 160–172.
World Health Organization. (2012, July). *Guidance on oral pre-exposure prophylaxis (PrEP) for serodiscordant couples, men and transgender women who have sex with men at high risk for HIV.* Retrieved from http://www.who.int/hiv/pub/ gidance_prep/en/index.html
Yancey, J., & Thomas, S. (2012). Chronic fatigue syndrome: Diagnosis and treatment. *American Family Physician, 86*(8), 74.

CHAPTER TWENTY-TWO

Neurologic Guidelines

Jill C. Cash, Julie Adkins, Karen M. Kress, Cheryl A. Glass, and Kimberly D. Waltrip

Alzheimer's Disease—*Jill C. Cash and Karen M. Kress*

Definition

A. Alzheimer's disease is a permanent, progressive neurocognitive disorder that is characterized by deficits in several dimensions of cognitive functioning, including memory disturbance, that severely interfere with the person's everyday living but produces no decrease in level of consciousness (LOC). Insidious onset, gradually progressive decline in intellectual functioning, and absence of other specific causes of dementia are also present.

Incidence

A. Alzheimer's disease is the most commonly occurring neurocognitive disorder. There are more than 5 million cases of Alzheimer's disease per 350 million people. Among the elderly, approximately 40% of those older than 85 years of age are affected. Of all types of dementias, Alzheimer's dementia includes 70% of those affected, with the other 30% affected by atypical dementia. Alzheimer's disease is the sixth leading cause of death in the United States.

Pathogenesis

A. The disease is a degenerative process involving cell loss from the basal forebrain, cerebral cortex, and other areas in which plaques and tangles build up and block the cell processes that are needed to survive, thereby destroying the nerve cells. Cortical atrophy is most prominent in the temporal and hippocampal regions of the brain. Death of the nerve cells causes memory loss, changes in personality, and other signs and symptoms of Alzheimer's disease. The Apo E epsilon 4 allele of chromosome 19 has been associated with familial and late onset Alzheimer's disease.

Predisposing Factors

A. Definite risks
   1. Advanced age older than 50 years
   2. Atrial fibrillation (AFib)
   3. Depression
   4. Abnormal genetic makeup, such as Down syndrome
   5. Positive family history of Alzheimer's disease
   6. Gender (females have a higher incidence; Alzheimer's is two thirds more common in females than in males).

B. Possible risks
   1. Delirium
   2. Head trauma
   3. Heavy smoking
   4. Hypertension (HTN)
   5. Hyperlipidemia
   6. Low educational level
   7. Postmenopausal hormone therapy (HT)

Common Complaints

A. Significant memory loss as reported by the patient, family, or caregiver

B. Change in behavior and ability to perform normal activities of self-care

Other Signs and Symptoms

A. The 10 warning signs of Alzheimer's disease:
   1. Memory loss interrupting daily living
   2. Loss of all intellectual capacities such as following plans, solving problems, and so on
   3. Difficulty completing daily tasks at home or work
   4. Confusion with time or place
   5. Having problems understanding visual images or spatial relationships
   6. Difficulty with speaking or writing words

7. Losing things and not being able to retrace steps to find them
8. Poor judgment in daily routine
9. Withdrawal from work or social activities
10. Change in mood or personality (www.alz.org/national/documents/checklist_10signs.pdf)

Subjective Data

Family members are a good resource for obtaining an accurate history.

A. Determine onset, course, and duration of symptoms.
B. Note loss of immediate, recent, or remote memory, such as trouble remembering appointments, difficulty recalling recent events, and inability to find personal belongings.
C. Determine the patient's ability to make reasonable judgments, such as answering the phone when it rings, and so forth.
D. Is the patient able to carry on daily functions of living, including cooking meals and cleaning house?
E. Discuss the patient's sleep–wake cycle.
F. Assess the patient for decreased appetite, lack of pleasure in usual activities, melancholy mood, or other symptoms associated with depression.
G. Note language difficulties and problems expressing self.
H. Note any recent physical illness.
I. Review the patient's medication history, specifically those medications with anticholinergic side effects, including over-the-counter (OTC) products such as diphenhydramine.
J. Discuss alcohol intake and abuse factors.
K. Review past medical history of head trauma, HTN, cerebrovascular accident (CVA), cancer, metabolic problems, neurologic disease, infections, gastric surgery (vitamin B_{12} deficiency), and emotional or psychiatric problems.
L. Note any recent major life events such as the death of a spouse, a move to a new living environment, or loss of purpose following retirement.

Physical Examination

A. Check blood pressure, pulse, respirations, and weight.
B. Inspect: Inspect overall appearance for hygiene and nutritional status.
C. Auscultate: Auscultate the heart, lungs, abdomen.
D. Neurologic exam: Perform a complete neurologic exam. Note facial asymmetry, distal weakness, and any focal neurologic findings.
E. Perform standardized mini-mental state examination (SMMSE) screening tool.
   1. Montreal Cognitive Assessment (MOCA). Available at www.mocatest.org
   2. Mini-Mental State Exam (MMSE). Available at: www.mountsinai.on.ca/care/psych/on-call-resources/on-call-resources/mmse.pdf
   3. Saint Louis University Mental Status Examination (SLUMS). Available at http://medschool.slu.edu/agingsuccessfully/pdfsurveys/slumsexam_05.pdf
   4. Mini-Cog. Available at: http://consultgerirn.org/uploads/File/trythis/try_this_3.pdf
   5. The Clock-Draw Test (CDT) may also be administered and used as a screening tool. The CDT is available at: www.healthcare.uiowa.edu/igec/tools/cognitive/clockDrawing.pdf

Rule out other specific causes of dementia, including cerebrovascular disease.

F. Complete depression screening with instrument of choice.
   1. Geriatric depression scale (GDS). Available at http://consultgerirn.org/uploads/File/trythis/try_this_4.pdf
   2. Patient Health Questionnaire-9 (PHQ-9). Available at www.phqscreeners.com/
   3. Beck depression scale. Available at www.med.navy.mil/sites/NMCP2/PatientServices/SleepClinicLab/Documents/Beck_Depression_Inventory.pdf
G. Assess functional status. May use a functional assessment tool such as the Physical Self-Maintenance Scale, Instrumental Activities of Daily Living Scale, or Reisberg Functional Assessment Staging Scale (FAST). Available at http://geriatrics.uthscsa.edu/tools/FAST.pdf
H. Palpate
   1. Neck and thyroid for goiter and lymphadenopathy

Diagnostic Tests

A. Complete blood count (CBC)
B. Chemistry profile
C. Thyroid function studies
D. Folate and B_{12} levels
E. Homocysteine
F. Methylmalonic acid
G. Vitamin D level
H. Venereal Disease Research Laboratory (VDRL) for syphilis
I. Computed tomography (CT) scan of the brain

Differential Diagnoses

A. Alzheimer's disease
B. Drug interactions
C. Delirium
D. Depression
E. Cerebrovascular disease

Plan

A. General interventions
  1. Identify the stage of impairment.
    Stage 1: No impairment—No evidence of symptoms
    Stage 2: Very mild decline—No symptoms of dementia, has memory lapses
    Stage 3: Mild decline—Difficulty in memory and concentration
    Stage 4: Moderate decline—Impairment with complex tasks, trouble with math solving problems, forgetting personal history.
    Stage 5: Moderately severe decline—Unable to remember phone number, address, confusion on the day of the week, difficulty with decisions on dressing self properly, and so forth.
    Stage 6: Severe decline—Difficulty with personal history, difficulty with naming family members, spouse, difficulty with dressing self, behavior changes, may wander and get lost.
    Stage 7: Very severe decline—Unable to communicate appropriately with others, requires assistance with activities of daily living (ADL), abnormal reflexes, difficulty swallowing
  2. Provide supportive measures for patient and family. Explain to family and the patient findings of exam and possible treatment options.
  3. Treatment may include treating coexisting diseases, thyroid disease, and vitamin B_{12} deficiency.
  4. Discuss therapy options such as musical therapy, occupational therapy, and mind-stimulating activities. Cognitive stimulation has been shown to slow down the degenerative process.
  5. Environment: Ensure that the patient has a safe environment; measures may need to be taken for environmental safety, such as locks on doors, alarms on doors, relinquishing driving privileges, and so on. See the Patient Teaching Guide for Chapter 3, "Safety Issues: Fall Prevention."
  6. Exercise: Daily exercise should be encouraged.

B. Patient teaching
  1. Support groups are encouraged for the patient, spouse, and/or family. Therapy sessions for each may be beneficial.
  2. Patient support group: Alzheimer's Association www.alz.org; 24/7 Helpline: 1-800-272-3900
  3. Families should seek out legal and financial advice early and not wait for a crisis. Alzheimer's Disease Family Relief Program 1-800-437-2423

C. Pharmaceutical therapy
  1. Cholinesterase inhibitors
    a. Rivastigmine (Exelon) 1.5 to 6 mg twice a day, increasing the dose by 1.5 mg every 4 weeks to a maximum of 6 mg twice daily. Exelon patch: Start at 4.6 mg/24 hr and then titrate up to 9.5 mg/24 hr. May be increased to the maximum effective dose of 13.3 mg/24 hr as indicated.
    b. Donepezil (Aricept) 5 mg at bedtime, then 10 mg/d may be given after 1 month.
    c. Galantamine (Razadyne) 4 mg twice a day with meals for 4 weeks, then may titrate to max of 12 mg twice a day. For missed doses, will need to retitrate doses. Razadyne ER: 8 mg once daily. After 4 weeks, may increase to 16 mg once daily, up to maximum of 24 mg daily titration.
  2. N-methyl-D-aspartate (NMDA) receptor antagonist
    a. Memantine (Namenda) XR is used for moderate to severe Alzheimer's disease: Namenda XR 7 mg daily, titrate up by 7 mg per week to a recommended dose of 28 mg daily.
  3. Assess the patient for secondary behaviors of dementia. Psychosis, delusions, hallucinations, anxiety, depression, and insomnia may occur and should be treated accordingly. Cognitive and behavioral interventions should be initiated in assisting the patient in controlling these behaviors. The benefits and risks must be weighted, and pharmacological treatment may be necessary for those patients exhibiting extreme, aggressive behaviors with irritability and/or insomnia. Treatment with antipsychotics is very controversial due to the side effects and extreme complications that may occur with these medications.
  4. Treatment of depression: Nortriptyline (Pamelor) 30 to 50 mg daily, sertraline (Zoloft), paroxetine (Paxil), or escitalopram (Lexapro). Monitor selective serotonin reuptake inhibitor (SSRI) for weight loss, decrease in seizure threshold, tremors. Do not use with monoamine oxidase (MAO)-I. Monitor Coumadin and lithium levels closely.

Follow-Up

A. Follow-up is variable, depending on patient status and needs of the patient and family. Follow-up is recommended every 3 months to follow the progression of disease. If medications are being introduced, monitor the patient monthly.

Consultation/Referral

A. Consider using a visiting nurse, social worker, or occupational and/or physical therapist.

B. Consult a physician for medication treatment for secondary behavioral symptoms.
C. Referral to geriatric psychiatry may be appropriate for treatment of behavioral and psychological symptoms.

Individual Considerations

A. Adults: Estrogen replacement therapy and antioxidant therapy (vitamin E) are being studied for their effectiveness in the prevention and delay of Alzheimer's disease.
B. Geriatrics
   1. Alzheimer's disease is primarily seen in this population.
   2. Long-term prognosis: Average patient lives 7 to 10 years after early symptoms, but life span while demented can be 20 years or more.

Resources

Alzheimer's Association: www.alz.org

Alzheimer's Disease Education and Referral Center: www.nia.nih.gov/alzheimers

Bell's Palsy

Definition

A. Bell's palsy, also known as idiopathic peripheral facial palsy, is characterized by an acute onset of unilateral facial paralysis. It accounts for approximately 75% of all cases of facial paralysis.

Incidence

A. Bell's palsy has an incidence of 25:100,000. Approximately 5% of those affected experience recurrence. Both sexes are affected, as well as all ages, but most patients are in their middle years, older than 30 years.

Pathogenesis

A. The pathogenesis of Bell's palsy is unknown, but some possible etiologies include genetic, metabolic, autoimmune, and vascular causes. An increasing body of evidence reveals that Bell's palsy may be a virally induced neuritis. A triggering event or stressor induces activation of a latent virus, most likely herpes simplex virus or herpes zoster virus, present within the geniculate ganglion of the facial nerve. Viral activation results in reexpression of dormant viral particles and neural inflammation, leading to entrapment, ischemia, and degeneration of the facial nerve.

Predisposing Factors

A. Diabetes
B. Pregnancy
C. Recent infection
D. Positive family history
E. HTN
F. Hypothyroidism

Common Complaints

A. Acute onset of unilateral facial weakness with inability to close one eye
B. Sagging of one eyebrow
C. Loss of nasolabial fold
D. Mouth drawn to affected side

Other Signs and Symptoms

A. Ipsilateral retroauricular pain with or preceding paralysis
B. Hyperacusis or hypersensitivity to sound
C. Dysgeusia, or perversion of taste, in the anterior two thirds of the tongue
D. Facial paresthesia
E. Drooling
F. Decreased tearing

Subjective Data

A. Elicit onset, duration, and course of symptoms.
B. Have the patient describe all neurologic symptoms present.
C. Note associated symptoms such as disruption of taste and disturbances in visual function or hearing.
D. Note predisposing factors such as trauma, infection, or pregnancy.
E. Review the patient's family history for presence of Bell's palsy.
F. Review the patient's medical history; especially note cerebrovascular or cardiac risk factors. A focused history should include contraindications to use of steroids.

Physical Examination

A. Check temperature, pulse, respirations, and blood pressure.
B. Inspect
   1. Note facial appearance.
   2. Observe symmetry of eyes. Check corneal reflex (decreased). Assess ears, nose, and throat; assess the skin for lesions. Assess in and behind ears for zosteriform lesions.
   3. Complete ear exam to rule out infection. **Assess paralysis of all the muscles supplied by one facial nerve. Paralysis may be of varying degrees and need not be complete.**
C. Auscultate: Auscultate the heart and lungs.
D. Neurologic exam: Perform a complete neurologic exam; test all cranial nerves (CNs).

Subjective decreased sensation may be present in the trigeminal distribution.

Diagnostic Tests

A. Lyme titer: Positive in patients with secondary facial weakness from Lyme disease

B. Skull radiography, CT scan, or magnetic resonance imaging (MRI): Negative in Bell's palsy, but may show evidence of fracture line, bony erosion by infection or neoplasm, stroke, or tumor
C. Electromyographic (EMG) studies: Occasionally performed to predict prognosis and progression. EMG is reserved for severe cases of paralysis lasting longer than 1 week.
D. Lumbar puncture (LP): Indicated only when other conditions are suspected. Cerebrospinal fluid (CSF) should be sent for cytology.

Differential Diagnoses

A. Bell's palsy
B. Sjögren's syndrome
C. Stroke
D. Lyme disease
E. Sarcoidosis
F. Ramsay Hunt syndrome, herpes zoster oticus
G. Acoustic neuroma
H. Middle ear disease such as purulent otitis media or neoplasms
I. Guillain–Barré syndrome (GBS)
J. Parotid gland tumor
K. Carcinomatous meningitis

Plan

A. General interventions
   1. Provide eye protection by means of the following.
      a. Apply methylcellulose drops as needed and ocular lubricant (Lacri-Lube) at bedtime and as needed.
      b. Tape eye closed, especially at night to avoid drying effect.
      c. Wear dark glasses when outdoors to minimize light exposure. May also be helpful indoors around bright overhead lights or lamps
   2. Physical therapy may be beneficial.
   3. Ensure that the patient gets reassurance and emotional support.

Recovery may take 3 to 6 months or longer and is complete in approximately 80% of the cases.

B. Patient teaching: See the Section III Patient Teaching Guide for this chapter, "Bell's Palsy."
   1. Consider operative decompression by an otologic surgeon; this technique is controversial.
   2. Operative anastomosis of the 12th CN to the 7th CN; this may cause difficulty with eating and has a limited role in facial restoration.

C. Pharmaceutical therapy
   1. Prednisone: Adults take 80 mg every day with breakfast for first 3 days, then decrease dosage to 40 mg for 3 days, then to 20 mg daily for 3 days, then stop.

Recent studies suggest that a brief course of prednisone conveys modest benefits with minimal risks.

   2. Use of oral acyclovir in conjunction with prednisone, at a dosage of 400 mg five times a day for 10 days. Consider acyclovir for patients without renal insufficiency and with no other contraindications to therapy. Valtrex 1g twice a day for 7 to 10 days is also available.
   3. Analgesics, such as acetaminophen, for ear pain or face pain.

Follow-Up

A. For patients with severe symptoms, follow up in 3 to 4 days, then again in 2 weeks.
B. If symptoms worsen or do not resolve within weeks, have the patient return to the clinic.

Consultation/Referral

A. Consult a neurologist for the following:
   1. Failure to resolve significantly after 4 to 6 weeks. Only 5% to 8% report distressing residual signs and symptoms, including contracture of facial muscles at rest and synergistic mass innervation due to defective nerve regeneration, manifested as either crocodile tears secondary to abnormal secretory fibers intended for the salivary glands or ipsilateral eyelid shutting.
   2. Other CN involvement or other abnormalities on neurologic exam
   3. Recurrence of facial palsy: About 5% to 7% of patients experience recurrence of symptoms. Known causes of recurrent palsy include sarcoidosis, diabetes, leukemia, and infectious mononucleosis.
   4. Bilateral facial palsies
B. Consult an ophthalmologist for persistent ocular pain or development of a corneal abrasion or ulceration.

Individual Considerations

A. Pregnancy: The incidence of Bell's palsy is increased in pregnancy, with the highest incidence in the third trimester or immediately postpartum. May treat with prednisone during pregnancy.

Carpal Tunnel Syndrome

Definition

A. Carpal tunnel syndrome (CTS) is a nerve entrapment condition of the median nerve of the wrist.

Incidence

A. CTS occurs in approximately 1% of the general population. It is primarily seen in 30- to 60-year-old adults.

Pathogenesis

A. CTS occurs from compression of the median nerve in the carpal canal. Compression occurs due to swelling of the flexor tenosynovium; the pressure blocks the nerve fibers, which produces numbness and discomfort in the digits/hands. Repetitive flexion and extension of the wrists create increased pressure in the carpal canal.
B. Potential causes of CTS include blunt trauma or structural changes; tumors; systemic diseases, such as rheumatoid disorders, diabetes mellitus, thyroid disorders, endocrine diseases, and so forth; mechanical overuse syndrome; and infectious diseases, such as tuberculosis (TB) and leprosy. Consider multifactorial causes of CTS.

Predisposing Factors

A. Women
B. Hobbies or jobs that require repetitive wrist or hand movement and the use of vibratory tools
C. Pregnancy

Common Complaints

A. Pain
B. Tingling/numbness sensation in the wrists, hands, and fingers that radiates up into the forearm

Other Signs and Symptoms

A. Paresthesia in wrists, hands, and fingers
B. Localized pain of radial three digits of the hand
C. Weakness with grasp
D. Decreased dexterity
E. Night pain in wrists
F. Referred pain to elbow and/or shoulder
G. Long-term pressure in the carpus can produce ischemic changes and may lead to axonal death, muscular atrophy, and pain. Long-term nerve compression may produce irreversible changes.

Subjective Data

A. Determine onset, duration, and course of presenting symptoms.
B. Note the progression of symptoms since the initial occurrence.
C. Assess whether the symptoms increase with hand or wrist activity and decrease with the joint at rest.
D. Identify factors that precipitate symptoms, that make symptoms worse, and that alleviate symptoms.
E. Inquire whether the patient awakens at night with numbness and tingling sensations.
F. Have the patient describe the pain, and note if radiation is present. Are symptoms bilateral?
G. Note the patient's occupation, hobby, and/or daily routines that require hand or wrist use.
H. Identify what treatment and/or relief measures have been used, and note results.

Physical Examination

A. Inspect: Inspect the hands for deformities. Note wasting or atrophy.
B. Palpate: Perform sensory motor evaluation of the hand and arm.
   1. Perform Tinel's test: Tap over transverse carpal ligament; result is positive if tingling in fingers is noted.
   2. Perform Phalen's test: Have patient place elbows on flat surface and hold forearms in vertical position, then flex wrists; result is positive if pain, numbness, or tingling is noted within the next 60 seconds.

Diagnostic Tests

A. EMG
B. Nerve conduction velocity studies
C. If an underlying systemic illness or condition exists, consider the following.
   1. Erythrocyte sedimentation rate (ESR)
   2. Blood glucose
   3. Thyroid profile
   4. Inflammatory disease studies

Differential Diagnoses

A. CTS
B. Peripheral neuropathy
C. Cervical spondylosis and cervical disk herniation
D. Brachial plexus lesion
E. Trauma
F. Thenar atrophy and neuropathy
G. Osteoarthritis
H. Neurologic disorders: Polyneuritis, multiple sclerosis (MS), tumors, and so on

Plan

A. General interventions
   1. Help the patient identify causative agents, eliminate activity if possible, decrease repetitive use, or use alternative methods to accomplish the same task.
   2. Advise resting arms and wrists as much as possible.
   3. Encourage performing daily stretching exercises.
   4. Give instructions on applying wrist splints, especially at bedtime, while sleeping.

B. Patient teaching
 1. Instruct the patient on splinting wrists.
 2. Demonstrate stretching exercises.
 3. Stress the importance of rest and elimination of the causative activity.
C. Pharmaceutical therapy
 1. Nonsteroidal anti-inflammatory drugs (NSAIDs) as needed. Ibuprofen (Motrin) 600 to 800 mg by mouth three times daily or naproxen (Naprosyn) 500 mg by mouth twice a day unless contraindicated.
 2. Vitamin B_6 100 mg/d
 3. Consider corticosteroid injections in carpal canal (40 mg/mL with 1% lidocaine 1 mL).

Follow-Up

A. Depending on treatment, consider follow-up in 1 month to evaluate status.

Consultation/Referral

A. Refer the patient to a physician for severe cases requiring evaluation for surgery.
B. Refer the patient to a surgeon for severe symptoms that could require carpal tunnel release.
C. Consider occupational therapy consult.
D. Consider physical therapy consult

Individual Considerations

A. Pregnancy: CTS is the most frequent complaint during pregnancy. About 15% of the cases will progress and continue several months postpartum.

Guillain–Barré Syndrome

Definition

A. GBS is an acute immune-mediated polyneuropathy of the peripheral nervous system. GBS often follows an infection.
B. GBS is not contagious, and there is no known cure.
C. GBS usually presents with ascending, progressive, multifocal, or symmetric muscle weakness, as well as paresthesia.
 1. The first symptom of GBS is weakness or tingling sensations of the legs. Most people reach the stage of greatest weakness within the first 2 weeks after symptoms appear.
 2. By the third week of GBS, 90% of patients are at their weakest.
D. GBS was considered monophasic and remits spontaneously but may also reoccur in 3% of patients. Twenty to thirty percent of patients will have persistent disability measured by tools such as the overall disability sum score (ODSS) (see Table 22.1). An electronic version of the ODSS is available online at http://farmacologiaclinica.info/scales/overall-disability-sum-score. This application grades the arm (range 0–5) and the leg (range 0–7) to provide an overall range score. A total score of 0 equals no disability and a total score of 12 equals maximum disability.

 There are several variants of GBS.
 1. Miller Fisher syndrome (MFS) often follows an infection, especially *Campylobacter jejuni (C. jejuni)* gastroenteritis.
 2. Acute inflammatory demyelinating polyradiculoneuropathy (AIDP): Approximately two thirds occur after an infection, including *C. jejuni*, cytomegalovirus (CMV), *Mycoplasma pneumonia*, or influenza virus.
 3. Acute motor axonal neuropathy (AMAN)
 4. Acute sensorimotor axonal neuropathy (AMSAN)
 5. Acute panautonomic neuropathy (rare)
 6. Bickerstaff's brainstem encephalitis (BBE)

Incidence

A. The incidence of GBS is 0.89 to 1.89 cases per 100,000 adults. A 20% increase is seen in every 10-year rise in age after the first year of life.
B. The lifetime individual incidence is 1:100,000.
C. GBS occurs in all age groups. GBS is more common in older adults, with those older than 50 years of age at greatest risk.
D. 80% to 90% become nonambulatory during the illness.
E. Relapses are not uncommon in adults who have been treated with intravenous immunoglobulin (IVIG) and plasma exchange.
F. Approximately 30% have a residual weakness after 3 years.
G. GBS severe enough to require mechanical ventilation is associated with both incomplete recovery and up to 20% mortality.
H. 5% of patients with GBS die from medical complications such as sepsis, pulmonary emboli, and cardiac arrest related to dysautonomia.
I. GBS is reported throughout the world.

Pathogenesis

A. GBS is believed to be an immune-mediated response linked to an antecedent infection wherein a patchy demyelination of the motor component of multiple peripheral nerves occurs. This causes a failure of neuromuscular transmission and leads to abrupt, distal weakness and symmetrical onset of paresthesias. The sensory disturbance is quickly followed by a rapid progressive limb weakness and sometimes paralysis. Most patients are able to identify a specific date of onset of sensory and motor symptoms.

TABLE 22.1 Overall Disability Sum Score

Area of Body	Activities	Functional Ability Scale for Each Activity	Disability Scale Grade
Arm disability	A. Dressing upper part of body (excludes buttons/zippers) B. Washing and brushing hair C. Turning a key in a lock D. Using a knife and fork (use of spoon applies if never used a fork/knife) E. Doing/undoing buttons and zippers	Not affected; affected but does not prevent activity; prevents activity	0 = Normal function for all activities 1 = Minor signs/symptoms (S/S) in one or both arms but does not affect the activity 2 = Moderate S/S in one or both arms affecting but not preventing any activity 3 = Severe S/S in one or both arms preventing at least one but not all activities 4 = Severe S/S in both arms preventing all functions, purposeful movements still possible 5 = Severe S/S in both arms preventing all purposeful movements
Leg disability	A. Do you have any problems walking? B. Do you walk with a walking aid? C. How do you get around for 25 feet (10 m)? 1. Without aid 2. With one stick or crutch or holding someone's arm 3. With two sticks or crutches or one stick and a crutch and holding someone's arm 4. With a wheelchair D. If you use a wheelchair, can you stand and walk a few steps with help? E. If you are restricted to bed most of the time, are you able to make some purposeful movements?	No; yes; does not apply	0 = Walking is not affected 1 = Walking is affected but does not look abnormal 2 = Walks independently but gait looks abnormal 3 = Usually uses unilateral support (stick, crutch, one arm) to walk 25 feet (10 m) 4 = Usually uses bilateral support (stick, crutch, two arms) to walk 25 feet (10 m) 5 = Usually uses a wheelchair to travel 25 feet (10 m) 6 = Restricted to wheelchair, unable to stand and walk a few steps with help but able to make some purposeful leg movements 7 = Restricted to wheelchair or bed most of the day, preventing all purposeful movements of the legs (e.g., unable to reposition legs in bed)

Adapted from Merkies, Schmitz, van der Meche, Samihn, and van Doorn (2002).

Predisposing Factors

A. Up to two thirds of patients with GBS have experienced a viral upper respiratory infection (URI) or gastroenteritis 10 to 14 days before onset.
   1. *C. jejuni* gastroenteritis (30% of infections)
   2. CMV (CMV is the second most common reported infection preceding GBS[10%].)
   3. Epstein–Barr virus (EBV)
   4. *Mycoplasma pneumonia*
   5. HIV
   6. *Haemophilus influenza*
   7. Enteroviruses
   8. Hepatitis A and B
   9. Herpes simplex
   10. Varicella-zoster virus
   11. *Chlamydophila* (formerly *Chlamydia*) pneumonia
B. Trauma
C. Surgery
D. Parturition
E. Immunization
   1. In 1976 there was a small increase in GBS following the flu vaccine formulated to protect against swine flu.
   2. Rabies vaccine is prepared from infected brain tissue.
F. There is no genetic factor for GBS.

Common Complaints

A. The classic clinical features
   1. Progressive, fairly symmetric muscle weakness (symmetric)
      a. Difficulty walking
      b. Nearly complete paralysis, including
         i. All extremities, generally starting in the proximal legs
         ii. Facial muscles/oropharyngeal weakness
         iii. Respiratory muscles (dyspnea on exertion and shortness of breath [SOB])
         iv. Bulbar (ocular) muscles
   2. Accompanying absent or depressed deep tendon reflexes (DTRs)
B. Acute weakness in hands, dropping things, trouble picking up small objects or buttoning buttons, inability to feel textures
C. Acute onset of persistent tingling or pins and needles, "crawling-skin" sensation in feet, possibly in hands, and inability to feel pain

D. Pain most severe in lower back pain, buttocks, thighs, and shoulder girdle

Other Signs and Symptoms

A. Sinus tachycardia or other arrhythmias
B. Bilateral, generally symmetric muscle weakness not improved by rest
C. Urinary retention
D. Ileus-gastric motility disorders
E. Severe residual fatigue that may persist for years
F. Loss of sweating
G. Facial or pharyngeal weakness

Subjective Data

A. Ask the patient about any dyspnea. If there is SOB, assess the need to go immediately by ambulance to a hospital.
B. Elicit information regarding the onset and duration of symptoms.
C. Question the patient regarding change or progression of symptoms.
D. Ascertain if the patient has had recent URI, flu, gastroenteritis, other infections, recent trauma, or surgery: Determine if there was an associated fever.
E. Look for paresthesias preceding weakness by approximately 24 to 48 hours.
F. Look for recent exposure to environmental hazards: Lead, pesticides, volatile solvents, or ticks.

Physical Examination

A. Check temperature (if indicated), pulse, respirations, and blood pressure (persistent hypotension, HTN alternating with hypotension, or orthostatic hypotension). HTN is seen in about one-third of patients with GBS and can be labile or followed by hypotension.
B. Inspect: Observe overall appearance; look for gait disturbance and respiratory distress.
C. Auscultate
   1. Note heart rate and rhythm: Tachycardia is common; bradycardia and other arrhythmias may be noted.
   2. Auscultate the lung fields.
   3. Abdomen assessment for bowel sounds/dysfunction. Gastrointestinal motility disorders occur in 15% of severely affected GBS patients.
D. Palpate
   1. Palpate the extremities.
   2. Note muscle tone, normal muscle bulk.
   3. Assess DTRs, muscle strength, areflexia (lack of reflexes), or hyporeflexia (diminished), although one third of patients may have hyperreflexia.
   4. Look for symmetric weakness. Incidence of weakness is greater in the ankle and knee than in biceps and triceps.
   5. Palpate the abdomen: Assess urinary retention.
E. Neurologic exam
   1. Perform complete neurologic exam: Generally no sensory deficits to touch or pinprick are noted. Decreased proprioception or vibration may be seen. In approximately 50% of clients, GBS may progress rapidly, sometimes within hours, to severe respiratory muscle weakness and respiratory failure.

Diagnostic Tests

Prompt treatment mandates that the clinician make the diagnosis of GBS solely on history and examination. The presence of distal paresthesia increases the likelihood that the diagnosis is GBS. Testing done in the inpatient setting includes:

A. LP
   1. The LP primarily rules out other infectious disease.
   2. Most GBS have elevated CSF protein levels with normal CSF cell counts
B. Needle electromyogram
C. Nerve conduction studies used to confirm the presence, pattern, and severity of neuropathy
D. Antibody testing
E. Seruwwm testing of electrolytes, liver function tests, creatine phosphokinase (CPK), and ESR

Differential Diagnoses

A. GBS
B. Myasthenia gravis (MG)
C. Poliomyelitis
D. Acute intermittent porphyria
E. West Nile encephalomyelitis
F. Tick paralysis: Lyme neuroborreliosis
G. Diphtheria
H. HIV
I. Cervical myelopathy
J. Sarcoidosis
K. Poisoning
   1. Heavy metal poisoning (arsenic, lead, thallium)
   2. Hexacarbon abuse (glue sniffing neuropathy)
   3. Organophosphate poisoning
   4. Botulism

Plan

A. **General interventions: Early diagnosis is crucial to appropriate management. A possible diagnosis of GBS requires *immediate* hospitalization at a facility with intensive care unit (ICU) capabilities and consultation with a neurologist who has experience managing GBS.**
B. Hospital medical management
   1. Plasmapheresis (plasma exchange)
   2. IVIG administration
   3. Steroids have not been shown to be helpful and may be detrimental.

4. Because of the associated autonomic instability, HTN should be treated with short-acting intravenous agents.
5. The presence of at least four of the six predictors indicates the need for support/mechanical ventilation:
   a. Onset of symptoms less than 7 days
   b. Inability to cough
   c. Inability to stand
   d. Inability to lift the elbows
   e. Inability to lift the head
   f. An increase in liver enzymes
6. Heparin and support/pressure stockings are used for nonambulatory patients due to the risk of deep vein thrombosis (DVT) and pulmonary embolus.

C. Pharmaceutical therapy
   1. Pain therapy
      a. Gabapentin (Neurontin) 15 mg/kg/d
      b. Carbamazepine (Tegretol) 300 mg/d
      c. Narcotics may be necessary.
      d. Tricyclic antidepressants (TCAs)
   2. Immunizations
      a. Immunizations are not recommended during the acute phase and up to approximately 1 year after the onset of GBS.
      b. Influenza, tetanus, and typhoid immunizations have been most commonly associated with relapse of GBS symptoms.

Follow-Up

A. Patients generally follow up with a neurologist once they have been discharged from the hospital or rehabilitation facility.
B. Full recovery can take up to 3 years with severe cases, and a small percentage of patients experience recurrence. Severe fatigue is a sequel of GBS in two thirds of adults.
C. The most critical part of treatment consists of keeping the patient's body functioning during recovery of the nervous system. Physical rehabilitation with a multidisciplinary team including occupational, speech, and physical therapists focuses on proper limb positioning, posture, orthotics, exercise, and strengthening swallowing muscles.
   1. Foot and wrist drop is not uncommon and may require orthotics.
   2. Joint contracture requires active and passive range of motion (ROM).
D. Psychological counseling may be required to help with adaptation.
E. The Centers for Disease Control (CDC) has set up the Vaccine Adverse Event Reporting system (VAERS) to monitor vaccine safety. The CDC and the U.S. Food and Drug Administration (FDA) comanage the VAERS as an early warning system about possible side effects noted following immunization.

Consultation/Referral

A. Consult with a physician if GBS is suspected.

Individual Considerations

A. Geriatrics
   1. Age older than 55 years is a poor prognostic factor.

Resources

CDC Vaccine Adverse Event Reporting System (VAERS): http://vaers.hhs.gov

GBS/CIDP Foundation International: www.gbs-cidp.org

Headache

Definition

A. Headache is a discomfort of the head that is produced from inflammation and/or tightness of the arteries, nerves, and/or muscles of the cranium. Primary headaches are a major cause for missed school and work, loss of productivity at work (presenteeism), and disability in adults.
B. There are multiple types of headaches: Tension-type headaches (TTHs); trigeminal autonomic cephalalgias, including cluster headaches; chronic daily headaches; and new daily-persistent headaches (NDPH) (see Table 22.2). Migraines are discussed in another section of this chapter; see Migraine Headaches. Posttraumatic headaches occur within 7 days after head trauma. Tension headaches are the most frequent type, occurring as part of the postconcussive syndrome. Hypnic headache occurs only in the elderly.
C. NDPHs have many similarities to TTHs and migraines. Other types of headaches, including posttraumatic headache, low CSF volume headache, raised CSF pressure headache, and headaches attributed to infection, should be ruled out. NDPH is unique in that the headache is daily and unremitting almost from the moment of onset, typically in individuals without a prior headache history. There are two subtypes.
   1. Self-limiting, which typically resolves without therapy within several months
   2. Refractory, which is resistant to aggressive treatment programs

Incidence

Headaches are very common, and their incidence depends on age, gender, and type of headache.

A. TTHs, the most common primary headaches, affect 31% to 74% of the population.

TABLE 22.2 International Headache Society Classification of Headaches (ICHD-II)

New Daily-Persistent Headache (NDPH)[a]	Tension-Type Headache (TTH)[b]	Cluster Headache	Medication Overuse Headache (MOH)[c]
Headache that is daily and unremitting from the moment of onset, or very rapidly builds up to continuous and unremitting pain. The pain is typically bilateral, pressing, or tightening in quality and of mild to moderate intensity. There may be photophobia, phonophobia, or mild nausea.	Episodic headache lasting minutes to days. Pain is mild to moderate, typically with bilateral, pressing, or tightening quality. Pain does not worsen with activity.	Episodic or chronic attacks separated by pain-free periods lasting a month or longer. Pain almost always recurs on the same side during a cluster period. May be provoked by alcohol, histamine, or nitroglycerine.	Variable headache that often has a peculiar pattern with characteristics shifting, even within the same day, from migraine-like to TTH.
Diagnostic Criteria	**Diagnostic Criteria**	**Diagnostic Criteria**	**Diagnostic Criteria**
A. Headache that within 3 days of onset fulfills B–D criteria. B. Headache is present daily and is unremitting for > 3 months	A. At least 10 episodes, < 1 day per month on average, and fulfills B–D criteria. B. Headache lasts 30 minutes to 7 days.	A. At least five attacks that fulfill B–D criteria. B. Severe or very severe unilateral, orbital, supraorbital, and/or temporal pain lasting 15–180 minutes if untreated.	A. Present 15 days per month, which fulfills B–D criteria. B. Regular overuse for 3 months of one or more drugs that can be taken for acute/or symptomatic treatment of headaches.
C. At least two of the following pain characteristics 1. Bilateral location 2. Pressing/tightening (non-pulsating) quality 3. Mild to moderate quality 4. Not aggravated by routine physical activity such as walking or climbing	C. At least two of the following characteristics 1. Bilateral location 2. Pressure/tightening, non-pulsating quality 3. Mild to moderate intensity 4. No increase with routine physical activity such as walking or climbing stairs	C. Accompanied by at least one of the following 1. Ipsilateral conjunctival infection and/or lacrimation 2. Ipsilateral nasal congestion and/or rhinorrhea 3. Ipsilateral eyelid edema 4. Ipsilateral forehead and facial sweating 5. Ipsilateral miosis and/or ptosis 6. Restlessness or agitation (usually unable to lie down and characteristically pace the floor)	C. Develops or markedly worsens during medication overuse.
D. Both of the following 1. No more than one of photophobia, phonophobia, or mild nausea 2. Neither moderate or severe nausea nor vomiting	D. Both of the following 1. No nausea or vomiting 2. No more than one photophobia or phonophobia	D. Attacks have a frequency from one every other day to eight per day.	D. Headache resolves or reverts to its previous pattern within 2 months after discontinuing the overused medication. Examples of medications include ergotamine, triptans, analgesics, opioids, and combination analgesics.
E. Not attributed to another disorder	E. Not attributed to another disorder	E. Not attributed to another disorder	

[a]The patient must clearly recall and unambiguously describe the daily headache as unremitting at the moment of onset and build to continuous/unremitting pain.
[b]Previously called common, muscle contraction, stress, ordinary, or psychogenic headache.
[c]Previously called rebound, drug-induced, or medication misuse headache.
Adapted from the International Headache Society Classification of Headaches (ICHD-II).

B. The prevalence of cluster headaches is less than 1% of the population, with men affected more than women.
C. Chronic daily headaches are more common in females than in males.
D. Medication overuse headaches (MOHs) are reported in 20% to 36% of adolescents with daily headaches.

Pathogenesis

A. Because there are different types of headaches, the origin of each type differs. Many people have a combination of the different types of headaches.

Headache causes range from systemic illness, such as infections; medical disorders, such as tumors or hemorrhage; medications; drug use; and/or stress. Tension headaches are headaches that occur due to contracted muscles of the scalp and neck. Cluster headaches have an uncertain etiology; however, they appear to be caused by extracerebral vasodilation.

B. Review environmental/seasonal factors. Headaches may be cyclic in the spring and summer months with allergic rhinitis and in the fall and winter for carbon monoxide poisoning from gas heaters.

C. Medications are associated with headaches; examples include:
   1. Nitroglycerine
   2. Nifedipine
   3. Dipyridamole
   4. SSRIs

Predisposing Factors

A. Tension, stress
B. Cervical, or back, disorders
C. Medications (e.g., nitroglycerine)
D. Bruxism
E. Sleep disorders (e.g., snoring, insomnia)
F. Foods/caffeine/alcohol
G. Hormonal changes
H. Family history of headaches
I. Sexual activity
J. Cough
K. Exertion/exercise
L. Viral/infectious etiologies
M. Poor-fitting dentures
N. Faulty/inefficient gas heating
O. Trigeminal neuralgia (TN)
P. Valsalva maneuvers
Q. Head trauma

Common Complaints

A. Pain and location depend on the type of headache.
B. Characteristics of the headache depend on the type of headache.
C. Depending on the type of headache, other symptoms may coexist, such as lacrimation, nasal congestion, restlessness, and visual changes.

Other Signs and Symptoms

A. Crying
B. Behavioral problems

Subjective Data

A. Use the acronym PQRST for subjective information.

   P: Provocation, or worsening of factors stimulating headaches

   Q: Quality of pain, severity of pain

   R: Region of headache

   S: Strength of pain, evaluate pain on scale of 0 to 10

   T: Time, including onset, frequency, and duration of headaches

B. Assess whether the patient has migraine headaches frequently. Is this the first or worst headache ever experienced by the patient?
C. If recurrent headaches exist, note frequency and patterns of similar headaches.
D. Note whether the patient has ever identified potential triggers of recurring headaches such as dietary, stressors, and odors (i.e., perfumes, cigarette smoke).
E. Identify the location of pain, along with radiation if present.
F. Describe the type of pain: Throbbing, constant, or burning.
G. Assess the presence of associated symptoms: Nausea or vomiting, photophobia, noise sensitivity, or the presence of halos around lights.
H. Determine whether the patient experiences any neurologic symptoms and/or prodromal symptoms prior to a headache.
I. Review the methods used in the past to abort and/or prevent headaches and the results.
J. Inquire about past diagnostic evaluations for headaches.
K. Note a family history of headaches.
L. List current medications, including OTC medications and herbals.
M. Review the patient's medical history for head trauma, allergies, presence of a ventriculoperitoneal (VP) shunt, or other neurologic diagnoses.
N. Is the patient in the second or third trimester of pregnancy?
O. Does the patient present with a fever or have a recent history of infection?
P. Rule out gas exposure.

Physical Examination

Physical exam may be normal unless patient presents with a headache.

A. Check blood pressure, pulse, and respirations (temperature if meningeal signs are present).
B. Inspect
   1. Observe overall appearance for the presence of discomfort, photosensitivity (use of sunglasses indoors), and LOC.
   2. Examine the eyes; perform funduscopic exam.
   3. Inspect the ears, nose, and throat.
C. Auscultate
   1. Listen for bruit at neck, eyes, and head for clinical signs of arteriovenous malformation (AVM).
D. Palpate
   1. Palpate the head, eyes, ears, temporomandibular joint (TMJ) syndrome, sinus cavities, temporal and neck arteries.

2. Palpate cervical vertebrae, cervical muscles, and shoulder regions. Identify potential trigger areas: Occipital nerves leave halfway between the middle of the neck at the back of the neck and lateral to this area. When palpating this trigger area, pain may be reproduced with palpation.
3. Examine the spine and neck muscles.
4. Assess cervical ROM.

E. Perform neurologic exam.
1. Extraocular movements (EOM)
2. Pupil response
3. Getting up from a seated position without any support
4. Walking on tiptoes and heels
5. Tandem gait
6. Romberg test
7. Symmetry on motor, sensory, DTRs, and coordination tests
8. Perform neck flexion for nuchal rigidity.

Diagnostic Tests

Tests are selected based on history and physical exam.

A. Sinus films to rule out sinusitis or a lesion
B. Sleep studies for obstructive sleep apnea
C. CT scan or MRI: Needed if headache is severe, no results are achieved with drug therapy, and/or aura is present.
D. People with any positive neurologic signs of an intracranial process should have neuroimaging.
E. Lab tests are rarely needed for headaches, unless an infectious process is suspected.

Differential Diagnoses

A. Headache
1. Tension
2. Cluster
3. MOH
4. Migraine
5. Combination headache
6. NDPH
7. Hypnic headache (occurs only in the elderly)
8. Cough headache

B. Sinusitis
C. Meningitis: Meningism, acute headache with fever, lethargy, nausea or vomiting, irritability, photophobia, and systemic infection
D. Space-occupying lesion: Subacute and progressive pain, new onset for adults older than 40 years
E. Temporal arteritis: New-onset progressive headache for adults older than 50 years, with presenting symptoms of temporal artery swelling, pain, pulselessness, visual changes, mental sluggishness, systemic symptoms (fever, anorexia, malaise), and ESR greater than 50 mm/hr
F. Carotid dissection: Sudden headache with neck pain, radiating to the face, ear, or eye; onset related to neck movement or trauma, Horner's syndrome, tinnitus, ipsilateral tongue weakness, cervical bruit or tenderness, diplopia, and syncope
G. TMJ syndrome: Jaw claudication, clicking, and locking sensation, ill-fitting dentures
H. Carbon monoxide poisoning
I. Temporal arteritis
J. Trigeminal neural
K. Pregnancy-induced hypertension (PIH)
L. Medication-induced headache: Review side effects of current medications (individual and/or combination of drugs).

Plan

A. General interventions
1. Encourage the patient to restrict associated triggers, such as food, alcohol, and exposure to odors.
2. Encourage the patient to exercise daily.
3. Have the patient begin a stress management routine, including yoga, meditation, and massage.
4. Tell the patient to take medications as prescribed.
5. Cluster headaches can be exacerbated by alcohol.
6. Use ice/heat for muscular tension.
7. Individual and/or family psychotherapy should be considered.
8. Complementary and alternative medicine (CAM)
   a. Nutraceutical options
      i. Magnesium 400 to 600 mg/d
      ii. Riboflavin 400 mg/d
      iii. Coenzyme Q10
      iv. Alpha lipoic acid
   b. Herbal preparations
      i. Feverfew 50 to 82 mg/d
      ii. *Petasites hybridus* (Butterbur)
      iii. *Cannabis* (Marijuana)
   c. Acupuncture
   d. Oxygen/hyperbaric oxygen therapy
   e. Transcutaneous electrical nerve stimulation (TENS) unit
   f. Chiropractic manipulation
   g. Physical therapy
   h. Continuous positive airway pressure (CPAP)
   i. Biofeedback
   j. Relaxation training

B. Patient teaching
  1. Encourage the patient to keep a diary of headaches and associated factors to try to pinpoint headache triggers.
  2. Teach patients who have menstrual headaches to avoid precipitating factors, such as alcohol, tyramine, or phenylethylamine foods; missed meals; and sleeping late.
  3. Discuss sleep hygiene guidelines (see "Sleep Disorders" in Chapter 24, "Psychiatric Guidelines").
  4. For muscular headaches that are nonmenstrual, biofeedback, breathing exercises, and visualization are helpful. Prevention must be stressed. Encourage lifestyle changes and daily exercise.
  5. When patients overuse various analgesics for headaches, paroxysmal migraines can convert into chronic daily headaches. Caution patients regarding this effect.
  6. MOHs occur with the highest incidence involving opioids, butalbital-containing combinations, and acetylsalicylic acid (aspirin)/acetaminophen/caffeine combinations, as well as triptans. Withdrawal of the overused medication is the treatment of choice for MOHs.

C. Pharmaceutical therapy: Therapy should be started at the lowest dosage and titrated up as tolerated, avoiding overuse.
  1. NSAIDs
     a. ASA 650 to 1,000 mg orally; maximal dose 4 g/d
     b. Ibuprofen (Advil) 400 to 800 mg every 8 hours; maximum dose 2.4 g/d
  2. Combination medications
     a. Acetaminophen, butalbital, and caffeine (Fioricet) with or without codeine one to two tablets every 4 hours as needed. Maximum dose is six tablets per day.
     b. ASA, butalbital, and caffeine (Fiorinal) one or two tablets every 4 hours as needed. Caution the patient regarding dependency patterns.
     c. Isometheptene mucate, dichloralphenazone, and acetaminophen (Epidrin or Migratine) one to two capsules every 4 hours if needed, up to eight capsules in a 24-hour period for tension headaches in adults
     d. Acetaminophen, ASA, and caffeine (Excedrin) two tablets every 6 hours. Maximal dose of 4 g of aspirin or acetaminophen.
  3. Cluster or vascular headaches
     a. Verapamil is the agent of choice for prevention therapy with cluster headaches.
     b. Propranolol (Inderal) or carbamazepine 80 mg daily in divided doses. Maximum range 160 to 240 mg daily.
     c. Oxygen 100% therapy has been effective for cluster headaches.
  4. Menstrual headaches
     a. Estrogen supplements or continuous cycling is used to decrease headaches. Have the patient start taking estrogen 2 days before expected migraine and use for 7 days.
     b. Naproxen 275 to 550 mg every 2 to 6 hours (maximum dose 1.5 mg/d) starting 7 days as needed before menses
     c. Ibuprofen 600 mg three times daily
     d. Fluoxetine (Prozac) 10 to 20 mg daily is also used for patients with premenstrual syndrome with luteal phase defect.
  5. Antidepressants may also be utilized for preventive treatment.
  6. Pharmaceutical therapies for chronic daily and NDPHs combine therapy that are used for tension type and migraine headaches.

Follow-Up

A. See the patient in 2 weeks to evaluate how therapies have worked.
B. Evaluate the patient's "headache log" to assist him or her in identifying headache triggers, if present.

Consultation/Referral

A. Consult a physician if headaches are caused by acute problems other than migraine and/or tension headaches.
B. Severe episodes need to be evaluated by a physician for opioid agonists and antagonists, narcotics, and neuroleptics.
C. If medications do not help with headaches, refer the patient to a neurologist.

Individual Considerations

A. Pregnancy
  1. PIH often presents with a headache.
B. Adults: Patients who are premenopausal may see improvement when their estrogen levels are constant, rather than cyclic.
C. Geriatrics
  1. The most common primary headache types in the elderly are tension, migraine, late-life migraine, cluster, and hypnic headaches.
  2. Headaches generally decrease with age; however, hypnic headaches only occur in the elderly. Hypnic headaches awaken patients from sleep and are short-lived.
  3. Serious secondary causes of headaches that increase with age include those associated with:
     a. Temporal arteritis
     b. TN
     c. Sleep apnea
     d. Postherpetic neuralgia
     e. Cervical spondylosis

f. Subarachnoid hemorrhage (SAH)
g. Intracerebral hemorrhage
h. Intracranial neoplasm
i. Postconcussive syndrome.

4. Consider imaging studies in the elderly with unusual presentations of headaches.
5. Consider chronic SDHs with patients who have frequent falls; perform CT scan or MRI for evaluation.
6. Elderly patients may not exhibit any symptoms other than a headache.
7. When medicating the elderly, start dosages low and increase as tolerated.
   a. Naproxen and hydroxyzine are commonly used oral rescue therapies for older adults with migraine or tension headaches.
   b. Oral agents for the prevention of hypnic headaches include caffeine and lithium.
   c. Cough headaches respond to indomethacin or acetazolamide.
8. Consider all contraindications when prescribing medications for headaches in the elderly.
   a. In the presence of cardiovascular disease, ergot derivatives are contraindicated.
   b. Amitriptyline and doxepin are not usually recommended for older individuals because of the risk of cognitive impairment, urinary retention, and cardiac arrhythmia.
   c. Consider renal function prior to prescribing NSAIDs.

Migraine Headache

Definition

A. Migraine headaches are a common medical complaint responsible for a significant disability and loss of quality of life. The economic impact involves loss of workdays, school, social interaction, and loss of productivity while at work (presenteeism). There are three types of migraines described by the International Headache Society (IHS) by type and diagnostic criteria (see Table 22.3).
B. Migraine headaches have been associated with increased risk of cerebral ischemia and an increased risk of cardiac ischemia.

Incidence

Headaches are one of the most common medical complaints. The exact incidence of migraines is unknown since patients self-treat, are underdiagnosed, and are commonly misdiagnosed. Ten to sixteen percent is the overall estimated incidence of migraines in North America and Europe; however, several subsets of migraineurs are noted in the literature.

A. 23% incidence in adolescents
B. 2% of the population has chronic migraines.
C. It is estimated that 38% of migraineurs need preventive therapy, but only 3% to 13% currently use preventive therapy.

Pathogenesis

A. Migraines have broad sensory processing dysfunction, with a prominent perception of pain in the dense somatosensory innervation of intracranial vessels. Current pathophysiologic concepts of migraine and migraine aura include a possible dysfunction of neuromodulatory structures in the brainstem and cortical spreading depression (CSD). Different receptors, including calcitonin gene-related peptide (CGRP), transient receptor potential cation channel subfamily V member (TrpVI [also known as the capsaicin receptor]), and glutamate receptors, are currently being targeted for migraine therapeutics.

Predisposing Factors

A. Family history of migraines
B. Chronic use of OTC analgesics (rebound)
C. Post head trauma
D. Food, odor, light, sound, sleep, weather changes, hormonal changes, and stress triggers
E. Menstruation
F. Obesity
G. Daily habitual snoring is a modest risk factor.
H. Estrogen use

Common Complaints

A. Unilateral headache
B. Frontotemporal area
C. Photophobia, or sensitivity to light
D. Phonophobia, or sensitivity to sound
E. Osmophobia, or hypersensitivity/aversion to smells/odors
F. Nausea with/without vomiting
G. Prodrome phase: Fatigue, reduced concentration, agitation, craving, irritability, depression, frequent yawning, or hyperexcitability hours to days before the onset of aura and headache

Other Signs and Symptoms

A. Muscle tension and neck pain
B. Cutaneous allodynia (pain from stimulus to normal skin or scalp)
C. Sinus congestion
D. Prodrome phase can last 25 hours accompanied by fatigue and a "hangover" headache

Subjective Data

A. Use the acronym PQRST for subjective information.

   P: Provocation, or worsening of factors stimulating headaches
   Q: Quality of pain, severity of pain
   R: Region of headache

TABLE 22.3 International Headache Society Classification of Migraines (ICHD-II)

Migraine Without Aura	Migraine With Aura (There Are Six Subtypes)	Chronic Migraine[a]
Recurrent headache attack lasting 4–72 hours meeting the diagnostic criteria	Recurrent disorder manifesting reversible focal neurological symptoms that usually develop gradually over 5–20 minutes and last for < 60 minutes. Typical aura consists of visual and/or sensory and/or speech symptoms	Chronic migraine that meets the criteria for migraine without aura that occurs with a frequency of at least 15 headache days per month for longer than 3-months duration
Diagnostic Criteria A. At least five attacks that fulfill criteria B–D B. Headache attacks last 4–72 hours (untreated or unsuccessfully treated) C. Has at least two of the following 1. Unilateral location 2. Pulsating quality 3. Moderate or severe intensity 4. Aggravated by or causing avoidance of routine physical activity D. During headache at least one of the following 1. Nausea and/or vomiting 2. Photophobia and phonophobia E. Not attributed to another disorder	**Diagnostic Criteria** A. At least two attacks that fulfill criteria B–D B. Aura consist of at least one of the following but no motor weakness 1. Fully reversible visual symptoms including positive features (e.g., flickering lights, spots, or lines) and/or negative features (i.e., loss of vision) 2. Fully reversible sensory symptoms including positive features (i.e., pins and needles) and/or negative features (i.e., numbness) 3. Fully reversible dysphasic speech disturbance C. At least two of the following 1. Homonymous visual symptoms (i.e., additional loss or blurring of central vision) and/or unilateral sensory symptoms 2. At least one aura symptom develops gradually over > 5 minutes and/or different aura symptoms occur in succession over > 5 minutes 3. Each symptom lasts > 5 minutes and < 60 minutes D. Headache fulfilling criteria B–C: Migraine without aura begins during the aura or follows the aura within 60 minutes E. Not attributed to another disorder	**Diagnostic Criteria** A. Headache, in the absence of medication overuse headache (MOH), on > 15 days per month for at least 3 months B. Occurring in a patient who has had at least 5 attacks fulfilling criteria for migraine without aura. C. On > 8 days per month for at least 3 months headache fulfills C1 and/or C2 criteria noted below. C1. Has at least two of the following 1. Unilateral location 2. Pulsating quality 3. Moderate or severe pain intensity 4. Aggravation by or causing avoidance of routine physical activity *and* at least one of the following a. Nausea and/or vomiting b. Photophobia and phonophobia C2. Treated and relieved by triptan(s) or ergot before the expected development of C1 symptoms D. No medication overuse and not attributed to another causative disorder

[a]A proposed alternative criteria is defined as a chronic headache for at least four migraine days and at least 15 total headache days, with at least 50% of headache days meeting criteria for migraine.
Adapted from the International Headache Society (ICHD-II).

S: Strength of pain; evaluate pain on a scale of 0 to 10

T: Time, including onset, frequency, and duration of headaches

B. Assess whether the patient has migraine headaches frequently. Is this the first or worst headache ever experienced by the patient?
C. If recurrent headaches exist, note frequency and patterns of similar headaches.
D. Note whether the patient has ever identified potential triggers of recurring headaches such as menstruation, diet, stressors, and odors (i.e., perfumes and cigarette smoke).
E. Identify the location of the pain, along with radiation if present.
F. Describe the type of pain: Throbbing, constant, or burning.
G. Assess the presence of associated symptoms: Nausea or vomiting, photophobia, and noise sensitivity.
H. Determine whether the patient experiences any neurologic symptoms and/or prodromal symptoms prior to headache.
I. Review the methods used in the past to abort and/or prevent headaches and the results.
J. Inquire about past diagnostic evaluations for headaches.
K. Note a family history of headaches.
L. List current medications, including OTC medications and herbal products.
M. Review the patient's medical history for head trauma, infection, allergies, presence of a VP shunt, or other neurologic diagnoses.

Physical Examination

Physical exam may be normal unless the patient presents with a headache.

A. Check blood pressure, pulse, and respirations (temperature if meningeal signs are present).
B. Inspect
   1. Observe overall appearance for the presence of discomfort, photosensitivity (use of sunglasses indoors), and LOC.
   2. Examine the eyes; perform funduscopic exam.
   3. Inspect the ears, nose, and throat.

C. Ausculate
   1. Listen for bruit at neck, eyes, and head for clinical signs of atrioventricular (AV) malformation.
D. Palpate
   1. Palpate the head, eyes, ears, TMJ, sinus cavities, temporal, and neck arteries.
   2. Palpate cervical vertebrae, cervical muscles, and shoulder regions. Identify potential trigger areas: Occipital nerves leave halfway between the middle of the neck at the back of the neck and lateral to this area. When palpating this trigger area, pain may be reproduced with palpation.
   3. Examine the spine and neck muscles.
   4. Assess the cervical ROM.
E. Perform neurologic exam.
   1. EOM
   2. Pupil response
   3. Getting up from a seated position without any support
   4. Walking on tiptoes and heels
   5. Tandem gait
   6. Romberg test
   7. Symmetry on motor, sensory, DTRs, and coordination tests

Diagnostic Tests

A. Neuroimaging, CT, and MRI are based on patient history and physical examination.
   1. Adults with stable headaches, a normal examination, and absence of seizures do not require neuroimaging.
   2. An emergent noncontrast CT should be obtained when the patient complains of "the worst headache ever" or when focal neurologic findings, nuchal rigidity, or altered mental status exist.
   3. The presence of personality changes, depression, and a migraine may indicate a temporal lobe tumor.
   4. The presence of orbital bruit requires neuroimaging.
   5. Neuroimaging is recommended for adults with onset of headache after age 40.
   6. Onset of headache with exertion, cough, or sexual activity should be considered for neuroimaging.
B. An LP may be indicated with altered mental status or focal findings.
C. Order sinus films to rule out sinusitis or a lesion.
D. Laboratory tests are not required for most patients with typical symptoms and a negative physical examination.
   1. Drug screen may be indicated.
   2. Complete metabolic panel (CMP)
   3. CBC
   4. Thyroid-stimulating hormone (TSH)
   5. Sedimentation rate

Differential Diagnoses

A. Migraine
   1. Migraine with aura
   2. Migraine without aura
B. Other types of headaches
   1. MOH
   2. Common headache
   3. Cluster headache
   4. Combination headache
   5. Chronic daily headache
   6. Tension headache
   7. Hypnic headaches (geriatrics)
C. Sinusitis
D. Space-occupying lesion: Subacute and progressive pain, new onset for adults older than 40 years
E. Temporal arteritis: New onset progressive headache for adults older than 50 years
F. Carotid dissection: Sudden headache with neck pain radiating to the face, ear, or eye
G. TMJ syndrome
H. Meningitis
I. Brain abscess
J. Encephalitis
K. Idiopathic intracranial HTN

Plan

A. General interventions: There are four main approaches to migraine therapy.
   1. Nonpharmacologic interventions
      a. Adjust habits to maintain a routine pattern of sleeping. This is especially important to maintain on weekends and vacations.
      b. Do not skip breakfast. Eat regular meals with one or two snacks.
      c. Avoid food triggers identified by the patient's migraine diary.
      d. Encourage drinking no more than two caffeinated beverages a day.
      e. Hydration is important.
      f. Encourage at least 30 minutes of exercise 3 to 7 days a week.
      g. Cold compresses
   2. Behavioral interventions
      a. Use relaxation techniques such as yoga, deep breathing, meditation, and guided imagery.
      b. Biofeedback is an adjunct to relaxation training.
      c. Cognitive behavioral therapy
      d. Psychiatric therapy
   3. Complementary and alternative interventions
      a. Acupuncture
      b. Nutraceuticals, including magnesium and coenzyme Q10

c. Vitamins: Riboflavin (B_2)
d. Herbal (nonregulated by the FDA), including feverfew, Petasites (purified extract of butterbur root extract), and MIG-99 (extract of *tanacetum parthenium* [feverfew])
e. Physical therapy
f. Hypnosis
g. Supraorbital transcutaneous stimulation (STS) was approved by the FDA in 2014 for patients 18 years and older.
   i. The precise mode of action is not known. The device is used daily, once per day for 20 minutes.
   ii. The stimulation electrole is placed on the forehead covering the supratrochlear and supraorbital nerves.
   iii. Side effects include intense paresthesia, sleepiness during the 20-minute session, and headache after the session
   iv. The STS device does not completely prevent migraines and did not reduce the intensity of migraines in studies. Therefore, the STS can be used concomitantly with medications
h. Chiropractic manipulation and occlusal adjustment are also noted in the literature.
i. Onabotulinumtoxin A has been tested extensively and has been found to be ineffective in episodic migraines but has been approved by the FDA in chronic headaches.

4. Pharmacologic interventions: Patients should be counseled to take medications as prescribed. When patients overuse various analgesics for headaches, paroxysmal migraines can convert into chronic daily headaches.

B. Patient teaching: Encourage the patient to keep a headache diary; an example of a migraine diary is available at www.webmd.com/migraines-headaches/guide/headache-diary.
   1. Examples of food triggers are aspartame, saccharin, red wine, alcohol, chocolate, aged cheese, oranges, tomatoes, avocado, nuts, onions, tyramine, phenylethylamine, monosodium glutamate (MSG), and nitrates and nitrites found in hot dogs, luncheon meat, and sausage.
   2. Examples of odor triggers are tobacco smoke, perfumes, and strong odors.
   3. Examples of visual triggers include strobe lights, bright lights/sunlight, fluorescent lights, and glare.
   4. Other triggers are medications, barometric weather changes, too much/too little sleep, and high altitude.

C. The 2014 American Heart Association/American Stroke Association guidelines for the prevention of strokes in women state that because of the increased stroke risk seen in women with migraine headaches with aura, and smoking, it is reasonable to strongly recommend smoking cessation.

D. Pharmaceutical therapy (see Table 22.4)

E. **The choice of drug therapy prophylactic agents depends on the patient's comorbid conditions such as cardiac, respiratory, psychiatric, sleep, and gastrointestinal disorders.**
   1. Many drugs commonly utilized for migraines are not FDA approved for migraine therapy, including amitriptyline, nortriptyline, and SSRIs.
   2. Antiepileptic medications, including valproic acid (Depakote) and topiramate (Topamax), are FDA approved for migraine prophylaxis. Topiramate should not be prescribed or should be discontinued for a history of kidney stones.
   3. Beta blockers are approved for migraine prophylaxis; however, they must be used with caution for patients with comorbidities such as asthma, depression, diabetes, and thyroid disease.
   4. There are currently several triptans and one triptan/NSAID combination. Triptans are widely used for menstrual migraines. Triptans should be used cautiously in patients with cardiovascular comorbidities. Triptans should not be given within 24 hours of an ergot.
   5. Dihydroergotamine mesylate (Migranal) is not to be used for patients during pregnancy or with heart disease, or for use with ischemic or vasospastic circulatory disease. Use ergot derivatives selectively. These medications are not to be used on a long-term basis or more than three times per week. There is an associated risk of strokes when using these medications due to the vasoconstrictive mechanisms of the medications.
   6. Ergots and triptans should not be given within 14 days of an MAO inhibitor.
   7. Antiemetics are prescribed as needed for nausea/vomiting associated with migraines.
   8. Multiple drugs are used off-label for migraines.

Follow-Up

A. See the patient in 2 weeks to evaluate how therapies have worked.

B. Evaluate the patient's headache diary to assist him or her in identifying headache triggers or patterns, such as prior to menstruation. Utilize the information documented in the diary as a tool for reevaluating the need for other tests and consultations.

C. Monitor liver enzymes and CBC periodically with antiseizure medication prophylaxis.

TABLE 22.4 Medications for Migraines

Medication	Class	Instructions for Adult Dosing	Acute vs. Prophylaxis
Sumatriptan (Imitrex)	Triptan	Initially 25–100 mg. May repeat at 2-hour intervals. (Maximum dose 200 mg/24 hours.) Also available subcutaneous and intranasal	Acute treatment
Sumatriptan (Alsuma)	Triptan	Initially 6 mg subcutaneous. May repeat in 1 hour. (Maximum of 12 mg/24 hours.)	Acute treatment and cluster headaches
Sumatriptan iontophoretic system (Zecuity)	Triptan	Transdermal system (TDS) that uses a low electrical current for drug delivery. Each patch delivers 6.5 mg of sumatriptan through the skin over 4 hours. No more than two should be used in a 24-hours period. The second TDS should be applied no sooner than 2 hours after activation of the first TDS.	Acute treatment migraine with and without aura
Rizatriptan (Maxalt)	Triptan	Initially 5–10 mg. May repeat at 2-hour intervals. (Maximum dose 30 mg/24 hours.) Available in oral or disintegrating tablets	Acute treatment
Zolmitriptan (Zomig)	Triptan	Initially 2.5–5 mg. May repeat in 2 hours. (Maximum dose 10 mg/24 hours.) Available in oral or disintegrating tablets	Acute treatment
Naratriptan (Amerge)	Triptan	Initially 1–2.5 mg. May repeat in 4 hours. (Maximum dose 5 mg/24 hours.)	Acute treatment
Almotriptan (Axert)	Triptan	Initially 6.25–12.5 mg. May repeat in 2 hours. (Maximum dose 25 mg/24 hours.)	Acute treatment
Eletriptan (Relpax)	Triptan	Initially 40 mg. May repeat in 2 hours. (Maximum dose 80 mg/24 hours.)	Acute treatment
Frovatriptan (Frova)	Triptan	Initially 2.5 mg. May repeat in 2 hours. (Maximum dose 7.5 mg/24 hours.)	Acute treatment
Sumatriptan with Naproxen sodium (Treximet)	Triptan + NSAID	1 tablet = sumatriptan 85 mg + 500 mg naproxen sodium. Initially 1 tablet. May repeat in 2 hours. (Maximum dose 2 tabs/24 hours.)	Acute treatment
Dihydroergotamine mesylate (Migranal)	Ergot derivative	Only available in intranasal spray. Initially 1 spray in each nostril. May repeat in 15 minutes. (Maximum 6 sprays/24 hours with a maximum of 8 sprays week.)	Acute treatment
Ergotamine tartrate + caffeine	Ergot derivative	Initially 2 tablets at onset. May repeat 1 tablet every 1/2 hour. (Maximum dose 6 tablets/24 hours with a maximum of 10 tablets week.) Also available in suppositories.	Acute treatment migraines and cluster headaches
Propranolol (Inderal)	Beta blocker	Initially 80 mg per day. May titrate up to 240 mg per day.	Migraine prophylaxis
Timolol	Beta blocker	10–15 mg twice a day: May titrate up to 30 mg per day.	Migraine prophylaxis
Topiramate (Topamax)	Antiseizure	Requires titration Week 1: 25 mg every bedtime Week 2: 25 mg/a.m. and 25 mg at bedtime Week 3: 25 mg/a.m. and 50 mg at bedtime Week 4: 50 mg/a.m. and 50 mg at bedtime (Maximum 100 mg/24 hours.)	Migraine prophylaxis
Valproic acid (Depakote)	Antiseizure	500 mg daily for 1 week, then increase up to 1 g per day	
Amitriptyline	Antidepressant	Initially 75 mg per day in divided doses *or* 50–100 mg at bedtime. (Maximum 150 mg/24 hours.)	Migraine prophylaxis
Nortriptyline (Pamelor)	Antidepressant	Initially 25 mg, three to four times a day. (Maximum dose 150 mg per day.)	Migraine prophylaxis
Fluoxetine (Prozac)	SSRI	Initially 20 mg/a.m. Increase if needed after several weeks. Doses > 20 mg per day should be given in divided doses in the a.m. and at noon. (Maximum 80 mg/24 hours.)	Migraine prophylaxis

Consultation/Referral

A. Consult a physician if headaches are caused by acute problems other than migraine and/or tension headaches.
B. If medications do not help with headaches, refer the patient to a neurologist.
C. Send the patient to the emergency department for any neurologic, life-threatening signs.

Individual Considerations

A. Pregnancy: Many medications are contraindicated in pregnancy.
B. Geriatrics
   1. Headaches decrease after age 50. Headache onset after age 50 is associated with epilepsy, essential tremor, ischemic stroke, mood disorders, asthma, and patent foramen ovale.
   2. Consider imaging studies for elderly patients that present with unusual headaches.
   3. Consider chronic SDHs with patients who have frequent falls; perform CT scan or MRI for evaluation. Elderly patients may not exhibit any symptoms other than a headache.
   4. Consider all contraindications when prescribing medications; many elderly patients have cardiovascular disease, which is contraindicated with ergot derivatives.

Mild Traumatic Brain Injury—*Kimberly D. Waltrip*

Definition

Head injury is defined as any external structural damage (i.e., a blow, a jolt, a bump) or functional impairment of cranial content, including the scalp, skull, meninges, blood vessels, or brain. Any of the following may occur immediately after the initial injury: Loss of consciousness or decreased LOC, memory loss specific to events immediately pre- or postinjury, altered mental status, and neuro deficits involving motor strength, balance, vision, sensation, and speech. Mild traumatic brain injury (MTBI) results in a disruption of brain function (altered mental status) indicating severity of the initial injury. MTBI-related deficits are often mild in nature without overt symptoms. Radiographic testing is negative for anatomic abnormality (e.g., cerebral edema, hemorrhage). *Concussion* is a commonly used term to describe MTBI, where a loss of consciousness may have occurred; confusion is also associated. Ninety percent of patients with concussive injuries do not experience decreased LOC. Serious complications of MTBI include asymptomatic extradural hematomas, fatal thrombosis of the basilar artery, and hemorrhage from existing conditions such as fibrous dysplasia or essential thrombocytopenia.

The American Academy of Neurology offers the following guidelines for grading the severity of concussions.

A. Grade I: Confusion, symptoms last less than 15 minutes, no loss of consciousness.
B. Grade II: Symptoms last longer than 15 minutes, no loss of consciousness.
C. Grade III: Loss of consciousness (IIIa, unresponsive period lasts seconds; IIIb, unresponsive period lasts minutes).

The Glasgow Coma Scale (GCS) can also be used to grade the severity of concussions. The GCS score of 13 to 15 that is measured approximately 30 minutes after the injury would be classified as a mild traumatic brain injury. The GCS can be found at www.bt.cdc.gov/masscasualties/pdf/glasgow-coma-scale.pdf.

Incidence

A. An estimated 1.7 million head injuries occur in the United States each year, with 275,000 hospital admissions and 52,000 deaths. Of these, approximately 75% to 90% are classified as MTBIs. Many individuals with MTBI do not seek medical attention, affecting the actual number of reported cases.
B. Elderly patients (> 65 years) represent 10% of patients with a MTBI; however, this population represents approximately 50% of traumatic brain injury (TBI)-related deaths.

Predisposing Factors

A. Motor vehicle accidents (MVAs)
B. Assaults
C. Sports- and recreation-related trauma
D. Male gender
E. Ages of increased incidence
   1. 0 to 4 years
   2. 15 to 19 years
   3. 65 years and older
F. Military occupation (i.e., exposure to blasts)
G. Falls

Pathogenesis

A. Head-injured patients can potentially sustain two different types of injuries: *Primary* (impact) injury and *secondary* injury.
   1. A primary injury is a direct result from the injury and occurs at the time of initial insult. This type of injury is purely mechanical and may be focal (contusion or laceration, bone fragmentation), or diffuse, as in concussion or diffuse axonal injury (DAI). These injuries do not require surgical intervention.
   2. Secondary injury is caused by a flow-metabolism mismatch. It is a complication of primary brain damage. This includes

ischemic and hypoxic damage, cerebral edema, intracranial hemorrhage (ICH), and the impact of prolonged increased intracranial pressure (ICP), hydrocephalus, and infection. Secondary injury has delayed onset, occurring in a matter of seconds, minutes, hours, or days.

Common Complaints

A. Headaches that are often constant, generalized, or frontal; may last days or weeks
B. Brief amnestic epoch surrounding impact
C. Faintness
D. Nausea/vomiting
E. Changes in vision, often slight blurring
F. Drowsiness
G. Loss of consciousness
H. Confusion

Other Signs and Symptoms

Other presenting symptoms and complaints are identified in four categories: Physical, emotional, cognitive, and sleep-cycle disturbances.

A. Physical
   1. Reported or observed injury to the head
   2. Dizziness
   3. Fatigue
   4. Decrease/change in balance
   5. Photophobia
   6. Sensitivity to noise
   7. Numbness/tingling
   8. Seizures, delayed onset status postinjury
B. Emotional
   1. Irritability
   2. Nervousness
   3. Depression
C. Cognitive
   1. Difficulty concentrating
   2. Memory impairment
      a. Short-term memory loss
      b. Repetition
   3. Confusion
   4. Slow responses/difficulty processing
   5. Changes in reaction time
   6. Changes in speech
   7. Disorientation
   8. Fatigue
D. Sleep-cycle disturbance
   1. Feeling "drowsy"
   2. Difficulty falling asleep
   3. Sleeping more or less than usual

Subjective Data

A. Obtain a description of injury from the patient or witness of the traumatic event, if possible. Identify the cause of the head injury, how it occurred (direct or indirect injury), and what type of force was exerted.
B. Confirm the patient's LOC at the time of injury and after injury. Inquire about amnesia (retrograde and anterograde), which might predict increased severity of the injury. Ask about the occurrence, whether it was observed by others, and duration.
C. Review initial and current symptoms (see Common Complaints, Signs and Symptoms). Include description, location, severity, and onset of symptoms. It is important to note what has happened since the actual injury. It is not uncommon for patients to report symptoms that reemerge or worsen with exertion.
D. Obtain the patient's medical history, especially of previous head injuries. Learning disabilities (e.g., attention deficit hyperactivity disorder [ADHD]), developmental disorders, depression, anxiety, sleep disorders, and mood disorders should also be noted since these can affect recovery.
E. Review current medications; certain medications like warfarin (Coumadin) can be a predisposing factor that can lead to complications.
F. Document any drug and alcohol history.
G. Ask significant others if they have noticed any additional signs or symptoms, behavioral changes, or evidence of seizure activity.

Physical Examination

A. Check pulse, respirations, and blood pressure.
B. Inspect
   1. Observe overall appearance. Note LOC.
   2. Inspect the skin and head for obvious injury. Periorbital ecchymosis ("raccoon's eyes"), postauricular/mastoid ecchymosis (Battle's sign), or evidence of a CSF leak (otorrhea, rhinorrhea) suggests a basilar skull fracture.
   3. Examine the eyes for the presence of papilledema (indicates increased ICP), proptosis, and periorbital edema.
   4. Examine the ears (hemotympanum or possible laceration to the external canal), nose, and throat.
   5. Examine for facial fractures.
   6. Examine for any trauma (e.g., malalignment, abnormal curvature) to the cervical spine.
C. Auscultate
   1. Auscultate over the globes of the eyes if warranted (bruit may indicate traumatic carotid-cavernous fistula).
   2. Auscultate carotid arteries bilaterally if warranted (bruit may indicate carotid dissection).
   3. Auscultate the heart and lungs if cardiovascular etiology is suspected.
   4. Auscultate the abdomen, if other injuries have occurred from incidental injury such as a contact sport or motor vehicle accident (MVA).

D. Palpate
  1. Palpate for instability of the facial bones, including the zygomatic arch: Can have a palpable step-off with orbital rim fractures.
  2. If appropriate, palpate the abdomen and the entire posterior spine to rule out any other incidental injury.

E. Neurologic examination
  1. Assess mental status and memory. Determine whether the patient is awake, alert, cooperative, and oriented (to person, place, time, and situation). Temporary impairment of memory is one of the most common deficits after a head injury.
  2. Assess CN function.
     a. Ophthalmoscopic/visual exam (CN II)
     b. Pupillary response (CN III)
     c. EOM (CNs III, IV, VI)
     d. Facial sensation and muscles of mastication (CN V)
     e. Facial expression and taste (CN VII)
  3. Perform a motor examination on all four extremities.
  4. Perform a sensory exam on all four extremities.

Diagnostic Tests

A. A plain film of the skull is usually not obtained for a minor traumatic injury. If the patient has suspected skull fracture or clinical indications for imaging, a CT scan is preferred. This type of imaging will usually reveal any linear or basilar skull fractures.

B. CT scan is indicated for patients with the following:
  1. Decreasing consciousness during or after the injury
  2. Focal neurologic deficits
  3. Potential, penetrating, or depressed skull fractures
  4. Increasing or persistent severe headache with nausea or vomiting
  5. Seizures postinjury
  6. Alcohol or substance intoxication
  7. Amnesia status postinjury
  8. Unreliable or questionable accuracy regarding the history of the injury

C. Consider anteroposterior (AP) and lateral spine films for suspected soft tissue injury or vertebral fracture, especially if the patient has experienced an amnestic episode or cannot recall the accident.

D. Drug screen

E. Blood alcohol level

Differential Diagnoses

A. Concussion (MTBI)
B. Contusion
C. ICH
D. Shearing injury
E. Skull fracture
F. SAH, traumatic
G. Subdural hematoma (SDH)
H. Epidural hematoma (EDH)
I. Vascular occlusion or dissection

Plan

A. General interventions
  1. Admit to the hospital for decreased LOC, seizure activity, focal deficits, penetrating or depressed skull fracture, vomiting, serious facial injuries, and positive head CT findings.
  2. Hospitalization may be required if the patient has an injured middle meningeal artery or if venous sinus or fractures posteriorly in the skull are suspected. Posterior fossa hematomas may present suddenly (will see a wide pulse pressure).
  3. Consider possible secondary injuries including cerebral edema, cerebral infarction, cerebral hemorrhage, hydrocephalus, and infection.
  4. The patient should not be impaired from alcohol or other drugs when leaving the clinic, which can impact and potentially mask neurologic function or emerging deficits.
  5. Hospital admission should be considered for patients without home observation/supervision.
  6. Discuss suspected abuse with the patient in a private setting.

B. Patient teaching
  1. See the Section III Patient Teaching Guide for this chapter, "Mild Head Injury."
  2. Provide instruction regarding safety and accident prevention, including the following.
     a. Use safety helmets.
     b. Use safety belts.
     c. Never drive or operate machinery under the influence.
     d. Remove scatter rugs and other objects that would increase fall risk.
     e. Use nonslip mats in the shower/bathtub.
     f. Install grab bars in the shower/bathtub.
     g. Always keep stairs, floors, and hallways clean and clear from clutter.
     h. Install handrails in stairways.
     i. Wear adequate, correct protective gear related to athletic games and work.
     j. Use helmets for biking and other sports.
  3. Recommend regular physical activity on most days of the week for elderly patients. Regular exercise will increase upper and lower body strength and balance. Improved strength and balance will help to prevent unintentional falls.

C. Pharmaceutical therapy
   1. Analgesics: Acetaminophen 650 mg every 6 to 8 hours as needed for headache (do not exceed 3,000 mg/d).
   2. TCAs may be used for posttraumatic migraines.

Follow-Up

A. Patients with injuries mild enough to be discharged may be observed. Patients with normal examinations in the outpatient setting generally do not require routine follow-up.
B. Assessment of driving ability of the elderly should be done after an MTBI from an MVA.
C. Postconcussion symptoms may continue for some period of time. The use of the Rivermead Post-Concussion Symptoms Questionnaire may be helpful for serial evaluation. The Rivermead tool is available at www.tbi-impact.org/cde/mod_templates/12_F_06_Rivermead.pdf.

Consultation/Referral

A. Refer all patients to the emergency department for the following:
   1. Focal neurologic deficit(s)
   2. Decreasing LOC
   3. Persistent headaches, nausea, and vomiting
   4. Seizures, any other evidence of skull fractures
   5. Neuropsychological dysfunction
B. Refer to a neurologist to evaluate postconcussive syndrome for continued complaints (i.e., irritability, fatigue, headaches, difficulty concentrating, dizziness, and memory problems). Further evaluation including MRI and electroencephalographic (EEG) testing may be needed.
C. Refer to a psychologist trained in neuropsychological testing (indicated for patients with mild head injury). The assessment tools evaluate brain function in the areas of attention/concentration, initiation/planning, motor/sensory skills, visual perception, learning and memory, language, speed of processing information/reaction time, and complex problem solving.

Individual Considerations

A. Geriatrics
   1. The number one risk factor in older adults for a head injury is unintentional falls. This is three times greater than in other age groups.
   2. The second highest risk factor for adults older than 65 years of age is MVAs due to slower vision problems, slower reflexes, alcohol, and medication.
   3. Medications such as aspirin and anticoagulant therapies increase the complication of a head injury.
   4. Limited studies exist on the elderly and MTBI. However, findings suggest that elderly patients who experience a MTBI have a higher mortality rate and increased frequency of intracerebral hematomas, and show an increased risk of cognitive deficits after a MTBI.
   5. Mortality is greatest among the elderly following an MTBI. MTBI increases their risk of premature death.

Resources

American Academy of Neurology 2013 evidence-based guideline update for the evaluation and management of concussions in sports is available at www.neurology.org/content/80/24/2250.full.html

Brain Injury Resource Center: www.headinjury.com

Brain Injury Resource Foundation, 1841 Montreal Road, Suite 220, Tucker, GA 30084, 678-937-1555 or toll free at 888334-2424, www.birf.info

Injury Association of America: www.biausa.org; About brain injury http://biausa.fyrian.com/about-brain-injury.htm

National Collegiate Athletic Association (NCAA) has concussion fact sheets for student athletes and for coaches. http://fs.ncaa.org/Docs/health_safety/ConFactSheetcoaches.pdf

TBI Resource Center: www.braininjuryresources.org

Multiple Sclerosis—*Kimberly D. Waltrip*

Definition

A. MS is an autoimmune degenerative disease that damages neuronal axons and breaks down myelin sheaths. The process of inflammatory demyelination varies in progression with recurrent relapse and remission of symptoms over time. The most common symptoms include visual disturbances, spastic paraparesis, and bladder dysfunction. The course of MS is typically intermittent with periodic exacerbations occurring in various areas of the central nervous system (CNS).
B. MS can also present more acutely in severity, progression, and variety of symptoms. Early diagnosis is difficult, but crucial for effective treatment. An MS attack or *exacerbation* lasts at least 24 hours, occurring without fever or any infectious process. Complete recovery after the first exacerbation is common, presenting as a clinically isolated syndrome, but typically converting to MS within 5 years. Subsequent progression of the disease with recurrent exacerbations diminishes physical function over time.
C. The loss of myelin leads to neurological deficits in vision, speech, gait, writing, and memory, and can affect the swallow or cough reflex. Individuals typically present to the emergency department upon relapse with 80% experiencing exacerbations of previous

deficits. Clinical diagnosis is supported when at least one reported exacerbation correlates with MS-related findings obtained during the neurological exam, with MRI, or with visual evoked potential (VEP) studies if visual disturbances are reported.

D. There are four categories of MS.
   1. *Relapsing-remitting (RRMS)* affects approximately 85% of individuals with MS; exacerbations of symptoms with periods of remission occur.
   2. *Primary progressive (PPMS)* is a less common form of MS that accounts for around 10% of MS cases; it progresses slowly without periods of exacerbations or remission.
   3. *Secondary progressive (SPMS)* is not unusual in individuals with RRMS. Progression of this particular disease process occurs over time with or without periods of remission. Symptoms do not decrease or stabilize in terms of severity.
   4. *Progressive-relapsing (PRMS)* involves patterns of RRMS and relapsing-progressive symptoms. PRMS is rare, affecting less than 5% that have MS of intermediate severity.

Incidence and Prevalence

A. Currently, the Multiple Sclerosis Foundation estimates 400,000 individuals in the United States have been diagnosed with MS and that there are a total of 2.3 million cases worldwide (as reported by other international organizations). It is one of the leading causes of disability in young adults. These statistics are challenged when U.S. physicians are not required to report new cases of MS and when diagnosis is questionably accurate. The signs and symptoms of MS may not be recognized or reported initially, nor when persisting over time; they may also be defined as other disease processes.

B. MS is typically diagnosed in adults between 20 and 50 years of age. Between 4% and 9% of individuals with MS experience onset of symptoms after age 50. However, "late-onset MS (LOMS)" has been diagnosed in adults older than age 55. The occurrence of MS is even less prevalent in those older than age 60. This may be associated with improved health care and longevity.

Pathogenesis

A. The cause of MS is unknown. A suspected combination of genetic predisposition and a trigger (chronic viral infections, environmental factors, metabolic issues) may create an autoimmune disorder that facilitates the degenerative disease process.

B. Autoimmune attacks on the myelin sheaths of neurons initiate an inflammatory response, followed by eventual plaque formation and scarring, the hallmark characteristic of the disease.

C. A loss of saltatory conduction is noted. Axonal death occurs during this acute inflammatory response, explaining any permanent disability. The associated inflammation and edema around a MS lesion, along with myelin and axonal loss, contribute to the associated neurologic deficit. A limited amount of remyelination and the eventual resolution of inflammation will allow a certain degree of recovery with remission. With each exacerbation, there is a lesser degree of recovery and subsequent decrease in function.

Predisposing Factors

A. Family history of MS
B. Female gender (two times more likely than men to develop MS)
C. Age 20 to 50 (onset can vary from age 10 to 70)
D. Caucasian race (Northern European ancestry)
E. Environment (living in temperate zones, e.g., Canada, northern areas of the United States, Europe). This is associated with prevalence, but no direct link has been established at this time; it is suspected that this distance from the equator causes a vitamin D deficiency secondary to a lack of direct sunlight, contributing to the development of MS.
F. Previous chronic viral infection *may* increase susceptibility.
G. Smoking

Common Complaints

A. Sensory loss (paresthesia) is often reported early in the course of the disease.
B. Visual disturbances: Diplopia upon lateral gaze (occurs in 33% of individuals with MS), blurred vision, loss of vision, and ocular pain
C. Urinary incontinence, frequency, hesitancy, or urgency (> 90% of individuals with MS report bladder dysfunction)
D. Fatigue (in up to 90% of individuals with MS)
E. Weakness in one or more extremities
F. Gait imbalance (within 15 years of onset, 50% will require assistance during ambulation)

Other Signs and Symptoms

A. Babinski response
B. Spasticity (usually in lower extremities)
C. Depression (nearly 50% of cases; also reported effects on memory, attention, and concentration)
D. Hyperreflexia
E. Loss of proprioception
F. Impotence (males)
G. Impaired cognition: Subjective difficulties with attention, concentration, short-term memory, planning, and judgment; dementia reported in 3% of individuals with late-stage MS.
H. Dysarthria
I. Reduced libido (in both males and females)

J. Constipation
K. Pain
L. TN (rare)
M. Dysphagia (may also have recurrent respiratory infections secondary to aspiration)
N. Vertigo (in 30%–50% of individuals with MS)

Subjective Data

A. Establish location and onset of symptoms. Is this the first time the patient has experienced the symptom in question? Was the onset acute or insidious?
B. Ask the patient to describe the quality and severity of the symptom and how it has evolved over time, including duration. Is there a relapse-remitting pattern? Is the symptom progressing in severity?
C. Ask the patient if any associated factors aggravate or alleviate the symptom. Does hot weather (as well as hot tubs, saunas, and overexertion) aggravate the condition? Does rest help? Did the symptom resolve spontaneously?
D. Establish if any viral or bacterial infections occurred prior to onset of symptoms.
E. Evaluate visual complaints, including the presence of scotoma, decreased color perception, diplopia, decreased acuity, or painful extraocular eye movements. Is visual deterioration induced by exercise, a hot meal, or a hot bath (the Uhthoff phenomenon)?

Physical Examination

A. Check blood pressure, pulse, and respirations.
B. Inspect
   1. Perform a complete eye exam (use Snellen eye chart; test CN II, III, IV, and VI).
      a. 50% of individuals with MS present with retrobulbar involvement but have no abnormal findings upon fundoscopic exam.
      b. Anterior involvement causes papillitis; look for the presence of macular star.
      c. Assess pupillary response bilaterally; look for pendular nystagmus or sinusoidal involuntary oscillations in one or both eyes, and/or loss of smooth eye pursuit.
   2. Perform a neurological and a musculoskeletal exam.
      a. Sensory: Test for perception of sharp versus dull stimulus, heat versus cold stimulus, ability to localize pain, proprioception, and vibratory sense, utilizing the tuning fork to evaluate.
      b. Motor strength (test all extremities); also observe for increased tone (spasticity), clonus, and tremors.
      c. Romberg test and heel-to-toe tandem gait testing. (Evaluate for ataxia, cerebellar involvement.)
      d. Finger-to-nose testing and heel-to-shin testing (rule out dystaxia)
      e. Check DTRs to assess for hyperreflexia; Babinski response may also be present in individuals with MS.
      f. Assess mental status (orientation to person, place, time, and situation); test short-term memory and the ability to plan—impaired planning is a cognitive deficit associated with MS.
      g. Assess for pain: Include location, descriptive characteristics, onset, duration, timing and setting, aggravating factors, alleviating factors, and any other associated information.
      h. Assess for depression, especially with progression of symptoms.

Diagnostic Tests

A. There is no specific confirmatory test for MS.
B. MRI is the test of choice supporting clinical diagnosis of MS. An MRI of the brain will reveal the associated plaques when present, but it cannot determine whether these particular lesions are specific to MS (similar radiographic findings are noted with other diseases).
   1. Transverse myelitis lesions identified with MRI may convert to MS over time.
C. CSF analysis: Characteristics of MS include the presence of oligoclonal bands (85%–90% of MS cases), increased IgG (greater than 12%), and increased white blood cells (WBCs) (greater than 5%).
D. Evoked response (ER) or evoked potential (EP): Several different tests evaluate brain function and nerve conduction with nerve velocity (NCV), detecting subtle changes in brainstem function with hearing (BAER), visual interpretation and perception (VEP), evoked visual response to flash and pattern reversal (VER), and sensation involving the peripheral and CNSs using somatosensory evoked potentials (SSEPs).
E. CBC with differential
F. Serum glucose to rule out hypoglycemia and chronic hyperglycemia as potential causes of neurologic findings

Differential Diagnoses

A. MS
B. CNS lymphoma
C. CNS infection
D. Acute disseminated encephalomyelitis (ADEM)
E. Tumor: Brainstem, cerebellar, or spinal cord
F. Amyotrophic lateral sclerosis (ALS)
G. Systemic lupus erythematosus (SLE)
H. Syringomyelia
I. Progressive multifocal leukoencephalopathy (PML)

J. Sarcoidosis
K. Sjogren's syndrome
L. Acute transverse myelitis
M. MG
N. GBS
O. CVA
P. DM
Q. Spinal cord compression (stenosis, ruptured disk)
R. Behcet's disease
S. Neuromyelitis optica (NMO)

Plan

A. Patient teaching
   1. Educate on heat sensitivity and how it can aggravate symptoms: Avoid hot tubs, saunas, prolonged exposure in hot/humid weather; choose appropriate clothing for the season. Around 60% of individuals with MS experience heat sensitivity, facilitating a *pseudoexacerbation* where MS symptoms may worsen, but do not necessarily indicate additional axon or myelin degeneration.
   2. For visual disturbances, offer advice on resting the eyes at various times during the day; for diplopia, an eye patch can be used temporarily.
   3. Stress the importance of exercise and its effect on MS-related fatigue and spasticity; overactivity/overexertion is another issue to address at this time. Rest periods are needed during exacerbations.
   4. Provide education on Kegel's exercises and timed voiding to improve bladder function; also advise to avoid alcohol and caffeinated beverages.
   5. Promote increased water intake, dietary fiber intake, and physical activity for increased bowel motility.
   6. Educate regarding the signs and symptoms of infection, especially urinary tract infections (UTIs), and how infection can trigger an exacerbation.
   7. Instruct safe performance of self-intermittent catheterization (SIC) for urinary retention and emphasize the importance of sterile technique.
   8. Discuss the purpose and availability of local MS support groups.
   9. Discuss counseling services for development of adaptive coping techniques, improved family dynamics and relationships with significant others, adjustment to physical disability, and any anticipatory grief issues.
   10. Educate on all medications, including side effects and associated laboratory tests with follow-up.
   11. Suggest strategies regarding short-term memory and planning ability: Individuals may choose to write things down, develop schedules and calendars, make lists, draw pictures, and take more time when devising plans.
B. Pharmacological therapy is prescribed specifically for the type of MS and may include a combination of the following.
   1. Disease-modifying drugs suppress the immune system to slow the progression of MS (lessen frequency and severity of exacerbations, reduce MS plaques).
      a. Interferon beta-1a agents: Avonex, Rebif
      b. Interferon beta-1b agents: Extavia, Betaseron
      c. Immunomodulators: glatiramer acetate (Copaxone)
      d. Spingosine 1-phosphate receptor modulator: fingolimod (Gilenya)
      e. Adrenocorticotropic hormone (ACTH) analogue: H.P. Acthar Gel
      f. Dimethyl fumarate (Tecfidera)
   2. The immunomodulator integrin-receptor antagonist, natalizumab (NTZ), or Tysabri may be considered for RRMS treatment. The FDA generally recommends Tysabri for those who cannot tolerate or who inadequately respond to other MS therapies.

NTZ (Tysabri) therapy includes a risk-minimization action plan utilized by neurologists who specialize in MS treatment under the TOUCH™ Prescribing Program. It is administered at infusion centers registered and authorized under TOUCH™, a distribution program designed to assess the risk of PML associated with Tysabri administration, minimize this risk, decrease PML-associated deaths and disability, and promote informed decision making regarding the risks and benefits of Tysabri use. Additional information is available on the FDA website at www.fda.gov/downloads/drugs/drugsafety/postmarketdrugsafetyinformationforpatientsandproviders/ucm107197.pdf

   3. Short-term steroid use (3- – 5-day course of methylprednisolone or dexamethasone) may shorten an exacerbation. Long-term use is not recommended. Intravenous steroids may be prescribed initially, then transitioned to oral steroids (prednisone, dexamethasone) that are tapered off over time.
   4. Dalfampridine is an FDA-approved drug that has been shown to improve ambulation in the MS population. It is a potassium-channel blocker that targets channels located on the outside of nerve fibers, possibly improving nerve conduction when the myelin sheaths are damaged.

5. Baclofen, zanaflex, valium (watch for sedation, dependence), Dantrium (would use only when other drugs are ineffective, as it can cause liver damage), and clonidine are drugs used for associated spasticity.
6. Botulinum toxin injections may be used for treatment of spasticity.
7. Intrathecal pump placement for administration of baclofen or clonidine may be considered for spasticity.
8. Stool softeners (Colace, Peri-Colace), bulk-forming agents (Metamucil), or laxatives (Milk of Magnesia, MiraLax) may be administered for complaints of constipation.
9. Flomax or hytrin may be prescribed to improve urine outflow.
10. Ditropan, tofranil, and detrol are drugs commonly prescribed for bladder spasms.
11. SSRIs (Zoloft, Prozac) or selective serotonin-norepinephrine reuptake inhibitors (SSNRIs) (Cymbalta, Effexor) for treatment of depression. Patients with protracted, painful, progressive medical conditions are at risk for suicide.
12. Provigil or symmetrel can be used to treat fatigue symptoms.
13. Stem-cell transplantation is emerging in the literature, with continued clinical trials that may determine it to be a possible treatment option for RRMS.

Follow-Up

A. A neurologist who specializes in MS management should coordinate and prescribe all necessary treatment and therapy for this population. Nurse practitioner comanagement with a primary care physician for follow-up care depends on the clinical presentation, type of diagnosis, and treatment involved.

Consultation and Referrals

A. Neurology referral and consultation for management of MS
B. Ophthalmology for visual disturbances, optic neuritis
C. Urology for genitourinary (GU) disturbances (impotence in males; urinary hesitancy, frequency, incontinence, and urgency; UTIs)
D. Occupational therapy can address any issues with fine motor skills (coordination, strength), performing ADL, and prescribe the necessary adaptive equipment.
E. Speech therapy can address any issues with language, cognition, or swallowing (including evaluations for feeding tube placement and diet recommendations).
F. Physical therapy can address gait imbalance, motor weakness, spasticity, and ROM, as well as prescribe assistive devices and equipment for impaired physical mobility.
G. Psychiatry referral and consultation for pharmacologic management of depression and dementia (if indicated); also consider psychology or licensed professional counselor referrals for counseling.
H. Social work referral for assistance with insurance issues, locating community resources, applying for disability, arranging home health care, obtaining placement in a skilled nursing facility (SNF), and providing counseling for the individual and the family.

Individual Considerations

A. Pregnancy
   1. Symptoms of MS may stabilize or remit during pregnancy, but 20% to 40% of patients have a relapse within 3 months after delivery.
   2. No evidence suggests that pregnancy affects the long-term course of MS. There is no acceleration in the rate of disability or disease progression postpartum.
   3. Neither epidural anesthesia nor breastfeeding has an adverse effect on the rate of relapse or progression of disability.
   4. There are no accepted guidelines for recommending for or against pregnancy in women with MS. MS history and current neurologic deficits should be considered independently per patient.
   5. Pregnancy may affect the treatment regimen; some of the drugs used to treat MS are known teratogens. Glucocorticoids may cause neonatal adrenal suppression and maternal glucose intolerance.
B. Geriatrics
   1. The occurrence of MS older than age 60 is not typical. Spinal infarcts are more commonly diagnosed when evaluating specific inflammatory lesions in this population.
   2. Clinical diagnosis of LOMS patients can be challenging due to the number of other age-associated diagnoses, atypical presentation of signs and symptoms, and lack of information on MS in older individuals. Hepatic and renal function decline with age as other comorbidities may increase, which also complicates diagnoses and treatment.

Resources

Multiple Sclerosis Association of America: http://www.mymsaa.org
Multiple Sclerosis Foundation: www.msfocus.org
National Multiple Sclerosis Society: www.nationalmssociety.org

Myasthenia Gravis

Definition

A. MG is a chronic autoimmune disorder that affects the neuromuscular junction and is characterized by fatigability and weakness of voluntary muscles.

Incidence

A. The prevalence is 0.5 to 11.5 cases per 1 million people. There are two peaks in MG incidence that are age- and gender-related: One is women in their 20s and 30s, and the other is men in their 60s and 70s.

Pathophysiology

A. MG is believed to be an antibody-mediated autoimmune attack that destroys variable numbers of acetylcholine receptors (AChR) at the postsynaptic junction. The decrease in AChRs results in weakness with repeated activities and recovery after rest. MG is often associated with thymic hyperplasia or tumors; the thymus plays an unclear role in the autoimmune process of MG.

Predisposing Factors

A. No predisposing factors have been identified.

Common Complaints

A. Classic triad: Ptosis, diplopia, and dysphagia
   1. Fluctuating symptoms such as droopy eyelid(s)
   2. Blurry or double vision
   3. Sense of choking
B. Difficulty chewing
C. Slurring of speech
D. Easy fatigability
E. Symptoms are more pronounced with fatigue or in the evening.

Other Signs and Symptoms

A. Selected voluntary muscles that fatigue with activity
B. Motor function that improves with rest but then decreases with use
C. Signs of impending MG crisis
   1. Sudden onset of inspiratory distress
   2. Difficulty swallowing
   3. Visual difficulty
   4. Tachycardia
   5. Rapid onset of weakness

Subjective Data

A. Establish onset of symptoms and possible progression
B. Ask the patient what makes the symptoms better or worse: Does rest help?
C. Ask if the patient feels better in the morning or in the afternoon or evening.
D. Look for difficulties with chewing or swallowing.
E. Investigate medications the patient is currently taking or has recently taken, such as antibiotics.

Physical Examination

> *The presentation and course of MG are both highly variable, and MG can therefore be very difficult to diagnose.*

A. Check pulse, respirations, and blood pressure.
B. Inspect
   1. Observe overall appearance.
   2. Perform complete eye exam. Subtleties of eye movement dysfunction are often key in differentiating MG from other disorders.
C. Palpate: Assess DTRs; note normal to increased reflexes.
D. Neurologic exam
   1. Perform complete neurologic exam.
   2. Test the following.
      a. Muscle strength: Weakness is increased with repetition or sustained activity; arm raise cannot be sustained.
      b. Eyes: Upward or lateral gaze cannot be maintained for longer than 30 seconds.
      c. Eyes: Ptosis occurs with repetitive lid closure.
      d. Ice pack test—fill a plastic bag or glove with ice and place over closed eyelid for 2 minutes. Remove ice and evaluate the degree of ptosis. Noted to be very sensitive with prominent ptosis.
      e. Voice: Voice quality or speech changes when counting out loud to 100.

> *Normal coordination, normal sensory perception, and normal pupillary response are noted in MG.*

Diagnostic Tests

A. Antibody titer for acetylcholine receptor (AChR-Ab) is positive in 90% of patients with MG. May also perform MuSK antibody titer. Approximately 6% to 12% of patients will have negative antibody titers for both titers.
B. Cholinesterase-inhibiting drug test: Improvement in strength following injection of edrophonium (Tensilon)
C. Repetitive muscle stimulation test: Decremental response
D. Single-fiber EMG and/or repetitive nerve stimulation (RNS) studies are diagnostic studies performed for diagnosis.

> *Initial diagnostic tests may be equivocal with some negative test results, but this does not absolutely rule out myasthenia.*

Differential Diagnoses

A. MG: The most common disorder of neuromuscular transmission. **It is important to maintain a high index of suspicion and include MG in the differential diagnosis of any patient presenting with variable muscle weakness even without eye signs.**
B. Incomplete extraocular nerve palsy
C. Polymyositis
D. Brainstem transient ischemic attack (TIA)
E. ALS
F. Brainstem vascular accident: "Dizziness" is a symptom rarely seen with MG but often associated with brainstem ischemia.
G. GBS
H. Brainstem tumor
I. Hyperthyroidism or hypothyroidism
J. **Cholinergic crisis: While it is useful to distinguish myasthenic crisis (weakness from MG exacerbation) from cholinergic crisis (weakness from too much medication), both can rapidly lead to respiratory failure. Transportation to an emergency room for evaluation should not be delayed by attempts to differentiate the two.**
K. Eaton-Lambert myasthenic syndrome: Often associated with bronchogenic carcinoma but may precede detection of the carcinoma by as many as 2 years.

Plan

A. General interventions
   1. MG is primarily managed by a neurologist, given the difficulty in diagnosing it, the variable course of the disease, and the highly individualized medication regimen required.
   2. The course of MG fluctuates most during the first 3 to 5 years after diagnosis.
   3. Autoimmune disorders, such as thyroid disease, rheumatoid arthritis, and SLE, should also be screened for in patients diagnosed with MG.
B. Patient teaching
   1. See the Section III Patient Teaching Guide for this chapter, "Myasthenia Gravis."
   2. Patients should have a MedicAlert tag and always carry a list of their medications and dosing schedules in case of an emergency.
C. Medical and surgical management
   1. Thymectomy is an early consideration; an MRI of the chest is obtained once the diagnosis is made to assess for thymic enlargement.

Thymectomy lessens the severity of MG but rarely results in complete elimination of the need for medication.

   2. Plasmapheresis, or plasma exchange to remove antibodies, is used emergently for the management of myasthenic crisis. Opinion is mixed regarding its use in the long-term management of myasthenia.
D. Pharmaceutical therapy
   1. **Many medications can worsen myasthenic symptoms, so changes and additions of any medication require consultation with the patient's neurologist.** Cholinesterase-inhibiting medications:
      a. Pyridostigmine (Mestinon) 60 mg and 180 mg sustained release (SR) titrate as needed, with usual dose up to 600 mg/d.
      b. Neostigmine methylsulfate (Prostigmin) 0.25 to 0.5 and 1.0 mg/mL concentrations titrated with starting dose 0.5 mg SC or IM every 3 to 4 hours.
   2. Steroids may be used when inpatient and then tapered on an outpatient basis, tapering every 3 days.
   3. Effectiveness of medication regimen is gauged by changes in ptosis, diplopia, dysphagia, chewing ability, and muscle fatigue.
   4. Care should be used with use of medications that may worsen symptoms of weakness.

Follow-Up

A. Patients with MG require lifelong management by a neurologist, given the variable course of both the disease and the patient's response to treatment.
B. The patient is initially followed every 1 to 2 months, then every 3 to 4 months.

Consultation/Referral

A. If MG is suspected, consult with a physician and consider neurologic referral.

Individual Considerations

A. Pregnancy
   1. MG is considered high risk for both the woman and the fetus.
      a. Pregnancy requires management by the patient's neurologist and a perinatologist.
   2. MG frequently manifests for the first time during pregnancy. Refer to a perinatologist.
B. Adults: Oral contraceptives may worsen myasthenic symptoms.

Neurocognitive Disorders (Dementia)

Definition

A. Neurocognitive disorders are characterized by deficits in cognitive function, with a significant decline from a previous level of function. Decline may be evident in one or more areas of function, including attention, language, memory, visuospatial skills, or executive function (complex tasks such as organizing, sequencing, judgment, and reasoning).

B. Neurocognitive disorders include Alzheimer's disease, vascular dementia, Lewy body dementia, and other dementias (frontotemporal dementia, Parkinson's dementia, HIV dementia, neurosyphilis, and Korsakoff's dementia).

C. Clinical features that differentiate these disorders
   1. Alzheimer's disease
      a. Gradual onset and a course of progressive decline
      b. Memory, language, and visuospatial deficits
      c. Depressive symptoms, which may precede diagnosis
      d. Delusions, hallucinations, agitation, and apathy
   2. Vascular dementia
      a. Abrupt onset and a stepwise course of progression
      b. Aphasia
   3. Lewy body dementia
      a. Visual hallucinations and delusions
      b. Extrapyramidal symptoms (muscle rigidity, parkinsonism)
      c. Fluctuating mental status
      d. Increased sensitivity to antipsychotic medications
   4. Frontotemporal dementia
      a. Change in personality
      b. Hyperorality
      c. Impairment in executive function, with relatively well-retained visuospatial skills
      d. Loss of social awareness

D. The diagnosis of dementia must be differentiated from delirium, a disturbance in cognition that develops over a short period of time and is characterized by an alteration in attention that fluctuates in severity during the course of the day. Delirium may be the consequence of an acute medical condition, hospitalization, or medication/substance induced. Delirium typically may last weeks to months, with gradual improvement in cognition.

Incidence

A. Dementia is present in 1% to 2% of persons aged 65 years, and up to 30% of those 85 years and older have a neurocognitive disorder. Alzheimer's disease is the most commonly occurring dementia (60%–70%), with the other cases due to mixed causes (30%), such as multi-infarct or vascular dementia. Alzheimer's accounts for more than 50% of nursing home admissions and is the condition most feared by aging adults. The Alzheimer's Association reports more than 5 million Americans have Alzheimer's disease. One in three senior adults will die with a diagnosis of Alzheimer's disease or another form of dementia. The incidence is higher in women, with almost two thirds of persons with Alzheimer's disease being female.

Pathogenesis

The following includes the pathogenesis of each type of dementia

A. Alzheimer's disease
   1. Cortical atrophy is most prominent in the temporal and hippocampal regions of the brain.
   2. There is extracellular deposition of beta-amyloid protein.
   3. Intracellular neurofibrillary tangles contribute to neuronal loss; tau proteins are a major component.
   4. Decreased levels of acetylcholine
   5. The Apo E epsilon 4 allele of chromosome 19 has been associated with familial and late-onset Alzheimer's disease.

B. Vascular dementia
   1. Microvascular changes of the brain.
   2. Cortical and subcortical infarctions.

C. Lewy body dementia
   1. Extensive cortical neuritic plaques.
   2. Presence of Lewy bodies (intraplasmic spherical neuronal inclusion bodies) in the brainstem, cortex, and neocortex.

D. Frontotemporal dementia
   1. Atrophy of the frontal and temporal regions of the brain.

E. A number of diseases alter cerebral metabolism resulting in dementia, such as Huntington's chorea and Parkinson's disease (PD). A variety of diseases that can produce or mimic dementia may be arrested or reversed. These are classified as pseudodementia, such as hypothyroidism or depression.

Predisposing Factors

A. Definite risks
   1. Advanced age
   2. AFib
   3. Depression
   4. Family history
   5. Down syndrome

B. Possible risks
   1. Delirium
   2. Head trauma
   3. Heavy smoking

Common Complaints

Interview the patient, family members, and /or friends/caretakers who spend quality time with the patient to assess for social, neurological, and cognitive changes experienced by the patient.

A. Memory impairment

B. Change in behavior and inability to perform normal activities of self-care

Other Signs and Symptoms

A. Disoriented to date and/or place
B. Naming difficulties (anomia)
C. Impaired recent recall
D. Decreased insight
E. Impaired judgment
F. Social withdrawal
G. Problems managing finances; inability to pay bills and to balance checkbook; spending money in unusual ways
H. Getting lost in familiar environments
I. Lack of safety awareness; leaving the stove on, taking medications incorrectly, increased vulnerability to strangers

Subjective Data

A. Elicit onset and duration of symptoms; commonly, this information comes from family members.
B. Question the family members and/or caregivers regarding personality changes in the patient or any changes in personal hygiene.
C. Review the patient's history, including history for sexually transmitted infections.
D. Review medications, specifically those medications with anticholinergic side effects, including OTC products such as diphenhydramine
E. Is there a loss of interest in things the patient used to find important?
F. Evaluate the patient's history for any recent major life events such as the death of a spouse, a move to a new living environment, or loss of purpose following retirement.

Physical Examination

A. Evaluate blood pressure, pulse, respirations, and weight.
B. Inspect
  1. Observe general appearance; note grooming, interest in conversation, and apathy.
  2. Note the presence of slurred speech and slowed body movements.
  3. Inspect the nail beds and mucous membranes for anemia.
C. Palpate: Palpate the thyroid.
D. Auscultate
  1. Auscultate heart, lungs, and abdomen
E. Neurologic exam: Perform a complete neurologic exam, including CNs, gait, motor function, and cerebellar function. Note facial asymmetry, distal weakness, and any focal neurologic findings.
  1. Complete mental status exam with instrument of choice: See Diagnostic Tests.
  2. Assess functional status. May use a functional assessment tool such as Physical Self-Maintenance Scale, Instrumental Activities of Daily Living Scale, or Reisberg FAST. Available at www.geriatricsatyourfingertips.org
  3. Complete depression screening with instrument of choice:
    a. GDS. Available at www.healthcre.uiowa.edu/.../depression/GDS
    b. PHQ-9. Available at www.phqscreeners.com/
    c. Beck depression scale. Available at www.nsand.ca/media/forms/EHNMC

Diagnostic Tests

A. MMSE. Complete mental status exam with instrument of choice.
  1. MOCA. Available at www.mocatest.org
  2. MMSE. Available at: www.mountsinai.on.ca/care/psych/on-call-resources/on-call-resources/mmse.pdf
  3. SLUMS. Available at: http://medschool.slu.edu/agingsuccessfully/pdfsurveys/slumsexam_05.pdf
  4. Mini-Cog. Available at: http://consultgerirn.org/uploads/File/trythis/try_this_3.pdf
  5. The CDT may also be administered and used as a screening tool. The CDT is available at www.rehabmeasures.org (see Section II "Procedures").
B. Rule out possible reversible causes of dementia; not all are required, so use discretion.
  1. Thyroid function tests, to rule out either hypothyroidism or hyperthyroidism
  2. CBC
  3. Vitamin B_{12} level: Anemia or B_{12} deficiency
  4. Serum chemistry profile: Hyponatremia
  5. Toxicology screen or serum drug screen: Toxicity or intoxication
  6. VDRL, fluorescent treponemal antibody absorption (FTA-ABS), or microhemagglutination assay for antibody to *T. pallidum* (MHA-TP) (CSF) to confirm syphilis
  7. HIV-1 antibody titer: AIDS dementia complex
  8. Liver function tests: Liver disease
  9. CT scan or MRI: Vascular dementia, tumor, chronic SDH, normal pressure hydrocephalus, and AIDS dementia complex
  10. EKG: Creutzfeldt–Jakob disease
  11. Neuropsychological evaluation

The history is the key to diagnosis of dementia. The physical exam may be normal. Dementia is not a normal part of aging; normal aging intelligence scores decrease by only about 10% by age 80. A thorough search for a potentially reversible cause is required.

Differential Diagnoses

A. Completely reversible dementia, rarely
B. Depression and adverse reactions to medications are the most common reversible causes of dementia. Use the DEMENTIA pneumonic:
   D: Drugs or depression
   E: Emotional upset
   M: Metabolic, for example, vitamin B_{12} deficiency or hypothyroidism
   E: Ear or eye impairment or sensory impairment
   N: Normal pressure hydrocephalus
   T: Tumors or masses, for example, SDH
   I: Infection or sepsis
   A: Anemia
C. Alzheimer's disease
D. Dementia with Lewy bodies
E. PD with dementia
F. Vascular dementia
G. Frontotemporal dementia

Plan

A. General interventions
   1. The goal is to treat identifiable abnormalities.
   2. Educate family and patient regarding the diagnosis, disease process, and progression.
   3. Encourage healthy behaviors including regular exercise, healthy diet, and stress management.
   4. Maintain brain function through involvement in stimulating social activities.
   5. Consider driving evaluation if the patient is still driving.
   6. Recommend the use of a safe-return bracelet.
   7. Evaluate the home for safety features.
   8. Arrange for supportive care for the family and patient.
   9. Information on support groups for the caregiver and family is very helpful.
   10. See Alzheimer's Disease section for treatment and care for families needing legal and/or financial assistance. Discuss advance directives and planning for future care needs.
B. Patient/family teaching
   1. See the Section III Patient Teaching Guide for this chapter, "Dementia."
   2. Educate regarding the diagnosis, disease process, and progression.
   3. Discuss advance directives and planning for future care needs.
   4. Encourage patient and family caregivers to become involved in dementia support groups.
   5. Consider driving evaluation, if patient is still driving.
   6. Recommend use of safe return bracelet.
   7. Evaluate the home for safety features.
   8. Avoid anticholinergic medications, including. diphenhydramine, hydroxyzine, TCAs, and oxybutynin.
C. Pharmaceutical therapy
   1. Patients with a diagnosis of mild-to-moderate Alzheimer's disease should receive a trial of a cholinesterase inhibitor. There is some evidence to support a trial of one of these medications for patients with vascular dementia, Lewy body dementia, and Parkinson's dementia.
      a. Donepezil (Aricept): Start 5 mg daily at bedtime for 4 weeks, then 10 mg at bedtime.
      b. Rivastigmine (Exelon): Start 1.5 mg twice daily, then increase by 1.5 mg every 4 weeks to maximum dose of 6 mg twice daily.
         Also Exelon patch: Start 4.6 mg topically daily; increase to 9.5 mg topically daily after 4 weeks.
      c. Galantamine (Razadyne): Start 4 mg twice a day for 4 weeks, then 8 mg twice a day. Maximum dose 12 mg twice daily.
   2. Patients with moderate-to-severe Alzheimer's disease:
      a. Memantine (Namenda): Namenda XR 7 mg daily, titrate by 7 mg per week to recommended dose of 28 mg daily.

Follow-Up

A. Follow-up visit at 1 month to evaluate patient's status, response to medication, and side effects.
B. Patients and families have an ongoing need for education and support in learning to deal with the diagnosis.
C. Subsequent follow-up visits can be scheduled every 3 to 6 months.

Consultation/Referral

A. Refer the patient to a neurocognitive specialist if the diagnosis is unclear.
B. Refer patients and families to support groups in the community.
C. Geriatric psychiatry may be appropriate for management and treatment of behavioral and psychological symptoms of dementia.
D. Refer to social services or geriatric case management for assistance with respite care and placement options.

Individual Considerations

A. Geriatrics: Irreversible dementia or Alzheimer's disease begins in the fourth to fifth decade of life and is characterized by loss of recent memory, inability to learn new information, language problems, mood swings, and personality changes.

Resources

Alzheimer's Association: www.alz.org

Alzheimer's Disease Education and Referral Center: www.nia.nih.gov/alzheimers

Frontotemporal dementia: National Institute of Neurological Disorders and Stroke: www.ninds.nih.gov

Lewy Body Dementia Association: www.lbda.org

Parkinson's Disease

Definition

A. PD is an idiopathic, progressive, chronic neurologic syndrome characterized by a combination of akinesia or bradykinesia, or reduction of spontaneous activity and movement; rigidity, or increase in spontaneous muscle tone and involuntary movements; tremor; and postural instability.

Incidence

A. One percent of the population older than age 50 has PD. The mean age of onset is 55 to 60 years. Only 5% is seen between the ages of 21 to 40. There is no gender difference in prevalence. PD is seen most frequently in people of European ancestry.

Pathophysiology

A. For reasons that are unclear, degenerative changes occur in the basal ganglia and deplete the dopaminergic neurons in the substantia nigra, resulting in dopamine reduction in the striatum. This interrupts neuronal circuits and produces akinesia and rigidity. The pathophysiology of tremor is less clear, but thalamic involvement is implicated.

Predisposing Factors

A. Antecedent encephalitis
B. Arteriosclerosis
C. Trauma
D. Toxins
E. Drugs, particularly phenothiazines
F. Familial neurodegenerative diseases in which parkinsonism is a prominent feature

Common Complaints

Cardinal symptoms

- A. Tremor at rest: May be intermittent but progresses over time
- B. Rigidity: Joints are more rigid. Increased resistance to passive movement. Appears unilaterally and then progresses to the opposite side. Usually asymmetrical. Appears as decreased movement in arm swing when ambulating, stooped posture, cogwheel rigidity—resistance with tremor.
- C. Bradykinesia, or slow voluntary movement, especially with daily activities such as cutting food, dressing self, and so forth. When walking, shorter steps are taken, shuffle-step, feeling of unsteadiness with walking. Postural instability.

Other Signs and Symptoms

A. Micrographia (handwriting that decreases in size when writing out name)
B. Voice changes: Fading, softness, hoarseness, and mumbling
C. Saliva escaping mouth, especially at night
D. Dysphagia
E. Neuropsychiatric changes: Cognitive impairment/dementia/memory loss, sleep disturbance, fatigue, anxiety, depression, pain, and sensory changes
F. Oily, greasy skin
G. Excessive perspiration
H. Constipation
I. Urinary hesitancy or frequency
J. Visual loss: Impaired vision, reflex, upward gaze, and convergence

Subjective Data

A. Elicit information regarding onset of symptoms. Note changes in progression of symptoms.
B. Talk with the patient and family to establish if there have been behavioral changes, problems with activities such as eating or getting out of chairs, or personality changes.
C. Determine if other family members have had similar symptoms.
D. Ascertain the patient's medical history, including current medications, both prescription and OTC.
E. Particularly in patients younger than 55 years, investigate substance abuse and exposure to herbicides or pesticides.

Physical Examination

A. Check pulse, respirations, blood pressure, and weight: Note orthostatic hypotension.
B. Inspect
   1. Observe overall appearance.
   2. Note asymmetric tremor at rest.
   3. Note subtle facial masking, decreased frequency, and amplitude of eye blinks.
   4. Note posture and gait disturbances: Festination, or shuffling, increasingly tiny steps; usually walking with arms down to side; difficulty turning; freezing, or inability to continue to move.
C. Palpate: Palpate extremities, noting increased tone in resting muscles.
D. Neurologic exam

1. Perform complete neurologic exam. Assess all CNs. Assess DTRs.
2. Assess rapid alternating movements. Note difficulty with rapid alternating movements such as tapping fingers or turning palm alternately up and down.
3. Check cogwheel phenomenon, which is stepwise rigidity of movement with passive ROM rather than anticipated smooth movement through ROM. Best tested in wrists.
4. Perform mental status exam.
5. Assess the progression of the disease state with the scale of choice. Scales commonly used include:
   a. Unified PD Rating Scale available: www.etas.ee/wp-content/uploads/2013/10/updrs.pdf
   b. The Movement Disorder Society. This site hosts a list of rating scales and questionnaires. www.movementdisorders.org/MDS.htm
   c. Hoehn and Yahr scale available at http://parkinsonsresource.org/wp-content/uploads/2012/01/The-FIVE-Stages-of-Parkinsons-Disease.pdf
   d. Scales for Outcomes in PD—Psychiatric Complications (nonmotor evaluation) and Nonmotor Symptom Screening Questionnaire available at www.neurology.org/cgi/content/abstract/61/9/1222

Diagnostic Tests

A. There is no definitive diagnostic test for PD.
B. Urinalysis to rule out urinary tract infection (UTI) with any urinary symptoms
C. Speech therapy evaluation of dysarthria and dysphagia to assess aspiration risk
D. Brain CT scan or MRI to exclude mass lesion, multiple infarcts, or normal pressure hydrocephalus
E. MRI of cervical spine if there is increased gait disturbance after a fall.

Differential Diagnoses

A. PD
B. Essential tremor
C. Multi-infarct dementia
D. Alzheimer's disease
E. Brain tumor
F. Progressive supranuclear palsy
G. Normal pressure hydrocephalus
H. Shy–Drager syndrome
I. Hypothyroidism
J. Hereditary disease such as Huntington's chorea or Wilson's disease
K. Chorea: Not generally seen in PD; its development in a patient with PD is generally a medication side effect and should be discussed with the patient's neurologist.

Plan

A. General interventions
   1. Encourage regular exercise to maintain or improve flexibility.
   2. The patient should follow a diet that is high in fiber and calcium, with adequate fluid intake, to limit complications due to constipation and osteoporosis. In some patients, protein intake may need to be timed to limit interactions with levodopa.
   3. Emphasize the importance of the nonmotor symptoms being addressed and adequately treated. Encourage the family to notify the provider if these symptoms are not being controlled. Anxiety, depression, fatigue, mood, and behavioral issues need to be addressed and controlled for quality of life for the patient and family.
   4. Home safety evaluations are recommended because the symptoms of PD place patients at high risk for falls and accidental injury.
   5. Surgery, such as pallidotomy or thalamotomy, is an option for severe PD in which tremor is poorly controlled with medications.
B. Patient teaching: See the Section III Patient Teaching Guide for this chapter, "Managing Your Parkinson's Disease."
C. Pharmaceutical therapy
   1. Polypharmacy is the hallmark rather than the exception with PD. Always comanage with a neurologist.
   2. Lower doses of several medications, rather than high doses of a single agent, aid in maximizing function while minimizing side effects.
   3. Drug dosages are always tapered, not stopped abruptly.
   4. First-line drug
      a. Levodopa, combined with a decarboxylase inhibitor, is the mainstay of treatment. Sinemet is the levodopa and carbidopa combination drug most often used.
         i. The dose and dosing frequency are very individualized.
         ii. Patients are often on a combination of sustained release and short-acting preparations.
         iii. See literature for individual dosing. Titrate dose up every 3 days for adjustments.
         iv. Long-term use is often associated with adverse effects requiring careful medication dosage.
   5. Second-line therapy: Dopamine agonists: Generally given in conjunction with levodopa, these allow use of lower doses of levodopa that can delay or reduce levodopa-associated

problems. Examples include pramipexole (Mirapex) and ropinirole (Requip).

6. Ergot derivatives include the following.
   a. Bromocriptine and pergolide are the two dopamine agonists most often used.
      i. Bromocriptine mesylate (Parlodel) is initiated at 1.25 mg daily or twice a day and slowly increased to 10 to 25 mg daily.
      ii. Pergolide mesylate (Permax) is initiated at 0.05 mg daily and increased slowly to 2 to 3 mg in divided doses three times a day.
   b. Nonergot drugs are preferred due to fewer side effects.
      i. Pramipexole (Mirapex) 0.125 mg three times daily up to 4.5 mg/d maximum useful for tremors or Ropinirole (ReQuip) 0.25 mg three times daily, maximum 24-hour period.
7. Neuroprotective agents: Selegiline (Eldepryl), MAO-B inhibitor 5 mg at breakfast and at lunch, may have neuroprotective effects and slow progression of symptoms.
   a. Often an initial treatment, a drug is usually continued throughout the course of the disease. Maximum dose is 10 mg/d.
   b. Amantadine (Symmetrel) is used as short-term monotherapy in patients younger than 60 years with mild–to-moderate PD in which akinesia and rigidity are more prominent than tremor.
      i. Its effects tend to wane, and it should be tapered once other antiparkinsonian drugs are started.
      ii. The usual dose is 100 to 300 mg twice daily. Adjust the dose gradually.
      iii. Caution should be used with these medications due to the interactions with other medications and foods that can precipitate high blood pressure to dangerous levels. Advise to avoid foods high in tyramine, such as some cheeses, tofu, and yeast extracts.
8. Anticholinergics: These are useful for treating resting tremor but not akinesia or impaired postural reflexes.
   a. The centrally acting drug trihexyphenidyl HCL (Artane) is the most common anticholinergic used.
      i. Drug is usually started at 0.5 to 1.0 mg twice daily with food and slowly increased to 2 to 3 mg three times daily.
      ii. Dosage should always be tapered, never stopped abruptly.
      iii. Use is not recommended in patients older than 60 or with dementia.
   b. Benztropine mesylate (Cogentin) 0.5 to 1 mg at bedtime may also be used in PD. Maximum is 6 mg/d. Increase every 6 to 7 days.
9. Sleep disorders are common in PD and respond well to TCAs, benzodiazepines, diphenhydramine, or low-dose chloral hydrate.
10. Excessive daytime sleepiness should first be evaluated as a symptom of depression before it is attributed to medications or effects of PD.

As PD progresses, patients often develop clear "on" and "off" times of medication effectiveness and functional ability, so medication schedules are very carefully customized to maximize "on" times.

Follow-Up

A. PD requires lifelong management by a neurologist.
B. Frequency of appointments depends on severity of disease and response to medication. Depression and neuropsychiatric side effects of medications are often seen in patients with PD, so any office visit should involve screening for these. Inquire particularly about memory loss, vivid dreams or nightmares, hallucinations, symptoms of depression or anxiety, and occurrence of panic attacks. Discuss findings with the patient's neurologist, as medication adjustments could be required.

Consultation/Referral

A. Managing PD requires referral to a neurologist to initiate and adjust medications.
B. If a PD patient requires the addition of medication for other conditions, consult the patient's neurologist to evaluate for possible serious adverse effects.
C. Involvement with a support group can be helpful for the patient and family. Information about PD and local support groups can be obtained from:
   1. The American Parkinson's Disease Association, Inc.
      135 Parkinson Avenue
      Staten Island, NY 10305
      www.apdaparkinson.org
      800-223-2732 Fax 718-981-4399
   2. National Parkinson Foundation
      1501 N.W 9th Ave./Bob Hope Road
      Miami, FL 33136-1494
      www.parkinson.org
      800-473-4636

Individual Considerations

A. Geriatrics: It is most commonly seen in this population.

Seizures

Definition

A. In 2013 the International League Against Epilepsy (ILAE) adopted its commissioned task force's definition of epilepsy to be utilized in clinical diagnosis. The official report of the ILAE was published in 2014 in the journal *Epilepsia*. Epilepsy is a disease of the brain that is defined by any of the three following conditions:
   1. At least two unprovoked (or reflex) seizures occurring more than 24 hours apart
   2. One unprovoked (or reflex) seizure and a probability of further seizures similar to the general recurrence risk (at least 60%) after two unprovoked seizures, occurring over the next 10 years
   3. Diagnosis of epilepsy syndrome

B. The ILAE's clinical definitions also state that epilepsy is considered to be resolved for individuals who had an age-dependent epilepsy syndrome but are now past the applicable age or those who have remained seizure-free for the past 10 years, with no seizure medications for the past 5 years.

C. Accurate classification of seizures is dependent on observations of witnessed seizures, full medical history including comorbidities, and clinical findings. The clinical signs and symptoms depend on the location of the epileptic discharges. Status epilepticus is a continuous state of seizure and is usually defined as 30 minutes of uninterrupted seizure activity.
   1. Partial (focal) seizures generally only involve one portion of the brain. They are the most common type of seizures and may be accompanied by visual or auditory hallucinations.
      a. Simple partial seizures (SPS) are not associated with altered consciousness or loss of consciousness.
      b. Common SPS includes jerking of a limb and may be preceded by an aura, including epigastric discomfort, fear, or unpleasant smells.
      c. Complex partial seizure (CPS) is notable for impaired consciousness. Confusion, fatigue, and headaches may follow a CPS.
      d. A SPS may last a few seconds and develop into a CPS with symptoms that include staring, repetitive motor behaviors, clouded consciousness, and automatisms (swallowing, chewing, or lip smacking).

D. Generalized seizures are notable for EEG changes since both hemispheres of the brain are involved. Almost all generalized seizures involve loss/impaired consciousness. There are four subtypes of generalized seizures:
   1. Tonic-clonic, also known as grand mal seizures, generally last 1 to 2 minutes and are notable for falls, cries, rigidity (tonicity), jerking (clonicity), and possible cyanosis.
   2. Absence seizures, also called petit mal seizures, last 2 to 15 seconds and are notable for beginning and ending abruptly. Symptoms noted include staring, eye flutters, and automatisms. First aid is not required.
   3. Myoclonic seizures are characterized by rapid, brief contraction of muscles (sudden jerks or clumsiness) usually on both sides of the body, arm, or sudden jerk of a foot during sleep. First aid is generally not required.
   4. Atonic seizures, also called drop seizures, are characterized by abrupt loss of muscle tone, loss of posture, or sudden collapse. These seizures tend to be resistant to medication. Protective headgear may be needed. Generally, first aid is not required unless an injury occurs.

E. Lennox–Gastaut syndrome (LGS) is a rare form of epilepsy consisting of multiple seizure types. Types include cognitive impairment and drop seizures. LGS patients may require antiseizure medications, steroids or immune globulin, vagus nerve stimulation, surgical resection, and ketogenic diet.

F. Eclampsia occurs anytime in pregnancy from the second trimester to the puerperium. It is notable for the occurrence of one or more generalized convulsions and/or coma in women with preeclampsia (in the absence of other neurologic conditions).
   1. Eclampsia is self-limited, and delivery is the treatment.
   2. The tonic-clonic seizure generally lasts 60 to 75 seconds.
   3. Fetal bradycardia lasts 3 to 5 minutes but does not necessitate an emergent cesarean section delivery. Compensatory fetal tachycardia and transient fetal heart rate decelerations occur. Delivery should be considered for the lack of improvement in 10 to 15 minutes after maternal/fetal resuscitative interventions.
   4. Seizures due to eclampsia generally resolve within a few hours to days postpartum. HELLP (hemolysis, elevated liver enzymes, low platelets) syndrome develops in approximately 10% to 20% of women with preeclampsia/eclampsia.

G. Idiopathic seizures, gelastic seizures, dacystic seizures, posttrauma, and nonepileptic seizures are other types noted in the literature.

Incidence

A. Three million Americans are affected by epilepsy. The prevalence of active epilepsy is about 0.8%.

B. Seniors: Most rapid population with comorbidity of epilepsy
   1. Stroke is the leading cause of new-onset epilepsy in adults after age 65.

C. Eclampsia
 1. Mild preeclampsia 0.5%
 2. Severe preeclampsia from 2% to 3%
 3. 48 hours postpartum up to 33%
D. Photosensitivity seizures are more common in children and adolescents.

Pathogenesis

A. Epilepsy is a functional disorder of the brain when neurons signal abnormally. The exact cause of epilepsy and eclampsia is unknown.

Predisposing Factors

A. Tumors
B. Alcohol/drugs
C. Cerebral infarction/stroke
D. Hypoglycemia
E. Alzheimer's disease
F. Posttrauma (head injury)
G. Surgery
H. Pregnancy (eclampsia)
I. Febrile illness
J. Photosensitivity
K. Risk factors for recurrent seizures
 1. Identifiable brain disease
 2. Mental retardation
 3. Abnormal neurologic examination/EEG
 4. Seizures onset after age 10
 5. Multiple types of seizures
 6. Family history/genetics
 7. Poor response to antiepileptic drugs (AEDs)/ combination therapy at time of withdrawal
 8. Chronic alcoholism
L. Eclampsia risk factors
 1. Nulliparous
 2. PIH
 3. Teens to lower 20s and again older than 35 years
 4. Other conditions to be ruled out.
  a. Stroke
  b. Hypertensive disease
  c. Space-occupying lesion
  d. Metabolic disorders (hypoglycemia, uremia, water intoxication)
  e. Meningitis or encephalitis
  f. Drug use (methamphetamine, cocaine)
  g. Idiopathic epilepsy
  h. Thrombotic thrombocytopenic purpura (TTP)

Common Complaints

A. Aura: Epigastric discomfort, fear, or unpleasant smells
B. Automatisms (swallowing, chewing, fumbling, picking clothes, or lip smacking)
C. Stiffening, then jerking of limbs
D. Staring with/without repetitive motor behaviors
E. Eclampsia
 1. Headache: Severe or persistent frontal or occipital
 2. Blurred vision
 3. Photophobia
 4. Right upper quadrant pain/epigastric pain
 5. Altered mental status
 6. Nausea and vomiting
 7. Hyperreflexia

Other Signs and Symptoms

A. Lack of memory of seizure
B. Impaired consciousness
C. Postictal
 1. Confusion
 2. Amnesia
 3. Fatigue
 4. Headaches
 5. Loss of urine or bowel control

Subjective Data

A. Obtain a history from the patient or a person who witnesses the seizure.
 1. Have the witness describe the duration, part of the body affected, and qualities of the seizure.
 2. Does the patient have a recollection of the seizure?
 3. How long did it take to feel better after the seizure?
B. Evaluate if the patient has ever had seizures, and ask whether this was an isolated event.
 1. Were there any warning symptoms prior to the seizure?
 2. What kind of warning was noted?
C. Did the patient have a fever or an active/recent infection?
D. Do a thorough review of the patient's medical history, including head injury, pregnancy, diabetes, and cancer.
E. Ask if there is a family history of seizures.
F. Take a full medication history including OTC and herbal products.
 1. Is the patient on an AED?
 2. Has the patient missed any doses?
 3. When was the last blood level checked to evaluate therapeutic dosing?
G. Review alcohol intake. Alcohol interferes with the efficacy of AEDs.

Physical Examination

A. Check blood pressure, pulse, respirations, and temperature (if indicated to rule out infection).
B. Inspect: LOC, orientation, general overall exam for secondary injuries from fall or striking objects.
C. Auscultate lungs for possible aspiration.
D. Palpation (if applicable for any injuries)
 1. Elevate neck for nuchal rigidity.

E. Neurologic examination
  1. CNS testing
    a. Wrinkle forehead/raise eyebrows.
    b. Smile and show teeth.
    c. Stick out the tongue/lateral tongue movement.
    d. Ocular movements
    e. Visual field
    f. Finger-to-nose test
  2. Motor strength
    a. Shrug shoulders.
    b. Test muscle strength: Grasp hands and squeeze.
    c. Check reflexes of biceps, triceps, patellar, brachioradial, and Achilles.
  3. Sensory testing: Pinprick
  4. Gait and posture

Diagnostic Tests

A. Diagnosis is confirmed by the patient's history, witness accounts, neurologic examination, blood work, and clinical testing, such as EEG.
B. EEG is essential in all cases of undiagnosed transient loss of consciousness, especially in the elderly, to rule out cardiac arrhythmias as the sudden loss of consciousness.
C. MRI is the gold standard for neuroimaging. The MRI is more accurate than a CT.
D. Blood glucose
E. Drug/alcohol screen
F. Serum level of anticonvulsant
G. LP if indicated for signs of infection/meningitis

Differential Diagnoses

A. Seizures
B. Brain tumor
C. CNS infection
D. Drug/alcohol use
E. Stroke/TIA
F. Hypoglycemia
G. Trauma
H. Migraine
I. Ménière's disease
J. Syncope
  1. Cardiac arrhythmic syncope
  2. Reflex
  3. Orthostatic
K. Psychogenic

Plan

A. **Emergency transport may be required. Seizures longer than 5 to 10 minutes require emergent care. If the patient has a persistent headache after a rest period, unconsciousness with failure to respond, unequal pupil size or excessively dilated pupils, or weakness of the limbs, immediate medical attention is essential.**
B. Obtain a consultation with a neurologist for a thorough evaluation.
C. States vary on the driving requirements/restrictions for patients with epilepsy. Individual state driving requirements are noted on the Epilepsy Foundation website: www.epilepsy.com/driving-laws.
  1. A person with epilepsy has the risk of an MVA while driving. It is considered similar or slightly higher than in patients with other medical conditions (diabetes, cardiovascular disease) and compares with the risk of MVA with persons with sleep apnea, alcoholism, dementia, and cellular phone use.
  2. Regulatory agents, as a measure of driving risk, require having a seizure-free interval of 3 to 12 months (state dependent). In studies, the seizure-free interval was the strongest predictor of MVA.
  3. Clinicians must warn patients about possible driving risks after reduction of medications or missing AED doses and must consider the patients' neurologic deficits other than seizures (e.g., cognition and visual field deficits) when making recommendations about driving. The risk factors for an MVA for persons with epilepsy are as follows.
    a. Medication noncompliance
    b. Recent history of alcohol or drug abuse
    c. Uncorrectable brain function or metabolic disorder
    d. Structural brain disease
    e. Frequent seizure recurrence after seizure-free intervals
    f. Prior crashes caused by seizures

Patient Teaching

A. Keeping a seizure diary is extremely helpful in identifying seizure trends, evaluating drug compliance, monitoring side effects, and evaluating the need for changing the course of therapy. The frequency or time of day that seizures occur is used in the adjustment of AED dosage and timing of administration.
B. Seizure triggers
  1. The most common cause is missed AED and/or sudden discontinuation of meds.
  2. Sleep deprivation
  3. Obstructive sleep apnea
  4. Alcohol/drug intake
  5. Stress
  6. Hormone fluctuations
  7. Pregnancy
  8. Photosensitivity/strobe or flashing light/intense lights
  9. TV and video games (flicker frequency)

10. Contrasting visual patterns (grids, checkerboard, and stripes)
11. Computer monitors
12. Visual fire alarms
13. Sunlight "shimmering off" water/through trees/ through window blinds

C. Review the importance of medication adherence.
1. Give oral and written dosing instructions.
2. Refill the prescription prior to running out.
3. Take the medication on a schedule (set a watch alarm, use a pill container, "mark off" the calendar). Taking an extra pill when a seizure aura occurs will not stop the seizure, since it is not absorbed fast enough.
4. New prescription interaction profiles should be evaluated before starting new drugs.
5. Patients should not use supplements, herbal, or OTC medications without checking with their health care provider.

D. Excessive alcohol use (> 3 drinks/d) increases the likelihood of seizures. Patients should have no more than 1 to 2 drinks a day.

E. First aid for grand mal seizure
1. Stay calm.
2. Time the seizure. Call 911 if the seizure lasts longer than 5 to 10 minutes.
3. Clear the area to prevent harm from surrounding objects.
4. Turn the person to the side and do not put anything in his or her mouth.
5. Do not hold the person down.
6. Place a soft object under the head to prevent head injury.
7. Cardiopulmonary resuscitation (CPR) is not necessary unless the person stops breathing after the seizure.
8. Stay with the person and reassure him or her.
9. Help get the person home; call family or friends.
10. Immediate transport to the emergency department is necessary for known conditions such as
a. Diabetes/hypoglycemia
b. Heat exhaustion
c. Pregnancy
d. Infection/high fever
e. Poisoning
f. Head injury

F. First aid for petit mal seizures
1. Stay calm.
2. Guide the patient away from any dangers.
3. Block access to hazards.
4. Do not restrain the person.
5. Stay with the person until full awareness returns.

Pharmaceutical Therapy

A. There is controversy concerning whether to start AED therapy for the first seizure. AEDs are generally started after a second seizure.

B. The prescription of AEDs should be individually weighed with a risk-versus-benefit decision that includes such factors as age; gender; family planning/desire for pregnancy; current driver; type/ recurrence of seizure; abnormal EEG; concurrent medications used for other comorbid conditions; history of depression, anxiety, suicidal ideation, and hepatic and renal disease; cost; patient preference and lifestyle issues; and side-effect profile of medication(s) (see Table 22.5).

C. A neurologist consultation should be obtained for full evaluation and prescription of AED with a neurologist or primary health care providers managing subsequent follow-up.

D. A single-agent AED is started and titrated slowly to the lowest dose that is the most effective in seizure control with the least number of side effects.
1. Ideally, the patient should be maintained on one AED; however, combination therapy may be required or the first agent discontinued.
2. When a second AED is required, the second additional medication is started by titration, a therapeutic level is achieved, and the first AED is subsequently tapered off. During this period of time there is an increase in side effects.
3. Switching to a generic formulation has been noted to increase seizure activity.
4. Rectal diazepam gel (Diastat) may be prescribed for use at home for patients with a history of prolonged seizures.

E. Medical marijuana has been used for uncontrolled seizures; however, there is a lack of research on the safety, consistent dose requirements, and potential side effects.

F. Stevens–Johnson syndrome (SJS) and TEN can occur up to 4 months after the institution of AEDs, including carbamazepine (Tegretol), oxcarbazepine (Trileptal), phenytoin (Dilantin), and lamotrigine (Lamictal).

G. Women should be routinely prescribed folate supplements of 0.4 to 0.8 mg/d. The folic acid recommendation is 4 mg/d for 1 to 3 months prior to conception when the patient is on valproate or carbamazepine (Tegretol).

Follow-Up

A. Follow-up by primary health care providers is dependent on the frequency of seizures, toxicity profile of AED, and other comorbid conditions.

B. Subsequent visits include the following evaluation.
1. Drug compliance

TABLE 22.5 Antiepileptic Medications

Drug	Seizure Type	First-Line Treatment
Carbamazepine (Tegretol)	Partial or mixed seizures. Generalized tonic-clonic seizures	First-line treatment
Clobazam (Onfi)	Lennox-Gastaut syndrome (LGS)	Adjunctive treatment
Clonazepam (Klonopin)	Absence seizures LGS	First-line treatment
	Myoclonic seizures	
Dibenzazepine (Oxtellar XR)	Partial seizures	Adjunctive treatment
Divalproex sodium (Depakote)	Absence seizures	First-line treatment
	Complex partial seizure	
Ethosuximide (Zarotin)	Absence seizures	Adjunctive treatment
Ezogabine (Potiga)	Partial seizures	Adjunctive treatment
Felbamate (Felbatol)	Partial seizures LGS	Not first line in partial seizures and used as an adjunctive for LGS
Gabapentin (Neurontin)	Partial seizures	Adjunctive treatment
Lacosamide (Vimpat)	Partial seizures	Adjunctive treatment
Lamotrigine (Lamictal)	Partial seizures LGS	First-line treatment LGS
Levetiracetam (Keppra)	Partial onset seizures	Adjunctive treatment for all types of seizures
	Myoclonic seizures	
	Generalized tonic-clonic seizures	
Magnesium sulfate (MgSO4)	Eclamptic tonic-clonic seizure	First-line treatment
Oxcarbazepine (Trileptal)	Partial seizures	Monotherapy or adjunct treatment
Perampanel (Fycompa)	Partial seizures	Adjunctive treatment
Phenytoin (Dilantin)	Tonic-clonic seizures	First-line treatment
	Psychomotor and neurosurgical-induced seizures	
Pregabalin (Lyrica)	Partial onset seizures	Adjunctive treatment
Primidone (Mysoline)	Focal and psychomotor seizures	Not first-line treatment
	Tonic-clonic seizures	
Rufinamide (Banzel)	LGS	Adjunctive treatment
Tiagabine (Gabitril)	Partial seizures	Adjunctive treatment
Topiramate (Topamax)	Partial onset seizures	First-line treatment and adjunctive for LGS
	Generalized tonic-clonic seizures LGS	
Topiramate (Trokendi XR)	Partial seizures	First-line treatment
	Primary tonic-clonic seizures or LGS	
Valproate	LGS	First-line treatment in LGS
Vigabatrin (Sabril)	Refractory complex partial seizures	Adjunctive treatment
Zonisamide (Zonegran)	Partial seizures	Adjunctive treatment

2. Seizure log/diary
   a. Epilepsy.com has the Seizure Severity Questionnaire available for download for individual use for patients to describe their most common type of seizure. The pdf is located at www.epilepsy.com/sites/core/files/atoms/files/ssq_0.pdf.
3. Drug concentrations, blood counts, and hepatic and renal function
4. Premenstrual serum levels when there is an increase in seizure activity the week before menstruation
5. Yearly drug levels are required for patients on a stable dose with no seizures.

C. There is an increased risk of suicide associated with several AEDs. Evaluation of the patient 1 week after institution of therapy is prudent. Instructions should be given to notify the office concerning depression.
   1. Perform serial depression/suicide screening.
   2. Psychiatric comorbid conditions should be treated promptly.

D. Bone loss is noted with long-term therapy with AEDs; therefore, a DEXA scan is warranted.
   1. Vitamin D and calcium may be prescribed with AEDs.

E. Patients taking AEDs need regular dental/oral care.

F. Each state has the legal prerogative to grant driving privileges. Clinicians cannot grant or suspend driving privileges.
   1. Six states require clinicians to report their patients with seizures (California, Delaware, Nevada, New Jersey, Oregon, and Pennsylvania).
   2. Some states require a letter sent to the motor vehicle department stating, "My patient has seizures and has been advised not to drive."
   3. All states require drivers with epilepsy or seizures to report their condition.
   4. Commercial driving restrictions are stricter. Restrictions for commercial vehicles involved in intrastate commerce vary among individual states.

G. Consider a sleep study to evaluate for obstructive sleep apnea.

Consultation/Referral

A. A neurology consultation is necessary for evaluation, medication initiation, and a discussion on the use of a ketogenic diet.

B. A neurosurgical consultation is necessary to evaluate a vagus nerve stimulator (VNS) or surgical options.
   1. The VNS has been approved for intractable epilepsy refractor to medications.

C. Refer to an obstetrician.

Individual Considerations

A. Women
   1. Preconception counseling and a planned pregnancy are imperative.
      a. Discuss the teratogenicity of AEDs.
         i. Attempt to decrease to monotherapy.
         ii. Taper doses of AEDs to the lowest possible dose.
         iii. If there is an absence of seizures for 2 to 5 years, consider a complete withdrawal of AEDs.
         iv. First-trimester use of one AED has been noted to have a two- to fivefold increase in major fetal anomalies such as neural tube defects, cleft lip and palate, and cardiac anomalies.
      b. Increase folic acid to 4 mg/d to help prevent neural tube defects.
      c. Stress the need for regular prenatal care.
      d. Offer maternal alpha-fetoprotein screening test.
      e. A fetal echocardiogram may be considered to diagnose cardiac defects.
      f. All care providers including nurses, pediatricians, and anesthesiologists should be aware that the patient has epilepsy on admission.
   2. Oral contraceptives are less effective on AEDs. The failure rate is 0.7 to 3.1 per 100 women. Women taking enzyme-inducing AEDs should use a backup method or alternative birth control. Enzyme-inducing AEDs include.
      a. Dilantin (phenytoin)
      b. Phenobarbital
      c. Tegretol (carbamazepine)
      d. Zarontin (ethosuximide)
      e. Felbatol (felbamate)
      f. Topamax (topiramate)
      g. Trileptal (oxcarbazepine)
   3. Estrogen and progesterone act on the temporal lobe where partial seizures often begin. Seizure patterns may change during menopause.

B. Geriatrics
   1. Seizures are likely to begin from 60 to 80 years of age.
   2. After stroke and dementia, epilepsy is the most common serious neurological disorder in the elderly.
   3. Focus on cardiovascular and neurologic systems in the clinical physical evaluation in the elderly.
   4. Management may be more difficult depending on comorbidities and the use of other medications.
   5. Commonly prescribed AEDs in the elderly include:
      a. Phenytoin
         i. Most commonly prescribed AED in the elderly
         ii. Use caution; phenytoin interacts with digoxin and warfarin
         iii. Causes sedation
      b. Sodium valproate
         i. Ataxia and tremor are not uncommon.
         ii. Can cause reversible extrapyramidal systems
      c. Carbamazepine
         i. Hyponatremia can occur, especially with coadministration of a diuretic
         ii. Increases warfarin metabolism
      d. Lamotrigine
         i. Requires a slow titration in the elderly
      e. Levetiracetam
         i. Mood and behavioral problems may occur
      f. Ginkgo biloba is the most commonly used herbal for seizures in the elderly

Stroke

Definition

Strokes are a medical emergency. Treatment for HTN is effective for the reduction of strokes across all ages and populations and is a major component of primary and secondary stroke prevention.

A. Due to the aging population, it is estimated that by the year 2030 approximately 4% of the population in the United States will have had a stroke. The risk of having a stroke increases with age 65 and older and is especially prominent in the population older than or equal to 80 years.

B. Strokes are the fifth leading cause of death for men, but the third leading cause of death in women.
C. Strokes are the leading cause of disability in the United States.
   1. Nearly half of stroke survivors have residual deficits, including weakness or cognitive dysfunction 6 months after stroke.
D. Stroke mortality varies by geographic location. The United States has a "Stroke Belt" in the southeastern states. Within this Stroke Belt there is an area described as the "buckle" region that has an approximate 40% increase in strokes. Georgia, North Carolina, and South Carolina are considered in the Stroke Belt Buckle area. The Pacific Northwestern states also have high stroke mortality rates.
E. Types of stroke include
   1. TIAs (see entry on TIAs in this chapter)
   2. Ischemic stroke
      a. Cerebral thrombosis
      b. Cerebral embolism
   3. Hemorrhagic
      a. Aneurysm
      b. AVM

Incidence

A. The incidence of stroke differs by race/ethnicity.
   1. Ischemic stroke is greater in Hispanics/Latinos and Blacks.
   2. Blacks and Hispanic/Latinos have a two to four times greater rate of stroke reoccurrence and stroke-related deaths.
B. Approximately 795,000 people in the United States have a stroke each year. One out of four people will have another stroke within 5 years.
C. The history of a stroke and/or TIA averages 10% yearly risk for a stroke.
D. The risk of a stroke within the first 7 days of a TIA is 3.5% to 10%.
E. The rate for ischemic stroke for patients with AFib is 5% yearly.
F. Hemorrhagic strokes account for 13% of strokes.
G. Women
   1. **Pregnancy-related HTN is the leading cause of both hemorrhagic and ischemic stroke in pregnant and postpartum women.**
   2. Presence of migraine with aura, contraceptive use, and smoking has a sevenfold higher odds of stroke in women.

Pathogenesis

A. Ischemic strokes are a complication related to atherosclerotic deposits. Plaque builds up and occludes the blood flow. The lack of blood flow to the brain causes ischemic changes. The symptoms exhibited are dependent on the location and severity of the ischemia. Ischemic strokes are also a complication of a cerebral embolism.
B. Hemorrhagic strokes are related to an aneurysm/rupture of a blood vessel or an AVM.

Predisposing Factors

A. Cardiac causes
   1. AFib (increases risk for stroke fivefold)
   2. Mitral and aortic valve disease
   3. Rheumatic heart disease
   4. Atrial and ventricular septal defects
   5. Carotid artery stenosis
   6. Thrombosis
   7. Embolism
B. Modifiable risk factors
   1. HTN
   2. Smoking/exposure to smoke
   3. Diabetes
   4. Dyslipidemia
   5. Obesity is an independent risk factor for stroke.
   6. Physical inactivity
   7. Sickle cell disease
C. Nonmodifiable risk factors
   1. Age
      a. The age of stroke onset is older for women, with the majority occurring after age 70.
   2. Gender
      a. Several factors are noted to increase the stroke risk for women.
         i. Pregnancy
         ii. Preeclampsia/eclampsia (twice the risk factor for stroke)
         iii. HT
         iv. Contraceptive use
         v. Migraine with aura
   3. Race/ethnicity
      a. Stroke risk is increased in Blacks and Hispanic/Latinos.
   4. Family history/genetic predisposition
      a. Inherited coagulopathies
D. TIA
E. Migraine with aura
F. Iatrogenic anticoagulation
G. Illicit drug use (i.e., cocaine or methamphetamines)
H. Postsurgical complications
I. Cerebral amyloidosis

Common Complaints

Signs and symptoms depend on the affected vessel and surrounding brain tissue.

A. Acute onset of focal neurologic deficit
   1. Partial or total loss of consciousness
   2. Headache (often described as the worst headache ever)

3. Limb weakness or numbness
4. Contralateral hemiparesis
5. Facial weakness/drooping
6. Speech difficulty (ranges from a total loss of speech to the inability to express and comprehend)
7. Dysphagia (ranges from an inability to chew and swallow to swallowing liquids that may lead to aspiration)
8. Visual changes (loss of vision, blurring, and double vision)
9. Ataxia

Other Signs and Symptoms

A. Cognitive changes
B. Behavioral changes
C. Nausea and vomiting
D. Fatigue
E. Seizures

Potential Complications

A. Long-term sequelae are dependent on the location and severity of the ischemia or hemorrhage.
B. Death

Subjective Data

If a stroke is suspected, call 911; symptoms of a TIA and a major stroke are not always distinguishable.

A. Ask detailed questions about symptoms before, during, and after the spell.
   1. Review the exact timing of onset of symptoms.
   2. How intense were the symptoms?
   3. What were the duration and the presence of any fluctuation of symptoms?
   4. Has there been a pattern that is becoming more frequent or escalating in symptoms?
B. Interview the patient, family members, witnesses, and emergency personnel for their description of behavior, speech, gait, memory, and movement.
C. Review the medical history.
   1. Previous TIA or stroke
   2. Previous/recent surgeries, specifically carotid or cardiac surgeries and any procedures such as coronary artery bypass graft (CABG) or stents
   3. AFib
   4. HTN
   5. Pregnancy or recent delivery history
   6. Migraine headaches
   7. Seizures
   8. CNS infection
   9. Illicit drug use
   10. Presence of any metabolic disorders
   11. Recent trauma (blunt or torsion injury to the neck)
D. Focus on precipitating factors and state of consciousness after the acute event.
E. Review all medications, including anticoagulants, oral contraceptives, HT, OTC, and particular review of substances not prescribed, as well as illicit drugs such as cocaine.
F. Herbals that alter bleeding time and interact with warfarin
   1. Feverfew
   2. Garlic
   3. Ginkgo biloba
   4. Ginger
   5. Ginseng

Physical Examination

> *Patients presenting with acute symptoms should be quickly assessed for the need to call emergency services 911 for immediate transport to the hospital. Time is of the essence for treatment with the drug tPA (tissue plasminogen activator).*

A. Check blood pressure, pulse, respirations, and pulse oximetry.
B. General observation
   1. Observe overall appearance, LOC, ability to interact, language, difficulty swallowing, tremors, and spasticity, as well as memory skills.
   2. Observe the patient walking (cerebellar system).
C. Inspect
   1. Dermal exam
      a. Overall hydration status
      b. Look for postcarotid endarterectomy scars, presence of a pacemaker, implantable cardioverter defibrillator, or other cardiac surgical scars.
   2. Check pupil size and reactivity to light.
   3. Perform a fundoscopic exam to evaluate optic disk margins, retinal plaques, and pigmentation. A "cherry red spot" may be evident in the macula in patients with central retinal artery occlusion.
D. Auscultate
   1. Heart for rate, rhythm, murmurs, or rubs
   2. Lungs: Note respiratory rate and pattern.
   3. Carotid arteries for the presence of bruit
E. Palpate
   1. Palpate extremities for pulses and peripheral edema.
F. Neurologic exam
   1. CN testing
      a. Wrinkle forehead/raise eyebrows.
      b. Smile and show teeth.
      c. Stick out the tongue/lateral tongue movement.
      d. Ocular movements
      e. Visual field

2. Motor strength
   a. Shrug shoulders
   b. Test muscle strength: Grasp hands and squeeze.
   c. Check reflexes of biceps, triceps, patellar, brachioradial, and Achilles.
3. Sensory testing: Pinprick
4. Gait and posture (cerebellar system evaluation)
   a. Ocular movements
   b. Gait
   c. Finger-to-nose test
   d. Heel-to-knee test

Diagnostic Tests

There is no "gold standard" for the diagnosis of CNS infarction.

A. CT scan
B. MRI
C. Other imaging
   1. Computed tomographic angiography (CTA) to look for abnormalities including aneurysm
   2. Magnetic resonance angiography (MRA) to locate a cerebral aneurysm
   3. Cerebral angiography/cerebral arteriography to locate size and location of blockages
   4. Duplex Doppler studies
D. Laboratory tests
   1. Emergent labs
      a. Glucose
      b. Serum chemistry profile
      c. Coagulation and hypercoagulability testing
      d. CBC
   2. Urgent labs
      a. ESR
      b. Cardiac enzymes
      c. Lipid profile
   3. Other laboratory tests based on history.
      a. Urine drug screen
      b. Blood alcohol level
      c. Antiphospholipid antibodies
E. EKG to identify cardiac dysrhythmia

Differential Diagnosis

A. Cardiovascular accident
   1. Ischemic stroke
   2. Hemorrhagic stroke
B. TIA
C. Aortic dissection
D. Thrombosis
E. CNS infection
F. Trauma
G. Brain tumor
H. Demyelination
I. Intoxication

Plan

A. General interventions
   1. Patient teaching
      a. Therapeutic lifestyle changes (TLCs), including exercise, diet, and weight management, are recommended for all patients.
      b. Increased physical activity. The 2013 American College of Cardiology/American Heart Association (ACC/AHA) guidelines on lifestyle management outline the newest physical activity recommendations advising adults to engage in 40 minutes of aerobic physical activity three to four times a week. The aerobic exercise should involve moderate-to-vigorous intensity to reduce blood pressure (BP), LDL-cholesterol (LDL-C), and non-HDL-C.
B. Dietary management
   1. Advise the patient that diet modification is the first line of therapy for hyperlipidemia.
   2. Explain cholesterol-lowering diet. Give dietary recommendation sheets. See Appendix B for low-fat/low-cholesterol and DASH dietary approaches to stop HTN.
C. Weight reduction
   1. Explain that weight reduction in patients greater than 20% over ideal body weight can lower LDL-C and triglyceride levels.
D. Other key dietary recommendations include:
   1. Reduce intake of saturated fats and trans fats. Aim for 5% to 6% of calories from saturated fat.
   2. Increase intake of poly-and monounsaturated fats.
   3. Increase intake of soluble fiber (psyllium supplement).
   4. Limit intake of alcohol: One drink per day for women and two drinks per day for men.
   5. Increase intake of plant stanols and sterols (1 oz of Promise Activ or Benecol spread per day).
   6. Follow the DASH, Mediterranean, or AHA diet.
   7. Lower sodium intake. Consume no more than 2,400 mg/d of sodium. Further reductions to 1,500 mg/d of sodium are associated with greater reduction in BP. Even a modest reduction in salt intake for more than or equal to 4 weeks leads to a reduction in BP.
   8. Discuss smoking cessation (see the Section III Patient Teaching Guide for Chapter 11, "Nicotine Dependence").
E. Carotid revascularization is a consideration for patients with ischemic stroke associated with carotid stenosis by doing a carotid endarterectomy. A cardiovascular procedure with a balloon angioplasty or a stent procedure is also utilized for revascularization.

F. People with hemorrhagic stroke secondary to a ruptured aneurysm may be surgical candidates.
G. Pharmaceutical therapy
   1. **Reperfusion therapy with intravenous thrombolytic drug r-tPA (recombinant tissue plasminogen activator) is utilized in the hospital setting for ischemic stroke. Use of r-tPA reduces the effects of stroke if administered within 3 hours of symptom onset. Delayed hospital arrival is the single most important reason for the failure to administer tPA within the window of 3 or 4.5 hours.**
      a. The 2012 American College of Chest Physicians Guidelines for Antithrombotic and Thrombolytic Therapy for Ischemic Stroke recommends:
         i. IV r-tPA to be initiated within 3 hours of symptom onset for patients with an acute ischemic stroke.
         ii. IV r-tPA can be initiated within 3 to 4.5 hours of acute symptom onset.
         iii. In patients with acute ischemic stroke in whom treatment cannot be initiated within 4.5 hours of symptom onset, the College recommends against IV r-tPA therapy.
   2. Aspirin (ASA) is the most commonly used antiplatelet therapy. Aspirin 75 to 100 mg daily is used for secondary stroke prevention.
      a. Gastrointestinal bleeding is a significant risk for prolonged ASA therapy.
      b. The 2014 American Heart Association/American Stroke Association (AHA/ASA) states aspirin therapy 81 mg/d or 100 mg every other day for women older than or equal to 65 years of age if blood pressure is controlled and the benefit of ischemic stroke and myocardial infarction prevention is likely to outweigh the risk of gastrointestinal bleeding and hemorrhagic stroke.
   3. Clopidogrel (Plavix) 75 mg once daily.
   4. The combination of aspirin and Clopidogrel may be considered for initiation after a minor ischemic stroke or TIA and for continuation for 90 days. Full recommendations are in the 2014 AHA/ASA Guideline for the Prevention of Stroke in Patients with Stroke and TIA available at http://stroke.ahajournals.org/content/early/2014/04/30/STR.0000000000000024
   5. Aspirin plus extended-release dipyridamole 25 mg/200 mg twice a day.
   6. Cilostazol 100 mg twice a day.
   7. **Ticlopidine 500 mg daily for secondary stroke prevention is rarely used. The most serious side effect/complication with ticlopidine is severe neutropenia requiring biweekly CBC.**
   8. Long-term anticoagulant therapy is required for the secondary prevention of AFib (see Chapter 12, "Cardiovascular Guidelines," for an in-depth review of AFib).
   9. Statin therapy is recommended to reduce the risk of stroke and cardiovascular events (see Chapter 12, "Cardiovascular Guidelines," "Atherosclerosis and Hyperlipidemia").
   10. Initiate or resume blood pressure therapy for prevention and reoccurrence of stroke to achieve a systolic pressure less than 140 mmHg and a diastolic pressure less than 90 mmHg (see Chapter 12, "Cardiovascular Guidelines," "Hypertension").
   11. Further adjuvant therapy must be had under the direction of a neurologist after a full evaluation.

Follow-Up

A. Follow-up is determined by patient's needs, severity of stroke, and whether complications are present.
B. Cardiac rhythm studies for more than 24 hours should be considered for nonvalvular AFib (NVAF).
C. Consider a sleep study and treatment with CPAP due to high prevalence of obstructive sleep apnea (OSA) with patients with strokes/TIA.
D. The AHA/ASA recommends that patients with sickle cell disease and prior strokes/TIA have chronic blood transfusions to reduce hemoglobin S to less than 30% of total hemoglobin.
E. Evaluate for depression at each office visit.
F. Stroke rehabilitation may include:
   1. Speech therapy
   2. Occupational therapy
   3. Physical therapy
G. Rehabilitation sites include:
   1. Nursing facility
   2. SNF
   3. Assisted living facility
   4. Home
H. Identify area support groups for the patient and/or caregivers.
I. Fitness for driving varies by state.

Consultation/Referral

A. Neurology
B. Cardiology, if applicable
C. Hematologist
D. Maternal–fetal medicine for high-risk pregnancy

Individual Considerations

A. Women
   1. Women older than 85 years of age have one of the highest risks of ischemic stroke. The

increased risk may be accounted for by women living longer than men.
2. Women have a higher rate of SAH as well as a higher risk of rupture.
3. Two major risk factors for stroke in women are oral contraceptives and pregnancy.
4. Prepregnancy HTN increases the risk for PIH and stroke during pregnancy.
5. The highest risk for stroke occurs in the third trimester of pregnancy.
6. Postmenopause
   a. Research indicates that natural menopause is not associated with a risk of stroke.
   b. Women with hysterectomy with bilateral oophorectomy have a slightly elevated risk of total stroke compared with women with hysterectomy with ovarian conservation.
   c. The 2014 American Heart Association/American Stroke Association guidelines for the prevention of stroke in women's HT recommendations include:
      i. HT, conjugated equine estrogen (CEE) with or without medroxyprogesterone should not be used for primary or secondary prevention of stroke in postmenopausal women.
      ii. Selective estrogen receptor modulators, such as raloxifene, tamoxifen, or tibolone should not be used for primary prevention of stroke.
7. Women with asymptomatic carotid stenosis should be screened for other treatable risk factors for stroke, and appropriate lifestyle changes and medical therapies should be instituted.

B. Geriatrics
1. 10% of intracerebral hemorrhages from cerebral amyloidosis occur in the elderly.
2. No dosage adjustment is necessary with Clopidogrel for elderly patients or patients with renal disease.

Resources

American Heart Association: https://www.heart.org/HEARTORG/GettingHealthy/GettingHealthy_UCM_001078_SubHomePage.jsp

National Stroke Association: http://www.stroke.org/site/PageNavigator/HOME

Stroke risk assessment tool: http://yourdiseaserisk.wustl.edu/YDRDefault.aspx?ScreenControl=YDRGeneral&ScreenName=YDRStroke

Transient Ischemic Attack

Definition

A. TIAs are brief focal brain deficits, spinal cord, or retinal ischemia (without acute infarction) caused by vascular occlusion. **TIAs are a medical emergency.**
Symptoms generally last less than an hour; however, they may have permanent sequelae. TIAs are a risk factor for recurrent risk of stroke. Approximately 15% of diagnosed strokes are preceded by TIAs. TIAs can be difficult to diagnose since symptoms are transient. Assume that all stroke-like symptoms signal an emergency.

B. **Persistence of neurologic deficit suggests a stroke rather than a TIA.**

Incidence

A. The prevalence of TIAs in the United States is between 200,000 and 500,000 per year. The population prevalence is about 2.3% or about 5 million Americans.
B. The early risk of stroke is approximately 5% at 2 days and as high as 11% at day 7 after a TIA.
C. The risk of a stroke within 3 months of a TIA is 10% to 15%.
D. More than one third of those who have a TIA will have a major stroke within a year if risk factors are not addressed.
E. The risk from death from coronary artery disease and stroke is as high as 6% to 10%, depending on other risk factors.

Pathogenesis

A. The pathogenesis is a neurologic event secondary to a temporary reduction of blood flow to the brain from a partially occluded vessel or related to an acute thromboembolic event.

Predisposing Factors

A. HTN
1. Systolic blood pressure greater than 140 mmHg
2. Diastolic blood pressure greater than 90 mmHg

B. Atherosclerosis
C. African American
D. Age older than 40 years
E. Hypotensive episodes
F. Oral contraceptives/HT
G. AFib
H. Smoking
I. Familial hyperlipidemia
J. Diabetes mellitus
K. Valvular heart disease
L. Infective endocarditis
M. Migraine with aura
N. Herbal medications alter bleeding time and interact with warfarin
1. Feverfew
2. Garlic
3. Ginkgo biloba

4. Ginger
5. Ginseng

Common Complaints

Signs and symptoms depend on the affected vessel and surrounding brain tissue.

A. Acute onset of focal neurologic deficit
   1. Limb weakness or numbness
   2. Facial weakness
   3. Speech difficulty to aphasia
   4. Visual loss/blurring
   5. Ataxia
B. Acute change in LOC or confusion
C. Posterior circulation TIAs may have a headache as one of the prodromal symptoms that precedes a stroke by days or weeks.
D. Basilar artery occlusion TIAs have vertigo, nausea, and headaches that may occur as early as 2 weeks or more prior to the onset of stroke.

Other Signs and Symptoms

A. Dysarthria
B. Dysphagia
C. Near syncope
D. Hemiparesis
E. Temporary monocular blindness
F. Behavior changes
G. Difficulty with balance and vertigo
H. Dizziness
I. Diplopia

Subjective Data

If a TIA is suspected, call 911; symptoms from a TIA and a major stroke are not always distinguishable.

A. Ask detailed questions about symptoms before, during, and after the spell.
   1. Review the exact timing of onset of symptoms.
   2. How intense were the symptoms?
   3. What was the duration of any fluctuation of symptoms?
   4. Has there been a pattern that is becoming more frequent or escalating in symptoms?
B. Interview the patient, family members, witnesses, and emergency personnel for their description of behavior, speech, gait, memory, and movement.
C. Focus on precipitating factors and state of consciousness after the acute event.
D. Question the patient about risk factors such as HTN, smoking, cardiac disease, and heredity.
E. Review all medications, including anticoagulants, OTC, and herbals and illicit drug use such as cocaine.
F. Review the medical history.
   1. Recent surgeries, specifically carotid or cardiac surgeries
   2. Seizures
   3. CNS infection
   4. Illicit drug use
   5. Presence of any metabolic disorders
   6. Recent trauma (blunt or torsion injury to the neck)
   7. AFib
   8. Migraine headaches

Physical Examination

A. Check temperature (if infectious process is suspected), pulse, respirations, and blood pressure, including orthostatic blood pressure, as well as pulse oximetry.
B. General observation
   1. Observe overall appearance, LOC, ability to interact, language, difficulty swallowing, tremors, and spasticity, as well as memory skills.
   2. Observe the patient walking (cerebellar system).
C. Inspect
   1. Dermal exam
      a. Overall hydration status
      b. Look for postcarotid endarterectomy scars, presence of a pacemaker, implantable cardioverter defibrillator, or other cardiac surgical scars.
   2. Check pupil size and reactivity to light.
   3. Perform a fundoscopic exam to evaluate optic disk margins, retinal plaques, and pigmentation.
D. Auscultate
   1. Heart for rate, rhythm, murmurs, or rubs
   2. Lungs: Note respiratory rate and pattern.
   3. Carotid arteries for the presence of bruit
E. Palpate
   1. Palpate extremities for pulses and peripheral edema.
F. Neurologic exam
   1. CN testing
      a. Wrinkle forehead/raise eyebrows.
      b. Smile and show teeth.
      c. Stick out the tongue/lateral tongue movement.
      d. Ocular movements
      e. Visual field
   2. Motor strength
      a. Shrug shoulders
      b. Test muscle strength: Grasp hands and squeeze.
      c. Check reflexes of biceps, triceps, patellar, brachioradial, and Achilles.
   3. Sensory testing: Pinprick
   4. Gait and posture (cerebellar system evaluation)
      a. Ocular movements
      b. Gait
      c. Finger-to-nose test
      d. Heel-to-knee test

Diagnostic Tests

A. Pulse oximetry
B. Laboratory tests
   1. Emergent labs
      a. Glucose
      b. Serum chemistry profile, including creatinine
      c. Coagulation and hypercoagulability testing
      d. CBC
   2. Urgent labs
      a. ESR
      b. Cardiac enzymes
      c. Lipid profile
   3. Other laboratory tests based on history.
      a. Urine drug screen
      b. Blood alcohol level
      c. Antiphospholipid antibodies
      d. Rapid plasma reagin (RPR) for syphilis
C. MRI or CT scan within 24 to 48 hours of symptom onset
D. Carotid Doppler ultrasonography identifies patients with urgent surgical needs.
E. Cardiac imaging to evaluate cardioembolic sources
F. EKG to evaluate dysrhythmias (i.e., AFib)
G. LP to rule out infection, demyelinating disease, and SAH
H. EEG as indicated for seizure activity
I. Consider Holter monitor for suspected intermittent AFib.

Differential Diagnoses

A. TIA
B. Ischemia stroke
C. SAH/SDH
D. Migraine
E. Hypoglycemia/HTN
F. Epilepsy-postictal period
G. Malignant HTN
H. Brain tumor
I. Bell's palsy
J. MS
K. Syncope
L. Drug induced
M. Concussion
N. Vertigo

Plan

A. General interventions
   1. Carefully assess the patient to timely diagnose.
   2. Perform a full workup to determine the underlying disease process.
   3. Prevent stroke by modification of risk factors.
B. Patient teaching: See the Section III Patient Teaching Guide for this chapter, "Transient Ischemic Attack."
C. Medical and surgical management
   1. Treat TIAs with antiplatelet drugs as soon as intracranial bleeding is ruled out.
   2. Consider carotid endarterectomy.
   3. Lipid control
   4. Glucose control
   5. Smoking cessation
   6. Eliminate or reduce alcohol consumption.
   7. Start an exercise plan for losing weight. Recommend starting with about 30 minutes of exercise three times per week.
D. Pharmaceutical therapy
E. **The mainstay of treatment for TIA is pharmacologic management with antithrombotic agents.**
   1. Antiplatelet therapy
      a. Aspirin 50 to 325 mg/d. **Aspirin should not be administered concomitantly with coumarin anticoagulants.**
      b. Dipyridamole (Persantine) 200 mg/d. May be given as an adjunct with warfarin therapy
      c. Aspirin + dipyridamole extended release (Aggrenox) 25/200 mg twice a day
      d. Clopidogrel (Plavix) 75 mg/d
         i. Aspirin is not routinely recommended with clopidogrel due to the risk of hemorrhage.
         ii. No dosage adjustment is necessary with Clopidogrel for elderly patients or patients with renal disease.
      e. Ticlopidine (Ticlid) 250 mg twice a day is a second-line antiplatelet therapy for patients who cannot tolerate or do not respond to aspirin therapy. In some circumstances, it can be an alternative to clopidogrel.
      f. Warfarin (Coumadin) 5 to 15 mg titrate for a goal international normalized ratio (INR) of 2.0 to 3.0
   2. Antihypertensive therapy as indicated to maintain blood pressure below 140/90 mmHg with an Ace inhibitor or an angiotensin receptor blocker alone or in combination with a diuretic.
   3. Initiate a daily statin to a goal LDL-C less than 100 mg/dL

Follow-Up

A. **Rapid transfer is essential for a patient with positive symptoms for risk stratification. Patients with a suspected TIA who are not admitted to the hospital should have rapid access (within 12 hours) for an urgent assessment and evaluation with CT or MRI brain scan, EKG, and carotid Doppler testing.**
B. Patients managed as outpatients should be fully educated about the need to return to the clinic or emergency department immediately if symptoms recur.
C. Specific follow-up depends on etiology, severity, frequency, and duration of TIAs.

D. Follow-up laboratory testing as indicated (i.e., CBC, cholesterol, INR)
E. Monitor the patient for occult bleeding if started on antiplatelet and/or antithrombotic medications.

Consultation/Referral

A. TIA should be viewed as a medical emergency because these patients have salvageable neurologic function; consult with a physician.
B. Cardiology and neurology consultations should be obtained when cardioembolic TIAs are treated with anticoagulation therapy.
C. Ophthalmologic consultation is indicated to assess the nature of transient visual symptoms.
D. Vascular surgeon consultation is necessary for patients with significant stenosis or occlusion. Patients with symptomatic carotid artery stenosis should have a surgical evaluation immediately.

Individual Considerations

A. Adults: TIAs that occur in the younger adult population should be evaluated for embolism.
B. Geriatrics
   1. TIAs are most commonly seen in this population.
   2. Screen for AFib in women, especially older than 75 years.
   3. Anticoagulation is not recommended for women younger than 65 years with AFib that are otherwise at low risk for stroke. Antiplatelet therapy is recommended for this population.

Resources

A. The National Institutes of Health Stroke Scale (NIHSS) is a stroke scale that evaluates the effect of an acute cerebral infarct. The 15-item stroke scale requires less than 10 minutes to complete.
   1. A free online training certification course for the NIHSS is available at www.nihstrokescale.org
   2. A hard copy of the NIHSS is located at www.ninds.nih.gov/doctors/NIH_Stroke_Scale.pdf
   3. An online NIHSS calculator is located at www.mdcalc.com/nih-stroke-scale-score-nihss
B. The ABCD2 Score for TIA estimates the risk of a stroke after a TIA.
   1. An online ABCD2 calculator is located at www.mdcalc.com/abcd2-score-for-tia
   2. A hard copy of the ABCD2 is available at www.stroke.org/site/DocServer/NSA_ABCD2_tool.pdf

Trigeminal Neuralgia

Definition

A. TN, also known as tic douloureux, is a chronic pain condition of the face. There are two types: Type I or TN1 and Type 2 or TN2.
   1. TN1 causes extreme, sporadic, sudden burning or shock-like facial pain that may last from a few seconds to as long as 2 minutes per episode. These attacks can occur in succession lasting as long as 2 hours.
   2. TN2 is characterized by constant aching, burning, or stabbing pain of somewhat lower intensity than TN1.
   3. Both can occur at the same time, in the same person. The pain can be physically and mentally incapacitating.

Incidence

A. TN occurs most often in people older than the age of 50, although it may occur at any age including infancy. The incidence of new cases is approximately 12 per 100,000 people per year. The disorder is more common in women than in men.

Pathogenesis

A. The trigeminal nerve is the fifth of 12 pairs of CNs in the head. It is the nerve responsible for providing sensation to the face. One trigeminal nerve runs to the right side of the head, whereas the other runs to the left. Each of these nerves branches off after the nerve leaves the brain and travels inside the skull. It divides into three smaller branches.
   1. The first branch controls sensation in the eye, upper eyelid, and forehead.
   2. The second branch controls sensation in the lower eyelid, cheek, nostril, upper lip, and upper gum.
   3. The third branch controls sensation in the jaw, lower lip, lower gum, and some of the muscles used in chewing.

Predisposing Factors

A. TN may be caused by a blood vessel pressing on the trigeminal nerve as it exits the brainstem causing the wearing away of the protective coating of the nerve (myelin sheath).
B. TN may occur in people with MS, a disease that causes deterioration of the trigeminal nerve sheath.
C. Injury to the trigeminal nerve resulting from sinus surgery, oral surgery, stroke, or facial trauma may produce neuropathic facial pain.
D. Rarely, TN may be caused by a tumor or tangle of arteries and veins known as anteriovenous malformation (AVM).

Common Complaints

A. Pain varies depending on the type of TN and may range from sudden, severe, and stabbing pain to a more constant, aching, and burning sensation. The usual pattern is for the attacks to intensify over time with shorter pain-free periods.

B. Flashes of pain may occur by vibration or contact with the cheek such as with shaving, washing the face, applying makeup, brushing teeth, eating, drinking, talking, or being exposed to the wind.
C. The pain may affect a small area of the face or it may spread.
D. Bouts of pain rarely occur at night when the patient is sleeping.

Other Signs and Symptoms

A. Classic pain occurs with definite periods of remission. The pain is intensely sharp, throbbing, and shocklike.
B. Atypical pain often presents as a constant, burning sensation affecting a more widespread area of the face. There may not be remission periods, and symptoms are more difficult to treat.
C. TN tends to run in cycles. Long stretches of frequent attacks will be followed by weeks, months, or even years with little or no pain.

Potential Complications

A. Uncontrollable facial twitching
B. Attacks becoming more frequent and intense
C. The attacks often worsen over time, eventually pain-free intervals disappear, and medication becomes less effective.
D. TN is not fatal, but it can be debilitating, causing patients to avoid daily activities or social contacts in fear of an impending attack.
E. TN may be caused by a tumor or MS.

Subjective Data

A. Ask patient what activity brought about or preceded the episode.
B. Have patient describe duration of pain and what time of day symptoms began.
C. Ask patient to describe pain—for example, crushing, stabbing, or burning—and affected areas.
D. Ask patient where sensation began and in what direction it radiates.
E. Have patient rate pain on a scale of 0 to 10, with 0 being no pain.
F. Ask patient to list all medications currently being taken, particularly substances not prescribed and illicit drugs such as cocaine.
G. Ask the patient about any other medical conditions he or she is being treated for.
H. Ask the patient if he or she has had sinus or dental surgery or facial trauma/injury.
I. What treatments have been tried so far and if anything helps the pain.
J. Ask how the pain impacts quality of life and ability to perform daily activities.

Physical Examination

A. Start with vital signs: Check temperature, pulse, respirations, and blood pressure.
B. Inspect
   1. Inspect general appearance, noting any patient discomfort.
   2. Note facial appearance and evidence of tics.
C. Ausculate
   1. Heart
   2. Lungs
D. Palpate
   1. Complete a full neurologic exam, testing all CNs.

Diagnostic Tests

A. MRI to rule out tumor or multiple sclerosis

Differential Diagnosis

A. TN
B. Brain tumor
C. MS
D. Temporal tendinitis (migraine mimic)
E. Ernest syndrome-injury of the stylomandibular ligament which connects the base of skull with the lower jaw.
F. Occipital neuralgia
G. Postherpetic neuralgia

Plan

A. General interventions
   1. Order MRI to rule out a tumor or MS as the cause of the pain.
   2. Surgery procedures are available if medications do not control the pain: Percutaneous (through the skin) or open. The benefits of surgery should always be weighed carefully against the risk involved. There is no guarantee that surgery will help every individual.
      a. Microvascular decompression involves exposure of the trigeminal nerve root with gentle movement of the blood vessel away from the point of compression.
      b. Rhizotomy involves the use of electrocoagulation (heat), destroying the part of the nerve that causes pain and suppressing the pain signal to the brain.
      c. Glycerol rhizotomy utilizes glycerol injection into the area where the nerve divides into the three branches hoping to damage the nerve, selectively interfering with the pain transmission to the brain.
      d. Radiosurgery (gamma knife) involves delivering a single highly concentrated dose of radiation to a small target of the trigeminal nerve. This procedure avoids many of the

risks and complications of open surgery and other treatments. The slow formation of a lesion in the nerve interrupts transmission of pain signals to the brain.

e. A last resort is the motor cortex stimulation. This is an open procedure with all the risks but without the high success rates.

B. Patient education
1. Provide patient with education regarding the disease process.
2. See the Section III Patient Teaching Guide for this chapter, "Trigeminal Neuralgia."

C. Pharmaceutical therapy
1. Carbamazepine, an anticonvulsant medication, is the most common medication used to treat TN. In the early stages, carbamazepine controls pain for most people but the effect of the drug decreases over time. Side effects include dizziness, double vision, drowsiness, and nausea.
2. Muscle relaxants such as baclofen, robaxin, norflex, or flexeril are especially effective when used with either carbamazepine or an anticonvulsant. Possible side effects include confusion, depression, and drowsiness.
3. Anticonvulsant medications such as phenytoin, which was the first medication used to treat TN, with possible side effects of gum overgrowth, balance disturbances, and drowsiness. Currently, more anticonvulsant medications are available for use.
4. Oxcarbazepine (Trileptal) has been used more recently as the first-line treatment and has fewer side effects, notably, dizziness and double vision.
5. Other medications include gabapentin, clonazepam, sodium valproate, lamotrigine, and topiramate.

Follow-Up

A. Follow-up is determined by patient needs, severity of symptoms, and whether complications are present. Monitor the patient for depression and sleep disturbance.

Consultation/Referral

A. Neurology referral is essential in confirming diagnosis of TN.
B. Medication initiation, titration, and management should be instituted by the neurologist.
C. Neurosurgeon referral per neurology recommendations due to medication failure and possible surgery
D. Some patients may require supportive counseling or therapy by a psychiatrist or psychologist.
E. Alternative therapy may include complementary techniques such as aroma therapy, meditation, acupuncture, chiropractic therapy, biofeedback, or botox injections.

Vertigo

Definition

A. Vertigo is the illusion of self or environmental movement, typically rotating, spinning, tilting, even a sensation that you are going to fall down. Older patients have an increased risk of falls and depression secondary to vertigo.
B. Vertigo is often classified as either central or peripheral in origin.

Incidence

A. Approximately 20% to 30% of the general population experience dizziness.
B. It is estimated that approximately 0.5% of the population consults their primary health care provider each year regarding vertigo.
C. Both sexes, as well as all age groups, are affected.
D. Benign paroxysmal positional vertigo (BPPV) is the most common cause of vertigo, excluding CNS lesions.
1. The prevalence of BPPV is 2.4%.
2. BPPV rarely occurs in people younger than 35 years unless there is a history of head trauma.
3. BPPV commonly presents in the ages between 50 and 70 years.
4. BPPV recurs in approximately one third of patients after 1 year and in about 50% in all patients treated after 5 years.

Pathogenesis

A. Distinguishing between peripheral and central vertigo is critical because the evaluation, treatment, and progress vary significantly. Central vertigo suggests brainstem dysfunction affecting the vestibular nuclei or their connections. This may be secondary to a structural lesion such as neoplasm or ischemia.
B. Vertigo due to vascular insufficiency is rarely isolated, and other symptoms of brainstem involvement are usually seen, such as diplopia, dysphagia, motor weakness, or disruption in sensation. Neoplasms are usually slow growing, and the vestibular dysfunction is often insidious. Other considerations for causes of central vertigo include MS, seizures, and migraines.
C. Vertigo of peripheral origin is more common and may be caused by dysfunction of the inner ear or vestibular nerve. BPPV is the most commonly diagnosed of peripheral vestibular disorders. The cause of BPPV is unknown. The most common explanation is free otoconia within the semicircular

canals that are dislodged by trauma, infection, or degeneration. The debris relocates when the head is repositioned and provokes vertigo. Causes of labyrinthine dysfunction include infection, trauma, ischemia, or toxins such as drugs or alcohol.

D. Ménière's disease causes vertigo, hearing loss, and ringing of the ears. The exact cause is unknown but a hypothesis is a buildup of fluid in the inner ear.

E. Viral infections may lead up to vestibular neuritis (labyrinthitis). The vertigo experienced with vestibular neuritis is sudden and severe and may last days.

F. Other possible causes of vertigo are psychogenic, cardiovascular, or metabolic conditions, as well as head trauma and migraines.

G. Medications that cause dizziness
   1. Anticonvulsants
   2. Antidepressants
   3. Antipsychotics
   4. Anxiolytic/sedatives
   5. Antihypertensives
   6. Nitrates
   7. Diuretics
   8. Insulin/oral hypoglycemic agents

Predisposing Factors

A. Head or body movement
   1. Rolling over in bed
   2. Getting out of bed
   3. Bending down from the waist
   4. Looking up

B. Fear or anxiety

C. Stress

D. Recent infection, usually upper respiratory in cases of vestibular neuronitis

E. Family history, especially in cases of vertiginous migraine

F. Head trauma

G. Migraines

H. Idiopathic with no cause identified

I. Hypoglycemia

J. Alcohol intoxication

K. Medication side effects

L. Cerebellar or brainstem stroke

M. Tumors

N. MS

O. Dehydration

Common Complaints

A. Dizziness with or without change in body positioning

B. Feeling of imbalance

C. Nausea/vomiting

D. Tinnitus

E. Aural fullness

F. Hearing loss

Other Signs and Symptoms

A. Central origin, including vascular insufficiencies, strokes, neoplasms, migraine, MS, seizures
   1. Double vision
   2. Dysarthria
   3. Dysphagia
   4. Paresthesias
   5. Changes in motor or sensory exam
   6. Mild to moderate vertigo
   7. Multiple episodes of vertigo lasting seconds to minutes in duration with vascular insufficiency and seizures
   8. Constant complaints of vertigo with neoplasms or strokes
   9. Multiple episodes of vertigo lasting hours with migraines
   10. Single episodes of vertigo with MS
   11. Dix–Hallpike test: Habituation common with delayed nystagmus

B. Peripheral origin, including BPPV, Ménière's disease, labyrinthitis, vestibular dysfunction, vestibular neuritis, and acoustic neuroma
   1. No associated signs of brainstem dysfunction
   2. Vertigo, usually described as severe
   3. Multiple episodes of vertigo lasting hours with Ménière's disease
   4. Single or multiple episodes of vertigo with labyrinthitis
   5. Vestibular dysfunction, described as constant vertigo
   6. Severe nausea or vomiting
   7. Hearing loss or tinnitus; aural fullness may be present, as well as a roaring sound.
   8. Triad of vertigo, tinnitus, and hearing loss is suggestive of Ménière's disease.
   9. Dix–Hallpike test: No habituation: nystagmus occurs immediately.

Subjective Data

A. Elicit onset, frequency, duration, and course of presenting symptoms.
   1. Is this recurrent or new?
      a. Acute vertigo is seen with trauma, stroke, meningitis, otitis media, mastoiditis, drug use, vestibular neuronitis, MS, and labyrinthitis.
      b. Recurrent vertigo is seen in migraines, BPPV, motion sickness, seizures, and Ménière's disease.

B. Elicit from the patient a verbal description of the sensation(s) experienced.

C. Note triggering and alleviating factors.

D. Query the patient regarding associated symptoms such as hearing loss, tinnitus, nausea, difficulty with gait, aural fullness, or other neurologic manifestations such as nystagmus. As a result of dizziness, ask the patient if he or she has ever fallen down when symptoms are present.

E. Review the patient's past medical history, including recent infections; trauma; risk factors for cardiovascular disease such as smoking, diabetes, and hyperlipidemia.
F. Review OTC, herbal products, and medication use: Aminoglycoside, antibiotics, diuretics, antihypertensives, and antidepressants.
G. Has the patient had any previous treatments for vertigo such as an Epley procedure?
H. Has the patient had any previous testing such as:
   1. Audiometric testing
   2. Electronystagmogram (ENG)/Videonystagmography (VNG) to evaluate balance
   3. Rotational/balance platform test
   4. CT or MRI
   5. Computerized dynamic posturography (CDP) to evaluate postural stability/motor control

Physical Examination

A. Check temperature (if indicated), pulse, respirations, and blood pressure; note orthostatic hypotension.
B. Inspect
   1. Observe overall appearance. Generalized muscle weakness may be observed.
   2. Note gait: Difficulty with tandem gait. Note global weakness.
   3. Inspect the eyes: Assess for nystagmus; a few beats of nystagmus on extreme lateral gaze may be normal.
   4. Ear examination: Rule out otitis media.
   5. Evaluate for aphasia that may indicate a stroke.
C. Palpate
   1. Palpate extremities; note pulses and edema.
   2. Perform Rinne test and Weber's test.
D. Neurologic exam
   1. Perform complete neurologic exam.
   2. Assess CNs.

      Brainstem involvement is frequently seen with detailed neurologic exam. Signs of cerebellar dysfunction include difficulty with finger-to-nose testing, rapid alternating supination or pronation of hands, and gait disturbance.

   3. Perform Romberg test: The patient stands with feet together and closes his or her eyes. Positive result is when the patient sways. This may be seen with vestibular disease and acoustic neuroma.
   4. The Dix–Hallpike test (also called the Nylen–Barany's maneuver test) is a provocative positional test.

      The Dix–Hallpike maneuver is considered the gold standard for diagnosing BPPV. However, a negative test does not rule out BPPV if the patient is asymptomatic on the date of the test. If a positive response is observed on the initial side, no further testing is required.

      a. Perform the Dix–Hallpike: While the patient is seated on the middle third of the examination table, turn the patient's head 45° toward the affected side (problem ear). While holding the head in that position, assist the patient to the reclining position past the supine position. BPPV has a distinctive nystagmus in which there is involuntary eye movement (predominately in a rotating fashion) starting slowly, progressing to a fast phase, and then reaching a resetting phase. The nystagmus generally lasts less than 20 seconds and reverses itself once the patient sits upright.
      b. Caution should be taken in performing the Dix–Hallpike test with patients who have cervical stenosis, severe kyphoscoliosis, spinal cord injuries, and significant vascular disease.
   5. Test for nuchal rigidity if fever is present.
E. Auscultate
   1. Auscultate the heart, neck, and carotid arteries.

      Physical examination may reveal cardiovascular abnormalities, such as a carotid bruit.

   2. Auscultate lungs: Pneumonia may cause dizziness.
   3. Auscultate the abdomen.

Diagnostic Tests

A. Laboratory testing
   1. Thyroid function studies: To rule out hypothyroidism
   2. VDRL: To rule out secondary or early tertiary syphilis, which can have symptoms similar to those of Ménière's disease.
   3. CBC: To rule out infection or severe anemia
   4. Electrolytes: To rule out hyponatremia, hypokalemia, and dehydration
   5. Urine drug screen (if indicated)
   6. Cardiac panel (if indicated)
   7. Urinalysis to rule out a UTI in the elderly
B. CT scan for head trauma
C. MRI with and without contrast to assess for mass, especially if a central origin is suspected
D. Caloric test: Definitive procedure for identifying vestibular pathology
E. Electronystagmography: Most useful in chronic peripheral disorders to determine the degree and progression of vestibular deficit
F. Audiogram: Test for possible hearing loss.

G. Rotating chair test: Interprets the slow component velocity of the nystagmus response with bilateral canals stimulated
H. LP if meningitis is suspected.

Differential Diagnoses

A. Vertigo
B. Vascular insufficiencies
C. Stroke
D. Neoplasms
E. Migraine
F. MS
G. Seizures
H. BPPV
I. Ménière's disease
J. Labyrinthitis
K. Vestibular dysfunction
L. Vestibular neuritis
M. Acoustic neuroma
N. Syncope
O. Multiple sensory defects
P. PD
Q. Adverse reaction to medications

Plan

A. General interventions: Treatment of vertigo depends on the underlying pathology and duration of the symptoms.
  1. Acute vertigo: Maintain the patient on bed rest, with the reassurance that most patients with acute vertigo recover spontaneously over a period of several weeks to months.
  2. Chronic vertigo: Refer the patient for physical therapy with emphasis on vestibular rehabilitation.
    a. Cawthorne Cooksey physical exercise regimen encourages eye, head, and body movements to facilitate recalibration of the vestibulo-ocular and vestibulospinal reflexes.
    b. Encourage ambulation when tolerated to induce central compensatory mechanism.
  3. Ménière's disease: The patient needs bed rest in the acute phase and nutritional therapy with restrictions of sodium, caffeine, alcohol, and tobacco.
  4. BPPV
    a. The patient needs bed rest for acute symptoms.
    b. Canalith repositioning procedures (CRP) provide immediate resolution of vertigo in 85% to 95% of patients. Epley procedure: The CRP is safe, simple, inexpensive, quick, and easy to perform. It is likely to be unsuccessful in patients with bilateral positional nystagmus, and it is not recommended for patients with acute vertigo, many of whom may have vestibular neuronitis. See the Section II Procedure, "Canalith Repositioning (Epley) Procedure for Vertigo." Contraindications to performing the Epley procedure are:
      i. Recent neck fracture or neck instability
      ii. A history of unstable carotid disease
      iii. Recent retinal detachment
      iv. Any physical condition that prevents the patient from lying down quickly or rolling over, which are required for the procedure.
    c. Instead, meclizine is used for 1 to 2 weeks, and then the patient is reassessed. Stop meclizine on the day the patient returns; it may suppress the positional nystagmus.
    d. For patients with severe positional vertigo during the Dix–Hallpike maneuver, premedicate with a prochlorperazine (Compazine) 25 mg suppository 1 hour prior to performance of the CRP.
    e. If the Dix–Hallpike is positive on the left, use a left-sided CRP. Conversely, if it is positive on the right, use a right-sided CRP. If the patient has bilateral disease, refer him or her to an otolaryngologist or treat the more symptomatic side first.
    f. After the Epley procedure, different types of recommendations are made to prevent the otoconia from returning to the posterior semicircular canal, including
      i. Wear a cervical collar for two nights after the maneuver.
      ii. Stay upright for 24 hours after the procedure or have the head elevated 30 degrees for one to two nights after the procedure.
      iii. Avoid sleeping with the affected ear down.
      iv. Counsel to avoid abrupt head changes for 1 week after the procedure.
      v. Avoid exercise such as yoga and sit-ups that would make similar motions.
      vi. Avoid looking up, such as looking at items on the top shelves at the grocery.
      vii. Symptoms may reoccur after tilting backward in dental chairs.
      viii. Symptoms may reoccur after turning in the hairdresser's chair and/or tilting backward for a shampoo.

B. Patient teaching: Encourage compliance with bed rest and exercises.
C. Pharmaceutical therapy

The American Academy of Otolaryngology—Head and Neck Surgery does not recommend the use of vestibular suppressant medications to control BPPV. The American Academy of Neurology also reports that there is no evidence

to support the routine use of vestibular suppressant therapy as treatment for BPPV.

1. Acute vertigo
   a. Metoclopramide (Reglan)
   b. Ondansetron (Zofran)
   c. Dimenhydrinate (Dramamine)
   d. Promethazine (Phenergan)
   e. Meclizine (Antivert)
   f. Dimenhydrinate (Dramamine)
   g. Diphenhydramine (Benadryl)
   h. Vestibular sedative
      i. Cinnarizine
      ii. Meclizine (Antivert)
      iii. Diazepam (Valium)
2. Chronic vertigo
   a. Cinnarizine
   b. Clonazepam (Klonopin)
   c. Carbamazepine (Tegretol)
3. Ménière's disease
   a. Considering diuretics such as hydrochlorothiazide and triamterene (Dyazide) together will help with vertigo but may not reduce hearing loss.
   b. TCAs may be used in resistant cases.
4. Antivirals are not useful for treatment of vestibular neuritis.
5. Steroids have been used in the treatment of vestibular neuritis.
6. Vestibular migraines respond to antimigraine medications.

D. Surgery
1. Pneumatic equalization tubes
2. BPPV surgery-canal partitioning or canal plugging
3. Vestibular nerve section (vestibular neurectomy) is a treatment for intractable violent episodes of BPPV.
4. Labyrinthectomy to remove the semicircular canals, utricle, and saccule, the balance organs. This procedure is considered only when a person has already lost all hearing function in the affected ear.
5. Chemical labyrinthectomy: Gentamicin infusion destroys the vestibular hair cells.

Follow-Up

A. The American Academy of Otolaryngology—Head and Neck Surgery Foundation recommends managing patients with BPPV as follows.
1. Canalith repositioning/Epley procedure should be offered unless there is a risk for impaired mobility or balance or the patient is at increased risk for falls.
2. Patients should be reevaluated in 1 month after an Epley procedure/CRP in order to confirm that the procedure resolved the symptoms of vertigo.
3. The recurrence rate after an Epley procedure is 30% to 50%.

B. Follow-up as needed according to the origin of the diagnosis and the patient's needs.

C. If indicated, transfer to the ER/call 911 for cardiovascular and cerebrovascular symptoms for treatment of stroke or cardiac events.

Consultation/Referral

A. Refer to a physician if the patient does not experience improvement in 2 to 4 weeks. If symptoms worsen, consider referring to an ear, nose, and throat specialist.

B. Refer to an otolaryngologist for testing, including
1. Audiometric testing
2. ENG to evaluate balance
3. Rotational/balance platform test

Individual Considerations

A. Geriatrics
1. **Many of the medications, individually and especially in combination, used for vestibular suppression are on the American Geriatrics Society Beers Criteria list of potentially inappropriate medications for older adults.**

Resources

American Speech-Language-Hearing Association (ASHA): www.asha.org

Vestibular Disorders Association: www.vestibular.org

Bibliography

Abbott, S. (2010). Diagnostic challenge: Myasthenia gravis in the emergency department. *Journal of the American Academy of Nurse Practitioners, 22*, 468–473.

American Academy of Neurology. (n.d.). *Guillain-Barré syndrome.* Retrieved from http://www.patients.aan.com/disorders/indexcfm?event=print&disorder_id=935

American Academy of Neurology Professional Association Model Policy. (n.d.). *Canalith Repositioning Procedure (CRP).* Retrieved from www.aan.com/globals/assets/7053.pdf

American Academy of Otolaryngology-Head and Neck Surgery. (2010, December). *Meniere's disease.* Retrieved from www.entnet.org/Healthinformation/menieresDisease.cfm

American Association of Neurological Surgeons. (2012). *Trigeminal neuralgia.* Retrieved from http://www.aans.org/Patient%20Information?Conditions$20and%20Treatment

American Speech-Language-Hearing Association. (2011). *Dizziness and balance.* Retrieved from www.asha.org/uploadedfiles/AIS-Dizziness-Balance.pdf

Andary, M. T. (2014, March 17). *Guillain-Barré syndrome. Medscape.* Retrieved from emedicine.medscape.com/article/315632-overview

Awad, A., & Stuve, O. (2010). Multiple sclerosis in the elderly patient. *Drugs & Aging, 27*(4), 283–294.

Baumann, R. J. (2012, March 27). *Febrile seizures. Medscape.* Retrieved from emedicine.medscape.com/article/1176205-overview

Bayer, A. (2012). Progress in diagnosis and management of Alzheimer's disease. *Quality in Aging & Older Adults, 13,* 189–196.

Bergman, K., Given, B., Fabiano, R., Schutte, D., von Eye, A., & Davidson, S. (2013, June). Symptoms associated with mild traumatic brain injury/concussion: The role of bother. *Journal of Neuroscience Nursing, 45,* 124–132.

Boissy, A., & Ford, P. (2012). A touch of MS: Therapeutic mislabeling. *Neurology, 78*(24), 1981–1985.

Bonnet, A. M., Jutras, M. F., Czernecki, V., Corvol, J. C., & Vidailhet, M. (2012). Nonmotor symptoms in Parkinson's disease in 2012: Relevant clinical aspects. *Parkinson's Disease.* Retrieved from www.hindawi.com/journals/pd/2012/198316/cta

Bove, R., Healy, B., Augustine, A., Musallam, S., Gholipour, T., & Chitnis, T. (2012). Effect of gender on late-onset multiple sclerosis. *Multiple Sclerosis Journal, 18*(10), 1472–1479.

Burns, T. M. (2008). Guillain-Barré syndrome. *Seminary in Neurology,* 28, 152–167.

Bushnell, C., McCullough, L. D., Awad, I. A., Chireau, M. V., Fedder, W. N., Furie, K. L., Howard, V.J., et. al. (2014). Guidelines for the prevention of stroke in women: A statement for healthcare professionals from the American Heart Association/American Stroke Association. Retrieved from http://stroke.ahajournals.org/content/early/2014/02/06/01.str.0000442009.06663.48.full.pdf+html

Casto, J., & Childers, J. (2014). A woman with sensory deficits, paresthesias, and ataxia. *Journal of the American Academy of Physician Assistants, 27*(3), 34–36.

Casye, G. (2012). Alzheimer's and other dementias. *Kai Tiaki Nursing New Zealand, 18,* 20–24.

Caughey, A. B. (2012, July 2). *Seizure disorders in pregnancy. Medscape.* Retrieved from emedicine.medscape.com/article/272050-overview

Cavazos, J. E. (2013, March 11). *Epilepsy and seizures. Medscape.* Retrieved from emedicine.medscape.com/article/1184846-overview

Centers for Disease Control and Prevention. (2012, August 23). *Guillain-Barré syndrome (GBS).* Retrieved from www.cdc.gov/flu/protect/vaccine/guillainbarré.htm

Centers for Disease Control and Prevention. (2014). *Injury prevention & control: Traumatic brain injury. May 29, 2014.* Retrieved from http://www.cdc.gov/concussion/

Centers for Disease Control and Prevention. (2014, March 17). *Stroke treatments.* Retrieved from http://www.cdc.gov/stroke/treatments.htm

Chawla, J. (2014, April 8). *Migraine headache. Medscape.* Retrieved from emedicine.medscape.com/article/114556-overview

ClinicalKey. (2012). *Transient ischemic attack.* Retrieved from https://www.clinicalkey.com/topics/neurology/transient-ischemic-attack.html

Collie, M. J. H. (2013, December). Vertigo diagnosis and management. *Clinician Reviews, 23*(12), 46–53.

Cucchiara, B. L., & Messé, S. R. (2013, October 7). Antiplatelet therapy for secondary prevention of stroke. *UpToDate.* Retrieved from http://www.uptodate.com/contents/antiplatelet-therapy-for-secondary-prevention-of-stroke?source=related_link

Culebras, A., Messé, S. R., Chaturveldi, S., Kase, C. S., & Gronseth, G. (2014). Summary of evidence-based guidelines update: Prevention of stroke in nonvascular atrial fibrillation: Report of the guideline subcommittee of the American Academy of Neurology. *Neurology, 82,* 716–724.

Donofrio, P. D., Berger, A., Brannagan, T. H., 3rd., Bromberg, M. B., Howard, J. F., Latov, N., ... Tandan, R. (2009). Consensus statement: The use of intravenous immunoglobulin in the treatment of neuromuscular conditions report of the AANEM ad hoc committee. *Muscle & Nerve, 40,* 890–900.

Eby, A. K. (2012). Myasthenia gravis: An update. *American Nurse Today.* Retrieved from www.americannursetoday.com/article.aspx?id=8950

Eckel, R. H., Jakicie, J. M., Ard, J. D., Hubbard, V. S., de Jesus, J. M., Lee, I. -Min., . . . Yanovsk, S. Z. (2013, November 12). AHA/ACC guideline on lifestyle management to reduce cardiovascular risk: A report of the American College of Cardiology/American Heart Association Task Force on practice guidelines. *Circulation.* Retrieved from http://circ.ahajournals.org

Engstrom, A., & Soderberg, S. (2011). Transition as experienced by close relatives of people with traumatic brain injury. *Journal of Neuroscience Nursing,* 43, 253–260.

Epilepsy Foundation. (n.d.a). *Diagnosis.* Retrieved from www.epilepsyfoundaton.org/aboutepilepsy/Diagnosis/index.cfm

Epilepsy Foundation. (n.d.b). *Driver and the law.* Retrieved from www.eplipsey.com/eplipsey/rights_driving

Epilepsy Foundation. (n.d.c). *First aid for seizures.* Retrieved from www.epilepsyfoundation.org/aboutepilepsy/firstaid/index.cfm

Epilepsy Foundation. (n.d.d). *Injuries from seizures.* Retrieved from www.epilepsyfoundation.org/aboutepilepsy/healthrisks/injuriesfrom seizures.cfm

Epilepsy Foundation. (n.d.e). *Photosensitivity and epilepsy.* Retrieved from www.epilepsyfoundation.org/aboutepilepsy/seizures/photosensitivity/index.cfm

Epilepsy Foundation. (n.d.f). *Seizures.* Retrieved from www.epilepsyfoundation.org/aboutepilepsy/seizures/index.cfm

Epilepsy Foundation. (n.d.g). *Seizure provoking triggers.* Retrieved from www.epilepsyfoundation.org/aboutepilepsy/Diagnosis/seizureprovkingtriggers.cfm

Epilepsy Foundation. (n.d.h). *Suicide risk.* Retrieved from www.epilepsyfoundation.org/aboutepilepsy/healthrisks/suicide.cfm

Epilepsy Foundation. (n.d.i). *Treatment.* Retrieved from www.epilepsyfoundation.org/aboutepilepsy/treatment/index.cfm

Evans, R.W. (2014). Concussion and mild traumatic brain injury. *UpToDate.* http://www.uptodate.com/contents/concussion-and-mild-traumatic-brain-injury?source=machineLearning&search=mild+traumatic+brain+injury&selectedTitle=1~150§ionRank=2&anchor=H25#H3

Family Doctor. (n.d.). *Headaches in elderly people.* Retrieved from www.familydoctor.co.uk/node/530

Fife, T. D., Iverson, D. J., Lempert, T., Furman, J. M., Baloh, R. W., Tusa, R. J., ... American Academy of Neurology. (2008). Practice parameter: Therapies for benign paroxysmal positional vertigo (an evidence-based review): Report of the quality standards subcommittee of the American Academy of Neurology. *Neurology, 70,* 2067–2074.

First Consult. (2011, April 22). *Migraine.* Retrieved from http://www.mdconsult.com.proxy.library.vanderbilt.edu/ds/pdxmd/body/405466689

Fisher, R. S., Acevedo, C., Arzimanoglou, A., Bogacz, A., Cross, H., Elger, C. E., et.al. (2014). A practical clinical definition of epilepsy. *Epilepsia, 55,* 475–482.

Fokke, C., van der Berg, B., Drenthen, J., Walgaar, C., Antoon van Doorn, P., & Jacobs, BC. (2014). Diagnosis of Guillain-Barré syndrome and validation of Brighton criteria. *Brain, 137,* 33–43.

fpnotebook. (2013). *Headache red flags.* Retrieved from www.fpnotebook.com/neuro/exam/HdchRdFlg.htm

Furman, J. M. (2013). Patient information: Dizziness and vertigo (beyond the basics). *UpToDate.* Retrieved from www.uptodate.com/contents/dizziness-and-vertigo-beyond-the-basics?view=print

Garza, I., & Schwedt, T. J. (2012, May 25). Chronic migraine. *UpToDate.* Retrieved from http:/www.upto-date.com/contents/chronic-migraine?topicKey=NEURO%2F3337

GBS/CIDP Foundation International. (2012). *Guillain-Barré syndrome, CIDP and variants: Guidelines for physical and occupational therapy.* Retrieved from www.gbs-cidp.org/wp-content/uploads/2012/01/PTOTGuidelines.pdf

GlobalRPh Inc. (n.d.). *Anti-platelet agents.* Retrieved from http://www.globalrph.com/antiplatelet.htm

Goff, D. C., Lloyd-Jones, D. M., Bennett, G., Coady, S., D'Agostino, Sr., R. B., Gibbons, R., ... Wilson, P. W. F. (2013, November 12). ACC/AHA guideline on the assessment of cardiovascular risk: A report of the American College of Cardiology/American Heart Association Task Force on practice guidelines. *Circulation.* Retrieved from http://circ.ahajournals.org

Goldenberg, M. M. (2012). Multiple sclerosis review. *P&T, 37,* 175–184.

González-Suárez, I., Sanz-Gallego, I., Rodríguez de Rivera, F., & Arpa, J. (2013). Guillain-Barré: Natural history and prognostic factors: a retrospective review of 106 cases. Retrieved from http://www.biomedcentral.com/1471-2377/13/95

Haight, T., & Jaquest, W. (2012). Relative contributions of biomarkers in Alzheimer's disease. *Annals of Epidemiology, 22,* 868–875.

Hain, T. C & The Vestibular Disorder Association. (2014). *Benign paroxysmal positional vertigo (BPPV).* Retrieved from http://vestibular.org/sites/default/files/page_files/Documents/BPPV.pdf

Hall, G. R., Gallagher, M., & Dougherty, J. (2009). Mental health: Integration roles for successful dementia management. *Nurse Practitioner: American Journal of Primary Health Care, 34*(11), 35–41.

Halloran, L. (2011, March). Dementia: Forget about it! Differentiation and diagnosis of dementias. *Journal of Nurse Practitioners, 7,* 242–243.

Halloran, L. (2013, April). Cognitive impairment: Pearls for practice. *The Journal for Nurse Practitioners, 9,* 254–255.

Hershey, L. A., & Bednarczyk, E. M. (2013). Treatment of headache in the elderly. *Current Treatment Options in Neurology,*15, 56–62.

Illinois Neurological Institute. (2013). *Headaches and sleep.* Retrieved from www.ini.org/services/sleep-disorders/conditions-treated/headaches-and-sleep.html

International Headache Society ICHD-II. (n.d.a). *Cluster headache.* Retrieved from http://www.ihs-classification .org/en/

International Headache Society ICHD-II. (n.d.b). *Migraine.* Retrieved from http://www.ihs-classification.org/en/02_klassifikation/02_tel1/01.00.00_migraine.html

International Headache Society ICHD-II. (n.d.c). *New daily-persistent headache (NDPH).* Retrieved from www.ihs-classification.org/en/02_klassifikation/02_teil1/04.08.00_other.html

International Headache Society ICHD-II. (n.d.d). *Tension-type headache (TTH).* Retrieved from http://www.ihs-classification. org/en/02/_klassifikation/02_teil1/02.00.00_tension.html

Jeffrey, S. (2014, March 11). *FDA approves first device to prevent migraine. Medscape.* Retrieved from http://www.medscape.com/viewarticle/821810

Johnson, A., & Smith, P. E. M. (2010). Epilepsy in the elderly. *Expert Reviews Neurotherapeutics,* 10, 1899–1910. Retrieved from http://www.medscape.com/viewarticle/733423

Kessing, L. (2012). Depression and the risk for dementia. *Current Opinion in Psychiatry,* 25, 457–461.

Kernan, W. N., Ovbiagele, B., Black, H. R., Bravata, D. M., Chimowitz, M., Ezekowitz, M. D., ... Wilson, J. A. (2014). *AHA/ASA guideline for the prevention of stroke in patients with stroke and transient ischemic attack.* Retrieved from http://stroke.ahajournals.org/content/early/2014/04/30/STR.0000000000000024

Khoo, T., Yarnell, A., Duncan, G., Coleman, S., O'Brien, J., Brooks, D., & Burn, D. (2013). The spectrum of nonmotor symptoms in early Parkinson disease. *Neurology, 80,* 276–281.

Kuitwaard, K., van Koningsveld, R., Ruts, L., Jacobs, B. C., & van Doorn, P. A. (2009). Recurrent Guillain–Barré syndrome. *Journal of Neurology Neurosurgery Psychiatry, 80,* 56–59.

Kutcher, J., Lee, M. J., & Hickenbottom, S. (2009, May 1). Neurologic disorders complicating pregnancy. *Online 16.3.* Retrieved from http://www.uptodate.com/online/content/topic.do?topicKey=medneuro/8805&view=print

Kutzin, J. M. (2012). Myasthenia gravis: A real emergency. *International Emergency Nursing, 20,* 102–105.

Lansberg, M. G., O'Donnell, M., Khatri, P., Lang, E. S., Nguyen-Huynh, M. N., Schwartz, N. E., Sonnenberg, F.A., et al. (2012). Antithrombotic and thrombolytic therapy for ischemic stroke. Antithrombotic therapy and prevention of thrombosis, 9th ed: American College of Chest Physicians Evidence-Based Clinical Practice Guidelines. *Chest, 141,* e601S–e634S.

Li, J. C. (2012, April 10). Benign paroxysmal positional vertigo. *Medscape.* Retrieved from emedicine.medscape.com/article884261-overview

Liebeskind, D. S. (2013, March 8). *Hemorrhagic stroke. Medscape.* Retrieved from http://emedicine.medscape.com/article/1916662-overview

Lo, A. X., & Harada, C. N. (2013). Geriatric dizziness: Evolving diagnostic and therapeutic approaches for the emergency department. *Clinics in Geriatric Medicine,* 29, 181–204.

Loder, R., Burch, R., & Rizzoli, P. (2012). The 2012 AHS/AAN guidelines for prevention of episodic migraine: A summary and comparison with other recent clinical practice guidelines. *Headache,* 52, 930–945.

Mayhew, M. (2010, March). Cholinesterase inhibitors and Alzheimer's Disease. *The Journal for Nurse Practitioners, 6,* 220–221.

Mayo Clinic. (2014). *Trigeminal neuralgia.* Retrieved from http://www.mayoclinic.org/diseases-conditions/trigeminal-neuralgia/basics/

MDGuidelines. (n.d.). *Guillain-Barré syndrome.* Retrieved from www.mdguidelines.com/guillain-barre-syndrome

Mollaoğlu, M., Fertelli, T., & Tuncay, F. (2011). Disability in elderly patients with chronic neurological illness: Stroke, multiple sclerosis and epilepsy. *Archives of Gerontology and Geriatrics,* 53(2), 227–231.

Moses, S. (2014, March 22). *Transient ischemic attack.* Retrieved from http://fpnotebook.com/Neuro/CV/TrnsntIschmcAtck.htm

Meena, A. K., Khadikar, S. V., & Muthy, J. M. K. (2011, July). Treatment guideline for Guillain–Barré syndrome. *Annals of Indian Academy of Neurology, 14*(Suppl 1), S73–S81.

Merck Manual. (2012). *Approach to the patient with headache: Headaches Merck manual professional.* Retrieved from www.merckmanuals.com/professional/print/neurologic_disorders/headache/approach_to_the-patient_withheadache.html

Merkies, I. S., Schmitz, P. I., van der Meche, F. G., Samijn, J. P., & van Doorn, P. A. (2002). Clinimetric evaluation of a new overall disability scale in immune mediated polyneuropathies. *Journal of Neurological Neurosurgery Psychiatry, 72,* 597.

Michoulas, A., & Farrell, K. (2010, May). Medical management of Lennox-Gastaut syndrome. *CNS Drugs, 24,* 363–74.

MPR Nurse Practitioner's Edition. (Summer 2014). New York, NY: Haymark Media, Inc.

Murray, T. J. (2006). Diagnosis and treatment of multiple sclerosis. *British Medical Journal, 332,* 523–527.

Nair, D. R. (2010, August 1). Epilepsy. *Cleveland Clinic Center for Continuing Education.* Retrieved from www.clevelandclinicmeded.com/medicalpubs/diseaemanagement/neurology/epileptic-syndrome/#s0035

Nanda, A. (2013, July 20). *Transient ischemic attack medication. Medscape.* Retrieved from http://emedicine.medscape.com/article/1910519-treatment

National Institute for Clinical Excellence. (2010, November). *EBP compendium: Summary of clinical practice guideline.* Retrieved from www.asha.org/Members/ebp/compendium/guidelines/Multiple-Sclerosis-National-Clinical-Guidelines-for-Diagnosis-and-Management-in-Primary-and-Secondary-Care.htm

National Institute on Deafness and Other Communication Disorders. (2010, July). *Meniere's disease* [NIDCD health information]. Retrieved from www.nidcd.nih.gov/health/balance/pages/meniere.aspx

National Institute of Neurological Disorders and Stroke. (2013, February 21). *Febrile seizures fact sheet.* Retrieved from www.ninds.nih.gov/disorders/febrile_seizures/detail_febirle_seizures.htm?css=print

National Institute of Neurological Disorders and Stroke. (2013, March 20). *NINDS transient ischemic attack information page.* Retrieved from www.ninds.nih.gov/disorders/tia/tia.htm?css=print

National Institute of Neurological Disorders and Stroke. (2014, April 16). *Guillain-Barré syndrome fact sheet.* Retrieved from http://www.ninds.nih.gov/disorders/gbs/detail_gbs.htm

National Institute of Neurological Disorders and Stroke. (2014, April 28). *Brain basics: Preventing stroke.* Retrieved from http://www.ninds.nih.gov/disorders/stroke/preventing_stroke.htm

National Institute of Neurological Disorders and Stroke. (2014). *Trigeminal neuralgia fact sheet.* Retrieved from http://www.ninds.nih.gov/disorders/trigeminal_neuralgia/detail_trigeminal

National Sleep Foundation. (n.d.). *Epilepsy and sleep.* Retrieved from http://sleepfoundation.org/sleep-disorders-problems/disease-and-sleep/epilepsy

National Stroke Association. (n.d.). *National Stroke Association guidelines for the management of TIA.* Retrieved from www.stroke.org/site/Docserver/TIA_Guidelines_070506_sm.pdf?docID=2361

National Stroke Association. (n.d.). *Transient ischemic attack (TIA): prognosis and key management considerations.* Retrieved from http://www.stroke.org/site/DocServer/NSA_ABCD2_tool.pdf

National Stroke Association. (2013, November 4). *TIA (Transient ischemic attack).* Retrieved from http://www.strokeassociation.org/STROKEORG/AboutStroke/TypesofStroke/TIA/TIA-Transient-Ischemic-Attack_UCM_310942_Article.jsp

Nentwich, L. M. (2013, March 4). *Transient ischemic attack. Medscape.* Retrieved from emedicine.medscape.com/article/1910519-overview

Orton, C. (2011, July). Vitamin B_{12} (cobalamin) deficiency in the older adult. *Journal for Nurse Practitioners, 8,* 547–553.

Ovbiagele, B. (2008). Antiplatelet therapy in management of transient ischemic attack: Overview and evidence-based rationale. *Journal of Emergency Medicine, 34,* 389–396.

Ovbiagele, B., Goldstein, L. B., Higashida, R. T., Howard, V. J., Johnson, S. C., Khavjou, O. A., …Lackland, D. T., Lichtman, J.H., Mohl, S., Sacco, R.L., Saver. J.L., & Trodgdon, J. G. (2013). Forecasting the future of stroke in the United States: A policy statement from the American Health Associations and American Stroke Association. *Stroke, 44,* 2361–2375.

Papas, L., Mendes, M., & Braga, C. (2012). Mild traumatic brain injury among the geriatric population. *Current Translational Geriatrics & Experimental Gerontology Reports, 1*(3), 135–142.

Perry, M. (2012). A guide to vascular dementia. *Practice Nurse, 42,* 25–29.

Polman, C. H., Reingold, S. C., Banwell, B., Clanet, M., Cohen, J. A., Filippi, M., … Wolinsky, J. S. (2011). Diagnostic criteria for multiple sclerosis: 2010 revisions to the McDonald criteria. *Annals of Neurology, 69,* 292–302.

Rabie, A. N. (2012, July 2). Canalith-repositioning maneuvers. *Medscape.* Retrieved from emedicine.medscape.com/article/82945-overview

Sacco, R. L., Kasner, S. E., Broderick, J. P., Caplan, L. R., Connor., J. J., Coulebras, A., … Viinters, H. V (2013). An updated definition of stroke for the 21st century: A statement for healthcare professionals from the American Heart Association/American Stroke Association. *Stroke, 44,* 2064–2089.

Sanders, D. B., & Scoppetta, C. (1994). The treatment of patients with myasthenia gravis. *Neurologic Clinics of North America, 12,* 343–367.

Schachter, S. C. (2012, October 5). Patient information: Seizures in adults (Beyond the basics) *UpToDate.* Retrieved from www.uptodate.com/contents/seizures-in-adults-beyond-the-basics?view=print

Schoenen, J., Vandermissen, B., Jeangette, S., Herroelen, L., Vanderheede, M., Gérard, P., & Magis, D. (2013). Migraine prevention with a supraorbital transcutaneous stimulator, a randomized controlled trial. *Neurology, 80,* 697–704.

Scott, B. L., & Stacy, M. A. (2009, June). The management of Parkinson's disease in the primary care setting. *Self Study Supplement to Clinician Reviews,* 1–12.

Scott, T. F., Frohman, E. M., & De Seze, J. (2011). Evidence-based guideline: Clinical evaluation and treatment of transverse myelitis. *Neurology, 77,* 2128–2134.

Silberstein, S. D., Holland, S., Freitag, F., Dodick, D. W., Argoff, C., & Ashman, E. (2012). Evidence-based guideline update: Pharmacologic treatments for episodic migraine prevention in adults. *Neurology, 78,* 1337–1345.

Stieman Cancer Center. (2013). *Your disease risk: Stroke.* Retrieved from http://yourdiseaserisk.wustl.edu/YDRDefault.aspx?ScreenControl=YDRGeneral&ScreenName=YDRStroke

Slade, S., & Ravert, P. (2012, October). Late-life body mass index and dementia: An integrative literature review. *The Journal for Nurse Practitioners, 8,* 725–728.

Smith, C., & Stickler, D. (2012). A collaborative approach to myasthenia gravis. *Clinical Advisor for Nurse Practitioners, 15,* 20–27.

Sorkin, L., Molton, I., Johnson, K., Smith, A., & Stern, M. (2012). Assessment and management of the elderly patient with multiple sclerosis. *Healthy Aging & Clinical Care in the Elderly, 4,* 1–11.

Stippler, M., Holguin, E., & Nemoto, E. (2012). Traumatic brain injury in elders. *Annals of Long-Term Care: Clinical Care and Aging., 20*(5), 41–46.

Stroke Awareness Foundation. (2014). *Transient ischemic attack (TIA).* Retrieved from http://strokeinfo.org/signsandsymptoms/stroke-facts/transient-ischemic-attack-tia/

Sun-Edelstein, C., & Mauskop, A. (2011, March). Alternative headache treatments: Nutraceuticals, behavioral, and physical treatments. *Headache Currents, 51*(3), 469–483.

Snyder, C. H., Facchiano, L., & Brewer, M. (2011, February). Using evidence-based practice to improve the recognition of anxiety in Parkinson's. *The Journal for Nurse Practitioners, 7,* 136–141.

Snyder, C. H., & Facchiano, L. (2011, March). An evidence-based critical appraisal of a topic: Effectiveness of high dose donepezil for advanced Alzheimer's disease. *The Journal for Nurse Practitioners, 7,* 201–206.

Snyder, C. H., & Facchiano, L. (2012, February). Evidence-based evaluation of cholinesterase inhibitors for mild cognitive impairment. *Journal for Nurse Practitioners, 8,* 136–144.

Sendon, J., Mena, M., & De Yebenes, J. (2012). Drug-induced Parkinsonism in the elderly. *Drugs & Aging, 29,* 105–116.

The White House.gov. (n.d.). *Ask the DEA to reschedule marijuana to a lower level to benefit greater access for research purposes.* Retrieved from https://petitions.whitehouse.gov/petition/ask-dea-reschedule-marijuana-lower-level-benefit-greater-access-research-purposes/vJVF409k

The Medical Letter, Inc. (2011, February). Drugs for migraine. *Treatment Guidelines from the Medical Letter, 9,* 7–12.

Uriri-Glover, J., McCarthy, M., & Cesarotti, E. (2012). Alzheimer disease: What new evidence shows. *Nurse Management, 43,* 26–32.

U.S. Headache Consortium. (n.d.a). *Evidence-based guidelines for migraine headache: Behavioral and physical treatments.* Retrieved from www.aan.com/professionals/practice/pdfs/g10089.pdf

U.S. Headache Consortium. (n.d.b). *Evidence-based guidelines for migraine headache in the primary care setting: Pharmacological management for prevention of migraine.* Retrieved from www.aan.com/professionals/practice/pdfs/g10090.pdf

U.S. Headache Consortium. (n.d.c). *Evidence-based guidelines in the primary care setting: Neuroimaging in patients with non-acute headache.* Retrieved from www.aan.com/professionals/practice/pdfs/g10088.pdf

U.S. Centers for Disease Control and Prevention. (n. d). *Heads up: Facts for physicians about mild traumatic brain injury.* Retrieved from http://www.cdc.gov/concussion/headsup/pdf/Facts_for_Physicians_booklet-a.pdf

Vernon, G. W. (2009, March). Parkinson disease and the nurse practitioner: Diagnostic and management challenges. *Journal for Nurse Practitioners, 5,* 195–206.

Vestibular Disorder Association. (n.d.a). *Benign paroxysmal positional vertical (BPPV).* Retrieved from vestibular.org/sites/default/files/page_files/BPPV_0.pdf

Vestibular Disorders Association. (n.d.b). *Diagnosis, how are vestibular disorders diagnosed?* Retrieved from http://vestibular .org/understanding-vestibular-disorder/diagnosis

Vestibular Disorder Association. (n.d.c). *Meniere's disease: How did Meniers's disease get its name.* Retrieved from vestibular .org/menieres-disease

Vestibular Disorder Association. (n.d.d). *Surgery for peripheral vestibular disorders.* Retrieved from vestibular.org/sites/default/page_files/surgery%20for%Peripheral%20Vestibular%20Disorders_1.pdf

Vestibular Disorder Association. (n.d.e). *Vestibular neuritis and labyrinthitis.* Retrieved from vestibular.org/sites/default/files/page_files/vestibular%20Neuritis%20%26%20Labyrinnitis_0pdf

Vriesendorp, F. J. (2013, March 20). Treatment and prognosis of Guillain-Barré syndrome in adults. *UpToDate.* Retrieved from www.uptodate.com/contents/treatment-and-prognosis-of-guillain-barre-syndrome-inadults?topicKey=NEURO%2F5172

Weeks, B. H. (2012). Myasthenia gravis. *Nurse Practitioner, 37,* 30–37.

Weintraub, D., & Burn, D. J. (2011, May). Parkinson's disease: The quintessential neuropsychiatric disorder. *Movement Disorders, 26,* 1022–1031. Retrieved from www.ncbi.nlm .nih.gov/pmc/articles/PMC3513835/

Yuki, M. & Hartung, H. P. (2012, June 14). Guillain-Barré Syndrome. *New England Journal of Medicine, 366,* 2294–2304.

CHAPTER TWENTY-THREE

Endocrine Guidelines

Julie Adkins, Jill C. Cash, Mellisa Hall, Cheryl A. Glass, and Angelito Tacderas

Addison's Disease

Definition

A. Primary adrenal insufficiency resulting in glucocorticoid and mineralocorticoid insufficiency.

Incidence

A. Approximately 40 to 60 cases per million; idiopathic autoimmune disease is more common in women and children. There is no racial predilection.

Pathogenesis

A. Autoimmune dysfunction of the adrenals accounts for up to 80% of cases; 10% to 20% of cases are attributed to tuberculosis. At least 90% of the adrenal gland is destroyed, resulting in chronic cortisol deficiency, reduced aldosterone, and decreased adrenal androgens. As a result, volume and sodium depletions occur with potassium excess. The risk of death in patients with Addison's disease is two times that of the general population due to higher rates of cardiovascular disease (CVD), cancer, and infectious disease.

Predisposing Factors

A. Other autoimmune disorders
   1. Insulin-dependent diabetes mellitus (IDDM)
   2. Pernicious anemia
   3. Thyroid disorders
B. Disseminated tuberculosis
C. Gonadal failure
D. Hypoparathyroidism
E. Vitiligo
F. Alopecia areata
G. Chronic active hepatitis
H. Metastatic disease (especially lung and breast cancer)
I. Acquired immunodeficiency syndrome (AIDS)
J. Certain medications (e.g., ketoconazole, anticoagulant)
K. Fungal disease
L. Bleeding diathesis (e.g., disseminated intravascular coagulation [DIC])
M. Sepsis
N. Metabolic stress
O. Trauma

Common Complaints*

A. Weakness
B. Fatigue
C. Anorexia
D. Nausea
E. Diarrhea
F. Abdominal pain
G. Weight loss
H. Hyperpigmentation

*Usually presenting as insidious and nonspecific

Other Signs and Symptoms

A. Proximal muscle weakness
B. Muscle and joint pain
C. Reduced axillary/pubic hair in women
D. Amenorrhea
E. Hypotension
F. Anemia with
   1. Lymphocytosis
   2. Eosinophilia
   3. Neutropenia
   4. Hyponatremia
   5. Hyperkalemia
   6. Hypoglycemia
   7. Hypercalcemia
G. Positive antiadrenal antibodies
H. Low plasma cortisol or failure to rise after corticotropin (adrenocorticotropic hormone [ACTH]) administration
I. EKG changes: Decreased voltage, prolonged PR and QT intervals, and general slowed rhythm

Missed or delayed diagnosis can lead to acute adrenal crisis, a medical emergency evidenced by sudden low back, abdominal, or leg pain; severe vomiting or diarrhea; hypotension; and loss of consciousness.

Subjective Data

A. Determine extent of fatigue.
B. Elicit degree and location of weakness.
C. Question the patient regarding appetite, nausea, or diarrhea.
D. Evaluate food intake.
E. Discuss hypopigmentation or hyperpigmentation and whether it occurs on unexposed areas as well as exposed areas of the skin.
F. Note presence of abdominal, muscle, and joint pain.
G. Assess for lightheadedness and/or fainting and when it occurs.
H. Inquire about the patient's history of cancer or fungal infections.
I. Note last date of tuberculosis evaluation (purified protein derivative [PPD]) and results.
J. Determine human immunodeficiency virus (HIV) status or risk.
K. For women, discuss pubic and axillary hair distribution and note menstrual patterns.
L. Inquire about libido.
M. Inquire regarding cold intolerance.

Physical Examination

A. Check pulse, respirations, and blood pressure (BP); pulse and BP seated and standing, weight.
B. Inspect
   1. Observe overall appearance.
   2. Note hair distribution and skin pigmentation, especially sun-exposed surfaces.
C. Auscultate
   1. Auscultate the heart, lungs, and abdomen.
D. Palpate
   1. Palpate the abdomen.
E. Musculoskeletal: Perform complete musculoskeletal examination.

Diagnostic Tests

A. Serum chemistry, electrolytes, blood urea nitrogen (BUN), creatinine, glomerular filtration rate (GER)
B. Complete blood count (CBC)
C. PPD
D. Rapid ACTH test: Rapid ACTH stimulation test excludes or establishes adrenal insufficiency but does not differentiate between primary and secondary adrenal insufficiency; with abnormal results (plasma cortisol < 18 to 20 mcg/dL), proceed to plasma ACTH levels.
E. Plasma ACTH level
F. Serum creatinine kinase (CK) levels

Plasma ACTH level differentiates between primary (adrenal) and secondary (pituitary) or tertiary (hypothalamus) etiologies (high plasma ACTH with primary insufficiency, whereas normal or low with secondary insufficiency). The clinician can use ACTH-releasing hormone (CRH) to distinguish between pituitary and hypothalamic etiologies.

G. Antiadrenal antibodies: A negative adrenal antibody test is observed in only 30% to 50% of persons with idiopathic Addison's disease and does not rule out adrenal insufficiency of autoimmune etiology.
H. Computed tomography (CT) scan of adrenals.

Differential Diagnoses

A. Secondary adrenal insufficiency (usually after exogenous glucocorticoid therapy)
B. Hypothalamic/pituitary lesions
C. Diabetic coma
D. Salt-losing nephritis
E. Acute infections
F. Occult cancer
G. Anorexia nervosa
H. Hemochromatosis
I. Acute poisoning
J. Myasthenia gravis
K. Pigmentation due to racial/ethnic variations
L. Premature primary ovarian failure
M. Testicular failure
N. Pernicious anemia
O. Cancer
P. Iatrogenic Cushing's syndrome

Plan

A. General interventions
   1. If primary adrenal insufficiency is established and the cause is not apparent, order an adrenal CT scan to look for metastatic disease, sarcoidosis, and tuberculosis.
B. Patient teaching
   1. See the Section III Patient Teaching Guide for this chapter, "Addison's Disease."
   2. Teach the patient regarding adrenal crisis and encourage treatment before symptoms begin.
   3. Encourage the patient to avoid contacts that predispose him or her to infections.
C. Pharmaceutical therapy
   1. Hydrocortisone (drug of choice) or prednisone in three doses (every 8 hours), or two thirds in the morning and the remainder in the afternoon or early evening; 12 to 15 mg cortisol/m^2 body surface area; most adults need a total of 20 to 30 mg/d.
   2. Increase hydrocortisone dose or add prednisone if ill; if accompanied by diarrhea, excessive

sweating, or fever, the patient should double the routine dose.

3. Simultaneously decrease fludrocortisone about 50% to avoid salt retention and elevated BP.
   a. Total daily stress dose is about 100 to 400 mg hydrocortisone.
4. If serum aldosterone is undetectable, mineralocorticoid replacement is likely necessary in addition to glucocorticoid.
5. Abrupt discontinuation of exogenous glucocorticoid administration after course as short as 3 weeks may induce temporary secondary adrenal insufficiency, leading to decreased cortisol but normal or near-normal aldosterone production. This may occur up to 12 months after discontinuation of glucocorticoid therapy.

Follow-Up

A. Plasma renin activity: When less than 10 ng/mL, this is a probable indication of adequate fludrocortisone dose.
B. Serum and urinary cortisol and serum ACTH to monitor hydrocortisone dose. Urinary free cortisol greater than 70 mcg/24 hr indicates excessive hydrocortisone dose, whereas values less than 20 mcg/24 hr indicate inadequate hydrocortisone dose.
C. Monitor BP and serum electrolytes to determine fludrocortisone dose.
D. Do annual adrenal function studies.

Consultation/Referral

A. If Addison's disease is suspected, consult with a physician.
B. Consider Addison's disease in any patient with hypotension and hyperkalemia.

Individual Considerations

A. Pregnancy
   1. Due to changes in plasma cortisol, diagnosis is based on lack of rise in plasma cortisol concentration after ACTH administration.
   2. If nausea and vomiting are problems, intramuscular glucocorticoid may be necessary.
   3. Delivery requires increased glucocorticoid dose similar to surgery.
B. Geriatrics
   1. Urinary excretion rate of cortisol decreases by about 25%; serum level and response to ACTH stimulation are unchanged.

Cushing's Syndrome

Definition

A. Cushing's syndrome is a cluster of symptoms, signs, and biochemical abnormalities arising from glucocorticoid overproduction. Iatrogenically induced Cushing's syndrome is the most common cause.

Incidence

A. For endogenous cases, two to four new cases per 1,000,000 annually; it is five times more frequent in women.

Pathogenesis

The cause is exogenous (chronic glucocorticoid or ACTH administration) or endogenous (increased ACTH secretion). The endogenous type is due to either excessive pituitary or ectopic ACTH secretion (ACTH dependent), resulting in signs of androgen excess or autonomous cortisol overproduction (ACTH independent [of ACTH regulation]), as well as depressed ACTH production and absent signs of androgen excess. The etiology of spontaneous Cushing's (adults) comprises

A. 70% to 80% pituitary ACTH hypersecretion (90% pituitary adenoma, 10% pituitary hyperplasia).
B. 10% to 15% autonomous adrenal tumor (adenoma or carcinoma).
C. 5% to 15% ectopic ACTH secretion (nonpituitary neoplasm, usually lung).
D. Less than 1% bilateral nodular hyperplasia without ACTH.

Predisposing Factors

A. Exogenous glucocorticoid administration
B. Excessive alcohol intake
C. Pituitary adenoma
D. Thoracic tumors
E. Adrenal neoplasms
F. Tumors of the pancreas
G. Thyroid and thymus disease
H. Pheochromocytoma

Common Complaints

A. Excessive coarse hair on face, chest, and back
B. Rapid weight gain
C. Easy bruising
D. Muscle weakness
E. Oligo- or amenorrhea
F. Impotence
G. Depression
H. Poorly controlled diabetes
I. Irregular menses

Other Signs and Symptoms

A. Cervicodorsal and supraclavicular fat pad
B. Hirsutism in women
C. Acne and/or folliculitis
D. Increased intraocular pressure
E. Purple striae
F. Increased BP

G. Polydipsia/polyuria, increased serum glucose, and glycosuria
H. Osteopenia/osteoporosis
I. Mood lability/changes
J. Spontaneous hypokalemia
K. Erythrocytosis

Subjective Data

A. Ask if the patient has taken exogenous glucocorticoids.
B. Determine whether the onset of complaints was acute or subacute.
C. Assess for bruising and determine if bruising was precipitated by trauma.
D. Assess for muscle weakness and, if present, whether it is proximal weakness.
E. Review the patient's menstrual history, including characteristics of menstrual periods.
F. Identify the patient's family history of similar problems.
G. Question the patient regarding any vision impairment.
H. Rule out the presence of abdominal pain.
I. Review the patient's history of neoplasms and location.
J. Identify the current pattern of sexual function.
K. Question the patient regarding mood swings or recent treatment for psychiatric disorder.
L. Identify the pattern of weight gain and effectiveness of weight loss interventions, if implemented.
M. Assess for the presence of leg or arm pain.
N. Review the patient's history of fractures, especially if postmenopausal.
O. Determine the amount of alcohol consumed.

Physical Examination

A. Check pulse, height, and weight.
B. Inspect
   1. Inspect the skin, noting hair distribution, lesions, bruising, and striae.
   2. Observe the face and note shape.
   3. Observe the neck.

Note that a "moon-shaped" face and fat pads in posterior neck ("buffalo hump") are characteristics of patients with Cushing's syndrome.

   4. Complete funduscopic examination. Be alert for cataracts, glaucoma, and/or signs of benign intracranial hypertension.
C. Auscultate
   1. Auscultate the heart and lungs.
D. Musculoskeletal exam
   1. Complete musculoskeletal examination. Be alert for septic necrosis of femoral and/or humeral head.

Initial Diagnostic Tests

A. Serum electrolytes
B. CBC and glucose
C. Urine-free cortisol (at least two measurements)
D. Late-night salivary cortisol (at least two measurements)
E. Overnight dexamethasone suppression test, 1 mg
F. Longer low-dose dexamethasone suppression test (2 mg/d for 48 hours)

The overnight dexamethasone suppression test has a false positive rate of 20% to 30%; false positives can occur with obesity, stress, depression, alcoholism, pregnancy, or medications that increase the hepatic metabolism of cortisol and dexamethasone (e.g., antiseizure drugs, estrogen, and rifampin). The false negative rate is less than 3%. Use the low-dose dexamethasone test as an alternative.

The 24-hour urinary free cortisol is the most sensitive and specific test and is the best choice for screening.

G. Bone density studies
   If any of the above initial screenings are positive, the patient should be referred to endocrinology for additional evaluation.

Differential Diagnoses

A. Iatrogenically induced Cushing's syndrome
B. Depression
C. Severe obesity
D. Chronic stress
E. Familial cortisol resistance
F. Medication induced (e.g., phenytoin, phenobarbital, primidone)
G. Pituitary adenoma
H. Adrenal and other neoplasms
I. Alcoholism
J. Nephrolithiasis
K. Psychosis

Plan

A. General interventions
   1. Taper glucocorticoid dose as appropriate for underlying disease.
   2. Begin alcohol detoxification if applicable.
   3. Consider hormone replacement therapy for postmenopausal women.
B. Patient teaching
   1. See the Section III Patient Teaching Guide for this chapter, "Cushing's Syndrome."
C. Medical-surgical management
   1. If noniatrogenic etiology, surgery is the treatment of choice, followed by irradiation and/or chemotherapy.
D. Pharmaceutical therapy
   1. Calcium 1,000 mg/d and vitamin D 400 IU/d.

2. Mitotane (Lysodren) 2 to 6 g daily for control of adrenocortical carcinoma progression.
3. Metyrapone inhibits adrenal steroid biosynthesis.
4. Ketoconazole (most useful for blocking adrenal steroidogenesis) and suramin inhibit adrenal steroid biosynthesis.
   a. Ketoconazole should be started at a dose of 200 mg two or three times daily and increased rapidly to 400 mg three times daily; higher doses are seldom more effective. Increase every 4 to 7 days. Avoid use in pregnancy.
5. Hydrocortisone may be given in physiologic doses to avoid adrenal insufficiency.

Most persons on daily steroid program for over 2 to 4 weeks have some degree of hypothalamic-pituitary-adrenal axis suppression.

6. Mifepristone (RU 486) is given for ectopic ACTH production or adrenal carcinoma. Mifepristone is an abortifacient.

Follow-Up

A. At the provider's discretion, 1 to 2 weeks after tests are complete, follow up to discuss results and possible therapy.

Consultation/Referral

A. If Cushing's syndrome is suspected, consult with an endocrinologist regarding treatment and therapy.

Individual Considerations

A. Pregnancy
   1. Urinary-free cortisol increases in the third trimester, but women still have normal 17-hydroxycorticosteroids and normal diurnal variability of serum cortisol. Dexamethasone testing is not recommended in the initial screening for Cushing's syndrome during pregnancy.

Resource

Addison and Cushing International Federation (ACIE)
PO Box 52137
2505 CC The Hague, The Netherlands
www.pslgroup.com/dg/6253e.htm

Diabetes Mellitus

Definition

Diabetes is a group of diseases characterized by high levels of blood glucose with a defect in insulin secretion or action caused by a chronic disorder of carbohydrate, fat, and protein metabolism. There are four categories of diabetes: type 1, type 2, gestational diabetes, and diabetes from secondary causes.

A. Type 1 diabetes, formerly referred to as insulin-dependent diabetes mellitus (IDDM), type 1, or juvenile-onset diabetes, is an endocrine condition in which there is complete destruction of pancreatic beta cells or a complete absence of insulin.
B. Type 2 diabetes, formerly referred to as noninsulin-dependent diabetes mellitus (NIDDM), type 2, or adult-onset diabetes, describes a condition in which individuals have an impairment in insulin production and/or insulin resistance.
C. Gestational diabetes is diagnosed during pregnancy. It usually disappears when the pregnancy is completed. It will increase the woman's risk of developing type 2 diabetes later in life.
D. Diabetes resulting from secondary causes is due to genetic defects and/or diseases of the pancreas, such as cystic fibrosis. Other causes of this type of diabetes can be drug/chemical-induced diabetes from medications or therapies used when treating HIV/AIDS and in patients who receive treatments after organ transplantation.
E. People with diabetes are more prone to have unhealthy low-density lipoprotein cholesterol (LDL-C) and, therefore, are at increased risk for atherosclerotic cardiovascular disease (ASCVD). The incidence of CVD is two to four times higher in adults with diabetes. The risk of stroke is two to four times higher because 60% to 65% of the patients have hypertension. In 2013, the American College of Cardiology (ACC) and the American Heart Association (AHA) published guidelines on the assessment of cardiovascular risk, lifestyle management, and treatment of cholesterol to reduce ASCVD risks. A downloadable spreadsheet enabling estimation of 10-year and lifetime risk for ASCVD and a web-based calculator are available at my.americanheart.org/cvriskcalculator and www.cardiosource.org/science-and-quality/practice-guidelines-andquality-standards/2013-prevention-guideline-tools.aspx. These risk tools are used to drive conversations on patient risk factors for ASCVD, potential benefits, and negative aspects of risk and patient preferences regarding initiation of relevant therapies. The assessment of ASCVD risk factors is recommended every 4 to 6 years in adults 20 to 79 years of age who are free from ASCVD. Long-term and lifetime risk information may be used to motivate therapeutic lifestyle changes and encourage adherence to lifestyle and pharmacological therapies.

Incidence

A. It is estimated that more than 25.8 million Americans, or 8.3% of the population, have diabetes. Diagnosed cases account for 18.8 million, with an estimated 7 million who have not been diagnosed. Type 1 diabetes accounts for less than 10% of diagnosed cases. There are 1.9 million new cases reported a year, not counting people 19 years old or younger.

Pathogenesis

A. Type 1 diabetes is an inherited defect causing an alteration in immunologic integrity, placing the beta cell at risk for inflammatory damage. The mechanism of damage is autoimmune. Environmental factors that may influence the etiology of diabetes include viral illnesses: mumps, coxsackievirus, cytomegalovirus, and hepatitis. Other factors that may influence the disease include diets high in dairy products, emotional and physical stress, and/or environmental toxins.
B. Type 2 diabetes involves impaired insulin secretion, insulin resistance, and/or an abnormally elevated glucose production by the liver. Genetics and obesity are major risk factors.
C. The severity of carbohydrate intolerance in gestational diabetes is unknown. Women identified at risk have screening done during the 24th and 28th weeks of gestation.
D. Genetic defects and medications/chemicals are thought to affect the beta-cell function and alter insulin function. Hemoglobin A1C levels may not be interpreted correctly in patients with blood disorders such as anemia/hemoglobinopathies. See www.ngsp.org/interf.asp for a complete list of laboratory methods recommended to be used to measure HgbA1C values for patients with hemoglobin variants (sickle cell trait, HbC, HbS, HbE, HbD trait, or elevated HbE).

Predisposing Factors

A. First-degree relative with type 1 or type 2 diabetes
B. Physical inactivity
C. Body mass index (BMI) greater than or equal to 27 kg/m^2
D. HbgA1C greater than or equal to 5.7%, impaired glucose tolerance (IGT) or IEG on previous testing
E. Native American, Hispanic, Asian, African American, and Pacific Islander heritage
F. Hypertension with systolic pressure greater than 140 mmHg and diastolic pressure greater than 90 mmHg
G. High-density lipoprotein (HDL) level of 35 mg/dL or less and/or triglyceride level of greater than or equal to 250 mg/dL
H. History of giving birth to babies larger than 9 pounds or gestational diabetes
I. History of IGT or fasting glucose
J. *Acanthosis nigricans* or severe obesity
K. Women with polycystic ovarian syndrome
L. History of CVD
M. All patients 45 years or older should be screened for diabetes. If negative, screening should occur every 3 years unless other risk factors develop.

Common Complaints

A. Classic triad of symptoms
   1. Polyuria
   2. Polydipsia
   3. Polyphagia
B. Weight loss
C. Lack of energy
D. Recurrent infections (urinary tract, vaginal, skin breakdown that is slow to heal)
E. Asymptomatic

Other Signs and Symptoms

A. Weakness
B. Fatigue
C. Nausea and vomiting
D. Abdominal pain
E. Anorexia
F. Sexual dysfunction, including impotence or dyspareunia
G. Itching
H. Visual disturbances
I. Signs and symptoms related to nephropathy, neuropathy, and/or retinopathy

Subjective Data

A. Obtain a detailed history regarding onset, duration, and course of presenting symptoms.
B. Question the patient regarding all characteristic signs and symptoms of diabetes.
C. Determine the patient's nutritional status, 24-hour recall, weight history, and eating patterns.
D. Review the family history of diabetes or other endocrine disorders.
E. Note predisposing factors to diabetes.
F. Review the patient's social history, including smoking, alcohol, and exercise.

Physical Examination

A. Check pulse, respirations, BP, and weight.
B. Inspect
   1. Observe overall appearance.
   2. Perform oral examination. Diabetic patients are prone to thrush, gingivitis, plaque, and infections. A dental examination should be done every 6 months.
   3. Complete funduscopic examination. Proliferative diabetic retinopathy is the leading cause of new blindness in adults in the United States. It occurs 60% of the time in those with type 1 and 30% of the time in those with type 2 diabetes. Patients with diabetes are 25 times more at

risk for blindness and have four to six times the increased risk for cataracts and twice an increased risk for glaucoma.
4. Inspect the skin, including feet, hands, fingers, and insulin injection sites.

C. Auscultate
1. Auscultate the heart.
2. Auscultate the lungs.

D. Percuss
1. Percuss the chest, abdomen, and deep tendon reflexes.

E. Palpate
1. Palpate the neck (thyroid).
2. Palpate the abdomen.
3. Palpate the extremities and check pulses.

Diagnostic Tests

A. Glycosylated hemoglobin (HgbA1c) of 6.5% or higher.
B. Fasting plasma glucose: Greater than or equal to 126 mg/dL. All patients should have a baseline fasting blood sugar (fasting for at least 8 hours) performed at 45 years of age, then repeated every 3 years. The baseline should be performed earlier if any predisposing factors exist.
C. Random plasma glucose: greater than or equal to 200 mg/dL with symptoms of diabetes
D. Oral Glucose Tolerance Test (OGTT): After 75 g glucose load, a 2-hour plasma glucose greater than or equal to 200 mg/dL; IGT is a fasting plasma glucose greater than or equal to 126 mg/dL.

According to the Diabetes Control and Complications Trial, an HgbAlc of 7.2% or below decreases the risk of retinopathy, neuropathy, and nephropathy by 50% to 70%.

Differential Diagnoses

A. Diabetes mellitus (DM)
B. Benign pancreatic insufficiency
C. Pheochromocytoma
D. Cushing's syndrome
E. History of corticosteroid use
F. Stress hyperglycemia
G. Acromegaly
H. Hemochromatosis
I. Somogyi phenomenon: Early morning hyperglycemia due to very early morning (2:00 a.m–3:00 a.m.) hypoglycemia

Plan

A. General interventions
1. Establish, review, and evaluate individual goals with the patient on a routine basis.
2. Center goals around normal metabolic control and the prevention and delay of complications while maintaining a flexible, normal, high-quality life.
3. After a new diagnosis is made and treatment has begun, be alert for an initial remission or honeymoon phase with decreased insulin needs and better control that may last 3 to 6 months.
4. Include the following in the treatment plan.
   a. Exercise plan
      i. Develop a consistent, individualized exercise plan with the patient to improve insulin sensitivity, blood sugars, weight reduction, and reduction of cardiovascular complications.
      ii. Evaluation by a health care provider, including a complete physical examination and EKG, must precede any exercise program.
      iii. Generally, the goals for physical activity are to reduce LDL-C and non-HDL-C and to lower BP. The exercise should involve moderate-to-vigorous intensity.
      iv. Exercise should not be done if the fasting blood sugar is greater than 250 mg/dL and ketones are present in the urine or if the glucose level is greater than 300 mg/dL at any time regardless of the presence of ketones.
      v. Because exercise can lower blood sugar concentration, special precautions such as medication adjustment and meal planning should be done before and after exercise if the patient is taking insulin or a glucose-lowering medication.
   b. Self-monitoring blood glucose (SMBG): The process of monitoring the patient's blood gives valuable information to the patient on a daily basis and assists the provider in identifying trends.
      i. Several different meters are available with a variety of options. A certified diabetes educator can show examples of different types before the patient purchases one.
      ii. Frequency of testing depends on the type of medication the patient is taking and the patient's compliance and motivation.
      iii. Additional testing should be done at times of changes in medication, meal plans, and/or exercise; and during illness or stress.
      iv. The Food and Drug Administration (FDA) has approved an automatic blood glucose suspend feature for continuous blood glucose monitoring

that is recommended for patients with hypoglycemia unawareness or frequent nocturnal hypoglycemia.

c. Psychosocial support: It is important from the beginning of treatment to give the patient a sense of control.
   i. Consistent involvement of family members will influence compliance.
   ii. Assess and discuss psychosocial issues at each visit.

B. Patient teaching
1. See the Section III Patient Teaching Guide for this chapter, "Diabetes."
2. Topics in the educational plan include the pathophysiology of diabetes, procedures for SMBG and medication therapies, recognition and treatment of hypoglycemia, and instructions for special situations such as illness and traveling.
3. Include preventive care, instructions for family members, and the importance of wearing a Medic Alert tag.
4. Smoking cessation and avoidance of all tobacco products should be advised to all patients. Counseling regarding smoking/tobacco cessation methods and classes should be offered.

C. Dietary/physical activity management
1. Nutritional plan: The patient should meet with a dietitian who has experience with diabetes nutritional therapy.
2. Eating patterns and ideal percentage of calories from protein, carbohydrates, and fat should be individualized for each patient and determined along with a dietitian.
3. Involve the family in improving compliance with the individualized meal plan.
4. Overweight/obese patients are encouraged to set a goal of healthy eating strategies to enhance weight loss. Along with dietary management, exercise programs should be encouraged as soon as the primary care provider has approved that the patient is safe to perform physical exercise on a routine basis. It is recommended to perform at least 150 minutes per week of moderate intensity physical exercise for at least 3 days a week, with not more than two consecutive days of rest. Resistance training is recommended for all patients with type 2 diabetes at least 2 days a week after authorization from the primary care provider.

D. Pharmaceutical therapy
1. Type 1 diabetes depends on exogenous insulin for treatment.
2. Type 2 diabetes is dependent on the severity of disease at diagnosis. If the glucose is less than 300 mg/dL, treatment is usually begun with an exercise program and nutrition plan. If glycemic goals are not reached in 2 or 3 months, monotherapy of medications is considered.
   a. Monotherapy for type 2 diabetes: Metformin is the preferred oral medication for type 2 diabetes. If monotherapy at the maximum dose is not achieved after 3 months, a second oral medication should be added. See www.care.diabetesjournals.org/content/37/Supplement_1/S14/E2.expansion.html for combination regimens. Insulin may eventually be required for patients who are not controlled on oral agents.
      i. Sulfonylurea (SU): First-generation (Orinase, Diabinese) and second-generation (Micronase, Glucotrol, Amaryl), Biguanide: metformin (Glucophage), Thiazolidinedione (TZD): rosiglitazone (Avandia) and pioglitazone (Actos), alpha-glucosidase inhibitor: acarbose (Precose)
   b. Combination therapy
      i. Two-drug combination
         Metformin + SU
         Metformin + TZD
         Metformin + DPP-4 inhibitor
         Metformin + GLP-1 receptor agonist (RA)
         Metformin + insulin (basal)
      ii. Three-drug combinations
         Metformin + SU + TZD, DPP-4 inhibitor, GLP-1 RA, or insulin
         Metformin + TZD + SU, DPP-4-I, GLP-1-RA, or insulin
         Metformin + DPP-4 inhibitor + SU, TZD, or insulin
         Metformin + GLP-1 receptor agonist + SU, TZD, or insulin
         Metformin + insulin (basal) + TZD, DPP-4-I, or GLP-1-RA
      iii. Complicated, uncontrolled patients on above therapy require insulin.
   c. Criteria for initiation of insulin therapy
      i. Glucose level at diagnosis of type 2 diabetes greater than 300 mg/dL
      ii. HgbA1c greater than or equal to 10%
      iii. Ketonuria

Although patients with type 2 diabetes do not depend on exogenous insulin, many will require supplemental insulin during times of stress, illness, or pregnancy or routinely along with oral medication (see Tables 23.1 and 23.2).

TABLE 23.1 Action Times of Insulin

Insulin	Onset	Peaks	Duration
Lispro/Aspart/Glulisine	10 minutes	1.5 hours	3 hours
Regular	20 minutes	3–4 hours	8 hours
NPH	1.5 hours	4–12 hours	22 hours
Lente	2.5 hours	7–15 hours	24 hours
Ultralente	4 hours	10–24 hours	36 hours
70 NPH/30 Reg	0–1 hour	Dual	12–20 hours
50 NPH/50 Reg	0–1 hour	Dual	12–20 hours
Detemir (Levemir)	1 hour	None	24 hours
Glargine (Lantus)	1 hour	None	24 hours

TABLE 23.2 Diabetes Medication/Class

Drug	Brand Name	Drug Classification
Acarbose	Precose	Alpha-glucosidase inhibitor
Pioglitazone + Metformin	ActoPlus Met	Thiazolidinedione (TZD) plus biguanide
Glimepiride	Amaryl	Sulfonylurea (SU)
Insulin glulisine	Apidra	Rapid-acting insulin
Rosiglitazone + Metformin	Avandamet	TZD plus biguanide
Rosiglitazone + Glimepiride	Avandaryl	TZD plus SU
Exenatide	Byetta	Incretin mimetic
Exenatide ER	Bydureon	GLP-1 receptor agonist
Glyburide	DiaBeta	SU (second generation)
Pioglitazone + Glimepiride	Duetact	TZD plus SU
Glucagon	–N/A–	Antihypoglycemic
Metformin ext. release	Glucophage	Biguanide
Glipizide ext. release	Glucotrol	SU (second generation)
Glyburide + metformin	Glucovance	SU plus biguanide
Glyburide micronized	Glynase PresTab	SU (second generation)
Miglitol	Glyset	Alpha-glucosidase inhibitor
Insulin lispro	Humalog	Rapid-acting insulin
NPH/Regular insulin	Humulin 70/30	Short- and intermediate-acting insulin
NPH/Regular insulin	Humulin 50/50	Short- and intermediate-acting insulin
Regular insulin	Humulin R	Rapid-acting insulin
NPH insulin	Humulin N	Intermediate-acting insulin
Sitagliptin + metformin	Janumet	Dipeptidyl peptidase-4 inhibitor plus biguanide
Sitagliptin	Januvia	Dipeptidyl peptidase-4 inhibitor
Insulin glargine	Lantus	Long-acting insulin
Insulin detemir	Levemir	Long-acting insulin
Linagliptin	Tradjenta	Dipeptidyl peptidase-4 inhibitor
Liraglutide	Victoza	Glucagon-like peptide-1 receptor agonist
Metformin + glipizide	Metaglip	Biguanide plus SU
Glyburide	Micronase	SU (second generation)

(continued)

TABLE 23.2 Diabetes Medication/Class (*continued*)

Drug	Brand Name	Drug Classification
Miglitol	Glyset	Alpha-glucosidase inhibitor
Nateglinide	Starlix	Amino acid derivative
Insulin isophane + regular insulin	Novolin 70/30	Short- and intermediate-acting insulin
Insulin aspart	NovoLog	Rapid-acting Insulin
Insulin aspart protamine/Insulin aspart	NovoLog Mix 70/30	Short- and intermediate-acting insulin
Insulin lispro protamine/insulin lispro	Humalog Mix 75/25	Short- and intermediate-acting insulin
Insulin lispro protamine/insulin lispro	Humalog Mix 50/50	Short- and intermediate-acting insulin
Nateglinide	Starlix	Insulin secretagogue
Insulin isophane suspension NPH	Novolin	Intermediate-acting insulin
Saxagliptin	Onglyza	Dipeptidyl peptidase-4 inhibitor
Pioglitazone	Actos	Thiazolidinedione (TZD)
Repaglinide + metformin	Prandimet	Meglitinide analogue plus biguanide meglitinide
Pramlintide	Symlin	Amylin analogue/amylinomimetic
Repaglinide	Prandin	Meglitinide analogue
Rosiglitazone	Avandia	TZD

d. Additional medications that may need to be considered
   i. Angiotensin-converting enzyme (ACE) inhibitors are the antihypertensive drug of choice to retard renal dysfunction associated with diabetes.
   ii. ACE inhibitors or angiotensin II receptor blockers (ARBs) are recommended for patients with an elevated urinary albumin excretion (30–299 mg/24 hr).
   iii. Calcium channel blockers may reduce microalbuminuria and proteinuria.
   iv. Aspirin therapy (75–162 mg/d) is recommended for primary prevention in patients with type 1 or type 2 diabetes with an increased risk of CVD (men > 50 years, women > 60 years with one or more risk factors, such as CVD, hypertension, smoking, dyslipidemia, or albuminuria). For patients who have a history of CVD with an allergy to aspirin, clopidogrel 75 mg/d should be used.

e. Some medications adversely affect diabetes.
   i. Nicotinic acids affect glycemic control by increasing insulin resistance.
   ii. Beta blockers increase the risk of hypoglycemia episodes in patients taking oral hypoglycemia agents.
   iii. Thiazide diuretics increase insulin resistance.

3. In 2013 the ACC/AHA published guidelines on the primary prevention of the treatment of cholesterol with people with DM and LDL-C of 70 to 189 mg/dL; they include:
   a. Moderate-intensity statin therapy initiated or continued for adults with DM 40 to 75 years of age.
   b. High-intensity statin therapy is reasonable for adults with DM 40 to 75 years of age with a greater than or equal to 7.5% estimated 10-year ASCVD risk unless contraindicated. (Utilize the lifetime risk calculator to define percentage of risk.)
   c. In adults with DM who are older than 75 years of age, it is reasonable to evaluate the potential for ASCVD benefits and for adverse effects, for drug–drug interactions, and to consider patient preferences when deciding to initiate, continue, or intensify statin therapy.

Follow-Up

A. Determine follow-up appointments by the type of diabetes, age, patient compliance, any treatment changes, and presence of any complications related to diabetes or other health problems.

B. A HgbA1c determination every 3 months can assist the provider in measuring control. There are several computer software packages that print the glucometer readings for assessing compliance; this can be done by the provider or the patient.

C. The American Diabetes Association management goals
   1. Preprandial glucose level 80 to 120 mg/dL
   2. 1 to 2 hours after meals, a glucose level less than 180 mg/dL
   3. A bedtime glucose level 100 to 140 mg/dL
   4. HgbA1c less than 7%
   5. In 2013, the American Diabetes Association recommended the BP goal for diabetics with hypertension should be a systolic blood pressure (SBP) of less than 140 mmHg and a diastolic blood pressure (DBP) of less than 80 mmHg. The 2014 report from the Eighth Joint National Committee (JNC VIII) recommends that in the diabetic population aged older than 18 years of age, pharmacologic treatment should be initiated at a SBP greater than 140 mmHg or a DBP greater than 90 mmHg and treated to a goal of SBP less than 140 mmHg and a goal of DBP less than 90 mmHg. The JNC VIII has the same recommendation for initiation of BP medication and treatment goals for patients older than 18 years of age with chronic kidney disease.
   6. Cholesterol less than 200 mg/dL, triglycerides less than 150 mg/dL, HDLs greater than 35 mg/dL, and LDLs less than 100 mg/dL, and less than 70 mg/dL if heart disease is present or patient is at high risk for atherosclerotic disease.

D. Annual tests or examinations should include a dilated funduscopic examination by an ophthalmologist to screen for retinopathy every 2 years, an annual EKG, monofilament foot examination, flu vaccination and other adult vaccines as recommended, thyroid studies, serum creatinine, BUN, GFR, lipid panel, urinalysis, and urine for albuminuria. Additional tests may be needed if complications develop.

Consultation/Referral

A. Refer to the physician if the patient experiences
   1. Diabetic ketoacidosis
   2. Severe or frequent hypoglycemia that is unresponsive to conventional pharmaceutical therapy.
   3. Hyperosmolar hyperglycemic nonketotic syndrome
   4. Pregnancy
   5. Symptoms from an acute complication related to retinopathy.
   6. Nephropathy develops 35% to 45% of the time in type 1 and 20% of the time in type 2 diabetes; it is the leading disease requiring kidney dialysis.
   7. Neuropathy: 60% to 70% of patients experience impaired sensation or pain in feet/hands, or carpal tunnel syndrome; over half of all amputations of lower extremities are related to diabetes. All patients should be screened for neuropathy at the diagnosis of type 2 diabetes and at 5 years after the diagnosis of type 1 diabetes, and then annually. Early diagnosis is imperative to prevent nerve damage from occurring. Tight control of the blood glucose levels can slow down the progression of nerve damage but cannot reverse neuronal loss. The pain experienced with neuropathy can be treated with oral medications. Pregabalin and duloxetine are both FDA-approved for neuropathic pain. Other medications that may be used include opioids such as tramadol or morphine, along with venlafaxine, amitriptyline, gabapentin, or valproate.
   8. Persistent uncontrolled diabetes

Individual Considerations

A. Pregnancy/preconceptual
   1. Women considering pregnancy should be switched to insulin before conception and during pregnancy.
      a. Fetal anomalies increase proportionally with uncontrolled diabetes.
      b. HgbA1c goal prior to conception is less than 7%.
      c. Gestational diabetes screening may be compléted by performing the "one-step" 2-hour 75 gm OGTT or a "two-step" approach with 1-hour 50 gm nonfasting Glucola followed by a 3-hour 100 gm OGTT for patients who test positive for the 1-hour screening.
   2. Hypertensive medications may need to be changed if considering pregnancy because ACE inhibitors, beta blockers, and diuretics are contraindicated during pregnancy.
   3. Increased monitoring of blood glucose is necessary during pregnancy.

Galactorrhea

Definition

A. The production of a milky discharge excreted from the nipple, occurring beyond the 6-month period of pregnancy and/or breastfeeding cessation.

Incidence

A. It is estimated that 1% to 50% of reproductive women will experience galactorrhea at some time in their life.

Pathogenesis

A. The pathogenesis depends on the etiology. Physiologic galactorrhea is caused by pregnancy. The anterior pituitary gland secretes prolactin, which stimulates milk production. Milk production is normal for 6 months after pregnancy and/or after breastfeeding has ceased. The majority of cases are from benign etiology. Malignancy is responsible for 5% to 10% of cases.

Predisposing Factors

A. Reproductive women
B. Medications: Oral contraceptions, phenothiazines, pimozide, risperidone, molindone, olanzapine, clomipramine, desipramine, haloperidol (Haldol), metoclopramide (Reglan), cimetidine, Isoniazid, methyldopa (Aldomet), reserpine, verapamil, codeine, morphine, and imipramine (Tofranil)

Common Complaints

A. Milky discharge from the nipple

Subjective Data

A. Note the onset, duration, and course of presenting symptoms.
B. Ask whether the patient has been pregnant and/or breastfed within the past 6 months. If so, how long did she nurse?
C. Review her menstrual history and pattern.
D. Ask her to describe the discharge, noting color, consistency, and/or presence of blood.
E. Determine the mechanism of production of discharge: Spontaneous or with manual expression.
F. Assess for any palpable mass in the breast.
G. Review current medications, including use of oral contraceptives.
H. Note any previous experience with galactorrhea. If so, discuss testing performed and treatment, if any.
I. Identify any family history of breast cancer or other tumors.

Physical Examination

A. Check pulse, respirations, and BP.
B. Inspect
   1. Inspect the breast.
   2. Assess the discharge.
   3. Inspect the skin; note dimpling, retraction, and irregularities.
   4. Eyes: Complete funduscopic examination.
   5. Perform visual field testing.
C. Palpate
   1. Palpate the breasts for masses and fibrocystic changes.
   2. Squeeze the nipple to induce discharge.
   3. Palpate the axillary lymph nodes.
   4. Palpate the neck, thyroid, and lymph nodes.

Diagnostic Tests

A. Prolactin level: Normal level is 1 to 20 ng/mL.
B. TSH

Many cases of galactorrhea are considered idiopathic. Usually endocrine studies will be normal.

C. Beta human chorionic gonadotropin (beta HCG)
D. Hemoccult of breast discharge
E. Breast discharge for pathology
F. Periareolar ultrasound (all ages)
G. CT/MRI of sella turcica if pituitary mass is suspected
H. Mammogram in women older than 30 years if tumor is suspected
I. Ductoscopy
J. Skin punch biopsy for abnormal skin presentations

Differential Diagnoses

A. Galactorrhea
B. Fibrocystic disease
C. Mastitis
D. Breast tumor
E. Medication induction
F. Breast cancer: Bloody nipple discharge, painless, firm fixed mass
G. Pituitary adenoma: Can produce permanent visual field loss and headaches
H. Hypothalamic disorders
I. Chiari-Frommel: Galactorrhea occurring after 6 months postpartum

Plan

A. General interventions
   1. Treat underlying cause of nipple discharge.
   2. If induced by medications, consider stopping medications if side effect outweighs benefits.
   3. If benign cause, no treatment is necessary with medication. Monitor symptoms. If symptoms progress, reevaluate.
B. Patient teaching
   1. Teach self-examination of the breast.
C. Pharmaceutical therapy
   1. No pharmaceuticals are advised with the exception of tapering or discontinuing medications that are causing the discharge. This is recommended only after cautious consideration of why the medication is being used (antipsychotics).

Follow-Up

A. Monitor prolactin level every 6 to 12 months.
B. Recommend yearly vision evaluation.
C. Order MRI at 1 year, then every 2 to 5 years if symptoms persist.

Consultation/Referral

A. Consult a physician regardless of normal imaging results if breast tumor is suspected with bloody discharge or palpable mass noted.

Individual Considerations

A. Pregnancy
   1. Galactorrhea during pregnancy is a normal physiologic response.

2. If galactorrhea persists after pregnancy/lactation has ceased for 6 months, a full workup evaluation is required.

B. Adults: Men: Galactorrhea is rare in men; however, it can occur with prolactinoma.

Gynecomastia

Definition

A. Gynecomastia is an enlargement of the breast tissue in males.

Incidence

A. Common in newborns and approximately 40% to 69% of adolescent boys will experience breast enlargement. It is also seen in men (between the ages of 50 and 80) with excessive weight gain.

Pathogenesis

A. Male breast duct proliferation occurs due to a hormonal imbalance of estrogen. Pathologic conditions such as pituitary tumors, systemic disorders, kidney disease, thyroid disorders, and liver disease can cause symptoms to occur. Medications can also induce symptoms. These medications include antiandrogens, antidepressants, cimetidine, ranitidine, omeprazole, aldactone, chemotherapeutic agents, amiodarone, diltiazem, nifedipine, digoxin, methyldopa, reserpine, hormones, and sedatives.

Predisposing Factors

A. Age (men older than 65 years) with excessive weight gain
B. Family history
C. Malnutrition with severe weight loss
D. Peutz–Jeghers syndrome

Common Complaints

A. Enlargement of breast tissue with or without discomfort

Other Signs and Symptoms

A. Asymptomatic
B. Type I: Nodule present under areola tissue area
C. Type II: Nodule palpable under and beyond areola area
D. Type III: Breast enlargement without contour separation of tissue

Subjective Data

A. Identify when breast development first appeared.
B. Determine whether enlargement is unilateral or bilateral.
C. Review the progression of enlargement.
D. Note any pain, discharge, or masses that are palpable.
E. List current medications, drugs, and alcohol and substance abuse.
F. Review the patient's medical history.
G. Note the patient's family history of gynecomastia.
H. Explore nutritional intake.
I. Discuss the patient's level of physical activity (sports, hobbies, etc.).
J. Note use of herbal products.

Objective Data

A. Inspect breasts bilaterally and surrounding nodes for enlargement or skin changes.
B. Palpate breast tissue systematically and surrounding nodes. Gynecomastia can usually be appreciated once the glandular tissue reaches 0.5 cm or larger.
C. Palpate testes for masses or atrophic changes.
D. BMI

Differential Diagnoses

A. Gynecomastia
B. Obesity: Fatty breast enlargement without glandular involvement
C. Breast cancer: Fixed, firm nodule in tissue with dimpling and/or breast discharge
D. Neurofibroma
E. Lipoma

Diagnostic Tests

A. Prolactin level
B. TSH
C. HCG
D. Serum luteinizing hormone (LH)
E. Testosterone level
F. Estradiol level
G. Mammography for suspicious breast masses in adult males

Plan

A. General interventions
   1. Identify any pathologic condition. If none is identified, reassure the patient that normal resolution will occur over time.
B. Patient teaching
   1. Reinforce weight reduction if weight gain is a factor in the condition.
C. Pharmaceutical therapy
   1. Antiestrogens (tamoxifen)
   2. Androgens (testosterone replacement)
   3. Aromatase inhibitors (anastrozole)
   4. Discontinue medications that may induce symptoms if possible.

Follow-Up

A. Follow-up is dependent on etiology and/or patient needs.

Consultation/Referral

A. Consult a physician or refer to an endocrinologist if the male patient is noted to have breast enlargement for longer than 2 years.

Individual Considerations

A. Adult men diagnosed with prostate cancer, who are treated with an antiandrogen monotherapy, are at higher risk for the development of gynecomastia.

Hypogonadism

Definition

A. Hypogonadism in men is failure of the testis to produce physiological levels of testosterone and a normal number of spermatozoa.

Incidence

A. An estimated 38.7% of men older than 45 years of age have below-normal values of serum testosterone.

Pathogenesis

A. Hypogonadism in men can be the result of testicular dysfunction or nondevelopment (primary hypogonadism) or dysfunction of the pituitary or hypothalamus (secondary hypogonadism). The two clinical manifestations of impaired spermatogenesis are infertility and decreased testicular size. There are several possible clinical manifestations of testosterone deficiency, which are determined by its time of onset during reproductive development.
   1. In utero first or second trimesters: Incomplete virilization of external genitalia, incomplete development of Wolffian ducts to form male internal genitalia
   2. Third trimester in utero: Micropenis
   3. Prepuberty: Incomplete pubertal maturation, eunuchoidal body habitus, poor muscle development, and reduced peak bone mass
   4. Postpuberty: Decreased energy, mood, and libido; decrease in sexual hair, hematocrit, muscle mass and strength, and bone mineral density

Predisposing Factors

A. Hypogonadism associated with Klinefelter syndrome
B. Chemotherapy
C. Radiation therapy
D. Excessive alcohol consumption
E. Painful testicular swelling
F. Anosmia associated with Kallmann syndrome
G. Use of medications that cause hypogonadism: Ketoconazole or extended-release opiates

Common Complaints

A. Decreased vigor and libido
B. Depression

Other Signs and Symptoms

A. Fatigue
B. Difficulty concentrating
C. Hot flashes
D. No change in deepening of the voice
E. Weight gain
F. Signs of metabolic syndrome
G. Erectile dysfunction

Subjective Data

A. Interview the patient, inquiring about the patient history of known chromosomal abnormalities in the family or patient.
B. Ask about a history of cryptorchidism.
C. Is there any history of muscular weakness?
D. Is there a history of varicocele unresolved within 6 months of birth?
E. Inquire about known infections affecting the scrotum and testes.
F. Has the patient had therapeutic radiation to the area or a history of chemotherapy?
G. Ask about a use of long-term ketoconazole, glucocorticoid, or long-acting opiate use.
H. Any known testicular trauma?
I. Is there any history of known torsion?
J. Evaluate for a history of autoimmune disorders and/or chronic illnesses including cirrhosis, chronic renal failure, or HIV.
K. Has the patient noted a decrease in spontaneous erections?

Physical Examination

A. Inspect
   1. Testes for appropriate size
   2. Upper and lower body musculature
   3. Full/dense male-pattern beard
   4. Testes should be bilaterally descended
   5. Rule out eunuchoid appearance
   6. Breasts for gynecomastia
   7. Inspection findings less valuable following puberty as changes due to hypogonadism are obvious to inspection and take years to develop
   8. Penis for hypospadias
B. Palpate
   1. The scrotum and testes for masses
   2. The breasts for masses (both male and females)

Diagnostic Tests

A. Serum testosterone (morning total), repeat to confirm
B. Measurement of free testosterone if total testosterone is not near the lower limit
C. Avoid lab tests during acute illness.

Differential Diagnoses

A. Hypogonadism
B. Moderate obesity
C. Nephrotic syndrome
D. Hypothyroidism
E. Use of glucocorticoids, progestins, and androgenic steroids

F. Acromegaly
G. DM
H. Hepatic cirrhosis
I. Hypopituitarism
J. Malnutrition
K. Klinefelter syndrome
L. Depression
M. Psychologic sexual dysfunction

Plan

A. General interventions
   1. Testosterone replacement's effect on reducing adverse health outcomes in the general population is unknown.
   2. Testosterone levels vary significantly with circadian rhythms, illness, and medications.
   3. Measurement of bone mineral density is recommended to assess fracture risk.
   4. LH and ESH concentrations can help distinguish between primary and secondary hypogonadism.
   5. Differentials for secondary hypogonadism should evaluate for pituitary neoplasia, hyperprolactinemia, hemochromatosis, obstructive sleep apnea (OSA), and genetic disorders.
   6. Testosterone replacement should be initiated only after a baseline prostate-specific antigen (PSA) and digital prostate exam. PSA levels should be followed routinely.
B. Patient teaching
   1. Both men and women with hypogonadism can lead normal lives with hormone replacement therapy.
   2. Hormone replacement should continue throughout life.
   3. Potential side effects of testosterone replacement therapy should be discussed prior to therapy.
   4. Patients using topically absorbed testosterone gel or creams can transfer testosterone to female partners or children by direct skin-to-skin contact. Advise the patient to use caution with topical gels/creams.
C. Pharmaceutical therapy
   1. Injectable testosterone replacement
   2. 1% testosterone gel: Androgel, Testim, Axiron
   3. Transdermal testosterone patch
   4. Buccal testosterone
   5. Implanted subcutaneous testosterone pellets

Follow-Up

A. Patients receiving hormone replacement should be reevaluated every 6 months or more frequently.
B. Testosterone replacement is contraindicated in metastatic prostate cancer and breast cancer. Routine screening should be performed.

Consultation/Referral

A. Physician consultation prior to initiating testosterone therapy is advised.
B. Endocrinology referral is recommended for males not responsive to the replacement therapy.
C. Patients with primary hypogonadism should be referred to an endocrinologist for initial workup and management.

Individual Considerations

A. Geriatrics: Current recommendations are *not* in favor of testosterone therapy for all older males. Providers should cautiously consider the benefits compared to the risks for older males. The benefits of testosterone replacement are unproven, and the long-term risks are unknown.
B. HIV patients: Short-term testosterone replacement should be considered for HIV men with low testosterone, weight loss, and muscular wasting.

Metabolic Syndrome/Insulin Resistance Syndrome

Definition

A. Metabolic syndrome is an association of several complex disorders: Obesity, insulin resistant type 2 diabetes, hypertension, and hyperlipidemia. This coexistence of conditions leads to atherosclerotic CVD. Metabolic syndrome is considered a proinflammatory and prothrombotic state. Elevated triglycerides and low HDL cholesterol are strong predictors of vascular events. Triglycerides and the waist circumference are considered the strongest predictors for the development of metabolic syndrome.
B. The inclusion of type 2 diabetes in the definition of metabolic syndrome is debated. The Adult Treatment Panel (ATP) III defines metabolic syndrome in adults as the coexistence of any three of five conditions (see Table 23.3).
C. Complications associated with metabolic syndrome include fatty liver disease, cirrhosis, chronic kidney disease, polycystic ovarian syndrome (PCOS), OSA, and gout.
D. Metabolic syndrome is noted in the literature under other names, including insulin resistance syndrome and obesity dyslipidemia syndrome. Previously, the term "Syndrome X" was used; however, Syndrome X is noted to have normal coronary arteries and the occurrence of angina.

Incidence

A. Age-dependent increase in incidence; overall incidence estimated at 22% of the population.
B. Asians living in the United States and Mexican Americans have the highest age-adjusted prevalence. Among African Americans and Mexican Americans, the prevalence is higher in women than in men.

TABLE 23.3 Adult Treatment Panel III Criteria for Metabolic Syndrome

Metabolic Syndrome Traits	Definition
Central/abdominal obesity	Adult waist circumference: Men > 40 inches (102 cm) Women > 35 inches (88 cm)
Serum triglycerides	Adults: > 150 mg/dL or drug treatment for elevated triglycerides
Serum HDL cholesterol	Adults: < 40 mg/dL in men; < 50 mg/dL in women
Blood pressure	Adults: > 130/85 or drug treatment for hypertension
Fasting plasma glucose (FPG)	Adults: > 100 mg/dL or drug treatment for elevated blood glucose

Source: National Institutes of Health. (2002). Third Report of the Expert Panel on Detection, Evaluation, and Treatment of High Blood Cholesterol in Adults (ATP III Final Report). Bethesda, MD: National Institutes of Health.

C. Ethnic background
   1. Native Americans are at the greatest risk (19% prevalence).
   2. Mexican Americans have the highest prevalence (31.9%).
   3. Black and Hispanic females are 1.5 times more likely than non-Hispanic White females.

Pathogenesis

A. The exact etiology is unknown; however, abdominal obesity has been associated with insulin resistance. Vascular endothelial dysfunction occurs secondary to insulin resistance, hyperglycemia, hyperinsulinemia, and adipokines. Along with high BP and abnormal lipids, vascular inflammation places the individual at high risk for a cardiovascular insult.

Predisposing Factors

A. Genetic predisposition
B. Weight gain, especially central/abdominal obesity
C. Females, especially postmenopausal
D. Smoking
E. High-carbohydrate diet, especially soft drink consumption
F. Lack of exercise
   1. Sedentary lifestyle
   2. Too much television watching by adults
G. Insulin resistance

Common Complaints

A. Complaints are all related to the individual coexisting comorbid symptoms.

Other Signs and Symptoms

A. All are related to the individual coexisting comorbid symptoms.

Subjective Data

A. Review the patient's medical history related to comorbid conditions, including obesity, hypertension, and any abnormal laboratory testing (lipids, triglycerides, and glucose tolerance tests [GTTs]).
B. Review the patient's family history.
C. Review all prescription medications, over-the-counter (OTC) drugs, and herbals.
D. Review the patient's current level of exercise.
E. Review the patient's usual diet (24-hour recall), noting high fat and high glucose consumption.
F. Review the patient's reproductive history.

Physical Examination

A. Check height, weight, waist circumference, BP, pulse, and respirations
B. Calculate the BMI and waist-to-hip measurement. Several Internet sites have BMI, body fat, and waist-to-hip ratio calculators.
C. Make general observations for acanthosis nigricans and skin tags (insulin resistance).
D. A full physical examination is guided by the patient's medical history and presenting signs and symptoms.

Diagnostic Tests

A. Fasting glucose
B. Fasting lipid panel
C. Triglycerides
D. Consider thyroid function.
E. Consider C-reactive protein (CRP) (optional).

Differential Diagnoses

A. Metabolic syndrome
   1. Obesity
   2. Hypertension
   3. Hyperlipidemia
   4. High-fasting plasma glucose

Plan

A. General interventions
   Aggressive lifestyle modification focusing on increased physical activity and weight reduction is a cornerstone for treatment.
B. Patient teaching
   1. Dietary recommendations include a low-fat, low-cholesterol, and/or dietary approaches to

stop hypertension (DASH) diet. Decrease simple sugar and saturated and trans fats and cholesterol (see Appendix B for dietary information).

2. Exercise recommendations include a minimum of 30 minutes a day of walking at a brisk pace or other activity at a moderate intensity. Start by using a pedometer, walking at breaks, or household work.
3. Weight loss of 5% to 10% or more; gradual weight loss of 1 to 2 kg per month. Even small losses are associated with health benefits.
4. BP control strategies include a low-sodium diet (DASH), smoking cessation, and alcohol in moderation.
5. Counsel on smoking cessation.
6. Abdominoplasties do not lower the risk for coronary artery disease (CAD) or insulin sensitivity.

C. Pharmaceutical therapy
1. Currently, the treatment for metabolic syndrome is to treat each individual component/diagnoses for the individual.
2. Insulin-resistant patients usually are not treated by insulin.
3. Statins are the most common classification used for elevated lipids.
4. A low-dose aspirin may be prescribed related to the patient's risk of CVDs or prothrombotic state.
5. Oral hypoglycemic agents used to treat type 2 diabetes are not currently recommended for the prevention of metabolic syndrome.
6. Hypertension should be controlled with appropriate antihypertensives.

Follow-Up

A. Follow-up involves assessing patients for metabolic syndrome at a minimum of 3-year intervals for anyone with one or more risk traits. Follow-up testing includes
1. BMI calculation
2. Waist-to-hip calculation
3. Fasting lipid profile
4. Fasting glucose
5. BP

Consultation/Referral

A. Refer to an obstetrician/gynecologist for consultation and management for infertility/pregnancy.
B. Refer to a specialist for any comorbid condition as needed.

Individual Considerations

A. Individual considerations for pregnancy and geriatrics are specific to their comorbid condition.

Obesity—*Mellisa Hall, Angelito Tacderas, and Cheryl A. Glass*

Definition

A. Obesity is a multifactorial disease with physical, psychological, and social consequences. The BMI is a standard measuring tool. The BMI is calculated by using the formula: weight in kilograms divided by height in meters squared (weight [kg]/height [m]^2). In adults, obesity is defined by a BMI greater than 30 kg/m^2 (see Table 23.4).

Incidence

A. More than two-thirds of the U.S. population is overweight (BMI of 27%); of those, one-third of the adults are obese, along with 16% of U.S. children. Obesity rates cross all groups in society, regardless of age, sex, race, ethnicity, socioeconomic status, educational level, or geographic group.

Pathogenesis

Numerous factors contribute to the development of obesity, including
A. Imbalance between energy intake and energy output
B. Genetics (40%–70% presumed explanation)
C. Environmental factors
D. Drug-induced obesity
1. Tricyclic antidepressants
2. Antipsychotics
3. SUs
4. Anticonvulsants (sodium valproate, carbamazepine)
5. Glucocorticoids

E. Sleep disturbance-induced obesity

Predisposing Factors

A. Consuming too many calories/high-fat diet
B. Poor dietary choices
C. Readily available food sources, especially fast foods
D. Lack of exercise/sedentary lifestyle
E. Decreased/elimination of physical education requirements in public schools

TABLE 23.4 Adult Obesity by Body Mass Index (BMI)

Classification of Adult Obesity by BMI	BMI (kg/m^2)
Underweight	< 18.5
Normal	18.5–24.9
Overweight (preobese)	25.0–29.9
Obesity	30.0–34.9
Severely obese	> 40.0
Morbidly obese	40.0–49.9
Super obese	> 50.0
Super-super obese (SSO)	> 60.0

F. Television, computer, and handheld game use more than 3 hours a day
G. Increased leisure time
H. Lack of funding and planning for community parks and recreation areas
I. Ethnic background: African American, Hispanic
J. Family history of obesity
K. Pregnancy
L. Insomnia, difficulty staying asleep, and frequent wakefulness

Common Complaints

A. Difficulties with activities of daily living (ADL) or functional impairment
B. Lack of interest/inability to tolerate exercise
C. Shortness of breath and/or asthma exacerbations
D. Difficulty with personal hygiene
E. Urinary incontinence
F. Desire to lose weight

Other Signs and Symptoms

A. OSA
B. Increased asthma symptoms
C. Infertility/PCOS
D. Symptoms associated with cholelithiasis
E. Hypertension
F. Early sexual maturity in girls

Subjective Data

A. Review onset of weight gain and duration of obesity. Identify when the patient first noticed the weight gain.
B. Ask the patient about other symptoms secondary to obesity.
C. Review full medical history.
D. Review medications, including OTC herbals and diet products.
E. Review the patient's previous history of weight loss attempts.
F. Assess ADL and function limitations and the presence of exercise intolerance.
G. Elicit history of sleep disorders (i.e., snoring and obstruction, sleep apnea).
H. Review 24-hour dietary recall. Review the patient's normal average meals per day, including snacks.
I. Review consumption of high-caloric drinks and alcohol intake.
J. Assess for history of binge eating, purging, lack of satiety, food-seeking behaviors, and other abnormal feeding habits.
K. Assess for depression.
L. Assess for readiness and commitment for weight loss. People who voluntarily enroll in a weight-loss program generally lose weight.
M. Ask the patient to describe his or her activity level, exercise routine, and daily activity (work activity).

Physical Examination

A. Check pulse, respirations, and BP: Supine, sitting, and standing
B. Measure height and weight to calculate BMI.
C. Measure waist and hip circumferences to calculate the waist-to-hip circumference ratio. The waist-to-hip ratio is the strongest anthropometric measure that is associated with myocardial infarction risk and is a better predictor than BMI. A waist-to-hip ratio that is greater than 0.8% usually has some form of premetabolic syndrome or insulin resistance.
D. Inspect
   1. Observe the overall appearance and note body fat distribution.
   2. Examine the skin.
   3. Mouth and teeth: Assess dental enamel for signs of purging.
E. Palpate the neck and thyroid.
F. Auscultate: Auscultate the carotid arteries, heart, lungs, and abdomen.
G. Palpate the extremities: Note edema.

Diagnostic Tests

A. Thyroid function
B. Lipid panel
C. Triglycerides
D. Pregnancy test
E. Fasting blood sugar/3-hour GTT
F. Sleep study (if indicated)
G. Nocturnal hypoxemia study

Differential Diagnoses

A. Obesity
B. Pseudotumor cerebri
C. Binge eating
D. Genetic syndrome (e.g., Prader–Willi syndrome)
E. Cushing syndrome
F. DM
G. Insulin resistance syndrome
H. Primary pulmonary hypertension

Plan

Manage obesity as a chronic relapsing disease, including the comanagement of other diseases secondary to obesity (i.e., diabetes, hypertension).

A. General interventions
   1. Reinforce the positive impact that weight-loss measures (diet, exercise) can have and the overall health benefits of weight loss.
   2. Identify and monitor any cardiovascular complications.
   3. Behavior modification: Intensive behavioral therapy has been shown with better success of weight loss and sustainable weight loss for longer periods of time. Behavioral therapy includes

weekly meeting with health care professionals for at least 6 to 8 weeks.

a. Dietary plan
   i. Low-calorie diet
   ii. Increase in fruits and vegetables
   iii. Eliminate alcohol and beverages containing sugar
   iv. Reduction of high-glycemic foods such as candy
   v. Reduction in high-caloric foods and drinks
   vi. Reduction of fat intake
   vii. Reduction of portion sizes
   viii. Reduction of the amount of processed foods in the diet
   ix. Increase in water intake
b. Exercise
   Encourage at least 60 minutes of exercise on most days. At least five times a week of moderate to vigorous exercise is recommended.
c. Wide range of benefits
   i. Helps lower BP
   ii. Improves cholesterol
   iii. Helps lower hemoglobin A1C in diabetes
   iv. Helps strengthen bones
   v. Weight loss
   vi. Improves depression
   vii. Boosts immune system
   viii. Reduces stress
   ix. Improves sense of well-being
   x. Believed to be a major driving force in lifestyle change
d. Obtain counseling on stimulus control, goal setting, self-monitoring, and contracts that reward behaviors.
e. Contraindication to exercise
f. There are several contraindications for beginning exercise: Individuals with recent myocardial infarction (2 weeks), unstable angina, severe aortic stenosis, decompensated congestive heart failure (low ejection fraction), left ventricular outflow obstruction, uncontrolled dysrhythmias, uncontrolled diabetes or diabetic complications, and uncontrolled hypertension.

B. Patient teaching on obesity treatment modalities
   1. Keep a food diary to identify food triggers.
   2. Counsel about pharmaceutical therapy drug side effects and the lack of long-term safety data. Stress to the patient the temporary nature of the weight-loss medication. Typical weight loss is modest, less than 5 kg (10–11 lbs) at 1 year.

C. Resources
   1. President's Council on Physical Fitness and Sports: www.fitness.gov
   2. Healthier US: www.healthierus.gov
   3. CDC Overweight and Obesity Resources: www.cdc.gov/obesity/resources.html
   4. Exercise: A Guide from the National Institute on Aging: www.nia.nih.gov/HealthInformation/Publications/ExerciseGuide
   5. NIH Exercise Videos: Exercise and Physical Activity for Older Adults: nihseniorhealth.gov/videolist.html#exercise
   6. Discovery Health: health.discovery.com
   7. National Association for Sport and Physical Education: www.aahperd.org/naspe
   8. American Heart Association: www.heart.org/HEARTORG/www.goredforwomen.org/BetterU/index.aspx
   9. Apps: MyFitnessPal: Useful app to track calories, exercise activity, and weight loss. Establish goals and projected weight loss based on food intake and exercise activity.

D. Pharmaceutical therapy
   1. After an adequate trial (minimum of 6 months) of diet and exercise therapy, consider pharmaceutical therapy. Pharmacologic intervention is not allowed in some states. State statutes should be considered prior to prescribing weight control products.
   2. Studies lack evidence to support whether one drug is more efficacious than another; nor does the literature support use of combination therapy for increased weight loss.
   3. The choice of a pharmaceutical agent depends on the side effect profile of the drug and tolerance of the side effects.
   4. The FDA has not approved any weight-loss medication for use beyond 2 years in adults. Appetite suppressants that are FDA approved:
      a. Qsymia, phentermine, diethylpropion, benzphetamine, and phendimetrazine are approved for short-term (12 weeks) use.
      b. Sibutramine (Reductil®) is FDA approved for 1-year use.
      c. Orlistat (Xenical®) is FDA approved for 2-year use.
   5. Appetite suppressants
      a. Qsymia (phentermine and topiramate extended release). Start with 3.75/23 mg extended release per day for initial BMI greater than 30 kg/m^2, or BMI greater than 27 kg/m^2 in the presence of risk factors. May gradually increase dose to 15/92 mg.
         i. Avoid evening dose.
         ii. Monitor for hypersensitivity to phentermine and topamax
         iii. These drugs are not recommended in the presence of hypertension, hyperthyroidism, CVD, and drug or alcohol abuse.

iv. Do not use if history of glaucoma, hyperthyroidism, or within 14 days of monoamine oxidase inhibitors (MAOIs).

b. Phentermine (Adipex-P) 37.5 mg orally once daily before or 1 to 2 hours after breakfast, or 18.75 mg one to two times per day for initial BMI greater than 30 kg/m^2, or BMI greater than 27 kg/m^2 in the presence of risk factors.
   i. Avoid late-evening dosing.
   ii. Not recommended in the presence of hypertension, hyperthyroidism, CVD, and drug or alcohol abuse.
   iii. Do not prescribe during or within 14 days of MAOIs.

c. Benzphetamine (Didrex) 25 to 50 mg orally initially in the midmorning or midafternoon. Increase if needed to 25 to 50 mg one to three times a day.
   i. Not recommended in the presence of hypertension, hyperthyroidism, CVD, and drug or alcohol abuse.
   ii. Not to be prescribed during or within 14 days of MAOIs.
   iii. Pregnancy category X: Known to cause fetal abnormalities or toxicity in animal and human studies.

d. Diethylpropion (Tenuate) 25 mg 1 tablet every 8 hours, 1 hour before meals. May add one additional dose for night hunger. Half-life of 4 to 6 hours.
   i. Avoid late evening dosing.
   ii. Not recommended in the presence of hypertension, hyperthyroidism, CVD, and drug or alcohol abuse.
   iii. Do not prescribe during or within 14 days of MAOIs.

e. Phendimetrazine (Bontril PDM) 35 mg orally two or three times daily 1 hour before meals. May reduce to 17.5 mg/dose. Maximum dose 210 mg/d in three evenly divided doses. Also available in slow-release 105 mg in the morning 30 to 60 minutes before breakfast.
   i. Not recommended in the presence of hypertension, hyperthyroidism, CVD, and drug or alcohol abuse.
   ii. Not to be prescribed during or within 14 days of MAOIs.

6. Lipase inhibitor
   a. Orlistat (Xenical) for use with a low-fat diet. Recommend 30% of calories spread over three main meals.
      i. Take one 120 mg capsule orally during or up to 1 hour after main meals up to three times per day.
      ii. If a meal is missed or had no fat, skip dosage.
      iii. May decrease absorption of fat-soluble vitamins and beta-carotene
      iv. Supplement diet with a multivitamin.
      v. FDA approved for up to 2 years use in adults
      vi. Gastrointestinal side effects include fatty/oily stools, oily spotting, flatus with discharge, fecal urgency, and fecal incontinence.
      vii. Contraindicated in chronic malabsorption syndrome and cholestasis.
      viii. May affect doses for antidiabetic medications.
      ix. Monitor warfarin and cyclosporine levels.
   b. Alli®, a lipase inhibitor, is the only FDA-available OTC weight-loss product.

7. Off-labeled medications used for obesity
   a. Metformin (Glucophage) is used to decrease central adiposity in weight loss, lower insulin levels, and slow down the process of gluconeogenesis.
      i. Start Metformin 500 mg at the evening meal. The dosage can be increased by 500 mg per week in divided doses up to the maximum of 2,000 mg/d.
      ii. Titrate slowly due to the gastrointestinal side effects.
      iii. Check a metabolic panel before and every 3 to 6 months to evaluate for lactic acidosis.
      iv. Metformin is contraindicated in patients with renal impairment; assess renal function prior to instituting metformin and monitor regularly.
      v. Metformin must be stopped prior to any procedure with radiographic dye.
      vi. Start on a patient with a waist-to-hip ratio greater than 0.8%.
   b. Topiramate (Topamax) is used to treat seizures and several types of headache. In small doses, it can be used alone or adjunct with phentermine to suppress appetite longer. Be familiar with the risks associated with the use of Topamax.
      i. If used alone, may start at 25 mg every day in the morning. Increase up to two or three times a day. Topamax has a longer half-life of 19 to 25 hours.
      ii. May be used as adjunct with phentermine. Start patient at 18.75 mg of phentermine and 12.5 mg of Topamax. Then gradually increase the dose to 37.5 mg of phentermine and 25 mg of Topamax.

iii. Always give the phentermine in the morning, preferably 30 minutes before meals. Topamax should be dosed in the afternoon or evening.
iv. Phentermine (Adipex-P) 37.5 mg orally once daily before or 1 to 2 hours after breakfast, or 18.75 mg one to two times per day for initial BMI greater than 30 kg/m^2, or BMI greater than 27 kg/m^2 in the presence of risk factors
v. Avoid late-evening dosing
vi. Not recommended in the presence of hypertension, hyperthyroidism, CVD, and drug or alcohol abuse
vii. Do not prescribe during or within 14 days of MAOIs.

Follow-Up

A. Reevaluate the patient every week for 6 to 8 weeks; then monthly either with or without pharmaceutical therapy until goal is achieved.
B. Maintain the recommended schedule for comorbid conditions.
C. If patient is a candidate for bariatric surgery, follow recommended pretreatment/reauthorization guidelines required by the payer and bariatric center.

Consultation/Referral

A. Refer for a nutrition/registered dietitian consultation.
B. Consider a referral to a bariatric center/surgical consultation and evaluation of bariatric surgery.
C. Consider a psychology consultation (may be required prior to bariatric surgery).
D. If the family is eligible, refer to the Women, Infant, and Children (WIC) Program.

Individual Considerations

A. Pregnancy
  1. Benzphetamine (Didrex) is a category X drug. Avoid use during pregnancy.
  2. Counsel patients regarding appropriate weight gain with pregnancy.
B. Geriatrics
  1. All adults should avoid inactivity. Some exercise is better than none.

Polycystic Ovarian Syndrome

Definition

PCOS is characterized by ovulatory dysfunction and hyperandrogenism. PCOS was previously called Stein–Leventhal syndrome. PCOS is a risk factor for metabolic syndrome, infertility, glucose intolerance, and type 2 DM. PCOS itself is not considered a disease; instead, it is a syndrome of coexisting conditions (see Table 23.5).

The Androgen Excess Society diagnostic criteria for PCOS

A. Hyperandrogenism
B. Ovarian dysfunction
C. Exclusion of other androgen excess or related disorders
D. Although obesity is one of the hallmarks of PCOS, lean women may also have insulin resistance/PCOS. The diagnosis of PCOS is based on medical history, physical examination, and laboratory tests. Aggressive lifestyle modification is the mainstay of all women with PCOS.

Incidence

A. The incidence of PCOS is 6.5% up to 12% in the literature. It is the most common worldwide endocrinopathy in women, with 5 to 7 million women in the United States experiencing its effects.

Pathogenesis

A. The exact etiology is unknown; however, PCOS is noted to have insulin resistance and abnormal pituitary function, as well as abnormal steroidogenesis.

Predisposing Factors

A. Obesity
B. Genetic predisposition, including Mexican American women
C. Metabolic syndrome
D. Women with oligo-ovulatory infertility
E. Type 1, type 2, or gestational diabetes
F. History of premature adrenarche
G. First-degree relatives with PCOS
H. Antiepileptic medications

TABLE 23.5 PCOS Associated Symptoms

Cutaneous signs	Hirsutism
	Severe acne
	Alopecia
Menstrual irregularity	Oligomenorrhea
	Amenorrhea
	Dysfunctional uterine bleeding
Obesity	> 35 inches (88-cm) waist circumference for women and adolescents > 16 y
	> 90% for ages 10 to < 16 y
Polycystic ovaries	Noted on ultrasound

Common Complaints

A. Hirsutism
B. Menstrual problems
C. Obesity
D. Infertility

Other Signs and Symptoms

A. Acne
B. Alopecia (male pattern)
C. Hyperhidrosis
D. Acanthosis nigricans
E. Seborrhea

Subjective Data

A. Review the patient's menstruation history.
   1. Premature puberty (younger than the age of 8)
   2. Primary amenorrhea: Lack of menses by age 15
   3. Oligomenorrhea: Missing four periods per year
   4. Dysfunctional uterine bleeding (DUB): Bleeding at irregular intervals, heavy cycles, periods longer than 7 days
B. Review the patient's history of weight gain, increased waist circumference, and obesity.
C. Review the patient's history of any skin/hair changes.
D. Review the family history for the presence of diabetes, metabolic syndrome, and infertility.

Physical Examination

A. Check height, weight, waist circumference, BP, pulse, and respirations.
B. Calculate the BMI and waist-to-hip measurement. Several Internet sites have BMI, body fat, and waist-to-hip ratio calculators.
C. Inspect
   1. Skin
      a. Evaluate hirsutism (upper lip, chin, nape of the neck, periareolar, abdomen-linea alba).
   2. Observe fat distribution.
D. Perform pelvic examination to evaluate enlarged ovaries and pelvic masses.

Diagnostic Tests

A. Fasting glucose
B. OGTT if fasting glucose is elevated between 100 mg/dL and 125 mg/dL
C. Thyroid function tests (TSH, free T_4)
D. Random serum cortisol to rule out Cushing syndrome
E. Serum LH and prolactin to rule out hypothalamic and pituitary diseases
F. Ultrasound to rule out ovarian pathology (as indicated: not required for definitive diagnosis)
G. Insulin-like growth factor (IGE-I)
H. DHEA-S to rule out adrenal hyperandrogenism
I. Free and total testosterone
J. Lipid profile
K. Endometrial biopsy if indicated for women without menses for 1 year
L. Pregnancy test prior to start of pharmaceutical therapy and history of an ovulation

Differential Diagnoses

A. PCOS
B. Adrenal disorders
   1. Congenital adrenal hyperplasia (CAH)
   2. Cushing syndrome
   3. Cortisol resistance
C. Hyperprolactinemia
D. Acromegaly
E. Insulin resistance (types 1 and 2 diabetes)
F. Thyroid dysfunction
G. Virilizing tumors
H. Drug-induced
   1. Anabolic steroids
   2. Valproic acid

Plan

A. General interventions
   1. Aggressive lifestyle modification focusing on increased physical activity and weight reduction is a cornerstone for treatment.
B. Patient education
   1. Exercise recommendations include a minimum of 30 minutes a day of walking at a brisk pace or other activity at a moderate intensity. Start by using a pedometer, walking at breaks, or household work.
   2. Weight loss of 5% to 10% or more. Gradual weight loss of 1 to 2 kg per month. Even small amounts of loss are associated with health benefits.
   3. Weight loss may cause a resumption of ovulation and the ability to get pregnant.
   4. High-fiber, low-fat diet, and reduction of refined sugar.
   5. Hair removal can be achieved with shaving, waxing, or use of depilatories. Electrolysis and laser treatment are more expensive therapies for hirsutism.
C. Pharmaceutical therapy
   1. OCPs are the most commonly used treatment for endometrial prevention and hirsutism.
      a. Due to sodium and water retention, weight reduction while on OCPs is more difficult.
      b. OCPs that contain 30 to 35 μ of ethinyl estradiol and progestins such as norethindrone (Ortho Micronor®), norgestimate

(Ortho-Tri-Cyclen®), desogestrel (Desogen® and Ortho-Cept®), or drospirenone (Yasmin®) are prescribed for PCOS

2. Metformin (Glucophage) is used to manage oligomenorrhea, cause weight loss, lower insulin levels, and induce ovulation for women with PCOS.
   a. Start metformin 500 mg at the evening meal. The dosage can be increased by 500 mg per week in divided doses up to the maximum of 2,000 mg/d.
   b. Titrate slowly due to the gastrointestinal side effects.
   c. Check a metabolic panel before and every 3 to 6 months to evaluate for lactic acidosis.
   d. Metformin is contraindicated in patients with renal impairment; assess renal function prior to instituting metformin and monitor regularly.
   e. Metformin must be stopped prior to any procedure with radiographic dye.
3. Medroxyprogesterone acetate (Provera) is used for a withdrawal bleed 5 to 10 mg daily for 10 days every 1 to 2 months, or micronized progesterone (Prometrium®) 100 to 200 mg by mouth at bedtime for 7 to 10 d/mo are used to protect the endometrium.
4. Spironolactone (Aldactone) 100 to 200 mg twice a day is utilized after a 4- to 6-month oral contraceptive trial as antiandrogen therapy.
   a. Spironolactone is also a good alternative when OCPs are contraindicated. However, spironolactone can be used in combination with OCPs.
   b. Alternative methods of birth control should be used when spironolactone is used alone secondary to abnormal development of the male fetus external genitalia.
   c. Monitor potassium during spironolactone therapy.
5. Eflornithine (Vaniqa) topical may be prescribed to prevent facial hair regrowth.
6. Clomiphene citrate (Clomid) is used to induce ovulation. Weight loss should be attempted prior to starting ovulation induction treatment.

Follow-Up

A. Glucose tolerance needs to be evaluated regularly for patients diagnosed with type 2 DM who are also diagnosed with PCOS (see Table 23.6).

Consultation/Referral

A. Refer to an obstetrician/gynecologist or a reproductive endocrinologist for consultation and management of
   1. Infertility/pregnancy
   2. Menstrual bleeding that is not controlled despite OCPs

B. An endocrinologist may be an appropriate consultation.

C. Consider a nutritional consultation.

Individual Considerations

A. Women who use OCPs are at increased risk for venous thromboembolism (VTE). Obese patients using OCPs are also at increased risk for VTE. Educate all patients regarding this risk factor and monitor the patient closely for this risk.

B. Obese women older than 40 years of age are at greater risk for VTE. Precautions should be used when prescribing OCPs to this population.

C. Chronic conditions of the patient should also be considered before prescribing OCPs for PCOS. Contraindications to the use of OCPs include patients with a previous history of VTE, hypertension, women 35 years or older who smoke 15 or more cigarettes per day, CVD, recent surgery, diabetes, rheumatic diseases, and so forth. The patient's medical history should be thoroughly evaluated.

TABLE 23.6 Androgen Excess Society Screening and Treatment Requirements for Impaired Glucose Tolerance (IGT)

All patients with PCOS, regardless of BMI, should be screened for IGT using a 2-hour OGTT.

Patients with a normal glucose test should be rescreened at least once every 2 years or earlier if additional risk factors are identified.

Patients with IGT should be screened annually for the development of type 2 DM.

Adolescents with PCOS should be screened for IGT using a 2-hour OGTT every 2 years. If IGT develops, the treatment with metformin should be considered.

The mainstay of treatment with PCOS and IGT is intensive lifestyle modification (diet, exercise, and weight loss). Insulin-sensitizing agents should be considered for patients with PCOS and IGT.

Source: Kelsey et al. (2007).

Thyroid Disease

Hyperthyroidism

Definition

A. Hyperthyroidism is a condition in which the thyroid hormone exerts greater than normal responses. Hyperthyroidism may be subclinical and may not be easily recognized or exhibit overt symptoms. The most common hyperthyroid conditions are Graves' disease and toxic multinodular goiter. The American Thyroid Association recommends that adults be screened for thyroid disease beginning at age 35 and every 5 years thereafter. However, Medicare at this time does not cover the charges for a screening thyroid test in an asymptomatic patient.

Incidence

A. Overall incidence of Graves' disease is 0.5 per 1,000. Graves' disease is responsible for 60% to 80% of cases of thyrotoxicosis.
B. Female gender
   1. 5:1 ratio higher in women than men
   2. Older women: 4% to 5% incidence
   3. Graves' disease is more common in younger women.
   4. Toxic nodular goiter is more common in older women.
C. Elderly: Toxic multinodular goiter (Plummer disease) occurs in 15% to 20% of patients with thyrotoxicosis.
D. Symptomatology incidence
   1. Ophthalmopathy is more common in smokers.
   2. Atrial fibrillation 10% to 25% incidence and is more common in the elderly.
   3. Autoimmune thyroid diseases have a peak incidence in people aged 20 to 40 years.

Pathogenesis

A. Hyperthyroidism is one form of thyrotoxicosis in which an excess of hormone is excreted by the thyroid gland. The diseases that can cause hyperthyroidism include Graves' disease, toxic multinodular goiter, thyroid cancer, and increased secretion of the TSH. Thyrotoxicosis not related to hyperthyroidism may be subacute thyroiditis, ectopic thyroid tissue, and ingestion of excessive thyroid hormone. Postpartum thyroiditis can precipitate a short-term mild hyperthyroidism, which has an onset at 2 to 6 months postpartum. Severe thyrotoxicosis of any cause is called thyrotoxic crisis or storm.
B. In Graves' disease, the normal feedback mechanisms that regulate hormone secretion are taken over by some abnormal thyroid-stimulating mechanism. Thyroid autoantibodies of the immunoglobulin G (IgG) class are present in more than 95% of patients with Graves' disease. The hyperfunctioning of the thyroid gland causes suppression of TSH and thyrotropin-releasing hormone (TRH). There are profound increases in iodine uptake and thyroid gland metabolism, which are believed to be the causes of the gland enlargement. The resulting increase in the level of circulating thyroid hormone is responsible for the thyrotoxic symptoms.
C. In the condition called toxic multinodular goiter, the thyroid gland enlarges in response to some bodily need such as puberty, pregnancy, iodine deficiency, and immunologic, viral, and genetic disorders. As TSH levels rise, the gland enlarges; when the condition demanding increased thyroid hormone resolves, TSH levels usually return to normal and the gland slowly assumes its original size.

Predisposing Factors

A. Graves' disease
   1. Women in the second through fifth decades of life
   2. Familial autoimmune thyroid disease
   3. Concomitant disorders believed to be autoimmune
   4. Increased in Trisomy 21
   5. Higher incidence in smokers
B. Toxic multinodular goiter
   1. Advanced age
   2. Recent exposure to iodine-containing medications (amiodarone and/or radio-contrast dye)
   3. Long-standing simple goiter
   4. Conditions such as puberty, pregnancy, iodine deficiency, immunologic, viral, or genetic disorders

Common Complaints

A. Graves' disease
   1. Prominence/protrusion of the eye (exophthalmos)
   2. Prominent "stare"
   3. Visual changes
      a. Diplopia
      b. Photophobia
      c. Eye irritation: Gritty feeling or pain
B. Weight loss with no change in diet or an increase in appetite
C. Anorexia (may be prominent in the elderly)
D. Weakness and fatigue
E. Tachycardia
F. Decreased tolerance to heat
G. Thinning scalp hair
H. Fingernail separation from the nail bed
I. Smooth, thin skin

J. Heart palpitations (atrial fibrillation)
K. Bowel symptoms
   1. Increase in frequency and loose bowel movements (not diarrhea)
   2. Constipation (more frequent in the elderly)
L. Swelling of feet and ankles

Other Signs and Symptoms

A. Goiter: **Approximately 50% of patients will not have an enlargement of the thyroid gland.** Elderly patients are less likely to have a goiter.
B. Periorbital edema
C. Flushing, warm skin
D. Fine hand tremors
E. Dyspnea (especially elderly)
F. Exertional fatigue/exercise intolerance
G. Insomnia
H. Irritability
I. Nervousness
J. Mood swings
K. Inability to concentrate
L. Depression and apathy (elderly)
M. Menses
N. Impotence and decreased libido in men
O. Gynecomastia
P. Galactorrhea (TSH-mediated hyperthyroidism)
Q. Atrial dysrhythmias (atrial fibrillation), left ventricular dilation (common in elderly)
R. Urinary frequency and nocturia
S. A combination of these noted symptoms should lead to the assessment of hyperthyroidism.

Subjective Data

A. Identify when symptoms began, duration, and any change or progression.
B. Identify whether the patient has noticed enlargement of the thyroid gland, difficulty swallowing, or change in voice.
C. Assess for change in weight over the past 3 months, past 6 months, and last year. Ask the patient whether his or her appetite has changed.
D. Explore the patient's family history of thyroid problems.
E. Obtain the patient's medical history of associated diseases (especially those of autoimmune pathogenesis: pernicious anemia, type 1 DM, myasthenia gravis, rheumatoid arthritis, ulcerative colitis).
F. Review the patient's medication history, including amiodarone, interferon alpha, levothyroxine (overdose), expectorants, and health food supplements containing seaweed.
G. Ask the patient to identify any changes in bowel habits, loose (nondiarrhea) stools, frequency of bowel movements, or constipation.
H. Ask about moods, changes in concentration, feelings of restlessness, nervousness, anxiety, and change in sleep habits.
I. Assess for any cardiac symptoms, such as palpitations, chest pain, shortness of breath, and decreased tolerance for activities previously done.
J. Ask whether the patient has noticed any swelling or puffiness anywhere.
K. Determine whether the patient has experienced changes in vision and/or eye irritation.
L. Assess for hand tremors, increase in the moistness and coolness of the skin, flushing, and blushing.
M. Ask the patient to identify any menstrual changes or whether the patient has had a recent pregnancy, or is in the postpartum period.
N. Review for a recent history of a viral infection.
O. Review recent trauma to the neck (significant trauma can cause thyrotoxicosis).

Physical Examination

A. Check temperature, if indicated; pulse (tachycardia); respirations (dyspnea); BP (systolic hypertension); and weight
B. Inspect
   1. Observe overall appearance: Does the patient have any difficulty with breathing, including dyspnea, or difficulty swallowing from tracheal obstruction secondary to a large goiter?
   2. Note eyelid retraction, lid lag, and exophthalmos. The clinician may see periorbital edema and an elevated upper eyelid, which leads to decreased blinking and a staring quality in Graves' disease.
   3. Note tremors that are best demonstrated from outstretched hands.
   4. Inspect the skin for temperature and texture.
   5. Inspect the fingernails for:
      a. Onycholysis, also known as Plummer's nails (loosening of the nails from the nail beds)
      b. Softening of the nails
   6. Inspect scalp/hair.
C. Auscultate
   1. Auscultate the thyroid for bruits.
   2. Auscultate the heart and pulse rate. Patients with subclinical hyperthyroidism frequently present with atrial fibrillation.
   3. Auscultate the carotid arteries for bruits.
   4. Auscultate bowel sounds.
D. Palpate
   1. Palpate the neck and thyroid for nodules, thrills, and enlargement. Depending on the etiology of the hyperthyroidism, the thyroid may range from normal to massive (Graves' disease or toxic multinodular goiter). Palpation of the

thyroid can induce the gland to release increased hormone; be alert for signs and symptoms of thyroid storm.
2. If the thyroid is tender and painful to palpation, granulomatous thyroiditis may be the etiology of hyperthyroidism.
3. Palpate the heart for thrills.
4. Palpate extremities for edema. Pretibial myxedema is noted in Graves' disease.

E. Neurologic examination
1. Assess DTRs.
2. Tests for lid lag
a. Have the patient follow your finger as it moves up and down.
b. Have the patient look down and observe if sclera can be seen above the iris.
3. Have the patient stick out the tongue to observe for presence of tremors.

Diagnostic Tests

A. TSH, free thyroxin (T4), triiodothyronine (T3) (see Table 23.7).
B. Radioactive iodine (^{131}I) uptake (RAIU), if needed. If the patient has ophthalmopathy, clinical symptoms of hyperthyroidism, and a diffusely enlarged thyroid gland, the RAIU test is not necessary to confirm Graves' disease. Pregnancy and breastfeeding are absolute contraindications to radionuclide imaging.
C. Consider additional laboratory testing.
1. CBC (may have normochromic, normocytic anemia)
2. Serum ferritin (may be high)
D. If T4 and T3 are high, but TSH is normal or high, a pituitary MRI should be ordered to look for a pituitary mass.
E. An echocardiogram should be considered if an irregular heart rate and signs of heart failure are noted on examination.

Differential Diagnoses

A. Hyperthyroidism
1. Graves' disease
2. T3-toxicosis
3. T4-toxicosis
4. Thyroid adenoma
5. Drug-induced hyperthyroidism, that is, iodine-rich amiodarone
6. Subclinical hyperthyroidism
7. TSH-induced hyperthyroidism (TSH-secreting pituitary adenoma)
8. Hyperthyroidism during pregnancy
9. Hashitoxicosis (combination of Hashimoto and thyrotoxicosis), rare autoimmune thyroid disease

B. CVD such as CAD and heart failure
C. Gastrointestinal disorders such as irritable bowel syndrome, ulcerative colitis, and Crohn's disease
D. Cancer: Testicular germ cell tumors
E. Neurologic disorder
F. Hydatidiform mole (molar pregnancy)
G. Psychological disorder

Plan

A. General interventions
1. Carefully assess for complications of hyperthyroidism: Cardiac, ophthalmologic, gastrointestinal, musculoskeletal, and psychological, and address each area identified.
2. Patients with tachycardia, palpitations, tremors, anxiety, and eyelid lag can be treated with a beta-adrenergic antagonist for some relief from those symptoms until they become euthyroid.
3. For infiltrative dermopathy over the lower extremities, occlusive wraps on the affected side are recommended.
4. Only 5% of patients with Graves' disease develop severe ophthalmopathy. An initial ophthalmologic exam is recommended as baseline, with follow-up determined by the ophthalmologist.

B. Patient teaching
1. Patients taking propylthiouracil (PTU) or methimazole (MMI) should be instructed to immediately report any side effects, including rash, hives, fever, jaundice, abdominal pain, and clay-colored stools.
2. Less than 1% of patients develop agranulocytosis, but all patients should be instructed to call the

TABLE 23.7 Test Results in Hyperthyroidism

Disorder	TSH	Free T4	T3	RAIU and Thyroid Scan
Overt hyperthyroidism	L	H	H	H
Graves' disease	L	H	H	H
Multinodular goiter	L	H	–	H
T3 thyrotoxicosis (may be caused by antithyroid drug therapy)	L	N or H	H	N or H

H, high; L, low; N, normal; RAIU, radioactive iodine uptake.

provider immediately if a fever, sore throat, or joint ache develops due to their susceptibility to serious infection.

3. Patients receiving radioactive iodine (RAI) should be informed that they most likely will need to take lifelong hormone replacement after the RAI treatment is completed.
4. Teach safety measures to guard against the possibility of fractures due to bone density loss secondary to hyperthyroidism. Get a baseline bone density scan (DEXA scan).
5. Inform patients that an episode of serious depression may follow successful treatment of hyperthyroidism.
6. No special diet is required; however, patients should be told to avoid herbal supplements and sushi that contains seaweed.

C. Medical–surgical management
  1. RAI is a common choice of therapy for adults. It is administered in capsule form or in water.
     a. One dose is usually sufficient; however, a second dose may be given if necessary.
     b. Permanent hypothyroidism requiring lifelong hormone replacement is the only notable complication.
  2. A thyroidectomy is seldom used except in limited patient conditions.
     a. Pregnancy—if women are noncompliant or cannot tolerate thionamides because of allergies or agranulocytosis
     b. Patients who refuse RAI therapy
     c. Refractory amiodarone-induced hyperthyroidism
     d. Patients with unstable cardiac conditions that require quick normalization of thyroid function

D. Pharmaceutical therapy
  1. Antithyroid drugs: The choice of drugs depends on clinician experience, the severity of the disease, and patient preference. Provide titration of antithyroid drug dose every 4 weeks until thyroid function normalizes and to ensure the patient does not become hypothyroid. Graves' disease may go into remission after treatment for 12 to 18 months, and drug therapy can be discontinued.
     a. PTU
        i. Initial dose 100 to 150 mg by mouth three times daily. Dosage decrease is almost always required at 4 to 8 weeks of start.
        ii. Thyroid storm: 150 to 200 mg orally every 4 to 6 hours
        iii. Except in thyroid storm, PTU is considered a second-line drug therapy. It is reserved for use in patients who are allergic to or intolerant of Tapazole (MMI) and in women who are in the first trimester of pregnancy or planning pregnancy.
     b. MMI (Tapazole)
        i. Adults: 20 to 40 mg/d or in divided twice-a-day dose. Maintenance doses are 2.5 to 15 mg/d.
        ii. Methimazole is more potent than PTU and has a longer duration of action.
        iii. Methimazole is not recommended for use in the first trimester of pregnancy.
  2. RAI therapy is one of the most common treatments in adults. It is administered orally as a single dose. RAI is contraindicated in pregnancy and lactation.
  3. Beta blockers such as propranolol (Inderal) are also used for hyperthyroidism.
  4. Atrial fibrillation treatment is directed toward restoring a euthyroid state. Other therapies include
     a. Beta blockers (unless contraindicated, including chronic obstructive pulmonary disease [COPD] and asthma)
     b. Calcium channel blockers if unable to utilize beta blocker
     c. Oral anticoagulation (keeping the INR [international normalized ratio] between 2 and 3)
     d. Antiarrhythmic drugs and cardioversion may be unsuccessful until euthyroid.

Follow-Up

A. Depending on the experience of the clinician, an endocrinologist best prescribes therapy, including RAI and antithyroid medication.
B. Patients receiving PTU or MMI should be seen in the office every 4 to 6 weeks for evaluation and have blood drawn for serum TSH and free T4 measurements until euthyroid state is achieved and maintained.
C. Patients are usually maintained on these drugs for 1 to 2 years, with office visits every 3 months. The drug is then gradually withdrawn, and 25% to 90% of patients experience permanent remission.
D. Patients with RAI therapy should be seen in the office to monitor thyroid levels. It is anticipated that most of them will require lifelong hormone replacement medication following treatment.
E. Perform bone density screening (DEXA scan) to evaluate for osteopenia/osteoporosis.
F. Consider testing for IGT.

Consultation/Referral

A. Ophthalmology consultation is recommended for patients with ophthalmologic involvement.

B. If surgery is the choice of treatment, refer the patient to an endocrinologist and a surgeon.
C. An experienced obstetrician or perinatologist should follow pregnant women.

Individual Considerations

A. Pregnancy
   1. Pregnant patients with mild hyperthyroidism may be followed with treatment.
   2. If an antithyroid drug is necessary, PTU is the drug of choice in the first trimester. MMI has been associated with congenital anomalies such as tracheoesophageal fistula and choanal atresia. After the first trimester, mothers may be switched to MMI.
   3. Monitor thyroid function every 4 weeks during pregnancy.
   4. RAI therapy is contraindicated during pregnancy and breastfeeding.
   5. Thyrotoxicosis may improve during pregnancy; however, symptoms may relapse during the postpartum period.
   6. Hyperthyroidism in the third trimester may increase the risk of low birth weight.
   7. Prolonged high-dose iodine therapy can cause fetal goiter.
   8. Ultrasounds should be performed to evaluate for fetal hyperthyroidism, assessing for goiter, poor growth, cardiac failure, and hydrops fetalis.
B. Adults: Sympathetic activation (anxiety, hyperactivity, etc.) is seen in adult years more commonly than in the elderly population.
C. Geriatrics
   1. Older patients exhibit only three clinical signs (tachycardia, fatigue, and weight loss), whereas younger patients may exhibit as many as 12 symptoms.
   2. Rare signs in this population include atrial fibrillation, hyperactive reflexes, increased sweating, heat intolerance, tremors, nervousness, polydipsia, and increased appetite. Goiter is much less common.
   3. Elderly women with hyperthyroidism are at increased risk for accelerated bone loss.

Hypothyroidism

Definition

A. Hypothyroidism is a condition in which the body does not produce enough thyroid hormone. In general, hypothyroidism is considered permanent, requiring lifelong therapy to restore a euthyroid state. The most common physical finding is a goiter. The most common worldwide cause of hypothyroidism is iodine deficiency, while the most common cause in the United States is Hashimoto thyroiditis, an autoimmune thyroid disease.

Incidence

A. Hypothyroidism occurs in 5% of the population.
B. It occurs in women more than men (5–8 times higher).
C. It may present in up to 15% of people older than 65 years.
D. In adolescents, approximately 6% have acquired hypothyroidism.
E. Approximately 10% of patients with type 1 DM will develop chronic thyroiditis.
F. Up to 10% develop lymphocytic thyroiditis in the postpartum period (up to 10 months postpartum).
G. Approximately 1:4,000 newborns have congenital hypothyroidism (cretinism).
H. The incidence is higher in Whites (5.1%) and Mexican Americans than in African Americans (1.7%).

Pathogenesis

Hypothyroidism is caused by an insufficient production of thyroid hormones by the thyroid gland, either by a primary or a secondary cause.

A. Primary causes include decreased hormone production caused by autoimmune thyroiditis, endemic iodine deficiency, congenital defects, or decreased thyroid activity after treatment for hyperthyroidism.
B. Secondary causes are much less common but may include insufficient stimulation from the pituitary or hypothalamus and peripheral resistance to thyroid hormones.
C. The most common cause of primary hypothyroidism is chronic autoimmune thyroiditis called Hashimoto thyroiditis. In this disease, circulating thyroid antibodies and the infiltration of lymphocytes destroy thyroid tissue. Autoimmune thyroiditis may also be a result of an inherited immune defect.
D. Acute thyroidism is a rare cause of hypothyroidism in which the cause is an acute bacterial infection. Subacute thyroiditis, a nonbacterial inflammation of the thyroid, is often preceded by a viral infection. Both of these conditions cause inflammation of the thyroid gland by lymphocytic and leukocytic infiltration into the thyroid tissue, resulting in hypothyroidism.

Predisposing Factors

A. Iodine deficiency
B. Women older than 40 years at highest risk
C. Presence of other autoimmune disorders (diagnosed and previously undiagnosed)
D. Recent acute bacterial or viral infection
E. Treatment with RAI for thyroid gland problems
F. Surgical removal of thyroid gland
G. Exposure to external radiation

H. Evidence of pituitary or hypothalamic disease
I. Postpartum
J. Type 1 (autoimmune) DM
K. Chromosomal disorders
  1. Down syndrome
  2. Turner syndrome
  3. Klinefelter syndrome
L. Celiac disease
M. Drug-induced
  1. Amiodarone
  2. Interferon alpha
  3. Thalidomide
  4. Lithium
  5. Stavudine
  6. Dopamine

Common Complaints

A. Weight gain/obesity
B. Fatigue/sluggishness
C. Cold intolerance
D. Constipation
E. Dry and flaky skin
F. Coarseness or loss of hair, inability of hair to hold a curl, hair loss at eyebrows, and reduced growth of hair
G. Reduced growth of nails
H. Hoarseness
I. Memory or mental impairment, difficulty concentrating, and slowed speech or thinking
J. Periorbital edema and facial puffiness
K. Irregular or heavy menses and infertility
L. Muscle aching and stiffness

Other Signs and Symptoms

A. Asymptomatic if subclinical hypothyroidism and have no overt symptoms
B. Delayed reflexes
C. Elevated BP
D. Hyperlipidemia
E. Jaundice
F. Painful subacute thyroiditis
  1. Sudden neck pain with sore throat, radiating to jaw and ears, and pain shifting to sides of the neck
  2. Late stage: Myxedema, thick scaly skin, muscle weakness/joint pain, enlarged tongue, hearing loss, bradycardia, cardiac hypertrophy, pleural effusion, and ascites
G. Pituitary or hypothalamic failure
  1. Loss of axillary and pubic hair
  2. Cessation of menses
  3. Postural hypotension
H. Exercise intolerance
I. Carpal tunnel syndrome is a common occurrence.
J. Depression
K. Ataxia
L. Decreased concentration/memory impairment

Subjective Data

A. Note history of recent illness and/or pregnancy.
B. Evaluate the patient's medical-surgical history for any treatment of hyperthyroidism, including radioactive treatment or thyroidectomy.
C. Review dietary and weight history, how much weight has been gained and over what period of time.
D. Review any changes in health status or symptoms associated with other body systems (thyroid symptoms usually involve multiple body systems).
E. Review any history of OSA.
F. Assess for pain or swelling of the neck or difficulty swallowing.
G. Inquire as to the patient's history of supervoltage x-ray therapy to the neck for nonthyroid cancer or for polio.
H. Identify family history.
  1. Does the patient have a first-degree relative with thyroid disease?
  2. Is there a family history of any endocrine problems, including thyroid, type 1 DM, and/or RA?
I. Review the patient's medication history for current medication, OTC medications, vitamins, or herbal supplements.
J. Review the patient's menstrual history or history of infertility.

Physical Examination

A. Check pulse (bradycardia), respirations, BP (decreased SBP and increased DBP), and weight
B. General observation
  1. Gait problems such as ataxia or rigidity and spasticity of the trunk and proximal extremities
  2. Quality of the patient's voice (hoarseness)
  3. Signs of depression, decreased concentration, or memory impairment
C. Inspect
  1. Inspect the skin (dry/flaky) for presence of jaundice.
  2. Inspect the hair (coarse, thin, brittle) and decrease in pubic/axillary hair pattern.
  3. Perform oral examination for evaluation of macroglossia (enlarged tongue).
  4. Inspect the face/eye for periorbital puffiness/edema.
  5. Inspect the neck for the presence of a goiter and surgical scar.
D. Auscultate
  1. Auscultate the thyroid and carotids.
  2. Auscultate the heart.
  3. Auscultate the lungs.
  4. Auscultate the abdomen for bowel sounds in each quadrant (hypoactive).

E. Palpate
   1. Palpate the neck, thyroid gland, and lymph nodes.
   2. Palpate the abdomen for presence of abdominal distension, ascites, and hepatomegaly.
   3. Palpate/evaluate extremities for edema.
F. Musculoskeletal examination: Perform a detailed musculoskeletal examination.
G. Neurologic examination
   1. Check visual fields (restricted with hypothyroidism).
   2. Test hearing.
      a. Whisper words and have the patient repeat.
      b. Use a ticking watch.
      c. Use a tuning fork.
         i. Weber test: Place vibrating fork on top midline of head (sound hearing equally in both ears).
         ii. Rinne test: Place vibrating tuning fork on mastoid, begin counting, and ask the patient to tell you when he/she no longer hears; then quickly reposition 1/2 to 1 inch from the ear and ask the patient when he/she no longer hears (hearing should be twice as long as bone conduction).
   3. Check for loss or reduction of DTRs.
   4. Evaluate proximal muscle weakness/strength.
   5. Test for abnormal tandem gait: Have the patient walk across the room in a heel-toe, heel-toe fashion.
   6. Check for sensory loss.
      a. Evaluate the first three fingers and one half of the fourth finger on testing loss of sensation from carpal tunnel syndrome.
      b. Evaluate sensory loss of the feet/legs (generally symmetrical in a "stocking-glove" distribution).

Diagnostic Tests

A. TSH
B. When a high TSH is noted, repeat the test and add a free T4.
C. T3 resin uptake
D. Thyroid antibodies (see Table 23.8)
E. TSH assay (if TSH assay is elevated, it indicates hypothyroidism)
F. Thyroid scan
G. CBC (anemia)
H. Lipid profile
I. Ultrasound of the neck and thyroid to detect nodules (not a first-line test)

Differential Diagnoses

A. Hypothyroidism
   1. Hashimoto thyroiditis
   2. Subclinical hypothyroidism
   3. Hypothyroidism secondary to treatment/intervention for hyperthyroidism
   4. De Quervain thyroiditis
   5. If TSH and free T4 are both low, consider hypothyroidism secondary to pituitary or hypothalamic failure.
B. Obesity: Patients with elevated total cholesterol levels or triglyceride levels are often misdiagnosed by assuming that these symptoms are caused by obesity and high-fat diets.
C. Depression
D. Ischemic heart disease
E. Nephrotic syndrome
F. Cirrhosis
G. Side effects/adverse effects of medications
H. Constipation
I. Sleep apnea/sleep disorder
J. Fibromyalgia
K. Infectious mononucleosis

Plan

A. General interventions
   1. The American Thyroid Association clinical practice guideline for detection of both subclinical and symptomatic hypothyroidism recommends that all adults aged 35 and older be screened for hypothyroidism every 5 years

TABLE 23.8 Test Results in Hypothyroidism

Disorder	TSH	Free T4	T3	RAIU and Thyroid Scan	Peroxidase Antibodies
Hypothyroid	H	L	Sometimes L	N or L	n/a
Hashimoto disease	H or variable	N or L	Not helpful	Variable	Positive
Subacute hypothyroidism	L	H	H or variable	L or absent	Usually thyroiditis
Silent lymphocytic	L when toxic	H when toxic	N/A	L when toxic	Positive
Thyroiditis (usually postpartum)	H when hypothyroid	L when hypothyroid			

H, high; L, low; N, normal; RAIU, radioactive iodine uptake.

to identify thyroid disease in the early stages. However, Medicare does not cover a screening TSH in an asymptomatic patient.
2. Patients with underactive thyroids require lifelong treatment with levothyroxine.
3. In patients with subacute thyroiditis, relatively large doses of NSAIDs or prednisone may be prescribed.
4. For patients with enlarged thyroid glands, surgery may be recommended if the gland begins obstructing the airway.
5. The treatment of patients with malignant thyroid nodules depends on the type of cancer.

B. Patient teaching
1. Teach the patient about the nature and course of the disease, as well as the signs and symptoms. Frequently, patients are relieved that perceived symptoms are real and that there is treatment. This may also improve patient compliance.
2. Teach the patient to report any side effects of the drug:
   a. Tachycardia
   b. Palpitations
   c. Chest pain
3. Emphasize the need for lifelong treatment with levothyroxine and the dangers of noncompliance.
4. Thyroid replacement should be taken on an empty stomach.
5. The beneficial effects of thyroid replacement occur in about 3 days to 1 week; the patient may not feel the clinical effects for several months.
6. When switching brands or using a generic version, the serum TSH should be checked in 6 weeks.

C. Pharmacological therapy
1. Patients requiring therapy with levothyroxine should be treated with the same brand/generic consistently since potency varies between brand and generics.
   a. Levothyroxine (Synthroid, Levoxyl, Levothroid, Unithroid)
      i. Adults 1.6 mcg/kg/d by mouth is administered as a single dose in the morning on an empty stomach.
      ii. Elderly with comorbid CAD or severe COPD should be started at 25 to 50 mcg/d.
      iii. Maintenance dose is 50 to 200 mcg by mouth every morning.
   b. Desiccated thyroid (Armor thyroid)
      i. Adult initial dosing is 15 to 30 mg/d by mouth and increased by 15 to 30 mg/d every 4 weeks.
      ii. Maintenance dose is 60 to 180 mg/d.
2. The medication should be titrated to the lowest dosage needed to maintain euthyroidism and a nonelevated serum TSH and a normal or slightly elevated T4.
3. Elderly patients and those with CVD should be started on very low doses (25 mcg/d) of levothyroxine; doses are increased very gradually over 8 to 12 weeks as tolerated. Close monitoring for the development of cardiac complications such as angina, arrhythmias, and myocardial infarction needs to be undertaken.
4. Thyroid hormones should be taken on an empty stomach in the mornings to avoid insomnia.
5. Other drugs can reduce the effectiveness/affect absorption of thyroid hormone:
   a. Cholesterol-reducing drugs
   b. Cholestyramine interferes with absorption in the gut
   c. Calcium carbonate
   d. Aluminum hydroxide
   e. Sucralfate (Carafate)
   f. If taking one of these drugs and levothyroxine, they should be taken 4 to 6 hours apart
6. Dietary fiber can interfere with levothyroxine absorption. Coffee reduces the absorption of levothyroxine.
7. Pharmacologic treatment of the patient with subclinical hypothyroidism is controversial. If a goiter is present, treatment may be considered.

Follow-Up

A. Patients who are not treated with medication should be seen every 6 to 12 months for reevaluation.
B. When medication is instituted, monitor laboratory values and patient well-being in the office every 4 to 6 weeks.
C. After the dosage is stabilized, the patient with an elevated serum TSH level should be seen every 6 to 12 months.
   1. Undetectable TSH levels are indicative of overmedication.
   2. High TSH levels are indicative of insufficient medication or patient noncompliance.
D. After the TSH is normalized, regular annual follow-up visits are required.
E. Order DEXA scan as indicated.

Consultation/Referral

A. Consultation with an endocrinologist is recommended for:
   1. Patients unresponsive to therapy
   2. Pregnant patients
   3. Presence of goiter, nodule, or other structural changes in the thyroid
   4. Compression symptoms of dysphagia
   5. Any patient with myxedema, significant cardiac disease, or involvement or hypothyroidism

secondary to pituitary or hypothalamic failure should be managed in consultation with a physician or should be referred to an endocrinologist for continued care

6. Refer to radiologist/physician if fine-needle aspiration biopsy is required.

Individual Considerations

A. Pregnancy
 1. Pregnancy: Monitor TSH levels monthly during the first trimester.
 2. Small increases in medication dosage may be required.
 3. Some women develop postpartum thyroiditis and hypothyroidism after taking hyperthyroid medication during pregnancy or immediately thereafter.
 4. Postpartum: Monitor TSH level at 6 weeks postpartum examination.
 5. A common cause of congenital hypothyroidism is maternal and infant iodine deficiency.
 6. Monitor the TSH to avoid overtreatment in postpartum women because excess thyroid hormone levels increase the risk of osteoporosis.
 7. Hypothyroidism in pregnancy is associated with preeclampsia, anemia, postpartum hemorrhage, cardiac ventricular dysfunction, spontaneous abortion, low birth weight, impaired cognitive development, and fetal mortality.

B. Geriatrics
 1. Some elderly patients who are actually hyperthyroid exhibit symptoms of hypothyroidism. Monitor these patients closely, especially when adjusting the medication dosage and/or adding medications that alter the absorption of the thyroid medication.

Thyrotoxicosis/Thyroid Storm

Definition

A. Severe thyrotoxicosis of any cause is called thyrotoxic crisis or storm.

Incidence

A. It is rare; the incidence varies, depending on the cause of the thyrotoxicosis.

Pathogenesis

A. Thyrotoxic crisis or storm usually develops in patients either undiagnosed as being hyperthyroid or those who are known to be severely hyperthyroid, are being treated insufficiently, and are subjected to excessive stress from other causes. Oversecretion of T3 and T4 is followed by a release of epinephrine. Metabolism is dramatically increased. The adrenal glands produce excessive corticosteroids, which is a response to stress.

Predisposing Factors

A. Severe, uncontrolled hyperthyroidism

B. Noncompliance with antihyperthyroid medication

C. Inadequate preparation for thyroid surgery

Common Complaints

A. Sudden onset of
 1. Hyperthermia
 2. Tachycardia (usually atrial tachydysrhythmias)
 3. High-output cardiac failure
 4. Altered sensorium (usually agitation, restlessness, delirium)
 5. Nausea, vomiting, and diarrhea

Subjective Data

A. Elicit information regarding the onset, duration, and nature of symptoms.

B. Determine the presence of cardiac symptoms.

C. Take a complete drug history, including whether or not patient has been taking antithyroid medication as prescribed.

D. Rule out any excessive acute stressors such as infection, pulmonary or cardiac problems, dialysis, plasmapheresis, and/or emotional stressors.

Physical Examination

A. Check temperature, pulse, respirations, and BP

B. Inspect
 1. Inspect the skin.

C. Auscultate
 1. Auscultate the heart and lungs.

D. Palpate the neck carefully for thyroid nodules and enlargement

Diagnostic Tests

A. Serum T3 and free T4

B. TSH

Differential Diagnoses

A. Thyroid storm

B. Thyrotoxic crisis

Plan

A. General interventions
 1. Closely monitor temperature, pulse, respirations, and BP.
 2. Assess the need to hospitalize the patient for supportive therapy: Intravenous fluids, medication treatment, antipyretics, and/or oxygen.

B. Patient teaching
 1. See Patient teaching in the "Hyperthyroidism" section.

C. Pharmaceutical therapy
 1. See Pharmaceutical therapy in the "Hyperthyroidism" section.

Follow-Up

A. Following resolution of the crisis, see the patient in the office every 3 to 4 weeks for evaluation and monitoring of serum TSH and free T4 levels.
B. See Follow-Up in the "Hyperthyroidism" section.

Consultation/Referral

A. Refer the patient to a physician immediately for possible hospitalization.

Individual Considerations

A. Pregnancy: See Individual Considerations in the "Hyperthyroidism" section.

Bibliography

Alberti, K. G. M. M., Eckel, R. H., Grundy, S. M., Zimmet, P. Z., Cleeman, J. L., Donato, K. A., ... International Association for the Study of Obesity. (2009). Harmonizing the metabolic syndrome: A joint interim statement of the International Diabetes Federation Task Force on Epidemiology and Prevention; National Heart, Lung, and Blood Institutes; American Heart Association; World Heart Federation; International Atherosclerosis Society; and International Association for the Study of Obesity. *Circulation, 120,* 1640–1645.

American Diabetes Association. (2013). Diagnosis and classification of diabetes mellitus. *Diabetes Care, 36*(Supplement 1), S67–S74.

American Diabetes Association. (2014). Standards of medical care in diabetes. *Diabetes Care, 37*(Supplement 1), S14–S80.

Azziz, R. (2012). Epidemiology and pathogenesis of polycystic ovarian syndrome in adults. Retrieved from http://www.uptodate.com

Barbieri, R. L. (2012). Treatment of hirsutism. *UpToDate.* Retrieved from http://www.uptodate.com

Barbieri, R. L., & Ehrmann, D. A. (2012a). Evaluation of premenopausal women with hirsutism. *UpToDate.* Retrieved from http://www.uptodate.com

Barbieri, R. L., & Ehrmann, D. A. (2012b). Pathogenesis and causes of hirsutism. *UpToDate.* Retrieved from www.uptodate.com/online/content/topic.do?topicKey=r_endo_f/24245&view=print

Barbieri, R. L., & Ehrmann, D. A. (2012c). Treatment of polycystic ovary syndrome in adults. *UpToDate.* Retrieved from http://www.uptodate.com/online/content/topic.do?topicKey=r_endo_f/24245&view=print

Bermas, B. L. (2012). Rheumatoid arthritis and pregnancy. *UpToDate.* Retrieved from http://www.uptodate.com/online/content/topic.do?topicKey=rheumart/7405&view=print

Bhasin, S., Cunningham, G. R., Hayes, F. J., Matsumoto, A. M., Snyder, P. J., Swerdloff, R. S., & Montori, V. M. (2010). Testosterone therapy in adult men with androgen deficiency syndromes: An endocrine society clinical practice guideline. *Journal of Clinical Endocrinology & Metabolism, 95*(6), 2536–2559.

BMI Calculator. (n.d.). *BMI calculator.* Retrieved from www.bmi-calculator.net

BMI Calculator. (n.d.). *Waist to hip ratio calculator.* Retrieved from http://www.bmi-calculator.net/waist-to-hip-ratio-calculator

Braunstein, G. D. (2012). Causes, evaluation, and management of gynecomastia. *UpToDate.* Retrieved from www.uptodate.com

Bray, G. A. (2013). Patient information: Weight loss treatments. *UpToDate Online 16.3.* Retrieved from http://www.uptodate.com

Centers for Disease Control and Prevention. (2011a). *Adult BMI calculator: English version.* Retrieved from http://www.cdc.gov/healthyweight/assessing/bmi/adult_bmi/english_bmi_calculator/bmi_calculator.html

Centers for Disease Control and Prevention. (2011b). *Obesity halting the epidemic by making health easier: At a glance 2011.* Retrieved from http://www.cdc.gov/NCCDPHP/publications/AAG/obesity.htm

Clemmons, D. R. (2012). Principles of endocrinology. In L. Goldman & A. I. Schafer (Eds.), *Goldman's cecil medicine.* Philadelphia, PA: Elsevier Saunders.

Eckel, R. H., Jakicie, J. M., Ard, J. D., Hubbard, V. S., de Jesus, J. M., Lee, I-Min., ... American College of Cardiology/American Heart Association Task Force on Practice Guidelines. (2014). AHA/ACC guideline on lifestyle management to reduce cardiovascular risk: A report of the American College of Cardiology/American Heart Association Task Force on practice guidelines. *Circulation, 129*(25 Suppl 2), S76-S99. doi: 10.1161/01.cir.0000437740.48606.d1

Ervin, B. (2009). Prevalence of metabolic syndrome among adults 20 years of age and older by sex, age, race, ethnicity, and body mass index United States 2003–2006. *National Health Statistics Reports.* Number 13. Retrieved from www.cdc.gov/nchs/data/nhsr/nhsr013.pdf

Foreyt, J. (2011, April). *Successful strategies for preventing weight regain following weight loss.* Slide presentation, American Academy of Bariatric Physicians. Baltimore, MD.

Goff, D. C., Lloyd-Jones, D. M., Bennett, G., Coady, S., D'Agostino, Sr., R. B., Gibbons, R., ... American College of Cardiology/American Heart Association Task Force on Practice Guidelines. (2014). ACC/AHA guideline on the assessment of cardiovascular risk: A report of the American College of Cardiology/American Heart Association Task Force on practice guidelines. *Circulation, 129*(25 Suppl 2), S49–73.

Golshan, M., & Iglehart, D. (2012). Nipple discharge. *UpToDate.* Retrieved from http://www.uptodate.com

Griffing, G. T., Odeke, S., Nagelberg, S. B., Einhorn, D., Talavera., F., & Chausmer, A. B. (2012). Addison disease treatment & management. *Medscape Drugs, Diseases and Disorders.* Retrieved from http://emedicine.medscape.com/article/116467

Grundy, S. M., Cleeman, J. L., Daniels, S. R., Donato, K. A., Eckel, R. H., Franklin, B. A., ... National Heart, Lung, and Blood Institute. (2005). Diagnosis and management of the metabolic syndrome: An American Heart Association/National Heart, Lung, and Blood Institute Scientific Statement: Executive summary. *Circulation, 112,* e285–e290.

James, P. A., Oparil, S., Carter, B. L., Cushman, W. C., Dennison-Himmelfarb, C., Handler, J., ... Ortiz E. (2014). 2014 Evidence-based guidelines for the management of high blood pressure in adults report from the panel members appointed to the eighth Joint National Committee (JNC 8). *Journal of the American Medical Association, 311*(5), 507–520.

Kelsey, E., Salley, S., Wickham, E. P., Cheang, K. I., Essah, P. A., Karjane, N. W., & Nestler, J. E. (2007). Position statement: Glucose intolerance in polycystic ovary syndrome: A position statement of the androgen excess society. *Journal of Clinical Endocrinology and Metabolism, 92*, 4546–4556.

Kemp, S., & Buehler, B. (2012). Hypogonadism. *Medscape Reference: Drugs, Diseases, and Procedures*. Retrieved from http://emedicine.medscape.com/article/922038-overview

Kim, M., & Ladenson, P. (2012). Thyroid. In L. Goldman & A. I. Schafer (Eds.), *Goldman's cecil medicine* (24th ed., pp. 1450–1462). Philadelphia, PA: Saunders-Elsevier.

King, J. (2008). Shouldering the weight of obesity. *The Nurse Practitioner, 33*, 45–51.

Klippel, J. H. (2008). *Primer on the rheumatic diseases* (13th ed.). New York, NY: Springer.

Lee, S. L. (2013). Hypothyroidism. *Medscape Drugs, Diseases & Procedures*. Retrieved from Medscape.com http://emedicine.medscape.com/article/121865-overview

Levi, J., Vinter, S., St. Laurent, R., & Segal, L. M. (2008). *F as in Fat: How obesity policies are failing in America*. (Issue Report 5th ed.). Washington, DC: Trust for America's Health.

Lin, J. S., O'Connor, E., Whitlock, E. P., & Beil, T. (2010). Behavioral counseling to promote physical activity and healthful diet to prevent cardiovascular disease in adults: A systematic review for the U.S. preventative task force. *Annals of Internal Medicine, 153*(11), 736–750.

Lindebaum, C. (2010). Polycystic ovarian syndrome: Where genetics and environment collide. *Advance for Nurse Practitioners, 18*, 20–27.

Mantzoros, C. (2012). Insulin resistance: Definition and clinical spectrum. *UpToDate*. Retrieved from http://www.uptodate.com/online/content/topic.do?topicKey=diabetes/14407&view=print

Meigs, J. B. (2013). The metabolic syndrome (insulin resistance syndrome or syndrome X). *UpToDate*. Retrieved from http://www.uptodate.com/online/content/topic.do?topicKey=diabetes/21989&view=print

Mulligan, T., Frick, M. F., Zuraw, Q. C., Stemhagen, A., & McWhirter, C. (2006). Prevalence of hypogonadism in males aged at least 45 years: The HIM study. *International Journal of Clinical Practice, 60*(7), 762–769. doi:10.1111/j.1742-1241.2006.00992.x

National Heart Lung and Blood Institute. (n.d.). Obesity education initiative: Calculate your body mass index. Retrieved from http://www.nhlbisupport.com/bmi

National Institutes of Health. (2002). *Third report of the expert panel on detection, evaluation, and treatment of high blood cholesterol in adults* (ATP III Final Report). Bethesda, MD: National Institutes of Health.

Neddeltcheva, A. V., Kilkus, J. M., Imperial, J., Schoeller, D. A., & Penev, P. D. (2010). Insufficient sleep undermines dietary efforts to reduce adiposity. *Annals of Internal Medicine, 153*(7), 435–441.

Nephorology News. (2012). Controlling obesity can lower cost of diabetes. *Nephrology News, 26*(28), 12.

Nieman, L. K. (2012). Adrenal cortex. In L. Goldman & A. I. Schafer (Eds.), *Goldman's cecil medicine* (24th ed., pp. 1463–1470). Philadelphia, PA: Saunders-Elsevier.

Nieman, L. K., Biller, B. M., Findling, J. W., Newell-Price, J., Savage, M. O., Stewart, P. M., & Montori, V. M. (2008). The diagnosis of Cushing's syndrome: The Endocrine Society clinical practice guideline. *Journal of Clinical Endocrinology & Metabolism, 93*(5), 1526–1540.

Nieman, L. K., Lacroix, A., & Martin, K. A. (2013). Medical therapy of hypocortisolism (Cushing's Syndrome). *UpToDate*. Retrieved from www.uptodate.com

NPPR. *Nurse practitioners' prescribing reference*. (2013, Spring). New York, NY: A Haymarket Media Publication.

O'Dell, J. R. (2012). Rheumatoid arthritis. In L. Goldman & A. I. Schafer (Eds.), *Goldman's cecil medicine* (24th ed., pp. 1681–1689). Philadelphia, PA: Saunders-Elsevier.

Orlander, P. R. (2013). Hypothyroidism. *Medscape Drugs, Diseases & Procedures*. Retrieved from emedicine.medscape.com/article/122393-overview

Rajki, M. (2011, December). Sleep problems in older adults. *NPs & PAs, 2*(12), 16–22. King of Prussia, PA: Merion Publication.

Ross, D. S. (2012a). Diagnosis and screening for hypothyroidism. *UpToDate*. Retrieved March 2013, from http://www.uptodate.com

Ross, D. S. (2012b). Diagnosis and treatment of hyperthyroidism during pregnancy. *UpToDate*. Retrieved from www.uptodate.com/online/content/topic.do?topicKey=thyroid/7568&view=print

Ross, D. S. (2012c). Treatment of hypothyroidism. *UpToDate*. Retrieved from http://www.uptodate.com/online/content/topic.do?topicKey=thyroid/2117&view=print

Rubin, D. I. (2012). Neurologic manifestations of hyperthyroidism. *UpToDate*. Retrieved from http://www.uptodate.com/online/content/topic.do?topicKey=medneuro/9866&view=print

Rubin, R. C., & Rubin, B. (2011). Adopting healthier habits: How to get started and follow through. *Diabetes Self-Management, 28*(5), 46–49. New York, NY: R. A. Rappaport Publishing.

Salem, A. (2013, April). *Controversy in diabetes prevention*. Slide Presentation, Southern Illinois School of Medicine, Updates in Primary Care. Carterville, IL.

Schur, P. H., & Cohen, S. (2012). Initial treatment of moderately to severely active rheumatoid arthritis in adults. *UpToDate*. Retrieved from uptodate.com

Schur, P. H, Matteson, P. H., & Turesson, C. (2013). Overview of the systemic and nonarticular manifestations of rheumatoid arthritis. *UpToDate*. Retrieved from uptodate.com

Stone, N. J., Robinson, J., Lichtenstein, A. H., Bairey Merz, C. N., Lloyd-Jones, D. M., & Blum, C. B. (2014). 2013 ACC/AHA guidelines on the treatment of blood cholesterol to reduce atherosclerotic cardiovascular risk in adults: A report of the American College of Cardiology/American Heart Association Task Force on practice guidelines. *Journal of American College of Cardiology, 63*, 2889–2934.

The Hormone Foundation. (2013). *PCOS overview*. Retrieved from http://www.hormone.org/polycystic/overview.cfm

U.S. Department of Health and Human Services. (2008). *2008 physical activity guidelines for Americans*. Retrieved from http://www.health.gov/paguidelines/pdf/paguide.pdf

U.S. Department of Health and Human Services. (2011). National diabetes fact sheet: National estimates and general information on diabetes and pre-diabetes in the United States, 2011. *Centers for Disease Control and Prevention*.

U.S. Department of Health and Human Services. (2012a). American Association of Clinical Endocrinologist and American Association of Endocrine Surgeons medical guidelines for the management of adrenal incidentalomas. *National Guideline Clearinghouse*. Guideline Summary: NGC-7474.

U.S. Department of Health and Human Services. (2012b). American Association of Clinical Endocrinologist medical guidelines for clinical practice for developing a diabetes mellitus comprehensive care plan. *National Guideline Clearinghouse*. Guideline Summary: NGC-8577.

U.S. Department of Health and Human Services. (2012c). Diagnosis and management of type 2 diabetes mellitus in adults. *National Guideline Clearinghouse.* Guideline Summary: NGC-9095.

Uwaifo, G. I., & Arloglu, E. (2013). Obesity [Electronic version]. Retrieved from emedicine.medscape.com/article/123702-overview

Venables, P. J. W., & Maini, R. N. (2012a). Clinical features of rheumatoid arthritis. *UpToDate.* Retrieved from www.uptodate.com/online/content/topic.do?topicKey=rheumart/3022&view=print

Venables, P. J. W., & Maini, R. N. (2012b). Diagnosis and differential diagnosis of rheumatoid arthritis. *UpToDate.* Retrieved from http://www.uptodate.com/online/content/topic.do?topicKey=rheumart/4741&view=print

Wang, S. S. (2012). Metabolic syndrome. Retrieved from http://emedicine.medscape.com/article/165124-print

Whyte, J. (2010, December). *What healthcare provider should know about exercise.* Retrieved from www.netce.com/courseoverview.php?courseid=689

Wigley, F. M. (2012a). Clinical manifestations and diagnosis of the Raynaud phenomenon. *UpToDate.* Retrieved from http://www.uptodate.com/online/content/topic.do?topicKey=sclerode/2595&view=print

Wigley, F. M. (2012b). Pharmacologic and surgical treatment of the Raynaud phenomenon. *UpToDate.* Retrieved from http://www.uptodate.com/online/content/topic.do?topicKey=sclerode/6308&view=print

Wjjeyaratne, C. N., Udayangani, S. A. D., & Balen, A. H. (2013). Ethnic-specific polyovarian syndrome. Epidemiology, significance, and implications. *Expert Review in Endocrinology and Metabolism, 8*(1), 71–79.

CHAPTER TWENTY-FOUR

Psychiatric Guidelines

Karen M. Kress, Jill C. Cash, and Cheryl A. Glass

Anxiety

Definition

A. Anxiety disorders are differentiated from transient fear and normal anxiety by persistence for 6 months or longer. Anxiety disorders are often comorbid with other psychiatric disorders, most often depression. They are characterized by excessive worry, tension, apprehension, and uneasiness from anticipated danger. Hypervigilance and avoidant behaviors are often features of anxiety disorder. It is the "fight-or-flight" response that is part of the survival instinct. The source of anxiety is largely unknown or unrecognized.

B. Anxiety in its chronic form is maladaptive and is considered a psychiatric disorder. Many cases of anxiety disorder in late life are chronic, having persisted from younger years. In its pathologic form, it interferes with developmental learning because it infers significant distress. Anxiety disorders include generalized anxiety disorder (GAD), panic disorder, agoraphobia, and specific phobias.

Incidence

A. Anxiety disorders affect approximately 40 million adults yearly. The lifetime prevalence of anxiety disorders is estimated to be from 5.7% to 28%. Prevalence of diagnosis peaks in middle age and tends to decline in later life. Increased prevalence is noted among persons who are widowed, separated, or divorced.

B. Anxiety is present in many medical illnesses and must be distinguished to treat it appropriately. GAD and panic disorder are also associated with frequent suicide attempts.

Pathogenesis

A. Some degree of familial transmission of GAD, as well as panic disorder, has been noted. Unconscious conflict is thought to be the underlying cause of anxiety, which signals the ego to be careful expressing unacceptable impulses. Behavioral anxiety is considered a conditioned response to a stimulus associated with danger.

B. Clinically, however, identifying specific anxiogenic stimuli is difficult. The onset of GAD is also thought to be the cumulative effect of several stressful life events. Many studies have found that phobic/anxiety symptoms predated clinical alcoholism by a number of years. t-Aminobutyric acid-benzodiazepine receptor complex, the locus coeruleus-norepinephrine system, and serotonin are three neurotransmitter systems implicated in the biologic basis of anxiety. These systems are thought to mediate "normal" anxiety and pathologic anxiety.

Predisposing Factors

A. Young to middle-aged women, onset usually at 20 to 30 years of age
B. Single
C. Lower socioeconomic status
D. A childhood overanxious disorder
E. Excessive worrying
F. Unresolved unconscious conflict

Common Complaints

A. Inability to control worrying
B. Motor tension
C. Autonomic hyperactivity vigilance
D. Sleep disturbance

Statements concerning self-medication with alcohol to help with sleep may indicate a coexistent alcohol abuse/dependence diagnosis that must be treated concomitantly.

E. Shortness of breath
F. Increased heart rate and respirations
G. Feelings of apprehension
H. Dizziness

I. Abdominal disturbances/nausea
J. Increased perspiration
K. Trembling

Other Signs and Symptoms

A. According to the *Diagnostic and Statistical Manual, of Mental Disorders, Fifth Edition (DSM-5),* excessive worry out of proportion to the likelihood or impact of the feared events that occurs for a period of 6 months or longer, during which the person has been bothered more days than not by these concerns.
B. At least three of the following six symptoms
   1. Muscle tension
   2. Restlessness or feeling keyed up or on edge
   3. Easy fatigability
   4. Difficulty concentrating or "mind going blank" because of anxiety
   5. Trouble falling or staying asleep
   6. Irritability
C. Impaired social or occupational function. The anxiety, worry, or physical symptoms significantly interfere with the person's normal routine or usual activities or cause marked distress.
D. The anxiety is not attributable to another medical condition or medication or substance effect.

Subjective Data

A. Review the onset, course, and duration of symptoms. How often does the anxiety occur (i.e., every day, week, month)?
B. Review any history of anxiety and age of onset. If treated, how was the previous anxiety treated and what was the success of the treatment?
C. Determine whether there is a history of suicide attempts. Does the patient have a current plan or vague ideas of suicide? Ask the patient, "Have you ever thought of hurting yourself or others?" If there is any concern regarding suicide/homicide, immediately refer the patient to a psychiatrist.
D. Review drug history for prescription, over-the-counter (OTC), and recreational/illicit drug use, and the patient's use of caffeine, which precipitates anxiety symptoms.
E. Review the patient's history of alcohol consumption. Mild or moderate alcohol withdrawal presents primarily with anxiety symptoms. In patients who have developed tolerance to the effects of alcohol or benzodiazepines, abrupt cessation of these agents may produce heightened anxiety over baseline, as well as a risk of seizure.
F. Review the patient's history for major stressors. Are these stressors new or chronic? If chronic problems, ask what made the patient come in today.
G. Determine how the patient has been coping with stress up until today (exercise, medication).
H. Review the patient's history of other medical problems.
I. Does anyone else in the family have the same problem? How are they treated?

Physical Examination

A. Check pulse, respirations, blood pressure, and weight.
B. Inspect
   1. Observe general appearance; note grooming, dress, ability to communicate, body movements, nail biting, playing with hair, and inability to sit still.
C. Administer mental exam of choice.
   1. *DSM-5-TR* Diagnostic Criteria for Generalized Anxiety Disorder available from the American Psychiatric Association (APA), *DSM-5* (2013).
   2. Beck Anxiety Scale
D. Physical examination as indicated by somatic complaints

Diagnostic Tests

A. Blood alcohol
B. Thyroid profile
C. Blood glucose
D. Medication level (theophylline, etc.) if applicable
E. Urine drug screen
F. Additional testing related to suspected physical pathology

Differential Diagnoses

A. Anxiety
B. Psychiatric syndrome
   1. Depressive disorders
   2. Psychotic disorders
   3. Somatoform disorders (characterized by physical complaints lacking known medical basis or demonstrable physical finding in the presence of psychological factors judged to be etiologic or important in the initiation, exacerbation, or maintenance of the disturbance)
   4. Personality disorders
   5. Alcoholism and drug abuse/dependence
   6. Adjustment disorders (posttraumatic stress disorder [PTSD])
C. Medical conditions. Anxiety syndromes mimic many medical illnesses, including intracranial tumors, menstrual irregularities, hypothyroidism, hyperparathyroidism and hypoparathyroidism, postconcussion syndrome, psychomotor epilepsy, and Cushing's disease.
   1. Hypoglycemia if anxiety is chronic
   2. Hypothyroidism
   3. Hyperthyroidism: Rapid-onset anxiety could be symptom of hyperthyroidism.
   4. Tumor
   5. Cushing's disease

Plan

A. General interventions
  1. Treat medical conditions as appropriate.
  2. Refer the patient for cognitive behavior therapy. Counseling is effective for learning new techniques to help with alleviating symptoms. Cognitive behavior therapy may be effective alone and/or may also be used as adjunct to medication treatment.
  3. Encourage the patient to perform self-calming techniques such as deep breathing/relaxation techniques and exercise.

B. Patient teaching: See the Section III Patient Teaching Guides for this chapter, as appropriate: "Sleep Disorders/Insomnia" and "Alcohol and Drug Dependence."

C. Pharmaceutical therapy
  1. Selective serotonin reuptake inhibitors (SSRIs) or selective serotonin norepinephrine reuptake inhibitors (SNRIs)
     a. Fluoxetine (Prozac), 5 to 10 mg/d orally initially; usual dose 20 to 80 mg/d; long half-life; alters metabolism of cytochrome P-450 2D6-cleared agents; use caution
     b. Paroxetine (Paxil), 10 mg/d orally initially; usual dose 25 to 50 mg/d
     c. Sertraline (Zoloft), 25 to 50 mg/d orally initially; usual dose 50 to 200 mg/d
     d. Venlafaxine (Effexor), 37.5 mg/d initially; usual dose 75 to 300 mg/d
     e. Citalopram (Celexa), 5 to 10 mg/d orally initially; usual dose 20 to 40 mg/d. Caution: Risk for QT prolongation, contraindicated in patients with congenital long QT syndrome and should not exceed 20 mg daily if prescribed to patients also taking CYP2C19 inhibitors (cimetidine, fluconazole, omeprazole).
     f. Escitalopram (Lexapro) 10 mg/d orally initially; usual dose 10 to 20 mg/d
     g. Duloxetine (Cymbalta), 20 mg/d orally initially; titrate to 30 to 60 mg/d.
     h. These medications can take 4 to 6 weeks to take full effect.
     i. Warn patients that they should not stop these medications abruptly; they should taper off gradually.
  2. Nonbenzodiazepine anxiolytic
     a. Buspirone (Buspar), 7.5 mg twice a day
     b. May increase by 5 mg/d orally every 2 to 3 days
     c. Usual range: 20 to 30 mg orally every day, maximum 60 mg orally every day
     d. Therapeutic effects may be delayed from 1 to 4 weeks.
  3. Short-acting benzodiazepines
     a. Alprazolam (Xanax), 0.25 to 0.5 mg orally two to three times daily
     b. Clonazepam 0.25 to 0.5 mg orally one or two times daily, titrated up to 1 mg two to three times daily as needed
     c. Lorazepam (Ativan), 0.5 to 2 mg, up to 6 mg orally every day in divided doses; maximum dose of 10 mg/d in divided doses
        i. Use for initial short-term stabilization while simultaneously prescribing buspirone or SSRI/serotonin-norepinephrine reuptake inhibitor (SNRI), because therapeutic effects are delayed from 1 to 4 weeks.
        ii. Limit use to several weeks to a few months to prevent dependence.

Follow-Up

A. Follow up in 1 to 2 weeks to assess the patient's status.

B. Follow up every 2 to 4 weeks after that to evaluate the patient's progress.

C. Assess suicide potential with every office visit.

Consultation/Referral

A. Refer to a psychiatric clinician for complex medication management and psychotherapy after initial assessment.

B. If the patient expresses suicidal thoughts, immediately refer to the emergency room (inpatient therapy) or psychiatric specialist for continuing psychotherapy.

Individual Considerations

A. Pregnancy
  1. Caution should be used in prescribing medications for anxiety during pregnancy; the benefits must be weighed against the risks.
  2. If the patient becomes pregnant while taking these medications, taper medication dose instead of ceasing abruptly.

B. Geriatrics
  1. Anxiety is often unrecognized and inadequately treated in this population because of concomitant medical illness, overlap with cognitive disorders, and comorbid depression, ageism, and cohort effects.
  2. Elderly patients may be hesitant to discuss mental health concerns and needs, due to the history of cultural stigma associated with mental illness.
  3. Start with the lowest dose of medication and increase slowly.
  4. Use of benzodiazepines in the elderly is known to increase fall risk, so if needed, use the lowest dose possible.

C. Partners
  1. If available in the community, provide resources for partners, such as the National Alliance for the Mentally Ill.
  2. Psychotherapy for the patient and partner is often helpful.

Depression

Definition

A. Depression is a mental health disorder that interferes with a person's daily life. Depressive disorders are characterized by sad, empty, or irritable mood lasting at least 2 weeks in duration. Depression may be mild or severe, depending on signs and symptoms expressed, as well as the length of time symptoms are present. Depression affects multiple body systems and may impact one emotionally, cognitively, or physically, as well as behaviorally. Symptoms of depression may include difficulty sleeping, depressed mood, inability to function at work, change in appetite, and inability to enjoy activities that bring one pleasure. There are many forms of depression, and treatment varies depending on the specific diagnosis. Types of depression include: Major depressive disorder, persistent depressive disorder (dysthymia), premenstrual dysphoric disorder, disruptive mood dysregulation disorder, and other specified depressive disorders.

B. Diagnostic criteria include: Depressed mood most of the day, decreased pleasure in activities, weight loss or weight gain, insomnia or hypersomnolence, psychomotor agitation or retardation, fatigue or loss of energy, feelings of worthlessness or guilt, decreased concentration, thoughts of death, suicidal ideation, and suicide attempt or plan for self-harm.

Incidence

A. One in 10 adults experiences one or more episodes of depression during his or her lifetime. Depression can occur at any age. In the United States, incidence of depression peaks in the 20s, but first onset in late life can occur. The lifetime risk is estimated to be as high as 30%. Women have a twofold to threefold higher rate of reported depression than men. Estimated rates of major depression in the elderly are 3% to 5% for those living in a community dwelling, 15% to 30% for those living in an institutional setting, and 13% for those living in nursing homes.

B. Only 10% to 25% of people with depressive disorders seek treatment. There is a high mortality from suicide if untreated (see "Suicide" section).

C. No single causal factor has been identified. Depressive syndromes are so varied in course and symptomatology that a single cause is unlikely. Several factors appear to contribute, including genetics, neurochemical abnormalities (reductions in adrenergic or serotonergic neurotransmission), electrolyte disturbances, and neuroendocrine abnormalities such as hypothalamic, pituitary, adrenal cortical, thyroid, and gonadal functions. Higher concentrations of proinflammatory cytokines, tumor necrosis factor (TNF)-alpha, and interleukin (IL)-6 have been found in depressed subjects, compared with control subjects.

D. Depression is frequently a concomitant diagnosis with other physical or mental disorders. Personality and psychodynamic factors of depression include low self-esteem, self-criticism, and interpersonal loss. A childhood history of emotional, physical, and/or sexual abuse can also contribute to adult-onset depression.

Predisposing Factors

A. Age (peak onset in 20s and the elderly)
B. Lack of social support/living alone
C. A history of early parental loss
D. Female gender
   1. Most common in childbearing years from ages 25 to 45 years
   2. Premenstrual
   3. Perimenopausal
   4. Postpartum
E. Family history of depression
F. Frequent exposure to stressful events
G. Nutritional disorders
   1. Vitamin B_{12} deficiency
   2. Pellagra
H. Personality characteristics that include absence of hardiness factors in response to stress (lack of resilience, flexibility, and optimism).
I. Anger not dealt with and turned in on the self
J. Negative interpretation of one's life experiences
K. Poor physical health
L. Postsurgical diagnosis of cancer
M. Chronic pain
N. Chronic medical problems such as hypothyroidism and hyperthyroidism, Cushing's syndrome, hypercalcemia, hyponatremia, diabetes mellitus, lupus erythematosus, fibromyalgia, rheumatoid disease, and chronic fatigue syndrome
O. Neurologic disorders such as stroke, subdural hematoma, multiple sclerosis, brain tumor, Parkinson's disease, epilepsy, dementias, and Huntington's disease
P. Alcoholism/drug abuse or dependence/withdrawal
Q. Infectious etiology such as mononucleosis and other viral infections, syphilis, HIV, and Lyme disease
R. Side effect of prescription drugs, such as alpha-methyldopa, antiarrhythmic, benzodiazepines, barbiturates/central nervous system (CNS) depressants, beta-blockers, cholinergic drugs, corticosteroids, digoxin, H_2-blockers, and reserpine.

Common Complaints

A. Lack of interest in pleasurable activities
B. Digestive problems
C. Chronic aches and pains that are not otherwise explained

Other Signs and Symptoms

A. Vegetative
   1. Changes (increased or decreased) in sleep, appetite, and weight
   2. Changes in appearance: Poor grooming and hygiene
   3. Poor eye contact, staring downward, flat affect
   4. Loss of energy
   5. Decreased interest in sex
   6. Psychomotor retardation or agitation
B. Cognitive
   1. Sense of guilt, worthlessness, low self-esteem
   2. Problems with attention span, concentration or memory, frustration tolerance, negative distortions, mild paranoia, and psychosis
C. Impulse control
   1. Suicidal or homicidal thoughts or acts. **Any statements made by the patient, such as "Life isn't worth living, I wish I were dead, I don't deserve to be alive, I can't deal with this," should be taken seriously. Refer the patient for counseling, assessment, and treatment.**
D. Behavioral
   1. Depressed mood, anxiety, and irritability
   2. Isolation, decreased motivation, fatigability, and anhedonia (inability to derive gratification from pleasurable activities)
E. Physical symptoms
   1. Digestion problems, nausea, constipation, diarrhea (less common), and dry mouth
   2. Fatigue, but difficulty sleeping
   3. Physical pain, chronic aches, and pains that cannot be explained
   4. Recurrent headaches, backaches, or stomachaches that have no cause
   5. Migrating pain that disappears when depression lifts
   6. Increased muscle tension

Subjective Data

A. Review the onset, duration, and course of presenting symptoms.
B. Review any previous history of depression (such as postpartum depression).
C. Determine how the previous depression was treated.
D. Evaluate the patient's suicide potential. Ask: "Have you ever thought of hurting yourself or others?" Does the patient have a current suicide plan or vague ideas of suicide? Has the patient had any previous history of suicide attempts? If so, evaluate how life threatening they were.
E. Review the patient's medical history (see Predisposing factors).
F. Review the patient's drug history for prescription, OTC, and recreational/illicit drug use (how much, how long, how often), and review his or her history of alcohol consumption (how much, how long, how often).
G. Review the patient's history for recent major life changes such as pregnancy, death, divorce, or any loss that may be normal throughout the stages of life. The *patient's perception* of the loss is what is important.
H. Review dietary intake since the symptoms have begun.
I. Establish usual weight, review weight gain/loss, and in what time span.
J. Review the patient's activities of daily living. Does the patient get up and dress daily, perform daily hygiene, put on makeup?
K. Review how many hours of sleep and quality of sleep per day.
L. Review the disruption of usual activities: Return to work, return to school, exercise.
M. Review the amount of crying per day, and for what length of time (days, weeks).
N. Assess whether the depression is cyclic/seasonal (starts in the fall, ends in the spring).
O. Review occupational/home exposure to lead and lead-based products.
P. Review any exposures to infectious diseases, including Lyme disease (refer to Chapter 18, "Infectious Disease Guidelines," for specific questions). Does anyone else such as family, friends, or coworkers have similar symptoms?
Q. If female, review for symptoms of menopause (sleep disturbances, irregular menses/amenorrhea, hot flashes, vaginal dryness, dyspareunia).

Physical Examination

A. Check pulse, respirations, blood pressure, and weight.
B. Inspect
   1. Observe overall appearance; note grooming, tone of voice, conduct of patient during communication, and breath (smell of alcohol).
   2. Complete neurologic examination with screening tool of choice.
   3. Complete dermal examination for signs of substance use (refer to "Substance Use Disorders" section).
C. Palpate
   1. Palpate the neck and thyroid; evaluate for presence of goiter.
   2. Palpate the axilla and groin for lymphadenopathy (infectious etiology).
   3. Check the joints for swelling, arthritis, and range of motion (ROM) (rule out musculoskeletal cause).
D. Auscultate
   1. Auscultate the heart, lungs, and abdomen (as applies to physical complaints).

Diagnostic Tests

A. Complete blood count (CBC) with differential
B. Electrolytes, serum calcium, and phosphorus
C. Thyroid profile
D. Liver profile
E. Lead level
F. Follicle-stimulating hormone/luteinizing hormone (FSH/LH)
G. Viral cultures
H. Blood alcohol
I. Urine drug screen
J. Monospot
K. CT and MRI scans
L. Dexamethasone suppression test
M. Perform mental state examination with depression rating scale of choice:
   1. Beck Depression Inventory Scale (Beck, Ward, Mendelson, Mock, & Erbaugh, 1961). Available at www.nsand.ca/media/forms/EHNMC-Beck DepressionInventory DSM-IV.doc
   2. Geriatric Depression Scale (GDS) (Yesavage et al., 1982 to 1983). Available at www.healthcare.uiowa.edu/.../depression/GDS
   3. Patient Health Questionnaire (PHQ-9) (PRIME-MD) (Spitzer, Williams, Kroenke, et al., 1999). Available online at www.phqscreeners.com

Differential Diagnoses

A. Depression
B. Chronic untreated anxiety disorders such as GAD, PTSD, or obsessive-compulsive disorder (OCD)
C. Personality disorders
D. Schizoaffective disorder
E. Seasonal affective disorder (SAD)
   1. Seasonal pattern: Starts in the fall, linked to lack of light exposure
   2. Women more than men
   3. Age typically in the 20s
F. Alcoholism and drug abuse/dependence
G. Early dementia
H. Endocrine etiologies (see Predisposing factors)
I. Infectious etiologies (see Predisposing factors)
J. Menopause
K. Side effect of medication (see Predisposing factors)
L. Cancer: 50% of patients with tumors, particularly of the brain and lung, and carcinoma of the pancreas develop symptoms of depression before the diagnosis of tumor is made.
M. Heavy metal poisoning
N. Nutritional deficit (see Predisposing Factors)

Plan

A. General interventions
   1. Keep the patient safe from self-harm.
   2. Treat physical/laboratory findings. Recommend dietary change, iron supplements, or hormone replacement therapy per findings (see related chapters).
B. Patient teaching
   1. Encourage the patient to take medications as prescribed. Educate the patient that some medications may take time to get into the system to work and time should be allowed to see the effects of the medication. Review side effects.
   2. Encourage the patient to express feelings or worsening of symptoms if this occurs prior to the next appointment. Have the patient make a client contract with you that he or she will not hurt himself or others; if he or she begins having these thoughts, the patient agrees to contact you or go to the nearest emergency room.
   3. Encourage exercise on a daily basis for 20 to 30 minutes to increase energy and enhance a feeling of well-being.
   4. Encourage the patient to get at least 7 to 8 hours of sleep each night. If sleep is a problem, address this issue with the client.
   5. Avoid caffeine at night and/or watching TV late at night.
   6. Encourage the patient to seek counseling with a professional counselor. Refer to appropriate site (psychologist, psychiatrist, group therapy, etc.). Offer local resources to the patient.
   7. Advise patient to participate in activities to enhance interpersonal relationships and build self-esteem. Include family and friends in recommended therapies and advise them to encourage the patient to participate in activities to enhance self-esteem.
   8. Once the patient is feeling better, encourage continued use of medication, activities, and resources for at least 6 months after the patient has started feeling better to prevent relapse.
C. Pharmaceutical therapy: Table 24.1 presents dosage information.
   1. Drugs of choice: SSRI antidepressants. Caution should be used when coadministering SSRIs and drugs with a narrow therapeutic window such as carbamazepine (Tegretol), warfarin, tricyclic antidepressants (TCAs), antiarrhythmics, and some antipsychotic medications (risperidone, haloperidol, and phenothiazine), and other drugs including diazepam (Valium) and monoamine oxidase (MAO) inhibitors. There are numerous SSRIs on the market today. Some of the newer agents, such as Pristiq and Viibryd, have fewer side effects.
      a. Most antidepressant therapy takes 3 to 4 weeks for onset of action to elicit visible changes.
      b. Never prescribe more than a week's supply or a total of 2 g of a TCA if there is a risk of suicide.

TABLE 24.1 Dosages for Common Antidepressant Drugs

Drug	Adults Aged 18–60 Years	Elderly >60 Years or Renal or Hepatic Patients
Fluoxetine hydrochloride (Prozac) Therapeutic onset occurs in 1–4 weeks. Serum levels peak in 4.5–8.5 hours.	20 mg daily in a.m., dosage increased according to patient response. May be given bid—in the morning and at noon. Maximum dosage is 80 mg/d.	10–20 mg daily in a.m. with clinical response monitored q 1–2 weeks. Gradual dose increases q 6 week until optimal therapeutic response is obtained.
Sertraline hydrochloride (Zoloft) Therapeutic onset occurs in 2–4 weeks. Serum levels peak in 4.5–8.5 hours.	50 mg daily in a.m. May increase to 100 mg. Dosage adjustments should be made at intervals of no <1 week. Maximum dosage is 200 mg/d.	25–50 mg daily in a.m. with clinical response monitored q 1–2 weeks and gradual increase.
Paroxetine hydrochloride (Paxil) Therapeutic onset occurs in 1–4 weeks. Serum levels peak in 2–8 hours.	10 mg daily in a.m., p.m., or @ HS. May increase 10 mg/d increments at weekly intervals. Maximum dosage is 50 mg/d.	10–20 mg daily in a.m., p.m., or @ HS with clinical response monitored q 1–2 weeks and gradual increase.
Nortriptyline hydrochloride (Pamelor) Therapeutic onset occurs in 2–4 weeks or longer. Serum levels peak in 7–8.5 hours.	25 mg tid or qid initially, gradually increase to maximum dose 150 mg qd.	30–50 mg daily tid or qid or in 1 day's dose.
Desipramine hydrochloride (Norpramin) Therapeutic onset occurs in 2–4 weeks or longer. Serum levels peak in 4–6 hours.	100–200 mg po in single or divided dose.	25–100 mg daily in divided doses, increase gradually to maximum of 150 mg qd.
Amitriptyline (Elavil) Therapeutic onset unknown—thought to take several weeks. Serum levels peak 2–12 hours.	75 mg po in divided doses initially or 50–100 mg @ HS. Dose not to exceed 150 mg/d.	10–20 mg po tid and 20 mg @ HS daily.

Note: Paxil works well for patients who have a component of anxiety to their depression. Monitor prothrombin time for patients taking warfarin, sertraline, and paroxetine.
@ HS, at bedtime; bid, twice a day; po, by mouth; q, every; qd, every day; qid, four times a day; tid, three times daily.

c. Medication should not be changed until it has been given a trial of 6 to 8 weeks to measure progress.
d. Before concluding that the antidepressant is ineffective, verify that the patient is taking the medication correctly.
e. First-line therapy in the elderly is SSRIs. The SSRIs have significantly fewer side effects than the traditional TCAs. Paroxetine and sertraline have short half-lives and can be withdrawn quickly.
f. Antidepressant therapy should be continued for 6 months to 1 year (up to 5 years if necessary) because of the risk of recurrence of depression.
g. Taper the medication off instead of abruptly withdrawing.

2. TCAs: Avoid administration after acute myocardial infarction. Men with prostatic hypertrophy do best with a nonsedating TCA that has a mild anticholinergic activity, such as desipramine (Norpramin) or nortriptyline (Pamelor).
3. Adrenergic modulators: A weak inhibitor of norepinephrine, dopamine, and serotonin reuptake: Bupropion hydrochloride (Wellbutrin).
   a. For patients older than age 18
   b. No dosage established for the elderly
   c. Therapeutic onset in 1 to 3 weeks
   d. Serum level peak within 2 hours
   e. Initially 100 mg twice a day for at least 3 days
   f. If well tolerated, increase to 375 or 400 mg daily.
   g. After 3 days more, 450 mg daily in four divided doses at least 4 hours apart
   h. Maximum single dosing 150 mg, maximum 450 mg daily
      i. Avoid bedtime dosing.
      ii. Do not give to patients with predisposition to seizures.
      iii. Give reduced dose to patients with renal or hepatic impairment.
4. Dual reuptake inhibitors: Blocks the reabsorption of the norepinephrine and serotonin into the neurons in the CNS. When this occurs, higher levels of norepinephrine and serotonin remain

and improve the nerve transmission in the brain, which then improves mood.

a. Venlafaxine hydrochloride (Effexor)
   i. For patients older than age 18
   ii. No dosage established for the elderly
   iii. Therapeutic onset unknown
   iv. Serum level peak and duration unknown
   v. Initially 75 mg every day in two to three divided doses with food
   vi. May increase at 4-day intervals in 75 mg/d increments to 150 mg every day. Maximum dosage is 375 mg every day in three divided doses.
   vii. With hepatic impairment, reduce dose by 50%.
   viii. Withdraw gradually over 2 weeks when discontinuing medication.
   ix. Interacts with MAO inhibitors. Do not start venlafaxine within 14 days of discontinuing an MAO inhibitor.
b. Duloxetine (Cymbalta) also blocks reuptake of serotonin and norepinephrine.
   i. Usual starting dose is 30 mg/d increasing to 60 mg/d. Maximum dose is 120 mg/d.
   ii. Patients should be warned about stopping the medication abruptly; have them taper down slowly.
   iii. Duloxetine is also helpful in treating the physical pain that accompanies some depression symptoms.

5. Tetracyclic antidepressant: Mirtazapine (Remeron). Potentiates noradrenergic and serotonergic activity.
   i. Starting dose is 15 mg at bedtime, with maximum dose of 45 mg.
   ii. Remeron stimulates appetite and may be used in patients with symptoms of weight loss.
   iii. Remeron is administered at bedtime; side effect of somnolence may be beneficial for patients with insomnia.
   iv. Contraindicated within 14 days of taking MAO inhibitor.
   v. Contraindicated with concomitant linezolid use.
6. **MAO inhibitors should only be prescribed by a psychiatrist.**

Follow-Up

A. Follow up in 1 to 2 weeks to assess patient's status, drug effectiveness, and adverse reactions.
B. Patients can become suicidal after the depression is treated and they begin to have more energy to act on the suicidal ideation. **Assess suicidality with every office visit.**
C. Follow up every 2 to 4 weeks afterward to check patient's progress.
D. Once positive change is seen, the patient can be seen monthly.
E. Refer to other applicable medical diagnosis for follow-up recommendations.

Consultation/Referral

A. If there is any potential for suicidal/homicidal behavior, refer patient immediately to a psychiatrist for possible emergency admission.
B. Consult with the physician, comanage with the physician, or the patient may need immediate referral/consult for continuing psychotherapy.
C. Patients who fail to respond to antidepressants after 1 to 2 months of appropriate antidepressant therapy should have a psychiatric consultation. Psychiatry may prescribe adjunctive medications including psychotropics and mood stabilizers.
D. Refractory depression should be managed by a psychiatrist. Other treatment options may include electroconvulsive therapy (ECT), transcranial magnetic stimulation, and deep brain stimulator (DBS).

Individual Considerations

A. Pregnancy
   1. A woman with a history of depression or previous postpartum depression is at high risk for postpartum depression (recurrent). Caution should be used in prescribing antidepressants during pregnancy. Review the benefits versus risks.
   2. Refer to Chapter 15, "Obstetrics Guidelines," for the section, "Postpartum Depression."
B. Partners
   1. If available in the community, provide resources for partners, such as the National Alliance for the Mentally Ill (listed in most telephone books).
   2. Frequently, partners will take too much responsibility for the depressed patient's state of mind and over time also become depressed. Relating to other people with depressed partners will assist them in dealing with their significant other's depression.
C. Geriatrics
   1. Dementia masked as "pseudodepression" is common in the elderly. Check for memory impairment and disorientation because delirium can often be mistaken for depression (see Chapter 22, "Neurologic Guidelines," "Dementia").
   2. Elderly patients who are depressed may experience agitation rather than retardation in psychomotor function.
   3. Persons age 65 and older account for 25% of all suicides. White men, age 80, have the highest

rate of suicide of any age group in the United States.
4. Assess for depression in caretakers of patients with Alzheimer disease.
5. Avoid use of Elavil in the elderly due to the high risk of anticholinergic side effects and risk for hypotension.

Elderly patients who are suicidal may present with atypical symptoms of depression and may not express their distress directly. Three identified behaviors include impaired ability to communicate, intractable tinnitus, and feelings of helplessness.

Failure to Thrive

Definition

Failure to thrive (FTT) is an abnormality in which an individual fails to maintain nutritional health. FTT is a manifestation of an underlying problem, whether the problem is mental, physical, or psychological.

A. Adults: FTT is seen in adults who have a weight less than 80% of the ideal average body weight for the adult.
B. Geriatrics: FTT in the geriatric population is defined as a deterioration in functional status disproportional to disease burden. Signs are decreased appetite, weight loss of greater than 5% of their weight, decreased physical activity, along with dehydration, depression, and compromised immune status.

Incidence

A. It is estimated to occur in 5% to 35% of the elderly population, with nursing home residents having an occurrence rate of 25% to 40%.

Pathogenesis

A. Organic causes for FTT
   1. Gastrointestinal (reflux, celiac disease, Hirschsprung's disease, and malabsorption)
   2. Cardiopulmonary (cardiac diseases, congestive heart failure)
   3. Pulmonary (asthma, bronchopulmonary dysplasia, cystic fibrosis)
   4. Renal (diabetes insipidus, renal insufficiency, urinary tract infections)
   5. Endocrine (hypothyroidism, adrenal diseases, parathyroid disorders, thyroid disorders, pituitary disorders)
   6. Neurologic (mental retardation, cerebral hemorrhages)
   7. Metabolic disorders (inborn errors of metabolism)
   8. Congenital (congenital syndromes such as fetal alcohol syndrome, chromosomal abnormalities, perinatal infections)
   9. Infectious (gastrointestinal infections, tuberculosis, HIV)
B. Inorganic (or psychosocial) causes pertain to family and social dynamics. It is common to see both organic and inorganic problems as causative factors for FTT.
C. Geriatric population
   1. Feel fuller with less food; this may be an endorphin response that decreases the adaptive relaxation of the fundus of the stomach.
   2. Increased number of cytokines, which contributes to anorexia
   3. Diminished sense of smell or taste
   4. Dysphagia
   5. Medications
   6. Depression, delirium, dementia
   7. Alcohol or substance abuse

Predisposing Factors

A. Geriatrics: Dementia, comorbidities (cancer, chronic infections, malabsorption syndromes, psychiatric disorders), limited mobility, despair
B. Poverty
C. Organic conditions with the major organs noted above
D. Parents with psychosocial disorders
E. Altered family processes

Common Complaints

A. Weight loss that is unintentional
B. Fatigue

Patients do not always present for this problem. Many patients are diagnosed at a routine examination in the ambulatory setting.

Other Signs and Symptoms

A. Loss of subcutaneous fat tissue
B. Muscle atrophy
C. Alopecia
D. Dermatitis
E. Marasmus
F. Kwashiorkor

Subjective Data

A. Obtain detailed history of the patient's diet. Note the differences between foods offered and foods eaten. If dietary supplements are used, note type, frequency, and amount taken.
B. Assess quality of nutrients offered to the patient. Consider knowledge deficit of care provider if inadequate.
   1. Geriatrics: Is patient able to chew and swallow food offered? Are dentures well fitting? Are supplements being offered?

C. Query regarding financial resources, and if needed, does the family participate in low-income opportunities (food stamp programs, meals on wheels, etc.)?
D. Evaluate whether religious or unusual dietary beliefs/habits contribute to the food preparation, if inadequate.
E. Rule out any difficulty in swallowing or retaining ingested food.
F. Note regular bowel/bladder habits.
G. Note any recent illness, chronic or acute.
H. Rule out family history of cystic fibrosis or lactose intolerance.
I. Geriatrics: Evaluate nutritional screening using the Mini Nutritional Assessment. This tool is available at www.mna-elderly.com

Physical Examination

A. Check temperature, pulse, respirations, blood pressure, height, and weight.
B. Inspect
   1. Observe overall appearance.
   2. Observe oral pathology: Check for ill-fitting dentures, dental and gum condition.
   3. Note muscle tone, strength, and movement.
   4. Note social interactions among family members.
   5. Note social skills of the patient.
C. Palpate
   1. Palpate abdomen, back, and extremities.
D. Percuss
   1. Percuss the abdomen
E. Auscultate
   1. Auscultate the heart and lungs.

Diagnostic Tests

A. CBC, urinalysis, electrolytes
B. Thyroid panel, if indicated
C. X-rays, if appropriate
D. Serum albumin in geriatrics

Differential Diagnoses

A. FTT: Inorganic versus organic etiology
B. Weight loss
C. Depression

Plan

A. General interventions
   1. The plan is based on the cause of FTT.
   2. Severe malnutrition requires hospitalization.
   3. Obtain nutritional consult to evaluate the dietary needs for protein, iron, and other nutrients according to age and size.
B. Patient teaching
   1. Reinforce positive eating habits and encourage dietary meal planning.
   2. Offer nutrition counseling with dietitian.
   3. Educate the patient and family about the importance of meeting the dietary requirements for protein, iron, calcium, and other nutrients to prevent weight loss, loss of muscle and bone mass, and to prevent infection and other complications that can stress the body.
C. Dietary management
   1. Meal suggestions: Offer adequate time for meals (20–30 minutes), offer solid food before drinks/juices, and provide a pleasant environment for eating.
   2. Socialization enhances mealtime. Encourage all family members to sit down and eat at least one meal a day together.
   3. Provide handout for high-calorie foods (peanut butter, cheese, whole milk, etc.).
   4. Consider exercise sessions for geriatrics to stimulate appetite.
   5. Encourage patients to attend centers where meals are served as a group or have meals delivered to the home.
   6. Encourage small, frequent meals with snacks between meals and before bedtime.

Weight gain with high-calorie supplements is commonly seen with patients who have a psychosocial etiology of FTT.

D. Pharmaceutical therapy
   1. High-calorie supplements are recommended for some patients (Polycose, Carnation Instant Breakfast, Ensure, Boost, Thrive).
   2. Geriatrics: Short-term aggressive caloric replacement has been shown to be effective in reversing FTT. Severe malnutrition may require hospitalization with total parental nutrition. Medications used to increase appetite:
      a. Megestrol 400 or 800 mg daily with meal
      b. SSRIs have been shown to be beneficial to help stimulate appetite and increase weight.
      c. Mirtazepine (Remeron) 15 mg at bedtime

Follow-Up

A. Two-week evaluation for weight measurements and to evaluate compliance with regimen at home. Routine visits recommended every 2 to 4 weeks to monitor progress.
B. Reevaluate patient in 1 to 2 months. After 2 months if no improvement or further loss is noted, refer to a specialist.

Consultation/Referral

A. A nutritional consult is helpful to assist the patient or food provider in providing adequate resources/calories for the patient.

B. Consider social services and visiting nurses for outpatient assistance in the home.
C. Occupational therapy may be useful to evaluate the patient's capacity to plan and prepare meals.

Individual Considerations

A. Geriatrics
   1. FTT in the elderly may lead to a decline in physical and mental function. Aggressive treatment should be employed to improve the nutritional status of these patients.
   2. FTT increases the risk of morbidity and mortality.
   3. FTT increases the risk of depression and social isolation in the elderly.

Grief

Definition

A. Grief is defined as the normal, appropriate emotional response caused by a loss. This feeling of loss is a response that has been caused by a particular event in one's life. It is unique to the individual experiencing it, and there is no general timetable for completing it. Grief is commonly seen following the death of a loved one, but grief also follows other losses (e.g., loss of independence, loss of affection, or loss of body parts, pain, and distress). Mourning is defined as the process by which grief is resolved. Mourning is individual and helps in reaching acceptance of a loss.
B. The process through which one resolves grief usually follows a typical course that can be viewed in five stages.
   1. Denial: Denial occurs when one refuses to accept the circumstance that has occurred. It is a natural defense mechanism that occurs to protect the body.
   2. Anger: Pain, tears, anxiousness, anger, and feelings of guilt may be seen.
   3. Bargaining: In this stage the person tries to negotiate alternatives that will make him or her feel better.
   4. Depression: One begins to understand what has happened and may show feelings of sadness and fear.
   5. Acceptance: One begins to rebuild life and think about the past with pleasure. In this phase one regains interest in activities and forms new relationships.
C. It is important to distinguish between the normal grief reaction to pathologic grief and major depression. Often, depressive symptoms are a pervasive part of the grief response, and a clear delineation of grief versus depression is not always possible. (Based on the Grief Cycle model first published in *On Death and Dying,* Elisabeth Kübler-Ross, 1969, Interpretation by Alan Chapman 2006–2009.) Retrieved from www.ekrfoundation.org/five-stages-of-grief

Incidence

Grief is a universal emotional response. Approximately 5% to 9% of the population will lose a close family member or friend each year. Grief is a normal emotional response that will follow this loss for an individual.

Pathogenesis

A. Grief is a normal emotional response to the loss of a loved one, pain, and/or distress. Abnormal, pathologic grief can occur if the mourner is not encouraged to grieve losses. Normal grief resolution begins to subside at approximately 6 months but may sometimes take longer.

Predisposing Factors

A. Sudden or terrible deaths
B. Excessive dependency on the deceased and feelings of ambivalence
C. Traumatic losses earlier in life
D. Social isolation
E. Actual or imagined responsibility for "causing" the death
F. Avoidance of grief and denial of loss
G. Survived a traumatic experience that killed the deceased

Common Complaints

A. Angry feelings at God or medical personnel for not doing more, anger at oneself for not seeing the warning signs, anger at the deceased for not taking better care of himself or herself. Common feelings of being left alone and not making proper financial/legal preparations may also occur.
B. Sleeping all the time or inability to sleep without medication
C. Change in eating habits with significant weight loss or gain
D. Fatigue, lethargy, or lack of motivation
E. Decreased concentration and memory, forgetfulness
F. Increased irritability
G. Unpredictable bouts of crying
H. Fears
   1. Of being alone or with people
   2. Of leaving the house
   3. Of staying in the house

Other Signs and Symptoms

A. Normal grief
   1. Protest, disbelief, shock, and denial
   2. Profound sadness and survivor guilt
   3. Multiple somatic symptoms without actual organic disease
   4. Sense of unreality and withdrawal from others
   5. Disruption of normal patterns of conduct, with restlessness and aimlessness

6. Preoccupation with memories of the deceased, dreams of the deceased, hallucinations, fear of going crazy, and transient psychotic symptoms
7. Response to support and ventilation improves over time.

B. Complicated or prolonged grief
1. Persistence of denial with delayed or absent grief
2. Depression with impaired self-esteem, suicidal thoughts, and impulses with self-destructive behavior
3. Actual organic disease and medical illness
4. Progressive social isolation
5. Persistent anger and hostility, leading to paranoid reactions, especially against those involved in medical care of the deceased, or suppression of any expression of anger and hostility
6. Continued disruption of normal patterns of conduct, often with a persistent hyperactivity unaccompanied by a sense of loss or grieving
7. Continued preoccupation with memories of the deceased to the point of searching for reunion (sustained depressive delusions)
8. Conversion symptoms similar to the symptoms of the deceased
9. Self-blame
10. Prolonged grief longer than 6 months is commonly linked to complications and impairment for the next 1 to 2 years.

Subjective Data

A. Review onset, duration, and course of presenting symptoms. Review the mourner's grief symptoms.
B. Obtain an in-depth personal history of the mourner and his or her relationship to the identified loss or with the deceased.

Understanding the bereaved's history is critical to understanding the individual's loss.

C. Identify anniversary dates pertinent to the mourner's relationship with the deceased/loss.
D. Determine whether the mourner has suicidal ideation (especially with a plan). **Be sure to ask: "Have you ever thought of hurting yourself or others?"**
E. Assess whether the mourner experiences self-blame.
F. Review the mourner's appetite.
G. Establish usual weight, review weight gain/loss, and in what time span.
H. Review the mourner's activities of daily living. Does the mourner get up and dress daily and perform daily hygiene?
I. Review the mourner's sleep quality.
J. Review the mourner's daily routines; return to work, return to school, and exercise.
K. Review the mourner's amount of crying per day, and note for what length of time (days, weeks).
L. Review the mourner's drug and alcohol consumption since the loss.

Statements suggesting self-medication with alcohol to facilitate sleep could indicate a coexistent alcohol abuse dependence diagnosis.

M. Review the mourner's usual medical problems and how the loss/grief has affected these problems.

Physical Examination

A. Check temperature, pulse, respirations, blood pressure, weight.
B. Inspect
1. Observe overall appearance. Note grooming habits, dress, appearance.
2. Note social interactions among family members.
3. Note social skills of the patient.

C. Auscultate
1. Auscultate the heart and lungs.

Diagnostic Tests

A. As indicated to rule out other pathology
B. Blood glucose
C. Thyroid studies
D. If depression is suspected, perform depression screening such as Beck's Depression Inventory Scale questionnaire (see "Depression" section).

Differential Diagnoses

A. Grief
B. Depressive disorder
C. PTSD
D. Somatoform disorders (characterized by physical complaints lacking known medical basis or demonstrable physical findings in the presence of psychological factors)
E. Alcoholism and drug abuse/dependence

Plan

A. General interventions
1. Evaluate the nature of the grief and any accompanying psychiatric symptoms.
2. Treat physical/laboratory findings as indicated.
3. Encourage the patient to eat a healthy diet, exercise daily, maintain normal sleep habits and activities.
4. Encourage family and friend support.
5. Offer counseling with professional psychologist or group sessions.
6. Assess for depression at each office visit and treat accordingly.

B. Patient teaching: See the Section III Patient Teaching Guide for this chapter, "Grief."

C. Pharmaceutical therapy: Antidepressants should not be prescribed for acute grief, but reserved for a possible subsequent major depression. Clinical data suggests that SSRIs may assist the patient with mobilizing the energy necessary to assist him or her through the grieving process.

Resist sedation of individuals suffering from acute grief because this tends to delay and prolong the mourning process. Refer to the "Depression" section for pharmaceutical therapy.

1. Drug of choice: Sedative to help sleep
    a. Sedative anxiolytic hypnotics may be prescribed for **no more than 2 weeks at a time.**
    b. Try initially for 1 week to establish a sleep pattern. If insomnia continues, refer the patient to a specialist.
    c. Temazepam (Restoril) 7.5 to 30 mg at bedtime *or* flurazepam (Dalmane) 15 to 30 mg at bedtime.
    d. Zolpidem (Ambien) 5 to 10 mg at bedtime (not to be used for more than 1 month).
2. Sedating antihistamines
    a. Hydroxyzine HCI (Atarax) 50 to 100 mg at bedtime
    b. Hydroxyzine pamoate (Vistaril) 50 to 100 mg at bedtime **(not to be used for more than 4 months)**
3. Antidepressant with sedating properties
    a. Trazodone HCI (Desyrel) 50 to 100 mg at bedtime
    b. Paroxetine (Paxil) 10 to 20 mg at bedtime
    c. Mirtazapine (Remeron) 15 mg every day at bedtime. Increase at 1 to 2 weeks: Usual range is 15 to 45 mg every day at bedtime.

Follow-Up

A. Follow up in 1 week to assess the patient's status and symptoms.
B. Then follow up every 2 weeks to assess the patient's progress.
C. Assess for depression and suicide at every office visit.
D. Once positive change is seen, the patient can be seen monthly.

Consultation/Referral

A. Provide immediate referral/consult for continuing psychotherapy for severe depression and/or suicidal threats.
B. Consult with a physician for evaluation of pharmacologic agents versus referral.

Individual Considerations

A. Pregnancy
    1. Miscarriage, stillbirth, and neonatal death should be considered a major loss and treated as a grief reaction.
    2. Grief is also seen in pregnancy termination. The woman who terminates a pregnancy (regardless of gestational age and reason for termination) may exhibit a major response to this loss.
    3. Hospitals often provide photographs, footprints, and identification bracelets and connect families with perinatal grief support groups.
    4. Use the baby's name when discussing feelings about the loss of a child.
    5. Suggest that friends and family not put away the clothes and bedroom furniture. The baby couple should do this as part of closure.

B. Adults: Grief responses vary from among individuals. Look for behaviors outside the norm.
C. Geriatrics:
    1. Grief in the elderly should be closely assessed to rule out medical diagnoses.
    2. Grief can be a very complicated and prolonged process for individuals who have dementia.
    3. Avoid use of sedating antihistamines in the elderly patient due to potential side effects.

D. Partners: Involvement in grief/loss psychotherapy groups is extremely helpful.

Intimate Partner Violence—*Cheryl A. Glass*

Definition

A. Intimate partner violence (IPV) is defined as intentional control or victimization of a person with whom the abuser has or is currently in an intimate, romantic, or spousal relationship. Domestic-IPV violence crosses all cultures and economic boundaries; it encompasses violence between both genders, including gay and lesbian relationships. Abusive behaviors can occur in a single event, sporadically, or can be continual. The Duluth Model Power and Control Wheel from the Domestic Abuse Intervention Project illustrates the abuser's power and control over the victim (see Figure 24.1).
B. Physical abuse, sexual assault, coercion, social isolation, emotional abuse, economic control, and deprivation are associated with IPV. There is no typical abuser, although all abusers tend to be violent in the home setting and their behavior at work is normal.
C. Forms of physical violence include threatening or assaulting with weapons, pushing, shoving, slapping, punching, choking, kicking, holding, throwing objects, and binding.
D. Psychological abuse includes threats of physical harm to the victim or others, humiliations, intimidation, degradation, ridicule, false accusations, isolation, and deprivation of food, money, access to health care, and transportation.
E. Psychological abuse in lesbian, bisexual, and transgender (LBTG) relationships includes the

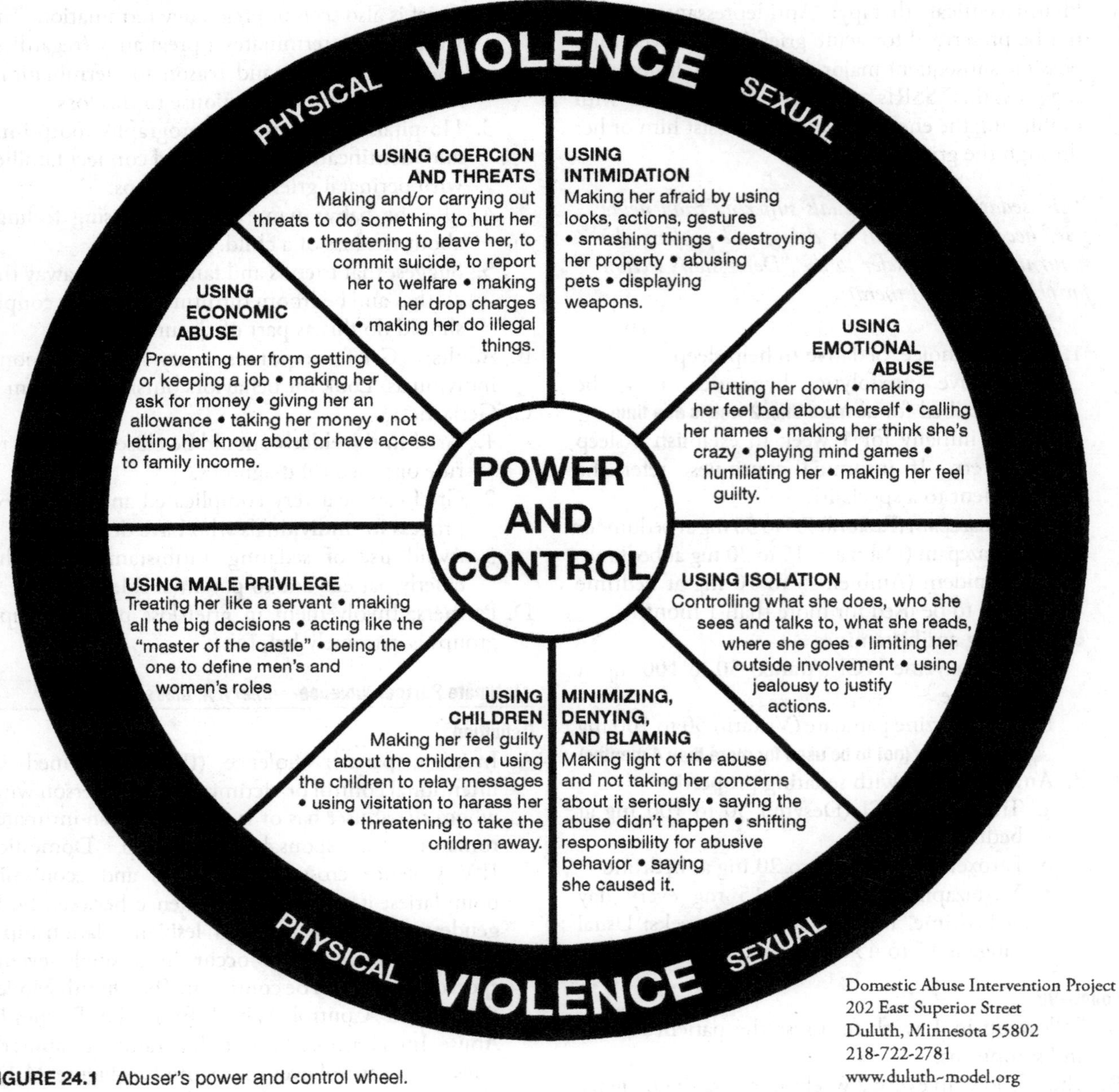

FIGURE 24.1 Abuser's power and control wheel.

threat to "out" their partner as well as threats related to custody of co-parented children.

F. Stalking as a form of IPV. Cyberstalking is psychological abuse via the Internet or texting. Intimate partner stalking occurs during a relationship or after the relationship ends.
   1. Monitoring cell phone and Internet activity
   2. Posting photographs or other types of humiliation on social media
G. Sexual abuse is nonconsensual (unwanted kissing or touching) or painful sexual acts.
H. Reproductive coercion is another form of IPV.
   1. Partner sabotage of safe sex practices (i.e., refusal to use condoms, thus exposing the patient to sexually transmitted infections)
   2. Refusal/control of contraception
   3. Forcing the woman to have an abortion, or utilizing physical violence to endanger a pregnancy
   4. Controlling access to health care

Incidence

The exact incidence of IPV is unknown due to the lack of reporting. The United Nations estimates that more than 600 million women live in countries where domestic violence is not considered a crime. The most significant reason for missing the diagnosis of IPV is failure to ask the patient.

A. **Girls and young women between the ages of 16 and 24 experience the highest rate of IPV.**

B. Domestic violence is the leading cause of homicide death in women globally.
C. Up to 75% of domestic assaults occur after separation; women are most likely to be murdered when reporting abuse or attempting to leave an abusive relationship.
D. An estimated 81% of women stalked by an intimate partner also suffer physical assault. Stalking by an intimate partner is estimated to occur among 1 million women and 317,000 men per year.
E. An estimated 4% to 15% women presenting in emergency rooms have situations related to domestic violence.
F. Women who separate have a risk of violence approximately three times that of divorced women.
   1. Over half of the children who witness domestic violence intervene in some way, including yelling to the abuser to stop, calling for help, and trying to get away.
G. The incidence of abused men is estimated as one in three. Men are also victims of attempted or complete rape, at approximately 3% during their lifetime.
H. Pregnancy has an increased incidence of violence.
   1. One in five young women and 35% of women have experienced pregnancy coercion.
   2. 53% of young women have experienced birth control sabotage.
   3. It is estimated that 5% to 20% of intimate partner abuse occurs against pregnant women.
I. Sexual violence, rape, physical assault, or stalking by an intimate partner occurs in 11% of lesbians and in 15% of men with male partners.
J. Among college women, 20% to 30% report violence during a date.
   1. Approximately 70% of college students say they have been sexually coerced.
K. Physical, emotional, or verbal abuse is estimated in one in three adolescent girls from a dating partner in the United States.
   1. The tween population from ages 11 to 14 years old reports that half of their friends have experienced dating violence.
   2. The tween population from ages 11 to 12 years old reports their friends are victims of verbal abuse.
   3. Teen victims are more likely to smoke, use drugs, and have other risky behaviors.
L. Women in the military are recognized as a vulnerable population susceptible to abuse due to their geographical location away from family and friends and the social isolation within the military culture.
   1. In 2010 the Department of Defense (DoD) estimated that 19,000 military assaults occurred.
      a. Only 191 resulted in court-martial convictions.
   2. One in three convicted military sex offenders remain in the military.
   3. The highest rates of abuse occur in the Army, followed by the Marines and Navy; the Air Force has the lowest rate of abuse in the service branches.

Pathogenesis

Intrapartner violence is not associated with an underlying medical condition. The cycle of abuse has three phases.

A. Tension building: The victim tries to avoid violence and is described as "walking on egg shells," unsure what will trigger an abusive incident.
B. Explosion and acute battering
C. "Honeymoon phase," noted for the absence of tension and reconciliation
D. Victims stay with their partners for multiple reasons, including fear, shame, denial, religious reasons, lack of resources, custody and other legal issues, fear of being "outed," and family pressures.

Predisposing Factors

A. Gender: Females are predominantly the victim.
B. Race: African American, American Indians, Hispanic women, and Alaskan Natives
C. Higher incidence in interracial couples
D. Pregnancy
E. History of violence
   1. Family domestic violence
   2. Abuse as a child: 50% report abuse as an adult.
F. History of drug use
G. PTSD
H. Lack of social support systems
I. Impulse control disorders
J. Poor economic status
K. Lesbian, gay, bisexual, and transgender (LGBT)

Common Complaints

A. Vague complaints
B. Sexual problems
C. Depression
D. Chronic pain inconsistent with organic disease
E. Chronic headaches/migraines
F. Stress
   1. Anxiety
   2. Panic attacks
G. Alcohol or drug abuse (the batterer, victim, or both)
H. Current or past self-mutilation
I. Gynecologic and obstetric complaints
   1. Dyspareunia
   2. Frequent vaginal or urinary tract infections
   3. Pelvic pain/infection
   4. Recurrent sexually transmitted infections
   5. Unintended pregnancy
   6. Late prenatal care
   7. Miscarriage
   8. Preterm bleeding/delivery
J. Complaints of falls and other recurrent accidents

K. Eating disorders
L. Gastrointestinal complaints/irritable bowel syndrome
M. Musculoskeletal complaints

Other Signs and Symptoms

A. Multiple prior visits to the emergency room for traumatic and nontraumatic complaints
B. A delay between injury and office visits (may result from lack of transportation or inability to leave the house)
C. Noncompliance with the treatment or missed appointments (lack of access to money or telephones)
D. Suicide attempt (25% higher in women with IPV)
E. The partner accompanies the patient at all visits.

Subjective Data

The "gold standard" research method to document the prevalence of women's exposure to violence includes conducting the interview one on one, in private, and asking specific direct questions.

A. The batterer often refuses to leave the patient alone and may answer questions for the patient. Translators should not be members of the patient's or suspected abuser's family.
B. Use direct questions: Women-validated Partner Violence Screen (PVS).
   1. Have you been hit, punched, kicked, or otherwise hurt by someone in the past year? If yes, by whom and were you injured?
   2. Do you feel safe in your current relationship?
   3. Is a partner from a previous relationship making you feel unsafe now?
   4. Are you here today due to injuries from a partner?
   5. Are you here today because of illness or stress related to threats, violent behavior, or fears due to a partner?
C. Assess if the patient has ever told family or friends, called hotlines, or attempted to leave the abuser.
D. Has the patient sought help with law enforcement or legal help, that is, filed a criminal complaint or got an order of protection?
E. Are there any weapons in the home?
   1. Has the abuser ever threatened or tried to kill you?
   2. Are you thinking of suicide? Have you ever considered or attempted to commit suicide because of problems in your relationship?
   3. Have you ever considered or attempted killing your batterer?
   4. Do you have a plan?

Physical Examination

A. Enforce the need to interview and do physical examinations in private. Do a full body examination, including the head/scalp.
   1. Most injuries are to the central (breast, chest, and abdomen) area, which is easily concealed by clothing.
   2. Other frequent sites of injury include the head, face, throat, and genitals.
   3. Explain the physical examination and touch with permission.
   4. Forensic exams need thorough documentation of injuries.
      a. Use color photographs before any treatment is started.
      b. Photograph damaged clothing.
      c. Take at least one full body photograph and a facial photograph.
      d. Take close-up photographs of all injuries.
      e. Use a ruler to identify/document the size of injuries.
      f. Documentation on the back of the photographs should include the patient's name, date, photographer's name, as well as any witnesses to the examination. The photographer should also sign each photograph.
      g. Use direct quotes of the patient's history of the violence.
B. Check blood pressure, pulse, and respirations.
C. General observation: Observe for depression/withdrawal, flat affect, anxiousness, fear, evasiveness, poor eye contact, and wearing of heavy makeup or clothing to conceal signs of abuse. Evaluate voice changes: Dysphonia and aphonia. Observe for difficulty breathing.
D. Inspect
   1. Dermal exam for the presence of cigarette burns, impression marks, rope burns, welts, abrasions, scratch marks, claw marks, bite marks, ligature marks, petechiae, and contusions at multiple sites (e.g., back, legs, buttocks).
   2. Eye exam
      a. Observe subconjunctival hemorrhages from strangulation/struggle.
      b. Perform a funduscopic examination (if indicated secondary to trauma).
   3. Evaluate the genitals for lacerations and hematomas of the vagina or labia.
E. Auscultate
   1. Auscultate all lung fields.
   2. Auscultate the bowel sounds in all four quadrants of the abdomen.
F. Palpate
   1. Evaluate skull/facial trauma to the maxillofacial area, eye orbits, mandible, and nasal bones. Facial injuries are reported in 94% of victims.
   2. Evaluate for dislocations, fractures (including spiral fractures), sprains, and contusions to the wrists, forearms, and shoulders.

G. Percuss: Abdomen, chest, and areas of injury (if indicated secondary to trauma).
H. Neurological examination (if indicated secondary to trauma).
I. Genital/rectal examination
   1. Evaluate genitals/anal area for redness, swelling, bruising, hematomas, abrasions, or lacerations.
   2. Perform bimanual examination (females).
   3. Perform an anoscopy (if indicated).
   4. Evaluate for evidence of sperm (recto/vaginal).
   5. Evaluate for the presence of condyloma (perineum, rectum, vagina).
   6. Evaluate for the presence of foreign bodies (recto/vaginal).

Diagnostic Tests

Diagnostic tests and x-rays are ordered dependent on the type of presenting complaints and physical examination.

A. Administer a domestic abuse assessment screening tool and have the victim mark a body map of injuries (see Figure 24.2).
B. CBC with differential and peripheral smear, bleeding evaluation, including prothrombin time/partial prothrombin time (PT/PTT), ALT, and AST to evaluate injury to the liver, serum amylase, or lipase to rule out pancreatic injury.
C. Urinalysis
D. Drug/toxicology screen (urine and blood).
E. Obtain forensic DNA samples from the skin, under nails, and within the vagina and rectum, as well as saliva from bite marks using sterile cotton-tipped applicators that have been moistened with sterile saline. These should be sent to a crime laboratory as soon as possible.
F. Test for sexually transmitted infections/HIV.
G. Pregnancy test (if indicated)
H. Radiographs: Facial injury, anteroposterior (AP) and lateral radiograph for any areas of bone tenderness, swelling, deformity, or limited ROM
I. Ultrasounds as indicated
J. Neuroimaging CT/MRI for any suspected nonaccidental head injury (i.e., head trauma, or scalp hematoma)

Differential Diagnoses

A. Domestic violence
   1. Intimate partner abuse
   2. Elder abuse
B. Rape
C. Other: Related to presenting symptoms

Plan

A. Provide a safe environment. Assess for immediate danger.
B. Clearly document the history, physical findings, and interventions.
C. Determine the risk to the victim and any children.
D. Evaluate the need for emergency room/hospital admission.
E. Battery is a crime; assess the victim's readiness for police intervention and need for a court order of protection.
F. Help develop a safety plan.
G. Assess readiness to leave: Collection of important papers (e.g., birth certificates, custody papers, divorce papers, legal agreements, address book, and copies of restraining orders), access to money/credit cards, and telling family and friends.
H. Provide contact numbers for shelters. Have the patient hide information in her shoes.
I. Counsel that violence may escalate.

Patient Teaching

A. Reinforce the fact that the violence is not the victim's fault. IPV is very common and the victims do not deserve to be abused. Discuss the cycle of abuse.
B. Violence increases in frequency and severity.
C. Help is available.
D. The DoD has a self-help phone app created by the Rape, Abuse, & Incest National Network (RAINN) for sexual assault survivors to create a customized self-care plan. This app is available through the iTunes store. The app is a resource for Active Duty, National Guard, and Reserve service members.
   1. **RAINN has adapted the National Sexual Online Hotline to provide specialized live help online at SafeHelpline.org to members of the DoD community who have been sexually assaulted.**
   2. **The Safe Helpline is also available by calling 877-995-5247.**
   3. **All Safe Helpline staff members have been trained to answer questions related to military-specific topics such as restricted and unrestricted reporting and how to contact relevant military resources such as the installation or base's Sexual Assault Response Coordinator (SARC) if their services are requested.**

Pharmaceutical Therapy

A. Prescriptions are related to physical injuries.
B. Treatment for sexually transmitted infections in the oral anal genital areas.
C. Tranquilizers may impair the victim's ability to flee or defend herself and should not be prescribed.

Follow-Up

A. Develop a follow-up plan.
   1. What type of help does the patient want?
   2. Does the patient have a plan for returning? Is the batterer home? Does she think it is safe?

ABUSE ASSESSMENT SCREEN

1. Have you ever been emotionally or physically abused by your partner or someone important to you?
   Yes ☐ No ☐
   If yes, by whom? ________________
   Total number of times ____________

2. Within the past year, have you been hit, slapped, kicked, or otherwise physically hurt by someone?
   Yes ☐ No ☐
   If yes, by whom? ________________
   Total number of times ____________

3. Since you've been pregnant, have you been hit, slapped, kicked, or otherwise physically hurt by someone?
   Yes ☐ No ☐
   If yes, by whom? ________________
   Total number of times ____________

4. Within the past year, has anyone forced you to have sexual activities?
   Yes ☐ No ☐
   If yes, by whom? ________________
   Total number of times ____________

5. Are you afraid of your partner or anyone you listed here?
   Yes ☐ No ☐

MARK THE AREA OF INJURY ON A BODY MAP AND SCORE EACH INCIDENT ACCORDING TO THE FOLLOWING SCALE

If any of the descriptions for the higher number apply, use the higher number.

1 = Threats of abuse including use of a weapon
2 = Slapping, pushing; no injury and/or lasting pain
3 = Punching, kicking, bruises, cuts, and/or continuing pain
4 = Beating up, severe contusions, burns, broken bones
5 = Head injury, internal injury, permanent injury
6 = Use of weapon; wound from weapon

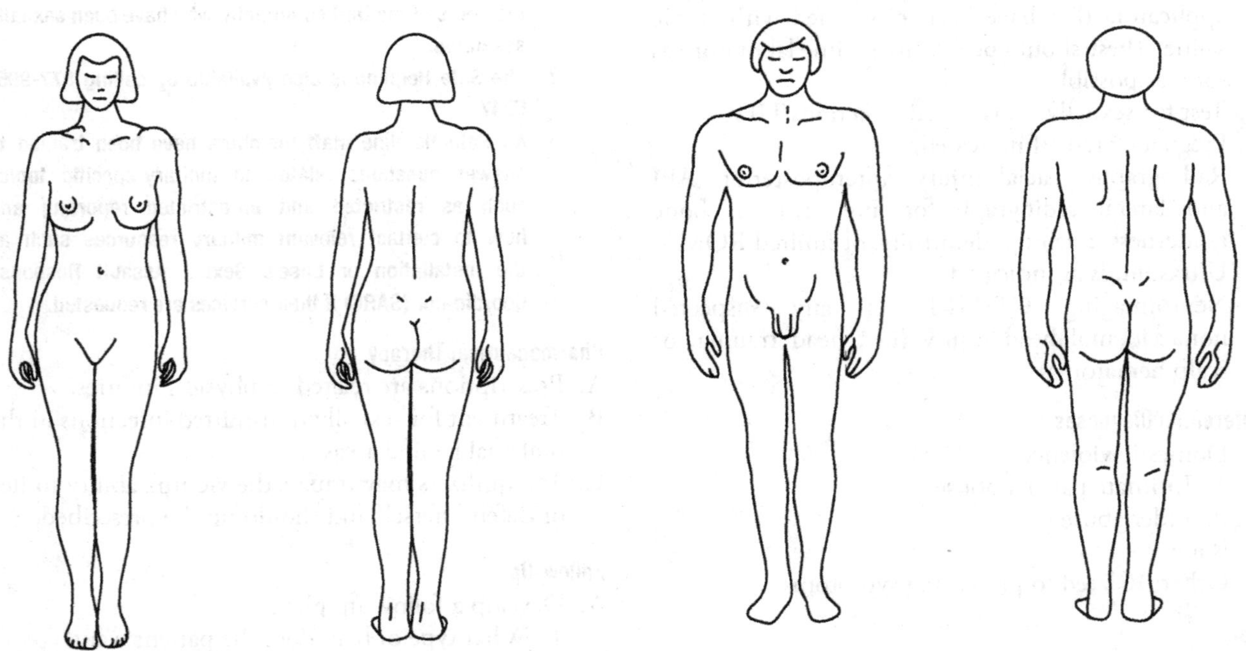

FIGURE 24.2 Abuse assessment screening tool with body map.
Reprinted with permission from Parker, McFarlane, Soeken, Torres, and Campbell (1993), Lippincott Williams & Wilkins.

3. Does she have a place to stay with family or friends; or does she want to go to a shelter?
4. Give the telephone numbers for shelters and crisis hotlines.

B. Screen the patient for abuse at all subsequent visits.
C. Mandatory reporting
   1. States require reporting when domestic violence involves a child under the age of 18 and abuse or neglect of the child is suspected.
   2. Abuse of a disabled person must be reported to the Disabled Persons Protection Commission.
   3. Reporting elder abuse may be mandatory in your state.
D. Your state may mandate reporting and intervention with law enforcement. Refer to the Domestic Violence, Sexual Assault, and Stalking Data Resource Center. www.jrsa.org/dvsa-drc/state-info.shtml
E. The 2013 National Protocol for Sexual Assault Medical Forensic Examination for Adults and Adolescents is available at ncjrs.gov/pdffiles1/ovw/241903.pdf

Consultation/Referral

A. Facilitate referrals to a shelter, counseling, and legal services.
B. Contact a SANE qualified health care provider if indicated.
C. Refer to community or private support groups and agencies.
D. Refer for a consultation with a psychiatrist if the victim is homicidal or suicidal.
E. Refer for a neurological or neurosurgical consultation for intracranial injuries or focal neurological findings.
F. Refer for an orthopedic consultation for fractures.

Individual Considerations

A. Pregnancy is a known period of increased risk of violence.
   1. The genitals, breast, and abdomen are common sites targeted for trauma.
   2. Women may present with a miscarriage or premature labor.
   3. Blunt trauma is a common injury in pregnancy.
   4. Perform universal screening at each trimester and postpartum since abuse often begins during pregnancy.

Resources

Dating Abuse Stops Here at www.datingabusestopshere.com

Domestic Violence, Sexual Assault and Stalking Data Resource Center: www.jrsainfo.org/dvsa-drc/state-summaries.shtml

Futures Without Violence *(Formerly Family Violence Prevention Fund):* www.futureswithoutviolence.org

National Domestic Violence Hotline: 1-800-799-7233

National TEEN Dating Abuse Helpline: 1-866-311-9474

Rape Abuse & Incest National Network (RAINN) Hotline: 1-800-656-4693

www.domesticviolence.org

Sleep Disorders

Definition

A. In normal sleepers, transient insomnia occurs in those who have traveled to another time zone (i.e., "jet lag"), are under situational stress, or are sleeping in unfamiliar surroundings. Treatment is not required in these situations because time takes care of the problem. With short-term insomnia, the normal sleeper experiences difficulty sleeping that does not resolve within a few days. This can be the result of stress, such as financial difficulty and divorce. These patients may require short-term symptomatic relief of insomnia.
B. Long-term insomnia is persistent and disabling. Studies suggest that almost all have an associated psychiatric disorder, especially depression; an associated drug use/abuse/withdrawal problem; or an associated medical disorder.

Incidence

A. Difficulties with sleep are among the most common complaints of medical patients and affect a large percentage of the population. From 10% to 20% of all adults express sleep-related complaints they consider to be serious. Sleep disorders also can affect proper mental functioning (53% of chronic insomniacs complain of memory difficulties). Sleep disorders are also implicated in decreased work efficiency, impaired industrial productivity, and increased risk of traffic accidents. They also seem to enhance the propensity for cardiovascular disease and increase the risk of death. Insomniacs are also at increased risk for the development of depression and anxiety disorders. Patients with obstructive sleep apnea (OSA) syndrome have significant performance impairments on complex motor tasks.

The risk of depression increases with time if insomnia is left untreated.

Pathogenesis

A. Other than situational stress, jet lag, and sleeping in unfamiliar surroundings, difficulty with sleep can be related to psychiatric illness or medical problems. It is most frequently due to chronic depression and/or anxiety. Antisocial and obsessive-compulsive features are also common among these patients. Patients may self-medicate, which produces more insomnia.

Predisposing Factors

A. Alcohol use: Initially assists with sleep but produces fragmented sleep
B. Hypnotic medications can produce tolerance, which causes sleep disruption and rebound insomnia with withdrawal from the medication.
C. Medications such as caffeine, nicotine cigarettes, amphetamines, steroids, methylphenidate, hallucinogens, aminophylline, ephedrine, decongestants, bronchodilators, weight loss/diet pills, thyroid preparations, MAO inhibitors, and anticancer agents
D. Persons with fibromyalgia syndrome
E. Women experiencing menopausal symptoms
F. Upper respiratory symptoms
G. OSA disorders such as nasal obstruction, large uvula, low-lying soft palate, craniofacial abnormalities, excessive pharyngeal tissue, pharyngeal masses (tumors, cysts), macroglossia, tonsillar hypertrophy, and vocal cord paralysis
H. Obesity
I. Hypothyroidism
J. Acromegaly
K. Chronic pain
L. Urinary frequency and nocturia due to prostatism, diabetes, diuretics, and infection

Common Complaints

A. Statements regarding impaired sleep pattern
   1. Inability to fall asleep
   2. Restless throughout the night
   3. Early morning awakening with inability to fall back to sleep
   4. Difficulty concentrating during the daytime hours
   5. Feels fatigued after 8 hours of sleep, no energy
   6. Partner complains of the patient's snoring

Other Signs and Symptoms

A. Excessive daytime sleepiness
B. Feels tense, irritable, and agitated
C. Heightened anxiety and aggressiveness (occasionally)
D. Reports of prolonged pauses in respiration during sleep
E. Weight gain
F. Frontal headaches on awakening
G. Difficulty with short-term recall

Subjective Data

A. Review the onset, course, and duration of problems and symptoms.
B. Take a thorough history of the sleep problem, including the 24-hour sleep–wake cycle: Sleep–wake habit history, sleep hygiene history, meal and exercise times, ambient noise, and light and temperature.
C. Identify the pattern: Trouble falling asleep, trouble staying asleep (frequent awakenings), and early morning awakenings.
D. Inquire about life stresses, drug and alcohol use, and marital and family problems.

> *Statements suggesting self-medication with alcohol to facilitate sleep could indicate a coexistent alcohol abuse/dependence diagnosis. In patients who have developed tolerance to alcohol or sleep medications, abrupt cessation of these agents may produce increased insomnia and anxiety.*

E. Determine whether the insomnia is simply normal sleep. Some "insomniacs" get ample sleep (pseudoinsomnia), and the problems are psychological.
F. Review the patient's smoking and caffeine intake history.
G. Review all medications, including prescribed and OTC medications, recreational drug use, and weight loss medications.
H. Review the patient's medical history: Thyroid problems, hypertension, steroid use, diabetes, and cancer.
I. Conduct an interview with the patient's bed partner to provide information about snoring, breathing pauses, and unusual body positions or movements. Is the partner concerned/frightened about the apneic pauses?
J. Review cardiopulmonary dysfunction: Orthopnea, paroxysmal nocturnal dyspnea, or nocturnal angina.
K. If female, establish last menses; rule out pregnancy or menopause. Are there regular menses, vaginal dryness, and/or hot flashes?
L. If male, review for signs of prostatism (> age 50, hesitancy, dribbling, nocturia, frequency, incomplete emptying, and so on. See section in Chapter 14, "Genitourinary Guidelines," "Benign Prostatic Hypertrophy").

Physical Examination

A. Check pulse, respirations, blood pressure, and weight.
B. Inspect
   1. Observe general overall appearance; note grooming and behaviors during interview.
   2. Evaluate eyes: Pupil dilation/constriction (may indicate recent medication/nonprescription drug use).
   3. Inspect nasal mucosa for erythema, edema, discharge, and nasal patency; look for septal deviation and polyps. Transilluminate sinus (if indicated).
   4. Inspect the mouth for erythema, the teeth for uneven surfaces (grinding), and the retropharynx for abnormality.
C. Auscultate
   1. Heart
   2. Lungs
   3. Abdomen

D. Palpate
   1. Conduct a neurologic examination.
   2. Palpate the neck and thyroid; evaluate for goiter.
   3. Check the joints for swelling and arthritis, and ROM (rule out musculoskeletal cause).
   4. Perform rectal examination if indicated for men with prostate symptoms.
   5. Perform speculum/bimanual examination if indicated to evaluate menopausal atrophy and bladder complaints.

Diagnostic Tests

A. CBC with differential
B. Electrolytes
C. Thyroid-stimulating hormone or full thyroid profile, FSH, LH
D. Prostate-specific antigen (PSA) for men
E. Serum creatinine and blood urea nitrogen
F. Urinalysis: Check hematuria.
G. Urine culture (if indicated)
H. Glucose tolerance test
I. Urine drug screen
J. Sinus x-rays
K. Urodynamics tests if bladder issues suspected
L. Postvoid residual (catheterization or ultrasound)
M. Nocturnal polysomnography or actigraphy
N. Administer psychiatric evaluation (if indicated).

Differential Diagnoses

A. Insomnia/sleep disorder
   1. Inadequate sleep hygiene: Habitual behaviors that harm sleep, such as delaying morning awakening time or napping
   2. Insufficient sleep syndrome: Curtailing time in bed in response to social and occupational demands, over long periods of time
   3. Adjustment sleep disorder: Acute emotional stressors (job loss or hospitalization) resulting in difficulty falling asleep because of tension and anxiety
   4. Psychophysiologic insomnia: Anticipatory anxiety over the prospect of another night of sleeplessness and the next day of fatigue
   5. Narcolepsy: Persistent daytime sleepiness with brief naps accompanied by vivid dreams
      a. Cataplexy or abrupt paralysis or paresis of skeletal muscles following anger, surprise, laughter, or physical exercise
      b. Hypnagogic hallucinations (vivid and often frightening dreams that occur shortly after falling asleep or on awakening)
      c. Sleep paralysis, a transient global paralysis of voluntary muscles that occurs shortly after falling asleep and lasts a few seconds or minutes
      d. Disturbed and restless sleep

B. Alcoholism and drug abuse/dependence
C. Major depressive disorder
D. Acute psychosis, mania, and hypomania
E. Medical problems such as chronic pain, anxiety, depression, hyperthyroidism, epilepsy, general paresis, diabetes, benign prostatic hypertrophy, urinary problems related to age/diuretic use, cardiopulmonary dysfunction, and menopause

Plan

A. General interventions
   1. Identify cause of insomnia.
   2. Treat physical/laboratory findings if underlying conditions exist. Treat conditions according to diagnosis made, that is, hormone replacement therapy, thyroid medications, diabetes, and so forth, as indicated. See related chapters for plans of care.
B. Patient teaching
   1. Have the patient record a 2-week log for sleep–wake habits. A sleep diary is available from the National Sleep Foundation at sleepfoundation.org/sleep-diary/sleepdiaryv6.pdf
   2. Advise the patient to avoid alcohol, caffeine, and stimulating agents during the evening hours.
   3. Avoid exercising prior to going to bed.
   4. Encourage smoking cessation. Avoid smoking in the evening hours (see the Section III Patient Teaching Guide for Chapter 11, "Nicotine Dependence").
   5. Encourage regular sleep habit/hygiene. Recommend going to bed the same time every night and waking up the same time every day.
   6. Recommend keeping the bedroom cool, quiet, and dark while sleeping.
   7. Encourage relaxation exercises prior to going to bed.
   8. If stress/anxiety contributes to sleeping disorder, recommend counseling with psychologist or counselor to identify and deal with issues.
   9. See the Section III Patient Teaching Guide for this chapter, "Sleep Disorders/Insomnia."
C. Pharmaceutical therapy
   1. Eliminate prescription medications (when possible) and OTC products as part of your management plan *before writing another prescription.*
   2. Only after making the assumption that the insomnia cannot be adequately treated by addressing the underlying medical problem responsible for causing the insomnia should medications for sleep be prescribed.

Do not prescribe medications for sleep to patients with alcohol/drug or depressive disorders.

3. Use short-term pharmaceutical therapy.
4. Drug of choice: *Sedative anxiolytic hypnotics:* Try initially for 1 week to establish a sleep pattern.

If insomnia continues for more than 1 month, refer the patient to a physician or specialist.

   a. Temazepam (Restoril) 7.5 to 30 mg at bedtime (1–2 weeks)
   b. Zolpidem (Ambien) 5 to 10 mg at bedtime (4 weeks maximum)
   c. Eszopiclone (Lunesta) 2 to 3 mg at bedtime. Start with 1 mg in the elderly.
   d. Ramelteon (Rozerem) 8 mg by mouth 30 minutes before bedtime. Do not take with meals.

Anxiolytic agents such as diazepam (Valium) and alprazolam (Xanax) tend to increase the duration and frequency of sleep apneas and are contraindicated for patients with possible/undiagnosed apnea spells.

5. **Sedating antihistamines are not recommended for use over 4 months. Side effects in elderly patients outweigh benefit.**
   a. Hydroxyzine HCI (Atarax) 50 to 100 mg at bedtime
   b. Hydroxyzine pamoate (Vistaril) 50 to 100 mg at bedtime
6. Antidepressants with sedating properties
   a. Trazodone HC1 (Desyrel) 50 to 100 mg at bedtime
   b. Mirtazapine (Remeron) 7.5 to 15 mg at bedtime

Follow-Up

A. Follow up in 1 week to assess the patient's status.
B. Then, follow up every 2 weeks to check the patient's progress.
C. Once positive change is seen, the patient can be seen monthly as needed.
D. Assess the patient's potential for suicide with every office visit.
E. If coexisting medication conditions exist, refer to medical diagnosis for follow-up recommendations.

Consultation/Referral

A. Refer to a psychiatric clinician for medication management and psychotherapy after initial assessment if psychiatric differential diagnosis is made.
B. Refer for psychological testing.
C. If insomnia continues for more than 1 month, refer to a physician if the patient requires a sedative anxiolytic hypnotic for more than 4 weeks.

Individual Considerations

A. Pregnancy: Sleep difficulties are more prevalent in second and third trimesters of pregnancy because of the growing size of the uterus and difficulty finding comfortable sleeping positions. Treat with comfort measures.
B. Adults
   1. The "right" amount of sleep results in optimal daytime alertness and a sense of mental efficiency and well-being.
   2. Daytime naps often interfere with the quality of night sleep. Encourage eliminating naps during the day.
   3. Nocturia and disturbed sleep are the symptoms that cause older men to seek medical help with prostatism.
C. Geriatrics
   1. With aging, it is normal for sleep time to decrease (< 7 hours), with a tendency toward sleep fragmentation and an increase in the frequency of awakenings and brief arousals. Explain this to older adults to avoid "worry over sleeplessness."
   2. Always assess for depression in elderly patients.
   3. Start with the lowest dose of pharmaceutical agents.
   4. Chronic pain is a leading cause for sleep disruption in elderly persons with degenerative joint pain.
   5. Review elderly patients' medications and dosage for insomnia because of known side effects or as a medication toxicity.
   6. Gastroesophageal reflux is commonly seen in geriatric patients at nighttime and causes them to wake up at night. Correcting the reflux with sleeping position, avoiding late night meals and spicy food, prescribing medications (PPIs), and making possible weight loss interventions could improve sleep disturbance in these patients.
   7. Patients with end-stage renal disease may have nocturnal leg movement disorders and anemia due to renal failure. Improving the anemia will improve the insomnia and will decrease the leg movements.
D. Partners: Those who find it necessary to sleep in another room because of their partner's snoring should refer the snorer to the primary care physician/advanced practice nurse to rule out an OSA syndrome.

Resource

National Sleep Foundation: www.sleepfoundation.org

Substance Use Disorders

Definition

A. Substance use disorders range from mild to severe forms of pathological patterns of behavior related to substance use. The *DSM-5* (APA, 2013) specifies 10 separate classes of drugs that are included in substance-related disorders: alcohol; caffeine; cannabis; hallucinogens; inhalants; opioids; sedatives, hypnotics, and anxiolytics; stimulants (amphetamine-type substances, cocaine, and other stimulants); tobacco; and other (or unknown) substances. All of these substances may be used in excess, producing an intense activation of the brain reward system.

B. The diagnosis of substance use disorders is based on impaired control over substance use, the use of larger amounts of a substance over a greater period of time, unsuccessful attempts to discontinue use of a substance, and spending a great amount of time to obtain, use the substance, and recover from its effects. Substance use may result in inability to maintain responsibilities at home, school, or work. Normal daily activities may be decreased or discontinued due to substance use. Risky behaviors may be exhibited, as continued substance use results in physical and psychological problems and the individual fails to abstain from the substance, despite the problems associated with its use.

Incidence

A. The National Institute on Drug Abuse (NIDA) estimates that 23.9 million persons, or 9.2% of the U.S. population, has used an illicit drug or abused a psychotherapeutic medication, including pain relievers, hypnotic/sedative medications, or stimulants. This is noted to be an increase of slightly more than 8% from findings in 2002. Marijuana use also increased, from about 14 million persons in 2007 to 19 million users in 2012.

B. The NIDA reports the abuse of tobacco, alcohol, and illicit drugs costs over $600 billion annually in costs related to health care, lost work productivity, and crime. Drug use tends to be highest among people in their teens to twenties; however, an increase has also been noted in persons in their fifties. This is thought to be secondary to the aging of "baby boomers," whose rate of illicit drug use has been higher than that of previous generations. Alcohol abuse is the primary substance abuse problem of those older than age 50.

C. The NIDA estimates that while 23.9 million Americans need treatment for substance use disorder, only 2.5 million have received treatment. See Table 24.2 for the NIDA list of commonly abused drugs and Table 24.3 for the NIDA list of abused prescription drugs.

D. Studies indicate that 8% of adults in the United States had a substance use disorder in the past 12 months. Approximately 40% of hospital admissions are related to substance abuse or to the effects of using substances.

E. Approximately 90% of the American population consumes some alcohol (at one time or another). Alcohol use is believed to be involved in 20% to 50% of all hospital admissions, but alcohol use disorders are formally diagnosed less than 5% of the time; 5% to 7% of Americans have alcoholism in a given year, and 13% will have it sometime during their life. Prevalence rates of alcoholism are 5% to 6% for men and 1% to 2% for women. It is highest in men aged 18 to 64 and women aged 18 to 24.

F. 25% of Americans use tobacco products. One study states that there is a link between early nicotine use and alcohol abuse and depression. Smoking before the age of 13 significantly increases the risk of drug dependence.

G. It is estimated that 37% of the population aged 12 or older has used an illicit psychoactive drug at least once in their lifetime.

A substance abuse problem is recognized in as few as 1 in 20 substance-abusing patients seeking medical attention.

Pathogenesis

A. No single gene has been identified as the culprit in the predisposition to substance dependence. Certain biologic features seem to be inherited by first-degree relatives (particularly males) of alcoholics, for example, a resistance to intoxication, a subnormal cortisol rise after drinking, and a subnormal epinephrine release following stress.

B. Some theories postulate alterations in metabolism of alcohol and drugs in people who are dependent. Studies pertaining to alcohol have included research into genetic heritability, flawed metabolism of alcohol by alcoholics, insensitivity to alcohol inherited by alcoholics (thus tending to increase tolerance or ability to know when to stop), and alterations in brain waves in alcoholics.

C. Although much of the research is specific to only one drug, much of what we know about the research can be applied to other drugs. There appears to be a higher rate of substance dependence, not limited to alcohol, in children of alcoholics.

Predisposing Factors

Factors vary among individuals, and no one factor can account entirely for the risk of substance abuse. Studies indicate a high correlation between substance use and the presence of psychiatric disorders, especially anxiety disorders, depression, schizophrenia, and, in women, eating disorders.

TABLE 24.2 Commonly Abused Drugs

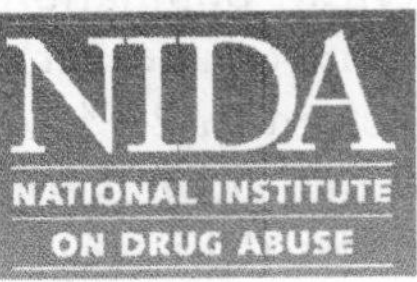

Visit NIDA at www.drugabuse.gov
National Institutes of Health
U.S. Department of Health and Human Services
NIH... Turning Discovery Into Health

Substances: Category and Name	Examples of Commercial and Street Names	DEA Schedule[a]/How Administered[b]	*Acute Effects*/Health Risks
Tobacco			Increased blood pressure and heart rate/chronic lung disease; cardiovascular disease; stroke; cancers of the mouth, pharynx, larynx, esophagus, stomach, pancreas, cervix, kidney, bladder, and acute myeloid leukemia; adverse pregnancy outcomes; addiction
Nicotine	Found in cigarettes, cigars, bidis, and smokeless tobacco (snuff, spit tobacco, chew)	Not scheduled/ smoked, snorted, chewed	
Alcohol			In low doses, euphoria, mild stimulation, relaxation, lowered inhibitions; in higher doses, drowsiness, slurred speech, nausea, emotional volatility, loss of coordination, visual distortions, impaired memory, sexual dysfunction, loss of consciousness/increased risk of injuries, violence, fetal damage (in pregnant women); depression; neurologic deficits; hypertension; liver and heart disease; addiction; fatal overdose
Alcohol (ethyl alcohol)	Found in liquor, beer, and wine	Not scheduled/ swallowed	
Cannabinoids			Euphoria; relaxation; slowed reaction time; distorted sensory perception; impaired balance and coordination; increased heart rate and appetite; impaired learning, memory; anxiety; panic attacks; psychosis/cough; frequent respiratory infections; possible mental health decline; addiction
Marijuana	Blunt, dope, ganja, grass, herb, joint, bud, Mary Jane, pot, reefer, green, trees, smoke, sinsemilla, skunk, weed	I/smoked, swallowed	
Hashish	Boom, gangster, hash, hash oil, hemp	I/smoked, swallowed	
Opioids			Euphoria; drowsiness; impaired coordination; dizziness; confusion; nausea; sedation; feeling of heaviness in the body; slowed or arrested breathing/constipation; endocarditis; hepatitis; HIV; addiction; fatal overdose
Heroin	*Diacetylmorphine:* smack, horse, brown sugar, dope, H, junk, skag, skunk, white horse, China white; cheese (with OTC cold medicine and antihistamine)	I/injected, smoked, snorted	
Opium	*Laudanum, paregoric:* big O, black stuff, block, gum, hop	II, III, V/swallowed, smoked	
Stimulants			Increased heart rate, blood pressure, body temperature, metabolism; feelings of exhilaration; increased energy, mental alertness; tremors; reduced appetite; irritability; anxiety; panic; paranoia; violent behavior; psychosis/ weight loss; insomnia; cardiac or cardiovascular complications; stroke; seizures; addiction Also, for cocaine—nasal damage from snorting Also, for methamphetamine—severe dental problems
Cocaine	*Cocaine hydrochloride:* blow, bump, C, candy, Charlie, coke, crack, flake, rock, snow, toot	II/snorted, smoked, injected	
Amphetamine	*Biphetamine, Dexedrine:* bennies, black beauties, crosses, hearts, LA turnaround speed, truck drivers, uppers	II/swallowed, snorted, smoked, injected	
Methamphetamine	*Desoxyn:* meth, ice, crank, chalk, crystal, fire, glass, go fast, speed	II/swallowed, snorted, smoked, injected	

(*continued*)

TABLE 24.2 Commonly Abused Drugs (*continued*)

Substances: Category and Name	Examples of Commercial and Street Names	DEA Schedule[a]/How Administered[b]	*Acute Effects*/Health Risks
Club Drugs			MDMA—mild hallucinogenic effects; increased tactile sensitivity, empathic feelings; lowered inhibition; anxiety; chills; sweating; teeth clenching; muscle cramping/sleep disturbances; depression; impaired memory; hyperthermia; addiction Flunitrazepam—sedation; muscle relaxation; confusion; memory loss; dizziness; impaired coordination/ addiction GHB—drowsiness; nausea; headache; disorientation; loss of coordination; memory loss/unconsciousness; seizures; coma
MDMA (methylenedioxymethamphetamine)	Ecstasy, Adam, clarity, Eve, lover's speed, peace, uppers	I/swallowed, snorted, injected	
Flunitrazepam[c]	*Rohypnol:* forget-me pill, Mexican Valium, R2, roach, Roche, roofies, roofinol, rope, rophies	IV/swallowed, snorted	
GHB[c]	*Gamma-hydroxybutyrate:* G, Georgia home boy, grievous bodily harm, liquid ecstasy, soap, scoop, goop, liquid X	I/swallowed	
Dissociative Drugs			Feelings of being separate from one's body and environment; impaired motor function/anxiety; tremors; numbness; memory loss; nausea Also, for ketamine—analgesia; impaired memory; delirium; respiratory depression and arrest; death Also, for *Pneumocystis carinii* pneumonia (PCP) and analogs—analgesia; psychosis; aggression; violence; slurred speech; loss of coordination; hallucinations Also, for DXM—euphoria; slurred speech; confusion; dizziness; distorted visual perceptions
Ketamine	*Ketalar SV:* cat Valium, K, Special K, vitamin K	III/injected, snorted, smoked	
PCP and analogs	*Phencyclidine:* angel dust, boat, hog, love boat, peace pill	I, II/swallowed, smoked, injected	
Salvia divinorum	Salvia, Shepherdess's Herb, Maria Pastora, magic mint, Sally-D	Not scheduled/ chewed, swallowed, smoked	
Dextromethorphan (DXM)	Found in some cough and cold medications: Robotripping, Robo, Triple C	Not scheduled/ swallowed	
Hallucinogens			Altered states of perception and feeling; hallucinations; nausea Also, for LSD and mescaline—increased body temperature, heart rate, blood pressure; loss of appetite; sweating; sleeplessness; numbness; dizziness; weakness; tremors; impulsive behavior; rapid shifts in emotion Also, for LSD—flashbacks, Hallucinogen Persisting Perception Disorder Also, for psilocybin—nervousness; paranoia; panic
Lysergic acid diethylamide (LSD)	*Lysergic acid diethylamide:* acid, blotter, cubes, microdot, yellow sunshine, blue heaven	I/swallowed, absorbed through mouth tissues	
Mescaline	Buttons, cactus, mesc, peyote	I/swallowed, smoked	
Psilocybin	Magic mushrooms, purple passion, shrooms, little smoke	I/swallowed	
Other Compounds			Steroids—no intoxication effects/hypertension; blood clotting and cholesterol changes; liver cysts; hostility and aggression; acne; in adolescents—premature stoppage of growth; in males—prostate cancer, reduced sperm production, shrunken testicles, breast enlargement; in females—menstrual irregularities, development of beard and other masculine characteristics Inhalants (varies by chemical)—stimulation; loss of inhibition; headache; nausea or vomiting; slurred speech; loss of motor coordination; wheezing/cramps; muscle weakness; depression; memory impairment; damage to cardiovascular and nervous systems; unconsciousness; sudden death
Anabolic steroids	*Anadrol, Oxandrin, Durabolin, Depo-Testosterone, Equipoise:* roids, juice, gym candy, pumpers	III/injected, swallowed, applied to skin	
Inhalants	*Solvents (paint thinners, gasoline, glues); gases (butane, propane, aerosol propellants, nitrous oxide); nitrites (isoamyl, isobutyl, cyclohexyl):* laughing gas, poppers, snappers, whippets	Not scheduled/ inhaled through nose or mouth	

(*continued*)

TABLE 24.2 Commonly Abused Drugs (*continued*)

Substances: Category and Name	Examples of Commercial and Street Names	DEA Schedule[a]/How Administered[b]	*Acute Effects*/Health Risks
Prescription Medications			
CNS depressants	For more information on prescription medications, please visit www.nida.nih.gov/DrugPages/PrescripDrugsChart.html		
Stimulants			
Opioid pain relievers			

[a]Schedule I and II drugs have a high potential for abuse. They require greater storage security and have a quota on manufacturing, among other restrictions. Schedule I drugs are available for research only and have no approved medical use; Schedule II drugs are available only by prescription (unrefillable) and require a form for ordering. Schedule III and IV drugs are available by prescription, may have five refills in 6 months, and may be ordered orally. Some Schedule V drugs are available over the counter.

[b]Some of the health risks are directly related to the route of drug administration. For example, injection drug use can increase the risk of infection through needle contamination with staphylococci, HIV, hepatitis, and other organisms.

[c]Associated with sexual assaults.

Principles of Drug Addiction Treatment

More than three decades of scientific research show that treatment can help drug-addicted individuals stop drug use, avoid relapse, and successfully recover their lives. Based on this research, 13 fundamental principles that characterize effective drug abuse treatment have been developed. These principles are detailed in *NIDA's Principles of Drug Addiction Treatment: A Research-Based Guide*. The guide also describes different types of science-based treatments and provides answers to commonly asked questions.

1. **Addiction is a complex but treatable disease that affects brain function and behavior.** Drugs alter the brain's structure and how it functions, resulting in changes that persist long after drug use has ceased. This may help explain why abusers are at risk for relapse even after long periods of abstinence.
2. **No single treatment is appropriate for everyone.** Matching treatment settings, interventions, and services to an individual's particular problems and needs is critical to his or her ultimate success.
3. **Treatment needs to be readily available.** Because drug-addicted individuals may be uncertain about entering treatment, taking advantage of available services the moment people are ready for treatment is critical. Potential patients can be lost if treatment is not immediately available or readily accessible.
4. **Effective treatment attends to multiple needs of the individual, not just his or her drug abuse.** To be effective, treatment must address the individual's drug abuse and any associated medical, psychological, social, vocational, and legal problems.
5. **Remaining in treatment for an adequate period of time is critical.** The appropriate duration for an individual depends on the type and degree of his or her problems and needs. Research indicates that most addicted individuals need at least 3 months in treatment to significantly reduce or stop their drug use and that the best outcomes occur with longer durations of treatment.
6. **Counseling—individual and/or group—and other behavioral therapies are the most commonly used forms of drug abuse treatment.** Behavioral therapies vary in their focus and may involve addressing a patient's motivations to change, building skills to resist drug use, replacing drug-using activities with constructive and rewarding activities, improving problem-solving skills, and facilitating better interpersonal relationships.
7. **Medications are an important element of treatment for many patients, especially when combined with counseling and other behavioral therapies.** For example, methadone and buprenorphine are effective in helping individuals addicted to heroin or other opioids stabilize their lives and reduce their illicit drug use. Also, for persons addicted to nicotine, a nicotine replacement product (nicotine patches or gum) or an oral medication (bupropion or varenicline) can be an effective component of treatment when part of a comprehensive behavioral treatment program.
8. **An individual's treatment and services plan must be assessed continually and modified as necessary to ensure it meets his or her changing needs.** A patient may require varying combinations of services and treatment components during the course of treatment and recovery. In addition to counseling or psychotherapy, a patient may require medication, medical services, family therapy, parenting instruction, vocational rehabilitation and/or social and legal services. For many patients, a continuing care approach provides the best results, with treatment intensity varying according to a person's changing needs.
9. **Many drug-addicted individuals also have other mental disorders.** Because drug abuse and addiction—both of which are mental disorders—often co-occur with other mental illnesses, patients presenting with one condition should be assessed for the other(s). And when these problems co-occur, treatment should address both (or all), including the use of medications as appropriate.
10. **Medically assisted detoxification is only the first stage of addiction treatment and by itself does little to change long-term drug abuse.** Although medically assisted detoxification can safely manage the acute physical symptoms of withdrawal, detoxification alone is rarely sufficient to help addicted individuals achieve long-term abstinence. Thus, patients should be encouraged to continue drug treatment following detoxification.
11. **Treatment does not need to be voluntary to be effective.** Sanctions or enticements from family, employment settings, and/or the criminal justice system can significantly increase treatment entry, retention rates, and the ultimate success of drug treatment interventions.
12. **Drug use during treatment must be monitored continuously, as lapses during treatment do occur.** Knowing their drug use is being monitored can be a powerful incentive for patients and can help them withstand urges to use drugs. Monitoring also provides an early indication of a return to drug use, signaling a possible need to adjust an individual's treatment plan to better meet his or her needs.
13. **Treatment programs should assess patients for the presence of HIV/AIDS, hepatitis B and C, tuberculosis, and other infectious diseases, as well as provide targeted risk-reduction counseling to help patients modify or change behaviors that place them at risk of contracting or spreading infectious diseases.** Targeted counseling specifically focused on reducing infectious disease risk can help patients further reduce or avoid substance-related and other high-risk behaviors. Treatment providers should encourage and support HIV screening and inform patients that highly active antiretroviral therapy (HAART) has proven effective in combating HIV, including among drug-abusing populations.

TABLE 24.3 Commonly Abused Prescription Drugs

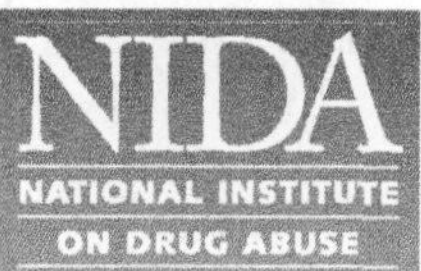

Visit NIDA at www.drugabuse.gov
National Institutes of Health
U.S. Department of Health and Human Services

Substances: Category and Name	Examples of *Commercial* and Street Names	DEA Schedule[a]/How Administered	*Intoxication Effects*/Health Risks
Depressants			Sedation/drowsiness, reduced anxiety, feelings of well-being, lowered inhibitions, slurred speech, poor concentration, confusion, dizziness, impaired coordination and memory/ slowed pulse, lowered blood pressure, slowed breathing, tolerance, withdrawal, addiction; increased risk of respiratory distress and death when combined with alcohol for barbiturates—euphoria, unusual excitement, fever, irritability/life-threatening withdrawal in chronic users
Barbiturates	*Amytal, Nembutal, Seconal, Phenobarbital:* barbs, reds, red birds, phennies, tooies, yellows, yellow jackets	II, III, IV/injected, swallowed	
Benzodiazepines	*Ativan, Halcion, Librium, Valium, Xanax, Klonopin:* candy, downers, sleeping pills, tranks	IV/swallowed	
Sleep medications	*Ambien (zolpidem), Sonata (zaleplon), Lunesta (eszopiclone)*	IV/swallowed	
Opioids and Morphine Derivatives[b]			Pain relief, euphoria, drowsiness, sedation, weakness, dizziness, nausea, impaired coordination, confusion, dry mouth, itching, sweating, clammy skin, constipation/slowed or arrested breathing, lowered pulse and blood pressure, tolerance, addiction, unconsciousness, coma, death; risk of death increased when combined with alcohol or other CNS depressants for fentanyl—80–100 times more potent analgesic than morphine for oxycodone—muscle relaxation/twice as potent analgesic as morphine; high abuse potential for codeine—less analgesia, sedation, and respiratory depression than morphine for methadone—used to treat opioid addiction and pain; significant overdose risk when used improperly
Codeine	*Empirin with Codeine, Fiorinal with Codeine, Robitussin A-C, Tylenol with Codeine:* Captain Cody, Cody, schoolboy (with glutethimide: doors & fours, loads, pancakes and syrup)	II, III, IV/injected, swallowed	
Morphine	*Roxanol, Duramorph:* M, Miss Emma, monkey, white stuff	II, III/injected, swallowed, smoked	
Methadone	*Methadone, Dolophine:* fizzies, amidone (with MDMA: chocolate chip cookies)	II/swallowed, injected	
Fentanyl and analogues	*Actiq, Duragesic, Sublimaze:* Apache, China girl, dance fever, friend, goodfella, jackpot, murder 8, TNT, Tango and Cash	II/injected, smoked, snorted	
Other opioid pain relievers: Oxycodone HCL Hydrocodone Bitartrate Hydromorphone Oxymorphone Meperidine Propoxyphene	*Tylox, Oxycontin, Percodan, Percocet:* Oxy, O.C., oxycontin, oxycet, hillbilly heroin, percs *Vicodin, Lortab, Lorcet:* vike, Watson-387 *Dilaudid:* juice, smack, D, footballs, dillies *Opana, Numorphan*	II, III, IV/chewed, swallowed, snorted, injected, suppositories	
	Numorphone: biscuits, blue heaven, blues, Mrs. O, octagons, stop signs, O Bomb *Demerol, meperidine hydrochloride:* demmies, pain killer *Darvon, Darvocet*		

(continued)

TABLE 24.3 Commonly Abused Prescription Drugs (*continued*)

Substances: Category and Name	Examples of *Commercial* and Street Names	DEA Schedule[a]/How Administered	*Intoxication Effects*/Health Risks
Stimulants			Feelings of exhilaration, increased energy, mental alertness/increased heart rate, blood pressure, and metabolism, reduced appetite, weight loss, nervousness, insomnia, seizures, heart attack, stroke for amphetamines—rapid breathing, tremor, loss of coordination, irritability, anxiousness, restlessness/delirium, panic, paranoia, hallucinations, impulsive behavior, aggressiveness, tolerance, addiction for methylphenidate—increase or decrease in blood pressure, digestive problems, loss of appetite, weight loss
Amphetamines	*Biphetamine, Dexedrine, Adderall:* bennies, black beauties, crosses, hearts, LA turnaround, speed, truck drivers, uppers	II/injected, swallowed, smoked, snorted	
Methylphenidate	*Concerta, Ritalin:* JIF, MPH, R-ball, Skippy, the smart drug, vitamin R	II/injected, swallowed, snorted	
Other Compounds			Euphoria, slurred speech/increased heart rate and blood pressure, dizziness, nausea, vomiting, confusion, paranoia, distorted visual perceptions, impaired motor function
Dextromethorphan (DXM)	*Found in some cough and cold medications:* Robotripping, Robo, Triple C	Not scheduled/ swallowed	

[a]Schedule I and II drugs have a high potential for abuse. They require greater storage security and have a quota on manufacturing, among other restrictions. Schedule I drugs are available for research only and have no approved medical use. Schedule II drugs are available only by prescription and require a new prescription for each refill. Schedule III and IV drugs are available by prescription, may have five refills in 6 months, and may be ordered orally. Most Schedule V drugs are available over the counter.
[b]Taking drugs by injection can increase the risk of infection through needle contamination with staphylococci, HIV, hepatitis, and other organisms. Injection is a more common practice for opioids, but risks apply to any medication taken by injection.

A. Genetic
B. Familial
C. Environmental
D. Occupational
E. Socioeconomic
F. Cultural
G. Personality
H. Life stress
I. Psychiatric comorbidity
J. Biologic
K. Social learning and behavioral conditioning

Common Complaints

Patients' complaints will be focused on the symptoms of the problem rather than the substance dependence. The problem itself will be avoided through the use of denial, minimization, blaming, and projection (all signs of the disease of substance dependence).

A. Chronic anxiety and tension
B. Insomnia
C. Chronic depression
D. Headaches and/or back pain

Consider patients who present frequently with somatic complaints, such as back pain or headache, as "drug seeking," especially when the patient knows what drugs work best or asks for specific narcotic analgesics.

E. Blackouts
F. Gastrointestinal problems
G. Tachycardia/palpitations
H. Frequent falls or minor injuries

Substance abuse should be suspected in all patients who present with accidents or signs of repeated trauma, especially to the head.

I. Problems with a loved one; problems at work or with friends

Other Signs and Symptoms

A. Defensiveness about alcohol/drug use or vagueness with answers
B. History of problems with family life, marital relationships, work, finances, and physical health
C. Change in spiritual beliefs (stops attending religious services)
D. Unexplained job changes and multiple traffic accidents
E. History of impulsive behavior, fighting, or unexplained falls
F. Arrest for public drunkenness, driving under the influence, or illegal activity when alcohol/drugs were involved
G. Tremors (shakes)
H. Delirium tremors (DTs)

I. Seizures related to drugs
J. Hallucinations
K. History of chronic family chaos and instability
L. Physical indications of chronic alcohol/drug use include spider angiomas, ruddy nose and face, nasal lesions, bruxism, swollen features, bruises, needle marks/tracks, cutaneous abscesses, malnourished, anemia, jaundice, and severe dental problems such as "meth mouth."
M. Active withdrawal symptoms include nausea and vomiting, malaise, weakness, tachycardia, diaphoresis, tremors, lightheadedness or dizziness, insomnia, irritability, confusion, perceptual abnormalities or hallucinations (auditory, visual, or tactile), paresthesia, blurred vision, diarrhea, anorexia, abdominal cramps, severe depression, severe anxiety, piloerection, fasciculation (muscle twitching), rhinorrhea, fever, elevated blood pressure and pulse, tinnitus, nystagmus, delirium, or seizures.
N. Overdose symptoms related to drug(s) include seizures, cardiovascular depression/collapse, and respiratory depression/collapse. Be prepared to provide cardiovascular and respirator support and supportive care until transport.

Subjective Data

A. Review the onset, duration, and course of presenting complaints.
B. The U.S. Preventive Services Task Force (USPSTF) recommends that all adults be screened in primary care for alcohol and drug use.
C. Question the patient regarding relatives with a history of alcohol, tobacco, or drug use or problems pertaining to use.
D. When questioning the patient, assume some use, for example, "At what age did you first start drinking?" Start with the least invasive questions first: Cigarettes, OTC medications, prescription medications, then alcohol, marijuana, stimulants, opiates, sedatives, hypnotics, benzodiazepines, barbiturates, hallucinogens, inhalants, steroids, and other drugs.
E. Review use of the following drugs concerning quantity and type (if cigarettes, brand smoked; if alcohol, type of alcohol: Beer, wine, hard liquor), and age at initiation. Query regarding previous attempts to stop use.
F. Start with the past and proceed to the present with use; include first use of the mood-altering substance, amounts, and the last use of the particular substance and amount.
G. Follow the CAGE test. The **CAGE** (2 out of 4) is highly predictive of addiction.
   1. Have you ever tried to **c**ut down on your alcohol/drug use?
   2. Do you get **a**nnoyed if someone mentions your use is a problem?
   3. Do you ever feel **g**uilty about your use?
   4. Do you ever have an "**e**ye-opener" first thing in the morning after you've been drinking or using the night before?
H. If patient admits drinking or drug use, ascertain specific amounts and last use of each substance.
I. Establish usual weight and recent loss and in what length of time.
J. Determine whether patient experiences suicidal ideation and if there is a history of past attempts (see section on "Suicide").

Physical Examination

A. Check temperature, pulse, respirations, blood pressure, and weight.
B. Inspect
   1. Observe general appearance, dress, grooming, breath odor, wasted appearance, attitude, sad affect, psychomotor retardation, or tremors.
   2. Conduct a dermal examination for spider angiomas, bruises, track marks, color, pallor, rash, jaundice, petechiae, and gynecomastia in men (hallucinogens).
   3. Examine the eyes for sclera color and features, pupil size, and reactivity.
   4. Inspect the nasal mucosa for erythema, edema, spider telangiectasis, and discharge; look for septal lesions or perforation, deviation, and polyps.
   5. Inspect the mouth/pharynx: Oral lesions, poor dental hygiene, erythema, and teeth for uneven surfaces, tooth decay, and gum erosion.
C. Palpate
   1. Palpate the neck and thyroid.
   2. Palpate the axilla and groin for lymphadenopathy.
   3. Palpate the abdomen; note hepatomegaly/tenderness.
D. Percuss
   1. Percuss the chest; note pulmonary consolidation.
   2. Percuss the abdomen for hepatosplenomegaly.
E. Auscultate
   1. Auscultate the heart for murmur, new S4 gallop, single S2, and arrhythmias.
   2. Auscultate the lungs for rales, effusion, and consolidation.
F. Perform neurologic examination/mental status.

Diagnostic Tests

A. Blood alcohol level
B. Cotinine level (nicotine) (where available)
C. Urine drug screen
D. CBC with differential
E. Platelet count
F. HIV or hepatitis

Intravenous drug use contributes strongly to the spread of AIDS, hepatitis B and hepatitis C, and other infectious diseases. Consider evaluation for sexually transmitted infections.

G. Antinuclear antibody, erythrocyte sedimentation rate, and rheumatoid factor
H. Electrolytes
I. Liver panel
   1. Elevated liver enzymes can also be attributed to overuse of acetaminophen (Tylenol), found in combination with opiates.
J. Blood cultures (fever)
K. Bone density studies
   1. Patients who have been drinking for years should have bone density studies done because alcohol increases the risk for osteoporosis.

Differential Diagnoses

A. Substance use disorder
B. Chronic pain syndrome
C. Anxiety
D. Depression

Plan

A. General interventions
   1. Discuss your concerns about alcohol, nicotine, or drug use and discuss addiction treatment with the patient.
   2. At each office visit, provide support to help prevent relapse. If relapse occurs, encourage the patient to try again immediately.
   3. Consider signing a contract with the patient to stop smoking, drinking, or using drugs.
   4. Assess potential for suicide with every office visit.
   5. If possible, obtain confirmation of the patient's abstinence from a family member.
   6. Stress the importance of 12-step meetings such as Alcoholics Anonymous (AA), Cocaine Anonymous (CA), and Narcotics Anonymous (NA).
   7. Have the patient sign a written release of information so that you can speak with a rehabilitation counselor. If the patient is willing, refer to an alcohol and drug treatment facility or smoking cessation program, after initial assessment and differential diagnosis is made.
   8. Treat physical/laboratory findings as indicated.
   9. Identify potential withdrawal symptoms from the cessation of stimulants, such as caffeine intake reduction, alcohol, and drug use.
   10. If malnourished, discuss dietary needs and treatment.
B. Patient teaching
   1. Educate the patient about the impact of alcohol, tobacco, and drugs on physical/emotional health. Provide information for the patient to read at home.
   2. See the Section III Patient Teaching Guide for this chapter, "Alcohol and Drug Dependence."
C. Pharmaceutical therapy
   1. Nicotine replacement
      Consider nicotine replacement for those who smoke more than one pack of cigarettes per day or who smoke their first cigarette within 30 minutes of waking. Stress that there is "no smoking" while using nicotine replacement.
      a. Nicotine patch
         i. 21 mg/24 hr for 4 weeks *then*
         ii. 14 mg/24 hr for 2 weeks *then*
         iii. 7 mg/24 hr for 2 weeks
      b. Nicotine gum
         i. 2 to 4 mg of nicotine gum per hour with maximum of 24 pieces/d for up to 12 weeks
      c. Nicotine lozenges
         i. 2 to 4 mg every 1 to 2 hours for 6 weeks
         ii. 2 mg every 2 to 4 hours for 3 weeks
         iii. 2 mg every 4 to 8 hours for 3 weeks
   2. Nonnicotine therapy
      a. Adults: Bupropion (Zyban, Wellbutrin) 150 mg daily for 3 days, then increase to 150 mg twice daily. Treat for 7 to 12 weeks. The patient may continue to smoke during the first 2 weeks of starting medication. This medication should not be given to patients with seizure disorders.
      b. Varenicline (Chantix): Start at 0.5 mg/d for the first 3 days, then for the next 4 days, 0.5 mg twice daily. After the first 7 days the dose is 1 mg twice daily.
         i. Encourage the patient to choose a stop date for smoking and start the Chantix 1 to 2 weeks prior to this stop date.
         ii. Patients should be encouraged to quit even if they have relapses.
         iii. Instruct patients that the most common side effects of Chantix are insomnia, vivid or strange dreams, and nausea. Advise that side effects are usually transient.
         iv. Give precautions to the patient regarding potential side effects of mood swings, aggression, homicidal thoughts, psychosis, anxiety, and panic disorder, which may occur on rare occasions.
         v. See package inserts or *Physicians' Desk Reference* for detailed instructions.
   3. Detoxification and methadone maintenance: Should be performed by specially licensed and trained professionals.
   4. Disulfiram (Antabuse) therapy is not recommended. Patients who consume alcohol after taking Antabuse can become extremely ill.

5. Refer patient to physician or specialist if patient is experiencing withdrawals; consider admission to rehabilitation center for detoxification and treatment.

Follow-Up

A. Make a follow-up appointment weekly. Make contact with the referral source (smoking cessation program, alcohol/drug rehabilitation program) before the next follow-up visit to check on the patient's progress. At weekly visit, question the patient regarding compliance.
B. Order blood alcohol, urine drug screen, or nicotine level (as appropriate) with every office visit while in outpatient treatment and throughout the year following treatment.
C. Once positive change is seen, the patient can be seen monthly. Discuss changes the patient has made, past relapses, circumstances under which they occurred, and any special concerns.
D. Refer to the medical diagnosis for other applicable follow-up recommendations.

Consultation/Referral

A. Refer patients with drug and/or alcohol dependence to a community mental health center that has an outpatient alcohol/drug rehabilitation program or to a specialist in the community who deals frequently with substance abuse/dependence.
B. Planning a family meeting to confront the patient is best done with the help of an experienced mental health professional.
C. Have referral numbers at close hand, so that the patient's moment of motivation is not lost.
D. Refer family members of alcoholics/drug addicts to Al-Anon, Nar-Anon, Co-dependents Anonymous, or Adult Children of Alcoholics (ACOA) meetings.

Individual Considerations

A. Pregnancy
   1. Substance-dependent pregnant women frequently avoid early prenatal care for fear of identification and reprisal.
   2. Cocaine use is associated with abruptio placenta and preterm labor. Consider drug screen for emergent admissions for patients in preterm labor and abruption.
   3. Notify the hospital nursery personnel/neonatologist before delivery to closely monitor the newborn for withdrawal and seizure precautions.
   4. Nicotine/smoking use is associated with intrauterine growth restriction, preterm delivery, and bleeding in pregnancy.
   5. Nicotine-dependent pregnant women should be encouraged to stop smoking without pharmacologic treatment. The nicotine patch should be used during pregnancy only if the increased likelihood of smoking cessation, with its potential benefits, outweighs the risk of nicotine replacement and potential concomitant smoking. Similar factors should be considered in lactating women.
   6. Pregnant women who use alcohol, tobacco, or drugs should always be classified as substance dependent rather than substance abusive.

B. Adults
   1. With women, tolerance can be established by asking the question, "How many drinks does it take to make you high?" More than two drinks indicates some tolerance.
   2. In considering a diagnosis of alcohol dependence, consider the following diagnostic findings: Hypertension; nonspecific EKG changes; cardiomyopathy; palpitations; increased mean cell volume; decreased red blood cell count; low platelet count; increased alanine aminotransferase (ALT), aspartate aminotransferase (AST), lactic dehydrogenase, g-glutamyltranspeptidase, alkaline phosphatase; type IV hyperlipoproteinemia; gout; and adult-onset diabetes mellitus.

C. Geriatrics
   1. Alcohol use disorders are often missed in this population because of reduced social and occupational functioning. Evaluate for signs of poor self-care, hygiene, and malnutrition.
   2. At-risk drinking for persons older than 65 is defined as more than three drinks on one occasion or greater than seven drinks per week.
   3. Pain medications and benzodiazepines, along with multiple medications for health problems, may contribute to a substance abuse problem.

D. Partners/family members
   1. For fear of retribution, the family may remain silent about the problem, even if accompanying the patient.
   2. Some studies by corporate business show that, per capita, business spends more money on the care of family members of substance-dependent patients than on the employee.
   3. Refer family members of alcoholics/drug addicts to Al-Anon, Nar-Anon, Co-dependents Anonymous, or ACOA meetings.

Resources

National Institute on Drug Abuse (NIDA): www.drugabuse.gov

Substance Abuse and Mental Health Services Administration: www.samhsa.gov/treatment. Offers free and downloadable publications for patient education, treatment, prevention, and recovery. Also includes professional and research topics and substance abuse treatment facility locator by state.

Suicide

Definition

A. Suicide is defined as the intentional destruction of one's own life. It is the most critical consequence of mental illness and occurs in all diagnostic psychiatric categories. Knowing the risk factors for suicide and eliciting key clinical features that differentiate the truly suicidal patient from the attention-seeker are of utmost importance. **Symptoms are often missed because they can be very subtle. Because there are important legal, social, and religious implications to suicide, the general health care practitioner should not attempt to treat these high-risk patients. This section focuses on identifying the suicidal patient for immediate referral to a psychiatrist or psychiatric inpatient facility.**

Incidence

A. The Rule of Sevens is helpful in the assessment of these patients:
   1. **One out of seven** with recurrent depressive illness commit suicide.
   2. **70%** of suicides have depressive illness.
   3. **70%** of suicides see their primary care physician within 6 weeks of suicide.
   4. Suicide is the **11th leading cause of death** in the United States; for young people between the ages of 15 to 24, it is the **third** leading cause of death.

B. The United States averages 10.6 suicides per 100,000 population annually. Every year between 30,000 and 35,000 people take their own lives, not including those individuals who die as a result of fatal accidents due to impaired concentration and attention, and death due to illnesses that may be sequelae (e.g., alcohol abuse).

C. According to the World Health Organization, by the year 2020, depression will be the number two cause, worldwide, of individuals losing healthy years of their lives to depression. Estimates associate 16,000 suicides in the United States annually with depressive disorder. Fifteen percent of those hospitalized for major depressive disorder attempt suicide. Fifteen percent of patients with severe primary major depressive disorder of at least 1 month's duration eventually commit suicide.

D. The rate of suicide in young adults has more than doubled since 1950. Little is known about midlife suicides compared to adolescent and elderly suicides. Midlife suicide rates tend to be highest among White men, although female suicide rates peak in midlife. Males exceed females in suicide completions but not in attempts. Whites are twice as likely as non-Whites to commit suicide, though in the 25- to 34-year age group their rates are equal. Rates for widowed, divorced, or separated individuals are higher than for those who are married. Rates are highest in Protestants, intermediate in Jews, and lowest in Catholics.

Pathogenesis

A. Recent studies confirm that some changes in the noradrenergic system along with reduced serotonin levels are associated with suicide. In recent studies independent of psychiatric diagnoses, one researcher identified a suicidality syndrome consisting of hopelessness, ruminative thinking, social withdrawal, and lack of activity as core symptoms.

B. Familial, genetic, early-life loss experiences, and comorbid alcoholism may be causal factors. In adolescence, depression is the largest single risk factor for suicidal behavior, although family relationship difficulties make a significant independent contribution to this. Environmental stressors in the presence of psychiatric disorders may also be responsible for initiating the impulsive behavior leading to suicide. The risk of suicidal behaviors is higher in those with mental disorders than in those with mood disorders.

Predisposing Factors "SAD PERSONAS"

S = sex
A = age
D = depression
P = previous attempts
E = ethanol abuse
R = rational thinking loss
S = social support loss
O = organized plan
N = no spouse
A = availability of lethal means
S = sickness

Also consider gender, race and ethnicity, medications, and other medical conditions.

Common Complaints

A. Overt or indirect suicide talk or threats: "You won't be bothered by me much longer."

Any mention of dying or ending one's life must be taken seriously.

B. Depressed or anxious mood due to depression

Every depressed patient must be assessed for suicide risk.

C. Significant recent loss such as spouse, job, or self-esteem

D. Unexpected change in behavior such as making a will, intense talks with friends, and giving away possessions

E. Unexpected change in attitude such as suddenly cheerful, angry, or withdrawn

F. Atypical symptoms of depression in the elderly such as impaired ability to communicate, intractable tinnitus, and feelings of helplessness

Other Signs and Symptoms

Indications for hospitalization of suicidal patients

A. Psychosis
B. Intoxication with drugs or alcohol that cannot be evaluated and treated over a period of time in the emergency department
C. No change in affect or symptoms despite the intervention of the physician, family, and friends
D. Command hallucinations
E. Lack of access to, or low availability of, outpatient resources
F. Family exhaustion
G. Escalating number of suicide attempts
H. Uncertainty about the risk of suicide
I. Severe psychic anxiety, anxious ruminations, and global insomnia are acute risk factors.

Subjective Data

A. Ascertain the patient's intention. Ask why he or she wants to die.
   1. Asking the patient about suicide does not give the patient any ideas about suicide.
B. Determine whether the patient has thought of a suicide plan. The more specific the plan, the more likely the act. A well-worked out, realistic, and potentially lethal plan suggests great risk.
C. Rule out the presence of psychiatric or organic factors such as psychotic depression, thought disorder, or sedative self-medication.
D. Determine whether the precipitating crisis is resolving satisfactorily to the patient.
E. Take an "inventory of loss." Determine the losses the patient has incurred in the last several months or years.
F. Review the patient's plans for the future.
G. Determine whether the patient thinks he or she is going to commit suicide.
H. Evaluate whether the patient has a caring family or other support systems.

Plan

A. General interventions
   1. If the patient is suicidal, refer immediately. Make sure there is someone with the patient at all times.
   2. If the patient came alone, call a family member or friend to accompany the patient to the hospital emergency room or treatment center.
   3. If you are fearful the patient will try to escape or leave unaccompanied, escort the patient to the hospital emergency room where commitment papers for involuntary hospital admission can be completed.

Be sure to advise the hospital staff of your concerns regarding the patient's suicidal status.

B. Patient teaching
   1. Educate patient and family regarding treatment with medication for depression. Discuss benefits/risks of medication and side effects.
   2. Encourage the patient to enroll in counseling with a psychologist/therapist to discuss current problems/needs.
   3. Determine if social services need to be contacted for patient for support services.
   4. Provide local resources for counseling and social services as appropriate.
   5. If patient is not hospitalized, make sure that family or friends are aware of the patient's status and that he or she has someone to talk to and monitor his or her condition until the next office appointment.
C. Pharmaceutical therapy: Patients with suicide potential should never be given more than 1 g or 1 week's supply of TCAs.
D. Documentation is critical. Make sure all statements are recorded and the decision-making process is followed.

Follow-Up

A. After emergency admission for suicidal ideation or threats, patients should be closely observed, especially in the first year after the serious suicide attempt.
B. With each visit, question the patient regarding suicidal ideation or a plan (see Subjective Data for important questions to ask).

Consultation/Referral

A. Consult with the patient's psychiatric practitioner. Obtain a release of information from the patient.
B. Be sure the patient continues to follow up with psychiatric counseling and medication management (see "Depression" section).

Individual Considerations

A. Pregnancy: A woman with a history of depression or previous postpartum depression is at high risk for postpartum depression (recurrent) (see "Postpartum Depression" section in Chapter 15, "Obstetrics Guidelines").
B. Geriatrics
   1. White men, age older than 80, have the highest rate of suicide of any age group in the United States.
   2. Older persons use the usual means for suicide as well as a slower plan including not eating, stopping prescription drugs or overmedicating, increasing alcohol intake, and refusing treatment.
   3. The elderly population is more susceptible to the adverse effects of medications.

4. Antidepressants should be started at the lowest doses and slowly increased for the elderly. The SSRIs are considered the first line of antidepressant therapy in the elderly population (see "Depression" section).

Violence Against the Older Adult—*Cheryl A. Glass*

Definition

Abuse of older individuals, defined as older than age 65, is associated with loss of functional capacity, depression, cognitive impairment, increased morbidity, and mortality. Perpetrators include partners, family members (of all ages), as well as strangers. There are several types of maltreatment in this population.

A. Physical abuse: Willful unnecessary restraint, the infliction of physical pain, or injury
B. Sexual abuse: Nonconsensual sexual contact
C. Psychological abuse: Infliction of emotional harm, bullying, ridicule, verbal abuse, terrorizing, and threatening to place in a long-term facility until the elder submits
D. Neglect: Failing to provide for needs and protection of a vulnerable adult
E. Self-neglect (subset of neglect): Malnutrition, dehydration, lack of personal hygiene, listlessness, hoarding
F. Abandonment: Desertion
G. Financial exploitation: Misappropriation of resources, utilities turned off for nonpayment, essential purchases including food or medicine not made, discrepancies in personal bookkeeping including unexplained credit card activities, recent changes in property titles, deeds, and refinanced mortages
H. Health care fraud and abuse: Not providing care, but charging for services; overmedicating; or undermedicating

Incidence

A. In 2011 the population age 65 and older was estimated to be 41.4 million. It is estimated that one in every eight people in the United States is an older person (65+). By 2040, the population of those 85+ is projected to be 14.1 million.
B. The exact incidence of elder abuse, neglect, exploitation, and self-neglect is unknown; however, it is believed to be common. The incidence is underreported due to the reluctance to report abuse, fear of implicating family members, and fear of being removed from the home.
C. Abuse is not uncommon in the institutional setting.
D. The highest rate of abuse is among elderly women older than age 80, with the abuser being the spouse or adult child. In the case of cognitive impairment, the victim may not remember or recognize abuse.

Pathogenesis

Maltreatment of vulnerable adults occurs by people who have an ongoing relationship with the older person when there is an expectation of responsibility; sons/daughters, spouses/intimate partners, other family members such as grandchildren, and others, including paid and unpaid caregivers. There are several identifying psychopathologies in the abuser.

A. Physical frailty and mental impairment of the victim plays an indirect role. The victim may have a decreased ability to defend or escape.
B. Caregiver stressors from caring for the elderly patient, including the patient's physical and verbal demands. Psychosocial factors of the caregiver, mental illness, and alcohol or drug abuse contribute.
C. The child who was once abused may continue the cycle of violence transferred to the parent.

Predisposing Factors

A. Age: 65 years and older (some studies indicate age 60)
B. Institutionalized
C. Cognitive impairment/diminished capacity
D. Decreased capacity for performing activities of daily living (ADL)
   1. Feeding themselves
   2. Bathing and dressing themselves
   3. Going to the toilet and performing hygiene themselves
E. Decreased capacity performing instrumental activities of daily living (IADL)
   1. Ability to prepare meals
   2. Ability to do household chores
   3. Ability to use the telephone
   4. Ability to manage personal finances
F. Females suffer a higher incidence of physical/sexual abuse.
G. Male gender is associated with self-neglect associated with impaired ADL and IADL
H. Family stressors involving the caretaker

Common Complaints

A. Depression
B. Falls
C. History of hip fracture
D. Pressure ulcers
E. Bruises, lacerations, and burns

Other Signs and Symptoms

A. Indications of healing spiral fractures on x-ray
B. Poor nutrition: Lack of resources/transportation to obtain food; caregiver not providing adequate nutrition/withholding food and/or dehydration
C. Multiple hospitalizations
D. Recurrent urinary tract infections

E. Noncompliance: May not be able to pay for medications; medications may be withheld or even given in excess by the caregiver.
F. Complaints of sexual abuse
  1. Pain or soreness in the genital area
  2. Bruises or lacerations on the perineum/rectum
  3. Vaginal or rectal bleeding
  4. Extremely upset when bathed, changed, or examined
G. Traumatic tooth and/or hair loss
H. Sedation from overmedicating
I. Changes in personality
J. Frequent unexplained injuries

Subjective Data

A. The caregiver often refuses to leave the patient alone and may answer questions for the patient.
B. The caregiver has a different explanation of the injury.
C. Ask the patient directly about abuse, neglect, or exploitation.
  1. Has anyone at home threatened or ever hurt you?
  2. Are you afraid of anyone at home?
  3. Are you left alone for long periods of time?
  4. Who cooks your meals? How often and what amounts of food do you eat?
  5. Who handles your financial business? Have you signed any documents that you didn't understand?
D. Assess the patient's living arrangements. Has the patient ever told family or friends, called hotlines, or attempted to leave the caregiver?

Physical Examination

A. Assessment
  1. Observation: If abuse is suspected, enforce the need to do the physical examination in private. Do a full body examination.
    a. Forensic exams need thorough documentation of injuries.
      i. Use color photographs before any treatment is started.
      ii. Make at least one full body photograph and a facial photograph.
      iii. Make close-up photographs of all injuries.
      iv. Use a ruler to identify/document the size of the injuries.
      v. Documentation on the back of the photographs should include the patient's name, date, photographer's name, as well as any witness to the examination. The photographer should also sign each photograph.
      vi. Use direct quotes of the victim's history.
  2. Check blood pressure, pulse, respirations, and weight.
  3. General observation: Observe for depression, withdrawn, flat affect, fearfulness, poor eye contact, inappropriate dress, and signs of malnutrition.
  4. Observe for poor hygiene, presence of urine and feces, matted or lice-infected hair, odors, dirty nails and skin, and soiled clothing.
  5. Assess cognitive abilities, depression, and functional ability of ADL and IADL.
B. Inspect
  1. Dermal examination for signs of burns, tears, lacerations, impression marks, and bruises in different stages of healing. Frequent areas of the body involved are the neck, arms, and/or legs. Evaluate for the presence of decubitus/pressure ulcers. Signs of dehydration include dry fragile skin, dry sore mouth, and mental confusion.
  2. Oral examination for poor oral hygiene, absence of dentures, and dry mucus membranes.
  3. Evaluate breasts and genitals for lacerations, and hematomas of the vagina or labia.
C. Auscultate
  1. Auscultate all lung fields.
  2. Auscultate bowel sounds in all four quadrants of the abdomen.
D. Palpate: Evaluate for dislocation, fractures, sprains, and contusions to the wrists, forearms, and shoulders.
E. Percuss: Abdomen and chest (if indicated).
F. Genital/rectal examination
  1. Evaluate genitals/anal area for redness, swelling, bruising, hematomas, abrasions, or lacerations.
  2. Evaluate for evidence of sperm.
  3. Evaluate for the presence of foreign bodies.

Diagnostic Tests

A. Diagnostic tests and x-rays are ordered dependent on the type of presenting complaints.
B. Obtain a CT for evaluation of injuries to the head and assault to the face, neck, or head. A CT or Doppler may be ordered for abdominal injuries.
C. Order laboratory testing to evaluate dehydration, malnutrition, electrolyte imbalance, and medication/substance abuse
  1. CBC
  2. Chemistry-7
  3. Urinalysis
  4. Calcium, magnesium, and phosphorus
  5. Drug/alcohol screen
  6. Serum levels for relevant medications
D. Obtain DNA samples if sexual abuse is present.

Differential Diagnoses

A. Elder abuse
B. Depression

C. Abdominal trauma
D. Sexual assault
E. Gait disturbance/fall
F. Pathologic fracture
G. Epidural/subdural hematoma

Plan

A. Provide a safe environment.
B. Clearly document the history, physical findings, and interventions.
C. Determine the perpetrator(s).
D. Evaluate the need for emergency room/hospital admission.

Patient Teaching

A. Reinforce that abuse/neglect is not the victim's fault. Elderly abuse is very common, and the aged do not deserve to be abused.
B. Help is available.

Pharmaceutical Therapy

A. Prescriptions are related to physical injuries.
B. Recommend treatment for sexually transmitted infections in the oral anal genital areas.

Follow-Up

The Department of Health and Human Services National Center on Elder Abuse Administration on Aging maintains a State-by-State Resource site that includes directories, helplines, hotlines, referral sources, state government agencies and laws, and regulations related to elder abuse located at ncea.aoa.gov/Stop_Abuse/Get_Help/State/index.aspx

A. Develop a follow-up plan. All states have legislation protecting against abuse, neglect, and exploitation of the older population.
B. Know if your state has mandatory requirements to report any suspicion of elder mistreatment.
C. Abuse of a disabled person must be reported to the Disabled Person Protection Commission.
D. Know if your state has additional regulations related to self-neglect. Contact adult protective services or law enforcement agencies.
E. At the present time, there is no recommendation for universal screening of all older adult patients except in nursing facilities.

Consultation/Referral

A. Arrange a social work consultation to coordinate an in-home geriatric assessment visit.
B. Facilitate referrals to a shelter, counseling, and legal services.
C. Contact a sexual assault nurse examiner (SANE) qualified health care provider, if indicated.
D. Refer to the community area agency for assistance.
E. Refer for a psychiatric consultation, if indicated.
F. Refer for a neurologic or neurosurgical consultation for intracranial injuries or focal neurologic findings.
G. Refer for an orthopedic consultation for fractures.

Resources

American Association of Retired Persons (AARP): www.aarp.org

Clearinghouse on Abuse and Neglect of the Elderly (CANE): www.cane.udel.edu

Help Hotline for suspected elder abuse, neglect, or exploitation: 1-800-677-1116

National Adult Protective Services Association (NAPSA): www.napsa-now.org

National Center on Elder Abuse Administration on Aging (NCEA): www.ncea.aoa.gov

Bibliography

Administration on Aging Administration for Community Living U.S. Department of Health and Human Services. (2012). *A profile of older Americans: 2012.* Retrieved from www.aoa.gov/AoARoot/Aging_Statistics/Profile/2012/docs/2012profile.pdf

Alzheimer's Disease International. *The prevalence of dementia worldwide.* London, Alzheimer's Disease International, December 2008. Retrieved from www.alz.co.uk/adi/pdf/prevalence.pdf

American College of Obstetricians and Gynecologists. (2012, February). Intimate partner violence. *Committee Opinion, 518,* 1–5.

American Psychiatric Association. (2013). *Diagnostic and statistical manual of mental disorders* (5th ed.). Arlington, VA: American Psychiatric Publishing.

Angstman, K. B., Pietruszewski, P., Rasmussen, N. H., Wilkinson, J. M., & Katzelnick, D. J. (2012). Depression remission after six months of collaborative care management: Role of initial severity of depression in outcome. *Mental Health in Family Medicine, 9*(2), 99–106.

Attention Deficit Disorder Association. Retrieved from www.add.org

Beck, A. T., Ward, C. H., Mendelson, M., Mock, J., & Erbaugh, J. (1961). An inventory for measuring depression. *Archives of General Psychiatry, 4,* 561–571.

Brandt, N. J., & Piechocki, J. M. (2013). Treatment of insomnia in older adults. *Journal of Gerontological Nursing, 39*(4), 48–54.

Buysse, D. (2013). Insomnia. *Journal of the American Medical Association, 309*(7), 706–716.

Cahoo, C. G. (2012). Depression in older adults. *American Journal of Nursing, 112*(11), 22–31.

Centers for Disease Control National Center for Injury Prevention and Control. (2010). *National intimate and partner and sexual violence survey 2010 summary report.* Retrieved from www.cdc.gov_violenceprevention_pdf_nisvs_report2010-a-pdf

Chan, D., Livingston, G., Jones, L., & Sampson, E. (2013). Grief reactions in dementia carers: A systematic review. *International Journal of Geriatric Psychiatry, 28*(1), 1–17.

Cole, S., & Lanham, J. (2011). Failure to thrive: An update. *American Family Physician, 83*(7), 829–834.

Dating Abuse Stops Here (DASH). (n.d.a). *Create a safety plan.* Retrieved from www.datingabusestopshere.com/create-a-safety-plan

Dating Abuse Stops Here (DASH). (n.d.b). *Warning signs in depth.* Retrieved from www.datingabusestopshere.com/warning-signs/warning-signs-in-depth

Department of Health and Human Services NCEA National Center on Elder Abuse Administration on Aging. (n.d.). *State resources.* Retrieved from http://ncea.aoa.gov/Stop_Abuse/Get_Help/State/index.aspx

Devries, K. M., Mak, J. Y. T., Garcia-Moreno, C., Petzold, M., Child, J. C., Falder, G., ... Watts, C. H. (2013, June 30). The global prevalence of intimate partner violence against women. *Sciencexpress.* Retrieved from http://www.sciencemag.org/content/early/recent

Dhekney, K., Faghih, S., & Secord, El. (2013). Fever and failure to thrive in toddler. *Contemporary Pediatrics, 30*(1), 35–40.

DoD Safe Helpline. (n.d.). *About RAINN.* Retrieved from https://m.safehelpline.org/about-rainn

Domestic Abuse Intervention Project. (n.d.). *Abuse of children wheel.* Retrieved from www.duluth-model.org

Domestic Violence, Sexual Assault and Stalking Data Resource Center. (n.d.). *State summaries.* Retrieved from http://www.jrsa.org/dvsa-drc/state-summaries.shtml

Domesticviolence.org. (n.d.). *Personalized safety plan-domestic violence.* Retrieved from www.domesticviolence.org/personalized_safety-plan/

Dowlati, Y., Hermann, N., Swordfager, W., Liu, H., Sham, L., Reim, E. K., & Lanctôt, K. L. (2010). A meta-analysis of cytokines in major depression. *Biological Psychiatry, 67*(5), 446–457.

Eldercare.gov. (n.d). *Protect your pocketbook, tips to avoid financial exploitation.* Retrieved from http://www.eldercare.gov/Eldercare.NET/Public/Resources/Brochures/docs/FinancialExploitationBrochure-508.pdf

Ewing, J. A. (1984). Detecting alcoholism: The CAGE questionnaire. *JAMA: Journal of the American Medical Association, 252,* 1905–1907.

Futures Without Violence, Formerly Family Violence Prevention Fund. (n.d.). The facts on the military and violence against women. Retrieved from http://www.futureswithoutviolence.org/userfiles/Military%20Factsheet%20update%2003%2003%2013.pdf

Geier, L. (2011, September). Identifying and managing generalized anxiety disorders in older adults. *The Journal for Nurse Practitioners, 7*(8), 693–694.

Ghio, L., Zanelli, E., Gotelli, S., Rossi, P., Natta, W., & Gabrielli, F. (2011). Involving patients who attempt suicide in suicide prevention: A focus groups study. *Journal of Psychiatric and Mental Health Nursing, 18*(6), 510–518.

Gilsenan, I. (2012). Nursing interventions to alleviate insomnia. *Nursing Older People, 24*(4), 14–18.

Hardy, S. (2013). Prevention and management of depression in primary care. *Nursing Standard, 27*(26), 51–56.

Haynes, P. L., Parthasarathy, S., Kersh, B., & Bootzin, R. R. (2011). Examination of insomnia and insomnia treatment in psychiatric inpatients. *International Journal of Mental Health Nursing, 20*(2), 130–136.

HealthyPlace America's Mental Health Channel. (n.d.). *Abuse test: Woman abuse screening tool.* Retrieved from www.healthyplace.com/psychological-tests/woman-abuse-screening-tool

HelpGuide.org. (n.d.). *Domestic violence and abuse: Signs of abuse and abusive relationships.* Retrieved from www.helpguide.org/mental/domestic_violence_abuse_types_signs_causes_effects.htm

HelpGuide.org. (n.d.). *Elder abuse and neglect: Warning signs, risk factors, prevention, help.* Retrieved from www.helpguide.org/mental/elder_abuse_physical_emotional_sexual_neglect.htm

HelpGuide.org. (n.d.). *Help for abused men: Escaping domestic violence by women or domestic partners.* Retrieved from www.helpguide.org/mental/domestic-violence-men-abused-by-women.htm

Ilse, S. (2008). *Empty arms: Coping with miscarriage, stillbirth, and infant death.* Maple Plain, MN: Wintergreen Press.

Ilse, S., & Burns, L. H. (2006). *Miscarriage: A shattered dream* (4th ed.). Maple Plain, MN: Wintergreen Press.

Juergens, T. M., & Barczi, S. R. (2007). Sleep. In E. H. Duthie & P. R. Katz (Eds.), *Practice of geriatrics* (3rd ed., Chap. 22, pp. 271–284). Philadelphia, PA: Saunders Elsevier.

Kessler, R. C., Petukhova, M., & Sampson, N. A. (2012). Twelve-month and lifetime prevalence and lifetime morbid risk of anxiety and mood disorders in the United States. *International Journal of Methods in Psychiatric Research, 21*(3), 169–184.

Lewiecki, E., & Miller, S. A. (2013). Suicide, guns and public policy. *American Journal of Public Health, 103*(1), 27–31.

Loveisrespect. (n.d.). *Dating abuse statistics.* Retrieved from http://www.loveisrespect.org/is-this-abuse/dating-violence-statistics

McCarney, S. B., & Bauer, A. B. (1995). *Parent's guide to attention deficit disorders: Intervention strategies for the home* (2nd ed.). Columbia, MO: Hawthorne Educational Services. Retrieved from http://www.hawthorne-ed.com/pages/adhd/ad3.html

Miller, E., Decker, M. R., McCauley, H. L., Tancredi, D. J., Levenson, R. R., Waldman, J., ... Silverman, J. G. (2010). Pregnancy coercion, intimate partner violence and unintended pregnancy. *Contraception, 81,* 316–322.

Minnesota Center Against Violence and Abuse (MINCAVA). (2010). *The facts about stalking.* Retrieved from www.vaw.umn.edu/documents/inbriefs/slalking/stalking.html

Morgan, J. P., & Yount, S. R. (2012). Postpartum depression in a primary-care setting. *Clinical Advisor for Nurse Practitioners, 15*(12), 28–40.

Moyer, V. A. (2013, March 19). Screening for intimate partner violence and abuse of elderly and vulnerable adults: A U.S. Preventive Services Task Force recommendation statement. *Annals of Internal Medicine, 158,* 478–486.

Muzik, M., & Borovska, S. (2010). Perinatal depression: Implications for child mental health. *Mental Health in Family Medicine, 7*(4), 239–247.

National Committee for the Prevention of Elder Abuse. (2008). *Elder abuse.* Retrieved from www.preventelderabuse.org/elderabuse

National Institute on Drug Abuse. (2011, March). *Commonly abused drugs chart.* Retrieved from www.drugabuse.gov/drugs-abuse/commonly-abused-drugs/commonly-abused-drugs-chart

National Institute on Drug Abuse. (2011, October). *Commonly abused prescription drug chart.* Retrieved from www.drugabuse.gov/drugs-abuse/commonly-abused-drugs/commonly-abused-prescrition-drugs-chart

National Sleep Foundation. (n.d.). *National Sleep Foundation sleep diary.* Retrieved from sleep.buffalo.edu/sleepdiary.pdf

NCPEA National Committee for the Prevention of Elder Abuse. (n.d.a). *Domestic violence.* Retrieved from http://www.preventelderabuse.org/elderabuse/domestic.html

NCPEA National Committee for the Prevention of Elder Abuse. (n.d.b). *Financial abuse.* Retrieved from http://www.preventelderabuse.org/elderabuse/fin_abuse.html

NCPEA National Committee for the Prevention of Elder Abuse. (n.d.c). *Neglect.* Retrieved from http://www.preventelderabuse.org/elderabuse/neglect.html

NCPEA National Committee for the Prevention of Elder Abuse. (n.d.d). *Physical abuse.* Retrieved from http://www.preventelderabuse.org/elderabuse/physical.html

NCPEA National Committee for the Prevention of Elder Abuse. (n.d.e). *Psychological abuse.* Retrieved from http://www.preventelderabuse.org/elderabuse/psychological.html

NCPEA National Committee for the Prevention of Elder Abuse. (n.d.f). *Sexual abuse.* Retrieved from http://www.preventelderabuse.org/elderabuse/s_abuse.html

NICHQ Vanderbilt Assessment Follow-up-TEACHER Informant. Retrieved from www.nichq.org/toolkis_ publications/complete_adhd/06VanAssessFollowUpTeachI nfor pdf

NICHQ Vanderbilt Assessment Scale-PARENT Informant. Retrieved from www.nichq.org/toolkits_publications/complete_adhd/03VanAssesScaleParent%20Infor.pdf

NICHQ Vanderbilt Assessment Scale-TEACHER Informant. Retrieved from www.nichq.org/toolkits_publications/complete_adhd/04VanAssesScaleTeachInfo.pdf

Nowrangi, M. A., Rao, V., & Lyketsos, C. (2011). Epidemiology, assessment, and treatment of dementia. *Psychiatric Clinics of North America, 34*(2), 275–294.

O'Malley, P. (2012). Baby boomers and substance abuse: The curse of youth again in old age: Implications for the clinical nurse specialist. *Clinical Nurse Specialist: The Journal for Advanced Nursing Practice, 26*(6), 305–307.

Parker, B., McFarlane, J., Soeken, K., Torres, S., & Campbell, D. (May/June 1993). Physical and emotional abuse in pregnancy: A comparison of adult and teenage women. *Nursing Research, 42*(3), 173–178.

Patterson, W. M., Dohn, H. H., Bird, J., & Patterson, G. A. (1983). Evaluation of suicidal patients: The Sad Persons Scale. *Psychosomatics, 24,* 343–345.

Posmontier, B., & Breiter, D. (2012, April). Managing generalized anxiety disorder in primary care. *Journal for Nurse Practitioners, 8*(4), 268–274.

Powers, C., Hart, V. A., & Shattell, J. (2012). The concept of "The Will to Thrive' in mental health. *Issues in Mental Health Nursing, 33*(11), 805–807.

RAINN Rape, Abuse & Incest National Network. (n.d.a). *State resources.* Retrieved from http://www.rainn.org/get-help/local-counseling-centers/state-sexual-assault-resources

RAINN Rape, Abuse & Incest Rational Network. (n.d.b). *Who are the victims?* Retrieved from www.rainn.org/get-information/statistics/sexual-assault-victims

Reuben, D. B., Herr, K. A., Pacala, J. T., Pollock, B. G., Potter, J. F., & Semla, T. P. (2012). *Geriatrics at your fingertips* (14th ed.). New York, NY: The American Geriatrics Society.

Richardson, L., & Puskar, K. (2012, June). Screening assessment for anxiety and depression in primary care. *Journal for Nurse Practitioners,* 8(6), 475–481.

Riedford, K. (2010, October). Recognizing anxiety disorders in children and adolescents. *Journal for Nurse Practitioners, 6*(9), 727–728.

Ross, R., Roller, C., Rusk, T., Martsolf, D., & Draucker, C. (2009). The SATELLITE sexual violence assessment and care guide for perinatal patients. *Women's Health Care: A Practical Journal for Nurse Practitioners, 8,* 25–31.

Saha, S., Deanne Wilson, J., Adger, R. J. (2012). K2, spice, and bath salts drugs of abuse commercially available. *Contemporary Pediatrics, 29*(10), 22–28.

Scoring Instructions for the NICHQ Vanderbilt Assessment Scales. Retrieved from http://www.uthsc.edu/pediatrics/general/clinical/behavior/aap_nichq_adhd_toolkit/07ScoringInstructions.pdf

Sellas, M. I. (2011, June 8). Elder abuse. *Medscape Reference.* Retrieved from emedicine.medscape.com/article/805727_overview.

Spar, J. E., & La Rue, A. (2002). *Geriatric psychiatry* (3rd ed.) Arlington, VA: American Psychiatric Publishing.

Spitzer, Williams, Kroenke, et al., 1999). Validation and utility of a self-report version of PRIME-MD: The PHQ Primary Care Study. *Journal of the American Medical Association, 282,* 1737–1744.

Suicide Awareness Voices of Education (SAVE). (2003–2013). *Suicide facts.* Retrieved from www.save.org/index.cfm?

Taur, F., Chai, S., Chen, M., Hou, J., Lin, S., & Tsai, S. (2012). Evaluating the suicide risk-screening scale used by general nurses on patients with chronic obstructive pulmonary disease and lung cancer: A questionnaire survey. *Journal of Clinical Nursing, 21*(3/4), 398–407.

Thomas, H., & Chan, T. (2012). Assessment and management of depression in primary care settings. *Nursing Older People, 24*(10), 32–40.

U.S. Department of Defense. (2012, September 17). *News Release, new DOD safe helpline mobile app now available.* Retrieved from http://www.defense.gov/utility/printitem.aspx?print=http://www.defense.gov/releases/release.aspx?releaseid=15571

U.S. Department of Justice Office on Violence Against Women. (2013). *A national protocol for sexual assault medical forensic examinations adults/adolescents* (2nd ed.). Retrieved from https://www.ncjrs.gov/pdffiles1/ovw/241903.pdf

Wendell, A. D. (2013). Overview and epidemiology of substance abuse in pregnancy. *Clinical Obstetrics & Gynecology, 56*(1), 91–96.

Widera, E., & Block, S. (2012). Managing grief and depression at the end of life. *American Family Physician, 86*(3), 259–264.

World Health Organization. (2011). *Intimate partner violence during pregnancy.* Retrieved from whqlibdoc.who.int/2001/WHO_RHR_11.35_eng.pdf.

World Health Organization. (2013). *Gender and women's mental health.* Retrieved from www.who.int/mental_health/prevention/genderwomen/en

Yesavage, J. A. (1986). The use of rating depression series in the elderly. In L. W. Poon (Ed.), *Clinical memory assessment of older adults.* Washington, DC: American Psychological Association.

Yesavage, J. A. et al. (1982–1983). Geriatric Depression Scale (GDS). Available at www.healthcare.uiowa.edu/.../depression/GDS.

Zoberi, K., & Pollard, A. (2010). Treating anxiety without SSRIs. *Journal of Family Practice, 59,* 148–154.bid,

SECTION II

Procedures

- Bimanual Examination: Cervical Evaluation During Pregnancy *Jill C. Cash and Rhonda Arthur*
- Canalith Repositioning (Epley) Procedure for Vertigo *Cheryl A. Glass*
- Clock-Draw Test *Cheryl A. Glass*
- Cystometry *Cheryl A. Glass*
- Establishing the Estimated Date of Delivery *Cheryl A. Glass*
- Evaluation of Sprains *Julie Adkins*
- Hernia Reduction (Inguinal/Groin) *Cheryl A. Glass*
- Inserting an Oral Airway *Cheryl A. Glass*
- Intrauterine Device (IUD) Insertion *Rhonda Arthur*
- Neurologic Examination *Cheryl A. Glass*
- Nonstress Test (NST) *Jill C. Cash*
- Pap Smear and Maturation Index Procedures *Rhonda Arthur*
- Pessary Insertion and Management *Amy Hull*
- Prostatic Massage Technique: 2-Glass Test *Cheryl A. Glass*
- Rectal Prolapse Reduction *Cheryl A. Glass*
- Removal of a Foreign Body From the Nose *Cheryl A. Glass*
- Removal of a Tick *Cheryl A. Glass*
- Trichloroacetic Acid (TCA)/Podophyllin Therapy *Rhonda Arthur*
- Wet Mount/Cervical Cultures *Jill C. Cash and Cheryl A. Glass*

BIMANUAL EXAMINATION: CERVICAL EVALUATION DURING PREGNANCY—*Jill C. Cash and Rhonda Arthur*

Description

A. The bimanual examination is a digital evaluation of the cervix with the index and middle fingers of the examiner's hand.

Indications

To assess cervical dilation, effacement, presentation of the fetus, and position and station of fetal presenting part.

The cervix may be assigned a Bishop score to evaluate cervical change and to determine difficulty/ease with induction of labor. There is an inherent subjective difference between examiners; however, the Bishop score can be used to evaluate preterm labor cervical changes over time (see Table II.1).

Precautions

A. **Bimanual exam should never be performed when there is suspicion of or history of documented placenta previa. Vaginal bleeding in second or third trimester of pregnancy should be treated as placenta previa until this is ruled out.**
B. **Suspicion of ruptured membranes with preterm contractions: First perform sterile speculum exam to assess for rupture.** Then, if membranes are intact, proceed with bimanual exam.
C. If membranes are ruptured in the absence of active labor, avoid bimanual examination until frequent, painful uterine contractions are present.

Equipment Required

A. Gloves (nonsterile if membranes are intact; sterile if suspicion of or documented ruptured membranes)
B. Water-soluble lubricant (sterile lubricant required if ruptured membranes)
C. Examination table or bed

Procedure

A. Stand at the foot of the examination table or sit near the foot of the bed and face the patient.
B. Place the patient in lithotomy position, or have the patient draw knees up and allow knees to drop to opposite sides.
C. Suggest relaxation techniques to reduce discomfort. If the patient is in active labor, the cervix will be tender.
D. Place lubricant on the index and middle fingers of the examining hand.
E. Inform the patient of each step prior to performance: Touch inner thigh first, then touch posterior portion of introitus and introduce gloved fingers into the vagina. Encourage the patient to relax pelvic muscles (a deep breath will often encourage relaxation).
F. Palpate the cervix and lower uterine segment evaluating (see Figure II.1):
   1. Dilatation
   2. Effacement
   3. Station
   4. Consistency (softness)

TABLE II.1 Bishop Scoring

Score	0	1	2	3
Dilation	0	1–2	3–4	5–6
% Effacement	0%–30%	40%–50%	60%–70%	80% or more
Station	–3	–2	–1 to 0	+1 to +2
Consistency	Firm	Medium	Soft	—
Position	Posterior	Mid	Anterior	—

Total score: 0 to 5, difficult induction; > 6, easy induction.

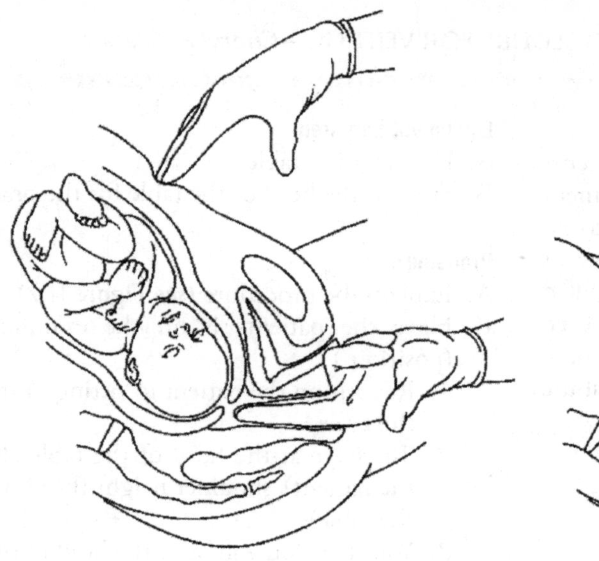
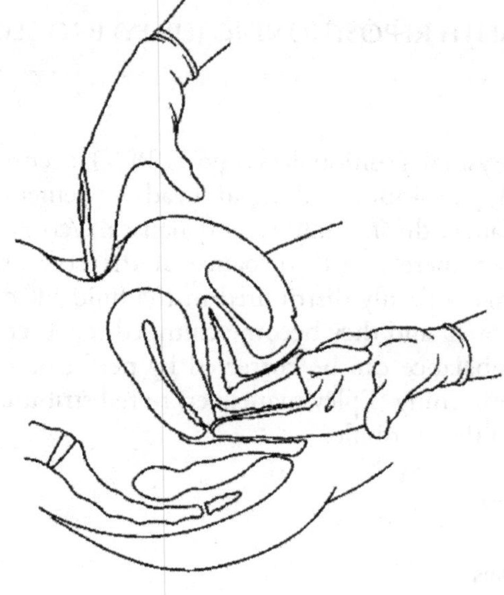
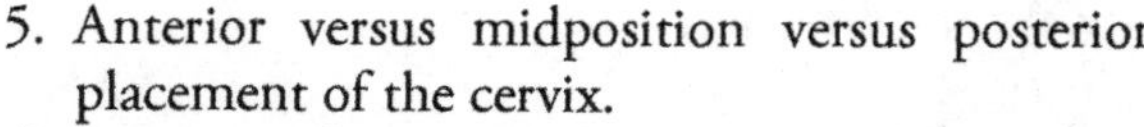

FIGURE II.1 Bimanual examination.

5. Anterior versus midposition versus posterior placement of the cervix.
6. In cases of preterm uterine contractions, it is helpful to assess the development of the lower uterine segment. A well-developed lower uterine segment (even in the absence of cervical dilation or effacement) is often a sign of preterm labor.
7. Note fetal presentation and station of the presenting part. Use ischial spines as landmarks to determine fetal descent through the pelvis.
8. If the fetus is sufficiently descended into the pelvis, determine the position of the presenting part.
9. If present, note bag of amniotic membranes. A bulging bag, known as a "forebag," may be present, even in the presence of documented ruptured membranes.

G. Following the exam, note if blood or vaginal discharge is on gloves.

CANALITH REPOSITIONING (EPLEY) PROCEDURE FOR VERTIGO—*Cheryl A. Glass*

Description

Benign paroxysmal positional vertigo (BPPV) occurs with changing position, and rapid head movement causes imbalance, disorientation, and nausea. Vertigo develops when there is a disturbance of the crystals that are normally evenly distributed in the fluid-filled semicircular canal and they become clumped together. Often the imbalance can be corrected by performing canalith repositioning (Epley maneuver) to redistribute the crystals in the vestibule.

Indications

A. BPPV

Contraindications

A. Testing should never be done in the case of head injury or suspected or confirmed cervical spine injury.

Equipment Required

A. Examination table
B. Stool at the head of the table for the practitioner

Procedure

A. Explain the procedure (see Figure II.2).
B. Have the patient sit on the examination table (position 1).
   1. Reposition the patient to sitting in the center of the table.
   2. The edge at the head of the table should be at the patient's shoulder height (head will hang off the table).
   3. Your position will be at the head of the examination table, and you use the stool for comfort while holding the patient's head with your hands.

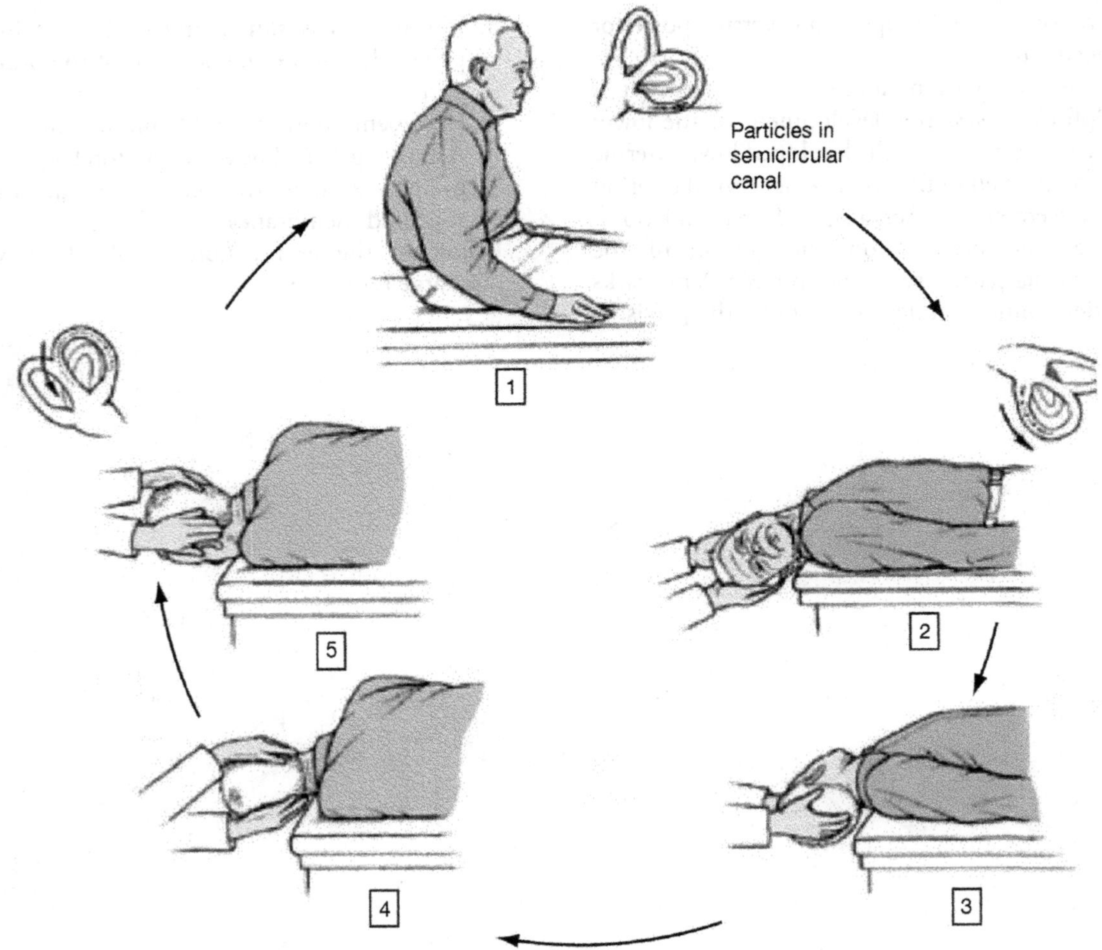

FIGURE II.2 Epley procedure for vertigo.
From the *Merck Manual of Diagnosis and Therapy*, edited by Robert Porter. Home Health Handbook, Copyright 2010-2013 by Merck Sharp & Dohme Corp., a subsidiary of Merck & Co., Inc. Whitehouse Station, NJ. Available at http://www.merckmanuals.com/professional.

C. Rapidly lay the patient down (position 2).
   1. The patient's head should be hanging over the table in a slightly downward tilt, supported by both of your hands.
   2. The patient should be instructed to keep his or her eyes open and try to focus on a stationary object on the wall throughout the positions on his or her back and sides.
   3. The patient's head is turned to the same side as the affected ear with the provider supporting the head.
      a. If the patient has vertigo affecting both inner ears, turn the patient's head to the dominantly affected side.
      b. As an alternative to just turning the head, the patient may quickly turn and lie down on the affected side while you support the head with both of your hands.
   4. After a few minutes the patient will be ready to be repositioned evidenced by his or her lack of nystagmus (rhythmic side-to-side eye movement) and confirmation that the dizziness has stabilized.

D. Turn the patient's head in the opposite direction while you continue to support the head (position 3). Again, the head should be in a slightly downward tilt.
   1. If the patient was using the side-lying position, have him or her turn to his or her back.
   2. Have the patient continue to keep the eyes open and focus on a stationary object on the wall.
   3. Again, the time lapse to repositioning is evidenced by the lack of nystagmus and subjective confirmation that the dizziness has stabilized/abated.

E. Ask the patient to roll from his or her back to the opposite side (or from the back to the opposition side) (position 4). The patient's head should be parallel to the floor.

F. With the patient side-lying (position 5), have him or her quickly turn only his or her face to the floor, while you are supporting the head.

G. After the patient verbalizes that the dizziness has abated from side-lying (position 5)
   1. The patient is to swing the legs to the edge of the table and quickly sit up.
   2. He or she will continue to feel vertigo at this point.

H. Assist the patient off the examination table.

I. The patient should be instructed to be in a sitting position or with the head no farther back than a 45-degree angle for the next 24 hours.

J. The Epley does not immediately stop the vertigo. The patient may begin to feel better within a few days.

K. If the Epley procedure needs to be repeated, allow 1 week between attempts.

CLOCK-DRAW TEST—*Cheryl A. Glass*

Description

The clock-draw test (CDT) is a quick screening tool to assess cognitive dysfunction. The tool can be used by itself or as a complement to other screening tests. The test is a component of the Mini-Cog and also the "7-Minute Neurocognitive Screening Battery." It can be administered repeatedly over time to evaluate deterioration of function. The CDT evaluates:

A. Orientation
B. Conceptualization of time
C. Visual spatial organization
D. Visual memory
E. Auditory comprehension
F. Numeric knowledge
G. Concentration
H. Frustration tolerance

Indications

A. Evaluation of dementia
B. Evaluation of delirium
C. Evaluation of neurologic insult
   1. Head trauma
   2. Stroke
   3. Alcohol and drug
D. Evaluation of psychiatric illness
   1. Schizophrenia
   2. Psychotic state

Administering the CDT

A number of variations can be used in administering the CDT.

This is not a timed test. There is no limitation to administration time; the test generally takes 1 to 2 minutes. However, in the Mini-Cog test, if the clock is not completed within 3 minutes, the patient should proceed with word recall.

General Information

Provide the patient with an 8.5- by 11-inch blank sheet of paper and a pencil.

Set-up

A. Equipment required includes a blank sheet of paper, a sheet of paper with a clock on one side, a pen, and a chair/table for ease of drawing.
B. A clock should not be visible to the patient during the CDT.

Patient Instructions (Rouleau et al., 1992)

The following instructions are given:

> "I would like you to draw a clock, put in all the numbers, and set the hands for 10 after 11."

Following this condition, the patient should be instructed to copy, as accurately as possible, a clock from a model. The model should contain all the numbers on the clock, be 3 inches in diameter, and be located on the upper part of an 8.5- by 11-inch sheet of paper. The hands on the model should be set for 10 after 11. The patient is then instructed to copy the model on the lower part of the same sheet of paper.

- Instructions can be repeated if necessary.
- Patients may use their nondominant hand for drawing the clock.

Scoring

There are several variations on scoring the CDT. The quickest scoring involves dividing the clock into four quadrants and counting the numbers in the correct quadrant. More complex assessment evaluates up to 20 traits or categorizes errors.

A. The placement of the arms of the clock is the most abstract feature and is useful in evaluating the early dementing process.
B. A normal clock suggests that multiple functions are intact and contributes to the assessment of the patient's ability to continue independently. Figure A is a "normal" clock draw.

A

C. A grossly abnormal clock is an indicator of potential problems that require attention (see Figures B and C).

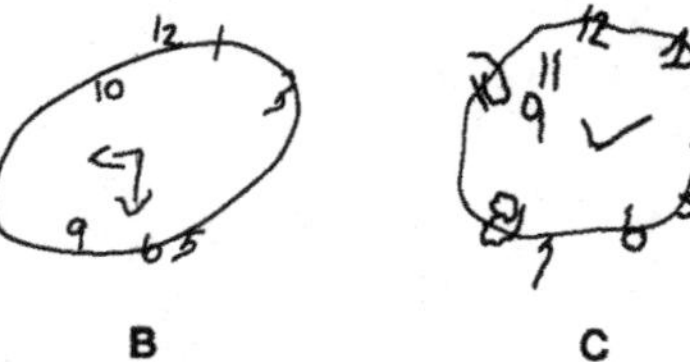

B C

D. There are several scoring systems for evaluating the CDT results. The most basic involves awarding 1 point for each of the following:
   1 point for the clock circle
   1 point for the numbers placed in the correct position
   1 point for the clock face numbers placed in their proper order around and inside the clock face
   1 point for the presence of the two clock hands
   1 point for the correct time as instructed

A normal score is 4 or 5 points.

Refusal to draw a clock is scored as abnormal.

Note: The next two pages may be used for serial testing.

Name: ______________________________ Date: ______________________________

Draw a clock with all the numbers, and set the hands for 10 after 11.

Clock-Draw Test

Name: ______________________ Date: ______________________

Copy this clock.

Reprinted from the Rehabilitation Measures Database, http://www.rehabmeasures.org, by Allen Heinemann, PhD, and Jennifer Moore, PT, DHS, NCS. Original instrument instructions published by Isabelle Rouleau, David Salmon, and colleagues in "Quantitative and Qualitative Analyses of Clock Drawings" in *Alzheimer's and Huntington's Disease, Brain and Cognition 18*, 70–87 (1992).

CYSTOMETRY—*Cheryl A. Glass*

Description

Cystometry testing is an office procedure to determine bladder capacity, post void residual (PVR), any fluid leak with stress maneuvers, or inhibited bladder capacity. Cystometry measures the intravesical bladder pressure during bladder filling. Many times cystometry is performed in conjunction with uroflowmetry. Cystometry of a female patient is described.

Indications

Patients presenting with complaints of urinary incontinence, stress incontinence (leaking), overactive bladder (OAB), and urinary retention (inability to empty bladder) are candidates for cystometry testing.

Prior to the Procedure

A. A thorough urogynecologic history should be taken and a physical examination should be performed, including a digital rectal examination.

Precautions

A. Rule out the presence of a urinary tract infection (UTI) as a cause of the incontinence prior to cystometry testing.
B. Use universal precautions. This is a sterile procedure and is contraindicated when infection or inflammation is present.
C. Risks of the procedure
 1. Discomfort
 2. Bleeding
 3. Infection
 4. Autonomic dysreflexia (AD) from bladder instrumentation and bladder distension
  a. Flushing
  b. Hypertension
  c. Reflex bradycardia
  d. Severe headache

Equipment Required

A. Sterile straight catheter (12–14 French catheter)
B. Catheter insertion kit
C. A 60-mL sterile syringe
D. 1,000 mL sterile water (CO_2, saline, or contrast medium may also be used)
E. Sterile measurement container
F. Urine collection device
G. A vaginal or rectal pressure catheter or insertion of a second catheter with a manometer to measure pressures
H. Light source for catheterization
I. Gown and drape for the patient

Procedure

A. Explain the procedure.
B. Obtain consent (if required).
C. Ask about any latex or Betadine allergies.
D. Throughout the procedure, ask the patient to speak to his or her feeling the sensation of the bladder filling, any discomfort, when the urge to void is sensed, and bladder fullness. Sensations noted by the patient are subject to the rate of bladder filling and temperature of the fluid.
E. During the initial physical exam, have the patient bear down and/or cough to evaluate urinary incontinence.
F. Have patient void, measure the urine, and collect the specimen for urinalysis.
 1. The measurement of the urine flow rate also screens abnormalities of micturition.
  a. A simple way to measure the flow rate is to time the duration of urination and measure the volume voided. A woman usually voids in a continuous flow rate until the bladder is empty. Intermittent flow patterns indicate dysfunction with voiding.
 2. The evaluation of urine speed and flow rate may be measured by uroflowmetry equipment utilizing a special toilet with a computer to record the flow rates.
G. Catheterize, using sterile technique.
 1. Measure urine drained from a catheter inserted post voiding; this amount is the PVR.
  a. Normal: Less than 100 mL PVR
  b. Abnormal: More than 100 mL PVR
  c. Differential diagnostic evaluation: Overflow incontinence secondary to retention
H. Attach the 60-mL syringe to the catheter.
 1. Observe if there was any difficulty passing the catheter.
  a. Normal findings: Catheter passes with ease.
  b. Abnormal findings: Catheter difficult or impossible to pass
  c. Differential diagnostic evaluation: Overflow incontinence possibly due to obstruction
I. Place the rectal or vaginal catheter to measure intra-abdominal pressure and involuntary/voluntary detrusor contractions.

J. Using gravity, fill the bladder slowly through catheter/syringe with sterile water (saline or contrast medium).
   1. Avoid instilling the sterile water too quickly; instill approximately 30 to 50 mL amounts at a time.
   2. Measure the amount of water instilled when the patient has the urge to void, different degrees of filling, and pain during filling.
      a. Normal: Bladder capacity usually at 300 mL when urge is sensed.
      b. Abnormal: Urge at less than 200 mL.
      c. Differential diagnostic evaluation: Urge incontinence due to small capacity.
   3. Continue to fill, noting if there is any fluctuation of the sterile water in the syringe during filling.
      a. Normal: Contractions or fluctuation occur around 200 to 250 mL from bladder into syringe (detrusor muscle contraction).
      b. Abnormal: Fluid moving into the syringe.
      c. Differential diagnostic evaluation: Urge incontinence related to bladder spasm.
   4. The rectal/vaginal probe measuring detrusor activity/overactivity notes phasic pressure increases associated with symptoms of urgency or urge incontinence, indicating detrusor overactivity.
   5. During the procedure, ask the patient to cough or bear down to help elicit involuntary bladder contractions. The Valsalva maneuver or cough assesses the sphincter competence.
   6. The instillation of sterile water should be stopped when the patient reports a full bladder. Measure the bladder capacity; that is, the patient reports perception that voiding can no longer be delayed.
   7. If the patient has not reported a full bladder prior to the instillation of 600 mL, the test should be discontinued.
   8. The urodynamic test is done until the point of leakage.
      a. Have patient cough or strain; observe for leaking, clamp catheter.
      b. Normal: Normal capacity 400 mL, no leaking with cough
      c. Abnormal: Urge prior to 400 mL, or leaking with pressure
      d. Differential diagnostic evaluation: Urge incontinence due to small capacity and/or stress incontinence due to leakage with pressure
      e. Coughing and straining during the procedure are also done to evaluate bladder pressure changes. The manometer also measures the pressure inside the bladder when leakage occurs.
   9. Remove catheter after bladder is filled to capacity (strong urge to void); have the patient cough.
      a. Normal: No leakage
      b. Abnormal: Leakage of fluid
      c. Differential diagnostic evaluation: Stress incontinence associated with weak pelvic muscles
   10. Have the patient void; measure output, compare with amount instilled.
      a. Normal: Return with a maximum of 100 mL retained (PVR)
      b. Abnormal: Greater than 100 mL retained after voiding
      c. Post procedure: While the patient is emptying the bladder, the manometer measures the bladder pressure and flow rate. Then remove the vaginal/rectal probe.
      d. Differential diagnostic evaluation: Overflow incontinence either from obstruction or an atonic bladder

K. Discuss treatment options, including pharmaceutical therapy and/or consultation with an urologist.

L. Postprocedure instruction and when to report problems are discussed.
   1. Expect some discomfort; it should lessen over time.
   2. Blood during urination may be expected after the procedure. The amount of blood lessens over time and with urination.
   3. Drinking additional fluids (noncaffeinated and noncarbonated beverages) will increase urination and ease discomfort and passage of blood.
   4. An antibiotic may be prescribed (per protocol).
   5. Anti-inflammatories such as ibuprofen may be discussed.
   6. Have the patient report
      a. Chills and fever
      b. Any abdominal pain
      c. Continued bloody urine 1 day postprocedure

ESTABLISHING THE ESTIMATED DATE OF DELIVERY—*Cheryl A. Glass*

The first 12 weeks of pregnancy are vital, as the fetal organ systems are developing.

Early Diagnosis of Pregnancy

A. Allows counseling about potential risks to the developing fetus
B. Enables the woman contemplating elective abortion to consider her options
C. Affords diagnosis/intervention in an ectopic pregnancy
D. Fosters early entry into prenatal care, which in turn may provide early identification of pregnancy complications

Obtain Menstrual History

A. Obtain sexual history.
B. Obtain fertility history.
   1. Length of cycles
   2. Regularity of cycles. Regularity of menstruation is influenced by
      a. Recent previous pregnancy and cycles, which have not yet reestablished themselves
      b. Breastfeeding
      c. Oral contraceptive pills
      d. Intramuscular contraceptive
      e. Polycystic ovarian syndrome (PCOS)
      f. Comorbid medical conditions
C. Is this a planned pregnancy? If so, how long did it take to conceive?
D. Has the patient been pregnant before? If so, what was the outcome of each pregnancy (miscarriage, stillbirth, live birth), delivery method, and fetal and/or pregnancy complications for each pregnancy?

Initial Assessment/Diagnosis of Pregnancy

A. Is the exact date of the last menstrual period (LMP) known, using the first day of the last period?
B. Was the LMP a normal period? If not, when was the most recent normal period?
C. Is there a known isolated sexual incident that could pinpoint a possible conception date?
D. Does the patient know when conception may have occurred?

Pregnancy Testing

Testing includes analysis of maternal blood or urine for the presence of human chorionic gonadotropin (HCG), a hormone produced by the trophoblastic cells of the developing placenta. **Positive testing is not diagnostic of a normal intrauterine pregnancy.**

A. Maternal blood: HCG
   1. Most accurate
   2. Earliest to become positive
   3. Negative test should be repeated in 2 weeks.
B. Urine
   1. More commonly used
   2. Accurate 4 to 7 days following conception
   3. Available over the counter
   4. First-voided morning specimen is best (most concentrated).
   5. Negative test should be repeated in 1 week to ensure that the first test was not done too early to detect urine HCG. HCG production decreases after 60 to 70 days, and thereafter declines below the sensitivity of some tests.

Presumptive Signs of Pregnancy

A. Amenorrhea
B. Has experienced pregnancy before and feels pregnant now
C. Nausea/vomiting: Nausea is not limited to "morning sickness."
D. Fatigue
E. Breast tenderness
F. Urinary frequency
G. Enlarging abdomen
H. Unexplained weight gain
I. Constipation

Probable Signs of Pregnancy

A. Positive Chadwick's sign: Purplish coloration of vagina and cervix; may be seen on speculum examination
B. Positive Hegar's sign: Softening of the lower uterine segment; may be palpated on bimanual examination.
C. Uterine enlargement
   1. 8 weeks gestation = 2 times nonpregnant size
   2. 10 weeks gestation = 3 times nonpregnant size
   3. 12 weeks gestation = 4 times nonpregnant size, uterine fundus (size of orange) palpable at symphysis pubis
   4. 16 weeks gestation = uterine fundus midway between symphysis pubis and umbilicus (size of grapefruit)
   5. 20 weeks gestation = uterine fundus at umbilicus (size of large honeydew melon)
D. Increased skin pigmentation (face [chloasma], nipples, abdomen [linea nigra])
E. Striae gravidarum: "Stretch marks"

Positive Diagnostic Signs

A. Fetal heart tones (FHTs)
   1. 10 to 12 weeks with ultrasonic Doppler (fetal doptone)
   2. If unable to hear FHTs with doptone at 12 weeks (by size and dates), have the patient return at 14 weeks.

3. If unable to hear FHTs at 14-week gestation, repeat visit; the patient needs ultrasound examination to confirm fetal viability. Consult with a physician if abnormal ultrasound results.
4. 18 to 20 weeks with fetoscope (helps verify estimated date of delivery [EDD])

B. Fetal movements palpated by the mother or health care provider

C. Ultrasound examination
   1. Gestational sac visualized by 6 weeks
   2. Fetal pole visualized by 8 weeks
   3. Fetal cardiac activity visualized by 8 weeks

EDD/Estimated Date of Confinement

A. 280 days (40 weeks) after LMP

B. 266 days (38 weeks) from last ovulation (in a 28-day cycle)

C. **Naegele's rule** for establishing estimated date of confinement (EDC): First day of the LMP plus 7 days minus 3 months = EDC.

D. Gestational calculator (in the form of a wheel) may be used to determine EDC. *Gestational wheels are based on a 28-day cycle.*

E. An online calculator is located online at www.perinatology.com/calculators/Due-Date.htm

EVALUATION OF SPRAINS—*Julie Adkins*

Evaluate each leg, comparing the injured with the uninjured and examining for signs of edema, deformity, tenderness, range of motion, strength, and discoloration.

McMurray Test for Knee Sprains

A. Explain the procedure.
B. Ask the patient to lie down on his or her back (supine).
C. The affected leg, right or left, should have hip flexed 60 to 70 degrees.
D. The injured knee is flexed 45 degrees.
E. Hold the foot in one hand and place the fingers of the other hand on the joint line.
F. Evaluate the patient's pain level when palpating the joint when the knee is flexed.
G. Apply valgus force by holding the femur steady and slowly move the lower leg laterally while still applying the valgus stress.
H. Then flex the knee to 135 degrees and switch to varus stress.
I. Finally, extend the knee in the varus position.
J. If the test is positive, a meniscus click or pop can be felt, which is characteristic of an anterior cruciate ligament tear or relocation.

Anterior Drawer Test for Evaluation of Lateral Ankle Sprain

A. Explain the procedure.
B. Perform this test on the uninjured ankle first, then repeat on the injured ankle.
C. Ask the patient to position the affected foot in the plantar flexion position (foot slightly at rest).
D. Grasp the lower portion of the uninjured leg for bracing. Use one hand at the shin and attempt to draw the heel anteriorly (forward) with your other hand.
E. Repeat the test on the injured ankle.
F. Anterior drawer test is positive for an ankle sprain if the talus at the injured point slides 4 mm or more than the same bone in the other joint.

Talar Tile Test for Evaluation of Lateral Ankle Sprain

A. Explain the procedure.
B. Perform this test on the uninjured ankle first, then repeat on the injured ankle.
C. To perform the talar test, grasp the lower heel with one hand while adducting or inverting the foot with your other hand.
D. The test is positive if the tilt is 5 to 10 degrees greater around the injured joint.

HERNIA REDUCTION (INGUINAL/GROIN)—*Cheryl A. Glass*

Description

A. A hernia reduction may be done by a manual technique used for external replacement of the bowel (occasionally omentum) from the hernia back into the abdomen/groin.

Indications

A. Herniation of bowel contents occurs secondary to pregnancy, straining, hard physical labor, or congenital defect.

Precautions

A. *Do not try to reduce a strangulated hernia.* This can cause gangrenous bowel to enter the peritoneal cavity. Strangulation symptoms include tenderness, discoloration, edema, fever, and signs of bowel obstruction.

Equipment Required

A. Gown/drape for the patient
B. Nonsterile gloves

Procedure

A. After doing a complete assessment, explain the reduction procedure to the patient, discussing each step just before performing it.
B. Obtain consent if required by protocol.
C. Ask the patient to void.
D. Apply nonsterile gloves.
E. Have the patient lie supine with slight flexion of the hips to relax abdominal muscles.
F. Ask the patient to take deep, slow, relaxing breaths. Hernia reduction should cause minimal discomfort.
   1. *Males:* Gently invaginate the scrotal skin, and replace the herniated contents back through the external/internal inguinal or femoral rings.
   2. *Females:* Gently invaginate the herniated bowel contents back through the external/internal inguinal or femoral rings.
G. Hernias should be easily reducible. Do not force any contents back into the abdominal wall defect.
H. After the reduction, ask the patient to cough and strain to evaluate successful reduction prior to discharge.

Evaluation/Results of Procedure

A. Consult a physician if unable to reduce the hernia. The hernia may be strangulated.
B. Have the patient return in 1 week for reexamination or sooner if needed.
C. Tell the patient not to strain with bowel movements, lift heavy objects, or exercise strenuously.
D. Review symptoms of obstruction or strangulation of entrapped bowel: Pain, nausea, and vomiting. At discharge, educate the patient to seek immediate medical attention for symptoms of strangulated bowel.
E. Recurrent hernias and congenital defects eventually require surgical repair.
F. Hernias secondary to pregnancy may not require surgery.

INSERTING AN ORAL AIRWAY—*Cheryl A. Glass*

Description
An oropharyngeal airway is a semicircular device used to hold the tongue away from the posterior wall of the pharynx. To insert this device, the mouth and pharynx should first be cleared of secretions, blood, or vomit, using a suction tip catheter (if available).

Indications
A. Oral airway insertion can be used to help control the airway, suction, ventilate, and provide oxygenation of the unconscious patient.

Precautions
A. If the patient is conscious, airway insertion may stimulate vomiting and laryngospasm. Oral airways should be inserted only if the patient is unconscious, unresponsive, and has no gag reflex.
B. If the airway is too long, it could press the epiglottis against the entrance of the larynx and produce a complete airway obstruction.
C. If the airway isn't inserted properly, it can push the tongue posteriorly and worsen an upper airway obstruction.
D. If the tongue and/or lips are between the teeth, trauma will result.
E. Oral airways should not be inserted if the patient has sustained oral trauma or has recently had oral surgery.

Equipment Required
A. An oropharyngeal airway (selection/measurement of the airway size is measured from the earlobe to the corner of the mouth)
B. A tongue blade
C. Gloves
D. A suction tip and canister (if available)

Procedure
A. Place head/neck in the correct position (see Figure II.3).
B. The best way to insert an oral airway is to turn it backward (upside down) as it enters the mouth.
C. As the airway transverses the oral cavity and approaches the posterior wall of the pharynx, rotate it into proper position.
D. Open the patient's mouth using a cross-finger technique. An alternate method is to move the tongue out of the way with a tongue blade before insertion of the airway.
E. The end flared flange of the airway should rest on the patient's lips.
F. Suction if necessary.

Evaluation/Results of Procedure
A. The airway is in the proper position and of the proper size when you hear clear breath sounds on auscultation of the lungs during ventilation.

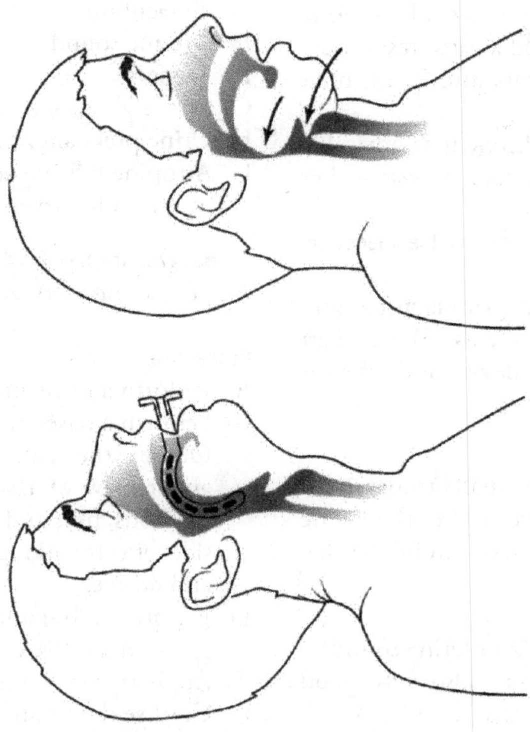

FIGURE II.3 Insertion of an oral airway.

INTRAUTERINE DEVICE (IUD) INSERTION—*Rhonda Arthur*

Note: Only trained health care providers who carefully reviewed the selected device's manufacturer's package insert for indications and use as well as specific insertion instructions should place intrauterine devices (IUDs).

Description

A. The IUD is a long-acting method of contraception that is inserted into the uterine cavity.
   1. Copper T 380 A (Paragard)
      a. T-shaped bound in fine copper wire
      b. **Approved for 10 years**
      c. Clear or white knotted double string
   2. Levonorgestrel (Mirena)
      a. T-shaped polyethylene frame with levonorgestrel reservoir coating
      b. **Approved for 5 years**
      c. Dark monofilament strings
      d. Indications also include use for treatment in women who have heavy menstrual bleeding and choose IUD for contraception.

Indications

A. To provide a long-acting method (5–10 years) of contraception
B. The Mirena IUD has been therapeutic with severe dysmenorrhea and severe menorrhagia.

Precautions

A. Pregnancy must be ruled out prior to insertion.
B. Risks at the time of insertion include uterine perforation and/or infection and a vagal response.
C. Small amounts of progestins pass into breast milk with Mirena.
D. To minimize the risk of expulsion, it is advisable to insert an IUD when the woman is *not* on her menstrual cycle.
E. **An existing IUD should be removed during the menstrual cycle.**
F. Consent(s) is required by the manufacturer and by individual institutional protocols. The patient should know the type of IUD device and when it should be replaced.

Contraindications

A. Women who have a history of sexually transmitted disease and/or currently have more than one sexual partner may not be good candidates for IUD use.
B. Uterine anomaly
C. Cervical stenosis (unable to pass a uterine sound)
D. Nulliparas (especially teens) are also not good candidates for the IUD.
E. Active pelvic infection (recent, acute, or subacute).
F. Purulent cervicitis.
G. History of ectopic pregnancy (strong relative risk)
H. Abnormal Pap smear/endometrial hyperplasia/cervical intraepithelial neoplasia (CIN)/cancer (review last recent Pap results); uterine or cervical neoplasm.
I. Concern for future fertility
J. Allergy to copper (Paragard) or allergy to component of Mirena as applies
K. Valvular heart disease

Insertion of an IUD may theoretically increase the woman's susceptibility to subacute bacterial endocarditis (SBE). No current evidence supports this. Optional therapy: Some clinicians require antibiotics for valvular coverage. High-risk patients may receive IV ampicillin and gentamicin, and moderate-risk patients may receive oral amoxicillin 2 g before insertion or removal.

L. Acute liver disease (Mirena)
M. Known or suspected breast carcinoma (Mirena)

Equipment Required

A. IUD
B. Speculum
C. Iodine solution
D. Tenaculum
E. Uterine sound
F. Scissors
G. Sterile gloves (two pair)
H. Urine pregnancy test kit
I. Atropine 0.5 mg should be available at the time of insertion for severe vasovagal response.

Backup staff should be available for complications such as vasovagal response and perforation of uterus.

Procedure

A. Perform a urine pregnancy test.
B. Perform a baseline blood pressure and pulse.
C. Obtain the patient's consent after full history and review of last Pap smear; discuss alternative methods, pros and cons of each method, procedure, side effects, and complications of IUD insertion and device.
D. Perform a bimanual exam to determine uterine position and size.
E. Apply sterile gloves.
F. Cleanse the vagina and cervix with iodine solution.

G. Use the tenaculum to grasp the anterior lip of the cervix approximately 1.5 to 2.0 cm from the os.
   1. Atropine should be readily available for severe vasovagal response.
   2. Lidocaine (Xylocaine) gel or benzocaine (Hurricane Spray) can be used to decrease discomfort with the application and use of the tenaculum.
H. Insert the uterine sound into the cervix/uterus slowly and gently.
   1. **Moisture mark on the sound will indicate the depth of insertion for the IUD. (Depth less than 6 cm is contraindication.)**
I. Change sterile gloves.
J. Load the IUD as directed by manufacturer.
K. Set indicator for depth of insertion as guided by the uterine sound.
L. While maintaining gentle traction with the tenaculum, insert the IUD gently to the predetermined mark on the guide sheath.
   1. Spasm of the internal cervical os may occur and will resolve by waiting a few minutes.
M. Gently push the IUD through the guide into position. **Excessive pain or bleeding is often a sign of perforation. Consult a physician immediately (most common perforation sites: Fundus, body of uterus, and cervical wall).**
N. Remove the guide sheath.
O. Remove the tenaculum.
P. Cut the IUD strings to approximately 1-inch length past the cervix.
Q. Remove the speculum.
R. Check the patient's blood pressure and pulse to rule out vasovagal potential.
S. Recommend a prostaglandin inhibitor if cramping occurs/persists (Motrin 400 mg by mouth four times a day).
T. Prophylactic antibiotics may be used for SBE prophylaxis. Amoxicillin is used unless there is an amoxicillin/penicillin allergy; then erythromycin (EES) or clindamycin may be prescribed. Amoxicillin 3.0 g by mouth 1 hour before the procedure, then 1.5 g by mouth 6 hours later.
   1. EES 800 mg by mouth 2 hours before the procedure, then 400 mg by mouth 6 hours later
   2. Clindamycin 300 mg by mouth 1 hour before the procedure, then 150 mg 6 hours later
U. Instruct the patient regarding string location and periodic checks. The patient should not have vaginal intercourse or use a tampon for 7 days (decreases infection).

Evaluation/Results of Procedure

A. See the patient after first menses to check for expulsion.
B. If the patient has missed two or more periods, perform a beta HCG test.
   1. Rule out ectopic pregnancy.
   2. Explore the canal for IUD.
   3. Consider ultrasound to rule out pregnancy/expulsion.
   4. Consider flat plate of abdomen.
   5. Consult a physician.
C. Yearly evaluation with Pap smear/annual checkup
D. Consider hemoglobin (Hgb) for reports of heavy bleeding with Paragard.
   1. If Hgb is less than 9, remove the IUD, provide an alternative method of contraception, and prescribe iron supplement for 2 months.
   2. Repeat Hgb in 1 month.

IUD Removal Procedure

A. Remove only during menses (cervix is more dilated).
B. Apply gentle, steady traction; remove slowly.
C. **Consider uterine embedding if unable to remove, needs consultation.**

Patient Should Call the Office For

A. A missed period
B. Abdominal pain (severe)
C. Temperature 100.4°F not associated with other problems (sinus infection, UTI)
D. Foul vaginal odor/discharge, especially if bloody or greenish color
E. Heavy bleeding with clots

NEUROLOGIC EXAMINATION—*Cheryl A. Glass*

Description

Performance of the neurologic examination is a diagnostic component of many physical examinations. Examination of all cranial nerves is not necessary for every patient; it should be performed based on patient-focused presenting complaints. The purpose of this support tool is to review the cranial nerves and review equipment needed for a neurologic examination.

A neurologic examination identifies dysfunction and assists in accurate diagnosis (see Table II.2).

Components of the Neurologic Examination

A. Thorough history
B. Assessment of mental status
C. Assessment of cranial nerve function
D. Assessment of motor function
E. Assessment of sensory function
F. Assessment of gait
G. Assessment of reflexes

Equipment Required

A. Multiple mental examinations are available. The clock-draw test and the Mini-Mental State Examination are two examples.
B. Pen light/ophthalmoscope: Light source
C. Ophthalmoscope
D. Snellen chart/Rosenbaum pocket card
E. Items to taste (salt, sugar)
F. Items to smell (vanilla, cinnamon)
G. Tongue depressor
H. Tuning fork
I. Ticking watch/clock
J. Cotton or soft tissue
K. Pin or other sharp object
L. Reflex hammer

TABLE II.2 Cranial Nerve Function

Cranial Nerve Number	Cranial Nerve	Functional Test
I	Olfactory	Smell reception and interpretation
II	Optic	Vision: Acuity and visual fields
III	Oculomotor	Motor: Eye/lid movement, pupil constriction, visual accommodation
IV	Trochlear	Eye movement up/down
V	Trigeminal	Chewing, jaw opening and clenching, facial sensation: Corneal, forehead, eyes, nose/mouth mucosa, teeth, tongue, and ears
VI	Abducens	Lateral gaze/eye movement
VII	Facial	Corneal reflex, facial expression, taste to the lateral two-thirds of tongue, and sensation to pharynx; parasympathetic secretion of tears and saliva
VIII	Acoustic	Hearing and equilibrium
IX	Glosso-medulla or Glossopharyngeal	Gag reflex, cough, swallow, taste on posterior third of tongue, parasympathetic secretion of salivary glands, and carotid reflex
X	Vagus	Laryngeal muscles—muscles of phonation, swallowing, sensation behind ear and part of external canal, parasympathetic secretion of digestive enzymes/peristalsis as well as involuntary action of heart and lungs
XI	Spinal accessory	Head and shoulder movement: shoulder shrug
XII	Hypoglossal	Tongue movement/muscles, swallowing, and sound articulation

Adapted from Seidel, Ball, Dains, and Benedict (1991).

NONSTRESS TEST (NST)—*Jill C. Cash*

Description

The nonstress test (NST) is a noninvasive antepartum fetal surveillance test to assess fetal well-being. A fetus with an intact central nervous system with adequate oxygenation will demonstrate transient fetal heart rate (FHR) accelerations in response to fetal movement. Results of the NST must be evaluated with consideration of gestational age. It is not uncommon for a neurologically intact fetus between the ages of 24 and 28 weeks gestation to have a nonreactive NST.

Indications

A. Patients at risk for adverse perinatal outcome
   1. Maternal indications
      a. Hypertension
      b. Maternal cardiac disease
      c. Diabetes (including gestational diabetes)
      d. Renal disease
      e. Hyperthyroidism
      f. Collagen vascular disease
      g. Sickle cell disease
      h. Previous stillbirth
   2. Fetal indications
      a. Intrauterine growth restriction (IUGR)
      b. Postdates (> 41 weeks)
      c. Decreased fetal movement
      d. Multiple gestation with complications
      e. Polyhydramnios
      f. Oligohydramnios
      g. Isoimmunization
      h. Previous fetal demise

B. Frequency of testing: One must consider prognosis for neonatal survival and severity of maternal disease. In general, most high-risk pregnant women should begin testing by 32 to 34 weeks estimated gestational age (EGA). In case of multiple or severe high-risk conditions, testing may begin at 26 to 28 weeks. Frequency may be weekly or biweekly. If clinical deterioration is noted, reducing the testing interval, as often as daily, is prudent.

Precautions

A. A reactive NST is reassuring. However, the significance of abnormal results is less clear. Loss of FHR reactivity may be benign, or it may be a sign of the metabolic consequences of hypoxemia.

Equipment Required

A. Electronic FHR monitor (EFM)
B. Reclining chair or bed/stretcher
C. Sphygmomanometer
D. Vibroacoustic stimulator (protocol dependent)

Procedure

A. Place the patient in the semi-Fowler's position in a recliner or on a stretcher. Optimal positioning includes the patient tilted to the left or right side to avoid vena caval compression. The patient is preferably nonfasting and has not recently smoked.
B. Measure the patient's blood pressure.
C. Apply EFM on the maternal abdomen.
D. Record FHR for 20 to 40 minutes. Ask the mother to record fetal movements with a marker button, if available. However, all accelerations may be counted as they probably have the same significance whether or not they occur in response to the fetal movement felt by the mother.
E. Interpret FHR tracing as reactive or nonreactive.
F. If the fetus is suspected to be in a sleep state, a vibroacoustic stimulation device may be applied, placed on the maternal abdomen, and used for a 3-second stimulation in an attempt to awaken the fetus.

Evaluation/Results of Procedure

A. Reactive NST: Baseline FHR 110 to 160 bpm with two or more accelerations of greater than or equal to 15 bpm amplitude that last at least 15 seconds or more, within a 20-minute period. **(Note: Before 32 weeks of gestation, accelerations are defined as two accelerations or more greater than 10 bpm amplitude that last at least longer than 10 seconds over a 20-minute period.)** If these criteria are met prior to 20 minutes, the test may be declared reactive. The FHR tracing may be continued for at least 40 minutes to account for the typical fetal sleep–wake cycle.
B. Nonreactive NST: Above criteria are not met within the 40-minute time frame.

Treatment

A. If the NST is a reactive, reassuring test, continue obstetrical prenatal care. Further testing is required for maternal and fetal indications as previously noted.

Consultation/Referral

A. Further evaluation is mandatory for a nonreactive NST.
B. Consult with a physician.
   1. Depending on the situation, the patient could be given juice or sent to eat and return later for a repeat NST.

2. Perform a modified NST, which includes a single 1- to 3-second sound (vibroacoustic) stimulation applied to the maternal abdomen, plus the assessment of amniotic fluid and/or biophysical profile (BPP).
3. Umbilical artery Doppler velocimetry is appropriate testing for IUGR, oligohydramnios, twin-to-twin transfusion, and/or discordant fetuses.
4. The patient may be sent to the hospital for another NST, modified NST, BPP, or a contraction stress test (CST).

The CST should only be performed in a setting where immediate delivery could occur if indicated for fetal distress.

PAP SMEAR AND MATURATION INDEX PROCEDURES—*Rhonda Arthur*

Description

A Pap smear is a cytological *screen* that is performed to detect the presence of cancerous and precancerous lesions of the uterine cervix. The procedure involves procuring a sample of both the ectocervix and endocervix. The maturation index (endocrine assessment) is a tool to evaluate atrophic vaginitis/estrogen deficiency.

Indications

According to the American Cancer Society (ACS) and the U.S. Preventative Task Force (USPTS) guidelines, all women should begin cervical cancer screening at age 21. From age 21 to 29, screen with conventional or liquid-based cytology every 3 years; from age 30 to 65, screen with conventional or liquid-based cytology every 3 years; or to extend testing time you can use conventional or liquid-based cytology *plus* human papillomavirus (HPV) co-test every 5 years. HPV co-testing should not be used in women under 30. Stop screening at age older than 65 with adequate screening history. Screening is not indicated for women who have had a total hysterectomy for benign indications.

A Pap smear may be obtained in pregnancy, or at the end of a period in the menses flow if light. If the patient is having a heavy menstrual flow, the procedure should be rescheduled.

A maturation index is obtained to evaluate decreased estrogenization of the vagina. Both liquid-based and conventional methods for collecting cervical cytology are acceptable.

Precautions

A. Ask the woman not to douche, use any antifungal or spermicides, or have intercourse the night prior to the procedure so that there will be nothing to interfere with obtaining a good sample.
B. Practitioners should be aware that some women experience discomfort during the Pap smear procedure and should be sensitive to this possibility.
C. In order to procure an adequate Pap smear, care must be taken to obtain a sample from the entire squamocolumnar junction of the cervical portio. (The squamocolumnar junction is more prominent in teens and women on oral contraceptives.)
D. Blood may obscure an adequate cytology interpretation. It is advisable, therefore, to obtain the endocervical sample following the ectocervical sample. Bleeding from the endocervix is common, particularly if a cytobrush is used. A cytobrush is recommended for sampling the endocervix as more cells are retrieved using this tool as compared to a Q-tip.

Equipment Required

A. Speculum (size appropriate for teen/woman)
B. Warm water for lubrication (excessive K-Y jelly may interfere with the smear and reading)
C. Spatula (wooden or plastic)
D. Q-tip or cytobrush
E. Glass slide (two if maturation index)
F. Container for slide(s)
G. Cytology fixative

Procedure (Conventional Method)

A. With the patient draped in a lithotomy position, insert the lightly lubricated speculum and visualize the cervix.
B. With the spatula, sample the entire (360-degree sweep) squamocolumnar junction using gentle pressure applied directly to this area (if visualized). The goal of the technique is to scrape exfoliated cells or those cells held loosely on the surface of the cervix. Vigorous scraping that abrades the cervix yields tissue that is virtually uninterpretable in the cytology smear.
C. **Insert the cytobrush or Q-tip until the brush or cotton swab is no longer visible. It is not necessary to insert further to obtain an adequate sample.** A fiber-tipped swab should be introduced in the canal and rotated clockwise several times to obtain cells. A cotton-tipped swab should first be moistened with saline to prevent cells from adhering to the cotton; a synthetic fiber swab is nonabsorbent and can be used without moistening. Pap smears taken with a brush have been found superior in containing endocervical cells.
D. Wipe the sample from the spatula and roll and twist the brush of the cytobrush or the Q-tip on the glass side as quickly as possible. The cytobrush sample can be rolled through the spatula sample. It is not necessary to separate these two areas or obtain two slides.
E. Spray the slide with cytology fixative held at a distance of approximately 12 inches to avoid "blasting" the cells from the slide. If held too far away, inadequate spray reaches the slide and drying distortion could result.
    1. Allow the slide to dry prior to covering in transport container.
    2. To obtain a cytology specimen from the vaginal cuff (post hysterectomy), use a spatula (rounded end) to scrape the upper lateral third of the vaginal wall. Spread on a slide and fix the slide with cytology fixative.

3. Vaginal pool specimens for a maturation index are often recommended in perimenopausal women; sampling is done by scraping the posterior fornix with the spatula. Spread on a separate slide from the Pap smear and fix the slide.

Procedure (Liquid-Based Cytology)

A. With the patient draped in a lithotomy position, insert the lightly lubricated speculum and visualize the cervix.

B. With the spatula, sample the entire (360-degree sweep) squamocolumnar junction using gentle pressure applied directly to this area (if visualized). The goal of the technique is to scrape exfoliated cells or those cells held loosely on the surface of the cervix. Rinse the spatula as quickly as possible in the solution by swirling vigorously 10 times and discard the spatula.

C. Insert the cytobrush until only the bottom-most fibers are visible. Rotate slowly one half-turn in one direction (do not over-rotate). Rinse the brush quickly by rotating the brush against the container wall and swirling. Place the cap on the specimen container and label properly (see Figure II.4).

D. Alternatively, you may use the broom device instead of the cytobrush. If so, insert the central bristles of the broom device into the endocervical canal (deep enough for the short bristles to contact the ectocervix) and rotate clockwise five times. Rinse the broom by quickly pushing against the bottom of the specimen container and swirling 10 times.

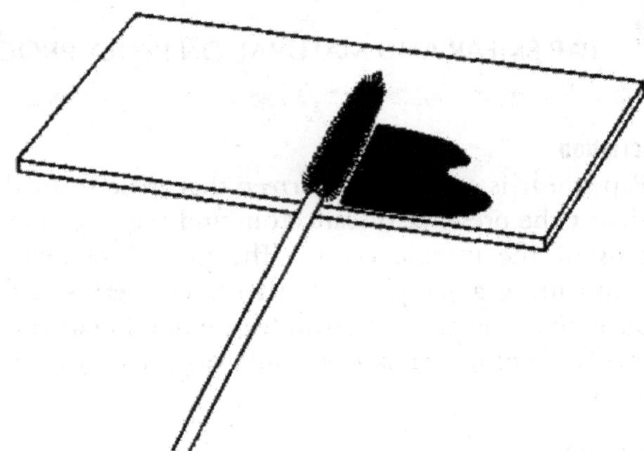

FIGURE II.4 Pap smear cytology brush.

Evaluation/Results of Procedure

A. A Pap smear may be classified as "inadequate" if no endocervical cells are present for interpretation (unless the patient has had a hysterectomy).

B. Pap smear adequacy may be compromised if the slide is allowed to air dry prior to spraying with cytology fixative.

C. A Pap smear reading may be compromised due to the presence of blood, lubricant, or certain vaginal infections creating an increase in vaginal discharge.

D. See Pap Smear Interpretation and American Society for Colposcopy and Cervical Pathology Consensus guidelines on the management of women with abnormal cervical cancer screening tests algorithms on the Internet at www.asccp.org/consensus.shtml.

PESSARY INSERTION AND MANAGEMENT—*Amy Hull*

Description

A. **This conservative therapy option is the gold standard for pelvic organ prolapse (POP) management.**
   1. Pessaries are made from medical-grade silicone.
   2. Many different styles and sizes are available to enable successful insertion. (Only four styles of pessaries are noted in this procedure.)
   3. Pessaries can be for temporary or long-term use.

Indications

A. POP
B. Stress urinary incontinence (SUI)
C. Patient frailty prevents surgical correction of POP or patient chooses to avoid surgery for personal reasons.
D. Can be used for diagnostic purposes when evaluating for potential SUI, or when symptoms described by patient do not fit with common POP symptoms.
E. Can serve as potential reduction of prolapse progression.

Precautions

A. Confirm patient is agreeable to a trial of pessary.
B. Confirm patient can be an active participant in her pessary care.
C. In the event of dementia or frailty, ensure patient has a caretaker who is willing to participate in the patient's care.
D. Patient and/or caregiver must be agreeable to frequent follow-up with the clinician.

Contraindications

A. Patient's inability or caregiver inability to collaborate in follow-up care and maintenance
B. Severe vaginal atrophy
C. Current vaginal infection
D. Prolapse ulcer

Equipment Required

A. Two to three different styles and sizes of pessaries
B. Latex-free gloves
C. Lubricating jelly

Procedure

A. Little evidence exists to determine the most appropriate pessary style choice.
B. Style is usually a subjective choice based on clinician comfort and familiarity.
C. Allow patient to hold pessary, becoming more comfortable with it.
D. Fit with patient in lithotomy position.
E. Apply water-based lubricant to gloved hand and carefully reduce the prolapse.
F. Assess vaginal length using gloved hand, two fingers in vagina with fingertips at the vaginal cuff or posterior fornix (see Figure II.5).
G. Separate the two intra-vaginal fingers to assess for width of the vaginal vault (see Figure II.6).
H. Select appropriate type and sized pessary, cleansing with soap and water prior to insertion (see Table II.3).
I. Insert pessary using gentle pressure toward the posterior vaginal wall.
   a. Insertion of a ring with support pessary: Fold in half; pessary will spring open in vaginal vault (see Figures II.7–II.9).
   b. Insertion of a Gellhorn pessary: Bend the stem or knob down against the dish (see Figures II.10–II.12).
   c. Insertion of a donut pessary: Compress the pessary, attempting to "squish" it (see Figures II.13–II.15).
   d. Insertion of a cube pessary: Compress the pessary, attempting to "squish" it (see Figures II.16–II.18).

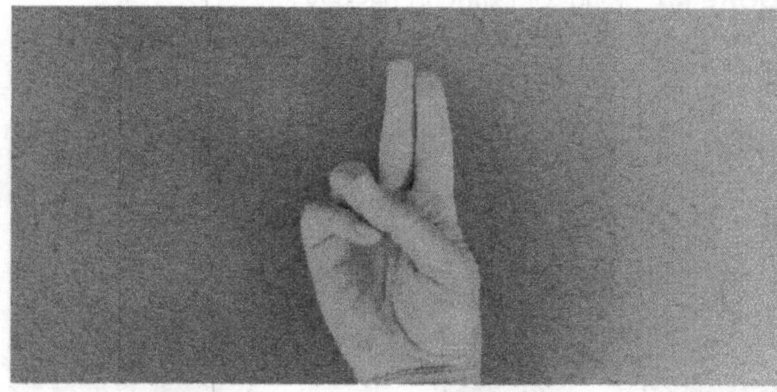

FIGURE II.5 Assessment of vaginal length using two fingers placed together in the vagina.

FIGURE II.6 Separate the two intra-vaginal fingers to assess the width of the vaginal vault.

TABLE II.3 Example of Types of Pessary and Use With POP and SUI

Pessary	Prolapse 1–2 Degree	Prolapse 3–4 Degree	Cystocele	Rectocele	SUI
Ring with support	X		X		X
Donut		X	X	X	
Cube	X	X	X	X	X
Gellhorn		X	X		

Modified from the Milex Pessary Guide www.incoshop.co.uk/milex-pessaries-50-c.asp.

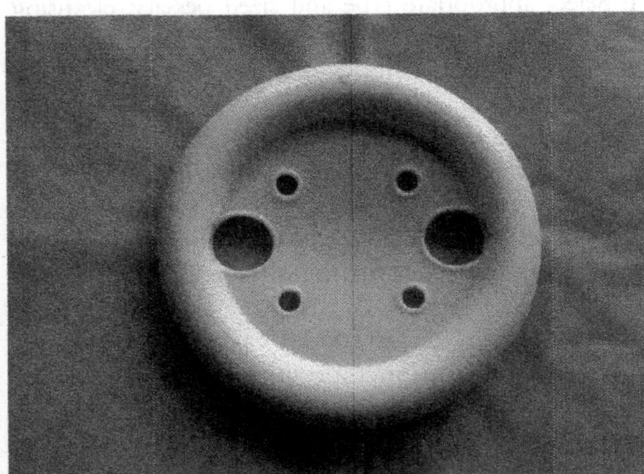

FIGURE II.7 Ring with support pessary.
Used with permission from CooperSurgical.coopersurgical.com.

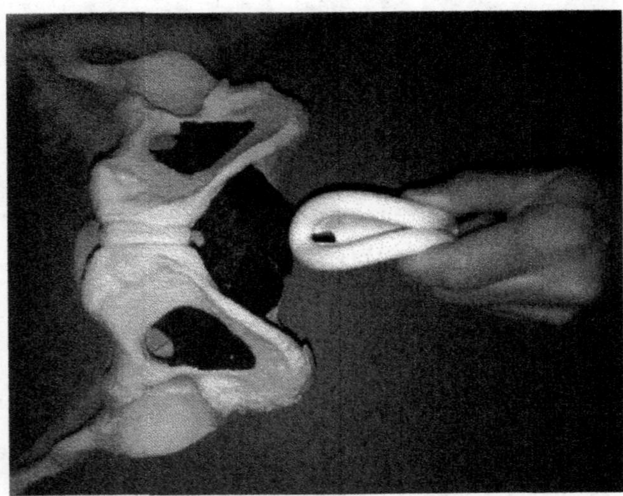

FIGURE II.8 Fold the ring pessary in half for insertion into the vaginal vault.
Photograph courtesy of Barry Jarnigan, MD, Center for Pelvic Health www.centerforpelvichealth.org/specialists.

J. Check for fit by asking the patient to Valsalva or cough. Perform with patient in both lithotomy and standing positions.
K. Ask patient to walk, sit, and bend to determine comfort of fit.

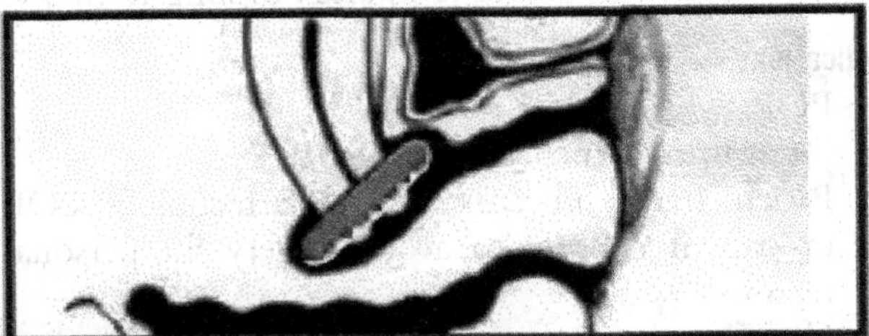

FIGURE II.9 Position of the ring pessary in the vaginal vault.
Used with permission from CooperSurgical. coopersurgical.com.

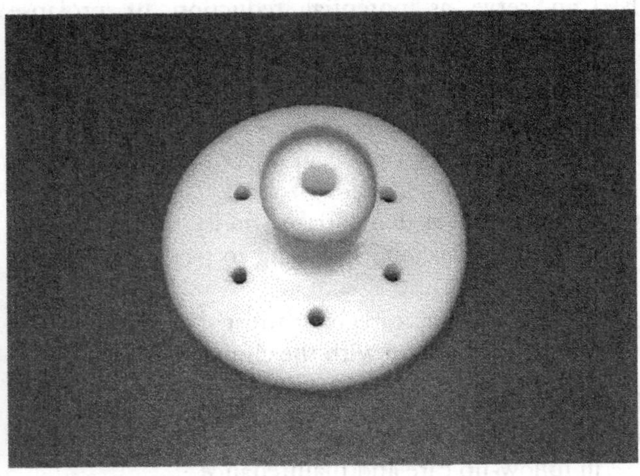

FIGURE II.10 Gellhorn pessary.
Used with permission from CooperSurgical. coopersurgical.com.

L. Instruct patient to attempt to void to determine ability to empty and to confirm proper fit.

Evaluation of Procedure

A. If the patient is comfortable with her new pessary, review removal procedures with her.
B. If the patient is comfortable with practicing in the office, have her practice removal and replacement in the exam room.

Removal Procedure

A. A ring with support pessary should be removed by inserting the index finger into the vagina, feeling for the hole, and pulling downward toward the introitus.

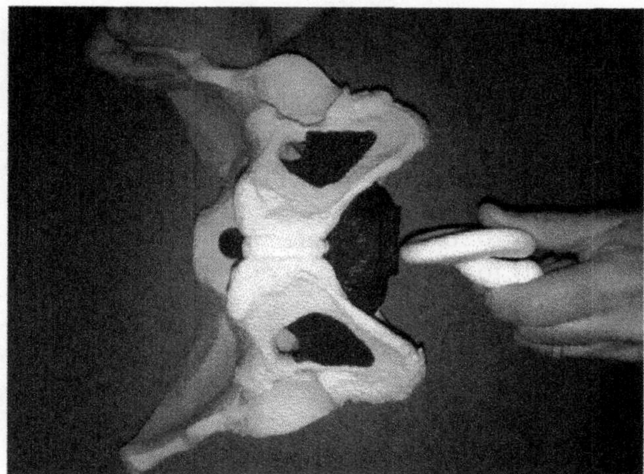

FIGURE II.11 Bend the stem or knob down against the dish for insertion of the Gellhorn pessary.

Photograph courtesy of Barry Jarnigan, MD, Center for Pelvic Health www.centerforpelvichealth.org/specialists.

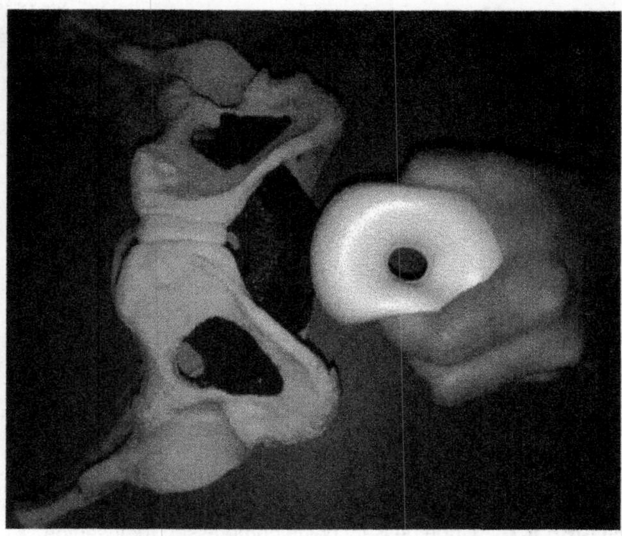

FIGURE II.14 **Squish** the Donut pessary for insertion into the vaginal vault.

Photograph courtesy of Barry Jarnigan, MD, Center for Pelvic Health www.centerforpelvichealth.org/specialists.

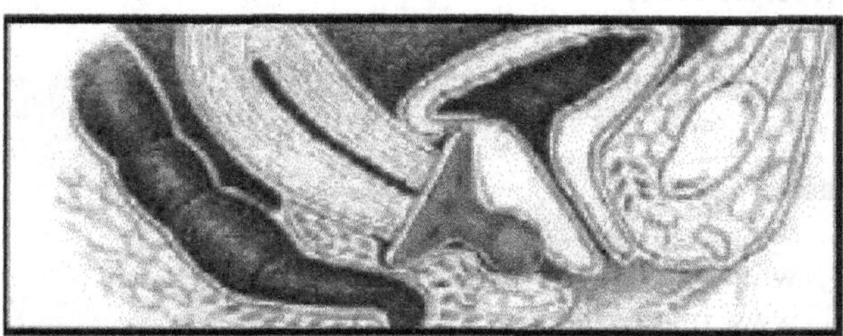

FIGURE II.12 Position of the Gellhorn pessary in the vaginal vault.

Used with permission from CooperSurgical.coopersurgical.com.

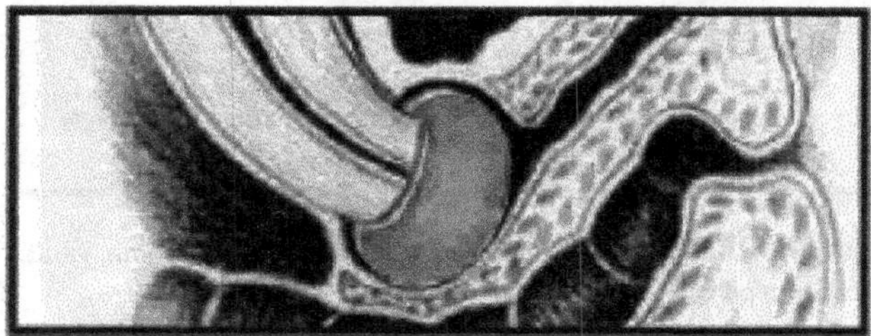

FIGURE II.15 Position of the Donut pessary in the vaginal vault.

Used with permission from CooperSurgical.coopersurgical.com.

FIGURE II.13 Donut pessary.

Used with permission from CooperSurgical.coopersurgical.com.

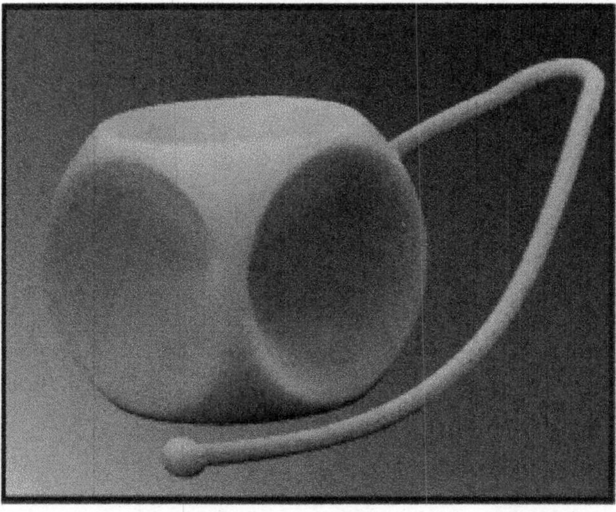

FIGURE II.16 Cube pessary.

Used with permission from CooperSurgical.coopersurgical.com.

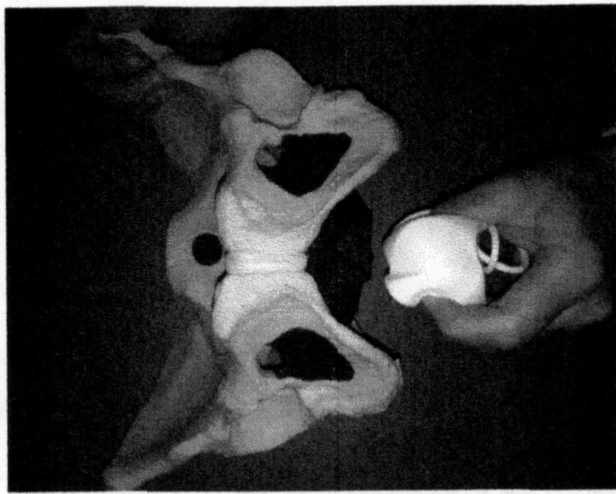

FIGURE II.17 Cube pessary being compressed for insertion.
Photograph courtesy of Barry Jarnigan, MD, Center for Pelvic Health www.centerforpelvichealth.org/specialists

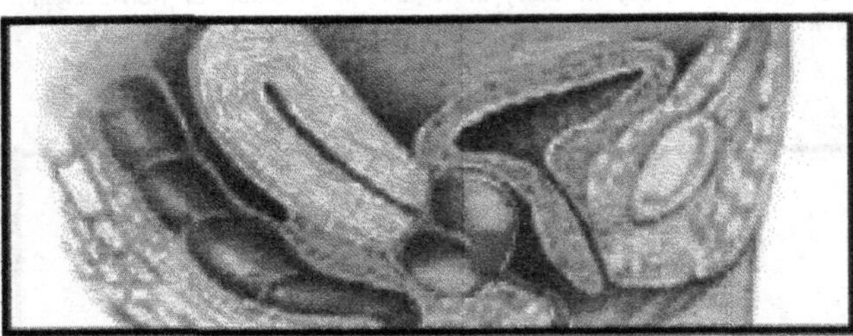

FIGURE II.18 Position of the cube pessary in the vaginal vault.
Used with permission from CooperSurgical.coopersurgical.com

B. A Gellhorn pessary can be removed by grasping the knob and gently pulling it laterally while also pulling downward toward the introitus. It may be helpful to ask the patient to Valsalva during the removal.

C. Removal of the Donut pessary can be done by inserting the index finger into the large hole in the center and gently pulling toward the introitus.

Patient Should Call the Office For

A. Pain when the pessary is in place
B. Vaginal bleeding
C. Inability to void or defecate
D. Inability to retain the pessary

Follow-Up

A. Follow-up after completion of fitting session
  1. Instruct patient to return for follow-up within 2 weeks if she is unable to remove the pessary.
  2. Instruct the patient to return for follow-up in 4 weeks if she can remove and replace the pessary.

B. Follow up for routine maintenance
  1. If the patient is unable to manage her pessary, follow-up should occur every 3 months with the clinician.
  2. If the patient can manage her pessary, follow-up can occur every 6 months to annually.

Procedure Codes

A. Pessary fitting: 57160
B. HCPCS code, nonrubber pessary: A4562
C. Follow-up 15-minute visit: 99213

Pessary Suppliers

A. www.bioteque.com
B. www.coopersurgical.com
C. www.medicalexpo.com

PROSTATIC MASSAGE TECHNIQUE: 2-GLASS TEST—*Cheryl A. Glass*

Description

A. Obtaining prostatic fluid by prostate massage using the 2-glass test known as the Nickel pre-massage and post-massage test. The Meares–Stamey, 4-glass test is considered too time consuming and is rarely used by urologists.

Indications

A. Expressed prostatic secretion (EPS) is used to distinguish chronic prostatitis from acute prostatitis or urinary tract infection.

Precautions

A. Do not perform in patients with acute prostatitis (swollen, tender, boggy prostate); may cause septicemia.

Equipment Required

A. Clean-catch specimen cups (2)
B. Labels (2) marked:
   1. Pre-massage
   2. Post-massage
C. Sterilized towelette

Procedure

A. Collection of a clean-catch midstream urine specimen for male patients: The patient should retract the foreskin (if applies) and cleanse the glans penis with a sterilized towelette in order to avoid contamination.
B. The patient should collect a midstream flow of urine by starting the flow of urination, then catch at least 10 mL urine specimen in the first clean-catch specimen cup marked pre-massage. The patient should be instructed to then stop the flow of urine.
C. The patient is asked to lean over the examining table for a digital rectal examination. With a lubricated index finger, gently enter the rectum. The prostate should be massaged by stroking it from the periphery toward the midline several times on each side (similar to a windshield wiper).
D. Following the massage, ask the patient to provide more urine in the second clean-catch specimen cup labeled post-massage.
E. Send both the pre-massage and post-massage urine specimens for urine cultures.

Treatment

A. See Table II.4.

TABLE II.4 Evaluation and Results of Prostatic Secretions

Diagnosis	Microscopic Evaluation	Treatment
Urethritis	WBC, bacteria in VB_1; in no other specimens	< 40 years, probably sexually transmitted infection (STI) RX: Rocephin and doxycycline > 40 years, probably coliform bacteria RX: Bactrim/septra DS po bid × 5–7 days
Cystitis	WBC, RBCs, bacteria in VB_2	Bactrim DS po bid × 5–7 days
Acute prostatitis	WBC, bacteria in VB_2 and/or EPS, VB_3	Bactrim DS po bid for 3–4 weeks Alternative: Quinolones: Cipro 500 mg bid for 3–4 weeks May need hospitalization for IV antibiotics
Chronic prostatitis	Bacteria in EPS and/or VB_3, but not in VB_1 or VB_2	Bactrim DS po bid *or* Cipro 500 mg bid for 3–4 months

bid, twice a day; EPS, expressed prostatic secretion; po, by mouth; RBC, red blood cells; WBC, white blood cells.

Description

There are three types of rectal prolapse.

A. *Partial.* Anus is inverted; rectal mucosa protrudes 1 to 3 cm out of rectal sphincter.
B. *Complete.* All layers of rectum have intussuscepted through the anus. (Rare in adults; most often seen in children and the elderly.)
C. *Internal.* Patient complains of a protrusion, but no protrusion is noted on examination.

Indications

A. Diagnosis of rectal prolapse is made by inspection. Several populations are at risk for rectal prolapse, including infants, women, and the elderly. Other factors associated with rectal prolapse include malnutrition, severe constipation, severe chronic diarrhea, obstetrical injuries, rectal intercourse, and multiple sclerosis as well as other neuromuscular diseases.
B. Hemorrhoids, mucosal prolapse, polyps, and cancer must be ruled out. Conditions associated with rectal prolapse include cystic fibrosis, ulcerative colitis, intussusception, and Hirschsprung disease.

Precautions

A. Refer patients with complete prolapse to a physician for evaluation and treatment. After a rectal prolapse reduction by proctoscope, follow-up testing by a barium enema or endoscopy is indicated.
B. Surgery may also be indicated, depending on the type of prolapse, recurrence, and risk of strangulation.
C. Patients with a history of surgery for rectal prolapse should be evaluated and assessed for hemorrhage, bowel obstruction, pelvic abscess, fecal impaction, and recurrent prolapse.
D. Instruct the patient on a high-residue diet, and warn him or her to avoid straining to induce a bowel movement.

Equipment Required

A. Sterile gauze
B. Normal saline
C. Anoscope
D. Water-soluble lubricant
E. Gloves
F. Chux pads and tissue
G. Light source
H. Examination table

Procedure

A. Explain the procedure to the patient and discuss all steps just before performing. Explain that during the procedure relaxation of the anal sphincter is key.
B. Obtain the patient's consent.
C. Ask the patient to void. (Urinary stress incontinence is common during the procedure.)
D. Apply gloves.
E. As the procedure is being done, give the patient and/or caregiver instructions on how reduction is done in the event of another prolapse.
   1. Provide the patients with gloves and lubricant for future need.
   2. Prolapses may also reduce spontaneously without any manual reduction.
F. Have the patient lie in the left lateral position and give extra tissues for urinary incontinence.
G. Ask the patient to strain (perform Valsalva maneuver). This allows the practitioner to fully evaluate the prolapse through the anal sphincter. If this does not produce the prolapse, have the patient squat and/or sit on the toilet to strain.
H. With a good light source, do a detailed visual examination to rule out hemorrhoids versus a complete/partial prolapse.
   1. Thrombosed hemorrhoids appear as blue, shiny masses.
   2. A normal hemorrhoid appears as a painless, flaccid skin tag.
   3. Anoscope reveals internal hemorrhoids as bright red to purplish bulges.
   4. Rectal prolapse looks like a pink doughnut or rosette; a complete prolapse involving the muscular wall is larger, red, and has circular folds.
I. After visual inspection/evaluation, reposition the patient into a knee–chest position. This allows the bowel to be pulled back into the anus.
J. If after changing positions the prolapse does not reduce with gravity, place a saline-soaked four-by-four gauze over the prolapse to prevent drying.
K. Apply gentle pressure with the saline gauze, and replace the rectal prolapse/protrusion back through the anus.
L. Using a lubricated gloved hand, perform a rectal examination to evaluate sphincter tone at rest and with some straining. This rectal exam should be painless. Pain raises suspicion for other pathology, such as incarceration or an unrelated lesion.

M. Apply lubricant to anoscope and slowly insert it anteriorly into the rectum. Remove inner cannula of anoscope, and slowly withdraw it to evaluate and identify any lesions. It is rare to see a polyp or carcinoma. Usually, erythema and edema will be noted.

Evaluation/Results of Procedure

A. If reduction of rectal prolapse occurs with minimal discomfort, have the patient return in 1 week to assess sphincter function.
B. If unable to reduce prolapse, send the patient for *immediate* evaluation by a physician. Keep prolapse covered with saline-soaked gauze during transport.
C. If prolapse was partial or complete, refer the patient to a physician after reduction.
D. Further evaluation may include a sigmoidoscopy, barium enema, or biopsy.
E. Presence of pain may indicate an incarceration with impending strangulation and requires *immediate* referral.
F. All patients need to follow a high-fiber diet and have instructions on avoiding straining.

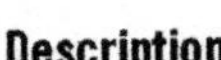

REMOVAL OF A FOREIGN BODY FROM THE NOSE—*Cheryl A. Glass*

Description

This is the technique for removing a nasal foreign body (NFB) that is anterior to the pharynx and can be visualized with a nasal speculum.

Indications

Patients with retained NFB often present with unilateral, foul rhinorrhea, nosebleeds, or the request for foreign body removal.

Precautions

A. Try to identify the type of object, organic or inorganic.
   1. Organic foreign objects include food items (e.g., peas and beans), sponges, or rubber.
   2. Inorganic foreign objects include a rock, pearl, battery, or small toy parts.

B. If you can't identify the object, don't irrigate the nares before removal.

C. Vegetable matter will swell if hydrated, so remove it in a dry environment when possible.

D. Small "button" batteries from toys are common obstructions and should not be irrigated due to the destruction from the low-volt current and potential spread of alkaline content.

E. When the object is too far into the nasal turbinate/cavity or when in doubt, do not attempt the procedure and refer to an otolaryngologist.
   1. The procedure may need to be done under sedation.
   2. The object may need to be surgically removed.

Equipment

A. Proper lighting (headlight or head mirror)

B. Nasal speculum

C. Topical anesthetic for use prior to procedure (topical 1% lidocaine with 0.5% phenylephrine)

D. Suction and several suction tips

E. Other equipment should be available, depending on the type of foreign body: Wire loop or curette, alligator or Hartman forceps, bayonet forceps, right-angle hooks, a Foley catheter, and suction.

Procedure

A. Determine the type of object in the nostril during history-taking in order to determine the best approach for removal.

B. Explain the procedure to the patient.

C. Obtain the patient's consent for removal.

D. To best visualize the nasal cavity, have the patient lie down or sit erect with the head slightly tilted.

E. Visualize the nostril with the nasal speculum.

F. If tissue edema is present in the nares, you may use a topical anesthetic with vasoconstrictor to the affected nares to help prevent bleeding.

G. If the patient is willing, have him or her dislodge the foreign body with forceful nose blowing while occluding the unaffected nostril and keeping the mouth closed.

H. The patient should be supine or with a slight elevation of the head with assistance to stabilize the patient's head.

I. If forceful blowing is not successful, attempt to remove the foreign object using the most appropriate instrument or technique (wire loop or curette, alligator or Hartman forceps, bayonet forceps, right-angle hooks and suctioning). The choice of instrument for removal is dependent upon the type of object, location, and how well the patient is able to cooperate during the procedure.

J. Use of a catheter involves lubricating the tip, inserting past the foreign body, and inflating the balloon.

K. Gentle withdrawal will pull the foreign object out.

L. Simple external pressure should be applied to prevent bleeding.

Evaluation/Results of Procedure

A. **Evaluate the other nares and ears if one foreign object is found.**

B. Bleeding is common after the removal of a foreign object. Pressure should be applied to stop the bleeding.

C. Follow up in 2 days to evaluate the mucosa.

D. Consult a physician if you are unable to dislodge or remove the object.

E. Button batteries require prompt removal and inspection due to the destruction to the mucosa.

REMOVAL OF A TICK—*Cheryl A. Glass*

Description

A. Ticks are vectors for Lyme disease and Rocky Mountain Spotted Fever. Ticks should be removed as soon as possible since they pass bacteria that cause the fevers and rashes.

Indications

A. There are several populations at risk for tick-borne transmission diseases, including hunters, campers, landscapers, persons in contact with dogs and other animals with ticks, and those in contact with heavy, brushy areas.

Equipment Required

A. Tweezers
B. Antiseptic or rubbing alcohol
C. Gloves, nonsterile may be used
D. Office setting: Scalpel if the tick head remains embedded

Procedure

A. Use gloves.
B. To remove the tick, care should be taken to avoid squeezing the body of the tick.
   1. It should be grasped with a fine-tip tweezer close to the skin.
   2. Remove by gently pulling the tick upward straight out without using any twisting motions (see illustrations).
   3. Do not crush the tick during removal.
C. Examine for the entire head and body removal; if the head is embedded, a small incision may be required for the removal.
D. Cleanse the skin with antiseptic or rubbing alcohol.
E. **Save the tick for identification. Write the patient's name, date of removal, and date of the tick bite on paper, and place the paper and the tick in a resealable baggie and place it in the freezer.**

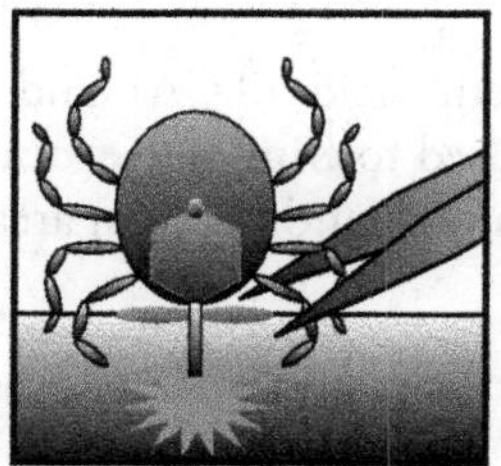

Grasp the tick's body close to the skin using a fine-tip tweezer. Avoid squeezing the body.

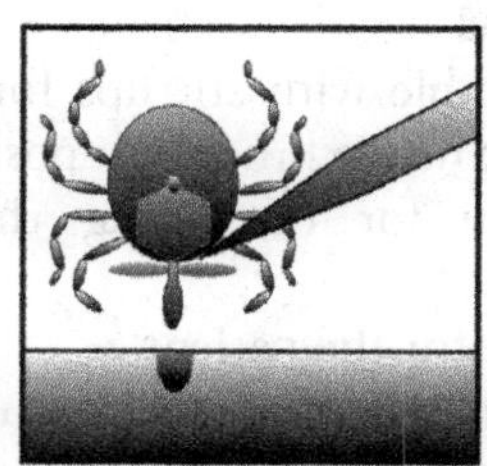

Remove by pulling the tick straight upward without using twisting motions.

Evaluation/Results of Procedure

A. Examine the rest of the body for other ticks.
B. Try to determine the length of time the tick was on the skin.
C. Assess for symptoms of Lyme disease and Rocky Mountain Spotted Fever.
D. Medications and consultants as applicable.

TRICHLOROACETIC ACID (TCA)/PODOPHYLLIN THERAPY—*Rhonda Arthur*

Description

A. Trichloroacetic acid (TCA) and podophyllin are substances used to eliminate exophytic warts on the external genitalia and perianal area.

Indications

A. External genitalia and perianal warts

Precautions

A. Podophyllin use is contraindicated in pregnancy.
B. Either substance should be applied sparingly to avoid contact with unaffected skin.

Equipment Required

A. Examining table with stirrups for positioning the female client in the lithotomy position
B. Light source for examining the genitalia and perianal area
C. Gown/drape for the patient
D. Gloves: Nonsterile glove may be used.
E. Cotton-tipped applicators
F. Petroleum jelly
G. Sodium bicarbonate (baking soda) or powder with talc
H. Plastic medicine cups
I. TCA 80% to 90% *or*
J. Podophyllin 10% to 25% in compound tincture of benzoin

Procedure

A. Assist the female client to the lithotomy position, the male client to a sitting or supine position, on the exam table.
B. Inspect the external genitalia and perianal areas for exophytic warts.
C. Pour small amount (0.5–1.0 mL) of solution (TCA or podophyllin) to be used in a plastic medicine cup.
D. Use the cotton-tipped applicator to apply petroleum jelly on unaffected skin surrounding areas identified for therapy.
E. Use the wooden end of the cotton-tipped applicator to apply a small amount of solution (TCA or podophyllin) to warts.
F. If TCA is used, apply sodium bicarbonate or powder with talc to absorb unreacted acid.
G. If podophyllin is used, instruct the client to thoroughly wash off solution in 1 to 4 hours.
H. Repeat weekly if necessary. If warts persist after six applications, consider other therapeutic methods.
I. Advise the client that mild to moderate pain or local irritation may occur after treatment.

WET MOUNT/CERVICAL CULTURES—*Jill C. Cash and Cheryl A. Glass*

Description

A. The wet mount procedure is a technique used to identify vulvovaginitis, commonly caused by trichomoniasis, bacterial vaginosis, and vulvovaginal candidiasis. Any patient complaining of vaginal discharge, irritation, vaginal pain, and/or a vaginal odor should have a wet mount performed to aid in identifying the organism to assist in the diagnosis.

Indications

A. Vaginal discharge
B. Vulvar/vaginal irritation or pain
C. Vaginal discharge with an odor
D. Prior to the examination: Take a thorough history prior to the physical examination to determine if other testing needs to be performed.
E. Presenting complaints (Refer to Table II.5 for a comparison of bacterial vaginosis, candidiasis, and trichomoniasis.)
   1. Bacterial vaginosis—complaints of a thin off-white "grayish" discharge, musty "fishy" amine odor. The odor increases after intercourse.
   2. Vulvovaginal candidiasis—thick, white "cottage cheese" discharge, no odor, pruritus, and some dysuria
   3. Trichomoniasis (parasite *Trichomonas vaginalis*)—copious, frothy, yellow-gray to green discolored, malodorous vaginal discharge, pruritus, and vaginal irritation. *The patient may also be asymptomatic.*

Precautions

A. Use universal precautions when obtaining specimens.
B. All specimens need to be disposed of as biohazard waste.

Equipment Required

A. Examining table with stirrups for positioning the patient in the lithotomy position
B. Light source for examining the cervix
C. Gown/drape for the patient
D. Gloves, two pairs (nonsterile)
E. Speculum: Always have several different types and sizes of speculums on hand for appropriate sizing, visualization, and comfort.
F. Condoms available, if needed
G. Q-tip/cotton-tipped applicators
H. Gen-probe, or other collecting tubes for *Neisseria gonorrhoeae* and *Chlamydia* specimens
I. Small test tube/plastic collection tube
J. Normal saline (NS) and 10% potassium hydroxide (KOH)
K. Glass slides (2): One marked KOH and one marked NS
L. Cover slips for slides (2)
M. Nitrazine pH test tape
N. Microscope with 10× and 40× objectives

Procedure

A. After the patient has voided and changed into a gown, assist the patient into the lithotomy position.
B. Apply gloves.
C. Prepare the test tube/specimen tube with 1 mm of NS. Prepare slides (one marked KOH and one marked NS); apply one drop of each solution to a clean slide and set aside.
D. Inspect the perineum for lesions, erythema, fissures, condyloma, and lacerations.
   1. Bacterial vaginosis—usually normal-appearing tissue
   2. Vulvovaginal candidiasis—vulvar and vaginal erythema, edema, and fissures
   3. Vulvar and vaginal edema and erythema
E. Gently insert the speculum into the vagina. Do not use lubricant since this may interfere with the quality of the specimen. Use warm water for lubrication.
F. While inserting the speculum, visualize the vaginal vault, walls, and cervix. Note any irregularities such as lesions, masses, and lacerations.
G. If the lateral sidewalls collapse and decrease visualization of the cervix, withdraw the speculum. Apply a condom to the speculum and cut the condom tip. Reinsert the condom-covered speculum to visualize the cervix.
H. Observe for vaginal discharge, noting the amount, color, consistency, and odor.
   1. Bacterial vaginosis—discolored discharge with odor, homogeneous discharge that adheres to the vaginal walls
   2. Vulvovaginal candidiasis—thick white discharge that adheres to the vaginal walls
   3. Frothy, purulent discharge and a "strawberry" cervix can be identified.
I. Collect a sample of discharge with the two Q-tips.
   1. Place one Q-tip into a prefilled test tube/specimen tube and make your slide later *or*
   2. Collect a sample of discharge with the Q-tip and roll the Q-tip into the NS-prepared slide cover with a cover slip.
   3. *Then* roll the Q-tip into the KOH-prepared slide.
   4. Note any "musty/fishy" amine odor prior to placing the cover slip on the slide. (Whiff test is positive if amine odor is noted.)

J. Using the second Q-tip, roll it over a strip of nitrazine test tape to evaluate pH.
K. Using the Gen-probe, insert the tip onto the cervical os and rotate the tip in the os several times to obtain an adequate specimen (sample for a minimum of about 30 seconds).
L. Withdraw the Gen-probe applicator and place in the appropriate specimen container.
M. Gently remove the speculum and perform a bimanual examination, assessing for cervical motion tenderness and pain.
N. After completing this exam, take the specimens to the lab area for evaluation (while the patient is dressing).
O. Prepare your slides (if you did not follow steps I.1–I.4).
   1. Slide 1: Place one drop of NS to the slide, roll the Q-tip, and apply cover slip.
   2. Slide 2: Place one drop of KOH to the slide and roll the Q-tip; note any "musty/fishy" amine odor from the slide prior to placing the cover slide.
P. Observe the NS slide, first under the microscope. Start on low power, 10×, and adjust the focus until the specimen is clearly seen under the microscope.
Q. Observe the entire field and note the number of squamous cells.
R. Switch to the high-powered field, 40×, making sure the light source and the visual focus are adequate.
S. Observe the slide for
   1. Vaginal squamous epithelial cells: Appear flat, with clear edges. Red blood cells (RBCs), sperm, or polymorphonuclear neutrophils (PMNs) may also be identified (see Figure II.19).
   2. Clue cells: Epithelial cells with irregular borders and a granular appearance; may see the presence of coccobacilli bacteria (not present on slide) (see Figure II.20).
   3. Bacteria
   4. *Lactobacilli:* Appear as rods (see Figure II.21).
   5. White blood cells (WBCs): Note, a large number of WBCs is not normal.
   6. Trichomonads: Appear as ovoid mobile organisms that dart around on the slide (see Figures II.22 and II.23).
   7. *Candida:* Appear as branching pseudohyphae or budding yeast (best seen under the KOH slide) (see Figure II.24).

Treatment

A. Refer to specific chapters for treatment recommendations and medication dosages.

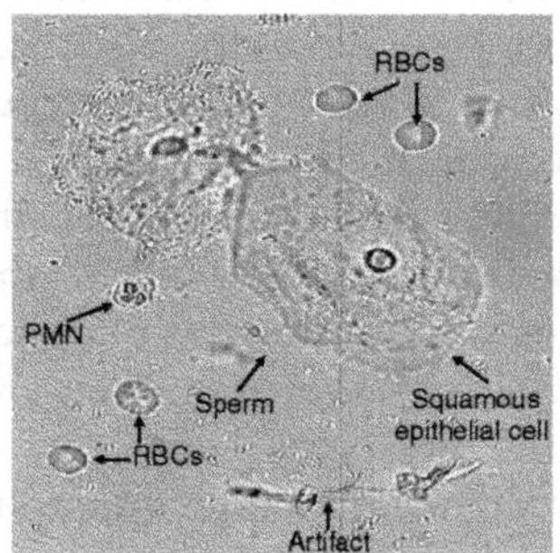

FIGURE II.19 Epithelial cells.
Used with permission from the Seattle STD/HIV Prevention Training Center at the University of Washington.

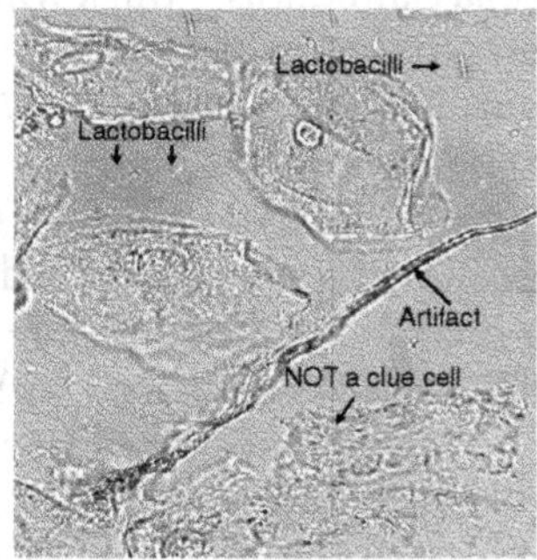

FIGURE II.21 *Lactobacilli*.
Used with permission from the Seattle STD/HIV Prevention Training Center at the University of Washington.

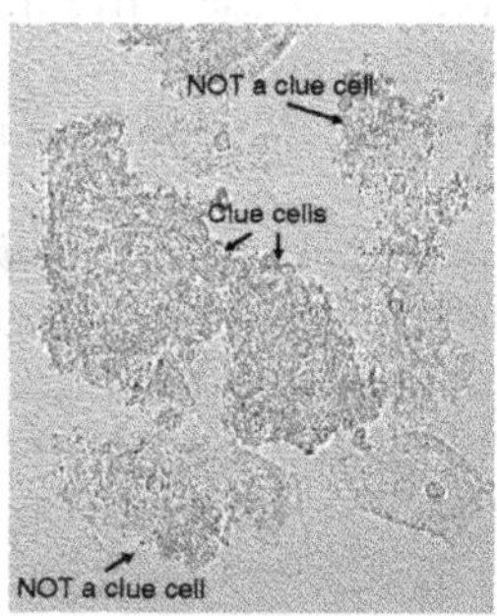

FIGURE II.20 Clue cells.
Used with permission from the Seattle STD/HIV Prevention Training Center at the University of Washington.

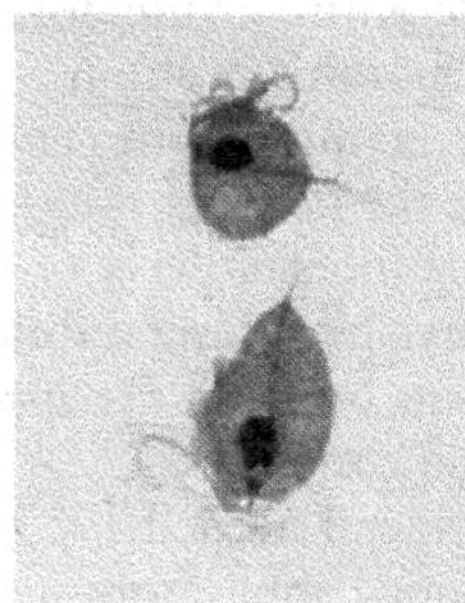

FIGURE II.22 *Trichomonas vaginalis*.
Used with permission from the Seattle STD/HIV Prevention Training Center at the University of Washington.

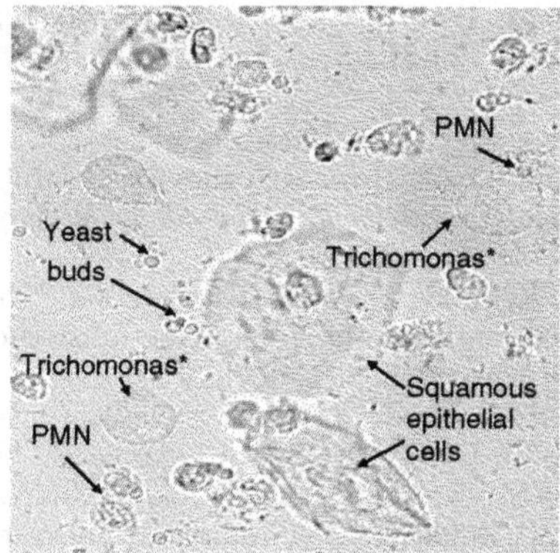

FIGURE II.23 *Trichomonas* (1,000×).
Note: Organism is enlarged.
Used with permission from the Seattle STD/HIV Prevention Training Center at the University of Washington.

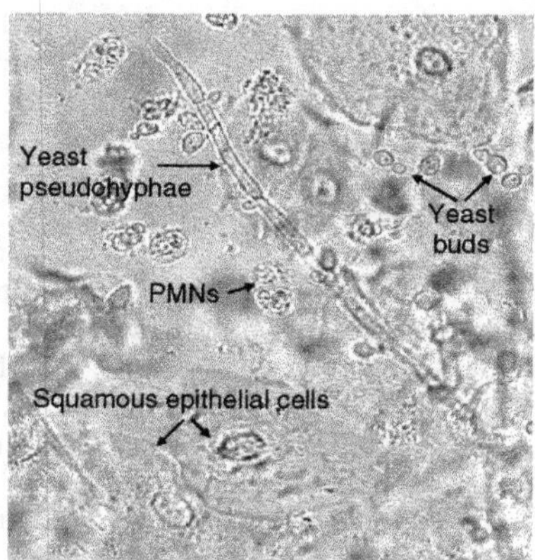

FIGURE II.24 Budding yeast cells, pseudohyphae, and septate hyphae and spores.
Used with permission from the Seattle STD/HIV Prevention Training Center at the University of Washington.

TABLE II.5 Vaginitis Differentiation

	Normal	Bacterial Vaginosis	Candidiasis	Trichomoniasis
Symptom presentation		Odor, discharge, itch	Itch, discomfort, dysuria, thick discharge	Itch, discharge, ~70% asymptomatic
Vaginal discharge	Clear to white	Homogeneous, adherent, thin, milky white; malodorous "foul fishy"	Thick, clumpy, white "cottage cheese"	Frothy, gray or yellow-green; malodorous
Clinical findings			Inflammation and erythema	Cervical petechiae "strawberry cervix"
Vaginal pH	3.8–4.2	> 4.5	Usually < 4.5	> 4.5
KOH "whiff" test	Negative	Positive	Negative	Often positive
NaCl wet mount	Lacto-bacilli	Clue cells (> 20%), no/few WBCs	Few to many WBCs	Motile flagellated protozoa, many WBCs
KOH wet mount			Pseudohyphae or spores if non-*albicans* species	

Bibliography

American Cancer Society. (2012). *Cervical cancer: Prevention and early detection.* Retrieved from http://www.cancer.org/cancer/cervicalcancer/moreinformation/cervicalcancerpreventionandearlydetection/cervical-cancer-prevention-andearly-detection-find-pre-cancer-changes

American College of Obstetricians and Gynecologists. (2009, July). ACOG Practice Bulletin No. 106: Intrapartum fetal heart rate monitoring: Nomenclature interpretation, and general management principles. *Obstetrics and Gynecology, 114*, 192–202.

American College of Obstetricians and Gynecologists. (2010, November). ACOG Practice Bulletin No.116: Management of intrapartum fetal heart rate tracing. *Obstetrics and Gynecology, 116*, 1232–1240.

American College of Obstetricians and Gynecologists. (2011). *Frequently asked questions FAQ028 gynecologic problems: Vaginitis.* Retrieved from www.acog.org/~/media/For%20Patients/faq028.pdf?dmc=1&ts=20130527T2155240385

American National Red Cross. (2011). *Airway adjunctions.* Retrieved from www.redcross.org/images/MEDIA_CustomProductCatalog/m4240191_AirwayAdjuncts FactsandSkill.pdf

American Society for Colposcopy and Cervical Pathology. (2013). 2-12 Updated consensus guidelines for the management of abnormal cervical cancer screening test and cancer precursors. *Journal of Lower Genital Tract Disease, 17*, S1–S27.

American Urological Association. (n.d.). *Adult urodynamics: AUA/SUFU guideline.* Retrieved from www.auanet.org/education/adult-urodynamics.cfm

Atnip, S., & O'Dell. (2012). Vaginal support pessaries: Indications for use and fitting strategies. *Urologic Nursing, 32*(5), 114–124.

Beattie, S. (2005, February 1). Placing an oropharyngeal airway. *Modern Medicine.* Retrieved from www.modernmedicine.com/node/40231

Blumenfeld, H. (n.d.). Neuroanatomy through clinical cases: Extraocular movements (CN III, IV, VI). Retrieved from http://www.neuroexam.com/content.php?p=20

Bradley, C. S., Smith, K. E., & Kreder, K. J. (2008). Urodynamic evaluation of the bladder and pelvic floor. *Gastroenterology Clinics of North America, 37*, 539–552.

Cheuck, L. (2014 January 7). Diagnostic prostatic massage technique. *Medscape Reference.* Retrieved from http://emedicine.medscape.com/article/1948091-overview

Davis, R., Jones, J. S., Barcocas, D. A., Castle, E. P., Lang, E. K., Leveillee, R. J., . . . Weitzel, W. (2012). Diagnosis, evaluation, and follow-up of asymptomatic microhematuria (AMH) in adults: AUA guideline. *American Urological Association (AUA).* Retrieved from www.auanet.org/content/media/asymptomic_microhematuria_guidelien.pdf

Epley Maneuver: A Simple Cure for a Common Cause of Vertigo. (2010–2013). In R. Porter (Ed.). *The Merck manual home health handbook.* Whitehouse Station, NJ: Merck Sharp & Dohme Corp., a subsidiary of Merck & Co. Retrieved from http://www.merckmanuals.com/home

Family Practice Notebook.com. Orthopedics Book. (n.d.). *Ankle anterior drawer test.* Retrieved from http://www.fpnotebook.com/Ortho/Exam/AnklAntrDrwrTst.htm

Family Practice Notebook.com. Orthopedics Book. (n.d.). *McMurray test.* Retrieved from http://www.fpnotebook.com/Ortho/Exam/McmryTst.htm

Family Practice Notebook.com. Orthopedics Book. (n.d.). *Talar tilt.* Retrieved from http://www.fpnotebook.com/Ortho/Exam/TlrTlt.htm

Fischer, J. I. (2013, October 15). Nasal foreign bodies. *Medscape Reference.* Retrieved from http://emedicine.medscape.com/article/763767-overview

Gray, M. (2011). Evaluation of bladder filling/storage functions. *Urologic Nursing, 31*, 149–153.

Hatcher, R. A., Trussell, J., Nelson, A. L., Cates, W., Kowal, D., & Policar, M. S. (Eds.). (2011). *Contraceptive technology* (20th ed.). New York: Ardent Media.

Heit, M., Rosenquist, C., Culligan, P., Graham, C., Murphy, M., & Shott, S. (2003). Predicting treatment choice for patients with pelvic organ prolapse. *Obstetrics & Gynecology, 101*(6), 1279–1284.

Hubbard, E. J., Santini, V., Blankevoot, C. G., Volker, K. M., Barrup, M. S., Byerly, L., ... Stern, R. A. (2008, May). Clock drawing performance in cognitively normal elderly. *Archives of Clinical Neuropsychology, 23*, 295–327.

Interstitial Cystitis Association. (2013). Urodyamics: What, when, why. Retrieved from www.idhelp.org/page. aspx?pid=990

Kennard, C. (2013). Clock drawing test. *About.com Alzheimer's/Dementia.* Retrieved from alzheimers.about.com/od/diagnosisissues/a/clock_test.htm?p=1

Krause, R. S. (2013, June 5). Reduction of rectal prolapse. *Medscape Reference.* Retrieved from http://emedicine.medscape.com/article/80982-overview

Lab Tests Online. (2013, May 9). Vaginitis and vaginosis. Retrieved from labtestsonline.org/understanding/conditions/vaginitis/start/2

Lowe, S., & Saxe, J. (1998). *Microscopic procedures for primary care providers.* Philadelphia, PA: Lippincott, Williams & Wilkins.

Markle, D., Skoczylas, L., Goldsmith, C., & Noblett, K. (2011). Patient characteristics associated with a successful pessary fitting. *Female Pelvic Medicine & Reconstructive Surgery, 17*(5), 249–252.

Murray, T. A., Kelly, N. R., & Jenkins, S. (2002). The complete neurological examination: What every nurse should know. *Advance for Nurse Practitioners, 10*, 25–29.

National Kidney and Urologic Diseases Information Clearinghouse (NKUDIC). (2012, January). Urodynamic testing. *NIH Publication No. 12-5106.* Retrieved from http://kidney.niddk.nih.gov/kudiseases/pubs/urodynamic/index.aspx

Nguyen, J. N., & Jones, C. R. (2005). Pessary treatment of pelvic relaxation: Factors affecting successful fitting and continued use. *Journal of Wound, Ostomy and Continence Nurses Society, 32*(4), 255–261.

O'Dell, K., & Atnip, S. (2012). Pessary care: Follow up and management of complications. *Urologic Nursing, 32*(3), 126–145.

Oregon Health & Science University. (n.d.). *OHSU health information: Cystometry.* Retrieved from https:www.ohsu.edu/xd/health/health-information/topic-by-id.cfm?ContentTypeId=92&ContentId=P07718

Preboth, M. (2000). Practice guidelines: ACOG guidelines on antepartum fetal surveillance. *American Family Physician, 62*, 1184–1188.

Public Health Laboratory. (2011, November 30). Vaginal wet preparation procedure. Retrieved from www.ok.gov/health2/documents/2012%20Vaginal%20Wet%Prep%Proc.pdf

Rehabilitation Institute of Chicago. (n.d.). *The clock draw test.* Available from www.rehabmeasures.org

Samara-Latif, O. M. (2014 March 7). Vulvovaginitis. *Medscape Reference.* Retrieved from http://emedicine.medscape.com/article/2188931-overview

Sand, P. K. (2008). Diagnostic procedures in the evaluation of female urinary incontinence and voiding dysfunction. *The Global Library of Women's Medicine.* Retrieved from www.glowm.com/section_view/heading/DiasnosticProceduresintheEvaluationofFemaleUrinaryIncontinenceandVoiding Dysfunction/item/55

Seidel, H. M., Ball, J. W., Dains, J. E., & Benedict, G. W. (1991). *Mosby's guide to physical examination* (2nd ed.). New York, NY: Mosby Year-Book.

Soddoqui, N. Y., & Edenfield, A. L. (2014). Clinical challenges in the management of vaginal prolapse. *International Journal of Women's Health, 6*, 83–94.

Weber, A. M., & Richter, H. E. (2005). Pelvic organ prolapse. *Obstetrics & Genecology, 106*(3), 615–634.

Wohlrab, K., & Pragana, M. (2013). Pessaries for pelvic organ prolapse. *Postgraduate Obstetrics & Gynecology, 33*(21), 1–7.

Young, B. K (2014, July 2). Antepartum fetal heart rate assessment. *UpToDate.* Retrieved from http://www.uptodate.com/contents/antepartum-fetal-heart-rate-assessment?source=search_result&search=fetal&selectedTitle=3%7E150

SECTION III

Patient Teaching Guides

- Adult-Geriatric Assessments
- Pain Management
- Dermatology Conditions
- Eye Disorders
- Ear Disorders
- Nasal Disorders
- Throat and Mouth Disorders
- Respiratory Disorders
- Cardiovascular Disorders
- Gastrointestinal Disorders
- Genitourinary Disorders
- Obstetrics
- Gynecology
- Sexually Transmitted Infections
- Infectious Diseases
- Systemic Disorders
- Musculoskeletal Disorders
- Rheumatology
- Neurologic Disorders
- Endocrine Disorders
- Psychiatric Disorders

Patient Teaching Guides for Chapter 3: Adult-Geriatric Assessments

- Safety Issues: Fall Prevention
- Safety Issues: Medication Safety

SAFETY ISSUES: FALL PREVENTION

PROBLEM

One third of people 65 years and older fall each year. A review of your home can help prevent falls. Complete a "My Falls-Free" Plan (see Table III.1) to help you and your caregiver identify problems and the need to have a referral to a specialist.

CAUSES

Your primary care provider and you should discuss your risk of falling. Most of the time it is a combination of factors that places you at risk for falls.

A. A previous fall makes you at the highest risk for another fall.

B. Medical problems that place you at risk for falls include arthritis, dizziness, blood pressure, diabetes, shortness of breath, heart problems, and having to go to the bathroom quickly.

C. Medicines including over-the-counter medicines and herbals may interact and cause problems with blood pressure, dizziness, and other side effects that put you at risk for falls.

D. Alcohol and use of recreational drugs also increase your risk for falls.

PREVENTION

A. A review of your home to identify items that place you at risk is essential.
   1. **General home safety review**
      a. Walk around each room to see if you have a clear path or if you have to walk around furniture. Your furniture may need to be moved to make a clear path.
      b. Remove clutter.
      c. Add side railings on both sides of stairs.
      d. Use nonslip rugs or even remove rugs to prevent tripping. Fix loose and torn carpeting.
      e. Increase lighting by using brighter watt bulbs and nightlights. Add an overhead light at the top and the bottom of the stairway.
      f. Wear shoes instead of slippers and wear shoes instead of going barefoot.
   2. **Bathroom safety review**
      a. Add grab bars on the inside and outside of the shower.
      b. Add at least one grab bar located at the toilet.
      c. Add a nonslip bath mat in your tub or shower.
      d. Use a nonslip mat to step on when getting out of the tub or shower.
      e. Use a raised toilet seat.
      f. Consider the need for a bedside commode.
   3. **Bedroom safety review**
      a. Add lamp close to the bed so that you don't have to reach from the edge of the bed.
      b. Use a nightlight.
      c. Use a comforter and blankets instead of long bed spreads that touch the floor.
   4. **Kitchen safety review**
      a. Place bowls, plates, and spices down on the lower level of your cabinets in order to get to them safely and not have to stand on your toes to reach for them.
      b. Never use a chair instead of a step stool.

B. **Other safety tips**
   1. Discuss the need for a Personal Emergency Response System.
   2. Carry a cell phone in your pocket.
   3. Keep emergency numbers near each phone and posted on the refrigerator.
   4. Limit alcohol to one drink a day to help prevent falls.

TREATMENT PLAN

A. Discuss the need for an eye examination.

B. Discuss the need for assistive devices such as canes and walkers.

C. Discuss the use of a Vial of Life to identify important information in case of an emergency. www.vialoflife.com/how_to_use_the_vial_of_life

Activity: Exercise is very important in maintaining balance.

A. Walk two or three times a week.

B. Do balance exercise such as Tai Chi.

TABLE III.1 **My Falls-Free Plan**

Name: _______________ **Date:** _______________

As we grow older, gradual health changes and some medications can cause falls, but many falls can be prevented. Use this to learn what to do to stay active, independent, and falls free.

Check "Yes" if you experience this (even if only sometimes)	No	Yes	What to do if you checked "Yes"
Have you had any falls in the last 6 months?			☐ Talk with your doctor(s) about your falls and/or concerns. ☐ Show this checklist to your doctor(s) to help understand and treat your risks, and protect yourself from falls.
Do you take four or more prescription or over-the-counter medications daily?			☐ Review your medications with your doctor(s) **and** your pharmacist at each visit, and with each new prescription. ☐ Ask which of your medications can cause drowsiness, dizziness, or weakness as a side effect. ☐ Talk with your doctor about anything that could be a medication side effect or interaction.
Do you have any difficulty walking or standing?			☐ Tell your doctor(s) if you have any pain, aching, soreness, stiffness, weakness, swelling, or numbness in your legs or feet—**don't ignore** these types of health problems. ☐ Tell your doctor(s) about **any** difficulty walking to discuss treatment. ☐ Ask your doctor(s) if physical therapy or treatment by a medical specialist would be helpful to your problem.
Do you use a cane, walker, or crutches, or have to hold onto things when you walk?			☐ Ask your doctor for training from a physical therapist to learn what type of device is best for you and how to safely use it.
Do you have to use your arms to be able to stand up from a chair?			☐ Ask your doctor for a physical therapy referral to learn exercises to strengthen your leg muscles. ☐ Exercise at least two or three times a week for 30 minutes.
Do you ever feel unsteady on your feet, weak, or dizzy?			☐ Tell your doctor, and ask if treatment by a specialist or physical therapist would help improve your condition. ☐ Review all of your medications with your doctor(s) or pharmacist if you notice **any** of these conditions.
Has it been more than 2 years since you had an eye exam?			☐ Schedule an eye exam every 2 years to protect your eyesight and your balance.
Has your hearing gotten worse with age, or do your family or friends say you have a hearing problem?			☐ Schedule a hearing test every 2 years. ☐ If hearing aids are recommended, learn **how** to use them to help protect and restore your hearing, which helps improve and protect your balance.
Do you usually exercise less than 2 days a week? (for 30 min total each of the days you exercise)			☐ Ask your doctor(s) what types of exercise would be good for improving your strength and balance. ☐ Find some activities that you enjoy and people to exercise with 2 or 3 days per week for 30 minutes.
Do you drink any alcohol daily?			☐ Limit your alcohol to one drink per day to avoid falls.
Do you have more than three chronic health conditions (such as heart or lung problems, diabetes, high blood pressure, arthritis, etc.)? Ask your doctor(s) if you are unsure.			☐ See your doctor(s) as often as recommended to keep your health in good condition. ☐ Ask your doctor(s) what you should do to stay healthy and active with your health conditions. ☐ Report any health changes that cause weakness or illness as soon as possible.

The more **Yes** answers you have, the greater your chance of having a fall. Be aware of what can cause falls, and take care of yourself to stay independent and falls-free!

Reviewed by: _______________

This information is public domain from the Washington State Department of Health, Injury & Violence Prevention Program.

SAFETY ISSUES: MEDICATION SAFETY

PROBLEM

Multiple problems may occur as a result of taking more than two medicines, including drug interactions and side effects. It is very important to ask questions and ask for written instructions to make sure that you understand your medicines.

CAUSES

The causes of problems with medications include:

A. Not understanding what each prescription is and how to take them

B. Seeing more than one doctor for different medical conditions

C. Using more than one pharmacy

D. Taking some prescription medication with herbal and over-the-counter medicines

E. Mixing other family members' medications with yours

F. Unable to remember if you have taken your medicine and take it again

G. Not having a system set up to take medications as prescribed

H. Taking someone else's medications

I. Some medicines need to be tapered off instead of just stopping them.

PREVENTION

A. Questions to ask your provider and pharmacist for medicines include:
   1. What is the medication for?
   2. What are the side effects of this medicine?
   3. How do you take it?
   4. When do you take it?
   5. What should you do if you miss any medicine?
   6. Can the medicine be taken with food or should it be taken on an empty stomach?
   7. Are there any foods that should not be eaten while on the medicine?
   8. Can the pill be cut in half?
   9. Can the pill be crushed or chewed?
   10. How long should it be taken?
   11. Should this medicine be stored in any special way, like keeping it in the refrigerator?
   12. Is there a generic medicine that costs less?

B. It is important to make a list of all of your medications, including any prescriptions, vitamins, herbal products, and any over-the-counter products that you take.
   1. Eye drops, creams, patches, and inhalers are medicines.
   2. Over-the-counter products that should be listed include medicines for your bowels, headaches, stomach, and sleep.
   3. Keep your medicine list up to date by adding new medicines, taking off medicines that are no longer taken, and updating your list if the medicine dose changes.
   4. Don't stop medicines just because you feel better.

C. Once or twice a year, take a bag of all of your medications into the office to have your health care provider review them.

D. Store your medicine in one place instead of multiple medications in the kitchen cabinets/shelves, bedroom, bathroom, and drawers.

E. Lock up your medications.
   1. Use a toolbox that can be locked.
   2. Others may go through medications due to their drug addiction.
   3. Children are curious about different color pills and containers.

F. Do not share medicines with anyone.

G. Keep individual family medicines separated by using a different shelf or basket.
   1. If you need to use inhalers for asthma or other lung problems, use one color basket for fast-acting inhalers and another color basket for the long-acting inhaler medicine.

H. Use a weekly pill container to prevent you from taking extra doses out of a bottle.
   1. Have someone help you set up your medicines.

I. Do not mix medicines in one bottle.

J. Medicine that comes in an amber container protects the medicine from light.

K. Before throwing out an old medicine bottle, scratch out or use a marker to make the information unreadable to protect personal information.

L. Ask the pharmacist how to dispose of unused and old medicines.

M. Throw out outdated medications and medications that are no longer taken. The Food and Drug Association (FDA) and the White House Office of National Drug Control Policy have developed guidelines for drug disposal.
   1. Do not flush medications down the sink or toilet unless there are specific labels on the medication.
      a. Narcotic pain medicine may have instructions to flush them to reduce the danger of unintentional use or overdose.
      b. Fentanyl patches for pain should be folded in half and flushed down the toilet.
   2. Use community drug takeback programs to bring any unused drugs to a central location for proper drug disposal. Often there are designated disposal containers in police stations.
   3. If the drug cannot be put down the drain/flushed and cannot be taken to a designated disposal, the following steps should be taken.
      a. Remove the medications from the original container and mix them with kitty litter, coffee grounds, or other undesirable substances.
      b. Place the mixture in a sealable bag, empty can, or other container to prevent leaking.

Patient Teaching Guides for Chapter 5: Pain Management

- Back Stretches
- Chronic Pain

BACK STRETCHES

You have been approved to do back-stretching exercises to help with your low-back pain. Follow the instructions, starting slowly to build up your strength.

EQUIPMENT

Use a mat or a towel on your floor for extra padding and comfort.

A. In the lying position
  1. Lie on your back with knees bent. Cross your arms over your chest.
  2. Raise your head and shoulders and curl your trunk upward, no more than 6 inches.
  3. Keep the small of your back pressed against the mat.
  4. Exhale during the curl up.
  5. Hold _____ seconds; do _____ repetitions _____ times a day (see Figure III.1).

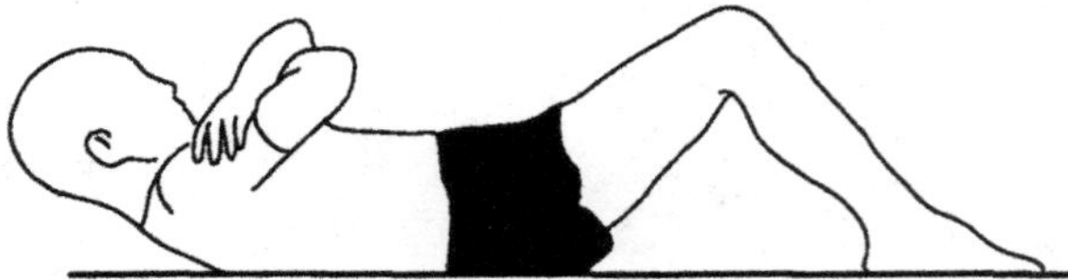

FIGURE III.1 Lie on a mat or towel.
Raise head and shoulders as demonstrated.

B. In the standing position
  1. Stand with your back against the wall.
  2. Place your feet shoulder width apart and 18 inches from the wall.
  3. Slowly slide down the wall until you are in the "chair" position.
  4. Hold for 10 seconds and relax, then slide back up the wall to a standing position.
  5. Do ____ repetitions ____ times a day (see Figure III.2).

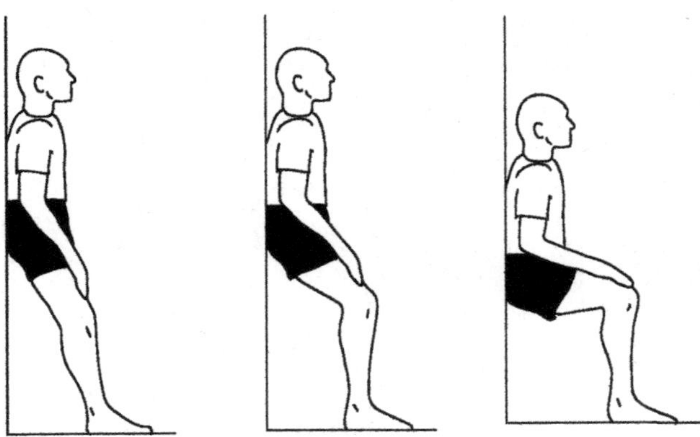

FIGURE III.2 Place your feet shoulder width apart.
Slide down against the wall to the "chair" position.

C. In the lying position
  1. Bring your right knee slowly to your chest, holding it in place with your hands on your knee.
  2. Relax the buttock and your back muscles.
  3. Hold ____ seconds, then relax with your right knee down.
  4. Repeat with your left knee.
  5. Now that you have stretched both legs, pull both of your knees up, holding them in place with your hands on your knees.
  6. You will be curled in the fetal position.
  7. Hold ____ seconds, then relax with your knees down.
  8. Do ______ repetitions, ______ times per day (see Figure III.3).

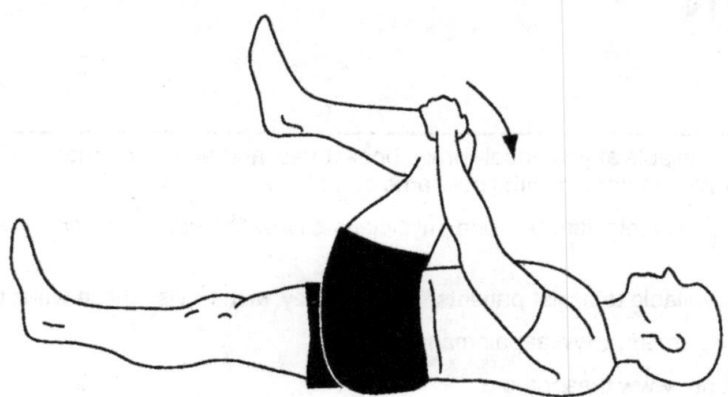

FIGURE III.3 Pull your left knee toward your chest to stretch, repeat with your right knee as demonstrated.

D. In the lying position
   1. Lie on your back with your knees bent.
   2. Tighten your abdominal muscles and squeeze. As you squeeze the buttocks muscles, flatten your back toward the mat/towel (as shown in Figure III.4). Relax.
   3. Tighten your buttocks muscles and lift your abdomen or "tummy" toward your knees while arching your back. Relax.
   4. Hold _____ seconds; do _____ repetitions _____ times a day (see Figure III.4).

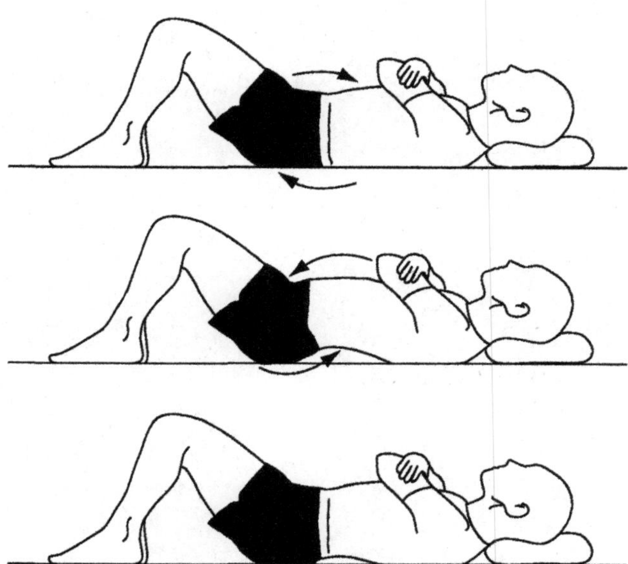

FIGURE III.4 Lie with knees bent, flatten your back, then lift your tummy toward knees with back arched.

CHRONIC PAIN

RESOURCES

Many patient resources on pain are available at your local library, bookstores, and on the Internet. Look for a local support group in your area to join and learn how other people are coping with your same condition.

An excellent resource book written for patients, families, and physicians is *How to Cope With Chronic Pain,* by Nelson Hendler, MD (Cool Hand Communications, 1993).

There are many pain organizations available to assist patients. Patients may wish to visit these websites for further information.

American Academy of Pain Management: www.aapainmanage.org

American Chronic Pain Association: www.theacpa.org

American Pain Society: www.americanpainsociety.org

Arthritis Foundation: www.arthritis.org

National Chronic Pain Outreach Association: www.healthcentral.com/chronic-pain/h/national-chronic-pain-outreach-association.html

National Fibromyalgia Association: www.fmaware.org

Patient Teaching Guides for Chapter 6: Dermatology Conditions

- Acne Rosacea
- Acne Vulgaris
- Dermatitis
- Eczema
- Erythema Multiforme
- Folliculitis
- Herpes Zoster (Shingles)
- Insect Bites and Stings
- Lice (Pediculosis)
- Lichen Planus
- Pityriasis Rosea
- Psoriasis
- Ringworm (Tinea)
- Scabies
- Seborrheic Dermatitis
- Skin Care Assessment
- Tinea Versicolor
- Warts
- Wound Care: Lower Extremity Ulcers
- Wound Care: Pressure Ulcers
- Wounds of the Skin
- Xerosis (Winter Itch)

ACNE ROSACEA

PROBLEM

Acne rosacea is a skin condition that affects primarily the nose and face, causing redness, flushing, pimples, and bumps. The blood vessels may be more prominent on the face, causing the skin to appear reddened.

CAUSE

The cause is not known. It is thought to be caused by the blood vessels in the face being too active, causing flushing and redness of the skin.

PREVENTION/CARE

A. Avoid rubbing or massaging the face, which can irritate the skin.

B. Avoid alcoholic beverages.

C. Avoid using harsh soaps/creams on face, including cosmetics that irritate the skin.

D. Wash face with a mild soap, such as Cetaphil or Purpose soap, daily. Other cleansers suggested are sulfa-based cleanser (Rosanil) or benzoyl peroxide cleanser daily.

E. Protect the skin when outdoors, wearing protective clothing, hats, and so on, to cover the face. Use a sunscreen with an SPF 30 or a zinc-based ointment, such as zinc oxide, on the skin for protection.

F. You may be prescribed an antibiotic by mouth or an antibiotic cream/gel to place on the skin. Use medications as prescribed by your provider.

G. Avoid using steroid creams on your face unless prescribed by your provider.

H. If your skin condition begins to affect your eyes, you need to notify your provider immediately. Do not apply any medications or creams on your eyes without being prescribed by your provider.

TREATMENT PLAN

A. Use antibiotics/medications as prescribed by your provider.

B. Wash face with mild cleanser daily.

Activity: As tolerated. No limitations in physical activity.

Diet:

A. Drink plenty of fluids daily.

B. Avoid alcoholic beverages.

Medications:

You Have Been Prescribed: ______________________________

You Need to Take: ______________________________

You Need to Notify the Office If:

A. You have a reaction to any of the medications or cleansers prescribed.

B. Rash appears on your eyes or other new places.

C. Symptoms worsen, or new signs or symptoms present before your next follow-up appointment.

D. Other: ______________________________

Phone: ____________________

RESOURCE

www.rosacea.org

ACNE VULGARIS

Acne vulgaris is blackheads, whiteheads, or red nodules noted on the face, back, chest, and arms.

CAUSE

Accumulation of cells and bacteria clog the pores and stimulate an inflammatory response, which results in papule or pustule (pimple or blackhead) formation.

PREVENTION/CARE

A. Wash area with mild soap (Purpose or Basis soap) no more than two times per day.

B. Avoid oil-based makeup and creams. Use matte-finished makeup or pore minimizer.

C. Use facial cleansers and moisturizers such as Cetaphil and Moisturel. These prevent the skin from drying out. Benzoyl peroxide 5% lotion or gel may be used at bedtime to help open pores and kill bacteria.

D. To prevent scarring, do not pick lesions.

E. Avoid excessive sun exposure. Use oil-free sunscreen with SPF 15 or greater.

F. Do not get frustrated if lesions return. Do not stop medications without the direction of your provider.

G. Stress can influence outbreaks of lesions. Practice routine exercise programs, stress management tactics, and other measures that decrease stress levels in your daily routine.

Activity: As tolerated. Physical activity encouraged.

Diet: Eat a well-balanced diet. Drink 8 to 10 glasses of water a day to help keep your skin well hydrated. Cocoa and chocolate do not have an effect on the development of acne vulgaris.

Medications: Antibiotics may need to be prescribed.

You Have Been Prescribed: ____________________

You Need to Take: ____________________

You Need to Notify the Office If:

A. You have a reaction to any of the medications prescribed.

B. You are unable to tolerate the prescribed medications.

Phone: ____________________

DERMATITIS

Inflammation of the skin that occurs from contact with an irritant substance (poison ivy, soaps, etc.).

CAUSE

Skin contact with irritating agent.

PREVENTION/TREATMENT PLAN

A. Avoid aggravating agents.

B. Learn to recognize all plants (poison ivy, poison oak, etc.).

C. Flare-ups are common.

D. Avoid all known stimuli (poison ivy, soaps, etc.).

E. Do not wear tight, restrictive clothing.

F. When around irritating substances, wear gloves for protection.

G. For poison ivy
   1. Wash all clothes, shoes, pets, or other substances that may have come in contact with the poison ivy oil.

Activity: As tolerated. Take cool baths as needed for itching. Oatmeal baths (Aveeno bath) help soothe the itching.

Diet: Regular diet.

Medications: Take Benadryl as needed for itching. Use calamine lotion as needed. Steroid creams may also be prescribed if reaction is severe. Steroid dose packs may be needed if you are not getting better.

You Have Been Prescribed: ______________________________

You Need to Take: ______________________________

You Need to Notify the Office If You Have:

A. Worsening symptoms

B. Sores on your face, eyes, or ears

C. More redness, swelling, pain, or drainage

D. Secondary bacterial infection

E. Fever

F. Other: ______________________________

Phone: ____________________

ECZEMA

PROBLEM

Red, itching, scaling, and thickening of skin occurs in patches. You may have papules (bumps) with vesicles (clear fluid) that can be found especially on the hands, scalp, face, back of the neck, or skin creases of elbows and knees.

CAUSE

The cause is unknown. If it is an allergic reaction, it may be caused by foods such as eggs, wheat, milk, or seafood; wool clothing; skin lotions and ointments; soaps; detergents; cleansers; plants; tanning agents used for shoe leather; dyes; and topical medications. The risk for developing eczema increases with stress, medical history of other allergic conditions, clothing made of synthetic fabric (which traps perspiration), and weather extremes (cold, hot).

PREVENTION/CARE

A. Avoid risk factors.

B. Wear rubber gloves for household cleaning tasks.

C. Wear loose, cotton clothing to help absorb perspiration.

D. Keep fingernails short and wear soft gloves during sleep.

E. Scratching worsens eczema.

F. Bathe less frequently to avoid excessive skin dryness.

G. Use special nonfat soaps (Purpose or Basis soap) and tepid water.

H. Do not use soap on inflamed areas.

I. Lubricate the skin after bathing; avoid lubricants with alcohol in the ingredients.

J. Recommended creams include Eucerin, Keri Lotion, and Lubriderm. Steroid creams may be prescribed.

K. Avoid extreme temperature changes.

L. Avoid anything that has previously worsened the condition.

Activity: No restrictions.

Diet: You may be told to try a special diet. Eliminate any foods known to cause flare-ups.

Medications:

You Have Been Prescribed: ______________________________

You Need to Take: ______________________________

You Need to Notify the Office If:

A. You have a reaction to any of the medications prescribed.

B. You cannot take the medications.

C. New symptoms develop.

Phone: ______________________

ERYTHEMA MULTIFORME

PROBLEM

An acute inflammatory disorder of the skin and mucous membranes, erythema multiforme is usually self-limited and benign.

A severe form is known as Stevens–Johnson syndrome or erythema multiforme majus, and the less severe form is referred to as erythema multiforme minus.

CAUSE

The cause is unknown in 50% of the cases. Erythema multiforme has been associated with viral infections, particularly the herpes simplex virus; bacterial and protozoan infections; an immunologic reaction of the skin; medications (sulfonamides, penicillins, anticonvulsants, salicylates, barbiturates), with reactions occurring up to 7 to 14 days after using the medication; pregnancy; premenstrual hormone changes; malignancy; or radiation therapy. Risk increases with previous history of erythema multiforme.

PREVENTION/CARE

A. Avoid suspected causes.

B. Seek prompt treatment of any illness or infection.

C. Prevent herpes simplex virus outbreaks by avoiding sun exposure and reducing stress.

D. Seek treatment immediately if at any time symptoms seem to be worsening or increasing.

E. Discontinue any implicated medication.

F. Apply wet dressings or soaks, with Burow's solution, or apply lotions to soothe the skin.

G. Bathe in lukewarm to cool water three times a day for 30 minutes.

H. Monitor yourself for any eye involvement and report it to your health care provider immediately.

I. If mouth sores are present, use good oral hygiene (brush two to three times a day using a soft brush) and rinse frequently with cool water.

J. Hospitalization may be required if there is extensive skin involvement.

Activity: As tolerated by the extent of the symptoms. Restrict yourself to bed rest if fever is present.

Diet: Usually no special diet is necessary, although if mouth sores are present, a soft or liquid diet may be better tolerated. Increase fluid intake above the general 8 to 10 glasses per day.

Medications: May be prescribed to control symptoms and pain.

You Have Been Prescribed: ______________________________

You Need to Take: ______________________________

You Need to Notify the Office If:

A. You have an adverse reaction to or cannot tolerate any of the prescribed medications.

B. Symptoms worsen during treatment, or the rash does not clear in 3 weeks (usual course: rash evolves over 1 to 2 weeks, usually clears in 2 to 3 weeks, but may take 5 to 6 weeks).

C. New or unexplained symptoms develop.

D. You have any questions or concerns.

Phone: ____________________

FOLLICULITIS

PROBLEM

A bacterial (or fungal) infection of the hair follicle. Folliculitis is seen when a pustule develops, commonly on the arms, legs, scalp, and face (beard).

CAUSE

A. Bacterial: Infection commonly caused by *Staphylococcus* bacteria.

B. Fungal: May be caused by yeast infection.

PREVENTION/TREATMENT PLAN

A. Keep skin clean and dry.

B. Avoid warm, moist conditions.

C. Healing generally occurs in 10 to 14 days after proper treatment with medications.

D. Practice good hand-washing technique, using antibacterial soaps.

E. Use clean razors daily.

F. Throw old razors away.

G. Do not share razors.

H. Shampoo scalp daily.

I. Folliculitis usually resolves within 4 to 6 weeks after proper treatment.

Activity: As tolerated.

Diet: Regular diet.

Medications: Topical and/or oral antibiotics as prescribed.

You Have Been Prescribed: ____________________

You Need to Take: ____________________

You Need to Notify the Office If:

A. You notice lesions worsening or spreading, despite adequate medication treatment.

B. You have a fever higher than 101°F.

C. Your condition is not getting better.

D. You have a reaction to your medication.

Phone: ____________________

HERPES ZOSTER (SHINGLES)

PROBLEM

Shingles is a reactivation of the viral infection common in childhood known as chickenpox. **The virus is contagious for those who have not had the chickenpox.**

CAUSE

Varicella-zoster virus is stimulated and produces a blister-like rash, commonly seen on the chest and trunk area. The rash is commonly confined to one side of the body.

PREVENTION

Zostavax is a vaccination for the prevention of shingles. The Centers for Disease Control and Prevention (CDC) recommends this one-time vaccine for anyone age 60 and older.

TREATMENT PLAN

A. Zostavax cannot be used to treat the shingles breakouts or the painful sensations (postherpetic neuralgia) after you develop shingles.

B. The shingles rash usually lasts 2 to 3 weeks; however, symptoms may persist beyond this period.

C. The goal is to relieve the itching.

D. Apply warm soaks of Burow's solution three times a day to lesions.

E. Notify family and friends of active virus. Advise anyone who has had contact with you that you have shingles, especially pregnant women and those who have never had the chickenpox.

Activity: Avoid touching the shingles. Wash your hands. Your partners should not touch the area, especially when blisters are present. Use separate bath towels.

Diet: There is no special diet for shingles.

Medications: Oral and topical medications may be prescribed to soothe the itching. Take acetaminophen (Tylenol) as needed for comfort. Antiviral medications are available to help slow down the virus if started within 48 to 72 hours after the initial outbreak. You may be prescribed medications to help with the painful sensations (neuralgia).

CDC Guidelines recommended all adults 60 years of age and older receive the Zostavax vaccine.

You Have Been Prescribed: ____________________

You Need to Take: ____________________

You Need to Notify the Office If You Have:

A. Severe pain at lesion sites.

B. Any new symptoms relating to the shingles, such as excruciating pain, headaches, numbness, tingling sensation, or other symptoms.

C. Any questions regarding the shingles.

Phone: ____________________

INSECT BITES AND STINGS

PROBLEM

Skin changes and insect bites or stings cause other reactions.

A. **Seek immediate help if you or a family member has any symptoms of allergic reaction or anaphylaxis, either immediately after the bite or 8 to 12 hours after the bite.**

B. You may need to call 911 or your local emergency response service.

C. If you have had a previous life-threatening allergic reaction, carry an anaphylaxis kit for emergency treatment.
   1. *Local skin reactions* include red bumps in the skin that usually appear within minutes after the bite or sting, but may not appear for 6 to 12 hours. Itching and discomfort may occur at the site.
   2. *Systemic (body) reactions* include nausea or vomiting; headache, fever, dizziness or lightheadedness; swelling; or convulsions.
   3. *Allergic reactions* include itchy eyes, facial flushing, dry cough, wheezing, or chest or throat constriction or tightness.

CAUSE

Bites or stings can be caused by mosquitoes, fleas, chiggers, bedbugs, ants, spiders, bees, scorpions, and other insects.

Risk increases with exposure to areas with heavy insect infestation, warm weather in spring and summer, lack of protective measures, use of perfumes or colognes, and previous sensitization.

PREVENTION/CARE

A. **Institute first-aid measures and activate emergency services if severe, life-threatening reactions occur.**

B. Avoid risk factors.

C. Wear protective clothing.

D. Use insect repellents with diethyltoluamide (DEET), avoiding the head, face, eyes, and mouth.

SPECIFIC INSECT CARE

A. For all stings: Remove stinger.

B. Bee, wasp, yellow jacket, or hornet stings: Rub a paste of meat tenderizer and water into the site.

C. Ant bites: Rub bite with ammonia, and repeat as often as necessary.

D. Spider and scorpion bites: Capture the arachnid if possible and seek medical attention.

E. Mites: Apply a petroleum product (Vaseline) until the animal withdraws from the skin.

F. Ticks: Remove the tick by following the instructions in the Patient Teaching Guides for Chapter 18, "Lyme Disease and Removal of a Tick."

GENERAL CARE FOR ALL BITES

A. Clean wound with soap and water.

B. Apply ice pack (no ice directly on skin, use towel or cloth to protect skin).

C. Elevate and rest the affected body part.

D. Immerse affected part or apply warm water soaks to site. However, if site itches, cool water feels best.

E. For minor discomfort, you may use nonprescription oral antihistamines (Benadryl) or topical steroid preparations (hydrocortisone cream).

F. Use only low-potency topical steroid products without fluorine on the face and groin area.

G. You may be prescribed more potent, prescription medications.

Activity: No restrictions.

Diet: Eat a regular diet. Maintain adequate hydration with 8 to 10 glasses of water per day.

Medications: You may be prescribed an EpiPen to use for future major reactions. You need to keep this with you at all times.

You Have Been Prescribed: ______________________________

You Need to Take: ______________________________

You Need to Notify the Office If:

A. Self-care treatment does not relieve symptoms or if no improvement is noticed after 2 to 3 days.

B. A bitten area becomes red, swollen, warm, and tender to the touch. These symptoms indicate infection.

C. You have a temperature higher than or equal to 101°F.

D. You have a reaction or cannot tolerate any of the prescribed medications.

Phone: ______________________________

LICE (PEDICULOSIS)

PROBLEM

A parasite called a louse has been found on your body or hair. Lice tend to live on the scalp, eyebrows, or genital area, or in warm moist areas of your skin. You may notice you have intense itching, swelling, or reddened areas of the skin, and sometimes even enlarged lymph glands.

CAUSE

The lice bite the skin and cause the intense itching. Lice and their eggs (called nits) may be difficult to see on the skin and shafts of hair. Lice look like small, 2- to 3-mm, tan-colored bugs. The eggs are tiny white eggs that stick to the hair shaft.

PREVENTION

You can prevent repeated episodes of lice if you bathe daily; avoid crowded living conditions; change the bed linens frequently; do not share hats, combs, brushes, or other belongings. When family members have been in contact with others diagnosed with lice, check family members closely for lice and treat as appropriate.

TREATMENT PLAN

A. Use medicated shampoo as directed.

B. Machine wash all linens, stuffed animals, or any other items with which the lice may have come in contact.

C. Wash clothes in hot, soapy water.

D. Dry all linens in a hot dryer for at least 30 minutes.

E. Items that cannot be washed must be taken to the dry cleaner or wrapped and sealed in a plastic bag for 14 days.

F. Boil all hair accessories and clean well.

G. Do not share hats and combs.

H. Spray all furniture with appropriate products that kill all nits and lice.

I. Vacuum.

Activity: There is no activity restriction.

Diet: There is no special diet.

Medications:

A. Food and Drug Administration (FDA) approved over-the-counter (OTC) products:
   1. Pyrethrins combined with piperonyl butoxide; brand name Rid, Triple X, A-200, Pronto, R & C. Approved for children 2 years and up. Avoid if allergic to ragweed or chrysanthemums.

B. FDA approved for children 2 months and older. Permethrin lotion 1%. Brand name: Nix. Repeat application on day 9 of initial dose.

You Have Been Prescribed to Use:

A. Treat as directed on the bottle.

B. After shampooing as directed, make sure to remove each single nit from each shaft of hair. Any nits left in the hair will hatch and start the cycle over again. Comb any dead or remaining live lice out of hair with a fine tooth comb.

C. Repeat in 24 hours, then again in 1 week.

D. Do not use a shampoo/conditioner or conditioner prior to use of the lice medications. Do not wash hair for 1 to 2 days after lice medication treatment.

You Need to Notify the Office If You Have:

A. Any questions regarding the removal of the nits and lice, or if you need any assistance. If other family members need to be evaluated, please let us know. If secondary infection occurs, please call the office.

B. Precautions: Do not overuse medications or combine different head lice medications. Use only as directed. These medications are insecticides and can be dangerous if used incorrectly.

Phone: ______________________________

LICHEN PLANUS

PROBLEM

A chronic skin eruption, lichen planus is not cancerous or contagious. It frequently appears as small, slightly raised, itchy, purplish bumps with a whitish surface. Sudden hair loss from the head may occur. Lichen planus may involve the skin of the legs, trunk, arms, wrists, scalp, or penis; the lining of the mouth or vagina; and the nail beds of the toenails and fingernails.

CAUSE

The cause is unknown, but it may be caused by a virus. In a few cases, this may be an adverse reaction to certain drugs. The risk of developing lichen planus increases with stress, fatigue, or exposure to drugs or chemicals.

PREVENTION/CARE

Currently, there are no known preventive measures.

A. The goal of treatment is to relieve symptoms.

B. Use cool-water soaks to relieve itching.

C. Reduce stress; this may help to prevent recurrences. Learn relaxation techniques or obtain counseling if necessary.

D. Speak with your health care provider if you suspect a drug to be the cause.

Activity: No restrictions.

Diet: Eat a well-balanced diet; drink 8 to 10 glasses of water every day.

Medications:

You Have Been Prescribed: ______________________________

You Need to Take: ______________________________

You Need to Notify the Office If:

A. You have a reaction to any of the prescribed medications.

B. You are unable to tolerate the prescribed medications.

C. Hair loss or nail destruction occurs.

D. New lesions appear as old lesions resolve.

E. Other: ______________________________

Phone: ______________________

PITYRIASIS ROSEA

PROBLEM

Pityriasis rosea is a very common condition characterized by a rash, which may or may not itch. You may have noticed a large scaly patch prior to breaking out with the more generalized rash. **It is not known to be contagious, and you do not need to isolate yourself.**

CAUSE

The cause of pityriasis rosea is unknown.

PREVENTION

Because the cause of pityriasis rosea is unknown, there are no recommended preventive measures.

TREATMENT PLAN

Good hygiene and avoidance of scratching are recommended to prevent a secondary infection.

Activity: It is not necessary for you to limit your activity. Sunlight exposure to skin for short periods of time daily for five consecutive days will decrease itching and improve rash. Care should be taken in not burning skin with short-term exposure to the sun.

Diet: No changes are required in your diet.

Medications: You may be prescribed an antihistamine medication to take by mouth and topical steroid creams to apply to the rash itself. If the itching is severe, you may have oral steroids prescribed.

You Have Been Prescribed: ______________________________

You Need to Take: ______________________________

You Need to Notify the Office If You Have:

A. Any new symptoms.

B. Any reaction to your medication.

Phone: ______________________________

PSORIASIS

PROBLEM

Psoriasis is a chronic, scaly, thickened skin disorder with frequent remissions and recurrences. The skin of the scalp, elbows, knees, chest, back, arms, legs, toenails, fingernails, and fold between the buttocks may be involved.

CAUSE

The cause of psoriasis is unknown.

PREVENTION/CARE

A. There is no known prevention, but symptoms can be controlled.

B. Moving to a warmer climate might be beneficial. Severity increases with cold.

C. Maintain good skin hygiene with daily baths or showers.

D. Avoid harsh soaps.

E. Avoid skin injury, including harsh scrubbing, which can trigger new outbreaks.

F. Avoid skin dryness.

G. To reduce scaling, use nonprescription, waterless cleansers, as well as hair preparations containing coal tar (Zetar, T/Gel, Pentrax), emollients (Eucerin Plus lotion or cream, Lubriderm, Moisture Plus, Moisturel), or products containing cortisone (often prescription strength).

H. Expose the skin to moderate amounts of sunlight as often as possible. Avoid long periods in the sun to prevent sunburn.

I. Oatmeal baths may loosen scales. Use 1 cup of oatmeal to a tub of warm water.

J. Stress may increase outbreaks of psoriasis. Consider counseling to assist in lifestyle changes, coping, or any psychological problems caused by psoriasis.

Activity: There are no activity restrictions.

Diet: Eat a well-balanced diet. You may be instructed to try a gluten-free diet. Drink 8 to 10 glasses of water per day. Avoid alcohol in your diet.

Medications: You may be prescribed the following types of medications:

A. Creams to rub on the skin
   1. Ointments containing coal tar. These may stain clothing.
   2. Salicylic acid cream, anthralin cream, or vitamin D-like cream (calcipotriene).
   3. Topical cortisone creams may also be used for short periods of time.

B. Psoralen plus ultraviolet light (PUVA) (combination of a medication and exposure to ultraviolet A light)

C. Combination of tar baths with ultraviolet B light.

D. Antihistamines to relieve itching.

You Have Been Prescribed: ____________________

You Need to Take: ____________________

You Need to Notify the Office If:

A. You have an adverse reaction to or cannot tolerate any of the prescribed medications.

B. Symptoms recur after treatment. Notify your health care provider if during an outbreak, pustules erupt on the skin and/or are accompanied by fever, muscle aches, and fatigue.

C. New, unexplained symptoms develop.

D. Other: ____________________

Phone: ____________________

For severe cases, you may be referred to a dermatologist (specialist for skin disorders).

RESOURCE

National Psoriasis Foundation
Suite 200
6415 SW Canyon Ct.
Portland, OR 97221
Phone: 800-723-9166
www.psoriasis.org

RINGWORM (TINEA)

PROBLEM

Ringworm is a fungal infection of the skin, which can be found on any part of the body. A worm does not cause ringworm. It gets the name because of the round ring shape that is red on the outside and normal on the inside. It is not uncommon to get more than one time. Other tinea fungal infections are:

A. Tinea pedis (athlete's foot)

B. Tinea cruris (jock itch)

C. Tinea capitis (ringworm on the head)

CAUSE

The fungus is transmitted by direct contact. It can be transmitted from objects, shoes, locker rooms, animals, and people.

PREVENTION/TREATMENT PLAN

A. Use good hygiene including not sharing hairbrushes and combs.

B. Keep skin cool and dry.

C. Wear shoes in locker rooms, and pools.

D. Wear loose-fitting clothing.

E. Treat pets' skin problems adequately. Ringworm is often blamed on cats but it can come from almost any animal, including horses, rabbits, dogs, and pigs.

F. Infections of fingernails and toenails may require prescription medications.

Activity: As tolerated. Some contact sports may increase getting tinea (football and wrestling).

Diet: There is no special diet.

Medications:

You Have Been Prescribed: ______________________________

You Need to Take: ______________________________

You Need to Notify the Office If:

A. Your symptoms get worse.

B. Other: ______________________________

Phone: ____________________

SCABIES

PROBLEM

Scabies is a common condition characterized by severe itching. You may have noticed small burrows between your fingers and in other locations, or you may have some redness and skin irritation that is aggravated by scratching.

CAUSE

Scabies is caused by an infestation of the skin by a mite. You have contracted scabies by coming in close contact with an individual who has the condition.

PREVENTION

You can prevent reinfection of scabies by following these measures:

A. Make sure all close contacts, sexual partners, family, and household contacts are treated.

B. All bedding and clothing that has touched infected skin should be machine washed and machine dried on the highest heat cycle.

C. Any clothing or bedding that cannot be laundered in the previously mentioned way should be placed in a plastic bag that is securely tied for at least a week. The mites cannot live this long away from human skin.

D. Coats, furniture, rugs, floors, and walls do not require any special cleaning or treatment.

TREATMENT PLAN

A. Most patients with scabies are successfully treated with only one overnight application of a cream known as a scabicide.

B. You should let your practitioner know if you are pregnant or breastfeeding.

C. You may itch for up to a week even with successful treatment.

D. If you still have symptoms after 2 weeks, you should see your practitioner, who will determine if you need a second treatment.

Activity: Affected children in day care or school can return the day after treatment is completed.

Diet: There is no special diet.

Medications: The most common medications used to treat scabies include:

A. Permethrin (Elimite cream), which is applied to all body areas from the neck down and washed off in 8 to 14 hours.

B. Lindane (Kwell cream), which is applied to all skin surfaces from the neck down and washed off in 8 to 12 hours.

C. You may be told to use Benadryl 25 to 50 mg if needed for itching.

D. Do not use it near your eyes.

You Have Been Prescribed: ____________________

You Need to Apply: ____________________

You Need to Notify the Office If:

A. You have new symptoms.

B. You have a reaction to the medication.

C. Other: ____________________

Phone: ____________________

SEBORRHEIC DERMATITIS

PROBLEM

Seborrheic dermatitis is a skin condition characterized by greasy or dry, white, flaking scales over reddish patches on the skin. The scales anchor to the hair shafts and may itch, but they are usually painless unless complicated by infection.

CAUSE

The cause is unknown. The risk of seborrheic dermatitis increases with stress; hot and humid, or cold and dry weather; infrequent shampoos; oily skin; and other skin disorders such as rosacea, acne, or psoriasis; obesity; Parkinson's disease; use of lotions that contain alcohol; and HIV/AIDS.

PREVENTION/CARE

A. There are no specific preventive measures.

B. The goal of care is to minimize the severity or frequency of symptoms.
   1. Shampoo vigorously and as often as once a day. The type of shampoo is not as important as the way you scrub your scalp. To loosen scales, scrub with your fingernails while shampooing, and scrub at least 5 minutes.
   2. If you suffer from minor dandruff, you may use nonprescription dandruff shampoos with selenium sulfide (Selsun Blue, Exsel) or zinc pyrithione (Zincon), as well as lubricating skin lotion.
   3. For severe problems, shampoos that contain coal tar or scalp creams that contain cortisone may be prescribed.
   4. To apply medication to the scalp, part the hair a few strands at a time, and rub the ointment or lotion vigorously into the scalp.
   5. Topical steroids may be prescribed for other affected parts of the skin.
   6. Be sure to dry skin folds thoroughly after bathing.
   7. Wear loose, ventilating clothing. Avoid constant cap wearing.

Activity: No restrictions. Outdoor activities in the summer may help alleviate symptoms.

Diet: Eat a well-balanced diet. Drink 8 to 10 glasses of water per day. Avoid foods that seem to worsen your condition.

Medications:

You Have Been Prescribed: ____________________

You Need to Take: ____________________

You Need to Notify the Office If:

A. You have an adverse reaction to any of the prescribed medications.

B. You are unable to tolerate any of the medications.

C. You have any secondary infection in the affected area.

D. Other: ____________________

Phone: ____________________

SKIN CARE ASSESSMENT

PROBLEM

Skin cancer is the most common type of cancer. In 2006, the Centers for Disease Control and Prevention noted that the rate of skin cancer varies by the state where you live. A state map is located on the Internet at www.cdc.gov/cancer/skin/statistics/state.htm.

CAUSE

Skin cancer is frequently caused by damage from the ultraviolet rays of the sun. Some people are at a higher risk for developing skin cancer. These risk factors include:

A. Fair complexion; blond/red hair; blue, green, or hazel eye color
B. Advanced age with sun-damaged skin
C. A history of a severe sunburn
D. A history of spending long hours outdoors
E. A history of x-ray procedures for skin conditions
F. Genetic susceptibility

PREVENTION/CARE

A. Protect yourself and prevent sun exposure to your skin by staying out of the harmful rays as much as possible, especially between the hours of 10:00 a.m. and 3:00 p.m. This time frame accounts for approximately 70% of the harmful ultraviolet radiation.
B. If you are exposed to the sun, wear a sunscreen product with an SPF of 15 or greater at all times.
C. Wear hats that screen your face and neck, as well as your ears.
D. Clothing is available with sun-protective materials. Regular long shirts and long pants also help to protect your skin.
E. Sit in the shade to rest.
F. Do not use a tanning booth.

STEPS TO TAKE TO PREVENT YOURSELF FROM BEING A VICTIM OF SKIN CANCER

A. Examine your skin monthly.
   1. Use a good light source and a mirror to see areas of your skin not clearly visible.
   2. Examine your entire body closely.
   3. Pay particular attention to areas that are frequently exposed to the sun, especially your face, lips, eyes, neck, scalp, and ears.
   4. Monthly screening allows you to familiarize yourself with birthmarks and moles. Note the size, shape, and color of these marks. Note any changes in these marks, using the "ABCDE" method:
      a. *Asymmetry:* The shape of the mark should be noted. Any change in shape or irregularity of the mark needs to be evaluated by your health care provider.
      b. *Border:* Look carefully at the border of the mark. If the border edge is ragged, notched, and not smooth, your health care provider needs to evaluate it.
      c. *Color:* Note the color of moles. If you notice any change in color, or if you notice the mole to have several colors (brown, black, tan, red, etc.), you need to alert your health care provider.
      d. *Diameter:* Measure the size of the mark and document it. Any change in size, especially if it is greater than 6 mm, should be brought to the attention of your health care provider.
      e. *Elevation:* Note elevation of lesion, change in size, and any evolving changes of the lesion. You need to alert your health care provider if changes occur.
   5. You should also evaluate lesions on your skin for any type of change. If the lesions begin bleeding or hurting, or change in texture or in any other way, your health care provider needs to evaluate the change.
   6. Be alerted to any skin ulcers that do not heal within 1 month. Also, any new moles or lesions need to be evaluated by your health care provider for proper diagnosis of the type of lesion.

Activity: As tolerated but protect yourself from sun exposure.

Diet: There is no special diet that will stop skin cancer.

Medications: There are no medications that prevent skin cancer.

You Need to Notify the Office If You Have:

A. Any of the skin changes mentioned here that need to be evaluated by your health care provider.

Phone: ______________________________

TINEA VERSICOLOR

PROBLEM

A yeast infection of the skin, tinea versicolor may cause color changes of the skin, commonly on the chest, back, shoulders, arms, and trunk. During the summer, these spots usually appear pale and do not tan. During the winter, the spots may appear pinker or darker than the normal skin color.

CAUSE

Tinea versicolor is caused by an increased production of yeast on the skin, which is influenced by warm, moist conditions. It is common to have recurring episodes.

PREVENTION/TREATMENT PLAN

A. Air dry skin as much as possible.

B. Apply medication as directed.

C. Patches on skin (color changes) may take several weeks to be resolved.

D. Monthly treatments may help prevent recurrences.

Activity: There are no activity restrictions with tinea versicolor.

Diet: There is no special diet.

Medications:

A. Apply Selsun Blue shampoo or other medication as directed.

B. Most medications may be washed off of skin 30 minutes after application.

C. Selsun Blue shampoo may be used daily on affected skin for 2 weeks.

D. Keep shampoo out of eyes and genital area.

E. Leave it on skin for about 20 minutes and then rinse it off.

You Have Been Prescribed: ______________________________

You Need to Take: ______________________________

You Need to Notify the Office If You:

A. Do not see improvement, despite proper treatment.

B. Develop new symptoms.

C. Other: ______________________________

Phone: ____________________

WARTS

PROBLEM

A wart is a raised, rough growth projecting from the skin, which can be contagious.

CAUSE

Warts are caused by a viral infection that stimulates the cells of the skin to multiply rapidly, which results in an outward growth.

PREVENTION/TREATMENT PLAN

A. Wash hands well.
B. Avoid scratching or picking warts. Warts bleed easily.
C. Some warts go away spontaneously without any treatment after time.
D. Medications may be prescribed.

TO ENHANCE DESTRUCTION

A. Soak wart in warm water 10 to 15 minutes a day.
B. After soaking, use an emery board to file wart down.
C. Apply over-the-counter medication as prescribed (Compound W) to site.
D. Duct tape may be applied over wart. Perform these steps every night until resolved.
E. Warts may reappear at the same spot or in other areas.
F. Cryotherapy "freezing" is another treatment option. Discuss this with your health care provider.

Activity: There are no activity restrictions for warts.

Diet: There are no special diets for warts.

Medications:

You Have Been Prescribed: ______________________________

You Need to Take: ______________________________

You Need to Notify the Office If:

A. You develop an infection at the site of the wart.
B. Other: ______________________________

Phone: ______________________________

WOUND CARE: LOWER EXTREMITY ULCERS

PROBLEM

An ulcer on the body that lies on the lower extremities.

CAUSE

Edema, trauma, ischemia, venous insufficiency

PREVENTION/CARE

A. Keep the area clean and free of foreign debris.

B. Dressing changes: ______________________________

C. You may be prescribed antibiotics; if so, take all antibiotics until they are completely gone.

Activity: Do not apply direct pressure to the site of ulcer. You may be prescribed to elevate your lower extremities: ______________________________

Diet: Eat a well-balanced diet. Increase protein intake.

Medications:

You Have Been Prescribed: ______________________________

You Need to Take: ______________________________

You Need to Notify the Office If You Have:

A. A reaction or cannot tolerate any of the prescribed medications

B. A fever and a general ill feeling

C. Any new or unexplained symptoms related to the ulcer
   1. Increase in size
   2. New odor
   3. Increased drainage
   4. Change in color of the drainage
   5. Increased pain at the site

D. Any questions or concerns

Phone: ______________________________

WOUND CARE: PRESSURE ULCERS

PROBLEMS

An ulcer on the body that lies over a bony surface.

CAUSE

Prolonged periods of pressure to the area of ulcer causing a breakdown of skin integrity.

PREVENTION/CARE

A. Keep the area clean and free of foreign debris.

B. You may be prescribed dressing changes.
   1. Remove dressing.
   2. Clean the ulcer with normal saline.
   3. Apply prescribed medication (see below).
   4. Cover with dry dressing, change as ordered.

C. You may be prescribed antibiotics, if so, take all antibiotics until they are completely gone.

Activity: Do not apply direct pressure to the site of the ulcer.

Diet: Eat a well-balanced diet. Drink 8 to 10 glasses of water per day. Increase protein intake.

Medications:

You Have Been Prescribed: ______________________________

You Need to Take: ______________________________

You Need to Notify the Office If You Have:

A. A reaction or cannot tolerate any of the prescribed medications.

B. A fever and a general ill feeling.

C. Any new or unexplained symptoms
   1. Increase in size
   2. New odor
   3. Increased drainage
   4. Change in color of the drainage
   5. Increased pain at the site

D. Any questions or concerns

Phone: ______________________

WOUNDS OF THE SKIN

PROBLEM

A wound is a break in the external surface of the body.

CAUSE

Wounds are often due to an accidental or intentional injury. Wound infection is usually caused by bacterial contamination of the site.

PREVENTION/CARE

A. Prevent accidental or intentional injury.

B. Immediately after injury, cleanse wound well with soap and water.

C. Remove all dirt and foreign material.

D. You may be prescribed antibiotics; if so, take all antibiotics until they are completely gone.

E. You may need a tetanus shot.

Activity: No restrictions. If infection is present, you may need to increase rest.

Diet: Eat a well-balanced diet. Drink 8 to 10 glasses of water per day.

Medications:

You Have Been Prescribed: ______________________________

You Need to Take: ______________________________

You Need to Notify the Office If You Have:

A. A reaction or cannot tolerate any of the prescribed medications.

B. A fever and a general ill feeling.

C. A wound/infection that seems to worsen.

D. Any new or unexplained symptoms.

E. Any questions or concerns.

Phone: ______________________________

XEROSIS (WINTER ITCH)

PROBLEM

Xerosis is severely chapped skin that becomes cracked, fissured, and inflamed. It can appear on skin anywhere on the body, but it is seen most commonly on the legs.

CAUSE

Xerosis is caused by insufficient oil on the skin's surface, which allows water to evaporate through the skin. Oil in the skin decreases with aging, excessive bathing, and excessive rubbing of the skin. An environment with low humidity also promotes dryness of the skin.

PREVENTION/CARE

A. Reduce water loss from the skin.
  1. Decrease the frequency and duration of baths or showers; use tepid water.
  2. Use soap sparingly.
  3. Avoid detergent soaps.
  4. Pat skin dry rather than rubbing.
  5. Apply skin lubricants (Lac-Hydrin, Eucerin, etc.) to dry skin before chapped areas become inflamed.
  6. Use ultrasonic, cool-mist humidifiers if the air is very dry.
  7. Clean the humidifier daily.
  8. Oil (such as Nivea) in the bath water may be helpful.
  9. Apply lubricants after bathing when possible to trap additional moisture before evaporation occurs.

B. Apply hand cream four to eight times a day to hands and twice daily on the trunk and extremities.

Activity: No restrictions. Avoid long-term exposure to drying environments.

Diet: Eat a well-balanced diet; drink 8 to 10 glasses of water per day.

Medications:

You Have Been Prescribed: ______________________________

You Need to Take: ______________________________

You Need to Notify the Office If You Have:

A. Severely chapped skin, and self-care does not relieve the symptoms in 1 week.
B. Chapped skin that becomes inflamed or if you see any oozing.
C. Any questions or concerns.

Phone: ______________________

Patient Teaching Guides for Chapter 7: Eye Disorders

- Conjunctivitis
- How to Administer Eye Medications

CONJUNCTIVITIS

PROBLEM

You have an infection of the eye, or conjunctivitis, which causes redness, itching, drainage from the eye, and crusting on the eyelids.

CAUSE

Bacteria, viruses, or allergies can cause eye infections.

PREVENTION

A. Wash your hands frequently.

B. Avoid persons with conjunctivitis such as pinkeye.

C. Avoid known allergens.

TREATMENT PLAN

A. All types:
   1. Wash your hands frequently, especially after touching the eyes, to avoid spread.
   2. Use cool compresses on the eyes as needed.
   3. Wash crusting eyelids with baby shampoo daily.
   4. Wipe the eyes from inner to outer corners.

B. *Bacterial:* Bacterial conjunctivitis is contagious until 24 hours after beginning medication.

C. *Viral:* Viral conjunctivitis is contagious for 48 to 72 hours, but it may last up to 2 weeks.

Activity: As tolerated

Diet: As tolerated

Medications: No medications are prescribed for viral infections. You will be given instructions on how to use eye drops or eye ointment.

You Have Been Prescribed: ____________________

You Need to Take: ____________________

You Need to Notify the Office If You Have:

A. A reaction to your medication.

B. Trouble seeing.

C. New symptoms.

D. Other: ____________________

Phone: ____________________

HOW TO ADMINISTER EYE MEDICATIONS

PROBLEM

You have been prescribed a medication for your eye(s). It is very important that you know the correct way to use your eye medication.

CAUSE

You have been diagnosed with______________________________.

PREVENTION

The health of your eyes is important.

A. Use good hand washing and try not to rub your eyes with your fingers.

B. Clean your contacts regularly with contact cleaning solution. Do not put your contacts in your mouth to moisten.

C. Wear sunglasses in bright sunshine.

D. Use eye goggles when working and playing sports to ensure extra protection.

E. Change your eye makeup often. Mascara, eye shadow, and eyeliner grow bacteria. Do not share makeup.

TREATMENT PLAN

A. Correct use of your medication is important.

B. You may or may not require an eye patch or shield.

HOW TO APPLY EYE OINTMENT

A. Always wash your hands before placing medication in your eyes.

B. Gently pull down the lower eyelid.

C. Make a small pocket between the eyeball and the eyelid.

D. If you have someone helping to put your eye ointment in the lower lid pocket, look up and away while he or she puts in the medicine.

E. Do not let the tube of medicine touch the eye or eyelid.

F. Squeeze a thin ribbon of the medication into the pocket of the eyelid.

G. Start at the inner fold of the eye going from the nose to the outer eye.

H. Let go of the eyelid and blink to spread the medication.

HOW TO INSTILL EYE DROPS

A. Always wash your hands before placing medication in your eyes.

B. Gently pull down the lower eyelid.

C. Make a small pocket between the eyelid and the eyeball.

D. If you have someone helping to put your eye drops in the lower lid pocket, look up and away while he or she puts in the medicine.

E. **Do not let the bottle of medication touch the eye or eyelid.**

F. Squeeze the prescribed number of drops of the medicine into the pocket of the eyelid.

G. Let go of the eyelid and blink (or tell the patient to blink) to spread the medication.

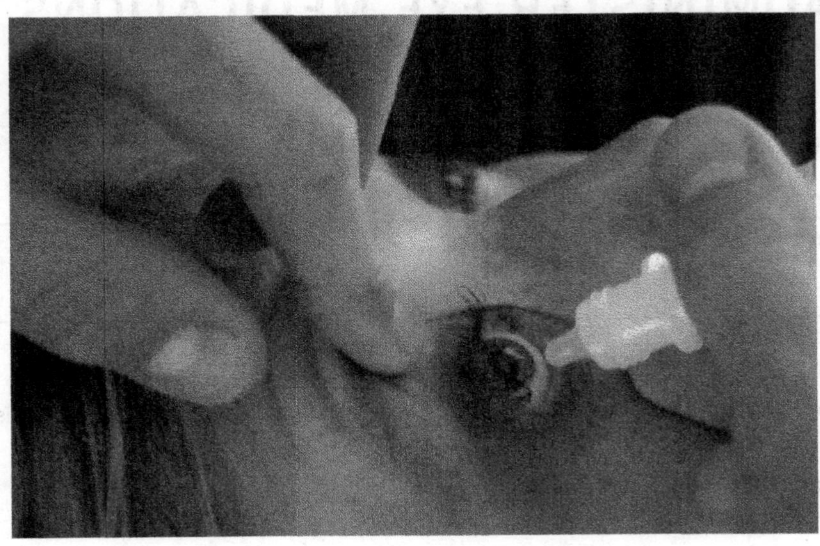

How to instill eye drops into the eye.

Activity: No restrictions are required unless you require eye surgery; then you will be given specific instructions about the amount of activity allowed.

Diet: No restrictions.

Medications:

You Have Been Prescribed: ____________________

You Need to Use the Medicine: ____________________

You Need to Notify the Office If:

A. You are unable to put in the medication yourself or get help from others.
B. You are not better 24 to 48 hours after starting the medication.
C. Your vision is worse after using the medication.
D. You have an allergic reaction to the medicine.
E. Other: ____________________

Phone: ____________________

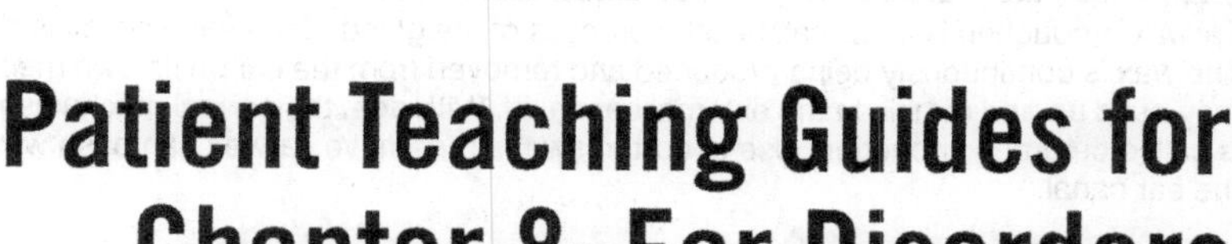

Patient Teaching Guides for Chapter 8: Ear Disorders

- Cerumen Impaction (Earwax)
- Otitis Externa
- Otitis Media With Effusion
- Tinnitus

CERUMEN IMPACTION (EARWAX)

PROBLEM

A buildup of earwax in the external ear canal that may cause itching, pain, and temporary hearing loss.

CAUSE

Earwax production is a normal, healthy process of the gland of the ear. Earwax is produced to protect the ear from infection and trauma. The wax is continuously being produced and removed from the ear on its own mechanism. However, at times, an overproduction of wax may build up and remain in the external ear canal. With age, the normal mechanisms of the ear for removing earwax are decreased. This is called cerumen impaction. Use of cotton swabs to remove earwax can push wax further into the ear and cause problems deeper into the ear canal.

PREVENTION

Do not use cotton swabs, paper clips, or other objects to clean your ears. These can damage the ear canal and lead to an external ear infection.

TREATMENT PLAN

A. **Use Debrox, mineral oil, or olive oil, two to three drops per day, gently placed into the external ear canal for 1 week. These oils will soften up the wax for easier removal.**

B. Clean ears with a wet washcloth. The external ear that is visible to the eye is the only part of the ear that should be cleaned with a wet washcloth.

C. Return to health care provider in 1 week for wax removal.

D. Do not try to remove the earwax on your own due to the chance of damaging your eardrum. Never stick any kind of tool into your ear. This will usually push the wax farther into your ear canal, making removal more difficult by your health care provider.

Activity: As tolerated.

Diet: As tolerated.

Medications: ____________________

You Have Been Prescribed: ____________________

You Need to Take: ____________________

You Need to Notify the Office If:

A. You are unable to hear.

B. You have colored drainage or fluid draining from your ears.

C. You run a fever.

D. You have dizziness.

E. Other: ____________________

Phone: ____________________

OTITIS EXTERNA

PROBLEM

Your practitioner has diagnosed you with a condition known as otitis externa, sometimes also referred to as "swimmer's ear." This is a common condition characterized by itching in the ear, sometimes followed by ear pain, swelling, and drainage of the ear canal. Difficulty hearing may also occur. The eardrum is rarely affected.

CAUSE

Otitis externa occurs from irritation to the external canal of the ear. The most common causes for otitis externa are long exposure to water in the ear canal after frequent swimming and too vigorous cleaning of the wax from your ears. It may involve either a bacterial or a fungal infection.

PREVENTION

You may prevent future problems with otitis externa by following these measures:

A. Clean the outer ear only as needed. Do not use cotton-tipped swabs or any other device to clean down into the ear canal. Usually, wax is just pushed deeper into the canal with this method, and the canal may be traumatized by the instrument used.

B. For swimmers or others susceptible to frequent recurrences of otitis externa, it may be helpful to dry the ear canals with a blow dryer on a low setting after exposure to water. You may also instill a solution of 50% isopropyl alcohol and 50% vinegar in the ear twice daily and after every submersion in water. Over-the-counter ear drops labeled for "swimmer's ear" may also be used as directed.

TREATMENT PLAN

For the most common bacterial infections associated with otitis externa, antibiotic/steroid ear drops are usually prescribed. In addition, you should keep water out of your ears during treatment. Your provider will give you specific instructions regarding how long you will need to keep the ear canal clean and dry. Bathing and shampooing your hair is fine as long as you prevent any water from getting in your ears. You can use earplugs or cotton balls with petroleum jelly to keep your ears dry.

Activity: Avoiding moisture accumulation in the ear is important. Activity restrictions are those involving submersion in water.

Diet: No changes are required in your diet.

Medications:

A. Ear drops are used to treat otitis externa.

B. The drops should be applied down the ear canal's opening, moving the earlobe back and forth to help the ear drops pass downward.

C. In severe cases, antibiotics may be given.

You Have Been Prescribed: ______________________________

You Need to Instill ____________ **Drops Into the Affected Ear** ____________ **Times Per Day.**

You Need to Notify the Office If You:

A. Have symptoms that worsen or do not seem to be improving.

B. Have a fever over 100.8°F.

C. Have increased pain, redness, or swelling in the ear or around the ear or face.

D. Are unable to instill ear drops into the ear due to swelling of the ear canal

E. Other: ______________________________

Phone: ______________________________

OTITIS MEDIA WITH EFFUSION

PROBLEM

You have inflammation of the middle ear with effusion, which is the presence of fluid in the middle ear without infection.

CAUSE

The middle ear fluid can remain behind the tympanic membrane after you have been treated for an ear infection (otitis media). The eustachian tube is blocked, and the fluid behind the ear is not draining out properly. Symptoms may include difficulty hearing and a feeling of fullness in the ear.

TREATMENT PLAN

A. Determine if you are having increased difficulty hearing.

B. Make accommodations for the hearing loss, such as reducing or eliminating external noises while having a conversation. Speak clearly and loudly.

C. If you have a buildup of fluid in the middle ear for longer than 12 weeks or you notice a significant or increasing hearing deficit, you should receive a hearing evaluation.

D. Follow up with a health care provider as instructed to avoid complications and/or permanent hearing loss.

Activity: There is no activity restriction.

Diet: There is no special diet.

Medications: There are not any medications that are used for fluid behind the ear. If infection is present, antibiotics are used to treat this infection.

You Have Been Prescribed: ______________________________

You Need to Take: ______________________________

You Need to Notify the Office If You Have:

A. Fever.
B. Decreased appetite.
C. Decreased activity level.
D. Ear pain.
E. Noticed a change in hearing loss or speech development.
F. Any other new symptoms that occur.
G. Other: ______________________________

Phone: ______________________________

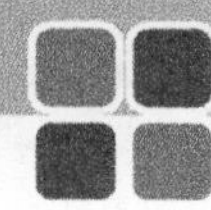

TINNITUS

PROBLEM

Tinnitus is an irritating noise or sound that is heard in one or both ears, commonly referred to as a buzzing, humming, or ringing noise.

CAUSE

Tinnitus is caused by a change in the normal hearing pathway of the ears. This can be caused from damage or irritation of the hearing pathway, which may be temporary or permanent. Damage to the nerves in the ear, fluid, wax buildup, and/or a mass in the middle ear are a few causes for tinnitus.

TREATMENT PLAN

A. Hearing evaluation will be performed to determine if there is hearing loss.

B. A CT or MRI may be performed to evaluate for the cause of the tinnitus.

C. Once the cause of the tinnitus is noted, treating the cause will begin.

D. There are some medications that are used to help decrease the "ringing, buzzing" noise that you are hearing. Ask your health care provider about these medications.

E. Surgery may be considered if a mass is noted on the CT or MRI scan.

F. Rest and exercise are encouraged to reduce the amount of stress that can worsen symptoms of tinnitus.

Activity: There is no activity restriction.

Diet: Some foods may make the tinnitus worsen. Therefore, reducing the amount of caffeine (tea, coffee, soft drinks) is encouraged.

Medications: Avoid aspirin. Aspirin has been known to aggravate the symptoms of tinnitus.

You Have Been Prescribed: ______________________________

You Need to Take: ______________________________

You Need to Notify the Office If You Have:

A. Fever

B. Ear pain

C. A change in hearing loss or speech development.

D. Any other new symptoms that occur.

E. Other: ______________________________

Phone: ______________________________

Patient Teaching Guides for Chapter 9: Nasal Disorders

- Allergic Rhinitis
- Nosebleeds
- Sinusitis

ALLERGIC RHINITIS

PROBLEM

Allergic rhinitis is a chronic or recurrent condition. Common symptoms are nasal congestion, sneezing, and clear nasal discharge. It's not contagious, so you can't catch it from anyone, and you can't spread it to others.

CAUSE

You are having an allergic response after being exposed to an allergen.

PREVENTION

A. The best prevention is to avoid things you know you're allergic to, for example, smoke (cigarette, cigar, wood smoke); pollens and molds; animal dander; dust mites; and indoor inhalants, such as hair spray and other aerosol spray products.

B. Target your bedroom as "allergy free" by removing carpets, damp mopping floors weekly, hanging washable curtains instead of blinds, removing books and stuffed animals, using foam pillows, and encasing the pillows and mattress in plastic.

C. Do not blow your nose too frequently or too hard. It may cause your eardrum to perforate (tear). Blow through both nostrils at the same time to equalize the pressure.

D. Use tissues when you blow your nose. Dispose of them and then wash your hands. If no tissue is available, do the "elbow sneeze" into the bend of your arm (away from your open hands). Always wash your hands.

TREATMENT PLAN

A. Use the air conditioner in your house and car to decrease exposure to pollens.

B. Use an air filtration system in your house or buy a small one for your bedroom.

C. Dust your house often, using a cloth and cleaner or polish to keep dust from flying.

D. Allergy testing may need to be done if you've had allergies for a long time. Ask your health care provider about a consultation with an allergist.

Activity: There are no activity restrictions. However, you may want to exercise indoors during the spring, summer, and fall when pollen counts are high.

Diet: Eat well-balanced meals. Drink at least six to eight glasses of liquid a day.

Medications: Common medications used include antihistamines, decongestants, and nasal sprays.

Antihistamines: Some antihistamines may cause drowsiness. Use with caution. You may consider using a different antihistamine during the day that does not cause drowsiness.

Decongestants: Decongestants may increase blood pressure and may also interact with other medications. Please consult with your provider before using these medications.

Nasal Sprays: Nasal saline spray is safe to use in the nose several times a day. Nasal decongestant sprays may be used for a short period of time. Do not use longer than 3 days to prevent causing rebound side effects from this medication. Consult with your provider if using a nasal decongestant spray.

You Have Been Prescribed: ____________________

You Need to Take: ____________________

You Need to Notify the Office If:

A. You experience trouble breathing or catching your breath.

B. You have asthma; call if your symptoms are worse.

C. Your symptoms aren't any better after using the medications for 3 complete days.

D. Your nasal discharge changes to a greenish color.

E. Other: ____________________

Phone: ____________________

NOSEBLEEDS

PROBLEM

Most nosebleeds stop within 10 minutes. **If you have trouble breathing with a nosebleed, *call 911*.**

CAUSE

Nosebleeds may be caused by several problems:

A. Trauma from nose picking or forcefully blowing the nose

B. Chronic sinus infections

C. Allergies

D. Drugs, including over-the-counter medications such as aspirin and Pepto-Bismol, or street drugs such as snorted cocaine

E. Exposure to irritants

PREVENTION

A. Avoid picking your nose. Keep fingernails trimmed short.

B. Don't blow your nose too frequently or too hard (it may also cause eardrum tearing).

C. Blow your nose through both nostrils at the same time to equalize pressure.

D. Use a humidifier in your home, or place a container of water near the radiator.

E. Use a lubricant such as petrolatum, A & D Ointment, or a skin barrier such as zinc oxide to add moisture to the inside of your nose with a Q-tip and promote healing.

F. Avoid smoking and secondhand smoke.

TREATMENT PLAN

A. If you experience a nosebleed, take these steps:
1. Sit up and lean forward.
2. Apply pressure to the bridge of your nose for 10 to 15 minutes to stop the blood flow.
3. If the bleeding continues, spray Afrin into your nostril.
4. If the bleeding still continues, lightly soak a cotton ball with the nasal spray, insert it into your nose, and press.
5. Apply zinc oxide, petrolatum, or A & D Ointment to prevent further drying and abrasion of the nasal septum (the partition between the two nostrils).

B. Gently blowing your nose also decreases or stops a nosebleed.

Activity: Avoid or limit the following activities for 3 to 5 days after a nosebleed:

A. Heavy lifting

B. Straining

C. Bending over from the waist

D. Very hot showers

Diet: Avoid hot, spicy foods for 3 to 5 days after a nosebleed.

Medications: Avoid medications that increase bleeding, such as aspirin and Pepto-Bismol.

You Have Been Prescribed: ______________________________

You Need to Take: ______________________________

You Need to Notify the Office If:

A. Bleeding doesn't stop with pressure or nasal spray applied to the bleeding site.

B. You keep having nosebleeds (more than two in a week or four in a month).

C. Other: ______________________________

Phone: ____________________

SINUSITIS

PROBLEM

Sinusitis (sinus infection) is classified as an acute, subacute, or chronic condition. In acute sinusitis, the infection is resolved after treatment. In subacute sinusitis, there is a persistent, yellow to green nasal discharge despite treatment. In chronic sinusitis, episodes of prolonged inflammation continue longer than 3 months despite treatment.

CAUSE

Sinusitis occurs when the mucous lining in your sinus cavities becomes inflamed and infected with bacteria or allergen. This can occur after a cold or tooth abscess.

PREVENTION

A. If you have a tooth abscess, see your dentist and finish all your antibiotics.

B. Don't blow your nose too frequently or too hard. It may cause your eardrum to perforate (tear). Blow through both nostrils at the same time to equalize pressure.

C. To prevent spreading germs to others, cover your mouth when you cough.
   1. Use tissues when you blow your nose. Dispose of them and then wash your hands.
   2. If no tissue is available, do the "elbow sneeze" into the bend of your arm (away from your open hands).

D. Always wash your hands after coughing or using tissues.

TREATMENT PLAN

A. Avoid smoking and secondhand smoke.

B. Use steam inhalation to liquefy secretions.

C. Use a room humidifier. Keep your humidifier clean—it can grow bacteria.

Activity: There are no activity restrictions; however, diving, swimming, and flying may increase the occurrence of symptoms or make them worse. Make sure to get plenty of rest each day.

Diet: Eat a healthy diet. Drink at least 8 to 10 glasses of liquid every day.

Medications: Take all of your prescribed antibiotics, even if you feel better.

Over-the-counter medications:

A. **Pain relievers:** Ibuprofen (Advil) or acetaminophen (Tylenol) as needed for facial pain.

B. **Antihistamines:** Some antihistamines may cause drowsiness. Use with caution. You may consider using a different antihistamine during the day, which does not cause drowsiness.

C. **Decongestants:** Decongestants may increase blood pressure and may also interact with other medications. Please consult with your provider before using these medications.

D. **Nasal sprays:** Nasal saline spray is safe to use in the nose several times a day. Nasal decongestant sprays may be used for a short period of time. Do not use longer than 3 days to prevent causing rebound side effects from this medication. Consult with your provider if you are using a nasal decongestant spray.

You Have Been Prescribed: ______________________________

You Need to Take: ______________________________

You Need to Call the Office If:

A. Your eyelids begin to swell or droop, or you experience decreased vision.

B. You have stiffness in your neck or increased fever.

C. You have asthma, and you are getting worse.

D. You begin vomiting and are unable to keep down your antibiotic.

E. You are a diabetic and your blood sugars are elevated, or you notice ketones in your urine.

F. Other: ______________________________

Phone: ______________________

Patient Teaching Guides for Chapter 10: Throat and Mouth Disorders

- Aphthous Stomatitis
- Pharyngitis
- Thrush

APHTHOUS STOMATITIS

PROBLEM

Aphthous stomatitis are tender ulcers in the mouth that recur.

CAUSE

The cause is unknown. Possible causes include diet (lack of iron, zinc, or B vitamins), menstrual or hormonal changes, and viruses.

TREATMENT PLAN

A. Use an over-the-counter gel such as Anbesol or Orajel four times daily.

B. You may be prescribed a mouthwash made of diphenhydramine (Benadryl), Maalox, and lidocaine or fluocinonide gel to "swish" in your mouth two to four times daily.

Activity: No restrictions are required.

Diet:

A. Avoiding spicy, salty, or hot foods may help.

B. Using a straw when drinking may decrease pain.

C. Cold foods may be easier to tolerate.

D. Avoid hard or sharp food.

E. Use a soft toothbrush.

Medications:

You Have Been Prescribed: ________________________________

You Need to Take: ________________________________

You Need to Notify the Office If You Have:

A. Worse symptoms than seen at the office visit today.

B. Ulcers that do not heal in approximately 1 to 2 weeks.

C. Other: ________________________________

Phone: ________________________________

PHARYNGITIS

PROBLEM

Pharyngitis (sore throat) is a condition that occurs when your throat becomes inflamed.

CAUSE

The inflammation can be due to a virus, a bacterium, or a fungus. Other noninfectious causes include postnasal drip, allergies, mouth breathing, and trauma.

PREVENTION

A. Avoid sick people and crowds. Stay at home if you are sick.

B. Cover your mouth when coughing.

C. Don't share a drinking glass, kiss, or have close contact with anyone who has an upper respiratory infection.

TREATMENT PLAN

A. Hot tea, soup, and throat lozenges soothe your throat.

B. Use disposable tissues when sneezing. Use tissues when you blow your nose. If no tissue is available, do the "elbow sneeze" into the bend of your arm (away from your open hands). Dispose of them and then wash your hands.

C. Avoid smoking and secondhand smoke.

Activity: If you have strep throat, don't return to school or work until you have completed a full 24 hours of antibiotic. Rest or nap as often as possible while you're sick.

Diet: Eat a healthy diet. If swallowing is difficult, eat soft foods such as ice cream, Jell-O, pudding, and soup. Avoid salt and spicy foods. Increase your fluid intake to 10 to 12 glasses a day.

Medications: You will be prescribed antibiotics if you have a bacterial infection. If your sore throat is due to a virus, antibiotics won't help. Don't share your prescription medications with other family members who are also sick. They need a full prescription, too. Many other medications are available over the counter, such as throat lozenges, cough suppressants, and so forth.

You Have Been Prescribed: ____________________

You Need to Take: ____________________

If You Are Prescribed Antibiotics, Complete All of the Doses.

You Need to Notify the Office If:

A. You have difficulty breathing because of the sore throat or enlarged tonsils.

B. Your symptoms are worse after 24 hours of antibiotics.

C. You are unable to keep down your antibiotic because of vomiting.

D. You develop a rash or itching after starting the antibiotic.

E. You are a diabetic and your blood glucose is high, or you have ketones in your urine.

F. Other: ____________________

Phone: ____________________

THRUSH

PROBLEM

Oral thrush is white patches that coat the inside of the mouth and tongue. It mainly affects adults with risk factors such as a compromised immune system, use of frequent antibiotics, and/or chronic use of steroid inhalers.

CAUSE

Thrush is caused by a yeast called *Candida* that grows rapidly on the lining of the mouth and tongue. It may also occur after a course of antibiotic medication.

PREVENTION

A. Avoid overuse of antibiotics.

B. Clean inhalers and dentures daily. Use a denture cleaner daily. You may soak the dentures overnight in the denture cleaner. Rinse dentures well before putting them into your mouth.

C. Practice good oral hygiene daily.

D. Change your toothbrush or sanitize the toothbrush when diagnosed with thrush to prevent reinfecting the mouth with yeast.

TREATMENT PLAN

A. Try to remove any large plaques with a moistened cotton-tipped applicator or gauze pad.

B. Cleanse the mouth before giving medication.

C. Place the medication in the front of the mouth on each side.

D. Rub it directly on the plaques with a cotton swab.

Diet: As tolerated. Limit foods high in sugar and yeast products such as beer, wine, and bread. Increase the diet to include yogurt and products that contain *acidophilus*.

Medications: Nystatin is an oral medication used to treat thrush. Nystatin 1 mL four times a day after meals or 30 minutes prior to eating. Patches should improve within 2 to 3 days of using the medication.

You Have Been Prescribed: ______________________________

You Need to Take: ______________________________

You Need to Notify the Office If:

A. You have difficulty with eating or drinking due to pain.

B. Symptoms don't improve or thrush lasts longer than 10 days.

C. Unexplained fever occurs.

D. Secondary infection occurs in the mouth (pain, tenderness, sores).

E. Other: ______________________________

Phone: ______________________________

Patient Teaching Guides for Chapter 11: Respiratory Disorders

- Asthma
    - Asthma Action Plan and Peak Flow Monitoring
    - How to Use a Metered-Dose Inhaler
- Bacterial Pneumonia
- Bronchitis, Acute
- Bronchitis, Chronic
- Chronic Obstructive Pulmonary Disease (COPD)
- Common Cold
- Cough
- Emphysema
- Influenza (Flu)
- Nicotine Dependence
- Pneumonia, Viral
- Sleep Apnea

ASTHMA

PROBLEM

Asthma is a chronic condition with wheezing, coughing, breathlessness, and chest tightness.

CAUSE

The most common cause is inflammation that results from exercise or exposure to environmental irritants, allergens, furry animals, cockroaches, dust mites, pollens and molds, cold air, or viral respiratory infections.

PREVENTION

You have asthma and so are encouraged to get the flu vaccine every year.

You may be able to prevent frequent recurrences of asthma by following these asthma trigger avoidance strategies:

A. *Dust mite allergens:* Wash bedding weekly in hot water and dry it in a hot dryer. Encase pillows and mattresses in airtight covers. Remove carpets, especially from your bedroom. Avoid use of fabric-covered furniture, especially for sleeping.

B. *Cockroach allergens:* Clean your house thoroughly. Use poison bait or traps. Don't leave food or garbage exposed.

C. *Animal fur allergens:* Avoid keeping house pets, or at least don't allow them in sleeping areas.

D. *Smoke allergens:* Avoid all of the following: Smoking, contact with tobacco smoke, smoke from wood-burning stoves or fireplaces, and unvented stoves or heaters.

E. *Outdoor pollens and molds:* Keep windows closed when pollen or mold counts are high.

F. *Indoor mold:* Reduce dampness in your home by using a dehumidifier. Clean damp areas often. Remove carpets that are laid on concrete.

G. *Other irritants:* Avoid perfumes, cleaning agents, and sprays.

TREATMENT PLAN

See the Patient Teaching Guides, "Asthma Action Plan and Peak Flow Monitoring" and "How to Use a Metered-Dose Inhaler."

Activity:

A. If cold air causes symptoms, wear a scarf over your mouth and nose if you must go outside during the winter.

B. Avoid vigorous exercise if this causes asthma symptoms. Learn to recognize activities that trigger your breathing problems.

C. Make an asthma action plan to follow. Copy the plan and place it on the refrigerator, take a copy of your action plan to school, and give each coach a copy of your asthma action plan.

D. Color code your inhalers with tape or markers; for example, use green tape for quick relief inhalers and blue tape for long-acting inhalers.

Diet: There are no diet restrictions unless you have found a food that causes an allergic reaction and trouble with breathing.

Medications: Cough medicines should not be used for asthma symptoms.

You Have Been Prescribed: ______________________________

You Need to Take: ______________________________

You Need to Notify the Office If You Have:

A. A peak flow reading below 60% of your personal best number that doesn't return to the yellow or green zone after taking your medication.

B. Other: ______________________________

Phone: ______________________________

ASTHMA ACTION PLAN AND PEAK FLOW MONITORING

A peak flow meter is a device that measures how well air moves out of your lungs. This measurement is referred to as your "peak expiratory flow," or PEF.

HOW TO USE A PEAK FLOW METER

A. Place the indicator at the bottom of the numbered scale.

B. Stand up.

C. Take a deep breath, filling your lungs as deeply as possible.

D. Place the mouthpiece in your mouth and close your lips around it. Don't put your tongue inside the hole.

E. Blow into the mouthpiece as hard and fast as you can. It is important to give this your best effort.

F. Write down the number on the indicator. If you cough or make a mistake, don't record that number—do it over again.

G. Repeat steps A through F two more times.

H. Write down the highest number of the three attempts. This is your PEF.

CALCULATING YOUR PERSONAL BEST PEAK FLOW NUMBER

This number is the highest peak flow number you can achieve over a 2- to 3-week period when your asthma is under good control (when you don't have any symptoms). To find this number, take peak flow readings:

A. Twice daily for 2 to 3 weeks.

B. When you wake up and between noon and 2 p.m.

C. Before and after taking your quick relief medication.

D. Or as directed by your health care provider.

THE PEAK FLOW ZONE SYSTEM

Once you have determined your personal best peak flow number, your health care provider can give you the numbers that let you know what medications to take based on your PEF. The numbers are set up like a traffic light system (red, yellow, and green).

Green Zone (80%–100% of your personal best number): Signals *good control*. No asthma symptoms are present, and you should take your medication as usual.

Yellow Zone (50%–80% of your personal best number): Signals *caution*. You may be having an episode of asthma that requires an increase in your medications.

Red Zone (below 50% of your personal best number): Signals a *medical alert*. You must use your "fast" inhaler to help open up your airways right away and call your health care provider immediately if your peak flow number doesn't return to the yellow or green zone and stay there.

Use the following "Asthma Action Plan," that specifies what medications you should take when you're in each zone and also use the self-assessment diary provided in Table III.2.

ASTHMA ACTION PLAN

A. My personal best PEF is ____________________.

B. When I am in the ***green zone***, PEF above ____________________, I should continue to take my regularly scheduled asthma medications. They are:
   1. ____________________
   2. ____________________
   3. ____________________

C. When I am in the ***yellow zone***, PEF between ____________ and ____________, I should add the following to my regularly scheduled medications:
   1. ____________________
   2. ____________________
   3. ____________________

TABLE III.2 **Asthma Diary Self-Assessment**

Symptom Codes: Rate your symptoms 1 (Mild); 2 (Moderate); or 3 (Severe)							
My Personal Best PEF Is __________							
Date	**PEAK FLOW ZONES** ***Green*** **= Good control** ***Yellow*** **= Caution** ***Red*** **= Emergency**			**Symptoms (Use Codes)** **W = Wheeze** **C = Cough** **S = Shortness of Breath**	**Quick Relief Medication (Include the Number of Times Needed for Relief)**	**Anti-Inflammatory Medication**	**Additional Medications or Activity**
Monday	a.m.	p.m.	Zone				

D. When I am in the ***red zone***, PEF below ________________________, I should immediately take the following rescue medication and contact my health care provider:

1. ____
2. ____
3. ____

Rescue Medication: ____

E. Other Directions: ____

____

____

HOW TO USE A METERED-DOSE INHALER

USING AN INHALER

To receive the proper dose from your inhaler, you must use good technique. Your health care practitioner may provide you with a drug-free practice inhaler. Practice the following steps until you are comfortable administering your inhalant:

A. Shake the inhaler well immediately before each use.

B. Using a spacer helps to deliver more medication.

C. Remove the cap from the mouthpiece. Hold the inhaler upright. Make sure the medication canister is firmly inserted into the plastic holder (actuator).

D. The first time you use your new inhaler (or if it has been 1 month or longer since the last use), test spray four times into the air.

E. Breathe out through your mouth to the end of a normal breath.

F. Position the mouthpiece about 1 to 2 inches in front of your open mouth. Or you may close your lips in a tight seal around the mouthpiece.

G. Open your mouth widely (unless you are using the second method), and position your head in a neutral position.

H. While breathing in slowly and deeply, firmly depress the container once.

I. Continue breathing in slowly until your lungs are full.

J. Once you have breathed in fully, hold your breath for 10 seconds or as long as you can.

K. If you need a second puff of the same medication, wait a minimum of 1 minute before repeating steps A through J. If you're using a different inhaler for the second puff, wait at least 5 minutes before using the second inhaler.

OTHER TIPS

A. If you're taking a steroid inhalant, rinse your mouth and throat with water after each dose.

B. When you are short of breath, use your bronchodilator ("rescue medicine") first; then wait about 5 minutes before using your steroid inhaler. The rescue inhaler opens your airways so more of the steroid medication reaches your lungs.

C. Keep the inhaler clean. Once a week, remove the medication canister from the actuator and wash the actuator in warm, soapy water. Rinse and allow to air dry. Replace the medication canister in the holder and recap the mouthpiece.

D. Always check the expiration date on your inhaler and make sure to refill your prescription before the medication expires.

E. Color code your inhalers with tape or markers; for example, use green tape for quick relief inhalers and blue tape for long-acting inhalers.

BACTERIAL PNEUMONIA

PROBLEM

Pneumonia is a lung infection that causes fluid to collect in the air sacs. You may have a fever, cough, or trouble breathing.

CAUSE

Respiratory bacteria or viruses cause pneumonia.

PREVENTION

People older than 65 years of age and younger people with severe lung disease may receive a vaccine to prevent pneumococcal pneumonia.

The flu vaccine is recommended to be taken every year.

TREATMENT PLAN

A. Use a cool-mist humidifier. Clean the humidifier daily.

B. Do not smoke, and avoid smoke-filled rooms.

C. Cover your mouth when you cough and cover your nose when you sneeze.

D. Use tissues when you blow your nose. Throw away tissues as soon as they are used.

E. If no tissue is available, do the "elbow sneeze" into the bend of your arm.

F. Wash your hands frequently with soap and water.

Activity: Rest during the early phase of the illness.

Diet: Eat a nutritious diet. Drink 8 to 10 glasses of water a day.

Medications:

A. Don't use cough suppressants if your cough produces sputum. Use them only for a dry, nonproductive cough.

B. Acetaminophen (Tylenol) may be used for fever or body aches.

C. Antibiotics are given for pneumonia that is caused by bacteria. Take your medication as directed.

D. Finish all of your antibiotics even though you may feel better.

You Have Been Prescribed: ______________________________

You Need to Take: ______________________________

You Need to Notify the Office If You Have:

A. Increased difficulty breathing.

B. Fever after 48 hours on an antibiotic.

C. Blood in your sputum.

D. Worsening discomfort or fatigue.

E. Unable to keep your antibiotic down.

F. Other: ______________________________

Phone: ______________________________

Follow-up appointment on: ______________________________

BRONCHITIS, ACUTE

PROBLEM

Acute bronchitis is a lung infection followed by a productive cough.

CAUSE

Respiratory viruses caused your bronchitis.

PREVENTION

A. Avoid exposure to other people with respiratory illnesses.
B. Don't smoke, and avoid secondhand smoke and other smoke-filled environments.
C. Avoid air pollutants, such as wood smoke, solvents, and cleaners.
D. Cover your nose and mouth with your sneeze or cough.
E. Use tissues when you blow your nose.
F. Throw away all tissues as soon as they are used. If no tissue is available, do the "elbow sneeze" into the bend of your arm.
G. Use good hand washing with soap and water.
H. You are encouraged to take the flu vaccine every year.

TREATMENT PLAN

A. Humidity and mist may be helpful.
B. Always clean the humidifier daily to prevent bacteria from growing.
C. Twenty minutes several times a day in a steamy bathroom may provide relief.

Activity: Rest is important since you have been diagnosed with bronchitis; then increase activity as tolerated when the fever subsides.

Diet: Eat a nutritious diet. Drink 8 to 10 glasses of water daily.

Medications:

A. Acetaminophen (Tylenol) may be used to relieve discomfort.
B. For a nonproductive cough, take cough suppressants if recommended. You may be prescribed a cough medicine or be told the best kind to buy in the drugstore.
C. Since a virus almost always causes acute bronchitis, **antibiotics will rarely be needed to get better.**

You Have Been Prescribed: ______________________________

You Need to Take: ______________________________

You Need to Notify the Office If You Have:

A. No improvement after 48 hours.
B. Worsening symptoms.
C. High fever, chills, chest tightness or pain, shortness of breath.
D. Symptoms that last longer than 3 weeks.
E. Other: ______________________________

Phone: ______________________________

BRONCHITIS, CHRONIC

PROBLEM

Chronic bronchitis is an upper respiratory infection followed by a productive cough. To be diagnosed as chronic bronchitis, you have had the symptoms 3 months for 2 years in a row.

CAUSE

Both viruses and bacterial infections cause chronic bronchitis.

PREVENTION

A. Avoid exposure to others with respiratory illnesses.

B. Don't smoke, and avoid secondhand smoke and smoke-filled environments.

C. Avoid other air pollutants, such as wood smoke, solvents, and cleaners.

D. Use good hand-washing techniques.

E. Use tissues for the mucus coughed up. Dispose of the tissues after use.

F. Cover your mouth when you cough. If you don't have a tissue, the "elbow sneeze" into the bend of your arm will prevent you from spreading your illness.

G. Although the flu vaccine does not prevent bronchitis, a yearly flu vaccine is recommended.

H. A pneumonia vaccine is recommended for people older than 65 years of age and for younger people with chronic respiratory conditions.

TREATMENT PLAN

A. Humidity and mist may be helpful.

B. Always clean the humidifier daily to prevent bacterial growth.

C. Twenty minutes several times a day in a steamy bathroom may provide relief.

D. If continuing to smoke, do your best to reduce the amount.

Activity: Rest during the early stage of the illness; then increase activity as tolerated when the fever subsides. It is not uncommon to feel tired for several weeks.

Diet: Eat a nutritious diet. Drink 8 to 10 glasses of water daily.

Medications:

A. Acetaminophen (Tylenol) may be used to relieve fever and discomfort.

B. You may be prescribed an inhaler to help your breathing.

C. You may be prescribed steroids to help with the inflammation of your lungs. The steroids may be given by an inhaler or as a pill.

D. It is very important that you use the inhaler properly so that the medicine can go into your lungs. A teaching sheet on how to use an inhaler is available.

E. You may also be prescribed an antibiotic for a bacterial infection. Take all of your antibiotics, even if you feel better.

F. You may be prescribed a cough suppressant to take at night to help you rest. However, coughing up the mucus is very important to clear out your "wind pipes."

You Have Been Prescribed: ______________________________

You Need to Take: ______________________________

You Need to Notify the Office If You Have:

A. No improvement after 48 hours.

B. Worsening symptoms.

C. High fever, chills, chest tightness or pain, shortness of breath.

D. Symptoms that last longer than 3 weeks after taking all of your antibiotics.

E. Other: ______________________________

CHRONIC OBSTRUCTIVE PULMONARY DISEASE (COPD)

PROBLEM

COPD is a chronic, progressive, debilitating disease of the lungs that doesn't have a cure. Most people have a combination of emphysema and chronic bronchitis. Persons with COPD usually have some of the following symptoms: cough (usually productive), shortness of breath at rest or with exertion, wheezing, decreased energy level, and weight loss.

CAUSE

COPD is most commonly associated with cigarette smoking and long-term exposure to pulmonary irritants in the environment (e.g., coal dust). Repeated respiratory infections may also contribute to the development of COPD.

PREVENTION

A. Avoid smoking and exposure to secondhand smoke.

B. Avoid exposure to environmental irritants, including pollution, household cleaning products, and smoke from fires.

TREATMENT PLAN

A. Stopping smoking is one of the most important treatments. Talk to your health care provider about support for stopping. **It is never too late to stop smoking.**

B. Reduce your exposure to lung irritants and extremely hot and cold air temperatures.

C. Begin an exercise program with your health care provider's approval. Walking is a good aerobic exercise. Begin with a pace that is tolerable and easy to maintain; then increase the duration and intensity of the exercise as tolerated. Stop if you experience shortness of breath or chest pain. A realistic goal may be 5 to 10 minutes a day, eventually increasing to 30 to 40 minutes a day.

D. Receive the flu vaccine every fall. The pneumococcal vaccine is recommended every 5 years and may be given at the same time as the flu vaccine.

E. Use a spacer/holding chamber to help you inhale all of your medicine. Spacers help you place more of your medicine in your lungs instead of at the back of your throat and mouth. Keep your spacer clean.

F. Use slow, deep breathing or pursed-lip breathing when you are short of breath. Breathe out like you are blowing out a candle.

G. Ask your health care provider if you are a candidate for low-flow oxygen treatment when shortness of breath occurs at night and causes insomnia and restlessness.

Activity: Group activities together such as planning shopping with going to the post office. Schedule rest periods throughout the day. Exercise programs should help increase activity tolerance.

Diet: Good nutrition is important. Six small, high-calorie meals a day are suggested. Avoid excessive intake of carbohydrates, especially simple carbohydrates like candy, soda, and potato chips. Milk and milk products do not increase the production of mucus. Ask your health care provider to refer you to a dietitian if nutritional problems persist.

Medications:

You Have Been Prescribed: ______________________________

You Need to Take: ______________________________

You Need to Notify the Office If:

A. Your mucus changes color, increases in amount, or the consistency is becoming thicker.

B. After you start your medication, call if your wheezing or shortness of breath is getting worse.

C. You are having trouble walking or talking due to your shortness of breath.

D. Other: ______________________________

Phone: ______________________________

You should have a follow-up appointment in 3 months unless you worsen before then.

COMMON COLD

PROBLEM

The common cold is swelling of the mucous membranes of the respiratory tract. Most people complain of feeling tired, have a runny or stopped-up nose, a sore throat, hoarseness, and watery and/or red eyes. You may have a low-grade fever or no fever at all.

CAUSE

A virus usually causes the common cold.

PREVENTION

A. Colds are spread from one person to another through hand-to-hand contact and contact with air droplets from sneezing, coughing, and talking.
B. Practice good hand-washing techniques with soap and water or hand sanitizers.
C. Do not drink from the same glass after others.
D. Cover your mouth and nose when you sneeze or cough.
E. Use tissues when you blow your nose. Dispose of them and then wash your hands.
F. If no tissue is available, do the "elbow sneeze" into the bend of your arm (away from your open hands). Always wash your hands.
G. The flu vaccine is recommended to be taken every year.

TREATMENT PLAN

A. Using a humidifier for your bedroom or inhaling steam helps keep the mucous membranes of your nose from drying.
B. Discuss using saline nose drops.
C. Secondary infections of the respiratory tract (sinuses, lungs) may occur. If these do occur, then antibiotic therapy may be needed.
D. Zinc preparations are not recommended for an acute cough due to the common cold.

Activity: There are no activity restrictions. Frequent rest periods or naps can help with fatigue.

Diet: Eat well-balanced meals and snacks. Drink extra liquids (10–12 glasses a day). Warm fluids, such as tea and soups, can increase the rate of mucus flow and provide some symptom relief.

Medications: Antibiotics aren't prescribed for a cold, but they may be prescribed for a secondary infection.

A. All cold medications are available over the counter. Please consider the side effects of these products as side effects can be greater than any benefit. If you choose to use them, take as directed.

You Have Been Prescribed: ______________________________

You Need to Take: ______________________________

You Need to Notify the Office If:

A. You experience pain that's getting worse in your ears, sinuses, throat, neck, or chest.
B. You have green or yellow nasal drainage.
C. Your temperature is higher than 100.4°F.
D. You are a diabetic and your blood sugars are elevated, or you notice ketones in your urine while you are sick.
E. Other: ______________________________

COUGH

PROBLEM

Coughing is an important defense mechanism your body uses to clear your airways of mucus and inhaled particles.

CAUSE

A cough is often associated with other respiratory symptoms and may be a sign of infection. Coughing is often related to environmental or chemical irritants such as smoking.

PREVENTION

A. Coughing can't be prevented, but you do have some voluntary control over it.

B. Occasionally, medications can cause a cough. Therefore, review all medications with your health care provider.

C. The flu vaccine is recommended each year; however, the flu vaccine does not prevent a cough.

TREATMENT PLAN

A. Stop smoking, including exposure to secondhand smoke. At the minimum, maintain a smoke-free bedroom.

B. Using a room humidifier may be helpful. Keep your humidifier clean—it can grow bacteria.

C. Change heating and air conditioning filters often to decrease environmental irritants.

D. Coughing for several minutes may tire you, so you may need extra rest.

Activity: No activity restrictions.

Diet: Drink at least 10 to 15 glasses of liquids a day.

Medications:

You Have Been Prescribed: ____________________

You Need to Take: ____________________

You Need to Notify the Office If:

A. You have difficulty breathing.

B. You cough up blood.

C. You develop other symptoms besides coughing, such as green sinus drainage and/or a sore throat.

D. You can't sleep because of coughing.

E. You develop a fever over 101°F.

F. Other: ____________________

Phone: ____________________

EMPHYSEMA

PROBLEM

Emphysema is a chronic lung disease, which is incurable. Emphysema can only be managed; the goal of treatment is to improve the activities of daily living and the quality of life by preventing symptoms and by preserving optimal lung function.

CAUSE

Cigarette smoking increases the risk of COPD (another name for several lung diseases) by about 30 times. Environmental irritants have also been linked with chronic lung diseases.

PREVENTION

Emphysema can't be prevented once lung changes have taken place.

TREATMENT PLAN

A. **Stop smoking—it causes more lung irritation, mucus/sputum production, and coughing. It is never too late to quit smoking.**

B. Eliminate other lung irritants, such as wood smoke; secondhand smoke; hair spray; and paint, bleach, and other chemicals found at home. Avoid sweeping and dusting, and stay indoors when air pollution or pollen counts are high.

C. Pulmonary rehabilitation may be ordered. Exercising is a very important component of pulmonary rehabilitation as well as learning breathing techniques.

D. Report respiratory infections to your health care provider as soon as possible.

E. Get a flu shot every year, and get a vaccination for pneumonia.

F. Use postural drainage: Lean over the side of the bed, rest your elbows on a pillow placed on the floor, and cough as someone gently pounds on your back.

G. Stay indoors during extremely hot or cold weather. If you must be outside in the cold, cover your nose and face. Use an air conditioner in hot weather.

H. Avoid people who have respiratory illnesses; also avoid crowds and poorly ventilated areas.

I. Oxygen therapy may be ordered if you have trouble breathing.

J. Use community resources such as Meals on Wheels, handicap tag, or parking stickers.

k. You may be asked to talk to a social worker.

Activity:

A. Pace yourself to avoid shortness of breath.

B. Follow a daily exercise plan. Start with 3 to 4 times a day, each lasting 5 to 15 minutes. Start at half-speed and build up.

C. Sexual dysfunction can occur because of lack of physical energy and trouble breathing. Find other ways to show affection such as kissing, hugging, or massage.

Diet:

A. If you do not have congestive heart failure, drink 3 liters of fluid a day—equal to one and a half large soda bottles.

B. Avoid dairy products; they increase mucus/sputum production.

C. Eat five to six small meals a day. Big meals feel like pressure on your stomach and lungs.

D. Avoid foods that cause gas and stomach discomfort.

E. Use oxygen during meals, if necessary; take your time eating, rest between bites, and avoid hard-to-chew foods, because eating may tire you. Rest before and after eating if you have shortness of breath.

F. Eat a high-protein diet with a good balance of vitamins and minerals.

G. Avoid excessively hot or cold foods and drinks that may start an irritating cough.

Medications:

You Have Been Prescribed: ____________________

You Need to Take: ____________________

Use of a Spacer/Chamber Device Improves Aerosol Delivery to Your Lungs and Reduces Side Effects.

You Need to Notify the Office If:

A. You have trouble breathing.
B. You develop an infection (signs are fever, change in sputum, sinus drainage).
C. Your inhaler does not help your symptoms.
D. Your symptoms don't improve within 48 hours of starting medication.
E. Other: ____________________

Phone: ____________________

You should have a follow-up appointment in 3 months unless you are worsening.

INFLUENZA (FLU)

PROBLEM

Influenza (flu) is an acute, self-limiting, febrile illness of the respiratory tract. You are contagious for 24 to 48 hours before feeling symptoms, and you are contagious up to 7 days after symptoms begin. Coughing and sneezing spread the flu.

CAUSE

There are many flu viruses. Stress, excessive fatigue, poor nutrition, recent illness, crowded places, and immunosuppression from drugs or illness lower your resistance to these viruses.

PREVENTION

A. Although the flu vaccine neither prevents nor causes the flu, the flu vaccine is recommended for almost everyone.

B. The flu vaccine should be taken yearly (in the fall) if you are at high risk:
   1. Health care worker
   2. Immunocompromised (transplant patients, HIV-positive patients, etc.)
   3. Pregnant (after the first trimester)
   4. Elderly (older than 65 years of age)

C. Avoid unnecessary contact with sick persons, including in crowded areas.

D. To keep the flu from spreading:
   1. Cover your mouth when coughing or sneezing.
   2. Use tissues when you blow your nose. Dispose of them and then wash your hands.
   3. If no tissue is available, do the "elbow sneeze" into the bend of your arm (away from your open hands).
   4. Do not share drinking glasses.
   5. Wash your hands with soap and water or use hand sanitizer.

TREATMENT PLAN

A. Rest.

B. Drink lots of fluids.

C. Run cool-mist vaporizer.

D. Take tepid sponge baths in warm water to prevent chilling and shivers.

E. Gargle with warm salt water for a sore throat.

F. Use warm compresses or heating pad on low for aching muscles.

Activity: Stay in bed for at least 24 hours after your fever is gone.

Diet: You may not be hungry, but you do not need to be on a special diet for the flu. Drink plenty of liquids (at least 10 glasses a day).

Medications:

A. **Antibiotics do not help the flu since it is a virus.**

B. Special medications shorten the flu. They must be started within 2 days of contracting the flu.

You Have Been Prescribed for Your Fever: ____________________

You Need to Take: ____________________

You Have Been Prescribed for Your Respiratory Symptoms: ____________________

You Need to Take: ____________________

You Have Been Prescribed for Your Respiratory (Cough Suppressant) Symptoms: ____________________

You Need to Take: ____________________

You Need to Notify the Office If You Have:

A. Thick, green nasal drainage.

B. Ear pain.

C. Increase in fever or cough.

D. Shortness of breath or chest pain.

E. Blood in your sputum.

F. Neck pain or stiffness.

G. New or unexplained symptoms.

H. Other: ____

Phone: __________________________________

NICOTINE DEPENDENCE

PROBLEM

Cigarette smoking is one of the most **preventable causes of death and disability in the United States.** Other forms of nicotine include chewing tobacco and pipe tobacco and can be just as harmful. Risks of lip, tongue, mouth, and throat cancer are associated with use of nicotine. Smoking may cause bleeding in pregnancy and may be responsible for the baby not growing well. It is well documented that infants and children who are exposed to long-term, secondhand smoke inhalation are at increased risk of **sudden infant death syndrome** and frequent **ear infections and chronic illnesses.**

Nicotine is addictive; therefore, stopping smoking is difficult.

CAUSE

Seeing your parents smoke and using tobacco may be one of the reasons that caused you to start using tobacco. Peer pressure is a big reason why you may have started smoking as a teenager. You may also feel nervous and use smoking for its instant calming effect.

REASONS TO QUIT

A. Quitting tobacco will add years to your life. **It is never too late to quit smoking.**

B. You will have healthier lungs, which will decrease your risk of developing cancer and having a heart attack or stroke.

C. You will also have more energy and feel better physically and mentally.

D. Smoking cessation will also decrease the secondhand smoke exposure around your family and friends, which will make them healthier, too.

E. Secondhand smoke causes asthma attacks and other health problems.

F. Some insurance plans are more expensive if you smoke.

G. You will save a lot of money by not buying cigarettes.

H. Don't quit for yourself: Quit for someone you love.

I. You will have fewer wrinkles.

J. Other treatment is available if you use smoking to help nervousness. Please talk to your health care provider if you feel this is the reason you smoke.

TREATMENT PLAN

1. Set a quit date within 2 to 4 weeks and get information/treatment from your provider.
2. Throw away all cigarettes, matches, lighters, and ashtrays in your home, car, and workplace.
3. Make smoking very inconvenient.
4. Ask your family/friends for support and encouragement to help you stop.
5. Stay in nonsmoking environments and avoid friends/family members who smoke.
6. If you get the urge to smoke, take deep cleansing breaths and try to occupy your time with something else, like chewing gum.
7. Leave the table and change the smoking routine you used to have, such as smoking with your coffee after meals.
8. Reward yourself often for staying smoke-free.
9. It is not unusual that you will go back to smoking; it is difficult to quit. Smoking even one less cigarette counts.
10. It may take several times to finally quit.
11. Use an alternative method to help during times of extreme stress (singing, music, prayer, reciting a favorite verse, taking deep abdominal breaths [5 times in over 1 minute]).

Activity:

1. Exercise daily to help alleviate the craving for nicotine.
2. Avoid caffeine if possible.
3. Chew gum or hard candy when you crave a cigarette.
4. Eat celery sticks or carrots in place of a cigarette.
5. Drink a lot of water and other fluids to keep hydrated.

Medications:

1. Discuss options available with your health care provider to help you quit.
2. Medications are available to help you quit.

3. The nicotine patch, inhaler, and gum are available and may be right for you. Discuss these options with your health care provider since they are good steps to quitting.
4. Many of the stop smoking medicines may be covered by your insurance.

You Have Been Prescribed: ______________________________

You Need to Take: ______________________________

You Need to Notify the Office If You Have:

1. Severe craving and the urge to smoke or chew tobacco even on medicines.
2. Feelings of impulsiveness, like you might do something you will later regret.
3. Started to smoke again after you have stepped down while using the nicotine patch.
4. ______________________________

Phone: ______________________________

RESOURCES

The American Cancer Society has some good tips on quitting smoking at www.cancer.org

The American Lung Association also has good guides to help stop smoking at www.lung.org

PNEUMONIA, VIRAL

PROBLEM

Viral pneumonia is an infection of the lung that causes fluid in the air sacs. You may have fever, cough, or difficulty breathing.

CAUSE

Respiratory viruses cause viral pneumonia and bacteria.

PREVENTION

A. Avoid contact with people with respiratory illnesses.

B. Although the flu vaccine does not prevent pneumonia, a yearly flu shot is recommended.

C. The pneumonia vaccine helps prevent pneumonia caused by bacteria. If you are older than 65 years or have other chronic respiratory illness, the pneumonia vaccine is recommended.

TREATMENT PLAN

A. Use a cool-mist humidifier and clean it daily.

B. Take deep breaths and cough frequently to clear secretions from lungs.

C. Avoid smoking and exposure to secondhand smoke.

D. Practice good hand washing or the use of hand sanitizers.

Activity: Rest frequently during the early phase of the illness. Fatigue may continue for up to 6 weeks.

Diet: Eat a nutritious diet. Drink 8 to 10 glasses of water a day.

Medications:

A. Take acetaminophen (Tylenol) for fever, discomfort, and headache.

B. Do not take cough suppressants. It is important for you to cough and get up any mucus.

C. Antibiotics are not given for a viral infection. If you have a bacterial infection, then you may be put on an antibiotic.

You Have Been Prescribed: ____________________

You Need to Take: ____________________

You Need to Notify the Office If You Have:

A. Increased difficulty breathing.

B. Fever over 101°F, or fever that persists after 48 hours of antibiotics.

C. Worsening discomfort.

D. Shortness of breath.

E. Blood in sputum.

F. Nausea, vomiting, or diarrhea.

G. Other: ____________________

Phone: ____________________

You should be seen for a follow-up appointment on: ____________________

SLEEP APNEA

PROBLEM

You have been diagnosed with sleep apnea. During your sleep your tongue and throat relax, causing less air to go down into your lungs. When you sleep and snore you have short periods when you stop breathing and may wake up gasping for breath. Your bed partner may shake you awake because of your loud snoring or may notice that you have stopped breathing. The sleep apnea makes you very tired, leading you to take daytime naps.

CAUSES

A. Being overweight and having a "thick neck" can cause sleep apnea.

B. As you get older you are more likely to have sleep apnea.

C. After menopause, women may start having sleep apnea.

D. If you have not had your tonsils removed, they may be part of the problem as your tongue and throat relaxes.

E. Alcohol and some medicines cause sleep apnea.

F. Allergies may also cause some sleep apnea.

PREVENTION

A. There is no way to prevent sleep apnea once you have it.

B. One way to help your sleep apnea is to lose weight.

TREATMENT PLAN

A. Review all of your medicines and any herbal products with your health care provider.

B. You may be told to sleep with your head up on two pillows, use a tennis ball under your pillow, or even sleep with a back pack under your pillow. This holds your head up higher and prevents your tongue from making your wind pipe smaller.

C. You may also need a mouthpiece to help your tongue from relaxing when you sleep. Your dentist will need to help you find the best one.

D. You may be sent to a lung specialist to help with your treatment.

E. You may be told you need to have a sleep study to check out and measure how often you stop breathing at night.

F. After your sleep study, your lung specialist may order you to have a sleep machine called continuous positive airway pressure (CPAP) or biphasic positive airway pressure (BiPAP).
1. The sleep machine uses nose tubing, a nasal mask, or a full face mask.
2. The machine is small and portable.
3. Your CPAP machine can be taken through the airport.
4. You will have a supplier send you more tubing, machine filters, and breathing tubes/masks on a regular schedule.

G. Continuing to use the prescribed treatment for sleep apnea is important to your overall health.

Activity:

A. You will continue to need to sleep with your head higher, use the mouthpiece, or use the sleep machine to keep from having sleep apnea.

B. Exercise; losing even a small amount of weight will help with sleep apnea.

C. Stop smoking.

D. Avoid alcohol, especially near your bedtime.

Diet: There is no special diet for sleep apnea, but losing weight helps.

Medications:

There are no medicines for sleep apnea.

You Need to Notify the Office If:

A. Your bed partner complains that your snoring or sleep apnea has worsened.

B. You want to make an appointment to discuss having a sleep study.

C. You are having difficulty with your sleep machine or other equipment.

D. Other: ______________________________

Phone: ______________________________

RESOURCE

The National Sleep Foundation at www.sleepfoundation.org

Patient Teaching Guides for Chapter 12: Cardiovascular Disorders

- Atherosclerosis and Hyperlipidemia
- Atrial Fibrillation
- Chronic Venous Insufficiency
- Deep Vein Thrombosis
- Lymphedema
- Peripheral Arterial Disease
- Superficial Thrombophlebitis
- Varicose Veins

ATHEROSCLEROSIS AND HYPERLIPIDEMIA

PROBLEM

Hyperlipidemia (excess lipids in the blood) is called "hardening of the arteries." The excess lipids increase your risk of developing heart disease and heart attacks.

CAUSE

Elevated blood cholesterol levels lead to plaque formation in the walls of the major arteries in the body. The higher the level of low-density lipoprotein (LDL), or "bad" cholesterol, the greater the chance of getting heart disease. On the other hand, the higher the level of high-density lipoprotein (HDL), or "good" cholesterol, the lower the risk of heart disease.

PREVENTION/TREATMENT PLAN

Lowering your risk of heart disease involves the following:

A. Diet changes to lower your bad cholesterol (LDL) and raise your good cholesterol (HDL).

B. Lose weight. Start with losing 5 to 10 pounds.

C. Start or increase your physical activity. Walking is a good exercise to start getting active.

D. Other ways to modify your risk factors:
  1. Stop smoking. **It is never too late to stop smoking.**
  2. Control your blood pressure.
  3. If you are a diabetic, control your blood sugar level.

Activity: Regular exercise, such as walking vigorously for 30 minutes three times a week, increases your good cholesterol levels, lowers blood sugar, and promotes weight loss.

Diet: Follow the dietary approaches to stop hypertension (DASH) and low-fat/low-cholesterol diet:

A. Decrease total fat calories and cholesterol.

B. Decrease total saturated fats, and replace with monounsaturated fats such as canola oil, olive oil, and margarine.

C. Increase fiber with oatmeal, bran, or fiber supplements.

D. Increase daily intake of fruits and vegetables.

E. Try garlic, soy protein, and vitamin C to help lower LDL cholesterol.

Medications: You may be prescribed a medicine to lower your cholesterol. You will need to come into the doctor's office and have your blood drawn to monitor your liver and cholesterol levels.

You Have Been Prescribed: ______________________________

You Need to Take: ______________________________

You Need to Notify the Office If You Have:

A. Chest pain.

B. Shortness of breath or trouble breathing while exercising.

C. Abdominal pain.

D. Muscle pain or weakness.

E. Other: ______________________________

Phone: ______________________________

ATRIAL FIBRILLATION

PROBLEM

Atrial fibrillation is the condition that causes the upper chambers of the heart (the atria) to beat faster and irregularly (also called fibrillation). The upper chambers of the heart do not beat at the same time as the lower chambers (the ventricles). When atrial fibrillation occurs, blood clots can form in the heart and then travel to the brain, causing a stroke.

CAUSES

Atrial fibrillation is caused by a malfunction of the heart's pacemaker. Many things can cause the heart's pacemaker to malfunction, including excessive alcohol intake, emotional stress, physical stress, recent heart surgery, medication side effects, and a long list of medical conditions. These medical conditions include coronary artery disease, leaky heart valves, high blood pressure, heart failure, heart attack, thyroid disease, infections, inflammation around the heart, sleep apnea, obesity, and lung diseases like chronic obstructive pulmonary disease, bronchitis, asthma, and emphysema.

PREVENTION

A. Stop smoking. Discuss smoking cessation with your health care provider. **It is never too late to stop smoking.**

B. Reduce or eliminate intake of alcohol and caffeine.

C. Lose weight. Discuss losing weight with your health care provider.

D. Make a list of your current medical conditions and current medications. Keep an updated copy in your wallet.

E. When traveling:
   1. Always travel with enough of your medication to last through your vacation plus an additional 3 days.

F. Take all of your medication as prescribed. If you become ill and are unable to take your medications, call your health care provider's office.

TREATMENT PLAN

A. Take your medications as ordered by your health care provider.

B. Effectively manage all other medical conditions, paying special attention to cholesterol, blood pressure, thyroid disease, sleep apnea, and any lung diseases.

C. Follow up with your primary health care provider and/or cardiologist on a regularly scheduled basis.

D. **If you are on a blood thinner that requires regular blood work, make sure you get your blood checked on the schedule set by your health care provider.**

Activity:

A. Get regular exercise, after discussing the type and frequency of exercise that is safe for you with your health care provider.

Diet:

A. Eat a balanced, low-fat, and low-salt diet in addition to dietary guidelines suggested by your health care provider.

Medications:

You Have Been Prescribed: ______________________________

You Need to Take: ______________________________

You Need to Notify the Office:

A. If you have any of the following symptoms:
   1. Palpitations or a fluttering in your chest
   2. Chest pain
   3. Weakness or extreme tiredness
   4. Shortness of breath at rest or with activity
   5. Dizziness
   6. Disorientation
   7. Confusion
   8. Passing out or losing consciousness
   9. Severe headache
   10. Frequent urination or a compelling urge to urinate
   11. Anxiety or panic symptoms

B. If vomiting or other illness causes you to miss more than one dose of your medications.

C. Other: ____________________

Phone: ____________________

RESOURCES

American Heart Association: www.heart.org

National Heart, Lung, and Blood Institute: www.nhli.nih.gov

CHRONIC VENOUS INSUFFICIENCY

PROBLEM

Chronic venous insufficiency (CVI) is a condition in which blood has difficulty flowing back to the heart from the arms or legs. This usually occurs when the valves along the inside of the veins are damaged and allow blood to flow backward. The pooling of blood leads to swelling, pain, a heavy feeling, darkening of the skin, and infections. Without treatment, CVI can lead to blood clots and serious infections that could lead to amputation.

CAUSES

Many things may increase the chance of having CVI. Some, like gender, age, or how tall you are, can't be changed. Others can be changed; these include prolonged standing or sitting and excessive weight.

PREVENTION

A. Avoid standing or sitting for long periods of time.

B. If overweight or obese, lose weight. Discuss what you can do to lose weight with your health care provider.

TREATMENT PLAN

A. Take your medications as ordered by your health care provider.

B. Wear compression stockings. Put them on before getting out of bed in the morning. Take them off just before going to bed at night.

C. Raise the affected arm or leg whenever lying down to improve pain and swelling.

D. Avoid standing or sitting for long periods of time.

E. Follow up with your primary health care provider on a regularly scheduled basis.

Activity:

A. Get regular exercise. Discuss what type and frequency of exercise is safe for you with your health care provider.

B. Exercise leg muscles by pumping ankles when sitting. Rocking in a rocking chair is another option.

Diet:

A. Discuss the type of diet that best suits your needs with your health care provider: diabetic diet, low-fat diet, low-cholesterol diet, and/or low-sodium diet.

Medications:

You Have Been Prescribed: ______________________________

You Need to Take: ______________________________

You Need to Notify the Office If You Have:

A. Fever over 101°F.

B. Increased redness, pain, tenderness to touch, swelling, and/or warmth.

C. Sudden shortness of breath.

D. Chest pain.

E. New wound or sore on the affected arm or leg.

F. If you are taking a blood-thinning medication and have any of these symptoms:
1. Vomit that is bright red or dark and looks like coffee grounds.
2. Bright red blood in your stools or black, tarry stools.
3. Severe headache.
4. Sudden weakness in an arm or leg.
5. Memory loss or confusion.
6. Sudden change in vision.
7. Trouble speaking or understanding others.

G. Other: ______________________________

Phone: ______________________________

RESOURCES

Vascular Disease Foundation: vasculardisease.org/flyers/chronic-venous-insufficiency-flyer.pdf

Vascular Web: www.vascularweb.org/vascularhealth/pages/chronic-venous-insufficiency.aspx

DEEP VEIN THROMBOSIS

PROBLEM

You have inflammation or a blood clot in one of the veins in your body. Phlebitis is inflammation, and thrombosis means a blood clot. Symptoms include:

A. Pain

B. Fever

C. Swelling

D. Tenderness in the affected leg or arm

E. The vein may feel somewhat "hard" to touch.

CAUSE

Blood clots form because of bed rest, surgery, a heart attack, a severe illness, and birth control pills. A blood clot can also form after breaking a hip or leg, pregnancy, cancer, and some medications.

TREATMENT PLAN/CARE

A. If you have phlebitis, you may be given an anti-inflammatory medicine.

B. Some patients need to go to the hospital and get intravenous (IV) medicine to break up the clot.

C. You may be given blood thinners either as a pill or by self-injection.

D. Be sure to take all of the medicine given as directed to help with the blood clot.

E. Do not smoke: This worsens your condition. **It is never too late to stop smoking.**

F. If you currently take any hormones, such as birth control pills, your health care provider may talk to you about stopping them.

G. Manage all other medical conditions, especially high blood pressure, diabetes, and high cholesterol, and try to lose any extra weight.

H. Follow up with your primary health care provider and/or cardiologist on a regularly scheduled basis.

Activity:

A. Get out of bed as soon as possible after surgery.

B. While in bed, perform range-of-motion exercises with your legs.

C. Exercise leg muscles by pumping your ankles when sitting.

D. Don't sit with your legs crossed.

E. Avoid standing or sitting for long periods of time.

F. Don't wear tight clothing such as knee-high hosiery.

G. Wear special supportive hosiery called compression stockings. Put them on before getting out of bed in the morning and take them off before going to bed at night.

H. When traveling:
1. Try to take rest breaks on a regular basis.
2. Continue to do the ankle pumping exercise when in the car or on the plane.
3. Wear loose-fitting clothes that are comfortable.
4. Avoid drinking alcohol.
5. Drink plenty of fluids unless you are instructed not to do so by your health care provider.
6. Ask your health care provider if you should wear compression stockings.

I. Wear a Medic Alert bracelet if you are put on blood thinners.

J. You will notice that you bruise easier while on your blood thinner.

K. You may need to come back to the office to have your labs drawn.

Diet:

A. Discuss the type of diet that best suits your needs: Diabetic diet, low-fat diet, low-cholesterol diet, and/or low-sodium diet.

B. If you are taking the blood thinner Coumadin, you will be given a list of foods that should not be eaten. These foods interfere with how the blood thinner works.

C. Avoid alcohol.

Medications: If you currently take birth control pills, ask your health care provider if you should stop taking them. You may be prescribed a blood thinner by injection or pills. Take this medicine even if you feel better.

You Have Been Prescribed: ___

You Need to Take: ___

You Need to Notify the Office If You Have:

A. Increased swelling, pain, or warmth in your leg or arm with the DVT.

B. Fever.

C. Sudden shortness of breath.

D. Chest pain.

E. If you are on a blood thinner medicine, call for signs of bleeding including:
 1. Nosebleed that will not stop with pressure.
 2. Coughing up blood.
 3. Vomit that is bright red or dark that looks like coffee grounds or grape jelly.
 4. Blood in your bowel movements that looks black or tarry in color.
 5. Heavy periods.
 6. Severe headache.
 7. Sudden weakness in an arm or leg.
 8. Sudden change in vision.
 9. Trouble speaking or understanding others.
 10. Memory loss or confusion.

F. Any new symptoms not present at your last office visit.

Phone: ___

You can build your own identification bracelets or neck chains from American Medical ID: http://www.americanmedical-id.com/category/medical-ID-bracelets-62

RESOURCES

Patient Education Center—Thromboembolism (DVT and Pulmonary Embolism): patienteducationcenter.org/articles/thromboembolism-deep-vein-thrombosis-and-pulmonary-embolism

Vascular Disease Foundation: vasculardisease.org/deep-vein-thrombosis-venous-disease

LYMPHEDEMA

PROBLEM

Lymphedema is the backup of fluid in the lymphatic system into an arm or leg. The fluid causes severe swelling, which restricts movement and can lead to infection and, in rare cases, a form of cancer called lymphangiosarcoma.

CAUSES

Many factors can cause lymphedema. These include a diagnosis of cancer treated with radiation, surgical removal of lymph nodes, infection, and disorders from birth, which affect the structure of the lymph system.

PREVENTION

A. Protect your arm or leg while recovering from cancer treatment.
   1. Avoid heavy lifting, if it involves an arm.
   2. Avoid strenuous exercise.
   3. Avoid heat on your arm or leg.
   4. Avoid tight clothing.

TREATMENT PLAN

A. Raise the affected arm or leg whenever lying down to improve pain and swelling.

B. Wear compression stockings. Put them on before getting out of bed in the morning. Take them off just before going to bed at night.

C. Apply lotion every day to the affected area.

D. Check the affected area every day and report any skin changes to your health care provider, especially any cracks or cuts.

E. Follow up with your primary health care provider and other specialty providers on a regularly scheduled basis.

Activity:

A. Get regular exercise. Discuss with your health care provider what type and frequency of exercise is safe for you.

B. Exercise leg muscles by pumping ankles when sitting. Rocking in a rocking chair is another option.

Diet:

A. Discuss with your health care provider the type of diet that best suits your needs: Diabetic diet, low-fat diet, low-cholesterol diet, and/or low-sodium diet.

Medications:

You Have Been Prescribed: ____________________

You Need to Take: ____________________

You Need to Notify the Office If You Have:

A. Fever over 101°F.

B. Increased redness, pain, tenderness to touch, and/or warmth in affected arm or leg.

C. New pain, swelling, or warmth in an arm or leg.

D. Other: ____________________

Phone: ____________________

RESOURCES

National Cancer Institute: www.cancer.gov/cancertopics/pdq/supportivecare/lymphedema/healthprofessional/page2

National Lymphedema Network: www.lymphnet.org

Patient Education Center—Lymphedema: patienteducationcenter.org/articles/lymphedema

PERIPHERAL ARTERIAL DISEASE

PROBLEM

Peripheral arterial disease is a condition in which fatty deposits build up on the inside of vessels that carry blood to the hands and feet. This makes it difficult for blood to travel to hands and feet, which causes pain with activity and when resting. If these blockages increase in size, the pain will also worsen; infections can also occur, which could lead to amputation.

CAUSES

Many things cause these fatty deposits to build up inside arteries. Some factors such as age, gender, and genetics can't be changed. Others can be changed; these include smoking, diabetes, high cholesterol, high blood pressure, and excessive weight.

PREVENTION

A. Stop smoking. **It is never too late to stop smoking.**

B. To prevent injury that could progress into an infection, do the following:
1. Wear well-fitting shoes that protect your feet.
2. Look and feel inside your shoes before putting them on.
3. Look at your feet daily for any signs of injury or infection.
4. Dry feet well after bathing, including between toes.
5. Do not trim your own toenails or shave off calluses. A health care provider should do this for you to prevent infection.
6. Do not use a heating pad or hot water on your hands or feet to keep warm. Wear gloves or socks instead.

TREATMENT PLAN

A. Take your medications as ordered by your health care provider.

B. Effectively manage all other medical conditions, paying special attention to cholesterol, blood pressure, diabetes, and obesity.

C. Follow up with your primary health care provider and/or cardiologist on a regularly scheduled basis.

Activity:

A. Get regular exercise, after discussing with your health care provider the type and frequency of exercise that is safe for you.

Diet:

A. Discuss the type of diet that best suits your needs: diabetic diet, low-fat diet, low-cholesterol diet, and/or low-sodium diet.

B. Follow the dietary guidelines suggested by your health care provider.

Medications:

You Have Been Prescribed: ____________________

You Need to Take: ____________________

You Need to Notify the Office If You Have:

A. Any of the following symptoms:
1. Worsening pain in your arm or leg
2. Fever of 101.5°F or greater
3. Any temperature change in a hand or foot
4. Any change in feeling of a hand or foot
5. Any change in the color of a hand or foot
6. Difficulty walking
7. Vomiting or other illness that causes you to miss more than one dose of your medications
8. Other: ____________________

Phone: ____________________

RESOURCE

Vascular Disease Foundation – Peripheral Artery Disease: http://vasculardisease.org/peripheral-artery-disease/

SUPERFICIAL THROMBOPHLEBITIS

PROBLEM

Superficial thrombophlebitis occurs when a vein is irritated or injured. The portion of the vein that is affected can develop a blood clot or become infected, causing redness, swelling, and pain. If untreated, the infection and/or blood clot can progress into a life-threatening condition like sepsis, deep vein thrombosis, or pulmonary embolism.

CAUSES

Many things can cause irritation and injury to veins. These include a recent intravenous line placed during a hospital stay, infection, some medications, and pregnancy. Some risk factors can't be changed, like genetics, whereas others can be changed, including inactivity and excessive weight.

PREVENTION

A. Avoid standing or sitting for long periods of time.

B. If you smoke, stop or reduce the amount you smoke. **It is never too late to stop smoking.**

C. If overweight or obese, lose weight. Discuss what you can do to lose weight with your health care provider.

TREATMENT PLAN

A. Take your medications as ordered by your health care provider.

B. Raise the affected arm or leg whenever lying down to improve pain and swelling.

C. Warm compresses to the affected area may improve pain.

D. Wear compression stockings. Put them on before getting out of bed in the morning. Take them off just before going to bed at night.

E. Avoid standing or sitting for long periods of time.

F. Follow up with your primary health care provider on a regularly scheduled basis.

Activity:

A. Get regular exercise. Discuss with your health care provider what type and frequency of exercise is safe for you.

B. Exercise leg muscles by pumping ankles when sitting. Rocking in a rocking chair is another option.

Diet:

A. Discuss with your health care provider the type of diet that best suits your needs: diabetic diet, low-fat diet, low-cholesterol diet, and/or low-sodium diet.

Medications:

You Have Been Prescribed: ______________________________

You Need to Take: ______________________________

You Need to Notify the Office If You Have:

A. Fever over 101°F.

B. Sudden shortness of breath.

C. Chest pain.

D. New pain, swelling, or warmth in an arm or leg.

E. Taken a blood-thinning medication and have any of these symptoms:
1. Vomit that is bright red or dark and looks like coffee grounds
2. Bright red blood in your stools or black, tarry stools
3. Severe headache
4. Sudden weakness in an arm or leg
5. Memory loss or confusion
6. Sudden change in vision
7. Trouble speaking or understanding others

F. Other: ______________________________

Phone: ______________________________

RESOURCES

Mayo Clinic—Thrombophlebitis: www.mayoclinic.com/health/thrombophlebitis/DS00223

Patient Education Center—Superficial Thrombophlebitis: patienteducationcenter.org/articles/superficial-thrombophlebitis

VARICOSE VEINS

PROBLEM

Varicose veins are caused when the valves inside of veins are damaged and allow blood to flow backward instead of toward the heart. This backflow of blood increases the pressure in the vein, leading to pain and swelling; this makes them more visible. Varicose veins can worsen and increase the risk of blood clots, infection, bleeding, and changes to the skin.

CAUSES

There are many factors that increase the chance of developing varicose veins. Some, like age and genetics, can't be changed. Some can be changed; these include prolonged standing, restrictive clothing, excessive weight, and smoking.

PREVENTION

A. Avoid prolonged standing. If prolonged standing is required, shift weight from one leg to the other.

B. Do not sit with legs dependent.

TREATMENT PLAN

A. Raise the affected arm or leg whenever lying down to improve pain and swelling.

B. Wear compression stockings. Put them on before getting out of bed in the morning. Take them off just before going to bed at night.

C. Avoid standing or sitting for long periods of time.

D. Follow up with your primary health care provider on a regularly scheduled basis.

Activity:

A. Get regular exercise. Discuss with your health care provider what type and frequency of exercise is safe for you.

B. Exercise leg muscles by pumping ankles when sitting. Rocking in a rocking chair is another option.

Diet:

A. Discuss with your health care provider the type of diet that best suits your needs: Diabetic diet, low-fat diet, low-cholesterol diet, and/or low-sodium diet.

B. If you are taking the blood thinner Coumadin, ask your health care provider about which foods are high in vitamin K and whether you should limit those foods in your diet.

Medications:

You Have Been Prescribed: ____________________

You Need to Take: ____________________

You Need to Notify the Office If You Have:

A. New pain, swelling, or warmth in an arm or leg.

B. Increased redness, pain, tenderness to touch, and/or warmth in the affected arm or leg.

C. Sudden shortness of breath.

D. Chest pain.

E. Other: ____________________

Phone: ____________________

RESOURCES

Patient Education Center—Varicose Veins: patienteducationcenter.org/articles/varicose-veins

Patient Handout—Varicose Veins: nursing.advanceweb.com/Article/Varicose-Veins-HTML.aspx

Patient Teaching Guides for Chapter 13: Gastrointestinal Disorders

- Abdominal Pain
- Crohn's Disease
- Diarrhea
- Fecal Incontinence
- Gastroesophageal Reflux Disease (GERD)
- Hemorrhoids
- Irritable Bowel Syndrome
- Jaundice and Hepatitis
- Lactose Intolerance and Malabsorption
- Management of Ulcers
- Tips to Relieve Constipation

ABDOMINAL PAIN

PROBLEM

Abdominal pain may range from simple gas to appendicitis. Acute pain is pain that has started recently; recurrent pain is present in three or more separate times over at least a 3-month period. It is important that you call if you have pain that lasts 3 hours or longer, have a fever, vomiting, or is unusually sharp or intense.

Suspect a medical emergency if abdominal pain lasts 3 hours or longer, there is fever or vomiting, or the pain is abnormal or unusually sharp or intense.

CAUSE

Pain may result from inflammation, ischemia (poor blood supply), bloating, constipation, or obstruction. Gastroenteritis is the most common cause of acute pain, and chronic stool retention (constipation) is the most common cause of chronic pain. Urinary tract infections can also cause abdominal pain.

A. Males: Torsion of the testicles or a strangulated inguinal hernia may cause abdominal pain.

B. Females: If you have missed a period or suspect you are pregnant, tell your health care provider; ectopic pregnancies are a medical emergency.

PREVENTION

The following suggestions can prevent abdominal pain from constipation:

A. Go to the bathroom as soon as you have the urge to have a bowel movement (BM).

B. Establishing a regular toilet time, such as after breakfast; 15 to 20 minutes after breakfast is a good time, because your gastrointestinal (GI) motility is greatest during that period.

TREATMENT PLAN

Do not take laxatives, use enemas, drugs, food, or liquids (including water) until consulting your health care provider for suspected abdominal pain and the following:

A. Increased or odd-looking vomit or stools

B. Hard, swollen abdomen

C. Lump in scrotum, groin, or lower abdomen

D. Missed period or suspected pregnancy

Activity: As tolerated. Abdominal pain with nausea and vomiting, with fever, or that lasts more than 3 hours and makes you stop doing daily activities should be reported.

Diet: Eat regular foods as tolerated. Do not eat food or drink liquids until you see a health care provider if you have pain with nausea and vomiting, with fever, or that lasts longer than 3 hours.

Medications:

You Have Been Prescribed: ______________________________

You Need to Take: ______________________________

You Need to Notify the Office If You Have:

A. Any change in first symptoms that brought you to the office.

B. Fever higher than ________ degrees.

C. Other: ______________________________

Phone: ______________________________

CROHN'S DISEASE

PROBLEM

Crohn's disease (CD) is an inflammatory disorder of the GI tract that produces ulceration, formation of fibrous tissue, and malabsorption. CD is chronic, relapsing, and incurable.

CAUSE

The cause is unknown, but it can be aggravated by bacterial infection or inflammation.

TREATMENT PLAN

A. Adequate nutrition is critical to the promotion of healing.

B. Vitamin, mineral, and folic acid are necessary for proper healing and avoid complications, such as bone disease and low blood counts.

C. To relieve pain, apply a heating pad or warm compress to your abdomen.

D. Check your BMs daily for signs of bleeding.

E. Surgery may be required to help control symptoms.

F. There may be a support group near where you live. The Crohn's and Colitis Foundation website has an area to find a support group at www.ccfa.org/living-with-crohns-colitis/find-a-support-group.

Activity: During acute attacks, rest in bed or in a chair. Get up only to go to the bathroom, bathe, or eat. Between attacks, resume normal activities, as tolerated.

Diet:

A. When you have diarrhea, increase the fiber content of your diet.

B. Restricting milk products may stop the diarrhea. Omit milk products for a short time, then try them again in a few weeks.

C. Reducing the amount of fat and gluten in your diet may help.

D. Ensure, Sustacal, and Isocal have been found to induce remission and improve symptoms.

E. Severe relapse may require partial bowel rest. Contact the office for instruction.

Medications: You may be prescribed vitamins and minerals, medicine to control pain and relieve diarrhea, and a steroid to reduce the inflammation. Don't stop taking the steroid abruptly. Your health care provider can tell you how to taper the dose over several days.

You Have Been Prescribed the Following Vitamins and Minerals: ______________________

You Need to Take: ______________________

You Have Been Prescribed the Following to Relieve Diarrhea: ______________________

You Need to Take: ______________________

You Have Been Prescribed the Following Steroid: ______________________

You Need to Take: ______________________

Other medications to treat CD include oral medication, intravenous infusions, and injectable medications to control the severity of symptoms. Your health care provider will discuss these with you and the need for close follow-up monitoring.

You Have Been Prescribed: ______________________

You Need to Take: ______________________

You Need to Return to the Office for Blood Work: ______________________

You Need to Notify the Office If You Have:

A. Black, tarry stools, or blood in the stool.

B. A swollen abdomen.

C. A temperature of 101.0°F or higher.

D. Other:____________________

Phone: ____________________

RESOURCE

Crohn's and Colitis Foundation of America: www.ccfa.org
386 Park Avenue South, 17th Floor
New York, NY 10013
800-932-2423
info@ccfa.org

DIARRHEA

PROBLEM

Diarrhea is loose, watery stools. If you are a diabetic and have more than 1 day of diarrhea, please contact the office.

CAUSE

There are many causes of diarrhea, including viral and bacterial infections and parasites.

PREVENTION

A. Avoid raw seafood and undercooked foods.

B. Store food in the refrigerator within 1 hour of cooking to prevent the growth of bacteria. Especially avoid buffet or picnic foods left out for several hours and food served by street vendors.

C. Wash your hands well before preparing foods, after going to the bathroom, and after handling diapers.

D. When traveling:
   1. Avoid local water supplies (including ice) when they are in question: Drink bottled water instead.
   2. Don't eat fresh vegetables that may have been washed in contaminated water.
   3. If possible, travel with antiseptic hand lotion and wipes.

E. When hiking or camping, don't drink from streams, springs, or untested wells. Boil all water used for drinking or cooking.

F. Don't allow people with diarrhea to handle food.

G. Thoroughly cook eggs and other foods of animal origin. Don't eat raw eggs or foods containing raw eggs, such as cookie dough.

H. Keep your child away from childcare centers if their diarrhea is too much for a diaper or they are unable to get to the toilet.

TREATMENT PLAN

A. Spontaneous recovery usually occurs in 24 to 48 hours.

B. Keep drinking liquids.

C. If you think a prescription drug is causing diarrhea, talk with your health care provider before stopping the medication.

D. Clean toys and hard surfaces with soap and water. Chlorine-based disinfectants inactivate rotavirus and may help prevent disease transmission in childcare centers.

Activity: Decrease activities until diarrhea stops.

Diet:

A. If diarrhea is accompanied by nausea, suck ice chips.

B. Drink clear liquids frequently, such as 7UP, Gatorade, ginger ale, broth, or gelatin, until diarrhea stops.

C. Use popsicles for added liquid.

D. After symptoms disappear, eat soft foods, such as cooked cereal, rice, baked potatoes, and yogurt, for 1 to 2 days.

E. You can eat normal foods in 2 to 3 days after the diarrhea stops.

F. Avoid fruit, alcohol, and highly seasoned foods for several more days.

Medications:

You Have Been Prescribed the Following Antidiarrheal Medication: ______________________________

You Need to Take: ______________________________

You Need to Notify the Office If:

A. You have diarrhea lasting more than 2 days or chronic diarrhea.

B. You have mucus, blood, or worms in the stool.

C. You have a fever of 101.0°F or higher.

D. You have severe pain in the stomach or rectum.

E. You have dehydration symptoms, including dry mouth, wrinkled skin, excessive thirst, and little or no urine.

F. Other: ______________________________

Phone: ______________________________

FECAL INCONTINENCE

PROBLEM

Fecal incontinence is losing mucus or stool while passing gas or completely losing stool before getting to a toilet.

CAUSES

There are many causes of fecal incontinence, including having diarrhea around a hard solid impacted stool from constipation, not being active, problems after delivery of a baby, taking too many laxatives, hemorrhoids, and radiation treatment.

PREVENTION

A. Go to the bathroom as soon as you feel that you need to have a BM.

B. Have a scheduled time to go to the toilet, after eating is a good time.

C. Tips to help deal with uncontrolled BMs.
   1. Use the toilet before leaving home.
   2. Identify public restrooms before they are needed.
   3. Carry a bag of supplies.
   4. Change your clothes as soon as possible.
   5. Pants with elastic bands are easier to pull down than pants that have buttons.
   6. Wear disposable underwear/absorbent pads.
   7. Use water without soap. Soap dries and irritates.
   8. Use baby wipes instead of toilet paper.
   9. Use a moisture-barrier cream such as zinc oxide.
   10. Use a special deodorant for your bowels.

TREATMENT PLAN

A. You may be asked to keep a stool diary for one week.

B. If you are constipated:
   1. You may need to have the hardened impacted stool removed
   2. Drink 8 to 10 glasses of water.

Activity: It is important to remain active, such as walking for exercise.

Diet:

A. You may be asked to keep a food diary for 1 week.

B. Eat foods like milk, not a lot of spices.

C. Eat more fiber in your diet. Fiber helps diarrhea and constipation. A separate diet sheet on fiber will be given to you.

You Have Been Instructed to Take the Following Fiber Supplement: ______________________

You Need to Take: ______________________

You Have Been Prescribed the Following Medication: ______________________

You Need to Take: ______________________

You Need to Notify the Office If You Have:

A. Blood in your BMs

B. Fever of 101.0°F or higher

C. Severe pain in the stomach or rectum

D. Other: ______________________

Phone: ______________________

TABLE III.3 Bowel-Control Stool Diary

PLEASE RECORD YOUR STOOL HABIT FOR 1 WEEK				Name				
Date	Time of BM	Incontinence	Stool Seepage or Staining	Stool Consistency (Type 1-5, see below)	Urgency-unable to postpone BM for more than 15 minutes	Use of pads	Medications	Comments
		Yes/No	Yes/No		Yes/No	Yes/No		

Type 1, Hard to pass—marble-like stool; **Type 2,** somewhat difficult to pass—stool is shaped like a chain; **Type 3,** easy to pass—stool comes out in a smooth long shape; **Type 4,** easy to pass—stool is in soft separate pieces; **Type 5,** diarrhea—with no formed pieces of stool, comes out like water.

Adapted from the NIH Let's Talk About Bowel Control diary.

GASTROESOPHAGEAL REFLUX DISEASE (GERD)

PROBLEM

You have stomach acid or a feeling of "heartburn" and "acid brash."

CAUSE

Heartburn occurs if stomach contents come back up into the throat. Diet, spicy foods, alcohol, pregnancy, and nervous tension can make it worse.

PREVENTION

A. Avoid smoking.

B. Avoid things that increase abdominal pressure:
   1. Do not wear tight clothes and belts.
   2. Do not lie down or bend over for 3 hours after eating.
   3. Coughing causes more pressure on your stomach.
   4. Straining causes more pressure on your stomach too.

C. Avoid medications, such as aspirin or ibuprofen, which may irritate your stomach.

D. Avoid alcohol.

TREATMENT PLAN

A. Weight loss is advised to relieve symptoms.

B. Stop smoking. **It is never too late to stop smoking.**

C. You may be instructed to elevate the head of your bed on 6-inch blocks, or sleep on a wedge bolster pillow.

D. Make a list of all of your medications, over-the-counter medications, and herbal products so that you can review them with your health care provider to help find any side effects that may cause your symptoms.

E. Take your medications at the correct times.

Activity: Postpone vigorous exercise until your stomach is likely to be empty, about 2 hours after eating.

Diet:

A. Eat a lower fat, bland diet.

B. Eat four to six small meals a day instead of three larger meals.

C. Don't eat 2 to 3 hours before bedtime.

D. Avoid chocolate, garlic, onions, citrus fruits, coffee (including decaffeinated), alcohol, highly seasoned foods, and carbonated beverages.

E. Eat slowly.

Medications: Sit or stand when taking solid medications (pills or capsules). Drink at least at least one cup of liquid to help swallow pills. When over-the-counter antacids and other medicines stop making your symptoms better, please call the office to make an appointment for medications that decrease gastric acid.

You Have Been Prescribed: ______________________

You Need to Take: ______________________

You Have Been Prescribed: ______________________

You Need to Take: ______________________

You Need to Notify the Office If You Have:

A. No relief from antacids or second medication, so that the next step of medication therapy may be prescribed.

B. New symptoms, such as blood in regurgitated stomach contents.

C. Other: ______________________

Phone: ______________________

HEMORRHOIDS

PROBLEM

A hemorrhoid is a varicose vein of the rectum. You may not know you have a hemorrhoid until bleeding occurs. Hemorrhoids are often found after painless rectal bleeding with a BM. They may cause rectal pain, itching, or a sensation that you have not emptied completely after a BM.

CAUSE

Repeated pressure in the anal or rectal veins causes hemorrhoids. Hemorrhoids are commonly seen with obesity, pregnancy, constipation, sedentary lifestyle, and liver disease.

PREVENTION

A. Avoid heavy lifting.
B. Try to prevent constipation or straining.
C. Eat a high-fiber diet.
D. Drink 8 to 10 glasses of water a day.
E. Lose weight if you're overweight.
F. Exercise regularly.

TREATMENT PLAN

A. Spend less time sitting on the toilet to reduce pressure in the veins around the anus.
B. Pat with toilet paper instead of rubbing.
C. Take sitz baths or soak in a warm bathtub three or four times a day for comfort.
D. Apply cold packs or witch hazel (Tucks) compresses for symptom relief.
E. Take a stool softener two to three times a day to prevent straining with BMs.
F. A hemorrhoid treatment may need to be done for severe cases.

Activity: No restrictions are required. Bowel function improves with good physical activity.

Medications:

You Have Been Prescribed the Following Stool Softener: ______________________

You Need to Take: ______________________

You Have Been Prescribed the Following Local Cream: ______________________

You Need to Apply: ______________________

You Need to Notify the Office If You Have:

A. A hard lump that develops where a hemorrhoid has been.
B. Hemorrhoids that cause severe pain that is not relieved by the above treatment.
C. Excessive rectal bleeding: More than a trace or streak on the toilet paper or BM. **Rectal bleeding may be an early sign of cancer.**
D. Other: ______________________

Phone: ______________________

IRRITABLE BOWEL SYNDROME

PROBLEM

Irritable bowel syndrome (IBS) is an irritative and inflammatory disorder of the intestine. You may have diarrhea, you may have constipation, or you may have problems with alternating constipation and diarrhea.

CAUSE

IBS is **not contagious.** IBS can flare with severe stress and may also be triggered by eating.

PREVENTION

A. Try to reduce stress or modify your response to it. Keep a stress diary to avoid stress triggers.

B. Good food habits also help.

C. No specific food has been identified as responsible for all IBS symptoms. Keep a food diary to identify and avoid your food triggers.

TREATMENT PLAN

A. Quit smoking: Nicotine may contribute to the problem. **It is never too late to stop smoking.**

B. Apply a warm heat compress to your abdomen for comfort.

Activity: Exercise, such as walking 20 minutes a day, improves bowel function and helps reduce stress. Other stress-reduction techniques include self-hypnosis and biofeedback.

Diet:

A. Eat a high-fiber diet. Fiber is good for both diarrhea and constipation.

B. Avoid sorbitol-containing (sugar-free) candies and gum as well as lactose-containing milk products to see if this eases your diarrhea symptoms.

C. Don't eat or drink anything that aggravates your symptoms such as the following:
   1. Coffee may be a major food trigger.
   2. Avoid spicy and gas-producing foods.
   3. Avoid large meals, but eat regularly.
   4. Limit alcohol.

Medications:

You Have Been Prescribed: ____________________

You Need to Take: ____________________

You Need to Notify the Office If You Have:

A. Fever.

B. Black or tarry-looking BMs.

C. Vomiting.

D. Unexplained weight loss of 5 pounds or more.

E. Symptoms that don't improve despite changes in diet, exercise, and medication.

F. Other: ____________________

Phone: ____________________

JAUNDICE AND HEPATITIS

PROBLEM

Jaundice is a yellow tinge of the skin. Your blood contains too much bilirubin—a yellow pigment found in bile, which is a fluid secreted by the liver.

Other symptoms that occur with jaundice are dark urine, light-colored BMs, fatigue, fever, chills, appetite loss, nausea, and vomiting.

CAUSE

Jaundice usually comes from a liver disorder, such as cirrhosis, hepatitis, or a disease of the gallbladder or pancreas. Sometimes jaundice results from taking a drug that damages the liver.

PREVENTION

Although hepatitis is considered contagious, you don't need to stay in your home. To help prevent the spread of hepatitis:

A. Do not prepare or handle food for others until cleared by your health care provider.
B. Wash your hands well after using the toilet and changing diapers.
C. If you have hepatitis A or B, avoid intimate sexual contact until cleared by your health care provider.
D. If you have hepatitis B or C, don't share razors, toothbrushes, and other personal items.
E. Never donate blood after a hepatitis B or C infection.
F. Your family and sex partners may need an injection or a vaccination, depending on the type of hepatitis you have.
G. School exposure to hepatitis A does not generally pose a risk to others.
H. Risk of hepatitis B transmission in day care centers appears to be extremely rare.

TREATMENT PLAN

Treatment for jaundice includes the following:

A. Use good hygiene with bathing, using the bathroom, and hand washing.
B. Apply anti-itch lotions, such as calamine.
C. Rest.
D. Make a list of all of the medications, over-the-counter medications, and herbal products that you are taking so that you and your health care provider can see if any of them are causing the jaundice.
E. A procedure may need to be done to crush a gall stone blocking the bile duct causing jaundice.
F. If you have hepatitis, you may need to be referred to a specialist.
G. The public health department will be notified by your health care provider for acute hepatitis.
H. Your health care provider may discuss the need for a liver biopsy.
I. Your health care provider may discuss treatment to help treat a virus that is causing hepatitis.
J. Avoid alcohol.

Activity: Plan rest periods throughout the day. Avoid strenuous exercise. Gradually resume activities and mild exercise during your convalescent period.

Diet: Eat small, frequent, low-fat, high-calorie meals. You may be instructed to limit protein during acute phases of some types of hepatitis. Sit down to eat to decrease pressure on your liver. Drink 8 to 10 glasses of liquids a day.

Medications:

You Have Been Prescribed: ________________________________

You Need to Take: ________________________________

You Have Been Prescribed: ________________________________

You Need to Take: ________________________________

You Need to Notify the Office If You Have:

A. Mild confusion.
B. Personality changes.
C. Worsening symptoms.
D. Tremors.
E. Other: ______________________________

Phone: ______________________________

RESOURCES

Centers for Disease Control and Prevention: www.cdc.gov/hepatitis

Hepatitis B information is available from the Hepatitis B Foundation: www.hepb.org

Hepatitis C information is available from American Liver Foundation: www.liverfoundation.org

LACTOSE INTOLERANCE AND MALABSORPTION

PROBLEM

You have problems digesting milk (lactose) products or have problems with malabsorption. Lactose intolerance can cause gas, bloating, abdominal cramps, diarrhea, and nausea or vomiting. You may be able to eat small portions without problems or be unable to tolerate any foods containing milk.

CAUSE

Lactose is the sugar present in milk. Lactose intolerance is very common; it occurs when the body is not able to digest this milk sugar content and causes diarrhea.

PREVENTION

Follow a lactose-free or lactose-controlled diet.

Activity: No restrictions are required. Resume normal activities as soon as diarrhea symptoms improve. You may be sent to see a registered dietitian to assist in your dietary plan.

Diet:

A. Limit or omit foods that contain milk, lactose, whey, or casein.

B. Lactose-controlled diets allow up to one cup of milk per day for cooking or drinking, if you can tolerate it.

C. If you can't tolerate any lactose, choose lactose-free foods with lactate, lactic acid, lactalbumin, whey protein, sodium caseinate, casein hydrolysates, and calcium compounds. Read labels carefully.

D. You may also choose kosher foods marked "pareve" or "parve," which don't contain lactose. Read labels carefully.

E. A low-fat diet is important if you have fat malabsorption.

F. To help with diarrhea due to malabsorption, avoid more than one serving a day of caffeine-containing drinks.

G. Beverages with high sugar content such as soft drinks and fruit juices may increase diarrhea. Juices and fruits with high amounts of fructose include apples, pears, sweet cherries, prunes, and dates.

H. Sugar-free (Sorbitol) candies and gums may cause diarrhea.

Medications: You may need the enzyme lactase to help you digest your food. You may need vitamins and minerals if you are having problems with malabsorption/diarrhea.

You Have Been Prescribed: ______________________________

You Need to Take: ______________________________

You Need to Notify the Office If You Have:

A. Severe abdominal pain.

B. Diarrhea causing dehydration.

C. Other: ______________________________

Phone: ______________________________

MANAGEMENT OF ULCERS

PROBLEM

An ulcer is a sore in the lining of the stomach or intestine occurring in areas exposed to acid and pepsin. Complications include bleeding ulcer and perforation, and obstruction can be life-threatening.

CAUSE

Although the cause of ulcer formation isn't completely understood, *Helicobacter pylori*, bacterium, and certain anti-inflammatory drugs have also been identified as causes.

PREVENTION

Modify your lifestyle to include health practices that prevent recurrences of ulcer pain and bleeding.

TREATMENT PLAN

A. If aspirin or a nonsteroidal anti-inflammatory drug like ibuprofen cause the ulcer you will have to stop taking it. If you need the medicine for other health problems, your health care provider will help with a new dose or therapy.

B. Avoid caffeine, colas, alcohol, and chocolate because they may increase acid production.

C. Stop smoking: It decreases the ulcer's healing rate and increases its recurrence. **It is never too late to stop smoking.**

D. Be sure to tell health care providers about your history of ulcer and GI pain if you need new prescriptions or are sent to the hospital.

E. Make a list of all of your medications, over-the-counter and herbal products so that you and your health care provider can review your list for possible causes or ulcer irritants.

Activity: Exercise daily. Plan rest periods, avoid fatigue, and learn to cope with or avoid stressful situations.

Diet:

A. Eat a well-balanced diet with high fiber content.

B. Eat meals at regular intervals. Frequent small feedings are unnecessary. Avoid bedtime snacks.

C. Eliminate foods that cause pain or distress; otherwise, your diet is usually not restricted. Examples of foods that cause worse pain are:
   1. Peppermint
   2. Spicy food
   3. Alcohol

D. Avoid extremely hot or cold food or fluids, chew thoroughly, and eat leisurely and relaxed for better digestion.

Medications:

A. Some of the medicines that help the pain and acid can be purchased at the drug store without a prescription. H_2 blockers and proton pump inhibitors (PPIs) reduce stomach acid.

B. Antibiotics fight *H. pylori* infection.

C. Other medications may be prescribed to coat the ulcer area. Antacids can be taken during the ulcer treatment but should not be used 1 hour before or 2 hours after the ulcer treatments because antacids can interfere with absorption.

D. Take the entire prescription: Don't stop when you feel better.

E. If you have been prescribed metronidazole (Flagyl) or clarithromycin, you may notice a metallic taste in your mouth.

F. Alcohol (including wine) should be avoided when taking Flagyl. The interaction can cause skin flushing, headache, nausea, and vomiting.

G. If you are prescribed bismuth, you may notice black BMs.

You Have Been Prescribed: ______________________________

You Need to Take: ______________________________

You Need to Notify the Office If You Have:

A. Worsening symptoms while taking your medication.

B. Vomiting that is bloody or looks like coffee grounds.

C. Tar-colored or "grape jelly" BMs. If this occurs, bring a stool sample to the office.

D. Diarrhea and/or severe pain despite treatment.

E. Unusual weakness or paleness.

F. Other: ______________________________

Phone: ______________________________

TIPS TO RELIEVE CONSTIPATION

PROBLEM

Constipation is an infrequent and difficult passing of hard stools and sensation of incomplete emptying or straining.

CAUSE

There are many reasons why you have constipation. You may have just one or a combination of causes:

A. Not drinking enough liquids
B. Eating a low-fiber diet
C. Sedentary lifestyle, lack of exercise
D. Ignoring the urge to go to the bathroom
E. Taking drugs, including blood pressure medications, antidepressants, pain medications, and antacids, or overusing laxatives. Make a list of all of your medicines, over-the-counter medicines, and herbals so that you and your health care provider can review them.
F. Depression
G. Other medical conditions

PREVENTION

A. Go to the bathroom as soon as you have the urge to have a BM. Do not wait.
B. Make a regular toilet time, such as after breakfast; 15 to 20 minutes after breakfast is a good time because spontaneous movement is greatest during that period.
C. Use a footrest during elimination to provide support and decrease straining.
D. Do not rely on laxatives; use prune juice as a natural substitute.
E. Stimulate the intestine by drinking hot or cold water or prune juice before eating.
F. Decrease eating sweets, which increase bacterial growth in the intestine and can lead to gas.
G. Stop taking enemas and drugs and herbals that are not needed.

TREATMENT PLAN

A. Follow the suggested prevention tips.
B. Change to a high-fiber diet.
C. Get daily exercise.

Activity: Daily exercise such as walking helps to maintain healthy bowel patterns.

Diet:

A. Eat a high-fiber diet.
B. Restrict cheese: It causes constipation.
C. Drink at least eight glasses of water each day.
D. Avoid refined cereals and breads, pastries, and sugar.
E. Coffee, tea, and alcohol decrease water to the colon. Limit to two drinks per day.

Medications: You may be prescribed a stool softener or a laxative for short-term use only. You may be prescribed a bulk-forming agent to take on a regular basis to increase the bulk of your stool.

You Have Been Prescribed: ____________________

You Need to Take: ____________________

You Need to Notify the Office If:

A. Constipation continues in spite of the self-care instructions, including diet and exercise.
B. You notice a change in your BMs. Changes in bowel patterns may be an early sign of cancer.
C. You develop a fever, or severe abdominal pain with your constipation.
D. Other: ____________________

Phone: ____________________

Patient Teaching Guides for Chapter 14: Genitourinary Disorders

- Benign Prostatic Hypertrophy (BPH)
- Chronic Kidney Disease (CKD)
- Epididymitis
- Nocturia
- Prostatitis
- Testicular Self-Examination
- Urinary Incontinence: Women
- Urinary Retention
- Urinary Tract Infection (UTI)

BENIGN PROSTATIC HYPERTROPHY (BPH)

PROBLEM

Enlargement of the prostate causes urinating. Symptoms include having to go to the bathroom more often, especially at night; trouble starting or stopping your urine; decreased stream; and feeling that you do not empty.

CAUSE

The cause is not known, but it may be due to change in your hormones as you get older.

PREVENTION

None

TREATMENT PLAN

Treatment depends on how bad the symptoms are. Medications can help, but an operation to fix the obstruction may be needed. Empty your bladder on a schedule every 2 to 3 hours to prevent overfilling of the bladder.

In some cases you may have to insert an intermittent urinary catheter to drain your urine and relieve the symptoms until you can follow up with your provider (see website resources noted below).

Activity: There are no restrictions. You may need to plan schedules with access to bathrooms in mind.

Diet: Avoid spicy foods that irritate the bladder. Caffeine and alcohol act as diuretics and increase your need to urinate.

Medications:

A. Medications that help relieve the blockage may block hormones or relax the muscles that control urination.
B. Antibiotics are used if there is also an infection in your bladder or prostate.
C. Do not take over-the-counter medications such as cold medications, decongestants, antihistamines (for allergies), and diarrhea medicines; they make symptoms worse.
D. Always read labels to check for advice: for example,"Do not take if you have prostate enlargement."
E. Avoid drinking liquids before bedtime or before going out.
F. Double void to empty your bladder more completely.

You Have Been Prescribed: ______________________________

You Need to Take: ______________________________

You Need to Notify the Office If:

A. You cannot urinate.
B. Your symptoms worsen.
C. You have a fever.
D. Other: ______________________________

Phone: ______________________________

RESOURCES

Urinary Catheterization Female: www.nlm.nih.gov/medlineplus/ency/patientinstructions/000144.htm

Urinary Catheterization Male: www.nlm.nih.gov/medlineplus/ency/patientinstructions/000143.htm

CHRONIC KIDNEY DISEASE (CKD)

PROBLEM

CKD means the kidney is having trouble performing its normal function to maintain health.

FUNCTIONS OF A NORMAL KIDNEY

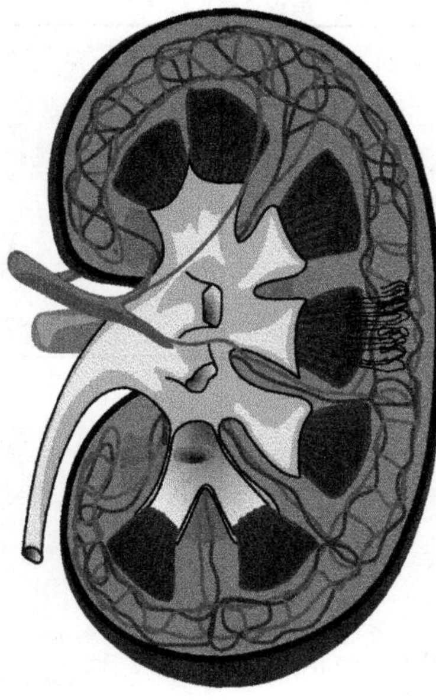

Source: Adapted from Piotr Michal Jaworski, Wikipedia.

The kidney has several functions:

A. Removal and absorption of fluids to maintain balance.

B. Filtration of blood to remove waste products.

C. Regulation of blood pressure.

D. Hormone regulation for blood production in the bone marrow.

E. Regulation of hormones and minerals.

F. Maintenance of healthy bones.

CAUSES

CKD has multiple causes.

A. Diabetes is the leading cause of CKD in the United States.

B. Hypertension is the second leading cause of CKD in the United States.

C. Other causes of CKD
   1. Glomerulonephritis
   2. Genetics (inherited) disease: Polycystic kidney disease and Alport's syndrome
   3. Congenital diseases
   4. Autoimmune disease
   5. Urinary tract infections (UTIs)
   6. Drugs (legal and illegal) and toxic substances

DETECTION

CKD can be detected by:

A. Blood tests: Blood urea nitrogen (BUN) and creatinine

B. Urinalysis (protein in urine and creatinine clearance)

C. Other (ultrasound, immunoassays, computed tomography scan, biopsies, etc.)

D. Glomerular filtration rate (GFR)
   1. Normal rate: 90 or higher without protein in the urine
   2. Gets lower with age
   3. An indicator on the function of the kidney
   4. Used to determine CKD stages
   5. Is lower as the kidney function worsens

STAGES OF CKD

Stage I (with protein in the urine)	GFR: 90 or higher
Stage II (mild)	60–89
Stage III (moderate)	30–59
Stage IV (severe)	15–29
Stage V (kidney failure)	14 or less

SYMPTOMS OF CKD

Symptoms can vary.

A. Usually unnoticed

B. More noticeable symptoms as CKD worsens (usually around Stage III).

C. It can include:
   1. Nausea
   2. Fatigue/weakness, no energy
   3. Decreased or lack of appetite
   4. Weight loss or rapid weight gain
   5. Shortness of breath, which may worsen with activity or at rest (when awakening in the morning)
   6. Swelling of the legs and feet and around the eyes
   7. Cloudy mind or difficulty with concentration
   8. Muscle cramps
   9. Frequent nighttime urination
   10. Difficulty sleeping or staying asleep

PROBLEMS CAUSED BY CKD

CKD can cause multiple problems:

A. Heart, including heart failure and other blood vessels
   1. High blood pressure
   2. Cholesterol abnormalities
   3. Heart attack
   4. Stroke

B. Poor nutritional status

C. Weak and unhealthy bones

D. Anemia

E. Water retention

F. Progression to kidney failure

LIFESTYLE CHANGES TO PREVENT PROGRESSION OF CKD

Ways you may slow down the progression of CKD and deal with other effects of CKD:

A. Take charge and be proactive.
   1. Be familiar with the health care team.
   2. Provide information on beliefs and practices relating to health.
   3. Inform the health care team about herbs and other alternative medicine being used.
   4. Be involved in the treatment plan.

B. Diet
   1. Meet with a registered dietitian.
   2. Eat a well-balanced meal.
   3. Some dietary restrictions may be necessary based on kidney function and stages of CKD.
   4. Follow dietary instructions regarding protein, fats, sodium, and minerals.

a. Dietary intake of protein is usually restricted to 0.8 to 1.0 g/kg/d.
b. Dietary sodium should be restricted to no more than 2 g daily.
c. Potassium should be restricted to 40 to 70 meq/d.
d. Calories should be restricted to 35 kcal/kg/d; if the body weight is greater than 120% of normal weight or the patient is older than 60 years of age, a lower amount may be prescribed.
e. Fat intake should be about 30% to 40% of total daily caloric intake.
f. Phosphorus should be restricted to 600 to 800 mg/d.
g. Calcium should be restricted to 1,400 to 1,600 mg/d.
h. Magnesium should be restricted to 200 to 300 mg/d.
i. Carbohydrates: The recommended normal intake is 225 to 358 g/d.

C. Exercise
1. Moderate exercise is recommended for at least 30 minutes, five times a week.
2. The benefits of exercise:
a. Lowers the blood pressure.
b. Improves cholesterol.
c. Lowers hemoglobin A1C in diabetes.
d. Strengthens bones.
e. Leads to weight loss.
f. Improves signs/symptoms of depression.
g. Boosts the immune system.
h. Reduces stress.
i. Provides an overall better feeling.

D. Target heart and blood vessels
1. Control blood pressure: Goal is less than 130/80 mmHg.
2. Lower your low-density lipoprotein.
3. Weight loss.
4. Lower hemoglobin A1C level with the goal less than 6.9% if you have diabetes.
a. Exercise.
b. Diet: No restriction, low-saturated-fat, low-carbohydrate diet.
c. Smoking cessation is essential.
d. Reduce or eliminate alcohol intake.
e. Medications may be necessary for the following:
i. Hypertension: Blood pressure medications.
ii. Hyperlipidemia: Cholesterol medications.
iii. Diabetes: Medications to control the blood sugar.

E. Target bones
1. Be familiar with your lab results (vitamin D level, calcium level, phosphorous level).
2. Supplements: Vitamin D, calcium supplements, and phosphate binders may be necessary.
3. Low phosphorous diet may be necessary.
4. Exercise: Weight-bearing exercise will help strengthen bones (walking, dancing, lifting weights, etc.).

F. Target anemia
1. Goal of the hemoglobin should be 11 g/dL or better.
2. Diet rich in iron.
3. Medication may be necessary (depends on the type of anemia)
a. Erythropoietin-stimulating agents
b. Vitamin B_{12}
c. Folic acid

G. Target water retention
1. Limit salt intake.
2. Diet (avoid processed foods/fast foods).
3. Medications may be needed (diuretics).

FOODS HIGH IN PHOSPHORUS

Amount of phosphorus in foods. Limit portions (registered dietitian consult is recommended).

Biscuits (mix) 1 (1 oz) 133 mg	Cheese (1 oz) 161 mg
Chocolate 1 bar (2 oz) 137 mg	Cola 1 can (12 oz) 60 mg
Cream soups (1 cup) 151 mg	Dried beans and peas (1 cup cooked) 206 mg
Hot dogs and sausage (2 each) 162/220 mg	Ice cream (1 cup) 157 mg
Liver and organ meats (3.5 oz) 400 mg	Macaroni and cheese (1 oz) 265 mg
Pancake mix 3 (4 inch pancakes) 368 mg	Peanut butter (3 tbsp) 172 mg
Pizza (1 slice) 259 mg	Pork and beans (1 cup) 266 mg
Yogurt (8 fl. oz) and pudding (1/2 cup) 292/280 mg	

POTASSIUM-FRIENDLY FOODS

Limit portion to 1/2 cup unless noted otherwise (registered dietitian consult is recommended).

Fruits	
Apple (1 small)	Canned pear
Cherries	Grapes (15 small)
Juices (apple, cranberry, grape, lemon, nectar, pear, peach, and pineapple)	Lemon (1/2)
Peach (1/2 cup canned or 1 small fresh)	Pineapple
Plum (1/2 cup canned or 1 medium)	Raspberries (blueberries, blackberries, and cranberries)
Strawberries	Watermelon (1 cup)
Vegetables	
Cabbage	Carrots (1/2 cup cooked or 1 small raw)
Celery (1 stalk)	Corn (1/2 canned or ear)
Cucumbers	Eggplant
Green (or wax) beans	Green peas
Lettuce (1 cup)	Onion
Radishes	Squash (Crookneck, Summer, and zucchini)

RESOURCES

American Diabetes Association: www.diabetes.org
1. Food and Fitness: www.diabetes.org/food-and-fitness/?loc=GlobalNavFF

BC Renal Agency: www.bcrenalagency.ca
1. Shopping Guide for kidney health: www.bcrenalagency.ca/NR/rdonlyres/B7525716-948F-41FD-9FAC-392CA628F1CD/54793/Shopping_Guide_For_Kidney_Health_WEB_Dec_11.pdf
2. Diabetes Kidney-friendly grocery list: www.bcrenalagency.ca/NR/rdonlyres/B7525716-948F-41FD-9FAC-392CA628F1CD/62687/DiabetesKidneyFriendlyShoppingList.pdf

National Kidney Foundation: www.kidney.org
1. Kidney Kitchen recipes: www.kidney.org/patients/kidneykitchen/recipes.cfm

EPIDIDYMITIS

PROBLEM

Epididymitis is infection of the gland that carries sperm.

CAUSE

The infection may be a urinary tract infection, or it may come from a sexually transmitted disease, including gonorrhea and chlamydia.

PREVENTION

A. Prevent UTIs with good hygiene.
  1. Clean under foreskin if uncircumcised.
  2. Wash your hands after each time you go to the bathroom (both urine and bowel movements).

B. Limit your sexual partners and use a condom to prevent all types of infection.

TREATMENT PLAN

A. Antibiotics to kill bacteria that cause infection.

B. Try one of the following comfort measures:
  1. Intermittent cold compresses for acute swelling and pain relief.
  2. Local heat or sitz bath after the initial discomfort.

C. Use an athletic supporter or elevate scrotum on a small rolled washcloth.

D. Your sexual partner(s) need(s) to be treated for sexually transmitted disease.

Activity:

A. Rest; do not engage in strenuous activity or heavy lifting.

B. Avoid sex until you finish the antibiotic.

Diet: Avoid foods that irritate the bladder: Caffeine, alcohol, and spicy foods.

Medications:

A. Antibiotics are used to kill bacteria causing infection.

B. Take all of the antibiotics prescribed for you; don't stop taking drugs after symptoms are gone.

C. Do not share your antibiotics with your sex partner(s); a full prescription of antibiotics is needed for both of you to get better.

D. Take pain medications or anti-inflammatory drugs such as acetaminophen (Tylenol) or ibuprofen as needed.

You Have Been Prescribed the Following Antibiotic: ______________________________

You Need to Take: ______________________________

Finish all of the antibiotics, even if you feel better.

You Have Been Prescribed the Following for Pain: ______________________________

You Need to Take: ______________________________

You Need to Notify the Office If:

A. You have a great increase in pain or swelling after going home.

B. You have worsening symptoms after starting the antibiotics.

C. You have fever over 101.0°F.

D. You get very constipated.

E. Other: ______________________________

Phone: ______________________________

NOCTURIA

PROBLEM

Nocturia is defined as having to urinate at night more than once or twice.

CAUSES

There are many causes of nocturia. Symptoms include having to go to the bathroom more often, especially at night, trouble starting or stopping your urine, decreased stream, and feeling that you do not empty.

PREVENTION

The causes vary with nocturia, and the condition may also be due to changes in your hormones as you get older.

TREATMENT PLAN

Treatment depends on how bad the symptoms are. Medications can help, but an operation may be necessary if there is an obstruction or other causes that may be fixed by an operation. Empty your bladder on a schedule every 2 to 3 hours to prevent overfilling of the bladder.

Activity: There are no restrictions. You may need to plan schedules with access to bathrooms in mind.

Diet: Avoid spicy foods that irritate the bladder. Caffeine and alcohol act as diuretics and increase your need to urinate.

Medications:

A. Medications that help relieve the blockage may block hormones or relax the muscles that control urination.

B. Antibiotics are used if there is also an infection in your bladder or prostate.

C. Do not take over-the-counter medications such as cold medications, decongestants, antihistamines (for allergies), and diarrhea medicines. They make symptoms worse.

D. Always read labels to check for advice: for example, "Do not take if you have prostate enlargement."

E. Avoid drinking liquids before bedtime or before going out.

F. Double void to empty your bladder more completely.

You Have Been Prescribed: ______________________________

You Need to Take: ______________________________

You Need to Notify the Office If: ______________________________

A. You cannot urinate.

B. Your symptoms worsen.

C. You have a fever.

D. Other: ______________________________

Phone: ______________________________

RESOURCES

American Urogynecologic Society: www.augs.org

American Urological Association: www.UrologyHealth.org

National Association for Continence: www.nafc.org

The Simon Foundation for Continence: www.simonfoundation.org

PROSTATITIS

PROBLEM

Prostatitis is infection and/or inflammation of the prostate. Symptoms can be problems with urinating, increased frequency or painful urination, fever, or chills. You may have pain in the scrotum and buttocks and blood in the urine or semen. Prostatitis can be treated and does not cause impotence.

CAUSE

An infection may be caused by bacteria from the bladder or reflux of urine, or it may have started from a rectal infection.

PREVENTION

A. Prevent prostate infection with good hygiene.
   1. Clean under foreskin if uncircumcised and wash your hands after each time you go to the bathroom (urine and bowel movements).
   2. Limit your sexual partners and use a condom to prevent all types of infection.
   3. Urinate when you have the urge. Do not hold your urine for long periods of time.

B. Staying sexually active with ejaculation may decrease the incidence.

TREATMENT PLAN

A. You may have to be in the hospital for severe infections.

B. At home, try the following comfort measures:
   1. Use a sitz bath or sit in warm bath water or a whirlpool three times a day to provide some relief.
   2. You may find you feel more comfortable when you empty your bladder in a warm water bath when your pelvic muscles relax.

C. Your sexual partner(s) may need to be evaluated and treated, too (ask your health care provider).

Activity: Rest; do not engage in strenuous physical activity or heavy lifting.

Diet: Increase fluid intake. ***Fluid Exception:*** **Decrease caffeine and alcohol, which can irritate the urethra.**

Medications: Antibiotics cure the infection by killing bacteria. You need to continue taking these drugs until infection is completely cured (usually about 1 month). You need to take all the antibiotics even if your symptoms are gone.

You Have Been Prescribed the Following Antibiotic: ______________________

You Need to Take: ______________________

Finish all of the antibiotic even if you feel better.

Pain medications combined with anti-inflammatory drugs to decrease pain are usually taken for 3 to 7 days. Take acetaminophen (Tylenol) to bring down fever.

You Have Been Prescribed the Following for Pain: ______________________

You Need to Take: ______________________

You Have Been Prescribed the Following for Fever: ______________________

You Need to Take: ______________________

You Need to Notify the Office If You Have:

A. Symptoms that get worse or do not improve during treatment.

B. Symptoms that recur after treatment.

C. Fever over 101.0°F.

D. Other: ______________________

Phone: ______________________

RESOURCES

American Urological Association Foundation: www.UrologyHealth.org

National Kidney and Urologic Disease Information Clearinghouse: www.kidney.niddk.nih.gov

National Urology Health Hotline Toll Free 1-800-828-7866

The Prostatitis Foundation: www.prostatitis.org

TESTICULAR SELF-EXAMINATION

The testicular self-examination is easy to do and does not take very much time to perform. Checking every month is a good way to become familiar with this area of your body and will help detect testicular cancer.

Set a date for the same day every month. An easy way to remember is choosing the first day of the month, the last day of the month, or your birth date. The best time to check your testicles is during or after a hot bath or shower. (Heat makes the testicles relax.)

Tumors can be felt. Boys and men from 15 to 35 years are at the highest risk because of hormonal activity.

PROCEDURE

A. If possible, do the self-examination in front of a mirror after a hot bath or shower.

B. Check for any swelling of the skin.

C. Support each testicle with one hand and examine it with the other hand.

D. Use both hands to feel all of the scrotal bag.
   1. With one hand, lift your penis, and check your sac with the other hand. Feel any change in shape or size.
   2. Look for red or blood veins that are bigger than they used to be.
   3. The left side may hang slightly lower than the right (this is normal).

E. Check each testicle.
   1. Place your left thumb on the front of your left testicle and your index and middle fingers behind it.
   2. Gently but firmly roll the testicle between your thumb and fingers.
   3. Then use your right hand to examine the right testicle the same way.
   4. The testicles should feel smooth, rubbery, oval shaped, and slightly tender. They should move freely.
   5. Locate the epididymis and spermatic cord. The epididymis is the irregular, cord-like structure on the top and the back of the testicle.
      a. Gently squeeze the spermatic cord above your left testicle between your thumb and the first two fingers of your left hand.
      b. Check for lumps and masses along the entire length of the cords.
      c. Repeat on the right side, using your right hand.

F. Call your health care provider if you notice:
   1. Any lumps, even small pea-sized ones.
   2. Any masses, like a bag of worms.
   3. A dull ache in the lower abdomen or in the groin.
   4. A feeling of heaviness in the scrotum.
   5. A significant loss of size in one of the testicles.
   6. Pain or discomfort in a testicle or in the scrotum.
   7. Any other changes you noticed since the last time you felt yourself for your examination.

G. Your health care provider may refer you to a urologist for further evaluation.

URINARY INCONTINENCE: WOMEN

PROBLEM

Urinary incontinence is when you are unable to hold your urine.

CAUSE

The cause depends on the type of incontinence you have.

PREVENTION

Exercise regularly, and practice pelvic floor exercises, commonly called Kegel exercises. Don't become constipated so you do not strain to have a bowel movement. Stop smoking. If you have a cough, you may need to see your health care provider to help treat it.

TREATMENT PLAN

Treatment depends on cause and type of incontinence. Fill out the bladder diary to help figure out what kind of problem you have. (see Table III.4.)

A. Pelvic floor exercises should be done every morning, afternoon, and evening; repeat the exercise five times for each set, and gradually increase to 10 times each set. To perform these exercises:
   1. Start by doing your pelvic muscles exercises lying down. When your muscles get stronger, do your exercises sitting or standing.
   2. Do not tighten your tummy, leg, or butt muscles: Just squeeze the muscles you use to start and stop the flow of urine.
   3. Do not hold your breath or practice while you are on the toilet urinating.
   4. Pull in pelvic muscles and hold it tight for a count of 5.
   5. Repeat five times.
   6. Work up to doing three sets of 10 repeats.
   7. Kegel exercises take just a few minutes a day, and most women notice an improvement after a few weeks of daily exercise.

B. Empty your bladder frequently. As soon as you feel the urge to urinate, go to the bathroom.

C. You may be taught relaxation techniques to control the feeling of having to go quickly.

D. Fill out your bladder diary and return it to your health care provider.

Activity: Try to get daily exercise. Use absorbent undergarments until your bladder leaking is under control.

Diet: Eat a well-balanced diet. If you are overweight, consider a weight-loss program. Avoid drinking lots of liquids, especially caffeinated beverages and alcohol.

Medications: What you take depends on the type of bladder leakage you have.

You Have Been Prescribed: ____________________

You Need to Take: ____________________

You Need to Notify the Office If You Have: ____________________

Phone: ____________________

RESOURCES

American Urogynecologic Society: www.augs.org

American Urological Association: www.UrologyHealth.org

National Association for Continence: www.nafc.org

The Simon Foundation for Continence: www.simonfoundation.org

TABLE III.4. **Bladder Control Diary**

Your Daily Bladder Diary

This diary will help you and your health care team figure out the causes of your bladder control trouble. The **sample** line shows you how to use the diary. Use this sheet as a master for making copies that you can use as a bladder diary for as many days as you need.

Your name: ____________________

Date: ____________________

Time	Drinks		Trips to the bathroom		Accidental leaks	Did you feel a strong urge to go?	What were you doing at the time?
	What kind?	*How much?*	*How many times?*	*How much urine? (circle one)*	*How much? (circle one)*	Circle one	*Sneezing, exercising, having sex, lifting, and so forth.*
Sample	Coffee	2 cups	✓✓	sm med lg	sm med lg	Yes No	Running
6–7 a.m.				sm med lg	sm med lg	Yes No	
7–8 a.m.				sm med lg	sm med lg	Yes No	
8–9 a.m.				sm med lg	sm med lg	Yes No	
9–10 a.m.				sm med lg	sm med lg	Yes No	
10–11 a.m.				sm med lg	sm med lg	Yes No	
11–12 noon				sm med lg	sm med lg	Yes No	
12–1 p.m.				sm med lg	sm med lg	Yes No	
1–2 p.m.				sm med lg	sm med lg	Yes No	
2–3 p.m.				sm med lg	sm med lg	Yes No	
3–4 p.m.				sm med lg	sm med lg	Yes No	
4–5 p.m.				sm med lg	sm med lg	Yes No	
5–6 p.m.				sm med lg	sm med lg	Yes No	
6–7 p.m.				sm med lg	sm med lg	Yes No	
7–8 p.m.				sm med lg	sm med lg	Yes No	
8–9 p.m.				sm med lg	sm med lg	Yes No	
9–10 p.m.				sm med lg	sm med lg	Yes No	
10–11 p.m.				sm med lg	sm med lg	Yes No	
11–12 midnight				sm med lg	sm med lg	Yes No	
12–1 a.m.				sm med lg	sm med lg	Yes No	
1–2 a.m.				sm med lg	sm med lg	Yes No	
2–3 a.m.				sm med lg	sm med lg	Yes No	
3–4 a.m.				sm med lg	sm med lg	Yes No	
4–5 a.m.				sm med lg	sm med lg	Yes No	
5–6 a.m.				sm med lg	sm med lg	Yes No	

I used _______ pads today. I used ______ diapers today (write number).

Questions to ask my health care team: ____________________

Let's Talk About Bladder Control for Women is a public health awareness campaign conducted by the National Kidney and Urologic Diseases Information Clearinghouse (NKUDIC), an information dissemination service of the National Institute of Diabetes and Digestive and Kidney Diseases (NIDDK), National Institutes of Health.

From NKUDIC, National Institutes of Health (NIH). kidney.niddk.nih.gov/kudiseases/pubs/bcw_ez/insertB.htm

URINARY RETENTION

PROBLEM

Urinary retention is the inability to empty your bladder completely. Symptoms include having to go to the bathroom more often, especially at night; trouble starting or stopping your urine; decreased stream; and feeling that you do not empty.

CAUSES

The cause depends on the type of incontinence you have.

PREVENTION

None

TREATMENT PLAN

Treatment depends on how bad the symptoms are. Medications can help, but an operation to fix the obstruction may be needed. Empty your bladder on a schedule every 2 to 3 hours to prevent overfilling of the bladder. In some cases you may have to insert an intermittent urinary catheter to relieve the symptoms until you can follow up with your provider (see Resources).

Activity: There are no restrictions. You may need to plan schedules with access to bathrooms in mind. Kegel exercise may help for some women.

Diet: Avoid spicy foods that irritate the bladder. Caffeine and alcohol act as diuretics and increase your need to urinate.

Medications:

A. Medications that help relieve the blockage may block hormones or relax the muscles that control urination.
B. Antibiotics are used if there is also an infection in your bladder or prostate.
C. Do not take over-the-counter medications such as cold medications, decongestants, antihistamines (for allergies), and diarrhea medicines. They make symptoms worse.
D. Always read labels to check for advice: for example, "Do not take if you have prostate enlargement."
E. Avoid drinking liquids before bedtime or before going out.
F. Double void to empty your bladder more completely.
G. Fill out your voiding diary and bring it to your next visit.
H. Call your physician immediately if you are unable to urinate.
I. Other: ____________________

Phone: ____________________

RESOURCES

American Urogynecologic Society: www.augs.org

American Urological Association: www.UrologyHealth.org

National Association for Continence: www.nafc.org

The Simon Foundation for Continence: www.simonfoundation.org

Urinary Catheterization Female: www.nlm.nih.gov/medlineplus/ency/patientinstructions/000144.htm

Urinary Catheterization Male: www.nlm.nih.gov/medlineplus/ency/patientinstructions/000143.htm

URINARY TRACT INFECTION (UTI)

PROBLEM

You have a bladder infection. The symptoms include painful, frequent urination and pain over bladder. Your symptoms may be mild, moderate, or painful.

CAUSE

Bacteria caused the infection of the bladder. A bladder infection is more common in women and in men who have prostate problems.

PREVENTION

A. Empty your bladder often:
   1. As soon as you feel the urge to go, empty your bladder at that time. Do not hold your urine.
   2. You may need to urinate on a schedule during the day, at least every 2 to 3 hours.

B. Wash your hands after going to the bathroom (both urine and bowel movements).

C. Good hygiene for females:
   1. Wipe front to back every time you empty your bladder and especially after bowel movements.
   2. Take showers instead of baths; do not take bubble baths.
   3. Empty your bladder before and after sex.
   4. Avoid feminine hygiene sprays and douches.

D. Wear cotton underwear. Do not wear tight underwear and clothes. Take off your underwear at night while sleeping.

TREATMENT PLAN

Treatment depends on how bad (severity) the infection is. Antibiotics are used to kill bacteria that cause infections. The most important thing is to finish all of your medications even if you feel better.

Activity: Rest; avoid strenuous activity. Avoid sexual activity until you finish the antibiotics.

Diet:

A. Increase fluids; drink at least one large glass of liquid every hour.

B. Avoid foods that irritate the bladder: Caffeine, alcohol, and spicy foods.

C. Drink cranberry juice to help fight bladder infections. If you do not like plain cranberry juice, mix it with another juice, such as orange juice.

Medications:

A. Antibiotics kill bacteria that cause infection. Make sure you take all of your medications, not just until you feel better.

B. Take acetaminophen (Tylenol) for fever.

C. You may be prescribed a medication to prevent bladder spasms and pain while urinating. This changes the color of your urine to orange or blue.

You Have Been Prescribed the Following Antibiotic: ______________________

You Need to Take: ______________________

Take all of your antibiotics, even if you feel better.

You Have Been Prescribed the Following for Discomfort: ______________________

You Need to Take: ______________________

You Need to Notify the Office If You Have:

A. Worsening symptoms or symptoms not improving during treatment.

B. Fever higher than 100.4°F.

C. Blood in your urine.

D. Symptoms that come back after you finish all of your medications: Painful urination, back pain, fever, chills, or nausea.

E. Other: ______________________

Phone: ______________________

Patient Teaching Guides for Chapter 15: Obstetrics

- Antepartum
  - First-Trimester Vaginal Bleeding
  - Gestational Diabetes
  - Insulin Therapy During Pregnancy
  - Iron-Deficiency Anemia (Pregnancy)
  - Preterm Labor
  - Urinary Tract Infection During Pregnancy: Pyelonephritis
  - Vaginal Bleeding: Second and Third Trimester
- Postpartum
  - Breast Engorgement and Sore Nipples
  - Endometritis
  - Mastitis
  - Wound Infection: Episiotomy and Cesarean Section

ANTEPARTUM: FIRST-TRIMESTER VAGINAL BLEEDING

PROBLEM

Vaginal bleeding may occur in the first trimester of pregnancy. The amount of bleeding may range from spotting to a complete miscarriage.

CAUSE

Bleeding may occur for a variety of reasons, including smoking, trauma, abnormal fetus, or other problems.

PREVENTION

In most cases, the cause of vaginal bleeding may not be preventable. If bleeding is light, it may lessen or stop. You need to avoid sexual intercourse, tampons, and douches. If you smoke, it is highly recommended that you cut down or stop smoking altogether.

TREATMENT PLAN

Treatment depends on the cause or suspected cause of your bleeding.

ACTIVITY

A. Many women experience less bleeding and cramping while on limited activities or bed rest. Unfortunately, activity restriction does not prevent miscarriage.

B. Avoid sexual intercourse until at least 2 weeks after the bleeding has stopped, or until your provider tells you.

C. If bed rest is prescribed, perform simple range-of-motion activities as directed by the practitioner. Examples are foot circles and moving legs in bed.

D. Do not use tampons during this period of time. Use pads so that you can evaluate how much you are bleeding.
   1. **Scant amount:** Blood only on tissue when wiped or less than 1-inch stain on peri pad.
   2. **Light amount:** Less than 4-inch stain on peri pad.
   3. **Moderate amount:** Less than 6-inch stain on peri pad.
   4. **Heavy amount:** Saturated peri pad within 1 hour.

Diet: As tolerated. If you are on bed rest, eat fresh vegetables, fruits, and bran cereal to avoid becoming constipated.

Medications: You may not be prescribed any medications.

You Need to Notify the Office If:

A. You develop a fever with your bleeding.

B. You have a gush of blood from your vagina that is more than a period.

C. You pass blood clots or tissue from your vagina.

D. Your vaginal bleeding has a foul odor.

E. You experience abdominal pain or uterine cramping not relieved by taking acetaminophen.

F. Other: ____________________

Phone: ____________________

GESTATIONAL DIABETES

PROBLEM

Gestational diabetes only develops during pregnancy; it occurs because of the new hormones being produced. The hormonal influence makes you "insulin resistant," meaning you still produce insulin but the hormones prevent it from working effectively.

Your blood sugar needs to be controlled so that the amount of sugar going to your baby is controlled, too. High blood sugar causes a big baby at delivery, increases your risk of a cesarean birth, causes the baby to have low blood sugar after delivery, increases jaundice, and causes other problems for the baby such as lung problems. It can also cause your baby to be overweight in childhood and increases the risk he will develop diabetes.

CAUSE

You are producing new hormones that cause insulin resistance. The likelihood of having gestational diabetes increases with other factors, such as the mother's age, and it is more common in certain groups, such as Latin Americans and Native Americans.

PREVENTION

Good control of your diet, exercise, and the possible use of medication and/or possibly insulin will help you to control your blood sugar during your pregnancy.

TREATMENT PLAN

A. You are asked to keep a record of your blood glucose values.
   1. You will be shown how to test your blood.
   2. You need to test your blood four times a day: First thing in the morning, after lunch, after dinner, and at bedtime.
   3. You will be given specific instructions before or after meals.
   4. Phone in your blood sugar values every week. Your insulin may be changed weekly.
   5. The goal of your fasting blood sugar before breakfast is 60 to 90 mg/dL.
   6. Your blood sugar goal before and 2 hours after meals is less than 120 mg/dL.

B. You need to test your urine for ketones every day.
   1. You will be shown how to test your urine.
   2. You need to test for ketones if you are unable to eat or if you have diarrhea.
   3. You need to test for ketones if you feel like you have a urinary tract infection, sinus infection, or any kind of infection.
   4. You need to test for ketones if your blood sugar is higher than 150 mg/dL.
   5. You must follow the diet given to you by the dietitian. If you have questions or do not understand what you should be eating, contact your dietitian.

Activity: Exercise lowers blood sugar—gestational diabetes control involves regular exercise. You need to walk at least 20 to 30 minutes a day. Try your local mall for a climate-controlled place to walk. Your heart rate should not get above 140 beats per minute.

Diet: You are placed on a _________ calorie diet. The amount of calories needs to be spread out over three meals and three snacks:

1. Breakfast, midmorning snack, lunch, midafternoon snack, dinner, and a snack at bedtime.
2. The time you eat is as important as what you eat. Try to keep on a regular schedule.

Medications: Depending on your blood sugar, you may require medication to control it. You will be instructed on how to take the medicine. If you are started on insulin, you will require extra testing for the rest of your pregnancy.

INSULIN THERAPY DURING PREGNANCY

You Have Been Prescribed Insulin Therapy:

A. Your insulin needs may change weekly because of the change in your hormones (you become more insulin resistant as your pregnancy progresses).

B. Insulin therapy is safe for your baby. Insulin does not cross the placenta like the sugar does.

C. The insulin lowers your blood sugar and therefore controls the amount of sugar that goes to your baby.

D. You may have been prescribed Humulin insulin, which works very much like your own body's insulin.

E. Some of the insulin therapies have a mix of short-term regular (clear) insulin with intermediate-acting (cloudy) insulin.
   1. You will be instructed in how to mix and give yourself your insulin.
   2. The first key to insulin therapy is to be able to recognize signs of too much and too little insulin. A chart is included to post on your refrigerator (see Table III.5).
   3. The second key is to let people know you are on insulin.
   4. You need a Medical Alert bracelet or necklace as well as information to put in your car and billfold.
   5. The third key is to have your baby and yourself evaluated more often when on insulin therapy.
      a. You need to be seen twice a week from 32 weeks gestation to delivery, or as recommended by your health care provider.
      b. You will have extra testing to make sure the baby is doing well and to make sure you are doing well, too.

F. You need to check your blood sugars four times a day. Your blood sugar target is ____________
   1. Fasting____________
   2. Before lunch____________
   3. Before dinner____________
   4. Before going to bed____________

G. You will be instructed to check your urine for ketones when you are sick or if you have high blood sugar.

Activity: It is important to continue to exercise.

Diet: Eat a good, healthy diet. You will be instructed on how many calories to eat. Eat six smaller meals a day; with insulin it is important to eat snacks. It is also important to try to eat at the same times each day.

TABLE III.5 Signs of High and Low Blood Sugar

Blood Sugar	What to Watch for	What to Do	Causes
HYPOGLYCEMIA Low blood sugar	Excessive sweating Feeling faint Feeling shaky Headache Impaired vision Hunger Irritable feelings Personality change Trouble awakening	**Call the provider immediately if your blood sugar is below ________** Take glucose tablets or eat Do not take your insulin Do not try to force any food or liquids by mouth if patient is not conscious	**Too much insulin** Not eating on time or enough food Unusual amounts of exercise
HYPERGLYCEMIA High blood sugar	Increased thirst Need to urinate more often Large amounts of sugar in your blood or urine Ketones in your urine Weakness and generalized aches Heavy, labored breathing with a fruity breath Nausea and vomiting	Test your blood sugar **Call your provider immediately if your blood sugar is ______** Test your urine for ketones Drink extra water if able to swallow	**Too little insulin** Eating more foods and foods not on your diet Infections and fever Stress

You Need to Notify the Office If:

A. You have moderate ketones in your urine.

B. You are unable to eat or you have loose diarrhea stool.

C. You have insulin reactions (blood sugar is below 50 mg/dL or you feel the symptoms of low blood sugar).

D. You have blood sugars higher than 175 mg/dL for two readings.

E. You have any signs of infection.

F. You have a decrease in fetal movement or do not feel your baby moving.

G. Other: ______________________________

Phone: ______________________________

IRON-DEFICIENCY ANEMIA (PREGNANCY)

PROBLEM

You have a "low blood count" called iron-deficiency anemia. Iron is needed for red blood formation.

CAUSE

This is caused by a deficiency of iron in your diet, and it is very common.

PREVENTION

Anemia may be prevented by increasing iron in your diet and by taking extra iron tablets.

TREATMENT PLAN

A. You need to increase the iron-rich food in your diet.

B. You will be prescribed an iron supplement.

C. Antacids for indigestion and dairy products interfere with iron absorption. Do not take your iron supplements with milk or just before or after an antacid.

D. If you are pregnant, you may be eligible for the WIC program (Women, Infants, and Children), which provides supplemental foods for pregnant women and young children. Ask your health care provider for information about its availability in your community.

Activity: You may feel more tired than usual due to anemia. You may need to rest more than usual; however, try to continue your current exercise routine as tolerated. Alternative exercise includes walking 20 minutes a day or swimming.

Diet: You need to increase the amount of iron in your diet. Generally, the redder the meat and the greener the vegetable, the richer it is as a source of iron. You also need to make sure you have adequate intake of vitamin C (this helps increase the absorption of iron into your body). Vitamin C is found in fresh, dark-green vegetables and citrus fruits. Drink 8 to 10 glasses of liquids every day.

Medications:

You Have Been Prescribed: ____________________

You Need to Take: ____________________

Special Instructions About Iron Supplements:

A. Take the iron medication as prescribed; higher doses are not better. You may need to be taking it for a longer time. High doses of iron can be toxic to children and adults.

B. Your body only absorbs a small portion of the iron pills you take.

C. You may notice green or black bowel movements. This is normal.

D. It is best to take the iron pills on an empty stomach.

E. Try taking your iron pill with a glass of orange juice. The vitamin C in the juice helps the iron be absorbed better.

F. You may have nausea or vomiting when you take iron pills, especially during early pregnancy. If this happens, try taking the pill with food. It is better to take your iron with food than to skip your pill altogether.

G. If you are not able to tolerate the iron in the morning, try taking it in the middle of the afternoon or at bedtime.

H. You may become constipated while taking iron pills. Increase your intake of fruits, vegetables, and water to avoid constipation.

You Need to Notify the Office If You:

A. Have nausea and vomiting while taking the iron supplement even after following the special instructions.

B. Become extremely constipated even after increasing the fiber and liquids in your diet.

C. Are unable to take the supplement at all.

D. Other: ____________________

Phone: ____________________

PRETERM LABOR

PROBLEM

Premature contractions and early labor put your baby at risk for premature delivery. Babies born too soon are at risk for breathing problems, bleeding into their brain, infection, and bowel problems, to name a few. Early recognition is the key to stopping premature labor and delivery.

CAUSE

There are several predisposing factors for preterm labor (PTL), including previous premature delivery, smoking, incompetent cervix, multiple gestation (twins or triplets), and infection. In most cases, the cause of PTL is unknown.

PREVENTION

You can decrease your risk for PTL by living a healthy lifestyle with a balanced diet, proper fluid consumption, and no smoking. Please review any previous PTL symptoms with your health care provider. Early recognition is a key to success.

TREATMENT PLAN

Treatment depends on the clinical picture. In general, you should remember:

A. Drink at least 8 to 10 glasses of noncaffeinated liquid a day; dehydration can increase contractions.
B. Empty your bladder every 2 to 3 hours.
C. Report any bladder infection symptoms, such as burning with urination, to your health care provider.
D. Avoid breast stimulation (including showers where the water stream is on your breasts); this can stimulate contractions.
E. Rest frequently. Rest means lying down on either side, not on your back.
F. Contractions and cramping happen more often in the evening and nighttime after having activity during the day.
G. Do not have intercourse or sexual stimulation without asking your nurse practitioner, certified nurse-midwife, or doctor. If intercourse is okay, use a condom to decrease infection.
H. Try to arrange for help with housework and childcare to help you maintain your bed-rest schedule.
I. Take medications to stop contractions as directed.

Activity: Activity at home is based on how significant your PTL has been. You should follow the following activity guidelines:

Level 1: As tolerated

A. Avoid heavy lifting above 20 pounds.

Level 2: Modified bed rest

A. You may be out of bed for breakfast.
B. Rest for 2 hours in the morning with only moderate activity until lunch.
C. Rest for 2 hours with only moderate activity until dinner.
D. Go to bed by 8 p.m.

Moderate activity consists of short periods of cooking, light housework (dusting and sweeping).

Level 3: Strict bed rest

A. You may be out of the bed only to go to the bathroom or to move to the couch.
B. You may take a shower, use the toilet, brush your teeth, then return immediately to bed.
C. You should not engage in lifting, bending, housework, or lengthy cooking.
D. You should not have sexual intercourse.
E. Perform range-of-motion exercises as directed by your practitioner to avoid muscle weakness and blood clots in your legs. Example: Make small circles with your feet, bend and straighten your legs.

Level 4: Hospitalization

Diet: Diet as tolerated, or follow your prescribed diet. Drink 8 to 10 glasses of water each day. Avoid beverages with caffeine. Eat fresh vegetables, fruits, and bran cereal to avoid becoming constipated.

Medications: Continue taking your prenatal vitamin every day.

You Have Been Prescribed the Following: ____________________

You Need to Take: ____________________

You Need to Notify the Office If You Have:

A. Contractions or cramping more frequent than four in 1 hour.

B. A gush of fluid or blood from your vagina (it is normal to have spotting after vaginal exam or intercourse).

C. Pelvic pressure or low, dull backache.

D. Noticed that your baby is not moving as much as usual: Less than 10 fetal movements in 2 hours after drinking and resting on your side.

E. Chest pain or difficulty breathing.

F. Other: ______________________________

Phone: ______________________________

URINARY TRACT INFECTION DURING PREGNANCY: PYELONEPHRITIS

PROBLEM

You have been diagnosed with an infection of the kidney (where urine is made). Bladder infections can spread to the kidney.

CAUSE

Bacteria from the bladder can move up to the kidney and cause a kidney infection. Other causes are blockage in the urine system or having a catheter, or tube, in the bladder.

PREVENTION

A. Urinate frequently. Don't hold urine for long periods of time.

B. Empty your bladder as soon as you feel it is filling.

C. Urinate before and after sexual intercourse.

D. After urinating, always wipe from front to back with toilet tissue.

E. Don't wear tight underwear or pants that can cause increased moistness and warmth in the perineal area.

F. Cotton panties are the best.

G. Wash your hands every time after going to the bathroom.

H. Do not use the same tissue that you blow your nose to wipe after emptying your bladder: This spreads infection.

TREATMENT PLAN

Antibiotics kill the bacteria that cause infection.

Activity: Rest; do not engage in strenuous physical activity.

Diet: Increase fluids; drink at least one large glass of water every hour while you are awake. Drink cranberry juice to help fight and prevent urinary tract infections. If you do not like the taste of cranberry juice, mix cranberry juice with another juice like grape juice.

Medications: You will be prescribed antibiotics to kill the bacteria causing infection. The drugs may be changed if your urine culture results show a different bacteria. You may need mild pain relievers if you have a lot of back pain. Medications such as Tylenol may be used to bring down fever. You may be prescribed a medicine to stop bladder spasm and pain.

You Have Been Prescribed an Antibiotic: ____________________

You Need to Take: ____________________

Finish all of your antibiotics even if you feel better.

You Have Been Prescribed the Following for Bladder Spasms: ____________________

You Need to Take: ____________________

This medicine will make your urine turn a different color.

You Need to Notify the Office If You Have:

A. Symptoms that worsen or don't get better during treatment.

B. New symptoms that develop during treatment, such as chest pain or shortness of breath.

C. Symptoms that return after treatment when you finish all of your antibiotics.

D. Difficulty taking your medication (you break out or vomit).

E. Other: ____________________

VAGINAL BLEEDING: SECOND AND THIRD TRIMESTER

PROBLEM

Vaginal bleeding may occur during the second and third trimesters of pregnancy (more than 12 weeks). The bleeding may range from spotting of blood on your panties to bleeding like a menstrual period.

CAUSE

A small amount of bloody mucous discharge or spotting may occur for about 1 day following a pelvic examination or sexual intercourse. This is normal if it is not associated with cramping or contractions.

Other causes of vaginal bleeding may be related to the location of the placenta (placenta previa) or premature separation (abruption) of the placenta from your womb. Placental abruption can be associated with cocaine use, cigarette smoking, and trauma (injuries from car wrecks or physical violence).

PREVENTION

There is no known way to prevent most types of vaginal bleeding. If you have been diagnosed by ultrasound with placenta previa, you may be able to prevent bleeding by avoiding sexual intercourse and maintaining bed rest.

There is no known method of preventing placenta previa. Smoking has been associated with placental abruption and placenta previa. You should not smoke or at least you should try to cut down and stop smoking during pregnancy. When you stop smoking, it is also good for your baby's health after delivery.

TREATMENT PLAN

A. Treatment depends on the cause of your vaginal bleeding. You may be placed on bed rest.
B. Stop smoking. Ask your provider for a handout on tips to stop smoking.
C. You may need to be on a rest schedule.
D. You may need to stop work.
E. You need to arrange help for childcare, grocery shopping, and housework.

Activity: The checked activity restriction(s) are prescribed by the provider.

Level 1: As tolerated, avoid heavy lifting above 20 pounds.

Level 2: Modified bed rest.

You may be out of bed for breakfast; rest (laying down) for 2 hours in the morning with moderate activity until lunch; rest for 2 hours with moderate activity until dinner.

Go to bed by 8 p.m.

Moderate activity consists of short periods of cooking and light housework.

Level 3: Strict bed rest.

You may be out of the bed only to go to the bathroom or to move to the couch.

You may take a shower, use the toilet, and brush your teeth, but then return immediately to bed.

No sexual intercourse.

Perform range-of-motion exercises as directed by your practitioner.

Diet: Eat fresh vegetables, fruits, and bran cereal to avoid becoming constipated on bed rest. Drinking extra liquids (especially water) also helps to prevent constipation.

Medications: Continue taking your prenatal vitamins every day.

You Need to Notify the Office If You Have:

A. Contractions or cramps, eight in 1 hour or four in 20 minutes.
B. Bloody, mucous discharge not associated with recent sexual intercourse or a pelvic examination.
C. Bright red or dark red vaginal spotting.
D. Bleeding like a period.
E. A gush of fluid or blood from your vagina.
F. Sharp, knifelike pain in your abdomen that does not go away.
G. Pelvic pressure or low backache not relieved with emptying your bladder and resting on one side.
H. Noticed decreased movement of the baby.
I. Other: ______________________________

POSTPARTUM: BREAST ENGORGEMENT AND SORE NIPPLES

PROBLEM

Engorgement causes swollen, tender breasts, which may have palpable nodular areas.

CAUSE

Engorgement may develop because of inadequate suckling by your baby.

PREVENTION

A. At first, nurse your baby every 2 hours.

B. Make sure your baby latches on to as much as possible of the areola (darkened area around the nipple). The baby suckling on the tip of the nipple does not provide the stimulation necessary to let down the milk and can make your nipples sore and cracked.

C. If your baby is not well attached to the breast, detach the baby and make sure he or she opens the mouth wide to accommodate most of the areola.

D. Wear a supporting nursing bra (avoid underwire bras as they can exert pressure on certain areas of the breast and cause milk stasis, which is a good medium for bacterial growth and infection); make sure that your bra does not squeeze your breasts too tightly.

E. Making sure that the baby is properly attached to the nipple helps to avoid cracking of nipples that can predispose you to an infection of the breast called mastitis.

F. After the baby feeds, express some milk and apply it to the nipple and areola.

G. Purified lanolin can also be very helpful for sore nipples and can prevent further cracking and infection. Apply routinely after each breastfeeding session for the first several days of nursing and longer if tender or cracked nipples occur. If the lanolin is purified, there is no need to wash it off prior to feedings.

TREATMENT PLAN

A. Engorgement
   1. Treatment of engorgement includes the application of heat, breast massage, and expression of milk for comfort only.
   2. A warm moist washcloth or a warm shower before massaging the breast decreases discomfort.
   3. Massage breast by making several gentle but firm stroking movements with the fingertips along the swollen ducts, moving toward the nipple. This should be done around the entire breast.
   4. After massaging, milk should be expressed or pumped until the breast softens enough for the baby to latch well. The baby should then be allowed to nurse from both breasts.
   5. The best strategy for engorgement is frequent breastfeeding (at least every 1/2 to 2 hours until engorgement resolves).

B. Sore Nipples
   1. Sore nipples are usually caused by the improper positioning of the baby on the nipple.
   2. Ensure your baby is grasping the areola when sucking and not just the nipple.
   3. Continuous suction pressure at the same spot of the nipple can be painful.
   4. Change the position of the baby to change the "latching on" position of your baby's mouth.
   5. If nipples become sore or cracked, start feeding on the less affected breast first.
   6. Apply purified lanolin to nipples after each feeding.
   7. Prevent mastitis with the following personal hygiene measures:
      a. Avoid using soap on nipples.
      b. Avoid decrusting the nipples of dried colostrum or milk.
      c. Change breast pads frequently.
      d. Wash hands before handling your breast and before breastfeeding.

Activity: As tolerated, extra rest is recommended after delivery.

Diet:

A. Breastfeeding mothers need extra liquids for milk production.

B. Drink 10 to 12 glasses of liquid a day.

C. Use caffeine in moderation (eliminate if possible).

D. Continue your regular diet and add about 500 extra calories per day.

E. Avoid gas-producing foods that may upset your baby's stomach.

Medications: Continue your prenatal vitamins while breastfeeding.

You Have Been Prescribed: Acetaminophen 500 mg or ibuprofen 600 mg every 3 to 4 hours for discomfort.

You Need to Notify the Office If You Have:

A. Temperature of 100.4°F or higher.

B. Pain that is not controlled with Tylenol or ibuprofen.

C. Flu-like symptoms (fever, chills, malaise).

D. Red streaks on breast.

E. Headache with the symptoms listed here.

F. Other: ______________________________

Phone: ______________________________

ENDOMETRITIS

PROBLEM

You have an infection of the inside of the uterus.

CAUSE

One or more types of bacteria that invaded damaged tissue following your delivery could cause endometritis. The bacteria may be from the vagina, the bowel, or the environment.

PREVENTION

A. Use careful perineal care:
  1. Wipe from front to back after voiding.
  2. Remove peri pad from front to back.
  3. Change peri pad at least every 4 hours.
  4. Use your squeeze bottle filled with warm water to cleanse after each time you urinate or have a bowel movement.
  5. Use good hand washing after changing your pads and the baby's diaper.

TREATMENT PLAN

A. You will need to be treated with antibiotic therapy.

B. Take your temperature three times a day for the first 3 days on the antibiotics.

C. Take Tylenol or ibuprofen as needed for fever or discomfort.

Activity: It is very important for you to increase rest with an infection. Try to get a nap when the baby is sleeping. You may continue to breastfeed on some antibiotic therapy. If you don't breastfeed while you are feeling bad, pump your breast milk to keep up your milk supply but dispose of it.

Diet: Eat well-balanced meals. Drink at least 10 to 12 glasses of liquid a day.

Medications: Continue your prenatal vitamins. Take all of your antibiotics even if you start feeling better.

You Have Been Prescribed: ____________________

You Need to Take: ____________________

You Need to Notify the Office If You Have:

A. Temperature that rises significantly or reaches 101°F.

B. Foul-smelling vaginal bleeding.

C. Increase in pain or tenderness.

D. Other: ____________________

Phone: ____________________

MASTITIS

PROBLEM

You have an infection in your breast tissue, not your breast milk.

CAUSE

The most common organism causing mastitis is *Staphylococcus aureus*. The immediate source of the organism is almost always the nursing infant's nose and mouth. Mastitis often develops in the presence of breast injury, such as cracked nipples.

PREVENTION

A. Prevent injury to the breast:
   1. Avoid overdistension of the breasts; feed infant or use the breast pump frequently (every 2–4 hours).
   2. Avoid clogged milk ducts by applying moist heat to the breasts and massage.
   3. Avoid rough manipulation of the breast; pump carefully.
   4. Avoid cracking of nipples by proper positioning of the infant's mouth on the nipple during feeding. The baby's mouth should cover the entire areola (dark brown part of the nipple area).
   5. Read the Patient Teaching Guide, "Breast Engorgement and Sore Nipples."

B. Personal hygiene measures:
   1. Avoid soap on the nipples; cleanse nipples with warm water only.
   2. Avoid decrusting the nipple of dried colostrum or milk.
   3. Use purified lanolin cream after each breastfeeding for sore, cracked nipples. (If lanolin is purified, there is no need to remove it prior to the next feeding.)
   4. Use good hand-washing techniques before handling the breast and before and after breastfeeding.

TREATMENT PLAN

A. Complete course of antibiotics. Be aware that antibiotics may cause a yeast infection.

B. Continue breastfeeding even on the antibiotics. It is not uncommon for your baby to develop "thrush" (looks like white patches on your baby's mouth and tongue). You may also be prescribed Nystatin cream to apply to your breasts to help prevent thrush.

C. Apply warm soaks to your breast (see the Patient Teaching Guide, "Breast Engorgement and Sore Nipples"). Breast massage may be needed, too.

D. Use Tylenol or ibuprofen for pain (see the Patient Teaching Guide, "Breast Engorgement and Sore Nipples").

Activity: Increased rest is recommended. Try to lie down for a nap when the baby goes to sleep.

Diet: There are no dietary restrictions; continue your regular diet and avoid gas-producing foods that may upset your baby's tummy (cabbage, chocolate, beans, pizza, and spicy foods). Increase fluid intake with elevated temperature. Drink at least 10 to 12 glasses of liquid a day. Use caffeine in moderation (eliminate if possible).

Medications: Continue your prenatal vitamins while breastfeeding.

You Have Been Prescribed: ____________________

You Need to Take: ____________________

Take all of your antibiotics even if you feel better.

You Have Been Prescribed: Nystatin cream for your breasts and nipples.

You Need to Apply It:

A. After each feeding, apply the Nystatin to each nipple and areola of your breast.

B. Before feeding, wipe off the excess cream with a warm washcloth (do not use soap for your breast because it causes excessive drying and cracking).

You Have Been Prescribed ____________ for a yeast infection.

You Need to Use It: ____________________

You Need to Notify the Office If:

A. You have a temperature that does not decrease within 2 days and resolve within 4 days of taking the antibiotics.
B. You have pain that is not controlled with acetaminophen or ibuprofen.
C. Your baby develops thrush. Notify your baby's health care provider for medication.
D. Other: ____.

Phone: ____

WOUND INFECTION: EPISIOTOMY AND CESAREAN SECTION

PROBLEM

You have an infection of your episiotomy site or cesarean section incision.

CAUSE

The cause is one or more types of bacteria that invaded the tissue following your delivery. The bacteria may be from the vagina, the bowel, or the environment.

TREATMENT

A. Take your temperature if you have fever and chills.

B. Episiotomy:
   1. Wash hands before and after changing your sanitary pads and your baby's diaper.
   2. Wipe or pat dry from front to back after every urination or bowel movement.
   3. Apply and remove perineal pad from front to back.
   4. Change perineal pad at least every 4 hours and after each voiding or bowel movement.
   5. Use squeeze bottle: Position nozzle between legs, empty entire bottle over perineum, blot dry with toilet paper, and avoid contamination from anal area.
   6. Use a blow dryer on the lowest setting to "air dry" your stitches.
   7. Wash perineum with mild soap and warm water at least once daily.

C. Cesarean section incision:
   1. Wash hands before and after dressing change and wound care.
   2. Follow all of the above directions (except 6) for your bleeding, too.
   3. After showering, gently pat dry your abdomen.
   4. If wound is draining, cover it with clean dressing and call the office for instructions. Otherwise, leave it open to air.
   5. Clean incision with warm soapy water and pat dry.
   6. If your incision opens, notify your practitioner for further instructions.

Activity: Increased rest is recommended; try to lie down for a nap when the baby goes to sleep.

Diet: There are no dietary restrictions; eat well-balanced meals. Increase your fluid intake with an infection. Drink at least 10 to 12 glasses of liquid a day.

Medications: Continue your prenatal vitamins. You may take acetaminophen one to two tablets every 4 to 6 hours for your fever and/or discomfort.

You Have Been Prescribed the Following Antibiotic: ____________________

You Need to Take: ____________________

Take all of your antibiotics, even if you feel better, unless you have an adverse reaction to them. Then call the office.

You Need to Notify the Office If You Have:

A. Temperature that rises significantly or reaches 101°F.

B. Foul-smelling drainage from the incision or episiotomy site.

C. Increased pain or tenderness.

D. Separation of wound or incision.

E. Other: ____________________

Phone: ____________________

Patient Teaching Guides for Chapter 16: Gynecology

- Amenorrhea
- Atrophic Vaginitis
- Bacterial Vaginosis
- Basal Body Temperature Measurement
- Cervicitis
- Contraception: How to Take Birth Control Pills (for a 28-Day Cycle)
- Dysmenorrhea (Painful Menstrual Cramps or Periods)
- Dyspareunia (Pain With Intercourse)
- Emergency Contraception
- Fibrocystic Breast Changes and Breast Pain
- Instructions for Postcoital Testing
- Menopause
- Pelvic Inflammatory Disease
- Premenstrual Syndrome
- Vaginal Yeast Infection

AMENORRHEA

PROBLEM

For some reason that we do not fully understand, you have stopped ovulating, or putting out an egg each month, and you have stopped having menstrual periods. This is a very common problem.

It is not immediately dangerous for you. However, it is not good for you to let this go on for a long period of time because the inside lining of your uterus is still being stimulated by estrogen, and over a long period of time, this could become cancerous.

CAUSE

Although the cause is usually unknown, amenorrhea is often associated with low thyroid activity, excessive exercise such as that of an athlete or dancer, or excessive weight loss.

PREVENTION

There is no specific prevention. However, if you notice a decreased frequency of menstrual periods or absence of menstrual periods when you increase your exercise, you should decrease the intensity of exercise. If you lose too much weight, you could stop having periods. Try to gain some weight.

TREATMENT PLAN

Decrease exercise, increase weight, and replace progesterone.

Activity: Decrease intensity of exercise. Take at least 2 days off each week, and decrease the amount of time during each exercise session.

Sexual Activity: You may have a return of fertility without warning. If pregnancy is undesired, be sure to use an effective birth control prevention method such as condoms and foam to prevent unintended pregnancy.

Diet: Increase calories and try to put on 5 pounds if you have lost a lot of weight.

Medications: Your health care provider will prescribe progesterone to replace what your ovaries are not making at the present time. Progesterone may be prescribed in the form of birth control pills.

You Have Been Prescribed: ______________________________

You Need to Take: ______________________________

You Need to Notify the Office If:

A. You have any new symptoms.
B. You have problems taking your medication.
C. You think you might be pregnant.
D. Other: ______________________________

Phone: ______________________________

ATROPHIC VAGINITIS

PROBLEM

You have been diagnosed with atrophic vaginitis. This means that the cells lining your vagina are thinner, less pliable, and less lubricated, and so are more prone to tears and abrasion. This is a natural part of aging, and it is also very common with breastfeeding.

CAUSE

Atrophic vaginitis is caused by an alteration in estrogen either from premature ovarian failure, breastfeeding, or naturally occurring menopause.

PREVENTION

A. This is a physical problem, *not* an emotional problem.
   1. If you are breastfeeding, your symptoms will decrease as weaning approaches.
   2. If you are menopausal or have premature ovarian failure, your symptoms will get better after starting a hormone replacement pill or using a hormonal vaginal cream.

B. You also can help your symptoms by doing the following:
   1. Use good hygiene; wipe yourself from front to back with every urination and bowel movement.
   2. Avoid perfumed hygiene sprays, talcs, and harsh soaps.
   3. Wear cotton underwear.
   4. Sleep without underwear.
   5. Use a water-soluble vaginal lubricant with sexual intercourse, such as K-Y jelly or Astroglide. **Do not use Vaseline.** Vaseline can contribute to infections.
   6. Regular sexual activity or masturbation facilitates the natural production of lubricating secretions of your body.
   7. Kegel exercise (using the muscles that start and stop the flow of the urine stream) improves the muscle tone and elasticity of the vagina.
   8. The female-superior "on top" or side-lying position for sexual intercourse gives you the ability to control the depth of thrusting with the penis, and this may make sex more comfortable.
   9. Yogurt douches or acidophilus tablets by mouth or inserted into your vagina can help maintain the vaginal pH to prevent vaginitis.

TREATMENT PLAN

A. Vitamin E oil may be used for vaginal dryness.

B. Use K-Y jelly or other water-soluble lubricants for intercourse.

C. You may be prescribed an estrogen cream or hormone replacements for menopause.

D. If you still have your uterus, hormones need to be balanced with estrogen and progesterone to prevent the lining of the uterus from overgrowing. Follow your hormone therapy instructions.

E. You still need regular pelvic examinations and Pap smears, even if you do not have a period.

Activity: Increase foreplay for increased lubrication. Try these suggestions on sexual positions for greater comfort and control.

Diet: As tolerated.

Medication:

You Have Been Prescribed: ____________________

You Need to Take It/Use It: ____________________

You Need to Notify the Office If You Have:

A. No relief of symptoms after following the preceding instructions.
B. No relief of symptoms after beginning the hormonal replacements.
C. Vaginal bleeding after intercourse.
D. A change in your symptoms.
E. Other: ____________________

Phone: ____________________

BACTERIAL VAGINOSIS

PROBLEM

You have been diagnosed with a vaginal infection, also known as bacterial vaginosis (BV). This is a very common problem that has a "fishy vaginal discharge." The odor increases after sexual intercourse, but it is not considered a sexually transmitted infection. Recurrence is common, and your partner may also need to be treated.

YOU CAN BE TREATED IN PREGNANCY

BV has been associated with premature rupture of the membranes and preterm labor.

CAUSE

BV is caused by an alteration in the normal flora of the vagina. There are many contributing pathogens and factors, including the routine use of douches, antibiotic use, menses, and pregnancy.

PREVENTION

A. Wear cotton panties or panties with a cotton crotch.

B. Do not wear tight restrictive clothes such as tight jeans.

C. Leave your underwear off during sleep.

D. Limit tub bathing and the use of hot tubs or whirlpools.

E. Avoid the use of bubble bath, feminine deodorant sprays, and perfumed sanitary products (sanitary pads, tampons, and toilet paper).

F. Use good hygiene:
   1. Wipe with toilet tissue from front to back after urinating and bowel movements.
   2. Wipe from front to back using clean towels with each bath or shower.
   3. Change your tampons and pads often during your period.

G. Routine douching destroys the normal vaginal flora. Avoid douching unless you are prescribed a medicated douche.

TREATMENT PLAN

A. Try the prevention tips to decrease the recurrence of BV.

B. You may be given a prescription for pills or vaginal creams.

C. Do not use a tampon with vaginal creams because it will absorb the medication.

D. Clindamycin is an oil-based, medicated cream used to treat BV and will weaken latex condoms for at least 72 hours after stopping the therapy.

E. All treatments (medications and douches) may be used during your period.

F. Metronidazole (Flagyl) oral tablets may be prescribed. The side effects include a sharp, unpleasant metallic taste in the mouth, furry tongue, and some urinary tract symptoms. Please remind your provider if you have a history of seizures or if you are on any blood-thinning drug.

OTHER METHODS OF TREATMENT

A. Vinegar and water douches: one tablespoon of white vinegar in one pint of water. Douche one to two times a week.

B. *Lactobacillus acidophilus* culture four to six tablets daily.

C. Garlic suppositories: Place one peeled clove of garlic wrapped in a cloth dipped in olive oil into your vagina overnight, and change daily for five nights. You will not smell like garlic.

Activity: As tolerated.

Diet: When taking the medicine metronidazole (Flagyl), you must **avoid alcohol during the entire week you are taking the medicine and 24 hours after your last dose.** The combination of the medicine and alcohol may cause nausea, vomiting, stomach upset, and a headache.

Medication:

You Have Been Prescribed: ______________________________

You Need to Take It/Use It: ______________________________

You Need to Notify the Office If:

A. You vomited your medication (Flagyl).

B. Your vaginal odor and discharge are not relieved after the medications.

C. You continue to have repeated infections after following the instructions.

D. Other: ____

Phone: ______________________________

BASAL BODY TEMPERATURE MEASUREMENT

DEFINITION

Basal body temperature (BBT) assessment is done to determine if and when a woman ovulates. It may be used to achieve or prevent pregnancy. During the follicular phase of the normal menstrual cycle (the first 2 weeks), one follicle and the oocyte it contains mature. The normal body temperature during the follicular phase when estrogen dominates ranges from 97.2°F to 97.6°F.

At midcycle, when progesterone dominates, the ovum is extruded from the ovary and may be fertilized any time from 12 to 24 hours later. Ovulation manifests as an increase in BBT from 0.6°F to 1°F above your baseline temperature. Some women have a dip in temperature just before the day of ovulation and then their temperature may rise.

Besides taking your temperature to predict ovulation (the best time to try to get pregnant or avoid sexual intercourse), another reason to take it is to check your cervical mucus.

CHECKING YOUR BBT

A. A BBT thermometer must be used. They are easily accessible in the contraceptive section of any pharmacy. If using any other type besides a basal body thermometer, such as a digital thermometer, it must be able to measure to 0.10 degree due to the slight changes that will be measured.

B. Record your temperature on the temperature chart provided in the thermometer packet or by a health care provider. The chart can be easily copied for as many months as needed.

C. Keeping your BBT calendar:
   1. Day 1 of the cycle is the first day of menstruation/bleeding.
   2. Mark the days of bleeding and other discharge, especially mucus, on the calendar.
   3. Mark any days that you are sick, stay up late, or sleep less than 6 hours since this will interfere with your temperature.
   4. Mark the days that you have sexual intercourse.
   5. Mark your medications on your BBT calendar.

D. **Each morning, prior to arising or any activity, place the thermometer under the tongue, leaving it in for 1 minute. Take your temperature consistently at the same time every morning.**

E. A temperature elevation that is 0.2°F or greater from your last 6 days of temperature (and that stays elevated) indicates an ovulatory pattern.
   1. This is the time when you are more likely to get pregnant.
      a. If pregnancy is desired, the standard recommendation is that sexual intercourse should be done 2 days before ovulation is expected and every 2 days thereafter until 2 to 4 days have passed following the rise in body temperature.
      b. If pregnancy is not desired, avoid sexual intercourse.

F. The record should be kept for 2 to 6 months minimum.

CHECKING YOUR CERVICAL MUCUS

Your cervical mucus ranges from a thick and tacky feeling to thin and slippery, the consistency of egg whites. The type of mucus you have also signals the time of ovulation.

A. Your mucus can be checked daily by touching yourself on the outside or, to be the most accurate, inserting one finger in your vagina to check the cervix.
   1. Wash your hands.
   2. Sit on the toilet and gently insert your finger to feel the cervix.
   3. The cervix feels firm, like the end of your nose.
   4. Check the thickness of the mucus and note it on your BBT chart.

B. After you have your period, the cervical mucus is thick and tacky; it is more difficult to get pregnant when the mucus is thick.

C. As ovulation approaches, you will notice the mucus getting thinner.

D. When the mucus is the consistency of egg whites, that signals ovulation and you are the most fertile.
   1. This is the time to have sexual intercourse/avoid intercourse.
   2. Continue until you see your BBT rise.
   3. You will notice the cervical mucus getting thicker.

CERVICITIS

PROBLEM

You are being treated for cervicitis. The cervix is the lower section of the uterus that opens into the vagina. Cervicitis is a condition or inflammation of the cervix.

CAUSE

Certain germs such as *C. trachomatis* or *N. gonorrhea* may cause cervicitis; however, in many cases no specific germ may be identified. In these cases, inflammation may be due to douching, chemical irritants, or altered vaginal flora. In many cases, no cause may be found.

Your health care provider will perform a physical evaluation, including pelvic examination, and obtain certain tests to diagnose the cause of cervicitis. If a sexually transmitted organism is found, you and your partner will need to be treated.

PREVENTION

In cases where cervicitis is caused by sexually transmitted organisms, use of condoms may prevent infection. Do not douche or use any other chemically irritating products.

TREATMENT PLAN

A. You may be prescribed an antibiotic by your health care provider.

B. **Depending on the cause of cervicitis, your sexual partner(s) may also need medical evaluation and treatment.**

Activity: Avoid sexual activity until treatment is completed.

Medications:

You Have Been Prescribed: ______________________________

You Need to Take It: ______________________________

You need to finish all of your antibiotics even though you may feel good.

You Need to Notify the Office If:

A. You are not able to take your medicine.

B. You have other new symptoms.

C. Other: ______________________________

Phone: ______________________________

CONTRACEPTION: HOW TO TAKE BIRTH CONTROL PILLS (FOR A 28-DAY CYCLE)

You have been prescribed an oral contraceptive, also known as a birth control pill. Most birth control pills contain a combination of synthetic estrogen and progestin.

A. Birth control pills suppress ovulation.

B. They make the lining of the uterus unreceptive for an egg to implant and grow. Birth control pills also alter the cervical mucus, making it thicker and harder for sperm to penetrate.

C. **A birth control pill does not prevent any sexually transmitted infection or HIV. A condom must still be used to protect yourself from the HIV virus or other infections.**

D. You will be asked to return to the office in 3 months after starting birth control pills to check your blood pressure and to check for other side effects of the pill, such as your potassium level and nausea.

E. If your blood pressure is normal and you are not having any other problems taking the pills, your prescription for birth control pills may be written for 1 year.

F. At the end of that time, you will need another physical examination and possibly a Pap smear. Then your prescription can be refilled for another year.

You Have Been Prescribed: ______________________________

A. This is a combination pill of estrogen and progestin.
   1. Your packet contains 28 pills. Notice that your pills are different colors. **You must take them in the order that they come in the packet**. There are 21 "active" pills, and the last 7 are "inactive or sugar pills" to keep you in the habit of taking a pill every day.
   2. You must take a pill **every day** at approximately the same time. Develop the habit of taking the pill with brushing your teeth, for example. You cannot share your birth control pills with anyone else.
   3. Start your packet on the Sunday of your period. Take the pill marked "1," "start here," or "Sunday."
   4. You take a pill every day for 21 days; when you start the last 7 pills, you will have a period or "withdrawal bleed."
   5. Your period may not start for 1 to 2 days into the last week of pills. This is normal. You generally have a shorter, lighter period on birth control pills.
   6. When you start your period, it is time to refill your prescription for your next month of pills.
   7. If this is your first packet of birth control pills, you are not considered protected and may get pregnant. Use a backup method of birth control for the first packet of pills.
   8. **Missed pills Instructions:**
      a. If you miss one pill: Take it as soon as you remember, then get back on your regular schedule (you take two pills in 1 day).
      b. If you miss two pills: Take two pills as soon as you remember, then get back on schedule (you take three pills in 1 day). You must use a **backup method of birth control**, such as a condom, until you finish that packet of pills. You may have spotting if you miss two pills. This is normal.
      c. If you miss three pills: You may have a period. Discard that packet of pills and start a new packet on Sunday. You must use a **backup method of birth control** such as a condom for the first 7 days of the new packet.
      d. If one or more birth control pills are missed, no backup method of contraception is used, and if you miss your period, you should do a pregnancy test.
   9. If you are prescribed antibiotics while taking birth control pills, you must use a **backup method of birth control** such as a condom. You can get pregnant. Antibiotics and other medications such as those used to prevent seizures make birth control pills less effective, making it possible to get pregnant.

You Need to Notify the Office If You:

A. Vomit your birth control pills.

B. Have a severe or migraine-like headache.

C. Are depressed (can't make yourself happy).

D. Have pain in your legs, especially if your calf hurts when walking or flexing your foot.

E. Break your leg and need to have a cast.

F. Think you are pregnant (skipped pills or are taking antibiotics).

G. Have blurred vision, loss of vision, or spots before your eyes.

H. Feel chest pain or shortness of breath.

I. Feel severe abdominal pain.

J. Have lots of swelling of the fingers, hands, ankles, or face.

K. Other: ______________________________

Phone: ______________________________

DYSMENORRHEA (PAINFUL MENSTRUAL CRAMPS OR PERIODS)

PROBLEM

Painful menstrual cramps, or dysmenorrhea, can cause occasional diarrhea, nausea or vomiting, and headache with menstrual periods.

CAUSE

A substance called prostaglandin causes most painful menstrual cramps. This substance is made in the uterus and causes the uterus to contract. Most menstrual cramps are normal and are not a sign of anything wrong. However, menstrual cramps may cause you to feel badly enough that you are unable to go to school or work. If that is the case, your health care provider can suggest medication to decrease the painful periods.

TREATMENT PLAN/CARE

A. Your health care provider may suggest a medicine such as a prostaglandin inhibitor. This medication helps decrease or eliminate the most likely substance that is causing the cramping of your uterus. The medications most often suggested are ibuprofen (Motrin, Advil) and naproxen (Aleve). Generic options for either of these are acceptable.
   1. These are available at your local drug store, grocery store, or convenience store.
   2. Take any of these with a snack or meal to protect your stomach lining and prevent nausea.
   3. If you usually have very painful menstrual cramps, begin your medication as soon as your period begins or even the day before your period. This helps stop the production of prostaglandin.

B. If your cramps are not better using over-the-counter (OTC) medications, your health care provider may write a prescription for a stronger medicine.

C. Many women take oral contraceptive pills to relieve menstrual cramps. A prescription is necessary.

D. Some women find that exercise such as walking helps ease the cramps.

E. Another idea is a warm bath, shower, or a warm heating pad on your abdomen.

F. General health practices such as regular exercise, yoga, routine sleep habits, and regular sexual activity are beneficial.

Activity: Try to continue your usual activity. Try taking a walk, swimming, or doing yoga. Try a warm bath or shower.

Diet: Eat your normal diet. If you are nauseated, drink a clear carbonated soda (7-UP or Sprite).

Medication:

You Have Been Prescribed: ______________________

You Need to Take: ______________________

You Need to Notify the Office If You Have:

A. Any questions concerning your condition.
B. Problems taking the medicine.
C. No relief when taking the medicine, and other measures do not help.
D. Any signs of infection, such as fever, chills, bad-smelling vaginal discharge, or burning sensation when you urinate.

Phone: ______________________

DYSPAREUNIA (PAIN WITH INTERCOURSE)

PROBLEM

As many as 60% of women complain of pain with sexual intercourse, also known as dyspareunia. Pain may occur with insertion of and/or with deep penetration of the penis into the vagina.

CAUSES

There are physical causes, such as episiotomy scars, a short vagina, and infections; musculoskeletal causes such as disk problems; hormonal causes such as the lack of estrogen in menopause; and poor communication with partners and lack of foreplay.

PREVENTION AND TREATMENT PLANS

A. Inadequate lubrication.
   1. More prolonged foreplay increases natural vaginal lubrication.
   2. Use a lubricant such as K-Y jelly or Astroglide.
   3. Do not use Vaseline as a lubricant.
   4. Do not use contraceptive creams for lubrication; they often cause dryness (dehydration) and may worsen soreness.

B. Pain on insertion of penis.
   1. Try different positions that give you more control.
   2. Guide the penis for insertion.
   3. If menopausal, you may be prescribed estrogen cream to use on an intermittent basis.

C. Pain with deep penetration.
   1. Use a side-lying position during intercourse; this may be more comfortable so that deep penetration is limited.
   2. You may need to be referred to a gynecologist for further treatment and/or surgery if you have any masses or scar tissue noted on a physical examination.

D. If you have or suspect an infection:
   1. Inform your provider that you may have an infection.
   2. A culture will be done.
   3. Antibiotics will be prescribed for you and possibly your partner(s).
   4. Refrain from sexual intercourse until all medications are gone (unless otherwise instructed).

E. If you have a very narrow vaginal opening, you may need to be evaluated for use of vaginal dilators.

F. Spasm of the muscles upon touching the vaginal area may be treated with medication, relaxation techniques, and Kegel exercises.

G. You and your partner may be referred to a sex counselor.

Medication:

You Have Been Prescribed: ______________________________

You Need to Take/Use It: ______________________________

You Need to Notify the Office If You Have:

A. No relief of your symptoms after your prescribed treatment.

B. Other: ______________________________

Phone: ______________________________

EMERGENCY CONTRACEPTION

You have indicated that you want to use an emergency contraception method. **Plan B One-Step** is an OTC brand of emergency contraceptive that is available without prescription in the United States.

TREATMENT PLAN

A. You must start levonorgestrel-based emergency contraception within 72 hours or ulipristal acetate within 120 hours of unprotected intercourse.

B. It is best to start within the first 12 to 24 hours.

C. You will be given a prescription or a supply of birth control pills.

D. The number of pills depends on the brand of the pill.

E. Your health care provider will give you clear instructions.

F. The sooner you begin emergency contraception, the more effective it will be.

G. The birth control pills and Plan B One-Step prevent pregnancy because the hormones cause the mucus in the cervix to thicken and the lining of the uterus and tubes to change.

H. You may not ovulate, but if you do ovulate, the egg will not be ready to be fertilized by a sperm.

I. Emergency contraception in the form of hormonal pills will *not* interrupt an already established pregnancy.

J. Because you are taking more female hormones than you are used to, you may become sick to your stomach.

K. Your health care provider will tell you what medication to buy or give you a prescription for medicine to keep you from being sick to your stomach.

L. Take this medicine at least 1 hour before you take the hormone pills.

M. Other common side effects include breast tenderness, headache, or dizziness. These side effects go away in a day or two.

N. You should have a menstrual period a week or so after you take the pills.

O. If you have not had a period by 3 weeks, call the office.

P. It is unlikely that you would get pregnant, but if you do and choose to have a baby, the emergency contraception is *not* associated with any increased chance of birth defects.

Medication:

You Have Been Prescribed the Following Emergency Contraception Medication: ____________________

You Have Been Prescribed the Following Nausea Medication: ____________________

You Need to Call Us If You Have Any Questions or Problems.

You Need to Notify the Office If You Have:

A. Serious side effects of medicine.

B. Severe chest pain.

C. Severe abdominal pain.

D. Headache.

E. Vision changes.

F. Shortness of breath.

Phone: ____________________

FIBROCYSTIC BREAST CHANGES AND BREAST PAIN

PROBLEM

You are being treated for breast pain or breast lumpiness that is from breast changes that are painful but not cancerous. You have probably had an extensive examination by your health care provider, perhaps a mammogram, sonogram, and/or a breast biopsy.

CAUSE

The cause is unknown, but probably related to estrogen changes that occur with menstrual periods.

PREVENTION

None known.

TREATMENT PLAN

Be fitted for a well-fitting bra. This helps to eliminate breast movement as a source of pain. Try ice packs on your breasts for 20 minutes every few hours. Some women find that heat on the breast can also relieve discomfort.

Activity: There are no activity restrictions. When exercising, wear a good, supportive bra.

Diet: Eliminate or decrease salt in your diet to decrease water retention if you have swelling of your breasts near your period. Some women have reported decreased breast pain with reduced caffeine and nicotine intake.

Medications: Several medications have been found to relieve breast pain from fibrocystic breast changes, such as medications that decrease or stabilize estrogen (oral contraceptive pills). Ask your health care provider which is best for you.

Complementary: Recent research has shown that flaxseed may reduce cyclic pain (flaxseed 25 mg a day).

You Have Been Prescribed: ________________________________

You Need to Take It/Use It: ________________________________

Phone: ________________________________

INSTRUCTIONS FOR POSTCOITAL TESTING

PROBLEM

This test is performed during an infertility evaluation to determine the presence of sperm and how they behave in cervical mucus. The postcoital test assists the clinician in determining possible causes for infertility that are often easy to correct. The test is performed on about day 14 of the menstrual cycle, or around the time of expected luteinizing hormone surge as determined by the rise of temperature seen on the BBT chart.

PROCEDURE

A. You and your partner should abstain from sexual intercourse for 48 hours prior to the test.
   1. Ideally, intercourse should take place the morning of or the night before the office visit.
   2. It is preferable to not use vaginal lubricants. If you must use a vaginal lubricant, use one that is water soluble, such as K-Y jelly or Astroglide.

B. At the office, you will have a speculum inserted into your vagina as if you were getting a Pap test.

C. Your cervix will be evaluated for the presence, amount, and consistency of mucus.

D. Mucus is taken from the cervix with a syringe and placed on a slide.

E. The clinician will evaluate the slide for presence of sperm, number of living sperm, and movement of sperm.

RESULTS

A. A normal test usually reveals the presence of 5 to 10 sperm moving deliberately.

B. A poor test may indicate that intercourse has been mistimed (there is a poor amount of cervical mucus).

C. Sperm should live at least 48 hours in good cervical mucus.

D. If your first test is abnormal, it will be repeated because a common problem is mistimed evaluation.

MENOPAUSE

DEFINITION

Menopause is the cessation of menses (stopping of menstrual periods) for 12 consecutive months and is generally experienced in women between 45 and 55 years of age; however, some women may be earlier or later.

A. Menopause before the age of 40 is considered premature.

B. Induced menopause is the abrupt cessation of menses related to chemical or surgical interventions.

Perimenopause is the time preceding menopause and may last several years. The average age of onset is usually in a woman's 40s but may occur earlier. Symptoms may occur during this time period due to fluctuations in hormone levels. **Pregnancy may still occur during this time and reliable contraception should be used.**

CAUSE

Menopause can be natural or induced. Natural menopause is a normal function of aging. Surgical or chemical intervention can result in induced menopause.

SYMPTOMS

Symptom occurrence and severity vary from very mild to moderate or severe. Symptoms may include:

A. Hot flashes

B. Night sweats

C. Insomnia

D. Vaginal dryness

E. Pain with intercourse

TREATMENT

Your care provider will work with you to develop a plan of treatment that is based on your individual symptom pattern. Inform your care provider if you have:

A. Acute liver disease

B. Cerebral vascular or coronary artery disease, myocardial infarction (MI), or stroke

C. History of or active thrombophlebitis or thromboembolic disorders

D. History of uterine or ovarian cancer

E. Known or suspected cancer of the breast

F. Known or suspected estrogen-dependent neoplasm

G. Pregnancy

H. Undiagnosed, abnormal vaginal bleeding

Activity:

A. Regular physical exercise can be beneficial for weight reduction and symptom control.

B. Dress in layers to accommodate hot flashes and avoid warm areas.

C. Avoid hot showers and baths.

D. Regular sexual intercourse is encouraged, and you may use vaginal lubricants (K-Y Jelly, Astroglide, Replens) helpful for vaginal dryness.

E. Be sure to use a reliable method of **birth control** to prevent undesired pregnancy if you have had a period within 1 year.

Diet: You need to eat a well-balanced diet (three meals). Supplement your diet to achieve calcium 1,200 mg/d and vitamin D 800 IU/d Avoid alcohol, caffeine, and spicy food as they may trigger hot flashes.

Medication:

You Have Been Prescribed: ______________________________

You Need to Take/Use It: ______________________________

You Need to Notify the Office If:

A. You experience unexpected vaginal bleeding.

B. Your symptoms worsen.

C. You are on hormone replacement therapy and you experience calf pain, chest pain, or shortness of breath; cough up blood, or have severe headaches, visual disturbances, breast pain, abdominal pain, or yellowing of the skin.

D. Other: ____

Phone: ______________________________

PELVIC INFLAMMATORY DISEASE

PROBLEM

You have been diagnosed as having pelvic inflammatory disease, also known as PID. This inflammation can involve the uterus, fallopian tubes, ovaries, broad ligament, and/or the pelvic vascular system or pelvic connective tissue.

CAUSE

Organisms that go up from the vagina and cervix into the uterus cause PID. The two most common organisms cultured from patients with PID are *Chlamydia trachomatis* and *Neisseria gonorrhoeae*. Your period increases the ability of gonococcal invasion into the upper genital tract. Infection and inflammation spread throughout the endometrium to the fallopian tubes. From there, it extends to the ovaries and peritoneal, or abdominal, cavity.

PREVENTION

A. Condoms and a spermicidal foam or cream with nonoxynol 9 are protective against PID.

B. Condoms must be used with *every* sexual intercourse.

C. Vaginal douching may lead to an increased risk for PID.
   1. Routine douching is *not recommended*; it eliminates the normal vaginal flora.

D. The more sex partners you have, the greater the chances are of contracting sexually transmitted infections.

TREATMENT

A. Your partner(s) need(s) to be evaluated and treated with antibiotic therapy, too.

B. Sexual abstinence
   1. **You should not have sexual intercourse until all of your symptoms are gone and your partner(s) has (have) completed antibiotic therapy.**
   2. If you do have sexual intercourse, you should use condoms consistently.

Activity: Limit yourself to bed rest for about 3 to 4 days, then pursue activity as tolerated.

Diet:

A. You need to drink at least 10 to 12 glasses of liquid every day.

B. You need to eat a well-balanced diet (three meals).

C. If you have been prescribed Flagyl (metronidazole), you must avoid all alcohol ingestion for at least 2 days after the last dose or you will experience severe nausea and vomiting.

Medications:

A. You will be prescribed *two or more* antibiotics; it is extremely important to **take all of the antibiotics**.

B. You may take acetaminophen (Tylenol) for fever.

C. You may be prescribed some pain medication.

You Have Been Prescribed: ______________________________

You Need to Take: ______________________________

Take all of your antibiotics, even if you feel better.

Your Second Prescribed Antibiotic Is: ______________________________

You Need to Take: ______________________________

You need to take all of both antibiotics, even if you feel better.

You Have Been Prescribed the Following for Your Pain: ______________________________

You Need to Take: ______________________________

You Need to Notify the Office If:

A. Your fever does not respond to acetaminophen (Tylenol).

B. Your symptoms worsen, even while taking both antibiotics.

C. You vomit or cannot tolerate your antibiotics.

D. You must return to the office 2 or 3 days after the antibiotics have been started for a repeat examination, or if you are unable to return for your follow-up office visit.

E. Other: ____

Phone: ____

Next Appointment: Date ______________ **Time** ______________

PREMENSTRUAL SYNDROME

DEFINITION

Premenstrual syndrome (PMS) is a common problem experienced by women in their reproductive years. You may have some or all of the following symptoms:

A. Cravings for food, particularly chocolate and salty foods
B. Irritability
C. Feelings of depression; crying spells
D. Bloated stomach
E. Weight gain and water retention
F. Difficulty concentrating
G. Tiredness
H. Feelings of faintness
I. Occasional clumsiness
J. Sore breasts

CAUSE

Although the cause is really not known, PMS is a response of your body to the changes in female hormones during the last half of your menstrual cycle.

PREVENTION

All of your symptoms probably cannot be prevented, but some of them may be made less severe.

TREATMENT PLAN

A. Keep track of your symptoms for at least 3 months so that your health care provider can determine if the symptoms always happen in the last half of your cycle.
B. Eat six small meals each day. Eat breakfast, have a morning snack like fruit or a glass of milk, eat lunch, have an afternoon snack, eat supper, and then have another evening snack. This helps keep your blood sugar even, to avoid low blood sugar.
C. Avoid candy, desserts, and other sugars. They may be associated with episodes of low blood sugar. Complex carbohydrates such as pasta, potatoes, fresh fruit, rice, and bread break down more slowly than sweets and keep your blood sugar steadier.
D. Stay away from salty foods such as chips, fast food, and pickles.
E. Avoid caffeine in soda, coffee, and chocolate. Caffeine makes you irritable and nervous.
F. Exercise daily. It is a good idea to do aerobic exercises or even walk. Exercise increases chemicals in your brain that help with your mood.
G. Join a PMS group so that you can get support from other women who have similar symptoms. You may get ideas of how other women handle PMS, and you can share your ideas, too.
H. If you smoke, try to cut down or quit.
I. Get a good night's rest and take naps during the day if possible.
J. Try stress reduction classes or yoga. Local community organizations usually have classes available.

Medications: There are a number of medications available that your health care provider may suggest for you.

You Have Been Prescribed: ____________________

You Need to Take: ____________________

You Have Also Been Prescribed: ____________________

You Need to Take: ____________________

You Need to Call to the Office If:

A. You have questions or concerns.

B. You feel that things are not improving.

C. Other: ____

Phone: ____

VAGINAL YEAST INFECTION

PROBLEM

You have been diagnosed with a vaginal yeast infection. This is an infection or inflammation of the vagina that is caused by a fungus known as yeast *(Monilia* or *Candida albicans)*.

CAUSE

Yeast cells *(Monilia)* are normally present on the skin in healthy people. These cells may be found in the vagina or rectal area. However, due to a disturbance in the body's hormones and pH, an overproduction of these cells has occurred and has caused an infection. Several factors can cause this disturbance, which include menstrual periods, pregnancy, diabetes, antibiotics or other medications, increased dietary intake of sugars and alcohol, and an increase in moisture and warmth in the vaginal or rectal area by wearing tight restrictive clothing.

PREVENTION

A. Keep the vaginal and rectal areas clean and dry.

B. Shower daily and avoid tub baths.

C. Avoid tight, restrictive clothing such as tight jeans and underwear.

D. Wear cotton panties that allow air to circulate. At bedtime, do not wear underwear with your pajamas.

E. Obesity can contribute to this problem too. If you have gained an excessive amount of weight, try to lose these extra pounds.

F. Avoid douching because this changes the normal flora and pH of the vagina, which can contribute to causing yeast infections.

TREATMENT PLAN

A pelvic exam may have been necessary to identify the source of your infection. Practice preventive tips to speed your recovery.

Activity: Avoid excessive exercise and activities that produce excessive sweating; also avoid sexual intercourse until your infection is gone. Your partner may also need to be treated for this same infection.

Diet: Drink plenty of water and other liquids. Avoid alcohol and excessive sugars. Increase the intake of yogurt and buttermilk in your diet.

Medications: Antifungal medications may be prescribed for you.

1. OTC medications may include Monistat vaginal suppositories and cream. This is also known as miconazole nitrate, which you may find in the drug store at a much lower price and which can be just as effective.
2. You must use the full days of the OTC medication. If you stop too early, the yeast can regrow.

If you have also been diagnosed with a bacterial infection of the vagina, other medications may also be prescribed. If your provider has prescribed Flagyl (metronidazole), **please do not drink any alcohol while taking this medication and for the next 3 days following this medication. The combination of this medication and alcohol can make you very sick**.

You Have Been Prescribed: ____________________

You Need to Take: ____________________

You Need to Notify the Office If:

A. OTC medications do not help your symptoms.

B. You develop other symptoms.

C. Other: ____________________

Phone: ____________________

Patient Teaching Guides for Chapter 17: Sexually Transmitted Infections

- Chlamydia
- Gonorrhea
- Herpes Simplex Virus
- Human Papillomavirus (HPV)
- Syphilis
- Trichomoniasis

CHLAMYDIA

PROBLEM

Chlamydia is a sexually transmitted infection. Often, no problems are present, but you may notice a yellowish discharge from the penis or vagina, burning during urination, frequent and urgent urination, or pelvic pain.

Untreated chlamydia in females may lead to a condition called pelvic inflammatory disease (PID). PID is a leading cause of infertility, increased ectopic pregnancies, and chronic pelvic pain in women.

CAUSE

Chlamydia is caused by a bacterium called *Chlamydia trachomatis*. This bacterium is spread through sexual contact and may infect the eyes, throat, vagina, penis, or rectum.

PREVENTION

A. Limit sexual partners.

B. Have routine screening tests for chlamydia prior to beginning a new sexual relationship.

C. Use condoms with sexual activity.

TREATMENT PLAN

Abstain from sexual activity until you and your partner(s) have completed your prescribed medication. Your health care provider is required to report this disease to the public health department. The health department may contact you.

Diet: As desired.

Medications: Chlamydia can be cured by the prescribed antibiotics.

You Have Been Prescribed: ______________________________

You Need to Take: ______________________________

You need to take all of your antibiotics. It is very important that you keep your follow-up appointment with your provider in 3 months: Your appointment has been scheduled for: ______________________________

You Need to Notify the Office If:

A. You are unable to take your antibiotics because of nausea, vomiting, or a reaction.

B. Other: ______________________________

Phone: ______________________________

GONORRHEA

PROBLEM

Gonorrhea is a sexually transmitted infection. You may have the following symptoms: burning during urination, yellowish discharge from the penis or vagina, heavier menstrual periods, or pelvic pain.

Untreated gonorrhea in females can lead to a condition called PID. PID is a leading cause of infertility, increased ectopic pregnancies, and chronic pelvic pain in women.

CAUSE

Gonorrhea is caused by an organism called *Neisseria gonorrhoeae*. This organism is spread through sexual contact and may infect the eyes, throat, vagina, penis, or rectum.

PREVENTION

A. Limit sexual partners.

B. Have routine screening tests for gonorrhea prior to beginning a new sexual relationship.

C. Use condoms when having intercourse.

TREATMENT PLAN

Your health care provider is required to report this disease to the public health department. The health department may contact you.

Abstain from sexual activity until you and your partner(s) have completed your prescribed medications.

Diet: There is no special diet that needs to be followed.

Medications: Gonorrhea can be cured by the prescribed antibiotics.

You Have Been Prescribed: ____________________

You Need to Take: ____________________

It is very important that you keep your follow-up appointment that has been scheduled for you on: ____________________

All of the antibiotics need to be taken.

You Need to Notify the Office If:

A. You have any new symptoms.

B. You are unable to take all of the antibiotics due to nausea or vomiting or a reaction.

C. Other: ____________________

HERPES SIMPLEX VIRUS

PROBLEM

You may experience oral or genital bumps or lesions (often painful), burning, itching, sensation of pressure, painful urination, painful lymph nodes (bumps along underwear line), flu-like symptoms (fever, headache, muscle aches, tired feeling).

CAUSE

A. The herpes simplex virus (HSV) is spread by direct contact with the secretions of someone who has the virus.

B. Viruses cannot be cured, but the problems or symptoms caused by them can often be managed with medication.

C. It is possible for someone to have HSV and have no symptoms. The first outbreak after contact with an infected individual usually occurs within 2 to 10 days, but it may take up to 3 weeks.

D. More severe symptoms are experienced with the first outbreak of HSV. The symptoms usually peak 4 to 5 days after the onset of infection and resolve after 2 to 3 weeks without medication.

E. Medication may decrease the severity and duration of the symptoms. Recurrent outbreaks usually last 5 to 7 days.

F. The virus may be spread even when symptoms are not present. This is known as viral shedding. Medication may also decrease the time of viral shedding.

G. Often, individuals with HSV experience itching, burning, or a feeling of pressure at the site 24 to 48 hours prior to an outbreak. This is known as prodrome.

H. Sexual activity should be avoided during this time because the viral shedding is occurring, which means the infection may be spread.

TREATMENT PLAN

A. Avoid sexual activity when lesions are present or when you feel the prodrome.

B. Use condoms with sexual activity.

C. Limit sexual partners.

D. Do not use any creams, lotions, or powders on lesions unless instructed to do so by your health care provider.

E. If urination is painful, pour water over the genital area while urinating.

F. Dry affected area thoroughly.

G. If you are pregnant at any time, notify your provider of your diagnosis of herpes to allow the provider to treat you accordingly prior to delivery to prevent spreading the herpes infection to your baby.

Activity: Stress is a trigger for an outbreak. Exercise may help with keeping your stress level down.

Diet: There is no special diet.

Medications: Antiviral medications are used to suppress the virus. They do not cure it but decrease the viral outbreaks.

You Have Been Prescribed: ______________________________

You Need to Take: ______________________________

You Need to Call the Office If:

A. You are unable to empty your bladder when you have an outbreak.

B. Other: ______________________________

Phone: ______________________________

HUMAN PAPILLOMAVIRUS (HPV)

PROBLEM

HPV, also known as condyloma, or genital or venereal warts, is a sexually transmitted infection.

A. You may experience "bumps" or lesions on the genitals or perianal area. They may be raised and rough appearing or flat and smooth. They are often wartlike in appearance.

B. Lesions may appear singly or in clusters and may be small or large. They are usually soft, painless, and pale pink to grayish in color, and they may itch.

C. **It is very important to get regular Pap smears.**

D. There are several treatment options that your health care provider will discuss.

CAUSE

HPV is acquired by having genital contact or intercourse with someone who has the infection.

PREVENTION/TREATMENT PLAN

There is no cure for HPV, but the following may decrease the spread of HPV:

A. Do not have genital contact or intercourse without a condom when the lesions are present. Some people who have the infection never have symptoms (bumps or warts). It is possible to spread the infection even when no symptoms are present.

B. Limit sexual partners and openly discuss the need to use a condom.

C. Examine new partners for bumps or warts.

D. Ask your provider about receiving the Gardasil vaccine for preventing the HPV virus. It is available for males and females ranging from 9 to 25 years of age.

Medications:

You Have Been Prescribed: ______________________________

You Need to Take: ______________________________

You Need to Notify the Office If:

A. You have any new symptoms.

B. It is time for your Pap smear.

C. Other: ______________________________

Phone: ______________________________

SYPHILIS

PROBLEM

You may have round or oval painless lesions, most commonly in the genital region, but they may occur anywhere on the body where transmission occurred.

A. You may experience a rash covering your body, including palms and soles.

B. **Flu-like symptoms** include fever; headache; sore throat; swollen, tender lymph nodes; and decreased appetite.

CAUSE

Syphilis is contracted by genital or oral contact with someone who has the infection. The infection is spread when lesions are present.

PREVENTION

A. Use condoms.

B. Limit sexual partners.

C. Screen new sexual partners by asking about any known infections.

TREATMENT PLAN

Do not engage in sexual activity while lesions are present. Notify all partners of the need for treatment. Keep follow-up appointments to determine if treatment has been effective.

Diet: There is no special diet.

Medications: Penicillin is the drug of choice for treating syphilis. Other antibiotics can be used if you are allergic to penicillin. Within 24 hours of antibiotic treatment, you may experience a fever or headache. Aspirin, acetaminophen (Tylenol), or ibuprofen may be taken if these symptoms occur.

You Have Been Prescribed: ____________________

You Need to Take: ____________________

You need to finish all of your antibiotics.

You Need to Notify the Office If You Have:

A. Any new symptoms.

B. Any reaction to your antibiotics.

C. Any other concerns about syphilis.

Phone: ____________________

TRICHOMONIASIS

PROBLEM

You may experience increased vaginal discharge, yellow-green or watery gray in color. It may have a foul odor. You may also have vaginal itching or irritation, burning during urination, discomfort during sexual intercourse, spotting or bleeding during or after sexual intercourse, or abdominal discomfort.

CAUSE

Trichomonas vaginalis is acquired by having sex with someone who has the infection.

PREVENTION

A. Use condom with each act of intercourse.

B. Limiting the number of sexual partners.

C. Screening new sexual partners.

TREATMENT PLAN

Do not have sexual activity until you and your partner have both completed medications. There are no limitations in other physical activity.

Diet: Do not drink alcohol during the use of medication and for 3 days after taking the last dose of your medicine. Alcohol use while taking this medication may result in nausea, vomiting, and severe upset stomach. You may have a metallic taste from the medicine that may slightly alter the taste of food. No other limitations in diet are required.

Medications: Metronidazole (Flagyl) is used to treat the infection.

You Have Been Prescribed: ______________________________

You Need to Take: ______________________________

Finish all of the medication.

You Need to Notify the Office If:

A. You are unable to tolerate the medicine.

B. Any new symptoms develop.

C. Other: ______________________________

Phone: ______________________________

Patient Teaching Guides for Chapter 18: Infectious Diseases

- Lyme Disease and Removal of a Tick
- Mononucleosis
- Rocky Mountain Spotted Fever and Removal of a Tick
- Toxoplasmosis

LYME DISEASE AND REMOVAL OF A TICK

PROBLEM

Ticks are vectors for Lyme disease and Rocky Mountain Spotted Fever. You have been diagnosed with Lyme disease.

CAUSE

Lyme disease is caused by a spirochete from ticks.

PREVENTION

A. Avoid areas with large deer populations.

B. Wear light-colored clothes to make ticks easier to spot. Wear long sleeves and tuck pants into the socks to form a barrier.

C. Stick to hiking trails. Avoid contact with overgrown foliage. Ticks prefer dense woods with thick growth of shrubs and small trees as well as along the edge of the woods.

D. Check for ticks after each outdoor activity, especially hairy regions of the body and beltline where ticks often attach. Check for ticks prior to bathing, especially at the back of the neck, knees, and ears.

E. Remove ticks promptly (see instructions that follow).

F. Inspect pets daily and remove ticks when present.

G. Some manufacturers currently offer permethrin-treated clothing that is effective for up to 20 washings. This clothing is not recommended for children.

H. Use tick repellent with diethyltoluamide (DEET) (except for small children younger than 2 years). As an alternative, picaridin and oil of eucalyptus preparations have been approved for use as repellents by the U.S. Environmental Protection Agency (EPA).

REMOVAL OF TICKS: PRECAUTIONS

A. Do not hold a lighted match or cigarette to the tick. Do not apply gasoline, kerosene, or oil to the tick's body.

B. Old treatments, including using nail polish and petroleum jelly, should not be used to remove ticks.

C. Avoid squeezing the body of the tick.

D. Grasp the tick with a fine-tip tweezer close to the skin. Remove by gently pulling the tick upward straight out without using any twisting motions (see illustrations that follow).

E. If you use your finger to remove ticks, protect your fingers with facial tissue or gloves. Wash your hands with soap and water or use rubbing alcohol after removal of the tick.

F. Do not crush the tick during removal.

G. **Save the tick for identification in case you become ill. Write the date of the tick bite on paper, place the paper and the tick in a resealable baggie, and place it in the freezer.**

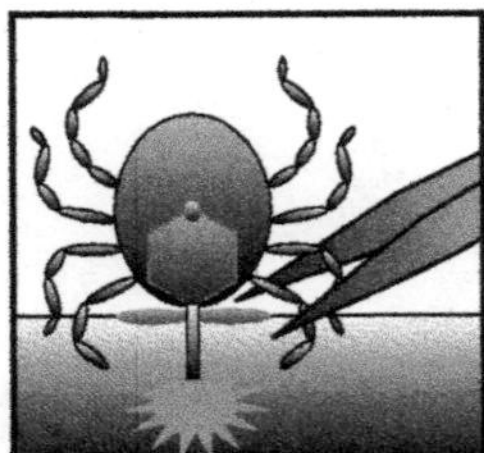

Grasp the tick's body close to the skin using a fine-tip tweezer. Avoid squeezing the body.

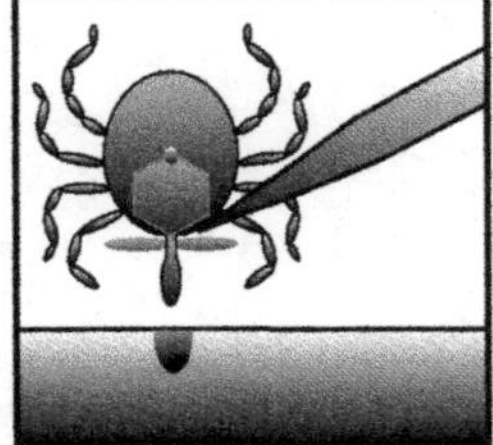

Remove by pulling the tick straight upward without using twisting motions.

TREATMENT PLAN

A. Antibiotics are effective against Lyme disease.

B. If you are prescribed doxycycline, avoid exposure to the sun because a rash may develop.

Activity: As tolerated.

Diet: Eat a regular diet.

Medications:

A. Acetaminophen may be taken for body aches and any fever.

B. You may be given an antibiotic for infection.

You Have Been Prescribed: ______________________________

You Need to Take: ______________________________

Take all of your antibiotics even if you feel better.

You Need to Notify the Office If You Have:

1. No signs of improvement with antibiotic therapy.
2. Red rash that develops.
3. Development of a high fever.
4. Other: ______________________________

Phone: ______________________________

MONONUCLEOSIS

PROBLEM

Mononucleosis (mono) is an acute, infectious, viral disease. Mono causes fever, sore throat, and swollen lymph glands.

CAUSE

Epstein–Barr virus causes mono and is spread to other persons by kissing, sharing food, and coughing without covering your mouth.

PREVENTION

A. Avoid contact with persons diagnosed with mono.

B. Cover your mouth and nose when you cough or sneeze to prevent the spread of infection.

C. Use tissues to blow your nose and throw it away.

D. If you do not have a tissue, use the "elbow sneeze" using the bend of your arm.

E. Wash your hands or use hand sanitizer.

TREATMENT PLAN

There is no specific cure. Gargle with warm salt water for a sore throat.

Activity:

A. Mono makes you very tired; rest in bed, then gradually return to normal activity.

B. You should not do any physical activity, especially contact sports (football, soccer, basketball, etc.), unless you have been cleared by your health care provider.

Diet: Eat a high-calorie diet. Drink plenty of liquids (at least 8 glasses a day).

Medications:

A. Acetaminophen may be taken for body aches.

B. You may be given an antibiotic for infection if indicated.

You Have Been Prescribed: ______________________________

You Need to Take: ______________________________

Take all of your antibiotics even if you feel better.

You Need to Notify the Office If You Have:

A. Fever more than 102°F.

B. Severe pain in the upper left abdomen (rupture of the spleen is a medical emergency).

C. Swallowing or breathing difficulty from a severe throat inflammation.

D. Rash: A rash may follow the use of antibiotics.

E. Other ______________________________

Phone: ______________________________

ROCKY MOUNTAIN SPOTTED FEVER AND REMOVAL OF A TICK

PROBLEM

Ticks are vectors for Lyme disease and Rocky Mountain Spotted Fever. You have been diagnosed with Rocky Mountain Spotted Fever.

CAUSE

Rocky Mountain Spotted Fever is caused by a bacterium from ticks.

PREVENTION

A. Avoid areas with large deer populations.

B. Wear light-colored clothes to make ticks easier to spot. Wear long sleeves and tuck pants into the socks to form a barrier.

C. Stick to hiking trails. Avoid contact with overgrown foliage. Ticks prefer dense woods with thick growth of shrubs and small trees as well as along the edge of the woods.

D. Check for ticks after each outdoor activity, especially hairy regions of the body and beltline where ticks often attach. Check for ticks prior to bathing, especially at the back of the neck, knees, and ears.

E. Remove ticks promptly (see instructions below).

F. Inspect pets daily and remove ticks when present.

G. Some manufacturers currently offer permethrin-treated clothing that is effective for up to 20 washings. This clothing is not recommended for children.

H. Antibiotic therapy to prevent Rocky Mountain Spotted Fever is not recommended for tick exposure. Instead, tell your health care provider if any symptom, especially fever and headache, occurs in the following 14 days.

I. Use tick repellent with DEET (except for small children younger than 2 years). As an alternative, picaridin and oil of eucalyptus preparations have been approved for use as repellents by the U.S. EPA.

REMOVAL OF TICKS PRECAUTIONS

A. Do not hold a lighted match or cigarette to the tick. Do not apply gasoline, kerosene, or oil to the tick's body.

B. Old treatments, including using nail polish, petroleum jelly should not be used to remove ticks.

C. Avoid squeezing the body of the tick.

D. Grasp the tick with a fine-tip tweezer close to the skin. Remove by gently pulling the tick upward straight out without using any twisting motions (see illustrations that follow).

E. If you use your fingers to remove ticks, protect your fingers with facial tissue or gloves. Wash your hands with soap and water or use rubbing alcohol after removal of the tick.

F. Do not crush the tick during removal.

G. **Save the tick for identification in case you become ill. Write the date of the tick bite on paper, place the paper and the tick in a resealable baggie, and place it in the freezer.**

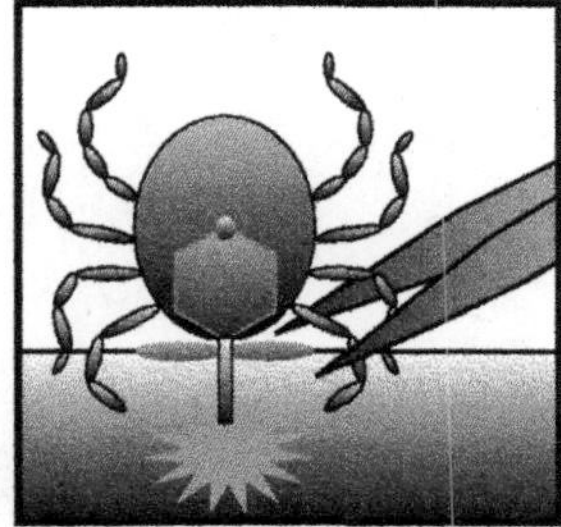

Grasp the tick's body close to the skin using a fine-tip tweezer. Avoid squeezing the body.

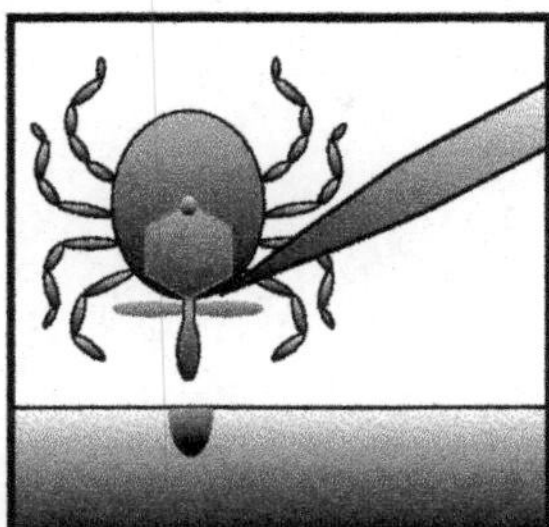

Remove by pulling the tick straight upward without using twisting motions.

TREATMENT PLAN

Activity: As tolerated, regular activity. Tepid sponge baths may be taken for fever.

Diet: Eat regular diet. Drink 8 to 10 glasses of water daily.

Medications:

A. Acetaminophen (Tylenol) may be taken for body aches.

B. You may be given an antibiotic for secondary infection, if needed.

You Have Been Prescribed: ______________________________

You Need to Take: ______________________________

Take all of your antibiotic even if you feel better.

You Need to Notify the Office If You Have:

A. No improvement while on antibiotic therapy.

B. Development of a high fever.

C. Red rash that develops, especially if it looks like a target's bullseye.

D. Decreased urinary output.

E. Dryness in your skin or mouth.

F. Other: ______________________________

Phone: ______________________________

TOXOPLASMOSIS

PROBLEM

Toxoplasmosis is an infection acquired through contact with infected cat feces or from eating raw or undercooked meat.

CAUSE

Toxoplasmosis is caused by a parasite. Cats are the primary host and humans are the intermediate host. **You do not need to destroy your cat.**

PREVENTION

A. Avoid uncooked eggs and unpasteurized milk.

B. Wash hands after handling raw meat.

C. Meat should be thoroughly cooked at 152°F or higher, or frozen for 24 hours in a household freezer before eating (smoked meats and meats cured in brine are considered safe). Avoid tasting meat while cooking.

D. Wash fruits and vegetables before eating.

E. Wash all kitchen surfaces that come into contact with uncooked meats.

F. Avoid drinking unfiltered water in any setting.

G. Use care in gardening where cats have access.

H. Wear gloves for gardening and landscaping.

I. Wear gloves for handling kitty litter, and wash hands after contact with cats. **Change kitty litter daily.**

J. Keep outdoor sandboxes covered.

K. Domestic cats can be protected from infection by feeding them commercially prepared cat food and preventing them from eating undercooked kitchen scraps and hunting wild rodents.

L. If you are not pregnant and have toxoplasmosis, you should not get pregnant for at least 6 months.

TREATMENT PLAN

A. If you are pregnant, you may be referred to a specialist.

B. If you have AIDS, you will be referred to a specialist.

Activity: There is no activity restriction for toxoplasmosis.

Diet: There is no special diet for toxoplasmosis. Avoid uncooked eggs and unpasteurized milk. Meat should be thoroughly cooked.

Medications: Depending on your risk, you may be prescribed one or two medications. You may be required to take the medication for several weeks.

You Have Been Prescribed: ____________________

You Need to Take: ____________________

You Need to Notify the Office If You Have:

A. Headache, dull and constant, with no relief from acetaminophen (Tylenol).

B. Abnormal speech.

C. Seizures.

D. Loss of visual acuity.

E. Poor concentration, forgetfulness.

F. Personality changes.

G. Other: ____________________

Phone: ____________________

Patient Teaching Guides for Chapter 19: Systemic Disorders

- Iron-Deficiency Anemia
- Pernicious Anemia
- Reference Resources for Patients With HIV/AIDS

IRON-DEFICIENCY ANEMIA

PROBLEM

You have been diagnosed with iron-deficiency anemia. Iron is an important building block for red cells. Red blood cells carry oxygen to the body.

CAUSES

Iron-deficiency anemia is the most common form of anemia. Your body may not be making enough iron, which means it is making fewer red blood cells that are too small.

Or you may have anemia from a loss of blood somewhere in your body.

Your body normally gets iron through your diet and by your body reusing old red blood cells. However, when these needs are not met, then the body becomes anemic.

Common causes of iron loss are:

A. History of heavy, long, or frequent menstrual periods or abnormal postmenopausal bleeding

B. Cancer of the esophagus, stomach, or colon

C. Esophageal varices

D. Use of aspirin, or arthritis medication, for a long period of time, which may cause gastrointestinal bleeding

E. Peptic ulcer disease

F. Celiac disease

G. Crohn's disease

H. Gastric bypass surgery

I. Taking too many antacids that contain calcium

J. Strict vegetarian diet

PREVENTION

A. Everyone's diet should include iron. Red meat, liver, and egg yolks are important sources of iron.

B. Increase the intake of iron-fortified flour, bread, and cereals.

C. Eat more foods that are higher in iron during periods of time when you are at risk for anemia, such as pregnancy and menstrual periods.

D. Elderly patients who have a poor appetite or do not eat three to four meals a day should also increase their dietary intake of iron.

TREATMENT PLAN

A. Initial treatment starts with finding the cause of your anemia. Blood work may be performed to measure your iron levels before starting treatment. Most of the time iron-deficiency anemia can be treated with iron supplementation.

B. Iron supplementation is needed to build up the iron stores in your body as directed by your health care provider. Ways to increase your iron stores include:
   1. Take iron supplements on an empty stomach.
   2. If you take antacids, you should take your iron supplement 2 hours before or 4 hours after your antacid to improve the iron absorption.
   3. Take iron supplements with vitamin C, which improves the absorption of iron.

C. Intravenous iron may be necessary if the iron is not well absorbed in the gastrointestinal tract.

Activity

Iron-deficiency anemia does not impair your activity unless you are experiencing extreme fatigue, weakness, shortness of breath, or dizziness. Fall precautions are essential if you are experiencing any of these symptoms.

Diet

A. It is recommended to increase your diet with iron-rich foods. Some suggestions of iron-rich foods may include:
   1. Meat: beef, pork, or lamb, especially liver
   2. Poultry: chicken, turkey, and duck, especially dark meats
   3. Fish—especially shellfish, sardines, and anchovies
   4. Leafy green cabbage family members such as broccoli, kale, turnip greens
   5. Legumes including lima beans, peas, pinto beans, and black-eyed peas
   6. Peanut butter
   7. Whole-grain bread, iron-enriched pastas, grains, rice, and cereals

You Have Been Prescribed the Following Medication: ______________________________

Iron supplements should be taken on an empty stomach.

Take iron supplements with a glass of orange juice or with a vitamin C tablet.

If you take antacids, take the iron supplement 2 hours before or 4 hours after the antacid to improve absorption.

Iron supplements may turn your stools black, which is a harmless side effect.

You Need to Notify the Office If You Have:

A. Shortness of breath, rapid heartbeat, or chest pain with activity

B. Constipation unresolved using over-the-counter preparations or if you have the need for daily use of preparation for constipation

C. Upcoming surgery

D. Other: ______________________________

Phone: ______________________________

PERNICIOUS ANEMIA

PROBLEM

You have been diagnosed with a condition called pernicious anemia. It is a condition in which vitamin B_{12} is not well absorbed. Vitamin B_{12} is necessary for red blood cell function.

CAUSE

Pernicious anemia is a common problem in pregnancy, with vegetarian diets, with previous stomach problems, and as you get older. Your condition may be due to the lack of a special factor in your stomach juices whereby your body cannot absorb the vitamin, or it may be from an autoimmune reaction.

PREVENTION

Pernicious anemia cannot always be prevented, but it is treatable once the cause is identified.

TREATMENT PLAN

A. You will need vitamin B_{12} injections for the rest of your life. This treatment cannot be given in pill form.
   1. After you have been on the shots for a while, the nurses can teach you or a family member to give the shot. Please ask your health care provider about this.
   2. Common side effects of vitamin B_{12} shots include:
      a. Pain and burning at the place the shot is given. This does not last very long.
      b. Some people experience diarrhea after taking the shot.

B. You may need to take iron tablets too.

C. You may be sent to see a nutritionist to help you review your diet and how you prepare foods.

Activity: Pernicious anemia may cause the loss of some senses and give you numbness and tingling, memory loss, loss of coordination, and some depression or irritability.

A. It is important to avoid extremely hot foods and drinks.

B. It is important to use caution in your home such as:
   1. Do not use loose "scatter" rugs, which can cause slips.
   2. Install shower or tub rails to help get in and out as well as toilet rails to get up and down easier.
   3. Use hand rails going up and down stairs.
   4. Do not use extremely hot water for bathing, showers, and doing dishes.
   5. Use nonslip surfaces in the tub and shower.
   6. **Do not use a heating pad if you do not have all your sensations in order to avoid burns.**

A home safety evaluation should be done to reduce the risk of falls. A checklist can be obtained from

National Safety Council: 1250 Eye Street, NW Suite 1000, Washington, DC 20005; www.homesafetycouncil.org.

Diet: A balanced, healthy diet is important. Increase your liquids to 8 to 10 glasses a day; iron supplements tend to cause constipation. Increase the fiber in your diet.

Medication:

You Have Been Prescribed the Following Iron Supplement: ______________________________

You Need to Take It: ______________________________

Your Next Vitamin B_{12} Shot Is Due: ______________________________

You Need to Notify the Office If: ______________________________

A. You feel worse the first week after the shot or have symptoms such as chest pain and shortness of breath.

B. You have worsening symptoms such as problems with balance and walking.

C. You have leg pain, especially when you put your weight on it.

D. You would like to make arrangements for home injections.

E. Other: ______________________________

Phone: ______________________________

REFERENCE RESOURCES FOR PATIENTS WITH HIV/AIDS

A. The Body, The Complete HIV/AIDS Resource is the most visited Internet site about HIV: www.thebody.com

B. The "well" project is designed for HIV-positive women, children, and family: www.thewellproject.org/hiv-information/women-children-family

C. The AIDS InfoNet provides reliable and up-to-date treatment information: www.aidsinfonet.org

D. HIVandHepatitis.com provides information about coinfection with hepatitis B and hepatitis C: www.hivandhepatitis.com

E. AIDS HEALTHCARE Foundation: www.aidshealth.org

F. HI-5 Information for Victory: www.aidsnetpa.org/onlineresources.html

G. Centers for Disease Control and Prevention (CDC) provides general information on HIV: www.cdc.gov/hiv

H. POZ Health Services Directory is a comprehensive guide to HIV care and services: directory.poz.com/napwa

I. Project Inform: Information, Inspiration, and Advocacy for People with HIV/AIDS and Hepatitis C
   1. Includes Spanish resources
   2. Provides multiple topics including the latest treatment options
   3. www.projectinform.org

Patient Teaching Guides for Chapter 20: Musculoskeletal Disorders

- Ankle Exercises
- Knee Exercises
- Neck Exercises
- RICE Therapy and Exercise Therapy

ANKLE EXERCISES

A. Education
 1. Exercise in your bare feet or in stocking feet.
 2. Count slowly (1,001, 1,002, etc.) when you must hold a position and count.
 3. Do each exercise 10 times the first day, and increase the repetitions by five each following day until you reach a maximum of 30, unless otherwise instructed.
 4. Repeat prescribed exercises three times a day.
 5. Exercise slowly and get the greatest stretch possible.
 6. Stop any exercise that causes new, unusual, or intense pain.
 7. You need to perform daily stretching exercises and toning to speed your recovery.
 8. It takes months to adequately heal these types of injuries. Therefore, do not be discouraged that it takes time for your ankle to heal.
 9. Sports to avoid: Stop-and-go activity, basketball, running, and impact aerobics.
 10. You may need to wear a velcro ankle brace or high-top tennis shoes for support.

B. Toe and foot bend (floor)
 1. Sit on the floor or bed with legs out straight.
 2. Bend the injured foot back toward the head and curl toes.
 3. Then point injured foot away and bend toes back.

C. Toe rise and foot slide (chair)
 1. Sit in a chair with knees bent at a right angle and feet flat on the floor.
 2. Raise all toes on the injured foot and slide the foot back 3 to 4 inches.
 3. Relax.
 4. Continue the sliding and toe raising until heel can no longer be kept on the floor.

D. Toe and foot bends (chair)
 1. Sit in a chair with knees bent at a right angle and feet flat on floor.
 2. Slide the foot on the injured side forward as far as possible while keeping the toes and heel in contact with the floor.
 3. From the straight-leg position, bend the foot toward the head as far as possible.
 4. Lower your foot back onto the floor.
 5. Bend the foot back and forth from the straight-leg position.

E. Heel-cord stretch
 1. Stand straight and face a wall with feet together, arms straight out, and palms flat against the wall.
 2. Lean toward the wall, bending the elbows, to stretch the cords above the heels.
 3. Continue leaning to a count of five and then straighten up again.

F. Inner-tube stretch (1)
 1. Sit with feet dangling side by side at a right angle to your legs.
 2. Tie stretch bands around your feet until they are snug.
 3. Keeping ankles together, move toes as far apart as possible.
 4. Hold the stretch for a count of five.

G. Inner-tube stretch (2)
 1. Sit with feet dangling.
 2. Cross your feet at the ankles.
 3. Tie bands snugly around feet.
 4. Move toes as far apart as possible.
 5. Hold the stretch for a count of five.

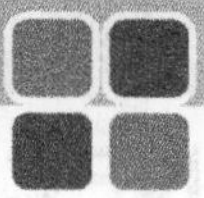

KNEE EXERCISES

CARE FOR YOUR KNEE

Please follow the type of exercises recommended for your knee. You may begin straight-leg raises after the pain resolves. Continue to wear your brace with activities as directed. It may take months for your knee to completely heal. You may gradually resume normal activity as directed by your provider. If you are not sure what activities you may perform, ask your provider before performing the activity.

A. Quad sets
   1. Exercise may be done while standing, sitting, or lying down.
   2. Straighten knee with intensity.
   3. Hold for 10 counts, then relax.
   4. Repeat the exercise three to four times per day.
   5. If a cast or splint is in place, straighten the knee until the front of the thigh and the cast pinch together.
   6. If the knee is bent, keep the foot planted and use the floor to push against.

B. Co-contractions
   1. Similar to quads, but the difference is to tighten the entire thigh while straightening the knee.
   2. Hold for 10 counts, then relax.
   3. Repeat the exercise approximately three to four times a day.

C. Hamstring sets
   1. Pull the leg back against the other foot, floor, or cast.
   2. Hold approximately 10 counts, then relax.
   3. Perform these sets three to four times a day.

D. Heel lifts
   1. Lie on back with support under the knee.
   2. Lift the heel while resting the knee on support.
   3. Make the knee as straight as possible.
   4. Hold for 10 counts, then relax.
   5. Do not use weights.
   6. Perform these exercises three to four times a day.

E. Straight-leg raises
   1. Straighten the knee.
   2. Lift and pause for 5 to 10 counts, then relax.
   3. Lower leg and relax, then repeat.
   4. Do three to five sets, three to four times a day. Rest between each set.
   5. Start with ____________ pounds of ankle weight and work up to ____________ pounds.
   6. Gradually increase weight used.

F. Hip flexors
   1. While sitting, lift the knee toward the chest.
   2. Hold for 10 counts, then relax.
   3. Lower the leg and relax. Repeat.
   4. Do 10 times, three to four times a day.
   5. Start with ____________ pounds of weight and work up gradually to ____________ pounds.
   6. The weights should be on the knee or ankle.

G. Hamstring stretches
   1. While seated on a sturdy table with the foot of your injured leg resting on the floor, lean forward with chin directed toward toes.
   2. Hold for at least 10 counts, then relax.
   3. The knee should be straight from your hips.
   4. **Do not do this exercise with bouncing or violent movements.**
   5. Do ____________ minutes, ____________ times a day.

NECK EXERCISES

Start each exercise slowly. Ease off the exercise if you start to have pain. Neck exercises are necessary for postural awareness, to prevent your muscles from becoming stiff, to stretch the neck muscles; relaxation techniques help prevent further injury of the neck. An overworked neck may cause pain in your head, upper back, shoulders, and arms. You may feel tingling or numbness of fingers.

PREVENTION: MEASURES TO PREVENT NECK PAIN

A. Avoid bending over a desk when working on computer, reading, or writing.

B. Raise your work to eye level, keeping you from bending your head down.

C. Change your position often. Take breaks when working on something for a long period of time and do some stretching exercises.

D. Putting too many pillows under your head can cause a "kink" in your neck. Avoid sleeping on your stomach.

TREATMENT PLAN

Neck exercises—try to do these exercises three times a day repeating each exercise 5 to 10 times each.

A. Active Range of Motion
   1. Turn head to each side as if you were looking over your shoulder.
   2. Bend head sideways, bringing ear toward each shoulder.
   3. Tuck chin, in bringing head forward toward chest.
   4. Shrug your shoulders and then roll them around as far as possible.

B. Stretching Exercise
   1. To stretch to the right side, place your right hand behind your head and bring your chin toward your chest.
   2. To stretch to the left side, drop the left shoulder down and tilt the right ear to the right shoulder.
   3. Lie on your back. Nod your head, bringing your chin toward your throat.
   4. Squeeze or pinch your shoulder blades together, keeping your chin tucked.

You Need to Notify the Office If You Have: (use A B C)

A. Increased pain in neck

B. Numbness and tingling of fingers and hands

C. Other physical symptoms (due to exercise)

D. Other____________________

Phone: ____________________

RESOURCES

Allina Hospitals and Clinics: Home Exercise Program for Neck Pain at www.allina.com

Exercise: A Guide From the National Institute on Aging. NIH Free Publication No. 01-4258. www.nih.gov.nia

Kaiser Permanente: Neck Arthritis-Exercises at www.kp.org. Enter V867 in the search box to learn more about neck exercises

RICE THERAPY AND EXERCISE THERAPY

RICE therapies are used for muscle injuries. RICE stands for **r**est, **i**ce, **c**ompression, and **e**levation.

REST

A. Take it easy; eliminate abuse; reduce regular exercise or activities of daily living as needed, but do not eliminate them.
B. Change activity or components of activity; for example, change running to walking.
C. Stop sports; restrict squatting, kneeling, and repetitious bending.
D. Limit weight bearing; immobilize with crutches for partial weight bearing.

ICE

A. Use cold in the acute phase of the injury (first 72 hours) to reduce pain and swelling.
B. Use cold in the form of ice in a plastic bag or even use frozen peas in a bag.
C. Apply cold four to eight times a day for 20 minutes at a time, with 45 to 60 minutes between applications.

COMPRESSION

A. Use elastic bandages, dry or wet, or open basket weave tape.
B. Avoid trying to provide support with elastic bandages; a brace, overlap taping, or a cast may be needed.

ELEVATION

A. Elevate the joint above the level of the heart to reduce swelling.
B. Apply cold compresses while the joint is elevated.

EXERCISE THERAPY

A. Begin exercise therapy after initial 48-hour period if pain and swelling begin to resolve.
B. Do gentle range-of-motion exercises several times a day within limits of pain for 7 to 10 days after knee ligament strain.
C. Exercise after 6 minutes of icing to take advantage of the cold's numbing effect.
D. Start with nonresistive, non-weight-bearing exercises.
E. Use exercises that improve range of motion and strength.
F. Maintain fitness of the extremity.

Patient Teaching Guides for Chapter 21: Rheumatology

- Fibromyalgia
- Gout
- Osteoarthritis
- Osteoporosis
- Polymyalgia Rheumatica
- Systemic Lupus Erythematous (SLE)

FIBROMYALGIA

PROBLEM

You have inflammation or pain in the muscles and connective tissues, usually noted in the lower back, shoulders, neck, chest, arms, hips, and thighs. This pain is chronic, and you may also have excessive fatigue and stiffness, difficulty with sleeping, and possibly other symptoms of anxiety, stress, and/or depression.

CAUSE

The cause is unknown. Fibromyalgia has been linked to anxiety, depression, and stress.

TREATMENT PLAN/CARE

A. Get regular exercise.

B. Get adequate amounts of sleep.

C. For symptoms of discomfort, you may try applying heat to the areas of pain, such as hot showers, heating pad, and whirlpools.

D. Gentle massages by a massage therapist may help with comfort.

E. Try to eliminate the daily stress in your life.

F. Consider alternatives to relieving stress, such as biofeedback, relaxation techniques, and yoga.

G. Notify your health care provider if you are having symptoms of anxiety or depression that need addressing and possibly treated with medications.

Activity: Regular exercise is recommended. Exercise at least 30 minutes for three to five times a week if possible. Even 5 minutes is better than no exercise. Establish a regular sleep time. Adequate and sound sleeping may decrease symptoms. You may require naps during the day.

Diet: Eat a nutritious regular diet. Increase your intake of fruits and vegetables. Avoid foods, caffeine, and alcohol that interfere with your normal sleep.

Medications: There are medications to help with your fibromyalgia. You may be prescribed one of these by your health care provider. Examples may include duloxetine (Cymbalta), milnacipran (Savella), or pregabalin (Lyrica).

You may also need to treat other symptoms accordingly:

1. Pain can be addressed with nonsteroidal anti-inflammatories such as ibuprofen or naproxen.
2. Sleep disorder: Address this with your health care provider for treatment.
3. Anxiety/stress/depression: Address this with your health care provider.

You Have Been Prescribed: ______________________________

You Need to Take: ______________________________

You Need to Notify the Office If You Have:

A. New or unexplained symptoms that have developed.

B. Fever higher than 100.0°F.

C. Other: ______________________________

Phone: ______________________________

RESOURCE

The National Fibromyalgia Association: www.fmaware.org

GOUT

PROBLEM

Gout is caused by high uric acid deposits in the joints, which produce pain and swelling at the joint. Gout commonly occurs in the big toe; however, other joints may be affected too. Other signs/symptoms include red, hot, and swollen joints, which may be tender to the touch. Gout also produces tophi, which are uric acid crystals that have formed under the skin, such as the edge of the ear, elbow, fingers and toes, and near the Achilles tendon.

Gout is the result of too much uric acid production or not enough uric acid excretion from the kidney.

PREVENTION/CARE

A. The goal is to prevent recurrences of the attacks.

B. Acute attacks: You may use warm or cool compresses to affected areas for comfort.

C. Avoid weight-bearing objects on the affected joint.

D. Take your medication as prescribed.

Activity: When you have an attack, resting the joint is the best treatment. Drinking large amounts of water will keep your urine diluted to help prevent kidney stones.

Diet:

A. Drink 10 to 12 glasses of water a day. Avoid dehydration.

B. Refrain from alcohol (beer, liquor). These will worsen your symptoms or trigger a new attack.

C. If overweight, you need to begin a weight-loss program appropriate for you.

D. Avoid crash diets. These will also precipitate an acute attack.

E. Foods to avoid: Purine-rich foods such as some seafood, sardines, anchovies, red meat and organ meats (liver, kidney), dried beans, shrimp, and sweet bread, as well as foods high in fructose corn syrup (soda, cakes, cookies, etc.).

F. Foods to increase: Dairy products, whole grains and vegetables, and coffee.

Medications: Medications to avoid: Salicylates (aspirin). This can interfere with the kidney trying to get rid of the high uric acid levels.

You may be prescribed medications for pain, such as anti-inflammatories (ibuprofen or naproxen), steroids, pain relievers (acetaminophen), or colchicine.

You Have Been Prescribed: ____________________

You Need to Take: ____________________

You Need to Notify the Office If You Have:

A. Acute attacks.

B. Fever higher than 101°F.

C. Rash.

D. Swelling of extremities.

E. Vomiting/diarrhea.

F. Signs/symptoms not improving within 3 to 4 days after starting therapy.

G. Any adverse effects from your medication.

Phone: ____________________

OSTEOARTHRITIS

PROBLEM

Osteoarthritis (OA) is a very common disorder that affects the weight-bearing and movable joints. OA damages the cartilage tissue in the joint. The cartilage provides the cushion around the joint. If the cartilage becomes damaged, it will become inflamed and irritated and start to thin. When this occurs, there is less cushion between the bones, and you will experience more pain and swelling. The joints most commonly involved are the finger and toe joints, knees, hips, and spine.

CAUSES

There are many causes of OA. A previous injury to the joint, repeated stress to the joint (like a bricklayer's hands), genetics, age, obesity, and other diseases (such as diabetes or infections) may cause OA.

TREATMENT

A. The goal of treatment is to prevent further joint damage.

B. Learn as much as you can about this disorder and ask your health care provider lots of questions.

C. Heat and massage may increase joint movement and decrease pain.

D. Physical or occupational therapy may be needed.

E. Heat or ice packs may be used for localized relief.

Activity:

Exercise:

1. Range-of-motion exercises increase the movement of the joint.
2. Careful exercise may also strengthen the muscles around the joint.
3. Ask your provider what's the best type of exercise for you.
4. Yoga and acupuncture have been shown to help relieve pain and stiffness.

Joint protection:

1. Don't overuse a joint.
2. If you work with your hands and have OA of the fingers, take frequent rest periods. This applies to all the other joints as well.

Diet: A low-fat, low-cholesterol diet may be suggested. Losing weight is recommended if you are overweight and if you have OA of the knees, hips, or spine.

Studies show that for every 1 pound of weight loss there is approximately a 4-pound weight stress reduction on the knees/joint.

Medications: Your health care provider may recommend that you take acetaminophen or an anti-inflammatory drug. This should help relieve the pain and stiffness. Special creams also sometimes help joint pain. In cases of severe OA, your health care provider may recommend an injection to the joint. For severe pain, surgery may be required.

Remember to take only the medicines prescribed for you.

You Have Been Prescribed: ______________________

You Need to Take: ______________________

You Need to Notify the Office If You Have:

A. Increased pain despite medication.

B. Fever higher than 100.4°F.

C. Abdominal pain or discomfort after taking medicine.

Phone: ______________________

RESOURCE

Arthritis Foundation
800-283-7800
www.arthritis.org

OSTEOPOROSIS

PROBLEM

Osteoporosis is a condition in which the bone loses its normal density, mass, and strength, which makes it weak and more vulnerable to fracture (break).

CAUSES

The weakening of the bone can be caused by several factors. Some of these risk factors include:

A. Inadequate amounts of calcium and vitamin D in the diet
B. Decreased exercise
C. Some chronic diseases such as thyroid disease, diabetes, and heart failure
D. Cancer
E. Smoking
F. Low estrogen levels (menopause)
G. Excessive alcohol intake
H. Advancing age
I. Ethnicity: Caucasian and Asian woman
J. Long-term use of certain medications such as steroids, thyroid medications, seizure medications, and some cancer treatment medications

PREVENTION

A. Calcium intake: Be sure to get adequate calcium intake.

Dietary intake of **calcium** is recommended for the following:

Men younger than 50 years: 1,000 mg/d

Men 50 to 69 years: 1,000 mg/d

Men older than 70 years: 1,200 mg/d

Women younger than or equal to 50 years: 1,000 mg/d

Women older than 50 years: 1,200 mg/d

Calcium supplements such as calcium carbonate or calcium citrate are recommended. Do not exceed more than 500 mg at one time. If taking two tablets to meet requirements, divided doses are recommended for best absorption.

Vitamin D intake: Be sure to get adequate vitamin D intake daily.

B. Dietary intake of vitamin D is recommended for the following:

Men younger than 50 years: 400 to 800 IU/d

Men 50 to 69 years: 800 to 1,000 IU/d

Men older than 70 years: 800 to 1,000 IU/d

Women younger than or equal to 50 years: 400 to 800 IU/d

Women older than 50 years: 800 to 1,000 IU/d

Food sources of vitamin D include milk fortified with vitamin D, salmon, egg yolks, cod liver oil, tuna, liver, and cereals fortified with vitamin D.

C. Avoid excessive alcohol intake.

D. Avoid smoking and/or encourage smoking cessation.

TREATMENT PLAN

A. If osteoporosis is suspected, your provider may order a bone density study of your bones. Goals are to prevent the disease from occurring.
B. If you have been diagnosed with osteoporosis, you need to prevent the disease from progressing and take measures to prevent all bone fractures.
C. Use caution when walking on wet, slippery surfaces.
D. Avoid risk of falls by making your home safe. Avoid throw rugs on floors and remove small items that are easily tripped over. Use caution when pets are around to prevent falling over your pet.

Activity:

A. Physical activity is vital to maintain and prevent further bone loss.

B. Weight-bearing activity is the best activity, such as walking or running for at least 30 minutes a day, 3 days a week.

C. Avoid high-impact sports and activities such as jumping and high-impact aerobics to prevent fracturing the bones.

D. Avoid any risk of falls.

E. Use walking devices, such as a cane or walker if needed.

F. Bathtubs should have nonskid protection.

Diet:

A. Eat a regular well-balanced diet. Increase food sources rich in calcium and vitamin D.

B. Sources of vitamin D include milk, some fish (salmon, tuna), egg yolks, cod liver oil, liver, and drinks and cereals fortified with vitamin D and minerals.

C. You can also get vitamin D from spending 20 to 30 minutes in the summer sunlight, exposing your skin to the sun without wearing sunscreen for this length of time.

D. Sources of calcium include dairy products, green leafy vegetables (kale and broccoli), almonds, tofu, milk, dairy products (cottage cheese, cheese, yogurt), and drinks fortified with calcium such as orange juice and soy milk.

E. If you are overweight, a low-fat, low-cholesterol diet is suggested to lose weight.

Medications:

A. You may be prescribed nonprescription medications like acetaminophen (Tylenol) as needed for pain.

B. Supplements: Calcium, vitamin D, and hormone replacement for women who are menopausal.

C. Bisphosphonates:
   1. If prescribed a bisphosphonate, take the medication with a full glass of water.
   2. Wait approximately 30 to 60 minutes before reclining or consuming other medications, beverages, or food to lower the risk of regurgitation or a burning sensation.

You Have Been Prescribed: ____________________

You Need to Take: ____________________

You Need to Notify the Office If You Have:

A. Been experiencing any pain; you need to have your provider assess this pain.

B. Other: ____________________

Phone: ____________________

RESOURCES

National Osteoporosis Foundation: www.nof.org

The National Women's Health Information Center: www.4women.gov/FAQ/osteoporosis.cfm

POLYMYALGIA RHEUMATICA

PROBLEM

Polymyalgia rheumatica (PMR) is a common disorder experienced by adults older than the age of 50 years in which complaints involve overall joint stiffness and pain. Common complaints include feeling fine one day and the next day having overall joint pain, with difficulty getting out of bed or standing up from a chair. Symptoms may occur gradually over a period of several days or weeks, or may appear abruptly over night. Symptoms are usually worse in the morning hours. The joints most commonly affected are the upper arms, thighs, hips, buttocks, and neck.

CAUSES

A. The cause of PMR is unknown.

B. Some theories maintain that PMR may be triggered by an infection; however, research does not identify any specific infection.

PREVENTION

There is not any way to prevent the onset of PMR.

TREATMENT PLAN

A. You may be treated with low dose steroids by mouth. Prednisone is a common medication used to treat this disorder. Stiffness and joint pain may quickly improve with the use of oral steroids. If improvement with steroids does not occur within 2 weeks of treatment, you should notify your provider.

B. Once improvement is noted, your provider will begin to lower the steroid dose gradually over time. This may take several weeks to months.

C. Do not change or taper your steroid dose on your own. Your provider will advise you on the tapering dose when appropriate.

Activity:

A. Once stiffness and pain have improved, you may resume normal activities. Exercise is encouraged on most days of the week.

Diet:

A. There is not any special diet to follow for this disorder.

B. Blood sugar: Side effects of the prednisone may include increased blood sugar. If you have concerns regarding your blood sugar values, or if you are diabetic, you need to discuss proper management and monitoring of your blood sugar while taking steroids.

Medications:

A. Oral steroids (prednisone) are commonly prescribed over a period of time. Discuss proper dosages and tapering of this medication with your provider.

You Have Been Prescribed: ______________________________

You Need to Take: ______________________________

You Need to Notify the Office If You Have:

A. Any new symptoms such as headache, jaw pain, or vision changes

B. Side effects from the prednisone or other medications prescribed

C. Increase in pain, or weakness while using prednisone

D. Any other concerns

Phone: ______________________________

RESOURCES

The Arthritis Foundation: www.arthritis.org

National Institute of Arthritis and Musculoskeletal and Skin Diseases Information Clearinghouse: www.niams.nih.gov/Health_info/Polymyalgia/default.asp

SYSTEMIC LUPUS ERYTHEMATOUS (SLE)

PROBLEM

You have been diagnosed with a condition called lupus. Lupus is a chronic, inflammatory, autoimmune disorder. There is currently no cure for lupus; however, it can be managed and can go into remission or a dormant state. Rashes, hair loss, arthritis-like joint pain, and fatigue are very common problems with lupus.

CAUSE

Lupus causes your body to attack its own cells. The exact cause is unknown. Lupus tends to run in families, but it is not contagious.

PREVENTION

There is no known prevention, only long-term management.

TREATMENT PLAN

A. Avoid sun exposure:
   1. Many lupus patients' eyes are sensitive to light; wear sunglasses and avoid direct exposure.
   2. Light exposure can make your rash worse.
   3. Apply a protective lotion or sunscreen to your skin while outside.
   4. Wear long sleeves and use hats.

B. You may be given steroids for your skin rashes or lesions.

C. Avoid exposure to drugs and chemicals.

D. Review all of your medications and over-the-counter drugs with your health care provider.

E. Avoid hair sprays and hair-coloring agents.

F. Mouth ulcers may occur with lupus:
   1. Avoid hot or spicy foods that might cause irritation to ulcers.
   2. Use good oral hygiene:
      a. Get regular dental exams.
      b. Floss your teeth daily.
      c. Brush your teeth at least twice a day.

G. Drugs called nonsteroidal anti-inflammatory drugs (NSAIDs) are used for minor joint pain.

H. It is very important for you to have your eyes examined **twice** a year to monitor eye changes.

I. Talk to your health care provider if you are planning a pregnancy.

Activity: You may get tired more easily; plan rest periods. However, you should still get some exercise as tolerated. Many people gain some weight from steroids.

Diet: Eat a regular diet as tolerated; you do not need any special foods.

Medications:

You Have Been Prescribed the Following Steroid: ______________________________

You Need to Take: ______________________________

A. Do not stop taking your steroid abruptly.

B. **Steroid medication should be tapered off (decreased until you are off of it).**

You Need to Notify the Office If:

A. You are unable to tolerate your medication.

B. You have any sign of infections, sinusitis, bronchitis, flu, urinary tract infections, and so forth.

C. You are getting worse or do not feel better.

D. You are planning a pregnancy or think you are pregnant.

E. Other: ______________________________

Phone: ______________________________

RESOURCES

Lupus Foundation of America: 800-558-0121 or www.lupus.org

Lupus Research Institute: www.lupusresearchinstitute.org

212-812-9881 e-mail: lupus@lupusny

Patient Teaching Guides for Chapter 22: Neurologic Disorders

- Bell's Palsy
- Dementia
- Managing Your Parkinson's Disease
- Migraine Headaches
- Mild Head Injury
- Myasthenia Gravis
- Transient Ischemic Attack
- Trigeminal Neuralgia

BELL'S PALSY

PROBLEM

Bell's palsy is a disorder that can occur at any age, but most frequently occurs between the ages of 20 and 60. The disorder affects the muscles associated with expression on one side of the face, including the muscles that allow the mouth to smile, the eyes to close, and the eyebrows to raise.

The exact cause of Bell's palsy remains unknown. Possible causes may include viral infections, a type of inflammatory process, or possibly an autoimmune disease.

PREVENTION/CARE

A. Bell's palsy is usually treated with a steroid, such as prednisone.

B. Pain is usually managed with acetaminophen (Tylenol) or another over-the-counter pain medication such as nonprescription anti-inflammatory medications (NSAIDs) such as ibuprofen or naproxen.

C. Sometimes it is helpful to use gentle massage or electrical stimulation of the nerve to help with the pain. Applying heat or cold packs for 15 to 20 minutes three to four times a day may also help with pain. When applying icepacks, do not directly apply ice to the skin and use caution on skin to avoid frostbite to the area.

D. Protection of the eye is very important if there is loss of lid function. Eye drops and lubricating ointment may be recommended along with taping the affected eye while sleeping. Wearing eyeglasses and/or sunglasses is recommended to protect the eye.

E. Physical therapy may also be helpful with recovering function of the muscles that are weak.

F. Symptoms usually resolve within 3 or 4 weeks to a few months. Occasionally, patients have symptoms lasting longer than this. The degree of paralysis varies in each person. If symptoms change or worsen, notify your health care provider immediately.

Activity: Engage in activities as tolerated. Use caution when performing activities requiring visual demands such as depth perception (driving, walking, etc.).

Diet: Eat a regular diet as tolerated.

Medications:

You Have Been Prescribed: ______________________________

You Need to Take: ______________________________

You Have Been Prescribed: ______________________________

You Need to Take: ______________________________

You Need to Notify the Office If You Have:

A. No relief in symptoms in 4 weeks.

B. New symptoms such as headaches, visual changes, or other problems such as trouble walking.

C. Other: ______________________________

Phone: ______________________________

RESOURCE

The Bell's Palsy Network: www.bellspalsy.ws

DEMENTIA

PROBLEM

Dementia is mental impairment due to a variety of disorders.

CAUSES

Dementia is caused by degeneration and loss of the gray matter from the brain; common causes are Alzheimer's disease, inadequate blood supply to the brain, alcoholism, chronic infections, inherited conditions, brain injury, or brain tumors.

PREVENTION

Early medical treatment is required for reversible causes of dementia. Prevention includes protection from head injury, eating a balanced diet, preventing alcoholism, avoiding drug abuse, and preventing atherosclerosis.

TREATMENT PLAN

A. Minimize changes in daily routines.

B. Provide simple memory reminders such as notes, calendars, and clocks.

C. Encourage social contacts.

D. Treat with respect.

E. Provide a safe environment.
   1. Remove scatter rugs.
   2. Install handrails and stairs.
   3. Discourage driving.
   4. Install stove cut-off switch.
   5. Lock closets.
   6. Lock up matches and firearms.

F. Encourage "thinking" games such as puzzles, word games, and reading.

G. Provide frequent gentle reorientation to surroundings.

Activity: Patient may engage in as much activity as possible with *supervision and direction*.

Diet: Eat a well-balanced diet low in saturated fat.

Medications: A variety of medications are available to treat symptoms.

You Have Been Prescribed: ______________________________

You Need to Take: ______________________________

You Need to Notify the Office If:

A. The symptoms/behaviors are getting worse.

B. You are unable to tolerate the medications due to side effects.

C. You need help with social services.

D. Other: ______________________________

Phone: ______________________________

RESOURCES

Alzheimer's Association: www.alz.org

The Alzheimer's Association's website includes information on locating the closest support group search by zip code: www.alz.org/apps/findus.aps

24/7 Helpline 1-800-272-3900

MANAGING YOUR PARKINSON'S DISEASE

PROBLEM

Parkinson's disease (PD) is a problem with the central nervous system that causes progressive muscle rigidity and tremors. The ability to move your muscles becomes difficult and you may also notice difficulty with walking and swallowing. Common symptoms you may experience include tremor at rest, rigidity (feeling stiff and finding it hard to start moving), bradykinesia (movements of your muscles slow down), and having a difficult time maintaining your posture, feeling like you are going to fall down. Other symptoms may also include difficulty speaking, swallowing, drooling more, changes in mood, and sleep patterns.

CAUSE

The brain is not able to produce or use the correct amount of a chemical, called dopamine, required by the body, and therefore the nervous system reacts by producing a loss in control of your muscles and movements.

TREATMENT PLAN/CARE

A. There is no cure for PD. However, medications may relieve a lot of your symptoms. Your health care provider will share the medications that are available to you.

B. People with PD can be very sensitive to heat. During hot weather, stay outside for very short periods of time, stay inside during the hottest part of the day, and increase your fluid intake.

C. Balance problems are common with PD and increase the risk of falls. Some ways to avoid injury are no loose rugs or other floor coverings; grab bars around the tub and toilet; a sturdy rail on stairs; adequate lighting so you can see where you are going; and straight-backed, firm chairs with arms.

D. Tremor increases the risk of accidents. Use sturdy plastic cups instead of glasses, use an electric razor to shave, and be cautious with sharp objects and power tools.

E. For clothes, Velcro fasteners, zippers, and snaps are easier to fasten than buttons. Loose clothing is also easier to put on and take off.

F. To avoid sleep problems, stay busy during the day and avoid naps. Discuss any problems you have with your neurologist; sometimes changes in your medication schedule can help.

G. If you have speech problems, work on ways to make your needs known. Practice speech exercises or consider speech therapy with a speech therapist.

H. Stay active in your daily work, hobbies, and other daily activities you enjoy.

I. If you are having signs of anxiety, depression, sleep problems, or other symptoms, please discuss these with your provider. These symptoms are common and can be addressed and treated with other medications.

Activity: Regular exercise helps maintain muscle flexibility and may reduce medication needs. Exercises to improve face, jaw, and tongue movement are encouraged.

Diet: Your diet should include plenty of fluids and adequate fiber to prevent or manage constipation. Have bran cereal in the morning and eat five or more servings of fruits and vegetables throughout the day. Bananas are low in fiber and should be avoided.

Plan medication schedules so that you are functioning well at meal times. Be sure you allow plenty of time to finish your meal.

If you need help planning your meals, your health care provider can suggest a dietitian with whom you can talk about food choices.

Alcoholic beverages are discouraged as alcohol can interfere with the effectiveness of your medications.

If you are having difficulty with swallowing, let your provider know. Take your time with eating meals. Sit upright. Thick liquids are easier to swallow than thin liquids.

Medications:

A. The medicines you are taking can improve your ability to carry out everyday activities, but they cannot totally eliminate your symptoms. It is important that you know why you are taking each medication as well as the possible side effects of each.

B. Check with your neurologist before starting any new medicine to be sure it does not interact with your PD medicines. Even vitamins can be a problem, so take only those recommended by your neurologist.

C. In case of emergency, keep with you a list of your medicines, including the amounts you take and your schedule for taking them.

You Have Been Prescribed: ______________________________

You Need to Take: ______________________________

You Need to Notify the Office If:

A. You have a reaction to your medication.

B. You are unable to tolerate your medication due to side effects.

C. Your symptoms become worse.

D. Other: ___

Phone: ___

RESOURCES

Michael J. Fox Foundation for Parkinson's Research
Grand Central Station
PO BOX 4777
New York, NY 10163-4777
www.michaeljfox.org

National Parkinson Foundation
1501 N.W. 9th Avenue/Bob Hope Road
Miami, Florida 33136-1494
1-800-473-4636
www.parkinson.org

Parkinson's Disease Foundation
1359 Broadway, Suite 1509
New York, NY 10018
212-923-4700
www.pdf.org

Worldwide Education and Awareness for Movement Disorders
www.wemove.org/par

MIGRAINE HEADACHES

PROBLEM

You have been diagnosed with migraine headaches. There are many ways that a migraine headache is described, including: pulsating, on one side of the head, behind one eye, seeing spots before your eyes, and a possible loss of vision for a short time.

Other symptoms of a migraine include nausea and vomiting; sensitivity to sound; sensitivity to light, especially to flickering lights; sensitivity to smells; and pain that gets worse with activity.

CAUSES

A. Migraines run in families; your mother or sister may also have migraines.

B. Head trauma may trigger headaches.

C. You may have a migraine headache when you start your period due to the change in your hormones.

D. Medicines, such as birth control pills and hormone replacement medicine, may cause migraines.

E. Many odors, such as smelling perfumes, cigarette smoke, scented candles, and food odors, may trigger a headache.

F. Changes in weather and high altitude may also make you have a migraine.

G. Alcohol and some foods trigger a headache.

H. Another cause of a migraine headache is a rebound from taking too many over-the-counter pain medications such as ibuprofen, Aleve, aspirin, and Excedrin products. The headache gets better with the pain products but comes back the next day so that you take the medicine again, causing a vicious cycle.

PREVENTION

A. Keep a diary to identify food triggers to your headache:
   1. Alcohol, especially red wine
   2. Foods such as hot dogs, ham, and bacon
   3. Aged cheese
   4. Citrus foods such as oranges, lemons, limes, and tomatoes
   5. Not eating

B. Read labels for the following preservatives:
   1. Aspartame—often found in yogurt
   2. Saccharin—often found in diet drinks and artificial sweeteners
   3. Tyramine—found in aged cheese such as feta, blue cheese, pickles, and olives
   4. Phenylethylamine—often found in sugarless gum and breath mints
   5. Monosodium glutamate (MSG)—often found in Chinese food
   6. Nitrates and nitrites—found in cured meats, such as ham and hot dogs

C. Keep a diary to identify visual triggers:
   1. Strobe lights
   2. Flickering light from going from sun into shade
   3. Fluorescent lights
   4. Sunlight glare off shiny objects and water

D. Keep a diary to identify other triggers, including:
   1. Too much sleep/too little sleep
   2. Strong odors
   3. Medicines
   4. Changes in weather

TREATMENT PLAN

A. One of the first things to look at is your diary of triggers in order to avoid or modify them.

B. You may be sent to a neurologist to evaluate if you need any special testing.

C. You may be sent to have your eyes examined for glasses.

D. Many medications are used to treat migraines:
   1. Over-the-counter pain medications, including Ibuprofen, Aleve, aspirin, and Excedrin in limited amounts
   2. Medications for depression are commonly used.
   3. Medications for seizures are also commonly used.
   4. Medications for blood pressure have been found to control migraines.
   5. Medications for nausea and vomiting

E. A special class of drugs called triptans is used to treat the migraine when it first starts. Some of the triptans are Imitrex, Maxalt, Zomig, Amerge, Relpax, and Frova. These medicines come in pill form and nasal spray, and are also given as a shot.

Activity: Relaxation training, such as yoga and biofeedback, helps headaches. Physical therapy and hypnosis have also helped migraine headaches.

Diet: There is no special diet for migraines.

A. Avoid the food triggers that you identified from your migraine diary.

B. Drink plenty of liquids.

You Have Been Prescribed the Following Medication for Acute Pain to Help Stop Migraines: ______________________

You Need to Take: ______________________

You Have Been Prescribed the Following Medication to Take Every Day to Manage Migraines: ______________________

You Need to Take: ______________________

You Have Been Prescribed the Following Medication for Nausea: ______________________

You Need to Take: ______________________

You Need to Notify the Office If:

A. You feel that this is the "worst headache you have ever had."

B. You have difficulty with speech.

C. You have fever with a stiff neck.

D. Other: ______________________

Phone: ______________________

RESOURCES

Mayo Clinic: www.mayoclinic.com/health/migraine-headache/DS00120

Migraine diaries are available for iPhones, iPod touch, and the iPad on iTunes.

National Institute of Neurological Disorders and Stroke: www.ninds.nih.gov/disorders/migraine/migraine.htm

WebMD Migraines & Headaches Health Center: www.webmd.com/migraines-headaches and a headache diary is located on the WebMD site: www.webmd.com/migraines-headaches/guide/headache-diary

MILD HEAD INJURY

PROBLEM

Mild head injury includes any bump, jolt, or blow to the head that affects normal brain function, possibly causing confusion or a loss of consciousness.

GUIDELINES FOR CARE AT HOME

Activity:

A. Have someone stay with you for the next 24 hours to be sure your injury does not worsen.

B. Limit physical activity, especially sports or heavy lifting.

C. Slowly increase your activities. Pace yourself, using rest periods whenever you are mentally or physically tired.

D. Do not drive or operate heavy machinery during the next 24 hours.

E. You must have approval from your primary care provider before returning to work or school.

F. Coaches or trainers must be notified of any head injury.

Diet: Do not eat or drink if you feel sick to your stomach. When you feel better, you can eat or drink anything except alcohol until cleared by your primary care provider and when your usual state of health has returned.

Medications: You should not take any medications, including those regularly taken, unless approved by your primary care provider.

INSTRUCTIONS FOR CAREGIVERS: OBSERVATION AFTER HEAD INJURY

Check the patient every 2 hours for the first 24 hours after discharge. If he or she is asleep, awaken him or her for testing.

HOW TO TEST THE PATIENT

A. Test orientation: Ask the patient to tell you his or her name, where he or she is, the year, and who you are.

B. Test the patient's strength: Ask the patient to squeeze one or two of your fingers as hard as he or she can, checking both hands at the same time, and compare them. Also have the patient lift one leg at a time off the bed and hold it up for a few seconds.

C. Have the patient open both eyes at the same time and check his or her pupils to make sure they are the same size. (The pupil is the black circular part in the center of the eye.)

D. If you are uncertain about these test results, repeat them every 5 minutes until you are sure of what you see.

WARNING SIGNS

Call the primary care provider's office or go to the emergency room if:

A. The patient cannot be easily awakened or sleeps constantly in between tests for no apparent reason.

B. The patient cannot answer orientation questions correctly or appears to be confused.

C. The patient has new or increasing weakness in any arm or leg.

D. The patient becomes very restless, agitated, is acting unusual, or has any other change in behavior.

E. One pupil is larger than the other.

F. You cannot understand what the patient is saying, or the patient has difficulty understanding what you have said.

G. The patient complains of a severe or worsening headache.

H. The patient continues to complain of nausea or begins vomiting.

I. The patient has a fever over 101.4°F.

J. The patient has a convulsion or seizure, or passes out.

K. The patient has fluid leaking from the nose or ear.

If any of the preceding events occurs or if you have any questions/concerns regarding any of the tests, please call the primary care provider or return the patient to the emergency room or clinic right away.

MYASTHENIA GRAVIS

PROBLEM

Myasthenia gravis (MG) is a chronic disorder in which the body's immune system mistakenly attacks and destroys proteins that help muscles respond to nerve impulses. This causes people to have muscle weakness that is worse with use and better with rest.

Eye muscles and muscles that help with chewing, swallowing, and talking tend to be affected the most. MG can be treated but not cured.

People with myasthenia generally have to take medicine for the rest of their lives to control the disorder. Surgery to remove their thymus gland may be necessary.

TREATMENT PLAN/CARE

A. Wear a Medic Alert tag and keep a list of medicines and the dosing schedule, along with the name and telephone number of your neurologist in case of emergency.

B. Dentists and any other health care providers should know that you have MG because many medicines can make your MG worse. Some examples of medicines that can be problems for people with MG are birth control pills, some antibiotics, and some local anesthetics. Many medicines can be problematic, so you should *never* start a new medicine without talking to your neurologist first, even if you took it in the past without having problems.

C. Any time you feel worse, particularly if you are having trouble with chewing and swallowing, you should contact your neurologist and plan to go to the hospital, because MG could possibly affect your breathing. You should have a plan for emergencies that includes how you will get to a hospital, childcare arrangements, and how to contact your neurologist.

D. An annual flu shot is recommended because infections can make MG worse.

E. Emotional upset and stress also can make MG worse. Your health care provider can supply you with information on handling stress effectively or assist in referring you to a counselor.

F. Surgery can make MG worse, so it should, when possible, be planned with your neurologist. Some changes in your medication schedules in the weeks before the surgery can make problems less likely.

G. Plasmaphoresis may be recommended to you. This procedure is performed to remove the antibodies that make the disease process worse. This procedure is similar to donating blood. Blood is removed from a vein, the antibodies are removed, and then the blood is donated back to you in another vein. This procedure may be offered to you many times since the effects are not permanent.

Activity: It is best to plan your activities to take advantage of the peak effects of your medicine and to avoid getting overtired.

Diet: A diet high in potassium-rich foods has been found by some to be helpful because low body potassium is associated with muscle weakness.

Medications:

You may be prescribed steroids or medications that improve muscle strength.

You Have Been Prescribed: ______________________

You Need to Take: ______________________

You Need to Notify the Office If:

A. You have worsening or new symptoms.

B. You are unable to tolerate your medicines due to side effects.

C. Other: ______________________

Phone: ______________________

RESOURCE

Myasthenia Gravis Foundation of America, Inc.: www.myasthenia.org

TRANSIENT ISCHEMIC ATTACK

PROBLEM/CAUSE

A transient ischemic attack (TIA) is a temporary loss of brain function due to a decrease of blood flow to the brain. It is considered a mini stroke. The symptoms may last only a few minutes, but the risk for a stroke is increased over the next week.

RISK FACTORS FOR TIAs

A. High blood pressure

B. Irregular heart beat (atrial fibrillation)

C. Smoking

D. High cholesterol

E. Being overweight

F. Diabetes

G. Obstructive sleep apnea

SUDDEN SIGNS AND SYMPTOMS OF A STROKE

F.A.S.T is an easy way to remember:

F. Face drooping

A. Arm weakness

S. Speech difficulty

T. Time to call 911

PREVENTION/CARE

A. A full workup is necessary to decide why you are having TIAs.

B. You may be referred to a neurologist—a doctor who specializes in medical problems involving the brain.

C. Special tests or surgery may be done to evaluate your heart and blood vessels. A carotid angioplasty or carotid endarterectomy are two procedures that may be performed to insert a stent into the artery or remove a blockage form the artery. Other treatment depends on your test results.

D. Treatment starts with modifying your risk factors:
   1. Lose weight.
   2. Eat a healthy diet.
   3. Lower your cholesterol.
   4. Eliminating alcohol is encouraged.
   5. If you are a diabetic, you must keep your diabetes under control to lower your risk.
   6. Do not smoke or use any tobacco products to lower your risk of a TIA and stoke.

E. Aspirin is commonly prescribed after a TIA. You may be prescribed a blood thinner. Some blood thinners require regular laboratory testing. Discuss treatment with your health care provider.

F. If you are taking a blood thinner, get a Medic Alert bracelet/necklace, or carry a card in your wallet and car in case you are in an accident. Medic Alert jewelry can be purchased at local drug stores, and there are multiple websites for ordering a Medic Alert identification. You can build your own identification bracelets or neck chains from American Medical ID: www.americanmedical-id.com/marketplace/build.php?buildwhat=bracelet

Activity: You need to exercise at least 30 minutes daily three to four times a week. Please make sure you have been released by your health care provider to begin exercising.

Diet: Eat a low-fat, low-cholesterol, and low-sodium diet.

Medications:

You Have Been Prescribed a Blood Thinner: ____________________

You Need to Take: ____________________

You Have Been Prescribed a Medicine to Lower Your Cholesterol: ____________________

You Need to Take: ____________________

WARNING SIGNS OF A TIA

If you experience any of these signs, seek medical attention (call 911) immediately.

A. Weakness or numbness of face, arm, or leg on one side of the body

B. Trouble talking or understanding others when they talk

C. Changes in eyesight such as dimness, double vision, or loss of vision

D. Dizziness, unsteadiness, or sudden falls

E. Sudden severe headaches

RESOURCES

American Heart Association
7272 Greenville Avenue
Dallas, TX 75231-4596
www.heart.org

National Stroke Association
9707 East Easter Lane, Suite B
Centennial, CO 80112-3747
www.stroke.org

There are many Stroke Risk Assessment tools including: www.yourdiseaserisk.wustl.edu/YDRDefault.aspx?ScreenControl=YDRGeneral&ScreenName=YDRStroke

TRIGEMINAL NEURALGIA

PROBLEM

Trigeminal neuralgia is a chronic condition causing extreme, sporadic, sudden burning or shock-like pain of the cheek area of the face. It occurs most often in people older than age 50. The symptoms arise from the trigeminal nerve that carries sensation from your face to your brain.

PREVENTION

A. Avoid triggers such as:
   1. Shaving
   2. Stroking face
   3. Too much pressure putting on makeup
   4. Avoiding wind exposure
   5. Vigorous washing of face
   6. Drinking too hot or cold beverages
   7. Eating tough meat or hard candies

B. If prescribed medication, take your medication as ordered and report any side effects to the primary care provider or neurologist. Avoid taking medications without provider input.

C. Pain varies and may be sudden and sporadic, affecting a small area of the face or more widespread. If pain worsens, notify your health care provider immediately.

Activity: Engage in activities as tolerated, avoiding triggers as much as possible. Use caution in activities if experiencing side effects of balance impairment, drowsiness, or dizziness.

Medications:

You Have Been Prescribed: ____________________

You Need to Notify the Office If You Are Experiencing:

A. Worsening pain

B. Side effects of medications

C. Any new symptoms

D. Other: ____________________

Phone: ____________________

RESOURCE

Mayo Clinic: Trigeminal neuralgia: www.mayoclinic.org/trigeminal-neuralgia/basics

Patient Teaching Guides for Chapter 23: Endocrine Disorders

- Addison's Disease
- Cushing's Syndrome
- Diabetes

ADDISON'S DISEASE

PROBLEM

Addison's disease has many symptoms, including weakness and fatigue, fainting or dizziness, poor appetite, weight loss, nausea, vomiting, diarrhea, abdominal discomfort, skin discoloration, and low blood pressure, as well as cravings for salty foods.

CAUSE

Addison's is most commonly caused by your body's unusual ability to attack its own tissues, called autoimmunity. This results in inadequate amounts of cortisol and/or aldosterone produced by the adrenal glands.

TREATMENT PLAN/CARE

A. Wear your identification band stating that you have Addison's disease and that lists treatment, as well as your health care provider's name and phone number.

B. Increased medication dosage will be required during any significant illness, especially with vomiting and/or diarrhea, before dental extractions, and before major surgical procedures. **These issues need to be discussed with your health care provider so you will know the correct dosage of medication to take.**

C. Have injectable cortisol available for emergencies when you are unconscious or otherwise unable to take pills.

Activity: As tolerated, avoid overexertion.

Diet: Eat a high-sodium, low-potassium, high-protein diet.

Medications:

You Have Been Prescribed: ______________________________

You Need To Take: ______________________________

You Need to Notify the Office If:

A. You have a reaction to your medications.
B. You cannot tolerate the prescribed medications.
C. You are having dental procedures or surgery to discuss adjusting your medicines.
D. You are sick with nausea and vomiting to discuss adjusting your medicines or coming into the office.
E. Other: ______________________________

Phone: ______________________________

RESOURCES

National Adrenal Diseases Foundation (NADF): www.nadf.us

You can build your own identification bracelets or neck chains from American Medical ID: www.americanmedical-id.com/marketplace/build.php?buildwhat=bracelet

CUSHING'S SYNDROME

PROBLEM

Cushing's syndrome has many symptoms, including weight gain, obesity, moon-shaped face, excessive hair growth, easy bruising, thin skin, muscle weakness, decreased or no menstrual periods, increased blood pressure, osteoporosis, and impaired wound healing.

CAUSE

Cushing's syndrome is caused by excessive cortisol production.

TREATMENT/CARE

A. Take medications precisely as directed.

B. Avoid excessive alcohol.

C. You may be instructed to purchase a Medic Alert bracelet or necklace for any emergencies. This can be used to list your treatment and health care provider's name and phone number.

Activity: Exercise is encouraged.

Diet: Eat a low-sodium, high-potassium, high-calcium diet.

Medications:

You Have Been Prescribed: ____________________

You Need to Take: ____________________

You Need to Notify the Office If You:

A. Have a reaction to the medications.

B. Cannot tolerate the prescribed medicines.

C. Other: ____________________

Phone: ____________________

RESOURCES

NADF: www.nadf.us

You can build your own identification bracelets or neck chains from American Medical ID: www.americanmedical-id.com/marketplace/build.php?buildwhat=bracelet

DIABETES

PROBLEM

You have been diagnosed as having diabetes. Diabetes does not go away; you have to manage it every day. It is a condition in which your body cannot use the glucose from food properly. Some signs that your blood sugar is too high and too low are listed here.

A. *Hyperglycemia* (high blood sugar) signs/symptoms: Fruity breath odor; abnormal breathing pattern; rapid, weak pulse; confusion; or stupor.

B. *Hypoglycemia* (low blood sugar) signs/symptoms: Hunger, weakness, sweating, headache, shaking, rapid heartbeat, paleness, fainting, seizures, or coma.

CAUSE

Your body has an organ close to the stomach called a pancreas. Your pancreas is not making enough insulin or your body is not using the insulin it is making properly.

TREATMENT/CARE

A. Lifestyle changes—exercise, stop smoking, follow your diet, and lose some weight—are necessary to control your diabetes.
   1. Stop smoking. Smoking doubles your risk of developing heart or blood vessel disease.
   2. Weight loss of even 5 to 10 pounds helps to control your diabetes.
   3. You need to wear an identification tag that tells others you have diabetes in case of an emergency.

B. Foot care is very important.
   1. Check feet every day.
   2. Wash with mild soap and lukewarm water.
   3. Apply lotion.
   4. File or clip nails after washing and drying.
   5. Do not tear skin around calluses.
   6. Wear clean socks daily.
   7. Wear well-fitted shoes at all times: No bare feet. You may not be able to feel or detect damage.
   8. Avoid crossing your legs.
   9. Take shoes off at every office visit.

C. Blood glucose monitoring: You will be instructed on how to check your blood sugar at home.

   Goals of Glycemia Control

   1. Fasting blood sugar: 80 to 120 mg/dL
   2. 2-h postprandial (after meal) glucose: Less than 180 mg/dL
   3. Bedtime glucose: 100 to 140 mg/dL
   4. Hemoglobin A1c: Less than 7%

D. For low blood sugar you need to follow the 15:15 rule:
   1. After having low blood sugar, you need to check your blood every 4 hours for the next 24 hours.
   2. 15:15 rule: Choose one to follow:
      a. Take three glucose tablets.
      b. Drink 1/2 cup orange juice.
      c. Drink 1/2 cup apple juice.
      d. Drink 1/3 cup grape juice.
      e. Drink 6 oz of regular Coke.
   3. If your blood sugar drops to less than 59, then you need to follow the 15:15 rule, drinking juice or taking glucose tablets, and then follow with 1/2 cup of milk and a starch and 1 ounce of protein.
   4. **If you have severe low blood sugar, you could pass out and go into a coma. You need to have glucagon for emergencies.**
      a. Glucagon is not glucose, but it helps the liver raise your blood glucose.
      b. Glucagon is a prescription drug and is given by injection; it usually works within 15 minutes.
      c. If you do not respond with the first shot of glucagon, your family needs to call 911.
      d. A second dose of glucagon should be given by your family if you do not awaken in 15 minutes.
      e. After receiving glucagon and you respond, you need to eat a snack.

REGULAR CARE

A. You will need to come to the office at regular times to have your diabetes checked and make sure you do not have any complications. Your provider will follow national standards of care, including:
   1. Order a dilated eye examination every year.
   2. Check your blood pressure and keep it less than 140/80.
   3. Check your cholesterol at least once a year.
   4. Do a special foot examination at least once a year.
   5. Check your A1c every 3 months to see if your blood sugar is under control.
   6. Check your urine for protein/kidney problems.
   7. Give you a flu vaccine every year.
   8. If you are older, you need a pneumonia vaccine, too.

SICK-DAY RULES

You will also need a special plan in the event you are sick or have a special occasion.

A. Test blood sugar more often up to every 2 to 4 hours.

B. Increase your fluids, even if you don't feel like eating.

C. Follow a meal plan if you can.

D. Call your health care provider if your blood sugar is less than 70 or greater than 240 for two readings in a row that can't be explained; if you are unable to retain food/fluids; and spilling urine ketones.

E. Check your ketones if your blood sugar is greater than 240. If your ketones are negative, keep testing if your blood sugar stays up.

F. Continue to take your usual insulin dose.

G. **Do not take glucophage if you are dehydrated.**

Activity: Exercise is very important in controlling your diabetes. It not only improves blood sugar by helping your insulin to work, but it also reduces your risk of heart attack, and stroke, and helps with losing weight.

Talk with your health care provider before starting an exercise plan. If you are currently doing some form of exercise, please continue; however, avoid any strenuous exercise.

Moderate exercise (walking, cycling, and swimming) is the best exercise. Your goal will be to develop a consistent exercise activity three to four times a week for 20 to 45 minutes. Drink plenty of fluids before and after you exercise to prevent dehydration.

Exercise causes a decrease in your blood sugar for up to 24 hours. Do not exercise if your fasting blood sugar is greater than 250 or your sugar at any time is over 300. Exercise is not recommended if you have ketones (burning fat instead of sugar).

Diet:

A. You will be seeing a dietitian to develop a nutritional plan that is suited for you.

B. Consistency with meal times and amounts and food from all the six major food groups is important.

C. Even though we stress carbohydrate counting, diabetes has abnormalities in carbohydrate, fat, and protein metabolism that cause hyperglycemia.

D. Dietary control includes control of fats such as cholesterol and saturated fat to help control blood lipid levels and prevent cardiovascular disease.

E. Eat a balanced diet, eat at regular times, and try not to skip meals; eat about the same amount of food at meal/snack times.

F. Use portion control, decrease the fats that you eat, and decrease fast simple sugars.

G. Decrease your alcohol consumption.

Medications:

A. You may need a combination of medications or insulin to help control your blood sugar to prevent complications.

B. If you use insulin injections or the insulin pump, the best place to give it is your stomach.

C. The American Diabetes Association recommends that you take an angiotensin-converting enzyme (ACE) inhibitor (blood pressure medicine) to help protect your kidneys.

D. You may be told to take an aspirin every day (if you are not allergic).

You Have Been Prescribed: ______________________________

You Need to Take: ______________________________

You Have Been Prescribed: ______________________________

You Need to Take: ______________________________

You Have Been Prescribed: ______________________________

You Need to Take: ______________________________

You Need to Notify the Office If:

A. You are sick and unable to keep foods/fluids down (vomiting) or have severe diarrhea.

B. You intend to take over-the-counter medications because they could react with your diabetes medication.

C. You are using Metformin (glucophage) and are going to have x-rays using any dyes. You must stop your medicine.

Phone: ______________________________

Remember to carry your ID and a carbohydrate source. Glucagon should be available for severe low blood glucose due to risk of aspiration and/or inability to swallow.

RESOURCES

American Diabetes Association (ADA): www.diabetes.org

You can build your own identification bracelets or neck chains from American Medical ID: www.americanmedical-id.com/marketplace/build.php?buildwhat=bracelet

Patient Teaching Guides for Chapter 24: Psychiatric Disorders

- Alcohol and Drug Dependence
- Coping Strategies for Teens and Adults With ADHD
- Grief
- Sleep Disorders/Insomnia

ALCOHOL AND DRUG DEPENDENCE

PROBLEM

Dependence on alcohol or drugs is a disease with signs and symptoms and a progressive course that requires treatment, just like diabetes or cancer.

CAUSES

Factors that contribute to dependence on alcohol and drugs may include inherited traits, the environment, occupation, socioeconomic status, family and upbringing, personality, life stress, and emotional stress. These factors vary among individuals, but no one factor can account entirely for the risk.

PREVENTION

The only way to prevent alcohol and/or drug abuse and dependence is not to start. Warning signs for needing help are not always dramatic. The following questions can help identify dependence.

A. **Are you or someone you know experiencing any of the following:**

1. Steadily drinking or using more at a time or more often?
2. Setting limits on how much, how often, when, or where you will drink or use other drugs and repeatedly violating your limits?
3. Keeping a large supply on hand or becoming concerned when you run low?
4. Drinking or using other drugs before going to activities where they won't be available (e.g., class or work)?
5. Drinking or using other drugs alone? Drinking or using other drugs every day?
6. Spending more money than you can afford on alcohol or other drugs?
7. Doing or saying things when you're under the influence that you regret later or don't remember?
8. Lying to friends and family about your drinking or other drug use?
9. Becoming accident prone when you're under the influence (spilling, dropping, or breaking things)?
10. Regularly hung over the morning after drinking?
11. Worrying about your drinking or other drug use?
12. Having work or school problems, such as tardiness or absenteeism?
13. Reducing contact with friends, or experiencing increasing problems with important relationships?

B. **If you answered "yes" to any of these questions, it suggests your drinking or drug use may be a problem.**

TREATMENT PLAN

A. There are no "quick cures" for alcohol and drug dependence, but early intervention is of utmost importance because it helps avoid the harmful effects of long-term alcohol or other drug use.

B. Your health care provider will be suggesting a plan of action for you to consider. You are strongly encouraged to follow the recommendations.

C. Don't hang around your drinking/drug-using friends. Instead, go to new areas, play new sports, and develop new hobbies.

D. Talk to your provider about seeking professional rehab treatment.

E. Ask about a support group in your area.

Activity: Daily exercise is helpful in alleviating the craving for alcohol and drugs. Walking daily and increasing your tolerance for distance are recommended.

Diet:

A. Avoid caffeine and nicotine, if possible.

B. Try to eat three meals a day and three snacks.

C. You may be given vitamin supplements to help restore the vitamins and minerals that have been depleted as a result of your alcohol or drug dependence.

Medications: Usually, medications are not prescribed because they may make the problem worse. If you are prescribed any medications, take them exactly as directed by your health care provider.

You Have Been Prescribed: ______________________________

Vitamins/Minerals: ______________________________

You Need to Take: ______________________________

You Need to Notify the Office If You Have:

A. Severe craving and the urge to use alcohol or drugs.
B. Any thoughts of hurting yourself or others.
C. Impulsive feelings, like you might do something you will later regret.

Phone: ____

RESOURCES

Al-Anon Family: 888-4AL-ANON and www.al-anon.alateen.org

Alcohol Help Line 24 hours a day, 7 days a week: 800-345-3552 and www.adcare.com

American Council for Drug Education: 800-488-3784 (DRUG) and www.health.gov/nhic

Cocaine Anonymous: 310-559-5833 and www.ca.org

Cocaine Hotline 24 hours a day, 7 days a week: 800-262-2463 and www.acde.org

Families Anonymous: 800-736-9805 and familiesanonymous.org

Mothers Against Drunk Driving (MADD) 24 hours a day, 7 days a week: 877-ASK-MADD and www.madd.org

New Life (Women for Sobriety): 215-536-8026 and www.womenforsobriety.org

Phoenix House: 1-888-286-5027

COPING STRATEGIES FOR TEENS AND ADULTS WITH ADHD

PROBLEM

Attention deficit hyperactivity disorder (ADHD) is a common mental health problem in which a person has difficulty with paying attention, has a short attention span, and frequently gets in trouble due to behavior issues. The patient may show signs of hyperactivity, difficulty with concentrating, reacting without thinking first, and may also have anger issues.

CAUSE

The cause of ADHD is unknown. However, it may be hereditary.

TREATMENT/PREVENTION PLAN

A. Identify coping skills. Identify what things help you to control your behavior and prevent outbursts.

B. Counseling and therapy are commonly encouraged to help you learn new coping skills to help with your problem. Make sure you keep all appointments with your counselor/therapist.

C. Make sure to clarify all assignments and tasks.

D. Keep simple lists of your chores for the day.

E. Attach reminder notes to logical items; for example, put a self-adhesive note on your bathroom mirror to remind yourself to do something.

F. Organize your things in a logical way. For example, put your medication bottle with your toothbrush so you will be sure to take it in the morning.

G. Establish a daily routine and stick to it.

H. Keep your environment as quiet and peaceful as possible. Seek out work and study sites that are quiet and peaceful.

I. Be good to yourself: Eat well, get enough rest, and exercise.

J. Take your medications as prescribed. If you feel that your medication is not improving your behavior, notify your parent and/or care provider so this can be evaluated.

RESOURCES

Children and Adults With Attention-Deficit Hyperactivity Disorder (CHADD): www.chadd.org

National Attention Deficit Disorder Association: www.add.org

National Resource Center for ADHD: www.help4adhd.org

GRIEF

PROBLEM

Normal grief resolution may take from 6 months up to as long as 2 years.

CAUSES

Grief can follow the death of a loved one, but grief also follows other losses such as a loss of independence, loss of affection, or loss of body parts after an accident.

TREATMENT PLAN

It is important that you talk about your loss and how it affects you. The more you are able to talk about your feelings related to the loss you are experiencing, the more you will be able to work through your feelings.

You may be encouraged to seek supportive therapy in the form of divorce groups, loss groups, or groups dealing specifically with death and dying.

Activity: Moderate exercise, such as daily walking, is encouraged. Vigorous, prolonged exercise, however, may precipitate anxiety attacks.

Diet: Avoid caffeinated beverages, including coffee, tea, and carbonated colas that do not specify "decaffeinated." Try to eat healthy food and avoid overeating or skipping meals.

Medications: Medications for loss and grief are usually avoided at first because the use of drugs can prolong the time it takes to work through your grief. However, your health care provider will discuss medications in more depth. If you are having signs of depression or think you may need treatment with medication, contact your health care provider.

You Have Been Prescribed: ______________________________

You Need to Take It: ______________________________

Do not stop antidepressants quickly. Talk to your health care provider if you want to discontinue them.

You Need to Notify the Office If:

A. You feel like you can't stop crying.
B. You are not eating and are losing weight.
C. You feel like you have no one to turn to and talk about your feelings.
D. You have difficulty sleeping after several weeks.
E. You have thoughts of hurting yourself or others.
F. You don't think you are getting better on the prescribed medication.

Phone: ______________________________
Local Support Group: ______________________________

SUGGESTED READING

Arnold, J. H., & Gemma, P. B. (1994). *A child dies: A portrait of family grief* (2nd ed.). Philadelphia, PA: Charles Press.

Fritsch, J., & Ilse, S. (1992). *The anguish of loss*. Maple Plain, MN: Wintergreen Press.

Ilse, S. (2008). *Empty arms: Coping with miscarriage, stillbirth, and infant death*. Maple Plain, MN: Wintergreen Press, Inc.

Smith, H. I. (2011). *A Decembered grief: Living with loss while others are celebrating*. Kansas City, MO: Beacon Hill Press. (Original work published 1999.)

Zonnebelt-Smeenge, S., & De Vries, R. C. (2001). *Empty chair: Handling grief on holidays and special occasions*. Grand Rapids, MI: Baker Books.

SLEEP DISORDERS/INSOMNIA

PROBLEM

Continued loss of sleep over a long period of time (several days to weeks) can produce a decrease in daytime awareness and functioning, as well as work and driving impairment.

CAUSE

Most sleep difficulties are related to situational problems and are best treated without medications. Medical illness may also predispose you to a sleeping disorder.

PREVENTION

A. Practice good "sleep hygiene." Here are a few tips:

1. Try to get to bed at the same time every night (even on weekends).
2. Plan for 8 hours of sleep.
3. Maintain the same waking time every morning (even on weekends).
4. Reserve the bedroom for sleeping. Do not do your work/homework in the bed. Do not watch TV in the bedroom, unless you sit in a chair. Do not read in bed.
5. Put your children in their own bed/bedroom.
6. Try a small bedtime snack.
7. Do not drink any liquids for at least 1 hour before going to bed. This helps prevent getting up to go to the bathroom during the night.
8. Review all of your prescription medications, over-the-counter drugs, and herbal products with your health care provider to evaluate if the drugs are making you stay awake.
9. Avoid alcohol and tobacco.

B. If you do not get a restful night's sleep, awaken yourself snoring, or your partner complains of your snoring, gasping, or stopping breathing, you may need to have a sleep study.

TREATMENT PLAN

A. Develop a "sleeping ritual." Wear your favorite pajamas and use your favorite pillows.

B. Keep the room dark and quiet. Try not to use a nightlight.

C. Run a small fan for background noise.

D. Arise promptly in the morning.

E. Avoid sleeping medication if possible.

F. Try some relaxation exercises, like yoga, self-hypnosis, or meditation. There are many books on these subjects that will assist you in developing good sleep hygiene. (Try your local library or bookstore.)

G. Keep a sleep diary to help identify the causes of your inability to sleep.

H. Discuss snoring and your partner's concerns about your breathing and the need for a sleep study.

Activity: Regular exercise during the day helps. (Do not exercise vigorously 1 hour before your bedtime—this could keep you awake.)

Relaxation techniques such as progressive relaxation, biofeedback, self-hypnosis, and meditation are helpful when done before bedtime. Avoid vigorous mental activities late in the evening.

Diet:

A. Avoid caffeinated drinks, including coffee, tea, and soda.

B. Avoid large meals in the evening.

C. Eat a nutritious balanced diet.

D. Limit your liquids to early evening. Do not drink water after 8 p.m.

Medications: Discuss the need for "short-term" medications to help you sleep.

You Have Been Prescribed: ______________________________

You Need to Take It: ______________________________

You Need to Notify the Office If You Have:

A. No relief of your symptoms and you are following the previous recommendations.

B. No relief of your symptoms and you are taking your medications as directed.

C. Feelings of depression or thoughts of hurting yourself or others.

D. Noticeable physical symptoms that were not mentioned in your office visit or any new symptoms that you are concerned about.

Phone: ____________________

RESOURCES

National Institutes of Health: health.nih.gov/topic/SleepDisorders

National Sleep Foundation: www.sleepfoundation.org

Appendices

- Normal Laboratory Values
- Diet Recommendations

APPENDIX A

Normal Laboratory Values

Cheryl A. Glass

Normal laboratory values are presented here. However, laboratory value ranges differ from laboratory to laboratory. They differ because of age and gender. Different values are presented; all normal values are listed under the Females column. Male values are the same unless otherwise noted. Legend: 10^6 = 1,000,000, 10^3 = 1,000.

Normal Laboratory Values

	FEMALES	MALES
Complete blood count		
Red blood cells (RBCs)	3.8–5.1 × 10^6/µL	4.2–5.6 × 10^6/µL
Hemoglobin (Hgb) ↑ polycythemia, dehydration, ↓ blood loss, severe anemia, low production or death of blood cell	11–16 g/dL	14–18 g/dL
Hematocrit (Hct) ↓ anemia, massive blood loss, ↑ dehydration or hemoconcentration with shock	34%–47%	39%–54%
Mean corpuscular volume (MCV) RBC size: Normocytic, microcytic, macrocytic	78–98 fL	
Mean corpuscular hemoglobin (MCH) RBC color: Normochromic, hypochromic	27–35 pg	
Mean corpuscular hemoglobin concentration (MCHC)	31–37 g/dL or %	
Reticulocyte count Measures the number of new RBCs produced by the bone marrow	33–137 × 10/µL	
White blood cells (WBCs) ↑ bacterial infections, infectious diseases (mononucleosis), ↓ stress tissue death, leukemia, cancer, hemorrhage	3.8–11.0 million/mm	3.8–11.0 × 10^3/mm^3
Differential Segmented neutrophils ↑ stress, trauma, inflammatory disorders, ↓ viral infections, severe bacterial infections, aplastic anemia	50%–81%	
Band neutrophils	1%–5%	
Lymphocytes ↑ chronic bacterial infection, viral infections, ↓ leukemia, AIDS, Lupus erythematosus	14%–44%	
Monocytes ↑ chronic inflammatory disorders, viral infections, chronic conditions, ↓ steroid therapy	2%–6%	
Eosinophils ↑ allergies, parasite infections, leukemia	1%–5%	

(*continued*)

Normal Laboratory Values (*continued*)

	FEMALES	MALES
Basophils ↑ leukemia ↓ allergic reactions, stress, hyperthyroidism	0%–1.0%	
Serum iron concentration of iron bound to transferrin	60–160 mcg/dL	80–180 mcg/dL
Total iron-binding capacity (TIBC) Amount of iron transferrin can bind	250–460 mcg/dL	
Erythrocyte sedimentation rate (ESR) ↑ pregnancy, inflammatory conditions, ↓ sickle cell anemia	Women < 50 < 20 mm/hr Women > 50 < 30 mm/hr	Males < 50 < 15 mm/hr Males > 50 < 20 mm/hr
BUN/creatinine-renal function tests		
Blood urea nitrogen (BUN)	6–23 mg/dL	0.2–0.6 mg/dL
Creatinine (Cr)	0.6–1.5 mg/dL	3.5–7.7 mg/dL
Creatine	0.6–1.0 mg/dL	
Uric acid	2.5–6.6 mg/dL	
Thyroid studies		
Thyroid-stimulating hormone (TSH)	2.0–10.5 μ/mL	
↑ hypothyroidism, ↓ hyperthyroidism	0.8–1.1 μ/dL	
T3 ↑ pregnancy and oral contraceptive use	5.0–13.0 μ/dL	
Thyroxine (T4) ↑ hyperthyroidism, ↓ hypothyroidism		
Aminotransferases		
↑ liver damage and medications	4–35 U/L	7–46 U/L
Alanine transaminase (ALT)	6–18 U/L	7–21 U/L
Aspartate aminotransferase (AST)		
Bilirubin (measures bile salt conjugation and excretion)		
Direct bilirubin	0.0–0.4 mg/dL	
Indirect bilirubin	Total bilirubin minus direct bilirubin	
Total bilirubin	0.21–1.0 mg/dL 3.0 mg/dL indicates hepatic disease, jaundice is visible	

Glucose

Fasting 65–110 mg/dL
2 hour postprandial 65–140 mg/dL

Serum albumin (measures protein synthesis)

3.5–5.0 g/dL
↑ dehydration, inflammatory illness, liver insufficiency, malnutrition, and cancer

Lipid profile

Fasting cholesterol: < 200 mg/dL
200–239 mg/dL: Borderline coronary heart disease (CHD)
> 240 mg/dL: High risk for CHD
Triglycerides:
Male > 40–170 mg/dL
Female > 35–135 mg/dL
High-density lipoprotein (HDL): > 45 mg/dL, desirable levels higher than 50 mg/dL
Low-density lipoprotein (LDL): < 130 mg/dL
130–159 mg/dL: Borderline CHD
> 160 mg/dL: High risk for CHD

Coagulation

Prothrombin time (PT): 10–14 sec
Partial thromboplastin time (PTT): 32–45 sec
Fibrinogen: 160–450 mg/dL
Bleeding time: 3–7 min
Thrombin time: 11–15 sec
Platelets: 140,000–450,000/mL
↓ thrombocytopenia, acute leukemia/aplastic anemia during chemotherapy, interferon, infections, and drug reactions
↑ myeloproliferative disease, cancer, and rheumatoid arthritis (RA)

Sickle cell disease

Sickle cell hemoglobin (HgbS): Normal, none present
Homozygous HgbS: Sickle cell disease
Heterozygous HgbS: Sickle cell trait
Hgb electrophoresis: Determines Hgb types and percentages

(*continued*)

Normal Laboratory Values (*continued*)

Hepatitis B
Hepatitis B surface antigen: Negative
Positive: Acute or chronic infection, further liver function tests needed
Hepatitis B surface antibody: Positive indicates immunity to infection (previous infection or HBV vaccine)

PSA (males)
0–4.0 mg/mL normal

Serum alkaline phosphatase (ALP) (marks liver disease)
30–120 IU/L
Pregnancy value 30–200 IU/L
↑ bile stones, biliary and pancreatic cancer, viral hepatitis, cirrhosis, Paget's disease, osteomalacia, bone metastasis

Vitamin D
25(OH)D ≥ 30 ng/mL: Optimal
25(OH)D 21–29 ng/mL: Vitamin D insufficiency
25(OH)D ≤ 20 ng/mL: Vitamin D deficiency
25(OH)D ≥ 150 ng/mL: Vitamin D toxicity

Urinalysis
Color: Pale yellow/straw to amber
Clarity: Clear
Specific gravity: 1.001–1.035
pH: Normal 4.6–8.0 (acidic)
Glucose: Absent
Ketones: Absent
Protein: Negative

Urine dipstick U/A
Nitrites: Negative (positive = bacteria, infection)
Leukocytes oxidase: Negative (positive = WBCs)

Arterial blood gas values (pH):
7.3–7.45 SAME
$PaCO_2$: 35–45 mmHg SAME
HCO_3: 22–26 mEq/L global 19–25
O_2 saturation: 96–100% global 90–95
PaO_2: 85–100 mmHg global 70–100
Base excess (BE): −2 to +2 mmol/L

Venous blood gas values (pH):
7.31–7.41 global rx has 7.32–7.42
$PaCO_2$: 41–51 mmHg global rx 38–52
HCO_3: 22–29 mEq/L global 19–25
O_2 saturation: 60%–85% global 40–70
PaO_2: 30–40 mmHg global 28–48
BE: 0 to +4 mmol/L

HIV
ELISA: Negative
ELISA: Positive: Repeat, if second ELISA positive perform Western blot
Western blot negative: No evidence of HIV
Western blot positive: Evidence of HIV

Rubella
Titer: > 1:10 Immune
Titer: < 1:8 Nonimmune administer Rubella vaccine

Female hormone levels
Testosterone: < 62 ng/dL

	Follicle-stimulating hormone (FSH)	**Luteinizing hormone (LH)**	**Progesterone**	**Prolactin**
Follicular phase	2–25 mIU/mL	5–30 mIU/mL	0.2–6.0 mIU/mL	< 23 ng/mL
Midcycle phase	10–90 mIU/mL	75–150 mIU/mL	6–30 mIU/mL	< 28 ng/mL
Luteal phase	2–25 mIU/mL	3–40 mIU/mL	5.7–28.1 mIU/mL	5–40 ng/mL
Postmenopausal	40–350 mIU/mL	30–200 mIU/mL	0–0.2 mIU/mL	< 12 ng/mL

Male testosterone by age range
14–15 years: 33–585 ng/dL
16–17 years: 185–886 ng/dL
18–39 years: 400–1,080 ng/dL
40–59 years: 350–890 ng/dL
≥ 60 years: 350–720 ng/dL

APPENDIX B

Diet Recommendations

Cheryl A. Glass and Deanna Tacderas

You have been prescribed a bland diet. This diet provides adequate nutrition along with the treatment of gastrointestinal problems, such as ulcerative conditions or inflammatory problems of the stomach and intestines. It is intended to decrease irritation in the lining of the stomach and intestines.

Food Tips

Foods to Avoid

Garlic, onions, alcohol, fatty foods, fried foods, chocolate, cocoa, coffee (even decaffeinated), dried fruits, citrus fruit and juices (orange, pineapple, and grapefruit), tomato products, peppermint, whole grain breads and cereals, prespiced foods such as processed lunch meats and ham, pepper, and chili powder. Avoid pepper, chili powder, and cocoa spices.

General Instructions

A. Eat at least three small meals a day.
B. Avoid alcohol and beer.
C. Avoid caffeinated drinks/colas.
D. Avoid fried, greasy foods.
E. Bake or broil your foods.
F. Trim the fat from meats before cooking.
G. Bake, broil, mash, or cream potatoes.
H. Avoid raw fruits and vegetables such as corn on the cob and other gas-forming vegetables such as cabbage, dried beans, and peas.
I. Avoid rich desserts.
J. Avoid bedtime snacks—they may increase acid production and cause discomfort at night.
K. Avoid eating 2 hours before you go to bed.
L. Ask your health care provider if nutritional supplements are necessary.

Approved Foods by Food Group

A. Dairy products
   1. Whole milk
   2. Low fat or 2% milk
   3. Skim milk
   4. Evaporated milk
   5. Buttermilk
   6. Cottage cheese
   7. Yogurt
   8. Cheese (avoid stronger cheeses that are darker yellow and blue cheese)

B. Meat
   1. Beef
   2. Veal
   3. Fresh pork
   4. Turkey
   5. Chicken
   6. Fish (canned or fresh)
   7. Liver
   8. Egg (as a meat substitute)
   9. Tofu
   10. Tempeh soy product

C. Breads/grains
   1. Enriched breads (plain toast)
   2. Oats
   3. Cereal
   4. Tortillas
   5. English muffins
   6. Saltine crackers
   7. Pasta (all types)

D. Fruits/vegetables
   1. All vegetables
   2. All fruits and juices (except citrus)

E. Desserts
   1. Custard
   2. Pudding
   3. Sherbet
   4. Ice cream (except peppermint and chocolate)
   5. Gelatin
   6. Angel food cake
   7. Pound cake
   8. Sugar cookies
   9. Jams and jellies
   10. Honey

F. Drinks
   1. Decaffeinated tea
   2. Juices (except citrus)
   3. Caffeine-free sodas

G. Spices
   1. Salt
   2. Thyme
   3. Sage
   4. Cinnamon
   5. Paprika
   6. Apple cider vinegar
   7. Prepared mustard
   8. Lemon and lime juices

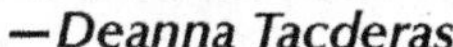

DASH DIET: DIETARY APPROACHES TO STOP HYPERTENSION

—Deanna Tacderas

The Dietary Approaches to Stop Hypertension (DASH) diet is based on a combination of different types of foods and is recommended to help control high blood pressure. It is a food plan that is based on foods that are low in cholesterol and high in dietary fiber, potassium, calcium, and magnesium; it is moderately high in protein. DASH eating has a reduction in lean red meats, added sugar, and sugar-containing sodas. The DASH diet's dairy food portions make the diet high in calcium and vitamin D. Overall, Americans, especially African Americans, are deficient in vitamin D.

The DASH diet, along with weight loss and exercise, is used to control other health problems such as type 2 diabetes and heart disease. If your ethnic background is Hawaiian, Native American, Eskimo, Hispanic, or African American, you are at higher risk for high blood pressure. Following a DASH eating plan also will help lower the bad cholesterol, or LDL, which can reduce heart disease.

A major way the DASH diet helps lower blood pressure is to limit the amount of salt (sodium). The recommendations are limiting sodium to 1,100 to 3,000 mg a day or less. If you have high blood pressure, you may be limited to 1,500 mg or less a day. **One teaspoon of salt contains 2,000 mg of sodium.**

Foods high in sodium make you retain extra fluid. If you notice that your hands are swelling (rings are tight) or your feet and legs swell (sock rings or shoes feel tight), you are getting too much salt. Fluid retention is bad if you have heart failure. This diet is rich in potassium, which can help you get rid of the extra sodium and decrease the fluid retention.

Sea salt, even though it may contain less sodium, is not low enough in sodium to use as a substitute for regular salt. Salt substitutes contain potassium chloride; this can cause more fluid retention. Potassium chloride salt substitutes may also interfere with your blood pressure medications, so check with your health care provider before using them.

Tips for Reducing Sodium

A. Slowly cut back on your salty foods and begin to use healthier products. Take the salt shaker off the table.

B. Eat fresh foods.
   1. Avoid prepackaged foods.
   2. Eat fresh vegetables instead of canned vegetables. If you use canned vegetables, choose the low-sodium option and/or rinse the vegetables.

C. Read food labels.
   1. Sodium is in almost all processed foods, including milk. Sodium is listed different ways on labels; see Table B.1.
   2. **Focus on the amount of sodium per food serving.**
   3. Don't forget to read labels on soda and sports drink bottles.
   4. Choose your favorite food brand with low-salt or low-sodium labels on the package instead of the same product with more salt.

D. Avoid salty snacks and foods, including:
   1. Crackers, chips, and pretzels
   2. Cheeses
   3. Olives, pickles, pickled okra, and other foods
   4. Processed foods, including jerky, hot dogs, bacon, deli meats, canned fish, and canned meats, which contain a large amount of sodium.

E. Limit using soy sauce, seasoned salts, and meat tenderizers.

F. Many seasonings, including ketchup and sauces, contain a lot of sodium. Substitute with other flavors such as fresh herbs (e.g., rosemary, thyme, oregano, cilantro, and basil). Use garlic powder, lemon and lime juice, crushed red peppers, as well as ginger.

G. Try making your own salt-free herb blend to use on your foods. Ingredients that can add flavor without adding salt include:
   1. Peppers such as cayenne, black pepper, and lemon pepper
   2. Dried herbs such as thyme
   3. Garlic powder
   4. Paprika
   5. Celery seed

H. Helpful websites for salt-free herb blends, products, and recipes are
   1. Salt-free seasoning recipes:
      a. busycooks.about.com/od/homemade_mixes/r/nosaltmix.htm
      b. www.tasteofhome.com/Recipes/Salt-Free-Seasoning-Mix
   2. Websites with low-salt recipes:
      a. homecooking.about.com/library/archive/blhelp13.htm
      b. McCormick: www.mccormick.com
      c. Mrs. Dash: www.mrsdash.com

Tips on Eating the DASH Way

A. Start small. Make gradual changes in your eating habits, such as eating smaller portions (see Tables B.2 and B.3).

B. Center your meal around carbohydrates, such as pasta, rice, beans, or vegetables.
C. Treat meat as only part of a whole meal instead of the main focus of the meal.
D. Use fruits or low-fat, low-calorie foods such as sugar-free gelatin for desserts and snacks.
E. Choose "whole" grains in breads and cereals.
F. Choose to eat vegetables without butter or sauce.
G. Choose lean cuts of meat. Use fresh poultry, for example, skinless turkey and chicken.
H. Choose ready-to-eat breakfast cereals that are lower in sodium.
I. Eat fruits for dessert. Use fruits that are canned in their own juice.
J. Add fruit to plain yogurt.
K. To increase eating vegetables, stir-fry with 2 oz of chicken and use 1½ cups of raw vegetables.
L. Snack on vegetables, bread sticks, graham crackers, or unbuttered/unsalted popcorn.
M. Drink water or club soda.
N. Eating out
   1. Ask the restaurant to prepare your meal without salt, if possible.
   2. Review the menu to avoid foods that are listed as pickled, cured, or smoked, or contain soy sauce or broth.
   3. Limit condiments, including mustard, ketchup, and pickles.
O. Table B.4 presents the number of servings, and Table B.5 illustrates the caloric adjustment for 2,000 calories a day using the DASH diet.

Resources

DASH Diet Calorie Adjustments for 1,200, 1,600, 2,000, and 2,400 Calorie Diets: dashdiet.org/images/ calories.pdf

DASH Diet Eating Plan: dashdiet.org/dash_diet_recipes.asp

DASH Diet Recipes: www.mayoclinic.com/health/dash-diet-recipes/RE00089

DASH for Health: www.dashforhealth.com/index.php

TABLE B.1 Ways Sodium Is Listed on a Food Label

Phrase on Label	Meaning of Sodium Content
Sodium free or salt free	<5 mg per serving
Very low sodium	35 mg or less of sodium per serving
Low sodium	140 mg or less of sodium per serving
Low-sodium meal	140 mg or less sodium per 3.5 oz (100 g)
Reduced or less sodium	At least 25% less sodium than the regular version
Light in sodium	50% less sodium than the regular version
Unsalted or no salt added	No salt added to the product during processing (this is not a sodium-free food)

Adapted from Food Facts from the U.S. Food and Drug Administration (2012).

TABLE B.2 Serving Portion Sizes

Food	Portion Size	Food	Portion Size
1 baked potato 1 cup of flaked cereal	Fist	½ cup of fresh fruit (k of baseball) ½ cup of pasta, rice, or potato (½ of baseball)	Baseball
1½ oz cheese (4 dice) 1 tsp of margarine (1 dice)	Dice	½ cup of ice cream	
¼ cup of raisins	Egg	3 oz of meat, includes fish, meat, and chicken	Deck of cards
½ cup almonds	Golf ball	1 pancake	Compact disc (CD)
2 tbsp peanut butter	Ping Pong ball	1 piece of cornbread	Bar of soap
1 cup of salad 1 cup of popcorn (unbuttered)	Baseball	3 oz of grilled or baked fish	Checkbook

Adapted from National Heart, Lung, and Blood Institute (2010).

TABLE B.3 DASH Diet Daily Servings

Food Group	Daily Servings	Serving Sizes	Examples and Notes	Significance of Each Food Group to the DASH Diet Pattern
Grains and grain product	6–8	1 slice bread ½ cup dry cereal ½ cup cooked rice, pasta, or cereal	Whole wheat bread, English muffin, pita bread, bagel, cereals, grits, oatmeal, couscous	Major sources of energy and fiber
Vegetables	4–5	1 cup raw leafy vegetables ½ cup cooked vegetables 6 oz vegetable juice	Tomatoes, potatoes, carrots, peas, squash, broccoli, turnip greens, collards, kale, spinach, artichokes, beans, sweet potatoes	Rich sources of potassium, magnesium, and fiber
Fruits	4–5	6 oz fruit juice 1 medium fruit ¼ cup dried fruit ¼ cup fresh, frozen, or canned fruit	Apricots, bananas, dates, grapes, oranges, orange juice, grapefruit, grapefruit juice, mangoes, melons, peaches, pineapples, prunes, raisins, strawberries, tangerines	Important sources of potassium, magnesium, and fiber
Low-fat or fat-free milk and dairy foods	2–3	1 cup milk 1 cup yogurt 1.5 oz cheese	Skim or 1% milk, skim or low-fat buttermilk, nonfat or low-fat yogurt, part-skim mozzarella cheese, nonfat cheese	Major sources of calcium and protein
Lean meats, poultry, and fish	6 or less	1 oz cooked meats, poultry, or fish 1 egg	Select only lean; trim away visible fat; broil, roast, or boil instead of frying. Remove skin from poultry	Rich sources of protein and magnesium
Nuts, seeds, and legumes	4–5 per week	1½ oz of nuts ½ oz or 2 tbsp seeds 2 tbsp of peanut butter ½ cup cooled legumes	Almonds, filberts, mixed nuts, peanuts, walnuts, sunflower seeds, kidney beans, lentils	Rich sources of energy, magnesium, potassium, protein, and fiber
Sweets and added sugars	5 or less per week	½ tbsp sugar 1 tbsp jelly or jam ½ cup sorbet or gelatin 1 cup lemonade	Fruit-flavored gelatin, fruit punch, hard candy, jelly, maple syrup, sugar	Sweets should be low in fat

Adapted from the NHLBI DASH Diet Eating Plan (n.d.a).

TABLE B.4 Total Number of Servings in 2,000 cal/d

Food Group	Servings
Grains	7–8
Vegetables	5
Fruits	5
Fat-free or low-fat milk and dairy foods	3
Lean meats, poultry, and fish	2
Nuts, seeds, and legumes	1
Fats and oils	2–3
Sweets and added sugars	1

TABLE B.5 DASH Example Menu (2,000 cal)

Food	Amount	Servings Provided
Breakfast		
Orange juice	6 oz	1 fruit
1% low-fat milk	8 oz (1 cup)	1 dairy
Cornflakes (with 1 tsp sugar)	1 cup	2 grains
Banana	1 medium	1 fruit
Whole wheat bread (with 1 tbsp jelly)	1 slice	1 grain
Soft margarine	1 tsp	1 fat
Lunch		
Chicken salad	¾ cup	1 poultry
Pita bread	½ large	1 grain
Raw vegetable medley:		
Carrot and celery sticks	3–4 sticks each	
Radishes	2	1 vegetable
Loose-leaf lettuce	2 leaves	
Part-skim mozzarella cheese	1.5 slice (1.5 oz)	1 dairy
1% low-fat milk	8 oz (1 cup)	1 dairy
Fruit cocktail in light syrup	½ cup	1 fruit
Dinner		
Herbed baked cod	3 oz	1 fish
Scallion rice	1 cup	2 grains
Steamed broccoli	½ cup	1 vegetable
Stewed tomatoes	½ cup	1 vegetable
Spinach salad:		
Raw spinach	½ cup	
Cherry tomatoes	2	1 vegetable
Cucumber	2 slices	
Light Italian salad dressing	1 tbsp	½ fat
Whole wheat dinner roll	1 small	1 grain
Soft margarine	1 tsp	1 fat
Melon balls	1/2 cup	1 fruit
Snacks		
Dried apricots	1 oz (¼ cup)	1 fruit
Mini-pretzels	1 oz (¾ cup)	1 grain
Mixed nuts	1.5 oz (½ cup)	1 nuts
Diet gingerale	12 oz	0

Gluten-Free Diet Tips

The symptoms from celiac disease are triggered from glutens in your diet. Three cereals that contain gluten are wheat, rye, and barley. **Glutens are also in other products, such as food additives, so it is very important to read all the ingredients on food labels** (see Table B.6).

Dietary Recommendation for Celiac Disease

A. You may also be told to follow a lactose-free diet for a short time to alleviate your symptoms.
B. Most bread sold in the grocery aisle is not allowed on a gluten-free eating plan.
C. All vegetables and fruits are gluten-free. However, frozen and canned fruits and vegetables may contain an additive with gluten.
D. Although you should not enjoy beer, wine is still on the menu when you go to dinner.
E. Specialty bakeries are able to make gluten-free cakes for special occasions. Plain hard candy, marshmallows, and other candies are usually gluten-free.
F. Caution should be taken when ordering any breaded foods such as chicken nuggets or breaded fish.
G. Deli meats may also contain gluten.
H. Gluten-free foods are often not fortified with vitamins and minerals. It is recommended to take a daily multivitamin.

Resources

Celiac Disease Foundation: www.celiac.org
Gluten-Free Recipes: allrecipes.com/Recipes/Healthy-Cooking/Gluten-Free/Main.aspx
www.BettyCrocker.com/glutenfree
www.celiac.com
www.celiacdisease.net/gluten-free-diet
www.chex.com/glutenfree

TABLE B.6 Examples of Foods That Are Allowed and Avoided on a Gluten-Free Diet

Allowed	Avoid
Fresh fruits and vegetables without any processing or additives	Wheat, wheat berry, wheat bran, wheat germ, wheat grass, whole wheat berries
Meat	Flours, bread flour
Soy, soybean, tofu	Bulgur (bulgur wheat, bulgur nuts)
Brown rice	Rye
Enriched rice/instant rice/wild rice	Barley
Buckwheat	Barley malt/barley extract
Millet	Oats, oat bran, oat fiber
Sorghum	Cereals
Alfalfa	Matzo
Almond	Beer, ale, porter, stout
Canola	Farina
Chickpea	Croutons
Corn, corn flour, cornmeal	Bran
Brown rice flour	Tabbouleh
Tapioca	Soy sauce
Coffee with no grains added	Bouillon cubes
Milk	Cold cut meats
Wine (check for preservatives and dyes)	Energy bars
Gluten-free beers	Instant coffee and teas
	Malted milk
	Malted wine coolers
	Beer, ales, and lagers

Fiber is a plant cell-wall component that is not broken down by the digestive system. An old term for fiber is "roughage" because it absorbs fluid and moves waste faster through the intestines in a bulky mass. The Food and Drug Administration defines as high-fiber those products that contain 20% of the daily fiber value. High-fiber diets are used to help prevent constipation as well as diarrhea. Fiber has been used to help several medical conditions such as diabetes, diverticulosis, irritable bowel syndrome (IBS), and high cholesterol, as well as weight loss. If you have a chronic health condition, check with your health care provider about starting any new dietary change.

Fiber provides a full feeling that can help with spacing meals further apart (3–4 hours). Fiber recommendations change with your age (see Table B.7).

Tips for Increasing Fiber in Your Diet

A. Read the Nutrition Facts food labels for fiber content per food serving.
   1. Cereals that provide 5 g of fiber per serving give you 20% of your daily fiber.
   2. Look for "whole grain" on the label. Just because bread is brown does not mean it is whole grain.

B. Increase fiber in your diet gradually to prevent gas. Adding too much fiber too quickly may give you abdominal pain, bloating, and constipation. Increase your fiber over several weeks so that it gives time for you to adjust.

C. As you increase fiber, it is also important to increase the amount of fluids you drink up to six to eight glasses a day, including tea, milk, fruit juices, coffee, and even soft drinks. The extra fluids that you drink along with the extra fiber makes you feel fuller, which can help control snacking.

D. Keep a food diary and review it periodically to decide on other diet adjustments needed to be made.

E. Several fiber supplements are available over the counter to help you get your daily recommendation of fiber.

Good Food Sources of Fiber

A. Bran: Add 1 teaspoon of whole-grain bran to food three times a day, or take an over-the-counter fiber supplement such as psyllium (Metamucil), as directed.

B. Whole-grain cereals and breads: Eat oat, bran, multigrain, light, wheat, or rye breads rather than pure white bread or breads that list eggs as a major ingredient. Grains are not only a good source of fiber but also contain vitamins and minerals. Folic acid has been added to breads and cereals to help reduce neural tube defects.

C. Fresh or frozen fruits and vegetables: Citrus fruits are especially good sources of fiber. Eat raw or minimally cooked vegetables, especially squash, cabbage, lettuce, other greens, and beans. Leave the skins on fruits and vegetables; eating the whole fruit is better than drinking the juice. Whole tomatoes offer more fiber than peeling the skin off. The more colorful the fruit and vegetable (dark green, reds, blue, yellow) the better; they provide a good source of antioxidants that are good for the heart and the prevention of some cancers. Apples are a good source of both fiber and water.

D. Legumes (pods): Peas and beans are a good source of fiber. Add chickpeas and kidney beans to salads for extra fiber and flavor. Add baked beans as a delicious side item to your meal.

E. Coffee is another source of fiber.

F. Nuts are an excellent source of fiber. They are considered nutrient-dense and are a good source of vitamins and folic acid. Sprinkle sunflower seeds on a salad to add flavor and fiber. The amount of nuts eaten should be limited to 1 to 2 ounces because they are also high in calories.

G. If you have diverticulosis: Avoid foods with seeds or indigestible material that may block the neck of a diverticulum, such as nuts, corn, popcorn, cucumbers, tomatoes, figs, strawberries, and caraway seeds.

TABLE B.7 Fiber Recommendations by Age

Group/Gender	Age	Fiber Recommendations
Men	19–50 years	38 g of fiber each day
Women	19–50 years	25 g of fiber each day
Men	51–70 years	30 g of fiber each day
Women	51–70 years	21 g of fiber each day
Men	>70 years	30 g of fiber each day
Women	>70 years	21 g of fiber each day

Adapted from the Institute of Medicine. (2005).

LACTOSE-INTOLERANCE DIET—*Cheryl A. Glass*

A. Lactose is the sugar present in milk. Lactose intolerance is very common; it occurs when the body is not able to appropriately digest the milk sugar content and the result is diarrhea. You have been diagnosed as having difficulty digesting milk (lactose) products or you have problems with malabsorption. Lactose intolerance can cause gas, bloating, abdominal cramps, diarrhea, and nausea or vomiting. You may be able to eat small portions without problems, or you may be unable to tolerate any foods containing lactose (see Table B.8).

B. Lactose intolerance with milk products often causes a problem with not getting enough calcium and vitamin D that are needed for bones and other health needs.

C. Lactose-free food is available in most grocery stores.

D. Keeping a food diary is important to see what kinds of foods cause the symptoms of stomach pain, diarrhea, gas, and bloating. Some symptoms start after 30 minutes of eating and other symptoms may not be felt for 2 hours.
   1. You may be instructed to take out all milk and lactose foods and slowly restart them.
   2. Yogurt may be better than milk.
   3. Small amounts of cheddar cheese on crackers may be tried.
   4. Small amounts of milk in cereal may be tolerated.

E. There are lactase medicines available that can be bought in grocery and drug stores.

Tips for Following a Lactose-Intolerant Diet

A. Limit or omit foods that contain milk, lactose, whey, or casein.

B. Lactose-controlled diets allow up to 1 cup of milk per day for cooking or drinking, if you can tolerate it.

TABLE B.8 Recommended Foods for Lactose Intolerance

Foods	Recommended	Not Recommended
Milk	Soybean milk, milk treated with lactase, nondairy creamers, whipped topping. Up to 1 cup/d of buttermilk, yogurt, sweet acidophilus milk, and whole, low-fat, or skim milk	Milk products in excess of 1 cup/d, malted milk, milk shakes, hot chocolate, cocoa
Meat and protein foods	All meats, fish, poultry, eggs, peanut butter, tofu, and hard, aged, and processed cheese, if tolerated	Sandwich meat, hot dogs that contain lactose, cottage cheese, any meat prepared with milk products
Vegetables	All fresh, frozen, canned, buttered, and/or breaded vegetables	Any vegetable prepared with milk or milk products in excess of allowance (1 cup)
Fruits	All fresh, frozen, or canned fruits	Any fruits processed with lactose
Breads, cereal, and starchy food	White, wheat, rye, or other yeast breads, crackers, macaroni, spaghetti, popcorn, dry or cooked cereals	Commercial bread products (French toast, bread mixes, pancakes, biscuits), cakes/cookies containing milk or milk products
Fats and oils	Butter/margarine, salad dressing, mayonnaise, all oils, nondairy creamers, bacon	Sour cream, salad dressings with milk products in excess of 1 cup allowance
Soups	Vegetable and meat soups, broth, and bullion	Dried soups, creamed soups made with milk
Desserts	Plain and fruit-flavored gelatins, sherbet, fruit pies, cakes, pudding, pastries, angel food cake, sponge cake	Ice cream, ice milk, cream pie, puddings, custards, cakes, and pastries with milk (unless counting as day's allowance)
Beverages	Coffee, tea, soft drinks, fruit juices, carbonated and mineral waters	Beverages with milk over the 1 cup allowance
Miscellaneous condiments	Catsup, mustard, soy sauce, vinegar, steak sauce, Worcestershire sauce, chili sauce	None
Seasonings	Salt, pepper, spices, herbs, and seasonings	None
Sweets	Sugar, jelly, honey, molasses, preserves, marmalade, syrups, hard candy, baker's cocoa, carob powder, artificial sweeteners	Cream or chocolate candies containing milk or milk products (unless counting as day's allowance), caramels, toffee, and butterscotch

C. **Read labels carefully.** If you can't tolerate any lactose, choose lactose-free foods with lactate, lactic acid, lactalbumin, whey protein, sodium caseinate, casein hydrolysates, and calcium compounds.
D. You may also choose kosher foods marked "pareve" or "parve," which do not contain lactose. Read labels carefully.
E. A low-fat diet is also important if you have fat malabsorption.
F. To help with diarrhea due to malabsorption, avoid more than one serving a day of caffeine-containing drinks.
G. Beverages with high sugar content, such as soft drinks and fruit juices, may increase diarrhea. Juices and fruits with high amounts of fructose include apples, pears, sweet cherries, prunes, and dates.
H. "Sugarless" sorbitol-containing candies and gums may cause diarrhea.

LOW-FAT/LOW-CHOLESTEROL DIET—*Cheryl A. Glass*

The connection between fat in the diet and heart attack is cholesterol. Cholesterol is a fatlike substance produced by your liver and also found in many foods. Too much cholesterol causes heart attacks by clogging the arteries that deliver blood to your heart.

Exercising and following a low-fat/low-cholesterol diet can help control your blood cholesterol and reduce your risk of heart attack.

Tips

A. **Read food labels.** Use the ingredient list on labels to identify products containing saturated fat. High-fat ingredients may have many names. Remember: Foods can say "no cholesterol" and still be high in saturated vegetable fat and calories.
B. Train yourself to think "low fat" in your food and cooking methods.
   1. Bake
   2. Broil
   3. Grill
   4. Stir-fry
C. Eat less fried food, fast food, and baked products.
D. Eat more fruits and vegetables.
E. Organize your shopping around low-fat foods.
F. Add flavor to foods by using herbs and spices instead of butter and sauces.
G. Choose coleslaw, sliced tomatoes, or a dill pickle instead of fries and chips.

Foods to Avoid or Limit

A. Proteins/meats
   1. Shrimp
   2. Fried meats, fish, or poultry
   3. Fatty ground meat
   4. Prime or heavily marbled meats
   5. Bacon, sausage, high-fat deli meats, and cheeses
   6. Liver and organ meats
B. Breads/cereals
   1. High-fat baked foods, such as Danish, croissants, and doughnuts
   2. Fried rice, crispy chow mein noodles
   3. Granola bars with coconut or coconut oil
   4. Chips, cheese, or butter crackers
   5. High-fat cookies and cakes
C. Fruits and vegetables
   1. Coconut
   2. Fried vegetables such as onion rings and breaded fried pickles, mushrooms, and okra
   3. Cream, cheese, or butter sauces on vegetables
D. Milk/dairy products
   1. Whole or 2% milk
   2. Cream, half-and-half, nondairy creamers
   3. Ice cream, whipped cream, nondairy whipped toppings
   4. Whole-milk yogurt, sour cream
   5. Cheeses: Cheddar, American, Swiss, cream cheese, brie, muenster
E. Very high-fat foods
   1. Butter or margarine made with partially hydrogenated oils
   2. Lard, meat fat, and coconut or palm oils
   3. Salad dressings made with sour cream or cheese
   4. Chocolate
   5. Beef tallow
   6. Hydrogenated or partially hydrogenated vegetable shortening
   7. Cream
   8. Cocoa butter

Foods That Are Allowed

A. Proteins/meats
   1. Fish and shellfish
   2. Chicken and turkey cooked without the skin
   3. Ground turkey
   4. Eggs: Limited to two yolks per week
   5. Dried beans, lentils, tofu
   6. Small amounts of meat and seafood
B. Breads/cereals
   1. Plain bread and English muffins and bagels
   2. Plain pasta, rice
   3. Cereals, oatmeal
   4. Pretzels, air-popped popcorn, rice cakes, Melba toast
   5. Low-fat baked goods: Angel food cake, graham crackers, fruit cookies, and gingersnaps
C. Fruits and vegetables
   1. Eat several servings per day of high-nutrition, low-fat fruits and vegetables.
   2. Prepare vegetables by steaming, broiling, baking, or stir-fry.
D. Milk/dairy products
   1. Skim or 1% milk
   2. Low-fat milk, evaporated milk, nonfat dry milk powder
   3. Frozen yogurt, ice milk, sherbet, sorbet
   4. Low-fat yogurt
   5. Low-fat cheeses: 1% cottage cheese, skim-milk ricotta, mozzarella, and American cheeses

E. Allowed high-fat foods
   1. Margarine made with liquid safflower, corn, or sunflower oils
   2. Olive, canola, or peanut oils
   3. Nut snacks in moderation (high fat and calories)
   4. Salad dressings made with saturated oils

Resources

The National Heart, Lung, and Blood Institute website has examples of low-fat and low-calorie food alternatives for dairy, meat, fish, poultry, snacks and sweets, fats, oils and salad dressings, and other miscellaneous foods at www.nhlbi.nih.gov/health/public/heart/obesity/lose_wt/lcal_fat.htm

For simple nausea and vomiting with an upset stomach, follow these steps:

Step 1: Replace lost fluids

A. Rest your stomach for 1 to 2 hours.
B. Older child and adults
   1. After vomiting stops, take sips of clear liquids at room temperature, such as flat ginger ale, flat cola, or gelatin.
   2. Suck on lollipops or popsicles.
   3. Gradually increase amount of liquids. If 4 hours pass without vomiting, progress to Step 2.

Step 2: Dry diet

The foods in this diet don't meet all daily food requirements and should be used only for a short period before adding foods or advancing to Step 3.

A. Cheerios
B. Crackers
C. Cornflakes
D. Graham crackers
E. Rice Krispies
F. Vanilla wafers
G. Toast
H. Dinner rolls

Step 3: More advanced carbohydrates

A. Oatmeal
B. Grits, unseasoned
C. Rice, unseasoned
D. Mashed potatoes
E. Baked potato
F. Noodles
G. Peanut butter
H. Pudding

Step 4: Bland foods with limited odors

After you are able to eat dry and more complex carbohydrates, a trial of bland foods may be tried. Foods with little or no odors are more easily tolerated after experiencing nausea and vomiting (see Table B.9).

BRAT Diet

You may be told to use a BRAT diet. This is a combination of foods that make up a bland diet and help with nausea and vomiting: **B**ananas, **R**ice, **A**pplesauce, and **T**oast as tolerated.

Side effects of cancer treatments require additional liquid nutrition in order to get enough calories, protein, and nutrition. Commercial liquid nutrition products are available over the counter; contact your oncologist to discuss the need for other treatments for managing the side effects of treatments.

TABLE B.9 Bland Foods With Limited Odors

Apple juice	Canned pears	Ice cream
Applesauce	Chicken noodle soup	Iced tea
Baked chicken	Cottage cheese	Low-fat milk
Baked turkey	Fresh apple	Sherbet
Canned peaches	Fresh banana	Turkey sandwich

Food is very important in healing wounds.

A. Foods from all food groups are needed, but foods loaded with protein are the best for healing.
B. Liquids are important too. You need 8 cups of liquids a day. You will need special instructions on how much you can drink if you have heart failure or kidney problems.
C. If you have diabetes, it is very important to check your blood sugar when you have a wound. Keeping your sugar under control will help you to heal. You may be instructed to check your urine for ketones.
D. You will need special instructions on eating extra protein foods if you have kidney problems.
E. You may be asked to write down all food that you eat in 24 hours to bring to your next visit.
F. You may be asked to weigh at home. Use the same scales and weigh yourself at the same time of the day.
G. You may be told to take extra vitamins if you do not eat very much fruit and vegetables.
H. You may be sent to see a dietitian to help plan meals.

Dietary Tips for Helping to Heal Your Wound

A. **Whole eggs are considered the "best" protein food.**
B. Eat three meals and snacks.
C. If possible, eat extra portions of protein.
D. You may find it easier to eat six smaller meals.
E. Shake-like drinks contain protein, vitamins, and minerals. These drinks are expensive.
F. If you use a protein powder, choose one that is made of 100% whey protein without all of the added sugars and other supplements.
G. Add powdered milk to your food to increase protein. Add powdered milk to scrambled eggs, milk, or cereal.
H. Add tuna to a salad.
I. Add beans to soups or salads.
J. Eat cottage cheese or yogurt with fruits.
K. Nuts make a good snack and may be added to salads.
L. Add eggs to salads and tuna.
M. The following list presents examples of high-protein foods.
   1. Whole eggs
   2. Meats:
      a. Red and white meat
      b. Liver
      c. Chicken or turkey
      d. Fish
   3. Nuts and seeds:
      a. Almond, cashews, peanuts, or walnuts
      b. Pumpkin or sunflower seeds
      c. Peanut butter
   4. Beans and peas:
      a. Black beans, kidney, pinto, white, lima, or soy beans
      b. Tofu
      c. Falafel patty
      d. Hummus
   5. Dairy:
      a. All types of milk
      b. Evaporated canned milk
      c. Cheese
      d. Plain or fruit yogurt
      e. Ice cream
      f. Cottage cheese
N. Foods that provide energy, vitamins, and minerals include:
   a. Any kind of fruit
   b. Any kind of vegetable
   c. Whole grain cereal and breads
   d. Rice and pasta
   e. Fats: Margarine/butter, oil and full fat dairy foods

FOOD SOURCES AND RECOMMENDATIONS FOR VITAMIN D AND CALCIUM—*Cheryl A. Glass and Deanna Tacderas*

Calcium-Rich Foods

Sunlight exposure to the skin is also recommended for approximately 20 to 30 minutes without sunscreen. Sun exposure provides an adequate source of vitamin D. Care should be taken not to burn skin.

1. Vitamin D assists with calcium absorption into the bones.
2. Research indicates that caffeine interferes with calcium absorption and lowers bone density. Carbonated beverages appear to be worse than coffee.
3. Vitamin D and calcium deficiency contribute to bone loss and, thus, osteoporosis.
4. Additional supplemental calcium and vitamin D are needed based on medical diagnoses and malabsorption from gastric bypass procedures (Table B.12).

TABLE B.10 Vitamin-D-Enriched Foods

Food Source	Serving Size	Food International Units (IU)
Fish liver oils, cod liver oil	15 mL	1,360
Mushrooms	3 oz	2,700
Fortified milk	8 oz	100
Herring	3 oz	1,383
Catfish	3 oz	425
Mackerel (cooked)	3.5 oz	345
Salmon (cooked)	3.5 oz	360
Sardines (canned in oil, drained)	1.75 oz	250
Fortified orange juice	8 oz	100
Fortified cereal	1 serving	100
Fortified cheese	3 oz	100

TABLE B.11 Foods That Are Calcium Rich

Food Source	Serving Size (mg)	International Units (IU)
Yogurt	1 cup	448
Orange juice	1 cup	350
Orange	1 medium size	52
Fat-free milk	1 cup	316
Soy milk (original and vanilla with calcium and vitamins A and D added)	1 cup	299
Soy milk (original and vanilla-unfortified)	1 cup	61
Yogurt, plain	8 oz	452
Skim milk	8 oz	452
Reduced fat milk (with vitamins A and D added)	1 cup	293
Ice cream (vanilla)	½ cup	84
Shrimp	3 oz	275
Salmon	3 oz	182
Tuna (canned)	3 oz	12
Instant oatmeal	1 packet	165
Tofu	½ cup	130
Broccoli	1 cup	94
Dried beans, cooked	½ cup	50
Cheddar cheese	1½ oz	306
Cottage cheese (low fat)	1 cup	206
Turnip greens	1 cup	197
Spinach (frozen)	1 cup	291
Cereal bars, snack bars (fortified)	1 bar	200

TABLE B.12 The Institute of Medicine Dietary Reference Intakes for Calcium and Vitamin D

Age Ranges	Calcium (mg/d)	Vitamin D (IU/d)
14–18 years old	1,100–1,300	400–600
19–30 years old	800–1,000	400–600
31–50 years old	800–1,000	400–600
51- to 70-year-old males	800–1,000	400–600
51- to 70-year-old females	1,000–1,200	400–600
> 70 years old	1,000–1,200	400–800
14–18 years old, pregnant/lactating	1,100–1,300	400–600
19–50 years old, pregnant/lactating	800–1,000	400–600

Adapted from Institute of Medicine of the National Academies (2011).

Bibliography

Academy of Nutrition and Dietetics. (2013, January). *Serving size vs. portion size: Is there a difference?* Retrieved from http://www.eatright.org/Public/content.aspx?id=4294967941&terms=serving%20size

Australian Wound Management Association. (2009). *Expert guide for healthcare professional: Nutrition & wound healing.* Retrieved from http://www.awma.com.au/publications/2009_vic_expert_guide_nutrition_wound_healing.pdf

Banks, D. (n.d.). Salt: Too much of a good thing. In *University of Illinois extension: Thrifty living.* Retrieved from http://urbanext.illinois.edu/thriftyliving/tl-salt.html

Boyle, M., & Long, S. (2013). *Personal nutrition* (8th ed.). Belmont, CA: Wadsworth CENGAGE Learning.

Collins, N., & Schnitzer, A. (2013, November/December). How dietary protein intake promotes wound healing. *Wound Care Advisor, 2*(6), 16–19

Combat Wound Initiative. (n.d.). *Nutrition and wound healing.* Retrieved from http://www.cwiprogram.org/patient-care/nutrition-and-wound-healing

Connected Wound Care. (2011). *Nutrition for people with wounds.* Retrieved from http://www.google.com/url?sa=t&rct=j&q=&esrc=s&source=web&cd=1&ved=0CB0QFjAA&url=http%3A%2F%2Fwww.grhc.org.au%2Fdocument-library%2Fdoc_download%2F280-cwc-nutrition-for-wounds-print-version&ei=MRvUU_GDAoyiyASLt4LoDw&usg=AFQjCNH5Jnigg_qk7fwkSpsL0ECNM9ueRg&bvm=bv.71778758,d.aWw

DASH Diet FAQ. (n.d.). Retrieved from http://dashdiet.org/dash_diet_faq.asp

Dietary Fiber Guide. (n.d.). *High fiber foods.* Retrieved from http://dietaryfiberguide.com

Friedrich, L., & Collins, N. (2013, November/December). Nutrition & wound healing in the older adult: Considerations for wound clinics. *Today's Wound Clinic.* Retrieved from http://www.todayswoundclinic.com/articles/nutrition-wound-healing-older-adult-considerations-wound-clinics

Institute of Medicine of the National Academies. (2005). *Dietary reference intakes for energy, carbohydrate, fiber, fat, fatty acids, cholesterol, protein, and amino acids.* Retrieved from http://www.nal.usda.gov/fnic/DRI/DRI_Energy/energy_full_report.pdf

Institute of Medicine of the National Academies. (2011). *Dietary reference intakes for calcium and vitamin D.* Retrieved from http://www.iom.edu/~/media/Files/Report%20Files/2010/Dietary-Reference-Intakes-for-Calcium-and-Vitamin-D/Vitamin%20D%20and%20Calcium%202010%20Report%20Brief.pdf

Low salt and the DASH diet. (n.d.). Retrieved from http://dashdiet.org/low_salt_diet.asp

National Heart, Lung, and Blood Institute. (2010). Keep an eye on portion size: What is the difference between portions and servings? *Servingcard7.pdf-food portion.* Retrieved from http://hp2010.nhlbihin.net/portion/servingcard7.pdf

National Heart, Lung, and Blood Institute. (n.d.a). Following the DASH eating plan. Retrieved from http://www.nhlbi.nig.gov/health/health=topics/topics/dash/follow dash

National Heart, Lung, and Blood Institute. (n.d.b). *Low-calorie, lower fat alternative foods.* Retrieved from http://www.nhlbi.nih.gov/health/public/heart/obesity/lose_wt/lcal_fat.htm

National Heart, Lung, and Blood Institute. (n.d.c). *Tips for reducing sodium in your diet.* Retrieved from www.nhlbi.nih.gov/hbp/prevent/sodium/tips.htm

National Heart, Lung, and Blood Institute. (n.d.d). *Tips on how to make healthier meals.* Retrieved from www.nhlbi.nih.gov/hbp/prevent/h_eating/tips.htm

National Osteoporosis Foundation. (n.d.). Calcium and vitamin D: What you need to know. Retrieved from www.nof.org/articles/10

Ross, A. C., Manison, J. E., Abrams, S. A., Aloia, J. F., Brannon, P. M., Clinton, S. K., . . . Shapses, S. A. (2011, January). The 2011 report on dietary reference intakes for calcium and vitamin D from the Institute of Medicine: What clinicians need to know. *Journal Clinical Endocrinology and Metabolism, 96*(1), 53–58.

The DASH Diet and African American Heart Health. (n.d.). Retrieved from http://dashdiet.org/dash_diet_and_african_american.asp

The DASH Diet Eating Plan. (n.d.). Retrieved from http://dashdiet.org/default.asp

Trans Tasman Dietetic Wound Care Group. (2011). *Evidence bases practice guidelines for the dietetic management of adults with pressure injuries.* Retrieved from http://daa.asn.au/wp-content/uploads/2011/09/Trans-Tasman-Dietetic-Wound-Care-Group-Pressure-Injury-Guidelines-2011.pdf

University of Chicago Celiac Disease Center. (n.d.). *Is a gluten free diet similar to a diabetic diet?* Retrieved from www.cureceliacdisease.org/?s=glutentfree+diet

U.S. Department of Health and Human Services, National Institutes of Health, National Heart, Lung, and Blood Institute. (2003, May). *Facts about the DASH eating plan (NIH Publication No. 03-4082).* Retrieved from www.ndhealth.gov/heartstroke/image/cache/Facts_About_The_

U.S. Department of Health and Human Services, National Institutes of Health, National Digestive Diseases Information Clearinghouse. (2014, May). *Lactose intolerance (NIH Publication No. 14-7994).* Retrieved from http://digestive.niddk.nih.gov/ddiseases/pubs/lactoseintolerance/Lactose_Intolerance_508.pdf

U.S. Department of Health and Human Services, National Institutes of Health, National Heart, Lung, and Blood Institute. (2006, April). *Your guide to lowering your blood pressure with DASH, DASH eating plan, Lower your blood pressure (NIH Publication No. 06-4082).* Retrieved from http://www.nhlbi.nih.gov/health/public/heart/hbp/dash/new_dash.pdf

U.S. Food and Drug Administration. (2014, June 20). *Sodium in your diet: Using the nutrition facts label to reduce your intake.* Retrieved from http://www.fda.gov/Food/IngredientsPackagingLabeling/LabelingNutrition/ucm315393.htm

Wild, T., Rahbarnia, A., Kllner, M., Sobotka, L., & Eberlein, T. (2010). Basics in nutrition and wound healing. *Nutrition, 26,* 862–866.

Index

Note: page numbers followed by f and t indicate material in figures and tables, respectively.